HOLY
BIBLE

THIS BIBLE BELONGS TO

PRESENTED BY

DATE

OCCASION

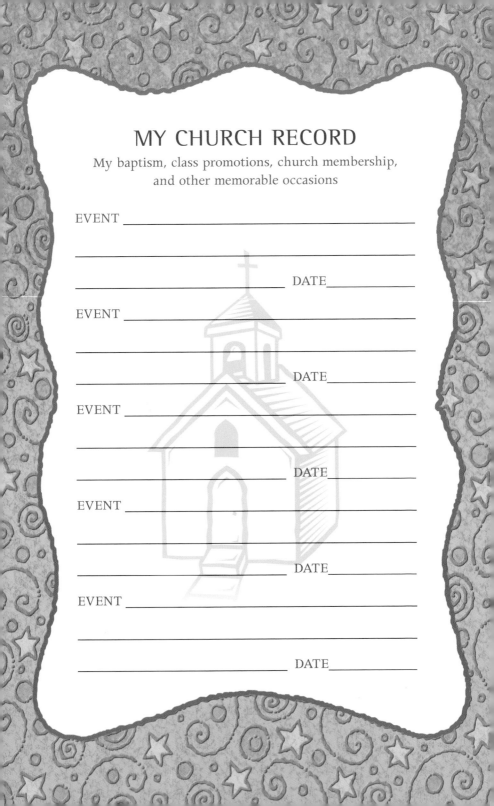

MY CHURCH RECORD

My baptism, class promotions, church membership,
and other memorable occasions

EVENT _____

_____

_____ DATE_____

EVENT _____

_____

_____ DATE_____

EVENT _____

_____

_____ DATE_____

EVENT _____

_____

_____ DATE_____

EVENT _____

_____

_____ DATE_____

EVENT _____

_____

_____ DATE_____

EVENT _____

_____

_____ DATE_____

EVENT _____

_____

_____ DATE_____

EVENT _____

_____

_____ DATE_____

EVENT _____

_____

_____ DATE_____

EVENT _____

_____

_____ DATE_____

MY FAMILY HISTORY

_____
MY NAME

_____
WHEN I WAS BORN

_____
MY FATHER   DATE BORN

_____
MY FATHER'S PARENTS

_____
MY MOTHER   DATE BORN

_____
MY MOTHER'S PARENTS

MY BROTHERS AND SISTERS

_____
NAME   DATE BORN

_____
NAME   DATE BORN

_____
NAME   DATE BORN

_____
NAME   DATE BORN

_____
NAME   DATE BORN

_____
NAME   DATE BORN

_____
NAME   DATE BORN

Holy Bible

International Children's Bible®

A Divsion of Thomas Nelson Publishers, Inc.
www.tommynelson.com

Holy Bible

International Children's Bible®

INTRODUCTION

Dear Parents and Children,

You have just picked up the most amazing and wonderful book of all time. No kidding—it's the greatest! The Bible is God's instruction book… his way to share all the things he wants you to know and do and learn. So many important lessons and mysteries and truths are inside these pages just waiting for you. Whether you are young or "young at heart," God's simple message of sharing, kindness, trust, faith, and love are here just for you.

We invite you to begin your journey to truly knowing God and the amazing gift of his Son Jesus by reading this Bible. Just as you eat, work, play, and sleep every day, take time to include God. Knowing God and his plan for you will make you a better person and the world a more wonderful place!

> God has made us what we are. In Christ Jesus, God made us new people so that we would do good works. God had planned in advance those good works for us. He had planned for us to live our lives doing them.
>
> Ephesians 2:10

TABLE OF CONTENTS

THE OLD TESTAMENT

THE NEW TESTAMENT

HOW TO USE THIS BIBLE

So you want to know how to get around in this Bible?
Let's get started. Take a look at the picture of a Bible page below.

Running Heads are at the top of the pages to show you where you are in the Bible. In other words you'll see the Bible book name and chapter(s). That way when you flip through the Bible, you'll always be able to tell where you are.

Subject Heads help to make it easier to know what is going on in the section of Bible verses you are reading.

Bible Verses are set in two columns and have small verse numbers at the beginning of each verse to help you find your way around. Sometimes they might have a small "*n*" or a small "*d*" included in the verse. The "*n*" tells you that there is a footnote at the bottom of the page that gives you more information about the verse. The "*d*" tells you that there is a definition for that word in the dictionary at the back of your Bible.

make their faces look strange to show people that they are giving up eating. I tell you the truth, those hypocrites already have their full reward. [17]So when you give up eating, comb your hair and wash your face. [18]Then people will not know that you are giving up eating. But your Father, whom you cannot see, will see you. Your Father sees what is done in secret, and he will reward you.

GOD IS MORE IMPORTANT THAN MONEY

[19]"Don't store treasures for yourselves here on earth. Moths and rust will destroy treasures here on earth. And thieves can break into your house and steal the things you have. [20]So store your treasure in heaven. The treasures in heaven cannot be destroyed by moths or rust. And thieves cannot break in and steal that treasure. [21]Your heart will be where your treasure is.

[22]"The eye is a light for the body. If your eyes are good, then your whole body will be full of light. [23]But if your eyes are evil, then your whole body will be full of darkness. And if the only light you have is really darkness, then you have the worst darkness.

[24]"No one can be a slave to two masters. He will hate one master and love the other. Or he will follow one master and refuse to follow the other. So you cannot serve God and money at the same time.

DON'T WORRY

[25]"So I tell you, don't worry about the food you need to live. And don't worry about the clothes you need for your body. Life is more important than food. And the body is more important than clothes. [26]Look at the birds in the air. They don't plant or harvest or store food in barns. But your heavenly Father feeds the birds. And you know that you are worth much more than the birds. [27]You cannot add any time to your life by worrying about it.

[28]"And why do you worry about clothes? Look at the flowers in the field. See how they grow. They don't work or make clothes for themselves. [29]But I tell you that even Solomon with his riches was not dressed as beautifully as one of these flowers. [30]God clothes the grass in the field like that. The grass is living today, but tomorrow it is thrown into the fire to be burned. So you can be even more sure that God will clothe you. Don't have so little faith! [31]Don't worry and say, 'What will we eat?' or 'What will we drink?' or 'What will we wear?' [32]All the people who don't know God keep trying to get these things. And your Father in heaven knows that you need them. [33]The thing you should want most is God's kingdom and doing what God wants. Then all these other things you need will be given to you. [34]So don't worry about tomorrow. Each day has enough trouble of its own. Tomorrow will have its own worries.

BE CAREFUL ABOUT JUDGING OTHERS

7 "Don't judge other people, and you will not be judged. [2]You will be judged in the same way that you judge others. And the forgiveness you give to others will be given to you.

[3]"Why do you notice the little piece of dust that is in your brother's eye, but you don't notice the big piece of wood that is in your own eye? [4]Why do you say to your brother, 'Let me take that little piece of dust out of your eye'? Look at yourself first! You still have that big piece of wood in your own eye. [5]You are a hypocrite!*d* First, take the wood out of your own eye. Then you will see clearly enough to take the dust out of your brother's eye.

[6]"Don't give holy things to dogs. Don't throw your pearls before pigs. Pigs will only trample on them. And the dogs will only turn to attack you.

ASK GOD FOR WHAT YOU NEED

[7]"Continue to ask, and God will give to you. Continue to search, and you will

1197

which he had made long ago. [24]God raised Jesus from death. God set him free from the pain of death. Death could not hold him. [25]For David said this about him:

'I keep the Lord before me always.
Because he is close by my side,
I will not be hurt.
[26]So I am glad, and I rejoice.
Even my body has hope.
[27]This is because you will not leave me
in the grave.
You will not let your Holy One rot.
[28]You will teach me God's way to live.
Being with you will fill me with joy.'

Psalm 16:8-11

[29]"Brothers, I can tell you truly about David, our ancestor. He died and was buried. His grave is still here with us today. [30]David was a prophet[d] and knew what God had said. God had promised David that he would make a person from David's family a king just as he was.[n] [31]David knew this before it happened. That is why he said:

'He was not left in the grave.
His body did not rot.'

David was talking about the Christ[d] rising from death. [32]So Jesus is the One who God raised from death! And we are all witnesses to this. [33]Jesus was lifted up to heaven and is now at God's right side. The Father has given the Holy Spirit[d] to Jesus as he promised. So now Jesus has poured out that Spirit. This is what you see and hear. [34]David was not the one who was lifted up to heaven. But he said:

'The Lord said to my Lord:
Sit by me at my right side,
[35] until I put your enemies under
your control.'[n]

Psalm 110:1

[36]"So, all the people of Israel should know this truly: God has made Jesus both Lord and Christ. He is the man you nailed to the cross!"

[37]When the people heard this, they were sick at heart. They asked Peter and the other apostles, "What shall we do?"

[38]Peter said to them, "Change your hearts and lives and be baptized, each one of you, in the name of Jesus Christ for the forgiveness of your sins. And you will receive the gift of the Holy Spirit. [39]This promise is for you. It is also for your children and for all who are far away. It is for everyone the Lord our God calls to himself."

[40]Peter warned them with many other words. He begged them, "Save yourselves from the evil of today's people!" [41]Then those people who accepted what Peter said were baptized. About 3,000 people were added to the number of believers that day. [42]They spent their time learning the apostles' teaching. And they continued to share, to break bread,[n] and to pray together.

THE BELIEVERS SHARE

[43]The apostles[d] were doing many miracles[d] and signs. And everyone felt great respect for God. [44]All the believers stayed together. They shared everything. [45]They sold their land and the things they owned. Then they divided the money and gave it to those people who needed it. [46]The believers met together in the Temple[d] every day. They all had the same purpose. They broke bread in their homes, happy to share their food with joyful hearts. [47]They praised God, and all the people liked them. More and more people were being saved every day; the Lord was adding those people to the group of believers.

PETER HEALS A CRIPPLED MAN

3 One day Peter and John went to the Temple.[d] It was three o'clock in the afternoon. This was the time for the daily

2:30 God . . . was See 2 Samuel 7:13; Psalm 132:11.
2:35 until . . . control Literally, "until I make your enemies a footstool for your feet."
2:42 break bread This may mean a meal as in verse 46, or the Lord's Supper, the special meal Jesus told his followers to eat to remember him (Luke 22:14-20).

Chapter Numbers are in bold type to help you find the chapters fast and easy.

Footnotes are helpful to give you more information about the verse. It might refer you to another verse in the Bible or explain what a certain word means.

STUDY HELPS

In the back of your Bible there are sections to help you learn about and love your Bible more.
- The Dictionary includes over 200 entries with information about people, places, and things.
- The "Where Do I Find It?" section helps you locate the stories and topics you might be interested in.
- The "What God Promises About . . ." section lists several of the many wonderful promises God has made for us.
- The "Memory Verses for My Life" is a section to help you study and memorize some of the key verses God gives us to help live a better life.

PREFACE

The *International Children's Bible*® is not a storybook or a paraphrased Bible. It is a translation of God's Word from the original Hebrew and Greek languages. It is the first translation of the Holy Scriptures prepared specifically for children. Until now children have had to learn God's truths either from Bible storybooks or adult-language Bibles. Many words and concepts, readily understood by adults, may leave children mystified or even with false impressions.

Yet, God intended for everyone to be able to understand his Word. Earliest Scriptures were in Hebrew, ideally suited for a barely literate society because of its economy of words, acrostic literary form and poetic parallelism. The New Testament was first written in the simple Greek of everyday life, not in the Latin of Roman courts or the classical Greek of the academies. Even Jesus, the Master Teacher, taught spiritual principles by comparing them to such familiar terms as pearls, seeds, rocks, trees and sheep. It is for this same purpose of making the Scriptures intelligible, even to children, that this translation was created.

A TRUSTWORTHY TRANSLATION

Two basic premises guided the translation process. The first concern was that the translation be faithful to the manuscripts in the original languages. A team composed of the World Bible Translation Center and twenty-one additional, highly qualified and experienced Bible scholars and translators was assembled. The team included men with translation experience on such accepted versions as the *New International Version*, the *New American Standard Bible* and the *New King James Version*. The most recent scholarship and the best available Hebrew and Greek texts were used, principally the third edition of the United Bible Societies' Greek text and the latest edition of the Biblia Hebraica, along with the Septuagint.

A CLEAR TRANSLATION

The second concern was to make the language simple enough for children to read and understand it for themselves. In maintaining language simplicity, several guidelines were followed. Sentences have been kept short and uncomplicated. Vocabulary choice has been based upon *The Living Word Vocabulary* by Dr. Edgar Dale and Dr. Joseph O'Rourke (Worldbook-Childcraft International, 1981) which is the standard used by the editors of *The World Book Encyclopedia* to determine appropriate vocabulary. For difficult words which have no simpler synonyms, footnotes and dictionary references are provided. Footnotes appear at the bottom of the page and are indicated in the text by an [n] (for "note"). The dictionary is located at the back of the Bible with references indicated in the text by a [d].

Dr. Charles K. Kinzer of Peabody College of Education, Vanderbilt University, did a comparative study of this base text and four other versions commonly used by children. The results showed that the *International Children's Bible*® was clearly the easiest version for children to comprehend on the literal level. The word choice in this version was also judged to be the most appropriate for the youngest students. It was, in fact, the only version that could be comprehended on a third-grade instructional level (Kinzer, Ransom and Hammond, 1983).

The *International Children's Bible*® aids a child's understanding by putting concepts into natural terms. Modern measurements and geographical locations have been used as much as possible. For instance, the traditional "shekels" and "cubits" have been converted to modern equivalents of weights and measures. Where geographical references are identical, the modern name has been used, such as the "Mediterranean Sea" instead of "Great Sea" or "Western Sea." Also, to minimize confusion, the most familiar name for a place is used consistently, instead of using variant names for the same place. "Lake Galilee" is used throughout rather than its variant forms, "Sea of Kinnereth," "Lake Gennesaret" and "Sea of Tiberias."

Ancient customs are often unfamiliar to modern readers. Customs such as shaving a man's beard to shame him or walking between the halves of a dead animal to seal an agreement are meaningless to children. So these are clarified either in the text or in a footnote.

Since *connotations* of words change with time, care has been taken to avoid potential misunderstandings. Instead of describing ancient citadels as "forts," which for modern children would likely conjure up pictures of wooden stockades in the Old West, the *International Children's Bible®* uses "strong, walled cities." Instead of using the phrase "God drove the nations out of Canaan," which could call up images in a child's mind of automobiles, the phrase is translated "forced them out of Canaan."

Rhetorical questions are obvious to adults, but not to children. To an adult, the implied answer to the psalmist's question, "Who is equal to our God?" is quite clear. To a child, the question remains unanswered. Therefore, rhetorical questions have been worded as statements, showing the implied meaning, as in this example: "No one is equal to our God."

Figures of speech can easily be misunderstood by children as literal statements. For instance, when Canaan is described as a land "flowing with milk and honey," children might literally see milk and honey running through the streets. To clarify, the *International Children's Bible®* has translated the meaning of the figures, while preserving the image as much as possible.

Idiomatic expressions of the biblical languages are translated to communicate the same meaning to today's child that would have been understood by the original audience. For example, the Hebrew idiom "he rested with his fathers" is translated by its meaning—"he died."

Every attempt has been made to maintain proper English style, while simplifying concepts and communications. The beauty of the Hebrew parallelism in poetry and the word plays have been retained. Images of the ancient languages have been captured in equivalent English images wherever possible.

OUR PRAYER

It is with great humility and prayerfulness that this Bible is presented to God's children. We acknowledge the infallibility of God's Word and our own human frailty. We pray that God has worked through us as his vessels so that his precious children might learn his truth for themselves and that it might richly grow in their lives. It is to his glory that this Bible is given.

THE PUBLISHER

THE OLD TESTAMENT

GENESIS

THE BEGINNING OF THE WORLD

1 In the beginning God created the sky and the earth. ²The earth was empty and had no form. Darkness covered the ocean, and God's Spirit*d* was moving over the water.

³Then God said, "Let there be light!" And there was light. ⁴God saw that the light was good. So he divided the light from the darkness. ⁵God named the light "day" and the darkness "night." Evening passed, and morning came. This was the first day.

⁶Then God said, "Let there be something to divide the water in two!" ⁷So God made the air to divide the water in two. Some of the water was above the air, and some of the water was below it. ⁸God named the air "sky." Evening passed, and morning came. This was the second day.

⁹Then God said, "Let the water under the sky be gathered together so the dry land will appear." And it happened. ¹⁰God named the dry land "earth." He named the water that was gathered together "seas." God saw that this was good.

¹¹Then God said, "Let the earth produce plants. Some plants will make grain for seeds. Others will make fruit with seeds in it. Every seed will produce more of its own kind of plant." And it happened. ¹²The earth produced plants. Some plants had grain for seeds. The trees made fruit with seeds in it. Each seed grew its own kind of plant. God saw that all this was good. ¹³Evening passed, and morning came. This was the third day.

¹⁴Then God said, "Let there be lights in the sky to separate day from night. These lights will be used for signs, seasons, days and years. ¹⁵They will be in the sky to give light to the earth." And it happened.

¹⁶So God made the two large lights. He made the brighter light to rule the day. He made the smaller light to rule the night. He also made the stars. ¹⁷God put all these in the sky to shine on the earth. ¹⁸They are to rule over the day and over the night. He put them there to separate the light from the darkness. God saw that all these things were good. ¹⁹Evening passed, and morning came. This was the fourth day.

²⁰Then God said, "Let the water be filled with living things. And let birds fly in the air above the earth."

²¹So God created the large sea animals. He created every living thing that moves in the sea. The sea is filled with these living things. Each one produces more of its own kind. God also made every bird that flies. And each bird produces more of its own kind. God saw that this was good. ²²God blessed them and said, "Have many young ones and grow in number. Fill the water of the seas, and let the birds grow in number on the earth." ²³Evening passed, and morning came. This was the fifth day.

²⁴Then God said, "Let the earth be filled with animals. And let each produce more of its own kind. Let there be tame animals and small crawling animals and wild animals. And let each produce more of its kind." And it happened.

²⁵So God made the wild animals, the tame animals and all the small crawling animals to produce more of their own kind. God saw that this was good.

²⁶Then God said, "Let us make human beings in our image and likeness. And let them rule over the fish in the sea and the birds in the sky. Let them rule over the tame animals, over all the earth and over all the small crawling animals on the earth."

²⁷So God created human beings in his image. In the image of God he created them. He created them male and female. ²⁸God blessed them and said, "Have

many children and grow in number. Fill the earth and be its master. Rule over the fish in the sea and over the birds in the sky. Rule over every living thing that moves on the earth."

²⁹God said, "Look, I have given you all the plants that have grain for seeds. And I have given you all the trees whose fruits have seeds in them. They will be food for you. ³⁰I have given all the green plants to all the animals to eat. They will be food for every wild animal, every bird of the air and every small crawling animal." And it happened. ³¹God looked at everything he had made, and it was very good. Evening passed, and morning came. This was the sixth day.

THE SEVENTH DAY—REST

2 So the sky, the earth and all that filled them were finished. ²By the seventh day God finished the work he had been doing. So on the seventh day he rested from all his work. ³God blessed the seventh day and made it a holy day. He made it holy because on that day he rested. He rested from all the work he had done in creating the world.

THE FIRST PEOPLE

⁴This is the story of the creation of the sky and the earth. When the Lord God made the earth and the sky, ⁵there were no plants on the earth. Nothing was growing in the fields. The Lord God had not yet made it rain on the land. And there was no man to care for the ground. ⁶But a mist often rose from the earth and watered all the ground.

⁷Then the Lord God took dust from the ground and formed man from it. The Lord breathed the breath of life into the man's nose. And the man became a living person. ⁸Then the Lord God planted a garden in the East, in a place called Eden. He put the man he had formed in that garden. ⁹The Lord God caused every beautiful tree and every tree that was good for food to grow out of the ground. In the middle of the garden, God put the tree that gives life. And he put there the tree that gives the knowledge of good and evil.

¹⁰A river flowed through Eden and watered the garden. From that point the river was divided. It had four streams flowing into it. ¹¹The name of the first stream is Pishon. It flows around the whole land of Havilah, where there is gold. ¹²That gold is good. Bdellium and onyx[n] are also there. ¹³The name of the second river is Gihon. It flows around the whole land of Cush. ¹⁴The name of the third river is Tigris. It flows out of Assyria toward the east. The fourth river is the Euphrates.

¹⁵The Lord God put the man in the garden of Eden to care for it and work it. ¹⁶The Lord God commanded him, "You may eat the fruit from any tree in the garden. ¹⁷But you must not eat the fruit from the tree which gives the knowledge of good and evil. If you ever eat fruit from that tree, you will die!"

THE FIRST WOMAN

¹⁸Then the Lord God said, "It is not good for the man to be alone. I will make a helper who is right for him."

¹⁹From the ground God formed every wild animal and every bird in the sky. He brought them to the man so the man could name them. Whatever the man called each living thing, that became its name. ²⁰The man gave names to all the tame animals, to the birds in the sky and to all the wild animals. But Adam[n] did not find a helper that was right for him. ²¹So the Lord God caused the man to sleep very deeply. While the man was asleep, God took one of the ribs from the man's body. Then God closed the man's skin at the place where he took the rib.

2:12 bdellium and onyx Bdellium is an expensive, sweet-smelling resin like myrrh. And onyx is a gem.
2:20 Adam This is the name of the first man. It also means "humans," including men and women.

²²The Lord God used the rib from the man to make a woman. Then the Lord brought the woman to the man.

²³And the man said,

"Now, this is someone whose bones
    came from my bones.
Her body came from my body.
I will call her 'woman,'
    because she was taken out of man."

²⁴So a man will leave his father and mother and be united with his wife. And the two people will become one body.

²⁵The man and his wife were naked, but they were not ashamed.

THE BEGINNING OF SIN

3 Now the snake was the most clever of all the wild animals the Lord God had made. One day the snake spoke to the woman. He said, "Did God really say that you must not eat fruit from any tree in the garden?"

²The woman answered the snake, "We may eat fruit from the trees in the garden. ³But God told us, 'You must not eat fruit from the tree that is in the middle of the garden. You must not even touch it, or you will die.'"

⁴But the snake said to the woman, "You will not die. ⁵God knows that if you eat the fruit from that tree, you will learn about good and evil. Then you will be like God!"

⁶The woman saw that the tree was beautiful. She saw that its fruit was good to eat and that it would make her wise. So she took some of its fruit and ate it. She also gave some of the fruit to her husband who was with her, and he ate it.

⁷Then, it was as if the man's and the woman's eyes were opened. They realized they were naked. So they sewed fig leaves together and made something to cover themselves.

⁸Then they heard the Lord God walking in the garden. This was during the cool part of the day. And the man and his wife hid from the Lord God among the trees in the garden. ⁹But the Lord God called to the man. The Lord said, "Where are you?"

¹⁰The man answered, "I heard you walking in the garden. I was afraid because I was naked. So I hid."

¹¹God said to the man, "Who told you that you were naked? Did you eat fruit from that tree? I commanded you not to eat from that tree."

¹²The man said, "You gave this woman to me. She gave me fruit from the tree. So I ate it."

¹³Then the Lord God said to the woman, "What have you done?"

She answered, "The snake tricked me. So I ate the fruit."

¹⁴The Lord God said to the snake,

"Because you did this,
    a curse will be put on you.
You will be cursed more than any
    tame animal or wild animal.
You will crawl on your stomach,
    and you will eat dust all the days of
        your life.
¹⁵I will make you and the woman
    enemies to each other.
Your descendants*d* and her
    descendants
    will be enemies.
Her child will crush your head.
    And you will bite his heel."

¹⁶Then God said to the woman,

"I will cause you to have much trouble
    when you are pregnant.
And when you give birth to children,
    you will have great pain.
You will greatly desire your husband,
    but he will rule over you."

¹⁷Then God said to the man, "You listened to what your wife said. And you ate fruit from the tree that I commanded you not to eat from.

"So I will put a curse on the ground.
    You will have to work very hard
        for food.
In pain you will eat its food
    all the days of your life.
¹⁸The ground will produce thorns and
    weeds for you.

And you will eat the plants of the
field.
19You will sweat and work hard
for your food.
Later you will return to the ground.
This is because you were taken
from the ground.
You are dust.
And when you die, you will return
to the dust."

20The man named his wife Eve.[n] This
is because she is the mother of everyone
who ever lived.

21The Lord God made clothes from
animal skins for the man and his wife.
And so the Lord dressed them. 22Then
the Lord God said, "Look, the man has
become like one of us. He knows good
and evil. And now we must keep him
from eating some of the fruit from the
tree of life. If he does, he will live forever."
23So the Lord God forced the man out of
the garden of Eden. He had to work the
ground he was taken from. 24God forced
the man out of the garden. Then God put
angels on the east side of the garden. He
also put a sword of fire there. It flashed
around in every direction. This kept
people from getting to the tree of life.

THE FIRST FAMILY

4 Adam had sexual relations with his
wife Eve. She became pregnant and
gave birth to Cain.[n] Eve said, "With the
Lord's help, I have given birth to a man."
2After that, Eve gave birth to Cain's
brother Abel. Abel took care of sheep.
Cain became a farmer.

3Later, Cain brought a gift to God. He
brought some food from the ground.
4Abel brought the best parts of his best
sheep. The Lord accepted Abel and his
gift. 5But God did not accept Cain and his
gift. Cain became very angry and looked
unhappy.

6The Lord asked Cain, "Why are you
angry? Why do you look so unhappy? 7If
you do good, I will accept you. But if you
do not do good, sin is ready to attack you.
Sin wants you. But you must rule over it."

8Cain said to his brother Abel, "Let's
go out into the field." So Cain and Abel
went into the field. Then Cain attacked
his brother Abel and killed him.

9Later, the Lord said to Cain, "Where
is your brother Abel?"

Cain answered, "I don't know. Is it my
job to take care of my brother?"

10Then the Lord said, "What have you
done? Your brother's blood is on the
ground. That blood is like a voice that tells
me what happened. 11And now you will be
cursed in your work with the ground. It is
the same ground where your brother's
blood fell. Your hands killed him. 12You
will work the ground. But it will not grow
good crops for you anymore. You will
wander around on the earth."

13Then Cain said to the Lord, "This
punishment is more than I can stand!
14Look! You have forced me to stop
working the ground. And now I must
hide from you. I will wander around on
the earth. And anyone who meets me
can kill me."

15Then the Lord said to Cain, "No! If
anyone kills you, I will punish that person
seven times more." Then the Lord put a
mark on Cain. It was a warning to anyone
who met him not to kill him.

CAIN'S FAMILY

16Then Cain went away from the Lord.
Cain lived in the land of Nod,[n] east of
Eden. 17Cain had sexual relations with his
wife. She became pregnant and gave birth
to Enoch. At that time Cain was building
a city. He named it after his son Enoch.
18Enoch had a son named Irad. Irad had a
son named Mehujael. Mehujael had a

3:20 **Eve** This name sounds like the Hebrew word meaning "alive."
4:1 **Cain** This name sounds like the Hebrew word for "I have given birth."
4:16 **Nod** This name sounds like the Hebrew word for "wander."

son named Methushael. And Methushael had a son named Lamech.

[19]Lamech married two women. One wife was named Adah, and the other was Zillah. [20]Adah gave birth to Jabal. He was the first person to live in tents and raise cattle. [21]Jabal's brother was Jubal. Jubal was the first person to play the harp and flute. [22]Zillah gave birth to Tubal-Cain. He made tools out of bronze and iron. The sister of Tubal-Cain was Naamah.

[23]Lamech said to his wives:

"Adah and Zillah, hear my voice!
    You wives of Lamech, listen to what
        I say.
I killed a man for wounding me.
    I killed a young man for hitting me.
[24]Cain's killer may be punished 7 times.
    Then Lamech's killer will be
        punished 77 times."

ADAM AND EVE HAVE A NEW SON

[25]Adam had sexual relations with his wife Eve again. And she gave birth to a son. She named him Seth.[n] Eve said, "God has given me another child. He will take the place of Abel, who was killed by Cain." [26]Seth also had a son. They named him Enosh. At that time people began to pray to the Lord.

ADAM'S FAMILY HISTORY

5 This is the family history of Adam. When God created human beings, he made them in God's likeness. [2]He created them male and female. And on that day he blessed them and named them human beings.

[3]When Adam was 130 years old, he became the father of another son. He was in the likeness and image of Adam. Adam named him Seth. [4]After Seth was born, Adam lived 800 years. During that time he had other sons and daughters. [5]So Adam lived a total of 930 years. Then he died.

[6]When Seth was 105 years old, he had a son named Enosh. [7]After Enosh was born,

Seth lived 807 years. During that time he had other sons and daughters. [8]So Seth lived a total of 912 years. Then he died.

[9]When Enosh was 90 years old, he had a son named Kenan. [10]After Kenan was born, Enosh lived 815 years. During that time he had other sons and daughters. [11]So Enosh lived a total of 905 years. Then he died.

[12]When Kenan was 70 years old, he had a son named Mahalalel. [13]After Mahalalel was born, Kenan lived 840 years. During that time he had other sons and daughters. [14]So Kenan lived a total of 910 years. Then he died.

[15]When Mahalalel was 65 years old, he had a son named Jared. [16]After Jared was born, Mahalalel lived 830 years. During that time he had other sons and daughters. [17]So Mahalalel lived a total of 895 years. Then he died.

[18]When Jared was 162 years old, he had a son named Enoch. [19]After Enoch was born, Jared lived 800 years. During that time he had other sons and daughters. [20]So Jared lived a total of 962 years. Then he died.

[21]When Enoch was 65 years old, he had a son named Methuselah. [22]After Methuselah was born, Enoch walked with God 300 years more. During that time he had other sons and daughters. [23]So Enoch lived a total of 365 years. [24]Enoch walked with God. One day Enoch could not be found, because God took him.

[25]When Methuselah was 187 years old, he had a son named Lamech. [26]After Lamech was born, Methuselah lived 782 years. During that time he had other sons and daughters. [27]So Methuselah lived a total of 969 years. Then he died.

[28]When Lamech was 182, he had a son. [29]Lamech named his son Noah.[n] Lamech said, "Noah will comfort us from the pain of our work. The pain is because God has

4:25 Seth This name sounds like the Hebrew word for "to give."
5:29 Noah This name sounds like the Hebrew word for "rest."

cursed the ground." [30]After Noah was born, Lamech lived 595 years. During that time he had other sons and daughters. [31]So Lamech lived a total of 777 years. Then he died.

[32]After Noah was 500 years old, he became the father of Shem, Ham and Japheth.

THE HUMAN RACE BECOMES EVIL

6 The number of people on earth began to grow. Daughters were born to these people. [2]The sons of God saw that these girls were beautiful. And they married any of them they chose. [3]The Lord said, "My Spirit[d] will not remain in human beings forever. This is because they are flesh. They will live only 120 years."

[4]The Nephilim[d] were on the earth in those days and also later. That was when the sons of God had sexual relations with the daughters of men. These women gave birth to children, who became famous. They were the mighty warriors of long ago.

[5]The Lord saw that the human beings on the earth were very wicked. He also saw that their thoughts were only about evil all the time. [6]The Lord was sorry he had made human beings on the earth. His heart was filled with pain. [7]So the Lord said, "I will destroy all human beings that I made on the earth. And I will destroy every animal and everything that crawls on the earth. I will also destroy the birds of the air. This is because I am sorry that I have made them." [8]But Noah pleased the Lord.

NOAH AND THE GREAT FLOOD

[9]This is the family history of Noah. Noah was a good man. He was the most innocent man of his time. He walked with God. [10]Noah had three sons: Shem, Ham and Japheth.

[11]People on earth did what God said was evil. Violence was everywhere. [12]And God saw this evil. All people on the earth did only evil. [13]So God said to Noah, "People have made the earth full of violence. So I will destroy all people from the earth. [14]Build a boat of cypress wood for yourself. Make rooms in it and cover it inside and outside with tar. [15]This is how big I want you to build the boat: 450 feet long, 75 feet wide and 45 feet high. [16]Make an opening around the top of the boat. Make it 18 inches high from the edge of the roof down. Put a door in the side of the boat. Make an upper, middle and lower deck in it. [17]I will bring a flood of water on the earth. I will destroy all living things that live under the sky. This includes everything that has the breath of life. Everything on the earth will die. [18]But I will make an agreement with you. You, your sons, your wife and your sons' wives will all go into the boat. [19]Also, you must bring into the boat two of every living thing, male and female. Keep them alive with you. [20]There will be two of every kind of bird, animal and crawling thing. They will come to you to be kept alive. [21]Also gather some of every kind of food. Store it on the boat as food for you and the animals."

[22]Noah did everything that God commanded him.

THE FLOOD BEGINS

7 Then the Lord said to Noah, "I have seen that you are the best man among the people of this time. So you and your family go into the boat. [2]Take with you seven pairs, each male with its female, of every kind of clean[d] animal. And take one pair, each male with its female, of every kind of unclean animal. [3]Take seven pairs of all the birds of the sky, each male with its female. This will allow all these animals to continue living on the earth after the flood. [4]Seven days from now I will send rain on the earth. It will rain 40 days and 40 nights. I will destroy from the earth every living thing that I made."

[5]Noah did everything that the Lord commanded him.

[6]Noah was 600 years old when the flood came. [7]He and his wife and his sons and their wives went into the boat. They went in to escape the waters of the flood. [8]The clean animals, the unclean animals, the birds and everything that crawls on the ground [9]came to Noah. They went into the boat in groups of two, male and female. This was just as God had commanded Noah. [10]Seven days later the flood started.

[11]Noah was now 600 years old. The flood started on the seventeenth day of the second month of that year. That day the underground springs split open. And the clouds in the sky poured out rain. [12]The rain fell on the earth for 40 days and 40 nights.

[13]On that same day Noah and his wife, his sons Shem, Ham and Japheth and their wives went into the boat. [14]They had every kind of wild animal and tame animal. There was every kind of animal that crawls on the earth. Every kind of bird was there. [15]They all came to Noah in the boat in groups of two. There was every creature that had the breath of life. [16]One male and one female of every living thing came. It was just as God had commanded Noah. Then the Lord closed the door behind them.

[17]Water flooded the earth for 40 days. As the water rose, it lifted the boat off the ground. [18]The water continued to rise, and the boat floated on the water above the earth. [19]The water rose so much that even the highest mountains under the sky were covered by it. [20]The water continued to rise until it was more than 20 feet above the mountains.

[21]All living things that moved on the earth died. This included all the birds, tame animals, wild animals and creatures that swarm on the earth. And all human beings died. [22]So everything on dry land died. This means everything that had the breath of life in its nose. [23]So God destroyed from the earth every living thing that was on the land. This was every man, animal, crawling thing and bird of the sky. All that was left was Noah and what was with him in the boat. [24]And the waters continued to cover the earth for 150 days.

THE FLOOD ENDS

8 But God remembered Noah and all the wild animals and tame animals with him in the boat. God made a wind blow over the earth. And the water went down. [2]The underground springs stopped flowing. And the clouds in the sky stopped pouring down rain. [3-4]The water that covered the earth began to go down. After 150 days the water had gone down so much that the boat touched land again. It came to rest on one of the mountains of Ararat.[n] This was on the seventeenth day of the seventh month. [5]The water continued to go down. By the first day of the tenth month the tops of the mountains could be seen.

[6]Forty days later Noah opened the window he had made in the boat. [7]He sent out a raven. It flew here and there until the water had dried up from the earth. [8]Then Noah sent out a dove. This was to find out if the water had dried up from the ground. [9]The dove could not find a place to land because water still covered the earth. So it came back to the boat. Noah reached out his hand and took the bird. And he brought it back into the boat.

[10]After seven days Noah again sent out the dove from the boat. [11]And that evening it came back to him with a fresh olive leaf in its mouth. Then Noah knew that the ground was almost dry. [12]Seven days later he sent the dove out again. But this time it did not come back.

[13]Noah was now 601 years old. It was the first day of the first month of that

8:3-4 **Ararat** The ancient land of Urartu, an area in Eastern Turkey.

year. The water was dried up from the land. Noah removed the covering of the boat and saw that the land was dry. ¹⁴By the twenty-seventh day of the second month the land was completely dry.

¹⁵Then God said to Noah, ¹⁶"You and your wife, your sons and their wives should go out of the boat. ¹⁷Bring every animal out of the boat with you—the birds, animals and everything that crawls on the earth. Let them have many young ones and let them grow in number."

¹⁸So Noah went out with his sons, his wife and his sons' wives. ¹⁹Every animal, everything that crawls on the earth and every bird went out of the boat. They left by families.

²⁰Then Noah built an altar to the Lord. Noah took some of all the clean*d* birds and animals. And he burned them on the altar as offerings to God. ²¹The Lord was pleased with these sacrifices. He said to himself, "I will never again curse the ground because of human beings. Their thoughts are evil even when they are young. But I will never again destroy every living thing on the earth as I did this time.

²²"As long as the earth continues,
there will be planting and harvest.
Cold and hot,
summer and winter,
day and night
will not stop."

THE NEW BEGINNING

9 Then God blessed Noah and his sons. He said to them, "Have many children. Grow in number and fill the earth. ²Every animal on earth and every bird in the sky will respect and fear you. So will every animal that crawls on the ground and every fish in the sea respect and fear you. I have given them to you. ³"Everything that moves, everything that is alive, is yours for food. Earlier I gave you the green plants. And now I give you everything for food. ⁴But you must not eat meat that still has blood in

it, because blood gives life. ⁵I will demand your blood for your lives. That is, I will demand the life of any animal that kills a person. And I will demand the life of anyone who takes another person's life.

⁶"Whoever kills a human being
will be killed by a human being.
This is because God made humans
in his own image.

⁷"Noah, I want you and your family to have many children. Grow in number on the earth and become many."

⁸Then God said to Noah and his sons, ⁹"Now I am making my agreement with you and your people who will live after you. ¹⁰And I also make it with every living thing that is with you. It is with the birds, the tame animals and the wild animals. It is with all that came out of the boat with you. I make my agreement with every living thing on earth. ¹¹I make this agreement with you: I will never again destroy all living things by flood-waters. A flood will never again destroy the earth."

¹²And God said, "I am making an agreement between me and you and every living creature that is with you. It will continue from now on. This is the sign: ¹³I am putting my rainbow in the clouds. It is the sign of the agreement between me and the earth. ¹⁴When I bring clouds over the earth, a rainbow appears in the clouds. ¹⁵Then I will remember my agreement. It is between me and you and every living thing. Floodwaters will never again destroy all life on the earth. ¹⁶When the rainbow appears in the clouds, I will see it. Then I will remember the agreement that continues forever. It is between me and every living thing on the earth."

¹⁷So God said to Noah, "That rainbow is a sign. It is the sign of the agreement that I made with all living things on earth."

NOAH AND HIS SONS

¹⁸The sons of Noah came out of the boat with him. They were Shem, Ham and Japheth. (Ham was the father of

Canaan.) ¹⁹These three men were Noah's sons. And all the people on earth came from these three sons.

²⁰Noah became a farmer and planted a vineyard. ²¹He drank wine made from his grapes. Then he became drunk and lay naked in his tent. ²²Ham, the father of Canaan, looked at his naked father. Ham told his brothers outside. ²³Then Shem and Japheth got a coat and carried it on both their shoulders. They walked backwards into the tent and covered their father. They turned their faces away. In this way they did not see their father without clothes.

²⁴Noah was sleeping because of the wine. Later he woke up. Then he learned what his youngest son, Ham, had done to him. ²⁵So Noah said,

"May there be a curse on Canaan!
    May he be the lowest slave to his
        brothers."
²⁶Noah also said,
"May the Lord, the God of Shem, be
        praised!
    May Canaan be Shem's slave.
²⁷May God give more land to Japheth.
    May Japheth live in Shem's tents,
        and may Canaan be their slave."

²⁸After the flood Noah lived 350 years. ²⁹He lived a total of 950 years. Then he died.

NATIONS GROW AND SPREAD

10 This is the family history of the sons of Noah: Shem, Ham and Japheth. After the flood these three men had sons.

JAPHETH'S SONS

²The sons of Japheth were Gomer, Magog, Madai, Javan, Tubal, Meshech and Tiras.

³The sons of Gomer were Ashkenaz, Riphath and Togarmah.

⁴The sons of Javan were Elishah, Tarshish, Kittim[n] and Rodanim. ⁵Those who lived in the lands around the Mediterranean Sea came from these sons of Japheth. All the families grew and became different nations. Each nation had its own land and its own language.

HAM'S SONS

⁶The sons of Ham were Cush, Mizraim,[n] Put and Canaan.

⁷The sons of Cush were Seba, Havilah, Sabtah, Raamah and Sabteca.

The sons of Raamah were Sheba and Dedan.

⁸Cush also had a descendant[d] named Nimrod. Nimrod became a very powerful man on earth. ⁹He was a great hunter before the Lord. That is why people say someone is "like Nimrod, a great hunter before the Lord." ¹⁰At first Nimrod's kingdom covered Babylon, Erech, Akkad and Calneh in the land of Babylonia. ¹¹From there he went to Assyria. There he built the cities of Nineveh, Rehoboth Ir and Calah. ¹²He also built Resen, the great city between Nineveh and Calah.

¹³Mizraim was the father of the Ludites, Anamites, Lehabites, Naphtuhites, ¹⁴Pathrusites, Casluhites and the people of Crete. (The Philistines came from the Casluhites.)

¹⁵Canaan was the father of Sidon his first son and of Heth. ¹⁶Canaan was also the father of the Jebusites, Amorites, Girgashites, ¹⁷Hivites, Arkites, Sinites, ¹⁸Arvadites, Zemarites and Hamathites. The families of the Canaanites scattered. ¹⁹The land of the Canaanites reached from Sidon to Gerar as far as Gaza. And it reached to Sodom, Gomorrah, Admah and Zeboiim, as far as Lasha.

²⁰All these people were the sons of Ham. All these families had their own languages, their own lands and their own nations.

SHEM'S SONS

²¹Shem, Japheth's older brother, also had sons. One of his descendants[d] was the father of all the sons of Eber.

10:4 Kittim His descendants were the people of Cyprus.
10:6 Mizraim This is another name for Egypt.

²²The sons of Shem were Elam, Asshur, Arphaxad, Lud and Aram.

²³The sons of Aram were Uz, Hul, Gether and Meshech.

²⁴Arphaxad was the father of Shelah. Shelah was the father of Eber. ²⁵Eber was the father of two sons. One son was named Peleg[n] because the earth was divided during his life. Eber's other son was named Joktan.

²⁶Joktan was the father of Almodad, Sheleph, Hazarmaveth, Jerah, ²⁷Hadoram, Uzal, Diklah, ²⁸Obal, Abimael, Sheba, ²⁹Ophir, Havilah and Jobab. All these people were the sons of Joktan. ³⁰These people lived in the area between Mesha and Sephar in the hill country in the East.

³¹These are the people from the family of Shem. They are arranged by families, languages, countries and nations.

³²This is the list of the families from the sons of Noah. They are arranged according to their nations. From these families came all the nations who spread across the earth after the flood.

THE LANGUAGES CONFUSED

11 At this time the whole world spoke one language. Everyone used the same words. ²As people moved from the East, they found a plain in the land of Babylonia. They settled there to live.

³They said to each other, "Let's make bricks and bake them to make them hard." So they used bricks instead of stones, and tar instead of mortar. ⁴Then they said to each other, "Let's build for ourselves a city and a tower. And let's make the top of the tower reach high into the sky. We will become famous. If we do this, we will not be scattered over all the earth."

⁵The Lord came down to see the city and the tower that the people had built. ⁶The Lord said, "Now, these people are united. They all speak the same language. This is only the beginning of what they will do. They will be able to do anything they want. ⁷Come, let us go down and confuse their language. Then they will not be able to understand each other."

⁸So the Lord scattered them from there over all the earth. And they stopped building the city. ⁹That is where the Lord confused the language of the whole world. So the place is called Babel.[n] So the Lord caused them to spread out from there over all the whole world.

THE STORY OF SHEM'S FAMILY

¹⁰This is the family history of Shem. Two years after the flood, when Shem was 100 years old, his son Arphaxad was born. ¹¹After that, Shem lived 500 years and had other sons and daughters.

¹²When Arphaxad was 35 years old, his son Shelah was born. ¹³After that, Arphaxad lived 403 years and had other sons and daughters.

¹⁴When Shelah was 30 years old, his son Eber was born. ¹⁵After that, Shelah lived 403 years and had other sons and daughters.

¹⁶When Eber was 34 years old, his son Peleg was born. ¹⁷After that, Eber lived 430 years and had other sons and daughters.

¹⁸When Peleg was 30 years old, his son Reu was born. ¹⁹After that, Peleg lived 209 years and had other sons and daughters.

²⁰When Reu was 32 years old, his son Serug was born. ²¹After that, Reu lived 207 years and had other sons and daughters.

²²When Serug was 30 years old, his son Nahor was born. ²³After that, Serug lived 200 years and had other sons and daughters.

²⁴When Nahor was 29 years old, his son Terah was born. ²⁵After that, Nahor lived 119 years and had other sons and daughters.

10:25 Peleg This name sounds like the Hebrew word for "divided."
11:9 Babel This name sounds like the Hebrew word for "confused."

[26]After Terah was 70 years old, his sons Abram, Nahor and Haran were born.

THE STORY OF TERAH'S FAMILY

[27]This is the family history of Terah. Terah was the father of Abram, Nahor and Haran. Haran was the father of Lot. [28]Haran died while his father, Terah, was still alive. This happened in Ur in Babylonia, where he was born. [29]Abram and Nahor both married. Abram's wife was named Sarai. Nahor's wife was named Milcah. She was the daughter of Haran. Haran was the father of Milcah and Iscah. [30]Sarai was not able to have children.

[31]Terah took his son Abram, his grandson Lot (Haran's son) and his daughter-in-law Sarai (Abram's wife). They moved out of Ur of Babylonia. They had planned to go to the land of Canaan. But when they reached the city of Haran, they settled there.

[32]Terah lived to be 205 years old. Then he died in Haran.

GOD CALLS ABRAM

12 Then the Lord said to Abram, "Leave your country, your relatives and your father's family. Go to the land I will show you.

[2]I will make you a great nation,
    and I will bless you.
I will make you famous.
    And you will be a blessing to others.
[3]I will bless those who bless you.
    I will place a curse on those who
        harm you.
And all the people on earth
    will be blessed through you."

[4]So Abram left Haran as the Lord had told him. And Lot went with him. At this time Abram was 75 years old. [5]Abram took his wife Sarai, his nephew Lot and everything they owned. They took all the servants they had gotten in Haran. They set out from Haran, planning to go to the land of Canaan. In time they arrived there.

[6]Abram traveled through that land. He went as far as the great tree of Moreh at Shechem. The Canaanites were living in the land at that time. [7]The Lord appeared to Abram. The Lord said, "I will give this land to your descendants."[d] So Abram built an altar there to the Lord, who had appeared to him. [8]Then Abram traveled from Shechem to the mountain east of Bethel. And he set up his tent there. Bethel was to the west, and Ai was to the east. There Abram built another altar to the Lord and worshiped him. [9]After this, he traveled on toward southern Canaan.

ABRAM GOES TO EGYPT

[10]At this time there was not much food in the land. So Abram went down to Egypt to live because there was so little food. [11]Just before they arrived in Egypt, Abram said to his wife Sarai, "I know you are a very beautiful woman. [12]When the Egyptians see you, they will say, 'This woman is his wife.' Then they will kill me but let you live. [13]Tell them you are my sister. Then things will go well with me. And I may be allowed to live because of you."

[14]So Abram went into Egypt. The people of Egypt saw that Sarai was very beautiful. [15]Some of the Egyptian officers saw her also. They told the king of Egypt how beautiful she was. They took her to the king's palace. [16]The king was kind to Abram because he thought Abram was Sarai's brother. He gave Abram sheep, cattle and male and female donkeys. Abram also was given male and female servants and camels.

[17]But the Lord sent terrible diseases on the king and all the people in his house. This was because of Abram's wife Sarai. [18]So the king sent for Abram. The king said, "What have you done to me? Why didn't you tell me Sarai was your wife? [19]Why did you say, 'She is my sister'? I made her my wife. But now here is your wife. Take her and leave!" [20]Then the king commanded his men to make Abram leave Egypt. So Abram and his wife left with everything they owned.

ABRAM AND LOT SEPARATE

13 So Abram, his wife and Lot left Egypt. They took everything they owned and traveled to southern Canaan. ²Abram was very rich in cattle, silver and gold.

³He left southern Canaan and went back to Bethel. He went where he had camped before, between Bethel and Ai. ⁴It was the place where Abram had built an altar before. So he worshiped the Lord there.

⁵During this time Lot was traveling with Abram. Lot also had many sheep, cattle and tents. ⁶Abram and Lot had so many animals that the land could not support both of them together. ⁷Abram's herders and Lot's herders began to argue. The Canaanites and the Perizzites were living in the land at this time.

⁸So Abram said to Lot, "There should be no arguing between you and me. Your herders and mine should not argue either. We are brothers. ⁹We should separate. The whole land is there in front of you. If you go to the left, I will go to the right. If you go to the right, I will go to the left."

¹⁰Lot looked all around and saw the whole Jordan Valley. He saw that there was much water there. It was like the Lord's garden, like the land of Egypt in the direction of Zoar. (This was before the Lord destroyed Sodom and Gomorrah.) ¹¹So Lot chose to move east and live in the Jordan Valley. In this way Abram and Lot separated. ¹²Abram lived in the land of Canaan. But Lot lived among the cities in the Jordan Valley. He moved very near to Sodom. ¹³Now the people of Sodom were very evil. They were always sinning against the Lord.

¹⁴After Lot left, the Lord said to Abram, "Look all around you. Look north and south and east and west. ¹⁵All this land that you see I will give to you and your descendants*d* forever. ¹⁶I will make your descendants as many as the dust of the earth. If anyone could count the dust on the earth, he could count your people. ¹⁷Get up! Walk through all this land. I am now giving it to you."

¹⁸So Abram moved his tents. He went to live near the great trees of Mamre. This was at the city of Hebron. There he built an altar to the Lord.

LOT IS CAPTURED

14 Now Amraphel was king of Babylonia. Arioch was king of Ellasar. Kedorlaomer was king of Elam. And Tidal was king of Goiim. ²All these kings went to war against several other kings: Bera king of Sodom, Birsha king of Gomorrah, Shinab king of Admah, Shemeber king of Zeboiim and the king of Bela. (Bela is also called Zoar.)

³These kings who were attacked united their armies in the Valley of Siddim. (The Valley of Siddim is now the Dead Sea.*d*) ⁴These kings had served Kedorlaomer for 12 years. But in the thirteenth year, they all turned against him. ⁵Then in the fourteenth year, Kedorlaomer and the kings with him came and defeated the Rephaites*d* in Ashteroth Karnaim. They also defeated the Zuzites in Ham and the Emites in Shaveh Kiriathaim. ⁶And they defeated the Horites in the mountains of Edom to El Paran. (El Paran is near the desert.) ⁷Then they turned back and went to En Mishpat (that is, Kadesh). They defeated all the Amalekites. They also defeated the Amorites who lived in Hazazon Tamar.

⁸At that time the kings of Sodom, Gomorrah, Admah, Zeboiim and Bela went out to fight in the Valley of Siddim. (Bela is called Zoar.) ⁹They fought against Kedorlaomer king of Elam, Tidal king of Goiim, Amraphel king of Babylonia, and Arioch king of Ellasar. So there were four kings fighting against five. ¹⁰There were many tar pits in the Valley of Siddim. The kings of Sodom and Gomorrah and their armies ran away. Some of the soldiers fell into the tar pits. But the others ran away to the mountains.

¹¹Now Kedorlaomer and his armies took everything the people of Sodom and Gomorrah owned. They also took all their food. ¹²They took Lot, Abram's nephew who was living in Sodom. The enemy also took everything he owned. Then they left. ¹³One of the men who was not captured went to Abram, the Hebrew. He told Abram what had happened. At that time Abram was camped near the great trees of Mamre the Amorite. Mamre was a brother of Eshcol and a brother of Aner. And they had all made an agreement to help Abram.

ABRAM RESCUES LOT

¹⁴Abram learned that Lot had been captured. So he called out his 318 trained men who had been born in his camp. Abram led the men and chased the enemy all the way to the town of Dan. ¹⁵That night he divided his men into groups. And they made a surprise attack against the enemy. They chased them all the way to Hobah, north of Damascus. ¹⁶Then Abram brought back everything the enemy had stolen. Abram brought back the women and the other people. And he also brought back Lot and everything Lot owned.

¹⁷After defeating Kedorlaomer and the kings who were with him, Abram went home. As Abram was returning, the king of Sodom came out to meet him in the Valley of Shaveh. (That is now called King's Valley.)

¹⁸Melchizedek king of Salem also went to meet Abram. Melchizedek was a priest for God Most High. He brought bread and wine. ¹⁹Melchizedek blessed Abram and said,

"Abram, may God Most High give you
    blessings.
God made heaven and earth.
²⁰And we praise God Most High.
He has helped you to defeat your
    enemies."

Then Abram gave Melchizedek a tenth of everything he had brought back from the battle.

²¹Then the king of Sodom said to Abram, "You may keep all these things for yourself. Just give me my people who were captured."

²²But Abram said to the king of Sodom, "I make a promise to the Lord. He is the God Most High, who made heaven and earth. ²³I promise that I will not keep anything that is yours. I will not keep even a thread or a sandal strap. That way you cannot say, 'I made Abram rich.' ²⁴I will keep nothing but the food my young men have eaten. But give Aner, Eshcol and Mamre their share of what we won. They went with me into battle."

GOD'S AGREEMENT WITH ABRAM

15 After these things happened, the Lord spoke his word to Abram in a vision. God said, "Abram, don't be afraid. I will defend you. And I will give you a great reward."

²But Abram said, "Lord God, what can you give me? I have no son. So my slave Eliezer from Damascus will get everything I own after I die." ³Abram said, "Look, you have given me no son. So a slave born in my house will inherit everything I have."

⁴Then the Lord spoke his word to Abram. He said, "That slave will not be the one to inherit what you have. You will have a son of your own. And your son will inherit what you have."

⁵Then God led Abram outside. God said, "Look at the sky. There are so many stars you cannot count them. And your descendants^d will be too many to count."

⁶Abram believed the Lord. And the Lord accepted Abram's faith, and that faith made him right with God.

⁷God said to Abram, "I am the Lord who led you out of Ur of Babylonia. I did that so I could give you this land to own."

⁸But Abram said, "Lord God, how can I be sure that I will own this land?"

⁹The Lord said to Abram, "Bring me a three-year-old cow, a three-year-old goat

and a three-year-old male sheep. Also bring me a dove and a young pigeon."

[10]Abram brought them all to God. Then Abram killed the animals and cut each of them into two pieces. He laid each half opposite the other half. But he did not cut the birds in half. [11]Later, large birds flew down to eat the animals. But Abram chased them away.

[12]As the sun was going down, Abram fell into a deep sleep. While he was asleep, a very terrible darkness came. [13]Then the Lord said to Abram, "You can be sure that your descendants will be strangers and travel in a land they don't own. The people there will make them slaves. And they will do cruel things to them for 400 years. [14]But I will punish the nation where they are slaves. Then your descendants will leave that land, taking great wealth with them. [15]Abram, you will live to be very old. You will die in peace and will be buried. [16]After your great-great-grand-children are born, your people will come to this land again. It will take that long, because the Amorites are not yet evil enough to punish."

[17]The sun went down, and it was very dark. Suddenly a smoking firepot and a blazing torch passed between the halves of the dead animals.[n] [18]So on that day the Lord made an agreement with Abram. The Lord said, "I will give this land to your descendants. I will give them the land between the river of Egypt and the great river Euphrates. [19]This is the land of the Kenites, Kenizzites, Kad-monites, [20]Hittites, Perizzites, Rephaites,[d] [21]Amorites, Canaanites, Girgashites and Jebusites."

HAGAR AND ISHMAEL

16 Sarai, Abram's wife, had no children. She had a slave girl from Egypt named Hagar. [2]Sarai said to Abram, "Look, the Lord has not allowed me to have children. So have sexual relations with my slave girl. If she has a child, maybe I can have my own family through her."

Abram did what Sarai said. [3]This was after Abram lived ten years in Canaan. And Sarai gave Hagar to her husband Abram. (Hagar was her slave girl from Egypt.)

[4]Abram had sexual relations with Hagar, and she became pregnant. When Hagar learned she was pregnant, she began to treat her mistress Sarai badly. [5]Then Sarai said to Abram, "This is your fault. I gave my slave girl to you. And when she became pregnant, she began to treat me badly. Let the Lord decide who is right—you or me."

[6]But Abram said to Sarai, "You are Hagar's mistress. Do anything you want to her." Then Sarai was hard on Hagar, and Hagar ran away.

[7]The angel of the Lord found Hagar beside a spring of water in the desert. The spring was by the road to Shur. [8]The angel said, "Hagar, you are Sarai's slave girl. Where have you come from? Where are you going?"

Hagar answered, "I am running from my mistress Sarai."

[9]The angel of the Lord said to her, "Go home to your mistress and obey her." [10]The angel of the Lord also said, "I will give you so many descendants[d] they cannot be counted."

[11]The angel also said to her,

"You are now pregnant,
    and you will have a son.
You will name him Ishmael,[n]
    because the Lord has heard your
        cries.
[12]Ishmael will be like a wild donkey.
    He will be against everyone.
    And everyone will be against him.
    He will attack all his brothers."

15:17 passed . . . animals This showed that God sealed the agreement between himself and Abram.
16:11 Ishmael The Hebrew words for "Ishmael" and "has heard" sound similar.

[13]The slave girl gave a name to the Lord who spoke to her. She said to him, "You are 'God who sees me.'" This is because she said to herself, "Have I really seen God who sees me?" [14]So the well there was called Beer Lahai Roi.[n] It is between Kadesh and Bered.

[15]Hagar gave birth to a son for Abram. And Abram named him Ishmael. [16]Abram was 86 years old when Hagar gave birth to Ishmael.

PROOF OF THE AGREEMENT

17 When Abram was 99 years old, the Lord appeared to him. The Lord said, "I am God All-Powerful. Obey me and do what is right. [2]I will make an agreement between us. I will make you the ancestor of many people."

[3]Then Abram bowed facedown on the ground. God said to him, [4]"I am making my agreement with you: I will make you the father of many nations. [5]I am changing your name from Abram[n] to Abraham.[n] This is because I am making you a father of many nations. [6]I will give you many descendants.[d] New nations will be born from you. Kings will come from you. [7]And I will make an agreement between me and you and all your descendants from now on: I will be your God and the God of all your descendants. [8]You live in the land of Canaan now as a stranger. But I will give you and your descendants all this land forever. And I will be the God of your descendants."

[9]Then God said to Abraham, "You and your descendants must keep this agreement from now on. [10]This is my agreement with you and all your descendants: Every male among you must be circumcised.[d] You must obey this agreement.

[11]Cut away the foreskin to show that you follow the agreement between me and you. [12]From now on when a baby boy is eight days old, you will circumcise him. This includes any boy born among your people or any who is your slave. (He would not be one of your descendants.) [13]So circumcise every baby boy. Circumcise him whether he is born in your family or bought as a slave. Your bodies will be marked. This will show that you are part of my agreement that lasts forever. [14]Any male who is not circumcised will be separated from his people. He has broken my agreement."

ISAAC—THE PROMISED SON

[15]God said to Abraham, "I will change the name of Sarai,[n] your wife. Her new name will be Sarah.[n] [16]I will bless her. I will give her a son, and you will be the father. She will be the mother of many nations. Kings of nations will come from her."

[17]Abraham bowed facedown on the ground and laughed. He said to himself, "Can a man have a child when he is 100 years old? Can Sarah give birth to a child when she is 90?" [18]Then Abraham said to God, "Please let Ishmael be the son you promised."

[19]God said, "No. Sarah your wife will have a son, and you will name him Isaac.[n] I will make my agreement with him. It will be an agreement that continues forever with all his descendants.[d]

[20]"You asked me about Ishmael, and I heard you. I will bless him. I will give him many descendants. And I will cause their numbers to grow very greatly. He will be the father of 12 great leaders. I will make him into a great nation. [21]But I will make

16:14 **Beer Lahai Roi** This means "the well of the Living One who sees me."
17:5 **Abram** This name means "honored father."
17:5 **Abraham** The end of the Hebrew word for "Abraham" sounds like the beginning of the Hebrew word for "many."
17:15 **Sarai** An Aramaic name meaning "princess."
17:15 **Sarah** A Hebrew name meaning "princess."
17:19 **Isaac** The Hebrew words for "he laughed" (vs. 17) and "Isaac" sound the same.

my agreement with Isaac. He is the son whom Sarah will have at this same time next year." ²²After God finished talking with Abraham, God rose and left him.

²³Then Abraham gathered Ishmael and all the males born in his camp. He also gathered the slaves he had bought. So that day Abraham circumcised every man and boy in his camp. This was what God had told him to do. ²⁴Abraham was 99 years old when he was circumcised. ²⁵And Ishmael, his son, was 13 years old when he was circumcised. ²⁶Abraham and his son were circumcised on that same day. ²⁷Also on that day all the men in Abraham's camp were circumcised. This included all those born in his camp and all the slaves he had bought from other nations.

THE THREE VISITORS

18 Later, the Lord again appeared to Abraham near the great trees of Mamre. At that time Abraham was sitting at the door of his tent. It was during the hottest part of the day. ²He looked up and saw three men standing near him. When Abraham saw them, he ran from his tent to meet them. He bowed facedown on the ground before them. ³Abraham said, "Sir, if you think well of me, please stay awhile with me, your servant. ⁴I will bring some water so all of you can wash your feet. You may rest under the tree. ⁵I will get some bread for you, so you can regain your strength. Then you may continue your journey."

The three men said, "That is fine. Do as you said."

⁶Abraham hurried to the tent where Sarah was. He said to her, "Hurry, prepare 20 quarts of fine flour. Make it into loaves of bread." ⁷Then Abraham ran to his cattle. He took one of his best calves and gave it to a servant. The servant hurried to kill the calf and to prepare it for food. ⁸Abraham gave the three men the calf that had been cooked. He also gave them milk curds and milk. While the

three men ate, he stood under the tree near them.

⁹The men asked Abraham, "Where is your wife Sarah?"

"There, in the tent," said Abraham.

¹⁰Then the Lord said, "I will certainly return to you about this time a year from now. At that time your wife Sarah will have a son."

Sarah was listening at the entrance of the tent which was behind him. ¹¹Abraham and Sarah were very old. Sarah was past the age when women normally have children. ¹²So she laughed to herself, "My husband and I are too old to have a baby."

¹³Then the Lord said to Abraham, "Why did Sarah laugh? Why did she say, 'I am too old to have a baby'? ¹⁴Is anything too hard for the Lord? No! I will return to you at the right time a year from now. And Sarah will have a son."

¹⁵Sarah was afraid. So she lied and said, "I didn't laugh."

But the Lord said, "No. You did laugh."

¹⁶Then the men got up to leave and started out toward Sodom. Abraham walked along with them a short time to send them on their way.

ABRAHAM'S BARGAIN WITH GOD

¹⁷The Lord said, "Should I tell Abraham what I am going to do now? ¹⁸Abraham's children will certainly become a great and powerful nation. And all nations on earth will be blessed through him. ¹⁹I have chosen him so he would command his children and his descendants^d to live the way the Lord wants them to. I did this so they would live right and be fair. Then I, the Lord, will give Abraham what I promised him."

²⁰Then the Lord said, "I have heard many things against the people of Sodom and Gomorrah. They are very evil. ²¹So I will go down and see if they are as bad as I have heard."

²²So the men turned and went toward Sodom. But Abraham stood there before

the Lord. ²³Then Abraham approached the Lord. Abraham asked, "Lord, do you plan to destroy the good persons along with the evil persons? ²⁴What if there are 50 good people in that city? Will you still destroy it? Surely you will save the city for the 50 good people living there. ²⁵Surely you will not destroy the good people along with the evil people. Then the good people and the evil people would be treated the same. You are the judge of all the earth. Won't you do what is right?"

²⁶Then the Lord said, "If I find 50 good people in the city of Sodom, I will save the whole city because of them."

²⁷Then Abraham said, "I am only dust and ashes. Yet I have been brave to speak to the Lord. ²⁸What if there are only 45 good people in the city? Will you destroy the whole city for the lack of 5 good people?"

The Lord said, "If I find 45 good people there, I will not destroy the city."

²⁹Again Abraham said to the Lord, "If you find only 40 good people there, will you destroy the city?"

The Lord said, "If I find 40 good people, I will not destroy the city."

³⁰Then Abraham said, "Lord, please don't be angry with me. Let me ask you this. If you find only 30 good people in the city, will you destroy it?"

The Lord said, "If I find 30 good people there, I will not destroy the city."

³¹Then Abraham said, "I have been brave to speak to the Lord. But what if there are 20 good people in the city?"

The Lord answered, "If I find 20 good people there, I will not destroy the city."

³²Then Abraham said, "Lord, please don't be angry with me. Let me bother you this one last time. What if you find 10 good people there?"

The Lord said, "If I find 10 good people there, I will not destroy it."

³³When the Lord finished speaking to Abraham, he left. And Abraham returned home.

LOT'S VISITORS

19 The two angels came to Sodom in the evening. Lot was sitting near the city gate and saw them. He got up and went to them and bowed facedown on the ground. ²Lot said, "Sirs, please come to my house and spend the night. There you can wash your feet. Then tomorrow you may continue your journey."

The angels answered, "No, we will spend the night in the city's public square."

³But Lot begged them to come to his house. So they agreed and went to his house. Then Lot prepared a meal for them. He baked bread without yeast, and they ate it.

⁴Before bedtime, all the men of the city surrounded Lot's house. These men were both young and old and came from every part of Sodom. ⁵They called to Lot, "Where are the two men who came to you tonight? Bring them out to us. We want to have sexual relations with them."

⁶Lot went outside to them, closing the door behind him. ⁷He said, "No, my brothers! Do not do this evil thing. ⁸Look! I have two daughters. They have never slept with a man. I will give them to you. You may do anything you want with them. But please don't do anything to these men. They have come to my house, and I must protect them."

⁹The men around the house answered, "Move out of the way!" Then they said to each other, "This man Lot came to our city as a stranger. Now he wants to tell us what to do!" They said to Lot, "We will do worse things to you than to them." So they started pushing Lot back. They were ready to break down the door.

¹⁰But the two men staying with Lot opened the door and pulled him back inside the house. Then they closed the door. ¹¹The two men struck the men outside the door with blindness. So these men, both young and old, could not find the door.

[12]The two men said to Lot, "Do you have any other relatives in this city? Do you have any sons-in-law, sons, daughters or any other relatives? If you do, tell them to leave now. [13]We are about to destroy this city. The Lord has heard of all the evil that is here. So he has sent us to destroy it."

[14]So Lot went out and spoke to his future sons-in-law. They were pledged to marry his daughters. Lot said, "Hurry and leave this city! The Lord is about to destroy it!" But they thought Lot was joking.

[15]At dawn the next morning, the angels begged Lot to hurry. They said, "Go! Take your wife and your two daughters with you. Then you will not be destroyed when the city is punished."

[16]But Lot delayed. So the two men took the hands of Lot, his wife and his two daughters. The men led them safely out of the city. So the Lord was merciful to Lot and his family. [17]The two men brought Lot and his family out of the city. Then one of the men said, "Run for your lives! Don't look back or stop anywhere in the valley. Run to the mountains or you will be destroyed."

[18]But Lot said to one of them, "Sir, please don't force me to go so far! [19]You have been merciful and kind to me. You have saved my life. But I can't run to the mountains. The disaster will catch me, and I will die. [20]Look, that little town over there is not too far away. Let me run there. It's really just a little town. I'll be safe there."

[21]The angel said to Lot, "Very well, I will allow you to do this also. I will not destroy that town. [22]But run there fast. I cannot destroy Sodom until you are safely in that town." (That town is named Zoar,[n] because it is little.)

SODOM AND GOMORRAH DESTROYED

[23]The sun had already come up when Lot entered Zoar. [24]The Lord sent a rain of burning sulfur down from the sky on Sodom and Gomorrah. [25]So the Lord destroyed those cities. He also destroyed the whole Jordan Valley, everyone living in the cities and even all the plants.

[26]At that point Lot's wife looked back. When she did, she became a pillar of salt.

[27]Early the next morning, Abraham got up and went to the place where he had stood before the Lord. [28]Abraham looked down toward Sodom and Gomorrah and all the Jordan Valley. He saw smoke rising from the land. It was like smoke from a furnace.

[29]God destroyed the cities in the valley. But he remembered what Abraham had asked. So God saved Lot's life. But he destroyed the city where Lot had lived.

LOT AND HIS DAUGHTERS

[30]Lot was afraid to continue living in Zoar. So he and his two daughters went to live in the mountains. They lived in a cave there. [31]One day the older daughter said to the younger, "Our father is old. Everywhere on the earth women and men marry. But there are no men around here for us to marry. [32]Let's get our father drunk. Then we can have sexual relations with him. We can use our father to have children. That way we can continue our family."

[33]That night the two girls got their father drunk. Then the older daughter went and had sexual relations with him. But Lot did not know when she lay down or when she got up.

[34]The next day the older daughter said to the younger, "Last night I had sexual relations with my father. Let's get him drunk again tonight. Then you can go and have sexual relations with him, too. In this way we can use our father to have children to continue our family." [35]So that night they got their father drunk again. Then the younger daughter went

---

19:22 Zoar This name sounds like the Hebrew word for "little."

and had sexual relations with him. Again, Lot did not know when she lay down or when she got up.

³⁶So both of Lot's daughters became pregnant by their father. ³⁷The older daughter gave birth to a son. She named him Moab. Moab is the ancestor of all the Moabite people who are still living today. ³⁸The younger daughter also gave birth to a son. She named him Ben-Ammi. He is the father of all the Ammonite people who are still living today.

ABRAHAM AND ABIMELECH

20 Abraham left Hebron and traveled to southern Canaan. He stayed awhile between Kadesh and Shur. Then he moved to Gerar. ²Abraham told people that his wife Sarah was his sister. Abimelech king of Gerar heard this. So he sent some servants to take her. ³But one night God spoke to Abimelech in a dream. God said, "You will die. That woman you took is married."

⁴But Abimelech had not slept with Sarah. So he said, "Lord, would you destroy an innocent nation? ⁵Abraham himself told me, 'This woman is my sister.' And she also said, 'He is my brother.' I am innocent. I did not know I was doing anything wrong."

⁶Then God said to Abimelech in the dream, "Yes, I know that you did not realize what you were doing. So I did not allow you to sin against me. I did not allow you to sleep with her. ⁷Give Abraham his wife back. He is a prophet.ᵈ He will pray for you, and you will not die. But if you do not give Sarah back, you will die. And all your family will surely die."

⁸So early the next morning, Abimelech called all his officers. He told them everything that had happened in the dream. They were very much afraid. ⁹Then Abimelech called Abraham to him. Abimelech said, "What have you done to us? What wrong did I do against you? Why did you bring this trouble to my kingdom? You

should not have done these things to me. ¹⁰What were you thinking that caused you to do this?"

¹¹Then Abraham answered, "I thought no one in this place respected God. I thought someone would kill me to get Sarah. ¹²And it is true that she is my sister. She is the daughter of my father. But she is not the daughter of my mother. ¹³God told me to leave my father's house and wander in many different places. When that happened, I told Sarah, 'You must do a special favor for me. Everywhere we go tell people I am your brother.'"

¹⁴Then Abimelech gave Abraham some sheep, cattle and male and female slaves. Abimelech also gave Sarah, his wife, back to him. ¹⁵And Abimelech said, "Look around you at my land. You may live anywhere you want."

¹⁶Abimelech said to Sarah, "I gave your brother Abraham 25 pounds of silver. I did this to make up for any wrong that people may think about you. I want everyone to know that you are innocent."

¹⁷Then Abraham prayed to God. And God healed Abimelech, his wife and his servant girls. Now they could have children. ¹⁸The Lord had kept all the women in Abimelech's house from having children. This was God's punishment on Abimelech for taking Abraham's wife Sarah.

A BABY FOR SARAH

21 The Lord cared for Sarah as he had said. He did for her what he had promised. ²Sarah became pregnant. And she gave birth to a son for Abraham in his old age. Everything happened at the time God had said it would. ³Abraham named his son Isaac. Sarah gave birth to this son of Abraham. ⁴Abraham circumcisedᵈ Isaac when he was eight days old as God had commanded.

⁵Abraham was 100 years old when his son Isaac was born. ⁶And Sarah said, "God has made me laugh.ⁿ Everyone who hears about this will laugh with me. ⁷No

---

21:6 laugh The Hebrew words for "he laughed" and "Isaac" sound the same.

one thought that I would be able to have Abraham's child. But I have given Abraham a son while he is old."

HAGAR AND ISHMAEL

[8]Isaac grew and became old enough to eat food. At that time Abraham gave a great feast. [9]But Sarah saw Ishmael making fun of Isaac. (Ishmael was the son of Abraham by Hagar, Sarah's Egyptian slave.) [10]So Sarah said to Abraham, "Throw out this slave woman and her son. When we die, our son Isaac will inherit everything we have. I don't want her son to inherit any of our things."

[11]This troubled Abraham very much because Ishmael was also his son. [12]But God said to Abraham, "Don't be troubled about the boy and the slave woman. Do whatever Sarah tells you. The descendants[d] I promised you will be from Isaac. [13]I will also make the descendants of Ishmael into a great nation. I will do this because he is your son, too."

[14]Early the next morning Abraham took some food and a leather bag full of water. He gave them to Hagar and sent her away. Hagar carried these things and her son. She went and wandered in the desert of Beersheba.

[15]Later, all the water was gone from the bag. So Hagar put her son under a bush. [16]Then she went away a short distance and sat down. Hagar thought, "My son will die. I cannot watch this happen." She sat there and began to cry.

[17]God heard the boy crying. And God's angel called to Hagar from heaven. He said, "What is wrong, Hagar? Don't be afraid! God has heard the boy crying there. [18]Help the boy up. Take him by the hand. I will make his descendants into a great nation."

[19]Then God showed Hagar a well of water. So she went to the well and filled her bag with water. Then she gave the boy a drink.

[20]God was with the boy as he grew up. Ishmael lived in the desert. He learned to shoot with a bow very well. [21]He lived in the Desert of Paran. His mother found a wife for him in Egypt.

ABRAHAM'S BARGAIN WITH ABIMELECH

[22]Then Abimelech came with Phicol, the commander of Abimelech's army. They said to Abraham, "God is with you in everything you do. [23]So make a promise to me here before God. Promise that you will be fair with me and my children and my descendants.[d] Be kind to me and to this land where you have lived as a stranger. Be as kind to me as I have been to you."

[24]And Abraham said, "I promise." [25]Then Abraham complained to Abimelech about Abimelech's servants. They had captured a well of water.

[26]But Abimelech said, "I don't know who did this. You never told me about this before today."

[27]Then Abraham gave Abimelech some sheep and cattle. And they made an agreement. [28]Abraham also put seven female lambs in front of Abimelech.

[29]Abimelech asked Abraham, "Why did you put these seven female lambs by themselves?"

[30]Abraham answered, "Accept these lambs from me. That will prove that you believe I dug this well."

[31]So that place was called Beersheba[n] because they made a promise to each other there.

[32]So Abraham and Abimelech made an agreement at Beersheba. Then Abimelech and Phicol, the commander of his army, went back to the land of the Philistines.

[33]Abraham planted a tamarisk tree at Beersheba. There Abraham prayed to the Lord, the God who lives forever. [34]And Abraham lived as a stranger in the land of the Philistines for a long time.

21:31 Beersheba This name means "well of the promise" or "well of seven."

GOD TESTS ABRAHAM

22 After these things God tested Abraham's faith. God said to him, "Abraham!"

And he answered, "Here I am."

²Then God said, "Take your only son, Isaac, the son you love. Go to the land of Moriah. There kill him and offer him as a whole burnt offering. Do this on one of the mountains there. I will tell you which one."

³Early in the morning Abraham got up and saddled his donkey. He took Isaac and two servants with him. He cut the wood for the sacrifice. Then they went to the place God had told them to go. ⁴On the third day Abraham looked up and saw the place in the distance. ⁵He said to his servants, "Stay here with the donkey. My son and I will go over there and worship. Then we will come back to you."

⁶Abraham took the wood for the sacrifice and gave it to his son to carry. Abraham took the knife and the fire. So Abraham and his son went on together.

⁷Isaac said to his father Abraham, "Father!"

Abraham answered, "Yes, my son."

Isaac said, "We have the fire and the wood. But where is the lamb we will burn as a sacrifice?"

⁸Abraham answered, "God will give us the lamb for the sacrifice, my son."

So Abraham and his son went on together. ⁹They came to the place God had told him about. There, Abraham built an altar. He laid the wood on it. Then he tied up his son Isaac. And he laid Isaac on the wood on the altar. ¹⁰Then Abraham took his knife and was about to kill his son.

¹¹But the angel of the Lord called to him from heaven. The angel said, "Abraham! Abraham!"

Abraham answered, "Yes."

¹²The angel said, "Don't kill your son or hurt him in any way. Now I can see that you respect God. I see that you have not kept your son, your only son, from me."

¹³Then Abraham looked up and saw a male sheep. Its horns were caught in a bush. So Abraham went and took the sheep and killed it. He offered it as a whole burnt offering to God. Abraham's son was saved. ¹⁴So Abraham named that place The Lord Gives. Even today people say, "On the mountain of the Lord it will be given."

¹⁵The angel of the Lord called to Abraham from heaven a second time. ¹⁶The angel said, "The Lord says, 'You did not keep back your son, your only son, from me. Because you did this, I make you this promise by my own name: ¹⁷I will surely bless you and give you many descendants.ᵈ They will be as many as the stars in the sky and the sand on the seashore. And they will capture the cities of their enemies. ¹⁸Through your descendants all the nations on the earth will be blessed. This is because you obeyed me.'"

¹⁹Then Abraham returned to his servants. They all traveled back to Beersheba, and Abraham stayed there.

²⁰After these things happened, someone told Abraham: "Your brother Nahor and his wife Milcah have children now. ²¹The first son is Uz. The second son is Buz. The third son is Kemuel (the father of Aram). ²²Then there are Kesed, Hazo, Pildash, Jidlaph and Bethuel." ²³Bethuel became the father of Rebekah. Milcah was the mother of these eight sons, and Nahor was the father. Nahor was Abraham's brother. ²⁴Also Nahor had four other sons by his slave womanᵈ Reumah. Their names were Tebah, Gaham, Tahash and Maacah.

SARAH DIES

23 Sarah lived to be 127 years old. ²She died in Kiriath Arba (that is, Hebron) in the land of Canaan. Abraham was very sad and cried because of her. ³After a while Abraham got up from the side of his wife's body. And he went to talk to the Hittites. He said, [4]"I am only a stranger and a foreigner here. Sell me some of your land so that I can bury my dead wife."

[5]The Hittites answered Abraham, [6]"Sir, you are a great leader among us. You may have the best place we have to bury your dead. You may have any of our burying places that you want. None of us will stop you from burying your dead wife."

[7]Abraham rose and bowed to the people of the land, the Hittites. [8]Abraham said to them, "If you truly want to help me bury my dead wife here, speak to Ephron for me. He is the son of Zohar. [9]Ask him to sell me the cave of Machpelah. It is at the edge of his field. I will pay him the full price. You can be the witnesses that I am buying it as a burial place."

[10]Ephron was sitting among the Hittites at the city gate. Ephron answered Abraham, [11]"No, sir. I will give you the land and the cave that is in it. I will give it to you with these people as witnesses. Bury your dead wife."

[12]Then Abraham bowed down before the Hittites. [13]He said to Ephron before all the people, "Please let me pay you the full price for the field. Accept my money, and I will bury my dead there."

[14]Ephron answered Abraham, [15]"Sir, the land is worth ten pounds of silver. But I won't argue with you over the price. Take the land, and bury your dead wife."

[16]Abraham agreed and paid Ephron in front of the Hittite witnesses. Abraham weighed out the full price: ten pounds of silver. They counted the weight as the traders normally did.

[17-18]So Ephron's field in Machpelah, east of Mamre, was sold. Abraham became the owner of the field, the cave in it and all the trees that were in the field. The sale was made at the city gate, with the Hittites as witnesses. [19]After

this, Abraham buried his wife Sarah in the cave. It was in that field of Machpelah, near Mamre. (Mamre was later called Hebron in the land of Canaan.) [20]Abraham bought the field and the cave on it from the Hittites. He used it as a burying place.

A WIFE FOR ISAAC

24 Abraham was now very old. The Lord had blessed him in every way. [2]Abraham's oldest servant was in charge of everything Abraham owned. Abraham called that servant to him and said, "Put your hand under my leg.[n] [3]Make a promise to me before the Lord, the God of heaven and earth. Don't get a wife for my son from the Canaanite girls who live around here. [4]Instead, go back to my country, to the land of my relatives. Get a wife for my son Isaac from there."

[5]The servant said to him, "What if this woman does not want to return with me to this land? Then, should I take your son with me back to your homeland?"

[6]Abraham said to him, "No! Don't take my son back there. [7]The Lord is the God of heaven. He brought me from the home of my father and the land of my relatives. But the Lord promised me, 'I will give this land to your descendants.'[d] The Lord will send his angel before you. The angel will help you get a wife for my son there. [8]But if the girl won't come back with you, you will be free from this promise. But you must not take my son back there." [9]So the servant put his hand under his master's leg. He made a promise to Abraham about this.

[10]The servant took ten of Abraham's camels and left. He carried with him many different kinds of beautiful gifts. He went to Northwest Mesopotamia to Nahor's city. [11]He made the camels kneel down at the well outside the city. It was in the evening when the women come out to get water.

24:2 **Put ... leg.** This showed that a person would keep the promise.

¹²The servant said, "Lord, you are the God of my master Abraham. Allow me to find a wife for his son today. Please show this kindness to my master Abraham. ¹³Here I am, standing by the spring of water. The girls from the city are coming out to get water. ¹⁴I will say to one of the girls, 'Please put your jar down so I can drink.' Then let her say, 'Drink, and I will also give water to your camels.' If that happens, I will know she is the right one for your servant Isaac. And I will know that you have shown kindness to my master."

¹⁵Before the servant had finished praying, Rebekah came out of the city. She was the daughter of Bethuel. (Bethuel was the son of Milcah and Nahor, Abraham's brother.) Rebekah was carrying her water jar on her shoulder. ¹⁶She was very pretty. She was a virgin;ᵈ she had never had sexual relations with a man. She went down to the spring and filled her jar. Then she came back up. ¹⁷The servant ran to her and said, "Please give me a little water from your jar."

¹⁸Rebekah said, "Drink, sir." She quickly lowered the jar from her shoulder and gave him a drink. ¹⁹After he finished drinking, Rebekah said, "I will also pour some water for your camels." ²⁰So she quickly poured all the water from her jar into the drinking trough for the camels. Then she kept running to the well until she had given all the camels enough to drink.

²¹The servant quietly watched her. He wanted to be sure the Lord had made his trip successful. ²²After the camels had finished drinking, he gave Rebekah a gold ring weighing one-fifth of an ounce. He also gave her two gold arm bracelets weighing about four ounces each. ²³The servant asked, "Who is your father? Is there a place in his house for me and my men to spend the night?"

²⁴Rebekah answered, "My father is Bethuel. He is the son of Milcah and Nahor." ²⁵Then she said, "And, yes, we have straw for your camels. We have a place for you to spend the night."

²⁶The servant bowed and worshiped the Lord. ²⁷He said, "Blessed is the Lord, the God of my master Abraham. The Lord has been kind and truthful to him. He has led me to my master's relatives."

²⁸Then Rebekah ran and told her mother's family about all these things. ²⁹She had a brother named Laban. He ran out to Abraham's servant, who was still at the spring. ³⁰Laban had heard what she had said. And he had seen the ring and the bracelets on his sister's arms. So he ran out to the well. And there was the man standing by the camels at the spring. ³¹Laban said, "Sir, you are welcome to come in. You don't have to stand outside. I have prepared the house for you and also a place for your camels."

³²So Abraham's servant went into the house. Laban unloaded the camels and gave them straw and food. Then Laban gave water to Abraham's servant so he and the men with him could wash their feet. ³³Then Laban gave the servant food. But the servant said, "I will not eat until I have told you why I came."

So Laban said, "Then tell us."

³⁴He said, "I am Abraham's servant. ³⁵The Lord has greatly blessed my master in everything. My master has become a rich man. The Lord has given him many flocks of sheep and herds of cattle. He has given Abraham silver and gold, male and female servants, camels and horses. ³⁶Sarah, my master's wife, gave birth to a son when she was old. My master has given everything he owns to that son. ³⁷My master had me make a promise to him. He said, 'Don't get a wife for my son from the Canaanite girls who live around here. ³⁸Instead you must go to my father's people and to my family. There you must get a wife for my son.' ³⁹I said to my master, 'What if the woman will not come back with me?' ⁴⁰But he said, 'I serve the Lord. He will send his angel

with you and will help you. You will get a wife for my son from my family and my father's people. ⁴¹Then you will be free from the promise. Or if they will not give you a wife for my son, you will be free from this promise.'

⁴²"Today I came to this spring. I said, 'Lord, God of my master Abraham, please make my trip successful. ⁴³Look, I am standing by this spring of water. I will wait for a young woman to come out to get water. Then I will say, "Please give me water from your jar to drink." ⁴⁴Then let her say, "Drink this water. I will also get water for your camels." By this I will know the Lord has chosen her for my master's son.'

⁴⁵"Before I finished my silent prayer, Rebekah came out of the city. She had her water jar on her shoulder. She went down to the spring and got water. I said to her, 'Please give me a drink.' ⁴⁶She quickly lowered the jar from her shoulder. She said, 'Drink this. I will also get water for your camels.' So I drank, and she gave water to my camels also. ⁴⁷Then I asked her, 'Who is your father?' She answered, 'My father is Bethuel son of Milcah and Nahor.' Then I put the ring in her nose and the bracelets on her arms. ⁴⁸At that time I bowed my head and thanked the Lord. I praised the Lord, the God of my master Abraham. I thanked him because he led me on the right road to get the granddaughter of my master's brother for his son. ⁴⁹Now, tell me, will you be kind and truthful to my master? And if not, tell me so. Then I will know what I should do."

⁵⁰Laban and Bethuel answered, "This is clearly from the Lord. We cannot change what must happen. ⁵¹Rebekah is yours. Take her and go. Let her marry your master's son as the Lord has commanded."

⁵²When Abraham's servant heard these words, he bowed facedown on the ground before the Lord. ⁵³Then the servant gave Rebekah gold and silver jewelry and clothes. He also gave expensive gifts to her brother and mother. ⁵⁴The servant and the men with him ate and drank. And they spent the night there. When they got up the next morning, the servant said, "Now let me go back to my master."

⁵⁵Rebekah's mother and her brother said, "Let Rebekah stay with us at least ten days. After that she may go."

⁵⁶But the servant said to them, "Do not make me wait. The Lord has made my trip successful. Now let me go back to my master."

⁵⁷Rebekah's brother and mother said, "We will call Rebekah and ask her what she wants to do." ⁵⁸They called her and asked her, "Do you want to go with this man now?"

She said, "Yes, I do."

⁵⁹So they allowed Rebekah and her nurse to go with Abraham's servant and his men. ⁶⁰They blessed Rebekah and said,

"Our sister, may you be the mother of
    thousands of people.
And may your descendants*ᵈ* capture
    the cities of their enemies."

⁶¹Then Rebekah and her servant girls got on the camels and followed the servant and his men. So the servant took Rebekah and left.

⁶²At this time Isaac had left Beer Lahai Roi. He was living in southern Canaan. ⁶³One evening he went out to the field to think. As he looked up, he saw camels coming. ⁶⁴Rebekah looked and saw Isaac. Then she jumped down from the camel. ⁶⁵She asked the servant, "Who is that man walking in the field to meet us?"

The servant answered, "That is my master." So Rebekah covered her face with her veil.

⁶⁶The servant told Isaac everything that had happened. ⁶⁷Then Isaac brought Rebekah into the tent of Sarah, his mother. And she became his wife. Isaac

loved her very much. So he was comforted after his mother's death.

ABRAHAM'S FAMILY

25 Abraham married again. His new wife was Keturah. [2]She gave birth to Zimran, Jokshan, Medan, Midian, Ishbak and Shuah. [3]Jokshan was the father of Sheba and Dedan. Dedan's descendants[d] were the people of Assyria, Letush and Leum. [4]The sons of Midian were Ephah, Epher, Hanoch, Abida and Eldaah. All these were descendants of Keturah. [5]Abraham left everything he owned to Isaac. [6]But before Abraham died, he did give gifts to the sons of his other wives. Abraham sent them to the East to be away from Isaac.

[7]Abraham lived to be 175 years old. [8]He breathed his last breath and died at an old age. He had lived a long and satisfying life. [9]His sons Isaac and Ishmael buried him in the cave of Machpelah. This cave is in the field of Ephron east of Mamre. Ephron was the son of Zohar the Hittite. [10]This is the same field that Abraham had bought from the Hittites. Abraham was buried there with his wife Sarah. [11]After Abraham died, God blessed his son Isaac. Isaac was now living at Beer Lahai Roi.

[12]This is the family history of Ishmael, Abraham's son. (Hagar, Sarah's Egyptian servant, was Ishmael's mother.) [13]These are the names of Ishmael's sons in the order they were born. The first son was Nebaioth. Then came Kedar, Adbeel, Mibsam, [14]Mishma, Dumah, Massa, [15]Hadad, Tema, Jetur, Naphish and Kedemah. [16]These were Ishmael's sons. And these are the names of the tribal leaders. They are listed according to their settlements and camps. [17]Ishmael lived 137 years. Then he breathed his last breath and died. [18]Ishmael's descendants lived from Havilah to Shur. This is east of Egypt stretching toward Assyria. Ishmael's descendants often attacked the descendants of his brothers.

ISAAC'S FAMILY

[19]This is the family history of Isaac. Abraham had a son named Isaac. [20]When Isaac was 40 years old, he married Rebekah. Rebekah was from Northwest Mesopotamia. She was Bethuel's daughter and the sister of Laban the Aramean. [21]Isaac's wife could not have children. So Isaac prayed to the Lord for her. The Lord heard Isaac's prayer, and Rebekah became pregnant.

[22]While she was pregnant, the babies struggled inside her. She asked, "Why is this happening to me?" Then she went to get an answer from the Lord.

[23]The Lord said to her,

"Two nations are in your body.
Two groups of people will be taken
    from you.
One group will be stronger than the
    other.
The older will serve the younger."

[24]And when the time came, Rebekah gave birth to twins. [25]The first baby was born red. His skin was like a hairy robe. So he was named Esau.[n] [26]When the second baby was born, he was holding on to Esau's heel. So that baby was named Jacob.[n] Isaac was 60 years old when they were born.

[27]When the boys grew up, Esau became a skilled hunter. He loved to be out in the fields. But Jacob was a quiet man. He stayed among the tents. [28]Isaac loved Esau. Esau hunted the wild animals that Isaac enjoyed eating. But Rebekah loved Jacob.

[29]One day Jacob was boiling a pot of vegetable soup. Esau came in from hunting in the fields. He was weak from

---

25:25 Esau This name may mean "hairy."
25:26 Jacob This name sounds like the Hebrew word for "heel." "Grabbing someone's heel" is a Hebrew saying for tricking someone.

hunger. [30]So Esau said to Jacob, "Let me eat some of that red soup. I am weak with hunger." (That is why people call him Edom.[n])

[31]But Jacob said, "You must sell me your rights as the firstborn son."[n]

[32]Esau said, "I am almost dead from hunger. If I die, all of my father's wealth will not help me."

[33]But Jacob said, "First, promise me that you will give it to me." So Esau made a promise to Jacob. In this way he sold his part of their father's wealth to Jacob. [34]Then Jacob gave Esau bread and vegetable soup. Esau ate and drank and then left. So Esau showed how little he cared about his rights as the firstborn son.

ISAAC LIES TO ABIMELECH

26 Once there was a time of hunger in the land. This was besides the time of hunger that happened during Abraham's life. So Isaac went to the town of Gerar. He went to see Abimelech king of the Philistines. [2]The Lord appeared to Isaac and said, "Don't go down to Egypt. Live in the land where I tell you to live. [3]Stay in this land, and I will be with you. I will bless you. I will give you and your descendants[d] all these lands. I will keep the agreement I made to Abraham your father. [4]I will give you many descendants. They will be as hard to count as the stars in the sky. And I will give them all these lands. Through your descendants all the nations on the earth will be blessed. [5]I will do this because your father Abraham obeyed me. He did what I said. He obeyed my commands, my teachings and my rules."

[6]So Isaac stayed in Gerar. [7]Isaac's wife Rebekah was very beautiful. The men of that place asked Isaac about her. Isaac said, "She is my sister." He was afraid to tell them she was his wife. He thought they might kill him so they could have her.

[8]Isaac lived there a long time. One day as Abimelech king of the Philistines looked out his window, he saw Isaac. Isaac was holding his wife Rebekah tenderly. [9]Abimelech called for Isaac and said, "This woman is your wife. Why did you say she was your sister?"

Isaac said to him, "I was afraid you would kill me so you could have her."

[10]Abimelech said, "What have you done to us? One of our men might have had sexual relations with your wife. Then we would have been guilty of a great sin."

[11]So Abimelech warned everyone. He said, "Anyone who touches this man or his wife will be put to death."

ISAAC BECOMES RICH

[12]Isaac planted seed in that land. And that year he gathered a great harvest. The Lord blessed him very much. [13]Isaac became rich. He gathered more wealth until he became a very rich man. [14]He had many slaves and many flocks and herds. The Philistines envied him. [15]So they stopped up all the wells the servants of Isaac's father Abraham had dug. (They had dug them when Abraham was alive.) The Philistines filled those wells with dirt. [16]And Abimelech said to Isaac, "Leave our country. You have become much more powerful than we are."

[17]So Isaac left that place. He camped in the Valley of Gerar and lived there. [18]Long before this time Abraham had dug many wells. After Abraham died, the Philistines filled them with dirt. So Isaac dug those wells again. He gave them the same names his father had given them. [19]Isaac's servants dug a well in the valley. From it a spring of water flowed. [20]But the men who herded sheep in Gerar argued with Isaac's servants.

25:30 Edom This name sounds like the Hebrew word for "red."
25:31 rights . . . son Usually the firstborn son had a high rank in the family. The firstborn son usually became the new head of the family.

They said, "This water is ours." So Isaac named that well Argue because they argued with him. [21]Then Isaac's servants dug another well. The people also argued about it. So Isaac named that well Fight. [22]Isaac moved from there and dug another well. No one argued about this one. So he named that well Room Enough. Isaac said, "Now the Lord has made room for us. We will be successful in this land."

[23]From there Isaac went to Beersheba. [24]The Lord appeared to Isaac that night. The Lord said, "I am the God of your father Abraham. Don't be afraid because I am with you. I will bless you and give you many descendants.[d] I will do this because of my servant Abraham." [25]So Isaac built an altar and worshiped the Lord there. He made a camp there, and his servants dug a well.

[26]Abimelech came from Gerar to see Isaac. Abimelech brought with him Ahuzzath, who advised him, and Phicol, the commander of his army. [27]Isaac asked them, "Why have you come to see me? You were my enemy. You forced me to leave your country."

[28]They answered, "Now we know that the Lord is with you. We will make a promise to you. And we would like you to make one to us. We would like to make an agreement with you. [29]We did not hurt you. So promise you will not hurt us. And we were good to you, and we sent you away in peace. Now the Lord has blessed you."

[30]So Isaac prepared food for them, and they all ate and drank. [31]Early the next morning the men made a promise to each other. Then Isaac sent them away, and they left in peace.

[32]That day Isaac's servants came and told him about the well they had dug. They said, "We found water in that well." [33]So Isaac named it Shibah[n] and that city is still called Beersheba even now.

[34]When Esau was 40 years old, he married two Hittite women. One was Judith daughter of Beeri. The other was Basemath daughter of Elon. [35]These women brought much sorrow to Isaac and Rebekah.

JACOB TRICKS ISAAC

27 When Isaac was old, his eyes were not good. He could not see clearly. One day he called his older son Esau to him. Isaac said, "Son."

Esau answered, "Here I am."

[2]Isaac said, "I am old. I don't know when I might die. [3]So take your bow and arrows, and go hunting in the field. Kill an animal for me to eat. [4]Prepare the tasty food that I love. Bring it to me, and I will eat. Then I will bless you before I die." [5]So Esau went out in the field to hunt.

Rebekah was listening as Isaac said this to his son Esau. [6]Rebekah said to her son Jacob, "Listen, I heard your father talking to your brother Esau. [7]Your father said, 'Kill an animal. Prepare some tasty food for me to eat. Then I will bless you before the Lord before I die.' [8]So obey me, my son. Do what I tell you. [9]Go out to our goats and bring me two young ones. I will prepare them just the way your father likes them. [10]Then you will take the food to your father. And he will bless you before he dies."

[11]But Jacob said to his mother Rebekah, "My brother Esau is a hairy man. I am smooth! [12]If my father touches me, he will know I am not Esau. Then he will not bless me. He will place a curse on me because I tried to trick him."

[13]So Rebekah said to him, "If your father puts a curse on you, I will accept the blame. Just do what I said. Go and get the goats for me."

[14]So Jacob went out and got two goats and brought them to his mother. Then she cooked them in the special way Isaac enjoyed. [15]She took the best clothes of her

---

26:33 **Shibah** This name sounds like the Hebrew words for "seven" and "promise."

older son Esau that were in the house. She put them on the younger son Jacob. ¹⁶She took the skins of the goats. And she put them on Jacob's hands and neck. ¹⁷Then she gave Jacob the tasty food and the bread she had made.

¹⁸Jacob went in to his father and said, "Father."

And his father said, "Yes, my son. Who are you?"

¹⁹Jacob said to him, "I am Esau, your first son. I have done what you told me. Now sit up and eat some meat of the animal I hunted for you. Then bless me."

²⁰But Isaac asked his son, "How did you find and kill the animal so quickly?"

Jacob answered, "Because the Lord your God led me to find it."

²¹Then Isaac said to Jacob, "Come near so I can touch you, my son. If I can touch you, I will know if you are really my son Esau."

²²So Jacob came near to Isaac his father. Isaac touched him and said, "Your voice sounds like Jacob's voice. But your hands are hairy like the hands of Esau." ²³Isaac did not know it was Jacob, because his hands were hairy like Esau's hands. So Isaac blessed Jacob. ²⁴Isaac asked, "Are you really my son Esau?"

Jacob answered, "Yes, I am."

²⁵Then Isaac said, "Bring me the food. I will eat it and bless you." So Jacob gave him the food, and Isaac ate. Jacob gave him wine, and he drank. ²⁶Then Isaac said to him, "My son, come near and kiss me." ²⁷So Jacob went to his father and kissed him. Isaac smelled Esau's clothes and blessed him. Isaac said,

"The smell of my son
    is like the smell of the field
    that the Lord has blessed.
²⁸May God give you plenty of rain
    and good soil.
Then you will have plenty of grain
    and wine.

²⁹May nations serve you.
    May peoples bow down to you.
May you be master over your
    brothers.
May your mother's sons bow down
    to you.
May everyone who curses you be
    cursed.
And may everyone who blesses you
    be blessed."

³⁰Isaac finished blessing Jacob. Then, just as Jacob left his father Isaac, Esau came in from hunting. ³¹Esau also prepared some tasty food and brought it to his father. He said, "Father, rise and eat the food that your son killed for you. Then bless me."

³²Isaac asked, "Who are you?"

He answered, "I am your son—your firstborn^d son—Esau."

³³Then Isaac trembled greatly. He said, "Then who was it that hunted the animals and brought me food before you came? I ate it, and I blessed him. And it is too late now to take back my blessing."

³⁴When Esau heard the words of his father, he let out a loud and bitter cry. He said to his father, "Bless me—me, too, my father!"

³⁵But Isaac said, "Your brother came and tricked me. He has taken your blessing."

³⁶Esau said, "Jacob^n is the right name for him. He has tricked me these two times. He took away my share of everything you own. And now he has taken away my blessing." Then Esau asked, "Haven't you saved a blessing for me?"

³⁷Isaac answered, "I gave Jacob the power to be master over you. And all his brothers will be his servants. And I kept him strong with grain and wine. There is nothing left to give you, my son."

³⁸But Esau continued, "Do you have only one blessing, Father? Bless me, too, Father!" Then Esau began to cry out loud.

27:36 Jacob This name sounds like the Hebrew word for "heel." "Grabbing someone's heel" is a Hebrew saying for tricking someone.

[39]Isaac said to him,
"You will live far away from the best
    land,
  far from the rain.
[40]You will live by using your sword
    and be a slave to your brother.
  But when you struggle,
    you will break free from him."

[41]After that Esau hated Jacob because of the blessing from Isaac. Esau thought to himself, "My father will soon die, and I will be sad for him. After that I will kill Jacob."

[42]Rebekah heard about Esau's plan to kill Jacob. So she sent for Jacob. She said to him, "Listen, your brother Esau is comforting himself by planning to kill you. [43]So, son, do what I say. My brother Laban is living in Haran. Go to him at once! [44]Stay with him for a while, until your brother is not so angry. [45]In time, your brother will not be angry. He will forget what you did to him. Then I will send a servant to bring you back. I don't want to lose both of my sons on the same day."

[46]Then Rebekah said to Isaac, "I am tired of Hittite women. If Jacob marries one of these Hittite women here in this land, I want to die."

JACOB SEARCHES FOR A WIFE

28 Isaac called Jacob and blessed him. Then Isaac commanded him, "You must not marry a Canaanite woman. [2]Go to the house of Bethuel, your mother's father, in Northwest Mesopotamia. Laban, your mother's brother, lives there. Marry one of his daughters. [3]May God All-Powerful bless you and give you many children. May you become the father of many peoples. [4]May the Lord give you and your descendants[d] the blessing of Abraham. Then you may own the land where you are now living as a stranger. This is the land God gave to Abraham."

[5]So Isaac sent Jacob to Northwest Mesopotamia. Jacob went to Laban, the brother of Rebekah. Bethuel, the Aramean, was the father of Laban and Rebekah. And Rebekah was the mother of Jacob and Esau.

[6]Esau learned that Isaac had blessed Jacob and sent him to Northwest Mesopotamia. Jacob went to find a wife there. Esau also learned that Isaac had commanded Jacob not to marry a Canaanite woman. [7]And Esau learned that Jacob had obeyed his father and mother. He had gone to Northwest Mesopotamia. [8]So Esau saw that his father Isaac did not want his sons to marry Canaanite women. [9]Now Esau already had wives. But he went to Ishmael son of Abraham. And he married Mahalath, Ishmael's daughter. Mahalath was the sister of Nebaioth.

JACOB'S DREAM AT BETHEL

[10]Jacob left Beersheba and set out for Haran. [11]He came to a place and spent the night there because the sun had set. He found a stone there and laid his head on it to go to sleep. [12]Jacob dreamed that there was a ladder resting on the earth and reaching up into heaven. And he saw angels of God going up and coming down the ladder. [13]And then Jacob saw the Lord standing above the ladder. The Lord said, "I am the Lord, the God of Abraham, your grandfather. And I am the God of Isaac. I will give you and your descendants[d] the land on which you are now sleeping. [14]Your descendants will be as many as the dust of the earth. They will spread west and east, north and south. All the families of the earth will be blessed through you and your descendants. [15]I am with you, and I will protect you everywhere you go. And I will bring you back to this land. I will not leave you until I have done what I have promised you."

[16]Then Jacob woke from his sleep. He said, "Surely the Lord is in this place. But I did not know it." [17]Jacob was afraid. He said, "This place frightens me! It is surely the house of God and the gate of heaven." [18]Jacob rose early in the morning. He took the stone he had slept on and set it

up on its end. Then he poured olive oil on the top of it. [19]At first, the name of that city was Luz. But Jacob named it Bethel.[n]

[20]Then Jacob made a promise. He said, "I want God to be with me and protect me on this journey. I want God to give me food to eat and clothes to wear. [21]Then I will be able to return in peace to my father's house. If the Lord does these things, he will be my God. [22]This stone which I have set up on its end will be the house of God. And I will give God one-tenth of all he gives me."

JACOB ARRIVES IN NORTHWEST MESOPOTAMIA

29 Then Jacob continued his journey. He came to the land of the people of the East. [2]He looked and saw a well in the field. Three flocks of sheep were lying nearby, because they drank water from this well. A large stone covered the mouth of the well. [3]All the flocks would gather there. The shepherds would roll the stone away from the well and water the sheep. Then they would put the stone back in its place.

[4]Jacob said to the shepherds there, "My brothers, where are you from?"

They answered, "We are from Haran."

[5]Then Jacob asked, "Do you know Laban grandson of Nahor?"

They answered, "We know him."

[6]Then Jacob asked, "How is he?"

They answered, "He is well. Look, his daughter Rachel is coming now with his sheep."

[7]Jacob said, "But look, it is still the middle part of the day. It is not time for the sheep to be gathered for the night. So give them water and let them go back into the pasture."

[8]But they said, "We cannot do that until all the flocks are gathered. Then we will roll away the stone from the mouth of the well and water the sheep."

[9]While Jacob was talking with the shepherds, Rachel came with her father's sheep. It was her job to take care of the sheep. [10]Then Jacob saw Laban's daughter Rachel and Laban's sheep. So he went to the well and rolled the stone from its mouth. Then he watered Laban's sheep. Now Laban was the brother of Rebekah, Jacob's mother. [11]Then Jacob kissed Rachel and cried. [12]He told her that he was from her father's family. He said that he was the son of Rebekah. So Rachel ran home and told her father.

[13]When Laban heard the news about his sister's son Jacob, Laban ran to meet him. Laban hugged him and kissed him and brought him to his house. Jacob told Laban everything that had happened. [14]Then Laban said, "You are my own flesh and blood."

JACOB IS TRICKED

So Jacob stayed there a month. [15]Then Laban said to Jacob, "You are my relative. But it is not right for you to keep on working for me without pay. What would you like me to pay you?"

[16]Now Laban had two daughters. The older was Leah, and the younger was Rachel. [17]Leah had weak eyes, but Rachel was very beautiful. [18]Jacob loved Rachel. So he said to Laban, "Let me marry your younger daughter Rachel. If you will, I will work seven years for you."

[19]Laban said, "It would be better for her to marry you than someone else. So stay here with me." [20]So Jacob worked for Laban seven years so he could marry Rachel. But they seemed to him like just a few days. This was because he loved Rachel very much.

[21]After seven years Jacob said to Laban, "Give me Rachel so that I may marry her. The time I promised to work for you is over."

[22]So Laban gave a feast for all the people there. [23]That evening Laban

---

28:19 **Bethel** This name means "house of God."

brought his daughter Leah to Jacob. Jacob and Leah had sexual relations together. [24](Laban gave his slave girl Zilpah to his daughter to be her servant.) [25]In the morning Jacob saw that he had had sexual relations with Leah! He said to Laban, "What have you done to me? I worked hard for you so that I could marry Rachel! Why did you trick me?"

[26]Laban said, "In our country we do not allow the younger daughter to marry before the older daughter. [27]But complete the full week of the marriage ceremony with Leah. I will give you Rachel to marry also. But you must serve me another seven years."

[28]So Jacob did this and completed the week with Leah. Then Laban gave him his daughter Rachel as a wife. [29](Laban gave his slave girl Bilhah to his daughter Rachel to be her servant.) [30]So Jacob had sexual relations with Rachel also. And Jacob loved Rachel more than Leah. Jacob worked for Laban for another seven years.

JACOB'S FAMILY GROWS

[31]The Lord saw that Jacob loved Rachel more than Leah. So the Lord made it possible for Leah to have children. But Rachel did not have any children. [32]Leah became pregnant and gave birth to a son. She named him Reuben,[n] because she said, "The Lord has seen my troubles. Surely now my husband will love me."

[33]Leah became pregnant again and gave birth to another son. She named him Simeon.[n] She said, "The Lord has heard that I am not loved. So he gave me this son."

[34]Leah became pregnant again and gave birth to another son. She named

him Levi.[n] Leah said, "Now, surely my husband will be close to me. I have given him three sons."

[35]Then Leah gave birth to another son. She named him Judah.[n] Leah named him this because she said, "Now I will praise the Lord." Then Leah stopped having children.

30 Rachel saw that she was not giving birth to children for Jacob. So she envied her sister Leah. Rachel said to Jacob, "Give me children, or I'll die!"

[2]Jacob became angry with her. He said, "Can I do what only God can do? He is the one who has kept you from having children."

[3]Then Rachel said, "Here is my slave girl Bilhah. Have sexual relations with her so she can give birth to a child for me. Then I can have my own family through her."

[4]So Rachel gave Bilhah, her slave girl, to Jacob as a wife. And he had sexual relations with her. [5]She became pregnant and gave Jacob a son. [6]Rachel said, "God has declared me innocent. He has listened to my prayer and has given me a son." So Rachel named this son Dan.[n]

[7]Bilhah became pregnant again and gave Jacob a second son. [8]Rachel said, "I have struggled hard with my sister. And I have won." So she named that son Naphtali.[n]

[9]Leah saw that she had stopped having children. So she gave her slave girl Zilpah to Jacob as a wife. [10]Then Zilpah had a son. [11]Leah said, "I am lucky." So she named her son Gad.[n] [12]Zilpah gave birth to another son. [13]Leah said, "I am very happy! Now women will call me happy." So she named that son Asher.[n]

29:32 Reuben This name sounds like the Hebrew word for "he has seen my troubles."
29:33 Simeon This name sounds like the Hebrew word for "has heard."
29:34 Levi This name sounds like the Hebrew word for "be close to."
29:35 Judah This name sounds like the Hebrew word for "praise."
30:6 Dan This name means "he has declared innocent."
30:8 Naphtali This name sounds like the Hebrew word for "my struggle."
30:11 Gad This name may mean "lucky."
30:13 Asher This name may mean "happy."

[14]During the wheat harvest Reuben went into the field and found some mandrake[n] plants. He brought them to his mother Leah. But Rachel said to Leah, "Please give me some of your son's mandrakes."

[15]Leah answered, "You have already taken away my husband. Now you are trying to take away my son's mandrakes."

But Rachel answered, "If you will give me your son's mandrakes, you may sleep with Jacob tonight."

[16]When Jacob came in from the field that night, Leah went out to meet him. She said, "You will have sexual relations with me tonight. I have paid for you with my son's mandrakes." So Jacob slept with her that night.

[17]Then God answered Leah's prayer, and she became pregnant again. She gave birth to a fifth son. [18]Leah said, "God has given me what I paid for, because I gave my slave girl to my husband." So Leah named her son Issachar.[n]

[19]Leah became pregnant again and gave birth to a sixth son. [20]She said, "God has given me a fine gift. Now surely Jacob will honor me, because I have given him six sons." So Leah named the son Zebulun.[n]

[21]Later Leah gave birth to a daughter. She named her Dinah.

[22]Then God remembered Rachel and answered her prayer. God made it possible for her to have children. [23]She became pregnant and gave birth to a son. She said, "God has taken away my shame." [24]She named him Joseph.[n] Rachel said, "I wish the Lord would give me another son."

JACOB TRICKS LABAN

[25]After the birth of Joseph, Jacob said to Laban, "Now let me go to my own home and country. [26]Give me my wives and my children, and let me go. I have earned them by working for you. You know that I served you well."

[27]Laban said to him, "If I have pleased you, please stay. I know the Lord has blessed me because of you. [28]Tell me what I should pay you, and I will give it to you."

[29]Jacob answered, "You know that I have worked hard for you. Your flocks have grown while I cared for them. [30]When I came, you had little. Now you have much. Every time I did something for you, the Lord blessed you. But when will I be able to do something for my own family?"

[31]Laban asked, "Then what should I give you?"

Jacob answered, "I don't want you to give me anything. Just do this one thing. Then I will come back and take care of your flocks. [32]Today let me go through all your flocks of white sheep and black goats. I will take every spotted or speckled lamb. I will take every black lamb and every spotted or speckled goat. That will be my pay. [33]In the future you can easily see if I am honest. You can come to look at my flocks. If I have any goat that isn't speckled or spotted or any sheep that isn't black, you will know I stole it."

[34]Laban answered, "Agreed! We will do what you ask." [35]But that day Laban took away all the male goats that had streaks or spots. And he took all the speckled and spotted female goats (all those that had white on them). And he took all the black sheep. He told his sons to watch over them. [36]Laban took these animals to a place that was three days' journey away from Jacob. Jacob took care of all the animals that were left.

30:14 **mandrake** A plant which was believed to cause a woman to become pregnant.
30:18 **Issachar** This name sounds like the Hebrew word for "paid for."
30:20 **Zebulun** This name sounds like the Hebrew word for "honor."
30:24 **Joseph** This name sounds like the Hebrew word for "he adds."

³⁷So Jacob cut green branches from poplar, almond and plane trees. He peeled off some of the bark so that the branches had white stripes on them. ³⁸He put the branches in front of the flocks at the watering places. When the animals came to drink, they also mated there. ³⁹So the goats mated in front of the branches. Then the young that were born were streaked, speckled or spotted. ⁴⁰Jacob separated the young animals from the others. And he made them face the streaked and dark animals in Laban's flock. Jacob kept his animals separate from Laban's. ⁴¹When the stronger animals in the flock were mating, Jacob put the branches before their eyes. This was so the animals would mate near the branches. ⁴²But when the weaker animals mated, Jacob did not put the branches there. So the animals born from the weaker animals were Laban's. And the animals born from the stronger animals were Jacob's. ⁴³In this way Jacob became very rich. He had large flocks, many male and female servants, camels and donkeys.

JACOB RUNS AWAY

31 One day Jacob heard Laban's sons talking. They said, "Jacob has taken everything our father owned. Jacob has become rich in this way." ²Then Jacob noticed that Laban was not as friendly as he had been before. ³The Lord said to Jacob, "Go back to the land where your ancestors lived. I will be with you."

⁴So Jacob told Rachel and Leah to meet him in the field where he kept his flocks. ⁵He said to them, "I have seen that your father is not as friendly with me as he used to be. But the God of my father has been with me. ⁶You both know that I have worked as hard as I could for your father. ⁷But he cheated me. He has changed my pay ten times. But God has not allowed your father to harm me. ⁸At one time Laban said, 'You can have all the speckled goats as your pay.' After that, all the animals gave birth to speckled young ones. But then Laban said, 'You can have all the streaked goats as your pay.' After that, all the animals gave birth to streaked babies. ⁹So God has taken the animals away from your father. And God has given them to me.

¹⁰"I had a dream during the season when the animals were mating. I saw that the only male goats who were mating were streaked, speckled or spotted. ¹¹The angel of God spoke to me in that dream. He said, 'Jacob!' I answered, 'Yes!' ¹²The angel said, 'Look! Only the streaked, speckled or spotted goats are mating. I have seen all the wrong things Laban does to you. ¹³I am the God who appeared to you at Bethel. There you poured olive oil on the stone you set up on end. There you made a promise to me. Now I want you to leave here. Go back to the land where you were born.'"

¹⁴Rachel and Leah answered Jacob, "Our father has nothing to give us when he dies. ¹⁵He has treated us like strangers. He sold us to you, and then he spent all of the money you paid for us. ¹⁶God took all this wealth from our father, and now it belongs to us and our children. So you do whatever God told you to do."

¹⁷So Jacob put his children and his wives on camels. ¹⁸Then they began their journey back to Isaac, his father. He lived in the land of Canaan. All the flocks of animals that Jacob owned walked ahead of them. He carried everything with him that he had gotten while he lived in Northwest Mesopotamia.

¹⁹Laban was gone to cut the wool from his sheep. While he was gone, Rachel stole the idols of false gods that belonged to him. ²⁰And Jacob tricked Laban the Aramean. He did not tell Laban he was leaving. ²¹Jacob and his family left quickly. They crossed the Euphrates River and traveled toward the mountains of Gilead.

²²Three days later Laban learned that Jacob had run away. ²³So Laban gathered

his relatives and began to chase Jacob. After seven days Laban found him in the mountains of Gilead. ²⁴That night God came to Laban the Aramean in a dream. The Lord said, "Be careful! Do not say anything to Jacob, good or bad."

THE SEARCH FOR THE STOLEN IDOLS

²⁵So Laban caught up with Jacob. Now Jacob had made his camp in the mountains. So Laban and his relatives set up their camp in the mountains of Gilead. ²⁶Laban said to Jacob, "What have you done? Why did you trick me? You took my daughters as if you had captured them in a war. ²⁷Why did you run away without telling me? Why did you trick me? Why didn't you tell me? Then I could send you away with joy and singing. There would be the music of tambourines*d* and harps. ²⁸You did not even let me kiss my grandchildren and my daughters good-bye. You were very foolish to do this! ²⁹I have the power to harm you. But last night the God of your father spoke to me. He warned me not to say anything to you, good or bad. ³⁰I know you want to go back to your home. But why did you steal my idols?"

³¹Jacob answered Laban, "I left without telling you, because I was afraid! I thought you would take your daughters away from me. ³²If you find anyone here who has taken your idols, he will be killed! Your relatives will be my witnesses. You may look for anything that belongs to you. Take anything that is yours." (Now Jacob did not know that Rachel had stolen Laban's idols.)

³³So Laban looked in Jacob's tent and in Leah's tent. He looked in the tent where the two slave women stayed. But he did not find his idols. When he left Leah's tent, he went into Rachel's tent. ³⁴Rachel had hidden the idols inside her camel's saddle. And she was sitting on them. Laban looked through the whole tent, but he did not find them.

³⁵Rachel said to her father, "Father, don't be angry with me. I am not able to stand up before you. I am having my monthly period." So Laban looked through the camp, but he did not find his idols.

³⁶Then Jacob became very angry. He said, "What wrong have I done? What law have I broken to cause you to chase me? ³⁷You have looked through everything I own. But you have found nothing that belongs to you. If you have found anything, show it to everyone. Put it in front of your relatives and my relatives. Then let them decide which one of us is right. ³⁸I have worked for you now for 20 years. During all that time none of the lambs and kids died during birth. And I have not eaten any of the male sheep from your flocks. ³⁹Any time a sheep was killed by wild animals, I did not bring it to you. I made up for the loss myself. You made me pay for any animal that was stolen during the day or night. ⁴⁰In the daytime the sun took away my strength. At night I was cold and could not sleep. ⁴¹I worked like a slave for you for 20 years. For the first 14 years I worked to get your two daughters. The last 6 years I worked to earn your animals. And during that time you changed my pay ten times. ⁴²But the God of my father was with me. He is the God of Abraham and the God of Isaac. If God had not been with me, you would have sent me away with nothing. But he saw the trouble I had and the hard work I did. And last night God corrected you."

JACOB AND LABAN'S AGREEMENT

⁴³Laban said to Jacob, "These girls are my daughters. Their children belong to me, and these animals are mine. Everything you see here belongs to me. But I can do nothing to keep my daughters and their children. ⁴⁴Let us make an agreement. Let us set up a pile of stones to remind us of our agreement."

⁴⁵So Jacob took a large rock and set it up on its end. ⁴⁶He told his relatives to

gather rocks. So they took the rocks and piled them up. Then they ate beside the pile of rocks. [47]Laban named that place in his language A Pile to Remind Us. And Jacob gave the place the same name in Hebrew.

[48]Laban said to Jacob, "This pile of rocks will remind us of the agreement between us." That is why the place was called A Pile to Remind Us. [49]It was also called Mizpah.[n] This was because Laban said, "Let the Lord watch over us while we are separated from each other. [50]Remember that God is our witness. This is true even if no one else is around us. He will know if you harm my daughters or marry other women. [51]Here is the pile of rocks that I have put between us. And here is the rock I set up on end. [52]This pile of rocks and this rock set on end will remind us of our agreement. I will never go past this pile to hurt you. And you must never come to my side of them to hurt me. [53]The God of Abraham is the God of Nahor and the God of their ancestors. Let God punish either of us if we break this agreement."

So Jacob made a promise in the name of God. This was the God of his father Isaac. [54]Then Jacob killed an animal and offered it as a sacrifice on the mountain. And he invited his relatives to share in the meal. After they finished eating, they spent the night on the mountain. [55]Early the next morning Laban kissed his grandchildren and his daughters. He blessed them, and then he left to return home.

JACOB MEETS ESAU

32 When Jacob also went his way, the angels of God met him. [2]When Jacob saw them, he said, "This is the camp of God!" So Jacob named that place Mahanaim.[n]

[3]Jacob's brother Esau was living in the area called Seir in the country of Edom.

Jacob sent messengers to Esau. [4]Jacob told the messengers, "Give this message to my master Esau: 'This is what Jacob, your servant, says: I have lived with Laban and have remained there until now. [5]I have cattle, donkeys, flocks, and male and female servants. I send this message to you and ask you to accept us.'"

[6]The messengers returned to Jacob and said, "We went to your brother Esau. He is coming to meet you. And he has 400 men with him."

[7]Then Jacob was very afraid and worried. He divided the people who were with him into two camps. He also divided all the flocks, herds and camels into two camps. [8]Jacob thought, "Esau might come and destroy one camp. But the other camp can run away and be saved."

[9]Jacob said, "God of my father Abraham! God of my father Isaac! Lord, you told me to return to my country and my family. You said that you would do good to me. [10]I am not worthy of the kindness and continual goodness you have shown me. The first time I traveled across the Jordan River, I had only my walking stick. But now I own enough to have two camps. [11]Please save me from my brother Esau. I am afraid he will come and kill all of us, even the mothers with the children. [12]You said to me, 'I will do good to you. I will make your children as many as the sand of the seashore. There will be too many to count.'"

[13]Jacob stayed there for the night. He prepared a gift for Esau from what he had with him. [14]It was 200 female goats and 20 male goats, 200 female sheep and 20 male sheep. [15]There were 30 female camels and their young, 40 cows and 10 bulls, 20 female donkeys and 10 male donkeys. [16]Jacob gave each separate flock of animals to one of his servants. Then he said to them, "Go ahead of me

---

31:49 Mizpah This name sounds like the Hebrew word for "watch."
32:2 Mahanaim This name means "two camps."

and keep some space between each herd." [17]Jacob gave them their orders. To the servant with the first group of animals he said, "My brother Esau will come to you. He will ask you, 'Whose servant are you? Where are you going? Whose animals are these?' [18]Then you will answer, 'These animals belong to your servant Jacob. He sent them as a gift to you my master, Esau. And Jacob also is coming behind us.'"

[19]Jacob ordered the second servant, the third servant and all the other servants to do the same thing. He said, "Say the same thing to Esau when you meet him. [20]Say, 'Your servant Jacob is coming behind us.'" Jacob thought, "If I send this gift ahead of me, maybe Esau will forgive me. Then when I see him, perhaps he will accept me." [21]So Jacob sent the gift to Esau. But Jacob stayed that night in the camp.

JACOB WRESTLES WITH GOD

[22]During the night Jacob rose and crossed the Jabbok River at the crossing. He took his 2 wives, his 2 slave girls and his 11 sons with him. [23]He sent his family and everything he had across the river. [24]But Jacob stayed behind alone. And a man came and wrestled with him until the sun came up. [25]The man saw that he could not defeat Jacob. So he struck Jacob's hip and put it out of joint. [26]Then the man said to Jacob, "Let me go. The sun is coming up."

But Jacob said, "I will let you go if you will bless me."

[27]The man said to him, "What is your name?"

And he answered, "Jacob."

[28]Then the man said, "Your name will no longer be Jacob. Your name will now be Israel,[n] because you have wrestled with God and with men. And you have won."

[29]Then Jacob asked him, "Please tell me your name."

But the man said, "Why do you ask my name?" Then he blessed Jacob there.

[30]So Jacob named that place Peniel.[n] He said, "I have seen God face to face. But my life was saved." [31]Then the sun rose as he was leaving that place. Jacob was limping because of his leg. [32]So even today the people of Israel do not eat the muscle that is on the hip joint of animals. This is because Jacob was touched there.

JACOB SHOWS HIS BRAVERY

33 Jacob looked up and saw Esau coming. With him were 400 men. So Jacob divided his children among Leah, Rachel and the two slave girls. [2]Jacob put the slave girls with their children first. Then he put Leah and her children behind them. And he put Rachel and Joseph last. [3]Jacob himself went out in front of them. He bowed down flat on the ground seven times as he was walking toward his brother.

[4]But Esau ran to meet Jacob. Esau put his arms around him and hugged him. Then Esau kissed him, and they both cried. [5]Esau looked up and saw the women and children. He asked, "Who are these people with you?"

Jacob answered, "These are the children God has given me. God has been good to me, your servant."

[6]Then the two slave girls and their children came up to Esau. They bowed down flat on the earth before him. [7]Then Leah and her children came up to Esau. They also bowed down flat on the earth. Last of all, Joseph and Rachel came up to Esau. And they, too, bowed down flat before him.

[8]Esau said, "I saw many herds as I was coming here. Why did you bring them?"

Jacob answered, "They were to please you, my master."

32:28 **Israel** This name means "he wrestles with God."
32:30 **Peniel** This name means "the face of God."

⁹But Esau said, "I already have enough, my brother. Keep what you have."

¹⁰Jacob said, "No! Please! If I have pleased you, then please accept the gift I give you. I am very happy to see your face again. It is like seeing the face of God because you have accepted me. ¹¹So I beg you to accept the gift I give you. God has been very good to me. And I have more than I need." And because Jacob begged, Esau accepted the gift.

¹²Then Esau said, "Let us get going. I will travel with you."

¹³But Jacob said to him, "My master, you know that the children are weak. And I must be careful with my flocks and their young ones. If I force them to go too far in one day, all the animals will die. ¹⁴So, my master, you go on ahead of me, your servant. I will follow you slowly. I will let the animals and the children set the speed at which we travel. I will meet you, my master, in Edom."

¹⁵So Esau said, "Then let me leave some of my men with you."

"No, thank you," said Jacob. "I only want to please you, my master." ¹⁶So that day Esau started back to Edom. ¹⁷But Jacob went to Succoth. There he built a house for himself. And he made shelters for his animals. That is why the place was named Succoth.ⁿ

¹⁸Jacob left Northwest Mesopotamia. And he arrived safely at the city of Shechem in the land of Canaan. He camped east of the city. ¹⁹He bought a part of the field where he had camped. He bought it from the sons of Hamor father of Shechem for 100 pieces of silver. ²⁰He built an altar there and named it after God, the God of Israel.

DINAH IS ATTACKED

34 Dinah was the daughter of Leah and Jacob. At this time Dinah went out to visit the women of that land. ²Shechem son of Hamor the Hivite, the ruler of that land, saw Dinah. He took

her and forced her to have sexual relations with him. ³Shechem fell in love with Dinah, and he spoke kindly to her. ⁴He told his father, Hamor, "Please get this girl for me so I can marry her."

⁵Jacob learned how Shechem had disgraced his daughter. But Jacob's sons were out in the field with the cattle. So Jacob said nothing until they came home. ⁶And Hamor father of Shechem went to talk with Jacob.

⁷When Jacob's sons heard what had happened, they came in from the field. They were very angry, because Shechem had done such a wicked thing to Israel. It was wrong for him to have sexual relations with Jacob's daughter. A thing like this should not be done.

⁸But Hamor talked to the brothers of Dinah. He said, "My son Shechem is deeply in love with Dinah. Please let him marry her. ⁹Marry our people. Give your women to our men as wives. And take our women for your men as wives. ¹⁰You can live in the same land with us. You will be free to own land and to trade here."

¹¹Shechem also talked to Jacob and to Dinah's brothers. He said, "Please accept my offer. I will give anything you ask. ¹²Ask as much as you want for the payment for the bride. I will give it to you. Just let me marry Dinah."

¹³The sons of Jacob answered Shechem and his father with lies. They were angry because Shechem had disgraced their sister Dinah. ¹⁴The brothers said to them, "We cannot allow you to marry our sister. You are not circumcised.ᵈ That would be a disgrace to us. ¹⁵But we will allow you to marry her if you do this one thing: Every man in your town must be circumcised like us. ¹⁶Then your men can marry our women, and our men can marry your women. Then we will live in your land and become one people. ¹⁷If you refuse to be circumcised, we will take Dinah and leave."

33:17 Succoth This name means "shelters."

[18]What they asked seemed fair to Hamor and Shechem. [19]So Shechem went quickly to be circumcised because he loved Jacob's daughter.

Now Shechem was the most respected man in his family. [20]So Hamor and Shechem went to the gate of their city. They spoke to the men of their city. They said, [21]"These people want to be friends with us. So let them live in our land and trade here. There is enough land for all of us. Let us marry their women. And we can let them marry our women. [22]But our men must agree to one thing. All our men must agree to be circumcised as they are. Then they will agree to live in our land. And we will be one people. [23]If we do this, their cattle and their animals will belong to us. Let us do what they say, and they will stay in our land." [24]All the men who had come to the city gate heard this. And they agreed with Hamor and Shechem. And every man was circumcised.

[25]Three days later the men who were circumcised were still in pain. Two of Jacob's sons, Simeon and Levi (Dinah's brothers), took their swords. They made a surprise attack on the city. And they killed all the men there. [26]Simeon and Levi killed Hamor and his son Shechem. Then they took Dinah out of Shechem's house and left. [27]Jacob's sons went among the dead bodies and stole everything that was in the city. This was to pay them back for what Shechem had done to their sister. [28]So the brothers took the flocks, herds and donkeys. And they took everything in the city and in the fields. [29]They took every valuable thing those people owned. They even took the wives and children and everything that was in the houses.

[30]Then Jacob said to Simeon and Levi, "You have caused me a lot of trouble. Now the Canaanites and the Perizzites who live in the land will hate me. There are only a few of us. If they join together to attack us, my people and I will be destroyed."

[31]But the brothers said, "We will not allow our sister to be treated like a prostitute."[d]

JACOB IN BETHEL

35 God said to Jacob, "Go to the city of Bethel and live there. Make an altar to the God who appeared to you there. This was when you were running away from your brother Esau."

[2]So Jacob said to his family and to all who were with him, "Put away the foreign gods you have. Make yourselves clean,[d] and change your clothes. [3]We will leave here and go to Bethel. There I will build an altar to God. He has helped me during my time of trouble. He has been with me everywhere I have gone." [4]So they gave Jacob all the foreign gods they had. And they gave him the earrings they were wearing. He hid them under the great tree near the town of Shechem. [5]Then Jacob and his sons left there. But God caused the people in the nearby cities to be afraid. So they did not follow the sons of Jacob. [6]And Jacob and all the people who were with him went to Luz. It is now called Bethel. It is in the land of Canaan. [7]There Jacob built an altar. He named the place Bethel, after God, because God had appeared to him there. That was when he was running from his brother.

[8]Deborah, Rebekah's nurse, died and was buried under the oak tree at Bethel. They named that place Oak of Crying.

JACOB'S NEW NAME

[9]When Jacob came back from Northwest Mesopotamia, God appeared to him again. And God blessed him. [10]God said to him, "Your name is Jacob. But you will not be called Jacob any longer. Your new name will be Israel." So he called him Israel. [11]God said to him, "I am God All-Powerful. Have many children and grow in number as a nation. You will be the ancestor of many nations and kings. [12]I gave Abraham and Isaac land. I will give that same land to you

and your descendants."[d] [13]Then God left him. [14]Jacob set up a stone on edge in that place where God had talked to him. And he poured a drink offering and olive oil on it to make it special for God. [15]And Jacob named the place Bethel.

RACHEL DIES GIVING BIRTH

[16]Jacob and his group left Bethel. Before they came to Ephrath, Rachel began giving birth to her baby. [17]But she was having much trouble with this birth. When Rachel's nurse saw this, she said, "Don't be afraid, Rachel. You are giving birth to another son." [18]Rachel gave birth to the son, but she died. As she lay dying, she named the boy Son of My Suffering. But Jacob called him Benjamin.[n]

[19]Rachel was buried on the road to Ephrath, a district of Bethlehem. [20]And Jacob set up a rock on her grave to honor her. That rock is still there today. [21]Then Israel, also called Jacob, continued his journey. He camped just south of Migdal Eder.

[22]While Israel was in that land Reuben had sexual relations with Israel's slave woman[d] Bilhah. And Israel heard about it.

THE FAMILY OF ISRAEL

Jacob had 12 sons. [23]He had 6 sons by his wife Leah. Reuben was his first son. Then Leah had Simeon, Levi, Judah, Issachar and Zebulun. [24]He had 2 sons by his wife Rachel: Joseph and Benjamin. [25]He had 2 sons by Rachel's slave girl Bilhah: Dan and Naphtali. [26]And he had 2 sons by Leah's slave girl Zilpah: Gad and Asher. These are Jacob's sons who were born in Northwest Mesopotamia.

[27]Jacob went to his father Isaac at Mamre near Hebron. This is where Abraham and Isaac had lived. [28]Isaac lived 180 years. [29]So Isaac breathed his last breath and died when he was very old. And his sons Esau and Jacob buried him.

ESAU'S FAMILY

36
This is the family history of Esau (also called Edom).

[2]Esau married women from the land of Canaan. He married Adah daughter of Elon the Hittite. And he married Oholibamah daughter of Anah. Anah was the son of Zibeon the Hivite. And he married [3]Basemath, Ishmael's daughter, the sister of Nebaioth.

[4]Adah gave Esau one son, Eliphaz. Basemath gave Esau Reuel. [5]And Oholibamah gave Esau Jeush, Jalam and Korah. These were Esau's sons who were born in the land of Canaan.

[6]Esau took his wives, his sons, his daughters and all the people who lived with him. He took his herds and other animals. And he took all the belongings he had gotten in Canaan. And he went to a land away from his brother Jacob. [7]Esau and Jacob's belongings were becoming too many for them to live in the same land. The land where they had lived could not support both of them. They had too many herds. [8]So Esau lived in the mountains of Edom. (Esau is also named Edom.)

[9]This is the family history of Esau. He is the ancestor of the Edomites, who live in the mountains of Edom.

[10]Esau's sons were Eliphaz son of Adah and Esau, and Reuel son of Basemath and Esau. [11]Eliphaz had five sons: Teman, Omar, Zepho, Gatam and Kenaz. [12]Eliphaz also had a slave woman[d] named Timna. Timna and Eliphaz gave birth to Amalek. These were Esau's grandsons by his wife Adah.

[13]Reuel had four sons: Nahath, Zerah, Shammah and Mizzah. These were Esau's grandsons by his wife Basemath.

[14]Esau's third wife was Oholibamah. She was the daughter of Anah. (Anah was the son of Zibeon.) Esau and

---

35:18 Benjamin This name means "right-hand son" or "favorite son."

Oholibamah gave birth to Jeush, Jalam and Korah.

¹⁵These were the leaders that came from Esau. Esau's first son was Eliphaz. From him came these leaders: Teman, Omar, Zepho, Kenaz, ¹⁶Korah, Gatam and Amalek. These were the leaders that came from Eliphaz in the land of Edom. They were the grandsons of Adah.

¹⁷Esau's son Reuel was the father of these leaders: Nahath, Zerah, Shammah and Mizzah. These were the leaders that came from Reuel in the land of Edom. They were the grandsons of Esau's wife Basemath.

¹⁸Esau's wife Oholibamah gave birth to these leaders: Jeush, Jalam and Korah. These are the leaders that came from Esau's wife Oholibamah. She was the daughter of Anah. ¹⁹These were the sons of Esau (also called Edom), and these were their leaders.

²⁰These were the sons of Seir the Horite, who were living in the land: Lotan, Shobal, Zibeon, Anah, ²¹Dishon, Ezer and Dishan. These sons of Seir were the leaders of the Horites in Edom.

²²The sons of Lotan were Hori and Homam. (Timna was Lotan's sister.)

²³The sons of Shobal were Alvan, Manahath, Ebal, Shepho and Onam.

²⁴The sons of Zibeon were Aiah and Anah. Anah is the man who found the hot springs in the desert. He found them while he was caring for his father's donkeys.

²⁵The children of Anah were Dishon and Oholibamah daughter of Anah.

²⁶The sons of Dishon were Hemdan, Eshban, Ithran and Keran.

²⁷The sons of Ezer were Bilhan, Zaavan and Akan.

²⁸The sons of Dishan were Uz and Aran.

²⁹These were the names of the Horite leaders: Lotan, Shobal, Zibeon, Anah, ³⁰Dishon, Ezer and Dishan.

These men were the leaders of the Horite families. They lived in the land of Edom.

³¹These are the kings who ruled in the land of Edom before the Israelites ever had a king.

³²Bela son of Beor was the king of Edom. He came from the city of Dinhabah.

³³When Bela died, Jobab son of Zerah became king. Jobab was from Bozrah.

³⁴When Jobab died, Husham became king. He was from the land of the Temanites.

³⁵When Husham died, Hadad son of Bedad became king. Hadad had defeated Midian in the country of Moab. Hadad was from the city of Avith.

³⁶When Hadad died, Samlah became king. He was from Masrekah.

³⁷When Samlah died, Shaul became king. He was from Rehoboth on the Euphrates River.

³⁸When Shaul died, Baal-Hanan son of Acbor became king.

³⁹When Baal-Hanan son of Acbor died, Hadad became king. He was from the city of Pau. His wife's name was Mehetabel daughter of Matred. Matred was the daughter of Me-Zahab.

⁴⁰These Edomite leaders came from Esau. They are listed by their families and regions. Their names were Timna, Alvah, Jetheth, ⁴¹Oholibamah, Elah, Pinon, ⁴²Kenaz, Teman, Mibzar, ⁴³Magdiel and Iram. These were the leaders of Edom. (Esau was the father of the Edomites.) The area where each of these families lived was named after that family.

JOSEPH THE DREAMER

37 Jacob lived in the land of Canaan, where his father had lived. ²This is the family history of Jacob.

Joseph was a young man, 17 years old. He and his brothers cared for the flocks. His brothers were the sons of Bilhah and Zilpah, his father's wives. Joseph gave his father bad reports about his brothers. ³Joseph was born when his father Israel, also called Jacob, was old. So Israel loved Joseph more than his other sons. He made Joseph a special robe with long sleeves. ⁴Joseph's brothers saw that their father loved Joseph more than he loved them. So they hated their brother and could not speak to him politely.

⁵One time Joseph had a dream. When he told his brothers about it, they hated him even more. ⁶Joseph said, "Listen to the dream I had. ⁷We were in the field tying bundles of wheat together. My bundle stood up, and your bundles of wheat gathered around mine. Your bundles bowed down to mine."

⁸His brothers said, "Do you really think you will be king over us? Do you truly think you will rule over us?" His brothers hated him even more now. They hated him because of his dreams and what he had said.

⁹Then Joseph had another dream. He told his brothers about it also. He said, "Listen, I had another dream. I saw the sun, moon and 11 stars bowing down to me."

¹⁰Joseph also told his father about this dream. But his father scolded him, saying, "What kind of dream is this? Do you really believe that your mother, your brothers and I will bow down to you?" ¹¹Joseph's brothers were jealous of him. But his father thought about what all these things could mean.

¹²One day Joseph's brothers went to Shechem to herd their father's sheep. ¹³Jacob said to Joseph, "Go to Shechem. Your brothers are there herding the sheep."

Joseph answered, "I will go."

¹⁴His father said, "Go and see if your brothers and the sheep are all right. Then come back and tell me." So Joseph's father sent him from the Valley of Hebron.

When Joseph came to Shechem, ¹⁵a man found him wandering in the field. He asked Joseph, "What are you looking for?"

¹⁶Joseph answered, "I am looking for my brothers. Can you tell me where they are herding the sheep?"

¹⁷The man said, "They have already gone. I heard them say they were going to Dothan." So Joseph went to look for his brothers and found them in Dothan.

JOSEPH SOLD INTO SLAVERY

¹⁸Joseph's brothers saw him coming from far away. Before he reached them, they made a plan to kill him. ¹⁹They said to each other, "Here comes that dreamer. ²⁰Let's kill him and throw his body into one of the wells. We can tell our father that a wild animal killed him. Then we will see what will become of his dreams."

²¹But Reuben heard their plan and saved Joseph. He said, "Let's not kill him. ²²Don't spill any blood. Throw him into this well here in the desert. But don't hurt him!" Reuben planned to save Joseph later and send him back to his father. ²³So when Joseph came to his brothers, they pulled off his robe with long sleeves. ²⁴Then they threw him into the well. It was empty. There was no water in it.

²⁵While Joseph was in the well, the brothers sat down to eat. When they looked up, they saw a group of Ishmaelites. They were traveling from Gilead to Egypt. Their camels were carrying spices, balm*ᵈ* and myrrh.*ᵈ*

²⁶Then Judah said to his brothers, "What will we gain if we kill our brother and hide his death? ²⁷Let's sell him to these Ishmaelites. Then we will not be guilty of killing our own brother. After all, he is our brother, our own flesh and blood." And the other brothers agreed. ²⁸So when the Midianite traders came by, the brothers took Joseph out of the well. They sold him to the Ishmaelites for eight ounces of silver. And the Ishmaelites took him to Egypt.

²⁹Reuben was not with his brothers when they sold Joseph to the Ishmaelites. When Reuben came back to the well, Joseph was not there. Reuben tore his clothes to show he was sad. ³⁰Then he went back to his brothers and said, "The

boy is not there! What will I do?" ³¹The brothers killed a goat and dipped Joseph's long-sleeved robe in its blood. ³²Then they brought the robe to their father. They said, "We found this robe. Look it over carefully. See if it is your son's robe."

³³Jacob looked it over and said, "It is my son's robe! Some savage animal has eaten him. My son Joseph has been torn to pieces!" ³⁴Then Jacob tore his clothes and put on rough cloth to show that he was sad. He continued to be sad about his son for a long time. ³⁵All of Jacob's sons and daughters tried to comfort him. But he could not be comforted. Jacob said, "I will be sad about my son until the day I die." So Jacob cried for his son Joseph.

³⁶Meanwhile the Midianites who had bought Joseph had taken him to Egypt. There they sold him to Potiphar. Potiphar was an officer to the king of Egypt and captain of the palace guard.

JUDAH AND TAMAR

38 About that time, Judah left his brothers. He went to stay with a man named Hirah. Hirah was from the town of Adullam. ²Judah met a Canaanite girl there and married her. Her father was named Shua. And Judah had sexual relations with her. ³She became pregnant and gave birth to a son. Judah named him Er. ⁴Later she gave birth to another son. She named him Onan. ⁵Later she had another son. She named him Shelah. She was at Kezib when this third son was born.

⁶Judah chose a girl named Tamar to be the wife of his first son Er. ⁷Er was Judah's oldest son. But he did what the Lord said was evil. So the Lord killed him. ⁸Then Judah said to Er's brother Onan, "Go and have sexual relations with your dead brother's wife.ⁿ It is your duty to provide children for your brother in this way."

⁹But Onan knew that the children would not belong to him. Onan was supposed to have sexual relations with Tamar. But he did not complete the sex act. This made it impossible for Tamar to become pregnant. So Er could not have descendants.ᵈ ¹⁰The Lord was displeased by this wicked thing Onan had done. So the Lord killed Onan also. ¹¹Then Judah said to his daughter-in-law Tamar, "Go back to live in your father's house. And don't marry until my young son Shelah grows up." Judah was afraid that Shelah also would die like his brothers. So Tamar returned to her father's home.

¹²After a long time Judah's wife, the daughter of Shua, died. After Judah had gotten over his sorrow, he went to Timnah. He went to his men who were cutting the wool from his sheep. His friend Hirah from Adullam went with him. ¹³Tamar learned that Judah, her father-in-law, was going to Timnah to cut the wool from his sheep. ¹⁴So she took off the clothes that showed she was a widow. Then she covered her face with a veil to hide who she was. She sat down by the gate of Enaim. It was on the road to Timnah. She did this because Judah's younger son Shelah had grown up. But Judah had not made plans for her to marry him.

¹⁵When Judah saw her, he thought she was a prostitute.ᵈ This was because she had covered her face with a veil. ¹⁶So Judah went to her and said, "Let me have sexual relations with you." He did not know that she was Tamar, his daughter-in-law.

She asked, "What will you give me if I let you have sexual relations with me?"

¹⁷Judah answered, "I will send you a young goat from my flock."

38:8 Go . . . wife. It was a custom in Israel that if a man died without children, one of his brothers would marry the widow. If a child was born, it would be considered the dead man's child.

She answered, "First give me something to keep as a deposit until you send the goat."

¹⁸Judah asked, "What do you want me to give you as a deposit?"

Tamar answered, "Give me your seal and its cord,ⁿ and give me your walking stick." So Judah gave these things to her. Then Judah and Tamar had sexual relations, and Tamar became pregnant. ¹⁹Tamar went home. She took off the veil that covered her face. And she put on the clothes that showed she was a widow.

²⁰Judah sent his friend Hirah with the young goat. Judah told Hirah to find the woman and get back his seal and the walking stick he had given her. But Hirah could not find her. ²¹Hirah asked some of the men at the town of Enaim, "Where is the prostitute who was here by the road?"

The men answered, "There has never been a prostitute here."

²²So he went back to Judah and said, "I could not find the woman. The men who lived there said, 'There has never been a prostitute here.'"

²³Judah said, "Let her keep the things. I don't want people to laugh at us. I sent her the goat as I promised. But you could not find her."

²⁴About three months later someone told Judah, "Tamar, your daughter-in-law, is guilty of acting like a prostitute. Now she is pregnant."

Then Judah said, "Bring her out and let her be burned to death."

²⁵When the men went to bring Tamar out, she sent a message to her father-in-law. She said, "The man who owns these things has made me pregnant. Look at this seal and its cord and this walking stick. Tell me whose they are."

²⁶Judah recognized them. He said, "She is more in the right than I. She did this because I did not give her to my son Shelah as I promised." And Judah did not have sexual relations with her again.

²⁷When time came for Tamar to give birth, there were twins in her body. ²⁸While she was giving birth, one baby put his hand out. The nurse tied a red string on his hand. She said, "This baby came out first." ²⁹But he pulled his hand back in. So the other baby was born first. The nurse said, "So you are able to break out first." And they named him Perez.ⁿ ³⁰After this, the baby with the red string on his hand was born. They named him Zerah.

JOSEPH IS SOLD TO POTIPHAR

39 Now Joseph had been taken down to Egypt. An Egyptian named Potiphar was an officer to the king of Egypt. He was the captain of the palace guard. He bought Joseph from the Ishmaelites who had brought him down there. ²The Lord was with Joseph, and he became a successful man. He lived in the house of his master, Potiphar the Egyptian.

³Potiphar saw that the Lord was with Joseph. He saw that the Lord made Joseph successful in everything he did. ⁴So Potiphar was very happy with Joseph. He allowed Joseph to be his personal servant. He put Joseph in charge of the house. Joseph was trusted with everything Potiphar owned. ⁵So Joseph was put in charge of the house. He was put in charge of everything Potiphar owned. Then the Lord blessed the people in Potiphar's house because of Joseph. And the Lord blessed everything that belonged to Potiphar, both in the house and in the field. ⁶So Potiphar put Joseph in charge of everything he owned. Potiphar was not concerned about anything, except the food he ate.

38:18 seal . . . cord A seal was used like a rubber stamp. People ran a string through it to tie around the neck. They wrote a contract, folded it, put wax or clay on the contract, and pressed the seal onto it as a signature.
38:29 Perez This name means "breaking out."

JOSEPH IS PUT INTO PRISON

Now Joseph was well built and handsome. [7]After some time the wife of Joseph's master began to desire Joseph. One day she said to him, "Have sexual relations with me."

[8]But Joseph refused. He said to her, "My master trusts me with everything in his house. He has put me in charge of everything he owns. [9]There is no one in his house greater than I. He has not kept anything from me, except you. And that is because you are his wife. How can I do such an evil thing? It is a sin against God."

[10]The woman talked to Joseph every day, but he refused to have sexual relations with her or even spend time with her.

[11]One day Joseph went into the house to do his work as usual. He was the only man in the house at that time. [12]His master's wife grabbed his coat. She said to him, "Come and have sexual relations with me." But Joseph left his coat in her hand and ran out of the house.

[13]She saw what Joseph had done. He had left his coat in her hands and had run outside. [14]So she called to the servants in her house. She said, "Look! This Hebrew slave was brought here to shame us. He came in and tried to have sexual relations with me. But I screamed. [15]My scream scared him, and he ran away. But he left his coat with me." [16]She kept his coat until her husband came home. [17]And she told her husband the same story. She said, "This Hebrew slave you brought here came in to shame me! [18]When he came near me, I screamed. He ran away, but he left his coat."

[19]When Joseph's master heard what his wife said Joseph had done, he became very angry. [20]So Potiphar arrested Joseph and put him into prison. This prison was where the king's prisoners were put. And Joseph stayed there in the prison. [21]But the Lord was with Joseph and showed him kindness. The Lord caused the prison warden to like Joseph. [22]The prison warden chose Joseph to take care of all the prisoners. He was responsible for whatever was done in the prison. [23]The warden paid no attention to anything that was in Joseph's care. This was because the Lord was with Joseph. The Lord made Joseph successful in everything he did.

JOSEPH INTERPRETS TWO DREAMS

40 After these things happened, two of the king's officers displeased the king. These officers were the man who served wine to the king and the king's baker. [2]The king became angry with his officer who served him wine and his baker. [3]So he put them in the prison of the captain of the guard. This was the same prison where Joseph was kept. [4]The captain of the guard put the two prisoners in Joseph's care. They stayed in prison for some time.

[5]One night both the king's officer who served him wine and the baker had a dream. Each had his own dream with its own meaning. [6]When Joseph came to them the next morning, he saw they were worried. [7]Joseph asked the king's officers who were with him, "Why do you look so unhappy today?"

[8]The two men answered, "We both had dreams last night. But no one can explain the meaning of them to us."

Joseph said to them, "God is the only One who can explain the meaning of dreams. So tell me your dreams."

[9]So the man who served wine to the king told Joseph his dream. He said, "I dreamed I saw a vine. [10]On the vine there were three branches. I watched the branches bud and blossom, and then the grapes ripened. [11]I was holding the king's cup. So I took the grapes and squeezed the juice into the cup. Then I gave it to the king."

[12]Then Joseph said, "I will explain the dream to you. The three branches stand for three days. [13]Before the end of three days the king will free you. He will allow

you to return to your work. You will serve the king his wine just as you did before. [14]But when you are free, remember me. Be kind to me. Tell the king about me so that I can get out of this prison. [15]I was taken by force from the land of the Hebrews. And I have done nothing here to deserve being put in prison."

[16]The baker saw that Joseph's explanation of the dream was good. So he said to Joseph, "I also had a dream. I dreamed there were three bread baskets on my head. [17]In the top basket there were all kinds of baked food for the king. But the birds were eating this food out of the basket on my head."

[18]Joseph answered, "I will tell you what the dream means. The three baskets stand for three days. [19]Before the end of three days, the king will cut off your head! He will hang your body on a pole. And the birds will eat your flesh."

[20]Three days later it was the king's birthday. So he gave a feast for all his officers. In front of his officers, he let the chief officer who served his wine and the chief baker out of prison. [21]The king gave his chief officer who served wine his old position. Once again he put the king's cup of wine into the king's hand. [22]But the king hanged the baker on a pole. Everything happened just as Joseph had said it would. [23]But the officer who served wine did not remember Joseph. He forgot all about him.

THE KING'S DREAMS

41 Two years later the king had a dream. He dreamed he was standing on the bank of the Nile River. [2]He saw seven fat and beautiful cows come up out of the river. They stood there, eating the grass. [3]Then seven more cows came up out of the river. But they were thin and ugly. They stood beside the seven beautiful cows on the bank of the Nile. [4]The seven thin and ugly cows ate the seven beautiful fat cows. Then the king woke up. [5]The king slept again and dreamed a second time. In his dream he saw seven full and good heads of grain growing on one stalk. [6]After that, seven more heads of grain sprang up. But they were thin and burned by the hot east wind. [7]The thin heads of grain ate the seven full and good heads. Then the king woke up again. And he realized it was only a dream. [8]The next morning the king was troubled about these dreams. So he sent for all the magicians and wise men of Egypt. The king told them his dreams. But no one could explain their meaning to him.

[9]Then the chief officer who served wine to the king said to him, "I remember something I promised to do. But I had forgotten about it. [10]There was a time when you were angry with me and the baker. You put us in prison in the house of the captain of the guard. [11]In prison we each had a dream on the same night. Each dream had a different meaning. [12]A young Hebrew man was in the prison with us. He was a servant of the captain of the guard. We told him our dreams, and he explained their meanings to us. He told each man the meaning of his dream. [13]Things happened exactly as he said they would: I was given back my old position, and the baker was hanged."

[14]So the king called for Joseph. The guards quickly brought him out of the prison. He shaved, put on clean clothes and went before the king.

[15]The king said to Joseph, "I have had a dream. But no one can explain its meaning to me. I have heard that you can explain a dream when someone tells it to you."

[16]Joseph answered the king, "I am not able to explain the meaning of dreams. God will do this for the king."

[17]Then the king said to Joseph, "In my dream I was standing on the bank of the Nile River. [18]I saw seven fat and beautiful cows. They came up out of the river and ate the grass. [19]Then I saw seven more

cows come out of the river. They were thin and lean and ugly. They were the worst looking cows I have seen in all the land of Egypt. [20]And these thin and ugly cows ate the first seven fat cows. [21]But after they had eaten the seven cows, no one could tell they had eaten them. They just looked as thin and ugly as they did in the beginning. Then I woke up.

[22]"I had another dream. I saw seven full and good heads of grain growing on one stalk. [23]Then seven more heads of grain sprang up after them. But these heads were thin and ugly. They were burned by the hot east wind. [24]Then the thin heads ate the seven good heads. I told this dream to the magicians. But no one could explain its meaning to me."

JOSEPH TELLS THE DREAMS' MEANING

[25]Then Joseph said to the king, "Both of these dreams mean the same thing. God is telling you what he is about to do. [26]The seven good cows stand for seven years. And the seven good heads of grain stand for seven years. Both dreams mean the same thing. [27]The seven thin and ugly cows stand for seven years. And the seven thin heads of grain burned by the hot east wind stand for seven years of hunger. [28]This will happen as I told you. God is showing the king what he is about to do. [29]You will have seven years of good crops and plenty to eat in all the land of Egypt. [30]But after those seven years, there will come seven years of hunger. All the food that grew in the land of Egypt will be forgotten. The time of hunger will eat up the land. [31]People will forget what it was like to have plenty of food. This is because the hunger that follows will be so great. [32]You had two dreams which mean the same thing. This shows that God has firmly decided that this will happen. And he will make it happen soon.

[33]"So let the king choose a man who is very wise and understanding. Let the king set him over the land of Egypt.

[34]And let the king also appoint officers over the land. They should take one-fifth of all the food that is grown during the seven good years. [35]They should gather all the food that is produced during the good years that are coming. Under the king's authority they should store the grain in the cities and guard it. [36]That food should be saved for later. It will be used during the seven years of hunger that will come on the land of Egypt. Then the people in Egypt will not die during the seven years of hunger."

JOSEPH IS MADE RULER OVER EGYPT

[37]This seemed like a very good idea to the king. All his officers agreed. [38]And the king asked them, "Can we find a better man than Joseph to take this job? God's spirit is truly in him!"

[39]So the king said to Joseph, "God has shown you all this. There is no one as wise and understanding as you are. [40]I will put you in charge of my palace. All the people will obey your orders. Only I will be greater than you."

[41]Then the king said to Joseph, "Look! I have put you in charge of all the land of Egypt." [42]Then the king took off from his own finger his ring with the royal seal on it. And he put it on Joseph's finger. He gave Joseph fine linen clothes to wear. And he put a gold chain around Joseph's neck. [43]The king had Joseph ride in the second royal chariot. Men walked ahead of his chariot calling, "Bow down!" By doing these things, the king put Joseph in charge of all of Egypt.

[44]The king said to him, "I am the king. And I say that no one in all the land of Egypt may lift a hand or a foot unless you say he may." [45]The king gave Joseph the name Zaphenath-Paneah. He also gave Joseph a wife named Asenath. She was the daughter of Potiphera, priest of On. So Joseph traveled through all the land of Egypt.

[46]Joseph was 30 years old when he began serving the king of Egypt. And he

left the king's court and traveled through all the land of Egypt. [47]During the seven good years, the crops in the land grew well. [48]And Joseph gathered all the food produced in Egypt during those seven years of good crops. He stored the food in the cities. In every city he stored grain that had been grown in the fields around that city. [49]Joseph stored much grain, as much as the sand of the seashore. He stored so much grain that he could not measure it.

[50]Joseph's wife was Asenath daughter of Potiphera, the priest of On. Before the years of hunger came, Joseph and Asenath had two sons. [51]Joseph named the first son Manasseh.[n] Joseph said, "God has made me forget all the troubles I have had and all my father's family." [52]Joseph named the second son Ephraim.[n] Joseph said, "God has given me children in the land of my troubles."

[53]The seven years of good crops came to an end in the land of Egypt. [54]Then the seven years of hunger began, just as Joseph had said. In all the lands people had nothing to eat. But in Egypt there was food. [55]The time of hunger became terrible in all of Egypt. The people cried to the king for food. He said to all the Egyptians, "Go to Joseph. Do whatever he tells you to do."

[56]The hunger was everywhere in that part of the world. And Joseph opened the storehouses and sold grain to the people of Egypt. This was because the time of hunger became terrible in Egypt. [57]And all the people in that part of the world came to Joseph in Egypt to buy grain. This was because the hunger was terrible everywhere in that part of the world.

THE DREAMS COME TRUE

42 Jacob learned that there was grain in Egypt. So he said to his sons, "Why are you just sitting here looking at one another? [2]I have heard that there is grain in Egypt. Go down there and buy grain for us to eat. Then we will live and not die."

[3]So ten of Joseph's brothers went down to buy grain from Egypt. [4]But Jacob did not send Benjamin, Joseph's brother, with them. Jacob was afraid that something terrible might happen to Benjamin. [5]Along with many other people, the sons of Jacob, also called Israel, went to Egypt to buy grain. This was because the people in the land of Canaan were hungry also.

[6]Now Joseph was governor over Egypt. He was the one who sold the grain to people who came to buy it. So Joseph's brothers came to him. They bowed face-down on the ground before him. [7]When Joseph saw his brothers, he knew who they were. But he acted as if he didn't know them. He asked unkindly, "Where do you come from?"

They answered, "We have come from the land of Canaan to buy food."

[8]Joseph knew they were his brothers. But they did not know who he was. [9]And Joseph remembered his dreams about his brothers bowing to him. He said to them, "You are spies! You came to learn where the nation is weak!"

[10]But his brothers said to him, "No, my master. We come as your servants just to buy food. [11]We are all sons of the same father. We are honest men, not spies."

[12]Then Joseph said to them, "No! You have come to learn where this nation is weak!"

[13]And they said, "We are 10 of 12 brothers. We are sons of the same father. We live in the land of Canaan. Our youngest brother is there with our father right now. And our other brother is gone."

[14]But Joseph said to them, "I can see I was right! You are spies! [15]But I will give

---

41:51 Manasseh This name sounds like the Hebrew word for "made me forget."
41:52 Ephraim This name sounds like the Hebrew word for "given me children."

you a way to prove you are telling the truth. As surely as the king lives, you will not leave this place until your youngest brother comes here. ¹⁶One of you must go and get your brother. The rest of you will stay here in prison. We will see if you are telling the truth. If not, as surely as the king lives, you are spies." ¹⁷Then Joseph put them all in prison for three days.

¹⁸On the third day Joseph said to them, "I am a God-fearing man. Do this thing, and I will let you live: ¹⁹If you are honest men, let one of your brothers stay here in prison. The rest of you go and carry grain back to feed your hungry families. ²⁰Then bring your youngest brother back here to me. If you do this, I will know you are telling the truth. Then you will not die."

The brothers agreed to this. ²¹They said to each other, "We are being punished for what we did to our brother. We saw his trouble. He begged us to save him, but we refused to listen. That is why we are in this trouble now."

²²Then Reuben said to them, "I told you not to harm the boy. But you refused to listen to me. So now we are being punished for what we did to him."

²³When Joseph talked to his brothers, he used an interpreter. So they did not know that Joseph understood what they were saying. ²⁴Then Joseph left them and cried. After a short time he went back and spoke to them. He took Simeon and tied him up while the other brothers watched. ²⁵Joseph told his servants to fill his brothers' bags with grain. They were to put the money the brothers had paid for the grain back in their bags. They were to give them things they would need for their trip back home. And the servants did this.

²⁶So the brothers put the grain on their donkeys and left. ²⁷When they stopped for the night, one of the brothers opened his sack. He was going to get food for his donkey. Then he saw his money in the top of the sack. ²⁸He said to the other brothers, "The money I paid for the grain has been put back. Here it is in my sack!"

The brothers were very frightened. They said to each other, "What has God done to us?"

THE BROTHERS RETURN TO JACOB

²⁹The brothers went to their father Jacob in the land of Canaan. They told him everything that had happened. ³⁰They said, "The master of that land spoke unkindly to us. He accused us of spying on his country. ³¹But we told him that we were honest men, not spies. ³²We told him that we were 10 of 12 brothers—sons of one father. We said that 1 of our brothers was gone. And we said that our youngest brother was with our father in Canaan.

³³"Then the master of the land said to us, 'Here is a way I can know you are honest men: Leave 1 of your brothers with me. Take back grain to feed your hungry families, and go. ³⁴And bring your youngest brother to me. Then I will know that you are not spies but honest men. And I will give you back your brother whom you leave with me. And you can move about freely in our land.'"

³⁵Then the brothers emptied their sacks. And each of them found his money in his sack. When they and their father saw it, they were afraid.

³⁶Their father Jacob said to them, "You are robbing me of all my children. Joseph is gone. Simeon is gone. And now you want to take Benjamin away, too. Everything is against me."

³⁷Then Reuben said to his father, "You may put my 2 sons to death if I don't bring Benjamin back to you. Trust him to my care. I will bring him back to you."

³⁸But Jacob said, "I will not allow Benjamin to go with you. His brother is dead. He is the only son left from my wife Rachel. I am afraid something terrible might happen to him during the

trip to Egypt. Then I would be sad until the day I die."

THE BROTHERS GO BACK TO EGYPT

43 Still no food grew in the land of Canaan. ²Jacob's family had eaten all the grain they had brought from Egypt. So Jacob said to them, "Go to Egypt again. Buy a little more grain for us to eat."

³But Judah said to Jacob, "The governor of that country strongly warned us. He said, 'Bring your brother back with you. If you don't, you will not be allowed to see me.' ⁴If you will send Benjamin with us, we will go down and buy food for you. ⁵But if you refuse to send Benjamin, we will not go. The governor of that country warned us. He said we would not see him if we didn't bring Benjamin with us."

⁶Jacob, also called Israel, said, "Why did you tell the man you had another brother? You have caused me a lot of trouble."

⁷The brothers answered, "He questioned us carefully about ourselves and our family. He asked us, 'Is your father still alive? Do you have another brother?' We just answered his questions. How could we know he would ask us to bring our other brother to him?"

⁸Then Judah said to his father Jacob, "Send Benjamin with me. Then we will go at once. Do this so that we, you and our children may live and not die. ⁹I will guarantee you that he will be safe. I will be personally responsible for him. If I don't bring him back to you, you can blame me all my life. ¹⁰If we had not wasted all this time, we could have already made two trips."

¹¹Then their father Jacob said to them, "If it has to be that way, then do this: Take some of the best foods in our land in your packs. Give them to the man as a gift: some balm,*ᵈ* some honey, spices, myrrh,*ᵈ* pistachio nuts and almonds. ¹²Take twice as much money with you this time. Take

back the money that was returned to you in your sacks last time. Maybe it was a mistake. ¹³And take Benjamin with you. Now leave and go to the man. ¹⁴I pray that God All-Powerful will cause the governor to be merciful to you. I pray that he will allow Simeon and Benjamin to come back with you. If I am robbed of my children, then I am robbed of them!"

¹⁵So the brothers took the gifts. They also took twice as much money as they had taken the first time. And they took Benjamin. They hurried down to Egypt and stood before Joseph.

¹⁶In Egypt Joseph saw Benjamin with them. Joseph said to the servant in charge of his house, "Bring those men into my house. Kill an animal and prepare a meal. Those men will eat with me today at noon." ¹⁷The servant did as Joseph told him. He brought the men to Joseph's house.

¹⁸The brothers were afraid when they were brought to Joseph's house. They thought, "We were brought here because of the money that was put in our sacks on the first trip. He wants to attack us, make us slaves and take our donkeys." ¹⁹So the brothers went to the servant in charge of Joseph's house. They spoke to him at the door of the house. ²⁰They said, "Sir, we came here once before to buy food. ²¹While we were going home, we stopped for the night and opened our sacks. Each of us found all his money in his sack. We brought that money with us to give it back to you. ²²And we have brought more money. It is to pay for the food we want to buy this time. We don't know who put that money in our sacks."

²³But the servant answered, "It's all right. Don't be afraid. Your God, the God of your father, must have put the money in your sacks. I got the money you paid me for the grain last time." Then the servant brought Simeon out to them.

²⁴The servant led the men into Joseph's house. He gave them water, and

they washed their feet. Then he gave their donkeys food to eat. 25The men prepared their gift to give to Joseph when he arrived at noon. They had heard they were going to eat with him there.

26When Joseph came home, the brothers gave him the gift they had brought into the house. Then they bowed down to the ground to him. 27Joseph asked them how they were doing. He said, "How is your aged father you told me about? Is he still alive?"

28The brothers answered, "Your servant, our father, is well. He is still alive." And they bowed low before Joseph to show him respect.

29Then Joseph saw his brother Benjamin, who had the same mother as he. Joseph asked, "Is this your youngest brother you told me about?" Then Joseph said to Benjamin, "God be good to you, my son!" 30Then Joseph hurried off. He had to hold back the tears when he saw his brother Benjamin. So Joseph went into his room and cried there. 31Then he washed his face and came out. He controlled himself and said, "Serve the meal."

32So they served Joseph at one table. They served his brothers at another table. And they served the Egyptians who ate with him at another table. This was because Egyptians did not like Hebrews and never ate with them. 33Joseph's brothers were seated in front of him. They were in order of their ages, from oldest to youngest. And they looked at each other because they were so amazed. 34Food from Joseph's table was taken to them. But Benjamin was given five times more food than the others. Joseph's brothers drank with him until they were very drunk.

JOSEPH SETS A TRAP

44 Then Joseph gave a command to the servant in charge of his house. Joseph said, "Fill the men's sacks with as much grain as they can carry. And put each man's money into his sack with the grain. 2Put my silver cup in the sack of the youngest brother. Also put his money for the grain in that sack." The servant did what Joseph told him.

3At dawn the brothers were sent away with their donkeys. 4They were not far from the city when Joseph said to the servant in charge of his house, "Go after the men. When you catch up with them, say, 'Why have you paid back evil for good? 5The cup you have stolen is the one my master uses for drinking. And he uses it for explaining dreams. You have done a very wicked thing!'"

6So the servant caught up with the brothers. He said to them what Joseph had told him to say.

7But the brothers said to the servant, "Why do you say these things? We would not do anything like that! 8We brought back to you the money we found in our sacks. We brought it back from the land of Canaan. So surely we would not steal silver or gold from your master's house. 9If you find that silver cup in the sack of one of us, then let him die. And we will be your slaves."

10The servant said, "We will do as you say. But only the man who has taken the cup will become my slave. The rest of you may go free."

11Then every brother quickly lowered his sack to the ground and opened it. 12The servant searched the sacks, going from the oldest brother to the youngest. He found the cup in Benjamin's sack. 13The brothers tore their clothes to show they were sad. Then they put their sacks back on the donkeys. And they returned to the city.

14When Judah and his brothers went back to Joseph's house, Joseph was still there. The brothers bowed facedown on the ground before him. 15Joseph said to them, "What have you done? Didn't you know that a man like me can learn things by signs and dreams?"

¹⁶Judah said, "Sir, what can we say? And how can we show we are not guilty? God has uncovered our guilt. So all of us will be your slaves, not just Benjamin."

¹⁷But Joseph said, "I will not make you all slaves! Only the man who stole the cup will be my slave. The rest of you may go back safely to your father."

¹⁸Then Judah went to Joseph and said, "Sir, please let me speak plainly to you. Please don't be angry with me. I know that you are as powerful as the king of Egypt himself. ¹⁹When we were here before, you asked us, 'Do you have a father or a brother?' ²⁰And we answered you, 'We have an old father. And we have a younger brother. He was born when our father was old. This youngest son's brother is dead. So he is the only one of his mother's children left alive. And our father loves him very much.' ²¹Then you said to us, 'Bring that brother to me. I want to see him.' ²²And we said to you, 'That young boy cannot leave his father. If he leaves him, his father would die.' ²³But you said to us, 'You must bring your youngest brother. If you don't, you will not be allowed to see me again.' ²⁴So we went back to our father and told him what you had said.

²⁵"Later, our father said, 'Go again. Buy us a little more food.' ²⁶We said to our father, 'We cannot go without our youngest brother. Without our youngest brother, we will not be allowed to see the governor.' ²⁷Then my father said to us, 'You know that my wife Rachel gave me two sons. ²⁸One son left me. I thought, "Surely he has been torn apart by a wild animal." And I haven't seen him since. ²⁹Now you want to take this son away from me also. But something terrible might happen to him. Then I would be sad until the day I die.' ³⁰Now what will happen if we go home to our father without our youngest brother? He is the most important thing in our father's life. ³¹When our father sees that the young boy is not with us, he will die. And it will be our fault. We will cause the great sorrow that kills our father.

³²"I gave my father a guarantee that the young boy would be safe. I said to my father, 'If I don't bring him back to you, you can blame me all my life.' ³³So now, please allow me to stay here and be your slave. And let the young boy go back home with his brothers. ³⁴I cannot go back to my father if the boy is not with me. I couldn't stand to see my father that sad."

JOSEPH REVEALS WHO HE IS

45 Joseph could not control himself in front of his servants any longer. He cried out, "Have everyone leave me." When only the brothers were left with Joseph, he told them who he was. ²Joseph cried so loudly that the Egyptians heard him. And the people in the king's palace heard about it. ³He said to his brothers, "I am Joseph. Is my father still alive?" But the brothers could not answer him, because they were very afraid of him.

⁴So Joseph said to them, "Come close to me." So the brothers came close to him. And he said to them, "I am your brother Joseph. You sold me as a slave to go to Egypt. ⁵Now don't be worried. Don't be angry with yourselves because you sold me here. God sent me here ahead of you to save people's lives. ⁶No food has grown on the land for two years now. And there will be five more years without planting or harvest. ⁷So God sent me here ahead of you. This was to make sure you have some descendants*ᵈ* left on earth. And it was to keep you alive in an amazing way. ⁸So it was not you who sent me here, but God. God has made me the highest officer of the king of Egypt. I am in charge of his palace. I am the master of all the land of Egypt.

⁹"So leave quickly and go to my father. Tell him, 'Your son Joseph says: God has made me master over all Egypt. Come

down to me quickly. [10]Live in the land of Goshen. You will be near me. Also your children, your grandchildren, your flocks and herds and all that you have will be near me. [11]I will care for you during the next five years of hunger. In this way, you and your family and all that you have will not starve.'

[12]"Now you can see for yourselves. The one speaking to you is really Joseph. And my brother Benjamin can see this. [13]So tell my father about how powerful I have become in Egypt. Tell him about everything you have seen. Now hurry and bring him back to me." [14]Then Joseph hugged his brother Benjamin and cried. And Benjamin cried also. [15]Then Joseph kissed all his brothers. He cried as he hugged them. After this, his brothers talked with him.

[16]The king of Egypt and his officers learned that Joseph's brothers had come. And they were very happy about this. [17]So the king said to Joseph, "Tell your brothers to load their animals and go back to the land of Canaan. [18]Tell them to bring their father and their families back here to me. I will give them the best land in Egypt. And they will eat the best food we have here. [19]Tell them to take some wagons from Egypt for their children and their wives. And tell them to bring their father back also. [20]Tell them not to worry about bringing any of their things with them. We will give them the best of what we have in Egypt."

[21]So the sons of Israel did this. Joseph gave them wagons as the king had ordered. And he gave them food for their trip. [22]He gave each brother a change of clothes. But he gave Benjamin five changes of clothes. And Joseph gave him about seven and one-half pounds of silver. [23]Joseph also sent his father ten donkeys loaded with the best things from Egypt. And he sent ten female donkeys. They were loaded with grain, bread and other food for his father on his trip

back. [24]Then Joseph told his brothers to go. As they were leaving, he said to them, "Don't quarrel on the way home."

[25]So the brothers left Egypt and went to their father Jacob in the land of Canaan. [26]They told him, "Joseph is still alive. He is the ruler over all the land of Egypt." Their father was shocked and did not believe them. [27]But the brothers told him everything Joseph had said. Then Jacob saw the wagons that Joseph had sent to carry him back to Egypt. Now Jacob felt better. [28]Jacob, also called Israel, said, "Now I believe you. My son Joseph is still alive. I will go and see him before I die."

JACOB GOES TO EGYPT

46 So Jacob, also called Israel, took all he had and started his trip. He went to Beersheba. There he offered sacrifices to the God of his father Isaac. [2]During the night God spoke to Israel in a vision. He said, "Jacob, Jacob."

And Jacob answered, "Here I am."

[3]Then God said, "I am God, the God of your father. Don't be afraid to go to Egypt. I will make your descendants[d] a great nation there. [4]I will go to Egypt with you. And I will bring you out of Egypt again. Joseph's own hands will close your eyes when you die."

[5]Then Jacob left Beersheba. The sons of Israel loaded their father, their children and their wives. They put them in the wagons the king of Egypt had sent. [6]They also took their farm animals and everything they had gotten in Canaan. So Jacob went to Egypt with all his descendants. [7]He took his sons and grandsons, his daughters and granddaughters. He took all his family to Egypt with him.

JACOB'S FAMILY

[8]Now these are the names of the children of Israel who went into Egypt. (They are Jacob and his descendants.[d])

Reuben was Jacob's first son. [9]Reuben's sons were Hanoch, Pallu, Hezron and Carmi.

[10]Simeon's sons were Jemuel, Jamin, Ohad, Jakin, Zohar and Shaul. (Shaul was Simeon's son by a Canaanite woman.)

[11]Levi's sons were Gershon, Kohath and Merari.

[12]Judah's sons were Er, Onan, Shelah, Perez and Zerah. (But Er and Onan had died in the land of Canaan.) Perez's sons were Hezron and Hamul.

[13]Issachar's sons were Tola, Puah, Jashub and Shimron.

[14]Zebulun's sons were Sered, Elon and Jahleel.

[15]These are the sons of Leah and Jacob born in Northwest Mesopotamia. His daughter Dinah was also born there. There were 33 persons in this part of Jacob's family.

[16]Gad's sons were Zephon, Haggi, Shuni, Ezbon, Eri, Arodi and Areli.

[17]Asher's sons were Imnah, Ishvah, Ishvi and Beriah. Their sister was Serah. Beriah's sons were Heber and Malkiel.

[18]These are Jacob's sons by Zilpah. She was the slave girl whom Laban gave to his daughter Leah. There were 16 persons in this part of Jacob's family.

[19]The sons of Jacob's wife Rachel were Joseph and Benjamin. [20]In Egypt, Joseph became the father of Manasseh and Ephraim by his wife Asenath. She was the daughter of Potiphera, priest of On.

[21]Benjamin's sons were Bela, Beker, Ashbel, Gera, Naaman, Ehi, Rosh, Muppim, Huppim and Ard.

[22]These are the sons of Jacob by his wife Rachel. There were 14 persons in this part of Jacob's family.

[23]Dan's son was Hushim.

[24]Naphtali's sons were Jahziel, Guni, Jezer and Shillem.

[25]These are Jacob's sons by Bilhah. She was the slave girl whom Laban gave to his daughter Rachel. There were 7 persons in this part of Jacob's family.

[26]So the total number of Jacob's direct descendants who went to Egypt was 66. (The wives of Jacob's sons were not counted in this number.) [27]Joseph had 2 sons born in Egypt. So the total number in the family of Jacob in Egypt was 70.

JACOB ARRIVES IN EGYPT

[28]Jacob sent Judah ahead of him to see Joseph in Goshen. Then Jacob and his people came into the land of Goshen. [29]Joseph prepared his chariot and went to meet his father Israel in Goshen. As soon as Joseph saw his father, he hugged his neck. And he cried there for a long time.

[30]Then Israel said to Joseph, "Now I am ready to die. I have seen your face. And I know that you are still alive."

[31]Joseph said to his brothers and his father's family, "I will go and tell the king you are here. I will say, 'My brothers and my father's family have left the land of Canaan. They have come here to me. [32]They are shepherds and take care of farm animals. And they have brought their flocks and their herds and everything they own with them.' [33]When the king calls you, he will ask, 'What work do you do?' [34]This is what you should tell him: 'We, your servants, have taken care of farm animals all our lives. Our ancestors did the same thing.' Then the king will allow you to settle in the land of Goshen. This is away from the Egyptians. They don't like to be near shepherds."

JACOB SETTLES IN GOSHEN

47 Joseph went in to the king and said, "My father and my brothers have arrived from Canaan. They have their flocks and herds and everything they own with them. They are now in the land of Goshen." [2]Joseph chose five of his brothers to introduce to the king.

[3]The king said to the brothers, "What work do you do?"

And they said to him, "We, your servants, are shepherds. Our ancestors were also shepherds." [4]They said to the king, "We have come to live in this land. There is no grass in the land of Canaan for our animals to eat. The hunger is very terrible there. So please allow us to live in the land of Goshen."

⁵Then the king said to Joseph, "Your father and your brothers have come to you. ⁶You may choose any place in Egypt for them to live. Give your father and your brothers the best land. Let them live in the land of Goshen. And if any of them are skilled shepherds, put them in charge of my sheep and cattle."

⁷Then Joseph brought in his father Jacob and introduced him to the king. And Jacob blessed the king.

⁸Then the king said to Jacob, "How old are you?"

⁹Jacob said to him, "My life has been spent wandering from place to place. It has been short, filled with trouble. I have lived only 130 years. My ancestors lived much longer than I." ¹⁰Then Jacob blessed the king and left.

¹¹Joseph obeyed the king. He gave his father and brothers the best land in Egypt. It was near the city of Rameses. ¹²And Joseph gave his father, his brothers and everyone who lived with them the food they needed.

JOSEPH BUYS LAND FOR THE KING

¹³The hunger became worse, and there was no food anywhere in the land. The land of Egypt and the land of Canaan became very poor because of this. ¹⁴Joseph collected all the money that was to be found in Egypt and Canaan. People paid him this money for the grain they were buying. He brought that money to the king's palace. ¹⁵After some time, the people in Egypt and Canaan had no money left. So they went to Joseph and said, "Please give us food. Our money is gone. If we don't eat, we will die here in front of you."

¹⁶Joseph answered, "Since you have no money, give me your farm animals. I will give you food in return." ¹⁷So people brought their farm animals to Joseph. And he gave them food in exchange for their horses, sheep, cattle and donkeys. So he kept them alive by trading food for their farm animals that year.

¹⁸The next year the people came to Joseph and said, "You know we have no money left. And all our animals belong to you. We have nothing left except our bodies and our land. ¹⁹Surely both we and our land will die here in front of you. Buy us and our land in exchange for food. And we will be slaves to the king, together with our land. Give us seed to plant. Then we will live and not die. And the land will not become a desert."

²⁰So Joseph bought all the land in Egypt for the king. Every Egyptian sold Joseph his field, because the hunger was very great. So the land became the king's. ²¹And Joseph made the people slaves from one end of Egypt to the other. ²²The only land he did not buy was the land the priests owned. They did not need to sell their land because the king paid them for their work. So they had money to buy food.

²³Joseph said to the people, "Now I have bought you and your land for the king. So I will give you seed. And you can plant your fields. ²⁴At harvest time you must give one-fifth to the king. You may keep four-fifths for yourselves. Use it as seed for the field and as food for yourselves, your families and your children."

²⁵The people said, "You have saved our lives. If you like, we will become slaves of the king."

²⁶So Joseph made a law in Egypt, which continues today: One-fifth of everything from the land belongs to the king. The only land the king did not get was the priests' land.

"DON'T BURY ME IN EGYPT"

²⁷The Israelites continued to live in the land of Goshen in Egypt. There they got possessions. They had many children and grew in number.

²⁸Jacob, also called Israel, lived in Egypt 17 years. So he lived to be 147

years old. [29]Israel knew he soon would die. So he called his son Joseph to him. He said to Joseph, "If you love me, put your hand under my leg.[n] Promise me you will not bury me in Egypt. [30]When I die, carry me out of Egypt. Bury me where my ancestors are buried."

Joseph answered, "I will do as you say." [31]Then Jacob said, "Promise me." And Joseph promised him that he would do this. Then Israel worshiped as he leaned on the top of his walking stick.

BLESSINGS FOR MANASSEH AND EPHRAIM

48 Some time later Joseph learned that his father was very sick. So he took his two sons Manasseh and Ephraim and went to his father. [2]When Joseph arrived, someone told Jacob, also called Israel, "Your son Joseph has come to see you." Jacob was weak. So he used all his strength and sat up on his bed.

[3]Then Jacob said to Joseph, "God All-Powerful appeared to me at Luz in the land of Canaan. God blessed me there. [4]He said to me, 'I will give you many children. I will make you the father of many peoples. And I will give your descendants[d] this land forever.' [5]Your two sons were born here in Egypt before I came. They will be counted as my own sons. Ephraim and Manasseh will be my sons just as Reuben and Simeon are my sons. [6]But if you have other children, they will be your own. But their land will be part of the land given to Ephraim and Manasseh. [7]When I came from Northwest Mesopotamia, Rachel died in the land of Canaan. We were traveling toward Ephrath. This made me very sad. I buried her there beside the road to Ephrath." (Today Ephrath is Bethlehem.)

[8]Then Israel saw Joseph's sons. He said, "Who are these boys?"

[9]Joseph said to his father, "They are my sons. God has given them to me here in Egypt."

Israel said, "Bring your sons to me so I may bless them."

[10]At this time Israel's eyesight was bad because he was old. So Joseph brought the boys close to him. Israel kissed the boys and put his arms around them. [11]He said to Joseph, "I thought I would never see you alive again. And now God has let me see you and also your children." [12]Then Joseph moved his sons off Israel's lap. Joseph bowed facedown to the ground. [13]He put Ephraim on his right side and Manasseh on his left. (So Ephraim was near Israel's left hand, and Manasseh was near Israel's right hand.) Joseph brought the boys close to Israel. [14]But Israel crossed his arms. He put his right hand on the head of Ephraim, who was younger. He put his left hand on the head of Manasseh. But he was the firstborn[d] son. [15]And Israel blessed Joseph and said,

"My ancestors Abraham and Isaac
    served our God.
And like a shepherd God has led me
    all my life.
[16]He was the Angel who saved me from
    all my troubles.
Now I pray that he will bless these
    boys.
May my name be known through
    these boys.
And may the names of my
    ancestors Abraham and Isaac be
    known through them.
May they have many descendants[d] on
    the earth."

[17]Joseph saw that his father put his right hand on Ephraim's head. Joseph didn't like it. So he took hold of his father's hand. He wanted to move it from Ephraim's head to Manasseh's head. [18]Joseph said to his father, "You are doing it wrong, Father. Manasseh is the firstborn son. Put your right hand on his head."

[19]But his father refused and said, "I know, my son, I know. Manasseh will be

great and have many descendants. But his younger brother will be greater. And his descendants will be enough to make a nation."

²⁰So Israel blessed them that day. He said,

"When a blessing is given in Israel,
    they will say:
  'May God make you like Ephraim
    and Manasseh.'"

In this way he made Ephraim greater than Manasseh.

²¹Then Israel said to Joseph, "Look at me. I am about to die. But God will be with you. He will take you back to the land of your fathers. ²²I have given you something that I did not give your brothers. I have given you the land of Shechem that I took from the Amorite people. I took it with my sword and my bow."

JACOB BLESSES HIS SONS

49 Then Jacob called his sons to him. He said, "Come here to me. I will tell you what will happen to you in the future.

²"Come together and listen, sons of
    Jacob.
  Listen to Israel, your father."

³"Reuben, my first son, you are my
    strength.
  Your birth showed I could be a
    father.
  You have the highest position among
    my sons.
  You are the most powerful.
⁴But you are uncontrolled like water.
  So you will no longer lead your
    brothers.
  This is because you got into your
    father's bed.
  You shamed me by having sexual
    relations with my slave girl.

⁵"Simeon and Levi are brothers.
  They used their swords to do
    violence.
⁶I will not join their secret talks.
  I will not meet with them to plan evil.

They killed men because they were
    angry.
  And they crippled oxen just for fun.
⁷May their anger be cursed, because it
    is too violent.
  May their violence be cursed,
    because it is too cruel.
  I will divide them up among the
    tribes*d* of Jacob.
  I will scatter them through all the
    tribes of Israel.

⁸"Judah, your brothers will praise you.
  You will grab your enemies by the
    neck.
  Your brothers will bow down to you.
⁹Judah is like a young lion.
  You have returned from killing, my
    son.
  Like a lion, he stretches out and lies
    down to rest.
  No one is brave enough to wake him.
¹⁰Men from Judah's family will be
    kings.
  Someone from Judah will always be
    on the throne.
  Judah will rule until the real king
    comes.
  And the nations will obey him.
¹¹He ties his donkey to a grapevine.
  He ties his young donkey to the best
    branch.
  He can afford to use wine to wash his
    clothes.
  He even uses grape juice to wash
    his robes.
¹²His eyes are bright from drinking
    wine.
  His teeth are white from drinking
    milk.

¹³"Zebulun will live near the sea.
  His shore will be a safe place for
    ships.
  His land will reach as far as Sidon.

¹⁴"Issachar is like a strong donkey.
  He lies down while carrying his
    load.

¹⁵He will see his resting place is good.
  He will see how pleasant his land is.
Then he will put his back to the load.
  He will become a slave.

¹⁶"Dan will rule his own people
  like the other tribes in Israel.
¹⁷Dan will be like a snake by the side of
  the road.
He will be like a dangerous snake
  lying near the path.
That snake bites a horse's leg.
  And the rider is thrown off
  backward.

¹⁸"Lord, I wait for your salvation.

¹⁹"Robbers will attack Gad.
  But he will defeat them and drive
  them away.

²⁰"Asher's land will grow much good
  food.
He will grow food fit for a king.

²¹"Naphtali is like a female deer that
  runs free.
She has beautiful fawns.

²²"Joseph is like a grapevine that
  produces much fruit.
He is like a healthy vine watered by
  a spring.
He is like a vine whose branches
  grow over the wall.
²³Men attack him violently with arrows.
  They shoot at him angrily.
²⁴But he aims his bow well.
  His arms are made strong.
He gets his power from the Mighty
  God of Jacob.
He gets his strength from the
  Shepherd, the Rock^d of Israel.
²⁵Your father's God helps you.
  God All-Powerful blesses you.
He blesses you with rain from above.
He blesses you with water from
  springs below.
He blesses you with many babies born
  to your wives.

He blesses you with many young
  ones born to your animals.
²⁶The blessings of your father are
  greater
than the blessings of the oldest
  mountains.
They are greater than the good
  things of the long-lasting hills.
May these blessings rest on the head
  of Joseph.
May they rest on the forehead of the
  one who was separated from his
  brothers.

²⁷"Benjamin is like a hungry wolf.
  In the morning he eats what he has
  caught.
In the evening he divides what he
  has taken."

²⁸These are the 12 tribes of Israel. And this is what their father said to them. He gave each son the blessing that was right for him. ²⁹Then Israel gave them a command. He said, "I am about to die. Bury me with my ancestors in the cave in the field of Ephron the Hittite. ³⁰That cave is in the field of Machpelah east of Mamre. It is in the land of Canaan. Abraham bought that field from Ephron the Hittite for a burying place. ³¹Abraham and Sarah his wife are buried there. Isaac and Rebekah his wife are buried there. I buried my wife Leah there. ³²The field and the cave in it were bought from the Hittite people." ³³After Jacob finished talking to his sons, he lay down. He put his feet back on the bed, took his last breath and died.

JACOB'S BURIAL

50 When Jacob died, Joseph hugged his father and cried over him and kissed him. ²He commanded the doctors who served him to prepare his father's body. So the doctors prepared Jacob's body to be buried. ³It took the doctors 40 days to prepare his body. This was the usual time it took. And the Egyptians had a time of sorrow for Jacob. It lasted 70 days.

⁴When this time of sorrow had ended, Joseph spoke to the king's officers. He said, "If you think well of me, please tell this to the king: ⁵'When my father was near death, I made a promise to him. I promised I would bury him in a cave in the land of Canaan. This is a burial place that he cut out for himself. So please let me go and bury my father. Then I will return.'"

⁶The king answered, "Keep your promise. Go and bury your father."

⁷So Joseph went to bury his father. All the king's officers, the elders of his court and all the elders of Egypt went with Joseph. ⁸Everyone who lived with Joseph and his brothers went with him. And everyone who lived with his father also went. They left only their children, their flocks and their herds in the land of Goshen. ⁹Men in chariots and on horses also went with Joseph. It was a very large group.

¹⁰They went to the threshing*d* floor of Atad, east of the Jordan River. There they cried loudly and bitterly for Jacob, also called Israel. Joseph's time of sorrow continued for seven days. ¹¹The people that lived in Canaan saw the sadness at the threshing floor of Atad. They said, "Those Egyptians are showing great sorrow!" So now that place is named Sorrow of the Egyptians.

¹²So Jacob's sons did what their father commanded. ¹³They carried his body to the land of Canaan. They buried it in the cave in the field of Machpelah near Mamre. Abraham had bought this cave and field from Ephron the Hittite. He bought the cave to use as a burial place. ¹⁴After Joseph buried his father, he returned to Egypt. His brothers and everyone who had gone with him to bury his father also returned.

THE BROTHERS FEAR JOSEPH

¹⁵After Jacob died, Joseph's brothers said, "What if Joseph is still angry with us? We did many wrong things to him. What if he plans to pay us back?" ¹⁶So they sent a message to Joseph. It said, "Your father gave this command before he died. ¹⁷He said to us, 'You have done wrong. You have sinned and done evil to Joseph. Tell Joseph to forgive you, his brothers.' So now, Joseph, we beg you to forgive our wrong. We are the servants of the God of your father." When Joseph received the message, he cried.

¹⁸And his brothers went to him and bowed low before him. They said, "We are your slaves."

¹⁹Then Joseph said to them, "Don't be afraid. Can I do what only God can do? ²⁰You meant to hurt me. But God turned your evil into good. It was to save the lives of many people. And it is being done. ²¹So don't be afraid. I will take care of you and your children." So Joseph comforted his brothers and spoke kind words to them.

²²Joseph continued to live in Egypt with all his father's family. He died when he was 110 years old. ²³During Joseph's life Ephraim had children and grandchildren. And Joseph's son Manasseh had a son named Makir. Joseph accepted Makir's children as his own.

THE DEATH OF JOSEPH

²⁴Joseph said to his brothers, "I am about to die. But God will take care of you. He will lead you out of this land. He will lead you to the land he promised to Abraham, Isaac and Jacob." ²⁵Then Joseph had the sons of Israel make a promise. He said, "Promise me that you will carry my bones with you out of Egypt."

²⁶Joseph died when he was 110 years old. Doctors prepared his body for burial. Then they put him in a coffin in Egypt.

EXODUS

JACOB'S FAMILY IN EGYPT

1 When Jacob, also called Israel, went to Egypt, he took his sons. And each son took his own family with him. These are the names of the sons of Israel: [2]Reuben, Simeon, Levi, Judah, [3]Issachar, Zebulun, Benjamin, [4]Dan, Naphtali, Gad and Asher. [5]There was a total of 70 people who were descendants[d] of Jacob. Jacob's son Joseph was already in Egypt.

[6]By some time later, Joseph and his brothers had died, along with all the people who had lived at that same time. [7]But the people of Israel had many children, and their number grew greatly. They became very strong, and the country of Egypt was filled with them.

TROUBLE FOR THE PEOPLE OF ISRAEL

[8]Then a new king began to rule Egypt. He did not know who Joseph was. [9]This king said to his people, "Look! The people of Israel are too many! And they are too strong for us to handle! [10]We must make plans against them. If we don't, the number of their people will grow even more. Then if there is a war, they might join our enemies. Then they could fight us and escape from the country!"

[11]So the Egyptians made life hard for the people of Israel. They put slave masters over the Israelites. The slave masters forced the Israelites to build the cities Pithom and Rameses for the king. These cities were supply centers in which the Egyptians stored things. [12]The Egyptians forced the Israelites to work even harder. But this made the Israelites grow in number and spread more. So the Egyptians became more afraid of them. [13]They forced the Israelites to work even harder. [14]The Egyptians made life hard for the Israelites. They forced the Israelites to work very hard making bricks and mortar. They also forced them to do all kinds of hard work in the fields. The Egyptians were not merciful to them in all their hard work.

[15]There were two Hebrew nurses named Shiphrah and Puah. These nurses helped the Israelite women give birth to their babies. The king of Egypt said to the nurses, [16]"When you are helping the Hebrew women give birth to their babies, watch! If the baby is a girl, let the baby live. But if it is a boy, kill it!" [17]But the nurses feared God. So they did not do as the king told them. They let all the boy babies live. [18]Then the king of Egypt sent for the nurses. He said, "Why did you do this? Why did you let the boys live?"

[19]The nurses said to him, "The Hebrew women are much stronger than the Egyptian women. They give birth to their babies before we can get there." [20]God was good to the nurses. And the Hebrew people continued to grow in number. So they became even stronger. [21]Because the nurses feared God, he gave them families of their own.

[22]So the king commanded all his people: "Every time a boy is born to the Hebrews, you must throw him into the Nile River. But let all the girl babies live."

BABY MOSES

2 There was a man from the family of Levi. He married a woman who was also from the family of Levi. [2]She became pregnant and gave birth to a son. She saw how wonderful the baby was, and she hid him for three months. [3]But after three months, she was not able to hide the baby any longer. So she got a basket made of reeds and covered it with tar so that it would float. She put the baby in the basket. Then she put the basket among the tall grass at the edge of the Nile River. [4]The baby's sister stood a short distance away. She wanted to see what would happen to him.

[5]Then the daughter of the king of Egypt came to the river. She was going to take

a bath. Her servant girls were walking beside the river. She saw the basket in the tall grass. So she sent her slave girl to get it. [6]The king's daughter opened the basket and saw the baby boy. He was crying, and she felt sorry for him. She said, "This is one of the Hebrew babies."

[7]Then the baby's sister asked the king's daughter, "Would you like me to find a Hebrew woman to nurse the baby for you?"

[8]The king's daughter said, "Yes, please." So the girl went and got the baby's own mother.

[9]The king's daughter said to the woman, "Take this baby and nurse him for me. I will pay you." So the woman took her baby and nursed him. [10]After the child had grown older, the woman took him to the king's daughter. She adopted the baby as her own son. The king's daughter named him Moses,[n] because she had pulled him out of the water.

MOSES HELPS HIS PEOPLE

[11]Moses grew and became a man. One day he visited his people, the Hebrews. He saw that they were forced to work very hard. He saw an Egyptian beating a Hebrew man, one of Moses' own people. [12]Moses looked all around and saw that no one was watching. So he killed the Egyptian and hid his body in the sand.

[13]The next day Moses returned and saw two Hebrew men fighting each other. He saw that one man was in the wrong. Moses said to that man, "Why are you hitting one of your own people?"

[14]The man answered, "Who made you our ruler and judge? Are you going to kill me as you killed the Egyptian?"

Then Moses was afraid. He thought, "Now everyone knows what I did."

[15]When the king heard about what Moses had done, he tried to kill Moses. But Moses ran away from the king and went to live in the land of Midian. There he sat down near a well.

MOSES IN MIDIAN

[16]There was a priest in Midian who had seven daughters. His daughters went to that well to get water for their father's sheep. They were trying to fill the water troughs for their father's sheep. [17]But some shepherds came and chased the girls away. Then Moses defended the girls and watered their sheep.

[18]Then they went back to their father, Reuel, also called Jethro. He asked them, "Why have you come home early today?"

[19]The girls answered, "The shepherds chased us away. But an Egyptian defended us. He got water for us and watered our sheep."

[20]He asked his daughters, "Where is this man? Why did you leave him? Invite him to eat with us."

[21]Moses agreed to stay with Jethro. And he gave his daughter Zipporah to Moses to be his wife. [22]Zipporah gave birth to a son, and Moses named him Gershom.[n] Moses named him this because Moses was a stranger in a land that was not his own.

[23]After a long time, the king of Egypt died. The people of Israel groaned because they were forced to work very hard. They cried for help. And God heard them. [24]God heard their cries, and he remembered the agreement he had made with Abraham, Isaac and Jacob. [25]God saw the troubles of the people of Israel, and he was concerned about them.

THE BURNING BUSH

3 One day Moses was taking care of Jethro's sheep. Jethro was the priest of Midian and also Moses' father-in-law. Moses led the sheep to the west side of the desert. He came to Sinai, the mountain of God. [2]There the angel of the Lord appeared to Moses in flames of fire

2:10 Moses The name Moses sounds like the Hebrew word for "to pull out."
2:22 Gershom This name sounds like the Hebrew word meaning "a stranger there."

coming out of a bush. Moses saw that the bush was on fire, but it was not burning up. ³So Moses said, "I will go closer to this strange thing. How can a bush continue burning without burning up?"

⁴The Lord saw Moses was coming to look at the bush. So God called to him from the bush, "Moses, Moses!"

And Moses said, "Here I am."

⁵Then God said, "Do not come any closer. Take off your sandals. You are standing on holy ground. ⁶I am the God of your ancestors. I am the God of Abraham, the God of Isaac and the God of Jacob." Moses covered his face because he was afraid to look at God.

⁷The Lord said, "I have seen the troubles my people have suffered in Egypt. And I have heard their cries when the Egyptian slave masters hurt them. I am concerned about their pain. ⁸I have come down to save them from the Egyptians. I will bring them out of that land. I will lead them to a good land with lots of room. This is a land where much food grows. This is the land of these people: the Canaanites, Hittites, Amorites, Perizzites, Hivites and Jebusites. ⁹I have heard the cries of the people of Israel. I have seen the way the Egyptians have made life hard for them. ¹⁰So now I am sending you to the king of Egypt. Go! Bring my people, the Israelites, out of Egypt!"

¹¹But Moses said to God, "I am not a great man! Why should I be the one to go to the king and lead the Israelites out of Egypt?"

¹²God said, "I will be with you. This will be the proof that I am sending you: You will lead the people out of Egypt. Then all of you will worship me on this mountain."

¹³Moses said to God, "When I go to the Israelites, I will say to them, 'The God of your ancestors sent me to you.' What if the people say, 'What is his name?' What should I tell them?"

¹⁴Then God said to Moses, "I AM WHO I AM.ⁿ When you go to the people of Israel, tell them, 'I AM sent me to you.'"

¹⁵God also said to Moses, "This is what you should tell the people: 'The Lord is the God of your ancestors. He is the God of Abraham, the God of Isaac and the God of Jacob. And he sent me to you.' This will always be my name. That is how people from now on will know me.

¹⁶"Go and gather the elders and tell them this: 'The Lord, the God of your ancestors, has appeared to me. The God of Abraham, Isaac and Jacob spoke to me. He says: I care about you, and I have seen what has happened to you in Egypt. ¹⁷I have decided that I will take you away from the troubles you are suffering in Egypt. I will lead you to the land of the Canaanites, Hittites, Amorites, Perizzites, Hivites and Jebusites. This land grows much food.'

¹⁸"The elders will listen to you. And then you and the elders of Israel will go to the king of Egypt. You will tell him, 'The Lord, the God of the Hebrews, appeared to us. Let us travel three days into the desert. There we must offer sacrifices to the Lord our God.'

¹⁹"But I know that the king of Egypt will not let you go. Only a great power will force him to let you go. ²⁰So I will use my great power against Egypt. I will make miracles*ᵈ* happen in that land. After I do this, he will let you go. ²¹And I will cause the Egyptian people to think well of the people of Israel. So when you leave, they will give gifts to your people. ²²Each Hebrew woman will ask her Egyptian neighbor and any Egyptian woman living in her house for gifts. Ask for silver, gold and clothing. You will put

3:14 I . . . I AM The Hebrew words are like the name "YAHWEH." This Hebrew name for God, usually called "Lord," shows that God always lives and is always with his people.

those gifts on your children when you leave Egypt. In this way you will take with you the riches of the Egyptians."

PROOF FOR MOSES

4 Then Moses answered, "What if the people of Israel do not believe me or listen to me? What if they say, 'The Lord did not appear to you'?"

[2]The Lord said to him, "What is that in your hand?"

Moses answered, "It is my walking stick."

[3]The Lord said, "Throw it on the ground."

So Moses threw it on the ground. And it became a snake. Moses ran from the snake. [4]But the Lord said to him, "Reach out and grab the snake by its tail." So Moses reached out and took hold of the snake. When he did this, it again became a stick in his hand. [5]The Lord said, "When this happens, the Israelites will believe that the Lord appeared to you. I am the God of their ancestors. I am the God of Abraham, the God of Isaac and the God of Jacob."

[6]Then the Lord said to Moses, "Put your hand inside your coat." So Moses put his hand inside his coat. When he took his hand out, it was white with a harmful skin disease.

[7]Then the Lord said, "Now put your hand inside your coat again." So Moses put his hand inside his coat again. When he took it out, his hand was healthy again. It was like the rest of his skin.

[8]Then the Lord said, "The people may not believe you or be convinced by the first miracle.[d] They may believe you when you show them this second miracle. [9]After these two miracles they still may not believe or listen to you. Then take some water from the Nile River. Pour it on the dry ground. The water will become blood when it touches the ground."

[10]But Moses said to the Lord, "But Lord, I am not a skilled speaker. I have never been able to speak well. And now,

even after talking to you, I am not a good speaker. I speak slowly and can't find the best words."

[11]Then the Lord said to him, "Who made man's mouth? And who makes him deaf or not able to speak? Or who gives a man sight or makes him blind? It is I, the Lord. [12]Now go! I will help you speak. I will tell you what to say."

[13]But Moses said, "Please, Lord, send someone else."

[14]The Lord became angry with Moses. He said, "Your brother Aaron, from the family of Levi, is a skilled speaker. He is already coming to meet you. And he will be happy when he sees you. [15]I will tell you what to say. Then you will tell Aaron. I will help both of you know what to say and do. [16]And Aaron will speak to the people for you. You will tell him what God says. And he will speak for you. [17]Take your walking stick with you. Use it to do the miracles."

MOSES RETURNS TO EGYPT

[18]Then Moses went back to Jethro, his father-in-law. Moses said to him, "Let me go back to my people in Egypt. I want to see if they are still alive."

Jethro said to Moses, "You may go. Have a safe trip."

[19]While Moses was still in Midian, the Lord said to him, "Go back to Egypt. The men who wanted to kill you are dead now."

[20]So Moses took his wife and his sons and put them on a donkey. Then he started back to Egypt. He took with him the walking stick of God.

[21]The Lord said to Moses, "When you get back to Egypt, do all the miracles.[d] I have given you the power to do them. Show them to the king of Egypt. But I will make the king very stubborn. He will not let the people go. [22]Then say to the king: 'This is what the Lord says: Israel is my firstborn[d] son. [23]And I told you to let my son go. Let him go so he may worship me. But you refused to let Israel go. So I will kill your firstborn son.'"

²⁴As Moses was on his way to Egypt, he stopped at a resting place for the night. The Lord met him there and tried to kill him. ²⁵But Zipporah took a flint knife and circumcised[d] her son. She took the skin and touched Moses' feet with it. Then she said to him, "You are a bridegroom of blood to me." ²⁶Zipporah said this because she had to circumcise her son. So the Lord did not kill Moses.

²⁷Meanwhile the Lord said to Aaron, "Go out into the desert to meet Moses." When Aaron went, he met Moses at Sinai, the mountain of God, and kissed him. ²⁸Moses told Aaron everything the Lord had said to him when he sent him to Egypt. And Moses told him about the miracles which the Lord had commanded him to do.

²⁹So Moses and Aaron gathered all the elders of the Israelites. ³⁰Aaron told them everything that the Lord had told Moses. Then Moses did the miracles for all the people to see. ³¹So the Israelites believed. They heard that the Lord was concerned about them and had seen their troubles. Then they bowed down and worshiped him.

MOSES AND AARON BEFORE THE KING

5 After Moses and Aaron talked to the people, they went to the king of Egypt. They said, "This is what the Lord, the God of Israel says: 'Let my people go so they may hold a feast for me in the desert.'"

²But the king of Egypt said, "Who is the Lord? Why should I obey him and let Israel go? I do not know the Lord. And I will not let Israel go."

³Then Aaron and Moses said, "The God of the Hebrews has talked with us. Now let us travel three days into the desert. There we will offer sacrifices to the Lord our God. If we don't do this, he may kill us with a disease or in war."

⁴But the king said to them, "Moses and Aaron, why are you taking the people away from their work? Go back to your hard work! ⁵There are very many Hebrews. And now you want them to quit their hard work!"

⁶That same day the king gave a command to the slave masters and foremen. ⁷He said, "Don't give the people straw to make bricks as you used to do. Let them gather their own straw. ⁸But they must still make the same number of bricks as they did before. Do not accept fewer. They have become lazy. That is why they are asking me, 'Let us go to offer sacrifices to our God.' ⁹Make these people work harder. Keep them busy. Then they will not have time to listen to the lies of Moses."

¹⁰So the slave masters and foremen went to the Israelites and said, "This is what the king says: I will no longer give you straw. ¹¹Go and get your own straw wherever you can find it. But you must make as many bricks as you made before." ¹²So the people went everywhere in Egypt looking for dry stalks to use for straw. ¹³The slave masters kept forcing the people to work harder. They said, "You must make just as many bricks as you did when you were given straw." ¹⁴The king's slave masters had chosen the Israelite foremen. They had made them responsible for the work the people did. The Egyptian slave masters beat these men and asked them, "Why aren't you making as many bricks as you made in the past?"

¹⁵Then the Israelite foremen went to the king. They complained and said, "Why are you treating us, your servants, this way? ¹⁶You give us no straw. But we are commanded to make bricks. Our slave masters beat us. But it is your own people's fault."

¹⁷The king answered, "You are lazy! You don't want to work! That is why you ask to leave here and make sacrifices to the Lord. ¹⁸Now, go back to work! We will not give you any straw. But you must make just as many bricks as you did before."

[19]The Israelite foremen knew they were in trouble. This was because the king had told them: "You must make just as many bricks each day as you did before." [20]As they were leaving the meeting with the king, they met Moses and Aaron. Moses and Aaron were waiting for them. [21]So they said to Moses and Aaron, "May the Lord punish you. You caused the king and his officers to hate us. You have given them an excuse to kill us."

MOSES COMPLAINS TO GOD

[22]Then Moses returned to the Lord and said, "Lord, why have you brought this trouble on your people? Is this why you sent me here? [23]I went to the king and said what you told me to say. But ever since that time he has made the people suffer. And you have done nothing to save them."

6 Then the Lord said to Moses, "Now you will see what I will do to the king of Egypt. I will use my great power against him, and he will let my people go. Because of my power, he will force them out of his country."

[2]Then God said to Moses, "I am the Lord. [3]I appeared to Abraham, Isaac and Jacob by the name, God All-Powerful. But they did not know me by my name, the Lord. [4]I also made my agreement with them to give them the land of Canaan. They lived in that land, but it was not their own land. [5]Now I have heard the cries of the Israelites. The Egyptians are treating them as slaves. And I remember my agreement. [6]So tell the people of Israel that I say to them, 'I am the Lord. I will save you from the hard work the Egyptians force you to do. I will make you free. You will not be slaves to the Egyptians. I will free you by my great power. And I will punish the Egyptians terribly. [7]I will make you my own people, and I will be your God. You will know that I am the Lord your God. I am the One who saves you from the hard work the Egyptians force you to do. [8]I will lead you to the land that I promised to Abraham, Isaac and Jacob. I will give you that land to own. I am the Lord.'"

[9]So Moses told this to the people of Israel. But they would not listen to him. They were discouraged, and their slavery was hard.

[10]Then the Lord said to Moses, [11]"Go tell the king of Egypt that he must let the Israelites leave his land."

[12]But Moses answered, "The Israelites will not listen to me. So surely the king will not listen to me, either. I am not a good speaker."

[13]But the Lord told Moses and Aaron to talk to the king. He commanded them to lead the Israelites out of Egypt.

FAMILIES OF ISRAEL

[14]These are the leaders of the families of Israel:

Israel's first son, Reuben, had four sons. They were Hanoch, Pallu, Hezron and Carmi. These are the family groups of Reuben.

[15]Simeon's sons were Jemuel, Jamin, Ohad, Jakin, Zohar and Shaul. Shaul was the son of a Canaanite woman. These are the family groups of Simeon.

[16]Levi lived 137 years. These are the names of his sons according to their family history: Gershon, Kohath and Merari.

[17]Gershon had two sons, Libni and Shimei, with their families.

[18]Kohath lived 133 years. The sons of Kohath were Amram, Izhar, Hebron and Uzziel.

[19]The sons of Merari were Mahli and Mushi.

These are the family groups of Levi, according to their family history.

[20]Amram married his father's sister Jochebed. Jochebed gave birth to Aaron and Moses. Amram lived 137 years.

[21]Izhar's sons were Korah, Nepheg and Zicri.

[22]Uzziel's sons were Mishael, Elzaphan and Sithri.

[23]Aaron married Elisheba. She was the daughter of Amminadab and the sister of Nahshon. Elisheba gave birth to Nadab, Abihu, Eleazar and Ithamar.

[24]The sons of Korah were Assir, Elkanah and Abiasaph. These are the family groups of the Korahites.

[25]Eleazar son of Aaron married a daughter of Putiel. And she gave birth to Phinehas.

These are the leaders of the family groups of the Levites.

[26]This was the Aaron and Moses to whom the Lord spoke. He said, "Lead my people out of Israel in their divisions." [27]Aaron and Moses are the ones who talked to the king of Egypt. They told him to let the people of Israel leave Egypt.

GOD REPEATS HIS CALL TO MOSES

[28]The Lord spoke to Moses in the land of Egypt. [29]He said, "I am the Lord. Tell the king of Egypt everything I tell you."

[30]But Moses answered, "I am not a good speaker. The king will not listen to me."

7 The Lord said to Moses, "I have made you like God to the king of Egypt. And your brother Aaron will be like a prophet[d] for you. [2]Tell Aaron your brother everything that I command you. Then let him tell the king of Egypt to let the Israelites leave his country. [3]But I will make the king stubborn. Then I will do many miracles[d] in Egypt. [4]But he will still refuse to listen. So then I will punish Egypt terribly. And I will lead my divisions, my people the Israelites, out of that land. [5]I will punish Egypt with my power. And I will bring the Israelites out of that land. Then they will know I am the Lord."

[6]Moses and Aaron did just as the Lord had commanded them. [7]Moses was 80 years old, and Aaron was 83, when they spoke to the king.

AARON'S WALKING STICK BECOMES A SNAKE

[8]The Lord said to Moses and Aaron, [9]"The king will ask you to do a miracle.[d] When he does, Moses, you tell Aaron to throw his walking stick down in front of the king. It will become a snake."

[10]So Moses and Aaron went to the king as the Lord had commanded. Aaron threw his walking stick down in front of the king and his officers. And it became a snake.

[11]So the king called in his wise men and his magicians. With their tricks the Egyptian magicians were able to do the same thing. [12]They threw their walking sticks on the ground, and their sticks became snakes. But then Aaron's stick swallowed theirs. [13]But the king was stubborn. He refused to listen to Moses and Aaron, just as the Lord had said.

THE WATER BECOMES BLOOD

[14]Then the Lord said to Moses, "The king is being stubborn. He refuses to let the people go. [15]In the morning the king will go out to the Nile River. Go meet him by the edge of the river. Take with you the walking stick that became a snake. [16]Tell him this: The Lord, the God of the Hebrews, sent me to you. He said, 'Let my people go worship me in the desert.' Until now you have not listened. [17]This is what the Lord says: 'This is how you will know that I am the Lord. I will strike the water of the Nile River with this stick in my hand. And the water will change into blood. [18]Then the fish in the Nile will die, and the river will begin to stink. And the Egyptians will not be able to drink the water from the Nile.'"

[19]The Lord said to Moses, "Tell Aaron to stretch the walking stick in his hand over the rivers, canals, ponds and pools in Egypt. The water will become blood everywhere in Egypt. There even will be blood in the wooden buckets and stone jars."

[20]So Moses and Aaron did just as the Lord had commanded. Aaron raised his walking stick and struck the water in the Nile River. He did this in front of the king and his officers. So all the water in

the Nile changed into blood. [21]The fish in the Nile died, and the river began to stink. So the Egyptians could not drink water from it. Blood was everywhere in the land of Egypt.

[22]Using their tricks, their magicians of Egypt did the same thing. So the king was stubborn and refused to listen to Moses and Aaron. This happened just as the Lord had said. [23]The king turned and went into his palace. He ignored what Moses and Aaron had done. [24]The Egyptians could not drink the water from the Nile. So all of them dug along the bank of the river. They were looking for water to drink.

THE FROGS

[25]Seven days passed after the Lord changed the Nile River.

8 Then the Lord told Moses, "Go to the king of Egypt and tell him, 'This is what the Lord says: Let my people go to worship me. [2]If you refuse, then I will punish Egypt with frogs. [3]The Nile River will be filled with frogs. They will come from the river and enter your palace. They will be in your bedroom and your bed. The frogs will enter the houses of your officers and your people. They will enter your ovens and your baking pans. [4]The frogs will jump up all over you, your people and your officers.'"

[5]Then the Lord said to Moses, "Tell Aaron to hold his walking stick in his hand over the rivers, canals and ponds. Make frogs come up out of the water onto the land of Egypt."

[6]So Aaron held his hand over all the waters of Egypt. The frogs came up out of the water and covered the land of Egypt. [7]The magicians used their tricks to do the same thing. So even more frogs came up onto the land of Egypt.

[8]So the king called for Moses and Aaron. He said, "Pray to the Lord to take the frogs away from me and my people. I will let your people go to offer sacrifices to the Lord."

[9]Moses said to the king, "Please set the time that I should pray for you, your people and your officers. Then the frogs will leave you and your houses. They will remain only in the Nile."

[10]The king answered, "Tomorrow."

Moses said, "What you want will happen. By this you will know that there is no one like the Lord our God. [11]The frogs will leave you, your houses, your officers and your people. They will remain only in the Nile."

[12]Moses and Aaron left the king. Moses asked the Lord about the frogs he had sent to the king. [13]And the Lord did as Moses asked. The frogs died in the houses, in the yards and in the fields. [14]The Egyptians put them in piles. The whole country began to stink. [15]When the king saw that they were free of the frogs, he became stubborn again. He did not listen to Moses and Aaron, just as the Lord had said.

THE GNATS

[16]Then the Lord said to Moses, "Tell Aaron to raise his walking stick and strike the dust on the ground. Then everywhere in Egypt the dust will change into gnats." [17]They did this. Aaron raised the walking stick that was in his hand and struck the dust on the ground. Then everywhere in Egypt the dust changed into gnats. The gnats got on the people and animals. [18]Using their tricks, the magicians tried to do the same thing. But they could not make the dust change into gnats. The gnats remained on the people and animals. [19]So the magicians told the king that the power of God had done this. But the king was stubborn and refused to listen to them. This happened just as the Lord had said.

THE FLIES

[20]The Lord told Moses, "Get up early in the morning. Meet the king of Egypt as he goes out to the river. Tell him, 'This is what the Lord says: Let my people go so

they can worship me. ²¹If you don't let them go, I will send swarms of flies. I will send them into your houses. The flies will be on you, your officers and your people. The houses of Egypt will be full of flies. And they will be all over the ground, too. ²²But I will not treat the people of Israel the same as the Egyptian people. There will not be any flies in the land of Goshen, where my people live. By this you will know that I, the Lord, am in this land. ²³I will treat my people differently from your people. This miracle*d* will happen tomorrow.'"

²⁴So the Lord did as he had said. Great swarms of flies came into the king's palace and his officers' houses. All over Egypt flies were ruining the land. ²⁵The king called for Moses and Aaron. He told them, "Offer sacrifices to your God here in this country."

²⁶But Moses said, "It wouldn't be right to do that. The Egyptians hate the sacrifices we offer to the Lord our God. They will see us offer sacrifices they hate. Then they will throw stones at us and kill us. ²⁷Let us make a three-day journey into the desert. We must offer sacrifices to the Lord our God there. This is what the Lord told us to do."

²⁸The king said, "I will let you go. Then you may offer sacrifices to the Lord your God in the desert. But you must not go very far away. Now go and pray for me."

²⁹Moses said, "I will leave and pray to the Lord. He will take the flies away from you, your officers and your people tomorrow. But do not try to trick us again. Do not stop the people from going to offer sacrifices to the Lord."

³⁰So Moses left the king and prayed to the Lord. ³¹And the Lord did as Moses asked. He removed the flies from the king, his officers and his people. Not one fly was left. ³²But the king became stubborn again and did not let the people go.

THE DISEASE ON THE FARM ANIMALS

9 Then the Lord told Moses, "Go to the king of Egypt. Tell him, 'This is what the Lord, the God of the Hebrews, says: Let my people go to worship me. ²You might refuse to let them go and continue to hold them. ³Then the Lord will punish you. He will send a terrible disease on all your farm animals. He will cause all of your horses, donkeys, camels, cattle and sheep to become sick. ⁴But the Lord will treat Israel's animals differently from the animals of Egypt. None of the animals that belong to the Israelites will die. ⁵The Lord has set tomorrow as the time he will do this in the land.'" ⁶The next day the Lord did as he promised. All the farm animals in Egypt died. But none of the animals belonging to Israelites died. ⁷The king sent people to see what had happened to the animals of Israel. They found that not one of them had died. But the king was still stubborn. He did not let the people go.

THE BOILS

⁸The Lord said to Moses and Aaron, "Fill your hands with the ashes from a furnace. Moses, throw the ashes into the air in front of the king of Egypt. ⁹The ashes will spread like dust through all the land of Egypt. The dust will cause boils to break out and become sores on the skin. These sores will be on people and animals everywhere in the land."

¹⁰So Moses and Aaron took ashes from a furnace. Then they went and stood before the king. Moses threw ashes into the air. It caused boils to break out and become sores on people and animals. ¹¹The magicians could not stand before Moses. This was because all the Egyptians had boils, even the magicians. ¹²But the Lord made the king stubborn. So he refused to listen to Moses and Aaron. This happened just as the Lord had said.

THE HAIL

¹³Then the Lord said to Moses, "Get up early in the morning and go to the king of Egypt. Tell him, 'This is what the Lord, the God of the Hebrews, says: Let

my people go to worship me. ¹⁴If you do not do this, this time I will punish you with all my power. I will punish you, your officers and your people. Then you will know that there is no one in the whole land like me. ¹⁵By now I could have used my power and caused a bad disease. It would have destroyed you and your people from the earth. ¹⁶But I have let you live for this reason: to show you my power. In this way my name will be talked about in all the earth. ¹⁷You are still against my people. You do not want to let them go.' ¹⁸So at this time tomorrow, I will send a terrible hailstorm. It will be the worst in Egypt since it became a nation. ¹⁹Now send for your animals and whatever you have in the fields. Bring them into a safe place. The hail will fall on every person or animal that is still in the fields. If they have not been brought in, they will die.'" ²⁰Some of the king's officers respected the word of the Lord. They hurried to bring their slaves and animals inside. ²¹But others ignored the Lord's message. They left their slaves and animals in the fields.

²²The Lord told Moses, "Raise your hand toward the sky. Then the hail will start falling over all the land of Egypt. It will fall on people, animals and on everything that grows in the fields of Egypt." ²³So Moses raised his walking stick toward the sky. And the Lord sent thunder and hail. And lightning flashed down to the earth. So he caused hail to fall upon the land of Egypt. ²⁴There was hail, and there was lightning flashing as it hailed. This was the worst hailstorm in Egypt since it had become a nation. ²⁵The hail destroyed everything that was in the fields in all the land of Egypt. The hail destroyed both people and animals. It also destroyed everything that grew in the fields. It broke all the trees in the fields. ²⁶The only place it did not hail was in the land of Goshen. The people of Israel lived there.

²⁷The king sent for Moses and Aaron. He told them, "This time I have sinned. The Lord is in the right. And I and my people are in the wrong. ²⁸Pray to the Lord. We have had enough of God's thunder and hail. I will let you go. You do not have to stay here any longer."

²⁹Moses told the king, "When I leave the city, I will raise my hands to the Lord in prayer. And the thunder and hail will stop. Then you will know that the earth belongs to the Lord. ³⁰But I know that you and your officers do not yet fear the Lord God."

³¹The flax was in bloom, and the barley had ripened. So these crops were destroyed. ³²But both wheat crops ripen later. So they were not destroyed.

³³Moses left the king and went outside the city. He raised his hands to the Lord. And the thunder and hail stopped. The rain also stopped falling to the ground. ³⁴The king saw that the rain, hail and thunder had stopped. Then he sinned again. He and his officers became stubborn again. ³⁵The king became stubborn and refused to let the Israelites go. This happened just as the Lord had said through Moses.

THE LOCUSTS

10 The Lord said to Moses, "Go to the king of Egypt. I have made him and his officers stubborn. I did this so I could show them my powerful miracles.ᵈ ²I also did this so you could tell your children and your grandchildren. Tell them how I made fools of the Egyptians. Tell them about the miracles I did among them. Then all of you will know that I am the Lord."

³So Moses and Aaron went to the king. They told him, "This is what the Lord, the God of the Hebrews, says: 'How long will you refuse to be sorry for what you have done? Let my people go to worship me. ⁴If you refuse to let my people go, tomorrow I will bring locustsᵈ into your country. ⁵They will cover the land, and

no one will be able to see the ground. They will eat anything that was left from the hailstorm. They will eat the leaves from every tree growing in the field. [6]They will fill your palaces and all your officers' houses. They will fill the houses of all the Egyptian people. There will be more locusts than your fathers or ancestors have ever seen. There will be more locusts than there have been since people began living in Egypt.'" Then Moses turned and walked away from the king.

[7]The king's officers asked him, "How long will this man make trouble for us? Let the Israelite men go to worship the Lord their God. Don't you know that Egypt is ruined?"

[8]So Moses and Aaron were brought back to the king. He said to them, "Go and worship the Lord your God. But tell me, just who is going?"

[9]Moses answered, "We will go with our young and our old people, our sons and daughters and sheep and cattle. This is because we are going to have a feast to honor the Lord."

[10]The king said to them, "The Lord really will have to be with you if ever I let you and all of your children leave Egypt. See, you are planning something evil. [11]No! Only the men may go and worship the Lord. That is what you have been asking for." Then the king forced Moses and Aaron out of his palace.

[12]The Lord told Moses, "Raise your hand over the land of Egypt, and the locusts will come. They will spread all over the land of Egypt. They will eat all the plants that the hail did not destroy."

[13]So Moses raised his walking stick over the land of Egypt. And the Lord caused a strong wind to blow from the east. It blew across the land all that day and night. When morning came, the east wind had brought the locusts. [14]Swarms of locusts covered all the land of Egypt and settled everywhere. There were more locusts than ever before or after.

[15]The locusts covered the whole land so that it was black. They ate everything that was left after the hail. They ate every plant in the field and all the fruit on the trees. Nothing green was left on any tree or plant anywhere in Egypt.

[16]The king quickly called for Moses and Aaron. He said, "I have sinned against the Lord your God and against you. [17]Now forgive my sin this time. Pray to the Lord your God. Ask him to stop this punishment that kills."

[18]Moses left the king and prayed to the Lord. [19]So the Lord changed the wind. He made a very strong wind to blow from the west. It blew the locusts away into the Red Sea.[d] Not one locust was left anywhere in Egypt. [20]But the Lord caused the king to be stubborn again. And he did not let the people of Israel go.

THE DARKNESS

[21]Then the Lord told Moses, "Raise your hand toward the sky, and darkness will cover the land of Egypt. It will be so dark you will be able to feel it." [22]So Moses raised his hand toward the sky. Then total darkness was everywhere in Egypt for three days. [23]No one could see anyone else. And no one could go anywhere for three days. But the Israelites had light where they lived.

[24]Again the king of Egypt called for Moses. He said, "All of you may go and worship the Lord. You may take your women and children with you. But you must leave your sheep and cattle here."

[25]Moses said, "You must let us have animals to use as sacrifices and burnt offerings. We have to offer them to the Lord our God. [26]So we must take our animals with us. Not a hoof will be left behind. We have to use some of the animals to worship the Lord our God. We do not yet know exactly what we will need to worship the Lord. We will know when we get there."

[27]But the Lord made the king stubborn again. So he refused to let them go.

28Then he told Moses, "Get out of here! Don't come here again! The next time you see me, you will die."

29Then Moses told the king, "I'll do what you say. I will not come to see you again."

THE DEATH OF THE FIRSTBORN

11 Now the Lord had told Moses, "I have one more way to punish the king and the people of Egypt. After this, the king will send all of you away from Egypt. When he does, he will force you to leave completely. 2Tell the men and women of Israel to ask their neighbors for things made of silver and gold." 3The Lord had caused the Egyptians to respect the Israelites. The king's officers and the Egyptian people already considered Moses to be a great man.

4So Moses said to the king, "This is what the Lord says: 'About midnight tonight I will go through all Egypt. 5Every firstborn*d* son in the land of Egypt will die. The firstborn son of the king, who sits on his throne, will die. Even the firstborn of the slave girl grinding grain will die. Also the firstborn farm animals will die. 6There will be loud crying everywhere in Egypt. It will be worse than any time before or after this. 7But not even a dog will bark at the Israelites or their animals.' Then you will know that the Lord treats Israel differently from Egypt. 8Then all your officers will come to me. They will bow facedown to the ground before me. They will say, 'Leave and take all your people with you.' After that, I will leave." Then Moses very angrily left the king.

9The Lord had told Moses, "The king will not listen to you and Aaron. This is so that I may do many miracles*d* in the land of Egypt." 10Moses and Aaron did all these great miracles in front of the king. But the Lord made him stubborn. And the king would not let the people of Israel leave his country.

PASSOVER

12 The Lord spoke to Moses and Aaron in the land of Egypt: 2"This month will be the first month of the year for you. 3Both of you are to tell the whole community of Israel: On the tenth day of this month each man must get one lamb. It is for the people in his house. 4There may not be enough people in his house to eat a whole lamb. Then he must share it with his closest neighbor. There must be enough lamb for everyone to eat. 5The lamb must be a one-year-old male. It must have nothing wrong with it. This animal can be either a young sheep or a young goat. 6Keep the animal with you to take care of it until the fourteenth day of the month. On that day all the people of the community of Israel will kill these animals. They will do this as soon as the sun goes down. 7The people must take some of the blood. They must put it on the sides and tops of the doorframes. These are the doorframes of the houses where they eat the lambs. 8On this night they must roast the lamb over a fire. Then they must eat it with bitter herbs and bread made without yeast. 9Do not eat the lamb raw or boiled in water. Roast the whole lamb over a fire—with its head, legs and inner organs. 10You must not leave any of it until morning. But if any of it is left over until morning, you must burn it with fire.

11"This is the way you must eat it: You must be fully dressed as if you were going on a trip. You must have your sandals on, and you must have your walking stick in your hand. You must eat it in a hurry. This is the Lord's Passover.*d*

12"That night I will go through the land of Egypt. I will kill all the firstborn*d* of animals and people in the land of Egypt. I will punish all the gods of Egypt. I am the Lord. 13But the blood will be a sign on the houses where you are. When I see the blood, I will pass over you. Nothing terrible will hurt you when I punish the land of Egypt.

[14]"You are always to remember this day. Celebrate it with a feast to the Lord. Your descendants[d] are to honor the Lord with this feast from now on. [15]For this feast you must eat bread made without yeast for seven days. On the first day of this feast, you are to remove all the yeast from your houses. No one should eat any yeast for the full seven days of the feast. If anyone eats yeast, then that person will be separated from Israel. [16]You are to have holy meetings on the first and last days of the feast. You must not do any work on these days. The only work you may do on these days is to prepare your meals. [17]You must celebrate the Feast[d] of Unleavened Bread. Do this because on this very day I brought your divisions of people out of Egypt. So all of your descendants must celebrate this day. This is a law that will last from now on. [18]You are to eat bread made without yeast. Start this on the evening of the fourteenth day of the first month of your year. Eat this until the evening of the twenty-first day. [19]For seven days there must not be any yeast in your houses. Anybody who eats yeast during this time must be separated from the community of Israel. This includes Israelites and non-Israelites. [20]During this feast you must not eat yeast. You must eat bread made without yeast wherever you live."

[21]Then Moses called all the elders of Israel together. He told them, "Get the animals for your families. Kill the animals for the Passover. [22]Take a branch of the hyssop plant and dip it into the bowl filled with blood. Wipe the blood on the sides and tops of the doorframes. No one may leave his house until morning. [23]The Lord will go through Egypt to kill the Egyptians. He will see the blood on the sides and tops of the doorframes. Then the Lord will pass over that house. He will not let the one who brings death come into your houses and kill you.

[24]"You must keep this command. This law is for you and your descendants from now on. [25]Do this when you go to the land the Lord has promised to give to you. [26]When your children ask you, 'Why are we doing these things?' [27]you will say, 'This is the Passover sacrifice to honor the Lord. When we were in Egypt, the Lord passed over the houses of Israel. The Lord killed the Egyptians, but he saved our homes.'" So now the people bowed down and worshiped the Lord. [28]They did just as the Lord commanded Moses and Aaron.

[29]At midnight the Lord killed all the firstborn sons in the land of Egypt. The firstborn of the king, who sat on the throne, died. Even the firstborn of the prisoner in jail died. Also all the firstborn farm animals died. [30]The king, his officers and all the Egyptians got up during the night. Someone had died in every house. So there was loud crying everywhere in Egypt.

ISRAEL LEAVES EGYPT

[31]During the night the king called for Moses and Aaron. He said to them, "Get up and leave my people. You and your people may do as you have asked. Go and worship the Lord. [32]Take all of your sheep and cattle as you have asked. Go. And also bless me." [33]The Egyptians also asked the Israelites to hurry and leave. They said, "If you don't leave, we will all die!"

[34]The people of Israel took their dough before the yeast was added. They wrapped the bowls for making dough in clothing and carried them on their shoulders. [35]The people of Israel did what Moses told them to do. They asked their Egyptian neighbors for things made of silver and gold and for clothing. [36]The Lord caused the Egyptians to think well of the Israelites. So the Israelites took rich gifts from the Egyptians.

[37]The Israelites traveled from Rameses to Succoth. There were about 600,000 men walking. This does not include the

women and children. ³⁸Many other people who were not Israelites went with them. A large number of sheep, goats and cattle went with them. ³⁹The Israelites used the dough they had brought out of Egypt. They baked loaves of bread without yeast. The dough had no yeast in it because they had been rushed out of Egypt. So they had no time to get food ready for their trip.

⁴⁰The people of Israel had lived in Egypt for 430 years. ⁴¹On the day the 430 years ended, the Lord's divisions of people left Egypt. ⁴²That night the Lord kept watch to bring them out of Egypt. So on this same night the Israelites are to keep watch. They are to do this to honor the Lord from now on.

⁴³The Lord told Moses and Aaron, "Here are the rules for Passover:ᵈ No foreigner is to eat the Passover. ⁴⁴Suppose a person buys a slave and circumcisesᵈ him. Then the slave may eat the Passover. ⁴⁵But no one who lives for a short time in your country may eat it. No hired worker may eat it.

⁴⁶"The meal must be eaten inside the house. None of the meat is to be taken outside the house. Don't break any of the bones. ⁴⁷The whole community of Israel must take part in this feast. ⁴⁸A foreigner who lives with you may share in the Lord's Passover. But first all the males in his house must be circumcised. Then, since he will be like a citizen of Israel, he may share in the meal. But a man who is not circumcised may not eat the Passover meal. ⁴⁹The same rules apply to an Israelite born in the country. And they apply to a foreigner living there."

⁵⁰So all the Israelites did just as the Lord had commanded Moses and Aaron. ⁵¹Then on that same day, the Lord led the Israelites out of Egypt. The people left by divisions.

THE LAW OF THE FIRSTBORN

13 Then the Lord said to Moses, ²"Give every firstbornᵈ male to me. Every firstborn male among the Israelites belongs to me, whether human or animal."

³Moses said to the people, "Remember this day, the day you left Egypt. You were slaves in that land. The Lord with his great power brought you out of it. You must not eat bread made with yeast. ⁴Today, in the month of Abib,ᵈ you are leaving Egypt. ⁵The Lord made a promise to your ancestors. The Lord promised to give you the land of these people: the Canaanites, Hittites, Amorites, Hivites and Jebusites. The Lord will lead you to this land where much food grows. There you must celebrate this feast during the first month of every year. ⁶For seven days you must eat bread made without yeast. On the seventh day there will be a feast to honor the Lord. ⁷So for seven days you must not eat any bread made with yeast. There must be no bread made with yeast anywhere in your land. ⁸On that day you should tell your son: 'We are having this feast because of what the Lord did for me when I came out of Egypt.' ⁹This feast will help you remember. It will be like a mark on your hand. It will be like a reminder on your forehead. This feast will remind you to speak the Lord's teachings. This is because the Lord used his great power to bring you out of Egypt. ¹⁰So celebrate this feast every year at the right time.

¹¹"The Lord will take you into the land of the Canaanites. He promised to give this land to you and your ancestors. ¹²Then you must give him every firstborn male. And every firstborn male animal must be given to the Lord. ¹³Buy back every firstborn donkey by offering a lamb. If you don't want to buy the donkey back, then break its neck. You must buy back from the Lord every firstborn of your sons.

¹⁴"From now on your son will ask you: 'What does this mean?' You will answer, 'With his great power, the Lord brought us out of Egypt. We were slaves in that

land. [15]In Egypt the king was stubborn. He refused to let us leave. But the Lord killed every firstborn male in Egypt, both human and animal. That is why I sacrifice every firstborn male animal to the Lord. And that is why I buy back each of my firstborn sons from the Lord.' [16]This feast is like a mark on your hand. And it is like a reminder on your forehead. It will help you remember that the Lord brought us out of Egypt with his great power."

THE WAY OUT OF EGYPT

[17]The king sent the people out of Egypt. God did not lead them on the road through the Philistine country. That road is the shortest way. But God said, "They might think they will have to fight. Then they might change their minds and go back to Egypt." [18]So God led them through the desert toward the Red Sea.[d] The Israelites were dressed for fighting when they left the land of Egypt.

[19]Moses carried the bones of Joseph with him. Before Joseph died, he had made the sons of Israel promise to do this. He had said, "When God saves you, remember to carry my bones with you out of Egypt."

[20]The people of Israel left Succoth and camped at Etham. Etham was on the edge of the desert. [21]The Lord showed them the way. During the day he went ahead of them in a pillar of cloud. And during the night the Lord was in a pillar of fire to give them light. They could travel during the day or night. [22]The pillar of cloud was always with them during the day. And the pillar of fire was always with them at night.

14 Then the Lord said to Moses, [2]"Tell the Israelites to turn back to Pi Hahiroth. Tell them to camp for the night between Migdol and the Red Sea. This is near Baal Zephon. [3]The king will think, 'The Israelites are lost, trapped by the desert.' [4]I will make the king stubborn again so he will chase after them.

But I will defeat the king and his army. This will bring honor to me. Then the people of Egypt will know that I am the Lord." The people of Israel did just as they were told.

THE KING CHASES THE ISRAELITES

[5]The king of Egypt was told that the people of Israel had already left. Then he and his officers changed their minds about them. They said, "What have we done? We have let the people of Israel leave. We have lost our slaves!" [6]So the king prepared his war chariot and took his army with him. [7]He took 600 of his best chariots. He also took all the other chariots of Egypt. Each chariot had an officer in it. [8]The Lord made the king of Egypt stubborn. So he chased the Israelites, who were leaving victoriously. [9]The king of Egypt came with his horses, chariot drivers and army. And they chased the Israelites. They caught up with the Israelites while they were camped by the Red Sea.[d] This was near Pi Hahiroth and Baal Zephon.

[10]The Israelites saw the king and his army coming after them. They were very frightened and cried to the Lord for help. [11]They said to Moses, "What have you done to us? Why did you bring us out of Egypt to die in the desert? There were plenty of graves for us in Egypt. [12]We told you in Egypt, 'Let us alone! Let us stay and serve the Egyptians.' Now we will die in the desert."

[13]But Moses answered, "Don't be afraid! Stand still and see the Lord save you today. You will never see these Egyptians again after today. [14]You will only need to remain calm. The Lord will fight for you."

[15]Then the Lord said to Moses, "Why are you crying out to me? Command the people of Israel to start moving. [16]Raise your walking stick and hold it over the sea. The sea will split. Then the people can cross the sea on dry land. [17]I have made the Egyptians stubborn so they

will chase the Israelites. But I will be honored when I defeat the king and all of his chariot drivers and chariots. [18]I will defeat the king, his chariot drivers and chariots. Then Egypt will know that I am the Lord."

[19]The angel of God usually traveled in front of Israel's army. Now the angel of God moved behind them. Also, the pillar of cloud moved from in front of the people and stood behind them. [20]So the cloud came between the Egyptians and the people of Israel. The cloud made it dark for the Egyptians. But it gave light to the Israelites. So the cloud kept the two armies apart all night.

[21]Moses held his hand over the sea. All that night the Lord drove back the sea with a strong east wind. And so he made the sea become dry ground. The water was split. [22]And the Israelites went through the sea on dry land. A wall of water was on both sides.

[23]Then all the king's horses, chariots and chariot drivers followed them into the sea. [24]Between two and six o'clock in the morning, the Lord looked down from the pillar of cloud and fire at the Egyptian army. He made them panic. [25]He kept the wheels of the chariots from turning. This made it hard to drive the chariots. The Egyptians shouted, "Let's get away from the Israelites! The Lord is fighting for them and against us Egyptians."

[26]Then the Lord told Moses, "Hold your hand over the sea. Then the water will come back over the Egyptians, their chariots and chariot drivers." [27]So Moses raised his hand over the sea. And at dawn the water became deep again. The Egyptians were trying to run from it. But the Lord swept them away into the sea. [28]The water became deep again. It covered the chariots and chariot drivers. So all the king's army that had followed the Israelites into the sea was covered. Not one of them survived.

[29]But the people of Israel crossed the sea on dry land. There was a wall of water on their right and on their left. [30]So that day the Lord saved the Israelites from the Egyptians. And the Israelites saw the Egyptians lying dead on the seashore. [31]When the people of Israel saw the great power that the Lord had used against the Egyptians, they feared the Lord. And they trusted the Lord and his servant Moses.

THE SONG OF MOSES

15 Then Moses and the Israelites sang this song to the Lord:
"I will sing to the Lord
　　because he is worthy of great honor.
He has thrown the horse and its rider
　　into the sea.
[2]The Lord gives me strength and
　　makes me sing.
He has saved me.
He is my God,
　　and I will praise him.
He is the God of my ancestors,
　　and I will honor him.
[3]The Lord is a great warrior.
　　The Lord is his name.
[4]The chariots and soldiers of the king
　　of Egypt
he has thrown into the sea.
The king's best officers
　　are drowned in the Red Sea.*d*
[5]The deep waters covered them.
　　They sank to the bottom like
　　　a rock.
[6]Your right hand, Lord,
　　is amazingly strong.
Lord, your right hand
　　broke the enemy into pieces.
[7]In your great victory
　　you destroyed those who were
　　　against you.
Your anger destroyed them,
　　like fire burning straw.
[8]Just a blast of your breath,
　　and the waters were blown back.
The moving water stood up like a
　　wall.

And the deep waters became solid
  in the middle of the sea.
[9]"The enemy bragged,
  'I'll chase them and catch them.
I'll take all their riches.
I'll take all I want.
I'll pull out my sword,
  and my hand will destroy them.'
[10]But you blew on them with your
    breath
  and covered them with the sea.
They sank like lead
  in the powerful water.

[11]"Are there any gods like you, Lord?
  No! There are no gods like you.
  You are wonderfully holy.
  You are amazingly powerful.
  You do great miracles.[d]
[12]You reached out with your right hand,
  and the earth swallowed our
    enemies.
[13]You keep your loving promise.
  You lead the people you have saved.
With your strength you will guide them
  to your holy land.

[14]"The other nations will hear this and
    tremble with fear.
  Terror will take hold of the
    Philistines.
[15]The leaders of the tribes[d] of Edom will
    be very frightened.
The powerful men of Moab will shake
  with fear.
The people of Canaan will lose all
  their courage.
[16]Those people will be filled with fear.
When they see your strength,
  they will be as still as a rock.
They will be still until your people
  pass by, Lord.
They will be still until the people
  you have bought from slavery
  pass by.

[17]You will lead your people and place
    them
  on your very own mountain.
Lord, that is the place that you made
    for yourself to live.
  Lord, that is the temple that your
    hands have made.
[18]The Lord will rule forever!"

[19]The horses, chariot drivers and chariots of the king of Egypt went into the sea. And the Lord covered them with water from the sea. But the Israelites walked through the sea on dry land. [20]Then Aaron's sister Miriam, who was a prophetess,[d] took a tambourine[d] in her hand. All the women followed her, playing tambourines and dancing. [21]Miriam told them:

  "Sing to the Lord
    because he is worthy of great honor.
  He has thrown the horse and its rider
    into the sea."

THE BITTER WATER

[22]Moses led the people of Israel away from the Red Sea.[d] The people went into the Desert of Shur. They traveled for three days in the desert but found no water. [23]Then they came to Marah, where there was water. But they could not drink it because it was too bitter. That is why the place was named Marah.[n] [24]The people grumbled to Moses. They asked, "What will we drink?"

[25]Moses cried out to the Lord. So the Lord showed him a tree. Moses threw the tree into the water. And the water became good to drink.

There the Lord gave the people a rule and a law to live by. There he also tested their loyalty to him. [26]He said, "You must obey the Lord, your God. You must do what the Lord said is right. You must obey all his laws and keep his rules. If you do these things, I will not give you any of the sicknesses I gave the Egyptians. I am the Lord. I am the Lord who heals you."

15:23 Marah This name means "bitter."

²⁷Then the people traveled to Elim. At Elim there were 12 springs of water and 70 palm trees. So the people camped there near the water.

THE PEOPLE DEMAND FOOD

16 Then the whole Israelite community left Elim. They came to the Desert of Sin. This place was between Elim and Sinai. They came to this place on the fifteenth day of the second month after they had left Egypt. ²Then the whole Israelite community grumbled to Moses and Aaron in the desert. ³The Israelites said to them, "It would have been better if the Lord had killed us in the land of Egypt. There we had meat to eat. We had all the food we wanted. But you have brought us into this desert. You will starve us to death here."

⁴Then the Lord said to Moses, "I will cause food to fall like rain from the sky. This food will be for all of you. Every day the people must go out and gather what they need for that day. I will do this to see if the people will do what I teach them. ⁵On the sixth day of each week, they are to gather twice as much as they gather on other days. Then they are to prepare it."

⁶So Moses and Aaron said to all the Israelites: "This evening you will know that the Lord is the one who brought you out of Egypt. ⁷Tomorrow morning you will see the greatness of the Lord. He has heard you grumble against him. We are nothing. You are not grumbling against us, but against the Lord." ⁸And Moses said, "Each evening the Lord will give you meat to eat. And every morning he will give you all the bread you want. He will do this because he has heard you grumble against him. You are not grumbling against Aaron and me. You are grumbling against the Lord."

⁹Then Moses said to Aaron, "Speak to the whole community of the Israelites. Say to them, 'Meet together in front of the Lord because he has heard your grumblings.'"

¹⁰So Aaron spoke to the whole community of the Israelites. While he was speaking, they looked toward the desert. There the greatness of the Lord appeared in a cloud.

¹¹The Lord said to Moses, ¹²"I have heard the grumblings of the people of Israel. So tell them, 'At twilight you will eat meat. And every morning you will eat all the bread you want. Then you will know I am the Lord, your God.'"

¹³That evening, quail came and covered the camp. And in the morning dew lay around the camp. ¹⁴When the dew was gone, thin flakes like frost were on the desert ground. ¹⁵When the Israelites saw it, they asked each other, "What is that?" They asked this question because they did not know what it was.

So Moses told them, "This is the bread the Lord has given you to eat. ¹⁶The Lord has commanded, 'Each one of you must gather what he needs. Gather about two quarts for every person in your family.'"

¹⁷So the people of Israel did this. Some people gathered much, and some gathered little. ¹⁸Then they measured it. The person who gathered more did not have too much. The person who gathered less did not have too little. Each person gathered just as much as he needed.

¹⁹Moses said to them, "Don't keep any of it to eat the next day." ²⁰But some of the people did not listen to Moses. They kept part of it to eat the next morning. But it became full of worms and began to stink. So Moses was angry with these people.

²¹Every morning each person gathered as much food as he needed. But when the sun became hot, it melted away.

²²On the sixth day the people gathered twice as much food. They gathered four quarts for every person. So all the leaders of the community came and told this to Moses. ²³Moses said to them, "This is what the Lord commanded. Tomorrow is the Sabbath,ᵈ the Lord's

holy day of rest. Bake what you want to bake, and boil what you want to boil today. But save the rest of the food until tomorrow morning."

[24]So the people saved it until the next morning, as Moses had commanded. And none of it began to stink or have worms in it. [25]Moses told the people, "Eat the food you gathered yesterday. Today is a Sabbath, the Lord's day of rest. So you will not find any out in the field today. [26]You should gather the food for six days. But the seventh day is a Sabbath day. On that day there will not be any food on the ground."

[27]On the seventh day some of the people went out to gather food, but they couldn't find any. [28]Then the Lord said to Moses, "How long will all you people refuse to obey my commands and teachings? [29]Look, the Lord has made the Sabbath a day of rest for all of you. So on the sixth day he will give you enough food for two days. But on the Sabbath each of you must stay where you are. Do not leave your house." [30]So the people rested on the Sabbath.

[31]The people of Israel called the food manna.[d] The manna was like small white seeds. It tasted like wafers made with honey.

[32]Then Moses said, "The Lord said, 'Save two quarts of this food for your descendants.[d] Then they can see the food that I gave you to eat. I did this in the desert when I brought you out of Egypt.'"

[33]Moses told Aaron, "Take a jar and fill it with two quarts of manna. And save this manna for your descendants."

[34]So Aaron did what the Lord had commanded Moses. Aaron put the jar of manna in front of the Box[d] of the Agreement. He did this so it could be kept. [35]The Israelites ate manna for 40 years. They ate it until they came to the land where they settled. They ate manna until they came to the edge of the land of Canaan. [36]The measure they used for the manna was two quarts. It was one-tenth of an ephah.[n]

WATER FROM A ROCK

17 The whole Israelite community left the Desert of Sin. They traveled from place to place as the Lord commanded. They camped at Rephidim. But there was no water there for the people to drink. [2]So they quarreled with Moses. They said, "Give us water to drink."

But Moses said to them, "Why do you quarrel with me? Why are you testing the Lord?"

[3]But the people were very thirsty for water. So they grumbled against Moses. They said, "Why did you bring us out of Egypt? Was it to kill us, our children and our farm animals with thirst?"

[4]So Moses cried to the Lord, "What can I do with these people? They are almost ready to kill me with stones."

[5]The Lord said to Moses, "Go ahead of the people of Israel. And take some of the elders of Israel with you. Carry with you the walking stick that you used to strike the Nile River. Now go! [6]I will stand in front of you on a rock at Mount Sinai. Hit that rock with the stick, and water will come out of it. Then the people can drink." Moses did these things as the elders of Israel watched. [7]Moses named that place Massah[n] because the Israelites tested the Lord. They asked, "Is the Lord with us or not?" He also named it Meribah[n] because they quarreled.

THE AMALEKITES FIGHT ISRAEL

[8]At Rephidim the Amalekites came and fought the Israelites. [9]So Moses said to Joshua, "Choose some men and go and fight the Amalekites. Tomorrow I

16:36 **ephah** An ephah was a measure that equaled 20 quarts.
17:7 **Massah** This name sounds like the Hebrew word for "testing."
17:7 **Meribah** This name sounds like the Hebrew word for "quarreled."

will stand on the top of the hill. I will hold the stick God gave me to carry."

¹⁰Joshua obeyed Moses and went to fight the Amalekites. At the same time Moses, Aaron and Hur went to the top of the hill. ¹¹As long as Moses held his hands up, the Israelites would win the fight. But when Moses put his hands down, the Amalekites would win. ¹²Later, Moses' arms became tired. So the men put a large rock under Moses, and he sat on it. Then Aaron and Hur held up Moses' hands. Aaron was on one side of Moses, and Hur was on the other side. They held his hands up like this until the sun went down. ¹³So Joshua defeated the Amalekites in this battle.

¹⁴Then the Lord said to Moses, "Write about this battle in a book so people will remember. And be sure to tell Joshua. Tell him because I will completely destroy the Amalekites from the earth."

¹⁵Then Moses built an altar. He named it The Lord is my Banner. ¹⁶Moses said, "I lifted my hands toward the Lord's throne. The Lord will fight against the Amalekites forever."

JETHRO VISITS MOSES

18 Jethro, Moses' father-in-law, was the priest of Midian. He heard about everything that God had done for Moses and his people, the Israelites. Jethro heard how the Lord had led the Israelites out of Egypt. ²Moses had sent his wife Zipporah to Jethro, his father-in-law. ³Moses had also sent his two sons. The first son was named Gershom.ⁿ When he was born, Moses said, "I am a stranger in a foreign country." ⁴The other son was named Eliezer.ⁿ When he was born, Moses said, "The God of my father is my help. He saved me from the king of Egypt."

⁵So Jethro, Moses' father-in-law, went to Moses. Moses was camped in the desert near Sinai, the mountain of God. Moses' wife and his two sons came with Jethro. ⁶Jethro had sent a message ahead to Moses. He said, "I am Jethro, your father-in-law. I am coming to you with your wife and her two sons."

⁷So Moses went out to meet his father-in-law. Moses bowed down and then kissed him. The two men asked about each other's health. Then they went into Moses' tent. ⁸Moses told his father-in-law everything the Lord had done to the king and the Egyptians. The Lord had done these things to help Israel. Moses told about all the problems they had faced along the way. And Moses told him how the Lord had saved them.

⁹Jethro was very happy when he heard all the good things the Lord had done for Israel. He was happy because the Lord had saved them from the Egyptians. ¹⁰Jethro said, "Praise the Lord. He has saved all of you from the Egyptians and their king. He has saved the people from the power of the Egyptians. ¹¹Now I know the Lord is greater than all gods. He did this to those who looked down on Israel." ¹²Then Jethro, Moses' father-in-law, gave a whole burnt offering and other sacrifices to God. Aaron and all the elders of Israel came to Moses' father-in-law. They ate the holy meal together before God.

¹³The next day Moses solved disagreements among the people. So the people stood around Moses from morning until night. ¹⁴Moses' father-in-law saw all that Moses was doing for the people. He asked, "What is all this you are doing for the people? Why are you the only one to solve disagreements? All the people are standing around you from morning until night!"

¹⁵Then Moses said to his father-in-law, "It is because the people come to me for God's help in solving their disagreements.

18:3 **Gershom** This name sounds like the Hebrew word for "a stranger there."
18:4 **Eliezer** This name sounds like the Hebrew word for "my help."

[16]When people have a disagreement, they come to me. I decide who is right. And I tell them God's laws and teachings."

[17]Moses' father-in-law said to him, "You are not doing this right. [18]You and the people who come to you will get too tired. This is too much work for you. You can't do it by yourself. [19]Now listen to me. I will give you some advice. I want God to be with you. You must talk to God for the people. You must tell him about their disagreements. [20]You should tell them the laws and teachings. Tell them the right way to live and what they should do. [21]But choose some capable men from among the people. Choose men who respect God and who can be trusted. They will not change their decisions for money. Make these men officers over groups of 1,000, 100, 50 and 10 people. [22]Let these officers solve the disagreements among the people all the time. They can bring the hard cases to you. But they can decide the simple cases themselves. That will make it easier for you. These men will share the work with you. [23]Do this if it is what God commands. Then you will be able to do your job. And all the people will go home with their disagreements solved."

[24]So Moses listened to his father-in-law and did everything he said. [25]He chose capable men from all the Israelites. He made them leaders over the people. They were officers over groups of 1,000, 100, 50 and 10 people. [26]These officers solved disagreements among the people all the time. They brought the hard cases to Moses. But they decided the simple cases themselves.

[27]Then Moses let his father-in-law leave. And Jethro went back to his own home.

ISRAEL AT SINAI

19 Exactly three months after the Israelites had left Egypt, they reached the Desert of Sinai. [2]They had left Rephidim and had come to the Desert of Sinai. The Israelites camped in the desert in front of Mount Sinai. [3]Then Moses went up on the mountain to God. The Lord called to him from the mountain. The Lord said, "Say this to the family of Jacob. And tell this to the people of Israel: [4]'Every one of you has seen what I did to the people of Egypt. You saw how I carried you out of Egypt. I did it as an eagle carries her young on her wings. And I brought you here to me. [5]So now obey me and keep my agreement. Do this, and you will be my own possession, chosen from all nations. Even though the whole earth is mine, [6]you will be my kingdom of priests. You will be a nation that belongs to me alone.' You must tell the Israelites these words."

[7]So Moses went down and called the elders of the people together. He told them all the words the Lord had commanded him to say. [8]And all the people answered together, "We will do everything he has said." Then Moses took their answer back to the Lord.

[9]And the Lord said to Moses, "I will come to you in a thick cloud. I will speak to you. The people will hear me talking to you. I will do this so the people will always trust you." Then Moses told the Lord what the people had said.

[10]The Lord said to Moses, "Go to the people and have them spend today and tomorrow preparing themselves. They must wash their clothes [11]and be ready by the day after tomorrow. On that day I, the Lord, will come down on Mount Sinai. And all the people will see me. [12]But you must set a limit around the mountain. The people are not to cross it. Tell the people not to go up on the mountain. Tell them not to touch the foot of it. Anyone who touches the mountain must be put to death. [13]He must be put to death with stones or shot with arrows. No one is allowed to touch him. Whether it is a person or an animal, he will not

live. But the trumpet will make a long blast. Only then may the people go up on the mountain."

14So Moses went down from the mountain to the people. He made them prepare themselves for service to God. And the people washed their clothes. 15Then Moses said to the people, "Be ready in three days. Do not have sexual relations during this time."

16It was the morning of the third day. There was thunder and lightning with a thick cloud on the mountain. And there was a very loud blast from a trumpet. All the people in the camp were frightened. 17Then Moses led the people out of the camp to meet God. They stood at the foot of the mountain. 18Mount Sinai was covered with smoke. This happened because the Lord came down on it in fire. The smoke rose from the mountain like smoke from a furnace. And the whole mountain shook wildly. 19The sound from the trumpet became louder. Then Moses spoke, and the voice of God answered him.

20So the Lord came down on the top of Mount Sinai. Then he called Moses to come up to the top of the mountain. So Moses went up. 21The Lord said to Moses, "Go down and warn the people. They must not force their way through to see me. If they do, many of them will die. 22Even the priests, who may come near me, must first prepare themselves. If they don't, I, the Lord, will punish them."

23Moses told the Lord, "The people cannot come up Mount Sinai. You yourself told us to set a limit around the mountain. We made it holy."

24The Lord said to him, "Go down and bring Aaron with you. But don't allow the priests or the people to force their way through. They must not come up to the Lord. If they do, I will punish them."

25So Moses went down to the people and told them these things.

THE TEN COMMANDMENTS

20 Then God spoke all these words: 2"I am the Lord your God. I brought you out of the land of Egypt where you were slaves.

3"You must not have any other gods except me.

4"You must not make for yourselves any idols. Don't make something that looks like anything in the sky above or on the earth below or in the water below the land. 5You must not worship or serve any idol. This is because I, the Lord your God, am a jealous God. A person may sin against me and hate me. I will punish his children, even his grandchildren and great-grandchildren. 6But I will be very kind to thousands who love me and obey my commands.

7"You must not use the name of the Lord your God thoughtlessly. The Lord will punish anyone who is guilty and misuses his name.

8"Remember to keep the Sabbath*d* as a holy day. 9You may work and get everything done during six days each week. 10But the seventh day is a day of rest to honor the Lord your God. On that day no one may do any work: not you, your son or daughter, or your men or women slaves. Neither your animals nor the foreigners living in your cities may work. 11The reason is that in six days the Lord made everything. He made the sky, earth, sea and everything in them. And on the seventh day, he rested. So the Lord blessed the Sabbath day and made it holy.

12"Honor your father and your mother. Then you will live a long time in the land. The Lord your God is going to give you this land.

13"You must not murder anyone.

14"You must not be guilty of adultery.*d*

15"You must not steal.

16"You must not tell lies about your neighbor in court.

17"You must not want to take your neighbor's house. You must not want his wife or his men or women slaves. You must not want his ox or his donkey. You must not want to take anything that belongs to your neighbor."

¹⁸The people heard the thunder and the trumpet. They saw the lightning on the mountain and smoke rising from the mountain. They shook with fear and stood far away from the mountain. ¹⁹Then they said to Moses, "Speak to us yourself. Then we will listen. But don't let God speak to us, or we will die."

²⁰Then Moses said to the people, "Don't be afraid. God has come to test you. He wants you to respect him so you will not sin."

²¹The people stood far away from the mountain while Moses went near the dark cloud where God was. ²²Then the Lord told Moses to say these things to the Israelites: "You yourselves have seen that I talked with you from heaven. ²³You must not use gold or silver to make idols for yourselves. You must not worship these false gods in addition to me.

²⁴"Make an altar of dirt for me. Offer your whole burnt offerings and fellowship offerings on this altar as a sacrifice to me. Use your sheep and your cattle to do this. Worship me in every place that I choose. Then I will come and bless you. ²⁵You may use stones to make an altar for me. But don't use stones that you have made smooth with tools. You must not use any tools on the stones. If you do, you make them unsuitable for use in worship. ²⁶And you must not make steps leading up to my altar. If you go up steps, people will be able to see under your clothes."

LAWS FOR LIVING

21 Then God said to Moses, "These are the laws for living that you will give to the Israelites:

²"If you buy a Hebrew slave, he will serve you for six years. In the seventh year you are to set him free. And he will have to pay nothing. ³He might not be married when he becomes your slave. Then he must leave without a wife. The man might be married when he becomes your slave. Then he may take his wife with him. ⁴The slave's master might give him a wife, and she might give birth to sons or daughters. Then the woman and her children will belong to the master. When the slave is set free, only he may leave.

⁵"But the slave might say, 'I love my master, my wife and my children. I don't want to go free.' ⁶Then the slave's master will take him to God. The master will take him to a door or doorframe. And he will punch a hole through the slave's ear using a sharp tool. Then the slave will serve that master all his life.

⁷"A man might sell his daughter as a slave. There are rules for setting her free. They are different from the rules for setting the men slaves free. ⁸Maybe the master wanted to marry her but then decided he was not pleased with her. He must let one of her close relatives buy her back. He has no right to sell her to foreigners. This is because he has treated her unfairly. ⁹The man who bought her might promise to let the woman marry his son. Then he must treat her as a daughter. ¹⁰The man who bought her might marry another woman. Then he must not keep his slave woman from having food or clothing or sexual relations. ¹¹If he does not give her these three things, she may go free. She owes him no money.

INJURIES

¹²"Anyone who hits a person and kills him must be put to death. ¹³But if a person kills someone accidentally, God allowed that to happen. So the person must go to a place I will choose. ¹⁴A person might plan and murder another person on purpose. Put him to death, even if he has run to my altar for safety.

¹⁵"Anyone who hits his father or his mother must be put to death.

¹⁶"A person might kidnap someone. Then he either sells him as a slave or still has him when he is caught. That person must be put to death.

¹⁷"Anyone who says cruel things to his father or mother must be put to death.

¹⁸"Two men might argue. And one might hit the other with a rock or with his fist. The hurt man might not be killed. But he might have to stay in bed. ¹⁹Later he might be able to get up. And he might be able to walk around outside with his walking stick. Then the one who hit him is not to be punished. But he must pay the injured man for the loss of his time. And he must support the injured man until he is completely healed.

²⁰"A man might beat his male or female slave with a stick. And the slave might die on the spot. Then the owner must be punished. ²¹But the slave might get well after a day or two. Then that owner will not be punished since the slave belongs to him.

²²"Two men might be fighting, and they might hit a pregnant woman so that the baby comes out. But there is no further injury. Then the man who caused the injury must pay money. He must pay what the woman's husband says and the court allows. ²³But if there is further injury, then the punishment is that life must be paid for life, ²⁴eye for eye, tooth for tooth. It is also hand for hand, foot for foot, ²⁵burn for burn, wound for wound and bruise for bruise.

²⁶"A man might hit his male or female slave in the eye. And the eye might be blinded. Then the man is to free the slave to pay for the eye. ²⁷A master might knock out a tooth of his male or female slave. Then the man is to free the slave to pay for the tooth.

²⁸"A man's bull might kill a man or woman. Then you must kill that bull with stones. You should not eat the bull. But the owner of the bull is not guilty. ²⁹But the bull might have hurt people in the past. The owner might have been warned. If he did not keep it in a pen and then it kills a man or woman, the bull must be killed with stones. And the owner must also be put to death. ³⁰But the family of the dead man might accept money. Then the man who owned the bull may buy back his life. But he must pay whatever is demanded. ³¹Use this same law if the bull kills a person's son or daughter. ³²But the bull might kill a male or female slave. Then the owner must pay the master the price for a new slave. That is 12 ounces of silver. And the bull must also be killed with stones.

³³"A man might take the cover off a pit. Or he might dig one and not cover it. Another man's ox or donkey might come and fall into it. ³⁴The owner of the pit must pay the owner of the animal for his loss. The dead animal will belong to the one who pays.

³⁵"One man's bull might kill another man's bull. Then they must sell the bull that is alive. Both men get half of the money. And both men will also get half of the bull that was killed. ³⁶A man's bull might have hurt other animals in the past. But the owner might not have kept it in a pen. Then that owner must pay bull for bull. And the dead animal is his.

PROPERTY LAWS

22 "A man might steal a bull or a sheep and kill or sell it. Then he must pay back five bulls for the one bull he stole. Or he must pay back four sheep for the one sheep he stole.

²⁻⁴"The robber who is caught must pay back what he stole. He might own nothing. Then he must be sold as a slave to pay for what he stole. The stolen animal might be found alive with the robber. Then he must give the owner two animals for every animal he stole. He must pay, whether he stole a bull, donkey or sheep.

"A thief might be killed while breaking into a house at night. Then the one who killed him is not guilty of murder. But if this happens during the day, he is guilty of murder.

⁵"A person might let his farm animal graze in his field or vineyard. And it might wander into another person's field or vineyard. Then the owner of the animal must pay back the loss. The payment must come from the best of his crop.

⁶"A man might start a fire that spreads through the thornbushes to his neighbor's field. The fire might burn his neighbor's growing grain or grain that has been stacked. Or it might burn his whole field. Then the person who started the fire must pay for what was burned.

⁷"A man might give his neighbor money or other things to keep for him. Those things might be stolen from the neighbor's house. And the thief might be caught. Then he must pay back twice as much as he stole. ⁸But maybe the thief is never found. Then the owner of the house must make a promise before God. He must promise that he has not stolen his neighbor's things.

⁹"Two men might disagree about who owns something. It might be an ox, donkey, sheep or clothing. Or it might be something else that is lost. Each says, 'This is mine.' Each man must bring his case to God. God's judges will decide who is guilty. Then he must pay the other man twice as much as the thing is worth.

¹⁰"A man might ask his neighbor to keep his animal for him. This animal might be a donkey, ox, sheep or some other animal. And that animal might die, be hurt or be taken away. And no one saw what happened. ¹¹That neighbor must promise before the Lord that he did not harm or kill the other man's animal. The owner of the animal must accept his promise made before God. The neighbor does not have to pay the owner for the animal. ¹²But the animal might have been stolen from the neighbor. Then he must pay the owner for it.

¹³Wild animals might have killed the animal. Then the neighbor must bring the body as proof. He will not have to pay for the animal that was killed.

¹⁴"A man might borrow an animal from his neighbor. It might get hurt or die while the owner is not there. Then the one who borrowed it must pay the owner for the animal. ¹⁵The owner might be with the animal. Then the one who borrowed it does not have to pay. If the animal was rented, the rental price covers the loss.

LAWS AND RELATIONSHIPS

¹⁶"A man might find a woman who is not pledged to be married. She has never had sexual relations with a man. He might trick her into having sexual relations with him. Then he must give her family the payment to marry her. And she will be his wife. ¹⁷But her father might refuse to allow his daughter to marry him. Then the man must still give the payment for a bride. He must pay the usual charge for a woman who has never had sexual relations.

¹⁸"Put to death any woman who does evil magic.

¹⁹"Put to death anyone who has sexual relations with an animal.

²⁰"Destroy completely any person who makes a sacrifice to any god except the Lord.

²¹"Do not cheat or hurt a foreigner. Remember that you were foreigners in the land of Egypt.

²²"Do not cheat a widow or an orphan. ²³If you do, they will cry out to me for help. I certainly will hear their cry. ²⁴And I will be very angry and kill you in war. Then your wives will become widows, and your children will become orphans.

²⁵"You might lend money to one of my people who is poor. Then do not treat him as a moneylender would. Charge him nothing for using your money. ²⁶Your neighbor might give you his coat as a promise. He is promising to

pay you the money he owes you. But you must give it back to him by sunset. [27]That coat is the only cover to keep his body warm. He has nothing else to sleep in. If he cries out to me for help, I will listen because I am merciful.

[28]"You must not speak against God. You must not curse a leader of your people.

[29]"Do not hold back your offering from the first of your harvest. Give me the first grain that you harvest. Give me the first wine that you make. Also, you must give me your firstborn[d] sons. [30]You must do the same with your bulls and your sheep. Let the firstborn males stay with their mothers for seven days. On the eighth day you must give them to me.

[31]"You are to be my holy people. You must not eat the meat of any animal that has been killed by wild animals. Instead, give it to the dogs.

LAWS ABOUT FAIRNESS

23 "You must not tell lies. You might be a witness in court. Don't help a bad person by telling lies.

[2]"You must not do wrong just because everyone else is doing it. You might be a witness in court. Then you must not ruin a fair trial. You must not tell lies just because everyone else is. [3]A poor man might be in court. You must not take his side just because he is poor.

[4]"You might see your enemy's ox or donkey wandering away. Then you must return it to him. [5]You might see that your enemy's donkey has fallen because its load is too heavy. You must not leave it there. You must help your enemy get the donkey back on its feet.

[6]"You must not be unfair to a poor man when he is in court. [7]You must not lie when you accuse someone in court. Never allow an innocent or honest person to be put to death as punishment. This is because I will not treat guilty people as if they were innocent.

[8]"You must not accept money from a person who wants you to lie in court. Such money will not let you see what is right. Such money makes good people tell lies.

[9]"You must not mistreat a foreigner. You know how it feels to be a foreigner. You were foreigners in Egypt.

LAWS FOR THE SABBATH

[10]"For six years you are to plant and harvest crops on your land. [11]Then during the seventh year, do not plow or plant your land. If any food grows there, allow the poor people to have it. And let the wild animals eat what is left. You should do the same with your vineyards and your orchards of olive trees.

[12]"You should work six days a week. But on the seventh day you must rest. This lets your ox and your donkey rest. This also lets the slave born in your house and the foreigner be refreshed.

[13]"Be sure to do all that I have said to you. You must not even say the names of other gods. The names of those gods must not come out of your mouth.

THREE YEARLY FEASTS

[14]"Three times each year you must hold a feast to honor me. [15]You must celebrate the Feast[d] of Unleavened Bread. Do this in the way I commanded you. For seven days you must eat bread that is made without yeast. You must do this at the set time during the month of Abib.[d] This is the month when you came out of Egypt. No one is to come to worship me without bringing an offering.

[16]"You must celebrate the Feast[d] of Harvest. Offer to God the first things you harvest. These are from the crops you planted in your fields.

"You must celebrate the Feast[d] of Tents in the fall. Do this when you gather all the crops from your fields.

[17]"So three times during every year all men must come to worship the Lord God.

[18]"You must not offer animal blood along with anything that has yeast in it.

"You must not save any of the fat from the sacrifice for the next day.

19"You must bring the best of the first-fruits[d] of your land. Bring them to the Holy Tent[n] of the Lord your God.

"You must not cook a young goat in its mother's milk.

PROMISES

20"I am sending an angel ahead of you. He will protect you as you travel. He will lead you to the place I have prepared. 21Pay attention to the angel and obey him. Do not turn against him. He will not forgive such turning against him because my power is in him. 22You must listen carefully to all he says. You must do everything that I tell you. If you do this, I will be an enemy to your enemies. I will fight all who fight against you. 23My angel will go ahead of you. He will take you into the land of these people: the Amorites, Hittites, Perizzites, Canaanites, Hivites and Jebusites. And I will destroy them.

24"You must not bow down to their gods or worship those gods. You must not live the way those people live. You must destroy their idols. And you must break into pieces stone pillars they use in worship. 25You must worship the Lord your God. If you do, I will bless your bread and your water. I will take away sickness from you. 26None of your women will have her baby die before it is born. All women will have children. I will allow you to live long lives.

27"I will make your enemies afraid of me. I will confuse any people you fight against. I will make all your enemies run away from you. 28I will send something like hornets ahead of you. They will force the Hivites, Canaanites and Hittites out of your way. 29But I will not force all those people out in only one year. If I did, the land would become a desert. Then the wild animals would become too many for you. 30Instead, I will force those people out of your land very slowly. I will wait until there are enough of you to take over the land.

31"I will give you the land from the Gulf of Aqaba to the Mediterranean Sea. And I will give you the land between the desert and the Euphrates River. I will give you power over the people who now live in the land. You will force them out ahead of you. 32You must not make an agreement with those people or with their gods. 33You must not let them live in your land. If they live there, they will make you sin against me. If you worship their gods, you will be like someone caught in a trap."

GOD AND ISRAEL MAKE THEIR AGREEMENT

24 The Lord told Moses, "You, Aaron, Nadab, Abihu and 70 of the elders of Israel must come up to me. You must worship me from a distance. 2Then Moses alone must come near me. The other men must not come near. And the rest of the people must not come up the mountain with Moses."

3So Moses told the people all the Lord's words and laws for living. Then all of the people answered out loud together. They said, "We will do all the things that the Lord has said." 4So Moses wrote down all the words of the Lord. And he got up early the next morning. He built an altar near the bottom of the mountain. He set up 12 stones, 1 stone for each of the 12 tribes[d] of Israel. 5Then Moses sent young Israelite men to offer whole burnt offerings. They also sacrificed young bulls as fellowship offerings to the Lord. 6Moses took the blood of these animals. He put half of it in bowls. And he sprinkled the other half of the blood on the altar. 7Then Moses took the book with the agreement written in it. He read it so the people could hear him. And they said, "We will do everything that the Lord has said. We will obey."

23:19 **Holy Tent** Literally, "house of the Lord your God." See Exodus 25:9.

⁸Then Moses took the blood from the bowls. He sprinkled it on the people. He said, "This is the blood that begins the agreement. This is the agreement which the Lord has made with you about all these things."

⁹Moses, Aaron, Nadab, Abihu and 70 of the elders of Israel went up the mountain. ¹⁰They saw the God of Israel. Under his feet was a surface. It looked as if it were paved with blue sapphire stones. And it was as clear as the sky! ¹¹These leaders of the Israelites saw God. But God did not destroy them. Then they ate and drank together.

MOSES GETS THE STONE TABLETS

¹²The Lord said to Moses, "Come up the mountain to me. Wait there, and I will give you two stone tablets. On these are the teachings and the commandments. I have written these to teach the people."

¹³So Moses and his helper Joshua set out. Moses went up Sinai, the mountain of God. ¹⁴Moses said to the elders, "Wait here for us until we come back to you. Aaron and Hur are with you. Anyone who has a disagreement with others can take it to them."

MOSES MEETS WITH GOD

¹⁵When Moses went up on the mountain, the cloud covered it. ¹⁶The greatness of the Lord came down on Mount Sinai. The cloud covered the mountain for six days. On the seventh day the Lord called to Moses from inside the cloud. ¹⁷The Israelites could see the greatness of the Lord. It looked like a fire burning on top of the mountain. ¹⁸Then Moses went into the cloud and went higher up the mountain. Moses was on the mountain for 40 days and 40 nights.

GIFTS FOR THE LORD

25 The Lord said to Moses, ²"Tell the Israelites to bring me gifts. Receive for me the gifts each man wants to give. ³These are the gifts that you should receive from them: gold, silver,

bronze, ⁴blue, purple and red thread, and fine linen. Receive cloth made of goat hair. ⁵Receive the male sheep skins that are dyed red. Receive fine leather, acacia wood ⁶and olive oil to burn in the lamps. And receive spices for sweet-smelling incense_d_ and the special olive oil poured on a person's head to make him a priest. ⁷Also accept onyx stones and other jewels to be put on the holy vest_d_ and the chest covering.

⁸"The people must build a holy place for me. Then I can live among them. ⁹Build this Holy Tent_d_ and everything in it by the plan I will show you.

THE BOX OF THE AGREEMENT

¹⁰"Use acacia wood and build a Holy Box._d_ It must be 45 inches long, 27 inches wide and 27 inches high. ¹¹Cover the Holy Box inside and out with pure gold. And put a gold strip all around it. ¹²Make four gold rings for the Holy Box. Attach the gold rings to its four feet, two rings on each side. ¹³Then make poles from acacia wood and cover them with gold. ¹⁴Put the poles through the rings on the sides of the Box. Use these poles to carry the Holy Box. ¹⁵These poles must always stay in the rings of the Holy Box. Do not take the poles out. ¹⁶Then put the two flat stones in the Holy Box. I will give you these stones on which the commands are written.

¹⁷"Then make a lid of pure gold for the Holy Box. This lid is the mercy seat._d_ Make it 45 inches long and 27 inches wide. ¹⁸Then hammer gold to make two creatures with wings. Put one on each end of the lid. ¹⁹Put one creature with wings on one end of the lid. And put the other creature with wings on the other end. Attach the creatures with wings to the lid so that they will all be one piece. ²⁰The creatures' wings should be spread out over the lid. The creatures are to face each other across the lid. ²¹Put this lid on top of the Holy Box. Also put in this Holy Box the agreement which I will make

with you. [22]I will meet with you there, above the lid between the two creatures with wings. These are on the Box of the Agreement. There I will give you all my commands for the Israelites.

THE TABLE

[23]"Make a table out of acacia wood. It must be 36 inches long, 18 inches wide and 27 inches high. [24]Cover it with pure gold. Put a gold strip around it. [25]Then make a frame three inches high that stands up all around the edge. Put a gold strip around the frame. [26]Then make four gold rings. Attach them to the four corners of the table where the four legs are. [27]Put the rings close to the frame around the top of the table. These rings will hold the poles for carrying the table. [28]Make the poles out of acacia wood and cover them with gold. Carry the table with these poles. [29]Make the plates and bowls for the table out of pure gold. Make the jars and cups out of pure gold. They will be used for pouring out the drink offerings. [30]On this table put the bread that shows you are in my presence. It must always be there in front of me.

THE LAMPSTAND

[31]"Hammer pure gold to make a lampstand. Its base, stand, flower-like cups, buds and petals must all be joined together in one piece. [32]The lampstand must have three branches on one side and three branches on the other. [33]Each branch must have three cups shaped like almond flowers on it. Each cup must have a bud and a petal. [34]And there must be four more cups made like almond flowers on the lampstand itself. These cups must also have buds and petals. [35]Put a bud under each pair of branches that goes out from the lampstand. [36]The branches, buds and lampstand must be one piece of pure, hammered gold.

[37]"Then make seven small oil lamps and put them on the lampstand. They will give light to the area in front of the lampstand. [38]The wick trimmers and trays must be made of pure gold. [39]Use 75 pounds of pure gold to make the lampstand and everything with it. [40]Be very careful to make them by the plan I showed you on the mountain.

THE HOLY TENT

26 "Make the Holy Tent[d] with ten pieces of cloth. These pieces must be made of fine linen and blue, purple and red thread. Have a skilled craftsman sew designs of creatures with wings on the pieces of cloth. [2]Make each piece the same size. Each piece should be 42 feet long and 6 feet wide. [3]Sew five pieces of cloth together for one set. Sew the other pieces together for the second set. [4]Make loops of blue cloth down the edge of the end piece of each set. [5]Make 50 loops on the end piece of the first set. And make 50 loops on the end piece of the second set. These loops must be opposite each other. [6]And make 50 gold hooks. Use these to join the two sets of cloth. This will make the Holy Tent one piece.

[7]"Then make another tent that will cover the Holy Tent. Make this tent of 11 pieces of cloth made from goat hair. [8]All these pieces of cloth must be the same size. They must be 45 feet long and 6 feet wide. [9]Sew five of the pieces together into one set. Then sew the other six pieces together into the second set. Fold the sixth piece double over the front of the Tent. [10]Make 50 loops down the edge of the end piece of one set. Do the same for the end piece of the other set. [11]Then make 50 bronze hooks. Put these in the loops to join the two sets of cloth. This will make the covering one piece. [12]Let the extra half piece of cloth hang over the back of the Holy Tent. [13]There will be 18 inches hanging over the sides of the Holy Tent. This will protect the Tent. [14]Make two more coverings for the Holy Tent. One should be made from male sheep skins colored red. The outer covering should be from fine leather.

15"Use acacia wood to make upright frames for the Holy Tent. 16Each frame must be 15 feet long and 27 inches wide. 17Every frame must be made the same way. There must be two pegs side by side in each frame. 18Make 20 frames for the south side of the Holy Tent. 19Each frame must have 2 silver bases to go under it. A peg fits into each silver base. You must make 40 silver bases for the frames. 20Make 20 more frames for the north side of the Holy Tent. 21Make 40 silver bases for them. Make 2 bases for each frame. 22You must make 6 frames for the rear or west end of the Holy Tent. 23Make 2 frames for each corner at the rear. 24The 2 frames at each corner are to be joined together. Hold them together from bottom to top with a metal ring. Both corner frames must be made this way. 25So there will be a total of 8 frames at the rear of the Tent. And there will be 16 silver bases—2 bases under each frame.

26"Make crossbars of acacia wood to connect the upright frames of the Holy Tent. Make five crossbars to hold the frames together on one side. 27Also make five crossbars to hold the frames together on the other side. And make crossbars to hold the frames together on the west end, at the rear. 28The middle crossbar is to be set halfway up the frames. It is to run along the entire length of each side and rear. 29Make gold rings on the sides of the frames. Pass the crossbars through the rings. Cover the frames and the crossbars with gold. 30Set up the Holy Tent by the plan shown to you on the mountain.

31"Make a curtain of fine linen and blue, purple and red thread. Have a skilled craftsman sew designs of creatures with wings on the curtain. 32Hang the curtain by gold hooks on four posts of acacia wood. Cover these posts with gold and set them in four silver bases. 33Hang the curtain from the hooks in the roof. Put the Holy Box*d* containing the two flat stones behind the curtain. This curtain will separate the Holy Place from the Most Holy Place. 34Put the lid on the Holy Box in the Most Holy Place.

35"Outside the curtain, put the table on the north side of the Holy Tent. And put the lampstand on the south side of the Holy Tent. This will be across from the table.

THE ENTRANCE OF THE HOLY TENT

36"Then make a curtain for the entrance of the Tent.*d* Make it with fine linen and blue, purple and red thread. Someone who can sew well is to sew designs on it. 37Make five posts of acacia wood covered with gold. Make five gold hooks on which to hang the curtain from the posts. And make five bronze bases for the five posts.

THE ALTAR

27 "Make an altar for burnt offerings out of acacia wood. Make it 4$\frac{1}{2}$ feet high. It should be square: 7$\frac{1}{2}$ feet long and 7$\frac{1}{2}$ feet wide. 2Make each of the four corners of the altar stick out like a horn. The corners with their horns must be all one piece. Then cover the whole altar with bronze.

3"Use bronze to make all the tools and dishes that will be used on the altar. Make pots to remove the ashes. Make shovels, bowls for sprinkling blood, meat forks and pans for carrying the burning wood. 4"Make a large, bronze screen to hold the burning wood. And put a bronze ring at each of the four corners of the screen. 5Put the screen inside the altar, under its rim, halfway up from the bottom.

6"Make poles of acacia wood for the altar. And cover them with bronze. 7Put the poles through the rings on both sides of the altar to carry it. 8Make the altar out of boards and leave the inside hollow. Make it as you were shown on the mountain.

THE COURTYARD OF THE HOLY TENT

⁹"Make a wall of curtains to form a courtyard around the Holy Tent.*ᵈ* The south side should have a wall of fine linen curtains 150 feet long. ¹⁰Hang the curtain with silver hooks and bands. Put these on 20 bronze posts on 20 bronze bases. ¹¹The north side must also be 150 feet long. Hang its curtains on silver hooks and bands. Put these on 20 bronze posts on 20 bronze bases.

¹²"The west end of the courtyard must have a wall of curtains 75 feet long. It must have 10 posts and 10 bases on that wall. ¹³The east end of the courtyard must also be 75 feet long. ¹⁴On one side of the entry, there is to be a wall of curtains. It is to be 22¹/₂ feet long. It is to be held up by 3 posts on 3 bases. ¹⁵On the other side of the entry, there is to be a wall of curtains. It is to be 22¹/₂ feet long. It is to be held up by 3 posts on 3 bases.

¹⁶"The entry to the courtyard is to be a curtain 30 feet wide. It is to be made of fine linen with blue, purple and red thread. Someone who can sew well is to sew designs on it. It is to be held up by 4 posts on 4 bases. ¹⁷All the posts around the courtyard must have silver bands and hooks and bronze bases. ¹⁸The courtyard must be 150 feet long and 75 feet wide. The wall of curtains around it should be 7¹/₂ feet high. They must be made of fine linen. The bases in which the posts are set must be bronze. ¹⁹All the things used in the Holy Tent must be made of bronze. And all the tent pegs for the Holy Tent and the wall around the courtyard must be made of bronze.

OIL FOR THE LAMP

²⁰"Command the people of Israel to bring you pure olive oil. It is to be made from pressed olives. This is to keep the lamps on the lampstand burning. ²¹Aaron and his sons must keep the lamps burning before the Lord from evening till morning. This will be in the Meeting Tent.*ᵈ* It is outside the curtain

which is in front of the Holy Box.*ᵈ* The Israelites and their descendants*ᵈ* must obey this rule from now on.

CLOTHES FOR THE PRIESTS

28 "Tell your brother Aaron to come to you. His sons Nadab, Abihu, Eleazar and Ithamar must come with him. Separate them from the other Israelites. These men must serve as priests. ²Make holy clothes for your brother Aaron to give him honor and beauty. ³Speak to all the people to whom I have given the ability to make clothes. Tell these skilled craftsmen to make the clothes for Aaron. Use these clothes to make him belong to me. Then he may serve me as a priest. ⁴These are the clothes they must make: a chest covering, a holy vest,*ᵈ* an outer robe, a woven inner robe, a turban and a cloth belt. The craftsmen must make these holy clothes. They are for your brother Aaron and his sons. Then Aaron and his sons may serve me as priests. ⁵The craftsmen must use gold and blue, purple and red thread, and fine linen.

THE HOLY VEST

⁶"Use gold and blue, purple and red thread, and fine linen to make the holy vest.*ᵈ* The craftsmen are to make this holy vest. ⁷At each top corner of this holy vest there will be a pair of shoulder straps. These are to be tied together over each shoulder.

⁸"The craftsmen will very carefully weave a belt on the holy vest. Make the belt with gold and blue, purple and red thread, and fine linen.

⁹"Take two onyx stones. Write the name of the 12 sons of Israel on these jewels. ¹⁰Write 6 names on one stone and 6 names on the other stone. Write the names in order, from the oldest son to the youngest. ¹¹Carve the names of the sons of Israel on these stones. Do this the same way a person carves words and designs on the seals.*ᵈ* Put gold around

the stones to hold them on the holy vest. [12]Put the two stones on the two straps of the holy vest. These stones are reminders of the 12 sons of Israel. Aaron is to wear their names on his shoulders. They are before the Lord as reminders of the sons of Israel. [13]Make two gold pieces to hold the stones. [14]Then make two chains of pure gold. Twist them together like a rope. Attach the chains to the two gold pieces that hold the stones.

THE CHEST COVERING

[15]"Make a chest covering to help in making decisions. The craftsmen should make it as they made the holy vest.[d] They must use gold and blue, purple and red thread, and fine linen. [16]The chest covering must be square. It should be nine inches long and nine inches wide. Fold it double to make a pocket. [17]Put four rows of beautiful gems on the chest covering. The first row of jewels must have a ruby, topaz and yellow quartz. [18]The second row must have turquoise, a sapphire and an emerald. [19]The third row must have a jacinth, an agate and an amethyst. [20]The fourth row must have a chrysolite, an onyx and a jasper. Put gold around these jewels to attach them to the chest covering. [21]There must be 12 jewels on the chest covering. That is 1 jewel for each of the names of the sons of Israel. Carve the name of one of the 12 tribes[d] on each of the stones. Carve them as you would carve a seal.[d]

[22]"Make chains of pure gold for the chest covering. Twist them together like rope. [23]Make two gold rings. Put them on the two upper corners of the chest covering. [24]Attach the two gold chains to the two rings. These are at the upper corners of the chest covering. [25]Attach the other ends of the two chains to the two gold pieces on the shoulder straps. This will tie the chains to the shoulder straps in the front of the holy vest.

[26]"Make two more gold rings. Put them at the two lower corners of the chest covering. Put them on the inside edge of the chest covering next to the holy vest. [27]Make two more gold rings. Attach them to the bottom of the shoulder straps in the front of the holy vest. Put the gold rings close to the seam above the woven belt of the holy vest. [28]Join the rings of the chest covering to the rings of the holy vest with blue ribbon. This will connect it to the woven belt. In this way the chest covering will not swing out from the holy vest.

[29]"When Aaron enters the Holy Place, he will wear the names of the sons of Israel over his heart. These names are on the chest covering that helps in making decisions. This will be a continual reminder before the Lord. [30]And put the Urim and Thummim[d] inside the chest covering. These things will be on Aaron's heart when he goes before the Lord. They will help in making decisions for the Israelites. So Aaron will always carry them with him when he is before the Lord.

[31]"Make the outer robe to be worn under the holy vest, using only blue cloth. [32]Make a hole in the center for Aaron's head. And there must be a woven collar around the hole so it will not tear. [33]Make balls like pomegranates[d] of blue, purple and red thread. Hang these pomegranate balls around the bottom of the outer robe. And hang gold bells between them. [34]So all around the bottom of the outer robe there should be a gold bell and a pomegranate ball, a gold bell and a pomegranate ball. [35]Aaron must wear this robe when he serves as priest. The ringing of the bells will be heard. They will ring when he enters and leaves the Holy Place before the Lord. This way Aaron will not be killed.

[36]"Make a strip of pure gold. Carve these words on the gold strip as you would carve on a seal:[d] 'Holy to the Lord.' [37]Use blue ribbon to tie a strip of gold to the turban. Put it on the front of the turban. [38]Aaron must wear this on his

forehead. In this way, he will be blamed if anything is wrong with the gifts of the Israelites. Aaron must always wear this on his head so the Lord will accept the gifts of the people.

39"Make the woven inner robe of fine linen. Make the turban of fine linen, also. Make the cloth belt with designs sewn on it. 40Also make woven inner robes, cloth belts and headbands for Aaron's sons. This will give them honor and beauty. 41Put these clothes on your brother Aaron and his sons. Then pour olive oil on their heads to appoint them as priests. Make them belong to me so they may serve me as priests.

42"Make for them linen underclothes to cover them from the waist to the upper parts of the legs. 43Aaron and his sons must wear these underclothes when they enter the Meeting Tent.*d* And they must wear these clothes anytime they come near the altar to serve as priests in the Holy Place. If they do not wear these clothes, they will be guilty of wrong. And they will be killed. This will be a law that will last from now on for Aaron and all his descendants.*d*

APPOINTING THE PRIESTS

29 "This is what you must do to appoint Aaron and his sons. Then they may serve me as priests. Take one young bull and two male sheep that have nothing wrong with them. 2Use fine wheat flour without yeast to make bread and cakes mixed with olive oil. Also use wheat flour without yeast to make wafers brushed with olive oil. 3Put these in one basket. Bring them in the basket along with the bull and two male sheep. 4Bring Aaron and his sons to the entrance of the Meeting Tent.*d* Then wash them with water. 5Take the clothes. Dress Aaron in the inner robe and the outer robe of the holy vest.*d* Then put on him the holy vest and the chest covering. Then tie the holy vest on him with its skillfully woven belt. 6Put the turban on

his head. Put the holy crown, the strip of gold, on the turban. 7Take the special olive oil and pour it on his head to make him a priest.

8"Then bring his sons and put the inner robes on them. 9Put the headbands on their heads. Then tie cloth belts around their waists. Aaron and his descendants*d* will be priests in Israel. This is by a rule that will continue from now on. This is how you will appoint Aaron and his sons as priests.

10"Bring the bull to the front of the Meeting Tent. Aaron and his sons must put their hands on the bull's head. 11Then kill the bull before the Lord at the entrance to the Meeting Tent. 12Take some of the bull's blood and go to the altar. Use your finger to put some blood on the corners of the altar. Pour the blood that is left at the bottom of the altar. 13Then take all the fat that covers the inner organs. Take the best part of the liver, and take both kidneys and the fat around them. Burn these on the altar. 14Take the bull's meat, skin and intestines. Burn these things outside the camp. This is an offering to take away sin.

15"Take one of the male sheep. Have Aaron and his sons put their hands on its head. 16Then kill that male sheep. Take its blood and sprinkle it on all four sides of the altar. 17Then cut the male sheep into pieces. Wash its inner organs and its legs. Put them with its head and its other pieces. 18Burn the whole male sheep on the altar. It is a burnt offering made by fire to the Lord. Its smell is pleasing to the Lord.

19"Take the other male sheep. Have Aaron and his sons put their hands on its head. 20Kill that male sheep and take some of its blood. Put it on the bottom of the right ears of Aaron and his sons. Also put it on the thumbs of their right hands. And put it on the big toes of their right feet. Then sprinkle the rest of the blood against all four sides of the altar.

²¹Then take some of the blood from the altar. Mix it with the special oil used in appointing priests. Sprinkle this on Aaron and his clothes. And sprinkle this on his sons and their clothes. This will show that Aaron and his sons and their clothes are given to my service.

²²"Then take the fat from the male sheep. Take the fat tail and the fat that covers the inner organs. Take the best part of the liver. Take both kidneys and the fat around them and the right thigh. This is the male sheep to be used in appointing priests.

²³"Then take the basket of bread that you made without yeast. This is the basket you put before the Lord. From it take a loaf of bread, a cake made with olive oil and a wafer. ²⁴Put these in the hands of Aaron and his sons. Tell them to present these things in their hands before the Lord. This will be an offering presented to the Lord. ²⁵Then take them from their hands. Burn them on the altar with the whole burnt offering. This is an offering made by fire to the Lord. Its smell is pleasing to the Lord. ²⁶Then take the breast of the male sheep used to appoint Aaron as priest. Present the breast of the male sheep before the Lord. It is an offering presented to the Lord. This part of the animal will be your share. ²⁷Then give to the service of the Lord the parts of the male sheep used to appoint them as priests. They belong to Aaron and his sons. They are the breast and the right thigh. These were presented to the Lord. ²⁸This is to be the regular share which the Israelites will always give to Aaron and his sons. This is the gift the Israelites must give to the Lord from their fellowship offerings.

²⁹"The holy clothes made for Aaron will belong to his descendants. They must wear these clothes when they are appointed as priests. ³⁰Aaron's son will become high priest after Aaron. He will come to the Meeting Tent to serve in the Holy Place. He is to wear these clothes for seven days.

³¹"Take the male sheep used to appoint priests. Boil its meat in a place made holy for serving me. ³²Then Aaron and his sons must eat the meat of the male sheep. They must do that at the entrance of the Meeting Tent. And they must also eat the bread that is in the basket. ³³These offerings were used to remove their sins when they were made priests so they would belong to God. Now they should eat these offerings. But no one else is to eat these things because they are holy. ³⁴If any of the meat from that male sheep or any of the bread is left the next morning, it must be burned. It shall not be eaten because it is holy.

³⁵"Do all these things that I commanded you to do to Aaron and his sons. You are to spend seven days appointing them. ³⁶Each day for seven days you are to offer a bull. This will remove the sins of Aaron and his sons so they will be given for service to the Lord. Make the altar ready for service to the Lord. Pour oil on it to make it holy. ³⁷Spend seven days making the altar ready for service to God and making it holy. Then the altar will become very holy. Anything that touches it must be holy.

THE DAILY SACRIFICES

³⁸"Every day from now on, offer on the altar two lambs that are one year old. ³⁹Offer one lamb in the morning and the other in the evening. ⁴⁰In the morning, when you offer the first lamb, offer also two quarts of fine flour. Mix it with one quart of oil from pressed olives. Pour out a quart of wine as a drink offering. ⁴¹Offer the second lamb in the evening. Also offer the same grain offering and drink offering as you did in the morning. This is an offering by fire to the Lord. And its smell is pleasing to the Lord.

⁴²"You must burn these things as an offering to the Lord every day. Do this at the entrance of the Meeting Tent*d* before

the Lord from now on. When you make the offering, I, the Lord, will meet you there and speak to you. [43]I will meet with the people of Israel there. And that place will be holy because of my greatness.

[44]"So I will make the Meeting Tent and the altar holy. And I will make Aaron and his sons holy so they may serve me as priests. [45]I will live with the people of Israel. I will be their God. [46]And they will know that I am the Lord their God. They will know that I am the one who led them out of Egypt. I did this so I could live with them. I am the Lord their God.

THE ALTAR FOR BURNING INCENSE

30 "Make an altar out of acacia wood for burning incense.[d] [2]Make it square—18 inches long and 18 inches wide. It must be 36 inches high. Make the corners stick out like horns. These must be one piece with the altar. [3]Cover its top, its sides and its corners with pure gold. And put a gold strip all around the altar. [4]Make two gold rings beneath the gold strip on opposite sides of the altar. Slide poles through these gold rings to carry the altar. [5]Make the poles from acacia wood and cover them with gold. [6]Put the altar of incense in front of the curtain. This curtain is in front of the Box[d] of the Agreement. Put the altar in front of the lid that covers that Holy Box. There I will meet with you.

[7]"Aaron must burn sweet-smelling incense on the altar every morning. He will do this when he comes to take care of the oil lamps. [8]He must burn incense again in the evening when he lights the lamps. So incense will burn before the Lord every day from now on. [9]Do not use this altar for offering any other incense or burnt offering. Do not use this altar to offer any kind of grain offering or drink offering. [10]Once a year Aaron must make the altar ready for service to God. He will do it by putting blood on its corners. This is blood of the animal offered to remove sins. He is to do this once a year from

now on. This altar belongs completely to God's service."

THE TAX FOR THE MEETING TENT

[11]The Lord said to Moses, [12]"Count the people of Israel. At that time every person must pay to buy back his life from the Lord. Then no terrible things will happen to the people when you number them. [13]Every person who is counted must pay one-fifth of an ounce of silver. This is set by the Holy Place measure, which weighs two-fifths of an ounce. This amount is a gift to the Lord. [14]Every person who is counted and is 20 years old or older must give this amount to the Lord. [15]A rich person must not give more than one-fifth of an ounce. And a poor person must not give less than one-fifth of an ounce. You are paying this to the Lord to buy back your lives. [16]Gather from the people of Israel this money paid to buy back their lives. Spend it to buy things for the service in the Meeting Tent.[d] This payment will remind the Lord that the Israelites' lives have been bought back."

THE BRONZE BOWL

[17]The Lord said to Moses, [18]"Make a bronze bowl for washing. Build it on a bronze stand. Put the bowl and stand between the Meeting Tent[d] and the altar. Put water in the bowl. [19]Aaron and his sons must wash their hands and feet with the water from this bowl. [20]Each time, before they enter the Meeting Tent, they must wash with water. This way they will not die. They approach the altar to serve as priests. They offer a sacrifice to the Lord by fire. [21]Each time they do this, they must wash their hands and their feet so they will not die. This is a rule which Aaron and his descendants[d] are to keep from now on."

OIL FOR APPOINTING

[22]Then the Lord said to Moses, [23]"Take the finest spices: 12 pounds of liquid myrrh,[d] half that amount (that is, 6 pounds) of sweet-smelling cinnamon, 6

pounds of sweet-smelling cane [24]and 12 pounds of cassia.[d] Weigh all these by the Holy Place measure. Also take 4 quarts of olive oil. [25]Mix all these things like a perfume to make a holy olive oil. This special oil must be put on people and things. Do this to make them ready for service to God. [26]Put this oil on the Meeting Tent[d] and the Holy Box[d] with my laws in it. [27]Put this oil on the table and all its dishes. And put this oil on the lampstand and all its tools. Put the oil on the incense[d] altar. [28]Also, put the oil on the altar for burning offerings and all its tools. Put this oil on the bowl and the stand under the bowl. Put oil on all these things to prepare them for service to God. [29]You will give these things for service to God. They will be very holy. Anything that touches these things must also be holy.

[30]"Put the oil on Aaron and his sons to make them priests. Give them for service to me. Then they may serve me as priests. [31]Tell the Israelites, 'This is to be my holy olive oil from now on. It is to be put on people and things to make them ready for service to God. [32]Do not pour it on the bodies of ordinary people. Do not make perfume the same way you make this oil. It is holy, and you must treat it as holy. [33]Someone might make perfume like it. Or he might put it on someone who is not a priest. Then that person must be separated from his people.'"

INCENSE

[34]Then the Lord said to Moses, "Take these sweet-smelling spices: resin, onycha, galbanum and pure frankincense.[d] Be sure that you have equal amounts of each. [35]You must make incense[d] as a man who makes perfume would do. Add salt to it to keep it pure and holy. [36]Beat some of the incense into a fine powder. Put some of it in front of the Holy Box[d] of the Agreement in the Meeting Tent.[d] There I will meet with you. You must use this incense powder only for its very special purpose. [37]Do

not make incense for yourselves the same way you make this incense. Treat it as holy to the Lord. [38]Whoever makes incense like this to use as perfume must be separated from his people."

BEZALEL AND OHOLIAB

31 Then the Lord said to Moses, [2]"See, I have chosen Bezalel son of Uri from the tribe[d] of Judah. Uri was the son of Hur. [3]I have filled Bezalel with the Spirit[d] of God. I have given him the skill, ability and knowledge to do all kinds of work. [4]He is able to design pieces to be made from gold, silver and bronze. [5]He is able to cut jewels and put them in metal. And he can carve wood. Bezalel can do all kinds of work. [6]I have also chosen Oholiab son of Ahisamach from the tribe of Dan. Oholiab will work with Bezalel. I have given skills to all skilled craftsmen. They will be able to make all these things I have commanded you: [7]the Meeting Tent,[d] the Box[d] of the Agreement, the lid that covers the Holy Box and everything in the Tent. [8]This includes the table and everything on it, the pure gold lampstand and everything with it and the altar of incense.[d] [9]It also includes the altar for burnt offerings and everything used with it, the bowl and the stand under it. [10]They will make the woven clothes and the holy clothes for Aaron and the clothes for his sons to wear when they serve as priests. [11]They will also make the special olive oil used in appointing people and things to the service of the Lord, and the sweet-smelling incense for the Holy Place.

"These workers will make all these things just as I have commanded you."

THE DAY OF REST

[12]Then the Lord said to Moses, [13]"Tell the Israelites, 'You must keep the rules about my Sabbaths.[d] This is because they will be a sign between you and me from now on. In this way you will know that I, the Lord, am making you holy.

[14]"'Make the Sabbath a holy day. If

anyone treats the Sabbath like any other day, that person must be put to death. Anyone who works on the Sabbath day must be separated from his people. [15]There are six days for working. But the seventh day is a day of rest. It is a day holy for the Lord. Anyone who works during the Sabbath day must be put to death. [16]The Israelites must remember the Sabbath day. It is an agreement between them and me that will continue from now on. [17]The Sabbath day will be a sign between me and the Israelites forever. This is because in six days I, the Lord, made the sky and the earth. And on the seventh day I did not work. I rested.'"

[18]So the Lord finished speaking to Moses on Mount Sinai. Then the Lord gave him the two stone tablets with the agreement written on them. The finger of God wrote the commands on the stones.

THE PEOPLE MAKE A GOLD CALF

32 The people saw that a long time had passed. And Moses had not come down from the mountain. So they gathered around Aaron. They said to him, "Moses led us out of Egypt. But we don't know what has happened to him. So make us gods who will lead us."

[2]Aaron said to the people, "Take off the gold earrings that your wives, sons and daughters are wearing. Bring them to me." [3]So all the people took their gold earrings and brought them to Aaron. [4]Aaron took the gold from the people. Then he melted it and made a statue of a calf. He finished it with a tool. Then the people said, "Israel! These are your gods who brought you out of the land of Egypt!"

[5]Aaron saw all this, and he built an altar before the calf. Then he made an announcement. He said, "Tomorrow there will be a special feast to honor the Lord." [6]The people got up early the next morning. They offered whole burnt offerings and fellowship offerings. First the people sat down to eat and drink. Then they got up and sinned sexually.

[7]And the Lord said to Moses, "Go down from this mountain. Your people, the people you brought out of the land of Egypt, have done a terrible sin. [8]They have quickly turned away from the things I commanded them to do. They have made for themselves a calf of melted gold. They have worshiped that calf and offered sacrifices to it. The people have said, 'Israel, these are your gods who brought you out of Egypt.'"

[9]The Lord said to Moses, "I have seen these people. I know that they are very stubborn people. [10]So now do not stop me. I am so angry with them that I am going to destroy them. Then I will make you and your descendants[d] a great nation."

[11]But Moses begged the Lord his God. Moses said, "Lord, don't let your anger destroy your people. You brought these people out of Egypt with your great power and strength. [12]Don't let the people of Egypt say, 'The Lord brought the Israelites out of Egypt. But he planned to kill them in the mountains and destroy them from the earth.' So stop being angry. Don't destroy your people. [13]Remember the men who served you— Abraham, Isaac and Israel. You promised with an oath to them. You said, 'I will make your descendants as many as the stars in the sky. I will give your descendants all this land that I have promised them. It will be theirs forever.'" [14]So the Lord changed his mind. He did not destroy the people as he had said he might.

[15]Then Moses went down the mountain. In his hands he had the two stone tablets with the agreement on them. The commands were written on both sides of each stone, front and back. [16]God himself had made the stones. And God himself had written the commands on the stones.

[17]Then Joshua heard the noise of the people shouting. He said to Moses, "It sounds like war down in the camp."

¹⁸Moses answered:

"It is not an army's shout of victory.

It is not an army's cry of defeat.

It is the sound of singing that I hear."

¹⁹When Moses came close to the camp, he saw the gold calf and the dancing. He became very angry. He threw down the stone tablets which he was carrying. He broke them at the bottom of the mountain. ²⁰Then he took the calf that the people had made. He melted it in the fire. And he ground the gold until it became powder. He threw the powder into the water. And he forced the Israelites to drink that water.

²¹Moses said to Aaron, "What did these people do to you? Why did you cause them to do such a terrible sin?"

²²Aaron answered, "Don't be angry, master. You know that these people are always ready to do wrong. ²³The people said to me, 'Moses led us out of Egypt. But we don't know what has happened to him. So make us gods who will lead us.' ²⁴So I told the people, 'Take off your gold jewelry.' So they gave me the gold. I threw it into the fire and out came this calf!"

²⁵Moses saw that the people were acting wildly. He saw that Aaron had let them get out of control. Their enemies would laugh at them. ²⁶So Moses stood at the entrance to the camp. He said, "Let anyone who wants to follow the Lord come to me." And all the people from the family of Levi gathered around Moses.

²⁷Then Moses said to them, "The Lord, the God of Israel, says this: 'Every man must put on his sword and go through the camp from one end to the other. Each man must kill his brother, his friend and his neighbor.'" ²⁸The people from the family of Levi obeyed Moses. That day about 3,000 of the people of Israel died. ²⁹Then Moses said, "Today you have been given for service to the Lord. You were willing to kill your own sons and brothers. And God has blessed you for this."

³⁰The next day Moses told the people, "You have done a terrible sin. But now I will go up to the Lord. Maybe I can do something so your sins will be removed. Then you will belong to God again." ³¹So Moses went back to the Lord and said, "How terrible it is! These people have sinned horribly. They have made for themselves gods from gold. ³²Now, forgive them of this sin. If you will not, then erase my name. Erase it from the book in which you have written the names of your people."

³³But the Lord told Moses, "I will erase from my book the names of the people who sin against me. ³⁴So now, go. Lead the people where I have told you. My angel will lead you. When the time comes to punish, I will punish them for their sin."

³⁵So the Lord caused terrible things to happen to the people. He did this because of what they did with the calf Aaron had made.

33 Then the Lord said to Moses, "You and the people you brought out of Egypt must leave this place. Go to the land that I promised with an oath to give to Abraham, Isaac and Jacob. I said, 'I will give that land to your descendants.' ²I will send an angel to lead you. And I will force these people out of the land: the Canaanites, Amorites, Hittites, Perizzites, Hivites and Jebusites. ³Go up to the land where much food grows. But I will not go with you. This is because I might destroy you on the way. You are such a stubborn people."

⁴The people heard this bad news, and they became very sad. None of them put on jewelry. ⁵This was because the Lord had said to Moses, "Tell the Israelites, 'You are a stubborn people. If I were to go with you even for a moment, I would destroy you. So take off all your jewelry. Then I will decide what to do with you.'" ⁶So the people of Israel took off their jewelry at Mount Sinai.

THE MEETING TENT

[7]Moses used to take a tent and set it up a long way outside the camp. Moses called it the "Meeting Tent."[d] A person might want to ask the Lord about something. Then he would go to the Meeting Tent outside the camp. [8]Anytime Moses went out to the Tent, all the people would rise. They stood at the entrances of their tents and watched Moses until he entered the Meeting Tent. [9]When Moses went into the Tent, the pillar of cloud would always come down. It would stay at the entrance of the Tent while the Lord spoke with Moses. [10]The people saw the pillar of cloud at the entrance of the Tent. Then they stood and worshiped, each person at the entrance of his own tent.

[11]The Lord spoke to Moses face to face as a man speaks with his friend. Then Moses would return to the camp. But Moses' young helper, Joshua son of Nun, did not leave the Tent.

[12]Moses said to the Lord, "You have told me to lead these people. But you did not say whom you would send with me. You have said to me, 'I know you very well. I am pleased with you.' [13]If I have truly pleased you, show me your plans. Then I may know you and continue to please you. Remember that this nation is your people."

[14]The Lord answered, "I myself will go with you. And I will give you victory."

[15]Then Moses said to him, "If you yourself don't go with us, then don't send us away from this place. [16]If you don't go with us, no one will know that you are pleased with me and your people. These people and I would be no different from any other people on earth."

[17]Then the Lord said to Moses, "I will do what you ask. This is because I know you very well, and I am pleased with you."

MOSES AND GOD'S GREATNESS

[18]Then Moses said, "Now, please show me your greatness."

[19]The Lord answered, "I will cause all my goodness to pass in front of you. I will announce my name, the Lord, so you can hear it. I will show kindness to anyone I want to show kindness. I will show mercy to anyone I want to show mercy. [20]But you cannot see my face. No one can see me and stay alive.

[21]"There is a place near me where you may stand on a rock. [22]My greatness will pass that place. I will put you in a large crack in that rock. And I will cover you with my hand until I have passed by. [23]Then I will take away my hand, and you will see my back. But my face must not be seen."

MOSES GETS NEW STONES

34 The Lord said to Moses, "Cut two more stone tablets like the first two. I will write the same words on them that were on the first two stones which you broke. [2]Be ready tomorrow morning. Then come up on Mount Sinai. Stand before me there on the top of the mountain. [3]No one may come with you. No one should even be seen any place on the mountain. Not even the sheep or cattle may eat grass near that mountain."

[4]So Moses cut two stone tablets like the first ones. Then early the next morning he went up Mount Sinai. He did this just as the Lord had commanded him. Moses carried the two stone tablets with him. [5]Then the Lord came down in the cloud and stood there with Moses. And the Lord called out his name, the Lord. [6]The Lord passed in front of Moses and said, "I am the Lord. The Lord is a God who shows mercy and is kind. The Lord doesn't become angry quickly. The Lord has great love and faithfulness. [7]The Lord is kind to thousands of people. The Lord forgives people for wrong and sin and turning against him. But the Lord does not forget to punish guilty people. The Lord will punish not only

the guilty people. He will also punish their children, their grandchildren, their great-grandchildren and their great-great-grandchildren."

⁸Then Moses quickly bowed to the ground and worshiped. ⁹Moses said, "Lord, if you are pleased with me, please go with us. I know that these are stubborn people. But forgive our evil and our sin. Take us as your own people."

¹⁰Then the Lord said, "I am making this agreement with you. I will do miracles*d* in front of all your people. These things have never before been done for any other nation on earth. The people with you will see my work. I, the Lord, will do wonderful things for you. ¹¹Obey the things I command you today, and I will force your enemies to leave your land. I will force out the Amorites, Canaanites, Hittites, Perizzites, Hivites and Jebusites ahead of you. ¹²Be careful. Don't make any agreement with the people who live in the land where you are going. It will bring you trouble. ¹³But destroy their altars. Break their stone pillars. Cut down their Asherah*d* idols. ¹⁴Don't worship any other god. This is because I, the Lord, the Jealous One, am a jealous God.

¹⁵"Be careful. Don't make any agreements with the people who live in that land. They will worship their false gods. And they will invite you to join them. Then you will join them, and you will eat their sacrifices. ¹⁶You might choose some of their daughters as wives for your sons. Those daughters worship false gods. They might lead your sons to do the same thing.

¹⁷"Do not make gods of melted metal.

¹⁸"Celebrate the Feast*d* of Unleavened Bread. For seven days you must eat bread made without yeast as I commanded you. Do this during the month I have chosen, the month of Abib.*d* This is because in that month you came out of Egypt.

¹⁹"Every firstborn*d* cow or sheep that is born to each animal belongs to me. ²⁰You may buy back a donkey by paying for it with a lamb. But if you don't want to buy back a donkey, you must break its neck. You must buy back all your firstborn sons.

"No one is to come before me without a gift.

²¹"You must work for six days. But on the seventh day you must rest. You must do this even during the planting season and harvest season.

²²"Celebrate the Feast*d* of Weeks when you gather the first grain of the wheat harvest. And celebrate the Feast*d* of Harvest in the fall.

²³"Three times each year all your men must come before the Master, the Lord, the God of Israel. ²⁴I will force out nations ahead of you. I will expand the borders of your land. You will go before the Lord your God three times each year. And at that time no one will try to take your land from you.

²⁵"Do not offer the blood of a sacrifice to me with anything containing yeast. And do not leave any of the sacrifice of the Feast*d* of Passover. It must not be left until the next morning.

²⁶"Bring the best first crops that you harvest from your ground. Bring those things to the Tent*d* of the Lord your God.

"You must not cook a young goat in its mother's milk."

²⁷Then the Lord said to Moses, "Write down these words. This is because with these words I have made an agreement with you and Israel."

²⁸Moses stayed there with the Lord 40 days and 40 nights. During that time he did not eat food or drink water. And Moses wrote the words of the agreement—the Ten Commandments—on the stone tablets.

THE FACE OF MOSES SHINES

²⁹Then Moses came down from Mount Sinai. In his hands he was carrying the

two stone tablets of the agreement. But Moses did not know that his face was shining because he had talked with the Lord. ³⁰Aaron and all the people of Israel saw that Moses' face was shining. So they were afraid to go near him. ³¹But Moses called to them. So Aaron and all the leaders of the people returned to Moses. Moses talked with them. ³²After that, all the people of Israel came near him. And he gave them all the commands that the Lord had given him on Mount Sinai.

³³When Moses finished speaking to the people, he put a covering over his face. ³⁴Anytime Moses went before the Lord to speak with him, Moses took off the covering until he came out. Then Moses would come out and tell the people of Israel the things the Lord had commanded. ³⁵The Israelites would see that Moses' face was shining. So he would cover his face again. He did this until the next time he went in to speak with the Lord.

RULES ABOUT THE SABBATH

35 Moses gathered all the Israelite community together. He said to them, "These are the things the Lord has commanded you to do. ²You are to work for six days. But the seventh day will be a holy day, a Sabbath*ᵈ* of rest to honor the Lord. Anyone who works on that day must be put to death. ³On the Sabbath day you must not light a fire in any of your houses."

⁴Moses said to all the Israelites, "This is what the Lord has commanded: ⁵From what you have, take an offering for the Lord. Let everyone who is willing bring this offering to the Lord: gold, silver, bronze, ⁶blue, purple and red thread, and fine linen, goat hair ⁷and male sheep skins, colored red. And they may bring fine leather and acacia wood. ⁸They may also bring olive oil for the lamps, spices for the special olive oil used for appointing priests and for the sweet-smelling incense.*ᵈ* ⁹And they may

bring onyx stones and other jewels to be put on the holy vest*ᵈ* and chest covering of the priests.

¹⁰"Let all the skilled workers come and make everything the Lord commanded: ¹¹the Holy Tent,*ᵈ* its outer tent and its covering, the hooks, frames, crossbars, posts and bases; ¹²the Box*ᵈ* of the Agreement, its poles, lid and the curtain in front of it; ¹³the table and its poles, all the things that go with the table and the bread that shows we are in God's presence; ¹⁴the lampstand for the light and all the things that go with it, the lamps and olive oil for the light; ¹⁵the altar of incense and its poles, the special oil and the sweet-smelling incense, the curtain for the entrance of the Meeting Tent; ¹⁶the altar of burnt offering and its bronze screen, its poles and all its tools, the bronze bowl and its base; ¹⁷the curtains around the courtyard, their posts and bases, and the curtain at the entry to the courtyard; ¹⁸the pegs of the Holy Tent and of the courtyard and their ropes; ¹⁹the special clothes that the priest will wear in the Holy Place. These are the holy clothes for Aaron the priest and his sons to wear when they serve as priests."

²⁰Then all the people of Israel went away from Moses. ²¹Everyone who wanted to give came and brought a gift to the Lord. These gifts were used for making the Meeting Tent, all the things in the Tent and the special clothes. ²²All the men and women who wanted to give brought gold jewelry of all kinds. They brought pins, earrings, rings and bracelets. They all presented their gold to the Lord. ²³Everyone who had blue, purple and red thread, and fine linen came and gave it to the Lord. Anyone who had goat hair or male sheep skins colored red or fine leather brought them to the Lord. ²⁴Everyone who could give silver or bronze brought that as a gift to the Lord. Everyone who had acacia wood to be used in the work brought it.

25Every skilled woman used her hands to make the blue, purple and red thread and fine linen. And they brought what they had made. 26All the women who were skilled and wanted to help made thread of the goat hair. 27The leaders brought onyx stones and other jewels. These stones and jewels were put on the holy vest and chest covering for the priest. 28They also brought spices and olive oil. These were used for the sweet-smelling incense, the special oil and the oil to burn in the lamps. 29All the men and women of Israel who wanted to help brought gifts to the Lord. They were used for all the work the Lord had commanded Moses and the people to do.

30Then Moses said to the people of Israel, "Look, the Lord has chosen Bezalel. He is the son of Uri the son of Hur, from the tribe*d* of Judah. 31The Lord has filled Bezalel with the Spirit*d* of God. The Lord has given Bezalel the skill, ability and knowledge to do all kinds of work. 32He is able to design pieces to be made of gold, silver and bronze. 33He is able to cut stones and jewels and put them in metal. Bezalel can carve wood and do all kinds of work. 34The Lord has given Bezalel and Oholiab the ability to teach others. Oholiab is the son of Ahisamach from the tribe of Dan. 35The Lord has given them the skill to do all kinds of work. They are able to cut designs in metal and stone. They can plan and sew designs in the fine linen with the blue, purple and red thread. And they are also able to weave things.

36 "So Bezalel, Oholiab and every skilled person will do the work the Lord has commanded. The Lord gave these people the wisdom and understanding to do all the skilled work needed to build the Holy Tent."

2Then Moses called Bezalel, Oholiab and all the other skilled people to whom the Lord had given skills. And they came because they wanted to help with the work. 3They received from Moses everything the people of Israel had brought as gifts to build the Holy Tent. The people continued to bring gifts each morning because they wanted to. 4So all the skilled workers left the work they were doing on the Holy Tent. And they went to speak to Moses. They said, 5"The people are bringing more than we need to do the work the Lord commanded."

6Then Moses sent this command throughout the camp: "No man or woman should make anything else as a gift for the Holy Tent." So the people were kept from giving more. 7What they had was already more than enough to do all the work.

THE HOLY TENT

8Then the skilled workers made the Holy Tent.*d* They made the ten pieces of blue, purple and red cloth. And they sewed designs of creatures with wings on the pieces. 9Each piece was the same size. It was 42 feet long and 6 feet wide. 10Five of the pieces were fastened together to make one set. The other five were fastened together to make another set. 11Then they made loops of blue cloth along the edge of the end piece on the first set of five. They did the same thing with the other set of five. 12There were 50 loops on one piece and 50 loops on the other piece. The loops were opposite each other. 13Then they made 50 gold hooks to join the two pieces together. So the Holy Tent was joined together as one piece.

14Then the workers made another tent of 11 pieces of cloth made of goat hair. This was to put over the Holy Tent. 15All 11 pieces were the same size. They were 45 feet long and 6 feet wide. 16The workers sewed five pieces together into one set. Then they sewed six together into another set. 17They made 50 loops along the edge of the outside piece of one set. And they made 50 loops along the edge of the outside piece of the other set. 18Then they made 50 bronze rings to join the two sets of cloth together and make the tent one piece. ¹⁹Then they made two more coverings for the outer tent. One covering was made of male sheep skin colored red. The other covering was made of fine leather.

²⁰Then they made upright frames of acacia wood. ²¹Each board was 15 feet tall and 27 inches wide. ²²There were two pegs side by side on each frame. Every frame of the Holy Tent was made this same way. ²³They made 20 frames for the south side of the Tent. ²⁴Then they made 40 silver bases that went under the 20 frames. There were two bases for every frame—one for each peg of each board. ²⁵They also made 20 frames for the north side of the Holy Tent. ²⁶They made 40 silver bases—2 to go under each frame. ²⁷They made 6 frames for the rear or west end of the Holy Tent ²⁸and 2 frames for the corners at the rear of the Holy Tent. ²⁹These 2 frames were joined together from the bottom to the top with a metal ring. They did this for each of these corners. ³⁰So there were 8 frames and 16 silver bases—2 bases under each frame.

³¹Then they made crossbars of acacia wood to connect the upright frames of the Holy Tent. Five crossbars held the frames together on one side of the Tent. ³²Five crossbars held the frames together on the other side. And five crossbars held the frames together on the west end, at the rear of the Tent. ³³They made the crossbar run along the entire length of each side and rear of the Tent. It was set halfway up the frames. ³⁴They made gold rings on the sides of the frames. They passed the crossbars through the rings. They covered the frames and the crossbars with gold.

³⁵Then they made the curtain with blue, purple and red thread, and fine linen. A skilled craftsman sewed designs of creatures with wings on it. ³⁶They made four posts of acacia wood and covered them with gold. Then they made gold hooks for the posts. And they made four silver bases in which to set the posts. ³⁷Then they made a curtain for the entrance to the Tent. They used blue, purple and red thread, and fine linen. A person who sewed well sewed designs on it. ³⁸Then they made five posts and hooks for it. They covered the tops of the posts and their bands with gold. And they made five bronze bases for the posts.

THE HOLY BOX

37 Bezalel made the Holy Box*d* of acacia wood. The Holy Box was 45 inches long, 27 inches wide and 27 inches high. ²He covered the inside and outside of the Holy Box with pure gold. Then he put a gold strip around it. ³He made four gold rings for it and attached them to its four feet. There were two rings on each side. ⁴Then he made poles of acacia wood and covered them with gold. ⁵He put the poles through the rings on each side of the Holy Box to carry it. ⁶Then he made a lid of pure gold. It was 45 inches long and 27 inches wide. ⁷Then Bezalel hammered gold to make two creatures with wings. He attached them to each end of the lid. ⁸He made one creature with wings on one end of the lid. He made the other creature with wings on the other end. He attached them to the lid so that it would be one piece. ⁹The creatures' wings were spread out over the lid. The creatures faced each other across the lid.

THE TABLE

¹⁰Then he made the table of acacia wood. The table was 36 inches long, 18 inches wide and 27 inches high. ¹¹He covered the table with pure gold. He put a gold strip around it. ¹²Then he made a frame 3 inches high that stood up all around the edge. He put a gold strip around the frame. ¹³Then he made four gold rings for the table. He attached them to the four corners of the table,

where the four legs were. [14]The rings were put close to the frame around the top of the table. The rings held the poles that were used to carry the table. [15]The poles for carrying the table were made of acacia wood. They were covered with gold. [16]Then he made of pure gold all the things that were used on the table: the plates, bowls, cups and jars used for pouring the drink offerings.

THE LAMPSTAND

[17]Then he made the lampstand of pure gold. He hammered out its base and stand. Its flower-like cups, buds and petals were joined together in one piece with the base and stand. [18]There were three branches on one side of the lampstand and three branches on the other. [19]Each branch had three cups shaped like almond flowers. Each cup had a bud and a petal. [20]There were four more cups shaped like almond flowers on the lampstand itself. Each cup had its buds and petals. [21]Three pairs of branches went out from the lampstand. A bud was under the place where each pair was attached to the lampstand. [22]The buds, branches and lampstand were all one piece of pure, hammered gold. [23]He made seven pure gold lamps for this lampstand. Then he made pure gold wick trimmers and trays. [24]He used about 75 pounds of pure gold to make the lampstand and all the things that go with it.

THE ALTAR FOR BURNING INCENSE

[25]Then he made the altar of incense[d] of acacia wood. The altar was square. It was 18 inches long, 18 inches wide and 36 inches high. Each corner stuck out like a horn. Each corner was joined into one piece with the altar. [26]He covered the top and all the sides and the corners with pure gold. Then he put gold trim around the altar. [27]He made two gold rings and put them below the trim on opposite sides of the altar. These rings held the poles for carrying the altar. [28]He made

the poles of acacia wood and covered them with gold.

[29]Then he made the holy olive oil for appointing the priests. He also made the pure, sweet-smelling incense. He made them like a person who mixes perfumes.

THE ALTAR

38 Then he built the altar for burning offerings. He made the altar of acacia wood. The altar was square. It was 7^1/$_2$ feet long, 7^1/$_2$ feet wide and 4^1/$_2$ feet high. [2]He made each corner stick out like a horn. The horns and the altar were joined together in one piece. Then he covered the altar with bronze. [3]He made all the tools of bronze to use on the altar: the pots, shovels, bowls for sprinkling blood, meat forks and pans for carrying the fire. [4]He made a large bronze screen to hold the burning wood for the altar. He put the screen inside the altar, under its rim, halfway up from the bottom. [5]He made bronze rings for holding the poles for carrying the altar. He put the rings at the four corners of the screen. [6]Then he made poles of acacia wood and covered them with bronze. [7]He put the poles through the rings on both sides of the altar. They were used for carrying the altar. He made the altar of boards and left the inside hollow.

THE BRONZE BOWL

[8]He made the bronze bowl for washing. He built it on a bronze stand. He used the bronze of mirrors. These mirrors belonged to the women who served at the entrance to the Meeting Tent.[d]

THE COURTYARD OF THE HOLY TENT

[9]Then he made a wall of curtains to form a courtyard around the Holy Tent.[d] On the south side the curtains were 150 feet long and were made of fine linen. [10]The curtains hung on silver hooks and bands. These were on 20 bronze posts on 20 bronze bases. [11]On the north side the wall of curtains was also 150 feet

long. It hung on silver hooks and bands on 20 posts with 20 bronze bases.

¹²On the west side of the courtyard, the wall of curtains was 75 feet long. It was held up by silver hooks and bands on 10 posts and 10 bases. ¹³The east side was 75 feet wide. ¹⁴On one side of the entry there was a wall of curtains that was 22¹/₂ feet long. It was held up by 3 posts and 3 bases. ¹⁵On the other side of the entry there was a wall of curtains 22¹/₂ feet long. It was held up by 3 posts and 3 bases. ¹⁶All the curtains around the courtyard were made of fine linen. ¹⁷The bases for the posts were made of bronze. The hooks and the bands on the posts were made of silver. The tops of the posts were covered with silver also. All the posts in the courtyard had silver bands.

¹⁸The curtain for the entry of the courtyard was made of blue, purple and red thread, and fine linen. It was sewn by a person who could sew well. The curtain was 30 feet long and 7¹/₂ feet high. It was the same height as the curtains around the courtyard. ¹⁹The curtain was held up by 4 posts and 4 bronze bases. The hooks and bands on the posts were made of silver. The tops on the posts were covered with silver. ²⁰All the tent pegs for the Holy Tent and for the curtains around the courtyard were made of bronze.

²¹This is a list of the metals used to make the Holy Tent. This is where the two flat stones with the Ten Commandments are kept. Moses ordered the Levites to make this list. Ithamar son of Aaron was in charge of keeping the list. ²²Bezalel son of Uri made everything the Lord commanded Moses. Uri was the son of Hur of the tribe*ᵈ* of Judah. ²³Oholiab son of Ahisamach of the tribe of Dan helped him. Oholiab could cut designs into metal and stone. He was a designer. He was also skilled at sewing the blue, purple and red thread, and fine linen.

²⁴The total amount of gold used to build the Holy Tent was presented to the Lord. It weighed over 2,000 pounds, as set by the Holy Place measure.

²⁵The silver was given by the members of the community who were counted. It weighed 7,550 pounds, as set by the Holy Place measure. ²⁶All the men 20 years old or older were counted. There were 603,550 men, and each man had to pay ¹/₅ ounce of silver. This is the weight as set by the Holy Place measure. ²⁷Of this silver, 7,500 pounds was used to make the 100 bases. These bases were for the Holy Tent and for the curtain. There was 75 pounds of silver in each base. ²⁸The other 50 pounds of silver was used to make the hooks for the posts. It was also used to cover the tops of the posts and to make the bands on the posts.

²⁹The bronze which was presented to the Lord weighed about 5,000 pounds. ³⁰They used the bronze to make the bases at the entrance of the Meeting Tent. They also used the bronze to make the altar and the bronze screen. And this bronze was used to make all the tools for the altar. ³¹This bronze was also used to make bases for the wall of curtains around the courtyard. It was used for the bases for the curtains at the entry to the courtyard. And this bronze was used to make the tent pegs for the Holy Tent and curtains that surrounded the courtyard.

CLOTHES FOR THE PRIESTS

39 They used blue, purple and red thread to make woven clothes for the priests. They were to wear these when they served in the Holy Place. They also made the holy clothes for Aaron as the Lord had commanded Moses.

²They made the holy vest*ᵈ* of gold and blue, purple and red thread, and fine linen. ³They hammered the gold into sheets. Then they cut the gold into long, thin strips. They worked the gold into

the blue, purple and red thread, and fine linen. This was done by a skilled craftsman. ⁴They made the shoulder straps for the holy vest. These straps were attached to the top corners of the vest. Then the shoulder straps were tied together over each shoulder. ⁵The skillfully woven belt was made in the same way. It was joined to the holy vest as one piece. It was made of gold and blue, purple and red thread, and fine linen. It was made the way the Lord commanded Moses.

⁶They put gold around the onyx stones. Then they wrote the names of the sons of Israel on these gems. They did that as a person carves words and designs on a seal.*ᵈ* ⁷Then they attached the gems on the shoulder straps of the holy vest. These gems are reminders of the 12 sons of Israel. This was done the way the Lord had commanded Moses.

⁸The skilled craftsmen made the chest covering. It was made like the holy vest. It was made of gold and blue, purple and red thread, and fine linen. ⁹The chest covering was square, nine inches long and nine inches wide. It was folded double to make a pocket. ¹⁰Then they put four rows of beautiful jewels on it. In the first row there was a ruby, a topaz and a yellow quartz. ¹¹In the second row there was a turquoise, a sapphire and an emerald. ¹²In the third row there was a jacinth, an agate and an amethyst. ¹³In the fourth row there was a chrysolite, an onyx and a jasper. Gold was put around these jewels to attach them to the chest covering. ¹⁴The names of the sons of Israel were carved on these 12 jewels as a person carves a seal. Each jewel had the name of 1 of the 12 tribes*ᵈ* of Israel.

¹⁵They made chains of pure gold for the chest covering. They were twisted together like a rope. ¹⁶The workers made two gold pieces and two gold rings. They put the two gold rings on the two upper corners of the chest covering. ¹⁷Then they put two gold chains in the two rings. These are at the ends of the chest covering. ¹⁸They fastened the other two ends of the chains to the two gold pieces. Then they attached these gold pieces to the two shoulder straps in the front of the holy vest. ¹⁹They made two more gold rings and put them at the lower corners of the chest covering. They put them on the inside edge next to the holy vest. ²⁰Then they made two more gold rings on the bottom of the shoulder straps in front of the holy vest. These rings were near the seam, just above the woven belt of the holy vest. ²¹They used a blue ribbon and tied the rings of the chest covering to the rings of the holy vest. This connected it to the woven belt. In this way the chest covering would not swing out from the holy vest. They did all these things the way the Lord commanded.

²²Then they made the outer robe to be worn under the holy vest. It was woven of blue cloth. ²³They made a hole in the center of the outer robe. A woven collar was sewn around this hole so it would not tear. ²⁴Then they made balls like pomegranates*ᵈ* of blue, purple and red thread, and fine linen. They hung them around the bottom of the outer robe. ²⁵They also made bells of pure gold. They hung these around the bottom of the outer robe between the balls. ²⁶So around the bottom of the outer robe there was a bell and a pomegranate ball, a bell and a pomegranate ball. The priest wore this outer robe when he served as priest, just as the Lord had commanded Moses.

²⁷They wove inner robes of fine linen for Aaron and his sons. ²⁸And they made turbans and underclothes of fine linen. ²⁹Then they made the cloth belt of fine linen and blue, purple and red thread. Designs were sewn onto the cloth. These things were made as the Lord had commanded Moses.

³⁰They made a strip of pure gold, which is the holy crown. They carved these words in the gold: "Holy to the Lord." They did it as one might carve on a seal. ³¹Then they tied this flat piece to the turban with a blue ribbon. This was done as the Lord had commanded Moses.

³²So all the work on the Meeting Tent*d* was finished. The Israelites did everything just as the Lord had commanded Moses. ³³Then they brought the Holy Tent to Moses: the Tent and all its furniture, hooks, frames, crossbars, posts and bases; ³⁴the covering made of male sheep skins colored red, the covering made of fine leather and the curtain that covered the entrance to the Most Holy Place; ³⁵the Box*d* of the Agreement, its poles and lid; ³⁶the table, all its containers and the bread that showed they were in God's presence; ³⁷the pure gold lampstand with its lamps in a row, all its tools and the olive oil for the light; ³⁸the gold altar, the special olive oil used for appointing priests, the sweet-smelling incense,*d* and the curtain that covered the entrance to the Tent; ³⁹the bronze altar and its screen, its poles and all its tools, the bowl and its stand; ⁴⁰the curtains for the courtyard with their posts and bases, the curtain that covered the entry to the courtyard, the cords, pegs and all the things in the Meeting Tent. ⁴¹They brought the clothes for the priests to wear when they served in the Holy Tent: the holy clothes for Aaron the priest and the clothes for his sons. They wore these when they served as priests.

⁴²The Israelites had done all this work just as the Lord had commanded Moses. ⁴³Moses looked closely at all the work. He saw they had done it just as the Lord had commanded. So Moses blessed them.

SETTING UP THE HOLY TENT

40 Then the Lord said this to Moses: ²"On the first day of the first month, set up the Holy Tent,*d* which is the Meeting Tent. ³Put the Box*d* of the Agreement in the Meeting Tent. Hang the curtain in front of the Holy Box. ⁴Then bring in the table. Arrange everything on the table that should be there. Then bring in the lampstand and set up its lamps. ⁵Put the gold altar for burning incense*d* in front of the Box of the Agreement. Then put the curtain at the entrance to the Holy Tent.

⁶"Put the altar of burnt offerings in front of the entrance of the Holy Tent, the Meeting Tent. ⁷Put the bowl between the Meeting Tent and the altar. Put water in the bowl. ⁸Set up the courtyard around the Holy Tent. Then put the curtain at the entry to the courtyard.

⁹"Use the special olive oil and pour it on the Holy Tent and everything in it. Give the Tent and all that is in it for service to the Lord. They will be holy. ¹⁰Pour the special oil on the altar for burning offerings. Pour it on all its tools. Give the altar for service to God. It will be very holy. ¹¹Then pour the special olive oil on the bowl and the base under it. When you do this, they will be given for service to God.

¹²"Bring Aaron and his sons to the entrance of the Meeting Tent. Wash them with water. ¹³Then put the holy clothes on Aaron. Pour the special oil on him, and give him for service to God. Then he may serve me as a priest. ¹⁴Bring Aaron's sons and put the inner robes on them. ¹⁵Pour the special oil on them to make them priests. Do this the same way that you appointed their father as priest. Then they may also serve me as priests. Pouring oil on them will make them a family of priests. They and their descendants*d* will be priests from now on." ¹⁶Moses did everything that the Lord commanded him.

¹⁷So the Holy Tent was set up. It was the first day of the first month during the second year after they left Egypt. ¹⁸When Moses set up the Holy Tent, he put the bases in place. Then he put the frames

on the bases. Next he put the crossbars through the rings of the frames and set up the posts. [19]After that, Moses spread the cloth over the Holy Tent. Then he put the covering over the Tent. He did these things just as the Lord commanded.

[20]Moses put the flat stones into the Box of the Agreement. These had God's law written on them. Moses put the poles through the rings of the Holy Box. Then he put the lid on it. [21]Next Moses brought the Holy Box into the Tent. He hung the curtain to cover the Holy Box. Moses did these things just as the Lord commanded him.

[22]Moses put the table in the Meeting Tent. He put it on the north side of the Holy Tent in front of the curtain. [23]Then he put the bread on the table before the Lord. He did this just as the Lord commanded him. [24]Moses put the lampstand in the Meeting Tent. He put it on the south side of the Holy Tent across from the table. [25]Then he put the lamps on the lampstand before the Lord. He did this just as the Lord commanded him.

[26]Moses put the gold altar for burning incense in the Meeting Tent. He put it in front of the curtain. [27]Then he burned sweet-smelling incense on it, just as the Lord commanded him. [28]Then he hung the curtain at the entrance to the Holy Tent.

[29]He put the altar for burning sacrifices at the entrance to the Holy Tent, the Meeting Tent. Then Moses offered a whole burnt offering and grain offerings on that altar. He did these things just as the Lord commanded him. [30]Moses put the bowl between the Meeting Tent and the altar for burning sacrifices. Moses put water in the bowl for washing. [31]Moses, Aaron and Aaron's sons used this water to wash their hands and feet. [32]They washed themselves every time they entered the Meeting Tent. They also washed themselves every time they went near the altar for burning sacrifices. They did these things just as the Lord commanded Moses.

[33]Then Moses set up the courtyard around the Holy Tent. He put the altar for burning sacrifices in the courtyard. Then he put up the curtain at the entry to the courtyard. So Moses finished the work.

THE CLOUD OVER THE HOLY TENT

[34]Then the cloud covered the Meeting Tent.[d] The greatness of the Lord filled the Holy Tent. [35]Moses could not enter the Meeting Tent. This was because the cloud had settled on it. And this was because the greatness of the Lord filled the Holy Tent.

[36]When the cloud rose from the Holy Tent, the Israelites would begin to travel. [37]But as long as the cloud stayed on the Holy Tent, the people did not travel. They stayed in that place until the cloud rose. [38]So the cloud of the Lord was over the Holy Tent during the day. And there was a fire in the cloud at night. So all the Israelites could see the cloud while they traveled.

LEVITICUS

THE BURNT OFFERING

1 The Lord called to Moses and spoke to him from the Meeting Tent.[d] The Lord said, [2]"Tell the people of Israel: 'When you bring an offering to the Lord, bring as your offering one of the cattle. Or you may bring one of the sheep or goats.

[3]"'If anyone offers a whole burnt offering from the cattle, it must be a male. It must have nothing wrong with it. The person must take the animal to the entrance of the Meeting Tent. Then the Lord will accept the offering. [4]The person must put his hand on the animal's head. Then the Lord will accept that burnt offering. It will remove the person's sin so he will belong to God. [5]The person must kill the young bull before the Lord. Then the priests must bring its blood to the altar. They must sprinkle the blood on all sides of the altar. This is the altar at the entrance to the Meeting Tent. [6]The person will cut the skin from that animal. Then he will cut the animal into pieces. [7]The priests must put wood and fire on the altar. [8]They must lay the head, the fat and other pieces on the wood. That wood is on the fire on the altar. [9]The priest must wash the animal's inner organs and legs with water. Then the priest must burn all the animal's parts on the altar. It is a whole burnt offering, an offering made by fire. And its smell is pleasing to the Lord.

[10]"'The burnt offering may be a sheep or goat. It must be a male animal that has nothing wrong with it. [11]The person must kill the animal on the north side of the altar. This is to be before the Lord. Then the priests must sprinkle its blood on the altar. They must sprinkle it on all sides. [12]The person must cut the animal into pieces. Then the priest must lay the pieces with the head and fat on the wood. The wood is on the fire on the altar. [13]The person must wash the animal's inner organs and legs with water. Then the priest must burn all its parts on the altar. It is a burnt offering, an offering made by fire. And its smell is pleasing to the Lord.

[14]"'The whole burnt offering may be a bird. It must be a dove or a young pigeon. [15]The priest will bring the offering to the altar. He will pull off the bird's head. Then he will burn it on the altar. The bird's blood must be drained out on the side of the altar. [16]The priest must remove the bird's crop[n] and its contents. He must throw them on the east side of the altar. This is where they put the ashes from the altar. [17]Then the priest must tear the bird open by its wings. But he must not divide the bird into two parts. Then the priest must burn the bird on the altar. He must place it on the wood which is on the fire. It is a burnt offering, an offering made by fire. Its smell is pleasing to the Lord.

THE GRAIN OFFERING

2 "'When anyone offers a grain offering to the Lord, it must be made from fine flour. The person must pour oil on it and put incense[d] on it. [2]Then he must take it to Aaron's sons and the priests. The priest must take a handful of the fine flour, with the oil and all the incense. He must burn it on the altar as a memorial portion. It is an offering made by fire. Its smell is pleasing to the Lord. [3]The rest of the grain offering will belong to Aaron and the priests. This offering is a most holy part of the offerings made by fire to the Lord.

[4]"'If you bring a grain offering that was baked in the oven, it must be made

---

1:16 crop A small bag inside a bird's throat. When a bird eats, its food goes into this part first. There, the food is made soft before it goes into the stomach.

from fine flour. It may be loaves made without yeast and mixed with oil. Or it may be wafers made without yeast. They are to have oil poured over them. ⁵If your grain offering is cooked on a griddle, it must be made without yeast. It must be made of fine flour mixed with oil. ⁶Crumble it and pour oil over it. It is a grain offering. ⁷If your grain offering is cooked in a pan, it must be made from fine flour and oil. ⁸Bring the grain offering made of these things to the Lord. Give it to the priest. He will take it to the altar. ⁹He will take out the memorial portion from the grain offering. He will burn it on the altar. This is an offering made by fire. Its smell is pleasing to the Lord. ¹⁰The rest of the grain offering belongs to Aaron and the priests. It is a most holy part of the offerings made to the Lord by fire.

¹¹"'Every grain offering you bring to the Lord must be made without yeast. You must not burn yeast or honey in an offering made by fire to the Lord. ¹²You may bring yeast and honey to the Lord as an offering from the first harvest. But yeast and honey must not be burned on the altar as a pleasing smell. ¹³You must also put salt on all your grain offerings. Salt stands for your agreement with God that will last forever. Do not leave it out of your grain offering. You must add salt to all your offerings.

¹⁴"'If you bring a grain offering from the first harvest to the Lord, bring crushed heads of new grain. They must be roasted in the fire. ¹⁵Put oil and incense on the grain. It is a grain offering. ¹⁶The priest will burn the memorial portion of the crushed grain and oil. It will have incense on it. It is an offering by fire to the Lord.

THE FELLOWSHIP OFFERING

3 "'A person's fellowship offering to the Lord may be from the cattle. It may be a male or female animal. But it must have nothing wrong with it. ²The person must put his hand on the animal's head. He must kill it at the entrance to the Meeting Tent.ᵈ Then the priests must sprinkle the blood on all sides of the altar. ³This person must make a sacrifice from the fellowship offering. The sacrifice must be made by fire to the Lord. He must offer the fat of the animal's inner organs. This is both the fat that is in them and that covers them. ⁴He must also offer both kidneys and the fat on them. They are near the lower back muscle. He must also offer the best part of the liver. He will remove it with the kidneys. ⁵Then the priests will burn these parts on the altar. They will put them on the burnt offering that is on the wood on the fire. It is an offering made by fire. Its smell is pleasing to the Lord.

⁶"'A person's fellowship offering to the Lord may be a lamb or a goat. He may offer a male or female animal. But it must have nothing wrong with it. ⁷If he offers a lamb, he must bring it before the Lord. ⁸He must put his hand on its head. Then he must kill the animal in front of the Meeting Tent. The priests will sprinkle its blood on all sides of the altar. ⁹Then the person must make a sacrifice from the fellowship offering. The sacrifice must be made by fire to the Lord. The person must bring the fat and the whole fat tail. The tail must be cut off close to the backbone. He must also offer the fat of the inner organs. This is both the fat that is in them and that covers them. ¹⁰He must offer both kidneys and the fat on them. They are near the lower back muscle. And he must offer the best part of the liver. He will remove it with the kidneys. ¹¹Then the priest will burn these parts on the altar as food. It will be an offering made by fire to the Lord.

¹²"'A person's fellowship offering may be a goat. He is to offer it before the Lord. ¹³He must put his hand on the goat's head. And he must kill it in front of the Meeting Tent. Then the priests must

sprinkle its blood on all sides of the altar. [14]From this fellowship offering the person must make a sacrifice. It will be an offering by fire to the Lord. The person must offer all the fat of the goat's inner organs. This is both the fat that is in them and that covers them. [15]He must offer both kidneys and the fat on them. They are near the lower back muscle. And he must offer the best part of the liver. He will remove it with the kidneys. [16]The priest will burn these parts on the altar as food. It is an offering made by fire. Its smell is pleasing to the Lord. All the fat belongs to the Lord.

[17]"'This law will continue for people from now on, wherever you live: You must not eat fat or blood.'"

THE SIN OFFERING

4 The Lord said to Moses, [2]"Tell the people of Israel this: 'A person might sin by accident. He might do some things the Lord has commanded not to be done. If so, that person must do these things:

[3]"'It may be the appointed priest who has sinned. If so, he has brought guilt on the people. So he must offer a young bull to the Lord. It must have nothing wrong with it. This will be a sin offering for the sin he has done. [4]He will bring the bull to the entrance of the Meeting Tent.[d] He must bring it in front of the Lord. Then he will put his hand on the bull's head. And he will kill the bull before the Lord. [5]Then the appointed priest must bring some of the bull's blood into the Meeting Tent. [6]The priest is to dip his finger into the blood. He must sprinkle it seven times before the Lord in front of the curtain. This curtain is in front of the Most Holy Place. [7]The priest must also put some of the blood on the corners of the altar of incense.[d] It stands before the Lord in the Meeting Tent. Then the priest must pour out the rest of the bull's blood. It must be poured at the bottom of the altar of burnt offering. That altar is at the door of the Meeting Tent. [8]He must remove all the fat from the bull of the sin offering. He must remove the fat on and around the inner organs. [9]He must remove both kidneys and the fat on them. They are near the lower back muscle. He must remove the best part of the liver with the kidneys. [10]He must do this in the same way the fat is removed from the bull of the fellowship offering. Then the priest must burn the animal parts on the altar of burnt offering. [11-12]But the priest must carry out the skin of the bull and all its meat. He must take these with the rest of the bull—its head, legs, intestines and other inner organs. He must take it outside the camp to the special clean[d] place where the ashes are poured out. He must burn it on a wood fire on the pile of ashes.

[13]"'The whole nation of Israel might sin without knowing it. They might do something the Lord has commanded not to be done. If this happens, they are guilty. [14]When they learn about the sin they have done, a young bull must be offered. It is a sin offering for the whole nation. They must bring it and give it before the Meeting Tent. [15]The elders of the group of people must put their hands on the bull's head. It must be done before the Lord. And the bull must be killed before the Lord. [16]Then the appointed priest must bring some of the bull's blood into the Meeting Tent. [17]The priest will dip his finger in the blood. He must sprinkle it seven times before the Lord in front of the curtain. [18]Then he must put some of the blood on the corners of the altar. The altar is before the Lord in the Meeting Tent. The priest must pour out the rest of the blood. He must pour it at the bottom of the altar of burnt offering. That altar is at the entrance to the Meeting Tent. [19]The priest must remove all the fat from the animal. And he must burn it on the altar. [20]He will do the same thing with this bull that he did with the first bull of the sin offering. In this way the

priest removes the sins of the people so they will belong to the Lord. And the Lord will forgive them. ²¹Then the priest must carry the bull outside the camp and burn it. He must do this just as he did with the first bull. This is the sin offering for the whole community.

²²"'A ruler might sin by accident. He might do something the Lord his God has commanded must not be done. If he does, he is guilty. ²³When he learns about his sin, he must bring a male goat. It must have nothing wrong with it. That will be his sin offering. ²⁴The ruler must put his hand on the goat's head and kill it. This must be done where they kill the whole burnt offering before the Lord. The goat is a sin offering. ²⁵The priest must take some of the blood of the sin offering on his finger. He must put it on the corners of the altar of burnt offering. He must pour out the rest of the blood at the bottom of the altar of burnt offering. ²⁶He must burn all the goat's fat on the altar. He must burn it in the same way he burns the fat of the fellowship offerings. In this way the priest removes the ruler's sin so he belongs to the Lord. And the Lord will forgive him.

²⁷"'A person in the community might sin by accident. He might do something which the Lord has commanded must not be done. He is guilty of sin. ²⁸When the person learns about his sin, he must bring a female goat. It must have nothing wrong with it. That will be his sin offering. ²⁹He must put his hand on the animal's head. He must kill it at the place of the whole burnt offering. ³⁰Then the priest must take some of the goat's blood on his finger. He must put it on the corners of the altar of burnt offering. He must pour out the rest of the goat's blood at the bottom of the altar. ³¹Then the priest must remove all the goat's fat. He must do it in the same way the fat is removed from the fellowship offerings. He must burn it on the altar. Its smell is pleasing

to the Lord. In this way the priest will remove that person's sin so he will belong to the Lord. And the Lord will forgive him.

³²"'This person may bring a lamb as his sin offering. If he does, he must bring a female. It must have nothing wrong with it. ³³The person must put his hand on the animal's head. He must kill it as a sin offering. He must kill it where they kill the whole burnt offering. ³⁴The priest must take some of the blood from the sin offering on his finger. He must put it on the corners of the altar of burnt offering. Then he must pour out the rest of the lamb's blood at the bottom of the altar. ³⁵The priest must remove all the lamb's fat. He must do it in the same way that the lamb's fat is removed from the fellowship offerings. He must burn the pieces on the altar. They go on top of the offerings made by fire for the Lord. In this way the priest will remove that person's sins so he will belong to the Lord. And the Lord will forgive him.

SPECIAL TYPES OF ACCIDENTAL SINS

5 "'These are things for which a sin offering must be made:

"'A person might be ordered to tell in court what he has seen or what he knows. If he does not tell the court, he is guilty of sin.

²"'Or someone might touch something unclean.ᵈ It might be the dead body of an unclean wild animal or an unclean farm animal or an unclean crawling animal. He might not know that he touched it. But he will still be unclean and guilty of sin.

³"'Many things come from a person which are not clean. Someone might touch one of these unclean things from a person and not know it. But when he learns about it, he will be guilty.

⁴"'Or someone might make a promise before the Lord without thinking. He might promise to do something bad or good. The promise might be about anything. He might even make a promise

before the Lord and forget about it. But when he remembers, he will be guilty.

⁵"When anyone is guilty of any of these things, he must tell how he sinned. ⁶He must bring an offering to the Lord. It is a penalty for his sin. It must be a female lamb or goat from the flock. The priest will perform the acts to remove that person's sin so he will belong to the Lord.

⁷"But perhaps the person cannot afford a lamb. Then he must bring two doves or two young pigeons to the Lord. These will be the penalty for his sin. One bird must be for a sin offering. The other must be for a burnt offering. ⁸He must bring them to the priest. First the priest will offer the one for the sin offering. He will pull the bird's head from its neck. But he will not pull it completely off. ⁹He must sprinkle the blood from the sin offering on the side of the altar. Then he must pour the rest of the blood at the bottom of the altar. It is a sin offering. ¹⁰Then the priest must offer the second bird as a burnt offering. This is what the law says. In this way the priest will remove the person's sin so he will belong to the Lord. And the Lord will forgive him.

¹¹"The person might not be able to afford two doves or two pigeons. If not, he must bring about two quarts of fine flour. This will be an offering for his sin. He must not put oil on the flour. And he must not put incense*d* on it, because it is a sin offering. ¹²He must bring the flour to the priest. The priest will take a handful of the flour as a memorial offering. He will burn it on the altar. It goes on top of the offerings made by fire to the Lord. It is a sin offering. ¹³In this way the priest will remove the person's sins so he will belong to the Lord. And the Lord will forgive him. What is left of the sin offering belongs to the priest. This is like the grain offering.'"

THE PENALTY OFFERING

¹⁴The Lord said to Moses, ¹⁵"A person might accidentally sin and do something against the holy things of the Lord. That person must bring a male sheep from the flock. It must have nothing wrong with it. This will be his penalty offering to the Lord. The value in silver of the male sheep must be correct. Use the proper value for silver as set by the Holy Place measure. ¹⁶That person must pay for the sin he did against the holy thing. He must add one-fifth to its value. Then he must give it all to the priest. In this way the priest will remove the person's sin so he will belong to the Lord. The priest does it by means of the male sheep of the penalty offering. And the Lord will forgive the person.

¹⁷"A person might sin and do something the Lord has commanded not to be done. It does not matter if that person knew or not. He is guilty. He is responsible for his sin. ¹⁸He must bring the priest a male sheep from the flock. It must have nothing wrong with it. It must be worth the correct amount. The male sheep will be a penalty offering. The person sinned without knowing it. But with this offering the priest will remove the sin so the person will belong to the Lord. And the Lord will forgive him. ¹⁹The person is guilty of doing wrong against the Lord. So he must give the penalty offering to the Lord."

6 The Lord said to Moses, ²"A person might sin against the Lord by doing one of these sins: He might lie about what happened to something he was taking care of for someone else. Or he might lie about a promise he made. Or he might steal something or cheat someone. ³He might find something that had been lost and then lie about it. He might make a promise before the Lord about something and not mean it. Or he might do some other sin. ⁴If he does any of these things, he is guilty of sin. He must bring back whatever he stole. Or he must bring back what he took by cheating. Or he must bring back the thing he took care of for someone else. Or he must bring back what he found and lied about. ⁵Or he must bring back what he made a false promise about. He must pay the full price. Then he must pay an extra one-fifth of the value of what he took. He must give the money to the true owner. This must be done on the day he brings his penalty offering. ⁶He must pay a penalty to the priest. It must be a male sheep from the flock. It must not have anything wrong with it. And it must be worth the correct amount. It will be a penalty offering to the Lord. ⁷Then the priest will perform the acts to remove that person's sin so he will belong to the Lord. And the Lord will forgive him for the sins that made him guilty."

THE WHOLE BURNT OFFERING

⁸The Lord said to Moses, ⁹"Give this command to Aaron and the priests: 'These are the teachings about the whole burnt offering. The burnt offering must stay on the altar all night until morning. The altar's fire must be kept burning. ¹⁰The priest must put on his linen robe. He must put on linen underclothes next to his body. Then he will remove the ashes from the burnt offering on the altar. He will put these ashes beside the altar. ¹¹Then he must take off those clothes and put on others. He must carry the ashes outside the camp to a special clean*ᵈ* place. ¹²But the fire must be kept burning on the altar. It must not be allowed to go out. The priest must put more firewood on the altar every morning. He must place the whole burnt offering on the fire. He must burn the fat of the fellowship offerings. ¹³The fire must be kept burning on the altar all the time. It must not go out.

THE GRAIN OFFERING

¹⁴"'These are the teachings about the grain offering: The priests must bring it to the Lord in front of the altar. ¹⁵The priest must take a handful of fine flour. The oil and incense*ᵈ* must be on it. The

priest must burn the grain offering on the altar. It will be a memorial offering to the Lord. Its smell is pleasing to him. ¹⁶Aaron and the priests may eat what is left. It must be eaten without yeast in a holy place. The priests must eat it in the courtyard of the Meeting Tent.*ᵈ* ¹⁷It must not be cooked with yeast. I have given it as their share of the offerings made to me by fire. It is most holy, like the sin offering and the penalty offering. ¹⁸Any male descendant*ᵈ* of Aaron may eat it. It is his share of the offerings made to the Lord by fire. This will continue from now on. Whatever touches these offerings must be holy.'"

¹⁹The Lord said to Moses, ²⁰"This is the offering Aaron and the priests must bring to the Lord. They must do this on the day they appoint Aaron as high priest. They must bring two quarts of fine flour for a grain offering. They must bring half of it in the morning and half in the evening. ²¹The fine flour must be mixed with oil and cooked on a griddle. Bring it when it is well mixed. You must break it into pieces. It will be a smell that is pleasing to the Lord. ²²One of the priests will be appointed to take Aaron's place as high priest. He must make the grain offering to the Lord. It is a rule forever. The grain offering must be completely burned to the Lord. ²³Every grain offering made by a priest must be completely burned. It must not be eaten."

THE SIN OFFERING

²⁴The Lord said to Moses, ²⁵"Tell Aaron and the priests: 'These are the teachings about the sin offering. The sin offering must be killed in front of the Lord. It must be killed in the same place the whole burnt offering is killed. It is most holy. ²⁶The priest who offers the sin offering must eat it. He must eat it in a holy place. It must be in the courtyard of the Meeting Tent.*ᵈ* ²⁷Whatever touches the meat of the sin offering must be holy. If the blood is sprinkled on any clothes,

you must wash them in a holy place.
²⁸The clay pot the meat is cooked in
must be broken. If a bronze pot is used,
it must be scrubbed and rinsed with
water. ²⁹Any male in a priest's family
may eat the offering. It is most holy.
³⁰The blood of the sin offering may be
taken into the Meeting Tent. It may be
used to remove sin in the Holy Place.
That sin offering must be burned with
fire. It must not be eaten.

THE PENALTY OFFERING

7 "'These are the teachings about
the penalty offering. It is most
holy. ²The penalty offering must be
killed where the whole burnt offering
is killed. Then the priest must sprinkle
its blood on all sides of the altar. ³He
must offer all the fat from the penalty
offering. He must offer the fat tail and
the fat that covers the inner organs.
⁴He must offer both kidneys and the
fat on them. They are near the lower
back muscle. And he must offer the
best part of the liver. This is to be
removed with the kidneys. ⁵The priest
must burn all these things on the altar.
They will be an offering made by fire to
the Lord. It is a penalty offering. ⁶Any
male in a priest's family may eat it. It
is most holy. So it must be eaten in a
holy place.

⁷"'The penalty offering is like the sin
offering. The teachings are the same for
both. The priest who offers the sacrifice
to remove sins will get the meat for food.
⁸The priest who offers the burnt offering
may also have the skin from it. ⁹Every
grain offering belongs to the priest who
offers it. This includes those baked in an
oven, cooked on a griddle or baked in a
dish. ¹⁰The grain offerings belong to the
priests. They may be dry or mixed with
oil. All priests will share alike.

FELLOWSHIP OFFERINGS

¹¹"'These are the teachings about the
fellowship offering a person may offer to
the Lord: ¹²He may bring the fellowship
offering to show his thanks. If he does,
he should also bring loaves of bread.
They must be made without yeast,
mixed with oil. And he should bring
wafers made without yeast. They must
have oil poured over them. He should
also bring loaves of fine flour mixed with
oil. ¹³He must also offer loaves of bread
made with yeast. These should be brought
with his fellowship offering, which he
gives to show thanks. ¹⁴One of each kind
of offering will be for the Lord. It will be
given to the priest who sprinkles the
blood of the fellowship offering. ¹⁵The
fellowship offering is to thank the Lord.
The meat from it must be eaten the same
day it is offered. None of it must be left
until morning.

¹⁶"'A person might bring a fellowship
offering just to give a gift to God. Or it
may be done because of a special
promise to God. Then, the sacrifice
should be eaten the same day he offers
it. If there is any left, it may be eaten the
next day. ¹⁷If any meat from this sacrifice is left on the third day, it must be
burned up. ¹⁸Any meat of the fellowship
offering eaten on the third day will not
be accepted. The Lord will not count the
sacrifice for the person who offered it. It
will become unclean.ᵈ Anyone who eats
the meat will be guilty of sin.

¹⁹"'People must not eat meat that
touches anything unclean. They must
burn this meat with fire. But anyone
who is clean may eat other meat. ²⁰But a
person who is unclean might eat the
meat from the fellowship offering that
belongs to the Lord. If he does, he must
be separated from his people.

²¹"'Someone might touch something
unclean that comes from people. Or the
unclean thing might be an animal or some
hated thing. Touching it will make him
unclean. If he then eats meat from the fellowship offering that belongs to the Lord,
he must be separated from his people.'"

²²The Lord said to Moses, ²³"Tell the people of Israel: 'You must not eat any of the fat from cattle, sheep or goats. ²⁴If an animal is found dead or torn by wild animals, you may use its fat for other things. But you must not eat it. ²⁵Someone might eat fat from an animal offering made by fire to the Lord. That person must be separated from his people. ²⁶It does not matter where you live. You must not eat blood from any bird or animal. ²⁷Anyone who eats blood must be separated from his people.'"

THE PRIESTS' SHARE

²⁸The Lord said to Moses, ²⁹"Tell the people of Israel: 'Someone may bring a fellowship offering to the Lord. He must give part of it as his sacrifice to the Lord. ³⁰He must carry that part of the gift in his own hands. It will be an offering made by fire to the Lord. He must carry the fat and the breast of the animal to the priest. The breast must be presented to the Lord as the priests' share. ³¹Then the priest must burn the fat on the altar. But the breast of the animal will belong to Aaron and the priests. ³²You must also give the right thigh from the fellowship offering to the priest as a gift. ³³It will belong to the priest who offers the blood and fat of the fellowship offering. ³⁴I have taken the breast and the thigh of the fellowship offering. And I have given these parts to Aaron and the priests as their share from the Israelites.'"

³⁵This is the portion that belongs to Aaron and his sons. It is from the offerings made by fire to the Lord. Aaron and his sons were given this share on the day they were presented to the Lord as priests. ³⁶On the day the Lord appointed the priests, he commanded Israel to give this share to them. It is to be given to the priests as their share from now on.

³⁷These are the teachings about the whole burnt offering, the grain offering, the sin offering and the penalty offering. They are the teachings about the appointment of priests. And they are the teachings about the fellowship offerings. ³⁸The Lord gave these teachings to Moses on Mount Sinai. It was on the day he commanded the Israelites to bring their offerings to him in the Sinai Desert.

AARON AND HIS SONS APPOINTED

8 The Lord said to Moses, ²"Bring Aaron and his sons and their clothes. Bring the special olive oil used in appointing people and things to the service of the Lord. Also bring the bull of the sin offering and the two male sheep. And bring the basket of bread made without yeast. ³Then gather the people together at the entrance to the Meeting Tent."ᵈ ⁴Moses did as the Lord commanded him. The people met together at the entrance to the Meeting Tent.

⁵Then Moses spoke to the people. He said, "This is what the Lord has commanded to be done." ⁶Then Moses brought Aaron and his sons forward. He washed them with water. ⁷He put the inner robe on Aaron. And he tied the cloth belt around Aaron. Then he put the outer robe on him. Next he put the holy vestᵈ on Aaron. Then he tied the skillfully woven belt around him. So the holy vest was tied to Aaron. ⁸Then Moses put the chest covering on him. And he put the Urim and the Thummimᵈ in the chest covering. ⁹He also put the turban on Aaron's head. He put the strip of gold on the front of the turban. This strip of gold is the holy crown. Moses did this as the Lord commanded him to do.

¹⁰Then Moses put the special oil on the Holy Tentᵈ and everything in it. In this way Moses made them holy for the Lord. ¹¹He sprinkled some oil on the altar seven times. He sprinkled the altar and all its tools. He also sprinkled special oil on the large bowl and its base. In this way he made them holy for the Lord. ¹²Then he poured some of the special oil on Aaron's head. In this way he made Aaron holy for the Lord. ¹³Then Moses

brought Aaron's sons forward. And he put the inner robes on them. He tied cloth belts around them. Then he put headbands on them. He did these things as the Lord had commanded him.

¹⁴Then Moses brought the bull for the sin offering. And Aaron and his sons put their hands on its head. ¹⁵Moses killed the bull and took some of the blood. With his finger he put some of the blood on all the corners of the altar. In this way he made the altar pure. Then he poured out the rest of the blood at the bottom of the altar. So he made it holy and ready for service to God. ¹⁶Moses took all the fat from the inner organs of the bull. He took the best part of the liver. And he took both kidneys and the fat on them. Then he burned them on the altar. ¹⁷But he took the bull's skin, its meat and its intestines outside the camp. He burned them in a fire outside the camp. Moses did all these things as the Lord had commanded him.

¹⁸Next Moses brought the male sheep of the burnt offering. Aaron and his sons put their hands on its head. ¹⁹Then Moses killed it. He sprinkled the blood on all sides of the altar. ²⁰Moses cut the male sheep into pieces. And he burned the head, the pieces and the fat. ²¹He washed the inner organs and legs with water. Then he burned the whole sheep on the altar. It was a burnt offering made by fire to the Lord. Its smell was pleasing to the Lord. Moses did these things as the Lord had commanded him.

²²Then Moses brought the other male sheep. It was used in appointing Aaron and his sons as priests. They put their hands on its head. ²³Then Moses killed the sheep. He put some of its blood on the bottom of Aaron's right ear. He put some on the thumb of Aaron's right hand. And he put some on the big toe of his right foot. ²⁴Then Moses brought Aaron's sons close to the altar. He put some of the blood on the bottom of their

right ears. He put it on the thumbs of their right hands. And he put it on the big toes of their right feet. Then he sprinkled blood on all sides of the altar. ²⁵He took the fat and the fat tail from the sheep. He took all the fat on the inner organs. He took the best part of the liver. He also took both kidneys, their fat and the right thigh. ²⁶A basket of bread made without yeast is put before the Lord each day. From the basket Moses took a loaf of bread. And he took a loaf made with oil and a wafer. He put these pieces of bread on the fat and right thigh of the male sheep. ²⁷He put all these things in the hands of Aaron and his sons. He presented the pieces as an offering before the Lord. ²⁸Then Moses took them from their hands. And he burned them on the altar on top of the burnt offering. So this was the offering for appointing Aaron and his sons as priests. It was an offering made by fire to the Lord. Its smell was pleasing to the Lord. ²⁹Moses took the breast and presented it as an offering before the Lord. It was Moses' share of the male sheep used in appointing the priests. This was as the Lord had commanded Moses.

³⁰Moses took some of the special oil and some of the blood which was on the altar. He sprinkled some of the oil on Aaron and Aaron's clothes. He also sprinkled some on Aaron's sons and their clothes. In this way Moses made Aaron, his clothes, his sons and their clothes holy for the Lord.

³¹Then Moses said to Aaron and his sons, "I gave you a command. I said, 'Aaron and his sons will eat these things.' So take the meat and basket of bread from the offering for appointing priests. Boil the meat at the door of the Meeting Tent. Eat it there with the bread. ³²If any of the meat or bread is left, burn it. ³³The time of appointing will last seven days. You must not go outside the entrance of the Meeting Tent

until that time is up. Stay there until the time of your appointing is finished. [34]The Lord commanded the things that were done today. He commanded these things to remove your sins so you will belong to him. [35]You must stay at the entrance of the Meeting Tent. Stay there day and night for seven days. If you don't obey the Lord's commands, you will die! The Lord has given me these commands."

[36]So Aaron and his sons did everything the Lord had commanded through Moses.

AARON AND HIS SONS OFFER SACRIFICES

9 On the eighth day after the time of appointing, Moses called for Aaron and his sons. He also called for the elders of Israel. [2]He said to Aaron, "Take a bull calf and a male sheep. There must be nothing wrong with these animals. The calf will be a sin offering. And the male sheep will be a whole burnt offering. Offer these animals to the Lord. [3]Tell the people of Israel, 'Take a male goat for a sin offering. And take a calf and a lamb for a whole burnt offering. The calf and the lamb must each be one year old. There must be nothing wrong with these animals. [4]Take a bull and a male sheep for fellowship offerings. Take with these animals a grain offering mixed with oil. Offer these things to the Lord. This is because the Lord will appear to you today.'"

[5]So all the people came to the front of the Meeting Tent.[d] They brought the things Moses had commanded them to bring. And they stood before the Lord. [6]Moses said, "You have done what the Lord commanded. So you will see the Lord's glory."

[7]Then Moses told Aaron, "Go to the altar. There offer sin offerings and whole burnt offerings. Do this to remove your sins and the people's sins so you will belong to God. Offer the sacrifices for the people. And perform the acts to remove their sins for them so they will belong to the Lord. Do this as the Lord has commanded."

[8]So Aaron went to the altar. He killed the bull calf as a sin offering for himself. [9]Then his sons brought the blood to him. Aaron dipped his finger in the blood and put it on the corners of the altar. Then he poured out the rest of the blood at the bottom of the altar. [10]Aaron took the fat, the kidneys and the best part of the liver from the sin offering. He burned these things on the altar. He did this the way the Lord had commanded Moses. [11]Aaron burned the meat and skin outside the camp.

[12]Then Aaron killed the animal for the whole burnt offering. Aaron's sons brought the blood to him. And he sprinkled it on all sides of the altar. [13]Aaron's sons gave the pieces and head of the burnt offering to Aaron. And he burned them on the altar. [14]Aaron also washed the inner organs and the legs of the burnt offering. And he burned them on the altar.

[15]Then Aaron brought the offering that was for the people. He took the goat of the people's sin offering. He killed and offered the goat of the sin offering. He did this just as he had done the first sin offering.

[16]Then Aaron brought the whole burnt offering and offered it. He did it as the Lord had commanded. [17]He also brought the grain offering to the altar. He took a handful of the grain and burned it on the altar. This was in addition to the morning's burnt offering.

[18]Aaron also killed the bull and the male sheep. These were the fellowship offerings for the people. Aaron's sons brought the blood from these animals to Aaron. He sprinkled it on all sides of the altar. [19]Aaron's sons also brought to Aaron the fat of the bull and the male sheep. They brought the fat tail and the fat covering the inner organs. They also

brought the kidneys and the best part of the liver. [20]Aaron's sons put these fat parts on the breasts of the bull and sheep. Then Aaron burned these fat parts on the altar. [21]He presented the breasts and the right thigh before the Lord as the priests' share of the offering. He did this as Moses had commanded.

[22]Then Aaron lifted up his hands toward the people and blessed them. Aaron had finished offering the sin offering, the burnt offering and the fellowship offering. Then he stepped down from the altar.

[23]Moses and Aaron went into the Meeting Tent. Then they came out and blessed the people. Then the Lord's glory came to all the people. [24]Fire came out from the Lord. It burned up the burnt offering and fat on the altar. When the people saw this, they shouted with joy. They bowed facedown on the ground.

GOD DESTROYS NADAB AND ABIHU

10 Aaron's sons Nadab and Abihu took their pans for burning incense.[d] They put fire in them and added incense. But they did not use the special fire Moses had commanded them to use. [2]So fire came down from the Lord and destroyed Nadab and Abihu. They died in front of the Lord. [3]Then Moses said to Aaron, "This is what the Lord was speaking about when he said,

'I must be respected as holy
    by those who come near me.
Before all the people
    I must be given honor.'"
So Aaron did not say anything about the death of his sons.

[4]Aaron's uncle Uzziel had two sons named Mishael and Elzaphan. Moses said to them, "Come here. Pick up your cousins' bodies. Carry them outside the camp away from the front of the Holy Place." [5]So Mishael and Elzaphan obeyed Moses. They carried the bodies of Nadab and Abihu outside the camp. Nadab and

Abihu were still wearing the special priest's inner robes.

[6]Then Moses spoke to Aaron and his other sons, Eleazar and Ithamar. Moses told them, "Don't show any sadness. Don't tear your clothes or leave your hair uncombed. If you do those things, you will die, and the Lord will be angry with all the people. All the people of Israel are your relatives. They may cry loudly about the Lord burning Nadab and Abihu. [7]But you must not even leave the Meeting Tent.[d] If you go out of the entrance, you will die! This is because the Lord has appointed you to his service." So Aaron, Eleazar and Ithamar obeyed Moses.

[8]Then the Lord said to Aaron, [9]"You and your sons must not drink wine or beer when you go into the Meeting Tent. If you do, you will die! This law will continue from now on. [10]You must keep what is holy separate from what is not holy. You must keep what is clean[d] separate from what is unclean. [11]The Lord gave his laws to Moses. And Moses gave them to the people. You must teach the people all the laws."

[12]Moses talked to Aaron and his remaining sons, Eleazar and Ithamar. Moses said, "Some of the grain offering is left from the sacrifices offered by fire to the Lord. Eat that part of the grain offering. But do not add yeast to it. Eat it near the altar because it is most holy. [13]The Law I gave you says this part belongs to you and your sons. But you must eat it in a holy place. It is part of the offerings made by fire to the Lord. I have been commanded to tell you this.

[14]"Also, you, your sons and daughters may eat the breast and thigh of the fellowship offering. They were presented to the Lord. You must eat them in a clean place. They are your share of the fellowship offerings given by the Israelites. [15]The people must bring the fat from their animals. It is part of the offering made by fire. They must also

bring the thigh and the breast of the fellowship offering. These will be presented to the Lord. They will be the regular share of the offerings for you and your children. The Lord has commanded it."

[16]Moses looked for the goat of the sin offering. But it had already been burned up. So he became very angry with Eleazar and Ithamar, Aaron's remaining sons. He said, [17]"You were supposed to eat that goat in a holy place before the Lord! It is most holy! He gave it to you to take away the guilt of the people. The goat was for removing the sins of the people so they will belong to the Lord. [18]You didn't bring the goat's blood inside the Holy Place. So you were supposed to eat the goat in a holy place, as I commanded!"

[19]But Aaron said to Moses, "Today they brought their sin offering and burnt offering before the Lord. But these terrible things have still happened to me today! Do you think the Lord would be any happier if I ate the sin offering today?" [20]When Moses heard this, he was satisfied.

RULES ABOUT WHAT MAY BE EATEN

11 The Lord spoke to Moses and Aaron. [2]He said, "Tell the people of Israel this: 'These are the land animals you may eat: [3]You may eat any animal that has split hoofs completely divided and chews the cud.[d]

[4]"'Some animals only chew the cud or only have split hoofs. Don't eat these animals. The camel chews the cud but does not have a split hoof. It is unclean[d] for you. [5]The rock badger chews the cud but does not have a split hoof. It is unclean for you. [6]The rabbit chews the cud but does not have a split hoof. It is unclean for you. [7]Now the pig has a split hoof that is completely divided. But it does not chew the cud. It is unclean for you. [8]You must not eat the meat from these animals. Don't even touch their dead bodies. They are unclean for you.

[9]"'Some animals live in the sea or in a river. If the animal has fins and scales, you may eat it. [10]But some animals live in the sea or in a river and do not have fins and scales. This includes the things that fill the water. And it includes all other things that live in the water. You should hate them. [11]You must not eat any meat from them. Don't even touch their dead bodies. This is because you should hate them. [12]You must hate any animal in the water that does not have fins and scales.

[13]"'Also, some birds should not be eaten. They should be hated. You must not eat any of these birds: eagles, vultures, black vultures, [14]kites or any kind of falcon. [15]Don't eat any kind of raven, [16]horned owls, screech owls, sea gulls or any kind of hawk. [17]Don't eat little owls, cormorants, great owls, [18]white owls, desert owls or ospreys. [19]Don't eat storks, any kind of heron, hoopoes or bats.

[20]"'Don't eat insects that have wings and walk on all four feet. They are also to be hated.

[21]"'But you may eat certain insects that have wings and walk on four feet. You may eat those that have legs with joints above their feet so they can jump. [22]These are the insects you may eat: all kinds of locusts, winged locusts, crickets and grasshoppers. [23]But all other insects that have wings and walk on four feet are hated. [24]Those insects will make you unclean. Anyone who touches the dead body of one of these insects will become unclean until evening. [25]If someone picks up one of these dead insects, he must wash his clothes. He will be unclean until evening.

[26]"'Some animals have split hoofs. But the hoofs are not completely divided. And some animals do not chew the cud. They are unclean for you. Anyone who touches the dead body of one of these animals will become unclean. [27]Other animals do not have hoofs at all. They walk on their paws. These animals are

unclean for you. Anyone who touches the dead body of one of these animals will become unclean. He will be unclean until evening. ²⁸Anyone who picks up their dead bodies must wash his clothes. He will be unclean until evening. These animals are unclean for you.

²⁹"'These crawling animals are unclean for you: moles, rats, all kinds of great lizards, ³⁰geckos, crocodiles, lizards, sand reptiles and chameleons. ³¹These crawling animals are unclean for you. Anyone who touches their dead bodies will be unclean until evening.

³²"'If an unclean animal dies and falls on something, that thing will also become unclean. The animal might fall on a thing made from wood, cloth, leather or rough cloth. It does not matter what the thing was used for. Whatever the animal falls on must be washed with water. It will be unclean until evening. Then it will become clean again. ³³The dead, unclean animal might fall into a clay bowl. If it does, anything in the bowl will become unclean. And you must break the bowl. ³⁴If water from the unclean clay bowl gets on any food, that food will become unclean. ³⁵If any dead, unclean animal falls on something, that thing becomes unclean. The animal may fall on a clay oven or a clay baking pan. If so, it must be broken into pieces. These things will be unclean. They are unclean for you.

³⁶"'A spring or well that collects water will stay clean. But anyone who touches the dead body of any unclean animal will become unclean. ³⁷A dead, unclean animal might fall on a seed to be planted. That seed is still clean. ³⁸But you might put water on some seeds. If a dead, unclean animal falls on those seeds, they are unclean for you.

³⁹"'Also, an animal which you use for food may die. If it does, anyone who touches its body will be unclean until evening. ⁴⁰Anyone who eats meat from this animal's dead body must wash his

clothes. He will be unclean until evening. Anyone who picks up the animal's dead body must wash his clothes. He will be unclean until evening.

⁴¹"'Every animal that crawls on the ground is one of the hated animals. It must not be eaten. Anyone who picks up the animal's dead body must wash his clothes. He will be unclean until evening. ⁴²You must not eat any of the animals that crawl on the ground. This includes animals that crawl on their stomachs. And it includes animals that walk on all four feet or on many feet. Those are hated animals to you. ⁴³Do not make yourself unclean by these hated animals. You must not become unclean by them. ⁴⁴I am the Lord your God. Keep yourselves holy for me because I am holy. Don't make yourselves unclean with these hated, crawling animals. ⁴⁵I am the Lord who brought you out of Egypt. I did it so I could be your God. You must be holy because I am holy.

⁴⁶"'These are the teachings about all of the cattle, birds and other animals on earth. These are the teachings about the animals in the sea. And these are the teachings about the animals that crawl on the ground. ⁴⁷These teachings help people know the difference between unclean animals and clean animals. They help people know which animals may be eaten and which ones must not be eaten.'"

RULES FOR NEW MOTHERS

12 The Lord said to Moses, ²"Tell the people of Israel this: 'If a woman gives birth to a son, she will become unclean^d for 7 days. This will be like her being unclean during her monthly period. ³On the eighth day the boy must be circumcised.^d ⁴Then it will be 33 days before she becomes clean from her loss of blood. She must not touch anything that is holy. She must not enter the holy place until her time of cleansing is finished. ⁵But a woman may give birth to a daughter. Then the mother will be unclean for 2 weeks. This is like her being unclean during her monthly period. It will be 66 days before she becomes clean from her loss of blood.

⁶"After she has a son or daughter, she must have a time of cleansing. When it is over, the new mother must bring certain sacrifices to the Meeting Tent.ᵈ She must give the priest at the entrance a year-old lamb for a burnt offering. And she must bring a dove or young pigeon for a sin offering. ⁷He will offer them before the Lord to make her clean so she will belong to the Lord again. Then she will be clean from her loss of blood. These are the teachings for a woman who gives birth to a boy or girl.

⁸"If she cannot afford a lamb, she is to bring two doves or two young pigeons. One bird will be for a burnt offering and one for a sin offering. In this way the priest will make her clean so she will belong to the Lord again. And she will be clean.'"

RULES ABOUT SKIN DISEASES

13 The Lord said to Moses and Aaron, ²"Someone might have a swelling on his skin. Or he might have a scab or a bright spot on his skin. If the sore looks like a harmful skin disease, the person must be brought to Aaron the priest. Or he must be brought to one of Aaron's sons, the priests. ³The priest must look at the sore on the person's skin. The hair in the sore may have become white. And the sore may seem deeper than the person's skin. If so, it is a harmful skin disease. When he has finished looking at the person, the priest must announce that the person is unclean.ᵈ

⁴"Sometimes there is a white spot on a person's skin, but the spot does not seem deeper than the skin. If that is true, and if the hair from the spot has not turned white, the priest must separate that person from other people for seven days. ⁵On the seventh day the priest

must look at the person again. He may see that the sore has not changed. It might not have spread on the skin. Then the priest must keep the person separated for seven more days. ⁶On the seventh day the priest must look at the person again. The sore may have faded. And it may not have spread on the skin. If that is true, the priest must announce that the person is clean. The sore is only a rash. The person must wash his clothes. Then he will become clean again.

⁷"But the sore may have spread again after the priest has announced him clean. Then the person must come again to the priest. ⁸The priest must look at him. If the rash has spread on the skin, the priest must announce that person is unclean. It is a harmful skin disease.

⁹"If a person has a harmful skin disease, he must be brought to the priest. ¹⁰The priest must look at him. There might be a white swelling in the skin. And the hair may have become white. And the skin may look raw in the swelling. ¹¹If these things are true, it is a harmful skin disease. It is one that he has had for a long time. The priest must announce that the person is unclean. He will not need to separate that person from other people. This is because everyone already knows that the person is unclean.

¹²"Sometimes skin disease spreads all over a person's body. The disease covers that person's skin from his head to his feet, as far as the priest can see. Then the priest must look at the person's whole body. ¹³The priest might see that the disease covers the whole body. It might have turned all of the person's skin white. Then the priest must announce that the person is clean.

¹⁴"But when the person has an open sore, he is not clean. ¹⁵When the priest sees the open sore, he must announce that the person is unclean. The open sore is not clean. It is a harmful skin disease. ¹⁶If the open sore becomes white

again, the person must come to the priest. [17]The priest must look at him. If the sores have become white, the priest must announce that the person with the sores is clean. Then he will be clean.

[18]"Someone may have a boil on his skin, but it is healed. [19]In the place where the boil was, there might be a white swelling. Or there might be a bright red spot. This place on the skin must be shown to the priest. [20]And the priest must look at it. The spot might seem deeper than the skin. And the hair on it might have become white. If these things are true, the priest must announce that the person is unclean. The spot is a harmful skin disease. It has broken out from inside the boil. [21]But the priest must look at the spot. There might be no white hairs in it. The spot may not be deeper than the skin. And it may have faded. Then the priest must separate the person from other people for seven days. [22]If the spot spreads on the skin, the priest must announce that the person is unclean. It is a disease that will spread. [23]But the bright spot might not spread or change. Then it is only the scar from the old boil. Then the priest must announce that the person is clean.

[24]"A person might get a burn on his skin. If the open sore becomes white or red, [25]the priest must look at it. The white spot might seem deeper than the skin. And the hair at that spot might have become white. If these things are true, it is a harmful skin disease. The disease has broken out in the burn. Then the priest must announce that the person is unclean. It is a harmful skin disease. [26]But the priest must look at the spot. There might be no white hair in the bright spot. And the spot may be no deeper than the skin. It may have faded. Then the priest must separate the person from other people for seven days. [27]On the seventh day the priest must look at him again. If the spot has spread on the skin, the priest must announce that the person is unclean. It is a harmful skin disease. [28]But the bright spot may not have spread on the skin. It may have faded. Then it is the swelling from the burn. And the priest must announce that the person is clean. The spot is only a scar from the burn.

[29]"Someone might get a sore on his scalp or on his chin. [30]A priest must look at the sore. It may seem to be deeper than the skin. And the hair around it may be thin and yellow. If these things are true, the priest must announce that the person is unclean. It is an itch, a harmful skin disease of the head or chin. [31]But when the priest looks at it, the sore might not seem deeper than the skin. There might not be any black hair in it. If that is true, the priest must separate the person from other people for seven days. [32]On the seventh day the priest must look at the sore. It may not have spread. There may be no yellow hairs growing in it. And the sore may not seem deeper than the skin. [33]If these things are true, the person must shave himself. But he must not shave the sore place. The priest must separate that person from other people for seven more days. [34]On the seventh day the priest must look at the sore. The sore may not have spread on the skin. And it may not seem deeper than the skin. If that is true, the priest must announce that the person is clean. So the person must wash his clothes and become clean. [35]But the sore might spread on the skin after the person has become clean. [36]Then the priest must look at him again. If the sore has spread on the skin, the priest doesn't need to look for the yellowish hair. The person is unclean. [37]But the priest might think the sore has stopped spreading. And black hair may be growing in it. Then the sore has healed. The person is clean. And the priest must announce that he is clean.

[38]"When a person has white spots on his skin, [39]a priest must look at them. If the spots on his skin are dull white, the disease is only a harmless rash. That person is clean.

[40]"A man might lose hair from his head and be bald. He is clean. [41]He might lose hair from the front of his head and have a bald forehead. He is clean. [42]But if there is a red-white sore on his scalp, it is a skin disease. [43]A priest must look at that person. The swelling of the sore might be red-white. It might look like a skin disease that spreads. [44]Then that person has a skin disease. He is unclean. And the priest must announce that the person is unclean because of the sore on his head.

[45]"If a person has a skin disease that spreads, he must warn other people. He must shout, 'Unclean, unclean!' His clothes must be torn at the seams. He must let his hair stay uncombed. And he must cover his mouth. [46]That person will be unclean the whole time he has the disease. He is unclean. He must live alone outside the camp.

RULES ABOUT MILDEW

[47]"Some clothing might have mildew[d] on it. The cloth might be linen or wool. [48]It might be woven or knitted. The mildew might be on a piece of leather or on something made from leather. [49]The mildew might be in the clothing, leather or woven or knitted material. If the mildew is green or red, it is a spreading mildew. Then it must be shown to the priest. [50]The priest must look at the mildew. And he must put that thing in a separate place for seven days. [51]On the seventh day he must look at the mildew. It doesn't matter if the mildew is on leather or cloth. It doesn't matter if the cloth is woven or knitted. It doesn't matter what it was used for. If the mildew has spread, it is a mildew that destroys. [52]The priest must burn it. It does not matter if it is woven or knitted, wool or linen or a leather article. The

mildew is spreading. The thing must be burned.

[53]"If the priest sees that the mildew has not spread, the cloth or leather must be washed. It does not matter if it is leather or cloth, knitted or woven. It must be washed. [54]The priest must order the people to wash that piece of leather or cloth. Then he must separate the clothing for seven more days. [55]After that time the priest must look at it again. If the mildew still looks the same, that thing is unclean.[d] It does not matter if the mildew has not spread. You must burn that cloth or piece of leather.

[56]"But when the priest looks at that piece of leather or cloth, the mildew might have faded. Then the priest must tear the mildew out of the piece of leather or cloth. It does not matter if the cloth is woven or knitted. [57]But the mildew might come back to that piece of leather or cloth. If that happens, the mildew is spreading. And that piece of leather or cloth must be burned. [58]The cloth, the woven or knitted material, or the leather may be washed. The mildew may then be gone. It must be washed again. Then it will be clean.

[59]"These are the teachings about mildew on pieces of leather or cloth. It doesn't matter if the cloth is woven or knitted."

RULES FOR CLEANSING FROM SKIN DISEASES

14 The Lord said to Moses, [2]"These are the teachings for people who had a harmful skin disease and have become well. These teachings are for making that person clean.[d]

[3]"A priest must look at the person who had the skin disease. He must go to that person outside the camp. He must see if the skin disease is healed. [4]If the person is healthy, the priest will tell him to do these things: He must get two living, clean birds. He must also get a piece of cedar wood, a piece of red cloth and a hyssop

plant. These things are for cleansing the person with the skin disease.

⁵"The priest must order one bird to be killed in a clay bowl containing fresh water. ⁶Then he will take the other bird that is still alive. He will take the piece of cedar wood, the red cloth and the hyssop. He will dip the living bird and other things into the blood. (This is the blood of the bird that was killed over the fresh water.) ⁷The priest will sprinkle the blood seven times on the person who had the skin disease. He must announce that the person is clean. Then the priest must go to an open field. He must let the living bird go free.

⁸"Next, that person must wash his clothes. He must shave off all his hair. And he must wash with water. Then he will be clean and may go into the camp. But at first he must stay outside his tent for seven days. ⁹On the seventh day he must shave off all his hair. He must shave off his hair, his beard and his eyebrows. He must wash his clothes and bathe his body in water. Then he will be clean.

¹⁰"On the eighth day the person who had the skin disease must take two male lambs. They must have nothing wrong with them. He must also take a year-old female lamb. It must have nothing wrong with it. The person must take six quarts of fine flour mixed with oil. This is for a grain offering. He must also take two-thirds of a pint of olive oil. ¹¹A priest must announce that the person is clean. Then he must bring that person and his sacrifices before the Lord. This is at the entrance of the Meeting Tent.ᵈ ¹²The priest will take one of the male lambs. He will offer it and the olive oil as a guilt offering. And he will present them before the Lord as an offering. ¹³Then he will kill the male lamb in the holy place. He will kill it where they kill the sin offering and the whole burnt offering. The penalty offering is like the sin offering. It belongs to the priest. It is most holy.

¹⁴"The priest will take some of the blood of the penalty offering. He will put some of it on the bottom of the right ear of the person to be made clean. He will put some of it on the thumb of the person's right hand. And he will put some on the big toe of the person's right foot. ¹⁵The priest will also take some of the oil and pour it into his own left hand. ¹⁶Then he will dip a finger of his right hand into the oil that is in his left hand. He will use his finger to sprinkle some of the oil seven times before the Lord. ¹⁷The priest will put some oil from his hand on the bottom of the right ear of the person to be made clean. He will put some of it on the thumb of the person's right hand. And he will put some of it on the big toe of the person's right foot. The oil will go on these places on top of the blood for the penalty offering. ¹⁸He will put the rest of the oil that is in his left hand on the head of the person to be made clean. In this way the priest will make that person clean so he can belong to the Lord again.

¹⁹"Next the priest will offer the sin offering. It will make that person clean so he can belong to the Lord again. After this the priest will kill the animal for the whole burnt offering. ²⁰Then he will offer the burnt offering and grain offering on the altar. In this way he will make that person clean so he can belong to the Lord again.

²¹"But the person may be poor and unable to afford these offerings. Then he must take one male lamb for a penalty offering. It will be presented to the Lord so the priest can make that person clean. Then he can belong to the Lord again. The person must take two quarts of fine flour mixed with oil. It will be used for a grain offering. He must also take two-thirds of a pint of olive oil. ²²He must take two doves or two young pigeons, which he can afford. One bird will be a sin offering. The other will be a whole

burnt offering. ²³On the eighth day the person will bring them to the priest at the entrance of the Meeting Tent. The gifts will be offered before the Lord. This is so the person can become clean. ²⁴The priest will take the lamb for the penalty offering and the oil. He will present them as an offering before the Lord. ²⁵Then he will kill the lamb of the penalty offering. He will take some of the blood of the penalty offering. He will put it on the bottom of the right ear of the person to be made clean. The priest will put some of this blood on the thumb of the person's right hand. And he will put some on the big toe of the person's right foot. ²⁶He will also pour some of the oil into his own left hand. ²⁷Then with a finger of his right hand, he will sprinkle some of the oil from his left hand. He will sprinkle it seven times before the Lord. ²⁸Then the priest will take some of the oil from his hand. He will put it on the bottom of the right ear of the person to be made clean. He will also put some of it on the thumb of the person's right hand. And he will put some on the big toe of the person's right foot. The oil will go on these places on top of the blood from the penalty offering. ²⁹The priest must put the rest of the oil that is in his hand on the head of the person to be made clean. In this way the priest will make the person clean so he can belong to the Lord again. ³⁰Then the priest will offer one of the doves or young pigeons. He must offer what the person can afford. ³¹He must offer one of the birds as a sin offering. And he must offer the other bird as a whole burnt offering. He must offer them with the grain offering. In this way the priest will make the person clean so he can belong to the Lord again. The person will become clean.

³²"These are the teachings for making a person clean. This is done after he has become well from a skin disease. These teachings are for people who cannot afford the regular sacrifices for becoming clean."

RULES FOR CLEANING MILDEW

³³The Lord also said to Moses and Aaron, ³⁴"I am giving the land of Canaan to your people. When they enter that land, I might cause mildew^d to grow in someone's house. ³⁵The owner of that house must come and tell the priest. He should say, 'I have seen something like mildew in my house.' ³⁶Then the priest must order the people to empty the house. They must do this before he goes in to look at the mildew. This is so he will not have to say that everything in the house is unclean.^d After the people have emptied the house, the priest will go in to look at it. ³⁷He will look at the mildew. The mildew on the walls of the house might be green or red. It might go into the wall's surface. ³⁸If these things are true, he must go out and close up the house for seven days. ³⁹On the seventh day the priest must come back and check the house. The mildew may have spread on the walls of the house. ⁴⁰If it has, the priest must order the people to tear out the stones with the mildew on them. They should throw the stones away. They must put the stones at a certain unclean place outside the city. ⁴¹Then the priest must have all the inside of the house scraped. The people must throw away the plaster they scraped off the walls. They must put the plaster at a certain unclean place outside the city. ⁴²Then the owner must put new stones in the walls. And he must cover the walls with new clay plaster.

⁴³"A person may have taken away the old stones and plaster. He may have put in new stones and plaster. But mildew may again appear in his house. ⁴⁴If it does, the priest must come back and check the house again. If the mildew has spread in the house, it is a mildew that destroys things. So the house is unclean. ⁴⁵Then the owner must tear down the

house. He must remove all its stones, plaster and wood. He must take them to the unclean place outside the city. [46]Anyone who goes into that house will be unclean until evening. [47]Anyone who eats in that house or lies down there must wash his clothes.

[48]"After new stones and plaster have been put in a house, the priest must check it again. The mildew may not have spread in the house. Then the priest will announce that the house is clean. This is because the mildew is gone.

[49]"Then, to make the house clean, the priest must take two birds. He must also take a piece of cedar wood, a piece of red cloth and a hyssop plant. [50]He will kill one bird in a clay bowl containing fresh water. [51]Then he will take the other bird that is still alive. He will also take the cedar wood, the hyssop and the red cloth. He will dip the living bird and other things into the blood. (This is the blood of the bird that was killed over the fresh water.) Then the priest will sprinkle the blood on the house seven times. [52]He will use the bird's blood, the fresh water and the live bird. And he will use the cedar wood, the hyssop and the red cloth. With these things he will make the house clean. [53]The priest will go to an open field outside the city. And he will let the living bird go free. This is how the priest makes the house clean and ready for service to the Lord."

[54]These are the teachings about any kind of skin disease. [55]These are the teachings for mildew on pieces of cloth or in a house. [56]These are also the teachings for swellings, rashes or bright spots on the skin. [57]They teach when things are unclean and when they are clean. These are the teachings about all these kinds of diseases.

RULES ABOUT A MAN'S BODY

15 The Lord also said to Moses and Aaron, [2]"Say to the people of Israel: 'When a fluid comes from a man's body, he is unclean.[d] [3]It doesn't matter if the fluid flows freely or if it is blocked from flowing.

[4]"'The man who discharges the body fluid may lie on a bed. If he does, that bed becomes unclean. Everything he sits on becomes unclean. [5]Also anyone who touches his bed must wash his clothes and bathe in water. This person will be unclean until evening. [6]Someone might sit on something that the man who discharges the fluid sat on. If he does, he must wash his clothes and bathe in water. He will be unclean until evening. [7]Anyone who touches the man who discharges the body fluid must wash his clothes and bathe in water. The person will be unclean until evening.

[8]"'The man who discharges the body fluid might spit on a clean person. If so, the person who was clean must wash his clothes. He must bathe in water. The person will be unclean until evening. [9]Everything on which the man who is unclean has ridden will become unclean. [10]Someone might touch something that was under the man who discharges a body fluid. If he does, he will be unclean until evening. Someone might carry these things that were under the man who discharges a body fluid. This person must wash his clothes and bathe in water. He will be unclean until evening.

[11]"'The man who discharges a body fluid may not have washed his hands in water. If he touches another person, that person must wash his clothes. That person must bathe in water. He will be unclean until evening.

[12]"'A man who discharges a body fluid may touch a clay bowl. That bowl must be broken. If he touches a wooden bowl, that bowl must be washed in water.

[13]"'A man who discharges a body fluid may be made clean. He must count seven days for himself for his cleansing. He must wash his clothes and bathe his body in fresh water. Then he will be

clean. [14]On the eighth day he must take two doves or two young pigeons. He must come before the Lord at the entrance of the Meeting Tent.[d] He will give the two birds to the priest. [15]The priest will offer the birds. One bird is for a sin offering. The other is for a burnt offering. So the priest will make that man clean so he can belong to the Lord again.

[16]"If semen[n] goes out from a man, he must bathe in water. He will be unclean until evening. [17]If the fluid gets on any clothing or leather, it must be washed with water. It will be unclean until evening.

[18]"If a man has sexual relations with a woman and semen comes out, both people must bathe in water. They will be unclean until evening.

RULES ABOUT A WOMAN'S BODY

[19]"When a woman has her monthly period, she is unclean[d] for seven days. Anyone who touches her will be unclean until evening. [20]Anything she lies on during this time will be unclean. Everything she sits on during that time will be unclean. [21]Anyone who touches her bed must wash his clothes and bathe in water. That person will be unclean until evening. [22]Anyone who touches something she has sat on must wash his clothes and bathe in water. That person will be unclean until evening. [23]It does not matter if the person touched the woman's bed or something she sat on. That person will be unclean until evening.

[24]"A man may have sexual relations with a woman during her monthly period. If he does, he will be unclean for seven days. Every bed he lies on will also be unclean.

[25]"A woman might have a loss of blood for many days. It may not be during her regular monthly period. Or she may continue to have a loss of blood after her regular period. If she does, she will be unclean, as she is during her monthly period. She will be unclean for as long as she continues to bleed. [26]Any bed she lies on during all the time of her bleeding will be like her bed during her regular monthly period. Everything she sits on will be unclean. It will be like during her regular monthly period.

[27]"If anyone touches those things, that person will be unclean. He must wash his clothes and bathe in water. He will be unclean until evening. [28]When the woman becomes clean from her bleeding, she must wait seven days. After this she will be clean. [29]Then on the eighth day she must take two doves or two young pigeons. She must bring them to the priest at the entrance of the Meeting Tent.[d] [30]Then the priest must offer one bird for a sin offering. He must offer the other bird for a whole burnt offering. So the priest will make her clean so she can belong to the Lord again.

[31]"So you must warn the people of Israel to stay separated from things that make them unclean. If you don't warn the people, they might make my Holy Tent[d] unclean. And then they would have to die!'"

[32]These are the teachings for the man who discharges a body fluid. These are the teachings for men who become unclean from semen[n] coming out of their bodies. [33]These are the teachings for women who become unclean from their monthly period. These are the teachings for anyone who becomes unclean by having sexual relations with another person who is unclean.

THE DAY OF CLEANSING

16 Now two of Aaron's sons had died while offering incense[d] to the Lord. At that time the Lord spoke to Moses. [2]He said, "Talk to your brother Aaron. Tell him there are times when he

---

15:16, 32 semen A man's body fluid by which he can make a woman pregnant.

cannot go behind the curtain into the Most Holy Place where the Holy Box*d* is. If he goes in when I appear in a cloud over the lid on the Holy Box, he will die.

³"Aaron may enter the Most Holy Place only on the Day of Cleansing. Before he enters, he must offer a bull for a sin offering. And he must offer a male sheep for a whole burnt offering. ⁴He must put on these clothes. He will put on the holy linen inner robe. The linen underclothes will be next to his body. His belt will be the cloth belt. And he will wear the linen turban. These are holy clothes. So he must wash his whole body with water before he puts them on.

⁵"Aaron must take from the people of Israel two male goats for a sin offering. And he must take one male sheep for a burnt offering. ⁶Then he will offer the bull for the sin offering. This sin offering is for himself. Then he will perform the acts to remove sins from him and his family so they will belong to the Lord.

⁷"Next Aaron will take the two goats. He will bring them before the Lord at the entrance to the Meeting Tent.*d* ⁸Aaron will throw lots*d* for the two goats. One lot will be for the Lord. The other lot will be for the goat that removes sin. ⁹Then Aaron will take the goat that was chosen for the Lord by throwing the lot. He must offer this goat as a sin offering. ¹⁰The other goat was chosen by lot to remove the sin. It must be brought alive before the Lord. The priest will use it to perform the acts to remove Israel's sin so they will belong to the Lord. Then this goat will be sent out into the desert.

¹¹"Then Aaron will offer the bull as a sin offering for himself. This will remove the sins of him and his family so they will belong to the Lord. He will kill the bull for the sin offering for himself. ¹²Then he must take a pan full of burning coals from the altar before the Lord. Aaron must take two handfuls of sweet incense that has been ground into

powder. He must bring it into the room behind the curtain. ¹³He must put the incense on the fire before the Lord. Then the cloud of incense will cover the lid on the Holy Box. Then when Aaron comes in, he will not die. ¹⁴Also, Aaron must take some of the blood from the bull. He must sprinkle it with his finger on the front of the lid. Then, with his finger he will sprinkle the blood seven times in front of the lid.

¹⁵"Then Aaron must kill the goat of the sin offering for the people. He must bring this goat's blood into the room behind the curtain. He must do with the goat's blood as he did with the bull's blood. He must sprinkle the goat's blood on the lid and in front of it. ¹⁶The people in Israel have been unclean.*d* So Aaron will perform the acts to make the Most Holy Place ready for service to the Lord. Then it will be clean from the sins and crimes of the people of Israel. He must do this because the Meeting Tent stays in the middle of unclean people. ¹⁷When Aaron makes the Most Holy Place ready for service to the Lord, no one is allowed in the Meeting Tent. No one must go in until Aaron comes out. So Aaron will perform the acts to remove sins from himself and his family so they will belong to the Lord. Then he will remove the sins of all the people of Israel so they will belong to the Lord. ¹⁸Afterward he will go out to the altar that is before the Lord. And he will make the altar ready for service to the Lord. Aaron will take some of the bull's blood and some of the goat's blood. He will put it on the corners of the altar on all sides. ¹⁹Then he will sprinkle some of the blood with his finger. He will sprinkle it on the altar seven times. In this way Aaron will make the altar holy for the Lord. And it will be clean from all the sins of the people of Israel.

²⁰"Aaron will make the Most Holy Place, the Meeting Tent and the altar clean. Then he will bring the goat alive to

the Lord. [21]He will put both his hands on the head of the living goat. Then he will confess all the sins and crimes of Israel over the goat. In this way Aaron will put the people's sins on the goat's head. Then he will send the goat away into the desert. A man who has been appointed will lead the goat away. [22]So the goat will carry all the people's sins on itself. It will go to a lonely place in the desert. The man who leads the goat will let it loose there.

[23]"Then Aaron will enter the Meeting Tent. He will take off the linen clothes. (He had put them on before he went into the Most Holy Place.) He must leave these clothes there. [24]He will wash his whole body with water in a holy place. Then he will put on his regular clothes. He will come out and offer the whole burnt offering for himself. And he will offer the whole burnt offering for the people. He will remove sins from himself and the people so they will belong to the Lord. [25]Then he will burn the fat of the sin offering on the altar.

[26]"The person who led the goat into the desert must wash his clothes. Then he must wash his whole body with water. After that, he may come back into the camp.

[27]"The bull and goat for the sin offerings must be taken outside the camp. The blood from these animals was brought into the Most Holy Place. It was to make the Holy Place ready for service to the Lord. The priests will burn the animals' skins, bodies and intestines in the fire. [28]Then the one who burns them must wash his clothes. And he must wash his whole body with water. After that, he may come back into the camp.

[29]"This law will always continue for you: On the tenth day of the seventh month, you must not eat. You must not do any work. The travelers or foreigners living with you must not work either. [30]On this day the priests make you clean so you will belong to the Lord again. All

your sins will be removed. [31]This is a very important day of rest for you. And you must not eat. This law will continue forever.

[32]"So the appointed priest will perform the acts for making things ready for service to the Lord. He is the priest on whom oil was poured. He is appointed to take his father's place. That priest must put on the holy linen clothes. [33]He must make the Most Holy Place ready for service to the Lord. He must make the Meeting Tent and the altar ready for service to the Lord. He must remove the sins of himself and all the people of Israel so they will belong to the Lord. [34]That law for removing the sins of the Israelites so they will belong to the Lord will continue forever. You will do these things once a year."

So they did the things the Lord had commanded Moses.

OFFERING SACRIFICES

17 The Lord said to Moses, [2]"Speak to Aaron, his sons and all the people of Israel. Tell them: 'This is what the Lord has commanded: [3]An Israelite might sacrifice an ox, a lamb or a goat. He might kill it inside the camp or outside it. [4]But he should have brought the animal to the entrance to the Meeting Tent.[d] He should have given the animal as a gift to the Lord. If he didn't, he is guilty of killing. He must be separated from his people. [5]This rule is so people will bring their sacrifices to the Lord. They have been sacrificing in the open fields. But they must bring those animals to the Lord at the entrance of the Meeting Tent. They must bring them to the priest and offer them as fellowship offerings. [6]Then the priest will sprinkle the blood from those animals on the Lord's altar. It is near the entrance to the Meeting Tent. And the priest will burn the fat from those animals on the altar. This smell will be pleasing to the Lord. [7]They must not offer any more sacrifices to their goat idols. They have chased after those other gods. In that way they have acted like prostitutes.*d* These rules will continue for people from now on.'

8"Tell the people this: 'Someone might offer a burnt offering or sacrifice. He might be a citizen of Israel. Or he might be a traveler or foreigner living with you. 9That person must take his sacrifice to the entrance to the Meeting Tent. There he may offer it to the Lord. If he does not do this, he must be separated from his people.

10"'I will be against anyone who eats blood. It does not matter if it is a citizen of Israel or a foreigner living with you. I will separate that person from his people. 11This is because the life of the body is in the blood. And I have given you rules for pouring that blood on the altar. You must do this to remove your sins so you will belong to the Lord. It is the blood that removes the sins from your life so you will belong to the Lord. 12So I tell the people of Israel this: "None of you may eat blood. And no foreigner living among you may eat blood."

13"'Someone may catch a wild animal or bird that can be eaten. The person may be a citizen of Israel or a foreigner living among you. He must pour the blood on the ground and cover it with dirt. 14This is because if blood is still in the meat, the animal's life is still in it. So I give this command to the people of Israel: "Don't eat meat that still has blood in it. Anyone who eats blood must be separated from his people."

15"'Someone may eat an animal that died by itself. Or he may eat an animal that was killed by another animal. The person may be a citizen of Israel or a foreigner living among you. If he eats the animal, he will be unclean until evening. He must wash his clothes and whole body with water. 16If he does not wash his clothes and bathe his body, he will be guilty of sin.'"

RULES ABOUT SEXUAL RELATIONS

18 The Lord said to Moses, 2"Tell the people of Israel: 'I am the Lord your God. 3In the past you lived in Egypt. You must not do what was done in that country. And you must not do as they do in the land of Canaan where I am bringing you. Do not follow their customs. 4You must obey my rules and follow them. I am the Lord your God. 5Obey my laws and rules. A person who obeys my laws and rules will live because of them. I am the Lord.

6"'You must never have sexual relations with your close relatives. I am the Lord.

7"'You must not shame your father by having sexual relations with your mother. She is your mother. Do not have sexual relations with her. 8You must not have sexual relations with your father's wife. That would shame your father.

9"'You must not have sexual relations with your sister. She may be the daughter of your father or your mother. It doesn't matter if she was born in your house or somewhere else.

10"'You must not have sexual relations with your granddaughter. She may be your son's daughter or your daughter's daughter. That would bring shame on you.

11"'If your father and his wife have a daughter, she is your sister. You must not have sexual relations with her.

12"'You must not have sexual relations with your father's sister. She is your father's close relative. 13You must not have sexual relations with your mother's sister. She is your mother's close relative. 14You must not have sexual relations with the wife of your father's brother. This would shame him. His wife is your aunt.

15"'You must not have sexual relations with your daughter-in-law. She is your son's wife. Do not have sexual relations with her.

16"'You must not have sexual relations with your brother's wife. That would shame your brother.

¹⁷"You must not have sexual relations with both a woman and her daughter. And do not have sexual relations with this woman's granddaughter. It may be the daughter of her son or her daughter. They are her close relatives. It is evil to do this.

¹⁸"While your wife is still living, you must not take her sister as another wife. Do not have sexual relations with her.

¹⁹"You must not go near a woman to have sexual relations with her during her monthly period. She is unclean^d during this time.

²⁰"You must not have sexual relations with your neighbor's wife and make yourself unclean with her.

²¹"You must not give any of your children to be sacrificed to Molech.^{d} This will show that you do not respect your God. I am the Lord.

²²"You must not have sexual relations with a man as you would a woman. That is a hated sin.

²³"You must not have sexual relations with an animal and make yourself unclean with it. Also a woman must not have sexual relations with an animal. It is not natural.

²⁴"Don't make yourself unclean by any of these wrong things. I am forcing nations out of their countries because they did these sins. And I am giving their land to you. ²⁵The land has become unclean. So I punished it for its sins. And the land is throwing out those people who live there.

²⁶"You must obey my laws and rules. You must not do any of these hated sins. These rules are for the citizens of Israel. They are also for the people who live with you. ²⁷The people who lived in the land before you did all these hated things. So the land became unclean. ²⁸If you do these things, you will also make the land unclean. And it will throw you out as it threw out the nations before you. ²⁹Anyone who does these hated sins

must be separated from his people. ³⁰The people who lived in the land before you have done these hated sins. But you must not do them. You must obey my laws. Don't make yourself unclean by these hated sins. I am the Lord your God.'"

OTHER LAWS

19 The Lord said to Moses, ²"Tell all the people of Israel: 'I am the Lord your God. You must be holy because I am holy.

³"Each person among you must respect his mother and father. And you must keep my Sabbaths.^{d} I am the Lord your God.

⁴"Do not worship idols. Do not make statues of gods for yourselves. I am the Lord your God.

⁵"You may sacrifice a fellowship offering to the Lord. If you do, you must offer it so you will be accepted. ⁶You may eat it the same day you offer it. And you may also eat it on the next day. But if any is left on the third day, you must burn it up. ⁷If any of it is eaten on the third day, it is unclean.^{d} It will not be accepted. ⁸Anyone who eats it then will be guilty of sin. This is because he did not respect the holy things that belong to the Lord. He must be separated from his people.

⁹"You harvest your crops on your land. But do not harvest all the way to the corners of your fields. If grain falls onto the ground, don't gather it up. ¹⁰Don't pick all the grapes in your vineyards. And don't pick up the grapes that fall to the ground. You must leave those things for poor people. You must also leave them for people traveling through your country. I am the Lord your God.

¹¹"You must not steal. You must not cheat people. You must not lie to each other. ¹²You must not make a false promise by my name. If you do that, you will show that you don't respect your God. I am the Lord.

¹³"You must not cheat your neighbor. You must not rob him. You must not

keep a hired worker's salary all night until morning. ¹⁴You must not curse a deaf man. And you must not put something in front of a blind person to make him fall. But you must respect your God. I am the Lord.

¹⁵"Be fair in your judging. You must not show special favor to poor people or great people. You must be fair when you judge your neighbor. ¹⁶You must not spread false stories against other people. You must not do anything that would put your neighbor's life in danger. I am the Lord.

¹⁷"You must not hate your brother in your heart. If your neighbor does something wrong, tell him about it. If you do not, you will be partly to blame. ¹⁸Forget about the wrong things people do to you. You must not try to get even. Love your neighbor as you love yourself. I am the Lord.

¹⁹"Obey my laws. You must not mate two different kinds of cattle. You must not sow your field with two different kinds of seed. You must not wear clothing made from two different kinds of material mixed together.

²⁰"A man might have sexual relations with a slave girl of another man. But this slave girl has not been bought or given her freedom. If this happens, there must be punishment. But they are not to be put to death. This is because the woman was not free. ²¹The man must bring a male sheep as his penalty offering. He must bring it to the Lord at the entrance to the Meeting Tent.*d* ²²The priest will offer the male sheep as a penalty offering before the Lord. It will be for the man's sin. The priest will perform the acts to remove the sins of the man so he will belong to the Lord. Then the man will be forgiven for his sin.

²³"In the future you will enter your country. You will plant many kinds of trees for food. After planting a tree, wait three years before using its fruit. ²⁴In the fourth year the fruit from the tree will be

the Lord's. It will be a holy offering of praise to him. ²⁵Then in the fifth year, you may eat the fruit from the tree. The tree will then produce more fruit for you. I am the Lord your God.

²⁶"You must not eat anything with the blood in it.

"You must not try to tell the future by signs or black magic.

²⁷"You must not cut the hair on the sides of your heads. And you must not cut the edges of your beard. ²⁸You must not cut your body to show sadness for someone who died. Do not put tattoo marks on yourselves. I am the Lord.

²⁹"You must not make your daughter become a prostitute.*d* That only shows you do not respect her. If you do this, the country will be filled with all kinds of sin.

³⁰"Obey the laws about Sabbaths. You must respect my Most Holy Place. I am the Lord.

³¹"Do not go to mediums*d* or fortune-tellers for advice. If you do, you will become unclean. I am the Lord your God.

³²"Show respect to old people. Stand up when they come into the room. Show respect also to your God. I am the Lord.

³³"Do not mistreat foreigners living in your country. ³⁴Treat them just as you treat your own citizens. Love foreigners as you love yourselves, because you were foreigners one time. That was in Egypt. I am the Lord your God.

³⁵"Be fair when you judge people. And be fair when you measure and weigh things. ³⁶Your weighing baskets should be the right size. And your jars should hold the right amount of liquid. Your weights and balances should weigh correctly. I am the Lord your God. I brought you out of the land of Egypt.

³⁷"Remember all my laws and rules, and obey them. I am the Lord.'"

WARNINGS ABOUT VARIOUS SINS

20 The Lord said to Moses, ²"You must also tell the people of Israel these things: 'A person in your country might give one of his children to Molech.*d* That person must be killed. It doesn't matter if he is a citizen or a foreigner living in Israel. You must throw stones at him and kill him. ³I will be against him. I will separate him from his people. This is because he gave his children to Molech. He showed that he did not respect my holy name. And he made my Holy Place unclean.*d* ⁴The people of the community might ignore that person. They might not kill the one who gave his children to Molech. ⁵But I will be against him and his family. I will separate him from his people. I will do this to anyone who is unfaithful to me and who worships Molech.

⁶"'I will be against anyone who goes to mediums*d* and fortune-tellers for advice. He is being unfaithful to me. So I will separate him from his people.

⁷"'Be my holy people. Be holy because I am holy. I am the Lord your God. ⁸Remember and obey my laws. I am the Lord, and I have made you holy.

⁹"'Anyone who curses his father or mother must be put to death. He has cursed his father or mother. So he must be punished.

PUNISHMENTS FOR SEXUAL SINS

¹⁰"'A man might have sexual relations with his neighbor's wife. If he does, both the man and the woman are guilty of adultery.*d* So they must be put to death. ¹¹A man might have sexual relations with his father's wife. If he does, both the man and his father's wife must be put to death. They have brought it on themselves. That man has shamed his father.

¹²"'A man might have sexual relations with his daughter-in-law. If he does, both of them must be put to death. What they have done is not natural. It must be punished.

¹³"'A man might have sexual relations with another man as a man does with a woman. If he does, these two men have done a hated sin. They must be put to death. They have brought it on themselves.

¹⁴"'A man might have sexual relations with both a woman and her mother. This is evil. The people must burn that man and the two women in fire. Do this so that your people will not be evil.

¹⁵"'A man might have sexual relations with an animal. If he does, he must be put to death. And you must also kill the animal. ¹⁶A woman might have sexual relations with an animal. If she does, you must kill the woman and the animal. They must be put to death. They have brought it on themselves.

¹⁷"'It is shameful for a brother to marry his sister and to have sexual relations with her. In front of everyone they must both be separated from their people. The man has shamed his sister. And he is guilty of sin.

¹⁸"'A man might have sexual relations with a woman during her monthly period. If he does, both the woman and the man must be separated from their people. They sinned because they showed the source of her blood.

¹⁹"'Do not have sexual relations with your mother's sister or your father's sister. That would shame a close relative. Both of you are guilty of this sin.

²⁰"'A man must not have sexual relations with his uncle's wife. That would shame his uncle. That man and his uncle's wife would die without children. They are guilty of sin.

²¹"'It is unclean for a man to marry his brother's wife. That man has shamed his brother. They would have no children.

²²"'Remember all my laws and rules, and obey them. I am leading you to your own land. If you obey my laws and rules, that land will not throw you out. ²³I am forcing the people who live there out of that country ahead of you. Because they did all these sins I have hated them. Do not live the way those people lived.

²⁴"'I have told you that you will get their land. I will give it to you as your

very own. It is a land where much food grows. I am the Lord your God. I have set you apart from other people and made you my own. ²⁵So you must treat clean animals and birds differently from unclean animals. Do not make yourselves unclean by any of these unclean birds or animals or things that crawl on the ground. I have made them unclean for you. ²⁶I have set you apart from other people. So you must be holy to me. This is because I am the Lord, and I am holy.

²⁷"'A man or woman who is a medium*d* or a fortune-teller must be put to death. You must kill them with stones. They have brought it on themselves.'"

HOW PRIESTS MUST BEHAVE

21 The Lord said to Moses, "Tell these things to Aaron's sons, the priests: 'A priest must not make himself unclean*d* by touching a dead person. ²But if the dead person was one of his close relatives, he may touch him. The priest may make himself unclean if the dead person is his mother or father, son or daughter, brother or ³unmarried sister. This sister is close to him because she has no husband. So the priest may make himself unclean for her if she dies. ⁴But a priest must not make himself unclean if the dead person was only related to him by marriage.

⁵"'Priests must not shave their heads. They must not shave off the edges of their beards. They must not cut their bodies. ⁶Priests must be holy to their God. They must show respect for God's name. This is because they present the offerings made by fire to the Lord. This is the food of their God. So they must be holy.

⁷"'A priest serves God in a special way. So he must not marry an unclean prostitute*d* or a divorced woman. ⁸Treat the priest in a special way. Think of him as holy. This is because he offers up the food of your God. I am the Lord. I make you holy. And I am holy.

⁹"'If a priest's daughter makes herself unclean by becoming a prostitute, she shames her father. She must be burned with fire.

¹⁰"'The high priest was chosen from among his brothers. The special olive oil used in appointing people and things to the service of the Lord was poured on his head. He was appointed to wear the priestly clothes. So he must not do things to show his sadness in public. He must not let his hair go uncombed. He must not tear his clothes. ¹¹He must not go into a house where there is a dead body. He must not make himself unclean, even if it is his own father or mother. ¹²The high priest must not go out of the Holy Place. If he does and becomes unclean, he would make God's Holy Place unclean. The special oil used in appointing priests was poured on the high priest's head. This separated him from the rest of the people. I am the Lord.

¹³"'The high priest must marry a woman who is a virgin.*d* ¹⁴He must not marry a widow, a divorced woman or a prostitute. He must marry a virgin from his own people. ¹⁵This is so the people will respect his children as his own. I am the Lord. I have set the high priest apart for his special job.'"

¹⁶The Lord said to Moses, ¹⁷"Tell Aaron: 'Some of your descendants*d* might have something wrong with them. If they do, they must never offer the special food of their God. ¹⁸Anyone who has something wrong with him must not serve as priest. And he must not bring sacrifices to me. These people cannot serve as priests: blind men, crippled men, men with damaged faces, deformed men, ¹⁹men with a crippled foot or hand, ²⁰hunchbacks, dwarfs, men who have something wrong with their eyes, men who have an itching disease or a skin disease or men who have damaged sex glands.

²¹"'One of Aaron's descendants*d* might have something wrong with him. If he

does, he cannot make the offerings made by fire to the Lord. He has something wrong with him. He cannot offer the food of his God. ²²But he is from the family of priests. So he may eat the most holy food. He may also eat the holy food. ²³But he may not go through the curtain into the Most Holy Place. He may not go near the altar. He has something wrong with him. He must not make my Holy Place unfit. I am the Lord. I make these things holy.'"

²⁴So Moses told these things to Aaron, Aaron's sons and all the people of Israel.

22 The Lord said to Moses, ²"Tell Aaron and his sons: 'The people of Israel will give offerings to me. These offerings are holy, and they are mine. So you must respect these offerings. This will show that you respect my holy name. I am the Lord. ³The people of Israel made the offerings holy for me. One of your descendants*d* might be unclean*d* and touch the offerings. From now on, anyone who does must be separated from appearing before me. I am the Lord.

⁴"'One of Aaron's descendants might have one of the harmful skin diseases. Or he might discharge a body fluid. He cannot eat the holy offerings until he becomes clean. He can become unclean from touching a dead body or from his own semen.*n* ⁵He will become unclean if he touches any unclean crawling animal. He will become unclean if he touches an unclean person. It doesn't matter what made him unclean. ⁶Anyone who touches those things will become unclean until evening. That person must not eat the holy offerings. But if he washes with water, he may eat the holy offerings. ⁷He will be clean only after the sun goes down. Then he may eat the holy offerings. The offerings are his food.

⁸"'A priest might find an animal that died by itself. Or he might find one that

was killed by some other animal. He must not eat that dead animal. If he eats it, he will become unclean. I am the Lord.

⁹"'The priests must keep all the rules I have given. That way they will not become guilty. If they are careful, they will not die. I am the Lord. I have made them holy. ¹⁰Only people in a priest's family may eat the holy offerings. A visitor staying with the priest must not eat it. A hired worker must not eat it. ¹¹But the priest might buy a slave with his own money. If he does, that slave may eat the holy offerings. Slaves who were born in the priest's house may also eat the priest's food. ¹²A priest's daughter might marry a person who is not a priest. If she does, she must not eat any of the holy offerings. ¹³The husband of a priest's daughter might die. Or the daughter might become divorced. She might not have children to support her. So she might go back to her father's house where she lived as a child. If this happens, she may eat some of her father's food. But only people from a priest's family may eat this food.

¹⁴"'Someone might eat some of the holy offering by mistake. That person must pay back the priest for that holy food. He must also pay the priest another one-fifth of the price of that food.

¹⁵"'The people of Israel will give offerings to the Lord. These gifts become holy. So the priest must not treat these holy things as though they were not holy. ¹⁶The priests might allow someone who is not a priest to eat the holy offerings. If they do, they are treating those offerings as though they were not holy. The person who eats will become guilty. He will have to pay for it. I am the Lord. I make them holy.'"

¹⁷The Lord said to Moses, ¹⁸"Tell Aaron and his sons and all the people of Israel: 'A citizen of Israel or a foreigner

---

22:4 **semen** A man's body fluid by which he can make a woman pregnant.

living in Israel might want to bring a whole burnt offering. It might be for some special promise he has made. Or it might be a special gift he wanted to give to the Lord. ¹⁹If he does, he must bring a male animal. It must have nothing wrong with it. The gift might be a bull, a sheep or a goat. This is so it might be accepted for him. ²⁰He must not bring an animal that has something wrong with it. It will not be accepted for him.

²¹"'Someone might bring a fellowship offering to the Lord. That offering might be payment for a special promise the person made. Or it may be a special gift the person wanted to give the Lord. It might be a bull or a sheep. But it must be healthy. There must be nothing wrong with it. This is so it might be accepted for him. ²²You must not offer to the Lord any animal that is blind. It must not have broken bones or be crippled. It must not have running sores or any sort of skin disease. You must not offer any animals like these on the altar. They cannot be used as an offering by fire to the Lord.

²³"'Sometimes a bull or lamb is smaller than normal. Or it may not be perfectly formed. If someone wants to give that animal as a special gift to the Lord, it will be accepted. But it will not be accepted as payment for a special promise the person made.

²⁴"'An animal might have bruised, crushed, torn or cut sex glands. If it does, you must not offer that animal to the Lord in your own land. ²⁵You must not take such animals from foreigners as sacrifices to the Lord. This is because the animals have been hurt in some way. They have something wrong with them. They will not be accepted for you.'"

²⁶The Lord said to Moses, ²⁷"When an ox, a sheep or a goat is born, it must stay seven days with its mother. But from the eighth day on, this animal will be accepted as a sacrifice. It may be offered by fire to the Lord. ²⁸But you must not

kill the animal and its mother on the same day. This rule is the same for an ox or a sheep.

²⁹"You might want to offer some special offering of thanks to the Lord. But you must do it in a way that pleases the Lord. ³⁰You must eat the whole animal that same day. You must not leave any of the meat for the next morning. I am the Lord.

³¹"Remember my commands and obey them. I am the Lord. ³²Show respect for my holy name. You Israelites must remember that I am holy. I am the Lord. I have made you holy. ³³I brought you out of Egypt. I became your God. I am the Lord."

SPECIAL HOLIDAYS

23 The Lord said to Moses, ²"Tell the people of Israel: 'You will announce the Lord's appointed feasts as holy meetings. These are my special feasts.

THE SABBATH

³"'There are six days for you to work. But the seventh day will be a special day of rest. It is a day for a holy meeting. You must not do any work. It is a Sabbath*d* to the Lord in all your homes.

THE PASSOVER AND UNLEAVENED BREAD

⁴"'These are the Lord's appointed feasts. You will announce the holy meetings at the times set for them. ⁵The Lord's Passover*d* is on the fourteenth day of the first month. It begins at twilight. ⁶The Feast*d* of Unleavened Bread begins on the fifteenth day of the same month. You will eat bread made without yeast for seven days. ⁷On the first day of this feast you will have a holy meeting. On that day you must not do any work. ⁸For seven days you will bring an offering made by fire to the Lord. There will be a holy meeting on the seventh day. And on that day you must not do any regular work.'"

THE FEAST OF HARVESTS

⁹The Lord said to Moses, ¹⁰"Tell the people of Israel: 'You will enter the land

I will give you. You will gather its harvest. At that time you must bring the first bundle of grain from your harvest to the priest. [11]The priest will present the bundle before the Lord. Then it will be accepted for you. He will present the bundle on the day after the Sabbath.*d*

[12]"On the day when you present the bundle of grain, offer a male lamb. It must be one year old. There must be nothing wrong with it. It will be a burnt offering to the Lord. [13]You must also offer a grain offering. It should be four quarts of fine flour mixed with olive oil. It is an offering made by fire to the Lord. Its smell will be pleasing to the Lord. You must also offer a quart of wine as a drink offering. [14]First bring your offering to your God. Until you do this, do not eat the new grain, roasted grain or bread made from the new grain. This law will always continue for people from now on, wherever you live.

THE FEAST OF PENTECOST

[15]"Count seven weeks from the morning after the Sabbath.*d* (This is the Sabbath that you bring the bundle of grain to present as an offering.) [16]On the fiftieth day, you will bring a new grain offering to the Lord. This is the first day after the seventh week. [17]On that day bring two loaves of bread from your homes. That bread will be presented as an offering. Use yeast and four quarts of flour to make those loaves of bread. They will be your gift to the Lord from the first wheat of your harvest.

[18]"Offer one bull, two male sheep and seven male lambs. The lambs must be one year old. There must be nothing wrong with them. Offer them with their grain offerings and drink offerings. They will be a burnt offering to the Lord. They will be an offering made by fire. And the smell will be pleasing to the Lord. [19]You must also offer one male goat for a sin offering. You must offer two male, one-year-old lambs as a fellowship offering.

[20]"The priest will present the two lambs as an offering. He will present them with the bread from the first wheat of the harvest. They are holy to the Lord. They will belong to the priest. [21]On that same day you will call a holy meeting. You must not do any work that day. This law will continue for you from now on, wherever you live.

[22]"You will harvest your crops on your land. But do not harvest all the way to the corners of your field. If grain falls onto the ground, don't gather it up. Leave it for poor people and foreigners in your country. I am the Lord your God.'"

THE FEAST OF TRUMPETS

[23]Again the Lord said to Moses, [24]"Tell the people of Israel: 'On the first day of the seventh month you must have a special day of rest. There will be a holy meeting. Blow the trumpet for a special time of remembering. [25]Do not do any work. And bring an offering made by fire to the Lord.'"

THE DAY OF CLEANSING

[26]The Lord said to Moses, [27]"The Day of Cleansing will be on the tenth day of the seventh month. There will be a holy meeting. You will give up eating and bring an offering made by fire to the Lord. [28]Do not do any work on that day. This is because it is the Day of Cleansing. On that day the priests will go before the Lord. They will perform the acts to make you clean*d* from sin so you will belong to the Lord.

[29]"If anyone refuses to give up food on this day, he must be separated from his people. [30]If anyone works on this day, I will destroy him from among his people. [31]You must not do any work at all. This law will continue for people from now on wherever you live. [32]It will be a special day of rest for you. And you must not eat. You will start this special day of rest on the evening after the ninth day of the month. It will continue from that evening until the next evening."

THE FEAST OF SHELTERS

³³Again the Lord said to Moses, ³⁴"Tell the people of Israel: 'On the fifteenth day of the seventh month is the Feast^d of Shelters. This feast to the Lord will continue for seven days. ³⁵There will be a holy meeting on the first day. Do not do any work. ³⁶You will bring an offering made by fire to the Lord each day for seven days. On the eighth day you will have another holy meeting. And you will bring an offering made by fire to the Lord. This will be a holy meeting. Do not do any work.

³⁷("'These are the Lord's special feasts. There will be holy meetings on these feast days. You will bring offerings made by fire to the Lord. They will be whole burnt offerings, grain offerings, sacrifices and drink offerings. You must bring these gifts at the right times. ³⁸You must bring these offerings in addition to those for the Lord's Sabbath^d days. You must offer them in addition to offerings you give as payment for special promises. They are also in addition to special offerings you want to give to the Lord.)

³⁹"'So on the fifteenth day of the seventh month, celebrate the Lord's festival for seven days. By then you will have gathered in the crops of the land. You must rest on the first day and the seventh day. ⁴⁰On the first day you will take good fruit from the fruit trees. And you will take branches from palm, poplars and other leafy trees. You will celebrate before the Lord your God for seven days. ⁴¹Celebrate this festival to the Lord for seven days each year. This law will continue from now on. You will celebrate it in the seventh month. ⁴²Live in shelters for seven days. All the people born in Israel must live in shelters. ⁴³This is so that all your descendants^d will know I made Israel live in shelters. It was during the time I brought them out of Egypt. I am the Lord your God.'"

⁴⁴So Moses told the people of Israel about all of the Lord's appointed feast days.

THE LAMPSTAND AND THE HOLY BREAD

24 The Lord said to Moses, ²"Command the people of Israel to bring you pure oil from crushed olives. That oil is for the lamps. These lamps must never go out. ³Aaron will keep the lamps burning in the Meeting Tent.^d They will burn from evening until morning before the Lord. This will be in front of the curtain of the Box^d of the Agreement. This law will continue from now on. ⁴Aaron must always keep the lamps burning. They are on the lampstands of pure gold before the Lord.

⁵"Take fine flour and bake 12 loaves of bread with it. Use four quarts of flour for each loaf. ⁶Put them in two rows on the golden table before the Lord. Six loaves will be in each row. ⁷Put pure incense^d on each row. This is the memorial portion to take the place of the bread. It is an offering made by fire to the Lord. ⁸Every Sabbath^d day Aaron will put the bread in order before the Lord. This agreement with the people of Israel will continue forever. ⁹That bread will belong to Aaron and his sons. They will eat it in a holy place. This is because it is a most holy part of the offerings made by fire to the Lord. That bread is their share forever."

THE MAN WHO CURSED GOD

¹⁰Now there was a son of an Israelite woman and an Egyptian father. The son was walking among the Israelites. And a fight broke out in the camp between him and an Israelite. ¹¹The son of the Israelite woman began cursing and speaking against the Lord. So the people took him to Moses. (The mother's name was Shelomith. She was the daughter of Debri from the family of Dan.) ¹²The people held him as a prisoner. They waited for the Lord's command to be made clear to them.

¹³Then the Lord said to Moses, ¹⁴"Take the one who spoke against me outside the camp. Then bring together all the people who heard him. They must put

their hands on his head.[n] Then all the people must throw stones at him and kill him. [15]Tell the people of Israel this: 'If anyone curses his God, he is guilty of sin. [16]Anyone who speaks against the Lord must be put to death. All the people must kill him by throwing stones at him. Foreigners must be punished just like the person born in Israel. If someone speaks against the Lord, he must be put to death.

[17]"'If someone kills another person, he must be put to death. [18]Someone might kill an animal that belongs to another person. If he does, he must give that person another animal to take its place. [19]And someone might cause an injury to his neighbor. If he does, the same kind of injury must be given back to him. [20]A broken bone must be paid for a broken bone, an eye for an eye and a tooth for a tooth. In the same way someone injures another person, he must be injured in return. [21]So anyone who kills another person's animal must give that person another animal to take its place. But the person who kills another person must be put to death.

[22]"'The law will be the same for the foreigner as for those from your own country. I am the Lord your God.'"

[23]Then Moses spoke to the people of Israel. And they took the person who had cursed outside the camp. Then they killed him with stones. So the people of Israel did as the Lord had commanded Moses.

THE TIME OF REST FOR THE LAND

25 The Lord spoke to Moses at Mount Sinai. He said, [2]"Tell the people of Israel this: 'I will give you land. When you enter it, let it have a special time of rest. This will be to honor the Lord. [3]You may plant seed in your field for six years. You may trim your vineyards for six years and bring in their

fruits. [4]But during the seventh year, you must let the land rest. This will be a special time to honor the Lord. You must not plant seed in your field or trim your vineyards. [5]You must not cut the crops that grow by themselves after harvest. You must not gather the grapes from your vines that are not trimmed. The land will have a year of rest.

[6]"'You may eat whatever the land produces during that year of rest. It will be food for your men and women servants. It will be food for your hired workers and the foreigners living in your country. [7]It will also be food for your cattle and the wild animals of your land. Whatever the land produces may be eaten.

THE YEAR OF JUBILEE

[8]"'Count off seven groups of 7 years. This will be 49 years. During that time there will be 7 years of rest for the land. [9]On the Day of Cleansing,[d] you must blow the horn of a male sheep. This will be on the tenth day of the seventh month. You must blow the horn through the whole country. [10]Make the fiftieth year a special year. Announce freedom for all the people living in your country. This time will be called Jubilee.[n] Each of you will go back to his own property. And each of you will go back to his own family and family group. [11]The fiftieth year will be a special time for you to celebrate. Don't plant seeds. Don't harvest the crops that grow by themselves. Don't gather grapes from the vines that are not trimmed. [12]That year is Jubilee. It will be a holy time for you. You may eat the crops that come from the field. [13]In the year of Jubilee each person will go back to his own property.

[14]"'Don't cheat your neighbor when you sell your land to him. And don't let him cheat you when you buy land from him. [15]You might want to buy your

24:14 put . . . head This shows that all these people were sharing in punishing the one who spoke against God.
25:10 Jubilee This word comes from the Hebrew word for a horn of a male sheep.

neighbor's land. If you do, count the number of years since the last Jubilee. Use that number to decide the right price. If he sells the land to you, count the number of years left for harvesting crops. Use that number to decide the right price. ¹⁶If there are many years, the price will be high. If there are only a few years, lower the price. This is because your neighbor is really selling only a few crops to you. At the next Jubilee the land will again belong to his family. ¹⁷You must not cheat each other. You respect your God. I am the Lord your God.

¹⁸"'Remember my laws and rules, and obey them. Then you will live safely in the land. ¹⁹The land will give good crops to you. You will eat as much as you want. And you will live safely in the land.

²⁰"'But you might ask, "If we don't plant seeds or gather crops, what will we eat the seventh year?" ²¹Don't worry. I will send you a great blessing during the sixth year. That year the land will produce enough crops for 3 years. ²²When you plant in the eighth year, you will still be eating from the old crop. You will eat the old crop until the harvest of the ninth year.

PROPERTY LAWS

²³"'The land really belongs to me. So you can't sell it forever. You are only foreigners and travelers living for a time on my land. ²⁴People might sell their land. But the family will always get its land back. ²⁵A person in your country might become very poor. He might be so poor that he must sell his land. So his close relatives must come and buy it back for him. ²⁶A person might not have a close relative to buy back his land for him. But he might get enough money to buy it back himself. ²⁷He must count the years since the land was sold. He must use that number to decide how much to pay for the land. Then he may buy it back. And the land will be his again. ²⁸But he might not find enough money to buy it back for

himself. Then the one who bought it will keep it until the year of Jubilee.ᵈ But during that celebration, the land will go back to the first owner's family.

²⁹"'Someone may sell a home in a walled city. But, for a full year after he sold it, he has the right to buy it back. ³⁰But the owner might not buy back the house before a full year is over. If he doesn't, the house in the walled city will belong to the one who bought it. It will belong to his future sons. The house will not go back to the first owner at Jubilee. ³¹But houses in small towns without walls are like open country. They can be bought back. And they must be returned to their first owner at Jubilee.

³²"'The Levites may always buy back their houses. This is true in the cities which belong to them. ³³Someone might buy a house from a Levite. But that house in the Levites' city will again belong to the Levites in the Jubilee. This is because houses in Levite cities belong to the people of Levi. The people of Israel gave these cities to the Levites. ³⁴Also the fields and pastures around the Levites' cities cannot be sold. Those fields belong to the Levites forever.

RULES FOR SLAVE OWNERS

³⁵"'Someone from your country might become too poor to support himself. Help him to live among you as you would a stranger or foreigner. ³⁶Do not charge him any interest on money you loan to him. Respect your God. And let the poor man live among you. ³⁷Don't lend him money for interest. Don't try to make a profit from the food he buys. ³⁸I am the Lord your God. I brought you out of the land of Egypt. I did it to give the land of Canaan to you and to become your God.

³⁹"'Someone from your country might become very poor. He might even sell himself as a slave to you. If he does, you must not make him work like a slave. ⁴⁰He will be like a hired worker. And he

will be like a visitor with you until the year of Jubilee.[d] [41]Then he may leave you. He may take his children and go back to his family and the land of his ancestors. [42]This is because the Israelites are my servants. I brought them out of slavery in Egypt. They must not become slaves again. [43]You must not rule this person cruelly. You must respect your God.

[44]"You may buy men and women slaves from other nations around you. [45]Also you may buy children as slaves. These children must come from the families of foreigners living in your land. These child slaves will belong to you. [46]You may even pass these foreign slaves on to your children after you die. You can make them slaves forever. But you must not rule cruelly over your own brothers, the Israelites.

[47]"A foreigner or visitor among you might become rich. And someone in your country might become poor. The poor man might sell himself as a slave to a foreigner living among you. Or he might sell himself to a member of a foreigner's family. [48]The poor man has the right to be bought back and become free. One of his relatives may buy him back. [49]His uncle or his uncle's son may buy him back. One of his close relatives may buy him back. Or if he gets enough money, he may pay the money himself. Then he will be free again.

[50]"How do you decide the price? You must count the years from the time he sold himself to the foreigner. And count up to the next year of Jubilee. Use that number to decide the price. This is because the person really only hired himself out for a certain number of years. [51]There might still be many years before the year of Jubilee. If so, the person must pay back a large part of the price. [52]There might only be a few years left until Jubilee. If so, the person must pay a small part of the first price. [53]But he will live like a hired man with the foreigner every year. Don't let the foreigner rule cruelly over him.

[54]"That person will become free, even if no one buys him back. At the year of Jubilee, he and his children will become free. [55]This is because the people of Israel are my servants. I brought them out of slavery in Egypt. I am the Lord your God.

REWARDS FOR OBEYING GOD

26 "Don't make idols for yourselves. Don't set up statues or memorials. Don't put stone statues in your land to bow down to. This is because I am the Lord your God.

[2]"Remember my Sabbaths,[d] and respect my Holy Place. I am the Lord.

[3]"Remember my laws and commands, and obey them. [4]If you do these things, I will give you rains at the right season. The land will produce crops. And the trees of the field will produce their fruit. [5]Your threshing[d] will continue until the grape harvest. And your grape harvest will continue until it is time to plant. Then you will have plenty to eat. You will live safely in your land. [6]I will give peace to your country. You will lie down in peace. No one will make you afraid. I will keep harmful animals out of your country. And armies will not pass through your country.

[7]"You will chase your enemies and defeat them. You will kill them with your sword. [8]Five of you will chase 100 men. And 100 of you will chase 10,000 men. You will defeat your enemies and kill them with your sword.

[9]"Then I will show kindness to you. I will let you have many children. I will keep my agreement with you. [10]You will have enough crops to last for more than a year. You will harvest the new crops. And you will have to throw out the old crops to make room for the new ones. [11]Also I will place my Holy Tent[d] among you. I will not turn away from you. [12]I will walk with you and be your God. And

you will be my people. 13I am the Lord your God. You were slaves in Egypt. You were bent low from the heavy weights you carried as slaves. But I broke the heavy weights that were on your shoulders. I let you walk proudly again.

PUNISHMENT FOR NOT OBEYING GOD

14"'But you must obey me. You must obey all my commands. 15If you refuse to obey all my laws and commands, you have broken our agreement. 16If you do that, I will cause terrible things to happen to you. I will cause you to have disease and fever. They will destroy your eyes and kill you. You will not have success when you plant your seed. And your enemy will eat your crops. 17I will be against you, and your enemies will defeat you. These enemies hate you. And they will rule over you. You will run away even when no one is chasing you.

18"'If you still do not obey me, I will punish you seven times more for your sins. 19And I will also break the great cities that make you proud. The skies will not give rain. The earth will not produce crops. 20You will work hard, but it will not help. Your land will not grow any crops. Your trees will not give their fruit.

21"'If you still turn against me and refuse to obey me, I will beat you seven times harder. The more you sin, the more you will be punished. 22I will send wild animals to attack you. They will take your children away from you. They will destroy your cattle. They will make you so few in number the roads will be empty.

23"'If you don't learn your lesson after all these things, and if you still turn against me, 24I will also turn against you. I will punish you seven more times for your sins. 25You broke my agreement, and I will punish you. I will bring armies against you. You will go into your cities for safety. But I will cause diseases to spread among you. Then your enemy will defeat you. 26There will be very little

bread to eat. Ten women will be able to cook all your bread in one oven. They will measure each piece of bread. You will eat, but you will still be hungry.

27"'If you still refuse to listen to me, and if you still turn against me, 28I will really show my anger. I will punish you seven more times for your sins. 29You will eat the bodies of your sons and daughters. 30I will destroy your places where false gods are worshiped. I will cut down your incense*d* altars. I will pile your dead bodies on the lifeless forms of your idols. I will hate you. 31I will destroy your cities. I will make your holy places empty. I will not smell the pleasing smell of your offerings. 32I will make the land empty. Your enemies who come to live in it will be shocked at it. 33I will scatter you among the nations. I will pull out my sword and destroy you. Your land will become empty. Your cities will become waste. 34You will be taken to your enemy's country. So your land will finally get its rest. It will enjoy its time of rest all the time it lies empty. 35During the time the land is empty, it will rest. It will have the rest you should have given it while you lived in it.

36"'Those who are left alive will lose their courage in the land of their enemies. They will be frightened of everything. They will be frightened by even the sound of a leaf being blown by the wind. They will run as if someone were chasing them with a sword. They will fall even when no one is chasing them. 37They will run as if someone were chasing them with a sword. They will fall over each other, even though no one is chasing them. You will not be strong enough to stand up against your enemies. 38You will die among other nations. You will disappear in your enemies' countries. 39So those who are left alive will rot away in their enemies' countries. They will rot away because of their sins and their ancestors' sins.

THERE IS ALWAYS HOPE

[40]"'But maybe the people will confess their sins and the sins of their ancestors. Maybe they will admit they turned against me and sinned against me. [41]That made me turn against them. So I sent them into the land of their enemies. These disobedient people might be sorry for what they did. They might accept punishment for their sin. [42]If they do, I will remember my agreement with Jacob. I will remember my agreement with Isaac and Abraham. And I will remember the land. [43]The land will be empty. It will enjoy its time of rest. Then those who are left alive will accept the punishment for their sins. They will learn that they were punished because they hated my laws. And they refused to obey my rules. [44]They truly sinned. But if they come to me for help, I will not turn away from them. I will listen to them even in the land of their enemies. I will not completely destroy them. I will not break my agreement with them. This is because I am the Lord their God. [45]For their good I will remember the agreement with their ancestors. I brought their ancestors out of the land of Egypt. I did it so I could become their God. The other nations saw these things. I am the Lord.'"

[46]These are the laws, rules and teachings the Lord gave the people of Israel. He gave these laws to the Israelites through Moses. This was at Mount Sinai.

PROMISES ARE IMPORTANT

27 The Lord said to Moses, [2]"Tell the people of Israel: 'Someone might make a special promise to the Lord. He might promise to give himself or another person as a servant to the Lord. That person will then begin to serve the Lord in a special way. The priest must set a certain price for that person. That is the price that would have to be paid to free the person from his special promise to the Lord. [3]The price for a man 20 to 60 years old is about 1 1/4

pounds of silver. (You must use the measure as set by the Holy Place.) [4]The price for a woman 20 to 60 years old is about 12 ounces of silver. [5]The price for a man 5 to 20 years old is about 8 ounces of silver. The price for a woman 5 to 20 years old is about 4 ounces of silver. [6]The price for a baby boy 1 month to 5 years old is about 2 ounces of silver. For a baby girl the price is about 1 1/2 ounces of silver. [7]The price for a man 60 years old or older is about 6 ounces of silver. The price for a woman 60 years old or older is about 4 ounces of silver.

[8]"'A person might be too poor to pay the price. If he is, bring him to the priest. The priest will decide how much money the person can afford to pay.

GIFTS TO THE LORD

[9]"'Some animals may be used as sacrifices to the Lord. If someone promises to bring one of these animals, it will become holy. [10]That person must not try to put another animal in its place. He must not try to exchange it for something else. He must not try to exchange a good animal for a bad animal. And he must not exchange a bad animal for a good animal. If he tries to exchange animals, both animals will become holy.

[11]"'Unclean[d] animals cannot be offered as sacrifices to the Lord. Someone might bring one of them to the Lord. If he does, that animal must be brought to the priest. [12]The priest will decide a price for the animal. The price will be according to whether the animal is good or bad. If the priest decides a price, that is the price for the animal. [13]If the person wants to buy back the animal, he must add an additional one-fifth to the price.

VALUE OF A HOUSE

[14]"'A person might give his house as holy to the Lord. If he does, the priest must decide its value. The price will be according to whether the house is good or bad. If the priest decides a price, that

is the price for the house. [15]But the person who gives the house might want to buy it back. If he does, he must add an additional one-fifth to the price. Then the house will belong to him again.

VALUE OF LAND

[16]"'A person might give part of his fields to the Lord. The value of those fields will depend on how much seed is needed to plant them. It will cost about one and one-fourth pounds of silver for each six bushels of barley seed needed. [17]The person might give his field at the year of Jubilee.[d] Then its value will be what the priest decides. [18]But he might give his field after the Jubilee. If he does, the priest must decide the exact price. He must count the number of years to the next year of Jubilee. Then he will use that number to decide the exact price. [19]The person who gave the field might want to buy it back. If he does, he must add one-fifth to that price. Then the field will belong to him again.

[20]"'If he does not buy back the field, it will always belong to the priest. If it is sold to someone else, the first person cannot buy it back. [21]But the person might not buy back the land. If he doesn't, at the year of Jubilee, it will remain holy to the Lord. It will belong to the priest forever. It will become the property of the priests.

[22]"'Someone may give a field he has bought to the Lord. But it may not be a part of his family land. [23]If he gives a field, the priest must count the years to the next Jubilee. He must decide the price for the land. Then that land will belong to the Lord. [24]At the year of Jubilee, the land will go back to its first owner. It will go back to the family who sold the land.

[25]"'You must use the measure as set by the Holy Place in paying these prices. It weighs two-fifths of an ounce.

VALUE OF ANIMALS

[26]"'People may give cattle and sheep to the Lord. But if an animal is the first one born to its parent, it already belongs to the Lord. So people may not give these animals again. [27]If the animal is unclean,[d] the person must buy it back. The priest will decide the price of the animal. And the person must add one-fifth to that price. If he does not buy it back, the priest must sell it. He will sell it for the price he had decided.

[28]"'There is a special kind of gift that people give to the Lord. It may be a person, animal or field from the family property. That gift cannot be bought back or sold. It is most holy to the Lord.

[29]"'If a person is given for the purpose of being destroyed, he cannot be bought back. He must be put to death.

[30]"'One-tenth of all crops belongs to the Lord. This includes the crops from fields and the fruit from trees. That one-tenth belongs to the Lord. [31]A person might want to get back his tenth. If he does, he must add one-fifth to its price and buy it back.

[32]"'The priest will take every tenth animal from a person's cattle or sheep. It will belong to the Lord. [33]The owner should not pick out the good animals from the bad. He should not exchange one animal for another. If he does exchange it, both animals will become holy. They cannot be bought back.'"

[34]These are the commands the Lord commanded at Mount Sinai. They are for the people of Israel.

NUMBERS

THE PEOPLE OF ISRAEL ARE COUNTED

1 The Lord spoke to Moses in the Meeting Tent.*d* This was in the Desert of Sinai. It was on the first day of the second month. This was in the second year after the people of Israel left Egypt. The Lord said to Moses: 2"Count all the people of Israel. List the name of each man with his family and family group. 3You and Aaron must count all the men of Israel 20 years old or older. They will serve in the army of Israel. List them by their divisions. 4One man from each tribe*d* will help you. He is to be the leader of his family. 5These are the names of the men who will help you:

from the tribe of Reuben—Elizur son of Shedeur;
6from the tribe of Simeon—Shelumiel son of Zurishaddai;
7from the tribe of Judah—Nahshon son of Amminadab;
8from the tribe of Issachar—Nethanel son of Zuar;
9from the tribe of Zebulun—Eliab son of Helon;
10from the tribe of Ephraim son of Joseph—Elishama son of Ammihud;
from the tribe of Manasseh son of Joseph—Gamaliel son of Pedahzur;
11from the tribe of Benjamin—Abidan son of Gideoni;
12from the tribe of Dan—Ahiezer son of Ammishaddai;
13from the tribe of Asher—Pagiel son of Ocran;
14from the tribe of Gad—Eliasaph son of Deuel;
15from the tribe of Naphtali—Ahira son of Enan."

16All these men were chosen by the people to be leaders of their tribes. They were the leaders of their family groups.

17Moses and Aaron took these men who had been picked. 18And Moses and Aaron called all the people of Israel together. This was the first day of the second month. Then the people were listed by their families and family groups. All the men who were 20 years old or older were listed by name. 19Moses did exactly what the Lord had commanded. Moses listed the people while they were in the Desert of Sinai.

20The tribe of Reuben was counted. Reuben was the first son born to Israel. All the men 20 years old or older who were able to serve in the army were listed. They were each listed by name with their families and family groups. 21The tribe of Reuben totaled 46,500 men.

22The tribe of Simeon was counted. All the men 20 years old or older who were able to serve in the army were listed. They were each listed by name with their families and family groups. 23The tribe of Simeon totaled 59,300 men.

24The tribe of Gad was counted. All the men 20 years old or older who were able to serve in the army were listed. They were listed by name with their families and family groups. 25The tribe of Gad totaled 45,650 men.

26The tribe of Judah was counted. All the men 20 years old or older who were able to serve in the army were listed. They were listed by name with their families and family groups. 27The tribe of Judah totaled 74,600 men.

28The tribe of Issachar was counted. All the men 20 years old or older who were able to serve in the army were listed. They were listed by name with their families and family groups. 29The tribe of Issachar totaled 54,400 men.

30The tribe of Zebulun was counted. All the men 20 years old or older who were able to serve in the army were listed. They were listed by name with their families and family groups. 31The tribe of Zebulun totaled 57,400 men.

32The tribe of Ephraim was counted. (Ephraim was a son of Joseph.) All the men 20 years old or older who were able to serve in the army were listed. They were listed by name with their families and family groups. 33The tribe of Ephraim totaled 40,500 men.

34The tribe of Manasseh was counted. (Manasseh was also a son of Joseph.) All the men 20 years old or older who were able to serve in the army were listed. They were listed by name with their families and family groups. 35The tribe of Manasseh totaled 32,200 men.

36The tribe of Benjamin was counted. All the men 20 years old or older who were able to serve in the army were listed. They were listed by name with their families and family groups. 37The tribe of Benjamin totaled 35,400 men.

38The tribe of Dan was counted. All the men 20 years old or older who were able to serve in the army were listed. They were listed by name with their families and family groups. 39The tribe of Dan totaled 62,700 men.

40The tribe of Asher was counted. All the men 20 years old or older who were able to serve in the army were listed. They were listed by name with their families and family groups. 41The tribe of Asher totaled 41,500 men.

42The tribe of Naphtali was counted. All the men 20 years old or older who were able to serve in the army were listed. They were listed by name with their families and family groups. 43The tribe of Naphtali totaled 53,400 men.

44Moses, Aaron and the 12 leaders of Israel counted these men. There was 1 leader from each of the families. 45Every man of Israel 20 years old or older who was able to serve in the army was counted. Each man was listed with his family. 46The total number of men was 603,550.

47The families from the tribe of Levi were not listed with the others. 48The Lord had told Moses: 49"Do not count the tribe of Levi or include them with the other Israelites. 50But make the Levites responsible for the Holy Tent*d* of the Agreement. They must take care of it and everything that is with it. They must carry the Holy Tent and everything in it. They must take care of it and make their camp around it. 51Any time the Holy Tent is moved, the Levites must take it down. Any time it is set up, the Levites must do it. If anyone else goes near the Holy Tent, he will be put to death. 52The Israelites will make their camps in separate divisions, each man near his family flag. 53But the Levites must make their camp around the Holy Tent of the Agreement. Then I will not be angry with the Israelites. The Levites will take care of the Holy Tent of the Agreement."

54So the Israelites did everything the Lord commanded Moses.

THE CAMP ARRANGEMENT

2 The Lord said to Moses and Aaron: 2"The Israelites should make their camps around the Meeting Tent.*d* But they should not camp too close to it. Each person should camp under the flag of his division near the banner of his family group."

3The camp of Judah will be on the east side, where the sun rises. They will camp by divisions there under their flag. The leader of the people of Judah is Nahshon son of Amminadab. 4There are 74,600 men in his division.

5Next to them the tribe*d* of Issachar will camp. The leader of the people of Issachar is Nethanel son of Zuar. 6There are 54,400 men in his division.

7Next is the tribe of Zebulun. The leader of the people of Zebulun is Eliab son of Helon. 8There are 57,400 men in his division.

9There are a total of 186,400 men in the camp of Judah. They are in their divisions. They will be the first to march out of camp.

10The divisions of the camp of Reuben will be south of the Holy Tent. They will camp under their flag. The leader of the people of Reuben is Elizur son of Shedeur. ¹¹There are 46,500 men in his division.

¹²Next to them the tribe of Simeon will camp. The leader of the people of Simeon is Shelumiel son of Zurishaddai. ¹³There are 59,300 men in his division.

¹⁴Next is the tribe of Gad. The leader of the people of Gad is Eliasaph son of Deuel. ¹⁵There are 45,650 men in his division.

¹⁶There are a total of 151,450 men in the camp of Reuben. They are in their divisions. They will be the second group to march out of camp.

¹⁷When the Levites move the Meeting Tent, they will be in between the other camps. The tribes will move in the same order as they camp. Each person will be with his family flag.

¹⁸The divisions of the camp of Ephraim will be on the west side. They will camp under their flag. The leader of the people of Ephraim is Elishama son of Ammihud. ¹⁹There are 40,500 men in his division.

²⁰Next to them the tribe of Manasseh will camp. The leader of the people of Manasseh is Gamaliel son of Pedahzur. ²¹There are 32,200 men in his division.

²²Next to them the tribe of Benjamin will camp. The leader of the people of Benjamin is Abidan son of Gideoni. ²³There are 35,400 men in his division.

²⁴There are a total of 108,100 men in the camp of Ephraim. They are in their divisions. They will be the third group to march out of camp.

²⁵The divisions of the camp of Dan will be on the north side. They will camp under their flag. The leader of the people of Dan is Ahiezer son of Ammishaddai. ²⁶There are 62,700 men in his division.

²⁷Next to them the tribe of Asher will camp. The leader of the people of Asher is Pagiel son of Ocran. ²⁸There are 41,500 men in his division.

²⁹Next is the tribe of Naphtali. The leader of the people of Naphtali is Ahira son of Enan. ³⁰There are 53,400 men in his division.

³¹There are 157,600 men in the camp of Dan. They will be the last to march out of camp. They will travel under their own flag.

³²These are the Israelites who were counted by families. The total number of Israelites in the camps, counted by divisions, is 603,550. ³³Moses did not count the Levites among the other people of Israel. This is what the Lord had commanded.

³⁴So the Israelites obeyed everything the Lord commanded Moses. They camped under their flags. Each person traveled with his family and family group.

AARON'S FAMILY, THE PRIESTS

3 This is the family history of Aaron and Moses. This was at the time the Lord talked to Moses on Mount Sinai.

²Aaron had four sons. Nadab was the oldest. Then Aaron had Abihu, Eleazar and Ithamar. ³Those were the names of Aaron's sons. They were appointed to serve as priests. ⁴But Nadab and Abihu died when they sinned in the presence of the Lord. They made an offering to the Lord in the Desert of Sinai. But they used the wrong kind of fire. They had no sons. So Eleazar and Ithamar served as priests during the lifetime of their father Aaron.

⁵The Lord said to Moses, ⁶"Bring the tribeᵈ of Levi to Aaron the priest. They must help him. ⁷They will help him and all the Israelites at the Meeting Tent.ᵈ They will do the work of the Holy Tent. ⁸The Levites must take care of everything in the Meeting Tent. They will serve the people of Israel by doing the work in the Holy Tent. ⁹Give the Levites to Aaron and his sons. Of all the Israelites, the Levites are given completely to him. ¹⁰Appoint Aaron and his sons to serve as priests. Anyone else who comes near the holy things must be put to death."

¹¹The Lord also said to Moses, ¹²"I am choosing the Levites from all the Israelites. They will take the place of all the firstbornᵈ children of Israel. The

Levites will be mine. [13]All the firstborn are mine. When you were in Egypt, I killed all the firstborn children of the Egyptians. I took all the firstborn of Israel to be mine. Firstborn animals and children are mine. I am the Lord."

[14]The Lord again talked to Moses in the Desert of Sinai. The Lord said, [15]"Count the Levites by families and family groups. Count every male one month old or older." [16]So Moses obeyed the Lord and counted them all.

[17]Levi had three sons. Their names were Gershon, Kohath and Merari. [18]The Gershonite family groups were Libni and Shimei. [19]The Kohathite family groups were Amram, Izhar, Hebron and Uzziel. [20]The Merarite family groups were Mahli and Mushi.

These were the family groups that belonged to the Levites.

[21]The family groups of Libni and Shimei belonged to Gershon. They were all the Gershonite family groups. [22]They had 7,500 males one month or older. [23]The Gershonite family groups camped on the west side, behind the Holy Tent. [24]The leader of the families of Gershon was Eliasaph son of Lael. [25]In the Meeting Tent the Gershonites were responsible for taking care of these things: the Holy Tent, its covering, the curtain at the entrance to the Meeting Tent, [26]the curtains in the courtyard, the curtain at the entry to the courtyard around the Holy Tent and the altar, the ropes and all the work connected with these things.

[27]The family groups of Amram, Izhar, Hebron and Uzziel belonged to Kohath. They were all the Kohathite family groups. [28]They had 8,600 males one month old or older. They were responsible for taking care of the Holy Place. [29]The Kohathite family groups camped south of the Holy Tent. [30]The leader of the Kohathite families was Elizaphan

son of Uzziel. [31]They were responsible for the Holy Box,[d] the table, the lampstand, the altars, the tools of the holy place, the curtain and all the work connected with these things. [32]The main leader of the Levites was Eleazar son of Aaron, the priest. Eleazar was in charge of all those responsible for the Holy Place.

[33]The family groups of Mahli and Mushi belonged to Merari. They were all the Merarite family groups. [34]They had 6,200 males one month old or older. [35]The leader of the Merari families was Zuriel son of Abihail. They were to camp north of the Holy Tent. [36]The Merarites were responsible for the frame of the Holy Tent, the braces, the posts, the bases and all the work connected with these things. [37]They were also responsible for the posts in the courtyard around the Holy Tent and their bases, tent pegs and ropes.

[38]Moses, Aaron and his sons camped east of the Holy Tent. They were in front of the Meeting Tent. They were responsible for the Holy Place. They did this for the Israelites. Anyone else who came near the Holy Place was to be put to death.

[39]Moses and Aaron counted the Levite men. The Lord commanded this. There were 22,000 males one month old or older.

LEVITES TAKE THE PLACE OF THE FIRSTBORN SONS

[40]The Lord said to Moses, "Count all the firstborn[d] sons in Israel one month old or older. List their names. [41]Take the Levites for me instead of the firstborn sons of Israel. Take the animals of the Levites instead of the firstborn animals from the rest of Israel. I am the Lord."

[42]So Moses did what the Lord commanded. Moses counted all the firstborn sons of the Israelites. [43]He listed all the firstborn sons one month old or older. There were 22,273 names.

[44]The Lord also said to Moses, [45]"Take the Levites instead of all the firstborn

sons of the Israelites. And take the animals of the Levites instead of the animals of the other people. The Levites are mine. I am the Lord. [46]There are 273 more firstborn sons than Levites. [47]So collect two ounces of silver for each of the 273 sons. Use the measure as set by the Holy Place. It weighs two-fifths of an ounce. [48]Give the silver to Aaron and his sons. It is the payment for the 273 Israelites."

[49]So Moses collected the money for the people the Levites could not replace. [50]Moses collected the silver from the firstborn of the Israelites. He collected 35 pounds of silver, using the measure set by the Holy Place. [51]So Moses obeyed the Lord. He gave the silver to Aaron and his sons.

THE JOBS OF THE KOHATH FAMILY

4 The Lord said to Moses and Aaron, [2]"Count the Kohathites among the Levites. Count them by family groups and families. [3]Count the men from 30 to 50 years old. They will serve in the Meeting Tent.[d]

[4]"They are responsible for the most holy things in the Meeting Tent. [5]When the Israelites move, Aaron and his sons must go into the Holy Tent. They are to take down the curtain. Then they must cover the Holy Box[d] of the Agreement with it. [6]Over this they must put a covering made from fine leather. Then they must spread the solid blue cloth over it. And they must put the poles in the rings on the Holy Box.

[7]"Then they must spread a blue cloth over the table. This is the table for the bread that shows we are in God's presence. They must put the plates, spoons, bowls and the jars for drink offerings on the table. They must leave the bread on the table. [8]Then they must put a red cloth over all of these things. They must cover everything with fine leather. Then they must put the poles in place.

[9]"With a blue cloth they must cover the lampstand, its lamps, its wick trimmers and trays. They must cover all the jars for the oil used in the lamps. [10]Then they must wrap everything in fine leather. They must put all these things on a frame for carrying them.

[11]"They must spread a blue cloth over the gold altar. Then they must cover it with fine leather. They must put its poles in place.

[12]"They must gather everything used for serving in the Holy Place. They must wrap them in a blue cloth. Then they must cover that with fine leather. They must put these things on a frame for carrying them.

[13]"They must clean the ashes off the bronze altar. Then they must spread a purple cloth over it. [14]They must gather all the things used for serving at the altar. These are the pans for carrying the fire, meat forks, shovels and bowls. They must put them on the bronze altar. Then they must spread a covering of fine leather over it. They must put the carrying poles in the rings on the altar.

[15]"When the camp is ready to move, have Aaron and his sons cover all the holy things. Then the Kohathites may go in and carry away those things. This way they won't touch the holy things and die. It is the Kohathites' job to carry the things that are in the Meeting Tent.

[16]"Eleazar son of Aaron, the priest, will be responsible for the Holy Tent. And he is responsible for everything in it: the oil for the lamp, the sweet-smelling incense,[d] the continual grain offering and the oil used to appoint priests and things to the Lord's service."

[17]The Lord said to Moses and Aaron, [18]"Don't let the Kohathites be destroyed from the Levites. [19]Do this for the Kohathites. Then they may go near the Most Holy Place and not die. Aaron and his sons must go in and show each Kohathite what to do. And they must show each man what to carry. [20]The Kohathites must not enter and look at

the holy things, even for a second. If they do, they will die."

THE JOBS OF THE GERSHON FAMILY

[21]The Lord said to Moses, [22]"Count the Gershonites by families and family groups. [23]Count the men from 30 to 50 years old. Everyone has a job to do in the Meeting Tent.[d]

[24]"This is what the Gershonite family groups must do and what they must carry. [25]They must carry the pieces of cloth of the Holy Tent[d] and Meeting Tent. They must also carry its covering and the covering made from fine leather. And they must carry the curtains for the entrance to the Meeting Tent. [26]They must carry the curtains of the courtyard that goes around the Holy Tent and the altar. They must carry the curtain for the entry to the courtyard and the ropes and all the things used with the curtains. They must do everything connected with these things. [27]Aaron and his sons are in charge of what the Gershonites do or carry. You tell them what they are responsible for carrying. [28]This is the work of the Gershonite family group at the Meeting Tent. Ithamar son of Aaron, the priest, will direct their work.

THE JOBS OF THE MERARI FAMILY

[29]"Count the Merarite families and family groups. [30]Count the men from 30 to 50 years old. They will work at the Meeting Tent.[d] [31]It is their job to carry the frame of the Meeting Tent, the crossbars, the posts and bases. [32]They must also carry the posts that go around the courtyard. They must carry the bases, tent pegs and ropes. And they must carry everything that is used with the poles around the courtyard. Tell each man exactly what to carry. [33]This is the work the Merarites will do for the Meeting Tent. Ithamar son of Aaron, the priest, will direct their work."

THE LEVITE FAMILIES

[34]Moses, Aaron and the leaders of Israel counted the Kohathites by families and family groups. [35]The men from 30 to 50 years old were to work at the Meeting Tent.[d] [36]The family group had 2,750 men. [37]This was the total of the Kohath family group who worked at the Meeting Tent. Moses and Aaron counted them as the Lord had commanded Moses.

[38]Also, the Gershon family group was counted by families and family groups. [39]The men from 30 to 50 years old were given work at the Meeting Tent. [40]The families and family groups had 2,630 men. [41]This was the total of the Gershon family group who worked at the Meeting Tent. Moses and Aaron counted them as the Lord had commanded.

[42]Also, the men in the families and family groups of the Merari family were counted. [43]The men from 30 to 50 years old were to work at the Meeting Tent. [44]The family group had 3,200 men. [45]This was the total of the Merari family group. Moses and Aaron counted them as the Lord had commanded Moses.

[46]So Moses, Aaron and the leaders of Israel counted all the Levites. They counted them by families and family groups. [47]The men from 30 to 50 were given work at the Meeting Tent. They also carried the Tent. [48]The total number of these men was 8,580. [49]Each man was counted as the Lord had commanded Moses. Each man was given his work and told what to carry. This was as the Lord had commanded Moses.

RULES ABOUT CLEANLINESS

5 The Lord said to Moses, [2]"Command the Israelites to send away from camp anyone with a harmful skin disease. Send away anyone who gives off body fluid. And send away anyone who has touched a dead body. [3]Send both men and women away from camp. Then they won't spread the disease there. I am living among you." [4]So Israel obeyed God's command. They sent those people outside the camp as the Lord had told Moses.

PAYING FOR DOING WRONG

5The Lord said to Moses, 6"Tell the Israelites: 'When a man or woman does something wrong to another person, that is really sinning against God. That person is guilty. 7He must tell what he has done wrong. And he must fully pay for the wrong he has done. Then he must add one-fifth to it. And he must give it to the person he wronged. 8But that person may be dead. That person may not have any close relatives to receive the payment. Then the one who did wrong owes the Lord. That person must pay the priest. The priest must sacrifice a male sheep to remove the wrong so that person will belong to God. 9When an Israelite brings a holy gift, he should give it to the priest. 10No one has to give these holy gifts. But if someone does give them, they belong to the priest.'"

SUSPICIOUS HUSBANDS

11Then the Lord said to Moses, 12"Tell the Israelites: 'A man's wife might be unfaithful to him. 13She might have sexual relations with another man. Her sin might be kept hidden from her husband. Her husband might not know about the wrong thing she did. Perhaps no one saw it, and she wasn't caught. 14But her husband might have feelings of jealousy whether she has sinned or not. 15He then should take her to the priest. The husband must also take an offering for her. This offering will be two quarts of barley flour. He must not pour oil or incense*d* on it. This is a grain offering for jealousy. It is to find out if she is guilty.

16"'The priest will bring in the woman and make her stand before the Lord. 17He will take some holy water in a clay jar. Then he will put some dirt from the floor of the Holy Tent into the water. 18The priest will make the woman stand before the Lord. Then he will loosen her hair. And he will hand her the grain offering for jealousy. He will hold the bitter water that brings a curse on her.

19The priest will tell her what the oath says will happen to her. He will ask her, "Has another man had sexual relations with you? Have you been unfaithful to your husband? If you haven't, then this water that brings a curse won't hurt you. 20But what if you have been unfaithful to your husband? What if you have had sexual relations with a man besides your husband?" 21The priest will tell her the curse that the oath will bring. He will say, "If you are guilty, the Lord will make the people curse you. Your stomach will get big, and you will not be able to have another baby. 22This water that brings a curse will go inside you. Your stomach will get big, and you will not be able to have another baby."

"'The woman must say, "I agree."

23"'The priest should write these curses on a scroll. Then he should wash the words off into the water. 24Then he will make the woman drink the water that brings a curse. When she does, it may make her sick. 25Then the priest will take the grain offering for jealousy from her. He will present it before the Lord. Then he will bring it to the altar. 26Then the priest will take a handful of the grain. This is a memorial offering. He will burn it on the altar. After that he will make the woman drink the water. 27He will make her drink it to see if she is not pure. He will know if she has sinned against her husband. When it goes into her, her stomach may get big. And she may not be able to have another baby. Her people will turn against her. 28But if the woman has not sinned, she is pure. She is not guilty. She will be able to have more babies.

29"'So this is the teaching about jealousy. This is what to do when a woman is unfaithful to her husband. 30It also should be done if the man gets jealous because he suspects his wife. The priest will have her stand before the Lord. Then he will do all these things. This is the teaching. ³¹If the husband is right, the woman will suffer.'"

THE NAZIRITES

6 The Lord said to Moses, ²"Tell the Israelites: 'A man or a woman might want to promise to belong to the Lord in a special way. This person will be called a Nazirite. ³During this time, he must not drink wine or beer. He must not drink vinegar made from wine or beer. He must not even drink grape juice or eat grapes or raisins. ⁴While he is a Nazirite, he must not eat anything that comes from the grapevine. He must not even eat the seeds or the skin.

⁵"During the time he promised to belong to the Lord, he must not cut his hair. He must be holy until this special time is over. He must let his hair grow long. ⁶During his special time of belonging to the Lord, a Nazirite must not go near a dead body. ⁷Even if his own father, mother, brother or sister dies, he must not touch them. This would make him unclean.ᵈ He must still keep his promise to belong to God in a special way. ⁸While he is a Nazirite, he belongs to the Lord.

⁹"If he is next to someone who dies suddenly, his hair has been made unclean. It was part of his promise. So he must shave his head seven days later to be clean. ¹⁰Then on the eighth day, he must bring two doves or two young pigeons to the priest. The priest will be at the entrance to the Holy Tent.ᵈ ¹¹The priest will offer one as a sin offering. He will offer the other as a burnt offering. This removes sin so the man will belong to God. He had sinned because he was near a dead body. That same day he will again promise to let his hair grow for the Lord. ¹²He must give himself to the Lord for another special time. He must bring a male lamb a year old. It will be a penalty offering. The days of the special time before don't count. This is because he became unclean during his first special time.

¹³"This is the teaching for a Nazirite. When the promised time is over, he must go to the entrance of the Meeting Tent.ᵈ ¹⁴There he will give his offerings to the Lord. He must offer a year-old male lamb as a burnt offering. It must have nothing wrong with it. He must also offer a year-old female lamb as a sin offering. There must be nothing wrong with it. And he must bring a male sheep for a fellowship offering. There must be nothing wrong with it. ¹⁵He must also bring the grain offerings and drink offerings that go with them. And he must bring a basket of bread made without yeast. There must be loaves made with fine flour mixed with oil. And there must be wafers made without yeast spread with oil.

¹⁶"The priest will give these offerings to the Lord. He will make the sin offering and the burnt offering. ¹⁷Then he will kill the male sheep as a fellowship offering to the Lord. Along with it, he will present the basket of bread. He will also make the grain offering and the drink offering along with it.

¹⁸"The Nazirite must go to the entrance of the Meeting Tent. There he must shave off his hair that he grew for his promise. The hair will be put in the fire that is under the sacrifice on the fellowship offering.

¹⁹"After the Nazirite cuts off his hair, the priest will give him a boiled shoulder from the male sheep. From the basket he will also give him a loaf and a wafer. Both are made without yeast. ²⁰Then the priest will present them to the Lord. This is an offering presented before the Lord. They are holy and belong to the priest. Also, he is to present the breast and the thigh from the male sheep to the Lord. They also belong to the priest. After that, the Nazirite may drink wine.

²¹"This is the teaching for the Nazirite promise. If a person makes the Nazirite promise, he must give all of these gifts to the Lord. If he promised to do more, he

must keep his promise. That is also the teaching of the Nazirite promise.'"

THE PRIESTS' BLESSINGS

²²The Lord said to Moses, ²³"Tell Aaron and his sons, 'This is how you should bless the Israelites. Say to them:

²⁴"May the Lord bless you and keep
  you.
²⁵May the Lord show you his kindness.
  May he have mercy on you.
²⁶May the Lord watch over you
  and give you peace.'"

²⁷"So Aaron and his sons will bless the Israelites with my name. And I will bless them."

THE HOLY TENT

7 When Moses finished setting up the Holy Tent,ᵈ he gave it for service to the Lord. Moses poured olive oil on the Tent and on everything used in the Tent. He also poured oil on the altar and all its tools. In this way he prepared them for service to the Lord. ²Then the leaders of Israel made offerings. These were the heads of the families and leaders of each tribe.ᵈ They were the men who counted the people. ³They brought to the Lord 6 covered carts and 12 oxen. Each leader gave an ox. Every two leaders gave a cart. They gave these to the Holy Tent.

⁴The Lord said to Moses, ⁵"Accept these gifts from the leaders. Use them in the work of the Meeting Tent. Give them to the Levites as they need them."

⁶So Moses accepted the carts and the oxen. He gave them to the Levites. ⁷He gave 2 carts and 4 oxen to the Gershonites. This is what they needed for their work. ⁸Then Moses gave 4 carts and 8 oxen to the Merarites. This is what they needed for their work. Ithamar son of Aaron, the priest, directed the work of all of them. ⁹Moses did not give any oxen or carts to the Kohathites. They were to carry the holy things on their shoulders. This was their job.

¹⁰The oil was poured on the altar. Then the leaders brought their offerings to it to give to the Lord's service. ¹¹The Lord had already told Moses, "Each day one leader must bring his gift. The gifts will make the altar ready for service to me."

¹²⁻⁸³Each of the 12 leaders brought these gifts. Each leader brought 1 silver plate that weighed about 3¼ pounds. And each one brought 1 silver bowl that weighed about 1¾ pounds. These weights were set by the Holy Place measure. Each bowl and plate were filled with fine flour mixed with oil. This was for a grain offering. Each leader also brought a large gold dish that weighed about 4 ounces. It was filled with incense.ᵈ

Each leader also brought 1 young bull, 1 male sheep and 1 male lamb a year old. These were for a burnt offering. Each leader also brought 1 male goat for a sin offering. Each leader brought 2 oxen, 5 male sheep, 5 male goats and 5 male lambs a year old. All of these were sacrificed for a fellowship offering.

On the first day Nahshon son of Amminadab brought his gifts. He was the leader of the tribe of Judah.

On the second day Nethanel son of Zuar brought his gifts. He was the leader of the tribe of Issachar.

On the third day Eliab son of Helon brought his gifts. He was the leader of the tribe of Zebulun.

On the fourth day Elizur son of Shedeur brought his gifts. He was the leader of the tribe of Reuben.

On the fifth day Shelumiel son of Zurishaddai brought his gifts. He was the leader of the tribe of Simeon.

On the sixth day Eliasaph son of Deuel brought his gifts. He was the leader of the tribe of Gad.

On the seventh day Elishama son of Ammihud brought his gifts. He was the leader of the tribe of Ephraim.

On the eighth day Gamaliel son of Pedahzur brought his gifts. He was the leader of the tribe of Manasseh.

On the ninth day Abidan son of Gideoni brought his gifts. He was the leader of the tribe of Benjamin.

On the tenth day Ahiezer son of Ammishaddai brought his gifts. He was the leader of the tribe of Dan.

On the eleventh day Pagiel son of Ocran brought his gifts. He was the leader of the tribe of Asher.

On the twelfth day Ahira son of Enan brought his gifts. He was the leader of the tribe of Naphtali.

[84]So these were the gifts from the Israelite leaders. Moses poured oil on the altar. And they brought their gifts to give the altar for service to the Lord. They brought 12 silver plates, 12 silver bowls and 12 gold dishes. [85]Each silver plate weighed about $3^1/4$ pounds. And each bowl weighed about $1^3/4$ pounds. All the silver plates and silver bowls together weighed about 60 pounds. This weight was set by the Holy Place measure. [86]The 12 gold dishes filled with incense weighed 4 ounces each. Together the gold dishes weighed about 3 pounds. [87]The total number of animals for the burnt offering was 12 bulls, 12 male sheep and 12 male lambs a year old. There was also a grain offering. And there were 12 male goats for a sin offering. [88]The total number of animals for the fellowship offering was 24 bulls, 60 male sheep, 60 male goats and 60 male lambs a year old. All these offerings were for giving the altar to the service of the Lord. This was after Moses had poured oil on it.

[89]Moses went into the Meeting Tent to speak with the Lord. He heard the Lord speaking to him. The voice was coming from between the two gold creatures with wings. They were above the lid of the Box[d] of the Agreement. And the Lord spoke with him.

THE LAMPSTAND

8 The Lord said to Moses, [2]"Speak to Aaron. Tell him, 'Put the seven lamps where they can light the area in front of the lampstand.'"

[3]Aaron did this. He put the lamps so they lighted the area in front of the lampstand. He obeyed the command the Lord gave Moses. [4]The lampstand was made from hammered gold. It was gold from its base to the flowers. It was made exactly the way the Lord had showed Moses.

THE LEVITES

[5]The Lord said to Moses, [6]"Take the Levites away from the other Israelites and make them clean.[d] [7]This is what you should do to make them clean. Sprinkle the cleansing water on them. Have them shave their bodies and wash their clothes. Then they will be clean. [8]They must take a young bull and the grain offering that goes with it. The grain offering will be flour mixed with oil. Then take another young bull for a sin offering. [9]Bring the Levites to the front of the Meeting Tent.[d] And gather all the Israelites around. [10]Bring the Levites before the Lord. Then the Israelites should put their hands on them.[n] [11]Aaron will present the Levites before the Lord. They will be like an offering presented from the Israelites. Then the Levites will be ready to do the work of the Lord.

[12]"The Levites will put their hands on the bulls' heads. One bull will be a sin offering to the Lord. The other will be a burnt offering. This will remove the sins of the Levites so they will belong to God. [13]Make the Levites stand in front of Aaron and his sons. Then present the Levites as an offering to the Lord. [14]In this way you must set apart the Levites from the other Israelites. The Levites will be mine.

[15]"So make the Levites pure. And present them as an offering. Then they may come to work at the Meeting Tent. [16]They will be given to me from the Israelites. I have taken them for myself. They are mine instead of the firstborn[d] son of

---

8:10 put ... them This showed that the people had a part in giving the Levites their special work.

every Israelite woman. [17]Every firstborn male in Israel—man or animal—is mine. I killed all the firstborn in Egypt. So now I set them aside for myself. [18]I have taken the Levites instead of all the first-born sons in Israel. [19]I have chosen the Levites from all the Israelites. And I have given them to Aaron and his sons. They will serve all the Israelites at the Meeting Tent. They will help remove the Israelites' sins so they will belong to God. Then no disaster will strike the Israelites when they approach the Holy Place."

[20]So Moses, Aaron and all the Israelites obeyed the Lord. They did with the Levites what the Lord commanded Moses. [21]The Levites made themselves clean and washed their clothes. Then Aaron presented them as an offering to the Lord. Aaron also removed their sins so they would be pure for the Lord. [22]After that, the Levites came to the Meeting Tent to work. Aaron and his sons told them what to do. They did with the Levites what the Lord commanded Moses.

[23]The Lord said to Moses, [24]"This command is for the Levites. Every man 25 years old or older must come to the Meeting Tent. They all have a job to do in the work there. [25]At the age of 50, he must retire from his job. He doesn't have to work again. [26]He may help his fellow Levites with their work at the Meeting Tent. But he must not do the work himself. This is the way you are to give the Levites their jobs."

THE PASSOVER

9 The Lord spoke to Moses in the Desert of Sinai. This was in the first month of the second year after the Israelites left Egypt. He said, [2]"Tell the Israelites to celebrate the Passover[d] at the appointed time. [3]That appointed time is the fourteenth day of this month. They should celebrate it at twilight. They must obey all the rules about it."

[4]So Moses told the Israelites to celebrate the Passover. [5]And so they did. It was in the Desert of Sinai at twilight. This was on the fourteenth day of the first month. The Israelites did everything just as the Lord commanded Moses.

[6]But some of the people could not celebrate the Passover on that day. They were unclean[d] because of a dead body. So they went to Moses and Aaron that day. [7]They said to Moses, "We are unclean because of a dead body. But why should we be kept from offering gifts to the Lord at this appointed time? Why can't we join the other Israelites?"

[8]Moses said to them, "Wait. I will find out what the Lord says about you."

[9]Then the Lord said to Moses, [10]"Tell the Israelites this: 'You or your descendants[d] might become unclean because of a dead body. Or, you might be away on a trip during the Passover. Still celebrate the Lord's Passover. [11]But celebrate it at twilight on the fourteenth day of the second month. Eat the lamb with bitter herbs and bread made without yeast. [12]Don't leave any of it until the next morning. Don't break any of its bones. When you celebrate the Passover, follow all the rules. [13]Anyone who is clean and is not away on a trip must eat the Passover. If he doesn't, he must be separated from his people. He did not give an offering to the Lord at the appointed time. He must be punished for his sin.

[14]"'A foreigner among you may celebrate the Lord's Passover. But he must follow all the rules. You must have the same rules for foreigners as you have for yourselves.'"

THE CLOUD ABOVE THE TENT

[15]On the day the Holy Tent[d] was set up, a cloud covered it. (The Holy Tent was also called the Tent of the Agreement.) From dusk until dawn the cloud above the Tent looked like fire. [16]The cloud stayed above the Tent. At night it

looked like fire. [17]When the cloud moved from its place over the Tent, the Israelites moved. Wherever the cloud stopped, the Israelites camped. [18]So the Israelites moved at the Lord's command. And they camped at his command. While the cloud stayed over the Tent, they stayed in place. [19]Sometimes the cloud stayed over the Tent for a long time. The Israelites obeyed the Lord and did not move. [20]Sometimes the cloud was over it only a few days. At the Lord's command the people camped. And at his command they moved. [21]Sometimes the cloud stayed only from dusk until dawn. When the cloud lifted the next morning, the people moved. When the cloud lifted, day or night, the people moved. [22]The cloud might stay over the Tent for two days, a month or a year. As long as it stayed, the people would camp. But when the cloud lifted, they moved. [23]At the Lord's command the people camped. And at his command they moved. They obeyed the Lord's order that he commanded through Moses.

THE SILVER TRUMPETS

10 The Lord said to Moses, [2]"Make two trumpets of hammered silver. Use them to call the people together and to march out of camp. [3]When both trumpets are blown, the people should gather. They should gather before you at the entrance to the Meeting Tent.[d] [4]If you blow only one trumpet, the leaders should meet before you. [5]When you blow the trumpets once, the tribes[d] camping on the east should move. [6]When you blow them again, the tribes camping on the south should move. The sound will tell them to move. [7]When you want to gather the people, blow the trumpets. But don't blow them the same way.

[8]"Aaron's sons, the priests, should blow the trumpets. This is a law for you and your descendants[d] from now on. [9]You might be fighting an enemy who attacks you in your own land. Blow the

trumpets. The Lord your God will remember you. He will save you from your enemies. [10]Also blow your trumpets at happy times. Blow them during your feasts and at New Moon[d] festivals. Blow them over your burnt offerings and fellowship offerings. They will help you remember your God. I am the Lord your God."

THE ISRAELITES MOVE CAMP

[11]The cloud lifted from the Tent[d] of the Agreement. This was on the twentieth day of the second month of the second year. [12]So the Israelites moved from the Desert of Sinai. They moved until the cloud stopped in the Desert of Paran. [13]This was their first time to move. They did it as the Lord had commanded Moses.

[14]The divisions from the camp of Judah moved first under their flag. Nahshon son of Amminadab was the commander. [15]Nethanel son of Zuar was over the division of the tribe[d] of Issachar. [16]Eliab son of Helon was over the division of the tribe of Zebulun. [17]Then the Meeting Tent was taken down. The Gershonites and Merarites, who carried it, moved next.

[18]Then came the divisions from the camp of Reuben under their flag. Elizur son of Shedeur was the commander. [19]Shelumiel son of Zurishaddai was over the division of the tribe of Simeon. [20]Eliasaph son of Deuel was over the division of the tribe of Gad. [21]Then came the Kohathites. They carried the holy things. The Holy Tent was to be set up before they arrived.

[22]Next came the divisions from the camp of Ephraim under their flag. Elishama son of Ammihud was the commander. [23]Gamaliel son of Pedahzur was over the division of the tribe of Manasseh. [24]Abidan son of Gideoni was over the division of the tribe of Benjamin.

[25]The last ones were the rear guard for all the tribes. These were the divisions from the camp of Dan under their flag.

Ahiezer son of Ammishaddai was the commander. ²⁶Pagiel son of Ocran was over the division of the tribe of Asher. ²⁷Ahira son of Enan was over the division of the tribe of Naphtali. ²⁸This was the order the Israelite divisions marched in when they moved.

²⁹Hobab was the son of Reuel the Midianite. Reuel, who is also called Jethro, was Moses' father-in-law. Moses said to Hobab, "We are moving to the land God promised to give us. Come with us. We will be good to you. The Lord has promised good things to Israel."

³⁰But Hobab answered, "No, I will not go. I will go back to my own land where I was born."

³¹But Moses said, "Please don't leave us. You know where we can camp in the desert. You can be our guide. ³²Come with us. We will share with you all the good things the Lord gives us." ³³So they left the mountain of the Lord. The Box^d of the Lord's Agreement went in front of the people. For three days they looked for a place to camp. ³⁴The Lord's cloud was over them during the day when they left their camp.

³⁵When the Holy Box left the camp, Moses always said,

"Rise up, Lord!
    Scatter your enemies.
Make those who are against you
    run from you."

³⁶And when the Holy Box was set down, Moses always said,

"Return, Lord,
    to the thousands of people of Israel."

FIRE FROM THE LORD

11 The people complained to the Lord about their troubles. When he heard them, he became angry. Fire from the Lord burned among the people. It burned the edge of the camp. ²So the people cried out to Moses. He prayed to the Lord, and the fire stopped burning.

³So that place was called Taberah.^n The people named it that because the Lord's fire had burned among them.

THE 70 OLDER LEADERS

⁴Some troublemakers among them wanted better food. Soon all the Israelites began complaining. They said, "We want meat! ⁵We remember the fish we ate for free in Egypt. We also had cucumbers, melons, leeks, onions and garlic. ⁶But now we have lost our appetite. We never see anything but this manna!"

⁷The manna was like small white seeds. ⁸The people would go to gather it. Then they ground it in handmills. Or they crushed it between stones. They cooked it in a pot or made cakes with it. It tasted like bread baked with olive oil. ⁹When the dew fell on the camp each night, so did the manna.

¹⁰Moses heard every family crying. They stood in the entrances of their tents. The Lord became very angry. And Moses got upset. ¹¹He asked the Lord, "Why have you brought me this trouble? I'm your servant. What have I done wrong? Why did you make me responsible for all these people? ¹²I am not the father of all these people. I didn't give birth to them. Why do you make me carry them to the land you promised to our ancestors? Must I carry them in my arms as a nurse carries a baby? ¹³Where can I get meat for all these people? They keep crying to me, 'We want meat!' ¹⁴I can't take care of all these people alone. It is too much for me. ¹⁵If you are going to continue doing this to me, then kill me now. If you like me, put me to death. Then I won't have any more troubles."

¹⁶The Lord said to Moses, "Bring me 70 of Israel's elders. Pick men you know are leaders among the people. Bring them to the Meeting Tent.^d Have them stand there with you. ¹⁷I will come down and speak with you there. I will take

11:3 Taberah This name means "burning."

some of the Spirit[d] that is in you. And I will give it to them. They will help you care for the people. Then you will not have to care for them alone.

[18]"Tell the people this: 'Make yourselves holy. Tomorrow you will eat meat. The Lord heard you cry, "We want meat! We were better off in Egypt!" So now the Lord will give you meat to eat. [19]You will not eat it for just 1, 2, 5, 10 or even 20 days. [20]You will eat that meat for a whole month. You will eat it until it comes out your nose. You will hate it. This is because you have rejected the Lord. He is here with you. But you have cried to him. You said, "Why did we ever leave Egypt?"'"

[21]Moses said, "Lord, here are 600,000 men standing around me. And you say, 'I will give them enough meat to eat for a month!' [22]If we killed all the sheep and cattle, that would not be enough. If we caught all the fish in the sea, that would not be enough."

[23]But the Lord said to Moses, "Do you think I'm weak? You will see if I can do what I say."

[24]So Moses went out to the people. He told them what the Lord had said. Moses gathered 70 of the elders together. He had them stand around the Tent. [25]Then the Lord came down in the cloud and spoke to Moses. The Lord took some of the Spirit Moses had. And he gave it to the 70 leaders. With the Spirit in them, they prophesied,[d] but just that one time.

[26]Two men named Eldad and Medad were also listed as leaders. But they did not go to the Tent. They stayed in the camp. The Spirit was given to them. So they prophesied in the camp. [27]A young man ran to Moses. He said, "Eldad and Medad are prophesying in the camp."

[28]Joshua son of Nun said, "Moses, my master, stop them!" (Since he was a young boy, Joshua had been Moses' assistant.)

[29]But Moses answered, "Are you afraid for me? I wish all the Lord's people could prophesy. I wish the Lord would give his Spirit to all of them!" [30]Then Moses and the leaders of Israel went back to the camp.

THE QUAILS COME

[31]The Lord sent a strong wind from the sea. It blew quail into the area all around the camp. The quail were about three feet above the ground. There were quail a day's walk in any direction. [32]The people went out and gathered quail. They gathered all that day, that night and the next day. Everyone gathered at least 60 bushels. Then they spread them around the camp. [33]But the Lord became very angry. He gave the people a terrible sickness. This came while the meat was still in their mouths. [34]So the people named that place Kibroth Hattaavah.[n] They named it that because there they buried those who wanted other food.

[35]From Kibroth Hattaavah the people went to stay at Hazeroth.

MIRIAM AND AARON SPEAK AGAINST MOSES' WIFE

12 Miriam and Aaron began to talk against Moses, who had married a Cushite. [2]They said to themselves, "Is Moses the only one the Lord speaks through? Doesn't he speak through us?" And the Lord heard this.

[3](Now Moses was very humble. He was the least proud person on earth.)

[4]So the Lord suddenly spoke to Moses, Aaron and Miriam. He said, "All three of you come to the Meeting Tent[d] now." So they went. [5]The Lord came down in a pillar of cloud. He stood at the entrance to the Tent. He called to Aaron and Miriam, and they both came near. [6]He said, "Listen to my words:

When a prophet[d] is among you,
   I, the Lord, will show myself to him
     in visions.
   I will speak to him in dreams.

11:34 Kibroth Hattaavah This name in Hebrew means "graves of craving."

[7]But this is not true with my servant
Moses.
I trust him to lead all my people.
[8]I speak face to face with him.
I speak clearly, not with hidden
meanings.
He has even seen the form of the
Lord.
You should be afraid
to speak against my servant Moses."

[9]The Lord was very angry with them,
but he left.

[10]The cloud lifted from the Tent. Then
Aaron turned toward Miriam. She was
as white as snow. She had a harmful skin
disease. [11]Aaron said to Moses, "Please,
my master, forgive us for our foolish sin.
[12]Don't let her be like a baby who is born
dead. (Sometimes a baby is born with
half of its flesh eaten away.)"

[13]So Moses cried out to the Lord, "God,
please heal her!"

[14]The Lord answered Moses, "If her
father had spit in her face, she would
have been shamed for seven days. So put
her outside the camp for seven days. After
that, she may come back." [15]So Miriam
was shut outside of the camp for seven
days. And the people did not move on
until she came back.

[16]After that, the people left Hazeroth.
And they camped in the Desert of Paran.

THE SPIES EXPLORE CANAAN

13 The Lord said to Moses, [2]"Send
men to explore the land of
Canaan. I will give that land to the Israelites. Send one leader from each tribe."[d]

[3]So Moses obeyed the Lord's command. He sent the Israelite leaders out
from the Desert of Paran. [4]These are
their names: from the tribe of Reuben,
Shammua son of Zaccur; [5]from the tribe
of Simeon, Shaphat son of Hori; [6]from
the tribe of Judah, Caleb son of Jephunneh; [7]from the tribe of Issachar, Igal son
of Joseph; [8]from the tribe of Ephraim,

Hoshea son of Nun; [9]from the tribe of
Benjamin, Palti son of Raphu; [10]from the
tribe of Zebulun, Gaddiel son of Sodi;
[11]from the tribe of Manasseh (a tribe of
Joseph), Gaddi son of Susi; [12]from the
tribe of Dan, Ammiel son of Gamalli;
[13]from the tribe of Asher, Sethur son of
Michael; [14]from the tribe of Naphtali,
Nahbi son of Vophsi; [15]from the tribe of
Gad, Geuel son of Maki.

[16]These are the names of the men
Moses sent to explore the land. (Moses
gave Hoshea son of Nun the new name
Joshua.)

[17]Moses sent them to explore Canaan.
He said, "Go through southern Canaan
and then into the mountains. [18]See what
the land looks like. Are the people who
live there strong or weak? Are there a few
or many? [19]What kind of land do they
live in? Is it good or bad? What about the
towns they live in—do they have walls,
or are they open like camps? [20]What
about the soil? Is it fertile or poor? Are
there trees there? Try to bring back some
of the fruit from that land." (It was the
season for the first grapes.)

[21]So they went up and explored the
land. They went from the Desert of Zin
all the way to Rehob by Lebo Hamath.
[22]They went through the southern area
to Hebron. That is where Ahiman,
Sheshai and Talmai lived. They were the
descendants[d] of Anak.[d] (The city of
Hebron had been built seven years
before Zoan in Egypt.) [23]In the Valley of
Eshcol, they cut off a branch of a
grapevine. It had one bunch of grapes on
it. They carried that branch on a pole
between two of them. They also got
some pomegranates[d] and figs. [24]They
call that place the Valley of Eshcol.[n] That
is because the Israelites cut off the
bunch of grapes there. [25]After 40 days of
exploring the land, the men returned to
the camp.

13:24 Eshcol This name in Hebrew means "bunch."

26They came back to Moses and Aaron and all the Israelites at Kadesh. This was in the Desert of Paran. The men reported to them and showed everybody the fruit from the land. 27They told Moses, "We went to the land where you sent us. It is a land where much food grows! Here is some of its fruit. 28But the people who live there are strong. Their cities are walled and large. We even saw some Anakites there. 29The Amalekites live in the southern area. The Hittites, Jebusites and Amorites live in the mountains. The Canaanites live near the sea and along the Jordan River."

30Then Caleb told the people near Moses to be quiet. Caleb said, "We should go up and take the land for ourselves. We can do it."

31But the men who had gone with him said, "We can't attack those people. They are stronger than we are." 32And those men gave the Israelites a bad report about the land they explored. They said, "The land would eat us up. All the people we saw are very tall. 33We saw the Nephilim*d* people there. (The Anakites come from the Nephilim people.) We felt like grasshoppers. And we looked like grasshoppers to them."

THE PEOPLE COMPLAIN AGAIN

14 That night all the people in the camp began crying loudly. 2All the Israelites complained against Moses and Aaron. All the people said to them, "We should have died in Egypt. Or we should have died in the desert. 3Why is the Lord bringing us to this land? We will be killed with swords. Our wives and children will be taken away. We would be better off going back to Egypt." 4They said to each other, "Let's get a leader and go back to Egypt."

5Then Moses and Aaron bowed facedown in front of all the Israelites gathered there. 6Joshua son of Nun and Caleb son of Jephunneh were among those who had explored the land. They tore their clothes. 7They said to all of the Israelites, "The land we went to explore is very good. 8If the Lord is pleased with us, he will lead us into that land. He will give us that land where much food grows. 9Don't turn against the Lord! Don't be afraid of the people in that land! We will chew them up. They have no protection, but we have the Lord. So don't be afraid of them."

10Then all the people talked about killing them with stones. But the glory of the Lord appeared at the Meeting Tent*d* to the Israelites. 11The Lord said to Moses, "How long will these people ignore me? How long will it be before they believe me? I have done miracles*d* among them. 12I will give them a terrible sickness. I will destroy them. But I will make you into a great nation. It will be stronger than they are."

13Then Moses said to the Lord, "The Egyptians will hear about it! You brought these people from there by your great power. 14And the Egyptians will tell this to those who live in this land. They have already heard about you, Lord. They know that you are with your people. And they know you were seen face to face. They know your cloud stays over your people. They know you lead your people with that cloud during the day and with fire at night. 15The nations have heard about your power. If you put to death your people all at once, the nations will talk. They will say, 16'The Lord was not able to bring them into the land he promised them. So he killed them in the desert.'

17"So show your strength now, my Lord. Do what you said. You said: 18'The Lord doesn't become angry quickly. The Lord has great love. The Lord forgives sin and law breaking. He has great mercy. But the Lord does not forget to punish guilty people. When parents sin, he will also punish their children. He will punish their grandchildren, great-grandchildren and great-great-grandchildren.' ¹⁹Show your great love. Forgive these people's sin. Forgive them as you have from the time they left Egypt until now."

²⁰The Lord answered, "I have forgiven them as you asked. ²¹But, as surely as I live, I make this promise. As surely as my glory fills the whole earth, I make this promise. ²²All these men saw my glory. They saw the miracles I did in Egypt and in the desert. But they disobeyed me and tested me 10 times. ²³So not one will see the land I promised to their ancestors. No one who angered me will see that land. ²⁴But my servant Caleb has a different spirit. He follows me completely. So I will bring him into the land he has already seen. And his children will own that land. ²⁵The Amalekites and the Canaanites are living in the valleys. So leave tomorrow and go back. Follow the desert road toward the Gulf of Aqaba."

THE LORD PUNISHES THE PEOPLE

²⁶The Lord said to Moses and Aaron, ²⁷"How long will these evil people complain about me? I have heard these Israelites' grumbling and complaining. ²⁸So tell them, 'This is what the Lord says. I heard what you said. As surely as I live, I will do those things to you. ²⁹You will die in this desert. Every one of you who is 20 years old or older and who was counted with the people will die. You complained against me, the Lord. ³⁰Not one of you will enter and live in the land I promised to you. Only Caleb son of Jephunneh and Joshua son of Nun will go in. ³¹You said that your children would be taken away. But I will bring them into the land. They will enjoy what you refused. ³²As for you, you will die in this desert. ³³Your children will be shepherds here for 40 years. They will suffer because you were not loyal. They will suffer until you lie dead in the desert. ³⁴For 40 years you will suffer for your sins. That is a year for each of the 40 days you explored the land. You will know me

as your enemy.' ³⁵I, the Lord, have spoken. I will certainly do these things to all these evil people. They have come together against me. So they will all die here in this desert."

³⁶The men Moses had sent to explore the land had returned. They had spread complaints among all the Israelites. They had given a bad report about the land. ³⁷They were responsible for the bad report. So the Lord killed them with a terrible sickness. ³⁸Only two of the men did not die. They were Joshua son of Nun and Caleb son of Jephunneh.

³⁹When Moses told these things to the Israelites, they were very sad. ⁴⁰Early the next morning they started to go toward the beginning of the mountains. They said, "We have sinned. We will go where the Lord told us."

⁴¹But Moses said, "Why are you disobeying the Lord's command? You will not win! ⁴²Don't go. The Lord is not with you. You will be beaten by your enemies. ⁴³You will run into the Amalekites and Canaanites. They will kill you with swords. You have turned away from the Lord. He will not be with you."

⁴⁴But they were proud. They went toward the beginning of the mountains. But Moses and the Box^d of the Agreement with the Lord did not leave the camp. ⁴⁵The Amalekites and the Canaanites who lived in those mountains came down. And they attacked the Israelites. They beat them back all the way to Hormah.

RULES ABOUT SACRIFICES

15 The Lord said to Moses, ²"Speak to the people of Israel. Say to them, 'You will enter a land that I am giving you as a home. ³There give the Lord offerings made by fire. These may be from your herds or flocks. And the smell will be pleasing to the Lord. These offerings may be burnt offerings or sacrifices for special promises. They may be offerings which are gifts to the Lord. Or they may be festival offerings. ⁴And the one who brings his offering shall also give the Lord a grain offering. It should be two quarts of fine flour mixed with one quart of olive oil. [5]Each time you offer a lamb as a burnt offering or sacrifice, also prepare a quart of wine. This is a drink offering.

[6]"If you are giving a male sheep, also prepare a grain offering. It should be four quarts of fine flour mixed with one and one-fourth quarts of olive oil. [7]Also prepare one and one-fourth quarts of wine. This is a drink offering. Offer it to the Lord. Its smell is pleasing to him.

[8]"You might prepare a young bull as a burnt offering or sacrifice. This might be for a fellowship offering or for a special promise to the Lord. [9]Bring a grain offering with the bull. It should be six quarts of fine flour mixed with two quarts of olive oil. [10]Also bring two quarts of wine as a drink offering. This offering is made by fire. And its smell will be pleasing to the Lord. [11]Prepare each bull or male sheep, lamb or young goat this way. [12]Do this for every one of the animals you bring.

[13]"All citizens must do these things in this way. And the smell of their offerings by fire will be pleasing to the Lord. [14]From now on foreigners will live among you. They will make offerings by fire so the smell will be pleasing to the Lord. They must offer them the same way you do. [15]The law is the same for you and for foreigners. It will be a law from now on. You and the foreigners are alike before the Lord. [16]The teachings and rules are the same for you and for the foreigners among you.'"

[17]The Lord said to Moses, [18]"Tell the Israelites: 'You are going to another land. I am taking you there. [19]When you eat the food there, offer part of it to the Lord. [20]Offer a loaf of bread from the first of your grain. That will be your offering from the threshing[d] floor. [21]From now on offer to the Lord the first part of your grain.

[22]"Now what if you forget to obey any of these commands the Lord gave Moses? [23]These are the Lord's commands given to you through Moses. They began the day the Lord gave them to you. And they will continue from now on. [24]But you might forget to obey one of these commands. The people might not remember the command. Then all the people must offer a young bull as a burnt offering. Its smell is pleasing to the Lord. By law you must also give the grain offering and the drink offering with it. And you must bring a male goat as a sin offering.

[25]"The priest will remove that sin for all the Israelites so they will belong to God. They are forgiven. They didn't know they were sinning. For the wrong they did they brought offerings to the Lord. They brought an offering by fire and a sin offering. [26]All of the people of Israel and the foreigners living among them will be forgiven. No one meant to do wrong.

[27]"Just one person might sin without meaning to. He must bring a year-old female goat for a sin offering. [28]The priest will remove the sin of the person who sinned without meaning to. That person will belong to the Lord again. He will be forgiven. [29]The same teaching is for everyone who sins without meaning to. It is the same for those born Israelites and for foreigners living among you.

[30]"But anyone who sins on purpose is against the Lord. That person must be separated from his people. It is the same for someone born among you or a foreigner. [31]That person has turned against the Lord's word. He has not obeyed the Lord's commands. He must surely be separated from the others. He is guilty.'"

A MAN WORKED ON THE SABBATH

[32]This happened when the Israelites were still in the desert. They found a man gathering wood on the Sabbath[d] day. [33]Those who found him gathering wood brought him to Moses and Aaron

and all the people. [34]They held the man under guard. They did not know what to do with him. [35]Then the Lord said to Moses, "The man must die. All the people must kill him with stones outside the camp." [36]So the people took him outside the camp. They killed him with stones as the Lord commanded Moses.

THE TASSELS

[37]The Lord said to Moses, [38]"Speak to the Israelites. Tell them this: 'Tie several pieces of thread together. And tie them to the corners of your clothes. Put a blue thread in each one of these tassels. Wear them from now on. [39]You will have these tassels to look at. They will remind you of the Lord's commands. Then you will obey them. And you won't follow what your bodies want and what your eyes wish for. [40]Remember to obey all my commands. Then you will be God's holy people. [41]I am the Lord your God. I brought you out of Egypt to be your God. I am the Lord your God.'"

KORAH, DATHAN, ABIRAM AND ON

16 Korah, Dathan, Abiram and On turned against Moses. (Korah was the son of Izhar. Izhar was the son of Kohath, and Kohath was the son of Levi. Dathan and Abiram were brothers, the sons of Eliab. And On was the son of Peleth.) Dathan, Abiram and On were from the tribe[d] of Reuben. [2]These 4 men gathered 250 other Israelite men and challenged Moses. They were well-known leaders chosen by the community. [3]They came as a group to speak to Moses and Aaron. The men said, "You have gone too far. All the people are holy. Every one of them is holy. And the Lord is with them. So why do you put yourselves above all the people?"

[4]When Moses heard this, he bowed facedown. [5]Then he said to Korah and all his followers: "Tomorrow morning the Lord will show who belongs to him. The Lord will bring the one who is holy near

to him. The Lord will bring to himself the person he chooses. [6]So Korah, you and all your followers do this: Get some pans for burning incense.[d] [7]Tomorrow put fire and incense in them. Then take them before the Lord. He will choose the man who is holy. You Levites have gone too far."

[8]Moses also said to Korah, "Listen, you Levites. [9]The God of Israel has separated you from the rest of the Israelites. He brought you near to himself. You do the work in the Lord's Holy Tent.[d] You stand before all the Israelites and serve them. Isn't that enough? [10]The Lord has brought you and all your fellow Levites near to himself. Now you want to be priests. [11]You and your followers have joined together against the Lord. Your complaint is not against Aaron."

[12]Then Moses called Dathan and Abiram, the sons of Eliab. But they said, "We will not come! [13]You have brought us out of a land where much food grows. You brought us to the desert to kill us. And now you want to order us around. [14]You haven't brought us into a land where much food grows. You haven't given us any land with fields and vineyards. Will you put out the eyes of these men? No! We will not come!"

[15]Then Moses became very angry. He said to the Lord, "Don't accept their gifts. I have not taken anything from them, not even a donkey. I have not done wrong to any of them."

[16]Then Moses said to Korah, "You and all your followers must stand before the Lord tomorrow. And Aaron will stand there with you and them. [17]Each of you must take your pan and put incense in it. Present these 250 pans before the Lord. You and Aaron must also present your pans." [18]So each man got his pan and put burning incense in it. Then they stood with Moses and Aaron at the entrance to the Meeting Tent. [19]Korah gathered all his followers who were against Moses

and Aaron. And they stood at the entrance to the Meeting Tent. Then the glory of the Lord appeared to everyone.

²⁰The Lord said to Moses and Aaron, ²¹"Move away from these men. In a minute I will destroy them."

²²But Moses and Aaron bowed facedown. They cried out, "God, you are the God over the spirits of all people. Please don't be angry with this whole group. Only one man has really sinned."

²³Then the Lord said to Moses, ²⁴"Tell everyone to move away from the tents of Korah, Dathan and Abiram."

²⁵Moses stood and went to Dathan and Abiram. The elders of Israel followed him. ²⁶Moses warned the people, "Move away from the tents of these evil men! Don't touch anything of theirs. If you do, you will be destroyed because of their sins." ²⁷So they moved away from the tents of Korah, Dathan and Abiram. Dathan and Abiram were standing outside their tents with their wives, children and little babies.

²⁸Then Moses said, "Now you will know that the Lord has sent me to do all these things. It was not my idea. ²⁹If these men die a normal death—the way men usually die—then the Lord did not really send me. ³⁰But if the Lord does something new, you will know they have insulted the Lord. The earth will open and swallow them. Alive, they will go to where the dead are. And everything that belongs to them will go with them."

³¹When Moses finished saying these things, the ground under the men opened up. ³²The earth seemed to open its mouth and swallow them. All their families, all Korah's men and everything they owned went down. ³³They were buried alive, going to where the dead are. And everything they owned went with them. Then the earth closed over them. They died and were gone from the community. ³⁴The people of Israel around them heard their screams. They ran away and said, "The earth will swallow us, too!"

³⁵Then a fire came down from the Lord. It destroyed the 250 men who had presented the incense.

³⁶The Lord said to Moses, ³⁷"Tell Eleazar son of Aaron, the priest, to take all the incense pans out of the fire. Have him scatter the coals. But the incense pans are still holy. ³⁸These men sinned and lost their lives. Take their pans and hammer them into flat sheets. Cover the altar with them. They are holy because they were presented to the Lord. It will be a sign to the Israelites."

³⁹So Eleazar the priest gathered all the bronze pans. These were the pans brought by the men who were burned up. Eleazar had the pans hammered into flat sheets to put on the altar. ⁴⁰This is what the Lord had commanded him through Moses. These sheets were to remind the Israelites that only descendantsᵈ of Aaron should burn incense before the Lord. Anyone else would die like Korah and his followers.

AARON SAVES THE PEOPLE

⁴¹The next day all the Israelites complained against Moses and Aaron. They said, "You have killed the Lord's people."

⁴²The people gathered to complain against Moses and Aaron. But when they turned toward the Meeting Tent,ᵈ the cloud covered it. The glory of the Lord appeared. ⁴³Then Moses and Aaron went in front of the Meeting Tent.

⁴⁴The Lord said to Moses, ⁴⁵"Move away from these people. In a minute I am going to destroy them." So Moses and Aaron bowed facedown.

⁴⁶Then Moses said to Aaron, "Get your pan. Put fire from the altar and incenseᵈ in it. Hurry to the people and remove their sin. The Lord is angry with them. The sickness has already started." ⁴⁷So Aaron did as Moses said. He ran to the middle of all the people. The sickness had already started among them. So Aaron offered the incense to remove their sin. ⁴⁸He stood between the living

and the dead. And the sickness stopped there. [49]But 14,700 people died from that sickness. There were also those who died because of Korah. [50]Then Aaron went back to Moses at the entrance to the Meeting Tent. The terrible sickness had been stopped.

AARON'S WALKING STICK BUDS

17 The Lord said to Moses, [2]"Speak to the people of Israel. Get 12 walking sticks from them. Get 1 from the leader of each tribe.[d] Write the name of each man on his stick. [3]On the stick from Levi, write Aaron's name. There must be 1 stick for the head of each tribe. [4]Put them in the Meeting Tent.[d] Place them in front of the Box[d] of the Agreement, where I meet with you. [5]I will choose one man. His stick will begin to grow leaves. And I will stop the Israelites from always complaining against you."

[6]So Moses spoke to the Israelites. Each of the 12 leaders gave him a walking stick. And Aaron's walking stick was among them. [7]Moses put them before the Lord in the Tent of the Agreement.

[8]The next day Moses entered the Tent. He saw that Aaron's stick had grown leaves. (It stood for the family of Levi.) It had even budded, blossomed and produced almonds. [9]So Moses brought out to the Israelites all the walking sticks from the Lord's presence. They all looked, and each man took back his stick.

[10]Then the Lord said to Moses, "Put Aaron's walking stick back. Put it in front of the Box of the Agreement. It will be a sign to these people who are always turning against me. This will stop their complaining against me. Now they won't die." [11]So Moses obeyed what the Lord commanded him.

[12]The people of Israel said to Moses, "We are going to die! We are lost. We are all lost! [13]Anyone who even comes near the Holy Tent of the Lord will die. Will we all die?"

THE WORK OF THE PRIESTS AND LEVITES

18 The Lord said to Aaron, "You, your sons and your family are now responsible for any wrongs done against the Holy Place. You and your sons are responsible for any wrongs done against the priests. [2]Bring with you your fellow Levites from your tribe.[d] They will help you and your sons serve in the Tent[d] of the Agreement. [3]They are under your control. They will do all the work that needs to be done in the Tent. But they must not go near the things in the Holy Place or near the altar. If they do, both you and they will die. [4]They will join you. They will take care of the Meeting Tent. They must do the work at the Tent. No one else may come near you.

[5]"You must take care of the Holy Place and the altar. Then I won't become angry with the Israelites again. [6]I myself chose your fellow Levites from among the Israelites. They are a gift given for you to the Lord. Their work is at the Meeting Tent. [7]But only you and your sons may serve as priests. Only you may serve at the altar or go behind the curtain. I am giving you this gift of serving as a priest. Anyone else who comes near the Holy Place will be put to death."

[8]Then the Lord said to Aaron, "I myself make you responsible for the offerings given to me. All the holy offerings that the Israelites give to me, I give to you. They are for you and your sons as your share. They will be your continual portion. [9]Your share of the holy offerings is that part which is not burned. The people will bring me gifts as most holy offerings. These are grain or sin or penalty offerings. These will be set apart for you and your sons. [10]You must eat it in a most holy place. Any male may eat it. But you must respect it as holy.

[11]"I also give you the offerings the Israelites present to me. I give these to you and your sons and daughters. This is your share. Anyone in your family who is clean[d] may eat it.

^{12}"And I give you all the best olive oil and all the best new wine and grain. This is what the Israelites give to me, the Lord. These are the first things they harvest. ^{13}They bring to the Lord all the first things they harvest. They will be yours. Anyone in your family who is clean may eat these things.

^{14}"Everything in Israel that is given to the Lord is yours. ^{15}The first one born to any family will be offered to the Lord. This is true for both men and animals. And that will be yours. But you must make a payment for every firstborn^d son and every firstborn animal that is unclean. ^{16}When they are one month old, you must make a payment for them. The cost will be two ounces of silver as set by the Holy Place measure.

^{17}"But you must not make a payment for the firstborn ox or sheep or goat. Those animals are holy. Sprinkle their blood on the altar and burn their fat. This is an offering made by fire. The smell is pleasing to the Lord. ^{18}But the meat will be yours. Also the breast that is presented and the right thigh will be yours. ^{19}Anything the Israelites present as holy gifts I, the Lord, give to you. It goes to you, your sons and daughters. It is your continual portion. This is a lasting promise before the Lord to you and your children forever."

^{20}The Lord also said to Aaron, "You will not inherit any of the land. And you will not own any land among the other people. I will be yours. Out of all the Israelites, only you will inherit me.

^{21}"The people of Israel will give a tenth of what they make. I give that tenth to the Levites. This is their payment for the work they do serving at the Meeting Tent. ^{22}But the other Israelites must never go near the Meeting Tent. If they do, they will die for their sin. ^{23}Only the Levites should work in the Meeting Tent. They are responsible for any sins against it. This is a rule from now on.

The Levites will not get any land among the other Israelites. ^{24}But the Israelites will give a tenth of everything they make to me. And I will give that tenth to the Levites. That is why I said about the Levites: 'They will not get any land among the Israelites.'"

^{25}The Lord said to Moses, ^{26}"Speak to the Levites. Tell them: 'You will receive a tenth of everything the Israelites make. I give that to you. But you must give a tenth of that back to the Lord. ^{27}I will accept your offering just as much as I accept the offerings from others. They give new grain or new wine. ^{28}In this way you will present an offering to the Lord as the other Israelites do. You will receive a tenth from the Israelites. Then you will give a tenth of that to Aaron the priest as the Lord's share. ^{29}Choose the best and holiest part from what you are given. This is the portion you must give to the Lord.'

^{30}"Say to the Levites: 'When you present the best it will be accepted as much as the grain and wine from the other people. ^{31}You and your families may eat all that is left anywhere. This is your pay for your work in the Meeting Tent. ^{32}And if you always give the best part to the Lord, you will never be guilty. If you do not sin against the holy offerings of the Israelites, you will not die.'"

THE OFFERING FOR CLEANSING

19 The Lord said to Moses and Aaron, ^{2}"These are the teachings that the Lord commanded. Tell the Israelites to get a young red cow. It must not have anything wrong with it. It must not have been worked. ^{3}Give the cow to Eleazar the priest. He will take it outside the camp and kill it. ^{4}Then Eleazar the priest must put some of the blood on his finger. He must sprinkle it seven times toward the front of the Meeting Tent.^{d} ^{5}Then the whole cow must be burned while he watches. The skin, the meat, the blood and the intestines must all be burned. ⁶Then the priest must take a cedar stick, a hyssop branch and a red string. He must throw them onto the burning cow. ⁷Then the priest must wash himself and his clothes with water. After that, he may come back into the camp. But he will be unclean*ᵈ* until evening. ⁸The man who burns the cow must wash himself and his clothes in water. He will be unclean until evening.

⁹"Then someone who is clean will collect the ashes from the cow. He will put them in a clean place outside the camp. The Israelites will use these ashes in a special ceremony to cleanse away sin. ¹⁰The man who collected the cow's ashes must wash his clothes. He will be unclean until evening. This is a lasting rule. It is for the Israelites and for the foreigners among them.

¹¹"Whoever touches a dead body will be unclean for seven days. ¹²He must wash himself with this water. He must do this on the third day and on the seventh day. Then he will be clean. But if he does not wash himself on the third day and the seventh day, he cannot be clean. ¹³Whoever touches a dead body is unclean. If he stays unclean and goes to the Lord's Holy Tent, it becomes unclean. So he must be separated from Israel. If the cleansing water is not sprinkled on him, he will stay unclean.

¹⁴"This is the teaching about someone who dies in his tent. Anyone in the tent or who enters it will be unclean for seven days. ¹⁵And every open jar or pot without a cover becomes unclean. ¹⁶If anyone touches someone who was killed by a sword or who died a natural death, he is unclean. If he touches a human bone or a grave, he is unclean. He will be unclean for seven days.

¹⁷"So you must use the ashes from the burnt offering to make that person clean again. Pour fresh water over the ashes into a jar. ¹⁸A clean person must take a hyssop branch and dip it into the water.

Then he must sprinkle it over the tent and its objects. And he must sprinkle the people who were there. He must sprinkle anyone who touched a bone or the body of someone who was killed. He must sprinkle anyone who touched a dead person or a grave. ¹⁹Then someone who is clean must sprinkle this water on the unclean person. He must do this on the third day and on the seventh day. On the seventh day that person becomes clean. He must wash his clothes and take a bath. He will be clean that evening. ²⁰If anyone who is unclean does not become clean, he must be separated from the community. He was not sprinkled with the cleansing water. He stays unclean. He could make the Holy Tent unclean. ²¹This is a lasting rule. Whoever sprinkles the cleansing water must also wash his clothes. Anyone who touches the water will be unclean until evening. ²²Anyone the unclean person touches becomes unclean. And whoever touches him will be unclean until evening."

WATER FROM THE ROCK

20 In the first month all the people of Israel arrived at the Desert of Zin. They stayed at Kadesh. There Miriam died and was buried. ²There was no water for the people. So they came together against Moses and Aaron. ³They argued with Moses. They said, "We should have died in front of the Lord as our brothers did. ⁴Why did you bring the Lord's people into this desert? Are we and our animals to die here? ⁵Why did you bring us from Egypt to this terrible place? It has no grain, figs or pomegranates.*ᵈ* And there's no water to drink!"

⁶So Moses and Aaron left the people. Then they went to the entrance of the Meeting Tent.*ᵈ* They bowed facedown. And the glory of the Lord appeared to them. ⁷The Lord said to Moses, ⁸"You and your brother Aaron should gather the people. Also take your walking stick. Speak to that rock in front of them. Then

water will flow from it. Give that water to the people and their animals."

⁹So Moses took the stick from in front of the Lord. He did as the Lord had said. ¹⁰He and Aaron gathered the people in front of the rock. Then Moses said, "Now listen to me, you complainers! Do you want us to bring water out of this rock?" ¹¹Then Moses lifted his hand and hit the rock twice with his stick. Water began pouring out. And the people and their animals drank it.

¹²But the Lord said to Moses and Aaron, "You did not believe me. You did not honor me as holy before the people. So you will not lead them into the land I will give them."

¹³These are the waters of Meribah.ⁿ Here the Israelites argued with the Lord. And the Lord showed them he was holy.

EDOM WILL NOT LET ISRAEL PASS

¹⁴From Kadesh, Moses sent messengers to the king of Edom. He said, "Your brothers, the Israelites, say to you: You know about all the troubles we have had. ¹⁵Our ancestors went down into Egypt. And we lived there for many years. The people of Egypt were cruel to our ancestors. ¹⁶But we cried out to the Lord. He heard us and sent us an angel to bring us out of Egypt.

"Now we are here at Kadesh, a town on the edge of your land. ¹⁷Please let us pass through your country. We will not touch any fields of grain or vineyards. We will not drink water from the wells. We will travel only along the king's road. We will not turn right or left until we have passed through your country."

¹⁸But the king of Edom answered: "You may not pass through here. If you try, I will come and meet you with swords."

¹⁹The Israelites answered: "We will go along the main road. If our animals drink any of your water, we will pay for it. We only want to walk through. That's all."

²⁰But he answered: "You may not pass through here."

Then the Edomites went out to meet the Israelites with a large and powerful army. ²¹The Edomites refused to let them pass through their country. So the Israelites turned back.

AARON DIES

²²All the Israelites moved from Kadesh to Mount Hor. ²³It was near the border of Edom. The Lord said to Moses and Aaron, ²⁴"Aaron will die. He will not enter the land that I'm giving to the Israelites. This is because you both acted against my command at the waters of Meribah. ²⁵Take Aaron and his son Eleazar up on Mount Hor. ²⁶Take off Aaron's special clothes and put them on his son Eleazar. Aaron will die there. He will join his ancestors."

²⁷Moses obeyed the Lord's command. They climbed up Mount Hor. All the people saw them go. ²⁸Moses took off Aaron's clothes. He put them on Aaron's son Eleazar. Then Aaron died there on top of the mountain. And Moses and Eleazar came back down the mountain. ²⁹Then all the people learned that Aaron was dead. So everyone in Israel cried for him for 30 days.

WAR WITH THE CANAANITES

21 The Canaanite king of Arad lived in the southern area. He heard that the Israelites were coming on the road to Atharim. So he attacked them and captured some of them. ²Then the Israelites made this promise to the Lord: "If you will help us defeat these people, we will completely destroy their cities." ³The Lord listened to the Israelites. And he let them defeat the Canaanites. The Israelites completely destroyed the Canaanites and their cities. So the place was named Hormah.ⁿ

20:13 **Meribah** This name in Hebrew means "argument."
21:3 **Hormah** This name in Hebrew means "completely destroyed."

THE BRONZE SNAKE

[4]The Israelites left Mount Hor and went on the road toward the Gulf of Aqaba. They did this to go around the country of Edom. But the people became impatient on the way. [5]They grumbled at God and Moses. They said, "Why did you bring us out of Egypt? We will die in this desert! There is no bread! There is no water! And we hate this terrible food!"

[6]So the Lord sent them poisonous snakes. They bit the people, and many of the Israelites died. [7]The people came to Moses and said, "We sinned when we grumbled at you and the Lord. Pray that the Lord will take away these snakes." So Moses prayed for the people.

[8]The Lord said to Moses, "Make a bronze snake. And put it on a pole. If anyone is bitten, he should look at it. Then he will live." [9]So Moses made a bronze snake. And he put it on a pole. Then when a snake bit anyone, he looked at the bronze snake and lived.

THE JOURNEY TO MOAB

[10]The Israelites went and camped at Oboth. [11]They went from Oboth to Iye Abarim. This was in the desert east of Moab. [12]From there they went and camped in the Zered Valley. [13]From there they went and camped across the Arnon. This was in the desert just inside the Amorite country. The Arnon is the border between the Moabites and the Amorites. [14]That is why the Book of the Wars of the Lord says:

> " . . . and Waheb in Suphah, and the ravines,
> the Arnon, [15]and the slopes of the ravines
> that lead to the settlement of Ar.
> These places are at the border of Moab."

[16]The Israelites went from there to Beer. A well is there where the Lord said to Moses, "Gather the people. I will give them water."

[17]Then the Israelites sang this song:

> "Pour out water, well!
> Sing about it.
> [18]Princes dug this well.
> Important men made this hole.
> With their scepters[d] and poles, they dug it."

The people went from the desert to Mattanah. [19]From Mattanah they went to Nahaliel and on to Bamoth. [20]From Bamoth they went to the valley of Moab. There the top of Mount Pisgah looks over the desert.

SIHON AND OG

[21]The people of Israel sent messengers to Sihon, king of the Amorites. They said to him, [22]"Let us pass through your country. We will not go through any fields of grain or vineyards. We will not drink water from the wells. We will travel only along the king's road. We will stay on it until we have passed through your country."

[23]But King Sihon would not let the Israelites pass through his country. He gathered his army together. They marched out to meet Israel in the desert. At Jahaz they fought the Israelites. [24]Israel killed the king. Then they captured his land from the Arnon River to the Jabbok River. They took the land as far as the Ammonite border. That border was strongly defended. [25]Israel captured all the Amorite cities and lived in them. They took Heshbon and all the towns around it. [26]Heshbon was the city where Sihon, the Amorite king, lived. In the past he had fought with the king of Moab. Sihon had taken all the land as far as the Arnon.

[27]That is why the poets say:

> "Come to Heshbon
> and rebuild it.
> Rebuild Sihon's city.
> [28]A fire began in Heshbon.
> Flames came from Sihon's city.
> It destroyed Ar in Moab.
> It burned the Arnon highlands.

²⁹How terrible for you, Moab!
The people of Chemosh*d* are ruined.
His sons ran away.
His daughters were captured
by Sihon, king of the Amorites.
³⁰But we defeated those Amorites.
We ruined their towns from
Heshbon to Dibon.
We destroyed them as far as
Nophah, near Medeba."

³¹So Israel lived in the land of the Amorites.

³²Moses sent spies to the town of Jazer. Then they captured the towns around it. They forced out the Amorites who lived there.

³³Then the Israelites went up the road toward Bashan. Og, the king of Bashan, and his army marched out to meet the Israelites. They fought at Edrei.

³⁴The Lord said to Moses, "Don't be afraid of him. I will hand him, his whole army and his land over to you. Do to him what you did to Sihon, the Amorite king who lived in Heshbon."

³⁵So the Israelites killed Og and his sons and all his army. No one was left alive. And they took his land.

BALAAM AND BALAK

22 Then the people of Israel went to the plains of Moab. They camped near the Jordan River across from Jericho.

²Balak son of Zippor saw everything the Israelites had done to the Amorites. ³And Moab was scared of so many Israelites. Truly, Moab was terrified by them.

⁴The Moabites said to the elders of Midian, "This mob will take everything around us. It will be like an ox eating grass."

Balak son of Zippor was the king of Moab at this time. ⁵He sent messengers to Balaam son of Beor at Pethor. It was near the Euphrates River in the land of Amaw. Balak said, "A nation has come out of Egypt. They cover the land. They have camped next to me. ⁶They are too powerful for me. So come and put a curse on them. Maybe then I can defeat them and make them leave the area. I know that if you bless someone, the blessings happen. And if you put a curse on someone, it happens."

⁷The elders of Moab and Midian went with payment in their hands. They found Balaam. Then they told him what Balak had said.

⁸Balaam said to them, "Stay here for the night. I will tell you what the Lord tells me." So the Moabite leaders stayed with him.

⁹God came to Balaam and asked, "Who are these men with you?"

¹⁰Balaam said to God, "The king of Moab, Balak son of Zippor, sent them. He sent me this message: ¹¹'A nation has come out of Egypt. They cover the land. So come and put a curse on them. Then maybe I can fight them and force them out of my land.'"

¹²But God said to Balaam, "Do not go with them. Don't put a curse on those people. I have blessed them."

¹³The next morning Balaam awoke and said to Balak's leaders, "Go back to your own country. The Lord will not let me go with you."

¹⁴So the Moabite leaders went back to Balak. They said, "Balaam refused to come with us."

¹⁵So Balak sent other leaders. He sent more leaders this time. And they were more important. ¹⁶They went to Balaam and said, "Balak son of Zippor says this: Please don't let anything stop you from coming to me. ¹⁷I will pay you well. I will do what you say. Come and put a curse on these people for me."

¹⁸But Balaam answered Balak's servants, "King Balak could give me his palace full of silver and gold. But I cannot disobey the Lord my God in anything, great or small. ¹⁹You stay here tonight as the other men did. I will find out what more the Lord tells me."

20That night God came to Balaam. He said, "These men have come to ask you to go with them. Go. But only do what I tell you."

BALAAM AND HIS DONKEY

21Balaam got up the next morning. He put a saddle on his donkey. Then he went with the Moabite leaders. 22But God became angry because Balaam went. So the angel of the Lord stood in the road to stop Balaam. Balaam was riding his donkey. And he had two servants with him. 23The donkey saw the angel of the Lord standing in the road. The angel had a sword in his hand. So the donkey left the road and went into the field. Balaam hit the donkey to force her back on the road.

24Later, the angel of the Lord stood on a narrow path between two vineyards. There were walls on both sides. 25Again the donkey saw the angel of the Lord. So the donkey walked close to one wall. This crushed Balaam's foot against the wall. So he hit her again.

26The angel of the Lord went ahead again. The angel stood at a narrow place. It was too narrow to turn left or right. 27The donkey saw the angel of the Lord. So she lay down under Balaam. Balaam was very angry and hit her with his stick. 28Then the Lord made the donkey talk. She said to Balaam, "What have I done to make you hit me three times?"

29Balaam answered the donkey, "You have made me look foolish! I wish I had a sword in my hand! I would kill you right now!"

30But the donkey said to Balaam, "I am your very own donkey. You have ridden me for years. Have I ever done this to you before?"

"No," Balaam said.

31Then the Lord let Balaam see the angel. The angel of the Lord was standing in the road with his sword drawn. Then Balaam bowed facedown on the ground.

32The angel of the Lord asked Balaam, "Why have you hit your donkey three times? I have stood here to stop you. What you are doing is wrong. 33The donkey saw me. She turned away from me three times. If she had not turned away, I would have killed you by now. But I would let her live."

34Then Balaam said to the angel of the Lord, "I have sinned. I did not know you were standing in the road to stop me. If I am wrong, I will go back."

35The angel of the Lord said to Balaam, "Go with these men. But say only what I tell you." So Balaam went with Balak's leaders.

36Balak heard that Balaam was coming. So he went out to meet him at Ar in Moab. It was beside the Arnon, at the edge of his country. 37Balak said to Balaam, "I had asked you before to come quickly. Why didn't you come to me? I am able to reward you well."

38But Balaam answered, "I have come to you now. But I can't say just anything. I can only say what God tells me to say."

39Then Balaam went with Balak to Kiriath Huzoth. 40Balak offered cattle and sheep as a sacrifice. He gave some meat to Balaam and the leaders with him.

41The next morning Balak took Balaam to Bamoth Baal. From there he could see the edge of the Israelite camp.

BALAAM'S FIRST MESSAGE

23 Balaam said, "Build me seven altars here. And prepare seven bulls and seven male sheep for me." 2Balak did what Balaam asked. Then they offered a male sheep and a bull on each of the altars.

3Then Balaam said to Balak, "Stay here beside your burnt offering. I will go. Maybe the Lord will come to me. I will tell you whatever he shows me." Then Balaam went to a higher place.

4God came to Balaam there. Balaam said to him, "I have prepared seven altars. And I have offered a bull and a male sheep on each altar."

5The Lord told Balaam what he should

say. Then the Lord said, "Go back to Balak and give him this message."

⁶So Balaam went back to Balak. Balak and all the leaders of Moab were still standing beside his burnt offering. ⁷Then Balaam gave them this message:

"Balak brought me here from Aram.
The king of Moab brought me from
   the eastern mountains.
Balak said, 'Come, put a curse on the
   people of Jacob for me.
Come, wish evil on the people
   of Israel.'
⁸But God has not cursed them.
So I cannot curse them.
The Lord has not wished evil on them.
So I cannot wish evil on them.
⁹I see them from the mountains.
I see them from the hills.
I see a people who live alone.
They think they are different
   from other nations.
¹⁰No one can number the people
   of Jacob.
No one can count a fourth of Israel.
Let me die like good men.
Let me end up like them!"

¹¹Balak said to Balaam, "What have you done to me? I brought you here to curse my enemies. But you have only blessed them!"

¹²But Balaam answered, "I must say what the Lord tells me to say."

BALAAM'S SECOND MESSAGE

¹³Then Balak said to him, "Come with me to another place. There you can also see the people. But you can only see part of them, not all of them. Curse them for me from there." ¹⁴So Balak took Balaam to the field of Zophim. This was on top of Mount Pisgah. There Balak built seven altars. And he offered a bull and a male sheep on each altar.

¹⁵So Balaam said to Balak, "Stay here by your burnt offering. I will meet with God over there."

¹⁶So the Lord came to Balaam. He told Balaam what to say. Then he said, "Go back to Balak and say such and such."

¹⁷So Balaam went to Balak. Balak and the leaders of Moab were standing beside his burnt offering. Balak asked him, "What did the Lord say?"

¹⁸Then Balaam gave this message:

"Stand up, Balak, and listen.
Hear me, son of Zippor.
¹⁹God is not a man. He will not lie.
God is not a human being. He does
   not change his mind.
What he says he will do, he does.
What he promises, he keeps.
²⁰He told me to bless them.
So I cannot change the blessing.
²¹He has found no wrong in the people
   of Jacob.
He saw no fault in Israel.
The Lord their God is with them.
They praise their King.
²²God brought them out of Egypt.
They are as strong as a wild ox.
²³No tricks will work on the people
   of Jacob.
No magic works against Israel.
People now say this about them,
'Look what God has done!'
²⁴The people are strong like a lioness.
They get up like a lion.
Lions don't rest until they have eaten.
They drink their enemies' blood."

²⁵Then Balak said to Balaam, "You haven't cursed these people. So at least don't bless them!"

²⁶Balaam answered Balak, "I told you before. I can only do what the Lord tells me."

BALAAM'S THIRD MESSAGE

²⁷Then Balak said to Balaam, "Come, I will take you to another place. Maybe God will be pleased. He may let you curse them from there." ²⁸So Balak took Balaam to the top of Peor. This mountain looks over the desert.

²⁹Balaam told Balak, "Build me seven altars here. Then prepare for me seven bulls and seven male sheep." ³⁰Balak did what Balaam asked. He offered a bull and a male sheep on each altar.

24 Balaam saw that the Lord wanted to bless Israel. So Balaam did not try to use any magic. He looked toward the desert. ²Balaam saw the Israelites camped in their tribes.*d* Then the Spirit*d* of God entered him. ³And Balaam gave this message:

"This is the message of Balaam son of Beor.

This is the message of a man who sees clearly.

⁴This is the message of a man who heard the words of God.

I see a vision from the All-Powerful One.

My eyes are open as I fall before him.

⁵Your tents are beautiful, people of Jacob!

So are your homes, Israel!

⁶Your tents spread out like valleys.

They are like gardens beside a river.

They are like spices planted by the Lord.

They are like cedar trees growing by the water.

⁷Israel's water buckets will always be full.

Their crops will have plenty of water.

Their king will be greater than Agag.

Their kingdom will be very great.

⁸God brought them out of Egypt.

They are as strong as a wild ox.

They will defeat their enemies.

They will break their enemies' bones.

They will shoot them with arrows.

⁹Like a lion, they lie waiting to attack.

No one would wake a sleeping lion.

Anyone who blesses you will be blessed.

And anyone who curses you will be cursed."

¹⁰Then Balak was angry with Balaam. Balak pounded his fist. He said to Balaam, "I called you here to curse my enemies. But you have blessed them three times. ¹¹Now go home! I said I would pay you well. But the Lord has made you lose your reward."

¹²Balaam said to Balak, "You sent messengers to me. I told them, ¹³'Balak could give me his palace filled with silver and gold. But I still cannot go against the Lord's commands. I could not do anything, good or bad, on my own. I must say what the Lord says.' ¹⁴Now I am going back to my own people. But I will tell you what these people will do to your people in the future."

BALAAM'S FINAL MESSAGE

¹⁵Then Balaam gave this message:

"This is the message of Balaam son of Beor.

This is the message of a man who sees clearly.

¹⁶This is the message of a man who hears the words of God.

I know the Most High God.

I see a vision from the All-Powerful One.

My eyes are open as I fall before him.

¹⁷I see someone who will come some day.

I see someone who will come, but not soon.

A star will come from Jacob.

A ruler will rise from Israel.

He will crush the heads of the Moabites.

He will smash the skulls of the sons of Sheth.

¹⁸Edom will be conquered.

His enemy Edom will be conquered.

But Israel will grow wealthy.

¹⁹The descendants*d* of Jacob will beat them down.

The Israelites will destroy those left in the city."

²⁰Then Balaam saw Amalek and gave this message:

"Amalek was the most important nation.

But Amalek will be destroyed at
    last."
²¹Then Balaam saw the Kenites and
gave this message:
"Your home is safe.
    It is like a nest on a cliff.
²²But you Kenites will be burned up.
    Assyria will keep you captive."
²³Then Balaam gave this message:
"No one can live when God does this.
²⁴   Ships will sail from the shores of
        Cyprus.
They will defeat Assyria and Eber.
    But they will also be destroyed."
²⁵Then Balaam got up and returned
home. Balak also went on his way.

ISRAEL AT PEOR

25 The people of Israel were still
camped at Acacia. The men began
sinning sexually with Moabite women.
²The women invited them to their sacrifices to their false gods. The Israelites ate
food there and worshiped these gods.
³So the Israelites began to worship Baal*d*
of Peor. And the Lord was very angry
with them.

⁴The Lord said to Moses, "Get all the
leaders of the people. Then kill them in
open daylight in the presence of the
Lord. Then the Lord will not be angry
with the people of Israel."

⁵So Moses said to Israel's judges,
"Each of you must put to death your
men who have become worshipers of
Baal of Peor."

⁶Moses and the Israelites were gathered at the entrance to the Meeting Tent.*d*
They were crying there. Then an Israelite
man brought a Midianite woman to his
brothers. This was in plain sight of Moses
and all the people. ⁷Phinehas son of
Eleazar, the son of Aaron, the priest, saw
this. So he left the meeting and got his
spear. ⁸He followed the Israelite into his
tent. And he drove his spear through
both the Israelite man and the Midianite
woman. Then the terrible sickness
among the Israelites stopped.

⁹This sickness had killed 24,000
people.
¹⁰The Lord said to Moses, ¹¹"Phinehas
son of Eleazar, the son of Aaron, the priest,
has saved the Israelites from my anger.
He is like I am in his concern for the
people. He tried to save my honor among
them. So I will not kill them. ¹²So tell
Phinehas that I am making my peace
agreement with him. ¹³He and all his
descendants*d* will have an agreement.
They will always be priests. This is because
he had great concern for the honor of his
God. He removed the sins of the Israelites so they would belong to God."

¹⁴The Israelite man who was killed
with the Midianite woman was named
Zimri son of Salu. He was the leader of a
family in the tribe*d* of Simeon. ¹⁵And the
name of the Midianite woman who was
put to death was Cozbi daughter of Zur.
Zur was the chief of a Midianite family.

¹⁶The Lord said to Moses, ¹⁷"The Midianites are your enemies. You should kill
them. ¹⁸They have already made you
their enemies. They tricked you at Peor.
Then there was Cozbi, the daughter of a
Midianite leader. She was the woman
who was killed when the sickness came.
It came because the people were worshiping the false god at Peor."

THE PEOPLE ARE COUNTED

26 After the great sickness, the Lord
spoke to Moses and Eleazar son
of Aaron, the priest. He said, ²"Count all
the people of Israel by families. Count all
the men who are 20 years old or older.
They will serve in the army of Israel."
³Moses and Eleazar the priest spoke to
the people. They were on the plains of
Moab near the Jordan River, across from
Jericho. They said, ⁴"Count the men 20
years old or older. This is what the Lord
commanded Moses."

Here are the Israelites who came out
of Egypt:
⁵The tribe*d* of Reuben was counted.
Reuben was the first son born to Israel.

From Hanoch came the Hanochite family group. From Pallu came the Palluite family group. ⁶From Hezron came the Hezronite family group. From Carmi came the Carmite family group. ⁷These were the family groups of Reuben. The total number of men was 43,730.

⁸The son of Pallu was Eliab. ⁹Eliab's sons were Nemuel, Dathan and Abiram. Dathan and Abiram were the leaders who turned against Moses and Aaron. They followed Korah when he turned against the Lord. ¹⁰The earth opened up and swallowed them and Korah. They died when the fire burned up the 250 men. This was a warning. ¹¹But the children of Korah did not die.

¹²These were the family groups in the tribe of Simeon. From Nemuel came the Nemuelite family group. From Jamin came the Jaminite family group. From Jakin came the Jakinite family group. ¹³From Zerah came the Zerahite family group. From Shaul came the Shaulite family group. ¹⁴These were the family groups of Simeon. The total number of men was 22,200.

¹⁵These were the family groups in the tribe of Gad. From Zephon came the Zephonite family group. From Haggi came the Haggite family group. From Shuni came the Shunite family group. ¹⁶From Ozni came the Oznite family group. From Eri came the Erite family group. ¹⁷From Arodi came the Arodite family group. From Areli came the Arelite family group. ¹⁸These were the family groups of Gad. The total number of men was 40,500.

¹⁹Two of Judah's sons, Er and Onan, died in Canaan.

²⁰These were the family groups in the tribe of Judah. From Shelah came the Shelanite family group. From Perez came the Perezite family group. From Zerah came the Zerahite family group. ²¹These were the family groups from Perez. From Hezron came the Hezronite family group. From Hamul came the Hamulite family group. ²²These were the family groups of Judah. The total number of men was 76,500.

²³These were the family groups in the tribe of Issachar. From Tola came the Tolaite family group. From Puah came the Puite family group. ²⁴From Jashub came the Jashubite family group. From Shimron came the Shimronite family group. ²⁵These were the family groups of Issachar. The total number of men was 64,300.

²⁶These were the family groups in the tribe of Zebulun. From Sered came the Seredite family group. From Elon came the Elonite family group. From Jahleel came the Jahleelite family group. ²⁷These were the family groups of Zebulun. The total number of men was 60,500.

²⁸These were the family groups of Joseph through Manasseh and Ephraim.

²⁹These were the family groups of Manasseh. From Makir came the Makirite family group. (Makir was the father of Gilead.) From Gilead came the Gileadite family group. ³⁰These were the family groups that came from Gilead. From Iezer came the Iezerite family group. From Helek came the Helekite family group. ³¹From Asriel came the Asrielite family group. From Shechem came the Shechemite family group. ³²From Shemida came the Shemidaite family group. From Hepher came the Hepherite family group. ³³(Zelophehad son of Hepher had no sons. He had only daughters. Their names were Mahlah, Noah, Hoglah, Milcah and Tirzah.) ³⁴These were the family groups of Manasseh. The total number of men was 52,700.

³⁵These were the family groups in the tribe of Ephraim. From Shuthelah came the Shuthelahite family group. From Beker came the Bekerite family group. From Tahan came the Tahanite family group. ³⁶This was the family group from Shuthelah. From Eran came the Eranite

family group. [37]These were the family groups of Ephraim. The total number of men was 32,500. These are the family groups that came from Joseph.

[38]These were the family groups in the tribe of Benjamin. From Bela came the Belaite family group. From Ashbel came the Ashbelite family group. From Ahiram came the Ahiramite family group. [39]From Shupham came the Shuphamite family group. From Hupham came the Huphamite family group. [40]These were the family groups from Bela through Ard and Naaman. From Ard came the Ardite family group. From Naaman came the Naamite family group. [41]These were the family groups of Benjamin. The total number of men was 45,600.

[42]This was the family group in the tribe of Dan. From Shuham came the Shuhamite family group. That was the family of Dan. [43]The total number of men in the Shuhamite family group of Dan was 64,400.

[44]These were the family groups in the tribe of Asher. From Imnah came the Imnite family group. From Ishvi came the Ishvite family group. From Beriah came the Beriite family group. [45]These were the family groups that came from Beriah. From Heber came the Heberite family group. From Malkiel came the Malkielite family group. [46](Asher also had a daughter named Serah.) [47]These were the family groups of Asher. The total number of men was 53,400.

[48]These were the family groups in the tribe of Naphtali. From Jahzeel came the Jahzeelite family group. From Guni came the Gunite family group. [49]From Jezer came the Jezerite family group. From Shillem came the Shillemite family group. [50]These were the family groups of Naphtali. The total number of men was 45,400.

[51]So the total number of the men of Israel was 601,730.

[52]The Lord said to Moses, [53]"Divide the land among these people by the number of names. [54]A large tribe will get more land. And a small tribe will get less land. The amount of land each tribe gets will depend on the number of its people. [55]Divide the land by drawing lots.[d] And the land each tribe gets will be named for that tribe. [56]Divide the land by drawing lots. Divide it between large and small groups."

[57]The tribe of Levi was also counted. These were the family groups of Levi. From Gershon came the Gershonite family group. From Kohath came the Kohathite family group. From Merari came the Merarite family group. [58]These also were Levite family groups: the Libnite family group, the Hebronite family group, the Mahlite family group, the Mushite family group and the Korahite family group. (Kohath was the ancestor of Amram. [59]Amram's wife was named Jochebed. She was from the tribe of Levi. She was born in Egypt. She and Amram had two sons, Aaron and Moses, and their sister Miriam. [60]Aaron was the father of Nadab, Abihu, Eleazar and Ithamar. [61]But Nadab and Abihu died. They died because they made an offering before the Lord with the wrong kind of fire.)

[62]The total number of male Levites one month old or older was 23,000. But these men were not counted with the other Israelites. They did not receive any of the land that the Lord gave the other Israelites.

[63]Moses and Eleazar the priest counted all these people. They counted the Israelites on the plains of Moab across the Jordan River from Jericho. [64]Moses and Aaron the priest had counted the Israelites in the Desert of Sinai. But no one Moses counted on the plains of Moab was in the first counting. [65]The Lord had told the Israelites they would all die in the desert. The only two left were Caleb son of Jephunneh and Joshua son of Nun.

ZELOPHEHAD'S DAUGHTERS

27 Zelophehad was the son of Hepher. Hepher was the son of Gilead. Gilead was the son of Makir. Makir was the son of Manasseh. Zelophehad's daughters belonged to the family groups of Manasseh son of Joseph. The daughters' names were Mahlah, Noah, Hoglah, Milcah and Tirzah. ²They went to the entrance of the Meeting Tent.*d* There they stood before Moses, Eleazar the priest, the leaders and all the people. They said, ³"Our father died in the desert. He was not one of Korah's followers who came against the Lord. Our father died because of his own sin. But he had no sons. ⁴Our father's name will die out because he had no sons. Give us property among our father's relatives."

⁵So Moses brought their case to the Lord. ⁶The Lord said to him, ⁷"The daughters of Zelophehad are right. They should get what their father owned. Give them property among their father's relatives.

⁸"Tell the Israelites, 'If a man dies and has no son, then everything he owned should go to his daughter. ⁹If he has no daughter, then everything he owned should go to his brothers. ¹⁰If he has no brothers, then everything he owned should go to his father's brothers. ¹¹If his father had no brothers, then everything he owned should go to the nearest relative in his family group. This should be a rule among the people of Israel as the Lord has given this command to Moses.'"

JOSHUA IS THE NEW LEADER

¹²Then the Lord said to Moses, "Climb this mountain in the Abarim Mountains. Look at the land I have given to the Israelites. ¹³After you have seen it, you will die as your brother Aaron did. ¹⁴You both acted against my command in the Desert of Zin. You did not honor me as holy before the people at the waters of Meribah." (This was at Meribah in Kadesh in the Desert of Zin.)

¹⁵Moses said to the Lord, ¹⁶"The Lord is the God of the spirits of all people. May he choose a good leader for these people. ¹⁷He must go in and out before them. He must lead them out like sheep and bring them in. The Lord's people must not be like sheep without a shepherd."

¹⁸So the Lord said to Moses, "Take Joshua son of Nun. My Spirit*d* is in him. Put your hand on him. ¹⁹Have him stand before Eleazar the priest and all the people. Then give him his orders as they watch. ²⁰Let him share your honor. Then all the Israelites will obey him. ²¹He must stand before Eleazar the priest. And Eleazar will get advice from the Lord by using the Urim.*d* At his command all the Israelites will go out. At his command they will all come in."

²²Moses did what the Lord told him. Moses had Joshua stand before Eleazar the priest and all the people. ²³Then Moses put his hands on him and gave him orders. This was just as the Lord had told him.

DAILY OFFERINGS

28 The Lord said to Moses, ²"Give this command to the Israelites. Tell them: 'Bring me food offerings made by fire. The smell is pleasing to me. Be sure to bring them at the right time.' ³Say to them: 'These are the offerings you must bring to the Lord. Bring two year-old lambs as a burnt offering each day. They must have nothing wrong with them. ⁴Offer one lamb in the morning and the other lamb at twilight. ⁵Also bring a grain offering of two quarts of fine flour. It must be mixed with one quart of oil from pressed olives. ⁶This is the daily burnt offering which began at Mount Sinai. The smell is pleasing to the Lord. ⁷Offer one quart of wine with each lamb as a drink offering. Pour it out to the Lord at the Holy Place. ⁸Offer the second lamb at twilight. As in the morning, also give a grain offering and a drink offering. This offering is made by fire. Its smell is pleasing to the Lord.

SABBATH OFFERINGS

9"On the Sabbath[d] day you must give two year-old lambs. They must have nothing wrong with them. Also give a drink offering and a grain offering. The grain offering must be four quarts of fine flour mixed with olive oil. 10This is the burnt offering for the Sabbath. It is in addition to the daily burnt offering and drink offering.

MONTHLY OFFERINGS

11"On the first day of each month bring a burnt offering to the Lord. This will be two young bulls, one male sheep and seven male lambs a year old. They all must have nothing wrong with them. 12Give a grain offering with each bull. It must be six quarts of fine flour mixed with olive oil. Also give a grain offering with the male sheep. It must be four quarts of fine flour mixed with olive oil. 13Also give a grain offering with each lamb. It must be two quarts of fine flour mixed with olive oil. This is a burnt offering. And its smell is pleasing to the Lord. 14The drink offering with each bull will be two quarts of wine. With the male sheep it will be one and one-half quarts. And with each lamb it will be one quart of wine. This is the burnt offering that must be offered each month of the year. 15Besides the daily burnt offerings and drink offerings, bring a sin offering to the Lord. It must be one male goat.

PASSOVER

16"The Lord's Passover[d] will be on the fourteenth day of the first month. 17The Feast[d] of Unleavened Bread begins on the fifteenth day of that month. It lasts for seven days. You may eat only bread made without yeast. 18Have a holy meeting on the first day of the festival. Don't work that day. 19Bring these burnt offerings to the Lord: two young bulls, one male sheep and seven male lambs a year old. They all must have nothing wrong with them. 20Also give a grain offering with each bull. It must be six quarts of fine flour mixed with olive oil. Give a grain offering with the male sheep. It must be four quarts of fine flour mixed with oil. 21Give a grain offering with each of the seven lambs. It must be two quarts of fine flour mixed with oil. 22Bring one goat as a sin offering. It will remove your sins so you will belong to God. 23Bring these offerings in addition to the burnt offerings you give every morning. 24So bring food offerings each day for seven days. The offering is made by fire. And its smell is pleasing to the Lord. Do it in addition to the daily burnt offering and its drink offering. 25On the seventh day have a holy meeting. Don't work that day.

FEAST OF WEEKS

26"On the day of firstfruits[d] offer new grain to the Lord. This is during the Feast[d] of Weeks. Have a holy meeting. Don't work that day. 27Give this burnt offering to the Lord: two young bulls, one male sheep and seven male lambs a year old. This smell is pleasing to the Lord. 28Also give a grain offering with each bull. It must be six quarts of fine flour mixed with oil. With the male sheep, it must be four quarts of flour. 29With each of the seven lambs offer two quarts of flour. 30Offer one male goat to remove your sins so you will belong to God. 31Bring these offerings and their drink offerings. These are in addition to the daily burnt offering and its grain offering. The animals must have nothing wrong with them.

FEAST OF TRUMPETS

29 "Have a holy meeting on the first day of the seventh month. Don't work on that day. That is the day you blow the trumpets. 2Bring these burnt offerings to the Lord: one young bull, one male sheep and seven male year-old lambs. They all must have nothing wrong with them. Their smell will be pleasing to the Lord. 3Give a grain offering with the bull. It must be six quarts of fine flour mixed with oil. With the male sheep offer four quarts. [4]And with each of the seven lambs offer two quarts. [5]Offer one male goat for a sin offering. It will remove your sins so you will belong to God. [6]These offerings are in addition to the monthly and daily burnt offerings. Their grain offerings and drink offerings must be done as you have been told. These offerings are made by fire to the Lord. And their smell is pleasing to him.

THE DAY OF CLEANSING

[7]"Have a holy meeting on the tenth day of the seventh month. On that day do not eat and do not work. [8]Bring these burnt offerings to the Lord: one young bull, one male sheep and seven male lambs a year old. They all must have nothing wrong with them. The smell will be pleasing to the Lord. [9]Give a grain offering with the bull. It must be six quarts of fine flour mixed with oil. With the male sheep it must be four quarts. [10]And with each of the seven lambs it must be two quarts. [11]Offer one male goat as a sin offering. This will be in addition to the sin offering which removes your sins. It will also be in addition to the daily burnt offering with its grain offering and the drink offerings.

FEAST OF TENTS

[12]"Have a holy meeting on the fifteenth day of the seventh month. Do not work on that day. Celebrate a festival to the Lord for seven days. [13]Give these burnt offerings to the Lord: 13 young bulls, 2 male sheep and 14 male lambs a year old. They all must have nothing wrong with them. The smell is pleasing to the Lord. [14]Also offer a grain offering with each of the 13 bulls. It must be six quarts of fine flour mixed with oil. With each of the 2 male sheep it must be four quarts. [15]And with each of the 14 lambs it must be two quarts. [16]Offer 1 male goat as a sin offering. This must be in addition

to the daily burnt offering with its grain and drink offerings.

[17]"On the second day of this festival give an offering. Offer 12 bulls, 2 male sheep and 14 male lambs a year old. They all must have nothing wrong with them. [18]Bring the grain and drink offerings for the bulls, sheep and lambs. [19]Offer 1 male goat as a sin offering. This must be in addition to the daily burnt offering with its grain and drink offerings.

[20]"On the third day offer 11 bulls, 2 male sheep and 14 male lambs a year old. They all must have nothing wrong with them. [21]Bring the grain and drink offerings for the bulls, sheep and lambs. [22]Offer 1 male goat as a sin offering. This must be in addition to the daily burnt offering with its grain and drink offerings.

[23]"On the fourth day offer 10 bulls, 2 male sheep and 14 male lambs a year old. They all must have nothing wrong with them. [24]Bring the grain and drink offerings for the bulls, sheep and lambs. [25]Offer 1 male goat as a sin offering. This must be in addition to the daily burnt offering with its grain and drink offerings.

[26]"On the fifth day offer 9 bulls, 2 male sheep and 14 male lambs a year old. They all must have nothing wrong with them. [27]Bring the grain and drink offerings for the bulls, sheep and lambs. [28]Offer 1 male goat as a sin offering. This must be in addition to the daily burnt offering with its grain and drink offerings.

[29]"On the sixth day offer 8 bulls, 2 male sheep and 14 male lambs a year old. They all must have nothing wrong with them. [30]Bring the grain and drink offerings for the bulls, sheep and lambs. [31]Offer 1 male goat as a sin offering. This must be in addition to the daily burnt offering with its grain and drink offerings.

[32]"On the seventh day offer 7 bulls, 2 male sheep and 14 male lambs a year old. They all must have nothing wrong with them. [33]Bring the grain and drink offerings for the bulls, sheep and lambs. [34]Offer

1 male goat as a sin offering. This must be in addition to the daily burnt offering with its grain and drink offerings. [35]"On the eighth day have a closing meeting. Do not work on that day. [36]Bring a burnt offering. Its smell will be pleasing to the Lord. Offer 1 bull, 1 male sheep and 7 male lambs a year old. They all must have nothing wrong with them. [37]Bring the grain and drink offerings for the bull, male sheep and lambs. [38]Offer 1 male goat as a sin offering. This must be in addition to the daily burnt offering with its grain and drink offerings.

[39]"At your festivals you should bring these to the Lord: your burnt offerings, grain offerings, drink offerings and fellowship offerings. These are in addition to other promised offerings and special gifts you want to give to the Lord.'"

[40]Moses told the Israelites everything the Lord had commanded him.

SPECIAL PROMISES

30 Moses spoke with the leaders of the Israelite tribes.[d] He told them these commands from the Lord.

[2]"A person might make a promise to the Lord. He might promise to do something special. If he does, he must keep his promise. He must do what he said. [3]A young woman still living at home might make a promise to the Lord. She might pledge to do something special. [4]Her father might hear about the promise or pledge and say nothing. Then she must do what she promised. She must keep her pledge. [5]But when her father hears about the promise or pledge, he might not allow it. Then the promise or pledge does not have to be kept. Her father would not allow them. So the Lord will free her from her promise.

[6]"A woman might make a pledge or a careless promise and then get married. [7]Her husband might hear about it and say nothing. Then she must keep her promise or the pledge she made. [8]But when her husband hears about it, he might not allow it. He cancels her pledge or the careless promise she made. The Lord will free her from keeping it.

[9]"A widow or divorced woman might make a promise. She must do whatever she promised.

[10]"A woman might make a promise or pledge while she was married. [11]When her husband hears about it, he might say nothing. He might not stop her. Then she must keep her promise or pledge. [12]But when her husband hears about it, he might cancel it. Then she does not have to do what she said. Her husband has canceled it. The Lord will free her from it. [13]A woman's husband may make her keep or cancel any promise or pledge she has made. [14]But her husband might say nothing to her about it for several days. Then she must keep her promises. If he hears about them and says nothing, she must keep her promises. [15]But he might cancel them long after he heard about them. Then he is responsible if she breaks her promise."

[16]These are commands that the Lord gave to Moses. They are for husbands and wives. And they are for fathers with daughters living at home.

ISRAEL ATTACKS THE MIDIANITES

31 The Lord spoke to Moses. He said, [2]"Pay back the Midianites for what they did to the Israelites. After that you will die."

[3]So Moses said to the people, "Get some men ready for war. The Lord will use them to pay back the Midianites. [4]Send to war 1,000 men from each of the tribes[d] of Israel." [5]So 12,000 men got ready for war. There were 1,000 men from each tribe. [6]Moses sent those 1,000 men from each tribe to war. Phinehas son of Eleazar the priest was with them. He took with him the holy things and the trumpets. [7]They fought the Midianites as the Lord had commanded Moses. And they killed every Midianite man. [8]Among those they killed were Evi,

Rekem, Zur, Hur and Reba. They were the five kings of Midian. They also killed Balaam son of Beor with a sword.

[9]The Israelites captured the Midianite women and children. They also took all their flocks, herds and goods. [10]Then they burned all the Midianite towns and camps. [11]They took all the people and animals and goods. [12]Then they went back to Moses and Eleazar the priest and all the Israelites. They brought back the captives, the animals and the goods. The camp was on the plains of Moab near the Jordan River. This was across from Jericho.

[13]Moses, Eleazar the priest and all the leaders of the people went outside the camp to meet them. [14]Moses was angry with the army officers who returned from war. He was angry with those commanders over 1,000 men and those over 100 men.

[15]He asked them, "Why did you let the women live? [16]They were the ones who followed Balaam's advice. They turned the Israelites from the Lord at Peor. Then a terrible sickness struck the Lord's people. [17]Kill all the Midianite boys. Kill all the Midianite women who have had sexual relations. [18]But save the girls for yourselves who have not had sexual relations with a man.

[19]"All you men who killed anyone or touched a dead body must stay outside the camp for seven days. On the third and seventh days you and your captives must make yourselves clean.[d] [20]You must clean all your clothes. And you must clean anything made of leather, wool or wood."

[21]Then Eleazar the priest spoke to the soldiers who had gone to war. He said, "These are the teachings that the Lord gave to Moses. [22]Put any gold, silver, bronze, iron, tin or lead into the fire. [23]Put into the fire anything that will not burn. Then wash those things with the cleansing water. Then they will be clean. If something cannot stand the fire, wash it with

the water. [24]On the seventh day wash your clothes. Then you will be clean. After that you may come into the camp."

DIVIDING THE GOODS

[25]The Lord said to Moses, [26]"You, Eleazar the priest and the leaders should take a count. Count the goods, the men and the animals that were taken. [27]Then divide those things between the soldiers who went to war and the rest of the people. [28]Tax the soldiers who went to war. The Lord's share is 1 thing out of every 500 things. This includes people, cattle, donkeys, sheep or goats. [29]Take it from the soldiers' half. And give it to Eleazar the priest. It is the Lord's share. [30]And from the people's half, take 1 thing out of every 50. This includes people, cattle, donkeys, sheep, goats or other animals. Give that to the Levites. They take care of the Lord's Holy Tent."[d] [31]So Moses and Eleazar did as the Lord commanded Moses.

[32]There remained from what the soldiers had taken 675,000 sheep, [33]72,000 cattle, [34]61,000 donkeys [35]and 32,000 women. These were the women who had not had sexual relations with a man. [36]The soldiers who went to war got 337,500 sheep. [37]They gave 675 of the sheep to the Lord. [38]They got 36,000 cattle. They gave 72 of them to the Lord. [39]They got 30,500 donkeys. They gave 61 of them to the Lord. [40]They got 16,000 people. And they gave 32 of them to the Lord. [41]Moses gave the Lord's share to Eleazar the priest. This was what the Lord had commanded him.

[42]Moses separated the people's half from the soldiers' half. [43]The people got 337,500 sheep, [44]36,000 cattle, [45]30,500 donkeys [46]and 16,000 people. [47]From the people's half Moses took 1 thing out of every 50 for the Lord. This included the animals and the people. Then he gave them to the Levites. They took care of the Lord's Holy Tent. This was what the Lord had commanded Moses.

⁴⁸Then the officers of the army came to Moses. They were the commanders of 1,000 men and commanders of 100 men. ⁴⁹They told Moses, "We, your servants, have counted our soldiers under our command. Not one of them is missing. ⁵⁰So we have brought the Lord a gift. We have brought the gold things that each of us found: arm bands, bracelets, signet*d* rings, earrings and necklaces. These are to remove our sins so we will belong to the Lord."

⁵¹So Moses and Eleazar the priest took the gold things from them. ⁵²The commanders of 1,000 men and the commanders of 100 men gave the Lord the gold. All of it together weighed about 420 pounds. ⁵³Each soldier had taken something for himself. ⁵⁴Moses and Eleazar the priest took the gold from the commanders of 1,000 men and the commanders of 100 men. Then they put it in the Meeting Tent.*d* It was a memorial before the Lord for the people of Israel.

THE TRIBES EAST OF THE JORDAN

32 The people of Reuben and Gad had many cattle. They saw that the lands of Jazer and Gilead were good for cattle. ²So they came to Moses, Eleazar the priest and the leaders of the people. ³⁻⁴They said, "We, your servants, have many cattle. The Lord has captured for the Israelites a land that is good for cattle. This is the land around Ataroth, Dibon, Jazer, Nimrah, Heshbon, Elealeh, Sebam, Nebo and Beon. ⁵If it pleases you, we would like this land to be given to us. Don't make us cross the Jordan River."

⁶Moses told the people of Gad and Reuben, "Shall your brothers go to war while you stay behind? ⁷You will discourage the Israelites. They will not want to go over to the land the Lord has given them. ⁸Your ancestors did the same thing. From Kadesh Barnea I sent them to look at the land. ⁹They went as far as the Valley of Eshcol. They saw the land.

And they discouraged the Israelites from going into the land the Lord had given them. ¹⁰The Lord became very angry that day. He made this promise: ¹¹'None of the people who came from Egypt and who are 20 years old or older will see this land. I promised it to Abraham, Isaac and Jacob. But these people have not followed me completely. ¹²Only Caleb son of Jephunneh the Kenizzite and Joshua son of Nun followed the Lord completely.'

¹³"The Lord was very angry with Israel. So he made them wander in the desert for 40 years. Finally all the people who had sinned against him had died. ¹⁴And now you are acting just like your fathers! You sinful people are making the Lord even more angry with Israel. ¹⁵If you quit following the Lord, it will add to their stay in the desert. So you will destroy all these people."

¹⁶But the Reubenites and Gadites came up to Moses. They said, "We will build pens for our animals. And we will build cities for our wives and children here. ¹⁷Then our families will be in strong, walled cities. They will be safe from the people who live in this land. Then we will prepare for war. We will help the other Israelites get their land. ¹⁸We will not return home until every Israelite has received his land. ¹⁹We won't take any of the land west of the Jordan River. Our part of the land is east of the Jordan."

²⁰So Moses told them, "You must do these things. You must go before the Lord into battle. ²¹You must cross the Jordan River armed. The Lord will force out the enemy. ²²After the Lord helps us take the land, you may return home. You will have done your duty to the Lord and Israel. Then you may have this land as your own.

²³"But if you don't do these things, you will be sinning against the Lord. And know for sure that you will be punished

for your sin. 24Build cities for your wives and children and pens for your animals. But then you must do what you promised."

25The Gadites and Reubenites said to Moses, "We are your servants. We will do what you, our master, command. 26Our wives, children and all our cattle will stay in the cities of Gilead. 27But we, your servants, will prepare for battle. We will go over and fight for the Lord, as you have said."

28So Moses gave orders about them to Eleazar the priest. And he gave them to Joshua son of Nun and the leaders of the tribes*d* of Israel. 29Moses said to them, "The Gadites and Reubenites will prepare for battle. They will cross the Jordan River with you. They will go before the Lord and help you take the land. If they do that, give them the land of Gilead for their own. 30But if they do not go over armed, they will not receive it. Their land will be in Canaan with you."

31The Gadites and Reubenites answered, "We are your servants. We will do as the Lord said. 32We will cross over into Canaan. We will go before the Lord ready for battle. But our land will be east of the Jordan River."

33So Moses gave that land to the Gadites, Reubenites and the eastern half-tribe of Manasseh. (Manasseh was Joseph's son.) That land had been the kingdom of Sihon, the king of the Amorites. And it included the kingdom of Og, king of Bashan. It also included all the cities and the land around them.

34The Gadites rebuilt the cities of Dibon, Ataroth, Aroer, 35Atroth Shophan, Jazer, Jogbehah, 36Beth Nimrah and Beth Haran. These were strong, walled cities. And they built sheep pens.

37The Reubenites built Heshbon, Elealeh, Kiriathaim, 38Nebo, Baal Meon and Sibmah. They renamed Nebo and Baal Meon when they rebuilt them.

39The descendants*d* of Makir son of Manasseh went and captured Gilead.

They forced out the Amorites who were there. 40So Moses gave Gilead to the family of Makir son of Manasseh. And they settled there. 41Jair son of Manasseh went out and captured the small towns there. He called them the Towns of Jair. 42Nobah went and captured Kenath and the small towns around it. Then he named it Nobah after himself.

ISRAEL'S JOURNEY FROM EGYPT

33 These are the places the Israelites went as Moses and Aaron led them out of Egypt in divisions. 2At the Lord's command Moses recorded the places they went. These are the places they went.

3On the fifteenth day of the first month, they left Rameses. That was the day after the Passover.*d* The Israelites marched out boldly in front of all the Egyptians. 4The Egyptians were burying their first-born*d* sons. The Lord had killed them. He showed that the gods of Egypt were false.

5The Israelites left Rameses and camped at Succoth.

6They left Succoth and camped at Etham. It was at the edge of the desert.

7They left Etham and went back to Pi Hahiroth. This was east of Baal Zephon. They camped near Migdol.

8They left Pi Hahiroth. They walked through the sea into the desert. After going three days through the Desert of Etham, they camped at Marah.

9They left Marah and went to Elim. There were 12 springs of water and 70 palm trees where they camped.

10They left Elim and camped near the Red Sea.*d*

11They left the Red Sea and camped in the Desert of Sin.

12They left the Desert of Sin and camped at Dophkah.

13They left Dophkah and camped at Alush.

14They left Alush and camped at Rephidim. The people had no water to drink there.

[15]They left Rephidim and camped in the Desert of Sinai.

[16]They left the Desert of Sinai and camped at Kibroth Hattaavah.

[17]They left Kibroth Hattaavah and camped at Hazeroth.

[18]They left Hazeroth and camped at Rithmah.

[19]They left Rithmah and camped at Rimmon Perez.

[20]They left Rimmon Perez and camped at Libnah.

[21]They left Libnah and camped at Rissah.

[22]They left Rissah and camped at Kehelathah.

[23]They left Kehelathah and camped at Mount Shepher.

[24]They left Mount Shepher and camped at Haradah.

[25]They left Haradah and camped at Makheloth.

[26]They left Makheloth and camped at Tahath.

[27]They left Tahath and camped at Terah.

[28]They left Terah and camped at Mithcah.

[29]They left Mithcah and camped at Hashmonah.

[30]They left Hashmonah and camped at Moseroth.

[31]They left Moseroth and camped at Bene Jaakan.

[32]They left Bene Jaakan and camped at Hor Haggidgad.

[33]They left Hor Haggidgad and camped at Jotbathah.

[34]They left Jotbathah and camped at Abronah.

[35]They left Abronah and camped at Ezion Geber.

[36]They left Ezion Geber and camped at Kadesh in the Desert of Zin.

[37]They left Kadesh and camped at Mount Hor. This was on the border of Edom. [38]Aaron the priest obeyed the Lord and went up Mount Hor. There he died. He died on the first day of the fifth month. This was in the fortieth year after the Israelites left Egypt. [39]Aaron was 123 years old when he died on Mount Hor.

[40]The king of Arad lived in the southern area of Canaan. He heard that the Israelites were coming.

[41]The people left Mount Hor and camped at Zalmonah.

[42]They left Zalmonah and camped at Punon.

[43]They left Punon and camped at Oboth.

[44]They left Oboth and camped at Iye Abarim. This was on the border of Moab.

[45]They left Iye Abarim and camped at Dibon Gad.

[46]They left Dibon Gad and camped at Almon Diblathaim.

[47]They left Almon Diblathaim and camped in the mountains of Abarim, near Nebo.

[48]They left the mountains of Abarim and camped on the plains of Moab. This was near the Jordan River across from Jericho. [49]They camped along the Jordan on the plains of Moab. Their camp went from Beth Jeshimoth to Abel Acacia.

[50]On the plains of Moab by the Jordan River across from Jericho, the Lord spoke to Moses. He said, [51]"Speak to the Israelites. Tell them, 'Cross the Jordan River and go into Canaan. [52]Force out the people who live there. Destroy all of their carved statues. Destroy their metal idols. Wreck all of their places of worship. [53]Take over the land and settle there. I have given this land to you to own. [54]Throw lots[d] to divide up the land by family groups. Give larger portions to larger family groups. Give smaller portions to smaller family groups. The land will be given as the lots decide. Each tribe[d] will get its own land.

[55]"'But if you don't force those people out of the land, they will bring you trouble. They will be like sharp hooks in your eyes. They will be like thorns in your sides. They will bring trouble to the

land where you live. ⁵⁶I will punish you as I had planned to punish them.'"

THE BORDERS OF CANAAN

34 The Lord said to Moses, ²"Give this command to the people of Israel: 'You will soon enter Canaan. It will be yours. These shall be the borders. ³On the south you will get part of the Desert of Zin. This is near the border of Edom. On the east side your southern border will start at the south end of the Dead Sea.ᵈ ⁴It will cross south of Scorpion Pass. It will go through the Desert of Zin and south of Kadesh Barnea. Then it will go to Hazar Addar and over to Azmon. ⁵From Azmon it will go to the brook of Egypt. It will end at the Mediterranean Sea.

⁶"'Your western border will be the Mediterranean Sea.

⁷"'Your northern border will begin at the Mediterranean Sea and go to Mount Hor. ⁸From Mount Hor it will go to Lebo Hamath. Then it will go to Zedad. ⁹Then the border will go to Ziphron and end at Hazar Enan. This will be your northern border.

¹⁰"'Your eastern border will begin at Hazar Enan and go to Shepham. ¹¹From Shepham the border will go east of Ain to Riblah. It will go along the hills east of Lake Galilee. ¹²Then the border will go down along the Jordan River. It will end at the Dead Sea.

"'These are the borders around your country.'"

¹³So Moses gave this command to the Israelites: "This is the land you will receive. Throw lotsᵈ to divide it among the nine and a half tribes.ᵈ The Lord commanded that it should be theirs. ¹⁴The tribes of Reuben and Gad and the eastern half-tribe of Manasseh have already received their land. ¹⁵These two and a half tribes received land east of the Jordan River. It is across from Jericho."

¹⁶Then the Lord said to Moses, ¹⁷"These are the men who will divide the land: Eleazar the priest and Joshua son of Nun. ¹⁸Also take one leader from each tribe. They will divide the land. ¹⁹These are the names of the leaders: from the tribe of Judah, Caleb son of Jephunneh; ²⁰from the tribe of Simeon, Shemuel son of Ammihud; ²¹from the tribe of Benjamin, Elidad son of Kislon; ²²from the tribe of Dan, Bukki son of Jogli; ²³from the tribe of Manasseh son of Joseph, Hanniel son of Ephod; ²⁴from the tribe of Ephraim son of Joseph, Kemuel son of Shiphtan; ²⁵from the tribe of Zebulun, Elizaphan son of Parnach; ²⁶from the tribe of Issachar, Paltiel son of Azzan; ²⁷from the tribe of Asher, Ahihud son of Shelomi; ²⁸from the tribe of Naphtali, Pedahel son of Ammihud."

²⁹The Lord commanded these men to divide the land of Canaan among the Israelites.

THE LEVITES' TOWNS

35 The Lord spoke to Moses on the plains of Moab. This was across from Jericho by the Jordan River. He said, ²"Command the Israelites to give the Levites cities to live in. These will be cities in the land they receive. Also give the Levites the pastureland around these cities. ³Then the Levites will have cities where they may live. And they will have pastureland for their cattle, sheep and other animals. ⁴The pastureland you give the Levites will extend 1,500 feet from the city wall. ⁵Also measure 3,000 feet in each direction from the city wall. Measure 3,000 feet east of the city. Measure 3,000 feet south of the city. Measure 3,000 feet west of the city. And measure 3,000 feet north of the city. The city will be in the center. This will be pastureland for the Levites' cities.

CITIES OF SAFETY

⁶"Six of the cities you give the Levites will be cities of safety.ᵈ A person might accidentally kill someone. If he does, he may run to one of those cities for safety.

You must also give 42 other cities to the Levites. ⁷Give the Levites a total of 48 cities and their pastures. ⁸The larger tribes^d of Israel must give more cities. The smaller tribes must give fewer cities. Each tribe must give some of its cities to the Levites. The number of cities they give will depend on the size of their land."

⁹Then the Lord said to Moses, ¹⁰"Tell the Israelites these things: 'You will cross the Jordan River and go into Canaan. ¹¹You must choose cities to be cities of safety. If a person accidentally kills someone, he may run to them for safety. ¹²There he will be safe from the dead person's relative who has the duty of punishing the killer. He will not die before he is judged in court. ¹³The six cities you give will be cities of safety. ¹⁴Give three cities east of the Jordan River. And give three cities in Canaan as cities of safety. ¹⁵These six cities will be places of safety for citizens of Israel. And they will be for foreigners and other people living with you. Any of these people may run to one of these cities if he accidentally kills someone.

¹⁶"'If a person uses an iron weapon to kill someone, he is a murderer. He must be put to death. ¹⁷A person might take a rock that could kill someone. If he kills a person with it, he is a murderer. He must be put to death. ¹⁸A person might pick up a piece of wood that could kill someone. If he kills someone with it, he is a murderer. He must be put to death. ¹⁹A relative of the dead person must put the murderer to death. When he finds the murderer, he must kill him. ²⁰A person might shove someone and kill him. Or he might throw something at someone and kill him. ²¹Or he might hit someone with his hand and kill him. If he did that from hate, he is a murderer. He must be put to death. A relative of the dead person must kill the murderer when he finds him.

²²"'But a person might suddenly shove someone. He did not hate the person. Or he might accidentally throw something and hit someone. ²³Or he might drop a rock that could kill someone. It might fall on someone he did not see. And it might kill that person. He didn't plan to hurt anyone. He didn't hate the person he killed. ²⁴If that happens, the community must decide what to do. They must decide between the relative of the dead person and the killer. Here are the rules. ²⁵They must protect the killer from the dead person's relative. They must send the killer back to the city of safety that he ran to. He must stay there until the high priest dies. The high priest had the holy oil poured on him.

²⁶"'That man must never go outside the limits of his city of safety. ²⁷If a relative of the dead person finds him outside the city, the relative may kill him. He will not be guilty of murder. ²⁸The killer must stay in his city of safety until the high priest dies. After the high priest dies, he may go back to his own land.

²⁹"'These laws are for you from now on, wherever you live.

³⁰"'A killer may be put to death only if he is a murderer. And there must be witnesses. No one may be put to death with only one witness.

³¹"'A murderer should die. Don't take money to spare his life. He must be put to death.

³²"'A person might run to a city of safety. Don't take money to let him go back home before the high priest dies.

³³"'Don't let murder spoil your land. There is only one way to remove the sin of killing an innocent person. The murderer must be put to death. ³⁴I am the Lord. I live among the Israelites. I live in that land with you. So do not spoil it with murder.'"

LAND FOR ZELOPHEHAD'S DAUGHTERS

36 The leaders of Gilead's family group went to talk to Moses and the leaders of the families of Israel. (Gilead was the son of Makir. Makir was

Manasseh's son, and Manasseh was Joseph's son.) ²They said, "The Lord commanded you, our master, to give the land to the Israelites by throwing lots.ᵈ And the Lord commanded you to give the land of Zelophehad, our brother, to his daughters. ³His daughters may marry men from other tribesᵈ of Israel. Then that land will leave our family. The people of the other tribes will get that land. So we will lose some of our land. ⁴The time of Jubileeᵈ will come for the Israelites. Then their land will go to other tribes. It will go to the tribes of the people they marry. So their land will be taken away from us. And that was land we received from our fathers."

⁵Then Moses gave the Israelites this command from the Lord: "These men from the tribe of Joseph are right. ⁶This is the Lord's command to Zelophehad's daughters: You may marry anyone you wish from your own tribe. ⁷In this way the Israelites' land will not pass from tribe to tribe. Each Israelite will keep the land in the tribe that belonged to his ancestors. ⁸A woman who inherits her father's land may marry. But she must marry someone from her own tribe. In this way every Israelite will keep the land that belonged to his ancestors. ⁹The land must not pass from tribe to tribe. Each Israelite tribe will keep the land it received from its ancestors."

¹⁰Zelophehad's daughters obeyed the Lord's command to Moses.

¹¹So Zelophehad's daughters—Mahlah, Tirzah, Hoglah, Milcah and Noah—married their cousins. These were their father's relatives. ¹²Their husbands were from the tribe of Manasseh son of Joseph. So their land stayed in their father's family group and tribe.

¹³These were the laws and commands that the Lord gave to the Israelites. He gave them through Moses. The Israelites were on the plains of Moab by the Jordan River, across from Jericho.

DEUTERONOMY

MOSES TALKS TO THE ISRAELITES

1 This is the message Moses gave the people of Israel. They were in the desert east of the Jordan River. They were in the Jordan Valley near Suph, between Paran and the towns of Tophel, Laban, Hazeroth and Dizahab. ²(The trip from Mount Sinai to Kadesh Barnea on the Mount Edom road takes 11 days.) ³But it was now 40 years after the Israelites had left Egypt. On the first day of the eleventh month, Moses spoke to the people. He told them everything the Lord had commanded him to tell them. ⁴This was after the Lord had defeated Sihon and Og. Sihon was king of the Amorite people and lived in Heshbon. Og was king of Bashan and lived in Ashteroth and Edrei.

⁵Now the Israelites were east of the Jordan River in the land of Moab. There Moses began to explain what God had commanded. Moses said:

⁶The Lord our God spoke to us at Mount Sinai. He said, "You have stayed long enough at this mountain. ⁷Get ready. Go to the mountain country of the Amorites. Go to all the places around there—the Jordan Valley, the mountains, the western slopes, the southern area, the seacoast, the land of Canaan and Lebanon. Go as far as the great river, the Euphrates. ⁸See, I have given you this land. Go in and take it for yourselves. The Lord promised it to your ancestors—Abraham, Isaac and Jacob and their descendants."ᵈ

MOSES APPOINTS LEADERS

⁹At that time I said, "I am not able to take care of you by myself. ¹⁰The Lord your God has made you grow in number. There are as many of you as there are stars in the sky. ¹¹I pray that the Lord, the God of your ancestors, will give you a thousand times more people. That's what he promised. ¹²But I cannot take care of your problems, your troubles and your arguments by myself. ¹³So choose some men from each tribe.ᵈ Choose wise men who have understanding and experience. I will make them leaders over you."

¹⁴And you said, "That's a good thing to do."

¹⁵So I took the wise and experienced leaders of your tribes. And I made them your leaders. I appointed commanders over 1,000 people, over 100 people, over 50 people and over 10 people. I made them officers over your tribes. ¹⁶Then I told your judges, "Listen to the arguments between your people. Judge fairly between two Israelites or between an Israelite and a foreigner. ¹⁷When you judge, be fair to everyone. Don't act as if one person is more important than another. Don't be afraid of anyone, because your decision comes from God. Bring the hard cases to me. I will judge them." ¹⁸At that time I told you everything you must do.

SPIES ENTER THE LAND

¹⁹Then, as the Lord our God commanded us, we left Mount Sinai. We went toward the mountain country of the Amorite people. We went through that large and terrible desert you saw. Then we came to Kadesh Barnea. ²⁰Then I said to you, "You have now come to the mountain country of the Amorites. The Lord our God will give us this land. ²¹Look, there it is! Go up. Take it. The Lord, the God of your ancestors, told you to do this. So don't be afraid. Don't worry."

²²Then all of you came to me. You said, "Let's send men before us to spy out the land. They can come back and tell us the way we should go. They can tell us about the cities we will find."

²³I thought that was a good idea. So I chose 12 of your men, 1 for each tribe.ᵈ

²⁴They left and went up to the mountains. They came to the Valley of Eshcol and explored it. ²⁵They took some of the fruit from that land. And they brought it down to us. They said, "It is a good land that the Lord our God is giving us."

ISRAEL REFUSES TO ENTER

²⁶But you refused to go. You would not obey the command of the Lord your God. ²⁷You grumbled in your tents. You said, "The Lord hates us. He brought us out of Egypt just to give us to the Amorites. They will destroy us. ²⁸Where can we go now? The spies we sent have made us afraid. They said, 'The people there are bigger and taller than we are. The cities are big. They have walls up to the sky. And we saw the Anakites^d there!' "

²⁹Then I said to you, "Don't be frightened. Don't be afraid of those people. ³⁰The Lord your God will go ahead of you. He will fight for you as he did in Egypt. You saw him do it. ³¹And in the desert you saw how the Lord your God carried you. He was like a man carrying his son. And he has brought you safely all the way to this place."

³²But you still did not trust the Lord your God. ³³As you moved, he went before you. He found places for you to camp. He went before you in a fire at night and in a cloud during the day. He showed you which way to go.

³⁴When the Lord heard what you said, he was angry. He made a promise. He said, ³⁵"I promised a good land to your ancestors. But none of you evil people will see it. ³⁶Only Caleb son of Jephunneh will see it. I will give him and his descendants^d the land he walked on. I will do this because he followed me completely."

³⁷Because of you, the Lord was also angry with me. He said to me, "You won't enter the land either. ³⁸But your assistant, Joshua son of Nun, will go there. Encourage Joshua, because he will lead Israel to take the land for their own."

³⁹The Lord said to us, "You said your babies would be captured. But they will go into the land. They are too young to know right from wrong. So I will give the land to them. And they will take it for their own. ⁴⁰But you must turn around. Follow the desert road toward the Gulf of Aqaba."

⁴¹Then you said to me, "We have sinned against the Lord. But now we will go up and fight, as the Lord our God commanded us." Then all of you put on weapons. You thought it would be easy to go into the mountains.

⁴²But the Lord said to me, "Tell them not to go up there and fight. I will not be with them. Their enemies will defeat them."

⁴³So I told you, but you would not listen. You would not obey the Lord's command. You were proud. So you went on up into the mountains. ⁴⁴The Amorites who lived there came out and fought you. They chased you like bees. They defeated you from Edom to Hormah. ⁴⁵So you came back and cried to the Lord. But the Lord did not hear you. He refused to listen to you. ⁴⁶So you stayed in Kadesh a long time.

ISRAEL WANDERS IN THE DESERT

2 Then we turned around. And we traveled on the desert road toward the Gulf of Aqaba. That is what the Lord had told me to do. We traveled through the mountains of Edom for many days.

²Then the Lord said to me, ³"You have traveled through these mountains long enough. Turn north. ⁴Tell the people this: 'You will soon go through the land of Edom. This land belongs to your relatives, the descendants^d of Esau. They will be afraid of you. But be very careful. ⁵Don't go to war against them. I am not giving you any of their land—not even a foot of it. I have given the mountains of Edom to Esau as his own. ⁶You must pay them in silver for any food you eat or water you drink.' "

[7]The Lord your God has blessed everything you have done. He has protected you while you traveled through this large desert. The Lord your God has been with you for these 40 years. You have had everything you needed.

[8]So we passed by our relatives, the people of Esau who lived in Edom. We turned off the Jordan Valley road. It comes from the towns of Elath and Ezion Geber. And we traveled along the desert road of Moab.

THE LAND OF AR

[9]Then the Lord said to me, "Don't bother the people of Moab. Don't go to war against them. I am not giving you any of their land. I have given Ar to the descendants[d] of Lot." [10](The Emites lived in Ar before. They were strong people, and there were many of them. They were very tall, like the Anakites.[d] [11]The Emites were thought to be Rephaites,[d] like the Anakites. But the Moabite people called them Emites. [12]The Horites also lived in Edom before. But the people of Esau forced them out. They destroyed the Horites and took their place. That is also what Israel did in the land the Lord gave them as their own.)

[13]And the Lord said to me, "Now get up and cross the Zered Valley." So we crossed the valley. [14]It had been 38 years since we left Kadesh Barnea until we crossed the Zered Valley. By then, all the fighting men from that time had died. This is what the Lord had promised would happen. [15]The Lord had continued to destroy them until they were all gone from the camp. [16]Now the last of those fighting men had died.

[17]Then the Lord said to me, [18]"Today you must go by Ar, on the border of Moab. [19]When you come near the people of Ammon, don't bother them. Don't go to war against them. I am not giving you their land. I have given that land to the descendants[d] of Lot."

[20](That land was also thought to be a land of Rephaites. Those people used to live there. But the Ammonites called them Zamzummites. [21]They were strong people, and there were many of them. They were very tall, like the Anakites. The Lord went before the Ammonites and destroyed the Zamzummites. The Ammonites forced them out of the land and took their place. [22]The Lord did the same thing for the descendants of Esau. They lived in Edom. He destroyed the Horites. The Edomites forced them out of the land and took their place. And they live there to this day. [23]The Caphtorite people came from Crete. They destroyed the Avvites. The Avvites lived in towns all the way to Gaza. But the Caphtorites destroyed them and took their place.)

FIGHTING THE AMORITES

[24]The Lord said, "Get up. Cross the Arnon Ravine. See, I am giving you the power to defeat Sihon the Amorite. He is king of Heshbon. I am giving you his land. So fight against him and begin taking his land. [25]Today I will begin to make all the people in the world afraid of you. They will hear reports about you. And they will shake with fear. They will be terrified of you."

[26]I sent messengers from the desert of Kedemoth to Sihon king of Heshbon. They offered him peace. They said, [27]"Let us pass through your country. We will stay on the road. We will not turn right or left. [28]We will pay you in silver for any food we eat or water we drink. We only want to walk through your country. [29]The descendants[d] of Esau in Edom let us go through their land. So did the Moabites in Ar. We want to cross the Jordan River into the land the Lord our God has given us." [30]But Sihon king of Heshbon would not let us pass. The Lord your God had made him stubborn. The Lord wanted you to defeat Sihon. And now this has happened.

³¹The Lord said to me, "See, I have begun to give Sihon and his country to you. Begin taking the land as your own."

³²Then Sihon and all his army came out. And they fought us at Jahaz. ³³But the Lord our God gave Sihon to us. We defeated him, his sons and all his army. ³⁴We captured all his cities. We completely destroyed them, the men, women and children. We left no one alive. ³⁵But we kept the cattle and valuable things from the cities for ourselves. ³⁶We defeated Aroer on the edge of the Arnon Ravine. And we defeated the town in the ravine, and even Gilead. No town was too strong for us. The Lord our God gave us all of them. ³⁷But you did not go near the land of the Ammonites. You did not go near the shores of the Jabbok River. You did not go near the towns in the mountains. This was what the Lord our God had commanded.

THE BATTLE AT BASHAN

3 Then we turned and went up the road toward Bashan. Og king of Bashan and all his army came out to fight us at Edrei. ²The Lord said to me, "Don't be afraid of Og. I will hand him, his whole army and his land over to you. Do to him what you did to Sihon king of the Amorites, who ruled in Heshbon."

³So the Lord our God gave us Og king of Bashan and all his army. We defeated them and left no one alive. ⁴Then we captured all of Og's cities. We captured all 60 of them. We took the whole area of Argob, Og's kingdom in Bashan. ⁵All these were strong cities. They had high walls and gates with bars. And there were also many small towns with no walls. ⁶We completely destroyed them. We destroyed them just like the cities of Sihon king of Heshbon. We killed all the men, women and children. ⁷But we kept all the cattle and valuable things from the cities for ourselves.

⁸So at that time we took the land east of the Jordan River. We took it from these two Amorite kings. It went from the Arnon Ravine to Mount Hermon. ⁹(Hermon is called Sirion by the Sidonian people. The Amorites call it Senir.) ¹⁰We captured all the cities on the high plain and all of Gilead. We took all of Bashan as far as Salecah and Edrei. These were towns in Og's kingdom of Bashan. ¹¹(Only Og king of Bashan was left of the few Rephaites.*ᵈ* His bed was made of iron. It was more than 13 feet long and 6 feet wide! It is still in the Ammonite city of Rabbah.)

THE LAND IS DIVIDED

¹²At that time we took this land to be our own. I gave the people of Reuben and Gad the land from Aroer by the Arnon Ravine. And I gave them half of the mountain country of Gilead and the cities in it. ¹³To the eastern half-tribe of Manasseh I gave the rest of Gilead. And I gave them all of Bashan, the kingdom of Og. (The area of Argob in Bashan was called the land of the Rephaites.*ᵈ* ¹⁴Jair, a descendant*ᵈ* of Manasseh, took the whole area of Argob. It went to the border of the Geshurites and Maacathites. That land was named for Jair. So even today Bashan is called the Towns of Jair.) ¹⁵I gave Gilead to Makir. ¹⁶I gave the Reubenites and the Gadites the land that begins at Gilead. It goes from the Arnon Ravine to the Jabbok River. (The middle of the Arnon is the border.) The Jabbok River is the Ammonite border. ¹⁷The border on the west was the Jordan River in the Jordan Valley. It goes from Lake Galilee to the Dead Sea*ᵈ* west of Mount Pisgah.

¹⁸At that time I gave you this command: "The Lord your God has given you this land as your own. Now your fighting men must take their weapons. And you must lead the other Israelites across the river. ¹⁹Your wives, your young children and your cattle may stay here. I know you have many cattle. They may stay here in the cities I have given

you. [20]Some day your Israelite relatives will also have a place to rest. They will receive the land the Lord your God has given them. It is on the other side of the Jordan River. After that, you may each return to the land I have given you."

[21]Then I gave this command to Joshua: "You have seen for yourself what the Lord your God has done to these two kings. The Lord will do the same thing to all the kingdoms where you are going. [22]Don't be afraid of them. The Lord your God will fight for you."

MOSES CANNOT ENTER THE LAND

[23]Then I begged the Lord: [24]"Lord God, you have begun to show me, your servant, how great you are. You have great strength. No other god in heaven or earth can do the powerful things you do. There is no other god like you. [25]Please let me cross the Jordan River. I want to see the beautiful mountains and Lebanon."

[26]But the Lord was angry with me because of you. He would not listen to me. The Lord said to me, "That's enough. Don't talk to me anymore about it. [27]Climb to the top of Mount Pisgah. Look west, north, south and east. You can look at the land. But you will not cross the Jordan River. [28]Appoint Joshua. Help him be brave and strong. He will lead the people across the river. He will give them the land that they are to inherit. You can only look at it." [29]So we stayed in the valley opposite Beth Peor.

MOSES TELLS ISRAEL TO OBEY

4 Now, Israel, listen to the laws and commands I will teach you. Obey them so you will live. Then you will go over and take the land. The Lord, the God of your ancestors, is giving it to you. [2]Don't add to these commands. And don't leave anything out. But obey the commands of the Lord your God that I give you.

[3]You have seen for yourselves what the Lord did at Baal Peor. The Lord your God destroyed everyone among you who

followed Baal[d] in Peor. [4]But you continued to follow the Lord your God. So you are still alive today.

[5]Look, I have taught you the laws and rules the Lord my God commanded me. Now you can obey the laws in the land you are entering. It is the land you will own. [6]Obey these laws carefully. This will show the other nations that you have wisdom and understanding. They will hear about these laws. And they will say, "This great nation of Israel is wise and understanding." [7]No other nation is as great as we are. Their gods do not come near them. But the Lord our God comes near when we pray to him. [8]And no other nation has such good teachings and commands. I am giving them to you today.

[9]But be careful! Watch out. Don't forget the things that you have seen. Don't forget them as long as you live. Teach them to your children and grandchildren. [10]Remember the day you stood before the Lord your God at Mount Sinai. He said to me, "Bring the people together to listen to what I say. Then they will respect me as long as they live in the land. And they will teach these things to their children." [11]Then you came and stood at the bottom of the mountain. It blazed with fire that reached to the sky. Black clouds made it very dark. [12]Then the Lord spoke to you from the fire. You heard the sound of words. But you did not see him. There was only a voice. [13]The Lord told you about his agreement. It was the Ten Commandments. And he told you to obey them. Then he wrote them on two stone tablets. [14]Then the Lord commanded me to teach you the laws and rules. You must obey them in the land you will own when you cross the Jordan River.

LAWS ABOUT IDOLS

[15]The Lord spoke to you from the fire at Mount Sinai. But you did not see him. So watch yourselves carefully! [16]Don't sin by making idols of any kind. Don't

make statues of men or women. [17]Don't make statues of animals on earth or birds that fly in the air. [18]Don't make statues of anything that crawls on the ground. Don't make statues of fish in the water below. [19]When you look up at the sky, you see the sun, moon and stars. You can see everything in the sky. But don't bow down and worship them. The Lord your God has made these things for all people everywhere. [20]Egypt tested you like a furnace for melting iron. The Lord brought you out of Egypt. And he made you his very own people, as you are now.

[21]The Lord was angry with me because of you. He made a strong promise that I would not cross the Jordan River. I could not go into the good land the Lord your God is giving you to own. [22]I will die here in this land. I will not cross the Jordan. But you will soon go across and take that good land. [23]Be careful. Don't forget the agreement of the Lord your God that he made with you. Don't make any idols for yourselves. The Lord your God has commanded you not to do that. [24]The Lord your God is a jealous God. He is like a fire that burns things up.

[25]You will live in the land a long time. You will have children and grandchildren. Even after that, don't do evil things. Don't make any kind of idol. Don't do what the Lord says is evil. That will make him angry. [26]I will ask heaven and earth to speak against you that day. Then you will quickly be removed from this land. You are crossing the Jordan River to take the land. But you will not live there long after that. You will be completely destroyed. [27]The Lord will scatter you among the other nations. Only a few of you will be left alive. And those few will be in other nations where the Lord will send you. [28]There you will worship gods made by men. They will be made of wood and stone. They cannot see, hear, eat or smell. [29]But even there

you can look for the Lord your God. And you will find him if you look. But you must look for him with your whole being. [30]It will be hard when all these things happen to you. But after that you will come back to the Lord your God. You will obey him. [31]The Lord your God is a merciful God. He will not leave you or destroy you. He will not forget the agreement he made with your ancestors. He made that agreement sure with his strong promise.

THE LORD IS GREAT

[32]Nothing like this has ever happened before! Look at the past, long before you were even born. Go all the way back to when God made man on the earth. Look from one end of heaven to the other. Nothing like this has ever been heard of! [33]No other people have ever heard God speak from a fire and still lived. But you have. [34]No other god has ever taken for himself one nation out of another. But the Lord your God did this for you in Egypt. He did it right before your own eyes. He did it with tests, signs, miracles,[d] war and great sights. He did it by his great power and strength.

[35]He showed you things so you would know that the Lord is God. There is no other God besides him. [36]He spoke to you from heaven to teach you. He showed you his great fire on earth. And you heard him speak from the fire. [37]The Lord loved your ancestors. That is why he chose you, their descendants.[d] He brought you out of Egypt himself by his great strength. [38]He forced nations out of their land ahead of you. And these nations were bigger and stronger than you were. But the Lord brought you into their land and gave it to you to own. And this land is yours today.

[39]Know and believe today that the Lord is God. He is God in heaven above and on the earth below. There is no other god! [40]Obey his laws and commands, which I am giving you today. Obey them

so that things will go well for you and your children. Then you will live a long time in this land. The Lord your God is giving it to you forever.

CITIES OF SAFETY

[41]Moses chose three cities east of the Jordan River. [42]A person who killed someone accidentally could go there. He did not hate the person he killed. So he could save his life by running to one of these cities. [43]These were the cities: Bezer in the desert high plain was for the Reubenites; Ramoth in Gilead was for the Gadites; Golan in Bashan was for the Manassites.

THE LAW MOSES GAVE

[44]These are the teachings Moses gave to the people of Israel. [45]They are the rules, commands and laws he gave them when they came out of Egypt. [46]They were in the valley near Beth Peor. That is east of the Jordan River in the land of Sihon. Sihon was king of the Amorites. He ruled in Heshbon. He was defeated by Moses and the Israelites as they came out of Egypt. [47]The Israelites captured his land. They also took the land of Og king of Bashan. These were the two Amorite kings east of the Jordan River. [48]This land went from Aroer to Mount Hermon. Aroer is on the edge of the Arnon Ravine. [49]It included all the Jordan Valley east of the Jordan River. And it went as far as the Dead Sea[d] below Mount Pisgah.

THE TEN COMMANDMENTS

5 Moses called all the people of Israel together and said: Listen, Israel, to the commands and laws I give you today. Learn them and obey them carefully. [2]The Lord our God made an agreement with us at Mount Sinai. [3]He did not make this agreement with our ancestors. He made it with us. He made it with all of us who are alive here today. [4]The Lord spoke to you face to face. He spoke from the fire on the mountain. [5](At that time I stood between you and the Lord. I told you what the Lord said. You were afraid of the fire. So you would not go up on the mountain.) The Lord said:

[6]"I am the Lord your God. I brought you out of the land of Egypt where you were slaves.

[7]"You must not have any other gods except me.

[8]"You must not make for yourselves any idols. Don't make something that looks like anything in the sky above or on the earth below or in the water below the land. [9]You must not worship or serve any idol. This is because I, the Lord your God, am a jealous God. A person may sin against me and hate me. I will punish his children, even his grandchildren and great-grandchildren. [10]But I will be very kind to thousands who love me and obey my commands.

[11]"You must not use the name of the Lord your God thoughtlessly. The Lord will punish anyone who is guilty and misuses his name.

[12]"Keep the Sabbath[d] as a holy day. The Lord your God has commanded you to do this. [13]You may work and get everything done during six days each week. [14]But the seventh day is a day of rest to honor the Lord your God. On that day no one may do any work: not you, your son or daughter, or your men or women slaves. Neither your ox, your donkey nor any of your animals may work. The foreigners living in your cities may not work. That way your servants may rest as you do. [15]Remember that you were slaves in Egypt. The Lord your God brought you out of Egypt by his great power and strength. So the Lord your God has commanded you to rest on the Sabbath day.

[16]"Honor your father and your mother. The Lord your God has commanded you to do this. Then you will live a long time. And things will go well for you in the land. The Lord your God is going to give you this land.

[17]"You must not murder anyone.

[18]"You must not be guilty of adultery.[d]

[19]"You must not steal.

[20]"You must not tell lies about your neighbor in court.

[21]"You must not want to take your neighbor's wife. You must not want to take your neighbor's house or land. You must not want to take his men or women slaves. You must not want to take his ox or his donkey. You must not want to take anything that belongs to your neighbor."

[22]The Lord gave these commands to all of you on the mountain. He spoke them in a loud voice out of the fire. He spoke from the cloud and the deep darkness. He did not say anything else. Then he wrote them on two stone tablets. And he gave them to me.

[23]You heard the voice from the darkness. The mountain was blazing with fire. Then all the leaders of your tribes[d] and your elders came to me. [24]And you said, "The Lord our God has shown us his glory and majesty. We have heard his voice from the fire. Today we have seen that a person can live even if God speaks to him. [25]But now, we will die! This great fire will burn us up. And we will die if we hear the Lord our God speak anymore. [26]No human being has ever heard the living God speaking from a fire and still lived. But we have. [27]Moses, you go near and listen to everything the Lord our God says. Then you tell us what the Lord our God tells you. We will listen and obey."

[28]The Lord heard what you said to me. And he said to me, "I have heard what the people said to you. Everything they said was good. [29]I wish their hearts would always respect me. I wish they would always obey my commands. Then things would go well for them and their children forever!

[30]"Go and tell the people to return to their tents. [31]But you stay here with me. I will give you all the commands, rules and laws. Teach the people to obey them in the land I am giving them to own."

[32]So be careful. Do what the Lord your God has commanded you. You must follow the commands exactly. [33]Live the way the Lord your God has commanded you. Then you will live and be successful. You will live a long time in the land you will own.

THE COMMAND TO LOVE GOD

6 These are the commands, rules and laws of the Lord your God. He told me to teach them to you. Obey them in the land you are crossing the Jordan River to own. [2]You, your children and grandchildren must respect the Lord your God. You must do this as long as you live. Obey all his rules and commands I give you. Then you will live a long time. [3]Listen, Israel, and carefully obey these laws. Then all will go well for you. You will become a great nation in a land where much food grows. The Lord, the God of your ancestors, has promised it to you.

[4]Listen, people of Israel! The Lord is our God. He is the only Lord. [5]Love the Lord your God with all your heart, soul and strength. [6]Always remember these commands I give you today. [7]Teach them to your children. Talk about them when you sit at home and walk along the road. Talk about them when you lie down and when you get up. [8]Write them down and tie them to your hands as a sign. Tie them on your forehead to remind you. [9]Write them on your doors and gates.

[10]The Lord your God will bring you into the land. He promised it to your ancestors, to Abraham, Isaac and Jacob. He will give it to you. The land has large, growing cities you did not build. [11]The houses there are full of good things that you did not buy. They have wells you did not dig. There are vineyards and olive trees you did not plant. You will eat as much as you want. [12]But be careful! Do not forget

the Lord. He brought you out of the land of Egypt where you were slaves.

[13]Respect the Lord your God. Serve only him. Make your promises in his name. [14]Do not worship other gods as the people around you do. [15]The Lord your God is a jealous God. He is present with you. If you worship other gods, he will become angry with you. And he will destroy you from the earth. [16]Do not test the Lord your God as you did at Massah. [17]Be sure to obey the commands of the Lord your God. Obey the rules and laws he has given you. [18]Do what the Lord says is good and right. Then things will go well for you. Then you may go in and take the good land the Lord promised to your ancestors. [19]He will force all your enemies out as you go in. This is what the Lord has said.

[20]In the future your son will ask you, "What do the laws, commands and rules the Lord our God gave us mean?" [21]Tell him, "We were slaves to the king of Egypt. But the Lord brought us out of Egypt by his great power. [22]The Lord showed us great and terrible signs and miracles.[d] He did them to Egypt, the king and his whole family. [23]The Lord brought us out of Egypt. He led us here. And he will give us the land he promised our ancestors. [24]The Lord ordered us to obey all these commands. And we must respect the Lord our God. Then we will always do well and stay alive as we are today. [25]The right thing for us to do is this: Obey all these rules in the presence of the Lord our God. He has commanded it."

GOD'S PEOPLE

7 The Lord your God will bring you into the land. You are entering that land to own it. As you go in, he will force out these nations: the Hittites, Girgashites, Amorites, Canaanites, Perizzites, Hivites and Jebusites. These seven nations are stronger than you. [2]The Lord your God will hand these nations over to you. You will defeat them. You must destroy them completely. Do not make a peace treaty with them. Do not show them any mercy. [3]Do not marry any of them. Don't let your daughters marry their sons. And don't let your sons marry their daughters. [4]Those people will turn your children away from me. Your children will begin serving other gods. The Lord will be very angry with you. And he will quickly destroy you. [5]This is what you must do to those people: Tear down their altars. Smash their holy stone pillars. Cut down their Asherah[d] idols and burn their idols in the fire. [6]You are holy people. You belong to the Lord your God. He has chosen you from all the people on earth. You are his very own.

[7]The Lord did not care for you and choose you because there were many of you. You are the smallest nation of all. [8]But the Lord chose you because he loved you. And he kept his promise to your ancestors. So he brought you out of Egypt by his great power. He brought you back from the land of slavery. He bought you back from the power of the king of Egypt. [9]So know that the Lord your God is God. He is the faithful God. He will keep his agreement of love for a thousand lifetimes. He does this for people who love him and obey his commands. [10]But he will pay back those people who hate him. He will destroy them. And he will not be slow to pay back those who hate him. [11]So be careful to obey the commands, rules and laws I give you today.

[12]Pay attention to these laws. Obey them carefully. Then the Lord your God will keep his agreement and show his love to you. He promised your ancestors he would. [13]He will love and bless you. He will make the number of your people grow. He will bless you with children. He will bless your fields with good crops. He will give you grain, new wine and oil. He will bless your cows with calves and your sheep with lambs. This is the way it will

be in the land he promised your ancestors he would give you. ¹⁴You will be blessed more than any other people. Every husband and wife will have children. All your cattle will have calves. ¹⁵The Lord will take away all disease from you. You will not have the terrible diseases that were in Egypt. But he will give them to your enemies. ¹⁶You must destroy all the people the Lord your God hands over to you. Do not feel sorry for them. Do not worship their gods. They will trap you.

¹⁷You might say to yourselves, "These nations are stronger than we are. We can't force them out." ¹⁸But don't be afraid of them. Remember what the Lord your God did to all of Egypt and its king. ¹⁹You saw for yourselves the troubles, signs and miracles*ᵈ* he did. You saw how the Lord's great power and strength brought you out of Egypt. The Lord your God will do the same thing to all the nations you now fear. ²⁰The Lord your God will also send hornets to attack them. Even those who are alive and hiding from you will die. ²¹Don't be afraid of them. The Lord your God is with you. He is a great God and people are afraid of him. ²²The Lord your God will force those nations out of the land. They will leave little by little ahead of you. Don't destroy them all at once. Otherwise, the wild animals will grow too many in number. ²³But the Lord your God will hand those nations over to you. He will confuse them until they are destroyed. ²⁴The Lord will help you defeat their kings. The world will forget who they were. No one will be able to stop you. You will destroy them all. ²⁵Burn up their idols in the fire. Do not wish for the silver and gold on them. Don't take it for yourselves, or you will be trapped by it. The Lord your God hates it. ²⁶Do not bring one of those hated things into your house. If you do, you will be completely destroyed along

with it. Hate and reject those things. They must be completely destroyed.

REMEMBER THE LORD

8 Carefully obey every command I give you today. Then you will live and grow in number. And you will enter and own the land the Lord promised your ancestors. ²Remember how the Lord your God has led you in the desert for these 40 years. He took away your pride. He tested you. He wanted to know what was in your heart. He wanted to know if you would obey his commands. ³He took away your pride. He let you get hungry. Then he fed you with manna.*ᵈ* Manna was something neither you nor your ancestors had ever seen. This was to teach you that a person does not live only by eating bread. But a person lives by everything the Lord says. ⁴During these 40 years, your clothes did not wear out. And your feet did not swell. ⁵Know in your heart that the Lord your God corrects you. He corrects you as a father does his son.

⁶Obey the commands of the Lord your God. Live as he has commanded you and respect him. ⁷The Lord your God is bringing you into a good land. The land has rivers and pools of water. Springs flow in the valleys and hills. ⁸The land has wheat and barley, vines, fig trees, pomegranates,*ᵈ* olive oil and honey. ⁹It is a land where you will have plenty of food. You will have everything you need there. The rocks are iron. You can dig copper out of the hills.

¹⁰You will have all you want to eat. Then praise the Lord your God. He has given you a good land. ¹¹Be careful not to forget the Lord your God. Do not fail to obey his commands, laws and rules. I am giving them to you today. ¹²You will eat all you want. You will build nice houses and live in them. ¹³Your herds of cattle and flocks of sheep will grow large. Your silver and gold will grow. You will have more of everything. ¹⁴Then your

heart will become proud. You will forget the Lord your God. He brought you out of the land of Egypt, where you were slaves. [15]He led you through the large and terrible desert. It was dry and had no water. It had poisonous snakes and stinging insects. He gave you water from a solid rock. [16]He gave you manna to eat in the desert. Manna was something your ancestors had never seen. He did this to take away your pride and to test you. He did it so things would go well for you in the end. [17]You might say to yourself, "I am rich because of my own strength and power." [18]But remember the Lord your God! It is he who gives you the power to become rich. He keeps the agreement he promised to your ancestors. So it is today.

[19]Never forget the Lord your God. Do not follow other gods. Do not worship them. Do not bow down to them. If you do, I warn you today that you will be destroyed. [20]The Lord destroyed the other nations for you. And you can be destroyed the same way if you do not obey the Lord your God.

THE LORD WILL BE WITH ISRAEL

9 Listen, Israel. You will soon cross the Jordan River. You will go in to force out nations that are bigger and stronger than you. They have large cities with walls up to the sky. [2]The people there are Anakites.[d] They are strong and tall. You know about them. You have heard it said: "No one can stop the Anakites." [3]But today remember that the Lord your God goes in before you. He will destroy them like a fire that burns things up. He will defeat them ahead of you. And you will force them out. You will destroy them quickly. It will happen just as the Lord has said.

[4]The Lord your God will force those nations out ahead of you. After that, don't say to yourself, "The Lord brought me here. I own this land because I am so good." No! It is because these nations

are evil. That is why the Lord will force them out ahead of you. [5]You are going in to own the land. But it is not because you are good and honest. It is because these nations are evil. That is why the Lord your God will force them out ahead of you. The Lord will keep his promise to your ancestors, to Abraham, Isaac and Jacob. [6]The Lord your God is giving you this good land to own. But know this: It is not because you are good. You are a stubborn people.

REMEMBER THE LORD'S ANGER

[7]Remember this. Do not forget it. You made the Lord your God angry in the desert. You would not obey the Lord from the day you left Egypt until you arrived here. [8]At Mount Sinai you made the Lord angry. He was angry enough to destroy you. [9]I went up on the mountain to receive the stone tablets. The tablets were the agreement the Lord had made with you. I stayed on the mountain for 40 days and 40 nights. I did not eat bread or drink water. [10]The Lord gave me two stone tablets. God had written on them with his own finger. On them were all the commands of the Lord. He gave them to you on the mountain out of the fire. This was on the day you were gathered there.

[11]Then the 40 days and 40 nights were over. And the Lord gave me the two stone tablets. Those tablets had the agreement on them. [12]Then the Lord told me, "Get up. Go down quickly from here. The people you brought out from Egypt are ruining themselves. They have quickly turned away from what I commanded. They have made an idol for themselves."

[13]The Lord said to me, "I have watched these people. They are very stubborn! [14]Get away. I will destroy them. I will make the whole world forget who they are. Then I will make another nation from you. It will be bigger and stronger than they are."

[15]So I turned and came down the mountain. The mountain was burning

with fire. And the two stone tablets with the agreement were in my hands. [16]When I looked, I saw you had sinned against the Lord your God. You had made an idol in the shape of a calf. You had quickly turned away from what the Lord had told you to do. [17]So I took the two stone tablets and threw them down. I broke them into pieces right in front of you.

[18]Then I again bowed facedown on the ground before the Lord. I did this for 40 days and 40 nights. I did not eat bread or drink water. You had sinned by doing what the Lord said was evil. You made him angry. [19]I was afraid of the Lord's anger and rage. He was angry enough with you to destroy you. But the Lord listened to me again. [20]And the Lord was angry enough with Aaron to destroy him. But then I prayed for Aaron, too. [21]I took that sinful calf idol you had made. And I burned it in the fire. I crushed it into a powder like dust. And I threw the dust into a stream that flowed down the mountain.

[22]You also made the Lord angry at Taberah, Massah and Kibroth Hattaavah. [23]Then the Lord sent you away from Kadesh Barnea. He said, "Go up and take the land I have given you." But you would not obey the command of the Lord your God. You did not trust him or obey him. [24]You have refused to obey the Lord as long as I have known you.

[25]The Lord had said he would destroy you. So I threw myself down in front of him for those 40 days and 40 nights. [26]I prayed to the Lord. I said, "Lord God, do not destroy your people. They are your own people. You freed them and brought them out of Egypt by your great power and strength. [27]Remember your servants Abraham, Isaac and Jacob. Don't look at how stubborn these people are. Don't look at their sin and evil. [28]Otherwise, Egypt will say, 'The Lord was not able to take his people into the land he promised them. He hated them. So he took them into the desert to kill them.' [29]But they are your people, Lord. They are your own people. You brought them out of Egypt with your great power and strength."

NEW STONE TABLETS

10 At that time the Lord said to me, "Cut two stone tablets like the first ones. Then come up to me on the mountain. Also make a wooden box. [2]I will write on the tablets the same words that were on the first tablets, which you broke. Put the new tablets in the box."

[3]So I made the box out of acacia wood. And I cut out two stone tablets like the first ones. Then I went up on the mountain. I had the two tablets in my hands. [4]The Lord wrote the same things on these tablets he had written before. He wrote the Ten Commandments. He had told them to you on the mountain from the fire. This was on the day you were gathered there. And the Lord gave them to me. [5]Then I turned and came down the mountain. I put the tablets in the box I had made. That is what the Lord had commanded. The tablets are still there in the box.

[6](The people of Israel went from the wells of the Jaakanites to Moserah. There Aaron died and was buried. Aaron's son Eleazar became priest in Aaron's place. [7]From Moserah they went to Gudgodah. From Gudgodah they went to Jotbathah, a place with streams of water. [8]At that time the Lord chose the tribe[d] of Levi. They were to carry the Box[d] of the Agreement with the Lord. They were to serve the Lord. They were to bless the people in the Lord's name. They still do this today. [9]That is why the Levites did not receive any land to own. Instead, they received the Lord himself as their gift. This is what the Lord your God told them.)

[10]I stayed on the mountain 40 days and 40 nights just like the first time. And the Lord listened to me this time also. He

did not want to destroy you. [11]The Lord said to me, "Go. Lead the people. They will go in and take the land I promised their ancestors."

WHAT THE LORD WANTS YOU TO DO

[12]Now, Israel, this is what the Lord wants you to do. Respect the Lord your God. Do what he has told you to do. Love him. Serve the Lord your God with your whole being. [13]And obey the Lord's commands and laws. I am giving them to you today for your own good.

[14]The Lord owns the world and everything in it. The heavens, even the highest heavens, are his. [15]But the Lord cared for and loved your ancestors. And he chose you, their descendants.[d] He chose you over all the other nations. And it is this way today. [16]Give yourselves to serving the Lord. Do not be stubborn any longer. [17]The Lord your God is God of all gods. He is the Lord of all lords. He is the great God. He is strong and wonderful. He does not take sides. And he will not be talked into doing evil. [18]He helps orphans and widows. He loves foreigners. He gives them food and clothes. [19]You also must love foreigners, because you were foreigners in Egypt. [20]Respect the Lord your God and serve him. Be loyal to him. Make your promises in his name. [21]You should praise him. He is your God. He has done great and wonderful things for you. You have seen them with your own eyes. [22]There were only 70 of your ancestors when they went down to Egypt. Now the Lord your God has made you as many as the stars in the sky.

GREAT THINGS ISRAEL SAW

11 Love the Lord your God. Obey his orders, rules, laws and commands. [2]Remember today it was not your children who saw and felt the correction of the Lord your God. They did not see his majesty, his power and his strength. [3]They did not see his signs and the things he did in Egypt to the king and

his whole country. [4]They did not see what he did to the Egyptian army, its horses and chariots. He drowned them in the Red Sea[d] when they were chasing you. The Lord ruined them forever. [5]They did not see what he did for you in the desert until you arrived here. [6]They did not see what he did to Dathan and Abiram, the sons of Eliab the Reubenite. The ground opened up and swallowed them, their families and their tents. And it swallowed up everyone who stood with them in Israel. [7]It was you who saw all these great things the Lord has done.

[8]So obey all the commands I am giving you today. Then you will be strong. Then you can go in and take the land you are going to own. [9]Then you will live a long time in that land. The Lord promised to give it to your ancestors and their descendants.[d] It is a land where much food grows. [10]The land you are going to take is not like Egypt, where you were. There you had to plant your seed. Then you had to water it, like a vegetable garden, by using your feet. [11]But you will soon cross the Jordan River and take the land. It is a land of hills and valleys. It drinks rain from heaven. [12]It is a land the Lord your God loves. His eyes are on it continually. He watches it from the beginning of the year to the end.

[13]Carefully obey the commands I am giving you today. Love the Lord your God. Serve him with your whole being. [14]Then he will send rain on your land at the right time, in the fall and spring. You will be able to gather your grain, new wine and oil. [15]He will put grass in the fields for your cattle. You will have plenty to eat.

[16]Be careful. Don't be fooled. Don't turn away and serve other gods. Don't worship them. [17]If you do, the Lord will become angry with you. He will shut the heavens so it will not rain. Then the land will not grow crops. And you will soon die in the

good land the Lord is giving you. [18]Remember my words in your hearts and souls. Write them down and tie them to your hands as a sign. Tie them on your foreheads to remind you. [19]Teach them well to your children. Talk about them when you sit at home and walk along the road. Talk about them when you lie down and when you get up. [20]Write them on your doors and gates. [21]Then both you and your children will live a long time in the land. This is the land the Lord promised your ancestors. You will live there for as long as the skies are above the earth.

[22]Be careful to obey every command I am giving you to follow. Love the Lord your God. Do what he has told you to do. And be loyal to him. [23]Then the Lord will force all those nations out of the land ahead of you. And you will take the land from nations that are bigger and stronger than you. [24]Everywhere you step will be yours. Your land will go from the desert to Lebanon. And it will go from the Euphrates River to the Mediterranean Sea. [25]No one will be able to stop you. The Lord your God will do what he promised. He will make the people afraid everywhere you go.

[26]See, today I am letting you choose a blessing or a curse. [27]You will be blessed if you obey the commands of the Lord your God. I am giving them to you today. [28]But you will be cursed if you disobey the commands of the Lord your God. So do not disobey the commands I am giving you today. Do not worship other gods you do not know. [29]The Lord your God will bring you into the land you will own. Then you are to announce the blessings from Mount Gerizim. Announce the curses from Mount Ebal. [30]These mountains are on the other side of the Jordan River. They are west, toward the sunset. They are near the great trees of Moreh. They are in the land of the Canaanites who live in the Jordan Valley opposite

Gilgal. [31]You will soon cross the Jordan River. You will enter and take the land the Lord your God is giving you. You will take it over and live there. [32]Then be careful to obey all the commands and laws I am giving you today.

THE PLACE FOR WORSHIP

12 These are the commands and laws you must carefully obey in the land the Lord your God is giving you. Obey them as long as you live in the land. [2]You will inherit the lands of these nations. You must completely destroy all the places where they serve their gods. These places are on high mountains and hills and under every green tree. [3]Tear down their altars. Smash their holy stone pillars. Burn their Asherah[d] idols. Cut down their idols. Destroy their names from those places.

[4]Don't worship the Lord your God that way. [5]But look for the place the Lord your God will choose. He will choose a place among your tribes[d] where he is to be worshiped. Go there. [6]Bring to that place your burnt offerings and sacrifices. Bring a tenth of what you gain and your special gifts. Bring what you have promised and the special gifts you want to give the Lord. And bring the first animals born to your herds and flocks.

[7]There you will be together with the Lord your God. There you and your families will eat. And you will enjoy all the good things for which you have worked. The Lord your God has blessed you.

[8]Do not worship the way we have been doing today. Each person does what he thinks is right. [9]You have not yet come to a resting place. The Lord your God will give you your own land. [10]But you will soon cross the Jordan River. And you will live in the land the Lord your God is giving you to own. And he will give you rest from all your enemies. You will live in safety. [11]Then the Lord your God will choose a place where he is to be worshiped. To that place you must bring

everything I tell you: your burnt offerings and sacrifices, your offerings of a tenth of what you gain, your special gifts and all your best things you promised to the Lord. ¹²There rejoice before the Lord your God. Everyone should rejoice: you, your sons and daughters, your male and female servants, and the Levites from your towns, who have no land of their own. ¹³Be careful. Don't sacrifice your burnt offerings just anywhere you please. ¹⁴Offer them only in the place the Lord will choose. He will choose a place in one of your tribes. And there you must do everything I am commanding you.

¹⁵But you may kill your animals in any of your towns. And you may eat as much of the meat as you want. Eat it as if it were a deer or a gazelle. This is the blessing the Lord your God is giving you. Anyone, clean*d* or unclean, may eat this meat. ¹⁶But do not eat the blood. Pour it out on the ground like water. ¹⁷Do not eat in your own towns what belongs to the Lord: one-tenth of your grain, new wine or oil; the first animals born to your herds or flocks; whatever you have promised to give; the special gifts you want to give to the Lord, or any other gifts. ¹⁸Eat these things when you are together with the Lord. Eat them in the place the Lord your God chooses to be worshiped. Everyone must do this: you, your sons and daughters, your male and female servants, and the Levites from your towns. Rejoice in the Lord's presence about the things you have worked for. ¹⁹Be careful not to forget the Levites as long as you live in the land.

²⁰The Lord your God will enlarge your country as he has promised. And you will want some meat. You will say, "I want some meat." Eat as much meat as you want. ²¹The Lord your God will choose a place where he is to be worshiped. But it may be too far away from you. If it is, you may kill animals from your herds and flocks. The Lord has given them to you. I have commanded that you may do this. You may eat as much of them as you want in your own towns. ²²Eat them as you would eat gazelle or deer meat. Both clean and unclean people may eat this meat. ²³But be sure you don't eat the blood. The life is in the blood. Don't eat the life with the meat. ²⁴Don't eat the blood. Pour it out on the ground like water. ²⁵Don't eat it. Then things will go well for you and your children. You will be doing what the Lord says is right.

²⁶Take your holy things and the things you have promised to give. And go to the place the Lord will choose. ²⁷Present your burnt offerings on the altar of the Lord your God. Offer both the meat and the blood. The blood of your sacrifices should be poured beside the altar. But you may eat the meat. ²⁸Be careful to obey all the rules I am giving you. Then things will always go well for you and your children. You will be doing what the Lord your God says is good and right.

²⁹You will enter the land and take it away from the nations there. The Lord your God will destroy those nations ahead of you. You will force them out and live in their land. ³⁰They will be destroyed for you. Be careful not to be trapped by asking about their gods. Don't say, "How do these nations worship? I will do the same." ³¹Don't worship the Lord your God that way. The Lord hates the evil ways they worship their gods. They even burn their sons and daughters as sacrifices to their gods!

³²Be sure to do everything I have commanded you. Do not add anything to it. And do not take anything away from it.

FALSE PROPHETS

13 A prophet*d* or someone who tells the future with dreams might come to you. He might say he will show you a miracle*d* or a sign. ²The miracle or sign might even happen. Then he might say, "Let's serve other gods." (These are gods you have not known.) "And let's worship them." ³But you must not listen to that prophet or dreamer. The Lord your God is testing you. He is finding out if you love him with your whole being. ⁴Serve only the Lord your God. Respect him. Keep his commands and obey him. Serve him and be loyal to him. ⁵That prophet or dreamer must be killed. He said you should turn against the Lord your God. The Lord brought you out of Egypt. He saved you from the land where you were slaves. That prophet tried to turn you from doing what the Lord your God commanded you to do. You must get rid of the evil among you.

⁶Some relative might try to lead you to serve other gods. It might be your brother, your son or daughter or the wife you love. Or it might be a close friend. He might say, "Let's go and worship other gods." (These are gods that neither you nor your ancestors have known. ⁷They are gods of the people who live around you. Some are nearby, and some are far away. They are from one end of the land to the other.) ⁸Do not give in to him. Do not listen. Do not feel sorry for him. Do not let him go free or protect him. ⁹You must put him to death. You must be the first one to start to kill him. Then everyone else must join in. ¹⁰You must throw stones at him until he dies. He tried to turn you away from the Lord your God. The Lord brought you out of the land of Egypt, where you were slaves. ¹¹Then everyone in Israel will hear about this. And they will be afraid. No one among you will ever do such an evil thing again.

CITIES TO DESTROY

¹²The Lord your God is giving you cities in which to live. You might hear something about one of them. Someone might say ¹³that evil men have moved in among you. And they might lead the people of that city away from God. They might say, "Let's go and worship other gods." (These are gods you have not known.) ¹⁴Then you must ask about it.

Look into the matter and check carefully. It might be true. It may be proved that a terrible thing has happened among you. ¹⁵If it has, then you must kill with a sword everyone who lives in that city. Destroy the city completely. Kill everyone in it, as well as the animals, with a sword. ¹⁶Gather up everything those people owned. Put it in the middle of the city square. Then completely burn the city and everything they owned. It will be a burnt offering to the Lord your God. That city should never be rebuilt. Let it be ruined forever. ¹⁷Don't keep any of the things found in that city for yourselves. Then the Lord will not be angry anymore. He will give you mercy. He will feel sorry for you. And he will make your nation grow larger. He promised this to your ancestors. ¹⁸You will have obeyed the Lord your God. You will be keeping all his commands. I am giving them to you today. And you will be doing what the Lord says is right.

GOD'S SPECIAL PEOPLE

14 You are the children of the Lord your God. When someone dies, do not cut yourselves or shave your heads to show your sadness. ²You are holy people. You belong to the Lord your God. He has chosen you from all the people on earth to be his very own.

³Do not eat anything the Lord hates. ⁴These are the animals you may eat: ox, sheep, goats, ⁵deer, gazelle, roe deer, wild goats, ibex, antelope and mountain sheep. ⁶You may eat any animal that has a split hoof and chews the cud.ᵈ ⁷But you may not eat camels, rabbits or rock badgers. These animals chew the cud, but their feet are not divided. So they are uncleanᵈ for you. ⁸Pigs are also unclean for you. They have split hoofs, but they do not chew the cud. Do not eat their meat or touch their dead bodies.

⁹There are many things that live in the water. You may eat anything that has fins and scales. ¹⁰But do not eat anything

that does not have fins and scales. It is unclean for you.

[11]You may eat any clean bird. [12]But do not eat these birds: eagles, vultures, black vultures, [13]red kites, falcons, any kind of kite, [14]any kind of raven, [15]horned owls, screech owls, seagulls, any kind of hawk, [16]little owls, great owls, white owls, [17]desert owls, ospreys, cormorants, [18]storks, any kind of heron, the hoopoes or bats.

[19]All insects with wings are unclean for you. Do not eat them. [20]Other things with wings are clean. You may eat them.

[21]Do not eat anything you find that is already dead. You may give it to a foreigner living in your town. He may eat it. Or you may sell it to a foreigner. But you are holy people. You belong to the Lord your God.

Do not cook a baby goat in its mother's milk.

GIVING ONE-TENTH

[22]Be sure to save one-tenth of all your crops each year. [23]Take it to the place the Lord your God will choose where he is to be worshiped. There you will be together with the Lord. There eat the tenth of your grain, new wine and oil. And eat the animals born first to your herds and flocks. Then you will learn to respect the Lord your God always. [24]But the place the Lord will choose to be worshiped might be too far away. And he may have blessed you so much you cannot carry a tenth. [25]If so, exchange your one-tenth for silver. Then take the silver with you to the place the Lord your God shall choose. [26]Use the silver to buy anything you wish. You may buy cattle, sheep, wine, beer or anything you wish. Then you and your family will eat and celebrate there before the Lord your God. [27]Do not forget the Levites in your town. They have no land of their own among you.

[28]At the end of every third year, everyone should bring one-tenth of that year's crop. Store it in your towns. [29]This is for the Levites so they may eat and be full. (They have no land of their own among you.) It is also for strangers, orphans and widows who live in your towns. All of them may eat and be full. Then the Lord your God will bless you and all the work you do.

THE SPECIAL SEVENTH YEAR

15 At the end of every seven years, you must forget about collecting what people owe you. [2]This is how you must do it: Everyone who has loaned money must forget the loan. He must not make his neighbor or brother pay it back. This is the Lord's time for canceling what people owe. [3]You may make a foreigner pay what he owes you. But you must not collect what your brother owes you. [4]But there should be no poor people among you. The Lord your God will richly bless you in the land he is giving you to own. [5]He will bless you if you obey him completely. But you must be careful to obey all the commands I am giving you today. [6]The Lord your God will bless you as he promised. You will lend to other nations. But you will not need to borrow from them. You will rule over many nations. But none will rule over you.

[7]There might be a poor man among you. He might be in one of the towns of the land the Lord your God is giving you. Do not be selfish or greedy toward your poor brother. [8]But give freely to him. Freely lend him whatever he needs. [9]Beware of evil thoughts. Don't think, "The seventh year is near. It's the year to forget what people owe." You might be mean to your needy brother. You might not give him anything. Then he will complain to the Lord about you. And the Lord will find you guilty of sin. [10]Give freely to the poor person. Do not wish that you didn't have to give. The Lord your God will bless your work and everything you touch. [11]There will always be poor people in the land. So I command

you to give freely to your brothers. Give freely to the poor and needy in your land.

LETTING SLAVES GO FREE

¹²One of your own people might sell himself to you as a slave. It may be a Hebrew man or woman. That person will serve you for six years. The seventh year you must let him go free. ¹³And when you let him go, don't send him away without anything. ¹⁴Give him some of your sheep, your grain and your wine. Give to him as the Lord has given to you. ¹⁵Remember that you were slaves in Egypt. And the Lord your God saved you. That is why I am commanding this to you today.

¹⁶But your slave might say to you, "I don't want to leave you." He might love you and your family. He might have a good life with you. ¹⁷If he does this, stick an awl[n] through his ear into the door. He will be your slave for life. Also do this to a woman slave.

¹⁸Do not think of it as a hard thing when you let your slave go free. After all, he served you six years. You paid him only half what a hired person would cost. The Lord your God will bless you in everything you do.

RULES ABOUT FIRSTBORN ANIMALS

¹⁹Save all the first male animals born to your herds and flocks. They are for the Lord your God. Do not work the first calf born to your oxen. And do not cut off the wool from the first lamb born to your sheep. ²⁰Each year you and your family are to eat these animals. Eat them in the presence of the Lord your God. Eat them in the place he will choose to be worshiped. ²¹An animal might have something wrong with it. It might be crippled or blind. It might have some other thing wrong with it. Do not sacrifice it to the Lord your God. ²²But you may eat that animal in your own town. Both clean[d] and unclean people may eat it. It would

be like eating a gazelle or a deer. ²³But don't eat its blood. Pour it out on the ground like water.

THE PASSOVER

16 Celebrate the Passover[d] of the Lord your God during the month of Abib.[d] It was during Abib that he brought you out of Egypt at night. ²Offer a sacrifice for the Passover to the Lord your God. It should be an animal from your flock or herd. Offer it at the place the Lord will choose to be worshiped. ³Do not eat it with bread made with yeast. But for seven days eat bread made without yeast. This is the bread of suffering because you left Egypt in a hurry. So all your life you will remember the time you left Egypt. ⁴There must be no yeast anywhere in your land for seven days. Offer the sacrifice on the evening of the first day. Eat all the meat before morning. Do not leave it overnight.

⁵Do not offer the Passover sacrifice in just any town the Lord your God gives you. ⁶Offer it in the place he will choose to be worshiped. Offer it in the evening as the sun goes down. That is when you left Egypt. ⁷Roast the meat. Then eat it at the place the Lord your God will choose. The next morning go back to your tents. ⁸Eat bread made without yeast for six days. On the seventh day have a special meeting for the Lord your God. Do not work that day.

FEAST OF WEEKS

⁹Count seven weeks from the time you begin to harvest the grain. ¹⁰Then celebrate the Feast[d] of Weeks for the Lord your God. Bring him an offering as a special gift to him. Give to him just as he has blessed you. ¹¹Rejoice before the Lord your God. Rejoice at the place he will choose to be worshiped. Everybody should rejoice: you, your sons and daughters, your male and female servants, the Levites in your town, the strangers,

---

15:17 awl A tool like a big needle with a handle at one end.

orphans and widows living among you. [12]Remember that you were slaves in Egypt. And carefully obey all these laws.

FEAST OF SHELTERS

[13]Celebrate the Feast[d] of Shelters for seven days. Do it after you have gathered your harvest from the threshing[d] floor and winepress.[d] [14]Everybody should rejoice at your Feast: you, your sons and daughters, your male and female servants, the Levites and strangers who live in your towns, orphans and widows in your towns. [15]Celebrate the Feast to the Lord your God for seven days. Celebrate it at the place he will choose. The Lord your God will bless all your harvest. He will bless all the work you do. And you will be completely happy.

[16]All your men must come before the Lord three times a year. They must come to the place he will choose. They must come at these times: the Feast[d] of Unleavened Bread, the Feast[d] of Weeks and the Feast of Shelters. No man should come before the Lord without a gift. [17]Each of you must bring a gift. It should show how much the Lord your God has blessed you.

JUDGES FOR THE PEOPLE

[18]Appoint judges and officers for your tribes.[d] Appoint them in every town the Lord your God is giving you. And they must judge the people fairly. [19]Do not judge unfairly or take sides. Do not let people pay you to make wrong decisions. That kind of payment makes wise people seem blind. And it changes the words of good people. [20]Always do what is right. Then you will live and own the land the Lord your God is giving you.

GOD HATES IDOLS

[21]Do not set up a wooden Asherah[d] idol next to the altar you build for the Lord your God. [22]And do not set up holy stone pillars. The Lord your God hates them.

17 An ox or sheep might have something wrong with it. Do not offer it as a sacrifice to the Lord your God. He would hate that.

[2]A man or woman might be found doing something evil in one of the towns the Lord gave you. That man or woman is breaking his agreement. [3]That person may have served other gods. He may have bowed down to them, to the sun or moon or stars of the sky. I have commanded that should not be done. [4]If someone has told you about it, you must look into the matter. It might be true. A terrible thing may have happened in Israel. [5]If it is true, take the man or woman who has done the evil thing to the city gate. Throw stones at that person until he dies. [6]There must be two or three witnesses that he did it. Then the person should be put to death. But if there is only one witness, the person should not be put to death. [7]The witnesses must be the first to throw stones at the person. Then everyone else will follow. You must get rid of the evil among you.

COURTS OF LAW

[8]Some cases that come before you may be too difficult to judge. It may be a case of murder, quarreling or attack. Take these cases to the place the Lord your God will choose. [9]Go to the priests who are Levites. And go to the judge who is on duty at that time. Ask them about the case, and they will decide. [10]You must follow the decision they give you. They will be at the place the Lord your God will choose. Be careful to do everything they tell you. [11]Follow the teachings they give you. Do whatever they decide. Do exactly what they tell you. [12]The person who does not show respect for the judge or priest must be put to death. They are there serving the Lord your God. You must get rid of that evil from Israel. [13]Then everyone will hear about this. And they will be afraid. They will not show disrespect anymore.

CHOOSING A KING

[14]You will enter the land the Lord your God is giving you. You will take it as your

own and live in it. Then you will say, "Let's appoint a king over us like the nations all around us." 15Be sure to appoint over you the king the Lord your God chooses. He must be one of your own people. Do not appoint a foreigner as your king. He is not a fellow Israelite. 16The king must not have too many horses for himself. He must not send people to Egypt to get more horses. The Lord has told you, "Don't return that way again." 17The king must not have many wives. If he does, his heart will be led away from God. He must not have too much silver and gold.

18When he becomes king, he should write a copy of the teachings on a scroll for himself. He should copy it from the priests and Levites. 19He should keep it with him all the time. He should read from it every day of his life. Then he will learn to respect the Lord his God. And he will obey all the teachings and commands. 20He should not think he is better than his brothers. He must not stop obeying the law in any way. Then he and his descendants*d* will rule the kingdom for a long time.

SHARES FOR PRIESTS AND LEVITES

18 The priests are from the tribe*d* of Levi. That tribe will not receive a share of the land with the Israelites. They will eat the offerings made to the Lord by fire. That is their share. 2They will not inherit any of the land like their brothers. They will inherit the Lord himself. This is what he promised them.

3When you offer a bull or sheep as a sacrifice, you must share with the priests. Give them the shoulder, the cheeks and the inner organs. 4Give them the first of your grain, new wine and oil. Give them the first wool you cut from your sheep. 5The Lord your God has chosen the priests and their descendants*d* out of all your tribes. They are to stand and serve the Lord always.

6A Levite might move from one of your towns anywhere in Israel where he

lives. He is sincere and comes to the place the Lord will choose. 7He may serve the Lord his God. He will be like his fellow Levites who serve there before the Lord. 8They all will have an equal share of the food. This is separate from what he has received from the sale of family possessions.

DO NOT FOLLOW OTHER NATIONS

9You will enter the land the Lord your God is giving you. But don't learn to do the terrible things the other nations do. 10Don't let anyone among you offer his son or daughter as a sacrifice in the fire. Don't let anyone use magic or witchcraft.*d* No one should try to explain the meaning of signs. 11Don't let anyone try to control others with magic. Don't let them be mediums*d* or try to talk with the spirits of dead people. 12The Lord hates anyone who does these things. The other nations do these things. That is why the Lord your God will force them out of the land ahead of you. 13You must be innocent in the presence of the Lord your God.

THE LORD'S SPECIAL PROPHET

14The nations you will force out listen to people who use magic and witchcraft.*d* But the Lord your God will not let you do those things. 15The Lord your God will give you a prophet*d* like me. He will be one of your own people. Listen to him. 16This is what you asked the Lord your God to do. You were gathered at Mount Sinai. You said, "Don't make us listen to the voice of the Lord our God again. Don't make us look at this terrible fire anymore. We will die."

17So the Lord said to me, "What they have said is good. 18So I will give them a prophet like you. He will be one of their own people. I will tell him what to say. And he will tell them everything I command. 19This prophet will speak for me. Anyone who does not listen when he speaks will answer to me. 20But a prophet might say something I did not tell him to say. And he might say he is speaking for me. Or a prophet might speak in the name of other gods. That prophet must be killed."

²¹You might be thinking, "How can we know if a message is not from the Lord?" ²²What a prophet says in the name of the Lord might not happen. If it doesn't, it is not the Lord's message. That prophet was speaking his own ideas. Don't be afraid of him.

CITIES OF SAFETY

19 The Lord your God is giving you land that belongs to other nations. He will destroy those nations. You will force them out and live in their cities and houses. ²Then choose three cities. They must be in the middle of the land the Lord your God is giving you to own. ³Build roads to those cities. And divide the land the Lord is giving you into three parts. Then someone who kills another person may run to these cities.

⁴This is the rule for someone who kills another person. He may run to one of these cities to save his life. But he must have killed his neighbor without meaning to kill him. He did not hate his neighbor. ⁵A man might go into the forest with his neighbor to cut wood. The man swings his ax to cut down a tree. But the ax head flies off the handle. It hits his neighbor and kills him. The man who killed him may run to one of these cities to save his life. ⁶Otherwise, the dead man's relative who has the duty of punishing a murderer might be angry and chase him. And the relative might catch him if the city is far away. The relative might kill the man. But the man should not be killed because he did not mean to kill his neighbor. ⁷This is why I command you to choose these three cities.

⁸⁻⁹Carefully obey all these laws I'm giving you today. Love the Lord your God. Always do what he wants you to do. Then the Lord your God will enlarge your land as he promised your ancestors. He will give you the whole land he promised to them. After that, choose three more cities of safety. ¹⁰This is so that innocent people will not be killed in your land. The Lord your God is giving it to you to own. By doing this you will not be guilty of murder.

¹¹But a person might hate his neighbor. And he might hide and wait for him. He might attack and kill him and then run to one of these cities for safety. ¹²The elders of his own city should send for him. They should bring him back from the city of safety. And they should hand him over to the relative who has the duty of punishing the murderer. ¹³Give him no mercy. You must remove from Israel the guilt of murdering innocent people. Then things will go well for you.

¹⁴Do not move the stone that marks the border of your neighbor's land. People long ago set them in place. They mark what you inherit in the land the Lord your God is giving you to own.

RULES ABOUT WITNESSES

¹⁵One witness is not enough to accuse a man of a crime or sin. A case must be proved by two or three witnesses.

¹⁶A witness might lie and accuse a person of a crime. ¹⁷The two people who are arguing must stand before the Lord. They must stand before the priests and judges who are on duty. ¹⁸The judges must check the matter carefully. The witness might be a liar. He might be lying about his fellow Israelite. ¹⁹If so, he must be punished as he wanted his brother punished. You must get rid of the evil among you. ²⁰The rest of the people will hear about this and be afraid. No one among you will ever do such an evil thing again. ²¹Give him no mercy. A life must be paid for a life. It must be an eye for an eye, a tooth for a tooth, a hand for a hand, a foot for a foot.

LAWS FOR WAR

20 When you go to war against your enemies, you might see horses and chariots. Their army might be bigger than yours. But don't be afraid of them. The Lord your God will be with you. He brought you out of Egypt. ²The priest must come and speak to the army before you go into battle. ³He should say, "Listen, Israel! Today you are going into battle against your enemies. Don't lose your courage or be afraid. Don't panic or be frightened. ⁴The Lord your God goes with you. He will fight for you against your enemies. And he will save you."

⁵The officers should say to the army, "Has anyone built a new house but not given it to God? He may go home. He might die in battle. Then someone else would get to give his house to God. ⁶Has anyone planted a vineyard and not begun to enjoy it? He may go home. He might die in battle. Then someone else would enjoy his vineyard. ⁷Is any man engaged to a woman and not yet married to her? He may go home. He might die in battle. Then someone else would marry her." ⁸Then the officers should also say, "Is anyone here afraid? Has anyone lost his courage? He may go home. Then he will not cause others to lose their courage, too." ⁹When the officers finish speaking to the army, they should appoint commanders to lead it.

¹⁰You will march up to attack a city. First, make them an offer of peace. ¹¹They might accept your offer and open their gates to you. If that happens, all the people of that city will become your slaves. They will work for you. ¹²But they might not make peace with you. They might fight you in battle. Then you should surround that city. ¹³The Lord your God will give you the city. Then kill all the men with your swords. ¹⁴You may take everything else in the city for yourselves. Take the women and children and animals. And you may use these things the Lord your God gives you from your enemies. ¹⁵Do this to all the cities that are far away. They do not belong to the nations nearby.

¹⁶But leave nothing alive in the cities of the land. This is the land the Lord your God is giving you. ¹⁷Completely destroy these people: the Hittites, Amorites, Canaanites, Perizzites, Hivites and Jebusites. The Lord your God has commanded you to do this. ¹⁸Otherwise, they will teach you what they do for their gods. And if you do these terrible things, you will sin against the Lord your God.

¹⁹You might surround and attack a city for a long time, trying to capture it. But do not destroy its trees with an ax. You can eat the fruit from the trees. Do not cut them down. These trees are not the enemy. So don't make war against them. ²⁰But you may cut down trees that you know are not fruit trees. You may use them to build devices to attack the city walls. You may do this until the city is captured.

A PERSON FOUND MURDERED

21 Someone might be found murdered. He might be lying in a field in the land the Lord your God is giving you to own. And no one knows who killed him. ²Your elders and judges should go to where he was found. And they should measure how far it is to the nearby cities. ³The elders of the city nearest the body are responsible. They must take a young cow that has never worked or worn a yoke.*ᵈ* ⁴And they must lead her down to a valley. It must never have been plowed or planted. It must have a stream flowing through it. There they must break the young cow's neck. ⁵The priests should come forward. They are the sons of Levi. They have been chosen by the Lord your God. They are to serve and give blessings in the Lord's name. And they are to decide cases of quarreling and attacks. ⁶Then all the elders of the city nearest the murdered man should wash their hands. They should do it over the young cow whose neck was broken in the valley. [7]They should declare: "We did not kill this man. And we did not see it happen. [8]Lord, remove this sin of your people Israel. You have saved them. Don't blame your people, the Israelites, for this innocent man's murder." And so the murder will be paid for. [9]Then you will have removed from yourselves the guilt of murdering an innocent person. You will be doing what the Lord says is right.

CAPTIVE WOMEN AS WIVES

[10]You will go to war against your enemies. The Lord will help you defeat them. You will take them captive. [11]You might see a beautiful woman among the captives. And you might be attracted to her. You may take her as your wife. [12]Bring her into your home. She must shave her head and cut her nails. [13]She must change out of the clothes she was wearing when you captured her. And she must live in your house and cry for her parents for a month. After that, you may marry her. You will be her husband, and she will be your wife. [14]But you might not be pleased with her. Then let her go anywhere she wants. You must not sell her for money. You must not make her a slave. You have taken away her honor.

THE OLDEST SON

[15]A man may have two wives. He might love one wife but not the other. Both wives might have sons by him. But the older son might be the son of the wife he does not love. [16]Someday that man must will his property to his sons. But he must not give the son of the wife he loves what belongs to the older son. The older son is the son of the wife the man does not love. [17]He must agree to give the older son two shares of everything he owns. The older son is from the wife he does not love. That son was the first to prove his father could have chil-

dren. So he has the rights that belong to the older son.

SONS WHO REFUSE TO OBEY

[18]A man might have a son who is stubborn. The son turns against his father and mother and doesn't obey them. He will not listen when they correct him. [19]His parents must take him to the elders at the city gate. [20]They will say to the leaders, "Our son is stubborn and turns against us. He will not obey us. He eats too much. And he is always drunk." [21]Then all the men in his town must throw stones at him until he dies. Get rid of the evil among you. All the people of Israel will hear about this and be afraid.

OTHER LAWS

[22]A man might be guilty of a sin worthy of death. He must be put to death and his body displayed on a tree. [23]But don't leave his body hanging on the tree overnight. Be sure to bury him that same day. Anyone whose body is displayed on a tree is cursed by God. You must not ruin the land the Lord your God is giving you to own.

22 You might see your fellow Israelite's ox or sheep wandering away. Don't ignore it. Take it back to its owner. [2]The owner might not live close to you. Or you might not know who he is. Then take the animal home with you. Keep it until the owner comes looking for it. Then give it back to him. [3]Do the same thing if you find his donkey or coat or anything he lost. Don't just ignore it.

[4]You might see your fellow Israelite's donkey or ox fallen on the road. Don't ignore it. Help him get it up.

[5]A woman must not wear men's clothes. And a man must not wear women's clothes. The Lord your God hates anyone who does that.

[6]You might find a bird's nest by the road. It might be in a tree or on the ground. And the mother bird might be sitting on the young birds or eggs. Do

not take the mother bird with the young birds. [7]You may take the young birds. But you must let the mother bird go free. Then things will go well for you. And you will live a long time.

[8]When you build a new house, build a wall around the roof.[n] Then you will not be guilty of murder if someone falls off the roof.

[9]Don't plant two different kinds of seeds in your vineyard. Otherwise, both crops will be ruined.

[10]Don't plow with an ox and a donkey tied together.

[11]Don't wear clothes made of wool and linen woven together.

[12]Tie several pieces of thread together. Then put these tassels on the four corners of your coat.

MARRIAGE LAWS

[13]A man might marry a girl and have sexual relations with her. But he might decide that he does not like her. [14]So he might lie about her and give her a bad name. He might say, "I married this woman. But when I had sexual relations with her, I did not find that she was a virgin."[d] [15]Then the girl's parents must bring proof that she was a virgin. They must bring it to the elders at the city gate. [16]The girl's father will say to the leaders, "I gave my daughter to this man to be his wife. But now he does not want her. [17]This man has told lies about my daughter. He has said, 'I did not find your daughter to be a virgin.' But here is the proof that my daughter was a virgin." Then her parents are to show the sheet to the city leaders. [18]Then the leaders must take the man and punish him. [19]They must make him pay about two and a half pounds of silver. The silver will go to the girl's father. This is because the man has given an Israelite girl a bad name. The girl must continue to be the man's wife. And he may not divorce her as long as he lives.

[20]But the things the husband said about his wife might be true. And there might be no proof that she was a virgin. [21]If so, the girl must be brought to the door of her father's house. Then the men of the town must put her to death by throwing stones at her. She has done a disgraceful thing in Israel. She had sexual relations before she was married. You must get rid of the evil among you.

[22]A man might be found having sexual relations with another man's wife. Both the woman and the man who had sexual relations with her must die. Get rid of this evil from Israel.

[23]A man might meet a virgin in a city and have sexual relations with her. But she might be engaged to another man. [24]You must take both of them to the city gate. Put them both to death by throwing stones at them. Kill the girl because she was in a city and did not scream for help. And kill the man for having sexual relations with another man's wife. You must get rid of the evil among you.

[25]But a man might meet a girl out in the country. He might force her to have sexual relations with him. But she might be engaged to another man. Only the man who had sexual relations with her must be put to death. [26]Don't do anything to the girl. She has not done a sin worthy of death. This is like the person who attacks and murders his neighbor. [27]The man found the engaged girl in the country. And she screamed. But no one was there to save her.

[28]A man might meet a virgin who is not engaged to be married. He might force her to have sexual relations with him. And people might find out about it. [29]The man must pay the girl's father about one and one-fourth pounds of silver. He must

---

22:8 roof In Bible times houses were built with flat roofs. The roof was used for drying things such as flax and fruit. And it was used as an extra room, as a place for worship and as a place to sleep in the summer.

also marry the girl because he has dishonored her. And he may never divorce her for as long as he lives.

³⁰A man must not marry his father's wife. He must not dishonor his father in this way.

THE LORD'S PEOPLE

23 No man who has had part of his sex organ cut off may come into the worship meeting of the Lord's people.

²No one born to parents who were forbidden by law to marry may come into the meeting to worship the Lord. His descendants for ten generations may not come in either.

³No Ammonite or Moabite may come into the meeting to worship the Lord. And none of their descendants for ten generations may come in. ⁴This is because the Ammonites and Moabites did not give you bread and water when you came out of Egypt. And they hired Balaam to put a curse on you. He was the son of Beor from Pethor in Northwest Mesopotamia. ⁵But the Lord your God would not listen to Balaam. He turned the curse into a blessing for you. The Lord your God loves you. ⁶Don't wish for their peace or success as long as you live.

⁷Don't hate Edomites. They are your relatives. Don't hate Egyptians, because you were foreigners in their country. ⁸The great-grandchildren of these two peoples may come into the meeting to worship the Lord.

KEEPING THE CAMP CLEAN

⁹When you are camped in time of war, keep away from unclean*ᵈ* things. ¹⁰A man might become unclean during the night. If he does, he must go outside the camp and not come back. ¹¹But when evening comes, he must wash himself. At sunset he may come back into the camp.

¹²Choose a place outside the camp where people may go to relieve themselves. ¹³Carry a stick with you. When you relieve yourself, dig a hole. Cover up your dung. ¹⁴The Lord your God moves around through your camp. He will protect you. He will help you defeat your enemies. So the camp must be holy. The Lord must not see anything unclean among you. Then he will not leave you.

OTHER LAWS

¹⁵An escaped slave might come to you. Do not hand him over to his master. ¹⁶Let the slave live with you anywhere he likes. He may live in any town he chooses. Do not mistreat him.

¹⁷No Israelite man or woman must ever become a temple prostitute.*ᵈ* ¹⁸Do not bring a male or female prostitute's pay to the Temple*ᵈ* of the Lord your God to pay what you have promised to the Lord. The Lord your God hates prostitution.

¹⁹You may loan your fellow Israelite money or food or anything else. But don't make him pay back more than what you loaned him. ²⁰You may charge a foreigner, but not a fellow Israelite. Then the Lord your God will bless everything you do. He will bless you in the land you are entering to take as your own.

²¹You might make a promise to give something to the Lord your God. Do not be slow to pay it. The Lord your God demands it from you. Do not be guilty of sin. ²²But if you do not make the promise, you will not be guilty. ²³You must do whatever you say you will do. You chose to make the promise to the Lord your God.

²⁴You might go into your neighbor's vineyard. You may eat as many grapes as you wish. But do not fill your basket with his grapes. ²⁵You might go into your neighbor's grainfield. You may pick grain with your hands. But you must not cut down his grain with your sickle.

24 A man might marry a woman. But he might decide she doesn't please him. He has found something bad about her. He writes out divorce papers for her. He gives them to her and sends her away from his house. ²After she leaves his house, she goes and marries another man. ³But her second husband does not like her either. So he writes out divorce papers for her. He gives them to her and sends her away from his house. Or the second husband might die. ⁴In either case, her first husband who divorced her must not marry her again. She has become unclean.ᵈ The Lord would hate this. Don't bring this sin into the land the Lord your God is giving you to own.

⁵A man who has just married must not be sent to war. And he must not be given any other duty. He should be free to stay home for a year to make his new wife happy.

⁶A man might owe you something. But do not take his two stones for grinding grain—not even the upper one—in place of what he owes. This is how he makes his living.

⁷A man might kidnap a fellow Israelite. He might make him a slave or sell him. The kidnapper must be killed. You must get rid of the evil among you.

⁸Be careful when someone has a harmful skin disease. Do exactly what the priests, the Levites, teach you. Be careful to do what I have commanded them. ⁹Remember what the Lord your God did to Miriam on your way out of Egypt.

¹⁰You might make a loan to your neighbor. But don't go into his house to get something in place of it. ¹¹Stay outside. Let the man himself go in and get what he promised you. ¹²A poor man might give you his coat to show he will pay the loan back. But don't keep his coat overnight. ¹³Give his coat back to him at sunset. He needs his coat to sleep in. He will thank you. And the Lord your God will see that you have done a good thing.

¹⁴Don't cheat a hired servant who is poor and needy. He might be a fellow Israelite. Or he might be a foreigner living in one of your towns. ¹⁵Pay him each day before sunset. He is poor and needs the money. Otherwise, he may complain to the Lord about you. And you will be guilty of sin.

¹⁶Fathers must not be put to death when their children do wrong. And children must not be put to death when their fathers do wrong. Each person must die for his own sin.

¹⁷Do not be unfair to a foreigner or an orphan. Don't take a widow's coat in place of a loan. ¹⁸Remember that you were slaves in Egypt. And the Lord your God saved you from there. That is why I am commanding you to do this.

¹⁹You might be gathering your harvest in the field. You might not see a bundle of grain. Don't go back and get it. Leave it there for foreigners, orphans and widows. Then the Lord your God can bless everything you do. ²⁰You may beat your olive trees to knock the olives off. But don't beat the trees a second time. Leave what is left for foreigners, orphans and widows. ²¹You may harvest the grapes in your vineyard. But don't pick the vines a second time. Leave what is left for foreigners, orphans and widows. ²²Remember that you were slaves in Egypt. That is why I am commanding you to do this.

25 Two people may have an argument. They should go to the court. And the judges will decide the case. They will declare one person to be right. And they will punish the one who is guilty. ²The guilty person might have to be punished with a beating. If so, the judge will make him lie down. They will beat him in front of the judge. The number of lashes should match the crime. ³But don't hit him more than 40 times. If he is beaten more than that, it would disgrace him before others.

⁴When an ox is working in the grain, do not cover its mouth to keep it from eating.

⁵Two brothers might be living together. One of them might die without having a son. His widow must not marry

someone outside her husband's family. Her husband's brother must marry her. This is his duty for her as a brother-in-law. ⁶The first son she has must be named for the dead brother. Then his name will not be forgotten in Israel.

⁷But a man might not want to marry his brother's widow. Then she should go to the elders at the town gate. And she should say, "My brother-in-law will not carry on his brother's name in Israel. He refuses to do his duty for me."

⁸Then the elders of the town must call for the man and talk to him. But he might be stubborn and say, "I don't want to marry her."

⁹If he does, the woman must go up to him in front of the leaders. She must take off one of his sandals. She must spit in his face and say, "This is for the man who won't continue his brother's family!" ¹⁰Then that man's family shall be known in Israel as the Family of the Unsandaled.

¹¹Two men might be fighting. And one man's wife comes to save her husband from his attacker. And she grabs the attacker by his sex organs. ¹²You must cut off her hand. Give her no mercy.

¹³Don't carry two sets of weights with you, one heavy and one light. ¹⁴Don't have two different sets of measures in your house, one large and one small. ¹⁵You must have true and honest weights and measures. Then you will live a long time in the land the Lord your God is giving you. ¹⁶The Lord your God hates anyone who is dishonest and uses dishonest measures.

¹⁷Remember what the Amalekites did to you when you came out of Egypt. ¹⁸You were tired and worn out. And they met you on the road. They killed all those lagging behind. They were not afraid of God. ¹⁹The Lord your God will give you rest from all the enemies around you. It will be in the land he is giving you to own. Then you shall destroy any memory of the Amalekites on the earth. Do not forget!

THE FIRST HARVEST

26 Soon you will go into the land the Lord your God is giving you to own. You will take it over and live in it. ²Then you must take some of the first harvest of crops. It will grow from the land the Lord your God is giving you. Put the food in a basket. Then go to the place where the Lord your God will choose to be worshiped. ³Say to the priest on duty at that time, "Today I declare this before the Lord your God. I have come into the land the Lord promised to give us. He promised this to our ancestors." ⁴The priest will take your basket. He will set it down in front of the altar of the Lord your God. ⁵Then you shall announce before the Lord your God: "My father was a wandering Aramean. He went down to Egypt. He stayed there with only a few people. But they became a great, powerful and large nation there. ⁶But the Egyptians were cruel to us. They made us suffer and work very hard. ⁷So we prayed to the Lord, the God of our ancestors. He heard us. He saw our trouble, hard work and suffering. ⁸Then the Lord brought us out of Egypt. He did it with his great power and strength. He used great terrors, signs and miracles.ᵈ ⁹Then he brought us to this place. He gave us this land where much food grows. ¹⁰Now I bring you part of the first harvest from this land. Lord, you have given me this land." Then place the basket before the Lord your God. And bow down before him. ¹¹Then you and the Levites and foreigners among you should rejoice. The Lord your God has given good things to you and your family.

¹²Bring a tenth of all your harvest the third year. This is the year to give a tenth of your harvest. Give it to the Levites, foreigners, orphans and widows. Then they may eat in your towns and be full. ¹³Then say to the Lord your God, "I have taken out of my house the part of my harvest that belongs to God. I have given

it to the Levites, foreigners, orphans and widows. I have done everything you commanded me. I have not broken your commands. And I have not forgotten any of them. [14]I have not eaten any of the holy part while I was in sorrow. I have not removed any of it while I was unclean.[d] I have not offered it for dead people. I have obeyed you, the Lord my God. I have done everything you commanded me. [15]So look down from heaven, your holy home. Bless your people Israel. And bless the land you have given us. You promised it to our ancestors. It is a land where much food grows."

OBEY THE LORD'S COMMANDS

[16]Today the Lord your God commands you to obey all these rules and laws. Be careful to do them with your whole being. [17]Today you have said that the Lord is your God. You have promised to do what he wants you to do. You have promised to keep his rules, commands and laws. You have said you will obey him. [18]And today the Lord has said that you are his very own people. He has promised it. But you must obey his commands. [19]The Lord will make you greater than all the other nations he made. He will give you praise, fame and honor. And you will be a holy people to the Lord your God. This is what he said.

THE LAW WRITTEN ON STONES

27 Moses and the elders of Israel commanded the people. They said, "Keep all the commands I have given you today. [2]Soon you will cross the Jordan River. You will go into the land the Lord your God is giving you. On that day set up some large stones. Cover them with plaster. [3]When you cross over, write all the words of these teachings on them. Then you may enter the land the Lord your God is giving you. It is a land where much food grows. It is just as the Lord, the God of your ancestors, promised. [4]After you have crossed the Jordan River, set up these stones. Set them on Mount Ebal as I command you today. And cover them with plaster. [5]Build an altar of stones there to the Lord your God. But don't use any iron tool to cut the stones. [6]Build the altar of the Lord your God with stones from the field. Offer burnt offerings on it to the Lord your God. [7]Offer fellowship offerings there. Eat them and rejoice before the Lord your God. [8]Then write clearly all the words of these teachings on the stones."

CURSES OF THE LAW

[9]Then Moses and the Levites, who are the priests, spoke to all Israel. They said, "Be quiet, Israel. Listen! Today you have become the people of the Lord your God. [10]Obey the Lord your God. Keep his commands and laws that I give you today."

[11]That day Moses also gave the people this command:

[12]You will cross the Jordan River. Then these tribes[d] must stand on Mount Gerizim to bless the people: Simeon, Levi, Judah, Issachar, Joseph and Benjamin. [13]And these tribes must stand on Mount Ebal to announce the curses: Reuben, Gad, Asher, Zebulun, Dan and Naphtali.

[14]The Levites will say to all the people of Israel in a loud voice:

[15]"Anyone will be cursed who makes an idol or statue and secretly sets it up. The Lord hates idols made by man."

Then all the people will say, "Amen!"

[16]"Anyone will be cursed who dishonors his father or his mother."

Then all the people will say, "Amen!"

[17]"Anyone will be cursed who moves the stone that marks his neighbor's border."

Then all the people will say, "Amen!"

[18]"Anyone will be cursed who leads a blind person away from the road."

Then all the people will say, "Amen!"

[19]"Anyone will be cursed who is unfair to foreigners, orphans or widows."

Then all the people will say, "Amen!"

[20]"A man will be cursed who has sexual relations with his father's wife. It is a dishonor to his father."

Then all the people will say, "Amen!"

²¹"Anyone will be cursed who has sexual relations with an animal."

Then all the people will say, "Amen!"

²²"A man will be cursed who has sexual relations with his sister. She may be his father's daughter or his mother's daughter."

Then all the people will say, "Amen!"

²³"A man will be cursed who has sexual relations with his mother-in-law."

Then all the people will say, "Amen!"

²⁴"Anyone will be cursed who kills his neighbor secretly."

Then all the people will say, "Amen!"

²⁵"Anyone will be cursed who takes money to murder an innocent person."

Then all the people will say, "Amen!"

²⁶"Anyone will be cursed who does not agree with the words of these teachings and does not obey them."

Then all the people will say, "Amen!"

BLESSINGS FOR OBEYING

28 You must completely obey the Lord your God. And you must carefully follow all his commands I am giving you today. Then the Lord your God will make you greater than any other nation on earth. ²Obey the Lord your God. Then all these blessings will come and stay with you:

³You will be blessed in the city. You will be blessed in the country.

⁴Your children will be blessed. Your crops will be blessed. Your cattle will be blessed with calves and your sheep with lambs.

⁵Your basket and your kitchen will be blessed.

⁶You will be blessed when you come in and when you go out.

⁷The Lord will let you defeat the enemies that come to fight you. They will attack you from one direction. But they will run from you in seven directions.

⁸The Lord your God will bless you with full barns. He will bless everything you do. He will bless the land he is giving you.

⁹The Lord will make you his holy people, as he promised. But you must obey his commands. You must do what he wants you to do. ¹⁰Then everyone on earth will see that you are the Lord's people. They will be afraid of you. ¹¹The Lord will make you rich. You will have many children. Your cattle will have many calves. Your land will give good crops. It is the land that the Lord promised your ancestors he would give to you.

¹²The Lord will open up his storehouse. The skies will send rain on your land at the right time. And he will bless everything you do. You will lend to other nations. But you will not need to borrow from them. ¹³The Lord will make you like the head and not like the tail. You will be on top and not on bottom. But you must obey the commands of the Lord your God that I am giving you today. Be careful to keep them. ¹⁴Do not disobey anything I command you today. Do exactly as I command. Do not follow other gods or serve them.

CURSES FOR DISOBEYING

¹⁵But you might not obey the Lord your God. You might not carefully follow all his commands and laws I am giving you today. Then all these curses will come upon you and stay:

¹⁶You will be cursed in the city. You will be cursed in the country.

¹⁷Your basket and your kitchen will be cursed.

¹⁸Your children will be cursed. Your crops will be cursed. The calves of your cattle will be cursed. And the lambs of your flocks will be cursed.

¹⁹You will be cursed when you go in and when you go out.

²⁰The Lord will send you curses, confusion and punishment in everything you do. You will be destroyed. You will suddenly be ruined. You did wrong when you left him. ²¹The Lord will give you terrible diseases. He will destroy you from the land you are going to take. ²²The Lord will

punish you with disease, fever, swelling, heat, no rain, plant diseases and mildew.*d* Then you will die. 23The sky above will look like bronze. And the ground below will be like iron. 24The Lord will turn the rain into dust and sand. It will fall from the skies until you are destroyed.

25The Lord will let your enemies defeat you. You will attack them from one direction. But you will run from them in seven directions. And you will become a thing of horror among all the kingdoms on earth. 26Your dead bodies will be food for all the birds and wild animals. There will be no one to scare them away. 27The Lord will punish you with boils like those the Egyptians had. You will have bad growths, sores and itches that can't be cured. 28The Lord will give you madness, blindness and a confused mind. 29You will have to feel around in the daylight like a blind man. You will fail in everything you do. People will hurt you and steal from you every day. There will be no one to save you.

30You will be engaged to a woman. But another man will force her to have sexual relations with him. You will build a house. But you will not live in it. You will plant a vineyard. But you will not get its grapes. 31Your ox will be killed before your eyes. But you will not eat any of it. Your donkey will be taken away from you. And it will not be brought back. Your sheep will be given to your enemies. And no one will rescue them. 32Your sons and daughters will be given to another nation. You will grow tired looking for them every day. But there is nothing you can do. 33People you don't know will eat the crops your land and hard work have produced. You will be mistreated and abused all your life. 34The things you see will cause you to go mad. 35The Lord will give you sore boils on your knees and legs. They cannot be cured. They will go from the soles of your feet to the tops of your heads.

36The Lord will send you and your king away to a nation you do not know. There you will serve other gods made of wood and stone. 37You will become a hated thing to the nations where the Lord sends you. They will laugh at you and make fun of you.

38You will plant much seed in your field. But your harvest will be small. Locusts*d* will eat the crop. 39You will plant vineyards and work hard in them. But you will not pick the grapes or drink the wine. The worms will eat them. 40You will have olive trees in all your land. But you will not get any olive oil. The olives will drop off the trees. 41You will have sons and daughters. But you will not be able to keep them. They will be taken captive. 42Locusts will destroy all your trees and crops.

43The foreigners who live among you will get stronger and stronger. And you will get weaker and weaker. 44Foreigners will lend money to you. But you will not be able to lend to them. They will be like the head. And you will be like the tail.

45All these curses will come upon you. They will chase you and catch you and destroy you. This will happen because you did not obey the Lord your God. You did not keep the commands and laws he gave you. 46The curses will be signs and miracles*d* to you and your descendants*d* forever. 47You had plenty of everything. But you did not serve the Lord your God with joy and a pure heart. 48So you will serve the enemies the Lord sends against you. You will be hungry, thirsty, naked and poor. The Lord will put a load on you until he has destroyed you.

THE CURSE OF AN ENEMY NATION

49The Lord will bring a nation against you from far away. It will be from the end of the world. The nation will swoop down like an eagle. You won't understand their language. 50They will look mean. They will not respect old people or feel sorry for the young. ⁵¹They will eat the calves from your cattle and the harvest of your field. And you will be destroyed. They will not leave you any grain, new wine or oil. They will not leave you any calves from your herds or lambs from your flocks. You will be ruined. ⁵²That nation will surround and attack all your cities. You trust in your high, strong walls. But they will fall down. That nation will surround all your cities everywhere in the land the Lord your God is giving you.

⁵³Your enemy will surround you. Those people will make you starve. You will eat your own babies. You will eat the bodies of the sons and daughters the Lord gave you. ⁵⁴Even the most gentle and kind man among you will become cruel. He will be cruel to his brother, his wife whom he loves and his children who are still alive. ⁵⁵He will not even give them any of the flesh of his children he is eating. It will be all he has left. Your enemy will surround you. Those people will make you starve in all your cities. ⁵⁶The most gentle and kind woman among you will become cruel. She is so gentle and kind she would hardly even walk on the ground. But she will be cruel to her husband whom she loves. And she will be cruel to her son and daughter. ⁵⁷She will give birth to a baby. But she will plan to eat the baby and what comes after the birth itself. She will eat them while the enemy surrounds the city. Those people will make you starve in all your cities.

⁵⁸Be careful to obey everything in these teachings. They are written in this book. You must respect the glorious and wonderful name of the Lord your God. ⁵⁹The Lord will give terrible diseases to you and your descendants.[d] You will have long and serious diseases. You will have long and miserable sicknesses. ⁶⁰And the Lord will give you all the diseases of Egypt that you dread. And the

diseases will stay with you. ⁶¹The Lord will also give you every disease and sickness not written in this Book of the Teachings. Then you will be destroyed. ⁶²You people may have outnumbered the stars. But only a few of you will be left. You did not obey the Lord your God. ⁶³Once the Lord was happy with you. He gave you good things. He made you grow in number. But now the Lord will be happy to ruin and destroy you. You will be removed from the land you are entering to own.

⁶⁴Then the Lord will scatter you among the nations. He will scatter you from one end of the earth to the other. There you will serve other gods of wood and stone. They are gods that neither you nor your ancestors have known. ⁶⁵You will have no rest among those nations. You will have no place that is yours. The Lord will make your mind worried, your sight weak and your soul sad. ⁶⁶You will live with danger. You will be afraid night and day. You will not be sure that you will live. ⁶⁷In the morning you will say, "I wish it were evening." And in the evening you will say, "I wish it were morning." Terror will be in your heart because of the things you have seen. ⁶⁸The Lord will send you back to Egypt in ships. I, Moses, said you would never go back to Egypt. And there you will try to sell yourselves as slaves to your enemies. But no one will buy you.

THE AGREEMENT IN MOAB

29 The Lord commanded Moses to make an agreement with the Israelites in Moab. This agreement was in addition to the agreement he had made with them at Mount Sinai.

²Moses called all the Israelites together. And he said to them:

You have seen everything the Lord did to the king of Egypt. You saw what he did to the king's leaders and to the whole country. ³With your own eyes you saw the great troubles, signs and miracles.[d]

[4]But to this day the Lord has not given you a mind that understands. You don't really understand what you see with your eyes or hear with your ears. [5]The Lord led you through the desert for 40 years. During that time neither your clothes nor sandals wore out. [6]You ate no bread. You drank no wine or beer. This was so you would understand that he is the Lord your God.

[7]You came to this place. Then Sihon king of Heshbon and Og king of Bashan came out to fight us. But we defeated them. [8]We captured their land. And we gave it to the Reubenites, the Gadites and the eastern half-tribe of Manasseh to own.

[9]You must carefully obey everything in this agreement. Then you will succeed in everything you do. [10]Today you are all standing here before the Lord your God. Here are your leaders and important men. Your elders, officers and all the other men of Israel are here. [11]Here are your wives and children and the foreigners who live among you. They chop your wood and carry your water. [12]You are all here to enter into an agreement and a promise with the Lord your God. The Lord is making this agreement with you today. [13]This will make you today the Lord's own people. He will be your God. This is what he told you. He promised it to your ancestors Abraham, Isaac and Jacob. [14]But the Lord is not just making this agreement and its promises with you. [15]You are standing here before the Lord your God today. But he is also making it with those who are not here today.

[16]You know how we lived in Egypt. You know how we passed through the countries when we came here. [17]You saw their hated idols made of wood, stone, silver and gold. [18]Make sure no man, woman, family group or tribe among you leaves the Lord. Don't let them go and serve the gods of those nations. That would be like a plant that grows bitter, poisonous fruit.

[19]That kind of person might hear these curses. But he blesses himself. And he thinks, "I will be safe. I will continue doing what I want to do." That person might destroy all of your land, both wet and dry. [20]The Lord will not forgive that person. His anger will be like a burning fire against that man. All the curses written in this book will come on him. And the Lord will destroy any memory of him on the earth. [21]The Lord will separate him from all the tribes of Israel for punishment. All the curses of the agreement will happen to him. They are written in this Book of the Teachings.

[22]Your children who will come after you will see this. And foreigners from faraway lands will see this. They will see the disasters that come to this land. And they will see the diseases the Lord will send on it. They will say, [23]"The land is nothing but burning cinders and salt. Nothing is planted. Nothing grows. Nothing blooms. It is like Sodom and Gomorrah, and Admah and Zeboiim. The Lord destroyed them because he was very angry." [24]All the other nations will ask, "Why has the Lord done this to the land? Why is he so angry?"

[25]And the answer will be, "It is because the people broke the agreement of the Lord, the God of their ancestors. He made it with them when he brought them out of Egypt. [26]They went and served other gods. They bowed down to gods they did not even know. The Lord did not allow that. [27]So the Lord became very angry at the land. And he brought all the curses on it that are written in this book. [28]The Lord became angry and furious with them. So he took them out of their land. And he put them in another land where they are today."

[29]There are some things the Lord our God has kept secret. But there are some things he has let us know. These things belong to us and our children forever. It is so we will do everything in these teachings.

THE ISRAELITES WILL RETURN

30 All these blessings and curses I have said will happen to you. The Lord your God will send you away to other nations. There you will think about these things. ²Then you and your children will return to the Lord your God. And you will obey him with your whole being. You will obey everything I command you today. ³Then the Lord your God will give you back your riches. He will feel sorry for you. And he will bring you back again from the nations where he sent you. ⁴He may send you to the ends of the earth. But he will gather you. He will bring you back from there. ⁵He will bring you back to the land that belonged to your ancestors. It will be yours. He will give you success. And there will be more of you than there were of your ancestors. ⁶The Lord your God will prepare you and your descendants*d* to serve him. You will love him with your whole being. Then you will live. ⁷The Lord your God will put all these curses on your enemies. They hate you and are cruel to you. ⁸And you will again obey the Lord. You will keep all his commands that I give you today. ⁹The Lord your God will make you successful in everything you do. You will have many children. Your cattle will have many calves. Your fields will produce good crops. He will again be happy with you, just as he was with your ancestors. ¹⁰But you must obey the Lord your God. You must obey his commands and rules that are written in this Book of the Teachings. You must follow the Lord your God with your whole being.

LIFE OR DEATH

¹¹This command I give you today is not too hard for you. It is not beyond what you can do. ¹²It is not up in heaven. You do not have to ask, "Who will go up to heaven and get it for us? Then we can obey it and keep it." ¹³It is not on the other side of the sea. You do not have to ask, "Who will go across the sea and get it? Who will tell it to us? Then we can keep it." ¹⁴No, the word is very near you. It is in your mouth and in your heart. So, you may obey it.

¹⁵Look, today I offer you life and success, death and destruction. ¹⁶I command you today to love the Lord your God. Do what he wants you to do. Keep his commands, his rules and his laws. Then you will live and grow in number. And the Lord your God will bless you in the land you are going to take as your own.

¹⁷But you might turn away from the Lord. You might not obey him. You might be led to bowing down and serving other gods. ¹⁸I tell you today that you will be destroyed. And you will not live long in the land you are crossing the Jordan River to enter and own.

¹⁹Today I ask heaven and earth to be witnesses. I am offering you life or death, blessings or curses. Now, choose life! Then you and your children may live. ²⁰Love the Lord your God. Obey him. Stay close to him. He is your life. And he will let you live many years in the land. This is the land he promised to give your ancestors Abraham, Isaac and Jacob.

JOSHUA TAKES MOSES' PLACE

31 Then Moses went and spoke these words to all the Israelites: ²"I am now 120 years old. I cannot lead you anymore. The Lord told me I would not cross the Jordan River. ³The Lord your God will lead you across himself. He will destroy those nations for you. You will take over their land. Joshua will also lead you across. This is what the Lord has said. ⁴The Lord will do to these nations what he did to Sihon and Og. They were the kings of the Amorites. He destroyed them and their land. ⁵The Lord will give those nations to you. Do to them everything I told you. ⁶Be strong and brave. Don't be afraid of them. Don't be frightened. The Lord your God will go with you. He will not leave you or forget you."

⁷Then Moses called Joshua and spoke to him in front of the people. Moses said, "Be strong and brave. Lead these people into the land the Lord promised to give their ancestors. Help the people take it as their own. ⁸The Lord himself will go before you. He will be with you. He will not leave you or forget you. Don't be afraid. Don't worry."

MOSES WRITES THE TEACHINGS

⁹So Moses wrote down the teachings. He gave them to the priests and all the elders of Israel. The priests are the sons of Levi. They carried the Box*d* of the Agreement with the Lord. ¹⁰⁻¹¹Then Moses commanded them: "Read these teachings for all Israel to hear. Do it at the end of every seven years. That is the year to forget what people owe. Do it during the Feast*d* of Shelters. All the Israelites will come to appear before the Lord your God. They will stand at the place the Lord will choose. ¹²Gather all the people: the men, women, children and foreigners living in your towns. Then they can listen and learn to respect the Lord your God. Then they can carefully obey everything in this law. ¹³Their children do not know this law. They must hear it. They must learn to respect the Lord your God for as long as they live in the land. It is the land you are crossing the Jordan River to own."

THE LORD CALLS MOSES AND JOSHUA

¹⁴The Lord said to Moses, "Soon you will die. Get Joshua and come to the Meeting Tent.*d* I will command him." So Moses and Joshua went to the Meeting Tent.

¹⁵The Lord appeared at the Meeting Tent in a cloud. The cloud stood over the entrance of the Tent. ¹⁶And the Lord said to Moses, "You will soon die. Then these people will not be loyal to me. They will worship the foreign gods of the land they are entering. They will leave me. And they will break the agreement I made with them. ¹⁷Then I will become very angry at them. I will leave them. I will turn away from them. And they will be destroyed. Many terrible things will happen to them. Then they will say, 'God is not with us. That is why these terrible things are happening.' ¹⁸I will turn away from them then. They have done wrong. They have turned to other gods.

¹⁹"Now write down this song. And teach it to the Israelites. Then have them sing it. It will testify against them. ²⁰I will bring them into the land I promised to their ancestors. It is a land where much food grows. They will eat as much as they want and get fat. But then they will turn to other gods and serve them. They will reject me and break my agreement. ²¹Then many troubles and terrible things will happen to them. And this song will testify against them. The song will not be forgotten by their descendants.*d* I know what they plan to do, even before I take them into the land I promised them." ²²So Moses wrote down the song that day. And he taught it to the Israelites.

²³Then the Lord gave this command to Joshua son of Nun: "Be strong and brave. Lead the people of Israel to the land I promised them. And I will be with you."

²⁴Moses wrote all the words of the teachings in a book. ²⁵Then he gave a command to the Levites. They carried the Box*d* of the Agreement with the Lord. ²⁶He said, "Take this Book of the Teachings. Put it beside the Box of the Agreement with the Lord your God. It must stay there as a witness against you. ²⁷I know how stubborn and disobedient you are. You have disobeyed the Lord while I am alive and with you. You will disobey even more after I die! ²⁸Gather all the older leaders of your tribes*d* and all your officers. I will say these things for them to hear. And I will ask heaven

and earth to testify against them. ²⁹I know that after I die you will become completely evil. You will turn away from the commands I have given you. Then terrible things will happen to you in the future. You will do what the Lord says is evil. You will make him angry with the idols you have made."

MOSES' SONG

³⁰And Moses spoke this whole song for all the people of Israel to hear:

32 Hear, heavens, and I will speak. Listen, earth, to what I say.
²My teaching will drop like rain.
My words will fall like dew.
They will be like showers on the grass.
They will pour down like rain on young plants.
³I will announce the name of the Lord.
Praise God because he is great!
⁴He is like a rock. What he does is perfect.
He is always fair.
He is a faithful God who does no wrong.
He is right and fair.

⁵They have done evil against him.
To their shame they are no longer his children.
They are an evil and lying people.
⁶This is not the way to repay the Lord.
You are foolish and unwise.
He is your Father and Maker.
He made you and formed you.

⁷Remember the old days.
Think of the years already passed.
Ask your father. He will tell you.
Ask your elders. They will inform you.
⁸The Most High God gave the nations their lands.
He divided up the human race.
He set up borders for the people.
He even numbered the Israelites.
⁹The Lord took his people as his share.
The people of Jacob were his very own.

¹⁰He found them in a desert.
It was a windy, empty land.
He surrounded them and brought them up.
He guarded them as those he loved very much.
¹¹He was like an eagle building its nest.
It flutters over its young.
It spreads its wings to catch them.
It carries them on its feathers.
¹²The Lord alone led them.
There were no foreign gods among them.

¹³The Lord brought them to the heights of the land.
He fed them the fruit of the fields.
He gave them honey from the rocks.
He brought oil from the solid rock.
¹⁴There were milk curds from the cows and milk from the sheep.
There were fat sheep and goats.
There were sheep and goats from Bashan.
There was the best of the wheat.
You drank the juice of grapes.

¹⁵Israel grew fat and kicked.
They were fat and full and firm.
They left the God who made them.
They rejected the Rock[d] who saved them.
¹⁶They made God jealous with foreign gods.
They made him angry with hated idols.
¹⁷They made sacrifices to demons,[d] not God.
They were gods they had never known.
They were new gods from nearby.
Your ancestors did not fear them.
¹⁸You left God who is the Rock, your Father.
You forgot the God who gave you birth.

¹⁹The Lord saw this and rejected them.

His sons and daughters had made
  him angry.
20He said, "I will turn away from them.
  I will see what will happen to them.
They are evil people.
  They are unfaithful children.
21They used things that are not gods to
    make me jealous.
  They used worthless idols to make
    me angry.
So I will use those who are not a
    nation to make them jealous.
  I will use a nation that does not
    understand to make them angry.
22My anger has started a fire.
  It burns down to where the dead
    are.
It will burn up the ground and its
    crops.
  And it will set fire to the mountains.

23"I will pile troubles upon them.
  I will shoot my arrows at them.
24They will be starved and sick.
  They will be destroyed by terrible
    diseases.
I will send them vicious animals
    and gliding, poisonous snakes.
25In the streets the sword will kill.
  In their homes there will be terror.
Young men and women will die.
  So will babies and gray-haired men.
26I will scatter them as I said.
  And no one will remember them.
27But I didn't want their enemy to brag.
  Their enemy might misunderstand.
They might say, 'We have won!
  The Lord has done none of this.'"

28Israel has no sense.
  They do not understand.
29I wish they were wise and understood
    this.
  I wish they could see what will
    happen to them.
30One person cannot chase 1,000
    people.
  And 2 people cannot fight 10,000.

This only happens if the Lord has sold
    them.
  Their Rock would have to give
    them up.
31The rock of these people is not like
    our Rock.
  Our enemies agree to that.
32Their vine comes from Sodom.
  Their fields are like Gomorrah.
Their grapes are full of poison.
  Their bunches of grapes are bitter.
33Their wine is like snake poison,
  like the deadly poison of cobras.

34"I have been saving this.
  I have it locked in my storehouses.
35I will punish those who do wrong.
  I will repay them.
Sometime their foot will slip.
Their day of trouble is near.
  And their punishment will come
    quickly."

36The Lord will defend his people.
  He will have mercy on his servants.
He will see that their strength is gone.
He will see that nobody is left,
  slaves or free.
37Then he will say, "Where are their
    gods?
  Where is the rock they trusted?
38Who ate the fat from their sacrifices?
  Who drank the wine of their drink
    offering?
Let those gods come to help you!
  Let them protect you!

39"Now you will see that I am the one
    God!
  There is no god but me.
I send life and death.
  I can hurt, and I can heal.
No one can escape from me.
40I raise my hand toward heaven and
    make this promise:
  As surely as I live forever,
41I will sharpen my flashing sword.
  And I will take it in my hand to
    judge.

I will punish my enemies.
I will pay back those who hate me.
42My arrows will be covered with their
blood.
My sword will eat their flesh.
The blood will flow from those who
are killed and the captives.
The heads of the enemy leaders will
be cut off."

43Be happy, nations, with his people.
He will repay you for the blood of
his servants.
He will punish his enemies.
And he will remove the sin of his
land and people.

44Moses came with Joshua son of Nun.
And they spoke all the words of this song
for the people to hear. 45When Moses finished speaking these words to all Israel,
46he said to them: "Pay attention to all the
words I have said to you today. Command
your children to obey carefully everything
in these teachings. 47These should not be
unimportant words for you. They mean
life for you! By these words you will live
a long time in the land you are crossing
the Jordan River to own."

MOSES GOES UP TO MOUNT NEBO

48The Lord spoke to Moses again that
same day. He said, 49"Go up the Abarim
Mountains. Go to Mount Nebo in the
country of Moab. It is across from
Jericho. Look at the land of Canaan. I am
giving it to the Israelites to own. 50You
will die on that mountain that you climb.
This is how your brother Aaron died on
Mount Hor. 51You both sinned against
me at the waters of Meribah Kadesh. That
is in the Desert of Zin. You did not honor
me as holy there among the Israelites.
52So now you will only look at the land
from far away. You will not enter the land
I am giving the people of Israel."

MOSES BLESSES THE PEOPLE

33 Moses, the man of God, gave this
blessing to the Israelites before
he died. 2He said:

"The Lord came from Mount Sinai.
He rose like the sun from Edom.
He showed his greatness from
Mount Paran.
He came with thousands of angels.
He came from the southern
mountains.
3The Lord surely loves his people.
He takes care of all those who
belong to him.
They bow down at his feet.
And they are taught by him.
4Moses gave us the teachings.
They belong to the people of Jacob.
5The Lord became king of Israel.
The leaders of the people gathered
then.
The tribes*d* of Israel came together.

6"Let the people of Reuben live and not
die.
But let the people be few."
7Moses said this about the people of
Judah:
"Lord, listen to Judah's prayer.
Bring them back to their people.
They defend themselves with their
hands.
Help them fight their enemies!"
8Moses said this about the people of
Levi:
"Lord, your Thummim and Urim*d*
belong
to Levi whom you love.
Lord, you tested him at Massah.
You argued with him at the waters
of Meribah.
9He said about his father and mother,
'I don't care about them.'
He did not recognize his brothers.
He did not know his children.
But he protected your word.
And he guarded your agreement.
10He teaches your laws to the people of
Jacob
and your teachings to the people of
Israel.
He burns incense*d* before you.

And he makes whole burnt
offerings on your altar.
¹¹Lord, make them strong.
Be pleased with the work they do.
Defeat those who attack them.
Don't let their enemies rise up
again."
¹²Moses said this about the people of
Benjamin:
"The Lord's loved ones will lie down
in safety.
The Lord protects them all day long.
The ones the Lord loves rest with
him."
¹³Moses said this about the people of
Joseph:
"May the Lord bless their land with
the best fruits.
Send rain from heaven above.
And bring the water from the
springs below.
¹⁴Let the sun produce the best fruits.
Let each month bring its best fruits.
¹⁵Let the old mountains give the finest
crops.
And let the everlasting hills give the
best fruits.
¹⁶Let the full earth give the best fruits.
Let the Lord who lived in the
burning bush be pleased.
May these blessings rest on the head
of Joseph.
May they rest on the forehead of the
one who was separated from his
brothers.
¹⁷Joseph has the majesty of a firstborn*d*
bull.
He is as strong as a wild ox.
He will stab other nations,
even those nations far away.
These are the ten thousands of
Ephraim.
And these are the thousands of
Manasseh."
¹⁸Moses said this about the people of
Zebulun:
"Be happy when you go out, Zebulun.
And be happy in your tents, Issachar.

¹⁹They will call the people to the
mountain.
And there they will offer the right
sacrifices.
They will do well from all that is in the
sea.
And they will do well from the
treasures hidden in the sand on
the shore."
²⁰Moses said this about the people of
Gad:
"Praise God who gives Gad more land!
Gad lives there like a lion.
He tears off arms and heads.
²¹They chose the best land for
themselves.
They received a large share, like
that given to an officer.
When the leaders of the people
gathered,
the people of Gad did what the Lord
said was right.
And they judged Israel fairly."
²²Moses said this about the people of
Dan:
"Dan is like a lion's cub,
who jumps out of Bashan."
²³Moses said this about the people of
Naphtali:
"Naphtali enjoys the Lord's special
kindnesses.
They are full of his blessings.
Their land goes south to Lake
Galilee."
²⁴Moses said this about the people of
Asher:
"Asher is the most blessed of the
sons.
He should be his brothers' favorite.
Let him bathe his feet in olive oil.
²⁵Your gates will have locks of iron and
bronze.
You will be strong as long as you live.

²⁶"There is no one like the God of Israel.
He rides through the skies to help
you.

He rides on the clouds in his
majesty.
27The everlasting God is your place of
safety.
His arms will hold you up forever.
He will force your enemy out ahead of
you.
He will say, 'Destroy the enemy!'
28The people of Israel will lie down in
safety.
Jacob's spring is theirs alone.
Theirs is a land full of grain and wine.
There the skies drop their dew.
29Israel, you are blessed!
No one else is like you.
You are a people saved by the Lord.
He is your shield and helper.
He is your glorious sword.
Your enemies will be afraid of you.
You will walk all over their holy
places."

MOSES DIES

34 Then Moses climbed up Mount
Nebo. He went from the plains
of Moab to the top of Mount Pisgah. It is
across from Jericho. From there the
Lord showed him all the land. He could
see from Gilead to Dan. 2He could see all
of Naphtali and the lands of Ephraim
and Manasseh. He could see all the land
of Judah as far as the Mediterranean Sea.

3He could see the southern desert and the
whole Valley of Jericho up to Zoar. Jericho
is called the city of palm trees. 4Then the
Lord said to Moses, "This is the land I
promised to Abraham, Isaac and Jacob. I
said to them, 'I will give this land to your
descendants.'d I have let you look at it,
Moses. But you will not cross over there."

5Then Moses, the servant of the Lord,
died there in Moab. It was as the Lord had
said. 6The Lord buried Moses in Moab in
the valley opposite Beth Peor. But even
today no one knows where his grave is.
7Moses was 120 years old when he died.
His eyes were not weak. And he was still
strong. 8The Israelites cried for Moses for
30 days. They stayed in the plains of
Moab until the time of sadness was over.

9Joshua son of Nun was then filled
with wisdom. Moses had put his hands
on Joshua. So the Israelites listened to
Joshua. And they did what the Lord had
commanded Moses.

10There has never been another prophetd
like Moses. The Lord knew Moses face to
face. 11The Lord sent Moses to do signs
and miraclesd in Egypt. He did them to
the king, to all his officers and to the
whole land of Egypt. 12Moses had great
power. He did wonderful things for all
the Israelites to see.

THE BOOK OF
JOSHUA

GOD'S COMMAND TO JOSHUA

1 Moses was the servant of the Lord. Joshua son of Nun was Moses' assistant. After Moses died, the Lord said to Joshua: [2]"My servant Moses is dead. Now you and all these people go across the Jordan River. Go into the land I am giving to the people of Israel. [3]I promised Moses I would give you this land. So I will give you every place you go in the land. [4]All the land from the desert in the south to Lebanon in the north will be yours. All the land from the great river, the Euphrates, in the east, to the Mediterranean Sea in the west will be yours. This includes the land of the Hittites. [5]Just as I was with Moses, so I will be with you. No one will be able to stop you all your life. I will not leave you. I will never leave you alone.

[6]"Joshua, be strong and brave! You must lead these people so they can take their land. This is the land I promised their fathers I would give them. [7]Be strong and brave. Be sure to obey all the teachings my servant Moses gave you. If you follow them exactly, you will be successful in everything you do. [8]Always remember what is written in the Book of the Teachings. Study it day and night. Then you will be sure to obey everything that is written there. If you do this, you will be wise and successful in everything. [9]Remember that I commanded you to be strong and brave. So don't be afraid. The Lord your God will be with you everywhere you go."

JOSHUA'S ORDERS TO THE PEOPLE

[10]So Joshua gave orders to the officers of the people. He said, [11]"Go through the camp and tell the people, 'Get your supplies ready. Three days from now you will cross the Jordan River. You will go and take the land the Lord your God is giving you.'"

[12]Then Joshua spoke to the people of Reuben, Gad and the eastern half-tribe of Manasseh. Joshua said, [13]"Remember what Moses, the servant of the Lord, told you. He said the Lord your God would give you rest. And he said the Lord would give you this land. [14]Now the Lord has given you this land east of the Jordan River. Your wives, your children and your animals may stay here. But your fighting men must dress for war and cross the Jordan River ahead of your brothers. You must help your brothers. [15]The Lord has given you a place to rest. He will do the same for your brothers. But you must help them until they take the land. This is the land the Lord their God is giving them. Then you may return to your own land east of the Jordan River. That is the land that Moses, the servant of the Lord, gave you."

[16]Then the people answered Joshua, "Anything you command us to do, we will do. Any place you send us, we will go. [17]Just as we fully obeyed Moses, we will obey you. We ask only that the Lord your God be with you just as he was with Moses. [18]Then, if anyone refuses to obey your commands or turns against you, he will be put to death. Just be strong and brave!"

SPIES SENT TO JERICHO

2 Joshua son of Nun secretly sent out two spies from Acacia. Joshua said to them, "Go and look at the land. Look closely at the city of Jericho."

So the men went to Jericho. They went to the house of a prostitute[d] and stayed there. This woman's name was Rahab.

[2]Someone told the king of Jericho, "Some men from Israel have come here tonight. They are spying out the land."

[3]So the king of Jericho sent this message to Rahab: "Bring out the men who came to you and entered your house. They have come to spy out our whole land."

[4]Now the woman had hidden the two men. She said, "They did come here. But I didn't know where they came from. [5]In the evening, when it was time to close the city gate, they left. I don't know where they went. Go quickly. Maybe you can catch them." [6](But the woman had taken the men up to the roof.[n] She had hidden them there under stalks of flax.[d] She had spread the flax out there to dry.) [7]So the king's men went out looking for the spies from Israel. They went to the places where people cross the Jordan River. The city gate was closed just after the king's men left the city.

[8]The spies were ready to sleep for the night. So Rahab went to the roof and talked to them. [9]She said, "I know the Lord has given this land to your people. You frighten us very much. Everyone living in this land is terribly afraid of you. [10]We are afraid because we have heard how the Lord helped you. We heard how he dried up the Red Sea[d] when you came out of Egypt. We heard how you destroyed Sihon and Og. They were the two Amorite kings who lived east of the Jordan. [11]When we heard this, we became very frightened. Now our men are afraid to fight you. This is because the Lord your God rules the heavens above and the earth below! [12]So now, make me a promise before the Lord. Promise that you will show kindness to my family just as I showed you kindness. Give me some proof that you will do this. [13]Promise me you will allow my family to live. Save my father, mother, brothers, sisters and all of their families from death."

[14]The men agreed. They said, "We will trade our lives for your lives. Don't tell anyone what we are doing. When the Lord gives us our land, we will be kind to you. You may trust us."

[15]The house Rahab lived in was built on the city wall. So she used a rope to let the men down through a window. [16]She said to them, "Go into the hills. The king's men will not find you there. Hide there for three days. After the king's men return, you may go on your way."

[17]The men said to her, "You must do as we say. If not, we cannot be responsible for keeping our promise. [18]You are using a red rope to help us escape. When we return to this land, you must tie it in the window through which you let us down. Bring your father, mother, brothers and all your family into your house. [19]We can keep everyone safe who stays in this house. If anyone in your house is hurt, we will be responsible. If anyone goes out of your house and is killed, it is his own fault. We cannot be responsible for him. [20]But you must not tell anyone about this agreement. If you do, we are free from it."

[21]Rahab answered, "I agree to this." So she sent them away, and they left. Then she tied the red rope in the window.

[22]The men left and went into the hills. There they stayed for three days. The king's men looked for them all along the road. But after three days, the king's men returned to the city without finding them. [23]Then the two men started back to Joshua. They left the hills and crossed the river. They went to Joshua son of Nun and told him everything that had happened to them. [24]They said to Joshua, "The Lord surely has given us all of the land. All the people in that land are terribly afraid of us."

CROSSING THE JORDAN

3 Early the next morning Joshua and all the people of Israel left Acacia. They traveled to the Jordan River and camped there before crossing it. [2]After three days the officers went through the camp. [3]They gave orders to the people. They said, "You will see the priests and

---

2:6 roof In Bible times houses were built with flat roofs. The roof was used for drying things such as flax and fruit. And it was used as an extra room, as a place for worship and as a place to sleep in the summer.

Levites carrying the Box[d] of the Agreement with the Lord your God. Then you should leave where you are and follow it. [4]That way you will know which way to go. You have never traveled this way before. But do not follow too closely. Stay about a thousand yards behind the Box of the Agreement."

[5]Then Joshua told the people, "Make yourselves holy for the Lord. Tomorrow the Lord will do amazing things among you."

[6]Joshua said to the priests, "Take the Box of the Agreement. Cross over the river ahead of the people." So the priests lifted the Holy Box and carried it ahead of the people.

[7]Then the Lord said to Joshua, "Today I will begin to make you a great man to all the Israelites. So the people will know I am with you just as I was with Moses. [8]The priests will carry the Box of the Agreement. Tell them this: 'Go to the edge of the Jordan River and stand in the water.'"

[9]Then Joshua said to the people of Israel, "Come here. Listen to the words of the Lord your God. [10]Here is proof that the living God is with you. Here is proof that he will drive out the Canaanites, Hittites, Hivites, Perizzites, Girgashites, Amorites and the Jebusites. [11]This is the proof: The Box of the Agreement will go ahead of you into the Jordan River. It is the Agreement with the Lord of the whole world. [12]Now choose 12 men from among you. Choose 1 from each of the 12 tribes[d] of Israel. [13]The priests will carry the Holy Box of the Lord, the Master of the whole world. They will carry it into the Jordan ahead of you. When they enter the water, the river will stop flowing. The water will be stopped. It will stand up in a heap as if a dam were there."

[14]So the priests carried the Box of the Agreement. And the people left the place where they had camped. Then they started across the Jordan River. [15]During harvest the Jordan is flooded. So the river was at its fullest. The priests who were carrying the Holy Box came to the edge of the river. And they stepped into the water. [16]Just at that moment, the water stopped flowing. It stood up in a heap a great distance away at Adam. This is a town near Zarethan. The water flowing down to the Sea of Arabah (the Dead Sea[d]) was completely cut off. So the people crossed the river near Jericho. [17]The ground there became dry. The priests carried the Box of the Agreement with the Lord to the middle of the river and stopped. They waited there while all the people of Israel walked across. They crossed the Jordan River on dry land.

ROCKS TO REMIND THE PEOPLE

4 All the people finished crossing the Jordan. Then the Lord said to Joshua, [2]"Choose 12 men from among the people. Choose 1 from each tribe.[d] [3]Tell the men to get 12 large rocks from the middle of the river. Take them from where the priests stood. Carry the rocks and put them down where you stay tonight."

[4]So Joshua chose 1 man from each tribe. Then he called the 12 men together. [5]He said to them, "Go out into the river where the Holy Box[d] of the Lord your God is. Each of you should find 1 large rock. There will be 1 rock for each tribe of Israel. Carry the rock on your shoulder. [6]They will be a sign among you. In the future your children will ask you, 'What do these rocks mean?' [7]Tell them the Lord stopped the water from flowing in the Jordan. When the Holy Box of the Agreement with the Lord crossed the river, the water was stopped. These rocks will help the Israelites remember this forever."

[8]So the Israelites obeyed Joshua. They carried 12 rocks from the middle of the Jordan River. There was 1 rock for each of the 12 tribes of Israel. They did this the way the Lord had commanded Joshua. They carried the rocks with them. And

they put them down where they made their camp. ⁹Joshua also put 12 rocks in the middle of the Jordan River. He put them where the priests had stood while carrying the Holy Box of the Lord. These rocks are still there today.

¹⁰The Lord had commanded Joshua to tell the people what to do. It was what Moses had said Joshua must do. So the priests carrying the Holy Box continued standing in the middle of the river until everything was done. And the people hurried across the river. ¹¹The people finished crossing the river. Then the priests carried the Holy Box of the Lord to the other side. As they carried it, the people watched. ¹²The men from the tribes of Reuben, Gad and the eastern half-tribe of Manasseh obeyed what Moses had told them. They were prepared for war. So they crossed the river ahead of the other people. ¹³About 40,000 soldiers were prepared for war. They passed before the Lord as they marched across the river. Then they went toward the plains of Jericho to go to war.

¹⁴That day the Lord made Joshua a great man to all the Israelites. They respected Joshua all his life, just as they had respected Moses.

¹⁵Then the Lord spoke to Joshua. ¹⁶He said, "Command the priests to bring the Box of the Agreement out of the river."

¹⁷So Joshua commanded the priests, "Come up out of the Jordan."

¹⁸So the priests carried the Box of the Agreement with the Lord out of the river. As soon as their feet touched dry land, the water began flowing again. The river again overflowed its banks. It was just as it had been before they crossed.

¹⁹The people crossed the Jordan on the tenth day of the first month. They camped at Gilgal, east of Jericho. ²⁰They carried with them the 12 rocks taken from the Jordan. And Joshua set them up at Gilgal. ²¹Then he spoke to the Israelites. He said, "In the future your children will

ask you, 'What do these rocks mean?' ²²Tell them, 'Israel crossed the Jordan River on dry land. ²³The Lord your God caused the water to stop flowing. The river was dry until the people finished crossing it. The Lord did the same thing for us at the Jordan that he did for the people at the Red Sea.ᵈ Remember that he stopped the water at the Red Sea so we could cross. ²⁴The Lord did this so all people would know he has great power. Then they will always respect the Lord your God.'"

5 So the Lord dried up the Jordan River until the Israelites had crossed it. Now all the kings of the Amorites west of the Jordan heard about it. And the Canaanite kings living by the Mediterranean Sea heard about it. They were very scared. After that they were too afraid to face the Israelites.

THE ISRAELITES ARE CIRCUMCISED

²At that time the Lord spoke to Joshua. He said, "Make knives from flint stones. Circumciseᵈ the Israelites again." ³So Joshua made knives from flint stones. Then he circumcised the Israelites at Gibeath Haaraloth.

⁴This is why Joshua circumcised the men: After the Israelites left Egypt, all the men old enough to serve in the army died. They died in the desert on the way out of Egypt. ⁵The men who had come out of Egypt had been circumcised. But many were born in the desert on the trip from Egypt. They had not been circumcised. ⁶The Israelites had moved about in the desert for 40 years. During that time all the fighting men who had left Egypt had died. This was because they had not obeyed the Lord. So the Lord swore they would not see the land. This was the land he had promised their ancestors to give them. It was a land where much food grows. ⁷So their sons took their places. But none of the sons born on the trip from Egypt had been circumcised. So Joshua circumcised

them. [8]After all the Israelites had been circumcised, they stayed in camp until they were healed.

[9]Then the Lord said to Joshua, "As slaves in Egypt you were ashamed. But today I have removed that shame." So Joshua named that place Gilgal. And it is still named Gilgal today.

[10]The people of Israel were still camped at Gilgal on the plains of Jericho. It was there, on the evening of the fourteenth day of the month, they celebrated the Passover[d] Feast. [11]The next day after the Passover, the people ate some of the food grown on that land: bread made without yeast and roasted grain. [12]The day they ate this food, the manna[d] stopped coming. The Israelites no longer got the manna from heaven. They ate the food grown in the land of Canaan that year.

[13]Joshua was near Jericho. He looked up and saw a man standing in front of him. The man had a sword in his hand. Joshua went to him and asked, "Are you a friend or an enemy?"

[14]The man answered, "I am neither one. I have come as the commander of the Lord's army."

Then Joshua bowed facedown on the ground. He asked, "Does my master have a command for me, his servant?"

[15]The commander of the Lord's army answered, "Take off your sandals. The place where you are standing is holy." So Joshua did.

THE FALL OF JERICHO

6 Now the people of Jericho were afraid because the Israelites were near. So they closed the city gates and guarded them. No one went into the city. And no one came out.

[2]Then the Lord spoke to Joshua. He said, "Look, I have given you Jericho, its king and all its fighting men. [3]March around the city with your army one time every day. Do this for six days. [4]Have seven priests carry trumpets made from horns of male sheep. Tell them to march

in front of the Holy Box.[d] On the seventh day march around the city seven times. On that day tell the priests to blow the trumpets as they march. [5]They will make one long blast on the trumpets. When you hear that sound, have all the people give a loud shout. Then the walls of the city will fall. And the people will go straight into the city."

[6]So Joshua son of Nun called the priests together. He said to them, "Carry the Box of the Agreement with the Lord. Tell seven priests to carry trumpets and march in front of it." [7]Then Joshua ordered the people, "Now go! March around the city. The soldiers with weapons should march in front of the Box of the Agreement with the Lord."

[8]So Joshua finished speaking to the people. Then the seven priests began marching before the Lord. They carried the seven trumpets and blew them as they marched. The priests carrying the Box of the Agreement with the Lord followed them. [9]The soldiers with weapons marched in front of the priests. And armed men walked behind the Holy Box. They were blowing their trumpets. [10]But Joshua had told the people not to give a war cry. He said, "Don't shout. Don't say a word until the day I tell you. Then shout!" [11]So Joshua had the Holy Box of the Lord carried around the city one time. Then they went back to camp for the night.

[12]Early the next morning Joshua got up. And the priests carried the Holy Box of the Lord again. [13]The seven priests carried the seven trumpets. They marched in front of the Holy Box of the Lord, blowing their trumpets. The soldiers with weapons marched in front of them. Other soldiers walked behind the Holy Box of the Lord. All this time the priests were blowing their trumpets. [14]So on the second day they marched around the city one time. Then they went back to camp. They did this every day for six days.

¹⁵On the seventh day they got up at dawn. They marched around the city seven times. They marched just as they had on the days before. But on that day they marched around the city seven times. ¹⁶The seventh time around the priests blew their trumpets. Then Joshua gave the command: "Now, shout! The Lord has given you this city! ¹⁷The city and everything in it are to be destroyed as an offering to the Lord. Only Rahab the prostitute*d* and everyone in her house should remain alive. They must not be killed. This is because Rahab hid the two spies we sent out. ¹⁸Don't take any of the things that are to be destroyed as an offering to the Lord. If you take them and bring them into our camp, then you yourselves will be destroyed. You will also bring trouble to all of Israel. ¹⁹All the silver and gold and things made from bronze and iron belong to the Lord. They must be saved for him."

²⁰When the priests blew the trumpets, the people shouted. At the sound of the trumpets and the people's shout, the walls fell. And everyone ran straight into the city. So the Israelites defeated that city. ²¹They completely destroyed every living thing in the city. They killed men and women, young and old. They killed cattle, sheep and donkeys.

²²Joshua spoke to the two men who had spied out the land. Joshua said, "Go into the prostitute's house. Bring her out. And bring out all the people who are with her. Do this because of the promise you made to her." ²³So the two men went into the house and brought out Rahab. They also brought out her father, mother, brothers and all those with her. They put all of her family in a safe place outside the camp of Israel.

²⁴Then Israel burned the whole city and everything in it. But they did not burn the things made from silver, gold, bronze and iron. These were saved for the Lord. ²⁵Joshua saved Rahab the prostitute, her family and all who were with her. He let them live. This was because Rahab had helped the men he had sent to spy out Jericho. Rahab still lives among the Israelites today.

²⁶Then Joshua made this important promise. He said:

"Anyone who tries to rebuild this city
  of Jericho
  will be punished by a curse from
    the Lord.
The man who lays the foundation of
    this city
  will lose his oldest son.
The man who sets up the gates
  will lose his youngest son."

²⁷So the Lord was with Joshua. And Joshua became famous through all the land.

THE SIN OF ACHAN

7 But the people of Israel did not obey the Lord. There was a man from the tribe*d* of Judah named Achan. (He was the son of Carmi and grandson of Zimri. And Zimri was the son of Zerah.) Achan kept some of the things that were to be given to the Lord. So the Lord became very angry at the Israelites.

²Joshua sent some men from Jericho to Ai. (Ai was near Beth Aven, east of Bethel.) He told them, "Go to Ai and spy out the area." So the men went to spy on Ai. ³Later they came back to Joshua. They said, "There are only a few men in Ai to fight against us. So we will not need all our people to defeat them. Send 2,000 or 3,000 men to fight there. There is no need to send all of our people." ⁴So about 3,000 men went to Ai. But the people of Ai beat them badly. ⁵The people of Ai chased the Israelites. They chased them from the city gate all the way to where stones were cut from the ground. They killed about 36 Israelites as they went down the hill. When the Israelites saw this, they became very afraid.

⁶Then Joshua tore his clothes to show how upset he was. He bowed facedown

on the ground before the Box*d* of the Lord. And he stayed there until evening. The leaders of Israel did the same thing. They also threw dirt on their heads to show they were upset. 7Then Joshua said, "Lord God, you brought our people across the Jordan River. Why did you bring us this far and then let the Amorites destroy us? We should have been happy to stay on the other side of the Jordan. 8Lord, there is nothing I can say now. Israel has been beaten by the enemy. 9The Canaanites and all the other people in this country will hear about this. They will surround and kill all of us! Then what will you do for your own great name?"

10The Lord said to Joshua, "Stand up! Why are you down on your face? 11The Israelites have sinned. They have broken the agreement I commanded them to obey. They took some of the things I commanded them to destroy. They have stolen from me. They have lied. They have taken those things for themselves. 12That is why the Israelites cannot face their enemies. They turn away from the fight and run. I have commanded that they be destroyed. You must destroy everything I commanded you to destroy. I will not help you anymore unless you do this.

13"Now go! Have the people make themselves holy for me. Tell them, 'Set yourselves apart to the Lord for tomorrow. The Lord, the God of Israel, says some of you are keeping things he commanded you to destroy. You will never defeat your enemies until you throw away those things.

14"'Tomorrow morning you must all stand before the Lord. All the tribes will stand before him. The Lord will choose one tribe. And that tribe must stand alone before him. Then the Lord will choose one family group from that tribe. And that family group must stand alone before him. Then the Lord will choose one family from that family group. And it must stand alone before him. Then the

Lord will look at that family man by man. 15The man who is keeping what should have been destroyed will himself be destroyed by fire. And everything he owns will be destroyed with him. He has broken the agreement with the Lord. He has done a disgraceful thing among the people of Israel!'"

16Early the next morning Joshua led all of Israel before the Lord. All of the tribes stood before him. And the Lord chose the tribe of Judah. 17So all the family groups of Judah stood before the Lord. The Lord then chose the family group of Zerah. And all the families of Zerah stood before the Lord. Then the family of Zimri was chosen. 18And Joshua told all the men in that family to come before the Lord. The Lord chose Achan son of Carmi. (Carmi was the son of Zimri. And Zimri was the son of Zerah.)

19Then Joshua said to Achan, "My son, you should tell the truth. Confess to the Lord, the God of Israel. Tell me what you did. Don't try to hide anything from me."

20Achan answered, "It is true! I have sinned against the Lord, the God of Israel. This is what I did: 21Among the things I saw was a beautiful coat from Babylonia. And I saw about five pounds of silver and more than one and one-quarter pounds of gold. I wanted these things very much for myself. So I took them. You will find them buried in the ground under my tent. The silver is under the coat."

22So Joshua sent some men to the tent. They ran to the tent and found the things hidden there. The silver was under the coat. 23The men brought them out of the tent. Then they took them to Joshua and all the Israelites. They spread them out on the ground before the Lord. 24Then Joshua and all the people led Achan son of Zerah to the Valley of Trouble. They also took the silver, the coat and the gold. They took Achan's sons, daughters, cattle, donkeys, sheep, tent and everything he owned. 25Joshua said, "I don't know why you caused so much trouble for us. But now the Lord will bring trouble to you." Then all the people threw stones at Achan until he died. They also killed his family with stones. Then the people burned them. ²⁶They piled rocks over Achan's body. And those rocks are still there today. That is why it is called the Valley of Trouble. After this the Lord was no longer angry.

AI IS DESTROYED

8 Then the Lord said to Joshua, "Don't be afraid. Don't give up. Lead all your fighting men to Ai. I will help you defeat the king of Ai. I am giving you his people, his city and his land. ²You will do to Ai and its king what you did to Jericho and its king. Only this time you may take all the wealth. You may keep it for yourselves. Now tell some of your soldiers to set up an ambush behind the city."

³So Joshua led his whole army toward Ai. Then he chose 30,000 of his best fighting men. He sent these men out at night. ⁴Joshua gave them these orders: "Listen carefully. You must set up an ambush behind the city. Don't go far from it. Continue to watch and be ready. ⁵I and the men who are with me will march toward the city. The men in the city will come out to fight us. Then we will turn and run away from them as we did before. ⁶They will chase us away from the city. They will think we are running away from them as we did before. When we run away, ⁷come out from your ambush and take the city. The Lord your God will give you the power to win. ⁸After you take the city, burn it. See to it! You have your orders."

⁹Then Joshua sent them to their place of ambush to wait. They went to a place between Bethel and Ai, to the west of Ai. But Joshua stayed the night with his people.

¹⁰Early the next morning Joshua gathered his men together. He and the older leaders of Israel led them to Ai. ¹¹All of the soldiers who were with Joshua marched to Ai. They stopped in front of the city and made camp north of Ai. There was a valley between them and the city. ¹²Then Joshua chose about 5,000 men. He set them in ambush in the area west of the city between Bethel and Ai. ¹³So the people took their positions. The main camp was north of the city. The other men were hiding to the west. That night Joshua went down into the valley.

¹⁴Now the king of Ai saw the army of Israel. So he and his people got up early the next morning and hurried out to fight them. They went out to a place east of the city. The king did not know soldiers were waiting in ambush behind the city. ¹⁵Joshua and all the men of Israel let the army of Ai push them back. Then they ran east toward the desert. ¹⁶The men in Ai were called to chase Joshua and his men. So they left the city and went after them. ¹⁷All the men of Ai and Bethel chased the army of Israel. The city was left open. Not a man stayed to protect it.

¹⁸Then the Lord said to Joshua, "Hold your spear toward Ai. I will give you that city." So Joshua held his spear toward the city of Ai. ¹⁹The men of Israel who were in ambush saw this. They quickly came out of their hiding place and hurried toward the city. They entered the city and took control of it. Then they quickly set it on fire.

²⁰When the men of Ai looked back, they saw smoke rising from their city. At the same time the men of Israel stopped running. They turned against the men of Ai. The men of Ai could not escape in any direction. ²¹Joshua and all his men saw that the army had taken control of the city. They saw the smoke rising from it. So they stopped running and turned to fight the men of Ai. ²²The men who were in ambush also came out of the city to help with the fight. The men of Ai were caught between the armies of Israel. The

Israelites fought until not one of the men of Ai was left alive. None of the enemy escaped. ²³But the king of Ai was left alive. And Joshua's men brought him to Joshua.

A REVIEW OF THE FIGHTING

²⁴During the fighting the army of Israel chased the men of Ai into the fields and desert. So the Israelites killed all of them in the fields and desert. Then they went back to Ai and killed everyone there. ²⁵All the people of Ai died that day, 12,000 men and women. ²⁶Joshua had held his spear toward Ai. It was a sign to his people to destroy the city. And Joshua held out his spear until all the people of Ai were destroyed. ²⁷The people of Israel kept the animals for themselves. They also kept the other things the people of Ai had owned. This is what the Lord told them to do when he gave Joshua the commands.

²⁸Then Joshua burned the city of Ai. It became an empty pile of ruins. And it is still like that today. ²⁹Joshua hung the king of Ai on a tree. He left him hanging there until evening. At sunset Joshua told his men to take the king's body down from the tree. He told them to throw it down at the city gate. Then they covered it with rocks. That pile of rocks is still there today.

³⁰Then Joshua built an altar for the Lord, the God of Israel. He built it on Mount Ebal, as ³¹Moses, the Lord's servant, had commanded. Joshua built the altar as it was explained in the Book of the Teachings of Moses. The altar was made from stones that were not cut. No tool was ever used on them. The Israelites offered burnt offerings to the Lord on that altar. They also offered fellowship offerings. ³²There Joshua wrote the teachings of Moses on stones. He did this for all the people of Israel to see. ³³The elders, officers, judges and all the Israelites were there. They were standing around the Box^d of the Agreement with the Lord. They stood before the priests, the Levites who had carried the Holy Box. Israelites and non-Israelites were all standing there. Half of the people stood in front of Mount Ebal. The other half stood in front of Mount Gerizim. This was the way the Lord's servant Moses had earlier commanded the people to be blessed.

³⁴Then Joshua read all the words of the teachings. He read the blessings and the curses. He read it exactly as they were written in the Book of the Teachings. ³⁵All the Israelites were gathered together. All the women and children were there. All the non-Israelites living with the Israelites were there. Joshua read every command that Moses had given.

THE GIBEONITE TRICKERY

9 All the kings west of the Jordan River heard about these things. These were the kings of the Hittites, Amorites, Canaanites, Perizzites, Hivites and Jebusites. They lived in the mountains and on the western mountain slopes. They also lived along the whole Mediterranean Sea coast. ²All these kings gathered to fight Joshua and the Israelites.

³The people of Gibeon heard how Joshua had defeated Jericho and Ai. ⁴So they decided to trick the Israelites. They gathered old leather wine bags that were cracked and mended. They put them on the backs of their donkeys. They also put old sacks on their donkeys. ⁵The men put old sandals on their feet and wore old clothes. They took some dry, moldy bread. ⁶Then they went to Joshua in the camp near Gilgal.

The men spoke to Joshua and the men of Israel. They said, "We have traveled from a faraway country. Make a peace agreement with us."

⁷The men of Israel said to these Hivites, "Maybe you live near us. How can we make a peace agreement with you?"

⁸The Hivites said to Joshua, "We are your servants."

But Joshua asked, "Who are you? Where do you come from?"

⁹The men answered, "We are your servants. We have come from a far country. We came because we heard of the fame of the Lord your God. We heard about what he has done. We heard about everything he did in Egypt. ¹⁰We heard that he defeated the two kings of the Amorites. They were from the east side of the Jordan River: Sihon king of Heshbon and Og king of Bashan who was king in Ashtaroth. ¹¹So our elders and our people spoke to us. They said, 'Take food for your journey. Go and meet the Israelites. Tell them, "We are your servants. Make a peace agreement with us."'

¹²"Look at our bread. When we left home it was warm and fresh. But now it is dry and moldy. ¹³Look at our leather winebags. When we left home they were new and filled with wine. Now they are cracked and old. Look at our clothes and sandals. The long journey has almost destroyed them."

¹⁴The men of Israel tasted the bread. But they did not ask the Lord what to do. ¹⁵So Joshua agreed to make peace with the Gibeonites. He agreed to let them live. The leaders of the Israelites made a promise to keep the agreement.

¹⁶Three days later the Israelites learned that the Gibeonites lived nearby. ¹⁷So the Israelites went to where they lived. On the third day the Israelites came to their cities. The cities were Gibeon, Kephirah, Beeroth and Kiriath Jearim. ¹⁸But the Israelites did not attack those cities. They had made a promise to them before the Lord, the God of Israel.

All the Israelites grumbled against the leaders who had made the agreement. ¹⁹But the leaders answered, "We have given our promise before the Lord, the God of Israel. We cannot attack them now. ²⁰This is what we must do. We must let them live. We cannot hurt them, or God's anger will be against us. We would be breaking the promise we made to them. ²¹So let them live. But they will cut wood and carry water for our people." So the leaders kept their promise of peace to them.

²²Joshua called for the Gibeonites. He said, "Why did you lie to us? Your land was near our camp. But you told us you were from a far country. ²³Now, you will be placed under a curse. You will be our slaves. You will have to cut wood and carry water for the people of the house of God."

²⁴The Gibeonites answered Joshua, "We lied to you because we were afraid you would kill us. We heard that God commanded his servant Moses to give you all of this land. And God told you to kill all the people who lived in the land. That is why we did this. ²⁵Now you can decide what to do with us. You can do anything to us that you think is right."

²⁶So Joshua saved their lives. He did not allow the Israelites to kill them. ²⁷But Joshua made the Gibeonites slaves to the Israelites. They cut wood and carried water for the Israelites. And they did it for the altar of the Lord—wherever he chose it to be. They are still doing this today.

THE SUN STANDS STILL

10 At this time Adoni-Zedek was the king of Jerusalem. He heard that Joshua had defeated Ai and completely destroyed it. He learned that Joshua had done the same thing to Jericho and its king. The king also learned that the Gibeonites had made a peace agreement with Israel. And they lived very near Jerusalem. ²So Adoni-Zedek and his people were very afraid because of this. Gibeon was not a little town like Ai. It was a large city. It was as big as a city that had a king. All its men were good fighters. ³So Adoni-Zedek king of Jerusalem sent a message to Hoham king of Hebron. He also sent it to Piram king of Jarmuth, Japhia king of Lachish, and Debir king of Eglon. The king of Jerusalem begged these men,

4"Come with me and help me attack Gibeon. Gibeon has made a peace agreement with Joshua and the Israelites."

5Then these five Amorite kings joined their armies. They were the kings of Jerusalem, Hebron, Jarmuth, Lachish and Eglon. These armies went to Gibeon, surrounded it and attacked it.

6The Gibeonites sent a message to Joshua in his camp at Gilgal. The message said: "We are your servants. Don't let us be destroyed. Come quickly and help us! Save us! All the Amorite kings from the mountains have joined their armies. They are fighting against us."

7So Joshua marched out of Gilgal with his whole army. His best fighting men were with him. 8The Lord said to Joshua, "Don't be afraid of those armies. I will allow you to defeat them. None of them will be able to defeat you."

9Joshua and his army marched all night to Gibeon. So Joshua surprised them when he attacked. 10The Lord confused those armies when Israel attacked. So Israel defeated them in a great victory. They chased them from Gibeon on the road going to Beth Horon. The army of Israel killed men all the way to Azekah and Makkedah. 11They chased the enemy down the road from Beth Horon to Azekah. While they were chasing them, the Lord threw large hailstones on them from the sky. Many of the enemy were killed by the hailstones. More men were killed by the hailstones than the Israelites killed with their swords.

12That day the Lord allowed the Israelites to defeat the Amorites. And that day Joshua stood before all the people of Israel and said to the Lord:

"Sun, stand still over Gibeon.

Moon, stand still over the Valley of Aijalon."

13So the sun stood still.

And the moon stopped

until the people defeated their enemies.

These words are written in the Book of Jashar.

The sun stopped in the middle of the sky. It waited to go down for a full day. 14That has never happened at any time before that day or since. That was the day the Lord listened to a man. Truly the Lord was fighting for Israel!

15After this, Joshua and his army went back to the camp at Gilgal.

16During the fight the five kings ran away. They hid in a cave near Makkedah. 17But someone found them hiding in the cave and told Joshua. 18So he said, "Cover the opening to the cave with large rocks. Put some men there to guard it. 19But don't stay there yourselves. Continue chasing the enemy. Continue attacking them from behind. Don't let them get to their cities safely. The Lord your God has given you the victory over them."

20So Joshua and the Israelites killed the enemy. But a few were able to get back to their strong, walled cities. 21After the fighting, Joshua's men came back safely to him at Makkedah. No one was brave enough to say a word against the Israelites.

22Joshua said, "Move the rocks that are covering the opening to the cave. Bring those five kings out to me." 23So Joshua's men brought the five kings out of the cave. They were the kings of Jerusalem, Hebron, Jarmuth, Lachish and Eglon. 24They brought the five kings out to Joshua. He called all his men to come to that place. He said to the commanders of his army, "Come here! Put your feet on the necks of these kings." So they came close and put their feet on their necks.

25Then Joshua said to his men, "Be strong and brave! Don't be afraid. I will show you what the Lord will do to the enemies you will fight in the future." 26Then Joshua killed the five kings. He hung their bodies on five trees. And he left them hanging on the trees until evening.

²⁷At sunset Joshua told his men to take the bodies down from the trees. Then they threw their bodies into the same cave where they had been hiding. They covered the opening to the cave with large rocks. They are still there today.

²⁸That day Joshua defeated Makkedah. He killed the king and completely destroyed all the people in that city. He killed them as an offering to the Lord. There was no one left alive. He did the same thing to the king of Makkedah as he had done to the king of Jericho.

DEFEATING SOUTHERN CITIES

²⁹Then Joshua and all the Israelites traveled from Makkedah. They went to Libnah and attacked it. ³⁰The Lord allowed them to defeat it and its king. They killed every person in the city. No one was left alive. And they did the same thing to that king as they had done to the king of Jericho.

³¹Then Joshua and all the Israelites left Libnah and went to Lachish. They camped around Lachish and attacked it. ³²The Lord allowed them to defeat Lachish. On the second day Joshua defeated it. The Israelites killed everyone in that city. This was the same thing they had done to Libnah. ³³During this same time Horam king of Gezer came to help Lachish. But Joshua also defeated him and his army. There was no one left alive.

³⁴Then Joshua and all the Israelites went from Lachish to Eglon. They camped around Eglon and attacked it. ³⁵That day they captured Eglon. They killed all its people and completely destroyed everything in it as an offering to the Lord. This is the same thing they had done to Lachish.

³⁶Then Joshua and the Israelites went from Eglon to Hebron and attacked it. ³⁷They captured it and all the little towns near it. The Israelites killed everyone in Hebron. No one was left alive there. This was the same thing they had done to Eglon. They completely destroyed the city and all its people as an offering to the Lord.

³⁸Then Joshua and the Israelites went back to Debir and attacked it. ³⁹They captured that city, its king and all the little towns near it. They completely destroyed everyone in Debir as an offering to the Lord. No one was left alive there. Israel did to Debir and its king the same thing they had done to Libnah and its king. This was what they had done to Hebron.

⁴⁰So Joshua defeated all the kings of the cities of these areas: the mountains, southern Canaan, the western mountain slopes and the eastern mountain slopes. The Lord, the God of Israel, had told Joshua to completely destroy all the people as an offering to the Lord. So he left no one alive in those places. ⁴¹Joshua captured all the cities from Kadesh Barnea to Gaza. And he captured all the cities from Goshen to Gibeon. ⁴²He captured all these cities and their kings on one trip. He did it because the Lord, the God of Israel, was fighting for Israel.

⁴³Then Joshua and all the Israelites returned to their camp at Gilgal.

DEFEATING NORTHERN KINGS

11 Jabin king of Hazor heard about all that had happened. He sent messages to Jobab king of Madon, to the king of Shimron and to the king of Acshaph. ²He sent one to the kings in the northern mountains. Jabin also sent a message to the kings in the Jordan Valley south of Lake Galilee and in the western mountain slopes. He sent a message to the king of Naphoth Dor in the west. ³Jabin also sent one to the kings of the Canaanites in the east and in the west. He sent messages to the Amorites, Hittites, Perizzites and Jebusites in the mountains. Jabin also sent one to the Hivites. They lived below Mount Hermon in the area of Mizpah. ⁴So the armies of all these kings came together. There were many fighting men, horses and chariots. It was a huge army. It looked like there were as many men as grains of sand on the seashore.

⁵All of these kings met together at the Waters of Merom. They joined their armies together into one camp. They made plans to fight against the Israelites.

⁶Then the Lord said to Joshua, "Don't be afraid of them. At this time tomorrow I will allow you to defeat them. You will kill all of them. You will cripple their horses and burn all their chariots."

⁷So Joshua and his whole army surprised the enemy. They attacked them at the Waters of Merom. ⁸The Lord allowed Israel to defeat them. They chased them to Greater Sidon, Misrephoth Maim and the Valley of Mizpah in the east. Israel fought until none of the enemy was left alive. ⁹Joshua did what the Lord said to do. He cut the legs of their horses and burned their chariots.

¹⁰Then Joshua went back and captured the city of Hazor. He killed the king of Hazor. (Hazor had been the leader of all the kingdoms that fought against Israel.) ¹¹Israel killed everyone in Hazor. They completely destroyed them. There was nothing left alive. Then they burned Hazor itself.

¹²Joshua captured all of these cities. He killed all of their kings. He completely destroyed everything in these cities. He did this the way Moses, the servant of the Lord, had commanded. ¹³But the Israelites did not burn any cities that were built on their hills, except Hazor. That city alone was burned by Joshua. ¹⁴The people of Israel kept for themselves everything they found in the cities. They kept all the animals they found. But they killed all the people there. They did not leave anyone alive. ¹⁵Long ago the Lord had commanded his servant Moses to do this. Then Moses had commanded Joshua to do it. So Joshua obeyed God. He did everything the Lord had commanded Moses.

¹⁶So Joshua defeated all the people in the land. He had control of the mountains and the area of southern Canaan. He controlled all the areas of Goshen, the western mountain slopes and the Jordan Valley. He controlled the mountains of Israel and all the hills near them. ¹⁷Joshua controlled all the land from Mount Halak near Edom to Baal Gad. Baal Gad was in the Valley of Lebanon, below Mount Hermon. Joshua captured all the kings in the land and killed them. ¹⁸He fought against them for many years. ¹⁹The people of only one city in all the land had made a peace agreement with Israel. They were the Hivites living in Gibeon. All the other cities were defeated in war. ²⁰The Lord made those people stubborn so they would fight against Israel. This way he could completely destroy them without mercy. This is what the Lord had commanded Moses to do.

²¹Now Joshua fought the Anakites[d] who lived in the mountains of Hebron, Debir, Anab, Judah and Israel. And he completely destroyed them and their towns. ²²There were no Anakites left living in the land of the Israelites. Only a few Anakites were left in Gaza, Gath and Ashdod. ²³Joshua took control of all the land of Israel. This was what the Lord had told Moses to do long ago. He gave the land to Israel because he had promised it to them. Then Joshua divided the land among the tribes[d] of Israel. The fighting had finally ended. And there was peace in the land.

KINGS DEFEATED BY ISRAEL

12 The Israelites took control of the land east of the Jordan River. They now had all the land from the Arnon Ravine to Mount Hermon. And they had all the land along the eastern side of the Jordan Valley. Here are all the kings the Israelites defeated to take this land:

²Sihon was the king of the Amorites. He lived in the city of Heshbon. He ruled the land from Aroer at the Arnon Ravine to the Jabbok River. His land started in

the middle of the ravine. This was their border with the Ammonites. Sihon ruled over half the land of Gilead. ³He also ruled over the eastern side of the Jordan Valley from Lake Galilee to the Dead Sea.*d* And he ruled from Beth Jeshimoth south to the hills of Pisgah.

⁴Og king of Bashan was one of the last of the Rephaites.*d* He ruled the land in Ashtaroth and Edrei. ⁵He ruled over Mount Hermon, Salecah and all the area of Bashan. His land ended where the people of Geshur and Maacah lived. Og also ruled half the land of Gilead. It stopped at the border of Sihon king of Heshbon.

⁶The Lord's servant Moses and the Israelites defeated all these kings. And Moses gave that land to the tribes*d* of Reuben and Gad and to the eastern half-tribe of Manasseh. This land was to be their own.

⁷The Israelites also defeated kings in the land that was west of the Jordan River. Joshua led the people in this land. He gave the people this land and divided it among the 12 tribes. This was the land that was promised to them. It was between Baal Gad in the Valley of Lebanon and Mount Halak near Edom. ⁸This included the mountains, the western mountain slopes and the Jordan Valley. It also included the eastern mountain slopes, the desert and southern Canaan. This was the land where the Hittites, Amorites, Canaanites, Perizzites, Hivites and Jebusites had lived. The people of Israel defeated the king of each of the following cities: ⁹Jericho, Ai (near Bethel), ¹⁰Jerusalem, Hebron, ¹¹Jarmuth, Lachish, ¹²Eglon, Gezer, ¹³Debir, Geder, ¹⁴Hormah, Arad, ¹⁵Libnah, Adullam, ¹⁶Makkedah, Bethel, ¹⁷Tappuah, Hepher, ¹⁸Aphek, Lasharon, ¹⁹Madon, Hazor, ²⁰Shimron Meron, Acshaph, ²¹Taanach, Megiddo, ²²Kedesh, Jokneam in Carmel, ²³Dor (in Naphoth Dor), Goyim in Gilgal, and ²⁴Tirzah.

The total number of kings was 31.

LAND STILL TO BE TAKEN

13 When Joshua was very old, the Lord spoke to him. He said, "Joshua, you have grown old. But there is still much land for you to take. ²You have not yet taken the land of Geshur and the land of the Philistines. ³You have not yet taken the area from the Shihor River at the border of Egypt to Ekron in the north. That belongs to the Canaanites. You must still defeat the five Philistine leaders. They are at Gaza, Ashdod, Ashkelon, Gath and Ekron. You must also defeat the Avvites. ⁴They live south of the Canaanite land. ⁵You have not yet defeated the Gebalites. And there is also the area of Lebanon east of Baal Gad below Mount Hermon to Lebo Hamath.

⁶"The Sidonians are living in the hill country from Lebanon to Misrephoth Maim. But I will force out all of them ahead of the Israelites. Be sure to remember this land when you divide the land among the Israelites. Do this as I told you.

⁷"Now divide the land among the nine tribes*d* and the western half-tribe of Manasseh."

DIVIDING THE LAND

⁸The eastern half-tribe of Manasseh and the tribes of Reuben and Gad had received their land. The Lord's servant Moses gave them the land east of the Jordan River. ⁹Their land started at Aroer at the Arnon Ravine. It continued to the town in the middle of the ravine. And it included the whole plain from Medeba to Dibon. ¹⁰All the towns that Sihon king of the Amorites ruled were in that land. He ruled in the city of Heshbon. The land continued to the area where the Ammonites lived. ¹¹Gilead was also there. And the area where the people of Geshur and Maacah lived was in that land. All of Mount Hermon and all of Bashan as far as Salecah was included. ¹²All the kingdom of Og king of Bashan

was in the land. In the past he ruled in Ashtaroth and Edrei. Og was one of the last of the Rephaites.*d* In the past Moses had defeated them and had taken their land. ¹³The Israelites did not force out the people of Geshur and Maacah. They still live among the Israelites today.

¹⁴The tribe of Levi was the only one that did not get any land. Instead, they were to be given all the burned sacrifices made to the Lord, the God of Israel. That is what the Lord had promised them.

¹⁵Moses had given each family group from the tribe of Reuben some land. This is the land they were given: ¹⁶It was the land from Aroer near the Arnon Ravine to the town of Medeba. This included the whole plain and the town in the middle of the ravine. ¹⁷The land continued to Heshbon. It included all the towns on the plain. These towns were Dibon, Bamoth Baal and Beth Baal Meon. ¹⁸They included Jahaz, Kedemoth, Mephaath, ¹⁹Kiriathaim, Sibmah and Zereth Shahar on the hill in the valley. ²⁰They also included Beth Peor, the hills of Pisgah and Beth Jeshimoth. ²¹So that land included all the towns on the plain and all the area that Sihon the king of the Amorites had ruled. He ruled from the town of Heshbon. But Moses had defeated him and the leaders of the Midianites. Those leaders included Evi, Rekem, Zur, Hur and Reba. All these leaders fought together with Sihon. And they lived in that country. ²²The Israelites killed many people during the fighting. They also killed Balaam of Beor. He tried to use magic to tell the future. ²³The land given to Reuben stopped at the shore of the Jordan River. So the land given to the family groups of Reuben included all these towns and their fields that were listed.

²⁴This is the land Moses gave to the tribe of Gad. He gave it to all the family groups: ²⁵He gave them the land of Jazar and all the towns of Gilead. He also gave them half the land of the Ammonites. It went as far as Aroer near Rabbah. ²⁶It included the area from Heshbon to Ramath Mizpah and Betonim. It included the area from Mahanaim to the land of Debir. ²⁷The land included the valley, Beth Haram, Beth Nimrah, Succoth and Zaphon. All the other land Sihon king of Heshbon had ruled was also included in it. This is the land on the east side of the Jordan River. It continued to the end of Lake Galilee. ²⁸All this is the land Moses gave to the tribe of Gad. It included all the towns that were listed. Moses gave it to all the family groups.

²⁹This is the land Moses had given to the eastern half-tribe of Manasseh. Half of all the family groups in the tribe of Manasseh were given this land: ³⁰The land started at Mahanaim. It included all of Bashan and the land ruled by Og king of Bashan. It also included all the Towns of Jair in Bashan. There were 60 cities in all. ³¹It also included half of Gilead, Ashtaroth and Edrei. (These were the cities where Og king of Bashan had ruled.) All this land had been given to the family of Makir son of Manasseh. Half of all his sons had been given this land.

³²Moses had given this land to these tribes on the plains of Moab. It was across the Jordan River east of Jericho. ³³But Moses had given no land to the tribe of Levi. The Lord, the God of Israel, promised that he himself would be the gift for the Levites.

14 Eleazar the priest, Joshua son of Nun and the leaders of all the tribes of Israel decided what land to give to the people. ²The Lord had commanded Moses long ago how he wanted the people to choose their land. The people of the nine-and-a-half tribes threw lots*d* to decide which land they would receive. ³Moses had already given the two-and-a-half tribes their land east of the Jordan River. But the tribe of Levi was not given any land like the others.

⁴The sons of Joseph had divided into two tribes—Manasseh and Ephraim. The tribe of Levi was not given any land. It was given only some towns in which to live. It was also given pastures for its animals. ⁵The Lord had told Moses how to give the land to the tribes of Israel. The Israelites divided the land as the Lord had commanded.

CALEB'S LAND

⁶One day some men from the tribe*ᵈ* of Judah went to Joshua at Gilgal. One of those men was Caleb son of Jephunneh the Kenizzite. He said to Joshua, "You remember what the Lord said at Kadesh Barnea. He was speaking to the prophet Moses about you and me. ⁷Moses, the Lord's servant, sent me to look at the land where we were going. I was 40 years old then. When I came back, I told Moses what I thought about the land. ⁸The other men who went with me told the people things that made them afraid. But I fully believed the Lord would allow us to take the land. ⁹So that day Moses promised me, 'The land where you went will become your land. Your children will own it forever. I will give you that land because you fully believed in the Lord, my God.'

¹⁰"Now then, the Lord has kept his promise. He has kept me alive for 45 years from the time he said this to Moses. During that time we all wandered in the desert. Now here I am, 85 years old. ¹¹I am still as strong today as I was the day Moses sent me out. I am just as ready to fight now as I was then. ¹²So give me the mountain country the Lord promised me that day long ago. Back then you heard that the Anakite*ᵈ* people lived there. And the cities were large and well protected. But now with the Lord helping me, I will force them out, just as the Lord said."

¹³Joshua blessed Caleb son of Jephunneh. He gave him the city of Hebron as his own. ¹⁴And Hebron still belongs to the family of Caleb son of Jephunneh the Kenizzite. It still belongs to his people because he had faith. He obeyed the Lord, the God of Israel. ¹⁵(In the past it was called Kiriath Arba. It was named for the greatest man among the Anakites. He was named Arba.)

After this there was peace in the land.

LAND FOR JUDAH

15 The land that was given to the tribe*ᵈ* of Judah was divided among all the family groups. It went all the way to the Desert of Zin in the far south, at the border of Edom.

²The southern border of Judah's land started at the south end of the Dead Sea.*ᵈ* ³It went south of Scorpion Pass to Zin. From there it passed to the south of Kadesh Barnea. It continued past Hezron to Addar. From Addar it turned and went to Karka. ⁴It continued to Azmon, the brook of Egypt and then to the Mediterranean Sea. This was the southern border.

⁵The eastern border was the shore of the Dead Sea. It went as far as the area where the Jordan River flowed into the sea.

The northern border started at the area where the Jordan River flowed into the Dead Sea. ⁶Then it went to Beth Hoglah and continued north of Beth Arabah. It continued to the stone of Bohan. Bohan was the son of Reuben. ⁷Then the northern border went through the Valley of Achor to Debir. There it turned toward the north and went to Gilgal. Gilgal is across from the road that goes through the mountain of Adummim. It is on the south side of the ravine. The border continued along the waters of En Shemesh. It stopped at En Rogel. ⁸Then it went through the Valley of Ben Hinnom. This is next to the southern side of the Jebusite city. (That city was called Jerusalem.) There the border went to the top of the hill on the west side of Hinnom Valley. This was at the northern end of the Valley of Giants. ⁹From there it went to the spring of the Waters of Nephtoah. Then it went to the cities near Mount Ephron. There it turned and went toward Baalah. (Baalah is also called Kiriath Jearim.) [10]At Baalah the border turned west and went toward Mount Edom. It continued along the north side of Mount Jearim (also called Kesalon) and came to Beth Shemesh. From there it went past Timnah. [11]Then it went to the hill north of Ekron. From there it turned toward Shikkeron and went past Mount Baalah. It continued on to Jabneel and ended at the sea.

[12]The Mediterranean Sea was the western border. Inside these borders lived the family groups of Judah.

[13]The Lord had commanded Joshua to give Caleb son of Jephunneh part of the land in Judah. So he gave Caleb the land God had commanded. He gave him the town of Kiriath Arba, also called Hebron. (Arba was the father of Anak.[d]) [14]Caleb forced out the three Anakite families living in Hebron. Those families were Sheshai, Ahiman and Talmai. They were descendants[d] of Anak. [15]Then he fought against the people living in Debir. (In the past Debir had been called Kiriath Sepher.) [16]Caleb said, "I want a man to attack and capture Kiriath Sepher. I will give him Acsah, my daughter, as a wife." [17]Othniel son of Kenaz defeated the city. So Caleb gave his daughter Acsah to Othniel to be his wife. [18]Acsah wanted Othniel to ask her father Caleb for more land.

So Acsah went to her father. When she got off her donkey, Caleb asked her, "What do you want?"

[19]Acsah answered, "I would like a special favor. The land you gave me is very dry. So also give me land with springs of water on it."

So Caleb gave her land with springs of water on the upper and lower part of it.

[20]The tribe of Judah got the land God had promised them. Each family group got part of the land.

[21]The tribe of Judah got all the towns in the southern part of Canaan. These towns were near the border of Edom. Here is a list of the towns: Kabzeel, Eder, Jagur, [22]Kinah, Dimonah, Adadah, [23]Kedesh, Hazor and Ithnan; [24]Ziph, Telem, Bealoth, [25]Hazor Hadattah and Kerioth Hezron (also called Hazor); [26]Amam, Shema, Moladah, [27]Hazar Gaddah, Heshmon and Beth Pelet; [28]Hazar Shual, Beersheba, Biziothiah, [29]Baalah, Iim, Ezem, [30]Eltolad, Kesil and Hormah; [31]Ziklag, Madmannah, Sansannah, [32]Lebaoth, Shilhim, Ain and Rimmon. There were 29 towns and all their fields.

[33]The tribe of Judah got these towns in the western mountain slopes: Eshtaol, Zorah, Ashnah, [34]Zanoah, En Gannim, Tappuah and Enam; [35]Jarmuth, Adullam, Socoh, Azekah, [36]Shaaraim, Adithaim and Gederah (also called Gederothaim). There were 14 towns and all their fields.

[37]Judah was also given these towns in the western mountain slopes: Zenan, Hadashah, Migdal Gad, [38]Dilean, Mizpah, Joktheel, [39]Lachish, Bozkath and Eglon; [40]Cabbon, Lahmas, Kitlish, [41]Gederoth, Beth Dagon, Naamah and Makkedah. There were 16 towns and all their fields.

[42]Judah was also given these towns in the western mountain slopes: Libnah, Ether, Ashan, [43]Iphtah, Ashnah, Nezib, [44]Keilah, Aczib and Mareshah. There were nine towns and all their fields.

[45]The tribe of Judah also got the town of Ekron and all the small towns and fields near it. [46]They also got the area west of Ekron and all the fields and towns near Ashdod. [47]Ashdod and all the small towns around it were part of the land of Judah. They also got the fields and towns around Gaza. Their land continued to the brook of Egypt. And it went on along the coast of the Mediterranean Sea.

[48]The tribe of Judah was also given these towns in the mountains: Shamir, Jattir, Socoh, [49]Dannah and Kiriath Sannah (also called Debir); [50]Anab, Eshtemoh, Anim, [51]Goshen, Holon and Giloh. There were 11 towns and all their fields.

⁵²They were also given these towns in the mountains: Arab, Dumah, Eshan, ⁵³Janim, Beth Tappuah and Aphekah; ⁵⁴Humtah, Kiriath Arba (also called Hebron) and Zior. There were 9 towns and all their fields.

⁵⁵Judah was also given these towns in the mountains: Maon, Carmel, Ziph, Juttah, ⁵⁶Jezreel, Jokdeam, Zanoah, ⁵⁷Kain, Gibeah and Timnah. There were 10 towns and all their fields.

⁵⁸They were also given these towns in the mountains: Halhul, Beth Zur, Gedor, ⁵⁹Maarath, Beth Anoth and Eltekon. There were 6 towns and all their fields.

⁶⁰The people of Judah were also given the 2 towns of Rabbah and Kiriath Baal (also called Kiriath Jearim).

⁶¹Judah was given towns in the desert. Here are those towns: Beth Arabah, Middin, Secacah, ⁶²Nibshan, the City of Salt and En Gedi. There were 6 towns and all their fields.

⁶³The army of Judah was not able to force out the Jebusites living in Jerusalem. So the Jebusites still live among the people of Judah in Jerusalem to this day.

LAND FOR EPHRAIM AND MANASSEH

16 This is the land the tribe*d* of Joseph received. It started at the Jordan River near Jericho. It continued to the waters of Jericho, just east of the city. The border went up from Jericho to the mountains of Bethel. ²Then it continued from Bethel (also called Luz) to the Arkite border at Ataroth. ³From there it went west to the border of the Japhletites. It continued to the area of the Lower Beth Horon. Then it went to Gezer and ended at the sea.

⁴So Manasseh and Ephraim received their land. They were sons of Joseph.

⁵This is the land that was given to the family groups of Ephraim: Their border started at Ataroth Addar in the east. It went to Upper Beth Horon ⁶and then to the sea. From Micmethath it turned eastward toward Taanath Shiloh and continued eastward to Janoah. ⁷Then it went down from Janoah to Ataroth and to Naarah. It continued until it touched Jericho and stopped at the Jordan River. ⁸The border went from Tappuah west to Kanah Ravine and went to the sea. This is all the land that was given to the Ephraimites. Each family group in the tribe got a part of this land. ⁹Many of the border towns of Ephraim were actually within Manasseh's borders. But the people of Ephraim got those towns and their fields. ¹⁰The Ephraimites could not force the Canaanites to leave Gezer. So the Canaanites still live among the Ephraimites today. But they became slaves of the Ephraimites.

17 Then land was given to the tribe of Manasseh. He was Joseph's first son. Manasseh's first son was Makir, the father of Gilead. Makir was a great soldier. So the lands of Gilead and Bashan were given to his family. ²Land was also given to the other family groups of Manasseh. They were Abiezer, Helek, Asriel, Shechem, Hepher and Shemida. These were all the other sons of Manasseh son of Joseph.

³Zelophehad was the son of Hepher. Hepher was the son of Gilead. Gilead was the son of Makir, and Makir was the son of Manasseh. But Zelophehad had no sons. He had five daughters. The daughters were named Mahlah, Noah, Hoglah, Milcah and Tirzah. ⁴The daughters went to Eleazar the priest. They also went to Joshua son of Nun and all the leaders. They said, "The Lord told Moses to give us land like the men received." So Eleazar obeyed the Lord and gave the daughters some land. These daughters received land just as the brothers of their father did. ⁵So the tribe of Manasseh had ten sections of land west of the Jordan River. They also had two more sections, Gilead and Bashan. These sections were on the other side of the Jordan River. ⁶The daughters of Manasseh got land

just as the sons did. Gilead was given to the rest of the families of Manasseh.

⁷The lands of Manasseh were in the area between Asher and Micmethath. This is near Shechem. The border went south to the En Tappuah area. ⁸The land of Tappuah belonged to Manasseh. But the town of Tappuah did not. It was along the border of Manasseh's land and belonged to the sons of Ephraim. ⁹The border of Manasseh continued south to Kanah Ravine. The cities in this area of Manasseh belonged to Ephraim. Manasseh's border was on the north side of the ravine and went to the sea. ¹⁰The land to the south belonged to Ephraim. And the land to the north belonged to Manasseh. The Mediterranean Sea was the western border. The border touched Asher's land on the north. And it touched Issachar's land on the east.

¹¹In the areas of Issachar and Asher, the people of Manasseh owned Beth Shan and its small towns. They also owned Ibleam and its small towns. And they owned all the people who lived in Dor and its small towns. They owned the people in Naphoth Dor and its small towns. And they owned all the people who lived in Taanach and its small towns. Manasseh also owned the people in Megiddo and its small towns. ¹²Manasseh was not able to defeat those cities. So the Canaanites continued to live there. ¹³But the Israelites grew strong. When this happened, they forced the Canaanites to work for them. But they did not force them to leave the land.

¹⁴The people from the tribes of Joseph spoke to Joshua. They said, "You gave us only one area of land. But we are many people. Why did you give us only one part of all the land the Lord gave his people?"

¹⁵And Joshua answered them, "You have many people. Go up to the forest. Make a place for yourselves to live there. This is in the land of the Perizzites and the Rephaites.ᵈ The mountain country of Ephraim is too small for you."

¹⁶The people of Joseph said, "It is true. The mountain country of Ephraim is not enough for us. But the land where the Canaanites live is dangerous. They are skilled fighters. They have powerful weapons in Beth Shan and all the small towns in that area. And they are also in the Valley of Jezreel."

¹⁷Then Joshua spoke to the people of Joseph—to Ephraim and to Manasseh. He said, "But there are many of you. And you have great power. You should be given more than one share of land. ¹⁸You also will have the mountain country. It is a forest. But you can cut down the trees and make it a good place to live. And you will own all of it. You will force the Canaanites to leave the land. You can defeat them even though they have powerful weapons and are strong."

THE REST OF THE LAND DIVIDED

18 All of the Israelites gathered together at Shiloh. There they set up the Meeting Tent.ᵈ The Israelites controlled that country. They had defeated all the enemies there. ²But there were still seven tribesᵈ of Israel that had not yet received the land God had promised them.

³So Joshua said to the Israelites: "Why do you wait so long to take your land? The Lord, the God of your fathers, has given this land to you. ⁴So each tribe should choose three men. I will send them out to study the land. They will describe in writing the land their tribe wants as its share. Then they will come back to me. ⁵They will divide the land into seven parts. The people of Judah will keep their land in the south. The people of Joseph will keep their land in the north. ⁶But you should divide the land into seven parts. Describe the seven parts in writing. Then bring what you have written to me. We will let the Lord our God decide which tribe will get

which land. [7]But the Levites do not get any part of these lands. They are priests, and their work is to serve the Lord. Gad, Reuben and the eastern half-tribe of Manasseh have received the land promised to them. They are on the east side of the Jordan River. Moses, the servant of the Lord, gave it to them."

[8]So the men who were chosen started into the land. Their plan was to describe it in writing and take it back to Joshua. Joshua told them, "Go and study the land. Describe it in writing. Then come back to me. Then I will ask the Lord to choose the land you should get. We will do this here in Shiloh." [9]So the men left and went into the land. They studied it and described it in writing for Joshua. They studied each town. They saw that the land had seven parts. They described it in writing and then came back to Joshua. He was still at the camp at Shiloh. [10]Then Joshua asked the Lord to help. He threw lots[d] to choose the lands that should be given to each tribe.

LAND FOR BENJAMIN

[11]The first part of the land was given to the tribe[d] of Benjamin. Each family group in the tribe of Benjamin received some land. They were given the land between the land of Judah and the land of Joseph. This is the land chosen for Benjamin:

[12]The northern border started at the Jordan River. It went along the northern edge of Jericho. Then it went west into the mountains. That boundary continued until it was just east of Beth Aven. [13]From there it went south to Luz (also called Bethel). Then it went down to Ataroth Addar. Ataroth Addar is on the hill south of Lower Beth Horon.

[14]There is a hill to the south of Beth Horon. At this hill the border turned and went south near the western side of the hill. It went to Kiriath Baal (also called Kiriath Jearim). This is a town where people of Judah lived. It was the western border.

[15]The southern border started near Kiriath Jearim and went to the Waters of Nephtoah. [16]Then it went down to the bottom of the hill. This was near the Valley of Ben Hinnom. It was the north side of the Valley of Rephaim. The border continued down the Hinnom Valley just south of the Jebusite city to En Rogel. [17]There it turned north and went to En Shemesh. It continued to Geliloth near the Adummim Pass in the mountains. Then it went down to the great Stone of Bohan. Bohan was the son of Reuben. [18]The border continued to the northern part of Beth Arabah. Then it went down into the Jordan Valley. [19]From there it went to the northern part of Beth Hoglah. It ended at the north shore of the Dead Sea.[d] This is where the Jordan River flows into the sea. This was the southern border.

[20]The Jordan River was the border on the eastern side. So this was the land given to the family groups of Benjamin. These were the borders on all sides.

[21]Each family group of Benjamin received some of this land. And these are the cities they owned: Jericho, Beth Hoglah, Emek Keziz, [22]Beth Arabah, Zemaraim and Bethel; [23]Avvim, Parah, Ophrah, [24]Kephar Ammoni, Ophni and Geba. There were 12 towns and all their villages.

[25]The tribe of Benjamin also owned Gibeon, Ramah and Beeroth. [26]They owned Mizpah, Kephirah, Mozah, [27]Rekem, Irpeel and Taralah. [28]They also owned Zelah, Haeleph, the Jebusite city (Jerusalem), Gibeah and Kiriath. There were 14 towns and all their villages. All these areas are the lands the tribe of Benjamin was given.

LAND FOR SIMEON

19 The second part of the land was given to the tribe[d] of Simeon. Each family group received some of the land. It was inside the area of Judah. [2]They received Beersheba (also called

Sheba), Moladah, [3]Hazar Shual, Balah, Ezem, [4]Eltolad, Bethul and Hormah. [5]They also received Ziklag, Beth Marcaboth, Hazar Susah, [6]Beth Lebaoth and Sharuhen. There were 13 towns and all their fields.

[7]They also received the towns of Ain, Rimmon, Ether and Ashan. There were 4 towns and all their fields. [8]They also received all the very small areas with people living in them as far as Baalath Beer. (This is the same as Ramah in southern Canaan.) So these were the lands given to the tribe of Simeon. Each family group received some of the land. [9]The land of the Simeonites was taken from part of the land of Judah. Judah had much more land than they needed. So the Simeonites received part of their land.

LAND FOR ZEBULUN

[10]The third part of the land was given to the tribe[d] of Zebulun. Each family group of Zebulun received some of the land. The border of Zebulun went as far as Sarid. [11]Then it went west to Maralah and came near Dabbesheth. Then it went near Jokneam. [12]Then it turned to the east. It went from Sarid to the area of Kisloth Tabor. From there it went on to Daberath and to Japhia. [13]It continued eastward to Gath Hepher and Eth Kazin. Then it ended at Rimmon. Then the border turned and went toward Neah. [14]At Neah it turned again and went to the north. It went to Hannathon and continued to the Valley of Iphtah El. [15]Inside this border were the cities of Kattath, Nahalal, Shimron, Idalah and Bethlehem. There were 12 towns and all their fields.

[16]So these are the towns and the areas that were given to Zebulun. Each family group received some of the land.

LAND FOR ISSACHAR

[17]The fourth part of the land was given to the tribe[d] of Issachar. Each family group of Issachar received some of the land. [18]Their land included Jezreel, Kesulloth, Shunem, [19]Hapharaim, Shion and Anaharath; [20]Rabbith, Kishion, Ebez, [21]Remeth, En Gannim, En Haddah and Beth Pazzez.

[22]The border of their land touched the area called Tabor, Shahazumah and Beth Shemesh. It stopped at the Jordan River. There were 16 towns and their fields.

[23]These cities and towns were part of the land that was given to the tribe of Issachar. Each family group received part of this land.

LAND FOR ASHER

[24]The fifth part of the land was given to the tribe[d] of Asher. Each family group of Asher received some of the land. [25]Their land included Helkath, Hali, Beten, Acshaph, [26]Allammelech, Amad and Mishal.

The western border touched Mount Carmel and Shihor Libnath. [27]Then it turned toward the east. It went to Beth Dagon. It touched Zebulun and the Valley of Iphtah El. Then it went north of Beth Emek and Neiel. It passed north to Cabul. [28]Then it went to Abdon, Rehob, Hammon and Kanah. It continued to Greater Sidon. [29]Then the border went back south toward Ramah. It continued to the strong, walled city of Tyre. Then it turned and went toward Hosah. It ended at the sea. This was in the area of Aczib, [30]Ummah, Aphek and Rehob. There were 22 towns and their fields.

[31]These cities and their fields were part of the land that was given to the tribe of Asher. Each family group in that tribe received some of this land.

LAND FOR NAPHTALI

[32]The sixth part of the land was given to the tribe[d] of Naphtali. Each family group of Naphtali received some of the land. [33]The border of their land started at the large tree in the area of Zaanannim. This is near Heleph. Then it went through Adami Nekeb and Jabneel. It continued to the area of Lakkum and ended at the

Jordan River. [34]Then it went to the west through Aznoth Tabor. It stopped at Hukkok. It went to the area of Zebulun on the south. And it went to the area of Asher on the west. It went to Judah, at the Jordan River, on the east. [35]There were some strong, walled cities inside these borders. Those cities were Ziddim, Zer, Hammath, Rakkath and Kinnereth; [36]Adamah, Ramah, Hazor, [37]Kedesh, Edrei and En Hazor; [38]Iron, Migdal El, Horem, Beth Anath and Beth Shemesh. There were 19 towns and all their fields.

[39]The cities and the towns around them were in the land that was given to the tribe of Naphtali. Each family group in that tribe got some of this land.

LAND FOR DAN

[40]The seventh part of the land was given to the tribe[d] of Dan. Each family group of Dan received some of the land. [41]Their land included Zorah, Eshtaol, Ir Shemesh, [42]Shaalabbin, Aijalon and Ithlah; [43]Elon, Timnah, Ekron, [44]Eltekeh, Gibbethon, Baalath, [45]Jehud, Bene Berak and Gath Rimmon; [46]Me Jarkon, Rakkon and the area near Joppa.

[47](But the Danites had trouble taking their land. There were strong enemies there. And the Danites could not easily defeat them. So the Danites went and fought against Leshem. They defeated Leshem and killed the people who lived there. So the Danites lived in the town of Leshem. They changed its name to Dan because he was the father of their tribe.) [48]All of these cities and towns were given to the tribe of Dan. Each family group got part of this land.

LAND FOR JOSHUA

[49]So the Israelite leaders finished dividing the land and giving it to the different tribes.[d] After they finished, all the Israelites decided to give Joshua son of Nun some land, too. This was land that had been promised to him. [50]The Lord had commanded that he be given this land. So they gave Joshua the town of Timnath Serah in the mountains of Ephraim. This was the town that Joshua told them he wanted. So he built up the town and lived there.

[51]So all of these lands were given to the different tribes of Israel. Eleazar the priest, Joshua son of Nun and the leaders of each tribe worked together. They divided up the land while they were at Shiloh. They met before the Lord at the entrance to the Meeting Tent[d] to do this. Now they had finished dividing the land.

CITIES OF SAFETY

20 Then the Lord said to Joshua: [2]"Tell the Israelites to choose the special cities of safety.[d] This is what I had Moses command you to do. [3]A person might kill someone accidentally and without meaning to kill him. He may go to a city of safety to hide. There he will be safe from the relative who has the duty of punishing a murderer.

[4]"This is what he must do. When he runs to one of those cities, he must stop at the entrance gate. He must stand there and tell the leaders of the people what happened. Then they will allow him to enter the city. They will give him a place to live among them. [5]But the one who is chasing him might follow him to that city. If this happens, the leaders of the city must not give him up. They must protect the person who came to them for safety. They must protect him because he killed that person accidentally. He was not angry and did not decide ahead of time to kill the person. [6]He should stay in the city until he has been judged by the court there. And he should stay until the high priest dies. Then he may go back to his own home in the town from which he ran away."

[7]So the Israelites chose some cities to be cities of safety. These cities were: Kedesh in Galilee in the mountains of Naphtali; Shechem in the mountains of Ephraim; Kiriath Arba (also called Hebron) in the

mountains of Judah; [8]Bezer on the east side of the Jordan River near Jericho in the desert in the land of Reuben; Ramoth in Gilead in the land of Gad; and Golan in Bashan in the land of Manasseh. [9]Any Israelite or anyone living among them who killed someone accidentally was included. He was to be allowed to run to one of these cities of safety. Then he could be safe there and would not be killed by the relative who had the duty of punishing a murderer. He would be judged by the court in that city.

TOWNS FOR THE LEVITES

21 The heads of the Levite families went to talk to Eleazar the priest. They also talked to Joshua son of Nun and to the heads of the families of all the tribes[d] of Israel. [2]This happened at the town of Shiloh in the land of Canaan. The heads of the Levite families said to them, "The Lord commanded Moses that you give us towns where we may live. And he commanded that you give us pastures." [3]So the Israelites obeyed this commandment of the Lord. They gave the Levite people these towns and pastures: [4]The Kohath family groups were part of the tribe of Levi. Some of the Levites in the Kohath family groups were from the family of Aaron the priest. To these Levites were given 13 towns. These towns were in the areas that belonged to Judah, Simeon and Benjamin. [5]The other family groups of Kohath were given 10 towns. These 10 towns were in the areas of Ephraim, Dan and West Manasseh.

[6]The people from the Gershon groups were given 13 towns. They were in the land that belonged to Issachar, Asher, Naphtali and the eastern half-tribe of Manasseh in Bashan.

[7]The family groups of Merari were given 12 towns. These 12 towns were in the area that belonged to Reuben, Gad and Zebulun.

[8]So the Israelites gave the Levites these towns and the pastures around them.

They did this to obey the commandment that the Lord had given Moses.

[9]These are the names of the towns that came from the lands of Judah and Simeon. [10]The first choice of towns was given to the Kohath family groups of the Levites. [11]They gave them Kiriath Arba (also called Hebron) and all its pastures. This was in the mountains of Judah. (Arba was the father of Anak.[d]) [12]But the fields and the small towns around the city of Kiriath Arba had been given to Caleb son of Jephunneh.

[13]So they gave the city of Hebron to the descendants[d] of Aaron. (Hebron was a city of safety.[d]) They also gave them these towns: Libnah, [14]Jattir, Eshtemoa, [15]Holon, Debir, [16]Ain, Juttah and Beth Shemesh. They also gave them all the pastures that were around these towns. There were 9 towns given to these two groups.

[17]They also gave the people of Aaron cities that belonged to the tribe of Benjamin. These cities were Gibeon, Geba, [18]Anathoth and Almon. They gave them these 4 towns and all the pastures around them.

[19]So these towns were given to the priests. These priests were from the family of Aaron. The total number of towns with their pastures was 13.

[20]The other Kohathite family groups of the Levites were given these towns from the tribe of Ephraim: [21]They gave them the city of Shechem from the mountains of Ephraim. (Shechem was a city of safety.) They also gave them Gezer, [22]Kibzaim and Beth Horon. There were 4 towns and their pastures.

[23]The tribe of Dan gave them Eltekeh, Gibbethon, [24]Aijalon and Gath Rimmon. There were 4 towns and their pastures.

[25]The western half-tribe of Manasseh gave them Taanach and Gath Rimmon. They were also given all the pastures around these 2 towns.

[26]So this was 10 more towns and all the pastures around the towns. These

were given to the rest of the Kohathite family groups.

27The Gershonite family groups of the Levite tribe were given these towns: The eastern half-tribe of Manasseh gave them Golan in Bashan. (Golan was a city of safety.) Manasseh also gave them Be Eshtarah. All the pastures around these two towns were also given to the Gershonites.

28The tribe of Issachar gave them Kishion, Daberath, 29Jarmuth and En Gannim. Issachar also gave them all the pastures around these 4 towns.

30The tribe of Asher gave them Mishal, Abdon, 31Helkath and Rehob. All the pastures around these 4 towns were also given to them.

32The tribe of Naphtali gave them Kedesh in Galilee. (Kedesh was a city of safety.) Naphtali also gave them Hammoth Dor and Kartan. All the pastures around these 2 towns were also given to the Gershonites.

33So the Gershonite family groups received 13 towns. They also received all the pastures around these towns.

34The Merarite family groups (the rest of the Levites) were given these towns: The tribe of Zebulun gave them Jokneam, Kartah, 35Dimnah and Nahalal. All the pastures around these 4 towns were also given to the Merarites.

36The tribe of Reuben gave them Bezer, Jahaz, 37Kedemoth and Mephaath. All the pastures around these 4 towns were also given to the Merarites.

38The tribe of Gad gave them Ramoth in Gilead. (Ramoth was a city of safety.) They also gave them Mahanaim, 39Heshbon and Jazer. Gad also gave them all the pastures around these 4 towns.

40So the total number of towns given to the Merarite family groups was 12.

41A total of 48 towns with their pastures were given to the Levites. All these towns were in the land controlled by the Israelites. 42Each town had pastures around it.

43So the Lord kept the promise he had made to the Israelites. He gave the people all the land he had promised. The people took the land and lived there. 44The Lord allowed them to have peace on all sides of their land. This is what he had promised to their people who lived long ago. None of their enemies defeated them. The Lord allowed the Israelites to defeat every enemy. 45He kept every promise he had made to the Israelites. No promises failed. Each one came true.

THREE TRIBES GO HOME

22 Then Joshua called a meeting of all the people from the tribes*d* of Reuben, Gad and the eastern half-tribe of Manasseh. 2He said to them, "You have obeyed everything Moses told you to do. He was a servant of the Lord. And also, you have obeyed all my commands. 3All this time you have supported all the other Israelites. You have been careful to obey all the commands the Lord your God gave you. 4The Lord your God promised to give the Israelites peace. Now he has kept his promise. Now you may go back to your homes. You may go to the land that Moses, the Lord's servant, gave you. It is the land on the east side of the Jordan River. 5But continue to obey the teachings Moses gave you. That law is to love the Lord your God and obey his commands. Continue to follow him and serve him the very best you can."

6Then Joshua said good-bye to them, and they left. They went away to their homes. 7Moses had given the land of Bashan to the eastern half-tribe of Manasseh. Joshua gave land on the west side of the Jordan River to the western half-tribe of Manasseh. And he sent them to their homes. He blessed them. 8He said, "Go back to your homes and your riches. You have many animals, silver, gold, bronze and iron. And you have many beautiful clothes. Also, you have taken many things from your enemies. You should divide these among yourselves."

⁹So the people from the tribes of Reuben, Gad and the eastern half-tribe of Manasseh left the other Israelites. They left Shiloh in Canaan and went back towards Gilead. This was their own land. Moses gave it to them as the Lord had commanded.

¹⁰The people of Reuben, Gad and the eastern half-tribe of Manasseh traveled to Geliloth. This was near the Jordan River in the land of Canaan. There they built a beautiful altar. ¹¹But the other Israelites still at Shiloh heard about the altar these three tribes had built. They heard that the altar was at the border of Canaan at Geliloth. It was near the Jordan River on Israel's side. ¹²All the Israelites became very angry at these three tribes. They met together and decided to fight them.

¹³So the Israelites sent some men to talk to the people of Reuben, Gad and the eastern half-tribe of Manasseh. The leader of these men was Phinehas son of Eleazar the priest. ¹⁴They also sent one leader of each of the ten tribes at Shiloh. Each of these men was a leader of his family group of Israelites.

¹⁵So these men went to Gilead. They went to talk to the people of Reuben, Gad and the eastern half-tribe of Manasseh. The men said to them: ¹⁶"All the Israelites ask you: 'Why did you turn against the God of Israel? Why did you build an altar for yourselves? You know that this is against God's law. ¹⁷Remember what happened at Peor? We still suffer today because of that sin. Because of it, God caused many of the Israelites to become very sick. ¹⁸And now are you doing the same thing? Are you turning against the Lord? Will you refuse to follow the Lord?

"'If you don't stop what you're doing, the Lord will be angry with everyone in Israel. ¹⁹Your land may not be a good enough place to worship. If not, come over into our land. The Lord's Tent is in our land. You may have some of our land and live there. But don't turn against the Lord by building another altar. We already have the altar of the Lord our God. ²⁰Remember Achan son of Zerah. He refused to obey the command about what must be completely destroyed. That one man broke God's law, but all the Israelites were punished. Achan died because of his sin. But many other people also died.'"

²¹The people from Reuben, Gad and the eastern half-tribe of Manasseh answered them. They said: ²²"The Lord is our God! Again we say that the Lord is our God! God knows why we did this. We want you to know also. You can judge what we did. If you believe we have done something wrong, you may kill us. ²³If we broke God's law, we ask the Lord himself to punish us. Do you think we built this altar to offer burnt offerings? And did we build it to use for offerings of grain and fellowship?

²⁴"No! We did not build it for that reason. We feared that some day your people would not accept us as part of your nation. Then they might say, 'You cannot worship the Lord, the God of Israel. ²⁵God gave you land on the other side of the Jordan River. It separates us from you people of Reuben and Gad. You cannot worship the Lord.' So we feared that your children might make our children stop worshiping the Lord.

²⁶"So we decided to build this altar. But we did not plan to use it for burning sacrifices and making offerings. ²⁷It was really to show our people that we worship the same God as you. This altar is proof to you and us. And it will prove to all our children who will come after us that we worship the Lord. We give our whole burnt offerings, grain and fellowship offerings to the Lord. This was to keep your children from saying that our children could not worship the Lord.

²⁸"In the future your children might say that we do not belong to Israel. Then

our children could say, 'Look! Our fathers who lived before us made an altar. It is exactly like the Lord's altar. We do not use it for sacrifices. This altar shows that we are part of Israel.'

²⁹"Truly, we don't want to be against the Lord. We don't want to stop following him. We know the only true altar is the one in front of the Holy Tent.[d] It belongs to the Lord our God."

³⁰Phinehas the priest and the ten leaders heard these things. They listened to the people of Reuben, Gad and Manasseh. And they were pleased. ³¹So Phinehas, son of Eleazar the priest, spoke. He said, "Now we know the Lord is with us. And we know you didn't turn against him. We're happy that the Israelites will not be punished by the Lord."

³²Then Phinehas and the leaders went home. They left the people of Reuben and Gad in Gilead. And they went back to Canaan. There they told the Israelites what had happened. ³³They were also pleased. They were happy and thanked God. And they decided not to fight against the people of Reuben and Gad. They decided not to destroy those lands.

³⁴And the people of Reuben and Gad gave the altar a name. They called it Proof that We Believe that the Lord Is God.

JOSHUA SAYS GOOD-BYE

23 The Lord gave Israel peace from their enemies around them. He made Israel safe. Many years passed, and Joshua became very old. ²So he called a meeting of all the elders, heads of families, judges and officers of the Israelites. He said, "I am now very old. ³You have seen what the Lord has done to our enemies. He did it to help us. The Lord your God fought for you. ⁴Remember that your people have been given their land. It's the land between the Jordan River and the Mediterranean Sea in the west. It's the land I promised to give you. But you don't control that land yet. ⁵The Lord your God will make the people

living there leave. You will enter the land. And the Lord will force them out ahead of you. He has promised you this.

⁶"Be strong. You must be careful to obey everything the Lord has commanded. Obey everything written in the Book of the Teachings of Moses. Do exactly as it says. ⁷There are still some people living among us who are not Israelites. They worship their own gods. Don't become friends with them. Don't serve or worship their gods. ⁸You must continue to follow the Lord your God. You have done this in the past. And you must continue to do it.

⁹"The Lord has helped you defeat many great and powerful nations. He has forced them to leave ahead of you. No nation has been able to defeat you. ¹⁰With his help, one Israelite could defeat a thousand enemies. This is because the Lord your God fights for you, as he promised to do. ¹¹So you must be careful to love the Lord your God.

¹²"Don't turn away from the way of the Lord. Don't become friends with these people who are not part of Israel. Don't marry them. If you do become their friends, ¹³the Lord your God will not help you defeat your enemies. So they will become like traps for you. They will cause you pain like a whip on your back and thorns in your eyes. And none of you will be left in this good land the Lord your God has given you.

¹⁴"It's almost time for me to die. You know and fully believe that the Lord has done great things for you. You know that he has not failed in any of his promises. He has kept every promise he has given. ¹⁵Every good promise that the Lord your God made has come true. And in the same way, his other promises will come true. He promised that evil will come to you. He will destroy you from this good land that he gave you. ¹⁶This will happen if you don't keep your agreement with the Lord your God. You will lose this land

if you go and serve other gods. You must not worship them. If you do, the Lord will become very angry with you. Then none of you will be left in this good land he has given you."

24 Then all the tribes[d] of Israel met together at Shechem. Joshua called them all together there. Then he called the elders, heads of families, judges and officers of Israel. These men stood before God.

²Then Joshua spoke to all the people. He said, "Here's what the Lord, the God of Israel, says to you: 'A long time ago your ancestors lived on the other side of the Euphrates River. I am talking about men like Terah, the father of Abraham and Nahor. They worshiped other gods. ³But I, the Lord, took your ancestor Abraham out of the land on the other side of the river. I led him through the land of Canaan. And I gave him many children. I gave him his son Isaac. ⁴And I gave Isaac two sons named Jacob and Esau. I gave the land around the mountains of Edom to Esau. But Jacob and his sons went down to Egypt. ⁵Then I sent Moses and Aaron to Egypt. I caused many terrible things to happen to the Egyptians. Then I brought you people out. ⁶When I brought your fathers out of Egypt, they came to the Red Sea.[d] And the Egyptians chased them. There were chariots and men on horses. ⁷So the people asked me, the Lord, for help. And I caused great trouble to come to the Egyptians. I caused the sea to cover them. You yourselves saw what I did to the army of Egypt. After that, you lived in the desert for a long time.

⁸"'Then I brought you to the land of the Amorites. This was east of the Jordan River. They fought against you, but I gave you the power to defeat them. I destroyed them before you. Then you took control of that land. ⁹But the king of Moab, Balak son of Zippor, prepared to fight against the Israelites. The king sent for Balaam son of Beor to curse you. ¹⁰But I, the Lord, refused to listen to Balaam. So he asked for good things to happen to you! He blessed you many times. I saved you and brought you out of his power.

¹¹"'Then you traveled across the Jordan River and came to Jericho. The people in the city of Jericho fought against you. Also, the Amorites, Perizzites, Canaanites, Hittites, Girgashites, Hivites and Jebusites fought against you. But I allowed you to defeat them all. ¹²While your army traveled forward, I sent hornets ahead of them. These hornets made the people leave before you came. So you took the land without using your swords and bows. ¹³It was I, the Lord, who gave you that land. I gave you land where you did not have to work. I gave you cities that you did not have to build. And now you live in that land and in those cities. You eat from vineyards and olive trees. But you did not have to plant them.'"

¹⁴Then Joshua spoke to the people. He said, "Now you have heard the Lord's words. So you must respect the Lord and serve him fully and sincerely. Throw away the false gods that your people worshiped. That happened on the other side of the Euphrates River and in Egypt. Now you must serve the Lord. ¹⁵But maybe you don't want to serve the Lord. You must choose for yourselves today. You must decide whom you will serve. You may serve the gods that your people worshiped when they lived on the other side of the Euphrates River. Or you may serve the gods of the Amorites who lived in this land. As for me and my family, we will serve the Lord."

¹⁶Then the people answered, "No! We will never stop following the Lord. We will never serve other gods! ¹⁷We know it was the Lord our God who brought our people out of Egypt. We were slaves in that land. But the Lord did great things for us there. He brought us out. He protected us while we traveled through other lands. ¹⁸Then he helped us defeat

the people living in these lands. He helped us defeat the Amorites who lived here. So we will continue to serve the Lord because he is our God."

[19]Then Joshua said, "You will not be able to serve the Lord well enough. He is a holy God. And he is a jealous God. If you turn against him and sin, he will not forgive you. [20]If you leave the Lord and serve other gods, he will cause great trouble to come to you. The Lord has been good to you. But if you turn against him, he will destroy you."

[21]But the people said to Joshua, "No! We will serve the Lord."

[22]Then Joshua said, "Look around at yourselves and the people with you here. Do you all know and agree that you have chosen to serve the Lord? Are you all witnesses to this?"

The people answered, "Yes, it's true! We all see that we have chosen to serve the Lord."

[23]Then Joshua said, "Now throw away the false gods that you have among you. Love the Lord, the God of Israel, with all your heart."

[24]Then the people said to Joshua, "We will serve the Lord our God. We will obey him."

[25]On that day Joshua made an agreement for the people. He made the agreement a law for them to follow. This happened at Shechem. [26]Joshua wrote these things in the Book of the Teachings of God. Then he found a large stone. He put the stone under the oak tree near the Lord's Holy Tent.[d]

[27]Then Joshua said to all the people, "See this stone! It will help you remember what we did today. It was here when the Lord was speaking to us today. It will help you remember what happened. It will stop you from turning against your God."

JOSHUA DIES

[28]Then Joshua told the people to go back to their homes. And everyone went back to his own land.

[29]After that, Joshua son of Nun died. He was 110 years old. [30]And they buried him in his own land at Timnath Serah. This was in the mountains of Ephraim, north of Mount Gaash.

[31]The Israelites had served the Lord during the time Joshua was living. And after he died, they continued to serve the Lord. They continued to serve him while their elders were still alive. These were the leaders who had seen what the Lord had done for the Israelites.

JOSEPH COMES HOME

[32]When the Israelites left Egypt, they carried the bones of Joseph with them. They buried them at Shechem, in the land Jacob had bought from the sons of Hamor. (Hamor was the father of Shechem.) Jacob had bought the land for 100 pieces of silver. This land belonged to Joseph's children.

[33]And Eleazar son of Aaron died. He was buried at Gibeah in the mountains of Ephraim. Gibeah had been given to Eleazar's son Phinehas.

THE BOOK OF
JUDGES

THE MEN OF JUDAH FIGHT THE CANAANITES

1 Joshua died. Then the people of Israel prayed to the Lord. They said, "Who will be first to go and fight for us against the Canaanite people?"

²The Lord said to them, "The tribe*d* of Judah will go. I have given them the power to take this land."

³The men of Judah asked for help from the men of Simeon, their relatives. The men of Judah said, "Come and help us fight the Canaanites for our land. If you do, we will go and help you fight for your land." So the men of Simeon went with them.

⁴The Lord gave the men of Judah the victory over the Canaanites and the Perizzites. The men of Judah defeated 10,000 men at the city of Bezek. ⁵There they found Adoni-Bezek, the ruler of the city, and fought him. The men of Judah defeated the Canaanites and the Perizzites. ⁶So Adoni-Bezek ran away. But the men of Judah chased him. When they caught him, they cut off his thumbs and big toes.

⁷Then Adoni-Bezek said, "I cut off the thumbs and big toes of 70 kings. And those kings had to eat scraps that fell from my table. Now God has paid me back for what I did to them." The men of Judah took Adoni-Bezek to Jerusalem, and he died there.

⁸Then the men of Judah fought against Jerusalem and captured it. They used their swords to kill the people of Jerusalem. And they burned the city.

⁹Later, they went down to fight against more of the Canaanites. Some of the Canaanites lived in the mountains. Others lived in the dry country to the south. And still others lived in the western mountain slopes. ¹⁰Then the men of Judah went to fight against the Canaanites in the city of Hebron. (Hebron used to be called Kiriath Arba.) The men of Judah defeated the descendants*d* of Sheshai, Ahiman and Talmai.

CALEB AND HIS DAUGHTER

¹¹Then the men of Judah left Hebron. They went to the city of Debir to fight against the people there. (Debir used to be called Kiriath Sepher.) ¹²Before attacking the city, Caleb said, "I want a man to attack and capture the city of Kiriath Sepher. I will give him Acsah, my daughter, as a wife." ¹³Caleb had a younger brother named Kenaz. Kenaz had a son named Othniel. Othniel captured the city of Kiriath Sepher. So Caleb gave his daughter Acsah to Othniel to be his wife. ¹⁴When Acsah came to Othniel, he told her to ask her father for some land. So she got down from her donkey, and Caleb said, "What do you want?"

¹⁵Acsah answered Caleb, "Do me a favor. You have put me in the dry land of southern Judah. Give me some land with springs of water." So Caleb gave her the upper and lower springs of water.

FIGHTS WITH THE CANAANITES

¹⁶The Kenite people left Jericho, the city of palm trees. They went with the men of Judah. The Kenites went to the Desert of Judah to live with the people there. This was in southern Judah near the city of Arad. (The Kenites were from the family of Moses' father-in-law.)

¹⁷Some Canaanite people also lived in the city of Zephath. So the men of Judah and the men of Simeon, their relatives, defeated those Canaanites. They completely destroyed the city. So they called the city Hormah.*n* ¹⁸The men of Judah captured Gaza, Ashkelon and Ekron and all the lands around them.

1:17 **Hormah** Hormah sounds like the Hebrew word meaning "to destroy completely."

¹⁹The Lord was on the side of the men of Judah. They took the land in the mountains. But they could not force out the people living on the plain. This was because those people had iron chariots. ²⁰As Moses had promised, Hebron was given to Caleb. Caleb forced out the three sons of Anak.ᵈ ²¹But the people of Benjamin could not make the Jebusite people leave Jerusalem. Since that time the Jebusites have lived with the Benjaminites in Jerusalem.

²²The men of Joseph went to fight against the city of Bethel. The Lord was on their side. ²³They sent some spies to Bethel. (Bethel used to be called Luz.) ²⁴The spies saw a man coming out of the city. They said to him, "Show us a way into the city. If you help us, we will be kind to you." ²⁵The man showed the spies the way into the city. The men of Joseph killed the people in Bethel. But the man who helped them and his family were allowed to go free. ²⁶He went to the land where the Hittite people lived, and he built a city. He named the city Luz, and it is called that today.

²⁷There were Canaanites living in the cities of Beth Shan, Taanach, Dor, Ibleam, Megiddo and the small towns around them. The people of Manasseh did not force those people out of their towns. The Canaanites were determined to stay there. ²⁸Later, the people of Israel grew strong. They forced the Canaanites to work as slaves for them. But the Israelites did not make all the Canaanites leave their land. ²⁹There were Canaanites living in Gezer. And the people of Ephraim did not make all of those Canaanites leave their land. So the Canaanite people continued to live in Gezer with the people of Ephraim. ³⁰Some Canaanites lived in the cities of Kitron and Nahalol. The people of Zebulun did not make them leave their land. They stayed and lived with the

people of Zebulun. But Zebulun made them work as slaves.

³¹The people of Asher did not make the Canaanites leave the cities of Acco, Sidon, Ahlab, Aczib, Helbah, Aphek and Rehob. ³²The people of Asher did not make them leave their land. So the Canaanites continued to live with the people of Asher. ³³The people of Naphtali did not make the people leave the cities of Beth Shemesh and Beth Anath. So the people of Naphtali continued to live with the Canaanites in those cities. Those people worked as slaves for the people of Naphtali. ³⁴The Amorites forced the Danites back into the mountains. The Amorites would not let them come down to live in the plain. ³⁵The Amorites were determined to stay in Mount Heres, Aijalon and Shaalbim. But the Israelites grew stronger. Then they made the Amorites work as slaves for them. ³⁶The land of the Amorites was from Scorpion Pass to Sela and beyond it.

THE ANGEL OF THE LORD AT BOKIM

2 The angel of the Lord went up from Gilgal to Bokim. He spoke to the people of Israel there and said: "I brought you up from Egypt. I led you to the land I promised to give to your ancestors. I said, 'I will never break my agreement with you. ²But in return, you must not make an agreement with the people who live in this land. You must destroy their altars.' But you did not obey me. How could you do this? ³Now I will tell you this: 'I will not force out the people in this land. They will become your enemies. Their gods will become a trap for you.'"

⁴After the angel gave Israel this message from the Lord, they cried loudly. ⁵So they named the place Bokim.ⁿ There they offered sacrifices to the Lord.

JOSHUA DIES

⁶Then Joshua told the people they could go home. So each one went to take

---

2:5 Bokim This name means "crying."

his own share of the land. [7]The people of Israel served the Lord as long as Joshua was alive. They continued serving the Lord during the lifetimes of the elders who lived on after Joshua. These men had seen all the great things the Lord had done for Israel. [8]Joshua son of Nun was the servant of the Lord. Joshua died at the age of 110. [9]So the Israelites buried him in the land he had been given. That land was at Timnath Heres. It was in the mountains of Ephraim, north of Mount Gaash.

THE PEOPLE DISOBEY

[10]After those people had died, their children grew up. They did not know the Lord or what he had done for Israel. [11]So they did evil and worshiped the Baal[d] idols. They did what the Lord said was wrong. [12]The Lord had brought the people of Israel out of Egypt. And the ancestors of these people had worshiped the Lord. But the Israelites quit following the Lord. They began to worship the gods of the people who lived around them. That made the Lord angry. [13]The Israelites quit following the Lord and worshiped Baal and Ashtoreth.[d] [14]The Lord was angry with the people of Israel. So he let robbers attack them and take their possessions. He let their enemies who lived around them defeat them. They could not protect themselves from their enemies. [15]When the Israelites went out to fight, they always lost. They lost because the Lord was not on their side. The Lord had sworn to them this would happen. So the Israelites suffered very much.

GOD CHOOSES JUDGES

[16]Then the Lord chose leaders called judges.[n] These leaders saved the people of Israel from the robbers. [17]But the Israelites did not listen to their judges. They were not faithful to God. They followed other gods instead. In the past the people of Israel obeyed the Lord's commands. But now the Israelites stopped obeying the Lord. [18]Many times the enemies of Israel hurt the Israelites. So the Israelites would cry for help. And each time the Lord felt sorry for them. Each time he sent a judge to save them from their enemies. The Lord was with those judges. [19]But when each judge died, the Israelites again sinned and worshiped the false gods. They became worse than their ancestors. The Israelites were very stubborn; they refused to change their evil ways.

[20]So the Lord became angry with the Israelites. He said, "These people have broken the agreement I made with their ancestors. They have not listened to me. [21]So I will no longer defeat the nations who were left when Joshua died. [22]I will use those nations to test Israel. I will see if Israel keeps the Lord's commands as their ancestors did." [23]In the past the Lord had permitted those nations to stay in the land. He did not quickly force them out. He did not help Joshua's army defeat them.

3 These are the nations the Lord did not force to leave. He wanted to test the Israelites who had not fought in the wars to take Canaan. [2]The only reason the Lord left those nations in the land was to teach the descendants[d] of the Israelites. He wanted to teach the people who had not fought in those wars how to fight. [3]These are the nations: the five rulers of the Philistines, all the Canaanites, the people of Sidon and the Hivites. The Hivites lived in the Lebanon mountains from Mount Baal Hermon to Lebo Hamath. [4]Those nations were in the land to test the Israelites. The Lord wanted to see if Israel would obey the commands he had given to their ancestors by Moses.

[5]The people of Israel lived with the Canaanites, Hittites, Amorites, Perizzites,

---

2:16 judges They were not judges in courts of law, but leaders of the people in times of emergency.

Hivites and Jebusites. ⁶The Israelites began to marry the daughters of those people. And the Israelites allowed their daughters to marry the sons of those people. Israel served the gods of those people.

OTHNIEL, THE FIRST JUDGE

⁷The people of Israel did what the Lord said was wrong. They forgot about the Lord their God. Instead, they served the idols of Baal*d* and Asherah.*d* ⁸The Lord was angry with Israel. He allowed Cushan-Rishathaim king of Northwest Mesopotamia to rule over the Israelites. They were under that king's rule for eight years. ⁹Then Israel cried to the Lord. So the Lord sent a man to save them. He was Othniel son of Kenaz. (Kenaz was Caleb's younger brother.) Othniel saved the Israelites. ¹⁰The Spirit*d* of the Lord entered Othniel. And he became Israel's judge and went to war. The Lord helped him to defeat Cushan-Rishathaim king of Northwest Mesopotamia. ¹¹So the land was at peace for 40 years. Then Othniel son of Kenaz died.

EHUD, THE JUDGE

¹²Again the people of Israel did what the Lord said was wrong. So the Lord gave Eglon king of Moab power to defeat Israel. This was because of the evil Israel did. ¹³Eglon got the Ammonite people and the Amalekite people to join him. Then he attacked Israel and took Jericho, the city of palm trees. ¹⁴The people of Israel were under the rule of Eglon king of Moab for 18 years.

¹⁵So the people cried to the Lord. And he sent a man to save them. That man was Ehud, who was left-handed. Ehud was the son of Gera from the people of Benjamin. Israel sent Ehud to give Eglon king of Moab the payment he demanded. ¹⁶Ehud made a sword for himself. The sword had two edges and was about 18 inches long. He tied the sword to his right upper leg under his clothes. ¹⁷So

Ehud came to Eglon king of Moab and gave him the payment he demanded. Eglon was a very fat man. ¹⁸After he had given Eglon the payment, Ehud sent home the men who had carried it. ¹⁹When he passed the statues near the city Gilgal, he turned around. Ehud said to Eglon, "I have a secret message for you, King Eglon."

The king said, "Be quiet!" Then he sent all of his servants out of the room. ²⁰Ehud went to King Eglon. Eglon was now sitting alone in the room on top of his summer palace.

Ehud said, "I have a message from God for you." As the king stood up from his chair, ²¹Ehud reached with his left hand. He took out the sword that was tied to his right upper leg. Then he stabbed the sword deep into the king's belly! ²²The sword went into Eglon's belly so far that even the handle sank in. And the blade came out his back. The king's fat covered the whole sword. So Ehud left the sword in Eglon. ²³He went out of the room and closed and locked the doors behind him.

²⁴The servants returned just after Ehud left. They found the doors to the room locked. So they thought the king was relieving himself. ²⁵They waited for a long time. Finally they became worried because he still had not opened the doors. So they got the key and unlocked them. When they entered, they saw their king lying dead on the floor!

²⁶While the servants were waiting, Ehud had escaped. He passed by the statues and went to Seirah. ²⁷When he arrived there, he blew a trumpet in the mountains of Ephraim. The people of Israel heard it and went down from the hills with Ehud leading them.

²⁸He said to them, "Follow me! The Lord has helped us to defeat our enemies, the people of Moab." So Israel followed Ehud. They took control of the places where the Jordan River could easily be

crossed. Israel did not allow the Moabites to come across the Jordan River. [29]Israel killed about 10,000 strong and able men from Moab. Not one Moabite man escaped. [30]So that day Moab was forced to be under the rule of Israel. And there was peace in the land for 80 years.

SHAMGAR, THE JUDGE

[31]After Ehud, another man saved Israel. His name was Shamgar son of Anath. Shamgar killed 600 Philistines with a sharp stick used to guide oxen.

DEBORAH, THE WOMAN JUDGE

4 After Ehud died, the people of Israel again did what the Lord said was wrong. [2]So he let Jabin, a king of Canaan, defeat Israel. Jabin ruled in the city of Hazor. Sisera was the commander of Jabin's army. Sisera lived in Harosheth Haggoyim. [3]He had 900 iron chariots and was very cruel to the people of Israel for 20 years. So they cried to the Lord for help.

[4]There was a prophetess[d] named Deborah. She was the wife of Lappidoth. She was judge of Israel at that time. [5]Deborah would sit under the Palm Tree of Deborah. This was between the cities of Ramah and Bethel, in the mountains of Ephraim. And the people of Israel would come to her to settle their arguments.

[6]Deborah sent a message to a man named Barak. He was the son of Abinoam. Barak lived in the city of Kedesh, which is in the area of Naphtali. Deborah said to Barak, "The Lord, the God of Israel, commands you: 'Go and gather 10,000 men of Naphtali and Zebulun. Lead them to Mount Tabor. [7]I will make Sisera, the commander of Jabin's army, come to you. Sisera, his chariots and his army will meet you at the Kishon River. I will help you to defeat Sisera there.'"

[8]Then Barak said to Deborah, "I will go if you will go with me. But if you will not go with me, I won't go."

[9]"Of course I will go with you," Deborah answered. "But you will not get credit for the victory. The Lord will let a woman defeat Sisera." So Deborah went with Barak to Kedesh. [10]At Kedesh, Barak called the people of Zebulun and Naphtali together. From them, he gathered 10,000 men to follow him. Deborah went with Barak also.

[11]Now Heber the Kenite had left the other Kenite people. (The Kenites were descendants[d] of Hobab, Moses' brother-in-law.) Heber had put up his tent by the great tree in Zaanannim. This is near Kedesh.

[12]Then Sisera was told that Barak son of Abinoam had gone up to Mount Tabor. [13]So Sisera gathered his 900 iron chariots and all the men with him. They went from Harosheth Haggoyim to the Kishon River.

[14]Then Deborah said to Barak, "Get up! Today is the day the Lord will help you defeat Sisera. You know the Lord has already cleared the way for you." So Barak led 10,000 men down from Mount Tabor. [15]He and his men attacked Sisera and his men. During the battle the Lord confused Sisera and his army and chariots. So Barak and his men used their swords to defeat Sisera's army. But Sisera left his chariot and ran away on foot. [16]Barak and his men chased Sisera's chariots and army to Harosheth Haggoyim. They used their swords to kill all of Sisera's men. Not one of them was left alive.

[17]But Sisera himself ran away. He came to the tent where Jael lived. She was the wife of Heber, one of the Kenite family groups. Heber's family was at peace with Jabin king of Hazor. [18]Jael went out to meet Sisera. She said to him, "Come into my tent, master! Come in. Don't be afraid." So Sisera went into Jael's tent, and she covered him with a rug.

[19]Sisera said to Jael, "I am thirsty. Please give me some water to drink." So she opened a leather bag in which she kept milk and gave him a drink. Then she covered him up.

²⁰Then Sisera said to Jael, "Go stand at the entrance to the tent. If anyone comes and asks you, 'Is anyone here?' say, 'No.'"

²¹But Jael, the wife of Heber, took a tent peg and a hammer. She quietly went to Sisera. Since he was very tired, he was sleeping. She hammered the tent peg through the side of Sisera's head and into the ground! And so Sisera died.

²²Then Barak came by Jael's tent, chasing Sisera. Jael went out to meet him and said, "Come. I will show you the man you are looking for." So Barak entered her tent. There Sisera lay dead, with the tent peg in his head.

²³On that day God defeated Jabin king of Canaan in the sight of Israel.

²⁴Israel became stronger and stronger against Jabin king of Canaan. Finally, they destroyed him.

THE SONG OF DEBORAH

5 On that day Deborah and Barak son of Abinoam sang this song:

²"The leaders led Israel.
The people volunteered to go to battle.
Praise the Lord!
³Listen, kings.
Pay attention, rulers!
I myself will sing to the Lord.
I will make music to the Lord, the God of Israel.

⁴"Lord, in the past you came from Edom.
You marched from the land of Edom,
and the earth shook.
The skies rained,
and the clouds dropped water.
⁵The mountains shook before the Lord, the God of Mount Sinai.
They shook before the Lord, the God of Israel!

⁶"In the days of Shamgar son of Anath, in the days of Jael, the main roads were empty.
Travelers went on the back roads.

⁷There were no warriors in Israel until I, Deborah, arose.
I arose to be a mother to Israel.
⁸At that time they chose to follow new gods.
Because of this, enemies fought us at our city gates.
No one could find a shield or a spear among the 40,000 men of Israel.
⁹My heart is with the commanders of Israel.
They volunteered freely from among the people.
Praise the Lord!

¹⁰"You who ride on white donkeys and sit on saddle blankets, listen!
And you who walk along the road, listen!
¹¹Listen to the sound of the singers at the watering holes.
There they tell about the victories of the Lord.
They tell about the victories of the Lord's warriors in Israel.
Then the Lord's people went down to the city gates.

¹²"Wake up, wake up, Deborah!
Wake up, wake up, sing a song!
Get up, Barak!
Go capture your enemies, son of Abinoam!

¹³"Then the men who were left came down to the important leaders.
The Lord's people came down to me with strong men.
¹⁴They came from Ephraim in the mountains of Amalek.
Benjamin was among the people who followed you.
From the family group of Makir in West Manasseh, the commanders came down.
And from Zebulun came those men who lead with an officer's staff.
¹⁵The princes of Issachar were with Deborah.

The people of Issachar were loyal to
  Barak.
They followed him into the valley.
The Reubenites thought hard
  about what they would do.
¹⁶Why did you stay by the sheepfold?
  Was it to hear the music played for
  your sheep?
The Reubenites thought hard
  about what they would do.
¹⁷The people of Gilead stayed east of the
  Jordan River.
People of Dan, why did you stay by
  the ships?
The people of Asher stayed at the
  seashore.
They stayed at their safe harbors.
¹⁸But the people of Zebulun risked their
  lives.
So did the people of Naphtali on the
  battlefield.

¹⁹"The kings came, and they fought.
  At that time the kings of Canaan
  fought
at Taanach, by the waters of Megiddo.
  But they took away no silver or
  possessions of Israel.
²⁰The stars fought from heaven.
  From their paths, they fought
  Sisera.
²¹The Kishon River swept Sisera's men
  away,
  that old river, the Kishon River.
March on, my soul, with strength!
²²Then the horses' hoofs beat the
  ground.
  Galloping, galloping go Sisera's
  mighty horses.
²³'May the town of Meroz be cursed,'
  said the angel of the Lord.
  'Bitterly curse its people,
because they did not come to help the
  Lord.
  They did not fight the strong enemy.'

²⁴"May Jael, the wife of Heber the Kenite,
  be blessed above all women who
  live in tents.

²⁵Sisera asked for water,
  but Jael gave him milk.
In a bowl fit for a ruler,
  she brought him cream.
²⁶Jael reached out and took the tent peg.
  Her right hand reached for the
  workman's hammer.
And she hit Sisera! She smashed his
  head!
  She crushed and pierced the side of
  his head!
²⁷At Jael's feet he sank.
  He fell, and he lay there.
At her feet he sank. He fell.
  Where Sisera sank, there he fell,
  dead!

²⁸"Sisera's mother looked out through
  the window.
  She looked through the curtains.
She asked, 'Why is Sisera's chariot so
  late in coming?
  Why are sounds of his chariots'
  horses delayed?'
²⁹The wisest of her servant ladies
  answer her.
  And Sisera's mother says to herself,
³⁰'Surely they are taking the possessions
  of the people they defeated!
  Surely they are dividing those
  things among themselves!
A girl or two is being given to each
  soldier.
  Maybe Sisera is taking pieces of
  dyed cloth.
Maybe they are even taking
  pieces of dyed, embroidered cloth
  for the necks of the victors!'

³¹"Let all your enemies die this way,
  Lord!
  But let all the people who love you
  be powerful like the rising sun!"
  So there was peace in the land for 40
years.

THE MIDIANITES ATTACK ISRAEL

6 Again the people of Israel did what
the Lord said was wrong. So for
seven years the Lord let the people of

Midian rule Israel. ²The Midianites were very powerful and were cruel to the Israelites. So the Israelites made hiding places in the mountains. They also hid in caves and safe places. ³Whenever the Israelites planted crops, the Midianites, Amalekites and other peoples from the east would come and attack them. ⁴These people camped in the land. And they destroyed the crops that the Israelites had planted. They did this as far as the land near Gaza. The people left nothing for Israel to eat. They left them no sheep, cattle or donkeys. ⁵The Midianites came up and camped in the land. They brought their tents and their animals with them. They were like swarms of locusts!ᵈ There were so many people and camels they could not be counted. These people came into the land to ruin it. ⁶Israel became very poor because of the Midianites. So the Israelites cried out to the Lord for help.

⁷The Israelites cried out to the Lord for help against the Midianites. ⁸So the Lord sent a prophetᵈ to them. The prophet said, "This is what the Lord, the God of Israel, says: I brought you out of Egypt, the land of slavery. ⁹I saved you from the people of Egypt. And I saved you from all the people of Canaan. I forced them out of their land. And I gave it to you. ¹⁰Then I said to you, 'I am the Lord your God. You will live in the land of the Amorites, but you must not worship their gods.' But you did not obey me."

THE ANGEL OF THE LORD VISITS GIDEON

¹¹The angel of the Lord came and sat down under an oak tree at Ophrah. The oak tree belonged to Joash, who was one of the Abiezrite people. Joash was the father of Gideon. Gideon was separating some wheat from the chaffᵈ in a winepress.ᵈ Gideon did this to keep the wheat from the Midianites. ¹²The angel of the Lord appeared to Gideon and said, "The Lord is with you, mighty warrior!"

¹³Then Gideon said, "Pardon me, sir. If the Lord is with us, why are we having so many troubles? Our ancestors told us he did miracles.ᵈ They told us the Lord brought them out of Egypt. But now he has left us. He has allowed the Midianites to defeat us."

¹⁴The Lord turned to Gideon and said, "You have the strength to save the people of Israel. Go and save them from the Midianites. I am the one who is sending you."

¹⁵But Gideon answered, "Pardon me, Lord. How can I save Israel? My family group is the weakest in Manasseh. And I am the least important member of my family."

¹⁶The Lord answered him, "I will be with you. It will seem as if you are fighting only one man."

¹⁷Then Gideon said to the Lord, "If you are pleased with me, give me proof. Show me that it is really you talking with me. ¹⁸Please wait here. Do not go away until I come back to you. Let me bring my offering and set it in front of you."

And the Lord said, "I will wait until you come back."

¹⁹So Gideon went in and cooked a young goat. He also took about 20 quarts of flour and made bread without yeast. Then he put the meat into a basket. And he put the broth from the boiled meat into a pot. He brought out the meat, the broth and the bread without yeast. He brought the food to the angel of the Lord. Gideon gave it to him under the oak tree.

²⁰The angel of God said to Gideon, "Put the meat and the bread without yeast on that rock over there. Then pour the broth on them." And Gideon did as he was told. ²¹The angel of the Lord had a stick in his hand. He touched the meat and the bread with the end of the stick. Then fire jumped up from the rock! The meat and the bread were completely burned up! And the angel of the Lord disappeared! ²²Then Gideon understood he had been talking to the angel of the Lord. So Gideon cried, "Lord God! I have seen the angel of the Lord face to face!"

23But the Lord said to Gideon, "Calm down! Don't be afraid! You will not die!"

24So Gideon built an altar there to worship the Lord. Gideon named the altar The Lord Is Peace. It still stands at Ophrah, where the Abiezrites live.

GIDEON TEARS DOWN THE ALTAR OF BAAL

25That same night the Lord spoke to Gideon. The Lord said, "Take the bull that belongs to your father and a second bull seven years old. Pull down your father's altar to Baal.d Cut down the Asherahd idol beside it. 26Then build an altar to the Lord your God. Build it on this high ground. Lay its stones in the right order. Then kill and burn the bull on this altar. Use the wood from the Asherah idol to burn your offering."

27So Gideon got ten of his servants. And he did what the Lord had told him to do. But Gideon was afraid that his family and the men of the city might see him. So he did it at night, not in the daytime.

28The men of the city got up the next morning. They saw that the altar for Baal had been destroyed! And they saw that the Asherah idol beside it had been cut down! They also saw the altar Gideon had built. And they saw the bull that had been sacrificed on it. 29The men of the city looked at each other and asked, "Who did this?" They asked many questions and looked for the person who had done those things.

Someone told them, "Gideon son of Joash did this."

30So they said to Joash, "Bring your son out. He has pulled down the altar of Baal. He has cut down the Asherah idol beside it. So your son must die!"

31But Joash spoke to the angry crowd around him. He said, "Are you going to take Baal's side? Are you going to defend Baal? Anyone who takes Baal's side will be killed by morning! If Baal is a god, let him fight for himself. It's his altar that has been pulled down." 32So on that day Gideon got the name Jerub-Baal. The name means "let Baal fight against him." They named him this because Gideon pulled down Baal's altar.

GIDEON DEFEATS MIDIAN

33All the Midianites, the Amalekites and other peoples from the east joined together. They came across the Jordan River and camped in the Valley of Jezreel. 34But the Spiritd of the Lord entered Gideon! Gideon blew a trumpet to call the Abiezrites to follow him. 35He sent messengers to all of Manasseh. The people of Manasseh were called to follow Gideon. Gideon also sent messengers to the people of Asher, Zebulun and Naphtali. They also went up to meet Gideon and his men.

36Then Gideon said to God, "You said you would help me save Israel. 37I will put some wool on the threshingd floor. Let there be dew only on the wool. But let all of the ground be dry. Then I will know what you said is true. I will know that you will use me to save Israel." 38And that is just what happened. Gideon got up early the next morning and squeezed the wool. He got a full bowl of water from the wool.

39Then Gideon said to God, "Don't be angry with me. Let me ask just one more thing. Please let me make one more test. Let the wool be dry while the ground around it gets wet with dew." 40That night God did that very thing. Just the wool was dry, but the ground around it was wet with dew.

7 Early in the morning Jerub-Baal and all his men set up their camp at the spring of Harod. (Jerub-Baal is also called Gideon.) The Midianites were camped north of them. The Midianites were camped in the valley at the bottom of the hill called Moreh. 2Then the Lord said to Gideon, "You have too many men to defeat the Midianites. I don't want the Israelites to brag that they saved themselves. 3So now, announce to the people, 'Anyone who is afraid may leave Mount Gilead. He may go back home.'" And

22,000 men went back home. But 10,000 remained.

⁴Then the Lord said to Gideon, "There are still too many men. Take the men down to the water, and I will test them for you there. If I say, 'This man will go with you,' he will go. But if I say, 'That one will not go with you,' he will not go."

⁵So Gideon led the men down to the water. There the Lord said to him, "Separate them. Those who drink water by lapping it up like a dog will be in one group. Those who bend down to drink will be in the other group." ⁶There were 300 men who used their hands to bring water to their mouths. They lapped it as a dog does. All the rest got down on their knees to drink.

⁷Then the Lord said to Gideon, "I will save you, using the 300 men who lapped the water. And I will allow you to defeat Midian. Let all the other men go to their homes." ⁸So Gideon sent the rest of Israel to their homes. But he kept 300 men. He took the jars and the trumpets of those who went home.

Now the camp of Midian was in the valley below Gideon. ⁹That night the Lord spoke to Gideon. He said, "Get up. Go down and attack the camp of the Midianites. I will allow you to defeat them. ¹⁰But if you are afraid to go down, take your servant Purah with you. ¹¹When you come to the camp of Midian, you will hear what they are saying. Then you will not be afraid to attack the camp."

GIDEON IS ENCOURAGED

So Gideon and his servant Purah went down to the edge of the enemy camp. ¹²The Midianites, the Amalekites and all the peoples from the east were camped in that valley. There were so many of them they seemed like locusts.ᵈ They had so many camels no one could count them. There were as many as there are grains of sand on the seashore!

¹³When Gideon came to the enemy camp, he heard a man talking. That man was telling his friend about a dream. He was saying, "Listen, I dreamed that a loaf of barley bread rolled into the camp of Midian. It hit the tent so hard that the tent turned over and fell flat!"

¹⁴The man's friend said, "Your dream is about the sword of Gideon son of Joash, a man of Israel. God will let Gideon defeat Midian and the whole army!"

¹⁵When Gideon heard about the dream and what it meant, he worshiped God. Then Gideon went back to the camp of Israel. He called out to them, "Get up! The Lord has defeated the army of Midian for you!" ¹⁶Then Gideon divided the 300 men into three groups. He gave each man a trumpet and an empty jar. A burning torch was inside each jar.

¹⁷Gideon told the men, "Watch me and do what I do. When I get to the edge of the camp, do what I do. ¹⁸Surround the enemy camp. I and everyone with me will blow our trumpets. When we blow our trumpets, you blow your trumpets, too. Then shout, 'For the Lord and for Gideon!'"

MIDIAN IS DEFEATED

¹⁹So Gideon and the 100 men with him came to the edge of the enemy camp. They came just after the enemy had changed guards. It was during the middle watch of the night. Then Gideon and his men blew their trumpets and smashed their jars. ²⁰All three groups of Gideon's men blew their trumpets and smashed their jars. They held the torches in their left hands and the trumpets in their right hands. Then they shouted, "A sword for the Lord and for Gideon!" ²¹Each of Gideon's men stayed in his place around the camp. But inside the camp, the men of Midian began shouting and running away.

²²When Gideon's 300 men blew their trumpets, the Lord caused all the men of Midian to fight each other with their swords! The enemy army ran away to the city of Beth Shittah. It is toward Zererah.

They ran as far as the border of the city of Abel Meholah. It is near the city of Tabbath. ²³Then men of Israel from Naphtali, Asher and all of Manasseh were called out to chase the Midianites. ²⁴Gideon sent messengers through all the mountains of Ephraim. They said, "Come down and attack the Midianites. Take control of the Jordan River as far as Beth Barah. Do this before the Midianites can get to the river and cross it."

So they called out all the men of Ephraim. They took control of the Jordan River as far as Beth Barah. ²⁵The men of Ephraim captured two princes of Midian named Oreb and Zeeb. The men of Ephraim killed Oreb at the rock of Oreb. They killed Zeeb at the winepress[d] of Zeeb. And they continued chasing the Midianites. They cut off the heads of Oreb and Zeeb and took them to Gideon. He was now east of the Jordan River.

8 The men of Ephraim asked Gideon, "Why did you treat us this way? Why didn't you call us when you went to fight against Midian?" They were very angry at Gideon.

²But he answered them, "I have not done as well as you! The small part you did was better than all that my people of Abiezer did. ³God allowed you to capture Oreb and Zeeb, the princes of Midian. How can I compare what I did with what you did?" When the men of Ephraim heard Gideon's answer, they were not as angry anymore.

GIDEON CAPTURES TWO KINGS

⁴Then Gideon and his 300 men came to the Jordan River. They were tired, but they chased the enemy across to the other side. ⁵Gideon said to the men of Succoth, "Please give my soldiers some bread. They are very tired. I am chasing Zebah and Zalmunna, the kings of Midian."

⁶But the leaders of Succoth said, "Why should we give your soldiers bread? You haven't caught Zebah and Zalmunna yet."

⁷Then Gideon said, "The Lord will help me capture Zebah and Zalmunna. After that, I will whip your skin with thorns and briers from the desert."

⁸Gideon left Succoth and went to the city of Peniel. He asked the men there for food. It was just as he had asked the men of Succoth. And the men of Peniel gave him the same answer as the men of Succoth. ⁹So Gideon said to the men of Peniel, "After I win the victory, I will come back here. And I will pull down this tower."

¹⁰Zebah and Zalmunna and their army were in the city of Karkor. Their army had about 15,000 men. They were all who were left of the army of the peoples of the east. Already 120,000 soldiers of that army had been killed. ¹¹Gideon used the road of those who live in tents. This road is east of Nobah and Jogbehah. Gideon attacked the enemy army when they did not expect it. ¹²Zebah and Zalmunna, the kings of Midian, ran away. But Gideon chased and captured them. Gideon and his men defeated the enemy army.

¹³Then Gideon son of Joash returned from the battle. He and his men returned by the Pass of Heres. ¹⁴Gideon captured a young man from Succoth and asked him some questions. The young man wrote down for Gideon the names of 77 men. They were the officers and elders of Succoth.

GIDEON PUNISHES SUCCOTH

¹⁵Then Gideon came to Succoth. He said to the men of that city, "Here are Zebah and Zalmunna. You made fun of me by saying, 'Why should we give bread to your tired men? You have not caught Zebah and Zalmunna yet.'" ¹⁶So Gideon took the elders of the city. He punished them with thorns and briers from the desert. ¹⁷He also pulled down the tower of Peniel. Then he killed the men in that city.

¹⁸Gideon spoke to Zebah and Zalmunna. He said, "You killed some men

on Mount Tabor. What were those men like?"

Zebah and Zalmunna answered, "They were like you. Each one of them seemed like a prince."

[19]Gideon said, "Those were my brothers, my mother's sons. As surely as the Lord lives, I would not kill you if you had spared them." [20]Then Gideon turned to Jether, his oldest son. Gideon said to him, "Kill them." But Jether was only a boy and was afraid. So he did not take out his sword.

[21]Then Zebah and Zalmunna said to Gideon, "Come on. Kill us yourself. As the saying goes, 'It takes a man to do a man's job.'" So Gideon got up and killed Zebah and Zalmunna. Then he took the decorations off their camels' necks.

GIDEON MAKES AN IDOL

[22]The people of Israel said to Gideon, "You saved us from the Midianites. So now, rule over us. We want you, your son and your grandson to rule over us."

[23]But Gideon told them, "The Lord will be your ruler. I will not rule over you. And my son will not rule over you." [24]He said, "I want you to do this one thing for me. I want each of you to give me a gold earring from the things you took in the fighting." (The Ishmaelite men wore gold earrings. And some Ishmaelites had been defeated in the battle.)

[25]So the people of Israel said to Gideon, "We will gladly give you what you want." So they put a coat down on the ground. Each man threw an earring onto the coat. [26]The gold earrings weighed about 43 pounds. This did not count the weight of the other gifts the people gave to Gideon. They gave him decorations, necklaces and purple robes. These were things that the kings of Midian had worn. The people also gave him chains from the camels of the kings of Midian. [27]Gideon used the gold to make an idol. He put the idol in his hometown of Ophrah. All the people of Israel were unfaithful to God and worshiped the idol. It became a trap that caused Gideon and his family to sin.

THE DEATH OF GIDEON

[28]So Midian was forced to be under the rule of Israel. Midian did not cause trouble anymore. And the land had peace for 40 years, as long as Gideon was alive.

[29]Gideon son of Joash went to his home to live. [30]He had 70 sons of his own. He had many sons because he had many wives. [31]Gideon had a slave woman[d] who lived in Shechem. He also had a son by her. He named that son Abimelech. [32]So Gideon son of Joash died at a good old age. He was buried in the tomb of Joash, his father. That tomb is in Ophrah, where the Abiezrites live.

[33]As soon as Gideon died, the people of Israel were again unfaithful to God. They followed the Baal[d] gods. They made Baal-of-the-Agreement their god. [34]The Israelites did not remember the Lord their God. He had saved them from all their enemies who were living all around them. [35]And Jerub-Baal, also called Gideon, had done many good things for Israel. But Israel was not kind to the family of Gideon for these things.

ABIMELECH BECOMES KING

9 Abimelech son of Jerub-Baal, also called Gideon, went to his uncles. They lived in the city of Shechem. He said to his uncles and all of his mother's family group, [2]"Ask the leaders of Shechem this question: 'Is it better for you to be ruled by the 70 sons of Jerub-Baal or to be ruled by only 1 man?' Remember, I am your relative."

[3]Abimelech's uncles spoke to all the leaders of Shechem. They asked them that question. All the leaders decided to follow Abimelech. They said, "He is our brother." [4]So the leaders of Shechem gave Abimelech about one and three-fourths pounds of silver. The silver was

from the temple of the god Baal*d*-of-the-Agreement. Abimelech used the silver to hire some worthless, reckless men. They followed Abimelech wherever he went. [5]Abimelech went to Ophrah, the hometown of his father. There Abimelech murdered his 70 brothers. They were the sons of Abimelech's father, Gideon. He killed them all on one stone. But Gideon's youngest son, Jotham, hid from Abimelech and escaped. [6]Then all of the leaders of Shechem and Beth Millo came together. They gathered beside the great tree at the stone pillar in Shechem. There they made Abimelech their king.

JOTHAM'S STORY

[7]When Jotham heard this, he went and stood on the top of Mount Gerizim. Jotham shouted to the people: "Listen to me, you leaders of Shechem. Then God may listen to you! [8]One day the trees decided to appoint a king to rule over them. They said to the olive tree, 'You be king over us!'

[9]"But the olive tree said, 'Men and gods are honored by my oil. Should I stop making it just to go and sway over the other trees?'

[10]"Then the trees said to the fig tree, 'Come and be our king!'

[11]"But the fig tree answered, 'Should I stop making my sweet and good fruit? Should I stop just to go and sway over the other trees?'

[12]"Then the trees said to the vine, 'Come and be our king!'

[13]"But the vine answered, 'My wine makes men and gods happy. Should I stop making it just to go and sway over the trees?'

[14]"Then all the trees said to the thornbush, 'Come and be our king.'

[15]"But the thornbush said to the trees, 'If you really want to appoint me king over you, come and find shelter in my shade! But if you do not want to do this, let fire come out of the thornbush. Let the fire burn up the cedars of Lebanon!'

[16]"Now, were you completely honest and sincere when you made Abimelech king? Have you been fair to Gideon and his family? Have you treated Gideon as you should? [17]Remember, my father fought for you. He risked his life to save you from the power of the Midianites. [18]But now you have turned against my father's family. You have killed my father's 70 sons on one stone. You have made Abimelech king over the people of Shechem. He is the son of my father's slave girl! You have made Abimelech king just because he is your relative. [19]So then, if you have been honest and sincere to Gideon and his family today, be happy with Abimelech as your king. And may he be happy with you! [20]But if you have not acted right, may fire come out of Abimelech! May that fire completely burn you leaders of Shechem and Beth Millo! Also may fire come out of the leaders of Shechem and burn up Abimelech!"

[21]Then Jotham ran away. He escaped to the city of Beer. He lived there because he was afraid of his brother Abimelech.

ABIMELECH FIGHTS AGAINST SHECHEM

[22]Abimelech ruled Israel for three years. [23]Then God sent an evil spirit to make trouble between Abimelech and the leaders of Shechem. So the leaders of Shechem turned against him. [24]Abimelech had killed Gideon's 70 sons. They were Abimelech's own brothers. And the leaders of Shechem had helped him kill them. So God sent the evil spirit to punish them. [25]The leaders of Shechem were against Abimelech then. They put men on the hilltops. These men attacked and robbed everyone who went by. Abimelech was told about these attacks.

[26]A man named Gaal and his brothers moved into Shechem. He was the son of Ebed. The leaders of Shechem decided to trust and follow Gaal. [27]The people of Shechem went out to the vineyards to pick grapes. They walked on the grapes to make wine. Then they had a feast in

the temple of their god. The people ate and drank and cursed Abimelech. [28]Then Gaal son of Ebed said, "We are the men of Shechem. Why should we obey Abimelech? Who does he think he is? Isn't Abimelech one of Gideon's sons? Didn't Abimelech make Zebul his officer? We should not obey Abimelech! We should obey the men of Hamor, Shechem's father. Why should we obey Abimelech? [29]If you made me commander of these people, I would get rid of Abimelech! I would say to him, 'Get your army ready and come out to battle!'"

[30]Now Zebul was the ruler of Shechem. He heard what Gaal son of Ebed said. And Zebul became very angry. [31]He sent messengers to Abimelech in the city of Arumah. The message said, "Gaal son of Ebed and Gaal's brothers have come to Shechem. Gaal is turning the city against you! [32]So now you and your men should get up in the night. Then go lie in the fields outside the city. [33]When the sun comes up in the morning, attack the city. Gaal and his men will come out to fight you. Then do what you can to them."

[34]So Abimelech and all his soldiers got up during the night. They went near Shechem and separated into four groups. There they hid. [35]Gaal son of Ebed went out and was standing at the entrance to the city gate. As he was standing there, Abimelech and his soldiers came out of their hiding places.

[36]When Gaal saw the soldiers, he said to Zebul, "Look! There are people coming down from the mountains!"

But Zebul said, "You are seeing the shadows of the mountains. The shadows just look like people."

[37]But again Gaal said, "Look, there are people coming down from the center of the land. And there is a group coming from the fortune-tellers' tree!"

[38]Zebul said to Gaal, "Where is your bragging now? You said, 'Who is Abimelech? Why should we obey him?' You made fun of these men. Now go out and fight them."

[39]So Gaal led the men of Shechem out to fight Abimelech. [40]Abimelech and his men chased them. Many of Gaal's men were killed before they could get back to the city gate. [41]Then Abimelech stayed at Arumah. Zebul forced Gaal and his brothers to leave Shechem.

[42]The next day the people of Shechem went out to the fields. Abimelech was told about it. [43]So he separated his men into three groups. And he hid them in the fields. When he saw the people coming out of the city, he jumped up and attacked them. [44]Abimelech and his group ran to the entrance gate to the city. The other two groups ran out to the people in the fields and killed them. [45]Abimelech and his men fought the city of Shechem all day. They captured it and killed its people. Then Abimelech tore down the city. And he threw salt[n] over the ruins so nothing would ever grow there.

THE TOWER OF SHECHEM

[46]The people who lived at the nearby Tower of Shechem heard what had happened to Shechem. So the leaders gathered in the safest room of the temple of the god Baal[d]-of-the-Agreement. [47]Abimelech heard that all the leaders of the Tower of Shechem had gathered there. [48]So he and all his men went up to Mount Zalmon, near Shechem. Abimelech took an ax and cut some branches. Then he put them on his shoulders. He said to all his men with him, "Hurry! Do what I have done!" [49]So all those men cut branches and followed Abimelech. They piled the branches against the safest room of the temple. Then they set them on fire and burned the people in the room. So all the

9:45 salt The salt would keep crops from growing there.

people who lived at the Tower of Shechem also died. There were about 1,000 men and women.

ABIMELECH'S DEATH

[50]Then Abimelech went to the city of Thebez. He surrounded the city, attacked it and captured it. [51]But inside the city was a strong tower. All the men and women of that city ran to the tower. When they got inside, they locked the door behind them. Then they climbed up to the roof of the tower. [52]Abimelech came to the tower and attacked it. He went up to the door of the tower to set it on fire. [53]As Abimelech came near, a woman dropped a large stone for grinding grain on his head. The stone crushed Abimelech's skull.

[54]He quickly called to the officer who carried his armor. He said, "Take out your sword and kill me. I don't want people to say, 'A woman killed Abimelech.'" So the officer stabbed Abimelech, and he died. [55]When the people of Israel saw Abimelech was dead, they all returned home.

[56]In that way God punished Abimelech for all the evil he had done. Abimelech had sinned against his own father by killing his 70 brothers. [57]God also punished the men of Shechem for the evil they had done. So the curse Jotham had spoken came true. (Jotham was the youngest son of Gideon.)

TOLA, THE JUDGE

10 After Abimelech died, another judge came to save the people of Israel. He was Tola son of Puah. (Puah was the son of Dodo.) Tola was from the people of Issachar. He lived in the city of Shamir in the mountains of Ephraim. [2]Tola was a judge for Israel for 23 years. Then he died and was buried in Shamir.

JAIR, THE JUDGE

[3]After Tola died, Jair became judge. He lived in the region of Gilead. He was a judge for Israel for 22 years. [4]Jair had 30 sons, who rode 30 donkeys. These 30 sons controlled 30 towns in Gilead. These towns are called the Towns of Jair to this day. [5]Jair died and was buried in the city of Kamon.

THE AMMONITES TROUBLE ISRAEL

[6]Again the Israelites did what the Lord said was wrong. They worshiped the Baal[d] and Ashtoreth[d] idols. They also worshiped the gods of the peoples of Aram, Sidon, Moab and Ammon. And they worshiped the gods of the Philistines. The Israelites left the Lord and stopped serving him. [7]So the Lord became angry with them. He allowed the Philistines and the Ammonites to defeat them. [8]In the same year those people destroyed the Israelites who lived east of the Jordan River. This is in the region of Gilead, where the Amorites lived. The Israelites suffered for 18 years. [9]The Ammonites then crossed the Jordan River to fight the people of Judah, Benjamin and Ephraim. The Ammonites caused much trouble to the people of Israel. [10]So the Israelites cried out to the Lord, "We have sinned against you. We left our God and worshiped the Baal idols."

[11]The Lord answered the Israelites, "You cried to me when the Egyptians, the Amorites, the Ammonites and the Philistines hurt you. I saved you from these people. [12]You cried to me when the Sidonians, Amalekites and Maonites hurt you. I also saved you from those people. [13]But you have left me. You have worshiped other gods. So I refuse to save you again! [14]You have chosen those gods. So go call to them for help. Let them save you when you are in trouble!"

[15]But the people of Israel said to the Lord, "We have sinned. Do to us whatever you want, but please save us today!" [16]Then the Israelites threw away the foreign gods among them. And they worshiped the Lord again. So he felt sorry for them when he saw their suffering.

[17]The Ammonite people gathered for war and camped in Gilead. The Israelites

gathered and camped at Mizpah. [18]The leaders of the people of Gilead said, "Who will lead us to attack the people of Ammon? He will become the head of all those who live in Gilead."

JEPHTHAH IS CHOSEN AS LEADER

11 Jephthah was from the people of Gilead. He was a strong soldier. His father was named Gilead, and his mother was a prostitute.[d] [2]Gilead's wife had several sons. When they grew up, they forced Jephthah to leave his home. They said to him, "You will not get any of our father's property. You are the son of another woman." [3]So Jephthah ran away from his brothers. He lived in the land of Tob. There some worthless men began to follow Jephthah.

[4]After a time the Ammonite people fought against Israel. [5]The Ammonites made war against Israel. At that time the elders of Gilead came to Jephthah. They wanted him to come back to Gilead. [6]They said to him, "Come and lead our army so we can fight the Ammonites."

[7]But Jephthah said to them, "Didn't you hate me? You forced me to leave my father's house! Why are you coming to me now that you are in trouble?"

[8]The elders of Gilead said to Jephthah, "That is the reason we come to you now. Please come with us and fight against the Ammonites! You will be the ruler over everyone who lives in Gilead."

[9]Then Jephthah answered, "Suppose you take me back to Gilead to fight the Ammonites. If the Lord helps me win, I will be your ruler."

[10]The elders of Gilead said to him, "The Lord is listening to everything we are saying. We promise to do all that you tell us to do." [11]So Jephthah went with the elders of Gilead. The people made him their leader and commander of their army. Jephthah repeated all of his words in front of the Lord at Mizpah.

JEPHTHAH SENDS MESSENGERS TO THE AMMONITE KING

[12]Jephthah sent messengers to the king of the Ammonites. The messengers asked the king, "What have you got against Israel? Why have you come to attack our land?"

[13]The king of the Ammonites answered the messengers of Jephthah. He said, "We are fighting Israel because you took our land when you came up from Egypt. You took our land from the Arnon River to the Jabbok River to the Jordan River. Now tell the people of Israel to give our land back to us in peace."

[14]Jephthah sent the messengers to the Ammonite king again. [15]They took this message:

"This is what Jephthah says: Israel did not take the land of the people of Moab or Ammon. [16]When the people of Israel came out of Egypt, they went into the desert. They went to the Gulf of Aqaba and then to Kadesh. [17]Israel sent messengers to the king of Edom. They asked, 'Let the people of Israel go across your land.' But the king of Edom didn't let us. We sent the same message to the king of Moab. But he would not let us go across his land either. So the Israelites stayed at Kadesh.

[18]"Then the Israelites went into the desert. They went around the borders of the lands of Edom and Moab. Israel walked east of the land of Moab. They camped on the other side of the Arnon River. It was the border of the land of Moab. They did not cross it to go into the land of Moab.

[19]"Then Israel sent messengers to Sihon king of the Amorites. Sihon was the king of the city of Heshbon. The messengers asked Sihon, 'Let the people of Israel pass through your land. We want to go to our land.' [20]But Sihon would not let the Israelites cross his land. He gathered all of his people and camped at Jahaz. Then the Amorites fought with Israel.

21"But the Lord, the God of Israel, helped the Israelites to defeat Sihon and his army. All the land of the Amorites became the property of Israel. 22So Israel took all the land of the Amorites. It went from the Arnon River to the Jabbok River. It also went from the desert to the Jordan River.

23"It was the Lord, the God of Israel, who forced out the Amorites ahead of the people of Israel. So do you think you can make the people of Israel leave this land? 24Surely you can live in the land which your god Chemosh[d] has given you. So we will live in the land the Lord our God has given us!

25"Are you any better than Balak son of Zippor? He was the king of Moab. Did he ever quarrel or fight with the people of Israel? 26For 300 years the Israelites have lived in Heshbon and Aroer and the towns around them. They have lived for 300 years in all the cities along the Arnon River. Why have you not taken these cities back in all that time? 27I have not sinned against you. But you are sinning against me by making war on me! May the Lord, the Judge, decide whether the Israelites or Ammonites are right."

28But the king of the Ammonites ignored this message from Jephthah.

JEPHTHAH'S PROMISE

29Then the Spirit[d] of the Lord entered Jephthah. Jephthah passed through Gilead and Manasseh. He came to the city of Mizpah in Gilead. From there, Jephthah passed through to the land of the Ammonites. 30Jephthah made a promise to the Lord. He said, "If you will let me defeat the Ammonites, 31I will give you a burnt offering. I will sacrifice the first thing that comes out of my house to meet me when I return from the victory. It will be the Lord's."

32Then Jephthah went over to fight the Ammonites. The Lord helped him defeat them. 33Jephthah defeated them from the city of Aroer to the area of Minnith.

He defeated them as far as the city of Abel Keramim. He defeated 20 cities in this area. The defeat was great. So the Ammonites were defeated by the Israelites.

34When Jephthah returned home to Mizpah, his daughter came out to meet him. She was playing a tambourine[d] and dancing. She was his only child. Jephthah did not have any other sons or daughters. 35When Jephthah saw his daughter, he tore his clothes to show how upset he was. He said, "My daughter! You have made me so sad! This is because I have made a promise to the Lord, and I cannot break it!"

36Then his daughter said, "Father, you made a promise to the Lord. So do to me just what you promised. The Lord helped you defeat your enemies, the Ammonites." 37Then she said, "But let me do one thing. Let me be alone for two months to go to the mountains. I will never marry. So let me and my friends go and cry together."

38Jephthah said, "Go." He sent her away for two months. She and her friends stayed in the mountains. There they cried for her because she would never marry. 39After two months she returned to her father. Jephthah did to her what he promised to the Lord. Now Jephthah's daughter had never had a husband.

So this became a custom in Israel. 40Every year the women of Israel would go out for four days. They did this to remember the daughter of Jephthah from Gilead.

JEPHTHAH AND EPHRAIM

12 The men of Ephraim called all their soldiers together. Then they crossed the river to the town of Zaphon. They said to Jephthah, "Why didn't you call us to help you fight the Ammonites? We will burn your house down with you in it!"

2Jephthah answered them, "My people and I fought a great battle against the

Ammonites. I called you, but you didn't come to help me. ³I saw that you would not help me. So I risked my own life! I went over to fight against the Ammonites. The Lord helped me to defeat them. Now why have you come to fight against me today?"

⁴Then Jephthah called the men of Gilead together. They fought the men of Ephraim. The men of Gilead attacked them because the Ephraimites had insulted them. They had said, "You men of Gilead are nothing but deserters from Ephraim and Manasseh." ⁵The men of Gilead captured the crossing places of the Jordan River. Those places led to the country of Ephraim. A man from Ephraim trying to escape would say, "Let me cross the river." Then the men of Gilead would ask him, "Are you from Ephraim?" If he said, "No," ⁶they would say to him, "Say the word 'Shibboleth.'" The men of Ephraim could not say that word correctly. They pronounced it "Sibboleth." If the man from Ephraim said, "Sibboleth," the men of Gilead would kill him at the crossing place. So 42,000 men from Ephraim were killed at that time.

⁷Jephthah was a judge for the people of Israel for six years. Then Jephthah, the man from Gilead, died. He was buried in a town in Gilead.

IBZAN, THE JUDGE

⁸After Jephthah died, Ibzan was a judge for Israel. He was from Bethlehem. ⁹He had 30 sons and 30 daughters. He let his daughters marry men who were not in his family group. And he brought 30 women who were not in his tribe to be wives for his sons. Ibzan judged Israel for seven years. ¹⁰Then he died and was buried in Bethlehem.

ELON, THE JUDGE

¹¹After Ibzan died, Elon was a judge for Israel. He was from the tribe*d* of Zebulun. He judged Israel for ten years.

¹²Then Elon, the man of Zebulun, died. He was buried in the city of Aijalon in the land of Zebulun.

ABDON, THE JUDGE

¹³After Elon died, Abdon was a judge for Israel. He was the son of Hillel. Abdon was from the city of Pirathon. ¹⁴He had 40 sons and 30 grandsons, who rode on 70 donkeys. He judged Israel for eight years. ¹⁵Then Abdon son of Hillel died. He was buried in Pirathon in the land of Ephraim. This is in the mountains where the Amalekites lived.

THE BIRTH OF SAMSON

13 Again the people of Israel did what the Lord said was wrong. So he let the Philistines rule over them for 40 years.

²There was a man named Manoah from the city of Zorah. Manoah was from the tribe*d* of Dan. He had a wife, but she could not have children. ³The angel of the Lord appeared to Manoah's wife. He said, "You have not been able to have children. But you will become pregnant and have a son! ⁴Don't drink wine or beer. Don't eat anything that is unclean.*d* ⁵You will become pregnant and have a son. You must never cut his hair because he will be a Nazirite.*d* He will be given to God from birth. He will begin the work of saving Israel from the power of the Philistines."

⁶Then Manoah's wife went to him and told him what had happened. She said, "A man from God came to me. He looked like an angel from God. His appearance was frightening. I didn't ask him where he was from. And he didn't tell me his name. ⁷But he said to me, 'You will be pregnant and will have a son. Don't drink wine or beer. Don't eat anything that is unclean. The reason is that the boy will be a Nazirite to God. He will be that from his birth until the day of his death.'"

⁸Then Manoah said a prayer to the Lord: "Lord, I beg you to let the man of

God come to us again. Let him teach us what we should do for the boy who will be born to us."

[9]God heard Manoah's prayer. The angel of God came to Manoah's wife again. This was while she was sitting in a field. But her husband Manoah was not with her. [10]So she ran to tell him, "He is here! The man who appeared to me the other day is here!"

[11]Manoah got up and followed his wife. When he came to the man, he said, "Are you the man who spoke to my wife?"

The man said, "I am."

[12]So Manoah asked, "When what you say happens, what kind of life should the boy live? What should he do?"

[13]The angel of the Lord said, "Your wife must do everything I told her to do. [14]She must not eat anything that grows on a grapevine. She must not drink any wine or beer. She must not eat anything that is unclean. She must do everything I have commanded her to do."

[15]Manoah said to the angel of the Lord, "We would like you to stay awhile. We want to cook a young goat for you."

[16]The angel of the Lord answered, "Even if I stay awhile, I would not eat your food. But if you want to prepare something, offer a burnt offering to the Lord." (Manoah did not understand that the man was really the angel of the Lord.)

[17]Then Manoah asked the angel of the Lord, "What is your name? We want to know. Then we may honor you when what you have said really happens."

[18]The angel of the Lord said, "Why do you ask my name? It is too wonderful for you to understand." [19]Then Manoah sacrificed a young goat on a rock. He also offered some grain as a gift to the Lord. The Lord did an amazing thing. Manoah and his wife watched what happened. [20]The flames went up to the sky from the altar. As the fire burned, the angel of the Lord went up to heaven in the fire! When Manoah and his wife saw

that, they bowed facedown on the ground. [21]The angel of the Lord did not appear to them again. Then Manoah understood that the man was really the angel of the Lord. [22]Manoah said, "We have seen God! Surely we will die because of this!"

[23]But his wife said to him, "The Lord does not want to kill us. If he wanted to kill us, he would not have accepted our burnt offering or grain offering. He would not have shown us all these things. And he would not have told us all this."

[24]So the woman gave birth to a boy. She named him Samson. Samson grew, and the Lord blessed him. [25]The Spirit[d] of the Lord began to work in Samson. This was while he was in the city of Mahaneh Dan. It is between the cities of Zorah and Eshtaol.

SAMSON'S MARRIAGE

14 Samson went down to the city of Timnah. There he saw a young Philistine woman. [2]When he returned home, he said to his father and mother, "I saw a Philistine woman in Timnah. I want you to get her for me. I want to marry her."

[3]His father and mother answered, "Surely there is a woman from Israel you can marry. Do you have to marry a woman from the Philistines? The Philistines are not even circumcised."[d]

But Samson said, "Get that woman for me! She is the one I want!" [4](Samson's parents did not know that the Lord wanted this to happen. He was looking for a way to start a fight with the Philistines. They were ruling over Israel at this time.) [5]Samson went down with his father and mother to Timnah. They went as far as the vineyard near there. Suddenly, a young lion came roaring toward Samson! [6]The Spirit[d] of the Lord entered Samson with great power. Samson tore the lion apart with his bare hands. For him it was as easy as tearing apart a young goat. But Samson did not tell his father or mother what he had done. [7]Then he went down to the city. There he talked to the Philistine woman, and he liked her.

[8]Several days later Samson went back to marry her. On his way he went over to look at the body of the dead lion. He found a swarm of bees in it. They had made some honey. [9]Samson got some of the honey with his hands. He walked along eating it. When he came to his parents, he gave some to them. They ate it, too. But Samson did not tell them he had taken the honey from the body of the dead lion.

[10]Samson's father went down to see the Philistine woman. The custom was for the bridegroom to give a feast. So Samson gave a feast. [11]When the people saw him, they sent 30 men to be with him.

SAMSON'S RIDDLE

[12]Then Samson said to the 30 men, "Let me tell you a riddle. This feast will last for seven days. Try to find the answer during that time. If you can, I will give you 30 linen shirts. I will also give you 30 changes of clothes. [13]But if you can't tell me the answer, you must pay me. You must give me 30 linen shirts and 30 changes of clothes."

So they said, "Tell us your riddle. We want to hear it."

[14]Samson said,

"Out of the eater comes something to eat.

Out of the strong comes something sweet."

The 30 men tried for three days to figure it out. But they could not find the answer. [15]On the fourth[n] day, they came to Samson's wife. They said, "Did you invite us here to make us poor? Trick your husband into telling us the answer to the riddle. If you don't, we will burn you and everyone in your father's house!"

[16]So Samson's wife went to him and began crying. She said, "You hate me!

You don't really love me! You told my people a riddle, but you won't tell me the answer."

Samson said, "I haven't even told my father or mother. Why should I tell you?"

[17]Samson's wife cried for the rest of the seven days of the feast. So he finally gave her the answer on the seventh day. He told her because she kept bothering him. Then she told her people the answer to the riddle.

[18]Before sunset on the seventh day of the feast, the Philistine men had the answer. They came to Samson and said,

"What is sweeter than honey?

What is stronger than a lion?"

Then Samson said to them,

"If you had not plowed with my little cow,

you would not have solved my riddle!"

[19]The Spirit[d] of the Lord entered Samson and gave him great power. Samson went down to the city of Ashkelon. He killed 30 of their men and took all their clothes and property. He gave those clothes to the men who had answered his riddle. Then he went to his father's house very angry. [20]And Samson's wife was given to his best man at the wedding.

SAMSON TROUBLES THE PHILISTINES

15 At the time of the wheat harvest, Samson went to visit his wife. He took a young goat with him. He said, "I'm going to my wife's room." But her father would not let Samson go in.

[2]He said to Samson, "I thought you really hated your wife. So I gave her to the best man from the wedding. Her younger sister is more beautiful. Take her."

[3]But Samson said to him, "Now I have a good reason to hurt you Philistines. No one will blame me!" [4]So Samson went out and caught 300 foxes. He took 2 foxes at a time and tied their tails together. Then he tied a torch to the tails

---

14:15 fourth The Hebrew word is "seventh." Some old translations say "fourth," which fits the order of events better.

of each pair of foxes. [5]Samson lit the torches. Then he let the foxes loose in the grainfields of the Philistines. In this way he burned up their standing grain and the piles of grain. He also burned up their vineyards and their olive trees.

[6]The Philistines asked, "Who did this?"

Someone told them, "Samson, the son-in-law of the man from Timnah, did. He did this because his father-in-law gave his wife to his best man."

So the Philistines burned Samson's wife and her father to death. [7]Then Samson said to the Philistines, "Since you did this, I will hurt you, too! I won't stop until I pay you back!" [8]Samson attacked the Philistines and killed many of them. Then he went down and stayed in a cave. It was in the rock of Etam.

[9]Then the Philistines went up and camped in the land of Judah. They stopped near a place named Lehi. [10]The men of Judah asked them, "Why have you come here to fight us?"

They answered, "We have come to make Samson our prisoner. We want to pay him back for what he did to our people."

[11]Then 3,000 men of Judah went to the cave in the rock of Etam. They said to Samson, "What have you done to us? Don't you know that the Philistines rule over us?"

Samson answered, "I only paid them back for what they did to me!"

[12]Then they said to him, "We have come to tie you up. We will give you to the Philistines."

Samson said to them, "Promise me you will not hurt me yourselves."

[13]The men from Judah said, "We agree. We will just tie you up and give you to the Philistines. We will not kill you." So they tied Samson with two new ropes. Then they led him up from the cave in the rock. [14]When Samson came to the place named Lehi, the Philistines came to meet him. They were shouting for joy. Then the Spirit[d] of the Lord entered Samson and gave him great power. The ropes on him became weak like strings that had been burned. They fell off his hands! [15]Samson found a jawbone of a donkey that had just died. He took it and killed 1,000 men with it!

[16]Then Samson said,

"With a donkey's jawbone
　I have made donkeys out of them.
With a donkey's jawbone
　I have killed 1,000 men!"

[17]When he finished speaking, he threw away the jawbone. So that place was named Ramath Lehi.[n]

[18]Samson was very thirsty. So he cried out to the Lord. He said, "I am your servant. You gave me this great victory. Do I have to die of thirst now? Do I have to be captured by people who are not circumcised?"[d] [19]Then God opened up a hole in the ground at Lehi, and water came out. When Samson drank that water, he felt better. He felt strong again. So he named that spring Caller's Spring. It is still there in Lehi to this day.

[20]So Samson judged Israel for 20 years. That was in the days of the Philistines.

SAMSON GOES TO THE CITY OF GAZA

16 One day Samson went to Gaza. He saw a prostitute[d] there. He went in to spend the night with her. [2]Someone told the people of Gaza, "Samson has come here!" So they surrounded the place and hid and waited for him. Remaining very quiet, they stayed near the city gate all night. They said to each other, "When dawn comes, we will kill Samson!"

[3]But Samson only stayed with the prostitute until midnight. Then he got up and took hold of the doors and the two posts of the city gate. He tore them loose, along with the bar. Then he put them on his

---

15:17 **Ramath Lehi** This name means Jawbone Hill.

shoulders. And he carried them to the top of the hill that faces the city of Hebron!

SAMSON AND DELILAH

[4]After this, Samson fell in love with a woman named Delilah. She lived in the Valley of Sorek. [5]The kings of the Philistines went to Delilah. They said, "Try to find out what makes Samson so strong. Try to trick him into telling you. Find out how we could capture him and tie him up. Then we will be able to control him. If you do this, each one of us will give you 28 pounds of silver."

[6]So Delilah said to Samson, "Tell me why you are so strong. How could someone tie you up and take control of you?"

[7]Samson answered, "Someone would have to tie me up. He would have to use seven new bowstrings that have not been dried. If he did that, I would be as weak as any other man."

[8]Then the kings of the Philistines brought seven new bowstrings to Delilah. They had not been dried. She tied Samson with them. [9]Some men were hiding in another room. Delilah said to Samson, "Samson, the Philistines are about to capture you!" But Samson easily broke the bowstrings. They broke like pieces of string burned in a fire. So the Philistines did not find out the secret of Samson's strength.

[10]Then Delilah said to Samson, "You've made me look foolish. You lied to me. Please tell me. How could someone tie you up?"

[11]Samson said, "They would have to tie me with new ropes that have not been used before. Then I would become as weak as any other man."

[12]So Delilah took new ropes and tied Samson. Some men were hiding in another room. Then she called out to him, "Samson, the Philistines are about to capture you!" But he broke the ropes as easily as if they were threads.

[13]Then Delilah said to Samson, "Until now, you have made me look foolish. You have lied to me. Tell me how someone could tie you up."

He said, "Use the loom.[n] Weave the seven braids of my hair into the cloth. Tighten it with a pin. Then I will become as weak as any other man."

Then Samson went to sleep. So Delilah wove the seven braids of his hair into the cloth. [14]Then she fastened it with a pin.

Again she called out to him, "Samson, the Philistines are about to capture you!" Samson woke up and pulled up the pin and the loom with the cloth.

[15]Then Delilah said to him, "How can you say, 'I love you,' when you don't even trust me? This is the third time you have made me look foolish. You haven't told me the secret of your great strength."

[16]She kept bothering Samson about his secret day after day. He became so tired of it he felt he was going to die!

[17]So he told her everything. He said, "I have never had my hair cut. I have been set apart to God as a Nazirite[d] since I was born. If someone shaved my head, then I would lose my strength. I would become as weak as any other man."

[18]Delilah saw that he had told her everything sincerely. So she sent a message to the kings of the Philistines. She said, "Come back one more time. He has told me everything." So the kings of the Philistines came back to Delilah. They brought the silver they had promised to give her. [19]Delilah got Samson to go to sleep. He was lying in her lap. Then she called in a man to shave off the seven braids of Samson's hair. In this way she began to make him weak. And Samson's strength left him.

[20]Then she called out to him, "Samson, the Philistines are about to capture you!"

He woke up and thought, "I'll get loose as I did before and shake myself free."

16:13 **loom** A machine for making cloth from thread.

But he did not know that the Lord had left him.

21Then the Philistines captured Samson. They tore out his eyes. And they took him down to Gaza. They put bronze chains on him. They put him in prison and made him grind grain. 22But his hair began to grow again.

SAMSON DIES

23The kings of the Philistines gathered to celebrate. They were going to offer a great sacrifice to their god Dagon.d They said, "Our god has given us Samson our enemy." 24When they saw him, they praised their god. They said,

"This man destroyed our country.
   He killed many of us!
But our god helped us
   capture our enemy."

25The people were having a good time at the celebration. They said, "Bring Samson out to perform for us." So they brought Samson from the prison. He performed for them. They made him stand between the pillars of the temple of Dagon. 26A servant was holding his hand. Samson said to him, "Let me feel the pillars that hold up the temple. I want to lean against them." 27Now the temple was full of men and women. All the kings of the Philistines were there. There were about 3,000 men and women on the roof.n They watched Samson perform. 28Then Samson prayed to the Lord. He said, "Lord God, remember me. God, please give me strength one more time. Let me pay these Philistines back for putting out my two eyes!" 29Then Samson held the two center pillars of the temple. These two pillars supported the whole temple. He braced himself between the two pillars. His right hand was on one, and his left hand was on the other. 30Samson said, "Let me die with these

Philistines!" Then he pushed as hard as he could. And the temple fell on the kings and all the people in it. So Samson killed more of the Philistines when he died than when he was alive.

31Samson's brothers and his whole family went down to get his body. They brought him back and buried him in the tomb of Manoah, his father. That tomb is between the cities of Zorah and Eshtaol. Samson was a judge for the people of Israel for 20 years.

MICAH'S IDOLS

17 There was a man named Micah. He lived in the mountains of Ephraim. 2He said to his mother, "You remember the 28 pounds of silver that were taken from you. I heard you say a curse about it. I have the silver with me. I took it."

His mother said, "The Lord bless you, my son!"

3Micah gave the 28 pounds of silver to his mother. Then she said, "I will give this silver to the Lord. I will have my son make a carved idol and an idol of melted silver. So I will give the silver back to you."

4So he gave the silver back to his mother. She took about 5 pounds of the silver and gave it to a silversmith. He used it to make a carved idol and an idol of melted silver. The idols were put in Micah's house. 5Micah had a temple for worshiping idols. He made a vestd for a priest and some household idols. Then Micah chose one of his sons to be his priest. 6At that time the Israelites did not have a king. So everyone did what he thought was right.

7There was a young man who was a Levite.n He was from the city of Bethlehem in the land of Judah. He had been living with the people of Judah. 8He left Bethlehem to look for another place to

---

16:27 **roof** In Bible times houses were built with flat roofs. The roof was used for drying things such as flax and fruit. And it was used as an extra room, as a place for worship and as a place to sleep in the summer.
17:7 **Levite** The Levites were the only ones God had appointed as priests.

live. On his way he came to Micah's house. It was in the mountains of Ephraim. [9]Micah asked him, "Where have you come from?"

He answered, "I'm a Levite from Bethlehem in Judah. I'm looking for a place to live."

[10]Then Micah said to him, "Live with me. Be my father and my priest. I will give you 4 ounces of silver each year. I will also give you clothes and food." So the Levite went in. [11]The young Levite agreed to live with Micah. He became like one of Micah's own sons. [12]Micah made him a priest. And he lived in Micah's house. [13]Then Micah said, "Now I know the Lord will be good to me. I know this because I have a Levite as my priest!"

DAN'S FAMILY CAPTURES LAISH

18 At that time the Israelites did not have a king. The people of Dan were still looking for a land where they could live. They wanted a land of their own. The other tribes[d] of Israel already had their own lands. But the Danites did not yet have their own land. [2]So they chose five soldiers from all their family groups. These five men were from the cities of Zorah and Eshtaol. They sent the men to spy out and explore the land. They were told, "Go, explore the land."

So they came to the mountains of Ephraim. They came to Micah's house, where they spent the night. [3]When they came near Micah's house, they recognized the voice of the young Levite.[n] So they stopped at Micah's house. They asked the young Levite, "Who brought you to this place? What are you doing here? Why are you here?"

[4]He told them what Micah had done for him. "He has hired me. I am his priest."

[5]They said to him, "Please ask God something for us. Will our search for a place to live be successful?"

[6]The priest said to them, "Go in peace. The Lord is pleased with your journey."

[7]So the five men left. They came to the city of Laish. They saw that the people there lived in safety. They were like the people of Sidon. They lived in peace and were not afraid of others. They had plenty of everything. They lived a long way from the Sidonians. And they had no dealings with anyone else.

[8]The five men went back to Zorah and Eshtaol. Their relatives asked them, "What did you find?"

[9]They answered, "We have seen the land. And it is very good. We should attack them. Aren't you going to do something? Don't wait! Let's go and take that land! [10]When you go, you will see there is plenty of land. There is plenty of everything! The people are not expecting an attack. Surely God has given that land to us!"

[11]So 600 men of Dan left Zorah and Eshtaol. They were ready for war. [12]On their way they stopped near the city of Kiriath Jearim in Judah. They set up camp there. That is why the place is named Mahaneh Dan[n] to this very day. It is west of Kiriath Jearim. [13]From there they traveled on to the mountains of Ephraim. Then they came to Micah's house.

[14]So the five men who had explored the land around Laish spoke. They said to their relatives, "There is a vest[d] for a priest in one of these houses. And there are household gods in these houses. There are also a carved idol and an idol of melted silver in these houses. You know what to do." [15]So they stopped at the Levite's house. This was also Micah's house. And they greeted the Levite. [16]The 600 men of Dan stood at the gate entrance. They wore their weapons of war. [17]The five spies went into the house.

18:3 **Levite** The Levites were the only ones God had appointed as priests.
18:12 **Mahaneh Dan** This name means "the camp of Dan."

They took the carved idol, the vest for a priest, the household idols and the silver idol. The priest and the 600 men ready for war stood by the gate entrance.

¹⁸When the spies went into Micah's house and took the carved image, the vest for a priest, the household idols and the silver idol, the priest asked them, "What are you doing?"

¹⁹They answered, "Be quiet! Don't say a word. Come with us. Be our father and our priest. Is it better for you to be a priest for the people in one man's house? Or is it better for you to be a priest for a tribe*d* and family group in Israel?" ²⁰This made the Levite happy. So he took the vest for a priest, the household idols and the carved idol. And he went with the men of Dan. ²¹They left Micah's house. They put their little children, their animals and everything they owned in front of them.

²²The men of Dan went a long way from Micah's house. Then the men who lived near Micah were called out. They chased the men of Dan and caught up with them. ²³The men with Micah shouted at the men of Dan. The men of Dan turned around. They said to Micah, "What's the matter with you? Why have you called out your men to fight?"

²⁴Micah answered, "You took my idols! I made those idols. You have also taken my priest. What do I have left? How can you ask me, 'What's the matter?'"

²⁵The men of Dan answered, "You should not argue with us. Some of our men have hot tempers. If you shout at us, they might attack you. You and your family might be killed." ²⁶Then the men of Dan went on their way. Micah knew they were too strong for him. So he turned and went back home.

²⁷So the men of Dan took what Micah had made. They also took his priest and went on to Laish. They attacked those peaceful people. The people of Laish had not expected an attack. The men of Dan killed them with their swords. Then they burned the city. ²⁸There was no one to save the people of Laish. They lived too far from Sidon. And they had no dealings with anyone else. Laish was in a valley near Beth Rehob.

The people of Dan rebuilt the city in that place. And they lived there. ²⁹They changed the name of Laish to Dan. They named it after their ancestor Dan. He was one of the sons of Israel.

³⁰The people of Dan set up the idols in the city of Dan. They made Jonathan son of Gershom their priest. Gershom was the son of Moses. Jonathan and his sons were priests for the tribe of Dan. They served as priests until the Israelites were taken captive. ³¹The people of Dan worshiped the idols Micah had made. They worshiped them as long as the Holy Tent*d* of God was in Shiloh.

A LEVITE AND HIS SERVANT

19 At that time the people of Israel did not have a king.

There was a Levite who lived in the faraway part of the mountains of Ephraim. He had taken a slave woman.*d* She was from the city of Bethlehem in the land of Judah. ²But she was unfaithful to him. She left him and went back to her father's house. It was in Bethlehem in Judah. She stayed there for four months. ³Then her husband went to ask her to come back to him. He took with him his servant and two donkeys. The Levite came to her father's house. And she invited the Levite to come in. Her father was happy to see him. ⁴The father-in-law, the young woman's father, asked him to stay. So he stayed for three days. He ate, drank and slept there.

⁵On the fourth day they got up early in the morning. The Levite was getting ready to leave. But the woman's father said to his son-in-law, "Refresh yourself by eating something. Then you may go." ⁶So the two men sat down to eat and drink together. After that, the father said to him, "Please stay tonight. Relax and

enjoy yourself." ⁷When the man got up to go, his father-in-law asked him to stay. So he stayed again that night. ⁸On the fifth day the man got up early in the morning to leave. The woman's father said, "Refresh yourself. Wait until this afternoon." So the two men ate together.

⁹Then the Levite, his slave woman and his servant got up to leave. His father-in-law, the young woman's father, said, "It's almost night. The day is almost gone. So spend the night here and enjoy yourself. Tomorrow morning you may get up early and go on your way home." ¹⁰But the Levite did not want to stay another night. He took his two saddled donkeys and his slave woman. He traveled toward the city of Jebus. (Jebus is another name for Jerusalem.)

¹¹The day was almost over. They were near Jebus. So the servant said to his master, "Let's stop at this city. It's the city of the Jebusite people. Let's spend the night here."

¹²But his master said, "No. We won't go inside a strange city. Those people are not Israelites. We will go on to the city of Gibeah." ¹³Then he said, "Come on. Let's try to make it to Gibeah or Ramah. We can spend the night in one of those cities." ¹⁴So they went on. And the sun went down as they came near Gibeah. Gibeah belongs to the tribeᵈ of Benjamin. ¹⁵So they stopped there to spend the night. They came to the public square in the middle of the city and sat down. But no one invited them home to spend the night.

¹⁶That evening an old man came into the city from his work in the fields. His home was in the mountains of Ephraim. But now he was living in Gibeah. (The men of Gibeah were from the tribe of Benjamin.) ¹⁷He saw the traveler, the Levite, in the public square. He asked, "Where are you going? Where did you come from?"

¹⁸The Levite answered, "We are traveling from Bethlehem in Judah. We're going to my home. I'm from a faraway part of the mountains of Ephraim. I have been to Bethlehem in Judah. Now I am going to the Holy Tentᵈ of the Lord. No one has invited me to stay in his house. ¹⁹We already have straw and food for our donkeys. There is bread and wine for me, the young woman and my servant. We don't need anything."

²⁰The old man said, "You are welcome to stay at my house. Let me give you anything you need. But don't spend the night in the public square." ²¹So the old man took the Levite into his house. He fed their donkeys, and they washed their feet. Then he gave them something to eat and drink.

²²While they were enjoying themselves, some wicked men of the city surrounded the house. They beat on the door. They shouted to the old man who owned the house. They said, "Bring out the man who came to your house. We want to have sexual relations with him."

²³The owner of the house went outside. And he said to them, "No, my friends. Don't be so evil. This man is a guest in my house. Don't do this terrible thing! ²⁴Look, here is my daughter. She has never had sexual relations before. And here is the man's slave woman. I will bring them out to you now. Do anything you want with them. But don't do such a terrible thing to this man."

²⁵But the men would not listen to him. So the Levite took his slave woman and sent her outside to them. They had sexual relations with her even though she didn't want to. They treated her very badly all night long. Then, at dawn, they let her go. ²⁶She came back to the house where her master was staying. She fell down at the door and lay there until daylight.

²⁷In the morning the Levite got up. He opened the door of the house. He went outside to go on his way. But there lay his slave woman. She had fallen down at the doorway of the house. Her hands

were on the doorsill. [28]Then the Levite said to her, "Get up; let's go." But she did not answer. So he put her on his donkey and went home.

[29]When the Levite got home, he took a knife and cut his slave woman into 12 parts. Then he sent a part to each of the areas where the people of Israel lived. [30]Everyone who saw this said, "Nothing like this has ever happened before. It has never happened since the people of Israel came out of Egypt. Think about it. Tell us what to do."

THE WAR BETWEEN ISRAEL AND BENJAMIN

20 So all the Israelites joined together. They came to stand before the Lord in the city of Mizpah. They came from as far away as the cities of Dan and Beersheba.[n] Even the Israelites from the land of Gilead were there. [2]The leaders of all the tribes[d] of Israel were there. They took their places in the meeting of the people of God. There were 400,000 soldiers with swords. [3](The people of Benjamin heard that the Israelites had gone up to Mizpah.) Then the Israelites said to the Levite, "Tell us how this evil thing happened."

[4]So the husband of the murdered woman answered: "My slave woman[d] and I came to Gibeah in Benjamin to spend the night. [5]During the night the men of Gibeah came after me. They surrounded the house and wanted to kill me. They had sexual relations with my slave woman even though she didn't want to. And she died! [6]So I took her and cut her into parts. Then I sent one part to each area of Israel's land. I did it because the people of Benjamin have done this wicked and terrible thing in Israel. [7]Now, all you men of Israel, speak up. Tell what you have decided we should do."

[8]Then all the people stood up at the same time. They said, "None of us will go home. Not one of us will go back to his house! [9]Now this is what we will do to Gibeah. We will throw lots[d] so that God can show us what to do. [10]We will choose 10 men from each 100 men. They will be from all the tribes of Israel. And we will choose 100 men from each 1,000. We will choose 1,000 men from each 10,000. These men will find supplies for the army. Then the army will go to the city of Gibeah of Benjamin. They will repay those people for the terrible thing they have done in Israel." [11]So all the men of Israel gathered against the city. They all agreed about what they were doing.

[12]The tribes of Israel sent men to all the family groups of Benjamin with a message. They said, "What is this evil thing some of your men have done? [13]Give up the evil men in Gibeah so that we can put them to death. We must remove this evil from Israel."

But the Benjaminites would not listen to their relatives, the people of Israel. [14]The Benjaminites left their own cities and met at Gibeah. They went to fight against the Israelites. [15]In only one day the Benjaminites got 26,000 soldiers together. These soldiers were trained with swords. They also had 700 chosen men from Gibeah. [16]Seven hundred of these trained soldiers were left-handed. Each of these left-handed soldiers could sling a stone at a hair and not miss!

[17]The Israelites, except for the Benjaminites, gathered 400,000 fighting men. These 400,000 men used swords and were trained soldiers.

[18]The Israelites went up to the city of Bethel. They asked God, "Which tribe shall be first to attack the Benjaminites?"

The Lord answered, "Judah shall go first."

[19]The next morning the Israelites got up. They made a camp near Gibeah.

20:1 **Dan ... Beersheba** Dan was the city farthest north in Israel. Beersheba was the city farthest south. So this means all the people of Israel.

[20]Then the men of Israel went out to fight the Benjaminites. The Israelites got into battle position at Gibeah. [21]Then the Benjaminites came out of Gibeah. They killed 22,000 Israelites during the battle that day. [22-23]The Israelites went before the Lord. They cried until evening. They asked the Lord, "Shall we go to fight our relatives, the Benjaminites, again?"

The Lord answered, "Go up and fight them." The men of Israel encouraged each other. So they took the same battle positions they had taken the first day.

[24]The Israelites brought their battle lines against the Benjaminites the second day. [25]The Benjaminites came out of Gibeah to attack the Israelites. This time, the Benjaminites killed 18,000 Israelites. All of these Israelites had been trained with swords.

[26]Then the Israelites went up to Bethel. There they sat down and cried to the Lord. They went without food all day until evening. They also brought burnt offerings and fellowship offerings to the Lord. [27]The Israelites asked the Lord a question. (In those days the Box[d] of the Agreement with God was there at Bethel. [28]A priest named Phinehas served before the Box of the Agreement. He was the son of Eleazar, who was the son of Aaron.) The people of Israel asked, "Shall we again go to fight against our relatives the Benjaminites? Or shall we stop fighting?"

The Lord answered, "Go, because tomorrow I will help you defeat them."

[29]Then the Israelites hid some men all around Gibeah. [30]They went to fight against the Benjaminites at Gibeah on the third day. They got into position for battle, as they had done before. [31]Then the Benjaminites came out of the city to fight them. The Israelites backed up and led the Benjaminites away from the city. The Benjaminites began to kill some of the Israelites as they had done before. About 30 men from Israel were killed.

Some of them were killed in the fields and some on the roads. One road led to Bethel. Another road led to Gibeah.

[32]The Benjaminites said, "We are winning as before!"

But the Israelites said, "Let's run. Let's trick them into going farther away from their city and onto the roads."

[33]All the men of Israel moved from their places. They got into battle positions at a place named Baal Tamar. Then the Israelites ran out from their hiding places west of Gibeah. [34]Ten thousand of the best trained soldiers from the army of Israel attacked Gibeah. The battle was very hard. The Benjaminites did not know disaster was about to come to them. [35]The Lord used the Israelites to defeat the Benjaminites. On that day the Israelites killed 25,100 Benjaminites. All these men were armed with swords. [36]Then the Benjaminites saw that they were defeated.

The men of Israel had moved back. They backed up because they were depending on the surprise attack. They had set it up near Gibeah. [37]The men in hiding rushed into Gibeah. They spread out and killed everyone in the city with their swords. [38]Now the men of Israel had made a plan with the men in hiding. The men in the surprise attack were to send up a signal. It was to be a big cloud of smoke from the city. [39]So the army of Israel turned around in the battle.

The Benjaminites had killed about 30 Israelites. They were saying, "We are winning, as in the first battle!" [40]But then the big cloud of smoke began to rise from the city. The Benjaminites turned around and saw it. The whole city was full of smoke that went up into the sky. [41]Then the Israelites turned and began to fight. The Benjaminites were terrified. Now they knew that disaster was coming to them. [42]So the Benjaminites ran away from the Israelites. They ran toward the desert. But they could not escape the battle. And the Israelites who came out of the cities killed them. [43]They surrounded the Benjaminites and chased them. They caught them in the area east of Gibeah. [44]So 18,000 brave and strong Benjaminite fighters were killed. [45]The Benjaminites ran toward the desert. They ran to a place called the rock of Rimmon. But the Israelites killed 5,000 Benjaminites along the roads. They kept chasing them as far as a place named Gidom. And they killed 2,000 more Benjaminites there.

[46]On that day 25,000 Benjaminites were killed. All of them had fought bravely with swords. [47]But 600 Benjaminites ran to the rock of Rimmon in the desert. They stayed there for four months. [48]Then the men of Israel went back to the land of Benjamin. They killed the people in every city. They also killed the animals. They destroyed everything they could find. And they burned every city they found.

WIVES FOR THE MEN OF BENJAMIN

21 At Mizpah the men of Israel had made a promise. This was their promise: "Not one of us will let his daughter marry a man from the tribe[d] of Benjamin."

[2]The people went to the city of Bethel. There they sat before God until evening, crying loudly. [3]They said, "Lord, you are the God of Israel. Why has this terrible thing happened to us? Why has one tribe of Israel been taken away?"

[4]Early the next day the people built an altar. They put burnt offerings and fellowship offerings to God on it.

[5]Then the Israelites asked, "Did any tribe of Israel not come here to meet with us before the Lord?" They asked this question because they had made a great promise. They had promised that anyone who did not meet with them at Mizpah would be killed.

[6]The Israelites felt sorry for their relatives, the Benjaminites. They said, "Today one tribe has been separated from Israel. [7]We made a promise before the Lord. We will not allow our daughters to marry a Benjaminite. How can we make sure that the men of Benjamin will have wives?" [8]Then they asked, "Which one of the tribes of Israel did not come here to Mizpah?" They found that no one from the city of Jabesh Gilead was there. [9]The people of Israel counted everyone, but no one from Jabesh Gilead was there.

[10]So the whole group of Israelites sent 12,000 soldiers to Jabesh Gilead. They told the soldiers to kill the people in Jabesh Gilead with their swords. Even the women and children were to be killed. [11]"This is what you must do: Kill every man in Jabesh Gilead. Also kill every woman who has had sexual relations with a man." [12]The soldiers found 400 young women in Jabesh Gilead who had never had sexual relations with a man. They brought these women to the camp at Shiloh in Canaan.

[13]Then the whole group of Israelites sent a message to the men of Benjamin. They offered to make peace with them. The men of Benjamin were at the rock of Rimmon. [14]So the men of Benjamin came back at that time. The Israelites gave them the women from Jabesh Gilead who had not been killed. But there were not enough women for all of them.

[15]The people of Israel felt sorry for the Benjaminites. This was because the Lord had separated the tribes of Israel. [16]The elders of the Israelites spoke. They said, "The women of Benjamin have been killed. Where can we get wives for the men of Benjamin who are still alive? [17]These men must have children to continue their families. This is so a tribe in Israel will not die out. [18]But we cannot allow our daughters to marry them. We have made this promise: 'Anyone who gives a wife to a man of Benjamin is cursed.' [19]We have an idea! There is a yearly festival of the Lord at Shiloh. Shiloh is north of the city of Bethel. It is east of the road that goes from Bethel to

Shechem. And it is south of the city of Lebonah."

²⁰So the elders told the men of Benjamin about their idea. They said, "Go and hide in the vineyards. ²¹Watch for the young women from Shiloh to come out. They will come to join the dancing. Then run out from the vineyards. Each of you take one of the young Shiloh women and go to the land of Benjamin. ²²The fathers or brothers of those young women will come to us. They will complain, but we will say: 'Be kind to the men of Benjamin. We did not get wives for Benjamin during the war. And you did not give the women to the men from Benjamin. So you are not guilty.'"

²³So that is what the Benjaminites did. While the young women were dancing, each man caught one of them. They took them away and married them. Then they went back to the land God had given them. They rebuilt their cities and lived there.

²⁴Then the Israelites went home. They went to their own tribes and family groups. They went to their own land that God had given them.

²⁵In those days the Israelites did not have a king. Everyone did what he thought was right.

RUTH

THE STORY OF A GIRL FROM MOAB

1 [1-2]Long ago the judges[n] ruled Israel. During their rule, there was a time in the land when there was not enough food to eat. A man named Elimelech left Bethlehem in Judah and moved to the country of Moab. He took his wife and his two sons with him. His wife was named Naomi, and his two sons were named Mahlon and Kilion. These people were from the Ephrathah district around Bethlehem in Judah. The family traveled to Moab and lived there.

[3]Later, Naomi's husband, Elimelech, died. So only Naomi and her two sons were left. [4]These sons married women from Moab. The name of one wife was Orpah. The name of the other wife was Ruth. Naomi and her sons lived in Moab about ten years. [5]Then Mahlon and Kilion also died. So Naomi was left alone without her husband or her two sons.

[6]While Naomi was in Moab, she heard that the Lord had taken care of his people. He had given food to them in Judah. So Naomi got ready to leave Moab and go back home. The wives of Naomi's sons also got ready to go with her. [7]So they left the place where they had lived. And they started back on the way to the land of Judah. [8]But Naomi said to her two daughters-in-law, "Go back home. Each of you go to your own mother's house. You have been very kind to me and to my sons who are now dead. I hope the Lord will also be kind to you in the same way. [9]I hope the Lord will give you another home and a new husband."

Then Naomi kissed the women. And they began to cry out loud. [10]Her daughters-in-law said to her, "No. We will go with you to your people."

[11]But Naomi said, "My daughters, go back to your own homes. Why do you want to go with me? I cannot give birth to more sons to give you new husbands. [12]So go back to your own homes. I am too old to have another husband. But even if I had another husband tonight and if I had more sons, it wouldn't help! [13]Would you wait until the babies were grown into men? Would you live for so many years without husbands? Don't do this thing. My life is much too sad for you to share. This is because the Lord is against me!"

[14]The women cried together again. Then Orpah kissed Naomi good-bye, but Ruth held on to her.

[15]Naomi said, "Look, your sister-in-law is going back to her own people and her own gods. Go back with her."

RUTH STAYS WITH NAOMI

[16]But Ruth said, "Don't ask me to leave you! Don't beg me not to follow you! Every place you go, I will go. Every place you live, I will live. Your people will be my people. Your God will be my God. [17]And where you die, I will die. And there I will be buried. I ask the Lord to punish me terribly if I do not keep this promise: Only death will separate us."

[18]Naomi saw that Ruth had made up her mind to go with her. So Naomi stopped arguing with her. [19]Naomi and Ruth went on until they came to the town of Bethlehem. When the two women entered Bethlehem, all the people became very excited. The women of the town said, "Is this Naomi?"

[20]But Naomi told the people, "Don't call me Naomi.[n] Call me Mara,[n] because God All-Powerful has made my life very sad. [21]When I left, I had all I wanted. But now, the Lord has brought me home

---

1:1-2 judges They were not judges in courts of law, but leaders of the people in times of emergency.
1:20 Naomi This name means "happy" or "pleasant."
1:20 Mara This name means "bitter" or "sad."

with nothing. So why should you call me Naomi when the Lord has spoken against me? God All-Powerful has given me much trouble."

²²So Naomi and her daughter-in-law Ruth, the woman from Moab, came back from Moab. They came to Bethlehem at the beginning of the barley harvest.

RUTH MEETS BOAZ

2 Now there was a rich man living in Bethlehem whose name was Boaz. Boaz was one of Naomi's close relatives from Elimelech's family.

²One day Ruth, the woman from Moab, said to Naomi, "Let me go to the fields. Maybe someone will be kind and let me gather the grain he leaves in his field."

Naomi said, "Go, my daughter."

³So Ruth went to the fields. She followed the workers who were cutting the grain. And she gathered the grain that they had left. It just so happened that the field belonged to Boaz. He was a close relative from Elimelech's family.

⁴When Boaz came from Bethlehem, he spoke to his workers: "The Lord be with you!"

And the workers answered, "May the Lord bless you!"

⁵Then Boaz spoke to his servant who was in charge of the workers. He asked, "Whose girl is that?"

⁶The servant answered, "She is the Moabite woman who came with Naomi from the country of Moab. ⁷She said, 'Please let me follow the workers and gather the grain that they leave on the ground.' She came and has remained here. From morning until just now, she has stopped only a few moments to rest in the shelter."

⁸Then Boaz said to Ruth, "Listen, my daughter. Stay here in my field to gather grain for yourself. Do not go to any other person's field. Continue following behind my women workers. ⁹Watch to see which fields they go to and follow them. I have warned the young men not to bother

you. When you are thirsty, you may go and drink. Take water from the water jugs that the servants have filled."

¹⁰Then Ruth bowed low with her face to the ground. She said to Boaz, "I am a stranger. Why have you been so kind to notice me?"

¹¹Boaz answered her, "I know about all the help you have given to Naomi, your mother-in-law. You helped her even after your husband died. You left your father and mother and your own country. You came to this nation where you did not know anyone. ¹²The Lord will reward you for all you have done. You will be paid in full by the Lord, the God of Israel. You have come to him as a little bird finds shelter under the wings of its mother."

¹³Then Ruth said, "You are very kind to me, sir. You have said kind words to me, your servant. You have given me hope. And I am not even good enough to be one of your servants."

¹⁴At mealtime Boaz told Ruth, "Come here! Eat some of our bread. Here, dip your bread in our vinegar."

So Ruth sat down with the workers. Boaz gave her some roasted grain. Ruth ate until she was full, and there was some food left over. ¹⁵Ruth rose and went back to work. Then Boaz told his servants, "Let her gather even around the bundles of grain. Don't tell her to go away. ¹⁶Drop some full heads of grain for her. Let her gather that grain, and don't tell her to stop."

¹⁷So Ruth gathered grain in the field until evening. Then she separated the grain from the chaff.ᵈ There was about one-half bushel of barley. ¹⁸Ruth carried the grain into town. And her mother-in-law saw what she had gathered. Ruth also gave her the food that was left over from lunch.

¹⁹Naomi asked her, "Where did you gather all this grain today? Where did you work? Blessed be the man who noticed you!"

Ruth told her about whose field she had worked in. She said, "The man I worked with today is named Boaz."

²⁰Naomi told her daughter-in-law, "The Lord bless him! The Lord still continues to be kind to all people—the living and the dead!" Then Naomi told Ruth, "Boaz is one of our close relatives,ⁿ one who will take care of us."

²¹Then Ruth said, "Boaz also told me to come back and continue working. He said, 'Keep close by my servants until they have finished the harvest.'"

²²Then Naomi said to her daughter-in-law Ruth, "It is good for you to continue working with his women servants. If you work in another field, someone might hurt you." ²³So Ruth continued working closely with the women servants of Boaz. She gathered grain until the barley harvest was finished. She also worked there through the end of the wheat harvest. And Ruth continued to live with Naomi, her mother-in-law.

NAOMI'S PLAN

3 Then Naomi, Ruth's mother-in-law, said to her, "My daughter, I must find a suitable home for you. That would be good for you. ²Now Boaz is our close relative.ⁿ You worked with his women servants. Tonight he will be working at the threshingᵈ floor. ³Go wash yourself and put on perfume. Change your clothes, and go down to the threshing floor. But don't let him see you until he has finished eating and drinking. ⁴Then he will lie down. Watch him so you will know the place where he lies down. Go there and lift the cover off his feetⁿ and lie down. He will tell you what you should do."

⁵Then Ruth answered, "I will do everything you say."

⁶So Ruth went down to the threshing floor. She did all her mother-in-law told her to do. ⁷After eating and drinking, Boaz was feeling good. He went to lie down beside the pile of grain. Then Ruth went to him quietly. She lifted the cover from his feet and lay down.

⁸About midnight Boaz woke up suddenly and rolled over. He was startled! There was a woman lying near his feet! ⁹Boaz asked, "Who are you?"

She said, "I am Ruth, your servant girl. Spread your cover over me because you are the one who is to take care of me."

¹⁰Then Boaz said, "The Lord bless you, my daughter. Your kindness to me is greater than the kindness you showed to Naomi in the beginning. You didn't look for a young man to marry, either rich or poor. ¹¹Now, my daughter, don't be afraid. I will do everything you ask. All the people in our town know you are a very good woman. ¹²And it is true, I am a relative who is to take care of you. But there is a man who is a closer relative to you than I. ¹³But stay here tonight. In the morning we will see if he will take care of you. If he decides to take care of you, that is fine. If he refuses to take care of you, I myself will marry you. Then I will buy back Elimelech's land for you. As surely as the Lord lives, I promise to do this. So lie here until morning."

¹⁴So Ruth lay near his feet until the morning. She rose while it was still too dark to be recognized. Boaz said to his servants, "Don't tell anyone that the woman came here to the threshingᵈ floor." ¹⁵Then Boaz said to Ruth, "Bring me your shawl. Now, hold it open."

So Ruth held her shawl open, and Boaz poured six portions of barley into it. Boaz then put it on her back, and she went to the city.

2:20; 3:2 close relatives In Bible times the closest relative could marry a widow without children so she could have children. He would care for this family, but they and their property would not belong to him. They would belong to the dead husband.
3:4 lift . . . feet This showed Ruth was asking him to be her husband.

[16]Ruth went to the home of her mother-in-law. And Naomi asked, "How did you do, my daughter?"

So Ruth told Naomi everything that Boaz did for her. [17]She said, "Boaz gave me these six portions of barley. He said, 'You must not go home without a gift for your mother-in-law.'"

[18]Naomi answered, "Ruth, my daughter, wait until you hear what happens. Boaz will not rest until he has finished doing what he should do this day."

BOAZ MARRIES RUTH

4 Boaz went to the city gate. He sat there until the close relative he had mentioned passed by. Boaz called to him, "Come here, friend! Sit down here!" So the man came over and sat down. [2]Boaz gathered ten of the old men who were leaders of the city. He told them, "Sit down here!" So they sat down.

[3]Then Boaz spoke to the close relative. He said, "Naomi has come back from the country of Moab. She wants to sell the piece of land that belonged to our relative Elimelech. [4]So I decided to say this to you: If you want to buy back the land, then buy it! Buy it in front of the people who live here and in front of the elders of my people. If you don't want to buy it, tell me. I am the only person after you who can buy back the land. If you don't buy it back, I will."

And the close relative said, "I will buy back the land."

[5]Then Boaz said, "When you buy the land from Naomi, you must marry Ruth, the dead man's wife. She is the woman from Moab. That way, the land will stay in her dead husband's family."

[6]The close relative answered, "Then I can't buy back the land. If I did, I might lose what I can pass on to my own sons. I cannot buy the land back. So you buy it yourself."

[7]Long ago in Israel when people traded or bought back something, one person took off his sandal and gave it to the other person. This was their proof of purchase.

[8]So the close relative said, "Buy the land yourself." And then he took off his sandal.

[9]Then Boaz spoke to the elders and to all the people. He said, "You are witnesses today of what I am buying from Naomi. I am buying everything that belonged to Elimelech and Kilion and Mahlon. [10]I am also taking Ruth as my wife. She is the Moabite who was the wife of Mahlon. I am doing this so her dead husband's property will stay with his family. This way, his name will not be separated from his family and his land. You are witnesses this day."

[11]So all the people and elders who were at the city gate said, "We are witnesses. This woman will be coming into your home. We hope the Lord will make her like Rachel and Leah. They had many children. So the people of Israel grew in number. May you become powerful in the district of Ephrathah. May you become famous in Bethlehem! [12]Tamar gave birth to Judah's son Perez.[n] In the same way, may the Lord give you many children through Ruth. And may your family be great like his."

[13]So Boaz took Ruth and married her. The Lord let her become pregnant, and she gave birth to a son. [14]The women told Naomi, "Praise the Lord who gave you this grandson. And may he become famous in Israel. [15]He will give you new life. And he will take care of you in your old age. This happened because of your daughter-in-law. She loves you. And she is better for you than seven sons. She has given birth to your grandson."

[16]Naomi took the boy, held him in her arms and cared for him. [17]The neighbors gave the boy his name. These women said, "This boy was born for Naomi."

4:12 Perez One of Boaz's ancestors.

The neighbors named him Obed. Obed was Jesse's father. And Jesse was the father of David.

¹⁸This is the family history of Perez. Perez was the father of Hezron. ¹⁹Hezron was the father of Ram. Ram was the father of Amminadab. ²⁰Amminadab was the father of Nahshon. Nahshon was the father of Salmon. ²¹Salmon was the father of Boaz. Boaz was the father of Obed. ²²Obed was the father of Jesse, and Jesse was the father of David.

SAMUEL'S BIRTH

1 There was a man named Elkanah son of Jeroham. He was from Ramathaim in the mountains of Ephraim. Elkanah was from the family of Zuph. (Jeroham was Elihu's son. Elihu was Tohu's son. And Tohu was the son of Zuph from the family group of Ephraim.) ²Elkanah had two wives. One was named Hannah, and the other was named Peninnah. Peninnah had children, but Hannah had none.

³Every year Elkanah left his town Ramah and went up to Shiloh. There he worshiped the Lord of heaven's armies and offered sacrifices to him. Shiloh was where Hophni and Phinehas served as priests of the Lord. They were the sons of Eli. ⁴When Elkanah offered sacrifices, he always gave a share of the meat to his wife Peninnah. He also gave shares of the meat to her sons and daughters. ⁵But Elkanah always gave a special share of the meat to Hannah. He did this because he loved Hannah and because the Lord had made Hannah unable to have children. ⁶Peninnah would upset Hannah and make her feel bad. She did this because the Lord had made Hannah unable to have children. ⁷This happened every year when they went up to the Tent[d] of the Lord at Shiloh. Peninnah would upset Hannah until Hannah would cry and not eat anything. ⁸Her husband Elkanah would say to her, "Hannah, why are you crying? Why won't you eat? Why are you sad? Don't I mean more to you than ten sons?"

⁹Once, after they had eaten their meal in Shiloh, Hannah got up. Now Eli the priest was sitting on a chair near the entrance to the Lord's Holy Tent. ¹⁰Hannah was very sad. She cried much and prayed to the Lord. ¹¹She made a promise. She said, "Lord of heaven's armies, see how bad I feel. Remember me! Don't forget me. If you will give me a son, I will give him back to you all his life. And no one will ever use a razor to cut his hair."[n]

¹²While Hannah kept praying, Eli watched her mouth. ¹³She was praying in her heart. Her lips moved, but her voice was not heard. So Eli thought she was drunk. ¹⁴He said to her, "Stop getting drunk! Throw away your wine!"

¹⁵Hannah answered, "No, master, I have not drunk any wine or beer. I am a woman who is deeply troubled. I was telling the Lord about all my problems. ¹⁶Don't think of me as an evil woman. I have been praying because of my many troubles and much sadness."

¹⁷Eli answered, "Go in peace. May the God of Israel give you what you asked of him."

¹⁸Hannah said, "I want to be pleasing to you always." Then she left and ate something. She was not sad anymore.

¹⁹Early the next morning Elkanah's family got up and worshiped the Lord. Then they went back home to Ramah. Elkanah had sexual relations with his wife Hannah. And the Lord remembered her. ²⁰So Hannah became pregnant, and in time she gave birth to a son. She named him Samuel.[n] She said, "His name is Samuel because I asked the Lord for him."

HANNAH GIVES SAMUEL TO GOD

²¹Every year Elkanah went to Shiloh to offer sacrifices. He went to keep the promise he had made to God. He brought his whole family with him. So once again he went up to Shiloh. ²²But

---

1:11 And . . . hair People who made special promises not to cut their hair or to drink wine or beer were called Nazirites. These people gave their lives to the Lord. See Numbers 6:1-5.
1:20 Samuel This name sounds like the Hebrew word for "God heard."

Hannah did not go with him. She told him, "When the boy is old enough to eat solid food, I will take him to Shiloh. Then I will give him to the Lord. He will become a Nazirite.*d* He will always live there at Shiloh."

23Elkanah, Hannah's husband, said to her, "Do what you think is best. You may stay home until the boy is old enough to eat. May the Lord do what you have said." So Hannah stayed at home to nurse her son until he was old enough to eat.

24When Samuel was old enough to eat, Hannah took him to the Tent*d* of the Lord at Shiloh. She also took a three-year-old bull, one-half bushel of flour and a leather bag filled with wine. 25They killed the bull for the sacrifice. Then Hannah brought Samuel to Eli. 26She said to Eli, "As surely as you live, my master, I am the same woman who stood near you praying to the Lord. 27I prayed for this child. The Lord answered my prayer and gave him to me. 28Now I give him back to the Lord. He will belong to the Lord all his life." And he worshiped the Lord there.

HANNAH GIVES THANKS

2 Hannah said:
"The Lord has filled my heart with joy.
I feel very strong in the Lord.
I can laugh at my enemies.
I am glad because you have helped me!

2"There is no one holy like the Lord.
There is no God but you.
There is no Rock*d* like our God.

3"Don't continue bragging.
Don't speak proud words.
The Lord is a God who knows everything.
He judges what people do.

4"The bows of warriors break,
but weak people become strong.

5Those who once had plenty of food now must work for food.
But people who once were hungry now grow fat on food.
The woman who was unable to have children now has had seven.
But the woman who had many sons now is sad.

6"The Lord causes people to die, and he causes them to live.
He brings people down to where the dead are,
and he raises them to life again.
7The Lord makes people poor,
and he makes people rich.
He makes people humble,
and he makes people great.
8The Lord raises the poor up from the dust.
And he picks needy people up from the ashes.
He lets the poor sit with princes.
He lets them sit on a throne of honor.

"The foundations of the earth belong to the Lord.
The Lord set the world upon them.
9He protects his holy people.
But those who do evil will be silenced in darkness.
Their power will not help them win.
10The Lord destroys his enemies.
He will thunder in heaven against them.
The Lord will judge all the earth.
He will give power to his king.
He will make his appointed king strong."

ELI'S EVIL SONS

11Then Elkanah went home to Ramah. But the boy continued to serve the Lord under Eli the priest.

12Now Eli's sons were evil men. They did not care about the Lord. 13This is what the priests would do to the people: Every time someone brought a sacrifice, the meat would be cooked in a pot. The priest's servant would then come with a fork in his hand. The fork had three prongs. [14]He would plunge the fork into the pot or the kettle. Whatever the fork brought out of the pot belonged to the priest. This is how they treated all the Israelites who came to Shiloh to offer sacrifices. [15]But even before the fat was burned, the priest's servant would come to the person offering sacrifices. The servant would say, "Give the priest some meat to roast. The priest won't accept boiled meat from you. He will only accept raw meat."

[16]But the man who offered the sacrifice might say, "Let the fat be burned up first as usual. Then you may take anything you want."

If so, the priest's servant would answer, "No, give me the meat now. If you don't, I'll take it by force."

[17]The Lord saw that the sin of the servants was very great. They did not show respect for the offerings made to the Lord.

SAMUEL GROWS UP

[18]But Samuel obeyed the Lord. He wore a linen holy vest.[d] [19]Every year Samuel's mother would make a little coat for him. She would take it to him when she went to Shiloh. She went there with her husband for the sacrifice. [20]Eli would bless Elkanah and his wife. Eli would say, "May the Lord repay you with children through Hannah. They will take the place of the boy Hannah prayed for and gave back to the Lord." Then Elkanah and Hannah would go home. [21]The Lord was kind to Hannah. She became the mother of three sons and two daughters. And the boy Samuel grew up serving the Lord.

[22]Now Eli was very old. He heard about everything his sons were doing to all the Israelites. He also heard about how his sons had sexual relations with the women who served at the entrance to the Meeting Tent.[d] [23]Eli said to his sons, "The people here tell me about the evil you do. Why do you do these evil things? [24]No, my sons. The Lord's people are saying bad things about you. [25]If someone sins against another person, God can help him. But if he sins against the Lord himself, no one can help him!" But Eli's sons would not listen to him. This was because the Lord had decided to put them to death.

[26]The boy Samuel kept growing. He pleased God and the people.

[27]A man of God came to Eli. He said, "This is what the Lord says: 'I clearly showed myself to the family of your ancestor Aaron. This was when they were slaves to the king of Egypt. [28]I chose them from all the tribes[d] of Israel to be my priests. I wanted them to go up to my altar, to burn incense[d] and to wear the holy vest. I also let the family of your ancestor have part of all the offerings sacrificed by the Israelites. [29]So why don't you respect the sacrifices and gifts? You honor your sons more than me. You become fat on the best parts of the meat the Israelites bring to me.'

[30]"Here's what the Lord, the God of Israel, says: 'I promised that your family and your ancestor's family would serve me forever.' But now the Lord says this: 'That will never be! I will honor those who honor me. But I will take honor away from those who do not honor me. [31]The time is coming when I will destroy the descendants[d] of both you and your ancestors. No man will grow old in your family. [32]You will see trouble in my house. Good things will be done to Israel. But there will never be an old man in your family. [33]I will save one man to serve as priest at my altar. He will wear out his eyes and use up his strength. The rest of your descendants will die by the sword.

[34]"'I will give you a sign. Both your sons, Hophni and Phinehas, will die on the same day. [35]I will choose a loyal priest for myself. He will listen to me and do what I want. I will make his family strong. He will always serve before my

appointed king. [36]Then everyone left in your family will come and bow down before him. They will beg for a little money or a little food. They will say, "Please give me a job as priest so I can have food to eat."'"

GOD CALLS SAMUEL

3 The boy Samuel served the Lord under Eli. In those days the Lord did not speak directly to people very often. There were very few visions.

[2]Eli's eyes were so weak he was almost blind. One night he was lying in bed. [3]Samuel was also in bed in the Lord's Holy Tent.[d] The Box[d] of the Agreement was in the Holy Tent. God's lamp was still burning.

[4]Then the Lord called Samuel. Samuel answered, "I am here!" [5]He ran to Eli and said, "I am here. You called me."

But Eli said, "I didn't call you. Go back to bed." So Samuel went back to bed.

[6]The Lord called again, "Samuel!"

Samuel again went to Eli and said, "I am here. You called me."

Again Eli said, "I didn't call you. Go back to bed."

[7]Samuel did not yet know the Lord. The Lord had not spoken directly to him yet.

[8]The Lord called Samuel for the third time. Samuel got up and went to Eli. He said, "I am here. You called me."

Then Eli realized the Lord was calling the boy. [9]So he told Samuel, "Go to bed. If he calls you again, say, 'Speak, Lord. I am your servant, and I am listening.'" So Samuel went and lay down in bed.

[10]The Lord came and stood there. He called as he had before. He said, "Samuel, Samuel!"

Samuel said, "Speak, Lord. I am your servant, and I am listening."

[11]The Lord said to Samuel, "See, I am going to do something in Israel. It will shock those who hear about it. [12]At that time I will do to Eli and his family everything I promised. I will not stop until I have finished. [13]I told Eli I would punish his family forever. I will do it because Eli knew his sons were evil. They spoke against me, but he did not control them. [14]So here is what I promised Eli's family: 'Your guilt will never be removed by sacrifice or offering.'"

[15]Samuel lay down until morning. Then he opened the doors of the Tent[d] of the Lord. He was afraid to tell Eli about the vision. [16]But Eli said to him, "Samuel, my son!"

Samuel answered, "I am here."

[17]Eli asked, "What did the Lord say to you? Don't hide it from me. May God punish you terribly if you hide from me anything he said to you." [18]So Samuel told Eli everything. He did not hide anything from him. Then Eli said, "He is the Lord. Let him do what he thinks is best."

[19]The Lord was with Samuel as he grew up. He did not let any of Samuel's messages fail to come true. [20]Then all Israel, from Dan to Beersheba,[n] knew Samuel was a prophet[d] of the Lord. [21]And the Lord continued to show himself to Samuel at Shiloh. He also showed himself to Samuel through his word.

4 News about Samuel spread through all of Israel.

THE PHILISTINES CAPTURE THE BOX OF THE AGREEMENT

At that time the Israelites went out to fight the Philistines. The Israelites camped at Ebenezer, and the Philistines camped at Aphek. [2]The Philistines went to meet the Israelites in battle. And as the battle spread, the Philistines defeated the Israelites. They killed about 4,000 soldiers of the Israelite army. [3]Then some Israelite soldiers went back to their camp. The elders of Israel asked, "Why did the Lord let the Philistines defeat us?

3:20 **Dan to Beersheba** Dan was the city farthest north in Israel. Beersheba was the city farthest south. So this means all the people of Israel.

Let's bring the Box[d] of the Agreement with the Lord here from Shiloh. In this way God will go with us into battle. He will save us from our enemies."

[4]So the people sent men to Shiloh. They brought back the Box of the Agreement with the Lord of heaven's armies. Eli's two sons, Hophni and Phinehas, were there with the Holy Box.

[5]The Box of the Agreement with the Lord came into the camp. And all the Israelites gave a great shout of joy. It made the ground shake. [6]The Philistines heard Israel's shout. They asked, "What's all this shouting in the Hebrew camp?"

Then the Philistines found out that the Holy Box of the Lord had come into the Hebrew camp. [7]They were afraid and said, "A god has come into the Hebrew camp! We're in trouble! This has never happened before! [8]How terrible it will be for us! Who can save us from these powerful gods? They are the ones who struck the Egyptians with all kinds of disasters in the desert. [9]Be brave, Philistines! Fight like men! In the past they were our slaves. So fight like men, or you will become their slaves."

[10]So the Philistines fought hard and defeated the Israelites. Every Israelite soldier ran away to his own home. It was a great defeat for Israel, because 30,000 Israelite soldiers were killed. [11]The Holy Box of God was taken by the Philistines. And Eli's two sons, Hophni and Phinehas, were killed.

[12]That same day a man from the tribe[d] of Benjamin ran from the battle. He tore his clothes and put dust on his head to show his great sadness. [13]When he arrived in Shiloh, Eli was by the side of the road. Eli was sitting there in a chair, watching. He was worried about the Holy Box of God. When the Benjaminite entered Shiloh, he told the bad news. Then all the people in town cried loudly.

[14]Eli heard the crying and asked, "What's all this noise?"

The Benjaminite ran to Eli and told him what had happened. [15]Eli was now 98 years old, and he was blind. [16]The Benjaminite told him, "I have come from the battle. I ran all the way here today."

Eli asked, "What happened, my son?"

[17]The Benjaminite answered, "Israel ran away from the Philistines. The Israelite army has lost many soldiers. Your two sons are both dead. And the Philistines have taken the Holy Box of God."

[18]When he mentioned the Holy Box of God, Eli fell backward off his chair. He fell beside the gate and broke his neck, because he was old and fat. And Eli died. He had led Israel for 40 years.

THE GLORY IS GONE

[19]Eli's daughter-in-law, the wife of Phinehas, was pregnant. It was nearly time for her baby to be born. She heard the news that the Holy Box[d] of God had been taken. She heard also that Eli, her father-in-law, and Phinehas, her husband, were both dead. So she began to give birth to her child. The child was born, but the mother had much trouble in giving birth. [20]As she was dying, the women who helped her give birth said, "Don't worry! You've given birth to a son!" But she did not answer or pay attention. She named the baby Ichabod.[n] [21]She named him Ichabod and said, "Israel's glory is gone." She said this because the Holy Box of God had been taken. It was also because her father-in-law and husband were dead. [22]She said, "Israel's glory is gone, because the Holy Box of God has been taken away."

TROUBLE FOR THE PHILISTINES

5 After the Philistines had captured the Holy Box[d] of God, they took it from Ebenezer to Ashdod. [2]They carried

---

4:20 Ichabod This name means "Where is the glory?"

it into Dagon's[d] temple and put it next to Dagon. [3]The people of Ashdod rose early the next morning. They found that Dagon had fallen on his face on the ground. He was lying before the Holy Box of the Lord. So the people of Ashdod put Dagon back in his place. [4]The next morning the people of Ashdod rose from sleep. And again they found Dagon on the ground! He had fallen down before the Holy Box of the Lord. His head and hands had broken off and were lying in the doorway. Only his body was still in one piece. [5]So, even today, Dagon's priests and others who enter his temple at Ashdod refuse to step on the doorsill.

[6]The Lord punished the people of Ashdod and their neighbors. He gave them much trouble. He gave them growths on their skin. [7]The people of Ashdod saw what was happening. They said, "The Holy Box of the God of Israel can't stay with us. God is punishing us and Dagon our god." [8]The people of Ashdod called all five Philistine kings together. They asked them, "What should we do with the Holy Box of the God of Israel?"

The rulers answered, "Move the Holy Box of the God of Israel to Gath." So the Philistines moved it to Gath.

[9]But after they had moved it to Gath, the Lord punished that city also. He made the people very afraid. God troubled both old and young people in Gath. He caused them to have growths on their skin. [10]Then the Philistines sent the Holy Box of God to Ekron.

But when it came into Ekron, the people of Ekron yelled. They said, "Why are you bringing the Holy Box of the God of Israel to our city? Do you want to kill us and our people?" [11]The people of Ekron called all the kings of the Philistines together. They said to the kings, "Send the Holy Box of the God of Israel back to its place. Do it before it kills us and our people!" They were very afraid. God's punishment was very terrible there.

[12]The people who did not die were troubled with growths on their skin. So the people of Ekron cried loudly to heaven.

THE HOLY BOX OF GOD IS SENT HOME

6 The Philistines kept the Holy Box[d] of God in their land seven months. [2]Then they called for their priests and magicians. They said, "What should we do with the Holy Box of the Lord? Tell us how to send it back home!"

[3]The priests and magicians answered them. They said, "If you send back the Holy Box of the God of Israel, don't send it away empty. You must offer a penalty offering so the God of Israel will forgive your sins. Then you will be healed. When God has forgiven you, he will stop punishing you."

[4]The Philistines asked, "What kind of penalty offering should we send to Israel's God?"

The priests and magicians answered, "Make five gold models of the growths on your skin. Also make five gold models of rats. The number of models must be the same as the number of Philistine kings. This is because the same sickness has come on you and your kings. [5]Make models of the growths and the rats that are ruining the country. Give them to Israel's God and honor him. Then maybe Israel's God will stop punishing you, your gods and your land. [6]Don't be stubborn like the king of Egypt and the Egyptians. God punished them terribly. That is why the Egyptians let the Israelites leave Egypt.

[7]"You must build a new cart. And get two cows that have just had calves. These must be cows that have never had yokes[d] on their necks. Then hitch the cows to the cart. Take the calves home. Don't let them follow their mothers. [8]Put the Holy Box of the Lord on the cart. And put the gold models in a box beside the Holy Box. They are your penalty offerings for God to forgive your sins. Send the cart straight on its way. [9]Watch the

cart. It may go toward Beth Shemesh in Israel's own land. If so, the Lord has given us this great sickness. But it may not go toward Beth Shemesh. Then we will know that Israel's God has not punished us. We will know that our sickness just happened by chance."

[10]The Philistines did what the priests and magicians said. They took two cows that had just had calves. They hitched them to the cart. But they kept their calves at home. [11]They put the Holy Box of the Lord on the cart. And they put the box with the gold rats and models of growths on the cart. [12]Then the cows went straight toward Beth Shemesh. They stayed on the road, mooing all the way. They did not turn right or left. The Philistine kings followed the cows as far as the border of Beth Shemesh.

[13]Now the people of Beth Shemesh were harvesting their wheat in the valley. They looked up and saw the Holy Box of the Lord. They were very happy to see it again. [14]The cart came to the field belonging to Joshua of Beth Shemesh. The cart stopped in this field near a large rock. The people of Beth Shemesh chopped up the wood of the cart. Then they killed the cows and sacrificed them to the Lord. [15]The Levites took down the Holy Box of the Lord. They also took down the box that had the gold models. They put both on the large rock. That day the people of Beth Shemesh offered whole burnt offerings and made sacrifices to the Lord. [16]The five Philistine kings watched them do all these things. Then they went back to Ekron the same day.

[17]The Philistines sent these gold models of the growths. They were penalty offerings to the Lord for their sins. They sent one model for each Philistine town. These towns were Ashdod, Gaza, Ashkelon, Gath and Ekron. [18]And the Philistines also sent gold models of rats. The number of rats was the same as the number of towns belonging to the Philistine kings. These towns included strong, walled cities and country villages. The large rock on which they put the Holy Box of the Lord is still there. It is in the field of Joshua of Beth Shemesh.

[19]But some of the men of Beth Shemesh looked into the Holy Box of the Lord. So God killed 70 of them. The people of Beth Shemesh cried because the Lord had punished them so terribly. [20]They said, "Who can stand before the Lord, this holy God? Where can the Holy Box go from here?"

[21]Then they sent messengers to the people of Kiriath Jearim. The messengers said, "The Philistines have brought back the Holy Box of the Lord. Come down and take it to your city."

7 The men of Kiriath Jearim came and took the Holy Box of the Lord. They took it to Abinadab's house on a hill. There they made Abinadab's son Eleazar holy for the Lord so he could guard the Holy Box.

THE LORD SAVES THE ISRAELITES

[2]The Holy Box[d] stayed at Kiriath Jearim a long time—20 years in all. And the people of Israel began to follow the Lord again. [3]Samuel spoke to the whole group of Israel. He said, "If you're turning back to the Lord with all your hearts, you must remove your foreign gods. You must remove your idols of Ashtoreth.[d] You must give yourselves fully to the Lord and serve only him. Then he will save you from the Philistines."

[4]So the Israelites put away their idols of Baal[d] and Ashtoreth. And they served only the Lord.

[5]Samuel said, "All Israel must meet at Mizpah. I will pray to the Lord for you." [6]So the Israelites met together at Mizpah. They drew water from the ground and poured it out before the Lord. They did not eat that day. They confessed, "We have sinned against the Lord." And Samuel served as judge of Israel at Mizpah.

⁷The Philistines heard the Israelites were meeting at Mizpah. So the Philistine kings came up to attack them. When the Israelites heard they were coming, they were afraid. ⁸They said to Samuel, "Don't stop praying to the Lord our God for us! Ask the Lord to save us from the Philistines!" ⁹Then Samuel took a baby lamb. He offered the lamb to the Lord as a whole burnt offering. He called to the Lord for Israel's sake. And the Lord answered him.

¹⁰While Samuel was burning the offering, the Philistines came near. They were going to attack Israel. But the Lord thundered against the Philistines with loud thunder. They were so frightened they became confused. So the Israelites defeated the Philistines in battle. ¹¹The men of Israel ran out of Mizpah and chased the Philistines. They went almost to Beth Car, killing the Philistines along the way.

PEACE COMES TO ISRAEL

¹²After this happened Samuel took a stone. He set it up between Mizpah and Shen. He named the stone Ebenezer.ⁿ Samuel said, "The Lord has helped us to this point." ¹³So the Philistines were defeated. They did not enter the Israelites' land again.

The Lord was against the Philistines all Samuel's life. ¹⁴Earlier the Philistines had taken towns from the Israelites. But the Israelites won them back, from Ekron to Gath. They also took back from the Philistines the neighboring lands of these towns. There was peace also between Israel and the Amorites.

¹⁵Samuel continued as judge of Israel all his life. ¹⁶Every year he went from Bethel to Gilgal to Mizpah. He judged the Israelites in all these towns. ¹⁷But Samuel always went back to Ramah, where his home was. He also judged Israel there. And there he built an altar to the Lord.

ISRAEL ASKS FOR A KING

8 When Samuel became old, he made his sons judges for Israel. ²His first son was named Joel, and his second son was named Abijah. Joel and Abijah were judges in Beersheba. ³But Samuel's sons did not live as he did. They tried to get money dishonestly. They took money secretly to be dishonest in their judging.

⁴So all the elders came together and met Samuel at Ramah. ⁵They said to him, "You're old, and your sons don't live as you do. Give us a king to rule over us like all the other nations."

⁶When the elders said that, Samuel was not pleased. He prayed to the Lord. ⁷The Lord told Samuel, "Listen to whatever the people say to you. They have not rejected you. They have rejected me from being their king. ⁸They are doing as they have always done. When I took them out of Egypt, they left me. They served other gods. They are doing the same to you. ⁹Now listen to the people. But give them a warning. Tell them what the king who rules over them will do."

¹⁰Samuel answered those who had asked him for a king. He told them all the words of the Lord. ¹¹Samuel said, "If you have a king ruling over you, this is what he will do: He will take your sons. He will make them serve with his chariots and his horses. They will run in front of the king's chariot. ¹²The king will make some of your sons commanders over 1,000 men or over 50 men. He will make some of your other sons plow his ground and reap his harvest. He will take others to make weapons of war and equipment for his chariots. ¹³This king will take your daughters. Some of your daughters will make perfume. Others will cook and bake for him. ¹⁴He will take your best fields, vineyards and olive groves. He will give them to his servants. ¹⁵He will take one-tenth of your grain

---

7:12 Ebenezer This name means "stone of help."

and grapes and give it to his officers and servants. [16]He will take your men servants and girl servants. He will take your best cattle and your donkeys. He will use them all for his own work. [17]He will take one-tenth of your flocks. And you yourselves will become his slaves. [18]When that time comes, you will cry out because of the king you chose. The Lord will not answer you then."

[19]But the people would not listen to Samuel. They said, "No! We want a king to rule over us. [20]Then we will be the same as all the other nations. Our king will judge us. He will go with us and fight our battles."

[21]Samuel heard all that the people said. Then he repeated all their words to the Lord. [22]The Lord answered, "You must listen to them. Give them a king."

Then Samuel told the people of Israel, "Everyone go back to his town."

SAUL LOOKS FOR HIS FATHER'S DONKEYS

9 Kish son of Abiel was from the tribe[d] of Benjamin. He was an important man. (Abiel was the son of Zeror. And Zeror was the son of Becorath. He was the son of Aphiah of Benjamin.) [2]Kish had a son named Saul. Saul was a fine young man. There was no Israelite better than he. Saul stood a head taller than any other man in Israel.

[3]Now the donkeys of Saul's father, Kish, were lost. So Kish said to Saul, his son, "Take one of the servants. Go and look for the donkeys." [4]Saul went through the mountains of Ephraim. And he went through the land of Shalisha. But he and the servant could not find the donkeys. They went into the land of Shaalim, but the donkeys were not there. They went through the land of Benjamin. But they still did not find the donkeys. [5]They arrived in the area of Zuph. Saul said to his servant, "Let's go back. My father will stop thinking about the donkeys. He will start worrying about us."

[6]But the servant answered, "A man of God is in this town. People respect him because everything he says comes true. Let's go into the town now. Maybe he can tell us something about the journey we have taken."

[7]Saul said to his servant, "If we go into the town, what can we give him? The food in our bags is gone. We have no gift to give him. Do we have anything at all to give him?"

[8]Again the servant answered Saul. "Look, I have one-tenth of an ounce of silver. Give it to the man of God. Then he will tell us about our journey." [9](In the past, someone in Israel might want to ask something from God. If so, he would say, "Let's go to the seer."[d] We call the person a man of God today. But in the past he was called a "seer.")

[10]Saul said to his servant, "That is a good idea. Come, let's go." So they went toward the town where the man of God was.

[11]Saul and the servant were going up the hill to the town. On the way they met some young women coming out to get water. Saul and the servant asked them, "Is the seer here?"

[12]The young women answered, "Yes, he's here. He's ahead of you. Hurry now. He has just come to our town today. This is because the people will offer a sacrifice at the place of worship. [13]When you enter the town, you will find him. He will be there before he goes up to the place of worship to eat. The people will not begin eating until the seer comes. He must bless the sacrifice. After that, the guests will eat. Go now, and you should find him."

SAUL MEETS SAMUEL

[14]Saul and the servant went up to the town. Just as they entered the town, they saw Samuel. He was on his way up to the place of worship. So he was coming out of the city toward them.

[15]The day before Saul came, the Lord had told Samuel: [16]"About this time

tomorrow I will send you a man. He will be from Benjamin. You must appoint him as leader over my people Israel. He will save my people from the Philistines. I have seen the suffering of my people. I have listened to their cry."

[17]When Samuel first saw Saul, the Lord spoke to Samuel. He said, "This is the man I told you about. He will rule my people."

[18]Saul came near Samuel at the gate. Saul said, "Please tell me where the seer's[d] house is."

[19]Samuel answered, "I am the seer. Go ahead of me to the place of worship. Today you and your servant are to eat with me. Tomorrow morning I will send you home. And I will answer all your questions. [20]Don't worry about the donkeys you lost three days ago. They have been found. Israel now wants you and all your father's family."

[21]Saul answered, "But I am from the tribe[d] of Benjamin. It's the smallest tribe in Israel. And my family group is the smallest in the tribe of Benjamin. Why do you say Israel wants me?"

[22]Then Samuel took Saul and his servant into a large room. He gave them a chief place at the table. About 30 guests were there. [23]Samuel said to the cook, "Bring the meat I gave you. It's the portion I told you to set aside."

[24]So the cook took the thigh and put it on the table in front of Saul. Samuel said, "This is the meat saved for you. Eat it because it was set aside for you for this special time. As I said, 'I have invited the people.'" So Saul ate with Samuel that day.

[25]After they finished eating, they came down from the place of worship. They went to the town. Then Samuel talked with Saul on the roof[n] of his house. [26]At dawn they got up, and Samuel called to Saul on the roof. He said, "Get up, and I will send you on your way." So Saul got up. He went out of the house with Samuel. [27]Saul, his servant and Samuel were getting near the edge of the city. Samuel said to Saul, "Tell the servant to go on ahead of us. I have a message from God for you."

SAMUEL APPOINTS SAUL

10 Samuel took a jar of olive oil. He poured the oil on Saul's head. He kissed Saul and said, "The Lord has appointed you to be leader of his people Israel. You will rule over the people of the Lord. You will save them from their enemies all around. This will be the sign that the Lord has appointed you as leader of his people. [2]After you leave me today, you will meet two men. They will be near Rachel's tomb on the border of Benjamin at Zelzah. They will say to you, 'The donkeys you were looking for have been found. But now your father has stopped thinking about his donkeys. He is worrying about you. He is asking, "What will I do about my son?"'

[3]"Then you will go on until you reach the great tree at Tabor. There three men will meet you. They will be on their way to worship God at Bethel. One man will be carrying three young goats. The second man will be carrying three loaves of bread. And the third one will have a leather bag full of wine. [4]They will greet you and offer you two loaves of bread. You will accept the bread from them. [5]Then you will go to Gibeah of God. There is a Philistine camp there. When you come near this town, a group of prophets[d] will come out. They will be coming from the place of worship. And they will be playing harps, tambourines,[d] flutes and lyres.[d] And they will be prophesying. [6]The Spirit[d] of the Lord will enter you with power. You will prophesy with these prophets. You will be changed into a different man. [7]After these signs

---

9:25 roof In Bible times houses were built with flat roofs. The roof was used for drying things such as flax and fruit. And it was used as an extra room, as a place for worship and as a place to sleep in the summer.

happen, do whatever you find to do. God will help you.

[8]"Go ahead of me to Gilgal. I will come down to you. Then I will offer whole burnt offerings and fellowship offerings. But you must wait seven days. Then I will come and tell you what to do."

SAUL MADE KING

[9]When Saul turned to leave Samuel, God changed Saul's heart. All these signs came true that day. [10]When Saul and his servant arrived at Gibeah, Saul met a group of prophets.[d] The Spirit[d] of God entered him. And he prophesied with the prophets. [11]People who had known Saul before saw him prophesying with the prophets. They asked each other, "What has happened to Kish's son? Is even Saul one of the prophets?"

[12]A man who lived there said, "Who is the father of these prophets?" This became a famous saying: "Is even Saul one of the prophets?" [13]When Saul finished prophesying, he went to the place of worship.

[14]Saul's uncle asked him and his servant, "Where have you been?"

Saul said, "We were looking for the donkeys. When we couldn't find them, we went to talk to Samuel."

[15]Saul's uncle asked, "Please tell me. What did Samuel say to you?"

[16]Saul answered, "He told us the donkeys had already been found." But Saul did not tell his uncle what Samuel had said about his becoming king.

[17]Samuel called all the people of Israel to meet with the Lord at Mizpah. [18]He said, "This is what the Lord, the God of Israel, says: 'I led Israel out of Egypt. I saved you from Egypt's control. And I saved you from other kingdoms that were troubling you.' [19]But now you have rejected your God. He saves you from all your troubles and problems. But you said, 'No! We want a king to rule over us.' Now come, stand before the Lord in your tribes[d] and family groups."

[20]Samuel brought all the tribes of Israel near. And the tribe of Benjamin was chosen. [21]Samuel had them pass by in family groups, and Matri's family was chosen. Then he had each man of Matri's family pass by. And Saul son of Kish was chosen. But when they looked for Saul, they could not find him. [22]Then they asked the Lord, "Has Saul come here yet?"

The Lord said, "Yes. He's hiding behind the baggage."

[23]So they ran and brought him out. When Saul stood among the people, he was a head taller than anyone else. [24]Then Samuel said to the people, "See the man the Lord has chosen. There is no one like him among all the people."

Then the people shouted, "Long live the king!"

[25]Samuel explained the rights and duties of the king. He wrote the rules in a book and put the book before the Lord. Then he told the people to go to their homes.

[26]Saul also went to his home in Gibeah. God touched the hearts of certain brave men who went along with him. [27]But some troublemakers said, "How can this man save us?" They hated Saul and refused to bring gifts to him. But Saul kept quiet.

NAHASH TROUBLES JABESH GILEAD

11 About a month later Nahash the Ammonite and his army surrounded the city of Jabesh in Gilead. All the people of Jabesh said to Nahash, "Make a treaty with us. And we will serve you."

[2]But he answered, "I will make a treaty with you. But I will only do it if I'm allowed to tear out the right eye of each of you. Then all Israel will be ashamed!"

[3]The elders of Jabesh said to Nahash, "Let us have seven days. We will send messengers through all Israel. If no one comes to help us, we will give ourselves up to you."

[4]The messengers came to Gibeah where Saul lived. When they told the people the news, the people cried loudly.

⁵Saul had finished plowing in the fields with his oxen. He was coming home when he heard the people crying. He asked, "What's wrong with the people? Why are they crying?" Then they told Saul what the messengers from Jabesh had said. ⁶When Saul heard their words, God's Spirit*ᵈ* entered him with power. Saul became very angry. ⁷So he took a pair of oxen and cut them into pieces. Then he gave the pieces of the oxen to messengers. He ordered them to carry the pieces through all the land of Israel.

The messengers made an announcement to the people. They said, "This is what will happen to the oxen of anyone who does not follow Saul and Samuel." So the people became very afraid of the Lord. They all came together as if they were one person. ⁸Saul gathered the people together at Bezek. There were 300,000 men from Israel and 30,000 men from Judah.

⁹They spoke to the messengers who had come. They said, "Tell the people at Jabesh Gilead this: 'Before the day becomes hot tomorrow, you will be saved.'" So the messengers went and reported this to the people at Jabesh. They were very happy. ¹⁰The people said to Nahash the Ammonite, "Tomorrow we will give ourselves up to you. Then you can do anything you want to us."

¹¹The next morning Saul divided his soldiers into three groups. At dawn they entered the Ammonite camp. And they defeated the Ammonites before the heat of the day. The Ammonites who were left alive were scattered. Not even two of them were still together.

¹²Then the people said to Samuel, "Who was it that didn't want Saul as king? Bring them here, and we will kill them!"

¹³But Saul said, "No! No one will be put to death today. The Lord has saved Israel today!"

¹⁴Then Samuel said to the people, "Come, let's go to Gilgal. At Gilgal we will again promise to obey the king." ¹⁵All the people went to Gilgal. And there, before the Lord, the people made Saul king. They offered fellowship offerings to the Lord. Saul and all the Israelites had a great celebration.

SAMUEL'S FAREWELL SPEECH

12 Samuel said to all Israel, "I have done everything you wanted me to do. I have put a king over you. ²Now you have a king to lead you. I am old and gray, and my sons are here with you. I have been your leader since I was young. ³Here I am. If I have done anything wrong, you must testify against me. Do this before the Lord and his appointed king. Did I steal anyone's ox or donkey? Did I hurt or cheat anyone? Did I ever secretly take money to pretend not to see something wrong? If I did any of these things, I will make it right."

⁴The Israelites answered, "You have not cheated us. You have not hurt us. You have not taken anything unfairly from anyone."

⁵Samuel said to them, "The Lord is a witness to what you have said. His appointed king is also a witness today. They are both witnesses that you did not find anything wrong in me."

"He is our witness," they said.

⁶Then Samuel said to the people, "The Lord is our witness. He chose Moses and Aaron. He brought your ancestors out of Egypt. ⁷Now, stand there. And I will talk with you about all the good things the Lord did for you and your ancestors.

⁸"After Jacob entered Egypt, his descendants*ᵈ* cried to the Lord for help. So the Lord sent Moses and Aaron. They took your ancestors out of Egypt and brought them to live in this place.

⁹"But they forgot the Lord their God. So he let them become the slaves of Sisera. He was the commander of the army of Hazor. The Lord let them become the slaves of the Philistines and the king of Moab. They all fought against your

ancestors. [10]Then your ancestors cried to the Lord. They said, 'We have sinned. We have left the Lord. We served the Baals[d] and the Ashtoreths.[d] But now save us from our enemies, and we will serve you.' [11]The Lord sent Gideon, who is also called Jerub-Baal. And he sent Barak, Jephthah and Samuel. Then he saved you from your enemies around you. And you lived in safety. [12]But then you saw Nahash king of the Ammonites coming against you. You said, 'No! We want a king to rule over us!' [13]Now here is the king you chose. The Lord has put him over you. [14]You must honor the Lord and serve him. You must obey his commands. Both you and the king ruling over you must follow the Lord your God. If you do, it will be well with you. [15]But if you don't obey the Lord, and if you fight against his commands, he will be against you. He will do to you what he did to your ancestors.

[16]"Now stand still and see the great thing the Lord will do before your eyes. [17]It is now the time of the wheat harvest.[n] I will pray for the Lord to send thunder and rain. Then you will know what an evil thing you did against the Lord when you asked for a king."

[18]Then Samuel prayed to the Lord. That same day the Lord sent thunder and rain. And the people became very afraid of the Lord and Samuel. [19]They said to Samuel, "Pray to the Lord your God for us, your servants! Don't let us die! We've added to all our sins the evil of asking for a king."

[20]Samuel answered, "Don't be afraid. It's true that you did wrong. But don't turn away from the Lord. Serve the Lord with all your heart. [21]Idols are of no use. So don't worship them. They can't help you or save you. They are useless! [22]For

his own sake, the Lord won't leave his people. Instead, he was pleased to make you his own people. [23]I will surely not stop praying for you. If I did, I would be sinning against the Lord. I will teach you what is good and right. [24]But you must honor the Lord. You must always serve him with all your heart. Remember the wonderful things he did for you! [25]But if you are stubborn and do evil, God will sweep you and your king away."

13 Saul was 30 years old when he became king. He was king over Israel 42 years.[n] [2]Saul chose 3,000 men from Israel. There were 2,000 men who stayed with him at Micmash in the mountains of Bethel. And 1,000 men stayed with Jonathan at Gibeah in Benjamin. Saul sent the other men in the army back home.

[3]Jonathan attacked the Philistine camp in Geba. And the other Philistines heard about it. Saul said, "Let the Hebrew people hear what happened." So he told the men to blow trumpets through all the land of Israel. [4]All the Israelites heard the news. The men said, "Saul has defeated the Philistine camp. Now the Philistines really hate us!" Then the Israelites were called to join Saul at Gilgal.

[5]The Philistines gathered to fight Israel. They had 3,000[n] chariots and 6,000 men to ride in the chariots. Their soldiers were many in number, like the grains of sand on the seashore. The Philistines went and camped at Micmash which is east of Beth Aven. [6]The Israelites saw that they were in trouble. So they went to hide in caves and bushes. They also hid among the rocks and in pits and wells. [7]Some Hebrews even went across the Jordan River to the land of Gad and Gilead.

But Saul stayed at Gilgal. All the men in his army were shaking with fear. [8]Saul

---

12:17 **time...harvest** This was a dry time in the summer when no rains fell.
13:1 **Saul...years** This is how the verse is worded in some early Greek copies. The Hebrew is not clear here.
13:5 **3,000** Some Greek copies say 3,000. The Hebrew copies say 30,000.

waited seven days, because Samuel had said he would meet him then. But Samuel did not come to Gilgal. And the soldiers began to leave.

⁹So Saul said, "Bring me the whole burnt offering and the fellowship offerings." Then Saul offered the whole burnt offering. ¹⁰Just as he finished, Samuel arrived. Saul went to meet him.

¹¹Samuel asked, "What have you done?"

Saul answered, "I saw the soldiers leaving me, and you were not here. The Philistines were gathering at Micmash. ¹²Then I thought, 'The Philistines will come against me at Gilgal. And I haven't asked for the Lord's approval.' So I forced myself to offer the whole burnt offering."

¹³Samuel said, "You acted foolishly! You haven't obeyed God's command. If you had obeyed him, God would make your kingdom continue in Israel forever. ¹⁴But now your kingdom will not continue. The Lord has looked for the kind of man he wants. The Lord has appointed him to become ruler of his people. He is doing this because you haven't obeyed his command."

¹⁵Then Samuel left Gilgal and went to Gibeah in Benjamin. The rest of the army followed Saul into battle. Saul counted the men still with him, and there were about 600.

HARD TIMES FOR ISRAEL

¹⁶Saul and his son Jonathan stayed in Geba in the land of Benjamin. The soldiers with them also stayed there. The Philistines made their camp at Micmash. ¹⁷Three groups went out from their camp to attack. One group went on the Ophrah road in the land of Shual. ¹⁸The second group went on the Beth Horon road. And the third group went on the border road. It overlooked the Valley of Zeboim toward the desert.

¹⁹The whole land of Israel had no blacksmith. This is because the Philistines had said, "The Hebrews might make swords and spears." ²⁰So all the Israelites went down to the Philistines. They went to have their plows, hoes, axes and sickles sharpened. ²¹The Philistine blacksmiths charged about one-fourth of an ounce of silver for sharpening plows and hoes. And they charged one-eighth of an ounce of silver for sharpening picks, axes and the sticks used to guide oxen.

²²So when the battle came, the soldiers with Saul and Jonathan had no swords or spears. Only Saul and his son Jonathan had them.

ISRAEL DEFEATS THE PHILISTINES

²³A group from the Philistine army had gone out to the mountain pass at Micmash.

14 One day Jonathan, Saul's son, spoke to the officer who carried his armor. Jonathan said, "Come, let's go over to the Philistine camp on the other side." But Jonathan did not tell his father.

²Saul was sitting under a pomegranate*d* tree at the threshing*d* floor near Gibeah. He had about 600 men with him. ³One man was Ahijah, who was a son of Ichabod's brother Ahitub. Ichabod was the son of Phinehas, Eli's son. Eli was the Lord's priest in Shiloh. He wore the holy vest.*d* No one knew Jonathan had left.

⁴There was a steep slope on each side of the pass. Jonathan planned to go through the pass to the Philistine camp. The cliff on one side was named Bozez. The other cliff was named Seneh. ⁵One cliff faced north toward Micmash. The other faced south toward Geba.

⁶Jonathan said to his officer who carried his armor, "Come. Let's go to the camp of those men who are not circumcised.*d* Maybe the Lord will help us. It doesn't matter if we have many people, or just a few. Nothing can keep the Lord from giving us victory."

⁷The officer who carried Jonathan's armor said to him, "Do whatever you think is best. Go ahead. I'm with you."

⁸Jonathan said, "Then come. We will

cross over to the Philistines. We will let them see us. [9]They may say to us, 'Stay there until we come to you.' If they do, we will stay where we are. We won't go up to them. [10]But they may say, 'Come up to us.' If so, we will climb up. And the Lord will allow us to defeat them. This will be the sign for us."

[11]Both Jonathan and his officer let the Philistines see them. The Philistines said, "Look! The Hebrews are crawling out of the holes they were hiding in!" [12]The Philistines in the camp shouted to Jonathan and his officer, "Come up to us. We'll teach you a lesson!"

Jonathan said to his officer, "Climb up behind me. The Lord has given the Philistines to Israel!" [13]So Jonathan climbed up, using his hands and feet. His officer climbed just behind him. Jonathan cut down the Philistines as he went. And his officer killed them as he followed behind Jonathan. [14]In that first fight Jonathan and his officer killed about 20 Philistines.

[15]All the Philistine soldiers panicked. Those in the camp and those in the raiding party were frightened. The ground itself shook! God caused the panic.

[16]Saul's guards were at Gibeah in the land of Benjamin. They saw the Philistine soldiers running in every direction. [17]Saul said to his army, "Check and find who has left our camp." When they checked, they learned that Jonathan and his officer were gone.

[18]So Saul said to Ahijah the priest, "Bring the Holy Box[d] of God." (At that time it was with the Israelites.) [19]While Saul was talking to the priest, the confusion in the Philistine camp was growing. Then Saul said to Ahijah, "Stop. There's not time to pray now!"

[20]Then Saul and the army with him gathered and entered the battle. They found the Philistines confused, even striking each other with their swords! [21]Earlier, there were Hebrews who had served the Philistines and had stayed in their camp. They now joined the Israelites with Saul and Jonathan. [22]All the Israelites hidden in the mountains of Ephraim heard that the Philistine soldiers were running away. They too joined the battle and chased the Philistines. [23]So the Lord saved the Israelites that day. And the battle moved on past Beth Aven.

SAUL MAKES ANOTHER MISTAKE

[24]The men of Israel were miserable that day. This was because Saul had made an oath for all of them. He had said, "No one should eat food before evening and before I finish defeating my enemies. If he does, he will be cursed!" So no Israelite soldier ate food.

[25]Now the army went into the woods. There was some honey on the ground. [26]They came to where the honey was. But no one took any because they were afraid of the oath. [27]But Jonathan had not heard the oath Saul had put on the people. So Jonathan dipped the end of his stick into the honey. He pulled out the honey and ate it. Then he felt better. [28]So one of the soldiers told Jonathan, "Your father made an oath for all the soldiers. He said any man who eats today will be cursed! That's why they are weak."

[29]Jonathan said, "My father has made trouble for the land! See how much better I feel after just tasting a little of this honey! [30]It would have been much better for the men to eat the food they took from their enemies today. We could have killed many more Philistines!"

[31]That day the Israelites defeated the Philistines from Micmash to Aijalon. After they did this, they were very tired. [32]They had taken sheep, cattle and calves from the Philistines. Now they were so hungry they killed the animals on the ground and ate them. But the blood was still in the animals! [33]Someone said to Saul, "Look! The men are sinning against the Lord. They're eating meat that still has blood in it!"

Saul said, "You have sinned! Roll a large stone over here now!" ³⁴Then he said, "Go to the men. Tell them that each person must bring his ox and sheep to me. They must kill and eat their ox and sheep here. Don't sin against the Lord. Don't eat meat with the blood still in it."

That night everyone brought his animals and killed them there. ³⁵Then Saul built an altar to the Lord. It was the first altar Saul had built to the Lord.

³⁶Saul said, "Let's go after the Philistines tonight. Let's take what they own. We won't let any of them live!"

The men answered, "Do whatever you think is best."

But the priest said, "Let's ask God."

³⁷So Saul asked God, "Should I chase the Philistines? Will you let us defeat them?" But that day God did not answer Saul. ³⁸That is why Saul said to all the leaders of his army, "Come here. Let's find what sin has been done today. ³⁹As surely as the Lord lives, even if my son Jonathan did the sin, he must die." But no one in the army answered.

⁴⁰Then Saul said to all the Israelites, "You stand on this side. I and my son Jonathan will stand on the other side."

The men answered, "Do whatever you think is best."

⁴¹Then Saul prayed to the Lord, the God of Israel, "Give me the right answer." And Saul and Jonathan were chosen by throwing lots.ᵈ The other men went free. ⁴²Saul said, "Throw the lot. It will show if it is I or Jonathan my son who is guilty." And Jonathan was chosen.

⁴³Saul said to Jonathan, "Tell me what you have done."

So Jonathan told Saul, "I only tasted a little honey from the end of my stick. And must I die now?"

⁴⁴Saul said, "Jonathan, if you don't die, may God punish me terribly."

⁴⁵But the soldiers said to Saul, "Must Jonathan die? Never! He is responsible for saving Israel today! As surely as the Lord lives, not even a hair of his head will fall to the ground! Today Jonathan fought against the Philistines with God's help!" So the army saved Jonathan, and he did not die.

⁴⁶Then Saul stopped chasing the Philistines. And they went back to their own land.

SAUL FIGHTS ISRAEL'S ENEMIES

⁴⁷When Saul became king over Israel, he fought against Israel's enemies all around. He fought Moab, the Ammonites, Edom, the king of Zobah and the Philistines. Everywhere Saul went he defeated Israel's enemies. ⁴⁸He became strong. He fought bravely and defeated the Amalekites. He saved Israel from the enemies who had taken what the Israelites owned.

⁴⁹Saul's sons were Jonathan, Ishvi and Malki-Shua. His older daughter was named Merab. His younger daughter was named Michal. ⁵⁰Saul's wife was Ahinoam daughter of Ahimaaz. The commander of his army was Abner son of Ner. Ner was Saul's uncle. ⁵¹Saul's father Kish and Abner's father Ner were sons of Abiel.

⁵²All Saul's life he fought hard against the Philistines. When he saw strong or brave men, he took them into his army.

SAUL REJECTED AS KING

15 Samuel said to Saul, "The Lord sent me to appoint you king over Israel. Now listen to his message. ²This is what the Lord of heaven's armies says: 'The Israelites came out of Egypt. But the Amalekites tried to stop them from going to Canaan. I saw what they did. ³Now go, attack the Amalekites. Destroy everything that belongs to them as an offering to the Lord. Don't let anything live. Put to death men and women, children and small babies. Kill the cattle and sheep, camels and donkeys.'"

⁴So Saul called the army together at Telaim. There were 200,000 soldiers and

10,000 men from Judah. [5]Then Saul went to the city of Amalek and set up an ambush in the ravine. [6]He said to the Kenites, "Go away. Leave the Amalekites so that I won't destroy you with them. You showed kindness to the Israelites when they came out of Egypt." So the Kenites moved away from the Amalekites.

[7]Then Saul defeated the Amalekites. He fought them all the way from Havilah to Shur, at the border of Egypt. [8]He took Agag king of the Amalekites alive. But he killed all of Agag's army with the sword. [9]But Saul and the army let Agag live. They also let the best sheep, fat cattle and lambs live. They let every good animal live. They did not want to destroy them. But when they found an animal that was weak or useless, they killed it.

[10]Then the Lord spoke his word to Samuel: [11]"Saul has stopped following me. And I am sorry I made him king. He has not obeyed my commands." Samuel was upset, and he cried out to the Lord all night long.

[12]Early the next morning Samuel got up and went to meet Saul. But the people told Samuel, "Saul has gone to Carmel. He has put up a monument in his own honor. Now he has gone down to Gilgal."

[13]Then Samuel came to Saul. And Saul said, "May the Lord bless you! I have obeyed the Lord's commands."

[14]But Samuel said, "Then why do I hear cattle mooing and sheep bleating?"

[15]Saul answered, "The soldiers took them from the Amalekites. They saved the best sheep and cattle to offer as sacrifices to the Lord your God. But we destroyed all the other animals."

[16]Samuel said to Saul, "Stop! Let me tell you what the Lord said to me last night."

Saul answered, "Tell me."

[17]Samuel said, "Once you didn't think much of yourself. But now you have become the leader of the tribes[d] of Israel. The Lord appointed you to be king over Israel. [18]And he told you to do something.

He said, 'Go and destroy those evil people, the Amalekites. Make war on them until all of them are dead.' [19]Why didn't you obey the Lord? Why did you take the best things? Why did you do what the Lord said was wrong?"

[20]Saul said, "But I did obey the Lord. I did what the Lord told me to do. I destroyed all the Amalekites. And I brought back Agag their king. [21]The soldiers took the best sheep and cattle to sacrifice to the Lord your God at Gilgal."

[22]But Samuel answered,

"What pleases the Lord more:
   burnt offerings and sacrifices or
   obedience?
It is better to obey God than to offer
   a sacrifice.
It is better to listen to God than to
   offer the fat of male sheep.
[23]Refusing to obey is as bad as the sin
   of sorcery.[d]
Being stubborn is as bad as the sin
   of worshiping idols.
You have rejected the Lord's
   command.
For this reason, he now rejects you
   as king."

[24]Then Saul said to Samuel, "I have sinned. I didn't obey the Lord's commands. I didn't do what you told me. I was afraid of the people, and I did what they said. [25]Now I beg you, forgive my sin. Come back with me so I may worship the Lord."

[26]But Samuel said to Saul, "I won't go back with you. You refused the Lord's command. And now he rejects you as king of Israel."

[27]As Samuel turned to leave, Saul caught his robe, and it tore. [28]Samuel said to him, "The Lord has torn the kingdom of Israel from you today. He has given it to one of your neighbors. He has given it to one better than you. [29]The Lord is the Eternal One of Israel. He does not lie or change his mind. He is not a man. So he does not change his mind as men do."

³⁰Saul answered, "I have sinned. But please honor me in front of my people's elders. Please honor me in front of the Israelites. Come back with me so that I may worship the Lord your God." ³¹So Samuel went back with Saul, and Saul worshiped the Lord.

³²Then Samuel said, "Bring me Agag king of the Amalekites."

Agag came to Samuel in chains. Yet Agag thought, "Surely the threat of death has passed."

³³Samuel said to him, "Your sword caused mothers to be without their children. Now your mother will have no children." And Samuel cut Agag to pieces before the Lord at Gilgal.

³⁴Then Samuel left and went to Ramah. But Saul went up to his home in Gibeah. ³⁵And Samuel never saw Saul again all the rest of his life. But he was sorry for Saul. And the Lord was very sorry he had made Saul king of Israel.

SAMUEL GOES TO BETHLEHEM

16 The Lord said to Samuel, "How long will you continue to feel sorry for Saul? I have rejected him as king of Israel. Fill your container with olive oil and go. I am sending you to Jesse who lives in Bethlehem. I have chosen one of his sons to be king."

²But Samuel said, "If I go, Saul will hear the news. And he will try to kill me."

The Lord said, "Take a young calf with you. Say, 'I have come to offer a sacrifice to the Lord.' ³Invite Jesse to the sacrifice. Then I will show you what to do. You must appoint the one I show you."

⁴Samuel did what the Lord told him to do. When he arrived at Bethlehem, the elders of Bethlehem shook with fear. They met him and asked, "Are you coming in peace?"

⁵Samuel answered, "Yes, I come in peace. I have come to make a sacrifice to the Lord. Make yourselves holy for the Lord and come to the sacrifice with me." Then he made Jesse and his sons holy for the Lord. And he invited them to come to the sacrifice.

⁶When they arrived, Samuel saw Eliab. Samuel thought, "Surely the Lord has appointed this person standing here before him."

⁷But the Lord said to Samuel, "Don't look at how handsome Eliab is. Don't look at how tall he is. I have not chosen him. God does not see the same way people see. People look at the outside of a person, but the Lord looks at the heart."

⁸Then Jesse called Abinadab and told him to pass by Samuel. But Samuel said, "The Lord has not chosen this man either." ⁹Then Jesse had Shammah pass by. But Samuel said, "No, the Lord has not chosen this one." ¹⁰Jesse had seven of his sons pass by Samuel. But Samuel said to him, "The Lord has not chosen any of these."

¹¹Then he asked Jesse, "Are these all the sons you have?"

Jesse answered, "I still have the youngest son. He is out taking care of the sheep."

Samuel said, "Send for him. We will not sit down to eat until he arrives."

¹²So Jesse sent and had his youngest son brought in. He was a fine boy, tanned and handsome.

The Lord said to Samuel, "Go! Appoint him. He is the one."

¹³So Samuel took the container of olive oil. Then he poured oil on Jesse's youngest son to appoint him in front of his brothers. From that day on, the Lord's Spirit^d entered David with power. Samuel then went back to Ramah.

DAVID SERVES SAUL

¹⁴But the Lord's Spirit^d had gone out of Saul. And an evil spirit from the Lord troubled him.

¹⁵Saul's servants said to him, "See, an evil spirit from God is troubling you. ¹⁶Give us the command. We will look for someone who can play the harp. When the evil spirit from the Lord enters you,

he will play. Then the evil spirit will leave you alone. And you will feel better."

17So Saul said to his servants, "Find someone. If he plays well, bring him to me."

18One of the servants said, "Jesse of Bethlehem has a son who plays the harp. I have seen him play it. He is a brave man and fights well. He is a good speaker and handsome. And the Lord is with him."

19Then Saul sent messengers to Jesse. The message said, "Send me your son David, who is with the sheep." 20So Jesse loaded a donkey with bread and a leather bag full of wine. He also took a young goat. He sent them all with his son David to Saul.

21When David came to Saul, he began to serve him. Saul loved David very much. And David became the officer who carried Saul's armor. 22Saul sent a message to Jesse. He said, "Let David stay and serve me. I like him."

23When the evil spirit from God entered Saul, David would take his harp and play. Then the evil spirit would go out of him. And Saul would feel relief. He would feel better again.

DAVID AND GOLIATH

17 The Philistines gathered their armies for war. They met at Socoh in Judah. Their camp was at Ephes Dammim between Socoh and Azekah. 2Saul and the Israelites gathered in the Valley of Elah. And they camped there. They took their positions to fight the Philistines. 3The Philistines controlled one hill. The Israelites controlled another. The valley was between them.

4The Philistines had a champion fighter named Goliath. He was from Gath. He was about nine feet four inches tall. He came out of the Philistine camp. 5He had a bronze helmet on his head. And he wore a coat of scale armor. It was made of bronze and weighed about 125 pounds. 6He wore bronze protectors on his legs. And he had a small spear of bronze tied on his back. 7The wooden part of his larger spear was like a weaver's rod. And its blade weighed about 15 pounds. The officer who carried his shield walked in front of him.

8Goliath stood and shouted to the Israelite soldiers, "Why have you taken positions for battle? I am a Philistine, and you are Saul's servants! Choose a man and send him to fight me. 9If he can fight and kill me, we will become your servants. But if I defeat and kill him, you will become our servants." 10Then he said, "Today I stand and dare the army of Israel! Send one of your men to fight me!" 11When Saul and the Israelites heard the Philistine's words, they were very afraid.

12Now David was the son of Jesse, an Ephrathite. Jesse was from Bethlehem in Judah. He had eight sons. In Saul's time Jesse was an old man. 13His three oldest sons followed Saul to the war. The first son was Eliab. The second son was Abinadab. And the third son was Shammah. 14David was the youngest son. Jesse's three oldest sons followed Saul. 15But David went back and forth from Saul to Bethlehem. There he took care of his father's sheep.

16The Philistine Goliath came out every morning and evening. He stood before the Israelite army. This continued for 40 days.

17Now Jesse said to his son David, "Take this half bushel of cooked grain. And take ten loaves of bread. Take them to your brothers in the camp. 18Also take ten pieces of cheese. Give them to the commander of your brothers' group of 1,000 soldiers. See how your brothers are. Bring back something to show me they are all right. 19Your brothers are with Saul and the army in the Valley of Elah. They are fighting against the Philistines."

20Early in the morning David left the sheep with another shepherd. He took the food and left as Jesse had told him.

When David arrived at the camp, the army was leaving. They were going out to their battle positions. The soldiers were shouting their war cry. ²¹The Israelites and Philistines were lining up their men to face each other in battle.

²²David left the food with the man who kept the supplies. Then he ran to the battle line and talked to his brothers. ²³While he was talking with them, Goliath came out. He was the Philistine champion from Gath. He shouted things against Israel as usual, and David heard it. ²⁴When the Israelites saw Goliath, they were very much afraid and ran away.

²⁵They said, "Look at this man Goliath. He keeps coming out to speak against Israel. The king will give much money to the man who kills Goliath. He will also give his daughter in marriage to whoever kills him. And his father's family will not have to pay taxes in Israel."

²⁶David asked the men who stood near him, "What will be done to reward the man who kills this Philistine? What will be done for whoever takes away the shame from Israel? Goliath is a Philistine. He is not circumcised.ᵈ Why does he think he can speak against the armies of the living God?"

²⁷The Israelites told David what they had been saying. They said, "This is what will be done for the man who kills Goliath."

²⁸David's oldest brother Eliab heard David talking with the soldiers. He became angry with David. He asked David, "Why did you come here? Who's taking care of those few sheep of yours in the desert? I know you are proud. Your attitude is very bad. You came down here just to watch the battle!"

²⁹David asked, "Now what have I done wrong? Can't I even talk?" ³⁰He then turned to other people and asked the same questions. And they gave him the same answer as before. ³¹Some men heard what David said and told Saul.

Then Saul ordered David to be sent to him.

³²David said to Saul, "Don't let anyone be discouraged. I, your servant, will go and fight this Philistine!"

³³Saul answered, "You can't go out against this Philistine and fight him. You're only a boy. Goliath has been a warrior since he was a young man."

³⁴But David said to Saul, "I, your servant, have been keeping my father's sheep. When a lion or bear came and took a sheep from the flock, ³⁵I would chase it. I would attack it and save the sheep from its mouth. When it attacked me, I caught it by its fur. I would hit it and kill it. ³⁶I, your servant, have killed both a lion and a bear! Goliath, the Philistine who is not circumcised, will be like the lion or bear I killed. He will die because he has stood against the armies of the living God. ³⁷The Lord saved me from a lion and a bear. He will also save me from this Philistine."

Saul said to David, "Go, and may the Lord be with you." ³⁸Saul put his own clothes on David. He put a bronze helmet on David's head and armor on his body. ³⁹David put on Saul's sword and tried to walk around. But he was not used to all the armor Saul had put on him.

He said to Saul, "I can't go in this. I'm not used to it." Then David took it all off. ⁴⁰He took his stick in his hand. And he chose five smooth stones from a stream. He put them in his pouch and held his sling in his hand. Then he went to meet Goliath.

⁴¹At the same time, the Philistine was coming closer to David. The man who held his shield walked in front of him. ⁴²Goliath looked at David. He saw that David was only a boy, tanned and handsome. He looked down at David with disgust. ⁴³He said, "Do you think I am a dog, that you come at me with a stick?" He used his gods' names to curse David. ⁴⁴He said to David, "Come here. I'll feed

your body to the birds of the air and the wild animals!"

⁴⁵But David said to him, "You come to me using a sword, a large spear and a small spear. But I come to you in the name of the Lord of heaven's armies. He's the God of the armies of Israel! You have spoken out against him. ⁴⁶Today the Lord will give you to me. I'll kill you, and I'll cut off your head. Today I'll feed the bodies of the Philistine soldiers to the birds of the air and the wild animals. Then all the world will know there is a God in Israel! ⁴⁷Everyone gathered here will know the Lord does not need swords or spears to save people. The battle belongs to him! And he will help us defeat all of you."

⁴⁸As Goliath came near to attack him, David ran quickly to meet him. ⁴⁹He took a stone from his pouch. He put it into his sling and slung it. The stone hit the Philistine on his forehead and sank into it. Goliath fell facedown on the ground.

⁵⁰So David defeated the Philistine with only a sling and a stone! He hit him and killed him. He did not even have a sword in his hand. ⁵¹David ran and stood beside the Philistine. He took Goliath's sword out of its holder and killed him. Then he cut off Goliath's head.

When the Philistines saw that their champion was dead, they turned and ran. ⁵²The men of Israel and Judah shouted and started chasing the Philistines. They chased them all the way to the entrance to the city of Gath. And they chased them to the gates of Ekron.

Many of the Philistines died. Their bodies lay on the Shaaraim road as far as Gath and Ekron. ⁵³The Israelites returned after chasing the Philistines. Then they took many things from the Philistine camp. ⁵⁴David took Goliath's head to Jerusalem. He also put Goliath's weapons in his own tent.

⁵⁵Saul had watched David go out to meet Goliath. Saul spoke to Abner, commander of the army. He said, "Abner, who is that young man's father?"

Abner answered, "As surely as you live, my king, I don't know."

⁵⁶The king said, "Find out whose son he is."

⁵⁷When David came back from killing Goliath, Abner brought him to Saul. David still held Goliath's head.

⁵⁸Saul asked him, "Young man, who is your father?"

David answered, "I am the son of your servant Jesse of Bethlehem."

SAUL FEARS DAVID

18 When David finished talking with Saul, Jonathan felt very close to David. He loved David as much as he loved himself. ²Saul kept David with him from that day on. He did not let David go home to his father's house. ³Jonathan made an agreement with David. He did this because he loved David as much as himself. ⁴He took off his coat and gave it to David. He also gave David his uniform, including his sword, bow and belt.

⁵Saul sent David to fight in different battles. And David was very successful. Then Saul put David over the soldiers. When he did this, Saul's officers and all the other people were pleased.

⁶After David had killed the Philistine, he and the men returned home. Women came out from all the towns of Israel to meet King Saul. They sang songs of joy, danced and played tambourines*d* and stringed instruments. ⁷As they played, they sang,

"Saul has killed thousands of his
    enemies.
But David has killed tens of
    thousands!"

⁸The women's song upset Saul, and he became very angry. He thought, "The women say David has killed tens of thousands of enemies. But they say I killed only thousands of enemies. The only thing left for him to have is the kingdom!" ⁹So Saul watched David closely from then on. He was jealous of him.

[10]The next day an evil spirit from God entered Saul with power. And he prophesied[d] in his house. David was playing the harp as he usually did. But Saul had a spear in his hand. [11]He raised the spear and thought, "I'll pin David to the wall." But David got away from him two times.

[12]The Lord was with David but had left Saul. So Saul was afraid of David. [13]He sent David away from him. He made David commander of 1,000 soldiers. So David led them in battle. [14]He had great success in everything he did because the Lord was with him. [15]Saul saw that David was very successful. And he became even more afraid of David. [16]But all the people of Israel and Judah loved David. This was because he led them well in battle.

SAUL'S DAUGHTER AND DAVID

[17]Saul said to David, "You're a brave soldier. And you fight the Lord's battles. Here is my older daughter Merab. I will let you marry her." Saul had decided, "I won't have to kill David. The Philistines will do that!"

[18]But David said, "I am not good enough for this honor. And my family is not important enough for me to become the king's son-in-law." [19]So when the time came for Saul's daughter Merab to marry David, Saul gave her instead to Adriel of Meholah.

[20]Now Saul's other daughter Michal loved David. When they told Saul about Michal loving David, he was pleased. [21]He thought, "I will let Michal marry David. Then she will become a trap for him. And the Philistines will defeat him." So Saul said to David a second time, "You may become my son-in-law."

[22]And Saul gave an order to his servants. He told them, "Speak to David in private. Say, 'Look, the king is pleased with you. His servants like you. You should become his son-in-law.'"

[23]Saul's servants said these words to David. But David answered, "Do you think it is easy to become the king's son-in-law? I'm only a poor man. Nobody knows me."

[24]Then Saul's servants told him what David had said. [25]Saul said, "Say to David, 'The king doesn't want you to pay a large price for the bride. All he wants is 100 Philistine foreskins. Then he will be even with his enemies.'" Saul planned to let the Philistines kill David.

[26]Saul's servants told David these words. David was pleased that he could become the king's son-in-law. [27]So he and his men went out and killed 200 Philistines. David took all their foreskins and brought them to Saul. He wanted to become the king's son-in-law. Then Saul gave him his daughter Michal for his wife. [28]Saul saw that the Lord was with David. He also saw that his daughter Michal loved David. [29]So he became even more afraid of David. And he was David's enemy all his life.

[30]The Philistine commanders continued to go out to fight the Israelites. But every time, David defeated them. He had more success than Saul's officers. And he became famous.

SAUL PLANS TO KILL DAVID

19 Saul told his son Jonathan and all his servants to kill David. But Jonathan cared very much for David. [2]So he warned David, "My father Saul is looking for a chance to kill you. Watch out in the morning. Hide in a secret place. [3]I will go out and stand with my father in the field where you are hiding. I'll talk to him about you. Then I'll let you know what I find out."

[4]Jonathan talked to Saul his father. He said good things about David. Jonathan said, "You are the king. Don't do wrong to your servant David. He did nothing wrong to you. What he did has helped you greatly. [5]David risked his life when he killed Goliath the Philistine. The Lord won a great victory for all Israel. You saw it, and you were happy. Why would you do wrong against David? He's innocent. There's no reason to kill him!"

⁶Saul listened to Jonathan. Then he made this promise: "As surely as the Lord lives, David won't be put to death."

⁷So Jonathan called to David. He told David everything that had been said. And he brought David to Saul. So David was with Saul as before.

⁸When war broke out again, David went out to fight the Philistines. He defeated them, and they ran away from him.

⁹But once again an evil spirit from the Lord entered Saul. He was sitting in his house, and he had his spear in his hand. David was playing the harp. ¹⁰Saul tried to pin David to the wall with his spear. But David moved away from him. So Saul's spear went into the wall. And David ran away that night.

¹¹Saul sent men to David's house. They watched it, wanting to kill him in the morning. But Michal, David's wife, warned him. She said, "Tonight you must run away to save your own life. If you don't, you will be killed tomorrow morning." ¹²Then she let David down out of a window. So he ran away and escaped. ¹³Then Michal took an idol and laid it on the bed. She covered it with clothes and put goats' hair at its head.

¹⁴Saul sent messengers to take David prisoner. But Michal said, "He is sick."

¹⁵The men went and told Saul, but he sent them back to see David. He told them, "Bring him to me on his bed so I can kill him."

¹⁶But when the messengers entered David's house, they found it was just an idol on the bed. Its hair was goats' hair.

¹⁷Saul said to Michal, "Why did you trick me this way? You let my enemy go. He has run away!"

Michal answered Saul, "David told me if I did not help him escape, he would kill me."

¹⁸After David had escaped from Saul, he went to Samuel at Ramah. He told Samuel everything Saul had done to him. Then David and Samuel went to Naioth

and stayed there. ¹⁹Saul heard that David was in Naioth at Ramah. ²⁰So he sent men to capture him. But they met a group of prophets*d* prophesying. Samuel was leading this group and was standing there. The Spirit*d* of God entered Saul's men, and they also prophesied.

²¹Saul heard the news. So he sent other men, but they also prophesied. Then he sent men a third time, but they also prophesied. ²²Finally, Saul himself went to Ramah. He came to the well at Secu. He asked, "Where are Samuel and David?"

The people answered, "In Naioth at Ramah."

²³Then Saul went to Naioth at Ramah. But the Spirit of God also entered him. And he walked on, prophesying until he came to Naioth at Ramah. ²⁴He took off his robes and prophesied in front of Samuel. He lay that way all day and all night. That is why people ask, "Is even Saul one of the prophets?"

DAVID AND JONATHAN

20 Then David ran away from Naioth in Ramah. He went to Jonathan and asked, "What have I done? What is my crime? How have I sinned against your father so that he's trying to kill me?"

²Jonathan answered, "No! You won't die! See, my father doesn't do anything without first telling me. It doesn't matter if it is very important or just a small thing. Why would he refuse to tell me he wants to kill you? No, it's not true!"

³But David took an oath. He said, "Your father knows very well that I'm your friend. He has said to himself, 'Jonathan must not know about it. If he knows, he will tell David.' But as surely as the Lord lives and as you live, I am very close to death!"

⁴Jonathan said to David, "I'll do anything you want me to do."

⁵So David said, "Look, tomorrow is the New Moon*d* festival. I am supposed to eat with the king. But let me hide in

the field until the third evening. ⁶Your father may notice I am gone. If he does, tell him, 'David begged me to let him go to his hometown of Bethlehem. Every year at this time, his family group offers a sacrifice.' ⁷If your father says, 'Fine,' I am safe. But if he becomes angry, you can believe he wants to hurt me. ⁸Jonathan, be kind to me, your servant. You have made an agreement with me before the Lord. If I am guilty, you may kill me yourself! Why hand me over to your father?"

⁹Jonathan answered, "No, never! If I learn that my father plans to harm you, I will warn you!"

¹⁰David asked, "Who will let me know if your father answers you unkindly?"

¹¹Then Jonathan said, "Come, let's go out into the field." So Jonathan and David went together into the field.

¹²Jonathan said to David, "I promise this before the Lord, the God of Israel: At this same time day after tomorrow, I will find out how my father feels. If he feels good toward you, I'll send word to you. I'll let you know. ¹³But my father may mean to hurt you. If so, I will let you know and send you away safely. May the Lord punish me terribly if I don't do this. And may the Lord be with you as he has been with my father. ¹⁴But show me the kindness of the Lord as long as I live. Do this so that I may not die. ¹⁵You must not stop showing your kindness to my family. Don't do this, even when the Lord has destroyed all your enemies from the earth."

¹⁶So Jonathan made an agreement with David. He said, "May the Lord punish David's enemies." ¹⁷And Jonathan asked David to repeat his promise of love for him. He did this because he loved David as much as he loved himself.

¹⁸Jonathan said to David, "Tomorrow is the New Moon festival. Your seat will be empty. So my father will notice you're gone. ¹⁹On the third day go to the place where you hid when this trouble began.

Wait by the rock Ezel. ²⁰On the third day I will shoot three arrows to the side of the rock. I will shoot as if I am shooting at a target. ²¹Then I will send a boy and tell him to go find the arrows. I may say to him, 'Look, the arrows are on this side of you. Bring them here.' If so, you may come out of hiding. You may do this as surely as the Lord lives because you are safe. There is no danger. ²²But I may say to the boy, 'Look, the arrows are beyond you.' If I do, you must go, because the Lord has sent you away. ²³Remember what we talked about. The Lord is a witness between you and me forever."

²⁴So David hid in the field. And when the New Moon festival came, the king sat down to eat. ²⁵He sat where he always sat, near the wall. Jonathan sat across from him, and Abner sat next to him. But David's place was empty. ²⁶That day Saul said nothing. He thought, "Maybe something has happened to David so that he is unclean."*d* ²⁷But the next day was the second day of the month. And David's place was empty again. So Saul said to Jonathan, "Why hasn't the son of Jesse come to the festival yesterday or today?"

²⁸Jonathan answered, "David begged me to let him go to Bethlehem. ²⁹He said, 'Let me go, because our family has a sacrifice in the town. And my brother has ordered me to be there. Now if I am your friend, please let me go and see my brothers.' That is why he has not come to the king's table."

³⁰Then Saul became very angry with Jonathan. He said, "You son of an evil and disobedient woman! I know you are on the side of David son of Jesse! You bring shame on yourself and on your mother who gave birth to you. ³¹As long as Jesse's son lives, you'll never be king or have a kingdom. Now send for David and bring him to me. He must die!"

³²Jonathan asked his father, "Why should David be killed? What wrong has he done?" ³³Then Saul threw his spear at

Jonathan, trying to kill him. So Jonathan knew that his father really wanted to kill David. 34Jonathan was very angry and left the table. That second day of the month he refused to eat. He was upset about what his father wanted to do to David.

35The next morning Jonathan went out to the field. He went to meet David as they had agreed. He had a young boy with him. 36Jonathan said to the boy, "Run and find the arrows I shoot." When he ran, Jonathan shot an arrow beyond him. 37The boy ran to the place where Jonathan's arrow fell. But Jonathan called, "The arrow is beyond you!" 38Then he shouted, "Hurry! Go quickly! Don't stop!" The boy picked up the arrow and brought it back to his master. 39(The boy knew nothing about what this meant. Only Jonathan and David knew.) 40Then Jonathan gave his weapons to the boy. He told him, "Go back to town."

41When the boy left, David came out from the south side of the rock. He bowed facedown on the ground before Jonathan. He did this three times. Then David and Jonathan kissed each other. They cried together, but David cried the most.

42Jonathan said to David, "Go in peace. We have promised by the Lord that we will be friends. We said, 'The Lord will be a witness between you and me, and between our descendants[d] forever.'" Then David left, and Jonathan went back to town.

DAVID GOES TO SEE AHIMELECH

21 David went to Nob to see Ahimelech the priest. Ahimelech shook with fear when he saw David. He asked David, "Why are you alone? Why is no one with you?"

2David answered him, "The king gave me a special order. He told me, 'No one must know about the work I am sending you to do. And no one must know what I

told you to do.' I told my men where to meet me. 3Now, what food do you have with you? Give me five loaves of bread or anything you find."

4The priest said to David, "I don't have any plain bread here. But I do have some holy bread[n] here. You may eat it if your men have kept themselves from women."

5David answered, "Women have been kept from us. My men always keep their bodies holy, even when we do ordinary work. And this is especially true when the work is holy."

6There was no bread except the bread made holy for the Lord. So the priest gave David the bread that showed the people were in the presence of God. This was the bread the priests had taken from the holy table before the Lord. Each day they took this bread away and put hot bread in its place.

7Now one of Saul's servants was there that day. He had been held there before the Lord. He was Doeg the Edomite, the chief of Saul's shepherds.

8David asked Ahimelech, "Do you have a spear or sword here? The king's business was very important. I had to leave quickly, and I didn't bring my sword or any other weapon."

9The priest answered, "The sword of Goliath the Philistine is here. He is the one you killed in the Valley of Elah. His sword is wrapped in a cloth. It is behind the holy vest.[d] If you want it, you may take it. There's no other sword here but that one."

David said, "There is no other sword like Goliath's. Give it to me."

DAVID GOES TO GATH

10That day David ran away from Saul. He went to Achish king of Gath. 11But the servants of Achish said to him, "This is David king of the Israelites. He's the man the Israelite women sing about when they dance. They sing:

21:4 **holy bread** This was the bread that showed the people were in the presence of God. Normally only the priests should eat this bread.

'Saul has killed thousands of his
    enemies.
  But David has killed tens of
    thousands.'"

[12]David paid attention to these words.
And he was very much afraid of Achish
king of Gath. [13]So he pretended to be
insane in front of Achish and his servants.
While he was with them, he acted like a
madman. He made marks on the doors of
the gate. He let spit run down his beard.

[14]Achish said to his servants, "Look at
the man! He's insane! Why do you bring
him to me? [15]I have enough madmen. I
don't need you to bring him here to act
like this in front of me! Don't leave him
in my house!"

DAVID AT ADULLAM AND MIZPAH

22 David left Gath and escaped to
the cave of Adullam. His brothers
and other relatives heard that he was
there. And they went to see him. [2]Many
people joined David. All those who were
in trouble, who owed money or who
were unsatisfied gathered around him.
And he became their leader. He had
about 400 men with him.

[3]From there David went to Mizpah in
Moab. He spoke to the king of Moab. He
said, "Please let my father and mother
come and stay with you. Let them stay
until I learn what God is going to do for
me." [4]So he left them with the king of
Moab. And they stayed with the king as
long as David was hiding in the protected place.

[5]But the prophet[d] Gad said to David,
"Don't stay in the protected place. Go to
the land of Judah." So David left and
went to the forest of Hereth.

SAUL DESTROYS AHIMELECH'S FAMILY

[6]Saul heard that David and his men
had been seen. He sat under the tamarisk
tree on the hill at Gibeah. All his officers
were standing around him. He had a
spear in his hand. [7]Saul said to them,
"Listen, men of Benjamin! Do you think

the son of Jesse will give all of you fields
and vineyards? Will David make you
commanders over thousands of men or
hundreds of men? [8]You have all made
plans against me! No one tells me when
my son makes an agreement with the
son of Jesse! No one cares about me! No
one tells me my son has encouraged my
servant to ambush me! And David is
doing this now!"

[9]Doeg the Edomite was standing there
with Saul's officers. He said, "I saw the
son of Jesse. He came to see Ahimelech
son of Ahitub at Nob. [10]Ahimelech prayed
to the Lord for David. He also gave him
food. And he gave him the sword of
Goliath the Philistine."

[11]Then the king sent for the priest
Ahimelech son of Ahitub. He sent for all
of Ahimelech's relatives who were priests
at Nob. And they all came to the king.
[12]Saul said to Ahimelech, "Listen now,
son of Ahitub."

Ahimelech answered, "Yes, master."

[13]Saul said, "Why have you and Jesse's
son made plans against me? You gave
him bread and a sword! You prayed to
God for him. David is waiting to attack
me. He is doing this now!"

[14]Ahimelech answered, "David is very
loyal to you. You have no other servant
who is as loyal as David. He is your own
son-in-law and captain of your bodyguards. All the people in your house
respect him. [15]That was not the first time
I prayed to God for David. Not at all!
Don't blame me or any of my relatives.
We are your servants. I know nothing
about what is going on."

[16]But the king said, "Ahimelech, you
and all your relatives must die!" [17]Then
he told the guards at his side, "Go and
kill the priests of the Lord. Do this
because they are on David's side. They
knew he was running away, but they
didn't tell me!"

But the king's officers refused to hurt
the priests of the Lord.

¹⁸Then the king ordered Doeg, "Go and kill the priests." So Doeg the Edomite went and killed the priests. That day he killed 85 men who wore the linen holy vest.ᵈ ¹⁹He also killed the people of Nob, the city of the priests. With the sword he killed men, women, children and small babies. And he killed cattle, donkeys and sheep.

²⁰But Abiathar escaped. He was a son of Ahimelech, who was the son of Ahitub. Abiathar ran away and joined David. ²¹He told David that Saul had killed the Lord's priests. ²²Then David told him, "Doeg the Edomite was there at Nob that day. I knew he would surely tell Saul. So I am responsible for the death of all your father's family. ²³The man who wants to kill you also wants to kill me. Stay with me. Don't be afraid. You will be safe with me."

DAVID AT KEILAH

23 Someone told David, "Look, the Philistines are fighting against Keilah. They are robbing grain from the threshingᵈ floors."

²David asked the Lord, "Should I go and fight these Philistines?"

The Lord answered him, "Go. Attack them, and save Keilah."

³But David's men said to him, "We're afraid here in Judah. We will be much more afraid if we go to Keilah where the Philistine army is."

⁴David again asked the Lord. And the Lord answered, "Go down to Keilah. I will help you defeat the Philistines." ⁵So David and his men went to Keilah. They fought the Philistines and took their cattle. David killed many Philistines and saved the people of Keilah. ⁶(Now Abiathar son of Ahimelech had brought the holy vestᵈ with him. He brought it when he came to David at Keilah.)

SAUL CHASES DAVID

⁷Someone told Saul that David was now at Keilah. Saul said, "God has given David to me! He has trapped himself because he has entered a town with gates and bars." ⁸Saul called all his army together for battle. They prepared to go down to Keilah to attack David and his men.

⁹David learned Saul was making evil plans against him. So he said to Abiathar the priest, "Bring the holy vest."ᵈ ¹⁰David prayed, "Lord, God of Israel, I have heard about Saul's plans. He is coming to Keilah to destroy the town because of me. ¹¹Will the people of Keilah give me to Saul? Will Saul come to Keilah, as I heard? Lord, God of Israel, tell me, your servant!"

The Lord answered, "Saul will come down."

¹²Again David asked, "Will the people of Keilah give me and my men to Saul?"

The Lord answered, "They will."

¹³So David and his men left Keilah. There were about 600 men who went with him. And they kept moving from place to place. When Saul found that David had escaped from Keilah, he did not go there.

¹⁴David stayed in the protected places in the desert. He also stayed in the hills of the Desert of Ziph. Every day Saul looked for David. But the Lord did not let him take David.

¹⁵David was at Horesh in the Desert of Ziph. He was afraid because Saul was coming to kill him. ¹⁶But Saul's son Jonathan went to David at Horesh. He helped David have stronger faith in God. ¹⁷Jonathan told him, "Don't be afraid. My father won't touch you. You will become king of Israel, and I will be second to you. Even my father Saul knows this." ¹⁸The two of them made an agreement before the Lord. Then Jonathan went home. But David stayed at Horesh.

¹⁹The people from Ziph went to Saul at Gibeah. They told him, "David is hiding in our land. He's at the protected places of Horesh. They are on the hill of Hakilah, south of Jeshimon. ²⁰Now, our king, come down anytime you want. It's our duty to give David to you."

²¹Saul answered, "The Lord bless you for helping me. ²²Go and learn more about him. Find out where he is staying. Find out who has seen him there. I have heard that he is clever. ²³Find all the hiding places he uses. And come back and tell me everything. Then I'll go with you. If David is in the area, I will find him. I will track him down among all the families in Judah."

²⁴So they went back to Ziph ahead of Saul. David and his men were in the Desert of Maon.ⁿ This was in the desert area south of Jeshimon. ²⁵Saul and his men went to look for David. But people warned David that Saul was looking for him. David then went down to a rock and stayed in the Desert of Maon. Saul heard that David had gone there. So he went after him into the Desert of Maon.

²⁶Saul was going along one side of the mountain. David and his men were on the other side. They were hurrying to get away from Saul. Saul and his soldiers were closing in on David and his men. ²⁷But a messenger came to Saul. He said, "Come quickly! The Philistines are attacking our land!" ²⁸So Saul stopped chasing David and went to fight the Philistines. That is why people call this place Rock of Parting. ²⁹David left the Desert of Maon and lived in the protected places of En Gedi.

DAVID SHAMES SAUL

24 Now Saul had chased the Philistines away. Then he was told, "David is in the Desert of En Gedi." ²So he chose 3,000 men from all Israel. He took these men and began looking for David and his men. They looked near the Rocks of the Wild Goats.

³Saul came to the sheep pens beside the road. A cave was there, and he went in to relieve himself. Now David and his men were hiding far back in the cave. ⁴The men said to David, "Today is the day the Lord talked about! The Lord told you, 'I will give your enemy to you. You can do anything you want with him.'"

Then David crawled near Saul. He cut off a corner of Saul's robe. But Saul did not notice him. ⁵Later David felt guilty because he had cut off a corner of Saul's robe. ⁶He said to his men, "May the Lord keep me from doing such a thing to my master! Saul is the Lord's appointed king. I should not do anything against him, because he is the Lord's appointed king!" ⁷David used these words to stop his men. He did not let them attack Saul. Then Saul left the cave and went his way.

⁸When David came out of the cave, he shouted to Saul, "My master and king!" Saul looked back, and David bowed facedown on the ground. ⁹He said to Saul, "Why do you listen when people say, 'David plans to harm you'? ¹⁰You have seen something with your own eyes today. You have seen how the Lord put you in my power in the cave. But I refused to kill you. I was merciful to you. I said, 'I won't harm my master, because he is the Lord's appointed king.' ¹¹My father, look at this piece of your robe in my hand! I cut off the corner of your robe, but I didn't kill you. Now understand and know I am not planning any evil against you. I did nothing wrong to you, but you are hunting me to kill me. ¹²May the Lord judge between us. And may he punish you for the wrong you have done to me! But I won't fight you. ¹³There is an old saying: 'Evil things come from evil people.' So I won't hurt you. ¹⁴Whom is the king of Israel coming out against? Whom are you chasing? You're not chasing someone who will hurt you! It's as if you are chasing a dead dog or a flea. ¹⁵May the Lord be our judge and decide between you and me. May the Lord support me and show that I am right. May he save me from you!"

23:24 **Maon** Some early Greek copies say "Maon." The Hebrew copies say "Paran."

[16]David finished saying these words. Then Saul asked, "Is that your voice, David my son?" And he cried loudly. [17]He said, "You are right, and I am wrong. You have been good to me. But I have done wrong to you. [18]You told me what good things you did. The Lord brought me to you, but you did not kill me. [19]If a man finds his enemy, he won't send him away with goodness, will he? May the Lord reward you because you were good to me today. [20]I know you will surely be king. You will rule the kingdom of Israel. [21]Now make a promise to me. Promise in the name of the Lord that you will not kill my descendants.[d] Promise me that you won't wipe out my name from my father's family."

[22]So David made the promise to Saul. Then Saul went back home. David and his men went up to the protected place.

DAVID AND NABAL

25 Now Samuel died. All the Israelites met and had a time of sadness for him. They buried him at his home in Ramah.

Then David moved to the Desert of Maon.[n] [2]A man in Maon who had land at Carmel was very rich. He had 3,000 sheep and 1,000 goats. He was cutting the wool off his sheep at Carmel. [3]His name was Nabal, and he was a descendant[d] of Caleb. His wife was named Abigail. She was a wise and beautiful woman. But Nabal was cruel and mean.

[4]David was in the desert. He heard that Nabal was cutting the wool from his sheep. [5]So he sent ten young men. He told them, "Go to Nabal at Carmel. Greet him for me. [6]Say to Nabal, 'May you and your family have good health! And may all who belong to you have good health. [7]I have heard that you are cutting the wool from your sheep. When your shepherds were with us, we did nothing wrong to them. All the time your shepherds

were at Carmel, we stole nothing from them. [8]Ask your servants, and they will tell you. We come at a happy time. So for this reason, be kind to my young men. Please give them anything you can find for them. Please do this for your son David.'"

[9]When the men arrived, they gave the message to Nabal. But Nabal insulted them. [10]He answered them, "Who is David? Who is this son of Jesse? Many slaves are running away from their masters today! [11]I have bread and water. And I have meat that I killed for my servants who cut the wool. But I won't give it to men I don't know."

[12]David's men went back and told him all Nabal had said. [13]Then David said to them, "Put on your swords!" So they put on their swords, and David put on his also. About 400 men went with David. But 200 men stayed with the supplies.

[14]One of Nabal's servants spoke to Abigail, Nabal's wife. He said, "David sent messengers from the desert to greet our master. But Nabal insulted them. [15]These men were very good to us. They did nothing wrong to us. They stole nothing from us during all the time we were out in the field with them. [16]Night and day they protected us. They were like a wall around us while we were with them caring for the sheep. [17]Now think about it, and decide what you can do. Terrible trouble is coming to our master and all his family. Nabal is such a wicked man that no one can even talk to him."

[18]Abigail hurried. She took 200 loaves of bread, 2 leather bags full of wine and 5 cooked sheep. She took about a bushel of cooked grain, 100 cakes of raisins and 200 cakes of pressed figs. She put all these on donkeys. [19]Then she told her servants, "Go on. I'll follow you." But she did not tell her husband.

[20]Abigail rode her donkey and came down into the mountain ravine. There

---

25:1 Maon Some early Greek copies say "Maon." The Hebrew copies say "Paran."

she met David and his men coming down toward her.

²¹David had just said, "It's been useless! I watched over Nabal's property in the desert. I made sure none of his sheep were missing. I did good to him, but he has paid me back with evil. ²²May God punish me terribly if I let just one of Nabal's family live until tomorrow."

²³When Abigail saw David, she quickly got off her donkey. She bowed facedown on the ground before David. ²⁴She lay at David's feet. She said, "My master, let the blame be on me! Please let me talk to you! Listen to what I say. ²⁵My master, don't pay attention to this worthless man Nabal. He is the same as his name. His name means 'fool,' and he is truly foolish. But I, your servant, didn't see the men you sent. ²⁶The Lord has kept you from killing and punishing people yourself. As surely as the Lord lives and as surely as you live, may your enemies become like Nabal! ²⁷I have brought a gift to you. Please give it to the men who follow you. ²⁸Please forgive my wrong. The Lord will certainly let your family have many kings. He will do this because you fight his battles. As long as you live, people will find nothing bad in you. ²⁹A man might chase you to kill you. But the Lord your God will keep you alive. He will throw away your enemies' lives as he would throw a stone from a sling. ³⁰The Lord will keep all his promises about good things for you. He will make you leader over Israel. ³¹Then you won't feel guilty. You won't have problems about killing innocent people and punishing them yourself. Please remember me when the Lord brings you success."

³²David answered Abigail, "Praise the Lord, the God of Israel. He sent you to meet me. ³³May you be blessed for your wisdom. You have kept me from killing or punishing people today. ³⁴As surely as the Lord, the God of Israel, lives, he has kept me from hurting you. If you hadn't come

quickly to meet me, no one belonging to Nabal would have lived until tomorrow."

³⁵Then David accepted Abigail's gifts. He told her, "Go home in peace. I have heard your words, and I will do what you have asked."

NABAL'S DEATH

³⁶When Abigail went back to Nabal, he was in the house. He was eating like a king. He was very drunk and in a good mood. So she told him nothing until the next morning. ³⁷In the morning he was not drunk. Then his wife told him everything. His heart failed him, and he became like a stone. ³⁸About ten days later the Lord struck Nabal and caused him to die.

³⁹When David heard that Nabal was dead, he said, "Praise the Lord! Nabal insulted me, but the Lord has supported me! He has kept me from doing wrong. And the Lord caused Nabal to die because he did wrong."

Then David sent a message to Abigail. He asked her to become his wife. ⁴⁰His servants went to Carmel and spoke to Abigail. They said, "David sent us to take you so you can become his wife."

⁴¹Abigail bowed facedown on the ground. She said, "I am your servant. I'm ready to serve you. I'm ready to wash the feet of my master's servants." ⁴²Abigail quickly got on a donkey and went with David's messengers. She had five maids following her. And she became David's wife.

⁴³David also had married Ahinoam of Jezreel. So they were both David's wives. ⁴⁴Saul's daughter Michal was also David's wife. But Saul had given her to Paltiel son of Laish. Paltiel was from Gallim.

DAVID SHAMES SAUL AGAIN

26 The people of Ziph went to see Saul at Gibeah. They said to him, "David is hiding on the hill of Hakilah opposite Jeshimon."

²So Saul went down to the Desert of Ziph. His 3,000 chosen men of Israel went

with him. They looked for David in the Desert of Ziph. ³Saul made his camp on the hill of Hakilah, beside the road opposite Jeshimon. But David stayed in the desert. He heard Saul had followed him. ⁴So David sent out spies and learned that Saul had come to Hakilah.

⁵Then David went to the place where Saul had camped. He saw where Saul and Abner son of Ner were sleeping. Abner was the commander of Saul's army. Saul was sleeping in the middle of the camp with all the army around him.

⁶David talked to Ahimelech the Hittite and Abishai son of Zeruiah. Abishai was Joab's brother. He asked them, "Who will go down into Saul's camp with me?"

Abishai answered, "I'll go with you."

⁷So that night David and Abishai went into Saul's camp. Saul was asleep in the middle of the camp. His spear was stuck in the ground near his head. Abner and the army were sleeping around Saul. ⁸Abishai said to David, "Today God has let you defeat your enemy! Let me pin Saul to the ground with the spear. I'll only do it once! I won't hit him twice."

⁹But David said to Abishai, "Don't kill Saul! No one can harm the Lord's appointed king and still be innocent! ¹⁰As surely as the Lord lives, the Lord himself will punish Saul. Maybe Saul will die naturally. Or maybe he will go into battle and be killed. ¹¹But may the Lord keep me from harming his appointed king! Now pick up the spear and water jug that are near Saul's head. Then let's go."

¹²So David took the spear and water jug that were near Saul's head. They left, and no one saw them. No one knew about it or woke up. The Lord had made them stay asleep.

¹³David crossed over to the other side of the hill. He stood on top of the mountain far from Saul's camp. David's and Saul's camps were far apart. ¹⁴David shouted to the army and to Abner son of Ner, "Answer me, Abner!"

Abner answered, "Who is calling for the king? Who are you?"

¹⁵David said, "You're the greatest man in Israel. Isn't that true? Then why didn't you guard your master the king? Someone came into your camp to kill your master the king! ¹⁶What you have done is not good. As surely as the Lord lives, you and your men should die. You haven't guarded your master, the Lord's appointed king. Look! Where are the king's spear and water jug that were near his head?"

¹⁷Saul knew David's voice. He said, "Is that your voice, David my son?"

David answered, "Yes, it is, my master and king." ¹⁸David also said, "Why are you chasing me, my master? What wrong have I done? What evil am I guilty of? ¹⁹My master and king, listen to me. If the Lord caused you to be angry with me, let him accept an offering. But if men caused you to be angry with me, let the Lord curse them! They have made me leave the land the Lord gave me. They have told me, 'Go and serve other gods.' ²⁰Now don't let me die far away from the Lord's presence. The king of Israel has come out looking for a flea! You're like a man hunting a partridge bird in the mountains!"

²¹Then Saul said, "I have sinned. Come back, David my son. Today you respected my life. So I will not try to hurt you. I have acted foolishly. I have made a big mistake."

²²David answered, "Here is your spear. Let one of your young men come here and get it. ²³The Lord rewards every man for the things he does right and for his loyalty to him. The Lord put you into my power today. But I wouldn't harm the Lord's appointed king. ²⁴I respected your life today. Surely, in the same way, the Lord will respect my life. Surely he will save me from all trouble."

²⁵Then Saul said to David, "You are blessed, my son David. You will do great things and succeed."

So David went on his way, and Saul went back home.

DAVID AND THE PHILISTINES

27 But David thought to himself, "Saul will catch me someday. The best thing I can do is escape to the land of the Philistines. Then he will give up looking for me in Israel. That way I can get away from him."

²So David and his 600 men left Israel. They went to Achish son of Maoch. Achish was king of Gath. ³David, his men and their families made their home in Gath with Achish. David had his two wives with him. Their names were Ahinoam of Jezreel and Abigail of Carmel. Abigail was the widow of Nabal. ⁴Now Saul was told that David had run away to Gath. So he stopped looking for him.

⁵Then David said to Achish, "If you are pleased with me, give me a place in one of the country towns. I can live there. I don't need to live in the royal city with you."

⁶That day Achish gave David the town of Ziklag. That is why Ziklag has belonged to the kings of Judah ever since. ⁷David lived in the Philistine land a year and four months.

⁸David and his men went to raid the people of Geshur, Girzi and Amalek. (These people had lived for a long time in the land that reached to Shur and Egypt.) ⁹When David fought them, he killed all the men and women. He took sheep, cattle, donkeys, camels and clothes. Then he returned to Achish.

¹⁰Many times Achish would ask David, "Where did you go raiding today?" And David would tell him that he had gone to the southern part of Judah. Or he would say he had gone to the territory of the Jerahmeelites or of the Kenites. ¹¹David never brought a man or woman alive to Gath. He thought, "If we bring anyone alive, he may tell Achish, 'This is what David really did.'" David did this all the time he lived in the Philistine land. ¹²Achish trusted David. He said to himself, "David's own people, the Israelites, now hate David very much. So David will serve me forever."

SAUL AND THE WITCH OF ENDOR

28 Later, the Philistines gathered their armies to fight against Israel. Achish said to David, "You understand that you and your men must join with me in my army."

²David answered, "Certainly! Then you can see for yourself what I, your servant, can do!"

Achish said, "Fine, I'll make you my bodyguard for life."

³Now Samuel was dead, and all the Israelites had shown their sadness for him. They had buried Samuel in his hometown of Ramah.

And Saul had forced out the mediums[d] and fortune-tellers from the land of Israel.

⁴The Philistines came together and made camp at Shunem. Saul gathered all the Israelites and made camp at Gilboa. ⁵When he saw the Philistine army, he was afraid. His heart pounded with fear. ⁶He prayed to the Lord, but the Lord did not answer him through dreams, Urim[d] or prophets.[d] ⁷Then Saul said to his servants, "Find me a woman who is a medium. I'll go and ask her what will happen."

His servants answered, "There is a medium in Endor."

⁸Then Saul put on other clothes so no one would know who he was. At night Saul and two of his men went to see the woman. Saul said to her, "Talk to a spirit for me. Call up the person I name."

⁹But the woman said to him, "Surely you know what Saul has done. He has forced the mediums and fortune-tellers out from the land of Israel. You are trying to trap me and kill me."

¹⁰Saul made a promise to the woman in the name of the Lord. He said, "As surely as the Lord lives, you won't be punished for doing this."

¹¹The woman asked, "Whom do you want me to bring up for you?"

He answered, "Bring up Samuel."

¹²When the woman saw Samuel, she screamed loudly. She said, "Why have you tricked me? You are Saul!"

¹³The king said to the woman, "Don't be afraid! What do you see?"

The woman said, "I see a spirit coming up out of the ground."

¹⁴Saul asked, "What does he look like?"

The woman answered, "An old man wearing a coat is coming up."

Then Saul knew it was Samuel, and he bowed facedown on the ground.

¹⁵Samuel asked Saul, "Why have you disturbed me by bringing me up?"

Saul said, "I am greatly troubled. The Philistines are fighting against me. God has left me. He won't answer me anymore, either by prophets or in dreams. That's why I called you. I want you to tell me what to do."

¹⁶Samuel said, "The Lord has left you. He has become your enemy. So why do you call on me? ¹⁷He has done what he said he would do. He said these things through me. He has torn the kingdom out of your hands. He has given it to one of your neighbors, David. ¹⁸You did not obey the Lord. You did not show the Amalekites how angry he was with them. That's why he has done this to you today. ¹⁹The Lord will give both Israel and you to the Philistines. Tomorrow you and your sons will be with me. The Lord will let the Philistines defeat the army of Israel."

²⁰Saul quickly fell to the ground and lay there. He was afraid because of what Samuel had said. He was also very weak because he had eaten nothing all that day and night.

²¹Then the woman came to Saul. She saw that he was really frightened. She said, "Look, I, your servant, have obeyed you. I have risked my life and done what you told me to do. ²²Now please listen to me. Let me give you some food. Then you may eat and have enough strength to go on your way."

²³But Saul refused. He said, "I won't eat."

His servants joined the woman in asking him to eat. And he listened to them. So he got up from the ground and sat on the bed.

²⁴The woman had a fat calf at the house. She quickly killed it. She took some flour and mixed dough with her hands. Then she baked some bread without yeast. ²⁵She put the food before them, and they ate. Then that same night they got up and left.

DAVID GOES BACK TO ZIKLAG

29 The Philistines gathered all their soldiers at Aphek. Israel camped by the spring at Jezreel. ²The Philistine kings were marching with their groups of 100 and 1,000 men. David and his men were marching at the back with Achish. ³The Philistine commanders asked, "What are these Hebrews doing here?"

Achish told them, "This is David. He was an officer to Saul king of Israel. But he has been with me for over a year now. I have found nothing wrong in David since the time he left Saul and came to me."

⁴But the Philistine commanders were angry with Achish. They said, "Send David back! He must go back to the city you gave him. He can't go with us into battle. If he's here, we'll have an enemy in our own camp. He would please his king by killing our own men. ⁵David is the one the Israelites sing about in their dances:

'Saul has killed thousands of his
   enemies.
But David has killed tens of
   thousands.'"

⁶So Achish called David. He said to him, "As surely as the Lord lives, you are loyal. I would be pleased to have you serve in my army. Since the day you came to me, I have found no wrong in you. But the Philistine kings don't trust you. ⁷Go back in peace. Don't do anything to displease the Philistine kings."

[8]David asked, "What wrong have I done? What evil have you found in me from the day I came to you until now? Why won't you allow me to fight your enemies, my lord and king?"

[9]Achish answered, "I know you are as pleasing to me as an angel from God. But the Philistine commanders have said, 'David can't go with us into battle.' [10]Early in the morning you and your master's servants, the Israelites, should go back. Go back to the city I gave you. Leave as soon as the sun comes up."

[11]So David and his men got up early in the morning. They went back to the country of the Philistines. And the Philistines went up to Jezreel.

DAVID'S WAR WITH THE AMALEKITES

30 On the third day David and his men arrived at Ziklag. The Amalekites had raided southern Judah and Ziklag. They had attacked Ziklag and burned it. [2]They took the women and everyone in Ziklag as prisoners, both young and old. But they did not kill any of the people. They only took them away.

[3]When David and his men came to Ziklag, they found the town had been burned. Their wives, sons and daughters had been taken as prisoners. [4]Then David and his army cried loudly until they were too weak to cry anymore. [5]David's two wives had also been taken. They were Ahinoam of Jezreel and Abigail the widow of Nabal from Carmel. [6]The men in the army were threatening to kill David with stones. This upset David very much. Each man was sad and angry because his sons and daughters had been taken as prisoners. But David found strength in the Lord his God. [7]David said to Abiathar the priest, "Bring me the holy vest."[d]

[8]Then David prayed to the Lord. He said, "Should I chase the people who took our families? Will I catch them?"

The Lord answered, "Chase them. You will catch them. You will succeed in saving your families."

[9]David and the 600 men with him came to the Besor Ravine. Some of the men stayed there. [10]David and 400 men kept up the chase. The other 200 men stayed behind because they were too tired and weak to cross the ravine.

[11]David's men found an Egyptian in a field. They took him to David. They gave the Egyptian some water to drink and some food to eat. [12]They gave him a piece of a fig cake and two clusters of raisins. He felt better after eating. He had not eaten any food or drunk any water for three days and nights.

[13]David asked him, "Who is your master? Where do you come from?"

He answered, "I'm an Egyptian. I'm the slave of an Amalekite. Three days ago my master left me, because I became sick. [14]We attacked the southern area of the Kerethites. We attacked the land of Judah and the southern area belonging to Caleb. We burned Ziklag, as well."

[15]David asked him, "Will you lead me to the people who took our families?"

He answered, "Yes, if you will make a promise to me before God. Promise that you won't kill me or give me back to my master. Then I will take you to them."

[16]So the Egyptian led David to the Amalekites. They were lying around on the ground, eating and drinking. They were celebrating with the things they had taken from the land of the Philistines and from Judah. [17]David fought them from sunset until evening the next day. None of them escaped, except 400 young men who rode off on their camels. [18]David got his two wives back. He also got back everything the Amalekites had taken. [19]Nothing was missing. David brought back everything: the young and old people, the sons and daughters, the valuable things and everything the Amalekites had taken. [20]David took all the sheep and cattle. His men made these animals go in front. They said, "They are David's prize."

²¹Then David came to the 200 men who had been too tired and weak to follow him. He had made them stay at the Besor Ravine. They came out to meet David and the army with him. When he came near, the men at the ravine greeted David and his army.

²²But there were evil men and troublemakers in the group that followed David. They said, "These 200 men didn't go with us. So we won't give them any of the things we took. But each man may take his wife and children and go."

²³David answered, "No, my brothers. Don't do that after what the Lord has given us. He has given us the enemy who attacked us. ²⁴Who will listen to what you say? The share will be the same for the man who stayed with the supplies as for the man who went into battle. All will share alike." ²⁵David made this an order and rule for Israel. This order and rule continues even today.

²⁶David arrived in Ziklag. Then he sent some of the things he had taken from the Amalekites to his friends, the leaders of Judah. He said, "Here is a present for you from the things we took from the Lord's enemies."

²⁷David sent some things from the Amalekites to the leaders in Bethel, Ramoth in the southern part of Judah, Jattir, ²⁸Aroer, Siphmoth, Eshtemoa ²⁹and Racal. He also sent some to the leaders of the cities of the Jerahmeelites and the Kenites, ³⁰to Hormah, Bor Ashan, Athach ³¹and Hebron. He sent some things to the people in all the other places where he and his men had been.

THE DEATH OF SAUL

31 The Philistines fought against Israel, and the Israelites ran away from them. Many Israelites were killed at Mount Gilboa. ²The Philistines fought hard against Saul and his sons.

They killed his sons Jonathan, Abinadab and Malki-Shua. ³The fighting became bad around Saul. When the archers shot at him, he was badly wounded. ⁴He said to the officer who carried his armor, "Pull out your sword and kill me. Then those uncircumcised[d] men won't make fun of me and kill me." But Saul's officer refused, because he was afraid. So Saul took his own sword and threw himself on it. ⁵The officer saw that Saul was dead. So he threw himself on his own sword. And he died with Saul. ⁶So Saul, his three sons and the officer who carried his armor died together that day.

⁷Now there were Israelites who lived on the other side of Jezreel Valley. And some lived across the Jordan River. They saw how the Israelite army had run away. And they saw that Saul and his sons were dead. So they left their cities and ran away. Then the Philistines came and lived there.

⁸The next day the Philistines came to take all the valuable things from the dead soldiers. They found Saul and his three sons dead on Mount Gilboa. ⁹They cut off Saul's head and took off his armor. Then they sent men to tell the news through all the land of the Philistines. They told it in the temple of their idols and to their people. ¹⁰They put Saul's armor in the temple of the Ashtoreths.[d] They also hung his body on the wall of Beth Shan.

¹¹The people living in Jabesh Gilead heard what the Philistines had done to Saul. ¹²So the brave soldiers of Jabesh marched all night and came to Beth Shan. They took the bodies of Saul and his sons off the wall of Beth Shan. Then they took them to Jabesh. There the people of Jabesh burned the bodies. ¹³They took their bones and buried them under the tamarisk tree in Jabesh. Then the people of Jabesh gave up eating for seven days.

SAMUEL

DAVID LEARNS ABOUT SAUL'S DEATH

1 Now Saul was dead. And after David had defeated the Amalekites, he returned to Ziklag. He stayed there two days. ²On the third day a young man came to Ziklag. He came from Saul's camp. To show his sadness his clothes were torn, and he had dirt on his head. He came and bowed facedown on the ground before David.

³David asked him, "Where did you come from?"

The man answered him, "I escaped from the Israelite camp."

⁴David asked him, "What happened? Please tell me!"

The man answered, "The people have run away from the battle. Many of them have fallen dead. Saul and his son Jonathan are dead also."

⁵David said to him, "How do you know Saul and his son Jonathan are dead?"

⁶The young man answered, "I happened to be on Mount Gilboa. There I saw Saul leaning on his spear. The Philistine chariots and the men riding in them were coming closer to Saul. ⁷When he looked back and saw me, he called to me. I answered him, 'Here I am!'

⁸"Then Saul asked me, 'Who are you?'

"I told him, 'I am an Amalekite.'

⁹"Then Saul said to me, 'Please come here and kill me. I am badly hurt and am almost dead already.'

¹⁰"So I went over and killed him. He had been hurt so badly I knew he couldn't live. Then I took the crown from his head and the bracelet from his arm. I have brought them here to you, my master."

¹¹Then David tore his clothes to show his sorrow. And all the men with him did also. ¹²They were very sad and cried. They did not eat until evening. They cried for Saul and his son Jonathan. And they cried for the Israelites who had been killed with swords.

DAVID ORDERS THE AMALEKITE KILLED

¹³David asked the young man who brought the report, "Where are you from?"

The young man answered, "I am the son of a foreigner. I am an Amalekite."

¹⁴David asked him, "Why were you not afraid to kill the Lord's appointed king?"

¹⁵Then David called one of his men. David told him, "Go! Kill the Amalekite!" So the Israelite killed the Amalekite. ¹⁶David had said to the Amalekite, "You are responsible for your own death. You have spoken against yourself! You said, 'I have killed the Lord's appointed king.'"

DAVID'S SONG ABOUT SAUL AND JONATHAN

¹⁷David sang a funeral song about Saul and his son Jonathan. ¹⁸David ordered that the people of Judah be taught this song. It is called "The Bow." This song is written in the Book of Jashar:

¹⁹"Israel, your leaders have been killed
on the hills.
How the mighty men have fallen in
battle!
²⁰Don't tell it in Gath.
Don't announce it in the streets of
Ashkelon.
If you do, the daughters of the
Philistines will be happy.
The daughters of the Philistines will
rejoice.

²¹"May there be no dew or rain on the
mountains of Gilboa.
May their fields produce no grain.
This is because there the mighty
warrior's shield was dishonored.
Saul's shield was no longer rubbed
with oil.
²²Jonathan's bow killed its share of
enemies.
And Saul's sword killed its share,
too.

Their weapons are stained with the
blood of dead men.
Their weapons have stabbed the
flesh of strong men.

23"We loved Saul and Jonathan.
We enjoyed them while they lived.
Saul and Jonathan are together
even in death.
They were faster than eagles.
They were stronger than lions.

24"You daughters of Israel, cry for Saul.
Saul clothed you with red dresses.
He put gold decorations on your
dresses.

25"How the mighty men have fallen in
battle!
Jonathan is dead on Gilboa's hills.
26I cry for you, my brother Jonathan.
I enjoyed your friendship so much.
Your love to me was wonderful,
more wonderful than the love of
women.

27"How the mighty men have fallen in
battle!
The weapons of war are gone."

DAVID IS MADE KING OF JUDAH

2 Later, David prayed to the Lord.
David said, "Should I go up to any
of the cities of Judah?"
The Lord said to David, "Go."
David asked, "Where should I go?"
The Lord answered, "To Hebron."
2So David went up to Hebron with his
two wives. One was Ahinoam from
Jezreel. The other was Abigail, the widow
of Nabal in Carmel. 3David also brought
his men and their families. They all made
their homes in the cities of Hebron.
4Then the men of Judah came to Hebron.
They appointed David king over Judah.
They told David that the men of
Jabesh Gilead had buried Saul. 5So David
sent messengers to the men of Jabesh
Gilead. They told David's message to the
men in Jabesh: "The Lord bless you. You
have shown kindness to your master

Saul by burying him. 6May the Lord now
be kind and true to you. I will also be
kind to you because you have done this.
7Now be strong and brave. Saul your
master is dead. The people of Judah have
appointed me their king."

WAR BETWEEN JUDAH AND ISRAEL

8Now Abner son of Ner was the commander of Saul's army. Abner took
Saul's son Ish-Bosheth to Mahanaim.
9There Abner made him king of Gilead,
Ashuri, Jezreel, Ephraim, Benjamin and
all Israel. 10Saul's son Ish-Bosheth was
40 years old when he became king over
Israel. He ruled two years. But the
people of Judah followed David. 11David
was king in Hebron for seven years and
six months.

12Abner son of Ner and the servants of
Ish-Bosheth son of Saul left Mahanaim.
They went to Gibeon. 13Joab son of
Zeruiah and David's men also went there.
They met Abner and Ish-Bosheth's men
at the pool of Gibeon. Abner's group sat
on one side of the pool. Joab's group sat
on the other side.

14Abner said to Joab, "Let's have the
young men get up and have a contest
here."
Joab said, "Yes, let them have a contest."
15Then the young men got up. The two
groups counted their men for the contest.
Twelve men were chosen from the people
of Benjamin for Ish-Bosheth son of Saul.
Twelve men were chosen from David's
men. 16Each man grabbed his enemy's
head. Then he stabbed his enemy's side
with a knife. And the men fell down
together. So that place in Gibeon is
called The Field of the Sharp Knives.
17That day the contest became a terrible
battle. And David's men defeated Abner
and the Israelites.

ABNER KILLS ASAHEL

18Zeruiah's three sons, Joab, Abishai
and Asahel, were there. Now Asahel was
a fast runner. He was as fast as a deer in

the field. ¹⁹Asahel chased Abner, going straight toward him. ²⁰Abner looked back and asked, "Are you Asahel?"

Asahel said, "Yes, I am."

²¹Then Abner said to Asahel, "Turn to your right or left. Catch one of the young men and take his armor." But Asahel refused to stop chasing him.

²²Abner again said to Asahel, "Stop chasing me! If you don't stop, I'll have to kill you! Then I won't be able to face your brother Joab again!"

²³But Asahel refused to stop chasing Abner. So Abner used the back end of his spear. He stabbed it into Asahel's stomach, and the spear came out of his back. Asahel died right there. Everyone stopped when they came to the place where Asahel's body lay.

²⁴But Joab and Abishai continued chasing Abner. The sun was going down when they arrived at the hill of Ammah. This is near Giah on the way to the empty land near Gibeon. ²⁵The men of Benjamin came to Abner. They all stood together at the top of the hill.

²⁶Abner shouted to Joab, "Must the sword kill forever? Surely you must know this will only end in sadness! Tell the people to stop chasing their own brothers!"

²⁷Then Joab said, "If you had not said anything, the people would have chased their brothers until morning. This is as sure as God is alive." ²⁸Then Joab blew a trumpet, and his people stopped chasing the Israelites. They did not try to fight them anymore.

²⁹Abner and his men marched all night through the Jordan Valley. They crossed the Jordan River. After marching all day, they arrived at Mahanaim.

³⁰Joab came back after he had stopped chasing Abner. Then Joab gathered the people together. Asahel and 19 of David's men were missing. ³¹But David's men had killed 360 Benjaminites who had followed Abner. ³²David's men took Asahel and buried him. They put him in the tomb of his father at Bethlehem. Then Joab and his men marched all night. The sun came up as they reached Hebron.

3 There was a long war between the people who supported Saul's family and those who supported David's family. The supporters of David's family became stronger and stronger. And the supporters of Saul's family became weaker and weaker.

DAVID'S SONS

²Sons were born to David at Hebron. The first son was Amnon. Amnon's mother was Ahinoam from Jezreel. ³The second son was Kileab. Kileab's mother was Abigail, the widow of Nabal from Carmel. The third son was Absalom. Absalom's mother was Maacah daughter of Talmai. Talmai was king of Geshur. ⁴The fourth son was Adonijah. His mother was Haggith. The fifth son was Shephatiah. His mother was Abital. ⁵The sixth son was Ithream. His mother was Eglah, David's wife. These sons were born to David at Hebron.

ABNER JOINS DAVID

⁶Abner made himself a main leader among the supporters of Saul. He did this during the war between the supporters of Saul's family and the supporters of David's family.

⁷Now Saul had once had a slave woman[d] named Rizpah. She was the daughter of Aiah. Ish-Bosheth said to Abner, "Why did you have sexual relations with my father's slave woman?"

⁸Abner was very angry because of what Ish-Bosheth said. Abner said, "I have been loyal to Saul and his family and friends! I didn't hand you over to David. I am not a traitor working for Judah! But now you are saying I did something wrong with this woman! ⁹May God punish me terribly if I don't

help David. I will make sure that what God promised does happen! [10]I will take the kingdom from the family of Saul. I will make David king of Israel and Judah! He will rule from Dan to Beersheba."[n]

[11]Ish-Bosheth couldn't say anything to Abner. He was too afraid of Abner.

[12]Then Abner sent messengers to David. Abner said, "Who is going to rule the land? Make an agreement with me, and I will help you become the king of all Israel."

[13]David answered, "Good! I will make an agreement with you. But I ask you one thing. I will not meet with you unless you bring Saul's daughter Michal to me."

[14]Then David sent messengers to Saul's son Ish-Bosheth. David said, "Give me my wife Michal. She was promised to me. I killed 100 Philistines to get her."

[15]So Ish-Bosheth sent men to take Michal from her husband. He was Paltiel son of Laish. [16]Michal's husband went with her, crying as he followed her to Bahurim. But Abner said to Paltiel, "Go back home." So he went home.

[17]Abner sent a message to the elders of Israel. He said, "You have been wanting to make David your king. [18]Now do it! The Lord has spoken about David. The Lord said, 'I will save my people the Israelites. I will save them from the Philistines and all their enemies. I will do this through my servant David.'"

[19]Abner also said these things to the people of Benjamin. He then went to Hebron to tell David what the Benjaminites and Israel wanted to do. [20]Abner came with 20 men to David at Hebron. There David prepared a feast for them. [21]Then Abner said to David, "My master and king, I will go and bring all the Israelites to you. Then they will make an agreement with you. You will rule over all Israel as you wanted." So David let Abner go, and he left in peace.

ABNER'S DEATH

[22]Just then Joab and David's men came from a battle. They had many valuable things they had taken from the enemy. David had let Abner leave in peace. So he was not with David at Hebron. [23]Joab and all his army arrived at Hebron. The army said to Joab, "Abner son of Ner came to King David. And David let him leave in peace."

[24]Joab came to the king and said, "What have you done? Abner came to you. Why did you let him go? Now he's gone. [25]You know Abner son of Ner! He came to trick you! He came to learn about everything you are doing!"

[26]Then Joab left David and sent messengers after Abner. They brought Abner back from the well of Sirah. But David did not know this. [27]When Abner arrived at Hebron, Joab took him aside into the gateway. Joab acted as though he wanted to talk with him in private. But Joab stabbed Abner in the stomach, and Abner died. Abner had killed Joab's brother Asahel. So Joab killed Abner to pay him back.

[28]Later David heard the news. He said, "My kingdom and I are innocent forever. We did not kill Abner son of Ner. The Lord knows this. [29]Joab and his family are responsible for this. I hope many troubles will come to his family. May his family always have someone with sores or with a harmful skin disease. May they always have someone who must lean on a crutch. May some of his family be killed in war. May they always have someone without food to eat."

[30](Joab and his brother Abishai had killed Abner, because he had killed their brother Asahel. This was in the battle at Gibeon.)

[31]Then David spoke to Joab and to all the people with Joab. He said, "Tear your clothes and put on rough cloth to

---

3:10 Dan to Beersheba Dan was the city farthest north in Israel. Beersheba was the city farthest south. So this means all the people of Israel.

show how sad you are. Cry for Abner." King David himself followed behind the body of Abner. [32]So they buried Abner in Hebron. David and all the people cried at Abner's grave.

[33]King David sang this funeral song for Abner.

"Did Abner die like a foolish man?
[34]   His hands were not tied.

His feet were not in chains.

He fell as a person falls before evil men."

Then all the people cried again for Abner. [35]They came to encourage David to eat while it was still day. But he made a promise. He said, "May God punish me terribly if I eat bread or any other food before the sun sets!"

[36]All the people saw what happened. They agreed with what the king was doing. [37]That day all the people of Judah and all the Israelites understood. They knew it was not David who had killed Abner son of Ner.

[38]David said to his officers, "You know that a very important leader died today in Israel. [39]Even though I am the appointed king, I am weak today. These sons of Zeruiah are too strong for me. May the Lord give them the punishment they should have."

ISH-BOSHETH'S DEATH

4 Ish-Bosheth son of Saul heard that Abner had died at Hebron. Then Ish-Bosheth and all Israel became very frightened. [2]Two men who were captains in Saul's army came to Ish-Bosheth. One man was named Baanah, and the other was named Recab. They were the sons of Rimmon of Beeroth, who was a Benjaminite. (The town Beeroth belonged to the tribe[d] of Benjamin.) [3]The people of Beeroth ran away to Gittaim. And they still live there today.

[4](Now Jonathan son of Saul had a son who was crippled in both feet. His name was Mephibosheth. He was five years old when the news came from Jezreel that Saul and Jonathan were dead.

Mephibosheth's nurse picked him up and ran away. But as she hurried to leave, he fell and became crippled.)

[5]Recab and Baanah, sons of Rimmon, were from Beeroth. They went to Ish-Bosheth's house at noon. [6-7]They came into the middle of the house. Recab and Baanah came as if they were going to get some wheat. Ish-Bosheth was lying on his bed in his bedroom. Recab and Baanah stabbed him in the stomach. Then they cut off his head and took it with them. They traveled all night through the Jordan Valley. [8]When they arrived at Hebron, they gave his head to David. They said to the king, "Here is the head of Ish-Bosheth son of Saul. He was your enemy. He tried to kill you! Today the Lord has paid back Saul and his family for what they did to you!"

[9]David answered Recab and his brother Baanah sons of Rimmon of Beeroth. David said, "As surely as the Lord lives, he has saved me from all trouble! [10]Once a man thought he was bringing me good news. He told me, 'Look! Saul is dead!' But I took hold of him and killed him at Ziklag. That was the reward I gave him for his news! [11]So even more I must require your death. This is because evil men have killed an innocent man. And he was on his own bed in his own house!"

[12]So David commanded his men to kill Recab and Baanah. Then they cut off the hands and feet of Recab and Baanah. They hung their hands and feet over the pool of Hebron. Then they took Ish-Bosheth's head and buried it in Abner's tomb at Hebron.

DAVID IS MADE KING OF ISRAEL

5 Then all the tribes[d] of Israel came to David at Hebron. They said to him, "Look, we are your own family. [2]In the past Saul was king over us. But you were the one leading us in battle for Israel. The Lord said to you, 'You will be like a shepherd for my people, the Israelites. You will become their ruler.'"

³All the elders of Israel came to King David at Hebron. Then he made an agreement with them in Hebron in front of the Lord. Then they poured oil on David to make him king over Israel.

⁴David was 30 years old when he became king. He ruled 40 years. ⁵He was king over Judah in Hebron for 7 years and 6 months. And he was king over all Israel and Judah in Jerusalem for 33 years.

⁶The king and his men went to Jerusalem to attack the Jebusites who lived there. The Jebusites said to David, "You can't come into our city. Even our people who are blind and crippled can stop you." They said this because they thought David could not enter their city. ⁷But David did take the city of Jerusalem with its strong walls. It became the City of David.

⁸That day David said to his men, "To defeat the Jebusites you must go through the water tunnel. Then you can reach those 'crippled' and 'blind' enemies. This is why people say, 'The blind and the crippled cannot enter the palace.'"

⁹So David lived in the city with its strong walls. He called it the City of David. David built more buildings around it. He began where the land was filled in on the east side of the city. He also built more buildings inside the city. ¹⁰He became stronger and stronger, because the Lord of heaven's armies was with him.

¹¹Hiram king of the city of Tyre sent messengers to David. He also sent cedar logs, carpenters and men to cut stone. They built a palace for David. ¹²Then David knew the Lord really had made him king of Israel. And he knew the Lord had made his kingdom very important. This was because the Lord loved his people, the Israelites.

¹³In Jerusalem David took for himself more slave women[d] and wives. This was after he moved there from Hebron. More sons and daughters were born to David. ¹⁴These are the names of the sons born to David in Jerusalem: Shammua, Shobab, Nathan, Solomon, ¹⁵Ibhar, Elishua, Nepheg, Japhia, ¹⁶Elishama, Eliada and Eliphelet.

DAVID DEFEATS THE PHILISTINES

¹⁷Now the Philistines heard that David had been made king over Israel. So all the Philistines went to look for him. But when David heard the news, he went down to a safe place. ¹⁸So the Philistines came and camped in the Valley of Rephaim. David asked the Lord, "Should I attack the Philistines? Will you help me defeat them?"

¹⁹The Lord said to David, "Go! I will certainly help you defeat them."

²⁰So David went to Baal Perazim and defeated the Philistines there. David said, "Like a flood of water, the Lord has broken through my enemies." So David named the place Baal Perazim.[n] ²¹The Philistines left their idols behind at Baal Perazim. And David and his men carried these idols away.

²²Once again the Philistines came and camped at the Valley of Rephaim. ²³David prayed to the Lord. This time the Lord told David, "Don't attack the Philistines from the front. Instead, go around them. Attack them opposite the balsam trees. ²⁴You will hear the sound of marching in the tops of the balsam trees. Then you must act quickly. I, the Lord, will have gone ahead of you and defeated the Philistine army." ²⁵So David did what the Lord commanded. He defeated the Philistines and chased them all the way from Gibeon to Gezer.

THE HOLY BOX IS BROUGHT TO JERUSALEM

6 David again gathered all the chosen men of Israel. There were 30,000 of them. ²Then David and all his people

---

5:20 Baal Perazim This name means "the Lord breaks through."

went to Baalah in Judah.[n] They took the Holy Box[d] of God from Baalah in Judah and moved it to Jerusalem. The Holy Box is called by the Name, the name of the Lord of heaven's armies. His throne is between the gold creatures with wings that are on the Holy Box. [3]David's men put the Holy Box of God on a new cart. Then they brought the Holy Box out of Abinadab's house on the hill. Uzzah and Ahio, sons of Abinadab, led the new cart. [4]This cart had the Holy Box of God on it. Ahio was walking in front of it. [5]David and all the Israelites were playing all kinds of musical instruments before the Lord. They were made of pine wood. There were lyres,[d] harps, tambourines,[d] rattles and cymbals.

[6]When David's men came to the threshing[d] floor of Nacon, the oxen stumbled. The Holy Box of God began to fall off the cart. So Uzzah reached out and took hold of it. [7]The Lord was angry with Uzzah and killed him. Uzzah had not honored God when he touched the Holy Box. So Uzzah died there beside it. [8]David was angry because the Lord had killed Uzzah. So that place is called The Punishment of Uzzah even today.

[9]David was afraid of the Lord that day. He said, "How can the Holy Box of the Lord come to me now?" [10]So David would not move the Holy Box of the Lord to be with him in Jerusalem. Instead, he took it to the house of Obed-Edom, a man from Gath. [11]The Holy Box of the Lord stayed in Obed-Edom's house for three months. And the Lord blessed Obed-Edom and all his family.

[12]The people told David, "The Lord has blessed the family of Obed-Edom. And all his things are blessed. This is because the Holy Box of God is there." So David went and brought it up from Obed-Edom's house to Jerusalem with joy. [13]When the men carrying the Holy Box of the Lord had walked six steps, David sacrificed a bull and a fat calf. [14]Then David danced with all his might before the Lord. He had on a holy linen vest.[d] [15]David and all the Israelites shouted with joy. They blew the trumpets as they brought the Holy Box of the Lord to the city.

[16]Saul's daughter Michal was looking out the window. She watched as the Holy Box of the Lord came into the city. When she saw David jumping and dancing before the Lord, she hated him.

[17]David put up a tent for the Holy Box. Then the Israelites put it in its place inside the tent. David offered whole burnt offerings and fellowship offerings before the Lord. [18]When David finished offering the whole burnt offerings and the fellowship offerings, he blessed the people in the name of the Lord of heaven's armies. [19]David gave a loaf of bread, a cake of dates and a cake of raisins to everyone. He gave them to all the Israelites, both men and women. Then all the people went home.

[20]David went back to bless the people in his home. But Saul's daughter Michal came out to meet him. She said, "The king of Israel did not honor himself today! You took off your clothes in front of the servant girls of your officers. You were like a foolish man who takes off his clothes without shame!"

[21]Then David said to Michal, "I did it before the Lord. The Lord chose me, not your father. He didn't choose anyone from Saul's family. The Lord appointed me to be leader of his people, the Israelites. So I will celebrate in front of the Lord. [22]Maybe I will lose even more honor. And you may think little of me. But the girls you talk about will honor me!"

[23]And Saul's daughter Michal had no children to the day she died.

6:2 Baalah in Judah Another name for Kiriath Jearim.

DAVID WANTS TO BUILD A TEMPLE

7 King David was living in his palace. And the Lord gave him peace from all his enemies around him. ²David said to Nathan the prophet,^d "Look, I am living in a palace made of cedar wood. But the Holy Box^d of God is still kept in a tent!"

³Nathan said to the king, "Go and do what you really want to do. The Lord is with you."

⁴But that night the Lord spoke his word to Nathan. The Lord said, ⁵"Go and tell my servant David, 'This is what the Lord says: You are not the person to build a house for me to live in. ⁶I did not live in a house when I brought the Israelites out of Egypt. I have been moving around all this time with a tent as my home. ⁷I have continued to move with the tribes^d of Israel. But I have never asked their leaders who take care of them to build me a house of cedar wood.'

⁸"You must tell my servant David, 'This is what the Lord of heaven's armies says: I took you from the pasture when you were following the sheep. I took you to become leader of my people, the Israelites. ⁹I have been with you everywhere you have gone. I have defeated your enemies for you. I will make you as famous as any of the great men on the earth. ¹⁰Also I will choose a place for my people, the Israelites. I will plant them so they can live in their own home. They will not be bothered anymore. Wicked people will no longer make them suffer as they have in the past. ¹¹Wicked people continued to do this even when I appointed judges. But I will give you peace from all your enemies. I also tell you that I will make your descendants^d kings of Israel after you.

¹²"'Your days will come to an end, and you will die. At that time I will make one of your sons the next king. ¹³He will build a temple^d for me. I will make his kingdom strong forever. ¹⁴I will be his father, and he will be my son. When he

sins, I will use other people to punish him. They will be my whips. ¹⁵But I will not stop loving him. I took away my love and kindness from Saul. I removed Saul when I turned to you. ¹⁶But your family and your kingdom will continue forever before me. Your rule will last forever.'"

¹⁷Nathan told David everything he had heard.

DAVID PRAYS TO GOD

¹⁸Then King David went in the tent and sat in front of the Lord. David said, "Lord God, why have you made me so important to you? Why have you made my family important? ¹⁹But that was not enough for you, Lord God. You have also said these kind things about my future family. I am your servant. Lord God, this is not the usual way you talk to people.

²⁰"What more can I say to you? Lord God, you love me, your servant, so much! ²¹You have done this wonderful thing because you said you would. You have done it because you wanted to. And you have decided to let me know all these great things. ²²This is why you are great, Lord God! There is no one like you. There is no God except you. We have heard all this ourselves! ²³And there are no others like your people, the Israelites. They are the one nation on earth that God chose to be his people. You used them to make your name well-known. You did great and wonderful miracles^d for them. You went ahead of them and forced other nations and their gods out of the land. You freed your people from slavery in Egypt. ²⁴You made the people of Israel your very own people forever. And, Lord, you became their God.

²⁵"Now, Lord God, keep the promise you made about my family and me, your servant. Do what you have promised. ²⁶Then you will be honored forever. And people will say, 'The Lord of heaven's armies is God over Israel!' And the family of your servant David will continue before you.

[27]"Lord of heaven's armies, the God of Israel, you have shown things to me. You have said, 'I will make your family great.' So I, your servant, am brave enough to pray to you. [28]Lord God, you are God, and your words are true. And you have promised these good things to me, your servant. [29]Please, bless my family. Let it continue before you forever. Lord God, you have said these wonderful things. With your blessing let my family be blessed forever."

DAVID WINS MANY WARS

8 Later, David defeated the Philistines. And he took control of their capital city.

[2]He also defeated the people of Moab. He forced them to lie on the ground. Then he used a rope to measure them. When two men were measured, David ordered them killed. But every third man was allowed to live. So the people of Moab became servants of David. They gave him the payments he demanded.

[3]As David went to take control again at the Euphrates River, he defeated Hadadezer. Hadadezer son of Rehob was king of Zobah. [4]David took from Hadadezer 1,700 men who rode in his chariots. He also captured 20,000 foot soldiers. David crippled all but 100 of the chariot horses. He saved those horses to pull chariots.

[5]Arameans from Damascus came to help Hadadezer king of Zobah. But David defeated those 22,000 Arameans. [6]Then David put groups of soldiers in Damascus in Aram. The Arameans became David's servants and gave him the payments he demanded. The Lord gave David victory everywhere he went.

[7]David took the shields of gold that had belonged to Hadadezer's officers. He brought them to Jerusalem. [8]David also took many things made of bronze from Tebah and Berothai. (They were cities that had belonged to Hadadezer.)

[9]Toi king of Hamath heard that David had defeated all the army of Hadadezer.

[10]So Toi sent his son Joram to greet and congratulate King David. Joram congratulated David for defeating Hadadezer. (Hadadezer had fought wars against Toi before.) Joram brought things made of silver, gold and bronze. [11]David took these things and gave them to the Lord. He also had given other silver and gold to the Lord. He had taken it from the nations he had defeated. [12]These nations were Edom, Moab, Ammon, Philistia and Amalek. David also defeated the king of Zobah who was Hadadezer son of Rehob.

[13]David was famous after he returned from the Valley of Salt. There he had defeated 18,000 Arameans. [14]David put groups of soldiers through all the land of Edom. All the people of Edom became servants for him. The Lord gave David victory everywhere he went.

[15]David was king over all Israel. His decisions were fair and right for all his people. [16]Joab son of Zeruiah was commander over the army. Jehoshaphat son of Ahilud was the recorder. [17]Zadok son of Ahitub and Ahimelech son of Abiathar were priests. Seraiah was the royal assistant. [18]Benaiah son of Jehoiada was over the Kerethites and Pelethites, the king's bodyguards. And David's sons were important leaders.

DAVID HELPS SAUL'S FAMILY

9 David asked, "Is there anyone still left in Saul's family? I want to show kindness to this person for Jonathan's sake!"

[2]Now there was a servant named Ziba from Saul's family. So David's servants called Ziba to him. King David said to him, "Are you Ziba?"

He answered, "Yes, I am Ziba, your servant."

[3]The king asked, "Is there anyone left in Saul's family? I want to show God's kindness to this person."

Ziba answered the king, "Jonathan has a son still living. He is crippled in both feet."

⁴The king asked Ziba, "Where is this son?"

Ziba answered, "He is at the house of Makir son of Ammiel in Lo Debar."

⁵Then King David had servants bring Jonathan's son from the house of Makir son of Ammiel in Lo Debar. ⁶Mephibosheth, Jonathan's son, came before David and bowed facedown on the floor.

David said, "Mephibosheth!"

Mephibosheth said, "I am your servant."

⁷David said to him, "Don't be afraid. I will be kind to you for your father Jonathan's sake. I will give you back all the land of your grandfather Saul. And you will always be able to eat at my table."

⁸Mephibosheth bowed to David again. Mephibosheth said, "You are being very kind to me, your servant! And I am no better than a dead dog!"

⁹Then King David called Saul's servant Ziba. David said to him, "I have given your master's grandson everything that belonged to Saul and his family. ¹⁰You, your sons and your servants will farm the land for Mephibosheth. You will harvest the crops. Then your master's grandson will have food to eat. But Mephibosheth, your master's grandson, will always be able to eat at my table."

(Now Ziba had 15 sons and 20 servants.) ¹¹Ziba said to King David, "I am your servant. I will do everything my master, the king, commands me."

So Mephibosheth ate at David's table as if he were one of the king's sons. ¹²Mephibosheth had a young son named Mica. Everyone in Ziba's family became Mephibosheth's servants. ¹³Mephibosheth was crippled in both feet. He lived in Jerusalem and always ate at the king's table.

WAR WITH THE AMMONITES AND ARAMEANS

10 Later Nahash king of the Ammonites died. His son Hanun became king after him. ²David said, "Nahash was kind to me. So I will be kind

to his son Hanun." So David sent his officers to comfort Hanun about his father's death.

David's servants went to the land of the Ammonites. ³But the important men of Ammon spoke to Hanun, their master. They said, "Do you think David wants to honor your father by sending men to comfort you? No! David sent them to study the city and to spy it out. They plan to capture it!" ⁴So Hanun took David's officers and shaved off half their beards to shame them. He cut their clothes off at the hips to insult them. Then he sent them away.

⁵When the people told David, he sent messengers to meet his officers. He did this because these men were very ashamed. King David said, "Wait at Jericho until your beards have grown out. Then come back to Jerusalem."

⁶Now the Ammonites saw that they had become David's enemies. So they hired 20,000 Aramean foot soldiers from Beth Rehob and Zobah. They also hired the king of Maacah with 1,000 men. And they hired 12,000 men from Tob.

⁷David heard about this. So he sent Joab with the whole army of warriors. ⁸The Ammonites came out and got ready for the battle. They stood at the city gate. The Arameans from Zobah and Rehob and the men from Tob and Maacah were out in the field. They were standing away from the Ammonites.

⁹Joab saw that there were enemies both in front of him and behind him. So he chose some of the best men from the Israelites. He got them ready for battle against the Arameans. ¹⁰Then Joab gave the other men to his brother Abishai to lead against the Ammonites. ¹¹Joab said to Abishai, "If the Arameans are too strong for me, come help me. If the Ammonites are too strong for you, I will come and help you. ¹²Be strong. Let us fight bravely for our people and for the cities of our God. The Lord will do what he decides is right."

[13]Then Joab and his men attacked the Arameans, and they ran away. [14]The Ammonites saw that the Arameans were running away. So they ran away from Abishai and went back to their city. So Joab returned from the battle with the Ammonites and came to Jerusalem.

[15]The Arameans saw that the Israelites had defeated them. So they came together into one big army. [16]Hadadezer sent messengers to bring the Arameans who lived on the other side of the Euphrates River. These Arameans went to Helam. Their leader was Shobach, the commander of Hadadezer's army.

[17]When David heard about this, he gathered all the Israelites together. They crossed over the Jordan River and went to Helam. There the Arameans prepared for battle and attacked. [18]But David defeated the Arameans, and they ran away from the Israelites. David killed 700 Aramean chariot drivers and 40,000 Aramean horsemen. He also killed Shobach, the commander of the Aramean army.

[19]The kings who served Hadadezer saw that the Israelites had defeated them. So they made peace with the Israelites and served them. And the Arameans were afraid to help the Ammonites again.

DAVID AND BATHSHEBA

11 In the spring the kings would go out to war. So in the spring David sent out Joab, his servants and all the Israelites. They destroyed the Ammonites and attacked the city of Rabbah. But David stayed in Jerusalem. [2]One evening David got up from his bed. He walked around on the roof[n] of his palace. While he was on the roof, he saw a woman bathing. She was very beautiful. [3]So David sent his servants to find out who she was. A servant answered, "That woman is Bathsheba daughter of Eliam. She is the wife of Uriah the Hittite." [4]David sent messengers to bring Bathsheba to him. When she came to him, he had sexual relations with her. (Now Bathsheba had purified herself from her monthly period.) Then she went back to her house. [5]But Bathsheba became pregnant. She sent word to David, saying, "I am pregnant."

[6]So David sent this message to Joab: "Send Uriah the Hittite to me." So Joab sent Uriah to David. [7]Uriah came to David. And David asked him how Joab was, how the soldiers were and how the war was going. [8]Then David said to Uriah, "Go home and rest."

So Uriah left the palace. The king also sent a gift to him. [9]But Uriah did not go home. He slept outside the door of the palace. He slept there as all the king's officers did.

[10]The officers told David, "Uriah did not go home."

Then David said to Uriah, "You came from a long trip. Why didn't you go home?"

[11]Uriah said to him, "The Holy Box[d] and the soldiers of Israel and Judah are staying in tents. My master Joab and his officers are camping out in the fields. It isn't right for me to go home to eat and drink and have sexual relations with my wife!"

[12]David said to Uriah, "Stay here today. Tomorrow I'll send you back to the battle." So Uriah stayed in Jerusalem that day and the next. [13]Then David called Uriah to come to see him. Uriah ate and drank with David. David made Uriah drunk, but he still did not go home. That evening Uriah went to sleep with the king's officers outside the king's door.

[14]The next morning David wrote a letter to Joab and sent it by Uriah. [15]In the letter David wrote, "Put Uriah on the front lines where the fighting is worst.

11:2 **roof** In Bible times houses were built with flat roofs. The roof was used for drying things such as flax and fruit. And it was used as an extra room, as a place for worship and as a place to sleep in the summer.

Then leave him there alone. Let him be killed in battle."

¹⁶Joab watched the city and saw where its strongest defenders were. He put Uriah there. ¹⁷The men of the city came out to fight against Joab. Some of David's men were killed. And Uriah the Hittite was one of them.

¹⁸Then Joab sent a report to David about everything that had happened in the war. ¹⁹Joab told the messenger, "Tell King David what happened in the war. ²⁰After you finish, the king may become angry. He may ask you, 'Why did you go so near the city to fight? Didn't you know they would shoot arrows from the city wall? ²¹Do you remember who killed Abimelech son of Jerub-Besheth?ⁿ It was a woman on the city wall. She threw a large stone for grinding grain on Abimelech. She killed him there in Thebez. Why did you go so near the wall?' If King David asks that, you must answer, 'Your servant Uriah the Hittite also died.'"

²²The messenger went in and told David everything Joab had told him to say. ²³The messenger told David, "The men of Ammon were winning. They came out and attacked us in the field. But we fought them back to the city gate. ²⁴The men on the city wall shot arrows at your servants. Some of your men were killed. Your servant Uriah the Hittite also died."

²⁵David said to the messenger, "Say this to Joab: 'Don't be upset about this. The sword kills everyone the same. Make a stronger attack against the city and capture it.' Encourage Joab with these words."

²⁶When Bathsheba heard that her husband was dead, she cried for him. ²⁷After she finished her time of sadness, David sent servants to bring her to his house. She became David's wife and gave birth to his son. But the Lord did not like what David had done.

DAVID'S SON DIES

12 The Lord sent Nathan to David. When Nathan came to David, Nathan said, "There were two men in a city. One man was rich, but the other was poor. ²The rich man had very many sheep and cattle. ³But the poor man had nothing except one little female lamb he had bought. The poor man fed the lamb. It grew up with him and his children. It shared his food and drank from his cup. It slept in his arms. The lamb was like a daughter to him.

⁴"Then a traveler stopped to visit the rich man. The rich man wanted to give food to the traveler. But he didn't want to take one of his own sheep or cattle to feed the traveler. Instead, he took the lamb from the poor man. The rich man killed the lamb and cooked it for his visitor."

⁵David became very angry at the rich man. He said to Nathan, "As surely as the Lord lives, the man who did this should die! ⁶He must pay for the lamb four times for doing such a thing. He had no mercy!"

⁷Then Nathan said to David, "You are the man! This is what the Lord, the God of Israel, says: 'I appointed you king of Israel. I saved you from Saul. ⁸I gave you his kingdom and his wives. And I made you king of Israel and Judah. And if that had not been enough, I would have given you even more. ⁹So why did you ignore the Lord's command? Why did you do what he says is wrong? You killed Uriah the Hittite with the sword of the Ammonites! And you took his wife to become your wife! ¹⁰So there will always be people in your family who will be killed by a sword. This is because you showed that you did not respect me! And you took the wife of Uriah the Hittite!'

¹¹"This is what the Lord says: 'I am bringing trouble to you from your own family. While you watch, I will take your wives from you. And I will give them to someone who is very close to you. He

---

11:21 **Jerub-Besheth** Another name for Gideon.

will have sexual relations with your wives, and everyone will know it. [12]You had sexual relations with Bathsheba in secret. But I will do this so all the people of Israel can see it.'"

[13]Then David said to Nathan, "I have sinned against the Lord."

Nathan answered, "The Lord has taken away your sin. You will not die. [14]But what you did caused the Lord's enemies to lose all respect for him. For this reason the son who was born to you will die."

[15]Then Nathan went home. And the Lord caused the son of David and Bathsheba, Uriah's widow, to become very sick. [16]David prayed to God for the baby. David refused to eat or drink. He went into his house and stayed there. He lay on the ground all night. [17]The elders of David's family came to him. They tried to pull him up from the ground. But he refused to get up. And he refused to eat food with them.

[18]On the seventh day the baby died. David's servants were afraid to tell him that the baby was dead. They said, "Look, we tried to talk to David while the baby was alive. But he refused to listen to us. If we tell him the baby is dead, he may harm himself."

[19]But David saw his servants whispering. Then he understood that the baby was dead. So he asked them, "Is the baby dead?"

They answered, "Yes, he is dead."

[20]Then David got up from the floor. He washed himself, put lotions on himself and changed his clothes. Then he went into the Lord's house to worship. After that, he went home and asked for something to eat. His servants gave him some food, and he ate.

[21]David's servants said to him, "Why are you doing this? When the baby was still alive, you refused to eat. You cried. But when the baby died, you got up and ate food."

[22]David said, "While the baby was still alive, I refused to eat, and I cried. I thought, 'Who knows? Maybe the Lord will feel sorry for me and let the baby live.' [23]But now the baby is dead. So why should I go without food? I can't bring him back to life. Some day I will go to him. But he cannot come back to me."

[24]Then David comforted Bathsheba his wife. He slept with her and had sexual relations with her. She became pregnant again and had another son. David named the boy Solomon. The Lord loved Solomon. [25]The Lord sent word through Nathan the prophet[d] to name the baby Jedidiah.[n] This was because the Lord loved the child.

DAVID CAPTURES RABBAH

[26]Now Joab fought against Rabbah, a city of the Ammonites. And he was about to capture the royal city. [27]Joab sent messengers to David and said, "I have fought against Rabbah. I have captured its water supply. [28]Now bring the other soldiers together and attack this city. Capture it before I capture it myself. If I capture this city, it will be called by my name!"

[29]So David gathered all the army and went to Rabbah. He fought against Rabbah and captured it. [30]David took the crown off their king's head. It was gold and weighed about 75 pounds. It also had gems in it. They put the crown on David's head. And David took many valuable things out of the city. [31]He also brought out the people of the city. He made them work with saws, iron picks and axes. He also forced them to build with bricks. David did this to all the Ammonite cities. Then David and all his army went back to Jerusalem.

AMNON AND TAMAR

13 Now David had a son named Absalom and a son named Amnon. Absalom had a beautiful sister

---

12:25 Jedidiah This name means "loved by the Lord."

named Tamar. And Amnon loved her. [2]Tamar was a virgin.[d] Amnon did not think he should do anything bad to her. But he wanted her very much. He made himself sick just thinking about her.

[3]Amnon had a friend named Jonadab son of Shimeah. (Shimeah was David's brother.) Jonadab was a very clever man. [4]He asked Amnon, "Why do you look so sad day after day? You are the king's son! Tell me what's wrong!"

Amnon told him, "I love Tamar. But she is the sister of my half-brother Absalom."

[5]Jonadab said to Amnon, "Go to bed. Act as if you are sick. Then your father will come to see you. Tell him, 'Please let my sister Tamar come in and give me food to eat. Let her make the food in front of me. Then I will see it and eat it from her hand.'"

[6]So Amnon lay down in bed and acted as if he were sick. King David came in to see him. Amnon said to him, "Please let my sister Tamar come in. Let her make two of her special cakes for me while I watch. Then I will eat them from her hands."

[7]David sent messengers to Tamar in the palace. They told her, "Go to your brother Amnon's house and make some food for him." [8]So Tamar went to her brother Amnon's house. He was in bed. Tamar took some dough and pressed it together with her hands. She made some special cakes while Amnon watched. Then she baked them. [9]Next she took the pan and took out the cakes for Amnon. But he refused to eat.

He said to his servants, "All of you, leave me alone!" So all his servants left the room. [10]Amnon said to Tamar, "Bring the food into the inner room. Then I'll eat from your hand."

Tamar took the cakes she had made. And she brought them to her brother Amnon in the inner room. [11]She went to him so he could eat from her hands. But Amnon grabbed her. He said, "Sister, come and have sexual relations with me."

[12]Tamar said to him, "No, brother! Don't force me! This should never be done in Israel! Don't do this shameful thing! [13]I could never get rid of my shame! And you will become like the shameful fools in Israel! Please talk with the king. He will let you marry me."

[14]But Amnon refused to listen to her. He was stronger than she was. So he forced her to have sexual relations with him. [15]After that, Amnon hated Tamar. He hated her much more than he had loved her before. Amnon said to her, "Get up and leave!"

[16]Tamar said to him, "No! Sending me away would be an even greater evil. That would be worse than what you've already done!"

But he refused to listen to her. [17]He called his young servant back in. Amnon said, "Get this girl out of here right now! Lock the door after her." [18]So his servant led her out of the room. And he bolted the door after her.

Now Tamar was wearing a special robe with long sleeves. The king's virgin daughters wore this kind of robe. [19]To show how upset she was Tamar took ashes and put them on her head. She tore her special robe. And she put her hand on her head. Then she went away, crying loudly.

[20]Absalom, Tamar's brother, said to her, "Has Amnon, that brother of yours, forced you to have sexual relations with him? He is your brother. So for now, sister, be quiet. Don't let this upset you so much!" So Tamar lived in her brother Absalom's house. She was sad and lonely.

[21]When King David heard the news, he was very angry. [22]Absalom did not say a word, good or bad, to Amnon. He hated Amnon for forcing his sister Tamar to have sexual relations with him.

ABSALOM'S REVENGE

[23]Two years later Absalom had some men come to Baal Hazor, near Ephraim.

They were to cut the wool from his sheep. Absalom invited all the king's sons to come also. ²⁴Absalom went to the king and said, "I have men coming to cut the wool. Please come with your officers and join me."

²⁵King David said to Absalom, "No, my son. We won't all go. It would be too much trouble for you." Absalom begged David to go. David did not go, but he did give his blessing.

²⁶Absalom said, "If you don't want to go, then please let my brother Amnon go with me."

King David asked Absalom, "Why should he go with you?"

²⁷Absalom kept begging David. Finally, David let Amnon and all the king's sons go with Absalom.

²⁸Then Absalom gave a command to his servants. He said, "Watch Amnon. When he is drunk, I will tell you, 'Kill Amnon.' Right then, kill him! Don't be afraid. I have commanded you! Be strong and brave!" ²⁹So Absalom's young men killed Amnon as Absalom commanded. But all of David's other sons got on their mules and escaped.

³⁰While the king's sons were on their way, the news came to David. The message was, "Absalom has killed all of the king's sons! Not one of them is left alive!" ³¹King David tore his clothes and lay on the ground to show his sadness. All his servants standing nearby tore their clothes also.

³²Jonadab was the son of Shimeah, David's brother. Jonadab said to David, "Don't think all the young men, your sons, are killed. No, only Amnon is dead! Absalom planned this because Amnon forced his sister Tamar to have sexual relations with him. ³³My master and king, don't think that all of the king's sons are dead. Only Amnon is dead!"

³⁴In the meantime Absalom had run away.

There was a guard standing on the city wall. He saw many people coming from the other side of the hill. ³⁵So Jonadab said to King David, "Look, I was right! The king's sons are coming!"

³⁶As soon as Jonadab had said this, the king's sons arrived. They were crying loudly. David and all his servants began crying also. They all cried very much. ³⁷David cried for his son every day.

But Absalom ran away to Talmaiⁿ son of Ammihud. Talmai was king of Geshur. ³⁸After Absalom ran away to Geshur, he stayed there for three years. ³⁹When King David got over Amnon's death, he missed Absalom greatly.

JOAB SENDS A WISE WOMAN TO DAVID

14 Joab son of Zeruiah knew that King David missed Absalom very much. ²So Joab sent messengers to Tekoa to bring a wise woman from there. Joab said to her, "Please pretend to be very sad for someone. Put on clothes to show your sadness. Don't put lotion on yourself. Act like a woman who has been crying many days for someone who died. ³Go to the king. Talk to him using the words that I tell you." Then Joab told the wise woman what to say.

⁴So the woman from Tekoa talked to the king. She bowed facedown on the ground to show respect. She said, "My king, help me!"

⁵King David asked her, "What is the matter?"

The woman said, "I am a widow. My husband is dead. ⁶I had two sons. They were out in the field fighting. No one was there to stop them. So one son killed the other son. ⁷Now all the family group is against me. They said to me, 'Bring the son who killed his brother. Then we will kill him for killing his brother. That way we will also get rid of the one who would receive what belonged to his father.' My son is like the last spark of a fire. He is all

13:37 Talmai He was Absalom's grandfather.

I have left. If they kill him, my husband's name and property will be gone from the earth."

⁸Then the king said to the woman, "Go home. I will take care of this for you."

⁹The woman of Tekoa said to him, "Let the blame be on me. My father's family and I are to blame, my master and king. But you and your throne are innocent."

¹⁰King David said, "Bring me anyone who says anything bad to you. Then he won't bother you again."

¹¹The woman said, "Please promise in the name of the Lord your God. Then my relative who has the duty of punishing a murderer won't add to the destruction. And he won't kill my son."

David said, "As surely as the Lord lives, no one will hurt your son. Not even one hair from your son's head will fall to the ground."

¹²The woman said, "Let me say something to you, my master and king."

The king said, "Speak."

¹³Then the woman said, "Why have you planned this? It is against the people of God. When you say this, you show that you are guilty. You have not brought back your son whom you forced to leave home. ¹⁴We will all die some day. We're like water spilled on the ground. No one can gather it back. But God doesn't take away life. Instead, he plans ways that those who have been sent away will not have to stay away from him! ¹⁵My master and king, I came to say this to you because the people have made me afraid! I thought, 'Let me talk to the king. Maybe he will do what I ask. ¹⁶Maybe he will listen. Perhaps he will save me from the man who wants to kill both me and my son. That man is trying to keep us from getting what God gave us.'

¹⁷"Now I say, 'May the words of my master the king give me rest. Like an angel of God, you know what is good and what is bad. May the Lord your God be with you!'"

¹⁸Then King David said, "You must answer the question I will ask you."

The woman said, "My master the king, please ask your question."

¹⁹The king said, "Did Joab tell you to say all these things?"

The woman answered, "As you live, my master the king, you are right. Your servant Joab did tell me to say these things. ²⁰Joab did it so you would see things differently. My master, you are wise like an angel of God. You know everything that happens on earth."

ABSALOM RETURNS TO JERUSALEM

²¹The king said to Joab, "Look, I will do what I promised. Now please bring back the young man Absalom."

²²Joab bowed facedown on the ground. He blessed the king. Then he said, "Today I know you are pleased with me. I know because you have done what I asked."

²³Then Joab got up and went to Geshur. And he brought Absalom back to Jerusalem. ²⁴But King David said, "Absalom must go to his own house. He may not come to see me." So Absalom went to his own house. He did not go to see the king.

²⁵Now Absalom was greatly praised for his handsome appearance. No man in Israel was as handsome as Absalom. No blemish was on him from his head to his foot. ²⁶At the end of every year, Absalom would cut the hair on his head. He cut it because it became too heavy. He would weigh it, and it would weigh about five pounds by the royal measure.

²⁷Absalom had three sons and one daughter. His daughter's name was Tamar. She was a beautiful woman.

²⁸So Absalom lived in Jerusalem for two full years without seeing King David. ²⁹Then Absalom sent for Joab. Absalom wanted to send Joab to the king. But Joab would not come. Absalom sent a message a second time. But Joab still refused to come. ³⁰Then Absalom said to his servants, "Look, Joab's field is next

to mine. He has barley growing there. Go burn it." So Absalom's servants set fire to Joab's field.

31Then Joab went to Absalom's house. Joab said to him, "Why did your servants burn my field?"

32Absalom said to Joab, "I sent a message to you, asking you to come here. I wanted to send you to the king. I wanted you to ask him why he brought me home from Geshur. It would have been better for me to stay there! Now let me see the king. If I have sinned, he can kill me!"

33So Joab went to the king and told him Absalom's words. The king called for Absalom, and Absalom came. He bowed facedown on the ground before the king. And the king kissed him.

ABSALOM PLANS TO TAKE DAVID'S KINGDOM

15 After this, Absalom got a chariot and horses for himself. He got 50 men to run before him. 2Absalom would get up early and stand near the city gate." If anyone had a problem he wanted the king to settle, he would come here. When he came, Absalom would call to the man. Absalom would say, "What city are you from?"

The man would answer, "I'm from one of the tribes*d* of Israel."

3Then Absalom would say to him, "Look, your claims are right. But the king has no one to listen to you." 4Absalom would also say, "I wish someone would make me judge in this land! Then I could help everyone who comes with a problem. I could help him get a fair decision for his problem!"

5People would come near Absalom to bow to him. When they did, Absalom would reach out his hand and take hold of them. Then he would kiss them. 6Absalom did that to all the Israelites who came to King David for decisions. In this way, Absalom won the hearts of all Israel.

7After four years Absalom said to King David, "Please let me go to Hebron. I want to carry out my promise that I made to the Lord. 8I made it while I was living in Geshur in Aram. I said, 'If the Lord takes me back to Jerusalem, I will worship him in Hebron.'"

9The king said, "Go in peace."

So Absalom went to Hebron. 10But he sent secret messengers through all the tribes of Israel. They told the people, "When you hear the trumpets, say this: 'Absalom has become the king at Hebron!'"

11Absalom had invited 200 men to go with him. So they went from Jerusalem with him. But they didn't know what he was planning. 12Ahithophel was one of the people who advised David. He was from the town of Giloh. While Absalom was offering sacrifices, he called Ahithophel to come from his hometown of Giloh. So Absalom's plans were working very well. More and more people began to support him.

13A man came in to tell the news to David. The man said, "The Israelites are beginning to follow Absalom."

14Then David spoke to all his officers who were with him in Jerusalem. He said, "We must leave quickly! If we don't, we won't be able to get away from Absalom. We must hurry before he catches us. He would destroy us and kill the people of Jerusalem."

15The king's officers said to him, "We will do anything you say."

16The king set out with everyone in his house. But he left ten slave women*d* to take care of the palace. 17The king left with all his people following him. They stopped at the last house. 18All the king's servants passed by him. All the Kerethites and Pelethites, the king's bodyguards, passed by him. All those from Gath, the 600 men who had followed him, passed by him.

15:2 city gate People came here to conduct business. Public meetings and court cases were also held here.

¹⁹The king spoke to Ittai, a man from Gath. He said, "Why are you also going with us? Turn back and stay with King Absalom. You are a foreigner. This is not your homeland. ²⁰Only a short time ago you came to join me. Today should I make you go with us to other places? I don't even know where I'm going. Turn back, and take your brothers with you. May kindness and loyalty be shown to you."

²¹But Ittai said to the king, "As surely as the Lord lives and as you live, I will stay with you. I'll be with you wherever you are. I'll be with you whether it means life or death."

²²David said to Ittai, "Go, march on." So Ittai from Gath and all his people with their children marched on. ²³All the people cried loudly as everyone passed by. King David also crossed the Kidron Valley. Then all the people went on to the desert. ²⁴Zadok and all the Levites with him were carrying the Box*d* of the Agreement with God. They set down the Holy Box. And Abiathar offered sacrifices until all the people had left the city.

²⁵The king said to Zadok, "Take the Holy Box of God back into the city. If the Lord is pleased with me, he will bring me back. He will let me see both it and Jerusalem again. ²⁶But if the Lord says he is not pleased with me, I am ready. He can do what he wants with me."

²⁷The king also said to Zadok the priest, "You are a seer.*d* Go back to the city in peace. Take your son Ahimaaz and Abiathar's son Jonathan with you. ²⁸I will wait near the crossings into the desert until I hear from you." ²⁹So Zadok and Abiathar took the Holy Box of God back to Jerusalem and stayed there.

³⁰David went up the Mount of Olives*d* crying as he went. He covered his head and went barefoot. All the people with David covered their heads also. And they were crying as they went. ³¹Someone told David, "Ahithophel is one of the people with Absalom who made secret plans against you."

So David prayed, "Lord, please make Ahithophel's advice foolish."

³²David came to the top of the mountain. This was where he used to worship God. Hushai the Arkite came to meet him. Hushai's coat was torn, and there was dirt on his head to show how sad he was. ³³David said to Hushai, "If you go with me, you will be just one more person to take care of. ³⁴But if you return to the city, you can make Ahithophel's advice useless. Tell Absalom, 'I am your servant, my king. In the past I served your father. But now I will serve you.' ³⁵The priests Zadok and Abiathar will be with you. You must tell them everything you hear in the king's palace. ³⁶Zadok's son Ahimaaz and Abiathar's son Jonathan are with them. Send them to tell me everything you hear." ³⁷So David's friend Hushai entered Jerusalem. About that time, Absalom also arrived there.

ZIBA MEETS DAVID

16 David passed a short way over the top of the Mount of Olives.*d* There Ziba, Mephibosheth's servant, met David. Ziba had two donkeys with saddles on them. They carried 200 loaves of bread, 100 cakes of raisins and 100 cakes of figs. They also carried leather bags full of wine. ²The king asked Ziba, "What are these things for?"

Ziba answered, "The donkeys are for your family to ride. The bread and cakes of figs are for the servants to eat. And the wine is for anyone to drink who becomes weak in the desert."

³The king asked, "Where is Mephibosheth?"

Ziba answered him, "Mephibosheth is staying in Jerusalem. He thinks, 'Today the Israelites will give my father's kingdom back to me!'"

⁴Then the king said to Ziba, "All right. Everything that belonged to Mephibosheth, I now give to you!"

Ziba said, "I bow to you. I hope I will always be able to please you."

SHIMEI CURSES DAVID

⁵As King David came to Bahurim, a man came out from there. He was from Saul's family group. His name was Shimei son of Gera. Shimei came out, cursing David as he came. ⁶He began throwing stones at David and his officers. But the people and soldiers gathered all around David. ⁷Shimei cursed David. He said, "Get out, get out, you murderer, you troublemaker. ⁸The Lord is punishing you for the people in Saul's family you killed! You took Saul's place as king! But now the Lord has given the kingdom to your son Absalom! Now you are ruined because you are a murderer!"

⁹Abishai son of Zeruiah said to the king, "Why should this dead dog curse you, the king? Let me go over and cut off his head!"

¹⁰But the king answered, "This does not concern you, sons of Zeruiah! If he is cursing me because the Lord told him to, who can question him?"

¹¹David also said to Abishai and all his officers, "My own son is trying to kill me! This man is a Benjaminite and has more right to kill me! Leave him alone. Let him curse me. The Lord told him to do this. ¹²Maybe the Lord will see my misery. Then maybe he will repay me with something good for the curses Shimei says today!"

¹³So David and his men went on down the road. But Shimei kept following David. Shimei walked on the hillside on the other side of the road. He kept cursing David and throwing stones and dirt at him. ¹⁴The king and all his people arrived at the Jordan. They were very tired. So they rested there.

¹⁵Meanwhile, Absalom, Ahithophel and all the men of Israel arrived at Jerusalem. ¹⁶David's friend Hushai the Arkite came to Absalom. He said to Absalom, "Long live the king! Long live the king!"

¹⁷Absalom asked, "Why are you not loyal to your friend David? Why didn't you leave Jerusalem with your friend?"

¹⁸Hushai said, "I belong to the one chosen by the Lord and by these people and all the men of Israel. I will stay with you. ¹⁹In the past I served your father. So whom should I serve now? David's son! I will serve you."

AHITHOPHEL'S ADVICE

²⁰Absalom said to Ahithophel, "Please tell us what we should do."

²¹Ahithophel said, "Your father left behind some of his slave women[d] who give birth to his children. He left them here to take care of the palace. Have sexual relations with them. Then all the Israelites will hear that your father is your enemy. And all your people will be encouraged to give you more support." ²²So they put up a tent for Absalom on the flat roof[n] of the palace. Everyone in Israel could see it. And Absalom had sexual relations with his father's slave women.

²³At that time people thought Ahithophel's advice was as reliable as God's own word. Both David and Absalom thought it was that reliable.

17 Ahithophel said to Absalom, "Let me choose 12,000 men. I'll chase David tonight. ²I'll catch him while he is tired and weak. I'll frighten him so all his people will run away. But I'll kill only King David. ³Then I'll bring everyone back to you. If the man you are looking for is dead, everyone else will return safely." ⁴This plan seemed good to Absalom and to all the leaders of Israel.

⁵But Absalom said, "Now call Hushai the Arkite. I also want to hear what he says." ⁶So Hushai came to Absalom. Absalom said to him, "This is the plan Ahithophel gave. Should we follow it? If not, tell us."

⁷Hushai said to Absalom, "Ahithophel's advice is not good this time."

16:22 roof In Bible times houses were built with flat roofs. The roof was used for drying things such as flax and fruit. And it was used as an extra room, as a place for worship and as a place to sleep in the summer.

[8]Hushai added, "You know your father and his men are strong. They are as angry as a bear that is robbed of its babies. Your father is a skilled fighter. He won't stay all night with the people. [9]He is probably already hiding in a cave or some other place. If your father attacks your men first, people will hear the news. And they will think, 'Absalom's followers are losing!' [10]Then even the men who are as brave as a lion will become frightened. This is because all the Israelites know your father is a fighter. They know his men are brave!

[11]"This is what I suggest: Gather all the Israelites from Dan to Beersheba.[n] There will be as many people as grains of sand by the sea. Then you yourself must go into the battle. [12]We will catch David where he is hiding. We will fall on him as dew falls on the ground. We will kill him and all of his men. No one will be left alive. [13]What if David escapes into a city? Then all the Israelites will bring ropes to that city. We'll pull that city into the valley. There won't be even a small stone left there!"

[14]Absalom and all the Israelites said, "The advice of Hushai the Arkite is better than that of Ahithophel." They said this because the Lord had planned to destroy the good advice of Ahithophel. In this way the Lord could bring disaster on Absalom.

[15]Hushai told these things to Zadok and Abiathar, the priests. He told them what Ahithophel had suggested to Absalom and the elders of Israel. He also reported to them what he himself had suggested. Hushai said, [16]"Quickly! Send a message to David. Tell him not to stay tonight at the crossings into the desert. Tell him to cross over the Jordan River at once. If he crosses the river, he and all his people won't be caught."

[17]Jonathan and Ahimaaz were waiting at En Rogel. They did not want to be seen going into the town. So a servant girl would go out to them and give them messages. Then Jonathan and Ahimaaz would go and tell King David. [18]But a boy saw Jonathan and Ahimaaz and told Absalom. So Jonathan and Ahimaaz ran away quickly. They went to a man's house in Bahurim. He had a well in his courtyard, and they climbed down into it. [19]The man's wife spread a sheet over the opening of the well. Then she covered it with grain. No one could tell that Jonathan and Ahimaaz were hiding there.

[20]Absalom's servants came to the woman at the house. They asked, "Where are Ahimaaz and Jonathan?"

She said to them, "They have already crossed the brook."

Absalom's servants then went to look for Jonathan and Ahimaaz. But they could not find them. So they went back to Jerusalem.

[21]After Absalom's servants had left, Jonathan and Ahimaaz climbed out of the well. Then they went to tell King David. They said, "Hurry, cross over the river! Ahithophel has said these things against you!" [22]So David and all his people crossed the Jordan River. By dawn, everyone had crossed the Jordan.

[23]Now Ahithophel saw that the Israelites did not accept his advice. So he saddled his donkey and went to his hometown. He gave orders for his family and property. Then he hung himself. After Ahithophel died, he was buried in his father's tomb.

WAR BETWEEN DAVID AND ABSALOM

[24]David arrived at Mahanaim. And Absalom and all his Israelites crossed over the Jordan River. [25]Now Absalom had made Amasa captain of the army

---

17:11 Dan to Beersheba Dan was the city farthest north in Israel. Beersheba was the city farthest south. So this means all the people of Israel.

instead of Joab. Amasa was the son of a man named Jether the Ishmaelite. Amasa's mother was Abigail daughter of Nahash and sister of Zeruiah. Zeruiah was Joab's mother. 26Absalom and the Israelites camped in the land of Gilead.

27Shobi, Makir and Barzillai were at Mahanaim when David arrived. Shobi son of Nahash was from the Ammonite town of Rabbah. Makir son of Ammiel was from Lo Debar. And Barzillai was from Rogelim in Gilead. 28They brought beds, bowls and clay pots. They brought wheat, barley, flour, roasted grain, beans and small peas. 29They also brought honey and milk curds, sheep, and cheese made from cows' milk. They brought these things for David and his people. They had said, "The people have become hungry and tired and thirsty in the desert."

18 David counted his men. He chose commanders over groups of 1,000 and commanders over groups of 100. 2He sent the troops out in three groups. Joab commanded one-third of the men. Joab's brother Abishai son of Zeruiah commanded another third. And Ittai from Gath commanded the last third. King David said to them, "I will also go with you."

3But the men said, "No! You must not go with us! If we run away in the battle, Absalom's men won't care. Even if half of us are killed, Absalom's men won't care. But you're worth 10,000 of us! It is better for you to stay in the city. Then, if we need help, you can send it."

4The king said to his people, "I will do what you think is best." So the king stood at the side of the gate as the army went out. They went out in groups of 100 and 1,000.

5The king gave a command to Joab, Abishai and Ittai. He said, "Be gentle with young Absalom for my sake." Everyone heard the king's orders about Absalom to the commanders.

6David's army went out into the field against Absalom's Israelites. They fought in the forest of Ephraim. 7There David's army defeated the Israelites. Many died that day—20,000 men. 8The battle spread through all the country. But that day more men died in the forest than in the fighting.

ABSALOM DIES

9Then Absalom happened to meet David's troops. As Absalom was riding his mule, it went under a large oak tree. The branches were thick, and Absalom's head got caught in the tree. His mule ran out from under him. So Absalom was left hanging above the ground.

10When one of the men saw it happen, he told Joab. He said, "I saw Absalom hanging in an oak tree!"

11Joab said to him, "You saw him? Why didn't you kill him and let him fall to the ground? I would have given you a belt and four ounces of silver!"

12The man answered, "I wouldn't try to hurt the king's son. I wouldn't even if you gave me 25 pounds of silver. We heard the king's command to you, Abishai and Ittai. The king said, 'Be careful not to hurt young Absalom.' 13If I had killed him, the king would have found out. And you would not have protected me!"

14Joab said, "I won't waste time here with you!" Now Absalom was still alive in the oak tree. So Joab took three spears and stabbed him in the heart. 15Ten young men who carried Joab's armor also gathered around Absalom. They struck him and killed him.

16Then Joab blew the trumpet. So the troops stopped chasing Absalom's Israelites. 17Then Joab's men took Absalom's body. They threw it into a large pit in the forest. Then they filled the pit with many stones. All the Israelites who followed Absalom ran away and went home.

18When Absalom was alive, he had put up a pillar in the King's Valley. It was a monument to himself. He said, "I have no son to keep my name alive." So he named the pillar after himself. That pillar is called Absalom's Monument even today.

¹⁹Ahimaaz son of Zadok spoke to Joab. He said, "Let me run and take the news to King David. I'll tell him the Lord has destroyed the enemy for him."

²⁰Joab answered Ahimaaz, "No, you are not the one to take the news today. You may do it another time. But do not take it today, because the king's son is dead."

²¹Then Joab said to a man from Cush, "Go. Tell the king what you have seen." The Cushite bowed to Joab and ran to tell David.

²²But Ahimaaz son of Zadok begged Joab again. He said, "No matter what happens, please let me go, along with the Cushite!"

Joab said, "Son, why do you want to carry the news? You won't get any reward for the news you bring!"

²³Ahimaaz answered, "No matter what happens, I will run."

So Joab said to Ahimaaz, "Run!" Then Ahimaaz ran by way of the Jordan Valley and passed the Cushite.

²⁴Now David was sitting between the inner and outer gates of the city. The watchman went up to the roof by the gate walls. As he looked up, he saw a man running alone. ²⁵He shouted to tell King David.

The king said, "If he is alone, he is bringing good news!"

The man came nearer and nearer to the city. ²⁶Then the watchman saw another man running. The watchman called to the gatekeeper, "Look! Another man is running alone!"

The king said, "He is also bringing good news!"

²⁷The watchman said, "I think the first man runs like Ahimaaz son of Zadok."

The king said, "Ahimaaz is a good man. He must be bringing good news!"

²⁸Then Ahimaaz called a greeting to the king. He bowed facedown on the ground to the king. He said, "Praise the Lord your God! The Lord has defeated the men who were against you, my king."

²⁹The king asked, "Is young Absalom all right?"

Ahimaaz answered, "When Joab sent me, I saw some great excitement. But I don't know what it was."

³⁰Then the king said, "Step over here and wait." So Ahimaaz stepped aside and stood there.

³¹Then the Cushite arrived. He said, "Master and king, hear the good news! Today the Lord has punished the people who were against you!"

³²The king asked the Cushite, "Is young Absalom all right?"

The Cushite answered, "May your enemies be like that young man. May all who come to hurt you be like that young man!"

³³Then the king knew Absalom was dead. He was very upset. He went to the room over the city gate and cried. As he went, he cried out, "My son Absalom, my son Absalom! I wish I had died for you. Absalom, my son, my son!"

JOAB SCOLDS DAVID

19 People told Joab, "Look, the king is crying. He is very sad because of Absalom." ²David's army had won the battle that day. But it became a very sad day for all the people. This was because they heard, "The king is very sad for his son." ³The people came into the city quietly. They were like people who had been defeated in battle and had run away. ⁴The king covered his face and cried loudly, "My son Absalom! Absalom, my son, my son!"

⁵Then Joab went into the king's house. He said to the king, "Today you have shamed all your men. They saved your life today! They saved the lives of your sons, daughters, wives and slave women.ᵈ ⁶You have shamed them because you love those who hate you. And you hate those people who love you. Today you've

made it clear that your commanders and men mean nothing to you. What if Absalom had lived and all of us were dead? I can see you would be very pleased. [7]Now go out and encourage your servants. I swear by the Lord that if you don't go out, no man will be left with you by tonight! That will be worse than all the troubles you have had from your youth until today."

[8]So the king went to the city gate.[n] The news spread that the king was at the gate. So everyone came to see him.

DAVID GOES BACK TO JERUSALEM

All the Israelites who had followed Absalom had run away to their homes. [9]People in all the tribes[d] of Israel began to argue. They said, "The king saved us from the Philistines and our other enemies. But he left the country because of Absalom. [10]We appointed Absalom to rule us, but now he has died in battle. We should make David the king again."

[11]King David sent a message to Zadok and Abiathar, the priests. David said, "Speak to the elders of Judah. Say, 'Even in my house I have heard what all the Israelites are saying. So why are you the last tribe to bring the king back to his palace? [12]You are my brothers, my own family. Then why are you the last tribe to bring back the king?' [13]And say to Amasa, 'You are part of my own family. May God punish me terribly if I don't make you commander of the army in Joab's place!'"

[14]David touched the hearts of all the people of Judah. They agreed as if they were one man. They sent a message to the king. They said, "Return with all your men." [15]Then the king returned as far as the Jordan River. The men of Judah came to Gilgal to meet him. They wanted to bring the king across the Jordan River.

[16]Shimei son of Gera was a Benjaminite. He lived in Bahurim. He hurried down with the men of Judah to meet King David. [17]With Shimei came 1,000 Benjaminites. Ziba, the servant from Saul's family, also came. He brought his 15 sons and 20 servants with him. They all hurried to the Jordan River to meet the king. [18]The people went across the Jordan River to help bring the king's family back to Judah. They did whatever the king wanted. As the king was about to cross the river, Shimei son of Gera came to him. Shimei bowed facedown on the ground in front of the king. [19]He said to the king, "My master, don't hold me guilty. Don't remember the wrong things I did when you left Jerusalem! Don't hold it against me. [20]I know I have sinned. That is why I am the first person from Joseph's family to come down and meet you today, my master and king!"

[21]But Abishai son of Zeruiah said, "Shimei should die. He cursed you, the Lord's appointed king!"

[22]David said, "This does not concern you, sons of Zeruiah! Today you're against me! No one will be put to death in Israel today. Today I know I am king over Israel!" [23]Then the king said to Shimei, "You won't die." The king made this promise to Shimei.

[24]Mephibosheth, Saul's grandson, also went down to meet King David. Mephibosheth had not cared for his feet, cut his beard or washed his clothes while David was gone. He had not done this from the time the king had left Jerusalem until he returned safely. [25]Mephibosheth came from Jerusalem to meet the king. The king asked him, "Mephibosheth, why didn't you go with me?"

[26]He answered, "My master, my servant Ziba tricked me! I said to Ziba, 'I am crippled. So saddle a donkey. Then I will ride it so I can go with the king.' [27]But he lied about me to you. You, my master and king, are like an angel from God. Do what you think is good. [28]You could have

---

19:8 city gate People came here to conduct business. Public meetings and court cases were also held here.

killed all my grandfather's family. Instead, you put me with the people who eat at your own table. So I don't have a right to ask anything more from the king!"

²⁹The king said to him, "Don't say anything more. I have decided that you and Ziba may divide the land."

³⁰Mephibosheth said to the king, "Let Ziba take all the land. I'm just happy that my master the king has arrived in peace at his own house."

³¹Barzillai of Gilead came down from Rogelim to cross the Jordan River with the king. ³²Now Barzillai was a very old man. He was 80 years old. He had taken care of the king when David was staying at Mahanaim. Barzillai could do this, because he was a very rich man. ³³David said to Barzillai, "Cross the river with me. Come with me to Jerusalem, and I will take care of you."

³⁴But Barzillai answered the king, "Do you know how old I am? Do you think I can go with you to Jerusalem? ³⁵I am 80 years old! I am too old to taste what I eat or drink. I am too old to hear the voices of men and women singers. Why should you be bothered with me? ³⁶I am not worthy of a reward from you. But I will cross the Jordan River with you. ³⁷Then please let me go back so I may die in my own city. Let me die near the grave of my father and mother. But here is Kimham. Let him go with you, my master and king. Do with him whatever you want."

³⁸The king answered, "Kimham will go with me. I will do for him anything you wish. And I will do anything for you that you wish." ³⁹The king kissed Barzillai and blessed him. Then Barzillai returned home. And the king and all the people crossed the Jordan.

⁴⁰When the king crossed the Jordan to Gilgal, Kimham went with him. All the troops of Judah and half the troops of Israel led David across the river.

⁴¹Soon all the men of Israel came to the king. They said to him, "Our brothers, the men of Judah, stole you away. They brought you and your family across the Jordan River with your men! Why did they do this?"

⁴²All the men of Judah answered the Israelites, "We did this because the king is our close relative. Why are you angry about it? We have not eaten food at the king's expense! He did not give us any gifts!"

⁴³The men of Israel answered the people of Judah, "We have ten tribes in the kingdom. So we have more right to David than you do! But you ignored us! We were the first ones to talk about bringing our king back!"

But the men of Judah spoke even more unkindly than the men of Israel.

SHEBA LEADS ISRAEL AWAY FROM DAVID

20 It happened that a troublemaker named Sheba son of Bicri was there. Sheba was from the tribe*d* of Benjamin. He blew the trumpet and said:

"We have no share in David!

We have no part in the son of Jesse!

People of Israel, let's go to our own homes!"

²So all the Israelites left David and followed Sheba son of Bicri. But the men of Judah stayed with their king all the way from the Jordan River to Jerusalem.

³David came to his palace in Jerusalem. Earlier he had left there ten of his slave women*d* who gave birth to his children. He had left them there to take care of the palace. Now he put them in a house where they would be guarded. They were kept there for the rest of their lives. David gave them food, but he did not have sexual relations with them. They lived like widows until they died.

⁴The king said to Amasa, "Tell the men of Judah to meet with me in three days. And you must also be here." ⁵So Amasa went to call the men of Judah together. But he took longer than the time the king had told him.

⁶David said to Abishai, "Sheba son of Bicri is more dangerous to us than Absalom was. Take my men and chase him. Hurry before he finds strong, walled cities. If he gets there, he will escape from us." ⁷So Joab's men, the Kerethites and the Pelethites, who were the king's bodyguards, and all the soldiers went with Abishai. They went out from Jerusalem to chase Sheba son of Bicri.

⁸When Joab and the army came to the great rock at Gibeon, Amasa came out to meet them. Joab was wearing his uniform. At his waist he wore a belt. It held his sword in its case. As Joab stepped forward, his sword fell out of its case. ⁹Joab asked Amasa, "Brother, is everything all right with you?" Then with his right hand he took Amasa by the beard to kiss him. ¹⁰Amasa did not guard against the sword that was in Joab's hand. So Joab pushed the sword into Amasa's stomach. This caused Amasa's insides to spill on the ground. Joab did not have to stab Amasa again. He was already dead. Then Joab and his brother Abishai continued to chase Sheba son of Bicri.

¹¹One of Joab's young men stood by Amasa's body. The young man said, "Everyone who is for Joab and David should follow Joab!" ¹²Amasa lay in the middle of the road, covered with his own blood. The young man saw that everyone was stopping to look at the body. So he dragged Amasa's body from the road and laid it in a field. Then he put a cloth over it. ¹³After Amasa's body was taken off the road, all the men followed Joab. They went with him to chase Sheba son of Bicri.

¹⁴Sheba went through all the tribes of Israel to Abel Beth Maacah. All the Berites also came together and followed him. ¹⁵So Joab and his men came to Abel Beth Maacah and surrounded it. They piled dirt up against the city wall so they could attack it. And they began digging under the city walls to make them fall down.

¹⁶But a wise woman shouted out from the city. She said, "Listen! Listen! Tell Joab to come here. I want to talk to him!" ¹⁷So Joab came near her. She asked him, "Are you Joab?"

He answered, "Yes, I am."

Then she said, "Listen to what I say!"

Joab said, "I'm listening."

¹⁸Then the woman said, "In the past people would say, 'Ask for advice at Abel.' Then the problem would be solved. ¹⁹I am one of the peaceful, loyal people of Israel. You are trying to destroy an important city of Israel. Why must you destroy what belongs to the Lord?"

²⁰Joab answered, "May I not destroy or ruin anything. ²¹That is not what I want. But there is a man here from the mountains of Ephraim. He is named Sheba son of Bicri. He has turned against King David. If you will bring him to me, I will leave the city alone."

The woman said to Joab, "His head will be thrown over the wall to you."

²²Then the woman spoke very wisely to all the people of the city. They cut off the head of Sheba son of Bicri. Then they threw it over the wall to Joab. So he blew the trumpet, and the army left the city. Every man returned home. And Joab went back to the king in Jerusalem.

²³Joab was commander of all the army of Israel. Benaiah son of Jehoiada led the Kerethites and Pelethites, the king's bodyguards. ²⁴Adoniram led the men who were forced to do hard work. Jehoshaphat son of Ahilud was the recorder. ²⁵Sheba was the royal assistant. Zadok and Abiathar were the priests. ²⁶And Ira the Jairite was David's priest.

THE GIBEONITES PUNISH SAUL'S FAMILY

21 During the time David was king, there was a time of hunger. It continued for three years. So David prayed to the Lord.

The Lord answered, "Saul and his family of murderers are the reason for this time of hunger. It has come because Saul killed the Gibeonites." ²(Now the Gibeonites were not Israelites. They were a group of Amorites who were left alive. The Israelites had promised not to hurt the Gibeonites. But Saul was very eager to help the people of Israel and Judah. So he tried to kill all the Gibeonites.)

King David called the Gibeonites together and talked to them. ³He asked them, "What can I do for you? What can I do to take away Israel's sin so you can bless the Lord's people?"

⁴The Gibeonites said to David, "Saul and his family don't have enough silver and gold to pay for what they did! And we don't have the right to kill anyone in Israel."

Then David asked, "What do you want me to do for you?"

⁵The Gibeonites said to him, "Saul made plans against us. He tried to destroy all our people who are left in the land of Israel. ⁶Saul was the Lord's chosen king. So bring seven of his sons to us. Then we will kill them and hang them on stakes. We will put them in front of the Lord at Gibeah, Saul's hometown."

The king said, "I will give them to you." ⁷But the king protected Jonathan's son Mephibosheth. (Jonathan was Saul's son.) David did this because of the promise he had made to Jonathan in the Lord's name. So the king did not let them hurt Mephibosheth. ⁸But the king did take Armoni and Mephibosheth,ⁿ sons of Rizpah and Saul. (Rizpah was the daughter of Aiah.) And the king took the five sons of Saul's daughter Merab. Adriel was the father of Merab's five sons. (Adriel was the son of Barzillai the Meholathite.) ⁹David gave these seven sons to the Gibeonites. Then the Gibeonites killed them and hung them on stakes on a hill before the Lord. All seven sons died together. They were put to death during the first days of the harvest

season. (The barley harvest was just beginning.)

¹⁰Aiah's daughter Rizpah took the rough cloth that was worn to show sadness. Then she put it on a rock for herself. She stayed there from the beginning of the harvest until the rain fell on her sons' bodies. During the day she did not let the birds of the sky touch her sons' bodies. At night she did not let the wild animals touch them.

¹¹People told David what Aiah's daughter Rizpah, Saul's slave woman,ᵈ was doing. ¹²Then David took the bones of Saul and Jonathan from the men of Jabesh Gilead. (They had taken these bones secretly from the public square of Beth Shan. The Philistines had hung the bodies of Saul and Jonathan there after they had killed Saul at Gilboa.) ¹³David brought the bones of Saul and his son Jonathan from Gilead. Then the people gathered the bodies of Saul's seven sons who were hanged on stakes. ¹⁴The people buried the bones of Saul and his son Jonathan at Zela in Benjamin. They buried them in the tomb of Saul's father Kish. The people did everything the king commanded.

Then God answered the prayers of the people in the land.

WARS WITH THE PHILISTINES

¹⁵Again there was war between the Philistines and Israel. David and his men went out to fight the Philistines. But David became tired and weak. ¹⁶Ishbi-Benob was one of the sons of Rapha.ᵈ His bronze spearhead weighed about seven and a half pounds. Ishbi-Benob had a new sword, and he planned to kill David. ¹⁷But Abishai son of Zeruiah killed the Philistine. So he saved David's life.

Then David's men made a promise to David. They said, "Never again will you go out with us to battle. If you were killed, Israel would lose its greatest leader."

21:8 Mephibosheth This is not Jonathan's son but another man with the same name.

[18]Later, at Gob, there was another battle with the Philistines. Sibbecai the Hushathite killed Saph, another one of the sons of Rapha.

[19]Later, there was another battle at Gob with the Philistines. Elhanan son of Jaare-Oregim from Bethlehem killed Goliath[n] from Gath. Goliath's spear was as large as a weaver's rod.

[20]At Gath another battle took place. A very large man was there. He had 6 fingers on each hand. And he had 6 toes on each foot. He had 24 fingers and toes in all. This man also was one of the sons of Rapha. [21]When he challenged Israel, Jonathan killed him. Jonathan was the son of Shimeah, David's brother.

[22]These four men were sons of Rapha from Gath. They all were killed by David and his men.

DAVID'S SONG OF PRAISE

22 David sang this song to the Lord. He sang it when the Lord had saved him from Saul and all his other enemies. [2]He said:

"The Lord is my rock, my place of
    safety, my Savior.
[3]My God is my rock.
    I can run to him for safety.
He is my shield and my saving
    strength.
The Lord is my high tower and my
    place of safety.
The Lord saves me from those who
    want to harm me.
[4]I will call to the Lord.
    He is worthy of praise.
And I will be saved from my
    enemies.

[5]"The waves of death came around me.
    The deadly rivers overwhelmed me.
[6]The ropes of death wrapped around
    me.
    The traps of death were before me.
[7]In my trouble I called to the Lord.
    I cried out to my God.

From his temple he heard my voice.
    My call for help reached his ears.

[8]"The earth trembled and shook.
    The foundations of heaven began to
      shake.
They shook because the Lord was
    angry.
[9]Smoke came out of his nose.
    Burning fire came out of his mouth.
    Burning coals went before him.
[10]He tore open the sky and came down.
    Dark clouds were under his feet.
[11]He rode a creature with wings and
    flew.
He flew on the wings of the wind.
[12]He made darkness his shelter around
    him,
    surrounded by fog and clouds.
[13]Out of the brightness of his presence
    came flashes of lightning.
[14]The Lord thundered from heaven.
    The Most High God raised his voice.
[15]He shot his arrows and scattered his
    enemies.
    His bolts of lightning confused
      them with fear.
[16]The Lord spoke strongly.
    The wind blew from his nose.
    The valleys of the sea appeared.
    The foundations of the earth were
      seen.

[17]"The Lord reached down from above
    and took me.
    He pulled me from the deep water.
[18]He saved me from my powerful
    enemies.
    Those who hated me were too
      strong for me.
[19]They attacked me at my time of
    trouble.
    But the Lord supported me.
[20]He took me to a safe place.
    Because he delights in me, he saved
    me.

21:19 Goliath In 1 Chronicles 20:5 he is called Lahmi brother of Goliath.

21"The Lord spared me because I did
   what was right.
   Because I have not done evil, he has
   rescued me.
22I have followed the ways of the Lord.
   I have not done evil by turning
   from my God.
23I remember all his laws.
   I have not broken his rules.
24I have kept myself innocent before
   him.
   I have kept myself from doing evil.
25The Lord rescued me because I did
   what was right.
   I did what the Lord said was right.

26"Lord, you are loyal to those who are
   loyal.
   You are good to those who are
   good.
27You are pure to those who are pure.
   But you are against those who are
   bad.
28You save those who are not proud.
   But you make humble those who
   are proud.
29Lord, you give light to my lamp.
   The Lord brightens the darkness
   around me.
30With your help, I can attack an army.
   With God's help, I can jump over a
   wall.

31"The ways of God are without fault.
   The Lord's words are pure.
   He is a shield to those who trust him.
32Who is God? Only the Lord.
   Who is the Rock?d Only our God.
33God is my protection.
   He makes my way free from fault.
34He makes me like a deer, which does
   not stumble.
   He helps me stand on the steep
   mountains.
35He trains my hands for battle.
   So my arms can bend a bronze bow.
36You protect me with your saving
   shield.

   You have stooped to make me
   great.
37You give me a better way to live.
   So I live as you want me to.
38I chased my enemies and destroyed
   them.
   I did not quit till they were
   destroyed.
39I destroyed and crushed them,
   so they couldn't rise up again.
   They fell beneath my feet.
40You gave me strength in battle.
   You made my enemies bow before
   me.
41You made my enemies turn back.
   I destroyed those who hated me.
42They called for help,
   but no one came to save them.
   They called to the Lord,
   but he did not answer them.
43I beat my enemies into pieces.
   They were like dust on the ground.
   I pounded them out and walked on
   them
   like mud in the streets.

44"You saved me when my people
   attacked me.
   You kept me as the leader of
   nations.
   People I never knew serve me.
45Foreigners obey me.
   As soon as they hear me, they obey
   me.
46They all become afraid.
   They tremble in their hiding places.

47"The Lord lives!
   May my Rock be praised!
   Praise God, the Rock, who saves
   me!
48God gives me victory over my
   enemies.
   He brings people under my rule.
49He frees me from my enemies.

   "You set me over those who hate me.
   You saved me from cruel men.

⁵⁰So I will praise you, Lord, among the
nations.
I will sing praises to your name.
⁵¹The Lord gives great victories to his
king.
He is loyal to his appointed king,
to David and his descendants*d*
forever."

DAVID'S LAST WORDS

23 These are the last words of David.
This is the message of David son
of Jesse.
The man made great by the Most
High God speaks.
He is the appointed king of the God of
Jacob.
He is the sweet singer of Israel.

²"The Lord's Spirit*d* spoke through me.
His word was on my tongue.
³The God of Israel spoke.
The Rock*d* of Israel said to me:
'The person who rules fairly over
people,
the person who rules with respect
for God,
⁴he is like the morning light at dawn.
He is like a morning without
clouds.
He is like sunshine after a rain.
The sunshine makes the tender
grass grow out of the ground.'

⁵"This is how God has cared for my
family.
God made a lasting agreement with
me,
good in every way and strong.
This agreement is my salvation.
This agreement is all I want.
Truly, the Lord will make it grow.

⁶"But all evil people will be thrown
away like thorns.
People cannot hold on to thorns.
⁷Anyone who touches them
uses a tool of iron or a spear.

They will be thrown in the fire and
burned where they lie."

DAVID'S ARMY

⁸These are the names of David's warriors:

Josheb-Basshebeth, the Tahkemonite,
was head of the Three.*n* He killed 800
men at one time.

⁹Next there was Eleazar son of Dodai
the Ahohite. Eleazar was one of the three
soldiers who were with David when they
challenged the Philistines. The Philistines
were gathered for battle, and the Israelites drew back. ¹⁰But Eleazar stayed
where he was. He fought the Philistines
until he was so tired he could not let go
of his sword. The Lord gave a great victory for the Israelites that day. The
people came back after Eleazar had won
the battle. But they came only to take
weapons and armor from the enemy.

¹¹Next there was Shammah son of
Agee the Hararite. The Philistines came
together to fight. They stood where there
was a field full of small peas. Israel's
troops ran away from the Philistines.
¹²But Shammah stood in the middle of
the field. He fought for the field and
killed the Philistines. And the Lord gave
a great victory.

¹³Once, three of the Thirty, David's
chief soldiers, came down to him during
harvest. Now David was at the cave of
Adullam. The Philistine army had
camped in the Valley of Rephaim. ¹⁴At
that time David was in a protected place.
And some of the Philistine soldiers were
in Bethlehem.

¹⁵David had a strong desire for some
water. He said, "Oh, I wish someone
would get me water from the well near
the city gate of Bethlehem!" ¹⁶So the three
warriors broke through the Philistine
army. They took water out of the well
near the city gate of Bethlehem. Then
they took it to David. But he refused to

23:8 Three These were David's most powerful soldiers. See 1 Chronicles 11:11.

drink it. He poured it out on the ground before the Lord. [17]David said, "Lord, I can't drink this! It would be like drinking the blood of the men who risked their lives!" So David refused to drink the water. These were the brave things that the three warriors did.

[18]Abishai was the brother of Joab son of Zeruiah. He was captain of the Three. Abishai used his spear against 300 enemies and killed them. He became as famous as the Three. [19]Abishai received even more honor than the Three. He became their commander. But he was not a member of them.

[20]Benaiah son of Jehoiada was a brave fighter from Kabzeel. He did many brave things. He killed two of the best soldiers from Moab. He also went down into a pit when it was snowing. There he killed a lion. [21]Benaiah killed a big Egyptian. The Egyptian had a spear in his hand. But Benaiah only had a club. Benaiah grabbed the spear from the Egyptian's hand. Then Benaiah killed him with his own spear. [22]These were the brave things that Benaiah son of Jehoiada did. He was as famous as the Three. [23]He received more honor than the Thirty. But he did not become a member of the Three. David made him leader of his bodyguard.

THE THIRTY CHIEF SOLDIERS

[24]The following men were among the Thirty:

Asahel the brother of Joab;

Elhanan son of Dodo from Bethlehem;
[25]Shammah the Harodite;

Elika the Harodite;
[26]Helez the Paltite;

Ira son of Ikkesh (from Tekoa);
[27]Abiezer the Anathothite;

Mebunnai the Hushathite;
[28]Zalmon the Ahohite;

Maharai the Netophathite;
[29]Heled son of Baanah the Netophathite;

Ithai son of Ribai from Gibeah of the land of Benjamin;
[30]Benaiah the Pirathonite;

Hiddai from the ravines of Gaash;
[31]Abi-Albon the Arbathite;

Azmaveth the Barhumite;
[32]Eliahba the Shaalbonite;

the sons of Jashen;

Jonathan [33]son of Shammah the Hararite;

Ahiam son of Sharar the Hararite;
[34]Eliphelet son of Ahasbai the Maacathite;

Eliam son of Ahithophel the Gilonite;
[35]Hezro the Carmelite;

Paarai the Arbite;
[36]Igal son of Nathan of Zobah;

the son of Hagri;
[37]Zelek the Ammonite;

Naharai the Beerothite, who carried the armor of Joab son of Zeruiah;
[38]Ira the Ithrite;

Gareb the Ithrite
[39]and Uriah the Hittite.

There were 37 in all.

DAVID COUNTS HIS ARMY

24 The Lord was angry with Israel again. He caused David to turn against the Israelites. David said, "Go, count the people of Israel and Judah."

[2]King David spoke to Joab, the commander of the army. David said, "Go through all the tribes[d] of Israel. Go from Dan to Beersheba[n] and count the people. Then I will know how many there are."

[3]But Joab said to the king, "May the Lord your God give you 100 times more people. And may you live to see this happen. But why do you want to do this?"

[4]But the king very strongly commanded Joab and the commanders of the army. So they left the king to count the people of Israel.

[5]After crossing the Jordan River, they camped near Aroer. They camped on the

---

24:2 Dan to Beersheba Dan was the city farthest north in Israel. Beersheba was the city farthest south. So this means all the people of Israel.

south side of the city in the ravine. They went through Gad and on to Jazer. 6Then they went to Gilead and the land of Tahtim Hodshi. Next they went to Dan Jaan and around to Sidon. 7They went to the strong, walled city of Tyre. They also went to all the cities of the Hivites and Canaanites. Finally, they went to southern Judah, to Beersheba. 8After 9 months and 20 days, they had gone through all the land. Then they came back to Jerusalem.

9Joab gave the list of the people to the king. There were 800,000 men in Israel who could use the sword. And there were 500,000 men in Judah.

10David felt ashamed after he had counted the people. He said to the Lord, "I have sinned greatly in what I have done! Lord, I beg you, forgive my sin! I have been very foolish."

11Before David got up in the morning, the Lord spoke his word to Gad. He was a prophet*d* and David's seer.*d* 12The Lord told Gad, "Go and tell David, 'This is what the Lord says: I offer you three choices. Choose one for me to do to you.'"

13Gad went to David and told him. Gad said, "Choose one of these three things. Should three years of hunger come to you and your land? Or should your enemies chase you for three months? Or should there be three days of disease in your country? Think about it. Then decide which of these things I should tell the Lord who sent me."

14David said to Gad, "I am really in trouble. But the Lord is very merciful. So let the Lord punish us. Don't let my punishment come from people!"

15So the Lord sent disease on Israel. It began in the morning. And it continued until the chosen time to stop. From Dan to Beersheba 70,000 people died. 16The angel raised his arm toward Jerusalem to destroy it also. But the Lord felt very sorry about the terrible things that had happened. He said to the angel who was destroying the people, "That's enough! Put down your arm!" At this time the angel of the Lord was by the threshing*d* floor of Araunah the Jebusite.

17David saw the angel that killed the people. Then he said to the Lord, "I've sinned! I've done wrong! But these people only followed me like sheep! They did nothing wrong! Please let your punishment be against me and my father's family!"

18That day Gad came to David. Gad told him, "Go and build an altar to the Lord. Build it on the threshing floor of Araunah the Jebusite." 19So David did what Gad told him to do. He obeyed the Lord's command and went to see Araunah.

20Araunah looked and saw the king and his servants coming to him. So he went out and bowed facedown on the ground. 21He said, "Why has my master the king come to me?"

David answered, "To buy the threshing floor from you. I want to build an altar to the Lord. Then the disease will stop."

22Araunah said to David, "My master and king, you may take anything you want for a sacrifice. Here are some oxen for the whole burnt offering. Here are the threshing boards and the yokes*d* for the wood! 23My king, I give everything to you!" Araunah also said to the king, "May the Lord your God be pleased with you!"

24But the king answered Araunah, "No. I will pay you for the land. I won't offer to the Lord my God burnt offerings which cost me nothing!"

So David bought the threshing floor and the oxen for one and one-fourth pounds of silver. 25Then he built an altar to the Lord there. And he offered whole burnt offerings and fellowship offerings. Then the Lord answered his prayer for the country. And the disease in Israel stopped.

THE FIRST BOOK OF THE
KINGS

ADONIJAH TRIES TO BECOME KING

1 At this time King David was very old. His servants covered him with blankets, but he could not keep warm. ²So they said to him, "We will find a young woman to care for you. She will lie close to you and keep you warm." ³So the king's servants looked everywhere in Israel for a beautiful young woman. They found a girl named Abishag from the Shunammite people. They brought her to the king. ⁴The girl was very beautiful. She cared for the king and served him. But King David did not have sexual relations with her.

⁵⁻⁶Adonijah was King David and Haggith's son. He was born next after Absalom. He was a very handsome man. He said, "I will be the king." So he got chariots and horses for himself. And he got 50 men to run ahead of him. Now David had never interfered with him by questioning what he did.

⁷Adonijah talked with Joab son of Zeruiah. He also talked with Abiathar the priest. They told him they would help him. ⁸But several men did not join Adonijah. These men were Zadok the priest, Benaiah son of Jehoiada, Nathan the prophet,ᵈ Shimei, Rei and King David's special guard.

⁹Then Adonijah killed some sheep, cows and fat calves for sacrifices. He made these sacrifices at the Stone of Zoheleth near the spring, En Rogel. He invited all his brothers, the other sons of King David, to come. He invited all the rulers and leaders of Judah also. ¹⁰But Adonijah did not invite Nathan the prophet, Benaiah, his father's special guard or his brother Solomon.

¹¹When Nathan heard about this, he went to Bathsheba. She was the mother of Solomon. Nathan asked her, "Have you heard what Adonijah, Haggith's son, is doing? He has made himself king. And our real king, David, does not know it. ¹²Your life and the life of your son Solomon may be in danger. But I will tell you how to save yourselves. ¹³Go to King David and say to him, 'My master and king, you made a promise to me. You promised that my son Solomon would be the king after you. You said he would rule on your throne. So why has Adonijah become king?' ¹⁴While you are still talking to him, I will come in. I will tell the king that what you have said about Adonijah is true."

¹⁵So Bathsheba went in to see the king in his bedroom. He was now very old. Abishag, the girl from Shunam, was caring for him there. ¹⁶Bathsheba bowed down before the king.

He asked, "What do you want?"

¹⁷She answered, "My master, you made a promise to me in the name of the Lord your God. You said, 'Your son Solomon will become king after me. He will rule on my throne.' ¹⁸But now Adonijah has become king. And you did not know it. ¹⁹Adonijah has killed many cows, fat calves and sheep for sacrifices. And he has invited all your sons. He also has invited Abiathar the priest and Joab the commander of your army. But he did not invite Solomon, your son who serves you. ²⁰My master and king, all the people of Israel are watching you. They are waiting for you to decide who will be king after you. ²¹As soon as you die, Solomon and I will be treated as criminals."

²²While Bathsheba was still talking with the king, Nathan the prophet arrived. ²³The servants told the king, "Nathan the prophet is here." So Nathan went to the king and bowed facedown on the ground before him. ²⁴Then Nathan said, "My master and king, have you said that Adonijah will be the king after you? Have you decided he will rule on your throne after you?

²⁵Today he has sacrificed many cows, fat calves and sheep. And he has invited all your other sons, the commanders of the army and Abiathar the priest. Right now they are eating and drinking with him. They are saying, 'Long live King Adonijah!' ²⁶But he did not invite me, Zadok the priest, Benaiah son of Jehoiada or your son Solomon. ²⁷Did you do this? We are your servants. Why didn't you tell us whom you chose to be the king after you?"

DAVID MAKES SOLOMON KING

²⁸Then King David said, "Tell Bathsheba to come in!" So she came in and stood before the king.

²⁹Then the king said, "The Lord has saved me from all trouble. As surely as he lives, I make this promise to you. ³⁰Today I will do what I promised you in the past. I made that promise in the name of the Lord, the God of Israel. I promised that your son Solomon would be king after me. I promised he would rule on my throne after me."

³¹Then Bathsheba bowed facedown on the ground before the king. She said, "Long live my master King David!"

³²Then King David said, "Tell Zadok the priest, Nathan the prophet*d* and Benaiah son of Jehoiada to come in here." So they came before the king. ³³Then the king said to them, "Take my servants with you and put my son Solomon on my own mule. Take him down to the spring called Gihon. ³⁴There Zadok the priest and Nathan the prophet should pour olive oil on him and make him king over Israel. Blow the trumpet and shout, 'Long live King Solomon!' ³⁵Then come back here with him. He will sit on my throne and rule in my place. I have chosen him to be the ruler over Israel and Judah."

³⁶Benaiah son of Jehoiada answered the king, "This is good! And may your God make it happen. ³⁷The Lord has always helped you, our king. Let the Lord also help Solomon. And let King Solomon be an even greater king than you."

³⁸So Zadok the priest, Nathan the prophet and Benaiah son of Jehoiada went down. The Kerethites and Pelethites, the king's bodyguards, went with them. They put Solomon on King David's mule and went with him to the spring called Gihon. ³⁹Zadok the priest took with him the container of olive oil from the Holy Tent.*d* He poured the olive oil on Solomon's head to show he was the king. Then they blew the trumpet. And all the people shouted, "Long live King Solomon!" ⁴⁰All the people followed Solomon into the city. They were playing flutes and shouting for joy. They made so much noise the ground shook.

⁴¹At this time Adonijah and all the guests with him were finishing their meal. They heard the sound from the trumpet. Joab asked, "What does all that noise from the city mean?"

⁴²While Joab was speaking, Jonathan son of Abiathar the priest arrived. Adonijah said, "Come in! You are an important man. So you must be bringing good news."

⁴³But Jonathan answered, "No! Our master King David has made Solomon the new king. ⁴⁴King David sent Zadok the priest, Nathan the prophet, Benaiah son of Jehoiada and all the king's bodyguards with him. They put Solomon on the king's own mule. ⁴⁵And Zadok the priest and Nathan the prophet poured olive oil on Solomon at Gihon to make him king. Then they went into the city, shouting with joy. Now the whole city is excited. That is the noise you hear. ⁴⁶Solomon has now become the king. ⁴⁷All the king's officers have come to tell King David that he has done a good thing. They are saying, 'May your God make Solomon even more famous than you. And may your God make Solomon an even greater king than you.'" Jonathan continued, "And King David bowed down on his bed to worship

God. [48]He said, 'Praise the Lord, the God of Israel. Today he has made one of my sons the king and allowed me to see it.'"

[49]Then all of Adonijah's guests were afraid, and they left quickly. [50]Adonijah was also afraid of Solomon. So he went and took hold of the corners of the altar.[n] [51]Then someone told Solomon, "Adonijah is afraid of you. He is at the altar, holding on to its corners. He says, 'Tell King Solomon to promise me today that he will not kill me.'"

[52]So Solomon answered, "Adonijah must show that he is a man of honor. If he does, I promise that he will not lose even a hair from his head. But if he does anything wrong, he will die." [53]Then King Solomon sent some men to get Adonijah. They brought him to King Solomon. So Adonijah came before King Solomon and bowed down. Then Solomon said, "Go home."

THE DEATH OF DAVID

2 It was almost time for David to die. So he talked to Solomon and gave him his last commands. [2]David said, "My time to die is near. Be a good and strong leader. [3]Obey everything that the Lord commands. Follow the commands he has given us. Obey all his laws, and do what he told us. Obey what is written in the teachings of Moses. If you do these things, you will be successful in all you do and wherever you go. [4]And if you obey the Lord, he will keep the promise he made to me. He promised: 'Your descendants[d] must live as I tell them. They must have complete faith in me. If they do this, then a man from your family will always be king over the people of Israel.'

[5]"Also, you remember what Joab son of Zeruiah did to me. He killed the two commanders of Israel's armies. He killed Abner son of Ner and Amasa son of Jether. He killed them as if he and they were at war. But this was in a time of peace. He killed innocent men. And their blood got on his belt and sandals. [6]You should punish him in the way you think is wisest. (But do not let him die peacefully of old age.)

[7]"Be kind to the children of Barzillai of Gilead. Allow them to eat at your table. They helped me when I ran away from your brother Absalom.

[8]"And remember, Shimei son of Gera is here with you. He is from the people of Benjamin in Bahurim. Remember he cursed me the day I went to Mahanaim. Then he came down to meet me at the Jordan River. I promised him before the Lord, 'Shimei, I will not kill you.' [9]But you should not leave him unpunished. You are a wise man. You will know what to do to him. But you must be sure he is killed."

[10]Then David died and was buried with his ancestors in Jerusalem. [11]He had ruled over Israel 40 years. Seven years were in Hebron, and 33 years were in Jerusalem.

SOLOMON TAKES CONTROL AS KING

[12]Now Solomon became king after David, his father. And he was in control of his kingdom.

[13]At this time Adonijah son of Haggith went to Bathsheba, Solomon's mother. Bathsheba asked, "Do you come in peace?"

Adonijah answered, "Yes. This is a peaceful visit. [14]I have something to say to you."

"You may speak," she said.

[15]Adonijah said, "You remember that at one time the kingdom was mine. All the people of Israel thought I was their king. But things changed. Now my brother is the king because the Lord chose him. [16]So now I have one thing to ask you. Please do not refuse me."

1:50 corners of the altar If a person were innocent of a crime, he could run into the Holy Place. If he held on to the corners of the altar there, he would not be punished. The corners looked like horns.

Bathsheba answered, "What do you want?"

¹⁷Adonijah said, "I know King Solomon will do anything you ask him. So please ask him to give me Abishag the Shunammite woman to be my wife."

¹⁸"Very well," she answered. "I will speak to the king for you."

¹⁹So Bathsheba went to King Solomon to talk to him for Adonijah. When Solomon saw her, he stood up to meet her. Then he bowed down to her and sat on the throne. He told some servants to bring another throne for his mother. Then she sat down at his right side.

²⁰Bathsheba said to him, "I have one small thing to ask you. Please do not refuse me."

The king answered, "Ask, mother. I will not refuse you."

²¹So she said, "Allow Abishag the Shunammite woman to marry your brother Adonijah."

²²King Solomon answered his mother, "Why do you ask me to give him Abishag? Why don't you ask for him to become the king also since he is my older brother? Abiathar the priest and Joab son of Zeruiah will support him!"

²³Then King Solomon made a promise in the name of the Lord. He said, "I promise Adonijah will pay for asking me this! May God punish me terribly if it doesn't cost Adonijah his life! ²⁴The Lord has given me the throne that belonged to my father David. The Lord has kept his promise and given the kingdom to me and my people. As surely as the Lord lives, Adonijah will die today!" ²⁵So King Solomon gave orders to Benaiah son of Jehoiada. And he went out and killed Adonijah.

²⁶Then King Solomon said to Abiathar the priest, "I should kill you. But I will allow you to go back to your home in Anathoth. I will not kill you now because you helped to carry the Holy Box[d] of the Lord God while marching with my father David. And I know you shared in all of the hard times with my father." ²⁷So Solomon removed Abiathar from being a priest to the Lord. This happened as the Lord had said it would. He had said this about the priest Eli and his family in Shiloh.

²⁸When Joab heard about this, he was afraid. He had supported Adonijah, but not Absalom. So Joab ran to the Tent[d] of the Lord and took hold of the corners of the altar.[n] ²⁹Someone told King Solomon that Joab had run to the Tent of the Lord and was beside the altar. So Solomon ordered Benaiah to go and kill him.

³⁰Benaiah went into the Tent of the Lord and said to Joab, "The king says, 'Come out!'"

But Joab answered, "No, I will die here."

So Benaiah went back to the king and told him what Joab had said. ³¹Then the king commanded Benaiah, "Do as he says! Kill him there and bury him. Then my family and I will be free of the guilt of Joab. Joab is guilty of killing innocent people. ³²He killed two men who were much better than he was. They were Abner son of Ner and Amasa son of Jether. Abner was the commander of Israel's army, and Amasa was the commander of Judah's army. My father David did not know that he killed them. So the Lord will pay him back for those men he killed. ³³He and his family will be forever guilty for their deaths. But there will be peace from God for David, his descendants,[d] his family and his rule forever."

³⁴So Benaiah son of Jehoiada killed Joab. And he was buried near his home in the desert. ³⁵Solomon then made Benaiah son of Jehoiada commander of the army in Joab's place. Solomon also

---

2:28 corners of the altar If a person were innocent of a crime, he could run into the Holy Place. If he held on to the corners of the altar there, he would not be punished. The corners looked like horns.

made Zadok the new high priest in Abiathar's place.

³⁶Next the king sent for Shimei. The king said to him, "Build a house for yourself here in Jerusalem. Live in the house, and don't leave the city. ³⁷If you leave and go past Kidron Valley, someone will kill you. And it will be your own fault."

³⁸So Shimei answered the king, "What you have said is good. I will obey you, my master and king." So Shimei lived in Jerusalem for a long time.

³⁹But three years later two of Shimei's slaves ran away. They went to Achish king of Gath. He was the son of Maacah. Shimei heard that his slaves were in Gath. ⁴⁰So he put his saddle on his donkey and left. He went to Achish at Gath to find his slaves. When he found them there, he brought them back to his home.

⁴¹Someone told Solomon that Shimei had gone from Jerusalem to Gath and had returned. ⁴²So Solomon sent for Shimei. Solomon said, "I made you promise in the name of the Lord not to leave Jerusalem. I warned you that if you went anywhere else you would die. And you agreed to what I said. You said you would obey me. ⁴³Why did you break your promise to the Lord? Why did you not obey my command? ⁴⁴You know the many wrong things you did against my father David. Now the Lord will punish you for those wrongs. ⁴⁵But the Lord will bless me. He will make the rule of David safe before the Lord forever."

⁴⁶Then the king ordered Benaiah to kill Shimei, and he did. Now Solomon was in full control of his kingdom.

SOLOMON ASKS FOR WISDOM

3 Solomon made an agreement with the king of Egypt by marrying his daughter. Solomon brought her to Jerusalem. At this time Solomon was still building his palace and the Temple*d* of the Lord. He was also building a wall around Jerusalem. ²The Temple had not yet been finished. So people were still offering animal sacrifices at altars in many places of worship. ³Solomon showed that he loved the Lord. He did this by following the commands his father David had given him. But Solomon still used the many places of worship to offer sacrifices and to burn incense.*d*

⁴King Solomon went to Gibeon to offer a sacrifice. He went there because it was the most important place of worship. He offered 1,000 burnt offerings on that altar. ⁵While he was at Gibeon, the Lord came to him in a dream during the night. God said, "Ask for anything you want. I will give it to you."

⁶Solomon answered, "You were very kind to your servant, my father David. He obeyed you. He was honest and lived right. And you showed great kindness to him when you allowed his son to be king after him. ⁷Lord my God, you have allowed me to be king in my father's place. But I am like a little child. I do not have the wisdom I need to do what I must do. ⁸I, your servant, am here among your chosen people. There are too many of them to count. ⁹So I ask that you give me wisdom. Then I can rule the people in the right way. Then I will know the difference between right and wrong. Without wisdom, it is impossible to rule this great people of yours."

¹⁰The Lord was pleased that Solomon had asked him for this. ¹¹So God said to him, "You did not ask for a long life. And you did not ask for riches for yourself. You did not ask for the death of your enemies. Since you asked for wisdom to make the right decisions, ¹²I will give you what you asked. I will give you wisdom and understanding. Your wisdom will be greater than anyone has had in the past. And there will never be anyone in the future like you. ¹³Also, I will give you what you did not ask for. You will have riches and honor. During your life no other king will be as great as you. ¹⁴I ask you to follow me and obey my laws and commands. Do

this as your father David did. If you do, I will also give you a long life."

¹⁵Then Solomon woke up. He knew that God had talked to him in the dream. Then he went to Jerusalem and stood before the Box^d of the Agreement with the Lord. There he gave burnt offerings and fellowship offerings to the Lord. After that, he gave a feast for all of his leaders and officers.

SOLOMON MAKES A WISE DECISION

¹⁶One day two women who were prostitutes^d came to Solomon. They stood before him. ¹⁷One of the women said, "My master, this woman and I live in the same house. I gave birth to a baby while she was there with me. ¹⁸Three days later this woman also gave birth to a baby. No one else was in the house with us. There were only the two of us. ¹⁹One night this woman rolled over on her baby, and it died. ²⁰So during the night she took my son from my bed while I was asleep. She carried him to her bed. Then she put the dead baby in my bed. ²¹The next morning I got up to feed my baby. But I saw that he was dead! Then I looked at him more closely. I saw that he was not my son."

²²But the other woman said, "No! The living baby is my son. The dead baby is yours!"

But the first woman said, "No! The dead baby is yours, and the living one is mine!" So the two women argued before the king.

²³Then King Solomon said, "Each of you says the living baby is your own. And each of you says the dead baby belongs to the other woman."

²⁴Then King Solomon sent his servants to get a sword. When they brought it to him, ²⁵he said, "Cut the living baby into two pieces. Give each woman half of the baby."

²⁶The real mother of the living child was full of love for her son. She said to the king, "Please, my master, don't kill him! Give the baby to her!"

But the other woman said, "Neither of us will have him. Cut him into two pieces!"

²⁷Then King Solomon said, "Give the baby to the first woman. Don't kill him. She is the real mother."

²⁸When the people of Israel heard about King Solomon's decision, they respected him very much. They saw he had wisdom from God to make the right decisions.

SOLOMON'S OFFICERS

4 King Solomon ruled over all Israel. ²These are the names of his leading officers:

Azariah son of Zadok was the priest;

³Elihoreph and Ahijah, sons of Shisha, recorded what happened in the courts;

Jehoshaphat son of Ahilud recorded the history of the people;

⁴Benaiah son of Jehoiada was commander of the army;

Zadok and Abiathar were priests;

⁵Azariah son of Nathan was in charge of the district governors;

Zabud son of Nathan was a priest and adviser to the king;

⁶Ahishar was responsible for everything in the palace;

Adoniram son of Abda was in charge of the slaves.

⁷Solomon placed 12 governors over the districts of Israel. They had to gather food from their districts. Then they were to give it to the king and his family. Each governor was responsible for giving food to the king one month of each year. ⁸These are the names of the 12 governors:

Ben-Hur was governor over the mountain country of Ephraim.

⁹Ben-Deker was governor over Makaz, Shaalbim, Beth Shemesh and Elon Bethhanan.

¹⁰Ben-Hesed was governor over Arubboth, Socoh and Hepher.

¹¹Ben-Abinadab was governor over Naphoth Dor. (He was married to Taphath daughter of Solomon.)

[12]Baana son of Ahilud was governor over Taanach, Megiddo and all of Beth Shan next to Zarethan. (This was below Jezreel from Beth Shan to Abel Meholah across Jokmeam.)

[13]Ben-Geber was governor over Ramoth in Gilead. (He was governor over all the Towns of Jair in Gilead. Jair was the son of Manasseh. Ben-Geber was also over the district of Argob in Bashan. It had 60 large, walled cities with bronze bars on their gates.)

[14]Ahinadab son of Iddo was governor over Mahanaim.

[15]Ahimaaz was governor over Naphtali. (He was married to Basemath daughter of Solomon.)

[16]Baana son of Hushai was governor over Asher and Aloth.

[17]Jehoshaphat son of Paruah was governor over Issachar.

[18]Shimei son of Ela was governor over Benjamin.

[19]Geber son of Uri was governor over Gilead. (Gilead was the country where Sihon king of the Amorite people lived. Og king of Bashan also lived there.) But Geber was the only governor over the district.

SOLOMON'S KINGDOM

[20]There were many people in Judah and Israel. There were as many people as there were grains of sand on the seashore. The people ate, drank and were happy. [21]Solomon ruled over all the kingdoms from the Euphrates River to the land of the Philistine people. His kingdom went as far as the border of Egypt. These countries brought Solomon the payments he demanded. And they obeyed him all his life.

[22]Solomon needed much food each day to feed himself and all the people who ate at his table. It took 185 bushels of fine flour and 375 bushels of meal. [23]It also took 10 cows that were fed good grain, 20 cows that were raised in the fields and 100 sheep. And it took 3 different kinds of deer and fat birds.

[24]Solomon ruled over all the countries west of the Euphrates River. This was the land from Tiphsah to Gaza. And Solomon had peace on all sides of his kingdom. [25]During Solomon's life Judah and Israel, from Dan to Beersheba,[n] lived in peace. Each man was able to sit under his own fig trees and grapevines.

[26]Solomon had 4,000 stalls for his chariot horses. And he had 12,000 chariot soldiers. [27]Each month one of the district governors gave King Solomon all the food he needed. This was enough for every person who ate at the king's table. The governors made sure he had everything he needed. [28]They also gave the king enough barley and straw for the chariot and work horses. Each person brought this grain to the required places.

SOLOMON'S WISDOM

[29]God gave great wisdom to Solomon. Solomon could understand many things. His wisdom was as hard to measure as the sand on the seashore. [30]His wisdom was greater than the wisdom of all the men in the East. And his wisdom was greater than all the wisdom of the men in Egypt. [31]He was wiser than any other man on earth. He was even wiser than Ethan the Ezrahite. He was wiser than Heman, Calcol and Darda. They were the sons of Mahol. King Solomon became famous in all the countries around Israel and Judah. [32]During his life King Solomon spoke 3,000 wise teachings. He also knew 1,005 songs. [33]He taught about many different kinds of plants. He taught about everything from the great cedar trees of Lebanon to the hyssop that grows out of the walls. He also taught about animals, birds, crawling things and fish. [34]People from all nations

---

4:25 Dan to Beersheba Dan was the city farthest north in Israel. Beersheba was the city farthest south. So this means all the people of Israel.

came to listen to King Solomon's wisdom. The kings of all nations sent them to listen to him. These kings had heard of Solomon's wisdom.

SOLOMON PREPARES TO BUILD THE TEMPLE

5 Now King Hiram was the king of Tyre. He had always been a friend of David. Hiram heard that Solomon had been made king in David's place. So he sent his messengers to Solomon. ²Then Solomon sent this message back to King Hiram: ³"You remember that my father David had to fight many wars with the countries around him. So he was never able to build a temple for worship to the Lord his God. David was waiting until the Lord allowed him to defeat all his enemies. ⁴But now the Lord my God has given me peace. There is peace on all sides of my country. I have no enemies now. My people are in no danger.

⁵"The Lord made a promise to my father David. The Lord said, 'I will make your son king after you. And he will build a temple for worship to me.' Now, I plan to build that temple for worship to the Lord my God. ⁶And so I ask for your help. Send your men to cut down cedar trees for me from Lebanon. My servants will work with yours. I will pay your servants whatever wages you decide. We don't have anyone who can cut down trees as well as the people of Sidon can."

⁷When Hiram heard what Solomon asked, he was very happy. He said, "I thank the Lord today! He has given David a wise son to rule over this great nation!" ⁸Then Hiram sent back this message to Solomon: "I received the message you sent. I will give you all the cedar and pine trees you want. ⁹My servants will bring them down from Lebanon to the sea. There I will tie them together. Then I will float them down the shore to the place you choose. There I will separate the logs, and you can take them away. In return you will give food

to all those who live with me." ¹⁰So Hiram gave Solomon as much cedar and pine as he wanted. ¹¹And Solomon gave Hiram about 125,000 bushels of wheat each year. It was to feed all those who lived with Hiram. And Solomon gave him about 115,000 gallons of pure olive oil every year.

¹²The Lord gave wisdom to Solomon as he had promised. And there was peace between Hiram and Solomon. These two kings made a treaty between themselves.

¹³King Solomon forced 30,000 men of Israel to help in this work. ¹⁴He put a man named Adoniram over them. Solomon sent a group of 10,000 men each month to Lebanon. So each group worked in Lebanon one month. Then it went home for two months. ¹⁵Solomon forced 80,000 men to work in the hill country, cutting stone. And he had 70,000 men to carry the stones. ¹⁶There were also 3,300 men who directed the workers. ¹⁷King Solomon commanded them to cut large blocks of fine stone. These were to be used for the foundation of the Temple.^d ¹⁸Solomon's and Hiram's builders and the men from Byblos carved the stones. They prepared the stones and the logs for building the Temple.

SOLOMON BUILDS THE TEMPLE

6 So Solomon began to build the Temple.^d This was 480 years after the people of Israel had left Egypt. (This was the fourth year of King Solomon's rule over Israel.) It was the second month, the month of Ziv.

²The Temple was 90 feet long and 30 feet wide. It was 45 feet high. ³The porch in front of the main room of the Temple was 15 feet deep and 30 feet wide. The room ran along the front of the Temple itself. Its width was equal to the width of the Temple. ⁴There were narrow windows in the Temple. These windows were narrow on the outside and larger on the inside. ⁵Then Solomon built some

side rooms against the walls of the main room of the Temple. These rooms were built on top of each other. [6]The rooms on the bottom floor were 7 1/2 feet wide. The rooms on the middle floor were 9 feet wide. The rooms above that were 10 1/2 feet wide. The Temple wall which made the side of each room was thinner than the wall in the room below. The rooms were pushed against the wall but did not have their main beams built into the wall.

[7]The stones were prepared at the same place they were cut from the ground. Only these stones were used to build the Temple. So there was no noise of hammers, axes or any other iron tools at the Temple.

[8]The entrance to the bottom rooms built beside the Temple was on the south side. From there, stairs went up to the second floor rooms. And from there, they went on to the third floor rooms. [9]Solomon put a roof made from beams and cedar boards on the Temple. So he finished building the Temple. [10]He also finished building the bottom floor that was beside the Temple. It was 7 1/2 feet high. It was attached to the Temple by cedar beams.

[11]The Lord spoke his word to Solomon: [12]"Obey all my laws and commands. If you do, I will do for you what I promised your father David. [13]And I will live among the children of Israel in this Temple you are building. I will never leave the people of Israel."

[14]So Solomon finished building the Temple. [15]The inside walls were covered from floor to ceiling with cedar boards. The floor was made from pine boards. [16]A room 30 feet long was built in the back part of the Temple. It was divided from the rest of the Temple by cedar boards reaching from floor to ceiling. It was called the Most Holy Place. [17]The main room, the room in front of the Most Holy Place, was 60 feet long. [18]Inside the

Temple was cedar. It was carved with pictures of flowers and plants. Everything inside was covered with cedar. So a person could not see the stones of the wall.

[19]He prepared the inner room at the back of the Temple to keep the Box[d] of the Agreement with the Lord. [20]This inner room was 30 feet long, 30 feet wide and 30 feet high. Solomon covered this room with pure gold. He built an altar of cedar and covered it also. [21]He covered the inside of the Temple with pure gold. And he placed gold chains across the front of the inner room. It was covered with gold. [22]So all the inside of the Temple was covered with gold. Also the altar in the Most Holy Place was covered with gold.

[23]Solomon made two creatures with wings from olive wood. Each creature was 15 feet tall. They were put in the Most Holy Place. [24]Each creature had two wings. Each wing was 7 1/2 feet long. So it was 15 feet from the end of one wing to the end of the other wing. [25]The creatures were the same size and shape. [26]And each was 15 feet tall. [27]These creatures were put beside each other in the Most Holy Place. Their wings were spread out. So one creature's wing touched one wall. The other creature's wing touched the other wall. And their wings touched each other in the middle of the room. [28]The two creatures were covered with gold.

[29]All the walls around the Temple were carved. They were carved with pictures of creatures with wings, palm trees and flowers. This was true for both the main room and the inner room. [30]The floors of both rooms were covered with gold.

[31]Doors made from olive wood were put at the entrance to the Most Holy Place. The doors were made to fit into an area with five sides. [32]Creatures with wings, palm trees and flowers were carved on the two olive wood doors. Then

the doors were covered with gold. And the creatures and the palm trees were covered with gold. 33At the entrance to the main room there was a door frame. It was square and was made of olive wood. 34Two doors were made from pine. Each door had two parts so that the doors folded. 35The doors were covered with pictures of creatures with wings, palm trees and flowers. And all of the carvings were covered with gold. The gold was smoothed over the carvings.

36The inner courtyard was built and enclosed with walls. The walls were made of three rows of cut stones and one row of cedar boards.

37Work began on the Temple in Ziv, the second month. This was during the fourth year Solomon ruled over Israel. 38The Temple was finished during the eleventh year Solomon ruled. It was finished in the eighth month, the month of Bul. It was finished exactly as it was planned. Solomon had worked seven years to build the Temple.

SOLOMON'S PALACE

7 King Solomon also built a palace for himself. It took him 13 years to finish building it. 2He built the Palace of the Forest of Lebanon. It was 150 feet long, 75 feet wide and 45 feet high. It had four rows of cedar columns. They supported the cedar beams. 3The ceiling was covered with cedar above the beams. There were 45 beams on the roof, with 15 beams in each row. 4Windows were placed in three rows facing each other. 5All the doors were square. The three doors at each end faced each other.

6Solomon also built the porch of pillars. It was 75 feet long and 45 feet wide. Along the front of the porch, there was a covering supported by pillars.

7Solomon also built a throne room where he judged people. He called this the Hall of Justice. The room was covered with cedar from the floor to the ceiling. 8The palace where Solomon was

to live was behind the Hall of Justice. And it was built like the Hall of Justice. Solomon also built the same kind of palace for his wife. She was the daughter of the king of Egypt.

9All these buildings were made with blocks of carefully cut fine stone. Then they were trimmed with a saw in the front and back. These fine stones went from the foundations of the buildings to the top of the walls. Even the courtyard was made with blocks of stone. 10The foundations were made with large blocks of fine stone. Some of the stones were 15 feet long. Others were 12 feet long. 11On top of those stones there were other cut blocks of fine stone and cedar beams. 12The palace courtyard, the courtyard inside the Temple[d] and the porch to the Temple were surrounded by walls. All of these walls had three rows of cut stone blocks and one row of cedar beams.

THE TEMPLE IS COMPLETED INSIDE

13King Solomon sent to Tyre and had Huram brought to him. 14Huram's mother was a widow from the tribe[d] of Naphtali. His father was from Tyre and had been skilled in making things from bronze. Huram was also very skilled and experienced in bronze work. So he came to King Solomon. And he did all the bronze work Solomon wanted.

15He made two bronze pillars. Each one was 27 feet tall and 18 feet around. 16He also made two bronze capitals[d] that were 7$\frac{1}{2}$ feet tall. He put them on top of the pillars. 17Then he made a net of seven chains for each capital. They covered the capitals on top of the two pillars. 18Then he made two rows of bronze pomegranates[d] to go on the nets. They were to cover the capitals at the top of the pillars. 19The capitals on top of the pillars in the porch were shaped like lilies. They were 6 feet tall. 20The capitals were on top of both pillars. They were above the bowl-shaped section and next to the nets. At that place there were 200 pomegranates in rows all around the capitals. [21]Huram put these two bronze pillars at the porch of the Temple.[d] He named the south pillar He Establishes. And he named the north pillar In Him Is Strength. [22]The capitals on top of the pillars were shaped like lilies. So the work on the pillars was finished.

[23]Then Huram made a large round bowl from bronze, which was called the Sea. It was 45 feet around. It was 15 feet across and 7¹/₂ feet deep. [24]There was a rim around the outer edge of the bowl. Under this rim there were two rows of bronze plants surrounding the bowl. There were ten plants in every 18 inches. They were made in one piece with the bowl. [25]The bowl rested on the backs of 12 bronze bulls. They faced outward from the center of the bowl. Three bulls faced north, 3 faced east, 3 faced south and 3 faced west. [26]The sides of the bowl were 4 inches thick. The rim was like the rim of a cup or like a lily blossom. The bowl held about 11,000 gallons.

[27]Then Huram made ten bronze stands. Each one was 6 feet long, 6 feet wide and 4¹/₂ feet high. [28]The stands were made from square sides, which were put on frames. [29]On the sides were bronze lions, bulls and creatures with wings. On the frames above and below the lions and bulls there were designs of flowers hammered into the bronze. [30]Each stand had four bronze wheels with bronze axles. At the corners there were bronze supports for a large bowl. The supports had designs of flowers. [31]There was a frame on top of the bowls. It was 18 inches high above the bowls. The opening of the bowl was round, 27 inches deep. There were designs carved into the bronze on the frame. The frame was square, not round. [32]The four wheels were under the frame. They were 27 inches high. The axles between the wheels were made as one piece with the stand. [33]The wheels were like a chariot's wheels. Everything on the wheels was made of bronze. The axles, rims, spokes and hubs were made of bronze.

[34]The four supports were on the four corners of each stand. They were made as one piece with the stand. [35]There was a strip of bronze around the top of each stand. It was 9 inches deep. It was made as one piece with the stand. [36]The sides of the stand and the frames were totally covered with carvings. They were carved with pictures of creatures with wings, lions and palm trees. There were also flowers carved all around. [37]So this is the way Huram made the ten stands. The bronze for each stand was melted and poured into a mold. So all of the stands were the same size and shape.

[38]Huram also made ten bronze bowls. There was one bowl for each of the ten stands. Each bowl was six feet across and could hold about 230 gallons. [39]Huram put five of the stands on the south side of the Temple. And he put the other five stands on the north side. He put the large bowl in the southeast corner of the Temple. [40]Huram also made bowls, shovels and small bowls.

So Huram finished making everything King Solomon wanted him to make. Here is a list of what Huram made for the Temple of the Lord:
[41]two pillars;
  two large bowls for the capitals on top of the pillars;
  two nets to cover the two large bowls for the capitals on top of the pillars;
[42]400 pomegranates for the two nets (there were two rows of pomegranates for each net covering the bowls for the capitals on top of the pillars);
[43]ten stands with a bowl on each stand;
[44]the large bowl with 12 bulls under it;
[45]the pots, shovels, small bowls and all the dishes for the Temple of the Lord.

Huram made everything King Solomon wanted. They were all made from polished bronze. ⁴⁶The king ordered these things to be made near the Jordan River between Succoth and Zarethan. They were made by melting and pouring bronze into clay molds. ⁴⁷Solomon never weighed the bronze used to make these things. There was too much to weigh. So the total weight of all the bronze was never known.

⁴⁸Solomon also commanded that many things be made of gold for the Temple:
the golden altar;
the golden table which held the bread
     that shows God's people are in
     his presence;
⁴⁹the lampstands of pure gold (five on
     the right side and five on the left
     side in front of the Most Holy
     Place);
the gold flowers, lamps and tongs;
⁵⁰the pure gold bowls, wick trimmers,
     small bowls, pans and dishes
     used to carry coals;
the hinges for the doors of the Most
     Holy Place and the main room of
     the Temple.

⁵¹So the work King Solomon did for the Temple of the Lord was finished. David, Solomon's father, had saved silver, gold and other articles for the Temple. So Solomon brought these things into the Temple. And he put them into the treasuries of the Temple of the Lord.

THE HOLY BOX IS BROUGHT INTO THE TEMPLE

8 Then King Solomon called for all the leaders of Israel to come to him in Jerusalem. He called for the elders, the heads of the tribes*d* and the leaders of the families. He wanted them to bring the Box*d* of the Agreement with the Lord from the older part of the city. ²So all the men of Israel came together with King Solomon. This was during a festival in the month of Ethanim. That is the seventh month.

³All of the elders of Israel arrived. Then the priests took up the Holy Box. ⁴They carried the Holy Box of the Lord, the Meeting Tent*d* and the holy things in it. The Levites helped the priests carry these things. ⁵King Solomon and all the people of Israel gathered before the Box of the Agreement. They sacrificed so many sheep and cattle no one could count them all. ⁶Then the priests put the Box of the Agreement with the Lord in its right place. This was inside the Most Holy Place in the Temple.*d* The Box of the Agreement was put under the wings of the golden creatures. ⁷The wings of the creatures were spread out over the place of the Holy Box. So they covered it and its carrying poles. ⁸The carrying poles were very long. Anyone standing in the Holy Place in front of the Most Holy Place could see the ends of the poles. But no one could see them from outside the Holy Place. The poles are still there today. ⁹The only things inside the Holy Box were two stone tablets.*n* Moses had put them in the Holy Box at Mount Sinai. That was where the Lord made his agreement with the Israelites after they came out of Egypt.

¹⁰When the priests left the Holy Place, the cloud filled the Temple of the Lord. ¹¹The priests could not continue their work. This was because the Temple was filled with the glory of the Lord.

SOLOMON SPEAKS TO THE PEOPLE

¹²Then Solomon said, "The Lord said he would live in a dark cloud. ¹³Lord, I have truly built a wonderful Temple*d* for you. It is a place for you to live forever."

¹⁴While all the people of Israel were standing there, King Solomon turned to them and blessed them.

¹⁵Then he prayed: "Praise the Lord, the God of Israel. He himself has done

---

8:9 stone tablets They were the two tablets on which God wrote the Ten Commandments.

what he promised to my father David. The Lord told my father, [16]'I brought my people Israel out of Egypt. But I have not yet chosen a city in any tribe[d] of Israel where a temple will be built for worshiping me. But I have chosen David to rule over my people Israel.'

[17]"My father David wanted to build a temple for worshiping the Lord, the God of Israel. [18]But the Lord said to my father David, 'I know you want to build a temple for worshiping me. And this is good. [19]But you are not the one to build the temple. It will be your son, who comes from your own body. He is the one who will build my temple.'

[20]"So the Lord has kept the promise that he gave. I am the king now in place of David my father. Now I rule Israel as the Lord promised. And I have built the Temple for worshiping the Lord, the God of Israel. [21]I have made a place in the Temple for the Holy Box. Inside that Box is the agreement the Lord made with our ancestors. He made that agreement when he brought them out of Egypt."

SOLOMON'S PRAYER

[22]Then Solomon stood facing the Lord's altar. All of the people of Israel were standing behind him. He spread out his hands and looked toward the sky. [23]He said:

"Lord, God of Israel, there is no god like you. There is no god like you in heaven above or on the earth below. You make agreements with your people because you love them. And you keep your agreements with those who truly follow you. [24]You have kept the promise you made to your servant David, my father. You made that promise with your own mouth. And with your great power you have made it come true today. [25]Now Lord, God of Israel, keep the other promises you made to your servant David, my father. You said, 'Your sons must be careful to obey me as you have obeyed me. If they do this, there will

always be someone from your family ruling Israel.' [26]Again, Lord, God of Israel, I ask you. Please continue to keep that promise you made to my father.

[27]"But, God, can you really live here on the earth? Even the sky and the highest place in heaven cannot contain you. Certainly this house which I have built cannot contain you either. [28]But please listen to my prayer and my request. I am your servant, and you are the Lord my God. Hear this prayer I am praying to you today. [29]In the past you said, 'I will be worshiped there.' So please watch over this Temple[d] night and day. Hear the prayer I pray to you here. [30]Hear my prayers and the prayers of your people Israel. Please hear us when we pray facing this place. Hear us from your home in heaven. And when you hear us, forgive us.

[31]"If a person does something wrong against someone else, he will be brought to the altar in this Temple. If he swears an oath that he is not guilty, [32]then hear in heaven. Judge the man. Punish the guilty person for what he has done. And declare that the innocent person is not guilty.

[33]"Sometimes your people of Israel will sin against you. Because of this their enemies will defeat them. Then the people will come back to you and praise you. They will pray to you in this Temple. [34]Please hear them in heaven. Forgive the sins of your people Israel. Allow them to have their land again. This is the land you gave to their ancestors.

[35]"Sometimes when they sin against you, you will stop the rain from falling on their land. Then they will pray, facing this place. They will praise you. They will stop sinning when you make them suffer. [36]When this happens, please hear their prayer in heaven. Then forgive the sins of your servant. And forgive the sins of the people of Israel. Teach them to do what is right. Then please send rain to this land you gave them.

³⁷"At times the land will become so dry that no food will grow. Or, a great sickness will spread among the people. Sometimes all the crops will be destroyed by locusts^d or grasshoppers. Your people will be attacked in their cities by their enemies. Your people will become sick. ³⁸When any of these things happen, the people will become truly sorry. If anyone of your people Israel spreads his hands in prayer toward this Temple, ³⁹please hear his prayer. Hear it from your home in heaven. Then forgive the people and help them. Only you know what people are really thinking. So judge each person, and do to him what is right. ⁴⁰Do this so your people will respect you all the time they live in this land. This is the land you gave to our ancestors.

⁴¹⁻⁴²"People who are not Israelites, who come from other lands, will hear about your greatness and power. They will come from far away to pray at this Temple. ⁴³Please hear their prayers from your home in heaven. Please do whatever they ask you. Then people everywhere will know you and respect you, as your people in Israel do. Then everyone will know I built this Temple for worship to you.

⁴⁴"Sometimes you will command your people to go and fight against their enemies. Then your people will pray to you facing this city which you have chosen. They will pray facing the Temple I have built for your worship. ⁴⁵When they pray, hear their prayers from your home in heaven. Then help them.

⁴⁶"Everyone sins. So your people will also sin against you. And you will become angry with your people. You will let their enemies defeat them. Their enemies will make them prisoners and carry them away to their own countries. ⁴⁷Your people might be sorry for their sins when they are held as prisoners in another country. Perhaps they will be sorry and pray to you in the land where they are held as prisoners. They might say, 'We have sinned and done wrong.' ⁴⁸They may truly turn back to you in the land of their enemies. Perhaps they will pray to you, facing this land you gave their fathers. They may pray to you, facing this city you have chosen. They may face this Temple I have built for your worship. ⁴⁹If they do, then please hear them from your home in heaven. Hear their prayers and do what is right. ⁵⁰Forgive your people of all their sins. And forgive them for turning against you. Make those who have taken them as prisoners show them mercy. ⁵¹Remember that they are your people. Remember that you brought them out of Egypt. It was as if you pulled them out of a blazing furnace!

⁵²"Please give your attention to my prayers. And please give your attention to the prayers of your people Israel. Listen to their prayers anytime they ask you for help. ⁵³You chose them from all the nations on earth to be your very own people. This is what you promised through Moses your servant. You promised it when you brought our ancestors out of Egypt, Lord God."

⁵⁴Solomon prayed this prayer to the Lord. He had been kneeling in front of the altar. And his arms had been raised toward heaven. When Solomon finished praying, he stood up. ⁵⁵Then, in a loud voice, he blessed all the people of Israel. Solomon said: ⁵⁶"Praise the Lord! He promised he would give rest to his people Israel. And he has given us rest! The Lord has kept all the good promises he gave through his servant Moses. ⁵⁷I ask that the Lord our God be with us. May he be with us as he was with our ancestors. May he never leave us. ⁵⁸May he cause us to turn to him and follow him. May we obey all the laws and commands he gave our ancestors. ⁵⁹I ask that the Lord our God always remember this prayer. I pray that he will help his

servant and his people Israel. I pray he will help us every day as we need it. ⁶⁰Then all the people of the world will know the Lord is the only true God. ⁶¹So you must fully obey the Lord our God. You must follow all his laws and commands. You must continue to obey in the future as you do now."

SACRIFICES ARE OFFERED

⁶²Then King Solomon and all Israel with him offered sacrifices to the Lord. ⁶³Solomon killed 22,000 cattle and 120,000 sheep. These were fellowship offerings. In this way the king and the Israelites showed they had given the Temple*d* to the Lord.

⁶⁴Also that day King Solomon made the courtyard before the Temple holy. He offered whole burnt sacrifices and grain offerings. He also offered the fat from the fellowship offerings. He had to make these offerings in the courtyard. This was because the bronze altar before the Lord was too small. It could not hold all the offerings.

⁶⁵So King Solomon and all the people of Israel also celebrated the other festival that came at that time. People came from as far away as Lebo Hamath in the north. And they came from as far as the brook of Egypt in the south. A great many people were there. They ate, drank and rejoiced before the Lord for a total of 14 days. ⁶⁶On the following day Solomon sent the people home. So they blessed the king and went home. They were happy because of all the good things the Lord had done for his servant David and for his people, Israel.

THE LORD APPEARS TO SOLOMON AGAIN

9 So Solomon finished building the Temple*d* of the Lord and his royal palace. Solomon finished building everything he wanted to build. ²Then the Lord appeared to him again. This was just as he had done before, in Gibeon. ³The Lord said to him: "I have heard

your prayer. I have heard what you asked me to do. You built this Temple. And I have made it a holy place. So I will be worshiped there forever. I will watch over it and protect it always.

⁴"But you must serve me as your father David did. He was fair and sincere. You must obey my laws and do everything I command. ⁵If you do these things, I will allow your family to rule Israel forever. I made this promise to your father David. I told him that someone from his family would always be king over Israel.

⁶"But you and your children must follow me. You must obey the laws and commands I have given you. You must not go off to serve or worship other gods. ⁷If you do, I will force Israel to leave the land I have given them. I made the Temple holy for people to worship me there. But if you don't obey me, I will tear it down. Then Israel will become a bad example, a joke, to other people. ⁸If the Temple is destroyed, everyone who sees it will be shocked. They will make fun of you and ask, 'Why did the Lord do this? Why did he do this terrible thing to this land and this Temple?' ⁹Other people will answer, 'This happened because they left the Lord their God. He brought their ancestors out of Egypt. But they decided to follow other gods. They worshiped and served those gods. That is why the Lord brought all this disaster to them.'"

SOLOMON'S OTHER ACTIVITIES

¹⁰By the end of 20 years, King Solomon had built the Temple*d* of the Lord. And he had built the royal palace. ¹¹At that time King Solomon gave 20 towns in Galilee to Hiram king of Tyre. Solomon did this because Hiram had helped with the buildings. Hiram had given him all the cedar, pine and gold he wanted. ¹²So Hiram traveled from Tyre to see the towns Solomon had given him. When Hiram saw them, he was not

pleased. [13]He asked, "What are these towns you have given me, my brother?" So he named that land the Land of Cabul.[n] And it is still called that today. [14]Hiram had sent to King Solomon about 9,000 pounds of gold.

[15]King Solomon had forced slaves to build the Temple and the palace. Then he had them fill in the land on the east side of the city. And he had them build the wall around Jerusalem. He also had them rebuild the cities of Hazor, Megiddo and Gezer. [16](In the past the king of Egypt had attacked Gezer and captured it. He had burned it and killed the Canaanites who lived there. Then he gave it to his daughter as a wedding present. His daughter married Solomon. [17]So Solomon rebuilt it.) He also built the cities of Lower Beth Horon, [18]Baalath and Tadmor, which is in the Judean desert. [19]King Solomon also built cities where he could store grain and supplies. And he built cities for his chariots and chariot soldiers. Solomon built whatever he wanted in Jerusalem, Lebanon and everywhere he ruled.

[20]There were people in the land who were not Israelites. There were some Amorites, Hittites, Perizzites, Hivites and Jebusites. [21]The Israelites had not been able to destroy them from the land. So Solomon forced them to work for him as slaves. And they are still slaves today. [22]But Solomon did not force any Israelites to be his slaves. The Israelites were his soldiers, government leaders, officers, captains and chariot commanders and drivers.

[23]There were 550 supervisors over Solomon's projects. They were supervisors over the men who did the work.

[24]The daughter of the king of Egypt moved from the old part of Jerusalem to the palace. This was the palace Solomon had built for her. Then Solomon filled in the land on the east side of the city.

[25]Three times each year Solomon offered whole burnt offerings and fellowship offerings on the altar. This is the altar he had built for the Lord. Solomon also burned incense[d] before the Lord. So he finished the work on the Temple.

[26]Solomon also built ships at Ezion Geber. This town is near Elath. It is on the shore of the Gulf of Aqaba, in the land of Edom. [27]King Hiram had sailors who knew much about the sea. So he sent them to serve in Solomon's ships with Solomon's men. [28]Solomon's ships sailed to Ophir. From there they brought back about 32,000 pounds of gold to King Solomon.

THE QUEEN OF SHEBA VISITS SOLOMON

10 Now the queen of Sheba heard about Solomon's fame. So she came to test him with hard questions. [2]She traveled to Jerusalem with a very large group of servants. There were many camels carrying spices, jewels and much gold. She came to Solomon and talked with him about all that she had in mind. [3]Solomon answered all her questions. Nothing was too hard for him to explain to her. [4]The queen of Sheba learned that Solomon was very wise. She saw the palace he had built. [5]She saw his many officers and the food on his table. She saw the palace servants and their good clothes. She was shown the servants who served him at feasts. And she was shown the whole burnt offerings he made in the Temple[d] of the Lord. All these things amazed her.

[6]So she said to King Solomon, "I heard in my own country about your achievements and wisdom. And all of it is true. [7]I could not believe it then. But now I have come and seen it with my own eyes. I was not told even half of it! Your wisdom and wealth are much greater than I had heard. [8]Your men and officers are very lucky! In always serving you, they are

---

9:13 Cabul This name sounds like the Hebrew word for "worthless."

able to hear your wisdom! ⁹Praise the Lord your God! He was pleased to make you king of Israel. The Lord has constant love for Israel. So he made you king to keep justice and to rule fairly."

¹⁰Then the queen of Sheba gave the king about 9,000 pounds of gold. She also gave him many spices and jewels. No one since that time has brought more spices into Israel than the queen of Sheba gave King Solomon.

¹¹(Hiram's ships brought gold from Ophir. They also brought from there very much juniper wood and jewels. ¹²Solomon used the juniper wood to build supports for the Temple of the Lord and the palace. He also used it to make harps and lyres*d* for the musicians. Such fine juniper wood has not been brought in or seen since that time.)

¹³King Solomon gave the queen of Sheba many gifts. He gave her gifts that a king would give to another ruler. Then he gave her whatever else she wanted and asked for. After this, she and her servants went back to her own country.

SOLOMON'S WEALTH

¹⁴Every year King Solomon received about 50,000 pounds of gold. ¹⁵Besides that he also received gold from the traders and merchants. And he received gold from the kings of Arabia and governors of the land.

¹⁶King Solomon made 200 large shields of hammered gold. Each shield contained about seven and one-half pounds of gold. ¹⁷He also made 300 smaller shields of hammered gold. They each contained about three and three-fourths pounds of gold. The king put them in the Palace of the Forest of Lebanon.

¹⁸Then King Solomon built a large throne of ivory. And he covered it with pure gold. ¹⁹There were six steps leading up to the throne. The back of the throne was round at the top. There were armrests on both sides of the chair. And beside each armrest was a statue of a lion.

²⁰Twelve lions stood on the six steps. There was one lion at each end of each step. Nothing like this had ever been made for any other kingdom. ²¹All of Solomon's drinking cups were made of gold. All of the dishes in the Palace of the Forest of Lebanon were pure gold. Nothing was made from silver. In Solomon's time people did not think silver was valuable.

²²King Solomon also had many trading ships at sea, along with Hiram's ships. Every three years the ships returned. They brought back gold, silver, ivory, apes and baboons.

²³So Solomon had more riches and wisdom than all the other kings on earth. ²⁴People everywhere wanted to see King Solomon. They wanted to hear the wisdom God had given him. ²⁵Every year everyone who came brought a gift. They brought things made of gold and silver, along with clothes, weapons, spices, horses and mules.

²⁶So Solomon had many chariots and horses. He had 1,400 chariots and 12,000 chariot soldiers. He kept some in special cities for the chariots. And he kept some with him in Jerusalem. ²⁷In Jerusalem silver was as common as stones while Solomon was king. Cedar trees were as common as the fig trees growing on the mountain slopes. ²⁸Solomon brought in horses from Egypt and Kue. His traders bought them in Kue and brought them to Israel. ²⁹A chariot from Egypt cost about 15 pounds of silver. And a horse cost about 3³/₄ pounds of silver. The traders also sold horses and chariots to the kings of the Hittites and the Arameans.

SOLOMON'S MANY WIVES

11 But King Solomon loved many women who were not from Israel. He loved the daughter of the king of Egypt. He also loved women of the Moabites, Ammonites, Edomites, Sidonians and Hittites. ²The Lord had told the Israelites, "You must not marry people of other nations. If you do, they will cause you to follow their gods." But Solomon fell in love with these women. ³He had 700 wives who were from royal families. He also had 300 slave women*d* who gave birth to his children. His wives caused him to turn away from God. ⁴As Solomon grew old, his wives caused him to follow other gods. He did not follow the Lord completely as his father David had done. ⁵Solomon worshiped Ashtoreth,*d* the goddess of the people of Sidon. And he worshiped Molech,*d* the hated god of the Ammonites. ⁶So Solomon did what the Lord said was wrong. He did not follow the Lord completely as his father David had done.

⁷On a hill east of Jerusalem, Solomon built two places for worship. He built a place to worship Chemosh,*d* the hated god of the Moabites. And he built a place to worship Molech, the hated god of the Ammonites. ⁸Solomon did the same thing for all of his foreign wives. So they burned incense*d* and gave sacrifices to their gods.

⁹The Lord had appeared to Solomon twice. But Solomon turned away from following the Lord, the God of Israel. So the Lord was angry with him. ¹⁰The Lord had commanded Solomon not to follow other gods. But Solomon did not obey the Lord's command. ¹¹So the Lord said to Solomon, "You have chosen to break your agreement with me. You have not obeyed my commands. So I promise I will tear your kingdom away from you. I will give it to one of your officers. ¹²But I will not take it away while you are alive. This is because of my love for your father David. I will tear it away from your son when he becomes king. ¹³But I will not tear away all the kingdom from him. I will leave him one tribe*d* to rule. I will do this because of David, my servant. And I will do it because of Jerusalem, the city I have chosen."

SOLOMON'S ENEMIES

¹⁴Now Hadad was a member of the family of the king of Edom. And the Lord caused Hadad the Edomite to become Solomon's enemy. ¹⁵Earlier, David had defeated Edom. Joab, the commander of David's army, went into Edom to bury the dead. While he was there, he killed all the males. ¹⁶Joab and all the Israelites stayed in Edom for six months. During that time they killed every male in Edom. ¹⁷But at that time Hadad was only a young boy. So he ran away to Egypt with some of his father's officers. ¹⁸They left Midian and went to Paran. In Paran other men joined them. Then they all went to Egypt to see the king. He gave Hadad a house, some land and food to eat.

¹⁹The king liked Hadad so much he gave Hadad a wife. She was the sister of Tahpenes, the king's wife. ²⁰They had a son named Genubath. Queen Tahpenes allowed him to grow up in the royal palace. So he grew up with the king's own children.

²¹While he was in Egypt, Hadad heard that David had died. He also heard that Joab, the commander of the army, was dead. So Hadad said to the king, "Let me go home. Let me return to my own country."

²²But the king said, "Why do you want to go back to your own country? What haven't I given you here?"

Hadad answered, "Nothing. But please, let me go."

²³God also caused another man to be an enemy to Solomon. This man was Rezon son of Eliada. Rezon had run away from his master, Hadadezer king of Zobah. ²⁴After David defeated the army of Zobah, Rezon gathered some men. He became the leader of a small army. They went to Damascus and settled there. And Rezon became king of Damascus. ²⁵Rezon ruled Aram, and he hated Israel. So he was an enemy of Israel all the time Solomon was alive. Rezon and Hadad caused some trouble for Israel.

²⁶Jeroboam son of Nebat was one of Solomon's officers. Jeroboam was one of

the Ephraimite people. He was from the town of Zeredah. His mother was a widow named Zeruah. He turned against the king.

²⁷This is the story of how Jeroboam turned against the king. Solomon was filling in the land on the east side of Jerusalem. He was also repairing the wall of Jerusalem. It was the city of David, his ancestor. ²⁸Jeroboam was a capable man. Solomon saw that this young man was a good worker. So Solomon put him over all the workers from the tribes*d* of Ephraim and Manasseh.

²⁹One day Jeroboam was leaving Jerusalem. Ahijah, the prophet*d* from Shiloh, met him on the road. Ahijah was wearing a new coat. The two men were alone out in the country. ³⁰Ahijah took his new coat and tore it into 12 pieces. ³¹Then he said to Jeroboam, "Take 10 pieces of this coat for yourself. The Lord, the God of Israel, says: 'I will tear the kingdom away from Solomon. Then I will give you 10 tribes. ³²But I will allow the family of David to control 1 tribe. I will do this for my servant David and for Jerusalem. Jerusalem is the city I have chosen from all the tribes of Israel. ³³I will do this because Solomon has stopped following me. He worships the Sidonian god Ashtoreth*d* and the Moabite god Chemosh.*d* He also worships Molech,*d* the Ammonite god. Solomon has not obeyed me. He has not done what I said is right. He has not obeyed my laws and commands. He is not living the way his father David lived.

³⁴"'But I will not take all the kingdom away from Solomon. I will let him rule all his life. I will do this because of my servant David. I chose David, and he obeyed all my commands and laws. ³⁵But I will take the kingdom away from his son. Jeroboam, I will allow you to rule over the 10 tribes. ³⁶I will allow Solomon's son to continue to rule over 1 tribe. I will do this so that David, my servant, will

always have a king before me in Jerusalem. It is the city where I chose to be worshiped. ³⁷But I will make you rule over everything you want. You will rule over all of Israel. ³⁸I will always be with you if you do what I say is right. You must obey all my commands. If you obey my laws and commands as David did, I will be with you. I will make your family a family of kings, as I did for David. I will give Israel to you. ³⁹I will punish David's children because of this. But I will not punish them forever.'"

SOLOMON'S DEATH

⁴⁰Solomon tried to kill Jeroboam. But Jeroboam ran away to Egypt. He went to Shishak king of Egypt. And Jeroboam stayed there until Solomon died.

⁴¹Everything else Solomon did is written down. He showed much wisdom. It is written in the book of the history of Solomon. ⁴²Solomon ruled in Jerusalem over all Israel for 40 years. ⁴³Then he died and was buried in Jerusalem, the city of David, his father. And his son Rehoboam became king after him.

ISRAEL TURNS AGAINST REHOBOAM

12 Rehoboam went to Shechem because all the Israelites had gone there to make him king. ²Jeroboam son of Nebat was still in Egypt. He had gone there to escape from Solomon. When Jeroboam heard about Rehoboam being made king, Jeroboam returned from Egypt. ³So the people sent for him. Then he and the people went to Rehoboam. They said to Rehoboam, ⁴"Your father forced us to work very hard. Now, make it easier for us. Don't make us work as hard as your father did. Then we will serve you."

⁵Rehoboam answered, "Come back to me in three days. Then I will answer you." So the people left.

⁶Some of the elders had helped Solomon make decisions during his lifetime. So King Rehoboam asked them

what he should do. He said, "How do you think I should answer these people?"

⁷They answered, "You should be like a servant to them today. Serve them, and give them a kind answer. If you do, they will serve you always."

⁸But Rehoboam did not listen to this advice. He asked the young men who had grown up with him. They advised him in making decisions. ⁹Rehoboam said, "The people said, 'Don't make us work as hard as your father did.' How do you think I should answer them? What is your advice?"

¹⁰The young men answered, "Those people came to you and said, 'Your father forced us to work very hard. Now make our work easier.' So you should tell them, 'My little finger is bigger than my father's whole body. ¹¹My father forced you to work hard. But I will make you work even harder! My father beat you with whips. But I will beat you with whips that have sharp points.'"

¹²Rehoboam had told the people, "Come back to me in three days." So after three days all the people returned to Rehoboam. ¹³At that time King Rehoboam spoke cruel words to them. He did not listen to the advice that the elders had given him. ¹⁴He did what the young men had told him to do. Rehoboam said, "My father forced you to work hard. So I will give you even more work. My father beat you with whips. But I will beat you with whips that have sharp points." ¹⁵So the king did not do what the people wanted. The Lord caused this to happen. He did this to keep the promise he had made to Jeroboam son of Nebat. He had made this promise through Ahijah, the prophet*d* from Shiloh.

¹⁶All the people of Israel saw that the new king refused to listen to them. So they said to the king,

"We have no share in David!
We have no part in the son of Jesse!

People of Israel, let's go to our own homes!
Let David's son rule his own people!"

So the Israelites went home. ¹⁷But Rehoboam still ruled over the Israelites who lived in the towns of Judah.

¹⁸Adoniram was in charge of the people who were forced to work. King Rehoboam sent him to the people. But they threw stones at him until he died. But King Rehoboam ran to his chariot and escaped to Jerusalem. ¹⁹Since then, Israel has been against the family of David.

²⁰All the Israelites heard that Jeroboam had returned. So they called him to a meeting. And they made him king over all Israel. But the tribe*d* of Judah continued to follow the family of David.

²¹When Rehoboam arrived in Jerusalem, he gathered the tribes of Judah and Benjamin. This was an army of 180,000 men. Rehoboam wanted to fight against the people of Israel. He wanted to take back his kingdom.

²²But God spoke his word to Shemaiah, a man of God. The Lord said, ²³"Talk to Solomon's son Rehoboam, the king of Judah. Talk also to all the people of Judah and Benjamin and to the rest of the people. ²⁴Say to them, 'The Lord says you must not go to war against your brothers, the Israelites. Every one of you should go home. I made all these things happen!'" So the men in Rehoboam's army obeyed the Lord's command. They all went home as the Lord had commanded.

²⁵Then Jeroboam made Shechem a very strong city. It is in the mountains of Ephraim. And Jeroboam lived there. He also went to the city of Peniel and made it stronger.

JEROBOAM BUILDS GOLDEN CALVES

²⁶Jeroboam said to himself, "The kingdom will probably go back to David's family. ²⁷The people will continue going to the Temple*d* of the Lord in Jerusalem. If they do, they will want to

be ruled again by Rehoboam. Then they will kill me and follow Rehoboam king of Judah."

²⁸King Jeroboam asked his men for advice. So he made two golden calves. He said to the people, "It is too hard for you to go to Jerusalem to worship. Israel, here are your gods who brought you out of Egypt." ²⁹King Jeroboam put one golden calf in the city of Bethel. And he put the other in the city of Dan. ³⁰And this became a very great sin. The people traveled as far as Dan to worship the calf there.

³¹Jeroboam built temples on the places of worship. He chose priests from all the people. (He did not choose priests only from the tribe of Levi.) ³²And he started a new festival. It was the fifteenth day of the eighth month. This was like the festival in Judah. During that time the king offered sacrifices on the altar. He offered sacrifices to the calves in Bethel he had made. He also chose priests in Bethel to serve at the places of worship he had made. ³³So Jeroboam chose his own time for a festival for the Israelites. It was the fifteenth day of the eighth month. During that time he offered sacrifices on the altar he had built in Bethel. So he set up a festival for the Israelites. And he offered sacrifices on the altar.

THE MAN OF GOD SPEAKS AGAINST BETHEL

13 The Lord commanded a man of God from Judah to go to Bethel. When he arrived, Jeroboam was standing by the altar to offer a sacrifice. ²The Lord had commanded the man of God to speak against the altar. The man said, "Altar, the Lord says to you: 'David's family will have a son named Josiah. He will kill the priests of the places of worship. They now make their sacrifices on you. But Josiah will sacrifice those priests on you. Human bones will be burned on you.'" ³The man of God gave proof that these things would happen. He said, "This is God's sign that this will happen. This

altar will break apart. And the ashes on it will fall onto the ground."

⁴King Jeroboam heard what the man of God said about the altar in Bethel. So Jeroboam raised his hand from the altar and pointed at the man. "Capture him!" he said. But when the king said this, his arm became paralyzed. He could not move it. ⁵Also, the altar broke into pieces. All its ashes fell onto the ground. This was the sign the Lord had told the man of God to give.

⁶Then the king said to the man of God, "Please pray to the Lord your God for me. Ask him to heal my arm."

So the man of God prayed to the Lord. And the king's arm was healed. It became as it was before.

⁷Then the king said to the man of God, "Please come home and eat with me. I will give you a gift."

⁸But the man of God answered the king, "I will not go home with you! Even if you gave me half of your kingdom, I would not go! I will not eat or drink anything in this place. ⁹The Lord commanded me not to eat or drink anything. He also commanded me not to return on the same road by which I came." ¹⁰So he traveled on a different road. He did not return on the same road by which he had come to Bethel.

¹¹Now there was an old prophet*d* living in Bethel. His sons came and told him what the man of God had done there that day. They told their father what he had said to King Jeroboam. ¹²The father asked, "Which road did he use when he left?" So his sons showed him which road the man of God from Judah had taken. ¹³The prophet told his sons to put a saddle on his donkey. So they saddled the donkey, and he left.

¹⁴He went after the man of God. He found the man sitting under an oak tree. The prophet asked, "Are you the man of God who came from Judah?"

The man answered, "Yes, I am."

¹⁵So the prophet said, "Please come home and eat with me."

¹⁶But the man of God answered, "I can't go home with you. I can't eat or drink with you in this place. ¹⁷The Lord said to me, 'You must not eat or drink anything there. And you must not return on the same road by which you came.'"

¹⁸Then the old prophet said, "But I also am a prophet like you." Then he told a lie. He said, "An angel from the Lord came to me. He told me to bring you to my home. He said you should eat and drink with me." ¹⁹So the man of God went to the old prophet's house. And he ate and drank with him there.

²⁰While they were sitting at the table, the Lord spoke his word to the old prophet. ²¹The old prophet cried out to the man of God from Judah. He said, "The Lord said you did not obey him! He said you did not do what the Lord your God commanded you. ²²The Lord commanded you not to eat or drink anything in this place. But you came back and ate and drank. So your body will not be buried in your family grave."

²³The man of God finished eating. Then the prophet put a saddle on his donkey for him. And the man left. ²⁴As he was traveling on the road home, a lion attacked and killed him. His body lay on the road. The donkey and the lion stood near it. ²⁵Some men were traveling on that road. They saw the body and the lion standing near it. So they went to the city where the old prophet lived. And they told what they had seen.

²⁶The old prophet who had brought the man of God back heard about what had happened. He said, "It is the man of God who did not obey the Lord's command. So the Lord sent a lion to kill him. The Lord said he would do this."

²⁷Then the prophet said to his sons, "Put a saddle on my donkey." So they did. ²⁸The old prophet went out and found the body lying on the road. The donkey and

the lion were still standing near it. The lion had not eaten the body. And it had not hurt the donkey. ²⁹So the prophet put the body on his donkey. And he carried it back to the city. There he would have a time of sadness for him and bury him. ³⁰The prophet buried the body in his own family grave. And he was sad for the man of God. He said, "Oh, my brother."

³¹So the prophet buried the body. Then he said to his sons, "When I die, bury me in this same grave. Put my bones next to his. ³²Through him the Lord spoke against the altar at Bethel. And he spoke against the places of worship in the towns of Samaria. And what the Lord spoke through him will certainly come true."

³³But King Jeroboam did not stop doing evil things. He continued to choose priests for the places of worship from all the people. Anyone who wanted to be a priest for the places of worship was allowed. ³⁴In this way the kingdom of Jeroboam sinned. And that sin caused its ruin and destruction from the earth.

JEROBOAM'S SON DIES

14 At that time Jeroboam's son Abijah became very sick. ²So Jeroboam said to his wife, "Go to Shiloh. Go to see the prophet*ᵈ* Ahijah. He is the one who said I would become king of Israel. But dress yourself so people won't know you are my wife. ³Give the prophet ten loaves of bread, some cakes and a jar of honey. Then ask him what will happen to our son. And he will tell you." ⁴So the king's wife did as he said. She went to Ahijah's home in Shiloh.

Now Ahijah was very old and had become blind. ⁵But the Lord had said to him, "Jeroboam's son is sick. So Jeroboam's wife is coming to ask you about him. When she arrives, she will pretend to be someone else." Then the Lord told Ahijah what to say.

⁶When Ahijah heard her walking to the door, he said, "Come in, wife of Jeroboam. Why are you pretending to be

someone else? I have bad news for you. [7]Go back and tell Jeroboam that this is what the Lord, the God of Israel, says: 'Jeroboam, I chose you from among all the people of Israel. I made you the leader of my people. [8]I took the kingdom away from David's family. And I gave it to you. But you are not like my servant David. He always obeyed my commands. He followed me with all his heart. He did only the things I said were right. [9]But you have done more evil things than anyone who ruled before you. You have quit following me. You have made other gods and idols of metal. This has made me very angry. [10]So I will bring disaster to the family of Jeroboam. I will kill all of the men in your family, both slaves and free men. I will destroy your family as completely as fire burns up manure. [11]Anyone from your family who dies in the city will be eaten by dogs. And anyone from your family who dies in the fields will be eaten by the birds. The Lord has spoken!'"

[12]Then Ahijah said to Jeroboam's wife, "Now go home. When you enter your city gate, your son will die. [13]All Israel will be sad for him and bury him. He will be the only one of Jeroboam's family who will be buried. This is because he is the only one in Jeroboam's family who pleased the Lord, the God of Israel.

[14]"The Lord will put a new king over Israel. That king will destroy Jeroboam's family. This will happen soon. [15]Then the Lord will punish Israel. The people of Israel will be like grass moving in the water. The Lord will pull up Israel from this good land. This is the land he gave their ancestors. But he will scatter Israel beyond the Euphrates River. This will happen because the Lord is angry with the people. They made him angry when they made idols to worship Asherah.[d] [16]Jeroboam sinned, and then he made the people of Israel sin. So the Lord will let the people of Israel be defeated."

[17]Then Jeroboam's wife traveled back to Tirzah. When she entered her home, the boy died. [18]They buried him. And all Israel had a time of sadness for him. This happened as the Lord said it would. The Lord had said these things through his servant, the prophet Ahijah.

[19]Everything else Jeroboam did is written down. He fought wars and continued to rule the people. It is all written in the book of the history of the kings of Israel. [20]Jeroboam ruled as king for 22 years. Then he died, and his son Nadab became king in his place.

THE DEATH OF REHOBOAM

[21]Solomon's son Rehoboam was 41 years old when he became king of Judah. His mother was Naamah from the land of Ammon. Rehoboam ruled in Jerusalem for 17 years. (The Lord had chosen that city from all the land of Israel. He chose to be worshiped there.) [22]The people of Judah did what the Lord said was wrong. The people's sins made the Lord very angry at them. They made the Lord even more angry than their ancestors had done. [23]The people built stone pillars and places to worship false gods and Asherah[d] idols. They built them on every high hill and under every green tree. [24]There were even male prostitutes[d] at the places of worship to the gods. The people who had lived in the land before the Israelites had done many evil things. And God had taken the land away from them. Now the people of Judah were doing the same evil things.

[25]During the fifth year Rehoboam was king, Shishak attacked Jerusalem. Shishak was king of Egypt. [26]He took the treasures from the Temple[d] of the Lord and the king's palace. He took everything, even the gold shields Solomon had made. [27]So King Rehoboam made bronze shields to put in their place. He gave them to the men who were guarding the palace gates. [28]Whenever the king went to the Temple of the Lord, the

guards carried the shields. After they were finished, they put the shields back in the guardroom.

²⁹Everything else King Rehoboam did is written down. It is in the book of the history of the kings of Judah. ³⁰Rehoboam and Jeroboam were always fighting a war with each other. ³¹Rehoboam died and was buried with his ancestors in Jerusalem. His mother was Naamah from Ammon. And Rehoboam's son Abijam[n] became king in his place.

ABIJAM KING OF JUDAH

15 Abijam became king of Judah. This was during the eighteenth year Jeroboam son of Nebat ruled Israel. ²And Abijam ruled in Jerusalem for three years. His mother was Maacah daughter of Abishalom. ³He did all the same sins his father before him had done. Abijam was not faithful to the Lord his God. In this way he was not like David, his great-grandfather. ⁴Because the Lord had loved David, the Lord gave Abijam a kingdom in Jerusalem. And the Lord allowed him to have a son to be king after him. The Lord also kept Jerusalem safe. ⁵David had always done what the Lord said was right. All his life he had always obeyed the Lord's commands. There was only one time David did not obey the Lord. This was when he sinned against Uriah the Hittite.

⁶Now there was war between Abijam and Jeroboam during Abijam's lifetime. ⁷Everything else Abijam did is written down. It is in the book of the history of the kings of Judah. During the time Abijam ruled, there was war between Abijam and Jeroboam. ⁸And Abijam died and was buried in Jerusalem. Abijam's son Asa became king in his place.

ASA KING OF JUDAH

⁹During the twentieth year Jeroboam was king of Israel, Asa became king of Judah. ¹⁰Asa ruled in Jerusalem for 41 years. His grandmother's name was Maacah. She was the daughter of Abishalom.

¹¹Asa did what the Lord said was right. This was as his ancestor David had done. ¹²There were male prostitutes[d] at the places where false gods were worshiped. Asa forced them to leave the country. He also took away the idols that his ancestors had made. ¹³His grandmother Maacah had made a terrible Asherah[d] idol. So Asa removed her from being queen. He cut down this idol and burned it in the Kidron Valley. ¹⁴Asa was faithful to the Lord all his life. But he did not destroy the places where false gods were worshiped. ¹⁵Asa and his father had given some things to God. They had given gifts of gold, silver and other objects. Asa put all these things in the Temple.[d]

¹⁶There was war between Asa and Baasha king of Israel. ¹⁷Baasha fought against Judah. He wanted to stop people from leaving or entering Asa's country, Judah. So he made the city of Ramah very strong.

¹⁸Then Asa took all the silver and gold from the treasuries of the Temple of the Lord and his own palace. He gave it to his officers. And he sent them to Ben-Hadad king of Aram. (Ben-Hadad was the son of Tabrimmon. And he was the son of Hezion.) Ben-Hadad was ruling in the city of Damascus. ¹⁹Asa sent this message: "My father and your father had a peace agreement. I am sending you a gift of gold and silver. Break your treaty with Baasha king of Israel so that he will leave my land."

²⁰Ben-Hadad agreed with King Asa. So he sent his army to fight against the towns of Israel. He defeated the towns of Ijon, Dan and Abel Bethmaacah. And he defeated all the land near Lake Galilee and the area of Naphtali. ²¹Baasha heard about these attacks. So he stopped

14:31 **Abijam** A negative name for Abijah. See 2 Chronicles 13.

building up Ramah and returned to Tirzah. ²²Then King Asa gave an order to all the people of Judah. Everyone had to help. They carried away all the stones and wood Baasha had been using in Ramah. King Asa used those things to build up Geba and Mizpah. (Geba was in the land of Benjamin.)

²³Everything else Asa did is written down. His victories and the cities he built are written down. They are in the book of the history of the kings of Judah. When he became old, he got a disease in his feet. ²⁴Then Asa died. And he was buried with his ancestors in Jerusalem. It was the city of David, his ancestor. Then Jehoshaphat, Asa's son, became king in his place.

NADAB KING OF ISRAEL

²⁵Nadab son of Jeroboam became king of Israel. This was during the second year Asa was king of Judah. And Nadab was king of Israel for two years. ²⁶He did what the Lord said was wrong. Jeroboam had caused the people of Israel to sin. Nadab sinned in the same way his father Jeroboam had sinned.

²⁷Baasha son of Ahijah was from the tribe[d] of Issachar. He made plans to kill Nadab. Nadab and all Israel were attacking the Philistine town of Gibbethon. So Baasha killed Nadab there. ²⁸This happened during Asa's third year as king of Judah. And Baasha became the next king of Israel.

BAASHA KING OF ISRAEL

²⁹As soon as Baasha became king, he killed all of Jeroboam's family. He left no one in Jeroboam's family alive. This happened as the Lord had said it would. The Lord had said this through his servant Ahijah from Shiloh. ³⁰This happened because King Jeroboam had sinned very much. And he had caused the people of Israel to sin. Jeroboam had made the Lord, the God of Israel, very angry.

³¹Everything else Nadab did is written down. It is in the book of the history of the kings of Israel. ³²There was war between Asa king of Judah and Baasha king of Israel all the time they were kings.

³³Baasha son of Ahijah became king of Israel. This was during Asa's third year as king of Judah. And Baasha ruled in Tirzah for 24 years. ³⁴But Baasha did what the Lord said was wrong. Jeroboam had caused the people of Israel to sin. And Baasha sinned in the same way Jeroboam had sinned.

16 Then Jehu son of Hanani spoke the word of the Lord against King Baasha. ²The Lord said, "You were nothing. Then I took you and made you a leader over my people Israel. But you have followed the ways of Jeroboam. You have caused my people Israel to sin. Their sins have made me angry. ³So, Baasha, I will destroy you and your family. I will do to you what I did to the family of Jeroboam son of Nebat. ⁴Anyone from your family who dies in the city will be eaten by dogs. And anyone from your family who dies in the fields will be eaten by birds."

⁵Everything else Baasha did and all his victories are written down. They are in the book of the history of the kings of Israel. ⁶So Baasha died and was buried in Tirzah. His son Elah became king in his place.

⁷The Lord spoke his word through the prophet[d] Jehu son of Hanani. The Lord's message was against Baasha and his family. Baasha had done many things the Lord said were wrong. This made the Lord very angry. Baasha did the same things that Jeroboam's family had done before him. The Lord was also angry because Baasha killed all of Jeroboam's family.

ELAH KING OF ISRAEL

⁸Elah son of Baasha became king of Israel. This was during Asa's twenty-sixth year as king of Judah. And Elah ruled in Tirzah for two years.

⁹Zimri was one of Elah's officers. He commanded half of Elah's chariots. But Zimri made plans against Elah.

Elah was in Tirzah, getting drunk at Arza's home. (Arza was the man in charge of the palace at Tirzah.) ¹⁰So Zimri went into Arza's house and killed Elah. This was during Asa's twenty-seventh year as king of Judah. Then Zimri became king of Israel in Elah's place.

ZIMRI KING OF ISRAEL

¹¹As soon as Zimri became king, he killed all of Baasha's family. He did not let any man of Baasha's family or friends live. ¹²So Zimri destroyed all of Baasha's family. This happened as the Lord had said it would. The Lord had spoken this against Baasha through the prophet[d] Jehu. ¹³This happened because of all the sins of Baasha and his son Elah. They sinned and caused the people of Israel to sin. They also made the Lord, the God of Israel, angry because they had made worthless idols.

¹⁴Everything else Elah did is written down. It is in the book of the history of the kings of Israel.

¹⁵So Zimri became king of Israel. This was during Asa's twenty-seventh year as king of Judah. Zimri ruled in Tirzah seven days. This is what happened:

The army of Israel was camped near Gibbethon, a Philistine town. ¹⁶The men in the camp heard that Zimri had made secret plans against the king. And they heard that Zimri had killed him. So that day in the camp they made Omri king over Israel. (Omri was commander of the army.) ¹⁷So Omri and all the Israelites left Gibbethon and attacked Tirzah. ¹⁸Zimri saw that the city had been captured. So he went into the palace and set it on fire. He burned the palace and himself with it. ¹⁹So Zimri died because he had sinned. He did what the Lord said was wrong. Jeroboam had caused the people of Israel to sin. And Zimri sinned in the same way Jeroboam had sinned.

²⁰Everything else Zimri did is written down. It is in the book of the history of the kings of Israel. The story of how Zimri turned against King Elah is also written there.

OMRI KING OF ISRAEL

²¹The people of Israel were divided into two groups. Half of the people wanted Tibni to be king. He was the son of Ginath. The other half of the people wanted Omri. ²²But Omri's followers were stronger than the followers of Tibni son of Ginath. So Tibni died, and Omri became king.

²³Omri became king of Israel. This was during the thirty-first year Asa was king of Judah. And Omri ruled Israel for 12 years. Six of those years he ruled in the town of Tirzah. ²⁴Omri bought the hill of Samaria from Shemer. He paid about 150 pounds of silver for it. Omri built a city on that hill. And he called it Samaria after the name of its earlier owner, Shemer.

²⁵But Omri did what the Lord said was wrong. He did more evil than all the kings who were before him. ²⁶Jeroboam son of Nebat had caused the people of Israel to sin. And Omri sinned in the same way Jeroboam had sinned. So the Israelites made the Lord, the God of Israel, very angry. He was angry because they worshiped worthless idols.

²⁷Everything else Omri did and all his successes are written down. They are all in the book of the history of the kings of Israel. ²⁸So Omri died and was buried in Samaria. His son Ahab became king in his place.

AHAB KING OF ISRAEL

²⁹So Ahab son of Omri became king of Israel. This was during Asa's thirty-eighth year as king of Judah. Ahab ruled Israel in the town of Samaria for 22 years. ³⁰Ahab did many things that the Lord said were wrong. He did more evil than any of the kings before him. ³¹He sinned in the same ways that Jeroboam son of

Nebat had sinned. But he did even worse things. He married Jezebel daughter of Ethbaal. (Ethbaal was king of the city of Sidon.) Then Ahab began to serve Baal[d] and worship him. [32]He built a temple in Samaria for worshiping Baal. And he put an altar there for Baal. [33]Ahab also made an idol for worshiping Asherah.[d] He did more things to make the Lord, the God of Israel, angry than all the other kings before him.

[34]During the time of Ahab, Hiel from Bethel rebuilt the town of Jericho. It cost Hiel the life of Abiram, his oldest son, to begin work on the city. And it cost the life of Segub, his youngest son, to build the city gates. The Lord had said, through Joshua, that this would happen.[n] (Joshua was the son of Nun.)

ELIJAH STOPS THE RAIN

17 Now Elijah was a prophet[d] from the town of Tishbe in Gilead. Elijah said to King Ahab, "I serve the Lord, the God of Israel. As surely as the Lord lives, I tell you the truth. No rain or dew will fall during the next few years unless I command it."

[2]Then the Lord spoke his word to Elijah: [3]"Leave this place. Go east and hide near Kerith Ravine. It is east of the Jordan River. [4]You may drink from the brook. And I have commanded ravens to bring you food there." [5]So Elijah did what the Lord told him to do. He went to Kerith Ravine, east of the Jordan, and lived there. [6]The birds brought Elijah bread and meat every morning and every evening. And he drank water from the brook.

[7]After a while the brook dried up because there was no rain. [8]Then the Lord spoke his word to Elijah, [9]"Go to Zarephath in Sidon. Live there. I have commanded a widow there to take care of you."

[10]So Elijah went to Zarephath. When he reached the town gate, he saw a widow there. She was gathering wood for a fire. Elijah asked her, "Would you bring me a little water in a cup? I would like to have a drink." [11]As she was going to get his water, Elijah said, "Please bring me a piece of bread, too."

[12]The woman answered, "As surely as the Lord your God lives, I tell you the truth. I have no bread. I have only a handful of flour in a jar. And I have only a little olive oil in a jug. I came here to gather some wood. I will take it home and cook our last meal. My son and I will eat it and then die from hunger."

[13]Elijah said to her, "Don't worry. Go home and cook your food as you have said. But first make a small loaf of bread from the flour you have. Bring it to me. Then cook something for yourself and your son. [14]The Lord, the God of Israel, says, 'That jar of flour will never become empty. The jug will always have oil in it. This will continue until the day the Lord sends rain to the land.'"

[15]So the woman went home. And she did what Elijah told her to do. So Elijah, the woman and her son had enough food every day. [16]The jar of flour and the jug of oil were never empty. This happened just as the Lord, through Elijah, said it would.

ELIJAH BRINGS A BOY BACK TO LIFE

[17]Some time later the son of the woman who owned the house became sick. He grew worse and worse. Finally he stopped breathing. [18]So the woman said to Elijah, "You are a man of God. What have you done to me? Did you come here to remind me of my sin? Did you come here to kill my son?"

[19]Elijah said to her, "Give me your son." So Elijah took the boy from her and carried him upstairs. Elijah laid the boy

---

16:34 The Lord ... happen When Joshua destroyed Jericho, he said whoever rebuilt the city would lose his oldest and youngest sons. See Joshua 6:26.

on the bed in the room where he was staying. ²⁰Then he prayed to the Lord. He said, "Lord my God, this widow is letting me stay in her house. Why have you done this terrible thing to her? Why have you caused her son to die?" ²¹Then Elijah lay on top of the boy three times. Elijah prayed to the Lord, "Lord my God, let this boy live again!"

²²The Lord answered Elijah's prayer. The boy began breathing again, and he was alive. ²³Elijah carried the boy downstairs. He gave the boy to his mother and said, "See! Your son is alive!"

²⁴The woman said to Elijah, "Now I know you really are a man from God. I know that the Lord truly speaks through you!"

ELIJAH AND THE PROPHETS OF BAAL

18 During the third year without rain, the Lord spoke his word to Elijah. The Lord said, "Go and meet King Ahab. I will soon send rain." ²So Elijah went to meet Ahab.

By this time there was no food in Samaria. ³So King Ahab sent for Obadiah. Obadiah was in charge of the king's palace. (Obadiah was a true follower of the Lord. ⁴One time Jezebel was killing all the Lord's prophets.ᵈ So Obadiah took 100 of them and hid them in two caves. He put 50 in one cave and 50 in another cave. And he brought them food and water.) ⁵King Ahab said to Obadiah, "Let's look at every spring and valley in the land. Maybe we can find enough grass to keep our horses and mules alive. Then we will not have to kill our animals." ⁶So each one chose a part of the country to search. Ahab went in one direction. Obadiah went in another direction.

⁷While Obadiah was walking along, Elijah met him. Obadiah knew who Elijah was. So he bowed down to the ground before Elijah. He said, "Elijah? Is it really you, master?"

⁸Elijah answered, "Yes. Go tell your master the king that I am here."

⁹Then Obadiah said, "If I tell Ahab that, he will kill me! I have done nothing wrong that I should be killed! ¹⁰As surely as the Lord your God lives, the king has looked everywhere for you! He has sent people to every country to look for you. If the ruler said you were not there, that was not enough. Ahab then forced the ruler to swear you could not be found in his country. ¹¹Now you want me to go to my master and tell him, 'Elijah is here'? ¹²The Spiritᵈ of the Lord may carry you to some other place after I leave. If I go tell King Ahab you are here, he will come. If he doesn't find you, he will kill me! I have followed the Lord since I was a boy. ¹³Haven't you heard what I did? When Jezebel was killing the Lord's prophets, I hid 100 of them. I put 50 prophets in one cave and 50 prophets in another cave. I brought them food and water. ¹⁴Now you want me to go and tell the king you are here. He will kill me!"

¹⁵Elijah answered, "I serve the Lord of heaven's armies. As surely as the Lord lives, I will stand before Ahab today."

¹⁶So Obadiah went to Ahab and told him where Elijah was. Then Ahab went to meet Elijah.

¹⁷When he saw Elijah, he said, "Is it you—the biggest troublemaker in Israel?"

¹⁸Elijah answered, "I have not caused trouble in Israel. You and your father's family have caused all this trouble. You have not obeyed the Lord's commands. You have followed the Baals.ᵈ ¹⁹Now tell all Israel to meet me at Mount Carmel. Also bring the 450 prophets of Baal there. And bring the 400 prophets of Asherah,ᵈ who eat at Jezebel's table."

²⁰So Ahab called all the Israelites and those prophets to Mount Carmel. ²¹Elijah stood before the people. He said, "How long will you try to serve both Baal and the Lord? If the Lord is the true God, follow him. But if Baal is the true God, follow him!"

But the people said nothing.

²²Elijah said, "I am the only prophet of the Lord here. But there are 450 prophets of Baal. ²³So bring two bulls. Let the prophets of Baal choose one bull. Let them kill it and cut it into pieces. Then let them put the meat on the wood. But they are not to set fire to it. Then I will do the same with the other bull. And I will put it on the wood. But I will not set fire to it. ²⁴You prophets of Baal, pray to your god. And I will pray to the Lord. The god who answers the prayer will set fire to his wood. He is the true God."

All the people agreed that this was a good idea.

²⁵Then Elijah said to the prophets of Baal, "There are many of you. So you go first. Choose a bull and prepare it. Pray to your god, but don't start the fire."

²⁶So they took the bull that was given to them and prepared it. They prayed to Baal from morning until noon. They shouted, "Baal, answer us!" But there was no sound. No one answered. They danced around the altar they had built.

²⁷At noon Elijah began to make fun of them. He said, "Pray louder! If Baal really is a god, maybe he is thinking. Or maybe he is busy or traveling! Maybe he is sleeping so you will have to wake him!" ²⁸So the prophets prayed louder. They cut themselves with swords and spears until their blood flowed. (This was the way they worshiped.) ²⁹The afternoon passed, and the prophets continued to act wildly. They continued until it was time for the evening sacrifice. But no voice was heard. Baal did not answer. No one paid attention.

³⁰Then Elijah said to all the people, "Now come to me." So they gathered around him. Elijah rebuilt the altar of the Lord because it had been torn down. ³¹He took 12 stones. He took 1 stone for each of the 12 tribes.ᵈ These 12 tribes were named for the 12 sons of Jacob. (Jacob was the man the Lord had called Israel.) ³²Elijah used these stones to rebuild the altar in honor of the Lord. Then he dug a small ditch around it. It was big enough to hold about 13 quarts of seed. ³³Elijah put the wood on the altar. He cut the bull into pieces and laid them on the wood. Then he said, "Fill four jars with water. Put the water on the meat and on the wood."

³⁴Then Elijah said, "Do it again." And they did it again.

Then he said, "Do it a third time." And they did it the third time. ³⁵So the water ran off of the altar and filled the ditch.

³⁶It was time for the evening sacrifice. So the prophet Elijah went near the altar. He prayed, "Lord, you are the God of Abraham, Isaac and Israel. I ask you now to prove that you are the God of Israel. And prove that I am your servant. Show these people that you commanded me to do all these things. ³⁷Lord, answer my prayer. Show these people that you, Lord, are God. Then the people will know that you are bringing them back to you."

³⁸Then fire from the Lord came down. It burned the sacrifice, the wood, the stones and the ground around the altar. It also dried up the water in the ditch. ³⁹When all the people saw this, they fell down to the ground. They cried, "The Lord is God! The Lord is God!"

⁴⁰Then Elijah said, "Capture the prophets of Baal! Don't let any of them run away!" So the people captured all the prophets. Then Elijah led them down to Kishon Valley. There he killed all the prophets.

THE RAIN COMES AGAIN

⁴¹Then Elijah said to Ahab, "Now, go, eat and drink. A heavy rain is coming." ⁴²So King Ahab went to eat and drink. At the same time Elijah climbed to the top of Mount Carmel. There he bent down to the ground with his head between his knees.

⁴³Then Elijah said to his servant, "Go and look toward the sea."

The servant went and looked. He said, "I see nothing."

Elijah told him to go and look again. This happened seven times. ⁴⁴The seventh time, the servant said, "I see a small cloud. It's the size of a man's fist. It's coming from the sea."

Elijah told the servant, "Go to Ahab. Tell him to get his chariot ready and to go home now. If he doesn't leave now, the rain will stop him."

⁴⁵After a short time the sky was covered with dark clouds. The wind began to blow. Then a heavy rain began to fall. Ahab got in his chariot and started back to Jezreel. ⁴⁶The Lord gave his power to Elijah. Elijah tightened his clothes around him. Then he ran ahead of King Ahab all the way to Jezreel.

ELIJAH AT MOUNT SINAI

19 King Ahab told Jezebel everything Elijah had done. Ahab told her how Elijah had killed all the prophets*d* with a sword. ²So Jezebel sent a messenger to Elijah. Jezebel said, "By this time tomorrow I will kill you. I will kill you as you killed those prophets. If I don't succeed, may the gods punish me terribly."

³When Elijah heard this, he was afraid. So he ran away to save his life. He took his servant with him. When they came to Beersheba in Judah, Elijah left his servant there. ⁴Then Elijah walked for a whole day into the desert. He sat down under a bush and asked to die. Elijah prayed, "I have had enough, Lord. Let me die. I am no better than my ancestors." ⁵Then Elijah lay down under the tree and slept.

Suddenly an angel came to him and touched him. The angel said, "Get up and eat." ⁶Elijah saw near his head a loaf baked over coals and a jar of water. So he ate and drank. Then he went back to sleep.

⁷Later the Lord's angel came to him a second time. The angel touched him and said, "Get up and eat. If you don't, the journey will be too hard for you." ⁸So Elijah got up and ate and drank. The food made him strong enough to walk for 40 days and nights. He walked to Mount Sinai, the mountain of God. ⁹There Elijah went into a cave and stayed all night.

Then the Lord spoke his word to him: "Elijah! Why are you here?"

¹⁰Elijah answered, "Lord, God of heaven's armies, I have always served you the best I could. But the people of Israel have broken their agreement with you. They have destroyed your altars. They have killed your prophets with swords. I am the only prophet left. And now they are trying to kill me, too!"

¹¹Then the Lord said to Elijah, "Go. Stand in front of me on the mountain. I will pass by you." Then a very strong wind blew. It caused the mountains to break apart. It broke apart large rocks in front of the Lord. But the Lord was not in the wind. After the wind, there was an earthquake. But the Lord was not in the earthquake. ¹²After the earthquake, there was a fire. But the Lord was not in the fire. After the fire, there was a quiet, gentle voice. ¹³When Elijah heard it, he covered his face with his coat. He went out and stood at the entrance to the cave.

Then a voice said to him, "Elijah! Why are you here?"

¹⁴Elijah answered, "Lord, God of heaven's armies, I have always served you the best I could. But the people of Israel have broken their agreement with you. They have destroyed your altars. They have killed your prophets with swords. I am the only prophet left. And now they are trying to kill me, too."

¹⁵The Lord said to him, "Go back on the road that leads to the desert around Damascus. Enter that city. There pour olive oil on Hazael to make him king over Aram. ¹⁶Then pour oil on Jehu son of Nimshi to make him king over Israel. Next, pour oil on Elisha son of Shaphat from Abel Meholah. He will be a prophet in your place. ¹⁷Jehu will kill anyone who

escapes from Hazael's sword. And Elisha will kill anyone who escapes from Jehu's sword. ¹⁸But I have left 7,000 people living in Israel. Those 7,000 have never bowed down before Baal.*ᵈ* Their mouths have never kissed his idol."

ELISHA BECOMES A PROPHET

¹⁹So Elijah left there and found Elisha son of Shaphat. He was plowing a field with a team of oxen. There were 11 teams ahead of him. Elisha was plowing with the twelfth team of oxen. Elijah came up to Elisha. Elijah took off his coat and put it on Elisha. ²⁰Then Elisha left his oxen and ran to follow Elijah. Elisha said, "Let me kiss my father and my mother goodbye. Then I will go with you."

Elijah answered, "That is fine. Go back. I won't stop you."

²¹So Elisha went back. He took his pair of oxen and killed them. He used the wooden yoke*ᵈ* for the fire. Then he cooked the meat and gave it to the people. And they ate it. Then Elisha went and followed Elijah and became his helper.

BEN-HADAD AND AHAB GO TO WAR

20 Now Ben-Hadad was king of Aram. He gathered together all his army. There were 32 kings with their horses and chariots. They went with him and surrounded Samaria and attacked it. ²The king sent messengers into the city to Ahab king of Israel. ³This was his message: "Ben-Hadad says, 'You must give me your silver and gold and the best of your wives and children.'"

⁴Ahab king of Israel answered, "My master and king, I agree to what you say. I and everything I have belongs to you."

⁵Then the messengers came to Ahab again. They said, "Ben-Hadad says, 'I told you before that you must give me your silver and gold, your wives and your children. ⁶About this time tomorrow I am going to send my men to you. They are to search everywhere in your palace. And they are to search the homes of the men who rule under you. My men will take anything they want.'"

⁷So Ahab called a meeting of all the elders of his country. He said, "Ben-Hadad is looking for trouble. First he said I had to give him my wives, my children, my silver and my gold. I agreed to that."

⁸But the elders and all the people said, "Pay no attention to him. Don't do what he says."

⁹So Ahab said to Ben-Hadad's messengers, "Tell my master the king this: 'I will do what you said at first. But I will not obey your second command.'" So King Ben-Hadad's men carried the message back to him.

¹⁰Then Ben-Hadad sent another message to Ahab: "I will completely destroy Samaria. There won't be even enough left for each of my men to get a handful of dust. May the gods punish me terribly if I don't do this!"

¹¹Ahab answered, "Tell Ben-Hadad this: 'The man who puts on his armor should not brag too soon. It's the man who lives long enough to take it off who has the right to brag.'"

¹²Now Ben-Hadad was drinking in his tent with the other rulers. The messengers came and gave him the message from Ahab. Ben-Hadad commanded his men to prepare to attack the city. So they moved into their places for the battle.

¹³At the same time a prophet*ᵈ* came to Ahab, king of Israel. The prophet said, "Ahab, the Lord says to you, 'Do you see that big army? I will let you defeat it today. Then you will know I am the Lord.'"

¹⁴Ahab said, "Who will you use to defeat them?"

The prophet answered, "The Lord says, 'The young officers of the district governors will defeat them.'"

Then the king asked, "Who will command the main army?"

The prophet answered, "You will."

15So Ahab gathered the young officers of the district governors. There were 232 of them. Then he called together the army of Israel. There were 7,000 of them.

16At noon Ben-Hadad and the 32 rulers helping him were getting drunk in their tents. At this time Ahab attacked them. 17The young officers of the district governors attacked first.

Ben-Hadad's scouts told him that soldiers were coming from Samaria. 18So Ben-Hadad said, "They may be coming to fight. Or they may be coming to ask for peace. In either case capture them alive."

19The young officers of the district governors led the attack. The army of Israel followed them. 20Then each officer of Israel killed the man who came against him. So the men from Aram ran away as Israel chased them. But Ben-Hadad king of Aram escaped on a horse with some of his horsemen. 21Ahab king of Israel led the army. He captured the Arameans' horses and chariots. So King Ahab caused a great defeat of the Aramean army.

22Then the prophet went to Ahab king of Israel and said, "The king of Aram will attack you again next spring. So you should go home now and make your army stronger. Make plans to defend yourself."

23The officers of Ben-Hadad king of Aram said to him, "The gods of Israel are mountain gods. Since we fought in a mountain area, Israel won. So let's fight them on the flat land. Then we will win. 24This is what you should do. Don't allow the 32 rulers to command the armies. Put commanders in their places. 25Gather an army like the one that was destroyed. Gather as many horses and chariots as it had. We will fight the Israelites on flat land. Then we will win." Ben-Hadad agreed with their advice and did what they said.

26The next spring Ben-Hadad gathered the people of Aram. He went to Aphek to fight against Israel.

27The Israelites also prepared for war. They marched out to meet the Arameans and camped opposite them. They looked like two small groups of goats. But the Arameans covered the area.

28A man of God came to the king of Israel with this message: "The Lord says, 'The people of Aram say that I, the Lord, am a god of the mountains. They think I am not a god of the valleys. So I will allow you to defeat this big army. Then you will know I am the Lord.'"

29The armies were camped across from each other for seven days. On the seventh day the battle began. The Israelites killed 100,000 Aramean soldiers in one day. 30The rest of them ran away to the city of Aphek. There a city wall fell on 27,000 of them. Ben-Hadad also ran away to the city and hid in a room.

31His officers said to him, "We have heard that the kings of Israel are merciful. Let's dress in rough cloth to show our sadness. And let's wear ropes on our heads as a sign of surrender. Then let's go to the king of Israel. Maybe he will let you live."

32So they dressed in rough cloth and wore ropes on their heads. Then they went to the king of Israel. They said, "Your servant Ben-Hadad says, 'Please let me live.'"

Ahab answered, "Is he still alive? He is my brother."

33Now Ben-Hadad's men had wanted a sign from Ahab. They wanted to know he would not kill Ben-Hadad. So when Ahab called Ben-Hadad his brother, they quickly said, "Yes! Ben-Hadad is your brother."

Ahab said, "Bring him to me." When Ben-Hadad came, Ahab asked him to join him in the chariot.

34Ben-Hadad said to him, "Ahab, I will give you back the towns my father took from your father. And you may put shops in Damascus, as my father did in Samaria."

Ahab said, "If you agree to this, I will allow you to go free." So the two kings made a peace agreement. Then Ahab let Ben-Hadad go free.

A PROPHET SPEAKS AGAINST AHAB

[35]One of the prophets[d] told another prophet, "Hit me!" He told him to do this because the Lord had commanded it. But the other prophet refused. [36]So the first prophet said, "You did not obey the Lord's command. So a lion will kill you as soon as you leave me." When the second prophet left, a lion found him and killed him.

[37]The first prophet went to another man and said, "Hit me, please!" So the man hit him and hurt him. [38]Then the prophet wrapped his face in a cloth. This way no one could tell who he was. Then he went and waited by the road for the king. [39]As Ahab king of Israel passed by, the prophet called out to him. The prophet said, "I went to fight in the battle. One of our men brought an enemy soldier to me. Our man said, 'Guard this man. If he runs away, you will have to give your life in his place. Or, you will have to pay a fine of 75 pounds of silver.' [40]But I became busy doing other things. So the man ran away."

The king of Israel answered, "You have said what the punishment is. You must do what the man said."

[41]Then the prophet quickly took the cloth from his face. When the king of Israel saw him, he knew he was one of the prophets. [42]Then the prophet said to the king, "This is what the Lord says: 'You set free the man I said should die. So your life will be taken in his place. And the lives of your people will be taken in place of the lives of his people.'"

[43]Then the king went back to his palace in Samaria. He was angry and upset.

NABOTH'S VINEYARD

21 A man named Naboth owned a vineyard. It was in Jezreel, near the palace of Ahab king of Israel. [2]One day Ahab said to Naboth, "Give me your vineyard. It is near my palace. I want to make it into a vegetable garden. I will give you a better vineyard in its place. Or, if you prefer, I will pay you what it is worth."

[3]Naboth answered, "May the Lord keep me from ever giving my land to you. It belongs to my family."

[4]So Ahab went home, angry and upset. He did not like what Naboth from Jezreel had said. (Naboth had said, "I will not give you my family's land.") So Ahab lay down on his bed. He turned his face to the wall and refused to eat.

[5]His wife, Jezebel, came in. She asked him, "Why are you upset? Why do you refuse to eat?"

[6]Ahab answered, "I talked to Naboth, the man from Jezreel. I said, 'Sell me your vineyard. Or, if you prefer, I will give you another vineyard for it.' But Naboth refused."

[7]Jezebel answered, "Is this how you rule as king over Israel? Get out of bed. Eat something. Cheer up. I will get Naboth's vineyard for you."

[8]So Jezebel wrote some letters and signed Ahab's name to them. And she used his own seal[d] to seal them. Then she sent them to the elders and important men who lived in Naboth's town. [9]The letter she wrote said: "Declare a day during which the people are to give up eating. Call the people together. And give Naboth a place of honor among them. [10]Seat two troublemakers across from him. Have them say they heard Naboth speak against God and the king. Then take Naboth out of the city and kill him with stones."

[11]So the elders and important men of Jezreel obeyed Jezebel's command. [12]They declared a special day. On that day the people were to give up eating. They called the people together. And they put Naboth in a place of honor before the people. [13]Then two troublemakers sat

across from Naboth. They said they had heard Naboth speak against God and the king. So the people carried Naboth out of the city. And they killed him with stones. ¹⁴Then the leaders sent a message to Jezebel. It said, "Naboth has been killed."

¹⁵When Jezebel heard that Naboth had been killed, she told Ahab. She said, "Naboth of Jezreel is dead. Now you may go and take for yourself his vineyard you wanted." ¹⁶When Ahab heard that Naboth was dead, he left. He went to the vineyard to take it for his own.

¹⁷At this time the Lord spoke his word to Elijah. (Elijah was the prophet[d] from Tishbe.) The Lord said, ¹⁸"Go to Ahab king of Israel, who rules in Samaria. He is at Naboth's vineyard to take it as his own. ¹⁹Tell Ahab that I, the Lord, say to him, 'Ahab! You have murdered Naboth and have taken his land. So I tell you this! In the same place that Naboth died, you will also die. The dogs that licked up Naboth's blood will lick up your blood in the same place!'"

²⁰When Ahab saw Elijah, he said, "So you have found me, my enemy!"

Elijah answered, "Yes, I have found you. You have always chosen to do what the Lord says is wrong. ²¹So the Lord says to you, 'I will destroy you. I will kill you and every male in your family, both slave and free. ²²Your family will be like the family of King Jeroboam son of Nebat. And it will be like the family of King Baasha son of Ahijah. Both of these families were completely destroyed. I will do this to you because you have made me angry. And you have caused the people of Israel to sin.'

²³"And the Lord also says, 'Dogs will eat the body of Jezebel in the city of Jezreel.'

²⁴"Anyone in your family who dies in the city will be eaten by dogs. Anyone who dies in the fields will be eaten by birds."

²⁵There was no one like Ahab. No one had so often chosen to do what the Lord said was wrong. His wife Jezebel influenced him to do evil. ²⁶Ahab sinned terribly by worshiping idols. This was the same thing the Amorite people did. So the Lord took their land away from them. And he gave it to the people of Israel.

²⁷After Elijah finished speaking, Ahab tore his clothes. He put on rough cloth and refused to eat. He even slept in the rough cloth. He did this to show how sad and upset he was.

²⁸The Lord spoke his word to Elijah from Tishbe: ²⁹"I see that Ahab is now sorry for what he has done. So I will not cause the trouble to come to him during his life. I will wait until his son is king. Then I will bring this trouble to Ahab's family."

THE DEATH OF AHAB

22 For three years there was peace between Israel and Aram. ²During the third year Jehoshaphat king of Judah went to visit Ahab king of Israel.

³At this same time Ahab asked his officers, "Remember that the king of Aram took Ramoth in Gilead from us? Why have we done nothing to get it back?" ⁴So Ahab asked King Jehoshaphat, "Will you go with us? Will you fight against the army of Aram at Ramoth in Gilead?"

Jehoshaphat answered, "I will go with you. My soldiers and my horses are ready to join with your army. ⁵But first we should ask the Lord to guide us."

⁶So Ahab called the prophets[d] together. There were about 400 men. He asked them, "Should I go to war against the army of Aram at Ramoth in Gilead? Or should I wait?"

The prophets answered, "Go, because the Lord will let you defeat them."

⁷But Jehoshaphat asked, "Isn't there a prophet of the Lord here? Let's ask him what we should do."

⁸King Ahab answered, "There is one other prophet. We could ask the Lord through him. But I hate him. When he

prophesies, he never says anything good about me. He always says something bad. He is Micaiah, Imlah's son."

Jehoshaphat said, "King Ahab, you shouldn't say that!"

⁹So Ahab king of Israel told one of his officers to bring Micaiah to him at once.

¹⁰Ahab king of Israel and Jehoshaphat king of Judah had on their royal robes. They were sitting on their thrones at the threshing*d* floor. This was near the entrance to the gate of Samaria. All the prophets were standing before them, speaking messages from the Lord. ¹¹One of the prophets was Zedekiah son of Kenaanah. He had made some iron horns. He said to Ahab, "This is what the Lord says, 'You will use these horns to fight the Arameans. And you will destroy them.'"

¹²All the other prophets said the same thing. They said, "Attack Ramoth in Gilead and win. The Lord will let you defeat the Arameans."

¹³The messenger who had gone to get Micaiah found him. He said to Micaiah, "All the other prophets are saying the king will succeed. You should agree with them. Give the king a good answer."

¹⁴But Micaiah answered, "As surely as the Lord lives, I can tell him only what the Lord tells me."

¹⁵Then Micaiah came to Ahab. The king asked him, "Micaiah, should we attack Ramoth in Gilead or not?"

Micaiah answered, "Attack and win! The Lord will let you defeat them."

¹⁶But Ahab said to Micaiah, "Tell me only the truth in the name of the Lord. How many times do I have to tell you this?"

¹⁷So Micaiah answered, "I saw the army of Israel. They were scattered over the hills like sheep without a shepherd. The Lord said, 'They have no leader. They should go home and not fight.'"

¹⁸Then Ahab king of Israel said to Jehoshaphat, "I told you! This prophet never says anything good about me. He only says bad things about me."

¹⁹But Micaiah continued to speak. He said, "Hear the message from the Lord: I saw the Lord sitting on his throne. His heavenly army was standing near him on his right and on his left. ²⁰The Lord said, 'Who will trick Ahab into attacking Ramoth in Gilead? Do this so he will go and be killed.'

"The spirits did not agree about what they should do. ²¹Then one spirit came and stood before the Lord. He said, 'I will trick him.'

²²"The Lord asked, 'How will you trick Ahab?'

"The spirit answered, 'I will go to Ahab's prophets. I will make them tell lies.'

"So the Lord said, 'You will succeed in tricking him. Go and do it.'"

²³Micaiah said, "Ahab, this has now happened. The Lord has caused your prophets to lie to you. The Lord has decided that great trouble should come to you."

²⁴Then Zedekiah son of Kenaanah went up to Micaiah. And he hit Micaiah in the face. Zedekiah said, "Do you really believe the Lord's spirit has left me and is now speaking through you?"

²⁵Micaiah answered, "You will find out on the day you go to hide in an inside room."

²⁶Then Ahab king of Israel ordered, "Take Micaiah. Send him to Amon, the governor of the city, and to Joash, the king's son. ²⁷Tell them I said to put Micaiah in prison. Give him only bread and water for food. Keep him there until I come home from the battle."

²⁸Micaiah said, "Ahab, if you come back safely from battle, the Lord has not spoken through me. Remember my words, all you people."

²⁹So Ahab king of Israel and Jehoshaphat king of Judah went to Ramoth in Gilead. ³⁰Ahab said to Jehoshaphat, "I will go into battle. But I will change my appearance so that no one will recognize

me. But you wear your royal clothes." So Ahab changed his appearance and went into battle.

³¹The king of Aram had 32 chariot commanders. He ordered them, "Don't fight with anyone but the king of Israel. It doesn't matter if they are important or unimportant." ³²When these commanders saw Jehoshaphat, they thought he was the king of Israel. So they turned to attack him. But Jehoshaphat began shouting. ³³Then the commanders saw he was not Ahab. So they stopped chasing him. ³⁴A soldier shot an arrow without aiming at anyone. But he hit Ahab king of Israel. The arrow hit him in a place not covered by his armor. King Ahab said to his chariot driver, "Turn the chariot around. Take me out of the battle. I am hurt!" ³⁵The battle continued all day. King Ahab was in his chariot, leaning against it to hold himself up. He was facing the Arameans. His blood flowed down and covered the bottom of the chariot. That evening he died. ³⁶Near sunset a cry went out through the army of Israel: "Each man go back to his own country and city."

³⁷So in that way King Ahab died. His body was carried to Samaria and buried there. ³⁸The men cleaned Ahab's chariot at a pool in Samaria. This was a pool where prostitutes*ᵈ* bathed. And the dogs licked King Ahab's blood from the chariot. These things happened as the Lord had said they would.

³⁹Everything else Ahab did is written down. It is in the book of the history of the kings of Israel. That book also tells about the palace Ahab built and decorated with ivory. And it tells about the cities he built. ⁴⁰So Ahab died, and his son Ahaziah became king in his place.

JEHOSHAPHAT KING OF JUDAH

⁴¹Jehoshaphat son of Asa became king of Judah. This was during Ahab's fourth year as king over Israel. ⁴²Jehoshaphat was 35 years old when he became king. And he ruled in Jerusalem for 25 years. His mother was the daughter of Shilhi. She was named Azubah. ⁴³Jehoshaphat was good like his father before him. He did what the Lord said was right. But Jehoshaphat did not destroy the places where false gods were worshiped. So the people continued offering sacrifices and burning incense*ᵈ* there. ⁴⁴Jehoshaphat was at peace with the king of Israel. ⁴⁵Jehoshaphat fought many wars. These wars and his successes are written down. They are in the book of the history of the kings of Judah. ⁴⁶There were prostitutes*ᵈ* in the places where false gods were worshiped. Jehoshaphat's father, Asa, had not forced all of them out. But Jehoshaphat forced the rest of them to leave.

⁴⁷During this time the land of Edom had no king. It was ruled by a governor.

⁴⁸King Jehoshaphat built trading ships to sail to Ophir for gold. But the ships were destroyed at Ezion Geber. So they never set sail. ⁴⁹Ahaziah son of Ahab went to help Jehoshaphat. Ahaziah said he would give Jehoshaphat some men to sail with his men. But Jehoshaphat refused.

⁵⁰Jehoshaphat died and was buried with his ancestors. He was buried in Jerusalem, the city of David, his ancestor. And his son Jehoram became king.

AHAZIAH KING OF ISRAEL

⁵¹Ahaziah son of Ahab became king of Israel in Samaria. This was during Jehoshaphat's seventeenth year as king over Judah. Ahaziah ruled Israel for two years. ⁵²Ahaziah did what the Lord said was wrong. He did the same things his father Ahab, his mother Jezebel and Jeroboam son of Nebat had done. All these rulers led the people of Israel into more sin. ⁵³Ahaziah worshiped and served the god Baal.*ᵈ* So Ahaziah made the Lord, the God of Israel, very angry. In these ways Ahaziah did what his father had done.

KINGS

ELIJAH AND KING AHAZIAH

1 After Ahab died, Moab broke away from Israel's rule. ²Ahaziah fell down through the wooden bars in his upstairs room in Samaria. He was badly hurt. He sent messengers and told them, "Go. Ask Baal-Zebub god of Ekron if I will get well from my injuries."

³But the Lord's angel said to Elijah the Tishbite, "Get up. Go meet the messengers sent by the king of Samaria. Say to them, 'Why are you going to ask questions of Baal-Zebub god of Ekron? Is it because you think there is no God in Israel?' ⁴So this is what the Lord says: 'You will not get up from the bed you are lying on. You will die.'" Then Elijah left.

⁵The messengers came back to Ahaziah. He asked them, "Why have you come back?"

⁶They said, "A man came to meet us. He said, 'Go back to the king who sent you. Tell him what the Lord says: "Why do you send men to ask questions of Baal-Zebub god of Ekron? Is it because you think there is no God in Israel? This is why you will not get up from your bed. You will die."'"

⁷Ahaziah asked them, "What did the man look like who met you and told you this?"

⁸They answered, "He wore a hairy coat and a leather belt around his waist."

Ahaziah said, "It was Elijah the Tishbite."

⁹Then he sent a captain with his 50 men to Elijah. The captain went to Elijah, who was sitting on top of the hill. He said to Elijah, "Man of God, the king says, 'Come down!'"

¹⁰Elijah answered the captain, "I am a man of God. So let fire come down from heaven and burn up you and your 50 men." Then fire came down from heaven. It burned up the captain and his 50 men.

¹¹Ahaziah sent another captain and 50 men to Elijah. The captain said to him, "Man of God, this is what the king says: 'Come down quickly!'"

¹²Elijah answered, "I am a man of God. So let fire come down from heaven and burn up you and your 50 men!" Then fire came down from heaven. It burned up the captain and his 50 men.

¹³Ahaziah sent a third captain with his 50 men. The third captain came and fell down on his knees before Elijah. He begged Elijah, "Man of God, I ask you. Please let my life and the lives of your 50 servants be valuable to you! ¹⁴See, fire came down from heaven. It burned up the first two captains of 50 with all their men. But now, let my life be valuable to you."

¹⁵The Lord's angel said to Elijah, "Go with him. Don't be afraid of him." So Elijah got up and went with him to see the king.

¹⁶Elijah told Ahaziah, "This is what the Lord says: 'You have sent messengers to ask questions of Baal-Zebub god of Ekron. Is it because you think there is no God in Israel to ask? Because of this, you will not get up from your bed. You will die.'" ¹⁷So he died, just as the Lord, through Elijah, had said he would.

Joram became king in Ahaziah's place. This was during the second year Jehoram son of Jehoshaphat was king of Judah. Joram ruled because Ahaziah had no son to take his place. ¹⁸The other things Ahaziah did are written down. They are in the book of the history of the kings of Israel.

ELIJAH IS TAKEN TO HEAVEN

2 It was near the time for the Lord to take Elijah. He was going to take him by a whirlwind up into heaven. Elijah and Elisha were at Gilgal. ²Elijah said to Elisha, "Please stay here. The Lord has told me to go to Bethel."

But Elisha said, "As the Lord lives, and as you live, I won't leave you." So they went down to Bethel. [3]A group of the prophets[d] at Bethel came to Elisha. They said to him, "Do you know the Lord will take your master away from you today?"

Elisha said, "Yes, I know. But don't talk about it."

[4]Elijah said to him, "Stay here, because the Lord has sent me to Jericho."

But Elisha said, "As the Lord lives, and as you live, I won't leave you."

So they went to Jericho. [5]A group of the prophets at Jericho came to Elisha. They said, "Do you know that the Lord will take your master away from you today?"

Elisha answered, "Yes, I know. But don't talk about it."

[6]Elijah said to Elisha, "Stay here. The Lord has sent me to the Jordan River."

Elisha answered, "As the Lord lives, and as you live, I won't leave you."

So the two of them went on. [7]Fifty men from a group of the prophets came. They stood far from where Elijah and Elisha were by the Jordan. [8]Elijah took off his coat. Then he rolled it up and hit the water. The water divided to the right and to the left. Then Elijah and Elisha crossed over on dry ground.

[9]After they had crossed over, Elijah said to Elisha, "What can I do for you before I am taken from you?"

Elisha said, "Leave me a double share of your spirit."[n]

[10]Elijah said, "You have asked a hard thing. But if you see me when I am taken from you, it will be yours. If you don't, it won't happen."

[11]Elijah and Elisha were still walking and talking. Then a chariot and horses of fire appeared. The chariot and horses of fire separated Elijah from Elisha. Then Elijah went up to heaven in a whirlwind.

[12]Elisha saw it and shouted, "My father! My father! The chariots of Israel and their horsemen!" Elisha did not see him anymore. Elisha grabbed his own clothes and tore them to show how sad he was.

[13]He picked up Elijah's coat that had fallen from him. Then Elisha returned and stood on the bank of the Jordan. [14]Elisha hit the water with Elijah's coat. He said, "Where is the Lord, the God of Elijah?" When he hit the water, it divided to the right and to the left. Then Elisha crossed over.

[15]A group of the prophets at Jericho were watching. They said, "Elisha now has the spirit Elijah had." They came to meet him. And they bowed down to the ground before him. [16]They said to him, "There are 50 strong men with us! Please let them go and look for your master. Maybe the Spirit[d] of the Lord has taken Elijah up and set him down. He may be on some mountain or in some valley."

But Elisha answered, "No. Don't send them."

[17]The group of prophets begged Elisha until he hated to refuse them anymore. Then he said, "Send them." So they sent 50 men who looked for three days. But they could not find Elijah. [18]Then they came back to Elisha at Jericho where he was staying. He said to them, "I told you not to go, didn't I?"

ELISHA MAKES THE WATER PURE

[19]The men of the city said to Elisha, "Look, master, this city is a nice place to live. You can see that. But the water is bad. That's why the land cannot grow crops."

[20]Elisha said, "Bring me a new bowl and put salt in it." So they brought it to him. [21]Then Elisha went out to the spring of water and threw the salt in it. He said, "This is what the Lord says: 'I have healed this water. From now on it won't cause death. And it won't keep the land

---

2:9 **"Leave ... spirit."** By law, the first son in a family would inherit a double share of his father's possessions. Elisha is asking to inherit a share of his master's power. He is not asking for twice as much power as Elijah had.

from growing crops.'" ²²The water was healed. It is still good today. It happened just as Elisha had said.

YOUNG PEOPLE MAKE FUN OF ELISHA

²³From there Elisha went up to Bethel. On the way some young men came out of the city. They made fun of Elisha. They said to him, "Go up, you baldhead! Go up, you baldhead!" ²⁴Elisha turned around and looked at them. He put a curse on them in the name of the Lord. Then two female bears came out of the woods. They tore to pieces 42 of the young men. ²⁵Then Elisha left and went on to Mount Carmel. From there he went back to Samaria.

WAR BETWEEN ISRAEL AND MOAB

3 Joram son of Ahab became king over Israel at Samaria. He began to rule in Jehoshaphat's eighteenth year as king of Judah. Joram ruled 12 years. ²Joram did what the Lord said was wrong. But he was not like his father and mother. He removed the stone pillars his father had made for Baal.ᵈ ³But he continued to do the same sins Jeroboam son of Nebat had done. Jeroboam had caused the people of Israel to sin. And Joram did not stop doing these same sins.

⁴Mesha king of Moab raised sheep. He had to give 100,000 lambs and the wool of 100,000 male sheep to the king of Israel. ⁵But when Ahab died, the king of Moab turned against the king of Israel. ⁶So King Joram went out from Samaria and gathered all Israel. ⁷He sent messengers to Jehoshaphat king of Judah. He said, "The king of Moab has turned against me. Will you go with me against Moab in battle?"

Jehoshaphat said, "I will go with you. I am ready to join you. My soldiers and my horses are ready to join with your army."

⁸Jehoshaphat asked, "Which way should we go to attack?"

Joram answered, "Through the Desert of Edom."

⁹So the king of Israel went with the king of Judah and the king of Edom. They marched seven days. There was no more water for the army or for their animals that were with them. ¹⁰The king of Israel said, "How terrible this is! Has the Lord called us three kings together so the Moabites can defeat us?"

¹¹But Jehoshaphat asked, "Is there a prophetᵈ of the Lord here? We can ask the Lord through a prophet."

An officer of the king of Israel answered, "Elisha son of Shaphat is here. He was Elijah's servant."

¹²Jehoshaphat said, "He speaks the Lord's truth." So the king of Israel and Jehoshaphat and the king of Edom went down to see Elisha.

¹³Elisha spoke to the king of Israel. He said, "I have nothing to do with you! Go to the prophets of your father and to the prophets of your mother!"

The king of Israel said to Elisha, "No. The Lord has called us three kings together to let the Moabites defeat us."

¹⁴Elisha said, "I serve the Lord of heaven's armies. As surely as he lives, I tell you the truth. I wouldn't even look at you or notice you if Jehoshaphat king of Judah were not here. I respect him! ¹⁵Now bring me someone who plays the harp."

While the harp was being played, the Lord gave Elisha power. ¹⁶Then Elisha said, "The Lord says to dig holes in the valley. ¹⁷He says that you won't see wind or rain. But the valley will be filled with water. Then you, your cattle and other animals will drink. ¹⁸This is easy for the Lord to do. He will also let you defeat Moab. ¹⁹You will destroy every strong, walled city and every important town. You will cut down every good tree. You will stop up all springs of water. You will ruin every good field with rocks."

²⁰The next morning, about the time the sacrifice was offered, there was water! It came from the direction of Edom and filled the valley.

²¹All the Moabites had heard that the kings had come up to fight against them. They gathered everyone old enough to put on armor. And they waited at the border. ²²But when the Moabites got up early in the morning, the sun was shining on the water. They saw the water across from them. It looked as red as blood. ²³The Moabites said, "This is blood! Surely the kings have fought and killed each other! Come, Moabites, let's take what is valuable from the dead bodies!"

²⁴The Moabites came to the camp of the Israelites. But the Israelites came out and fought them until they ran away. The Israelites went on into the land to fight the Moabites. ²⁵They tore down the cities. They threw rocks on every good field and filled it. They stopped up all the springs of water. And they cut down all the good trees. Kir Hareseth was the only city with its stones still in place. But the men with slings surrounded Kir Hareseth and conquered it, too.

²⁶The king of Moab saw that the battle was too strong for him. So he took 700 men with swords to break through to the king of Edom. But they could not break through. ²⁷Then the king of Moab took his oldest son, who would have become king after him. And he offered his son as a burnt offering on the wall. So there was great anger against the Israelites. They left and went back to their own land.

A WIDOW ASKS ELISHA FOR HELP

4 The wife of a man from a group of the prophets*ᵈ* came to Elisha. She said, "Your servant, my husband, is dead! You know he honored the Lord. But now the man he owes money to is coming to take my two boys. He will make them his slaves!"

²Elisha answered, "How can I help you? Tell me, what do you have in your house?"

The woman said, "I don't have anything there except a pot of oil."

³Then Elisha said, "Go and get empty jars from all your neighbors. Don't ask for just a few. ⁴Then you must go into your house and close the door. Only you and your sons will be there. Then pour oil into all the jars. Set the full ones to one side."

⁵She left Elisha and shut the door. Only she and her sons were in the house. As they brought the jars to her, she poured the oil. ⁶When the jars were all full, she said to her son, "Bring me another jar."

But he said, "There are no more jars." Then the oil stopped flowing.

⁷She went and told Elisha. Elisha said to her, "Go. Sell the oil and pay what you owe. You and your sons can live on what is left."

THE SHUNAMMITE WOMAN

⁸One day Elisha went to Shunem. An important woman lived there. She begged Elisha to stay and eat. So every time Elisha passed by, he stopped there to eat. ⁹The woman said to her husband, "I know that Elisha is a holy man of God. He passes by our house all the time. ¹⁰Let's make a small room on the roof.*ⁿ* Let's put a bed in the room for Elisha. And we can put a table, a chair and a lampstand there. Then when he comes by, he can stay there."

¹¹One day Elisha came to the woman's house. He went to his room and rested. ¹²He said to his servant Gehazi, "Call the Shunammite."

When the servant called her, she stood in front of him. ¹³Elisha told his servant, "Now say to her, 'You have gone to all this trouble for us. What can I do for you? Do you want me to speak to the king or the commander of the army for you?'"

The woman answered, "I live among my own people."

4:10 roof In Bible times houses were built with flat roofs. The roof was used for drying things such as flax and fruit. And it was used as an extra room, as a place for worship and as a place to sleep in the summer.

¹⁴Elisha said, "But what can we do for her?"

Gehazi answered, "She has no son, and her husband is old."

¹⁵Then Elisha said, "Call her." So he called her, and she stood in the doorway. ¹⁶Then Elisha said, "About this time next year, you will hold a son in your arms."

The woman said, "No, master, man of God. Don't lie to me!"

¹⁷But the woman became pregnant. And she gave birth to a son at that time the next year as Elisha had told her.

¹⁸The child grew. One day he went out to his father, who was with the men harvesting grain. ¹⁹The boy said to his father, "My head! My head!"

The father said to his servant, "Carry him to his mother!" ²⁰The servant took him to his mother. He lay on his mother's lap until noon. Then he died. ²¹She took him up and laid him on Elisha's bed. Then she shut the door and went out.

²²She called to her husband. She said, "Send me one of the servants and one of the donkeys. Then I can go quickly to the man of God and come back."

²³The woman's husband said, "Why do you want to go to him today? It isn't the New Moon*d* or the Sabbath*d* day."

She said, "It will be all right."

²⁴Then she saddled the donkey and said to her servant, "Lead on. Don't slow down for me unless I tell you." ²⁵So she went to Elisha at Mount Carmel.

He saw her coming from far away. So he said to his servant Gehazi, "Look, there's the Shunammite woman! ²⁶Run to meet her! Say to her, 'Are you all right? Is your husband all right? Is the child all right?'"

She answered, "Everything is all right."

²⁷Then she came to Elisha at the hill. She caught hold of his feet. Gehazi came near to pull her away. But Elisha said to him, "Let her alone. She's very upset, and the Lord has not told me about it. He has hidden it from me."

²⁸She said, "Master, I didn't tell you I wanted a son. I told you, 'Don't fool me.'"

²⁹Then Elisha said to Gehazi, "Get ready. Take my walking stick in your hand and go quickly. If you meet anyone, don't greet him. If anyone greets you, don't answer him. Lay my walking stick on the face of the boy."

³⁰But the child's mother said, "As surely as the Lord lives and as you live, I won't leave you!" So he got up and followed her.

³¹Gehazi went on ahead. He laid the walking stick on the child's face. But the child did not talk or move. Then Gehazi went back to meet Elisha. He told Elisha, "The child has not awakened."

³²Elisha came into the house. There was the child, lying dead on his bed. ³³When Elisha entered the room, he shut the door. Only he and the child were in the room. Then Elisha prayed to the Lord. ³⁴He went to the bed and lay on the child. He put his mouth on the child's mouth. He put his eyes on the child's eyes and his hands on the child's hands. He stretched himself out on top of the child. Then the child's skin became warm. ³⁵Elisha turned away and walked around the room. Then he went back and put himself on the child again. Then the child sneezed seven times and opened his eyes.

³⁶Elisha called Gehazi and said, "Call the Shunammite!" And he did. When she came, Elisha said, "Pick up your son." ³⁷She came in and fell at Elisha's feet. She bowed facedown to the floor. Then she picked up her son and went out.

ELISHA AND THE POISON

³⁸Elisha came to Gilgal again. There was a time of hunger in the land. A group of prophets*d* was sitting in front of him. He said to his servant, "Put the

large pot on the fire. Boil some stew for these men."

³⁹One of them went out into the field to gather plants. He found a wild vine. He picked fruit from the vine and filled his robe with it. Then he came and cut up the fruit into the pot. But they did not know what kind of fruit it was. ⁴⁰Then they poured out the stew for the men to eat. But when they began to eat it, they shouted out, "Man of God! There's death in the pot!" They could not eat it.

⁴¹Elisha told them to bring some flour. Then he threw it into the pot. He said, "Pour it out for the people to eat." And there was nothing harmful in the pot.

ELISHA MULTIPLIES BREAD

⁴²A man from Baal Shalishah came to Elisha. He brought 20 loaves of barley bread from the first harvest to Elisha. He also brought fresh grain in his sack. Then Elisha said, "Give it to the people to eat."

⁴³Elisha's servant said, "How can I feed 100 men with so little?"

But Elisha said, "Give the bread to the people to eat. This is what the Lord says: 'They will eat and will have food left over.'" ⁴⁴Then he gave it to them. The people ate and had food left over, as the Lord had said.

NAAMAN IS HEALED

5 Naaman was commander of the army of the king of Aram. He was a great man to his master. He had much honor because the Lord had used him to give victory to Aram. He was a mighty and brave man. But he had a harmful skin disease.

²The Arameans had gone out to steal from the Israelites. And they had taken a little girl as a captive from Israel. This little girl served Naaman's wife. ³She said to her mistress, "I wish that my master would meet the prophet^d who lives in Samaria. He would heal Naaman of his disease."

⁴Naaman went to the king. He told him what the girl from Israel had said. ⁵The king of Aram said, "Go now. And I will send a letter to the king of Israel." So Naaman left and took about 750 pounds of silver. He also took about 150 pounds of gold and ten changes of clothes with him. ⁶He brought the letter to the king of Israel. It read, "I am sending my servant Naaman to you. I'm sending him so you can heal him of his skin disease."

⁷The king of Israel read the letter. Then he tore his clothes to show how upset he was. He said, "I'm not God! I can't kill and make alive again! Why does this man send someone with a harmful skin disease for me to heal? You can see that the king of Aram is trying to start trouble with me!"

⁸Elisha, the man of God, heard that the king of Israel had torn his clothes. So he sent a message to the king. It said, "Why have you become so upset that you tore your clothes? Let Naaman come to me. Then he will know there is a prophet in Israel!" ⁹So Naaman went with his horses and chariots to Elisha's house. And he stood outside the door.

¹⁰Elisha sent a messenger to Naaman. The messenger said, "Go and wash in the Jordan River seven times. Then your skin will be healed, and you will be clean."

¹¹Naaman became angry and left. He said, "I thought Elisha would surely come out and stand before me. I thought he would call on the name of the Lord his God. I thought he would wave his hand over the place and heal the disease! ¹²Abana and Pharpar, the rivers of Damascus, are better than all the waters of Israel! Why can't I wash in them and become clean?" So Naaman went away very angry.

¹³But Naaman's servants came near and talked to him. They said, "My father, if the prophet had told you to do some great thing, wouldn't you have done it? Doesn't it make more sense just to do it?

After all, he only told you, 'Wash, and you will be clean.'" [14]So Naaman went down and dipped in the Jordan seven times. He did just as Elisha had said. Then Naaman's skin became new again. It was like the skin of a little boy. And Naaman was clean!

[15]Naaman and all his group came back to Elisha. He stood before Elisha and said, "Look. I now know there is no God in all the earth except in Israel! Now please accept a gift from me."

[16]But Elisha said, "I serve the Lord. As surely as the Lord lives, I won't accept anything." Naaman urged him to take the gift, but he refused.

[17]Then Naaman said, "If you won't take the gift, then please give me some dirt. Give me as much as two of my mules can carry. From now on I'll not offer any burnt offering or sacrifice to any other gods. I'll only offer sacrifices to the Lord. [18]But let the Lord pardon me for this: My master goes into the temple of Rimmon[n] to worship. When he goes, he will lean on my arm. Then I must bow in that temple. May the Lord pardon me when I do that."

[19]Elisha said to him, "Go in peace."

Naaman left Elisha and went a short way. [20]Gehazi was the servant of Elisha the man of God. Gehazi thought, "My master has not accepted what Naaman the Aramean brought. As surely as the Lord lives, I'll run after him. I'll get something from him." [21]So he went after him.

Naaman saw someone running after him. So he got off the chariot to meet Gehazi. He said, "Is everything all right?"

[22]Gehazi said, "Everything is all right. My master has sent me. He said, 'Two young men just came to me. They are from the group of the prophets in the mountains of Ephraim. Please give them 75 pounds of silver and two changes of clothes.'"

[23]Naaman said, "Please take 150 pounds." He urged Gehazi to take it. He tied 150 pounds of silver in two bags with two changes of clothes. Then he gave them to two of his servants. They carried them for Gehazi. [24]When they came to the hill, Gehazi took these things from Naaman's servants. And he put them in the house. He let Naaman's servants go, and they left.

[25]Then he came in and stood before his master. Elisha said to him, "Where have you been, Gehazi?"

Gehazi said, "I didn't go anywhere."

[26]But Elisha said to him, "My spirit was with you. I knew when the man turned from his chariot to meet you. This isn't a time to receive money, clothes, olives and grapes. It isn't a time to receive sheep, oxen, male servants and female servants. [27]Naaman's skin disease will come on you and your children forever." When Gehazi left Elisha, he had the disease. He was as white as snow.

AN AXHEAD FLOATS

6 The group of the prophets[d] said to Elisha, "The place where we meet with you is too small for us. [2]Let's go to the Jordan River. There every man can get a pole. And let's build a place there to live."

Elisha said, "Go."

[3]One of them said, "Please go with us."

Elisha said, "I will go." [4]So he went with them. When they arrived at the Jordan, they cut down some trees. [5]As one man was cutting down a tree, the head of his ax fell into the water. He yelled, "Oh, my master! I borrowed that ax!"

[6]Elisha asked, "Where did it fall?" The man showed Elisha the place. Then Elisha cut down a stick and threw it into the water. It made the iron head float. [7]Elisha said, "Pick up the axhead." Then the man reached out and took it.

5:18 temple of Rimmon The place where the Aramean people worshiped the false god Rimmon.

ELISHA AND THE BLINDED ARAMEANS

[8]The king of Aram was at war with Israel. He had a council meeting with his officers. He said, "I will set up my camp in this place."

[9]But Elisha sent a message to the king of Israel. It said, "Be careful! Don't pass that place. The Arameans are going down there!"

[10]The king of Israel checked the place about which Elisha had warned him. Elisha warned him several times. So the king added guards in those places.

[11]The king of Aram was angry about this. He called his officers together. He said to them, "Tell me who of us is working for the king of Israel."

[12]One of the officers of the king of Aram said, "No, my master and king. It's Elisha, the prophet[d] from Israel. He can tell you what you speak in your bedroom."

[13]The king said, "Go and find him. Then I can send men and catch him."

The servants came back and reported, "He is in Dothan."

[14]Then the king sent horses, chariots and a large army to Dothan. They arrived at night and surrounded the city.

[15]The servant of Elisha got up early. When he went out, he saw an army with horses and chariots all around the city. The servant said to Elisha, "Oh, my master, what can we do?"

[16]Elisha said, "Don't be afraid. The army that fights for us is larger than the one against us."

[17]Then Elisha prayed, "Lord, open my servant's eyes. Let him see."

The Lord opened the eyes of the young man. And he saw that the mountain was full of horses and chariots of fire all around Elisha.

[18]As the enemy came down toward Elisha, he prayed to the Lord. He said, "Make these people blind." So the Lord made the Aramean army blind, as Elisha had asked.

[19]Elisha said to them, "This is not the right road. This is not the right city. Follow me. I'll take you to the man you are looking for." Then Elisha led them to Samaria.

[20]After they entered Samaria, Elisha said, "Lord, open these men's eyes so they can see." So the Lord opened their eyes. And the Aramean army saw that they were inside the city of Samaria!

[21]The king of Israel saw the Aramean army. He said to Elisha, "My father, should I kill them? Should I kill them?"

[22]Elisha answered, "Don't kill them. You wouldn't kill people whom you captured with your sword and bow. Give them food and water. And let them eat and drink. Then let them go home to their master." [23]So he prepared a great feast for the Aramean army. They ate and drank. Then the king sent them away. They went home to their master. The soldiers of Aram did not come anymore into the land of Israel.

A TIME OF HUNGER

[24]Later, Ben-Hadad king of Aram gathered all his army. He went to surround and attack Samaria. [25]There was a time of terrible hunger in Samaria. It was so bad that a donkey's head was sold for about two pounds of silver. Half of a pint of dove's dung sold for about two ounces of silver.

[26]The king of Israel was passing by on the wall. A woman yelled out to him, "Help me, my master and king!"

[27]The king said, "If the Lord doesn't help you, how can I? Can I get help from the threshing[d] floor or from the winepress?"[d] [28]Then the king said to her, "What is your trouble?"

She answered, "This woman said to me, 'Give up your son so we can eat him today. Then we will eat my son tomorrow.' [29]So we boiled my son and ate him. Then the next day I said to her, 'Give up your son so we can eat him.' But she had hidden him."

³⁰When the king heard the woman's words, he tore his clothes to show how upset he was. He walked along the wall. The people looked and saw he had on rough cloth under his clothes. This was to show his sadness. ³¹He said, "The head of Elisha son of Shaphat will be taken from his body today! May God punish me terribly if this doesn't happen!"

³²The king sent a messenger to Elisha. Elisha was sitting in his house. And the elders were sitting with him. But before the messenger arrived, Elisha spoke to them. He said, "See, this murderer is sending men to take off my head. When the messenger arrives, shut the door. Hold it and don't let him in. The sound of his master's feet is behind him."

³³While Elisha was still talking with the leaders, the king came. He said, "This trouble has come from the Lord. Why should I wait for the Lord any longer?"

7 Elisha said, "Listen to the Lord's word. This is what he says: 'About this time tomorrow 7 quarts of fine flour will be sold for two-fifths of an ounce of silver. And 13 quarts of barley will be sold for two-fifths of an ounce of silver. This will happen at the gate of Samaria.'"

²Then the officer who was close to the king answered Elisha. He said, "Even if the Lord opened windows in heaven, that couldn't happen."

Elisha said, "Because you have said that, you will see it with your eyes. But you will not eat any of it."

³There were four men with a harmful skin disease at the entrance to the city gate. They said to each other, "Why do we sit here until we die? ⁴A time of hunger is in the city. So if we go into the city, we will die there. If we stay here, we will die. So let's go to the Aramean camp. If they let us live, we will live. If they kill us, then we die."

⁵So they got up at twilight. And they went to the Aramean camp. But when they arrived, no one was there. ⁶The Lord had caused the Aramean army to hear the sound of chariots, horses and a large army. They had said to each other, "The king of Israel has hired the Hittite and Egyptian kings to attack us!" ⁷So they ran away in the twilight. They left their tents, horses and donkeys. They left the camp standing and ran for their lives.

⁸The men with the skin disease came to the edge of the camp. Then they went into one of the tents. They ate and drank. They carried silver, gold and clothes out of the camp and hid them. Then they came back and entered another tent. They carried things from this tent and hid them, also. ⁹Then they said to each other, "We're doing wrong. Today we have good news, but we are silent. If we wait until the sun comes up, we'll be punished. Let's go now and tell the people in the king's palace."

¹⁰So they went and called to the gatekeepers of the city. They said, "We went to the Aramean camp. But no one is there. We didn't hear anyone. The horses and donkeys were still tied up, and the tents were still standing." ¹¹Then the gatekeepers shouted out and told the people in the palace.

¹²So the king got up in the night. He said to his officers, "I'll tell you what the Arameans are doing to us. They know we are hungry. They have gone out of the camp to hide in the field. They're saying, 'When the Israelites come out of the city, we'll capture them alive. Then we'll enter the city.'"

¹³One of his officers answered, "Let some men take five horses still left in the city. These men are like all the Israelites who are left. They are also about to die. Let's send them to see what has happened."

¹⁴So the men took two chariots with horses. The king sent them after the Aramean army. He told them, "Go and see what has happened." ¹⁵The men followed the Aramean army as

far as the Jordan River. The road was full of clothes and equipment. The Arameans had thrown these things away as they had hurried away. So the messengers came back and told the king. [16]Then the people went out and took valuable things from the Aramean camp. So 7 quarts of fine flour were sold for two-fifths of an ounce of silver. And 13 quarts of barley were sold for two-fifths of an ounce of silver. It happened just as the Lord had said.

[17]The king chose the officer who was close to him to guard the gate. But the people ran over the officer so that he died. This happened just as the man of God had told the king. Elisha had said it when the king came to his house. [18]He had said, "Thirteen quarts of barley and 7 quarts of fine flour will each sell for two-fifths of an ounce of silver. It will happen about this time tomorrow at the gate of Samaria."

[19]But the officer had answered, "Even if the Lord opened windows in heaven, that couldn't happen." And Elisha had told him, "Because you have said that, you will see it with your eyes. But you won't eat any of it." [20]It happened to the officer just that way. The people ran over him in the gate, and he died.

THE SHUNAMMITE REGAINS HER LAND

8 Elisha talked to the woman whose son he had brought back to life. He said, "Get up and go with your family. Stay any place you can. This is because the Lord has called for a time of hunger. It will last seven years." [2]So the woman got up and did as the man of God said. She left with her family. And they stayed in the land of the Philistines for seven years. [3]After seven years she came back from the land of the Philistines. She went to beg the king for her house and land back. [4]The king was talking with Gehazi. He was the servant of the man of God. The king had said to Gehazi, "Please

tell me all the great things Elisha has done." [5]Now Gehazi was telling the king how Elisha had brought a dead person back to life. Just then the woman whose son Elisha had brought back to life came and begged the king for her house and land.

Gehazi said, "My master and king, this is the woman. And this is the son Elisha brought back to life."

[6]The king asked the woman, and she told him about it. Then the king chose an officer to help her. The king said, "Give the woman everything that is hers. Give her all the money made from her land from the day she left until now."

BEN-HADAD IS KILLED

[7]Elisha went to Damascus. Now Ben-Hadad king of Aram was sick. Someone told him, "The man of God has come here."

[8]Then the king said to Hazael, "Take a gift in your hand and go meet him. Ask the Lord through him if I will get well from my sickness."

[9]So Hazael went to meet Elisha. He took with him a gift. It was 40 camels loaded with every good thing in Damascus. He came and stood before Elisha. Hazael said, "Your son Ben-Hadad king of Aram sent me to you. He asks if he will get well from his sickness."

[10]Then Elisha said to Hazael, "Go and tell Ben-Hadad, 'You will surely get well.' But the Lord has told me he will really die." [11]Elisha stared at Hazael until Hazael felt ashamed. Then Elisha cried.

[12]Hazael asked, "Why are you crying, master?"

Elisha answered, "Because I know what evil you will do to the Israelites. You will burn their strong, walled cities with fire. You will kill their young men with swords. You will throw their babies to the ground. You will split open their pregnant women."

[13]Hazael said, "I, your servant, am only a dog. How could I do such things?"

Elisha answered, "The Lord has shown me that you will be king over Aram."

¹⁴Then Hazael left Elisha and came to his master. Ben-Hadad said to Hazael, "What did Elisha say to you?"

Hazael answered, "He told me that you will surely get well." ¹⁵But the next day Hazael took a blanket and dipped it in water. Then he put it over Ben-Hadad's face, and he died. So Hazael became king in Ben-Hadad's place.

JEHORAM KING OF JUDAH

¹⁶Jehoram son of Jehoshaphat became king of Judah. This was during Joram's fifth year as king of Israel. Joram was the son of Ahab. ¹⁷Jehoram was 32 years old when he began to rule. He ruled eight years in Jerusalem. ¹⁸But Jehoram followed the ways of the kings of Israel. This was just as the family of Ahab had done. It was because Ahab's daughter was Jehoram's wife. Jehoram did what the Lord said was wrong. ¹⁹But the Lord would not destroy Judah because of his servant David. The Lord had promised that David and his children would always have a kingdom.

²⁰In Jehoram's time Edom broke away from Judah's rule. The people of Edom chose their own king. ²¹So Jehoram and all his chariots went to Zair. At night the Edomites came around him and his chariot commanders. Jehoram got up and attacked the Edomites. But his army ran away to their tents. ²²So the Edomites broke away from the rule of Judah. And they are still separate today. At the same time Libnah also broke away from Judah's rule.

²³The other acts of Jehoram and all the things he did are written down. They are in the book of the history of the kings of Judah. ²⁴Jehoram died and was buried with his ancestors in Jerusalem. Jehoram's son Ahaziah ruled in his place.

²⁵Ahaziah son of Jehoram became king of Judah. This was during Joram's twelfth year as king of Israel. Joram was the son of Ahab. ²⁶Ahaziah was 22 years old when he became king. He ruled one year in Jerusalem. His mother's name was Athaliah. She was a granddaughter of Omri king of Israel. ²⁷Ahaziah followed the ways of Ahab's family. He did what the Lord said was wrong, as Ahab's family had done. He did this because he was a son-in-law in Ahab's family.

²⁸Ahaziah went with Joram son of Ahab to Ramoth in Gilead. There they fought against Hazael king of Aram. The Arameans wounded Joram. ²⁹So King Joram returned to Jezreel to heal from the injuries. (He had been wounded by the Arameans at Ramoth. This was when he fought Hazael king of Aram.) And Ahaziah son of Jehoram king of Judah went down to see Joram. He went to see Joram son of Ahab at Jezreel because he had been wounded.

JEHU IS CHOSEN KING

9 Elisha called a man from the group of the prophets.*ᵈ* Elisha said, "Tighten your clothes around you. And take this small bottle of olive oil in your hand. Go to Ramoth in Gilead. ²When you arrive, find Jehu son of Jehoshaphat. Jehoshaphat is the son of Nimshi. Go in and make Jehu get up from among his brothers. Take him to an inner room. ³Take the bottle and pour the oil on Jehu's head. Say, 'This is what the Lord says: I have appointed you king over Israel.' Then open the door and run away. Don't wait!"

⁴So the young man, the prophet, went to Ramoth in Gilead. ⁵When he arrived, he saw the officers of the army sitting together. He said, "Commander, I have a message for you."

Jehu asked, "For which one of us?"

The young man said, "For you, commander."

⁶Jehu got up and went into the house. Then the young prophet poured the olive oil on Jehu's head. He said to Jehu, "This is what the Lord of Israel says: 'I

have appointed you king over the Lord's people, Israel. [7]You must destroy the family of Ahab your master. I will punish Jezebel for the deaths of my servants the prophets. And I will punish her for all the Lord's servants who were murdered. [8]So all Ahab's family will die. I will not let any male child in Ahab's family live in Israel. It does not matter if he is a slave or a free person. [9]I will make Ahab's family like the family of Jeroboam son of Nebat. They will be like the family of Baasha son of Ahijah. [10]The dogs will eat Jezebel in the portion of land at Jezreel. And no one will bury her.'"

Then the young prophet opened the door and ran away.

[11]Jehu went back to his master's officers. One of them said to Jehu, "Is everything all right? Why did this crazy man come to you?"

Jehu answered, "You know the man and how he talks."

[12]They answered, "That's not true! Tell us."

Jehu said, "He said, 'This is what the Lord says: I have appointed you to be king over Israel.'"

[13]Then the officers hurried. Each man took off his own coat. They put them on the stairs for Jehu. Then they blew the trumpet. They said, "Jehu is king!"

JORAM AND AHAZIAH ARE KILLED

[14]So Jehu son of Jehoshaphat made plans against Joram. (Jehoshaphat was the son of Nimshi.) Now Joram and all Israel had been defending Ramoth in Gilead from Hazael king of Aram. [15]But King Joram had to return to Israel to heal from the injuries the Arameans had given him. He received these injuries when he fought against Hazael king of Aram.

Jehu said, "If you agree with this, don't let anyone leave the city. They might tell the news in Jezreel." [16]Then he got into his chariot and set out for Jezreel. Joram was resting there. And

Ahaziah king of Judah had gone down to see him.

[17]The lookout was standing on the watchtower in Jezreel. He saw Jehu's troops coming. He said, "I see some soldiers!"

Joram said, "Take a horseman and send him to meet them. Tell him to ask, 'Do you bring good news?'"

[18]So the horseman rode out to meet Jehu. The horseman said, "This is what the king says: 'Do you bring good news?'"

Jehu said, "That's none of your business! Come along behind me."

The lookout reported, "The messenger reached them. But he is not coming back."

[19]So Joram sent out a second horseman. This rider came to Jehu's group and said, "This is what the king says: 'Do you bring good news?'"

Jehu answered, "That's none of your business! Come along behind me."

[20]The lookout reported, "The second man reached them. But he is not coming back. The man in the chariot is driving like Jehu son of Nimshi. He drives as if he were crazy!"

[21]Joram said, "Get my chariot ready." Then the servant got Joram's chariot ready. Joram and Ahaziah king of Judah went out. Each king went in his own chariot to meet Jehu. And they met him at the property of Naboth the Jezreelite.

[22]When Joram saw Jehu, he said, "Do you bring good news, Jehu?"

Jehu answered, "There will never be any good news as long as your mother Jezebel worships idols and uses witchcraft."[d]

[23]Joram turned the horses to run away. He yelled to Ahaziah, "It's a trick, Ahaziah!"

[24]Then Jehu drew his bow and shot Joram between his shoulders. The arrow went through Joram's heart. And he fell down in his chariot.

[25]Jehu ordered Bidkar, his chariot officer, "Pick up Joram's body. Throw it into the field of Naboth the Jezreelite.

Remember when you and I rode together with Joram's father Ahab. The Lord made this prophecy[d] against him: [26]"Yesterday I saw the blood of Naboth and his sons, says the Lord. So I will punish Ahab in his field, says the Lord.' So take Joram's body and throw it into the field, as the Lord has said."

[27]When Ahaziah king of Judah saw this, he ran away toward Beth Haggan. Jehu chased him, saying, "Shoot Ahaziah, too!" Ahaziah was wounded in his chariot on the way up to Gur near Ibleam. Ahaziah got as far as Megiddo but died there. [28]His servants carried his body in a chariot to Jerusalem. They buried him with his ancestors in his tomb in Jerusalem. [29](Ahaziah had become king over Judah in Joram's eleventh year as king. Joram was the son of Ahab.)

DEATH OF JEZEBEL

[30]When Jehu came to Jezreel, Jezebel heard about it. She put paint on her eyes and fixed her hair. Then she looked out the window. [31]Jehu entered the city gate. And Jezebel said, "Have you come in peace, you Zimri,[n] you who killed your master?"

[32]Jehu looked up at the window. He said, "Who is on my side? Who?" Two or three eunuchs[d] looked out from the window at Jehu. [33]Jehu said to them, "Throw her down!" So they threw Jezebel down. And the horses ran over her body. Some of her blood splashed on the wall and on the horses.

[34]Jehu went into the house and ate and drank. Then he said, "Now see about this cursed woman. Bury her, because she is a king's daughter."

[35]The men went to bury Jezebel. But they could not find her body. They could only find the skull, feet and palms of her hands. [36]So they came back and told Jehu. Then Jehu said, "The Lord said this through his servant Elijah the Tishbite:

'The dogs will eat the body of Jezebel in the portion of land at Jezreel. [37]Her body will be like manure on the field in the land at Jezreel. Then people cannot say that the body is Jezebel.'"

FAMILIES OF AHAB AND AHAZIAH KILLED

10 Ahab's family had 70 sons in Samaria. Jehu wrote letters and sent them to Samaria. He sent them to the officers and elders of Jezreel. He also sent them to the guardians of the sons of Ahab. Jehu said, [2]"You have chariots, horses and a city with strong walls. You also have weapons. When you get this letter, [3]choose the best and most worthy person among your master's sons. Make him king. Then fight for your master's family."

[4]But the officers and older leaders of Jezreel were very frightened. They said, "The two kings could not stop Jehu. So, surely we can't either."

[5]The palace manager, the city governor, the older leaders and the guardians sent a message to Jehu. They said, "We are your servants. We will do everything you tell us to do. We won't make any man king. Do whatever you think is best."

[6]Then Jehu wrote a second letter. It said, "If you are on my side and will obey me, cut off the heads of your master's sons. And come to me at Jezreel tomorrow about this time."

Now there were 70 sons of the king's family. They were with the leading men of the city who were their guardians. [7]The leaders received the letter. Then they took the king's sons and killed all 70 of them. They put their heads in baskets. And they sent them to Jehu at Jezreel. [8]The messenger came to Jehu. He told Jehu, "They have brought the heads of the king's sons!"

Then Jehu said, "Lay the heads in two piles at the city gate until morning."

9:31 Zimri He was the man who killed Elah and the family of Baasha. Read 1 Kings 16:8-12.

⁹In the morning, Jehu went out and stood before the people. He said to them, "You are innocent. Look, I made plans against my master. I killed him. But who killed all these? ¹⁰You should know that nothing the Lord said will fail. Everything the Lord said about Ahab's family will come true. The Lord has spoken through his servant Elijah. And the Lord has done what he said." ¹¹So Jehu killed everyone of Ahab's family in Jezreel who was still alive. He also killed all Ahab's leading men, close friends and priests. No one was left alive who had helped Ahab.

¹²Then Jehu left and went to Samaria. He went on the road to Beth Eked of the Shepherds. ¹³There Jehu met some relatives of Ahaziah king of Judah. Jehu said, "Who are you?"

They answered, "We are relatives of Ahaziah. We have come down to visit the families of the king and the king's mother."

¹⁴Then Jehu said, "Take them alive!" So they captured Ahaziah's relatives alive. But they killed them at the well near Beth Eked. There were 42 of them. Jehu did not leave anyone alive.

¹⁵After Jehu left there, he met Jehonadab son of Recab. He was also on his way to meet Jehu. Jehu greeted him and said, "Are you as good a friend to me as I am to you?"

Jehonadab answered, "Yes, I am."

Jehu said, "If you are, then give me your hand." So Jehonadab gave him his hand, and Jehu pulled him into the chariot. ¹⁶Jehu said, "Come with me. You can see how strong my feelings are for the Lord." So Jehu had Jehonadab ride in his chariot.

¹⁷When Jehu came to Samaria, he killed all of Ahab's family. He did this until he had destroyed all of those who were left. Jehu did what the Lord had told Elijah would happen.

BAAL WORSHIPERS KILLED

¹⁸Then Jehu gathered all the people together. He said to them, "Ahab served Baal[d] a little. But Jehu will serve Baal much. ¹⁹Now call for me all Baal's prophets and priests. Call all the people who worship Baal. Don't let anyone miss this meeting. I have a great sacrifice for Baal. Anyone who is not there will not remain alive." But Jehu was tricking them so he could destroy the worshipers of Baal. ²⁰He said, "Prepare a holy meeting for Baal." So they announced the meeting. ²¹Then Jehu sent word through all Israel. All the worshipers of Baal came. Not one stayed home. They came into the temple of Baal. The temple was filled from one side to the other.

²²Jehu spoke to the man who kept the robes. He said, "Bring out robes for all the worshipers of Baal." So he brought out robes for them. ²³Then Jehu and Jehonadab son of Recab went into the temple of Baal. Jehu said to the worshipers of Baal, "Look around. Be sure there are no servants of the Lord with you. Be sure there are only people here who worship Baal." ²⁴So the worshipers of Baal went in to offer sacrifices and burnt offerings.

But Jehu had 80 men waiting outside. He told them, "Don't let anyone escape. If you let anyone escape, you must pay with your own life."

²⁵Jehu finished offering the burnt offering. Then he spoke to the guards and the captains. He said, "Go in and kill the worshipers of Baal! Don't let anyone come out." So the guards and captains killed the worshipers of Baal with the sword. They threw the bodies of the worshipers of Baal out. Then they went to the inner rooms of the temple. ²⁶They brought out the pillars of the temple of Baal and burned them. ²⁷Then they tore down the stone pillar of Baal. They also tore down the temple of Baal. They made it into a sewage pit, and it is still one today.

²⁸So Jehu destroyed Baal worship in Israel. ²⁹But he did not stop doing the

sins Jeroboam son of Nebat had done. Jeroboam had caused Israel to sin. They worshiped the golden calves in Bethel and Dan.

³⁰The Lord said to Jehu, "You have done well. You have done what I said was right. You have done to the family of Ahab as I wanted. Your descendants*d* as far as your great-great-grandchildren will be kings of Israel." ³¹But Jehu was not careful to keep the teachings of the Lord with all his heart. He did not stop doing the same sins Jeroboam had done. Jeroboam had caused Israel to sin.

³²At that time the Lord began to make Israel smaller. Hazael defeated the Israelites in all the land of Israel. ³³He took all the land on the east side of the Jordan. This was the land of Gilead. (It was the region of Gad, Reuben and Manasseh.) He took land from Aroer by the Arnon Ravine through Gilead to Bashan.

³⁴The other things Jehu did are written down. Everything he did and all his victories are recorded. They are in the book of the history of the kings of Israel. ³⁵Jehu died and was buried in Samaria. Jehu's son Jehoahaz became king in his place. ³⁶Jehu was king over Israel in Samaria for 28 years.

ATHALIAH AND JOASH

11 Now Ahaziah's mother, Athaliah, saw that her son was dead. Then she killed all the royal family. ²But Jehosheba took Joash, Ahaziah's son. She stole him from among the other sons of the king who were about to be murdered. (Jehosheba was King Jehoram's daughter and Ahaziah's sister.) She put Joash and his nurse in a bedroom. She hid Joash from Athaliah. So he was not killed. ³He was hidden with her in the Temple*d* of the Lord for six years. During that time Athaliah ruled the land.

⁴In the seventh year Jehoiada sent for the commanders of groups of 100 men. He sent for guards and the Carites, the royal bodyguards. He brought them together in the Temple of the Lord. Then he made an agreement with them. There, in the Temple of the Lord, he made them promise loyalty. Then he showed them the king's son. ⁵He commanded them, "This is what you must do. A third of you who come in on the Sabbath*d* will guard the king's palace. ⁶Another third of you will be at the Sur Gate. And another third will be at the gate behind the guard. This way you will guard the Temple. ⁷Two groups will go off duty on the Sabbath. They must protect the Temple of the Lord for the king. ⁸All of you must stand around the king. Each man must have his weapon in his hand. If anyone comes near, kill him. Stay close to the king when he goes out and when he comes in."

⁹The commanders over 100 men obeyed everything Jehoiada the priest had commanded. Each one took his men who were beginning their Sabbath duty. Each one also took those who were ending their Sabbath duty. Both groups came to Jehoiada the priest. ¹⁰And he gave spears and shields to the commanders. They used to belong to King David. They were kept in the Temple of the Lord.

JOASH BECOMES KING

¹¹Then each of the guards took his place. Each man had his weapon in his hand. There were guards from the south side of the Temple*d* to the north side. They stood by the altar and the Temple and around the king. ¹²Jehoiada brought out the king's son. He put the crown on Joash. Then he gave Joash a copy of the Agreement with the Lord. They appointed him king and poured olive oil on him. They clapped their hands and said, "Long live the king!"

¹³Athaliah heard the noise of the guards and the people. So she came to the people at the Temple of the Lord. ¹⁴She looked, and there was the king. He was standing by the pillar, as the custom

was. The officers and trumpeters were standing beside him. All the people of the land were very happy and were blowing trumpets. Then Athaliah tore her clothes to show how upset she was. She screamed, "Traitors! Traitors!"

15Jehoiada the priest gave orders to the commanders of 100 men who led the army. He said, "Surround her with soldiers. Kill with a sword anyone who follows her." He said this because he had said, "Don't put Athaliah to death in the Temple of the Lord." 16So they caught her when she came to where the horses enter the palace grounds. There she was put to death.

17Then Jehoiada made an agreement. It was between the Lord and the king and the people. They agreed to be the Lord's special people. He also made an agreement between the king and the people. 18All the people of the land went to the temple of Baal*d* and tore it down. They smashed the altars and idols into small pieces. And they killed Mattan, the priest of Baal, in front of the altars.

Then Jehoiada the priest placed guards at the Temple of the Lord. 19He took with him the commanders of 100 men and the Carites, the royal bodyguards. He took the guards and all the people of the land. Together they took the king out of the Temple of the Lord. They went into the palace through the gate of the guards. Then the king sat on the royal throne. 20So all the people of Judah were very happy. And Jerusalem had peace because Athaliah had been put to death with the sword at the palace.

21Joash was seven years old when he became king.

12 Joash became king of Judah in Jehu's seventh year as king of Israel. Joash ruled for 40 years in Jerusalem. His mother's name was Zibiah. She was from Beersheba. 2Joash did what the Lord said was right all the time Jehoiada the priest taught him. 3But the places where false gods were worshiped were not removed. The people still made sacrifices and burned incense*d* there.

THE TEMPLE TO BE REPAIRED

4Joash said to the priests, "Take all the money brought as offerings to the Temple*d* of the Lord. This includes the money each person owes in taxes. It also includes the money each person promises or brings to the Lord because he wants to. 5Each priest must take the money from the people he serves. Then the priests must repair any damage they find in the Temple."

6But by the twenty-third year of Joash the priests still had not repaired the Temple. 7So King Joash called for Jehoiada the priest and the other priests. He said to them, "Why are you not repairing the damage of the Temple? Don't take any more money from the people you serve. But hand over the money for the repair of the Temple." 8The priests agreed not to take any more money from the people. And they agreed not to repair the Temple themselves.

9But Jehoiada the priest took a box and made a hole in the top of it. Then he put it by the altar. It was on the right side as the people came into the Temple of the Lord. The priests guarding the doorway put all the money brought to the Temple of the Lord into the box.

10Each time the priests saw that the box was full of money, the king's royal assistant and the high priest came. They counted the money that had been brought to the Temple of the Lord. Then they put it into bags. 11Next they weighed the money. They gave it to the men who were in charge of the work on the Temple. With it they paid the carpenters and the builders who worked on the Temple of the Lord. 12They also paid the stoneworkers and stonecutters. They used the money to buy timber and cut stone. The money was used to repair the damage of the Temple of the Lord. It paid for everything.

[13]The money brought into the Temple of the Lord was not used to make silver cups. It was not used for wick trimmers, bowls or trumpets. And it wasn't used for any gold or silver vessels. [14]They paid the money to the workers. And the workers used it to repair the Temple of the Lord. [15]They did not make the men tell how the money was spent. This was because the men were honest. [16]The money from the penalty offerings and sin offerings was not brought into the Temple of the Lord. It belonged to the priests.

JOASH SAVES JERUSALEM

[17]About this time Hazael king of Aram attacked Gath and captured it. Then he went to attack Jerusalem. [18]But Joash king of Judah took all the holy things his ancestors had given. His ancestors were the kings of Judah—Jehoshaphat, Jehoram and Ahaziah. He also took his own holy things. He took the gold that was found in the treasuries of the Temple[d] of the Lord. And he took the gold from the palace. Joash sent all this treasure to Hazael king of Aram. Then Hazael turned away from Jerusalem.

[19]Everything else Joash did is written down. It is in the book of the history of the kings of Judah. [20]His officers made plans against him. They killed him at Beth Millo on the road to Silla. [21]The officers who killed him were Jozabad son of Shimeath and Jehozabad son of Shomer. Joash was buried with his ancestors in Jerusalem. And Amaziah, his son, became king in his place.

JEHOAHAZ KING OF ISRAEL

13 Jehoahaz son of Jehu became king over Israel in Samaria. This was during Joash's twenty-third year as king of Judah. Joash was the son of Ahaziah. And Jehoahaz ruled 17 years. [2]He did what the Lord said was wrong. Jehoahaz did the same sins Jeroboam son of Nebat had done. Jeroboam had caused Israel to sin. And Jehoahaz did not stop doing these same sins. [3]So the Lord was angry with Israel. And he gave them into the power of Hazael king of Aram and his son Ben-Hadad.

[4]Then Jehoahaz begged the Lord, and the Lord listened to him. The Lord had seen the troubles of Israel. He saw how terribly the king of Aram was treating the Israelites. [5]So he gave Israel a man to save them. And they escaped from the Arameans. So the Israelites lived in their own homes as they had before. [6]But the Israelites still did not stop doing the same sins that the family of Jeroboam had done. He had caused Israel to sin. They continued doing those sins. The Asherah[d] idol also was left standing in Samaria.

[7]Nothing was left of Jehoahaz's army except 50 horsemen, 10 chariots and 10,000 foot soldiers. The king of Aram had destroyed them. He had made them like dust at the time of threshing.[d]

[8]Everything else Jehoahaz did and all his victories are written down. They are in the book of history of the kings of Israel. [9]Jehoahaz died and was buried in Samaria. His son Jehoash became king in his place.

JEHOASH KING OF ISRAEL

[10]Jehoash son of Jehoahaz became king of Israel in Samaria. This was during Joash's thirty-seventh year as king of Judah. Jehoash ruled 16 years. [11]He did what the Lord said was wrong. He did not stop doing the same sins Jeroboam son of Nebat had done. Jeroboam had caused Israel to sin. And Jehoash continued to do the same thing. [12]Everything else he did and all his victories are written down. This includes his war against Amaziah king of Judah. All this is written in the book of the history of the kings of Israel. [13]Jehoash died, and Jeroboam took his place on the throne. Jehoash was buried in Samaria with the kings of Israel.

THE DEATH OF ELISHA

[14]At this time Elisha became sick. (Later, he died from this illness.) Jehoash king of Israel went to Elisha and cried for him. Jehoash said, "My father, my father! The chariots of Israel and their horsemen!"

[15]Elisha said to Jehoash, "Take a bow and arrows." So he took a bow and arrows. [16]Then Elisha said to him, "Put your hand on the bow." So Jehoash put his hand on the bow. Then Elisha put his hands on the king's hands. [17]Elisha said, "Open the east window." So Jehoash opened the window. Then Elisha said, "Shoot," and Jehoash shot. Elisha said, "The Lord's arrow of victory over Aram! You will defeat the Arameans at Aphek until you destroy them."

[18]Elisha said, "Take the arrows." So Jehoash took them. Then Elisha said to him, "Hit the ground." So Jehoash hit the ground three times. Then he stopped. [19]The man of God was angry with him. Elisha said, "You should have hit five or six times! Then you would have defeated Aram until you had completely destroyed it! But now you will defeat it only three times."

[20]So Elisha died and was buried.

At that time groups of Moabites would rob the land in the springtime. [21]Once the Israelites were burying a man. Suddenly they saw a group of Moabites coming. The Israelites threw the dead man into Elisha's grave. When the man touched Elisha's bones, the man came back to life. And he stood up on his feet.

WAR WITH ARAM

[22]During all the days Jehoahaz was king, Hazael king of Aram troubled Israel. [23]But the Lord was kind to the Israelites. He had mercy on them. And he helped them because of his agreement with Abraham, Isaac and Jacob. He did not destroy them or reject them.

[24]Hazael king of Aram died. And his son Ben-Hadad became king in his place. [25]During a war Hazael had taken some cities from Jehoahaz, Jehoash's father. But now Jehoash took back those cities from Hazael's son Ben-Hadad. He defeated Ben-Hadad three times and took back the cities of Israel.

AMAZIAH KING OF JUDAH

14 Amaziah son of Joash became king of Judah. This was during the second year Jehoash son of Jehoahaz was king of Israel. [2]Amaziah was 25 years old when he became king. He ruled 29 years in Jerusalem. His mother was Jehoaddin. She was from Jerusalem. [3]Amaziah did what the Lord said was right. Amaziah did everything his father Joash had done. But he did not do as David his ancestor had done. [4]The places where false gods were worshiped were not removed. The people still sacrificed and burned incense[d] there.

[5]Amaziah took strong control of the kingdom. Then he put the officers to death who had killed his father the king. [6]But he did not put to death the children of the murderers. This is because of the rule written in the Book of the Teachings of Moses. The Lord had commanded: "Fathers must not be put to death when their children do wrong. And children must not be put to death when their fathers do wrong. Each person must die for his own sins."[n]

[7]Amaziah killed 10,000 Edomites in the Valley of Salt. In a battle Amaziah took the city of Sela. He called it Joktheel, and it is still called that today.

[8]Amaziah sent messengers to Jehoash son of Jehoahaz. (Jehoahaz was the son of Jehu, king of Israel.) The message read, "Come, let's meet face to face in battle."

[9]Then Jehoash king of Israel answered Amaziah king of Judah. Jehoash said, "A little thornbush in Lebanon sent

---

14:6 "Fathers . . . sins." See Deuteronomy 24:16.

a message to a big cedar tree in Lebanon. It said, 'Let your daughter marry my son.' But then a wild animal from Lebanon came by. It walked on and crushed the thornbush. [10]Yes, you have defeated Edom. But you have become proud because of your victory over Edom. Stay at home and brag! Don't ask for trouble by fighting me. If you do, you and Judah will be defeated."

[11]But Amaziah would not listen. So Jehoash king of Israel went to attack. He and Amaziah king of Judah faced each other in battle at Beth Shemesh in Judah. [12]Israel defeated Judah. Every man of Judah ran away to his home. [13]At Beth Shemesh Jehoash king of Israel captured Amaziah king of Judah. Amaziah was the son of Joash, who was the son of Ahaziah. Then Jehoash went to Jerusalem. He broke down the wall of Jerusalem from the Gate of Ephraim to the Corner Gate. This part of the wall was about 600 feet long. [14]Then he took all the gold and silver and everything in the Temple[d] of the Lord. And he took the treasuries of the palace. He also took some hostages and returned to Samaria.

[15]The other acts of Jehoash and his victories are written down. This includes his war against Amaziah king of Judah. All this is in the book of the history of the kings of Israel. [16]Jehoash died and was buried in Samaria with the kings of Israel. And his son Jeroboam became king in his place.

[17]Amaziah son of Joash was king of Judah. He lived 15 years after Jehoash king of Israel died. Jehoash was the son of Jehoahaz. [18]The other things Amaziah did as king are written down. They are in the book of the history of the kings of Judah. [19]The people made plans in Jerusalem against Amaziah. So he ran away to the town of Lachish. But they sent men after him to Lachish and killed

him. [20]They brought his body back on horses. And he was buried with his ancestors in Jerusalem, the city of David.

[21]Then all the people of Judah chose Azariah[n] to be king. He became king in place of his father Amaziah. Azariah was 16 years old. [22]He rebuilt the town of Elath and made it part of Judah again. He did this after Amaziah died.

JEROBOAM KING OF ISRAEL

[23]Jeroboam son of Jehoash became king of Israel in Samaria. This was during the fifteenth year Amaziah was king of Judah. (Amaziah was the son of Joash.) And Jeroboam ruled 41 years. [24]He did what the Lord said was wrong. Jeroboam son of Nebat had caused Israel to sin. And Jeroboam son of Jehoash did not stop doing the same sins. [25]Jeroboam won back Israel's border from Lebo Hamath to the Dead Sea.[d] This happened as the Lord of Israel had said. He said it through his servant Jonah son of Amittai. He was the prophet[d] from Gath Hepher. [26]The Lord had seen how the Israelites, both slave and free, were suffering terribly. No one was left who could help Israel. [27]But the Lord had not said that he would completely destroy Israel from the world. So he saved the Israelites through Jeroboam son of Jehoash.

[28]Everything else Jeroboam did is written down. All his victories are recorded. He won back Damascus and Hamath for Israel. (They had belonged to Judah.) All this is written in the book of the history of the kings of Israel. [29]Jeroboam died and was buried with his ancestors, the kings of Israel. Jeroboam's son Zechariah became king in his place.

AZARIAH KING OF JUDAH

15 Azariah[n] son of Amaziah became king of Judah. This was during Jeroboam's twenty-seventh year as king of Israel. [2]Azariah was 16 years

14:21; 15:1 **Azariah** Also called Uzziah in 2 Chronicles.

old when he became king. He ruled 52 years in Jerusalem. His mother was named Jecoliah, and she was from Jerusalem. [3]He did what the Lord said was right. He obeyed God just as his father Amaziah had done. [4]But the places where false gods were worshiped were not removed. So the people still made sacrifices and burned incense[d] there.

[5]The Lord struck Azariah with a harmful skin disease. He had this disease until the day he died. He lived in a separate house. Jotham, the king's son, was in charge of the palace. He governed the people of the land.

[6]All the other things Azariah did are written down. They are in the book of the history of the kings of Judah. [7]Azariah died and was buried near his ancestors in Jerusalem. And his son Jotham became king in his place.

ZECHARIAH KING OF ISRAEL

[8]Zechariah son of Jeroboam was king over Israel in Samaria. He ruled for six months. This was during Azariah's thirty-eighth year as king of Judah. [9]Zechariah did what the Lord said was wrong. He did just as his ancestors had done. Jeroboam son of Nebat had caused the people of Israel to sin. And Zechariah did not stop doing the same sins.

[10]Shallum son of Jabesh made plans against Zechariah. He killed Zechariah in Ibleam. And Shallum became king in Zechariah's place. [11]The other acts of Zechariah are written down. They are in the book of the history of the kings of Israel. [12]Now the Lord had told Jehu: "Your sons down to your great-great-grandchildren will be kings of Israel." And the Lord's word came true.

SHALLUM KING OF ISRAEL

[13]Then Shallum son of Jabesh became king. This was during Uzziah's thirty-ninth year as king of Judah. Shallum ruled for a month in Samaria. [14]Then Menahem son of Gadi came up from Tirzah to Samaria. He attacked Shallum son of Jabesh in Samaria. He killed him and became king in Shallum's place.

[15]The other acts of Shallum and his secret plans are written down. They are in the book of the history of the kings of Israel.

MENAHEM KING OF ISRAEL

[16]Menahem started out from Tirzah and attacked Tiphsah. He destroyed the city and the area nearby. This was because the people had refused to open the city gate for him. So he defeated them and ripped open all their pregnant women.

[17]Menahem son of Gadi became king over Israel. This was during Azariah's thirty-ninth year as king of Judah. And Menahem ruled ten years in Samaria. [18]He did what the Lord said was wrong. Jeroboam son of Nebat had caused Israel to sin. And all the time Menahem was king, he did not stop doing the same sins.

[19]Pul king of Assyria came to attack the land. Menahem gave him about 74,000 pounds of silver. This was so Pul would support Menahem and make his hold on the kingdom stronger. [20]Menahem raised the money by taxing all the rich men of Israel. He taxed each man about 1¼ pounds of silver. Then he gave the money to the king of Assyria. So the king of Assyria left and did not stay in the land.

[21]Everything else Menahem did is written down. It is in the book of the history of the kings of Israel. [22]Then Menahem died. And his son Pekahiah became king in his place.

PEKAHIAH KING OF ISRAEL

[23]Pekahiah son of Menahem became king over Israel in Samaria. This was during Azariah's fiftieth year as king of Judah. Pekahiah ruled two years. [24]He did what the Lord said was wrong. Jeroboam son of Nebat had caused Israel to sin. And Pekahiah did not stop doing the same sins.

²⁵Pekah son of Remaliah was one of Pekahiah's captains. He made plans against Pekahiah. He took 50 men of Gilead with him and killed Pekahiah. They killed him, Argob and Arieh in the palace at Samaria. Then Pekah became king in Pekahiah's place.

²⁶Everything else Pekahiah did is written down. It is in the book of the history of the kings of Israel.

PEKAH KING OF ISRAEL

²⁷Pekah son of Remaliah became king over Israel in Samaria. This was during Azariah's fifty-second year as king of Judah. And Pekah ruled 20 years. ²⁸He did what the Lord said was wrong. Jeroboam son of Nebat had caused Israel to sin. And Pekah did not stop doing the same sins.

²⁹Tiglath-Pileser, also called Pul, was king of Assyria. He attacked while Pekah was king of Israel. Tiglath-Pileser captured the cities of Ijon, Abel Beth Maacah, Janoah, Kedesh and Hazor. He also captured Gilead and Galilee. And he captured all the land of Naphtali. He sent the people from these places away to Assyria. ³⁰Then Hoshea son of Elah made plans against Pekah son of Remaliah. Hoshea attacked and killed Pekah. Then he became king in Pekah's place. This was during the twentieth year Jotham son of Uzziah was king.

³¹Everything else Pekah did is written down. It is in the book of the history of the kings of Israel.

JOTHAM KING OF JUDAH

³²Then Jotham son of Uzziah became king of Judah. This was during the second year Pekah son of Remaliah was king of Israel. ³³Jotham was 25 years old when he became king. He ruled 16 years in Jerusalem. His mother's name was Jerusha daughter of Zadok. ³⁴Jotham did what the Lord said was right. He obeyed God just as his father Uzziah had done. ³⁵But the places where false gods were worshiped were not removed. And the people still made sacrifices and burned incense*d* there. Jotham rebuilt the Upper Gate of the Temple*d* of the Lord.

³⁶The other things Jotham did while he was king are written down. They are in the book of the history of the kings of Judah. ³⁷At that time the Lord began to send Rezin king of Aram against Judah. He also sent Pekah son of Remaliah against them. ³⁸Jotham died and was buried with his ancestors in Jerusalem. It was the city of David, his ancestor. And Jotham's son Ahaz became king in his place.

AHAZ KING OF JUDAH

16 Ahaz was the son of Jotham king of Judah. Ahaz became king of Judah in the seventeenth year Pekah was king of Israel. Pekah was the son of Remaliah. ²Ahaz was 20 years old when he became king. He ruled 16 years in Jerusalem. He was not like his ancestor David. He did not do what the Lord his God said was right. ³Ahaz did the same things the kings of Israel had done. He even sacrificed his sons by burning them in the fire. He did the same hated sins as the other nations had done. And the Lord had forced these nations out of the land ahead of the Israelites. ⁴Ahaz offered sacrifices and burned incense*d* at the places where false gods were worshiped. And he did this on the hills and under every green tree.

⁵Rezin king of Aram and Pekah king of Israel came up to Jerusalem to attack it. (Pekah was the son of Remaliah.) They surrounded Ahaz but could not defeat him. ⁶At that time Rezin king of Aram took back the city of Elath for Aram. He forced out all the people of Judah. Then Edomites moved into Elath. And they still live there today.

⁷Ahaz sent messengers to Tiglath-Pileser king of Assyria. Ahaz said, "I am your servant. Come and save me from the king of Aram and the king of Israel.

They are attacking me." [8]Ahaz took the silver and gold that was in the Temple[d] of the Lord. He also took the treasuries of the palace. He sent these as a gift to the king of Assyria. [9]So the king of Assyria listened to Ahaz. He attacked Damascus and captured it. Then he sent all the people of Damascus to Kir. And he killed Rezin.

[10]Then King Ahaz went to Damascus to meet Tiglath-Pileser king of Assyria. Ahaz saw an altar at Damascus. He sent plans and a pattern of this altar to Uriah the priest. [11]So Uriah the priest built an altar. It was just like the plans King Ahaz had sent him from Damascus. Uriah finished the altar before King Ahaz came back from Damascus. [12]When the king arrived from Damascus, he saw the altar. He went near and offered sacrifices on it. [13]He burned his burnt offerings and grain offerings. He poured out his drink offering. He also sprinkled the blood of his fellowship offerings on the altar.

[14]Ahaz moved the bronze altar that was before the Lord at the front of the Temple. It was between Ahaz's altar and the Temple of the Lord. He put it on the north side of his altar. [15]King Ahaz gave a command to Uriah the priest. Ahaz said, "Burn the morning burnt offering and the evening grain offering on the large altar. Also offer the king's burnt offering and his grain offering. Offer the whole burnt offering for all the people of the land. And offer their grain offering and drink offering. Sprinkle on the altar all the blood of the burnt offering and of the sacrifice. But I will use the bronze altar to ask questions of God." [16]Uriah the priest did everything King Ahaz commanded him to do.

[17]Then King Ahaz took off the side panels from the bases. He took the washing bowls off the top of the bases. He also took the large bowl, which was called the Sea, off the bronze bulls that held it up. And he put it on a stone base.

[18]Ahaz took away the platform for the royal throne. It had been built at the Temple. He also took away the outside entrance for the king. He did these things because of the king of Assyria.

[19]The other things Ahaz did as king are written down. They are in the book of the history of the kings of Judah. [20]Ahaz died and was buried with his ancestors in Jerusalem. Ahaz's son Hezekiah became king in his place.

HOSHEA, LAST KING OF ISRAEL

17 Hoshea son of Elah became king over Israel. This was during Ahaz's twelfth year as king of Judah. Hoshea ruled in Samaria nine years. [2]He did what the Lord said was wrong. But he was not as bad as the kings of Israel who had ruled before him.

[3]Shalmaneser king of Assyria came to attack Hoshea. Hoshea had been Shalmaneser's servant. He had made the payments to Shalmaneser that he had demanded. [4]But the king of Assyria found out that Hoshea had made plans against him. Hoshea had sent messengers to So, the king of Egypt. And Hoshea had quit giving Shalmaneser the payments he demanded. In the past Hoshea had paid him every year. So the king put Hoshea in prison. [5]Then the king of Assyria came and attacked all the land of Israel. He surrounded Samaria and attacked it for three years. [6]He defeated Samaria in the ninth year Hoshea was king. He took the Israelites away to Assyria. He settled some of them in Halah. Some were made to settle in Gozan on the Habor River. Others were settled in the cities of the Medes.

ISRAELITES PUNISHED FOR SIN

[7]All these things happened because the Israelites had sinned against the Lord their God. He had brought them out of Egypt. He had rescued them from the power of the king of Egypt. But the Israelites had honored other gods. [8]They

lived like the nations the Lord had forced out of the land ahead of them. They also lived as the evil kings had shown them. ⁹They secretly sinned against the Lord their God. They built places in all their cities where false gods were worshiped. They built them everywhere from the watchtower to the strong, walled city. ¹⁰They put up stone pillars for worshiping false gods. And they put up Asherah*d* idols on every high hill and under every green tree. ¹¹The Israelites burned incense*d* everywhere false gods were worshiped. The nations who lived there before them had done this. And the Lord had forced them out of the land. The Israelites did wicked things that made the Lord angry. ¹²They served idols. And the Lord had said, "You must not do this." ¹³The Lord used every prophet*d* and seer*d* to warn Israel and Judah. He said, "Stop your evil ways. Obey my commands and laws. Follow all the teachings that I commanded your ancestors to obey. I sent you this law through my servants the prophets."

¹⁴But the people would not listen. They were stubborn, just as their ancestors had been. Their ancestors did not believe in the Lord their God. ¹⁵They rejected the Lord's laws and the agreement he had made with their ancestors. And they refused to listen to his warnings. They worshiped useless idols and became useless themselves. They did what the nations around them did. And the Lord had warned them not to do this. ¹⁶The people disobeyed all the commands of the Lord their God. They made statues of two calves from melted metal. And they made an Asherah idol. They worshiped all the stars of heaven and served Baal.*d* ¹⁷They sacrificed their sons and daughters in the fire. And they tried to find out the future by magic and witchcraft.*d* They always chose to do what the Lord said was wrong. And this made him angry. ¹⁸So he was very angry

with the people of Israel. He removed them from his presence. Only the tribe*d* of Judah was left.

JUDAH IS ALSO GUILTY

¹⁹But even Judah did not obey the commands of the Lord their God. They did what the Israelites had done. ²⁰So the Lord rejected all the people of Israel. He punished them and let people destroy them. He threw them out of his presence. ²¹The Lord separated them from the family of David. And the Israelites made Jeroboam son of Nebat their king. Jeroboam led the Israelites away from following the Lord. He caused them to sin greatly. ²²So they continued to do all the sins Jeroboam did. They did not stop doing these sins ²³until the Lord removed the people from his presence. This was just as he had said he would do. He had said this through all his servants the prophets.*d* So the Israelites were taken out of their land to Assyria. And they have been there to this day.

THE BEGINNING OF THE SAMARITAN PEOPLE

²⁴The king of Assyria brought people from Babylon, Cuthah, Avva, Hamath and Sepharvaim. He put them in the cities of Samaria to replace the Israelites. These people took over Samaria and lived in the cities. ²⁵At first they did not worship the Lord. So he sent lions among them. The lions killed some of them. ²⁶The king of Assyria was told this. It was said, "You sent foreigners into the cities of Samaria. They do not know the law of the god of the land. This is why that land's god has sent lions among them. The lions are killing them because they don't know what the god wants."

²⁷Then the king of Assyria gave a command. He said, "You took Samaria's priests away. Send back one of the priests to live there. Let him teach them what the god wants." ²⁸So one of the

priests who had been carried away from Samaria returned. He came to live in Bethel. And he taught the people how to worship the Lord.

²⁹But each nation made gods of its own. They put them in the cities where they lived. They put them in the temples where false gods were worshiped. These temples had been made by the Samaritans. ³⁰The men from Babylon made Succoth Benoth their god. The men from Cuthah worshiped Nergal. The men of Hamath worshiped Ashima. ³¹The Avites worshiped Nibhaz and Tartak. And the Sepharvites burned their children in the fire. They sacrificed them to Adrammelech and Anammelech, the gods of Sepharvaim. ³²They also worshiped the Lord. But they chose priests for the places where false gods were worshiped. The priests were chosen from among themselves. And they made sacrifices for the people. ³³The people worshiped the Lord but also served their own gods. They served their gods as the nations did from which they had been brought. ³⁴Even today they do as they did in the past. They do not worship the Lord. They do not obey his rules and commands. They do not obey the teachings or the commands of the Lord. He gave these commands to the children of Jacob, whom the Lord had named Israel. ³⁵The Lord had made an agreement with them. He had commanded them, "Do not worship other gods. Do not bow down to them or serve them. Do not give sacrifices to them. ³⁶Worship the Lord who brought you up out of the land of Egypt. He did it with great power and strength. Bow to the Lord and make sacrifices to him. ³⁷Obey the rules, orders and the teachings. Obey the commands the Lord wrote for you. Obey and always do them. Do not worship other gods. ³⁸Do not forget the agreement I made with you. And do not worship other gods. ³⁹Instead worship the Lord your God. He will save you from all your enemies."

⁴⁰But the Israelites did not listen. They kept on doing the same things they had done before. ⁴¹So these nations worshiped the Lord but served their idols. And their children and grandchildren still do as their ancestors did.

HEZEKIAH KING OF JUDAH

18 Hezekiah son of Ahaz king of Judah became king. This was during the third year Hoshea son of Elah was king of Israel. ²Hezekiah was 25 years old when he became king. And he ruled 29 years in Jerusalem. His mother's name was Abijah daughter of Zechariah. ³Hezekiah did what the Lord said was right. He did just as his ancestor David had done. ⁴He removed the places where false gods were worshiped. He broke the stone pillars they worshiped. He cut down the Asherah^d idols. Also the Israelites had been burning incense^d to the bronze snake made by Moses. (It was called Nehushtan.) But Hezekiah broke it into pieces.

⁵Hezekiah trusted in the Lord, the God of Israel. There was no one like him among all the kings of Judah. There was no king like him, before him or after him. ⁶Hezekiah was loyal to the Lord. He did not stop following the Lord. He obeyed the commands the Lord had given Moses. ⁷And the Lord was with Hezekiah. He had success in everything he did. He turned against the king of Assyria and stopped serving him. ⁸Hezekiah defeated the Philistines all the way to Gaza and its borders. He defeated them everywhere, from the watchtower to the strong, walled city.

THE ASSYRIANS CAPTURE SAMARIA

⁹Shalmaneser king of Assyria surrounded Samaria and attacked it. This was in the fourth year Hezekiah was king. And it was the seventh year Hoshea son of Elah was king of Israel. ¹⁰After three years the Assyrians captured Samaria. This was in the sixth year Hezekiah

was king. And it was Hoshea's ninth year as king of Israel. [11]The king of Assyria took the Israelites away to Assyria. He put them in Halah and in Gozan on the Habor River. He also put them in the cities of the Medes. [12]This happened because they did not obey the Lord their God. They broke his agreement. They did not obey all that Moses, the Lord's servant, had commanded. They would not listen to the commands or do them.

ASSYRIA ATTACKS JUDAH

[13]During Hezekiah's fourteenth year as king, Sennacherib king of Assyria attacked Judah. He attacked all the strong, walled cities of Judah and defeated them. [14]Then Hezekiah king of Judah sent a message to the king of Assyria at Lachish. He said, "I have done wrong. Leave me alone. Then I will pay anything you demand of me." So the king of Assyria told Hezekiah how much to pay. It was about 22,000 pounds of silver and 2,000 pounds of gold. [15]Hezekiah gave him all the silver that was in the Temple[d] of the Lord. And he gave him all the silver in the palace treasuries. [16]Hezekiah cut off all the gold that covered the doors of the Temple of the Lord. He also removed the gold from the doorposts. Hezekiah had put gold on these doors himself. He gave it all to the king of Assyria.

ASSYRIA TROUBLES HEZEKIAH

[17]The king of Assyria sent out his supreme commander, his chief officer and his field commander. They went with a large army from Lachish to King Hezekiah in Jerusalem. When they came near the waterway from the upper pool, they stopped. The upper pool is on the road to the Washerman's Field. [18]They called for the king. So Eliakim, Shebna and Joah went out to meet them. Eliakim son of Hilkiah was the palace manager. Shebna was the royal assistant. And Joah son of Asaph was the recorder.

[19]The field commander said to them, "Tell Hezekiah this:

"'The great king, the king of Assyria, says: You have nothing to trust in to help you. [20]You say you have battle plans and power for war. But your words mean nothing. Whom are you trusting for help so that you turn against me? [21]Look, you are depending on Egypt to help you. Egypt is like a splintered walking stick. If you lean on it for help, it will stab you and hurt you. The king of Egypt will hurt those who depend on him. [22]You might say, "We are depending on the Lord our God." But Hezekiah destroyed the Lord's altars and the places of worship. Hezekiah told Judah and Jerusalem, "You must worship only at this one altar in Jerusalem."

[23]"'Now make an agreement with my master, the king of Assyria: I will give you 2,000 horses if you can find enough men to ride them. [24]You cannot defeat one of my master's least important officers. So why do you depend on Egypt to give you chariots and horsemen? [25]I have not come to attack and destroy this place without an order from the Lord. The Lord himself told me to come to this country and destroy it.'"

[26]Then Eliakim son of Hilkiah, Shebna and Joah spoke to the field commander. They said, "Please speak to us in the Aramaic language. We understand it. Don't speak to us in Hebrew because the people on the city wall can hear you."

[27]But the commander said, "No. My master did not send me to tell these things only to you and your king. My master sent me to tell them also to those people sitting on the wall. They will have to eat their own dung and drink their own urine like you."

[28]Then the commander stood and shouted loudly in the Hebrew language. He said, "Listen to the word from the great king, the king of Assyria! [29]The king says you should not let Hezekiah

fool you. Hezekiah can't save you from my power. ³⁰Don't let Hezekiah talk you into trusting the Lord. Hezekiah says, 'The Lord will surely save us. This city won't be given over to the king of Assyria.'

³¹"Don't listen to Hezekiah. The king of Assyria says, 'Make peace with me. Come out of the city to me. Then everyone will be free to eat the fruit from his own grapevine and fig tree. Everyone will be free to drink water from his own well. ³²Then I will come and take you to a land like your own. It is a land with grain and new wine. It has bread and vineyards. It is a land of olives and honey. Then you can choose to live and not to die!'

"Don't listen to Hezekiah. He is fooling you when he says, 'The Lord will save us.' ³³The god of any other nation has not saved his people from the power of the king of Assyria. ³⁴Where are the gods of Hamath and Arpad? Where are the gods of Sepharvaim, Hena and Ivvah? They did not save Samaria from my power. ³⁵Not one of all the gods of these countries has saved his people from me. Then the Lord cannot save Jerusalem from my power."

³⁶The people were silent. They didn't answer the commander at all. This was because King Hezekiah had ordered, "Don't answer him."

³⁷Then Eliakim, Shebna and Joah tore their clothes to show how upset they were. (Eliakim son of Hilkiah was the palace manager. Shebna was the royal assistant. And Joah son of Asaph was the recorder.) The three men went to Hezekiah and told him what the field commander had said.

JERUSALEM WILL BE SAVED

19 When King Hezekiah heard the message, he tore his clothes. And he put on rough cloth to show how sad he was. Then he went into the Temple*ᵈ* of the Lord. ²Hezekiah sent Eliakim, Shebna and the older priests to Isaiah. Eliakim was the palace manager, and Shebna was the royal assistant. The men were all wearing the rough cloth when they came to Isaiah. He was a prophet,*ᵈ* the son of Amoz. ³These men told Isaiah, "This is what Hezekiah says: Today is a day of sorrow and punishment and disgrace. It is sad, as when a child should be born, but the mother is not strong enough to give birth to it. ⁴The king of Assyria sent his field commander to make fun of the living God. Maybe the Lord your God will hear what the commander said. Maybe the Lord your God will punish him for what he said. So pray for the few people of Israel who are left alive."

⁵When Hezekiah's officers came to Isaiah, ⁶he said to them, "Tell your master this: The Lord says, 'Don't be afraid of what you have heard. Don't be frightened by the words the servants of the king of Assyria said against me. ⁷Listen! I am going to put a spirit in the king of Assyria. He will hear a report that will make him return to his own country. And I will cause him to die by the sword there.'"

⁸The field commander heard that the king of Assyria had left Lachish. So the commander left and found the king fighting against the city of Libnah.

⁹The king received a report that Tirhakah was coming to attack him. Tirhakah was the Cushite king of Egypt. When the king of Assyria heard this, he sent messengers to Hezekiah. The king said: ¹⁰"Say this to Hezekiah king of Judah: Don't be fooled by the god you trust. Don't believe him when he says Jerusalem will not be defeated by the king of Assyria. ¹¹You have heard what the kings of Assyria have done. They have completely defeated every country. Do not think you will be saved. ¹²The gods of those people did not save them. My ancestors destroyed them. My ancestors defeated the cities of Gozan,

Haran and Rezeph. They defeated the people of Eden living in Tel Assar. ¹³Where are the kings of Hamath and Arpad? Where is the king of the city of Sepharvaim? Where are the kings of Hena and Ivvah?"

HEZEKIAH PRAYS TO THE LORD

¹⁴Hezekiah received the letter from the messengers and read it. Then he went up to the Temple*d* of the Lord. Hezekiah spread the letter out before the Lord. ¹⁵And he prayed to the Lord: "Lord, God of Israel, your throne is between the gold creatures with wings! Only you are God of all the kingdoms of the earth. You made the heavens and the earth. ¹⁶Hear, Lord, and listen. Open your eyes, Lord, and see. Listen to the word Sennacherib has said to insult the living God. ¹⁷It is true, Lord. The kings of Assyria have destroyed these countries and their lands. ¹⁸These kings have thrown the gods of these nations into the fire. But they were only wood and rock statues that men made. So the kings have destroyed them. ¹⁹Now, Lord our God, save us from the king's power. Then all the kingdoms of the earth will know that you, Lord, are the only God."

GOD ANSWERS HEZEKIAH

²⁰Then Isaiah son of Amoz sent a message to Hezekiah. Isaiah said, "The Lord, the God of Israel, says this: I have heard your prayer to me about Sennacherib king of Assyria. ²¹So this is what the Lord has said against Sennacherib:

'The people of Jerusalem
　hate you and make fun of you.
The people of Jerusalem
　laugh at you as you run away.
²²You have insulted me and spoken
　against me.
　You have raised your voice against
　　me.
　You have a proud look on your face.
　You disobey me, the Holy One of
　　Israel!

²³You have used your messengers to
　insult the Lord.
　You have said, "I have many
　　chariots.
With them I have gone to the tops of
　the mountains.
I have climbed the highest
　mountains of Lebanon.
I have cut down its tallest cedars.
　I have cut down its best pine trees.
I have reached its farthest places.
　I have gone to its best forests.
²⁴I have dug wells in foreign countries.
　I have drunk water there.
By the soles of my feet,
　I have dried up all the rivers of
　　Egypt."

²⁵"King of Assyria, surely you have
　heard.
　Long ago I, the Lord, planned these
　　things.
Long ago I planned them.
　Now I have made them happen.
I allowed you to turn those strong,
　walled cities
　into piles of rocks.
²⁶The people living in those cities were
　weak.
　They were frightened and put to
　　shame.
They were like grass in the field.
　They were like tender, young grass.
They were like grass that grows on the
　housetop.
　It is burned by the wind before it
　　can grow.

²⁷"I know when you rest and when you
　come and go.
　I know how you speak against me.
²⁸You speak strongly against me.
　And I have heard your proud words.
So I will put my hook in your nose.
　And I will put my bit in your
　　mouth.
Then I will force you to leave my
　country
　the same way that you came.'

29"Then the Lord said, 'Hezekiah, I will give you this sign:

This year you will eat the grain that grows wild.
And the second year you will eat what grows wild from that.
But in the third year, plant grain and harvest it.
Plant vineyards and eat their fruit.
30Some of the people in the family of Judah
will be saved.
Like plants that take root,
they will grow strong and have many children.
31A few people will come out of Jerusalem alive.
There will be a few from Mount Zion^d who will live.
The strong love of the Lord of heaven's armies
will cause this to happen.'
32"So this is what the Lord says about the king of Assyria:
'He will not enter this city.
He will not even shoot an arrow here.
He will not fight against it with shields.
He will not build a ramp to attack the city walls.
33He will return to his country the same way he came.
He will not enter this city,'
says the Lord.
34The Lord says, 'I will defend and save this city.
I will do this for myself and for David, my servant.'"

35That night the angel of the Lord went out. He killed 185,000 men in the Assyrian camp. The people got up early the next morning. And they saw all the dead bodies! 36So Sennacherib king of Assyria left. He went back to Nineveh and stayed there.

37One day Sennacherib was worshiping in the temple of his god Nisroch. While he was there, his sons Adram-melech and Sharezer killed him with a sword. Then they escaped to the land of Ararat. So Sennacherib's son Esarhaddon became king of Assyria.

HEZEKIAH'S ILLNESS

20 At that time Hezekiah became very sick. He was almost dead. The prophet^d Isaiah son of Amoz went to see him. Isaiah told him, "This is what the Lord says: You are going to die. So you should give your last orders to everyone. You will not get well."

2Hezekiah turned toward the wall and prayed to the Lord. He said, 3"Lord, please remember that I have always obeyed you. I have given myself completely to you. I have done what you said was right." And Hezekiah cried loudly.

4Before Isaiah had left the middle courtyard, the Lord spoke his word to Isaiah: 5"Go back and tell Hezekiah, the leader of my people: 'This is what the Lord, the God of your ancestor David, says: I have heard your prayer. And I have seen your tears. So I will heal you. Three days from now you will go up to the Temple^d of the Lord. 6I will add 15 years to your life. I will save you and this city from the king of Assyria. And I will protect the city for myself and for my servant David.'"

7Then Isaiah said, "Make a paste from figs." So they made it and put it on Hezekiah's boil. And he got well.

8Hezekiah asked Isaiah, "What will be the sign that the Lord will heal me? What is the sign that I will go up to the Temple^d of the Lord on the third day?"

9Isaiah said, "The Lord will do what he says. This is the sign from the Lord to show you: Do you want the shadow to go forward ten steps? Or do you want it to go back ten steps?"

10Hezekiah answered, "It's easy for the shadow to go forward ten steps. Instead, let it go back ten steps."

11Then Isaiah the prophet called to the Lord. And the Lord brought the shadow back ten steps. It went back up the stairway of Ahaz that it had gone down.

MESSENGERS FROM BABYLON

[12]At that time Merodach-Baladan, son of Baladan, was king of Babylon. He sent letters and a gift to Hezekiah. He did this because he had heard that Hezekiah had been sick. [13]Hezekiah was happy to see the messengers. So he showed them what was in his storehouses: the silver, gold, spices and expensive perfumes. He showed them his swords and shields. He showed them all his wealth. He showed them everything in his palace and his kingdom.

[14]Then Isaiah the prophet[d] went to King Hezekiah. Isaiah asked him, "What did these men say? Where did they come from?"

Hezekiah said, "They came from a faraway country. They came to me from Babylon."

[15]So Isaiah asked him, "What did they see in your palace?"

Hezekiah said, "They saw everything in my palace. I showed them all my wealth."

[16]Then Isaiah said to Hezekiah, "Listen to the words of the Lord: [17]'In the future everything in your palace will be taken away to Babylon. Everything your ancestors have stored up until this day will be taken away. Nothing will be left,' says the Lord. [18]'Some of your own children will be taken away. Those who will be born to you will be taken away. And they will become eunuchs[d] in the palace of the king of Babylon.'"

[19]Hezekiah told Isaiah, "These words from the Lord are good." He said this because he thought, "There will be peace and security while I am king."

[20]Everything else Hezekiah did is written down. All his victories and his work on the pool are written down. And his work on the tunnel to bring water into the city is recorded. They are all written in the book of the history of the kings of Judah. [21]Then Hezekiah died. And his son Manasseh became king in his place.

MANASSEH KING OF JUDAH

21 Manasseh was 12 years old when he became king. And he was king 55 years in Jerusalem. His mother's name was Hephzibah. [2]He did what the Lord said was wrong. He did the hated things the other nations had done. And the Lord had forced these nations out of the land ahead of the Israelites. [3]Manasseh's father, Hezekiah, had destroyed the places where false gods were worshiped. But Manasseh rebuilt them. He built altars for Baal.[d] And he made an Asherah[d] idol as Ahab king of Israel had done. Manasseh worshiped all the stars of heaven and served them. [4]The Lord had said about the Temple,[d] "I will be worshiped in Jerusalem." But Manasseh built altars in the Temple of the Lord. [5]He built altars to worship the stars in the two courtyards of the Temple of the Lord. [6]He burned his own son as a sacrifice. He practiced magic and told the future by explaining signs and dreams. He got advice from mediums[d] and fortune-tellers. He did many things that the Lord said were wrong. And this made the Lord angry.

[7]Manasseh carved an Asherah idol and put it in the Temple. The Lord had spoken to David and his son Solomon about the Temple. He had said, "I will be worshiped in this Temple and in Jerusalem forever. I have chosen Jerusalem from all the tribes[d] of Israel. [8]I will never again make the Israelites wander out of the land I gave their ancestors. But they must obey everything I have commanded them. And they must obey all the teachings my servant Moses gave them." [9]But the people did not listen. Manasseh led them to do wrong. They did more evil than the nations the Lord had destroyed ahead of the Israelites.

[10]The Lord spoke through his servants the prophets.[d] He said, [11]"Manasseh

king of Judah has done these hated things. He has done more evil than the Amorites before him. Manasseh also has caused Judah to sin with his idols. [12]So this is what the Lord, the God of Israel, says: 'I will bring much trouble on Jerusalem and Judah. Anyone who hears about it will be shocked. [13]I will stretch the measuring line of Samaria over Jerusalem. And the plumb line[d] used against Ahab's family will be used on Jerusalem. I will wipe out Jerusalem as a man wipes a dish. He wipes it and turns it upside down. [14]I will go away from the rest of my people who are left. I will give them to their enemies. They will be robbed by all their enemies. [15]My people did what I said was wrong. They have made me angry from the day their ancestors left Egypt until now.'"

[16]Manasseh also killed many innocent people. He filled Jerusalem from one end to the other with their blood. This was besides the sin he caused Judah to do. He caused Judah to do what the Lord said was wrong.

[17]The other things Manasseh did as king are written down, even the sin he did. They are in the book of the history of the kings of Judah. [18]Manasseh died and was buried in the garden of his own palace. It is the garden of Uzza. Then Manasseh's son Amon became king in his place.

AMON KING OF JUDAH

[19]Amon was 22 years old when he became king. He was king for two years in Jerusalem. His mother's name was Meshullemeth daughter of Haruz. She was from Jotbah. [20]Amon did what the Lord said was wrong. He did as his father Manasseh had done. [21]Amon lived in the same way his father had lived. He worshiped the idols his father had worshiped. And he bowed down before them. [22]Amon rejected the Lord, the God of his ancestors. He did not follow the ways of the Lord.

[23]Amon's officers made plans against him and killed him in his palace. [24]Then the people of Judah killed all those who had made plans to kill King Amon. And they made his son Josiah king in his place.

[25]Everything else Amon did is written down. It is in the book of the history of the kings of Judah. [26]He was buried in his grave in the garden of Uzza. And his son Josiah became king in his place.

JOSIAH KING OF JUDAH

22 Josiah was eight years old when he became king. He ruled 31 years in Jerusalem. His mother's name was Jedidah daughter of Adaiah. Adaiah was from Bozkath. [2]Josiah did what the Lord said was right. He did good things as his ancestor David had done. Josiah did not stop doing what was right.

[3]In Josiah's eighteenth year as king, he sent Shaphan to the Temple[d] of the Lord. Shaphan was the son of Azaliah, who was the son of Meshullam. Shaphan was the royal assistant. Josiah said, [4]"Go up to Hilkiah the high priest. Have him empty out the money the gatekeepers have gathered from the people. This is the money they have brought into the Temple of the Lord. [5]Have him give the money to the supervisors of the work on the Temple. They must pay the men who work to repair the Temple of the Lord. [6]The workers are carpenters, builders and stoneworkers. Also use the money to buy timber and cut stone to repair the Temple. [7]They do not need to report how they use the money given to them. They are working honestly."

THE BOOK OF THE LAW IS FOUND

[8]Hilkiah the high priest said to Shaphan the royal assistant, "I've found the Book of the Teachings. It was in the Temple[d] of the Lord." He gave it to Shaphan, who read it.

[9]Then Shaphan the royal assistant went to the king and reported to Josiah, "Your officers have paid out the money

that was in the Temple of the Lord. They have given it to the workers and supervisors at the Temple." [10]Then Shaphan the royal assistant told the king, "Hilkiah the priest has given me a book." And Shaphan read from the book to the king. [11]The king heard the words of the Book of the Teachings. Then he tore his clothes to show how upset he was. [12]He gave these orders to Hilkiah the priest and Ahikam son of Shaphan. He also gave them to Acbor son of Micaiah, Shaphan and Asaiah. Shaphan was the royal assistant. And Asaiah was the king's servant. These were the orders: [13]"Go and ask the Lord about the words in the book that has been found. Ask for me and for all the people and for all Judah. The Lord's anger is burning against us because our ancestors did not obey the words of this book. They did not do all the things written for us to do!"

[14]So Hilkiah the priest, Ahikam, Acbor, Shaphan and Asaiah left. They went to talk to Huldah the prophetess.[d] She was the wife of Shallum son of Tikvah, the son of Harhas. Harhas took care of the king's clothes. Huldah lived in Jerusalem, in the new area of the city. [15]She said to them, "This is what the Lord, the God of Israel, says: Tell the man who sent you to me, [16]'This is what the Lord says: I will bring trouble to this place and to the people living here. It is in the words of the book which the king of Judah has read. [17]The people of Judah have left me. They have burned incense[d] to other gods. They have made me angry by all the idols they have made. My anger burns against this place like a fire. It will not be put out.' [18]Tell the king of Judah, who sent you to ask the Lord, 'This is what the Lord, the God of Israel, says about the words you heard: [19]You heard my words against this place and its people. You became sorry in the Lord's presence for what you had done. I said they would become cursed and

would be destroyed. Then you tore your clothes to show how upset you were. And you cried in my presence. This is why I have heard you, says the Lord. [20]So I will cause you to die. You will be buried in peace. You won't see all the trouble I will bring to this place.'"

So they took her message back to the king.

THE PEOPLE HEAR THE LAW

23 Then the king gathered all the elders of Judah and Jerusalem together. [2]He went up to the Temple[d] of the Lord. All the men from Judah and Jerusalem went with him. The priests, prophets[d] and all the people—from the least important to the most important—went with him. He read to them all the words of the Book of the Agreement. That book was found in the Temple of the Lord. [3]The king stood by the pillar. He made an agreement in the presence of the Lord. He agreed to follow the Lord and obey his commands, rules and laws with his whole being. He agreed to do what was written in this book. Then all the people promised to obey the agreement.

JOSIAH DESTROYS THE PLACES FOR IDOL WORSHIP

[4]The king gave a command to Hilkiah the high priest. He also gave it to the priests of the next rank and the gatekeepers. He told them to bring out of the Temple of the Lord everything made for Baal,[d] Asherah[d] and all the stars of heaven. Then Josiah burned them outside Jerusalem in the fields of the Kidron Valley. And he carried the ashes to Bethel. [5]The kings of Judah had chosen priests for these gods. These priests burned incense[d] on the places where false gods were worshiped. These places were in the cities of Judah and the towns around Jerusalem. The priests burned incense to Baal, the sun and the moon. And they burned incense to the planets

and all the stars of heaven. But Josiah took those priests away. [6]He removed the Asherah idol from the Temple of the Lord. He took it outside Jerusalem to the Kidron Valley. There he burned it and beat it into dust. And he threw the dust on the graves of the common people. [7]Then he tore down the houses of the male prostitutes[d] who were in the Temple of the Lord. This was where the women did weaving for Asherah.

[8]King Josiah brought all the false priests from the cities of Judah. He made the places where false gods were worshiped impure. This is where the priests had burned incense. These places of worship were everywhere, from Geba to Beersheba. He destroyed the places of worship at the entrance to the Gate of Joshua. (Joshua was the ruler of the city.) This gate was on the left side of the city gate. [9]The priests at the places where false gods were worshiped were not allowed to serve at the Lord's altar in Jerusalem. But they could eat bread made without yeast with their brothers.

[10]Topheth was in the Valley of Ben Hinnom. Josiah made it impure so no one could sacrifice his son or daughter to Molech.[d] [11]Judah's kings had placed horses at the front door of the Temple of the Lord. This was in the courtyard near the room of Nathan-Melech, an officer. These horses were for the worship of the sun. But Josiah removed them. Then he burned the chariots that were for sun worship.

[12]The kings of Judah had also built altars on the roof[n] of the upstairs room of Ahaz. Josiah broke down these altars. He also broke down the altars Manasseh had made. These were in the two courtyards of the Temple of the Lord. He smashed them to pieces. Then he threw their dust into the Kidron Valley. [13]King Josiah made impure the places east of Jerusalem where false gods were worshiped. These were south of the Mount of Olives.[n] Solomon king of Israel had built these places. One was for Ashtoreth,[d] the hated goddess of the Sidonians. One was for Chemosh,[d] the hated god of Moab. And one was for Molech, the hated god of the Ammonites. [14]Josiah smashed into pieces the stone pillars they worshiped. He cut down the Asherah idols. And he covered the places with human bones.

[15]Josiah also broke down the altar at Bethel. This was the place of worship Jeroboam son of Nebat had made. Jeroboam had caused Israel to sin. Josiah burned that place. He broke the stones of the altar to pieces. Then he beat them into dust. And he burned the Asherah idol. [16]When he turned around, he saw the graves on the mountain. He had the bones taken from the graves. Then he burned the bones on the altar to make it impure. This happened as the Lord had said it would through the man of God.

[17]Josiah asked, "What is that monument to the dead I see?"

The people of the city answered, "It's the grave of the man of God who came from Judah. This prophet announced the things you have done against the altar of Bethel."

[18]Josiah said, "Leave the grave alone. No person may move this man's bones." So they left his bones. And they left the bones of the prophet who had come from Samaria.

[19]The kings of Israel had built temples for worshiping false gods in the cities of Samaria. That had caused the Lord to be angry. Josiah removed all those temples. He did the same things as he had done at

---

23:12 **roof** In Bible times houses were built with flat roofs. The roof was used for drying things such as flax and fruit. And it was used as an extra room, as a place for worship and as a place to sleep in the summer.
23:13 **Mount of Olives** Literally, "The Mountain of Ruin."

Bethel. [20]Josiah killed all the priests of those places of worship. He killed them on the altars. And he burned human bones on the altars. Then he went back to Jerusalem.

THE PASSOVER IS BROUGHT BACK

[21]The king gave a command to all the people. He said, "Celebrate the Passover[d] to the Lord your God. Do it as it is written in this Book of the Agreement." [22]No Passover like this one had been celebrated since the judges led Israel. Nor had one like it happened while there were kings of Israel and kings of Judah. [23]This Passover was celebrated to the Lord in Jerusalem. It was the eighteenth year of King Josiah's rule.

[24]Josiah destroyed the mediums,[d] fortune-tellers, house gods and idols. He destroyed all the hated gods seen in the land of Judah and Jerusalem. He did this to obey the words of the teachings. They were written in the book Hilkiah the priest had found in the Temple[d] of the Lord.

[25]There was no king like Josiah before or after him. He obeyed the Lord with all his heart, soul and strength. He followed all the Teachings of Moses.

[26]Even so, the Lord did not stop his strong and terrible anger. His anger burned against Judah. It was because of all that Manasseh had done to make him angry. [27]The Lord said, "I have taken Israel away. I will do the same to Judah. I will take them out of my sight. I will reject Jerusalem which I chose. I will take away the Temple about which I said, 'I will be honored there.'"

[28]Everything else Josiah did is written down. It is in the book of the history of the kings of Judah.

[29]While Josiah was king, Neco king of Egypt went to help the king of Assyria. Neco was at the Euphrates River. King Josiah marched out to fight against Neco. But at Megiddo, Neco faced Josiah and killed him. [30]Josiah's servants carried his body in a chariot from Megiddo. They brought him to Jerusalem and buried him in his own grave. Then the people of Judah chose Josiah's son Jehoahaz. They poured olive oil on him to appoint him king in his father's place.

JEHOAHAZ KING OF JUDAH

[31]Jehoahaz was 23 years old when he became king. And he was king in Jerusalem for three months. His mother's name was Hamutal. She was the daughter of Jeremiah from Libnah. [32]Jehoahaz did what the Lord said was wrong. He did just as his ancestors had done.

[33]King Neco took Jehoahaz prisoner at Riblah in the land of Hamath. He did this so Jehoahaz could not rule in Jerusalem. Neco made the people of Judah pay about 7,500 pounds of silver and about 75 pounds of gold.

[34]King Neco made Josiah's son Eliakim the king in place of Josiah his father. Then Neco changed Eliakim's name to Jehoiakim. But Neco took Jehoahaz to Egypt, and he died there. [35]Jehoiakim gave King Neco the silver and gold he demanded. But Jehoiakim taxed the land so he could pay the king. He took silver and gold from the people of the land. The amount he took from each person depended on how much he had.

JEHOIAKIM KING OF JUDAH

[36]Jehoiakim was 25 years old when he became king. He was king in Jerusalem for 11 years. His mother's name was Zebidah daughter of Pedaiah. She was from Rumah. [37]Jehoiakim did what the Lord said was wrong, just as his ancestors had done.

24 While Jehoiakim was king, Nebuchadnezzar king of Babylon attacked the land of Judah. So Jehoiakim became Nebuchadnezzar's servant for three years. Then Jehoiakim turned against Nebuchadnezzar. And he broke away from his rule. [2]The Lord sent men from Babylon, Aram, Moab and Ammon against Jehoiakim. He sent them to destroy Judah. This happened the way the Lord had said it would through his servants the prophets.[d]

[3]The Lord commanded this to happen to the people of Judah. He did it to remove them from his presence. This was because of all the sins Manasseh had done. [4]He had killed many innocent people. He had filled Jerusalem with their blood. And the Lord would not forgive these sins.

[5]The other things that happened while Jehoiakim was king and all he did are written down. They are in the book of the history of the kings of Judah. [6]Jehoiakim died, and his son Jehoiachin became king in his place.

[7]The king of Egypt did not come out of his land again. This was because of the king of Babylon. He had captured all that belonged to the king of Egypt. He took all the land from the brook of Egypt to the Euphrates River.

JEHOIACHIN KING OF JUDAH

[8]Jehoiachin was 18 years old when he became king. He was king three months in Jerusalem. His mother's name was Nehushta daughter of Elnathan. She was from Jerusalem. [9]Jehoiachin did what the Lord said was wrong, just as his father had done.

[10]At that time the officers of Nebuchadnezzar king of Babylon came up to Jerusalem. They surrounded the city and attacked it. [11]Nebuchadnezzar himself came to the city while his officers were attacking it. [12]Jehoiachin king of Judah surrendered to the king of Babylon. Jehoiachin's mother, servants, elders and officers also surrendered. Then the king of Babylon made Jehoiachin a prisoner. This was in the eighth year Nebuchadnezzar was king. [13]Nebuchadnezzar took all the treasures from the Temple[d] of the Lord. He also removed the treasures from the palace.

He took all the gold objects Solomon king of Israel had made for the Temple. This happened as the Lord had said it would. [14]Nebuchadnezzar took away all the people of Jerusalem. This included all the leaders and all the wealthy people. He also took all the craftsmen and metal workers. There were 10,000 prisoners in all. Only the poorest people in the land were left. [15]Nebuchadnezzar carried away Jehoiachin to Babylon. He took the king's mother and his wives. He also took the officers and leading men of the land. They were taken captive from Jerusalem to Babylon. [16]The king of Babylon also took all 7,000 soldiers. These men were all strong and able to fight in war. And 1,000 craftsmen and metal workers were taken, too. Nebuchadnezzar took them as prisoners to Babylon. [17]He made Mattaniah king in Jehoiachin's place. Mattaniah was Jehoiachin's uncle. He also changed Mattaniah's name to Zedekiah.

ZEDEKIAH KING OF JUDAH

[18]Zedekiah was 21 years old when he became king. And he was king in Jerusalem for 11 years. His mother's name was Hamutal daughter of Jeremiah.[n] She was from Libnah. [19]Zedekiah did what the Lord said was wrong, just as Jehoiakim had done. [20]All this happened in Jerusalem and Judah because the Lord was angry with them. Finally, he threw them out of his presence.

THE FALL OF JERUSALEM

Zedekiah turned against the king of Babylon.

25 Then Nebuchadnezzar king of Babylon marched against Jerusalem with his whole army. This happened during Zedekiah's ninth year, tenth month and tenth day as king. He made a camp around the city. Then he built devices all around the city walls to attack it. [2]The city was under attack until

---

24:18 Jeremiah This is not the prophet Jeremiah but a different man with the same name.

Zedekiah's eleventh year as king. [3]By the ninth day of the fourth month, the hunger was terrible in the city. There was no food for the people to eat. [4]Then the city wall was broken through. And the whole army ran away at night. They went through the gate between the two walls by the king's garden. The Babylonians were still surrounding the city. Zedekiah and his men ran toward the Jordan Valley. [5]But the Babylonian army chased King Zedekiah. They caught up with him in the plains of Jericho. All of his army was scattered from him. [6]So they captured Zedekiah and took him to the king of Babylon at Riblah. There he passed sentence on Zedekiah. [7]They killed Zedekiah's sons as he watched. Then they put out his eyes. They put bronze chains on him and took him to Babylon.

[8]Nebuzaradan was the commander of the king's special guards. This officer of the king of Babylon came to Jerusalem. This was on the seventh day of the fifth month. This was in Nebuchadnezzar's nineteenth year as king of Babylon. [9]Nebuzaradan set fire to the Temple[d] of the Lord and the palace. He also set fire to all the houses of Jerusalem. Every important building was burned.

[10]The whole Babylonian army broke down the walls around Jerusalem. That army was led by the commander of the king's special guards. [11]Nebuzaradan, the commander of the guards, took captive the people left in Jerusalem. And he took captive those who had surrendered to the king of Babylon. The rest of the people were also taken away. [12]But the commander left behind some of the poorest people of the land. They were to take care of the vineyards and fields.

[13]The Babylonians broke up the bronze pillars, the bronze stands and the large bronze bowl, which was called the Sea. These were in the Temple of the Lord. Then they carried the bronze to Babylon. [14]They also took the pots, shovels, wick trimmers, dishes and all the bronze objects. These were used to serve in the Temple. [15]The commander of the king's special guards took away the pans for carrying hot coals. He also took the bowls and everything made of pure gold or silver. [16]There was so much bronze that it could not be weighed. There were two pillars and the large bronze bowl. There were also the movable stands which Solomon had made for the Temple of the Lord. [17]Each pillar was about 27 feet high. The bronze capital[d] on top of the pillar was about 4½ feet high. It was decorated with a net design and bronze pomegranates[d] all around it. The other pillar also had a net design. It was like the first pillar.

JUDAH IS TAKEN PRISONER

[18]The commander of the guards took some prisoners. He took Seraiah the chief priest, Zephaniah the priest next in rank, and the three doorkeepers. [19]The commander also took other people who were still in the city. He took the officer in charge of the fighting men. He also took five people who advised the king. And he took the royal assistant who selected people for the army. And he took 60 other men who were in the city. [20]Nebuzaradan, the commander, took all these people. And he brought them to the king of Babylon at Riblah. [21]There at Riblah, in the land of Hamath, the king had them killed. So the people of Judah were led away from their country as captives.

GEDALIAH BECOMES GOVERNOR

[22]Nebuchadnezzar king of Babylon left some people in the land of Judah. He appointed Gedaliah son of Ahikam as governor. (Ahikam was the son of Shaphan.)

[23]The army captains and their men heard that the king of Babylon had made Gedaliah governor. So they all came to Gedaliah at Mizpah. They were Ishmael son of Nethaniah and Johanan son of

Kareah. Also there were Seraiah son of Tanhumeth the Netophathite, Jaazaniah son of the Maacathite and their men. ²⁴Then Gedaliah made promises to these army captains and their men. He said, "Don't be afraid of the Babylonian officers. Live in the land and serve the king of Babylon. Then everything will go well for you."

²⁵Ishmael was the son of Nethaniah. Nethaniah was the son of Elishama from the king's family. In the seventh month Ishmael came with ten men and killed Gedaliah. They also killed the men of Judah and Babylon who were with Gedaliah at Mizpah. ²⁶Then all the people, from the least important to the most important, ran away to Egypt. The army leaders also went. This was because they were afraid of the Babylonians.

JEHOIACHIN IS SET FREE

²⁷Jehoiachin king of Judah was held in Babylon for 37 years. In the thirty-seventh year Evil-Merodach became king of Babylon. He let Jehoiachin out of prison on the twenty-seventh day of the twelfth month. ²⁸Evil-Merodach spoke kindly to Jehoiachin. He gave Jehoiachin a seat of honor. It was above the seats of the other kings who were with him in Babylon. ²⁹So Jehoiachin put away his prison clothes. For the rest of his life, he ate at the king's table. ³⁰Every day the king gave Jehoiachin an allowance. This lasted as long as he lived.

THE FIRST BOOK OF THE
CHRONICLES

FROM ADAM TO ABRAHAM

1 Adam was the father of Seth. Seth was the father of Enosh. Enosh was the father of Kenan. [2]Kenan was the father of Mahalalel. Mahalalel was the father of Jared. Jared was the father of Enoch. [3]Enoch was the father of Methuselah. Methuselah was the father of Lamech. And he was the father of Noah.

[4]The sons of Noah were Shem, Ham and Japheth.

[5]Japheth's sons were Gomer, Magog, Madai, Javan, Tubal, Meshech and Tiras.

[6]Gomer's sons were Ashkenaz, Riphath and Togarmah.

[7]Javan's sons were Elishah, Tarshish, Kittim[n] and Rodanim.

[8]Ham's sons were Cush, Mizraim,[n] Put and Canaan.

[9]Cush's sons were Seba, Havilah, Sabta, Raamah and Sabteca.

Raamah's sons were Sheba and Dedan.

[10]Cush was the father of Nimrod. Nimrod grew up to become a mighty warrior on the earth.

[11]Mizraim was the father of the people living in Lud, Anam, Lehab and Naphtuh. [12]Mizraim was also the father of the people living in Pathrus, Casluh and Crete. (The Philistine people came from Casluh.)

[13]Canaan's first child was Sidon. Canaan was also the father of the Hittites, [14]Jebusites, Amorites and the Girgashites. [15]He was the father of the Hivites, Arkites, Sinites, [16]Arvadites, Zemarites and the Hamathites.

[17]Shem's sons were Elam, Asshur, Arphaxad, Lud and Aram.

Aram's sons were Uz, Hul, Gether and Meshech.

[18]Arphaxad was the father of Shelah. Shelah was the father of Eber.

[19]Eber had two sons. One son was named Peleg.[n] He was named this because the people on the earth were divided into different languages during his life. Peleg's brother was named Joktan.

[20]Joktan was the father of Almodad, Sheleph, Hazarmaveth, Jerah, [21]Hadoram, Uzal and Diklah. [22]He was also the father of Obal, Abimael, Sheba, [23]Ophir, Havilah and Jobab. All these were Joktan's sons. [24]The family line went from Shem to Abraham. It included Shem, Arphaxad, Shelah, [25]Eber, Peleg, Reu, [26]Serug, Nahor, Terah [27]and Abram, who is called Abraham.

ABRAHAM'S FAMILY

[28]Abraham's sons were Isaac and Ishmael.

[29]These were the sons of Isaac and Ishmael. Ishmael's first son was Nebaioth. Ishmael's other sons were Kedar, Adbeel, Mibsam, [30]Mishma, Dumah, Massa, Hadad, Tema, [31]Jetur, Naphish and Kedemah. These were Ishmael's sons. [32]Keturah was Abraham's slave woman.[d] She gave birth to Zimran, Jokshan, Medan, Midian, Ishbak and Shuah.

Jokshan's sons were Sheba and Dedan.

[33]Midian's sons were Ephah, Epher, Hanoch, Abida and Eldaah. All these people were descendants[d] of Keturah.

[34]Abraham was the father of Isaac. Isaac's sons were Esau and Israel.

[35]Esau's sons were Eliphaz, Reuel, Jeush, Jalam and Korah.

[36]Eliphaz's sons were Teman, Omar, Zepho, Gatam, Kenaz, Timna and Amalek.

[37]Reuel's sons were Nahath, Zerah, Shammah and Mizzah.

1:7 Kittim His descendants were the people of Cyprus.
1:8 Mizraim This is another name for Egypt.
1:19 Peleg This name sounds like the Hebrew word for "divided."

THE EDOMITES FROM SEIR

38Seir's sons were Lotan, Shobal, Zibeon, Anah, Dishon, Ezer and Dishan.

39Lotan's sons were Hori and Homam. Lotan had a sister named Timna.

40Shobal's sons were Alvan, Manahath, Ebal, Shepho and Onam.

Zibeon's sons were Aiah and Anah.

41Anah's son was Dishon.

Dishon's sons were Hemdan, Eshban, Ithran and Keran.

42Ezer's sons were Bilhan, Zaavan and Akan.

Dishan's sons were Uz and Aran.

THE KINGS OF EDOM

43There were kings ruling in Edom before there were kings in Israel. Bela son of Beor was king of Edom. Bela's city was named Dinhabah.

44When Bela died, Jobab son of Zerah became king. Jobab was from Bozrah.

45When Jobab died, Husham became king. He was from Teman.

46When Husham died, Hadad son of Bedad became king. Hadad's city was named Avith. Hadad defeated Midian in the country of Moab.

47When Hadad died, Samlah became king. He was from Masrekah.

48When Samlah died, Shaul became king. He was from Rehoboth by the River.

49When Shaul died, Baal-Hanan son of Acbor became king.

50When Baal-Hanan died, Hadad became king. Hadad's city was named Pau. Hadad's wife was named Mehetabel, and she was Matred's daughter. Matred was the daughter of Me-Zahab. 51Then Hadad died.

The leaders of the family groups of Edom were Timna, Alvah, Jetheth, 52Oholibamah, Elah, Pinon, 53Kenaz, Teman, Mibzar, 54Magdiel and Iram. These were the leaders of Edom.

ISRAEL'S FAMILY

2 The sons of Israel, also called Jacob, were Reuben, Simeon, Levi, Judah, Issachar, Zebulun, 2Dan, Joseph, Benjamin, Naphtali, Gad and Asher.

JUDAH'S FAMILY

3Judah's sons were Er, Onan and Shelah. A Canaanite woman, the daughter of Shua, was their mother. Judah's first son, Er, did what the Lord said was wicked. So the Lord put him to death. 4Judah's daughter-in-law Tamar gave birth to Perez and Zerah. Judah was the father. So Judah had five sons.

5Perez's sons were Hezron and Hamul.

6Zerah had five sons. They were Zimri, Ethan, Heman, Calcol and Darda.

7Carmi's son was Achan. He caused trouble for Israel because he took things that had been given to the Lord to be destroyed.

8Ethan's son was Azariah.

9Hezron's sons were Jerahmeel, Ram and Caleb.

10Ram was Amminadab's father. And Amminadab was Nashon's father. Nahshon was the leader of the people of Judah. 11Nahshon was the father of Salmon. Salmon was the father of Boaz. 12Boaz was the father of Obed. Obed was the father of Jesse.

13Jesse's first son was Eliab. His second son was Abinadab. His third son was Shimea. 14His fourth son was Nethanel. His fifth son was Raddai. 15Jesse's sixth son was Ozem, and his seventh son was David. 16Their sisters were Zeruiah and Abigail. Zeruiah's three sons were Abishai, Joab and Asahel. 17Abigail was the mother of Amasa. Amasa's father was an Ishmaelite named Jether.

CALEB'S FAMILY

18Caleb son of Hezron had children by his wife Azubah and by Jerioth. Caleb and Azubah's sons were Jesher, Shobab and Ardon. 19When Azubah died, Caleb married Ephrath. They had a son named Hur. 20Hur was the father of Uri. Uri was the father of Bezalel.

²¹Later, when Hezron was 60 years old, he married the daughter of Makir. Makir was Gilead's father. Hezron had sexual relations with Makir's daughter, and she had a son named Segub. ²²Segub was the father of Jair. Jair controlled 23 cities in the country of Gilead. ²³(But Geshur and Aram captured the Towns of Jair. They also captured Kenath and the small towns around it. There were 60 towns in all.) All these were descendants*d* of Makir, the father of Gilead.

²⁴After Hezron died in Caleb Ephrathah, his wife Abijah had his son. He was named Ashur. Ashur became the father of Tekoa.

JERAHMEEL'S FAMILY

²⁵Jerahmeel was Hezron's first son. Jerahmeel's sons were Ram, Bunah, Oren, Ozem and Ahijah. Ram was Jerahmeel's first son. ²⁶Jerahmeel had another wife, who was named Atarah. She was the mother of Onam.

²⁷Jerahmeel's first son, Ram, had sons. They were Maaz, Jamin and Eker. ²⁸Onam's sons were Shammai and Jada.

Shammai's sons were Nadab and Abishur. ²⁹Abishur's wife was named Abihail. Abishur and Abihail's sons were Ahban and Molid. ³⁰Nadab's sons were Seled and Appaim. Seled died without having children. ³¹Appaim's son was Ishi. Ishi was the father of Sheshan.

Sheshan was the father of Ahlai.

³²Jada was Shammai's brother. Jada's sons were Jether and Jonathan. Jether died without having children. ³³Jonathan's sons were Peleth and Zaza.

These were Jerahmeel's descendants.*d*

³⁴Sheshan did not have any sons, only daughters. He had a servant from Egypt named Jarha. ³⁵Sheshan let his daughter marry his servant Jarha. Then she had a son named Attai.

³⁶Attai was the father of Nathan. Nathan was the father of Zabad. ³⁷Zabad was the father of Ephlal. Ephlal was the father of Obed. ³⁸Obed was the father of Jehu. Jehu was the father of Azariah. ³⁹Azariah was the father of Helez. Helez was the father of Eleasah. ⁴⁰Eleasah was the father of Sismai. Sismai was the father of Shallum. ⁴¹Shallum was the father of Jekamiah. And Jekamiah was the father of Elishama.

CALEB'S FAMILY

⁴²Caleb was Jerahmeel's brother. Caleb's first son was Mesha. Mesha was the father of Ziph. And his son Mareshah was the father of Hebron.

⁴³Hebron's sons were Korah, Tappuah, Rekem and Shema. ⁴⁴Shema was the father of Raham. Raham was the father of Jorkeam. Rekem was the father of Shammai. ⁴⁵Shammai's son was Maon. Maon was the father of Beth Zur.

⁴⁶Caleb's slave woman*d* was named Ephah. She was the mother of Haran, Moza and Gazez. Haran was the father of Gazez.

⁴⁷Jahdai's sons were Regem, Jotham, Geshan, Pelet, Ephah and Shaaph.

⁴⁸Caleb had another slave woman named Maacah. She was the mother of Sheber and Tirhanah. ⁴⁹She was also the mother of Shaaph and Sheva. Shaaph was the father of Madmannah. Sheva was the father of Macbenah and Gibea. Caleb's daughter was Acsah.

⁵⁰⁻⁵¹These were Caleb's descendants:*d* Caleb's son Hur was the first son of his mother Ephrathah. Hur's sons were Shobal, Salma and Hareph. Shobal was the father of Kiriath Jearim. Salma was the father of Bethlehem. And Hareph was the father of Beth Gader.

⁵²Shobal was the father of Kiriath Jearim. These were Shobal's descendants: Haroeh, half the Manahathites, ⁵³and the family groups of Kiriath Jearim. Shobal was also the ancestor of the Ithrites, Puthites, Shumathites and

the Mishraites. The Zorathites and the Eshtaolites came from the Mishraite people.

⁵⁴Salma's descendants were Bethlehem, the Netophathites, Atroth Beth Joab, half the Manahathites and the Zorites. ⁵⁵His descendants were also the families who lived at Jabez. These were the people who wrote and copied important papers. These people were the Tirathites, Shimeathites and Sucathites. They were from the Kenite family group who came from Hammath. He was the father of the people living in Recab.

DAVID'S FAMILY

3 These are David's sons who were born in Hebron. David's first son was Amnon. Amnon's mother was Ahinoam from the town of Jezreel. David's second son was Daniel. His mother was Abigail from Carmel. ²David's third son was Absalom. His mother was Maacah, the daughter of Talmai king of Geshur. David's fourth son was Adonijah. His mother was Haggith. ³David's fifth son was Shephatiah. His mother was Abital. David's sixth son was Ithream. David's wife Eglah was his mother. ⁴These six sons of David were born to him in Hebron. David ruled there 7 years and 6 months.

David ruled in Jerusalem 33 years. ⁵These were David's children who were born in Jerusalem: David and Bathsheba, Ammiel's daughter, had four children. They were Shammua, Shobab, Nathan and Solomon. ⁶⁻⁸David's other nine children were Ibhar, Elishua, Eliphelet, Nogah, Nepheg, Japhia, Elishama, Eliada and Eliphelet. ⁹Those are all of David's sons, except for those born to his slave women.*ᵈ* David also had a daughter named Tamar.

THE KINGS OF JUDAH

¹⁰Solomon's son was Rehoboam. Rehoboam's son was Abijah. Abijah's son was Asa. Asa's son was Jehoshaphat.

¹¹Jehoshaphat's son was Jehoram. Jehoram's son was Ahaziah. Ahaziah's son was Joash. ¹²Joash's son was Amaziah. Amaziah's son was Azariah. Azariah's son was Jotham. ¹³Jotham's son was Ahaz. Ahaz's son was Hezekiah. Hezekiah's son was Manasseh. ¹⁴Manasseh's son was Amon. Amon's son was Josiah.

¹⁵These were Josiah's sons: Josiah's first son was Johanan. His second son was Jehoiakim. His third son was Zedekiah. His fourth son was Shallum.

¹⁶Jehoiakim was followed by Jehoiachin. Jehoiachin was followed by Zedekiah.

DAVID'S DESCENDANTS AFTER THE BABYLONIAN CAPTIVITY

¹⁷Jehoiachin was taken as a prisoner. His sons were Shealtiel, ¹⁸Malkiram, Pedaiah, Shenazzar, Jekamiah, Hoshama and Nedabiah.

¹⁹Pedaiah's sons were Zerubbabel and Shimei.

Zerubbabel's sons were Meshullam and Hananiah. Their sister was Shelomith. ²⁰Zerubbabel also had five other sons. Their names were Hashubah, Ohel, Berekiah, Hasadiah and Jushab-Hesed.

²¹Hananiah's descendants*ᵈ* were Pelatiah and Jeshaiah, and the sons of Rephaiah, Arnan, Obadiah and Shecaniah.

²²Shecaniah's son was Shemaiah. Shemaiah's sons were Hattush, Igal, Bariah, Neariah and Shaphat. There were six in all.

²³Neariah had three sons. They were Elioenai, Hizkiah and Azrikam.

²⁴Elioenai had seven sons. They were Hodaviah, Eliashib, Pelaiah, Akkub, Johanan, Delaiah and Anani.

OTHER FAMILY GROUPS OF JUDAH

4 Judah's descendants*ᵈ* were Perez, Hezron, Carmi, Hur and Shobal. ²Reaiah was Shobal's son. Reaiah was the father of Jahath. Jahath was the father of Ahumai and Lahad. They were the family groups of the Zorathite people.

3-4Hur was the oldest son of Caleb and his wife Ephrath. Hur was the leader of Bethlehem. Hur's three sons were Etam, Penuel and Ezer. Etam's sons were Jezreel, Ishma and Idbash. They had a sister named Hazzelelponi. Penuel was the father of Gedor. Ezer was the father of Hushah.

5Tekoa's father was Ashhur. Ashhur had two wives named Helah and Naarah.

6The sons of Ashhur and Naarah were Ahuzzam, Hepher, Temeni and Haahash-tari. These were the descendants of Naarah.

7Helah's sons were Zereth, Zohar, Ethnan 8and Koz. Koz was the father of Anub and Hazzobebah. He was also the father of the Aharhel family group. Aharhel was the son of Harum.

9There was a man named Jabez. He was respected more than his brothers. His mother named him Jabez[n] because she said, "I was in much pain when I gave birth to him." 10Jabez prayed to the God of Israel. Jabez said, "Please do good things for me. Please give me more land. Stay with me, and don't let anyone hurt me. Then I won't have any pain." And God did what Jabez had asked.

11Kelub was Shuhah's brother. Kelub was the father of Mehir. Mehir was the father of Eshton. 12Eshton was the father of Beth Rapha, Paseah and Tehinnah. Tehinnah was the father of the people from the town of Nahash. These people were from Recah.

13The sons of Kenaz were Othniel and Seraiah.

Othniel's sons were Hathath and Meonothai. 14Meonothai was the father of Ophrah.

Seraiah was the father of Joab. Joab was the ancestor of the people from Craftsmen's Valley. It is called Crafts-men's Valley because the people living there were craftsmen.

15Caleb was Jephunneh's son. Caleb's sons were Iru, Elah and Naam. Elah's son was Kenaz.

16Jehallelel's sons were Ziph, Ziphah, Tiria and Asarel.

17-18Ezrah's sons were Jether, Mered, Epher and Jalon. Mered married Bithiah, the daughter of the king of Egypt. The children of Mered and Bithiah were Miriam, Shammai and Ishbah. Ishbah was the father of Eshtemoa. Mered also had a wife from Judah. She gave birth to Jered, Heber and Jekuthiel. Jered be-came the father of Gedor. Heber became the father of Soco. And Jekuthiel became the father of Zanoah.

19Hodiah's wife was Naham's sister. The sons of Hodiah's wife were Eshte-moa and the father of Keilah. Keilah was from the Garmite people. And Eshtemoa was from the Maacathite people.

20Shimon's sons were Amnon, Rinnah, Ben-Hanan and Tilon.

Ishi's sons were Zoheth and Ben-Zoheth.

21-22Shelah was Judah's son. Shelah's sons were Er, Laadah, Jokim, the men from Cozeba, Joash and Saraph. Er was the father of Lecah. Laadah was the father of Mareshah and the family groups of linen workers at Beth Ashbea. Joash and Saraph ruled in Moab and Jashubi Lehem. The writings about this family are very old. 23These sons of Shelah made things from clay. They lived in Netaim and Gederah. They stayed there and worked for the king.

SIMEON'S CHILDREN

24Simeon's sons were Nemuel, Jamin, Jarib, Zerah and Shaul. 25Shaul's son was Shallum. Shallum's son was Mibsam. Mibsam's son was Mishma.

26Mishma's son was Hammuel. Ham-muel's son was Zaccur. Zaccur's son was Shimei. 27Shimei had 16 sons and 6 daughters. But his brothers did not have

4:9 Jabez This name in Hebrew sounds like the word for "pain."

many children. So there were not as many people in their family group as there were in Judah.

²⁸Shimei's children lived in Beersheba, Moladah, Hazar Shual, ²⁹Bilhah, Ezem and Tolad. ³⁰They also lived in Bethuel, Hormah, Ziklag, ³¹Beth Marcaboth, Hazar Susim, Beth Biri and Shaaraim. They lived in these cities until David became king. ³²The five villages near these cities were Etam, Ain, Rimmon, Token and Ashan. ³³There were also other villages as far away as Baalath. This is where they lived. And they wrote the history of their family.

³⁴⁻³⁸This is the list of men who were leaders of their family groups. There were Meshobab, Jamlech, Joshah son of Amaziah, Joel and Jehu son of Joshibiah. (Joshibiah was the son of Seraiah, who was the son of Asiel.) There were also Elioenai, Jaakobah, Jeshohaiah, Asaiah, Adiel, Jesimiel, Benaiah and Ziza. (Ziza was the son of Shiphi, who was the son of Allon. Allon was the son of Jedaiah, who was the son of Shimri. And Shimri was the son of Shemaiah.)

These men's families grew to be very large. ³⁹They went to the area outside the city of Gedor to the east side of the valley. They went there to look for pasture for their sheep. ⁴⁰They found good pastures with plenty of grass. The land was open country and peaceful and quiet. Ham's descendants*d* had lived there in the past.

⁴¹These men listed above came to Gedor while Hezekiah was king of Judah. They fought against the Hamite people and destroyed their tents. They also fought against the Meunite people who lived there and completely destroyed them. So there are no Meunites there even today. Then these men began to live there, because there was pasture for their sheep. ⁴²Ishi's sons, Pelatiah, Neariah, Rephaiah and Uzziel, led 500 of the Simeonite people. They attacked the

people living in the mountains of Edom. ⁴³They killed the few Amalekite people who were still alive. From that time until now these Simeonites have lived in Edom.

REUBEN'S CHILDREN

5 Reuben was Israel's first son. Reuben should have received the special privileges of the oldest son. But he had sexual relations with his father's slave woman.*d* So those special privileges were given to Joseph's sons. (Joseph was a son of Israel.) In the family history Reuben's name is not listed as the first son. ²Judah became stronger than his brothers. And a leader came from his family. But Joseph's family received the privileges that belonged to the oldest son. ³Reuben was the first son born to Israel. Reuben's sons were Hanoch, Pallu, Hezron and Carmi.

⁴These were the children of Joel: Shemaiah was Joel's son. Gog was Shemaiah's son. Shimei was Gog's son. ⁵Micah was Shimei's son. Reaiah was Micah's son. Baal was Reaiah's son. ⁶Beerah was Baal's son. Beerah was a leader of the tribe*d* of Reuben. Tiglath-Pileser king of Assyria captured Beerah and took him away.

⁷Joel's brothers and all his family groups are listed just as they are written in their family histories: Jeiel was the first, then Zechariah ⁸and Bela. (Bela was the son of Azaz. Azaz was Shema's son. Shema was Joel's son.) They lived in the area of Aroer all the way to Nebo and Baal Meon. ⁹Bela's people lived to the east. Their land went as far as the edge of the desert, which is beside the Euphrates River. They lived there because they had too many cattle for the land of Gilead.

¹⁰When Saul was king, Bela's people fought a war against the Hagrite people. And they defeated the Hagrites. Then Bela's people lived in the tents that had belonged to the Hagrites. They lived in all the area east of Gilead.

GAD'S CHILDREN

[11]The people from the tribe[d] of Gad lived near the Reubenite people. The Gadites lived in the area of Bashan all the way to Salecah. [12]Joel was the main leader in Bashan. Shapham was the second leader. Then Janai and Shaphat were leaders.

[13]The seven relatives in their families were Michael, Meshullam, Sheba, Jorai, Jacan, Zia and Eber. [14]They were the descendants[d] of Abihail. Abihail was Huri's son. Huri was Jaroah's son. Jaroah was Gilead's son. Gilead was Michael's son. Michael was Jeshishai's son. Jeshishai was Jahdo's son. Jahdo was the son of Buz. [15]Ahi was Abdiel's son. Abdiel was Guni's son. Ahi was the leader of their family.

[16]The Gadite people lived in Gilead, Bashan and in the small towns around Bashan. They also lived on all the pasturelands in the Plain of Sharon all the way to the borders.

[17]All these people's names were written in the family history of Gad. This was done during the time Jotham was king of Judah and Jeroboam was king of Israel.

SOLDIERS SKILLED IN WAR

[18]There were 44,760 fighters from the tribes[d] of Reuben and Gad and the eastern half-tribe of Manasseh. They were brave men who could use shields and swords. They could use their bows well. They were skilled in war. [19]They started a war against the Hagrites and the people of Jetur, Naphish and Nodab. [20]The men from the tribes of Manasseh, Reuben and Gad prayed to God in the war. They asked God to help them. So he helped them because they trusted him. He allowed them to defeat the Hagrites. And they also defeated all those who were with the Hagrites. [21]They took the animals that belonged to the Hagrites. They took 50,000 camels, 250,000 sheep and 2,000 donkeys. They also captured 100,000 people. [22]Many Hagrites were killed. This is because God helped the people of Reuben, Gad and Manasseh. Then they lived there until Babylon captured them and took them away.

THE EASTERN HALF-TRIBE OF MANASSEH

[23]There were many people in the eastern half-tribe of Manasseh. They lived in the area of Bashan all the way to Baal Hermon, Senir and Mount Hermon.

[24]These were the family leaders: Epher, Ishi, Eliel, Azriel, Jeremiah, Hodaviah and Jahdiel. They were all strong, brave and famous men. And they were leaders in their families. [25]But they sinned against the God that their ancestors had worshiped. They began worshiping the gods of the people in that land. And those were the people God was destroying. [26]So the God of Israel made Pul king of Assyria want to go to war. Pul was also called Tiglath-Pileser. He captured the people of Reuben, Gad and the eastern half-tribe of Manasseh. And he took them away to Halah, Habor, Hara and near the Gozan River. And they have lived there from that time until this day.

LEVI'S CHILDREN

6 Levi's sons were Gershon, Kohath and Merari.

[2]Kohath's sons were Amram, Izhar, Hebron and Uzziel.

[3]Amram's children were Aaron, Moses and Miriam.

Aaron's sons were Nadab, Abihu, Eleazar and Ithamar. [4]Eleazar was the father of Phinehas. Phinehas was the father of Abishua. [5]Abishua was the father of Bukki. Bukki was the father of Uzzi. [6]Uzzi was the father of Zerahiah. Zerahiah was the father of Meraioth. [7]Meraioth was the father of Amariah. Amariah was the father of Ahitub. [8]Ahitub was the father of Zadok. Zadok was the father of Ahimaaz. [9]Ahimaaz was the father of Azariah. Azariah was the father of Johanan.

[10]Johanan was the father of Azariah. (Azariah was a priest in the Temple[d] Solomon built in Jerusalem.) [11]Azariah was the father of Amariah. Amariah was the father of Ahitub. [12]Ahitub was the father of Zadok. Zadok was the father of Shallum. [13]Shallum was the father of Hilkiah. Hilkiah was the father of Azariah. [14]Azariah was the father of Seraiah. Seraiah was the father of Jehozadak.

[15]Jehozadak was forced to leave his home when the Lord sent Judah and Jerusalem into captivity. That was when Nebuchadnezzar captured them and took them away.

[16]Levi's sons were Gershon, Kohath and Merari.

[17]The names of Gershon's sons were Libni and Shimei.

[18]Kohath's sons were Amram, Izhar, Hebron and Uzziel.

[19]Merari's sons were Mahli and Mushi. This is a list of the family groups of Levi. They are listed by the name of the father of each group.

[20]Gershon's son was Libni. Libni's son was Jehath. Jehath's son was Zimmah. [21]Zimmah's son was Joah. Joah's son was Iddo. Iddo's son was Zerah. And Zerah's son was Jeatherai.

[22]Kohath's son was Amminadab. Amminadab's son was Korah. Korah's son was Assir. [23]Assir's son was Elkanah. Elkanah's son was Ebiasaph. Ebiasaph's son was Assir. [24]Assir's son was Tahath. Tahath's son was Uriel. Uriel's son was Uzziah, and Uzziah's son was Shaul.

[25]Elkanah's sons were Amasai and Ahimoth. [26]Ahimoth's son was Elkanah. Elkanah's son was Zophai. Zophai's son was Nahath. [27]Nahath's son was Eliab. Eliab's son was Jeroham. Jeroham's son was Elkanah, and Elkanah's son was Samuel.

[28]Samuel's sons were Joel, the first son, and Abijah, the second son.

[29]Merari's son was Mahli. Mahli's son was Libni. Libni's son was Shimei. Shimei's son was Uzzah. [30]Uzzah's son was Shimea. Shimea's son was Haggiah, and Haggiah's son was Asaiah.

THE TEMPLE MUSICIANS

[31]David chose some men to be in charge of the music in the house of the Lord. They began their work after the Box[d] of the Agreement was put there. [32]They served by making music at the Holy Tent.[d] (It is also called the Meeting Tent.) And they served until Solomon built the Temple[d] of the Lord in Jerusalem. They followed the rules for their work.

[33]These are the musicians and their sons:

From Kohath's family there was Heman the singer. Heman was Joel's son. Joel was Samuel's son. [34]Samuel was Elkanah's son. Elkanah was Jeroham's son. Jeroham was Eliel's son. Eliel was Toah's son. [35]Toah was Zuph's son. Zuph was Elkanah's son. Elkanah was Mahath's son. Mahath was Amasai's son. [36]Amasai was Elkanah's son. Elkanah was Joel's son. Joel was Azariah's son. Azariah was Zephaniah's son. [37]Zephaniah was Tahath's son. Tahath was Assir's son. Assir was Ebiasaph's son. Ebiasaph was Korah's son. [38]Korah was Izhar's son. Izhar was Kohath's son. Kohath was Levi's son. Levi was Israel's son.

[39]There was Heman's helper Asaph. Asaph's group stood by Heman's right side. Asaph was Berekiah's son. Berekiah was Shimea's son. [40]Shimea was Michael's son. Michael was Baaseiah's son. Baaseiah was Malkijah's son. [41]Malkijah was Ethni's son. Ethni was Zerah's son. Zerah was Adaiah's son. [42]Adaiah was Ethan's son. Ethan was Zimmah's son. Zimmah was Shimei's son. [43]Shimei was Jahath's son. Jahath was Gershon's son. Gershon was Levi's son.

[44]Merari's family were the helpers of Heman and Asaph. Merari's family stood by Heman's left side. In this group was Ethan son of Kishi. Kishi was Abdi's

son. Abdi was Malluch's son. ⁴⁵Malluch was Hashabiah's son. Hashabiah was Amaziah's son. Amaziah was Hilkiah's son. ⁴⁶Hilkiah was Amzi's son. Amzi was Bani's son. Bani was Shemer's son. ⁴⁷Shemer was Mahli's son. Mahli was Mushi's son. Mushi was Merari's son. Merari was Levi's son.

⁴⁸The other Levites served by doing their own special work in the Holy Tent. It is the house of God. ⁴⁹Aaron and his descendants*d* offered the sacrifices on the altar of burnt offering. They also burned the incense on the altar of incense. They offered the sacrifices that removed the Israelites' sins so they could belong to God. They did all the work in the Most Holy Place. They followed all the laws that Moses, God's servant, had commanded.

⁵⁰These were Aaron's sons: Eleazar was Aaron's son. Phinehas was Eleazar's son. Abishua was Phinehas' son. ⁵¹Bukki was Abishua's son. Uzzi was Bukki's son. Zerahiah was Uzzi's son. ⁵²Meraioth was Zerahiah's son. Amariah was Meraioth's son. Ahitub was Amariah's son. ⁵³Zadok was Ahitub's son. Ahimaaz was Zadok's son.

LAND FOR THE LEVITES

⁵⁴These are the places where Aaron's descendants*d* lived. Aaron's descendants from the Kohath family group were given this land to live in. They received the first share of the land that was given to the Levites.

⁵⁵They were given the city of Hebron in Judah and the pastures around it. ⁵⁶But the fields farther from the city were given to Caleb son of Jephunneh. And the villages near Hebron were given to Caleb. ⁵⁷So the descendants of Aaron were given Hebron. It was one of the cities of safety.*n* They also received the cities of Libnah, Jattir, Eshtemoa,

⁵⁸Hilen, Debir, ⁵⁹Ashan, Juttah and Beth Shemesh. They received all these cities and the pastures around them. ⁶⁰They also received cities from the tribe of Benjamin. They received Gibeon, Geba, Alemeth, Anathoth and their pastures. The Kohath family groups received a total of 13 cities.

⁶¹The rest of the Kohath family group was given 10 cities. These cities were from the family groups of the western half-tribe of Manasseh. The cities were chosen by throwing lots.*d*

⁶²The Gershon family group received 13 cities. They were from the tribes of Issachar, Asher, Naphtali and the part of Manasseh living in Bashan.

⁶³The Merari family group received 12 cities from the tribes of Reuben, Gad and Zebulun. Those cities were chosen by throwing lots.

⁶⁴So the Israelites gave these cities and their pastures to the Levites. ⁶⁵The cities from the tribes of Judah, Simeon and Benjamin were chosen by throwing lots. They are the cities named above.

⁶⁶Some of the Kohath family groups received cities and pastures from the tribe of Ephraim. ⁶⁷They received Shechem in the mountains of Ephraim. It was one of the cities of safety. They also received the cities of Gezer, ⁶⁸Jokmeam, Beth Horon, ⁶⁹Aijalon and Gath Rimmon. They received the cities and the pastures around them.

⁷⁰The rest of the people in the Kohath family group received cities from the western half-tribe of Manasseh. They received the cities of Aner and Bileam and their pastures.

⁷¹From the eastern half-tribe of Manasseh, the Gershon family received towns and pastures. They received Golan in Bashan, Ashtaroth and the pastures around them.

6:57 cities of safety A person who had accidentally killed someone could go to one of the six cities of safety. There he would receive protection and a fair trial.

[72-73]From the tribe of Issachar, the Gershon family received towns and pastures. They received Kedesh, Daberath, Ramoth, Anem and their pastures.

[74-75]From the tribe of Asher, the Gershon family received towns and pastures. They received Mashal, Abdon, Hukok, Rehob and their pastures.

[76]From the tribe of Naphtali, the Gershon family received towns and pastures. They received Kedesh in Galilee, Hammon, Kiriathaim and their pastures.

[77]The rest of the Levites, the people from the Merari family, also received towns and pastures. They received Jokneam, Kartah, Rimmono and Tabor from the tribe of Zebulun. They also received the pastures around those cities.

[78-79]From the tribe of Reuben, the Merari family received towns and pastures. They received Bezer in the desert, Jahzah, Kedemoth, Mephaath and their pastures. (The tribe of Reuben lived east of the Jordan River, across from Jericho.)

[80-81]From the tribe of Gad, the Merari family received towns and pastures. They received Ramoth in Gilead, Mahanaim, Heshbon, Jazer and their pastures.

ISSACHAR'S CHILDREN

7 Issachar had four sons. Their names were Tola, Puah, Jashub and Shimron.

[2]Tola's sons were Uzzi, Rephaiah, Jeriel, Jahmai, Ibsam and Samuel. They were leaders of their families. In the family history of Tola's descendants,[d] 22,600 men were listed as fighting men. This was during the time David was king.

[3]Uzzi's son was Izrahiah.

Izrahiah's sons were Michael, Obadiah, Joel and Isshiah. All five of them were leaders. [4]Their family history shows they had 36,000 men ready to serve in the army. This was because they had many women and children.

[5]The records of the family groups of Issachar show there were 87,000 fighting men.

BENJAMIN'S CHILDREN

[6]Benjamin had three sons. Their names were Bela, Beker and Jediael.

[7]Bela had five sons. Their names were Ezbon, Uzzi, Uzziel, Jerimoth and Iri. They were leaders of their families. Their family history shows they had 22,034 fighting men.

[8]Beker's sons were Zemirah, Joash, Eliezer, Elioenai, Omri, Jeremoth, Abijah, Anathoth and Alemeth. They all were Beker's sons. [9]Their family history listed the family leaders and 20,200 fighting men.

[10]Jediael's son was Bilhan.

Bilhan's sons were Jeush, Benjamin, Ehud, Kenaanah, Zethan, Tarshish and Ahishahar. [11]All these sons of Jediael were leaders of their families. They had 17,200 fighting men ready to serve in the army.

[12]The Shuppites and Huppites were descendants[d] of Ir. And the Hushites were descendants of Aher.

NAPHTALI'S CHILDREN

[13]Naphtali's sons were Jahziel, Guni, Jezer and Shillem. They were Bilhah's grandsons.

MANASSEH'S CHILDREN

[14]These are Manasseh's descendants:[d] Manasseh had an Aramean slave woman.[d] She was the mother of Asriel and Makir. Makir was Gilead's father. [15]Makir took a wife from the Huppites and Shuppites. His sister was named Maacah. His second son was named Zelophehad. Zelophehad had only daughters. [16]Makir's wife Maacah had a son whom she named Peresh. Peresh's brother was named Sheresh. Sheresh's sons were Ulam and Rakem.

[17]Ulam's son was Bedan.

These were the sons of Gilead. Gilead was Makir's son. Makir was Manasseh's son. [18]Makir's sister Hammoleketh gave birth to Ishhod, Abiezer and Mahlah.

[19]The sons of Shemida were Ahian, Shechem, Likhi and Aniam.

EPHRAIM'S CHILDREN

[20] These are the names of Ephraim's descendants.[d] Ephraim's son was Shuthelah. Shuthelah's son was Bered. Bered's son was Tahath. Tahath's son was Eleadah. Eleadah's son was Tahath. [21] Tahath's son was Zabad. Zabad's son was Shuthelah.

Ezer and Elead went to Gath to steal the people's cows and sheep. So some men who grew up in that city killed Ezer and Elead. [22] Their father Ephraim cried for them many days. And his family came to comfort him. [23] Then he had sexual relations with his wife again. She became pregnant and gave birth to a son. Ephraim named his son Beriah[n] because of the bad things that had happened to his family. [24] Ephraim's daughter was Sheerah. She built Lower Beth Horon and Upper Beth Horon and Uzzen Sheerah.

[25] Rephah was Ephraim's son. Resheph was Rephah's son. Telah was Resheph's son. Tahan was Telah's son. [26] Ladan was Tahan's son. Ammihud was Ladan's son. Elishama was Ammihud's son. [27] Nun was Elishama's son. Joshua was the son of Nun.

[28] Ephraim's descendants lived in these lands and cities: Bethel and the villages near it, Naaran on the east, Gezer and the villages near it on the west, and Shechem and the villages near it. These villages went all the way to Ayyah and its villages. [29] Along the borders of Manasseh's land were the towns of Beth Shan, Taanach, Megiddo and Dor. There were also villages near them. The descendants of Joseph son of Israel lived in these towns.

ASHER'S CHILDREN

[30] Asher's sons were Imnah, Ishvah, Ishvi and Beriah. Their sister was Serah. [31] Beriah's sons were Heber and Malkiel. Malkiel was Birzaith's father.

[32] Heber was the father of Japhlet, Shomer and Hotham and their sister Shua. [33] Japhlet's sons were Pasach, Bimhal and Ashvath. They were Japhlet's children. [34] Japhlet's brother was Shomer. Shomer's sons were Rohgah, Hubbah and Aram. [35] Shomer's brother was Hotham. Hotham's sons were Zophah, Imna, Shelesh and Amal. [36] Zophah's sons were Suah, Harnepher, Shual, Beri, Imrah, [37] Bezer, Hod, Shamma, Shilshah, Ithran and Beera. [38] Jether's sons were Jephunneh, Pispah and Ara. [39] Ulla's sons were Arah, Hanniel and Rizia.

[40] All these men were descendants of Asher. They were leaders of their families. They were powerful warriors and outstanding leaders. Their family history lists that they had 26,000 soldiers ready to serve in the army.

THE FAMILY HISTORY OF KING SAUL

8 Benjamin was the father of Bela. Bela was Benjamin's first son. Ashbel was his second son. Aharah was his third son. [2] Nohah was Benjamin's fourth son, and Rapha was his fifth son.

[3] Bela's sons were Addar, Gera, Abihud, [4] Abishua, Naaman, Ahoah, [5] Gera, Shephuphan and Huram.

[6] These were the descendants[d] of Ehud. They were leaders of their families in Geba. They were forced to leave their homes and move to Manahath. [7] Ehud's descendants were Naaman, Ahijah and Gera. Gera forced them to leave their homes. He was the father of Uzza and Ahihud.

[8-11] Shaharaim and his wife Hushim had sons named Abitub and Elpaal. In Moab Shaharaim divorced his wives Hushim and Baara. Shaharaim and his

---

7:23 Beriah This name sounds like the Hebrew word for "trouble."

wife Hodesh had these children: Jobab, Zibia, Mesha, Malcam, Jeuz, Sakia and Mirmah. These sons were leaders of their families.

12-13Elpaal's sons were Eber, Misham, Shemed, Beriah and Shema. Shemed built the towns of Ono and Lod and the villages around them. Beriah and Shema were leaders of the families living in Aijalon. These sons forced the people who lived in Gath to leave.

14Beriah's sons were Ahio, Shashak, Jeremoth, 15Zebadiah, Arad, Eder, 16Michael, Ishpah and Joha.

17Elpaal's sons were Zebadiah, Meshullam, Hizki, Heber, 18Ishmerai, Izliah and Jobab.

19Shimei's sons were Jakim, Zicri, Zabdi, 20Elienai, Zillethai, Eliel, 21Adaiah, Beraiah and Shimrath.

22Shashak's sons were Ishpan, Eber, Eliel, 23Abdon, Zicri, Hanan, 24Hananiah, Elam, Anthothijah, 25Iphdeiah and Penuel.

26Jeroham's sons were Shamsherai, Shehariah, Athaliah, 27Jaareshiah, Elijah and Zicri.

28The family histories show that all these men were leaders of their families. They lived in Jerusalem.

29Jeiel lived in the town of Gibeon, where he was the leader. His wife was named Maacah. 30Jeiel's first son was Abdon. His other sons were Zur, Kish, Baal, Ner, Nadab, 31Gedor, Ahio, Zeker 32and Mikloth. Mikloth was the father of Shimeah. These sons also lived near their relatives in Jerusalem.

33Ner was the father of Kish. Kish was the father of Saul. And Saul was the father of Jonathan, Malki-Shua, Abinadab and Esh-Baal.

34Jonathan's son was Merib-Baal. Merib-Baal was Micah's father.

35Micah's sons were Pithon, Melech, Tarea and Ahaz. 36Ahaz was the father of Jehoaddah. Jehoaddah was the father of Alemeth, Azmaveth and Zimri. Zimri was the father of Moza. 37Moza was the father of Binea. Raphah was Binea's son. Eleasah was Raphah's son. And Azel was Eleasah's son.

38Azel had six sons. Their names were Azrikam, Bokeru, Ishmael, Sheariah, Obadiah and Hanan. All these were Azel's sons.

39Azel's brother was Eshek. Eshek's first son was Ulam. Jeush was his second son, and Eliphelet was his third son. 40Ulam's sons were mighty warriors who could use a bow and arrow well. They had many sons and grandsons. There were 150 of them in all.

All these men were Benjamin's descendants.

9 The names of all the people of Israel were listed in their family histories. Those family histories were put in the book of the kings of Israel.

THE PEOPLE IN JERUSALEM

The people of Judah were captured and forced to go to Babylon. This is because they were not faithful to God. 2The first people to come back and live in their own lands and towns were some Israelites, priests, Levites and Temple[d] servants.

3People from the tribes[d] of Judah, Benjamin, Ephraim and Manasseh lived in Jerusalem. This is a list of those people.

4There was Uthai son of Ammihud. (Ammihud was Omri's son. Omri was Imri's son. Imri was Bani's son. Bani was a descendant[d] of Perez. Perez was Judah's son.)

5Of the Shilonite people there were Asaiah and his sons. Asaiah was the oldest son in his family.

6Of the Zerahite people there were Jeuel and other relatives of Zerah. There were 690 of them in all.

7From the tribe of Benjamin there was Sallu son of Meshullam. (Meshullam was Hodaviah's son. Hodaviah was Hassenuah's son.) 8There was also Ibneiah son of Jeroham and Elah son of

Uzzi. (Uzzi was Micri's son.) And there was Meshullam son of Shephatiah. (Shephatiah was Reuel's son, and Reuel was Ibnijah's son.) [9]The family history of Benjamin lists 956 people living in Jerusalem. All these men were leaders of their families.

[10]Of the priests there were Jedaiah, Jehoiarib, Jakin and [11]Azariah son of Hilkiah. (Hilkiah was Meshullam's son. Meshullam was Zadok's son. Zadok was Meraioth's son. Meraioth was Ahitub's son. Ahitub was the officer who was responsible for the Temple of God.) [12]Also there was Adaiah son of Jeroham. (Jeroham was Pashhur's son, and Pashhur was Malkijah's son.) And there was Maasai son of Adiel. (Adiel was Jahzerah's son. Jahzerah was Meshullam's son. Meshullam was Meshillemith's son, and Meshillemith was Immer's son.) [13]There were 1,760 priests. They were leaders of their families. They were responsible for serving in the Temple of God.

[14]Of the Levites there was Semaiah son of Hasshub. (Hasshub was Azrikam's son. Azrikam was Hashabiah's son. Hashabiah was from the family of Merari.) [15]There were also Bakbakkar, Heresh, Galal and Mattaniah son of Mica. (Mica was Zicri's son. Zicri was Asaph's son.) [16]There was also Obadiah son of Shemaiah. (Shemaiah was Galal's son, and Galal was Jeduthun's son.) And there was Berekiah son of Asa. (Asa was Elkanah's son. Elkanah lived in the villages of the Netophathite people.)

[17]Of the gatekeepers there were Shallum, Akkub, Talmon, Ahiman and their relatives. Shallum was their leader. [18]These gatekeepers from the tribe of Levi still stand next to the King's Gate on the east side of the city. [19]Shallum was Kore's son. Kore was Ebiasaph's son. Ebiasaph was Korah's son. Shallum and his relatives from the family of Korah were gatekeepers. They were responsible for guarding the gates of the Temple. Their ancestors had also been responsible for guarding the entrance to the Temple. [20]In the past Phinehas was in charge of the gatekeepers. He was Eleazar's son. The Lord was with Phinehas. [21]Zechariah was the gatekeeper at the entrance to the Temple. He was the son of Meshelemiah.

[22]In all, 212 men were chosen to guard the gates. Their names were written in their family histories in their villages. David and Samuel the seer[d] chose these men because they were dependable. [23]The gatekeepers and their descendants had the responsibility of guarding the gates of the Temple of the Lord. (The Temple took the place of the Holy Tent.[d]) [24]There were gatekeepers on all four sides of the Temple: east, west, north and south. [25]The gatekeepers' relatives who lived in the villages had to come and help them at certain times. Each time they came they helped the gatekeepers for seven days. [26]Because they were dependable, four gatekeepers were made the leaders of all the gatekeepers. They were Levites. They were responsible for the rooms and treasures in the Temple of God. [27]They stayed up all night guarding the Temple of God. And they opened it every morning.

[28]Some of the gatekeepers were responsible for the tools and dishes used in the Temple services. They counted these tools and dishes when people took them out. And they counted them when people brought them back. [29]Other gatekeepers were chosen to take care of the things in the Holy Place. They also took care of the flour, wine, oil, incense[d] and spices. [30]But some of the priests took care of mixing the spices. [31]There was a Levite named Mattithiah. Because he was dependable, he had the job of baking the bread used for the offerings. He was Shallum's first son. Shallum was from the family of Korah. [32]Some of the gatekeepers had the job of preparing the

special bread. This was the bread that was put on the table every Sabbath.*d* These people were from the Kohath family.

³³Some of the Levites were musicians in the Temple. The leaders of these families stayed in the rooms of the Temple. They were on duty day and night. So they did not do other work in the Temple.

³⁴These are the leaders of the Levite families. Their names were listed in their family histories. They lived in Jerusalem.

THE FAMILY HISTORY OF KING SAUL

³⁵Jeiel lived in the town of Gibeon, where he was the leader. His wife was named Maacah. ³⁶Jeiel's first son was Abdon. His other sons were Zur, Kish, Baal, Ner, Nadab, ³⁷Gedor, Ahio, Zechariah and Mikloth. ³⁸Mikloth was Shimeam's father. Jeiel's family lived near their relatives in Jerusalem.

³⁹Ner was Kish's father. Kish was Saul's father. And Saul was the father of Jonathan, Malki-Shua, Abinadab and Esh-Baal.

⁴⁰Jonathan's son was Merib-Baal. Merib-Baal was Micah's father.

⁴¹Micah's sons were Pithon, Melech, Tahrea and Ahaz. ⁴²Ahaz was Jadah's father. Jadah was the father of Alemeth, Azmaveth and Zimri. Zimri was Moza's father. ⁴³Moza was Binea's father. Rephaiah was Binea's son. Eleasah was Rephaiah's son, and Azel was Eleasah's son.

⁴⁴Azel had six sons. Their names were Azrikam, Bokeru, Ishmael, Sheariah, Obadiah and Hanan. They were Azel's sons.

THE DEATH OF KING SAUL

10 The Philistine people fought against the people of Israel. The Israelites ran away from them. And many Israelites were killed on Mount Gilboa. ²The Philistines continued chasing Saul and his sons. And they killed Saul's sons Jonathan, Abinadab and Malki-Shua. ³The fighting became

heavy around Saul. The archers shot him with their arrows and wounded him.

⁴Then Saul said to the officer who carried his armor, "Pull out your sword and kill me. If you don't, these men who are not circumcised will come and hurt me." But the officer was afraid. So he refused to kill Saul. Then Saul took his own sword and fell on it. ⁵The officer saw that Saul was dead. So he fell on his own sword and died. ⁶So Saul and three of his sons died. All his family died together.

⁷The Israelites living in the valley saw that their army had run away. And they saw that Saul and his sons were dead. So they left their towns and ran away. Then the Philistines came and lived in those towns.

⁸The next day the Philistines came to take valuable things from the dead bodies. On Mount Gilboa they found the bodies of Saul and his sons. ⁹The Philistines stripped Saul's body. And they took his head and his armor. They sent messengers through all their country to tell the news to their idols and their people. ¹⁰The Philistines put Saul's armor in the temple of their idols. And they hung his head in the temple of Dagon.*d*

¹¹All the people living in Jabesh Gilead heard what the Philistines had done to Saul. ¹²So all the brave men from Jabesh Gilead went and got the bodies of Saul and his sons. They brought them to Jabesh Gilead. Then they buried the bones of Saul and his sons under the large tree in Jabesh. And they gave up eating for seven days.

¹³Saul died because he was not faithful to the Lord. He did not obey the Lord. He even went to a medium*d* and asked her for advice. ¹⁴He did this instead of asking the Lord for help. This is why the Lord put Saul to death and gave the kingdom to Jesse's son David.

DAVID BECOMES KING

11 All the people of Israel came to David at the town of Hebron. They said, "We are your people. ²Even when Saul was king, you were the man who led Israel in battle. The Lord your God spoke to you. He said, 'David, you will be the shepherd of my people, the people of Israel. You will become their leader.'"

³All the elders of Israel came to King David at Hebron. He made an agreement with them before the Lord in Hebron. The leaders poured olive oil on David to appoint him king over Israel. The Lord had promised this would happen. He had made this promise through Samuel.

DAVID DEFEATS JERUSALEM

⁴David and all the Israelites went to the city of Jerusalem. At that time Jerusalem was called Jebus. The people living there were named Jebusites. ⁵They said to David, "You can't get inside our city." But David captured their strong city of Jerusalem, the City of David.

⁶David had said, "The person who leads the attack against the Jebusites will become the commander over all my army." Joab son of Zeruiah led the attack. So he became the commander of the army.

⁷Then David made his home in the strong, walled city. That is why it was named the City of David. ⁸David rebuilt the city. He started where the land was filled in and went to the wall that was around the city. Joab repaired the other parts of the city. ⁹David became more and more powerful. And the Lord of heaven's armies was with him.

DAVID'S MIGHTY WARRIORS

¹⁰This is a list of the leaders over David's warriors. These warriors helped make David's kingdom strong. All the people of Israel also supported David's kingdom. These heroes and all the people of Israel made David king. This happened as the Lord had promised.

¹¹This is a list of David's warriors:

Jashobeam was from the Hacmonite people. He was the leader of the Three,ⁿ David's most powerful soldiers. He used his spear to fight 300 men at one time. And he killed them all.

¹²Next was Eleazar. He was one of the Three. Eleazar was Dodai's son. Dodai was from the Ahohite people. ¹³Eleazar was with David at Pas-Dammim. The Philistines came there to fight the Israelites. There was a field of barley at that place. The Israelites ran away from the Philistines. ¹⁴But they stopped in the middle of that field and fought the Philistines. And they killed the Philistines. The Lord gave Israel a great victory.

¹⁵Three of the 30 leaders went to David. He was at the rock by the cave near Adullam. At the same time a group from the Philistine army was camped in the Valley of Rephaim.

¹⁶David was in a protected place at that time. The Philistine army was staying in the town of Bethlehem. ¹⁷David had a strong desire for some water. He said, "Oh, I wish someone would get me water from the well near the city gate of Bethlehem!" ¹⁸So the Three fought their way through the Philistine army. And they took water out of the well near the city gate in Bethlehem. Then they took it back to David. But he refused to drink it. He poured it out before the Lord. ¹⁹David said, "May God keep me from drinking this water! It would be like drinking the blood of the men who risked their lives to bring me this water." So David refused to drink it.

These were the brave things the Three did.

²⁰Abishai brother of Joab was the leader of the Three. Abishai fought 300 men with his spear and killed them. He became as famous as the Three. ²¹He was more honored than the Three. He

---

11:11 Three Or maybe "Thirty." These were David's most powerful soldiers. See 2 Samuel 23:8.

became their commander even though he was not one of them.

²²Benaiah son of Jehoiada was a brave fighter from Kabzeel. Benaiah did many brave things. He killed two of the best warriors from Moab. He also went down into a pit when it was snowing. There he killed a lion. ²³Benaiah also killed an Egyptian who was about seven and a half feet tall. The Egyptian had a spear as large as a weaver's rod. Benaiah had a club. But he grabbed the spear from the Egyptian's hand. And he used the Egyptian's own spear to kill him. ²⁴These were the things Benaiah son of Jehoiada did. Benaiah became as famous as the Three. ²⁵He received more honor than the Thirty, David's most powerful soldiers. But he did not become a member of the Three. David chose Benaiah to be the leader of his bodyguards.

²⁶These were also mighty warriors:
Asahel brother of Joab;
Elhanan son of Dodo from Bethlehem;
²⁷Shammoth from the Harorites;
Helez from the Pelonites;
²⁸Ira son of Ikkesh from Tekoa;
Abiezer from the Anathothites;
²⁹Sibbecai from the Hushathites;
Ilai from the Ahohites;
³⁰Maharai from the Netophathites;
Heled son of Baanah from the Netophathites;
³¹Ithai son of Ribai from Gibeah in Benjamin.
Benaiah from the Pirathonites;
³²Hurai from the ravines of Gaash;
Abiel from the Arbathites;
³³Azmaveth from the Baharumites;
Eliahba from the Shaalbonites;
³⁴the sons of Hashem from the Gizonites;
Jonathan son of Shagee from the Hararites;
³⁵Ahiam son of Sacar from the Hararites;
Eliphal son of Ur;
³⁶Hepher from the Mekerathites;
Ahijah from the Pelonites;
³⁷Hezro from the Carmelites;
Naarai son of Ezbai;
³⁸Joel brother of Nathan;
Mibhar son of Hagri;
³⁹Zelek from the Ammonites;
Naharai, from the Berothites, the officer who carried the armor for Joab son of Zeruiah;
⁴⁰Ira from the Ithrites;
Gareb from the Ithrites;
⁴¹Uriah from the Hittites;
Zabad son of Ahlai;
⁴²Adina son of Shiza the Reubenite, who was the leader of the Reubenites, and his 30 soldiers;
⁴³Hanan son of Maacah;
Joshaphat from the Mithnites;
⁴⁴Uzzia from the Ashterathites;
Shama and Jeiel sons of Hotham from the Aroer;
⁴⁵Jediael son of Shimri;
Joha, Jediael's brother, from the Tizites;
⁴⁶Eliel from the Mahavites;
Jeribai and Joshaviah, Elnaam's sons;
Ithmah from the Moabites;
⁴⁷Eliel, Obed and Jaasiel from the Mezobaites.

WARRIORS JOIN DAVID

12 These were the men who came to David at Ziklag. David was hiding from Saul son of Kish at that time. These were the men who helped David in battle. ²They came with bows for weapons. They could use either their right or left hands to shoot arrows or to sling rocks. They were Saul's relatives from the tribe*d* of Benjamin. ³Ahiezer was their leader. And there was Joash. (Ahiezer and Joash were Shemaah's sons. He was from the town of Gibeah.) There were also Jeziel and Pelet the sons of Azmaveth. There were Beracah and Jehu from the town of Anathoth. ⁴And there was Ishmaiah from the town of Gibeon. Ishmaiah was one of the Thirty. In fact, he was the leader of the Thirty.

There were Jeremiah, Jahaziel, Johanan and Jozabad from Gederah. [5]There were Eluzai, Jerimoth, Bealiah and Shemariah. There was Shephatiah from Haruph. [6]There were Elkanah, Isshiah, Azarel, Joezer and Jashobeam. They were from the family group of Korah. [7]And there were Joelah and Zebadiah the sons of Jeroham. They were from the town of Gedor.

[8]Part of the people of Gad joined David at his protected place in the desert. They were brave warriors trained for war. They were skilled with shields and spears. They were as fierce as lions. And they could run as fast as gazelles[d] over the hills.

[9]Ezer was the leader of Gad's army. Obadiah was second in command. Eliab was third. [10]Mishmannah was fourth, and Jeremiah was fifth. [11]Attai was sixth, and Eliel was seventh. [12]Johanan was eighth, and Elzabad was ninth. [13]Jeremiah was tenth, and Macbannai was eleventh in command.

[14]They were the commanders of the army from Gad. The weakest of these leaders was in charge of 100 soldiers. The strongest was in charge of 1,000 soldiers. [15]They crossed the Jordan River and chased away the people living in the valleys. They chased them to the east and to the west. This happened in the first month of the year when the Jordan floods the valley.

[16]Other people from the tribes[d] of Benjamin and Judah also came to David at his protected place. [17]David went out to meet them. He said to them, "If you have come peacefully to help me, I welcome you. Join me. But you might have come to turn me over to my enemies, even though I have done nothing wrong. If you do this, the God of our ancestors will see this and punish you."

[18]Then the Spirit[d] entered Amasai, the leader of the Thirty. Amasai said:

"We belong to you, David.
    We are with you, son of Jesse.

Success, success to you.
    Success to those who help you,
    because your God helps you."

So David welcomed these men. He made them leaders of his army.

[19]Some of the men from Manasseh also joined David. They joined him when he went with the Philistines to fight Saul. But David and his men did not really help the Philistines. After talking about it, the Philistine leaders decided to send David away. They said, "If David goes back to his master Saul, we will be killed!" [20]The men from Manasseh joined David when he went to Ziklag. These were the men: Adnah, Jozabad, Jediael, Michael, Jozabad, Elihu and Zillethai. Each of these men was a leader of a thousand men from Manasseh. [21]All these men of Manasseh were brave soldiers. They helped David fight against groups of men who went around the country robbing people. These soldiers became commanders in David's army. [22]Every day more men joined David. So his army became large. It was like the army of God.

OTHERS JOIN DAVID AT HEBRON

[23]These are the numbers of the men who joined David at Hebron. They came ready for battle. They came to help turn the kingdom of Saul over to David. The Lord had said this would happen.

[24]There were 6,800 men with their weapons from the people of Judah. They carried shields and spears.

[25]There were 7,100 men from the people of Simeon. They were warriors ready for war.

[26]There were 4,600 men from the people of Levi. [27]Jehoiada, a leader from Aaron's family, was in that group. There were 3,700 with him. [28]Zadok was also in that group. He was a strong young warrior. He came with 22 leaders from his family.

[29]There were 3,000 men from the people of Benjamin. They were Saul's relatives. And most of them had remained loyal to Saul's family until then.

³⁰There were 20,800 men from the people of Ephraim. They were brave warriors. They were famous men in their own family groups.

³¹There were 18,000 men from the western half-tribe of Manasseh. Each man was especially chosen to make David king.

³²There were 200 leaders from the family of Issachar. They knew what Israel should do. And they knew the right time to do it. Their relatives were with them and under their command.

³³There were 50,000 men from the people of Zebulun. They were trained soldiers. They were trained to use every kind of weapon of war. They followed David completely.

³⁴There were 1,000 officers from the people of Naphtali. They had 37,000 men with them who carried shields and spears.

³⁵There were 28,600 men from the people of Dan. They were ready for war.

³⁶There were 40,000 trained soldiers from the people of Asher. They were ready for war.

³⁷There were 120,000 men from the east side of the Jordan River. They were from the people of Reuben, Gad and the eastern half-tribe of Manasseh. They had every kind of weapon.

³⁸All these fighting men were ready to go to war. They came to Hebron fully agreed to make David king of all Israel. All the other Israelites also agreed to make David king. ³⁹The men spent three days there with David. They ate and drank, because their relatives had prepared food for them. ⁴⁰Also, their neighbors brought food. They came from as far as the areas belonging to Issachar, Zebulun and Naphtali. They brought food on donkeys, camels, mules and oxen. They brought much flour, fig cakes, raisins, wine, oil, cows and sheep. This was because the people of Israel were very happy.

BRINGING BACK THE HOLY BOX

13 David talked with all the officers of his army. He talked with the commanders of 100 men and the commanders of 1,000 men. ²Then David called the people of Israel together. He said, "If you think it is a good idea, and if it is what the Lord our God wants, let's send a message. Let's send it to our fellow Israelites in all the areas of Israel. Let's also send it to the priests and Levites living with them in their towns and pastures. Tell them to come and join us. ³Let's bring the Holy Box*d* of our God back to us. We did not use it to ask God for help while Saul was king." ⁴So all the people agreed with David. They all thought it was the right thing to do.

⁵So David gathered all the Israelites from the Shihor River in Egypt to Lebo Hamath. They were to bring the Holy Box of God back from the town of Kiriath Jearim. ⁶David and all the Israelites with him went to Baalah of Judah. (Baalah is another name for Kiriath Jearim.) They went there to get the Holy Box of God the Lord. His throne is between the golden creatures with wings on the Holy Box. It is called by the Lord's name.

⁷The people moved the Holy Box of God from Abinadab's house. They put it on a new cart. And Uzzah and Ahio guided the cart. ⁸David and all the Israelites were celebrating with all their strength before God. They were singing and playing harps, lyres,*d* tambourines,*d* cymbals and trumpets.

⁹They came to the threshing*d* floor of Kidon. The oxen pulling the cart stumbled. And Uzzah reached out his hand to steady the Holy Box. ¹⁰The Lord became very angry with Uzzah. And he killed Uzzah because Uzzah had touched the Holy Box. So Uzzah died there in the presence of God.

¹¹David became angry because the Lord had punished Uzzah in his anger.

So even today that place is called the Punishment of Uzzah.

[12]David was afraid of God that day. David asked, "How can I bring the Holy Box of God home to me?" [13]So David did not take the Holy Box with him to Jerusalem. Instead, he took it to the house of Obed-Edom of Gath. [14]The Holy Box of God stayed with Obed-Edom's family in his house for three months. And the Lord blessed Obed-Edom's family and everything he owned.

DAVID'S KINGDOM GROWS

14 Hiram king of the city of Tyre sent messengers to David. He also sent cedar logs, stonecutters and carpenters. He sent them to build a palace for David. [2]Then David knew that the Lord really had made him king of Israel. And he knew the Lord had made his kingdom very important. The Lord did this because he loved his people, the Israelites.

[3]David married more women in Jerusalem. And he had more sons and daughters. [4]These are the names of David's children born in Jerusalem: Shammua, Shobab, Nathan, Solomon, [5]Ibhar, Elishua, Elpelet, [6]Nogah, Nepheg, Japhia, [7]Elishama, Beeliada and Eliphelet.

DAVID DEFEATS THE PHILISTINES

[8]The Philistine people heard that David had been appointed king of all Israel. So all the Philistines went to look for him. When David heard about it, he went out to fight them. [9]The Philistines had attacked and robbed the people in the Valley of Rephaim. [10]David asked God, "Should I go and attack the Philistines? Will you let me defeat them?"

The Lord answered him, "Go. I will let you defeat them."

[11]So David and his men went up to the town of Baal Perazim. There he defeated the Philistines. David said, "Like a flood of water, God has broken through my enemies. He has done this through me." So that place was named Baal Perazim.[n] [12]The Philistines had left their idols there. So David ordered his men to burn them.

[13]Soon the Philistines attacked the people in the valley again. [14]So David prayed to God again, and God answered him. God said, "Don't attack the Philistines from the front. Instead, go around them. Attack them in front of the balsam trees. [15]You will hear the sound of marching in the tops of the balsam trees. Then quickly attack the Philistines. I, God, will have gone out before you to defeat the Philistine army." [16]David did what God commanded him to do. So David and his men defeated the Philistine army. They killed the Philistines all the way from Gibeon to Gezer.

[17]So David became famous in all the countries. And the Lord made all nations afraid of David.

THE HOLY BOX IS BROUGHT TO JERUSALEM

15 David built houses for himself in Jerusalem. Then he built a place for the Holy Box[d] of God. And he set up a tent for it. [2]Then David said, "Only the Levites may carry the Holy Box of God. The Lord chose them to carry the Holy Box of the Lord. He chose them to serve him forever."

[3]David called all the people of Israel to come to Jerusalem. He wanted to bring the Holy Box of the Lord to the place he had made for it. [4]David called together the descendants[d] of Aaron and the Levites. [5]There were 120 people from Kohath's family group. Uriel was their leader. [6]There were 220 people from Merari's family group. Asaiah was their leader. [7]There were 130 people from Gershon's family group. Joel was their leader. [8]There were 200 people from Elizaphan's family

---

14:11 Baal Perazim This name means "the Lord breaks through."

group. Shemaiah was their leader. ⁹There were 80 people from Hebron's family group. Eliel was their leader. ¹⁰There were 112 people from Uzziel's family group. Amminadab was their leader.

¹¹Then David asked the priests Zadok and Abiathar to come to him. He also asked these Levites to come: Uriel, Asaiah, Joel, Shemaiah, Eliel and Amminadab. ¹²David said to them, "You are the leaders of the families of Levi. You and the other Levites must give yourselves for service to the Lord. Then bring up the Holy Box of the Lord, the God of Israel. Bring it to the place I have made for it. ¹³The last time we did not ask the Lord how to carry it. You Levites didn't carry it. So the Lord our God punished us."

¹⁴Then the priests and Levites prepared themselves for service to the Lord. They did this so they could carry the Holy Box of the Lord, the God of Israel. ¹⁵The Levites used special poles to carry the Holy Box of God on their shoulders. This was the way Moses had commanded. They carried it just as the Lord had said they should.

¹⁶David told the leaders of the Levites to appoint their brothers as singers. The singers were to play their lyres,ᵈ harps and cymbals. And they were to sing happy songs.

¹⁷So the Levites appointed Heman and his relatives Asaph and Ethan. Heman was Joel's son. Asaph was Berekiah's son. And Ethan, from the Merari family group, was Kushaiah's son. ¹⁸There was also a second group of Levites. They were Zechariah, Jaaziel, Shemiramoth, Jehiel, Unni, Eliab, Benaiah, Maaseiah, Mattithiah, Eliphelehu, Mikneiah, Obed-Edom and Jeiel. They were the Levite guards.

¹⁹The singers Heman, Asaph and Ethan played bronze cymbals. ²⁰Zechariah, Jaaziel, Shemiramoth, Jehiel, Unni, Eliab, Maaseiah and Benaiah played the high-pitched lyres. ²¹Mattithiah, Eliphelehu, Mikneiah, Obed-Edom, Jeiel and Azaziah played the low-pitched harps. ²²The Levite leader Kenaniah was in charge of the singing. He had this job because he was very good at singing.

²³Berekiah and Elkanah were two of the guards for the Box of the Agreement. ²⁴The priests Shebaniah, Joshaphat, Nethanel, Amasai, Zechariah, Benaiah and Eliezer had the job of blowing trumpets. They did this in front of the Box of the Agreement. Obed-Edom and Jehiah were also guards for the Box of the Agreement.

²⁵David, the leaders of Israel, and the commanders went to get the Box of the Agreement with the Lord. Each of the commanders was over a group of 1,000 soldiers. They all went to bring the Holy Box from Obed-Edom's house. And they were very happy. ²⁶God helped the Levites who carried the Box of the Agreement with the Lord. So they sacrificed seven bulls and seven male sheep. ²⁷All the Levites who carried the Holy Box wore robes of fine linen. Kenaniah, the man in charge of the singing, and all the singers wore robes of fine linen. David wore a robe of fine linen. And he also wore a holy vestᵈ of fine linen. ²⁸So all the people of Israel brought up the Box of the Agreement with the Lord. They shouted and blew sheep horns and trumpets. They played cymbals, lyres, and harps.

²⁹So the Box of the Agreement with the Lord entered Jerusalem. As it entered, Saul's daughter Michal watched from a window. When she saw King David dancing and celebrating, she hated him.

16 They brought the Holy Box of God and put it inside the tent. This was the tent David had set up for it. Then they offered burnt offerings and fellowship offerings to God. ²David finished giving the burnt offerings and fellowship offerings. Then he used the Lord's name to bless the people. ³He gave a loaf of bread, some dates and raisins to every Israelite man and woman.

⁴Then David appointed some of the Levites to serve before the Holy Box of the Lord. They had the job of leading the worship. They gave thanks and praise to the Lord, the God of Israel. ⁵Asaph was the leader. He played the cymbals. Zechariah was second to him. The other Levites were Jaaziel, Shemiramoth, Jehiel, Mattithiah, Eliab, Benaiah, Obed-Edom and Jeiel. They played the lyres and harps. ⁶Benaiah and Jahaziel were priests. They blew the trumpets regularly before the Box of the Agreement with God. ⁷That day David first gave Asaph and his relatives the job of singing praises to the Lord.

DAVID'S SONG OF THANKS

⁸Give thanks to the Lord and pray to
    him.
  Tell the nations what he has done.
⁹Sing to him. Sing praises to him.
  Tell about all the wonderful things
    he has done.
¹⁰Be glad that you are his.
  Let those who ask the Lord for help
    be happy.
¹¹Depend on the Lord and his strength.
  Always go to him for help.
¹²Remember the wonderful things he
    has done.
  Remember his miracles*d* and his
    decisions.
¹³You are the descendants*d* of Israel, the
    Lord's servant.
  You are the children of Jacob, his
    chosen people.
¹⁴He is the Lord our God.
  His laws are for all the world.
¹⁵He will keep his agreement forever.
  He will keep his promises always.
¹⁶He will keep the agreement he made
    with Abraham.
  He will keep the promise he made
    to Isaac.

¹⁷The Lord made it a law for the people
    of Jacob.
  He made it an agreement with
    Israel to last forever.
¹⁸The Lord said, "I will give you the
    land of Canaan. The promised
    land will belong to you."

¹⁹Then God's people were few in
    number.
  They were strangers in the land.
²⁰They went from one nation to
    another.
  They went from one kingdom to
    another.
²¹But the Lord did not let anyone hurt
    them.
  He warned kings not to harm them.
²²He said, "Don't hurt my chosen people.
  Don't harm my prophets."*d*

²³Sing to the Lord, all the earth.
  Every day tell how he saves us.
²⁴Tell the nations about the Lord's
    glory.
  Tell all peoples about his wonderful
    works.
²⁵The Lord is great; he should be
    praised.
  He should be honored more than all
    the gods.
²⁶All the gods of the nations are only
    idols.
  But the Lord made the skies.
²⁷The Lord has glory and majesty.
  He has power and joy in his
    Temple.*d*

²⁸Praise the Lord, all nations on earth.
  Praise the Lord's glory and power.
²⁹ Praise the Lord for the glory of his
    name.
  Bring your offering to him.
  Worship the Lord because he is
    holy.
³⁰The whole earth should tremble
    before the Lord.
  The earth is set, and it cannot be
    moved.

³¹Let the skies rejoice and the earth be
   glad.
   Let people everywhere say, "The
      Lord is king!"
³²Let the sea and everything in it shout.
   Let the fields and everything in
      them show their joy.
³³Then the trees of the forest will sing.
   They will sing with joy before the
      Lord.
   They will sing because the Lord is
      coming to judge the world.

³⁴Thank the Lord because he is good.
   His love continues forever.
³⁵Say to him, "Save us, God our Savior.
   Bring us back and save us from the
      nations.
   Then we will thank you.
   Then we will gladly praise you."
³⁶Praise the Lord, the God of Israel,
   forever and forever.

All the people said, "Amen" and "Praise
the Lord."

³⁷Then David left Asaph and the other
Levites there in front of the Box*d* of the
Agreement with the Lord. They were to
serve there every day. ³⁸David also left
Obed-Edom and 68 other Levites to
serve with them. Hosah and Obed-Edom
son of Jeduthun were guards.

³⁹David left Zadok the priest and the
other priests who served with him in
front of the Tent of the Lord. This was at
the place of worship in Gibeon. ⁴⁰Every
morning and evening they offered burnt
offerings on the altar of burnt offerings.
They did this to follow the rules written
in the Teachings of the Lord. These were
the Teachings he had given Israel.
⁴¹With them were Heman and Jeduthun
and other Levites. They were chosen by
name to sing praises to the Lord because
the Lord's love continues forever.
⁴²Heman and Jeduthun also had the job
of playing the trumpets and cymbals.
They also played other musical instruments when songs were sung to God.
Jeduthun's sons guarded the gates.

⁴³Then all the people left. Each person
went to his own home. And David also
went home to bless his family.

GOD'S PROMISE TO DAVID

17 David moved into his palace.
Then he said to Nathan the
prophet, "Look, I am living in a palace
made of cedar. But the Box*d* of the
Agreement with the Lord sits in a tent."

²Nathan answered David, "Do what
you want to do. God is with you."

³But that night God spoke his word to
Nathan. God said, ⁴"Go and tell my servant David: 'This is what the Lord says:
David, you are not the person to build a
house for me to live in. ⁵From the time I
brought Israel out of Egypt until now I
have not lived in a house. I have moved
from one tent site to another. I have
gone from one place to another. ⁶I have
moved with the Israelites to different
places. I commanded leaders to take
care of my people. I never said to any of
those leaders, "Why haven't you built
me a house of cedar?"'

⁷"Now, tell my servant David: 'The
Lord of heaven's armies says: I took you
from the pasture and from tending the
sheep. I made you king of my people
Israel. ⁸I have been with you everywhere
you have gone. I have killed your enemies for you. Now I will make you one of
the most famous men on earth. ⁹I will
give this place to my people Israel. I will
settle them here. Then they will have a
home of their own. They won't be bothered anymore. Evil people won't hurt
them as they have done since the first.
¹⁰Evil people have hurt them since I
chose leaders for my people Israel. I will
also defeat all your enemies.

"'I tell you that the Lord will make
your descendants*d* kings of Israel after
you. ¹¹When you die and join your
ancestors, I will let your child be the new
king. He will be one of your own sons.
And I will make his kingdom strong.
¹²He will build a house for me. And I will

let his family rule forever. [13]I will be his father, and he will be my son. I took away my love from Saul, who ruled before you. But I will never stop loving your son. [14]I will put him in charge of my house and kingdom forever. His family will rule forever.'"

[15]Nathan told David everything God had said in this vision.

DAVID'S PRAYER

[16]Then King David went in and sat in front of the Lord. David said, "Lord God, why have you made me so important to you? Why have you made my family important? [17]But that was not enough for you, God. You have also said these kind things about my future family. I am your servant. Lord God, you have treated me like a very important man.

[18]"What more can I say to you? You have done so much for me, your servant. You love me so much. [19]Lord, you have done this wonderful thing for me for my sake. And you have done it because you wanted to. You have let me know all these great promises.

[20]"There is no one like you, Lord. There is no God except you. We have heard all this ourselves. [21]There is no one like your people, the Israelites. It is the one nation on earth that God chose to be his people. You used them to make your name well-known. You did great and wonderful things for them. You went ahead of them and forced other nations out of the land. You freed your people from slavery in Egypt. [22]You made the people of Israel your very own people forever. And, Lord, you became their God.

[23]"Lord, you made this promise about my family and me, your servant. Now, keep your promise forever. Do what you have promised. [24]Then people will know you and honor you forever. And people will say, 'The Lord of heaven's armies, the God over Israel, is Israel's God!' And the family of your servant David will continue before you.

[25]"My God, you have told me that you would make my family great. So I, your servant, am brave enough to pray to you. [26]Lord, you are God. You have promised these good things to me, your servant. [27]You have chosen to bless my family. Let it continue before you forever. Lord, you have blessed my family. So it will be blessed forever."

DAVID DEFEATS NATIONS

18 Later, David attacked the Philistine people and defeated them. He took Gath and the small towns around it from the Philistines.

[2]Then David defeated the country of Moab. So the Moabites became David's servants. And they brought the payments he demanded from them.

[3]David also fought against Hadadezer king of Zobah. David fought Hadadezer's army all the way to the town of Hamath. He did this because Hadadezer tried to spread his kingdom all the way to the Euphrates River. [4]David took from Hadadezer 1,000 chariots and 7,000 chariot drivers. And he took 20,000 soldiers on foot. David also crippled most of Hadadezer's horses used for pulling chariots. He saved only 100 of the chariot horses.

[5]The Aramean people from Damascus came to help Hadadezer king of Zobah. But David killed 22,000 of them. [6]Then David put camps of troops in Damascus in Aram. The Arameans became David's servants and brought him the payments he demanded. So the Lord gave David victory everywhere he went.

[7]David took the gold shields from Hadadezer's army leaders. And he brought them to Jerusalem. [8]David also took much bronze from the towns of Tebah and Cun. These towns belonged to Hadadezer. Later, Solomon used this bronze to make things for the Temple:[d] the large bronze bowl, which was called the Sea, the pillars and other bronze things.

9Toi was king of the city of Hamath. He heard that David had defeated the whole army of Hadadezer king of Zobah. 10So Toi sent his son Hadoram to greet King David. Hadoram also congratulated David for fighting and defeating Hadadezer. Hadadezer had been at war with Toi before. Hadoram gave David all kinds of things made of gold, silver and bronze. 11King David gave these things to the Lord. David had done the same thing with the silver and gold he had taken from these nations: Edom, Moab, the Ammonites, the Philistines and Amalek.

12Abishai son of Zeruiah killed 18,000 Edomite people in the Valley of Salt. 13Abishai also put camps of troops in Edom. And all the Edomites became David's servants. The Lord gave David victory everywhere he went.

DAVID'S IMPORTANT OFFICERS

14David was king over all of Israel. He did what was right and fair for everyone. 15Joab son of Zeruiah was commander of David's army. Jehoshaphat son of Ahilud was the recorder. 16Zadok son of Ahitub and Ahimelech son of Abiathar were priests. Shavsha was the royal assistant. 17Benaiah was responsible for leading the Kerethites and Pelethites, the king's bodyguards. Benaiah was Jehoiada's son. And David's sons were important officers. They served at King David's side.

DAVID FIGHTS THE AMMONITES

19 Nahash was king of the Ammonite people. When Nahash died, his son became the king. 2David said, "Nahash was kind to me. So I will be kind to Hanun son of Nahash." Then David sent a group to comfort Hanun about the death of his father.

David's men went to comfort Hanun in the country of Ammon. 3But the Ammonite leaders said to Hanun, "Don't be fooled. David didn't send these men to comfort you. They are not here to honor your dead father. David sent his men to spy on you and your land. He wants to destroy your country." 4So Hanun arrested David's men. To shame them he cut off their beards and cut off their clothes at the hips. Then he sent them away.

5David's men were too ashamed to go home. Some people came to David and told him what had happened to his men. So he sent messengers to meet them. He said, "Stay in Jericho until your beards have grown back. Then come home."

6The Ammonite people saw they had caused David to hate them. So Hanun and the Ammonites sent about 74,000 pounds of silver to hire chariots and chariot drivers. They hired Arameans from Northwest Mesopotamia, Aram Maacah and Zobah. 7The Ammonites hired 32,000 chariots and chariot drivers. They also hired the king of Maacah and his army. So he and his army came and set up camp near the town of Medeba. The Ammonites themselves came out of their towns and got ready for battle.

8David heard about this. So he sent out Joab and the whole army of Israel. 9The Ammonites came out and got ready for battle. They were near the city gate. The kings who had come to help stayed out in the fields by themselves.

10Joab saw that there were enemy troops in front of him and behind him. So Joab chose some of the best soldiers of Israel. And he sent them out to fight the Arameans. 11Joab put the rest of the army of Israel under the command of Abishai, his brother. Then they went out to fight the Ammonites. 12Joab said to Abishai, "The Arameans may be too strong for me. If they are, then you must help me. Or, the Ammonites may be too strong for you. If they are, then I will help you. 13Let's be strong. We must fight bravely for our people and the cities of our God. The Lord will do what he thinks is right."

¹⁴Then Joab and the army with him went to attack the Arameans. And the Arameans ran away from them. ¹⁵The Ammonite army saw that the Arameans were running away. So they also ran away from Abishai and his army. The Ammonites went back inside their city. And Joab went back to Jerusalem.

¹⁶The Arameans saw that Israel had defeated them. So they sent messengers to bring other Arameans from east of the Euphrates River. Shophach the commander of Hadadezer's army led them. ¹⁷When David heard about this, he gathered all the Israelites. And he led them across the Jordan River. He lined them up for battle, facing the Arameans. And they attacked the Arameans. ¹⁸But the Arameans ran away from the Israelites. David and his army killed 7,000 Aramean chariot drivers. And they killed 40,000 Aramean foot soldiers. They also killed Shophach, the commander of the Aramean army.

¹⁹Hadadezer's officers saw that Israel had defeated them. So they made peace with David. They became his servants. So the Arameans refused to help the Ammonites again.

JOAB DESTROYS THE AMMONITES

20 In the spring Joab led the army of Israel out to battle. This was the time of year when kings went out to battle. But David stayed in Jerusalem. The army of Israel destroyed the land of Ammon. Then they went to the city of Rabbah. They surrounded it and attacked it until they destroyed it. ²David took the crown from the head of their king.ⁿ That gold crown weighed about 75 pounds. And it had valuable gems in it. The crown was put on David's head. Then David took many valuable things from the city. ³David brought out the people from Rabbah. And he forced them to work with saws, iron picks and axes. David did the same thing to all the Ammonite towns. Then David and all the army returned to Jerusalem.

PHILISTINE GIANTS ARE KILLED

⁴Later, war broke out between Israel and the Philistines at Gezer. At this time Sibbecai from Hushah killed Sippai. Sippai was one of the descendantsᵈ of the Rephaites.ᵈ So those Philistines were defeated.

⁵Another time, the Israelites again fought the Philistines. Elhanan son of Jair killed Lahmi, the brother of Goliath. Goliath was from the town of Gath. Lahmi's spear was as large as a weaver's rod.

⁶Later, the Israelites fought another war with the Philistines at Gath. In this town there was a very large man. He had 6 fingers on each hand and 6 toes on each foot. So he had 24 fingers and toes in all. He also was a descendant of Rapha.ᵈ ⁷When he made fun of Israel, Jonathan killed him. Jonathan was the son of Shimea, David's brother.

⁸These Philistines were descendants of Rapha from Gath. David and his men killed them.

DAVID COUNTS ISRAEL

21 Satan was against Israel. He encouraged David to count the people of Israel. ²So David gave an order to Joab and the commanders of the troops. He said, "Go and count all the Israelites. Count everyone from Beersheba to Dan.ⁿ Then tell me so I will know how many people there are."

³But Joab answered, "May the Lord make the nation 100 times as large. My master the king, all the Israelites are your servants. Why do you want to do this, my master? You will make Israel guilty of sin."

20:2 king Or, "Milcom," the god of the Ammonite people.
21:2 Beersheba to Dan Beersheba was the city farthest south in Israel. Dan was the city farthest north. So this means all the people of Israel.

⁴But King David made Joab follow his order. So Joab left and went through all Israel, counting the people. Then he returned to Jerusalem. ⁵He told David how many people there were. In Israel there were 1,100,000 men who could use a sword. And there were 470,000 men in Judah who could use a sword. ⁶But Joab did not count the tribes*d* of Levi and Benjamin. He didn't count them because he didn't like King David's order. ⁷David had done something God had said was wrong. So God punished Israel.

⁸Then David said to God, "I have done something very foolish. It was a terrible sin. Now, I beg you to forgive me, your servant."

⁹Gad was David's seer.*d* The Lord said to Gad, ¹⁰"Go and tell David: 'This is what the Lord says: I am going to give you three choices. Choose one, and I will punish you in that way.'"

¹¹So Gad went to David and said to him, "This is what the Lord says: 'Choose which punishment you want. ¹²You may choose three years without enough food for the nation. Or choose three months of running from your enemies as they chase you with their swords. Or choose three days of punishment from the Lord. A terrible disease will spread through the country. The angel of the Lord will go through Israel destroying the people.' Now, David, decide which answer I will give to the Lord, who sent me."

¹³David said to Gad, "I am in trouble. I don't want some man to punish me. The Lord is very merciful. So let the Lord punish me."

¹⁴So the Lord sent a terrible disease on Israel, and 70,000 people died. ¹⁵God sent an angel to destroy Jerusalem. But when the angel started to destroy it, the Lord saw it and felt sorry. So he said to the angel who was destroying, "That is enough! Stop!" The angel of the Lord was then standing at the threshing*d* floor of Araunah the Jebusite.

¹⁶David looked up and saw the angel of the Lord in the sky. The angel was holding his sword over Jerusalem. Then David and the elders bowed facedown on the ground. They were wearing rough cloth to show their sadness. ¹⁷David said to God, "I am the one who sinned. I gave the order for the people to be counted. I have done wrong. These people are only sheep. What wrong have they done? Lord my God, punish me and my family. But stop the terrible disease that is killing your people."

¹⁸Then the angel of the Lord gave an order to Gad. He told Gad to tell David to build an altar to worship the Lord. It was to be at the threshing floor of Araunah the Jebusite. ¹⁹Gad told David these things from the Lord. So David went to Araunah's threshing floor.

²⁰Araunah was separating the straw from the wheat. When he turned around, he saw the angel. Araunah's four sons who were with him hid. ²¹David went to Araunah. When Araunah saw David, he left the threshing floor. He bowed facedown on the ground before David.

²²David said to him, "Sell me your threshing floor. Then I can build an altar to worship the Lord here. Then the terrible disease will be stopped. Sell it to me for the full price."

²³Araunah said to David, "Take this threshing floor. You are my master the king. Do anything you want. Look, I will also give you oxen for the burnt offering. I will give you boards as wood for the fire. And I will give the wheat for the grain offering. I will give all this to you."

²⁴But King David answered Araunah, "No, I must pay the full price. I won't take anything that is yours and give it to the Lord. I won't give an offering that costs me nothing."

²⁵So David paid Araunah about 15 pounds of gold for the place. ²⁶David built an altar to worship the Lord there. He offered burnt offerings and fellowship

offerings. David prayed to the Lord. And the Lord answered him by sending down fire from heaven. It came down on the altar of burnt offering. [27]Then the Lord commanded the angel to put his sword back into its holder.

[28]David saw that the Lord had answered him on the threshing floor of Araunah. So he offered sacrifices to the Lord there. [29]The Holy Tent[d] and the altar of burnt offerings were in Gibeon. They were at the place of worship there. Moses had made the Holy Tent while the Israelites were in the desert. [30]But David could not go to the Holy Tent to speak with God. He was afraid of the angel of the Lord and his sword.

22 David said, "The Temple[d] of the Lord God will be built here. And the altar for burnt offerings for Israel will be built here."

DAVID MAKES PLANS FOR THE TEMPLE

[2]So David gave an order for all foreigners living in Israel to be gathered together. From that group David chose stonecutters. Their job was to cut stones to be used in building the Temple[d] of God. [3]David supplied a large amount of iron. It was used for making nails and hinges for the gate doors. He also supplied more bronze than could be weighed. [4]And he supplied more cedar logs than could be counted. Much of the cedar had been brought to David by the people from Sidon and Tyre.

[5]David said, "We should build a great Temple for the Lord. It should be famous everywhere for its greatness and beauty. But my son Solomon is young. He hasn't yet learned what he needs to know. So I will prepare for the building of it." So David got many of the materials ready before he died.

[6]Then David called for his son Solomon. He told Solomon to build the Temple for the Lord, the God of Israel.

[7]David said to him, "My son, I wanted to build a temple for worshiping the Lord my God. [8]But the Lord spoke his word to me, 'David, you have killed too many people. You have fought too many wars. So you cannot build a temple for worship to me. You have killed too many people. [9]But, you will have a son. He will be a man of peace and rest. I will give him rest from all his enemies around him. His name will be Solomon.[n] And I will give Israel peace and quiet while he is king. [10]Solomon will build a temple for worship to me. He will be my son, and I will be his father. I will make his kingdom strong. Someone from his family will rule Israel forever.'"

[11]David also said, "Now, my son, may the Lord be with you. May you build a temple for the Lord your God, as he said you would. [12]The Lord will make you the king of Israel. May the Lord give you wisdom and understanding. Then you will be able to obey the teachings of the Lord your God. [13]Be careful to obey the rules and laws the Lord gave Moses for Israel. If you obey them, you will have success. Be strong and brave. Don't be afraid or discouraged.

[14]"Solomon, I have worked hard getting many of the materials for building the Temple of the Lord. I have supplied about seven and a half million pounds of gold. And I have supplied about seventy-five million pounds of silver. I have supplied so much bronze and iron it cannot be weighed. And I have supplied wood and stone. And you may add to them. [15]You have many workmen. You have stonecutters, stoneworkers and carpenters. You have men skilled in every kind of work. [16]They are skilled in working with gold, silver, bronze and iron. You have more craftsmen than can be counted. Now begin the work. And may the Lord be with you."

22:9 Solomon This name sounds like the Hebrew word for "peace."

[17]Then David ordered all the leaders of Israel to help his son Solomon. [18]David said to them, "The Lord your God is with you. He has given you rest from our enemies. He helped me to defeat the people living around us. The Lord and his people are in control of this land. [19]Now give yourself completely to obeying the Lord your God. Build the holy place of the Lord God. Build the Temple for worship to the Lord. Then bring the Box[d] of the Agreement with the Lord into the Temple. And bring in the holy things that belong to God."

THE LEVITES

23 David had lived long and was old. Then he made his son Solomon the new king of Israel. [2]David gathered all the leaders of Israel, along with the priests and Levites. [3]David counted the Levites who were 30 years old and older. In all, there were 38,000 Levites. [4]David said, "Of these, 24,000 Levites will direct the work of the Temple[d] of the Lord. And 6,000 Levites will be officers and judges. [5]And 4,000 Levites will be gatekeepers. And 4,000 Levites will praise the Lord with musical instruments. I made these instruments for them to use for praise."

[6]David separated the Levites into three groups. These groups were led by Levi's three sons: Gershon, Kohath and Merari.

THE PEOPLE OF GERSHON

[7]From the people of Gershon, there were Ladan and Shimei.

[8]Ladan had three sons. His first son was Jehiel. His other sons were Zetham and Joel.

[9]Shimei's sons were Shelomoth, Haziel and Haran. These three sons were leaders of Ladan's families. [10]Shimei had four sons. They were Jahath, Ziza, Jeush and Beriah. [11]Jahath was the first son, and Ziza was the second son. But Jeush and Beriah did not have many children.

So they were counted as if they were one family.

THE PEOPLE OF KOHATH

[12]Kohath had four sons. They were Amram, Izhar, Hebron and Uzziel.

[13]Amram's sons were Aaron and Moses. Aaron and his descendants[d] were chosen to be special forever. They were chosen to prepare the holy things for the Lord's service. They were to offer sacrifices before the Lord. They were to serve him as priests. They were to give blessings in the Lord's name forever.

[14]Moses was the man of God. Moses' sons were counted as part of the tribe[d] of Levi. [15]Moses' sons were Gershom and Eliezer. [16]Gershom's first son was Shubael. [17]Eliezer's first son was Rehabiah. Eliezer had no other sons, but Rehabiah had many sons.

[18]Izhar's first son was Shelomith.

[19]Hebron's first son was Jeriah. His second son was Amariah. Jahaziel was the third son. And Jekameam was the fourth son.

[20]Uzziel's first son was Micah. And Isshiah was his second son.

THE PEOPLE OF MERARI

[21]Merari's sons were Mahli and Mushi. Mahli's sons were Eleazar and Kish. [22]Eleazar died without having sons. He had only daughters. Eleazar's daughters married their cousins, the sons of Kish. [23]Mushi's three sons were Mahli, Eder and Jerimoth.

THE LEVITES' WORK

[24]These were Levi's descendants[d] listed by their families. They were the leaders of families. Each person who was 20 years old or older was listed. They served in the Lord's Temple.[d]

[25]David had said, "The Lord is the God of Israel. He has given rest to his people. He has come to live in Jerusalem forever. [26]So the Levites don't need to carry the Holy Tent.[d] They don't need to carry any of the things used in its services any-

more." [27]David's last instructions were to count the Levites. All who were 20 years old and older were counted.

[28]The Levites had the job of helping Aaron's descendants. They helped in the service of the Temple of the Lord. They cared for the Temple courtyard and side rooms. They had the job of making all the holy things pure. Their job was to serve in the Temple of God. [29]They were responsible for putting the holy bread on the table. They also were responsible for the flour in the grain offerings. And they were responsible for the bread made without yeast. They were also responsible for the baking and mixing. And they did all the measuring. [30]The Levites also stood every morning and gave thanks and praise to the Lord. They also did this every evening. [31]The Levites offered all the burnt offerings to the Lord on the special days of rest. And they offered them at the New Moon[d] festivals and at all appointed feasts. They served before the Lord every day. They were to follow the rules for how many Levites should serve each time. [32]So the Levites took care of the Meeting Tent. They also took care of the Holy Place. And they helped their relatives, Aaron's descendants, with the services at the Temple of the Lord.

THE GROUPS OF THE PRIESTS

24 These were the groups of Aaron's sons:

Aaron's sons were Nadab, Abihu, Eleazar and Ithamar. [2]But Nadab and Abihu died before their father did. And they had no sons. So Eleazar and Ithamar served as the priests. [3]David separated the family groups of Eleazar and Ithamar into two different groups. Each group had certain duties it had been given. Zadok and Ahimelech helped David. Zadok was a descendant[d] of Eleazar. And Ahimelech was a descendant of Ithamar. [4]There were more leaders from Eleazar's family than from Ithamar's. There were 16 leaders from Eleazar's family. And there were 8 leaders from Ithamar's family. [5]Men were chosen from Eleazar's and Ithamar's families by throwing lots.[d] Some men from each family were chosen to be in charge of the Holy Place. And some men from each family were chosen to serve as priests.

[6]Shemaiah son of Nethanel was the secretary. He was from the tribe[d] of Levi. Shemaiah recorded the names of those descendants in front of King David and these officers: Zadok the priest, Ahimelech son of Abiathar, and the leaders of the families of the priests and Levites. The work was divided by lots among the families of Eleazar and Ithamar. The following men with their groups were chosen.

[7]The first one chosen was Jehoiarib. The second was Jedaiah. [8]The third was Harim. The fourth was Seorim. [9]The fifth was Malkijah. The sixth was Mijamin. [10]The seventh was Hakkoz. The eighth was Abijah. [11]The ninth was Jeshua. The tenth was Shecaniah. [12]The eleventh was Eliashib. The twelfth was Jakim. [13]The thirteenth was Huppah. The fourteenth was Jeshebeab. [14]The fifteenth was Bilgah. The sixteenth was Immer. [15]The seventeenth was Hezir. The eighteenth was Happizzez. [16]The nineteenth was Pethahiah. The twentieth was Jehezkel. [17]The twenty-first was Jakin. The twenty-second was Gamul. [18]The twenty-third was Delaiah. The twenty-fourth was Maaziah.

[19]These were the groups chosen to serve in the Temple of the Lord. They obeyed the rules Aaron had given them. The Lord, the God of Israel, had given those rules to Aaron.

THE OTHER LEVITES

[20]These are the names of the rest of Levi's descendants:[d]

Shubael was a descendant of Amram. And Jehdeiah was a descendant of Shubael.

²¹Isshiah was the first son of Rehabiah.

²²From the Izhar family group, there was Shelomoth. And Jahath was a descendant of Shelomoth.

²³Hebron's first son was Jeriah. Amariah was his second son. Jahaziel was his third son, and Jekameam was his fourth.

²⁴Uzziel's son was Micah. Micah's son was Shamir. ²⁵Isshiah was Micah's brother. Isshiah's son was Zechariah.

²⁶Merari's descendants were Mahli and Mushi. Merari's son was Jaaziah. ²⁷Jaaziah son of Merari had sons named Shoham, Zaccur and Ibri. ²⁸Mahli's son was Eleazar. But Eleazar did not have any sons.

²⁹Kish's son was Jerahmeel.

³⁰Mushi's sons were Mahli, Eder and Jerimoth.

These are the Levites, listed by their families. ³¹They were chosen for special jobs by throwing lots.ᵈ They did this just as their relatives, the priests, had done. The priests were Aaron's descendants. They threw lots in front of King David, Zadok and Ahimelech. The leaders of the families of the priests and Levites were also there. The families of the oldest brother and the youngest brother were treated the same.

THE MUSIC GROUPS

25 David and the commanders of the army chose some men to preach. They chose some of the sons of Asaph, Heman and Jeduthun. They were to preach God's message and play harps, lyresᵈ and cymbals. Here is a list of the men who served in this way:

²Asaph's sons who served were Zaccur, Joseph, Nethaniah and Asarelah. King David chose Asaph to preach. And Asaph directed his sons.

³Jeduthun's sons who served were Gedaliah, Zeri, Jeshaiah, Shimei, Hashabiah and Mattithiah. There were six of them, and Jeduthun directed them. He preached. And he used a harp to give thanks and praise to the Lord.

⁴Heman's sons who served were Bukkiah, Mattaniah, Uzziel, Shubael and Jerimoth. There were also Hananiah, Hanani, Eliathah, Giddalti and Romamti-Ezer. And there were Joshbekashah, Mallothi, Hothir and Mahazioth. ⁵All these men were sons of Heman, David's seer.ᵈ God promised to make Heman strong. So Heman had many sons. God gave him 14 sons and 3 daughters. ⁶Heman directed all his sons in making music for the Templeᵈ of the Lord. They used cymbals, lyres and harps. That was their way of serving in the Temple of God. And King David was in charge of Asaph, Jeduthun and Heman. ⁷These men and their relatives from the Levites were trained in music. They were skilled in making music for the Lord. There were 288 of them. ⁸Everyone threw lotsᵈ to choose the time his family was to serve at the Temple. The young and the old had to throw lots. The teacher and the student had to throw lots.

⁹First, 12 men were chosen from Joseph, his sons and relatives. Joseph was from the family of Asaph.

Second, 12 men were chosen from Gedaliah, his sons and relatives.

¹⁰Third, 12 men were chosen from Zaccur, his sons and relatives.

¹¹Fourth, 12 men were chosen from Izri, his sons and relatives.

¹²Fifth, 12 men were chosen from Nethaniah, his sons and relatives.

¹³Sixth, 12 men were chosen from Bukkiah, his sons and relatives.

¹⁴Seventh, 12 men were chosen from Jesarelah, his sons and relatives.

¹⁵Eighth, 12 men were chosen from Jeshaiah, his sons and relatives.

¹⁶Ninth, 12 men were chosen from Mattaniah, his sons and relatives.

¹⁷Tenth, 12 men were chosen from Shimei, his sons and relatives.

¹⁸Eleventh, 12 men were chosen from Azarel, his sons and relatives.

¹⁹Twelfth, 12 men were chosen from Hashabiah, his sons and relatives.

²⁰Thirteenth, 12 men were chosen from Shubael, his sons and relatives. ²¹Fourteenth, 12 men were chosen from Mattithiah, his sons and relatives. ²²Fifteenth, 12 men were chosen from Jerimoth, his sons and relatives. ²³Sixteenth, 12 men were chosen from Hananiah, his sons and relatives. ²⁴Seventeenth, 12 men were chosen from Joshbekashah, his sons and relatives. ²⁵Eighteenth, 12 men were chosen from Hanani, his sons and relatives. ²⁶Nineteenth, 12 men were chosen from Mallothi, his sons and relatives. ²⁷Twentieth, 12 men were chosen from Eliathah, his sons and relatives. ²⁸Twenty-first, 12 men were chosen from Hothir, his sons and relatives. ²⁹Twenty-second, 12 men were chosen from Giddalti, his sons and relatives. ³⁰Twenty-third, 12 men were chosen from Mahazioth, his sons and relatives. ³¹Twenty-fourth, 12 men were chosen from Romamti-Ezer, his sons and relatives.

THE GATEKEEPERS

26 These are the groups of the gatekeepers.

From the family of Korah, there was Meshelemiah and his sons. (Meshelemiah son of Kore was from Asaph's family.) ²Meshelemiah had sons. Zechariah was his first son. Jediael was his second son. Zebadiah was his third son. Jathniel was his fourth son. ³Elam was his fifth son. Jehohanan was his sixth son, and Eliehoenai was his seventh son.

⁴There were also Obed-Edom and his sons. Obed-Edom's first son was Shemaiah. Jehozabad was his second son. Joah was his third son. Sacar was his fourth son. Nethanel was his fifth son. ⁵Ammiel was his sixth son. Issachar was his seventh son, and Peullethai was his eighth son. God had blessed Obed-Edom with children.

⁶Obed-Edom's son Shemaiah also had sons. They were leaders in their father's family because they were capable men. ⁷Shemaiah's sons were Othni, Rephael, Obed, Elzabad, Elihu and Semakiah. Elihu and Semakiah were skilled workers. ⁸All these men were Obed-Edom's descendants.ᵈ They and their sons and relatives were capable men. They were strong enough to do the work. Obed-Edom had 62 descendants in all.

⁹Meshelemiah had sons and relatives. They were skilled workers. In all, there were 18 sons and relatives.

¹⁰These are the gatekeepers from the Merari family. Hosah had sons. Shimri was chosen to be in charge. He was not the oldest son, but his father chose him to be in charge. ¹¹Hilkiah was his second son. Tabaliah was his third son, and Zechariah was his fourth son. In all, Hosah had 13 sons and relatives.

¹²These were the leaders of the groups of the gatekeepers. They had jobs for serving in the Templeᵈ of the Lord. Their relatives also had jobs in the Temple. ¹³Each family was given a gate to guard. They were chosen by throwing lots.ᵈ Young and old threw lots.

¹⁴Meshelemiah was chosen by lot to guard the East Gate. Then lots were thrown for Meshelemiah's son Zechariah. He was a wise counselor. He was chosen for the North Gate. ¹⁵Obed-Edom was chosen for the South Gate. And Obed-Edom's sons were chosen to guard the storehouse. ¹⁶Shuppim and Hosah were chosen for the West Gate. They also were to guard the Shalleketh Gate on the upper road.

Guards stood side by side with guards. ¹⁷Six Levites stood guard every day at the East Gate. Four Levites stood guard every day at the North Gate. Four Levites stood guard every day at the South Gate. And two Levites at a time guarded the storehouse. ¹⁸There were two guards at the western court. And there were four guards on the road to the court.

[19]These were the groups of the gatekeepers. They were from the families of Korah and Merari.

OTHER LEADERS

[20]Other Levites were responsible for taking care of the treasuries of the Temple[d] of God. They were also responsible for the places where the holy things were kept.

[21]Ladan was Gershon's son. Ladan was the ancestor of several family groups. Jehiel was a leader of one of the family groups. [22]Jehiel's sons were Zetham and his brother Joel. They were responsible for the treasuries of the Temple of the Lord.

[23]Other leaders were chosen from the family groups of Amram, Izhar, Hebron and Uzziel. [24]Shubael was the leader responsible for the treasuries of the Temple of the Lord. Shubael was the descendant[d] of Gershom, who was Moses' son. [25]These were Shubael's relatives from Eliezer: Eliezer's son Rehabiah, Rehabiah's son Jeshaiah, Jeshaiah's son Joram, Joram's son Zicri and Zicri's son Shelomith. [26]Shelomith and his relatives were responsible for everything that had been collected for the Temple. Things had been collected by King David and the heads of families. They had been collected by commanders of 1,000 men and of 100 men and other army commanders. [27]They also gave some of the things they had taken in wars. They gave them to be used in repairing the Temple of the Lord. [28]Shelomith and his relatives took care of all the holy things. Some had been given by Samuel the seer[d] and Saul son of Kish. Some had been given by Abner son of Ner and Joab son of Zeruiah.

[29]Kenaniah was from the Izhar family. He and his sons worked outside the Temple. They worked as officers and judges in different places in Israel.

[30]Hashabiah was from the Hebron family. He and his relatives were responsible for the Lord's work and the king's business in Israel west of the Jordan River. There were 1,700 skilled men in Hashabiah's group. [31]The history of the Hebron family shows that Jeriah was their leader. In David's fortieth year as king, the records were searched. Some capable men of the Hebron family were found living at Jazer in Gilead. [32]Jeriah had 2,700 relatives who were skilled men. They were leaders of families. King David gave them the responsibility of directing the tribes[d] of Reuben, Gad and the eastern half-tribe of Manasseh. They took care of the Lord's work and the king's business for them.

ARMY DIVISIONS

27 This is the list of the Israelite people who served the king in the army. Each division was on duty one month each year. There were leaders of families, commanders of 100 men, commanders of 1,000 men and other officers. Each division had 24,000 men.

[2]Jashobeam son of Zabdiel was in charge of the first division for the first month. There were 24,000 men in his division. [3]He was one of the descendants[d] of Perez. Jashobeam was leader of all the army officers for the first month.

[4]Dodai was in charge of the division for the second month. He was from the Ahohites. Mikloth was a leader in the division. There were 24,000 men in Dodai's division.

[5]The third commander was Benaiah son of Jehoiada the priest. He was the commander for the third month. There were 24,000 men in Benaiah's division. [6]He was the Benaiah who was one of the Thirty[n] soldiers. Benaiah was a brave warrior who led those men. Benaiah's son Ammizabad was in charge of Benaiah's division.

27:6 **Thirty** These were David's most powerful soldiers. See 2 Samuel 23:24.

[7]The fourth commander was Asahel, the brother of Joab. He was the commander for the fourth month. Later, Asahel's son Zebadiah took his place as commander. There were 24,000 men in his division.

[8]The fifth commander was Shamhuth, from Izrah's family. He was the commander for the fifth month. There were 24,000 men in his division.

[9]The sixth commander was Ira son of Ikkesh. He was the commander for the sixth month. He was from the town of Tekoa. There were 24,000 men in his division.

[10]The seventh commander was Helez. He was the commander for the seventh month. He was from the Pelonites and a descendant of Ephraim. There were 24,000 men in his division.

[11]The eighth commander was Sibbecai. He was the commander for the eighth month. He was from Hushah and was from Zerah's family. There were 24,000 men in his division.

[12]The ninth commander was Abiezer, from the town of Anathoth. He was the commander for the ninth month. He was from the tribe[d] of Benjamin. There were 24,000 men in his division.

[13]The tenth commander was Maharai. He was the commander for the tenth month. He was from Netophah and was from Zerah's family. There were 24,000 men in his division.

[14]The eleventh commander was Benaiah. He was the commander for the eleventh month. He was from Pirathon and was from the tribe of Ephraim. There were 24,000 men in his division.

[15]The twelfth commander was Heldai. He was the commander for the twelfth month. He was from Netophah and was from Othniel's family. There were 24,000 men in his division.

LEADERS OF THE TRIBES

[16]These were the leaders of the tribes[d] of Israel. Eliezer son of Zicri was over the tribe of Reuben. Shephatiah son of Maacah was over the tribe of Simeon. [17]Hashabiah son of Kemuel was over the tribe of Levi. Zadok was over the people of Aaron. [18]Elihu, one of David's brothers, was over the tribe of Judah. Omri son of Michael was over the tribe of Issachar. [19]Ishmaiah son of Obadiah was over the tribe of Zebulun. Jerimoth son of Azriel was over the tribe of Naphtali. [20]Hoshea son of Azaziah was over the tribe of Ephraim. Joel son of Pedaiah was over the western half-tribe of Manasseh. [21]Iddo son of Zechariah was over the eastern half-tribe of Manasseh. Jaasiel son of Abner was over the tribe of Benjamin. [22]Azarel son of Jeroham was over the tribe of Dan.

These were the leaders of the tribes of Israel.

[23]The Lord had promised to make the Israelites as many as the stars in the sky. So David only counted the men who were 20 years old and older. [24]Joab son of Zeruiah began to count the people. But he did not finish. God became angry with Israel for counting the people. So the number of the people was not put in the history book about King David's rule.

THE KING'S DIRECTORS

[25]Azmaveth son of Adiel was in charge of the royal storehouses.

Jonathan was in charge of the storehouses in the towns, villages and towers. He was the son of Uzziah.

[26]Ezri son of Kelub was in charge of the field workers. They farmed the land.

[27]Shimei was in charge of the vineyards. He was from the town of Ramah.

Zabdi was in charge of storing the wine that came from the vineyards. Zabdi was from Shepham.

[28]Baal-Hanan was in charge of the olive trees and sycamore trees in the western mountain slopes. He was from Geder.

Joash was in charge of storing the olive oil.

²⁹Shitrai was in charge of the cows that fed in the Plain of Sharon. He was from Sharon.

Shaphat son of Adlai was in charge of the cows in the valleys.

³⁰Obil was in charge of the camels. He was an Ishmaelite.

Jehdeiah was in charge of the donkeys. He was from Meronoth.

³¹Jaziz was in charge of the sheep. He was from the Hagrites.

All these men were the officers who took care of King David's property.

³²Jonathan was David's uncle. He advised David. Jonathan was a wise man and a teacher of the law. Jehiel son of Hacmoni took care of the king's sons. ³³Ahithophel advised the king. Hushai was the king's friend. He was from the Arkite people. ³⁴Jehoiada and Abiathar later took Ahithophel's place in advising the king. Jehoiada was Benaiah's son. Joab was the commander of the king's army.

DAVID'S PLANS FOR THE TEMPLE

28 David commanded all the leaders of Israel to come to Jerusalem. There were the leaders of the tribes*d* and the commanders of the divisions serving the king. There were the commanders of 1,000 men and of 100 men. There were the leaders who took care of the property and animals that belonged to the king and his sons. There were the men over the palace, the powerful men and all the brave warriors.

²King David stood up and said, "Listen to me, my relatives and my people. I wanted to build a place to keep the Box*d* of the Agreement with the Lord. I wanted it to be God's footstool. And I made plans to build a temple for worship to God. ³But God said to me, 'You must not build a temple for worship to me. You must not do that because you are a soldier. You have killed many men.'

⁴"But the Lord, the God of Israel, chose me from my whole family. He chose me

to be king of Israel forever. The Lord chose the tribe of Judah to be a leader. And from the people of Judah, he chose my father's family. And from that family God was pleased to make me king of Israel. ⁵The Lord has given me many sons. And from those sons he has chosen Solomon. Solomon will be the new king of Israel. Israel is the Lord's kingdom. ⁶The Lord said to me, 'Your son Solomon will build my Temple.*d* And he will build the area around it. This is because I have chosen Solomon to be my son. And I will be his father. ⁷He is obeying my laws and commands now. If he continues to obey them, I will make his kingdom strong forever.'"

⁸David said, "Now, in front of all Israel and God, I tell you these things: Be careful to obey all the commands of the Lord your God. Then you may keep this good land. And you may pass it on to your descendants*d* forever.

⁹"And you, my son Solomon, accept the God of your father. Serve him completely. Be happy to serve him. Do this because the Lord knows what is in every person's mind. He understands everything you think. If you go to him for help, you will get an answer. But if you turn away from the Lord, he will leave you forever. ¹⁰Solomon, you must understand this. The Lord has chosen you to build the Temple as his holy place. Be strong and finish the job."

¹¹Then David gave his son Solomon the plans for building the Temple. Those plans were also for the porch around the Temple. They were for its buildings, its storerooms, its upper rooms and its inside rooms. They also were the plans for the place where the people's sins were removed. ¹²David gave him plans for everything he had in mind. David gave him plans for the courtyards around the Lord's Temple and all the rooms around it. He gave him plans for the Temple treasuries. And he gave him

plans for the treasuries of the holy things used in the Temple. [13]David gave Solomon directions for the groups of the priests and Levites. David told him about all the work of serving in the Temple of the Lord. He told him about the things to be used in the Temple service. [14]Many things made of gold or silver would be used in the Temple. David told Solomon how much gold or silver should be used to make each thing. [15]David told him how much gold to use for each gold lampstand and its lamps. He told him how much silver to use for each silver lampstand and its lamps. The different lampstands were to be used where needed. [16]David told how much gold should be used for each table that held the holy bread. And he told how much silver should be used for the silver tables. [17]He told how much pure gold should be used to make the forks, bowls and pitchers. He told how much gold should be used to make each gold dish. He told how much silver should be used to make each silver dish. [18]David told how much pure gold should be used for the altar of incense.[d] He also gave Solomon the plans for the chariot. This is where the golden creatures spread their wings over the Box[d] of the Agreement with the Lord.

[19]David said, "All these plans were written with the Lord guiding me. He helped me understand everything in the plans."

[20]David also said to his son Solomon, "Be strong and brave. Do the work. Don't be afraid or discouraged. The Lord God, my God, is with you. He will help you until all the work is finished. He will not leave you. You will build the Temple of the Lord. [21]The groups of the priests and Levites are ready for all the work on the Temple of God. Every skilled worker is ready to help you with all the work. The leaders and all the people will obey every command you give."

GIFTS FOR BUILDING THE TEMPLE

29 King David spoke to all the Israelites who were gathered. He said, "God chose my son Solomon. Solomon is young and hasn't yet learned what he needs to know. But the work is important. This palace is not for people. It is for the Lord God. [2]I have done my best to prepare for building the Temple[d] of God. I have given gold for the things made of gold. I have given silver for the things made of silver. I have given bronze for the things made of bronze. I have given iron for the things made of iron. I have given wood for the things made of wood. I have given onyx for the settings and turquoise. I have given gems of many different colors. I have given valuable stones and white marble. I have given much of all these things. [3]I have already given this for the Temple. But now I am also giving my own treasures of gold and silver. I am doing this because I really want the Temple of my God to be built. [4]I have given about 220,000 pounds of pure gold from Ophir. And I have given about 520,000 pounds of pure silver. They will be used to cover the walls of the buildings. [5]They will also be used for all the gold and silver work. Skilled men may use the gold and silver to make things for the Temple. Now, who is ready to give himself to the service of the Lord today?"

[6]The family leaders and the leaders of the tribes of Israel gave their valuable things. The commanders of 1,000 men and of 100 men gave their valuable things. And the leaders responsible for the king's work gave their valuable things. [7]These are the things they gave for the Temple of God: about 380,000 pounds of gold, about 750,000 pounds of silver, about 1,350,000 pounds of bronze and about 7,500,000 pounds of iron. [8]People who had valuable gems gave them to the treasury of the Temple of the Lord. Jehiel, from the Gershon family, took care of the

valuable gems. ⁹The leaders gave freely and completely to the Lord. The people were happy to see their leaders give so gladly. King David was also very happy.

DAVID'S PRAYER

¹⁰David praised the Lord in front of all of the people who were gathered. He said: "We praise you, Lord.
You are the God of our father Israel.
We praise you forever and ever.
¹¹Lord, you are great and powerful.
You have glory, victory and honor.
Everything in heaven and on earth belongs to you.
The kingdom belongs to you, Lord.
You are the ruler over everything.
¹²Riches and honor come from you.
You rule everything.
You have the power and strength to make anyone great and strong.
¹³Now, our God, we thank you.
And we praise your glorious name.

¹⁴"These things did not really come from me and my people.
Everything comes from you.
We have given you back what you gave us.
¹⁵We are like foreigners and strangers.
All our ancestors were also foreigners and strangers.
Our time on earth is like a shadow.
There is no hope.
¹⁶Lord our God, we have gathered all this to build your Temple.
We will build it for worship to you.
But everything has come from you.
Everything belongs to you.
¹⁷I know, my God, that you test people's hearts.
You are happy when people do what is right.
I was happy to give all these things.
I gave with an honest heart.
Your people gathered here are happy to give to you.
I am happy to see their giving.
¹⁸Lord, you are the God of our ancestors.

You are the God of Abraham, Isaac and Jacob.
Please help your people to want to serve you always.
And help them to want to obey you always.
¹⁹Give my son Solomon a strong desire to serve you.
Help him always obey your commands, laws and rules.
Help him build the Temple for which I have prepared."
²⁰Then David said to all the people who were gathered, "Praise the Lord your God." So they all praised the Lord, the God their ancestors worshiped. They bowed to the ground to give honor to the Lord and the king.

SOLOMON BECOMES KING

²¹The next day the people made sacrifices to the Lord. They offered burnt offerings to him. They offered 1,000 bulls, 1,000 male sheep and 1,000 male lambs. They also brought drink offerings. Many sacrifices were made for all the people of Israel. ²²That day the people ate and drank with much joy. And the Lord was with them.

And they made David's son Solomon king for the second time. They poured olive oil on Solomon to appoint him king. And they poured oil on Zadok to appoint him as priest. They did this in the presence of the Lord. ²³Then Solomon sat on the Lord's throne as king. He took his father David's place. Solomon was very successful. And all the people of Israel obeyed him. ²⁴All the leaders and soldiers and King David's sons accepted Solomon as king. They promised to obey him. ²⁵The Lord made Solomon great before all the Israelites. The Lord gave Solomon much honor. No king of Israel before Solomon had such honor.

DAVID'S DEATH

²⁶David son of Jesse was king over all Israel. ²⁷He was king for 40 years. He ruled in the city of Hebron for 7 years.

And he ruled in Jerusalem for 33 years. [28]David died when he was old. He had lived a good, long life. He had received many riches and honors. And David's son Solomon became king after him.

[29]Everything King David did as king, from beginning to end, is recorded. Those things are written in the records of Samuel the seer.[d] And they are in the records of Nathan the prophet and the records of Gad the seer. [30]Those writings tell what David did as king of Israel. They tell about his power and all that happened to him. And they tell what happened to Israel and all the kingdoms around them.

CHRONICLES

SOLOMON ASKS FOR WISDOM

1 Solomon was David's son, and he became a powerful king. This was because the Lord his God was with him. The Lord made Solomon very great.

²Solomon spoke to all the people of Israel. He spoke to the commanders of 100 men and of 1,000 men. He spoke to the judges, to every leader in all Israel and to the leaders of the families. ³Then Solomon and all the people gathered with him went to the place of worship. This was at the town of Gibeon. God's Meeting Tent*d* was there. Moses, the Lord's servant, had made that Tent in the desert. ⁴David had brought the Box*d* of the Agreement with God from Kiriath Jearim to Jerusalem. David had made a place for it there. He had set up a tent for it in Jerusalem. ⁵Bezalel was Uri's son, and Uri was Hur's son. Bezalel had made a bronze altar. It was in Gibeon in front of the Holy Tent. So Solomon and the people worshiped the Lord there. ⁶Solomon went up to the bronze altar before the Lord at the Meeting Tent. He offered 1,000 burnt offerings on the altar.

⁷That night God appeared to Solomon. God said, "Solomon, ask for whatever you want me to give you."

⁸Solomon answered, "You have been very kind to my father David. You have chosen me to be the king in his place. ⁹Now, Lord God, may your promise to my father David come true. You have made me king of a very large nation. There are so many of them they are like the dust of the earth. ¹⁰Now give me wisdom and knowledge so I can lead these people in the right way. No one can rule them without your help."

¹¹God said to Solomon, "What you want is good. I have chosen you to be king of these people. You have not asked for wealth or riches or honor. You have not asked for your enemies to be killed.

You have not asked for a long life. But you have asked for wisdom and knowledge to lead my people. ¹²So I will give you wisdom and knowledge. I will also give you more wealth, riches and honor than any king who has lived before you. And the kings who will live after you will not have as much."

¹³Then Solomon left the place of worship at Gibeon. He left the Meeting Tent and went back to Jerusalem. There King Solomon ruled over Israel.

SOLOMON'S WEALTH

¹⁴Solomon gathered horses and chariots. He had 1,400 chariots and 12,000 horses. He put some horses and chariots in the cities where the chariots were kept. And he kept some with him in Jerusalem. ¹⁵In Jerusalem, Solomon gathered much silver and gold. He got so much it was as common as rocks. He also gathered much cedar wood. It became as plentiful as the sycamore trees on the western mountain slopes. ¹⁶Solomon imported horses from Egypt and Kue. The king's traders bought the horses in Kue. ¹⁷They imported a chariot from Egypt for about 15 pounds of silver. And they imported a horse for nearly 4 pounds of silver. Then they sold the horses and chariots to all the kings of the Hittites and the Arameans.

SOLOMON PREPARES FOR THE TEMPLE

2 Solomon decided to build a temple*d* as a place to worship the Lord. He also decided to build a palace for himself. ²He chose 70,000 men to carry things. He chose 80,000 men to cut stone in the mountains. And he chose 3,600 men to direct the workers.

³Then Solomon sent a message to Hiram king of the city of Tyre. Solomon said:

Help me as you helped my father David. You sent him cedar logs so he could build himself a palace to live in. ⁴I will build a temple as a place to worship the Lord my God. And I will give this temple to the Lord. There we will burn sweet-smelling spices in his presence. We will set out the bread that shows we are in God's presence. And we will burn sacrifices every morning and evening. We will worship him on Sabbath^d days and New Moons.^d And we will worship him on the other feast days the Lord our God has commanded us to celebrate. This is a rule for Israel to obey forever.

⁵The temple I build will be great. This is because our God is greater than all gods. ⁶But no one can really build a house for our God. Not even the highest of heavens can hold God. How then can I build a temple for him? I can only build a place to burn sacrifices to God.

⁷Now send me a man skilled in working with gold, silver, bronze and iron. He must know how to work with purple, red and blue thread. He must know how to make engravings. He will work with my skilled craftsmen in Judah and Jerusalem. These are the men my father David chose.

⁸Also send me cedar, pine and juniper logs from Lebanon. I know your servants are experienced at cutting down the trees in Lebanon. My servants will help them. ⁹Send me a lot of wood. The temple I am going to build will be large and wonderful. ¹⁰I will give your servants who cut the wood 125,000 bushels of wheat. And I will give them 125,000 bushels of barley, 115,000 gallons of wine and 115,000 gallons of oil.

¹¹Then Hiram king of Tyre answered Solomon with this letter:

Solomon, the Lord loves his people. That is why he chose you to be their king.

¹²Hiram also said:

Praise the Lord, the God of Israel! He made heaven and earth! He gave King David a wise son. Solomon, you have wisdom and understanding. You will build a temple for the Lord and a palace for yourself.

¹³I will send you a skilled and wise man named Huram-Abi. ¹⁴His mother was from the people of Dan. And his father was from Tyre. Huram-Abi has skill in working with gold, silver, bronze, iron, stone and wood. He has skill in working with purple, blue and red thread and expensive linen. And he is skilled in making engravings. He can make any design you show him. He will help your craftsmen and the craftsmen of your father David.

¹⁵Now send my servants the wheat, barley, oil and wine you promised. ¹⁶We will cut as much wood from Lebanon as you need. We will use rafts to carry it by sea to Joppa. Then you may carry it to Jerusalem.

¹⁷Solomon counted all the foreigners living in Israel. This was after the time his father David had counted the people. There were 153,600 foreigners in the country. ¹⁸Solomon chose 70,000 of them to carry things. He chose 80,000 of them to cut stone in the mountains. And he chose 3,600 of them to direct the workers. They were to keep the people working.

SOLOMON BUILDS THE TEMPLE

3 Solomon began to build the Temple^d of the Lord. He built it in Jerusalem on Mount Moriah. This was where the Lord had appeared to David, Solomon's father. Solomon built the Temple on the place David had prepared. This place was the threshing^d floor of Araunah the Jebusite. ²Solomon began building in the second month of the fourth year he ruled Israel.

³Solomon used these measurements for building the Temple of God. It was 90

feet long and 30 feet wide. (Solomon used the old measurement.) [4]The porch in front of the Temple was 30 feet long and 30 feet high.

Solomon covered the inside of the porch with pure gold. [5]He put panels of pine on the walls of the main room. Then he covered them with pure gold. And he put designs of palm trees and chains in the gold. [6]He put gems in the Temple for beauty. And he used gold from Parvaim.[n] [7]Solomon put gold on the Temple's ceiling beams, doorposts, walls and doors. And he carved creatures with wings on the walls.

[8]Then Solomon made the Most Holy Place. It was 30 feet long and 30 feet wide. It was as wide as the Temple. He covered its walls with about 46,000 pounds of pure gold. [9]The gold nails weighed over a pound. Solomon also covered the upper rooms with gold.

[10]He made two creatures with wings for the Most Holy Place. He made them out of hot liquid gold. [11]The wings of the gold creatures were spread out. Together, they were 30 feet across. One wing of one creature touched the Temple wall. The wing was 7 1/2 feet long. The creature's other wing touched a wing of the second creature. This wing was also 7 1/2 feet long. [12]One wing of the second creature touched the other side of the room. It was also 7 1/2 feet long. The second creature's other wing touched the first creature's wing. This wing was also 7 1/2 feet long. [13]Together, the creatures' wings were 30 feet across. The creatures stood on their feet. They looked inside toward the main room.

[14]Solomon made the curtain of blue, purple and red thread and expensive linen. And he put designs of creatures with wings in it.

[15]Solomon made two pillars to stand in front of the Temple. They were about 52 feet tall. The capital[d] of each pillar was over 7 feet tall. [16]Solomon made a net of chains. He put them on the tops of the pillars. He made 100 pomegranates[d] and put them on the chains. [17]Then Solomon put the pillars up in front of the Temple. One pillar stood on the south side. The other stood on the north. He named the south pillar He Establishes. And he named the north pillar In Him Is Strength.

THINGS FOR THE TEMPLE

4 Solomon made a bronze altar. It was 30 feet long, 30 feet wide and 15 feet tall. [2]Then Solomon used melted bronze to make a large bowl, which was called the Sea. It was round and measured 15 feet across from edge to edge. It was over 7 feet tall, and it measured 45 feet around. [3]There were carvings of bulls under the rim of the bowl. There were 10 bulls in every 1 1/2 feet. They were put in two rows around the bowl when it was made.

[4]The bowl rested on 12 statues of bulls. Three bulls faced north, 3 faced west, 3 faced south and 3 faced east. The bowl was on top of them. They faced outward from the center of the bowl. [5]The bowl was 3 inches thick. Its rim was like the rim of a cup. It looked like a lily blossom. It could hold about 17,500 gallons.

[6]Solomon made 10 smaller bowls. He put 5 of them on the south side. And he put 5 of them on the north. They were to be used to wash the animals for the burnt offerings. But the large bowl was to be used by the priests for washing.

[7]Solomon made 10 lampstands of gold, following the plans for them. He put them in the Temple.[d] He put 5 on the south side and 5 on the north.

[8]Solomon made 10 tables and put them in the Temple. He put 5 on the south side and 5 on the north. And he used gold to make 100 other bowls.

⁹Solomon also made the priests' courtyard and the large courtyard. He made the doors that opened to the courtyard and covered them with bronze. ¹⁰Then he put the large bowl on the south side. He put it in the Temple's southeast corner.

¹¹He made the pots, shovels and bowls. So Huram finished his work for King Solomon on the Temple of God. He had made these things:

¹²two pillars;

two large bowls for the capitals on top of the pillars;

two nets to cover the two large bowls for the capitals on top of the pillars;

¹³400 pomegranates*d* for the two nets (there were two rows of pomegranates for each net covering the bowls for the capitals on top of the pillars);

¹⁴the stands with a bowl on each stand;

¹⁵the large bowl with 12 bulls under it;

¹⁶the pots, shovels, forks and all the things to go with them.

All the things Huram-Abi made King Solomon for the Temple of the Lord were made of polished bronze. ¹⁷King Solomon first had these things poured into clay molds. The molds were made in the plain of the Jordan between Succoth and Zarethan. ¹⁸Solomon had so many things made no one even tried to weigh all the bronze used.

¹⁹Solomon also made all the things for God's Temple. He made the gold altar. He made tables to hold the bread that shows we are in God's presence. ²⁰He made the lampstands and their lamps of pure gold. They were to burn in front of the Most Holy Place as planned. ²¹Solomon used pure gold to make the flowers, lamps and tongs. ²²He used pure gold to make the wick trimmers. He used pure gold for the bowls, pans and dishes used to carry coals. He used

pure gold to make the doors for the Temple. And he used pure gold for the inside doors for the Most Holy Place and the doors for the main room.

5 Then all the work Solomon had done for the Temple of the Lord was finished. He brought in everything his father David had given for the Temple. He brought in all the silver and gold and all the furniture. And he put everything in the treasuries of God's Temple.

THE HOLY BOX IS CARRIED INTO THE TEMPLE

²Then Solomon called for all the elders of Israel. He asked them to come to him in Jerusalem. He called for all the older leaders, the heads of the tribes*d* and the leaders of the families. He wanted them to bring the Box*d* of the Agreement with the Lord from the older part of the city. ³All the men of Israel came together with King Solomon. This was during the festival that was held in the seventh month.

⁴All the elders of Israel arrived. Then the Levites picked up the Holy Box. ⁵The priests and the Levites carried the Box of the Agreement. They also carried the Meeting Tent*d* and the holy things in it. ⁶King Solomon and all the Israelites met in front of the Box of the Agreement. They sacrificed so many sheep and bulls no one could count them.

⁷Then the priests put the Box of the Agreement with the Lord in its place. This was inside the Most Holy Place in the Temple.*d* They put it under the wings of the gold creatures. ⁸The wings of the creatures were spread out over the place for the Holy Box. They covered it and its carrying poles. ⁹The carrying poles were very long. Anyone standing in the Holy Place in front of the Most Holy Place could see the ends of the poles. But no one could see the poles from outside the Holy Place. The poles are still there today. ¹⁰The only things inside the Holy Box were two stone tablets.*n* Moses had put

---

5:10 stone tablets They were the two stone tablets on which God wrote the Ten Commandments.

them in the Holy Box at Mount Sinai. That was where the Lord made an agreement with the Israelites after they came out of Egypt. ¹¹Then all the priests left the Holy Place. All the priests from each group made themselves ready to serve the Lord. ¹²All the Levite musicians stood on the east side of the altar. They were Asaph, Heman, Jeduthun and all their sons and relatives. They were dressed in white linen and played cymbals, lyres*d* and harps. With them were 120 priests who blew trumpets. ¹³Those who blew the trumpets and those who sang together sounded like one person. They praised and thanked the Lord. They sang as they played their trumpets, cymbals and other instruments. They praised the Lord with this song:

"The Lord is good.

His love continues forever."

Then the Temple of the Lord was filled with a cloud. ¹⁴The priests could not continue their work because of the cloud. This was because the Lord's glory filled the Temple of God.

6 Then Solomon said, "The Lord said he would live in the dark cloud. ²I have built a great Temple for you, Lord. It is a place for you to live forever."

SOLOMON'S SPEECH

³King Solomon turned around and blessed all the Israelites gathered in front of him. ⁴He said, "Praise the Lord, the God of Israel. He has done what he promised my father David. The Lord said, ⁵'I brought my people out of Egypt. But I have not yet chosen a city in any tribe*d* of Israel for my temple.*d* This is where I have chosen to be worshiped. I have not chosen a man to lead my people, the Israelites. ⁶But now I have chosen Jerusalem as the place I am to be worshiped. And I have chosen David to lead my people Israel.'

⁷"My father David wanted to build a temple as a place to worship the Lord,

the God of Israel. ⁸But the Lord said to my father, 'David, it was good that you wanted to build a temple as a place to worship me. ⁹But you are not the one who will build the temple. Your own son will build my temple.'

¹⁰"Now the Lord has kept his promise. I have taken my father David's place. Now I am Israel's king. This is what the Lord promised. And I have built the Temple where the Lord, the God of Israel, will be worshiped. ¹¹I have put the Box*d* of the Agreement there. The agreement that the Lord made with the people of Israel is kept in the Holy Box."

SOLOMON'S PRAYER

¹²Solomon stood in front of the Lord's altar. He was standing before all the people gathered there. Then he spread his arms out. ¹³He had made a bronze platform. It was 7¹/₂ feet long, 7¹/₂ feet wide and 7¹/₂ feet high. And he had placed it in the middle of the outer courtyard. Solomon stood on the platform. Then he kneeled in front of all the people of Israel who were gathered there. Solomon spread his hands out toward the sky. ¹⁴He said, "Lord, God of Israel, there is no god like you in heaven or on earth. You keep your agreement of love with your servants who completely obey you. ¹⁵You have kept your promise to my father David, your servant. With your words you made a promise. And with the work of your hands, you have made that promise come true today.

¹⁶"Now, Lord, God of Israel, also keep this promise you made to my father David, your servant. You said, 'David, you will always have someone from your family rule Israel. But this will happen only if they are careful to obey my teachings in everything they do. They must obey my teachings just as you have.' ¹⁷Now, Lord, God of Israel, keep your promise. Let this promise to your servant David come true.

¹⁸"But, God, can you really live here on the earth with people? Not even the highest of heavens can hold you. And this Temple[d] I built cannot hold you. ¹⁹But pay attention to my prayer and my cry for mercy. Lord my God, listen to my cry. Listen to the prayer I, your servant, pray to you. ²⁰I pray that you will watch over this Temple day and night. You said you would make this the place to worship you. I pray that you will hear my prayers when I pray facing this Temple. ²¹Hear my prayers and the prayers of your people Israel. Hear us when we pray facing this Temple. Hear from your home in heaven. And when you hear our prayers, forgive us.

²²"A person might do something wrong against someone else. The person who did the wrong will have to swear he is innocent. He will come to swear this before your altar in the Temple. ²³When he does this, listen from heaven and act. Judge your servants. Punish the one who did wrong. Make him suffer the same things he made others suffer. Prove that the person who has done right is innocent.

²⁴"An enemy might defeat your people Israel because they have sinned against you. Then the people of Israel will return to you and say you are God. They will pray and beg you for help in this Temple. ²⁵When this happens, listen from heaven. Forgive the sin of your people, the Israelites. Bring them back into the land you gave to them and their ancestors.

²⁶"The sky might not let it rain because your people have sinned against you. Then they will pray, facing this Temple. They will say you are God. They will stop doing their sin because you are punishing them. ²⁷When that happens, then listen from heaven. Forgive the sins of your servants, the Israelites. Then teach them the right way to live. And send rain on your land. This is the land you gave your people as their own.

²⁸"There might be a time without food in the land. Or there might be terrible sicknesses, disease in the crops, mildew,[d] locusts[d] or grasshoppers. Or enemies might attack Israel's cities. There might be a disaster in Israel. ²⁹Then one of your people, an Israelite, will pray or cry for help. Each person knows his own trouble and pain. He will spread his arms out, facing this Temple. ³⁰When that happens, then listen from heaven, your home. Forgive and treat each person as he should be treated. You know what is in his heart. (Only you know what is in a person's heart.) ³¹Then the people will fear and obey you as long as they live in this land. This is the land you gave our ancestors.

³²"A foreigner might come here from a country far away. He is not one of your people, the people of Israel. But he will come because he has heard about your greatness and power. He knows about the things you have done. When he comes and prays, facing this Temple, ³³then listen. Listen from heaven, your home. And do what he asks you to do. Then all the peoples of the earth will know you and respect you, just as your people Israel do. And they will know that this Temple I built is for worshiping you.

³⁴"You might send your people to fight their enemies. They will pray to you, facing this city you chose and the Temple I built for worshiping you. ³⁵If they do, then listen from heaven to their prayer. Listen to their cry and help them.

³⁶"People will sin against you. There is not a person who does not sin. And you will become angry with them. You will let an enemy defeat them. The enemy will capture them and take them away. It may be to a land far away or near. ³⁷But then they will be sorry for what they have done. As captives in that land, they will cry out to you. They will say, 'We have sinned. We have done wrong and acted wickedly.' ³⁸In the land where they

are captives, they will come back to you. They will want to obey you completely. They will pray, facing their land, the land you gave their ancestors. They will pray, facing the city you chose and the Temple I built for you. ³⁹When this happens, listen from your home in heaven. Listen to their cries and help them. Forgive your people who have sinned against you.

⁴⁰"Now, my God, look at us. Listen to the prayers we will pray in this place.
⁴¹Now, rise, Lord God, and come to
your resting place.
Come with the Box*ᵈ* of the
Agreement that shows your
strength.
Let your priests receive your
salvation, Lord God.
And may your holy people be happy
because of your goodness.
⁴²Lord God, do not reject your
appointed one.
Remember your love for your
servant David."

THE TEMPLE IS GIVEN TO THE LORD

7 When Solomon finished praying, fire came down from the sky. It burned up the burnt offering and the sacrifices. The Lord's glory filled the Temple.*ᵈ* ²The priests could not enter the Temple of the Lord because the Lord's glory filled it. ³All the people of Israel saw the fire come down from heaven. They also saw the Lord's glory on the Temple. Then they bowed down on the pavement with their faces to the ground. They worshiped and thanked the Lord. They said,
"The Lord is good.
His love continues forever."
⁴Then King Solomon and all the Israelites offered sacrifices before the Lord. ⁵King Solomon offered a sacrifice of 22,000 cattle and 120,000 sheep. So the king and all the people gave the Temple for the worship of God. ⁶The priests stood ready to do their work. The Levites also stood with the instruments

of the Lord's music. King David had made these instruments for praising the Lord. The priests and Levites were saying, "The Lord's love continues forever." The priests, who stood across from the Levites, blew their trumpets. And all the Israelites were standing.

⁷Solomon made the middle part of the courtyard holy for the Lord. That courtyard is in front of the Temple of the Lord. There Solomon offered burnt offerings and the fat of the fellowship offerings. He used the middle of the courtyard because the bronze altar he had made could not hold everything. It couldn't hold the burnt offerings, grain offerings and fat.

⁸Solomon and all the Israelites celebrated the festival for seven days. There were many people. They came from as far away as Lebo Hamath. And they came all the way from the brook of Egypt. ⁹They had given the altar for the worship of the Lord. And they celebrated that for seven days. Then they celebrated the festival for seven days. On the eighth day they had a meeting. ¹⁰On the twenty-third day of the seventh month Solomon sent the people home. They were full of joy. They were happy because the Lord had been so good to David, Solomon and his people the Israelites.

THE LORD APPEARS TO SOLOMON

¹¹Solomon finished the Temple*ᵈ* of the Lord and the king's palace. He had success in doing everything he planned in the Temple of the Lord and his own palace. ¹²Then the Lord appeared to Solomon at night. The Lord said, "Solomon, I have heard your prayer. And I have chosen this place for myself to be a Temple for sacrifices.

¹³"I may stop the sky from sending rain. I may command the locusts*ᵈ* to destroy the land. I may send sicknesses to my people. ¹⁴Then my people, who are called by my name, will be sorry for what they have done. They will pray and obey

me and stop their evil ways. If they do, I will hear them from heaven. I will forgive their sin, and I will heal their land. [15]Now I will see them. And I will listen to the prayers prayed in this place. [16]I have chosen this Temple and made it holy. So I will be worshiped here forever. Yes, I will always watch over it and love it.

[17]"Solomon, obey me as your father David did. Obey all I have commanded. Obey my laws and rules. [18]If you do, I will make your kingdom strong. This is the agreement I made with your father David. I told him, 'David, someone from your family will always be king in Israel.'

[19]"But you must not turn away from me. You must not stop obeying the laws and commands I gave you. You must not serve and worship other gods. [20]If you do, I will take the Israelites out of my land, the land I gave them. And I will leave this Temple that I have made holy. All the nations will make fun of it and speak evil about it. [21]This Temple is honored now. But then, everyone who passes by will be surprised. They will say, 'Why has the Lord done this terrible thing to this land and this Temple?' [22]Then people will answer, 'It's because the Israelites left the Lord, the God their ancestors obeyed. He is the God who led them out of Egypt. But they accepted other gods and worshiped and served them. That is why the Lord brought this disaster on them.'"

SOLOMON'S OTHER ACHIEVEMENTS

8 It took Solomon 20 years to build the Temple[d] of the Lord and his own palace. [2]Then Solomon rebuilt the towns that Hiram had given him. And Solomon sent Israelites to live in them. [3]Then he went to Hamath Zobah and captured it. [4]Solomon also built the town of Tadmor in the desert. He built all the towns in Hamath as towns for storing things. [5]He rebuilt the towns of Upper Beth Horon and Lower Beth Horon. He made them protected towns with strong walls, gates and bars in the gates. [6]He also rebuilt the town of Baalath. And he built all the other towns where he stored things. He built all the cities where the chariots and horses were kept. Solomon built all he wanted in Jerusalem, Lebanon and in all the country he ruled.

[7-8]Many people who were not Israelites were left living in the country. These people were the Hittites, Amorites, Perizzites, Hivites and Jebusites. They were descendants[d] of the people that the Israelites had not destroyed. Solomon forced all of them to be slave workers. This is still true today. [9]But Solomon did not force any of the Israelites to be slave workers. They were his fighting men. They were the commanders of his army officers, his chariots and his chariot drivers. [10]Some of them were his most important officers. There were 250 of them to direct the people.

[11]Solomon brought the daughter of the king of Egypt from the older part of Jerusalem. He brought her to the palace he had built for her. Solomon said, "My wife must not live in King David's palace. This is because the places where the Box[d] of the Agreement has been are holy places."

[12]Then Solomon offered burnt offerings to the Lord on the Lord's altar. Solomon built that altar in front of the Temple porch. [13]He offered sacrifices every day as Moses had commanded. Sacrifices were to be offered on the Sabbath[d] days, New Moons[d] and the three yearly feasts. The three yearly feasts were the Feast[d] of Unleavened Bread, the Feast of Weeks and the Feast of Shelters. [14]Solomon followed his father David's instructions. Solomon chose the groups of priests for their service. He chose the Levites to lead the praise. And they were to help the priests do their daily work. And he chose the gatekeepers by their groups to serve at each gate. This is what

David, the man of God, had commanded. [15]They obeyed all of Solomon's commands to the priests and Levites. And they obeyed his commands about the treasuries.

[16]All Solomon's work was done. Everything was done as he had said from the day the Temple of the Lord was begun until it was finished. So the Temple was finished.

[17]Then Solomon went to the towns of Ezion Geber and Elath. They were near the Red Sea[d] in the country of Edom. [18]Hiram sent to Solomon ships commanded by his own men. They were skilled sailors. Hiram's men went with Solomon's men to Ophir. And they brought back about 34,000 pounds of gold to King Solomon.

THE QUEEN OF SHEBA VISITS SOLOMON

9 The queen of Sheba heard about Solomon's fame. So she came to Jerusalem to test him with hard questions. She had a very large group of people with her. She had camels that carried spices, much gold and many gems. She came to Solomon and talked with him about all her questions. [2]And Solomon answered all her questions. Nothing was too hard for him to explain to her. [3]The queen of Sheba saw that Solomon was very wise. She also saw the palace he had built. [4]She saw the food on his table and his many officers. She saw the palace servants and their good clothes. She saw the servants who served Solomon his wine. And she saw their good clothes. She saw the burnt offerings he made in the Temple[d] of the Lord. All these things amazed her. [5]So she said to King Solomon, "I heard in my own country about your achievements and wisdom. And all of it is true. [6]I did not believe it then. But now I have come and seen it with my own eyes. Not even half of your great wisdom was told to me! You are much greater than I had heard. [7]Your men and officers are very lucky!

Since they are always serving you, they are able to hear your wisdom! [8]Praise the Lord your God! He was pleased to make you king. He has put you on his throne to rule for the Lord your God. Your God loves Israel and supports Israel forever. So the Lord has made you king of Israel to keep law and order and to rule fairly."

[9]Then the queen of Sheba gave King Solomon about 9,000 pounds of gold. She also gave him many spices and gems. No one had ever given such fine spices as she gave to King Solomon.

[10]Hiram's men and Solomon's men brought in gold from Ophir. They also brought in juniper wood and gems. [11]King Solomon used the juniper wood to make steps for the Temple of the Lord and the palace. He also used it to make lyres[d] and harps for the singers. No one in Judah had ever seen such beautiful things as these.

[12]King Solomon gave the queen of Sheba everything she wanted and asked for. He gave her more than she had brought to him. Then she and her servants left and returned to their own country.

SOLOMON'S GREAT WEALTH

[13]The amount of gold that Solomon received in one year weighed about 50,000 pounds. [14]Besides that, he also received gold from merchants and traders. All the kings of Arabia and the rulers of the land also brought gold and silver to Solomon.

[15]King Solomon made 200 large shields from hammered gold. Each shield contained about 7$\frac{1}{2}$ pounds of hammered gold. [16]Solomon also made 300 small shields of hammered gold. Each shield contained about 4 pounds of gold. King Solomon put them in the Palace of the Forest of Lebanon.

[17]Then he built a large throne of ivory. And he covered it with pure gold. [18]The throne had six steps on it. And it had a

gold footstool on it. There were armrests on both sides of the chair. And beside each armrest was a statue of a lion. [19]Twelve lions stood on the six steps. There was one lion at each end of each step. Nothing like this had ever been made for any other kingdom. [20]All King Solomon's drinking cups were made of gold. All of the dishes in the Palace of the Forest of Lebanon were pure gold. In Solomon's time people did not think silver was valuable. So nothing was made of silver. [21]King Solomon had many ships that he sent out to trade. Hiram's men sailed Solomon's ships. Every three years the ships returned. They brought back gold, silver, ivory, apes and baboons.

[22]King Solomon had more riches and wisdom than all the other kings on earth. [23]All the kings of the earth came to see Solomon. They wanted to hear the wisdom God had given him. [24]Every year everyone who came brought a gift. They brought things made of silver and gold, clothes, weapons, spices, horses and mules.

[25]Solomon had 4,000 stalls to hold his horses and chariots. He had 12,000 horses. He kept them in special cities for the chariots. And he kept some with him in Jerusalem. [26]Solomon was king over all the kings from the Euphrates River to the Philistine country to the border of Egypt. [27]In Jerusalem silver was as common as stones while Solomon was king. Cedar trees were as common as the fig trees growing on the western mountain slopes. [28]Solomon imported horses from Egypt and all other countries.

SOLOMON'S DEATH

[29]The other things Solomon did as king, from the beginning to the end, are written down. They are in the writings of Nathan the prophet.[d] And they are in the prophecy of Ahijah and the visions of Iddo. Ahijah was from Shiloh. Iddo was a seer[d] who wrote about Jeroboam,

Nebat's son. [30]Solomon was king in Jerusalem over all Israel for 40 years. [31]Then Solomon died and was buried in Jerusalem. This was the city of his father David. And Solomon's son Rehoboam became king in his place.

REHOBOAM ACTS FOOLISHLY

10 Rehoboam went to Shechem because all the Israelites had gone there to make him king. [2]Jeroboam son of Nebat was in Egypt. He had gone there to run away from King Solomon. Jeroboam heard that Rehoboam was going to be the new king. So he returned from Egypt. [3]The people sent for Jeroboam. Then he and the people went to Rehoboam. They said to Rehoboam, [4]"Your father forced us to work very hard. Now, make it easier for us. Don't make us work as hard as your father did. Then we will serve you."

[5]Rehoboam answered, "Come back to me in three days." So the people left.

[6]There were some elders who had helped Solomon make decisions during his lifetime. So King Rehoboam asked them what he should do. He said, "How do you think I should answer these people?"

[7]They answered, "Be kind to these people. Please them and give them a kind answer. If you do, they will serve you always."

[8]But Rehoboam did not listen to the advice the older leaders gave him. He talked with the young men who had grown up with him. They advised him in making decisions. [9]Rehoboam asked them, "What is your advice? How should we answer these people? They said, 'Don't make us work as hard as your father did.'"

[10]Then the young men who had grown up with him said, "The people said to you, 'Your father forced us to work very hard. Now make our work easier.' But you should tell those people, 'My little finger is thicker than my father's waist.

[11]My father forced you to work hard. But I will make you work even harder. My father beat you with whips. But I will beat you with whips that have sharp points.'"

[12]King Rehoboam had told the people, "Come back to me in three days." So three days later Jeroboam and all the people returned to Rehoboam. [13]Then King Rehoboam spoke to them in a cruel way. He did not take the advice of the elders. [14]He followed the advice of the young men. He said, "My father forced you to work hard. But I will give you even more work. My father beat you with whips. But I will beat you with whips that have sharp points." [15]So King Rehoboam did not do what the people wanted. God caused this to happen. He did this so the Lord could keep his promise to Jeroboam son of Nebat. The Lord had made this promise through Ahijah, a prophet[d] from Shiloh.

[16]The people of Israel saw that King Rehoboam did not listen to them. So they said to the king,

"We have no share in David.
We have no part in the son of Jesse.
People of Israel, let's go to our own
    homes!
Let David's son rule his own
    people."

So all the Israelites went home. [17]But Rehoboam still ruled over the Israelites who lived in the towns of Judah.

[18]Adoniram was in charge of the people who were forced to work. Rehoboam sent him to the people. But they threw stones at Adoniram until he died. But King Rehoboam was able to run to his chariot and escape to Jerusalem. [19]Since then, Israel has always turned against the family of David.

11 When Rehoboam came to Jerusalem, he gathered 180,000 of the best soldiers. They were from the people of Judah and Benjamin. He gathered them to fight Israel. He wanted to bring the kingdom back under his control. [2]But the Lord spoke his word to Shemaiah, the man of God. The Lord said, [3]"Shemaiah, talk to Solomon's son Rehoboam, the king of Judah. Talk also to all the Israelites living in Judah and Benjamin. Say to them, [4]'The Lord says you must not go to war against your brothers. Every one of you should go home. I made all these things happen.'" So King Rehoboam and his army obeyed the Lord's command. They turned back and did not attack Jeroboam.

REHOBOAM MAKES JUDAH STRONG

[5]Rehoboam lived in Jerusalem. He built strong cities in Judah to defend it against attacks. [6]He built up the cities of Bethlehem, Etam, Tekoa, [7]Beth Zur, Soco, Adullam, [8]Gath, Mareshah, Ziph, [9]Adoraim, Lachish, Azekah, [10]Zorah, Aijalon and Hebron. These were strong, walled cities in Judah and Benjamin. [11]When Rehoboam made those cities strong, he put commanders in them. He also put supplies of food, oil and wine in them. [12]Also, Rehoboam put shields and spears in all the cities. So he made them very strong. Rehoboam kept the peoples and cities of Judah and Benjamin under his control.

[13]The priests and the Levites from all over Israel joined Rehoboam. [14]The Levites even left their pasturelands and fields and came to Judah and Jerusalem. They did this because Jeroboam and his sons refused to let them serve as priests to the Lord. [15]Jeroboam chose his own priests to serve in the places of worship. He chose his own priests for the goat and calf idols he had made. [16]There were people from all the tribes[d] of Israel who wanted to obey the Lord, the God of Israel. They went to Jerusalem with the Levites. They went to sacrifice to the Lord, the God of their ancestors. [17]These people made the kingdom of Judah strong. And they supported Solomon's son Rehoboam for three years. During this time they lived the way David and Solomon had lived.

REHOBOAM'S FAMILY

[18]Rehoboam married Mahalath. She was the daughter of Jerimoth and Abihail. Jerimoth was David's son. Abihail was Eliab's daughter, and Eliab was Jesse's son. [19]Mahalath gave Rehoboam these sons: Jeush, Shemariah and Zaham. [20]Then Rehoboam married Absalom's daughter Maacah. And she gave Rehoboam these children: Abijah, Attai, Ziza and Shelomith. [21]Rehoboam loved Maacah more than his other wives and slave women.[d] Rehoboam had 18 wives and 60 slave women. He was the father of 28 sons and 60 daughters.

[22]Rehoboam chose Abijah to be the leader of his own brothers. He did this because he planned to make Abijah king. [23]Rehoboam acted wisely. He spread his sons through all the areas of Judah and Benjamin. He sent them to every strong, walled city. And he gave plenty of supplies to his sons. He also found wives for them.

SHISHAK ATTACKS JERUSALEM

12 Rehoboam became a strong king. He also made his kingdom strong. Then he and the people of Judah stopped obeying the teachings of the Lord. [2]Shishak was the king of Egypt. He attacked Jerusalem in the fifth year Rehoboam was king. This happened because Rehoboam and the people were unfaithful to the Lord. [3]Shishak had 1,200 chariots and 60,000 horsemen. He brought troops of Libyans, Sukkites and Cushites from Egypt with him. There were so many they couldn't be counted. [4]Shishak captured the strong, walled cities of Judah. And he came as far as Jerusalem.

[5]Then Shemaiah the prophet[d] came to Rehoboam and the leaders of Judah. They had gathered in Jerusalem because they were afraid of Shishak. Shemaiah said to them, "This is what the Lord says: 'You have left me. So now I will leave you to face Shishak alone.'"

[6]Then the leaders of Judah and King Rehoboam were sorry for what they had done. They said, "The Lord does what is right."

[7]The Lord saw that they were sorry for what they had done. So the Lord spoke his word to Shemaiah. The Lord said, "The king and the leaders are sorry. So I will not destroy them but will save them soon. I will not use Shishak to punish Jerusalem in my anger. [8]But the people of Jerusalem will become Shishak's servants. Then they may learn that serving me is different than serving the kings of other nations."

[9]Shishak king of Egypt attacked Jerusalem. He took the treasures from the Temple[d] of the Lord and from the king's palace. He took everything, even the gold shields Solomon had made. [10]So King Rehoboam made bronze shields to take their place. He gave them to the commanders of the guards for the entrance to the king's palace. [11]Whenever the king entered the Temple of the Lord, the guards went with him. They would carry the shields. Later, they would put them back in the guard room.

[12]When Rehoboam was sorry for what he had done, the Lord held his anger back. So the Lord did not fully destroy Rehoboam. There was some good in Judah.

[13]King Rehoboam made himself a strong king in Jerusalem. He was 41 years old when he became king. And he was king in Jerusalem for 17 years. Jerusalem is the city that the Lord chose from all the tribes[d] of Israel. He chose to be worshiped in Jerusalem. Rehoboam's mother was Naamah from the country of Ammon. [14]Rehoboam did evil things because he did not want to ask the Lord for help.

[15]The things Rehoboam did as king, from the beginning to the end, are written down. They are in the records of Shemaiah the prophet. And they are in

the records of Iddo the seer.*d* These men wrote family histories. There were wars between Rehoboam and Jeroboam all the time they ruled. ¹⁶Rehoboam died and was buried in Jerusalem. Then Rehoboam's son Abijah became king.

ABIJAH KING OF JUDAH

13 Abijah became the king of Judah. This was during the eighteenth year Jeroboam was king of Israel. ²Abijah was king in Jerusalem for three years. Abijah's mother was Maacah daughter of Uriel. Uriel was from the town of Gibeah.

And there was war between Abijah and Jeroboam. ³Abijah led an army of 400,000 capable soldiers into battle. And Jeroboam prepared to fight him with 800,000 capable soldiers.

⁴Abijah stood on Mount Zemaraim in the mountains of Ephraim. He said, "Jeroboam and all Israel, listen to me! ⁵You should know this: The Lord, the God of Israel, gave David and his sons the right to be king over Israel forever. God gave this right to David with an agreement which will last forever. ⁶But Jeroboam turned against his master. Jeroboam was the son of Nebat, one of Solomon's officers. Solomon was David's son. ⁷Then worthless, evil men became friends with Jeroboam. They were against Rehoboam, Solomon's son. Rehoboam was young and didn't know what to do. So he could not stop them.

⁸"Now you people are making plans against the Lord's kingdom. The Lord's kingdom belongs to David's sons! There are many of you. And you have the gold calves Jeroboam made for you as gods. ⁹You have thrown out the Lord's priests and the Levites. The priests are Aaron's sons. You have chosen your own priests as people in other countries do. Anyone who comes to make himself ready to serve the Lord with a young bull and seven male sheep can become a priest. He may become a priest of idols that are not gods.

¹⁰"But as for us, the Lord is our God. We have not left him. The priests who serve the Lord are Aaron's sons. And the Levites help the priests serve the Lord. ¹¹They offer burnt offerings and sweet-smelling incense*d* to the Lord every morning and evening. They also put the bread on the special table in the Temple.*d* And they light the lamps on the gold lampstand every evening. We obey the command of the Lord our God. But you have left the Lord. ¹²God himself is with us. He is our ruler, and his priests are with us. The priests blow the trumpet to call us to war against you. Men of Israel, don't fight against the Lord because you won't succeed. He is the God of your ancestors."

¹³But Jeroboam had sent some troops to sneak behind Abijah's army. So while Jeroboam was in front of Abijah's army, Jeroboam's soldiers were behind them. ¹⁴The soldiers in Abijah's army looked around. Then they saw Jeroboam's army attacking both in front and back. They cried out to the Lord. And the priests blew the trumpets. ¹⁵Then the men of Judah gave a battle cry. When they shouted, God defeated Jeroboam and the army of Israel. They ran away from Abijah and the army of Judah. ¹⁶The men of Israel ran away from the men of Judah. God let the army from Judah defeat them. ¹⁷Abijah's army killed many of Israel's men. Of Israel's best men 500,000 were killed. ¹⁸So at that time the people of Israel were defeated. And the people of Judah won. They won because they depended on the Lord, the God of their ancestors.

¹⁹Abijah's army chased Jeroboam's army. Abijah's army captured from Jeroboam the towns of Bethel, Jeshanah and Ephron. They also captured the small villages near these towns. ²⁰Jeroboam never became strong again while Abijah was alive. The Lord struck Jeroboam, and he died.

²¹But Abijah became strong. He married 14 women. And he was the father of 22 sons and 16 daughters. ²²All the other things Abijah did as king are written down. What he said and did are recorded in what the prophet Iddo has written.

14 Abijah died and was buried in Jerusalem. Then Abijah's son Asa became king in his place. There was peace in the country for 10 years in Asa's time.

ASA KING OF JUDAH

²Asa did what the Lord said was good and right. ³He removed the foreign altars used for idol worship. He removed the places where false gods were worshiped. He smashed the stone pillars that honored false gods. And he tore down the Asherah*ᵈ* idols. ⁴Asa commanded the people of Judah to obey the Lord, the God their ancestors followed. Asa commanded them to obey the Lord's teachings and commandments. ⁵He also removed the places where false gods were worshiped and the incense altars from every town in Judah. So the kingdom had peace while Asa was king. ⁶Asa built strong, walled cities in Judah during the time of peace. He had no war in these years because the Lord gave him peace.

⁷Asa said to the people of Judah, "Let's build up these towns and put walls around them. Let's make towers, gates and bars in the gates. This country is ours because we have obeyed the Lord our God. We have tried to obey him, and he has given us peace all around." So they built and had success.

⁸Asa had an army of 300,000 men from the people of Judah. And he had 280,000 men from the people of Benjamin. The men from Judah carried large shields and spears. The men from Benjamin carried small shields and bows and arrows. All these men were brave fighting men.

⁹Then Zerah from Cush came out to fight Asa's army. Zerah had a large army and 300 chariots. They came as far as the town of Mareshah. ¹⁰Asa went out to fight Zerah. Asa's army prepared for battle in the Valley of Zephathah at Mareshah.

¹¹Asa called out to the Lord his God. He said, "Lord, only you can help weak people against the strong. Help us, Lord our God. We depend on you. We fight against this large army in your name. Lord, you are our God. Don't let anyone win against you."

¹²Then the Lord defeated the Cushites when Asa's army from Judah attacked them. And the Cushites ran away. ¹³Asa's army chased them as far as the town of Gerar. So many Cushites were killed that the army could not fight again. They were crushed by the Lord and his army. Asa and his army carried many valuable things away from the enemy. ¹⁴They destroyed all the towns near Gerar. The people living in these towns were afraid of the Lord. These towns had many valuable things. So Asa's army took these things away. ¹⁵Asa's army also attacked the camps where the shepherds lived. And they took many sheep and camels. Then they went back to Jerusalem.

ASA'S CHANGES

15 The Spirit*ᵈ* of God entered Azariah son of Oded. ²Azariah went to meet Asa. Azariah said, "Listen to me, Asa and all you people of Judah and Benjamin. The Lord is with you when you are with him. If you obey the Lord, you will find him. But if you leave him, he will leave you. ³For a long time Israel was without the true God. And they were without a priest to teach them and without the teachings. ⁴But when they were in trouble, they turned to the Lord again. He is the God of Israel. They looked for the Lord and found him. ⁵In those days no one could travel safely. There was much trouble in all the nations. ⁶One nation would destroy another nation. And one city would destroy another city. This happened because God troubled them with all kinds of trouble. [7]But you should be strong. Don't give up, because you will get a reward for your good work."

[8]Asa felt brave when he heard these words and the message from Azariah. Azariah was the son of Oded the prophet.[d] So he removed the hated idols from all of Judah and Benjamin. And he removed them from the towns he had captured in the hills of Ephraim. He repaired the Lord's altar that was in front of the porch of the Temple[d] of the Lord.

[9]Then Asa gathered all the people from Judah and Benjamin. He also gathered the people of the tribes[d] of Ephraim, Manasseh and Simeon who were living in Judah. Many people came to Asa from Israel. They came because they saw that the Lord, Asa's God, was with him.

[10]Asa and these people gathered in Jerusalem. This was in the third month of the fifteenth year of Asa's rule. [11]At that time they sacrificed to the Lord 700 bulls and 7,000 sheep and goats. Asa's army had taken these animals and other valuable things from their enemies. [12]Then they made an agreement. They promised to obey the Lord with their whole being. He is the God their ancestors served. [13]Anyone who refused to obey the Lord, the God of Israel, was to be killed. It did not matter if that person was important or unimportant. It did not matter if that person was a man or woman. [14]Then Asa and the people made a promise before the Lord. They shouted with a loud voice. They also blew on trumpets and sheep's horns. [15]All the people of Judah were happy about the promise. They had promised with all their heart. They looked for God and found him. So the Lord gave them peace in all the country.

[16]King Asa also removed Maacah, his mother, from being queen mother. He did this because she had made an Asherah[d] idol, which the Lord hated. Asa cut down that idol and smashed it into pieces. Then he burned it in the Kidron Valley. [17]The places of worship to false gods were not removed from Judah. Asa desired very much to obey the Lord all his life.

[18]And Asa put the holy gifts that he and his father had given into the Temple of God. These things were made of silver and gold.

[19]There was no more war until the thirty-fifth year of Asa's rule.

ASA'S LAST YEARS

16 In the thirty-sixth year of Asa's rule, Baasha king of Israel attacked Judah. He went to the town of Ramah and made it strong. He used it to keep people from going in or out of the country of Judah.

[2]Asa took silver and gold out of the treasuries of the Temple[d] of the Lord. And he took silver and gold out of his own palace. Then he sent it with messengers to Ben-Hadad king of Aram. Ben-Hadad was living in Damascus. Asa's message said: [3]"Let's make an agreement between you and me. Let's make it like the agreement between your father and mine. See, I am sending you silver and gold. Now break your agreement with Baasha king of Israel. Then he will take his army away from my country."

[4]Ben-Hadad agreed with King Asa. So Ben-Hadad sent the commanders of his armies to attack the towns of Israel. These commanders defeated the towns of Ijon, Dan and Abel Beth Maacah. They also defeated all the towns in Naphtali where treasures were stored. [5]When Baasha heard about this, he stopped building Ramah. He left his work. [6]Then King Asa called all the men of Judah together. They went to Ramah and took away the rocks and wood that Baasha had used. And they used the rocks and wood to build up Geba and Mizpah.

[7]At that time Hanani the seer[d] came to Asa king of Judah. Hanani said to him, "You depended on the king of Aram to help you. You did not depend on the Lord your God. So the king of Aram's army escaped from you. [8]The Cushites and Libyans had a large and powerful army. They had many chariots and horsemen. But you depended on the Lord to help you. So he let you defeat them. [9]The Lord searches all the earth for people who have given themselves completely to him. He wants to make them strong. Asa, you did a foolish thing. From now on you will have wars."

[10]Asa was angry with Hanani the seer because of what he had said. Asa was so angry that he put Hanani in prison. Asa was cruel with some of the people at that same time.

[11]The things Asa did as king, from the beginning to the end, are written down. They are in the book of the kings of Judah and Israel. [12]In the thirty-ninth year of his rule, Asa got a disease in his feet. His disease was very bad. But he did not ask for help from the Lord. He only asked for help from the doctors. [13]Then Asa died in the forty-first year of his rule. [14]The people buried Asa in the tomb he had made for himself in Jerusalem. They laid him on a bed. It was filled with spices and different kinds of mixed perfumes. And they made a large fire to honor Asa.

JEHOSHAPHAT KING OF JUDAH

17 Jehoshaphat, Asa's son, became king of Judah in Asa's place. Jehoshaphat made Judah strong so they could fight against Israel. [2]He put troops in all the strong, walled cities of Judah. And he put troops in Judah and in the towns of Ephraim his father Asa had captured.

[3]The Lord was with Jehoshaphat because he did good things. He lived as his father Asa did when he first became king. Jehoshaphat did not ask for help from the Baal[d] idols. [4]He asked for help from the God his father had followed. He obeyed God's commands. He did not live as the people of Israel lived. [5]The Lord made Jehoshaphat a strong king over Judah. All the people of Judah brought gifts to Jehoshaphat. So he had much wealth and honor. [6]He wanted very much to obey the Lord. He also removed the places for worshiping false gods and the Asherah[d] idols from Judah.

[7]Jehoshaphat sent his officers to teach in the towns of Judah. This happened in the third year of his rule. These officers were Ben-Hail, Obadiah, Zechariah, Nethanel and Micaiah. [8]Jehoshaphat sent with them these Levites: Shemaiah, Nethaniah, Zebadiah, Asahel, Shemiramoth, Jehonathan, Adonijah, Tobijah and Tob-Adonijah. He also sent the priests Elishama and Jehoram. [9]These leaders, Levites and priests taught the people in Judah. They took the Book of the Teachings of the Lord with them. And they went through all the towns of Judah and taught the people.

[10]The nations near Judah were afraid of the Lord. So they did not start a war against Jehoshaphat. [11]Some of the Philistines brought gifts and silver to Jehoshaphat as forced payments. Some Arabs brought him flocks. They brought him 7,700 male sheep and 7,700 goats.

[12]Jehoshaphat became more and more powerful. He built strong, walled cities and storage towns in Judah. [13]He kept many supplies in the towns of Judah. And he kept trained soldiers in Jerusalem. [14]These soldiers were listed by families.

From the families of Judah, these were the commanders of groups of 1,000 men: Adnah was the commander of 300,000 soldiers. [15]Jehohanan was the commander of 280,000 soldiers. [16]And Amasiah was the commander of 200,000 soldiers. Amasiah son of Zicri had volunteered to serve the Lord.

[17]These were the commanders from the families of Benjamin: Eliada had 200,000 soldiers who used bows and shields. Eliada was a brave soldier. [18]And Jehozabad had 180,000 men armed for war.

[19]All these soldiers served King Jehoshaphat. The king also put other men in the strong, walled cities through all of Judah.

MICAIAH WARNS KING AHAB

18 Jehoshaphat had much wealth and honor. He made an agreement with King Ahab through marriage.[n] [2]A few years later Jehoshaphat visited Ahab in Samaria. Ahab sacrificed many sheep and cattle as a great feast to honor Jehoshaphat and the people with him. He encouraged Jehoshaphat to attack Ramoth in Gilead. [3]Ahab king of Israel asked Jehoshaphat king of Judah, "Will you go with me to attack Ramoth in Gilead?"

Jehoshaphat answered, "I will be with you. And my soldiers will be like your own soldiers. We will join you in the battle." [4]Jehoshaphat also said to Ahab, "But first we should ask the Lord to guide us."

[5]So King Ahab called a meeting of the prophets.[d] There were 400 men. Ahab asked them, "Should we go to war against Ramoth in Gilead or not?"

They answered, "Go, because God will let you defeat it."

[6]But Jehoshaphat asked, "Is there a prophet of the Lord here? If there is, let's ask him what we should do."

[7]Then King Ahab said to Jehoshaphat, "There is one other prophet. We could ask the Lord through him. But I hate him. When he prophesies, he never says anything good about me. He always says something bad. He is Micaiah, Imlah's son."

Jehoshaphat said, "King Ahab, you shouldn't say that."

[8]So King Ahab told one of his officers to bring Micaiah to him at once.

[9]King Ahab of Israel and King Jehoshaphat of Judah had on their royal robes. They were sitting on their thrones at the threshing[d] floor. This was near the entrance to the gate of Samaria. All the prophets were speaking messages in front of the two kings. [10]One of the prophets was Zedekiah son of Kenaanah. He had made some iron horns. He said to Ahab, "This is what the Lord says: 'You will use these horns to fight the Arameans. And you will destroy them.'"

[11]All the other prophets said the same thing. They said, "Attack Ramoth in Gilead and win. The Lord will let you defeat the Arameans."

[12]The messenger who had gone to get Micaiah found him. He said to Micaiah, "All the other prophets are saying the same thing. They are saying that King Ahab will win against the Arameans. You had better agree with them. Give the king a good answer."

[13]But Micaiah said, "As surely as the Lord lives, I can tell him only what my God says."

[14]Then Micaiah came to King Ahab. The king asked him, "Micaiah, should we attack Ramoth in Gilead or not?"

Micaiah answered, "Attack and win. You will defeat it."

[15]King Ahab said to Micaiah, "Tell me only the truth by the power of the Lord. How many times do I have to tell you this?"

[16]Then Micaiah answered, "I saw the army of Israel. They were scattered over the hills like sheep without a shepherd. The Lord said, 'They have no leaders. Let each one go home and not fight.'"

[17]Then King Ahab of Israel said to Jehoshaphat, "I told you! This prophet never says anything good about me. He only says bad things about me."

18:1 agreement ... through marriage Jehoshaphat's son Jehoram married Athaliah, Ahab's daughter. See 2 Chronicles 21:6.

[18]But Micaiah continued to speak. He said, "Hear the message from the Lord: I saw the Lord sitting on his throne. His heavenly army was standing on his right and on his left. [19]The Lord said, 'Who will trick King Ahab of Israel into attacking Ramoth in Gilead? Do this so he will go and be killed.' The spirits did not agree about what they should do. [20]Then a spirit came and stood before the Lord. He said, 'I will trick him.' The Lord asked, 'How will you do it?' [21]The spirit answered, 'I will go to Ahab's prophets. I will make them tell lies.' So the Lord said, 'You will succeed in tricking him. Go and do it.'"

[22]Micaiah said, "Ahab, this has now happened. The Lord has caused your prophets to lie to you. The Lord has decided that great trouble should come to you."

[23]Then Zedekiah son of Kenaanah went up to Micaiah. And he slapped Micaiah in the face. Zedekiah said, "Do you really believe that the Lord's Spirit[d] has left me and is now speaking through you?"

[24]Micaiah answered, "You will find out on the day you go to hide in an inside room."

[25]Then King Ahab ordered, "Take Micaiah. Send him to Amon, the governor of the city, and to Joash, the king's son. [26]Tell them I said to put Micaiah in prison. Give him only bread and water. Keep him there until I come back safely from the battle."

[27]Micaiah said, "Ahab, if you come back safely from the battle, the Lord has not spoken through me. Remember my words, all you people!"

AHAB IS KILLED

[28]So Ahab king of Israel and Jehoshaphat king of Judah went to Ramoth in Gilead. [29]King Ahab said to Jehoshaphat, "I will go into battle. But I will wear other clothes so no one will know who I am. But you wear your royal clothes." So King Ahab of Israel wore other clothes and went into battle.

[30]The king of Aram gave an order to his chariot commanders. He said, "Don't fight with anyone but the king of Israel. It doesn't matter if they are important or unimportant." [31]When these commanders saw Jehoshaphat, they thought he was the king of Israel. So they turned to attack him. But Jehoshaphat called out, and the Lord helped him. God made the chariot commanders turn away from Jehoshaphat. [32]When they saw he was not King Ahab, they stopped chasing him.

[33]By chance, a soldier shot an arrow. And it hit Ahab king of Israel. The arrow went in between the pieces of his armor. King Ahab said to his chariot driver, "Turn around and get me out of the battle. I've been wounded." [34]The battle went on all day. King Ahab held himself up in his chariot. He faced the Arameans until evening. Then Ahab died at sunset.

19 Jehoshaphat king of Judah came back safely to his palace in Jerusalem. [2]Jehu son of Hanani went out to meet him. Jehu was a seer.[d] He said to King Jehoshaphat, "Why did you help evil people? Why do you love those who hate the Lord? That is the reason the Lord is angry with you. [3]But there is some good in you. You took the Asherah[d] idols out of this country. And you have wanted to obey God."

JEHOSHAPHAT CHOOSES JUDGES

[4]Jehoshaphat lived in Jerusalem. He went out again to be with the people. He went from Beersheba to the mountains of Ephraim. He brought these people back to the Lord, the God their ancestors followed. [5]Jehoshaphat appointed judges in all the land. He appointed judges for each of the strong, walled cities of Judah. [6]Jehoshaphat said to them, "Be careful in what you do. This is because you are not judging for people but for the Lord. He will be with you when you make a

decision. [7]Now let each of you fear the Lord. Be careful in what you do because the Lord our God wants people to be fair. He wants all people to be treated the same. And he doesn't want people to accept money to change their judgments."

[8]And in Jerusalem Jehoshaphat appointed some of the Levites, priests and leaders of Israelite families to be judges. They were to decide cases about the law of the Lord. And they were to settle problems between the people who lived in Jerusalem. [9]Jehoshaphat gave them commands. He said, "You must always serve the Lord completely. You must fear him. [10]You will have cases about killing, about the teachings, commands, rules or some other law. These cases will come from your people living in the cities. In all these cases you must warn the people not to sin against the Lord. If you don't, the Lord will be angry with you and your people. But if you warn them, you won't be guilty.

[11]"Amariah is the leading priest. He will be over you in all cases about the Lord. Zebadiah son of Ishmael is a leader in the tribe[d] of Judah. He will be over you in all cases about the king. Also, the Levites will serve as officers for you. Have courage. May the Lord be with those who do what is right."

JEHOSHAPHAT FACES WAR

20 Later some people came to start a war with Jehoshaphat. They were the Moabites, Ammonites and some Meunites. [2]Some men came and told Jehoshaphat, "A large army is coming against you from Edom. They are coming from the other side of the Dead Sea.[d] They are already in Hazazon Tamar!" (Hazazon Tamar is also called En Gedi.) [3]Jehoshaphat was afraid. So he decided to ask the Lord what to do. He announced that no one in Judah should eat during this special time of prayer to God. [4]The people of Judah came together

to ask the Lord for help. They came from every town in Judah to ask for his help.

[5]The people of Judah and Jerusalem met in front of the new courtyard in the Temple[d] of the Lord. Then Jehoshaphat stood up before them. [6]He said, "Lord, you are the God of our ancestors. You are the God in heaven. You rule over all the kingdoms of the nations. You have power and strength. No one can stand against you. [7]Our God, you forced out the people who lived in this land. You forced them out as your people Israel moved in. And you gave this land forever to the descendants[d] of your friend Abraham. [8]They lived in this land and built a Temple for worshiping you. They said, [9]"Trouble may come to us. It may be war, punishment, sickness or a time of hunger. If it comes, we will stand before you and before this Temple where you have chosen to be worshiped. We will cry out to you when we are in trouble. Then you will hear and save us.'

[10]"But now here are men from Ammon, Moab and Edom. You wouldn't let the Israelites enter their lands when the Israelites came from Egypt. So the Israelites turned away and did not destroy them. [11]But see how they repay us for not destroying them! They have come to force us out of your land. And you gave us this land as our own. [12]Our God, punish those people. We have no power against this large army that is attacking us. We don't know what to do. So we look to you for help."

[13]All the men of Judah stood before the Lord. Their babies, wives and children were with them. [14]Then the Spirit[d] of the Lord entered Jahaziel. (Jahaziel was Zechariah's son. Zechariah was Benaiah's son. Benaiah was Jeiel's son, and Jeiel was Mattaniah's son.) Jahaziel was a Levite and a descendant of Asaph. He stood up in the meeting. [15]And he said: "Listen to me, King Jehoshaphat! Listen, all you people living in Judah and

Jerusalem! The Lord says this to you: 'Don't be afraid or discouraged because of this large army. The battle is not your battle. It is God's battle. [16]Tomorrow go down there and fight those people. They will come up through the Pass of Ziz. You will find them at the end of the ravine that leads to the Desert of Jeruel. [17]You won't need to fight in this battle. Just stand strong in your places. You will see the Lord save you. Judah and Jerusalem, don't be afraid. Don't be discouraged. The Lord is with you. So go out against those people tomorrow!'"

[18]Jehoshaphat bowed facedown on the ground. All the people of Judah and Jerusalem bowed down before the Lord. And they worshiped him. [19]Then some Levites from the Kohathite and Korahite people stood up and praised the Lord. They praised the God of Israel with very loud voices.

[20]Jehoshaphat's army went out into the Desert of Tekoa early in the morning. As they were starting out, Jehoshaphat stood and said, "Listen to me, people of Judah and Jerusalem! Have faith in the Lord your God. Then you will stand strong. Have faith in the Lord's prophets.[d] Then you will succeed." [21]Jehoshaphat listened to the people's advice. Then he chose men to be singers to the Lord. They were to praise the Lord because he is holy and wonderful. They marched in front of the army. They said,

"Thank the Lord.
    His love continues forever."

[22]As they began to sing and praise God, the Lord set ambushes. He set them for the people of Ammon, Moab and Edom. They were the ones who came to attack Judah. And they were defeated. [23]The men of Ammon and Moab started to attack the men from Edom. They killed and destroyed them. After they had killed the men from Edom, they killed each other.

[24]The men from Judah came to a place where they could see the desert. They looked at the enemy's large army. But they only saw dead bodies lying on the ground. No one had escaped. [25]Jehoshaphat and his army came to take valuable things from the dead bodies. They found many supplies, much clothing, and other valuable things. There was more than they could carry away. There was so much it took three days to gather it all. [26]On the fourth day Jehoshaphat and his army met in the Valley of Beracah. There they praised the Lord. That is why that place has been called the Valley of Beracah[n] to this day.

[27]Then Jehoshaphat led all the men from Judah and Jerusalem back to Jerusalem. The Lord had made them happy because their enemies were defeated. [28]They entered Jerusalem with lyres,[d] harps and trumpets and went to the Temple of the Lord.

[29]All the kingdoms of the lands around them heard how the Lord had fought Israel's enemies. So they feared the Lord. [30]So Jehoshaphat's kingdom was not at war. His God gave him peace from all the countries around him.

JEHOSHAPHAT'S RULE ENDS

[31]Jehoshaphat ruled over the country of Judah. He was 35 years old when he began to rule. And he ruled 25 years in Jerusalem. His mother's name was Azubah daughter of Shilhi. [32]Jehoshaphat lived as his father Asa had lived. He followed what Asa had done. He did what the Lord said was right. [33]But the places where false gods were worshiped were not removed. And the people did not strongly desire to follow the God their ancestors had followed.

[34]The other things Jehoshaphat did as king, from the beginning to the end, are written down. They are in the writings of Jehu son of Hanani. These writings are in the book of the kings of Israel.

20:26 Beracah This name means "blessing" or "praise."

[35]Later, Jehoshaphat king of Judah made an agreement with Ahaziah king of Israel. It was wrong for him to do this. [36]Jehoshaphat agreed with Ahaziah to build trading ships. They built them in the town of Ezion Geber. [37]Then Eliezer son of Dodavahu spoke against Jehoshaphat. Eliezer was from the town of Mareshah. He said, "Jehoshaphat, because you joined with Ahaziah, the Lord will destroy what you have made." The ships were wrecked. So Jehoshaphat and Ahaziah could not send them out to trade.

21

Then Jehoshaphat died and was buried with his ancestors in Jerusalem. Jehoshaphat's son Jehoram became king in his place. [2]Jehoram's brothers were Azariah, Jehiel, Zechariah, Azariahu, Michael and Shephatiah. They were the sons of Jehoshaphat king of Judah. [3]Jehoshaphat gave his sons many gifts of silver, gold and valuable things. He also gave them strong, walled cities in Judah. But Jehoshaphat gave the kingdom to Jehoram because he was the first son.

JEHORAM KING OF JUDAH

[4]Jehoram took control of his father's kingdom. Then he killed all his brothers with a sword. He also killed some of the leaders of Israel. [5]He was 32 years old when he began to rule. And he ruled eight years in Jerusalem. [6]He lived as the kings of Israel had lived. He lived as Ahab's family had lived. This was because he married Ahab's daughter. Jehoram did what the Lord said was wrong. [7]But the Lord would not destroy David's family. This was because of the agreement he had made with David. The Lord had promised that one of David's descendants[d] would always rule.

[8]While Jehoram was king, Edom turned against Judah's rule. The people of Edom chose their own king. [9]So Jehoram went to Edom with all his commanders and chariots. The Edomite army surrounded Jehoram and his chariot commanders. But Jehoram fought his way out at night. [10]From then until now the country of Edom has fought against Judah.

At the same time the people of Libnah also turned against Jehoram. This happened because Jehoram left the Lord, the God his ancestors followed. [11]Jehoram also had built places to worship false gods on the hills in Judah. He had led the people of Jerusalem into sinning. And he had led the people of Judah away from the Lord. [12]Jehoram received a letter from Elijah the prophet. The letter said:

This is what the Lord says. He is the God your father David followed. The Lord says, "Jehoram, you have not lived as your father Jehoshaphat lived. You have not lived as Asa king of Judah lived. [13]But you have lived as the kings of Israel lived. You have led the people of Judah and Jerusalem into sinning against God. That is what Ahab and his family did. You have killed your brothers. And they were better than you. [14]So now the Lord is about to punish your people terribly. He will punish your children, wives and everything you own. [15]You will have a terrible disease in your intestines. It will become worse every day. Finally it will cause your intestines to come out."

[16]The Lord caused the Philistines and the Arabs to be angry with Jehoram. They lived near the Cushites. [17]So the Philistines and Arabs attacked Judah. They took away all the wealth of Jehoram's palace, as well as his sons and wives. Only Jehoram's youngest son, Ahaziah, was left.

[18]After these things happened, the Lord gave Jehoram a disease in his intestines. It could not be cured. [19]After he was sick for two years, Jehoram's intestines fell out because of the disease. He died in terrible pain. The people did not

make a large fire to honor Jehoram as they had done for his ancestors.

²⁰Jehoram was 32 years old when he became king. And he ruled eight years in Jerusalem. No one was sad when he died. He was buried in Jerusalem, but not in the graves for the kings.

AHAZIAH KING OF JUDAH

22 The people of Jerusalem chose Ahaziah to be king in Jehoram's place. Ahaziah was Jehoram's youngest son. The robbers who had come with the Arabs to attack Jehoram's camp had killed all of Jehoram's older sons. So Ahaziah began to rule Judah. ²He was 22 years old when he began to rule. And he ruled one year in Jerusalem. His mother's name was Athaliah, a granddaughter of Omri. ³Ahaziah also lived as Ahab's family had lived. This was because his mother encouraged him to do wrong things. ⁴Ahaziah did what the Lord said was wrong. That is what Ahab's family had done. And they gave advice to Ahaziah after his father died. Their bad advice led to his death. ⁵Ahaziah followed their advice when he went to fight King Hazael of Aram. King Joram of Israel, Ahab's son, went with him. They met Hazael at the town of Ramoth in Gilead. The Arameans wounded Joram in battle. ⁶So Joram returned to the town of Jezreel to get well. He was wounded at Ramoth when he fought Hazael king of Aram.

Then King Ahaziah of Judah, son of Jehoram, went to Jezreel. He went there to visit Joram son of Ahab because he was wounded.

⁷God caused Ahaziah's death when he went to visit Joram. Ahaziah arrived and went out with Joram to meet Jehu son of Nimshi. The Lord had appointed Jehu to destroy Ahab's family. ⁸While Jehu was punishing Ahab's family, he found the leaders of Judah. He also found Ahaziah's relatives who served Ahaziah. Jehu killed them all. ⁹Then Jehu looked for Ahaziah. Jehu's men caught him hiding in Samaria. So they brought him to Jehu. Then they killed and buried him. They said, "Ahaziah is a descendant[d] of Jehoshaphat. And Jehoshaphat obeyed the Lord with all his heart." No one in Ahaziah's family had the power to take control of the kingdom of Judah.

ATHALIAH QUEEN OF JUDAH

¹⁰Now Ahaziah's mother, Athaliah, saw that her son was dead. Then she killed all the royal family in Judah. ¹¹But Jehosheba took Joash, Ahaziah's son. She stole him from among the other sons of the king. Those sons were going to be murdered. She put Joash and his nurse in a bedroom. Jehosheba was King Jehoram's daughter and Ahaziah's sister. She was also the wife of Jehoiada the priest. She hid Joash so Athaliah could not kill him. ¹²Joash was hidden with them in the Temple[d] of God for six years. During that time Athaliah ruled the land.

23 In the seventh year Jehoiada decided to do something. He made an agreement with the commanders of the groups of 100 men. These were the commanders: Azariah son of Jeroham, Ishmael son of Jehohanan, Azariah son of Obed, Maaseiah son of Adaiah, and Elishaphat son of Zicri. ²They went around in Judah and gathered the Levites from all the towns. They also gathered the leaders of the families of Israel. Then they went to Jerusalem. ³All the people together made an agreement with the king in the Temple of God.

Jehoiada said to them, "The king's son will rule. That is what the Lord promised about David's descendants.[d] ⁴Now this is what you must do: You priests and Levites go on duty on the Sabbath.[d] A third of you will guard the doors. ⁵A third of you will be at the king's palace. And a third of you will be at the Foundation Gate. All the other people will stay in the courtyards of the Temple of the Lord.

⁶Don't let anyone come into the Temple of the Lord. Only the priests and Levites who serve may come in. They may come because they have been made ready to serve the Lord. But all the other men must do the job the Lord has given them. ⁷The Levites must stay near the king. Every man must have his sword with him. If anyone tries to enter the Temple, kill him. You must stay with the king everywhere he goes."

⁸The Levites and all the people of Judah obeyed everything Jehoiada the priest had commanded. He did not excuse anyone from the groups of the priests. So each commander took the men who came on duty on the Sabbath with those who went off duty on the Sabbath. ⁹Jehoiada gave the commanders of the groups of 100 men the spears and the large and small shields. They had belonged to King David. They were kept in the Temple of God. ¹⁰Then Jehoiada told the men where to stand. Every man had his weapon in his hand. They stood around the king, near the altar and the Temple. They stood from the south side of the Temple to the north side.

¹¹Jehoiada and his sons brought out the king's son. And they put the crown on him. They gave him a copy of the law. Then they appointed him king and poured olive oil on him. Then they shouted, "Long live the king!"

¹²Athaliah heard the noise of the people running and praising the king. So she went to them at the Temple of the Lord. ¹³She looked and saw the king standing by his pillar at the entrance. The officers and the men who blew trumpets were near him. All the people of the land were happy and blowing trumpets. The singers were playing musical instruments and leading praises. Then Athaliah tore her clothes to show how upset she was. She shouted, "Traitors! Traitors!"

¹⁴Jehoiada the priest sent out the commanders of 100 men who led the army.

He said to them, "Surround her with soldiers and take her out of the Temple area. Kill with a sword anyone who follows her." He had said, "Don't put Athaliah to death in the Temple of the Lord." ¹⁵So they caught her when she came to the entrance of the Horse Gate near the palace. And they put her to death there.

¹⁶Then Jehoiada made an agreement with the people and the king. They agreed that they would be the Lord's special people. ¹⁷All the people went to the temple of Baal[d] and tore it down. They smashed the altars and idols there. And they killed Mattan the priest of Baal in front of the altars.

¹⁸Then Jehoiada chose the priests to be responsible for the Temple of the Lord. These priests were Levites. David had given them duties in the Temple of the Lord. They were to offer the burnt offerings to the Lord as the Teachings of Moses commanded. They offered the sacrifices with much joy and singing as David had commanded. ¹⁹Jehoiada put guards at the gates of the Temple of the Lord. Then anyone who was unclean[d] in any way could not enter the Temple.

²⁰Jehoiada took with him the commanders of 100 men, the important men, the rulers of the people and all the people of the land. They brought the king down from the Temple of the Lord. They went through the Upper Gate into the palace. Then they seated the king on the throne. ²¹All the people of Judah were very happy. And Jerusalem had peace because Athaliah had been put to death with the sword.

JOASH REBUILDS THE TEMPLE

24 Joash was seven years old when he became king. And he ruled 40 years in Jerusalem. His mother's name was Zibiah. She was from Beersheba. ²Joash did what the Lord said was right as long as Jehoiada the priest was alive. ³Jehoiada chose two wives for Joash. And Joash had sons and daughters.

⁴Later, Joash decided to repair the Temple^d of the Lord. ⁵He called the priests and the Levites together. He said to them, "Go to the towns of Judah. Gather the money all the Israelites have to pay every year. Use it to repair the Temple of your God. Do this now." But the Levites did not hurry.

⁶So King Joash called Jehoiada the leading priest. Joash said to him, "Why haven't you made the Levites bring in the tax money from Judah and Jerusalem? Moses the Lord's servant and the people of Israel used that money for the Holy Tent."^d

⁷In the past the sons of wicked Athaliah had broken into the Temple of God. They had used its holy things for worshiping the Baal^d idols.

⁸King Joash commanded that a box for contributions be made. It was to be put outside, at the gate of the Temple of the Lord. ⁹Then the Levites made an announcement in Judah and Jerusalem. They told the people to bring the tax money to the Lord. Moses the servant of God had made the Israelites give it while they were in the desert. ¹⁰All the officers and people were happy to give their money. They put it in the box until the box was full. ¹¹Then the Levites would take the box to the king's officers. They would see that it was full of money. Then the king's royal assistant and the leading priest's officer would come and take out the money. Then they would take the box back to its place. They did this often and gathered much money. ¹²King Joash and Jehoiada gave the money to the people who worked on the Temple of the Lord. And they hired stoneworkers and carpenters to repair the Temple of the Lord. They also hired people to work with iron and bronze to repair the Temple.

¹³The people worked hard. And the work to repair the Temple went well. They rebuilt the Temple of God to be as it was before. And they made it stronger.

¹⁴When the workers finished, they brought the money that was left to King Joash and Jehoiada. They used that money to make things for the Temple of the Lord. They made things for the service in the Temple and for the burnt offerings. They also made bowls and other things from gold and silver. Burnt offerings were given every day in the Temple of the Lord while Jehoiada was alive.

¹⁵Jehoiada grew old. He had lived many years. Then he died when he was 130 years old. ¹⁶Jehoiada was buried in Jerusalem with the kings. He was buried there because he had done much good in Israel for God and his Temple.

JOASH DOES EVIL

¹⁷After Jehoiada died, the officers of Judah came and bowed down to King Joash. The king listened to them. ¹⁸The king and these leaders stopped worshiping in the Temple^d of the Lord. He is the God their ancestors obeyed. The king and the officers began to worship the Asherah^d idols and other idols. Because they did wrong, God was angry with the people of Judah and Jerusalem. ¹⁹The Lord sent prophets^d to the people to turn them back to him. The prophets warned them, but the people refused to listen.

²⁰Then the Spirit^d of God entered Zechariah son of Jehoiada the priest. Zechariah stood before the people and said, "This is what God says: 'Why do you disobey the Lord's commands? You will not be successful. You have left the Lord. So the Lord has also left you.'"

²¹But the king and his officers made plans against Zechariah. The king commanded them to kill Zechariah. So they threw stones at him in the Temple courtyard until he died. ²²King Joash did not remember Jehoiada's kindness to him. So Joash killed Zechariah, Jehoiada's son. Before Zechariah died, he said, "May the Lord see what you are doing and punish you."

²³At the end of the year, the Aramean army came against Joash. They attacked

Judah and Jerusalem and killed all the leaders of the people. Then they sent all the valuable things to their king in Damascus. 24The Aramean army came with only a small group of men. But the Lord let them defeat a very large army from Judah. He did this because the people of Judah had left the Lord. He is the God their ancestors followed. So Joash was punished. 25When the Arameans left, Joash was badly wounded. His own officers made plans against him. They did this because he had killed Zechariah son of Jehoiada the priest. So they killed Joash in his own bed. He died and was buried in Jerusalem. But he was not buried in the graves of the kings.

26The officers who made plans against Joash were Jozabad and Jehozabad. Jozabad was the son of Shimeath, a woman from Ammon. And Jehozabad was the son of Shimrith, a woman from Moab. 27The story of Joash's sons, the great prophecies*d* against him, and how he rebuilt the Temple of God are written down. They are in the book of the kings. Joash's son Amaziah became king in his place.

AMAZIAH KING OF JUDAH

25 Amaziah was 25 years old when he became king. He ruled for 29 years in Jerusalem. His mother's name was Jehoaddin. She was from Jerusalem. 2Amaziah did what the Lord said was right. But he did not really want to obey the Lord. 3Amaziah took strong control of the kingdom. Then he put to death the officers who had murdered his father the king. 4But Amaziah did not put their children to death. He obeyed what was written in the Book of Moses. There the Lord commanded, "Fathers must not be put to death when their children do wrong. And children must not be put to death when their fathers do wrong. Each person must die for his own sins."*n*

5Amaziah gathered the people of Judah together. He grouped all the people of Judah and Benjamin by families. And he put commanders over groups of 1,000 and over groups of 100. He counted the men who were 20 years old and older. In all there were 300,000 soldiers ready to fight. They were skilled with spears and shields. 6Amaziah also hired 100,000 soldiers from Israel. He paid about 7,500 pounds of silver for them. 7But a man of God came to Amaziah and said, "My king, don't let the army of Israel go with you. The Lord is not with Israel. He is not with the people from the tribes*d* of Israel. 8You can make yourself strong for war. But God will defeat you. He has the power to help you or to defeat you."

9Amaziah said to the man of God, "But what about the 7,500 pounds of silver I paid to the Israelite army?"

The man of God answered, "The Lord can give you much more than that!"

10So Amaziah sent the Israelite army back home to Israel. They were very angry with the people of Judah. And they went home angry.

11Then Amaziah became very brave and led his army to the Valley of Salt. It is in the country of Edom. There Amaziah's army killed 10,000 men from Edom. 12The army of Judah also captured 10,000 men. They took those men to the top of a cliff and threw them off. And they were broken to pieces.

13At the same time the Israelite army was robbing some towns in Judah. These were troops that Amaziah had not let fight in the war. They robbed towns from Samaria to Beth Horon. They killed 3,000 people and took many valuable things.

14Amaziah came home after he had defeated the Edomites. He brought back the idols they worshiped. And he started to worship them also. He bowed down to them and offered sacrifices to them.

25:4 "Fathers ... sins." See Deuteronomy 24:16.

[15]The Lord was very angry with Amaziah. The Lord sent a prophet[d] to him. The prophet said, "Why have you asked their gods for help? They could not even save their own people from you!"

[16]As the prophet spoke, Amaziah said to him, "We never gave you the job of advising the king! Stop, or you will be killed."

The prophet stopped speaking. Then he said, "I know that God has decided to destroy you because you have done this. You did not listen to my advice."

[17]Amaziah king of Judah talked with his men who gave him advice. Then he sent a message to Jehoash son of Jehoahaz. (Jehoahaz was the son of Jehu king of Israel.) Amaziah said to Jehoash, "Come, let's meet face to face in battle."

[18]Then Jehoash king of Israel answered Amaziah king of Judah. Jehoash said, "A little thornbush in Lebanon sent a message to a big cedar tree in Lebanon. It said, 'Let your daughter marry my son.' But then a wild animal from Lebanon came by. It walked on and crushed the thornbush. [19]You say to yourself that you have defeated Edom. You are proud, and you brag. But you stay at home! Don't ask for trouble by fighting me. If you do, you and Judah will be defeated."

[20]But Amaziah would not listen. God caused this to happen. He planned to let Jehoash of Israel defeat Judah. This was because Judah asked for help from the gods of Edom. [21]So Jehoash king of Israel went to attack. He and Amaziah king of Judah faced each other in battle at Beth Shemesh in Judah. [22]Israel defeated Judah. Every man of Judah ran away to his home. [23]At Beth Shemesh Jehoash king of Israel captured Amaziah king of Judah. (Amaziah was the son of Joash, who was the son of Ahaziah.) Then Jehoash brought him to Jerusalem. Jehoash broke down the wall of Jerusalem

from the Gate of Ephraim to the Corner Gate. This part of the wall was about 600 feet long. [24]Then he took all the gold and silver and everything in the Temple[d] of God. Obed-Edom had taken care of these things. Jehoash also took the treasures from the king's palace. Then he took some hostages and returned to Samaria. [25]Amaziah son of Joash was king of Judah. He lived 15 years after Jehoash king of Israel died. Jehoash was the son of Jehoahaz. [26]The other things Amaziah did as king, from the beginning to the end, are written down. They are in the book of the kings of Judah and Israel. [27]When Amaziah stopped obeying the Lord, the people in Jerusalem made plans against him. So he ran away to the town of Lachish. But they sent men after him to Lachish and killed him there. [28]They brought his body back on horses. And he was buried with his ancestors in Jerusalem.

UZZIAH KING OF JUDAH

26 Then all the people of Judah chose Uzziah[n] to be king. He became king in place of Amaziah, his father. Uzziah was 16 years old. [2]He rebuilt the town of Elath and made it part of Judah again. He did this after Amaziah died.

[3]Uzziah was 16 years old when he became king. And he ruled 52 years in Jerusalem. His mother's name was Jecoliah, and she was from Jerusalem. [4]He did what the Lord said was right. He obeyed God just as his father Amaziah had done. [5]Uzziah obeyed God while Zechariah was alive. Zechariah taught Uzziah how to respect and obey God. As long as Uzziah obeyed the Lord, God gave him success.

[6]Uzziah fought a war against the Philistine people. He tore down the walls around their towns of Gath, Jabneh and Ashdod. He built new towns near Ashdod

---

26:1 Uzziah Also called Azariah in 2 Kings.

and in other places among the Philistines. [7]God helped Uzziah fight the Philistines, the Arabs living in Gur Baal and the Meunites. [8]The Ammonites made payments Uzziah demanded. Uzziah was very powerful. So his name became famous all the way to the border of Egypt.

[9]Uzziah built towers in Jerusalem and made them strong. He built them at the Corner Gate, the Valley Gate and where the wall turned. [10]He also built towers in the desert and dug many wells. He had many cattle on the western mountain slopes and in the plains. He had people who worked his fields and vineyards. They worked in the hills and in the fertile lands. Uzziah loved the land.

[11]He had an army of trained soldiers. They were counted and put in groups by Jeiel the royal assistant and Maaseiah the officer. Hananiah, one of the king's commanders, was their leader. [12]There were 2,600 leaders over the soldiers. [13]They were in charge of an army of 307,500 men. The army fought with great power. And they helped the king against the enemy. [14]Uzziah gave his army shields, spears, helmets, armor, bows and stones for their slings. [15]In Jerusalem Uzziah made devices that were invented by clever men. These devices were put on the towers and corners of the city walls. They were used to shoot arrows and large rocks. So Uzziah became famous in faraway places. He had much help until he became powerful.

[16]But when Uzziah became strong, his pride caused him to be destroyed. He was unfaithful to the Lord his God. He went into the Temple[d] of the Lord to burn incense[d] on the altar for incense. [17]Azariah and 80 other brave priests who served the Lord followed Uzziah into the Temple. [18]They told Uzziah he was wrong. They said to him, "You don't have the right to burn incense to the Lord. Only the priests, Aaron's descendants,[d] should burn the incense. They have been made holy for the Lord to do this special duty. Leave this holy place. You have been unfaithful to God. The Lord God will not honor you for this."

[19]Uzziah was standing beside the altar for incense in the Temple of the Lord. He had in his hand a pan for burning incense. He was very angry with the priests. As he was standing in front of the priests, a harmful skin disease broke out on his forehead. [20]Azariah the leading priest and all the other priests looked at him. They could see the harmful skin disease on his forehead. So they hurried him out of the Temple. Uzziah rushed out, because the Lord had punished him. [21]So King Uzziah had the skin disease until the day he died. He had to live in a separate house. He could not enter the Temple of the Lord. His son Jotham was in charge of the palace. He governed the people of the land.

[22]The other things Uzziah did as king were written down by the prophet Isaiah. Isaiah son of Amoz wrote about Uzziah's rule from beginning to end. [23]Uzziah died and was buried near his ancestors in a graveyard that belonged to the kings. This was because people said, "He had a harmful skin disease." And his son Jotham became king in his place.

JOTHAM KING OF JUDAH

27 Jotham was 25 years old when he became king. He ruled 16 years in Jerusalem. His mother's name was Jerusha daughter of Zadok. [2]Jotham did what the Lord said was right. He obeyed God just as his father Uzziah had done. But Jotham did not enter the Temple[d] of the Lord to burn incense[d] as his father had. But the people continued doing wrong. [3]Jotham rebuilt the Upper Gate of the Temple of the Lord. He did much building on the wall at the place named Ophel. [4]He also built towns in the hill country of Judah. And he built walled cities and towers in the forests.

⁵Jotham also fought the king of the Ammonite people. And Jotham defeated the Ammonites. So each year for three years they gave Jotham about 7,500 pounds of silver. They also gave him about 62,000 bushels of wheat and about 62,000 bushels of barley. ⁶Jotham became powerful because he always obeyed the Lord his God.

⁷The other things Jotham did while he was king and all his wars are written down. They are in the book of the kings of Israel and Judah. ⁸Jotham was 25 years old when he became king. And he ruled 16 years in Jerusalem. ⁹Jotham died and was buried in Jerusalem. And Jotham's son Ahaz became king in his place.

AHAZ KING OF JUDAH

28 Ahaz was 20 years old when he became king. And he ruled 16 years in Jerusalem. He was not like his ancestor David. He did not do what the Lord said was right. ²Ahaz did the same things the kings of Israel had done. He made metal idols to worship Baal.ᵈ ³He burned incenseᵈ in the Valley of Ben Hinnom. He sacrificed his own sons by burning them in the fire. He did the same terrible sins as the other nations had done. And the Lord had forced these nations out of the land ahead of the Israelites. ⁴Ahaz offered sacrifices and burned incense at the places where false gods were worshiped. And he did this on the hills and under every green tree.

⁵So the Lord his God let the king of Aram defeat Ahaz. The Arameans defeated Ahaz and took many people of Judah as prisoners. The Arameans took them to Damascus.

The Lord also let Pekah king of Israel defeat Ahaz. Pekah's army killed many soldiers of Ahaz. ⁶Pekah was the son of Remaliah. Pekah's army killed 120,000 brave soldiers from Judah in one day. Pekah defeated them because they had left the Lord. He is the God their ancestors obeyed. ⁷Zicri was a warrior from Ephraim. He killed King Ahaz's son Maaseiah. He also killed Azrikam, the officer in charge of the palace and Elkanah, second in command to the king. ⁸The Israelite army captured 200,000 of their own relatives. They took women, sons and daughters and many valuable things from Judah. Then they carried them back to Samaria. ⁹But a prophetᵈ of the Lord named Oded was there. He met the Israelite army when it returned to Samaria. He said to them, "The Lord is the God your ancestors obeyed. He let you defeat Judah because he was angry with those people. But God has seen the cruel way you killed them. ¹⁰Now you plan to make the people of Judah and Jerusalem your slaves. But you also have sinned against the Lord your God. ¹¹Now listen to me. Send back your brothers and sisters whom you captured. Do this because the Lord is very angry with you."

¹²Then some of the leaders in Israel met the Israelite soldiers coming home from war. These leaders were Azariah son of Jehohanan, Berekiah son of Meshillemoth, Jehizkiah son of Shallum and Amasa son of Hadlai. ¹³They warned the soldiers, "Don't bring the prisoners from Judah here. If you do, we will be guilty of sin. That will make our sin and guilt even worse. And our guilt is already so much that the Lord is angry with Israel."

¹⁴So the soldiers left the prisoners and valuable things in front of the officers and people there. ¹⁵The leaders who were named took the prisoners. These four men got the clothes that the Israelite army had taken. And they gave them to these people who were naked. They gave the prisoners clothes, sandals, food, drink and medicine. They put the weak prisoners on donkeys. Then they took them back to their families in Jericho, the city of palm trees. Then they returned home to Samaria.

¹⁶⁻¹⁷At that same time the Edomites came again. They attacked Judah and

carried away prisoners. So King Ahaz asked the king of Assyria for help. [18]The Philistines also robbed the towns in the western mountain slopes and in southern Judah. They captured the towns of Beth Shemesh, Aijalon, Gederoth, Soco, Timnah and Gimzo. They also captured the villages around them. Then the Philistines lived in those towns. [19]The Lord brought trouble on Judah because of Ahaz their king. Ahaz had caused the people of Judah to sin. And he had been unfaithful to the Lord. [20]Tiglath-Pileser king of Assyria came to Ahaz. But he gave Ahaz trouble instead of help. [21]Ahaz took some valuable things from the Temple[d] of the Lord. He also took some from the king's palace and from the princes. Ahaz gave them to the king of Assyria, but it did not help.

[22]In Ahaz's troubles he was even more unfaithful to the Lord. [23]He offered sacrifices to the gods the people of Damascus worshiped. These people had defeated him. So he thought, "The gods of the kings of Aram helped them. If I offer sacrifices to them, they will help me also." But this brought ruin to Ahaz and all Israel.

[24]Ahaz gathered the things from the Temple of God and broke them into pieces. Then he closed the doors of the Temple of the Lord. He made altars and put them on every street corner in Jerusalem. [25]In every town in Judah, Ahaz made places for burning sacrifices to worship other gods. He made the Lord, the God his ancestors worshiped, very angry.

[26]The other things Ahaz did as king, from the beginning to the end, are written down. They are in the book of the kings of Judah and Israel. [27]Ahaz died and was buried in the city of Jerusalem. But he was not buried in the graves of the kings of Israel. Ahaz's son Hezekiah became king in his place.

HEZEKIAH PURIFIES THE TEMPLE

29 Hezekiah was 25 years old when he became king. And he ruled 29 years in Jerusalem. His mother's name was Abijah daughter of Zechariah. [2]Hezekiah did what the Lord said was right. He did just as his ancestor David had done.

[3]Hezekiah opened the doors of the Temple[d] of the Lord and repaired them. He did this in the first month of the first year he was king. [4]Hezekiah brought the priests and Levites together in a group. He met with them in the courtyard on the east side of the Temple. [5]Hezekiah said, "Listen to me, Levites! Make yourselves ready for the Lord's service. And make the Temple of the Lord holy. He is the God your ancestors obeyed. Remove from the Temple the things that make it impure. [6]Our ancestors were unfaithful to God. They did what the Lord said was wrong. They left the Lord. They stopped worshiping at the Temple where he lives. They rejected him. [7]They shut the doors of the porch of the Temple. They let the fire go out in the lamps. They stopped burning incense[d] and offering burnt offerings in the holy place to the God of Israel. [8]So the Lord became very angry with the people of Judah and Jerusalem. And he punished them. Other peoples are frightened and shocked by what the Lord did to Judah and Jerusalem. They insult the people of Judah. You know these things are true. [9]That is why our ancestors were killed in battle. That is why our sons, daughters and wives were taken prisoner. [10]So now I, Hezekiah, have decided to make an agreement with the Lord, the God of Israel. Then he will not be angry with us anymore. [11]My sons, don't waste any more time. The Lord chose you to serve him. You should serve him and burn incense to him."

[12]These are the Levites who started to work. From the Kohathite family there were Mahath son of Amasai and Joel son

of Azariah. From the Merarite family there were Kish son of Abdi and Azariah son of Jehallelel. From the Gershonite family there were Joah son of Zimmah and Eden son of Joah. [13]From Elizaphan's family there were Shimri and Jeiel. From Asaph's family there were Zechariah and Mattaniah. [14]From Heman's family there were Jehiel and Shimei. From Jeduthun's family there were Shemaiah and Uzziel.

[15]These Levites gathered their brothers together. Then they made themselves holy for service in the Temple. They obeyed the king's command that had come from the Lord. They went into the Temple of the Lord to purify it. [16]The priests went into the Temple of the Lord to purify it. They took out all the unclean[d] things they found in the Temple of the Lord. And they put them in the Temple courtyard. Then the Levites took these things out to the Kidron Valley. [17]They made the Temple holy for the Lord's service. They began on the first day of the first month. On the eighth day of the month, they came to the porch of the Temple. For eight more days they made the Temple of the Lord holy. They finished on the sixteenth day of the first month.

[18]Then they went to King Hezekiah. They said to him, "We have purified all the Temple of the Lord. We have purified the altar for burnt offerings and its things. We have purified the table for the holy bread and all its things. [19]When Ahaz was king, he was unfaithful to God. He removed some things from the Temple. But we have put them back and made them holy for the Lord. They are now in front of the Lord's altar."

[20]Early the next morning King Hezekiah gathered the leaders of the city. They went up to the Temple of the Lord. [21]They brought seven bulls, seven male sheep, seven male lambs and seven male goats. These animals were an offering to remove the sin of the people and the kingdom of Judah. And this offering made the Temple ready for service to God. King Hezekiah commanded the priests to offer these animals on the Lord's altar. The priests were from the family of Aaron. [22]So the priests killed the bulls. Then they sprinkled the bulls' blood on the altar. They killed the male sheep and sprinkled their blood on the altar. Then they killed the lambs. And they sprinkled the lambs' blood on the altar. [23]Then the priests brought the male goats before the king and the people there. The goats were for the sin offering. The king and the people put their hands on the goats. [24]Then the priests killed the goats. They made a sin offering with the goats' blood on the altar. They did this to remove the sins of the Israelites so they would belong to the Lord. The king had said that the burnt offering and sin offering should be made for all Israel.

[25]King Hezekiah put the Levites in the Temple of the Lord with cymbals, harps and lyres.[d] He did this as David, Gad and Nathan had commanded. (Gad was the king's seer,[d] and Nathan was a prophet.[d]) This command came from the Lord through his prophets. [26]So the Levites stood ready with David's instruments of music. And the priests stood ready with their trumpets.

[27]Then Hezekiah gave the order to sacrifice the burnt offering on the altar. When the burnt offering began, the singing to the Lord also began. The trumpets were blown. And the musical instruments of David king of Israel were played. [28]All the people worshiped, the singers sang, and the trumpet players blew their trumpets. They did this until the burnt offering was finished.

[29]When the sacrifices were finished, King Hezekiah and everyone with him bowed down and worshiped. [30]King Hezekiah and his officers ordered the

Levites to praise the Lord. They were to use the words David and Asaph the seer used. They praised God with joy. And they bowed down and worshiped.

31 Then Hezekiah said, "Now you people of Judah have given yourselves to the Lord. Come near to the Temple of the Lord. Bring sacrifices and offerings to show thanks to the Lord." So the people brought sacrifices and offerings to show thanks to the Lord. Anyone who wanted to also brought burnt offerings. 32 For burnt offerings they brought a total of 70 bulls, 100 male sheep and 200 lambs. All these animals were sacrificed as burnt offerings to the Lord. 33 The offerings made holy for the Lord totaled 600 bulls and 3,000 sheep and goats. 34 There were not enough priests to skin all the animals for the burnt offerings. So their relatives the Levites helped them. They helped until the work was finished and other priests could be made holy for the Lord's service. The Levites had been more careful to make themselves holy for the Lord's service than the priests. 35 There were many burnt offerings. With them were the fat of fellowship offerings and drink offerings. So the service in the Temple of the Lord began again. 36 And Hezekiah and the people were very happy. They were happy that God had made it happen so quickly for his people.

HEZEKIAH CELEBRATES THE PASSOVER

30 King Hezekiah sent messages to all the people of Israel and Judah. He also wrote letters to the people of Ephraim and Manasseh. Hezekiah invited all these people to come to the Temple[d] of the Lord in Jerusalem. There they could celebrate the Passover[d] for the Lord, the God of Israel. 2 King Hezekiah, his officers and all the people in Jerusalem agreed to celebrate the Passover in the second month. 3 They could not celebrate it at the normal time. This was because not enough priests had made themselves ready to serve the Lord. And the people had not gathered yet in Jerusalem. 4 This plan satisfied King Hezekiah and all the people. 5 So they made an announcement everywhere in Israel, from Beersheba to Dan.[n] They told the people to come to Jerusalem. There they would celebrate the Passover for the Lord, the God of Israel. For a long time most of the people had not celebrated the Passover as the law commanded. 6 So the messengers took letters from the king and his officers all through Israel and Judah. This is what the letters said:

People of Israel, come back to obeying the Lord. He is the God that Abraham, Isaac and Israel obeyed. Then God will come back to you who are still alive. You have escaped from the kings of Assyria. 7 Don't be like your ancestors or your relatives. They turned against the Lord, the God their fathers obeyed. So the Lord caused other people to be disgusted with them. You know this is true. 8 Don't be stubborn as your ancestors were. Obey the Lord willingly. Come to the Temple, which the Lord has made holy for his service forever. Serve the Lord your God. Then he will not be angry with you. 9 Come back and obey the Lord. Then the people who captured your relatives and children will be kind to them. They will let them return to this land. The Lord your God is kind and merciful. He will not turn away from you if you come back to him.

10 The messengers went to every town in Ephraim and Manasseh. They went all

---

30:5 Beersheba to Dan Dan was the city farthest north in Israel. Beersheba was the city farthest south. So this means all the people of Israel.

the way to Zebulun. But the people laughed at the messengers and made fun of them. [11]But some men from Asher, Manasseh and Zebulun were sorry for what they had done and went to Jerusalem. [12]And God caused all the people of Judah to agree to obey King Hezekiah and his officers. Their command had come from the Lord.

[13]A large crowd came together in Jerusalem to celebrate the Feast[d] of Unleavened Bread. This was in the second month. [14]The people removed the altars and incense[d] altars to false gods in Jerusalem. And they threw them into the Kidron Valley.

[15]They killed the Passover lamb on the fourteenth day of the second month. The priests and the Levites were ashamed. So they made themselves holy for the Lord. They brought burnt offerings into the Temple of the Lord. [16]They took their regular places in the Temple as the Teachings of Moses the man of God commanded. The Levites gave the blood of the sacrifices to the priests. Then the priests sprinkled the blood on the altar. [17]Many people in the crowd had not made themselves holy for the Lord. So they were not permitted to kill the Passover lambs. So the Levites were responsible for killing the Passover lambs for everyone who was not clean.[d] The Levites made each lamb holy for the Lord. [18-19]Many people from Ephraim, Manasseh, Issachar and Zebulun had not purified themselves for the feast. But they ate the Passover even though it was against the law. So Hezekiah prayed for them. He said, "Lord, you are good. You are the Lord, the God our ancestors obeyed. Please forgive everyone who tries to obey you. Forgive them even if they did not make themselves clean as the rules of the Temple command." [20]The Lord listened to Hezekiah's prayer, and he healed the people. [21]The Israelites in Jerusalem celebrated the Feast of Unleavened Bread for seven days. And they were very happy. The Levites and priests praised the Lord every day with loud music. [22]Some of the Levites understood well how to do their service for the Lord. And Hezekiah encouraged them. The people ate the feast for seven days. And they offered fellowship offerings. They praised the Lord, the God their ancestors worshiped.

[23]Then all the people agreed to stay seven more days. So they celebrated the Passover with joy for seven more days. [24]Hezekiah king of Judah gave 1,000 bulls and 7,000 sheep to the people. The officers gave 1,000 bulls and 10,000 sheep to the people. Many priests made themselves holy for the Lord. [25]All the people of Judah, the priests, the Levites, those who came from Israel, the foreigners from Israel and the foreigners living in Judah were very happy. [26]There was much joy in Jerusalem. There had not been a celebration like this since Solomon's time. He was the son of David and king of Israel. [27]The priests and Levites stood up and blessed the people. And God heard them because their prayer reached heaven, which is his holy home.

THE COLLECTION FOR THE PRIESTS

31 The Passover[d] celebration was finished. All the Israelites in Jerusalem went out to the towns of Judah. There they smashed the stone pillars used to worship false gods. They cut down the Asherah[d] idols. They destroyed the altars and places for worshiping false gods. They destroyed all of them in the areas of Judah, Benjamin, Ephraim and Manasseh. They destroyed everything used for worshiping the false gods. Then all the Israelites returned to their own towns and homes.

[2]King Hezekiah appointed groups of priests and Levites for their special duties. They were to offer burnt offerings and fellowship offerings. They were to worship and to give thanks and praise

at the gates where the Lord lives. [3]Hezekiah gave some of his own animals for the burnt offerings. Burnt offerings were given every morning and evening. They were also given on Sabbath[d] days and during New Moons[d] and other feasts commanded by the Lord's Teachings.

[4]Hezekiah commanded the people living in Jerusalem to give the priests and Levites the portion that belonged to them. Then the priests and Levites could give all their time to the Lord's Teachings. [5]Soon the king's command went out to the Israelites. And they gave quickly and freely. They gave the first portion of their grain, wine, oil and honey. They gave the first portion of everything they grew in their fields. They brought a large amount, one-tenth of everything. [6]The men of Israel and Judah who lived in Judah also gave. They brought one-tenth of their cattle and sheep. And they brought one-tenth of the holy things that were given to the Lord their God. They put all these things in piles. [7]The people began bringing their things in the third month. And they finished in the seventh month. [8]Hezekiah and his officers came and saw the piles. Then they praised the Lord and his people, the people of Israel. [9]Hezekiah asked the priests and Levites about the piles. [10]Azariah was the leading priest from Zadok's family. He answered Hezekiah, "Since the people began to bring their offerings to the Temple[d] of the Lord, we have had plenty to eat. We have had plenty left over. The Lord has blessed his people. So we have all this left over."

[11]Then Hezekiah commanded the priests to prepare the storerooms in the Temple of the Lord. So this was done. [12]Then the priests brought the offerings and the things given to the Lord. They also brought the tenth of everything the people had given. All these things were put in the storerooms. Conaniah the Levite was in charge of these things.

Conaniah's brother Shimei was second to him. [13]Conaniah and his brother Shimei were over these supervisors: Jehiel, Azaziah, Nahath, Asahel, Jerimoth, Jozabad, Eliel, Ismakiah, Mahath and Benaiah. King Hezekiah and Azariah the officer in charge of the Temple of God chose those men.

[14]Kore was in charge of the special gifts the people wanted to give to God. He was responsible for giving out the contributions made to the Lord and the holy gifts. Kore was the son of Imnah the Levite. Kore was the guard at the East Gate. [15]Eden, Miniamin, Jeshua, Shemaiah, Amariah and Shecaniah helped Kore. They served well in the towns where the priests lived. They gave from what was collected to the other groups of priests. They gave both to the young and the old.

[16]These men also gave from what was collected to the males 3 years old and older. These were males who had their names in the Levite family histories. They were to enter the Temple of the Lord for their daily service. Each group had its own responsibilities. [17]The priests were given their part of the collection. This was done by families, as listed in the family histories. The Levites 20 years old and older were given their part of the collection. This was done by their responsibilities and by their groups. [18]The Levites' babies, wives, sons and daughters also got part of the collection. This was done for all the Levites who were listed in the family histories. This was because the Levites always kept themselves ready to serve the Lord.

[19]Some of Aaron's descendants,[d] the priests, lived on the farmland near the towns. Some also lived in the towns. Men were chosen by name to give part of the collection to these priests. All the males and those named in the family histories of the Levites received part of the collection.

²⁰This is what King Hezekiah did in Judah. He did what was good and right and obedient before the Lord his God. ²¹Hezekiah tried to obey God in his service of the Temple of God. He tried to obey God's teachings and commands. He gave himself fully to his work for God. So he had success.

ASSYRIA TROUBLES HEZEKIAH

32 Hezekiah did all these things to serve the Lord. Sennacherib king of Assyria came to attack Judah. He and his army surrounded and attacked the strong, walled cities. He wanted to take them for himself. ²Hezekiah knew that Sennacherib had come to Jerusalem to attack it. ³So Hezekiah talked to his officers and army commanders. They decided to cut off the waters from the springs outside the city. So the officers and commanders helped Hezekiah. ⁴Many people came to help. They cut off all the springs and the stream that flowed through the land. They said, "The king of Assyria will not find much water when he comes here." ⁵Then Hezekiah made Jerusalem stronger. He rebuilt all the broken parts of the wall. And he built towers on the wall. He also built another wall outside the first one. And he made the area that was filled in on the east side of the old part of Jerusalem stronger. He made many weapons and shields.

⁶Hezekiah put army commanders over the people. He met with these commanders at the open place near the city gate. Hezekiah encouraged them, saying, ⁷"Be strong and brave. Don't be afraid or worried because of the king of Assyria or his large army. There is a greater power with us than with him. ⁸He only has men, but we have the Lord our God. He will help us. He will fight our battles." The people were encouraged by the words of Hezekiah king of Judah.

⁹King Sennacherib of Assyria and all his army surrounded and attacked Lachish. Then he sent his officers to Jerusalem with a message. The message was for King Hezekiah of Judah and all the people of Judah in Jerusalem. This was the message:

¹⁰Sennacherib king of Assyria says this: "You have nothing to trust in to help you. It is no use for you to stay in Jerusalem under attack. ¹¹Hezekiah says to you, 'The Lord our God will save us from the king of Assyria.' But he is fooling you. If you stay in Jerusalem, you will die from hunger and thirst. ¹²Hezekiah himself removed your Lord's places of worship and altars. He told you people of Judah and Jerusalem that you must worship and burn incense^d on only one altar.

¹³"You know what my ancestors and I have done to all the people in other nations. The gods of those nations could not save their people from my power. ¹⁴My ancestors destroyed those nations. None of their gods could save them from me. So your god cannot save you from my power. ¹⁵Do not let Hezekiah fool you or trick you. Do not believe him. No god of any nation or kingdom has been able to save his people from me or my ancestors. Your god is even less able to save you from me."

¹⁶Sennacherib's officers said worse things against the Lord God and his servant Hezekiah. ¹⁷King Sennacherib also wrote letters insulting the Lord, the God of Israel. This is what his letters said: "The gods of the other nations could not save their people from me. In the same way Hezekiah's god won't be able to save his people from me." ¹⁸Then the king's officers shouted out in Hebrew. They called out to the people of Jerusalem who were on the city wall. The officers wanted to scare the people away so they could capture Jerusalem. ¹⁹They said evil things about the gods the people of

the world worshiped. They are only things people have made with their hands. In the same way the officers said evil things about the God of Jerusalem.

²⁰King Hezekiah and the prophet*d* Isaiah son of Amoz prayed to heaven about this. ²¹Then the Lord sent an angel to the king of Assyria's camp. That angel killed all the soldiers, leaders and officers of the Assyrian army. So the king of Assyria returned to his own country in disgrace. He went into the temple of his god. There some of his own sons killed him with a sword.

²²So the Lord saved Hezekiah and the people in Jerusalem. He saved them from Sennacherib king of Assyria and from all other people. The Lord took care of Hezekiah and the people of Jerusalem. ²³Many people brought gifts for the Lord to Jerusalem. They also brought valuable gifts to King Hezekiah of Judah. From then on all the nations respected Hezekiah.

HEZEKIAH DIES

²⁴At that time Hezekiah became very sick. He was almost dead. He prayed to the Lord. And the Lord spoke to him and gave him a sign.*n* ²⁵But Hezekiah was proud. So he did not thank God for his kindness. So the Lord was angry with him and the people of Judah and Jerusalem. ²⁶But later Hezekiah and the people of Jerusalem were sorry and stopped being proud. So the Lord did not punish them while Hezekiah was alive.

²⁷Hezekiah had many riches and much honor. He made treasuries for his silver, gold, gems, spices, shields and other valuable things. ²⁸Hezekiah built storage buildings for grain, new wine and oil. He built stalls for all the cattle and pens for the sheep. ²⁹He also built many towns. He had many flocks of sheep and

herds of cattle. God gave Hezekiah much wealth.

³⁰It was Hezekiah who cut off the upper pool of the Gihon spring. He made those waters flow straight down on the west side of the older part of Jerusalem. And Hezekiah was successful in everything he did. ³¹But one time the leaders of Babylon sent messengers to Hezekiah. They asked him about a strange sign*n* that had happened in the land. When they came, God left Hezekiah alone to test him. He wanted to know everything that was in Hezekiah's heart.*n*

³²Hezekiah's love for the Lord and the other things he did as king are recorded. They are written in the vision of the prophet*d* Isaiah son of Amoz. This is in the book of the kings of Judah and Israel. ³³Hezekiah died and was buried on a hill. It is where the graves of David's ancestors are. All the people of Judah and Jerusalem honored Hezekiah when he died. And Hezekiah's son Manasseh became king in his place.

MANASSEH KING OF JUDAH

33 Manasseh was 12 years old when he became king of Judah. And he was king for 55 years in Jerusalem. ²He did what the Lord said was wrong. He did the hated things the other nations had done. And the Lord had forced these nations out of the land ahead of Israel. ³Manasseh's father, Hezekiah, had torn down the places where false gods were worshiped. But Manasseh rebuilt them. Manasseh also built altars for the Baal*d* gods and made Asherah*d* idols. He bowed down to the stars and worshiped them. ⁴The Lord had said about the Temple,*d* "I will be worshiped in Jerusalem forever." But Manasseh built altars for false gods in the Temple of the Lord. ⁵He built altars

---

32:24, 31 sign See Isaiah 38:1-8. It tells the story about the sign and how the Lord gave Hezekiah 15 more years to live.
32:31 God . . . heart See 2 Kings 20:12-19.

to worship the stars in the two court-yards of the Temple of the Lord. [6]He burned his sons as sacrifices in the Valley of Ben Hinnom. He practiced magic and witchcraft.[d] He told the future by explaining signs and dreams. He got advice from mediums[d] and fortune-tellers. He did many things the Lord said were wrong. And this made the Lord angry.

[7]He carved an idol and put it in the Temple of God. God had spoken to David and his son Solomon about the Temple. He had said, "I will be worshiped in this Temple and in Jerusalem forever. I have chosen Jerusalem from all the tribes[d] of Israel. [8]I will never again make the Israelites leave the land I gave to their ancestors. But they must obey every-thing I commanded them. They must obey all the teachings, rules and com-mands I gave them through Moses." [9]But Manasseh led the people of Judah and Jerusalem to do wrong. They did more evil than the nations the Lord had destroyed ahead of the Israelites.

[10]The Lord spoke to Manasseh and his people, but they did not listen. [11]So the Lord brought the king of Assyria's army commanders to attack Judah. They cap-tured Manasseh and put hooks in him. They put bronze chains on his hands. They made him their prisoner and took him to Babylon. [12]As Manasseh suffered, he begged the Lord his God for help. He became very sorry for what he had done before the God of his ancestors. [13]When Manasseh prayed, the Lord heard him and had pity for him. So the Lord let him return to Jerusalem and to his kingdom. Then Manasseh knew that the Lord is the true God.

[14]After that happened, Manasseh rebuilt the outer wall for Jerusalem. It was in the valley on the west side of the Gihon spring. It went to the entrance of the Fish Gate and around the hill of Ophel. He also made the wall higher. Then he put commanders in all the strong, walled cities in Judah.

[15]Manasseh removed the idols of other nations. And he took the idol out of the Temple of the Lord. He removed all the altars he had built on the Temple hill and in Jerusalem. And he threw them out of the city. [16]Then he set up the Lord's altar. And he sacrificed on it fel-lowship offerings and offerings to show thanks to the Lord. Manasseh com-manded all the people of Judah to serve the Lord, the God of Israel. [17]The people continued to offer sacrifices at the places of worship. But their sacrifices were only to the Lord their God. [18]The other things Manasseh did as king are written down. His prayer to his God is recorded. And what the seers[d] said to him in the name of the Lord, the God of Israel, is recorded. They are all in the book of the history of the kings of Israel. [19]Manasseh's prayer and God's pity for him are written down. Also all of Manasseh's sins and how he was unfaithful to the Lord are recorded. The places he built for worshiping false gods and for the Asherah[d] idols are recorded. He did all these things but later became sorry for them. They are all in the book of the seers. [20]Manasseh died and was buried in his palace. Then Manasseh's son Amon became king in his place.

AMON KING OF JUDAH

[21]Amon was 22 years old when he became king. And he was king for two years in Jerusalem. [22]He did what the Lord said was wrong. He did as his father Manasseh had done. Amon worshiped and offered sacrifices to all the carved idols Manasseh had made. [23]Amon was not sorry for what he did wrong before the Lord. He was not sorry as his father Manasseh had been. Instead, Amon sinned even more.

[24]Amon's officers made plans against him and killed him in his palace. [25]But the people of Judah killed all those who

had made plans to kill King Amon. And they made his son Josiah to be king in his place.

JOSIAH KING OF JUDAH

34 Josiah was eight years old when he became king. He ruled 31 years in Jerusalem. [2]He did what the Lord said was right. He did good things as his ancestor David had done. Josiah did not stop doing what was right.

[3]In his eighth year as king, Josiah began to obey the God his ancestor David had followed. This was while Josiah was still young. In his twelfth year as king, Josiah began to remove the false gods from Judah and Jerusalem. He destroyed the places for worshiping false gods. He removed the Asherah[d] idols and the wooden and metal idols. [4]The people tore down the altars for the Baal[d] gods as Josiah directed. Then Josiah cut down the incense[d] altars that were above them. He broke up the Asherah idols and the wooden and metal idols. He beat them into powder. Then he sprinkled the powder on the graves of the people who had offered sacrifices to these gods. [5]He burned the bones of their priests on their own altars. So Josiah removed idol worship from Judah and Jerusalem. [6]He did the same for the towns in the areas of Manasseh, Ephraim and Simeon. He did this all the way to Naphtali. And he did the same for the ruins near these towns. [7]Josiah broke down the altars and Asherah idols. Then he beat the idols into powder. He cut down all the incense altars in all of Israel. Then he went back to Jerusalem.

[8]In Josiah's eighteenth year as king, he made Judah and the Temple[d] pure again. He sent Shaphan son of Azaliah, Maaseiah the city leader and Joah son of Joahaz the recorder. They were to repair the Temple of the Lord, the God of Josiah. [9]These men went to Hilkiah the high priest. They gave him the money the people had given for the Temple of God. The Levite doorkeepers had collected this money from the people of Manasseh, Ephraim and all the Israelites who were left alive. They also collected this money from all the people of Judah, Benjamin and Jerusalem. [10]Then the Levites gave it to the men who directed the work on the Temple of the Lord. And these supervisors paid the workers that rebuilt and repaired the Temple. [11]They gave money to carpenters and builders to buy cut rocks and wood. The wood was used to rebuild the buildings and to make beams for them. The kings of Judah had let the buildings become ruins. [12]The men did their work well. Their supervisors were Jahath, Obadiah, Zechariah and Meshullam. Jahath and Obadiah were Levites from the family of Merari. Zechariah and Meshullam were from the family of Kohath. These Levites were all skilled musicians. [13]They were in charge of the workers who carried things and all the other workers. Some Levites worked as secretaries, officers and doorkeepers.

THE LAW IS FOUND

[14]The Levites brought out the money that was in the Temple[d] of the Lord. As they were doing this, Hilkiah the priest found the Book of the Lord's Teachings. These teachings had been given through Moses. [15]Hilkiah said to Shaphan the royal assistant, "I've found the Book of the Teachings. It was in the Temple of the Lord!" He gave it to Shaphan.

[16]Then Shaphan took the book to the king and reported to Josiah: "Your officers are doing everything you told them to do. [17]They have paid out the money that was in the Temple of the Lord. They have given it to the supervisors and the workers." [18]Then Shaphan the royal assistant told the king, "Hilkiah the priest has given me a book." And Shaphan read from the book to the king.

[19]The king heard the words of the Teachings. Then he tore his clothes to

show how upset he was. [20]He gave these orders to Hilkiah, Ahikam son of Shaphan. He also gave them to Acbor son of Micaiah, Shaphan and Asaiah. Shaphan was the royal assistant. And Asaiah was the king's servant. These were the orders: [21]"Go and ask the Lord about the words in the book that was found. Ask for me and for the people who are left alive in Israel and Judah. The Lord is very angry with us because our ancestors did not obey the Lord's word. They did not do everything this book says to do."

[22]So Hilkiah and those the king sent with him left. They went to talk to Huldah the prophetess.[d] She was the wife of Shallum son of Tikvah, the son of Harhas. Harhas took care of the king's clothes. Huldah lived in Jerusalem, in the new area of the city.

[23]She said to them, "This is what the Lord, the God of Israel, says: Tell the man who sent you to me, [24]'This is what the Lord says: I will bring trouble to this place and to the people living here. I will bring all the curses that are written in the book that was read to the king of Judah. [25]The people of Judah have left me. They have burned incense[d] to other gods. They have made me angry by all the bad things they have made. So I will punish them in my anger. My anger will not be stopped.' [26]Tell the king of Judah who sent you to ask the Lord, 'This is what the Lord, the God of Israel, says about the words you heard: [27]You heard my words against this place and its people. And you became sorry for what you had done. You became sorry in my presence. You tore your clothes to show how upset you were. And you cried in my presence. This is why I have heard you, says the Lord. [28]So I will let you die. You will be buried in peace. You won't see all the trouble that I will bring to this place and the people living here.'"

So they took her message back to the king.

[29]Then the king gathered all the elders of Judah and Jerusalem together. [30]He went up to the Temple of the Lord. All the men from Judah and the people from Jerusalem went with him. The priests and the Levites and all the people—from the most important to the least important—went with him. He read to them all the words in the Book of the Agreement. That book was found in the Temple of the Lord. [31]Then the king stood by his pillar. He made an agreement in the presence of the Lord. He agreed to follow the Lord and to obey his commands, rules and laws with his whole being. And he agreed to obey the words of the agreement written in this book. [32]Then Josiah made all the people in Jerusalem and Benjamin promise to accept the agreement. The people of Jerusalem obeyed the agreement of God, the God their ancestors obeyed.

[33]And Josiah threw out the hated idols from all the land that belonged to the Israelites. He led everyone in Israel to serve the Lord their God. While Josiah lived, the people obeyed the Lord, the God their ancestors obeyed.

JOSIAH CELEBRATES THE PASSOVER

35 King Josiah celebrated the Passover[d] to the Lord in Jerusalem. The Passover lamb was killed on the fourteenth day of the first month. [2]Josiah chose the priests to do their duties. And he encouraged them as they served in the Temple[d] of the Lord. [3]The Levites taught the Israelites and were made holy for service to the Lord. Josiah said to them: "When David's son Solomon was king of Israel, he built the Temple. Put the Holy Box[d] in that Temple. Do not carry it from place to place on your shoulders anymore. Now serve the Lord your God and his people the Israelites. [4]Prepare yourselves by your family groups for service. Do the jobs that King David and his son Solomon gave you to do.

⁵"Stand in the holy place with a group of the Levites. Do this for each family group of the people so you may help them. ⁶Kill the Passover lambs. Make yourselves holy to the Lord. And prepare the lambs for your relatives, the people of Israel. Do everything the Lord through Moses commanded us to do."

⁷Josiah gave the Israelites 30,000 sheep and goats to kill for the Passover sacrifices. He also gave them 3,000 cattle. They were all King Josiah's own animals.

⁸Josiah's officers also gave willingly to the people, the priests and the Levites. Hilkiah, Zechariah and Jehiel were the officers in charge of the Temple. They gave the priests 2,600 lambs and goats and 300 cattle for Passover sacrifices. ⁹Also Conaniah, his brothers Shemaiah and Nethanel, and Hashabiah, Jeiel and Jozabad gave the Levites animals. They gave 5,000 sheep and goats and 500 cattle for Passover sacrifices. These men were leaders of the Levites.

¹⁰When everything was ready for the Passover service, the priests and Levites went to their places. This is what the king had commanded. ¹¹The Passover lambs were killed. Then the Levites skinned the animals and gave the blood to the priests. The priests sprinkled the blood on the altar. ¹²Then they gave the animals for the burnt offerings to the different family groups. This was done so the burnt offerings could be offered to the Lord as the Law of Moses taught. They also did this with the cattle. ¹³The Levites roasted the Passover sacrifices over the fire as they were commanded. And they boiled the holy offerings in pots, kettles and pans. Then they quickly gave the meat to the people. ¹⁴After this was finished, the Levites prepared meat for themselves and for the priests. The priests were the descendants[d] of Aaron. The priests worked until night, offering the burnt offerings and burning the fat of the sacrifices.

¹⁵The Levite singers were from Asaph's family. They stood in the places King David had chosen for them. They were Asaph, Heman and Jeduthun, the king's seer.[d] The gatekeepers at each gate did not have to leave their places. This was because their fellow Levites had prepared everything for them for the Passover.

¹⁶So everything was done that day for the worship of the Lord. And it was done as King Josiah commanded. The Passover was celebrated, and the burnt offerings were offered on the Lord's altar. ¹⁷The Israelites who were there celebrated the Passover and the Feast[d] of Unleavened Bread for seven days. ¹⁸The Passover had not been celebrated like this in Israel since the prophet[d] Samuel was alive. None of the kings of Israel had ever celebrated a Passover like this. King Josiah, the priests and the Levites celebrated it. And the people of Judah and Israel who were there with the people of Jerusalem celebrated it. ¹⁹This Passover was celebrated in the eighteenth year Josiah was king.

THE DEATH OF JOSIAH

²⁰So Josiah did all this for the Temple.[d] After this, King Neco of Egypt led an army to attack Carchemish. It was a town on the Euphrates River. And Josiah marched out to fight against Neco. ²¹But Neco sent messengers to Josiah. They said, "King Josiah, there should not be war between us. I did not come to fight you, but my enemies. God told me to hurry, and he is on my side. So don't fight God, or he will destroy you."

²²But Josiah did not go away. He wore different clothes so no one would know who he was. He refused to listen to what Neco said at God's command. So Josiah went to fight on the plain of Megiddo. ²³In the battle King Josiah was shot by arrows. He told his servants, "Take me away. I am badly wounded." ²⁴So they took him out of his chariot. And they put him in another chariot he had brought

to the battle. Then they took him to Jerusalem where he died. He was buried in the graves where his ancestors were buried. All the people of Judah and Jerusalem were very sad because he was dead.

25Jeremiah wrote some sad songs about Josiah. Even to this day all the men and women singers remember and honor Josiah with these songs. It became a custom in Israel to sing these songs. They are written in the collection of sad songs.

26-27The other things Josiah did as king, from the beginning to the end, are written down. They are in the book of the kings of Israel and Judah. It tells how he loved the Lord and obeyed the Lord's teachings.

JEHOAHAZ KING OF JUDAH

36 The people of Judah chose Josiah's son Jehoahaz. They made him king in Jerusalem in his father's place.

2Jehoahaz was 23 years old when he became king. And he was king in Jerusalem for three months. 3Then King Neco of Egypt made Jehoahaz no longer a king in Jerusalem. Neco made the people of Judah pay about 7,500 pounds of silver and about 75 pounds of gold. 4The king of Egypt made Jehoahaz's brother Eliakim the king of Judah and Jerusalem. Then Neco changed Eliakim's name to Jehoiakim. But Neco took Eliakim's brother Jehoahaz to Egypt.

JEHOIAKIM KING OF JUDAH

5Jehoiakim was 25 years old when he became king. And he was king in Jerusalem for 11 years. He did what the Lord his God said was wrong. 6King Nebuchadnezzar of Babylon attacked Judah. He captured Jehoiakim and put bronze chains on him. Then Nebuchadnezzar took him to Babylon. 7Nebuchadnezzar took some of the things from the Temple*d* of the Lord. And he took them to Babylon and put them in his own palace.

8The other things Jehoiakim did as king are written down. The hated things he did and everything he was guilty of doing are recorded. They are in the book of the kings of Israel and Judah. Jehoiakim's son Jehoiachin became king in his place.

JEHOIACHIN KING OF JUDAH

9Jehoiachin was 18 years old when he became king of Judah. And he was king in Jerusalem for three months and ten days. He did what the Lord said was wrong. 10In the spring King Nebuchadnezzar sent some servants to get Jehoiachin. They took him and some valuable treasures from the Temple*d* of the Lord to Babylon. Then Nebuchadnezzar made Jehoiachin's relative Zedekiah the king of Judah and Jerusalem.

ZEDEKIAH KING OF JUDAH

11Zedekiah was 21 years old when he became king of Judah. And he was king in Jerusalem for 11 years. 12Zedekiah did what the Lord his God said was wrong. The prophet*d* Jeremiah spoke messages from the Lord. But Zedekiah did not obey.

JERUSALEM IS DESTROYED

13Zedekiah turned against King Nebuchadnezzar. Nebuchadnezzar had forced Zedekiah to promise to be loyal to him. And Zedekiah had promised, using God's name. But Zedekiah became stubborn. He refused to obey the Lord, the God of Israel. 14Also, all the leaders of the priests and the people of Judah became more wicked. They followed the evil example of the other nations. The Lord had made the Temple*d* in Jerusalem holy. But the leaders made the Temple unholy.

THE FALL OF JERUSALEM

15The Lord, the God of their ancestors, sent prophets*d* again and again to warn his people. He did this because he had pity for them and for his Temple. 16But they made fun of God's prophets. They hated God's messages. So they refused to listen to the prophets. Finally God became so angry with his people that he could not be stopped. [17]So God brought the king of Babylon to attack them. The king killed the young men even when they were in the Temple. He did not have mercy on the people. He killed both young men and women. He even killed the old men and those who were sick. God permitted Nebuchadnezzar to punish the people of Judah and Jerusalem. [18]Nebuchadnezzar carried away to Babylon all the things from the Temple of God, both large and small. He took all the treasures from the Temple of the Lord and from the king and his officers. [19]Nebuchadnezzar and his army set fire to God's Temple. They broke down Jerusalem's wall. And they burned all the palaces. They took or destroyed every valuable thing in Jerusalem.

[20]Nebuchadnezzar took captive to Babylon the people who were left alive. And he forced them to be slaves for him and his descendants.[d] They remained there as slaves until the Persian kingdom defeated Babylon. [21]And so what the Lord had told Israel through the prophet Jeremiah happened. The Lord had said that place would be an empty wasteland for 70 years. This happened to make up for the years of Sabbath rests[n] that the people had not kept.

[22]It was the first year Cyrus was king of Persia. The Lord caused Cyrus to write an announcement and send it everywhere in his kingdom. This happened so the Lord's message spoken by Jeremiah would come true. [23]This is what Cyrus king of Persia says:

"The Lord, the God of heaven, has given all the kingdoms of the earth to me. And he has appointed me to build a Temple for him at Jerusalem in Judah. Now all of you who are God's people are free to go to Jerusalem. May the Lord your God be with you."

36:21 **Sabbath rests** The Law said that every seventh year the land was not to be farmed. See Leviticus 25:1–7.

THE BOOK OF
EZRA

CYRUS HELPS THE CAPTIVES RETURN

1 It was the first year Cyrus was king of Persia. The Lord caused Cyrus to write an announcement and send it everywhere in his kingdom. And he also put it in writing. This happened so the Lord's message spoken by Jeremiah would come true. The announcement said:

²This is what Cyrus king of Persia says:

The Lord, the God of heaven, has given all the kingdoms of the earth to me. And he has appointed me to build a Temple*d* for him at Jerusalem in Judah. ³Now all of you who are God's people are free to go to Jerusalem. May your God be with you. And you may build the Temple of the Lord. He is the God of Israel, who is in Jerusalem. ⁴Those who stay behind should support anyone who wants to go. Give them silver and gold, supplies and cattle. And give them special gifts for the Temple of God in Jerusalem.

⁵Then the family leaders of Judah and Benjamin got ready to go to Jerusalem. So did the priests and the Levites. They were going to Jerusalem to build the Temple of the Lord. God made all these people want to go. ⁶All their neighbors helped them. They gave them things made of silver and gold, along with supplies, cattle and valuable gifts. And they gave them the special gifts for the Temple. ⁷Also, King Cyrus brought out the bowls and pans that belonged in the Temple of the Lord. Nebuchadnezzar had taken them from Jerusalem. And he had put them in the temple of his own god. ⁸Cyrus king of Persia had Mithredath the treasurer get them out. So he made a list of the things for Sheshbazzar the prince of Judah.

⁹There were 30 gold dishes, 1,000 silver dishes, 29 silver pans, ¹⁰30 gold bowls, 410 matching silver bowls and 1,000 other pieces.

¹¹There was a total of 5,400 pieces of gold and silver. Sheshbazzar brought all these things along when the captives went from Babylon to Jerusalem.

THE CAPTIVES WHO RETURNED

2 These are the people of the area who returned from captivity. Nebuchadnezzar king of Babylon had taken them captive to Babylon. Now they returned to Jerusalem and Judah. Each one went back to his own town. ²These people returned with Zerubbabel, Jeshua, Nehemiah, Seraiah, Reelaiah, Mordecai, Bilshan, Mispar, Bigvai, Rehum and Baanah.

These are the men from Israel: ³the descendants*d* of Parosh—2,172; ⁴the descendants of Shephatiah—372; ⁵the descendants of Arah—775; ⁶the descendants of Pahath-Moab (through the family of Jeshua and Joab)—2,812; ⁷the descendants of Elam—1,254; ⁸the descendants of Zattu—945; ⁹the descendants of Zaccai—760; ¹⁰the descendants of Bani—642; ¹¹the descendants of Bebai—623; ¹²the descendants of Azgad—1,222; ¹³the descendants of Adonikam—666; ¹⁴the descendants of Bigvai—2,056; ¹⁵the descendants of Adin—454; ¹⁶the descendants of Ater (through the family of Hezekiah)—98; ¹⁷the descendants of Bezai—323; ¹⁸the descendants of Jorah—112; ¹⁹the descendants of Hashum—223; ²⁰the descendants of Gibbar—95.

²¹These are the men from the town of Bethlehem—123; ²²from Netophah—56; ²³from Anathoth—128; ²⁴from Azmaveth—42; ²⁵from Kiriath Jearim, Kephirah and Beeroth—743; ²⁶from Ramah and Geba—621; ²⁷from Micmash—122; ²⁸from Bethel and Ai—223; ²⁹from Nebo—52; ³⁰from Magbish—156; ³¹from the other town of Elam—1,254; ³²from Harim—320; ³³from Lod, Hadid and

Ono—725; [34]from Jericho—345; [35]from Senaah—3,630.

[36]These are the priests: the descendants of Jedaiah (through the family of Jeshua)—973; [37]the descendants of Immer—1,052; [38]the descendants of Pashhur—1,247; [39]the descendants of Harim—1,017.

[40]These are the Levites: the descendants of Jeshua and Kadmiel (through the family of Hodaviah)—74.

[41]These are the singers: the descendants of Asaph—128.

[42]These are the gatekeepers of the Temple:[d] the descendants of Shallum, Ater, Talmon, Akkub, Hatita and Shobai—139.

[43]These are the Temple servants: the descendants of Ziha, Hasupha, Tabbaoth, [44]Keros, Siaha, Padon, [45]Lebanah, Hagabah, Akkub, [46]Hagab, Shalmai, Hanan, [47]Giddel, Gahar, Reaiah, [48]Rezin, Nekoda, Gazzam, [49]Uzza, Paseah, Besai, [50]Asnah, Meunim, Nephussim, [51]Bakbuk, Hakupha, Harhur, [52]Bazluth, Mehida, Harsha, [53]Barkos, Sisera, Temah, [54]Neziah and Hatipha.

[55]These are the descendants of the servants of Solomon: the descendants of Sotai, Hassophereth, Peruda, [56]Jaala, Darkon, Giddel, [57]Shephatiah, Hattil, Pokereth-Hazzebaim and Ami.

[58]The Temple servants and the descendants of the servants of Solomon numbered 392.

[59]Some people came to Jerusalem from these towns: Tel Melah, Tel Harsha, Kerub, Addon and Immer. But they could not prove that their families came from the family of Israel. Here are their names and their number: [60]the descendants of Delaiah, Tobiah and Nekoda—652.

[61]And these priests could not prove that their families came from Israel: the descendants of Hobaiah, Hakkoz and Barzillai. (He had married a daughter of Barzillai from Gilead and was called by her family name.)

[62]These people searched for their family records. But they could not find them. So they could not be priests because they were thought to be unclean.[d] [63]The governor ordered them not to eat any of the food offered to God. First a priest had to settle this matter by using the Urim and Thummim.[d]

[64]The total number of those who returned was 42,360. [65]This is not counting their 7,337 male and female servants. They also had 200 men and women singers with them. [66]They had 736 horses, 245 mules, [67]435 camels and 6,720 donkeys.

[68]That group arrived at the Temple of the Lord in Jerusalem. Some of the leaders of families gave special offerings. Those offerings were given to rebuild the Temple of God. It would be on the same site as before. [69]Those people gave as much as they could to the treasury. It was to rebuild the Temple. They gave about 1,100 pounds of gold, about 6,000 pounds of silver and 100 pieces of clothing for the priests.

[70]All the Israelites settled in their hometowns. The priests, Levites, singers, gatekeepers and temple servants, along with some of the other people, settled in their own towns.

REBUILDING THE ALTAR

3 By the seventh month, the Israelites were settled in their hometowns. They met together in Jerusalem. [2]Then Jeshua son of Jozadak and his fellow priests joined Zerubbabel son of Shealtiel. They began to build the altar of the God of Israel. That's where they offered burnt offerings just as it is written in the Teachings of Moses. Moses was the man of God. [3]They were afraid of the people living around them. But they still built the altar where it had been before. They offered burnt offerings on it to the Lord morning and evening. [4]Then, to obey what was written, they celebrated the Feast[d] of Shelters. They offered the right

number of sacrifices for each day of the festival. [5]After the Feast of Shelters, they had regular sacrifices every day. They had sacrifices for the New Moon[d] and all the festivals commanded by the Lord. Also there were special offerings brought as gifts to the Lord. [6]On the first day of the seventh month they began to bring burnt offerings to the Lord. But the foundation of the Lord's Temple[d] had not yet been laid.

REBUILDING THE TEMPLE

[7]Then they gave money to the stone-workers and carpenters. They also gave food, wine and oil to the cities of Sidon and Tyre. This was so they would float cedar logs from Lebanon to the seacoast town of Joppa. Cyrus king of Persia had given permission for this.

[8]It was in the second year after their arrival at the Temple[d] of God in Jerusalem. In the second month Zerubbabel and Jeshua began the work. So did the rest of their fellow priests and Levites. And all who had returned from captivity to Jerusalem began to work. They chose Levites 20 years old and older to be in charge of the building of the Temple of the Lord. [9]These men were in charge of the work of building the Temple of God: Jeshua and his sons and brothers; Kadmiel and his sons who were the descendants of Hodaviah; and the sons of Henadad and their sons and brothers. They were all Levites.

[10]The builders finished laying the foundation of the Temple of the Lord. Then the priests, dressed in their robes, got trumpets. And the Levites, the sons of Asaph, had cymbals. They all took their places. They praised the Lord just as David king of Israel had said to do. [11]With praise and thanksgiving, they sang to the Lord:

"He is good;

his love for Israel continues forever."

And then all the people shouted loudly, "Praise the Lord! The foundation of his Temple has been laid." [12]But many of the older priests, Levites and family leaders cried aloud. They had seen the first Temple. Now they saw the foundation of this Temple. But most of the other people were shouting with joy. [13]The people made so much noise no one could tell the difference between the joyful shouting and the sad crying. It could be heard far away.

ENEMIES OF THE REBUILDING

4 The people of Judah and Benjamin had enemies. They heard that the returned captives were building a Temple[d] for the Lord, the God of Israel. [2]So the enemies came to Zerubbabel and the leaders of the families. The enemies said, "Let us help you build. We are like you. We want to worship your God. We have been offering sacrifices to him since the time of Esarhaddon. He was king of Assyria, and he brought us here."

[3]But Zerubbabel, Jeshua and the leaders of Israel answered, "No. You people will not help us build a Temple to our God. We will build it ourselves. It is for the Lord, the God of Israel. This is what King Cyrus, the king of Persia, commanded us to do."

[4]Then the people around them tried to discourage the people of Judah. They tried to make them afraid to build. [5]Their enemies hired others to delay the building plans. This went on during the time Cyrus was king of Persia. And it continued to the time Darius was king of Persia.

MORE PROBLEMS FOR THE BUILDERS

[6]When Xerxes became king, those enemies wrote a letter against the people of Judah and Jerusalem.

[7]Later Artaxerxes became king of Persia. Then Bishlam, Mithredath, Tabeel and those with them wrote a letter to Artaxerxes. The letter was written in the Aramaic language.

[8]Also Rehum the governor and Shimshai the governor's assistant wrote a

letter. It was to Artaxerxes the king. And it was against Jerusalem. It said:

⁹This letter is from Rehum the governor, Shimshai the assistant and others. They are judges and important officers. They are over the men who came from Tripolis, Persia, Erech and Babylon. They are over the Elamite people of Susa. ¹⁰And they are over those whom the great and honorable Ashurbanipal forced out of their countries. He forced them to move and settle in the city of Samaria. And he forced them to settle in other places west of the Euphrates River.

¹¹(This is a copy of the letter they sent to Artaxerxes:)

To King Artaxerxes.

From your servants who live west of the Euphrates River.

¹²King Artaxerxes, you remember the Jews who came to us from you. You should know they have gone to Jerusalem. They are rebuilding that evil city that refuses to obey. They are fixing the walls and repairing the foundations of the buildings.

¹³Now, King Artaxerxes, you should know what could happen. If Jerusalem is built and its walls are fixed, Jerusalem will pay no taxes of any kind. Then the amount of money your government collects will be less. ¹⁴Since we must be loyal to the government, we don't want to see the king dishonored. So we are writing to let the king know. ¹⁵We suggest you search the records of the kings who ruled before you. You will find out that the city of Jerusalem refuses to obey. It makes trouble for kings and areas controlled by Persia. Since long ago it has been a place where disobedience started. That is why it was destroyed. ¹⁶We want you to know this, King Artaxerxes. This city should

not be rebuilt and its walls fixed. If it is, you will be left with nothing west of the Euphrates River.

¹⁷King Artaxerxes sent this answer:

To Rehum the governor and Shimshai the assistant. To all the people with them living in Samaria. And to those in other places west of the Euphrates.

Greetings.
¹⁸The letter you sent to us has been translated and read to me. ¹⁹I ordered the records to be searched, and it was done. We found that Jerusalem has a long history of disobedience to kings. It has been a place of problems and trouble. ²⁰Jerusalem has had powerful kings. They have ruled over the whole area west of the Euphrates. Taxes of all kinds have been paid to them. ²¹Now, give an order for those men to stop work. The city of Jerusalem will not be rebuilt until I say so. ²²Make sure you do this. If it continues, it will hurt the government.

²³A copy of the letter that King Artaxerxes sent was read. It was read to Rehum and Shimshai the assistant and the others. Then they quickly went to the Jews in Jerusalem. They forced them to stop building.

²⁴So the work on the Temple*d* of God in Jerusalem stopped. It stopped until the second year Darius was king of Persia.

TATTENAI'S LETTER TO DARIUS

5 Haggai and Zechariah son of Iddo were prophets.*d* They prophesied to the Jews in Judah and Jerusalem. They prophesied in the name of the God of Israel. ²Then Zerubbabel son of Shealtiel and Jeshua son of Jozadak started working again. They worked to rebuild the Temple*d* of God in Jerusalem. The prophets of God were there, helping them.

³At that time Tattenai was the governor west of the Euphrates. He and

Shethar-Bozenai and others went to the Jews. They asked, "Who gave you permission to rebuild this Temple and fix these walls?" 4They also asked, "What are the names of these men working on this building?" 5But their God was watching over the elders of the Jews. The builders were not stopped until a report could go to King Darius. And then his written answer had to be received.

6This is a copy of the letter that Tattenai, Shethar-Bozenai and the others sent to King Darius. Tattenai was governor west of the Euphrates River. The other people were important officers west of the Euphrates. 7This is what the report they sent to him said:

To King Darius.

Greetings. May you have peace.
8King Darius, you should know that we went to the district of Judah. That is where the Temple of the great God is. The people there are building that Temple with large stones. They are putting timbers in the walls. The people are working very hard. And they are building very fast.

9We asked their elders, "Who gave you permission to rebuild this Temple and these walls?" 10We also asked for their names. We wrote down the names of their leaders so you would know who they are.

11This is the answer they gave to us: "We are the servants of the God of heaven and earth. We are rebuilding the Temple that a great king of Israel built. He finished it many years ago. 12But our ancestors made the God of heaven angry. So God let them be defeated by Nebuchadnezzar king of Babylon. He destroyed this Temple. And he took the people to Babylon as captives.

13"Later, Cyrus was in his first year as king of Babylon. He gave a special order for this Temple to be rebuilt.

14And Cyrus brought out things from the temple in Babylon. They were the gold and silver bowls and pans that came from the Temple of God. Nebuchadnezzar had taken them from the Temple in Jerusalem. And he had put them in the temple in Babylon.

"Then King Cyrus gave them to Sheshbazzar. He had appointed Sheshbazzar as governor. 15Cyrus said to him, 'Take these gold and silver bowls and pans. Put them back in the Temple in Jerusalem. And rebuild the Temple of God where it was.' 16So Sheshbazzar came. He laid the foundations of the Temple of God in Jerusalem. From that day until now the work has been going on. But it is not yet finished."

17Now, if the king wishes, let a search be made. Search the royal records of Babylon to see if King Cyrus gave such an order. See if he gave an order to rebuild this Temple in Jerusalem. Then let the king write us and tell us what he has decided.

THE ORDER OF DARIUS

6 So King Darius gave an order to search the records. They were kept in the treasury in Babylon. 2A scroll was found in the capital city, Ecbatana. It is in the area of Media. This is what was written on it:

Note:

3King Cyrus gave an order about the Templed of God in Jerusalem. This was in the first year he was king. This was the order:

"Let the Temple be rebuilt. It will be a place to present sacrifices. Let its foundations be laid. The Temple should be 90 feet high and 90 feet wide. 4It must have three layers of large stones, then one layer of timbers. The costs should be paid from the king's treasury. 5The gold and silver things from the Temple of God should be put back in their places. Nebuchadnezzar took those things from the Temple in Jerusalem. And he brought them to Babylon. They are to be put back in the Temple of God in Jerusalem."

⁶Now then, I, Darius, give this order to you, Tattenai, governor west of the Euphrates. And I give it to Shethar-Bozenai and all the officers of that area. Stay away from there. ⁷Do not bother or interrupt the work on that Temple of God. Let the governor of the Jews and the Jewish elders rebuild this Temple. Let them build it where it was before.

⁸Also, I order you to do this for those elders of the Jews. They are building this Temple. The cost of the building is to be fully paid from the royal treasury. The money will come from taxes collected west of the Euphrates River. Do this so the work will not stop. ⁹Give those people anything they need. Give them young bulls, male sheep or male lambs for burnt offerings to the God of heaven. Give them wheat, salt, wine or olive oil. Give the priests in Jerusalem anything they ask for. Give it every day without fail. ¹⁰Then they may offer sacrifices pleasing to the God of heaven. And they can pray for the life of the king and his sons.

¹¹Also, I give this order: If anyone changes this order, a wood beam is to be pulled from his house. Drive one end of the beam through his body. And because he did this crime, make his house a pile of ruins. ¹²God has chosen Jerusalem as the place he is to be worshiped. May he defeat any king or person who tries to change this order. May God destroy anyone who tries to destroy this Temple.

I, Darius, have given this order. Let it be obeyed quickly and carefully.

COMPLETION OF THE TEMPLE

¹³So, Tattenai, the governor west of the Euphrates, Shethar-Bozenai and the others obeyed. They carried out King Darius' order quickly and carefully. ¹⁴So the Jewish elders continued to build. And they were successful because of the preaching of Haggai the prophet*d* and Zechariah son of Iddo. They finished building the Temple*d* as the God of Israel had said. It was also done to obey the kings Cyrus, Darius and Artaxerxes of Persia. ¹⁵The Temple was finished on the third day of the month Adar. It was the sixth year that Darius was king.

¹⁶Then the people of Israel celebrated. They gave the Temple to God to honor him. Everybody was happy: the priests, the Levites and the rest of the Jews who had returned from captivity. ¹⁷This is how they gave the Temple to God for worshiping him: They offered 100 bulls, 200 male sheep and 400 male lambs as sacrifices. And as an offering to forgive the sins of all Israel, they offered 12 male goats. That is 1 goat for each tribe*d* in Israel. ¹⁸Then they put the priests and the Levites into their separate groups. Each group had a certain time to serve God in the Temple at Jerusalem. This was done just as it is written in the Book of Moses.

THE PASSOVER

¹⁹The Jews who returned from captivity celebrated the Passover.*d* This was on the fourteenth day of the first month. ²⁰The priests and Levites had made themselves clean.*d* The Levites killed the Passover lambs for all the Jews who had returned from captivity. They also did it for their relatives the priests and for themselves. ²¹So all the people of Israel who returned from captivity ate the Passover lamb. So did those who had given up the unclean ways of their non-Jewish neighbors. They worshiped the Lord, the God of Israel. ²²For seven days they celebrated the Feast*d* of Unleavened

Bread in a very joyful way. The Lord had made them happy by changing the mind of the King of Assyria. So the king had helped them in the work on the Temple of the God of Israel.

EZRA COMES TO JERUSALEM

7 After these things[n] during the rule of Artaxerxes king of Persia, Ezra came up from Babylon. Ezra was the son of Seraiah. Seraiah was the son of Azariah. Azariah was the son of Hilkiah. [2]Hilkiah was the son of Shallum. Shallum was the son of Zadok. Zadok was the son of Ahitub. [3]Ahitub was the son of Amariah. Amariah was the son of Azariah. Azariah was the son of Meraioth. [4]Meraioth was the son of Zerahiah. Zerahiah was the son of Uzzi. Uzzi was the son of Bukki. [5]Bukki was the son of Abishua. Abishua was the son of Phinehas. Phinehas was the son of Eleazar. Eleazar was the son of Aaron the high priest. [6]This Ezra came to Jerusalem from Babylon. He was a teacher. He knew the Teachings of Moses well. The Teachings had been given by the Lord, the God of Israel. Ezra received everything he asked for from the king. This was because the Lord his God was helping him. [7]In the seventh year of King Artaxerxes more Israelites came to Jerusalem. Among them were priests, Levites, singers, gatekeepers and Temple[d] servants.

[8]Ezra also arrived in Jerusalem. It was the fifth month of Artaxerxes' seventh year as king. [9]Ezra had left Babylon on the first day of the first month. And he arrived in Jerusalem on the first day of the fifth month. God was helping Ezra. [10]Ezra had worked hard to know and obey the Teachings of the Lord. He also taught the rules and commands of the Lord to the Israelites.

ARTAXERXES' LETTER TO EZRA

[11]King Artaxerxes had given a letter to Ezra. Ezra was a priest and teacher. He taught about the commands and laws the Lord gave Israel. This is a copy of the letter:

[12]From Artaxerxes, king of kings. To Ezra the priest, a teacher of the Law of the God of heaven.

Greetings.

[13]Now I give this order: Any Israelite in my kingdom who wishes may go with you to Jerusalem. This includes priests and Levites. [14]Ezra, you are sent by the king and the seven people who advise him. You are to ask about how Judah and Jerusalem are obeying the Law of your God, which you are carrying with you. [15]Also take with you the silver and gold the king and those who advise him have given freely. It's for the God of Israel, whose Temple[d] is in Jerusalem. [16]Also take the silver and gold you receive from the area of Babylon. And take the offerings the Israelites and their priests have given as gifts to the Lord. They are for the Temple of their God in Jerusalem. [17]With this money buy bulls, male sheep and male lambs. Buy the grain offerings and drink offerings that go with those sacrifices. Then sacrifice them on the altar in the Temple of your God in Jerusalem.

[18]Then you and your fellow Jews may spend the silver and gold left over. Use it as you want and as God wishes. [19]Take to the God of Jerusalem all the things put in your care. They are for the worship in the Temple of your God. [20]And you may get anything else you need for the Temple of your God. Pay for it from the royal treasury.

[21]Now I, King Artaxerxes, give this order to all the men in charge of the treasury west of the Euphrates: Give

7:1 **After these things** There is a time period of about 60 years between chapters six and seven.

Ezra anything he asks for right away. Ezra is a priest and a teacher of the Law of the God of heaven. ²²Give him up to 7,500 pounds of silver, 600 bushels of wheat, 600 gallons of wine and 600 gallons of olive oil. And give him as much salt as he wants. ²³Carefully give him whatever the God of heaven wants. Do it for the Temple of the God of heaven. We do not want God to be angry with the king and his sons. ²⁴Remember, you must not make these people pay taxes of any kind: priests, Levites, singers, gatekeepers, Temple servants and other workers in this Temple of God.

²⁵And you, Ezra, use the wisdom you have from your God. Choose judges and lawmakers to rule the Jews west of the Euphrates. They know the laws of your God. And teach anyone who does not know them. ²⁶Whoever does not obey the law of your God or of the king must be punished. He will be killed or sent away. He will have his property taken away or be put in jail.

²⁷Praise the Lord, the God of our ancestors. He caused the king to want to honor the Temple of the Lord in Jerusalem. ²⁸The Lord has shown me, Ezra, his love. He did this before the king, those who advise the king and the royal officers. The Lord my God was helping me. So I had courage. I gathered the leaders of Israel to return with me.

LEADERS WHO RETURNED WITH EZRA

8 These are the leaders of the family groups who returned with me. And it is a listing of those who were with them. They came back from Babylon during the rule of King Artaxerxes.

²From the descendants*d* of Phinehas, there was Gershom.

From the descendants of Ithamar, there was Daniel.

From the descendants of David, there was Hattush ³of the descendants of Shecaniah.

From the descendants of Parosh, there was Zechariah. And 150 men came with him.

⁴From the descendants of Pahath-Moab, there was Eliehoenai son of Zerahiah, with 200 men.

⁵From the descendants of Zattu, there was Shecaniah son of Jahaziel, with 300 men.

⁶From the descendants of Adin, there was Ebed son of Jonathan, with 50 men.

⁷From the descendants of Elam, there was Jeshaiah son of Athaliah, with 70 men.

⁸From the descendants of Shephatiah, there was Zebadiah son of Michael, with 80 men.

⁹From the descendants of Joab, there was Obadiah son of Jehiel, with 218 men.

¹⁰From the descendants of Bani, there was Shelomith son of Josiphiah, with 160 men.

¹¹From the descendants of Bebai, there was Zechariah son of Bebai, with 28 men.

¹²From the descendants of Azgad, there was Johanan son of Hakkatan, with 110 men.

¹³From the descendants of Adonikam, these were the last ones: Eliphelet, Jeuel and Shemaiah. With them were 60 men.

¹⁴From the descendants of Bigvai, there were Uthai and Zaccur, with 70 men.

THE RETURN TO JERUSALEM

¹⁵I, Ezra, called all those people together at the canal. It flows toward Ahava. We camped there for three days. I checked all the people and the priests. But I did not find any Levites. ¹⁶So I called these leaders: Eliezer, Ariel, Shemaiah, Elnathan, Jarib, Elnathan, Nathan, Zechariah and Meshullam. And I called Joiarib and Elnathan, who were teachers. ¹⁷I sent those men to Iddo, the leader at Casiphia. I told them what to say to Iddo and his relatives, who are the Temple*d* servants in Casiphia. I sent them to bring servants to us for the Temple*d* of our God. ¹⁸Our God was

helping us. So Iddo's relatives gave us Sherebiah, a wise man from the descendants of Mahli. Mahli was the son of Levi. And Levi was the son of Israel. And they brought Sherebiah's sons and brothers. In all there were 18 men. ¹⁹And they brought to us Hashabiah and Jeshaiah from the descendants of Merari. And they also brought his brothers and nephews. In all there were 20 men. ²⁰They also brought 220 of the Temple servants. This is a group David and the officers had set up to help the Levites. All of those men were listed by name.

²¹There by the Ahava Canal, I announced we would all give up eating. We would make ourselves humble before our God. And we would ask God for a safe trip for ourselves, our children and all our possessions. ²²I was ashamed to ask the king for soldiers and horsemen. They could have protected us from enemies on the road. But we had said to the king, "Our God helps everyone who obeys him. But God is very angry with all who reject him." ²³So we gave up eating and prayed to our God about our trip. He answered our prayers.

²⁴Then I chose 12 of the priests who were leaders. They were Sherebiah and Hashabiah and 10 of their relatives. ²⁵I weighed the offering of silver and gold. And I weighed the things given for the Temple of our God. I gave them to the 12 priests I had chosen. The king, the people who advised him, his officers and all the Israelites there with us had given these things for the Temple. ²⁶I weighed out and gave them about 50,000 pounds of silver, about 7,500 pounds of silver objects and about 7,500 pounds of gold. ²⁷I gave them 20 gold bowls that weighed about 19 pounds. And I gave them 2 fine pieces of polished bronze that were as valuable as gold.

²⁸Then I said to the priests, "You and these things belong to the Lord for his service. The silver and gold are gifts to the Lord, the God of your ancestors. ²⁹Guard these things carefully. In Jerusalem, weigh them in front of the leading priests, Levites and the leaders of the family groups of Israel. Do this in the rooms of the Temple of the Lord." ³⁰So the priests and Levites took the silver, the gold and the special things that had been weighed out. They were to take them to the Temple of our God in Jerusalem.

³¹On the twelfth day of the first month we left the Ahava Canal. We started toward Jerusalem. Our God helped us. He protected us from enemies and robbers along the way. ³²Then we arrived in Jerusalem. We rested there three days.

³³On the fourth day we weighed out the silver, the gold and the special things in the Temple of our God. We handed them to the priest Meremoth son of Uriah. Eleazar son of Phinehas was with Meremoth. Also the Levites Jozabad son of Jeshua and Noadiah son of Binnui were with them. ³⁴We checked everything by number and by weight. And the total weight was written down at that time.

³⁵Then the captives who returned made burnt offerings to the God of Israel. They sacrificed 12 bulls for all Israel, 96 male sheep and 77 male lambs. All these animals were burned as sacrifices to the Lord. For a sin offering to the Lord there were 12 male goats. ³⁶They took King Artaxerxes' orders to the royal officers and to the governors west of the Euphrates. Then these men gave help to the people and the Temple of God.

EZRA'S PRAYER

9 After these things had been done, the leaders came to me. They said, "Ezra, the Israelites, including the priests and Levites, have not kept themselves separate from the people around us. Those neighbors do evil things as the Canaanites, Hittites, Perizzites, Jebusites, Ammonites, Moabites, Egyptians and Amorites did. ²The Israelite men and their sons have married the women of these non-Jewish people. They have mixed the people who belong to God with the people around them. The leaders and officers of Israel did this first. And they caused the rest of the Israelites to do this unfaithful thing."

³When I heard this, I angrily tore my robe and coat. I pulled hair from my head and beard and sat down in shock. ⁴Then everyone who trembled in fear at the word of the God of Israel gathered around me. This was because of the unfaithfulness of the captives who had returned. I sat there in shock until the evening sacrifice.

⁵Then, at the evening sacrifice, I got up from where I had shown my disgrace. My inner robe and coat were torn. And I fell on my knees with my hands spread out to the Lord my God. ⁶I prayed,

"My God, I am too ashamed and embarrassed to lift up my face to you. I am in disgrace because our sins are so many they are higher than our heads. Our sins even reach up to the sky. ⁷From the days of our ancestors until now, we have been very guilty. Because of our sins, we, our kings and priests have suffered punishment. We have been punished by the sword and captivity. Foreign kings have taken away our things and shamed us. It is that way today.

⁸"But now, for a short time, the Lord our God has been kind to us. He has let some of us come back from captivity. He has let us live in safety in his holy place. And so our God gives us hope and a little relief from our slavery. ⁹Even though we are slaves, our God has not left us. He caused the kings of Persia to be kind to us. He has given us new life. So we can rebuild the Temple*ᵈ* and repair its ruins. And he has given us a wall to protect us in Judah and Jerusalem.

¹⁰"But now, our God, what can we say after you have done all this? We have disobeyed your commands. ¹¹You gave these commands through your servants the prophets.*ᵈ* You said, 'The land you are entering to own is ruined. The people living there have spoiled it by the evil they do. Their evil filled the land with uncleanness*ᵈ* from one end to the other. ¹²So do not let your daughters marry their sons. And do not let their daughters marry your sons. Do not wish for their peace or success. Then you may be strong and eat the good things of the land. And then you can leave this land to your descendants*ᵈ* forever.'

¹³"What has happened to us is our own fault. We have done evil things. Our guilt is great. But you, our God, have punished us less than we deserve. You have left a few of us alive. ¹⁴We should not again break your commands by allowing marriages with these wicked people. If we did, you would get angry enough to destroy us. Then none of us would be left alive. ¹⁵Lord, God of Israel, by your goodness a few of us are left alive today. We admit that we are guilty. None of us should be allowed to stand before you."

THE PEOPLE CONFESS SIN

10 Ezra was praying and confessing. He was crying and throwing himself down in front of the Temple.*ᵈ* A large group of Israelite men, women and children gathered around him. They were also crying loudly. ²Then Shecaniah son of Jehiel the Elamite spoke to Ezra. Shecaniah said, "We have been unfaithful to our God. We have been marrying women from the peoples around us. But even so, there is still hope for Israel. ³Now let us make an agreement before our God. We will send away all these women and their children. This is your advice. It is also the advice of those who respect the commands of our God. Let it be done to obey his Teachings. ⁴Get up, Ezra. You are in charge. But we will support you. So have courage and do it."

[5]So Ezra got up. He made these people make a promise: the priests, the Levites and all the people of Israel. They promised to do what was suggested. [6]Then Ezra left the Temple. He went to the room of Jehohanan son of Eliashib. While Ezra was there, he did not eat or drink. He was still sad about the unfaithfulness of the captives who had returned.

[7]Then an order was sent everywhere in Judah and Jerusalem. All the captives who had returned had to meet together in Jerusalem. [8]Whoever did not come to Jerusalem within three days would lose his property. And he would no longer be a member of the community of the returned captives. That was the decision of the officers and elders.

[9]So within three days all the men of Judah and Benjamin gathered in Jerusalem. It was the twentieth day of the ninth month. All the people were sitting in the open place in front of the Temple. They were upset because of the meeting and because it was raining. [10]Then Ezra the priest stood up and said to them, "You have been unfaithful. You have married non-Jewish women. You have made Israel more guilty. [11]Now, confess it to the Lord, the God of your ancestors. Do the Lord's will. Separate yourselves from the people living around you and from your non-Jewish wives."

[12]Then the whole group answered Ezra. They shouted, "Ezra, you're right! We must do what you say. [13]But there are many people here. It's the rainy season. We can't stand outside. Also, this problem can't be solved in a day or two. We have sinned badly. [14]Let our officers make a decision for the whole group. Then let everyone in our towns who has married a non-Jewish woman meet with the elders and judges of each town. Let them meet at a planned time. Then the hot anger of our God will turn away from us." [15]Only these men were against the plan: Jonathan son of Asahel,

Jahzeiah son of Tikvah, Meshullam and Shabbethai the Levite.

[16]So the returned captives did what was suggested. Ezra the priest chose men who were leaders of the family groups. He named one from each family division. On the first day of the tenth month they sat down to study each case. [17]By the first day of the first month, they had finished. They had dealt with all the men who had married non-Jewish women.

THOSE GUILTY OF MARRYING NON-JEWISH WOMEN

[18]These are the descendants[d] of the priests who had married foreign women:

From the descendants of Jeshua son of Jozadak and Jeshua's brothers, there were Maaseiah, Eliezer, Jarib and Gedaliah. [19](They all promised to divorce their wives. Then each one brought a male sheep from the flock as a penalty offering.)

[20]From the descendants of Immer, there were Hanani and Zebadiah.

[21]From the descendants of Harim, there were Maaseiah, Elijah, Shemaiah, Jehiel and Uzziah.

[22]From the descendants of Pashhur, there were Elioenai, Maaseiah, Ishmael, Nethanel, Jozabad and Elasah.

[23]Among the Levites, there were Jozabad, Shimei, Kelaiah (also called Kelita), Pethahiah, Judah and Eliezer.

[24]Among the singers, there was Eliashib.

Among the gatekeepers, there were Shallum, Telem and Uri.

[25]And among the other Israelites, these married non-Jewish women:

From the descendants of Parosh, there were Ramiah, Izziah, Malkijah, Mijamin, Eleazar, Malkijah and Benaiah.

[26]From the descendants of Elam, there were Mattaniah, Zechariah, Jehiel, Abdi, Jeremoth and Elijah.

[27]From the descendants of Zattu, there were Elioenai, Eliashib, Mattaniah, Jeremoth, Zabad and Aziza.

²⁸From the descendants of Bebai, there were Jehohanan, Hananiah, Zabbai and Athlai.

²⁹From the descendants of Bani, there were Meshullam, Malluch, Adaiah, Jashub, Sheal and Jeremoth.

³⁰From the descendants of Pahath-Moab, there were Adna, Kelal, Benaiah, Maaseiah, Mattaniah, Bezalel, Binnui and Manasseh.

³¹From the descendants of Harim, there were Eliezer, Ishijah, Malkijah, Shemaiah, Shimeon, ³²Benjamin, Malluch and Shemariah.

³³From the descendants of Hashum, there were Mattenai, Mattattah, Zabad, Eliphelet, Jeremai, Manasseh and Shimei.

³⁴From the descendants of Bani, there were Maadai, Amram, Uel, ³⁵Benaiah, Bedeiah, Keluhi, ³⁶Vaniah, Meremoth, Eliashib, ³⁷Mattaniah, Mattenai and Jaasu.

³⁸From the descendants of Binnui, there were Shimei, ³⁹Shelemiah, Nathan, Adaiah, ⁴⁰Macnadebai, Shashai, Sharai, ⁴¹Azarel, Shelemiah, Shemariah, ⁴²Shallum, Amariah and Joseph.

⁴³From the descendants of Nebo, there were Jeiel, Mattithiah, Zabad, Zebina, Jaddai, Joel and Benaiah.

⁴⁴All these men had married non-Jewish women. And some of them had children by these wives.

THE BOOK OF
NEHEMIAH

NEHEMIAH'S PRAYER

1 These are the words of Nehemiah son of Hacaliah.

I, Nehemiah, was in the capital city of Susa. It was in the month of Kislev. This was in the twentieth year.[n] ²One of my brothers named Hanani came from Judah. Some other men were with him. I asked them about the Jews who lived through the captivity. And I also asked about Jerusalem.

³They answered, "Nehemiah, those who are left from the captivity are back in the area of Judah. But they are in much trouble and are full of shame. The wall around Jerusalem is broken down. And its gates have been burned."

⁴When I heard these things, I sat down and cried for several days. I was sad and did not eat food. I prayed to the God of heaven. ⁵I said, "Lord, God of heaven, you are the great God who is to be respected. You keep your agreement of love with those who love you and obey your commands. ⁶Listen carefully. Look at me. Hear the prayer your servant is praying to you day and night. I am praying for your servants, the people of Israel. I confess the sins we Israelites have done against you. My father's family and I have sinned against you. ⁷We have been wicked toward you. We have not obeyed the commands, rules and laws you gave your servant Moses.

⁸"Remember what you taught your servant Moses. You said, 'If you are unfaithful, I will scatter you among the nations. ⁹But if you come back to me and obey my commands, I will gather your people. I will gather them from the far ends of the earth. And I will bring them from captivity to where I have chosen to be worshiped.'

¹⁰"They are your servants and your people. You have saved them with your great strength and power. ¹¹Lord, listen carefully to my prayer. I am your servant. And listen to the prayers of your servants who love to honor you. Give me, your servant, success today. Allow this king to show kindness to me."

I was the one who served wine to the king.

NEHEMIAH IS SENT TO JERUSALEM

2 It was the month of Nisan. It was in the twentieth year King Artaxerxes was king. He wanted some wine. So I took some and gave it to the king. I had not been sad in his presence before. ²So the king said, "Why does your face look sad? You are not sick. Your heart must be sad."

Then I was very afraid. ³I said to the king, "May the king live forever! My face is sad because the city where my ancestors are buried lies in ruins. And its gates have been destroyed by fire."

⁴Then the king said to me, "What do you want?"

First I prayed to the God of heaven. ⁵Then I answered the king, "Send me to the city in Judah where my ancestors are buried. I will rebuild it. Do this if you are willing and if I have pleased you."

⁶The queen was sitting next to the king. He asked me, "How long will your trip take? When will you get back?" It pleased the king to send me. So I set a time.

⁷I also said to him, "If you are willing, give me letters for the governors west of the Euphrates River. Tell them to let me pass safely through their lands on my way to Judah. ⁸And may I have a letter for Asaph? He is the keeper of the king's forest. Tell him to give me timber. I will need it to make boards for the gates of

---

1:1 twentieth year This is probably referring to the twentieth year King Artaxerxes I ruled Persia.

the palace. It is by the Temple.^d The wood is also for the city wall and the house I will live in." So the king gave me the letters. This was because God was showing kindness to me. ⁹So I went to the governors west of the Euphrates River. I gave them the king's letters. The king had also sent army officers and soldiers on horses with me.

¹⁰Sanballat the Horonite and Tobiah the Ammonite leader heard about this. They were upset that someone had come to help the Israelites.

NEHEMIAH INSPECTS JERUSALEM

¹¹I went to Jerusalem and stayed there three days. ¹²Then at night I started out with a few men. I had not told anyone what God had caused me to do for Jerusalem. There were no animals with me except the one I was riding.

¹³It was night. I went out through the Valley Gate. I rode toward the Dragon Well and the Trash Gate. I was inspecting the walls of Jerusalem. They had been broken down. And the gates had been destroyed by fire. ¹⁴Then I rode on toward the Fountain Gate and the King's Pool. But there was not enough room for the animal I was riding to get through. ¹⁵So I went up the valley at night. I was inspecting the wall. Finally, I turned and went back in through the Valley Gate. ¹⁶The officers did not know where I had gone or what I was doing. I had not yet said anything to the Jews, the priests, the important men or the officers. I had not said anything to any of the others who would do the work.

¹⁷Then I said to them, "You can see the trouble we have here. Jerusalem is a pile of ruins. And its gates have been burned. Come, let's rebuild the wall of Jerusalem. Then we won't be full of shame any longer." ¹⁸I also told them how God had been kind to me. And I told them what the king had said to me.

Then they answered, "Let's start rebuilding." So they began to work hard.

¹⁹But Sanballat the Horonite, Tobiah the Ammonite leader and Geshem the Arab heard about it. They made fun of us and laughed at us. They said, "What are you doing? Are you turning against the king?"

²⁰But I answered them, "The God of heaven will give us success. We are God's servants. We will start rebuilding. But you have no share in Jerusalem. You have no claim or past right to it."

BUILDERS OF THE WALL

3 Eliashib the high priest and his fellow priests went to work. They rebuilt the Sheep Gate. They gave it to the Lord's service and set its doors in place. They worked as far as the Tower of the Hundred, and they gave it to the Lord's service. Then they went on to the Tower of Hananel. ²The men of Jericho built the part of the wall next to the priests. And Zaccur son of Imri built next to them.

³The sons of Hassenaah rebuilt the Fish Gate. They set the boards in place. And they put its doors, bolts and bars in place. ⁴Meremoth son of Uriah made repairs next to them. (Uriah was the son of Hakkoz.) Meshullam son of Berekiah worked next to Meremoth. (Berekiah was the son of Meshezabel.) And Zadok son of Baana worked next to Meshullam. ⁵The men from Tekoa made repairs next to them. But the leading men of Tekoa would not work under their supervisors.

⁶Joiada son of Paseah and Meshullam son of Besodeiah repaired the Old Gate. They set its boards in place. And they put its doors, bolts and bars in place. ⁷Next to them, men from Gibeon and Mizpah made repairs. Melatiah was from Gibeon, and Jadon was from Meronoth. These places were ruled by the governor west of the Euphrates River. ⁸Next to them, Uzziel son of Harhaiah made repairs. He was a goldsmith. And next to him, Hananiah made repairs. He was one of the people who made perfume.

These men rebuilt Jerusalem as far as the Broad Wall. [9]The next part of the wall was repaired by Rephaiah son of Hur. He was ruler of half of the district of Jerusalem. [10]Next to him, Jedaiah son of Harumaph made repairs. He worked opposite his own house. And next to him, Hattush son of Hashabneiah made repairs. [11]Malkijah son of Harim and Hasshub son of Pahath-Moab repaired another part of the wall. And they repaired the Tower of the Ovens. [12]Next to them, Shallum son of Hallohesh made repairs. He was ruler of half of the district of Jerusalem. His daughters helped him.

[13]Hanun and the people of Zanoah repaired the Valley Gate. They rebuilt it and put its doors, bolts and bars in place. They also repaired the 500 yards of the wall to the Trash Gate.

[14]Malkijah son of Recab repaired the Trash Gate. He was ruler of the district of Beth Hakkerem. He rebuilt that gate and put its doors, bolts and bars in place.

[15]Shallun son of Col-Hozeh repaired the Fountain Gate. He was ruler of the district of Mizpah. He rebuilt it and put a roof over it. And he put its doors, bolts and bars in place. He also repaired the wall of the Pool of Siloam. It is next to the King's Garden. He repaired the wall all the way to the steps. They went down from the older part of the city. [16]Next to Shallun, Nehemiah[n] son of Azbuk made repairs. He was ruler of half of the district of Beth Zur. He made repairs up to a place opposite the tombs of David. He made repairs as far as the man-made pool and the House of the Heroes.

[17]Next to him, the Levites made repairs. Some worked under Rehum son of Bani. Next to him, Hashabiah made repairs for his district. He was ruler of half of the district of Keilah. [18]Next to him, Binnui son of Henadad and his relatives made repairs. Binnui was the ruler of the other half of the district of Keilah. [19]Next to them, Ezer son of Jeshua worked. He was ruler of Mizpah. He repaired another part of the wall. He worked across from the way up to the storehouse for weapons. And he worked to the place where the wall turns. [20]Next to him, Baruch son of Zabbai worked very hard to repair another part of the wall. It went from the place where the wall turns to the entrance of the house of Eliashib. He was the high priest. [21]Next to him, Meremoth son of Uriah worked. (Uriah was the son of Hakkoz.) He repaired another part of the wall. It went from the entrance to Eliashib's house to the far end of it.

[22]Next to him worked the priests from the surrounding area. [23]Next to them, Benjamin and Hasshub made repairs in front of their own house. Next to them, Azariah son of Maaseiah made repairs beside his own house. (Maaseiah was the son of Ananiah.) [24]Next to him, Binnui son of Henadad repaired another part of the wall. It went from Azariah's house to the place where the wall turned. And it went to the corner. [25]Palal son of Uzai worked across from the place where the wall turned. And he worked by the tower on the upper palace. That is near the courtyard of the king's guard. Next to Palal, Pedaiah son of Parosh made repairs. [26]The Temple[d] servants lived on the hill of Ophel. They made repairs as far as a point opposite the Water Gate. They worked toward the east and the tower that extends from the palace. [27]Next to them, the men of Tekoa made repairs. They worked on the wall from the great tower that extends from the palace to the wall of Ophel.

[28]The priests made repairs above the Horse Gate. Each worked in front of his own house. [29]Next to them, Zadok son of Immer made repairs across from his

---

3:16 Nehemiah This is a different Nehemiah than the one who wrote this book.

own house. Next to him, Shemaiah son of Shecaniah made repairs. He was the guard of the East Gate. [30]Next to him, Hananiah son of Shelemiah and Hanun, the sixth son of Zalaph, made repairs. They worked on another part of the wall. Next to them, Meshullam son of Berekiah made repairs. It was across from where he lived. [31]Next to him, Malkijah made repairs. He was one of the goldsmiths. He worked as far as the house of the Temple servants and the traders. That is across from the Inspection Gate. And he worked as far as the room above the corner of the wall. [32]The goldsmiths and the traders made repairs on another part of the wall. It was between the room above the corner of the wall and the Sheep Gate.

THOSE AGAINST THE REBUILDING

4 Sanballat heard we were rebuilding the wall. He was very angry, even furious. He made fun of the Jews. [2]He said to his friends and the army of Samaria, "What are these weak Jews doing? They think they can rebuild the wall. They think they will offer sacrifices. Maybe they think they can finish rebuilding it in only one day. They can't bring stones back to life. These are piles of trash and ashes."

[3]Tobiah the Ammonite was next to Sanballat. Tobiah said, "A fox could climb up on what they are building. Even it could break down their stone wall."

[4]I prayed, "Hear us, our God. We are hated. Turn the insults of Sanballat and Tobiah back on their own heads. Let them be captured and taken away like valuables that are stolen. [5]Do not hide their guilt. Do not take away their sins so you can't see them. The builders have seen them make you angry."

[6]So we rebuilt the wall until all of it went halfway up. The people were willing to work hard.

[7]But Sanballat, Tobiah, the Arabs, the Ammonites and the men from Ashdod were very angry. They heard that the repairs to Jerusalem's walls were continuing. And they heard that the holes in the wall were being closed. [8]So they all made plans against Jerusalem. They planned to come and fight and stir up trouble. [9]But we prayed to our God. And we appointed guards to watch for them day and night.

[10]The people of Judah said, "The workers are getting tired. There is too much dirt and trash. We cannot rebuild the wall."

[11]And our enemies said, "The Jews won't know it or see us. But we will come among them and kill them. We will stop the work."

[12]Then the Jews who lived near our enemies came. They told us ten times, "Everywhere you turn, the enemy will attack us." [13]So I put some of the people behind the lowest places along the wall. And I put some at the open places. I put families together with their swords, spears and bows. [14]Then I looked around. I stood up and spoke to the important men, the leaders and the rest of the people. I said, "Don't be afraid of them. Remember the Lord. He is great and others are afraid of him. And fight for your brothers, your sons and daughters, your wives and your homes."

[15]Then our enemies heard that we knew about their plans. God had ruined their plans. So we all went back to the wall. Each person went back to his own work.

[16]From that day on, half my men worked on the wall. The other half was ready with spears, shields, bows and armor. The officers stood in back of the people of Judah [17]who were building the wall. Those who carried materials did their work with one hand. They carried a weapon in the other hand. [18]Each builder wore his sword at his side as he worked. The man who blew the trumpet to warn the people stayed next to me.

[19]Then I spoke to the important men, the leaders and the rest of the people. I said, "This is a very big job. We are spreading out along the wall. We are far apart. [20]So wherever you hear the sound of the trumpet, assemble there. Our God will fight for us."

[21]So we continued to work. Half the men held spears. We worked from sunrise till the stars came out. [22]At that time I also said to the people, "Let every man and his helper stay inside Jerusalem at night. They can be our guards at night. And they can be workmen during the day." [23]Neither I, my brothers, my men nor the guards with me ever took off our clothes. Each person carried his weapon even when he went for water.

NEHEMIAH HELPS POOR PEOPLE

5 The men and their wives complained loudly against their fellow Jews. [2]Some of them were saying, "We have many sons and daughters in our families. To eat and stay alive, we need grain."

[3]Others were saying, "We are borrowing money to get grain. There is not much food. We might not be able to pay back the money we've borrowed. Then we will have to pay with our fields, vineyards and homes."

[4]And still others were saying, "We are having to borrow money. We have to pay the king's tax on our fields and vineyards. [5]We are just like our fellow Jews. Our sons are like their sons. But we have to sell our sons and daughters as slaves. Some of our daughters have already been sold. But there is nothing we can do. Our fields and vineyards already belong to other people."

[6]When I heard their complaints about these things, I was very angry. [7]I thought about it. Then I accused the important people and the leaders. I told them, "You are charging your own brothers too much interest." So I called a large meeting to deal with them. [8]I said to them, "Our fellow Jews had been sold to non-Jewish nations. But, as much as possible, we have bought them back. Now you are making your fellow Jews sell themselves to us!" The leaders were quiet. They had nothing to say.

[9]Then I said, "What you are doing is not right. You should live in fear of God. Don't let our non-Jewish enemies shame us. [10]I, my brothers and my men are also lending money and grain to the people. But stop charging them too much for this! [11]Give back their fields, vineyards, olive trees and houses right now. Also give them back the extra amount you charged them. That is the hundredth part of the money, grain, new wine and oil."

[12]They said, "We will give it back. And we will not demand anything more from them. We will do as you say."

Then I called for the priests. And I made the important men and leaders promise to do what they had said. [13]Also I shook out the folds of my robe. I said, "In this way may God shake out every man who does not keep his promise. May God shake him out of his house. And may he shake him out of the things that are his. Let that man be shaken out and emptied!"

Then the whole group said, "Amen." And they praised the Lord. So the people did what they had promised.

[14]I was appointed governor in the land of Judah. This was in the twentieth year of King Artaxerxes' rule. I was governor till his thirty-second year. So I was governor of Judah for 12 years. During that time neither my brothers nor I ate the food that was allowed for the governor. [15]But the governors before me placed a heavy load on the people. They took about one pound of silver from each person. And they took food and wine. The governors' helpers before me also controlled the people. But I did not do that because I feared God. [16]I worked on the wall. So did all my men who were gathered there. We did not buy any fields.

¹⁷Also, I fed 150 Jews and officers at my table. And I fed those who came from the nations around us. ¹⁸This is what was prepared every day for me and those who ate with me: one ox, six good sheep, and birds. And every ten days there were all kinds of wine. But I never demanded the food that was allowed for the governor. This was because the people were already working very hard.

¹⁹Remember, my God, to be kind to me. Remember all the good I have done for these people.

MORE PROBLEMS FOR NEHEMIAH

6 Then Sanballat, Tobiah, Geshem the Arab and our other enemies heard that I had rebuilt the wall. There was not one gap in it. But I had not yet set the doors in the gates. ²So Sanballat and Geshem sent me this message: "Come, Nehemiah, let's meet together in Kephirim on the plain of Ono."

But they were planning to harm me. ³So I sent messengers to them with this answer: "I am doing a great work. I can't come down. I don't want the work to stop while I leave to meet you." ⁴Sanballat and Geshem sent the same message to me four times. And I sent back the same answer each time.

⁵The fifth time Sanballat sent his helper to me with the message. And in his hand was an unsealed letter. ⁶This is what was written:

A report is going around to all the nations. And Geshem says it is true. It says you and the Jews are planning to turn against the king. That's why you are rebuilding the wall. They say you are going to be their king. ⁷They say you have appointed prophets^d to announce in Jerusalem: "There is a king of Judah!" The king will hear about this. So come, let's discuss this together.

⁸So I sent him back this answer: "Nothing you are saying is really happening. You are just making it up in your own mind."

⁹Our enemies were trying to scare us. They were thinking, "They will get too weak to work. Then the wall will not be finished."

But I prayed, "God, make me strong."

¹⁰One day I went to the house of Shemaiah son of Delaiah. Delaiah was the son of Mehetabel. Shemaiah had to stay at home. He said, "Nehemiah, let's meet in the Temple^d of God. Let's go inside the Temple and close the doors. Men are coming at night to kill you."

¹¹But I said, "Should a man like me run away? Should I run into the Temple to save my life? I will not go." ¹²I knew that God had not sent him. Tobiah and Sanballat had paid him to prophesy against me. ¹³They paid him to frighten me so I would do this and sin. Then they could give me a bad name to shame me.

¹⁴I prayed, "Remember Tobiah and Sanballat, my God. Remember what they have done. Also remember the prophetess Noadiah and the other prophets who have been trying to frighten me."

THE WALL IS FINISHED

¹⁵So the wall of Jerusalem was completed. It was on the twenty-fifth day of the month of Elul. It took 52 days to rebuild. ¹⁶Then all our enemies heard about it. And all the nations around us saw it. So they were shamed. They understood that the work had been done with the help of our God.

¹⁷Also in those days the important men of Judah sent many letters to Tobiah. And Tobiah answered them. ¹⁸Many Jews had promised to be faithful to Tobiah. This was because Tobiah was the son-in-law of Shecaniah son of Arah. And Tobiah's son Jehohanan had married the daughter of Meshullam son of Berekiah. ¹⁹Those important men kept telling me about the good things Tobiah was doing. Then they would tell Tobiah what I said about him. So Tobiah sent letters to frighten me.

7 After the wall had been rebuilt, I had set the doors in place. Then the gatekeepers, singers and Levites were chosen. ²I put my brother Hanani, along with Hananiah, in charge of Jerusalem. Hananiah was commander of the palace. He was honest, and he feared God more than most men. ³I said to them, "The gates of Jerusalem should not be opened until the sun is hot. While the gatekeepers are still on duty, have them shut and bolt the doors. Appoint people who live in Jerusalem as guards. Put some at guard posts and some near their own houses."

THE CAPTIVES WHO RETURNED

⁴The city was large and full of room. But there were few people in it. And the houses had not yet been rebuilt. ⁵So my God caused me to gather the people. I gathered the important men, the leaders and the common people. This was so I could register them by families. I found the family history of those who had returned first. This is what I found written there:

⁶These are the people of the area who returned from captivity. Nebuchadnezzar king of Babylon had taken them captive. Now they returned to Jerusalem and Judah. Each one went back to his own town. ⁷These people returned with Zerubbabel, Jeshua, Nehemiah, Azariah, Raamiah, Nahamani, Mordecai, Bilshan, Mispereth, Bigvai, Nehum and Baanah.

These are the men from Israel: ⁸the descendants*d* of Parosh—2,172; ⁹the descendants of Shephatiah—372; ¹⁰the descendants of Arah—652; ¹¹the descendants of Pahath-Moab (through the family of Jeshua and Joab)—2,818; ¹²the descendants of Elam—1,254; ¹³the descendants of Zattu—845; ¹⁴the descendants of Zaccai—760; ¹⁵the descendants of Binnui—648; ¹⁶the descendants of Bebai—628; ¹⁷the descendants of Azgad—2,322; ¹⁸the descendants of Adonikam—667; ¹⁹the descendants of Bigvai—2,067; ²⁰the descendants of Adin—655; ²¹the descendants of Ater (through Hezekiah)—98; ²²the descendants of Hashum—328; ²³the descendants of Bezai—324; ²⁴the descendants of Hariph—112; ²⁵the descendants of Gibeon—95.

²⁶These are the men from the towns of Bethlehem and Netophah—188; ²⁷the men from Anathoth—128; ²⁸the men from Beth Azmaveth—42; ²⁹the men from Kiriath Jearim, Kephirah and Beeroth—743; ³⁰the men from Ramah and Geba—621; ³¹the men from Micmash—122; ³²the men from Bethel and Ai—123; ³³the men from the other Nebo—52; ³⁴the men from the other Elam—1,254; ³⁵the men from Harim—320; ³⁶the men from Jericho—345; ³⁷the men from Lod, Hadid and Ono—721; ³⁸the men from Senaah—3,930.

³⁹These are the priests: the descendants of Jedaiah (through the family of Jeshua)—973; ⁴⁰the descendants of Immer—1,052; ⁴¹the descendants of Pashhur—1,247; ⁴²the descendants of Harim—1,017.

⁴³These are the Levites: the descendants of Jeshua (through Kadmiel through the family of Hodaviah)—74.

⁴⁴These are the singers: the descendants of Asaph—148.

⁴⁵These are the gatekeepers: the descendants of Shallum, Ater, Talmon, Akkub, Hatita and Shobai—138.

⁴⁶These are the Temple*d* servants: the descendants of Ziha, Hasupha, Tabbaoth, ⁴⁷Keros, Sia, Padon, ⁴⁸Lebana, Hagaba, Shalmai, ⁴⁹Hanan, Giddel, Gahar, ⁵⁰Reaiah, Rezin, Nekoda, ⁵¹Gazzam, Uzza, Paseah, ⁵²Besai, Meunim, Nephussim, ⁵³Bakbuk, Hakupha, Harhur, ⁵⁴Bazluth, Mehida, Harsha, ⁵⁵Barkos, Sisera, Temah, ⁵⁶Neziah and Hatipha.

⁵⁷These are the descendants of the servants of Solomon: the descendants of Sotai, Sophereth, Perida, ⁵⁸Jaala, Darkon, Giddel, ⁵⁹Shephatiah, Hattil, Pokereth-Hazzebaim and Amon.

⁶⁰The Temple servants and the descendants of the servants of Solomon totaled 392 people.

⁶¹Some people came to Jerusalem from these towns: Tel Melah, Tel Harsha, Kerub, Addon and Immer. But they could not prove that their families came from the family of Israel. Here are their names and their number: ⁶²the descendants of Delaiah, Tobiah and Nekoda—642.

⁶³And these priests could not prove that their families came from Israel: the descendants of Hobaiah, Hakkoz and Barzillai. (He had married a daughter of Barzillai from Gilead and was called by her family name.)

⁶⁴These people searched for their family records. But they could not find them. So they could not be priests because they were thought to be unclean.*d* ⁶⁵So the governor ordered them not to eat any of the food offered to God. First a priest had to settle this matter by using the Urim and Thummim.*d*

⁶⁶The total number of those who returned was 42,360. ⁶⁷This is not counting their 7,337 male and female servants. They also had 245 men and women singers with them. ⁶⁸They had 736 horses, 245 mules, ⁶⁹435 camels and 6,720 donkeys.

⁷⁰Some of the family leaders gave to the work. The governor gave to the treasury about 19 pounds of gold. He also gave 50 bowls and 530 pieces of clothing for the priests. ⁷¹Some of the family leaders gave about 375 pounds of gold to the treasury for the work. They also gave about 2,660 pounds of silver. ⁷²This is the total of what the other people gave: about 375 pounds of gold, about 2,250 pounds of silver and 67 pieces of clothing for the priests. ⁷³So these people all settled in their own towns: the priests, the Levites, the gatekeepers, the singers, the Temple servants and all the other people of Israel.

EZRA READS THE TEACHINGS

By the seventh month the Israelites were settled in their own towns.

8 All the people of Israel gathered together in the square by the Water Gate. They asked Ezra the teacher to bring out the Book of the Teachings of Moses. These are the Teachings the Lord had given to Israel.

²So Ezra the priest brought out the Teachings for the crowd. This was on the first day of the seventh month. Men, women and all who could listen and understand had gathered. ³Ezra read the Teachings out loud. He read from early morning until noon. He was facing the square by the Water Gate. He read to the men, women and everyone who could listen and understand. All the people listened carefully to the Book of the Teachings.

⁴Ezra the teacher stood on a high wooden platform. It had been built just for this time. On his right were Mattithiah, Shema, Anaiah, Uriah, Hilkiah and Maaseiah. And on his left were Pedaiah, Mishael, Malkijah, Hashum, Hashbaddanah, Zechariah and Meshullam.

5Ezra opened the book. All the people could see him because he was above them. As he opened it, all the people stood up. ⁶Ezra praised the Lord, the great God. And all the people held up their hands and said, "Amen! Amen!" Then they bowed down and worshiped the Lord with their faces to the ground.

⁷These Levites taught the people the Teachings as they stood there: Jeshua, Bani, Sherebiah, Jamin, Akkub, Shabbethai, Hodiah, Maaseiah, Kelita, Azariah, Jozabad, Hanan and Pelaiah. ⁸They read the Book of the Teachings of God. They read so the people could understand. And they explained what it meant. Then the people understood what was being read.

⁹Then Nehemiah the governor and Ezra the priest and teacher spoke up.

And the Levites who were teaching spoke up. They said to all the people, "This is a holy day to the Lord your God. Don't be sad or cry." All the people had been crying as they listened to the words of the Teachings.

[10]Nehemiah said, "Go and enjoy good food and sweet drinks. Send some to people who have none. Today is a holy day to the Lord. Don't be sad. The joy of the Lord will make you strong."

[11]The Levites helped calm the people. They said, "Be quiet. This is a holy day. Don't be sad."

[12]Then all the people went away to eat and drink. They sent some of their food to others. And they celebrated with great joy. They finally understood what they had been taught.

[13]On the second day of the month, the leaders of all the families met with Ezra the teacher. The priests and Levites also met with him. They gathered to study the words of the Teachings. [14]This is what they found written in the Teachings: The Lord had commanded through Moses that the people of Israel were to live in shelters. This was during the feast of the seventh month. [15]The people were supposed to preach this message. They were to spread it through all of their towns and in Jerusalem: "Go out into the mountains. Bring back branches from olive and wild olive trees, myrtle trees, palms and shade trees. Make shelters with them. It is written in the Law."

[16]So the people went out and got tree branches. They built shelters on their roofs[n] and in their courtyards. They built shelters in the courtyards of the Temple.[d] And they built them in the square by the Water Gate and the square next to the Gate of Ephraim. [17]The whole group that had come back from captivity built shelters. And they lived in them. The Israelites had not done this since the time of Joshua son of Nun. And they were very happy.

[18]Ezra read to them from the Book of the Teachings. He read every day, from the first day to the last. The people of Israel celebrated the feast for seven days. Then on the eighth day the people gathered as the law said.

ISRAEL CONFESSES SINS

9 It was on the twenty-fourth day of that same month. The people of Israel gathered together. They did not eat. And they put on rough cloth and put dust on their heads. This was to show their sadness. [2]Those people whose ancestors were from Israel had separated themselves from all foreigners. They stood and confessed their sins and their ancestors' sins. [3]For a fourth of the day they stood where they were. And they read from the Book of the Teachings of the Lord their God. Then they spent another fourth of the day confessing their sins. And they worshiped the Lord their God. [4]These Levites were standing on the stairs: Jeshua, Bani, Kadmiel, Shebaniah, Bunni, Sherebiah, Bani and Kanani. They called out to the Lord their God with loud voices. [5]And these Levites spoke: Jeshua, Kadmiel, Bani, Hashabneiah, Sherebiah, Hodiah, Shebaniah and Pethahiah. They said, "Stand up and praise the Lord your God. He lives forever and ever."

THE PEOPLE'S PRAYER

"Blessed be your wonderful name.
    It is more wonderful than all
        blessing and praise.
  [6]You are the only Lord.
    You made the heavens, even the
        highest heavens.
    You made all the stars.
  You made the earth and everything
    that is on it.

8:16 roofs In Bible times houses were built with flat roofs. The roof was used for drying things such as flax and fruit. And it was used as an extra room, as a place for worship and as a place to sleep in the summer.

You made the seas and everything
that is in them.
You give life to everything.
The heavenly army worships you.

⁷"You are the Lord God.
You chose Abram.
You brought him out of Ur of the
Babylonians.
You named him Abraham.
⁸You found that he was faithful to you.
So you made an agreement with
him.
You promised to give his
descendants*d* the land of the
Canaanites,
Hittites, Amorites,
Perizzites, Jebusites and
Girgashites.
You have kept your promise.
You are fair.

⁹"You saw our ancestors suffering in
Egypt.
You heard them cry out at the Red
Sea.*d*
¹⁰You did signs and miracles*d* against
the king of Egypt.
And you did them against all his
officers and all the people of
Egypt.
You knew how proud they were.
You made everyone know your name.
And it is still known today.
¹¹You divided the sea in front of our
ancestors.
They walked through it on dry
ground.
But you threw the people chasing
them into the deep water.
They were like a stone being thrown
into mighty waters.
¹²You led our ancestors with a pillar of
cloud in the daytime.
And you led them with a pillar of
fire at night.
It lit the way
they were supposed to go.
¹³You came down to Mount Sinai.

You talked to our ancestors from
heaven.
You gave them fair rules and true
teachings.
You gave them good orders and
commands.
¹⁴You told them about your holy
Sabbath.*d*
You gave commands, orders and
teachings to them
through your servant Moses.
¹⁵When they were hungry, you gave
them bread from heaven.
When they were thirsty, you
brought them water from the
rock.
You told them to go into the land and
take it over.
You had promised to give it to
them.

¹⁶"But our ancestors were proud and
stubborn.
They did not obey your commands.
¹⁷They refused to listen.
They forgot the miracles*d* you did
for them.
They became stubborn and turned
against you.
They chose a leader to lead them
back to their slavery.
But you are a forgiving God.
You are kind and full of mercy.
You do not become angry quickly.
And you have great love.
So you did not leave them.
¹⁸Our ancestors even made an idol of a
calf for themselves.
They said, 'This is your god, Israel.
It brought you up out of Egypt.'
They spoke against you.

¹⁹"You have great mercy.
So you did not leave them in the
desert.
During the day the pillar of cloud
guided them on their way.
And the pillar of fire led them at
night.

It lit the way they were supposed
to go.
20You gave your good Spirit^d to teach
them.
You gave them manna^d to eat.
And you gave them water when
they were thirsty.
21You took care of them for 40 years
in the desert.
They needed nothing.
Their clothes did not wear out.
And their feet did not swell.

22"You gave them kingdoms and
nations.
You gave them more land.
They took over the country of Sihon
king of Heshbon.
And they took over the country of
Og king of Bashan.
23You made their children as many as
the stars in the sky.
And you brought them into the
land.
This was where you had told their
ancestors to enter and take over.
24So their children went into the land
and took over.
The Canaanites lived there.
But you defeated them for our
ancestors.
You handed over to them the
Canaanites, their kings and the
people of the land.
Our ancestors could do what they
wanted with them.
25Our ancestors captured strong, walled
cities and fertile land.
They took over houses full of good
things.
They took over wells that were already
dug.
They took vineyards, olive trees and
many fruit trees.
They ate until they were full and
became fat.
They enjoyed your great goodness.

26"But they were disobedient and
turned against you.
They ignored your teachings.
Your prophets^d warned them to come
back to you.
But they killed those prophets.
And they spoke against you.
27So you allowed their enemies to defeat
them.
Their enemies treated them badly.
But in this time of trouble our
ancestors cried out to you.
And you heard from heaven.
You had great mercy.
You gave them saviors who saved
them from the power of their
enemies.
28But as soon as they had rest,
they again did what was evil.
So you left them to their enemies
who ruled over them.
But they cried out to you again.
And you heard from heaven.
Because of your mercy, you saved
them again and again.
29You warned them to return to obeying
your teachings.
But they were proud. They did not
obey your commands.
If a man obeys your laws, he will live.
But they sinned against your laws.
They were stubborn and disobedient.
They would not listen.
30You were patient with them for many
years.
You warned them by your Spirit
through the prophets.
But they did not pay attention.
So you allowed them to be defeated
by other countries.
31But because your mercy is great, you
did not kill them all.
You did not leave them.
You are a kind and merciful God.

32"And so, our God, you are the great
and mighty and wonderful God.
You keep your agreement of love.

Do not let all our trouble seem
　　unimportant in your eyes.
This trouble has come to us, to our
　　kings and to our leaders.
It has come to our priests and
　　prophets.
It has come to our ancestors and all
　　your people.
This trouble has come to us since the
　　days of the kings of Assyria.
And it has lasted until today.
33You have been fair in everything that
　　has happened to us.
You have been loyal, but we have
　　been wicked.
34Our kings, leaders, priests and
　　ancestors did not obey your
　　teachings.
They did not pay attention to the
　　commands and warnings you
　　gave them.
35Even when our ancestors were living
　　in their kingdom,
they did not serve you.
They were enjoying all the good
　　things you had given them.
They were enjoying the land that
　　was fertile and full of room.
But they did not stop their evil
　　ways.
36"Look, we are slaves today
　　in the land you gave our ancestors.
They were to enjoy its fruit and its
　　good things.
But look, we are slaves here.
37The land's great harvest belongs to the
　　kings you have put over us.
This is because of our sins.
Those kings rule over us and our
　　cattle as they please.
And we are in much trouble.

THE PEOPLE'S AGREEMENT

38"Because of all this, we are making
an agreement in writing. Our leaders, Levites and priests are putting their seals*d*
on it."

10 These are the men who sealed
the agreement:

Nehemiah the governor, son of Hacaliah, sealed it.

These men also sealed it: Zedekiah,
2Seraiah, Azariah, Jeremiah, 3Pashhur,
Amariah, Malkijah, 4Hattush, Shebaniah,
Malluch, 5Harim, Meremoth, Obadiah,
6Daniel, Ginnethon, Baruch, 7Meshullam,
Abijah, Mijamin, 8Maaziah, Bilgai and
Shemaiah. These are the priests.

9These are the Levites who sealed it:
Jeshua son of Azaniah, Binnui of the
sons of Henadad, Kadmiel, 10and their
fellow Levites: Shebaniah, Hodiah,
Kelita, Pelaiah, Hanan, 11Mica, Rehob,
Hashabiah, 12Zaccur, Sherebiah, Shebaniah, 13Hodiah, Bani and Beninu.

14These are the leaders of the people
who sealed the agreement: Parosh,
Pahath-Moab, Elam, Zattu, Bani, 15Bunni,
Azgad, Bebai, 16Adonijah, Bigvai, Adin,
17Ater, Hezekiah, Azzur, 18Hodiah,
Hashum, Bezai, 19Hariph, Anathoth,
Nebai, 20Magpiash, Meshullam, Hezir,
21Meshezabel, Zadok, Jaddua, 22Pelatiah,
Hanan, Anaiah, 23Hoshea, Hananiah,
Hasshub, 24Hallohesh, Pilha, Shobek,
25Rehum, Hashabnah, Maaseiah, 26Ahiah,
Hanan, Anan, 27Malluch, Harim and
Baanah.

28The rest of the people took an oath.
They were the priests, Levites, gatekeepers, singers and Temple*d* servants.
And they were all those who separated
themselves from foreigners to keep the
Teachings of God. It was also their wives
and their sons and daughters who could
understand. 29They joined their fellow
Israelites and their leading men. They
took an oath, which was tied to a curse in
case they broke the oath. They promised
to follow the Teachings of God, which
they had been given through Moses the
servant of God. These people also promised to obey all the commands, rules and
laws of the Lord our Master.

[30]They said:

We promise not to let our daughters marry foreigners. And we promise not to let our sons marry their daughters. [31]The foreigners might bring goods or grain to sell on the Sabbath.[d] But we will not buy on the Sabbath day or any holy day. Every seventh year we will not plant. And that year we will forget all that people owe us.

[32]We will be responsible for obeying the commands. We will pay for the service of the Temple of our God. We will give an eighth of an ounce of silver each year. [33]It is to pay for the bread that is set out on the table. It is to pay for the regular grain offerings and burnt offerings. It is for the offerings on the Sabbaths, New Moon[d] festivals and special feasts. It is for the holy offerings. And it is for the offerings to remove the sins of the Israelites so they will belong to God. It is for the work of the Temple of our God.

[34]We are the priests, the Levites and the people. We have thrown lots[d] to decide when each family must bring wood to the Temple. This is to be done at certain times each year. The wood is for burning on the altar of the Lord our God. We will do this as it is written in the Teachings.

[35]We also will bring the first fruits from our crops. And we will bring the first fruits of every tree to the Temple each year.

[36]We will bring our firstborn[d] sons and cattle to the Temple. We will bring the firstborn of our herds and flocks. We will do this as it is written in the Teachings. We will bring them to the priests who are serving in the Temple.

[37]We will bring things to the priests at the storerooms of the Temple. We will bring the first of our ground meal, our offerings, the fruit from all our trees and our new wine and oil. And we will bring a tenth of our crops to the Levites. The Levites will collect these things in all the towns where we work. [38]A priest of Aaron's family must be with the Levites when they receive the tenth of the people's crops. The Levites must bring a tenth of all they receive to the Temple of our God. Then they will put it in the storerooms of the treasury. [39]The people of Israel and the Levites are to bring their gifts to the storerooms. These are the gifts of grain, new wine and oil. The things for the Temple are kept in the storerooms. It is also where the priests, who are serving, the gatekeepers and singers stay.

We will not ignore the Temple of our God.

NEW PEOPLE MOVE INTO JERUSALEM

11 The leaders of Israel lived in Jerusalem. The rest of the people threw lots.[d] One person out of every ten was to come and live in Jerusalem. It was the holy city. The other nine could stay in their own cities. [2]The people blessed those who volunteered to live in Jerusalem.

[3]These are the area leaders who lived in Jerusalem. (Some people lived on their own land in the cities of Judah. These included Israelites, priests, Levites, Temple servants and descendants[d] of Solomon's servants. [4]Others from the families of Judah and Benjamin lived in Jerusalem.)

These are descendants of Judah who moved into Jerusalem. There was Athaiah son of Uzziah. (Uzziah was the son of Zechariah, who was the son of Amariah. Amariah was the son of Shephatiah, who was the son of Mahalalel. Mahalalel was a descendant of Perez.) [5]There was also Masseiah son of Baruch. (Baruch was the son of Col-Hozeh, who was the son of Hazaiah. Hazaiah was the son of Adaiah, who was the son of Joiarib. Joiarib was the son of Zechariah, who was a descendant of Shelah.) [6]All the descendants of Perez who lived in Jerusalem totaled 468 men. They were soldiers.

⁷These are descendants of Benjamin who moved into Jerusalem. There was Sallu son of Meshullam. (Meshullam was the son of Joed, who was the son of Pedaiah. Pedaiah was the son of Kolaiah, who was the son of Maaseiah. Maaseiah was the son of Ithiel, who was the son of Jeshaiah.) ⁸Following him were Gabbai and Sallai. All together there were 928 men. ⁹Joel son of Zicri was appointed over them. And Judah son of Hassenuah was second in charge of the new area of the city.

¹⁰These are the priests who moved into Jerusalem. There was Jedaiah son of Joiarib, Jakin ¹¹and Seraiah son of Hilkiah. (Hilkiah was the son of Meshullam, who was the son of Zadok. Zadok was the son of Meraioth, who was the son of Ahitub. Seraiah was the supervisor in the Temple.) ¹²And there were others with them who did the work for the Temple. All together there were 822 men. Also there was Adaiah son of Jeroham. (Jeroham was the son of Pelaliah, who was the son of Amzi. Amzi was the son of Zechariah, who was the son of Pashhur. Pashhur was the son of Malkijah.) ¹³And there were family heads with him. All together there were 242 men. Also there was Amashsai son of Azarel. (Azarel was the son of Ahzai, who was the son of Meshillemoth. Meshillemoth was the son of Immer.) ¹⁴And there were brave men with Amashsai. All together there were 128 men. Zabdiel son of Haggedolim was appointed over them.

¹⁵These are the Levites who moved into Jerusalem. There was Shemaiah son of Hasshub. (Hasshub was the son of Azrikam, who was the son of Hashabiah. Hashabiah was the son of Bunni.) ¹⁶And there were Shabbethai and Jozabad. They were two of the leaders of the Levites. They were in charge of the work outside the Temple. ¹⁷There was Mattaniah son of Mica. (Mica was the son of Zabdi, who was the son of Asaph.) Mattaniah was the director. He led the people in thanksgiving and prayer. There was Bakbukiah, who was second in charge over his fellow Levites. And there was Abda son of Shammua. (Shammua was the son of Galal, who was the son of Jeduthun.) ¹⁸All together 284 Levites lived in the holy city of Jerusalem.

¹⁹These are the gatekeepers who moved into Jerusalem. There were Akkub, Talmon and others with them. There was a total of 172 men. They guarded the city gates.

²⁰The other Israelites, priests and Levites lived on their own land. They were in all the cities of Judah.

²¹The Temple servants lived on the hill of Ophel. Ziha and Gishpa were in charge of them.

²²Uzzi son of Bani was appointed over the Levites in Jerusalem. (Bani was the son of Hashabiah, who was the son of Mattaniah. Mattaniah was the son of Mica.) Uzzi was one of Asaph's descendants. They were the singers. They were responsible for the service of the Temple. ²³The singers took orders from the king. Those orders told the singers what to do each day.

²⁴Pethahiah son of Meshezabel was the king's spokesman. Meshezabel was a descendant of Zerah, the son of Judah.

²⁵Some of the people of Judah lived in villages with their surrounding fields. Some lived in Kiriath Arba and its surroundings. Some lived in Dibon and its surroundings. Some lived in Jekabzeel and its surroundings. ²⁶Others lived in Jeshua, Moladah, Beth Pelet, ²⁷Hazar Shual, Beersheba and its surroundings. ²⁸Others were in Ziklag and Meconah and its surroundings. ²⁹Some people lived in En Rimmon, Zorah, Jarmuth, ³⁰Zanoah, Adullam and their villages. Some were in Lachish and the fields around it. Some lived in Azekah and its surroundings. So they settled from Beersheba all the way to the Valley of Hinnom.

³¹The descendants of the Benjaminites from Geba lived in Micmash, Aija, Bethel and its surroundings. ³²They lived in Anathoth, Nob, Ananiah, ³³Hazor, Ramah and Gittaim. ³⁴They lived in Hadid, Zeboim, Neballat, ³⁵Lod, Ono and in the Valley of the Craftsmen.

³⁶Some groups of the Levites from Judah settled in the land of Benjamin.

PRIESTS AND LEVITES

12 These are the priests and Levites who returned with Zerubbabel son of Shealtiel and with Jeshua. There were Seraiah, Jeremiah, Ezra, ²Amariah, Malluch, Hattush, ³Shecaniah, Rehum, Meremoth, ⁴Iddo, Ginnethon, Abijah, ⁵Mijamin, Moadiah, Bilgah, ⁶Shemaiah, Joiarib, Jedaiah, ⁷Sallu, Amok, Hilkiah and Jedaiah. They were the leaders of the priests and their relatives. This was in the days of Jeshua.

⁸The Levites were Jeshua, Binnui, Kadmiel, Sherebiah, Judah and also Mattaniah. He and his relatives were in charge of the songs of thanksgiving. ⁹Bakbukiah and Unni, their relatives, stood across from them in the services.

¹⁰Jeshua was the father of Joiakim. Joiakim was the father of Eliashib. Eliashib was the father of Joiada. ¹¹Joiada was the father of Jonathan. And Jonathan was the father of Jaddua.

¹²In the days of Joiakim, these priests were the leaders of the families of priests. Meraiah was over Seraiah's family. Hananiah was over Jeremiah's family. ¹³Meshullam was over Ezra's family. Jehohanan was over Amariah's family. ¹⁴Jonathan was over Malluch's family. Joseph was over Shecaniah's family. ¹⁵Adna was over Harim's family. Helkai was over Meremoth's family. ¹⁶Zechariah was over Iddo's family. Meshullam was over Ginnethon's family. ¹⁷Zicri was over Abijah's family. Piltai was over Miniamin's and Moadiah's families. ¹⁸Shammua was over Bilgah's family. Jehonathan was over Shemaiah's family.

¹⁹Mattenai was over Joiarib's family. Uzzi was over Jedaiah's family. ²⁰Kallai was over Sallu's family. Eber was over Amok's family. ²¹Hashabiah was over Hilkiah's family. Nethanel was over Jedaiah's family.

²²The leaders of the families of the Levites and the priests were written down. This was in the days of Eliashib, Joiada, Johanan and Jaddua. They were written down while Darius the Persian was king. ²³The family leaders among the Levites were written down in the history book. These were only up to the time of Johanan son of Eliashib. ²⁴The leaders of the Levites were Hashabiah, Sherebiah, Jeshua son of Kadmiel and their relatives. Their relatives stood across from them. They gave praise and thanksgiving to God. One group answered the other group. That is what David, the man of God, had commanded.

²⁵These were the gatekeepers who guarded the storerooms next to the gates: Mattaniah, Bakbukiah, Obadiah, Meshullam, Talmon and Akkub. ²⁶They served in the days of Joiakim son of Jeshua. (Jeshua was the son of Jozadak.) They also served in the days of Nehemiah the governor and Ezra the priest and teacher.

GIVING OF THE WALL OF JERUSALEM

²⁷The wall of Jerusalem was offered as a gift to God. The Levites were found in the places where they lived. And they were brought to Jerusalem to celebrate with joy the giving of the wall. They were to celebrate with songs of thanksgiving and with the music of cymbals, harps and lyres.ᵈ ²⁸They also brought together singers. They came from all around Jerusalem and from the Netophathite villages. ²⁹They came from Beth Gilgal and the areas of Geba and Azmaveth. The singers had built villages for themselves around Jerusalem. ³⁰The priests and Levites made themselves pure. They also made the people, the gates and the wall of Jerusalem pure.

³¹I had the leaders of Judah go up on top of the wall. I appointed two large choruses to give thanks. One chorus went to the right on top of the wall. This was toward the Trash Gate. ³²Behind them went Hoshaiah and half the leaders of Judah. ³³Azariah, Ezra, Meshullam, ³⁴Judah, Benjamin, Shemaiah and Jeremiah also went. ³⁵Some priests with trumpets also went, along with Zechariah son of Jonathan. (Jonathan was the son of Shemaiah, who was the son of Mattaniah. Mattaniah was the son of Micaiah, who was the son of Zaccur. Zaccur was the son of Asaph.) ³⁶Zechariah's relatives also went. They were Shemaiah, Azarel, Milalai, Gilalai, Maai, Nethanel, Judah and Hanani. These men played the musical instruments of David, the man of God. Ezra the teacher walked in front of them. ³⁷They went from the Fountain Gate straight up the steps to the older part of the city. They went on to the slope of the wall. They went above the house of David to the Water Gate on the east.

³⁸The second chorus went to the left. I followed them on top of the wall. Half the people were with me. We went from the Tower of the Ovens to the Broad Wall. ³⁹We went over the Gate of Ephraim to the Old Gate and the Fish Gate. We went to the Tower of Hananel and the Tower of the Hundred. We went as far as the Sheep Gate. We stopped at the Gate of the Guard.

⁴⁰The two choruses took their places at the Temple.ᵈ Half of the leaders and I did also. ⁴¹These priests were there with their trumpets: Eliakim, Maaseiah, Miniamin, Micaiah, Elioenai, Zechariah and Hananiah. ⁴²These people were also there: Maaseiah, Shemaiah, Eleazar, Uzzi, Jehohanan, Malkijah, Elam and Ezer. The choruses sang, led by Jezrahiah. ⁴³The people offered many sacrifices that day. They were happy because God made them very happy. The women and children were happy. The sound of happiness in Jerusalem could be heard far away.

⁴⁴At that time the leaders appointed men to be in charge of the storerooms. These rooms were for the gifts, the first fruits and a tenth of what the people gained. The Teachings said they should bring a share for the priests and Levites. These were to come from the fields around the towns. The people of Judah were happy to do this for the priests and Levites who served. ⁴⁵They performed the service of their God. They had the service of purifying things. The singers and gatekeepers also did their jobs as David had commanded his son Solomon. ⁴⁶Earlier, in the time of David and Asaph, there was a leader of the singers. There were songs of praise and thanksgiving to God. ⁴⁷So it was in the days of Zerubbabel and Nehemiah. All the people of Israel gave something to the singers and gatekeepers. They also set aside things for the Levites. The Levites set aside things for the descendantsᵈ of Aaron.

FOREIGN PEOPLE ARE SENT AWAY

13 On that day they read the Book of Moses to the people. They found that it said no Ammonite or Moabite should ever be allowed in the meeting to worship. ²The Ammonites and Moabites had not welcomed the Israelites with food and water. Instead, they hired Balaam to put a curse on Israel. (But our God turned the curse into a blessing.) ³The people heard this teaching. So they separated all foreigners from Israel.

NEHEMIAH RETURNS TO JERUSALEM

⁴Before that happened, Eliashib the priest was in charge of the Templeᵈ storerooms. He was friendly with Tobiah. ⁵Eliashib let Tobiah use one of the large storerooms. That storeroom had been used for grain offerings, incenseᵈ and other things for the Temple. It was also

used for the tenth offerings of grain, new wine and olive oil. These belonged to the Levites, singers and gatekeepers. It had also been used for gifts for the priests.

⁶I was not in Jerusalem when this happened. I had gone back to Artaxerxes king of Babylon. I went back in the thirty-second year he was king. Finally I asked the king to let me leave. ⁷I came to Jerusalem. Then I found out the evil thing Eliashib had done. He had let Tobiah have a room in the Temple courtyard. ⁸I was very upset at this. I threw all of Tobiah's goods out of the room. ⁹I ordered the rooms to be purified. And I brought back the things for God's Temple, the grain offerings and the incense.ᵈ

¹⁰Then I found out the people were not giving the Levites their shares. So the Levites and singers who served had gone to their own farms. ¹¹So I argued with the officers. I said, "Why haven't you taken care of the Temple?" Then I gathered the Levites and singers. I put them back at their places.

¹²Then all the people of Judah brought a tenth of what they had gained in grain, new wine and olive oil. And they brought it to the storerooms. ¹³I put these men in charge of the storerooms: Shelemiah the priest, Zadok the teacher and Pedaiah a Levite. I made Hanan son of Zaccur their helper. (Zaccur was the son of Mattaniah.) Everyone knew they were honest men. They gave out the portions that went to their relatives.

¹⁴Remember me, my God, for this. Do not ignore my love for the Temple and its service.

¹⁵In those days I saw people in Judah working in the winepressesᵈ on the Sabbathᵈ day. People were bringing in grain and loading it on donkeys on the Sabbath day. People were bringing loads of wine, grapes and figs into Jerusalem on the Sabbath day. I warned them about selling food on that day. ¹⁶Men from the city of Tyre were living in Jerusalem. They brought in fish and other things. They sold them in Jerusalem on the Sabbath day to the people of Judah. ¹⁷I argued with the important men of Judah. I said to them, "What is this evil thing you are doing? You are ruining the Sabbath day. ¹⁸This is just what your ancestors did. So our God did terrible things to us and this city. Now you are making him even more angry at Israel. You are ruining the Sabbath day."

¹⁹So I ordered the doors shut at sunset before the Sabbath. The gates were not to be opened until the Sabbath was over. I put my servants at the gates. So no load could come in on the Sabbath. ²⁰Once or twice traders and sellers of all kinds of goods spent the night outside Jerusalem. ²¹So I warned them. I said, "Why are you spending the night by the wall? If you do it again, I will force you away." After that, they did not come back on the Sabbath. ²²Then I ordered the Levites to purify themselves. I told them to go and guard the city gates. They were to make sure the Sabbath remained holy.

Remember me, my God, for this. Have mercy on me because of your great love.

²³In those days I saw men of Judah who had married women from Ashdod, Ammon and Moab. ²⁴Half their children were speaking the language of Ashdod or some other place. They couldn't speak the language of Judah. ²⁵I argued with those people. I put curses on them. I hit some of them and pulled out their hair. I forced them to make a promise to God. I said, "Do not let your daughters marry the sons of foreigners. Do not take the daughters of foreigners as wives for your sons or yourselves. ²⁶Foreign women made King Solomon of Israel sin. There was never a king like him in any of the nations. God loved Solomon. God made him king over all Israel. But foreign women made Solomon sin. ²⁷And now you are not obedient when you do this

evil thing. You are unfaithful to our God when you marry foreign wives."

²⁸Joiada was the son of Eliashib the high priest. One of Joiada's sons married a daughter of Sanballat the Horonite, who was not a Jew. So I forced Joiada's son away from me.

²⁹Remember them, my God. They made the priesthood unclean.ᵈ They made the agreement of the priests and Levites unclean.

³⁰So I purified them of everything that was foreign. I appointed duties for the priests and Levites. Each man had his own job. ³¹I also made sure wood was brought for the altar at regular times. And I made sure the first fruits were brought.

Remember, my God, to be kind to me.

ESTHER

QUEEN VASHTI DISOBEYS THE KING

1 This is what happened during the time of King Xerxes. He was the king who ruled the 127 areas from India to Cush. ²In those days King Xerxes ruled from his capital city of Susa. ³In the third year of his rule, he gave a banquet. It was for all his important men and royal officers. The army leaders from the countries of Persia and Media were there. And the important men from all Xerxes' empire were there.

⁴The banquet lasted 180 days. All during that time King Xerxes was showing off the great wealth of his kingdom. And he was showing his own honor and greatness. ⁵When the 180 days were over, the king gave another banquet. It was held in the courtyard of the palace garden for 7 days. It was for everybody in the palace at Susa, from the greatest to the least important. ⁶The courtyard had fine white curtains and purple drapes. These were tied to silver rings on marble pillars by white and purple cords. And there were gold and silver couches. These were on a floor set with tiles of white marble, shells and gems. ⁷Wine was served in gold cups of various kinds. And there was plenty of the king's wine because he was very generous. ⁸The king commanded that each guest be permitted to drink as much as he wished. He had told the wine servers to serve each man what he wanted.

⁹Queen Vashti also gave a banquet. It was for the women in the royal palace of King Xerxes.

¹⁰On the seventh day of the banquet, King Xerxes was very happy because he had been drinking much wine. He gave a command to the seven eunuchs*d* who served him. They were Mehuman, Biztha, Harbona, Bigtha, Abagtha, Zethar and Carcas. ¹¹He commanded them to bring him Queen Vashti, wearing her royal crown. She was to come to show her beauty to the people and important men. She was very beautiful. ¹²The eunuchs told Queen Vashti about the king's command. But she refused to come. Then the king became very angry. His anger was like a burning fire.

¹³It was a custom for the king to ask advice from experts about law and order. So King Xerxes spoke with the wise men. They would know the right thing to do. ¹⁴The wise men the king usually talked to were Carshena, Shethar, Admatha, Tarshish, Meres, Marsena and Memucan. They were seven of the important men of Persia and Media. These seven had special privileges to see the king. They had the highest rank in the kingdom.

¹⁵The king asked those men, "What does the law say must be done to Queen Vashti? She has not obeyed the command of King Xerxes, which the eunuchs took to her."

¹⁶Then Memucan spoke to the king and the other important men. He said, "Queen Vashti has not done wrong to the king alone. She has also done wrong to all the important men and all the people in all the empire of King Xerxes. ¹⁷All the wives of the important men of Persia and Media will hear about the queen's actions. Then they will no longer honor their husbands. They will say, 'King Xerxes commanded Queen Vashti to be brought to him. But she refused to come.' ¹⁸Today the wives of the important men of Persia and Media have heard about the queen's actions. And they will speak in the same way to their husbands. And there will be no end to disrespect and anger.

¹⁹"So, our king, if it pleases you, give a royal order. And let it be written in the laws of Persia and Media, which cannot be changed. The law should say Vashti is

never again to enter the presence of King Xerxes. Also let the king give her place as queen to someone who is better than she is. [20]And let the king's order be announced everywhere in his large kingdom. Then all the women will respect their husbands, from the greatest to the least important."

[21]The king and his important men were happy with this advice. So King Xerxes did as Memucan suggested. [22]He sent letters to all the areas of the kingdom. A letter was sent to each area, written in its own form of writing. And a letter was sent to each group of people, written in their own language. These letters announced that each man was to be the ruler of his own family. Also, each family was to speak the language of the man.

ESTHER IS MADE QUEEN

2 Later, King Xerxes was not so angry. Then he remembered Vashti and what she had done. And he remembered his order about her. [2]Then the king's personal servants had a suggestion. They said, "Let a search be made for beautiful young virgins[d] for the king. [3]Let the king choose supervisors in every area of his kingdom. Let them bring every beautiful young virgin to the palace at Susa. These women should be taken to the women's quarters and put under the care of Hegai. He is the king's eunuch[d] in charge of the women. And let beauty treatments be given to them. [4]Then let the girl who most pleases the king become queen in place of Vashti." The king liked this advice. So he did as they said.

[5]Now there was a Jewish man in the palace of Susa. His name was Mordecai son of Jair. Jair was the son of Shimei. And Shimei was the son of Kish. Mordecai was from the tribe[d] of Benjamin. [6]Mordecai had been taken captive from Jerusalem by Nebuchadnezzar king of Babylon. Mordecai was part of the group taken into captivity with Jehoiachin king of Judah. [7]Mordecai had a cousin named Hadassah, who had no father or mother. So Mordecai took care of her. Hadassah was also called Esther, and she had a very pretty figure and face. Mordecai had adopted her as his own daughter when her father and mother died.

[8]The king's command and order had been heard. And many girls had been brought to the palace in Susa. They had been put under the care of Hegai. When this happened, Esther was also taken to the king's palace. She was put into the care of Hegai, who was in charge of the women. [9]Esther pleased Hegai, and he liked her. So Hegai quickly began giving Esther her beauty treatments and special food. He gave her seven servant girls chosen from the king's palace. Then Hegai moved Esther and her seven servant girls to the best part of the women's quarters.

[10]Esther did not tell anyone about her family or who her people were. Mordecai had told her not to. [11]Every day Mordecai walked back and forth near the courtyard. This was where the king's women lived. He wanted to find out how Esther was and what was happening to her.

[12]Before a girl could take her turn with King Xerxes, she had to complete 12 months of beauty treatments. These were ordered for the women. For 6 months she was treated with oil and myrrh.[d] And she spent 6 months with perfumes and cosmetics. [13]Then she was ready to go to the king. Anything she asked for was given to her. She could take it with her from the women's quarters to the king's palace. [14]In the evening she would go to the king's palace. And in the morning she would return to another part of the women's quarters. There she would be placed under the care of a man named Shaashgaz. Shaashgaz was the king's eunuch in charge of the slave women.[d] The girl would not go back to the king again unless he was pleased

with her. Then he would call her by name to come back to him.

[15]Esther daughter of Abihail, Mordecai's uncle, had been adopted by Mordecai. The time came for Esther to go to the king. She asked for only what Hegai suggested she should take. (Hegai was the king's eunuch who was in charge of the women.) And everyone who saw Esther liked her. [16]So Esther was taken to King Xerxes in the royal palace. This happened in the tenth month, the month of Tebeth. It was in Xerxes' seventh year as king.

[17]And the king was pleased with Esther more than with any of the other virgins. And he liked her more than any of the others. So King Xerxes put a royal crown on Esther's head. And he made her queen in place of Vashti. [18]Then the king gave a great banquet for Esther. He invited all his important men and royal officers. He announced a holiday in all the empire. And he was generous and gave everyone a gift.

MORDECAI DISCOVERS AN EVIL PLAN

[19]Now Mordecai was sitting at the king's gate. This was when the virgins[d] were gathered the second time. [20]And Esther had still not told anyone about her family or who her people were. That is what Mordecai had told her to do. She still obeyed Mordecai just as she had done when he was bringing her up.

[21]Now Bigthana and Teresh were two of the king's officers who guarded the doorway. While Mordecai was sitting at the king's gate, Bigthana and Teresh became angry at the king. And they began to make plans to kill King Xerxes. [22]But Mordecai found out about their plans and told Queen Esther. Then Queen Esther told the king. She also told him that Mordecai had found out about the evil plan. [23]When the report was investigated, it was found to be true. The two officers who had planned to kill the king were hanged. And all this was written down in the daily court record in the king's presence.

HAMAN PLANS TO DESTROY THE JEWS

3 After these things happened, King Xerxes honored Haman son of Hammedatha the Agagite. He gave Haman a new rank that was higher than all the important men. [2]And all the royal officers at the king's gate would bow down and kneel before Haman. This was what the king had ordered. But Mordecai would not bow down, and he did not kneel.

[3]Then the royal officers at the king's gate asked Mordecai, "Why don't you obey the king's command?" [4]And they said this to him every day. When he did not listen to them, they told Haman about it. They wanted to see if Haman would accept Mordecai's behavior because Mordecai had told them that he was a Jew.

[5]Then Haman saw that Mordecai would not bow down to him or kneel before him. And he became very angry. [6]He had been told who the people of Mordecai were. And he thought of himself as too important to try to kill only Mordecai. So he looked for a way to destroy all of Mordecai's people, the Jews, in all of Xerxes' kingdom.

[7]It was in the first month of the twelfth year of King Xerxes' rule. That is the month of Nisan. Pur (that is, the lot[d]) was thrown before Haman. The lot was used to choose a day and a month. So the twelfth month, the month of Adar, was chosen.

[8]Then Haman said to King Xerxes, "There is a certain group of people in all the areas of your kingdom. They are scattered among the other people. They keep themselves separate. Their customs are different from those of all the other people. And they do not obey the king's laws. It is not right for you to allow them to continue living in your kingdom. [9]If it pleases the king, let an order be given to destroy those people.

Then I will pay 375 tons of silver to those who do the king's business. They will put it into the royal treasury."

¹⁰So the king took his signet*d* ring off and gave it to Haman. Haman son of Hammedatha, the Agagite, was the enemy of the Jews. ¹¹Then the king said to Haman, "The money and the people are yours. Do with them as you please."

¹²On the thirteenth day of the first month, the royal secretaries were called. They wrote out all of Haman's orders. They wrote to the king's governors and to the captains of the soldiers in each area. And they wrote to the important men of each group of people. The orders were written to each area in its own form of writing. And they were written to each group of people in their own language. They were written in the name of King Xerxes and sealed with his signet ring. ¹³Letters were sent by messengers to all the king's empire. They stated the king's order to destroy, kill and completely wipe out all the Jews. That meant young and old, women and little children, too. The order said to kill all the Jews on a single day. That was to be the thirteenth day of the twelfth month, which was Adar. And it said to take all the things that belonged to the Jews. ¹⁴A copy of the order was to be given out as a law in every area. It was to be made known to all the people so that they would be ready for that day.

¹⁵The messengers set out, hurried by the king's command. At the same time the order was given in the palace at Susa. And the king and Haman sat down to drink. But the city of Susa was in confusion.

MORDECAI ASKS ESTHER TO HELP

4 Now Mordecai heard about all that had been done. To show how upset he was, he tore his clothes. Then he put on rough cloth and ashes. And he went out into the city crying loudly and very sadly. ²But Mordecai went only as far as the king's gate. This was because no one

was allowed to enter that gate dressed in rough cloth. ³The king's order reached every area. And there was great sadness and loud crying among the Jews. They gave up eating and cried out loudly. Many Jews lay down on rough cloth and ashes to show how sad they were.

⁴Esther's servant girls and eunuchs*d* came to her and told her about Mordecai. Esther was very upset and afraid. She sent clothes for Mordecai to put on instead of the rough cloth. But he would not wear them. ⁵Then Esther called for Hathach. He was one of the king's eunuchs chosen by the king to serve her. Esther ordered him to find out what was bothering Mordecai and why.

⁶So Hathach went to Mordecai. Mordecai was in the city square in front of the king's gate. ⁷Then Mordecai told Hathach everything that had happened to him. And he told Hathach about the amount of money Haman had promised to pay into the king's treasury for the killing of the Jews. ⁸Mordecai also gave him a copy of the order to kill the Jews, which had been given in Susa. He wanted Hathach to show it to Esther and to tell her about it. And Mordecai told him to order Esther to go into the king's presence. He wanted her to beg for mercy and to plead with him for her people.

⁹Hathach went back and reported to Esther everything Mordecai had said. ¹⁰Then Esther told Hathach to say to Mordecai, ¹¹"All the royal officers and people of the royal areas know this: No man or woman may go to the king in the inner courtyard without being called. There is only one law about this. Anyone who enters must be put to death. But if the king holds out his gold scepter,*d* that person may live. And I have not been called to go to the king for 30 days."

¹²And Esther's message was given to Mordecai. ¹³Then Mordecai gave orders to say to Esther: "Just because you live in the king's palace, don't think that out of

all the Jews you alone will escape. [14]You might keep quiet at this time. Then someone else will help and save the Jews. But you and your father's family will all die. And who knows, you may have been chosen queen for just such a time as this."

[15]Then Esther sent this answer to Mordecai: [16]"Go and get all the Jews in Susa together. For my sake, give up eating. Do not eat or drink for three days, night and day. I and my servant girls will also give up eating. Then I will go to the king, even though it is against the law. And if I die, I die."

[17]So Mordecai went away. He did everything Esther had told him to do.

ESTHER SPEAKS TO THE KING

5 On the third day Esther put on her royal robes. Then she stood in the inner courtyard of the king's palace, facing the king's hall. The king was sitting on his royal throne in the hall, facing the doorway. [2]The king saw Queen Esther standing in the courtyard. When he saw her, he was very pleased. He held out to her the gold scepter[d] that was in his hand. So Esther went up to him and touched the end of the scepter.

[3]Then the king asked, "What is it, Queen Esther? What do you want to ask me? I will give you as much as half of my kingdom."

[4]Esther answered, "My king, if it pleases you, come today with Haman to a banquet. I have prepared it for you."

[5]Then the king said, "Bring Haman quickly so we may do what Esther asks."

So the king and Haman went to the banquet Esther had prepared for them. [6]As they were drinking wine, the king said to Esther, "Now, Esther, what are you asking for? I will give it to you. What is it you want? I will give you as much as half of my kingdom."

[7]Esther answered, "This is what I want and ask for. [8]My king, I hope you are pleased with me. If it pleases you,

give me what I ask for and do what I want. Come with Haman tomorrow to the banquet I will prepare for you. Then I will answer your question about what I want."

HAMAN'S PLANS AGAINST MORDECAI

[9]Haman left the king's palace that day happy and content. Then he saw Mordecai at the king's gate. And he saw that Mordecai did not stand up nor did he tremble with fear before him. So Haman became very angry with Mordecai. [10]But he controlled his anger and went home.

Then Haman called his friends and Zeresh, his wife, together. [11]And he told them about how wealthy he was and how many sons he had. He also told them about all the ways the king had honored him. And he told them how the king had placed him higher than his important men and his royal officers. [12]"And that's not all," Haman added. "I'm the only person Queen Esther invited to come with the king to the banquet she gave. And tomorrow also the queen has asked me to be her guest with the king. [13]But all this does not really make me happy. I'm not happy as long as I see that Jew Mordecai sitting at the king's gate."

[14]Then Haman's wife Zeresh and all his friends said, "Have a platform built to hang someone. Build it 75 feet high. And in the morning ask the king to have Mordecai hanged on it. Then go to the banquet with the king and be happy." Haman liked this suggestion. So he ordered the platform to be built.

MORDECAI IS HONORED

6 That same night the king could not sleep. So he gave an order for the daily court record to be brought in and read to him. [2]And it was found recorded that Mordecai had warned the king about Bigthana and Teresh. These men had planned to kill the king. They were two of the king's officers who guarded the doorway.

³Then the king asked, "What honor and reward have been given to Mordecai for this?"

The king's personal servants answered, "Nothing has been done for Mordecai."

⁴The king said, "Who is in the courtyard?" Now Haman had just entered the outer court of the king's palace. He had come to ask the king about hanging Mordecai on the platform he had prepared.

⁵The king's personal servants said, "Haman is standing in the courtyard."

So the king said, "Bring him in."

⁶So Haman came in. And the king asked him, "What should be done for a man that the king wants very much to honor?"

And Haman thought to himself, "Whom would the king want to honor more than me?" ⁷So he answered the king, "This is what you could do for the man you want very much to honor. ⁸Have the servants bring a royal robe that the king himself has worn. And also bring a horse with a royal crown on its head. The horse should be one the king himself has ridden. ⁹Then let the robe and the horse be given to one of the king's most important men. Let the servants put the robe on the man the king wants very much to honor. And let them lead him on the horse through the city streets. As they are leading him, let them announce: 'This is what is done for the man the king wants very much to honor!'"

¹⁰The king commanded Haman, "Go quickly. Take the robe and the horse just as you have said. And do all this for Mordecai the Jew who sits at the king's gate. Do not leave out anything that you have suggested."

¹¹So Haman took the robe and the horse. And he put the robe on Mordecai. Then he led him on horseback through the city streets. Haman announced before Mordecai: "This is what is done for the man the king wants very much to honor!"

¹²Then Mordecai went back to the king's gate. But Haman hurried home with his head covered. He was embarrassed and ashamed. ¹³He told his wife Zeresh and all his friends everything that had happened to him.

Haman's wife and the men who gave him advice said, "You are starting to lose power to Mordecai. Since he is a Jew, you cannot win against him. You will surely be ruined." ¹⁴While they were still talking, the king's eunuchs*d* came to Haman's house. They made Haman hurry to the banquet Esther had prepared.

HAMAN IS HANGED

7 So the king and Haman went in to eat with Queen Esther. ²They were drinking wine. And the king said to Esther on this second day also, "What are you asking for? I will give it to you. What is it you want? I will give you as much as half of my kingdom."

³Then Queen Esther answered, "My king, I hope you are pleased with me. If it pleases you, let me live. This is what I ask. And let my people live, too. This is what I want. ⁴I ask this because my people and I have been sold to be destroyed. We are to be killed and completely wiped out. If we had been sold as male and female slaves, I would have kept quiet. That would not be enough of a problem to bother the king."

⁵Then King Xerxes asked Queen Esther, "Who is he? Where is he? Who has done such a thing?"

⁶Esther said, "A man who is against us! Our enemy is this wicked Haman!"

Then Haman was filled with terror before the king and queen. ⁷The king was very angry. He got up, left his wine and went out into the palace garden. But Haman stayed inside to beg Queen Esther to save his life. He could see that the king had already decided to kill him.

⁸The king came back from the palace garden to the banquet hall. And he saw Haman falling on the couch where Esther

was lying. The king said, "Will he even attack the queen while I am in the house?"

As soon as the king said that, servants came in and covered Haman's face. [9]Harbona was one of the eunuchs[d] there serving the king. He said, "Look, a platform for hanging people stands near Haman's house. It is 75 feet high. This is the one Haman had prepared for Mordecai, who gave the warning that saved the king."

The king said, "Hang Haman on it!" [10]So they hanged Haman on the platform he had prepared for Mordecai. Then the king was not so angry anymore.

THE KING HELPS THE JEWS

8 That same day King Xerxes gave Queen Esther everything Haman had left when he died. Haman had been the enemy of the Jews. And Mordecai came in to see the king. He came because Esther had told the king how he was related to her. [2]Then the king took off his signet[d] ring, which he had taken back from Haman. And he gave it to Mordecai. Then Esther put Mordecai in charge of everything Haman had left when he died.

[3]Once again Esther spoke to the king. She fell at the king's feet and cried. She begged the king to stop the evil plan of Haman the Agagite. Haman had thought up the plan against the Jews. [4]The king held out the gold scepter[d] to Esther. Esther got up and stood in front of the king.

[5]She said, "My king, I hope you are pleased with me. And maybe it will please you to do this. You might think it is the right thing to do. And maybe you are happy with me. If so, let an order be written to cancel the letters Haman wrote. [6]I could not stand to see that terrible thing happen to my people. I could not stand to see my family killed."

[7]King Xerxes answered Queen Esther and Mordecai the Jew. He said, "Because Haman was against the Jews, I have

given his things to Esther. And my soldiers have hanged him. [8]Now write another order in the king's name. Write it to the Jews as it seems best to you. Then seal the order with the king's signet[d] ring. No letter written in the king's name and sealed with his signet ring can be canceled."

[9]At that time the king's secretaries were called. This was done on the twenty-third day of the third month, which is Sivan. The secretaries wrote out all of Mordecai's orders. They wrote to the Jews and to the governors and to the captains of the soldiers in each area. And they wrote to the important men of the 127 areas which reached from India to Cush. They wrote to each area in its own form of writing. And they wrote to each group of people in their own language. They also wrote to the Jews in their own form of writing and their own language. [10]Mordecai wrote orders in the name of King Xerxes. And he sealed the letters with the king's signet ring. Then he sent the king's orders by messengers on horses. The messengers rode fast horses, which were raised just for the king.

[11]These were the king's orders: The Jews in every city have the right to gather together to protect themselves. They have the right to destroy, kill and completely wipe out the army of any area or people who attack them. And they are to do the same to the women and children of that army. The Jews also have the right to take by force the property of the enemies. [12]The one day set for the Jews to do this was the thirteenth day of the twelfth month. This was the month of Adar. They were allowed to do this in all the empire of King Xerxes. [13]A copy of the king's order was to be sent out as a law in every area. It was to be made known to the people of every nation living in the kingdom. This was so the Jews would be ready on that set day. The Jews would be allowed to pay back their enemies.

[14]The messengers hurried out, riding on the royal horses. The king commanded those messengers to hurry. And the order was also given in the palace at Susa.

[15]Mordecai left the king's presence wearing royal clothes. They were blue and white. And he had on a large gold crown. He also had a purple robe made of the best linen. And the people of Susa shouted for joy. [16]It was a time of happiness, joy, gladness and honor for the Jews. [17]The king's order went to every area and city. And there was joy and gladness among the Jews. This happened in every area and city to which the king's order went. The Jews were having feasts and celebrating. And many people through all the empire became Jews. They did that because they were afraid of the Jews.

VICTORY FOR THE JEWS

9 The order the king had commanded was to be done on the thirteenth day of the twelfth month. That was the month of Adar. That was the day the enemies of the Jews had hoped to defeat them. But that was changed. So the Jews themselves defeated those who hated them. [2]The Jews met in their cities in all the empire of King Xerxes. They met in order to attack those who wanted to harm them. And no one was strong enough to fight against them. This was because all the other people living in the empire were afraid of the Jews. [3]And all the important men of the areas, the governors, captains of the soldiers, and the king's officers helped the Jews. They helped because they were afraid of Mordecai. [4]Mordecai was very important in the king's palace. He was famous in all the empire. This was because he was becoming a leader of more and more people.

[5]And, with their swords, the Jews defeated all their enemies, killing and destroying them. And the Jews did what they wanted with those people who hated

them. [6]In the palace at Susa, they killed and destroyed 500 men. [7]They also killed these men: Parshandatha, Dalphon, Aspatha, [8]Poratha, Adalia, Aridatha, [9]Parmashta, Arisai, Aridai and Vaizatha. [10]They were the ten sons of Haman, son of Hammedatha, the enemy of the Jews. But the Jews did not take their belongings.

[11]And on that day the number of the men killed in the palace at Susa was reported to the king. [12]The king said to Queen Esther, "The Jews have killed and destroyed 500 men in the palace at Susa. And they have also killed Haman's ten sons. What have they done in the rest of the king's empire! Now what else are you asking? I will do it! And what else do you want? It will be done."

[13]Esther answered, "If it pleases the king, give the Jews who are in Susa permission to do this. Let them do again tomorrow what the king ordered for today. And let the bodies of Haman's ten sons be hanged on the platform built for hanging people to death."

[14]So the king ordered that it be done. A law was given in Susa, and the bodies of the ten sons of Haman were hanged. [15]The Jews in Susa came together. It was on the fourteenth day of the month of Adar. And they killed 300 men in Susa. But they did not take their belongings.

[16]At that same time, the other Jews in the king's empire also met. They met in order to protect themselves and get rid of their enemies. And they killed 75,000 of those who hated them. But they did not take their belongings. [17]This happened on the thirteenth day of the month of Adar. And on the fourteenth day the Jews rested. They made it a day of joyful feasting.

THE FEAST OF PURIM

[18]But the Jews in Susa met on the thirteenth and fourteenth days of the month of Adar. Then they rested on the fifteenth day. They made it a day of joyful feasting.

¹⁹This is why the Jews who live in the country and small villages celebrate on the fourteenth day. They keep the fourteenth day of the month of Adar as a day of joyful feasting. And it is also a day for giving presents to each other.

²⁰Mordecai wrote down everything that had happened. Then he sent letters to all the Jews in all the empire of King Xerxes. He sent letters to places far and near. ²¹Mordecai did this to have the Jews celebrate every year. They were to celebrate on the fourteenth and fifteenth days of the month of Adar. ²²It was to celebrate a time when the Jews got rid of their enemies. They were also to celebrate it as the month their sadness was turned to joy. It was the month when their crying for the dead was turned into celebration. Mordecai wrote letters to all the Jews. He wrote to tell them to celebrate those days as days of joyful feasting. It was to be a time of giving food to each other. And it was a time of giving presents to the poor.

²³So the Jews agreed to do what Mordecai had written to them. And they agreed to hold the celebration every year. ²⁴Haman son of Hammedatha, the Agagite, was the enemy of all the Jews. He had made an evil plan against the Jews to destroy them. And Haman had thrown the pur (that is, the lot*d*) to choose a day to ruin and destroy the Jews. ²⁵But when the king learned of the evil plan, he sent out written orders. This was so the evil plans Haman had made against the Jews would be used against him. And those orders said that Haman and his sons should be hanged on the platform for hanging. ²⁶So these days were called Purim. The name Purim comes from the word "pur" (the lot). ²⁷And so the Jews set up this custom. They and their descendants*d* would celebrate these two days every year. The Jews and all those who join them are to celebrate these two days. They should do it without fail every year. They should do it in the right way and at the time Mordecai had ordered them in the letter. ²⁸These two days should be remembered and celebrated from now on in every family. And they must be celebrated in every area and every city. These days of Purim should never stop being celebrated by the Jews. And the descendants of the Jews should always remember to celebrate these two days of Purim.

²⁹So Queen Esther daughter of Abihail, along with Mordecai the Jew, wrote this second letter about Purim. Using the power they had, they wrote to prove the first letter was true. ³⁰And Mordecai sent letters to all the Jews in the 127 areas of the kingdom of Xerxes. Mordecai wrote a message of peace and truth. ³¹He wrote to set up these days of Purim. They are to be celebrated at their chosen times. Mordecai the Jew and Queen Esther had sent out the order for the Jews. They had set up for themselves and their descendants these two days. They set them up so the Jews would give up eating and cry loudly. ³²Esther's letter showed that these practices about Purim were correct. They were written down in the records.

THE GREATNESS OF MORDECAI

10 King Xerxes made people pay taxes. Even the cities far away on the seacoast had to pay taxes. ²And all the great things that Xerxes did are written down. They tell of his power and strength. They are written in the record books of the kings of Media and Persia. Also written in those record books are all the things that Mordecai did. The king had made Mordecai a great man. ³Mordecai the Jew was second in importance to King Xerxes. He was the most important man among the Jews. And his fellow Jews respected him very much. They respected Mordecai because he worked for the good of his people. And they respected him because he spoke up for the safety of all the Jews.

JOB

JOB, THE GOOD MAN

1 A man named Job lived in the land of Uz. He was an honest man and innocent of any wrong. He honored God and stayed away from evil. [2]Job had seven sons and three daughters. [3]He owned 7,000 sheep, 3,000 camels, 500 pairs of oxen and 500 female donkeys. And he had a large number of servants. He was the greatest man among all the people of the East.

[4]Job's sons took turns holding feasts in their homes. And they invited their sisters to eat and drink with them. [5]After a feast was over, Job would send and have them made clean.[d] Early in the morning Job would offer a burnt offering for each of them. He thought, "My children may have sinned and cursed God in their hearts." Job did this every time.

SATAN APPEARS BEFORE GOD

[6]One day the angels came to show themselves before the Lord. Satan[n] also came with them. [7]The Lord said to Satan, "Where have you come from?"

Satan answered the Lord, "I have been wandering around the earth. I have been going back and forth in it."

[8]Then the Lord said to Satan, "Have you noticed my servant Job? No one else on earth is like him. He is an honest man and innocent of any wrong. He honors God and stays away from evil."

[9]But Satan answered God, "Job honors God for a good reason. [10]You have put a wall around him, his family and everything he owns. You have blessed the things he has done. So his flocks of sheep and herds of cattle are large. They almost cover the land. [11]But reach out your hand and destroy everything he has. Then he will curse you to your face."

[12]The Lord said to Satan, "All right, then. Everything Job has is in your power. But you must not touch Job himself." Then Satan left the Lord's presence.

[13]One day Job's sons and daughters were eating and drinking wine together. They were at the oldest brother's house. [14]A messenger came to Job and said, "The oxen were plowing. And the donkeys were eating grass nearby. [15]And the Sabeans attacked and carried them away. They killed the servants with swords. And I am the only one who escaped to tell you!"

[16]The messenger was still speaking when another messenger came in. He said, "Lightning from God fell from the sky. It burned up the sheep and the servants. And I am the only one who escaped to tell you!"

[17]The second messenger was still speaking when another messenger came in. He said, "The Babylonians sent three groups of attackers. They swept down and stole your camels. They killed the servants. And I am the only one who escaped to tell you!"

[18]The third messenger was still speaking when another messenger came in. He said, "Your sons and daughters were eating and drinking wine together. They were at the oldest brother's house. [19]Suddenly a great wind came in from the desert. It struck all four corners of the house at once. The house fell in on your sons and daughters. And they are all dead. I am the only one who escaped to tell you!"

[20]When Job heard this, he got up. To show how sad he was he tore his robe and shaved his head. Then he bowed down to the ground to worship God. [21]He said:

"I was naked when I was born.
  And I will be naked when I die.

1:6 Satan Or "the accuser."

The Lord gave these things to me.
And he has taken them away.
Praise the name of the Lord."

[22]In all this Job did not sin. He did not blame God.

SATAN APPEARS BEFORE GOD AGAIN

2 On another day the angels came to show themselves before the Lord. And Satan also came with them. [2]The Lord said to Satan, "Where have you come from?"

Satan answered the Lord, "I have been wandering around the earth. I have been going back and forth in it."

[3]Then the Lord said to Satan, "Have you noticed my servant Job? No one else on earth is like him. He is an honest man, innocent of any wrong. He honors God and stays away from evil. You caused me to ruin him for no good reason. But he continues to be without blame."

[4]"One skin for another!" Satan answered. "A man will give all he has to save his own life. [5]But reach out your hand and destroy his own flesh and bones. Then he will curse you to your face."

[6]The Lord said to Satan, "All right, then. Job is in your power. But you must let him live."

[7]So Satan left the Lord's presence. And he put painful sores all over Job's body. They went from the top of his head to the soles of his feet. [8]Then Job took a piece of broken pottery. And he used it to scrape himself. He sat in ashes to show how upset he was.

[9]Job's wife said to him, "Are you still trying to stay innocent? You should just curse God and die!"

[10]Job answered, "You are talking like a foolish woman. Should we take only good things from God and not trouble?" In all this Job did not sin in what he said.

JOB'S THREE FRIENDS

[11]Now Job had three friends. They were Eliphaz the Temanite, Bildad the Shuhite and Zophar the Naamathite. These friends heard about the troubles that had happened to Job. So they agreed to meet and go see Job. They wanted to show him they were upset for him, too. And they wanted to comfort him. [12]They saw Job from far away. But he looked so different they almost didn't recognize him. They began to cry loudly. They tore their robes and put dirt on their heads to show how sad they were. [13]Then they sat on the ground with Job seven days and seven nights. No one said a word to him. This was because they saw how much he was suffering.

JOB CURSES HIS BIRTH

3 After seven days Job spoke. He cursed the day he had been born. [2]Job said:

[3]"Let the day I was born be destroyed.
And destroy the night when it was
said, 'A boy is born!'
[4]Let that day turn to darkness.
Let God not even care about it.
Don't let light shine on that day.
[5]Let darkness and gloom have that day.
Let a cloud hide that day.
Let darkness cover its light.
[6]Let thick darkness capture that night.
Don't count it among the days of
the year.
Don't put it in any of the months.
[7]Let that night be empty.
Let no shout of joy be heard in it.
[8]Let the people who curse days curse
that day.
They know how to wake up the sea
monster Leviathan.[d]
[9]Let that day's morning stars become
dark.
Let it wait for daylight, but don't let
it come.
Don't let it see the first light of
dawn.
[10]This is because it allowed me to be
born.

That day did not hide trouble from
my eyes.

11"Why didn't I die as soon as I was
born?
Why didn't I die when I came out of
the womb?
12Why did my mother's knees receive
me?
Why did my mother's breasts feed
me?
13If they had not been there, I would be
lying dead in peace.
I would be asleep and at rest.
14I would be asleep with kings and wise
men of the earth.
They built places for themselves
that are now ruined.
15I would be asleep with rulers who had
gold.
They filled their houses with silver!
16Or why was I not buried like a child
born dead?
I wish I were like a baby who never
saw the light of day.
17In the grave the wicked stop causing
trouble.
And people who are tired are at
rest.
18In the grave there is rest for the
captives.
They no longer hear the shout of
the slave driver.
19People great and small are in the
grave.
And the slave is freed from his
master.

20"Why is life given to those who are in
misery?
Why is it given to those who are so
unhappy?
21Some people want to die, but death
does not come.
They search for death more than for
hidden treasure.
22They are very happy
when they get to the grave.

23Life shouldn't be given to a man who
doesn't know what will happen
to him.
It shouldn't be given to a man who
feels trapped by God.
24I make sad sounds as I eat.
My groans pour out like water.
25The thing I was afraid of has
happened to me.
And the thing I dreaded has
happened.
26I have no peace. I have no quietness.
I have no rest. I only have trouble."

ELIPHAZ SPEAKS

4 Then Eliphaz the Temanite answered:

2"If someone tried to speak with you,
would you be upset?
I cannot keep from speaking.
3Think about how many people you
have taught.
Think about how you have made
weak hands strong.
4Your words have comforted those
who fell.
And you have given strength to
those who could not stand.
5But now trouble comes to you. And
you are discouraged.
Trouble hits you, and you are
terrified.
6You should trust in your respect for
God.
You should have hope because you
are innocent.

7"Think about this now: A person who
has not done wrong will not die.
Honest people were never
destroyed.
8I have noticed that people who plow
evil
and plant trouble harvest it.
9God's breath destroys them.
A blast of his anger kills them.
10The lions roar and growl.
But the teeth of great lions are
broken.

[11]The lion dies because he can't find an animal to eat.
So the cubs of the female lion are scattered.

[12]"A word was brought to me in secret.
My ears heard a whisper of it.
[13]It was during troublesome dreams in the night
when men are in deep sleep.
[14]I was shaking with fear.
All my bones were shaking.
[15]A spirit glided past my face.
The hair on my body stood up in fear.
[16]The spirit stopped,
but I could not see what it was.
A shape stood before my eyes.
And I heard a quiet voice.
[17]It said, 'Can a man be holy in the presence of God?
Can a man be pure before the one who made him?
[18]God does not trust his servants.
He even blames his angels for mistakes.
[19]So he puts even more blame on people who live in clay houses.[n]
The foundations of these houses are made of dust.
They can be crushed more easily than a moth.
[20]Between dawn and sunset they are broken to pieces.
They are not noticed. They die and are gone forever.
[21]The ropes of their tents are pulled up.
And they die without wisdom.'

5 "Call if you want to, but no one will answer you.
You can't turn to any of the holy ones.
[2]Foolish anger kills a person.
And jealousy kills a weak-minded person.

[3]I have seen a fool have success like a tree taking root.
But suddenly his home was destroyed.
[4]His children are far away from safety.
They are crushed in court with no one to defend them.
[5]Hungry people eat this fool's harvest.
They even take what grew up among the thorns.
And thirsty people want his wealth.
[6]Hard times do not come up from the ground.
And trouble does not grow from the earth.
[7]But man is born to have trouble as surely as sparks fly upward.

[8]"But if I were you, I would call on God.
I would bring my problem before him.
[9]God does wonderful things that cannot be understood.
He does so many miracles[d] they cannot be counted.
[10]God gives rain to the earth.
He sends water on the fields.
[11]God makes the humble person important.
He lifts to places of safety those who are sad.
[12]God ruins the plans of those who trick others.
Then they have no success.
[13]He catches wise men in their own clever traps.
And the plans of those who try to trick others are swept away.
[14]Darkness covers them up in the daytime.
At noon they feel around in the dark.
[15]God saves needy people from their lies.
He saves them from the harm done by powerful people.
[16]So the poor people have hope.

4:19 clay houses This is probably talking about people's bodies.

And those who are unfair are silenced.

17"The person whom God corrects is happy.
So do not hate being corrected by God All-Powerful.
18God hurts, but he also bandages up.
He injures, but his hands also heal.
19He will save you from six troubles.
Even seven troubles will not harm you.
20God will buy you back from death in times of hunger.
And in battle he will save you from death by the sword.
21You will be hidden from the tongue that hits like a whip.
You will not need to be afraid when destruction comes.
22You will laugh at destruction and hunger.
You do not need to fear the wild animals.
23This is because you will have an agreement with the animals born in the wild.
And the wild animals will be at peace with you.
24You will know that your tent is safe.
You will check the things you own and find nothing missing.
25You will know that you will have many children.
Your descendants^d will be as many as the blades of grass on the earth.
26You will come to the grave with all your strength.
You will be like bundles of grain gathered at the right time.
27"We have checked this, and it is true.
So hear it and decide what it means to you."

JOB ANSWERS ELIPHAZ

6 Then Job answered:

2"I wish my suffering could be weighed.
And I wish my misery could be put on the scales.
3My sadness would be heavier than the sand of the seas.
No wonder my words seem careless.
4The arrows of God All-Powerful are in me.
My spirit drinks in their poison.
God's terrors are gathered against me.
5A wild donkey does not bray when it has grass to eat.
An ox is quiet when it has feed.
6Tasteless food is not eaten without salt.
There is no flavor in the white part of an egg.
7I refuse to touch it.
Such food makes me sick.

8"How I wish I might have what I ask for.
How I wish God would give me what I hope for.
9I wish God would be willing to crush me
and reach out his hand to destroy me.
10Then I would have this comfort.
I would be glad even in this unending pain.
I would know I did not reject the words of the Holy One.

11"I do not have the strength to wait.
There is nothing to hope for so how can I be patient?
12I do not have the strength of stone.
My flesh is not bronze.
13I have no power to help myself.
This is because success has been taken away from me.

14"They say, 'A man's friends should be kind to him when he is in trouble.
This should be done even if he stops fearing God All-Powerful.'

¹⁵But my brothers cannot be counted
on.
They are like streams that do not
flow regularly,
streams that sometimes run over.
¹⁶They are like streams made dark by
melting ice,
that rise with melting snow.
¹⁷But they stop flowing when it is the
dry season.
They go away when it is hot.
¹⁸Groups of travelers turn away from
their paths.
They go into the desert and die.
¹⁹The groups of travelers from Tema
look for water.
The traders of Sheba who travel
look hopefully.
²⁰They are upset because they had been
sure.
But when they arrive, they are
disappointed.
²¹You also have been no help.
You see something terrible, and you
are afraid.
²²I have never said, 'Give me a gift.
Use your wealth to pay my debt.
²³Save me from the enemy's power.
Buy me back from the clutches of
cruel people.'

²⁴"Teach me, and I will be quiet.
Show me where I have been wrong.
²⁵Honest words are painful!
But your arguments prove nothing.
²⁶Do you mean to correct what I say?
Will you treat the words of a
troubled man as if they were only
wind?
²⁷You would even throw lots_d_ for
orphans.
And you would trade away your
friend.

²⁸"But now please look at me.
I would not lie to your face.
²⁹Change your mind. Do not be unfair.
Think again, because my innocence
is being questioned.

³⁰What I am saying is not wicked.
I can tell the difference between
right and wrong.

7 "Man has a hard task on earth.
His days are like those of a hired man.
²Man is like a slave wishing for the
evening shadows.
Or he is like a hired man who wants
his pay.
³But I am given months that are empty.
Nights of misery have been given to
me.
⁴When I lie down, I think, 'How long is
it until I get up?'
The night is long, and I toss until
dawn.
⁵My body is covered with worms and
scabs.
My skin is broken and full of
running sores.

⁶"My days go by faster than a weaver
moves his tool.
And they come to an end without
hope.
⁷Remember, God, that my life is only
as long as a breath.
My eyes will never see happy times
again.
⁸Those who see me now will see me no
more.
You will look for me, but I will be
gone.
⁹A cloud disappears and is gone.
In the same way, a person who goes
where the dead are does not
return.
¹⁰He will never come back to his house
again.
His place will not know him
anymore.

¹¹"So I will not stay quiet.
I will speak out in the suffering of
my spirit.
I will complain because I am so
unhappy.

¹²I am not the sea or the sea monster.
  So why have you set a guard over
  me?
¹³Sometimes I think my bed will
  comfort me.
  Or I think my couch will stop my
  complaint.
¹⁴Then you frighten me with dreams.
  You terrify me with visions.
¹⁵My throat prefers to be choked.
  My bones welcome death.
¹⁶I hate my life. I don't want to live
  forever.
  Let me alone. My days have no
  meaning.
¹⁷"Why do you make man so important?
  Why do you give him so much
  attention?
¹⁸Will you examine him every morning?
  Why do you test him every
  moment?
¹⁹Will you never look away from me?
  Will you not let me alone even long
  enough to swallow?
²⁰If I have sinned, what have I done to
  you,
  you watcher of men?
  Why have you made me your target?
  Have I become a heavy load for
  you?
²¹Why don't you pardon my wrongs
  and forgive my sins?
  I will soon lie down in the dust and
  die.
  You will search for me, but I will be
  no more."

BILDAD SPEAKS TO JOB

8 Then Bildad the Shuhite answered:

²"How long will you say such things?
  Your words are no more than a
  strong wind.
³God does not twist fairness.
  God All-Powerful does not make
  wrong what is right.
⁴Your children sinned against God.

And he punished them for their
  sins.
⁵But you should ask God for help.
  Pray to God All-Powerful for mercy.
⁶You must be good and honest.
  Then he will start doing something
  for you.
  And he will bring you back where
  you belong.
⁷The place you began will seem
  unimportant
  because your future will be so
  successful.

⁸"Ask old people
  and find out what their ancestors
  learned.
⁹We were only born yesterday and
  know nothing.
  Our days on earth are like only a
  shadow.
¹⁰Those people will teach you and tell
  you.
  They will tell you what they know.
¹¹Papyrus plants cannot grow tall where
  there is no wet land.
  Reeds cannot grow tall without
  water.
¹²While they are still growing and not
  yet cut,
  they will dry up more quickly than
  grass.
¹³That is what will happen to everyone
  who forgets God.
  The hope of the person without God
  will be gone.
¹⁴What he trusts in is easily broken.
  It is as easily broken as a spider's
  web.
¹⁵He leans on the spider's web, but it
  breaks.
  He holds on to it, but it does not
  hold him up.
¹⁶He is like a well-watered plant in the
  sunshine.
  The plant spreads its roots all
  through the garden.

[17]It wraps its roots around a pile of
  rocks.
  And it looks for a place among the
  stones.
[18]But the plant may be torn from its
  place.
  Then that place rejects it and says,
  'I never saw you.'
[19]Then its life dries up.
  And other plants grow up from the
  dirt in its place.

[20]"Surely God does not reject innocent
  men.
  He does not give strength to those
  who do evil.
[21]God will yet fill your mouth with
  laughter.
  And he will fill your lips with shouts
  of joy.
[22]Your enemies will be covered in shame.
  And the tents of the wicked will be
  gone."

JOB ANSWERS BILDAD

9 Then Job answered:

[2]"Yes, I know that this is true.
  But how can man be right in the
  presence of God?
[3]A person might want to argue with
  God.
  But he could not answer God one
  time out of a thousand.
[4]God's wisdom is deep, and his power
  is great.
  No one can fight God without being
  hurt.
[5]God moves mountains without
  anyone knowing it.
  He turns mountains over when he
  is angry.
[6]God shakes the earth out of its place.
  And he makes the earth's
  foundations shake.
[7]God commands the sun not to shine.
  He shuts off the light of the stars.

[8]God alone stretches out the skies.
  And he walks on the waves of the
  sea.
[9]It is God who made the Bear, Orion
  and the Pleiades[n]
  and the groups of stars in the
  southern sky.
[10]God does wonderful things that
  people cannot understand.
  He does so many miracles[d] they
  cannot be counted.
[11]When he passes me, I cannot see him.
  When he goes by me, I cannot
  recognize him.
[12]If God snatches something away, no
  one can stop him.
  No one can say to him, 'What are
  you doing?'
[13]God will not hold back his anger.
  Even the helpers of the monster
  Rahab[d] lie at God's feet in fear.
[14]So how can I argue with God?
  I cannot find words to argue with
  him.
[15]Even if I was right, I could not answer
  him.
  I could only beg God, my Judge, for
  mercy.
[16]I might call to him. But even if he
  answered,
  I still would not believe he would
  listen to me.
[17]God would crush me with a storm.
  He would multiply my hurts for no
  reason.
[18]He would not let me catch my breath.
  He would overwhelm me with
  misery.
[19]When it comes to strength, God is
  stronger than I.
  And when it comes to justice, no
  one can accuse him!
[20]Even if I were right, my own mouth
  would say I was wrong.
  If I were innocent, my mouth would
  say I was guilty.

9:9 Bear . . . Pleiades Names of well-known groups of stars.

21"I am innocent.
   But I don't think about myself.
   I hate my own life.
22It is all the same. That is why I say,
   'God destroys both the innocent
   and the evil people.'
23A whip may bring sudden death.
   And God will laugh when good
   people suffer.
24When land falls into the hands of evil
   people,
   God covers the judges' faces so they
   can't see it.
   If it is not God who does this, then
   who is it?

25"My days go by faster than a runner.
   They fly away without my seeing
   even a little joy.
26They glide past like boats made of
   papyrus plants.
   My days are like eagles that swoop
   down on animals they attack.
27I might say, 'I will forget my
   complaint.
   I will change the look on my face,
   and smile.'
28But I will still dread all my suffering.
   I know you will hold me guilty.
29I have already been found guilty.
   So why should I struggle for no
   reason?
30I might wash myself with soap.
   And I might even wash my hands
   with strong soap.
31But you would push me into a dirty
   pit.
   And even my clothes would hate
   me.

32"God is not a man like me. So I cannot
   answer him.
   We cannot meet each other in
   court.
33I wish there was someone to make
   peace between us.
   I wish someone could decide our
   case.

34I wish someone could remove God's
   punishment from me.
   Then his terror would not frighten
   me anymore.
35Then I could speak up without being
   afraid of God.
   But I am not able to do that.

10 "I hate my own life.
      So I will complain without
   holding back.
   And I will speak because I am so
   unhappy.
2I will say to God: Do not hold me
   guilty.
   But tell me what you have against
   me.
3Does it make you happy to trouble
   me?
   Don't you care about me, the work
   of your own hands?
   Are you happy with the plans of evil
   people?
4Do you have human eyes?
   Do you see as a man sees?
5Are your days like the days of man?
   Are your years like the years of a
   man?
6You look for evil I have done
   and search for my sin.
7But you know I am not guilty.
   And you know no one can save me
   from your power.

8"Your hands shaped me and made
   me.
   But now you turn around and
   destroy me.
9Remember that you molded me like a
   piece of clay.
   Now will you turn me back into
   dust?
10You formed me in my mother's womb
   as cheese is formed from milk.
11You put skin and flesh on me like
   clothing.
   You sewed me together with bones
   and muscles.

¹²You gave me life and showed me
　　kindness.
　　And in your care you watched over
　　　my life.

¹³"But in your heart you hid other plans.
　　I know this is what was in your
　　　mind:
¹⁴If I sinned, you would be watching me.
　　You would not let my sin go
　　　unpunished.
¹⁵How terrible it will be for me if I am
　　guilty!
　　But even if I am right, I cannot lift
　　　my head.
　I am full of shame.
　　It is as if I am drowning in my pain.
¹⁶If I hold up my head, you hunt me like
　　a lion.
　　And again you show your terrible
　　　power against me.
¹⁷You bring new witnesses against me.
　　You increase your anger against me.
　　Your armies come against me like
　　　waves of the sea.

¹⁸"So why did you allow me to be born?
　　I wish I had died before anyone saw
　　　me.
¹⁹I wish I had never been born.
　　Or I wish I had been carried straight
　　　from birth to the grave!
²⁰My few days of life are almost over.
　　Leave me alone so I can have a
　　　moment of joy.
²¹Soon I will leave and not return.
　　I will go to the land of darkness and
　　　gloom.
²²It is the land of darkest night.
　　It is the land of gloom and
　　　confusion.
　　Even the light is darkness there."

ZOPHAR SPEAKS TO JOB

11 Then Zophar the Naamathite
answered:

²"All these words should not go without
　　an answer.
　　Is this talker to be judged as right?

³Your talk should not make people be
　　quiet.
　　People should shame you when you
　　　make fun of God.
⁴You say to God, 'My teachings are
　　right.
　　And I am clean^d in God's sight.'
⁵I wish God would speak.
　　I wish he would open his lips to
　　　speak against you.
⁶I wish he would tell you the secrets of
　　wisdom.
　　This is because wisdom has two
　　　sides.
　Know this: God has even forgotten
　　some of your sin.

⁷"Can you understand the secrets of
　　God?
　　Can you search the limits of the God
　　　All-Powerful?
⁸God's limits are higher than the
　　heavens. You cannot reach them!
　　They are deeper than where the
　　　dead are. You cannot know
　　　them!
⁹His limits are longer than the earth
　　and wider than the sea.

¹⁰"God might come along and put you
　　in prison.
　　If he calls you into court, no one
　　　can stop him.
¹¹God knows which men are evil.
　　And when he sees evil, he notices it.
¹²A stupid person cannot become wise.
　　That is as impossible as a wild
　　　donkey being born tame.

¹³"You must give your whole heart to
　　him.
　　You must hold out your hands to
　　　him for help.
¹⁴Put away the sin that is in your hand.
　　Let no evil live in your tent.
¹⁵Then you can lift up your face without
　　shame.
　　You can stand strong without fear.
¹⁶You will forget your trouble.

You will remember your troubles
   only as water that has passed by.
17Your life will be as bright as the
   noonday sun.
   And darkness will seem like
      morning.
18You will feel safe because there is
      hope.
   You will look around and rest in
      safety.
19You will lie down, and no one will
   make you afraid.
   Many people will want favor from
      you.
20But the wicked people will not be able
      to see.
   So they will not be able to find the
      way to escape.
   Their only hope will be to die."

JOB ANSWERS ZOPHAR

12 Then Job answered:

2"You really think you are the only
   wise people.
   You think when you die wisdom
      will die with you.
3But my mind is as good as yours.
   You are not better than I am.
   Everyone knows all these things.
4My friends all laugh at me
   when I call on God and expect him
      to answer me.
   They laugh at me even though I am
      right and innocent!
5People who are comfortable don't care
      that others have trouble.
   They think that people who are in
      trouble should have more
      troubles.
6The tents of robbers are not bothered.
   Those who make God angry are
      safe.
   They have their god in their pocket.

7"But ask the animals, and they will
   teach you.
   Or ask the birds of the air, and they
      will tell you.

8Speak to the earth, and it will teach
   you.
   Or let the fish of the sea tell you.
9Every one of these knows
   that the hand of the Lord has done
      this.
10The life of every creature
   and the breath of all people are in
      God's hand.
11The ear tests words
   as the tongue tastes food.
12Older people are supposed to be wise.
   Long life is supposed to bring
      understanding.

13"But God has wisdom and power.
   He has good advice and
      understanding.
14What God tears down cannot be
      rebuilt.
   The man God puts in prison cannot
      be let out.
15If God holds back the waters, there is
   a time without rain.
   But if he lets the waters go, they
      flood the land.
16God is strong and victorious.
   Both the person who fools others
      and the one who is fooled belong
      to him.
17God leads wise men away as captives.
   He turns wise judges into fools.
18God takes the royal belt off of kings.
   And he dresses them like prisoners
      with only a cloth around their
      waist.
19He leads priests away as captives.
   He destroys the power of those who
      have been powerful.
20God makes trusted people be silent.
   And he takes away the wisdom of
      elders.
21God brings disgrace on important
      people.
   And he takes away the weapons of
      the strong.
22God uncovers the deep things of
      darkness.

He brings dark shadows into the
light.
23He makes nations great, and he
destroys them.
He makes nations large, and he
scatters them.
24He takes understanding away from
the leaders of the earth.
He makes them wander through a
desert with no paths.
25They feel around in darkness with no
light.
God makes them stumble around
like drunken people.

13

"My eyes have seen all this.
My ears have heard and
understood it.
2What you know, I also know.
You are not better than I am.
3But I want to speak to God
All-Powerful.
I want to argue my case with God.
4But you smear me with lies.
You are worthless doctors, all of
you!
5I wish you would just stop talking.
Then you would really be wise!
6Listen to my argument.
Hear my lips begging.
7You should not speak for God by
saying evil things.
You cannot speak God's truth by
telling lies.
8You should not unfairly choose his
side against mine.
You should not argue the case for
God.
9You will not do well if he examines
you.
You cannot fool God as you might
fool men.
10God would surely scold you
if you unfairly took one person's
side.
11His bright glory would scare you.

You would be very much afraid of
him.
12Your wise sayings are worth no more
than ashes.
Your arguments are as weak as clay.
13"Be quiet and let me speak.
Then let things happen to me as
they will.
14I will put myself in danger
and take my life in my own hands.
15He will kill me. I have no hope.[n]
But I still will defend my ways to his
face.
16This might really save me,
because a wicked man would not be
brave enough to come before
him.
17Listen carefully to what I say.
Let your ears hear what I say.
18See now, I have prepared my case.
I know I will be proved right.
19No one can blame me for doing wrong.
If someone can, I will be quiet and
die.
20"God, please just give me these two
things.
Then I will not hide from you.
21Take your punishment away from me.
And stop frightening me with your
terrors.
22Then call me, and I will answer.
Or let me speak and you answer.
23How many evil things and sins have I
done?
Show me my wrong and my sin.
24Don't hide your face from me.
Don't think of me as your enemy.
25Don't punish a leaf that is blown by
the wind.
Don't chase after dry chaff.[d]
26You write down cruel things against
me.
You make me suffer for sins I did
when I was young.
27You put my feet in chains.

13:15 He ... hope. Or "Even if God kills me, I will still put my hope in him."

You keep close watch on
everywhere I go.
And you mark the soles of my feet.
²⁸So man wears out like something
rotten.
He is like clothing that has been
eaten by moths.

14 "All of us born to women
live only a few days and have
a lot of trouble.
²We grow up like flowers and then dry
up and go away.
We are like a passing shadow that
does not last.
³Lord, do you need to watch someone
like this?
Do you need to bring him before
you to be judged?
⁴I wish something clean*d* could come
from something unclean.
But it never can!
⁵Our time is limited.
You have given us only so many
months to live.
You have set limits we cannot go
beyond.
⁶So look away from us and leave us
alone.
Leave us alone until we put in our
time like a hired man.

⁷"There is hope for a tree.
If you cut it down, it will grow
again.
It will keep sending out new
branches.
⁸Its roots may grow old in the ground.
And its stump may die in the dirt.
⁹But at the smell of water it will bud.
It will put out new shoots like a
plant.
¹⁰But we die, and our bodies are laid in
the ground.
We take our last breath and are
gone.
¹¹Water disappears from a lake.
And a river loses its water and dries
up.

¹²In the same way we lie down and do
not rise again.
We will not get up or be awakened
until the heavens disappear.
¹³"I wish you would hide me where the
dead are.
Hide me until your anger is gone.
I wish you would set a time
and then remember me!
¹⁴Will the dead live again?
I will wait, struggling hard
until things change for me.
¹⁵You will call, and I will answer you.
You will desire the creature your
hands have made.
¹⁶Then you will count my steps.
But you will not keep track of my
sin.
¹⁷My wrongs will be closed up in a bag.
And you will cover up my sin.

¹⁸"A mountain washes away and
crumbles.
And a rock can be moved from its
place.
¹⁹Water washes over stones and wears
them down.
And rushing waters wash away the
dirt.
In the same way, you destroy hope.
²⁰You defeat man forever, and he is
gone.
You change his appearance and
send him away.
²¹His sons are honored, but he does not
know it.
His sons are disgraced, but he does
not see it.
²²He only feels the pain of his body.
And he feels sorry only for himself."

ELIPHAZ ANSWERS JOB

15 Then Eliphaz the Temanite answered:

²"A wise man would not answer with
empty words.
He would not fill his stomach with
hot, east wind.

3He would not argue with useless
words.
He would not make speeches that
have no value.
4But you even break down the worship
of God.
You stand in the way of those who
pray to him.
5Your sin teaches your mouth what to
say.
You use the same words as people
who trick others.
6It is your own mouth, not mine, that
shows you are wicked.
Your own lips speak as a witness
against you.

7"You are not the first man ever born.
You were not born before the hills
were made.
8You cannot listen in on God's secret
advice.
You cannot limit wisdom to
yourself.
9You don't know any more than we
know.
You don't understand any more
than we understand.
10Old people with gray hair are on our
side.
They are men even older than your
father.
11The comfort God gives you is not
enough for you,
even when words are spoken gently
to you.
12Your heart has carried you away from
God.
Your eyes flash with anger.
13You speak out your anger against
God.
And these words pour out of your
mouth.

14"How can man be pure?
How can a person born to a woman
be good?
15God places no trust in his holy ones.

Even the heavens are not pure in
his eyes.
16And man is even less than they are.
He is terrible and rotten.
He drinks up evil as if it were water!

17"Job, listen to me, and I will tell you
about it.
I will tell you what I have seen.
18These are things wise men have told.
Their ancestors told them these
things, and they have hidden
nothing.
19(The land was given to their fathers
only.
No foreigner lived among them.)
20The evil man suffers pain all his life.
The cruel man suffers during all the
years saved up for him.
21Terrible sounds fill his ears.
When things seem to be going well,
robbers attack him.
22The evil person gives up trying to
escape from the darkness.
It has been decided that he will die
by the sword.
23He wanders around. He will become
food for vultures.
He knows death will soon come.
24Worry and suffering terrify him.
They overwhelm him. They seem
like a king ready to attack.
25This is because he shakes his fist at
God.
He tries to get his own way against
God All-Powerful.
26He stubbornly charges at God
with a thick, strong shield.

27"The evil person's face is covered with
fat.
His waist is fat with flesh.
28He will live in towns that are ruined.
He will live in houses where no one
lives.
They are houses that are crumbling
into ruins.
29The evil person will no longer get rich.
And the riches he has will not last.

The things he owns will no longer
spread over the land.
³⁰He will not escape the darkness.
A flame will dry up his branches.
God's breath will carry that evil
person away.
³¹The evil person should not fool
himself by trusting what is
useless.
If he does, he will get nothing in
return.
³²His branch will dry up before it
finishes growing.
It will not even become green.
³³He will be like a vine whose grapes are
pulled off before they are ripe.
He will be like an olive tree that
loses its blossoms.
³⁴People without God can produce
nothing.
Fire will destroy the tents of people
who take money to do evil.
³⁵They plan trouble and give birth to
evil.
Their hearts plan ways to trick
people."

JOB ANSWERS ELIPHAZ

16 Then Job answered:

²"I have heard many things like these.
You are all painful comforters!
³Will your long, useless speeches never
end?
What makes you keep on arguing?
⁴I also could speak as you do
if you were in my place.
I could make great speeches against
you.
And I could shake my head at you.
⁵But, instead, my words would
encourage you.
I would speak words of comfort to
bring you relief.

⁶"But if I speak, my pain does not
become less.
And if I don't speak, it still does not
go away.

⁷God, you have surely taken away my
strength.
You have destroyed my whole
family.
⁸You have made me thin and weak.
And people feel that this shows I
have done wrong.
⁹God attacks me and tears me with
anger.
He grinds his teeth at me.
My enemy stares at me with his
angry eyes.
¹⁰People open their mouths to make fun
of me.
They hit my cheeks to insult me.
They join together against me.
¹¹God has turned me over to evil men.
He has thrown me into the clutches
of the wicked.
¹²Everything was fine with me.
But then God broke me into pieces.
He held me by the neck and
crushed me.
He has made me his target.
¹³   God's archers surround me.
He stabs my kidneys and has no
mercy.
He spills my blood on the ground.
¹⁴Again and again God attacks me.
He runs at me like a soldier.

¹⁵"I have sewed rough cloth over my
skin to show my sadness.
I have buried my face in the dust.
¹⁶My face is red from crying.
I have dark circles around my eyes.
¹⁷And yet my hands have never done
anything cruel.
And my prayer is pure.

¹⁸"Earth, please do not cover up my
blood.
Don't let my cry ever stop being
heard!
¹⁹Even now I have one who speaks for
me in heaven.
The one who is on my side is high
above.

²⁰The one who speaks for me is my
friend.
While he does this, my eyes pour
out tears to God.
²¹He begs God on behalf of a man
as a man begs for his friend.

²²"Only a few years will pass
before I go on the journey from
which I cannot return.

17
My spirit is broken.
The days of my life are almost
gone.
The grave is waiting for me.
²Those who laugh at me surround me.
I watch them insult me.

³"God, make me a promise.
No one else will make a promise for
me.
⁴You have closed the minds of my
friends so they do not
understand.
So you will not let them win over
me.
⁵A man might speak against his friends
for money.
But if he does, the eyes of his
children go blind.

⁶"God has caused people to use my
name as a curse word.
People spit in my face.
⁷My sight has grown weak because of
my sadness.
My body is so thin it's like a
shadow.
⁸Honest people are upset about this.
Innocent people are upset with
people who do wrong.
⁹But people who do right will continue
to do right.
And those whose hands are not
dirty with sin will grow stronger.

¹⁰"But, all of you, come and try again!
I do not find a wise man among
you!
¹¹My days are gone, and my plans have
been destroyed.

The desires of my heart are also
destroyed.
¹²These men think night is day.
When it is dark, they say, 'Light is
near.'
¹³It might be that the only home I hope
for is where the dead are.
I might spread out my bed in
darkness.
¹⁴I might say to the grave, 'You are my
father.'
And I might say to the worm, 'You
are my mother' or 'You are my
sister.'
¹⁵If these things are true, I have no
hope.
No one can see any hope for me.
¹⁶Hope will go down to the gates of
death.
We will go down together into the
dust."

BILDAD ANSWERS JOB

18
Then Bildad the Shuhite answered:

²"When will you stop these speeches?
Be sensible, and then we can talk.
³You think of us as only cattle.
You think we are stupid.
⁴You tear yourself to pieces in your
anger.
Does everyone have to leave the
earth just for you?
Do the rocks have to be moved
from their place for you?

⁵"The lamp of the wicked person will
be put out.
The flame in his lamp will stop
burning.
⁶The light in his tent will become dark.
The lamp by his side will go out.
⁷His footsteps will become weak and
lose their strength.
He will fall into his own evil trap.
⁸His feet are caught in a net
when he walks into its web.
⁹A trap will catch him by the heel.
And it will hold him tight.

10A trap for him is hidden on the
     ground.
   It lies in his path.
11Terrible things startle him from every
     side.
   They chase him at every step.
12Hunger takes away his strength.
   Disaster is at his side.
13Disease eats away parts of his skin.
   The signs of death begin to eat away
     at his arms and legs.
14The evil person is torn from the safety
     of his tent.
   He is dragged off to Death, the King
     of Terrors.
15His tent is set on fire.
   Burning sulfur is scattered over his
     home.
16His roots dry up below ground,
   and his branches above ground die.
17People on earth will not remember
     him.
   His name will be forgotten in the
     land.
18He will be driven from the light into
     darkness.
   He will be chased out of the world.
19He has no children or descendants*d*
     among his people.
   No one will be left alive where he
     once lived.
20People of the west are shocked at what
     has happened to him.
   People of the east are very
     frightened.
21This is surely what will happen to the
     home of an evil person.
   This is the place of one who does
     not know God."

JOB ANSWERS BILDAD

19
Then Job answered:

2"How long will you hurt me
   and crush me with your words?
3You have insulted me ten times now.
   You attack me without shame.
4If I have sinned,
   it is my worry alone.

5Maybe you want to make yourselves
     look better than I do
   so you can blame me for my
     suffering.
6Then know that God has wronged me.
   He has pulled his net around me.

7"I shout, 'I have been wronged!'
   But I get no answer.
   I call loudly for help,
     but I receive no justice.
8God has blocked my way so I cannot
     pass.
   He has covered my paths with
     darkness.
9He has taken away my honor.
   He has removed the crown from my
     head.
10He beats me down on every side until
     I am gone.
   He pulls up my hope as a tree is
     pulled up by its roots.
11His anger burns against me.
   And he treats me as one of his
     enemies.
12His armies gather.
   They prepare a way to attack me.
   They camp around my tent.

13"God has made my brothers my
     enemies.
   My friends have become complete
     strangers.
14My relatives have gone away.
   My friends have forgotten me.
15My guests and my women servants
     think of me as a stranger.
   They look at me as if I were a
     foreigner.
16I call for my servant, but he does not
     answer.
   I even beg him with my own mouth.
17My wife hates my breath.
   My own family hates me.
18Even the little boys hate me.
   When I leave, they talk about me.
19All my close friends hate me.
   Even those I love have turned
     against me.

²⁰I am nothing but skin and bones.
  I have escaped with only the skin of
    my teeth.
²¹Pity me, my friends. Pity me!
  The hand of God has hit me.
²²Why do you chase me as God does?
  Haven't you had enough of hurting
    my body?

²³"How I wish my words were written
    down.
  I wish they were written on a scroll.
²⁴I wish they were carved with an iron
    pen into lead,
  or carved into stone forever!
²⁵I know that my Defender lives.
  And in the end he will come to
    show that I am right.
²⁶Even after my skin has been
    destroyed,
  in my flesh I will still see God.
²⁷I will see him myself.
  I myself will see him with my own
    eyes.
  How my heart wants that to
    happen!

²⁸"You may say, 'We will continue to
    trouble Job.
  The problem lies with him.'
²⁹But you should be afraid of the sword
    yourselves.
  God's anger will bring punishment
    by the sword.
  Then you will know that there is
    judgment."

ZOPHAR ANSWERS

20 Then Zophar the Naamathite
        answered:

²"My troubled thoughts cause me to
    answer.
  I am very upset.
³I hear you criticize, and I am insulted.
  But I understand how to answer
    you.

⁴"You know how it has been for a long
    time.

It has been this way since man was
    put on the earth.
⁵The happiness of an evil person is
    very short.
  The joy of a person without God
    lasts only a moment.
⁶His pride may be as high as the
    heavens.
  His head may touch the clouds.
⁷But he will be gone forever, like his
    own dung.
  People who knew him will say,
    'Where is he?'
⁸He will fly away like a dream.
  He will not be found again.
  He will be chased away like a vision
    in the night.
⁹Those who saw him will not see him
    again.
  The place where he lived will see
    him no more.
¹⁰His children will have to make up for
    how he mistreated the poor.
  He will have to give his wealth back
    with his own hands.
¹¹He has the strength of his youth in his
    bones.
  But it will lie with him in the dust of
    death.

¹²"Evil may taste sweet in the evil
    person's mouth.
  He may hide it under his tongue.
¹³He cannot stand to let go of it.
  So he keeps it in his mouth.
¹⁴But his food will turn sour in his
    stomach.
  It will be like the poison of a snake
    inside him.
¹⁵He has swallowed riches, but he will
    spit them out.
  God will make the evil person's
    stomach vomit them up.
¹⁶He will suck the poison of snakes.
  The snake's poisonous fangs will
    kill him.
¹⁷He will not admire the sparkling
    streams

or the rivers flowing with honey
and cream.
¹⁸He must give back what he worked for
without eating it.
He will not enjoy the money he
made from his trading.
¹⁹This is because he has troubled the poor
people and left them with nothing.
He has taken houses he did not build.

²⁰"The evil person has no rest from his
desire.
Nothing escapes his selfishness.
²¹But nothing will be left for him to eat.
His riches will not continue.
²²When he still has plenty, trouble will
catch up to him.
Great misery will come down on him.
²³The evil person may eat until his
stomach is full.
But then God will send his burning
anger against him.
God will send blows of punishment
down on him like rain.
²⁴The evil person may run away from
an iron weapon.
But then a bronze arrow will stab
him.
²⁵He will pull the arrow out of his back.
He will pull its point out of his liver.
Terrors will come over him.
²⁶   Total darkness waits for his treasure.
A fire not fanned by people will
destroy him.
That fire will burn up what is left of
his tent.
²⁷The heavens will show his guilt.
The earth will rise up against him.
²⁸A flood will carry his house away.
The rushing waters will come on
the day of God's anger.
²⁹This is what God plans for evil people.
This is what he has decided they
will receive."

JOB ANSWERS ZOPHAR

21 Then Job answered:

²"Listen carefully to my words.

Let this be the way you comfort
me.
³Be patient while I speak.
After I have finished, you may
continue to make fun of me if
you wish .

⁴"My complaint is not just against
people.
I have reason to be impatient.
⁵Look at me then and be shocked.
Put your hand over your mouth in
shock.
⁶When I think about this, I am terribly
afraid.
My body shakes!
⁷Why do evil people live a long time?
They grow old and become more
powerful.
⁸They see their children become strong
around them.
They watch their children grow up.
⁹Their homes are safe and without
fear.
God does not punish them.
¹⁰Their bulls never fail to mate.
Their cows have healthy calves.
¹¹Their children run and play like flocks
of lambs.
Their little ones dance about.
¹²They sing to the music of
tambourines*d* and harps.
The sound of the flute makes them
happy.
¹³Evil people enjoy success during their
lives.
Then they go down in peace to
where the dead are.
¹⁴But they say to God, 'Leave us alone!
We don't want to know your ways.
¹⁵Who is God All-Powerful that we
should serve him?
We would gain nothing by praying
to him.'
¹⁶But the wicked think they succeed by
their own strength.
Their way of thinking is not godly.

[17]Yet how often is the lamp of evil
people turned off?
How often does trouble come to
them?
How often do they suffer the
punishment God plans in his
anger?
[18]How often are they like straw in the
wind
or like chaff[d] that is blown away by
a storm?
[19]It is said, 'God saves up a man's
punishment for the man's
children.'
God should punish the evil person
himself so he will know it.
[20]His eyes should see his own
destruction.
He should suffer the anger of God
All-Powerful.
[21]He does not care about the family he
leaves behind
when his life has come to an end.

[22]"No one can teach knowledge to God.
He is the one who judges even the
most important people.
[23]One man dies while he still has all his
strength.
He feels completely safe and
comfortable.
[24]His body was well fed.
And his bones were strong and
healthy.
[25]But another man dies with an
unhappy heart.
He never had any happiness.
[26]These two men are buried next to
each other.
And worms cover both of them.

[27]"I know very well what you are
thinking.
I know your plans to do wrong to
me.
[28]You say about me, 'Now where is this
great man's house?
And where are the tents where the
evil men lived?'

[29]You have never asked those who
travel.
You have not listened to their
stories.
[30]On the day of God's anger and
punishment,
it is the evil man who is spared.
[31]Who will accuse him to his face?
No one pays him back for the evil
he has done.
[32]He is carried to his grave.
And someone keeps watch over his
tomb.
[33]The dirt in the valley will seem sweet
to him.
Everybody follows after him.
Many people go before him.

[34]"So you cannot comfort me with this
nonsense.
Your answers are still only lies!"

ELIPHAZ ANSWERS

22 Then Eliphaz the Temanite answered:

[2]"A man cannot be of any real use to
God.
Even a wise man does him no good.
[3]It does not help God All-Powerful for
you to be good.
He gains nothing if you are
innocent.
[4]God does not punish you for
respecting him.
He does not bring you into court for
this.
[5]No! It is because your evil is without
limits.
And your sins have no end.
[6]You took your brothers' things to pay
a debt they didn't owe.
You took clothes from people and
left them naked.
[7]You did not give water to tired people.
And you kept food away from the
hungry.
[8]You were a powerful man who owned
land.

You were honored and lived in the
　　land.
⁹But you sent widows away without
　　giving them anything.
　　You even mistreated orphans.
¹⁰That is why traps are all around you.
　　That is why sudden danger
　　frightens you.
¹¹That is why it is so dark you cannot
　　see.
　　And that is why a flood of water
　　covers you.

¹²"God is in the highest part of heaven.
　　See how high the highest stars are!
¹³But you say, 'God knows nothing.
　　He cannot judge us through the
　　dark clouds.
¹⁴Thick clouds cover him so he cannot
　　see us.
　　He walks around high up in the
　　sky.'
¹⁵Are you going to stay on the old path
　　where evil people walk?
¹⁶They were carried away before their
　　time was up.
　　Their foundations were washed
　　away by a flood.
¹⁷They said to God, 'Leave us alone!
　　God All-Powerful can do nothing to
　　us.'
¹⁸But it was God who filled their houses
　　with good things.
　　He did this even though their way
　　of thinking was not godly.

¹⁹"Good people can watch and be glad.
　　Innocent people can laugh at them
　　and say,
²⁰'Surely our enemies are destroyed.
　　And fire burns up their wealth.'

²¹"Obey God, and then you will be at
　　peace with him.
　　This way you can be happy.
²²Accept teaching from his mouth.
　　Keep his words in your heart.
²³If you return to God All-Powerful, you
　　will be blessed again.

Remove evil from your house.
²⁴Throw your gold nuggets into the dust.
　　Throw your fine gold to the rocks in
　　the ravines.
²⁵Then God All-Powerful will be your
　　gold.
　　He will be the best silver for you.
²⁶You will find pleasure in God All-
　　Powerful.
　　And you will look up to him.
²⁷You will pray to him, and he will hear
　　you.
　　And you will keep your promises to
　　him.
²⁸Anything you decide will be done.
　　And light will shine on your ways.
²⁹When terrible things happen to
　　people, you will say, 'Have
　　courage.'
　　Then those who are humble will be
　　saved.
³⁰Even the guilty will escape.
　　They will be saved because your
　　hands are clean."[d]

JOB ANSWERS

23

Then Job answered:

²"My complaint is still strong today.
　　God's hand is heavy against me
　　even though I am groaning.
³I wish I knew where to find God.
　　I wish I could go to where he lives.
⁴I would present my case before him.
　　I would fill my mouth with
　　arguments.
⁵I would know the words of his
　　answer.
　　And I would think about what he
　　would say.
⁶He would not come against me with
　　great power.
　　He would really listen to me.
⁷Then an honest person could present
　　his case to God.
　　And I would be saved forever from
　　my judge.

⁸"If I go to the east, God is not there.

And if I go to the west, I do not see
  him there.
⁹When he is at work in the north,
  I catch no sight of him.
And when he turns to the south,
  I cannot see him.
¹⁰But God knows the way that I take.
  When he has tested me, I will come
  out pure as gold.
¹¹My feet have closely followed his
  steps.
  I have stayed in his way without
  turning aside.
¹²I have never left the commands he has
  spoken.
  I have treasured his words more
  than my food.

¹³"But he is the only God.
  No one can come against him.
  He does anything he wants.
¹⁴He will do to me what he said he
  would do.
  And he has many plans like this.
¹⁵That is why I am so afraid before him.
  When I think of all this, I am afraid
  of him.
¹⁶God has made me afraid.
  God All-Powerful has made me
  terribly afraid.
¹⁷But I am not cut off by the darkness,
  by the thick darkness that covers
  my face.

24 "I wish God All-Powerful would
  set a time for judging.
  People who know God look for such
  a day, but they do not see it.
²Wicked people take other people's
  land.
  They steal flocks of sheep and take
  them to new pastures.
³They chase away the orphan's donkey.
  And they take the widow's ox when
  she cannot pay what she owes.
⁴They push needy people off the path.
  So all the poor people of the land
  hide from them.

⁵The poor become like wild donkeys in
  the desert.
  They go about their job of finding
  food.
  The desert gives them food for their
  children.
⁶They gather hay and straw in the
  fields.
  And they pick up leftover grapes
  from the evil man's vineyard.
⁷They spend the night naked, because
  they have no clothes.
  They have nothing to cover
  themselves in the cold.
⁸They are soaked from mountain rains.
  They stay near the large rocks
  because they have no shelter.
⁹The child who has no father is
  grabbed from its mother's
  breast.
  They take a poor mother's baby to
  pay for what she owes.
¹⁰So the poor go around naked because
  they have no clothes.
  They carry bundles of grain for evil
  people, but they still go hungry.
¹¹They crush olives to get oil.
  And they crush grapes in the
  winepresses,ᵈ but they still are
  thirsty.
¹²Dying people groan in the city.
  People who are injured cry out for
  help.
  But God accuses no one of doing
  wrong.

¹³"There are people who fight against
  the light.
  God's ways are strange to them.
  And they do not stay in the lighted
  path.
¹⁴When the light of day is gone, the
  murderer gets up.
  He kills poor and needy people.
  At night he goes about like a thief.
¹⁵The person who is guilty of adulteryᵈ
  watches for the night.
  He thinks, 'No one will see me.'

And he keeps his face covered.
16In the dark, evil people break into
houses.
But in the daytime they shut
themselves up in their own
houses.
They want nothing to do with the
light.
17Darkness is like morning to all these
evil people.
They make friends with the terrors
of darkness.

18"They are like foam floating on the
water.
Their part of the land is cursed.
No one uses the road that goes by
their vineyards.
19Heat and dryness quickly take away
the melted snow.
In the same way, the place for the
dead quickly takes away those
who have sinned.
20The evil person's mother will even
forget him.
The worms will eat his body.
He will no longer be remembered.
So wickedness is broken in pieces
like a stick.
21These evil men are unfair to women
who cannot have children.
And they show no kindness to
widows.
22God drags away strong men by his
power.
But even though they seem strong,
they do not know how long they
will live.
23God may let these evil people feel safe.
But he is watching their ways.
24For a little while they are important,
and then they are gone.
They are made unimportant and
gathered up like everyone else.
They are cut off like the tops of
stalks of grain.
25If this is not true, who can prove I am
wrong?

And who can show that my words
are worth nothing?"

BILDAD ANSWERS

25 Then Bildad the Shuhite answered:

2"God rules and must be honored.
He set up order in his high heaven.
3No one can count God's armies.
His light shines on all people.
4So no man can be good in the
presence of God.
No one born to a woman can be
pure.
5Even the moon is not bright,
and the stars are not pure in his
eyes.
6Man is much less! He is like an insect.
He is only a worm!"

JOB ANSWERS BILDAD

26 Then Job answered:

2"You are no help to a person who has
no strength!
You have given no help to one
whose arm is weak!
3You have given advice to me as if I
had no wisdom!
This is not great wisdom you have
shown!
4Who has helped you say these words?
And where did you get these words
you speak?

5"The spirits of the dead beneath the
waters shake.
And so do those that live in the
waters.
6Death is naked before God.
Destruction is uncovered before
him.
7God stretches the northern sky out
over empty space.
And he hangs the earth on nothing.
8God wraps up the waters in his thick
clouds.
But the clouds do not break under
the weight of the water.

9God covers the face of the full moon.
    He spreads his clouds over it.
10God draws the horizon like a circle on
    the water
    at the place where light and
    darkness meet.
11Heaven's foundations shake
    when he thunders at them.
12God's power controls the sea.
    By his wisdom he destroyed
    Rahab,*d* the sea monster.
13God breathes, and the sky becomes
    clear.
    God's hand stabs the gliding snake.
14And these are only a small part of
    God's works.
    We only hear a small whisper of
    him.
    So who can understand God's
    thundering power?"

27 And Job continued speaking:

2"As surely as God lives, he has taken
    away my rights.
    God All-Powerful has made me
    unhappy.
3As long as I am alive
    and God's breath of life is in my
    nose,
4My lips will not speak evil.
    And my tongue will not tell a lie.
5I will never agree you are right.
    Until I die, I will never stop saying I
    was innocent.
6I will hold tightly to the right things I
    said.
    My sense of right and wrong does
    not bother me at all.

7"Let my enemies be like evil people.
    Let them be like those who are not
    fair!
8What hope does a wicked person have
    when he dies?
    He has no hope when God takes his
    life away.
9God will not listen to his cry
    when trouble comes to him.

10He will not find joy in God
    All-Powerful,
    even though he calls out to God all
    the time.

11"I will teach you about the power of
    God.
    I will not hide the ways of God
    All-Powerful.
12You have all seen this yourselves.
    So why are we having all this talk
    that means nothing?

13"Here is what God has planned for
    evil people.
    This is what cruel people will get
    from God All-Powerful:
14They may have many children, but the
    sword will kill them.
    The children who are left will never
    have enough to eat.
15Then they will die and be buried.
    And the widows will not even cry
    for them.
16The evil person may heap up silver
    like piles of dirt.
    He may have so many clothes they
    are like piles of clay.
17But good people will wear what the
    evil person has gathered.
    And those who are not guilty of
    wrong will divide up his silver.
18The house the evil person builds is
    like a spider's web.
    It is like a hut that a guard builds.
19The evil person is rich when he goes
    to bed, but he is rich for the last
    time.
    When he opens his eyes, everything
    is gone.
20Fears come over him like a flood.
    A storm snatches him away in the
    night.
21The east wind will carry him away,
    and then he is gone.
    It sweeps him out of his place.
22The wind will hit the evil person
    without mercy

as he tries to run away from its power.

²³It will be as if the wind is clapping its hands at him.
It will whistle at him as he runs from his place.

28 "There are mines where people dig silver.
And there are places where gold is made pure.
²Iron is taken out of the ground.
And copper is melted out of rocks.
³Miners bring light into the mines.
They search even the deepest parts of the mines.
They look for metal in places of thick darkness.
⁴Miners dig a tunnel far away from where people live.
They dig it where people never go.
They work far away from people, swinging and swaying from ropes.
⁵Food grows on top of the earth.
But below ground things are changed as if by fire.
⁶Sapphires are found in rocks.
And the dust of the earth contains gold.
⁷No hawk knows the path.
The falcon has not seen it.
⁸Proud animals have not walked on this path.
And no lions cross over it.
⁹Men hit the rocks of flint.
They dig away at the bottom of the mountains.
¹⁰Miners cut tunnels through the rock.
They see all the treasures there.
¹¹They search the places where rivers begin.
And they bring things hidden there out into the light.

¹²"But where can wisdom be found.
Where does understanding live?
¹³People do not understand the value of wisdom.

It cannot be found among living people.
¹⁴The deep ocean says, 'It's not in me.'
The sea says, 'It's not in me.'
¹⁵Wisdom cannot be bought with the best gold.
Its cost cannot be weighed in silver.
¹⁶Wisdom cannot be bought with fine gold.
It cannot be bought with valuable onyx or sapphire gems.
¹⁷Gold and crystal are not as valuable as wisdom.
And you cannot buy it with jewels of gold.
¹⁸Coral and jasper are not even worth talking about.
The price of wisdom is much greater than rubies.
¹⁹The topaz from Cush cannot compare to wisdom.
It cannot even be bought with the purest gold.

²⁰"So from where does wisdom come?
And where does understanding live?
²¹It is hidden from the eyes of every living thing.
It is hidden even from the birds of the air.
²²The places of destruction and death say,
'We have only heard reports about it.'
²³God understands the way to wisdom.
And he is the only one who knows where it lives.
²⁴This is because God sees to the farthest parts of the earth.
And he sees everything under the heavens.
²⁵Wisdom began when God gave power to the wind.
It was when he measured the water and put limits on it.
²⁶It was when God made rules for the rain.

And he set a path for a
thunderstorm to follow.
²⁷Then God looked at wisdom and
decided its worth.
He set wisdom up and tested it.
²⁸Then he said to man,
'The fear of the Lord is wisdom,
and to stay away from evil is
understanding.'"

JOB CONTINUES

29 Job continued to speak:

²"How I wish for the months that have
passed.
I wish for the days when God
watched over me.
³I wish for the days when God's lamp
shined on my head.
And I wish for the time I walked
through darkness by his light.
⁴I wish for the days when I was at my
strongest,
when God's close friendship blessed
my house.
⁵That was when my children were all
around me.
And God All-Powerful was still with
me.
⁶Life was so good. It was as if my path
were covered with cream.
It was as if even the rocks poured
out streams of olive oil for me.
⁷I would go to the city gate
and sit in the public square.
⁸When the young men saw me, they
would step out of my way.
And the old men would stand up in
respect for me.
⁹The leading men stopped speaking
and covered their mouths with their
hands.
¹⁰The voices of the important men were
quiet.
It was as if each man's tongue stuck
to the roof of his mouth.
¹¹Anyone who heard me said good
things about me.
And those who saw me praised me.

¹²This was because I saved the poor
who cried for help.
And I saved the orphan who had no
one to help him.
¹³The dying person blessed me.
And I made the widow's heart sing.
¹⁴I put on right living as if it were
clothing.
I wore fairness as if it were my robe
and my turban.
¹⁵I tried to be eyes for the blind.
And I tried to be feet for those who
were crippled.
¹⁶I was like a father to needy people.
And I took the side of strangers
when they were in trouble.
¹⁷I broke the fangs of evil people.
And I snatched from their teeth the
people they wanted to hurt.

¹⁸"I thought, 'I will live for as many
days as there are grains of sand.
And I will die in my own house.
¹⁹I will be like a tree whose roots reach
down to the water.
The dew will lie on the branches all
night.
²⁰New honors will come to me
continually.
I will always have great strength.'

²¹"People listened to me carefully.
They waited quietly for my advice.
²²After I finished speaking, they spoke
no more.
My words fell very gently on their
ears.
²³They waited for me as they would for
rain.
They drank in my words as if they
were spring rain.
²⁴I smiled at them when they doubted.
And my approval was important to
them.
²⁵I chose the right way for them and
was their leader.
I lived like a king among his army.
I was like a person who gives
comfort to sad people.

30

"But now men who are younger than I
make fun of me.
I would not have even let their fathers
sit with my sheep dogs.
²Their hands had no strength to help me.
They had even lost their strength to
work.
³They were thin from being hungry
and in need.
They wandered through the dry and
ruined land at night.
⁴They gathered desert plants by the
brush for food.
They even ate the root of the broom
tree.
⁵They were forced to live away from
other people.
People shouted at them as if they
were thieves.
⁶These young men had to live in dried
up streambeds.
They lived in caves and among the
rocks.
⁷They howled like animals out among
the bushes.
And they huddled together in the
brush.
⁸They are worthless people without
names.
They were forced to leave the land.

⁹"Now they make fun of me with
songs.
My name has become a joke among
them.
¹⁰They hate me and stay far away from
me.
But they do not mind spitting in my
face.
¹¹God has taken away my strength and
made me suffer.
So they attack me with all their
anger.
¹²On my right side they attack me like a
mob.
They lay traps for my feet.
They prepare to attack me.

¹³They break up my road.
They work to destroy me
without anyone stopping them.
¹⁴They go forward as if through a hole
in the wall.
They roll in among the ruins.
¹⁵Great fears overwhelm me.
They blow my honor away as if by a
great wind.
My safety disappears like a cloud.

¹⁶"Now my life is almost over.
My days are full of suffering.
¹⁷At night my bones ache.
Gnawing pains never stop.
¹⁸In his great power God grabs hold of
my clothing.
He chokes me with the collar of my
coat.
¹⁹He throws me into the mud.
And I become like dirt and ashes.

²⁰"I cry out to you, God, but you do not
answer.
I stand up, but you just look at me.
²¹You turn on me without mercy.
You attack me with your powerful
hand.
²²You snatch me up and throw me into
the wind.
You toss me about in the storm.
²³I know you will bring me down to
death.
You will bring me to the place
where all living people must go.

²⁴"Surely no one would hurt a ruined
man
when he cries for help in his time of
trouble.
²⁵I have cried for those who are in
trouble.
My soul has been very sad for poor
people.
²⁶But when I hoped for good, only evil
came to me.
When I looked for light, darkness
came.
²⁷I never stop being upset inside.
Days of suffering are ahead of me.

28I have become black, but not by the
sun.
I stand up in public and cry for
help.
29It is as if I have become a brother to
wild dogs
and a friend to ostriches.
30My skin becomes black and peels off.
My body burns with fever.
31My harp is tuned for singing a sad
song.
And my flute is tuned for the sound
of loud crying.

31

"But I made an agreement with
my eyes
not to look with desire at a girl.
2What has God above promised those
who do this?
What has God All-Powerful on high
planned for them?
3It is ruin for the evil people.
It is disaster for those who do
wrong.
4God sees my ways,
and he counts every step I take.

5"I have not been a dishonest person.
I have not lied to others.
6Let God weigh me on honest scales.
Then he will know I have done
nothing wrong.
7I have not turned away from doing
what is right.
My heart has not been led by my
eyes to do wrong.
My hands have not been made
unclean.*d*
8If I have done these things, then let
other people eat what I have
planted.
And let my crops be plowed up.

9"I have not desired another woman.
I have never waited at my
neighbor's door to have sexual
relations with his wife.

10If I have done these things, then let
my wife grind another man's
grain.
And let other men have sexual
relations with her.
11Sexual sin is shameful.
It is a sin which must be punished.
12It is like a fire that burns and destroys
forever.
It would destroy all I have.

13"I have been fair to my male and
female slaves
when they had a complaint against
me.
14If I have not, how could I tell God
what I did?
What will I answer when God asks
me to explain what I've done?
15God made me in my mother's womb,
and he also made them.
The same God formed both of us in
our mothers' wombs.

16"I have never refused anything the
poor wanted.
I have never let widows give up
hope while looking for help.
17I have not kept my food to myself.
I have also given it to the orphans.
18Since I was young, I have been like a
father to the orphans.
And from my birth I guided the
widows.
19I have not let a person die because he
had no clothes.
I have not let a needy person go
without a coat.
20That person's heart blessed me.
This was because I warmed him
with the wool of my sheep.
21I have never hurt an orphan
even when I knew I could win in
court.
22If I have, then let my arm fall off my
shoulder.
Let it be broken at the joint.
23This is because I dread destruction
from God.

I could not do such things because
I fear his majesty.

24"I have not put my trust in gold.
I have not said to pure gold, 'You
are my safety.'
25I have not celebrated my great wealth.
I have not celebrated that my hands
had gained riches.
26I have not thought about worshiping
the sun in its brightness.
I have not admired the moon
moving in glory
27so that my heart was pulled away
from God.
My hand has never offered the sun
and moon a kiss of worship.
28If I had, these also would have been
sins to be punished.
I would have been unfaithful to God
if I had done these things.

29"I have not been happy when my
enemy was ruined.
I have not laughed when he had
trouble.
30I have not let my mouth sin
by cursing my enemy's life.
31The men of my house have always
said,
'Everyone has eaten all he wants of
Job's food.'
32No stranger ever had to spend the
night in the street.
I always let the traveler stay in my
home.
33I have not hidden my sin as other
men do.
I did not hide my guilt in my heart.
34I was not so afraid of the crowd.
I did not keep quiet and stay inside
because I feared being hated by
other families.

35("How I wish a court would hear my
case!
Here I sign my name to show I have
told the truth.
Now let God All-Powerful answer me.

Let the one who is against me write
down what he accuses me of.
36I would surely wear the writing on my
shoulder.
I would put it on like a crown.
37I would explain to God every step
I took.
I would come near to God like a
prince.)

38"My land did not cry out against me.
Its plowed rows were not wet with
tears.
39I did not take the land's harvest
without paying.
I did not break the spirit of those
who took care of the land.
40If I did, then let thorns come up
instead of wheat.
And let weeds come up instead of
barley."

The words of Job are finished.

ELIHU SPEAKS

32 These three men stopped answering Job. This is because Job
was so sure he was right. 2But Elihu son
of Barakel the Buzite became very angry
with Job. (Elihu was from the family of
Ram.) He was angry because Job
claimed he was right instead of God.
3Elihu was also angry with Job's three
friends. They had no answer to show
that Job was wrong. And yet they continued to blame him. 4Now Elihu had
waited before speaking to Job. This is
because the three friends were older
than he was. 5But when Elihu saw that
the three men had nothing more to say,
he became very angry.

6So Elihu son of Barakel the Buzite
said this:

"I am young,
and you are old.
That is why I was afraid
to tell you what I know.
7I thought, 'Older people should speak.

Those who have lived many years should teach wisdom.'

⁸But it is the spirit in a person that gives him understanding.
It is the breath of God All-Powerful in him.

⁹It is not just older people who are wise.
Older people are not the only ones who understand what is right.

¹⁰So I say, listen to me!
I will also tell you what I know.

¹¹I waited while you spoke.
I listened to your explanations.
I waited while you looked for words to use.

¹² I paid close attention to you.
But not one of you has proved Job wrong.
Not one of you has answered his arguments.

¹³Don't you say, 'We have found wisdom.
Only God will show Job to be wrong, not people.'

¹⁴Job has not spoken his words against me.
So I will not use your arguments to answer Job.

¹⁵"These three friends are defeated and have no more to say.
Words have failed them.

¹⁶Now they are standing there with no answer for Job.
Now that they are quiet, must I wait to speak?

¹⁷No, I also will speak.
I will also tell what I know.

¹⁸I am full of words.
And the spirit in me causes me to speak.

¹⁹I am like wine that has been bottled up.
I am ready to burst like a new leather bag for holding wine.

²⁰I must speak. Then I will feel relief.
I must open my mouth and answer.

²¹I will be fair to everyone.
I will not flatter anyone.

²²I don't know how to flatter.
If I did, God, my Maker, would quickly take me away.

33

"But now, Job, listen to my words.
Pay attention to everything I say.

²I open my mouth.
I am ready to speak.

³My words come from an honest heart.
I am sincere when I speak what I know.

⁴The Spirit^d of God created me.
The breath of God All-Powerful gave me life.

⁵Answer me if you can.
Get yourself ready and stand before me.

⁶I am just like you before God.
I was also made out of clay.

⁷Don't be afraid of me.
I will not be hard on you.

⁸"But I heard what you have said.
I heard every word.

⁹You said, 'I am pure and without sin.
I am innocent and free from guilt.

¹⁰But God has found fault with me.
He considers me his enemy.

¹¹He locks my feet in chains.
He closely watches everywhere I go.'

¹²"But I tell you, you are not right in saying this.
God is greater than we are!

¹³Why do you accuse God
of not answering man's complaints?

¹⁴God does speak—sometimes one way and sometimes another.
He speaks even though men may not understand it.

¹⁵God may speak in a dream or a vision of the night.
This is when men are in a deep sleep
and lying in their beds.

[16]He may speak in their ears
  and frighten them with warnings.
[17]He warns them to turn away from
    doing wrong.
  And he warns them not to be proud.
[18]God does this to save a man's soul
    from death.
  He does it to keep him from dying.
[19]A man may be corrected while on his
    bed in great pain.
  He may have continual pain in his
    very bones.
[20]He may be in such pain that he even
    hates food.
  He may hate even the very best
    meal.
[21]His body becomes so thin there is
    almost nothing left of it.
  And his bones that were hidden by
    flesh now stick out.
[22]His soul is near the place of death.
  His life is almost over.

[23]"But there may be an angel on his
    side.
  The angel may be one out of a
    thousand who will speak for the
    man.
  He will tell the man what he should
    do.
[24]The angel will beg for mercy and say:
  'Save this man from the place of
    death.
  I have found a way to pay for his life.'
[25]Then his body is made new like a
    child's body.
  It will be returned to the way it was
    when he was young.
[26]That person will pray to God, and God
    will listen to him.
  He will see God's face and will shout
    with happiness.
  And God will set things right for
    him again.
[27]Then the man will say to other people,
  'I sinned and twisted what was
    right.

But I did not receive the punishment
    I should have received.
[28]God bought back my life from death.
  And I will continue to enjoy life.'

[29]"God does all these things to a man.
  He does them two times or even
    three.
[30]He does them so a person won't die as
    punishment for his sins.
  He does it so the man may still
    enjoy life.

[31]"Job, pay attention and listen to me.
  Be quiet, and I will speak.
[32]If you have anything to say, answer
    me.
  Speak up, because I want you to be
    shown as right.
[33]But if you have nothing to say, then
    listen to me.
  Be quiet, and I will teach you
    wisdom."

34 Then Elihu said:

[2]"Hear my words, you men who think
    you are wise.
  Listen to me, you men who think
    you know a lot.
[3]The ear tests words
  as the tongue tastes food.
[4]Let's decide for ourselves what is right.
  And let's learn together what is
    good.

[5]"Job says, 'I am not guilty.
  But God has refused me a fair trial.
[6]Instead of getting a fair trial,
  I am called a liar.
  I have been seriously hurt,
    even though I have not sinned.'
[7]There is no other man like Job.
  He takes insults as if he were
    drinking water.
[8]He is around people who do evil.
  He spends time with wicked men.
[9]This is because he says, 'It does not
    help a man
  to try and please God.'

¹⁰"So listen to me, you who can
    understand.
    God All-Powerful can never do
        wrong!
    It is impossible for God to do evil.
¹¹God pays a person back for what he
        has done.
    God gives him what his actions
        deserve.
¹²Truly God will never do wrong!
    God All-Powerful will never twist
        what is right.
¹³No one chose God to rule over the
        earth.
    No one put him in charge of the
        whole world.
¹⁴God could decide
    to take away his spirit and breath.
¹⁵If he did, all people would die
        together.
    And they would all turn back into
        dust.

¹⁶"If you can understand, hear this.
    Listen to what I have to say.
¹⁷Can anyone govern who hates what is
        right?
    How can you blame God who is
        both fair and powerful?
¹⁸God is the one who says to kings, 'You
        are worth nothing.'
    And he says to important people,
        'You are evil.'
¹⁹God is not better to princes than other
        people.
    He is not better to rich people than
        poor people.
    This is because he made them all
        with his own hands.
²⁰They can die in a moment, in the
        middle of the night.
    The rich are struck down, and then
        they pass away.
    Powerful people die without man's
        help.

²¹"God watches where people go.
    He sees every step they take.

²²There is no dark place or deep shadow
    where those who do evil can hide
        from God.
²³God does not need to watch people
        more closely.
    He does not need for men to come
        before him for judging.
²⁴Without asking questions, God breaks
        powerful people into pieces.
    And he puts other people in their
        place.
²⁵This is because God knows what
        people do.
    He defeats them in the night, and
        they are crushed.
²⁶He punishes them for the evil things
        they do.
    He does it so that everyone else can
        watch.
²⁷This is because they stopped following
        God.
    They did not care about any of his
        ways.
²⁸God lets the cry of poor people reach
        him.
    He hears the cry of the needy.
²⁹But if God keeps quiet, who can blame
        him?
    If he hides his face, no one can see
        him.
    But God still rules over both men and
        nations.
³⁰He still keeps wicked men from ruling.
    And he keeps them from trapping
        others.

³¹"But suppose such a man says to God,
    'I am guilty, but I will not sin
        anymore.
³²Teach me what I cannot see.
    If I have done wrong, I will not do it
        again.'
³³So, Job, should God reward you the
        way you want
    when you will not change your
        heart and life?
    You must decide, not I.
    So tell me what you know.

³⁴"Men who understand speak.
    And wise men who hear me say,

35'Job speaks without knowing what is
true.
His words show he does not
understand.'
36I wish Job would be tested completely
because he answered like an evil
man!
37Job has sinned, and now he turns
against God.
He claps his hands as an insult.
And he speaks more and more
against God."

35

Then Elihu said:

2"Do you think this is fair?
You say, 'God will show that I am
right.'
3But you say to him, 'What good is it to
me?
I don't gain anything by not sinning.'

4"I would like to answer you.
And I want to answer your friends
who are with you.
5Look up at the sky and see.
Look at the clouds so high above
you.
6If you sin, it does nothing to God.
Even if your sins are many, they do
nothing to God.
7If you are good, you give nothing to
God.
He receives nothing from your
hand.
8Your evil ways only hurt a man like
yourself.
And the good you do only helps
other human beings.

9"People cry out for help when they are
in trouble.
They beg for relief from powerful
people.
10But no one asks, 'Where is God, my
Maker?
He gives us songs in the night.
11He makes us more clever than the
animals of the earth.

He makes us wiser than the birds of
the air.'
12God does not answer evil people when
they cry for help.
This is because they are too proud.
13He does not listen to their useless
begging.
God All-Powerful pays no attention
to them.
14He will listen to you even less
when you say you do not see him.
He will not listen when you say your
case is before him
and you must wait for him.
15He will not listen when you say his
anger never punishes
and that he doesn't notice evil.
16So Job is only speaking useless words.
He says many words without
knowing what is true."

ELIHU'S SPEECH CONTINUES

36

Elihu continued:

2"Listen to me a little longer. Then I
will show you
that there is more to be said for
God's side.
3What I know comes from far away.
I will show that God, my Maker, is
right.
4You can be sure that my words are
not false.
One who really knows is with you.

5"God is powerful, but he does not hate
people.
He is powerful and sure of what he
wants to do.
6God will not keep evil people alive.
But he gives troubled people their
rights.
7God does not stop watching over
those who do right.
He sets them on thrones with kings.
And he lifts them up on high
forever.
8People may be bound in chains.

Or trouble may tie them up like
ropes around them.
⁹But then God tells them what they
have done.
He tells them they have sinned by
being too proud.
¹⁰God makes them listen to his warning.
He commands them to change from
doing evil.
¹¹If they obey and serve him,
the rest of their lives will be
successful.
And the rest of their years will be
happy.
¹²But if they do not listen,
they will die by the sword.
And they will die without knowing
better.

¹³"People who have wicked hearts hold
on to anger.
Even when God ties them down
with trouble, they do not cry for
help.
¹⁴They die while they are still young.
They die among the male
prostitutes*ᵈ* at the places of
worship.
¹⁵But God will save suffering people by
their suffering.
He gets them to listen through their
pain.

¹⁶"God is gently calling you from the
jaws of trouble.
He is calling you to an open place of
freedom.
There he has set your table full of
the best food.
¹⁷But now you are given the
punishment evil people should
have.
Now you are being punished.
¹⁸Be careful! Don't be led away from
God by riches.
Don't let a promise of much money
turn you away.
¹⁹Neither your wealth nor all your great
strength
will keep you out of trouble.

²⁰Don't wish for the night.
That is when people are taken from
their homes.
²¹Be careful not to turn to evil,
which you seem to want more than
suffering.

²²"God does great things by his power.
No other teacher is like him.
²³No one has planned his ways for him.
No one has said to God, 'You have
done wrong.'
²⁴Remember to praise his work.
Men sing about it.
²⁵Everybody has seen it.
People look at it from far off.
²⁶God is so great! He is greater than we
can understand!
No one can discover how many
years he has been alive.

²⁷"God takes up the drops of water from
the earth.
And he turns them into drops of
rain.
²⁸Then the rain pours down from the
clouds.
And showers fall on people.
²⁹No one understands how God spreads
out the clouds.
No one understands how he
thunders from where he lives.
³⁰Watch how God scatters his lightning
around him.
It even lights up the deepest parts
of the sea.
³¹This is the way God governs the
nations.
This is how he gives us enough food.
³²God fills his hands with lightning.
And he commands it to strike its
target.
³³His thunder announces that a storm is
coming.
Even the cattle show that the storm
is coming.

37 "At the sound of his thunder,
my heart pounds.

It is as if my heart will jump out of
my chest.
[2]Listen! Listen to the thunder of God's
voice.
Listen to the rumbling that comes
from his mouth.
[3]He turns his lightning loose under the
whole sky.
And he sends it to the farthest parts
of the earth.
[4]After that you can hear the roar
when he thunders with a great
sound.
He does not hold back the flashing
when his voice is heard.
[5]God's voice thunders in wonderful
ways.
He does great things we cannot
understand.
[6]God says to the snow, 'Fall on the
earth.'
And he says to the rain shower, 'Be
a heavy rain.'
[7]With it, God stops everyone from
working.
That way, everyone knows it is the
work of God.
[8]The animals take cover from the rain.
They stay in their dens.
[9]The storm comes from where it was
stored.
The cold comes from the strong
winds.
[10]The breath of God makes ice.
And the wide waters become
frozen.
[11]God fills the clouds up with water.
And he scatters his lightning
through them.
[12]At God's command they swirl around
over the whole earth.
They do whatever he commands.
[13]God uses the clouds to punish people
or to water his earth and show his
love.

[14]"Job, listen to this.
Stop and notice God's miracles.[d]

[15]Do you know how God controls the
clouds
and makes his lightning flash?
[16]Do you know how the clouds hang in
the sky?
They are the miracles of God, who
knows everything.
[17]You suffer in your clothes
when the land is made quiet by the
hot, south wind.
[18]You cannot stretch out the sky like God
and make it look as hard as
polished bronze.
[19]Tell us what we should say to God.
We cannot get our arguments ready
because we do not have enough
understanding.
[20]Should God be told that I want to
speak?
A man might try to speak to God,
but he would surely be
swallowed up.
[21]No one can look at the sun
when it is bright in the sky
after the wind has blown all the
clouds away.
[22]God comes out of the north in golden
light.
He comes in overwhelming
greatness.
[23]God All-Powerful is too high for us to
reach.
He has great strength.
He is always right and never
punishes unfairly.
[24]That is why people honor God.
He does not respect those who say
they are wise."

THE LORD QUESTIONS JOB

38 Then the Lord answered Job
from the storm. He said:

[2]"Who is this that makes my purpose
unclear
by saying things that are not true?
[3]Be strong like a man.
I will ask you questions,
and you must answer me.

⁴Where were you when I made the
  earth's foundation?
Tell me, if you understand.
⁵Who marked off how big it should be?
  Surely you know!
⁶What were the earth's foundations set
  on?
  Or who put its cornerstone*d* in
  place?
⁷Who did all this while the morning
  stars sang together?
  Who did this while the angels
  shouted with joy?

⁸"Who shut the doors to keep the sea
  in
  when it broke through and was
  born?
⁹This was when I made the clouds like
  a coat for the sea.
  And I wrapped the sea in dark
  clouds.
¹⁰It was when I put limits on the sea.
  And I put its doors and bars in
  place.
¹¹It was when I said to the sea, 'You
  may come this far, but no
  farther.
  This is where your proud waves
  must stop.'

¹²"Have you ever given orders for
  morning to begin?
  Or have you shown the dawn where
  its place was?
¹³The dawn takes hold of earth by its
  edges
  and shakes evil people out of it.
¹⁴At dawn the earth changes like clay
  being pressed by a seal.*d*
  The hills and valleys stand out like
  folds in a coat.
¹⁵Light is not given to evil people.
  Their arm is raised to do harm, but
  it is broken.

¹⁶"Have you ever gone to where the sea
  begins?

Or have you walked in the valleys
  under the sea?
¹⁷Have the gates of death been opened
  to you?
  Or have you seen the gates of the
  deep darkness?
¹⁸Do you understand the great width of
  the earth?
  Tell me, if you know all these
  things.

¹⁹"What is the path to light's home?
  And where does darkness live?
²⁰Can you take them to their places?
  Do you know the way to their
  homes?
²¹Surely you know, if you were already
  born when all this happened!
  Have you lived that many years?

²²"Have you ever gone into the
  storehouse where snow is kept?
  Or have you seen the storehouses
  for hail?
²³I save the snow and hail for times of
  trouble.
  I save them for days of war and
  battle.
²⁴How do you get to the place where
  light comes from?
  Or where is the place from which
  the east winds are scattered over
  the earth?
²⁵Who cuts a waterway for the heavy
  rains?
  And who sets a path for the
  thunderstorm to follow?
²⁶Who waters the land where no one
  lives?
  Who waters the desert that has no
  one in it?
²⁷Who sends rain to satisfy the empty
  land
  so the grass begins to grow?
²⁸Does the rain have a father?
  Who is father to the drops of dew?
²⁹Who is the mother of the ice?
  Who gives birth to the frost from
  the sky?

³⁰The waters become hard as stone.
　　Even the surface of the deep ocean
　　　is frozen.

³¹"Can you tie up the stars of the
　　Pleiades?
　　Can you loosen the ropes of the
　　　stars in Orion?
³²Can you bring out the stars at the
　　right times?
　　Or can you lead out the stars of the
　　　Bear with its cubs?
³³Do you know the laws of the sky?
　　Can you understand their rule over
　　　the earth?

³⁴"Can you shout an order to the clouds
　　and cover yourself with a flood of
　　　water?
³⁵Can you send lightning bolts on their
　　way?
　　Do the flashes of lightning report to
　　　you and say, 'Here we are'?
³⁶Who put wisdom inside the mind?
　　Or who put understanding in the
　　　heart?
³⁷Who has the wisdom to count the
　　clouds?
　　Who can pour water from the jars
　　　of heaven?
³⁸Who can do this when the dust
　　becomes hard
　　and the clumps of dirt stick
　　　together?

³⁹"Do you hunt food for the female lion
　　to satisfy the hunger of the young
　　　lions?
⁴⁰Do you hunt for them while they lie in
　　their dens
　　or hide in the bushes waiting to
　　　attack?
⁴¹Who gives food to the birds
　　when their young cry out to God?
　　And who gives them food when
　　　they wander about without any?

39 "Do you know when the
　　mountain goats give birth?

Do you watch when the deer gives
　　birth to her fawn?
²Do you count the months until they
　　give birth?
　　Do you know when the time is right
　　　for them to give birth?
³They lie down, and their young are
　　born.
　　Then the pain of giving birth is over.
⁴Their young ones grow and become
　　strong in the wild country.
　　Then they leave their homes and do
　　　not come back.

⁵"Who let the wild donkey go free?
　　Who untied his ropes?
⁶I am the one who gave the donkey the
　　desert as his home.
　　I gave him the desert lands as a
　　　place to live.
⁷The wild donkey laughs at the
　　confusion in the city.
　　He does not hear the drivers shout.
⁸He roams the hills looking for pasture.
　　And he looks for anything green to
　　　eat.

⁹"Will the wild ox agree to serve you?
　　Will he stay by your feeding box at
　　　night?
¹⁰Can you hold him to the plowed row
　　with a harness?
　　Will he plow the valleys for you?
¹¹Will you depend on the wild ox for his
　　great strength?
　　Will you leave your heavy work for
　　　him to do?
¹²Can you trust the ox to bring in your
　　grain?
　　Will he gather it to your threshing^d
　　　floor?

¹³"The wings of the ostrich flap happily.
　　But the ostrich's wings are not as
　　　beautiful as the feathers of the
　　　stork.
¹⁴The ostrich lays her eggs on the
　　ground
　　and lets them warm in the sand.

¹⁵She does not stop to think that a foot
    might step on them and crush
    them.
  She does not care that some animal
    might walk on them.
¹⁶The ostrich is cruel to her young, as if
    they were not even hers.
  She does not care that her work is
    for nothing.
¹⁷This is because God did not give the
    ostrich wisdom.
  God did not give her a share of good
    sense.
¹⁸But when the ostrich gets up to run,
    she is so fast
  that she laughs at the horse and its
    rider.

¹⁹"Job, are you the one who gives the
    horse his strength?
  Or do you put a flowing mane on
    his neck?
²⁰Do you make the horse jump like a
    locust?ᵈ
  He scares people with his proud
    snorting.
²¹He paws wildly, enjoying his strength.
  And he charges into the battle.
²²He laughs at fear and is afraid of
    nothing.
  He will not run away from the
    sword.
²³The bag of arrows rattles against the
    horse's side.
  It is there with the flashing spears.
²⁴With great excitement, the horse races
    over the ground.
  He cannot stand still when he hears
    the trumpet.
²⁵When the trumpet blows, the horse
    snorts, 'Aha!'
  He smells the battle from far away.
  He hears the thunder of
    commanders and the shouts of
    battle.

²⁶"Is it through your wisdom that the
    hawk flies?

  Is this why he spreads his wings
    toward the south?
²⁷Are you the one that commands the
    eagle to fly
  and build his nest so high?
²⁸The eagle lives on a high cliff and
    stays there at night.
  The rocky peak is his protected
    place.
²⁹From there he looks for his food.
  His eyes can see it from far away.
³⁰His young eat blood.
  And where there is something dead,
    the eagle is there."

40 The Lord said to Job:

²"Will the person who argues with God
    All-Powerful correct him?
  Let the person who accuses God
    answer him!"

³Then Job answered the Lord:

⁴"I am not worthy. I cannot answer
    you anything.
  I will put my hand over my mouth.
⁵I spoke one time, but I will not answer
    again.
  I even spoke two times, but I will
    say nothing more."

⁶Then the Lord spoke to Job from the
storm:

⁷"Be strong, like a man.
  I will ask you questions.
  And you must answer me.
⁸Would you say that I am unfair?
  Would you blame me to make
    yourself look right?
⁹Are you as strong as God?
  And can your voice thunder like
    his?
¹⁰If so, then decorate yourself with glory
    and beauty.
  And put on honor and greatness as
    if they were clothing.
¹¹Let your great anger punish.

Look at everyone who is proud and
make him feel unimportant.
[12]Look at everyone who is proud and
bring him under your control.
Crush the wicked wherever they are.
[13]Bury them all in the dirt together.
Cover their faces in the grave.
[14]If you can do that, then I myself will
praise you
because you are strong enough to
save yourself.

[15]"Look at Behemoth.[n]
I made him just as I made you.
He eats grass like an ox.
[16]Look at the strength he has in his body.
The muscles of his stomach are
powerful!
[17]His tail extends like a cedar tree.
The muscles of his thighs are woven
together.
[18]His bones are like tubes of bronze
metal.
His legs are like bars of iron.
[19]He is one of the first of God's works.
But God, his Maker, can destroy
him.
[20]The hills, where the wild animals play,
provide food for him.
[21]He lies under the lotus plants
hidden by the tall grass in the swamp.
[22]The lotus plants hide him in their
shadow.
The poplar trees by the streams
surround him.
[23]If the river floods, he will not be afraid.
He is not afraid even if the Jordan
River rushes to his mouth.
[24]Can anyone blind his eyes and capture
him?
Can anyone put hooks in his nose?

41
"Can you catch Leviathan[n] on a
fishhook?
Or can you tie his tongue down with
a rope?

[2]Can you put a cord through his nose
or put a hook in his jaw?
[3]Will he keep begging you for mercy?
Will he speak to you with gentle
words?
[4]Will he make an agreement with you?
Will he let you take him as your
slave for life?
[5]Can you make a pet of Leviathan as
you would a bird?
Or can you put him on a leash for
your girls?
[6]Will traders try to bargain with you
for him?
Will they divide him up among the
traders?
[7]Can you stick him with darts until his
skin is full of them?
Or can you fill his head with fishing
spears?
[8]If you put one hand on him,
you will never forget the battle.
And you will never do it again!
[9]There is no hope of defeating him.
Just seeing him overwhelms people.
[10]No one is brave enough to make him
angry.
So who would be able to stand up
against me?
[11]No one has ever given me anything
that I must pay back.
Everything under heaven belongs to
me.

[12]"I can silence his bragging.
I can silence his brave words and
powerful arguments.
[13]No one can tear off his outer hide.
No one can poke through his
double armor.
[14]No one can force open his great jaws.
There are frightening teeth all
around his jaws.
[15]He has rows of shields on his back.
They are tightly sealed together.
[16]Each shield is so close to the next one
that no air can go between them.

40:15 Behemoth A large land animal, exact identity unknown.
41:1 Leviathan A sea creature, exact identity unknown.

¹⁷They are joined strongly to one
  another.
  They hold on to each other and
  cannot be broken apart.
¹⁸When he snorts, flashes of light are
  thrown out.
  His eyes look like the light at dawn.
¹⁹Flames blaze from his mouth.
  Sparks of fire shoot out.
²⁰Smoke pours out of his nose
  as if coming from a large pot over a
  hot fire.
²¹His breath sets coals on fire.
  And flames come out of his mouth.
²²There is great strength in his neck.
  People are afraid and run away
  from him.
²³The folds of his skin are tightly joined.
  They are set and cannot be moved.
²⁴His chest is as hard as a rock.
  It is as hard as a stone used to grind
  grain.
²⁵Powerful creatures fear his terrible
  looks.
  They draw back in fear as he moves.
²⁶The sword that hits him does not hurt
  him.
  The darts and spears, small and
  large, do not hurt him.
²⁷He treats iron as if it were straw.
  And he treats bronze metal as if it
  were rotten wood.
²⁸He does not run away from arrows.
  Stones from slings are like chaff*d* to
  him.
²⁹Clubs feel like pieces of straw to him.
  And he laughs when they shake a
  spear at him.
³⁰The underside of his body is like
  broken pieces of pottery.
  It leaves a trail in the mud like a
  threshing*d* board.
³¹He makes the deep sea bubble like a
  boiling pot.
  And he stirs up the sea like a pot of
  oil.
³²When he swims, he leaves a shining
  path in the water.

It makes the sea look as if it had
  white hair.
³³Nothing else on earth is equal to him.
  He is a creature without fear.
³⁴He looks down on all those who are
  too proud.
  He is king over all proud creatures."

JOB ANSWERS THE LORD

42 Then Job answered the Lord:

²"I know that you can do all things.
  No plan of yours can be ruined.
³You asked, 'Who is this that made my
  purpose unclear by saying things
  that are not true?'
  Surely I talked about things I did
  not understand.
  I spoke of things too wonderful for
  me to know.

⁴You said, 'Listen now, and I will
  speak.
  I will ask you questions.
  And you must answer me.'
⁵My ears had heard of you before.
  But now my eyes have seen you.
⁶So now I hate myself.
  I will change my heart and life and
  sit in the dust and ashes."

END OF THE STORY

⁷After the Lord had said these things
to Job, he spoke to Eliphaz the Temanite.
The Lord said to him, "I am angry with
you and your two friends. This is because
you have not said what is right about me.
But my servant Job did. ⁸So now take
seven bulls and seven male sheep. Go to
my servant Job. And offer a burnt offering
for yourselves. My servant Job will pray
for you. And I will listen to his prayer.
Then I will not punish you for being
foolish. You have not said what is right
about me. But my servant Job did." ⁹So
Eliphaz the Temanite did as the Lord told
him to do. Bildad the Shuhite and Zophar
the Naamathite also did as the Lord said.
And the Lord listened to Job's prayer.

¹⁰After Job had prayed for his friends,
God gave him success again. God gave

Job twice as much as he had owned before. ¹¹Job's brothers and sisters came to his house. Everyone who had known him before came to his house. And they all ate with him there. They comforted Job and spoke kindly to him. They made him feel better about the trouble the Lord had brought on him. And each one gave Job a piece of silver and a gold ring.

¹²The Lord blessed the last part of Job's life even more than the first part. Job had 14,000 sheep and 6,000 camels. He had 1,000 pairs of oxen and 1,000 female donkeys. ¹³Job also had seven sons and three daughters. ¹⁴He named the first daughter Jemimah. The second daughter he named Keziah. And his third daughter he named Keren-Happuch. ¹⁵There were no other women in all the land as beautiful as Job's daughters. And their father Job gave them land to own along with their brothers.

¹⁶After this, Job lived 140 years. He lived to see his children, grandchildren, great-grandchildren and great-great-grandchildren. ¹⁷Then Job died. He was old and had lived many years.

THE BOOK OF
PSALMS

Book 1

TWO WAYS TO LIVE

1 Happy is the person who doesn't listen to the wicked.
He doesn't go where sinners go.
He doesn't do what bad people do.
[2] He loves the Lord's teachings.
He thinks about those teachings day and night.
[3] He is strong, like a tree planted by a river.
It produces fruit in season.
Its leaves don't die.
Everything he does will succeed.

[4] But wicked people are not like that.
They are like useless chaff[d]
that the wind blows away.
[5] So the wicked will not escape God's punishment.
Sinners will not worship God with good people.
[6] This is because the Lord protects good people.
But the wicked will be destroyed.

GOD'S CHOSEN KING

2 Why are the nations so angry?
Why are the people making useless plans?
[2] The kings of the earth prepare to fight.
Their leaders make plans together against the Lord
and his appointed king.
[3] "Let's break the chains that hold us prisoners.
Let's throw off the ropes that tie us," the nations say.

[4] But the Lord in heaven laughs.
He makes fun of them.
[5] Then the Lord warns them.
He frightens them with his anger.
[6] He says, "I have appointed my own king!

He will rule in Jerusalem on my holy mountain."
[7] Now I will tell you what the Lord has declared:
He said to me, "You are my son.
Today I have become your father.
[8] If you ask me, I will give you the nations.
All the people on earth will be yours.
[9] You will make them obey you by punishing them with an iron rod.
You will break them into pieces like pottery."

[10] So, kings, be wise.
Rulers, learn this lesson.
[11] Obey the Lord with great fear.
Be happy, but tremble.
[12] Show that you are loyal to his son.
Otherwise you will be destroyed.
He can quickly become angry.
But happy are those who trust him for protection.

A MORNING PRAYER

David sang this when he ran away from his son Absalom.

3 Lord, I have many enemies!
Many people have turned against me.
[2] Many people are talking about me.
They say, "God won't rescue him."   *Selah*[d]

[3] But, Lord, you are my shield.
You are my wonderful God who gives me courage.
[4] I will pray to the Lord.
And he will answer me from his holy mountain.   *Selah*

[5] I can lie down and go to sleep.
And I will wake up again because the Lord protects me.
[6] Thousands of enemies may surround me.
But I am not afraid.

⁷Lord, rise up!
　My God, come save me!
　You have hit my enemies on the
　　cheek.
　　You have broken the teeth of the
　　wicked.
⁸The Lord can save his people.
　Lord, bless your people.　　　*Selah*

AN EVENING PRAYER

For the director of music. With stringed
　instruments. A song of David.

4 Answer me when I pray to you,
　my God who does what is right.
Lift the load that I carry.
　Be kind to me and hear my prayer.

²People, how long will you turn my
　　honor into shame?
　You love what is false, and you look
　　for new lies.　　　*Selah*[d]
³You know that the Lord has chosen
　　for himself those who are loyal to
　　him.
　The Lord listens when I pray to
　　him.
⁴When you are angry, do not sin.
　Think about these things quietly
　　as you go to bed.　　　*Selah*
⁵Do what is right as a sacrifice to the
　　Lord.
　And trust the Lord.

⁶Many people ask,
　"Who will give us anything good?
　Lord, be kind to us."
⁷But you have made me very happy.
　I am happier than they are,
　　even with all their grain and wine.
⁸I go to bed and sleep in peace.
　Lord, only you keep me safe.

A MORNING PRAYER FOR PROTECTION

For the director of music. For flutes.
　A song of David.

5 Lord, listen to my words.
　Understand what I am thinking.
²Listen to my cry for help.
　My king and my God, I pray to you.

³Lord, every morning you hear my
　　voice.
　Every morning, I tell you what I need.
　And I wait for your answer.

⁴You are not a God who is pleased with
　　what is wicked.
　You do not live with those who do
　　evil.
⁵Those people who make fun of you
　　cannot stand before you.
　You hate all those who do wrong.
⁶You destroy liars.
　The Lord hates those who kill and
　　trick others.

⁷Because of your great love,
　I can come into your Temple.[d]
Because I fear and respect you,
　I can worship in your holy
　　Temple.
⁸Lord, since I have many enemies,
　show me the right thing to do.
　Show me clearly how you want me
　　to live.

⁹With their mouths my enemies do not
　　tell the truth.
　In their hearts they want to destroy
　　people.
Their throats are like open graves.
　They use their tongues for telling
　　lies.
¹⁰God, declare them guilty!
　Let them fall into their own traps.
Send them away because their sins
　　are many.
　They have turned against you.

¹¹But let everyone who trusts you be
　　happy.
　Let them sing glad songs forever.
Protect those who love you.
　They are happy because of you.
¹²Lord, you bless those who do what is
　　right.
　You protect them like a soldier's
　　shield.

A PRAYER FOR MERCY IN TROUBLED TIMES

For the director of music.
With stringed instruments.
By the sheminith.[d] A song of David.

6 Lord, don't correct me when you
are angry.
Don't punish me when you are very
angry.
[2] Lord, be kind to me because I am
weak.
Heal me, Lord, because my bones
ache.
[3] I am very upset.
Lord, how long will it be?

[4] Lord, return and save me.
Save me because of your kindness.
[5] Dead people don't remember you.
Those in the grave don't praise you.

[6] I am tired of crying to you.
Every night my bed is wet with
tears.
My bed is soaked from my crying.
[7] My eyes are weak from so much
crying.
They are weak from crying about
my enemies.

[8] Get away from me, all you who do
evil.
The Lord has heard my crying.
[9] The Lord has heard my cry for help.
The Lord will answer my prayer.
[10] All my enemies will be ashamed and
troubled.
They will turn and suddenly leave
in shame.

A PRAYER FOR FAIRNESS

A shiggaion[d] of David which he sang to the
Lord about Cush, from the tribe of Benjamin.

7 Lord my God, I trust in you for
protection.
Save me and rescue me
from those who are chasing me.
[2] Otherwise, they will tear me apart like
a lion.

They will rip me to pieces, and no
one can save me.

[3] Lord my God, what have I done?
Have my hands done something
wrong?
[4] Have I done wrong to my friend?
Have I stolen from my enemy?
[5] If I have, let my enemy chase me and
capture me.
Let him trample me into the dust.
Let him bury me in the ground.
Selah[d]

[6] Lord, rise up in your anger.
Stand up against my enemies'
anger.
Get up and demand fairness.
[7] Gather the nations around you,
and rule them from above.
[8] Lord, judge the people.
Lord, defend me.
Prove that I am right.
Show that I have done no wrong,
God Most High.
[9] God, you do what is right.
You know our thoughts and
feelings.
Stop those wicked actions done by
evil people.
And help those who do what is
right.

[10] God Most High protects me like a
shield.
He saves those whose hearts are
right.
[11] God judges by what is right.
And God is always ready to punish
the wicked.
[12] If they do not change their lives,
God will sharpen his sword.
He will string his bow and take aim.
[13] He has prepared his deadly weapons.
He has made his flaming arrows.

[14] There are people who think up evil.
They plan trouble and tell lies.
[15] They dig a hole to trap other people.
But they will fall into it themselves.

¹⁶They themselves will get into trouble.
  The violence they cause will hurt
    only themselves.

¹⁷I praise the Lord because he does
    what is right.
  I sing praises to the name of the
    Lord Most High.

GOD'S GREATNESS AND MAN'S WORTH

For the director of music.
By the gittith.ᵈ A song of David.

8 Lord our Master,
  your name is the most wonderful
    name in all the earth!
  It brings you praise in heaven
    above.
²You have taught children and babies
    to sing praises to you.
  This is because of your enemies.
And so you silence your enemies
    and destroy those who try to get
      even.

³I look at the heavens,
    which you made with your hands.
  I see the moon and stars,
    which you created.
⁴But why is man important to you?
    Why do you take care of human
      beings?
⁵You made man a little lower than the
    angels.
  And you crowned him with glory
    and honor.
⁶You put him in charge of everything
    you made.
  You put all things under his
    control:
⁷all the sheep, the cattle
    and the wild animals,
⁸the birds in the sky,
    the fish in the sea,
    and everything that lives under
      water.

⁹Lord our Master,
  your name is the most wonderful
    name in all the earth!

THANKSGIVING FOR VICTORY

For the director of music. To the tune of
"The Death of the Son." A song of David.

9 I will praise you, Lord, with all my
    heart.
  I will tell all the miraclesᵈ you have
    done.
²I will be happy because of you.
  God Most High, I will sing praises
    to your name.

³My enemies turn back.
  They are overwhelmed and die
    because of you.
⁴You have heard what I complained to
    you about.
  You sat on your throne and judged
    by what was right.
⁵You spoke strongly against the foreign
    nations
  and destroyed the wicked people.
  You wiped out their names forever
    and ever.
⁶The enemy is gone forever.
  You destroyed their cities.
  No one even remembers them.

⁷But the Lord rules forever.
  He sits on his throne to judge.
⁸The Lord will judge the world by what
    is right.
  He will decide what is fair for the
    nations.
⁹The Lord defends those who suffer.
  He protects them in times of
    trouble.
¹⁰Those who know the Lord trust him.
  He will not leave those who come to
    him.

¹¹Sing praises to the Lord who is king
    on Mount Zion.ᵈ
  Tell the nations what he has done.
¹²He remembers who the murderers
    are.
  He will not forget the cries of those
    who suffer.
¹³Lord, be kind to me.
  See how my enemies hurt me.

Do not let me go through the gates
of death.
¹⁴Then, at the gates of Jerusalem, I will
praise you.
I will rejoice because you saved me.

¹⁵The nations have fallen into the pit
they dug.
Their feet are caught in the nets
they laid.
¹⁶The Lord has made himself known by
his fair decisions.
The wicked get trapped by what
they do.   *Higgaion.ᵈ Selahᵈ*

¹⁷Wicked people will go to the grave.
So will all those who forget God.
¹⁸Those who have troubles will not be
forgotten.
The hopes of the poor will not die.

¹⁹Lord, rise up and judge the nations.
Don't let humans think they are
strong.
²⁰Teach them to fear you, Lord.
The nations must learn that they
are only human.   *Selah*

A COMPLAINT ABOUT EVIL PEOPLE

10 Lord, why are you so far away?
Why do you hide when there is
trouble?
²Proudly the wicked chase down those
who suffer.
The wicked set traps to catch them.
³They brag about the things they want.
They bless the greedy but hate the
Lord.
⁴The wicked people are too proud.
They do not look for God.
There is no room for God in their
thoughts.
⁵They always succeed.
They are far from keeping your
laws.
They make fun of their enemies.
⁶They say to themselves, "Nothing bad
will ever happen to me.
I will never be ruined."

⁷Their mouths are full of curses, lies
and threats.
They use their tongues for sin and
evil.
⁸They hide near the villages.
They look for innocent people to kill.
They watch in secret for the helpless.
⁹They wait in hiding like a lion.
They wait to catch poor people.
They catch the poor in nets.
¹⁰The poor are thrown down and
crushed.
They are defeated because the
others are stronger.
¹¹The wicked think,
"God has forgotten us.
He doesn't see what is happening."

¹²Lord, rise up and punish the wicked.
Don't forget those who need help.
¹³Why do wicked people hate God?
They say to themselves, "God won't
punish us."
¹⁴Lord, surely you see these cruel and
evil things.
Look at them and do something.
People in trouble look to you for help.
You are the one who helps the
orphans.
¹⁵Break the power of wicked men.
Punish them for the evil they have
done.

¹⁶The Lord is King forever and ever.
Remove from your land those
nations that do not worship you.
¹⁷Lord, you have heard what the poor
people want.
Do what they ask. Listen to them.
¹⁸Protect the orphans. Put an end to
suffering.
Then they will no longer be afraid
of evil people.

A STATEMENT ABOUT TRUST IN GOD

For the director of music. Of David.

11 I trust in the Lord for protection.
So why do you say to me,
"Fly like a bird to your mountain.

[2]Like hunters, the wicked string their
  bows.
  They set their arrows on the
  bowstrings.
They shoot from dark places
  at those who are honest.
[3]When all that is good falls apart,
  what can good people do?"

[4]The Lord is in his holy temple.
  The Lord sits on his throne in
  heaven.
And he sees what people do.
  He keeps his eye on them.
[5]The Lord tests those who do right.
  But he hates the wicked and those
  who love to hurt others.
[6]He will send hot coals on the wicked.
  Burning sulfur and a whirlwind is
  what they will get.
[7]The Lord does what is right, and he
  loves justice.
  So honest people will see his face.

A PRAYER AGAINST LIARS

For the director of music. By the sheminith.[d]
            A song of David.

12 Save me, Lord, because the
      good people are all gone.
  No true believers are left on earth.
[2]Everyone lies to his neighbors.
  They say one thing and mean
  another.

[3]The Lord will stop those lying lips.
  He will cut off those bragging
  tongues.
[4]They say, "Our tongues will help us
  win.
  We can say what we wish. No one is
  our master."

[5]But the Lord says,
  "I will now rise up
  because the poor are being hurt.
Because of the moans of the helpless,
  I will give them the help they want."
[6]The Lord's words are pure.
  They are like silver purified by fire,
  like silver purified seven times over.

[7]Lord, keep us safe.
  Always protect us from such
  people.
[8]The wicked are all around us.
  Everyone loves what is wrong.

A PRAYER FOR GOD TO BE NEAR

For the director of music. A song of David.

13 How long will you forget me,
      Lord?
How long will you hide from me?
  Forever?
[2]How long must I worry?
  How long must I feel sad in my
  heart?
  How long will my enemy win over
  me?

[3]Lord, look at me.
  Answer me, my God.
  Tell me, or I will die.
[4]Otherwise my enemy will say, "I have
  won!"
  Those against me will rejoice that
  I've been defeated.

[5]I trust in your love.
  My heart is happy because you
  saved me.
[6]I sing to the Lord
  because he has taken care of me.

THE UNBELIEVING FOOL

For the director of music. Of David.

14 A wicked fool says to himself,
      "There is no God."
Fools are evil. They do terrible things.
  None of them does anything good.

[2]The Lord looked down from heaven at
  all the people.
  He looked to see if anyone was wise,
  if anyone was looking to God for
  help.
[3]But all have turned away.
  Together, everyone has become evil.
  None of them does anything good.

[4]Don't the wicked understand?
  They destroy my people as if they
  were eating bread.
  They do not ask the Lord for help.

5But the wicked are filled with terror
     because God is with those who do
       what is right.
6The wicked upset the plans of the
       poor.
   But the Lord will protect the poor.

7I pray that victory will come to Israel
     from Mount Zion![d]
   May the Lord give them back their
       riches.
   Then the people of Jacob will rejoice.
   And the people of Israel will be glad.

WHAT GOD DEMANDS

A song of David.

15 Lord, who may enter your Holy
       Tent?[d]
   Who may live on your holy
       mountain?

2Only a person who is innocent
     and who does what is right.
   He must speak the truth from his
       heart.
3 He must not tell lies about others.
   He must do no wrong to his
       neighbors.
   He must not gossip.
4He must not respect hateful people.
   He must honor those who honor
       the Lord.
   He must keep his promises to his
       neighbor,
     even when it hurts.
5He must not charge interest on money
       he lends.
   And he must not take money to
       hurt innocent people.

Whoever does all these things will
     never be destroyed.

THE LORD TAKES CARE OF HIS PEOPLE

A miktam[d] of David.

16 Protect me, God,
       because I trust in you.
2I said to the Lord, "You are my Lord.
   Every good thing I have comes
       from you."

3There are godly people in the world.
   I enjoy them.
4But those who turn to idols will have
       much pain.
   I will not offer blood to those idols.
   I won't even speak their names.

5No, the Lord is all I need.
   He takes care of me.
6My share in life has been pleasant.
   My part has been beautiful.

7I praise the Lord because he guides me.
   Even at night, I feel his leading.
8I keep the Lord before me always.
   Because he is close by my side
   I will not be hurt.
9So I rejoice, and I am glad.
   Even my body has hope.
10This is because you will not leave me
       in the grave.
   You will not let your holy one rot.
11You will teach me God's way to live.
   Being with you will fill me with joy.
   At your right hand I will find
       pleasure forever.

A PRAYER FOR PROTECTION

A prayer of David.

17 Lord, hear me begging for
       fairness.
   Listen to my cry for help.
   Pay attention to my prayer.
   I speak the truth.
2You will judge that I am right.
   Your eyes can see what is true.
3You have examined my heart.
   You have tested me all night.
   You questioned me without finding
       anything wrong.
   I did not plan any evil.
4I have obeyed your commands.
   I have not done what evil people do.
5I have done what you told me to do.
   I have not failed.

6I call to you, God,
     and you answer me.
   Listen to me now.
   Hear what I say.

⁷Your love is wonderful.
  By your power you save
  from their enemies those who trust
    you.
⁸Protect me as you would protect your
    own eye.
  Protect me as a bird hides her
    young under her wings.
⁹Keep me from the wicked who attack
    me.
  Protect me from my enemies who
    surround me.
¹⁰They are selfish.
  They brag about themselves.
¹¹They have chased me.
  Now they surround me.
  They plan to throw me to the
    ground.
¹²They are like lions ready to kill.
  Like lions, they sit in hiding.

¹³Lord, rise up and face the enemy.
  Throw them down.
  Save me from the wicked
  with your sword.
¹⁴Lord, save me from them by your
    power.
  Their reward is in this life.
  They have plenty of food.
  They have many sons.
  They leave money to their children.

¹⁵Because I have lived right, I will see
    your face.
  When I wake up, I will see your
    likeness and be satisfied.

A SONG OF VICTORY

For the director of music. By the Lord's
servant, David. David sang this song to the
Lord. He sang it when the Lord had saved him
from Saul and all his other enemies.

18 I love you, Lord. You are my
    strength.
²The Lord is my rock, my protection,
    my Savior.
  My God is my rock.
  I can run to him for safety.
  He is my shield and my saving
    strength, my high tower.

³I will call to the Lord.
  He is worthy of praise.
  And I will be saved from my
    enemies.

⁴The ropes of death bound me.
  The deadly rivers overwhelmed
    me.
⁵The ropes of death wrapped around
    me.
  The traps of death were before
    me.
⁶In my trouble I called to the Lord.
  I cried out to my God for help.
  From his temple he heard my voice.
  My call for help reached his ears.

⁷The earth trembled and shook.
  The foundations of the mountains
    began to shake.
  They shook because the Lord was
    angry.
⁸Smoke came out of his nose.
  Burning fire came out of his mouth.
  Burning coals went before him.
⁹He tore open the sky and came down.
  Dark clouds were under his feet.
¹⁰He rode a creature with wings and
    flew.
  He flew on the wings of the wind.
¹¹He made darkness his covering, his
    shelter around him,
  surrounded by fog and clouds.
¹²Out of the brightness of his presence
    came clouds.
  They came with hail and lightning.
¹³The Lord thundered from heaven.
  God Most High raised his voice.
  And there was hail and lightning.
¹⁴He shot his arrows and scattered his
    enemies.
  His many bolts of lightning
    confused them with fear.
¹⁵Lord, you spoke strongly.
  The wind blew from your nose.
  The valleys of the sea appeared.
  The foundations of the earth were
    seen.

[16]The Lord reached down from above
and took me.
He pulled me from the deep water.
[17]He saved me from my powerful
enemies.
Those who hated me were too
strong for me.
[18]They attacked me at my time of
trouble.
But the Lord supported me.
[19]He took me to a safe place.
Because he delights in me,
he saved me.

[20]The Lord spared me because I did
what was right.
Because I have not done evil, he has
rewarded me.
[21]I have followed the ways of the Lord.
I have not done evil by turning
away from my God.
[22]I remember all his laws.
I have not broken his rules.
[23]I am innocent before him.
I have kept myself from doing evil.
[24]The Lord rewarded me because I did
what was right.
I did what the Lord said was right.

[25]Lord, you are loyal to those who are
loyal.
You are good to those who are
good.
[26]You are pure to those who are pure.
But you are against those who are
bad.
[27]You save those who are not proud.
But you make humble those who
are proud.
[28]Lord, you give light to my lamp.
My God brightens the darkness
around me.
[29]With your help I can attack an army.
With God's help I can jump over a
wall.

[30]The ways of God are without fault.
The Lord's words are pure.
He is a shield to those who trust him.

[31]Who is God? Only the Lord.
Who is the Rock?[d] Only our God.
[32]God is my protection.
He makes my way free from fault.
[33]He makes me like a deer, which does
not stumble.
He helps me stand on the steep
mountains.
[34]He trains my hands for battle.
So my arms can bend a bronze bow.
[35]You protect me with your saving shield.
You support me with your right
hand.
You have stooped to make me
great.
[36]You give me a wide path on which to
walk.
My feet have not slipped.
[37]I chased my enemies and caught
them.
I did not quit till they were
destroyed.
[38]I crushed them so they couldn't rise
up again.
They fell beneath my feet.
[39]You gave me strength in battle.
You made my enemies bow before
me.
[40]You made my enemies turn back.
I destroyed those who hated me.
[41]They called for help,
but no one came to save them.
They called to the Lord,
but he did not answer them.
[42]I beat my enemies into pieces.
They were like dust in the wind.
I poured them out like mud in the
streets.

[43]You saved me when the people
attacked me.
You made me the leader of nations.
People I never knew serve me.
[44]As soon as they hear me, they obey
me.
Foreigners obey me.
[45]They all become afraid.
They tremble in their hiding places.

46 The Lord lives!
　　May my Rock be praised.
　　Praise the God who saves me!
47 God gives me victory over my
　　　enemies.
　　He brings people under my rule.
48 He saves me from my enemies.

　　You set me over those who hate me.
　　You saved me from cruel men.
49 So I will praise you, Lord, among the
　　　nations.
　　I will sing praises to your name.
50 The Lord gives great victories to his
　　　king.
　　He is loyal to his appointed king,
　　to David and his descendants[d]
　　　forever.

GOD'S WORKS AND WORD

For the director of music. A song of David.

19 The heavens tell the glory of
　　God.
　　And the skies announce what his
　　　hands have made.
2 Day after day they tell the story.
　　Night after night they tell it again.
3 They have no speech or words.
　　They don't make any sound to be
　　　heard.
4 But their message goes out through all
　　　the world.
　　It goes everywhere on earth.
　　The sky is like a home for the sun.
5 　The sun comes out like a
　　　bridegroom from his bedroom.
　　It rejoices like an athlete eager to
　　　run a race.
6 The sun rises at one end of the sky,
　　and it follows its path to the other
　　　end.
　　Nothing hides from its heat.

7 The Lord's teachings are perfect.
　　They give new strength.
　　The Lord's rules can be trusted.
　　They make plain people wise.
8 The Lord's orders are right.
　　They make people happy.

The Lord's commands are pure.
　　They light up the way.
9 It is good to respect the Lord.
　　That respect will last forever.
　　The Lord's judgments are true.
　　They are completely right.
10 They are worth more than gold,
　　even the purest gold.
　　They are sweeter than honey,
　　even the finest honey.
11 They tell your servant what to do.
　　Keeping them brings great reward.

12 No one can see all his own mistakes.
　　Forgive me for my secret sins.
13 Keep me from the sins that I want to
　　　do.
　　Don't let them rule me.
　　Then I can be pure
　　and free from the greatest of sins.

14 I hope my words and thoughts please
　　　you.
　　Lord, you are my Rock,[d] the one
　　　who saves me.

A PRAYER FOR THE KING

For the director of music. A song of David.

20 May the Lord answer you in
　　times of trouble.
　　May the God of Jacob protect you.
2 May he send you help from his
　　　Temple.[d]
　　May he support you from Mount
　　　Zion.[d]
3 May he remember all your offerings.
　　May he accept all your sacrifices.
　　　　　　　　　　　　　　Selah[d]
4 May he give you what you want.
　　May all your plans succeed.
5 We will shout for joy when you
　　　succeed.
　　We will raise a flag in the name of
　　　our God.
　　May the Lord give you all that you ask
　　　for.

6 Now I know the Lord helps his
　　appointed king.

He answers him from his holy
heaven.
He saves him with his strong right
hand.
⁷Some trust in chariots, others in
horses.
But we trust the Lord our God.
⁸They are overwhelmed and defeated.
But we march forward and win.
⁹Lord, save the king!
Answer us when we call for help.

THANKSGIVING FOR THE KING

For the director of music. A song of David.

21 Lord, the king rejoices because
of your strength.
He is so happy when you save him!
²You gave the king what he wanted.
You did not refuse what he asked
for.   *Selah*ᵈ
³You put good things before him.
You placed a gold crown on his
head.
⁴He asked you for life.
And you gave it to him.
His years go on and on.
⁵He has great glory because you gave
him victories.
You gave him honor and praise.
⁶You always gave him blessings.
You made him glad because you
were with him.
⁷The king truly trusts the Lord.
Because God Most High always
loves him,
he will not be overwhelmed.
⁸Your hand is against all your enemies.
Those who hate you will feel your
power.
⁹When you appear, you will burn them
like wood in a furnace.
In your anger you will eat them up.
Your fire will burn them up.
¹⁰You will destroy their families from
the earth.
Their children will not live.
¹¹They made evil plans against you.
But their traps won't work.

¹²You will make them turn their backs
when you aim your arrows at them.
¹³Be supreme, Lord, in your power.
We sing and praise your greatness.

THE PRAYER OF A SUFFERING MAN

For the director of music. To the tune
of "The Doe of Dawn." A song of David.

22 My God, my God, why have you
left me alone?
You are too far away to save me.
You are too far away to hear my
moans.
²My God, I call to you during the day.
But you do not answer.
And I call at night.
I am not silent.

³You sit as the Holy One.
The praises of Israel are your throne.
⁴Our ancestors trusted you.
They trusted you, and you saved
them.
⁵They called to you for help.
And they were rescued.
They trusted you.
And they were not disappointed.

⁶But I am like a worm instead of a
man.
Men make fun of me.
They look down on me.
⁷Everyone who looks at me laughs.
They stick out their tongues.
They shake their heads.
⁸They say, "Turn to the Lord for help.
Maybe he will save you.
If he likes you,
maybe he will rescue you."

⁹You had my mother give birth to me.
You made me trust you
while I was just a baby.
¹⁰I have leaned on you since the day
I was born.
You have been my God since my
mother gave birth to me.
¹¹So don't be far away from me.
Now trouble is near,
and there is no one to help.

[12]Men have surrounded me like angry
bulls.
The strong bulls of Bashan are on
every side.
[13]Like hungry, roaring lions
they open their jaws at me.
[14]My strength is gone
like water poured out onto the
ground.
All my bones are out of joint.
My heart is like wax.
It has melted inside me.
[15]My strength has dried up like a piece
of a broken pot.
My tongue sticks to the top of my
mouth.
You laid me in the dust of death.
[16]Evil men have surrounded me.
Like dogs they have trapped me.
They have bitten my arms and legs.
[17]I can count all my bones.
People look and stare at me.
[18]They divided my clothes among them,
and they threw lots[d] for my
clothing.

[19]But, Lord, don't be far away.
You are my power. Hurry to help me.
[20]Save me from the sword.
Save my life from the dogs.
[21]Rescue me from the lion's mouth.
Save me from the horns of the bulls.

[22]Then I will tell my brothers and
sisters about you.
I will praise you when your people
meet to worship you.
[23]Praise the Lord, all you who worship
him.
All you descendants[d] of Jacob,
honor him.
Fear him, all you Israelites.
[24]The Lord does not ignore
the one who is in trouble.
He doesn't hide from him.
He listens when the one in trouble
calls out to him.

[25]Lord, I praise you in the great meeting
of your people.
These worshipers will see me do
what I promised.
[26]Poor people will eat until they are full.
Those who look to the Lord will
praise him.
May your hearts live forever!
[27]People everywhere will remember
and will turn to the Lord.
All the families of the nations
will worship him.
[28]This is because the Lord is King.
He rules the nations.

[29]All the powerful people on earth will
eat and worship.
Everyone will bow down to him.
[30]The people in the future will serve
him.
They will always be told about the
Lord.
[31]They will tell that he does what is
right.
People who are not yet born
will hear what God has done.

THE LORD THE SHEPHERD

A song of David.

23 The Lord is my shepherd.
I have everything I need.
[2]He gives me rest in green pastures.
He leads me to calm water.
[3]He gives me new strength.
For the good of his name,
he leads me on paths that are right.
[4]Even if I walk
through a very dark valley,
I will not be afraid
because you are with me.
Your rod and your shepherd's staff
comfort me.

[5]You prepare a meal for me
in front of my enemies.
You pour oil of blessing on my head.[n]
You give me more than I can hold.

23:5 **pour oil ... head** This can mean that God gave him great wealth and blessed him.

6Surely your goodness and love will be
with me
all my life.
And I will live in the house of the Lord
forever.

A WELCOME FOR GOD INTO THE TEMPLE

A song of David.

24 The earth and everything in it
belong to the Lord.
The world and all its people belong
to him.
2He built it on the waters.
He set it on the rivers.

3Who may go up on the mountain of
the Lord?
Who may stand in his holy
Temple?[d]
4Only those with clean hands and pure
hearts.
They must not have worshiped
idols.
They must not have made promises
in the name of a false god.
5It is they who will receive a blessing
from the Lord.
The God who saves them will
declare them right.
6They try to follow God.
They look to the God of Jacob for
help.   *Selah*[d]

7Open up, you gates.
Open wide, you aged doors.
Then the glorious king will come in.
8Who is this glorious king?
The Lord, strong and mighty.
The Lord, the powerful warrior.
9Open up, you gates.
Open wide, you aged doors.
Then the glorious king will come in.
10Who is this glorious king?
The Lord of heaven's armies—
he is the glorious king.   *Selah*

A PRAYER FOR GOD TO GUIDE

Of David.

25 Lord, I give myself to you.
2   My God, I trust you.

Do not let me be disgraced.
Do not let my enemies laugh at me.
3No one who trusts you will be
disgraced.
But those who sin without excuse
will be disgraced.

4Lord, tell me your ways.
Show me how to live.
5Guide me in your truth.
Teach me, my God, my Savior.
I trust you all day long.
6Lord, remember your mercy and love.
You have shown them since long
ago.
7Do not remember the sins
and wrong things I did when I was
young.
But remember to love me always
because you are good, Lord.

8The Lord is good and right.
He points sinners to the right way.
9He shows those who are not proud
how to do right.
He teaches them his ways.
10All the Lord's ways are loving and true
for those who follow the demands
of his agreement.
11For the sake of your name, Lord,
forgive my many sins.
12Is there someone who worships the
Lord?
The Lord will point him to the best
way.
13He will enjoy a good life.
His children will inherit the land.
14The Lord tells his secrets to those who
respect him.
He tells them about his agreement.
15My eyes are always looking to the
Lord for help.
He will keep me from any traps.
16Turn to me and be kind to me.
I am lonely and hurting.
17My troubles have grown larger.
Free me from my problems.
18Look at my suffering and troubles.
Take away all my sins.

[19]Look at how many enemies I have!
See how much they hate me!
[20]Protect me and save me.
I trust you.
Do not let me be disgraced.
[21]My hope is in you.
So may goodness and honesty
guard me.
[22]God, save Israel from all their troubles!

THE PRAYER OF AN INNOCENT MAN

Of David.

26 Lord, defend me.
I have lived an innocent life.
I trusted the Lord and never doubted.
[2]Lord, try me and test me.
Look closely into my heart and
mind.
[3]I see your love.
I live by your truth.
[4]I do not spend time with liars.
I do not make friends with people
who hide their sin.
[5]I hate the company of evil people.
I won't sit with the wicked.
[6]I wash my hands to show I am
innocent.
I come to your altar, Lord.
[7]I raise my voice in praise.
I tell of all the miracles[d] you have
done.
[8]Lord, I love the Temple[d] where you live.
It is where your greatness is.
[9]Do not kill me with those sinners.
Do not take my life with those
murderers.
[10]Evil is in their hands.
They do wrong for money.
[11]But I have lived an innocent life.
So save me and be kind to me.
[12]I stand in a safe place.
Lord, I praise you in the great
meeting.

A SONG OF TRUST IN GOD

Of David.

27 The Lord is my light and the
one who saves me.
So why should I fear anyone?

The Lord protects my life.
So why should I be afraid?
[2]Evil people may try to destroy my body.
My enemies and those who hate me
attack me.
But they are overwhelmed and
defeated.
[3]If an army surrounds me,
I will not be afraid.
If war breaks out,
I will trust the Lord.

[4]I ask only one thing from the Lord.
This is what I want:
Let me live in the Lord's house
all my life.
Let me see the Lord's beauty.
Let me look around in his Temple.[d]
[5]During danger he will keep me safe in
his shelter.
He will hide me in his Holy Tent.[d]
Or he will keep me safe on a high
mountain.
[6]My head is higher
than my enemies around me.
I will offer joyful sacrifices in his Holy
Tent.
I will sing and praise the Lord.

[7]Lord, hear me when I call.
Be kind and answer me.
[8]My heart said of you, "Go, worship
him."
So I come to worship you, Lord.
[9]Do not turn away from me.
Do not turn your servant away in
anger.
You have helped me.
Do not push me away or leave me
alone,
God, my Savior.
[10]If my father and mother leave me,
the Lord will take me in.
[11]Lord, teach me your ways.
Guide me to do what is right
because I have enemies.
[12]Do not let my enemies defeat me.
They tell lies about me.
They say they will hurt me.

[13]I truly believe
  I will live to see the Lord's
    goodness.
[14]Wait for the Lord's help.
  Be strong and brave
  and wait for the Lord's help.

A PRAYER IN TROUBLED TIMES
Of David.

28 Lord, my Rock,[d] I call out to
      you for help.
  Do not be deaf to me.
  If you are silent,
    I will be like those in the grave.
[2]Hear the sound of my prayer,
  when I cry out to you for help.
  I raise my hands
    toward your Most Holy Place.
[3]Don't drag me away with the
    wicked,
  with those who do evil.
  They say, "Peace" to their
    neighbors.
  But evil is in their hearts.
[4]Pay them back for what they have
    done.
  They have done evil.
  Pay them back for what they have
    done.
  Give them their reward.
[5]They don't understand what the Lord
    has done
  or what he has made.
  So he will knock them down
  and not lift them up.

[6]Praise the Lord.
  He heard my prayer for help.
[7]The Lord is my strength and shield.
  I trust him, and he helps me.
  I am very happy.
  And I praise him with my song.
[8]The Lord is powerful.
  He gives power and victory to his
    chosen one.
[9]Save your people.
  Bless those who are your own.
  Be their shepherd and carry them
    forever.

GOD IN THE THUNDERSTORM
A song of David.

29 Praise the Lord, you angels.
      Praise the Lord's glory and
        power.
[2]Praise the Lord for the glory of his
    name.
  Worship the Lord because he is holy.

[3]The Lord's voice is heard over the sea.
  The glorious God thunders.
  The Lord thunders over the great
    ocean.
[4]The Lord's voice is powerful.
  The Lord's voice is majestic.
[5]The Lord's voice breaks the trees.
  The Lord breaks the cedars of
    Lebanon.
[6]He makes the land of Lebanon dance
    like a calf.
  He makes Mount Hermon jump
    like a baby bull.
[7]The Lord's voice makes the lightning
    flash.
[8]The Lord's voice shakes the desert.
  The Lord shakes the Desert of
    Kadesh.
[9]The Lord's voice shakes the oaks.
  The leaves fall off the trees.
  In his Temple[d] everyone says,
    "Glory to God!"

[10]The Lord controls the flood.
  The Lord will be King forever.
[11]The Lord gives strength to his people.
  The Lord blesses his people with
    peace.

THANKSGIVING FOR ESCAPING DEATH
A song of David. A song for giving the
Temple[d] to the Lord.

30 I will praise you, Lord,
      because you rescued me.
  You did not let my enemies laugh
    at me.
[2]Lord, my God, I prayed to you.
  And you healed me.
[3]You lifted me out of the grave.

You spared me from going down
    where the dead are.

4Sing praises to the Lord, you who
    belong to him.
    Praise his holy name.
5His anger lasts only a moment.
    But his kindness lasts for a lifetime.
    Crying may last for a night.
    But joy comes in the morning.

6When I felt safe, I said,
    "I will never fail."
7Lord, in your kindness you made my
    mountain safe.
    But when you turned away, I was
    frightened.

8I called to you, Lord.
    I asked you to have mercy on me.
9I said, "What good will it do if I die
    or if I go down to the grave?
    Dust cannot praise you.
    It cannot speak about your truth.
10Lord, hear me and be merciful to me.
    Lord, help me."

11You changed my sorrow into dancing.
    You took away my rough cloth,
    which shows sadness, and
    clothed me in happiness.
12I will sing to you and not be silent.
    Lord, my God, I will praise you
    forever.

A PRAYER OF FAITH IN TROUBLED TIMES

For the director of music. A song of David.

31 Lord, I trust in you.
    Let me never be disgraced.
    Save me because you do what is right.
2Listen to me.
    Save me quickly.
    Be my rock of protection,
    a strong city to save me.
3You are my rock and my protection.
    For the good of your name, lead me
    and guide me.
4Set me free from the trap they set
    for me.
    You are my protection.

5I give you my life.
    Save me, Lord, God of truth.
6I hate those who worship false gods.
    I trust only in the Lord.
7I will be glad because of your love.
    You saw my suffering.
    You knew my troubles.
8You have not let my enemies defeat
    me.
    You have set me in a safe place.

9Lord, have mercy. I am in misery.
    My eyes are weak from so much
    crying.
    My whole being is tired from grief.
10My life is ending in sadness.
    My years are spent in crying.
    My troubles are using up my strength.
    My bones are getting weaker.
11Because of all my troubles, my
    enemies hate me.
    Even my neighbors look down on
    me.
    When my friends see me,
    they are afraid and run.
12I am like a piece of a broken pot.
    I am forgotten as if I were dead.
13I have heard many insults.
    Terror is all around me.
    They make plans against me.
    They want to kill me.

14Lord, I trust you.
    I have said, "You are my God."
15My life is in your hands.
    Save me from my enemies' grasp.
    Save me from those who are
    chasing me.
16Show your kindness to me, your
    servant.
    Save me because of your love.
17Lord, I called to you.
    So do not let me be disgraced.
    Let the wicked be disgraced.
    Let them lie silent in the grave.
18With pride and hatred
    they speak against the righteous.
    So shut their lying lips.

[19]How great is your goodness!
You have stored it up for those who
fear you.
You do good things for those who
trust you.
You do this for all to see.
[20]You protect them by your presence
from what people plan against them.
You keep them safe in your shelter
from evil words.
[21]Praise the Lord.
His love to me was wonderful
when my city was attacked.
[22]In my distress, I said,
"God cannot see me!"
But you heard my prayer
when I cried out to you for help.
[23]Love the Lord, all you who belong to
him.
The Lord protects those who truly
believe.
But he punishes the proud as much
as they have sinned.
[24]All you who put your hope in the Lord
be strong and brave.

IT IS BETTER TO CONFESS SIN

A maskil[d] of David.

32 Happy is the person
whose sins are forgiven,
whose wrongs are pardoned.
[2]Happy is the person
whom the Lord does not consider
guilty.
In that person there is nothing
false.

[3]When I kept things to myself,
I felt weak deep inside me.
I moaned all day long.
[4]Day and night
you punished me.
My strength was gone
as in the summer heat.   *Selah*[d]
[5]Then I confessed my sins to you.
I didn't hide my guilt.
I said, "I will confess my sins to the
Lord."
And you forgave my guilt.   *Selah*

[6]For this reason, all who obey you
should pray to you while they still
can.
When troubles rise like a flood,
they will not reach them.
[7]You are my hiding place.
You protect me from my troubles.
You fill me with songs of salvation.
          Selah

[8]The Lord says, "I will make you wise.
I will show you where to go.
I will guide you and watch over you.
[9]So don't be like a horse or donkey.
They don't understand.
They must be led with bits and reins,
or they will not come near you."

[10]Wicked people have many troubles.
But the Lord's love surrounds those
who trust him.
[11]Good people, rejoice and be happy in
the Lord.
All you whose hearts are right, sing.

PRAISE GOD WHO CREATES AND SAVES

33 Sing to the Lord, you who do
what is right.

Honest people should praise him.
[2]Praise the Lord on the harp.
Make music for him on the
ten-stringed lyre.[d]
[3]Sing a new song to him.
Play well and joyfully.

[4]God's word is true.
Everything he does is right.
[5]He loves what is right and fair.
The Lord's love fills the earth.

[6]The sky was made at the Lord's
command.
By the breath from his mouth, he
made all the stars.
[7]He gathered the water in the sea into a
heap.
He made the great ocean stay in its
place.
[8]All the earth should worship the Lord.
The whole world should fear him.

⁹He spoke, and it happened.
    He commanded, and it appeared.
¹⁰The Lord upsets the plans of nations.
    He ruins all their plans.
¹¹But the Lord's plans will stand
        forever.
    His ideas will last from now on.
¹²Happy is the nation whose God is the
        Lord.
    Happy are the people he chose for
        his very own.
¹³The Lord looks down from heaven.
    He sees every person.
¹⁴From his throne he watches
    everyone who lives on earth.
¹⁵He made their hearts.
    He understands everything they do.
¹⁶No king is saved by his great army.
    No warrior escapes by his great
        strength.
¹⁷Horses can't bring victory.
    They can't save by their strength.
¹⁸But the Lord looks after those who
        fear him.
    He watches over those who put
        their hope in his love.
¹⁹He saves them from death.
    He spares their lives in times of
        hunger.
²⁰So our hope is in the Lord.
    He is our help, our shield to protect
        us.
²¹We rejoice in him.
    We trust his holy name.
²²Lord, show your love to us
    as we put our hope in you.

PRAISE GOD WHO JUDGES AND SAVES

David's song from the time he acted crazy
so Abimelech would send him away.
And David did leave.

34 I will praise the Lord at all
        times.
    His praise is always on my lips.
²My whole being praises the Lord.
    The poor will hear and be glad.
³Tell the greatness of the Lord with me.
    Let us praise his name together.

⁴I asked the Lord for help, and he
        answered me.
    He saved me from all that I feared.
⁵Those who go to him for help are
        happy.
    They are never disgraced.
⁶This poor man called, and the Lord
        heard him.
    The Lord saved him from all his
        troubles.
⁷The Lord saves those who fear him.
    His angel camps around them.

⁸Examine and see how good the Lord
        is.
    Happy is the person who trusts the
        Lord.
⁹People who belong to the Lord, fear
        him!
    Those who fear him will have
        everything they need.
¹⁰Even lions may become weak and
        hungry.
    But those people who go to the Lord
        for help will have every good
        thing.
¹¹Children, come and listen to me.
    I will teach you to worship the Lord.
¹²You must do these things
    to enjoy life and have many happy
        days.
¹³You must not say evil things.
    You must not tell lies.
¹⁴Stop doing evil and do good.
    Look for peace and work for it.

¹⁵The Lord sees the good people.
    He listens to their prayers.
¹⁶But the Lord is against those who do
        evil.
    He makes the world forget them.
¹⁷The Lord hears good people when
        they cry out to him.
    He saves them from all their
        troubles.
¹⁸The Lord is close to the
        brokenhearted.
    He saves those whose spirits have
        been crushed.

¹⁹People who do what is right may have
many problems.
But the Lord will solve them all.
²⁰He will protect their very bones.
Not one of them will be broken.
²¹Evil will kill the wicked people.
Those who hate good people will be
judged guilty.
²²But the Lord saves his servants' lives.
No one who trusts him will be
judged guilty.

A PRAYER FOR HELP
Of David.

35 Lord, battle with those who
battle with me.
Fight against those who fight
against me.
²Pick up the shield and armor.
Rise up and help me.
³Lift up your spears, both large and
small,
against those who chase me.
Tell me, "I will save you."

⁴Make those who want to kill me
be ashamed and disgraced.
Make those who plan to harm me
turn back and run away.
⁵Make them like chaff^d blown by the
wind.
Let the angel of the Lord chase
them away.
⁶Let their road be dark and slippery
as the angel of the Lord chases
them.
⁷For no reason they spread out their
net to trap me.
For no reason they dug a pit for me.
⁸So let ruin strike them suddenly.
Let them be caught in their own
nets.
Let them fall into the pit and die.
⁹Then I will rejoice in the Lord.
I will be happy when he saves me.
¹⁰Even my bones will say,
"Lord, who is like you?
You save the weak from the strong.

You save the weak and poor from
robbers."

¹¹Men without mercy stand up to testify.
They ask me things I do not know.
¹²They repay me with evil for the good
I have done.
They make me very sad.
¹³Yet when they were sick, I put on
rough cloth to show my sadness.
I showed my sorrow by going
without food.
But my prayers were not answered.
¹⁴ I acted as if they were my friends or
brothers.
I bowed in sadness as if I were crying
for my mother.
¹⁵But when I was in trouble, they
gathered and laughed.
They gathered to attack before
I knew it.
They insulted me without stopping.
¹⁶They made fun of me and were cruel
to me.
They ground their teeth at me in
anger.

¹⁷Lord, how long will you watch this
happen?
Save my life from their attacks.
Save me from these people who are
like lions.
¹⁸I will praise you in the great meeting.
I will praise you among crowds of
people.
¹⁹Do not let my enemies laugh at me.
They hate me for no reason.
Do not let them make fun of me.
They have no reason to hate me.
²⁰Their words are not friendly.
They think up lies about peace-
loving people.
²¹They speak against me.
They say, "Aha! We saw what you
did!"
²²Lord, you have been watching. Do not
keep quiet.
Lord, do not leave me alone.

²³Wake up! Come and defend me!
   My God and Lord, fight for me!
²⁴Lord my God, defend me with your
   justice.
   Don't let them laugh at me.
²⁵Don't let them think, "Aha! We got
   what we wanted!"
   Don't let them say, "We destroyed
   him."
²⁶Let them be ashamed and
   embarrassed.
   They were happy when I hurt.
Cover them with shame and disgrace.
   They thought they were better than
   I was.
²⁷May my friends sing and shout for
   joy.
   May they always say, "Praise the
   greatness of the Lord.
   He loves to see his servants do
   well."
²⁸I will tell of your goodness.
   I will praise you every day.

WICKED MEN AND A GOOD GOD

For the director of music.
Of David, the servant of the Lord.

36 Sin speaks to the wicked man
      in his heart.
   He has no fear of or respect for God.
²He thinks too much of himself.
   He doesn't see his sin and hate it.
³His words are wicked lies.
   He is no longer wise or good.
⁴At night he makes evil plans.
   What he does leads to nothing
   good.
   He doesn't refuse things that are
   evil.
⁵Lord, your love reaches to the
   heavens.
   Your loyalty goes to the skies.
⁶Your goodness is as high as the
   mountains.
   Your justice is as deep as the great
   ocean.
   Lord, you protect both men and
   animals.

⁷God, your love is so precious!
   You protect people as a bird protects
   her young under her wings.
⁸They eat the rich food in your house.
   You let them drink from your river
   of pleasure.
⁹You are the giver of life.
   Your light lets us enjoy life.

¹⁰Continue to love those who know you.
   And continue to do good to those
   who are good.
¹¹Don't let proud people attack me.
   Don't let the wicked force me away.
¹²Those who do evil have been defeated.
   They are overwhelmed; they cannot
   do evil any longer.

GOD WILL REWARD FAIRLY

Of David.

37 Don't be upset because of evil
      people.
   Don't be jealous of those who do
   wrong.
²Like the grass, they will soon dry up.
   Like green plants, they will soon die
   away.

³Trust the Lord and do good.
   Live in the land and enjoy its safety.
⁴Enjoy serving the Lord.
   And he will give you what you want.
⁵Depend on the Lord.
   Trust him, and he will take care of
   you.
⁶Then your goodness will shine like the
   sun.
   Your fairness will shine like the
   noonday sun.

⁷Wait and trust the Lord.
   Don't be upset when others get rich
   or when someone else's plans
   succeed.
⁸Don't get angry.
   Don't be upset; it only leads to
   trouble.
⁹Evil people will be sent away.
   But people who trust the Lord will
   inherit the land.

¹⁰In a little while there will be no more
    wicked people.
  You may look for them, but they
    will be gone.
¹¹People who are not proud will inherit
    the land.
  They will enjoy complete peace.

¹²The wicked make evil plans against
    good people.
  They grind their teeth at them in
    anger.
¹³But the Lord laughs at the wicked.
  He sees that their day is coming.
¹⁴The wicked draw their swords.
  They bend their bows.
  They try to kill the poor and helpless.
  They want to kill those who are
    honest.
¹⁵But their swords will stab their own
    hearts.
  Their bows will break.

¹⁶It's better to have little and be right
    than to have much and be wrong.
¹⁷The power of the wicked will be
    broken.
  But the Lord supports those who do
    right.
¹⁸The Lord watches over the lives of the
    innocent.
  Their reward will last forever.
¹⁹They will not be ashamed when
    trouble comes.
  They will be full in times of hunger.
²⁰But the wicked will die.
  The Lord's enemies will be like the
    flowers of the fields.
  They will disappear like smoke.
²¹The wicked people borrow but don't
    pay back.
  But those who do right give freely to
    others.
²²Those people the Lord blesses will
    inherit the land.
  But those he curses will be sent away.

²³When a man's steps follow the Lord,
  God is pleased with his ways.

²⁴If he stumbles, he will not fall,
  because the Lord holds his hand.

²⁵I was young, and now I am old.
  But I have never seen the Lord leave
    good people helpless.
  I have never seen their children
    begging for food.
²⁶Good people always lend freely to
    others.
  And their children are a blessing.

²⁷Stop doing evil and do good.
  Then you will live forever.
²⁸The Lord loves justice.
  He will not leave those who worship
    him.
  He will always protect them.
  But the children of the wicked will
    die.
²⁹Good people will inherit the land.
  They will live in it forever.

³⁰A good person speaks with wisdom.
  He says what is fair.
³¹The teachings of his God are in his
    heart.
  He does not fail to keep them.
³²The wicked watch for good people.
  They want to kill them.
³³The Lord will not take away his
    protection.
  He will not judge good people
    guilty.

³⁴Wait for the Lord's help
  and follow him.
  He will honor you and give you the
    land.
  And you will see the wicked people
    sent away.

³⁵I saw a wicked and cruel man.
  He looked strong like a healthy tree
    in good soil.
³⁶But he died and was gone.
  I looked for him, but he couldn't be
    found.

³⁷Think of the innocent person.
  Watch the honest one.

The man who has peace
  will have children to live after him.
[38]But sinners will be destroyed.
  In the end the wicked will die.

[39]The Lord saves good people.
  He is their strong city in times of
    trouble.
[40]The Lord helps them and saves them.
  He saves them from the wicked
    because they trust in him for
    protection.

A PRAYER IN TIME OF SICKNESS

A song of David to remember.

38 Lord, don't correct me when
       you are angry.
  Don't punish me when you are very
    angry.
[2]Your arrows have wounded me.
  Your hand has come down on me.
[3]My body is sick from your
    punishment.
  Even my bones are not healthy
    because of my sin.
[4]My guilt has overwhelmed me.
  Like a load it weighs me down.

[5]My sores stink and become infected
    because I was foolish.
[6]I am bent over and bowed down.
  I am sad all day long.
[7]I am burning with fever.
  My whole body is sore.
[8]I am weak and faint.
  I moan from the pain I feel.

[9]Lord, you know everything I want.
  My cries are not hidden from you.
[10]My heart pounds, and my strength is
    gone.
  I am losing my sight.
[11]Because of my wounds, my friends
    and neighbors leave me alone.
  My relatives stay far away.
[12]Some people set traps to kill me.
  Those who want to hurt me plan
    trouble.
  All day long they think up lies.

[13]I am like a deaf man; I cannot hear.
  Like a mute, I cannot speak.
[14]I am like a person who does not hear.
  I have no answer to give.
[15]I trust you, Lord.
  You will answer, my God and Lord.
[16]I said, "Don't let them laugh at me.
  Don't let them brag when I am
    defeated."
[17]I am about to die.
  I cannot forget my pain.
[18]I confess my guilt.
  I am troubled by my sin.
[19]My enemies are strong and healthy.
  Many people hate me for no reason.
[20]They repay me with evil for the good
    I did.
  They lie about me because I try to
    do good.

[21]Lord, don't leave me.
  My God, don't go away.
[22]Quickly come and help me,
  my Lord and Savior.

LIFE IS SHORT

For the director of music.
For Jeduthun. A song of David.

39 I said, "I will be careful how I act.
       I will not sin by what I say.
  I will be careful what I say
    around wicked people."
[2]So I kept very quiet.
  I didn't even say anything good.
  But I became even more upset.
[3]I became very angry inside.
  And the more I thought about it,
    the angrier I became.
  So I spoke:
[4]"Lord, tell me when the end will come.
  How long will I live?
  Let me know how long I have.
[5]You have given me only a short life.
  My lifetime is like nothing to you.
  Everyone's life is only a breath.
                              Selah[d]
[6]A person is like a shadow moving
    about.
  All his work is for nothing.

He collects things, but he doesn't
   know who will get them.

7"So, Lord, what hope do I have?
   You are my hope.
8Save me from all my sins.
   Don't let wicked fools make fun of
      me.
9I am quiet. I do not open my mouth.
   You are the one who has done this.
10Quit punishing me.
   Your beating is about to kill me.
11You correct and punish people for
      their sins.
   Like a moth, you destroy what they
      love.
   Everyone's life is only a breath.
                                              Selah

12"Lord, hear my prayer.
   Listen to my cry.
   Do not ignore my tears.
I am like a visitor with you.
   Like my ancestors, I'm only here a
      short time.
13Leave me alone so I can be happy.
   Soon I will leave and be no more."

PRAISE AND PRAYER FOR HELP

For the director of music. A song of David.

40 I waited patiently for the Lord.
      He turned to me and heard
         my cry.
2He lifted me out of the pit of
      destruction,
   out of the sticky mud.
He stood me on a rock.
   He made my feet steady.
3He put a new song in my mouth.
   It was a song of praise to our God.
Many people will see this and worship
      him.
   Then they will trust the Lord.

4Happy is the person
   who trusts the Lord.
He doesn't turn to those who are
      proud,
   to those who worship false gods.

5Lord our God, you have done many
      miracles.*d*
   Your plans for us are many.
If I tried to tell them all,
   there would be too many to count.

6You do not want sacrifices and
      offerings.
   But you have made a hole in my ear
   to show that my body and life are
      yours.
You do not ask for burnt offerings
   and offerings to take away sins.
7Then I said, "Look, I have come.
   It is written about me in the book.
8My God, I want to do what you want.
   Your teachings are in my heart."

9I will tell about your goodness in the
      great meeting of your people.
   Lord, you know my lips are not
      silent.
10I do not hide your goodness in my
      heart.
   I speak about your loyalty and
      salvation.
I do not hide your love and truth
   from the people in the great
      meeting.

11Lord, do not hold back your mercy
      from me.
   Let your love and truth always
      protect me.
12Troubles have gathered around me.
   There are too many to count.
My sins have caught me.
   I cannot see a way to escape.
I have more sins than hairs on my
      head.
   I have lost my courage.
13Please, Lord, save me.
   Hurry, Lord, to help me.
14People are trying to kill me.
   Shame them and disgrace them.
People want to hurt me.
   Let them run away in disgrace.
15People are making fun of me.
   Let them be shamed into silence.

16But let those who follow you
   be happy and glad.
They love you for saving them.
   May they always say, "Praise the
   Lord!"

17Lord, I am poor and helpless.
   But please remember me.
You are my helper and savior.
   My God, do not wait.

A PRAYER IN TIME OF SICKNESS

For the director of music. A song of David.

41 Happy is the person who thinks
      about the poor.
   When trouble comes, the Lord will
   save him.
2The Lord will protect him and spare
   his life.
   The Lord will bless him in the land.
   The Lord will not let his enemies
   take him.
3The Lord will give him strength when
   he is sick.
   The Lord will make him well
   again.

4I said, "Lord, be kind to me.
   Heal me because I have sinned
   against you."
5My enemies are saying bad things
   about me.
   They say, "When will he die and be
   forgotten?"
6Some people come to see me.
   But they lie.
They just come to get bad news.
   Then they go and gossip.
7All my enemies whisper about me.
   They think the worst about me.
8They say, "He has a terrible disease.
   He will never get out of bed again."
9My best and truest friend ate at my
   table.
   Now even he has turned against
   me.

10Lord, have mercy on me.
   Give me strength so I can pay them
   back.

11My enemies do not defeat me.
   That's how I know you are pleased
   with me.
12Because I am innocent, you support me.
   You will let me be with you forever.

13Praise the Lord, the God of Israel.
   He has always been,
   and he will always be.
         Amen and amen.

Book 2

WISHING TO BE NEAR GOD

For the director of music.
A maskil[d] of the sons of Korah.

42 A deer thirsts for a stream
      of water.
   In the same way, I thirst for you,
   God.
2I thirst for the living God.
   When can I go to meet with him?
3Day and night, my tears have been my
   food.
People are always saying,
   "Where is your God?"
4When I remember these things,
   I speak with a broken heart.
I used to walk with the crowd.
   I led the happy crowd to God's
   Temple,[d]
   with songs of praise.

5Why am I so sad?
   Why am I so upset?
I should put my hope in God.
   I should keep praising him,
   My Savior and 6my God.

I am very sad.
   So I remember you while I am in
   the land where the Jordan River
   begins.
I will remember you while I am near
   the Hermon mountains
   and on the mountain of Mizar.
7Troubles have come again and again.
   They sound like waterfalls.
Your waves are crashing
   all around me.

⁸The Lord shows his true love every day.
At night I have a song,
and I pray to my living God.
⁹I say to God, my Rock,ᵈ
"Why have you forgotten me?
Why am I sad
and troubled by my enemies?"
¹⁰My enemies' insults make me feel
as if my bones were broken.
They are always saying,
"Where is your God?"

¹¹Why am I so sad?
Why am I so upset?
I should put my hope in God.
I should keep praising him,
my Savior and my God.

A PRAYER FOR PROTECTION

43 God, defend me.
Argue my case against those
who don't follow you.
Save me from liars and those who
do evil.
²God, you are my strength.
Why have you rejected me?
Why am I sad
and troubled by my enemies?
³Send me your light and truth.
They will guide me.
Lead me to your holy mountain.
Lead me to where you live.
⁴I will go to the altar of God,
to God who is my joy and happiness.
I will praise you with a harp,
God, my God.

⁵Why am I so sad?
Why am I so upset?
I should put my hope in God.
I should keep praising him,
my Savior and my God.

A PRAYER FOR HELP

For the director of music.
A maskilᵈ of the sons of Korah.

44 God, we have heard about you.
Our ancestors told us
what you did in their days,
in days long ago.

²With your power you forced the
nations out of the land.
You placed our ancestors here.
You destroyed those other nations.
But you made our ancestors grow
strong.
³It wasn't their swords that took the
land.
It wasn't their power that gave
them victory.
But it was your great power and
strength.
You were with them because you
loved them.

⁴My God, you are my King.
Your commands led Jacob's people
to victory.
⁵With your help we pushed back our
enemies.
In your name we walked on those
who came against us.
⁶I don't trust my bow to help me.
My sword can't save me.
⁷You saved us from Egypt.
You made our enemies ashamed.
⁸We will praise God every day.
We will praise your name forever.
Selahᵈ

⁹But you have rejected us and shamed
us.
You don't march with our armies
anymore.
¹⁰You let our enemies push us back.
Our enemies have taken our wealth.
¹¹You gave us away like sheep to be
eaten.
You scattered us among the
nations.
¹²You sold your people for nothing.
You made no profit on the sale.

¹³You made us a joke to our neighbors.
The community laughs and makes
fun of us.
¹⁴You made us a joke to the other
nations.
People shake their heads.

¹⁵I am always in disgrace.
  I am covered with shame.
¹⁶My enemy is getting even
  with insults and curses.

¹⁷All these things have happened to us,
  but we have not forgotten you.
  We have kept our agreement with
    you.
¹⁸Our hearts haven't turned away from
    you.
  We haven't stopped following you.
¹⁹But you crushed us in this place
  where wild dogs live.
  You covered us with deep darkness.

²⁰We did not forget our God.
  We did not lift our hands in prayer
    to foreign gods.
²¹God would have known if we had.
  He knows what is in our hearts.
²²But for you we are in danger of death
    all the time.
  People think we are worth no more
    than sheep to be killed.

²³Wake up, Lord! Why are you sleeping?
  Get up! Don't reject us forever.
²⁴Why are you hidden from us?
  Have you forgotten our pain and
    troubles?

²⁵We have been pushed down into the
    dirt.
  We are flat on the ground.
²⁶Get up and help us.
  Because of your love, save us.

A SONG FOR THE KING'S WEDDING

For the director of music.
To the tune of "Lilies." A maskil.ᵈ
A love song of the sons of Korah.

45 Beautiful words fill my mind.
  I am speaking of royal things.
My tongue is like the pen of a
    skilled writer.

²You are more handsome than anyone.
  You are a very good speaker.
  God has blessed you forever.

³Put on your sword, powerful warrior.
  Show your glory and majesty.
⁴In your majesty win the victory.
  Defend what is true and right.
  Your power will do amazing things.
⁵Your sharp arrows will enter
  the hearts of the king's enemies.
  Nations will be defeated before you.
⁶God, your throne will last forever and
    ever.
  You will rule your kingdom with
    fairness.
⁷You love right and hate evil.
  So God has chosen you to rule those
    with you.
  Your God has given you much joy.
⁸Your clothes smell like myrrh,ᵈ aloesᵈ
    and cassia.ᵈ
  From palaces of ivory
  music comes to make you happy.
⁹Kings' daughters are among your
    honored women.
  Your bride stands at your right side
  wearing gold from Ophir.

¹⁰Listen to me, daughter. Look and pay
    attention.
  Forget your people and your
    father's family.
¹¹The king loves your beauty.
  Because he is your master, you
    should obey him.
¹²People from the city of Tyre have
    brought a gift.
  Wealthy people will want to meet
    you.

¹³The princess is very beautiful.
  Her gown is woven with gold.
¹⁴In her beautiful clothes she is brought
    to the king.
  Her bridesmaids follow behind her.
  And they are also brought to him.
¹⁵They come with happiness and joy.
  They enter the king's palace.

¹⁶You will have sons to take the place of
    your ancestors.

You will make them rulers through
all the land.
¹⁷I will make your name famous from
now on.
People will praise you forever and
ever.

GOD PROTECTS HIS PEOPLE

For the director of music. By alamoth.^d
A song of the sons of Korah.

46 God is our protection and our
strength.
He always helps in times of trouble.
²So we will not be afraid if the earth
shakes,
or if the mountains fall into the sea.
³We will not fear even if the oceans
roar and foam,
or if the mountains shake at the
raging sea.   *Selah^d*

⁴There is a river which brings joy to the
city of God.
This is the holy place where God
Most High lives.
⁵God is in that city, and so it will not be
shaken.
God will help her at dawn.
⁶Nations tremble, and kingdoms
shake.
God shouts, and the earth
crumbles.

⁷The Lord of heaven's armies is with
us.
The God of Jacob is our protection.
        Selah

⁸Come and see what the Lord has
done.
He has done amazing things on the
earth.
⁹He stops wars everywhere on the
earth.
He breaks all bows and spears
and burns up the chariots with fire.
¹⁰God says, "Be quiet and know that I
am God.
I will be praised in all the nations.

I will be praised throughout the
earth."
¹¹The Lord of heaven's armies is with
us.
The God of Jacob is our protection.
        Selah

GOD, THE KING OF THE WORLD

For the director of music.
A song of the sons of Korah.

47 Clap your hands, all you people.
Shout to God with joy.
²The Lord Most High is wonderful.
He is the great King over all the
earth!
³He defeated nations for us
and put them under our control.
⁴He chose the land we would inherit.
We are the children of Jacob, whom
he loved.   *Selah^d*

⁵God has risen with a shout of joy.
The Lord has risen as the trumpets
sounded.
⁶Sing praises to God. Sing praises.
Sing praises to our King. Sing
praises.
⁷God is King of all the earth.
So sing a song of praise to him.
⁸God is King over the nations.
God sits on his holy throne.
⁹The leaders of the nations meet
with the people of the God of
Abraham.
Even the leaders of the earth belong to
God.
He is supreme.

JERUSALEM, THE CITY OF GOD

A song of the sons of Korah.

48 The Lord is great; he should be
praised
in the city of our God, on his holy
mountain.
²It is high and beautiful.
It brings joy to the whole world.
Mount Zion^d is like the high
mountains of the north.
It is the city of the Great King.

³God is within its palaces.
  He is known as its protection.
⁴Kings joined together
  and came together to attack the
    city.
⁵But when they saw it, they were
    amazed.
  They ran away in fear.
⁶Fear took hold of them.
  They hurt like a woman having a
    baby.
⁷You destroyed the large trading ships
  with an east wind.

⁸First we heard.
  And now we have seen that
God will always keep his city safe.
  It is the city of the Lord of heaven's
    armies,
  the city of our God.   *Selah*ᵈ

⁹God, we come into your Temple.ᵈ
  There we think about your love.
¹⁰God, your name is known everywhere.
  Everywhere on earth people praise
    you.
  Your right hand is full of goodness.
¹¹Mount Zion is happy.
  All the towns of Judah rejoice
because your decisions are fair.

¹²Walk around Jerusalem
  and count its towers.
¹³Notice how strong they are. Look at
    the palaces.
  Then you will be able to tell your
    children about them.
¹⁴This God is our God forever and ever.
  He will guide us from now on.

TRUSTING MONEY IS FOOLISH

For the director of music.
A song of the sons of Korah.

49 Listen to this, all you nations.
  Listen, all you who live on earth.
²Listen, both great and small,
  rich and poor together.
³What I say is wise.
  My heart speaks with
    understanding.

⁴I will pay attention to a wise saying.
  I will explain my riddle on the harp.

⁵Why should I be afraid of bad days?
  Why should I fear when evil men
    surround me?
⁶They trust in their money.
  They brag about their riches.
⁷No one can buy back the life of
    another person.
  No one can pay God for his own life.
⁸The price of a life is high.
  No payment is ever enough.
⁹Do people live forever?
  Don't they all face death?

¹⁰See, even wise men die.
  Fools and stupid people also die.
  They leave their wealth to others.
¹¹Their graves will always be their
    homes.
  They will live there from now on,
    even though they named places
    after themselves.
¹²Even rich people do not live forever.
  Like the animals, people die.

¹³This is what will happen to people
  who trust in themselves.
  And this will happen to their
    followers who believe them.
                                      *Selah*ᵈ

¹⁴Like sheep, they must die.
  And death will be their shepherd.
Honest people will rule over them in
    the morning.
  Their bodies will rot in a grave far
    from home.
¹⁵But God will save my life.
  He will take me from the grave.
                                      Selah

¹⁶Don't be afraid of a rich man
  because his house is more beautiful.
¹⁷He won't take anything to the grave.
  His wealth won't die with him.
¹⁸He was praised when he was alive.
  (And people may praise you when
    you succeed.)

¹⁹But he will go to where his ancestors
    are.
He will never see light again.
²⁰Rich people with no understanding
    are just like animals that die.

GOD WANTS TRUE WORSHIP

A song of Asaph.

50 The God of gods, the Lord,
        speaks.
He calls the earth from the rising to
    the setting sun.
²God shines from Jerusalem,
    whose beauty is perfect.
³Our God comes, and he will not be
    silent.
A fire burns in front of him,
and a storm surrounds him.
⁴He calls to the sky and to the earth
    to see him judge his people.
⁵He says, "You who worship me,
    gather around.
You have made an agreement with
    me, using a sacrifice."
⁶God is the judge.
    Even the skies say he is right. *Selah*^d

⁷God says, "My people, listen to me.
Israel, I will testify against you.
I am God, your God.
⁸I do not scold you for your sacrifices.
You always bring me your burnt
    offerings.
⁹But I do not need the bulls from your
    stalls
or the goats from your pens.
¹⁰Every animal of the forest is already
    mine.
The cattle on a thousand hills are
    mine.
¹¹I know every bird on the mountains.
Every living thing in the fields is
    mine.
¹²If I were hungry, I would not tell you.
The earth and everything on it are
    mine.
¹³I don't eat the meat of bulls
or drink the blood of goats.

¹⁴Give an offering to show thanks to
    God.
Give God Most High what you have
    promised.
¹⁵Call to me in times of trouble.
I will save you, and you will honor
    me."

¹⁶But God says to the wicked people,
    "Why do you talk about my laws?
Why do you mention my agreement?
¹⁷You hate my teachings.
You turn your back on what I say.
¹⁸When you see a thief, you join him.
You take part in adultery.^d
¹⁹You don't stop your mouth from
    speaking evil.
Your tongue makes up lies.
²⁰You speak against your brother.
You lie about your mother's son.
²¹I have kept quiet while you did these
    things.
So you thought I was just like you.
But I will scold you.
I will accuse you to your face.

²²"Think about this, you people who
    forget God.
Otherwise, I will tear you apart,
and no one will save you.
²³Those people honor me
who give me offerings to show
    thanks.
And I, God, will save those who do
    that."

A PRAYER FOR FORGIVENESS

For the director of music. A song of David
    when the prophet^d Nathan came to David
    after David's sin with Bathsheba.

51 God, be merciful to me
        because you are loving.
Because you are always ready to be
    merciful,
wipe out all my wrongs.
²Wash away all my guilt
and make me clean again.

³I know about my wrongs.
I can't forget my sin.

[4]You are the one I have sinned against.
   I have done what you say is wrong.
So you are right when you speak.
   You are fair when you judge me.
[5]I was brought into this world in sin.
   In sin my mother gave birth to me.

[6]You want me to be completely
      truthful.
   So teach me wisdom.
[7]Take away my sin, and I will be clean.
   Wash me, and I will be whiter than
      snow.
[8]Make me hear sounds of joy and
      gladness.
   Let the bones you crushed be happy
      again.
[9]Turn your face from my sins.
   Wipe out all my guilt.

[10]Create in me a pure heart, God.
   Make my spirit right again.
[11]Do not send me away from you.
   Do not take your Holy Spirit[d] away
      from me.
[12]Give me back the joy that comes when
      you save me.
   Keep me strong by giving me a
      willing spirit.
[13]Then I will teach your ways to those
      who do wrong.
   And sinners will turn back to you.

[14]God, save me from the guilt of
      murder.
   God, you are the one who saves me.
   I will sing about your goodness.
[15]Lord, let me speak
   so I may praise you.
[16]You are not pleased by sacrifices.
   Otherwise, I would give them.
   You don't want burnt offerings.
[17]The sacrifice God wants is a willing
      spirit.
   God, you will not reject
   a heart that is broken and sorry for
      its sin.

[18]Do whatever good you wish for
      Jerusalem.
   Rebuild the walls of Jerusalem.

[19]Then you will be pleased with right
      sacrifices and whole burnt
      offerings.
   And bulls will be offered on your
      altar.

GOD WILL PUNISH THE PROUD

For the director of music. A maskil[d] of David.
When Doeg the Edomite came to Saul and
said to him, "David is in Ahimelech's house."

52 Mighty warrior, why do you
      brag about the evil you do?
   God's love will continue forever.
[2]You think up evil plans.
   Your tongue is like a sharp razor,
      making up lies.
[3]You love wrong more than right
   and lies more than truth.   Selah[d]
[4]You love words that bite
   and tongues that lie.

[5]But God will ruin you forever.
   He will grab you and throw you out
      of your tent.
   He will tear you away from the land
      of the living.   Selah
[6]Those who do right will see this and
      fear God.
   They will laugh at you and say,
[7]"Look what happened to the man
   who did not depend on God.
Instead, he depended on his money.
   He grew strong by his evil plans."

[8]But I am like an olive tree
   growing in God's Temple.[d]
I trust God's love
   forever and ever.
[9]God, I will thank you forever for what
      you have done.
   With those who worship you, I will
      trust you because you are good.

THE UNBELIEVING FOOL

For the director of music. By mahalath.[d]
      A maskil[d] of David.

53 A wicked fool says to himself,
      "There is no God."
Fools are evil. They do terrible things.
   None of them does anything good.

²God looked down from heaven at all
the people.
He looked to see if anyone was wise,
if anyone was looking to God for
help.
³But everyone has turned away.
Together, everyone has become evil.
None of them does anything good.

⁴Don't the wicked understand?
They destroy my people as if they
were eating bread.
They have not asked God for help.
⁵The wicked became filled with terror
where there had been nothing to be
terrified of.
God will scatter the bones of your
enemies.
You will defeat them,
because God has rejected them.

⁶I pray that victory will come to Israel
from Mount Zion!ᵈ
May God give them back their
riches.
Then the people of Jacob will
rejoice.
And the people of Israel will be glad.

A PRAYER FOR HELP

For the director of music. With stringed
instruments. A maskilᵈ of David when the
Ziphites went to Saul and said, "We think
David is hiding among our people."

54 God, save me because of who
you are.
By your strength show that I am
innocent.
²Hear my prayer, God.
Listen to what I say.
³Strangers turn against me.
Cruel men want to kill me.
They do not care about God.   *Selah*ᵈ

⁴See, God will help me.
The Lord will spare my life.
⁵Let my enemies be punished with
their own evil.
Destroy them because you are loyal
to me.

⁶I will offer a sacrifice as a special gift
to you.
I will thank you, Lord, because you
are good.
⁷You have saved me from all my
troubles.
I have seen my enemies defeated.

A PRAYER ABOUT A FALSE FRIEND

For the director of music. With stringed
instruments. A maskilᵈ of David.

55 God, listen to my prayer.
Do not ignore my prayer.
²Pay attention to me and answer me.
I am troubled and upset
³by what the enemy says
and how the wicked look at me.
They bring troubles down on me.
In anger they attack me.

⁴I am frightened inside.
The terror of death has attacked me.
⁵I am scared and shaking.
Terror grips me.
⁶I said, "I wish I had wings like a dove.
Then I would fly away and rest.
⁷I would wander far away.
I would stay in the desert.   *Selah*ᵈ
⁸I would hurry to my place of escape,
far away from the wind and storm."

⁹Lord, destroy and confuse their words.
I see violence and fighting in the city.
¹⁰Day and night they are all around its
walls.
Evil and trouble are everywhere
inside.
¹¹Destruction is everywhere in the city.
Trouble and lying never leave its
streets.

¹²It was not an enemy insulting me.
I could stand that.
It was not someone who hated me.
I could hide from him.
¹³But it is you, a person like me.
You were my companion and good
friend.
¹⁴We had a good friendship.
We went together to God's Temple.ᵈ

¹⁵Let death take away my enemies.
Let them die while they are still
young
because evil lives with them.
¹⁶But I will call to God for help.
And the Lord will save me.
¹⁷Morning, noon and night I am
troubled and upset.
But he will listen to me.
¹⁸Many are against me.
But he keeps me safe in battle.
¹⁹God who lives forever
will hear me and punish them.
But they will not change.
They do not fear God.   *Selah*

²⁰The one who was my friend attacks
his friends.
He breaks his promises.
²¹His words are slippery like butter.
But war is in his heart.
His words are smoother than oil,
but they cut like knives.

²²Give your worries to the Lord.
He will take care of you.
He will never let good people down.
²³But, God, you will bring down
the wicked to the grave.
Murderers and liars will live
only half a lifetime.
But I will trust in you.

TRUSTING GOD FOR HELP

For the director of music. To the tune of "The
Dove in the Distant Oak." A miktam*d* of David
when the Philistines captured him in Gath.

56 God, be merciful to me because
people are chasing me.
The battle has pressed me all day
long.
²My enemies have chased me all day.
There are many of them fighting
me.
³When I am afraid,
I will trust you.
⁴I praise God for his word.
I trust God. So I am not afraid.
What can human beings do to me?

⁵All day long they twist my words.
All their evil plans are against me.
⁶They wait. They hide.
They watch my steps.
They hope to kill me.
⁷God, do not let them escape.
Punish the foreign nations in your
anger.
⁸You have recorded my troubles.
You have kept a list of my tears.
Aren't they in your records?

⁹On the day I call for help, my enemies
will be defeated.
I know that God is on my side.
¹⁰I praise God for his word to me.
I praise the Lord for his word.
¹¹I trust in God. I will not be afraid.
What can people do to me?

¹²God, I must keep my promises to you.
I will give you my offerings to thank
you.
¹³You have saved me from death.
You have kept me from being
defeated.
So I will walk with God
in light among the living.

A PRAYER IN TROUBLED TIMES

For the director of music. To the tune of "Do
Not Destroy." A miktam*d* of David when he
escaped from Saul in a cave.

57 Be merciful to me, God.
Be merciful to me
because I come to you for
protection.
I will come to you as a bird comes for
protection under its mother's
wings
until the trouble has passed.

²I cry out to God Most High,
to the God who does everything for
me.
³He sends help from heaven and saves
me.
He punishes those who attack me.
*Selah*d
God sends me his love and truth.

⁴Enemies are like lions all around me.
  I must lie down among them.
Their teeth are like spears and arrows.
  Their tongues are as sharp as swords.

⁵God is supreme over the skies.
  His greatness covers the earth.

⁶They set a trap for me.
  I am very worried.
They dug a pit in my path.
  But they fell into it themselves. *Selah*

⁷My heart is right, God. My heart is
    right.
  I will sing and praise you.

⁸Wake up, my soul.
  Wake up, harp and lyre!ᵈ
  I will wake up the dawn.

⁹Lord, I will praise you among the
    nations.
  I will sing songs of praise about you
    to all the nations.

¹⁰Your love is so great it reaches to the
    skies.
  Your truth reaches to the clouds.

¹¹God, you are supreme over the skies.
  Let your glory be over all the earth.

UNFAIR JUDGES

For the director of music. To the tune of "Do
Not Destroy." A miktamᵈ of David.

58 Do you rulers really say what is
      right?
  Do you judge people fairly?

²No, in your heart you plan evil.
  You think up violent crimes in the
    land.

³From birth evil men start doing bad
    things.
  They tell lies and do wrong as soon
    as they are born.

⁴They are like poisonous snakes,
  like deaf cobras that can't hear.

⁵They cannot hear the music of the
    snake charmer
  no matter how well he plays for them.

⁶God, break the teeth out of their
    mouths!

Tear out the fangs of those lions,
    Lord!

⁷Let them disappear like water that
    flows away.
  Let them be cut short like a broken
    arrow.

⁸Let them be like snails that melt as
    they move.
  Let them be like a child born dead
    who never saw the sun.

⁹His anger will blow them away alive.
  It will happen faster than burning
    thorns can heat a pot.

¹⁰Good people will be glad when they
    see him get even.
  They will wash their feet in the
    blood of the wicked.

¹¹Then people will say,
  "There really are rewards for doing
    what is right.
  There really is a God who judges the
    world."

A PRAYER FOR PROTECTION

For the director of music. To the tune of "Do
Not Destroy." A miktamᵈ of David when Saul
sent men to watch David's house to kill him.

59 God, save me from my
      enemies.
  Protect me from those who come
    against me.

²Save me from those who do evil.
  Save me from murderers.

³Look, men are waiting to attack me.
  Cruel men attack me.
  But I have not sinned or done
    wrong, Lord.

⁴I have done nothing wrong, but they
    are ready to attack me.
  Wake up to help me and look.

⁵You are the Lord God of heaven's
    armies, the God of Israel.
  Come and punish those people.
  Do not give those traitors any
    mercy.   *Selah*ᵈ

⁶They come back at night.
  Like dogs they growl and roam
    around the city.

⁷Notice what comes from their mouths.
    Insults come from their lips.
    They say, "Who's listening?"
⁸But, Lord, you laugh at them.
    You make fun of all of them.

⁹God, my strength, I wait for you.
    God, you are my protection.
¹⁰My God loves me, and he will be with
    me.
    He will help me defeat my enemies.
¹¹Lord, our protector, do not kill them.
    If you do, my people will forget.
    With your power scatter them
    and defeat them.
¹²They sin by what they say.
    They sin with their words.
    They curse and tell lies.
    So let their pride trap them.
¹³Destroy them in your anger.
    Destroy them completely!
    Then they will know
        that God rules over Israel
        and to the ends of the earth.   *Selah*

¹⁴They come back at night.
    Like dogs they growl
    and roam around the city.
¹⁵They wander about looking for food.
    And they howl if they do not find
        enough.
¹⁶But I will sing about your strength.
    In the morning I will sing about
        your love.
    You are my protection,
        my place of safety in times of trouble.
¹⁷God, my strength, I will sing praises to
    you.
    God, my protection, you are the
    God who loves me.

A PRAYER AFTER A DEFEAT

For the director of music. To the tune of "Lily
of the Agreement." A miktam*d* of David. For
teaching. When David fought the Arameans of
Northwest Mesopotamia and Zobah, and
when Joab returned and defeated 12,000
Edomites at the Valley of Salt.

60 God, you have rejected us and
        scattered us.

You have been angry, but please
    come back to us.
²You made the earth shake and crack.
    Fix its breaks because it is shaking.
³You have given your people trouble.
    You made us unable to walk
        straight, like people drunk with
        wine.
⁴You have raised a banner to gather
        those who fear you.
    Now they can escape the enemy.
                                    *Selah*d

⁵Answer us and save us by your power.
    Then the people you love will be
        rescued.

⁶God has said from his Temple,*d*
    "When I win, I will divide Shechem
    and cut up the Valley of Succoth.
⁷Gilead and Manasseh are mine.
    Ephraim is like my helmet.
    Judah holds my royal scepter.*d*
⁸Moab is like my washbowl.
    I throw my sandals at Edom.
    I shout at Philistia."

⁹Who will bring me to the strong,
        walled city?
    Who will lead me to Edom?
¹⁰God, surely you have rejected us.
    You do not go out with our armies.
¹¹Help us fight the enemy.
    Human help is useless.
¹²But we can win with God's help.
    He will defeat our enemies.

A PRAYER FOR PROTECTION

For the director of music.
With stringed instruments. Of David.

61 God, hear my cry.
        Listen to my prayer.
²I call to you from the ends of the
        earth.
    I am afraid.
    Carry me away to a high mountain.
³You have been my protection,
    like a strong tower against my
        enemies.

⁴Let me live in your Holy Tent^d forever.
Protect me as a bird protects its
young under its wings. *Selah*^d
⁵God, you have heard my promises.
You have given me the things that
belong to those who fear you.

⁶Give the king a long life.
Let him live many years.
⁷Let him rule in the presence of God
forever.
Protect him with your love and truth.
⁸Then I will praise your name forever.
And every day I will keep my
promises.

TRUST ONLY IN GOD

For the director of music.
For Jeduthun. A song of David.

62 I wait patiently for God.
Only he can save me.
²He is my rock, who saves me.
He protects me like a strong, walled
city.
I will not be defeated.

³How long will you attack me?
Will all of you throw me down?
I am like a leaning wall, like a fence
ready to fall.
⁴You are planning to make me fall.
You enjoy telling lies about me.
With your mouth you bless me.
But in your heart you curse me.
Selah^d

⁵I wait patiently for God to save me.
Only he gives me hope.
⁶He is my rock, who saves me.
He protects me like a strong, walled
city.
I will not be defeated.
⁷My honor and salvation come from
God.
He is my mighty rock and my
protection.
⁸People, trust God all the time.
Tell him all your problems.
God is our protection. *Selah*

⁹People are only a breath.
Even the greatest men are just a lie.
On the scales, they weigh nothing.
Together they are only a breath.
¹⁰Do not trust in force.
Stealing is of no use.
Even if you gain more riches,
don't put your trust in them.

¹¹God has said this,
and I have heard it over and over:
God, you are strong.
¹²Lord, you are loving.
You reward a person for what he
does.

WISHING TO BE NEAR GOD

A song of David when he was
in the desert of Judah.

63 God, you are my God.
I want to follow you.
My whole being
thirsts for you,
like a man in a dry, empty land
where there is no water.
²I have seen you in the Temple.^d
I have seen your strength and glory.
³Your love is better than life.
I will praise you.
⁴I will praise you as long as I live.
I will lift up my hands in prayer to
your name.
⁵I will be content as if I had eaten the
best foods.
My lips will sing. My mouth will
praise you.

⁶I remember you while I'm lying in
bed.
I think about you through the night.
⁷You are my help.
Because of your protection, I sing.
⁸I stay close to you.
You support me with your right
hand.

⁹Some people are trying to kill me.
But they will go down to the grave.
¹⁰They will be killed with swords.
They will be eaten by wild dogs.

[11]But the king will rejoice in his God.
  All who make promises in his name
    will praise him.
  But the mouths of liars will be shut.

A PRAYER AGAINST ENEMIES

For the director of music. A song of David.

64 God, listen to my complaint.
  I am afraid of my enemies.
  Protect my life from them.
[2]Hide me from those wicked people,
  from that gang who does evil.
[3]They sharpen their tongues like swords.
  They shoot bitter words like arrows.
[4]They hide and shoot at innocent
    people.
  They shoot suddenly and are not
    afraid.
[5]They encourage each other to do wrong.
  They talk about setting traps.
  They think no one will see them.
[6]They plan wicked things and say,
  "We have a perfect plan."
  The mind of man is hard to
    understand.

[7]But God will shoot them with arrows.
  They will suddenly be struck down.
[8]Their own words will be used against
    them.
  All who see them will shake their
    heads.
[9]Then everyone will fear God.
  They will tell what God has done.
  They will learn from what he has
    done.
[10]Good people will be happy in the
    Lord.
  They will find protection in him.
  Let everyone who is honest praise
    the Lord.

A HYMN OF THANKSGIVING

For the director of music. A song of David.

65 God, you will be praised in
  Jerusalem.
  We will keep our promises to you.
[2]You hear our prayers.
  All people will come to you.

[3]Our guilt overwhelms us.
  But you forgive our sins.
[4]Happy are the people you choose.
  You have them stay in your
    courtyards.
  We are filled with good things in your
    house,
  your holy Temple.[d]

[5]You answer us in amazing ways,
  God our Savior.
  People everywhere on the earth
    and beyond the sea trust you.
[6]You made the mountains by your
    strength.
  You have great power.
[7]You stopped the roaring seas,
  the roaring waves and the uproar of
    the nations.
[8]Even those people at the ends of the
    earth fear your miracles.[d]
  You are praised from where the sun
    rises to where it sets.

[9]You take care of the land and water it.
  You make it very fertile.
  The rivers of God are full of water.
  Grain grows because you make it
    grow.
[10]You cause rain to fall on the plowed
    fields.
  You soak them with water.
  You soften the ground with rain.
  And then you bless it.
[11]You give the year a good harvest.
  You load the wagons with many
    crops.
[12]The desert is covered with grass.
  The hills are covered with
    happiness.
[13]The pastures are full of sheep.
  The valleys are covered with grain.
  Everything shouts and sings for joy.

PRAISE GOD FOR ANSWERING PRAYERS

For the director of music. A song of praise.

66 Everything on earth, shout
  with joy to God!
[2]Sing about his glory!
  Make his praise glorious!

³Say to God, "Your works are amazing!
  Your power is great.
  Your enemies fall before you.
⁴All the earth worships you.
  They sing praises to you.
  They sing praises to your name."
                                      Selah^d

⁵Come and see what God has done.
  See what amazing things he has
    done for people.
⁶He turned the sea into dry land.
  The people crossed the river on foot.
  So let us rejoice because of what he
    did.
⁷He rules forever with his power.
  He keeps his eye on the nations.
  So people should not turn against
    him.   *Selah*

⁸You people, praise our God.
  Loudly sing his praise.
⁹He protects our lives
  and does not let us be defeated.
¹⁰God, you have tested us.
  You have purified us like silver.
¹¹You let us be trapped.
  You put a heavy load on us.
¹²You let our enemies walk on our
    heads.
  We went through fire and flood.
  But you brought us to a place with
    good things.

¹³I will come to your Temple^d with
    burnt offerings.
  I will give you what I promised.
¹⁴I promised to give you these things
  when I was in trouble.
¹⁵I will bring you offerings of fat
    animals.
  And I will offer male sheep, bulls
    and goats.   *Selah*

¹⁶All of you who fear God, come and
    listen.
  I will tell you what he has done for
    me.
¹⁷I cried out to him with my mouth.
  I praised him with my tongue.

¹⁸If I had known of any sin in my heart,
  the Lord would not have listened
    to me.
¹⁹But God has listened.
  He has heard my prayer.
²⁰Praise God.
  He did not ignore my prayer.
  He did not hold back his love from
    me.

EVERYONE SHOULD PRAISE GOD

For the director of music. With stringed
  instruments. A song of praise.

67 God, have mercy on us and
      bless us.
  Show your kindness to us.   *Selah*^d
²Then the world will learn your ways.
  All nations will learn that you can
    save.

³God, the people should praise you.
  All people should praise you.
⁴The nations should be glad and sing
  because you judge people fairly.
  You guide all the nations on earth.
                                      Selah
⁵God, the people should praise you.
  All people should praise you.

⁶The land has given its crops.
  God, our God, blesses us.
⁷God blesses us
  so people to the ends of the earth
    will fear him.

PRAISE GOD WHO SAVED THE NATION

For the director of music. A song of David.

68 Let God come and scatter his
      enemies.
  Let those who hate him run away.
²Blow them away as smoke
  is driven away by the wind.
  As wax melts before a fire,
    let the wicked be destroyed before
    God.
³But those who do right should be glad.
  They should rejoice before God.
  They should be happy and glad.

⁴Sing to God. Sing praises to his name.
  Prepare the way for him
    who rides through the desert.

His name is the Lord.
Rejoice before him.
[5]God is in his holy Temple.[d]
He is a father to orphans.
He defends the widows.
[6]God gives the lonely a home.
He leads prisoners out with joy.
But those who turn against God will
live in a dry land.

[7]God, you led your people out.
You marched through the desert.
Selah[d]

[8]The ground shook,
and the sky poured down rain
before God, the God of Mount Sinai,
before God, the God of Israel.
[9]God, you sent much rain.
You refreshed your tired land.
[10]Your people settled there.
God, in your goodness
you took care of the poor.

[11]The Lord gave the command.
And a great army told the news:
[12]"Kings and their armies run away.
The women at home divide the
wealth taken in war."
[13]Those who stayed behind by the
sheepfold
will get the riches taken in battle.
[14]God scattered kings
like snow on Mount Zalmon.

[15]The mountains of Bashan are great
mountains.
Mount Bashan has many peaks.
[16]Why do you mountains with many
peaks look down
on Mount Zion,[d] which God chose
for his home?
The Lord will live there forever.
[17]God comes with millions of chariots.
The Lord comes from Mount Sinai
to his holy place.
[18]He went up to the heights.
He led a parade of captives.
He received the payment he
demanded from the people,

even from those who turned against
him.
And the Lord God will live there.

[19]Praise the Lord, day by day.
God our Savior helps us.   *Selah*
[20]Our God is a God who saves us.
The Lord God saves us from death.

[21]God will crush his enemies' heads,
the hairy skulls of those who
continue to sin.
[22]The Lord said, "I will bring the enemy
back from Bashan.
I will bring them back from the
depths of the sea.
[23]Then you can stick your feet in their
blood.
And your dogs can lick their share."

[24]God, people have seen your victory
march.
God my King marched into the holy
place.
[25]The singers are in front, and the
instruments are behind.
In the middle are the girls with the
tambourines.[d]
[26]Praise God in the meeting place.
Praise the Lord in the gathering of
Israel.
[27]There is the smallest tribe,[d] Benjamin,
leading them.
And there are the leaders of Judah
with their group.
There also are the leaders of
Zebulun and of Naphtali.

[28]God, order up your power.
Show the mighty power you have
used for us before.
[29]Kings will bring their wealth to you,
to your Temple in Jerusalem.
[30]Punish Egypt, the beast among the tall
grass along the river.
Punish the leaders of nations, those
bulls among the cows.
Then they will bring you their silver.
Scatter those nations that love war.

³¹Messengers will come from Egypt
    with forced payment.
    The people of Cush will pray to God.

³²Kingdoms of the earth, sing to God.
    Sing praises to the Lord.   *Selah*
³³Sing to the one who rides through the
    skies, which are from long ago.
    He speaks with a thundering voice.
³⁴Announce that God is powerful.
    He rules over Israel.
    His power is in the skies.
³⁵God, you are wonderful in your
    Temple.
    The God of Israel gives his people
    strength and power.

    Praise God!

A CRY FOR HELP

For the director of music. To the tune of
    "Lilies." A song of David.

69 God, save me.
    The water has risen to my neck.
²I'm sinking down into the mud.
    There is nothing to stand on.
I am in deep water.
    The flood covers me.
³I am tired from calling for help.
    My throat is sore.
My eyes are tired from waiting
    for God to help me.
⁴There are more people who hate me
    for no reason
    than hairs on my head.
Those who want to destroy me are
    powerful.
    My enemies are liars.
They make me pay back
    what I did not steal.

⁵God, you know what I have done
    wrong.
    I cannot hide my guilt from you.
⁶Master, the Lord of heaven's armies,
    do not let those who hope in you be
    ashamed because of me.
God of Israel,
    do not let your worshipers
    be disgraced because of me.

⁷For you, I carry this shame.
    My face is covered with disgrace.
⁸I am like a stranger to my brothers.
    I am like a foreigner to my mother's
    sons.
⁹My strong love for your Temple*d*
    completely controls me.
    When people insult you, it hurts
    me.
¹⁰When I cry and go without food,
    they make fun of me.
¹¹When I wear rough cloth to show my
    sadness,
    they joke about me.
¹²They make fun of me in public places.
    The drunkards make up songs
    about me.

¹³But I pray to you, Lord.
    I pray that you will accept me.
God, because of your great love,
    answer me.
    You are truly able to save.
¹⁴Pull me from the mud.
    Do not let me sink.
Save me from those who hate me
    and from the deep water.
¹⁵Do not let the flood drown me.
    Do not let the deep water swallow
    me.
    Do not let the grave close its mouth
    over me.
¹⁶Lord, answer me because your love is
    so good.
    Because of your great kindness,
    turn to me.
¹⁷Do not hide from me, your servant.
    I am in trouble. Hurry to help me!
¹⁸Come near and save me.
    Rescue me from my enemies.

¹⁹You see my shame and disgrace.
    You know all my enemies and what
    they have said.
²⁰Insults have broken my heart.
    I am weak.
I looked for sympathy, but there was
    none.
    I found no one to comfort me.

²¹They put poison in my food.
  They gave me vinegar to drink.

²²Let their own feasts cause their ruin.
  Let their feasts trap them and pay
    them back.
²³Let their eyes be closed so they cannot
    see.
  Let their backs be forever weak
    from troubles.
²⁴Pour your anger out on them.
  Show them how angry you are.
²⁵May their place be empty.
  Leave no one to live in their tents.
²⁶They chase after those you have hurt.
  They talk about the pain of those
    you have wounded.
²⁷Charge them with crime after crime.
  Do not let them have anything
    good.
²⁸Wipe their names from the book of
    life.
  Do not list them with those who do
    what is right.

²⁹I am sad and hurting.
  God, save me and protect me.

³⁰I will praise God in a song.
  I will honor him by giving thanks.
³¹That will please the Lord more than
    offering him cattle.
  It will please him more than the
    sacrifice of a bull with horns and
    hoofs.
³²People who are not proud will see this
    and be glad.
  Be encouraged, you who worship
    God.
³³The Lord listens to those in need.
  He does not look down on captives.

³⁴Heaven and earth should praise him.
  The seas and everything in them
    should also.
³⁵God will save Jerusalem.
  He will rebuild the cities of Judah.
  Then people will live there and own
    the land.

³⁶ The descendants[d] of his servants will
    inherit that land.
  Those who love him will live there.

A CRY FOR GOD TO HELP QUICKLY

For the director of music. A song of David.
  To help people remember.

70 God, save me.
  Lord, hurry to help me.
²People are trying to kill me.
  Shame them and disgrace them.
People want to hurt me.
  Let them run away in disgrace.
³People make fun of me.
  Stop them and make them
    ashamed.
⁴But let all the people who worship you
    rejoice and be glad.
Let the people who love your salvation
    always say, "Praise the greatness of
    God."
⁵I am poor and helpless.
  God, hurry to me.
You help me and save me.
  Lord, do not wait.

AN OLD PERSON'S PRAYER

71 In you, Lord, is my protection.
  Never let me be ashamed.
²Because you do what is right, save and
    rescue me.
  Listen to me and save me.
³Be my place of safety
  where I can always come.
Give the command to save me.
  You are my rock and my strong,
    walled city.
⁴My God, save me from the power of
    the wicked.
  Save me from the hold of evil and
    cruel people.
⁵Lord God, you are my hope.
  I have trusted you since I was
    young.
⁶I have depended on you since I was
    born.
  You have been my help from the
    day I was born.
  I will always praise you.

⁷I am an example to many people.
  You are my strong protection.
⁸I am always praising you.
  All day long I honor you.
⁹Do not reject me when I am old.
  Do not leave me when my strength
    is gone.
¹⁰My enemies have made plans against
    me.
  They meet together to kill me.
¹¹They say, "God has left him.
  Go after him and take him.
  No one will save him."

¹²God, don't be far off.
  My God, hurry to help me.
¹³Let them be ashamed.
  Destroy those who accuse me.
  They are trying to hurt me.
  Cover them with shame and
    disgrace.
¹⁴But I will always have hope.
  And I will praise you more and
    more.
¹⁵I will tell about how you do what is
    right.
  I will tell about your salvation all
    day long,
  even though it is more than I can
    tell.
¹⁶I will come and tell about your
    powerful works, Lord God.
  I will tell only about you and how
    you do what is right.

¹⁷God, you have taught me since I was
    young.
  Even until today I tell about the
    miracles[d] you do.
¹⁸Even though I am old and gray,
  do not leave me, God.
  I will tell the children about your
    power.
  I will tell those who will live after
    me about your might.

¹⁹God, your justice reaches to the skies.
  You have done great things.
  God, there is no one like you.

²⁰You have given me many troubles and
    bad times.
  But you will give me life again.
  When I am almost dead,
    you will keep me alive.
²¹You will make me greater than ever.
  And you will comfort me again.

²²I will praise you with the harp.
  I trust you, my God.
  I will sing to you with the lyre.[d]
  You are the Holy One of Israel.
²³I will shout for joy when I sing praises
    to you.
  You have saved me.
²⁴I will tell about your justice all day long.
  And those who want to hurt me
  will be ashamed and disgraced.

A PRAYER FOR THE KING
Of Solomon.

72 God, give the king your good
  judgment
  and the king's son your goodness.
²Help him judge your people fairly.
  Help him decide what is right for
    the poor.
³Let there be peace on the mountains
  and goodness on the hills.
⁴Help him be fair to the poor.
  Help him save the needy
  and punish those who hurt them.

⁵Help him live as long as the sun
    shines.
  Help him rule as long as the moon
    glows.
  Let him be king from now on!
⁶Let him be like rain on the grass,
  like showers that water the earth.
⁷Let goodness be plentiful while he
    lives.
  Let peace continue as long as there
    is a moon.

⁸Let his kingdom go from sea to sea,
  and from the Euphrates River to the
    ends of the earth.
⁹Let the people of the desert bow down
    to him.
  And make his enemies lick the dust.

¹⁰Let the kings of Tarshish and the
faraway lands
bring him gifts.
Let the kings of Sheba and Seba
bring their presents to him.
¹¹Let all kings bow down to him.
Let all nations serve him.

¹²He will help the poor when they cry
for help.
He will help the needy when no one
else will help them.
¹³He will be kind to the weak and poor.
He will save their lives.
¹⁴He will save them from cruel people
who try to hurt them.
Their lives are precious to him.

¹⁵Long live the king!
Let him receive gold from Sheba.
Let people always pray for him.
Let them bless him all day long.
¹⁶Let the fields grow plenty of grain.
Let the hills be covered with crops.
Let the land be as fertile as Lebanon.
Let the cities grow like the grass in a
field.
¹⁷Let the king be famous forever.
Let him be remembered as long as
the sun shines.
Let the nations be blessed because of
him.
And may they all bless him.

¹⁸Praise the Lord God, the God of Israel.
Only he does such miracles.ᵈ
¹⁹Praise his glorious name forever.
Let his glory fill the whole world.
Amen and amen.
²⁰This ends the prayers of David son of
Jesse.

Book 3

SHOULD THE WICKED BE RICH?

A song of Asaph.

73 God is truly good to Israel,
to those who have pure hearts.
²But I had almost stopped believing
this truth.
I had almost lost my faith

³because I was jealous of proud people.
I saw wicked people doing well.

⁴They are not suffering.
They are healthy and strong.
⁵They don't have troubles like the rest
of us.
They don't have problems like other
people.
⁶So they wear pride like a necklace.
They put on violence as their
clothing.
⁷They are looking for profits.
They do not control their selfish
desires.
⁸They make fun of others and speak
evil.
Proudly they speak of hurting
others.
⁹They brag to the sky.
Their mouths gossip on the earth.
¹⁰So their people turn to them
and give them whatever they want.
¹¹They say, "How can God know?
What does God Most High know?"
¹²These people are wicked,
always at ease and getting richer.
¹³So why have I kept my heart pure?
Why have I kept my hands from
doing wrong?
¹⁴I have suffered all day long.
I have been punished every
morning.

¹⁵God, if I had decided to talk about
this,
I would have let your people down.
¹⁶I tried to understand all this.
But it was too hard for me to see
¹⁷until I went to the Templeᵈ of God.
Then I understood what will
happen to them.
¹⁸You have put them in danger.
You cause them to be destroyed.
¹⁹They are destroyed in a moment.
They are swept away by terrors.
²⁰It will be like waking from a dream.
Lord, when you come, they will
disappear.

²¹When my heart was sad and
   I was angry,
²²I was senseless and stupid.
   I acted like an animal toward you.
²³But I am always with you.
   You have held my hand.
²⁴You guide me with your advice.
   And later you will receive me in
      honor.
²⁵I have no one in heaven but you.
   I want nothing on earth besides
      you.
²⁶My mind and my body may become
      weak.
   But God is my strength.
   He is mine forever.

²⁷Those who are far from God will die.
   You destroy those who are
      unfaithful.
²⁸But I am close to God, and that is
      good.
   The Lord God is my protection.
   I will tell all that you have done.

A NATION IN TROUBLE PRAYS

A maskil*ᵈ* of Asaph.

74 God, why have you rejected us
         for so long?
   Why are you angry with us, the
      sheep of your pasture?
²Remember the people you bought
      long ago.
   You saved us. We are your very
      own.
   You live on Mount Zion.*ᵈ*
³Make your way through these old
      ruins.
   The enemy wrecked everything in
      the Temple.*ᵈ*

⁴Those who were against you shouted
      in your meeting place.
   They raised their flags there.
⁵They came with axes raised
      as if to cut down a forest of trees.
⁶They smashed the carved panels
      with their axes and hatchets.

⁷They burned your Temple to the
      ground.
   They have made the place where
      you live unclean.*ᵈ*
⁸They thought, "We will completely
      crush them!"
   They burned every place where God
      was worshiped in the land.
⁹We do not see any signs.
   There are no more prophets.
   And no one knows how long this
      will last.
¹⁰God, how much longer will the enemy
      make fun of you?
   Will they insult you forever?
¹¹Why do you hold back your power?
   Bring your power out in the open
      and destroy them!

¹²God, you have been our king for a
      long time.
   You have saved this country.
¹³You split open the sea by your power.
   You broke the heads of the sea
      monster.
¹⁴You smashed the heads of the
      monster Leviathan.*ᵈ*
   You gave him to the desert
      creatures as food.
¹⁵You opened up the springs and
      streams.
   And you made the rivers run dry.
¹⁶Both the day and the night are yours.
   You made the sun and the moon.
¹⁷You made all the limits on the earth.
   You created summer and winter.

¹⁸Lord, remember how the enemy
      insulted you.
   Remember how those foolish
      people turned away from you.
¹⁹Do not give us, your doves, to those
      wild animals.
   Never forget your poor people.
²⁰Remember the agreement you made
      with us
   because violence fills every dark
      corner of this land.

²¹Do not let your suffering people be
　　disgraced.
　　The poor and helpless people praise
　　you.

²²God, come and defend yourself.
　　Remember the insults that come
　　from those foolish people all
　　day long.
²³Don't forget what your enemies said.
　　Don't forget their roar as they rise
　　against you always.

GOD THE JUDGE

For the director of music. To the tune
of "Do Not Destroy." A song of Asaph.

75 God, we thank you.
　　We thank you because you are
　　near.
　　We tell about the wonderful things
　　you do.

²You say, "I set the time for trial.
　　I will judge fairly.
³The earth with all its people may shake.
　　I am the one who holds it steady.
　　　　　　　　　　　　　　　*Selah*ᵈ
⁴I say to those who are proud, 'Don't
　　brag.'
　　I say to the wicked, 'Don't show
　　your power.
⁵Don't try to use your power against
　　heaven.
　　Don't be stubborn.'"

⁶No one from the east or the west
　　or the desert can judge you.
⁷God is the judge.
　　He judges one person as guilty, and
　　another as innocent.
⁸The Lord holds a cup of anger in his
　　hand.
　　It is full of wine mixed with spices.
　　He pours it out even to the last drop.
　　And the wicked drink it all.

⁹I will tell about this forever.
　　I will sing praise to the God of Jacob.
¹⁰He will take all power away from the
　　wicked.
　　But the power of good people will
　　grow.

THE GOD WHO ALWAYS WINS

For the director of music. With stringed
instruments. A song of Asaph.

76 People in Judah know God.
　　People in Israel know he is
　　great.
²He lives in Jerusalem.
　　His home is on Mount Zion.ᵈ
³There God broke the flaming arrows,
　　the shields and swords of war.
　　　　　　　　　　　　　　　*Selah*ᵈ

⁴God, how wonderful you are!
　　You are more wonderful than the
　　hills full of animals.
⁵The brave soldiers were stripped
　　as they lay asleep in death.
　Not one warrior
　　had the strength to stop it.
⁶God of Jacob, when you spoke
　　strongly,
　　horses and riders fell dead.
⁷You should be feared.
　　Who can stand against you when
　　you are angry?
⁸From heaven you gave the decision.
　　And the earth was afraid and silent.
⁹God, you stood up to judge
　　and to save the people of the earth
　　who were not proud.　　　*Selah*
¹⁰People praise you for your anger
　　against evil.
　　Those who live through your anger
　　are stopped from doing more
　　evil.

¹¹Keep your promises to the Lord your
　　God.
　　From all around gifts should come
　　to the God we worship.
¹²God defeats great leaders.
　　The kings on earth fear him.

REMEMBERING GOD'S HELP

For the director of music. For Jeduthun.
A song of Asaph.

77 I cry out loud to God.
　　I call to God, and he will
　　hear me.

²I looked for the Lord on the day of
trouble.
All night long I reached out my
hands.
I cannot be comforted.
³When I remember God, I become
upset.
When I think, I become afraid.
Selahᵈ

⁴You keep my eyes from closing.
I am too upset to say anything.
⁵I keep thinking about the old days,
the years of long ago.
⁶At night I remember my songs.
I think, and I ask myself:
⁷"Will the Lord reject us forever?
Will he never be kind to us again?
⁸Is his love gone forever?
Has he stopped speaking for all
time?
⁹Has God forgotten mercy?
Is he too angry to pity us?"   *Selah*
¹⁰Then I said, "This is what makes me
sad:
For years the power of God Most
High was with us."

¹¹I remember what the Lord did.
I remember the miraclesᵈ you did
long ago.
¹²I think about all the things you did.
I think about what you have done.

¹³God, your ways are holy.
No god is as great as our God.
¹⁴You are the God who did miracles.
You showed people your power.
¹⁵By your power you have saved your
people,
the descendantsᵈ of Jacob and
Joseph.   *Selah*

¹⁶God, the waters saw you.
They saw you and became afraid.
The deep waters shook with fear.
¹⁷The clouds poured down their rain.
The sky thundered.
Your lightning flashed back and
forth.

¹⁸Your thunder sounded in the
whirlwind.
Lightning lit up the world.
The earth trembled and shook.
¹⁹You made a way through the sea
and paths through the deep waters.
But your footprints were not seen.
²⁰You led your people like a flock of
sheep.
You led them by using Moses and
Aaron.

GOD SAVED ISRAEL FROM EGYPT

A maskilᵈ of Asaph.

78 My people, listen to my
teaching.
Listen to what I say.
²I will speak using stories.
I will tell things that have been
secret since long ago.
³We have heard them and know them.
Our fathers told them to us.
⁴We will not keep them from our
children.
We will tell those who come later
about the praises of the Lord.
We will tell about his power
and the miraclesᵈ he has done.

⁵The Lord made an agreement with
Jacob.
He gave the teachings to Israel.
And he commanded our ancestors
to teach them to their children.
⁶Then their children would know
them,
even their children not yet born.
And they would tell their children.
⁷So they would all trust God.
They would not forget what God
had done.
Instead, they would obey his
commands.
⁸They would not be like their ancestors
who were stubborn and
disobedient.
Their hearts were not loyal to God.
They were not true to him.

⁹The men of Ephraim had bows for
  weapons.
  But they ran away on the day of
    battle.
¹⁰They didn't keep their agreement with
  God.
  They refused to live by his
    teachings.
¹¹They forgot what he had done
  and the miracles he had shown
    them.
¹²He did miracles while their ancestors
  watched,
  in the fields of Zoan in Egypt.
¹³He divided the Red Sea*d* and led them
  through.
  He made the water stand up like a
    wall.
¹⁴He led them with a cloud by day.
  And he led them at night by the
    light of a fire.
¹⁵He split the rocks in the desert.
  And he gave them much water, as if
    it were from the deep ocean.
¹⁶He brought streams out of the rock.
  The water flowed down like rivers.

¹⁷But the people continued to sin
  against him.
  In the desert they turned against
    God Most High.
¹⁸They decided to test God
  by asking for the food they wanted.
¹⁹Then they spoke against God.
  They said, "Can God prepare food
    in the desert?
²⁰When he hit the rock, water poured
    out.
  Rivers flowed down.
  But can he give us bread also?
  Will he provide his people with
    meat?"
²¹When the Lord heard them, he was
  very angry.
  His anger was like fire to the people
    of Jacob.
  His anger grew against the people
    of Israel.

²²They had not believed God.
  They had not trusted him to save
    them.
²³But he gave a command to the clouds
  above.
  The doors of heaven opened.
²⁴He rained manna*d* down on them to
  eat.
  He gave them grain from heaven.
²⁵So they ate the bread of angels.
  He sent them all the food they could
    eat.
²⁶He sent the east wind from heaven.
  He led the south wind by his power.
²⁷He rained meat on them like dust.
  The birds were as many as the sand
    of the sea.
²⁸He made the birds fall inside the camp,
  all around the tents.
²⁹So the people ate and became very
  full.
  God had given them what they
    wanted.
³⁰While they were still eating,
  and while the food was still in their
    mouths,
³¹God became angry with them.
  He killed some of the healthiest of
    them.
  He struck down the best young men
    of Israel.
³²But they kept on sinning.
  They did not believe even with the
    miracles.
³³So he ended their days without
  meaning
  and their years in terror.
³⁴Anytime he killed them, some would
  look to him for help.
  They would come back to God and
    follow him.
³⁵They would remember that God was
  their Rock,*d*
  that God Most High had saved
    them.
³⁶But their words were false.
  Their tongues lied to him.

37Their hearts were not really loyal to
   God.
   They did not keep his agreement.
38Still God was merciful.
   He forgave their sins.
   He did not destroy them.
   Many times he held back his anger.
   He did not stir up all his anger.
39He remembered that they were only
   human.
   They were like a wind that blows
   and does not come back.

40They turned against God so often in
   the desert!
   There they made him very sad.
41Again and again they tested God.
   They brought pain to the Holy One
   of Israel.
42They did not remember his power
   or the time he saved them from the
   enemy.
43They forgot the signs he did in Egypt
   and his miracles in the fields of
   Zoan.
44He turned the rivers to blood.
   So no one could drink the water.
45He sent flies that bit the people.
   He sent frogs that destroyed them.
46He gave their crops to grasshoppers
   and what they worked for to locusts.*d*
47He destroyed their vines with hail
   and their sycamore trees with sleet.
48He killed their animals with hail
   and their cattle with lightning.
49He showed them his hot anger.
   He sent his strong anger against
   them.
   He sent his destroying angels.
50He found a way to show his anger.
   He did not keep them from dying.
   He let them die by a terrible disease.
51God killed all the firstborn*d* sons in
   Egypt,
   the oldest son of each family of
   Ham.*n*

52But God led out his people like sheep.
   He guided them like a flock through
   the desert.
53He led them to safety. They had
   nothing to fear.
   But their enemies drowned in the
   sea.
54So God brought them to his holy land.
   He brought them to the mountain
   country he took with his own
   power.
55He forced out the other nations.
   And he had his people inherit the
   land.
   He let the tribes*d* of Israel settle
   there in tents.

56But they tested God
   and turned against the Most High.
   They did not keep his rules.
57They turned away and sinned just like
   their ancestors.
   They were like a crooked bow that
   does not shoot straight.
58They made God angry by building
   places to worship false gods.
   They made him jealous with their
   idols.
59When God heard them, he became
   very angry.
   And he rejected the people of Israel
   completely.
60He left his dwelling at Shiloh,
   the tent where he lived among men.
61He let his Holy Box*d* be captured.
   He let the Holy Box, which was his
   glory, be taken by enemies.
62He let his people be killed.
   He was very angry with his
   children.
63The young men died by fire.
   The young women had no one to
   marry.
64Their priests fell by the sword.
   But their widows were not allowed
   to cry.

78:51 Ham The people in Egypt were descendants of Ham, one of Noah's sons. See Genesis 10:6.

⁶⁵Then the Lord got up as if he had been
asleep.
He awoke like a man who was
drunk with wine.
⁶⁶He struck down his enemies.
He disgraced them forever.
⁶⁷But God rejected the family of Joseph.
He did not choose the tribe of
Ephraim.
⁶⁸Instead, he chose the tribe of Judah
and Mount Zion,ᵈ which he loves.
⁶⁹And he built his Templeᵈ high like the
mountains.
Like the earth, he built it to last
forever.
⁷⁰He chose David to be his servant.
He took him from the sheep pens.
⁷¹He brought him from tending the
sheep
so he could lead the flock, the
people of Jacob.
This flock was his own people, the
people of Israel.
⁷²And David led them with an innocent
heart.
He guided them with skillful hands.

THE NATION CRIES FOR JERUSALEM

A song of Asaph.

79 God, nations have come against
your people.
They have ruined your holy
Temple.ᵈ
They have turned Jerusalem into
ruins.
²They have given the bodies of your
servants
as food to the wild birds.
They have given the bodies of those
who worship you
to the wild animals.
³They have spilled blood like water
all around Jerusalem.
No one was left to bury the dead.
⁴We are a bad joke to the other
nations.
They laugh and make fun of us.

⁵Lord, how long will this last? Will you
be angry forever?
How long will your jealousy burn
like a fire?
⁶Be angry with the nations that do not
know you.
Be angry with the kingdoms that do
not honor you.
⁷They have destroyed the people of
Jacob.
Those nations have destroyed the
people's land.
⁸Don't punish us for the sins of our
ancestors.
Show your mercy to us soon.
We are helpless!
⁹God our Savior, help us
so people will praise you.
Save us and forgive our sins
so people will honor you.
¹⁰Why should the nations say,
"Where is their God?"
Tell the other nations in our presence
that you punish those who kill your
servants.
¹¹Hear the moans of the prisoners.
Use your great power
to save those sentenced to die.
¹²Repay those around us seven times
over
for their insults to you, Lord.
¹³We are your people, the sheep of your
flock.
We will thank you always.
Forever and ever we will praise you.

A PRAYER TO BRING ISRAEL BACK

For the director of music. To the tune of
"Lilies of the Agreement." A song of Asaph.

80 Shepherd of Israel, listen to us.
You lead the people of Joseph
like a flock.
You sit on your throne between the
gold creatures with wings.
Show your greatness ²to the people
of Ephraim, Benjamin and
Manasseh.
Use your strength.
Come and save us.

³God, take us back.
Show us your kindness so we can
be saved.

⁴Lord God of heaven's armies,
how long will you be angry
at the prayers of your people?
⁵You have fed your people tears.
You have made them drink many
tears.
⁶You made those around us fight over
us.
Our enemies make fun of us.

⁷God of heaven's armies, take us back.
Show us your kindness so we can
be saved.

⁸You brought us out of Egypt as if we
were a vine.
You forced out other nations and
planted us in the land.
⁹You cleared the land for us.
Like a vine, we took root and filled
the land.
¹⁰We covered the mountains with our
shade.
We had limbs like the mighty cedar
tree.
¹¹Our branches reached the
Mediterranean Sea.
And our shoots went to the
Euphrates River.

¹²So why did you pull down our walls?
Now everyone who passes by steals
from us.
¹³Like wild pigs they walk over us.
Like wild animals they feed on us.

¹⁴God of heaven's armies, come back.
Look down from heaven and see.
Take care of us, your vine.
¹⁵ You planted this shoot with your
own hands.
You raised and strengthened this
child.
¹⁶Now it is cut down and burned with fire.
You destroyed us by your angry
looks.

¹⁷Help the man you have chosen.
Make this human being strong for
your service.
¹⁸Then we will not turn away from you.
Give us life again, and we will call to
you for help.

¹⁹Lord God of heaven's armies, take us
back.
Show us your kindness so we can
be saved.

A SONG FOR A HOLIDAY

For the director of music. By the gittith.ᵈ
A song of Asaph.

81 Sing for joy to God, our
strength.
Shout out loud to the God of Jacob.
²Begin the music. Play the
tambourines.ᵈ
Play pleasant music on the harps
and lyres.ᵈ
³Blow the sheep's horn at the time of
the New Moon.ᵈ
Blow it when the moon is full, when
our feast begins.
⁴This is the law for Israel.
It is God's command to the people
of Jacob.
⁵He made this agreement with the
people of Joseph
when they went out of the land of
Egypt.

I heard a language I did not know,
saying:
⁶"I took the load off your shoulders.
I let you put down your baskets.
⁷When you were in trouble, you called,
and I saved you.
I answered you with thunder.
I tested you at the waters of
Meribah.   Selahᵈ
⁸My people, listen. I am warning you.
Israel, please listen to me!
⁹You must not have foreign gods
among you.
You must not worship any false
god.

¹⁰I, the Lord, am your God.
    I brought you out of Egypt.
    Open your mouth, and I will feed
        you.
¹¹"But my people did not listen to me.
    Israel did not want me.
¹²So I let them go their stubborn way.
    They followed their own advice.
¹³I wish my people would listen to me.
    I wish Israel would live my way.
¹⁴Then I would quickly defeat their
        enemies.
    I would turn my hand against those
        who are against them.
¹⁵Those who hate the Lord would bow
        before him.
    Their punishment would continue
        forever.
¹⁶But I would give you the finest wheat.
    I would fill you with honey from the
        rocks."

GOD JUDGES THE JUDGES

A song of Asaph.

82 God is in charge of the great
        meeting of his people.
    He judges the judges.
²He says, "How long will you defend
        evil people?
    How long will you show greater
        kindness to the wicked?   *Selah*ᵈ
³Defend the orphans and the weak.
    Defend the rights of the poor and
        suffering.
⁴Save the weak and helpless
    from the power of the wicked.

⁵"You know nothing. You don't
        understand.
    You walk in the dark,
        while the world is falling apart.
⁶I said, 'You are gods.
    You are all sons of the Most High
        God.'
⁷But you will die like any other person.
    You will die like all the leaders."

⁸God, come and judge the earth.
    You own all the nations.

A PRAYER AGAINST THE ENEMIES

A song of Asaph.

83 God, do not keep quiet.
        God, do not be silent or still.
²Your enemies are making plans.
    Those who hate you are getting
        ready to attack.
³They are making plans against your
        people.
    They plan to hurt those you love.
⁴They say, "Come, let's destroy them as
        a nation.
    Then no one will remember the
        name 'Israel' anymore."
⁵They are united in their plan.
    These have made an agreement
        against you:
⁶the families of Edom and the
        Ishmaelites,
    Moab and the Hagrites,
⁷the people of Byblos, Ammon,
        Amalek,
    Philistia and Tyre.
⁸Even Assyria has joined them
    to help Ammon and Moab, the
        descendantsᵈ of Lot.   *Selah*ᵈ

⁹God, do to them what you did to
        Midian.
    Do what you did to Sisera and Jabin
        at the Kishon River.
¹⁰They died at Endor.
    Their bodies rotted on the ground.
¹¹Do to their important leaders what
        you did to Oreb and Zeeb.
    Do to their princes what you did to
        Zebah and Zalmunna.
¹²They said, "Let's take for ourselves
    the pasturelands that belong to
        God."
¹³My God, make them like the
        tumbleweed,
    like chaffᵈ blown away by the wind.
¹⁴Be like a fire that burns a forest
    or like flames that blaze through the
        hills.
¹⁵Chase them with your storm.
    Frighten them with your wind.

¹⁶Cover them with shame.
>   Then people will look for you, Lord.
¹⁷Make them afraid and ashamed
>   forever.
>   Disgrace them and destroy them.
¹⁸Then they will know that you are the
>   Lord.
>   They will know that only you are
>   God Most High over all the earth.

WISHING TO BE IN THE TEMPLE

For the director of music. By the gittith.^d
A song of the sons of Korah.

84
Lord of heaven's armies,
how lovely is your Temple!^d
²I want to be in
>   the courtyards of the Lord's Temple.
>   My whole being wants
>   to be with the living God.
³The sparrows have found a home.
>   And the swallows have nests.
>   They raise their young near your altars,
>   Lord of heaven's armies, my King
>   and my God.
⁴Happy are the people who live at your
>   Temple.
>   They are always praising you. Selah^d

⁵Happy are those whose strength
>   comes from you.
>   They want to travel to Jerusalem.
⁶As they pass through the Valley of
>   Baca,
>   they make it like a spring.
>   The autumn rains fill it with pools
>   of water.
⁷The people get stronger as they go.
>   And everyone meets with God in
>   Jerusalem.

⁸Lord God of heaven's armies, hear my
>   prayer.
>   God of Jacob, listen to me.   Selah
⁹God, look at our shield.
>   Be kind to your appointed king.

¹⁰One day in the courtyards of your
>   Temple is better
>   than a thousand days anywhere
>   else.

I would rather be a doorkeeper in the
>   Temple of my God
>   than live in the homes of the
>   wicked.
¹¹The Lord God is like our sun and
>   shield.
>   The Lord gives us kindness and
>   glory.
>   He does not hold back anything good
>   from those whose life is innocent.
¹²Lord of heaven's armies,
>   happy are the people who trust you!

A PRAYER FOR THE NATION

For the director of music.
A song of the sons of Korah.

85
Lord, you have been kind to
your land.
>   You gave the people of Jacob back
>   their riches.
²You forgave the guilt of the people.
>   You covered all their sins.   Selah^d
³You stopped all your anger.
>   You stopped your strong anger.

⁴God our Savior, bring us back again.
>   Stop being angry with us.
⁵Will you be angry with us forever?
>   Will you stay angry from now on?
⁶Won't you give us life again?
>   Your people would rejoice in you.
⁷Lord, show us your love.
>   Save us.

⁸I will listen to God the Lord.
>   He has ordered peace for his people
>   who worship him.
>   Don't let them go back to
>   foolishness.
⁹God will soon save those who respect
>   him.
>   And his greatness will be seen in
>   our land.
¹⁰Love and truth will belong to God's
>   people.
>   Goodness and peace will be theirs.
¹¹On earth people will be loyal to God.
>   And God's goodness will shine
>   down from heaven.

¹²The Lord will give his goodness.
  And the land will give its crops.
¹³Goodness will go before God
  and prepare the way for him.

A CRY FOR HELP

A prayer of David.

86 Lord, listen to me and answer
      me.
  I am poor and helpless.
²Protect me, because I worship you.
  My God, save me, your servant.
  I trust in you.
³Lord, be merciful to me.
  I have called to you all day.
⁴Give happiness to me, your servant.
  Lord, I give my life to you.
⁵Lord, you are kind and forgiving.
  You have great love for those who
    call to you.
⁶Lord, hear my prayer.
  Listen when I ask for mercy.
⁷I call to you in times of trouble.
  You certainly will answer me.

⁸Lord, there is no god like you.
  There are no works like yours.
⁹Lord, all the nations you have made
  will come and worship you.
  They will honor you.
¹⁰You are great, and you do miracles.ᵈ
  Only you are God.

¹¹Lord, teach me what you want me to do.
  And I will live by your truth.
  Teach me to respect you completely.
¹²Lord, my God, I will praise you with
    all my heart.
  I will honor your name forever.
¹³You have great love for me.
  You have saved me from death.

¹⁴God, proud men turn against me.
  A gang of cruel men are trying to
    kill me.
  They do not respect you.
¹⁵But Lord, you are a God who shows
    mercy and is kind.
  You don't become angry quickly.
  You have great love and
    faithfulness.

¹⁶Turn to me and be merciful.
  Give me, your servant, strength.
  Save me, the son of your female
    servant.
¹⁷Show me a sign of your goodness.
  When my enemies look, they will be
    ashamed.
  You, Lord, have helped me and
    comforted me.

GOD LOVES JERUSALEM

A song of the sons of Korah.

87 The Lord built Jerusalem on the
      holy mountain.
² He loves its gates
  more than any other place in Israel.
³City of God,
  wonderful things are said about
    you.   *Selah*ᵈ
⁴God says, "I will put Egypt and
    Babylonia
  on the list of nations that know me.
  People from Philistia, Tyre and Cush
  will be born there."

⁵They will say about Jerusalem,
  "This one and that one were born
    there.
  God Most High will strengthen
    her."
⁶The Lord will keep a list of the
    nations.
  He will note, "This person was born
    there."   *Selah*
⁷They will dance and sing,
  "All good things come from
    Jerusalem."

A SAD COMPLAINT

A song of the sons of Korah. For the director
of music. By the mahalath leannoth.ᵈ
A maskilᵈ of Heman the Ezrahite.

88 Lord, you are the God who
      saves me.
  I cry out to you day and night.
²Accept my prayer.
  Listen to my cry.

³My life is full of troubles.
  I am nearly dead.

⁴They think I am on the way to my grave.
  I am like a man with no strength.
⁵I have been left as dead,
  like a body lying in a grave.
You don't remember dead people.
  They are cut off from your care.
⁶You have brought me close to death.
  I am almost in the dark place of the
    dead.
⁷You have been very angry with me.
  All your waves crush me.   *Selahᵈ*
⁸You have taken my friends away from
    me.
You have made them hate me.
I am trapped and cannot escape.
⁹ My eyes are weak from crying.
Lord, I have prayed to you every day.
  I have lifted my hands in prayer to
    you.

¹⁰Do you show your miraclesᵈ for the
    dead?
  Do their spirits rise up and praise
    you?   *Selah*
¹¹Will your love be told in the grave?
  Will your loyalty be told in the place
    of death?
¹²Will your miracles be known in the
    dark grave?
  Will your goodness be known in the
    land where the dead are
    forgotten?

¹³But, Lord, I have called out to you for
    help.
  Every morning I pray to you.
¹⁴Lord, why do you reject me?
  Why do you hide from me?
¹⁵I have been weak and dying since I
    was young.
  I suffer from your terrors, and I am
    helpless.
¹⁶You have been angry with me.
  Your terrors have destroyed me.
¹⁷They surround me daily like a flood.
  They are all around me.
¹⁸You have taken away my loved ones
    and friends.
  Darkness is my only friend.

A SONG ABOUT GOD'S LOYALTY

A maskilᵈ of Ethan the Ezrahite.

89 I will always sing about the
      Lord's love.
  I will tell of his loyalty from now on.
²I will say, "Your love continues
    forever.
  Your loyalty goes on and on like the
    sky."
³You said, "I made an agreement with
    the man of my choice.
  I made a promise to my servant
    David.
⁴I told him, 'I will make your family
    continue forever.
  Your kingdom will continue from
    now on.'"   *Selahᵈ*

⁵Lord, the heavens praise you for your
    miraclesᵈ
  and for your loyalty in the meeting
    of your holy ones.
⁶Who in heaven is equal to the Lord?
  None of the angels is like the Lord.
⁷When the holy ones meet, it is God
    they fear.
  He is more frightening than all who
    surround him.
⁸Lord God of heaven's armies, who is
    like you?
  Lord, you are powerful and
    completely to be trusted.
⁹You rule the mighty sea.
  You calm the stormy waves.
¹⁰You crushed the sea monster Rahab.ᵈ
  By your power you scattered your
    enemies.
¹¹The skies and the earth belong
    to you.
  You made the world and everything
    in it.
¹²You created the north and the south.
  Mount Tabor and Mount Hermon
    sing for joy at your name.
¹³Your arm has great power.
  Your hand is strong. Your right
    hand is lifted up.

14Your kingdom is built on what is right
and fair.
Love and truth are in all you do.

15Happy are the people who know how
to praise you.
Lord, let them live in the light of
your presence.
16In your name they rejoice all the time.
They praise your goodness.
17You are their glorious strength.
In your kindness you honor our king.
18Our king, our shield, belongs to the
Lord.
Our king belongs to the Holy One of
Israel.

19Once, in a vision, you spoke
to those who worship you.
You said, "I have given strength to a
warrior.
I have selected a young man from
my people.
20I have found my servant David.
I appointed him by pouring holy oil
on him.
21I will steady him with my hand.
I will strengthen him with my arm.
22No enemy will make him give forced
payments.
Wicked people will not defeat him.
23I will crush his enemies in front of
him.
I will defeat those who hate him.
24My loyalty and love will be with him.
Through me he will be strong.
25I will give him power over the sea
and control over the rivers.
26He will say to me, 'You are my father,
my God, the Rock,d the one who
saves me.'
27I will make him my firstbornd son.
He will be the greatest king on
earth.
28My love will watch over him forever.
My agreement with him will never
end.
29I will make his family continue.
His kingdom will last as long as the
skies.

30"But his descendantsd might reject my
teachings
and not follow my rules.
31They might break my laws
and disobey my commands.
32Then I will punish their sins with a rod
and their wrongs with a whip.
33But I will not hold back my love from
David.
I will not stop being loyal.
34I will not break my agreement.
I will not change what I have said.
35It is certain that I am a holy God.
So it is certain I will not lie to David.
36His family will continue forever.
His kingdom will continue before
me like the sun.
37It will last forever, like the moon,
like a lasting witness in the sky."

Selah

38But now, you have rejected your
appointed king.
You have been angry with him.
39You have broken the agreement with
your servant.
You threw his crown to the ground.
40You have torn down all the city walls.
You have turned his strong, walled
cities into ruins.
41Everyone who passes by steals from
him.
His neighbors insult him.
42You have given strength to his
enemies.
You have made them all happy.
43You have made his sword useless.
You did not help him stand in
battle.
44You have kept him from winning.
You threw his throne to the ground.
45You have cut his life short.
You have covered him with shame.

Selah

46Lord, how long will this go on?
Will you ignore us forever?
How long will your anger burn like
a fire?

⁴⁷Remember how short my life is.
Why did you create us anyway?
⁴⁸What man alive will not die?
Can he escape the grave?   *Selah*

⁴⁹Lord, where is your love from times
past?
With loyalty you promised it to
David.
⁵⁰Lord, remember how they insulted
your servant.
Remember how I have suffered the
insults of the nations.
⁵¹Lord, remember how your enemies
insulted you.
Remember how they insulted your
appointed king wherever he went.

⁵²Praise the Lord forever!
Amen and amen.

Book 4

GOD IS ETERNAL, AND WE ARE NOT

A prayer of Moses, the man of God.

90 Lord, you have been our home
since the beginning.
²Before the mountains were born,
and before you created the earth
and the world,
you are God.
You have always been, and you will
always be.

³You turn people back into dust.
You say, "Go back into dust, human
beings."
⁴To you, a thousand years
is like the passing of a day.
It passes like an hour in the night.
⁵While people sleep, you take their
lives.
They are like weeds that grow in the
morning.
⁶In the morning they are fresh and
new.
But by evening they dry up and die.

⁷We are destroyed by your anger.
We are terrified by your hot anger.

⁸You have put the evil we have done
right in front of you.
You clearly see our secret sins.
⁹All our days pass while you are angry.
Our years end with a moan.
¹⁰Our lifetime is 70 years.
If we are strong, we may live to be 80.
But the years are full of hard work
and pain.
They pass quickly, and then we are
gone.

¹¹Who knows the full power of your
anger?
Your anger is as great as our fear of
you should be.
¹²Teach us how short our lives really are
so that we may be wise.

¹³Lord, how long before you return
and show kindness to your servants?
¹⁴Fill us with your love every morning.
Then we will sing and rejoice all our
lives.
¹⁵We have seen years of trouble.
Now give us joy as you gave us
sorrow.
¹⁶Show your servants the wonderful
things you do.
Show your greatness to their
children.
¹⁷Lord our God, be pleased with us.
Give us success in what we do.
Yes, give us success in what we do.

SAFE IN THE LORD

91 Those who go to God Most High
for safety
will be protected by God
All-Powerful.
²I will say to the Lord, "You are my
place of safety and protection.
You are my God, and I trust you."

³God will save you from hidden traps
and from deadly diseases.
⁴He will protect you like a bird
spreading its wings over its young.
His truth will be like your armor
and shield.

⁵You will not fear any danger by night
or an arrow during the day.
⁶You will not be afraid of diseases that
come in the dark
or sickness that strikes at noon.
⁷At your side 1,000 people may die,
or even 10,000 right beside you.
But you will not be hurt.
⁸You will only watch what happens.
You will see the wicked punished.

⁹The Lord is your protection.
You have made God Most High
your place of safety.
¹⁰Nothing bad will happen to you.
No disaster will come to your home.
¹¹He has put his angels in charge of you.
They will watch over you wherever
you go.
¹²They will catch you with their hands.
And you will not hit your foot on a
rock.
¹³You will walk on lions and cobras.
You will step on strong lions and
snakes.

¹⁴The Lord says, "If someone loves me,
I will save him.
I will protect those who know me.
¹⁵They will call to me, and I will answer
them.
I will be with them in trouble.
I will rescue them and honor them.
¹⁶I will give them a long, full life.
They will see how I can save."

THANKSGIVING FOR GOD'S GOODNESS

A song for the Sabbath[d] day.

92 It is good to praise the Lord,
to sing praises to God Most
High.
²It is good to tell of your love in the
morning
and of your loyalty at night.
³It is good to praise you with the ten-
stringed lyre[d]
and with the soft-sounding harp.

⁴Lord, you have made me happy by
what you have done.

I will sing for joy about what your
hands have done.
⁵Lord, you have done such great
things!
How deep are your thoughts!
⁶Stupid people don't know these
things.
Fools don't understand.
⁷Wicked people grow like the grass.
Evil people seem to do well.
But they will be destroyed forever.
⁸But, Lord, you will be honored
forever.

⁹Lord, surely your enemies,
surely your enemies will be
destroyed.
All who do evil will be scattered.
¹⁰But you have made me as strong as a
wild ox.
You have poured fine oils on me.
¹¹When I looked, I saw my enemies.
I heard the cries of those who are
against me.

¹²But good people will grow like palm
trees.
They will be tall like the cedar trees
of Lebanon.
¹³They will be like trees planted in the
courtyards of the Lord.
They will grow strong in the
courtyards of our God.
¹⁴When they are old, they will still
produce fruit.
They will be healthy and fresh.
¹⁵They will say that the Lord is good.
He is my Rock,[d] and there is no
wrong in him.

THE MAJESTY OF GOD

93 The Lord is king. He is clothed
with majesty.
The Lord is clothed in majesty
and armed with strength.
The world is set,
and it cannot be moved.
²Lord, your kingdom was set up long
ago.
You are everlasting.

³Lord, the seas rise up.
  The seas raise their voice.
  The seas lift up their pounding
    waves.
⁴The sound of the water is loud.
  The ocean waves are powerful.
  But the Lord above is much greater.

⁵Lord, your laws will stand forever.
  Your Temple*d* will be holy
    forevermore.

GOD WILL PAY BACK HIS ENEMIES

94 The Lord is a God who gives
        people what they should get.
  God, show your greatness and
    punish!
²Rise up, Judge of the earth.
  Give the proud what they should get.
³How long will the wicked be happy?
  How long, Lord?

⁴They are full of proud words.
  Those who do evil brag about what
    they have done.
⁵Lord, they crush your people.
  They make your children suffer.
⁶They kill widows and foreigners.
  They murder orphans.
⁷They say, "The Lord doesn't see.
  The God of Jacob doesn't notice."

⁸You stupid ones among the people,
    pay attention.
  You fools, when will you
    understand?
⁹Can't the creator of ears hear?
  Can't the maker of eyes see?
¹⁰Won't the one who corrects nations
    punish you?
  Doesn't the teacher of men know
    everything?
¹¹The Lord knows what people think.
  He knows they are just a puff of
    wind.

¹²Lord, those you correct are happy.
  You give them your teachings.
¹³You give them rest from times of
    trouble
  until a grave is dug for the wicked.

¹⁴The Lord won't leave his people.
  He will not give up his children.
¹⁵Judgment will again be fair.
  And all who are honest will follow
    it.

¹⁶Who will help me fight against the
    wicked?
  Who will stand with me against
    those who do evil?
¹⁷If the Lord had not helped me,
  I would have died soon.
¹⁸I said, "I am about to be
    overwhelmed."
  But, Lord, your love kept me safe.
¹⁹I was very worried.
  But you comforted me and made
    me happy.

²⁰Crooked leaders cannot be your
    friends.
  They use the law to cause suffering.
²¹They join forces against people who
    do right.
  They sentence to death the
    innocent.
²²But the Lord protects me like a strong,
    walled city.
  My God is the rock of my
    protection.
²³God will pay them back for their sins.
  He will destroy them for their evil.
  The Lord our God will destroy
    them.

A CALL TO PRAISE AND OBEDIENCE

95 Come, let's sing for joy to the
        Lord.
  Let's shout praises to the Rock*d*
    who saves us.
²Let's come to him with thanksgiving.
  Let's sing songs to him.
³The Lord is the great God.
  He is the great King over all gods.
⁴The deepest places on earth are his.
  And the highest mountains belong
    to him.
⁵The sea is his because he made it.
  He created the land with his own
    hands.

⁶Come, let's bow down and worship
  him.
  Let's kneel before the Lord who
    made us.
⁷He is our God.
  And we are the people he takes
    care of
  and the sheep that he tends.

Today listen to what he says:
⁸ "Do not be stubborn, as your
    ancestors were at Meribah,
  as they were that day at Massah in
    the desert.
⁹There your ancestors tested me.
  They put me to the test even though
    they saw what I did.
¹⁰I was angry with those people for 40
    years.
  I said, 'They are not loyal to me.
  They have not understood my ways.'
¹¹I was angry and made a promise,
  'They will never enter my land of
    rest.'"

PRAISE FOR GOD'S GLORY

96 Sing to the Lord a new song.
  Sing to the Lord, all the earth.
²Sing to the Lord and praise his name.
  Every day tell how he saves us.
³Tell the nations of his glory.
  Tell all peoples the miracles*ᵈ* he
    does.

⁴The Lord is great; he should be
    praised.
  He should be honored more than all
    the gods.
⁵All the gods of the nations are only
    idols.
  But the Lord made the skies.
⁶The Lord has glory and majesty.
  He has power and beauty in his
    Temple.*ᵈ*

⁷Praise the Lord, all nations on earth.
  Praise the Lord's glory and power.
⁸Praise the glory of the Lord's name.
  Bring an offering and come into his
    Temple courtyards.

⁹Worship the Lord because he is holy.
  The whole earth should tremble
    before the Lord.
¹⁰Tell the nations, "The Lord is king."
  The earth is set, and it cannot be
    moved.
  He will judge the people fairly.
¹¹Let the skies rejoice and the earth be
    glad.
  Let the sea and everything in it
    shout.
¹²Let the fields and everything in them
    show their joy.
  Then all the trees of the forest will
    sing for joy.
¹³ They will sing before the Lord
    because he is coming.
  He is coming to judge the world.
  He will judge the world with fairness
    and the nations with truth.

A HYMN ABOUT GOD'S POWER

97 The Lord is king. Let the earth
    rejoice.
  Faraway lands should be glad.
²Thick, dark clouds surround him.
  His kingdom is built on what is
    right and fair.
³A fire goes before him
  and burns up his enemies all
    around.
⁴His lightning flashes in the sky.
  When the people see it, they
    tremble.
⁵The mountains melt like wax before
    the Lord.
  He is Lord of all the earth.
⁶The skies tell about his goodness.
  And all the people see his glory.

⁷Those who worship idols should be
    ashamed.
  They brag about their false gods.
  All the gods should worship the
    Lord.
⁸When Jerusalem hears this, she is glad.
  The towns of Judah rejoice.
  They are happy because of your
    judgments, Lord.

9You are the Lord Most High over all
the earth.
You are supreme over all gods.

10People who love the Lord should hate
evil.
The Lord watches over those who
follow him.
He frees them from the power of
the wicked.
11Light shines on those who do right.
Joy belongs to those who are
honest.
12Rejoice in the Lord, you who do right.
Praise his holy name.

THE GOD OF POWER AND JUSTICE

A song.

98 Sing to the Lord a new song
because he has done miracles.*d*
By his right hand and holy arm
he has won the victory.
2The Lord has told about his power to
save.
He has shown the other nations his
victory for his people.
3He has remembered his love
and his loyalty to the people of Israel.
All the ends of the earth have seen
God's power to save.

4Shout with joy to the Lord, all the
earth.
Burst into songs and praise.
5Make music to the Lord with harps,
with harps and the sound of
singing.
6Blow the trumpets and the sheep's
horns.
Shout for joy to the Lord the King.

7Let the sea and everything in it shout.
Let the world and everyone on it
sing.
8Let the rivers clap their hands.
Let the mountains sing together for
joy.
9Let them sing before the Lord
because he is coming to judge the
world.

He will judge the world fairly.
He will judge the nations with
fairness.

GOD THE FAIR AND HOLY KING

99 The Lord is king.
Let the nations shake with fear.
He sits between the gold creatures
with wings.
Let the earth shake.
2The Lord in Jerusalem is great.
He is supreme over all the nations.
3Let them praise your name.
It is great, holy and to be feared.

4The King is powerful and loves justice.
Lord, you made things fair.
You have done what is fair and right
for the people of Jacob.
5Praise the Lord our God.
Worship at the Temple,*d* his
footstool.
He is holy.

6Moses and Aaron were among his
priests.
And Samuel was among his
worshipers.
They called to the Lord,
and he answered them.
7He spoke to them from the pillar of
cloud.
They kept the rules and laws he
gave them.

8Lord our God, you answered them.
You showed them that you are a
forgiving God.
But you punished them for their
wrongs.
9Praise the Lord our God.
Worship at his holy mountain.
The Lord our God is holy.

A CALL TO PRAISE GOD

A song of thanks.

100 Shout to the Lord, all the
earth.
2   Serve the Lord with joy.
Come before him with singing.

³Know that the Lord is God.
He made us, and we belong
to him.
We are his people, the sheep he
tends.

⁴Come into his city with songs of
thanksgiving.
Come into his courtyards with
songs of praise.
Thank him, and praise his name.
⁵The Lord is good. His love continues
forever.
His loyalty continues from now on.

A PROMISE TO RULE WELL

A song of David.

101 I will sing of love and
fairness.
Lord, I will sing praises to you.
²I will be careful to live an innocent
life.
When will you come to me?

I will live an innocent life in my
house.
³ I will not look at anything wicked.
I hate those who turn against you.
They will not be found near me.
⁴Let those who want to do wrong stay
away from me.
I will have nothing to do with evil.
⁵If anyone secretly says things against
his neighbor,
I will stop him.
I will not allow people
to be proud and look down on
others.
⁶I will look for trustworthy people
so I can live with them in the land.
Only those who live innocent lives
will be my servants.
⁷No one who is dishonest will live in
my house.
No liars will stay around me.
⁸Every morning I will destroy
the wicked in the land.
I will rid the Lord's city
of people who do evil.

A CRY FOR HELP

A prayer of a person who is suffering when he
is discouraged and tells the Lord his
complaints.

102 Lord, listen to my prayer.
Let my cry for help come
to you.
²Do not hide from me
in my time of trouble.
Pay attention to me.
When I cry for help, answer me
quickly.

³My life is passing away like smoke.
My bones are burned up with fire.
⁴My heart is like grass
that has been cut and dried.
I forget to eat.
⁵Because of my grief,
my skin hangs on my bones.
⁶I am like a desert owl.
I am like an owl living among the
ruins.
⁷I lie awake.
I am like a lonely bird on a
housetop.
⁸All day long enemies insult me.
Those who make fun of me use my
name as a curse.
⁹I eat ashes as my food.
My tears fall into my drinks.
¹⁰Because of your great anger,
you have picked me up and thrown
me away.
¹¹My days are like a passing shadow.
I am like dried grass.

¹²But, Lord, you rule forever.
Your fame continues from now on.
¹³You will come and have mercy on
Jerusalem.
The time has now come to be kind
to her.
¹⁴Your servants love even her stones.
They even care about her dust.
¹⁵Nations will fear the name of the
Lord.
All the kings on earth will honor
him.

¹⁶The Lord will rebuild Jerusalem.
　　There his glory will be seen.
¹⁷He will answer the prayers of the needy.
　　He will not reject their prayers.

¹⁸Write these things for the future.
　　Then people who are not yet born
　　　will praise the Lord.
¹⁹The Lord looked down from his holy
　　place above.
　　From heaven he looked down at the
　　　earth.
²⁰He heard the moans of the prisoners.
　　And he freed those sentenced to die.
²¹The name of the Lord will be heard in
　　Jerusalem.
　　His praise will be heard in
　　　Jerusalem.
²²People will come together.
　　Kingdoms will serve the Lord.

²³God has made me tired of living.
　　He has cut short my life.
²⁴So I said, "My God, do not take me in
　　the middle of my life.
　　Your years go on and on.
²⁵In the beginning you made the earth.
　　And your hands made the skies.
²⁶They will be destroyed, but you will
　　remain.
　　They will all wear out like clothes.
　　And, like clothes, you will change
　　　them.
　　And they will be thrown away.
²⁷But you never change.
　　And your life will never end.
²⁸Our children will live in your
　　presence.
　　And their children will remain with
　　　you."

PRAISE TO THE GOD OF LOVE

Of David.

103 All that I am, praise the
Lord.
Everything in me, praise his holy
　　name.
²My whole being, praise the Lord.
　　Do not forget all his kindnesses.

³The Lord forgives me for all my
　　sins.
　　He heals all my diseases.
⁴He saves my life from the grave.
　　He loads me with love and mercy.
⁵He satisfies me with good things.
　　He makes me young again, like the
　　　eagle.

⁶The Lord does what is right and fair
　　for all who are wronged by others.
⁷He showed his ways to Moses
　　and his miracles[d] to the people of
　　　Israel.
⁸The Lord shows mercy and is kind.
　　He does not become angry quickly,
　　and he has great love.
⁹He will not always scold us.
　　He will not be angry forever.
¹⁰He has not punished us as our sins
　　should be punished.
　　He has not repaid us for the evil we
　　　have done.
¹¹As high as the sky is above the earth,
　　so great is his love for those who
　　　respect him.
¹²He has taken our sins away from us
　　as far as the east is from west.
¹³The Lord has mercy on those who fear
　　him,
　　as a father has mercy on his
　　　children.
¹⁴He knows how we were made.
　　He remembers that we are dust.

¹⁵Human life is like grass.
　　We grow like a flower in the field.
¹⁶After the wind blows, the flower is
　　gone.
　　There is no sign of where it was.
¹⁷But the Lord's love for those who fear
　　him
　　continues forever and ever.
　　And his goodness continues to their
　　　grandchildren
¹⁸and to those who keep his agreement
　　and who remember to obey his
　　　orders.

¹⁹The Lord has set his throne in heaven.
  And his kingdom rules over
    everything.
²⁰You who are his angels, praise the
    Lord.
  You are the mighty warriors who do
    what he says.
  Listen to what he says.
²¹You, his armies, praise the Lord.
  You are his servants who do what
    he wants.
²²Everything the Lord has made
  should praise him in all the places
    he rules.
  My whole being, praise the Lord.

PRAISE TO GOD WHO MADE THE WORLD

104 My whole being, praise
        the Lord.
  Lord my God, you are very great.
  You are clothed with glory and
    majesty.
² You wear light like a robe.
  You stretch out the skies like a tent.
³ You build your room above the
    clouds.
  You make the clouds your chariot.
  You ride on the wings of the wind.
⁴You make the winds your messengers.
  Flames of fire are your servants.

⁵You built the earth on its foundations.
  So it can never be moved.
⁶You covered the earth with oceans.
  The water was above the
    mountains.
⁷But at your command, the water
    rushed away.
  When you gave your orders like
    thunder, it hurried away.
⁸The mountains rose.
  The valleys sank.
  The water went to the places you
    made for it.
⁹You set borders for the seas that they
    cannot cross.
  The water will never cover the earth
    again.

¹⁰You make springs pour into the
    ravines.
  They flow between the mountains.
¹¹They water all the wild animals.
  The wild donkeys come there to
    drink.
¹²Wild birds make nests by the water.
  They sing among the tree branches.
¹³You water the mountains from above.
  The earth is full of the things you
    made.
¹⁴You make the grass for cattle
  and vegetables for the use of man.
  You make food grow from the earth.
¹⁵You give us wine that makes happy
    hearts.
  And you give us olive oil that makes
    our faces shine.
  You give us bread that gives us
    strength.
¹⁶The Lord's trees have plenty of water.
  They are the cedar trees of
    Lebanon, which he planted.
¹⁷The birds make their nests there.
  The stork's home is in the fir trees.
¹⁸The high mountains belong to the
    wild goats.
  The rocks are hiding places for the
    badgers.

¹⁹You made the moon to mark the
    seasons.
  And the sun always knows when to
    set.
²⁰You make it dark, and it becomes
    night.
  Then all the wild animals creep
    around.
²¹The lions roar as they attack.
  They look to God for food.
²²When the sun rises, they leave.
  They go back to their dens to lie
    down.
²³Then people go to work.
  And they work until evening.

²⁴Lord, you have made many things.
  With your wisdom you made
    them all.
  The earth is full of your riches.

25Look at the sea, so big and wide.
  Its creatures large and small cannot
    be counted.
26Ships travel over the ocean.
  And there is the sea monster
    Leviathan,*d*
  which you made to play there.

27All these things depend on you
    to give them their food at the right
      time.
28When you give it to them,
    they gather it up.
  When you open your hand, they are
    filled with good food.
29When you turn away from them,
    they become frightened.
  When you take away their breath,
    they die and turn into dust.
30When you breathe on them,
    they are created.
  You make the land new again.

31May the glory of the Lord be forever.
  May the Lord enjoy what he has
    made.
32He just looks at the earth, and it
    shakes.
  He touches the mountains, and they
    smoke.

33I will sing to the Lord all my life.
  I will sing praises to my God as long
    as I live.
34May my thoughts please him.
  I am happy in the Lord.
35Let sinners be destroyed from the
    earth.
  Let the wicked people live no
    longer.

My whole being, praise the Lord.
  Praise the Lord.

GOD'S LOVE FOR ISRAEL

105
Give thanks to the Lord and
  pray to him.
Tell the nations what he has done.
2Sing to him. Sing praises to him.
  Tell about all the wonderful things
    he has done.

3Be glad that you are his.
  Let those who ask the Lord for help
    be happy.
4Depend on the Lord and his strength.
  Always go to him for help.
5Remember the wonderful things he
    has done.
  Remember his miracles*d* and his
    decisions.
6You are descendants*d* of his servant
    Abraham,
  the children of Jacob, his chosen
    people.
7He is the Lord our God.
  His laws are for all the world.

8He will keep his agreement forever.
  He will keep his promises always.
9He will keep his agreement he made
    with Abraham.
  He will keep the promise he made
    to Isaac.
10He made it a law for the people of Jacob.
  He made it an agreement with
    Israel to last forever.
11The Lord said, "I will give you the
    land of Canaan.
  The promised land will belong to
    you."

12Then God's people were few in number.
  They were strangers in the land.
13They went from one nation to
    another.
  They went from one kingdom to
    another.
14But the Lord did not let anyone hurt
    them.
  He warned kings not to harm them.
15He said, "Don't hurt my chosen
    people.
  Don't harm my prophets."*d*

16God ordered a time of hunger in the
    land.
  And he destroyed all the food.
17Then he sent a man ahead of them.
  It was Joseph, who was sold as a
    slave.

18They put chains around his feet
and an iron ring around his neck.
19Then the time he had spoken of came.
The Lord's words proved that
Joseph was right.
20The king of Egypt sent for Joseph and
freed him.
The ruler of the people set him free.
21He made him the master of his house.
Joseph was in charge of his riches.
22He could order the princes as he
wished.
He taught the older men to be wise.
23Then his father Israel came to Egypt.
Jacob, also called Israel, lived in
Egypt.*n*
24The Lord made his people grow in
number.
He made them stronger than their
enemies.
25And he caused the Egyptians to hate
his people.
They made plans against the Lord's
servants.
26Then he sent his servant Moses,
and Aaron, whom he had chosen.
27They did many signs among the
Egyptians.
They worked miracles in Egypt.
28The Lord sent darkness and made the
land dark.
But the Egyptians turned against
what he said.
29So he changed their water into blood
and made their fish die.
30Then their country was filled with frogs.
They were even in the bedrooms of
their rulers.
31The Lord spoke, and flies came.
Gnats were everywhere in the
country.
32He made hail fall like rain.
And he sent lightning through their
land.

33He struck down their grapevines and
fig trees.
He destroyed every tree in the
country.
34He spoke, and grasshoppers came.
The locusts*d* were too many to
count.
35They ate all the plants in the land.
They ate what the earth produced.
36The Lord also killed all the firstborn*d*
sons in the land,
the oldest son of each family.

37Then he brought his people out,
and they carried with them silver
and gold.
Not one of his people stumbled.
38The Egyptians were glad when they
left
because the Egyptians were afraid
of them.
39The Lord covered them with a cloud
and lit up the night with fire.
40When they asked, he brought them
quail.
He filled them with bread from
heaven.
41God split the rock, and water flowed
out.
It ran like a river through the
desert.
42He remembered his holy promise
to his servant Abraham.

43So God brought his people out with
joy.
He brought out his chosen ones
with singing.
44He gave them lands that belonged to
other nations.
They received what others had
worked for.
45This was so they would keep his
orders
and obey his teachings.

Praise the Lord!

105:23 Egypt Literally, "the land of Ham." Also in verse 27. The people in Egypt were descendants of Ham, one of
Noah's sons. See Genesis 10:6.

ISRAEL'S FAILURE TO TRUST GOD

106 Praise the Lord!
Thank the Lord because he
is good.
His love continues forever.
²No one can tell all the mighty things
the Lord has done.
No one can speak all his praise.
³Happy are those people who are fair,
who do what is right at all times.

⁴Lord, remember me when you are
kind to your people.
Help me when you save them.
⁵Let me see the good things you do for
your chosen people.
Let me be happy along with your
happy nation.
Let me join your own people in
praising you.

⁶We have sinned just as our ancestors
did.
We have done wrong. We have
done evil.
⁷Our ancestors in Egypt
did not learn from your miracles.ᵈ
They did not remember all your
kindnesses.
So they turned against you at the
Red Sea.ᵈ
⁸But the Lord saved them for his own
sake,
to show his great power.
⁹He commanded the Red Sea, and it
dried up.
He led them through the deep sea
as if it were a desert.
¹⁰He saved them from those who hated
them.
He saved them from their enemies.
¹¹And the water covered their enemies.
Not one of them escaped.
¹²Then the people believed what the
Lord said.
They sang praises to him.

¹³But they quickly forgot what he had
done.
They did not wait for his advice.
¹⁴They became greedy for food in the
desert.
And they tested God there.
¹⁵So he gave them what they wanted.
But he also sent a terrible disease
among them.

¹⁶The people in the camp became
jealous of Moses
and of Aaron, the holy priest of the
Lord.
¹⁷Then the ground opened up and
swallowed Dathan.
It closed over Abiram's group.
¹⁸Then a fire burned among their
followers.
Flames burned up the wicked
people.

¹⁹The people made a gold calf at Mount
Sinai.
They worshiped a metal statue.
²⁰They exchanged their glorious God
for a statue of a bull, which eats
grass.
²¹They forgot the God who saved them,
who had done great things in Egypt.
²²He did miracles in Egypt.ⁿ
He did amazing things by the Red
Sea.
²³So God said he would destroy them.
But Moses, his chosen one, stood
before him.
He stopped God's anger from
destroying them.

²⁴Then they refused to go into the
beautiful land of Canaan.
They did not believe what God
promised.
²⁵They grumbled in their tents
and did not obey the Lord.
²⁶So he swore to them
that they would die in the desert.

106:22 Egypt Literally, "the land of Ham." The people in Egypt were descendants of Ham, one of Noah's sons. See
Genesis 10:6.

²⁷He said their children would be killed
      by other nations
   and that they would be scattered
      among other countries.

²⁸They joined in worshiping Baal*d* at
      Peor.
   They ate meat that had been
      sacrificed to lifeless statues.
²⁹They made the Lord angry by what
      they did.
   So many people became sick with a
      terrible disease.
³⁰But Phinehas prayed to the Lord,
   and the disease stopped.
³¹The Lord will remember that
      Phinehas did what was right.
   And God will remember this from
      now on.

³²The people also made the Lord angry
      at Meribah.
   And Moses was in trouble because
      of them.
³³The people turned against the Spirit*d*
      of God.
   So Moses spoke without stopping to
      think.

³⁴The people did not destroy the other
      nations
   as the Lord had told them to do.
³⁵Instead, they mixed with the other
      nations.
   And they learned their customs.
³⁶They worshiped other nations' idols.
   And they were trapped by them.
³⁷They even killed their sons and
      daughters
   as sacrifices to demons.*d*
³⁸They killed innocent people.
   They killed their own sons and
      daughters
   as sacrifices to the idols of Canaan.
   So the land was made unholy by
      their blood.
³⁹The people became unholy by their sins.
   They were unfaithful to God in what
      they did.

⁴⁰So the Lord became angry with his
      people.
   He hated his own children.
⁴¹He let other nations defeat them.
   He let their enemies rule over them.
⁴²Their enemies were cruel to them.
   Their enemies kept them under
      their power.
⁴³The Lord saved his people many times.
   But they continued to turn against
      him.
   So they became even more wicked.

⁴⁴But God saw their misery.
   He heard their cry.
⁴⁵He remembered his agreement with
      them.
   And he felt sorry for them because
      of his great love.
⁴⁶He caused them to be pitied
   by those who held them captive.

⁴⁷Lord our God, save us.
   Bring us back from other nations.
   Then we will thank you.
   Then we will gladly praise you.

⁴⁸Praise the Lord, the God of Israel.
   He always was and always will be.
   Let all the people say, "Amen!"

Praise the Lord!

Book 5

GOD SAVES FROM MANY DANGERS

107 Thank the Lord because he
         is good.
   His love continues forever.
²That is what the people the Lord has
      saved should say.
   They are the ones he has saved
      from the enemy.
³He has gathered them from other
      lands,
   from east and west, north and
      south.

⁴Some people had wandered in the
      desert lands.
   They found no city to live in.

⁵They were hungry and thirsty.
  They were discouraged.
⁶In their misery they cried out to the
  Lord.
  And he saved them from their
  troubles.
⁷He led them on a straight road
  to a city where they could live.
⁸Let them give thanks to the Lord for
  his love
  and for the miracles*d* he does for
  people.
⁹He satisfies the thirsty.
  He fills up the hungry.

¹⁰Some sat in gloom and darkness.
  They were prisoners suffering in
  chains.
¹¹They had turned against the words of
  God.
  They had refused the advice of God
  Most High.
¹²So he broke their pride by hard work.
  They stumbled, and no one helped.
¹³In their misery they cried out to the
  Lord.
  And he saved them from their
  troubles.
¹⁴He brought them out of their gloom
  and darkness.
  He broke their chains.
¹⁵Let them give thanks to the Lord for
  his love
  and for the miracles he does for
  people.
¹⁶He breaks down bronze gates.
  And he cuts apart iron bars.

¹⁷Some became fools who turned
  against God.
  They suffered for the evil they did.
¹⁸They refused to eat anything.
  So they almost died.
¹⁹In their misery they cried out to the
  Lord.
  And he saved them from their
  troubles.
²⁰God gave the command and healed
  them.
  So they were saved from dying.

²¹Let them give thanks to the Lord for
  his love
  and for the miracles he does for
  people.
²²Let them offer sacrifices to thank him.
  With joy they should tell what he
  has done.

²³Others went out to sea in ships.
  They did business on the great
  oceans.
²⁴They saw what the Lord could do.
  They saw the miracles he did.
²⁵He spoke, and a storm came up.
  It blew up high waves.
²⁶The ships tossed as high as the sky
  and fell low in the waves.
  The storm was so bad the men lost
  their courage.
²⁷They stumbled and fell like men who
  were drunk.
  They did not know what to do.
²⁸In their misery they cried out to the
  Lord.
  And he saved them from their
  troubles.
²⁹He made the storm be still.
  He calmed the waves.
³⁰They were happy that it was quiet.
  And God guided them to the port
  they wanted.
³¹Let them give thanks to the Lord for
  his love
  and for the miracles he does for
  people.
³²Let them praise his greatness in the
  meeting of the people.
  They should praise him in the
  meeting of the elders.

³³He changed rivers into a desert,
  and springs of water into dry ground.
³⁴He made fertile land salty
  because the people there did evil.
³⁵He changed the desert into pools of
  water
  and dry ground into springs of water.
³⁶He had the hungry settle there.
  They built a city to live in.

³⁷They planted seeds in the fields and
vineyards.
And they had a good harvest.
³⁸God blessed them, and they grew in
number.
Their cattle did not become fewer.

³⁹Because of disaster, troubles and
sadness,
their families grew smaller and
weaker.
⁴⁰He showed he was displeased with
their important men.
He made them wander in a pathless
desert.
⁴¹But he lifted the poor out of their
suffering.
And he made their families grow
like flocks of sheep.
⁴²Good people see this and are happy.
But the wicked say nothing.

⁴³Whoever is wise will remember these
things.
He will think about the love of the
Lord.

A PRAYER FOR VICTORY

A song of David.

108 God, my heart is right.
I will sing and praise you
with all my being.
²Wake up, harp and lyre!ᵈ
I will wake up the dawn.
³Lord, I will praise you among the
nations.
I will sing songs of praise about you
to all the nations.
⁴Your love is so great that it is higher
than the skies.
Your truth reaches to the clouds.
⁵God, you are supreme over the skies.
Let your glory be over all the earth.

⁶Answer us and save us by your power.
Then the people you love will be
rescued.
⁷God has said from his Temple,ᵈ
"When I win, I will divide Shechem
and cut up the Valley of Succoth.

⁸Gilead and Manasseh are mine.
Ephraim is like my helmet.
Judah holds my royal scepter.ᵈ
⁹Moab is like my washbowl.
I throw my sandals at Edom.
I shout at Philistia."

¹⁰Who will bring me to the strong,
walled city?
Who will lead me to Edom?
¹¹God, surely you have rejected us.
You do not go out with our armies.
¹²Help us fight the enemy.
Human help is useless.
¹³But we can win with God's help.
He will defeat our enemies.

A PRAYER AGAINST AN ENEMY

For the director of music. A song of David.

109 God, I praise you.
Do not be silent.
²Wicked people and liars have spoken
against me.
They have told lies about me.
³They have said hateful things about
me.
They attack me for no reason.
⁴They attacked me, even though I
loved them
and prayed for them.
⁵I was good to them, but they repay me
with evil.
I loved them, but they hate me in
return.

⁶They say about me, "Have the Evil
One work against him.
Let the devil accuse him.
⁷When he is judged, let him be found
guilty.
Let even his prayers show that he is
guilty.
⁸Let his life be cut short.
Let another man replace him as
leader.
⁹Let his children become orphans.
Let his wife become a widow.
¹⁰Make his children wander around,
begging for food.

Let them be forced out of the ruins
they live in.
[11]Let the people he owes money to take
everything he owns.
Let strangers steal everything he
has worked for.
[12]Let no one show him love.
Let no one have mercy on his
children.
[13]Let all his descendants[d] die.
Let him be forgotten by people who
live after him.
[14]Let the Lord remember how wicked
his ancestors were.
Don't let the sins of his mother be
wiped out.
[15]Let the Lord always remember their
sins.
Then he will make people forget
about them completely.

[16]"He did not remember to be loving.
He hurt the poor, the needy and
those who were sad
until they were nearly dead.
[17]He loved to put curses on others.
So let those same curses fall on him.
He did not like to bless others.
So do not let good things happen to
him.
[18]He cursed others as often as he wore
clothes.
Cursing others filled his body and
his life,
like drinking water and using olive
oil.
[19]So let curses cover him like clothes.
Let them wrap around him like a
belt."
[20]May the Lord do these things to those
who accuse me,
to those who speak evil against me.

[21]But you, Lord God,
be kind to me so others will know
you are good.
Because your love is good, save me.
[22]I am poor and helpless.
And I am very sad.

[23]I am dying like an evening shadow.
I am shaken off like a locust.[d]
[24]My knees are weak from hunger.
I have become thin.
[25]My enemies insult me.
They look at me and shake their
heads.

[26]Lord my God, help me.
Because you are loving, save me.
[27]Then they will know that you have
saved me.
They will know it was your power,
Lord.
[28]They may curse me, but you bless me.
They may attack me, but they will
be disgraced.
Then I, your servant, will be glad.
[29]Let those who accuse me be
disgraced.
Let them be covered with shame
like a coat.

[30]I will thank the Lord very much.
I will praise him in front of many
people.
[31]He defends the helpless.
He saved me from those who
accuse me.

THE LORD APPOINTS A KING

A song of David.

110 The Lord said to my Master,
"Sit by me at my right side
until I put your enemies under your
control."
[2]The Lord will make you king in
Jerusalem over all nations.
And you will rule your enemies in
their own countries.
[3]Your people will join you on the day
you come to power.
You have been dressed in holiness
from birth.
You have the freshness of a child.

[4]The Lord has made a promise
and will not change his mind.
He said, "You are a priest forever,
a priest like Melchizedek."

⁵The Lord is beside you to help you.
When he becomes angry, he will
crush kings.
⁶He will judge those nations, filling
them with dead bodies.
He will defeat rulers all over the
world.
⁷The king will drink from the brook on
the way.
Then he will be strengthened and
win the battle.

PRAISE FOR GOD'S GOODNESS

111 Praise the Lord!

I will thank the Lord with all my heart
in the meeting of his good people.
²The Lord does great things.
Those people who love them think
about them.
³What he does is glorious and splendid.
His goodness continues forever.
⁴His miracles*d* are unforgettable.
The Lord is kind and merciful.
⁵He gives food to those who fear him.
He remembers his agreement
forever.
⁶He has shown his people his power
when he gave them the lands of
other nations.

⁷Everything he does is good and fair.
All his orders can be trusted.
⁸They will continue forever.
They were made true and right.
⁹He sets his people free.
He made his agreement everlasting.
He is holy and wonderful.

¹⁰Wisdom begins with respect for the
Lord.
Those who obey his orders have
good understanding.
He should be praised forever.

HONEST PEOPLE ARE BLESSED

112 Praise the Lord!

Happy is the person who fears the Lord.
He loves what the Lord commands.

²His descendants*d* will be powerful in
the land.
The children of honest people will
be blessed.
³His house will be full of wealth and
riches.
His goodness will continue forever.

⁴A light shines in the dark for honest
people.
It shines for those who are good
and kind and merciful.
⁵It is good to be kind and generous.
Whoever is fair in his business
⁶will never be defeated.
A good person will be remembered
from now on.
⁷He won't be afraid of bad news.
He is safe because he trusts the Lord.
⁸That person is confident. He will not
be afraid.
He will look down on his enemies.
⁹He gives freely to the poor.
The things he does are right and
will continue forever.
He will be given great honor.

¹⁰The wicked will see this and become
angry.
They will grind their teeth in anger
and then disappear.
The wishes of the wicked will come
to nothing.

PRAISE FOR GOD'S KINDNESS

113 Praise the Lord!

Praise him, you servants of the Lord.
Praise the name of the Lord.
²The Lord's name should be praised
now and forever.
³The Lord's name should be praised
from where the sun rises to where it
sets.
⁴The Lord is supreme over all the
nations.
His glory reaches to the skies.

⁵No one is like the Lord our God.
He rules from heaven.

⁶He bends down to look
  at the skies and the earth.
⁷The Lord lifts the poor from the dirt.
  He takes the helpless from the
    ashes.
⁸And he seats them with princes,
  the princes of his people.
⁹He gives children to the woman who
    has none.
  He makes her a happy mother.

Praise the Lord!

GOD BROUGHT ISRAEL FROM EGYPT

114 The Israelites went out of
    Egypt.
  The people of Jacob left that foreign
    country.
²Then Judah became God's holy place.
  Israel became the land he ruled.

³The Red Sea^d looked and ran away.
  The Jordan River turned back.
⁴The mountains danced like sheep
  and the hills like little lambs.
⁵Sea, why did you run away?
  Jordan, why did you turn back?
⁶Mountains, why did you dance like
    sheep?
  Hills, why did you dance like little
    lambs?

⁷Earth, shake with fear before the Lord.
  Tremble in the presence of the God
    of Jacob.
⁸He turned a rock into a pool of water.
  He changed a hard rock into a
    spring of water.

THE ONE TRUE GOD

115 It does not belong to us,
    Lord.
  The praise belongs to you
  because of your love and loyalty.

²Why do the nations ask,
  "Where is their God?"
³Our God is in heaven.
  He does what he wants.
⁴Their idols are made of silver and gold.
  They are made by human hands.

⁵They have mouths, but they cannot
    speak.
  They have eyes, but they cannot
    see.
⁶They have ears, but they cannot hear.
  They have noses, but they cannot
    smell.
⁷They have hands, but they cannot
    feel.
  They have feet, but they cannot
    walk.
  And no sounds come from their
    throats.
⁸The people who make idols and trust
    them
  are all like them.

⁹Family of Israel, trust the Lord.
  He is your helper and your
    protection.
¹⁰Family of Aaron, trust the Lord.
  He is your helper and your
    protection.
¹¹You people who fear the Lord should
    trust him.
  He is your helper and your
    protection.

¹²The Lord remembers us and will bless
    us.
  He will bless the family of Israel.
  He will bless the family of Aaron.
¹³The Lord will bless those who fear
    him,
  from the smallest to the greatest.

¹⁴May the Lord give you many children.
  And may he give them children
    also.
¹⁵May the Lord bless you.
  He made heaven and earth.

¹⁶Heaven belongs to the Lord.
  But he gave the earth to people.
¹⁷Dead people do not praise the Lord.
  Those in the grave are silent.
¹⁸But we will praise the Lord
  now and forever.

Praise the Lord!

THANKSGIVING FOR ESCAPING DEATH

116

¹I love the Lord because he listens
to my prayers for help.
²He paid attention to me.
So I will call to him for help as long
as I live.
³The ropes of death bound me.
The fear of death took hold of me.
I was troubled and sad.
⁴Then I called out the name of the
Lord.
I said, "Please, Lord, save me!"

⁵The Lord is kind and does what is
right.
Our God is merciful.
⁶The Lord watches over the foolish.
When I was helpless, he saved me.
⁷I said to myself, "Relax,
because the Lord takes care of you."
⁸Lord, you have saved me from death.
You have stopped my eyes from
crying.
You have kept me from being
defeated.
⁹So I will walk with the Lord
in the land of the living.
¹⁰I believed, so I said,
"I am completely ruined."
¹¹In my distress I said,
"All people are liars."

¹²What can I give the Lord
for all the good things he has given
to me?
¹³I will give him a drink offering for
saving me.
And I will pray to the Lord.
¹⁴In front of all his people,
I will give the Lord what I
promised.

¹⁵The death of one that belongs to him
is precious to the Lord.
¹⁶Lord, I am your servant.
I am your servant and the son of
your female servant.
You have freed me from my chains.

¹⁷I will give an offering to show thanks
to you.
And I will worship the Lord.
¹⁸In front of all his people,
I will give the Lord what I
promised.
¹⁹I will do this in the Temple[d] courtyards
in Jerusalem.

Praise the Lord!

A HYMN OF PRAISE

117

¹All you nations, praise the Lord.
All you people, praise him.
²The Lord loves us very much.
His truth is everlasting.

Praise the Lord!

THANKSGIVING FOR VICTORY

118

¹Thank the Lord because he is good.
His love continues forever.
²Let the people of Israel say,
"His love continues forever."
³Let the family of Aaron say,
"His love continues forever."
⁴Let those who fear the Lord say,
"His love continues forever."

⁵I was in trouble. So I called to the
Lord.
The Lord answered me and set me
free.
⁶I will not be afraid because the Lord is
with me.
People can't do anything to me.
⁷The Lord is with me to help me.
I will see my enemies defeated.
⁸It is better to trust the Lord
than to trust people.
⁹It is better to trust the Lord
than to trust princes.

¹⁰All the nations surrounded me.
But I defeated them in the name of
the Lord.
¹¹They surrounded me on every side.
But with the Lord's power,
I defeated them.

¹²They surrounded me like a swarm of
bees.
But they died as quickly as thorns
burn.
By the Lord's power, I defeated
them.
¹³They chased me until I was almost
defeated.
But the Lord helped me.
¹⁴The Lord gives me strength and
makes me sing.
He has saved me.

¹⁵Shouts of joy and victory
come from the tents of those who
do right:
"The Lord has done powerful things."
¹⁶The power of the Lord has won the
victory.
With his power the Lord has done
mighty things.

¹⁷I will not die, but live.
And I will tell what the Lord has
done.
¹⁸The Lord has taught me a hard lesson.
But he did not let me die.

¹⁹Open for me the Temple*d* gates.
Then I will come in and thank the
Lord.
²⁰This is the Lord's gate.
Only those who are good may enter
it.
²¹Lord, I thank you for answering me.
You have saved me.

²²The stone that the builders did not want
became the cornerstone.*d*
²³The Lord did this,
and it is wonderful to us.
²⁴This is the day that the Lord has made.
Let us rejoice and be glad today!

²⁵Please, Lord, save us.
Please, Lord, give us success.
²⁶God bless the one who comes in the
name of the Lord.
We bless all of you from the Temple
of the Lord.

²⁷The Lord is God.
And he has shown kindness to us.
With branches in your hands, join the
feast.
Come to the corners of the altar.

²⁸You are my God, and I will thank you.
You are my God, and I will praise
your greatness.

²⁹Thank the Lord because he is good.
His love continues forever.

THE WORD OF GOD

119 Happy are the people who
live pure lives.
They follow the Lord's teachings.
²Happy are the people who keep his
rules.
They ask him for help with their
whole heart.
³They don't do what is wrong.
They follow his ways.
⁴Lord, you gave your orders
to be followed completely.
⁵I wish I were more loyal
in meeting your demands.
⁶Then I would not be ashamed
when I think of your commands.
⁷When I learned that your laws are fair,
I praised you with an honest heart.
⁸I will meet your demands.
So please don't ever leave me.

⁹How can a young person live a pure
life?
He can do it by obeying your word.
¹⁰With all my heart I try to obey you,
God.
Don't let me break your commands.
¹¹I have taken your words to heart
so I would not sin against you.
¹²Lord, you should be praised.
Teach me your demands.
¹³My lips will tell about
all the laws you have spoken.
¹⁴I enjoy living by your rules
as people enjoy great riches.
¹⁵I think about your orders
and study your ways.

16I enjoy obeying your demands.
  And I will not forget your word.

17Do good to me, your servant, so I can
     live,
  so I can obey your word.
18Open my eyes to see the wonderful
     things
  in your teachings.
19I am a stranger on earth.
  Do not hide your commands from
     me.
20I want to study
  your laws all the time.
21You scold proud people.
  Those who ignore your commands
     are cursed.
22Don't let me be insulted and hated
  because I obey your rules.
23Even if princes speak against me,
  I, your servant, will think about
     your demands.
24Your rules give me pleasure.
  They give me good advice.

25I am about to die.
  Give me life, as you have promised.
26I told you about my life, and you
     answered me.
  Teach me your demands.
27Help me understand your orders.
  Then I will think about your
     miracles.d
28I am sad and tired.
  Make me strong again as you have
     promised.
29Don't let me be dishonest.
  Be kind to me by helping me obey
     your teachings.
30I have chosen to obey you.
  I have obeyed your laws.
31I hold on to your rules.
  Lord, do not let me be disgraced.
32I will obey your commands
  because you have made me happy.

33Lord, teach me your demands.
  Then I will obey them until the end.

34Help me understand, so I can obey
     your teachings.
  I will obey them with all my heart.
35Help me obey your commands
  because that makes me happy.
36Help me want to obey your rules
  instead of selfishly wanting riches.
37Keep me from looking at worthless
     things.
  Let me live by your word.
38Keep your promise to me, your
     servant,
  so you will be feared.
39Take away the shame I fear.
  Your laws are good.
40How I want to follow your orders.
  Give me life because of your
     goodness.

41Lord, show me your love.
  Save me as you have promised.
42Then I will have an answer for people
     who insult me.
  I trust what you say.
43Never keep me from speaking your
     truth.
  I depend on your fair laws.
44I will obey your teachings
  forever and ever.
45So I will live in freedom
  because I want to follow your
     orders.
46I will discuss your rules with kings.
  And I will not be ashamed.
47I enjoy obeying your commands.
  I love them.
48I praise your commands, which I love.
  And I think about your demands.

49Remember your promise to me, your
     servant.
  It gives me hope.
50When I suffer, this comforts me:
  Your promise gives me life.
51Proud people make fun of me all the
     time.
  But I do not reject your teachings.
52I remember your laws from long ago.
  They comfort me, Lord.

⁵³I become angry with wicked people.
   They have not kept your teachings.
⁵⁴I sing about your demands
   wherever I live.
⁵⁵Lord, I remember you at night.
   I will obey your teachings.
⁵⁶This is what I do:
   I follow your orders.

⁵⁷Lord, you are my share in life.
   I have promised to obey your words.
⁵⁸I prayed to you with all my heart.
   Be kind to me as you have
      promised.
⁵⁹I thought about my life,
   and I decided to obey your rules.
⁶⁰I hurried and did not wait
   to obey your commands.
⁶¹Wicked people have surrounded me.
   But I have not forgotten your
      teachings.
⁶²In the middle of the night, I get up to
      thank you
   because your laws are right.
⁶³I am a friend to everyone who fears
      you.
   I am a friend to anyone who follows
      your orders.
⁶⁴Lord, your love fills the earth.
   Teach me your demands.

⁶⁵You have done good things for me,
      your servant,
   as you have promised, Lord.
⁶⁶Teach me wisdom and knowledge
   because I trust your commands.
⁶⁷Before I suffered, I did wrong.
   But now I obey your word.
⁶⁸You are good, and you do what is
      good.
   Teach me your demands.
⁶⁹Proud people have made up lies about
      me.
   But I will follow your orders with all
      my heart.
⁷⁰Those people have no feelings,
   but I love your teachings.
⁷¹It was good for me to suffer
   so I would learn your demands.

⁷²Your teachings are worth more to me
   than thousands of pieces of gold
      and silver.

⁷³You made me and formed me with
      your hands.
   Give me understanding so I can
      learn your commands.
⁷⁴Let those who fear you rejoice when
      they see me
   because I put my hope in your
      word.
⁷⁵Lord, I know that your laws are right.
   And it was right for you to punish
      me.
⁷⁶Comfort me with your love,
   as you promised me, your servant.
⁷⁷Have mercy on me so that I may live.
   I love your teachings.
⁷⁸Make the proud people ashamed
   because they lied about me.
   But I will think about your orders.
⁷⁹Let those who fear you come to me.
   They know your rules.
⁸⁰Let me obey your demands perfectly.
   Then I will not be ashamed.

⁸¹I am weak from waiting for you to
      save me.
   But I trust your word.
⁸²My eyes are tired from looking for
      your promise.
   When will you comfort me?
⁸³Even though I am like a leather wine
      bag going up in smoke,
   I do not forget your demands.
⁸⁴How long will I live?
   When will you judge those who are
      hurting me?
⁸⁵Proud people have dug pits to trap me.
   They have nothing to do with your
      teachings.
⁸⁶All of your commands can be trusted.
   Liars are hurting me. Help me!
⁸⁷They have almost put me in the
      grave.
   But I have not rejected your orders.
⁸⁸Give me life by your love
   so I can obey your rules.

[89]Lord, your word is everlasting.
It continues forever in heaven.
[90]Your loyalty will continue from now
on.
You made the earth, and it still
stands.
[91]All things continue to this day
because of your laws.
All things serve you.
[92]If I had not loved your teachings,
I would have died from my
sufferings.
[93]I will never forget your orders
because you have given me life by
them.
[94]I am yours. Save me.
I have wanted to know your orders.
[95]Wicked people are waiting to destroy
me.
But I will think about your rules.
[96]Everything I see has its limits.
But your commands have none.

[97]How I love your teachings!
I think about them all day long.
[98]Your commands make me wiser than
my enemies
because they are mine forever.
[99]I am wiser than all my teachers
because I think about your rules.
[100]I have more understanding than the
elders
because I follow your orders.
[101]I have avoided every evil way
so I could obey your word.
[102]I haven't stopped obeying your laws
because you yourself are my
teacher.
[103]Your promises are so sweet to me.
They are like honey to my mouth!
[104]Your orders give me understanding.
So I hate lying ways.

[105]Your word is like a lamp for my feet
and a light for my way.
[106]I will do what I have promised
and obey your fair laws.
[107]I have suffered for a long time.
Lord, give me life by your word.

[108]Lord, accept my willing praise.
And teach me your laws.
[109]My life is always in danger.
But I haven't forgotten your
teachings.
[110]Wicked people have set a trap for me.
But I haven't disobeyed your
orders.
[111]I will follow your rules forever.
They make me happy.
[112]I will try to do what you demand
forever, until the end.
[113]I hate people who are not completely
loyal to you.
But I love your teachings.
[114]You are my hiding place and my
shield.
I trust your word.
[115]Get away from me, you people who
do evil,
so I can keep my God's commands.
[116]Support me as you promised so I can
live.
Don't let me be embarrassed
because of my hopes.
[117]Help me, and I will be saved.
I will always respect your demands.
[118]You reject everyone who ignores
your demands.
Their lies mislead them.
[119]You throw away the wicked of the
world like trash.
So I will love your rules.
[120]I shake in fear of you.
I fear your laws.

[121]I have done what is fair and right.
Don't leave me to my enemies.
[122]Promise that you will help me, your
servant.
Don't let proud people hurt me.
[123]My eyes are tired from looking for
your salvation
and for your good promise.
[124]Show your love to me, your servant.
Teach me your demands.
[125]I am your servant. Give me wisdom
so I can understand your rules.

126Lord, it is time for you to do
something.
People have disobeyed your
teachings.
127I love your commands
more than the purest gold.
128I respect all your orders.
So I hate lying ways.

129Your rules are wonderful.
That is why I obey them.
130Learning your words gives wisdom
and understanding for the foolish.
131I want to learn your commands.
I am like a person breathing hard
and waiting impatiently.
132Look at me and have mercy on me
as you do for those who love you.
133Guide my steps as you promised.
Don't let any sin control me.
134Save me from harmful people.
Then I will obey your orders.
135Show your kindness to me, your
servant.
Teach me your demands.
136Tears stream from my eyes
because people do not obey your
teachings.

137Lord, you do what is right.
And your laws are fair.
138The rules you commanded are right
and completely trustworthy.
139I am so upset I am worn out.
This is because my enemies have
forgotten your words.
140Your promises are proven.
I, your servant, love them.
141I am unimportant and hated.
But I have not forgotten your orders.
142Your goodness continues forever.
And your teachings are true.
143I have had troubles and misery.
But I love your commands.
144Your rules are good forever.
Help me understand so I can live.

145Lord, I call to you with all my heart.
Answer me,
and I will keep your demands.

146I call to you. Save me
so I can obey your rules.
147I wake up early in the morning and
cry out.
I trust your word.
148I stay awake all night
so I can think about your promises.
149Listen to me because of your love.
Lord, give me life by your laws.
150Those who love evil are near.
They are far from your teachings.
151But, Lord, you are also near.
And all your commands are true.
152Long ago I learned from your rules
that you made them to continue
forever.

153See my suffering and save me
because I have not forgotten your
teachings.
154Argue my case and save me.
Let me live by your promises.
155Wicked people are far from being
saved
because they do not want to obey
your demands.
156Lord, you are very kind.
Give me life by your laws.
157Many enemies are after me.
But I have not rejected your rules.
158I see those traitors, and I hate them
because they do not obey what you
say.
159See how I love your orders.
Lord, give me life by your love.
160Your words are true from the start.
And all your laws will be fair forever.

161Leaders attack me for no reason.
But I fear your law in my heart.
162I am as happy over your promises
as if I had found a great treasure.
163I hate and despise lies.
But I love your teachings.
164Seven times a day I praise you
for your fair laws.
165Those who love your teachings will
find true peace.
Nothing will defeat them.

166I am waiting for you to save me, Lord.
   I will obey your commands.
167I keep your rules.
   I love them very much.
168I keep your orders and rules.
   You know everything I do.

169Hear my cry to you, Lord.
   Let your word help me understand.
170Listen to my prayer.
   Save me as you promised.
171Let me speak your praise.
   You have taught me your demands.
172Let me sing about your promises.
   All your commands are fair.
173Always be ready to help me
   because I have chosen to obey your
   commands.
174I want you to save me, Lord.
   I love your teachings.
175Let me live so I can praise you.
   Your laws will help me.
176I have wandered like a lost sheep.
   Look for your servant because I
   have not forgotten your
   commands.

A PRAYER OF SOMEONE FAR FROM HOME

A song for going up to worship.

120 When I was in trouble,
   I called to the Lord.
And he answered me.
2Lord, save me from liars
   and from those who plan evil.

3You who plan evil, what will God do to
   you?
   How will he punish you?
4He will punish you with the sharp
   arrows of a warrior
   and with burning coals of wood.

5How terrible it is to live in the land of
   Meshech.
   I have to live among the people of
   Kedar.
6I have lived too long
   with people who hate peace.
7I want peace and try to talk peace,
   but they want war.

THE LORD GUARDS HIS PEOPLE

A song for going up to worship.

121 I look up to the hills.
   But where does my help
      come from?
2My help comes from the Lord.
   He made heaven and earth.

3He will not let you be defeated.
   He who guards you never sleeps.
4He who guards Israel
   never rests or sleeps.
5The Lord guards you.
   The Lord protects you as the shade
   protects you from the sun.
6The sun cannot hurt you during the
   day.
   And the moon cannot hurt you at
   night.
7The Lord will guard you from all
   dangers.
   He will guard your life.
8The Lord will guard you as you come
   and go,
   both now and forever.

HAPPY PEOPLE IN JERUSALEM

A song for going up to worship. Of David.

122 I was happy when they said
   to me,
   "Let's go to the Temple*d* of the
   Lord."
2Jerusalem, we are standing
   at your gates.

3Jerusalem is built as a city
   where friends can come together.
4The people from the tribes*d* go up
   there.
   The tribes belong to the Lord.
   It is the rule to praise
   the Lord at Jerusalem.
5There the descendants*d* of David
   set their thrones to judge the
   people.

6Pray for peace in Jerusalem:
   "May those who love her be safe.
7May there be peace within her walls
   and safety within her strong towers."

8To help my relatives and friends,
  I repeat, "Let Jerusalem have
    peace."
9For the sake of the Temple of the Lord
    our God,
  I wish good for her.

A PRAYER FOR MERCY

A song for going up to worship.

123 Lord, I look up to you.
  You live in heaven.
2Slaves depend on their masters.
  And a female servant depends on
    her mistress.
In the same way, we depend on our
    God.
  We wait for him to show us mercy.

3Be kind to us, Lord. Be kind to us
  because we have been insulted.
4We have suffered many insults from
    lazy people
  and much cruelty from the proud.

THE LORD SAVES HIS PEOPLE

A song for going up to worship. Of David.

124 What if the Lord had not
  been on our side?
(Let Israel repeat this.)
2What if the Lord had not been on our
    side
  when men attacked us?
3When they were angry with us,
  they would have swallowed us alive.
4They would have been like a flood
    drowning us.
  They would have poured over us
    like a river.
5 They would have swept us away like
    a mighty stream.

6Praise the Lord.
  He did not let them chew us up.
7We have escaped like a bird
  from the hunter's trap.
The trap has been broken,
  and we have escaped.
8Our help comes from the Lord,
  who made heaven and earth.

GOD PROTECTS THOSE WHO TRUST HIM

A song for going up to worship.

125 Those who trust the Lord
  are like Mount Zion.d
It sits unmoved forever.
2The mountains surround Jerusalem.
  And the Lord surrounds his people
    now and forever.

3The wicked will not rule
  over those who do right.
If they did, the people who do right
  might use their power to do evil.

4Lord, be good to those who are good,
  whose hearts are honest.
5But, Lord, when you punish those
    who do evil,
  also punish those who stop
    following you.

Let there be peace in Israel.

LORD, GIVE OUR RICHES BACK

A song for going up to worship.

126 When the Lord gave the
  riches back to Jerusalem,
it seemed as if we were dreaming.
2Then we were filled with laughter,
  and we sang happy songs.
Then the other nations said,
  "The Lord has done great things for
    them."
3The Lord has done great things for us,
  and we are very glad.

4Lord, give us back our riches again.
  Do this as you bring streams to the
    desert.
5Those who cry as they plant crops
  will sing at harvesttime.
6Those who cry
  as they carry out the seeds
will return singing
  and carrying bundles of grain.

ALL GOOD THINGS COME FROM GOD

A song for going up to worship. Of Solomon.

127 If the Lord doesn't build the
  house,
the builders are working for nothing.

If the Lord doesn't guard the city,
  the guards are watching for
    nothing.
[2]It is no use for you to get up early
  and stay up late,
working for a living.
  The Lord gives sleep to those he
    loves.
[3]Children are a gift from the Lord.
  Babies are a reward.
[4]Sons who are born to a young man
  are like arrows in the hand of a
    warrior.
[5]Happy is the man
  who has his bag full of arrows.
They will not be defeated
  when they fight their enemies in
    court.

THE HAPPY HOME

A song for going up to worship.

128 Happy are those who
         respect the Lord
and obey him.
[2]You will enjoy what you work for.
  You will be blessed with good things.
[3]Your wife will give you many children.
  She will be like a vine that produces
    a lot of fruit.
  Your children will bring you much
    good.
  They will be like olive branches that
    produce many olives.
[4]This is how the man who respects the
    Lord
  will be blessed.
[5]May the Lord bless you from Mount
    Zion.[d]
  May you enjoy the good things of
    Jerusalem all your life.
[6]May you see your grandchildren.

Let there be peace in Israel.

A PRAYER AGAINST THE ENEMIES

A song for going up to worship.

129 They have treated me badly
         all my life.
(Let Israel repeat this.)

[2]They have treated me badly all my
    life.
  But they have not defeated me.
[3]Like farmers plowing, they plowed
    over my back,
  making long wounds.
[4]But the Lord does what is right.
  He has set me free from those
    wicked people.

[5]Let those who hate Jerusalem
  be turned back in shame.
[6]Let them be like the grass on the
    roof.
  It dries up before it has grown.
[7]There is not enough of it to fill a
    man's hand
  or to make into a bundle to fill his
    arms.
[8]Let those who pass by them not say,
  "May the Lord bless you.
  We bless you by the power of the
    Lord."

A PRAYER FOR MERCY

A song for going up to worship.

130 Lord, I am in great trouble.
         So I call out to you for help.
[2]Lord, hear my voice.
  Listen to my prayer for help.
[3]Lord, if you punished people for all
    their sins,
  no one would be left.
[4]But you forgive us.
  So you are respected.

[5]I wait for the Lord to help me.
  I trust his word.
[6]I wait for the Lord to help me
  more than night watchmen wait for
    the dawn,
  more than night watchmen wait for
    the dawn.

[7]People of Israel, put your hope in the
    Lord
  because he is loving
  and able to save.
[8]He will save Israel
  from all their sins.

CHILDLIKE TRUST IN GOD

A song for going up to worship. Of David.

131 Lord, my heart is not proud.
I don't look down on others.
I don't do great things,
and I can't do miracles.*d*
2But I am calm and quiet.
I am like a baby with its mother.
I am at peace, like a baby with its
mother.

3People of Israel, put your hope in the
Lord
now and forever.

IN PRAISE OF THE TEMPLE

A song for going up to worship.

132 Lord, remember David
and all his suffering.
2He made a promise to the Lord.
He made a promise to the Mighty
God of Jacob.
3He said, "I will not go home to my
house.
I will not lie down on my bed.
4I will not close my eyes
or let myself sleep
5until I find a place for the Lord.
I want to provide a home for the
Mighty God of Jacob."

6We heard about the Box*d* of the
Agreement in Bethlehem.
We found it at Kiriath Jearim.
7Let's go to the Lord's house.
Let's worship at his footstool.
8Rise, Lord, and come to your resting
place.
Come with the Holy Box that shows
your strength.
9May your priests do what is right.
May your people sing for joy.

10For the sake of your servant David,
do not reject your appointed king.
11The Lord made a promise to David.
It was a sure promise that he will
not take back.
He promised, "I will make one of your
descendants*d*
rule as king after you.

12But your sons must keep my agreement
and the rules that I teach them.
Then their sons after them will rule
on your throne forever and ever."

13The Lord has chosen Jerusalem.
He wants it for his home.
14He says, "This is my resting place
forever.
Here is where I want to stay.
15I will bless her with plenty of food.
I will fill her poor with food.
16I will let her priests receive salvation.
And those who worship me will
really sing for joy.

17"I will make a king come from the
family of David.
I will provide my appointed one
descendants*d* to rule after him.
18I will cover his enemies with shame.
But his crown will shine."

THE LOVE OF GOD'S PEOPLE

A song for going up to worship. Of David.

133 It is good and pleasant when
God's people live together in
peace!
2It is like having perfumed oil poured
on the priest's head
and running down his beard.
It ran down Aaron's beard
and on to the collar of his robes.
3It is like the dew of Mount Hermon
falling on the hills of Jerusalem.
There the Lord gives his blessing
of life forever.

TEMPLE GUARDS, PRAISE THE LORD

A song for going up to worship.

134 Praise the Lord, all you
servants of the Lord.
You serve at night in the Temple*d* of
the Lord.
2Raise your hands in the Temple
and praise the Lord.

3May the Lord bless you from Mount
Zion.*d*
He made heaven and earth.

GOD SAVES, IDOLS DO NOT

135 Praise the Lord!

Praise the name of the Lord.
Praise him, you servants of the
Lord.
[2]Praise him, you who stand in the
Lord's Temple[d]
and in the Temple courtyards.
[3]Praise the Lord, because he is good.
Sing praises to him, because it is
pleasant.

[4]The Lord has chosen the people of
Jacob for himself.
He has chosen the people of Israel
for his very own.
[5]I know that the Lord is great.
Our Lord is greater than all the
gods.
[6]The Lord does what he wants,
in heaven and on earth,
in the seas and the deep oceans.
[7]He brings the clouds from the ends of
the earth.
He sends the lightning with the
rain.
He brings out the wind from his
storehouses.

[8]He destroyed the firstborn[d] sons in
Egypt,
the firstborn of both men and
animals.
[9]He did many signs and miracles[d] in
Egypt.
He did amazing things to the king
and his servants.
[10]He defeated many nations
and killed powerful kings:
[11]Sihon king of the Amorites,
Og king of Bashan
and all the kings of Canaan.
[12]Then he gave their land as a gift.
It was a gift to his people, the
Israelites.

[13]Lord, your name is everlasting.
Lord, you will be remembered from
now on.

[14]You defend your people.
You have mercy on your servants.

[15]The idols of other nations are made of
silver and gold.
They are made by human hands.
[16]They have mouths, but they cannot
speak.
They have eyes, but they cannot see.
[17]They have ears, but they cannot hear.
They have no breath in their mouths.
[18]The people who make idols and trust
them
are all like them.

[19]Family of Israel, praise the Lord.
Family of Aaron, praise the Lord.
[20]Family of Levi, praise the Lord.
You people who fear the Lord
should praise him.
[21]You people of Jerusalem, praise the
Lord on Mount Zion.[d]

Praise the Lord!

GOD'S LOVE CONTINUES FOREVER

136 Give thanks to the Lord
because he is good.
His love continues forever.
[2]Give thanks to the God over all gods.
His love continues forever.
[3]Give thanks to the Lord of all lords.
His love continues forever.

[4]Only he can do great miracles.[d]
His love continues forever.
[5]With his wisdom he made the skies.
His love continues forever.
[6]He spread out the earth on the seas.
His love continues forever.
[7]He made the sun and the moon.
His love continues forever.
[8]He made the sun to rule the day.
His love continues forever.
[9]He made the moon and stars to rule
the night.
His love continues forever.

[10]He killed the firstborn[d] sons of the
Egyptians.
His love continues forever.

¹¹He brought the people of Israel out of
    Egypt.
    His love continues forever.
¹²He did it with his great power and
    strength.
    His love continues forever.
¹³He parted the water of the Red Sea.ᵈ
    His love continues forever.
¹⁴He brought the Israelites through the
    middle of it.
    His love continues forever.
¹⁵But the king of Egypt and his army
    drowned in the Red Sea.
    His love continues forever.

¹⁶He led his people through the desert.
    His love continues forever.
¹⁷He defeated great kings.
    His love continues forever.
¹⁸He killed powerful kings.
    His love continues forever.
¹⁹He defeated Sihon king of the
    Amorites.
    His love continues forever.
²⁰He defeated Og king of Bashan.
    His love continues forever.
²¹He gave their land as a gift.
    His love continues forever.
²²It was a gift to his servants, the
    Israelites.
    His love continues forever.

²³He remembered us when we were in
    trouble.
    His love continues forever.
²⁴He freed us from our enemies.
    His love continues forever.
²⁵He gives food to every living creature.
    His love continues forever.

²⁶Give thanks to the God of heaven.
    His love continues forever.

ISRAELITES IN CAPTIVITY

137 By the rivers in Babylon we
        sat and cried
when we remembered Jerusalem.
²On the poplar trees nearby
    we hung our harps.

³Those who captured us asked us to
    sing.
    Our enemies wanted happy songs.
    They said, "Sing us a Templeᵈ song
        from Jerusalem!"

⁴But we cannot sing songs about the
    Lord
    while we are in this foreign country!
⁵Jerusalem, if I forget you,
    let my right hand lose its skill.
⁶Let my tongue stick to the roof of my
    mouth
    if I do not remember you.
Let these things happen if I do not
    think about Jerusalem
    as my greatest joy.

⁷Lord, remember what the Edomites
    did
    on the day Jerusalem fell.
They said, "Tear it down!
    Tear it down to its foundations!"

⁸People of Babylon, you will be
    destroyed.
    The people who pay you back will
        be happy.
    They will punish you for what you
        did to us.
⁹They will grab your babies
    and throw them against the rocks.

A HYMN OF THANKSGIVING

A song of David.

138 Lord, I will thank you with
        all my heart.
    I will sing to you before the false
        gods.
²I will bow down facing your holy
    Temple.ᵈ
    And I will thank you for your love
        and loyalty.
You have made your name and your
    word
    greater than anything.
³On the day I called to you, you
    answered me.
    You made me strong and brave.

⁴Lord, let all the kings of the earth
praise you.
They have heard the words you
speak.
⁵They will sing about what the Lord
has done
because the Lord's glory is great.

⁶Though the Lord is supreme
he takes care of those who are not
proud.
But he stays away from those who
are proud.
⁷Lord, even when I have trouble all
around me,
you will keep me alive.
When my enemies are angry,
you will reach down and save me by
your power.
⁸Lord, you do everything for me.
Lord, your love continues forever.
You made us. Do not leave us.

GOD KNOWS EVERYTHING

For the director of music. A song of David.

139 Lord, you have examined me.
You know all about me.
²You know when I sit down and when I
get up.
You know my thoughts before I
think them.
³You know where I go and where I lie
down.
You know well everything I do.
⁴Lord, even before I say a word,
you already know what I am going
to say.
⁵You are all around me—in front and
in back.
You have put your hand on me.
⁶Your knowledge is amazing to me.
It is more than I can understand.

⁷Where can I go to get away from your
Spirit?^d
Where can I run from you?
⁸If I go up to the skies, you are there.
If I lie down where the dead are,
you are there.

⁹If I rise with the sun in the east,
and settle in the west beyond the sea,
¹⁰even there you would guide me.
With your right hand you would
hold me.

¹¹I could say, "The darkness will hide me.
The light around me will turn into
night."
¹²But even the darkness is not dark to
you.
The night is as light as the day.
Darkness and light are the same to
you.

¹³You made my whole being.
You formed me in my mother's
body.
¹⁴I praise you because you made me in
an amazing and wonderful way.
What you have done is wonderful.
I know this very well.
¹⁵You saw my bones being formed
as I took shape in my mother's body.
When I was put together there,
¹⁶ you saw my body as it was formed.
All the days planned for me
were written in your book
before I was one day old.

¹⁷God, your thoughts are precious to
me.
They are so many!
¹⁸If I could count them,
they would be more than all the
grains of sand.
When I wake up,
I am still with you.

¹⁹God, I wish you would kill the
wicked!
Get away from me, you murderers!
²⁰These men say evil things about you.
Your enemies use your name
thoughtlessly.
²¹Lord, I hate those who hate you.
I hate those who rise up against
you.
²²I feel only hate for them.
They are my enemies.

²³God, examine me and know my heart.
Test me and know my thoughts.
²⁴See if there is any bad thing in me.
Lead me in the way you set long ago.

A PRAYER FOR PROTECTION

For the director of music. A song of David.

140
Lord, rescue me from evil
people.
Save me from cruel men.
²They make evil plans.
They always start fights.
³They make their tongues sharp as a
snake's.
Their words are like snake poison.

Selah^d

⁴Lord, guard me from the power of
wicked people.
Save me from cruel men
who plan to trip me up.
⁵Proud men have hidden a trap for me.
They have spread out a net beside
the road.
They have set traps for me.   *Selah*

⁶I said to the Lord, "You are my God."
Lord, listen to my prayer for help.
⁷Lord God, my mighty savior,
you protect me in battle.
⁸Lord, do not give the wicked what
they want.
Don't let their plans succeed,
or they will become proud.   *Selah*

⁹Those around me have planned
trouble.
Now let it come to them.
¹⁰Let burning coals fall on them.
Throw them into the fire
or into pits from which they cannot
escape.
¹¹Don't let liars settle in the land.
Let evil quickly hunt down cruel men.

¹²I know the Lord will get justice for the
poor.
He will defend the needy in court.
¹³Good people will praise his name.
Honest people will live in his
presence.

A PRAYER NOT TO SIN

A song of David.

141
Lord, I call to you. Come
quickly.
Listen to me when I call to you.
²Let my prayer be like incense^d placed
before you.
Let my praise be like the evening
sacrifice.

³Lord, help me control my tongue.
Help me be careful about what I say.
⁴Don't let me want to do evil
or join others in doing wrong.
Don't let me eat
with those who do evil.

⁵If a good man punished me, that
would be kind.
If he corrected me,
that would be like having perfumed
oil on my head.
I shouldn't refuse it.
But I pray against those who do evil.
⁶ Let their leaders be thrown down
the cliffs.
Then people will know that I have
spoken the truth:
⁷"The ground is plowed and broken up.
In the same way, our bones have
been scattered at the grave."

⁸Lord God, I look to you for help.
I trust in you. Don't let me die.
⁹Protect me from the traps they set for
me
and from the net evil people have
spread.
¹⁰Let the wicked fall into their own pits.
And let me pass by safely.

A PRAYER FOR SAFETY

A maskil^d of David when he was in the cave.
A prayer.

142
I cry out to the Lord.
I pray to the Lord for mercy.
²I pour out my problems to him.
I tell him my troubles.
³When I am afraid,
you, Lord, know the way out.

In the path where I walk,
a trap is hidden for me.
[4]Look around me and see.
No one cares about me.
I have no place of safety.
No one cares if I live.

[5]Lord, I cry out to you.
I say, "You are my protection.
You are all I want in this life."
[6]Listen to my cry
because I am helpless.
Save me from those who are chasing
me.
They are too strong for me.
[7]Free me from my prison.
Then I will praise your name.
Then the good people will surround me
because you have taken care of me.

A PRAYER NOT TO BE KILLED

A song of David.

143 Lord, hear my prayer.
Listen to my cry for mercy.
Come to help me
because you are loyal and good.
[2]Don't judge me, your servant,
because no one alive is right before
you.
[3]My enemies are chasing me.
They have crushed me to the ground.
They have made me live in darkness
like those who are long dead.
[4]I am afraid.
My courage is gone.

[5]I remember what happened long ago.
I recall everything you have done.
I think about all you have made.
[6]I lift my hands to you in prayer.
As a dry land needs rain, I thirst
for you.   *Selah*[d]

[7]Lord, answer me quickly.
I am getting weak.
Don't turn away from me,
or I will be like those who are dead.
[8]Tell me in the morning about your love.
I trust you.
Show me what I should do
because my prayers go up to you.

[9]Lord, save me from my enemies.
I come to you for safety.
[10]Teach me to do what you want,
because you are my God.
Let your good Spirit[d]
lead me on level ground.

[11]Lord, let me live
so people will praise you.
In your goodness
save me from my troubles.
[12]In your love defeat my enemies.
Destroy all those who trouble me
because I am your servant.

A PRAYER FOR VICTORY

Of David.

144 Praise the Lord, my Rock.[d]
He trains me for war.
He trains me for battle.
[2]He gives me love and protects me like
a strong, walled city.
He is my place of safety and my
Savior.
He is my shield and my protection.
He helps me rule my people.

[3]Lord, why is man important to you?
Why do you even think about a
human being?
[4]A man is like a breath.
His life is like a passing shadow.

[5]Lord, tear open the sky and come
down.
Touch the mountains so they will
smoke.
[6]Send the lightning and scatter my
enemies.
Shoot your arrows and force them
away.
[7]Reach down from above.
Pull me out of this sea of enemies.
Rescue me from these foreigners.
[8]They are liars.
They are dishonest.

[9]God, I will sing a new song to you.
I will play to you on the
ten-stringed harp.

¹⁰You give victory to kings.
　　You save your servant David from
　　　cruel swords.
¹¹Save me, rescue me from these
　　foreigners.
　　They are liars.
　　They are dishonest.

¹²Let our sons in their youth
　　grow like strong trees.
　Let our daughters be
　　like the decorated stones in the
　　　Temple.ᵈ
¹³Let our barns be filled
　　with crops of all kinds.
　Let our sheep in the fields have
　　thousands and thousands of lambs.
¹⁴　Let our cattle be strong.
　Let no one break in.
　　Let there be no war.
　　Let there be no screams in our
　　　streets.

¹⁵Happy are those who are like this.
　　Happy are the people whose God is
　　　the Lord.

PRAISE TO GOD THE KING

A song of praise. Of David.

145 I praise your greatness, my
　　　　　God the King.
　I will praise you forever and ever.
²I will praise you every day.
　I will praise you forever and ever.
³The Lord is great. He is worthy of our
　　praise.
　No one can understand how great
　　he is.

⁴Parents will tell their children what
　　you have done.
　They will retell your mighty acts,
⁵wonderful majesty and glory.
　And I will think about your
　　miracles.ᵈ
⁶They will tell about the amazing
　　things you do.
　I will tell how great you are.
⁷They will remember your great
　　goodness.
　They will sing about your fairness.

⁸The Lord is kind and shows mercy.
　　He does not become angry quickly
　　　but is full of love.
⁹The Lord is good to everyone.
　　He is merciful to all he has made.
¹⁰Lord, everything you have made will
　　praise you.
　Those who belong to you will bless
　　you.
¹¹They will tell about the glory of your
　　kingdom.
　They will speak about your power.
¹²Then everyone will know what
　　powerful things you do.
　They will know about the glory and
　　majesty of your kingdom.
¹³Your kingdom will continue forever.
　　And you will be King from now on.

The Lord will keep his promises.
　　With love he takes care of all he has
　　　made.
¹⁴The Lord helps those who have been
　　defeated.
　He takes care of those who are in
　　trouble.
¹⁵All living things look to you for food.
　　And you give it to them at the right
　　　time.
¹⁶You open your hand,
　　and you satisfy all living things.

¹⁷Everything the Lord does is right.
　　With love he takes care of all he has
　　　made.
¹⁸The Lord is close to everyone who
　　prays to him,
　to all who truly pray to him.
¹⁹He gives those who fear him what
　　they want.
　He listens when they cry, and he
　　saves them.
²⁰The Lord protects everyone who loves
　　him.
　But he will destroy the wicked.

²¹I will praise the Lord.
　　Let everyone praise his holy name
　　　forever.

PRAISE GOD WHO HELPS THE WEAK

146
Praise the Lord!
My whole being, praise the
Lord.
2I will praise the Lord all my life.
I will sing praises to my God as long
as I live.

3Do not put your trust in princes
or other people, who cannot save
you.
4When people die, they are buried.
Then all of their plans come to an
end.
5Happy are those who are helped by
the God of Jacob.
Their hope is in the Lord their God.
6He made heaven and earth,
the sea and everything in it.
He remains loyal forever.
7The Lord does what is fair for those
who have been wronged.
He gives food to the hungry.
The Lord sets the prisoners free.
8 The Lord gives sight to the blind.
The Lord lifts up people who are in
trouble.
The Lord loves those who do right.
9The Lord protects the foreigners.
He defends the orphans and widows.
But he overthrows the wicked.

10The Lord will be King forever.
Jerusalem, your God is everlasting.

Praise the Lord!

PRAISE GOD WHO HELPS HIS PEOPLE

147
Praise the Lord!

It is good to sing praises to our God.
It is good and pleasant to praise him.
2The Lord rebuilds Jerusalem.
He brings back the scattered
Israelites who were taken captive.
3He heals the brokenhearted.
He bandages their wounds.

4He counts the stars
and names each one.
5Our Lord is great and very powerful.
There is no limit to what he knows.

6The Lord defends those who are not
proud.
But he throws the wicked to the
ground.

7Sing praises to the Lord.
Praise our God with harps.
8He fills the sky with clouds.
He sends rain to the earth.
He makes grass grow on the hills.
9He gives food to cattle
and to the little birds that call.

10He is not pleased by the strength of a
horse
or the power of a man.
11The Lord is pleased with those who
fear him,
with those who trust his love.

12Jerusalem, praise the Lord.
Jerusalem, praise your God.
13He makes your city gates strong.
He blesses the people inside.
14He brings peace to your country.
He fills you with the finest grain.

15He gives a command to the earth,
and it quickly obeys him.
16He spreads the snow like wool.
He scatters the frost like ashes.
17He throws down hail like rocks.
No one can stand the cold he sends.
18Then he gives a command, and it
melts.
He sends the breezes, and the
waters flow.

19He gave his word to Jacob.
He gave his laws and demands to
Israel.
20He didn't do this for any other
nation.
They don't know his laws.

Praise the Lord!

THE WORLD SHOULD PRAISE THE LORD

148
Praise the Lord!

Praise the Lord from the heavens.
Praise him high above the earth.

[2]Praise him, all you angels.
  Praise him, all you armies of
    heaven.
[3]Praise him, sun and moon.
  Praise him, all you shining stars.
[4]Praise him, highest heavens
  and you waters above the sky.
[5]Let them praise the Lord
  because they were created by his
    command.
[6]He set them in place forever and ever.
  He made a law that will never end.

[7]Praise the Lord from the earth.
  Praise him, you large sea animals
    and all the oceans.
[8]Praise him, lightning and hail, snow
    and clouds,
  and stormy winds that obey him.
[9]Praise him, mountains and all hills,
  fruit trees and all cedar trees.
[10]Praise him, you wild animals and all
    cattle,
  small crawling animals and birds.
[11]Praise him, you kings of the earth and
    all nations,
  princes and all rulers of the earth.
[12]Praise him, you young men and
    women,
  old people and children.

[13]Praise the Lord.
  He alone is great.
  He is greater than heaven and
    earth.
[14]God has given his people a king.
  He should be praised by all who
    belong to him.
  He should be praised by the
    Israelites, the people closest to
    his heart.

Praise the Lord!

PRAISE THE GOD OF ISRAEL

149
Praise the Lord!

Sing a new song to the Lord.
  Sing his praise in the meeting of his
    people.

[2]Let the Israelites be happy because of
    God, their Maker.
  Let the people of Jerusalem rejoice
    because of their King.
[3]They should praise him with
    dancing.
  They should praise him with
    tambourines[d] and harps.
[4]The Lord is pleased with his people.
  He saves those who are not proud.
[5]Let those who worship him rejoice in
    his glory.
  Let them sing for joy even in bed!

[6]Let them shout his praise
  with their two-edged swords in
    their hands.
[7]They will punish the nations.
  They will defeat the people.
[8]They will put those kings in chains
  and those important men in iron
    bands.
[9]They will punish them as God has
    written.
  God is honored by all who worship
    him.

Praise the Lord!

PRAISE THE LORD WITH MUSIC

150
Praise the Lord!

Praise God in his Temple.[d]
  Praise him in his mighty heaven.
[2]Praise him for his strength.
  Praise him for his greatness.
[3]Praise him with trumpet blasts.
  Praise him with harps and lyres.[d]
[4]Praise him with tambourines[d] and
    dancing.
  Praise him with stringed
    instruments and flutes.
[5]Praise him with loud cymbals.
  Praise him with crashing cymbals.
[6]Let everything that breathes praise
    the Lord.

Praise the Lord!

PROVERBS

WHY PROVERBS IS IMPORTANT

1 These are the wise words of Solomon son of David. Solomon was king of Israel.

² They teach wisdom and self-control.
They give understanding.
³ They will teach you how to be wise and self-controlled.
They will teach you what is honest and fair and right.
⁴ They give the ability to think to those with little knowledge.
They give knowledge and good sense to the young.
⁵ Wise people should also listen to them and learn even more.
Even they can find good advice in these words.
⁶ Then they will be able to understand wise words and stories.
They will understand the words of wise men and their riddles.

⁷ Knowledge begins with respect for the Lord.
But foolish people hate wisdom and discipline.

WARNINGS AGAINST EVIL

⁸ My child, listen to your father's teaching.
And do not forget your mother's advice.
⁹ Their teaching will beautify your life.
It will be like flowers in your hair or a chain around your neck.

¹⁰ My child, sinners will try to lead you into sin.
But do not follow them.
¹¹ They might say, "Come with us.
Let's ambush and kill someone.
Let's attack some harmless person just for fun.
¹² Let's swallow them alive, as death does.
Let's swallow them whole, as the grave does.

¹³ We will take all kinds of valuable things.
We will fill our houses with what we steal.
¹⁴ Come join us,
and we will share with you what we steal."
¹⁵ My child, do not go along with them.
Do not do what they do.
¹⁶ They run to do evil.
They are quick to kill.
¹⁷ It is useless to spread out a net right where the birds can see it!
¹⁸ These men are setting their own trap.
They will only catch themselves!
¹⁹ All greedy people end up this way.
Greed takes away the life of the greedy person.

WISDOM SPEAKS

²⁰ Wisdom is like a good woman who shouts in the street.
She raises her voice in the city squares.
²¹ She cries out in the noisy street.
She makes her speech at the city gates:
²² "You foolish people! How long do you want to stay foolish?
How long will you make fun of wisdom?
How long will you hate knowledge?
²³ Listen when I correct you.
I will tell you what's in my heart.
I will tell you what I am thinking.
²⁴ I called, but you refused to listen.
I held out my hand, but you paid no attention.
²⁵ You did not follow my advice.
You did not want me to correct you.
²⁶ So I will laugh when you are in trouble.
I will make fun when disaster happens to you.
²⁷ Disaster will come over you like a storm.

Trouble will strike you like a
  whirlwind.
Pain and trouble will overwhelm
  you.

28"Then you will call out to me.
  But I will not answer.
You will look for me.
  But you will not find me.
29You rejected knowledge.
  You did not choose to respect the
    Lord.
30You did not accept my advice.
  You rejected my correction.
31So you will get what you deserve.
  You will get what you planned for
    others.
32Fools wander away and get killed.
  They are destroyed because they do
    not care.
33But those who listen to me will live in
    safety.
  They will be safe, without fear of
    being hurt."

REWARDS OF WISDOM

2 My child, believe what I say.
  And remember what I command
    you.
2Listen to wisdom.
  Try with all your heart to gain
    understanding.
3Cry out for wisdom.
  Beg for understanding.
4Search for it as you would for silver.
  Hunt for it like hidden treasure.
5Then you will understand what it
    means to respect the Lord.
  Then you will begin to know God.
6Only the Lord gives wisdom.
  Knowledge and understanding
    come from him.
7He stores up wisdom for those who
    are honest.
  Like a shield he protects those who
    are innocent.
8He guards those who are fair to others.
  He protects those who are loyal to
    him.

9Then you will understand what is
    honest and fair and right.
  You will understand what is good
    to do.
10You will have wisdom in your heart.
  And knowledge will be pleasing to
    you.
11Good sense will protect you.
  Understanding will guard you.
12It will keep you from doing evil.
  It will save you from people whose
    words are bad.
13Such people do not do what is right.
  They do what is evil.
14They enjoy doing wrong.
  They are happy to do what is
    crooked and evil.
15What they do is wrong.
  Their ways are dishonest.

16It will save you from the unfaithful
    wife
  who tries to lead you into adultery*d*
    with pleasing words.
17Such women leave the husbands they
    married when they were young.
  They forget the promise they made
    before God.
18If you go to her house, you are on
    your way to death.
  What she does leads to death.
19No one who goes to her comes back.
  He will not continue to live.

20But wisdom will help you be a good
    person.
  It will help you do what is right.
21Those who are honest will stay in the
    land.
  Those who are innocent will remain
    in it.
22But evil people will be removed from
    the land.
  The unfaithful will be thrown out
    of it.

ADVICE TO CHILDREN

3 My child, do not forget my
  teaching.
  Keep my commands in mind.

²Then you will live a long time.
And your life will be successful.

³Don't ever stop being kind and
truthful.
Let kindness and truth show in all
you do.
Write them down in your mind as if
on a tablet.
⁴Then you will be respected
and pleasing to both God and men.

⁵Trust the Lord with all your heart.
Don't depend on your own
understanding.
⁶Remember the Lord in everything you
do.
And he will give you success.

⁷Don't depend on your own wisdom.
Respect the Lord and refuse to do
wrong.
⁸Then your body will be healthy.
And your bones will be strong.

⁹Honor the Lord by giving him part of
your wealth.
Give him the firstfruits*d* from all
your crops.
¹⁰Then your barns will be full.
And your wine barrels will overflow
with new wine.

¹¹My child, do not reject the Lord's
discipline.
And don't become angry when he
corrects you.
¹²The Lord corrects those he loves,
just as a father corrects the child
that he likes.

¹³Happy is the person who finds
wisdom.
And happy is the person who gets
understanding.
¹⁴Wisdom is worth more than silver.
It brings more profit than gold.
¹⁵Wisdom is more precious than rubies.
Nothing you want is equal to it.
¹⁶With her right hand wisdom offers
you a long life.

With her left hand she gives you
riches and honor.
¹⁷Wisdom will make your life pleasant.
It will bring you peace.
¹⁸As a tree makes fruit, wisdom gives
life to those who use it.
Everyone who uses wisdom will be
happy.

¹⁹Using his wisdom, the Lord made the
earth.
Using his understanding, he set the
sky in place.
²⁰Using his knowledge, he made rivers
flow from underground springs.
And he made the clouds drop rain
on the earth.

²¹My child, hold on to wisdom and
reason.
Don't let them out of your sight!
²²They will give you life.
Like a necklace, they will beautify
your life.
²³Then you will go on your way in
safety.
And you will not get hurt.
²⁴You won't need to be afraid when you
lie down.
When you lie down, your sleep will
be peaceful.
²⁵You won't need to be afraid of trouble
coming suddenly.
You won't need to fear the ruin that
comes to the wicked.
²⁶The Lord will keep you safe.
He will keep you from being
trapped.

²⁷Whenever you are able,
do good to people who need help.
²⁸If you have what your neighbor asks
for,
don't say to him,
"Come back later. I will give it to
you tomorrow."
²⁹Don't make plans to hurt your
neighbor.
He lives nearby and trusts you.

³⁰Don't accuse a man for no good reason.
  Don't accuse him if he has not
  harmed you.

³¹Don't be jealous of men who use
  violence.
  And don't choose to be like them.
³²The Lord hates those who do wrong.
  But he is a friend to those who are
  honest.
³³The Lord will put a curse on the evil
  person's house.
  But he will bless the home of people
  who do what is right.
³⁴The Lord laughs at those who laugh at
  him.
  But he is kind to those who are not
  proud.
³⁵Wise people will receive honor.
  But foolish people will be disgraced.

WISDOM IS IMPORTANT

4 My children, listen to your father's
  teaching.
  Pay attention so you will
  understand.
²What I am telling you is good.
  Do not forget what I teach you.
³I was once a young boy in my father's
  house.
  I was like an only child to my
  mother.
⁴And my father taught me and said,
  "Hold on to my words with all your
  heart.
  Keep my commands and you will
  live.
⁵Get wisdom and understanding.
  Don't forget or ignore my words.
⁶Use wisdom, and it will take care of you.
  Love wisdom, and it will keep you
  safe.
⁷Wisdom is the most important thing.
  So get wisdom.
  If it costs everything you have, get
  understanding.
⁸Believe in the value of wisdom, and it
  will make you great.
  Use it, and it will bring honor to you.

⁹Like flowers in your hair, it will
  beautify your life.
  Like a crown, it will make you look
  beautiful."

¹⁰My child, listen and accept what I say.
  Then you will have a long life.
¹¹I am guiding you in wisdom.
  And I am leading you to do what is
  right.
¹²Nothing will hold you back.
  You will not be overwhelmed.
¹³Always remember what you have
  been taught.
  Don't let go of it.
  Keep safe all that you have learned.
  It is the most important thing in
  your life.
¹⁴Don't follow the ways of the wicked.
  Don't do what evil people do.
¹⁵Avoid their ways. Don't go near what
  they do.
  Stay away from them and keep on
  going.
¹⁶They cannot sleep until they do evil.
  They cannot rest until they hurt
  someone.
¹⁷They fill themselves with wickedness
  and cruelty
  as if they were eating bread and
  drinking wine.
¹⁸The way of the good person is like the
  light of dawn.
  It grows brighter and brighter until
  it is full daylight.
¹⁹But the wicked are like those who
  stumble in the dark.
  They can't even see what has hurt
  them.

²⁰My child, pay attention to my words.
  Listen closely to what I say.
²¹Don't ever forget my words.
  Keep them deep within your heart.
²²These words are the secret to life for
  those who find them.
  They bring health to the whole body.

²³Be very careful about what you think.
Your thoughts run your life.
²⁴Don't use your mouth to tell lies.
Don't ever say things that are not
true.
²⁵Keep your eyes focused on what is
right.
Keep looking straight ahead to what
is good.
²⁶Be careful what you do.
Always do what is right.
²⁷Do not do anything unless it is right.
Stay away from evil.

WARNING ABOUT ADULTERY

5 My son, pay attention to my
wisdom.
Listen to my words of understanding.
²Be careful to use good sense.
Watch what you say.
³The words of another man's wife may
seem sweet as honey.
Her words may be as pleasant as
olive oil.
⁴But in the end she will bring you
sorrow.
She will cause you pain like a two-
edged sword.
⁵She is on the way to death.
Her steps are headed straight to the
grave.
⁶She gives no thought to life.
She does not know that her ways
are wrong.

⁷Now, my sons, listen to me.
Don't ignore what I say.
⁸Stay away from such a woman.
Don't even go near the door of her
house.
⁹If you do, you will give your riches to
others.
And the best years of your life will
be given to someone who is cruel.
¹⁰Strangers will enjoy your wealth.
And what you worked so hard for
will go to someone else.
¹¹You will groan at the end of your life.
Then your health will be gone.

¹²Then you will say, "I hated self-control!
I would not listen when I was
corrected!
¹³I would not listen to my teachers.
I paid no attention to what they
taught me.
¹⁴I have come very close to being
completely ruined
in front of a whole group of people."

¹⁵Be faithful to your own wife.
She is like your own well of water
from which you drink.
¹⁶You wouldn't drink from streams
flowing in the city streets or
squares.
So be satisfied with your wife,
not those outside your home.
¹⁷These things are yours alone.
Don't share them with strangers.
¹⁸Be happy with the wife
you married when you were young.
She gives you joys
as your fountain gives you water.
¹⁹She is as lovely and graceful as a deer.
Let her love always make you
happy.
Let her love always hold you
captive.
²⁰My son, don't be held captive by a
woman who takes part in
adultery.ᵈ
Don't hold another man's wife.

²¹The Lord sees everything you do.
He watches where you go.
²²An evil man will be caught in his evil
ways.
He will be tied up by his sins as if
they were ropes.
²³He will die because he does not
control himself.
He will be held captive by his own
foolishness.

DANGERS OF BEING FOOLISH

6 My child, be careful about giving a
guarantee for somebody else.
Be careful about promising to pay
what someone else owes.

²You might get trapped by what you
say.
You might be caught by your own
words.
³My child, you might do this and be
under somebody's control.
Then here is how to get free.
Go to your neighbor and don't be
proud.
Beg him to free you from your
promise.
⁴Don't go to sleep.
Don't even rest your eyes.
⁵But free yourself like a deer running
from a hunter.
Free yourself like a bird flying away
from a trapper.

⁶Go watch the ants, you lazy person.
Watch what they do and be wise.
⁷Ants have no commander.
They have no leader or ruler.
⁸But they store up food in the summer.
They gather their supplies at
harvest.
⁹How long will you lie there, you lazy
person?
When will you get up from
sleeping?
¹⁰You sleep a little; you take a nap.
You fold your hands and rest.
¹¹So you will be as poor as if you had
been robbed.
You will have as little as if you had
been held up.

¹²Some people are wicked and no
good.
They go around telling lies.
¹³They wink with their eyes and signal
with their feet.
They make signs with their fingers.
¹⁴They make evil plans in their hearts.
They are always causing trouble.
¹⁵So trouble will strike them in an
instant.
Suddenly they will be hurt beyond
cure.

¹⁶There are six things the Lord hates.
There are seven things he cannot
stand:
¹⁷ a proud look,
a lying tongue,
hands that kill innocent people,
¹⁸ a mind that thinks up evil plans,
feet that are quick to do evil,
¹⁹ a witness who tells lies
and a man who causes trouble
among brothers.

WARNING ABOUT ADULTERY
²⁰My son, keep your father's commands.
Don't forget your mother's
teaching.
²¹Remember their words forever.
Let it be as if they were tied around
your neck.
²²They will guide you when you walk.
They will guard you while you
sleep.
They will speak to you when you
are awake.
²³Their commands are like a lamp.
Their teaching is like a light.
And the correction that comes from
them
helps you have life.
²⁴Such teaching will keep you from
sinful women
and from the pleasing words of
another man's unfaithful wife.
²⁵Don't want her because she is
beautiful.
Don't let her capture you by the way
she looks at you.
²⁶A prostitute*d* may leave you with only
a loaf of bread.
And a woman who takes part in
adultery*d* may cost you your life.
²⁷You cannot carry hot coals against
your chest
without burning your clothes.
²⁸And you cannot walk on hot coals
without burning your feet.
²⁹The same thing happens if you have
sexual relations with another
man's wife.

Anyone who does so will be
punished.

³⁰People do not hate a thief
when he steals because he is
hungry.
³¹But if he is caught, he must pay back
seven times what he stole.
It may cost him everything he owns.
³²A man who takes part in adultery
doesn't have any sense.
He will destroy himself.
³³He will be beaten up and disgraced.
And his shame will never go away.
³⁴Jealousy makes a husband very angry.
He will have no mercy when he gets
even.
³⁵He will accept no payment for the
wrong.
He will take no money, no matter
how much it is.

THE WOMAN OF ADULTERY

7 My son, remember what I say.
Treasure my commands.
²Obey my commands, and you will
live.
Protect my teachings as you would
your own eyes.
³Remind yourself of them.
Write them down in your mind as if
on a tablet.
⁴Be good to wisdom as if she were your
sister.
Make understanding your closest
friend.
⁵Wisdom and understanding will keep
you away from adultery.ᵈ
They will keep you away from the
unfaithful wife and her pleasing
words.
⁶I once was standing at the window of
my house.
I looked out through the shutters.
⁷I saw some foolish, young men.
I noticed one of them who had no
wisdom.
⁸He was walking down the street near
the corner.

He was on the road leading to her
house.
⁹It was the twilight of the evening.
The darkness of the night was just
beginning.
¹⁰Then the woman approached him.
She was dressed like a prostituteᵈ
and was planning to trick him.
¹¹She was a loud and stubborn woman.
She never stayed at home.
¹²She was always out in the streets or in
the city squares.
She was always waiting around on
the street corners.
¹³She grabbed him and kissed him.
Without shame she said to him,
¹⁴"I made my fellowship offering and
have the meat at home.
I have kept my special promises.
¹⁵So I have come out to meet you.
I have been looking for you and
have found you!
¹⁶I have covered my bed
with colored sheets from Egypt.
¹⁷I have made my bed smell sweet
with myrrh,ᵈ aloesᵈ and cinnamon.
¹⁸Come, let's make love until morning.
Let's enjoy each other's love!
¹⁹My husband is not home.
He has gone on a long trip.
²⁰He took a lot of money with him.
And he won't be home for weeks."
²¹By her clever words she made him
give in.
By her pleasing words she led him
into doing wrong.
²²All at once he followed her.
He was like an ox being led to the
butcher.
He was like a deer caught in a trap.
²³   But quickly an arrow shot through
his liver.
He was like a bird caught in a trap.
He didn't know what he did would
kill him.

²⁴Now, my sons, listen to me.
Pay attention to what I say.

²⁵Don't let yourself be tricked by the
  woman who is guilty of adultery.
  Don't join her in her evil actions.
²⁶She has ruined many good men.
  Many have died because of her.
²⁷Going to her house is like taking the
  road to death.
  That road leads down to where the
  dead are.

LISTEN TO WISDOM

8 Like a person, wisdom calls out
  to you.
  Understanding raises her voice.
²On the hilltops along the road
  and at the crossroads, she stands
  calling.
³She stands beside the city gates.
  At the entrances into the city, she
  calls out:
⁴"People, I'm calling out to you.
  I am shouting to all people.
⁵You who do not know better, get the
  ability to think.
  You who are foolish, get
  understanding.
⁶Listen. I have important things to say.
  What I tell you is right.
⁷What I say is true.
  I hate it when people speak evil.
⁸Everything I say is honest.
  Nothing I say is crooked or false.
⁹People with good sense know that
  what I say is true.
  People with knowledge know that
  my words are right.
¹⁰Choose my teachings instead of silver.
  Choose knowledge rather than the
  finest gold.
¹¹Wisdom is more precious than rubies.
  Nothing you want is equal to it.

¹²"I am wisdom, and I have the ability
  to think.
  I also have knowledge and good
  sense.
¹³If you respect the Lord, you also will
  hate evil.
  It is wise to hate pride and bragging,
  evil ways and lies.

¹⁴I have good sense and advice.
  I have understanding and power.
¹⁵Kings use me to govern.
  And rulers use me to make fair laws.
¹⁶Princes use me to lead.
  So do important men and all good
  judges.
¹⁷I love those who love me.
  Those who want me find me.
¹⁸Riches and honor are mine.
  So are wealth and lasting success.
¹⁹What I give is better than the finest
  gold.
  What I give is better than pure
  silver.
²⁰I do what is right.
  I do what is fair.
²¹I give wealth to those who love me.
  I fill them with treasures.

²²"I, wisdom, was with God when he
  began his work.
  This was before he made anything
  else long ago.
²³I was appointed in the very beginning,
  even before the world began.
²⁴I began before there were oceans.
  There were no springs overflowing
  with water.
²⁵I began before the hills were there.
  The mountains had not even been
  put in place.
²⁶God still had not made the earth or
  fields.
  He had not even made the first dust
  of the earth.
²⁷I was there when God put the skies in
  place,
  when he stretched the horizon over
  the oceans.
²⁸I was there when he made the clouds
  above.
  I was there when he put the
  fountains in the oceans.
²⁹I was there when he ordered the sea
  not to go beyond the borders he
  had set for it.

I was there when he laid the earth's
  foundation.
30 I was like a child by his side.
I was happy every day
  and enjoyed being in his presence.
31I enjoyed the whole world.
  And I was happy with all its people.

32"Now, my children, listen to me.
  Those who follow my ways are
    happy.
33Listen to my teaching, and you will be
    wise.
  Do not ignore it.
34Those who listen to me are happy.
  They stand watching at my door
    every day.
  They are at my open doorway,
    wanting to be with me.
35Whoever finds me finds life.
  And the Lord will be pleased with
    him.
36Whoever does not find me hurts
    himself.
  Those who hate me love death."

BEING WISE OR FOOLISH

9 Wisdom has built her house.
  She has made its seven columns.
2She has prepared her food and wine.
  She has set her table.
3She has sent out her servant girls.
  She calls out from the highest place
    in the city.
4She says to those who are not wise,
  "Come in here, you foolish people!
5Come and eat my food.
  And drink the wine I have
    prepared.
6Stop your foolish ways, and you will
    live.
  Be a person of understanding.

7"If you correct someone who makes fun
    of wisdom, you will get insulted.
  If you correct an evil person, you
    will get hurt.
8Do not correct someone who makes
    fun of wisdom, or he will hate you.

But correct a wise man, and he will
    love you.
9Teach a wise man, and he will become
    even wiser.
  Teach a good man, and he will learn
    even more.

10"Wisdom begins with respect for the
    Lord.
  And understanding begins with
    knowing God, the Holy One.
11If you live wisely, you will live a long
    time.
  Wisdom will add years to your life.
12The wise person is rewarded by his
    wisdom.
  But a person who makes fun of
    wisdom will suffer for it."

13Foolishness is like a loud woman.
  She does not have wisdom or
    knowledge.
14She sits at the door of her house.
  It is at the highest place in the city.
15She calls out to those who are passing
    by.
  They are minding their own
    business.
16She says to those who are not wise,
  "Come in here, you foolish people!
17Stolen water is sweeter.
  Stolen food tastes better."
18But these people don't know that
    everyone dies who goes there.
  They don't realize that her guests
    are deep in the grave.

THE PROVERBS OF SOLOMON

10 These are the wise words of Sol-
    omon:

A wise son makes his father happy.
  But a foolish son makes his mother
    sad.

2Riches gotten by doing wrong have no
    value.
  But right living will save you from
    death.

³The Lord does not let people who live
   right go hungry.
But he does not let evil people get
   what they hunger for.

⁴A lazy person will end up poor.
But a hard worker will become
   rich.

⁵A son who gathers crops when they
   are ready is wise.
But the son who sleeps through the
   harvest is a disgrace.

⁶People who do what is right will have
   rich blessings.
But the wicked will be overwhelmed
   by violence.

⁷Good people will be remembered as a
   blessing.
But evil people will soon be
   forgotten.

⁸A wise person does what he is told.
But a talkative fool will be ruined.

⁹The honest person will live safely.
But the one who is dishonest will be
   caught.

¹⁰A wink may get you into trouble.
And foolish talk will lead to your
   ruin.

¹¹Like a fountain of water, the words of
   a good person give life.
But the words of the wicked contain
   nothing but violence.

¹²Hatred stirs up trouble.
But love forgives all wrongs.

¹³You can expect wise people to speak
   with understanding.
But people without wisdom can
   expect to be punished.

¹⁴Wise people don't tell everything they
   know.
But a foolish person talks too much
   and is ruined.

¹⁵Having lots of money protects the rich.
But having no money destroys the
   poor.

¹⁶Good people are rewarded with life.
But evil people are paid back with
   punishment.

¹⁷The person who accepts correction is
   on the way to life.
But the person who ignores
   correction will be ruined.

¹⁸Whoever hides his hate is a liar.
Whoever tells lies is a fool.

¹⁹If you talk a lot, you are sure to sin.
If you are wise, you will keep quiet.

²⁰The words of a good person are like
   pure silver.
But an evil person's thoughts are
   worth little.

²¹A good person's words will help many
   others.
But a foolish person dies because he
   doesn't have wisdom.

²²The Lord's blessing brings wealth.
And with it comes no sorrow.

²³A foolish person enjoys doing wrong.
But a person with understanding
   enjoys doing what is wise.

²⁴An evil person will get what he fears
   most.
But a good person will receive what
   he wants most.

²⁵A storm will blow the evil person away.
But a good person will always be
   safe.

²⁶A lazy person brings trouble to the
   one he works for.
He bothers others like vinegar on
   the teeth or smoke in the eyes.

²⁷Whoever respects the Lord will have a
   long life.
But an evil person will have his life
   cut short.

²⁸A good person can look forward to
   happiness.
   But an evil person can expect
   nothing.

²⁹The Lord will protect good people.
   But he will ruin those who do evil.

³⁰Good people will always be safe.
   But evil people will not remain in
   the land.

³¹A good person says wise things.
   But a liar's tongue will be stopped.

³²Good people say the right thing.
   But the wicked tell lies.

11
The Lord hates dishonest
   scales.
   But he is pleased with correct
   weights.

²Pride leads only to shame.
   It is wise not to be proud.

³Good people will be guided by
   honesty.
   But dishonesty will destroy those
   who are not trustworthy.

⁴Riches will not help when it's time to
   die.
   But doing what is right will save
   you from dying too soon.

⁵The goodness of an innocent person
   makes his life easier.
   But a wicked person will be
   destroyed by his wickedness.

⁶Doing what is right brings freedom to
   honest people.
   But those who are not trustworthy
   will be caught by their own
   desires.

⁷When a wicked person dies, his hope
   is gone.
   The hopes he placed in his riches
   will come to nothing.

⁸The good man is saved from trouble.
   It comes to the wicked instead.

⁹By his words an evil person can
   destroy his neighbor.
   But a good person will escape by
   being smart.

¹⁰When good people succeed, the city is
   happy.
   When evil people die, there are
   shouts of joy.

¹¹The influence of good people makes a
   city great.
   But the wicked can destroy it with
   their words.

¹²A person without good sense finds
   fault with his neighbor.
   But a person with understanding
   keeps quiet.

¹³A person who gossips can't keep
   secrets.
   But a trustworthy person can keep
   a secret.

¹⁴Without leadership a nation will be
   defeated.
   But when many people give advice,
   it will be safe.

¹⁵Whoever guarantees to pay what
   somebody else owes will suffer.
   It is safer to avoid such promises.

¹⁶A kind woman is respected.
   But cruel men get wealth.

¹⁷A kind person is doing himself a
   favor.
   But a cruel person brings trouble
   on himself.

¹⁸An evil person really gains nothing
   from what he earns.
   But a good person will surely be
   rewarded.

¹⁹Those who are truly good will live.
   But those who chase after evil will
   die.

²⁰The Lord hates those with evil hearts.
   But he is pleased with those who
   are innocent.

21You can be sure that evil people will
be punished.
But those who do what is right will
not be punished.

22A beautiful woman without good
sense
is like a gold ring in a pig's snout.

23The wishes of those who do right will
come true.
But the hopes of the wicked will be
defeated by God's anger.

24Some people give much but get back
even more.
But others don't give what they
should, and they end up poor.
25A person who gives to others will get
richer.
Whoever helps others will himself
be helped.

26People curse someone who keeps all
the grain for himself.
But they bless a person who is
willing to sell it.

27Whoever looks for good will find
kindness.
But whoever looks for evil will find
trouble.

28Those who trust in riches will be
ruined.
But a good person will be as healthy
as a green leaf.

29Whoever brings trouble to his family
will be left with nothing but the
wind.
And a foolish person will become a
servant to the wise.

30As a tree makes fruit, a good person
gives life to others.
The wise person shows others how
to be wise.

31Good people will be rewarded on
earth.

So the wicked and the sinners will
also be punished.

12 Anyone who loves learning
accepts being corrected.
But a person who hates being
corrected is stupid.

2The Lord is pleased with a good
person.
But he will punish anyone who
plans evil.

3Doing evil brings a person no safety
at all.
But a good person has safety and
security.

4A good wife is like a crown for her
husband.
But a disgraceful wife is like a
disease in his bones.

5The plans that good people make are
fair.
But the advice of the wicked will
trick you.

6The wicked talk of killing people.
But the words of good people will
save them.

7Wicked people die and leave nothing
behind.
But a good man's family goes on.

8A wise person is praised.
But a stupid person is not
respected.

9A person might not be important but
still have a servant.
He is better off than someone who
acts important but has no food.

10A good man takes care of his animals.
But even the kindest acts of the
wicked are cruel.

11The person who works his land will
have plenty of food.
But the one who chases useless
dreams isn't wise.

¹²Evil people want what other evil
    people have stolen.
But good people want to give to
    others.

¹³Evil people are trapped by their evil
    talk.
But good people stay out of trouble.

¹⁴A person will be rewarded for what he
    says.
And he will also be rewarded for
    what he does.

¹⁵A foolish person thinks he is doing
    right.
But a wise person listens to advice.

¹⁶A foolish person quickly shows that
    he is upset.
But a wise person ignores an insult.

¹⁷An honest witness tells the truth.
But a dishonest witness tells lies.

¹⁸Careless words stab like a sword.
But wise words bring healing.

¹⁹Truth will last forever.
But lies last only a moment.

²⁰Those who plan evil mean to lie.
But those who plan peace will be
    happy.

²¹No harm comes to a good person.
But an evil person's life is full of
    trouble.

²²The Lord hates those who tell lies.
But he is pleased with those who do
    what they promise.

²³A wise person keeps what he knows to
    himself.
But a foolish person shows how
    foolish he is.

²⁴Hard workers will become leaders.
But those who are lazy will be
    slaves.

²⁵Worry makes a person feel as if he is
    carrying a heavy load.

But a kind word cheers up
    a person.

²⁶A good person takes advice from his
    friends.
But an evil person is easily led to do
    wrong.

²⁷A lazy person catches no food to cook.
But a hard worker will have great
    wealth.

²⁸Doing what is right is the way to life.
But there is another way that leads
    to death.

13 A wise son takes his father's
        advice.
But a person who makes fun of
    wisdom won't listen to correction.

²A person will be rewarded for what he
    says.
But those who can't be trusted want
    only violence.

³Whoever is careful about what he says
    protects his life.
But anyone who speaks without
    thinking will be ruined.

⁴The lazy person will not get what he
    wants.
But a hard worker gets everything
    he wants.

⁵Good people hate what is false.
But wicked people do shameful and
    disgraceful things.

⁶Doing what is right protects the
    honest person.
But evil ruins the sinner.

⁷Some people pretend to be rich but
    really have nothing.
Other people pretend to be poor but
    really are wealthy.

⁸A rich man may have to pay a ransom
    for his life.
But a poor person will never have to
    face such a danger.

⁹Good people will live long like bright
flames.
But the wicked will die like a flame
going out.

¹⁰Pride leads to arguments.
But those who take advice are wise.

¹¹Money that comes easily disappears
quickly.
But money that is gathered little by
little will slowly grow.

¹²It is sad when you don't get what you
hoped for.
But when wishes come true, it's like
eating fruit from the tree of life.

¹³Whoever rejects what he is taught will
pay for it.
But whoever does what he is told
will be rewarded.

¹⁴The teaching of a wise person gives life.
It is like a fountain of water that can
save people from death.

¹⁵People with good understanding will
be liked.
But the lives of those who are not
trustworthy are hard.

¹⁶Every wise person acts with good
sense.
But a foolish person shows how
foolish he is.

¹⁷A wicked messenger brings nothing
but trouble.
But a trustworthy one makes
everything right.

¹⁸A person who refuses correction will
end up poor and disgraced.
But a person who accepts
correction will be honored.

¹⁹It is so good when wishes come true.
But foolish people still refuse to
stop doing evil.

²⁰Whoever spends time with wise
people will become wise.

But whoever makes friends with
fools will suffer.

²¹Trouble always comes to sinners.
But good people enjoy success.

²²Good people's wealth will be inherited
by their grandchildren.
And a sinner's wealth will be saved
for good people.

²³A poor man's field might have plenty
of food.
But unfair people steal it from him.

²⁴If a person does not punish his
children, he does not love them.
But the person who loves his
children is careful to correct them.

²⁵Good people have enough to eat.
But the wicked will go hungry.

14 A wise woman strengthens her
family.
But a foolish woman destroys hers
by what she does.

²People who live good lives show
respect for the Lord.
But those who live evil lives show
no respect for him.

³A foolish person will be punished for
his proud words.
But a wise person's words will
protect him.

⁴When there are no oxen, there is no
food in the barn.
But with the strength of an ox,
much grain can be grown.

⁵A truthful witness does not lie.
But a false witness tells nothing but
lies.

⁶Those who make fun of wisdom look
for it but do not find it.
But the person with understanding
easily finds knowledge.

⁷Stay away from a foolish person.
You won't learn anything from him.

⁸What makes a person wise is
  understanding what to do.
  But what makes a person foolish is
    dishonesty.

⁹Foolish people don't care if they sin.
  But honest people work at being
    right with others.

¹⁰No one else can know your sadness.
  Strangers cannot share your joy.

¹¹The wicked person's house will be
    destroyed.
  But a good person's tent will still be
    standing.

¹²Some people think they are doing
    what's right.
  But what they are doing will really
    kill them.

¹³When someone is laughing, he may be
    sad inside.
  And when the laughter is over,
    there is sorrow.

¹⁴Evil people will be paid back for their
    evil ways.
  And good people will be rewarded
    for their good ones.

¹⁵A foolish person will believe anything.
  But a wise person thinks about
    what he does.

¹⁶A wise person is careful and stays out
    of trouble.
  But a foolish person is quick to act
    and careless.

¹⁷A person who quickly loses his
    temper does foolish things.
  But a person with understanding
    remains calm.

¹⁸Foolish people get nothing for their
    work but more foolishness.
  But wise people are rewarded with
    knowledge.

¹⁹Evil people will have to bow down to
    good people.

The wicked will bow down at the
    door of those who do right.

²⁰The poor are rejected, even by their
    neighbors.
  But rich people have many friends.

²¹It is a sin to hate your neighbor.
  But being kind to the needy brings
    happiness.

²²Those who make evil plans will be
    ruined.
  But people love and trust those who
    plan to do good.

²³Those who work hard make a profit.
  But those who only talk will be
    poor.

²⁴Wise people are rewarded with
    wealth.
  But foolish people will only be
    rewarded with more foolishness.

²⁵A truthful witness saves lives.
  But a false witness is a traitor.

²⁶A person who respects the Lord will
    have security.
  And his children will be protected.

²⁷Respect for the Lord gives life.
  It is like a fountain of water that can
    save people from death.

²⁸A king is honored when he has many
    people to rule.
  But a prince is ruined if he has
    none.

²⁹A person who does not quickly get
    angry shows that he has
    understanding.
  But a person who quickly loses his
    temper shows his foolishness.

³⁰Peace of mind means a healthy body.
  But jealousy will rot your bones.

³¹Whoever is cruel to the poor insults
    their Maker.
  But anyone who is kind to the
    needy honors God.

³²The wicked are ruined by their own
  evil.
  But those who do what is right are
  protected by their honesty.

³³The person who has understanding
  has wisdom.
  And even fools recognize it.

³⁴Doing what is right makes a nation
  great.
  But sin will bring disgrace to any
  people.

³⁵A king is pleased with a wise servant.
  But he will become angry with one
  who causes him shame.

15 A gentle answer will calm
  a person's anger.
  But an unkind answer will cause
  more anger.

²Wise people use knowledge when they
  speak.
  But fools speak only foolishness.

³The Lord's eyes see everything that
  happens.
  He watches both evil and good
  people.

⁴As a tree gives us fruit, healing words
  give us life.
  But evil words crush the spirit.

⁵A foolish person rejects his father's
  correction.
  But anyone who accepts correction
  is wise.

⁶There is much wealth in the houses of
  good people.
  But evil people are paid only with
  trouble.

⁷With their words wise people spread
  knowledge.
  But there is no knowledge in the
  thoughts of the foolish.

⁸The Lord hates the sacrifice that the
  wicked person offers.

But he is pleased with an honest
  person's prayer.

⁹The Lord hates what evil people do.
  But he loves those who do what is
  right.

¹⁰The person who quits doing what is
  right will really be punished.
  The one who hates to be corrected
  will die.

¹¹The Lord knows what is happening
  where the dead people are.
  So he can surely know what living
  people are thinking.

¹²A person who laughs at wisdom does
  not like to be corrected.
  He will not ask advice from the wise.

¹³Happiness makes a person smile.
  But sadness breaks a person's spirit.

¹⁴Smart people want more knowledge.
  But a foolish person just wants
  more foolishness.

¹⁵Every day is hard for those who suffer.
  But a happy heart makes it like a
  continual feast.

¹⁶It is better to be poor and respect the
  Lord
  than to be wealthy and have much
  trouble.

¹⁷It is better to eat vegetables with those
  who love you
  than to eat meat with those who
  hate you.

¹⁸A person who quickly gets angry
  causes trouble.
  But a person who controls his
  temper stops a quarrel.

¹⁹A lazy person's life is as difficult as
  walking through a patch of
  thorns.
  But an honest person's life is as
  easy as walking down a smooth
  highway.

20 A wise son makes his father happy.
But a foolish person hates his
mother.

21 A man without wisdom enjoys being
foolish.
But a man with understanding does
what is right.

22 Plans fail without good advice.
But plans succeed when you get
advice from many others.

23 People enjoy giving good answers!
Saying the right word at the right
time is so pleasing!

24 A wise person does things that will
make his life better.
He avoids whatever would cause
his death.

25 The Lord will tear down the proud
person's house.
But he will protect the property
of a widow.

26 The Lord hates evil thoughts.
But he is pleased with kind words.

27 A greedy person brings trouble to his
family.
But the person who can't be paid
to do wrong will live.

28 Good people think before they
answer.
But the wicked simply give evil
answers.

29 The Lord does not listen to the
wicked.
But he hears the prayers of those
who do right.

30 Good news makes you feel better.
Your happiness will show in your
eyes.

31 A wise person pays attention to
correction
that will improve his life.

32 A person who refuses correction hates
himself.
But a person who accepts correction
gains understanding.

33 Respect for the Lord will teach you
wisdom.
If you want to be honored, you
must not be proud.

16 People make plans in their
hearts.
But only the Lord can make those
plans come true.

2 A person may believe he is doing
right.
But the Lord will judge his reasons.

3 Depend on the Lord in whatever you
do.
Then your plans will succeed.

4 The Lord makes everything work the
way he wants it.
He even has a day of disaster for
evil people.

5 The Lord hates those who are proud.
You can be sure that they will be
punished.

6 Love and truth bring forgiveness of
sin.
By respecting the Lord you will
avoid evil.

7 A person should live so that he
pleases the Lord.
If he does, even his enemies will
make peace with him.

8 It is better to be poor and do what is
right
than to be wealthy and be unfair.

9 A person may think up plans.
But the Lord decides what he will do.

10 The words of a king are like a message
from God.
So his decisions should be fair.

11The Lord wants honest balances and scales to be used.
He wants all weights to be honest.

12Kings hate those who do wrong because governments only last if they are fair.

13Kings are pleased with those who speak honest words.
They value a person who speaks the truth.

14If a king becomes angry, he may put someone to death.
So a wise man will try to keep peace.

15A king's kindness can give people life.
His kindness is like a spring shower.

16It is better to get wisdom than gold.
It is better to choose understanding than silver!

17A good person stays away from evil.
A person who watches what he does protects his life.

18Pride leads to destruction.
A proud attitude brings ruin.

19It is better not to be proud and to be with those who suffer
than to share stolen property with proud people.

20Whoever pays attention to what he is taught will succeed.
And whoever trusts the Lord will be happy.

21A wise person is known for his understanding.
He wins people to his side with pleasant words.

22Understanding is like a fountain of water which gives life to those who use it.
But foolishness will cause foolish people to be punished.

23A wise person's mind tells him what to say.
This helps him to teach others better.

24Pleasant words are like a honeycomb.
They make a person happy and healthy.

25Some people think they are doing what's right.
But in the end it causes them to die.

26The worker's hunger helps him.
His desire to eat makes him work.

27An evil person makes evil plans.
And his words are like a burning fire.

28An evil person causes trouble.
And a person who gossips ruins friendships.

29A cruel man tricks his neighbor.
He leads him to do wrong.

30Someone who winks at you is planning evil.
And the one who grins at you is about to do something wrong.

31Gray hair is like a crown of honor.
You earn it by living a good life.

32Patience is better than strength.
Controlling your temper is better than capturing a city.

33People throw lots*d* to make a decision.
But the answer comes from the Lord.

17 It is better to eat a dry crust of bread in peace
than to have a feast where there is quarreling.

2A wise servant will rule over his master's disgraceful son.
And he will even inherit a share of what the master leaves his sons.

3A hot furnace tests silver and gold.
In the same way, the Lord tests a person's heart.

⁴An evil person listens to evil words.
  A liar pays attention to cruel words.

⁵If you make fun of the poor,
  you insult God, who made them.
 If you laugh at someone's trouble,
  you will be punished.

⁶Grandchildren are the reward of old
    people.
  And children are proud of their
    parents.

⁷Foolish people should not be proud.
  And rulers should not be liars!

⁸A person might think he can pay
    people and they will do anything
    he asks.
  He thinks it will succeed every time.

⁹Whoever forgives someone's sin
    makes a friend.
  But the one who tells about the sin
    breaks up friendships.

¹⁰A wise man will learn more from a
    warning
  than a foolish person will learn
    from 100 lashings.

¹¹A disobedient person is only looking
    for trouble.
  So a cruel messenger will be sent
    against him.

¹²It is better to meet a bear robbed of
    her cubs
  than to meet a foolish person doing
    foolish things.

¹³If a person gives evil in return for good,
  his house will always be full of
    trouble.

¹⁴Starting a quarrel is like a leak in a dam.
  So stop the quarrel before a fight
    breaks out.

¹⁵The Lord hates both these things:
  letting guilty people go free and
    punishing those who are not
    guilty.

¹⁶It won't do a fool any good to try to
    buy wisdom.
  He doesn't really want to be wise.

¹⁷A friend loves you all the time.
  A brother is always there to help
    you.

¹⁸It is not wise to promise
  to pay what your neighbor owes.

¹⁹Whoever loves to quarrel loves to sin.
  Whoever is proud is asking for
    trouble.

²⁰A person with an evil heart will find
    no success.
  And the person whose words are
    evil will get into trouble.

²¹It is sad to have a foolish son.
  There is no joy in being the father
    of a fool.

²²A happy heart is like good medicine.
  But a broken spirit drains your
    strength.

²³A wicked person secretly accepts
    money to do wrong.
  Then there will be no fairness.

²⁴The person with understanding looks
    for wisdom.
  But a foolish person lets his mind
    wander everywhere.

²⁵A foolish son makes his father sad.
  And he causes his mother great
    sorrow.

²⁶It is not good to punish those who
    have done what is right.
  Nor is it good to punish leaders for
    being honest.

²⁷The person who has knowledge says
    very little.
  And a person with understanding
    stays calm.

²⁸Even a foolish person seems to be
    wise if he keeps quiet.

He appears to have understanding
if he doesn't speak.

18 An unfriendly person cares only
about himself.
He makes fun of all wisdom.

²A foolish person does not want to
understand anything.
He only enjoys telling others what
he thinks.

³Do something evil, and people won't
like you.
Do something shameful, and they
will make fun of you.

⁴Understanding people's words is as
hard as getting water out of a
deep well.
But understanding wisdom is as
easy as getting water from a
flowing stream.

⁵It is not good to honor the wicked.
Nor is it good to be unfair to the
innocent.

⁶A fool's words start quarrels.
They make people want to give him
a beating.

⁷A fool's words will ruin him.
He will be trapped by his own
words.

⁸The words of a gossip are like tasty
bits of food.
People take them all in.

⁹A person who doesn't work hard
is just like a person who destroys
things.

¹⁰The Lord is like a strong tower.
Those who do what is right can run
to him for safety.

¹¹Rich people trust their wealth to
protect them.
They think it is like the high walls of
a city.

¹²People who are proud will be ruined.
But those who are not proud will be
honored.

¹³A person who answers without
listening
is foolish and disgraceful.

¹⁴The will to live can get you through
sickness.
But no one can live with a broken
spirit.

¹⁵The mind of a smart person is ready
to get knowledge.
The wise person listens to learn
more.

¹⁶Taking a gift to an important person
will help get you in to see him.

¹⁷The first person to tell his side of a
story seems right.
But that may change when
somebody comes and asks him
questions.

¹⁸Throwing lots^d settles arguments.
It keeps the two sides from
fighting.

¹⁹A brother who has been insulted is
harder to win back than a walled
city.
And arguments separate people like
the barred gates of a palace.

²⁰What you say affects how you live.
You will be rewarded by how you
speak.

²¹What you say can mean life or death.
Those who love to talk will be
rewarded for what they say.

²²A man who finds a wife finds
something good.
She shows that the Lord is pleased
with him.

²³Poor people beg for mercy.
Rich people give rude answers.

24Some friends may ruin you.
  But a real friend will be more loyal
    than a brother.

19 It is better to be poor and
      honest
  than to be foolish and tell lies.

2Enthusiasm without knowledge is not
    good.
  If you act too quickly, you might
    make a mistake.

3A person's own foolishness ruins his
    life.
  But in his mind he blames the Lord
    for it.

4Wealthy people are always finding
    more friends.
  But the poor lose their friends.

5A witness who lies will be punished.
  An untruthful person will not be
    left unpunished.

6Many people want to please a leader.
  And everyone is friends with those
    who give gifts.

7A poor person's relatives avoid him.
  Even his friends stay far away!
He runs after them, begging.
  But they are gone.

8The person who gets wisdom is good
    to himself.
  And the one who has
    understanding will succeed.

9A witness who lies will be punished.
  An untruthful person will die.

10No foolish person should live in
    luxury.
  No slave should rule over princes!

11A wise person is patient.
  He will be honored if he ignores a
    wrong done against him.

12A king's anger scares people like the
    roar of a lion.
  But his kindness is as pleasant as
    the dew on the grass.

13A foolish son will ruin his father.
  And a quarreling wife is as
    bothersome as dripping water.

14Houses and wealth are inherited from
    parents.
  But a wise wife is a gift from the
    Lord.

15Lazy people sleep a lot.
  Idle people will go hungry.

16Whoever obeys the commands
    protects his life.
  Whoever is careless in what he does
    will die.

17Being kind to the poor is like lending
    to the Lord.
  The Lord will reward you for what
    you have done.

18Correct your son while there is still
    hope.
  Do not help him destroy himself.

19A person who is always getting angry
    will pay for it.
  If you help him, you will have to do
    it again and again.

20Listen to advice and accept correction.
  Then in the end you will be wise.

21People can make many different plans.
  But only the Lord's plan will
    happen.

22People want others to be loyal.
  So it is better to be poor than to be a
    liar.

23Those who respect the Lord will live
    and be content, unbothered by
    trouble.

24The lazy person may put his hand in
    the dish,
  but he won't lift the food to his
    mouth!

25Whip a person who makes fun of
    wisdom, and then foolish people
    will learn how to think.

Just correct a smart man, and he
will gain knowledge.

26 A son who robs his father and sends
away his mother
brings shame and disgrace on
himself.

27 Don't stop listening to correction, my
child.
If you do, you will not obey what
you have already learned.

28 An evil witness makes fun of
fairness.
And wicked people love what
is evil.

29 People who make fun of wisdom will
be punished.
And the backs of foolish people will
be beaten.

20 Wine and beer make people
loud and uncontrolled.
It is not wise to get drunk on them.

2 A king's anger is like the roar of a lion.
Making him angry may cost you
your life.

3 Foolish people are always getting into
quarrels.
But avoiding quarrels will bring you
honor.

4 A lazy farmer doesn't plow when he
should.
So at harvest time he has no crop.

5 Understanding a person's thoughts is
as hard as getting water from a
deep well.
But someone with understanding
can find the wisdom there.

6 Many people claim to be loyal.
But it is hard to find someone who
really can be trusted.

7 The good person who lives an honest
life
is a blessing to his children.

8 A king sits on his throne and judges
people.
He knows evil when he sees it.

9 No one can say, "I am innocent.
I have never done anything wrong."

10 The Lord hates both these things:
dishonest weights and dishonest
measures.

11 Even a child is known by his behavior.
His actions show if he is innocent
and good.

12 The Lord has made both these things:
Ears that can hear and eyes that
can see.

13 If you love to sleep, you will be poor.
If you stay awake, you will have
plenty of food.

14 The buyer says, "This is bad. It's no
good."
Then he goes away and brags about
what he bought.

15 There is plenty of gold, and there are
many rubies.
But there are only a few people who
speak with knowledge.

16 Take the coat of someone who promises
to pay what a stranger owes.
Keep it until he pays the stranger's
bills.

17 When a person gets food dishonestly,
it may taste sweet at first.
But later he will feel as if he has a
mouth full of gravel.

18 Get advice if you want your plans to
work.
If you go to war, get the advice of
others.

19 Gossips can't keep secrets.
So avoid people who talk too much.

20 Whoever curses his father or mother
will die like a light going out in
darkness.

²¹Wealth that is gotten quickly in the
    beginning
  will do you no good in the end.

²²Don't say, "I'll pay you back for the
    evil you did."
  Wait for the Lord. He will make
    things right.

²³The Lord hates dishonest weights.
  And dishonest scales do not please
    him.

²⁴The Lord decides what a person does.
  So no one can understand what his
    life is all about.

²⁵It's dangerous to promise something
    to God too quickly.
  After you've thought about it, it
    may be too late.

²⁶A wise king finds out who the evil
    people are.
  Then he punishes them.

²⁷The Lord looks into a person's
    feelings.
  He searches through a person's
    thoughts.

²⁸Loyalty and truth keep a king in power.
  He continues to rule if he is loyal.

²⁹Young men are admired for their
    strength.
  Old men are honored for their
    experience.

³⁰Hard punishment will get rid of evil.
  Whippings can change the evil
    person's heart.

21 The Lord can control a king's
    mind as easily as he
    controls a river.
  He can direct it as he pleases.

²A person may believe he is doing
    right.
  But the Lord judges his reasons.

³Do what is right and fair.
  That is more important to the Lord
    than animal sacrifices.

⁴Proud looks, proud thoughts
  and evil actions are sin.

⁵Those who plan and work hard earn a
    profit.
  But those who act too quickly
    become poor.

⁶Wealth that comes from telling lies
  vanishes like a mist and leads to
    death.

⁷The violence of the wicked will
    destroy them
  because they refuse to do what is
    right.

⁸Guilty people live dishonest lives.
  But honest people do what is right.

⁹It is better to live in a corner on the
    roof[n]
  than inside the house with a
    quarreling wife.

¹⁰An evil person only wants to harm
    others.
  His neighbor will get no mercy
    from him.

¹¹Punish a person who makes fun of
    wisdom, and he will become wise.
  But just teach a wise person, and he
    will get knowledge.

¹²God, who is always right, sees the
    house of the wicked.
  And he brings about the ruin of
    every evil person.

¹³If you ignore the poor when they cry
    for help,
  you also will cry for help and not be
    answered.

¹⁴A gift given secretly will calm an
    angry man.

21:9 roof In Bible times houses were built with flat roofs. The roof was used for drying things such as flax and
fruit. And it was used as an extra room, as a place for worship and as a place to sleep in the summer.

A present given in secrecy will calm
even great anger.

¹⁵When things are done fairly, good
people are happy,
but evil people are frightened.

¹⁶A person who does not use
understanding
will join the dead.

¹⁷Whoever loves pleasure will become
poor.
Whoever loves wine and rich food
will never be wealthy.

¹⁸Wicked people will suffer instead of
good people.
And those who cannot be trusted
will suffer instead of those who
can.

¹⁹It is better to live alone in the desert
than with a quarreling and
complaining wife.

²⁰Wise people store up the best foods
and olive oil.
But a foolish person eats up
everything he has.

²¹A person who tries to live right and be
loyal
finds life, success and honor.

²²A wise person can defeat a city full of
strong men.
He can tear down the defenses they
trust.

²³A person who is careful about what he
says
keeps himself out of trouble.

²⁴People who act with stubborn pride
are called "proud" and "bragger."

²⁵The lazy person's desire for sleep will
kill him
because he refuses to work.

²⁶All day long the lazy person wishes for
more.

But the good person gives without
holding back.

²⁷The Lord hates sacrifices made by evil
people,
particularly when they make them
for the wrong reasons.

²⁸The words of a lying witness will die.
But the words of an obedient man
will always be remembered.

²⁹A wicked person is stubborn.
But an honest person thinks
carefully about what he does.

³⁰There is no wisdom, understanding or
advice
that can succeed against the Lord.

³¹You can get the horses ready for
battle.
But it is the Lord who gives the
victory.

22 Being respected is more
important than having great
riches.
To be well thought of is better than
owning silver or gold.

²The rich and the poor are alike
in that the Lord made them all.

³When a wise person sees danger
ahead, he avoids it.
But a foolish person keeps going
and gets into trouble.

⁴Respecting the Lord and not being
proud
will bring you wealth, honor and
life.

⁵The lives of evil people are like
paths covered with thorns and
traps.
People who protect themselves
don't have such problems.

⁶Train a child how to live the right way.
Then even when he is old, he will
still live that way.

⁷The rich rule over the poor.
    And borrowers become servants to
        those who lend.

⁸A person who does evil things will
        receive trouble in return.
    Then he won't be cruel to others
        any longer.

⁹A generous person will be blessed
    because he shares his food with the
        poor.

¹⁰Get rid of the person who makes fun
        of wisdom.
    Then fighting, quarrels and insults
        will stop.

¹¹A person who loves innocent thoughts
        and kind words
    will have even the king as a friend.

¹²The Lord protects knowledge from
        being lost.
    But he destroys false words.

¹³The lazy person says, "There's a lion
        outside!
    I might get killed out in the street!"

¹⁴The words of an unfaithful wife are
        like a deep trap.
    Those who make the Lord angry
        will get caught by them.

¹⁵Every child is full of foolishness.
    But punishment can get rid of it.

¹⁶The one who gets rich by being cruel
        to the poor will become poor.
    And so will the one who gives
        presents to the wealthy.

OTHER WISE SAYINGS

¹⁷Pay attention and listen to what wise
        people say.
    Remember what I am teaching you.
¹⁸It will be good to keep these things in
        mind.
    Be prepared to repeat them.
¹⁹I am teaching them to you now
    so that you will put your trust in the
        Lord.

²⁰I have written down 30 sayings for you.
    They give knowledge and good
        advice.
²¹I am teaching you true and reliable
        words.
    Then you can give true answers to
        anyone who asks.

²²Do not abuse poor people because
        they are poor.
    And do not take away the rights of
        the needy in court.
²³The Lord will defend them in court.
    And he will take the life of those
        who take away their rights.

²⁴Don't make friends with someone
        who easily gets angry.
    Don't spend time with someone
        who has a bad temper.
²⁵If you do, you may learn to be like
        him.
    Then you will be in real danger.

²⁶Don't promise to pay what someone
        else owes.
    And don't give guarantees that you
        will pay what he owes.
²⁷If you cannot pay what he owes,
    your own bed will be taken and
        sold.

²⁸Don't move an old stone that shows
        where a person's land is.
    These stones were set up by your
        ancestors.

²⁹Do you see a man skilled in his work?
    That man will work for kings.
    He won't have to work for ordinary
        people.

23 If you sit down to eat with
        a ruler,
    notice the food that is in front of
        you.
²Control yourself
    if you have a big appetite.
³Don't be greedy for his fine foods.
    He might use that rich food to trick
        you.

⁴Don't wear yourself out trying to get
rich.
  Be wise enough to control yourself.
⁵Wealth can vanish in the wink of an
eye.
  It seems to grow wings
  and fly away like an eagle in the sky.

⁶Don't eat the food of a selfish person.
  Don't be greedy for his fine foods.
⁷A selfish person is always worrying
about how much the food costs.
  He tells you, "Eat and drink."
  But he doesn't really mean it.
⁸So you will feel like throwing up the
little bit you have eaten.
  And you will have wasted your kind
words.

⁹Don't speak to a foolish person.
  He will only ignore your wise words.

¹⁰Don't move an old stone that shows
where somebody's land is.
  And don't take fields that belong to
orphans.
¹¹God, their defender, is strong.
  He will take their side against you.

¹²Remember what you are taught.
  And listen carefully to words of
knowledge.

¹³Don't fail to punish a child.
  If you spank him, you will keep him
from dying.
¹⁴If you punish him with a spanking,
you will save him from a fool's death.

¹⁵My child, if you are wise,
  then I will be happy.
¹⁶I will be so pleased
  if you speak what is right.

¹⁷Don't envy sinners.
  But always respect the Lord.
¹⁸If you do, you will have hope for the
future.
  Your wishes will come true.

¹⁹Listen, my child, and be wise.
  Keep your mind on what is right.

²⁰Don't be one of those who drink too
much wine
  or who eat too much food.
²¹Those who drink too much and eat
too much become poor.
  They sleep too much and end up
wearing rags.

²²Listen to your father, who gave you
life.
  And do not forget your mother
when she is old.
²³Learn the truth and never reject it.
  Get wisdom, self-control and
understanding.
²⁴The father of a good child is very
happy.
  The person who has a wise son is
glad because of him.
²⁵Make your father and mother happy.
  Give your mother a reason to be
glad.

²⁶My son, pay attention to me.
  And watch closely what I do.
²⁷A prostitute[d] is as dangerous as a
deep pit.
  And an unfaithful wife is like a
narrow well.
²⁸They ambush you like robbers.
  And they cause many men to be
unfaithful to their wives.

²⁹⁻³⁰Some people drink too much wine.
  They try out all the different kinds
of drinks.
  So they have trouble. They are sad.
  They fight. They complain.
  They have unnecessary bruises.
  They have bloodshot eyes.
³¹Don't stare at the wine's pretty, red
color.
  It may sparkle in the cup.
  It may go down your throat
smoothly.
³²But later it bites like a snake.
  Like a snake, it poisons you.
³³Your eyes will see strange sights.
  And your mind will be confused.

³⁴You will feel dizzy, as if you're out on
the stormy ocean.
You will feel as if you're on top of a
ship's sails.
³⁵You will think, "They hit me, but I'm
not hurt!
They have beaten me up, but I don't
remember it.
I wish I could wake up.
Then I would get another drink."

24 Don't envy evil people.
Don't try to be friends with them.
²In their minds they plan cruel things.
And they always talk about making
trouble.

³It takes wisdom to have a good family.
It takes understanding to make it
strong.
⁴It takes knowledge to fill a home
with rare and beautiful treasures.

⁵A wise man has great power.
And a man who has knowledge is
very strong.
⁶So you need the advice of others when
you go to war.
If you have many people to give
advice, you will win.

⁷A foolish person cannot understand
wisdom.
He has nothing to say in court.

⁸Whoever makes evil plans
will be known as a troublemaker.
⁹Making foolish plans is sinful.
And making fun of others is hateful.

¹⁰If you give up when trouble comes,
it shows that you have very little
strength.

¹¹Save those who are being led to their
death.
Rescue those who are about to be
killed.
¹²You may say, "We don't know
anything about this."

But God knows what is in your
mind, and he will notice.
He is watching you, and he will know.
He will pay each person back for
what he has done.

¹³My child, eat honey because it is good.
Honey from the honeycomb tastes
sweet.
¹⁴In the same way, wisdom is pleasing
to you.
If you find it, you have hope for the
future.
Your wishes will come true.

¹⁵Don't be like the wicked and attack a
good man's house.
Don't rob the place where he lives.
¹⁶A good man may be bothered by
trouble seven times, but he does
not give up.
But the wicked are overwhelmed by
trouble.

¹⁷Don't be happy when your enemy is
defeated.
Don't be glad when he is
overwhelmed.
¹⁸The Lord will notice and be displeased.
Then the Lord may not be angry
with him anymore.

¹⁹Don't envy evil people.
And don't be jealous of the wicked.
²⁰An evil person has nothing to hope
for.
The wicked will die like a flame that
is put out.

²¹My child, respect the Lord and the
king.
Don't join those people who refuse
to obey them.
²²The Lord and the king will quickly
destroy such people.
Those two can cause great trouble!

MORE WORDS OF WISDOM
²³These are also wise sayings:

It is not good to take sides when you
are the judge.

²⁴Don't say that the wicked have done
    right.
  People will curse you, and nations
    will hate you.
²⁵But things will go well for judges who
    punish the guilty.
  And they will receive good things
    from God.

²⁶An honest answer is as pleasing
    as a kiss on the lips.

²⁷First, you should work outside
    and prepare your fields.
  After that, you can start having your
    family.

²⁸Don't testify against your neighbor for
    no good reason.
  Don't say things that are false.
²⁹Don't say, "I'll get even with that man.
  I'll do to him what he did to me."

³⁰I passed by a lazy person's field.
  I went by the vineyard of a man
    who had no sense.
³¹Thorns had grown up everywhere.
  The ground was covered with
    weeds.
  And the stone walls had fallen
    down.
³²I thought about what I had seen.
  I learned this lesson from what I
    saw.
³³You sleep a little; you take a nap.
  You fold your hands and rest.
³⁴Soon you will be poor, as if you had
    been robbed.
  You will have as little as if you had
    been held up.

MORE WISE SAYINGS OF SOLOMON

25 These are more wise sayings of
    Solomon. They were copied by
the men of Hezekiah king of Judah.

²God is honored for what he keeps
    secret.
  Kings are honored for what they
    can discover.

³No one can measure the height of the
    skies or the depth of the earth.
  So also no one can understand the
    mind of a king.

⁴Remove the scum from the silver.
  Then the silver can be used by the
    silversmith.
⁵Remove wicked people from the king's
    presence.
  Then his government will be honest
    and last a long time.

⁶Don't brag to the king.
  Don't act as if you are a great man.
⁷It is better for him to promote you to
    a higher job
  than to give you a less important
    position.

  Because of something you have seen,
⁸ do not quickly take someone to
    court.
  What will you do later
    when your neighbor proves you are
    wrong?

⁹If you have an argument with your
    neighbor,
  don't tell other people what was
    said.
¹⁰Whoever hears it might say bad
    things about you.
  And you might not ever be
    respected again.

¹¹The right word spoken at the right
    time
  is as beautiful as gold apples in a
    silver bowl.

¹²The warning of a wise person is
    valuable to someone who will
    listen.
  It is worth as much as gold earrings
    or fine gold jewelry.

¹³A trustworthy messenger refreshes
    those who send him.
  He is like the coolness of snow in
    the summertime.

[14]People who brag about gifts they
    never give
  are like clouds and wind that give
    no rain.

[15]With patience you can convince a ruler.
  And a gentle word can get through
    to the hard-headed.

[16]If you find honey, don't eat too much.
  Too much of it will make you sick.
[17]Don't go to your neighbor's house too
    often.
  Too much of you will make him
    hate you.

[18]Anyone who lies about his neighbor
  hurts him as a club, a sword or a
    sharp arrow would.

[19]Don't trust unfaithful people when
    you are in trouble.
  It's like eating with a broken tooth
    or walking with a crippled foot.

[20]Don't sing songs to someone who is
    sad.
  It's like taking off a coat on a cold
    day
  or pouring vinegar on soda.

[21]If your enemy is hungry, feed him.
  If he is thirsty, give him a drink.
[22]Doing this will be like pouring
    burning coals on his head.
  And the Lord will reward you.

[23]The north wind brings rain.
  In the same way, telling gossip
    brings angry looks.

[24]It is better to live in a corner on the
    roof[n]
  than inside the house with a
    quarreling wife.

[25]Hearing good news from a faraway
    place
  is like having a cool drink when you
    are tired.

[26]A good person who gives in to evil
  is like a muddy spring or a dirty well.

[27]It is not good to eat too much honey.
  In the same way, it is not good to
    brag about yourself.

[28]A person who does not control himself
  is like a city whose walls have been
    broken down.

26 It shouldn't snow in summer
    or rain at harvest.
  Neither should a foolish person
    ever be honored.

[2]Curses will not harm someone who is
    innocent.
  They are like sparrows or swallows
    that fly around and never land.

[3]A whip is used to guide a horse, and a
    harness is used for a donkey.
  In the same way, a paddle is used
    on a foolish person to guide him.

[4]Don't give a foolish person a foolish
    answer.
  If you do, you will be just like him.

[5]But answer a foolish person as he
    should be answered.
  If you don't, he will think he is
    really wise.

[6]Don't send a message by a foolish
    person.
  That would be like cutting off your
    feet or drinking poison.

[7]A wise saying spoken by a fool does
    no good.
  It is like the legs of a crippled person.

[8]Giving honor to a foolish person does
    no good.
  It is like tying a stone in a slingshot.

[9]A wise saying spoken by a fool
  is like a thorn stuck in the hand of a
    drunk.

25:24 roof In Bible times houses were built with flat roofs. The roof was used for drying things such as flax and
fruit. And it was used as an extra room, as a place for worship and as a place to sleep in the summer.

¹⁰Someone might employ a foolish
person or anyone just passing by.
That employer is like an archer who
shoots at anything he sees.

¹¹A dog eats what it throws up.
And a foolish person repeats his
foolishness.

¹²Some people think they are wise.
There is more hope for a foolish
person than for them.

¹³The lazy person says, "There's a lion
in the road.
There's a lion in the streets!"

¹⁴The lazy person is like a door that turns
back and forth on its hinges.
He stays in bed and turns over and
over.

¹⁵The lazy person may put his hand in
the dish.
But he's too tired to lift the food to
his mouth.

¹⁶The lazy person thinks he is wiser
than seven people who give sensible
answers.

¹⁷To grab a dog by the ears is asking for
trouble.
So is interfering in someone else's
quarrel if you're just passing by.

¹⁸⁻¹⁹A person shouldn't trick his
neighbor
and then say, "I was just joking!"
That is like a madman shooting
deadly, burning arrows.

²⁰Without wood, a fire will go out.
And without gossip, quarreling will
stop.

²¹Charcoal and wood keep a fire going.
In the same way, a quarrelsome
person keeps an argument going.

²²The words of a gossip are like tasty
bits of food.
People take them all in.

²³Kind words from a wicked mind
are like a shiny coating on a clay
pot.

²⁴A person who hates you may fool you
with his words.
But in his mind he is planning evil.

²⁵His words are kind, but don't believe
him.
His mind is full of evil thoughts.

²⁶He hides his hate with lies.
But his evil will be plain to
everyone.

²⁷Whoever digs a deep trap for others
will fall into it himself.
Whoever tries to roll a boulder over
others will be crushed by it.

²⁸A liar hates the people he hurts.
And false praise can ruin others.

27 Don't brag about what will
happen tomorrow.
You don't really know what will
happen then.

²Don't praise yourself. Let someone
else do it.
Let the praise come from a stranger
and not from your own mouth.

³Stone is heavy, and sand is hard to
carry.
But the complaining of a foolish
person causes more trouble than
either.

⁴Anger is cruel. It destroys like a flood.
But who can put up with jealousy!

⁵It is better to correct someone openly
than to love him and not show it.

⁶The slap of a friend can be trusted to
help you.
But the kisses of an enemy are
nothing but lies.

⁷When someone is full, not even honey
tastes good.
But when he is hungry, even
something bitter tastes sweet.

⁸A man who leaves his home
is like a bird that leaves its nest.

⁹Perfume and oils make you happy.
And good advice from a friend is
sweet.

¹⁰Don't forget your friend or your
father's friend.
Don't always go to your brother for
help when trouble comes.
A neighbor close by is better than a
brother far away.

¹¹Be wise, my child, and you will make
me happy.
Then I can respond to any insult.

¹²When a wise person sees danger
ahead, he avoids it.
But a foolish person keeps going
and gets into trouble.

¹³Take the coat of someone who
promises to pay what a stranger
owes.
Keep it until he pays the stranger's
bills.

¹⁴Don't greet your neighbor loudly early
in the morning.
He will think of it as a curse.

¹⁵A quarreling wife is as bothersome
as a continual dripping on a rainy
day.
¹⁶Stopping her is like stopping the
wind.
It's like trying to grab oil in your
hand.

¹⁷Iron can sharpen iron.
In the same way, people can help
each other.

¹⁸The person who tends a fig tree will
eat its fruit.
And the person who takes care of
his master will be honored.

¹⁹As water shows you your face,
so your mind shows you what kind
of person you are.

²⁰People will never stop dying and
being destroyed.
In the same way, people will never
stop wanting more than they
have.

²¹A hot furnace tests silver and gold.
And people are tested by the praise
they receive.

²²Even if you ground up a foolish
person like grain in a bowl,
you couldn't remove his
foolishness.

²³Be sure you know how your sheep are
doing.
Pay close attention to the condition
of your cattle.
²⁴Riches will not continue forever.
Nor do governments continue
forever.
²⁵Bring in the hay. Let the new grass
appear.
Gather the grass from the hills.
²⁶Make clothes from the lambs' wool.
Sell some goats to buy a field.
²⁷There will be plenty of goat milk
to feed you and your family.
It will make your servant girls
healthy.

28

Evil people run even though no
one is chasing them.
But good people are as brave as a
lion.

²When a country is disobedient, it has
one ruler after another.
But when it is led by a man with
understanding and knowledge, it
continues strong.

³Rulers who are cruel to the poor
are like a hard rain that destroys
the crops.

⁴People who disobey what they have
been taught praise the wicked.

But those who obey what they have been taught are against the wicked.

⁵Evil people do not understand fairness.
But those who follow the Lord understand it completely.

⁶It is better to be poor and innocent than to be rich and wicked.

⁷The son who obeys what he has been taught
shows he is wise.
But the son who makes friends with those who have no self-control disgraces his father.

⁸Some people get rich by overcharging others.
But their wealth will be given to those who are kind to the poor.

⁹If you refuse to obey what you have been taught,
your prayers will not be heard.

¹⁰Those who lead honest people to do wrong
will be ruined by their own evil.
But the innocent will be rewarded with good things.

¹¹A rich man may think he is wise.
But a poor man who has understanding knows the rich man is wrong.

¹²When good people win, there is great happiness.
But when the wicked get power, everybody hides.

¹³If you hide your sins, you will not succeed.
If you confess and reject them, you will receive mercy.

¹⁴Those who always respect the Lord will be happy.

But those who are stubborn will get into trouble.

¹⁵A wicked ruler is as dangerous to poor people
as a roaring lion or a charging bear.

¹⁶A ruler who is cruel does not have wisdom.
But the one who hates money taken dishonestly will live a long time.

¹⁷A man who is guilty of murder
will run until he dies.
So do not stop him.

¹⁸Innocent people will be kept safe.
But those who are dishonest will suddenly be ruined.

¹⁹The person who works his land will have plenty of food.
But the one who chases useless dreams instead will end up very poor.

²⁰A truthful man will have many blessings.
But those eager to get rich will be punished.

²¹It is not good for a judge to take sides.
But some will sin for just a piece of bread.

²²A selfish person is in a hurry to get rich.
He does not realize his selfishness will make him poor.

²³Those who correct others will later be liked
more than those who give false praise.

²⁴Some people rob their fathers or mothers
and say, "It's not wrong."
Such people are just like those who destroy things.

²⁵A greedy person causes trouble.
But the one who trusts the Lord will succeed.

²⁶The person who trusts in himself is
foolish.
But the person who lives wisely will
be kept safe.

²⁷The person who gives to the poor will
have everything he needs.
But the one who ignores the poor
will have many curses put on
him.

²⁸When the wicked get power,
everybody hides.
But when the wicked die, the good
people do well.

29 Some people are still stubborn
after they have been corrected
many times.
But they will suddenly be hurt
beyond cure.

²When good people do well, everyone
is happy.
But when evil people rule, everyone
groans.

³Whoever loves wisdom makes his
father happy.
But the one who makes friends with
prostitutes*d* wastes his money.

⁴If a king is fair, he makes his country
strong.
But if he takes money dishonestly,
he tears his country down.

⁵Anyone who gives false praise to his
neighbor
is setting a trap for him.

⁶An evil person is trapped by his own
sin.
But a good person can sing and be
happy.

⁷Good people are concerned that the
poor are treated fairly.
But the wicked don't care.

⁸People who make fun of others cause
trouble in a city.
But wise people calm anger down.

⁹A wise man should not take a foolish
person to court.
The fool will only shout or laugh at
him. There will be no peace.

¹⁰Murderers hate honest people.
But those who do right try to
protect them.

¹¹A foolish person loses his temper.
But a wise person controls his
anger.

¹²If a ruler pays attention to lies,
then all his officers will become
wicked.

¹³The poor person and the cruel person
are alike in this way:
The Lord gave eyes to both of them.

¹⁴A king should judge poor people
fairly.
Then his government will continue
forever.

¹⁵Punishment and correction make a
child wise.
If he is left to do as he pleases, he
will disgrace his mother.

¹⁶When there are many wicked people,
there is much sin.
But those who do right will see
them destroyed.

¹⁷Correct your child, and you will be
proud of him.
He will give you pleasure.

¹⁸Where there is no word from God,
people are uncontrolled.
But those who obey what they have
been taught are happy.

¹⁹Words alone cannot correct a servant.
Even if he understands, he won't
respond.

²⁰Sometimes you see people who speak
too quickly.
There is more hope for a foolish
person than for them.

²¹Don't spoil your servant when he is
young.
   If you do, he will bring you grief
later on.

²²An angry person causes trouble.
   A person who easily gets angry sins
a lot.

²³A man's pride will ruin him.
   But a person who is humble will be
honored.

²⁴The partner of a thief is his own worst
enemy.
   He has to testify in court, but he is
afraid to say anything.

²⁵Being afraid of people can get you into
trouble.
   But if you trust the Lord, you will be
safe.

²⁶Many people want to be heard by a
ruler.
   But fairness comes from the Lord.

²⁷Good people hate those who are
dishonest.
   And the wicked hate those who are
honest.

WISE WORDS FROM AGUR

30 These are the words of Agur son
of Jakeh.

This is his message to Ithiel and Ucal:

²"I am the most stupid person there is.
   I have no understanding.
³I have not learned to be wise.
   And I don't know much about God,
the Holy One.
⁴Who has gone up to heaven and come
back down?
   Who can hold the wind in his hand?
Who can gather up the waters in his
coat?
   Who has decided where the ends of
the earth will be?
What is his name? And what is his
son's name?
   Surely, you know!

⁵"Every word of God can be trusted.
   He protects those who come to him
for safety.
⁶Do not add to his words.
   If you do, he will correct you and
prove that you are a liar.

⁷"I ask two things from you, Lord.
   Don't refuse me before I die.
⁸Keep me from lying and being
dishonest.
   And don't make me either rich or
poor.
   Just give me enough food for each
day.
⁹If I have too much, I might reject you.
   I might say, 'I don't know the Lord.'
If I am poor, I might steal.
   Then I would disgrace the name of
my God.

¹⁰"Do not say bad things about a
servant to his master.
   If you do, he will curse you, and you
will suffer for it.

¹¹"Some people curse their fathers.
   And they do not bless their
mothers.
¹²Some people think they are pure.
   But they are not really free from
evil.
¹³Some people have such a proud look!
   They look down on others.
¹⁴Some people have teeth like swords.
   It is as if their jaws are full of
knives.
They want to remove the poor people
from the earth.
   They want to get rid of the needy.

¹⁵"Greed has two daughters.
   Their names are 'Give me. Give me.'
There are three things that are never
satisfied.
   There are really four that never say,
'I've had enough!'
¹⁶These things are the cemetery, the
childless mother,
   the land that never gets enough rain,

and fire that never says, 'I've had
enough!'

17"Don't make fun of your father.
Don't refuse to obey your mother.
If you do, your eye will be pecked out
by the birds of the valley.
You will be eaten by hawks.

18"There are three things that are too
hard for me.
There are really four that I don't
understand:
19the way an eagle flies in the sky,
the way a snake slides over a rock,
the way a ship sails on the sea
and the way a man acts with a girl.

20"This is the way a woman who takes
part in adultery*d* acts:
She sins and doesn't care.
She says, 'I haven't done anything
wrong.'

21"There are three things that make the
earth tremble.
There are really four that it cannot
stand:
22a servant who becomes a king,
a foolish person who has plenty to
eat,
23a hateful woman who gets married
and a maid who replaces her
mistress.

24"There are four things on earth that
are small.
But they are very wise:
25Ants are not very strong.
But they store up food in the
summer.
26Rock badgers are not powerful
animals.
But they can live among the rocks.
27Locusts*d* have no king.
But they all go out in formation.
28And lizards can be caught in the hand.
But they are found even in kings'
palaces.

29"There are three things that strut
proudly.
There are really four that walk as if
they are important:
30Lions are the proudest animals.
They are strong and run from
nothing.
31Roosters and male goats strut proudly.
And so does a king when his army
is around him.

32"You may have been foolish and
proud.
If you planned evil, cover your
mouth.
33Stirring milk makes butter.
Twisting noses makes them bleed.
And stirring up anger makes
trouble."

WISE WORDS OF KING LEMUEL

31 These are the words of King
Lemuel. This is the message his
mother taught him:

2"My son, I gave birth to you.
You are the son I prayed for.
3Don't waste your strength on women.
Don't waste your time on those who
ruin kings.

4"Kings should not drink wine,
Lemuel.
Rulers should not desire beer.
5If they drink, they might forget the
law.
They might keep the needy from
getting their rights.
6Give beer to people who are dying.
And give wine to those who are sad.
7Let them drink and forget their need.
Then they won't remember their
misery anymore.

8"Speak up for those who cannot speak
for themselves.
Defend the rights of all those who
have nothing.
9Speak up and judge fairly.
Defend the rights of the poor and
needy."

THE GOOD WIFE

¹⁰It is hard to find an excellent wife.
> She is worth more than rubies.

¹¹Her husband trusts her completely.
> With her, he has everything he
> needs.

¹²She does him good and not harm
> for as long as she lives.

¹³She looks for wool and linen.
> She likes to work with her hands.

¹⁴She is like a trader's ship.
> She goes far to get food.

¹⁵She gets up while it is still dark.
> She prepares food for her family.
> She also feeds her servant girls.

¹⁶She looks at a field and buys it.
> With money she has earned, she
> plants a vineyard.

¹⁷She does her work with energy.
> Her arms are strong.

¹⁸She makes sure that what she makes
> is good.
> She works by her lamp late into the
> night.

¹⁹She makes thread with her hands
> and weaves her own cloth.

²⁰She welcomes the poor.
> She helps the needy.

²¹She does not worry about her family
> when it snows.
> They all have fine clothes to keep
> them warm.

²²She makes coverings for her bed.
> Her clothes are made of linen and
> other expensive material.

²³Her husband is recognized at the city
> meetings.
> He makes decisions as one of the
> leaders of the land.

²⁴She makes linen clothes and sells
> them.
> She provides belts to the
> merchants.

²⁵She is strong and is respected by the
> people.
> She looks forward to the future with
> joy.

²⁶She speaks wise words.
> And she teaches others to be kind.

²⁷She watches over her family.
> And she is always busy.

²⁸Her children bless her.
> Her husband also praises her.

²⁹He says, "There are many excellent
> wives,
> but you are better than all of
> them."

³⁰Charm can fool you, and beauty can
> trick you.
> But a woman who respects the Lord
> should be praised.

³¹Give her the reward she has earned.
> She should be openly praised for
> what she has done.

ECCLESIASTES

1 These are the words of the Teacher. He is a son of David, king in Jerusalem.
²The Teacher says,

"Useless! Useless!
Completely useless!
All things are useless."

³What do people really gain
from all the hard work they do here
on earth?

THINGS NEVER CHANGE

⁴People live, and people die.
But the earth continues forever.
⁵The sun rises, and the sun sets.
Then it hurries back to the place
where it rises again.
⁶The wind blows to the south.
Then it blows to the north.
It blows from one direction and then
another.
Then it turns around and repeats
the same pattern, going nowhere.
⁷All the rivers flow to the sea.
But the sea never becomes full.
⁸Everything is boring.
It makes you so tired you don't
even want to talk about it.
Words come again and again to our
ears.
But we never can hear enough.
Nor can we ever really see all we
want to see.
⁹All things continue the way they have
been since the beginning.
The same things will be done that
have always been done.
There is nothing new here on earth.
¹⁰A person might say,
"Look, this is new!"
But really it has always been here.
It was here before we were!
¹¹People don't remember what
happened long ago.
In the future, people will not
remember what happens now.

And later, other people will not
remember what was done before
them.

DOES WISDOM BRING HAPPINESS?

¹²I, the Teacher, was king over Israel in Jerusalem. ¹³I decided to use my wisdom. I wanted to learn about everything that happens here on earth. I learned that God has given us terrible things to face here on earth. ¹⁴I looked at everything done here on earth. I saw that it is all a waste of time. It is like chasing the wind.

¹⁵If something is crooked,
you can't make it straight.
If something is missing,
you can't say it is there.

¹⁶I said to myself, "I have become very wise. I am now wiser than anyone who ruled Jerusalem before me. I know what wisdom and knowledge really are." ¹⁷So I decided to find out how wisdom and knowledge are better than foolish thinking. But I learned that trying to become wise is also like chasing the wind.

¹⁸With much wisdom comes much
disappointment.
The person who gains more
knowledge also gains more
sorrow.

DOES "HAVING FUN" BRING HAPPINESS?

2 I said to myself, "I will try having fun. I will enjoy myself." But I found that this is also useless. ²It is foolish to laugh all the time. Having fun gets nothing done. ³I decided to cheer myself up with wine. At the same time my mind was still thinking wisely. I wanted to find a way to enjoy myself. I wanted to see what was good for people to do during their few days of life.

DOES HARD WORK BRING HAPPINESS?

⁴Then I did great things. I built houses, and I planted vineyards for myself. ⁵I

planted gardens, and I made parks. I planted all kinds of fruit trees in them. ⁶I made pools of water for myself. And I used them to water my growing trees. ⁷I bought men and women slaves. Slaves were also born in my house. I had large herds of cattle and flocks of sheep. I had more than anyone in Jerusalem before me. ⁸I also gathered silver and gold for myself. I took treasures from kings and other areas. I had men and women singers. I had all the wives a man could ever want. ⁹I became very famous. I was greater than anyone who had lived in Jerusalem before me. My wisdom helped me in all this.

¹⁰Anything I saw and wanted, I got for
   myself.
I did not miss any pleasure
   I desired.
I was pleased with everything I did.
And this pleasure was the reward
   for all my hard work.
¹¹But then I looked at what I had done.
I thought about all the hard work.
Suddenly I realized it was just a waste
   of time, like chasing the wind!
There is nothing to gain from
   anything we do here on earth.

MAYBE WISDOM IS THE ANSWER

¹²Then I began to think again about
   being wise.
And I thought also about being
   foolish and doing crazy things.
But after all, what more can any king
   do?
He can only do what some other
   king has already done.
¹³I saw that being wise is certainly
   better than being foolish,
just as light is better than darkness.
¹⁴A wise man sees where he is going.
But a foolish person is like someone
   walking around in the dark.
Yet I saw that
   both the foolish person and the
   wise man end the same way.

¹⁵I thought to myself,
   "What happens to a foolish person
     will happen to me, too.
   So what do I get for being so
     wise?"
I said to myself,
   "Being wise is also useless."
¹⁶The wise man and the foolish
   person
   will both die!
People will not remember either one
   forever.
In the future, both will be
   forgotten.

IS THERE REAL HAPPINESS IN LIFE?

¹⁷So I hated life. It made me sad to think that everything here on earth is useless. It is like chasing the wind. ¹⁸I hated all the things I had worked for here on earth. I hated them because I must leave them to someone who will live after me. ¹⁹Someone else will control everything for which I worked so hard here on earth. And I don't know if he will be wise or foolish. This is also useless. ²⁰So I became sad about all the hard work I had done here on earth. ²¹A person can work hard using all his wisdom, knowledge and skill. But he will die, and other people will get the things he worked for. They did not do the work, but they will get everything. This is also unfair and useless. ²²What does a person get for all his work and struggling here on earth? ²³All his life his work is full of pain and sorrow. Even at night his mind doesn't rest. This is also useless.

²⁴The best a person can do is eat, drink and enjoy his work. I saw that even this comes from God. ²⁵No one can eat or enjoy life without God. ²⁶If a person pleases God, God will give him wisdom, knowledge and joy. But the sinner will get only the work of gathering and storing wealth. Then he will have to give it to the one who pleases God. So all his work is useless. It is like chasing the wind.

THERE IS A TIME FOR EVERYTHING

3 There is a right time for everything. Everything on earth has its special season.

[2]There is a time to be born
and a time to die.
There is a time to plant
and a time to pull up plants.
[3]There is a time to kill
and a time to heal.
There is a time to destroy
and a time to build.
[4]There is a time to cry
and a time to laugh.
There is a time to be sad
and a time to dance.
[5]There is a time to throw away stones
and a time to gather them.
There is a time to hug
and a time not to hug.
[6]There is a time to look for something
and a time to stop looking for it.
There is a time to keep things
and a time to throw things away.
[7]There is a time to tear apart
and a time to sew together.
There is a time to be silent
and a time to speak.
[8]There is a time to love
and a time to hate.
There is a time for war
and a time for peace.

GOD CONTROLS HIS WORLD

[9]Does a person really gain anything from his work? [10]I saw the hard work God has given us to do. [11]God has also given us a desire to know the future. God certainly does everything at just the right time. But we can never completely understand what he is doing. [12]So I realize that the best thing for people is to be happy. They should enjoy themselves as long as they live. [13]God wants everyone to eat and drink and be happy in his work. These are gifts from God. [14]I know anything God does will continue forever. People cannot add anything to what God has done. And they cannot take anything away from it.

God does it this way to cause people to honor him.

[15]What happens now has also happened in the past.
Things that will happen in the future have also happened before.
God makes the same things happen again and again.

GOD ALLOWS UNFAIRNESS

[16]I also saw this here on earth:
Where there should have been justice, there was evil.
Where there should have been fairness, there was wickedness.
[17]I certainly believe that
God has planned a time for every thing and every action.
He will judge both good people and bad people.

[18]But I decided that God leaves it the way it is to test people. He wants to show them they are just like animals. [19]The same thing happens to animals and to people. They both have the same breath. So they both die. People are no better off than the animals. The lives of both are soon gone. [20]Both end up the same way. Both came from dust. And both will go back to dust. [21]Who can be sure that the spirit of man goes up to God? Or who can be sure that the spirit of an animal goes down into the ground? [22]So I saw the best thing a person can do is to enjoy his work. That is all he has. No one can help a person see what will happen in the future.

IS IT BETTER TO BE DEAD?

4 Again I saw all the people who were treated badly here on earth.
I saw their tears.
I saw that they had no one to comfort them.
Cruel people had all the power.
There was no one to comfort the people they hurt.

²I decided that the dead
   are better off than the living.
³But those who have never been born
   are better off still.
They have not seen the evil
   that is done here on earth.

WHY WORK SO HARD?
⁴I realized the reason people work hard
and try to succeed: They are jealous of
each other. This, too, is useless. It is like
chasing the wind.

⁵Some say that it is foolish to fold your
      hands and do nothing.
   You will starve to death!
⁶Maybe so, but I say it is better to be
      content
   with what little you have.
Otherwise, you will always be
      struggling for more.
   That is like chasing the wind.

⁷Again I saw something here on earth
      that was senseless:
⁸I saw a person who had no family.
   He had no son or brother.
He always worked hard.
   But he was never satisfied with
      what he had.
He never asked himself, "For whom
      am I working so hard?
   Why don't I let myself enjoy life?"
This also is very sad and senseless.

FRIENDS AND FAMILY GIVE STRENGTH
⁹Two people are better than one.
   They get more done by working
      together.
¹⁰If one person falls,
   the other can help him up.
But it is bad for the person who is
      alone when he falls.
   No one is there to help him.
¹¹If two lie down together, they will be
      warm.
   But a person alone will not be warm.
¹²An enemy might defeat one person,
   but two people together can defend
      themselves.

A rope that has three parts wrapped
      together
   is hard to break.

FAME AND POWER ARE USELESS
¹³A young person may be poor but
wise. He is better than a foolish, old king
who doesn't listen to advice. ¹⁴I saw such
a young person become king. He had
been born poor in the kingdom. He had
even gone to prison before becoming
king. ¹⁵I watched some of the people who
live on earth follow him. They made him
their king. ¹⁶Yes, a great many people followed him at first. But later, they did not
like him, either. So fame and power are
shown to be useless. They are like chasing
the wind.

BE CAREFUL ABOUT MAKING PROMISES
5 Be careful when you go to worship at
   the Temple.ᵈ It is better to listen than
to offer foolish sacrifices. People who do
this don't even know they are doing
wrong.

²Think before you speak.
   Be careful about what you promise
      to God.
God is in heaven,
   and you are on the earth.
   So say only a few words to God.
³The saying is true: Bad dreams come
      from too much worrying.
   So too many words come from
      foolish people.

⁴If you make a promise to God, don't
be slow to keep it. God is not happy with
foolish people. Give God what you promised. ⁵It is better not to promise anything
than to promise something and not do it.
⁶So don't let your words cause you to sin.
Also, don't say to the priest at the Temple,
"I didn't mean what I promised!" If you
do, God will become angry with your
words. He will destroy everything you
have worked for. ⁷Many empty promises
are like many foolish dreams. They mean
nothing. You should honor God.

OFFICERS CHEAT EACH OTHER

8In some countries you will see poor people treated badly. They are not treated fairly or given their rights. Don't be surprised! One officer is cheated by a higher officer. They in turn are cheated by even higher officers. 9The wealth of the country is divided up among them all. Even the king makes sure he gets his share of the profits.

WEALTH CANNOT BUY HAPPINESS

10The person who loves money
    will never have all the money he
        wants.
The person who loves wealth
    will not be satisfied when he gets it.
    This is also useless.
11The more wealth a person has,
    the more friends he has to help him
        spend it.
So what does he really gain?
    He gains nothing except to look at
        his riches.
12A man who works hard sleeps in
        peace.
    It is not important if he has little or
        much to eat.
But a rich person worries about his
        wealth.
    He cannot sleep.

13I have seen something unfair here on
        earth:
    A person suffers harm from saving
        up his money.
14   Then he loses it all in a bad deal.
So he has nothing
    to give to his son.
15A person comes into this world with
        nothing.
    And when he dies, he leaves with
        nothing.
In spite of all his hard work,
    he leaves exactly as he came.
16This, too, is unfair:
He leaves exactly as he came.
    So what does he gain from chasing
        the wind?

17All he gets are days filled with sadness
        and sorrow.
    He ends up sick, defeated and
        angry.

ENJOY YOUR LIFE'S WORK

18I have seen what is best for a person to do here on earth. He should eat and drink and enjoy his work. This is because the life God has given him on earth is short. 19God gives some people the ability to enjoy the wealth and property he gives them. He also gives them the ability to accept their state in life and enjoy their work. 20Such people do not worry much about how short life is. This is because God keeps them busy with the things they love to do.

6 I have seen something else unfair here on earth. It causes serious problems for people. 2God gives some people great wealth, riches and honor. They have everything they want. But God does not let them enjoy such things. Someone else enjoys them instead. This is unfair and senseless. 3It is sad when a person can't enjoy the good things God gives him. Such a person might have 100 children. He might live a long time. But what good is it if he can't enjoy the good God gives him? I say a baby who is born dead is better off than he is. 4It is useless for such a baby to be born. It ends up in the darkness of the grave without even a name. 5That baby never saw the sun. It never knew anything. But it finds more rest than the person who never gets to enjoy the good things God gives him. 6Even if he lives 2,000 years, it is sad if a person can't enjoy the good things God gives him. After all, both he and the baby born dead go to the same place—the grave.

7A person works just to feed himself.
    But he never seems to get enough
        to eat.
8In this way a wise man
    is no better off than a foolish
        person.

Then, too, it does a poor man little
good
to know how to get along in life.
[9]So it is better to be happy with what
you have
than always to be wanting more.
Always wanting more is useless—
like chasing the wind.

WHO CAN UNDERSTAND GOD'S PLAN?

[10]Everything that happens was planned
long ago.
A man is only what he was created
to be.
It is useless to argue with God about it.
This is because God is more
powerful than man is.
[11]The more you argue,
the more useless it is.
You gain nothing at all by arguing.

[12]A person has only a few days of life
on the earth. His short life passes like a
shadow. And who knows what is best for
him while he lives? Who can tell him
what will happen after his time on earth?

SOME BENEFITS OF SERIOUS THINKING

7 It is better to have respect than
good perfume.
The day a person dies is better than
the day he was born.
[2]It is better to go to a funeral
than to a party.
We all must die.
Everyone living should think about
this.
[3]Sorrow is better than laughter.
Sadness has a good influence on
you.
[4]A wise man thinks about death,
but a foolish person thinks only
about having a good time.
[5]It is better to be criticized by a wise
man
than to be praised by a foolish
person.
[6]The laughter of foolish people is
useless.

It is like heating a pot by burning
straw.
There is a lot of fire but no heat.

[7]Even a wise man will become foolish
if he lets money change his
thinking.

[8]It is better to finish something
than to start it.
It is better to be patient
than to be proud.
[9]Don't become mad quickly,
because getting angry is foolish.

[10]Don't ask, "Why was life better in the
'good old days'?"
It is not wise to ask such questions.

[11]Wisdom is as good to have as
inheriting property.
It helps people see what to do.
[12]Wisdom is like money.
They both help a person.
But wisdom is better than money,
because it can save a person's life.

[13]Stop and think about everything that
God causes to happen.
You cannot change a thing,
even if you think it is wrong.
[14]When life is good, enjoy it.
But when life is hard, remember:
God gives us good times and hard
times.
And no one knows what tomorrow
will bring.

IT IS IMPOSSIBLE TO BE TRULY GOOD

[15]In my short life I have seen both of
these:
I have seen good men die being good.
And I have seen evil men living a
long time.
[16]Don't try to be too right all the time.
Don't try to be too wise, either.
Why should you destroy yourself
this way?
[17]Don't be too wicked.
And don't be a foolish person.
You will die young if you do so.

[18]Try to avoid going too far in doing
  anything.
    Those who honor God will avoid
      doing too much of anything.

[19]Wisdom gives a person strength.
    One wise man is stronger than ten
      leaders in a city.

[20]Surely there is not a good man on
  earth
    who always does good and never
      sins.

[21]Don't listen to everything people say.
    You might hear your servant
      insulting you.
[22]You know that many times
    you also have insulted others.

[23]I used wisdom to test all these things.
    I wanted to be wise,
      but it was too hard for me.
[24]I cannot understand why things are as
  they are.
    It is too hard for anyone to
      understand.
[25]I studied and tried very hard to find
  wisdom.
    I tried to find some meaning for
      everything.
    I learned that it is foolish to be evil.
      And it is crazy to act like a fool.

[26]I found that some women are worse
  than death.
    They are as dangerous as traps.
    Their love is like a net.
    Their arms hold men like chains.
    A man who follows God will run away
      from them.
    But a sinner will be caught by them.

[27]The Teacher says, "This is what I
  learned:
    I added all these things together
      to see if I could find some meaning
        for everything.
[28]I am still looking for it,
    but I have not found it.

But I did discover that truly good
  people are hard to find.
    Such people are one in a million!
[29]One thing I have learned:
    God made people good.
      But people have found all kinds of
        ways to be bad."

OBEY THE KING

8 No one is like the wise man.
    He can understand what things
      mean.
    His wisdom makes him happy.
    It makes his sad face happy.

  [2]I advise you always to obey the king's
command. Do this because you made a
promise to God. [3]Don't be too quick to
quit the job the king gave you. But don't
support something that is wrong. Remember, the king does whatever he
pleases. [4]The king is the highest power.
No one can tell him what to do.

[5]A person will be safe if he obeys the
    king's command.
    A wise man knows how to do the
      right thing at the right time.
[6]And there is a right time and a right
    way for everything.
    Yet people often have many
      troubles.
[7]They do not know what the future
  holds.
    No one can tell them what will
      happen.
[8]No one has the power to keep the
    wind from blowing.
    No one has the power to stop his
      own death.
    During war a soldier cannot go home.
    So also, the person who does evil
      will not get away free.

JUSTICE, REWARDS AND PUNISHMENT
[9]I saw all of this as I studied. I considered all that is done here on earth. And I
saw men rule others and hurt them. [10]I
saw evil people being buried. They used
to go in and out of the holy place. Good

things were said about them in the same towns where they had done evil. This is senseless, too.

[11]Sometimes people are not punished right away for the bad things they do. That makes other people want to do bad things, too. [12]A sinner might do a hundred evil things. And he might live a long time. Even so, I know it will be better for those who honor God. They fear him, and he sees it. [13]And I also know it will not go well for evil people. Their lives will be like a brief shadow. They will not live very long. [14]But sometimes something senseless happens on earth. Bad things happen to good people. Good things happen to bad people. This is truly senseless. [15]So I decided it was more important to enjoy life. The best that people can do here on earth is to eat, drink and enjoy life. These joys will help people do the hard work God gives them here on earth.

WE CANNOT UNDERSTAND ALL GOD DOES

[16]I used my mind to learn about all that happens on earth. I saw how busy people are. They work day and night and hardly ever sleep. [17]I also saw all that God has done. Nobody can understand what God does here on earth. No matter how hard a person tries to understand it, he cannot. Even if a wise man says he understands, he really cannot. No one at all can really understand it.

IS DEATH FAIR?

9 I thought about something else and tried hard to understand it. I saw that God takes care of both good people and wise people and what they do. But no one knows if he will see good or bad times.

[2]Both good and bad things happen to everyone.
They happen to those who are fair
    and to those who are wicked.
They happen to those who are good
    and to those who are evil.

They happen to those who sacrifice
    and to those who do not.
The same things happen to a good person
    as happen to a sinner.
The same things happen to a person
    who makes promises to God
    as to one who does not.

[3]This is something unfair that happens here on earth. The same things happen to everyone. So men's minds are full of evil and foolish thoughts while they live. After that, they join the dead. [4]But anyone still alive has hope. Even a live dog is better off than a dead lion!

[5]The living know they will die.
    But the dead no longer think about
        such things.
Dead people have no more reward.
    People forget them.
[6]After a person is dead,
    he can no longer show love or hate
        or jealousy.
And he will never again share
    in the things that happen here on
        earth.

ENJOY LIFE WHILE YOU CAN

[7]So go eat your food and enjoy it.
    Drink your wine and be happy.
It is all right with God
    if you do this.
[8]Put on nice clothes
    and make yourself look good.

[9]Enjoy life with the wife you love. Enjoy all the days of this short life God has given you here on earth. It is all you have. So enjoy the work you have to do here on earth. [10]Whatever work you do, do your best. This is because you are going to the grave. There is no working, no planning, no knowledge and no wisdom there.

TIME AND CHANCE

[11]I also realized something else here on earth that is senseless:
    The fast runner does not always win
        the race.

The strong army does not always
    win the battle.
The wise man does not always have
    food.
The smart man does not always
    become wealthy.
And the man with special skills
    does not always receive praise.
Bad things happen to everyone.
12A person never knows what will
    happen to him next.
He is like a fish caught in a cruel net.
He is like a bird caught in a trap.
In the same way, a person is trapped
    by bad things
    that suddenly happen to him.

WISDOM DOES NOT ALWAYS WIN

13I also saw something wise happen here on earth. And it was very impressive to me. 14There was a small town with only a few people in it. A great king fought against it and put his armies all around it. 15Now there was a wise man in the town. He was poor, but he used his wisdom to save his town. But later on, everyone forgot about him. 16I still think wisdom is better than strength. But those people forgot about the poor man's wisdom. And they stopped listening to what he said.

17The quiet words of a wise man are
    better
    than the shouts of a foolish ruler.
18Wisdom is better than weapons of
    war.
    But one sinner can destroy much
    good.

10 Dead flies will make even
    perfume smell bad.
In the same way, a little foolishness
    can ruin
    a wise man's fame for wisdom.
2A wise man's heart leads him in the
    right way.
But the heart of a foolish person
    leads him in the wrong way.
3A foolish person is not wise.
    It shows in everything he does.

Even as he walks along the road,
    he shows everyone how stupid he is.
4Don't leave your job
    just because the ruler is angry with
    you.
Remain calm.
    It will help correct your mistakes.

5Here is something else unfair that
    happens here on earth.
It is the kind of mistake rulers
    make:
6Foolish people are given important
    positions
    while rich people are given less
    important ones.
7I have seen servants ride on horses
    while princes walk beside them on
    foot.
8Anyone who digs a pit might fall into
    it.
    Anyone who knocks down a wall
    might be bitten by a snake.
9Anyone who moves large stones
    might be hurt by them.
    And anyone who cuts logs might
    get hurt while doing it.
10Cutting logs with a dull ax
    makes you work harder.
A wise man will sharpen his ax.
    In the same way, wisdom can make
    any job easier.
11Someone might know how to control
    snakes.
    But what good is such wisdom if the
    snake has already bitten him?

12A wise man's words bring him praise.
    But a foolish person's words will
    destroy him.
13A foolish person begins by saying
    something foolish.
    In the end he is saying even crazier
    things.
14A foolish person talks too much about
    what he will do.
No one knows the future.
    No one can tell him what will
    happen after he dies.

¹⁵A foolish person doesn't know even
   the most obvious things.
   He can't even find his way back to
      town.
   So he has to wear himself out
      working.

THE VALUE OF WORK

¹⁶How terrible it will be for a country
   if its king is a child.
   How terrible it will be for that country
   if its leaders have parties all the
      time.
¹⁷A country is well off
   if its king comes from a good
      family.
   It is good for a country
   if its leaders control their eating
      and drinking.
   They should eat and drink for
      strength,
   not to get drunk.

¹⁸If a person is lazy and doesn't repair
   the roof,
   it will begin to fall.
   If he refuses to fix it,
   the house will leak.

¹⁹A party makes you feel good.
   And wine makes you feel happy.
   But both cost you a lot of money.

²⁰Don't say or think bad things about
   the king.
   And don't say bad things about rich
   people even alone in your
      bedroom.
   A little bird might report it to others.
   A bird might fly to them and tell all
   you said.

BOLDLY FACE THE FUTURE

11 Do good things everywhere you
   go.ⁿ
   After a while the good you do will
      return to help you.
²Invest what you have in several
   different businesses.

You don't know what bad things
   might happen on earth.
³If clouds are full of rain,
   they will pour water on the earth.
   A tree can fall to the north or south.
   But it will stay where it falls.
⁴If a person waits for perfect weather,
   he will never plant his seeds.
   And if he is afraid that every cloud
   will bring rain,
   he will never harvest his crops.

⁵You don't know where the wind will
      blow.
   And you don't know how a baby
   grows in its mother's body.
   In the same way, God certainly made
      all things.
   But you can't understand what he is
      doing.
⁶Begin planting early in the morning,
   and don't stop working until
      evening.
   This is because you don't know which
   things you do will succeed.
   It is even possible that everything
   you do will succeed.

SERVE GOD WHILE YOU ARE YOUNG

⁷It is good to be alive
   to enjoy the light of day.
⁸A person ought to enjoy every day of
   his life.
   This is true no matter how long he
      lives.
   But he should also remember this:
   You will be dead much longer than
   you live.
   After you are dead, you accomplish
      nothing.
⁹Young people, enjoy yourselves while
   you are young.
   Be happy while you are young.
   Do whatever your heart desires.
   Do whatever you want to do.
   But remember that God will judge you
   for everything you do.

11:1 Do good . . . go Literally, "Throw your bread upon the water."

[10]So avoid sorrow and sadness.
Forget about all the bad things that
happen to you.
This is because the joys of youth
pass quickly away.

THE PROBLEMS OF OLD AGE

12 Remember your Creator while
you are young.
Your old age is coming
when you will have many troubles.
When that time comes,
you won't have much to enjoy.
[2]When you become old,
the light from the sun, moon and
stars will seem dark to you.
It will seem as if the rain clouds
never go away.
[3]At that time your arms will lose their
strength.
Your strong legs will become weak
and bent.
Your teeth will fall out so you cannot
chew.
Your eyes will not see clearly.
[4]Your ears will be deaf to the noise in
the streets.
You will barely hear singing.
The sound of the millstone grinding
your grain will seem very quiet.
But you'll wake up when a bird first
starts singing!
[5]You will fear high places.
And you will be afraid to go for a
walk because you may fall.
Your hair will become white like the
flowers on an almond tree.
You will limp along like a
grasshopper when you walk.
Your desires will be gone.
Then you will go to your everlasting
home.
And people will go to your funeral.

[6]Remember God before your life is
snapped like a silver chain.
Remember God before your life is
broken like a golden bowl.
It will be as useless as a broken bucket
at the spring.
It will be no good, like a broken
wheel at a water well.
[7]Your body will become part of the
dust of the earth again.
But your spirit will return to God
who gave it.

[8]Everything is useless!
The Teacher says that everything is
useless.

CONCLUSION

[9]The Teacher was very wise. He taught
the people what he knew. The Teacher
very carefully thought about, studied and
set in order many wise teachings. [10]The
Teacher looked for just the right words.
He wrote teachings that are dependable
and true.

[11]Words from wise men are like sharp
sticks used to guide animals. These words
are like nails that have been driven in
firmly. They are wise teachings that come
from God the Shepherd. [12]So be careful,
my son, about other teachings. People
are always writing books. And too much
study will make you very tired.

[13]Now, everything has been heard.
Here is my final advice:
Honor God and obey his commands.
This is the most important thing
people can do.
[14]God knows everything people do,
even the things done in secret.
He knows all the good and all
the bad.
He will judge everything people do.

SONG OF SONGS

1 Solomon's Song of Songs.

THE WOMAN SPEAKS TO THE MAN SHE LOVES

²Kiss me with the kisses of your mouth!
  Your love is better than wine.
³The smell of your perfume is pleasant.
  Your name is pleasant like
    expensive perfume!
  That's why the young women love
    you.
⁴Take me with you; let's run.
  The king takes me into his rooms.

FRIENDS SPEAK TO THE MAN

 We will rejoice and be happy with
    you.
  We praise your love more than
    wine.

THE WOMAN SPEAKS

 With good reason, the young women
    love you, my lover.
⁵I'm dark but lovely,
  women of Jerusalem.
  I'm dark like the tents of Kedar,
  like the curtains of Solomon.
⁶Don't look at how dark I am,
  at how dark the sun has made me.
 My brothers were angry with me.
  They made me tend the vineyards.
  So I haven't tended my own
    vineyard!
⁷Tell me, you whom I love,
  where do you feed your sheep?
  Where do you make them rest at
    noon?
 Why should I look for you near your
    friend's sheep?
  Am I like a woman who wears a
    veil?ⁿ

THE MAN SPEAKS TO THE WOMAN

⁸You are the most beautiful of women.
  Surely you know to follow the sheep.

 Feed your young goats
  near the shepherds' tents.
⁹My darling, you are like a mare
  that pulls the king's chariots.
¹⁰Your cheeks are beautiful with
    ornaments.
  Your neck is beautiful with jewels.
¹¹We will make for you gold earrings
  with silver hooks.

THE WOMAN SPEAKS

¹²The smell of my perfume spreads out
  to the king on his couch.
¹³My lover is like a bag of myrrh*d*
  that lies all night between my
    breasts.
¹⁴My lover is like a bunch of flowers
  from the vineyards at En Gedi.

THE MAN SPEAKS

¹⁵My darling, you are beautiful!
  Oh, you are beautiful!
  Your eyes are like doves!

THE WOMAN ANSWERS THE MAN

¹⁶You are so handsome, my lover.
  You are so pleasant!
  Our bed is the grass.
¹⁷The boards of our house are cedar
    trees.
  And the wood of our ceiling is
    juniper trees.

THE WOMAN SPEAKS AGAIN

2 I am a rose in the Plain of Sharon.
  I am a lily in the valleys.

THE MAN SPEAKS AGAIN

 ²Among the young women, my darling
  is like a lily among thorns!

THE WOMAN ANSWERS

 ³Among young men, my lover
  is like an apple tree among the trees
    in the woods!
 I enjoy sitting in his shadow.
  His fruit is sweet to my taste.

1:7 **veil** This was the way a prostitute usually dressed.

⁴He brought me to the banquet room.
  His banner over me is love.
⁵Strengthen me with raisins.
  Refresh me with apples,
  because I am weak with love.
⁶My lover's left hand is under my head.
  And his right arm holds me tight!

THE WOMAN SPEAKS TO THE FRIENDS
⁷Women of Jerusalem, promise me
  by the gazelles*d* and the deer.
  Promise not to wake love.
  Don't excite my feelings of love
  until I'm ready.

THE WOMAN SPEAKS AGAIN
⁸I hear my lover's voice.
  He comes jumping across the
    mountains.
  He comes skipping over the hills!
⁹My lover is like a gazelle*d* or a young
    deer.
  Look, he stands behind our wall.
  He stares in through the windows,
  looking through the blinds.
¹⁰My lover spoke. He said to me,
  "Get up, my darling.
  Let's go away, my beautiful one.
¹¹Look, the winter is past.
  The rains are over and gone.
¹²Blossoms appear through all the land.
  The time has come to sing.
  The cooing of doves is heard in our
    land.
¹³There are young figs on the fig trees.
  The blossoms on the vines smell
    sweet.
  Get up, my darling.
  Let's go away, my beautiful one."

THE MAN SPEAKS
¹⁴My beloved is like a dove that hides in
    the cracks of the rock.
  She hides in the secret places of the
    cliff.
  Show me your face.
  Let me hear your voice.
  Your voice is very sweet,
  and your face is lovely.

¹⁵Catch the foxes for us—
  the little foxes that ruin the vineyards.
  Our vineyards are in blossom.

THE WOMAN SPEAKS
¹⁶My lover is mine, and I am his.
  He feeds among the lilies
¹⁷until the day dawns
  and the shadows disappear.
  Turn, my lover.
  Be like a gazelle*d* or a young deer
  on the rugged mountains.

THE WOMAN DREAMS
3 At night on my bed,
  I looked for the one I love.
  I looked for him, but I could not find
    him.
²I will get up now. I will go around the
    city,
  in the streets and squares.
  I will look for the one I love.
  I looked for him, but I could not
    find him.
³The watchmen found me as they
    patrolled the city.
  I asked, "Have you seen the one
    I love?"
⁴As soon as I had left them
  I found the one I love.
  I held him. I would not let him go
  until I had brought him to my
    mother's house.
  I brought him into the room where
    I was born.

THE WOMAN SPEAKS TO THE FRIENDS
⁵Women of Jerusalem, promise me
  by the gazelles*d* and the deer.
  Promise not to wake love.
  Don't excite my feelings of love
  until I'm ready.
⁶Who is this coming out of the desert
  like a cloud of smoke?
  Who is this that smells like myrrh,*d*
    incense*d*
  and other spices?
⁷Look, it's Solomon's couch*n*
  with 60 soldiers around it.

3:7 couch Something like a bed carried by slaves on which the king lay or sat while traveling.

They are the finest soldiers of
   Israel.
[8]These soldiers all carry swords.
   They have been trained in war.
Every man wears his sword at his
   side.
He is ready for the dangers of the
   night.
[9]King Solomon had a couch made for
   himself.
   It is made of wood from Lebanon.
[10]He made its posts of silver
   and its braces of gold.
The seat was covered with purple
   cloth.
   The women of Jerusalem wove it
   with love.
[11]Women of Jerusalem, go out and see
   King Solomon.
   He is wearing the crown his mother
   put on his head.
It was his wedding day,
   when his heart was happy!

THE MAN SPEAKS TO THE WOMAN

4 How beautiful you are, my darling!
   Oh, you are beautiful!
Your eyes behind your veil are like
   doves.
   Your hair is like a flock of goats
   streaming down Mount Gilead.
[2]Your teeth are white like newly-
   sheared sheep
   just coming from their bath.
Each one has a twin.
   None of them is alone.
[3]Your lips are like red silk thread.
   Your mouth is lovely.
Your cheeks behind your veil
   are like slices of a pomegranate.[d]
[4]Your neck looks like David's tower.
   The tower was built with rows of
   stones.
A thousand shields hang on its walls.
   Each shield belongs to a strong
   soldier.
[5]Your breasts are like two fawns.
   They are like twins of a gazelle,[d]
   eating among the lilies.

[6]Until the day dawns
   and the shadows disappear,
I will go to that mountain of myrrh.[d]
   And I will go to that hill
   of incense.[d]
[7]My darling, everything about you is
   beautiful.
   There is nothing at all wrong with
   you.
[8]Come with me from Lebanon, my
   bride.
   Come with me from Lebanon.
Come from the top of Mount
   Amana,
   from the tops of Mount Senir and
   Mount Hermon.
Come from the lions' dens
   and from the leopards' hills.
[9]My sister, my bride,
   you have thrilled my heart.
You have thrilled my heart
   with a glance of your eyes,
   with one jewel from your necklace.
[10]Your love is so sweet, my sister, my
   bride!
   Your love is better than wine.
   Your perfume smells better than
   any spice.
[11]My bride, your lips drip honey.
   Honey and milk are under your
   tongue.
   Your clothes smell like the cedars of
   Lebanon.
[12]My sister, my bride, you are like a
   garden locked up.
   You are like a spring with a wall
   around it, a fountain that is
   closed.
[13]Your limbs are like an orchard
   of pomegranates and all the best
   fruit.
   It is filled with flowers and nard.[d]
[14]It also has saffron,[d] calamus[d] and
   cinnamon.
   It is filled with trees of incense,
   myrrh and aloes[d]—
   all the best spices.

¹⁵You are like a garden fountain—
    a well of fresh water
    flowing down from the mountains
        of Lebanon.

THE WOMAN SPEAKS

¹⁶Awake, north wind!
    Come, you south wind!
Blow on my garden.
    Let its sweet smells flow out.
Let my lover enter the garden.
    And let him eat its best fruits.

THE MAN SPEAKS

5 I have entered my garden,
    my sister, my bride.
    I have gathered my myrrh*ᵈ* with my
        spice.
    I have eaten my honeycomb and my
        honey.
    I have drunk my wine and my milk.

THE FRIENDS SPEAK

Eat, friends, and drink.
    Yes, drink deeply, lovers.

THE WOMAN DREAMS

²I sleep, but my heart is awake.
    I hear my lover knocking.
"Open to me, my sister, my darling,
    my dove, my perfect one.
My head is wet with dew.
    And my hair is wet with the
        dampness of the night."
³I have taken off my garment.
    I don't want to put it on again!
I have washed my feet.
    I don't want to get them dirty again!
⁴My lover put his hand through the
        door opening.
    I felt excited inside.
⁵I got up to open the door for my lover.
    Myrrh*ᵈ* was dripping from my
        hands.
Myrrh was flowing from my fingers,
    onto the handles of the lock.
⁶I opened the door for my lover.
    But my lover had left. He was gone.
When he had spoken, he had taken
    my breath away.

I looked for him, but I could not find
        him.
    I called for him, but he did not
        answer me.
⁷The watchmen found me
    as they patrolled the city.
They hit me; they hurt me.
    The guards on the wall took away
        my coat.
⁸I tell you, women of Jerusalem,
    if you find my lover,
    tell him I am weak with love.

THE FRIENDS ANSWER THE WOMAN

⁹Is your lover better than other lovers,
    you, the most beautiful of women?
Is your lover better than other lovers?
    Is that why you talk like this?

THE WOMAN ANSWERS THE FRIENDS

¹⁰My lover is clean and tanned.
    He's the best of 10,000 men.
¹¹His head is like the finest gold.
    His hair is wavy and black like a
        raven.
¹²His eyes are like doves
    by springs of water.
They seem to be bathed in cream.
    They are set like jewels.
¹³His cheeks are like garden beds of
        spices.
    They smell like mounds of
        perfume.
His lips are like lilies
    flowing with myrrh.*ᵈ*
¹⁴His hands are like gold hinges,
    filled with jewels.
His body is like smooth ivory
    covered with sapphires.
¹⁵His legs are like large marble posts,
    standing on bases of fine gold.
He is tall like a cedar of Lebanon—
    like the best cedar trees.
¹⁶His mouth is sweet to kiss.
    I desire him very much.
Yes, daughters of Jerusalem,
    this is my lover.
    This is my friend.

THE FRIENDS SPEAK TO THE WOMAN

6 Where has your lover gone,
most beautiful of women?
Which way did your lover turn?
We will look for him with you.

THE WOMAN ANSWERS THE FRIENDS

²My lover has gone down to his garden.
He has gone to the garden beds of
spices
to feed in the gardens
and to gather lilies.
³I belong to my lover.
And my lover belongs to me.
He feeds among the lilies.

THE MAN SPEAKS TO THE WOMAN

⁴My darling, you are as beautiful as the
city of Tirzah.
You are as lovely as the city of
Jerusalem.
You are as wonderful as an army
flying flags.
⁵Turn your eyes from me.
They excite me too much!
Your hair is like a flock of goats
streaming down Mount Gilead.
⁶Your teeth are white like sheep
just coming from their bath.
Each one has a twin.
None of them is alone.
⁷Your cheeks behind your veil
are like slices of a pomegranate.ᵈ
⁸There may be 60 queens and 80 slave
womenᵈ
and so many girls you cannot count
them.
⁹But there is only one like my dove, my
perfect one.
She is her mother's only daughter,
the brightest of the one who gave
her birth.
The young women saw her and called
her happy.
The queens and the slave women
also praised her.

THE YOUNG WOMEN PRAISE THE WOMAN

¹⁰Who is that young woman?
She shines out like the dawn.
She's as pretty as the moon.
She's as bright as the sun.
And she's as wonderful
as an army flying flags.

THE MAN SPEAKS

¹¹I went down into the orchard of nut
trees.
I went to see the blossoms of the
valley.
I went to look for buds on the vines,
to see if the pomegranateᵈ trees had
bloomed.
¹²My desire for you makes me feel
like a prince in a chariot.

THE FRIENDS CALL TO THE WOMAN

¹³Come back, come back, woman of
Shulam.
Come back, come back,
so we may look at you!

THE WOMAN ANSWERS THE FRIENDS

Why do you want to look at the
woman of Shulam
as you would at the dance of two
groups?

THE MAN SPEAKS TO THE WOMAN

7 Your feet are beautiful in sandals,
you daughter of a prince.
Your round thighs are like jewels
shaped by an artist.
²Your navel is like a round drinking
cup
always filled with wine.
Your stomach is like a pile of wheat
with lilies around it like a fence.
³Your breasts are like two fawns.
They are like twins of a gazelle.ᵈ
⁴Your neck is like an ivory tower.
Your eyes are like the pools in
Heshbon
near the gate of Bath Rabbim.
Your nose is like a tower of Lebanon
which looks toward Damascus.
⁵Your head is like Mount Carmel.
And your hair is like purple cloth.
The king is captured in its folds.
⁶You are beautiful.
You are very pleasant.
My love, you are full of delights!

[7]You are tall like a palm tree.
>Your breasts are like its bunches of
>fruit.

[8]I said, "I will climb up the palm tree.
>I will take hold of its fruit."
Let your breasts be like bunches of
>grapes.
Let the smell of your breath be like
>apples.

[9] And let your mouth be like the best
>wine.

THE WOMAN SPEAKS TO THE MAN

Let this wine go down sweetly for my
>lover.
>May it flow gently past the lips and
>teeth.

[10]I belong to my lover,
>and he desires only me.

[11]Come, my lover.
>Let's go out into the country.
>Let's spend the night in the fields.

[12]Let's go early to the vineyards.
>Let's see if the buds are on the vines.
Let's see if the blossoms have already
>opened
>and if the pomegranates[d] have
>bloomed.
There I will give you my love.

[13]The mandrake flowers give their
>sweet smell.
>And at our gates there are all the
>best fruits.
I have saved them for you, my lover,
>the old delights and the new.

8 I wish you were like my brother
>who was fed at my mother's
>breasts!
If I found you outside,
>I would kiss you.
>And no one would look down on
>me.

[2]I would lead you and bring you
>to my mother's house.
>She is the one who has taught me.
I would give you a drink of spiced
>wine
>from my pomegranates.

THE WOMAN SPEAKS TO THE FRIENDS

[3]My lover's left hand is under
>my head.
>And his right arm holds me tight!

[4]Women of Jerusalem, promise me.
>Promise not to wake love.
Don't excite my feelings of love
>until I'm ready.

THE FRIENDS SPEAK

[5]Who is this coming out of the desert,
>leaning on her lover?

THE MAN SPEAKS TO THE WOMAN

I woke you under the apple tree.
>It was there that you were born.
>There your mother gave birth
>to you.

[6]Put me like a seal on your heart,
>like a seal on your arm.
Love is as strong as death.
>Desire is as strong as the grave.
Love bursts into flames.
>It burns like a very hot fire.

[7]Even much water cannot put out the
>flame of love.
>Floods cannot drown love.
If a man offered everything in his
>house for love,
>people would totally reject it.

THE WOMAN'S BROTHERS SPEAK

[8]We have a little sister,
>and her breasts are not yet
>grown.
What should we do for our sister
>on the day she becomes engaged?

[9]If she is a wall,
>we will put silver towers on her.
If she is a door,
>we will protect her with cedar
>boards.

THE WOMAN SPEAKS

[10]I am a wall,
>and my breasts are like towers.
So I was to him,
>as one who brings happiness.

[11]Solomon had a vineyard at Baal
>Hamon.

He rented the vineyards for others
    to tend.
Everyone who rented had to pay
    25 pounds of silver for the fruit.
[12]But my own vineyard is mine
    to give.
Solomon, the 25 pounds of silver
    are for you.
And 5 pounds are for those who
    tend the fruit.

THE MAN SPEAKS TO THE WOMAN

[13]You who live in the gardens,
    my friends are listening for your
      voice.
    Let me hear it!

THE WOMAN SPEAKS TO THE MAN

[14]Hurry, my lover.
    Be like a gazelle[d]
or a young deer
    on the mountains where spices grow.

ISAIAH

1 This is the vision Isaiah son of Amoz saw. God showed Isaiah what would happen to Judah and Jerusalem. Isaiah saw these things while Uzziah, Jotham, Ahaz and Hezekiah were kings of Judah.

GOD FINDS FAULT WITH HIS PEOPLE

²Heaven and earth, listen,
   because the Lord is speaking:
"I raised my children and helped
      them grow.
   But they have turned against me.
³An ox knows its master.
      And a donkey knows where its
         owner feeds it.
   But the people of Israel do not know me.
   My people do not understand."

⁴Terrible times are coming for Israel,
      a nation of sin.
   The people are loaded down with
      guilt.
They are like a group of children
      doing evil.
   They are full of evil.
They have left the Lord.
   They hate God, the Holy One of
      Israel.
   They have turned away from him.

⁵Why should you continue to be
      punished?
   Why do you continue to turn
      against him?
Your whole head is hurt.
   And your whole heart is sick.
⁶There is no healthy spot
   from the bottom of your foot to the
      top of your head.
   You are covered with wounds, hurts
      and open sores.
Your wounds are not cleaned and
      covered.
   No medicine takes away the pain.

⁷Your land is ruined.
   Your cities have been burned with
      fire.

While you watch,
   your enemies are stealing
      everything from your land.
   Your land is ruined like a country
      destroyed by enemies.
⁸Jerusalem is left alone
   like an empty shelter in a vineyard.
It is like a hut left in a field of
      melons.
   It is like a city surrounded by
      enemies.
⁹The Lord of heaven's armies
   allowed a few of our people to live.
   Otherwise we would have been
      completely destroyed
   like the cities of Sodom and
      Gomorrah.

¹⁰Jerusalem, your rulers are like those
      of Sodom.
   Your people are like those of
      Gomorrah.
Hear the word of the Lord.
   Listen to the teachings of our God!
¹¹The Lord says,
   "I do not want all these sacrifices
      you give me.
I have had enough of your sacrifices
   of male sheep and fat from fine
      animals.
I am not pleased
   by the blood of bulls, sheep and
      goats.
¹²You come to meet with me.
   But who asked you to do
      all this running in and out?
¹³Don't continue bringing me worthless
      sacrifices!
   I hate the incense*d* you burn.
I can't stand your New Moons,*d*
      Sabbaths*d* and other feast days.
   I can't stand the evil you do in
      holding your holy meetings.
¹⁴I hate your New Moon feasts
   and your other yearly feasts.

They have become like heavy weights
　　on me.
　　I am tired of carrying them.
¹⁵You will raise your arms in prayer to
　　me.
　　But I will refuse to look at you.
Even if you say many prayers,
　　I will not listen to you.
It's because your hands are full of
　　blood.
¹⁶Wash yourselves and make yourselves
　　clean.^d
　　Stop doing the evil things I see you
　　do.
Stop doing wrong!
¹⁷　Learn to do good.
Be fair to other people.
　　Punish those who hurt others.
Help the orphans.
　　Stand up for the rights of widows."

¹⁸The Lord says,
　　"Come, we will talk these things
　　over.
Your sins are red like deep red cloth.
　　But they can be as white as snow.
Your sins are bright red.
　　But you can be white like wool.
¹⁹If you will obey me,
　　you will eat good crops from the
　　land.
²⁰But if you refuse to obey and if you
　　turn against me,
　　you will be destroyed by your
　　enemies' swords."
The Lord himself said these things.

JERUSALEM IS NOT LOYAL TO GOD
²¹The city of Jerusalem once followed
　　the Lord.
　　But she is no longer loyal to the
　　Lord.
She used to be filled with fairness.
　　People there lived the way God
　　wanted.
　　But now, murderers live there.
²²Jerusalem, you have become like the
　　scum left when silver is purified.
　　You are like wine mixed with water.

²³Your rulers are rebels.
　　They are friends of thieves.
They all accept money for doing
　　wrong things.
　　They are paid to cheat people.
They don't try to help the orphans.
　　And they don't listen to the widows'
　　needs.
²⁴The Master, the Lord of heaven's
　　armies,
　　the Mighty One of Israel, says:
"You, my enemies, will not cause me
　　any more trouble.
　　I will pay you back for what you did.
²⁵I will turn against you.
　　I will clean away all your wrongs as
　　if with soap.
　　I will take all the worthless things
　　out of you.
²⁶I will bring back judges as you had
　　long ago.
　　Your counselors will be like the
　　ones you had in the beginning.
Then you will be called the City That
　　Is Right with God.
　　You will be called the Loyal City."

²⁷Because the Lord does what is fair,
　　he will rescue Jerusalem.
Because the Lord does what is right,
　　he will save her people who come
　　back to him.
²⁸But sinners and those who turn
　　against him will be destroyed.
　　Those who have left the Lord will
　　die.

²⁹"You will be ashamed
　　because you have worshiped false
　　gods under the oak trees.
You will be disgraced
　　because you have worshiped idols
　　in your gardens.
³⁰You will be like an oak whose leaves
　　are dying.
　　You will be like a garden without
　　water.
³¹Powerful people will be like small, dry
　　pieces of wood.

And what they do will be like
　　sparks.
The people and what they do will
　　burn together.
And no one will be able to stop that
　　fire."

THE MESSAGE ABOUT JERUSALEM

2 Isaiah son of Amoz saw this message about Judah and Jerusalem.
[2] In the last days
　the mountain on which the Lord's
　　Temple[d] stands
　will become the most important of
　　all mountains.
It will be raised above the hills.
　And people from all nations will
　　come streaming to it.
[3] Many nations will come and say,
　"Come, let us go up to the
　　mountain of the Lord.
　Let us go to the Temple of the God
　　of Jacob.
Then God will teach us his ways.
　And we will obey his teachings."
The Lord's teachings will go out from
　　Jerusalem.
　The Lord's message will go out
　　from Jerusalem.
[4] Then the Lord will settle arguments
　　among many nations.
　He will make decisions for strong
　　nations that are far away.
Then the nations will make their
　　swords into plows.
　They will make their spears into
　　hooks for trimming trees.
Nations will no longer fight other
　　nations.
　They will not even train for war
　　anymore.

[5] Come, family of Jacob.
　We should follow the way of the
　　Lord.

A TERRIBLE DAY IS COMING

[6] Lord, you have left your people,
　the family of Jacob.

They have become filled with wrong
　　ideas from people in the East.
　Your people try to tell the future
　　like the Philistines.
They have completely accepted
　　those foreign ideas.
[7] Their land has been filled with silver
　　and gold.
　There are a great many treasures
　　there.
Their land has been filled with horses.
　There are many chariots there.
[8] Their land is full of idols.
　The people worship these idols that
　　they made with their own hands.
They worship statues shaped by
　　their fingers.
[9] People will not be proud any longer.
　They will bow low with shame.
　God, do not forgive them.

[10] Go into the caves of the cliffs.
　Dig holes and hide in the ground.
Hide from the anger of the Lord
　and from his great power!
[11] Proud people will stop being proud.
　They will bow low with shame.
At that time only the Lord will still be
　　praised.

[12] The Lord of heaven's armies has a
　　certain day planned.
　On that day he will punish the
　　proud and those who brag.
They will no longer be important.
[13] He will bring down the tall cedar trees
　　from Lebanon.
　He will destroy the great oak trees
　　of Bashan.
[14] He will destroy all the tall mountains
　　and the high hills.
[15] He will knock down every tall tower
　　and every high, strong wall.
[16] He will sink all the trading ships.
　And he will destroy the beautiful
　　ships.
[17] At that time proud people will stop
　　being proud.
　They will bow low with shame.

And at that time only the Lord will be
  praised.
18 But all the idols will be gone.

19People will run to caves in the rocky
    cliffs.
  They will dig holes and hide in the
    ground.
  They will hide from the anger of the
    Lord
    and his great power.
  They will do this when the Lord
    stands to shake the earth.
20At that time people will throw away
    their gold and silver idols.
  They made these idols for themselves
    to worship.
  But they will throw them away to
    the bats and moles.
21Then the people will hide in caves
    and cracks in the rocks.
  They will hide from the anger of the
    Lord
    and his great power.
  They will do this when the Lord
    stands to shake the earth.

22You should stop trusting in people to
    save you.
  People are only human.
  They aren't able to help you.

GOD WILL PUNISH JUDAH AND JERUSALEM

3 Understand what I am telling you.
  The Master, the Lord of heaven's
    armies,
  will take away everything Judah and
    Jerusalem need.
  He will take away all the food and
    water.
2He will take away all the heroes and
    great soldiers.
  He will take away all the judges,
    prophets,d
  people who do magic and elders.
3He will take away the military leaders
    and government leaders.

He will take away the counselors,
  the skilled craftsmen and those
  who try to tell the future.
4The Lord says, "I will cause young
    boys to be your leaders.
  Foolish children will rule over you.
5Everyone will be against everyone
    else.
  Young people will not respect older
    people.
  Common people will not respect
    important people."
6At that time a man will grab one of his
    brothers
  from his own family and say,
"You have a coat. So you will be our
    leader.
  You will be the leader over all these
    ruins."
7But that brother will stand up and say,
  "I cannot help you.
  I do not have food or clothes in my
    house.
  You will not make me your
    leader."
8This will happen because Jerusalem
    has stumbled
  and Judah has fallen.
  The things they say and do are against
    the Lord.
  They sin openly against the Lord.
9The look on their faces shows they are
    guilty of doing wrong.
  Like the people of Sodom, they are
    proud of their sin.
  They don't care who sees it.
  How terrible it will be for them!
  They have brought much trouble to
    themselves.
10Tell the good people that good things
    will happen to them.
  They will receive a reward for the
    good they do.
11But how terrible it will be for wicked
    people!
  They will be punished for all the
    wrong they have done.

[12]Children treat my people cruelly.
　Women rule over them.
My people, your guides lead you in
　the wrong way.
　They turn you away from what is
　　right.

[13]The Lord takes his place in court.
　He stands to judge the people.
[14]The Lord presents his case
　against the elders and other leaders
　　of his people.
He says, "You have burned my
　vineyard.
　Your houses are full of what you
　　took from the poor.
[15]What gives you the right to crush my
　people?
　How can you grind the faces of the
　　poor into the dirt?"
The Master, the Lord of heaven's
　armies, said this.

A WARNING TO WOMEN OF JERUSALEM

[16]The Lord says,
　"The women of Jerusalem are proud.
They walk around with their heads
　held high.
　They flirt with their eyes.
They take quick, short steps,
　making noise with their ankle
　　bracelets."
[17]So the Lord will put sores on the
　heads of those women in
　　Jerusalem.
　He will make them lose all their hair.

[18]At that time the Lord will take away everything that makes them proud. He will take away their beautiful ankle bracelets, their headbands and their necklaces shaped like the moon. [19]He will take away their earrings, bracelets and veils. [20]He will take away their scarves, ankle chains, the cloth belts worn around their waists, their bottles of perfume and charms. [21]He will take away their signet[d] rings, nose rings, [22]their fine robes, capes, shawls and purses. [23]And he will take away their mirrors, linen dresses, turbans and long shawls.

[24]Instead of having sweet-smelling
　perfume, they will stink.
Instead of fine cloth belts, they will
　have ropes of captives to wear.
Instead of having their hair fixed in
　fancy ways, they will be bald.
Instead of fine clothes, they will
　have rough clothes of sadness.
Instead of having beauty, they will
　have the brand of a captive.
[25]At that time your men will be killed
　with swords.
　Your heroes will die in war.
[26]There will be crying and sadness in the
　meeting places near the city gates.
Jerusalem will be like a woman who
　has lost everything and sits on
　　the ground.

4 At that time seven women
　will grab one man.
They will say, "We will make our own
　bread.
　And we will make our own clothes.
But please marry us!
　Please, take away our shame."

THE BRANCH OF THE LORD

[2]At that time the Lord's branch will be very beautiful and great. The people still living in Israel will be proud of what the land grows. [3]All the people who are still living in Jerusalem will be called holy. This will be all the people whose names are recorded among the living in Jerusalem. [4]The Lord will wash away the filth from the women of Jerusalem. He will wash the bloodstains out of Jerusalem. He will clean Jerusalem with the spirit of fairness and the spirit of fire. [5]As he did when Israel left Egypt, the Lord will cover them with a cloud of smoke during the day. And he will cover them with a bright, flaming fire at night. These proofs will be over Mount Zion.[d] They will be over every meeting of the people there. There will be a covering over every person. [6]This covering will be a place of safety. It will protect the people from the heat of the sun.

It will be a safe place to hide from the storm and rain.

ISRAEL, GOD'S SPECIAL FIELD

5 Now I will sing a song to my friend.
This song is about his vineyard.
My friend had a vineyard
on a hill with very rich soil.
²He dug and cleared the field of stones.
He planted the best grapevines
there.
And he built a tower in the middle
of it.
He cut out a winepress*d* as well.
He hoped good grapes would grow
there.
But only bad grapes grew.

³My friend says, "You people living in
Jerusalem,
and you men of Judah,
judge between me and my
vineyard.
⁴What more could I have done for my
vineyard?
I did everything I could.
I hoped for good grapes to grow.
But why were there only bad
grapes?
⁵Now I will tell you
what I will do to my vineyard:
I will remove the hedge,
and it will be burned.
I will break down the stone wall,
and it will be walked on.
⁶I will ruin my field.
It will not be trimmed or hoed.
Weeds and thorns will grow there.
I will command the clouds
not to rain on it."

⁷The vineyard belonging to the Lord of
heaven's armies
is the nation of Israel.
The garden that the Lord loves
is the men of Judah.
The Lord looked for justice, but there
was only killing.
The Lord hoped for right living, but
there were only cries of pain.

⁸How terrible it will be for you who
add more houses to your houses
and more fields to your fields.
Finally there is no room left for other
people.
Then you are left alone in the land.

⁹The Lord of heaven's armies said this
to me:
"The fine houses will be destroyed.
The large and beautiful houses will
be left empty.
¹⁰At that time a ten-acre vineyard will
make only six gallons of wine.
And ten bushels of seed will grow
only half a bushel of grain."

¹¹How terrible it will be for people who
rise early in the morning
to look for strong drink.
They stay awake late at night,
becoming drunk with wine.
¹²At their parties they have lyres,*d* harps,
tambourines,*d* flutes and wine.
They don't see what the Lord has
done.
They don't notice the work of his
hands.
¹³So my people will be captured and
taken away
because they don't really know me.
All the great men will die of hunger.
The common people will die of
thirst.
¹⁴So the place where the dead are wants
more and more people.
It opens its mouth wide.
Jerusalem's important men will go
down into it.
And the common people will go
down into it.
¹⁵So the common people and the great
people will be humbled.
Those who are proud will be
humbled.
¹⁶The Lord of heaven's armies will
receive glory by judging fairly.
The holy God will show himself
holy by doing what is right.

¹⁷Then the sheep will go anywhere they
want.
  Lambs will feed on the land that
  rich people once owned.

¹⁸How terrible it will be for those people!
  They pull their guilt and sins behind
  them
  as people pull wagons with ropes.
¹⁹They say, "Let's see God hurry.
  Let's see him do his work soon.
  We want to see it.
Let's see the plan of the Holy One of
  Israel happen soon.
  Then we would know what it really
  is."

²⁰How terrible it will be for people who
  call good things bad
  and bad things good.
They think darkness is light
  and light is darkness.
They think sour is sweet
  and sweet is sour.

²¹How terrible it will be for people who
  think they are wise.
  They think they are clever.

²²How terrible it will be for people who
  are famous for drinking wine.
  They are champions at mixing
  drinks.
²³They take money to set the guilty free.
  But they don't allow good people to
  be judged fairly.
²⁴They will be destroyed
  just as fire burns straw or dry grass.
They will be destroyed
  like a plant whose roots rot
and whose flower dies and blows
  away like dust.
They have refused to obey the
  teachings of the Lord of heaven's
  armies.
  They hated the message from the
  Holy God of Israel.
²⁵So the Lord has become very angry
  with his people.

And he has raised his hand to
  punish them.
Even the mountains are frightened.
  Dead bodies lie in the streets like
  garbage.

But the Lord is still angry.
  His hand is still raised to strike
  down the people.

²⁶God raises a banner for the nations far
  away.
  He is whistling to call those people.
The enemy comes quickly!
²⁷Not one of them becomes tired or falls
  down.
  Not one of them gets sleepy and
  falls asleep.
Their weapons are close at hand.
  Their sandal straps are not broken.
²⁸Their arrows are sharp.
  All of their bows are ready to shoot.
The horses' hoofs are hard as rock.
  Their chariot wheels move like a
  whirlwind.
²⁹Their shout is like the roar of a lion.
  It is loud like a young lion.
The enemy growls as they grab their
  captives.
  There is no one to stop them from
  taking their captives away.
³⁰On that day they will roar
  like the waves of the sea.
And when people look at the land,
  they will see only darkness and
  pain.
  All light will become dark in this
  thick cloud.

ISAIAH BECOMES A PROPHET

6 In the year that King Uzziah died, I
saw the Lord. He was sitting on a
very high throne. His long robe filled the
Temple.ᵈ ²Burning heavenly creatures
stood above him. Each creature had six
wings. They used two wings to cover their
faces. They used two wings to cover their
feet. And they used two wings for flying.
³Each creature was calling to the others:

"Holy, holy, holy is the Lord of
  heaven's armies.
His glory fills the whole earth."
[4]Their voices caused the frame around
the door to shake. The Temple filled with
smoke.

[5]I said, "Oh, no! I will be destroyed. I
am not pure. And I live among people
who are not pure. But I have seen the
King, the Lord of heaven's armies."

[6]On the altar there was a fire. One of
the burning heavenly creatures used a
pair of tongs to take a hot coal from the
fire. Then he flew to me with the hot coal
in his hand. [7]The creature touched my
mouth with the hot coal. Then he said,
"Look. Your guilt is taken away because
this hot coal has touched your lips. Your
sin is taken away."

[8]Then I heard the Lord's voice. He said,
"Whom can I send? Who will go for us?"

So I said, "Here I am. Send me!"

[9]Then the Lord said, "Go and tell this
to the people:

'You will listen and listen, but you will
  not understand.
You will look and look, but you will
  not learn.'
[10]Make these people stubborn.
Make them not able to understand
  what they hear and see.
Otherwise, they might really
  understand
what they see with their eyes
and hear with their ears.
They might really understand in their
  minds.
If they did this, they would come
  back to me and be forgiven."

[11]Then I asked, "Lord, how long should
I do this?"

He answered,
"Do this until the cities are destroyed
  and the people are gone.

Do this until there are no people left
  living in the houses.
Do this until the land is destroyed
  and left empty.
[12]I will send the people far away.
And the land will be left empty.
[13]One-tenth of the people will be left in
  the land.
But the land will be destroyed
  again.
These people will be like an oak tree.
When the tree is chopped down, a
  stump is left.
The people who remain will be like
  a stump that will sprout again."

TROUBLE WITH ARAM

7 Now Ahaz was the son of Jotham,
who was the son of Uzziah. When
Ahaz was king of Judah, Rezin and Pekah
went up to Jerusalem to fight against it.
Rezin was king of Aram. And Pekah son
of Remaliah was king of Israel. But they
were not able to defeat the city.

[2]A message was told to Ahaz king of
Judah. It said, "The armies of Aram and
Israel[n] have joined together."

When Ahaz heard this, he and the
people became very frightened. They
shook with fear like trees of the forest
blown by the wind.

[3]Then the Lord told Isaiah, "You and
your son Shear-Jashub should go out and
talk to Ahaz. Go to the place where the
water flows into the upper pool. This is on
the road to the Washerman's Field. [4]Tell
Ahaz, 'Be careful. Be calm, and don't be
afraid. Don't let those two men, Rezin and
Remaliah's son Pekah, scare you. Don't be
afraid of their anger and Aram's anger.
Those two men are as weak as two barely
burning sticks that are ready to go out.
[5]They have made plans against you. They
said, [6]"Let's fight against Judah and tear it
apart. We will divide Judah for ourselves.
We will make the son of Tabeel the new
king of Judah." [7]But I, the Lord God, say,

7:2 Israel Literally, "Ephraim." Isaiah often uses "Ephraim" to mean all of Israel.

Their plan will not succeed.
　It will not happen.
⁸That is because Aram is led by the city
　of Damascus.
　And Damascus is led by its weak
　　king, Rezin.
Within 65 years Israel will no longer
　be a nation.
⁹Israel is led by the city of Samaria,
　and Samaria is led by its weak king,
　　the son of Remaliah.
If your faith is not strong,
　then you will not have strength to
　　last.'"

IMMANUEL—GOD IS WITH US

¹⁰Then the Lord spoke to Ahaz again.
¹¹The Lord said, "Ask for a sign to prove
to yourself that these things are true. It
may be a sign from as deep as the place
where the dead are or as high as the
heavens."

¹²But Ahaz said, "I will not ask for a
sign. I will not test the Lord."

¹³Then Isaiah said, "Ahaz, descendant[d] of David, listen very carefully! Isn't
it bad enough that you wear out the
patience of people? Do you have to wear
out the patience of my God also? ¹⁴But
the Lord himself will give you a sign: The
virgin[n] will be pregnant. She will have a
son, and she will name him Immanuel.[n]
¹⁵He will be eating milk curds and honey
when he learns to reject what is evil and
to choose what is good. ¹⁶You are afraid
of the kings of Israel and Aram now. But
before the child learns what is good and
what is evil, the lands of Israel and Aram
will be empty. ¹⁷The Lord will bring
some troubled times to you. Those troubles will come to your people and to the
people of your father's family. The Lord
will bring the king of Assyria to fight
against you.

¹⁸"At that time the Lord will whistle to
call for the Egyptians. And they will come
like flies from the streams of Egypt. The
Lord will call for the Assyrians. And they
will come like bees from the land of Assyria. ¹⁹These enemies will camp in the
deep ravines and in the cliffs. They will
camp by the thornbushes and watering
holes. ²⁰The Lord will use Assyria to
punish Judah. Assyria will be hired and
used like a razor. It will be as if the Lord
is shaving the hair from Judah's head
and legs and is shaving off Judah's beard.

²¹"At that time a person will be able to
keep only one young cow and two sheep
alive. ²²There will be only enough milk
for that person to eat milk curds. All who
remain in the land will go back to eating
only milk curds and honey. ²³In this land
there are now vineyards that have 1,000
grapevines. These grapevines are worth
about 25 pounds of silver. But these fields
will become full of weeds and thorns. ²⁴The
land will become wild and useful only as a
hunting ground. ²⁵People once worked
and grew food on these hills. But at that
time people will not go there. The land
will be filled with weeds and thorns.
Only sheep and cattle will go to those
places."

ASSYRIA WILL COME SOON

8 The Lord told me, "Take a large
scroll on which to write. Use a pen to
write these words: 'Maher-Shalal-Hash-
Baz.'[n] ²I will gather some men to be reliable witnesses. They will be Uriah the
priest and Zechariah son of Jeberekiah."

³Then I went to the prophetess.[d] She
became pregnant and had a son. Then
the Lord told me, "Name the boy Maher-
Shalal-Hash-Baz. ⁴The king of Assyria
will take away all the wealth and possessions of Damascus and Samaria. This

---

7:14 virgin The Hebrew word means "a young woman." Often this meant a girl who was not married and had not
　yet had sexual relations with anyone.
7:14 Immanuel This name means "God is with us."
8:1 Maher-Shalal-Hash-Baz This name means "there will soon be looting and stealing."

will happen before the boy learns to say 'my father' or 'my mother.'"

⁵Again the Lord spoke to me. ⁶He said, "These people refuse to accept
the slow-moving waters of the pool of Shiloah.
These people are terrified of Rezin and Remaliah's son Pekah.
⁷So I, the Lord, will bring
the king of Assyria and all his power against them.
They will come like a powerful flood of water from the Euphrates River.
The Assyrians will be like water rising over the banks of the river,
flowing over the land.
⁸That water will flow into Judah and pass through it.
It will rise to Judah's throat.
Immanuel, this army will spread its wings like a bird
until it covers your whole country."

⁹Be broken, all you nations.
Be smashed to pieces.
Listen, all you faraway countries.
Prepare for battle and be smashed to pieces!
Prepare for battle and be smashed to pieces!
¹⁰Make your plans for the fight.
But your plans will be defeated.
Give orders to your armies.
But your orders will be useless.
This is because God is with us.

WARNINGS TO ISAIAH

¹¹The Lord spoke to me with his great power. He warned me not to follow the lead of the rest of the people. The Lord said,
¹²"People are saying that others make plans against them.
You should not believe those things.
Don't be afraid of the things they fear.
Do not dread those things.

¹³But remember that the Lord of heaven's armies is holy.
He is the one you should fear.
He is the one you should dread.
¹⁴Then he would be a place of safety for you.
But for the two families of Israel, he will be like a stone that causes people to stumble.
He will be like a rock that makes them fall.
He will be like a trap for the people of Jerusalem.
He will catch them in his trap.
¹⁵Many people will fall over this rock.
They will fall and be broken.
They will be trapped and caught."

¹⁶Make an agreement.
Seal up the teaching while my followers are watching.
¹⁷I will wait for the Lord to help us.
The Lord is ashamed of the family of Israel.
I will trust the Lord.

¹⁸I am here. And with me are the children the Lord has given me. We are signs and proofs for the people of Israel. We have been sent by the Lord of heaven's armies. He lives on Mount Zion.ᵈ
¹⁹Some people say, "Ask the mediumsᵈ and fortune-tellers what to do. They whisper and mutter and ask dead people what to do." But I tell you that people should ask their God for help. Why should people who are still alive ask something from the dead? ²⁰You should follow the teachings and the agreement with the Lord. The mediums and fortune-tellers do not speak the word of the Lord. Their words are worth nothing.
²¹People will wander through the land troubled and hungry. When they become hungry, they will become angry. Then they will look up and curse their king and their God. ²²They will look around them at their land. And they will see only trouble and darkness and awful gloom. And they will be forced into the darkness.

A NEW DAY IS COMING

9 But suddenly there will be no more gloom for the land that suffered. In the past God made the lands of Zebulun and Naphtali hang their heads in shame. But in the future that land will be made great. That land stretches from the way along the Mediterranean Sea to the land along the Jordan River. And it goes north to Galilee where the people who are not Israelites live.

2Now those people live in darkness.
But they will see a great light.
They live in a place that is very dark.
But a light will shine on them.
3God, you will cause the nation to
grow.
You will make the people happy.
And they will show their happiness
to you.
It will be like the joy during harvest
time.
It will be like the joy of people
taking what they have won in war.
4Like the time you defeated Midian,
you will take away their heavy load.
You will take away the heavy pole
from their backs.
You will take away the rod the enemy
uses to punish your people.
5Every boot that marched in battle will
be destroyed.
Every uniform stained with blood
will be destroyed.
They will be thrown into the fire.
6A child will be born to us.
God will give a son to us.
He will be responsible for leading
the people.
His name will be Wonderful
Counselor, Powerful God,
Father Who Lives Forever, Prince of
Peace.
7Power and peace will be in his
kingdom.
It will continue to grow.
He will rule as king on David's throne
and over David's kingdom.

He will make it strong,
by ruling with goodness and fair
judgment.
He will rule it forever and ever.
The Lord of heaven's armies will do
this
because of his strong love for his
people.

GOD WILL PUNISH ISRAEL

8The Lord sent a message against the
people of Jacob.
That message says that God will
judge Israel.
9Then everyone in Israel, even the
leaders in Samaria,
will know that God punished them.
Those people, who are proud and who
brag now, say this:
10"These bricks have fallen,
but we will build again with cut
stones.
These small trees have been chopped
down.
But we will put great cedars there."
11But the Lord will make the enemies of
Rezin strong against them.
He will stir up their enemies against
them.
12The Arameans come from the east
and the Philistines from the west.
They will eat up Israel with their
armies.

But the Lord is still angry.
His hand is still raised to punish the
people.

13But the people do not return to the
one who struck them.
They do not follow the Lord of
heaven's armies.
14So the Lord will cut off Israel's head
and tail.
He will take away both the branch
and stalk in one day.
15The elders and important men are the
head.
The prophets[d] who speak lies are
the tail.

16Those who lead the people lead them
in the wrong direction.
And those who follow them will be
destroyed.
17So the Lord is not happy with the
young men.
He will not show mercy to the
widows and orphans.
All the people are separated from God
and are very evil.
They all speak lies.

But the Lord is still angry.
His hand is still raised to strike
down the people.

18Evil is like a small fire.
First, it burns weeds and thorns.
Next, it burns the larger bushes in the
forest.
They all go up in a column of smoke.
19The Lord of heaven's armies is angry.
So the land will be burned.
All the people will be burned in that fire.
No one will try to save his brother.
20People will grab something on the
right,
but they will still be hungry.
They will eat something on the left,
but they will not be filled.
Then each person will turn and eat his
own children.
21The people of Manasseh will fight
against the people of Ephraim.
And Ephraim will fight against
Manasseh.
Then both of them will turn against
Judah.

But the Lord is still angry.
His hand is still raised to strike
down the people.

10 How terrible it will be for the
lawmakers who write evil
laws.
They write laws that make life hard
for people.
2They are not fair to the poor.
They rob my people of their rights.

They allow people to steal from
widows
and to take from orphans what they
should get.
3Lawmakers, how will you explain the
things you have done?
What will you do when your
destruction comes from far
away?
Where will you run for help?
Where will you hide your money
and your riches then?
4You will have to bow down among the
captives.
You will fall down among the dead
bodies.

But the Lord is still angry.
His hand is still raised to strike
down the people.

GOD WILL PUNISH ASSYRIA
5God says, "How terrible it will be for
the king of Assyria.
I use him like a stick.
In anger I use Assyria like a club.
6I send it to fight against a nation that is
separated from God.
I am angry with those people.
So I command Assyria to fight
against them.
Assyria will take their wealth from
them.
Judah will become like dirt for them
to walk on in the streets.
7But Assyria's king doesn't understand
that I am using him.
He doesn't know he is a tool for me.
He only wants to destroy other
people.
He plans to destroy many nations.
8The king of Assyria says to himself,
'All of my commanders are like
kings.
9The city Calno is like the city
Carchemish.
And the city Hamath is like the city
Arpad.

The city Samaria is like the city
Damascus.
¹⁰I defeated those kingdoms that
worship idols.
And those idols were more than the
idols of Jerusalem and Samaria.
¹¹I defeated Samaria and her idols.
So I will also defeat Jerusalem and
her idols.'"

¹²The Lord will finish doing what he
planned to Mount Zion*d* and Jerusalem.
Then he will punish Assyria. The king of
Assyria is very proud. His pride made him
do these bad things. So God will punish
him. ¹³The king of Assyria says this:
"By my own power I have done these
things.
By my wisdom I have defeated
many nations.
I have taken their wealth.
And like a mighty one, I have taken
their people.
¹⁴I have taken the riches of all these
people,
like one who reaches into a bird's
nest.
I have taken these nations,
like a person taking eggs.
No one raised a hand against me.
No one opened his mouth to stop
me."

¹⁵An ax is not better than the person
who swings it.
A saw is not better than the person
who uses it.
A stick cannot control the person who
picks it up.
A club cannot pick up the person!
¹⁶So the Master, the Lord of heaven's
armies,
will send a terrible disease against
Assyria's soldiers.
The strength of Assyria will be burned
up.
It will be like a fire burning until
everything is gone.

¹⁷God, the Light of Israel, will be like a
fire.
The Holy One will be like a flame.
He will be like a fire
that suddenly burns the weeds and
thorns.
¹⁸The fire burns away the great trees
and rich farmlands.
It will destroy everything.
Things will be like a sick man who
wastes away.
¹⁹Only a few trees will be left standing.
There will be so few even a child
will be able to count them.

²⁰At that time some people will be left
alive in Israel
from the family of Jacob.
They will not continue to depend
on the person who defeated them.
They will learn truly to depend on the
Lord,
the Holy One of Israel.
²¹The people who are left alive in
Jacob's family
will again follow the powerful God.
²²Israel, your people are very many.
They are like the grains of sand by
the sea.
But only a few of them will be left
alive to return to the Lord.
God has announced that he will
destroy the land
completely and fairly.
²³The Master, the Lord of heaven's
armies, will certainly destroy this
land.
He will destroy it as he has
announced.

²⁴This is what the Master, the Lord of
heaven's armies, says:
"My people living in Jerusalem,
don't be afraid of the Assyrians.
They beat you with a rod.
They raise a stick to hurt you, as
Egypt did.
²⁵But after a short time my anger will
stop.

Then I will turn my anger to
destroying them."

26Then the Lord of heaven's armies
will beat the Assyrians with a
whip.
He will defeat them as he defeated
Midian at the rock of Oreb.
He will raise his stick over the waters
as he did in Egypt.
27Then the troubles that Assyria puts
on you
will be removed.
The load they make you carry
will be taken away.

ASSYRIA INVADES ISRAEL

28The army of Assyria will enter near
Aiath.
They will walk through Migron.
They will store their food in
Micmash.
29The army will go over the pass.
They will sleep at Geba.
The people of Ramah will be afraid.
The people at Gibeah of Saul will
run away.
30Cry out, Bath Gallim!
Laishah, listen!
Poor Anathoth!
31The people of Madmenah are running
away.
The people of Gebim are hiding.
32This day the army will stop at Nob.
And the army will shake their fist at
Mount Zion,d
at the hill of Jerusalem.

33Watch! The Master, the Lord of
heaven's armies,
will chop them down like a great
tree.
He will do this with his great power.
Those who are great will be cut down.
Those who are important will fall to
the ground.
34The Lord will cut them down
as a forest is cut down with an ax.

And the great trees of Lebanon
will fall by the power of the Mighty
One.

THE KING OF PEACE IS COMING

11 A branch will grow
from a stump of a tree that was
cut down.
So a new king will come
from the family of Jesse.n
2The Spiritd of the Lord will rest upon
that king.
The Spirit gives him wisdom,
understanding, guidance and
power.
And the Spirit teaches him to know
and respect the Lord.
3This king will be glad to obey the
Lord.
He will not judge by the way things
look.
He will not judge by what people
say.
4He will judge the poor honestly.
He will be fair in his decisions for
the poor people of the land.
At his command evil people will be
punished.
By his words the wicked will be put
to death.
5Goodness and fairness will give him
strength.
They will be like a belt around his
waist.

6Then wolves will live in peace with
lambs.
And leopards will lie down to rest
with goats.
Calves, lions and young bulls will eat
together.
And a little child will lead them.
7Cows and bears will eat together in
peace.
Their young will lie down together.
Lions will eat hay as oxen do.

11:1 Jesse King David's father.

⁸A baby will be able to play near a
cobra's hole.
A child will be able to put his hand
into the nest of a poisonous
snake.
⁹They will not hurt or destroy each
other
on all my holy mountain.
The earth will be full of the knowledge
of the Lord,
as the sea is full of water.

¹⁰At that time the new king from the
family of Jesse will stand as a banner for
the people. The nations will come together around him. And the place where
he lives will be filled with glory. ¹¹At that
time the Lord will again reach out and
take his people who are left alive. These
are God's people who are left alive in
Assyria, North Egypt, South Egypt, Cush,
Elam, Babylonia, Hamath and all the
islands of the sea.

¹²God will raise a banner as a sign for all
people.
He will gather the people of Israel
who were forced from their
country.
He will gather the scattered people of
Judah
from all parts of the earth.
¹³At that time Israel will not be jealous
anymore.
Judah will have no enemies left.
Israel will not be jealous of Judah.
And Judah will not hate Israel.
¹⁴But Israel and Judah will attack the
Philistines on the west.
Together they will take the riches
from the people of the east.
They will conquer Edom and Moab.
And the people of Ammon will be
under their control.
¹⁵The Lord will dry up
the Red Sea*d* of Egypt.
He will wave his arm over the
Euphrates River.

He will dry it up with a scorching
wind.
He will divide it into seven small rivers.
And people will be able to walk
across them with their sandals on.
¹⁶So God's people who are left alive
will have a way to leave Assyria.
It will be like the time the Israelites
went out of Egypt.

A SONG OF PRAISE TO GOD

12 At that time you will say:
"I praise you, Lord!
You were angry with me.
But you are not angry with me now!
You have comforted me.
²God is the one who saves me.
I trust him. I am not afraid.
The Lord, the Lord, gives me strength
and makes me sing.
He has saved me."
³You will receive your salvation with
joy.
You will take it as you would draw
water from a well.

⁴At that time you will say,
"Praise the Lord, and worship him.
Tell everyone what he has done.
Tell them how great he is.
⁵Sing praise to the Lord, because he
has done great things.
Let all the world know what he has
done.
⁶Shout and sing for joy, you people of
Jerusalem.
The Holy One of Israel does great
things before your eyes."

GOD'S MESSAGE TO BABYLON

13 God showed Isaiah son of Amoz
this message about Babylon:
²Raise a flag on the bare mountain.
Call out to the men.
Raise your hand to signal them.
Tell them to enter through the gates
for important people.
³I myself have commanded those
people
whom I have separated as mine.

I have called those warriors to carry
out my anger.
> They rejoice and are glad to do my
> will.

4Listen to the loud noise in the
mountains.
> It sounds like many people.
Listen to the noise among the
kingdoms.
> Nations are gathering together.
The Lord of heaven's armies is calling
his army together for battle.
5This army is coming from a faraway
land.
> It is coming from the edge of the
> horizon.
In anger the Lord is using this army
like a weapon.
> And it will destroy the whole
> country.

6Cry, because the Lord's day of judging
is near.
> God All-Powerful is sending
> destruction.
7People will be weak with fear.
> Their courage will melt away.
8Everyone will be afraid.
> Pain and hurt will grab them.
> They will hurt like a woman giving
> birth to a baby.
They will look at each other in fear.
> Their faces will become red like fire.

9Look, the Lord's day of judging is
coming.
> It will be a terrible day. God will be
> very angry,
and he will destroy the country.
> God will destroy the sinners who
> live in the land.
10The stars will not show their light.
> The skies will be dark.
The sun will grow dark as it rises.
> And the moon will not give its light.

11The Lord says, "I will punish the
world for its evil.
> I will punish wicked people for their
> sins.
I will cause the proud people to lose
their pride.
> I will destroy the pride of those who
> are cruel to others.
12People will be harder to find than
pure gold.
> There will be fewer people than
> there is fine gold in Ophir.
13I will make the sky shake.
> And the earth will be moved from
> its place.
The Lord of heaven's armies will be
very angry.
> His anger will burn at that time.

14"Then the people from Babylon will
run away like hunted deer.
> They will run like sheep who have
> no shepherd.
Everyone will turn back to his own
people.
> Each will run back to his own land.
15Anyone who is captured will be killed.
> Everyone who is caught will be
> killed with a sword.
16Their little children will be beaten to
death as their parents watch.
> Everything in their houses will be
> stolen.
> And their wives will be raped.
17Look, I will cause the armies of Media
to attack Babylon.
> They do not care about silver.
> They do not delight in gold.
18Their soldiers will shoot the young
men with arrows.
> The soldiers will show no mercy on
> the children.
> They will not feel sorry for the little
> boys.
19Babylon is the most beautiful of all
kingdoms.
> The Babylonians are very proud
> of it.
But God will destroy it
like Sodom and Gomorrah.

²⁰No one will ever live there.
   No one will settle there again.
No Arab will put his tent there.
   No shepherd will bring his sheep
     there.
²¹Only animals from the desert will live
     there.
   The houses of Babylon will be full of
     wild dogs.
Owls will live there.
   Wild goats will leap about in the
     houses.
²²Wolves will howl within the strong
     walls.
   Wild dogs will bark in the beautiful
     buildings.
The end of Babylon is near.
   Its time is almost over."

ISRAEL WILL RETURN HOME

14 The Lord will again show mercy to the people of Jacob. The Lord will again choose the people of Israel. He will settle them in their own land. Then non-Israelite people will join the Israelites. The non-Israelite people will become a part of the family of Jacob. ²Nations will take the Israelites back to their land. Those men and women from the other nations will become slaves to Israel. In the past the Israelites were their slaves. But now the Israelites will defeat those nations and rule over them.

THE KING OF BABYLON WILL FALL

³The Lord will take away the Israelites' hard work, and he will comfort them. They will no longer have to work as slaves. ⁴On that day Israel will sing this song about the king of Babylon:
   The cruel king who ruled us is
     finished.
     His rule is finished!
⁵The Lord breaks the scepter*ᵈ* of evil
     rulers.
   He takes away their power.
⁶The king of Babylon beat people in
     anger.
   He beat them again and again.

He ruled the people in anger.
   He kept on doing terrible things to
     the people.
⁷But now, the whole land rests and is
     quiet.
   Now the people begin to sing.
⁸Even the pine trees are happy.
   And the cedar trees of Lebanon
     rejoice.
They say, "The king has fallen.
   No one will ever cut us down again."

⁹The place of the dead is excited
   to meet you when you come.
It wakes the spirits of the dead to
     greet you.
   They were the leaders of the world.
It makes dead kings stand up from
     their thrones to greet you.
   They were rulers of nations.
¹⁰All these leaders will make fun of you.
   They will say,
"Now you are weak, as we are.
   Now you are just like us."
¹¹Your pride has been sent down to
     where the dead are.
   The music from your harps goes
     with it.
Flies are spread out like your bed
     beneath you.
   And worms cover your body like a
     blanket.

¹²King of Babylon, morning star, you
     have fallen from heaven,
     even though you were as bright as
      the rising sun!
In the past all the nations on earth
     bowed down before you.
   But now you have been cut down.
¹³You told yourself,
   "I will go up to heaven.
I will put my throne
   above God's stars.
I will sit on the mountain of the gods.
   I will sit on the slopes of the sacred
     mountain.
¹⁴I will go up above the tops of the
     clouds.
   I will be like God Most High."

[15]But you were brought down to the
grave.
You were brought down to the deep
places where the dead are.

[16]Those who see you stare at you.
They think about what has
happened to you.
They say, "Is this the same man who
caused great fear on earth?
Is he the one who shook the
kingdoms?
[17]Is this the man who turned the land
into a desert?
Is he the one who destroyed its
cities?
Is he the one who captured people
in war
and would not let them go home?"

[18]Every king of the earth has been
buried with honor.
Every king has his own grave.
[19]But you are thrown out of your grave,
like an unwanted branch is cut
from a tree and thrown away.
You are covered by bodies
that died in battle.
You have been thrown into a rocky pit.
And other soldiers walk on you.
[20]   You will not be buried like other
people.
This is because you ruined your own
country.
And you killed your own people.
So your children will never
be mentioned again.

[21]Prepare to kill his children.
Kill them because their father is
guilty.
They will never again take control of
the earth.
They will never again fill the world
with their cities.

[22]The Lord of heaven's armies says this:
"I will fight against those people.
I will destroy Babylon and its people.

I will destroy its people and their
descendants,"[d] says the Lord.
[23]"I will make Babylon fit only for owls.
It will become a swamp.
I will sweep Babylon as with a broom
of destruction,"
says the Lord of heaven's armies.

GOD WILL PUNISH ASSYRIA

[24]The Lord of heaven's armies has
made this promise:
"These things will happen exactly as I
planned them.
These things will happen exactly as
I set them up.
[25]I will destroy the king of Assyria in
my country.
I will trample him on my mountains.
He put a heavy load on my people.
But that weight will be removed.

[26]"This is what I plan to do against all
the earth.
I will raise my hand to strike down
all nations."
[27]When the Lord of heaven's armies
makes a plan,
no one can stop it.
When the Lord raises his hand to
punish people,
no one can stop him.

GOD'S MESSAGE TO PHILISTIA

[28]This message was given the year
King Ahaz died:
[29]Country of Philistia, don't be so
happy.
The king who beat you is now dead.
But he is like a snake that will give
birth to another dangerous
snake.
The new king will be like a quick,
dangerous snake to bite you.
[30]Even the poorest of my people will be
able to eat safely.
People in need will be able to lie
down in safety.
But I will kill your family with hunger.
And all your people who are left will
die.

31People near the city gates, cry out!
  Philistines, be frightened!
A cloud of dust comes from the north.
  It is an army, full of men ready to
    fight.
32What shall we tell the messengers
    from Philistia?
Say that the Lord has made
  Jerusalem strong.
Say that his poor people will go
  there for safety.

GOD'S MESSAGE TO MOAB

15 This is a message about Moab:
  In one night armies took the
    wealth from Ar in Moab.
That night the city was destroyed.
In one night armies took the wealth
    from Kir in Moab.
That night the city was destroyed.
2The people of Dibon go to the places
    of worship to cry.
The people of Moab cry for the
  cities of Nebo and Medeba.
Everyone has shaved his head and
  beard to show how sad he is.
3In the streets at Moab they wear
    rough cloth to show their
      sadness.
On the roofs[n] and in the public
    squares,
they are crying loudly.
4People in the cities Heshbon and
    Elealeh cry out loud.
You can hear their voices far away
  in the city Jahaz.
Even the soldiers are frightened.
  They are shaking from fear.

5My heart cries with sorrow for Moab.
  Its people run away to Zoar for
    safety.
They run to Eglath Shelishiyah.
People are going up the mountain
  road to Luhith.
They are crying as they go.

People are going on the road to
  Horonaim.
They cry out loud over their
  destruction.
6But the water of Nimrim has dried up.
  The grass has dried up.
All the plants are dead.
  Nothing green is left.
7So the people gather up what they
    have saved.
They carry those things and cross
  the Ravine of the Poplars.
8Crying is heard everywhere in Moab.
  Their crying is heard as far away as
    the city Eglaim.
Their crying is heard as far away as
  Beer Elim.
9The water of the city Dibon is full of
    blood.
And I, the Lord, will bring even
  more troubles to Dibon.
A few people living in Moab have
  escaped the enemy.
But I will send lions to kill them.

16 Send the king of the land
  the payment he demands.
Send a lamb from Sela through the
    desert
to the mountain of Jerusalem.
2The women of Moab
  try to cross the river Arnon.
They are like little birds
  that have fallen from their nest.

3They say: "Help us.
  Tell us what to do.
Protect us from our enemies
  as shade protects us from the noon
    sun.
Hide us because we are running for
    safety!
Don't give us to our enemies.
4Let those of us who were forced out of
    Moab live in your land.
Hide us from our enemies."

15:3 roofs In Bible times houses were built with flat roofs. The roof was used for drying things such as flax and
fruit. And it was used as an extra room, as a place for worship and as a place to sleep in the summer.

The robbing of Moab will stop.
The enemy will be defeated.
The men who hurt others will
disappear from the land.
⁵Then a new loyal king will come.
This faithful king will be from the
family of David.
He will judge fairly.
He wants to do what is right.

⁶We have heard that the people of
Moab are proud
and very conceited.
They are very proud and angry.
But their bragging means nothing.
⁷So the people of Moab will cry.
They will all be sad.
They will moan and groan
for the raisin cakes they had in Kir
Hareseth.
⁸But the fields of Heshbon and the
vines of Sibmah cannot grow
grapes.
Foreign rulers have destroyed the
grapevines.
The grapevines once spread as far as
the city of Jazer and into the
desert.
They had spread as far as the sea.
⁹I cry with the people of Jazer
for the grapevines of Sibmah.
I will cry with the people of Heshbon
and Elealeh.
There will be no shouts of joy,
because there will be no harvest or
ripe fruit.
¹⁰There will be no joy and happiness in
the orchards.
There will be no songs or shouts of
joy in the vineyards.
No one makes wine in the
winepresses.ᵈ
I have put an end to shouts of joy.
¹¹My heart cries for Moab like a harp
playing a funeral song.
I am very sad for Kir Hareseth.
¹²The people of Moab will go to their
places of worship.
They will try to pray.

But when they go to their temple to
pray,
they will not be able.

¹³The Lord said these things about
Moab before. ¹⁴And now the Lord says,
"In three years all those people and what
they are proud of will be hated. (This is
three years as a hired helper would count
time.) There will be a few people left, but
they will be weak."

GOD'S MESSAGE TO ARAM

17 This is the message for Damascus:
"The city of Damascus will be
destroyed.
Only ruins will be left there.
²People will leave the cities of Aroer.
Flocks of sheep will wander freely
in those empty towns.
There will be no one to bother
them.
³The strong, walled cities of Israel will
be destroyed.
The government in Damascus will
end.
Those left alive of Aram will be
like the glory of Israel," says the
Lord of heaven's armies.

⁴"At that time Israel's wealth will all be
gone.
Israel will be like a man who has
lost much weight from sickness.
⁵That time will be like the grain harvest
in the Valley of Rephaim.
The workers cut the wheat.
Then they cut the heads of grain from
the plants.
And they collect the grain.
⁶That time will also be like the olive
harvest,
when a few olives are left.
Two or three olives are left in the top
branches.
Four or five olives are left on full
branches," says the Lord, the
God of Israel.

7At that time people will look to God,
     their Maker.
   Their eyes will see the Holy One of
     Israel.
8They will not trust the altars they have
     made.
   They will not trust what their hands
     have made.
   They will not respect the Asherah*d*
     idols
   and altars they have made.

9In that day all their strong cities will
be empty. They will be like the cities that
the Hivites and the Amorites left. They
left their cities when the Israelites came to
take the land. Everything will be ruined.

10You have forgotten the God who saves
     you.
   You have not remembered that God
     is your place of safety.
   You plant the finest grapevines.
   You plant grapevines from faraway
     places.
11You will plant your grapevines one
     day and try to make them grow.
   The next day they will begin to grow.
   But at harvest time everything will be
     dead.
   A sickness will kill all the plants.

12Listen to the many people!
   They are crying loud like the noise
     from the sea.
   Listen to the noise!
   The crying is like the crashing of
     great waves.
13The people roar like those waves.
   But when God speaks harshly to
     them, they will run away.
   They will be like chaff*d* on the hills
     being blown by the wind.
   They will be like tumbleweeds
     blown away by a storm.
14At night the people will be very
     frightened.
   Before morning, no one will be left.
   So our enemies will come to our land,
     but they will become nothing.

GOD'S MESSAGE TO CUSH

18 How terrible it will be for the
     land beyond the rivers of
     Cush.
   It is filled with the sound of wings.
2That land sends people across the sea.
   They go on the water in boats made
     of reeds.

   Quick messengers, go
     to the people who are tall and
       smooth-skinned.
   They are feared everywhere.
   They are a powerful nation with
     strange speech.
   They defeat the other nations.
   Their land is divided by rivers.

3All you people of the world, look!
   Everyone who lives in the world,
     look!
   You will see a banner raised on a
     mountain.
   You will hear a trumpet sound.
4The Lord said to me,
   "I will quietly watch from where
     I live.
   I will be like heat in the sunshine.
   I will be like the dew in the heat of
     harvest time."
5The time will be after the flowers have
     bloomed and before the harvest.
   The new grapes will be budding and
     growing.
   Then the enemy will cut the plants
     with knives.
   He will cut down the vines and take
     them away.
6They will be left for the birds of the
     mountains to eat.
   They will be left for the wild
     animals to eat.
   Birds will feed on them all summer.
   And that winter wild animals will
     eat them.

7At that time gifts will be brought to
     the Lord of heaven's armies.
   They will come from the people
     who are tall and smooth-skinned.
   They are feared everywhere.

They are a powerful nation with
    strange speech.
Their land is divided by rivers.
These gifts will be brought to the
    place of the Lord of heaven's
    armies.
They will be brought to Mount
    Zion.*d*

GOD'S MESSAGE TO EGYPT

19 The message about Egypt:
    Look, the Lord is coming on a
    fast cloud.
He will enter Egypt.
And the idols of Egypt will tremble
    before him.
Egypt's courage will melt away.

²The Lord says, "I will cause the
    Egyptians to fight against
    themselves.
Men will fight with their brothers.
Neighbors will fight neighbors.
Cities will fight cities.
Kingdoms will fight kingdoms.
³The Egyptians will be afraid.
I will ruin their plans.
They will ask their idols and spirits of
    the dead what they should do.
They will ask their mediums*d* and
    fortune-tellers."
⁴The Master, the Lord of heaven's
    armies, says,
"I will give Egypt to a hard master.
A powerful king will rule over
    them."

⁵The sea will become dry.
    The water will disappear from the
    Nile River.
⁶The canals will stink.
    The streams of Egypt will decrease
    and dry up.
All the water plants will rot.
⁷   All the plants along the banks of the
    Nile will die.
Even the planted fields by the Nile
    will dry up, blow away and
    disappear.

⁸The fishermen, all those who catch
    fish from the Nile,
    will groan and cry.
Those who depend on the Nile for
    food will be sad.
⁹All the people who make cloth from
    flax will be sad.
Those who weave linen will lose
    hope.
¹⁰Those who weave cloth will be broken.
All those who work for money will
    be sad.

¹¹The officers of the city of Zoan are
    fools.
The wise men who advise the king
    of Egypt give wrong advice.
How can they say to him they are
    wise?
How can they say they are from the
    old family of the kings?
¹²Egypt, where are your wise men?
Let them show you
what the Lord of heaven's armies has
    planned for Egypt.
¹³The officers of Zoan have been fooled.
The leaders of Memphis have
    believed false things.
So the leaders of Egypt
lead her the wrong way.
¹⁴The Lord has made the leaders
    confused.
They wander and lead Egypt in the
    wrong ways.
They are like drunk people
    stumbling in their own vomit.
¹⁵There is nothing Egypt can do.
No one in Egypt can help.

¹⁶In that day the people of Egypt will
be like frightened women. They will be
afraid of the Lord of heaven's armies. He
will raise his hand to strike them down.
¹⁷The land of Judah will bring fear to the
people in Egypt. Anyone in Egypt who
hears the name Judah will be afraid. This
will happen because the Lord of heaven's
armies has planned terrible things for
Egypt. ¹⁸At that time five cities in Egypt

will speak Hebrew, the language of Canaan. They will promise to be loyal to the Lord of heaven's armies. One of these cities will be named the City of Destruction. 19At that time there will be an altar for the Lord in the middle of Egypt. At the border of Egypt there will be a monument to the Lord. 20This will be a sign. It will show that the Lord of heaven's armies is powerful. When the people cry to the Lord for help, he will send help. He will send someone to save and defend the people. He will rescue them from those who hurt them.

21So the Lord will show himself to the Egyptians. Then they will say he is the Lord. They will serve God and offer many sacrifices. They will make promises to the Lord, and they will keep them. 22The Lord will punish the Egyptians. Then he will heal them. They will come back to the Lord. He will listen to their prayers and heal them.

23At that time there will be a highway from Egypt to Assyria. Then people from Assyria will go to Egypt. And the Egyptians will go to Assyria. The Egyptians and Assyrians will worship God together. 24At that time Israel, Assyria and Egypt will join together. This will be a blessing for the earth. 25The Lord of heaven's armies will bless them. He will say, "Egypt, you are my people. Assyria, I made you. Israel, I own you. You are all blessed!"

ASSYRIA WILL DEFEAT EGYPT AND CUSH

20 Sargon was the king of Assyria. He sent a military commander to Ashdod to attack that city. So the commander attacked and captured it. 2Then the Lord spoke through Isaiah son of Amoz. The Lord said, "Take the rough cloth off your body. Take your sandals off your feet." So Isaiah obeyed the Lord. He walked around without his clothes of rough cloth or his sandals.

3Then the Lord said, "Isaiah my servant has walked around without his clothes of rough cloth or his sandals for three years. This is a sign for Egypt and Cush. 4The king of Assyria will defeat Egypt and Cush. Assyria will take prisoners and lead them away from their countries. The old people and young people will be led away naked. They will go without clothes and without sandals. So the Egyptians will be shamed. 5People who looked to Cush for help will be afraid. People who were amazed by Egypt's glory will be shamed. 6Those people who live near the sea will say, 'We trusted those countries to help us. We ran to them so they would save us from the king of Assyria. But look at them. They have been captured. So how will we be able to escape?'"

GOD'S MESSAGE TO BABYLON

21 The message about the Desert by the Sea:[n]

Disaster is coming from the desert.
　　It is coming like wind blowing in
　　　the south.
　　It is coming from a terrible
　　　country.
2I have seen a terrible vision.
　　I see traitors turning against you.
　　I see people taking your wealth.

Elam, attack the people!
　　Media, surround the city and
　　　attack it!
　　I will bring an end to the pain the
　　　city causes.

3I saw those terrible things, and now
　　I am in pain.
　　My pains are like the pains of giving
　　　birth.
　　What I hear makes me very afraid.
　　What I see causes me to shake
　　　with fear.
4I am worried,
　　and I am shaking with fear.
　　My pleasant evening
　　has become a night of fear.

21:1 **Desert by the Sea** Probably Babylon.

⁵They set the table.
    They spread the rugs.
    They eat and drink!
Leaders, stand up.
    Prepare the shields for battle!

⁶The Lord said to me,
    "Go. Have a man be a lookout for the
        city.
    Have him report what he sees.
⁷If he sees chariots and teams of
        horses,
    donkeys or camels,
he should pay very close attention."

⁸Then the lookout called out,
    "My Master, each day I stand in the
        watchtower watching.
    Every night I have been on guard.
⁹Look. I see a man coming in a
        chariot
    with a team of horses."
The man gives back the answer,
    "Babylon has fallen. It has fallen!
All the statues of her gods
    lie broken on the ground."

¹⁰My people are crushed like grain on
        the threshing[d] floor.
    My people, I tell you what I have
        heard from the Lord.
He is the Lord of heaven's armies,
    the God of Israel.

GOD'S MESSAGE TO EDOM

¹¹The message about Dumah:[n]
Someone calls to me from Edom.
    He says, "Watchman, how much of
        the night is left?
    Watchman, how much longer will it
        be night?"
¹²The watchman answered,
    "Morning is coming, but then night
        will come again.
    If you have something to ask,
        then come back and ask."

GOD'S MESSAGE TO ARABIA

¹³The message about Arabia:
A group of traders from Dedan
    spent the night near some trees in
        Arabia.
¹⁴   They gave water to thirsty travelers.
The people of Tema gave food
    to those who were escaping.
¹⁵They were running from swords.
    The swords were ready to kill.
They were running from bows ready
    to shoot.
They were running from a hard
    battle.

¹⁶This is what the Lord said to me: "In
one year all the glory of the country of
Kedar will be gone. (This is a year as a
hired helper counts time.) ¹⁷At that time
only a few of the archers will be left. Only
a few of the soldiers of Kedar will be left
alive." The Lord, the God of Israel, has
spoken.

GOD'S MESSAGE TO JERUSALEM

22 The message about the Valley of
    Vision:[n]
What is wrong with you people?
    Why are you on your roofs?[n]
²This city was a very busy city.
    It was full of noise and wild parties.
But your people have been killed,
    but not with swords.
    They did not die in battle.
³All your leaders ran away together.
    But they all have been captured
        without using a bow.
All you who were captured
    tried to run away before the enemy
        came near.
⁴So I say, "Don't look at me.
    Let me cry loudly.
Don't hurry to comfort me
    about the destruction of
        Jerusalem."

21:11 **Dumah** Another name for Edom.
22:1 **Valley of Vision** This probably means a valley near Jerusalem.
22:1 **roofs** In Bible times houses were built with flat roofs. The roof was used for drying things such as flax and
    fruit. And it was used as an extra room, as a place for worship and as a place to sleep in the summer.

⁵The Master, the Lord of heaven's
armies, has chosen a special day.
There will be riots and confusion.
People will trample each other in
the Valley of Vision.
The city walls will be knocked down.
The people will cry out to the
mountain.
⁶The soldiers from Elam will take their
bags of arrows.
Men in chariots and on horses will
attack.
Kir will prepare their shields.
⁷Your nicest valleys will be filled with
chariots.
Horsemen will be ordered to guard
the gates of the city.
⁸ The walls protecting Judah will fall.

At that time the people of Jerusalem
depended on
the weapons kept at the Palace of
the Forest.
⁹You saw that the walls of Jerusalem
had many cracks that needed
repairing.
You stored up water in the lower
pool.
¹⁰You counted the houses of Jerusalem.
You tore them down to fix the walls
with their stones.
¹¹You made a pool between the two
walls.
It was to save water from the old
pool.
But you did not trust the God who
made these things.
You did not respect the One who
planned them long ago.

¹²The Master, the Lord of heaven's
armies, told the people
to cry and be sad.
He told them to shave their heads
and wear rough cloth.
¹³But look. The people are happy.
There are wild parties.
They kill the cattle and the sheep.
They eat the food and drink the wine.

They say, "Let us eat and drink,
because tomorrow we will die."

¹⁴The Lord of heaven's armies said to
me: "You people will die before this guilt
is forgiven." The Master, the Lord of
heaven's armies, said this.

GOD'S MESSAGE TO SHEBNA

¹⁵This is what the Master, the Lord of
heaven's armies, says:
"Go to this servant Shebna.
He is the manager of the palace.
¹⁶Say to him, 'What are you doing here?
Who said you could cut out a tomb
for yourself here?
Why are you preparing your tomb in
a high place?
Why are you carving out a tomb
from the rock?
¹⁷Look, mighty man! The Lord will
throw you away.
He will take firm hold of you.
¹⁸He will roll you tightly into a ball
and throw you into another
country.
There you will die.
Your fine chariots will remain
there.
You are a disgrace to your master's
house.
¹⁹I will force you out of your important
job here.
You will be thrown down from your
important place.'

²⁰"At that time I will call for my servant Eliakim son of Hilkiah. ²¹I will take
your robe and put it on him. I will give
him your belt. I will give him the important job you have. He will be like a father
to the people of Jerusalem and the
family of Judah. ²²I will put the key to the
house of David around his neck. If he
opens a door, no one will be able to close
it. If he closes a door, no one will be able
to open it. ²³He will be like an honored
chair in his father's house. I will make
him strong like a peg that is hammered

into a strong board. ²⁴All the honored and important things of his family will depend on him. All the adults and little children will depend on him. They will be like bowls and jars hanging on him.

²⁵"At that time," says the Lord of heaven's armies, "the peg hammered into the strong board will weaken. It will break and fall. And everything hanging on it will be destroyed." The Lord says this.

GOD'S MESSAGE TO LEBANON

23 The message about Tyre:
You ships of Tarshish, cry!
The houses and harbor of Tyre are
destroyed.
This news came to the ships
from the land of Cyprus.
²Be silent, you who live on the island of
Tyre.
You merchants of Sidon, be silent.
Seamen have made you rich.
³They traveled the sea to bring grain
from Egypt.
The men of Tyre brought grain
from the Nile Valley
and sold it to other nations.

⁴Sidon, be ashamed.
Strong city of the sea, be ashamed.
The sea says:
"I have not felt the pain of giving
birth.
I have not reared young men or
women."
⁵Egypt will hear the news about Tyre.
And it will make Egypt hurt with
sorrow.

⁶You ships should return to Tarshish.
You people living near the sea
should be sad.
⁷Look at your once happy city!
Look at your old, old city!
People from that city have traveled
far away to live.
⁸Who planned Tyre's destruction?
Tyre made others rich.

Her merchants were treated like
princes.
Her traders were greatly respected.
⁹It was the Lord of heaven's armies
who planned this!
He decided to make these proud
men unimportant.
He decided to disgrace those who
were greatly respected.
¹⁰Go through your land,
Tarshish, like the Nile goes through
Egypt.
There is no harbor for you now!
¹¹The Lord has stretched his hand over
the sea.
He makes its kingdoms tremble.
He commands that Canaan's
places of safety be destroyed.
¹²The Lord said, "Sidon, you will not
rejoice any longer.
You are destroyed.
Even if you cross the sea to Cyprus,
you will not find a place to rest."
¹³Look at the land of the Babylonians.
Babylonia is not a country now.
Assyria has made it a place for wild
animals.
Assyria built towers to attack it.
The soldiers took all the treasures
from its cities.
They turned it into ruins.
¹⁴So be sad, you trading ships.
Your place of safety is destroyed.

¹⁵At that time people will forget about Tyre for 70 years. That is the length of a king's life. After 70 years, Tyre will be like the prostitute*ᵈ* in this song:

¹⁶"Oh woman, you are forgotten.
Take your harp and walk through
the city.
Play your harp well. Sing your song
often.
Then people will remember you."

¹⁷After 70 years the Lord will deal with Tyre. Tyre will again have trade. It will be like a prostitute for all the nations of the earth. ¹⁸The profits will be saved for

the Lord. Tyre will not keep the money she earns. It will give them to the people who serve the Lord. So they will have plenty of food and nice clothes.

GOD WILL PUNISH THE WORLD

24 Look! The Lord will destroy the earth and leave it empty.
He will ruin the surface of the land
and scatter its people.

2 At that time the same thing will
happen to everyone:
to common people and priests,
to slaves and masters,
to women slaves and their women
masters,
to buyers and sellers,
to those who borrow and those who
lend,
and to bankers and those who owe
the bank.

3 The earth will be completely empty.
The wealth will all be taken.
This will happen because the Lord
commanded it.

4 The earth will dry up and die.
The world will grow weak and die.
The great leaders in this land will
become weak.

5 The people of the earth have ruined it.
They do not follow God's teachings.
They do not obey God's laws.
They break their agreement with
God that was to last forever.

6 A curse will destroy the earth.
The people of the world are guilty.
So they will be burned up.
Only a few will be left.

7 The new wine will be bad, and the
grapevines will die.
People who were happy will be sad.

8 The happy music of the tambourines*d*
will end.
The happy sounds of wild parties
will stop.
The joyful music from the harps
will end.

9 People will no longer sing while they
drink their wine.

The beer will taste bitter to those
who drink it.

10 The ruined city will be empty.
People will hide behind closed
doors.

11 People in the streets will ask for wine.
But joy will have turned to sadness.
All the happiness will have left.

12 The city will be left in ruins.
Its gates will be smashed to pieces.

13 This is what will happen all over the
earth.
This will happen to all the nations.
The earth will be like an olive tree
after the harvest.
It will be like the few grapes left on
a vine after harvest.

14 The people shout for joy.
From the west they praise the
greatness of the Lord.

15 People in the east, praise the Lord.
People in the islands of the sea,
praise the name of the Lord, the
God of Israel.

16 We hear songs from every part of the
earth.
These songs praise God, the
Righteous One.

But I said, "I am dying! I am dying!
How terrible it will be for me!
Traitors turn against people.
With their dishonesty, they turn
against people."

17 There are terrors, holes and traps
for the people of the earth.

18 Anyone who tries to escape from the
sound of terror
will fall into a hole.
Anyone who climbs out of the hole
will be caught in a trap.
The clouds in the sky will pour out
rain.
The foundations of the earth will
shake.

19 The earth will be broken up.
And the earth will split open.
The earth will shake violently.

²⁰The earth will stumble around like a
   man who is drunk.
  It will shake like a hut in a storm.
Its sin is like a heavy weight on its
   back.
  The earth will fall and never rise
   again.

²¹At that time the Lord will punish
   the powers in the sky above
  and the rulers on earth below.
²²They will be gathered together.
   They will be thrown into a pit as
    prisoners.
  They will be shut up in prison.
   After much time they will be
    punished.
²³The moon will be embarrassed.
   The sun will be ashamed.
  This will happen because the Lord
   of heaven's armies will rule as
   king
  on Mount Zion_d_ in Jerusalem.
  Jerusalem's leaders will see his
   greatness.

A SONG OF PRAISE TO GOD

25 Lord, you are my God.
    I honor you and praise you.
  You have done amazing things.
   You have always done what you
    said you would.
   You have done what you planned
    long ago.
²You have made the city a pile of rocks.
   You have destroyed her walls.
  The city our enemies built with strong
   walls is gone.
  It will never be built again.
³People from powerful nations will
   honor you.
  Cruel people from strong cities will
   fear you.
⁴You help the poor people.
   You help the helpless when they are
    in danger.
  You are like a shelter from storms.
   You are like shade that protects
    them from the heat.

  The cruel people attack
   like a rainstorm beating against the
    wall.
⁵ The cruel people burn like the heat
   in the desert.
But you, God, stop their violent
   attack.
  As a cloud cools a hot day,
   Lord, you silence the songs of those
    who have no mercy.

GOD'S BANQUET FOR HIS SERVANTS

⁶The Lord of heaven's armies will give
   a feast.
  It will be on this mountain for all
    people.
  It will be a feast with the best food
   and wine.
  The meat and wine will be the
    finest.
⁷On this mountain God will destroy
   the veil that covers all nations.
  This veil, called "death," covers all
    peoples.
⁸But God will destroy death forever.
   The Lord God will wipe away every
    tear from every face.
God will take away the shame
   of his people from the earth.
  The Lord has spoken.

⁹At that time people will say,
   "Our God is doing this!
We have trusted in him, and he has
   come to save us.
  We have been trusting our Lord.
  So we will rejoice and be happy when
    he saves us."
¹⁰The Lord will protect Jerusalem.
   But the Lord will crush our enemy
    Moab.
Moab will be like straw that is
   trampled down in the manure.
¹¹They will spread their arms in it
   like a person who is swimming.
  The Lord will bring down their
    pride.
  All the clever things they have made
    will mean nothing.

¹²Moab's high walls protect them.
  But the Lord will destroy these
    walls.
The Lord will throw them down on
    the ground.
The stones will lie in the dust.

A SONG OF PRAISE TO GOD

26 At that time people will sing this
    song in Judah:
We have a strong city.
  God protects us with its strong
    walls and defenses.
²Open the gates,
  and the good people will enter.
  They follow God's good way of
    living.
³You, Lord, give true peace.
  You give peace to those who
    depend on you.
  You give peace to those who trust
    you.
⁴So, trust the Lord always.
  Trust the Lord because he is our
    Rock^d forever.
⁵But the Lord will destroy the proud
    city.
  And he will punish the people living
    there.
He will bring that high city down to
    the ground.
He throws it down into the dust.
⁶Then those who were hurt by the city
    will walk on its ruins.
  Those who were made poor by the
    city will trample it under their
    feet.

⁷The path of life of the people who are
    right with God is level.
  Lord, you make the way of life
    smooth for those people.
⁸But, Lord, we are waiting
  for your way of justice.
  Our souls want to remember
    you and your name.
⁹My soul wants to be with you at night.
  And my spirit wants to be with you
    at the dawn of every day.

When your way of justice comes to
    the land,
  people of the world will learn the
    right way of living.
¹⁰An evil person will not learn to do good
    even if you show him kindness.
He will continue doing evil, even if he
    lives in a good world.
He never sees the Lord's greatness.
¹¹Lord, you are ready to punish those
    people.
  But they do not see that.
Lord, show them your strong love for
    your people.
  Then the evil people will be
    ashamed.
Burn them in the fire
  you have prepared for your
    enemies.
¹²Lord, all our success is because of
    what you have done.
  So give us peace.
¹³Lord, our God, other masters besides
    you have ruled us.
  But we honor only you.
¹⁴Those masters are now dead.
  Their ghosts will not rise from
    death.
You decided to destroy them.
  And you destroyed any memory of
    them.
¹⁵Lord, you multiplied the number of
    your people.
  You multiplied them and brought
    honor to yourself.
You made the borders of the land
    wide.
¹⁶Lord, people remember you when
    they are in trouble.
  They say quiet prayers to you when
    you punish them.
¹⁷Lord, when we are with you,
  we are like a woman giving birth to
    a baby.
  She cries and has pain from the
    birth.
¹⁸In the same way, we had pain.
  We gave birth, but only to wind.

We don't bring salvation to the land.
We don't make new people for the
world.
[19]Your people have died, but they will
live again.
Their bodies will rise from death.
Dead people in the ground,
get up and be happy!
The dew covering you is like the dew
of a new day.
The ground will give birth to the
dead buried in it.

JUDGMENT: REWARD OR PUNISHMENT
[20]My people, go into your rooms.
Shut your doors behind you.
Hide in your rooms for a short time.
Hide until God's anger is finished.
[21]The Lord will leave his place.
He will punish the people of the
world for their sins.
The earth will show the blood of the
people who have been killed.
It will not cover the dead any
longer.

27 At that time the Lord will judge
Leviathan,[d] the gliding snake.
He will punish Leviathan, the coiled
snake.
The Lord will use his great sword,
his hard and powerful sword.
He will kill the monster in the sea.

[2]In that day
people will sing about the pleasant
vineyard.
[3]"I, the Lord, will care for that
vineyard.
I will water it at the right time.
No one will hurt it.
I will guard it day and night.
[4]I am not angry.
If anyone builds a wall of thornbushes
in war,
I will march to it and burn it.
[5]But if anyone comes to me for safety
and wants to make peace with me,
he should come and make peace
with me."

[6]In the days to come, the people of
Jacob will be like a plant with
good roots.
Israel will grow like a plant
beginning to bloom.
Then the world will be filled with
their children.

GOD "DIVORCES" ISRAEL
[7]The Lord has not hurt his people as he
hurt their enemies.
His people have not been killed like
those who tried to kill them.
[8]The Lord will settle his argument with
Israel by sending it far away.
Like a hot desert wind, he will drive
Israel away.
[9]This is how Israel's guilt will be
forgiven.
This is how its sins will be taken
away.
Israel will crush the rocks of the altar
to dust.
No statues or altars will be left
standing for the Asherah[d] idols.
[10]At that time the strong, walled city
will be empty.
It will be like a desert.
Calves will eat grass there.
They will lie down there.
They will eat leaves from the
branches.
[11]The limbs will become dry and break
off.
Women will use them for firewood.
The people refuse to understand.
So God will not comfort them.
Their Maker will not be kind to
them.

[12]At that time the Lord will begin gathering his people one by one. He will gather all his people from the Euphrates River to the brook of Egypt. He will separate them from others as grain is separated from chaff.[d] [13]Many of my people are now lost in Assyria. Some of my people have run away to Egypt. But at that time a great trumpet will be blown. And all

those people will come back to Jerusalem. They will bow down before the Lord on that holy mountain.

WARNINGS TO NORTH ISRAEL

28 How terrible it will be for Samaria, the pride of Israel's drunken people!
That beautiful crown of flowers is just a dying plant.
It sits on a hill above a rich valley where drunkards live.
²Look, the Lord has someone who is strong and full of power.
That person will come like a storm of hail and strong wind.
He will come like a sudden flood of water pouring over the country.
He will throw Samaria down to the ground.
³That city, the pride of Israel's drunken people,
will be trampled underfoot.
⁴That beautiful crown of flowers is just a dying plant.
It sits on a hill above a rich valley.
That city will be like the first fig of summer.
When a person sees it,
he quickly picks it and eats it.

⁵At that time the Lord of heaven's armies
will be like a beautiful crown.
He will be like a wonderful crown of flowers
for his people who are left alive.
⁶Then the Lord will give wisdom
to the judges who rule his people.
The Lord will give strength
to those who battle at the city gate.
⁷But now those leaders are drunk with wine.
They stumble from drinking too much beer.
The priests and prophets*d* are drunk with beer.
They are filled with wine.
They stumble from too much beer.

The prophets are drunk when they see their visions.
The judges stumble when they make their decisions.
⁸Every table is covered with vomit.
There is not a clean place anywhere.

⁹The Lord is trying to teach the people a lesson.
He is trying to make them understand his teachings.
But the people are like little babies.
They are like babies who just nursed at their mother's breast.
¹⁰So they make fun of the Lord's prophet and say:
"A command here, a command there.
A rule here, a rule there.
A lesson here, a lesson there."
¹¹So the Lord will use strange words and foreign languages
to speak to these people.
¹²God said to them,
"Here is a place of rest.
Let the tired people come and rest.
This is the place of peace."
But the people would not listen.
¹³So the words of the Lord will be,
"A command here, a command there.
A rule here, a rule there.
A lesson here, a lesson there."
They will fall back and will be defeated.
They will be trapped and captured.

¹⁴You who brag should listen to the Lord's message.
Pay attention, you leaders in Jerusalem.
¹⁵You say, "We have made an agreement with death.
We have a contract with death.
When punishment passes by,
it won't hurt us.
We will be safe with our lies.
We will hide behind our tricks."

[16]Because of these things, this is what
the Lord God says:
"I will put a stone in the ground in
    Jerusalem.
  This will be a tested stone.
Everything will be built on this
    important and precious rock.
  Anyone who trusts in it will never
    be disappointed.
[17]I will use justice as a measuring line.
  I will use goodness to measure by.
The lies you hide behind will be
    destroyed as if by hail.
  They will be washed away as if in a
    flood.
[18]Your agreement with death will be
    erased.
  Your contract with death will not
    help you.
When punishment comes,
  you will be crushed by it.
[19]Whenever punishment comes, it will
    take you away.
  It will come morning after morning.
  It will defeat you by day and by
    night.
Those who hear of this punishment
    will be terrified."
[20]You will be like the man who tried to
    sleep
  on a bed that was too short for him.
And his blanket was too narrow
  to wrap around himself.
[21]The Lord will fight as he did at Mount
    Perazim.
  He will be angry as he was in the
    Valley of Gibeon.
Then the Lord will do his work, his
    strange work.
  He will finish his job, his strange job.
[22]Now, you must not make fun of these
    things.
  If you do, the ropes around you will
    become tighter.
The Lord of heaven's armies has told
    me these things.
  He has told me how the whole earth
    will be destroyed.

THE LORD PUNISHES FAIRLY

[23]Listen closely to what I tell you.
  Listen carefully to what I say.
[24]A farmer does not plow his field all
    the time.
  He does not go on working the soil.
[25]He prepares the ground.
  Then he plants the dill seed and
    scatters the cummin seed.
He plants the wheat in rows.
  He plants barley in its special place,
    and other wheat in its own field.
[26]His God teaches him
  and shows him the right way.
[27]A farmer doesn't use heavy boards to
    crush dill.
  He doesn't use a wagon to crush
    cummin.
He uses a small stick to break open
    the dill.
  With a stick he opens the cummin.
[28]The grain is ground to make bread.
  People do not ruin it by crushing it
    forever.
The farmer separates the wheat from
    the chaff[d] with his cart.
  But he does not let his horses
    grind it.
[29]This lesson comes from the Lord of
    heaven's armies.
  He gives wonderful advice. He is
    very wise.

WARNINGS TO JERUSALEM

29 How terrible it will be for you,
        Jerusalem.
  You are the city where David
    camped.
Her festivals have continued
  year after year.
[2]I will attack Jerusalem.
  That city will be filled with sadness
    and crying.
  It will be like an altar to me.
[3]I will put armies all around you,
    Jerusalem.
  I will surround you with towers.
  I will build devices around you to
    attack you.

⁴You will be pulled down and will
    speak from the ground.
I will hear your voice rising from
    the ground.
It will sound like the voice of a ghost.
Your words will come like a
    whisper from the dirt.

⁵Your many enemies will become like
    fine dust.
The groups of cruel people will be
    like chaff*d* that is blown away.
Everything will happen very quickly.
6   The Lord of heaven's armies will
    come.
He will come with thunder,
    earthquakes and great noises.
He will come with storms, strong
    winds and a fire that destroys.
⁷Then all the nations that fight against
    Jerusalem
will be like a dream.
All the nations that surround and
    attack her
will be like a vision in the night.
⁸They will be like a hungry man who
    dreams he is eating.
But when he wakes up, he is still
    hungry.
They will be like a thirsty man who
    dreams he is drinking.
But when he wakes up, he is still
    weak and thirsty.
It will be the same way with all the
    nations
who fight against Mount Zion.*d*

⁹Be surprised and amazed.
Blind yourselves so that you cannot
    see.
Become drunk, but not from wine.
Trip and fall, but not from beer.
¹⁰The Lord has made you go into a deep
    sleep.
He has closed your eyes. (The
    prophets are your eyes.)
He has covered your heads. (The
    seers*d* are your heads.)

¹¹This vision is like the words of a book
that is closed and sealed. You may give
the book to someone who can read. And
you may tell that person to read it. But he
will say, "I can't read the book. It is closed,
and I can't open it." ¹²Or you may give the
book to someone who cannot read. You
may tell him to read the book. But he will
say, "I can't read it because I don't know
how to read."

¹³The Lord says:
"These people say they love me.
They show honor to me with words.
But their hearts are far from me.
The honor they show me
is nothing but human rules they
    have memorized.
¹⁴So I will continue to amaze these
    people
by doing more and more miracles.*d*
Their wise men will lose their wisdom.
Their wise men will not be able to
    understand."

WARNINGS ABOUT OTHER NATIONS
¹⁵How terrible it will be for those who
    try
to hide things from the Lord.
How terrible it will be for those who
    do their work in darkness.
They think no one will see them or
    know what they do.
¹⁶You are confused.
You think the clay is equal to the
    potter.
You think that an object can tell the
    person who made it,
"You didn't make me."
This is like a pot telling its maker,
"You don't know anything."

A BETTER TIME IS COMING
¹⁷In a very short time, Lebanon will
    become rich farmland.
And the rich farmland will seem
    like a forest.
¹⁸At that time the deaf will hear the
    words in a book.

Instead of having darkness and
gloom, the blind will see.
[19]The Lord will make the poor people
happy.
They will rejoice in the Holy One of
Israel.
[20]Then the people without mercy will
come to an end.
Those who do not respect God will
disappear.
Those who enjoy doing evil will be
gone.
[21]Those who lie about others in court
will be gone.
Those who trap people in court will
be gone.
Those who lie and take justice from
innocent people in court will be
gone.

[22]The Lord set Abraham free. This Lord
speaks to the family of Jacob.
"Now the people of Jacob will not be
ashamed.
They will not be disgraced any
longer.
[23]They will see all their children,
the children I made with my hands.
And they will say my name is holy.
The people will agree that the Holy
One of Jacob is holy.
They will respect the God of Israel.
[24]People who do wrong will now
understand.
Those who complain will accept
being taught."

WARNINGS TO THE STUBBORN NATION

30 The Lord said,
"How terrible it will be for these
stubborn children.
They make plans, but they don't ask
me to help them.
They make agreements with other
nations, without asking my
Spirit.[d]
They are adding more and more
sins to themselves.
[2]They go down to Egypt for help,
but they didn't ask me about it first.
They hope they will be saved by the
king of Egypt.
They want Egypt to protect them.
[3]But hiding in Egypt will bring you
only shame.
Egypt's protection will only
disappoint you.
[4]Your officers have gone to Zoan.
Your messengers have gone to
Hanes.
[5]But they will be put to shame,
because Egypt is useless to them.
Egypt will give no help and be of no
use.
It will cause them only shame and
embarrassment."

GOD'S MESSAGE TO JUDAH

[6]This is the message about the animals in southern Judah:
Southern Judah is a dangerous place.
It is full of lions and lionesses,
poisonous snakes and darting
snakes.
The messengers travel through there
with their wealth on donkeys'
backs.
They have put their treasure on the
backs of camels.
They carry them to a nation that
cannot help them.
[7] They go to Egypt whose help is
useless.
So I call that country Rahab[d]
the Do-Nothing.

[8]Now write this on a sign for the people.
Write this on a scroll.
Write these things for the days to
come.
Write them so they will last forever.
[9]These people are like children who lie
and refuse to obey.
They refuse to listen to the Lord's
teachings.
[10]They tell the seers,[d]
"Don't see any more visions!"
They say to the prophets,[d]

"Don't tell us the truth!
Say things that will make us feel good.
See only good things for us.
¹¹Stop blocking our path.
Get out of our way.
Stop telling us
about God, the Holy One of Israel."

¹²So this is what the Holy One of Israel
says:
"You people have refused to accept
this message from the Lord.
You depended on cruelty and lies to
help you.
¹³You are guilty of these things.
So you are like a high wall with
cracks in it.
It will fall suddenly and break into
small pieces.
¹⁴You will be like a clay jar that breaks.
It breaks into many pieces.
Those pieces will be too small
to take coals from the fire
or to get water from a well."

¹⁵This is what the Lord God, the Holy
One of Israel, says:
"If you come back to me and trust
me, you will be saved.
If you will be calm and trust me,
you will be strong."
But you don't want to do that.
¹⁶You say, "No, we need horses to run
away on."
So you will run away on horses.
You say, "We will ride away on fast
horses."
So those who chase you will be fast.
¹⁷One enemy will make threats,
and 1,000 of your men will run
away.
Five enemies will make threats,
and all of you will run from them.
You will be left alone like a flagpole on
a hilltop.
You will be like a banner on a hill.
¹⁸The Lord wants to show his mercy
to you.
He wants to rise and comfort you.
The Lord is a fair God.

And everyone who waits for his
help will be happy.

GOD WILL HELP HIS PEOPLE

¹⁹You people who live on Mount Zion*d*
in Jerusalem will not cry anymore. The
Lord will hear your crying, and he will
comfort you. The Lord will hear you, and
he will help you. ²⁰The Lord has given you
sorrow and hurt. It was like the bread and
water you ate every day. But he is your
teacher, and he will not continue to hide
from you. You will see your teacher with
your own eyes. ²¹If you go the wrong
way—to the right or to the left—you will
hear a voice behind you. It will say, "This
is the right way. You should go this way."
²²You have statues covered with silver
and gold. But you will ruin them for further use. You will throw them away like
filthy rags. You will say, "Go away!"

²³At that time the Lord will send rain for
you. You will plant seeds in the ground,
and the ground will grow food for you.
The harvest will be very great. You will
have plenty of food in the fields for your
animals. There will be large fields for
your sheep. ²⁴Your oxen and donkeys
will work the soil. They will have all the
food they need. You will have to use
shovels and pitchforks to spread all the
food for your animals to eat. ²⁵Every
mountain and hill will have streams filled
with water. These things will happen after
many people are killed and the towers are
pulled down. ²⁶At that time the light from
the moon will be bright like the sun. The
light from the sun will be seven times
brighter than now. The light from the
sun in one day will be like a full week.
These things will happen when the Lord
bandages his broken people and heals
the hurts he gave them.

²⁷Look! The Lord comes from far away.
His anger is like a fire with thick
clouds of smoke.
His mouth is filled with anger,
and his tongue is like a burning fire.

28The Lord's breath is like a rushing
river.
It rises until it reaches the throat.
He will judge the nations as if he is
sifting them through the strainer
of destruction.
He will place in their mouths a bit
that will lead them the wrong way.
29You will sing happy songs
as on the nights you begin a festival.
You will be happy as people listening
to flutes
as they go to the mountain of the
Lord.
The Lord is the Rock[d] of Israel.
30The Lord will cause all people to hear
his great voice.
He will cause them to see his
powerful arm come down.
It will come with anger like a great fire
that burns everything.
It will be like a great storm with
much rain and hail.
31Assyria will be afraid when it hears
the voice of the Lord.
The Lord will beat Assyria with a rod.
32The Lord will punish Assyria with a
rod.
He will beat them to the music of
tambourines[d] and harps.
The Lord will fight against them
with his mighty weapons.
33Topheth[n] has been made ready for a
long time.
It is ready for the king.
It was made deep and wide.
There is much wood and fire there.
And the Lord's breath will come
like a stream of burning sulfur and
burn it.

WARNINGS ABOUT RELYING ON EGYPT

31 How terrible it will be for those
people who go down to Egypt
for help.
They think horses will save them.

They think their many chariots
and strong horsemen will save
them.
They don't trust God, the Holy One of
Israel.
They don't ask the Lord for help.
2But it is the Lord who is wise and who
can bring them trouble.
He does not change his warnings.
He will rise up and fight against the
evil people.
And he will fight against those who
try to help evil people.
3The Egyptians are only people and are
not God.
Their horses are only animals and
are not spirit.
The Lord will stretch out his arm,
and the one who helps will
stumble.
The people who wanted help will
fall.
All of them will be destroyed
together.

4The Lord says this to me:
"When a lion or a lion's cub kills an
animal to eat,
it stands over the dead animal and
roars.
A band of shepherds
may be assembled against it.
But the lion will not be afraid of their
yelling.
It will not be upset by their noise.
So the Lord of heaven's armies will
come down
to fight on Mount Zion[d] and on its
hill.
5The Lord of heaven's armies will
defend Jerusalem.
He will defend it like birds flying
over their nests.
He will defend and save it.
He will 'pass over' and save
Jerusalem."

30:33 Topheth Gehenna; the Valley of Hinnom. Here people burned the bodies of criminals and animals, along
with garbage.

⁶You children of Israel, come back to the God that you fought against. ⁷The time is coming when each of you will stop worshiping the idols of gold and silver that you made. You truly sinned when you made them.

⁸"Assyria will be defeated by a sword,
  but not the sword of a man.
Assyria will be destroyed, but not
  by a man's sword.
Assyria will run away from the sword
  of God.
But their young men will be caught
  and made slaves.
⁹They will panic, and their place of
  safety will be destroyed.
  Their commanders will be terrified
  when they see God's battle flag."
The Lord said all these things.
  The Lord's fire is in Jerusalem.
  His furnace is in Jerusalem.

A GOOD KINGDOM IS COMING

32 A king will rule in a way that
  brings justice.
  Leaders will make fair decisions.
²Then each ruler will be like a shelter
  from the wind.
He will be like a safe place in a storm.
He will be like streams of water in a
  dry land.
He will be like a cool shadow from a
  large rock in a hot land.

³People will look to the king for help.
  And they will truly listen to what he
  says.
⁴People who are now worried will be
  able to understand.
  Those who cannot speak clearly
  now will then be able to speak
  clearly and quickly.
⁵Fools will not be called great men.
  People will not respect wicked men.
⁶A fool says foolish things.
  And in his mind he plans to do evil
  things.
A fool wants to do things that are
  wrong.

He says wrong things about the
  Lord.
A fool does not feed the hungry.
  He does not let thirsty people drink
  water.
⁷The wicked man uses evil like a tool.
  He plans ways to take everything
  from poor people.
He destroys the poor with lies,
  even when the poor man is in the
  right.
⁸But a good leader plans good things to
  do.
  And those good things make him a
  good leader.

HARD TIMES ARE COMING

⁹You women who are calm now,
  stand up and listen to me.
You women who feel safe now,
  hear what I say.
¹⁰You women feel safe now,
  but after one year you will be afraid.
There will be no grape harvest.
  There will not be any summer fruit
  to gather.
¹¹Women, you are calm now, but you
  should shake with fear.
  Women, you feel safe now, but you
  should tremble.
Take off your nice clothes.
  Then put rough cloth around your
  waist to show your sadness.
¹²Beat your breasts in grief because the
  fields that were pleasant are now
  empty.
  Cry because the vines that once had
  fruit now have no more grapes.
¹³Cry for the land of my people.
  Cry because only thorns and weeds
  grow there now.
Cry for the city that once was happy.
  And cry for all the houses that once
  were filled with joy.
¹⁴The palace will be empty.
  People will leave the noisy city.
Strong cities and towers will be empty.
  Wild donkeys will love to live there.
  Sheep will go there to eat.

THINGS WILL GET BETTER

¹⁵This will continue until God puts his
Spirit^d from above into us.
Then the desert will be like a fertile
field.
And the fertile field will be like a
forest.
¹⁶Justice will be found even in the desert.
And fairness will be found in the
fertile fields.
¹⁷That fairness will bring peace.
And fairness will bring calm and
safety forever.
¹⁸My people will live in peaceful places.
They will have safe homes.
They will live in calm places of rest.
¹⁹Hail will destroy the forest.
And the city will be completely
destroyed.
²⁰But you will be happy as you plant
seeds near every stream.
You will let your cattle and donkeys
wander freely.

WARNINGS TO ASSYRIA AND PROMISES
TO GOD'S PEOPLE

33 How terrible it will be for you
who destroy others.
But you have not been destroyed
yet.
How terrible it will be for you, traitor.
But no one has turned against you
yet.
When you stop destroying,
others will destroy you.
When you stop turning against
others,
they will turn against you.

²Lord, be kind to us.
We have waited for your help.
Lord, give us strength every morning.
Save us when we are in trouble.
³Your powerful voice makes people
run away in fear.
Your greatness causes the nations
to run away.
⁴Like locusts,^d your enemies will take
away the things you stole in war.

Like locusts rushing about, they will
take your wealth.
⁵The Lord is very great. He lives in a
high place.
He fills Jerusalem with fairness and
justice.
⁶The Lord will be your safety.
He is full of salvation, wisdom and
knowledge.
Respect for the Lord is the greatest
treasure.

⁷See, brave men are crying out in the
streets.
Those who tried to bring peace are
crying loudly.
⁸There is no one on the roads.
No one is walking in the paths.
People have broken the agreements
they made.
People refuse to believe the proof
from witnesses.
No one respects other people.
⁹The land is sick and dying.
Lebanon is ashamed and dying.
The Plain of Sharon is dry like the
desert.
The trees of Bashan and Carmel are
dying.

¹⁰The Lord says, "Now, I will stand up
and show my greatness.
Now, I will become important to the
people.
¹¹You people do useless things.
These things are like hay and straw.
A destructive wind will burn you
like fire.
¹²People will be burned until their
bones become like lime.
They will burn quickly like dry
thornbushes."

¹³You people in faraway lands, hear
what I have done.
You people who are near me, learn
about my power.
¹⁴The sinners in Jerusalem are afraid.

The people who are separated from
　　God shake with fear.
They say, "Can any of us live through
　　this fire that destroys?
Who can live near this fire that
　　burns on and on?"
¹⁵A person might do what is right.
　　He might speak what is right.
He might refuse to take money
　　unfairly.
　　He might refuse to take money to
　　　　hurt others.
　　He might not listen to plans of
　　　　murder.
　　He might refuse to think about evil.
¹⁶This is the kind of person who will be
　　safe.
　　He will be protected as he would be
　　　　in a high, walled city.
　　He will always have bread,
　　　　and he will not run out of water.
¹⁷Your eyes will see the king in his
　　beauty.
　　You will see the land that stretches
　　　　far away.
¹⁸You will think about the terror of the
　　past.
　　You will think, "Where is that
　　　　officer?
　　Where is the one who collected the
　　　　taxes?
　　Where is the officer in charge of our
　　　　defense towers?"
¹⁹You will not see those proud people
　　from other countries anymore.
　　No more will you hear their strange
　　　　language
　　that you couldn't understand.

GOD WILL PROTECT JERUSALEM

²⁰Look at Jerusalem, the city of our
　　festivals.
　　Look at Jerusalem, that beautiful
　　　　place of rest.
It is like a tent that will never be
　　moved.
　　The pegs that hold her in place will
　　　　never be moved.
　　Her ropes will never be broken.

²¹There the Lord will be our Mighty One.
　　That land is a place with streams
　　　　and wide rivers.
But there will be no enemy boats on
　　those rivers.
　　No powerful ship will sail on those
　　　　rivers.
²²This is because the Lord is our judge.
　　The Lord makes our laws.
The Lord is our king.
　　He will save us.
²³You sailors from other lands, hear:
　　The ropes on your boats hang loose.
　　The mast is not held firm.
　　The sails are not spread open.
The Lord will give us your wealth.
　　There will be so much wealth even
　　　　the crippled people will carry off
　　　　a share.
²⁴No one living in Jerusalem will say,
　　"I am sick."
　　The people who live there will have
　　　　their sins forgiven.

GOD WILL PUNISH HIS ENEMIES

34

All you nations, come near
　　and listen.
　　Pay attention, you peoples!
The earth and all the people in it
　　should listen.
　　The world and everything in it
　　　　should listen.
²The Lord is angry with all the nations.
　　He is angry with their armies.
He will destroy them and kill them all.
³Their bodies will be thrown outside.
　　The stink will rise from the bodies,
　　and the blood will flow down the
　　　　mountains.
⁴The sun, moon and stars will dissolve.
　　The sky will be rolled up like a scroll.
The stars will fall
　　like dead leaves from a vine
　　or dried-up figs from a fig tree.
⁵The Lord's sword in the sky is covered
　　with blood.
　　It will cut through Edom.
　　He will destroy these people as an
　　　　offering to the Lord.

[6]The Lord's sword will be covered with
 blood.
It will be covered with fat.
It is the blood from lambs and goats.
It is the fat from the kidneys of
 male sheep.
This is because the Lord decided there
 will be a sacrifice in Bozrah.
He has decided there will be much
 killing in Edom.
[7]The oxen will be killed.
And the cattle and the strong bulls
 will be killed.
The land will be filled with their blood.
The dirt will be covered with their
 fat.

[8]The Lord has chosen a time for
 punishment.
He has chosen a year when people
 must pay for the wrongs they did
 to Jerusalem.
[9]Edom's rivers will be like hot tar.
The dirt of Edom will be like
 burning sulfur.
The land of Edom will be like
 burning tar.
[10]The fires will burn night and day.
The smoke will rise from Edom
 forever.
Year after year that land will be
 empty.
No one will ever travel through that
 land again.
[11]Birds and small animals will own that
 land.
Owls and ravens will live there.
God will make it an empty wasteland.
It will have nothing left in it.
[12]The important men will have no one
 left to rule them.
The leaders will all be gone.
[13]Thorns will take over the strong
 towers.
Wild bushes will grow in the walled
 cities.
Wild dogs will live there.
Owls will live in those homes.

[14]Desert animals will live with the
 hyenas there.
And wild goats will call to their
 friends.
Night animals will live there.
They will find a place of rest there.
[15]Owls will nest there and lay eggs.
When the eggs open, the owls will
 gather their young under their
 wings.
Hawks will gather
with their own kind.

[16]Look at the Lord's scroll. Read what
is written there:
None of these will be missing.
Every one will have its mate.
God said he will gather them together.
So his Spirit[d] will gather them
 together.
[17]God has divided the land among
 them.
And he has given them each their
 land.
So they will own that land forever.
They will live there year after year.

GOD WILL COMFORT HIS PEOPLE

35 The desert and dry land will
become happy.
The desert will be glad and will
 produce flowers.
Like a flower, [2]it will have many
 blooms.
It will show its happiness, as if it is
 shouting with joy.
It will be beautiful like the forest of
 Lebanon.
It will be as beautiful as the hill of
 Carmel and the Plain of Sharon.
All people will see the glory of the
 Lord.
They will see the splendor of our
 God.

[3]Make the weak hands strong.
Make the weak knees strong.
[4]Say to people who are afraid and
 confused,
"Be strong. Don't be afraid.

Look, your God will come,
and he will punish your enemies.
He will make them pay for the wrongs
they did.
He will come and save you."

5Then the blind people will see again.
Then the deaf will hear.
6Crippled people will jump like deer.
And those who can't talk now will
shout with joy.
Springs of water will flow in the
desert.
Streams will flow in the dry land.
7The burning desert will have pools of
water.
The dry ground will have springs.
Where wild dogs once lived,
grass and water plants will grow.
8A road will be there.
This highway will be called "The
Road to Being Holy."
Evil people will not be allowed to walk
on that road.
Only good people will walk on that
road.
No fools will go on it.
9No lions will be there.
No dangerous animals will be on
that road.
They will not be found there.
That road will be for the people God
saves.
10   The people the Lord has freed will
return there.
They will enter Jerusalem with joy.
Their happiness will last forever.
Their gladness and joy will fill them
completely.
Sorrow and sadness will go far
away.

THE ASSYRIANS INVADE JUDAH

36 During Hezekiah's fourteenth
year as king, Sennacherib king
of Assyria attacked Judah. He attacked
all the strong, walled cities of Judah and
defeated them. 2The king of Assyria sent
out his field commander. He went with a

large army from Lachish to King Hezekiah in Jerusalem. When the commander
came near the waterway from the upper
pool, he stopped. The upper pool is on the
road to the Washerman's Field. 3Eliakim,
Shebna and Joah went out to meet him.
Eliakim son of Hilkiah was the palace
manager. Shebna was the royal assistant.
And Joah son of Asaph was the recorder.
4The field commander said to them,
"Tell Hezekiah this:

"'The great king, the king of Assyria,
says: You have nothing to trust in to help
you. 5You say you have battle plans and
power for war. But your words mean
nothing. Whom are you trusting for help
so that you turn against me? 6Look, you
are depending on Egypt to help you.
Egypt is like a splintered walking stick. If
you lean on it for help, it will stab you and
hurt you. The king of Egypt will hurt
those who depend on him. 7You might
say, "We are depending on the Lord our
God." But Hezekiah destroyed the Lord's
altars and the places of worship. Hezekiah told Judah and Jerusalem, "You
must worship only at this one altar."

8"'Now make an agreement with my
master, the king of Assyria: I will give
you 2,000 horses if you can find enough
men to ride them. 9You cannot defeat
one of my master's least important officers. So why do you depend on Egypt to
give you chariots and horsemen? 10I
have not come to attack and destroy this
country without an order from the Lord.
The Lord himself told me to come to this
country and destroy it.'"

11Then Eliakim, Shebna and Joah
spoke to the field commander. They said,
"Please speak to us in the Aramaic language. We understand it. Don't speak to
us in Hebrew because the people on the
city wall can hear you."

12But the commander said, "No. My
master did not send me to tell these
things only to you and your king. My
master sent me to tell them also to those

people sitting on the wall. They will have to eat their own dung and drink their own urine like you."

¹³Then the commander stood and shouted loudly in the Hebrew language. He said, "Listen to the words from the great king, the king of Assyria! ¹⁴The king says you should not let Hezekiah fool you. Hezekiah can't save you. ¹⁵Don't let Hezekiah talk you into trusting the Lord. Hezekiah says, 'The Lord will surely save us. This city won't be given over to the king of Assyria.'

¹⁶"Don't listen to Hezekiah. The king of Assyria says, 'Make peace with me. Come out of the city to me. Then everyone will be free to eat the fruit from his own grapevine and fig tree. Everyone will be free to drink water from his own well. ¹⁷Then I will come and take you to a land like your own. It is a land with grain and new wine. It has bread and vineyards.'

¹⁸"Don't let Hezekiah fool you. He says, 'The Lord will save us.' The god of any other nation has not saved his people from the power of the king of Assyria. ¹⁹Where are the gods of Hamath and Arpad? Where are the gods of Sepharvaim? They did not save Samaria from my power. ²⁰Not one of all the gods of these countries has saved his people from me. Then the Lord cannot save Jerusalem from my power."

²¹The people were silent. They didn't answer the commander at all. This was because King Hezekiah had ordered, "Don't answer him."

²²Then Eliakim, Shebna and Joah tore their clothes to show how upset they were. (Eliakim son of Hilkiah was the palace manager. Shebna was the royal assistant. And Joah son of Asaph was the recorder.) The three men went to Hezekiah and told him what the field commander had said.

HEZEKIAH ASKS GOD TO HELP

37 When King Hezekiah heard the message, he tore his clothes. And he put on rough cloth to show how sad he was. Then he went into the Temple[d] of the Lord. ²Hezekiah sent Eliakim, Shebna and the older priests to Isaiah. Eliakim was the palace manager, and Shebna was the royal assistant. The men were all wearing the rough cloth when they came to Isaiah. He was a prophet,[d] the son of Amoz. ³These men told Isaiah, "This is what Hezekiah says: Today is a day of sorrow and punishment and disgrace. It is sad, as when a child should be born, but the mother is not strong enough to give birth to it. ⁴The king of Assyria sent his field commander to make fun of the living God. Maybe the Lord your God will hear what the commander said. Maybe the Lord your God will punish him for what he said. So pray for the few people of Israel who are left alive."

⁵When Hezekiah's officers came to Isaiah, ⁶he said to them, "Tell your master this: The Lord says, 'Don't be afraid of what you have heard. Don't be frightened by the words the servants of the king of Assyria said against me. ⁷Listen! I am going to put a spirit in the king of Assyria. He will hear a report that will make him return to his own country. And I will cause him to die by the sword there.'"

⁸The field commander heard that the king of Assyria had left Lachish. So the commander left and found the king fighting against the city of Libnah.

⁹The king received a report that Tirhakah was coming to attack him. Tirhakah was the Cushite king of Egypt. When the king of Assyria heard this, he sent messengers to Hezekiah. The king said: ¹⁰"Say this to Hezekiah king of Judah: Don't be fooled by the god you trust. Don't believe him when he says Jerusalem will not be defeated by the king of Assyria. ¹¹You have heard what the kings of Assyria have done. They have completely defeated every country. Do not think you will be saved. ¹²The gods of those people did not save them. My ancestors destroyed them. My ancestors

defeated the cities of Gozan, Haran and Rezeph. They defeated the people of Eden living in Tel Assar. [13]Where are the kings of Hamath and Arpad? Where is the king of the city of Sepharvaim? Where are the kings of Hena and Ivvah?"

HEZEKIAH PRAYS TO THE LORD

[14]Hezekiah received the letter from the messengers and read it. Then he went up to the Temple[d] of the Lord. Hezekiah spread the letter out before the Lord. [15]And he prayed to the Lord: [16]"Lord of heaven's armies, you are the God of Israel. Your throne is between the gold creatures with wings. Only you are the God of all the kingdoms of the earth. You made the heavens and the earth. [17]Hear, Lord, and listen. Open your eyes, Lord, and see. Listen to all the words Sennacherib has said to insult the living God.

[18]"It is true, Lord. The kings of Assyria have destroyed all these countries and their lands. [19]These kings have thrown the gods of these nations into the fire. But they were only wood and rock statues that men made. So the kings have destroyed them. [20]Now, Lord our God, save us from the king's power. Then all the kingdoms of the earth will know that you, Lord, are the only God."

GOD ANSWERS HEZEKIAH

[21]Then Isaiah son of Amoz sent a message to Hezekiah. Isaiah said, "The Lord, the God of Israel, says this: 'You prayed to me about Sennacherib king of Assyria. [22]So this is what the Lord has said against Sennacherib:

The people of Jerusalem
  hate you and make fun of you.
The people of Jerusalem
  laugh at you as you run away.
[23]You have insulted me and spoken
    against me.
  You have raised your voice against
    me.
  You have a proud look on your face.

You disobey me, the Holy One of
    Israel!
[24]You have used your messengers to
    insult the Lord.
  You have said, "I have many
    chariots.
With them I have gone to the tops of
    the mountains.
  I have climbed the highest
    mountains of Lebanon.
I have cut down its tallest cedars.
  I have cut down its best pine trees.
I have gone to its greatest heights.
  I have gone to its best forests.
[25]I have dug wells in foreign countries.
  I have drunk water there.
By the soles of my feet,
  I have dried up all the rivers of
    Egypt."

[26]"King of Assyria, surely you have
    heard.
  Long ago I, the Lord, planned these
    things.
Long ago I planned them.
  Now I have made them happen.
I allowed you to turn those strong,
    walled cities
  into piles of rocks.
[27]The people living in those cities were
    weak.
  They were frightened and put to
    shame.
They were like grass in the field.
  They were like tender, young grass.
They were like grass that grows on the
    housetop.
  It is burned by the wind before it
    can grow.

[28]"I know when you rest and when you
    come and go.
  I know how you speak against me.
[29]You speak strongly against me.
  And I have heard your proud
    words.
So I will put my hook in your nose.
  And I will put my bit in your
    mouth.

Then I will force you to leave my
country
the same way that you came.'

[30]"Then the Lord said, 'Hezekiah, I will
give you this sign:
This year you will eat the grain that
grows wild.
And the second year you will eat
what grows wild from that.
But in the third year, plant grain and
harvest it.
Plant vineyards and eat their fruit.
[31]The people left alive in the family of
Judah
will be saved.
Like plants that take root,
they will grow strong and have
many children.
[32]A few people will come out of
Jerusalem alive.
There will be a few from Mount
Zion[d] who will live.
The strong love of the Lord of
heaven's armies
will cause this to happen.'

[33]"So this is what the Lord says about
the king of Assyria:
'He will not enter this city.
He will not even shoot an arrow
here.
He will not fight against it with
shields.
He will not build a ramp to attack
the city walls.
[34]He will return to his country the same
way he came.
He will not enter this city,'
says the Lord.
[35]The Lord says, 'I will defend and save
this city.
I will do this for myself and for
David, my servant.'"

[36]Then the angel of the Lord went out.
He killed 185,000 men in the Assyrian
camp. When the people got up early the
next morning, they saw all the dead
bodies! [37]So Sennacherib king of Assyria
left. He went back to Nineveh and stayed
there.

[38]One day Sennacherib was worshiping in the temple of his god Nisroch.
While he was there, his sons Adram-
melech and Sharezer killed him with a
sword. Then they escaped to the land of
Ararat. So Sennacherib's son Esarhaddon
became king of Assyria.

HEZEKIAH'S ILLNESS

38 At that time Hezekiah became
very sick. He was almost dead.
The prophet[d] Isaiah son of Amoz went to
see him. Isaiah told him, "This is what
the Lord says: You are going to die. So
you should give your last orders to
everyone. You will not get well."

[2]Hezekiah turned toward the wall and
prayed to the Lord. [3]He said, "Lord, please
remember that I have always obeyed you.
I have given myself completely to you. I
have done what you said was right." And
Hezekiah cried loudly.

[4]Then the Lord spoke his word to
Isaiah: [5]"Go to Hezekiah and tell him:
'This is what the Lord, the God of your
ancestor David, says: I have heard your
prayer. And I have seen your tears. I will
add 15 years to your life. [6]I will save you
and this city from the king of Assyria. I
will defend this city.'"

[21n] Then Isaiah said, "Make a paste
from figs. Put it on Hezekiah's boil. Then
he will get well."

[22]Hezekiah asked Isaiah, "What will
be the sign? What will show that I will go
up to the Temple[d] of the Lord?"

[7]Isaiah said, "The Lord will do what
he says. This is the sign from the Lord to
show you: [8]The sun has made a shadow
go down the stairway of Ahaz. I will make
it go back ten steps." So the shadow made

38:21-22 These verses are generally found at the end of chapter 38. But the same story in 2 Kings 20:6-9 shows the
events happened in this order.

by the sun went back up the ten steps it had gone down.

⁹After Hezekiah king of Judah got well, he wrote this song:

¹⁰I said, "I am in the middle of my life.
Do I have to go through the gates
where the dead are now?
Will I have the rest of my life taken
away from me?"

¹¹I said, "I will not see the Lord
in the land of the living again.
I will not again see the people
who live on the earth.

¹²Like a shepherd's tent,
my home has been pulled down
and taken from me.
I am finished like the cloth
a weaver rolls up and cuts from the
loom.
In one day you brought me to this
end.

¹³All night I cried loudly.
Like a lion, he crushed all my
bones.
In one day you brought me to this
end.

¹⁴I cried like a bird.
I moaned like a dove.
My eyes became tired as I looked to
the heavens.
Lord, I have troubles. Please help
me."

¹⁵What can I say?
The Lord told me what would
happen and then made it
happen.
I have had these troubles in my soul.
So now I will be humble all my life.

¹⁶Lord, because of you, men live.
Because of you, my spirit also lives.
You made me well and let me live.

¹⁷It was for my own good
that I had such troubles.
Because you love me very much,
you did not let me die.
You threw my sins
far away.

¹⁸People in the place where the dead are
cannot praise you.
Those who have died cannot sing
praises to you.
Those who die don't trust you
to help them.

¹⁹The people who are alive are the ones
who praise you.
They praise you as I praise you
today.
A father should tell his children
that you provide help.

²⁰The Lord saved me.
So we will sing and play songs.
We will make music in the Temple of
the Lord
all the days of our lives.

MESSENGERS FROM BABYLON

39 At that time Merodach-Baladan son of Baladan was king of Babylon. He sent letters and a gift to Hezekiah. He did this because he had heard that Hezekiah had been sick and was now well. ²Hezekiah was happy to see the messengers. So he showed them what was in his storehouses: the silver, gold, spices and expensive perfumes. He showed them his swords and shields. He showed them all his wealth. He showed them everything in his palace and in his kingdom.

³Then Isaiah the prophet[d] went to King Hezekiah. He asked Hezekiah, "What did these men say? Where did they come from?"

Hezekiah said, "They came from a far-away country. They came to me from Babylon."

⁴So Isaiah asked him, "What did they see in your palace?"

Hezekiah said, "They saw everything in my palace. I showed them all my wealth."

⁵Then Isaiah said to Hezekiah: "Listen to the words of the Lord of heaven's armies: ⁶'In the future everything in your palace will be taken away to Babylon. Everything your ancestors have stored up

until this day will be taken away. Nothing will be left,' says the Lord. ⁷Some of your own children will be taken away. Those who will be born to you will be taken away. And they will become eunuchs*d* in the palace of the king of Babylon."

⁸Hezekiah told Isaiah, "These words from the Lord are good." He said this because he thought, "There will be peace and security while I am king."

ISRAEL'S PUNISHMENT WILL END

40 Your God says,
"Comfort, comfort my people.
²Speak kindly to the people of
   Jerusalem.
   Tell them
that their time of service is finished.
   Tell them that they have paid for
      their sins.
   Tell them that the Lord has punished
      Jerusalem
   twice for every sin they did."

³This is the voice of a man who calls out:
"Prepare in the desert
   the way for the Lord.
Make the road in the dry lands
   straight for our God.
⁴Every valley should be raised up.
   Every mountain and hill should be
      made flat.
The rough ground should be made
   level.
   The rugged ground should be made
      smooth.
⁵Then the glory of the Lord will be
   shown.
   All people together will see it.
The Lord himself said these things."

⁶A voice says, "Cry out!"
   Then I said, "What shall I cry out?"

"Say all people are like the grass.
   And all their strength is like the
      flowers of the field.
⁷The grass dies, and the flowers fall.
   This is because the breath of the
      Lord blows on them.
   Surely the people are like grass.

⁸The grass dies, and the flowers fall.
   But the word of our God will live
      forever."

⁹Jerusalem, you have good news to tell.
   Go up on a high mountain.
Jerusalem, you have good news to tell.
   Shout out loud the good news.
Shout it out and don't be afraid.
   Say to the towns of Judah,
   "Here is your God."
¹⁰Look, the Lord God is coming with
      power.
   He will use his power to rule all the
      people.
Look, he will bring reward for his
      people.
   He will have their payment with
      him.
¹¹The Lord takes care of his people like
      a shepherd.
   He gathers the people like lambs in
      his arms.
   He carries them close to him.
He gently leads the mothers of the
      lambs.

GOD IS SUPREME

¹²Who has measured the oceans in the
      palm of his hand?
   Who has used his hand to measure
      the sky?
Who has used a bowl to measure all
      the dust of the earth?
   Who has used scales to weigh the
      mountains and hills?
¹³Who has known the mind of the Lord?
   Who has been able to give the Lord
      advice?
¹⁴Whom did the Lord ask for help?
   Who taught him the right way?
Who taught the Lord knowledge?
   Who showed him the way to
      understanding?

¹⁵The nations are like one small drop in
      a bucket.
   They are no more than the dust on
      his measuring scales.

To him the islands are no more
than fine dust on his scales.
¹⁶All the trees in Lebanon are not
enough for the altar fires.
And all the animals in Lebanon are
not enough for burnt offerings.
¹⁷Compared to the Lord all the nations
are worth nothing.
To him they are less than nothing.

¹⁸Can you compare God to anything?
Can you compare him to an image
of anything?
¹⁹An idol is formed by a man.
And another man covers it with
gold.
And he makes silver chains for it.
²⁰A poor man cannot buy those
expensive statues.
So he finds a tree that will not rot.
And he finds a skilled workman
to make it into an idol that will not
fall over.

²¹Surely you know. Surely you have
heard.
Surely in the beginning someone
told you.
Surely you understand how the
earth was created.
²²God sits on his throne above the circle
of the earth.
And compared to him, people are
like grasshoppers.
He stretches out the skies like a piece
of cloth.
He spreads them out like a tent to
sit under.
²³He makes rulers unimportant.
He makes the judges of this world
worth nothing.
²⁴They are like plants that are placed in
the ground.
They are like seeds that are planted.
As soon as they begin to grow strong,
he blows on them and they die.
The wind blows them away like
chaff.^d

²⁵God, the Holy One, says, "Can you
compare me to anyone?
Is anyone equal to me?"
²⁶Look up to the skies.
Who created all these stars?
He leads out all the army of heaven
one by one.
He calls all the stars by name.
He is very strong and full of power.
So not one of them is missing.

²⁷People of Jacob, why do you
complain?
People of Israel, why do you say,
"The Lord does not see what happens
to me.
He does not care if I am treated
fairly"?
²⁸Surely you know.
Surely you have heard.
The Lord is the God who lives forever.
He created all the world.
He does not become tired or need to
rest.
No one can understand how great
his wisdom is.
²⁹The Lord gives strength to those who
are tired.
He gives more power to those who
are weak.
³⁰Even boys become tired and need to
rest.
Even young men trip and fall.
³¹But the people who trust the Lord will
become strong again.
They will be able to rise up as an eagle
in the sky.
They will run without needing rest.
They will walk without becoming
tired.

THE LORD WILL HELP ISRAEL

41 The Lord says, "Faraway
countries, listen to me.
Let the nations become strong.
Come to me and speak.
We will meet together to decide
who is right.

2"Who caused the man to come from
the east?
Who gives the man victories
everywhere he goes?
The one who brought him gives
nations over to him.
He defeats kings for him.
The man uses his sword, and the
kings become like dust.
He uses his bow, and they are
blown away like chaff.[d]
3He chases them and is never hurt.
He goes places where he has never
been before.
4Who caused this to happen?
Who has controlled history since
the beginning?
I, the Lord, am the one. I was here at
the beginning.
And I will be here when all things
are finished."

5All you faraway places, look and be
afraid.
All you places far away on the earth,
shake with fear.
Come close and listen to me.
6   The workers help each other.
They say to each other, "Be strong!"
7The man who carves wood
encourages the man who works
with gold.
The workman who smooths the
metal with a hammer encourages
the man who shapes the metal.
This last workman says, "This metal
work is good."
He nails the statue to a base so it
can't fall over.

ONLY THE LORD CAN SAVE US
8The Lord says, "People of Israel, you
are my servants.
People of Jacob, I chose you.
You are from the family of my friend
Abraham.
9You were far away on the earth.
I called you from a faraway country.
I said, 'You are my servants.'

I have chosen you, and I have not
turned against you.
10So don't worry, because I am with
you.
Don't be afraid, because I am your
God.
I will make you strong and will help
you.
I will support you with my right
hand that saves you.

11"All those people who are angry with
you
will be ashamed and disgraced.
Those who are against you
will disappear and be lost.
12You will look for your enemies.
But you will not find them.
Those who fought against you
will vanish completely.
13I am the Lord your God.
I am holding your right hand.
And I tell you, 'Don't be afraid.
I will help you.'
14You few people of Israel who are left,
do not be afraid even though you
are weak as a worm.
I myself will help you," says the Lord.
"I am the one who saves you, the
Holy One of Israel.
15Look, I have made you like a
threshing[d] board.
You are new, with many sharp
teeth.
So you will walk on mountains and
crush them.
You will make the hills like chaff.[d]
16You will throw them into the air. And
the wind will carry them away.
A windstorm will scatter them.
Then you will be happy in the Lord.
You will be proud of the Holy One
of Israel.

17"The poor and needy people look for
water.
But they can't find any.
Their tongues are dry with thirst.

But I, the Lord, will answer their
prayers.
I, the God of Israel, will not leave
them to die.
18I will make rivers flow on the dry hills.
I will make springs of water flow
through the valleys.
I will change the desert into a lake of
water.
I will change the dry land into
springs of water.
19I will make trees grow in the desert.
There will be cedars, acacia, myrtle
and olive trees.
I will put pine, fir and cypress trees
growing together in the desert.
20People will see these things and
understand.
Together they will think carefully
about these things.
They will know that the Lord's power
did this.
They will know that the Holy One of
Israel made these things."

THE LORD CHALLENGES FALSE GODS

21The Lord says, "Present your case."
The Lord, the King of Jacob, says,
"Tell me your arguments.
22Bring in your idols to tell us
what is going to happen.
Have them tell us what happened in
the beginning.
Then we will think about these
things.
Then we will know how they will
turn out.
Tell us what will happen in the future.
23 Tell us what is coming next.
Then we will believe that you are
gods.
Do something, whether it is good or
bad.
Make us afraid of you.
24You false gods are less than nothing.
You can't do anything.

Those who worship you should
be hated."
25"I have brought someone to come out
of the north.[n]
I have called by name a man from
the east, and he knows me.
He walks on kings as if they were
mud.
He walks on them as a potter walks
on the clay.
26Who told us about this before it
happened?
Who told us ahead of time so we
could say, 'He was right'?
None of you told us anything.
None of you told us before it
happened.
No one heard you tell about it.
27I, the Lord, was the first one to tell
Jerusalem that the people were
coming home.
I sent a messenger to Jerusalem
with the good news.
28I look at the idols, but there is not one
that can answer.
None of them can give advice.
None of them can answer my
questions.
29Look, all these idols are false gods.
They cannot do anything.
They are worth nothing.

THE LORD'S SPECIAL SERVANT

42 "Here is my servant, the one
I support.
He is the one I chose, and I am
pleased with him.
I will put my Spirit[d] in him.
And he will bring justice to all
nations.
2He will not cry out or yell.
He will not speak loudly in the
streets.
3He will not break a crushed blade of
grass.

41:25 someone . . . north This probably means Cyrus, a king of Persia.

He will not put out even a weak
　　flame.
He will bring justice and find what is
　　true.
⁴　He will not lose hope or give up
until he brings justice to the world.
　　And people far away will trust his
　　　teachings."

⁵God, the Lord, said these things.
He created the skies and stretched
　　them out.
He spread out the earth and
　　everything on it.
He gives life to all people on earth.
He gives life to everyone who walks
　　on the earth.
⁶The Lord says, "I called you to do
　　right.
And I will hold your hand.
I will protect you.
　　You will be the sign of my
　　　agreement with the people.
　　You will be a light to shine for all
　　　people.
⁷You will help the blind to see.
　　You will free those who are in
　　　prison.
　　You will lead those who live in
　　　darkness out of their prison.

⁸"I am the Lord. That is my name.
　　I will not give my glory to another.
　　I will not let idols take the praise
　　　that should be mine.
⁹The things I said would happen have
　　happened.
　　And now I tell you about new
　　　things.
Before those things happen,
　　I tell you about them."

A SONG OF PRAISE TO THE LORD
¹⁰Sing a new song to the Lord.
　　Sing his praise everywhere on the
　　　earth.
Praise him, you people who sail on
　　the seas and you animals who
　　live in them.

Praise him, you people living in
　　faraway places.
¹¹The deserts and their cities should
　　praise him.
The settlements of Kedar should
　　praise him.
The people living in Sela should sing
　　for joy.
　　They should sing from the
　　　mountaintops.
¹²They should give glory to the Lord.
People in faraway lands should
　　praise him.
¹³The Lord will march out like a strong
　　soldier.
He will be excited like a man ready
　　to fight a war.
He will shout out the battle cry.
And he will defeat his enemies.

¹⁴The Lord says, "For a long time I have
　　said nothing.
I have been quiet and held myself
　　back.
But now I will cry out.
　　I will strain like a woman giving
　　　birth to a child.
¹⁵I will destroy the hills and mountains.
　　I will dry up all the plants that grow
　　　there.
I will make the rivers become dry
　　land.
　　I will dry up the pools of water.
¹⁶Then I will lead the blind along a way
　　they never knew.
I will guide them along paths they
　　have not known.
I will make the darkness become light
　　for them.
　　And I will make the rough ground
　　　smooth.
These are the things I will do.
　　I will not leave my people.
¹⁷But some people trust in idols.
　　They say to their statues,
'You are our gods.'
　　Those people will be rejected in
　　　disgrace.

ISRAEL REFUSED TO LISTEN TO GOD

18"You who are deaf, hear me.
   You who are blind, look and see.
19No one is more blind than my servant
      Israel.
   The messenger I send is the most
      deaf.
   No one is more blind than the person
      I own.
   No one is more blind than the
      servant of the Lord.
20Israel, you have seen much, but you
      have not obeyed.
   You have heard, but you refuse to
      listen."
21The Lord made his teachings
      wonderful.
   He did this because he is good.
22These people have been defeated and
      robbed.
   They are trapped in pits.
   They are locked up in prison.
   Like robbers, enemies have taken
      them away.
   There is no one to save them.
   Enemies carried them off.
   And no one said, "Bring them
      back."

23Will any of you listen to this?
   Will you listen carefully in the
      future?
24Who let the people of Jacob be carried
      off?
   Who let robbers take Israel away?
   The Lord allowed this to happen
      because we sinned against him.
   We did not live the way the Lord
      wanted us to live.
   We did not obey his teaching.
25So the Lord became very angry with
      us.
   He brought terrible wars against us.
   It was as if the people of Israel had
      fire all around them.
   But they didn't know what was
      happening.
   It was as if they were burning.
   But they didn't pay any attention.

GOD IS ALWAYS WITH HIS PEOPLE

43 Now this is what the Lord says.
      He created you, people of Jacob.
   He formed you, people of Israel.
   He says, "Don't be afraid, because I
      have saved you.
   I have called you by name, and you
      are mine.
2When you pass through the waters, I
      will be with you.
   When you cross rivers, you will not
      drown.
   When you walk through fire, you will
      not be burned.
   The flames will not hurt you.
3This is because I, the Lord, am your
      God.
   I, the Holy One of Israel, am your
      Savior.
   I gave Egypt to pay for you.
   I gave Cush and Seba to make you
      mine.
4You are precious to me.
   I give you honor, and I love you.
   So I will give other people in your
      place.
   I will give other nations to save
      your life.
5So don't be afraid. I am with you.
   I will gather your children from the
      east.
   I will gather you from the west.
6I will tell the north: Give my people to
      me.
   I will tell the south: Don't keep my
      people in prison.
   Bring my sons from far away.
   Bring my daughters from faraway
      places.
7Bring to me all the people who are
      mine.
   I made them for my glory.
   I formed them; I made them."

JUDAH IS GOD'S WITNESS

8Bring out the people who have eyes
      but don't see.
   Bring out those who have ears but
      don't hear.

⁹All the nations should gather together.
  All the people should come together.
Which of their gods said that this
  would happen?
Which of their gods can tell what
  happened in the beginning?
They should bring their witnesses to
  prove they were right.
Then others will say, "It is true."
¹⁰The Lord says, "You are my
  witnesses.
You are the servant I chose.
I chose you so you would know and
  believe me.
  I chose you so you would
  understand that I am the true
  God.
There was no God before me,
  and there will be no God after me.
¹¹I myself am the Lord.
  I am the only Savior.
¹²I myself have spoken to you, saved
  you and told you these things.
  It was not some foreign god among
  you.
You are my witnesses, and I am God,"
  says the Lord.
¹³ "I have always been God.
No one can save people from my
  power.
  When I do something, no one can
  change it."

¹⁴This is what the Lord says.
  He is the Holy One of Israel who
  saves you.
He says, "I will send armies to
  Babylon for you.
  All the Babylonians will be
  captured.
They will be taken away in their ships
  they are proud of.
¹⁵I am the Lord, your Holy One.
  I made Israel. I am your king."

GOD WILL SAVE HIS PEOPLE AGAIN
¹⁶This is what the Lord says.
  He is the one who made a road
  through the sea.

Even through rough waters he
  made a path for his people.
¹⁷He is the one who defeated the
  chariots and horses.
He defeated the mighty armies.
They fell together, and they will never
  rise again.
  They were destroyed as a flame is
  put out.
¹⁸The Lord says, "Forget what
  happened before.
  Do not think about the past.
¹⁹Look at the new thing I am going to
  do.
  It is already happening. Don't you
  see it?
I will make a road in the desert.
  I will make rivers in the dry land.
²⁰Even the wild animals will be thankful
  to me.
  The wild dogs and owls will honor
  me.
They will honor me when I put water
  in the desert.
  They will honor me when I make
  rivers in the dry land.
I will do this to give water to my
  people, the ones I chose.
²¹These are the people I made.
  And they will sing songs to praise
  me.

²²"People of Jacob, you have not called
  to me.
  People of Israel, you have become
  tired of me.
²³You have not brought your sacrifices
  of sheep to me.
  You have not honored me by
  bringing sacrifices to me.
I did not force you to give sacrifices
  to me.
  I did not force you to burn incense[d]
  until you became tired.
²⁴So you did not buy incense for me.
  You did not freely bring fat from
  your sacrifices to me.

Instead you have weighed me down
  with your many sins.
You have made me tired of your
  many wrongs.

25"I, I am the One who forgives all your
  sins.
I do this to please myself.
I will not remember your sins.
26But you should remind me.
Let's meet and decide what is right.
Tell what you have done and show
  you are right.
27Your first father sinned.
And your leaders have turned
  against me.
28So I will make your holy rulers not holy.
And I will bring destruction on the
  people of Jacob.
And I will let Israel be insulted."

THE LORD IS THE ONLY GOD

44 The Lord says, "People of
Jacob, you are my servants.
Listen to me!
People of Israel, I chose you."
2This is what the Lord says. He made
  you.
He formed you when you were in
  your mother's body.
And he will help you.
The Lord says, "People of Jacob, my
  servants, don't be afraid.
Israel, I chose you.
3I will pour out water for the thirsty
  land.
I will make streams flow on dry
  land.
I will put my Spirit^d into your
  children.
My blessing will be like a stream of
  water flowing over your family.
4Your children will grow like a tree in
  the grass.
They will be like poplar trees
  growing beside streams of water.
5One person will say, 'I belong to the
  Lord.'
Another will use the name Jacob.

Another will sign his name 'I am the
  Lord's.'
And another will use the name
  Israel."

6The Lord is the king of Israel.
The Lord of heaven's armies saves
  Israel.
The Lord says, "I am the beginning
  and the end.
I am the only God.
7There is no other God like me.
If there is, then that god should
  come and prove it.
Who has announced coming events
  from the beginning?
He should tell what will happen in
  the future.
8Don't be afraid! Don't worry!
I have always told you what will
  happen.
You are my witnesses.
There is no other God.
I know of no other Rock.^d I am the
  only One."

FALSE GODS ARE USELESS

9Some people make idols, but they are
  worth nothing.
People love them, but they are
  useless.
Those people are witnesses for the
  statues. But those people cannot
  see.
They know nothing. They don't
  know enough to be ashamed.
10Who made these false gods?
Who made these useless idols?
11The workmen who made those gods
  will be ashamed!
Those workmen are only human.
If they all would come together,
  they would all be ashamed and
  afraid.

12One workman uses tools to heat iron.
He works over hot coals.
He uses his hammer to beat the metal
  and make a statue.
He uses his powerful arms.

But when he becomes hungry, he
loses his power.
If he does not drink water, he
becomes tired.

[13] Another workman uses a line and a
compass
to draw lines on the wood.
Then he uses his chisels to cut a statue
from wood.
He uses his calipers to measure the
statue.
This way, the workman makes the
wood look exactly like a man.
And this statue of a man sits in the
house.
[14] A man cuts down cedar
or gets cypress or oak trees.
Those trees grew by their own power
in the forest.
Or he plants a pine tree, and the
rain makes it grow.
[15] Then he burns the tree.
He uses some of the wood for a fire
to keep himself warm.
He also starts a fire to bake his
bread.
But he uses part of the wood to make
a god. Then he worships it!
He makes the idol and bows down
to it!
[16] The man burns half of the wood in the
fire.
He uses the fire to cook his meat.
And he eats the meat until he is full.
He burns the wood to keep himself
warm. He says,
"Good! Now I am warm. I can see
because of the fire's light."
[17] But the man makes a statue from the
wood that is left. He calls it his
god.
He bows down to it and worships it.
He prays to it and says,
"You are my god. Save me!"
[18] Those people don't know what they
are doing. They don't
understand!

It is as if their eyes are covered so
they can't see.
Their minds don't understand.
[19] They have not thought about these
things.
They don't understand.
They have never thought to themselves,
"I burned half of the wood in the
fire.
I used the hot coals to bake my
bread.
I cooked and ate my meat.
And I used the wood that was left to
make this hated thing.
I am worshiping a block of wood!"
[20] He doesn't know what he is doing.
His confused mind leads him the
wrong way.
He cannot save himself.
He cannot say, "This statue I am
holding is a false god."

THE LORD IS THE TRUE GOD
[21] The Lord says, "People of Jacob,
remember these things!
People of Israel, remember you are
my servants.
I made you. You are my servants.
So Israel, I will not forget you.
[22] I have swept away your sins like a big
cloud.
I have removed your sins like a
cloud that disappears into the air.
Come back to me because I saved
you."

[23] Skies, sing for joy because the Lord
did great things!
Earth, shout for joy, even in your
deepest parts!
Sing, you mountains, with thanks to
God.
Sing, too, you trees in the forest!
The Lord saved the people of Jacob!
The Lord showed his greatness
when he saved Israel.
[24] The Lord saved you.
He formed you while you were still
in your mother's body.

The Lord says, "I, the Lord, made
   everything!
I alone stretched out the skies.
I spread out the earth by myself.
25I show that the lying prophets'[d] signs
   are false.
I make fools of those who do magic.
I confuse even wise men.
   They think they know much, but I
   make them look foolish.
26I make the messages of my servants
   come true.
I make the advice of my messengers
   come true.
I say to Jerusalem,
   'People will live in you again!'
I say to the towns of Judah,
   'You will be built again!'
I say to Jerusalem's ruins,
   'I will repair you.'
27I tell the deep waters, 'Become dry!
I will make your streams become
   dry!'
28I say of Cyrus,[n] 'He is my shepherd.
He will do all that I want him to do.
He will say to Jerusalem, "You will
   be built again!"
He will tell the Temple,[d] "Your
   foundations will be rebuilt."'"

GOD CHOOSES CYRUS TO FREE ISRAEL

45 This is what the Lord says to
Cyrus, his appointed king:
"I hold your right hand.
I will help you defeat nations.
I will help you take other kings'
   power away.
I will open doors for you
   so city gates will not stop you.
2I will go before you.
   And I will make the mountains flat.
I will break down the bronze gates of
   the cities.
I will cut through the iron bars on
   the gates.
3I will give you the wealth that is stored
   away.
And I will give you hidden riches.

I will do this so you will know I am
   the Lord.
I, the God of Israel, call you by name.
4I do these things for my servants, the
   people of Jacob.
I do these things for my chosen
   people, the Israelites.
Cyrus, I call you by name.
I give you a title of honor even
   though you don't know me.
5I am the Lord. There is no other God.
I am the only God.
I will make you strong
   even though you don't know me.
6I do these things so everyone will
   know
   there is no other God.
From the east to the west they will
   know
I alone am the Lord.
7I made the light and the darkness.
I bring peace, and I cause troubles.
I, the Lord, do all these things.

8"Sky above, make victory fall like rain.
Clouds, pour down victory.
May the earth receive it.
   May salvation grow.
May victory grow with it.
I, the Lord, have created it.

9"How terrible it will be for those who
   argue with the God who made
   them.
   They are like one piece of broken
   pottery among many pieces.
The clay does not ask the potter,
   'What are you doing?'
The thing that is made doesn't say to
   its maker,
   'You have no hands.'
10How terrible it will be for the child
   who says to his father,
   'Why are you giving me life?'
How terrible it will be for the child
   who says to his mother,
   'Why are you giving birth to me?'"

44:28 Cyrus A king of Persia. He ruled from about 550-530 B.C.

[11]The Lord is the Holy One of Israel,
and its Maker.
He says this:
"You ask me about what will happen.
You question me about my
children.
You give me orders about what I
have made.
[12]I made the earth.
And I made all the people living on it.
With my own hands I stretched out
the skies.
I command all the armies in the sky.
[13]I will bring Cyrus to do good things.
And I will make his work easy.
Cyrus will rebuild my city,
and he will set my people free.
Cyrus has not been paid to do these
things.
The Lord of heaven's armies says
this."

[14]The Lord says,
"The things made in Egypt and Cush
and the tall people of Seba
will come to you.
They will become yours.
The Sabeans will walk behind you.
They will come along in chains.
They will bow down before you.
They will pray to you, saying,
'God is with you.
And there is no other God.'"

[15]You are a God that people cannot see.
You are the God and Savior of Israel.
[16]All the people who make idols will be
put to great shame.
They will go off together in
disgrace.
[17]But Israel will be saved by the Lord.
That salvation will continue forever.
Never again will Israel be put to
shame.

[18]The Lord created the heavens.
He is the God
who formed the earth.
He made the earth.

But he did not want it to be empty.
He wanted life to be on the earth.
This is what the Lord says:
"I am the Lord. There is no other
God.
[19]I did not speak in secret.
I did not hide my words somewhere
in a dark place.
I did not tell the family of Jacob
to look for me in empty places.
I am the Lord, and I speak the truth.
I say what is right.

[20]"You people have escaped from other
nations.
So gather together and come before
me.
Come near together.
People who carry idols of wood don't
know what they are doing.
They pray to a god who cannot save
them.
[21]Tell these people to come to me.
Let them talk about these things
together.
Who told you long ago that this would
happen?
Who told about it long ago?
I, the Lord, said these things.
There is no other God besides me.
I am the only good God. I am the
Savior.
There is no other God.

[22]"All people everywhere,
follow me and be saved.
I am God. There is no other God.
[23]I will make a promise by my own
power.
And my promise is true.
What I say will not be changed.
I promise that everyone will bow
before me.
Everyone will promise to follow me.
[24]People will say, 'Goodness and power
come only from the Lord.'"
Everyone who has been angry with
the Lord
will come to him and be ashamed.

25But with the Lord's help, the people
of Israel
will be found to be good.
And they will praise him.

FALSE GODS ARE USELESS

46 Bel[d] and Nebo[d] bow down.
Their idols are carried by
animals.
The statues are only heavy loads that
must be carried.
They only make people tired.
2These false gods will all bow down.
They cannot save themselves.
They will all be carried away like
prisoners.

3"Family of Jacob, listen to me!
All you people from Israel who are
still alive, listen!
I have carried you since you were born.
I have taken care of you from your
birth.
4Even when you are old, I will take care
of you.
Even when your hair has turned
gray, I will take care of you.
I made you and will take care of you.
I will carry you, and I will save you.

5"Can you compare me to anyone?
No one is equal to me or like me.
6Some people are rich with gold.
They weigh their silver on the
scales.
They hire a goldsmith, and he makes
it into a god.
Then they bow down and worship it.
7They put it on their shoulders and
carry it.
They set it in its place, and there it
stands.
It cannot move from its place.
People may yell at it, but it cannot
answer.
It cannot save people from their
troubles.

8"Remember this, and do not forget it!
Think about these things, you who
turn against God.

9Remember what happened long ago.
Remember that I am God. There is
no other God.
I am God. There is no one like me.
10From the beginning I told you what
would happen in the end.
A long time ago I told you things
that have not yet happened.
When I plan something, it happens.
I do the things I want to do.
11I am calling a man from the east to
carry out my plan.
He will come like a hawk from a
country far away.
I will make what I have said come true.
I will do what I have planned.
12Listen to me, you stubborn people.
You are far from what is right.
13I will soon do the things that are right.
I will bring salvation soon.
I will save Jerusalem.
And I will bring glory to Israel."

GOD WILL DESTROY BABYLON

47 The Lord says, "City of
Babylon, go down and sit in
the dirt.
People of Babylon, sit on the ground.
You are no longer the ruler.
You will no longer be called
tender or beautiful.
2 You must use large stones to grind
grain into flour.
Remove your veil and your nice
skirts.
Uncover your legs and cross the
rivers.
3Men will see your nakedness.
They will see your shame.
I will punish you.
I will punish every one of you."

4Our Savior is named the Lord of
heaven's armies.
He is the Holy One of Israel.

5"Babylon, sit in darkness and say
nothing.
You will no longer be called the
queen of kingdoms.

⁶I was angry with my people.
  So I rejected those people who
    belonged to me.
I gave them to you,
  but you showed them no mercy.
You even made the old people
  work very hard.
⁷You said, 'I will live forever.
  I will always be the queen.'
You did not think about these things.
  You did not think about what
    would happen.

⁸"Now, listen, you lover of pleasure.
  You think you are safe.
You tell yourself,
  'I am the only important person.
I will never be a widow.
  I will never lose my children.'
⁹Two things will happen to you
  suddenly in a single day.
  You will lose your children and
    your husband.
These things will truly happen to you.
  All your magic and powerful tricks
    will not save you.
¹⁰You do evil things, but you feel safe.
  You say, 'No one sees what I do.'
Your wisdom and knowledge
  have fooled you.
You say to yourself,
  'I am God. No one is equal to me.'
¹¹But troubles will come to you.
  You will not know how to stop
    them.
Disaster will fall on you.
  And you will not be able to keep it
    away.
You will be destroyed quickly.
  You will not even see it coming.

¹²"Keep on using your tricks.
  Continue doing all your magic.
  You have done these things since
    you were young.
Maybe they will help you.
  Maybe you will be able to scare
    someone.

¹³You are tired of the advice you have
  received.
So let those who study the sky come.
  They tell the future by looking at the
    stars.
So let them save you from what is
  about to happen to you.
¹⁴But they are like straw.
  Fire will quickly burn them up.
They cannot save themselves
  from the power of the fire.
They are not like coals that give
  warmth.
  They are not like a fire you may sit
    beside.
¹⁵You have worked with these people.
  They have been with you since you
    were young.
But they will not be able to help
  you.
Everyone will go his own way.
  And there will be no one left to save
    you."

GOD CONTROLS THE FUTURE

48 The Lord says, "Family of
      Jacob, listen to me.
  You are called Israel.
  You come from the family of Judah.
You use the Lord's name to make
  promises.
  You praise the God of Israel,
  but you are not honest or sincere.
²You call yourselves people of the holy
  city.
  You depend on the God of Israel.
  He is named the Lord of heaven's
    armies.
³Long ago I told you what would
  happen.
  I said these things and made them
    known.
  Suddenly I acted, and these things
    happened.
⁴I did that because I knew you were
  stubborn.
  Your neck was like an iron muscle.
  It was as if your head were made of
    bronze.

[5]So a long time ago I told you about
    these things.
  I told you about them before they
    happened.
  I did this so you couldn't say, 'My
    idols did this.
  My wooden and metal statues made
    these things happen.'

[6]"You heard and saw all the things that
    happened.
  So you should tell this news to others.
  Now I will tell you about new things.
  These are hidden things that you
    don't know yet.
[7]These things are happening now, not
    long ago.
  You have not heard about them
    before today.
  So you cannot say, 'We already knew
    about that.'
[8]But you have not heard me. You have
    not understood.
  Even long ago you did not listen to
    me.
  I knew you would surely turn against
    me.
  You have fought against me since
    you were born.
[9]But for my own sake I will be patient.
  People will praise me for not
    becoming angry
  and destroying you.
[10]I have made you pure, but not by fire,
    as silver is made pure.
  I have purified you by giving you
    troubles.
[11]I do this for myself, for my own sake.
  I will not let people speak evil
    against me.
  I will not let some false god take my
    glory.

ISRAEL WILL BE FREE
[12]"People of Jacob, listen to me.
  People of Israel, I have called you to
    be my people.

I am God.
  I am the beginning and the end.
[13]I made the earth with my own hands.
  With my right hand I spread out
    the skies.
  When I call them,
    they come together before me.

[14]"All of you, come together and listen.
  None of the false gods said these
    things would happen.
  I, the Lord, have chosen someone
    to attack the Babylonians.
  He will carry out my wishes against
    Babylon.
[15]I have spoken. I have called him.[n]
  I have brought him, and I will make
    him successful.
[16]Come to me and listen to this.
  From the beginning I have spoken
    openly.
  From the time it began, I was
    there."

Now, the Lord God
  has sent me with his Spirit.[d]

[17]The Lord is your close relative who
    saves you, the Holy One of Israel.
  The Lord says,
  "I am the Lord your God.
  I teach you to do what is good.
  I lead you in the way you should go.
[18]If you had obeyed me,
  you would have had peace like a
    full-flowing river.
  Good things would have flowed to
    you like the waves of the sea.
[19]You would have had many children.
  They would have been as many as
    the grains of sand.
  They would never have died out.
  They would not have been
    destroyed."

[20]My people, leave Babylon!
  Run from the Babylonians!

48:15 him This probably refers to Cyrus king of Persia.

Tell this news with shouts of joy to the
people.
Spread it everywhere on earth.
Say, "The Lord has saved
his servants, the people of Jacob."
²¹They did not become thirsty when he
led them through the deserts.
He made water flow from a rock for
them.
He split the rock,
and water flowed out.

²²"There is no peace for evil people,"
says the Lord.

GOD CALLS HIS SPECIAL SERVANT

49 All of you people in faraway
places, listen to me.
Listen, all you nations far away.
Before I was born, the Lord called me
to serve him.
The Lord named me while I was
still in my mother's body.
²The Lord made my tongue like a
sharp sword.
He hid me in the shadow of his
hand.
The Lord made me like a sharp arrow.
He hid me in the holder for his
arrows.
³The Lord told me, "Israel, you are my
servant.
I will show my glory through you."
⁴But I said, "I have worked hard for
nothing.
I have used all my power, but I did
nothing useful.
But the Lord will decide what my
work is worth.
God will decide my reward."
⁵The Lord made me in the body of my
mother
so I would be his servant.
He made me to lead the people of
Jacob back to him.
He made me so that Israel might be
gathered to him.
The Lord will honor me.
I will get my strength from my God.

⁶The Lord told me,
"You are an important servant to me.
You will bring back the tribes^d of
Jacob.
You will bring back the people of
Israel who are left alive.
But, more importantly, I will make
you a light for all nations.
You will show people all over the
world the way to be saved."

⁷The Lord is your close relative who
saves you.
He is the Holy One of Israel.
He speaks to the one who is hated by
the people.
He speaks to the servant of rulers.
The Lord says, "Kings will see you
and stand to honor you.
Great leaders will bow down before
you.
This is because the Lord can be
trusted.
He is the Holy One of Israel, who
has chosen you."

THE DAY OF SALVATION

⁸This is what the Lord says:
"At the right time I will hear your
prayers.
On the day of salvation I will help
you.
I will protect you.
And you will be the sign of my
agreement with the people.
You will bring back the people to the
land.
You will give the land that is now
ruined back to its owners.
⁹You will tell the prisoners, 'Come out
of your prison.'
You will tell those in darkness,
'Come into the light.'
The people will eat beside the roads.
They will find food even on bare
hills.
¹⁰They will not be hungry or thirsty.
Neither the hot sun nor the desert
wind will hurt them.

The God who comforts them will lead
them.
He will lead them by springs of
water.
[11]I will make my mountains into roads
for my people.
And the roads will be raised up.
[12]Look, people are coming to me from
far away.
They are coming from the north
and from the west.
They are coming from Aswan in
southern Egypt."

[13]Heavens and earth, be happy.
Mountains, shout with joy.
Be happy because the Lord comforts
his people.
He will comfort those who suffer.

JERUSALEM AND HER CHILDREN

[14]But Jerusalem said, "The Lord has left
me.
The Lord has forgotten me."

[15]The Lord answers, "Can a woman
forget the baby she nurses?
Can she feel no kindness for the
child she gave birth to?
Even if she could forget her children,
I will not forget you.
[16]See, I have written your name on my
hand.
Jerusalem, I always think about
your walls.
[17]Your children will soon return to you.
And the people who defeated you
and destroyed you will leave.
[18]Look up and look around you.
All your children are gathering to
return to you."
The Lord says, "As surely as I live,
your children will be like jewels.
You will be as proud of them as a
bride is of her jewels.

[19]"You were destroyed and defeated.
Your land was made useless.
But now you will have more people
than the land can hold.

And those people who destroyed
you will be far away.
[20]Children were born to you while you
were sad.
But they will say to you,
'This place is too small for us.
Give us a bigger place to live.'
[21]Then you will say to yourself,
'Who gave me all these children?
I was sad and lonely.
I was defeated and away from my
people.
So who reared these children?
I was left all alone.
Where did all these children come
from?'"

[22]This is what the Lord God says:
"See, I will lift my hand to signal the
nations.
I will raise my banner for all people
to see.
Then they will bring your sons back to
you in their arms.
They will carry your daughters on
their shoulders.
[23]Kings will teach your children.
Daughters of kings will take care of
those children.
They will bow down before you.
They will kiss the dirt at your feet.
Then you will know I am the Lord.
Anyone who trusts in me will not be
disappointed."

[24]Can the wealth a soldier wins in war
be taken away from him?
Can a prisoner be freed from a
powerful soldier?
[25]But this is what the Lord says:
"The prisoners will be taken from the
strong soldiers.
What the soldiers have taken will be
saved.
I will fight your enemies.
I will save your children.
[26]I will force those who trouble you to
eat their own flesh.

Their own blood will be the wine
  that makes them drunk.
Then everyone will know
  I, the Lord, am the One who saves
  you.
  I am the Powerful One of Jacob who
  saves you."

ISRAEL WAS PUNISHED FOR ITS SIN

50 This is what the Lord says:
  "People of Israel, you say
    I divorced your mother.
  Then where is the paper that proves
  it?
  Or do you think I sold you to pay a
  debt?
No! It was because of the evil things
  you did that I sold you.
  It was because of the times she
  turned against me that your
  mother was sent away.
²I came home and found no one there.
  I called, but no one answered.
  Do you think I am not able to save
  you?
  Do I not have the power to save
  you?
Look, I need only to shout, and the
  sea becomes dry.
  I change rivers into a desert.
Their fish rot because there is no
  water.
  The fish die of thirst.
³I can make the skies dark.
  I can make them black like clothes
  of sadness."

GOD'S SERVANT OBEYS

⁴The Lord God gave me the ability to
  teach.
  He has taught me what to say to
  make the weak strong.
Every morning he wakes me.
  He teaches me to listen like a
  student.
⁵The Lord God helps me learn.
  And I have not turned against him.
  I have not stopped following him.

⁶I offered my back to those who beat
  me.
  I offered my cheeks to those who
  pulled my beard.
  I won't hide my face from them
  when they make fun of me and spit
  at me.
⁷The Lord God helps me.
  So I will not be ashamed.
  I will be determined.
  I know I will not be disgraced.
⁸The Lord shows that I am innocent,
  and he is close to me.
  So who can accuse me?
  If there is someone, let us go to
  court together.
If someone wants to prove I have
  done wrong,
  he should come and tell me.
⁹It is the Lord God who helps me.
  So who can prove me guilty?
All those who try will become useless
  like old clothes.
  Moths will eat them.

¹⁰Who among you fears the Lord
  and obeys his servant?
That person may walk in the dark
  and have no light.
Then let him trust in the Lord.
  Let him depend on his God.
¹¹But instead, some of you want to light
  your own fires.
  You want to make your own light.
So, go, walk in the light of your fires.
  Trust your own light to guide you.
But this is what you will receive from
  me:
  You will lie down in a place of pain.

JERUSALEM WILL BE SAVED

51 The Lord says, "Listen to me,
  those of you who try to live
  right and follow the Lord.
Look at the rock from which you were
  cut.
  Look at the stone quarry from
  which you were dug.
²Look at Abraham, your ancestor.

Look at Sarah, who gave birth to
your ancestors.
Abraham had no children when I called
him.
But I blessed him and gave him
many descendants.[d]
[3]So the Lord will comfort Jerusalem.
He will show mercy to those who
live in her ruins.
He will change her deserts into a
garden like Eden.
He will make her empty lands like
the garden of the Lord.
People there will be very happy.
They will give thanks and sing songs.

[4]"My people, listen to me.
My nation, pay attention to me.
I will give the people my teachings.
And my decisions will be like a light
to all people.
[5]I will soon show I do what is right.
I will soon save you.
I will use my power and judge all
nations.
All the faraway places are waiting for
me.
They wait for my power to help
them.
[6]Look up to the heavens.
Look around you at the earth below.
The skies will disappear like clouds of
smoke.
The earth will become useless like
old clothes.
Its people will die like flies.
But my salvation will continue
forever.
My goodness will never end.

[7]"You people who know what is right
should listen to me.
You people who follow my
teachings should hear what I say.
Don't be afraid of the evil things
people say.
Don't be upset by their insults.
[8]Moths will eat those people as if they
were clothes.

Worms will eat them as if they were
wool.
But my goodness will continue
forever.
My salvation will continue from
now on."

[9]Wake up, wake up, and use your
strength,
powerful Lord.
Wake up as you did in the old times.
Wake up as you did a long time ago.
With your own power, you cut Rahab[d]
into pieces.
You killed that sea monster.
[10]You caused the sea to become dry.
You dried the waters of the deep
ocean.
You made the deepest parts of the sea
into a road.
Your people crossed over on that
road and were saved.
[11]The people the Lord has freed will
return.
They will enter Jerusalem with joy.
Their happiness will last forever.
They will have joy and gladness.
All sadness and sorrow will be gone
far away.

[12]The Lord says, "I am the one who
comforts you.
So why should you be afraid of
people, who die?
Why should you fear people who
die like the grass?
[13]Have you forgotten that the Lord
made you?
He stretched out the skies.
He made the earth.
Why are you always afraid
of those angry people who trouble
you?
They want to destroy.
But where are those angry people
now?
[14]   People in prison will soon be set free.
They will not die in prison.
They will have enough food.

¹⁵This is because I am the Lord your God.
  I stir the sea and make the waves
    roar.
  My name is the Lord of heaven's
    armies.
¹⁶I will give you the words I want you to
    say.
  I will cover you with my hands and
    protect you.
  I made the heavens and the earth.
  And I say to Jerusalem, 'You are my
    people.'"

GOD PUNISHED ISRAEL

¹⁷The Lord was very angry with you.
  Your punishment was like wine in a
    cup.
  The Lord made you drink that wine
    until you stumbled.
¹⁸Jerusalem had many people.
  But there was not a person to lead
    her.
  Of all the people who grew up there,
    no one was there to guide her.
¹⁹Troubles came to you in groups of
    two.
  No one will feel sorry for you.
  There was ruin and disaster, great
    hunger and fighting.
  No one can comfort you.
²⁰Your people have become weak.
  They fall down and lie on every
    street corner.
  They are like animals caught in a
    net.
  They have felt the full anger of the
    Lord.
  They have heard God's angry shout.

²¹So listen to me, poor Jerusalem,
  you who are drunk but not from
    wine.
²²Your God will fight for his people.
  This is what the Lord your God
    says:
  "The punishment I gave you is like a
    cup of wine.
  You drank it and could not walk
    straight.

  I am taking that cup of my anger
    away from you.
  You will never be punished by my
    anger again.
²³I will now give that cup of
    punishment to those who gave
    you pain.
  They told you,
  'Bow down so we can walk over
    you.'
  They made your back like dirt for
    them to walk on.
  You were like a street for them to
    travel on."

JERUSALEM WILL BE SAVED

52 Wake up, wake up, Jerusalem!
    Become strong!
Be beautiful again,
  holy city of Jerusalem.
The people who do not worship God
  and who are not pure
  will not enter you again.
²Jerusalem, you once were a prisoner.
  Now shake off the dust and stand up.
Jerusalem, you once were a prisoner.
  But now free yourself from the
    chains around your neck.
³This is what the Lord says:
  "You were not sold for a price.
  So you will be saved without cost."
⁴This is what the Lord God says:
  "First my people went down to Egypt
    to live.
  Later Assyria made them slaves.

⁵"Now see what has happened," says
    the Lord.
  "Another nation has taken away my
    people for nothing.
  This nation who rules them makes
    fun of me," says the Lord.
  "All day long they speak against
    me.
⁶But this has happened so my people
    will know who I am.
  They will know I am God.
  And they will know that I am the
    one speaking to them."

⁷How beautiful is the person
　who comes over the mountains to
　　bring good news.
How beautiful is the one who
　announces peace.
He brings good news
　and announces salvation.
How beautiful are the feet of the one
　who says to Jerusalem,
"Your God is king."
⁸Listen! Your guards are shouting.
　They are all shouting for joy!
They all will see with their own eyes
　when the Lord returns to
　　Jerusalem.
⁹Jerusalem, your buildings are
　destroyed now.
But shout and rejoice together.
You can rejoice because the Lord has
　comforted his people.
He has saved Jerusalem.
¹⁰The Lord will show his holy power
　to all the nations.
Then everyone on earth
　will see the salvation of our God.

¹¹You people, leave, leave; get out of
　Babylon!
Touch nothing that is unclean.*d*
You men who carry the things used in
　worship,
　leave there and make yourselves
　　pure.
¹²You will not be forced to leave
　Babylon quickly.
You will not be forced to run away.
The Lord will go before you.
　And the God of Israel will guard you
　　from behind.

GOD'S SUFFERING SERVANT

¹³The Lord says, "See, my servant will
　act wisely.
People will greatly honor and
　respect him.
¹⁴Many people were shocked when they
　saw him.
His appearance was so damaged he
　did not look like a man.

His form was changed so much they
　could barely tell he was human.
¹⁵But now he will sprinkle many people.
Kings will be amazed and shut their
　mouths.
They will see the things they had not
　been told about my servant.
They will understand the things
　they had not heard."

53 Who would have believed what
we heard?
Who saw the Lord's power in this?
²He grew up like a small plant before
　the Lord.
He was like a root growing in a dry
　land.
He had no special beauty or form to
　make us notice him.
There was nothing in his appearance
　to make us desire him.
³He was hated and rejected by people.
He had much pain and suffering.
People would not even look at him.
He was hated, and we didn't even
　notice him.

⁴But he took our suffering on him
　and felt our pain for us.
We saw his suffering.
We thought God was punishing
　him.
⁵But he was wounded for the wrong
　things we did.
He was crushed for the evil things
　we did.
The punishment, which made us well,
　was given to him.
And we are healed because of his
　wounds.
⁶We all have wandered away like
　sheep.
Each of us has gone his own way.
But the Lord has put on him the
　punishment
for all the evil we have done.

⁷He was beaten down and punished.
But he didn't say a word.

He was like a lamb being led to be
  killed.
He was quiet, as a sheep is quiet
  while its wool is being cut.
He never opened his mouth.
[8]Men took him away roughly and
  unfairly.
He died without children to
  continue his family.
He was put to death.
He was punished for the sins of my
  people.
[9]He was buried with wicked men.
He died with the rich.
He had done nothing wrong.
He had never lied.

[10]But it was the Lord who decided
  to crush him and make him suffer.
So the Lord made his life a penalty
  offering.
But he will see his descendants[d] and
  live a long life.
He will complete the things the
  Lord wants him to do.
[11]He will suffer many things in his soul.
But then he will see life and be
  satisfied.
My good servant will make many
  people right with God.
He carried away their sins.
[12]For this reason I will make him a
  great man among people.
He will share in all things with
  those who are strong.
He willingly gave his life.
He was treated like a criminal.
But he carried away the sins of many
  people.
And he asked forgiveness for those
  who sinned.

PEOPLE WILL RETURN TO JERUSALEM

54 The Lord says, "Sing, Jerusalem.
  You are like a woman who
      never gave birth to children.
Start singing and shout for joy.
You never felt the pain of giving
  birth.

But you will have more children
  than the woman who has a husband.
[2]Make your tent bigger.
Stretch it out and make it wider.
Do not hold back.
Make the ropes longer.
Make its stakes stronger.
[3]Do this because you will begin
  growing very much.
Your children will take over other
  nations.
And they will again live in cities
  that once were destroyed.

[4]"Don't be afraid because you will not
  be ashamed.
Don't be embarrassed because you
  will not be disgraced.
You will forget the shame you felt
  earlier.
You will not remember the shame
  you felt when you lost your
  husband.
[5]This is because the God who made
  you is like your husband.
His name is the Lord of heaven's
  armies.
The Holy One of Israel is the one who
  saves you.
He is called the God of all the earth.
[6]You were like a woman whose
  husband left her.
And you were very sad.
You were like a wife who married
  young
and then her husband left her.
But the Lord called you to be his,"
  says your God.
[7]God says, "I left you, but only for a
  short time.
But with great kindness I will bring
  you back again.
[8]I became very angry
  and hid from you for a short time.
But I will show you mercy with
  kindness forever,"
says the Lord your close relative
  who saves you.

[9]The Lord says, "This is like the time of
  Noah.
I promised then
    that I would never flood the world
      again.
In the same way, I promise
    I will not be angry with you or
      punish you again.
[10]The mountains may disappear,
    and the hills may come to an end.
But my love will never disappear.
    My promise of peace will not come
      to an end,"
    says the Lord who shows mercy to
      you.

[11]"You poor city. Storms have hurt you,
    and you have not been comforted.
But I will rebuild you using turquoise
      stones.
    I will build your foundations with
      sapphires.
[12]I will use rubies to build your walls.
    I will use shining jewels for the
      gates.
    I will build all your outer walls from
      precious jewels.
[13]All your children will be taught by the
      Lord.
    And they will have much peace.
[14]I will build you using fairness.
  You will be safe from those who
      would hurt you.
    So you will have nothing to fear.
    Nothing will come to make you
      afraid.
[15]I will not send anyone to attack you.
    And you will defeat those who do
      attack you.

[16]"See, I made the blacksmith.
    He fans the fire to make it hotter.
    And he makes the kind of tool he
      wants.
  In the same way I have made the
      destroyer to destroy.
[17] So no weapon that is used against you
    will defeat you.

You will show that those who speak
      against you are wrong.
These are the good things my servants
      receive.
    Their victory comes from me," says
      the Lord.

GOD GIVES WHAT IS GOOD

55 The Lord says, "All you who are
      thirsty,
  come and drink.
Those of you who do not have money,
      come, buy and eat!
Come buy wine and milk.
    You don't need money; it will cost
      you nothing.
[2]Why spend your money on something
      that is not real food?
  Why work for something that
      doesn't really satisfy you?
  Listen closely to me, and you will eat
      what is good.
    You will enjoy the food that satisfies
      your soul.
[3]Come to me and listen.
    Listen to me so you may live.
  I will make an agreement with you
      that will last forever.
    I will give you the blessings I
      promised to David.
[4]I made David a witness of my power
      for all nations.
    I made him a ruler and commander
      of many nations.
[5]You will call for nations that you don't
      yet know.
    And these nations will run to you.
  This will happen because of the Lord
      your God.
    The Holy One of Israel honors you."

[6]So you should look for the Lord before
      it is too late.
    You should call to him while he is
      near.
[7]Evil people should stop being evil.
    They should stop thinking bad
      thoughts.

They should return to the Lord, and
   he will have mercy on them.
They should come to our God,
   because he will freely forgive
   them.

[8]The Lord says, "Your thoughts are not
   like my thoughts.
Your ways are not like my ways.
[9]Just as the heavens are higher than
   the earth,
   so are my ways higher than your
   ways.
And my thoughts are higher than
   your thoughts.
[10]Rain and snow fall from the sky.
   They don't return without watering
   the ground.
They cause the plants to sprout and
   grow.
And the plants make seeds for the
   farmer.
And from these seeds people have
   bread to eat.
[11]The words I say do the same thing.
   They will not return to me empty.
They make the things happen that I
   want to happen.
They succeed in doing what I send
   them to do.

[12]"So you will go out with joy.
   You will be led out in peace.
The mountains and hills will burst
   into song before you.
All the trees in the fields will clap
   their hands.
[13]Large cypress trees will grow where
   thornbushes were.
Myrtle trees will grow where weeds
   were.
These things will be a reminder of the
   Lord's promise.
And this reminder will never be
   destroyed."

ALL NATIONS WILL OBEY THE LORD

56 This is what the Lord says:
   "Give justice to all people.
Do what is right.

Do this because my salvation will
   come to you soon.
Soon everyone will know that I do
   what is right.
[2]The person who obeys the law about
   the Sabbath[d]
will be blessed.
And the person who does no evil
will be blessed."

[3]Foreigners have joined the Lord. They
   should not say,
   "The Lord will not accept me with
   his people."
The eunuch[d] should not say,
   "Because I cannot have children the
   Lord will not accept me."
[4]This is what the Lord says:
   "The eunuchs should obey the law
   about the Sabbath.
They should do what I want.
They should keep my agreement.
[5]If they do, I will make their names
   remembered
   within my Temple[d] and its walls.
It will be better for them than
   children.
I will give them a name that will last
   forever.
It will never be forgotten.
[6]Foreigners will join the Lord to serve
   him.
They will worship and love him.
They will worship him.
They will obey the law about the
   Sabbath.
They will keep the agreement with
   the Lord.
[7]I will bring these people to my holy
   mountain.
I will give them joy in my house of
   prayer.
The offerings and sacrifices
   they place on my altar will please me.
This is because my Temple will be
   called
   a house for prayer for people from
   all nations."

[8]The Lord gathers the Israelites who
　　were forced to leave their country.
　This is what the Lord God says,
　"I will bring other people to those
　　who are already gathered."

ISRAEL'S LEADERS ARE EVIL

[9]All you animals of the field, come to
　　eat.
　All you animals of the forest, come
　　to eat.
[10]The leaders who are to guard the
　　people are blind.
　They don't know what they are
　　doing.
　All of them are like quiet dogs.
　They don't know how to bark.
　They lie down and dream.
　They love to sleep.
[11]They are like hungry dogs.
　They are never satisfied.
　They are like shepherds
　　who don't know what they are
　　doing.
　They each have gone their own way.
　All they want to do is satisfy
　　themselves.
[12]They say, "Come, let's drink some
　　wine.
　Let's drink all the beer we want.
　And tomorrow we will do this again.
　Or, maybe we will have even a
　　better time."

ISRAEL DOES NOT FOLLOW GOD

57 Those right with God may die,
　　but no one pays attention.
　Good people are taken away,
　　but no one understands.
　The people who do right are being
　　taken away because of evil.
[2]　But they are given peace.
　The people who live the way God
　　wants them to
　find rest in death.

[3]"Come here, you magicians!
　Come here, you sons of prostitutes[d]
　　and those who take part in
　　adultery![d]

[4]Whom are you making fun of?
　Whom are you insulting?
　At whom do you stick out your
　　tongue?
　You turn against God,
　　and you are liars.
[5]You have sexual relations under every
　　green tree
　to worship your false gods.
　You kill children in the ravines
　　and sacrifice them in the rocky
　　places.
[6]You take the smooth rocks from the
　　ravines.
　They are your portion.
　You pour drink offerings on them to
　　worship them.
　You give grain offerings to them.
　Do you think this makes me want
　　to forgive you?
[7]You make your bed on every hill and
　　mountain.
　And there you offer sacrifices.
[8]You have hidden your idols
　　behind your doors and doorposts.
　You have left me, and you have
　　uncovered yourself.
　You have pulled back the covers
　　and climbed into bed.
　You have made an agreement with
　　the ones whose beds you love.
　And you have looked at their
　　nakedness.
[9]You use your oils and perfumes
　　to look nice for Molech.[d]
　You have sent your messengers to
　　faraway lands.
　You even tried to send them to
　　where the dead are.
[10]You have worked hard to do these
　　things.
　But you never gave up.
　You found new strength.
　So you did not quit.

[11]"Whom were you so afraid of
　　that you lied to me?
　You have not remembered me
　　or even thought about me.

I have been quiet for a long time.
  Is that why you are not afraid of me?
[12]I will tell about your 'goodness' and
  what you do.
  And those things will do you no
    good.
[13]When you cry out for help,
  let the false gods you have gathered
    help you.
The wind will blow them all away.
  Just a puff of wind will take them
    away.
But the person who depends on me
  will receive the land.
  He will have my holy mountain."

THE LORD WILL SAVE HIS PEOPLE

[14]The Lord says, "Build a road! Build a
  road! Prepare the way!
  Make the way clear for my people."
[15]God lives forever and is holy.
  He is high and lifted up, and he
    says,
"I live in a high and holy place.
  But I also live with people who are
    sad and humble.
I give new life to those who are
    humble.
  I give new life to those whose hearts
    are broken.
[16]I will not accuse forever.
  I will not always be angry.
If I continued to be angry, man's life
    would grow weak.
  Man, whom I created, would die.
[17]I was angry because they were
    dishonest in order to make
    money.
  I punished them and turned away
    from them in anger.
  But they continued to do evil.
[18]I have seen what they have done,
  but I will heal them.
I will guide them and comfort them.
  And those who were sad will praise
    me.
[19]I will give peace, real peace, to those
    far and near.
  And I will heal them," says the Lord.

[20]But evil people are like the angry sea.
  It cannot rest.
  Its waves toss up waste and mud.
[21]"There is no peace for evil people,"
  says my God.

HOW TO HONOR GOD

58 The Lord says, "Shout out loud.
    Don't hold back.
  Shout out loud like a trumpet.
Tell the people about the things they
  have done against God.
  Tell the family of Jacob about their
    sins.
[2]Then they will come every day looking
    for me.
  And they will want to learn my
    ways.
They will become a nation that does
    what is right.
  They will obey the commands of
    their God.
They will ask me to judge them fairly.
  They will want God to be near them.
[3]They say, 'To honor you we had
    special days when we gave up
    eating.
  But you didn't see.
We humbled ourselves to honor you.
  But you didn't notice.'"

But the Lord says, "You do what
    pleases yourselves on these
    special days.
  And you are unfair to your workers.
[4]On these special days when you do
    not eat, you argue and fight.
  You hit each other with your fists.
You cannot do these things as you do
    now
  and believe I will listen to your
    prayers.
[5]This kind of special day is not what I
    want.
  This is not the way I want people to
    be sorry for what they have done.
I don't want people just to bow their
    heads like a plant.

I don't want them to wear rough
cloth and lie in ashes to show
their sadness.
This is what you do on your special
days when you do not eat.
But do you think this is what the
Lord wants?

⁶"I will tell you the kind of special day
I want.
I want you to free the people you have
put in prison unfairly.
Undo their chains.
Free those to whom you are unfair.
Free them from their hard labor.
⁷I want you to share your food with
hungry people.
I want you to bring poor, homeless
people into your own homes.
When you see someone who has no
clothes, give him yours.
Don't refuse to help your own
relatives.
⁸If you do these things, your light will
shine like the dawn.
Then your wounds will quickly heal.
Your God will walk before you,
and the glory of the Lord will
protect you from behind.
⁹Then you will call to the Lord, and the
Lord will answer you.
You will cry out to the Lord, and he
will say, 'Here I am.'

"You should stop making trouble for
others.
You should stop using cruel words
and pointing your finger at others.
¹⁰You should feed those who are hungry.
You should take care of the needs of
those who are troubled.
Then your light will shine in the
darkness.
And you will be bright like sunshine
at noon.
¹¹The Lord will always lead you.
He will satisfy your needs in dry
lands.
He will give strength to your bones.

You will be like a garden that has
much water.
You will be like a spring that never
runs dry.
¹²Your people will rebuild the old cities
that are now in ruins.
You will rebuild the foundations of
these ancient cities.
You will be known for repairing the
broken places.
You will be known for rebuilding
the roads and houses.

¹³"You must obey God's law about the
Sabbath.ᵈ
You must not do what pleases
yourselves on that holy day.
You should call the Sabbath a joyful
day.
You should honor the Lord's holy
day.
You should honor it by not doing
whatever you please on that day.
You should not say whatever you
please on that day.
¹⁴Then you will find joy in the Lord.
And I, the Lord, will carry you to
the high places above the earth.
I will let you eat the crops of the
land your ancestor Jacob had."
The Lord has said these things.

THE EVIL THAT PEOPLE DO

59 Surely the Lord's power is
enough to save you.
He can hear you when you ask him
for help.
²It is your evil that has separated
you from your God.
Your sins cause him to turn away
from you.
And then he does not hear you.
³With your hands you have killed
others.
Your fingers are covered with blood
from killing people.
With your lips you have lied.
With your tongue you say evil
things.

⁴People take each other to court
   unfairly.
   No one tells the truth in arguing his
      case.
   They accuse each other falsely and tell
      lies.
   They cause trouble and create more
      evil.
⁵They hatch evil like eggs from
   poisonous snakes.
   If you eat one of those eggs, you will
      die.
   And if you break one open, a
      poisonous snake comes out.
   People tell lies as they would spin a
      spider's web.
⁶   The webs they make cannot be used
      for clothes.
   You can't cover yourself with those
      webs.
   The things they do are evil.
   They use their hands to hurt others.
⁷They eagerly run to do evil.
   They are always ready to kill
      innocent people.
   They think evil thoughts.
   Everywhere they go they cause ruin
      and destruction.
⁸They don't know how to live in peace.
   There is no fairness in their lives.
   They are dishonest.
   Anyone who lives as they live will
      never have peace.

ISRAEL'S SIN BRINGS TROUBLE

⁹Fairness has gone far away.
   Goodness is nowhere to be found.
   We wait for the light, but there is only
      darkness now.
   We hope for a bright light, but all
      we have is darkness.
¹⁰We are like blind people feeling our
   way along a wall.
   We have to feel our way as if we had
      no eyes.
   In the brightness of day we trip as if it
      were night.
   We are like dead men among the
      strong.

¹¹All of us growl like the bears.
   We call out sadly like the doves.
   We look for justice, but there isn't
      any.
   We want to be saved, but salvation
      is far away.
¹²We have done many wrong things
   against our God.
   Our sins show we are wrong.
   We know we have turned against God.
   We know the evil things we have
      done.
¹³We have sinned and turned against
   the Lord.
   We have turned away from our
      God.
   We have planned to hurt others and
      to disobey God.
   We have planned and spoken lies.
¹⁴We have driven away justice.
   We have kept away from what is
      right.
   Truth is not spoken in the streets.
   What is honest is not allowed to
      enter the city.
¹⁵Truth cannot be found anywhere.
   And people who refuse to do evil
      are attacked.

   The Lord looked and could not find
      any justice.
   And he was displeased.
¹⁶He could not find anyone to help the
      people.
   He was surprised that there was no
      one to help.
   So the Lord used his own power to
      save the people.
   His own goodness gave him
      strength.
¹⁷The Lord covered himself with
      goodness like armor.
   He put on the helmet of salvation.
   He put on the clothes of punishment.
   And he put on the coat of his strong
      love.
¹⁸The Lord will pay back his enemies
      for what they have done.

He will show his anger to those who
were against him.
He will punish the people in faraway
places.
He will give them the punishment
they should have.
19Then people from the west will fear
the Lord.
People in the east will fear his glory.
The Lord will come quickly like a fast-
flowing river,
driven by the breath of the Lord.

20"Then a close relative who will save
you will come to Jerusalem.
He will come to the people of Jacob
who sinned but turned back to
God,"
says the Lord.

21The Lord says, "I will make an agreement with these people. I promise that
my Spirit[d] and my words that I give you
will never leave you. They will be with
your children and your grandchildren.
They will be with you now and forever."

JERUSALEM WILL BE GREAT

60 "Jerusalem, get up and shine.
Your light has come.
The glory of the Lord shines on you.
2Darkness now covers the earth.
Deep darkness covers her people.
But the Lord shines on you,
and people see his glory around you.
3Nations will come to your light.
Kings will come to the brightness of
your sunrise.

4"Look around you.
People are gathering and coming to
you.
They are your sons coming from far
away.
And your daughters are coming
with them.
5When you see them, you will shine
with happiness.
You will be excited and full of joy.

The wealth of the nations across the
seas will be given to you.
The riches of the nations will come
to you.
6Herds of camels will cover your land.
Young camels will come from
Midian and Ephah.
People will come from Sheba
bringing gold and incense.[d]
And they will sing praises to the
Lord.
7All the sheep from Kedar will be given
to you.
The male sheep from Nebaioth will
be brought to you.
They will be pleasing sacrifices on my
altar.
And I will make my beautiful
Temple[d] more beautiful.

8"The people are returning to you like
clouds.
They are like doves flying to their
nests.
9People in faraway lands are waiting
for me.
The great trading ships will come
first.
They are bringing your children from
faraway lands.
And with them they bring silver
and gold.
This will happen to honor the Lord
your God.
He is the Holy One of Israel.
And he does wonderful things for
you.

10"Jerusalem, foreigners will rebuild
your walls.
Their kings will serve you.
When I was angry, I hurt you.
But now I want to be kind to you
and comfort you.
11Your gates will always be open.
They will not be closed day or night
so the nations can bring their wealth
to you.
And their kings will be led to you.

¹²If a nation or kingdom doesn't serve
      you,
    it will be destroyed.
    It will be completely ruined.

¹³"The great trees of Lebanon will be
      given to you.
    Its pine, fir and cypress trees will
      come to you.
  You will use these trees to make my
      Temple beautiful.
    And I will give much honor to this
      place where I rest my feet.
¹⁴The people who have hurt you will
      bow down to you.
    Those who hated you will bow
      down at your feet.
  They will call you The City of the
      Lord.
    They will call you Jerusalem, city of
      the Holy One of Israel.

¹⁵"You have been hated and left empty.
    No one has even passed through.
  But I will make you great from now on.
    You will be a place of happiness
      forever and ever.
¹⁶Nations will give you what you need.
    It will be like a child drinking milk
      from its mother.
  Then you will know that it is I, the
      Lord, who saves you.
    You will know that the Powerful
      One of Jacob protects you.
¹⁷I will bring you gold in place of
      bronze.
    I will bring you silver in place of
      iron.
  I will bring you bronze in place of
      wood.
    I will bring you iron in place of
      rocks.
  I will change your punishment into
      peace.
    And you will be ruled by what is
      right.
¹⁸There will be no more violence in your
      country.
    It will not be ruined or destroyed.

You will name your walls Salvation.
    And you will name your gates
      Praise.
¹⁹The sun will no longer be your light
      during the day.
    The light from the moon will no
      longer be your light.
  This is because the Lord will be your
      light forever.
    Your God will be your glory.
²⁰Your sun will never set again.
    Your moon will never be dark
      again.
  This is because the Lord will be your
      light forever.
    And your time of sadness will end.
²¹All of your people will do what is
      right.
    They will receive the earth forever.
  They are the plant I have planted.
    I made them with my own hands to
      show my greatness.
²²The smallest family will grow to a
      thousand.
    The least important of you will
      become a powerful nation.
  I am the Lord,
    and when it is time, I will make
      these things happen quickly."

THE LORD'S MESSAGE OF FREEDOM

61 The Lord God has put his Spirit[d]
      in me.
  This is because he has appointed
      me to tell the good news to the
      poor.
  He has sent me to comfort those
      whose hearts are broken.
  He has sent me to tell the captives
      they are free.
  He has sent me to tell the prisoners
      that they are released.
²He has sent me to announce the time
      when the Lord will show his
      kindness
  and the time when our God will
      punish evil people.
  He has sent me to comfort all those
      who are sad.

³He has sent me to the sorrowing
   people of Jerusalem.
 I will give them a crown to replace
   their ashes.
 I will give them the oil of gladness to
   replace their sorrow.
 I will give them clothes of praise to
   replace their spirit of sadness.
 Then they will be called Trees of
   Goodness.
 They will be like trees planted by
   the Lord and will show his
   greatness.

⁴They will rebuild the old ruins.
 They will build up the places
   destroyed long ago.
 They will repair the ruined cities
   that were destroyed for so long.

⁵My people, foreigners will come to
   tend your sheep.
 People from other countries will
   tend your vineyards.
⁶You will be called priests of the Lord.
 You will be named the servants of
   our God.
 You will have riches from all the
   nations on earth.
 And you will take pride in them.
⁷Instead of being ashamed, you will
   receive twice as much wealth.
 Instead of being disgraced, you will
   be happy because of what you
   receive.
 You will receive a double share of the
   land.
 So your happiness will continue
   forever.
⁸The Lord says, "I love justice.
 I hate stealing and everything that
   is wrong.
 I will be fair and give my people what
   they should have.
 I will make an agreement with them
   that will continue forever.
⁹Everyone in all nations will know the
   children of my people.

And their children will be known
   among the nations.
 Anyone who sees them will know
   that the Lord blesses them."

¹⁰The Lord makes me very happy.
 All that I am rejoices in my God.
 The Lord has covered me with clothes
   of salvation.
 He has covered me with a coat of
   goodness.
 I am like a bridegroom dressed for his
   wedding.
 I am like a bride dressed in jewels.
¹¹The earth causes plants to grow.
 And a garden causes the seeds
   planted there to grow.
 In the same way the Lord God will
   make grow what is right.
 He will make praise come from all
   the nations.

NEW JERUSALEM

62 Because I love Jerusalem, I will
     continue to speak for her.
 For Jerusalem's sake I will not stop
   speaking.
 I will speak until her goodness shines
   like a bright light.
 I will speak until her salvation
   burns bright like a flame.
²Jerusalem, the nations will see your
   goodness.
 All kings will see your honor.
 Then you will have a new name.
 The Lord himself will give you that
   new name.
³You will be like a beautiful crown in
   the Lord's hand.
 You will be like a king's crown in
   your God's hand.
⁴You will never again be called the
   People that God Left.
 Your land will never again be called
   the Land that God Destroyed.
 You will be called the People God
   Loves.
 Your land will be called the Bride
   of God.

This is because the Lord loves you.
 And your land will belong to him as
  a bride belongs to her husband.
⁵As a young man marries a woman,
 so your children will marry your
  land.
As a man is very happy about his new
  wife,
 so your God will be happy with you.

⁶Jerusalem, I have put guards on the
  walls to watch.
 They must not be silent day or
  night.
You people who remind the Lord
 should never be quiet.
⁷You should not stop praying to the
  Lord until he builds up
  Jerusalem.
 Don't stop until he makes Jerusalem
  a city all people will praise.

⁸The Lord has made a promise.
 And by his power he will keep his
  promise.
He said, "I will never again give your
  grain
 as food to your enemies.
I will not let your enemies drink the
  wine
 that you have worked to make.
⁹The person who gathers food will eat it.
 And he will praise the Lord.
The person who gathers the grapes
  will drink the wine
 in the courts of my Temple."ᵈ

¹⁰Go through, go through the gates!
 Make the way ready for the people.
Build up, build up the road!
 Move all the stones off the road.
Raise the banner as a sign for the
  people.

¹¹The Lord is speaking
 to all the faraway lands:
"Tell the people of Jerusalem,
 'Look, your Savior is coming.
He is bringing your reward to you.
 He is bringing his payment with
  him.'"

¹²His people will be called the Holy
  People.
 They will be called the Saved People
  of the Lord.
And Jerusalem will be called the City
  God Wants.
 It will be named the City God Has
  Not Rejected.

THE LORD JUDGES HIS PEOPLE

63 Who is this coming from Edom?
  He comes from the city of
   Bozrah dressed in red.
Who is this dressed in fine clothes?
 He marches forward with his great
  power.

He says, "I, the Lord, speak what is
  right.
 I have the power to save you."

²Why are your clothes bright red
 as if you had walked on the grapes
  to make wine?

³The Lord answers, "I have walked in
  the winepressᵈ alone.
 No one among the nations helped
  me.
I was angry and walked on the
  nations.
 I crushed them because of my
  anger.
Blood splashed on my clothes.
 I stained all my clothing.
⁴I chose a time to punish people.
 And the time has come for me to
  save my people.
⁵I looked around, but I saw no one to
  help me.
 I was surprised that no one
  supported me.
So I used my own power to save my
  people.
 My own anger supported me.
⁶While I was angry, I walked on the
  nations.
 In my anger I punished them
  and poured their blood on the
  ground."

THE LORD'S KINDNESS TO HIS PEOPLE

7I will tell about the Lord's kindness.
  And I will praise him for what he
    has done.
He has given many good things to us.
  He has been very good to the people
    of Israel.
The Lord has shown mercy to us.
  And he has been kind to us.
8The Lord said, "These are my people.
  My children will not lie to me."
So the Lord saved them.
9When they suffered, he suffered also.
  He sent his own angel to save them.
Because of his love and kindness, the
    Lord saved them.
  Since long ago he has picked them
    up and carried them.
10But they turned against the Lord.
  They made his Holy Spirit*d* very sad.
So the Lord became their enemy.
  And he fought against them.

11But then his people remembered what
    happened long ago.
  They remembered Moses.
Where is the Lord who brought the
    people through the sea?
  Where is the one who brought them
    with the leaders of his people?
Where is the one
  who put his Holy Spirit among
    them?
12The Lord led Moses by the right hand.
  The Lord led him by his wonderful
    power.
The Lord divided the water before
    them so the people could walk
    through the sea.
  And by this the Lord made his
    name famous forever.
13The Lord led the people through the
    deep waters.
  Like a horse walking through a desert,
    the people did not stumble.
14Like cattle that go down to the valley,
    the Spirit of the Lord led the people
    to a place of rest.

Lord, that is the way you led your
    people.
  And by this you made your name
    wonderful.

A PRAYER FOR HELP

15Lord, look down from the heavens
    and see.
  Look at us from your wonderful
    holy home in heaven.
Where is your strong love and power?
  Why are you keeping your love and
    mercy from us?
16You are our father.
  Abraham doesn't know we are his
    children.
  Israel doesn't know who we are.
Lord, you are our father.
  You are called "the one who has
    always saved us."
17Lord, why are you making us wander
    from your ways?
  Why do you make us stubborn so
    that we don't honor you?
For our sake come back to us.
  We are your servants, and we
    belong to you.
18Your people had your Temple*d* for a
    while.
  But now our enemies have walked
    on your holy place and crushed it.
19You have never ruled over some
    people.
  They have never worn your name.
And we have become like those
    people.

64 Tear open the skies and come
    down to earth.
  The mountains would tremble
    before you.
2Be like a fire that burns twigs.
  Be like a fire that makes water boil.
Do this so that your enemies will
    know who you are.
  Then all nations will shake with fear
    when they see you.
3You have done amazing things that
    we did not expect.

You came down, and the
  mountains trembled before you.
[4]From long ago no one has ever heard
  of a God like you.
No one has ever seen a God besides
  you.
You help the people who trust you.
[5]You help those who enjoy doing good.
You help those who remember how
  you want them to live.
But you were angry because we sinned.
For a long time we disobeyed.
How will we be saved?
[6]All of us are dirty with sin.
All the right things we have done
  are like filthy pieces of cloth.
All of us are like dead leaves.
Like the wind our sins have carried
  us away.
[7]No one worships you.
No one even asks you to help us.
So you have turned away from us.
And we are destroyed because of
  our sins.

[8]But Lord, you are our father.
We are like clay, and you are the
  potter.
Your hands made us all.
[9]Lord, don't continue to be angry with
  us.
Don't remember our sins forever.
Please, look at us
  because we are your people.
[10]Your holy cities are empty like the
  desert.
Jerusalem is like a desert;
Jerusalem is destroyed.
[11]Our ancestors worshiped you
  in our holy and wonderful Temple.
But now it has been burned with fire.
All our precious things have been
  destroyed.
[12]When you see these things, will you
  hold yourself back from helping
  us, Lord?
Will you be silent and punish us
  beyond what we can stand?

ALL PEOPLE WILL LEARN ABOUT GOD

65 The Lord says, "I made myself
  known to people who were
  not looking for me.
I was found by those who were not
  asking me for help.
I spoke to a nation that was not
  praying to me.
I said, 'Here I am. Here I am.'
[2]All day long I stood ready to accept
  people who turned against me.
But the way they continue to live is
  not good.
They do anything they want to do.
[3]Right in front of me they continue
  to do things that make me angry.
They offer sacrifices to their false
  gods in their gardens.
They burn incense[d] on altars of
  brick.
[4]They sit among the graves.
They spend their nights waiting to
  get messages from the dead.
They eat the meat of pigs.
Their pots are full of soup made
  from meat that is wrong to eat.
[5]But they tell others, 'Stay away. Don't
  come near me.
I am too holy for you.'
These people are like smoke in my
  nose.
Like a fire that burns all the time,
  they continue to make me
  angry.

[6]"Look, it is written here before me.
I will not be quiet. Instead, I will
  repay you in full.
I will punish you for what you have
  done.
[7]I will punish you for your sins and
  your ancestors' sins,"
  says the Lord.
"They burned incense to false gods on
  the mountains.
They shamed me on those hills.
So I will punish them as they should
  be punished
  for what they did."

[8]This is what the Lord says:
"When there is juice left in the grapes,
    people do not destroy them.
They know there is good left in
    them.
I will do the same thing to my servants.
    I will not completely destroy them.
[9]I will leave some of the children of
    Jacob.
    Some of the people of Judah will
        receive my mountain.
I will choose the people who will live
    there.
    My servants will live there.
[10]Then the Plain of Sharon will be a
    field for sheep.
    The Valley of Achor will be a place
        for cattle to rest.
    They will be for the people who
        want to follow me.

[11]"But you who left the Lord will be
    punished.
    You forgot about my holy
        mountain.
You worship the false god Luck.
    You hold religious feasts for the
        false god Fate.
[12]But I decide your fate, and I will
    punish you with my sword.
    You will all be killed.
This is because I called you, but you
    refused to answer.
    I spoke to you, but you wouldn't
        listen.
You did the things I said were evil.
    You chose to do things that
        displease me."

[13]So the Lord God said these things:
"My servants will eat.
    But you evil people will be hungry.
My servants will drink.
    But you evil people will be thirsty.
My servants will be happy.
    But you evil people will be shamed.
[14]My servants will shout for joy
    because of the goodness of their
        hearts.

But you evil people will cry,
    because you will be sad.
You will cry loudly because your
    spirits will be broken.
[15]Your names will be like curses to my
    servants.
    And the Lord God will put you to
        death.
But he will call his servants by
    another name.
[16]People in the land who ask for
    blessings
    will ask for them from the faithful
        God.
People in the land who make a
    promise
    will promise in the name of the
        faithful God.
This is because the troubles of the
    past will be forgotten.
    I will make those troubles go away.

A NEW TIME IS COMING

[17]"Look, I will make new heavens and a
    new earth.
    And people will not remember the
        past.
    They will not think about those
        things.
[18]My people will be happy forever
    because of the things I will make.
I will make a Jerusalem that is full of
    joy.
    And I will make her people a
        delight.
[19]Then I will rejoice over Jerusalem.
    I will be delighted with my people.
There will never again be
    crying and sadness in that city.
[20]There will never be a baby from that
    city
    who lives only a few days.
And there will never be an older
    person
    who doesn't have a long life.
A person who lives 100 years will be
    called young.
    And the person who dies before he is
        100 will be thought of as a sinner.

[21]In that city the person who builds a
house will live there.
The person who plants vineyards
will get to eat grapes.
[22]No more will one person build a house
and someone else live there.
One person will not plant a garden
and someone else eat its fruit.
My people will live a long time
as trees live long.
My chosen people will live there
and enjoy the things they make.
[23]People will never again work for
nothing.
They will never again give birth to
children who die young.
All my people will be blessed by the
Lord.
My people and their children will be
blessed.
[24]I will provide for their needs before
they ask.
I will help them while they are still
asking for help.
[25]Wolves and lambs will eat together in
peace.
Lions will eat hay like oxen.
A snake on the ground will not hurt
anyone.
They will not hurt or destroy each
other
on all my holy mountain,"
says the Lord.

GOD WILL JUDGE ALL NATIONS

66 This is what the Lord says:
"The skies are my throne.
The earth is my footstool.
So do you think you can build a house
for me?
There is no place where I need to
rest.
[2]My hand made all things.
All things are here because I made
them,"
says the Lord.

"These are the people I am pleased
with.
They are those who are not proud
or stubborn.
They fear me and obey me.
[3]But those people who kill bulls as a
sacrifice to me
are like those who kill men.
Those who kill sheep as a sacrifice to
me
are like those who break the necks
of dogs.
Those who give me grain offerings
are like those who offer me the
blood of pigs.[n]
Those who burn incense[d]
are like those who worship idols.
These people choose their own
ways—not mine.
They love the terrible things they
do.
[4]So I will punish them.
I will punish them using what they
fear most.
I called to them, but they did not
listen.
I spoke to them, but they did not
hear me.
They did things I said were evil.
They chose to do things I did not
like."

[5]You people who obey the words of the
Lord,
listen to what he says:
"Your brothers hated you.
They turned against you because
you followed me.
Your brothers said, 'When the Lord is
honored,
we will come back and rejoice with
you.'
But they will be punished.
[6]Listen to the loud noise coming from
the city.
Hear the noise from the Temple.[d]

66:3 dogs . . . pigs God did not want his people to offer dogs and pigs as sacrifices because they were unclean animals.

It is the Lord punishing his enemies.
He is giving them the punishment
they should have.

7"A woman does not give birth before
she feels the pain.
She does not give birth to a son
before she feels the pain of birth.
8No one has ever heard of that
happening.
No one has ever seen that happen.
In the same way no one ever saw a
country begin in one day.
No one has ever heard of a new
nation beginning in one day.
But Jerusalem will give birth to her
children
just as soon as she feels the birth
pains.
9In the same way I will not cause pain
without allowing something new to
be born," says the Lord.
"If I cause you the pain,
I will not stop you from giving birth
to your new nation," says your
God.
10"Jerusalem, rejoice.
All you people who love Jerusalem,
be happy.
Those of you who felt sad for
Jerusalem
should now feel happy with her.
11You will enjoy her good things and be
satisfied
as a child is nursed by its mother.
You will receive her good things
and enjoy her wealth."

12This is what the Lord says:

"I will give her peace that will flow to
her like a river.
The wealth of the nations will come
flowing to her.
Like babies you will be nursed and
held in my arms.
You will be bounced on my knees.
13I will comfort you
as a mother comforts her child.
You will be comforted in Jerusalem."

14When you see these things, you will be
happy.
You will grow like the grass.
The Lord's servants will see his
power.
But the Lord's enemies will see his
anger.
15Look, the Lord is coming with fire.
The Lord's armies are coming with
clouds of dust.
He will punish those people with his
anger.
He will punish them with flames of
fire.
16The Lord will judge the people with
fire.
He will destroy many people with
his sword.
He will kill many people.

17"These people make themselves holy
and pure to go to worship their false gods
in their gardens. They follow each other
into their special gardens. They eat the
meat of pigs and rats and other hated
things. But they will all be destroyed
together," says the Lord.

18"I know they have evil thoughts and
do evil things. So I am coming to punish
them. I will gather all nations and all
people. All people will come together
and see my glory.

19"I will put a mark on some of the
people. And I will send some of these
saved people to the nations. I will send
them to Tarshish, Libya, Lud (the land of
archers), Tubal, Greece and all the faraway lands. These people have never
heard about what I have done. They have
never seen my glory. So the saved people
will tell the nations about my glory. 20And
they will bring all your fellow Israelites
from all nations. They will bring them to
my holy mountain in Jerusalem. Your
fellow Israelites will come on horses, donkeys, camels and in chariots and wagons.
They will be like the grain offerings that
the people bring in clean containers to

the Temple," says the Lord. [21]"And I will choose some of these people to be priests and Levites," says the Lord.

[22]"I will make new heavens and the new earth. And they will last forever," says the Lord. "In the same way, your names and your children will always be with me. [23]All people will come to worship me. They will come to worship me every Sabbath[d] and every New Moon,"[d] says the Lord. [24]"They will go out and see the dead bodies of the people who sinned against me. The worms that eat them will never die. The fires that burn them will never stop. And everyone will hate to see those bodies."

THE BOOK OF
JEREMIAH

1 These are the words of Jeremiah son of Hilkiah. He belonged to the family of priests who lived in the town of Anathoth. That town is in the land that belongs to the tribe*d* of Benjamin. ²The Lord spoke his word to Jeremiah. This happened during the thirteenth year that Josiah son of Amon was king of Judah. ³The Lord also spoke to Jeremiah while Jehoiakim son of Josiah was king of Judah. And the Lord spoke to Jeremiah during the 11 years and 5 months Zedekiah son of Josiah was king of Judah. After that, the people who lived in Jerusalem were taken away as captives out of their country.

GOD CALLS JEREMIAH

⁴The Lord spoke these words to me:
⁵"Before I made you in your mother's
womb, I chose you.
Before you were born, I set you
apart for a special work.
I appointed you as a prophet*d* to the
nations."

⁶Then I said, "But Lord God, I don't know how to speak. I am only a boy."

⁷But the Lord said to me, "Don't say, 'I am only a boy.' You must go everywhere that I send you. You must say everything I tell you to say. ⁸Don't be afraid of anyone, because I am with you. I will protect you," says the Lord.

⁹Then the Lord reached out with his hand and touched my mouth. He said to me, "See, I am putting my words in your mouth. ¹⁰Today I have put you in charge of nations and kingdoms. You will pull up and tear down, destroy and overthrow. You will build up and plant."

TWO VISIONS

¹¹The Lord spoke this word to me: "Jeremiah, what do you see?"

I answered the Lord and said, "I see a stick of almond wood."

¹²The Lord said to me, "You have seen correctly! And I am watching to make sure my words come true."

¹³The Lord spoke his word to me again: "Jeremiah, what do you see?"

I answered the Lord and said, "I see a pot of boiling water. It is tipping over from the north!"

¹⁴The Lord said to me, "Disaster will come from the north. It will happen to all the people who live in this country. ¹⁵In a short time I will call all of the people in the northern kingdoms," said the Lord.
"Those kings will come and set up
their thrones
near the entrance of the gates of
Jerusalem.
They will attack the city walls around
Jerusalem.
They will attack all the cities in
Judah.
¹⁶And I will announce my judgments
against my people.
I will do this because of their evil in
turning away from me.
They offered sacrifices to other gods.
And they worshiped idols they had
made with their own hands.

¹⁷"Jeremiah, get ready. Stand up and speak to the people. Tell them everything I tell you to say. Don't be afraid of the people. If you are afraid of them, I will give you good reason to be afraid of them. ¹⁸Today I am going to make you a strong city, an iron pillar, a bronze wall. You will be able to stand against everyone in the land: Judah's kings, officers, priests and the people of the land. ¹⁹They will fight against you. But they will not defeat you. This is because I am with you, and I will save you!" says the Lord.

ISRAEL TURNS FROM GOD

2 The Lord spoke this word to me: ²"Go and speak to the people of Jerusalem. Say to them: This is what the Lord says:

'When you were a young nation, you
were faithful to me.
You loved me like a young bride.
You followed me through the desert.
It was a land that had never been
planted.
³The people of Israel were holy to the
Lord.
They were like the first fruits from
his harvest.
Those who tried to hurt Israel were
judged guilty.
Disasters happened to them,'" says
the Lord.

⁴Hear the word of the Lord, family of
Jacob.
Hear the message, all you family
groups of Israel.
⁵This is what the Lord says:
"I was fair to your ancestors.
Why did they turn away from me?
Your ancestors worshiped useless
idols.
And they became useless
themselves.
⁶Your ancestors didn't say,
'The Lord brought us out of Egypt.
He led us through the desert.
He led us through a dry and rocky
land.
He led us through a dark and
dangerous land.
He led us where no one travels or
lives.
But where is he now?'
⁷I brought you into a fertile land.
I did this so you could eat its fruit
and produce.
But you came and made my land
unclean.ᵈ
You made it a hated place.
⁸The priests didn't ask,
'Where is the Lord?'
The people who know the teachings
didn't know me.
The leaders turned against me.

The prophetsᵈ prophesied in the
name of Baal.ᵈ
They worshiped useless idols.

⁹"So now I will again tell what I have
against you," says the Lord.
"And I will tell what I have against
your grandchildren.
¹⁰Go across the sea to the island of
Cyprus and see.
Send someone to the land of Kedar
to look closely.
See if there has ever been anything
like this!
¹¹Has a nation ever exchanged their old
gods for new ones?
(Of course, their gods are not really
gods at all.)
But my people have exchanged their
glorious God
for idols worth nothing!
¹²Skies, be shocked at the things that
have happened.
Shake with great fear!" says the
Lord.
¹³"My people have done two sins.
They have turned away from me.
And I am the spring of living water.
And they have dug their own wells.
But they are broken wells that
cannot hold water.
¹⁴Have the people of Israel become
slaves?
Have they become like someone
who was born a slave?
Why was their wealth stolen?
¹⁵Enemies roar like lions at Israel.
They growl at Israel.
They have destroyed the land of
Israel.
The cities of Israel have been
burned,
and all the people have left.
¹⁶The men from the Egyptian cities of
Memphis and Tahpanhes
have disgraced you by shaving the
top of your head.
¹⁷You have brought this on yourselves.

You turned away from me, the Lord
your God,
when I led you in the way.
¹⁸It did not help to go to Egypt
and drink from the Shihor River.
It did not help to go to Assyria
and drink from the Euphrates
River.
¹⁹Your evil will bring punishment to you.
The wrong you have done will teach
you a lesson.
Think about it and understand.
It is a terrible evil to turn away from
the Lord your God.
It is wrong not to fear me,"
says the Lord, the Lord of heaven's
armies.

²⁰"A long time ago you refused to obey
me as an ox breaks its yoke.ᵈ
You broke the ropes I used to hold
you to me.
You said to me, 'I will not serve
you!'
In fact, on every high hill
and under every green tree
you lay down as a prostitute.ᵈ
²¹I planted you as a special vine.
You were like very good seed.
How then did you turn
into a wild vine that grows bad
fruit?
²²You might wash yourself with
cleanser.
And you might use much soap.
But I can still see the stain of your
guilt," says the Lord God.
²³"How can you say to me, 'I am not
guilty.
I have not worshiped the Baalᵈ
idols'?
Think about the things you did in the
valley.
Think about what you have done.
You are like a she-camel in mating
season
that runs from place to place.

²⁴You are like a wild donkey that lives
in the desert.
At mating time she sniffs the wind.
At that time no one can hold her
back.
Any male who chases her will easily
catch her.
At mating time, it is easy to find
her.
²⁵Don't run until your feet are bare
or until your throat is dry.
But you say, 'It's no use!
I love those other gods.
I must worship them!'

²⁶"A thief is ashamed when someone
catches him stealing.
In the same way the family of Israel
is ashamed.
The kings and the officers,
the priests and the prophets are
ashamed.
²⁷They say to things of wood, 'You are
my father.'
They say to idols of stone, 'You gave
birth to me.'
Those people won't look at me.
They have turned their backs to me.
But when they get into trouble,
they say,
'Come and save us!'
²⁸Where are the idols you have made
for yourselves?
Let them come and save you
when you are in trouble!
People of Judah, you have as many
idols
as you have towns!

²⁹"Why do you accuse me?
All of you have turned against me,"
says the Lord.
³⁰"I punished your people, but it did
not help.
They didn't come back when they
were punished.
You killed with your swords the
prophets who came to you.
You were like a dangerous lion.

³¹"People of Judah, pay attention to
the word of the Lord:
  Have I been like a desert to the people
    of Israel?
    Have I been like a dark and
      dangerous land to them?
  Why do my people say, 'We are free to
    wander.
    We won't come to you anymore'?
³²A young woman does not forget her
    jewelry.
    A bride does not forget the
      decorations for her dress.
  But my people have forgotten me
    for more days than can be counted!
³³You really know how to chase after
    love.
    Even the worst women can learn
      evil ways from you.
³⁴You have blood on your clothes.
    It is the blood of the poor and
      innocent people.
  You killed them,
    but they weren't thieves you had
      caught breaking in.
  You do all these things,
³⁵   but you say, 'I am innocent.
    God is not angry with me.'
  But I will judge you guilty of lying.
    It is because you say, 'I have not
      sinned.'
³⁶It is so easy for you to change your
    mind.
    Assyria let you down.
    And Egypt will let you down, too.
³⁷You will eventually leave that place.
    And, like captives, your hands will
      be on your head.
  You trusted those countries.
    But you will not be helped by them.
  This is because the Lord has rejected
    them.

JUDAH IS UNFAITHFUL

3 "Now a man might divorce his
    wife.
    And she might leave him and marry
      another man.

Should her first husband come back
    to her again?
  If he went back to her, the land
    would become completely
    unclean.ᵈ
  But you have acted like a prostituteᵈ
    with many lovers.
    And now you want to come back to
      me?" says the Lord.
²"Look up to the bare hilltops, Judah.
    Is there any place where you have
      not been a prostitute?
  You have sat by the road waiting for
    lovers.
    You sat there like an Arab in the
      desert.
  You made the land unclean.
    This was because you did evil and
      were like a prostitute.
³So the rain has not come.
    There have not been any spring
      rains.
  But your face still looks like the face of
    a prostitute.
    You refuse even to be ashamed of
      what you did.
⁴But now you are calling to me.
    You say, 'My father, you have been
      my friend since I was young.
⁵Will you always be angry at me?
    Will your anger last forever?'
  Judah, you say this,
    but you do as much evil as you can!"

JUDAH AND ISRAEL ARE LIKE SISTERS

⁶When King Josiah was ruling Judah,
the Lord spoke to me. He said: "Jeremiah,
you saw what unfaithful Israel did. She
was guilty of adultery.ᵈ She had idols on
every hill and under every green tree. ⁷I
said to myself, 'Israel will come back to
me after she does this evil.' But she didn't
come back to me. And Israel's wicked
sister Judah saw what Israel did. ⁸Un-
faithful Israel knew that I divorced her
because of her adultery. But that didn't
make her wicked sister Judah afraid. She
also went out and acted like a prostitute!ᵈ ⁹And she didn't care that she was

acting like a prostitute. So she made her country unclean.*d* She was guilty of adultery. This was because she worshiped idols made of stone and wood. [10]Israel's wicked sister didn't come back to me with her whole heart. She only pretended to come back to me," says the Lord.

[11]The Lord said to me, "Unfaithful Israel had a better excuse than wicked Judah. [12]Go and speak this message toward the north:

'Come back, unfaithful people of Israel,'
     says the Lord.
'I will stop frowning at you.
I am full of mercy,' says the Lord.
'I will not be angry with you
     forever.
[13]All you have to do is admit your sin.
     You turned against the Lord your
          God.
     You worshiped the false gods of other
          nations.
     You worshiped them under every
          green tree.
     You didn't obey me,'" says the Lord.

[14]"Come back to me, you unfaithful people," says the Lord. "I am your husband. I will take one person from every city. And I will take two people from every family group. And I will bring you to Jerusalem. [15]Then I will give you new rulers. They will be faithful to me. They will lead you with knowledge and understanding. [16]In those days there will be many of you in the land," says the Lord. "At that time people will no longer say, 'I remember the Box*d* of the Agreement.' They won't even think about the Holy Box anymore. They won't even remember or miss it or make another one. [17]At that time Jerusalem will be called The Throne of the Lord. All nations will come together in Jerusalem to show respect to the Lord. They will not follow their stubborn, evil hearts anymore. [18]In those days the family of Judah will join the family of Israel. They will come together

from a land in the north. They will come to the land I gave to their ancestors.

[19]"I, the Lord, said,
'How happy I would be to treat you as
     sons!
     I would be glad to give you a
          pleasant land.
     It's a land more beautiful than that
          of any other nation.'
I thought you would call me 'Father'
     and not turn away from me.
[20]But like a woman who is unfaithful to
     her husband,
     family of Israel, you have been
          unfaithful to me," says the Lord.

[21]You can hear crying on the bare
     hilltops.
     The people of Israel are crying and
          praying for mercy.
They have become very evil.
     They have forgotten the Lord their
          God.

[22]"Come back to me, you unfaithful
     people of Israel.
     Come back, and I will forgive you
          for being unfaithful."

"Yes, we will come to you.
     You are the Lord our God.
[23]It was foolish to worship idols on the
     hills.
     All the loud noises on the
          mountains were a lie.
Surely the salvation of Israel
     comes from the Lord our God.
[24]Since we were young, shameful gods
     have eaten up in sacrifice
          everything our fathers worked
               for.
The shameful gods have taken our
     fathers' sheep and cattle.
     They have taken our fathers' sons
          and daughters.
[25]Let us lie down in our shame.
     And let our shame cover us like a
          blanket.

We have sinned against the Lord our
  God.
Both we and our fathers have
  sinned.
Since we were children and until now,
  we have not obeyed the Lord our
  God."

4 "If you will come back, Israel,
  then come back to me," says the
  Lord.
"Throw away your idols that I hate.
  Don't wander away from me.
²Then you may say when you make a
  promise,
  'As surely as the Lord lives.'
And you can say it in a truthful,
  honest and right way.
Then the nations will be blessed by
  the Lord.
And they will praise the Lord for
  what he has done."

³This is what the Lord says to the men
of Judah and Jerusalem:
"Plow your unplowed fields.
  Don't plant seeds among the
  thorns.
⁴Give yourselves to the service of the
  Lord.
  Decide to obey him.
Do this, men of Judah and people
  of Jerusalem.
If you don't, my anger will spread
  among you like a fire.
No one will be able to put it out
  because of the evil you have done.

TROUBLE FROM THE NORTH
⁵"Announce this message to Judah and
  say it in Jerusalem:
  'Blow the trumpet throughout the
  country!'
Shout out loud and say,
  'Come together!
  Let's all escape to the strong, walled
  cities!'
⁶Raise the signal flag toward
  Jerusalem!
  Run for your lives! And don't wait!

Do this because I am bringing disaster
  from the north.
It will be terrible destruction."

⁷A lion has come out of his den.
  A destroyer of nations has begun to
  march.
He has left his home
  to destroy your land.
Your towns will be destroyed.
  There will be no people left to live
  in them.
⁸So put on rough cloth,
  show how sad you are and cry
  loudly.
The terrible anger of the Lord
  has not turned away from us.

⁹"When this happens," says the Lord,
  "the king and officers will lose their
  courage.
The priests will be terribly afraid.
  And the prophets*d* will be shocked!"

¹⁰Then I, Jeremiah, said, "Lord God,
you have tricked the people of Judah and
Jerusalem. You said, 'You will have
peace.' But now the sword is pointing at
our throats!"
  ¹¹At that time this message will be given
to Judah and Jerusalem: "A hot wind
blows from the bare hilltops. It comes out
of the desert toward the Lord's people. It
is not like the gentle wind farmers use to
separate grain from chaff.*d* ¹²It's a stronger
wind than that. And it comes from the
Lord. Now he will announce his judgment against the people of Judah."

¹³Look! The enemy rises up like a cloud.
  His chariots come like a windstorm.
His horses are faster than eagles.
  How terrible it will be for us! We
  are ruined!
¹⁴People of Jerusalem, clean the evil
  from your hearts and be saved.
  Don't continue making evil plans.
¹⁵A voice from Dan makes an
  announcement.

From the mountains of Ephraim
        someone brings bad news.
16"Report this to the nations.
        Spread this news in Jerusalem:
    'Enemies are coming from a faraway
        country.
    They are shouting words of war
        against the cities of Judah.
17The enemy has surrounded Jerusalem
        as men guard a field.
    This is because Judah turned
        against me,'" says the Lord.
18"The way you have lived and acted
        has brought this trouble to you.
    This is your punishment.
        How terrible it is!
        The pain stabs your heart!"

JEREMIAH'S CRY

19Oh, how I hurt! How I hurt!
        I am bent over in pain.
    Oh, the torture in my heart!
        My heart is pounding inside me.
        I cannot keep quiet.
    This is because I have heard the
        sound of the trumpet.
    I have heard the words of war.
20Disaster follows disaster.
        The whole country has been
            destroyed.
    My tents are destroyed in only a
        moment.
        My curtains are torn down quickly.
21How long must I look at the war
        flag?
    How long must I listen to the war
        trumpets?

22The Lord says, "My people are foolish.
        They do not know me.
    They are stupid children.
        They don't understand.
    They are skillful at doing evil.
        They don't know how to do good."

DISASTER IS COMING

23I looked at the earth.
        It was empty and had no shape!
    I looked at the sky.
        And its light was gone.

24I looked at the mountains,
        and they were shaking!
    All the hills were trembling.
25I looked, and there were no people!
        Every bird in the sky had flown
            away.
26I looked, and the good, rich land had
        become a desert!
    All its towns had been destroyed.
    The Lord and his great anger has
        caused this.

27This is what the Lord says:
    "All the land will be ruined.
    But I will not completely destroy it.
28So the people in the land will cry
        loudly.
    And the sky will grow dark.
    This is because I have spoken and will
        not change my mind.
    I have made a decision, and I will
        not change it."

29The towns will hear the sound of the
        horsemen and soldiers with
        bows.
    All the people will run away.
    Some of them will hide in the thick
        bushes.
    Some will climb up into the rocks.
    All of the cities of Judah are empty.
        No one lives in them.
30Judah, you destroyed nation, what are
        you doing?
    Why do you put on your finest
        dress?
    Why do you put on your gold
        jewelry?
    Why do you put on your eye shadow?
        You make yourself beautiful, but it
            is all useless.
    Your lovers hate you.
        They want to kill you.

31I hear a cry like a woman having a
        baby.
    It is a cry like a woman having her
        first child.

It is the voice of Jerusalem gasping for
breath.
She lifts her hands in prayer and
says,
"Oh! I am about to faint.
They are about to murder me!"

NO ONE IS RIGHT

5 The Lord says, "Walk up and down
the streets of Jerusalem.
Look around and think about these
things.
Search the public squares of the
city.
See if you can find one person who
does honest things.
Find just one who searches for the
truth.
If you can, I will forgive this city.
²The people say, 'As surely as the Lord
lives!'
But they don't really mean it."

³Lord, don't you look for truth in
people?
You hit the people of Judah.
But they didn't feel any pain.
You crushed them,
but they refused to learn what is
right.
They became more stubborn than a
rock.
They refused to turn back to God.
⁴But I thought,
"These are only the poor, foolish
people.
They have not learned the way of the
Lord.
They do not know what their God
wants them to do.
⁵So I will go to the leaders of Judah.
I will talk to them.
Surely they understand the way of the
Lord.
They know what God wants them to
do."
But the leaders had all joined together
to break away from the Lord.
They broke their ties with him.

⁶So a lion from the forest will attack
them.
A wolf from the desert will kill them.
A leopard is hiding and waiting for
them near their towns.
It will tear to pieces anyone who
comes out of the city.
This will happen because the people
of Judah have sinned greatly.
They have wandered away from the
Lord many times.

⁷The Lord said, "Tell me why I should
forgive you.
Your children have left me.
They have made promises to idols
that are not gods at all.
I gave your children everything they
needed.
But they still were like an unfaithful
wife to me.
They spent much time in houses of
prostitutes.ᵈ
⁸They are like well-fed, male horses
filled with sexual desire.
Each one wants another man's wife.
⁹Shouldn't I punish the people of
Judah for doing these things?"
says the Lord.
"I should give a nation such as this
the punishment it deserves.

¹⁰"Go along and cut down Judah's
vineyards.
But do not completely destroy them.
Cut off all her people as if they were
branches.
Do it because they do not belong to
the Lord.
¹¹The families of Israel and Judah
have been completely unfaithful to
me," says the Lord!

¹²Those people have lied about the
Lord.
They have said, "The Lord will not
do anything to us!
Nothing bad will happen to us.
We will never see war or hunger.

¹³The prophets*d* are like an empty wind.
    The word of God is not in them.
    Let these bad things they say
        happen to them.”

¹⁴So this is what the Lord of heaven's
armies says:
    “The people said I would not punish
        them.
    So, Jeremiah, the words I give you
        will be like fire.
    And these people will be like wood
        the fire burns up.
¹⁵Listen, family of Israel,” says the
    Lord.
    “I will soon bring a nation from far
        away to attack you.
    It is an old nation that has lasted a
        long time.
    The people there speak a language
        you do not know.
    You cannot understand what they
        say.
¹⁶Their arrows bring death.
    All their men are strong warriors.
¹⁷They will eat your crops and your
        food.
    They will eat your sons and
        daughters.
    They will eat your flocks and herds.
    They will eat your grapes and figs.
    They will destroy with their swords
        the strong, walled cities you trust in!

¹⁸“Yet even then,” says the Lord, “I will
not destroy you completely. ¹⁹The people
of Judah will ask, ‘Why has the Lord our
God done this terrible thing to us?’ Give
them this answer: ‘You have left the Lord.
You have served foreign idols in your own
land. So now you will serve foreigners in
a land that does not belong to you!’

²⁰“Announce this message to the family
        of Jacob.
    And tell it to the nation of Judah:
²¹Hear this message, you foolish people
        who have no sense.

    You have eyes, but you don't really
        see.
    You have ears, but you don't really
        listen.
²²Surely you are afraid of me,” says the
    Lord.
    “You should shake with fear in my
        presence.
I am the one who made the beaches to
        be a border for the sea.
    They keep the water in its place
        forever.
The waves may pound the beach, but
        they can't win over it.
    The waves may roar,
    but they cannot go beyond it.
²³But the people of Judah are stubborn
        and have turned against me.
    They have turned aside and gone
        away from me.
²⁴They do not say to themselves,
    ‘We should fear the Lord our God.
He gives us autumn and spring rains
        in their seasons.
    He makes sure we have the harvest
        at the right time.’
²⁵But your evil has kept away both rain
        and harvest.
    Your sins have kept you from
        enjoying good things.
²⁶There are wicked men among my
        people.
    They are like men who make nets
        for catching birds.
    But they set their traps to catch
        men instead of birds.
²⁷Like cages full of birds,
    their houses are full of lies.
    They have become rich and powerful.
²⁸   They have grown big and fat.
    There is no end to the evil things they
        do.
    They won't plead the case of the
        orphan.
    They won't help the poor be judged
        fairly.

[29]Shouldn't I punish the people of
 Judah for doing these things?"
 says the Lord.
 "I should give a nation such as this
 the punishment it deserves.

[30]"A terrible and shocking thing
 has happened in the land of Judah:
[31]The prophets tell lies.
 The priests take power into their
 own hands.
 And my people love it this way.
 But what will you do when the end
 comes?

JERUSALEM IS SURROUNDED

6 "Run for your lives, people of
 Benjamin!
 Run away from Jerusalem!
 Blow the war trumpet in the town of
 Tekoa!
 Raise the warning flag over the
 town of Beth Hakkerem!
 Disaster is coming from the north.
 Terrible destruction is coming to
 you.
[2]Jerusalem, I will destroy you.
 You are fragile and gentle.
[3]Shepherds with their flocks will come
 against Jerusalem.
 They will set up their tents all
 around her.
 Each shepherd will take care of his
 own section."
[4]They say, "Get ready to fight against
 Jerusalem!
 Get up! We will attack at noon!
 But it is already getting late.
 The evening shadows are growing
 long.
[5]So get up! We will attack at night.
 We will destroy the strong towers of
 Jerusalem!"

[6]This is what the Lord of heaven's
armies says:
 "Cut down the trees around
 Jerusalem.
 Build an attack ramp to the top of
 Jerusalem's walls.

This city must be punished!
 Inside this city is nothing but
 slavery.
[7]Jerusalem pours out her evil
 as a well pours out its water.
 The sounds of violence and
 destruction are heard within her.
 I can see the sickness and hurts of
 Jerusalem.
[8]Listen to this warning, Jerusalem.
 If you don't listen, I will turn my
 back on you.
 I will make your land an empty desert.
 No one will be able to live there!"

[9]This is what the Lord of heaven's
armies says:
 "Gather the few people of Israel who
 are left alive.
 Gather them as you would the last
 grapes on a grapevine.
 Check each vine again,
 like someone who gathers grapes."

[10]To whom can I speak? Whom can I
 warn?
 Who will listen to me?
 The people of Israel have closed ears!
 So they cannot hear my warnings.
 They don't like the word of the Lord.
 They don't want to listen to it!
[11]But I am full of the anger of the Lord.
 I am tired of holding it in.

"Pour out the Lord's anger on the
 children who play in the street.
 Pour it out on the young men
 gathered together.
 A husband and his wife will both be
 caught in his anger.
 The very old people will be caught
 in it.
[12]Their houses will be turned over to
 others.
 Their fields and wives will be given
 away.
 I will raise my hand
 and punish the people of Judah,"
 says the Lord.

13"Everyone, from the least important
     to the greatest,
   is greedy for money.
 Even the prophets[d] and priests
   all tell lies.
14They try to heal my people's serious
     injuries
   as if they were small wounds.
 They say, 'It's all right, it's all right!'
   But really, it is not all right.
15They should be ashamed of the
     terrible way they act.
   But they are not ashamed at all.
   They don't even know how to blush
     about their sins.
 So they will fall, along with everyone
     else.
   They will be thrown to the ground
     when I punish them," says the
     Lord.

16This is what the Lord says:
 "Stand where the roads cross and
     look.
   Ask where the old way is.
 Ask where the good way is, and walk
     on it.
   If you do, you will find rest for
     yourselves.
   But you have said, 'We will not walk
     on the good way!'
17I chose watchmen to watch over you.
   I told you, 'Listen for the sound of
     the war trumpet!'
   But you said, 'We will not listen.'
18So listen, all you nations.
   Pay attention, you witnesses.
   Watch what I will do to the people
     of Judah.
19Hear this, people of the earth:
   I am going to bring disaster to the
     people of Judah!
   It will happen because of the evil
     they plan.
 They have not listened to my
     messages.
   They have rejected my teachings.

20Why do you bring me offerings of
     incense[d] from the land of Sheba?
   Why do you bring me sweet-smelling
     cane from a faraway land?
 Your burnt offerings will not be
     accepted.
   Your sacrifices do not please me."

21So this is what the Lord says:
 "I will put problems in front of Judah.
   Fathers and sons will stumble over
     them.
   Neighbors and friends will die."

22This is what the Lord says:
 "Look, an army is coming
   from the land of the north.
 A great nation is coming
   from the far sides of the earth.
23The soldiers carry bows and spears.
   They are cruel and show no mercy.
 They sound like the roaring ocean
   when they ride their horses.
 That army is coming lined up for
     battle.
   It is coming to attack you,
     Jerusalem."

24We have heard the news about that
     army.
   We are helpless from fear.
 We feel trapped by our troubles.
   We are in pain like a woman having
     a baby.
25Don't go out into the fields.
   Don't walk down the roads!
 This is because the enemy has swords.
   There is terror on every side.
26My people, put on rough cloth
   and roll in the ashes to show how
     sad you are.
 Cry loudly for those who are dead.
   Cry as if your only son had died.
 Do it because the destroyer
   will soon come against us.

27"Jeremiah, I have made you like a
     worker who tests metal.
   And my people are like the ore for
     the metal.

You must observe their ways.
And you must test them.
[28]My people have turned against me
and are stubborn.
They go around telling lies about
people.
They are like bronze and iron,
that became covered with rust.
[29]The fire is fanned to make it hotter.
But the lead does not melt.
The pure silver does not come out.
And the evil is not removed from
my people.
[30]My people will be called rejected
silver.
They will be given that name
because the Lord has rejected
them."

JEREMIAH'S TEMPLE SERMON

7 This is the word that the Lord spoke
to Jeremiah: [2]"Stand at the gate of
the Temple.[d] Preach this message there:
"'Hear the word of the Lord, all you
people of the nation of Judah! All you
who come through these gates to worship
the Lord, listen to this message! [3]This is
what the Lord of heaven's armies, the
God of Israel, says: Change your lives
and do what is right! If you do, I will let
you live in this place. [4]Don't trust the lies
that some people say! They say, "This is
the Temple of the Lord. This is the
Temple of the Lord. This is the Temple of
the Lord!" [5]You must change your lives
and do what is right. You must be fair to
each other. [6]You must not be hard on the
strangers, the orphans and widows.
Don't kill innocent people in this place!
Don't follow other gods, or they will ruin
your lives. [7]If you do these things, I will
let you live in this land. This is the land I
gave to your ancestors to keep forever.
[8]"'But look! You are trusting lies. Such
trust is useless. [9]Will you steal and
murder? Will you be guilty of adultery?[d]
Will you falsely accuse other people? Will
you worship the false god Baal?[d] And will
you follow other gods you have not

known? [10]If you do that, do you think you
can come before me? Can you stand in
this place where I have chosen to be worshiped? Do you think you can say, "We
are safe!" Are you safe to do all these
hated things? [11]This is the place where I
have chosen to be worshiped. Is it nothing
more to you than a hideout for robbers? I
have been watching you, says the Lord!
[12]"'You people of Judah, go now to the
town of Shiloh. It was there that I first
made a place to be worshiped. Go there
and see what I did because of the evil
things they had done. [13]You people of
Israel were doing all these evil things,
says the Lord. I spoke to you again and
again. But you did not listen to me. I
called you, but you did not answer. [14]So I
will destroy the place where I have chosen
to be worshiped in Jerusalem. You trust
in that place. I gave it to you and your
ancestors. But I will destroy it just as I
destroyed Shiloh. [15]I will push you away
from me. I will do it just as I pushed
away your brothers, the people of Israel!'
[16]"As for you, Jeremiah, don't pray for
these people. Don't cry out for them or
ask anything for them. Don't beg me to
help them. I will not listen to you. [17]Don't
you see what they are doing in the towns
of Judah? Don't you see what they are
doing in the streets of Jerusalem? [18]This
is what the people of Judah are doing:
The children gather wood. The fathers
use the wood to make a fire. The women
make the dough for cakes of bread. And
they offer them to the Queen Goddess.[d]
They pour out drink offerings to worship other gods. They do this to make
me angry. [19]But I am not the one the
people of Judah are really hurting, says
the Lord. They are only hurting themselves. They are bringing shame upon
themselves.
[20]"'So this is what the Lord says: I will
pour out my anger on this place. I will
pour it out on man and animal. I will pour
out my anger on the trees in the field. And

I will pour it out on the crops in the ground. My anger will be like a hot fire. And no one will be able to put it out.

OBEDIENCE IS MORE THAN SACRIFICE

²¹"This is what the Lord of heaven's armies, the God of Israel, says: Go and offer as many burnt offerings and sacrifices as you want! Eat the meat of those sacrifices yourselves! ²²I brought your ancestors out of Egypt. I spoke to them. But I did not give them commands only about burnt offerings and sacrifices. ²³I also gave them this command: Obey me, and I will be your God and you will be my people. Do all that I command, and good things will happen to you. ²⁴But your ancestors did not listen or pay attention to me. They were stubborn and did whatever their evil hearts wanted. They went backward, not forward. ²⁵Since the day your ancestors left Egypt, I have sent you my servants, the prophets.ᵈ I sent them to you again and again. ²⁶But your ancestors did not listen or pay attention to me. They were very stubborn. And they did more evil than their ancestors.'

²⁷"Jeremiah, you will tell these things to the people of Judah. But they will not listen to you! You will call to them, but they will not answer you. ²⁸So say to them, 'This is the nation that has not obeyed the Lord its God. These people do nothing when I correct them. They do not tell the truth. It has disappeared from their lips.

THE VALLEY OF KILLING

²⁹"Cut off your hair and throw it away. Go up to the bare hilltop and cry. Do it because I, the Lord, have rejected these people. I have turned my back on them. And in my anger I will punish them! ³⁰The people of Judah have done what I said was evil, says the Lord. They have set up their hated idols in the place where I have chosen to be worshiped. They have made it unclean!ᵈ ³¹The people

of Judah have built places of worship at Topheth in the Valley of Ben Hinnom. There the people offered their own sons and daughters as sacrifices. This is something I never commanded. It never even entered my mind! ³²So, I warn you. The days are coming, says the Lord, when people will not call this place Topheth. They will not call it the Valley of Ben Hinnom anymore. They will call it the Valley of Killing. They will bury dead people in Topheth until there is no room to bury anyone else! ³³Then the bodies of the dead will lie on top of the ground. They will become food for the birds of the sky. Wild animals will eat the bodies. There will be no one left alive to chase the birds or animals away. ³⁴I will end the happy sounds of the bride and bridegroom. There will be no happy sounds in Judah or in the streets of Jerusalem. The land will become an empty desert!

8 "'The Lord says: At that time the bones will be removed from the tombs. The bones of Judah's kings and officers, priests and prophetsᵈ and the people of Jerusalem will be removed. ²The bones will be spread on the ground under the sun, moon and stars the people loved and served. They went after these gods, searched them out and worshiped them. No one will gather up the bones and bury them. So they will be like dung thrown on the ground. ³I will force the people of Judah to leave their homes and their land. Those of this evil family who are not dead will wish they were dead, says the Lord.'

SIN AND PUNISHMENT

⁴"Say to the people of Judah: 'This is what the Lord says:

When a man falls down, doesn't he
    get up again?
And when a man goes the wrong
    way, doesn't he come back again?

5Why, then, have the people of Judah
        gone the wrong way?
    And why do the people of Jerusalem
        not turn back?
They believe their own lies.
    They refuse to turn around and
        come back.
6I have listened to them very carefully.
    But they do not say what is right.
They do not feel sorry about their
        wicked ways.
    The people don't think about the
        bad things they have done.
Each person goes his own way.
    He is like a horse charging into a
        battle.
7Even the birds in the sky
    know the right times to do things.
The storks, doves, swifts and thrushes
    know when it is time to migrate.
But my people don't know
    what the Lord wants them to do!

8"You keep saying, "We are wise.
    This is because we have the
        teachings of the Lord."
But actually, those who copy the
        Scriptures
    have written lies with their pens.
9These wise men refused to listen to
        the word of the Lord.
    So they are not really wise at all.
They will be ashamed.
    They will be shocked and trapped.
10So I will give their wives to other men.
    I will give their fields to new
        owners.
Everyone, from the least important to
        the greatest,
    is greedy for money.
Even the prophets*d* and priests
    all tell lies.
11They try to heal my people's serious
        injuries
    as if they were small wounds.
They say, "It's all right, it's all right!"
    But really, it is not all right.

12They should be ashamed of the
        terrible way they act.
    But they are not ashamed at all.
    They don't even know how to blush
        about their sins.
So they will fall, along with everyone
        else.
    They will be thrown to the ground
        when I punish them, says the
        Lord.

13"I will take away their crops, says the
        Lord.
    There will be no grapes on the
        vine.
There will be no figs on the fig tree.
    Even the leaves will dry up and die.
I will take away what I gave them!'"

14"Why are we just sitting here?
    Let's get together!
We have sinned against the Lord.
    So he has given us poisoned water
        to drink.
Come, let's run to the strong, walled
        cities.
    The Lord our God has decided that
        we must die.
    So let's die there.
15We hoped to have peace.
    But nothing good has come.
We hoped for a time when he would
        heal us.
    But only disaster has come!
16From the land of the tribe*d* of Dan,
    the snorting of the enemy's horses
        is heard.
    The ground shakes from the
        neighing of their large horses.
They have come to destroy
    the land and everything in it.
They have come to destroy
    the city and all the people who live
        there."

17"Look! I am sending poisonous
        snakes to attack you.
    These snakes cannot be charmed.
    They will bite you," says the Lord.

JEREMIAH'S SADNESS

18God, you are my comfort when I am
  very sad.
  You are my comfort when I'm afraid.
19Listen to my people!
  They are crying for help from a
  faraway land.
  They say, "Is the Lord still in
  Jerusalem?
  Is Jerusalem's king still there?"

But God says, "Why did the people
  make me angry by worshiping
  idols?
  They worshiped their useless
  foreign idols."

20And the people say, "Harvest time is
  over.
  Summer has ended.
  And we have not been saved."

21My people are crushed. So I am
  crushed.
  I cry loudly, and I am afraid for
  them.
22Surely there is a balm*d* in the land of
  Gilead.
  Surely there is a doctor there.
  So why aren't the hurts of my people
  healed?

9 I wish my head were like a spring
  of water.
  And I wish my eyes were a fountain
  of tears!
  Then I could cry day and night
  for my people who have been killed.
2I wish I had a place in the desert—
  a house where travelers spend the
  night.
  Then I could leave my people.
  I could go away from them.
  This is because they are all unfaithful
  to God.
  They are all turning against him.

JUDAH'S FAILURES

3"They use their tongues like a bow.
  They shoot lies from their mouths
  like arrows.

Lies, not truth,
  have grown strong in the land.
  They go from one evil thing to
  another.
  They do not know who I am," says
  the Lord.
4"Watch your friends.
  Don't trust your own brothers.
  This is because every brother is a
  cheater.
  And every friend tells lies about
  you.
5Everyone lies to his friend.
  No one speaks the truth.
  The people of Judah have taught their
  tongues to lie.
  They become tired from sinning.
6Jeremiah, you live in the middle of evil.
  And lies follow lies.
  The people have refused to know me,"
  says the Lord.

7So this is what the Lord of heaven's
armies says:
  "I will test the people of Judah as a
  person tests metal in a fire.
  I have no other choice.
  My people have sinned.
8Their tongues are like sharp arrows.
  Their mouths speak lies.
  Everyone speaks nicely to his
  neighbor.
  But he is secretly planning to attack
  him.
9Shouldn't I punish the people for
  doing this?" says the Lord.
  "Shouldn't I give them the
  punishment they deserve?"

10I, Jeremiah, will cry loudly for the
  mountains.
  I will sing a funeral song for the
  empty fields.
  They are empty, and no one passes
  through.
  The mooing of cattle cannot be
  heard.
  The birds have flown away,
  and the animals are gone.

11"I, the Lord, will make the city of
  Jerusalem a heap of ruins.
  It will become a home for wild dogs.
I will destroy the cities in the land of
  Judah
  so no one can live there."

12What man is wise enough to understand these things? Is there someone who has been taught by the Lord who can explain them? Why was the land ruined? Why has it been made like an empty desert where no one goes?
13The Lord answered, "It is because Judah quit following my teachings that I gave them. They have not obeyed me. They have not done what I told them to do. 14Instead, the people of Judah were stubborn. They followed the false god Baal.*d* Their fathers taught them to do this!" 15So this is what the Lord of heaven's armies, God of Israel, says: "I will soon make the people of Judah eat bitter food. I will make them drink poisoned water. 16I will scatter them through other nations. They will live in strange nations that they and their ancestors never knew about. I will chase the people of Judah with the sword until they are all killed."
17This is what the Lord of heaven's armies says:
"Now, think about these things!
  Call for the women who cry at
    funerals.
  Send for those women who are
    good at that job.
18Let them come quickly
  and cry loudly for us.
Then our eyes will fill with tears.
  And streams of water will come out
    of our eyes.
19The sound of loud crying is heard
    from Jerusalem:
  'We are truly ruined!
  We are truly ashamed!
  We must leave our land,
    because our houses are in ruins.'"

20Now, women of Judah, listen to the
    word of the Lord.
  Open your ears to hear the words of
    his mouth.
Teach your daughters how to cry
    loudly.
  Teach one another a funeral song!
21Death has climbed in through our
    windows.
  It has entered our strong cities.
Death has taken away our children
    who play in the streets.
  It has taken the young men who
    meet in the city squares.

22Say, "This is what the Lord says:
  'The dead bodies of men will lie
    in the open field like dung.
  They will lie on the ground like grain
    a farmer has cut.
  But there will be no one to gather
    them.'"

23This is what the Lord says:
"Wise men must not brag about their
    wisdom.
  Strong men must not brag about
    their strength.
  Rich men must not brag about their
    money.
24But if someone wants to brag, let him
    brag about this:
  Let him brag that he understands
    and knows me.
Let him brag that I am the Lord.
  Let him brag that I am kind and
    fair.
  Let him brag that I do things that
    are right on earth.
This kind of bragging pleases me,"
  says the Lord.

25The Lord says, "The time is coming when I will punish all those who are circumcised*d* only in the flesh. 26That is the people of Egypt, Judah, Edom, Ammon and Moab. I will also punish the desert people who cut their hair short. The men in all those countries have not given themselves to serving me. And the men of Israel do not give themselves to serving me."

THE LORD AND THE IDOLS

10 Family of Israel, listen to what the Lord says to you. ²This is what he says:

"Don't live like the people from other
    nations.
Don't be afraid of special signs in
    the sky,
even though the other nations are
    afraid of them.
³The customs of other people are
    worth nothing.
Their idols are nothing but wood
    from the forest.
They are made by a worker with his
    chisel.
⁴They decorate their idols with silver
    and gold.
With hammers and nails they
    fasten them down.
That keeps them from falling over.
⁵Their idols are like scarecrows in
    melon fields.
They cannot talk.
They cannot walk.
They must be carried.
Do not be afraid of those idols.
They can't hurt you.
And they can't help you either!"

⁶Lord, there is no one like you.
You are great.
Your name is great and powerful.
⁷Everyone should respect you, King of
    all nations.
You deserve their respect.
There are many wise men among the
    nations.
And there are wise men in all the
    kingdoms.
But none of them are as wise as
    you.
⁸Those wise men are stupid and
    foolish.
Their teachings come from
    worthless wooden idols.

⁹They use silver from Tarshish
    and gold from Uphaz.
Their idols are made by craftsmen
    and goldsmiths.
They put blue and purple clothes on
    the idols.
All these things are made by skilled
    workers.
¹⁰But the Lord is the only true God.
He is the only living God, King
    forever.
The earth shakes when he is angry.
The nations cannot stand up to his
    anger.

¹¹"Tell them this message: 'These false gods did not make heaven and earth. But they will be destroyed and disappear from heaven and earth.'"

¹²God made the earth by his power.
He used his wisdom to build the
    world.
He used his understanding to
    stretch out the skies.
¹³When he thunders, the waters in the
    skies roar.
He makes clouds rise in the sky all
    over the earth.
He sends lightning with the rain.
He brings out the wind from his
    storehouses.

¹⁴People are so stupid and know so
    little.
Goldsmiths are made ashamed by
    their idols.
Those statues are only false gods.
They have no breath in them.
¹⁵They are worth nothing.
People make fun of them.
When they are judged, they will be
    destroyed.
¹⁶But God, who is Jacob's Portion,ᵈ is
    not like the idols.
God made everything.
And he made Israel to be his special
    people.

The Lord of heaven's armies is his
name.

DESTRUCTION IS COMING

[17]Get everything you own and prepare
to leave.
You people of Judah are trapped in
the city by your enemies.
[18]This is what the Lord says:
"At this time I will throw out the
people of Judah who live in this
land.
I will bring pain and trouble to them.
And they will really feel it."

[19]How terrible it will be for me because
of my injury.
I am injured and cannot be healed.
Yet I told myself,
"This is my sickness; I must suffer
through it."
[20]My tent is ruined.
All its ropes are broken.
My children have gone away and left
me.
No one is left to put up my tent.
No one is left to set up a shelter
for me.
[21]The shepherds are stupid.
They don't ask the Lord.
So they do not have success.
Their flocks are scattered and lost.
[22]Listen! The news is coming.
The loud noise is coming from the
north.
It will make the towns of Judah an
empty desert.
They will become a home for wild
dogs!

JEREMIAH'S PRAYER

[23]Lord, I know that a person's life
doesn't really belong to him.
No one can control his own life.
[24]Lord, correct me, but be fair.
Don't punish me in anger.
If you do, you will destroy me.
[25]Pour out your anger on other nations.
They do not know you.
They do not pray to you.

Those nations have destroyed Jacob's
family.
They have eaten him up.
They destroyed his homeland.

THE AGREEMENT IS BROKEN

11 These are the words that the
Lord spoke to Jeremiah: [2]"Listen
to the words of this agreement. Tell the
people of Judah about it. Tell it to those
living in Jerusalem. [3]Tell them this is
what the Lord, the God of Israel, says:
'Trouble will come to anyone who does
not obey this agreement. [4]I am talking
about the agreement I made with your
ancestors. I made it with them when I
brought them out of Egypt. Egypt was like
a furnace for melting iron!' I told them,
'Obey me and do everything I command
you. If you do this, you will be my people.
And I will be your God. [5]Then I will keep
the promise I made to your ancestors. I
promised to give them a land where
much food grows.' And you are living in
that country today!"

I, Jeremiah, answered, "Amen, Lord."

[6]The Lord said this to me: "Prophesy[d]
this message in the towns of Judah and
in the streets of Jerusalem: 'Listen to the
words of this agreement. Then obey
them! [7]I warned your ancestors to obey
me when I brought them out of Egypt. I
have warned them again and again to
this very day! [8]But your ancestors did
not listen to me. They were stubborn
and did what their own evil hearts
wanted. The agreement says curses will
come upon them if they don't obey it. So
I made all those curses come upon them!
I commanded them to obey the agreement, but they did not.'"

[9]Then the Lord said to me, "I know
the people of Judah and those living in
Jerusalem have made secret plans. [10]They
are doing the same sins their ancestors
did! Their ancestors refused to listen to
my message. They followed and worshiped other gods. The families of Israel
and Judah have broken the agreement I

made with their ancestors. [11]So this is what the Lord says: 'I will soon bring a disaster on the people of Judah. They will not be able to escape! And they will cry to me for help. But I will not listen to them! [12]The people living in the towns of Judah and the city of Jerusalem will pray to their idols for help. They will burn incense[d] to their idols. But those idols will not be able to help when that terrible time comes! [13]The people of Judah have as many idols as there are towns in Judah. They have built many altars for worshiping that shameful god Baal.[d] There are as many altars as there are streets in Jerusalem!'

[14]"As for you, Jeremiah, don't pray for these people. Don't cry out for them or ask anything for them. I will not listen when they call to me in the time of their trouble.

[15]"What is my lover, Judah, doing in my
    Temple?[d]
She makes many evil plans.
Does she think animal sacrifices
    will stop her punishment?
When you do your evil, then you are
    happy."
[16]The Lord called you "a leafy olive tree,
    with beautiful fruit to look at."
But with a strong storm
    the Lord will set that tree on fire.
    And its branches will be burned up.

[17]The Lord of heaven's armies planted you. And he has announced that disaster will come to you. This is because the families of Israel and Judah have done evil things. They have made him angry by offering sacrifices to Baal.

EVIL PLANS AGAINST JEREMIAH

[18]The Lord showed me that men were making plans against me. The Lord showed me what they were doing. So I knew they were against me. [19]Before this, I was like a gentle lamb waiting to be butchered. I did not know they had made plans against me. They said:
"Let us destroy the tree and its fruit!
    Let's kill him!
    Then people will forget him!"

[20]But, Lord of heaven's armies, you are
    a fair judge.
You know how to test peoples'
    hearts and minds.
I will tell you what I have against
    them.
And I will let you give them the
    punishment they should have!

[21]So the Lord speaks about the men from Anathoth who were planning to kill Jeremiah. Those men say, "Don't prophesy[d] in the name of the Lord. If you do, we will kill you!" [22]So this is what the Lord of heaven's armies says: "I will soon punish the men from Anathoth. Their young men will die in war. Their sons and daughters will die from hunger. [23]No one from the city of Anathoth will be left alive. I will cause a disaster to happen to them that year."

JEREMIAH'S FIRST COMPLAINT

12 Lord, if I complain to you,
    you are always right.
But I want to ask you about the justice
    you give.
Why are evil people successful?
Why do dishonest people have such
    easy lives?
[2]You have put the evil people here.
    They are like plants with strong
    roots.
    They grow and produce fruit.
With their mouths they speak well of
    you.
    But their hearts are really far away
    from you.
[3]But you know my heart, Lord.
    You see me and test my mind.
Drag the evil people away like sheep
    to be butchered.
    Set them aside for the day of killing.
[4]How much longer will the land stay
    dried up?
    How long will the grass in every
    field be dead?
The animals and birds in the land
    have died.

And it is because the people are evil.
Yet, they are saying,
"God does not see what happens to
us!"

GOD'S ANSWER TO JEREMIAH

5"If you get tired racing against men,
how can you race against horses?
You stumble in a country that is safe.
What will you do in the thick
thornbushes along the Jordan
River?
6These men are your own brothers.
Members of your own family are
making plans against you.
People from your own family are
crying out against you.
Don't trust them,
even when they speak to you like
friends!

7"I have left Israel.
I have left my people.
I have given the people I love
to their enemies.
8My people have become
like a lion in the forest to me.
They roar at me.
So I hate them.
9My people have become to me
like a speckled bird attacked by
hawks.
Go, gather the wild animals!
Bring them to get something to eat.
10Many shepherds will ruin my
vineyards.
They will walk on the plants in my
field.
They will turn my beautiful field
into an empty desert.
11They will turn my field into a desert.
It will be wilted and dead.
The whole country is an empty desert.
This is because no one who lives
there cares.
12Many soldiers will march over those
barren hills.
The Lord will use the armies to
punish that land.

People from one end of the land to the
other will be punished.
No one will be safe.
13The people will plant wheat.
But they will harvest only thorns.
They will work hard until they are
very tired.
But they will get nothing for all
their work.
You will be ashamed of your poor
harvest.
The Lord's terrible anger has
caused this."

14This is what the Lord said to me:
"Here is what I will do to those wicked
people who take the land I gave my
people, the Israelites. I will pull them up
and throw them out of their land. And I
will pull up the people of Judah from
among them. 15But after I pull them up,
I will feel sorry for them. I will bring each
person back to his own property. And I
will bring him back to his own land. 16I
want them to learn their lessons well. In
the past they taught my people to use
Baal's*d* name to make promises. Now I
want them to learn to use my name! I
want them to say, 'As surely as the Lord
lives . . .' If they do, I will allow them to
be successful. And I will let them live
among my people. 17But a nation might
not listen to my message. If it doesn't, I
will pull it up completely and destroy it,"
says the Lord.

JEREMIAH'S LINEN BELT

13 This is what the Lord said to me:
"Go and buy a linen belt. Then
put it around your waist. Don't let the
belt get wet."
2So I bought a linen belt, just as the
Lord told me. And I put it around my
waist. 3Then the Lord spoke his word to
me a second time: 4"Take the belt you
bought and are wearing. Go to Perath.
Hide the belt there in a crack in the rocks."
5So I went to Perath and hid the belt
there, just as the Lord told me.

⁶Many days later the Lord said to me, "Now go to Perath. Get the belt that I told you to hide there." ⁷So I went to Perath and dug up the belt. I took it from where I had hidden it. But now it was ruined. It was good for nothing.

⁸Then the Lord spoke his word to me. ⁹This is what the Lord said: "In the same way I will ruin the pride of the people of Judah and the great pride of Jerusalem. ¹⁰These evil people refuse to listen to my warnings. They stubbornly do only what they want to do. They follow other gods to serve and worship them. So they will become like this linen belt. They will be good for nothing. ¹¹A belt is wrapped tightly around a man's waist. In the same way I wrapped the families of Israel and Judah around me," says the Lord. "I did that so they would be my people. Then they would bring fame, praise and honor to me. But my people would not listen to me.

WARNINGS ABOUT LEATHER WINE BAGS

¹²"Say to them: 'This is what the Lord, the God of Israel, says: All leather bags for holding wine should be filled with wine.' People will say to you: 'Of course, we know all wine bags should be filled with wine.' ¹³Then you will say to them, 'This is what the Lord says: I will make everyone in this land like a drunken man. I am talking about the kings who sit on David's throne. I am also talking about the priests and the prophets.ᵈ I am talking about all the people who live in Jerusalem. ¹⁴I will make the people of Judah stumble and fall into one another. Fathers and sons will fall into one another, says the Lord. I will not feel sorry or have pity for them. My mercy will not stop me from destroying them!'"

THREAT OF SLAVERY

¹⁵Listen and pay attention.
  Don't be too proud.
  The Lord has spoken to you.
¹⁶Honor the Lord your God.
  Give him glory before he brings
    darkness.
Praise him before you fall
  on the dark hills.
You hope for light.
  But the Lord will turn it into thick
    darkness.
  He will change it into deep gloom.
¹⁷If you don't listen to the Lord,
  I will cry secretly.
  Your pride will cause me to cry.
I will cry painfully.
  My eyes will overflow with tears.
  This is because the Lord's people
    will be captured.

¹⁸Tell this to the king and queen mother:
  "Come down from your thrones.
Your beautiful crowns
  have fallen from your heads."
¹⁹The cities in the desert of southern
    Judah are shut up.
  No one can open them.
All Judah will be taken as captives to a
    foreign land.
  They will be carried away
    completely.

²⁰Jerusalem, look up and see.
  Someone comes from the north.
Where is the flock God gave to you to
    care for?
  It is the flock you bragged about.
²¹What will you say when they appoint
    as your heads
  those you had thought were your
    friends?
Won't you have much pain and
    trouble?
  Your pain will be like that of a
    woman having a baby.
²²You might ask yourself,
  "Why has this happened to me?"
It happened because of your many sins.
  Because of your sins, your skirt was
    torn off
  and your body has been treated
    badly.

²³A black man from Cush cannot
  change the color of his skin.
A leopard cannot change his spots.
In the same way, Jerusalem, you
  cannot change and do good.
You always do evil.

²⁴"I will scatter you like chaff*d* that is
  blown away by the desert wind.
²⁵This is what will happen to you.
This is your part in my plans," says
  the Lord.
"This will happen because you forgot
  me.
You have trusted in false gods.
²⁶Jerusalem, I will pull your skirts up
  over your face.
Everyone will see you, and you will
  be ashamed.
²⁷I have seen the terrible things you
  have done.
I know your acts of adultery*d* and
  your snorting.
I have seen you acting like a
  prostitute.*d*
I have seen your hated acts
on the hills and in the fields.
How terrible it will be for you,
  Jerusalem.
How long will you continue being
  unclean?"*d*

A TIME WITHOUT RAIN

14 These are the words that the Lord
spoke to Jeremiah about the time
when there was no rain:
²"The nation of Judah cries.
  Her cities are dying.
They cry out for the land.
A cry goes up to God from
  Jerusalem.
³The important men send their
  servants to get water.
The servants go to the wells,
but they find no water.
So they return with empty jars.
They are ashamed and
  embarrassed.
They cover their heads in shame.

⁴The ground is dry and cracked open
  because no rain falls on the land.
The farmers are upset and sad.
So they cover their heads in shame.
⁵Even the mother deer in the field
  leaves her fawn.
She does this because there is no
  grass.
⁶Wild donkeys stand on the bare hills.
They sniff the wind like wild dogs.
But their eyes are dull because
  there is no food."

⁷We know that we suffer because of
  our sins.
Lord, do something to help us for
  the good of your name.
We have left you many times.
We have sinned against you.
⁸God, you are the Hope of Israel.
You have saved Israel in times of
  trouble.
But now you are like a stranger in the
  land.
You are like a traveler who only
  stays one night.
⁹You seem like a man who has been
  attacked by surprise.
You seem like a warrior who is not
  able to save anyone.
But you are among us, Lord.
And we are called by your name.
So don't leave us without help!

¹⁰This is what the Lord says about the
people of Judah:
"They really love to wander from me.
They don't stop themselves from
  leaving me.
So now I, the Lord, will not accept
  them.
I will now remember the evil they do.
I will punish them for their sins."

¹¹Then the Lord said this to me: "Don't
pray for good things to happen to the
people of Judah. ¹²Even if they give up
eating, I will not listen to their prayers.
Even if they offer burnt offerings and

grain offerings to me, I will not accept them. I will destroy the people of Judah with war, hunger and terrible diseases."

¹³But I said, "Oh! Lord God, the false prophets*d* keep telling the people something different! They are saying, 'You will not suffer from an enemy's sword. You will never suffer from hunger. The Lord will give you peace in this land.'"

¹⁴Then the Lord said to me, "Those prophets are prophesying lies in my name. I did not send them. I did not appoint them or speak to them. They have been prophesying false visions, idolatries and worthless magic. And they have been prophesying their own wishful thinking. ¹⁵So this is what I say about the prophets who are prophesying in my name. I did not send them. They said, 'No enemy with swords will ever attack this country. There will never be hunger in this land.' Those prophets will die from hunger. And an enemy's sword will kill them. ¹⁶And the people the prophets spoke to will be thrown into the streets of Jerusalem. They will die from hunger and from an enemy's sword. No one will be there to bury them. And no one will bury their wives, their sons or their daughters. I will punish them.

¹⁷"Speak this message to the people of Judah:

'Let my eyes be filled with tears.
    I will cry night and day, without
        stopping.
I will cry for my people.
    They have received a terrible blow.
    They have been hurt very badly.
¹⁸If I go into the country,
    I see people killed by swords.
If I go into the city,
    I see much sickness because the
        people have no food.
Both the priests and the prophets
    have been taken to a foreign
        land.'"

¹⁹Lord, have you completely rejected
        the nation of Judah?
    Do you hate Jerusalem?
Why have you hurt us so badly
    that we cannot be made well again?
We hoped for peace,
    but nothing good has come.
We looked for a time of healing,
    but only terror came.
²⁰Lord, we admit that we are very
        wicked.
    We admit that our ancestors did
        evil things.
    We have sinned against you.
²¹For your sake, do not hate us.
    Do not take away the honor from
        your glorious throne.
    Remember your agreement with us.
    Do not break it.
²²Do foreign idols have the power to
        bring rain?
    Does the sky itself have the power
        to send down showers of rain?
No, it is you, Lord our God.
    You are our only hope.
    You are the one who made all these
        things.

15 The Lord said to me: "I would not feel sorry for the people of Judah even if Moses and Samuel prayed for them. Send the people away from me! Tell them to go! ²They might ask you, 'Where will we go?' You tell them this: 'This is what the Lord says:

Some people are meant to die.
    And they will die.
Some are meant to die in war.
    And they will die in war.
Some are meant to die from hunger.
    And they will die from hunger.
Some are meant to be taken as slaves
        to a foreign country.
    And they will become slaves in that
        foreign country.'

³"I will send four kinds of destroyers against them," says the Lord. "I will send war to kill. I will send dogs to drag the

bodies away. I will send birds of the air and wild animals. They will eat and destroy the bodies. ⁴I will make the people of Judah hated by everyone on earth. I will do this because of what Manasseh did in Jerusalem. (Manasseh son of Hezekiah was king of the nation of Judah.)

⁵"Who will feel sorry for you, Jerusalem?
    Who will be sad and cry for you?
    Who will go out of his way to ask
        how you are?
⁶Jerusalem, you have left me," says the
        Lord.
    "You keep going farther and farther
        away.
So I will take hold of you and destroy
        you.
    I am tired of holding back my
        anger.
⁷I will separate the people of Judah
        with my pitchfork.
    I will scatter them at the city gates
        of the land.
My people haven't changed their
        ways.
    So I will destroy them.
    I will take away their children.
⁸Many women will lose their
        husbands.
    There will be more widows than the
        sand of the sea.
I will bring a destroyer at noontime
    against the mothers of the young
        men of Judah.
I will suddenly bring pain and fear
    on the people of Judah.
⁹The enemy will attack.
    I will still hand over to the killers
        those who are left alive from
        Judah.
A woman might have seven sons, but
        they will all die.
    She will cry until she becomes weak
        and unable to breathe.
She will be upset and confused.
    Her bright day will become dark
        from sadness!" says the Lord.

JEREMIAH'S SECOND COMPLAINT

¹⁰Mother, I am sorry that you gave birth
        to me.
    I am the one who must accuse and
        criticize the whole land.
I have not loaned or borrowed
        anything.
    But everyone curses me.
¹¹The Lord said,
    "I will save you for a good reason.
I will make your enemies beg you
    in times of disaster and trouble.
¹²No one can smash a piece of iron or
        bronze.
    I mean the kind of iron and bronze
        that comes from the north.
¹³The people of Judah have wealth and
        treasures.
    But I will freely give those riches to
        others.
This is because the people of Judah
        have sinned
    throughout the country.
¹⁴I will make you slaves to your enemies.
    You will be slaves in a land that you
        have never known.
My anger is like a hot fire.
    And it will burn against you."

¹⁵Lord, you understand.
    Remember me and take care of me.
    Punish for me the people who are
        hurting me.
Don't destroy me while you remain
        patient with them.
    Think about the pain I suffer for
        you, Lord.
¹⁶Your words came to me, and I
        listened carefully to them.
    Your words made me very happy.
I was happy because I am called by
        your name.
    Your name is the Lord God of
        heaven's armies.
¹⁷I never sat with the crowd
    as they laughed and had fun.
    I sat by myself because you were
        there.

You filled me with anger at the evil around me.

[18] I don't understand why my pain has no end.

I don't understand why my injury is not cured or healed!

Lord, will you be like a brook that goes dry?

Will you be like a spring whose water stops flowing?

[19] So this is what the Lord says:

"If you change your heart and come back to me, I will take you back.

Then you may serve me.

You must speak things that have worth.

You must not speak useless words.

Then you may speak for me.

Let the people of Judah turn to you.

But you must not change and be like them.

[20] I will make you as strong as a wall to this people.

You will be as strong as a wall of bronze.

They will fight against you.

But they will not defeat you.

This is because I am with you.

I will rescue you and save you," says the Lord.

[21] "I will save you from these evil people.

I will save you from these cruel people."

THE DAY OF DISASTER

16 Then the Lord spoke his word to me: [2] "You must not get married. You must not have sons or daughters in this place."

[3] The Lord says this about the sons and daughters born in this land. And he says this about the mothers and fathers of those children: [4] "They will die of terrible diseases. No one will cry for them. No one will bury them. Their bodies will lie on the ground like dung. They will die in war, or they will starve to death. Their dead bodies will be food for the birds of the sky. And they will be food for the wild animals."

[5] So this is what the Lord says: "Jeremiah, do not go into a house where there is a funeral meal. Do not go there to cry for the dead or to show your sorrow. Do not do this because I have taken back my blessing, my love and my pity from these people," says the Lord. [6] "Important people and common people will die in the land of Judah. No one will bury them or cry for them. No one will cut himself for them. And no one will shave his head to show sorrow for them. [7] No one will bring food to the people who are crying for the dead. No one will comfort one whose mother or father has died. No one will offer a drink to comfort them.

[8] "Do not go into a house where the people are having a feast. Do not go there and sit down to eat and drink. [9] This is what the Lord of heaven's armies, the God of Israel, says: I will soon stop the sounds of joy and gladness in this place! I will stop the happy sounds of brides and bridegrooms! This will happen during your lifetime.

[10] "You will tell the people of Judah these things. And they will ask you, 'Why has the Lord said these terrible things to us? What have we done wrong? What sin have we done against the Lord our God?'

[11] "Then say to them: 'This is because your ancestors quit following me,' says the Lord. 'And they began to follow other gods. They served and worshiped other gods. Your ancestors left me. And they quit obeying my teaching. [12] But you have done even more evil than your ancestors. You are very stubborn. You do only what you want to do. You have not obeyed me. [13] So I will throw you out of this country. You will go to a land that you and your ancestors never knew. There you can serve false gods day and night. I will not help you or show you any favors.'

[14] "People say, 'As surely as the Lord lives, who brought the people of Israel

out of Egypt...' But the time is coming," says the Lord, "when people will not say this anymore. [15]They will say instead, 'As surely as the Lord lives, who brought the Israelites from the northern land and from all the countries where he had sent them...' And I will bring them back to the land I gave to their ancestors.

[16]"I will soon send for many fishermen to come to this land," says the Lord. "The fishermen will catch the people of Judah. After that, I will send for many hunters to come to this land. Those hunters will hunt the people of Judah on every mountain and hill. And they will hunt Judah in the cracks of the rocks. [17]I see everything they do. They cannot hide the things they do from me. Their sin is not hidden from my eyes! [18]I will pay back the people of Judah for the evil they have done. I will punish them two times for every one of their sins. I will do this because they have made my land unclean.[d] They have done it with their hated idols. They have filled my country with them!"

[19]Lord, you are my strength and my
        protection.
    You are a safe place for me to run to
        in times of trouble.
    The nations will come to you from all
        over the world.
    They will say, "Our fathers had only
        false gods.
    They worshiped useless idols that
        didn't help them.
[20]Can people make gods for themselves?
    They will not really be gods!"
[21]The Lord says, "So I will teach those
        who make idols.
    Right now I will teach them
    about my power and my strength.
    Then they will know
        that my name is the Lord.

JUDAH'S GUILTY HEART

17 "The sin of the people of Judah
        is written with an iron tool.
    Their sins were cut into stone with
        a hard point.

That stone is their hearts.
    Their sins were cut into the corners
        of their altars.
[2]Even their children remember
    their altars to idols and their
        Asherah[d] idols.
They remember the altars under the
        green trees
    and on the high hills.
[3]They remember the altars on my
        mountain and in the open
        country.
I will give your wealth and treasures
        to other people.
And they will destroy the places of
        worship in your country.
    You sinned by worshiping at those
        places.
[4]You will lose the land I gave you.
    And it is your own fault.
I will let your enemies take you as
        their slaves.
    You will be slaves in a land you
        have never known.
This is because you have made my
        anger burn like a hot fire.
    And it will burn forever."

TRUSTING IN MAN OR GOD

[5]This is what the Lord says:
"A curse will be placed on those who
        trust other people.
    It will happen to those who depend
        on people for strength.
    Those are the ones who have
        stopped trusting the Lord.
[6]They are like a bush in a desert.
    It grows in a land where no one
        lives.
    It is in a hot and dry land with bad
        soil.
They don't know about the good
        things that God can give.

[7]"But the person who trusts in the
        Lord will be blessed.
    The Lord will show him that he can
        be trusted.

[8]He will be strong, like a tree planted
near water.
That tree has large roots that find
the water.
It is not afraid when the days are hot.
Its leaves are always green.
It does not worry in a year when no
rain comes.
That tree always produces fruit."

[9]"More than anything else, a person's
mind is evil.
It cannot be healed.
Who can understand it?
[10]But I am the Lord, and I can look into
a person's heart.
I can test a person's mind.
So I can decide what each one deserves.
I can give each one the right
payment for what he does."

[11]Sometimes a bird will hatch an egg
that it did not lay.
That bird is like the man who gets
rich by cheating.
When that man's life is half finished,
he will lose his riches.
At the end of his life, it will be clear
he was a fool.

[12]From the beginning, our Temple[d] has
been honored
as a glorious throne for God.
[13]Lord, you are the hope of Israel.
Those who leave you will be shamed.
A person who quits following the
Lord will be like a name written
in the dust.
That is because he has left the Lord.
The Lord is the spring of living
water.

JEREMIAH'S THIRD COMPLAINT

[14]Lord, heal me, and I will truly be
healed.
Save me, and I will truly be saved.
Lord, you are the one I praise.
[15]The people of Judah keep asking me,
"Where is the word from the Lord?
Let's see that message come true!"

[16]Lord, I didn't run away from being
the shepherd you wanted.
I didn't want the terrible day to
come.
You know everything I have said.
You see all that is happening.
[17]Lord, don't bring terror to me.
I run to you for safety in times of
trouble.
[18]Make those who are hurting me be
ashamed.
But don't bring shame to me.
Let them be terrified,
but keep me from terror.
Bring the day of disaster on my
enemies.
Destroy them, and destroy them
again.

KEEPING THE SABBATH HOLY

[19]This is what the Lord said to me: "Go
and stand at the People's Gate of Jerusalem. This is where the kings of Judah
go in and out. And then go to all the
other gates of Jerusalem. [20]Say to them
there: 'Hear the word of the Lord. Listen,
kings of Judah. Listen, all you people of
Judah and all who come through these
gates into Jerusalem! [21]This is what the
Lord says: Be careful not to carry a load
on the Sabbath[d] day. And don't bring it
through the gates of Jerusalem on the
Sabbath. [22]Don't take a load out of your
houses on the Sabbath. Don't do any
work on that day. Keep the Sabbath as a
holy day. I gave this same command to
your ancestors. [23]But your ancestors did
not listen. They did not pay attention to
me. They were very stubborn. I punished
them, but it didn't do any good. They did
not listen to me. [24]But you must be
careful to obey me, says the Lord. You
must not bring a load through the gates
of Jerusalem on the Sabbath. You must
keep the Sabbath as a holy day. You
must not do any work on that day.

[25]"If you obey this command, this is
what will happen: Kings who sit on
David's throne will come through the

gates of Jerusalem with their officers. They will come riding in chariots and on horses. The people of Judah and Jerusalem will be with them. And the city of Jerusalem will have people living in it forever! ²⁶People will come to Jerusalem from the villages around it and from the towns of Judah. They will come from the land of Benjamin. They will come from the western mountain slopes and from the mountains. And they will come from southern Judah. They will all bring burnt offerings, sacrifices, grain offerings, incense*d* and offerings to show thanks to God. They will bring these to the Temple*d* of the Lord. ²⁷But you must obey me and keep the Sabbath day as a holy day. You must not carry any loads into Jerusalem on the Sabbath. If you do, I will start a fire that cannot be put out. It will start at the gates of Jerusalem. And it will burn until it burns even the strong towers!'"

THE POTTER AND THE CLAY

18 This is the word the Lord spoke to Jeremiah: ²"Go down to the potter's house. I will give you my message there." ³So I went down to the potter's house. I saw him working at the potter's wheel. ⁴He was making a pot from clay. But something went wrong with it. So the potter used that clay to make another pot. He used his hands to shape the pot the way that he wanted it to be.

⁵Then the Lord spoke his word to me: ⁶"Family of Israel, can't I do the same thing with you?" says the Lord. "You are like the clay in the potter's hands. ⁷There may come a time when I will speak about a nation or a kingdom. I might say I will pull that nation up by its roots. Or I might say I will pull that nation down and destroy it. ⁸But if the people of that nation are sorry for the evil they have done, I would change my mind. I would not carry out my plans to bring disaster to them. ⁹There may come another time when I will speak about a nation. I might say that I will build up and plant that

nation. ¹⁰But if I see it doing evil by not obeying me, I would change my mind. I would not carry out my plans to do good for them.

¹¹"So, say this to the people of Judah and those who live in Jerusalem: 'This is what the Lord says: I am preparing disaster for you right now. I am making plans against you. So stop doing the evil you are doing. Change your ways and do what is right.' ¹²But the people of Judah will answer, 'It won't do any good to try! We will continue to do what we want. Each of us will do what his stubborn, evil heart wants!'"

¹³So this is what the Lord says:
"Ask the people in other nations this
    question:
  'Have you ever heard anything like
    this?'
  The people of Israel have done a
    horrible thing.
¹⁴The snow on the mountains of
    Lebanon
  never melts from the rocks.
Its cool, flowing streams
  do not dry up.
¹⁵But my people have forgotten me.
  They make offerings to worthless
    idols.
This makes them stumble in what
    they do.
  They stumble about in the old ways
    of their ancestors.
They walk along back roads
  and on poor highways.
¹⁶So Judah's country will become an
    empty desert.
  People will not stop making fun of it.
They will shake their heads as they
    pass by.
  They will be shocked at how the
    country was destroyed.
¹⁷I will scatter them before their
    enemies
  as a strong east wind blows things
    away.

At that awful time they will not see me
coming to help them.
They will see me leaving."

JEREMIAH'S FOURTH COMPLAINT

18Then the people said, "Come, let's
make plans against Jeremiah. Surely the
teaching of the law by the priest will not
be lost. And the advice from the wise
men will still be with us. We will still
have the words of the prophets.*d* So let's
ruin him by telling lies about him! We
won't pay attention to anything he says."

19Lord, listen to me.
Listen to what my accusers are
saying!
20Good should not be paid back with evil.
But they have dug a pit in order to
kill me.
Lord, remember that I stood before
you
and asked you to do good things for
these people.
I asked you to turn your anger away
from them.
21So now, let their children starve.
Let their enemies defeat them with
swords.
Let their wives lose their children and
husbands.
Let the men from Judah be put to
death.
Let the young men be killed in
battle.
22Let them cry out in their houses.
Bring an enemy against them
suddenly.
Let all this happen because my
enemies have dug a pit to
trap me.
And they have hidden traps for me
to step in.
23Lord, you know
about their plans to kill me.
Don't forgive their crimes.
Don't erase their sins.
Make them fall from their places.
Punish them while you are angry.

THE BROKEN JAR

19 This is what the Lord said to me:
"Go and buy a clay jar from a
potter. 2Go out to the Valley of Ben
Hinnom. Go near the front of the Pot-
sherd Gate. Take some of the elders of
the people and priests with you. There
speak the words I tell you. 3Say, 'King of
Judah and people of Jerusalem, listen to
this message from the Lord. This is what
the Lord of heaven's armies, the God of
Israel, says: I will soon bring a disaster
on this place! Everyone who hears about
it will be amazed and full of fear. 4I will
do this because the people of Judah have
quit following me. They have made this
a place for foreign gods. They have
burned sacrifices to other gods. They did
not worship these gods long ago! Their
ancestors didn't worship these gods.
The kings of Judah filled this place with
the blood of the innocent people. 5The
kings of Judah have built places to worship Baal.*d* There they burn their sons in
the fire to Baal. I did not speak about it or
tell them to do that. I never even thought
of such a thing. 6Now people call this
place the Valley of Ben Hinnom or
Topheth. But watch out! The days are
coming, says the Lord, when people will
call this place the Valley of Killing.

7"'At this place I will ruin the plans of
the people of Judah and Jerusalem. The
enemy will chase them. And I will let the
people of Judah be killed with swords. I
will make their dead bodies food for the
birds and wild animals. 8I will completely destroy this city. People will
make fun of it and hiss at it. And they
will shake their heads when they pass by
Jerusalem. They will be shocked when
they see how the city was destroyed. 9An
enemy army will surround the city. They
will not let anyone go out to get food.
The people will become so hungry they
will eat the bodies of their own sons and
daughters. And then they will begin to
eat each other.'"

¹⁰The Lord said, "While the people with you are watching, break that jar. ¹¹Then say this: 'The Lord of heaven's armies says: I will break this nation and this city just as someone breaks a clay jar. It cannot be put back together again. The dead people will be buried here in Topheth. We will bury bodies until there is no more room. ¹²This is what I will do to these people and to this place, says the Lord. I will make this city like Topheth. ¹³The houses in Jerusalem and the king's palaces will become as unclean*d* as this place, Topheth. This is because the people worshiped false gods on the roofs*n* of their houses. They worshiped the stars and burned incense*d* to honor them. They gave drink offerings to false gods.'"

¹⁴Then Jeremiah left Topheth where the Lord had told him to prophesy.*d* He went to the Lord's Temple,*d* stood in the courtyard and said to all the people: ¹⁵"This is what the Lord of heaven's armies, the God of Israel, says: 'I said I would bring disaster to Jerusalem and the villages around it. I will make it happen soon! This is because the people are very stubborn. They do not listen at all to what I say.'"

JEREMIAH AND PASHHUR

20 Pashhur son of Immer was a priest. He was the highest officer in the Temple*d* of the Lord. He heard Jeremiah prophesying*d* in the Temple courtyard. ²So he had Jeremiah the prophet beaten. And he had Jeremiah's hands and feet locked between large blocks of wood. This was at the Upper Gate of Benjamin of the Lord's Temple. ³The next day Pashhur took Jeremiah out from between the blocks of wood. Then Jeremiah said to him, "The Lord's name for you is not Pashhur. Now the Lord's name for you is Terror on Every Side. ⁴That is your name because this is what the Lord says: 'I will soon make you a terror to yourself and to all your friends. You will watch enemies killing your friends with swords. And I will give all the people of Judah to the king of Babylon. He will take them away as captives to Babylon. Then his army will kill them with swords. ⁵I will give all the wealth of this city to its enemies. I will give them its goods and its valuables. I will give the treasures of the kings of Judah to their enemies. The enemies will carry Judah and all its valuables off to Babylon. ⁶And Pashhur, you and everyone in your house will be taken away. You will be forced to go as a captive to Babylon. You will die and be buried there. Your friends you have prophesied lies to will also die and be buried in Babylon!'"

JEREMIAH'S FIFTH COMPLAINT

⁷Lord, you tricked me, and I was
  fooled.
  You are stronger than I am. So you
    won.
  I have become a joke.
  Everyone makes fun of me all day
    long.
⁸Every time I speak, I shout.
  I am always shouting about
    violence and destruction.
  I tell the people about the message
  I received from the Lord.
  But this only brings me insults.
  The people make fun of me all
    day long.
⁹Sometimes I say to myself,
  "I will forget about the Lord.
  I will not speak anymore in his
    name."
  But then the Lord's message becomes
    like a burning fire inside me.
  It feels like it burns deep within my
    bones.

19:13 roofs In Bible times houses were built with flat roofs. The roof was used for drying things such as flax and fruit. And it was used as an extra room, as a place for worship and as a place to sleep in the summer.

I get tired of trying to hold the Lord's
message inside of me.
And finally, I cannot hold it in.
¹⁰I hear many people whispering
about me:
"Terror on every side!
Let's tell the rulers about him."
My friends are all just waiting for me
to make some mistake.
They are saying,
"Maybe we can trick Jeremiah.
Then we can defeat him.
Then we can pay him back."

¹¹But the Lord is with me like a strong
warrior.
So those who are chasing me will
trip and fall.
They will not defeat me.
They will be very disappointed and
ashamed.
Their shame will never be
forgotten.

¹²Lord of heaven's armies, you test
good people.
You look deeply into the heart and
mind of a person.
I have told you my arguments against
these people.
So let me see you give them the
punishment they deserve.

¹³Sing to the Lord!
Praise the Lord!
He saves the life of the poor.
He saves them from the power of
wicked people.

JEREMIAH'S SIXTH COMPLAINT

¹⁴Let there be a curse on the day I was
born.
Let there be no blessing on the day
when my mother gave birth to me.
¹⁵Let there be a curse on the man
who brought my father the news:
"You have a son!"
This made my father glad.
¹⁶Let that man be like the towns
the Lord destroyed without pity.

Let that man hear loud crying in the
morning.
And let him hear battle cries at
noon.
¹⁷This is because he did not kill me
before I was born.
Then my mother would have been
my grave.
I would never have been born.
¹⁸Why did I have to come out of my
mother's body?
All I have known is trouble and
sorrow.
And my life will end in shame.

GOD REJECTS KING ZEDEKIAH'S REQUEST

21 This is the word that the Lord
spoke to Jeremiah. It came when
Zedekiah king of Judah sent Pashhur
son of Malkijah to Jeremiah. He also sent
the priest Zephaniah son of Maaseiah.
²They said, "Ask the Lord for us what
will happen. We want to know because
Nebuchadnezzar king of Babylon is
attacking us. Maybe the Lord will do
miracles*d* for us as he did in the past.
Maybe he will make Nebuchadnezzar
stop attacking us and leave."

³But Jeremiah answered them, "Tell
King Zedekiah this: ⁴'Here is what the
Lord, the God of Israel, says: You have
weapons of war in your hands. You are
using them to defend yourselves against
the king of Babylon and the Babylonians.
But I will make those weapons useless.
The army from Babylon is all around the
outside of the city wall. Soon I will bring
that army into the center of the city. ⁵I
myself will fight against you with my great
power and strength. I am very angry with
you. So I will fight against you with my
own powerful arm. I will fight very hard
against you in my very great anger. ⁶I
will kill everything living in Jerusalem—
both people and animals. They will die
from terrible diseases. ⁷Then, says the
Lord, I'll give Zedekiah king of Judah
to Nebuchadnezzar king of Babylon. I
will also give Zedekiah's officers to

Nebuchadnezzar. Some of the people in Jerusalem will not die from the terrible diseases. Some will not die in battle or from hunger. I will give them also to Nebuchadnezzar king of Babylon. I will let those win who want to kill the people of Judah. So the people of Judah and Jerusalem will be killed in war. Nebuchadnezzar will not show any mercy or pity or feel sorry for them!'

⁸"Also tell this to the people of Jerusalem: 'This is what the Lord says: I will let you choose to live or die. ⁹Anyone who stays in Jerusalem will die. He will die in war or from hunger or from a terrible disease. But anyone who goes out of Jerusalem and surrenders to the Babylonians who are around the city will live. Anyone who leaves the city will save his life. ¹⁰I have decided to make trouble for this city and not to help it, says the Lord. I will give it to the king of Babylon. He will burn it with fire.'

¹¹"Tell these things to Judah's royal family: 'Hear the word of the Lord! ¹²Family of David, the Lord says these things:

You must judge people fairly every day.
    Protect from criminals
    the person who has been robbed.
If you don't do that, I will become
    very angry.
My anger will be like a fire that no
    one can put out.
This will happen because you have
    done evil things.

¹³"'Jerusalem, I am against you.
    You sit on top of the mountain.
    You sit over this valley, says the
    Lord.
You say, "No one can attack us.
    No one can come into our strong
    city."
¹⁴But I will give you the punishment
    you deserve, says the Lord.
I will start a fire in your forests.
    It will burn up everything around
    you!'"

JUDGMENT AGAINST EVIL KINGS

22 This is what the Lord says: "Go down to the palace of the king of Judah. Prophesy*ᵈ* this message there: ²'Hear the word of the Lord, king of Judah. You rule from David's throne. You and your officers, listen well! All of your people who come through these gates, listen! ³This is what the Lord says: Do what is fair and right. Protect those who have been robbed from those who robbed them. Don't do any wrong to the orphans or widows. Don't hurt them. Don't kill innocent people here. ⁴If you carefully obey these commands, this is what will happen: Kings who sit on David's throne will come through the gates of this palace. They will come with their officers and people. They will all come riding in chariots and on horses. ⁵But if you don't obey these commands, this is what the Lord says: I promise in my own name that this king's palace will become a ruin.'"

⁶This is what the Lord says about the palace where the king of Judah lives:

"This palace is tall like the forests of
    Gilead.
    It is high like the mountains of
    Lebanon.
But I will truly make it like a desert.
    It will be empty like towns where no
    one lives.
⁷I will send men to destroy the palace.
    Each man will have his weapons
    with him.
They will cut up your strong, beautiful
    cedar beams.
    And they will throw them into
    the fire.

⁸"People from many nations will pass by this city. They will ask each other, 'Why has the Lord done such a terrible thing to Jerusalem? This was such a great city.' ⁹And the answer will be: 'It was because the people of Judah quit following the agreement with the Lord their God. They worshiped and served other gods.'"

JUDGMENT AGAINST JEHOAHAZ

[10]Don't cry for the king who has died.
  Don't cry loudly for him.
  But cry painfully for the king who is
    being taken away from here.
  Cry for him because he will never
    come back again.
  He will never see his homeland
    again.

[11]This is what the Lord says about Jehoahaz son of Josiah. Jehoahaz became king
of Judah after his father died. He has left
this place. The Lord says, "He will never
come back again. [12]He will die where those
who captured him have taken him. He
will not see this land again."

JUDGMENT AGAINST JEHOIAKIM

[13]"How terrible it will be for him who
    builds his palace by doing evil.
  He cheats people so he can build its
    upper rooms.
  He is making his own people work for
    nothing.
  He is not paying them for their
    work.
[14]He says, 'I will build a great palace for
    myself.
  I will have large upper rooms.'
  So he builds the palace with large
    windows.
  He uses cedar wood for the walls.
  And he paints it red.

[15]"Does having a lot of cedar in your
    house
    make you a great king?
  Your father was satisfied to have food
    and drink.
  He did what was right and fair.
  So everything went well for him.
[16]He helped those who were poor and
    needy.
  So everything went well for him.
  That's what it means to know God,"
    says the Lord.
[17]"But your eyes only look for what you
    can get dishonestly.

You are always thinking about
    getting more for yourself.
  You are even willing to kill innocent
    people to get it.
  You are making it hard for people.
  You even steal things from them."
[18]So this is what the Lord says to Jehoi-
akim son of Josiah king of Judah:
  "The people of Judah will not cry
    loudly when Jehoiakim dies.
  They will not say, 'Oh, my brother,
    I am so sad!
  Oh, my sister, I am so sad!'
  The people of Judah will not cry for
    him, saying:
  'Oh, master, oh, my king.'
[19]The people of Jerusalem will bury him
    like a donkey.
  They will just drag his body away.
  Then they will throw it outside the
    gates of Jerusalem.

[20]"Judah, go up to Lebanon and cry out.
  Let your voice be heard in Bashan.
  Cry out from Abarim.
  All your friends are destroyed!
[21]Judah, when you were successful,
    I warned you.
  But you refused to listen.
  You have acted like this since you
    were young.
  You have not obeyed me.
[22]My punishment will come like a
    storm.
  And it will blow all your shepherds
    away.
  Your friends will be taken away as
    captives.
  Then you will really be ashamed.
  You will be disgraced because of all
    the wicked things you did.
[23]King, you live in your palace.
  You are cozy in your rooms of
    cedar.
  But you will groan when your
    punishment comes.
  You will hurt like a woman giving
    birth to a baby!

JUDGMENT UPON JEHOIACHIN

[24]"As surely as I live," says the Lord, "I will do this to you, Jehoiachin son of Jehoiakim king of Judah: Even if you were a signet[d] ring on my right hand, I would still pull you off. [25]Jehoiachin, I will give you to Nebuchadnezzar king of Babylon. And I will hand you over to the Babylonians. Those are the people you are afraid of because they want to kill you. [26]I will throw you and your mother into another country. Neither of you was born there. But both of you will die there. [27]You will want to come back. But you will never be able to return."

[28]Jehoiachin is like a broken pot
　　someone threw away.
　He is like something no one wants.
　Why will Jehoiachin and his children
　　be thrown out?
　Why will they be thrown into a
　　foreign land?
[29]Land, land, land of Judah,
　hear the word of the Lord!
[30]This is what the Lord says:
　"Write this down about Jehoiachin:
　He is a man who is to have no
　　children.
　He will not be successful in his
　　lifetime.
　And none of his children will be
　　successful.
　None of his children will sit on the
　　throne of David.
　They will not rule in Judah."

THE EVIL LEADERS

23 "How terrible it will be for the leaders of Judah. They are destroying my people. They are making them run in all directions," says the Lord. [2]They are responsible for the people. And the Lord, the God of Israel, says to them: "You have made my people run away in all directions. You have forced them away. And you have not taken care of them. So I will punish you for the evil things you have done," says the Lord. [3]"I

sent my people to other countries. But I will gather my people who are left alive. And I will bring them back to their own country. When they are back in their own land, they will have many children. And they will grow in number. [4]I will place new leaders over my people. They will take care of my people. And my people will not be afraid or terrified. None of them will be lost," says the Lord.

THE GOOD DESCENDANT

[5]"The days are coming," says the Lord,
　"when I will raise up a good
　　descendant[d] in David's family.
This descendant will be a king who
　　will rule in a wise way.
And he will do what is fair and right
　　in the land.
[6]In his time Judah will be saved.
　Israel will live in safety.
This will be his name:
　The Lord Does What Is Right.
[7]"So the days are coming," says the Lord, "when people will not say: 'As surely as the Lord lives, who brought Israel out of Egypt . . .' [8]But people will say something new: 'As surely as the Lord lives, who brought Israel from the land of the north and from all the countries where he had sent them away . . .' Then the people of Israel will live in their own land."

FALSE PROPHETS

[9]A message to the prophets:[d]
My heart is broken.
　All my bones shake.
I'm like a man who is drunk.
　I'm like a man who has been
　　overcome with wine.
This is because of the Lord
　and his holy words.
[10]The land of Judah is full of people who
　　are guilty of adultery.[d]
　Because of this, the Lord cursed the
　　land.
　And it has become very dry.
　The pastures have dried up.

The people are evil.
They use their power in the wrong
way.

[11] "Both the prophets and the priests are
evil.
I have seen them doing evil things
even in my own Temple,"[d] says
the Lord.
[12] "So they will be in danger.
They will be forced into darkness.
There they will be defeated.
I will bring disaster on them.
At that time I will punish those
prophets and priests," says the
Lord.

[13] "I saw the prophets of Samaria
do something wrong.
I saw those prophets prophesy by the
false god Baal.[d]
And they led my people, the
Israelites, away.
[14] And I have seen the prophets of
Jerusalem
do some terrible things.
These prophets are guilty of adultery
and live by lies.
They encourage evil people to keep on
doing evil.
So the people don't stop sinning.
All of those people are like the city of
Sodom.
The people of Jerusalem are like the
city of Gomorrah to me!"

[15] So this is what the Lord of heaven's
armies says about the prophets:
"I will make those prophets eat bitter
food.
I will make them drink poisoned
water.
This is because the prophets of
Jerusalem spread wickedness
through the whole country."

[16] This is what the Lord of heaven's
armies says:
"Don't pay attention to the things
those prophets are saying to you.
They are trying to fool you.

Those prophets talk of visions from
their own minds.
But they did not get their visions
from me.
[17] They say to those who hate me:
'The Lord says: You will have
peace.'
They say to those who are stubborn
and do as they please:
'Nothing bad will happen to you!'
[18] But none of these prophets has stood
in the meeting of angels.
None of them has seen or heard the
message of the Lord.
None of them has paid close
attention to the Lord's message.
[19] Look, the punishment from the Lord
will come like a storm.
His anger will be like a hurricane.
It will come crashing down on the
heads of those wicked people.
[20] The Lord's anger will not stop
until he finishes what he plans to do.
When that day is over,
you will understand this clearly.
[21] I did not send those prophets.
But they ran to tell their message.
I did not speak to them.
But they prophesied anyway.
[22] But if they had stood in the meeting of
angels,
they would have told my message
to my people.
They would have turned the people
from their evil ways.
They would have turned them from
doing evil.

[23] "I am a God who is near," says the Lord.
"I am also a God who is far away."
[24] "No one can hide
where I cannot see him," says the
Lord.
"I fill all of heaven and earth," says
the Lord.

[25] "I have heard the prophets who
prophesy lies in my name. They say, 'I
have had a dream! I have had a dream!'

26How long will this continue in the minds of these lying prophets? They prophesy from their own wishful thinking. 27They are trying to make the people of Judah forget me. They are doing this by telling each other these dreams. They are trying to make my people forget me in the same way that their ancestors forgot me. Their ancestors forgot me and worshiped Baal. 28Straw is not the same thing as wheat!" says the Lord. "If a prophet wants to tell about his dreams, let him! But let the person who hears my message speak it truthfully! 29My message is like a fire," says the Lord. "It is like a hammer that smashes a rock!

30"So I am against the false prophets," says the Lord. "These prophets keep stealing words from each other. They say these words are from me. 31I am against the false prophets," says the Lord. "They use their own words and pretend it is a message from me. 32I am against the prophets who prophesy false dreams," says the Lord. "They mislead my people with their lies and false teachings! I did not send those prophets to teach the people. I never commanded them to do anything for me. They can't help the people of Judah at all," says the Lord.

THE SAD MESSAGE FROM THE LORD

33"The people of Judah, a prophet*d* or a priest may ask you: 'Jeremiah, what is the message from the Lord?' You will answer them and say, 'You are a heavy load to the Lord. And I will throw down this heavy load, says the Lord!' 34A prophet or a priest or one of the people might say, 'This is a message from the Lord!' That person has lied. So I will punish him and his whole family. 35This is what you will say to each other: 'What did the Lord answer?' or 'What did the Lord say?' 36But you will never again say, 'The message of the Lord.' This is because the only message you speak is your own words. You used to change the words of our God. He is the living God,

the Lord of heaven's armies. 37This is how you speak to the prophets: 'What answer did the Lord give you?' or 'What did the Lord say?' 38But don't say, 'What was the message from the Lord?' If you use these words, the Lord will say this to you: You should not have called it a message from the Lord. I told you not to use those words. 39I will pick you up like a heavy load. And I'll throw you away from me. I gave the city of Jerusalem to your ancestors and to you. But I will throw you and that city away from me. 40And I will make a disgrace of you forever. You will never forget your shame."

THE GOOD AND BAD FIGS

24 I saw a vision after Nebuchadnezzar king of Babylon took Jehoiachin son of Jehoiakim as a prisoner. Jehoiachin king of Judah and his officers were taken away from Jerusalem. They were taken to Babylon. Nebuchadnezzar also took away all the craftsmen and metalworkers of Judah. It was then that the Lord showed me these things: I saw two baskets of figs. They were arranged in front of the Temple*d* of the Lord. 2One of the baskets had very good figs in it. They were like figs that ripen early in the season. But the other basket had rotten figs. They were too rotten to eat.

3The Lord said to me, "What do you see, Jeremiah?"

I answered, "I see figs. The good figs are very good. But the rotten figs are too rotten to eat."

4Then the Lord spoke his word to me. 5This is what the Lord, the God of Israel, said: "I sent the people of Judah out of their country into Babylon. Those people will be like these good figs. I think of them as good. 6I will look after them. I will bring them back to the land of Judah. I will not tear them down. I will build them up. I will not pull them up. I will plant them so they can grow. 7I will make them want to know me. They will know that I am the Lord. They will be my people, and I will be their God. This is because they will return to me with their whole hearts.

⁸"But the bad figs are too rotten to eat," says the Lord. "Zedekiah king of Judah and his officers will be like those rotten figs. All the people from Jerusalem who are left alive will be like that. This will be true even if those people now live in Egypt. ⁹I will make those people hated as an evil people by all the kingdoms of the earth. People will make fun of the people from Judah and tell jokes about them. People will point fingers at them. They will curse them everywhere I scatter them. ¹⁰I will send war, hunger and disease against them. I will attack them until they have all been killed. Then they will no longer be in the land I gave to them and their ancestors."

A SUMMARY OF JEREMIAH'S PREACHING

25 This is the message that came to Jeremiah concerning all the people of Judah. It came in the fourth year that Jehoiakim son of Josiah was king of Judah. This was the first year Nebuchadnezzar was king of Babylon. ²This is the message Jeremiah the prophet*ᵈ* spoke to all the people of Judah and Jerusalem:

³The Lord has spoken his word to me again and again for these past 23 years. I have been a prophet since the thirteenth year of Josiah. Josiah was the son of Amon king of Judah. I have spoken messages from the Lord to you from that time until today. But you have not listened.

⁴The Lord has sent his servants the prophets to you over and over again. But you have not listened to them. You have not paid any attention to them. ⁵They have said, "Stop your evil ways. Stop doing what is wrong. Do this so you can stay in the land. This is the land that the Lord gave to you and your ancestors long ago. He gave it to you to live in forever. ⁶Don't follow other gods to serve them or to worship them. You must not worship idols that are the work of

someone's hands. That makes the Lord angry, and he will punish you."

⁷"But you did not listen to me," says the Lord. "You worshiped idols that were the work of someone's hands. That made me angry. So I punished you."

⁸So this is what the Lord of heaven's armies says: "You have not listened to my messages. ⁹So I will soon send for all the peoples of the north," says the Lord. "I will soon send for my servant Nebuchadnezzar king of Babylon. I will bring them all against Judah and all the nations around you, too. I will completely destroy all those countries. I will leave them in ruins forever. People will be shocked when they see how badly they will be destroyed. ¹⁰I will bring an end to the sounds of joy and happiness. There will be no more happy sounds of brides and bridegrooms. I will take away the sound of people grinding meal. And I will take away the light of the lamp. ¹¹That whole area will be an empty desert. And these nations will be slaves of the king of Babylon for 70 years.

¹²"But when the 70 years have passed, I will punish the king of Babylon and his nation," says the Lord. "I will punish the Babylonians for their evil. I will make that land a desert forever. ¹³I have said many terrible things will happen to Babylonia. All of them will happen. Jeremiah prophesied about those foreign nations. And the warnings are written in this book. ¹⁴The Babylonians will have to serve many nations and many great kings. I will give them the punishment they deserve. They will be punished for all the things they do."

JUDGMENT ON THE NATIONS

¹⁵The Lord, the God of Israel, said this to me: "My anger is like the wine in a cup. Take it from my hand. I am sending you to all the nations. Make them drink all of my anger from this cup. ¹⁶They will drink my anger like wine. Then they will not be able to walk straight. They will act

like madmen. They will do this because of the war that I am going to send among them."

¹⁷So I took the cup from the Lord's hand. I went to those nations. And I made them drink from the cup. ¹⁸I poured this wine for the people of Jerusalem and the towns of Judah. I made the kings and officers of Judah drink from the cup. I did it so that they would become a ruin. People would be shocked when they saw how badly they were destroyed. People would insult them and speak evil of them. And it happened. Judah is like that now. ¹⁹I also made these people drink from that cup of my anger: the king of Egypt, his servants, his officers and all his people; ²⁰all the Arabs, and all the kings of the land of Uz; all the kings of the Philistines (the kings of the cities of Ashkelon, Gaza, Ekron and the people left at Ashdod); ²¹the people of Edom, Moab and Ammon; ²²all the kings of Tyre and Sidon; all the kings of the faraway countries; ²³the people of Dedan and Tema and Buz; all who cut their hair short; ²⁴all the kings of Arabia; and the kings of the people who live in the desert; ²⁵all the kings of Zimri, Elam and Media; ²⁶and all the kings of the north, near and far, one after the other. I made all the kingdoms on earth drink from the cup of the Lord's anger. But the king of Babylon will drink from this cup after all the others.

²⁷"Then say this to them: 'This is what the Lord of heaven's armies, the God of Israel, says: Drink this cup of my anger. Get drunk from it and vomit. Fall down and don't get up. Don't get up because I am sending a war to kill you!'

²⁸"They will refuse to take the cup from your hand. They will refuse to drink it. Then say this to them: 'The Lord of heaven's armies says this: You must drink from this cup. ²⁹I am already bringing disaster on Jerusalem. And it is the city that is called by my name. And do you think you will not be punished?

You will be punished! I am sending war on all the people of the earth, says the Lord of heaven's armies.'

³⁰"You will prophesy*d* against them with these words. Say to them:
'The Lord roars from heaven.
  He shouts from his Holy Temple.*d*
  He roars against his land.
He will shout like people who walk on
    grapes to make wine.
He will shout against all who live on
    the earth.
³¹The noise will spread all over the
    earth.
  This is because the Lord is
    punishing all the nations.
He judges and tells what is wrong
    with all people.
And he is killing the evil people
    with a sword,'" says the Lord.

³²This is what the Lord of heaven's armies says:
"Disasters will soon spread
    from nation to nation.
They will come like a powerful storm
    to all the faraway places on earth."

³³At that time the dead bodies will reach from one end of the earth to the other. No one will cry for them. No one will gather up their bodies and bury them. They will be left lying on the ground like dung.

³⁴Cry, you leaders! Cry out loud!
  Roll around in the dust, leaders of
    the people!
It is now time for you to be killed.
  You will fall and be scattered
    everywhere, like pieces of a
    broken jar.
³⁵There will be no place for the leaders
    to hide.
  These leaders will not escape.
³⁶I hear the leaders shouting.
  I hear the leaders of the people
    crying loudly.
  This is because the Lord is
    destroying their land.

³⁷Those peaceful pastures will be like an
empty desert.
This happened because the Lord is
very angry.
³⁸The Lord, like a lion, has left his den.
Their land has been destroyed.
It is because of his destroying anger.
It is because of his fierce anger.

JEREMIAH'S LESSON AT THE TEMPLE

26 This message came from the
Lord. It was during the first year
Jehoiakim son of Josiah was king of
Judah. ²This is what the Lord said: "Jeremiah, stand in the courtyard of the
Temple*ᵈ* of the Lord. Give this message
to all the people of the towns of Judah.
They are coming to worship at the
Temple of the Lord. Tell them everything I tell you to say. Don't leave out
any part of my message. ³Maybe they
will listen and stop their evil ways. I have
plans to bring disaster on them because
of the evil they have done. But if they
change, I will change my mind about
bringing disaster on them. ⁴Say to them:
'This is what the Lord says: I gave my
teachings to you. You must obey me and
follow my teachings. ⁵You must listen to
what my servants the prophets*ᵈ* say to
you. I have sent prophets to you again
and again. But you did not listen to them.
⁶If you don't obey me, I will destroy my
Temple in Jerusalem. I will destroy it as I
destroyed my Holy Tent*ᵈ* at Shiloh. People
all over the world will curse Jerusalem.'"

⁷The priests, the prophets and all the
people heard Jeremiah. He said all of
these words in the Temple of the Lord.
⁸Jeremiah finished speaking everything
the Lord had commanded him to say.
Then the priests, prophets and all the
people grabbed Jeremiah. They said,
"You must die! ⁹How dare you prophesy
such a thing in the name of the Lord!
How dare you say that this Temple will
be destroyed like the one at Shiloh! How
dare you say that Jerusalem will become
a desert without anyone to live in it!" All

the people crowded around Jeremiah in
the Temple of the Lord.

¹⁰Now the officers of Judah heard
about what was happening. So they came
out of the king's palace and went up to the
Temple of the Lord. There they took their
places at the entrance of the New Gate.
¹¹Then the priests and prophets spoke to
the officers and all the other people. They
said, "Jeremiah should be killed. He said
bad things about Jerusalem! You heard
him say it."

¹²Then Jeremiah spoke to all the officers of Judah and all the other people. He
said, "The Lord sent me to say these
things about this Temple and this city.
Everything that you have heard is from
the Lord. ¹³Now change your lives! You
must start doing good things. You must
obey the Lord your God. If you do that,
the Lord will change his mind. He will
not bring on you the disaster he has told
you about. ¹⁴As for me, I am in your
power. Do to me what you think is good
and right. ¹⁵But if you kill me, be sure of
one thing. You will be guilty of killing an
innocent person. You will make this city
and everyone who lives in it guilty, too!
The Lord sent me to you. The message
you heard is from the Lord!"

¹⁶Then the officers and all the people
spoke. They said to the priests and the
prophets, "Jeremiah must not be killed.
What he told us comes from the Lord
our God."

¹⁷Then some of the elders stood up.
They spoke to all the people. ¹⁸They said,
"Micah the prophet was from the city of
Moresheth. He was a prophet during the
time Hezekiah was king of Judah. Micah
said these things to all the people of
Judah: 'This is what the Lord of heaven's
armies says:

Jerusalem will be plowed like a field.
Jerusalem will become a pile of
rocks.
The hill where the Temple stands
will be covered with bushes.'

[19]"Hezekiah was the king of Judah. And he did not kill Micah. No one else in Judah killed him. You know that Hezekiah feared the Lord. He wanted to please the Lord. So the Lord changed his mind. He did not bring on Judah the disaster he had promised. If we hurt Jeremiah, we will bring a terrible disaster on ourselves!"

[20](Now there was another man who prophesied in the name of the Lord. His name was Uriah the son of Shemaiah. Uriah was from the city of Kiriath Jearim. He preached the same things against this city and land that Jeremiah did. [21]King Jehoiakim, all his army officers and all the leaders of Judah heard Uriah preach. King Jehoiakim wanted to kill Uriah. But Uriah heard about it and was afraid. So he escaped to Egypt. [22]But King Jehoiakim sent Elnathan son of Acbor and some other men to Egypt. [23]They brought Uriah back from Egypt. Then they took him to King Jehoiakim. Jehoiakim ordered Uriah to be killed with a sword. His body was thrown into the burial place where poor people are buried.)

[24]There was an important man named Ahikam son of Shaphan. Ahikam supported Jeremiah. So Ahikam kept Jeremiah from being killed by the people.

NEBUCHADNEZZAR IS MADE RULER

27 The Lord spoke his word to Jeremiah. This happened when Zedekiah son of Josiah was king of Judah. [2]This is what the Lord said to me: "Make a yoke[d] out of straps and poles. Put it on the back of your neck. [3]Then send messages to the kings of Edom, Moab, Ammon, Tyre and Sidon. Send the messages through the messengers of these kings. Those messengers have come to Jerusalem to see Zedekiah king of Judah. [4]Tell them to give this message to their masters. Tell them, 'The Lord of heaven's armies, the God of Israel, says: "Tell your masters: [5]I made the earth and everyone on it. I made all the animals on the earth. I did this with my great power and my strong arm. I can give the earth to anyone I want. [6]Now I have given all these lands to Nebuchadnezzar king of Babylon. He is my servant. I will make even the wild animals obey him. [7]All nations will serve Nebuchadnezzar and his son and grandson. Then the time will come for Babylon to be defeated. Many nations and great kings will make Babylon their servant.

[8]"""But now some nations or kingdoms might refuse to serve Nebuchadnezzar king of Babylon. They might refuse to be under his control. If that happens, I will punish that nation with war, hunger and terrible sickness, says the Lord. I will do it until I destroy that nation. I will use Nebuchadnezzar to destroy the nation that fights against him. [9]So don't listen to your false prophets.[d] Don't listen to people who use magic to tell what will happen in the future. Don't listen to those who say they can tell what dreams mean. Don't listen to mediums[d] or magicians. They all tell you, 'You will not be slaves to the king of Babylon.' [10]They are telling you lies! They will only cause you to be taken far from your homeland. I will force you to leave your homes. And you will die in another land. [11]But some nations will put themselves under the control of the king of Babylon. They will serve him. I will let those nations stay in their own country, says the Lord. The people from those nations will live in their own land and farm it.""'

[12]I gave the same message to Zedekiah king of Judah. I said, "You must put yourself under the control of the king of Babylon and serve him. If you serve him and his people, you will live. [13]Why should you and your people die like those who do not serve the king of Babylon? Why should you die because of war, hunger and sickness? The Lord said this will happen. [14]But the false prophets are saying this: 'You will never be slaves to the king of Babylon.' Don't listen to

them because they are prophesying lies to you! [15]'I did not send them,' says the Lord. 'They are prophesying lies. And they are saying the message is from me. So I will send Judah away. You will die! And those prophets who prophesy to you will die also.'"

[16]Then I, Jeremiah, said to the priests and all the people, "This is what the Lord says: Those false prophets are saying that what the Babylonians took from the Temple[d] of the Lord will be brought back soon. Don't listen to them! They are prophesying lies to you. [17]Don't listen to those prophets. But serve the king of Babylon, and you will live. There is no reason for you to cause Jerusalem to become a ruin. [18]They might be prophets and have the message from the Lord. If so, let them pray to the Lord of heaven's armies. Let them pray about the things that are still in the Temple of the Lord. Let them pray about the things that are still in the king's palace and in Jerusalem. Let them pray that all this will not be taken away to Babylon.

[19]"This is what the Lord of heaven's armies says about those things left in Jerusalem. In the Temple there are the pillars, the large bronze bowl, which is called the Sea, the stands that can be moved and other things. Nebuchadnezzar king of Babylon left them in Jerusalem. [20]Nebuchadnezzar did not take these away when he took Jehoiachin king of Judah captive. Jehoiachin was the son of King Jehoiakim. Nebuchadnezzar also took other important people away from Judah and Jerusalem. [21]This is what the Lord of heaven's armies, the God of Israel, says about the things left in the Temple of the Lord and in the king's palace and in Jerusalem: 'All of this will also be taken to Babylon. [22]And they will stay there until the day I go to get them,' says the Lord. 'Then I will bring them back and return them to this place.'"

THE FALSE PROPHET HANANIAH

28 It was the fifth month of King Zedekiah's fourth year as king of Judah. This was at the beginning of the king's rule. At that time Hananiah the prophet[d] spoke to me. He was the son of Azzur. And he was from the town of Gibeon. He was in the Temple[d] of the Lord when he spoke to me. In front of the priests and all the people, Hananiah said: [2]"The Lord of heaven's armies, the God of Israel, says: 'I will break the yoke[d] the king of Babylon has put on Judah. [3]Before two years are over, I will bring back everything that Nebuchadnezzar king of Babylon took from the Lord's Temple. [4]I will also bring Jehoiachin son of Jehoiakim king of Judah back here. And I will bring back all the other people of Judah as captives to Babylon,' says the Lord. 'So I will break the yoke the king of Babylon put on Judah.'"

[5]Then the prophet Jeremiah answered the prophet Hananiah. They were standing in the Temple[d] of the Lord. The priests and all the people there could hear Jeremiah's answer. [6]He said, "Amen! Let the Lord really do that! May the Lord make the message you prophesy come true. May the Lord bring everything from the Lord's Temple back from Babylon. And may he bring back to their homes all the people who were taken as captives.

[7]"But listen to what I must say to you and all the people. [8]There were prophets long before we became prophets, Hananiah. They prophesied that war, hunger and terrible sicknesses would come. They would come to many countries and great kingdoms. [9]But a prophet might prophesy that we will have peace. The message of that prophet might come true. If it does, only then can he be recognized as one truly sent by the Lord!"

[10]Then the prophet Hananiah took the yoke off Jeremiah's neck and broke it. [11]Hananiah said in front of all the people, "This is what the Lord says: 'In

the same way I will break the yoke of Nebuchadnezzar king of Babylon. He put that yoke on all the nations of the world. But I will break it before two years are over.'" After Hananiah had said that, Jeremiah left the Temple.

¹²Then the Lord spoke his word to Jeremiah. This was not long after the prophet Hananiah had broken the yoke off of the prophet Jeremiah's neck. ¹³The Lord said, "Go and tell Hananiah, 'This is what the Lord says: You have broken a wooden yoke. But I will make a yoke of iron in the place of the wooden one! ¹⁴The Lord of heaven's armies, the God of Israel, says: I will put a yoke of iron on the necks of all these nations. I will do that to make them serve Nebuchadnezzar king of Babylon. And they will be slaves to him. I will even give Nebuchadnezzar control over the wild animals.'"

¹⁵Then the prophet Jeremiah said to the prophet Hananiah, "Listen, Hananiah! The Lord did not send you. And you have made the people of Judah trust in lies. ¹⁶So this is what the Lord says: 'Soon I will remove you from the earth. You will die this year. This is because you taught the people to turn against the Lord.'"

¹⁷Hananiah died in the seventh month of that same year.

A LETTER TO THE JEWS IN BABYLON

29 Jeremiah the prophet*d* sent a letter to the people taken as captives to Babylon. He sent it to the elders who were among the captives, the priests and the prophets. And he sent it to all the other people Nebuchadnezzar had taken from Jerusalem to Babylon. ²(This letter was sent after all these people were taken away: Jehoiachin and the queen mother; the officers and leaders of Judah and Jerusalem; and the craftsmen and metalworkers.) ³Zedekiah king of Judah had sent Elasah son of Shaphan and Gemariah son of Hilkiah to King Nebuchadnezzar. So Jeremiah gave the letter to them to take to Babylon. This is what the letter said:

⁴This is what the Lord of heaven's armies, the God of Israel, says to all those people he sent away from Jerusalem as captives to Babylon: ⁵"Build houses and settle in the land. Plant gardens and eat the food you grow. ⁶Get married and have sons and daughters. Find wives for your sons. Let your daughters be married so they may also have sons and daughters. Have many children and grow in number in Babylon. Don't become fewer in number. ⁷Also do good things for the city where I sent you as captives. Pray to the Lord for the city where you are living. If there is peace in that city, you will have peace also." ⁸The Lord of heaven's armies, the God of Israel, says: "Don't let your prophets and the people who do magic fool you. Don't listen to their dreams. ⁹They are prophesying lies. And they are saying that their message is from me. But I did not send them," says the Lord.

¹⁰This is what the Lord says: "Babylon will be powerful for 70 years. After that time I will come to you who are living in Babylon. I will keep my promise to bring you back to Jerusalem. ¹¹I say this because I know what I have planned for you," says the Lord. "I have good plans for you. I don't plan to hurt you. I plan to give you hope and a good future. ¹²Then you will call my name. You will come to me and pray to me. And I will listen to you. ¹³You will search for me. And when you search for me with all your heart, you will find me! ¹⁴I will let you find me," says the Lord. "And I will bring you back from your captivity. I forced you to leave this place. But I will gather you from all the nations. I will gather you from the places I have sent you as captives," says the Lord. "And I will bring you back to this place."

¹⁵You might say, "The Lord has given us prophets here in Babylon."

¹⁶But the Lord says this about the king who is sitting on David's throne now. And I'm also talking about all the other people still in Jerusalem. These are your relatives who did not go to Babylon with you. ¹⁷The Lord of heaven's armies says: "I will soon send war, hunger and terrible diseases against those still in Jerusalem. I will make them like bad figs that are too rotten to eat. ¹⁸I will chase them with war, hunger and terrible diseases. I will make them a hated people by all the kingdoms of the earth. People will speak evil of them. They will be shocked when they hear what has happened. And people will use them as a shameful example wherever I make them go. ¹⁹This is because those in Jerusalem have not listened to my message," says the Lord. "I sent my message to them again and again. I used my servants, the prophets, to give my messages to them. But they did not listen," says the Lord.

²⁰You captives, I forced you to leave Jerusalem and go to Babylon. So listen to the message from the Lord. ²¹The Lord of heaven's armies says this about Ahab son of Kolaiah. And he says it about Zedekiah son of Maaseiah: "These two men have been prophesying lies to you. They have said that their message is from me. But I will hand over those two prophets to Nebuchadnezzar king of Babylon. And Nebuchadnezzar will kill them in front of you who are captives in Babylon. ²²Because of this, all the captives from Judah will use this curse: 'May the Lord treat you like Zedekiah and Ahab. The king of Babylon burned them with fire.' ²³They have done evil things among the people of Israel. They are guilty of adultery*d* with their neighbors' wives.

They have also spoken lies. And they said those lies were a message from me, the Lord. I did not tell them to do that. I know what they have done. I am a witness!" says the Lord.

²⁴Also give a message to Shemaiah. He is from the Nehelamite family. ²⁵The Lord of heaven's armies, the God of Israel, says: "Shemaiah, you sent letters to all the people in Jerusalem. And you sent letters to the priest Zephaniah son of Maaseiah. You also sent letters to all the priests. You sent those letters in your own name. ²⁶You said to Zephaniah, 'The Lord has made you priest in place of Jehoiada. You are to be in charge of the Temple*d* of the Lord. You should arrest any madman who acts like a prophet. You should lock the hands and feet of that person between wooden blocks. And put iron rings around his neck. ²⁷Now Jeremiah from Anathoth is acting like a prophet. So why haven't you arrested him? ²⁸Jeremiah has sent this message to us in Babylon: You will be there for a long time. So build houses and settle down. Plant gardens and eat what you grow.'"

²⁹Zephaniah the priest read the letter to Jeremiah the prophet. ³⁰Then the Lord spoke his word to Jeremiah: ³¹"Send this message to all the captives in Babylon: 'This is what the Lord says about Shemaiah the Nehelamite: Shemaiah has prophesied to you, but I did not send him. He has made you believe a lie. ³²Because Shemaiah has done that, this is what the Lord says: I will soon punish Shemaiah the Nehelamite. He will not see the good things I will do for my people, says the Lord. None of his family will be left alive among the people. This is because he has taught the people to turn against me.'"

PROMISES OF HOPE

30 These are the words that the Lord spoke to Jeremiah. ²The Lord, the God of Israel, said: "Jeremiah, write in a book all the words I have spoken to you. ³The days will come when I will make everything as good as it was before," says the Lord. "I will bring Israel and Judah back from captivity," says the Lord. "I will return them to the land I gave their ancestors. Then my people will own that land again!"

⁴The Lord spoke this message about the people of Israel and Judah: ⁵This is what the Lord said:

"We hear people crying from fear.
  They are afraid. There is no peace.
⁶Ask this question, and consider it:
  A man cannot have a baby.
So why do I see every strong man
  holding his stomach in pain like a
    woman having a baby?
Why is everyone's face turning
  white like a dead man's face?
⁷This will be a terrible day!
  There will never be another time
    like this.
This is a time of great trouble for the
  people of Jacob.
But they will be saved from it."

⁸The Lord of heaven's armies says,
  "At that time
I will break the yoke[d] from their
  necks.
And I will break the ropes holding
  them.
Foreign people will never again
  make my people slaves!
⁹They will serve the Lord their God.
  And they will serve David their
    king.
I will send that king to them.

¹⁰"So people of Jacob, my servants,
  don't be afraid!
Israel, don't be frightened," says the
  Lord.
"I will save you from that faraway
  place where you are captives.
I will save your family from that
  land.

The people of Jacob will be safe and
  have peace again.
There will be no enemy to frighten
  them.
¹¹I am with you and will save you,"
  says the Lord.
"I scattered you among those nations.
Even if I completely destroy all
  those nations,
I will not destroy you.
You will be punished fairly.
But I will punish you."

¹²This is what the Lord said:
"You people have a wound that
  cannot be cured.
  Your injury will not heal.
¹³There is no one to argue your case.
  There is no cure for your sores.
  So you will not be healed.
¹⁴All those nations who were your
  friends have forgotten you.
  They don't care about you.
I hurt you as an enemy would.
  I punished you very hard.
I did this because your guilt was so
  great.
I did this because your sins were so
  many.
¹⁵Why are you crying about your
  injury?
  There is no cure for your pain.
I, the Lord, did these things to you
  because of your great guilt.
I did these things because of your
  many sins.
¹⁶But those nations that destroyed you
  will now be destroyed.
  Your enemies will become captives.
Those who stole from you will have
  their own things stolen.
Those who took things from you in
  war will have their own things
    taken.
¹⁷I will bring back your health.
  And I will heal your injuries," says
    the Lord.

"This is because other people forced
    you out from among them.
Those people said about you, 'No
    one cares about Jerusalem!'"

¹⁸This is what the Lord said:
"I will make the tents of Jacob's
    people as they used to be.
And I will have pity on Israel's
    houses.
The city will be rebuilt on its hill of
    ruins.
And the king's palace will stand in
    its proper place.
¹⁹People in those places will sing songs
    of praise.
There will also be the sound of
    laughter.
I will give them many children.
    They will not be small.
I will bring honor to them.
    No one will look down on them.
²⁰Their descendants^d will be like they
    were in the old days.
I will make their people strong
    before me.
And I will punish the nations who
    have hurt them.
²¹One of their own people will lead them.
    Their ruler will come from among
    them.
He will come near to me when I invite
    him.
Who would dare to come
    uninvited?" says the Lord.
²²"So you will be my people,
    and I will be your God."

²³The Lord was very angry.
    He punished the people.
And the punishment came like a storm.
    It came like a hurricane against the
    evil people.
²⁴The Lord will stay angry
    until he finishes punishing the
    people.
He will stay angry
    until he finishes the punishment he
    planned.

When that day comes,
    you will understand this.

THE NEW ISRAEL

31 The Lord says, "At that time I
will be God of all Israel's family
groups. And they will be my people."
²This is what the Lord says:
"Some of the people were not killed
    by the enemy's sword.
Those people will find help in the
    desert.
I have come to give rest to Israel."

³And from far away the Lord appeared
to his people. He said,
"I love you people
    with a love that will last forever.
I became your friend
    because of my love and kindness.
⁴People of Israel, I will build you up
    again,
    and you will be rebuilt.
You will pick up your tambourines^d
    again.
You will dance with those who are
    joyful.
⁵You will plant vineyards again
    on the hills around Samaria.
The farmers will plant them
    and enjoy their fruit.
⁶There will be a time when watchmen
    in the mountains of Ephraim
    shout this message:
'Come, let's go up to Jerusalem to
    worship the Lord our God!'"

⁷This is what the Lord says:
"Be happy and sing for the people of
    Jacob.
Shout for Israel, the greatest of the
    nations.
Sing your praises and shout this:
'Lord, save your people!
Save those who are left alive from
    the nation of Israel!'
⁸Look, I will bring Israel from the
    country in the north.
I will gather them from the faraway
    places on earth.

Some of the people are blind and
  crippled.
    Some of the women will be
      pregnant and ready to give birth.
    A great many people will come
      back.
⁹Those people will be crying as they
  come back.
    But they will pray as I bring them
      back.
I will lead those people by streams of
  water.
    I will lead them on an even road
      where they will not stumble.
This is because I am Israel's father.
    And Israel is my firstborn^d son.

¹⁰"Nations, listen to the message from
  the Lord.
    Tell this message in the faraway
      lands by the sea:
'The one who scattered the people of
  Israel will bring them back
  together.
    And he will watch over his people
      like a shepherd.'
¹¹The Lord will bring the people of
  Jacob back.
    The Lord will buy them back from
      people stronger than they were.
¹²The people of Israel will come to the
  high points of Jerusalem.
    There they will shout for joy.
Their faces will shine with happiness
  about all the good things from
  the Lord:
    the grain, new wine, oil, young
      sheep and cows.
They will be like a garden that has
  plenty of water.
    And the people of Israel will not be
      troubled anymore.
¹³Then young women of Israel will be
  happy and dance.
    The young men and old men will
      also dance.
I will change their sadness into
  happiness.

I will give them comfort and joy
  instead of sadness.
¹⁴The priests will have more than
  enough sacrifices.
    And my people will be filled with
      the good things I give them!"
    says the Lord.

¹⁵This is what the Lord says:
"A sound was heard in Ramah.
    It was painful crying and much
      sadness.
Rachel cries for her children.
    And she cannot be comforted,
      because her children are dead!"

¹⁶But this is what the Lord says:
"Stop crying.
    Don't let your eyes fill with tears.
You will be rewarded for your work!"
    says the Lord.
    "The people will come back from
      their enemy's land.
¹⁷So there is hope for you!" says the
  Lord.
    "Your children will come back to
      their own land.

¹⁸"I have heard Israel moaning:
'Lord, you punished me, and I have
  learned my lesson.
    I was like a calf that had never been
      trained.
Take me back, and I will come back.
    You truly are the Lord my God.
¹⁹Lord, I wandered away from you.
    But I changed my heart and life.
Once I understood,
    I beat my breast with sorrow.
I am ashamed and disgraced
    because of the foolish things I did
      when I was young.'

²⁰"You know that Israel is my dear son.
    I love that child.
Yes, I often speak against Israel,
    but I still remember him.
I love him very much.
    And I want to comfort him," says
      the Lord.

21"People of Israel, fix the road signs.
    Put up the signs that show you the
        way home.
Watch the road.
    Pay attention to the road on which
        you travel.
People of Israel, come home.
    Come back to your towns.
22You are an unfaithful daughter.
    How long will you wander before
        you come home?
The Lord will make something new
    happen in the land:
A woman will go seeking a man."

23The Lord of heaven's armies, the
God of Israel, says: "I will again do good
things for the people of Judah. At that
time the people in the land of Judah and
its towns will again say: 'May the Lord
bless you. You are a righteous dwelling.
You are a holy mountain.' 24People in all
the towns of Judah will live together in
peace. Farmers and those who move
around with their flocks will live together
in peace. 25I will give rest and strength to
those who are weak and tired."

26After hearing that, I, Jeremiah, woke
up and looked around. My sleep had
been very pleasant.

27The Lord says, "The days are coming
when I will help the families of Israel and
Judah to grow. I will help their children
and animals to grow, too. It will be like
planting and caring for a plant. 28In the
past I watched over Israel and Judah, but
I watched for the time to pull them up. I
tore them down. I destroyed them. I
brought disaster to them. But now I will
watch over them to build them up and
make them strong," says the Lord.

29"At that time people will no longer
say:
'The fathers have eaten sour grapes.
    And that caused the children to
        grind their teeth from the sour
            taste.'

30But each person will die for his own
sin. The person who eats sour grapes
will grind his own teeth.

THE NEW AGREEMENT

31"Look, the time is coming," says the
    Lord,
    "when I will make a new agreement.
It will be with the people of Israel
    and the people of Judah.
32It will not be like the agreement
    I made with their ancestors.
That was when I took them by the
        hand
    to bring them out of Egypt.
I was a husband to them,
    but they broke that agreement,"
        says the Lord.
33"I will make this agreement
    with the people of Israel," says the
        Lord.
"I will put my teachings in their minds.
    And I will write them on their
        hearts.
I will be their God,
    and they will be my people.
34People will no longer have to teach
        their neighbors and relatives
    to know the Lord.
This is because all people will know me,
    from the least to the most
        important," says the Lord.
"I will forgive them for the wicked
        things they did.
    I will not remember their sins
        anymore."

THE LORD WILL NEVER LEAVE ISRAEL

35This is what the Lord says:
"The Lord makes the sun shine in the
        day.
    And he makes the moon and stars
        shine at night.
He stirs up the sea so that its waves
        crash on the shore.
    The Lord of heaven's armies is his
        name.
36"Only if these laws should ever fail,"
    says the Lord,

"will Israel's descendants[d] stop
being a nation before me."

[37]This is what the Lord says:

"There's only one way I will reject all
the descendants of Israel.

That is if people can measure the
sky above.

It is if they can learn the secrets of
the earth below.

Then I will reject them because of
what they have done," says the
Lord.

THE NEW JERUSALEM

[38]The Lord says, "The days are coming
when Jerusalem will be rebuilt for me.
Everything from the Tower of Hananel
to the Corner Gate will be rebuilt. [39]The
measuring line will stretch from the
Corner Gate straight to the hill of Gareb.
Then it will turn to the place named
Goah. [40]There is the whole valley where
dead bodies and ashes are thrown. It will
be holy to the Lord. And all the terraces
out to the Kidron Valley will be included.
They are on the east as far as the corner of
the Horse Gate. All that area will be holy
to the Lord. The city of Jerusalem will
never again be torn down or destroyed."

JEREMIAH BUYS A FIELD

32 This is the word the Lord spoke
to Jeremiah. It was in the tenth
year that Zedekiah was king of Judah.
The tenth year of Zedekiah was the eighteenth year of Nebuchadnezzar. [2]At that
time the army of Babylon was surrounding
Jerusalem. Jeremiah was under arrest in
the courtyard of the guard. This courtyard
was at the palace of the king of Judah.

[3]Zedekiah king of Judah had put Jeremiah in prison there. Zedekiah had asked,
"Why have you prophesied[d] the things
you have?" (Jeremiah had said, "This is
what the Lord says: 'I will soon give the
city of Jerusalem to the king of Babylon.
Nebuchadnezzar will capture this city.
[4]Zedekiah king of Judah will not escape
from the army of the Babylonians. But

he will surely be given to the king of
Babylon. And Zedekiah will speak to the
king of Babylon face to face. Zedekiah
will see him with his own eyes. [5]The king
of Babylon will take Zedekiah to Babylon.
Zedekiah will stay there until I have punished him,' says the Lord. 'If you fight
against the Babylonians, you will not
succeed.'")

[6]While Jeremiah was prisoner, he
said, "The Lord spoke his word to me. He
said: [7]Jeremiah, your cousin Hanamel
will come to you soon. He is the son of
your uncle Shallum. Hanamel will say to
you, 'Jeremiah, you are my nearest relative. So buy my field near the town of
Anathoth. It is your right and your
responsibility to buy that field.'

[8]"Then it happened just as the Lord
had said. My cousin Hanamel came to
me in the courtyard of the guard. He said
to me, 'Buy my field near Anathoth in
the land of Benjamin. Buy that land for
yourself. It is your right to buy it and
own it.' So I knew this was a message
from the Lord.

[9]"I bought the field at Anathoth from
my cousin Hanamel. I weighed out
seven ounces of silver for him. [10]I signed
the record that showed I now owned the
field. And I had a copy of the record sealed
up. Some men witnessed it and signed it
also. And I weighed out the silver on the
scales. [11]Then I took the sealed copy of the
record of ownership. And I took the copy
that was not sealed. [12]And I gave them to
Baruch son of Neriah. Neriah was the son
of Mahseiah. The sealed copy of the
record of ownership had all the demands
and limits of my purchase. I gave this
paper of ownership to Baruch. It was
while my cousin Hanamel and the other
witnesses were there. Those witnesses
also signed the record of ownership.
There were also many Jews sitting in the
courtyard. And they saw me give the
record of ownership to Baruch.

[13]"With all the people watching, I said to Baruch, [14]'This is what the Lord of heaven's armies, the God of Israel, says: Take both copies of the record of ownership. Take both the sealed copy and the copy that was not sealed. And put them in a clay jar. Do this so that they will last a long time. [15]This is what the Lord of heaven's armies, the God of Israel, says: In the future my people will once again buy houses. They will also buy fields for grain and vineyards in the land of Israel.'

[16]"I gave the record of ownership to Baruch son of Neriah. Then I prayed to the Lord. I said: [17]Oh, Lord God, you made the skies and the earth. You made them with your very great power. There is nothing too wonderful for you to do. [18]Lord, you show love and kindness to thousands of people. But you also bring punishment to children for their fathers' sins. Great and powerful God, your name is the Lord of heaven's armies. [19]You plan and do great things, Lord. You see everything that people do. You reward people for the way they live and for what they do. [20]Lord, you did miracles[d] and wonderful things in the land of Egypt. You have kept on doing them even until today. You did miracles in Israel and among the other nations. You have become well known. [21]Lord, you used signs and miracles and brought your people, the Israelites, out of Egypt. You used your great power and strength to do those things. You brought great terror on everyone. [22]Lord, you gave this land to the people of Israel. This is the land you promised to their ancestors long ago. It's a land where much food grows. [23]The people of Israel came into this land and took it for their own. But those people did not obey you. They did not follow your teachings. They did not do the things you commanded. So you made all these terrible things happen to them.

[24]"And now, the enemy has surrounded the city. They are building roads to the top of the walls. There will be war, hunger and terrible diseases. These will cause the city to be handed over to the Babylonians. They are attacking the city now. Lord, you said this would happen. And now you see it is happening. [25]But now, Lord God, you are telling me, 'Buy the field with silver. Choose some men to watch while I purchase it.' You are telling me this while the Babylonian army is ready to capture the city."

[26]Then the Lord spoke his word to Jeremiah: [27]"I am the Lord. I am the God of every person on the earth. You know that nothing is impossible for me. [28]So this is what I say: I will soon give the city of Jerusalem to the Babylonian army. And I will give it to Nebuchadnezzar king of Babylon. That army will capture the city. [29]The Babylonian army is already attacking the city of Jerusalem. They will soon enter the city and start a fire to burn down the city. They will also burn down the houses. The people of Jerusalem made me angry. They offered sacrifices to Baal[d] on the roofs[n] of their houses. And the people poured out drink offerings to other idols. [30]The people of Israel and Judah have done only the things I said were wrong. They have done this since they were young. They have made me angry by worshiping idols made with their own hands," says the Lord. [31]"From the day Jerusalem was built until now, they have made me very angry. Jerusalem has made me so angry I must remove it from my sight. [32]I will destroy it. This is because of the evil the people of Israel and Judah have done. The people, their kings and officers have made me angry. Their priests and prophets have

---

32:29 roofs In Bible times houses were built with flat roofs. The roof was used for drying things such as flax and fruit. And it was used as an extra room, as a place for worship and as a place to sleep in the summer.

made me angry. All the men of Judah and the people of Jerusalem have made me angry. ³³They turned their backs to me. I tried to teach them again and again. But they wouldn't listen to me. I tried to correct them, but they wouldn't listen. ³⁴They put their hated idols in the place where I have chosen to be worshiped. In this way they made it unclean.ᵈ ³⁵In the Valley of Ben Hinnom those people built places to worship Baal. They built them so they could burn their sons and daughters as sacrifices to Molech.ᵈ But I never commanded them to do such a hated thing. I never even thought of it! This would make Judah sin.

³⁶"You are saying, 'There will be war, hunger and terrible diseases. So the city will be handed over to the king of Babylon.' But the Lord, the God of Israel, says: ³⁷I have forced the people of Israel and Judah to leave their land. I was very furious and angry with them. But I will gather them from the land where I forced them to go. I will bring them back to this place. I will let them live in peace and safety. ³⁸The people of Israel and Judah will be my people. And I will be their God. ³⁹I will make them want to be truly one people. They will have one goal. They will truly want to worship me all their lives. They will do this for their own good and for their children after them.

⁴⁰"I will make an agreement with them. This agreement will last forever. And I will never turn away from them. I will always be good to them. I will make them want to respect me. Then they will never turn away from me. ⁴¹I will enjoy doing good to them. And I will surely plant them in this land and make them grow. I will do this with my whole being."

⁴²This is what the Lord says: "I have brought this great disaster to the people of Israel and Judah. In the same way I will bring good things to them. I promise to do good things for them. ⁴³You are

saying, 'This land is an empty desert. There are no people or animals here. The Babylonian army defeated this country.' But in the future, people will once again buy fields in this land. ⁴⁴They will use their money and buy fields. They will sign and seal their agreements. People will witness their signing records of ownership. They will again buy fields in the land of Benjamin and in the area around Jerusalem. They will buy fields in the towns of Judah and in the mountains. They will buy them in the western mountain slopes and in southern Judah. This is because I will make everything as good as it once was," says the Lord.

THE PROMISE OF GOD

33 Now Jeremiah was still locked up in the courtyard of the guards. And the Lord spoke his word to him a second time: ²"The Lord made the earth. He made it, and he keeps it safe. The Lord is his name. This is what the Lord says: ³'Judah, pray to me, and I will answer you. I will tell you important secrets. You have never heard these things before.' ⁴The Lord is the God of Israel. He says these things about the houses in Jerusalem and the royal palaces of Judah. They have been torn down to be used against the attack by the Babylonian army. ⁵The Lord says, 'Some people will come to fight against the Babylonians. They will fill these houses with dead bodies. I killed those people in my hot anger. I have turned away from this city because of all the evil its people have done.

⁶"'But then I will bring health and heal the people there. I will let them enjoy peace and safety. ⁷I will make good things happen to Judah and Israel again. I will make them strong as in the past. ⁸They sinned against me. But I will wash away that sin. They did evil and turned away from me, but I will forgive them. ⁹Then Jerusalem will be a wonderful place! People who live there will be

happy. And people from all nations will praise it. This will happen because they will hear about the good things I am doing there. They will be surprised and shocked at the good things and peace I will bring to Jerusalem.'

¹⁰"You are saying, 'Our country is an empty desert. There are no people or animals living there.' It is now quiet in the streets of Jerusalem and in the towns of Judah. There are no people or animals there either. But it will be noisy there soon! ¹¹There will be sounds of joy and gladness. There will be the happy sounds of brides and bridegrooms. There will be the sounds of people bringing their offerings to the Temple*d* of the Lord. Their offerings will be to show thanks to the Lord. They will say,

'Praise the Lord of heaven's armies!
    The Lord is good!
    His love continues forever!'

They will say this because I will again do good things for Judah. It will be as in the beginning," says the Lord.

¹²This is what the Lord of heaven's armies says: "This place is empty now. There are no people or animals living here. But there will be shepherds in all the towns of Judah. And there will be pastures where they let their flocks of sheep rest. ¹³Shepherds will again count their sheep as the sheep walk in front of them. People will be counting their sheep all around the country. They will count them in the mountains and in the western mountain slopes. They will count them in southern Judah and the land of Benjamin. They will count them around Jerusalem and the other towns of Judah!"

THE GOOD BRANCH

¹⁴The Lord says, "The time is coming when I will do the things I promised. I made a special promise to the people of Israel and Judah.
¹⁵In those days and at that time,
    I will make a righteous branch
        sprout from David's family.

He will do what is fair and right in
    the land.
¹⁶At this time Judah will be saved.
    The people of Jerusalem will live in
        safety.
    The branch will be named:
        The Lord Does What Is Right."

¹⁷This is what the Lord says: "Someone from David's family will always sit on the throne. And he will rule the family of Israel. ¹⁸And there will always be priests from the family of Levi. Those priests will always stand before me. And they will offer burnt offerings and grain offerings. And they will offer sacrifices to me."

¹⁹The Lord spoke his word to Jeremiah. ²⁰"This is what the Lord says: I have an agreement with day and night. I agreed that they will continue forever. Day and night will always come at the right times. If you could change that agreement, ²¹you could also change my agreement with David and Levi. Only then would descendants*d* from my servant David not be the kings on their thrones. And only then would the family of Levi not be priests serving me in the Temple.*d* ²²But I will give many descendants to my servant David. And I will give them to the family group of Levi who serve me in the Temple. They will be as many as the stars in the sky that no one can count. And they will be as many as the grains of sand on the seashore that no one can count."

²³The Lord spoke his word to Jeremiah: ²⁴"Jeremiah, have you heard what the people are saying? They are saying: 'The Lord turned away from the two families of Israel and Judah. He chose those people. But now he doesn't think of them as a nation anymore!'"

²⁵This is what the Lord says: "If I had not made my agreement with day and night, and if I had not made the laws for the sky and earth, ²⁶only then might I turn away from Jacob's descendants.

And only then I might not let the descendants of David my servant rule over the descendants of Abraham, Isaac and Jacob. And I will be kind to those people. I will cause good things to happen to them again."

A WARNING TO ZEDEKIAH

34 The Lord spoke his word to Jeremiah. It came when Nebuchadnezzar king of Babylon was fighting against Jerusalem and all the towns around it. Nebuchadnezzar had with him all his army. And he had the armies of all the kingdoms and peoples he ruled. [2]This is what the Lord, the God of Israel, said: "Jeremiah, go to Zedekiah king of Judah and tell him: 'This is what the Lord says: I will hand the city of Jerusalem over to the king of Babylon very soon. And he will burn it down! [3]You will not escape from the king of Babylon. You will surely be caught and given to him. You will see the king of Babylon with your own eyes. He will talk to you face to face. And you will go to Babylon. [4]But, Zedekiah king of Judah, listen to the promise of the Lord. This is what the Lord says about you: You will not be killed with a sword. [5]You will die in a peaceful way. People made funeral fires to honor your ancestors, who ruled before you. In the same way, people will make a funeral fire to honor you. They will cry for you. They will sadly say, "Ah, master!" I myself make this promise to you, says the Lord.'"

[6]So Jeremiah the prophet[d] gave the message from the Lord to Zedekiah in Jerusalem. [7]This was while the army of the king of Babylon was fighting against Jerusalem. It was also fighting against the cities of Judah that had not been taken prisoners—Lachish and Azekah. These were the only strong, walled cities left in the land of Judah.

SLAVES ARE FREE

[8]King Zedekiah had made an agreement with all the people in Jerusalem. He agreed to give freedom to all the Hebrew slaves. After Zedekiah made that agreement, the Lord spoke his word to Jeremiah. [9]Everyone was supposed to free his Hebrew slaves. This included all male and female Hebrew slaves. No one was to keep a fellow Jew as a slave. [10]So the officers and all the people accepted this agreement. Everyone would free their male and female slaves. They would no longer keep them as slaves. So all the slaves were set free. [11]But after that, the people who had slaves changed their minds. So they took back the people they had set free. And they made them slaves again.

[12]Then the Lord spoke his word to Jeremiah: [13]"This is what the Lord, the God of Israel, says: I brought your ancestors out of Egypt where they were slaves. When I did that, I made an agreement with them. [14]I said to your ancestors: 'At the end of every seven years, each one of you must set his Hebrew slaves free. You might have a fellow Hebrew who has sold himself to you. You must let him go free after he has served you for six years.' But your ancestors did not listen or pay attention to me. [15]A short time ago you changed your hearts and did what is right. Each of you gave freedom to his fellow Hebrews who were slaves. And you even made an agreement before me. You made it in the place where I have chosen to be worshiped. [16]But now you have changed your minds. You have shown you do not honor me. Each of you has taken back the male and female slaves you had set free. You have forced them to become slaves again.

[17]"So this is what the Lord says: You have not obeyed me. You have not given freedom to your fellow Hebrews. Because you have not kept the agreement, I will give freedom, says the Lord. I will give freedom to war. And I will give freedom to terrible diseases and to hunger to kill you. I will make you hated

by all the kingdoms of the earth. [18]I will hand over the men who broke my agreement. They have not kept the promises they made before me. These men cut a calf into two pieces before me. And they walked between the two pieces.[n] [19]These people made the agreement before me: the leaders of Judah and Jerusalem; the officers of the court; the priests and all the people of the land. [20]So I will hand those people over to their enemies. I will hand them over to everyone who wants to kill them. Their bodies will become food for the birds of the air. And they will become food for the wild animals of the earth. [21]I will hand Zedekiah king of Judah and his officers over to their enemies. I will hand them over to everyone who wants to kill them. I will hand Zedekiah and his people over to the army of the king of Babylon. I will do this even though that army has left Jerusalem. [22]I will give the order, says the Lord, to bring the Babylonian army back to Jerusalem. That army will fight against Jerusalem. They will capture it, set it on fire and burn it down. I will destroy the towns in the land of Judah. And they will become empty ruins. No one will live there!"

THE RECABITE FAMILY

35 When Jehoiakim son of Josiah was king of Judah, the Lord spoke his word to Jeremiah. This was his message: [2]"Jeremiah, go to the family of Recab. Invite them to come to one of the side rooms of the Temple[d] of the Lord. Offer them wine to drink."

[3]So I went to get Jaazaniah son of Jeremiah.[n] Jeremiah was the son of Habazziniah. And I gathered all of Jaazaniah's brothers and sons. I gathered the whole family of the Recabites together. [4]Then I brought them into the Temple of the Lord. We went into the room of the sons

of Hanan son of Igdaliah. Hanan was a man of God. The room was next to the one where the officers stay. It was over the room of Maaseiah son of Shallum. Maaseiah was the doorkeeper in the Temple. [5]Then I put some bowls full of wine and some cups before the Recabite family. And I said to them, "Drink some wine."

[6]But the Recabite people answered, "We never drink wine. It is because of our ancestor Jonadab son of Recab. He gave us this command: 'You and your descendants[d] must never drink wine. [7]Also you must never build houses, plant seeds or plant vineyards. You must never do any of those things. You must live only in tents. Then you will live a long time in the land where you are a wanderer.' [8]So we Recabites have obeyed everything Jonadab our ancestor commanded us. We never drink wine. And our wives, sons and daughters never drink wine. [9]We never build houses in which to live. And we never own fields or vineyards. And we never plant crops. [10]We have lived in tents. And we have obeyed everything our ancestor Jonadab commanded us. [11]But Nebuchadnezzar king of Babylon attacked the country of Judah. We said to each other, 'Come, we must enter Jerusalem. This is so we can escape the Babylonian army and the Aramean army.' So we have stayed in Jerusalem."

[12]Then the Lord spoke his word to Jeremiah: [13]"This is what the Lord of heaven's armies, the God of Israel, says: Jeremiah, go and tell the men of Judah and the people of Jerusalem: 'You should learn a lesson and obey my message,' says the Lord. [14]'Jonadab son of Recab ordered his sons not to drink wine. And that command has

---

34:18 **they walked ... pieces** This showed that the men were willing to be killed, like this animal, if they did not keep their agreement.
35:3 **Jeremiah** Not the prophet Jeremiah, but a different man with the same name.

been obeyed. Until today the descendants of Jonadab obeyed their ancestor's command. They do not drink wine. But I am the Lord. I have given you messages again and again. But you did not obey me. ¹⁵I sent my servants the prophets to you again and again. They said to you, "Each of you must stop doing evil. You must change and be good. Do not follow other gods to serve them. If you obey me, you will live in the land I have given to you and your ancestors." But you have not listened or paid attention to my message. ¹⁶The descendants of Jonadab obeyed the commands that their ancestor gave them. But the people of Judah have not obeyed me.'

¹⁷"So the Lord God of heaven's armies, the God of Israel, says: 'I said many disasters would come to Judah and on everyone living in Jerusalem. I will soon bring every one of those disasters on them. I spoke to those people, but they refused to listen. I called out to them, but they did not answer me.'"

¹⁸Then Jeremiah said to the Recabites, "This is what the Lord of heaven's armies, the God of Israel, says: 'You have obeyed the commands of your ancestor Jonadab. You have followed all of Jonadab's teachings. You have done everything he commanded.' ¹⁹So this is what the Lord of heaven's armies, the God of Israel, says: 'There will always be a descendant of Jonadab son of Recab to serve me.'"

JEHOIAKIM BURNS JEREMIAH'S SCROLL

36 The Lord spoke his word to Jeremiah. This was during the fourth year that Jehoiakim son of Josiah was king of Judah. This was his message: ²"Jeremiah, get a scroll. Write on it all the words I have spoken to you about Israel and Judah and all the nations. Write everything I have spoken to you since Josiah was king until now. ³Maybe the family of Judah will hear what disasters I

am planning to bring on them. And maybe they will stop doing wicked things. Then I would forgive them for the sins and the evil things they have done."

⁴So Jeremiah called for Baruch son of Neriah. Jeremiah spoke the messages the Lord had given him. And Baruch wrote those messages on the scroll. ⁵Then Jeremiah said to Baruch, "I cannot go to the Temple^d of the Lord. I must stay here. ⁶So I want you to go to the Temple of the Lord. Go there on a day when the people are giving up eating. Read to all the people of Judah from the scroll. These people come into Jerusalem from the towns where they live. Read the messages from the Lord. Read the words that you wrote on the scroll as I spoke them to you. ⁷Perhaps they will ask the Lord to help them. Perhaps each one will stop doing wicked things. The Lord has announced that he is very angry with them." ⁸So Baruch son of Neriah did everything Jeremiah the prophet^d told him to do. He read aloud the scroll that had the Lord's messages written on it. He read it in the Lord's Temple.

⁹It was the ninth month of the fifth year that Jehoiakim son of Josiah was king. A special time to give up eating was announced. All the people of Jerusalem were supposed to give up eating to honor the Lord. And everyone who had come into Jerusalem from the towns of Judah was supposed to give up eating. ¹⁰At that time Baruch read the scroll that contained Jeremiah's words. Baruch read the scroll in the Temple of the Lord to all the people there. He was in the room of Gemariah son of Shaphan. Gemariah was a royal assistant. That room was in the upper courtyard at the entrance of the New Gate of the Temple.

¹¹A man named Micaiah son of Gemariah, the son of Shaphan, heard all the messages from the Lord. Baruch read them from the scroll. ¹²Micaiah went down to the royal assistant's room in the

king's palace. All of the officers were sitting there: Elishama the royal assistant; Delaiah son of Shemaiah; Elnathan son of Acbor; Gemariah son of Shaphan; Zedekiah son of Hananiah; and all the other officers. ¹³Micaiah told those officers everything he had heard Baruch read from the scroll.

¹⁴Then the officers sent a man named Jehudi son of Nethaniah to Baruch. (Nethaniah was the son of Shelemiah, who was the son of Cushi.) Jehudi said to Baruch, "Bring the scroll that you read to the people and come with me."

So Baruch son of Neriah took the scroll and went with Jehudi to the officers. ¹⁵Then the officers said to Baruch, "Sit down and read the scroll to us."

So Baruch read the scroll to them. ¹⁶When the officers heard all the words, they became afraid. And they looked at one another. They said to Baruch, "We must certainly tell the king about these words." ¹⁷Then the officers asked Baruch, "Tell us, Baruch, where did you get these words you wrote on the scroll? Did you write down what Jeremiah said to you?"

¹⁸"Yes," Baruch answered. "Jeremiah spoke, and I wrote down all the words with ink on this scroll."

¹⁹Then the officers said to Baruch, "You and Jeremiah must go and hide. Don't tell anyone where you are hiding."

²⁰Then the officers put the scroll in the room of Elishama the royal assistant. Then they went to the king in the courtyard and told him all about the scroll. ²¹So King Jehoiakim sent Jehudi to get the scroll. Jehudi brought the scroll from the room of Elishama the royal assistant. Then Jehudi read the scroll to the king. And he read it to all the officers who stood around the king. ²²This happened in the ninth month of the year. So King Jehoiakim was sitting in the winter apartment. There was a fire burning in a small firepot in front of him. ²³Jehudi began to read from the scroll. But after

he had read three or four columns, the king cut those columns off of the scroll with a pen knife. And he threw them into the firepot. Finally, the whole scroll was burned in the fire. ²⁴King Jehoiakim and his servants heard the message from the scroll. But they were not frightened! They did not tear their clothes to show their sorrow. ²⁵Elnathan, Delaiah and Gemariah tried to talk King Jehoiakim into not burning the scroll. But the king would not listen to them. ²⁶Instead, the king ordered some men to arrest Baruch the secretary and Jeremiah the prophet. Those men were Jerahmeel son of the king, Seraiah son of Azriel and Shelemiah son of Abdeel. But the Lord had hidden Baruch and Jeremiah.

²⁷The Lord spoke his word to Jeremiah. This happened after King Jehoiakim had burned the scroll. This was the scroll where Baruch had written all the words Jeremiah had spoken to him. The Lord said: ²⁸"Jeremiah, get another scroll. Write all the words on it that were on the first scroll. That was the scroll that Jehoiakim king of Judah burned up. ²⁹Also say this to Jehoiakim king of Judah: 'This is what the Lord says: You burned up that scroll. You said, "Why did Jeremiah write that the king of Babylon will come and destroy this land? Why did he say the king of Babylon will destroy both men and animals in it?" ³⁰So the Lord says this about Jehoiakim king of Judah: Jehoiakim's descendants*d* will not sit on David's throne. When Jehoiakim dies, his body will be thrown out on the ground. It will be left out in the heat of the day. And it will also be left in the cold frost of the night. ³¹I, the Lord, will punish Jehoiakim and his children. And I will punish his servants. I will do this because they have done evil things. I have promised to bring disasters upon them. And I will bring them upon all the people in Jerusalem and Judah, just as I promised. This is because they have not listened to me.'"

³²So Jeremiah took another scroll and gave it to Baruch. Baruch son of Neriah was his secretary. As Jeremiah spoke, Baruch wrote on the scroll. He wrote the same words that were on the scroll Jehoiakim king of Judah had burned in the fire. And many other words like those words were added to the second scroll.

JEREMIAH IN PRISON

37 Nebuchadnezzar was king of Babylon. He appointed Zedekiah son of Josiah as king of Judah. Zedekiah took the place of Jehoiachin son of Jehoiakim. ²But Zedekiah, his servants and the people of Judah did not listen to the words of the Lord. The Lord had spoken his words through Jeremiah the prophet.^d

³Now King Zedekiah sent Jehucal and Zephaniah with a message to Jeremiah the prophet. Jehucal was the son of Shelemiah. And Zephaniah the priest was the son of Maaseiah. This was the message: "Jeremiah, pray to the Lord our God for us."

⁴At that time Jeremiah had not yet been put into prison. So he was free to go anywhere he wanted. ⁵The army of the king of Egypt had marched from Egypt toward Judah. Now the Babylonian army had surrounded the city of Jerusalem so they could attack it. Then they had heard about the Egyptian army marching toward them. So the Babylonian army left Jerusalem to fight the Egyptian army.

⁶The Lord spoke his word to Jeremiah the prophet: ⁷"This is what the Lord, the God of Israel, says: Jehucal and Zephaniah, I know Zedekiah king of Judah sent you to ask me questions. Tell this to King Zedekiah: 'The army of the king of Egypt marched out of Egypt. They came here to help you against the Babylonian army. But that army will go back to Egypt. ⁸After that, the Babylonian army will come back here. And they will attack Jerusalem. Then the Babylonian army will take and burn Jerusalem.'

⁹"This is what the Lord says: People of Jerusalem, do not fool yourselves. Do not say to yourselves: 'The Babylonian army will surely leave us alone.' They will not! ¹⁰You might defeat all of the Babylonian army that is attacking you. But there would still be a few injured men left in their tents. Even those injured men would come from their tents and burn down Jerusalem!"

¹¹So the Babylonian army left Jerusalem. They left to fight the army of the king of Egypt. ¹²Now Jeremiah wanted to travel from Jerusalem to his home in the land of Benjamin. He was going there to get his share of the property that belonged to his family. ¹³Jeremiah got to the Benjamin Gate of Jerusalem. But then the captain in charge of the guards arrested him. The captain's name was Irijah son of Shelemiah son of Hananiah. So Irijah the captain arrested Jeremiah. Irijah said, "You are leaving us to join the Babylonian side!"

¹⁴Jeremiah said to Irijah, "That's not true! I am not leaving to join the Babylonians." But Irijah refused to listen to Jeremiah. So he arrested Jeremiah and took him to the officers of Jerusalem. ¹⁵Those rulers were very angry with Jeremiah. They gave an order for him to be beaten. Then they put him in prison in the house of Jonathan the royal assistant. Jonathan's house had been made into a prison. ¹⁶So those people put Jeremiah into a cell in a dungeon. And Jeremiah was there for a long time.

¹⁷Then King Zedekiah sent for Jeremiah and had him brought to the palace. Zedekiah talked to Jeremiah in private. He asked Jeremiah, "Is there any message from the Lord?"

Jeremiah answered, "Yes, there is a message from the Lord. Zedekiah, you will be handed over to the king of Babylon." ¹⁸Then Jeremiah said to King Zedekiah, "What crime have I done against you? What crime have I done to your officers or the people of Jerusalem? Why have you thrown me into prison? [19]Where are your prophets now? Those prophets prophesied this message to you: 'The king of Babylon will not attack you or this land of Judah.' [20]But now, my master, king of Judah, please listen to me. And please do what I ask of you. Do not send me back to the house of Jonathan the royal assistant. If you do, I will die there!"

[21]So King Zedekiah gave orders for Jeremiah to be put under guard in the courtyard. And he ordered that Jeremiah be given bread from the street of the bakers. Jeremiah was to be given bread until there was no more bread in the city. So he stayed under guard in the courtyard.

JEREMIAH IS THROWN INTO A WELL

38 Some of the officers heard what Jeremiah was prophesying.[d] They were Shephatiah son of Mattan, Gedaliah son of Pashhur, Jehucal son of Shelemiah and Pashhur son of Malkijah. Jeremiah was telling all the people this message: [2]"This is what the Lord says: 'Everyone who stays in Jerusalem will die in war. Or he will die of hunger or terrible diseases. But everyone who surrenders to the Babylonian army will live. They will escape with their lives and live.' [3]And this is what the Lord says: 'This city of Jerusalem will surely be handed over to the army of the king of Babylon. He will capture this city!'"

[4]Then the officers said to the king, "Jeremiah must be put to death! He is making the soldiers who are still in the city become discouraged. He is discouraging everyone by the things he is saying. He does not want good to happen to us. He wants to ruin the people of Jerusalem."

[5]King Zedekiah said to them, "Jeremiah is in your control. I cannot do anything to stop you!"

[6]So the officers took Jeremiah and put him into the well of Malkijah, the king's son. That well was in the courtyard of the guards. The officers used ropes to lower Jeremiah into the well. It did not have any water in it, only mud. And Jeremiah sank down into the mud.

[7]But Ebed-Melech heard that the officers had put Jeremiah into the well. Ebed-Melech was a Cushite, and he was a eunuch[d] in the palace. King Zedekiah was sitting at the Benjamin Gate. [8]So Ebed-Melech left the palace and went to the king. Ebed-Melech said, [9]"My master and king, the rulers have acted in an evil way. They have treated Jeremiah the prophet badly! They have thrown him into a well! They have left him there to die! When there is no more bread in the city, he will starve."

[10]Then King Zedekiah commanded Ebed-Melech the Cushite: "Ebed-Melech, take 30 men from the palace with you. Go and lift Jeremiah the prophet out of the well before he dies."

[11]So Ebed-Melech took the men with him. And he went to a room under the storeroom in the palace. He took some old rags and worn-out clothes from that room. Then he let those rags down with some ropes to Jeremiah in the well. [12]Ebed-Melech the Cushite said to Jeremiah, "Put these old rags and worn-out clothes under your arms. They will be pads for the ropes." So Jeremiah did as Ebed-Melech said. [13]The men pulled Jeremiah up with the ropes and lifted him out of the well. And Jeremiah stayed under guard in the courtyard.

ZEDEKIAH QUESTIONS JEREMIAH

[14]Then King Zedekiah sent someone to get Jeremiah the prophet.[d] He had Jeremiah brought to the third entrance to the Temple[d] of the Lord. Then the king said to Jeremiah, "I am going to ask you something. Do not hide anything from me. But tell me everything honestly."

[15]Jeremiah said to Zedekiah, "If I give you an answer, you will probably kill me.

And even if I give you advice, you will not listen to me."

¹⁶But King Zedekiah made a secret promise to Jeremiah. He said, "As surely as the Lord lives who has given us breath and life, I will not kill you. And I promise not to give you to the officers who want to kill you."

¹⁷Then Jeremiah said to Zedekiah, "This is what the Lord God of heaven's armies, the God of Israel, says: 'You must surrender to the officers of the king of Babylon. Then your life will be saved. And Jerusalem will not be burned down. And you and your family will live. ¹⁸You must not refuse to surrender to the officers of the king of Babylon. If you do, Jerusalem will be given to the Babylonian army. They will burn Jerusalem down. And you will not escape from them.'"

¹⁹Then King Zedekiah said to Jeremiah, "I'm afraid of some of the Jews. They have already gone over to the side of the Babylonian army. I'm afraid the Babylonians may hand me over to them. And they will treat me badly."

²⁰But Jeremiah answered, "The Babylonians will not hand you over to the Jews. Obey the Lord by doing what I tell you. Then things will go well for you. And your life will be saved. ²¹But if you refuse to surrender to the Babylonians, the Lord has shown me what will happen. ²²All the women left in the palace of the king of Judah will be brought out. They will be taken to the important officers of the king of Babylon. Your women will make fun of you with this song:

'Your good friends led you the wrong
	way and were stronger than you.
Those were friends that you trusted.
Your feet are stuck in the mud.
Your friends have left you.'

²³"All your wives and children will be brought out. They will be given to the Babylonian army. You yourself will not even escape from them. You will be taken prisoner by the king of Babylon. And Jerusalem will be burned down."

²⁴Then Zedekiah said to Jeremiah, "Do not tell anyone that I have been talking to you. If you do, you will die. ²⁵Those officers might find out that I talked to you. Then they will come to you and say, 'Tell us what you said to King Zedekiah. And tell us what King Zedekiah said to you. Don't keep any secrets from us. If you don't tell us everything, we will kill you.' ²⁶If they ask you, tell them this: 'I was begging the king not to send me back to Jonathan's house to die.'"

²⁷The officers did come to question Jeremiah. So he told them everything the king had ordered him to say. Then the officers said no more to Jeremiah. This was because no one had heard what Jeremiah and the king had discussed. ²⁸So Jeremiah stayed under guard in the courtyard until the day Jerusalem was captured.

THE FALL OF JERUSALEM

39 This is how Jerusalem was captured: Nebuchadnezzar king of Babylon marched against Jerusalem with his whole army. He surrounded the city to attack it. This was during the tenth month of the ninth year Zedekiah was king of Judah. ²This lasted until the ninth day of the fourth month in Zedekiah's eleventh year. Then the city wall was broken through. ³And all the officers of the king of Babylon came into Jerusalem. They sat down at the Middle Gate. They were Nergal-Sharezer of the district of Samgar; Nebo-Sarsekim, a chief officer; Nergal-Sharezer, an important leader; and all the other important officers.

⁴When Zedekiah king of Judah and all his soldiers saw them, they ran away. They left Jerusalem at night and went out from the king's garden. They went through the gate that was between the two walls. Then they headed toward the Jordan Valley. ⁵But the Babylonian army

chased them. They caught up with Zedekiah in the plains of Jericho. They captured him and took him to Nebuchadnezzar king of Babylon. Nebuchadnezzar was at Riblah in the land of Hamath. There Nebuchadnezzar passed his sentence on Zedekiah. 6There at Riblah the king of Babylon killed Zedekiah's sons as he watched. And Nebuchadnezzar killed all the important officers of Judah as Zedekiah watched. 7Then he put out Zedekiah's eyes. He put bronze chains on Zedekiah and took him to Babylon.

8The Babylonians set fire to the palace. And they set fire to the houses of the people of Jerusalem. And they broke down the walls around Jerusalem. 9Nebuzaradan was commander of the king's special guards. He took the people left in Jerusalem as captives. He also took those captives who had surrendered to him earlier. And he took the rest of the people of Jerusalem. He carried them all away to Babylon. 10But Nebuzaradan, commander of the guard, left some of the poor people of Judah behind. They were the people who owned nothing. So on that day he gave them vineyards and fields.

11Nebuchadnezzar had given these orders about Jeremiah through Nebuzaradan, commander of the guard: 12"Find Jeremiah and take care of him. Do not hurt him. Give him whatever he asks for." 13So these men sent for Jeremiah: Nebuzaradan, commander of the guards; Nebushazban, a chief officer; Nergal-Sharezer, an important leader; and all the other officers of the king of Babylon. 14They had Jeremiah taken out of the courtyard of the guard. They turned him over to Gedaliah son of Ahikam son of Shaphan. Gedaliah had orders to take Jeremiah back home. So they took him home, and he stayed among his own people.

15While Jeremiah was guarded in the courtyard, the Lord spoke his word to him: 16"Jeremiah, go and tell Ebed-Melech the Cushite this message: 'This is what the Lord of heaven's armies, the God of Israel, says: Very soon I will make my words about Jerusalem come true. They will come true through disaster, not through good times. You will see everything come true with your own eyes. 17But I will save you on that day, Ebed-Melech, says the Lord. You will not be handed over to the people you fear. 18I will surely save you, Ebed-Melech. You will not die from a sword. But you will escape and live. This will happen because you have trusted in me, says the Lord.'"

JEREMIAH IS SET FREE

40 The Lord spoke his word to Jeremiah. This was after Nebuzaradan, commander of the guards, had set Jeremiah free at the city of Ramah. He had found Jeremiah in Ramah bound in chains. He was with all the captives from Jerusalem and Judah. They were being taken away to Babylon. 2When commander Nebuzaradan found Jeremiah, Nebuzaradan said to him, "The Lord your God announced this disaster would come to this place. 3And now the Lord has done everything he said he would do. This disaster happened because the people of Judah sinned against the Lord. You people did not obey the Lord. 4But now I will set you free. I am taking the chains off your wrists. If you want to, come with me to Babylon. And I will take good care of you. But if you don't want to come, then don't. Look, the whole country is open to you." 5Before Jeremiah turned to leave, Nebuzaradan said, "Or go back to Gedaliah son of Ahikam, the son of Shaphan. The king of Babylon has chosen Gedaliah to be governor over the towns of Judah. Go and live with Gedaliah among the people. Or go anywhere you want."

Then Nebuzaradan gave Jeremiah some food and a present and let him go.

[6]So Jeremiah went to Gedaliah son of Ahikam at Mizpah. And Jeremiah stayed with him there. He lived among the people who were left behind in Judah.

THE SHORT RULE OF GEDALIAH

[7]There were some officers and their men from the army of Judah. These men were still out in the open country. They heard that the king of Babylon had put Gedaliah son of Ahikam in charge. He was put in charge of the people who were left in the land: the men, women and children who were very poor. They were the ones who were not carried off to Babylon as captives. [8]So these soldiers came to Gedaliah at Mizpah. They were Ishmael son of Nethaniah, and Johanan and Jonathan sons of Kareah. Also Seraiah son of Tanhumeth and the sons of Ephai the Netophathite came. And Jaazaniah son of the Maacathite and their men came.

[9]Gedaliah son of Ahikam, the son of Shaphan, made a promise to them. Gedaliah said, "Do not be afraid to serve the Babylonians. Live in the land and serve the king of Babylon. Then everything will go well for you. [10]I myself will live in Mizpah. I will speak for you before the Babylonians who come here. You harvest the wine, the summer fruit and the oil. Put what you harvest in your storage jars. Live in the towns you control."

[11]Some Jews were in Moab, Ammon, Edom and other countries. They heard that the king of Babylon had left a few Jews alive in the land. And they heard the king of Babylon had chosen Gedaliah as governor over them. (Gedaliah was the son of Ahikam, the son of Shaphan.) [12]When the people of Judah heard this news, they came back to Judah. They came back to Gedaliah at Mizpah. They came from all the countries where they had been scattered. They gathered a large harvest of wine and summer fruit.

[13]Johanan son of Kareah came to Gedaliah at Mizpah. All the army officers of Judah still in the open country also came. [14]Johanan and the officers with him said to Gedaliah, "Don't you know that Baalis king of the Ammonite people wants you dead? He has sent Ishmael son of Nethaniah to kill you." But Gedaliah son of Ahikam did not believe them.

[15]Then Johanan son of Kareah spoke to Gedaliah in private at Mizpah. He said to Gedaliah, "Let me go and kill Ishmael son of Nethaniah. No one will know anything about it. We should not let Ishmael kill you. All the Jews gathered around you would be scattered to different countries again. Then the few people of Judah who are left alive would be lost."

[16]But Gedaliah son of Ahikam said to Johanan son of Kareah, "Do not kill Ishmael! The things you are saying about Ishmael are not true!"

41 In the seventh month Ishmael son of Nethaniah came to Gedaliah son of Ahikam. (Nethaniah was the son of Elishama.) Ishmael came with ten of his men to Mizpah. Now Ishmael was a member of the king's family. He had been one of the officers of the king of Judah. Ishmael and his men ate a meal with Gedaliah at Mizpah. [2]While they were eating together, Ishmael and his ten men got up. They killed Gedaliah son of Ahikam with a sword. Gedaliah was the man the king of Babylon had chosen as governor over Judah. [3]Ishmael killed all the Jews with Gedaliah at Mizpah, too. He also killed the Babylonian soldiers who were there with Gedaliah.

[4-5]The day after Gedaliah was murdered, 80 men came to Mizpah. They were bringing grain offerings and incense[d] to the Temple[d] of the Lord. Those 80 men had shaved off their beards, torn their clothes and cut themselves.[n] They came

---

41:4-5 **shaved ... themselves** The men did this to show they were sad about the Temple in Jerusalem being destroyed.

from Shechem, Shiloh and Samaria. None of them knew that Gedaliah had been murdered. [6]Ishmael son of Nethaniah went out from Mizpah to meet them. He cried as he walked. When he met them, he said, "Come with me to meet Gedaliah son of Ahikam." [7]So they went into Mizpah. Then Ishmael son of Nethaniah and his men killed 70 of them! They threw the bodies into a deep well. [8]But the 10 men who were left alive said to Ishmael, "Don't kill us! We have wheat and barley. And we have oil and honey. We have hidden these things in a field." So Ishmael let those 10 men alone. He did not kill them with the others. [9]Now the well where he had thrown the bodies had been made by King Asa. Asa had made the well as a part of his defenses against Baasha king of Israel. But Ishmael son of Nethaniah put dead bodies in it until it was full.

[10]Ishmael captured all the other people in Mizpah. He captured the king's daughters and all the other people who were left there. They were the people whom Nebuzaradan commander of the guard had chosen Gedaliah son of Ahikam to take care of. So Ishmael son of Nethaniah captured those people. And he started to cross over to the country of the Ammonites.

[11]Johanan son of Kareah heard about all the evil things Ishmael son of Nethaniah had done. All the army officers with him heard it, too. [12]So Johanan and the army officers took their men and went to fight Ishmael son of Nethaniah. They caught him near the big pool of water at Gibeon. [13]The captives Ishmael had taken saw Johanan and the army officers. And they became very happy. [14]Then all the people Ishmael had taken captive turned around. They ran to Johanan son of Kareah. [15]But Ishmael son of Nethaniah and eight of his men escaped from Johanan. And they ran away to the Ammonites.

[16]So Johanan son of Kareah and all his army officers saved the captives. Ishmael son of Nethaniah had murdered Gedaliah son of Ahikam. Then he had taken those people from Mizpah. Among those left alive were soldiers, women, children and court officers. Johanan brought them back from the town of Gibeon.

THE ESCAPE TO EGYPT

[17-18]Johanan and the other army officers were afraid of the Babylonians. The king of Babylon had chosen Gedaliah son of Ahikam to be governor of Judah. But Ishmael son of Nethaniah had murdered Gedaliah. So Johanan was afraid that the Babylonians would be angry. They decided to run away to Egypt. On the way they stayed at Geruth Kimham, near the town of Bethlehem.

42 While there, Johanan son of Kareah and Jezaniah son of Hoshaiah went to Jeremiah the prophet.[d] All the army officers went with Johanan and Jezaniah. All the people, from the least important to the greatest, all went along, too. [2]They said to him, "Jeremiah, please listen to what we ask. Pray to the Lord your God. Pray for all the people left alive from the family of Judah. At one time there were many of us. You can see that there are few of us now. [3]So pray that the Lord your God will tell us where we should go. And pray he will tell us what we should do."

[4]Then Jeremiah the prophet answered, "I understand what you want me to do. I will pray to the Lord your God as you have asked. I will tell you everything he says. I will not hide anything from you."

[5]Then the people said to Jeremiah, "We will do everything the Lord your God tells us. If we don't, may the Lord be a true and loyal witness against us. We know he will send you to tell us what to do. [6]It does not matter if we like the message or not. We will obey the Lord our God. We are sending you to the Lord for a message from him. We will obey

what he says. Then good things will happen to us."

⁷Ten days later the Lord spoke his word to Jeremiah. ⁸Then Jeremiah called for Johanan son of Kareah and the army officers who were with him. Jeremiah also called all the other people, from the least important to the greatest. ⁹Then Jeremiah said to them, "You sent me to ask the Lord for what you wanted. This is what the Lord, the God of Israel, says: ¹⁰'If you will stay in Judah, I will make you strong. I will not destroy you. I will plant you, and I will not pull you up. This is because I am sad about the disaster I brought on you. ¹¹Now you are afraid of the king of Babylon. But don't be afraid of him. Don't be afraid of the king of Babylon,' says the Lord. 'I am with you. I will save you. I will rescue you from his power. ¹²I will be kind to you. And the king of Babylon will also treat you with mercy. He will bring you back to your land.'

¹³"But you might say, 'We will not stay in Judah.' If you say that, you will disobey the Lord your God. ¹⁴Or you might say, 'No, we will go and live in Egypt. We will not be bothered with war there. We will not hear the trumpets of war. And in Egypt we will not be hungry.' ¹⁵If you say that, listen to the message of the Lord. It is to you who are left alive from Judah. This is what the Lord of heaven's armies, the God of Israel, says: 'If you make up your mind to go and live in Egypt, these things will happen: ¹⁶You are afraid of war. But it will defeat you in the land of Egypt. And you are worried about hunger. But you will be hungry in Egypt. You will die there. ¹⁷Everyone who goes to live in Egypt will die in war. Or he will die from hunger or terrible disease. No one who goes to Egypt will live. No one will escape the terrible things I will bring to them.'

¹⁸"This is what the Lord of heaven's armies, the God of Israel, says: 'I showed my anger against Jerusalem. I punished the people who lived in Jerusalem. In the same way I will show my anger against you when you go to Egypt. Other nations will speak evil of you. People will be shocked by what has happened to you. You will become a curse word. People will insult you. And you will never see Judah again.'

¹⁹"You who are left alive in Judah, the Lord has told you, 'Don't go to Egypt.' I warn you today. ²⁰You are making a mistake that will cause your deaths. You sent me to the Lord your God. You said to me, 'Pray to the Lord our God for us. Tell us everything the Lord says, and we will do it.' ²¹So today I have told you the message from the Lord. But you have not obeyed the Lord your God. You have not done all that he sent me to tell you to do. ²²So now be sure you understand this: You want to go to live in Egypt. But you will die by war, hunger or terrible diseases."

43 So Jeremiah finished telling the people the message from the Lord their God. He told them everything the Lord their God had sent him to tell them.

²Azariah son of Hoshaiah, Johanan son of Kareah and some other men were too proud. They said to Jeremiah, "Jeremiah, you are lying! The Lord our God did not send you to say, 'You must not go to Egypt to live there.' ³Baruch son of Neriah is causing you to be against us. He wants you to hand us over to the Babylonians. Then they will kill us. Or they will capture us and take us to Babylon."

⁴So Johanan, the army officers and all the people disobeyed the Lord's command. He had commanded them to stay in Judah. ⁵But Johanan son of Kareah and the army officers took those who were left alive from Judah to Egypt. These were the people who had run away from the Babylonians to other countries. But they had come back to Judah. ⁶Now Johanan and the army officers took the men,

women and children. Among those people were the king's daughters. And they led them to Egypt. Nebuzaradan commander of the guard had put Gedaliah in charge of those people. (Gedaliah was the son of Ahikam son of Shaphan.) Johanan also took Jeremiah the prophet[d] and Baruch son of Neriah. [7]These people did not listen to the Lord. So they all went to Egypt to the town of Tahpanhes.

[8]In Tahpanhes the Lord spoke his word to Jeremiah: [9]"Take some large stones. Bury them in the clay in the brick pavement. This is in front of the king of Egypt's palace in Tahpanhes. Do this while the Jews are watching you. [10]Then say to them, 'This is what the Lord of heaven's armies, the God of Israel, says: I will send for my servant, Nebuchadnezzar king of Babylon. And I will set his throne over these stones I have buried. He will spread his covering for shade above these stones. [11]He will come here and attack Egypt. He will bring death to those who are supposed to die. He will make prisoners of those who are to be taken captive. And he will bring war to those who are to be killed with a sword. [12]Nebuchadnezzar will set fire to the temples of the gods of Egypt. He will burn those temples. And he will take the idols away. A shepherd wraps himself in his clothes. In the same way Nebuchadnezzar will wrap Egypt around him. Then he will safely leave Egypt. [13]He will destroy the stone pillars in the temple of the sun god in Egypt. And he will burn down the temples of the gods of Egypt.'"

DISASTER IN EGYPT

44 Jeremiah received a message from the Lord. It was for all the Jews living in Egypt. It was for the Jews in Migdol, Tahpanhes, Memphis and southern Egypt. This was the message: [2]"The Lord of heaven's armies, the God of Israel, says: You saw the terrible things I brought on Jerusalem and the towns of Judah. Those towns are empty ruins today. [3]And it is because the people who lived there did evil. Those people burned incense[d] to other gods. And that made me angry! Your people and your ancestors did not worship those gods before. [4]I sent my prophets[d] to them again and again. Those prophets were my servants. They spoke my message and said to the people, 'Don't do this terrible thing. The Lord hates for you to worship other gods.' [5]But they did not listen to the prophets. They did not pay attention. They did not stop doing evil things. They did not stop burning incense to other gods. [6]So I showed my great anger against them. I punished the towns of Judah and the streets of Jerusalem. My anger made Jerusalem and the towns of Judah empty. They are only ruins and piles of stones today.

[7]"So the Lord of heaven's armies, the God of Israel, says: Why are you doing such great harm to yourselves by continuing to worship other gods? You are cutting off the men and women, children and babies from the family of Judah. So you leave yourselves without anyone from the family of Judah. [8]Why do you want to make me angry by making idols? Why do you burn incense to the gods of Egypt, where you have come to live? You will destroy yourselves. Other nations will speak evil of you. And all the other nations on the earth will make fun of you. [9]Have you forgotten about the evil things your ancestors did? And have you forgotten the evil the kings and queens of Judah did? Have you forgotten about the evil you and your wives did? They did these things in Judah and in the streets of Jerusalem. [10]Even to this day the people of Judah are still too proud. They have not learned to respect me. And they have not followed my teachings. They have not obeyed the laws I gave you and your ancestors!

¹¹"So this is what the Lord of heaven's armies, the God of Israel, says: I am determined to bring disasters on you. I will destroy the whole family of Judah. ¹²There were a few left alive from Judah. They were determined to go to Egypt and settle there. But they will all die in Egypt. They will be killed in war or die from hunger. From the least important to the greatest, they will be killed in war or die from hunger. Other nations will speak evil about them. People will be shocked by what has happened to them. They will become a curse word. People will insult them. ¹³I will punish those people who have gone to live in Egypt. I will use swords, hunger and terrible diseases to punish them. I will punish them just as I punished Jerusalem. ¹⁴Of the people of Judah who were left alive and have gone to Egypt none will escape my punishment. They want to return to Judah and live there. But none of them will live to return to Judah. None of them will return to Judah, except a few people who escape."

¹⁵A large group of the people of Judah, who lived in southern Egypt, were meeting together. Among them were many women of Judah who lived in Egypt. They were burning incense to other gods, and their husbands knew it. All these people said to Jeremiah, ¹⁶"We will not listen to the message from the Lord that you spoke to us. ¹⁷We promised to make sacrifices to the Queen Goddess!ᵈ And we will do everything we promised. We will burn incense and pour out drink offerings to worship her. We did that in the past. And our ancestors, kings and officers did that in the past. All of us did those things in the towns of Judah and in the streets of Jerusalem. At that time we had plenty of food. We were successful. Nothing bad happened to us. ¹⁸But then we stopped making sacrifices to the Queen Goddess. And we stopped pouring out drink offerings to her. Since then we have had

problems. Our people have been killed in war and by hunger."

¹⁹The women said, "Our husbands knew what we were doing. We had their permission to burn incense to the Queen Goddess! We had their permission to pour out drink offerings to her. Our husbands knew we were making cakes that looked like her and that we poured out drink offerings to her."

²⁰Then Jeremiah spoke to all the people—men and women—who answered him. ²¹He said to them, "The Lord remembered that you burned incense. You burned it in the towns of Judah and in the streets of Jerusalem. You and your ancestors, kings and officers did that. And the people of the land did that. The Lord remembered and thought about it. ²²Then he could not be patient with you any longer. He hated the terrible things you did. So he made your country an empty desert. No one lives there now. Other people curse that country. ²³All this happened because you burned incense to other gods. You sinned against the Lord. You did not obey him. You did not follow his teachings or the laws he gave you. You did not keep your part of the agreement. This disaster has happened. It is there for you to see."

²⁴Then Jeremiah spoke to all those men and also to the women. He said, "People of Judah who are now in Egypt, hear the word of the Lord: ²⁵The Lord of heaven's armies, the God of Israel, says: You women did what you said you would do. You said, 'We will keep the promises we made. We promised to make sacrifices to the Queen Goddess. And we promised to pour out drink offerings to her.' So, go ahead. Do the things you promised you would do. Keep your promises. ²⁶But hear the word of the Lord. Listen, all you Jews living in Egypt. The Lord says, 'I use my great name and make this promise: The people of Judah now living in Egypt will never again use

my name to make promises. They will never again say, "As surely as the Lord God lives..." [27]I am watching over them. I am not watching over them to take care of them, but to hurt them. The Jews who live in Egypt will die from swords or hunger until they are all destroyed. [28]Some people will escape being killed by the sword. They will come back to Judah from Egypt. But there will only be a very few who escape. Then, of the people of Judah who came to live in Egypt, those who are left alive will know. They will know whether my word or their word came true. [29]I will give you a sign that I will punish you here in Egypt,' says the Lord. 'Then you will know my promises to hurt you will really happen.' [30]This is what the Lord says: 'Hophra king of Egypt has enemies who want to kill him. I will hand over King Hophra to his enemies. I will do this just as I handed Zedekiah king of Judah over to Nebuchadnezzar king of Babylon. Nebuchadnezzar wanted to kill Zedekiah.'"

A MESSAGE TO BARUCH

45 It was the fourth year that Jehoiakim son of Josiah was king of Judah. Jeremiah the prophet[d] told these things to Baruch son of Neriah. And Baruch wrote them on a scroll. This is what Jeremiah said to Baruch: [2]"This is what the Lord, the God of Israel, says to you: [3]Baruch, you have said, 'How terrible it is for me! The Lord has given me sorrow along with my pain. I am tired because of my suffering. I cannot rest.'"

[4]The Lord said, "Say this to Baruch: 'This is what the Lord says: I will tear down what I have built. And I will pull up what I have planted. I will do that everywhere in Judah. [5]Baruch, you are looking for great things for yourself. Don't do that! Don't look for them because I will bring disaster on all the people. The Lord says these things! You will have to go many places. But I will let you escape alive wherever you go.'"

MESSAGES ABOUT THE NATIONS

46 The Lord spoke this word to Jeremiah the prophet[d] about the nations:

[2]This message is about Egypt: This message is about the army of King Neco, king of Egypt. His army was defeated at the city of Carchemish on the Euphrates River. It was defeated by Nebuchadnezzar king of Babylon. This was in the fourth year that Jehoiakim son of Josiah was king of Judah. This is the Lord's message to Egypt:

[3]"Prepare your shields, large and
　　small.
　　March out for battle!
[4]Harness the horses.
　　Soldiers, get on your horses!
　　Go to your places for battle.
　　Put on your helmets!
　　Polish your spears.
　　Put on your armor!
[5]What do I see?
　　That army is terrified.
　　The soldiers are running away.
　　Their warriors are defeated.
　　They run away quickly.
　　They don't look back.
　　There is terror on every side!"
　　says the Lord.
[6]"The fast runners cannot run away.
　　The strong soldiers cannot escape.
　　They will stumble and fall
　　in the north, by the Euphrates
　　　River.
[7]Who is this, rising up like the Nile
　　　River?
　　Who comes like that strong, fast
　　　river?
[8]Egypt rises up like the Nile River.
　　It is Egypt that comes like that
　　　strong, fast river.
　　Egypt says, 'I will rise up and cover
　　　the earth.
　　I will destroy cities and the people
　　　in them!'
[9]Horsemen, charge into battle!
　　Chariot drivers, drive hard!

March on, brave soldiers—
   soldiers from Cush and Put who
    carry shields.
   March on, soldiers from Lydia who
    use bows.

¹⁰"But that day belongs to the Master,
   the Lord of heaven's armies.
   At that time he will give those people
    the punishment they deserve.
   The sword will kill until it is finished.
   The sword will kill until it satisfies
    its thirst for blood.
   This is because the Master, the Lord
    of heaven's armies, will offer a
    sacrifice.
   That sacrifice is Egypt's army in the
    land of the north, by the
    Euphrates River.

¹¹"Go to Gilead and get some balm.ᵈ
   Go up, people of Egypt!
   You will make up many medicines,
    but you will not be healed.
¹²The nations will hear of your shame.
   Your cries will fill all the earth.
   One warrior will run into another.
   And both of them will fall down
    together!"

¹³This is the message the Lord spoke
to Jeremiah the prophet.ᵈ This message is
about Nebuchadnezzar king of Babylon
as he came to attack Egypt:
¹⁴"Announce this message in Egypt,
   and prophesy it in Migdol.
   Preach this message also in
    Memphis and Tahpanhes:
  'Get ready for war.
   The battle is all around you.'
¹⁵Egypt, why will your warriors be
   killed?
   They cannot stand because the
    Lord will push them down.
¹⁶Those soldiers will stumble again and
   again.
   They will fall over each other.
   They will say, 'Get up. Let's go back
    to our own people and our
    homeland.

We must get away from our
    enemy's sword!'
¹⁷In their homelands those soldiers will
   say,
  'The king of Egypt is only a lot of
    noise.
   His time of glory is over!'"

¹⁸The King's name is the Lord of
   heaven's armies.
   He says, "As surely as I live,
  a powerful leader will come.
   He will be strong as great Mount
    Tabor is higher than other
    mountains.
   He will be mighty as Mount Carmel
    is higher than the sea.
¹⁹People of Egypt, pack your things
   to be taken away as captives.
   This is because Memphis will be
    destroyed.
   The cities will be ruins, and no one
    will live there.

²⁰"Egypt is like a beautiful young cow.
   But a horsefly is coming
    from the north to attack her.
²¹The hired soldiers in Egypt's army
   are like fat calves.
   They will all turn and run away
    together.
   They will not stand strong against
    the attack.
   Their time of destruction is coming.
   They will soon be punished.
²²Egypt is like a hissing snake that is
   trying to escape.
   The enemy comes closer and closer.
   They will come against Egypt with
    axes.
   They are like men who cut down
    trees.
²³They will chop down Egypt's army
   as if it were a great forest," says the
    Lord.
  "There are more enemy soldiers than
    locusts.ᵈ
   There are too many soldiers to
    count.

²⁴The people of Egypt will be ashamed.
They will be handed over to the
enemy from the north."

²⁵The Lord of heaven's armies, the God of Israel, says: "Very soon I will punish Amon, the god of Thebes. And I will punish Egypt, her king and her gods. And I will punish the people who depend on the king. ²⁶I will let all those people be defeated by their enemies. And those enemies want to kill them. I will give them to Nebuchadnezzar king of Babylon and his officers. But in the future, Egypt will live in peace as it once did," says the Lord.

A MESSAGE TO ISRAEL

²⁷"People of Jacob, my servants, don't
be afraid.
Don't be frightened, Israel.
I will surely save you from those
faraway places.
I will save your children from the
lands where they are captives.
The people of Jacob will have peace
and safety again.
And no one will make them afraid.
²⁸People of Jacob, my servants, do not
be afraid.
I am with you," says the Lord.
"I scattered you to many different
nations.
And I will completely destroy all
those nations.
But I will not completely destroy
you.
I will punish you fairly.
But I cannot let you escape your
punishment."

A MESSAGE ABOUT THE PHILISTINES

47 The Lord spoke his word to Jeremiah the prophet.ᵈ This message is about the Philistine people. It came before the king of Egypt attacked the city of Gaza.
²This is what the Lord says:
"See, the enemy is gathering in the
north like rising waters.

They will become like an
overflowing stream.
They will cover the whole country like
a flood.
They will cover the towns and the
people living in them.
Everyone living in that country
will cry for help.
The people will cry painfully.
³They will hear the sound of the
running horses.
They will hear the noisy
chariots.
They will hear the rumbling chariot
wheels.
Fathers will not help their children to
safety.
Those fathers will be too weak to
help.
⁴The time has come
to destroy all the Philistines.
It's time to destroy all who are left
alive
who could help Tyre and Sidon.
The Lord will soon destroy the
Philistines.
He will destroy those left alive from
the island of Crete.
⁵The people from Gaza will be sad and
shave their heads.
The people from Ashkelon will be
made silent.
Those left alive from the valley,
how long will you cut
yourselves?ⁿ

⁶"You cry, 'Sword of the Lord,
how long will you keep fighting?
Return to your holder.
Stop! Be still.'
⁷But how can the sword of the Lord
rest?
The Lord gave it a command.
The Lord has ordered it
to attack the city of Ashkelon and
the seacoast.'"

47:5 sad and . . . yourselves? The people did these things to show their sadness.

A MESSAGE ABOUT MOAB

48 This message is about the country of Moab. This is what the Lord of heaven's armies, the God of Israel, says:

"How terrible it will be for Nebo.
  It will be ruined.
The town of Kiriathaim will be
  disgraced and captured.
The strong city will be disgraced
  and shattered.
²Moab will not be praised again.
  Men in the town of Heshbon plan
    Moab's defeat.
  They say, 'Come, let us put an end
    to that nation!'
Town of Madmen, you will also be
  silenced.
  The sword will chase you.
³Listen to the cries from the town of
  Horonaim.
  They are cries of much confusion
    and destruction.
⁴Moab will be broken up.
  Her little children will cry for help.
⁵Moab's people go up the path to
  Luhith.
  They cry loudly as they go.
On the road down to the town of
  Horonaim,
  cries of pain and suffering can be
    heard.
⁶Run! Run for your lives!
  Go like a bush being blown through
    the desert.
⁷You trust in the things you do and in
  your wealth.
  So you also will be captured.
The god Chemosh*d* will be taken into
  captivity.
  And his priests and officers will be
    taken with him.
⁸The destroyer will come against every
  town.
  Not one town will escape.

The valley will be ruined.
  The high plain will be destroyed.
  The Lord said this would happen.
⁹Spread salt*n* over the fields in Moab.
  The country will be an empty
    desert.
Moab's towns will become empty.
  No one will live in them.
¹⁰A curse will be on anyone who doesn't
  do what the Lord says.
  A curse will be on anyone who keeps
    back his sword from killing.

¹¹"The people of Moab have never
  known trouble.
  They are like wine left to settle.
They have never been poured like
  wine from one jar to another.
  They have not been taken into
    captivity.
So they taste as they did before.
  And their smell has not changed.
¹²A time is coming," says the Lord.
  "And I will soon send men to pour
    you from your jars.
Those men will empty Moab's jars.
  And they will smash their jugs.
¹³The people of Israel trusted that god
  in Bethel.
  They were ashamed when there was
    no help.
In the same way Moab will be
  ashamed of their god Chemosh.

¹⁴"You cannot say, 'We are warriors!
  We are brave men in battle!'
¹⁵The enemy will attack Moab and
  destroy their towns.
  Their best young men will be
    killed!" says the King.
  The King's name is the Lord of
    heaven's armies.
¹⁶"The end of Moab is near.
  They will soon be destroyed.
¹⁷All you who live around Moab, cry
  for her.

48:9 salt The salt would keep crops from growing there.

All you who know about her, cry for
   her.
Say, 'The ruler's power is broken.
   Moab's power and glory are gone.'

¹⁸"You people living in Dibon, come
      down from your place of honor.
   Sit on the dry ground.
This is because the destroyer of Moab
      is coming against you.
   And he will destroy your strong,
      walled cities.
¹⁹You people living in Aroer,
   stand next to the road and watch.
See the man running away and the
      woman escaping.
   Ask them what happened.
²⁰Moab will be ruined and filled with
      shame.
   Cry, Moab, cry out!
Announce at the Arnon River
   that Moab is destroyed.
²¹People on the high plain have been
      punished.
   Judgment has come to these towns:
      Holon, Jahzah and Mephaath;
²²   Dibon, Nebo and Beth Diblathaim;
²³   Kiriathaim, Beth Gamul and Beth
         Meon;
²⁴   Kerioth and Bozrah.
   Judgment has come to all the towns
      of Moab, far and near.
²⁵Moab's strength has been cut off.
   Moab's arm is broken!" says the
      Lord.

²⁶"The people of Moab thought they
      were greater than the Lord.
   So punish Moab until they act as if
      they are drunk.
Moab will fall and roll around in their
      own vomit.
   People will make fun of them.
²⁷Moab, you made fun of Israel.
   Israel was caught in the middle of a
      gang of thieves.
You often spoke about Israel.
   And you shook your head and acted
      as if you were better than Israel.

²⁸People in Moab, leave your towns
      empty.
   Go live among the rocks.
Be like a dove that makes its nest
   at the entrance of a cave!

²⁹"We have heard that the people of
      Moab are proud
   and very conceited.
They are proud and think they are
      important.
   They were very proud in their
      hearts."
³⁰The Lord says,
   "I know Moab's quick anger, but it
      is useless.
   Moab's bragging accomplishes
      nothing.
³¹So I cry sadly for Moab.
   I cry out for everyone in Moab.
   I moan for the men from Kir
      Hareseth.
³²I cry with the people of Jazer
   for the grapevines of Sibmah.
In the past your vines spread all the
      way to the sea.
   They reached as far as the sea of
      Jazer.
But the destroyer has taken
   your fruit and grapes.
³³Joy and happiness are gone
   from the large fields of Moab.
I have stopped the flow of wine from
      the winepresses.ᵈ
   No one walks on the grapes with
      shouts of joy.
There are shouts,
   but not shouts of joy.

³⁴"Their crying can be heard
   from Heshbon to Elealeh and Jahaz.
It can be heard from Zoar as far away
   as Horonaim and Eglath
      Shelishiyah.
   Even the waters of Nimrim are
      dried up.
³⁵I will stop Moab
   from making burnt offerings at the
      places of worship.

I will stop them from burning incense[d]
  to their gods," says the Lord.

36"My heart cries for Moab like a flute
  playing a funeral song.
It cries for the people from Kir
  Hareseth.
Their money and riches have all
  been taken away.
37Everyone has a shaved head.
  Everyone's beard is cut off.
Everyone's hands are cut.
  Everyone wears rough cloth around
  his waist.[n]
38People are crying on every roof[n] in
  Moab
  and in every public square.
There is nothing but sadness
  because I have broken Moab
  like a jar no one wants," says the
  Lord.
39"Moab is shattered! The people are
  crying!
  Moab turns away in shame!
People all around her make fun of
  her.
  The things that happened fill them
  with fear."

40This is what the Lord says:
  "Look! An eagle is diving down
  from the sky.
  It spreads its wings over Moab.
41The towns of Moab will be captured.
  The strong, walled cities will be
  defeated.
At that time Moab's warriors will be
  frightened.
  They will feel pain like a woman
  who is having a baby.
42The nation of Moab will be destroyed.
  This is because they thought they
  were greater than the Lord.
43Fear, deep pits and traps wait for you,
  people of Moab," says the Lord.

44"People will run from fear.
  But they will fall into the pits.
Anyone who climbs out of the pits
  will be caught in the traps.
I will bring the year of punishment to
  Moab," says the Lord.

45"People have run from the powerful
  enemy.
  They ran to Heshbon for safety.
But fire started in Heshbon.
  A blaze broke out in Sihon's town.
And it burns the leaders of Moab.
  It destroys those proud people.
46How terrible it will be for you, Moab!
  Chemosh's people are being
  destroyed.
Your sons and daughters are being
  taken away as captives.

47"But in days to come,
  I will make good things happen
  again to Moab," says the Lord.

This ends the judgment on Moab.

A MESSAGE ABOUT AMMON

49 This message is about the Ammonite people. This is what the
Lord says:
  "Do you think that Israel has no sons?
  Do you think there is no one to take
  the land when the parents die?
Maybe that is why Molech[d] took Gad's
  land.
  Maybe that is why Molech's people
  live in Gad's towns."
2The Lord says,
"The time will come when I will make
  the capital city of Rabbah Ammon
  hear the battle cry.
It will be a hill covered with ruins.
  And the towns around it will be
  burned.
Those people forced Israel out of that
  land.

48:37 **shaved head . . . waist** The people did these things to show their sadness for those who had died.
48:38 **roof** In Bible times houses were built with flat roofs. The roof was used for drying things such as flax and
  fruit. And it was used as an extra room, as a place for worship and as a place to sleep in the summer.

But now the people of Israel will
    force them out!" says the Lord.
³"People in Heshbon, cry because the
    town of Ai is destroyed!
Those who live in Rabbah Ammon,
    cry out!
Put on your rough cloth to show your
    sadness, and cry loudly.
Run here and there for safety inside
    the walls.
This is because the enemy will take
    Molech away as a captive.
They will also take away his priests
    and officers with him.
⁴You brag about your valleys.
You brag about the fruit in your
    valleys.
You are like an unfaithful child.
You believe your treasures will save
    you.
You think, 'Who would attack me?'
⁵I will bring terror on you
    from every side,"
says the Master, the Lord of
    heaven's armies.
"You will all be forced away.
No one will be able to gather you.

⁶"But the time will come
    when I will make good things
      happen to the Ammonites again,"
says the Lord.

A MESSAGE ABOUT EDOM

⁷This message is about Edom. This is
what the Lord of heaven's armies says:
"Is there no more wisdom in Teman?
Can the wise men of Edom no
    longer give good advice?
Have they lost their wisdom?
⁸You people living in Dedan,
    run away and hide in deep caves.
This is because I will punish
    the people of Esau with disaster for
    what they did.
⁹If workers came and picked the
    grapes from your vines,
    they would leave a few grapes
    behind.

If robbers came at night,
    they would steal only enough for
    themselves.
¹⁰But I will strip Esau bare.
I will find all their hiding places.
They will not be able to hide from
    me.
The children, relatives and neighbors
    will die.
¹¹Leave the orphans, and I will take care
    of them.
Your widows also can trust in me."

¹²This is what the Lord says: "Some
people did not deserve to be punished.
But they had to drink from the cup of
suffering anyway. People of Edom, you
deserve to be punished. So you will not
escape punishment. You must drink from
the cup of suffering." ¹³The Lord says, "I
make this promise in my own name. The
city of Bozrah will become a pile of ruins!
People will be shocked by what happened
there. People will insult that city and
speak evil of it. And all the towns around
Bozrah will become ruins forever."

¹⁴I have heard a message from the Lord.
    A messenger has been sent among
      the nations, saying,
"Gather your armies to attack it!
    Get ready for battle!"

¹⁵"Soon I will make you the smallest of
    nations!
You will be greatly hated.
¹⁶Edom, you frightened other nations.
Your pride has fooled you.
You live in the hollow places of the cliff.
You live on the high places of the
    hills.
Even if you build your home as high
    as an eagle's nest,
I will bring you down from there!"
    says the Lord.

¹⁷"Edom will be destroyed.
People will be shocked to see the
    destroyed cities.
They will be amazed at the injuries.

¹⁸Edom will be destroyed like the cities
    of Sodom and Gomorrah
    and the towns around them," says
    the Lord.
"No one will live there!
    No man will stay in Edom."

¹⁹"A lion will come from the thick
    bushes near the Jordan River.
    And it will go into the rich pastures
    where people feed their flocks.
I am like that lion! I will suddenly
    chase Edom from their land.
    Who is the one I have chosen to do
    this?
There is no one like me.
    There is no one who can challenge
    me.
    None of their leaders can stand up
    against me."

²⁰So listen to what the Lord has planned
    to do against Edom.
    Listen to what he has decided to do
    to the people in Teman.
The Lord will surely drag away the
    young ones of Edom.
    Edom's pastures will surely be
    destroyed because of them.
²¹At the sound of Edom's fall, the earth
    will shake.
    Their cry will be heard all the way
    to the Gulf of Aqaba.
²²The Lord is like an eagle swooping
    down.
    He is like an eagle spreading its
    wings over the city of Bozrah.
At that time Edom's soldiers will
    become very frightened.
    They will be crying from fear like a
    woman having a baby.

A MESSAGE ABOUT DAMASCUS

²³This message is about the city of Da-
mascus:
"The towns of Hamath and Arpad are
    put to shame.
    They are afraid because they have
    heard bad news.
They are discouraged.

They are troubled like the tossing sea.
²⁴The city of Damascus has become
    weak.
    The people want to run away.
    The people are ready to panic.
The people feel pain and suffering
    like a woman having a baby.
²⁵Damascus was a city of my joy.
    Why have the people not left that
    famous city yet?
²⁶Surely the young men will die in the
    public squares of that city.
    All of her soldiers will be killed at
    that time," says the Lord of
    heaven's armies.
²⁷"I will set fire to the walls of
    Damascus.
    The fire will completely burn the
    strong cities of Ben-Hadad."

A MESSAGE ABOUT KEDAR AND HAZOR

²⁸This message is about the tribe[d] of
Kedar and the kingdoms of Hazor. Nebuchadnezzar king of Babylon defeated
them. This is what the Lord says:
"Go and attack the people of Kedar.
    Destroy the people of the East.
²⁹Their tents and flocks will be taken
    away.
    Their tents and all their things will
    be carried off.
    Their enemy will take away their
    goods and camels.
Men will shout to them,
    'Terror on every side!'

³⁰"Run away quickly!
    People in Hazor, find a good place
    to hide!" says the Lord.
"Nebuchadnezzar king of Babylon has
    made plans against you.
    He has made plans to defeat you!

³¹"There is a nation that is comfortable.
    It is sure that no one will defeat it,"
    says the Lord.
"That nation does not have gates or
    fences to protect it.
    Its people live alone.
Attack that nation!

³²The enemy will steal their camels
    and their large herds of cattle.
I will scatter the Arabs to every part of
    the earth.
And I will bring disaster on them
    from everywhere," says the Lord.
³³"Hazor will become a place where
    wild dogs live.
It will become an empty desert
    forever.
No one will live there.
    No man will stay in it."

A MESSAGE ABOUT ELAM

³⁴It was early in the time when Zedekiah was king of Judah. The Lord spoke
this word to Jeremiah the prophet.ᵈ This
message is about the nation of Elam.

³⁵This is what the Lord of heaven's
armies says:
"I will break Elam's bow.
    I will break its strength.
³⁶I will bring the four winds against Elam.
    I will bring them from the four
        corners of the skies.
I will scatter the people of Elam
    everywhere the four winds blow.
And its captives will go to every
    nation.
³⁷I will break Elam to pieces in front of
    their enemies.
The enemies want to destroy Elam.
I will bring disaster to Elam.
    I will show them how angry I am!"
        says the Lord.
"I will send a sword to chase Elam.
    It will chase them until I have killed
        them all.
³⁸I will show Elam that I am king.
    And I will destroy her king and her
        officers!" says the Lord.

³⁹"But I will make good things happen
        to Elam again
    in the future," says the Lord.

A MESSAGE ABOUT BABYLON

50 This is the message the Lord
spoke about Babylon and the
Babylonian people. He spoke this message through Jeremiah the prophet.ᵈ

²"Announce this to the nations.
    Lift up a banner and tell them.
    Speak the whole message and say:
'Babylon will be captured.
    The god Belᵈ will be put to shame.
    The god Mardukᵈ will be very
        afraid.
Babylon's idols will be put to shame.
    Her idols will be filled with terror!'
³A nation from the north will attack
    Babylon.
That nation will make Babylon like
    an empty desert.
No people will live there.
    Both men and animals will run
        away from there."

⁴The Lord says, "At that time
    the people of Israel and Judah will
        be together.
They will cry and look for the Lord
    their God.
⁵Those people will ask how to go to
    Jerusalem.
They will start to go in that
    direction.
They will come and join themselves to
    the Lord.
They will make an agreement that
    will last forever.
It will be an agreement that will
    never be forgotten.

⁶"My people have been like lost sheep.
    Their leaders have led them in the
        wrong way.
Their leaders made them wander
    around in the mountains and
        hills.
They forgot where their resting
    place was.
⁷Whoever found my people hurt
    them.
And those enemies said, 'We did
    nothing wrong.
Those people sinned against the Lord,
    their true resting place.
He was the God their fathers
    trusted.'

8"Run away from Babylon.
    Leave the land of the Babylonians.
    Be like the goats that lead the flock.
9I will bring against Babylon
    many nations from the north.
This group of nations will take their
        places for war against Babylon.
    Babylon will be captured by people
        from the north.
Their arrows are like trained soldiers
        who do not return from war with
        empty hands.
10The enemy will take all the wealth
        from the Babylonians.
    Those enemy soldiers will get all
        they want!" says the Lord.

11"Babylon, you are excited and happy.
    You took my land.
You dance around like a young cow in
        the grain.
    Your laughter is like the neighing of
        male horses.
12Your mother will be very ashamed.
    The woman who gave you birth will
        be disgraced.
Babylonia will be the least important
        of all the nations.
    She will be an empty, dry desert.
13The Lord will show his anger.
    No people will live there.
Babylon will be completely empty.
Everyone who passes by Babylon will
        be afraid.
    They will shake their heads when
        they see how it has been
        destroyed.

14"Take your positions for war against
        Babylon,
    all you soldiers with bows.
Shoot your arrows at Babylon! Do not
        save any of them.
    This is because Babylon has sinned
        against the Lord.
15Soldiers around Babylon, shout the
        war cry!
    Babylon has surrendered. Her
        towers have fallen.
    Her walls have been torn down.

The Lord is giving them the
        punishment they deserve.
    You nations should give Babylon
        what she deserves.
    Do to her what she has done to
        others.
16Don't let the people from Babylon
        plant their crops.
    Don't let them gather the harvest.
The soldiers of Babylon treated their
        captives cruelly.
    Now, let everyone go back
        home!
    Let everyone run to his own
        country.

17"The people of Israel are like a flock of
        sheep that are scattered.
    They are like sheep that have been
        chased away by lions.
The first lion to eat them up
    was the king of Assyria.
The last lion to crush their bones
    was Nebuchadnezzar king of
        Babylon."

18So this is what the Lord of heaven's
armies, the God of Israel, says:
    "I will punish the king of Babylon and
        his country.
    I will punish him as I punished the
        king of Assyria.
19But I will bring the people of Israel
        back to their own pasture.
    They will eat on Mount Carmel and
        in Bashan.
    They will eat and be full.
    They will eat on the hills of Ephraim
        and Gilead."
20The Lord says,
    "At that time people will try to find
        Israel's guilt.
    But there will be no guilt.
People will try to find Judah's sins.
    But no sins will be found.
This is because I am saving the few
        people left alive from Israel and
        Judah.
    And I am forgiving their sins.

²¹"Attack the land of Merathaim.
    Attack the people who live in Pekod.
Chase them, kill them and completely
    destroy them.
    Do everything I commanded you!"
    says the Lord.

²²"The noise of battle can be heard all
    over the country.
    It is the noise of much destruction.
²³Babylon was the hammer of the whole
    earth.
    But how broken and shattered that
    hammer is now!
Babylon is truly the most ruined
    of all the nations.
²⁴Babylon, I set a trap for you.
    And you were caught before you
    knew it.
You fought against the Lord.
    So you were found and taken
    prisoner.
²⁵The Lord has opened up his storeroom.
    He has brought out the weapons of
    his anger.
This is because the Lord God of
    heaven's armies has work to do.
    He has work to do in the land of the
    Babylonians.
²⁶Come against Babylon from far away.
    Break open her storehouses of
    grain.
Pile up her dead bodies like big
    piles of grain.
Completely destroy Babylon
    and do not leave anyone alive.
²⁷Kill all the young men in Babylon.
    Let them be killed.
The time has come for their defeat.
    How terrible it will be for them!
    It is time for them to be punished.
²⁸Listen to the people running from the
    country of Babylon!
    They are telling Jerusalem
how the Lord our God is punishing
    Babylon as it deserves.
This is because Babylon destroyed
    his Temple.^d

²⁹"Call for the men who shoot arrows
    to come against Babylon.
Tell them to surround the city.
    Don't let anyone escape.
Pay her back for the bad things she
    has done.
    Do to her what she has done to
    other nations.
Babylon acted with pride against the
    Lord,
    the Holy One of Israel.
³⁰So Babylon's young men will be killed
    in the streets.
    All her soldiers will die on that
    day," says the Lord.
³¹"Babylon, you are too proud. And
    I am against you,"
    says the Master, the Lord of
    heaven's armies.
"This is because the time has come
    for you to be punished.
³²Proud Babylon will stumble and fall.
    And no one will help her get up.
I will start a fire in her towns.
    It will completely burn up
    everything around her."

³³This is what the Lord of heaven's
armies says:
    "The people of Israel
    and Judah both are slaves.
The enemy took them as prisoners.
    And they won't let them go.
³⁴But God is strong and will buy them
    back.
    His name is the Lord of heaven's
    armies.
He will defend them with power
    so he can give rest to their land.
    But he will not give rest to those
    living in Babylon."

³⁵The Lord says,
"Let a sword kill the people living in
    Babylon!
    Let a sword kill its officers and wise
    men!
³⁶Let a sword kill its false prophets!^d
    They will become fools.

Let a sword kill Babylon's warriors!
　They will be full of terror.
[37] Let a sword kill its horses and
　　chariots.
　Let a sword kill all the soldiers
　　hired from other countries!
　They will be like frightened women.
　Let there be a sword against Babylon's
　　treasures!
　They will be taken away.
[38] Let there be a sword against its
　　waters!
　They will be dried up.
　It is a land of idols.
　Those idols will go crazy with fear.

[39] "Babylon will never be filled with
　　people again.
　Desert animals and hyenas will live
　　there.
　Owls will live there.
　But no people will live there ever
　　again.
[40] God completely destroyed the cities of
　　Sodom and Gomorrah
　and the towns around them," says
　　the Lord.
　"In the same way no people will live
　　in Babylon.
　No man will stay there.

[41] "Look! An army is coming from the
　　north.
　It comes from a powerful nation.
　Many kings are coming together
　　from all around the world.
[42] Their armies have bows and spears.
　The soldiers are cruel and have no
　　mercy.
　The soldiers come riding on their
　　horses.
　And the sound is loud like the
　　roaring sea.
　They stand in their places, ready for
　　battle.
　They are ready to attack you, city of
　　Babylon.
[43] The king of Babylon heard about
　　those armies.

And he became helpless because of
　　his fear.
　His fear is like pain.
　It is like the pain of a woman
　　having a baby.

[44] "A lion will come from the thick
　　bushes near the Jordan River.
　It will go into the rich pastures
　　where people feed their flocks.
　I am like that lion! I will suddenly
　　chase the people of Babylon from
　　their land.
　Who is the one I have chosen to do
　　this?
　There is no one like me.
　There is no one who can challenge
　　me.
　None of their leaders can stand up
　　against me."

[45] So listen to what the Lord has planned
　　to do against Babylon.
　Listen to what he has decided to do
　　to the people in Babylon.
　He will surely drag away the young
　　ones of Babylon.
　Babylon's pastures will be
　　destroyed because of them.
[46] At the sound of Babylon's fall, the
　　earth will shake.
　People in all nations will hear about
　　their destruction.

51

This is what the Lord says:
　"I will cause a destroying wind
　　to blow.
　It will blow against Babylon and the
　　Babylonian people.
[2] I will send foreign people to destroy
　　Babylon
　like a wind that blows chaff[d] away.
　Those people will make Babylon
　　empty.
　Armies will surround the city
　　when disaster comes upon her.
[3] The Babylonian soldiers will not use
　　their bows and arrows.
　Those soldiers will not even put on
　　their armor.

Don't feel sorry for the young men of
  Babylon.
  Completely destroy her army.
⁴Babylon's soldiers will be killed in
  Babylon.
  They will be badly injured in
  Babylon's streets.
⁵The Lord God of heaven's armies
  did not leave Israel and Judah alone.
  They are fully guilty of leaving the
  Holy One of Israel.
  But he has not left them.

⁶"Run away from Babylon!
  Run to save your lives!
  Don't stay and be killed because of
  Babylon's sins.
  It is time for the Lord to punish
  Babylon.
  Babylon will get the punishment it
  deserves.
⁷Babylon was like a gold cup in the
  Lord's hand.
  It made the whole earth drunk.
  The nations drank Babylon's wine.
  So they went crazy.
⁸Babylon will suddenly fall and be
  broken.
  Cry for her!
Get balm*d* for her pain.
  Maybe she can be healed.

⁹"Foreigners in Babylon say, 'We tried
  to heal Babylon.
  But she cannot be healed.
So let us leave her and each go to his
  own country.
  Babylon's guilt is as high as the
  clouds.
  Babylon's guilt reaches to the sky.'

¹⁰"The people of Judah say, 'The Lord
  has shown us to be right.
  Come, let us tell about it in
  Jerusalem.
  Let us tell about what the Lord our
  God has done.'

¹¹"Sharpen the arrows.
  Pick up your shields!

The Lord has stirred up the kings of
  the Medes.
  He has stirred them up because he
  wants to destroy Babylon.
  The Lord will give the people of
  Babylon the punishment they
  deserve.
  This is because Babylon destroyed
  his Temple*d* in Jerusalem.
¹²Lift up a banner against the walls of
  Babylon!
  Bring more guards.
  Put the watchmen in their places.
  Get ready for a secret attack!
  The Lord will do what he has planned.
  He will do what he said he would do
  against the people of Babylon.
¹³People of Babylon, you live near much
  water.
  You are rich with treasures.
  But your end as a nation has come.
  It is time for you to be destroyed.
¹⁴The Lord of heaven's armies has
  promised in his own name:
  'Babylon, I will surely fill you with
  so many enemy soldiers they will
  be like a swarm of locusts.*d*
  They will stand over you and shout
  their victory.'

¹⁵"The Lord made the earth by his
  power.
  He used his wisdom to build the
  world.
  He used his understanding to
  stretch out the skies.
¹⁶When he thunders, the waters in the
  skies roar.
  He makes clouds rise in the sky all
  over the earth.
  He sends lightning with the rain.
  He brings out the wind from his
  storehouses.

¹⁷"People are so stupid and know so
  little.
  Goldsmiths are made ashamed by
  their idols.
  Those statues are only false gods.
  They have no breath in them.

¹⁸They are worth nothing.
　People make fun of them.
When they are judged, they will be
　destroyed.
¹⁹But God, who is Jacob's Portion,^d is
　not like the idols.
God made everything.
And he made Israel to be his special
　people.
The Lord of heaven's armies is his
　name.

²⁰"You are my war club.
　You are my battle weapon.
I use you to smash nations.
　I use you to destroy kingdoms.
²¹I use you to smash horse and rider.
　I use you to smash chariot and
　　driver.
²²I use you to smash men and women.
　I use you to smash old men and
　　young men.
I use you to smash young men and
　young women.
²³I use you to smash shepherds and
　flocks.
I use you to smash farmers and
　oxen.
I use you to smash governors and
　officers.

²⁴"But I will pay Babylon back, and I
will pay back all the Babylonians for all
the evil things they did to Jerusalem," says
the Lord.

²⁵The Lord says,
　"Babylon, you are a destroying
　　mountain.
　And I am against you.
　You have destroyed the whole land.
I will put my hand out against you.
　I will roll you off the cliffs.
I will make you a burned-out
　mountain.
²⁶People will not find any rocks in
　Babylon big enough for
　cornerstones.^d

People will not take any rocks from
　Babylon to use for the
　foundation of a building.
This is because your city will be just
　a pile of ruins forever," says the
　Lord.

²⁷"Lift up the banner in the land!
　Blow the trumpet among the
　　nations!
Get the nations ready for battle
　against Babylon.
Call these kingdoms to come fight
　against Babylon:
Ararat, Minni and Ashkenaz.
Choose a commander to lead the
　army against Babylon.
Send so many horses that they are
　like a swarm of locusts.
²⁸Get the nations ready for battle
　against Babylon.
Get the kings of the Medes ready.
Get their governors and all their
　officers ready.
Get all the countries they rule ready
　for battle against Babylon.
²⁹The land shakes and moves like it is in
　pain.
It will shake when the Lord does
　what he planned to Babylon.
His plan is to make Babylon into an
　empty desert.
No one will live there.
³⁰Babylon's warriors have stopped
　fighting.
They stay in their protected cities.
Their strength is gone.
They have become like frightened
　women.
Babylon's houses are burning.
The bars of her gates are broken.
³¹One messenger follows another.
　Messenger follows messenger.
They announce to the king of Babylon
　that his whole city has been
　captured.
³²The river crossings have been
　captured.

The swamplands are burning.
All of Babylon's soldiers are terribly
afraid."

33This is what the Lord of heaven's
armies, the God of Israel, says:
"The city of Babylon is like a
threshing*d* floor,
where people crush the grain at
harvest time.
The time to harvest Babylon is
coming soon."

34"Nebuchadnezzar king of Babylon has
destroyed us.
In the past he took our people away.
And we became like an empty jar.
He was like a giant snake that
swallowed us.
He ate everything until he was full
of our best things.
Then he spit us out.
35Babylon did terrible things to hurt us.
Now let those things happen to
Babylon,"
say the people of Jerusalem.
"The people of Babylon are guilty of
killing our people.
Now let them be punished for the
evil they did," says Jerusalem.

36So this is what the Lord says:
"I will defend you, Judah.
I will make sure that Babylon is
punished.
I will dry up Babylon's sea.
And I will make her springs become
dry.
37Babylon will become a pile of ruins.
Wild dogs will live there.
People will be shocked by what
happened there.
No one lives there anymore.
38Babylon's people are like roaring
young lions.
They growl like baby lions.
39While they are stirred up,
I will give a feast for them.
I will make them drunk.

They will shout and laugh.
And they will sleep forever and
never wake up!" says the Lord.
40"I will take the people of Babylon to
be killed.
They will be like lambs,
like male sheep and goats waiting
to be killed.

41"How Babylon will be defeated!
The pride of the whole earth will be
taken captive.
People from other nations will be
shocked at what happened to
Babylon.
And the things they see will make
them afraid.
42The sea will rise over Babylon.
Its roaring waves will cover her.
43Babylon's towns will be ruined and
empty.
Babylon will become a dry, desert
land.
It will become a land where no one
lives.
People will not even travel through
Babylon.
44I will punish the god Bel*d* in Babylon.
I will make him spit out what he
has swallowed.
Nations will no longer come to
Babylon.
And the wall around the city will
fall.

45"Come out of Babylon, my people!
Run for your lives!
Run from the Lord's great anger.
46Don't lose courage.
Rumors will spread, but don't be
afraid.
One rumor comes this year, and
another comes the next year.
There will be rumors of terrible
fighting in the country.
There will be rumors of rulers
fighting against rulers.
47The time will surely come
when I will punish the idols of
Babylon.

And the whole land will be disgraced.
  There will be many dead people
    lying all around.
⁴⁸Then heaven and earth and all that is
    in them
  will shout for joy about Babylon.
They will shout because the army
    came from the north
  and fought against Babylon," says
    the Lord.

⁴⁹"Babylon killed people from Israel.
  Babylon killed people from
    everywhere on earth.
  So Babylon must fall.
⁵⁰You people escaped being killed with
    swords.
  You must hurry and leave Babylon.
Don't wait!
  Remember the Lord in the faraway
    land where you are.
  And think about Jerusalem."

⁵¹"We people of Judah are disgraced.
  We have been insulted.
  We have been shamed.
This is because strangers have gone
    into
  the holy places of the Lord's
    Temple!"ᵈ

⁵²The Lord says, "The time is coming
    when I will punish the idols of
    Babylon.
  Wounded people will cry with pain
    all over that land.
⁵³Babylon might grow until she touches
    the sky.
  She might make her cities strong.
But I will send people to destroy
    that city," says the Lord.

⁵⁴"We can hear people crying in
    Babylon.
  We hear the sound of people
    destroying things
    in the land of the Babylonians.
⁵⁵The Lord will destroy Babylon.
  He will make the loud sounds of the
    city become silent.

Enemies will come roaring in like
    ocean waves.
  People all around will hear that roar.
⁵⁶The army will come and destroy
    Babylon.
  Babylon's soldiers will be taken
    captive.
  Their bows will be broken.
This is because the Lord is a God
    who punishes people for the
    evil they do.
  He gives them the full punishment
    they deserve.
⁵⁷I will make Babylon's rulers and wise
    men drunk.
  I will make her governors, officers
    and soldiers drunk, too.
Then they will sleep forever and never
    wake up," says the King.
  His name is the Lord of heaven's
    armies.

⁵⁸This is what the Lord of heaven's
armies says:
"Babylon's thick wall will be pulled
    down.
  Her high gates will be burned.
The people will work hard, but it
    won't help.
  Their work will only become fuel
    for the flames!"

A MESSAGE TO BABYLON

⁵⁹This is the message that Jeremiah
the prophetᵈ gave to the officer Seraiah.
Seraiah was the son of Neriah, who was
the son of Mahseiah. Seraiah went to
Babylon with Zedekiah king of Judah.
This happened in the fourth year Zedekiah was king of Judah. ⁶⁰Jeremiah had
written on a scroll all the terrible things
that would happen to Babylon. He had
written all these words about Babylon.
⁶¹Jeremiah said to Seraiah, "Go to Babylon. Be sure to read this message so all
the people can hear you. ⁶²Then say,
'Lord, you have said that you will destroy
this place. You will destroy it so that no
people or animals will live in it. It will be

an empty ruin forever.' [63]After you finish reading this scroll, tie a stone to it. And throw it into the Euphrates River. [64]Then say, 'In the same way Babylon will sink. It will not rise again. It will sink because of the terrible things I will make happen here. Her people will fall.'"

The words of Jeremiah end here.

THE FALL OF JERUSALEM

52 Zedekiah was 21 years old when he became king. And he was king in Jerusalem for 11 years. His mother's name was Hamutal daughter of Jeremiah.[n] She was from Libnah. [2]Zedekiah did what the Lord said was wrong, just as Jehoiakim had done. [3]All this happened in Jerusalem and Judah because the Lord was angry with them. Finally, he threw them out of his presence.

Zedekiah turned against the king of Babylon.

[4]Then Nebuchadnezzar king of Babylon marched against Jerusalem with his whole army. They made a camp around the city. Then they built devices all around the city walls to attack it. This happened during Zedekiah's ninth year, tenth month and tenth day as king. [5]The city was under attack until Zedekiah's eleventh year as king.

[6]By the ninth day of the fourth month, the hunger was terrible in the city. There was no food for the people to eat. [7]Then the city wall was broken through. And the whole army ran away at night. They went through the gate between the two walls by the king's garden. The Babylonians were still surrounding the city. Zedekiah and his men ran toward the Jordan Valley.

[8]But the Babylonian army chased King Zedekiah. They caught up with him in the plains of Jericho. All of his army was scattered from him. [9]So they captured Zedekiah and took him to the king of Babylon at Riblah. Riblah is in the land

of Hamath. There he passed sentence on Zedekiah. [10]There at Riblah the king of Babylon killed Zedekiah's sons as he watched. The king also killed all the officers of Judah. [11]Then he put out Zedekiah's eyes. He put bronze chains on him and took him to Babylon. And the king kept Zedekiah in prison there until the day he died.

[12]Nebuzaradan was the commander of the king's special guards. This servant of the king of Babylon came to Jerusalem. This was on the tenth day of the fifth month. This was in Nebuchadnezzar's nineteenth year as king of Babylon. [13]Nebuzaradan set fire to the Temple[d] of the Lord and the palace. He also set fire to all the houses of Jerusalem. Every important building was burned. [14]The whole Babylonian army broke down the walls around Jerusalem. That army was led by the commander of the king's special guards. [15]Nebuzaradan, the commander of the guards, took captive some of the poorest people. And he took those who were left in Jerusalem. He took captive those who had surrendered to the king of Babylon. And he took away the skilled craftsmen who were left in Jerusalem. [16]But Nebuzaradan left behind the rest of the poorest people of the land. They were to take care of the vineyards and fields.

[17]The Babylonians broke up the bronze pillars, the bronze stands and the large bronze bowl, which was called the Sea. These were in the Temple of the Lord. Then they carried all the bronze to Babylon. [18]They also took the pots, shovels, wick trimmers, bowls, dishes and all the bronze objects. They were used to serve in the Temple. [19]The commander of the king's special guards took these things away: bowls, pans for carrying hot coals and large bowls; pots, lampstands, pans and bowls used for drink

---

52:1 **Jeremiah** This is not the prophet Jeremiah but a different man with the same name.

offerings. He took everything that was made of pure gold or silver.

²⁰There was so much bronze that it could not be weighed. There were two pillars. There was the large bronze bowl with the 12 bronze bulls under it. And there were the movable stands, which King Solomon had made for the Temple of the Lord.

²¹Each of the pillars was about 27 feet high. Each pillar was 18 feet around and hollow. The wall of each pillar was 3 inches thick. ²²The bronze capital[d] on top of the pillar was about 7¹/₂ feet high. It was decorated with a net design and bronze pomegranates[d] all around it. The other pillar also had pomegranates. It was like the first pillar. ²³There were 96 pomegranates on the sides of the pillars. There was a total of 100 pomegranates above the net design.

²⁴The commander of the guards took some prisoners. He took Seraiah the chief priest, Zephaniah the priest next in rank, and the three doorkeepers. ²⁵The commander also took other people who were still in the city. He took the officer in charge of the fighting men. He also took seven people who advised the king. He also took the royal assistant who selected people for the army. And he took 60 other men who were in the city.

²⁶Nebuzaradan, the commander, took all these people. And he brought them to the king of Babylon at Riblah. ²⁷There at Riblah, in the land of Hamath, the king had them killed.

So the people of Judah were led away from their country as captives. ²⁸This is how many people Nebuchadnezzar took away as captives: in the seventh year, 3,023 Jews; ²⁹in Nebuchadnezzar's eighteenth year, 832 people from Jerusalem; ³⁰in Nebuchadnezzar's twenty-third year, Nebuzaradan took 745 Jews as captives. Nebuzaradan was the commander of the king's special guards.

In all 4,600 people were taken captive.

JEHOIACHIN IS SET FREE

³¹Jehoiachin king of Judah was in prison in Babylon for 37 years. That year Evil-Merodach became king of Babylon. He let Jehoiachin king of Judah out of prison that year. He set Jehoiachin free on the twenty-fifth day of the twelfth month. ³²Evil-Merodach spoke kindly to Jehoiachin. He gave Jehoiachin a seat of honor. It was above the seats of the other kings who were with him in Babylon. ³³So Jehoiachin put away his prison clothes. For the rest of his life, he ate at the king's table. ³⁴Every day the king of Babylon gave Jehoiachin an allowance. This lasted as long as he lived, until Jehoiachin died.

LAMENTATIONS

JERUSALEM CRIES OVER HER DESTRUCTION

1 Jerusalem once was full of people.
But now the city is empty.
Jerusalem once was a great city
among the nations.
But now she[n] has become like a
widow.
She was like a queen of all the other
cities.
But now she is a slave.

[2] She cries loudly at night.
Tears are on her cheeks.
There is no one to comfort her.
All her lovers are gone.
All her friends have turned against
her.
They have become her enemies.

[3] Judah has gone into captivity.
She has suffered and worked hard.
She lives among other nations.
But she has found no rest.
Those who chased her caught her.
They caught her when she was in
trouble.

[4] The roads to Jerusalem are sad.
No one comes to Jerusalem for the
feasts.
No one passes through her gates.
And her priests groan.
Her young women are suffering.
And Jerusalem suffers terribly.

[5] Her enemies have become her
masters.
Her enemies enjoy the wealth they
have won.
The Lord is punishing her
for her many sins.
Her children have gone away.
They are captives of the enemy in a
foreign land.

[6] The beauty of Jerusalem
has gone away.
Her rulers are like deer
that cannot find food.
They are weak and have run away
from those who chased them.

[7] Jerusalem is suffering and homeless.
She remembers all the precious
things
she had in the past.
She remembers when her people were
defeated by the enemy.
There was no one to help her.
When her enemies saw her,
they laughed to see her ruined.

[8] Jerusalem sinned terribly.
So she has become unclean.[d]
Those who honored her hate her now
because they have seen her
nakedness.
Jerusalem groans
and turns away.

[9] Jerusalem made herself dirty by her
sins.
She did not think about what would
happen to her.
Her defeat was surprising.
There was no one to comfort her.
She says, "Lord, see how I suffer.
The enemy has won."

[10] The enemy reached out and took
all her precious things.
She even saw foreigners
enter her Temple.[d]
Lord, you had commanded
that they should not enter the
meeting of your people.

[11] All of Jerusalem's people are
groaning.
They are looking for bread.

1:1 she In this poem the city of Jerusalem is described as a woman.

They are giving away their precious
    things for food
  so they can stay alive.
The city says, "Look, Lord, and see.
  I am hated."

12Jerusalem says, "You who pass by on
    the road don't seem to care.
  Come, look at me and see.
Is there any pain like mine?
  Is there any pain like that he has
    caused me?
The Lord has punished me
  on the day of his great anger.

13"The Lord sent fire from above.
  It went down into my bones.
He stretched out a net for my feet.
  He turned me back.
He made me sad and lonely.
  I am weak all day.

14"He has noticed my sins.
  They are tied together by his hands.
They hang around my neck.
  He has turned my strength into
    weakness.
The Lord has let me be defeated
  by those who are stronger than I am.

15"The Lord has rejected
  all my mighty men inside my walls.
He brought an army against me
  to destroy my young men.
As if in a winepress,d the Lord has
    crushed
  the capital city of Judah.

16"I cry about these things.
  My eyes overflow with tears.
There is no one near to comfort me.
  There is no one who can give me
    strength again.
My children are left sad and lonely
  because the enemy has won."

17Jerusalem reaches out her hands,
  but there is no one to comfort her.
The Lord has commanded for the
    people of Jacob
  that their enemies surround them.

Jerusalem has become unclean
  like those around her.

18Jerusalem says, "The Lord is right.
  But I refused to obey him.
Listen, all you people.
  Look at my pain.
My young women and men
  have gone into captivity.

19"I called out to my friends,
  but they turned against me.
My priests and my elders
  have died in the city.
They were looking for food
  so they could stay alive.

20"Look at me, Lord. I am upset.
  I am troubled.
My heart is troubled
  because I have been so stubborn.
Out in the streets, the sword kills.
  Inside the houses, death destroys.

21"People have heard my groaning.
  There is no one to comfort me.
All my enemies have heard of my
    trouble.
  They are happy that you have done
    this to me.
Now bring that day you have
    announced.
  Let my enemies be like me.

22"Look at all their evil.
  Do to them what you have done to
    me
  because of all my sins.
I groan over and over again,
  and I am afraid."

THE LORD DESTROYED JERUSALEM

2 Look how the Lord in his anger
  has brought Jerusalem to shame.
He has thrown down the greatness
    of Israel
  from the sky to the earth.
He did not remember the Temple,d
    his footstool,
  on the day of his anger.

²The Lord swallowed up without
  mercy
  all the houses of the people of
    Jacob.
In his anger he pulled down
  the strong places of Judah.
He threw her kingdom and its rulers
  down to the ground in dishonor.

³In his anger the Lord has removed
  all the strength of Israel.
He took away his power from Israel
  when the enemy came.
He burned against the people of Jacob
  like a flaming fire
  that burns up everything around it.

⁴Like an enemy, the Lord prepared to
    shoot his bow.
  He took hold of his sword.
Like an enemy, he killed
  all the good-looking people.
He poured out his anger like fire
  on the tents of Jerusalem.

⁵The Lord has become like an enemy.
  He has swallowed up Israel.
He has swallowed up all her palaces.
He has destroyed all her strong
    places.
He has caused more moaning and
    groaning
  for Judah.

⁶He has destroyed his Temple as if it
    were a garden tent.
  He has destroyed the place where
    he met with his people.
The Lord has made Jerusalem forget
  the set feasts and Sabbath*ᵈ* days.
He has rejected the king and the priest
  in his great anger.

⁷The Lord has rejected his altar
  and abandoned his Temple.
He has given to the enemy
  the walls of Jerusalem's palaces.
The enemy shouted in the Lord's
    Temple
  as if it were a feast day.

⁸The Lord planned to destroy
  the wall around Jerusalem.
He marked the wall off with a
  measuring line.
He did not stop himself from
  destroying it.
He made the walls and defenses sad.
  Together they have fallen.

⁹Jerusalem's gates have fallen to the
    ground.
  He destroyed and smashed the bars
    of the gates.
Her king and her princes are sent
  away among the nations.
The teaching of the Lord has
  stopped.
The prophets*ᵈ* have not had
  any visions from the Lord.

¹⁰The elders of Jerusalem
  sit on the ground and are silent.
They pour dust on their heads
  and put on rough cloth to show
    how sad they are.
The young women of Jerusalem
  bow their heads to the ground in
    sorrow.

¹¹My eyes are weak from crying.
  I am troubled.
I feel as if I have been poured out on
    the ground
  because my people have been
    destroyed.
Children and babies are fainting
  in the streets of the city.

¹²They say to their mothers,
  "Where is some bread and wine?"
They faint like wounded soldiers
  in the streets of the city.
They die in their mothers' arms.

¹³What can I say about you, Jerusalem?
  What can I compare you to?
What can I say you are like?
  How can I comfort you, Jerusalem?
Your ruin is as big as the sea.
  No one can heal you.

14Your prophets saw visions about you.
But they were false and worth
nothing.
They did not expose your sins.
They did not keep you from being
captured.
The messages they preached to you
were false.
They fooled you.

15All who pass by on the road
clap their hands at you.
They make fun and shake their heads
at Jerusalem.
They ask, "Is this the city that people
called
the most beautiful city,
the happiest city on earth?"

16All your enemies open their mouths
to say things against you.
They make fun and grind their teeth
in anger.
They say, "We have swallowed her
up.
This is the day we were waiting for.
We have finally seen it happen."

17The Lord has done what he planned.
He has carried out the order
that he commanded long ago.
He has destroyed without mercy.
He has made your enemies happy
because of what happened to you.
He has strengthened your enemies.

18The people
cry out to the Lord.
Wall of Jerusalem,
let your tears flow
like a river day and night.
Do not stop.
Do not let your eyes rest.

19Get up, cry out in the night.
Cry all through the night.
Pour out your heart like water
in prayer to the Lord.
Lift up your hands in prayer to him.
Pray for the life of your children.

They are fainting with hunger
on every street corner.

20Jerusalem says: "Look, Lord, and see.
You have never done this to anyone
else.
Women eat their own babies,
the children they have cared for.
Priests and prophets
are killed in the Temple of the Lord.

21"Young men and old men
lie on the ground in the streets of
the city.
My young women and young men
have been killed by the sword.
You, Lord, killed them on the day of
your anger.
You killed them without mercy.

22"You invited terrors to come against
me on every side.
It was as if you were inviting them
to a feast.
No one escaped or remained alive
on the day of the Lord's anger.
My enemy has killed
those whom I gave birth to and
brought up."

THE MEANING OF SUFFERING

3 I am a man who has seen the
suffering
that comes from the rod of the
Lord's anger.
2He led me
into darkness, not light.
3He turned his hand against me
again and again, all day long.

4He caused my flesh and skin to wear
out.
He broke my bones.
5He surrounded me and attacked me
with sadness and grief.
6He made me sit in the dark,
like someone who has been dead a
long time.

7He shut me in so I could not get out.
He put heavy chains on me.

⁸I cry out and beg for help.
  But he ignores my prayer.
⁹He has blocked my way with stones.
  He has made my life difficult.

¹⁰The Lord is like a bear ready to attack
    me.
  He is like a lion in hiding.
¹¹He led me the wrong way and tore me
    to pieces.
  He left me without help.
¹²He prepared to shoot his bow.
  He made me the target for his
    arrows.

¹³He shot me in the kidneys
  with the arrows from his arrow bag.
¹⁴I have become a joke to all my people.
  All day long they make fun of me
    with songs.
¹⁵The Lord filled me with misery.
  He filled me with suffering.

¹⁶The Lord broke my teeth with gravel.
  He crushed me into the dirt.
¹⁷I have no more peace.
  I have forgotten what happiness is.
¹⁸I said, "My strength is gone.
  I have no more hope that the Lord
    will help me."

¹⁹Lord, remember my suffering and
    how I have no home.
  Remember the misery and
    suffering.
²⁰I remember them well.
  And I am very sad.
²¹But I have hope
  when I think of this:

²²The Lord's love never ends.
  His mercies never stop.
²³They are new every morning.
  Lord, your loyalty is great.
²⁴I say to myself, "The Lord is what I
    have left.
  So I have hope."

²⁵The Lord is good to those who put
    their hope in him.

He is good to those who look to him
    for help.
²⁶It is good to wait quietly
  for the Lord to save.
²⁷It is good for a man to work hard
  while he is young.

²⁸He should sit alone and be quiet
  because the Lord has given him
    hard work to do.
²⁹He should bow to the Lord with his
    face to the ground.
  Maybe there is still hope.
³⁰He should offer his cheek if someone
    wants to hit him.
  He should be filled with shame.

³¹The Lord will not reject
  his people forever.
³²Although the Lord brings sorrow, he
    also has mercy.
  His love is great.
³³The Lord does not like to punish
    people
  or make them sad.

³⁴The Lord sees if any prisoner of the
    earth
  is crushed under his feet.
³⁵He sees if someone is treated unfairly
  before the Most High God.
³⁶The Lord sees
  if someone is cheated in his case in
    court.

³⁷Nobody can speak and have it happen
  unless the Lord commands it.
³⁸Both bad and good things
  come by the command of the Most
    High God.
³⁹No man should complain
  when he is punished for his sins.

⁴⁰Let us examine and look at what we
    have done.
  Then let us return to the Lord.
⁴¹Let us lift up our hands and pray from
    our hearts.
  Let us say to God in heaven,

⁴²"We have sinned and turned against
you.
And you have not forgiven us.

⁴³"You wrapped yourself in anger and
chased us.
You killed us without mercy.
⁴⁴You wrapped yourself in a cloud.
No prayer could get through.
⁴⁵You made us like scum and trash
among the other nations.

⁴⁶"All of our enemies
open their mouths and say things
against us.
⁴⁷We have been frightened and fearful.
We have been ruined and
destroyed."
⁴⁸Streams of tears flow from my eyes
because my people are destroyed.

⁴⁹My tears flow continually,
without stopping,
⁵⁰until the Lord looks down
and sees from heaven.
⁵¹I am sad when I see
what has happened to all the
women of my city.

⁵²Those who are my enemies for no
reason
hunted me like a bird.
⁵³They threw me alive into a pit.
They threw stones at me.
⁵⁴Water came up over my head.
I said to myself, "I am going to die."
⁵⁵I called out to you, Lord,
from the bottom of the pit.
⁵⁶You heard me calling, "Do not close
your ears.
Do not ignore my cry for help."
⁵⁷You came close when I called out to
you.
You said, "Don't be afraid."

⁵⁸Lord, you have taken my case.
You have given me back my life.
⁵⁹Lord, you have seen how I have been
wronged.
Now judge my case for me.

⁶⁰You have seen how my enemies took
revenge on me.
You have seen all their evil plans
against me.

⁶¹Lord, you have heard their insults
and all their evil plans against me.
⁶²The words and thoughts of my
enemies
are against me all the time.
⁶³Look! In everything they do
they make fun of me with songs.

⁶⁴Punish them as they should be
punished, Lord.
Pay them back for what they have
done.
⁶⁵Make them stubborn.
Put your curse on them.
⁶⁶Chase them in anger.
Destroy them from the Lord's earth.

THE ATTACK ON JERUSALEM

4 See how the gold has lost its shine!
See how the good gold has changed!
The stones of the Temple^d are
scattered
at every street corner.

²The precious people of Jerusalem
were more valuable than gold.
But now they are thought of as clay
jars
made by the hands of a potter.

³Even wild dogs give their milk
to feed their young.
But my people are cruel
like ostriches in the desert.

⁴The baby is so thirsty
that his tongue sticks to the roof of
his mouth.
Children beg for bread.
But no one breaks off a piece to
share with them.

⁵Those who once ate fine foods
are now starving in the streets.
The people who grew up wearing nice
clothes
now pick through trash piles.

⁶My people have been punished
    more than Sodom was.
Sodom was destroyed suddenly.
    No hands reached out to help her.

⁷Our princes were purer than snow.
    They were whiter than milk.
Their bodies were redder than rubies.
    Their faces shined like sapphires.

⁸But now they are blacker than coal.
    No one even recognizes them in the
        streets.
Their skin is stretched over their
        bones.
    It is as dry as wood.

⁹Those people who were killed by the
        sword had it better
    than those killed by hunger.
They starved in pain and died
    because there was no food from the
        field.

¹⁰With their own hands kind women
        cooked their own children.
The children became food for their
        parents.
    This happened when my people
        were destroyed.

¹¹The Lord turned loose all of his anger.
    He poured out his strong anger.
He set fire to Jerusalem.
    It burned down to the foundations.

¹²Kings of the earth and people of the
        world
    could not believe it.
They could not believe that enemies
    could come through the gates of
        Jerusalem.

¹³But it happened because her
        prophets[d] had sinned.
    And her priests had done evil.
They killed in the city
    the people who did what was right.

¹⁴They wandered in the streets
    like blind men.
They became dirty with blood.
    So no one could touch their clothes.

¹⁵"Go away! You are unclean,"[d] people
        shouted at them.
    "Get away! Get away! Do not touch
        us!"
So they left and wandered around.
    The other nations said, "Don't stay
        here."

¹⁶The Lord himself scattered them.
    He did not look after them
        anymore.
He did not respect the priests.
    He showed no mercy to the elders.

¹⁷Also, our eyes grew tired
    looking for help that never came.
We kept watch from our towers
    for a nation to save us.

¹⁸Our enemies hunted us
    so we could not even walk in the
        streets.
Our end came near. Our time was up.
    Our end came.

¹⁹The men who chased us
    were faster than eagles in the sky.
They ran us into the mountains.
    They ambushed us in the desert.

²⁰The Lord's appointed king, who was
        our very breath,
    was caught in their traps.
We had said about him, "We will be
        protected by him
    among the nations."

²¹Be happy and glad, people of Edom,
    you who live in the land of Uz.
But the Lord's anger is like a cup of
    wine that you also will have to
        drink.
Then you will get drunk on it and
    make yourselves naked.

²²Your punishment is complete,
        Jerusalem.
    He will not keep you in captivity
        any longer.
But the Lord will punish your wrongs,
    people of Edom.
    He will uncover your sins.

A PRAYER TO THE LORD

5 Remember, Lord, what happened
to us.
Look and see our disgrace.
²Our land has been turned over to
strangers.
Our houses have been given to
foreigners.
³We have become orphans with no
father.
Our mothers have become like
widows.
⁴We have to buy the water we drink.
We must pay for the wood for our
fires.
⁵They work us hard as if we were
animals with a yoke*d* on our
necks.
We get tired and have no rest.
⁶We made an agreement with Egypt
and with Assyria to get enough
food.
⁷Our ancestors sinned against you. But
they are gone.
Now we must suffer because of
their sins.
⁸Slaves have become our rulers.
There is no one who can save us
from them.
⁹We risk our lives to get our food
because there are men with swords
in the desert.
¹⁰Our skin is hot like an oven.
We burn with fever because of the
terrible hunger.

¹¹The enemy attacked the women of
Jerusalem
and the girls in the cities of Judah.
¹²The enemy hung our princes by the
hands.
They do not honor our elders.
¹³The young men grind grain at the
mill.
Boys stumble while carrying loads
of wood.
¹⁴The elders no longer sit at the city
gates.
The young men no longer make
music.
¹⁵We have no more joy in our hearts.
Our dancing has turned into
sadness.
¹⁶The glory has gone from Jerusalem.
How terrible it is for us because we
have sinned.
¹⁷Because of this we are afraid.
Because of these things our eyes are
dim.
¹⁸Mount Zion*d* is empty.
Now wild dogs wander around it.

¹⁹But you rule forever, Lord.
You will be King from now on.
²⁰Why have you forgotten us for so long?
Why have you left us for so long?
²¹Bring us back to you, Lord. We will
return.
Make our days as they were before.
²²Or have you completely rejected us?
Will your anger never end?

EZEKIEL

EZEKIEL'S VISION OF LIVING THINGS

1 It was the thirtieth year, on the fifth day of the fourth month of our captivity. I, Ezekiel, was by the Kebar River in Babylon. I was among the people who had been carried away as captives from the land of Judah. The sky opened, and I saw visions of God.

²It was the fifth year that King Jehoiachin had been a prisoner. It was on the fifth day of the month. ³The Lord spoke his word to Ezekiel son of Buzi. This was in the land of the Babylonians by the Kebar River. There he felt the power of the Lord.

⁴When I looked, I saw a stormy wind coming from the north. There was a great cloud with a bright light around it. Fire was flashing out of it. And there was something that looked like glowing metal in the center of the fire. ⁵Inside the cloud were what looked like four living creatures. They were shaped like men. ⁶Each of them had four faces. And each of them had four wings. ⁷Their legs were straight. Their feet were like a calf's hoofs. And they sparkled like polished bronze. ⁸The living creatures had men's hands. They were under their wings on their four sides. All four of them had faces and wings. ⁹And their wings touched each other. The living creatures did not turn when they moved. Each went straight ahead.

¹⁰Their faces looked like this: In front each living creature had the face of a man. Each one had the face of a lion on the right side. Each one had the face of an ox on the left side. And in back each one had the face of an eagle. ¹¹This was what their faces looked like. Their wings were spread out above. Each had two wings that touched one of the other living creatures. Each living creature had two wings that covered its body. ¹²Each went straight ahead. Wherever the spirit would go, the living creatures would also go. When they went, they did not turn. ¹³The living creatures looked like burning coals of fire. They were like torches. Fire went back and forth among the living creatures. It was bright, and lightning flashed from it. ¹⁴The living creatures ran back and forth like bolts of lightning.

¹⁵Now I looked at the living creatures. And I saw a wheel on the ground by each of the living creatures with its four faces. ¹⁶The wheels and the way they were made were like this: They looked like sparkling chrysolite. All four of them looked the same. The wheels looked like one wheel crossways inside another wheel. ¹⁷When they moved, they went in any one of the four directions. They did not turn as they went. ¹⁸I saw the rims of the wheels. The rims were full of eyes all around.

¹⁹When the living creatures moved, the wheels moved beside them. When the living creatures were lifted up from the ground, the wheels also were lifted up. ²⁰Wherever the spirit would go, the living creatures would go. And the wheels were lifted up beside them. This is because the spirit of the living creatures was in the wheels. ²¹When the living creatures moved, the wheels moved. When the living creatures stopped, the wheels stopped. And when the living creatures were lifted from the ground, the wheels were lifted beside them. This is because the spirit of the living creatures was in the wheels.

²²Now there was something like a dome over the heads of the living creatures. It sparkled like ice and was frightening. ²³And under the dome the wings of the living creatures were stretched out straight toward one another. Each living creature also had two wings covering its body. ²⁴I heard the sound of their wings as they moved. It was like the roaring sound of the sea. It was like the voice of

God All-Powerful. It was a roaring sound like a noisy army. When the living creatures stood still, they lowered their wings. 25And a voice came from above the dome over the heads of the living creatures. When the living creatures stood still, they lowered their wings. 26Now above the dome there was something that looked like a throne. It looked like a sapphire gem. And on the throne was a shape like a man. 27Then I noticed what he looked like from the waist up. He looked like glowing metal with fire inside it. And from his waist down he looked like fire. I saw a bright light all around him. 28The glow around him looked like the rainbow in the clouds on a rainy day. It seemed to look like the glory of the Lord. So when I saw it, I bowed facedown on the ground. And I heard a voice speaking.

THE LORD SPEAKS TO EZEKIEL

2 He said to me, "Human being, stand up on your feet. Then I will speak with you." 2While he spoke to me, the Spirit*d* entered me and put me on my feet. Then I heard the Lord speaking to me.

3He said, "Human being, I am sending you to the people of Israel. They are a nation of people who turned against me. They broke away from me. They and their ancestors have sinned against me until this very day. 4And I am sending you to people who are stubborn. They do not obey. You will say this to them, 'This is what the Lord God says.' 5The people may listen, or they may not. They are a people who turn against me. But whatever they do, they will know that a prophet*d* has been among them. 6You, human being, don't be afraid of the people or their words. Thorny branches and thorns may be all around you. And you may live with insects that sting with poison. Don't be afraid of their words. Don't be afraid of their looks. They are a people who turn against me. 7But speak my words to them. They may listen, or they may not, because they turn against

me. 8But you, human being, listen to what I say to you. Don't turn against me as those people do. Open your mouth and eat what I am giving you."

9I looked and saw a hand stretched out to me. A scroll was in the hand. 10The Lord opened the scroll in front of me. The scroll was written on the front and back. Funeral songs, sad writings and troubles were written on the scroll.

3 Then the Lord said to me, "Human being, eat what you find. Eat this scroll. Then go and speak to the people of Israel." 2So I opened my mouth, and the Lord gave me the scroll.

3The Lord said to me, "Human being, eat this scroll which I am giving you. Fill your stomach with it." Then I ate it. And it was sweet like honey in my mouth.

4Then the Lord said to me, "Human being, go to the people of Israel. Speak my words to them. 5You are not being sent to people whose speech you can't understand. Their language is not difficult. You are being sent to Israel. 6You are not being sent to many nations whose speech you can't understand. The language of Israel is not difficult. You are not being sent to people whose words you cannot understand. If I had sent you to them, they would have listened to you. 7But the people of Israel are not willing to listen to you. This is because they are not willing to listen to me. Yes, all the people of Israel are stubborn and will not obey. 8See, I have made you as stubborn as they are. You will be as hard as they are. 9I have made you as hard as a diamond, harder than stone. Don't be afraid of them. Don't be frightened by them. They are a people who turn against me."

10Also, the Lord said to me, "Human being, believe all the words that I will speak to you. And listen carefully. 11Go to the captives, your people. And speak to them, whether they listen or not. Tell them, 'The Lord God says this.'"

¹²Then the Spirit lifted me up. And I heard a loud rumbling sound behind me. A voice said, "Praise God in heaven." ¹³I heard the wings of the living creatures touching each other. And I heard the sound of the wheels by them. It was a loud rumbling sound. ¹⁴So the Spirit lifted me up and took me away. I was unhappy and angry. I felt the great power of the Lord. ¹⁵I came to the captives from Judah. They lived by the Kebar River at Tel Abib. I sat there seven days where these people lived. I was shocked.

ISRAEL'S WARNING

¹⁶After seven days the Lord spoke his word to me again. He said, ¹⁷"Human being, I have made you a watchman for Israel. Any time you hear a word from my mouth, warn them for me. ¹⁸When I say to an evil person, 'You will surely die,' you must warn him. If you don't speak out to warn the evil person to leave his evil way, he will die in his sin. But I will hold you responsible for his death. ¹⁹You must warn the evil person. Then if he does not turn from his wickedness or his evil ways, he will die because of his sin. But you will have saved yourself.

²⁰"Again, a person who does right may turn away from his goodness. He may do evil. If I caused him to sin, he will die. Because you have not warned him, he will die because of his sin. And the good he did will not be remembered. But I will hold you responsible for his death. ²¹But if you do warn that good person not to sin, he may not sin. Then he will surely live. This is because he was warned. And you will save yourself."

²²Then I felt the power of the Lord there. He said to me, "Get up and go out to the plain. There I will speak to you." ²³So I got up and went out to the plain. I saw the glory of the Lord standing there. It was like the glory I saw by the Kebar River. And I bowed facedown on the ground.

²⁴Then the Spirit*ᵈ* entered me and made me stand on my feet. He spoke to me and said, "Go, shut yourself up in your house. ²⁵As for you, human being, the people will tie you up with ropes. They will tie you up, and you will not be able to go out among them. ²⁶Also, I will make your tongue stick to the roof of your mouth. Then you will be silent. And you will not be able to argue with the people, even though they turn against me. ²⁷But when I speak to you, I will open your mouth. And you will say, 'The Lord God says this.' Whoever will listen, let him listen. Whoever refuses, let him refuse. They are a people who turn against me.

THE MAP OF JERUSALEM

4 "Now, human being, get yourself a brick. Put it in front of you and draw a map of Jerusalem on it. ²Then surround it with an army. Build battle works against the city. Build a road of earth to the top of the city walls. Set up camps around it. Put heavy logs in place to break down the walls. ³Then get yourself an iron plate. Put it up like an iron wall between you and the city. Turn your face toward the city as if to attack it. Then surround it and attack it. This is a sign to Israel.

⁴"Then lie down on your left side. Take the guilt of Israel on yourself. Their guilt will be on you for the number of days you lie on your left side. ⁵I have given you the same number of days as the years of the people's sin. So you will have the guilt of Israel's sin on you for 390 days.

⁶"When you have finished these 390 days, lie down a second time. This time lie on your right side. You will then have the guilt of Judah on you. I have given it to you for 40 days. This is a day for each year of their sin. ⁷Then you will turn your face toward the army attacking Jerusalem. With your arm bare, you will prophesy*ᵈ* against Jerusalem. ⁸I will put ropes on you so you cannot turn from one side to the other. This will last until you have finished the days of your attack on Jerusalem.

⁹"Take wheat, barley, beans, small peas and millet seeds. And put them in one bowl. Make them into bread for yourself. You will eat it the 390 days you lie on your side. ¹⁰You will eat eight ounces of food every day. You will eat it at set times. ¹¹You will drink about two-thirds of a quart of water every day. Drink it at set times. ¹²Eat your food as you would eat a barley cake. Bake it over human dung where the people can see." ¹³Then the Lord said, "In the same way Israel will eat unclean*d* food. They will eat it among the nations where I force them to go."

¹⁴But I said, "No, Lord God! I have never been made unclean. From the time I was young until now I've never eaten anything that died by itself. And I've never eaten anything torn by animals. Unclean meat has never entered my mouth."

¹⁵"Very well," he said. "Then I will give you cow's dung instead of human dung. You may use it for your fire to bake your bread."

¹⁶Then the Lord said to me, "Human being, look! I am going to cut off the supply of bread to Jerusalem. They will eat the bread that is measured out to them. And they will worry as they eat it. They will drink water that is measured out to them. And they will be in shock as they drink it. ¹⁷This is because bread and water will be hard to find. And the people will be shocked at the sight of each other. They will become weak because of their sin.

EZEKIEL CUTS HIS HAIR

5 "Now, human being, take a sharp sword. Use it like a barber's razor to shave your head and beard. Then take scales and weigh and divide the hair. ²Burn one-third with fire when the days of the attack on Jerusalem are over. Burn it in the middle of the city. Then take one-third and cut it up with the knife all around the city. And scatter one-third to the wind. This is how I will chase them with a sword. ³Also take a few of these hairs and tie them in the folds of your clothes. ⁴Take a few more and throw them into the fire and burn them up. From there a fire will spread to all the people of Israel.

⁵"This is what the Lord says: This is Jerusalem. I have put her at the center of the nations with countries all around her. ⁶But she has refused to obey my laws. She has been more evil than the nations. She has refused to obey my rules even more than those around her. The people of Jerusalem have rejected my laws and have not lived by my rules.

⁷"So this is what the Lord God says: You caused more confusion than the nations around you. You did not follow my rules or obey my laws. You have not even obeyed the laws of the nations around you.

⁸"So this is what the Lord God says: I myself am against you. I will punish you and the nations will watch. ⁹I will do things among you that I have not done before. I will never do anything like them again. I will do them because you do the things I hate. ¹⁰So fathers among you will eat their children. And children will eat their fathers. I will punish you. I will scatter to the winds all who are left alive. ¹¹So the Lord God says: As surely as I live, you have made my Temple*d* unclean.*d* You have done it with all your evil idols and the hated things you do. Because of this I will cut you off. I will have no pity. I will show no mercy. ¹²A third of you will die by disease or be destroyed by hunger inside your walls. A third will fall dead by the sword outside your walls. And a third I will scatter in every direction. I will chase them with a sword. ¹³Then my anger will come to an end. I will use it up against them. Then I will be satisfied. Then they will know that I, the Lord God, have spoken. After I have carried out my anger against them, they will know how strongly I felt.

14"I will make you a ruin. And I will make you a shame among the nations around you. All who pass by will see this. 15Then you will be shamed by the nations around you. They will make fun of you. You will be a warning to them. They will be terrified. This will happen when I punish you in my great anger. I, the Lord, have spoken. 16I will send a time of hunger to destroy you. Then I will make your hunger get even worse. I will cut off your supply of food. 17I will send a time of hunger and wild animals against you. They will kill your children. Disease and death will sweep through your people. I will bring the sword against you to kill you. I, the Lord, have spoken."

PROPHECIES AGAINST THE MOUNTAINS

6 Again the Lord spoke his word to me. The Lord said, 2"Human being, look toward the mountains of Israel. Prophesy*d* against them. 3Say, 'Mountains of Israel, listen to the word of the Lord God. The Lord God says this to the mountains, the hills, the ravines and the valleys: I will bring a sword against you. I will destroy your places of idol worship. 4Your altars will be destroyed. Your incense*d* altars will be broken down. Your people will be killed in front of your idols. 5I will lay the dead bodies of the Israelites before their idols. And I will scatter your bones around your altars. 6In all the places you live, cities will become empty. And the places of idol worship will be ruined. Your altars will become lonely ruins. Your idols will be broken and brought to an end. Your incense altars will be cut down. And the things you made will be wiped out. 7Your people will be killed and fall among you. Then you will know that I am the Lord God.

8"'But I will leave some people alive. Some will not be killed by the nations when you are scattered among the foreign lands. 9Then those who have escaped will remember me. They will be living among the nations where they have been taken as captives. They will remember how I was hurt because they were unfaithful to me. They had turned away from me. They will remember how I was hurt because they desired to worship their idols. They will hate themselves because of the evil things they did that I hate. 10Then they will know that I am the Lord. I did not bring this terrible thing on them for no reason.

11"'This is what the Lord God says: Clap your hands, stamp your feet. Say, "Oh!" because the people of Israel have done terrible things. So they will die by war, hunger and disease. 12The person who is far away will die by disease. The one who is nearby will die in war. The person who is still alive and has escaped these will die from hunger. So I will carry out my anger on them. 13Their people will lie dead among their idols around the altars. They will be on every high hill, on all the mountain tops and under every green tree and leafy oak. These are the places where they offered sweet-smelling incense to their idols. Then you will know that I am the Lord. 14I will use my power against them. I will make the land empty and wasted from the desert to Diblah, wherever they live. Then they will know that I am the Lord.'"

EZEKIEL TELLS OF THE END

7 Again the Lord spoke his word to me. He said: 2"Human being, the Lord says this to the land of Israel: An end! The end has come on the four corners of the land. 3Now the end has come for you. I will send my anger against you. I will judge you for the way you have lived. I will make you pay for your terrible actions. 4I will have no pity on you. I will not hold back punishment from you. I will make you pay for your ways and for your terrible actions. Then you will know that I am the Lord.

5"This is what the Lord God says: Disaster on top of disaster is coming.

⁶The end has come! The end has come! It has stirred itself up against you! Look! It has come! ⁷The end has come for you who live in the land! The time has come. The day of confusion is near. There will be no happy shouting on the mountains. ⁸Soon I will pour out my anger against you. I will carry out my anger against you. I will judge you for the way you have lived. I will make you pay for all the things you have done that I hate. ⁹I will show no pity. I will not hold back punishment. I will pay you back for the way you have lived and the terrible things you have done. Then you will know that I am the Lord who punishes.

¹⁰"Look, the day is here. It has come. Destruction has come. Violence has grown. There is more pride than ever. ¹¹Violence has grown into a weapon for punishing wickedness. None of the people will be left. None of that crowd, none of their wealth, and nothing of value will be left among them. ¹²The time has come. The day has arrived. Don't let the buyer be happy or the seller be sad. My burning anger is against the whole crowd. ¹³Sellers will not return to the land they have sold as long as they live. This is because the vision against all that crowd will not be changed. Because of their sins, no one will save his life. ¹⁴They have blown the trumpet, and everything is ready. But no one is going to the battle. My anger is against all that crowd.

¹⁵"The sword is outside. Disease and hunger are inside. The person who is in the field will die by the sword. Hunger and disease will destroy those in the city. ¹⁶Those who are left alive and who escape will be on the mountains. They will moan like doves of the valleys. Each person will groan about his own sin. ¹⁷All hands will hang weakly. All knees will become as weak as water. ¹⁸They will put on rough cloth to show how sad they are. They will tremble all over with fear. Their faces will show their shame.

And all their heads will be shaved. ¹⁹The people will throw their silver into the streets. Their gold will be like trash. Their silver and gold will not save them from the Lord's anger. It will not satisfy their hunger or fill their stomachs. It was what caused them to fall into sin. ²⁰They were proud of their beautiful jewelry. They used it to make their idols, which I hate, and their evil statues. So I will turn their wealth into something they hate. ²¹And I will give it to the foreigners as treasures from war. I will give it to the evil people of the earth as treasure. These foreigners and evil people will dishonor the people's jewelry. ²²I will also turn away from the people of Israel. They will dishonor my treasured place. Then robbers will enter and dishonor it.

²³"Make chains for captives. The land is full of bloody crimes. And the city is full of violence. ²⁴So I will bring the worst of the nations to take over the people's houses. I will also end the pride of the rich. And their holy places will be dishonored. ²⁵When the people are suffering greatly, they will look for peace. But there will be none. ²⁶Disaster will come on top of disaster. Rumor will be added to rumor. Then they will try to get a vision from a prophet.ᵈ Even the teachings of God from the priest will be lost. And advice from the elders will also be lost. ²⁷The king will cry greatly. The prince will give up hope. The hands of the people who owned land will shake with fear. I will punish them for the way they have lived. The way they have judged others is the way I will judge them. Then they will know that I am the Lord."

EZEKIEL'S VISION OF JERUSALEM

8 It was the sixth year, on the fifth day of the sixth month of our captivity. I was sitting in my house with the elders of Judah before me. There I felt the power of the Lord God. ²I looked and saw something that looked like a man. From his waist down he looked like fire.

From his waist up he looked like bright glowing metal. ³He stretched out the shape of a hand. And he caught me by the hair on my head. The Spirit*d* lifted me up between the earth and the sky. He took me in the visions of God to Jerusalem. He took me to the entrance to the north gate of the inner courtyard of the Temple.*d* The courtyard was where the idol was that caused God to be jealous. ⁴The glory of the God of Israel was there. It was like what I had seen on the plain.

⁵Then God said to me, "Human being, now look toward the north." So I looked up toward the north. I saw an altar to the north of the gate. The idol that caused God to be jealous was in the entrance.

⁶The Lord said to me, "Human being, do you see what they are doing? Do you see how many hated things the people of Israel are doing here? This will drive me far away from my Temple. But you will see things more hated than these."

⁷Then the Lord brought me to the entry of the courtyard. When I looked, I saw a hole in the wall. ⁸The Lord said to me, "Human being, dig through the wall." So I dug through the wall and saw an entrance.

⁹Then the Lord said to me, "Go in and see the terrible, evil things they are doing here." ¹⁰So I entered and looked. And I saw pictures of every kind of crawling thing. I saw awful beasts and all the idols of the people of Israel. They were carved on the wall all around. ¹¹Seventy of the elders of Israel were standing there. They were in front of these carvings and idols. Jaazaniah son of Shaphan stood with them. Each man had his pan for burning incense*d* in his hand. A sweet-smelling cloud of incense was rising.

¹²Then the Lord said to me, "Human being, have you seen what the elders of Israel are doing in the dark? Have you

seen each man in the room of his own idol? They say, 'The Lord doesn't see us. The Lord has left the land.'" ¹³And he said to me, "You will see even more terrible things that they are doing."

¹⁴Then the Lord brought me to the opening of the north gate of the Temple. And I saw women sitting there crying for Tammuz.*n* ¹⁵The Lord said to me, "Do you see, human being? You will see things even more terrible than these."

¹⁶Then the Lord brought me into the inner courtyard of the Temple. And I saw about 25 men. They were at the entrance to the Temple, between the porch and the altar. Their backs were turned to the Temple of the Lord. They faced east. They were worshiping the sun in the east.

¹⁷The Lord said to me, "Do you see, human being? Is it unimportant that the people of Judah are doing the terrible things they have done here? They have filled the land with violence. They continually make me angry. Look, they are insulting me every way they can. ¹⁸So I will act in anger. I will have no pity. I will not show mercy. Even if they shout in my ears, I won't listen to them."

VISION OF THE ANGELS

9 The Lord shouted with a loud voice in my ears. He said, "You who are chosen to punish this city, come near. Bring your weapon in your hand." ²Then six men came from the direction of the upper gate, which faces north. Each had his powerful weapon in his hand. Among them was a man dressed in linen. At his side he had things to write with. The men went in and stood by the bronze altar.

³Then the glory of the God of Israel went up. It had been above the creatures with wings. It moved to the place in the Temple*d* where the door opened. Then the Lord called the man dressed in linen. He had the things to write with at his

---

8:14 Tammuz Tammuz was a false god in Babylon. Every year people thought this god died when the plants died. After they cried for him, they believed he came back to life and the plants lived again.

side. [4]The Lord said to him, "Go through Jerusalem. Put a mark on the foreheads of the people who groan and cry about all the terrible things being done among them."

[5]As I listened, the Lord spoke to the other men. He said, "Go through the city behind the man dressed in linen and kill. Don't pity anyone. Don't show mercy. [6]Kill and destroy old men, young men and women, little children and older women. But don't touch anyone who has the mark on him. Start at my Temple." So they started with the elders who were in front of the Temple.

[7]And the Lord said to the men, "Make the Temple unclean.[d] Fill the courtyards with those who have been killed. Go out!" Then the men went out and killed the people in the city. [8]While the men were killing the people, I was left alone. I bowed facedown on the ground. I cried out, "Oh, Lord God! Will you destroy everyone left alive in Israel when you turn loose your anger on Jerusalem?"

[9]Then the Lord said to me, "The sin of the people of Israel and Judah is very great. The land is filled with people who murder. And the city is full of people who are not fair. The people say, 'The Lord has left the land. And the Lord does not see.' [10]But I will have no pity. I will show no mercy. But I will bring their evil acts back on their heads."

[11]Then the man dressed in linen reported to the Lord. He was the man who had things to write with at his side. He said, "I have done just as you have commanded me."

THE COALS OF FIRE

10 Then I looked and saw the sky above the heads of the living creatures. I saw something like a sapphire gem. It looked like a throne. [2]The Lord said to the man dressed in linen, "Go in between the wheels under the living creatures. And fill your hands with coals of fire from between the living creatures. Scatter the coals over the city."

As I watched, the man with linen clothes went in. [3]Now the living creatures were standing on the south side of the Temple[d] when the man went in. And the cloud from the Lord filled the inner courtyard. [4]Then the glory of the Lord went up from the living creatures. And it stood over the door of the Temple. The Temple was filled with the cloud. And the courtyard was full of the brightness from the glory of the Lord. [5]The sound of the wings of the living creatures was heard all the way to the outer courtyard. It was like the voice of God All-Powerful when he speaks.

[6]The Lord commanded the man dressed in linen, "Take fire from between the wheels, from between the living creatures." Then the man went in and stood by a wheel. [7]One living creature put out his hand to the fire that was among them. The living creature took some of the fire. And he put it in the hands of the man dressed in linen. The man took the fire and went out.

THE WHEELS AND THE CREATURES

[8]Something that looked like a man's hand appeared under the wings of the living creatures. [9]I saw the four wheels by the living creatures. One wheel was by each living creature. The wheels looked like shining chrysolite. [10]All four wheels looked alike. Each looked like a wheel crossways inside another wheel. [11]When the wheels moved, they went in any of the directions that the four living creatures faced. The wheels did not turn about. The living creatures did not turn their bodies as they went. But they followed wherever their faces pointed. [12]All their bodies, their backs, hands, wings and the wheels were full of eyes all over. Now each of the four living creatures had a wheel. [13]I heard the wheels being called "whirling wheels." [14]Each living creature had four faces. The first face was the face of a creature with wings. The second face was the face of a man.

The third was the face of a lion. And the fourth was the face of an eagle.

¹⁵The living creatures flew up. They were the same living creatures I had seen by the Kebar River. ¹⁶And when the living creatures moved, the wheels moved by their sides. The living creatures lifted their wings to fly up from the ground. And the wheels did not leave their sides. ¹⁷When the living creatures stopped, the wheels stopped. When the creatures went up, the wheels went up also. This was because the spirit of the living creatures was in the wheels.

¹⁸Then the glory of the Lord left the door of the Temple*d* and stood over the living creatures. ¹⁹The living creatures spread their wings. And they flew up from the ground while I watched. As they went up, the wheels stayed by their sides. They stood where the east gate of the Temple of the Lord opened. The glory of the God of Israel was over them.

²⁰These are the living creatures I had seen under the God of Israel. This was by the Kebar River. I knew they were called cherubim. ²¹Each one had four faces. Each one had four wings. Things that looked like a man's hands were under their wings. ²²Their faces looked the same as the ones I had seen by the Kebar River. They each went straight ahead.

PROPHECIES AGAINST EVIL LEADERS

11 The Spirit*d* lifted me up. And he brought me to the front gate of the Temple*d* of the Lord. This gate faces east. I saw 25 men where the gate opens. I saw Jaazaniah son of Azzur and Pelatiah son of Benaiah. They were leaders of the people. They were among these 25 men. ²Then the Lord said to me, "Human being, these are the men who plan evil. And they give wicked advice in this city of Jerusalem. ³They say, 'It is almost time for us to build houses. This city is like a cooking pot. And we are like the best meat.' ⁴So prophesy*d* against them. Prophesy, human being."

⁵Then the Spirit of the Lord entered me. He told me to say: "This is what the Lord says: You have said these things, people of Israel. But I know what is going through your mind. ⁶You have killed many people in this city. You have filled its streets with their bodies.

⁷"So this is what the Lord God says: Those people you have killed and left in the middle of the city are like the best meat. And this city is like the cooking pot. But I will force you out of the city. ⁸You have feared the sword. But I will bring a sword against you, says the Lord God. ⁹I will force you out of the city. I will hand you over to strangers. I will surely punish you. ¹⁰You will die by the sword. I will punish you at the border of Israel. Then you will know that I am the Lord. ¹¹This city will not be your cooking pot. You will not be the best meat in the middle of the city. I will punish you at the border of Israel. ¹²Then you will know that I am the Lord. You did not live by my rules. You did not obey my laws. You did the same things that the nations around you do."

¹³As I prophesied, Pelatiah son of Benaiah died. Then I bowed facedown on the ground. I shouted with a loud voice and said, "Oh no, Lord God! Will you completely destroy the Israelites who are left alive?"

PROMISE TO THOSE REMAINING

¹⁴The Lord spoke his word to me. He said, ¹⁵"Human being, the people still in Jerusalem have spoken about your relatives. And they have spoken about all the people of Israel who are captives with you. The people still in Jerusalem have said, 'They are far from the Lord. This land was given to us as our property.'

¹⁶"So say, 'This is what the Lord God says: I sent the people far away among the nations. I scattered them among the countries. But for a little while I have become a Temple*d* to them in the countries where they have gone.'

¹⁷"So say: 'This is what the Lord God says: I will gather you from the nations. And I will bring you together from the countries where you have been scattered. Then I will give you back the land of Israel.'

¹⁸"They will come to this land. Then they will take away all the hated idols from the land. They will take all the terrible images from there. ¹⁹I will give them a desire to respect me completely. I will put a new way to think inside them. I will take out the stubborn heart like stone from their bodies. Then I will give them an obedient heart of flesh. ²⁰Then they will live by my rules. They will obey my laws and keep them. They will be my people, and I will be their God. ²¹But some people will want to serve their evil statues and hated idols. And I will pay them back for their evil ways, says the Lord God."

EZEKIEL'S VISION ENDS

²²Then the living creatures lifted their wings. The wheels went beside them. And the glory of the God of Israel was above them. ²³The glory of the Lord went up from inside Jerusalem. And it stopped on the mountain on the east side of the city. ²⁴The Spirit^d lifted me up. And he brought me to the captives who had been taken from Judah to Babylonia. He did this in a vision given by the Spirit of God. Then the vision I had seen ended. ²⁵And I told the things that the Lord had shown me. I told it to the captives from Judah.

EZEKIEL MOVES OUT

12 Again the Lord spoke his word to me. He said: ²"Human being, you are living among a people who refuse to obey. They have eyes to see, but they do not see. They have ears to hear, but they do not hear. This is because they are a family that refuses to obey.

³"So, human being, pack your things as if you will be taken away captive. And walk away like a captive. Do this in the daytime with the people watching. Move from your place to another with the people watching. Maybe they will understand, even though they are a people who refuse to obey. ⁴Bring out the things you would pack as a captive. Do it during the day when the people are watching. At evening go out with the people watching. Go like those who are taken away as captives from their country. ⁵Dig a hole through the wall while they watch. Bring your things out through the hole. ⁶Lift them onto your shoulders with the people watching. Carry them out in the dark. Cover your face so you cannot see the ground. I have made you a sign to the people of Israel."

⁷I did these things as I was commanded. In the daytime I brought out my things. I was packed, ready to go away as a captive. Then in the evening I dug through the wall with my hands. I brought my things out in the dark. I carried them on my shoulders. And the people saw all this.

⁸Then in the morning the Lord spoke his word to me. He said: ⁹"Human being, Israel refuses to obey. Didn't those people ask you, 'What are you doing?'

¹⁰"Say to them, 'This is what the Lord God says: This message is about the king in Jerusalem. And it is about all the people of Israel who live there.' ¹¹Say, 'I am a sign to you.'

"The same things I have done will be done to the people in Jerusalem. They will be taken away from their country as captives. ¹²The king among them will put his things on his shoulder in the dark. And he will leave. The people will dig a hole through the wall to bring him out. He will cover his face so he cannot see the ground. ¹³But I will spread my net over him. He will be caught in my trap. Then I will bring him to Babylon in the land of the Babylonians. He will not see that land, but he will die there. ¹⁴All who are around the king I will scatter in every direction. I will scatter his helpers and all his army. I will chase them with a sword.

¹⁵"Then they will know that I am the Lord. I will scatter them among the nations. And I will spread them among the countries. ¹⁶But I will save a few of them from the sword. I will save a few from hunger and disease. Then they can tell about their hated actions among the nations where they go. Then they will know that I am the Lord."

THE LESSON OF EZEKIEL'S SHAKING

¹⁷The Lord spoke his word to me. He said: ¹⁸"Human being, shake as you eat your food. Shake with fear as you drink your water. ¹⁹Then say to the people of the land: 'This is what the Lord God says about the people who live in Jerusalem in the land of Israel: They will eat their food with fear. And they will drink their water in shock. This is because their land will be made empty. This is because of the violence of the people who live in it. ²⁰And the cities where people live will become ruins. The land will become empty. Then you will know that I am the Lord.'"

THE VISIONS WILL COME TRUE

²¹The Lord spoke his word to me. He said: ²²"Human being, what is this saying you have in the land of Israel: 'The days go by and every vision comes to nothing'? ²³So say to them, 'This is what the Lord God says: I will make them stop saying this. Then nobody in Israel will use it anymore.' But tell them, 'The time is near when every vision will come true. ²⁴There will be no more false visions or pleasing prophecies*d* inside the nation of Israel. ²⁵This is because I, the Lord God, will speak. What I say will be done. It will not be delayed. You are a people who refuse to obey. And in your time I will say the word and do it, says the Lord God.'"

²⁶The Lord spoke his word to me. He said: ²⁷"Human being, look! The people of Israel are saying this: 'The vision that Ezekiel sees is for a time many years

from now. He is prophesying about times far away.'

²⁸"So say to them: 'The Lord God says this: None of my words will be delayed anymore. What I have said will be done, says the Lord God.'"

EZEKIEL SPEAKS AGAINST FALSE PROPHETS

13 The Lord spoke his word to me. He said: ²"Human being, prophesy*d* against the prophets of Israel. Say to those who make up their own prophecies: 'Listen to the word of the Lord. ³This is what the Lord God says: How terrible it will be for the foolish prophets. They are the ones who follow their own ideas. And they have not seen a vision from me. ⁴People of Israel, your prophets have been like wild dogs hunting to kill and eat among ruins. ⁵Israel is like a house in ruins. But you have not gone up into the broken places. Your prophets have not repaired the wall. So how can Israel hold back the enemy in the battle on the Lord's day of judging? ⁶Your prophets see false visions. They prophesy lies. They say, "This is the message of the Lord." The Lord has not sent them. But they still hope their words will come true. ⁷You said, "This is the message of the Lord." But that is a false vision. Your prophecies are lies because I have not spoken.

⁸"'So this is what the Lord God says: You prophets spoke things that are false. You saw visions that do not come true. That is why I am against you, says the Lord God. ⁹So I will punish the prophets who see false visions and prophesy lies. They will have no place among my people. Their names will not be written on the list of the people of Israel. They will not enter the land of Israel. Then you will know that I am the Lord God.

¹⁰"'It is because they led my people away. They said, "Peace!" but there is no peace. When the people build a weak wall, the prophets cover it with whitewash to

make it look strong. [11]So tell those who cover a weak wall with whitewash that it will fall down. Rain will pour down. Hailstones will fall. And a stormy wind will break the wall down. [12]When the wall has fallen, people will ask you, "Where is the whitewash you used on the wall?"

[13]"'So this is what the Lord God says: I will break the wall with a stormy wind. In my anger rain will pour down. And hailstones will destroy the wall. [14]I will tear down the wall on which you put whitewash. I will level it to the ground. Then people will see the wall's foundation. And when the wall falls, you will be destroyed under it. Then you will know that I am the Lord. [15]So I will carry out my anger on the wall and against those who covered it with whitewash. Then I will tell you, "The wall is gone. And those who covered it with whitewash are also gone. [16]The prophets of Israel who prophesy to Jerusalem will be gone. And those who see visions of peace for Jerusalem will be gone also. There will be no peace, says the Lord God."'

FALSE WOMEN PROPHETS

[17]"Now, human being, reject the women among your people who make up their own prophecies.[d] Prophesy against them. [18]Say, 'This is what the Lord God says: How terrible it will be for women who sew magic charms on their wrists. How terrible it will be for those who make veils of every length. These women do this to trap people. You ruin the lives of my people but try to save your own lives! [19]And you have dishonored me among my people. You have done it for handfuls of barley and pieces of bread. You have killed people who should not die. And you have kept alive those who should die. You have done this by lying to my people. And my people are willing to listen to lies.

[20]"'So this is what the Lord God says: I am against your magic charms. You use them to trap people as if they were birds.

I will tear these charms off your arms. I will free those people you have trapped like birds. [21]I will also tear off your veils. I will save my people from your hands. They will no longer be in your power. You will not trap them. Then you will know that I am the Lord. [22]By your lies you caused the heart of the person who did right to be sad. I did not make him sad. You have encouraged the evil person not to stop being evil. And that would have saved his life. [23]So you will not see any more false visions. You will not prophesy anymore. And I will save my people from your power. Then you will know that I am the Lord.'"

STOP WORSHIPING IDOLS

14 Some of the elders of Israel came to me and sat down before me. [2]Then the Lord spoke his word to me. He said: [3]"Human being, these men love to worship idols. They put up evil things that cause people to sin. Should I allow them to ask me for help? [4]So speak to them. Tell them, 'This is what the Lord God says: Any person in Israel might want to worship idols. He might even put up evil things that cause people to sin. Then he might come to the prophet.[d] When he does, I, the Lord, will answer him. I will put him to death because he worshiped idols. [5]Then I will win back my people Israel. They have left me because of all their idols.'

[6]"So say this to the people of Israel: 'This is what the Lord God says: Change your hearts and lives. Stop worshiping idols. Stop doing all the things I hate. [7]Any Israelite or any foreigner in Israel can separate himself from me. He can do this by wanting to worship idols. Or he can put up the things that cause people to sin. Then if he comes to the prophet to ask me questions, I, the Lord, will answer him myself. [8]I will reject him. I will make him a sign and an example. I will separate him from my people. Then you will know that I am the Lord.

⁹"'But the prophet may be tricked into giving a prophecy. Then it is because I, the Lord, have tricked that prophet to speak. Then I will use my power against him. I will destroy him from among my people Israel. ¹⁰The prophet will be as guilty as the one who asks him for help. They both will be responsible for their guilt. ¹¹Then the nation of Israel will not leave me anymore. And they will not make themselves unclean*d* anymore with all their sins. Then they will be my people. And I will be their God, says the Lord God.'"

JERUSALEM WILL NOT BE SPARED

¹²The Lord spoke his word to me. He said: ¹³"Human being, sometimes the people of a country will sin against me by not being loyal. When that happens, I will use my power against them. I will cut off their supply of food. I will send them a time of hunger. I will destroy both their people and animals. ¹⁴Three great men like Noah, Daniel and Job might be in that country. But their goodness could save only themselves, says the Lord God.

¹⁵"I might even send wild animals into that land. They would leave the land empty and without children. Then no one would pass through it because of the animals. ¹⁶As surely as I live, says the Lord God, not even Noah, Daniel and Job could help. Even if they were in the land, they could not save their own sons or daughters. They could only save themselves. And that country would remain empty.

¹⁷"Or, I might bring a war against that country. I might say, 'Let a war be fought in that land. Let it destroy its men and animals.' ¹⁸As surely as I live, says the Lord God, not even these three men could help. Even if they were in the land, they could not save their sons or daughters. They could only save themselves.

¹⁹"Or, I might cause a disease to spread in that country. I might pour out my anger against that country, destroying and killing people and animals. ²⁰As surely as I live, says the Lord God, not even Noah, Daniel and Job could help. Even if they were in the land, they could not save their son or daughter. They could save only themselves because they did what was right.

²¹"This is what the Lord God says: I will send my four terrible punishments against Jerusalem. They are war, hunger, wild animals and disease. They will destroy people and animals from Jerusalem. ²²But some people will escape. Some sons and daughters will be led out. They will come out to you. You will see how they live. Then you will be comforted after the disasters I have brought against Jerusalem. You will be comforted after all the things I will bring against it. ²³You will be comforted when you see how they live. You will know there was a good reason for what I did to Jerusalem, says the Lord God."

STORY OF THE VINE

15 The Lord spoke his word to me. He said: ²"Human being, what good is the wood of the vine? Is it better than the wood of a tree in the forest? ³Can wood be taken from the vine to make anything? Can you use it to make a peg on which to hang something? ⁴The vine is thrown into the fire for fuel. The fire burns up both ends and starts to burn the middle. Then is it useful for anything? ⁵When the vine was whole, it couldn't be made into anything. When the fire has burned it completely, it certainly cannot be made into anything."

⁶So this is what the Lord God says: "Out of all the trees in the forest, I gave the wood of the vine as fuel for fire. In the same way I have given up the people who live in Jerusalem. ⁷I will turn against them. They came through one fire. But fire will still destroy them. When I turn against them, you will know that I am the Lord. ⁸So I will make the land empty.

This is because the people have not been loyal, says the Lord God."

THE LORD'S KINDNESS TO JERUSALEM

16 The Lord spoke his word to me. He said: [2]"Human being, tell Jerusalem about her hated actions. [3]Say, 'This is what the Lord God says to Jerusalem: Your beginnings and your ancestors were in the land of the Canaanites. Your father was an Amorite. And your mother was a Hittite. [4]On the day you were born, your cord[n] was not cut. You were not washed with water for cleansing. You were not rubbed with salt. You were not wrapped in cloths. [5]No one felt sorry for you. No one would do any of these things for you. No, you were thrown out into the open field. This is because you were hated on the day you were born.

[6]"Then I passed by and saw you kicking about in your blood. I said to you, "Live!" [7]I made you grow like a plant in the field. You grew up and became tall. You grew up and became like a beautiful jewel. Your breasts formed. Your hair grew. But you were naked and without clothes.

[8]"Later I passed by you and looked at you. I saw that you were at the time for love. So I spread my robe over you and covered your nakedness. I also made a marriage promise to you. I entered into an agreement with you. Then you became mine, says the Lord God.

[9]"Then I bathed you with water and washed all the blood off of you. I put oil on you. [10]I put beautiful clothes made with needlework on you. I put sandals of fine leather on your feet. I wrapped you in fine linen and covered you with silk. [11]I put jewelry on you. I put bracelets on your arms and a necklace around your neck. [12]I also put a ring in your nose and earrings in your ears. And I put a beautiful crown on your head. [13]So you wore gold and silver. Your dress was made of fine linen, silk and beautiful needlework.

You ate fine flour, honey and olive oil. You were very beautiful and became a queen. [14]Then you became famous among the nations because you were so beautiful. Your beauty was perfect, because of the glory I gave you, says the Lord God.

JERUSALEM BECOMES A PROSTITUTE

[15]"But you trusted in your beauty. You became a prostitute[d] because you were so famous. You had sexual relations with anyone who passed by. [16]And you took some of your clothes and made your places of worship colorful. This is where you carried on your prostitution. These things should not have happened. They should never happen again. [17]You also took your beautiful jewelry. It was made from gold and silver I had given you. Then you made for yourselves male idols. And you were a prostitute with them. [18]Then you took your clothes with beautiful needlework and covered the idols. You gave my oil and incense[d] as an offering to them. [19]Also, you took the bread I gave you. You took the fine flour, oil and honey I gave you to eat. And you offered them before the false gods as a pleasing smell. This is what happened, says the Lord God.

[20]"Also, you took your sons and daughters who were my children. And you sacrificed them to idols as food. Your sexual sins were not enough for you. [21]You killed my children and offered them up in fire to idols. [22]You did all your hated acts and sexual sins. But you did not remember when you were young. At that time you were naked and had no clothes. You were left in your blood.

[23]"How terrible! How terrible it will be for you, says the Lord God. This is what you did after all these evil things. [24]You built yourself a place to worship false gods. You made for yourself a place of worship in every city square. [25]You built a place of worship at the head of

---

16:4 cord The umbilical cord that gives the unborn baby food and air from its mother.

every street. You made your beauty hateful. You offered your body for sex to anyone who passed by. Your sexual sins became worse and worse. ²⁶You also had sexual relations with the Egyptians. They were your neighbors and partners in sexual sin. Your sexual sins became even worse. And they caused me to be angry. ²⁷So then, I used my power against you. I took away some of your land. I let those who hated you defeat you. They were the Philistine women. Even they were ashamed of your evil ways. ²⁸Also, you had sexual relations with the Assyrians because you could not be satisfied. You had sexual relations with them, but you still were not satisfied. ²⁹You did even more sexual sins in the land of Babylonia. The Babylonians were traders. But you were not satisfied even with this.

³⁰"Truly your will is weak, says the Lord God. You do all the things a stubborn prostitute does. ³¹You built your place to worship false gods at the beginning of every street. And you made places of worship in every city square. But you were not like a prostitute because you refused payment.

³²"You are a wife who is guilty of adultery.ᵈ You desire strangers instead of your husband. ³³Men pay prostitutes, but you pay all your lovers. You pay them to come to you. And they come from all around for sexual relations. ³⁴So you are different from other prostitutes. No one acts like a prostitute the same way you do. You give money, and no money is given to you. Yes, you are different.

THE PROSTITUTE IS JUDGED

³⁵"So, prostitute,ᵈ hear the word of the Lord. ³⁶This is what the Lord God says: You showed your riches to other countries. And you uncovered your body in your sexual sins with your lovers. And you even did it with all your hated idols. You killed your children and offered their blood to your idols. ³⁷So I will gather all your lovers with whom you found pleasure. Yes, I will gather all those you loved and those you hated. Yes, I will gather them against you from all around. I will strip you naked in front of them. Then they will be able to see your nakedness. ³⁸So I will punish you as judges punish women guilty of adultery.ᵈ I will punish you as murderers are punished. I will put you to death because I am angry and jealous. ³⁹I will also hand you over to your lovers. They will tear down your places of worship. They will destroy the places where you worship false gods. They will tear off your clothes and take away your jewelry. They will leave you naked and bare. ⁴⁰They will bring a crowd against you. They will throw stones at you and cut you into pieces with their swords. ⁴¹They will burn your houses with fire. They will punish you in front of many women. Then I will put an end to your sexual sins. And you will no longer pay your lovers. ⁴²Then I will rest from my anger against you. I will stop being jealous. I will be quiet and not angry anymore.

⁴³"You didn't remember when you were young. So you have made me angry in all these ways. And I will repay you for what you have done, says the Lord God. Didn't you add sexual sins to all your other acts which I hate?

⁴⁴"Everyone who uses wise sayings will say this about you: "The daughter is like her mother." ⁴⁵You are like your mother. She hated her husband and children. You are also like your sisters. They hated their husbands and children. Your mother was a Hittite. And your father was an Amorite. ⁴⁶Now your older sister is Samaria. She lived north of you with her daughters. And your younger sister Sodom lived south of you with her daughters. ⁴⁷You followed their ways. And you did what they did. But you were even worse than they were in everything you did. ⁴⁸As surely as I live, says the Lord God, this is true. Your sister Sodom

and her daughters never did what you and your daughters have done.

⁴⁹"'This was the sin of your sister Sodom: She and her daughters were proud. They had plenty of food. They lived in great comfort. But she did not help the poor and needy. ⁵⁰So Sodom and her daughters were proud. And they did things I hate in front of me. So I got rid of them when I saw what they did. ⁵¹Also, Samaria did not do half the sins you do. You have done more hated things than they did. So you make your sisters look good because of all the hated things you have done. ⁵²You will suffer disgrace because you have provided an excuse for your sisters. They are more right than you are. Your sins were even more terrible than theirs. Be ashamed and suffer disgrace because you made your sisters seem right.

⁵³"'But I will give Sodom and her daughters their riches back. I will give Samaria and her daughters their riches back. And with them I will also give you back your riches. ⁵⁴But you will have to suffer disgrace. You will feel ashamed for all the things you have done. You even gave comfort to your sisters in their sins. ⁵⁵Your sisters are Sodom with her daughters and Samaria with her daughters. They will return to what they were before. You and your daughters will also return to what you were before. ⁵⁶You would not even mention your sister Samaria when you were proud. ⁵⁷Nor would you mention her before your evil was uncovered. And now the Edomite women and their neighbors say bad things about you. Even the Philistine women say bad things about you. Those around you hate you. ⁵⁸You will be punished for your sexual sins and actions that I hate, says the Lord.

GOD KEEPS HIS PROMISES

⁵⁹"'This is what the Lord God says: I will give you what you should have. You hated and broke the marriage agreement. ⁶⁰But I will remember my agreement I made with you when you were young. I will make an agreement that will continue forever with you. ⁶¹Then you will remember what you have done. You will be ashamed when you receive your sisters—both your older and your younger sisters. I will give them to you like daughters. But it will not be because of my agreement with you. ⁶²I will set up my agreement with you. And you will know that I am the Lord. ⁶³You will remember and be ashamed. You will not open your mouth again because of your shame. This is because I will forgive you for all the things you have done, says the Lord God.'"

THE EAGLE AND THE VINE

17 The Lord spoke his word to me. He said: ²"Human being, give a riddle. Tell a story to the people of Israel. ³Say, 'This is what the Lord God says: A great eagle came to Lebanon. He had great wings with long feathers of many different colors. The eagle took hold of the top of a cedar tree. ⁴He pulled off the top branch. And he brought it to a land of traders. The eagle planted it in a city of traders.

⁵"'The eagle took a young plant from the land. And he planted it in a good field near plenty of water. He planted it to grow like a willow tree. ⁶The plant grew and became a low vine that spread over the ground. The vine's branches turned toward the eagle. The vine's roots were under the eagle. So the plant became a vine. And its branches grew, sending out leaves.

⁷"'But there was another eagle with great wings and many feathers. The vine then bent its roots toward this eagle. The vine also sent out its branches toward the eagle so he could water it. The vine turned away from the area where it was planted. ⁸It was planted in a good field. It was by plenty of water so it could grow branches and give fruit. It could have become a fine vine.'

[9]"Say to them, 'This is what the Lord God says: The vine will not continue to grow. The first eagle will pull up the vine's roots and strip off its fruit. Then the vine will dry up. All its new leaves will dry up and die. It will not take a strong arm or many people to pull the vine up by its roots. [10]It might be planted again. But it will not continue to grow. It will completely die when the east wind hits it. It will dry up in the area where it grew.'"

ZEDEKIAH AGAINST NEBUCHADNEZZAR

[11]Then the Lord spoke his word to me. He said: [12]"Say now to the people who refuse to obey: 'Do you know what these things mean?' Say: 'The king of Babylon came to Jerusalem. He took the king and important men of Jerusalem and brought them to Babylon. [13]Then he took a member of the family of the king of Judah. He made an agreement with him. The king of Babylon made this person promise to support him. The king also took away the leaders of Judah. [14]He did this to make the kingdom of Judah weak so it would not be strong again. Then the kingdom of Judah could continue only by keeping its agreement with the king of Babylon. [15]But the king of Judah turned against the king of Babylon. The king of Judah sent his messengers to Egypt. He asked the Egyptians for horses and many soldiers. Will the king of Judah succeed? Will the one who does such things escape? He cannot break the agreement and escape.

[16]"As surely as I live, says the Lord God, he will die in Babylon. He will die in the land of the king who made him king of Judah. The king of Judah hated his promise. He broke his agreement with the king of Babylon. [17]The king of Egypt will not help the king of Judah in the war. He will not help with his mighty army and many people. The Babylonians will build devices to attack the cities and to kill many people. [18]The king of Judah showed that he hated the promise by breaking the agreement. He promised to support Babylon, but he did all these things. So he will not escape.

[19]"So this is what the Lord God says: As surely as I live, this is true: I will pay back the king of Judah for hating my promise and breaking my agreement. [20]I will spread my net over him. He will be caught in my trap. Then I will bring him to Babylon. There I will judge him for the unfaithful acts he did against me. [21]And all the best of his soldiers who escape will die by the sword. Those who live will be scattered to every wind. Then you will know that I, the Lord, have spoken.

[22]"This is what the Lord God says: I myself will also take a young branch from the top of a cedar tree. And I will plant it. I will cut off a small twig. It will be from the top of the tree's young branches. I will plant it on a high and great mountain. [23]I will plant it on the high mountain of Israel. Then it will grow branches and give fruit. And it will become a great cedar tree. Birds of every kind will build nests in it. They will live in the shelter of the tree's branches. [24]Then all the trees of the field will know that I am the Lord. I am the one who brings down the high tree. I make the low tree tall. I dry up the green tree. And I make the dry tree grow. I am the Lord. I have spoken, and I will do it.'"

GOD IS FAIR

18 The Lord spoke his word to me. He said: [2]"What do you mean by using this saying about the land of Israel:
'The fathers have eaten sour grapes.
And that caused the children to
grind their teeth from the sour
taste'?

[3]"As surely as I live, says the Lord God, this is true: You will not use this saying in Israel anymore. [4]Every living thing belongs to me. The life of the father is mine. And the life of the son is mine. The person who sins will die.

⁵"There may be a good person. This person does what is fair and right. ⁶He does not eat at the mountain places of worship. He does not look to the idols of Israel for help. He does not have sexual relations with his neighbor's wife. He does not have sexual relations with a woman during her time of monthly bleeding. ⁷He does not mistreat anyone. But he returns what was given as a promise for a loan. He does not rob other people. He gives bread to hungry people. He gives clothes to those who have no clothes. ⁸He does not lend money to get too much interest or profit. He keeps his hand from doing wrong. He judges fairly between men. ⁹He lives by my rules and obeys my laws faithfully. The person who does all these things is good. He will surely live, says the Lord God.

¹⁰"But this person might have a wild son who murders people. This son may do any of these other bad things. ¹¹(But the father himself has not done any of these things.) This son eats at the mountain places of worship. He has sexual relations with his neighbor's wife. ¹²He mistreats the poor and needy. He steals things. He refuses to return what was promised for a loan. He looks to idols for help. He does things which I hate. ¹³He lends money for too much interest and profit. Will this son live? No, he will not live! He has done all these hated things. He will surely be put to death. He will be responsible for his own sins.

¹⁴"But this son might have a son who has seen the sins his father did. But after seeing them, he does not do those things. ¹⁵He does not eat at the mountain places of worship. He does not look to the idols of Israel for help. He does not have sexual relations with his neighbor's wife. ¹⁶He does not mistreat anyone. He does not keep something promised for a loan. He does not steal. But he gives bread to the hungry people. He gives clothes to people without clothes. ¹⁷He keeps his hand

from doing wrong. He does not take too much interest or profit when he lends money. He obeys my laws and lives by my rules. He will not die for his father's sin. He will surely live. ¹⁸But his father took other people's money unfairly. He robbed his brother. He did what was wrong among his people. So he will die for his own sin.

¹⁹"But you ask, 'Why is the son not punished for the father's sin?' The son has done what is fair and right. He obeys all my rules. So he will surely live. ²⁰It is the person who sins that will die. The son will not be punished for the father's sin. The father will not be punished for the son's sin. The person who does right is responsible for his own goodness. The evil person is responsible for his own evil.

²¹"But the evil person might stop doing all the sins he has done. And he might obey all my rules and do what is fair and right. Then he will surely live. He will not die. ²²His sins will be forgotten. Now he does what is right. So he will live. ²³I do not really want the evil person to die, says the Lord God. I want him to stop his bad ways and live.

²⁴"But a person who does right might stop doing good and do wrong. And he might do the same hated things an evil person does. Will he live? All his good acts will be forgotten. This is because he became unfaithful. He has sinned. So he will die because of his sins.

²⁵"But you say, 'What the Lord does isn't fair.' Hear now, people of Israel. I am fair. It is what you do that is not fair! ²⁶A good person might stop doing good. He might do wrong and die because of it. He will die because he did wrong. ²⁷An evil person might stop doing the evil things he has done. And he might do what is fair and right. He will save his life. ²⁸He thought about it and stopped doing all the sins he had done. He will surely live. He will not die. ²⁹But the people of Israel still say, 'What the Lord does isn't

fair.' People of Israel, I am fair. It is what you do that is not fair.

³⁰"So I will judge you, people of Israel. I will judge each person by what he does, says the Lord God. Change your hearts. Stop all your sinning. Then sin will not bring your ruin. ³¹Get rid of all the sins you have done. And get for yourselves a new heart and a new way to think. Why do you want to die, people of Israel? ³²I do not want anyone to die. So change your hearts and lives so you may live.

A SAD SONG FOR ISRAEL

19 "Sing a funeral song for the leaders of Israel. ²Say:

'Your mother was like a female lion.
She lay down among the young lions.
    She had many cubs.
³She brought up one of her cubs.
    And he became a strong lion.
He learned to tear the animals he
    hunted.
    And he ate people.
⁴The nations heard about him.
    He was trapped in their pit.
And they brought him with hooks
    to the land of Egypt.

⁵"The mother lion waited and saw
    that there was no hope for her cub.
So she took another one of her cubs
    and made him a strong lion.
⁶This cub roamed among the lions.
    He was now a strong lion.
He learned to tear the animals he
    hunted.
    And he ate people.
⁷He destroyed their strong places.
    He destroyed their cities.
The land and everything in it
    were terrified by the sound of his
    roar.
⁸Then the nations came against him
    from areas all around.
And they spread their net over him.
    He was trapped in their pit.
⁹Then they put him into a cage with
    chains.

And they brought him to the king
    of Babylon.
They put him into prison.
Then his roar could not be heard
    again
    on the mountains of Israel.

¹⁰"Your mother was like a vine in your
    vineyard.
    It was planted beside the water.
The vine had many branches and gave
    much fruit
    because there was plenty of water.
¹¹The vine had strong branches.
    They were good enough for a king's
    scepter.ᵈ
The vine became tall
    among the thick branches.
And it was seen because it was tall
    with many branches.
¹²But it was pulled up by its roots in
    anger.
    It was thrown down to the ground.
The east wind dried it up.
    Its fruit was torn off.
Its strong branches were broken off.
    They were burned up.
¹³Now the vine is planted in the desert,
    in a dry and thirsty land.
¹⁴And fire has spread from the vine's
    main branch.
    It has destroyed its fruit.
There is not a strong branch left on it
    that could become a scepter for a
    king.'

This is a funeral song. It is to be used as a funeral song."

ISRAEL HAS REFUSED GOD

20 It was the seventh year, in the fifth month of our captivity. It was the tenth day of the month. Some of the elders of Israel came to ask about the Lord. They sat down before me.

²The Lord spoke his word to me. He said: ³"Human being, speak to the elders of Israel. Say to them: 'This is what the Lord God says: Did you come to ask me questions? As surely as I live, I will not let you ask me questions.'

⁴"Will you judge them? Will you judge them, human being? Let them know the hated things their fathers did. ⁵Say to them: 'This is what the Lord God says: I chose Israel and made a promise to the descendants*d* of Jacob. At that time I made myself known to them in Egypt. I promised them, "I am the Lord your God." ⁶At that time I promised them I would bring them out of Egypt. I promised to bring them into a land I had chosen for them. This is a land where much food grows. It is the best of all lands. ⁷I said to them, "Each one of you must throw away the hateful idols you have set your eyes on. Don't make yourselves unclean*d* with the idols of Egypt. I am the Lord your God."

⁸"But they turned against me and refused to listen to me. They did not throw away the hated idols which they saw and liked. They did not leave the idols of Egypt. Then I decided to pour out my anger against them in the land of Egypt. ⁹But I acted to show who I am. I did not allow myself to be dishonored before the nations where the Israelites lived. I made myself known to the Israelites. I did this by bringing them out of Egypt while the nations were watching. ¹⁰So I took them out of Egypt and brought them into the desert. ¹¹I gave them my rules. I told them about my laws. If a person obeys them, he will live. ¹²I also gave them my Sabbaths.*d* They were to be a sign between us. Then they would know that I am the Lord. I make them holy.

¹³"But in the desert Israel turned against me. They did not follow my rules. They rejected my laws. But if a person obeys them, he will live. They dishonored my Sabbaths. Then I decided to pour out my anger against them and destroy them in the desert. ¹⁴But I acted for the sake of my name. I did not allow it to be dishonored before the nations. As the nations watched, I had brought the Israelites out of Egypt. ¹⁵But in the desert I had to make another promise to the Israelites. I had to promise I would not bring them into the land I had given them. It is a land where much food grows. It is the best of all the lands. ¹⁶This is because they rejected my laws. They did not follow my rules. They dishonored my Sabbaths. They would rather worship their idols. ¹⁷But I had pity on them. I did not destroy them. I did not put an end to them in the desert. ¹⁸I said to their children in the desert, "Don't live by the rules of your fathers. Don't obey their laws. Don't make yourselves unclean with their idols. ¹⁹I am the Lord your God. Live by my rules. Obey my laws and do them. ²⁰Keep my Sabbaths holy. They will be a sign between me and you. Then you will know that I am the Lord your God."

²¹"But the people turned against me. If a person obeys my laws, he will live. But they did not live by my rules. They were not careful to obey my laws. They dishonored my Sabbaths. So I decided to pour out my anger against them. I decided to carry out my anger against them in the desert. ²²But I held back my anger. I acted for the sake of my name. Then my name would not be dishonored with the nations watching. As the nations watched, I had brought the Israelites out from Egypt. ²³Also in the desert I had to make a promise to the Israelites. I had to promise to scatter them among the nations and spread them among the countries. ²⁴This is because they did not obey my laws. They had rejected my rules and dishonored my Sabbaths. And they worshiped the idols of their ancestors. ²⁵I also allowed them to follow rules that were not good. And they followed laws by which they could not live. ²⁶I let the Israelites make themselves unclean by the gifts they brought to their false gods. They sacrificed their oldest children in the fire.

This is how I shocked them so they would know that I am the Lord.'

27"So, human being, speak to the people of Israel. Say to them, 'This is what the Lord God says: Your ancestors spoke against me by being unfaithful to me in this way: 28I had brought them into the land I promised to give them. They saw every high hill and every leafy tree. There they offered their sacrifices to false gods. They brought offerings that made me angry. There, also, they burned their incense.[d] There they poured out their drink offerings. 29Then I said to them: What is this place where you go to worship false gods?'" (It is still called High Place today.)

30"So say to the people of Israel: 'This is what the Lord God says: Will you make yourselves unclean as your ancestors did? Will you be unfaithful and desire their hated idols? 31You offer your children as gifts to the false gods. You sacrifice them in the fire. You make yourselves unclean with all your idols even today. So, people of Israel, should I let you ask me questions? As surely as I live, says the Lord God, I will not accept questions from you.

32"'What you want will not come true. You say, "We want to be like the other nations and the people in other lands. We want to worship idols made of wood and stone." 33As surely as I live, says the Lord God, I will rule you. I will rule you with my great power and strength and anger. 34I will bring you out from the foreign nations. I will gather you from the lands where you are scattered. I will do this with my great power and strength and anger. 35I will bring you among the nations as I brought your ancestors into the desert with Moses. There I will judge you face to face. 36I will judge you the same way I judged your ancestors. That was in the desert of the land of Egypt. So I will judge you, says the Lord God. 37I will take control of you. I will punish you

by my agreement. 38I will get rid of those who refuse to obey me and who turn against me. I will bring them out of the land where they are now living. But they will never enter the land of Israel. Then you will know that I am the Lord.

39"'This is what the Lord God says: People of Israel, go serve your idols for now. But later you will listen to me. You will not continue to dishonor my holy name with your gifts and false gods. 40My holy mountain is the high mountain of Israel. There all Israel will serve me in the land, says the Lord God. There I will accept you. There I will look for your offerings. I will look for the first harvest of your offerings and all your holy gifts. 41I will accept you like a pleasing smell. This will happen when I bring you out from the foreign nations. It will take place when I gather you from the lands where you are scattered. Then through you I will show how holy I am. The nations will see it. 42When I bring you into the land of Israel, you will know that I am the Lord. I will bring you into the land I promised your ancestors. 43There you will remember everything you did that made you unclean. Then you will hate yourselves for all the evil things you have done. 44I will deal with you to show who I am. Then you will know I am the Lord, people of Israel. But it's not because of your evil ways or unclean actions, says the Lord God.'"

45Now the Lord spoke his word to me. He said: 46"Human being, look toward the south. Prophesy[d] against the south. Prophesy against the forest of the southern area. 47Say to that forest: 'Hear the word of the Lord. This is what the Lord God says: I am ready to start a fire in you. The fire will destroy all your green trees and all your dry trees. The flame that burns will not be put out. All the land from south to north will be burned by the fire. 48Then all the people will see that I, the Lord, have started the fire. It will not be put out.'"

⁴⁹Then I said, "Ah, Lord God! The people are saying about me, 'He is only telling stories.'"

BABYLON, THE LORD'S SWORD

21 Then the Lord spoke his word to me. He said: ²"Human being, look toward Jerusalem and speak against their holy place. Prophesy^d against the land of Israel. ³Say to Israel: 'This is what the Lord says: I am against you. I will pull my sword out of its holder. I will separate you from both wicked people and those who do right. ⁴I am going to separate the wicked and those who do right. So my sword will come out from its holder. And it will come against all people from south to north. ⁵Then all people will know that I, the Lord, have pulled my sword out from its holder. My sword will not go back in again.'

⁶"So, human being, groan with breaking heart and great sadness. Make these sad sounds in front of the people. ⁷They will ask you, 'Why do you make these sad sounds?' Then you will say, 'Because of the news that is coming. Every heart will melt with fear. All hands will become weak. Everyone will be afraid. All knees will become weak as water. Look, it is coming. It will happen, says the Lord God.'"

⁸The Lord spoke his word to me. He said, ⁹"Human being, prophesy and say, 'This is what the Lord says:

A sword, a sword,
    made sharp and polished.
¹⁰It is made sharp for the killing.
    It is polished to flash like lightning.

"'You are not happy about this horrible punishment by the sword. But my son, Judah, you did not change when you were only beaten with a rod.
¹¹The sword should be polished.
    The sword is meant to be held in
        the hand.
    It is made sharp and polished.

It is made ready for the hand of the
    killer.
¹²Shout and yell, human being.
    This is because the sword is against
        my people.
    It is against all the rulers of Israel.
They will be killed by the sword,
    along with my people.
    So beat your chest in sadness.

¹³"'The test will come. And Judah, who is hated by the armies of Babylon, will not last, says the Lord God.'

¹⁴"So, human being, prophesy.
    And clap your hands.
Let the sword hit
    two or three times.
It is the sword for killing.
    It is the sword for much killing.
    This sword surrounds the people.
¹⁵Their hearts will melt with fear.
    And many people will die.
I have placed the killing sword
    at all their gates.
Oh! The sword is made to flash like
    lightning.
    It is held, ready for killing.
¹⁶Sword, cut on the right side.
    Then cut on the left side.
    Cut anywhere your blade is turned.
¹⁷I will also clap my hands.
    Then my anger will rest.
I, the Lord, have spoken."

JERUSALEM TO BE DESTROYED
¹⁸The Lord spoke his word to me. He said: ¹⁹"Human being, mark two roads that the king of Babylon and his sword can follow. Both of these roads will start from the same country. And make signs where the road divides and one way goes toward the city. ²⁰One sign shows the road he can take with his sword to Rabbah. It is in the land of the Ammonites. And the other sign shows the road he can take to Judah and Jerusalem. Jerusalem is protected with strong walls. ²¹The king of Babylon will come to where the road divides into two. He will use magic. He

will throw lots*d* with arrows. He will ask questions of his family idols. He will look at the liver of a sacrificed animal to learn where he should go. ²²The lots will tell him to go toward his right to Jerusalem. They will tell him these things: Use logs to break down the city gates. Shout the battle cry and give the order to kill. Build a dirt road to the top of the walls and devices to attack the walls. ²³The people of Jerusalem have made agreements with other nations to help them fight Babylon. So they will think this prediction is wrong. But the king of Babylon will remind them of their sin. And he will capture them.

²⁴"So this is what the Lord God says: 'You have shown how sinful you are by turning against the Lord. Your sins are seen in all the things you do. So you will be taken captive by the enemy.

²⁵"'You unclean*d* and evil leader of Israel, you will be killed! The time of your final punishment has come. ²⁶This is what the Lord God says: Take off the turban. Take off the crown. Things will change. Those who are important now will be made unimportant. And those who are unimportant now will be made important. ²⁷A ruin! A ruin! I will make it a ruin! This place will not be rebuilt until the one comes who has a right to be king. Then I will give it to him.'

THE PUNISHMENT OF AMMON

²⁸"And you, human being, prophesy*d* and say: 'This is what the Lord God says about the people of Ammon and their insults:

A sword, a sword
   is pulled out of its holder.
It is polished to kill and destroy.
   It will flash like lightning!
²⁹Prophets*d* see false visions about you
   and prophesy lies about you.
The sword will be put on the necks
   of these evil people who are to be
   killed.
Their day has come.

The time of your final punishment
   has come.
³⁰Put the sword back in its holder.
I will judge you in the place where
   you were created.
I will judge you in the land where you
   were born.
³¹I will pour out my anger against
   you.
I will breathe on you with the fire of
   my anger.
I will hand you over to cruel men
   who are skilled in destruction.
³²You will be like fuel for the fire.
You will die in the land.
You will not be remembered.
I, the Lord, have spoken.'"

THE SINS OF JERUSALEM

22 The Lord spoke his word to me. He said: ²"And you, human being, will you judge? Will you judge the city of murderers? Then tell her about all her hated acts. ³You will say: 'This is what the Lord God says: You are a city that kills those who come to live there. You make yourself unclean*d* by making idols. ⁴You have become guilty of murder. And you have become unclean by your idols which you have made. So you have brought your time of punishment near. You have come to the end of your years. So I have made you a thing of shame to the nations. All lands will laugh at you. ⁵Those near and those far away will laugh at you. You will have a bad name. You will be full of confusion.

⁶"'Jerusalem, see how each ruler of Israel in you has been trying to kill people. ⁷The people in you hate their fathers and mothers. They mistreat the foreigners in you. They wrong the orphans and widows in you. ⁸You hate my holy things. You dishonor my Sabbaths.*d* ⁹The men in you tell lies to cause the death of others. The people in you eat food offered to idols at the mountain places of worship. They do sexual sins in you. ¹⁰The people in you have sexual relations with their fathers'

wives. The men in you have sexual relations with women who are unclean, during their time of monthly bleeding. [11]One person in you does a hated act with his neighbor's wife. Another has shamefully made his daughter-in-law unclean sexually. And another forces his half sister to have sexual relations with him. [12]The people in you take money to kill people. You take unfair interest and profits. You make profits by mistreating your neighbor. And you have forgotten me, says the Lord God.

[13]"'So with my fists I will hit you who have stolen money and you who have murdered people. [14]Will you still be brave and strong when I punish you? I, the Lord, have spoken, and I will act. [15]I will scatter you among the nations. I will spread you through the countries. I will get rid of your uncleanness. [16]But you, yourself, will be dishonored in the sight of the nations. Then you will know that I am the Lord.'"

ISRAEL IS WORTHLESS

[17]The Lord spoke his word to me. He said: [18]"Human being, the people of Israel have become useless like scum to me. They are like the copper, tin, iron and lead left in the furnace. These are left when silver is purified by melting. [19]So this is what the Lord God says: 'You have become useless like scum. I am going to gather you into Jerusalem. [20]People gather silver, copper, iron, lead and tin into a furnace. Then they melt it in a blazing fire. In the same way I will gather you in my hot anger. I will put you in Jerusalem and melt you. [21]I will gather you. And I will make you feel the heat of my anger. You will be melted in the fire. [22]Silver is melted in the furnace. In the same way you will be melted in the city. Then you will know that I, the Lord, have poured out my anger against you.'"

SINS OF THE PEOPLE

[23]The Lord spoke his word to me. He said: [24]"Human being, say to the land,

'You are a land that has not had rain or showers in a day of anger.' [25]Israel's rulers make evil plans. They are like a roaring lion that tears the animal it has caught. They have destroyed lives. They have taken treasure and valuable things. They have caused many women to become widows. [26]Israel's priests do cruel things to my teachings. They do not honor my holy things. They make no difference between holy and unholy things. They teach there is no difference between clean[d] and unclean things. They do not remember my Sabbaths.[d] So I am dishonored by them. [27]Jerusalem's leaders are like wolves tearing a dead animal. They have killed people for profit. [28]And the prophets[d] try to cover this up by false visions and by lying. They say, 'This is what the Lord God says' when the Lord has not spoken. [29]The people cheat others. They steal. They hurt people who are poor and needy. They cheat foreigners and don't treat them fairly.

[30]"I looked for someone to build up the walls. I looked for someone to stand before me where the walls are broken to defend these people. Then I would not have to destroy them. But I did not find anyone. [31]So I will let them see my anger. I will destroy them with an anger that is like fire. This is because of all the things they have done, says the Lord God."

SAMARIA AND JERUSALEM

23 The Lord spoke his word to me. He said: [2]"Human being, a woman had two daughters. [3]While they were young, they went to Egypt and became prostitutes.[d] They let men touch and hold their breasts. [4]The older girl was named Oholah, and her sister was named Oholibah. They were mine and had sons and daughters. Oholah is Samaria, and Oholibah is Jerusalem.

[5]"Samaria left me. She went to her lover, Assyria. The Assyrians were warriors. [6]They wore blue uniforms. And all of them—governors, commanders and

horsemen—were handsome. ⁷Samaria became a prostitute for all the important men in Assyria. And she made herself unclean*ᵈ* with all the idols of everyone she desired. ⁸She continued the prostitution she began in Egypt. When she was young, she slept with men. They touched her breasts and had sexual relations with her.

⁹"So I gave her to her lovers, the Assyrians, that she wanted so badly. ¹⁰They stripped her naked and took away her sons and daughters. Then they killed her with a sword. Women everywhere began talking about how she had been punished.

¹¹"Her sister Jerusalem saw what happened to Samaria. And so Jerusalem became worse than her sister in her sexual desire and prostitution. ¹²She also desired the Assyrians. All of them—governors, commanders, warriors dressed in uniform, and horsemen—were handsome. ¹³I saw that both girls were alike. Both of them were prostitutes.

¹⁴"But Jerusalem went even further. She saw carvings of Babylonian men on a wall. They wore red ¹⁵and had belts around their waists. They wore turbans on their heads. They all looked like chariot officers born in Babylonia. ¹⁶When she saw them, she wanted to have sexual relations with them. So she sent messengers to them in Babylonia. ¹⁷So these Babylonian men came and had sexual relations with her. They made her unclean. After that, she became sick of them. ¹⁸But she continued her prostitution so that everyone knew about it. And I finally became sick of her, as I had her sister. ¹⁹But she remembered how she was a young prostitute in Egypt. So she took part in even more prostitution. ²⁰She wanted men who behaved like animals in their sexual desire. ²¹In the same way you desired to do the sinful things you had done in Egypt. There men touched and held your young breasts.

GOD'S JUDGMENT ON JERUSALEM

²²"So, Jerusalem, this is what the Lord God says: You have tired of your lovers. So now I will make them angry with you. And they will surround you. ²³Men from Babylon and all Babylonia and men from Pekod, Shoa and Koa will come against you. All the Assyrians will come against you. They are governors, commanders, chariot drivers and important men, all riding horses. ²⁴Those men will come with great armies. They will come with their weapons, chariots and wagons. They will surround you with large and small shields and with helmets. And I will hand you over to them for punishment. And they will punish you with their own kind of punishment. ²⁵Then you will see how strong my anger can be. They will punish you in their anger. They will cut off your noses and ears. They will take away your sons and daughters. Those who are left will be burned. ²⁶They will take off your clothes and steal your jewelry. ²⁷I will put a stop to the sinful life you began when you were in Egypt. You will not desire these things anymore. And you will not remember Egypt anymore.

²⁸"This is what the Lord God says: You became sick of your lovers. But I am giving you to those men you now hate. ²⁹They will treat you with hate and take away everything you worked for. They will leave you empty and naked. Everyone will know about the sinful things you did. Your sexual sins ³⁰have brought this on you. You have made yourselves unclean*ᵈ* by worshiping their idols. ³¹You did the same things your sister did. So you will get the same punishment.

³²"This is what the Lord God says:
You will drink the same cup your
    sister did.
And that cup is deep and wide.
Everyone will make fun of you,
    because the cup is full.
³³It will make you miserable and
    drunk.
It is the cup of fear and ruin.
It is the cup of your sister Samaria.

³⁴You will drink everything in it.
  Then you will smash it
  and tear at your breasts.
I have spoken, says the Lord God.

³⁵"So this is what the Lord God says:
You have forgotten me and turned your
back on me. So you will be punished for
your sexual sins."

JUDGMENT ON SAMARIA AND JERUSALEM

³⁶The Lord said to me: "Human being,
will you judge Samaria and Jerusalem?
Then show them their hated acts. ³⁷They
are guilty of adultery*d* and murder. They
have taken part in adultery with their
idols. They even offered their children as
sacrifices in the fire. They were to be food
for these idols. ³⁸They have also done this
to me: They made my Temple*d* unclean*d*
at the same time they dishonored my
Sabbaths.*d* ³⁹They offered their children
to their idols. Then they entered my
Temple at that very time to dishonor it.
That is what they did inside my Temple.

⁴⁰"They even sent for men from far
away. A messenger was sent to them,
and they came. The two sisters bathed
themselves for them, painted their eyes
and put on jewelry. ⁴¹They sat on a fine
bed with a table set before it. They put
my incense*d* and my oil on the table.

⁴²"There was the noise of a reckless
crowd in the city. Common people gathered, and drunkards were brought from
the desert. They put bracelets on the
hands of the two sisters. And they put
beautiful crowns on their heads. ⁴³Then
I said about the one who was worn out
by her acts of adultery, 'Let them continue their sexual sins with her. She is
nothing but a prostitute.'*d* ⁴⁴They kept
going to her as they would go to a prostitute. So they continued to go to Oholah,
which was Samaria, and Oholibah, which
was Jerusalem. These were the shameful
women. ⁴⁵But men who do right will
judge them as they judge women who
take part in adultery. And they will judge
them as they judge women who murder

people. This is because Samaria and Jerusalem are guilty of adultery and murder.

⁴⁶"This is what the Lord God says:
Bring together a mob against Samaria
and Jerusalem. And hand them over to
be frightened and robbed. ⁴⁷Let the mob
kill them by throwing stones at them. Let
the mob cut them down with their
swords. Let them kill their sons and
daughters and burn their houses with fire.

⁴⁸"So I will put an end to sexual sins in
the land. Then all women will be warned.
And they will not do the sexual sins you
have done. ⁴⁹You will be punished for
your sexual sins and the sin of worshiping idols. Then you will know that I
am the Lord God."

THE POT AND THE MEAT

24 The Lord spoke his word to me.
It was in the ninth year, in the
tenth month of our captivity. It was on
the tenth day of the month. He said:
²"Human being, write for yourself this
date, this very date. The king of Babylon
has surrounded Jerusalem this very day.
³And tell a story to the people who refuse
to obey me. Say to them: 'This is what
the Lord God says:

Put on the pot. Put it on
  and pour water in it.
⁴Put in the pieces of meat.
  Put in the best pieces—the legs
    and the shoulders.
Fill it with the best bones.
⁵ Take the best of the flock.
Pile wood under the pot.
  Boil the pieces of meat
  until even the bones are cooked.

⁶"'This is what the Lord God says:
How terrible it will be for the city of
    murderers!
  How terrible it will be for the rusty
    pot!
  Its rust will not go away!
Take the meat out of it, piece by piece.
  Don't choose any special piece.

7"'The blood from her killings is still in
the city.
She poured the blood on the bare
rock.
She did not pour it on the ground
where dust would cover it.
8To stir up my anger and revenge,
I put the blood she spilled on the
bare rock.
So it will not be covered.

9"'So this is what the Lord God says:
How terrible it will be for the city of
murderers!
I will also pile the wood high for
burning.
10Pile up the wood
and light the fire.
Finish cooking the meat.
Mix in the spices.
And let the bones burn.
11Then set the empty pot on the coals.
It will become hot, and its copper
sides will glow.
The dirty scum stuck inside it may
then melt
and its rust burn away.
12But efforts to clean the pot have failed.
Its heavy rust cannot be removed,
even in the fire.

13"'In your sinful action there is
shame. I wanted to cleanse you, but you
are still unclean.*d* You will never be
cleansed from your sin until my anger
against you is carried out.

14"'I, the Lord, have spoken. The time
has come for me to act. I will not hold
back punishment. I will not feel pity. I
will judge you by your ways and actions,
says the Lord God.'"

THE DEATH OF EZEKIEL'S WIFE

15Then the Lord spoke his word to me.
He said: 16"Human being, I am going to
take your wife from you. She is the desire
of your eyes. She will die suddenly. But
you must not be sad or cry loudly for her.
You must not shed any tears. 17Groan
silently. Do not cry loudly for the dead.

Tie on your turban, and put your sandals on your feet. Do not cover your face.
And do not eat the food people eat when
they are sad about a death."

18So I spoke to the people in the
morning. Then my wife died in the
evening. The next morning I did as I had
been commanded.

19Then the people asked me, "Tell us,
what do the things you are doing mean
for us?"

20Then I said to them, "The Lord spoke
his word to me. He said, 21'Say to the
people of Israel, This is what the Lord God
says: I am going to dishonor my Temple.*d*
You think it gives you strength. You are
proud of it. You love to look at it. It
makes you happy. But your sons and
daughters that you left behind in Jerusalem will fall dead by the sword. 22And
you will do as I have done. You will not
cover your face. You will not eat the food
people eat when they are sad about a
death. 23Your turbans will be on your
heads. And your sandals will be on your
feet. You will not cry loudly. But you will
rot away in your sins. You will groan to
each other. 24So Ezekiel will be a sign for
you. You will do all the same things he
did. When it happens, you will know
that I am the Lord God.'

25"And as for you, human being, this
is how it will be. I will take away the
Temple that gives them strength. It
makes them happy and proud. They
love to look at it. It makes them happy.
And I will take away their sons and
daughters also. 26At that time the person
who escapes will come to you. He will
have information for you to hear. 27At
that time your mouth will be opened.
You will speak and be silent no more. So
you will be a sign for them. Then they
will know that I am the Lord."

PROPHECY AGAINST AMMON

25 The Lord spoke his word to me.
He said: 2"Human being, look
toward the people of Ammon and

prophesy*d* against them. ³Say to them, 'Hear the word of the Lord God. This is what the Lord God says: You were glad when my Temple*d* was dishonored. You were glad when the land of Israel was ruined. And you were glad when the people of Judah were taken away as captives. ⁴So I am going to give you to the people of the East to be theirs. They will set up their camps among you. They will make their homes among you. They will eat your fruit and drink your milk. ⁵And I will make the city of Rabbah a pasture for camels. And the land of Ammon will become a resting place for sheep. Then you will know that I am the Lord. ⁶This is what the Lord God says: You clapped your hands and stamped your feet. You are happy about all the insults you have made against the land of Israel. ⁷So I will use my power against you. I will give you to the nations as if you were valuables taken in war. I will wipe you out of the lands so you will no longer be a nation. I will destroy you. And you will know that I am the Lord.'"

PROPHECY AGAINST MOAB AND EDOM

⁸"This is what the Lord God says: 'Moab and Edom say, "The people of Judah are like all the other nations." ⁹So I am going to take away the cities that protect Moab's borders. They are the best cities in that land. They are Beth Jeshimoth, Baal Meon and Kiriathaim. ¹⁰Then I will give Moab, along with the Ammonites, to the people of the East. They will take over these people. Then along with the Ammonites, Moab will not be a nation anymore. ¹¹So I will punish the people of Moab. And they will know that I am the Lord.'"

PROPHECY AGAINST EDOM

¹²"This is what the Lord God says: 'Edom took revenge on the people of Judah. And the Edomites became guilty because of it. ¹³So this is what the Lord God says: I will use my power against Edom. I will kill every man and animal in Edom. And I will destroy Edom all the way from Teman to Dedan. The Edomites will die in battle. ¹⁴I will take revenge on Edom through my people Israel. So the Israelites will do to Edom what my hot anger demands. Then the Edomites will know my revenge, says the Lord God.'"

PROPHECY AGAINST PHILISTIA

¹⁵"This is what the Lord God says: 'The Philistines have taken revenge with hateful hearts. Because of their strong hatred, they have tried to destroy Judah. ¹⁶So this is what the Lord God says: I will use my power against the Philistines. I will remove the Kerethites. I will destroy those people still alive on the coast of the Mediterranean Sea. ¹⁷I will punish them in my anger until they have had enough. They will know that I am the Lord when I punish them.'"

PROPHECY AGAINST TYRE

26 It was the eleventh year, on the first day of the month of our captivity. The Lord spoke his word to me. He said: ²"Human being, the city of Tyre has spoken against Jerusalem: 'The city that traded with the nations is destroyed. Now we can be the trading center. The city Jerusalem is ruined. Now we can make money.' ³So this is what the Lord God says: I am against you, Tyre. I will bring many nations against you. They will come like the sea beating its waves on your island shores. ⁴They will destroy the walls of Tyre and pull down her towers. I will also scrape away her ruins. I will make Tyre a bare rock. ⁵Tyre will be an island where fishermen dry their nets. I have spoken, says the Lord God. The nations will steal valuable things from Tyre. ⁶Also, her villages on the shore across from the island will be destroyed by war. Then they will know that I am the Lord.

NEBUCHADNEZZAR TO ATTACK TYRE

⁷"This is what the Lord God says: I will bring a king from the north against Tyre.

He is Nebuchadnezzar king of Babylon, the greatest king. He will bring horses, chariots, horsemen and a great army. ⁸He will fight a battle and destroy your villages on the shore across from the island. He will set up devices to attack you. He will build a road of earth to the top of the walls. He will raise his shields against you. ⁹He will bring logs to pound through your city walls. And he will break down your towers with his iron bars. ¹⁰His horses will be so many that they will cover you with their dust. Your walls will shake at the noise of horsemen, wagons and chariots. The king of Babylon will enter your city gates. He will enter as men enter a city where the walls are broken through. ¹¹The hoofs of his horses will run over your streets. He will kill your people with the sword. Your strong pillars will fall down to the ground. ¹²Also, his men will take away your riches. They will steal the things you sell. They will break down your walls and destroy your nice houses. They will throw your stones, wood and trash into the sea. ¹³So I will stop your songs. The music of your harps will not be heard anymore. ¹⁴I will make you a bare rock. You will be a place for drying fishing nets. You will not be built again. This is because I, the Lord, have spoken, says the Lord God.

¹⁵"This is what the Lord God says to Tyre: The people who live along the seacoast will shake with fear when they hear your defeat. Those of you who are injured and dying will groan. ¹⁶Then all the leaders of the seacoast will go down from their thrones. They will take off their beautiful needlework clothes. They will clothe themselves with fear. They will sit on the ground. They will shake with fear all the time. They will be shocked when they see you. ¹⁷They will begin singing a funeral song about you. They will say to you:

'Tyre, you famous city, you have been destroyed!
  Once seamen lived in you.

You and your people
  had great power on the seas.
All the people around you
  were afraid of you.
¹⁸Now the people who live by the coast
  will shake with fear on the day you fall.
The islands of the sea
  will be afraid because you have been defeated.'

¹⁹"This is what the Lord God says: I will make you an empty city. You will be like the cities that have no people living in them. I will bring the deep ocean waters over you. The Mediterranean Sea will cover you. ²⁰At that time I will send you down to the place of the dead. You will join the people who died long ago. I will make you live with the dead below the earth among old ruined places. You will not come back from there. People will never live in you again. ²¹Other people will be afraid of what happened to you. It will be the end of you. People will look for you. But they will never find you again, says the Lord God."

A FUNERAL SONG FOR TYRE

27 The Lord spoke his word to me. He said: ²"Human being, sing a funeral song for the city of Tyre. ³Speak to Tyre that is at the entrance to the Mediterranean Sea. For the people of many lands along the seacoast, Tyre is a place for trade. This is what the Lord God says:

Tyre, you have said,
  "I am like a beautiful ship."
⁴You were at home on the high seas.
  Your builders have made your
    beauty perfect.
⁵Your builders made all your boards
  of fir trees from Mount Hermon.
They have taken a cedar tree from
    Lebanon.
  They took it to make a ship's mast
    for you.
⁶They made your oars
  from oak trees in Bashan.

They made your deck
    from cypress trees from the coast of
        Cyprus.
    Your deck has ivory set into it.
[7]Your sail of linen with designs sewed
        on it came from Egypt.
    Your sail became like a flag for you.
    Your cloth shades over the deck were
        blue and purple.
    They came from the island of
        Cyprus.
[8]Men from Sidon and Arvad used oars
        to row you.
    Tyre, your skilled men were the
        sailors on your deck.
[9]Workers of Byblos were on board ship
        with you.
    They put caulk[n] in your ship's seams.
    All the ships of the sea and their sailors
        came alongside to trade with you.

[10]"Men of Persia, Lydia and Put
        were soldiers in your army.
    They hung their shields and helmets
        on your walls.
    Their victories made you famous.
[11]Men of Arvad and Celicia
        guarded your city walls all around.
    Men of Gammad
        were in your watchtowers.
    They hung their shields around your
        walls.
    They made your beauty perfect.

[12]"Tarshish traded with you for many
kinds of things. They paid for them with
silver, iron, tin and lead. [13]"People of Greece, Tubal and Meshech traded with you. They traded slaves
and bronze things for the things you sell.
[14]"People of Beth Togarmah traded
work horses, war horses and mules for
the things you sell. [15]"People of Rhodes traded with you.
You sold your things on many coast-
lands. They paid you with ivory tusks and
valuable black wood.

[16]"Aram traded with you because you
had so many good things to sell. They
traded turquoise, purple cloth and cloth
with designs sewed on. They also traded
fine linen, coral and rubies for the things
you sell. [17]"Judah and Israel traded with you.
They paid for the things you sell with
wheat from Minnith. They also paid with
honey, olive oil and balm.[d] [18]"Damascus traded with you because you have many good things. They
paid for them with wine from Helbon
and wool from Zahar. [19]"The Greeks from Uzal traded for the
things you sold. They paid with wrought
iron, cassia[d] and sugar cane for your
good things. [20]"Dedan traded saddle blankets to
you. [21]"Arabia and all the rulers of Kedar
traded with you. They traded lambs,
male sheep and goats to you. [22]"The traders of Sheba and Raamah
traded with you. They paid with all the
best spices, valuable gems and gold. [23]"Haran, Canneh, Eden and the
traders of Sheba, Asshur and Kilmad
traded with you. [24]They paid with the
best clothes, blue cloth and cloth with
designs sewed on. They traded carpets
of many colors and tightly wound ropes.

[25]"Trading ships
        carried the things you sold.
    You were like a ship full of heavy
        cargo
        in the middle of the sea.
[26]The men who rowed you
        brought you out into the high seas.
    But the east wind has broken you to
        pieces
        in the middle of the sea.
[27]Your wealth, your trade and the
        things you sell will sink.

27:9 caulk Something like tar put between the boards of a ship to make it waterproof so it will not sink.

Your seamen, your sailors and your
    workers will sink.
Your traders, your soldiers,
    and everyone else on board
will sink into the sea.
    This will happen on the day your
      ship is wrecked.
28The people on the shore will shake
    with fear
    when your sailors cry out.
29All the men who row
    will leave their ships.
The seamen and the sailors of other
    ships
    will stand on the shore.
30They will cry loudly about you.
    They will cry very much.
They will throw dust on their heads.
    They will roll in ashes to show they
      are sad.
31They will shave their heads for you.
    And they will put on rough cloth to
      show they are upset.
They will cry very much for you.
    They will cry loudly.
32And in their loud crying
    they will sing a funeral song for you.
    "No one was ever destroyed like Tyre,
      surrounded by the sea."
33The things you traded went out over
    the seas.
    You met the needs of many nations.
With your great wealth and things
    you sold,
    you made kings of the earth rich.
34But now you are broken by the sea.
    You have sunk to the bottom.
The things you sell and all your people
    have gone down with you.
35All those who live along the shore
    are shocked by what happened to
      you.
Their kings are terribly afraid.
    Their faces show their fear.
36The traders among the nations hiss at
    you.
    You have come to a terrible end.
    And you are gone forever.'"

PROPHECY AGAINST THE KING OF TYRE

28 The Lord spoke his word to me.
He said: 2"Human being, say to
the ruler of Tyre: 'This is what the Lord
God says:
You are too proud.
    And you say, "I am a god.
I sit on the throne of a god
    in the middle of the seas."
You think you are as wise as a god.
    But you are a man, not a god.
3You think you are wiser than Daniel.
    You think you can find out all secrets.
4Through your wisdom and
    understanding
    you have made yourself rich.
You have gained gold and silver.
    And you have saved it in your
      storerooms.
5Through your great skill in trading,
    you have made your riches grow.
You are too proud
    because of your riches.

6"'So this is what the Lord God says:
You think you are wise
    like a god.
7But I will bring foreign people against
    you.
    They will be the cruelest nation.
They will pull out their swords
    and destroy all that your wisdom
      has built.
    And they will dishonor your
      greatness.
8They will kill you.
    You will die a terrible death
    like those who are killed at sea.
9While they are killing you,
    you will not be able to say anymore,
    "I am a god."
You will be only a man, not a god,
    when your murderers kill you.
10You will die like an unclean*d* person.
    Foreigners will kill you.

I have spoken, says the Lord God.'"

11The Lord spoke his word to me. He
said: 12"Human being, sing a funeral song

for the king of Tyre. Say to him: 'This is
what the Lord God says:

You were an example of what was
    perfect.
You were full of wisdom and perfect
    in beauty.
[13]You had a wonderful life,
    like those in Eden, the garden of
        God.
Every valuable gem was on you:
    ruby, topaz and emerald,
    yellow quartz, onyx and jasper,
    sapphire, turquoise and chrysolite.
Your jewelry was made of gold.
    It was prepared on the day you
        were created.
[14]I appointed a living creature to guard
    you.
    I put you on the holy mountain of
        God.
    You walked among the gems of fire.
[15]Your life was right and good.
    This was from the day you were
        created,
    until evil was found in you.
[16]Because you traded with countries far
    away,
    you learned to be cruel, and you
        sinned.
So I threw you down in disgrace from
    the mountain of God.
    And the living creature who
        guarded you
    forced you out from among the
        gems of fire.
[17]You became too proud
    because of your beauty.
You ruined your wisdom
    because of your greatness.
I threw you down to the ground.
    Your example taught a lesson to
        other kings.
[18]You dishonored your places of
    worship
    through your many sins and
        dishonest trade.
So I set your city on fire.
    And it burned up.

I turned you into ashes on the ground
    for all those watching to see.
[19]All the nations who knew you
    are shocked about you.
Your punishment was so terrible.
    And you are gone forever.'"

PROPHECY AGAINST SIDON

[20]The Lord spoke his word to me. He
said: [21]"Human being, look toward the
city of Sidon and prophesy[d] against her.
[22]Say: 'This is what the Lord God says:

I am against you, Sidon.
    I will show my greatness among you.
Then people will know that I am the
        Lord
    when I have punished Sidon.
    I will show my holiness by
        defeating her.
[23]I will send diseases to Sidon,
    and blood will flow in her streets.
Those who are wounded in Sidon will
    fall dead.
    She will be attacked from all sides.
Then they will know that I am the
        Lord.

GOD WILL HELP ISRAEL

[24]"'No more will neighboring nations
be like thorny branches or sharp stickers
to hurt Israel. Then they will know that I
am the Lord God.

[25]"'This is what the Lord God says: I
will gather the people of Israel from the
nations where they are scattered. I will
show my holiness when the nations see
what I do to my people. Then they will
live in their own land—the land I gave
to my servant Jacob. [26]Then they will live
safely in the land. They will build houses
and plant vineyards. They will live in
safety after I have punished all the nations
around who hate them. Then they will
know that I am the Lord their God.'"

PROPHECY AGAINST EGYPT

29 It was the tenth year, in the tenth
month of our captivity. It was on
the twelfth day of the month. The Lord
spoke his word to me. He said: [2]"Human

being, look toward the king of Egypt. And prophesy[d] against him and all Egypt. [3]Say: 'This is what the Lord God says:

I am against you, king of Egypt.
You are like a great crocodile that
lies in the Nile River.
You say, "The Nile is mine.
I made it for myself."
[4]But I will put hooks in your jaws.
I will make the fish of the Nile stick
to your sides.
I will pull you up out of your rivers,
with all the fish sticking to your sides.
[5]I will leave you in the desert.
I will leave you and all the fish from
your rivers.
You will fall on the open field.
You will not be picked up or buried.
I have given you to the wild animals.
And I have given you to the birds of
the sky for food.

[6]Then all the people who live in Egypt will know that I am the Lord.

"'Israel tried to lean on you for help. But you were like a crutch made out of a weak stalk of grass. [7]When their hands grabbed you, you splintered and tore open their shoulders. When they leaned on you, you broke and made all their backs twist.

[8]"'So this is what the Lord God says: I will cause an enemy to attack you. He will kill your men and animals. [9]Then Egypt will become an empty desert. They will know that I am the Lord.

"'This is because you said, "The Nile River is mine. And I have made it." [10]So, I am against you. I am against your rivers. I will destroy the land of Egypt. It will be empty desert from Migdol in the north to Aswan in the south. It will be empty all the way to the southern border of Cush. [11]No man or animal will walk through it. No one will live in Egypt for 40 years. [12]I will make the land of Egypt the emptiest country of all. And her cities will be the emptiest of all ruined cities for 40 years. And I will scatter the

Egyptians among the nations. And I will spread them among the countries.

[13]"'This is what the Lord God says: After 40 years I will gather Egypt from the nations where they have been scattered. [14]I will bring back the Egyptian captives. I will make the Egyptians return to southern Egypt. They will return to the land that they came from. They will become a weak kingdom there. [15]It will be the weakest kingdom. It will never again rule other nations. I will make it so weak it will never again rule over the nations. [16]The Israelites will never again depend on Egypt. Egypt's punishment will remind the Israelites of their sin. They turned to Egypt for help and not to God. Then they will know that I am the Lord God.'"

EGYPT IS GIVEN TO BABYLON

[17]It was the twenty-seventh year of our captivity, in the first month. It was on the first day of the month. The Lord spoke his word to me. He said: [18]"Human being, Nebuchadnezzar king of Babylon made his army fight hard against Tyre. Every soldier's head was rubbed bare. Every shoulder was rubbed raw. But Nebuchadnezzar and his army gained nothing from fighting Tyre. [19]So this is what the Lord God says: I will give the land of Egypt to Nebuchadnezzar king of Babylon. And Nebuchadnezzar will take away Egypt's people. He will take Egypt's wealth and its valuable things as pay for his army. [20]I have given Nebuchadnezzar the land of Egypt. It is a reward for working hard to defeat Egypt for me. That is what the Lord God says.

[21]"On that day I will make Israel grow strong again. I will let you, Ezekiel, speak to them. Then they will know that I am the Lord God."

EGYPT WILL BE PUNISHED

30 The Lord spoke his word to me. He said, [2]"Human being, prophesy[d] and say, 'This is what the Lord God says:

Cry and say,
"The terrible day is coming."
³The day is near.
The Lord's day of judging is near.
It is a cloudy day.
It is a time when the nations will be
judged.
⁴An enemy will attack Egypt.
And Cush will tremble with fear.
When the killing begins in Egypt,
her wealth will be taken away.
Egypt's foundations will be torn
down.

⁵Cush, Put, Lydia, Arabia, Libya and my
people will die. All these who made an
agreement with Egypt will fall dead in
war.
⁶"This is what the Lord God says:
Those who fight on Egypt's side will
fall.
The power she is proud of will go
down.
The people in Egypt will fall dead in
war
from Migdol in the north to Aswan
in the south,
says the Lord God.
7They will be
the emptiest land.
Egypt's cities will be
like other cities that lie in ruin.
⁸Then they will know that I am the
Lord.
This will happen when I set fire to
Egypt
and when all those nations on her
side are crushed.
⁹"At that time I will send messengers
in ships. They will frighten Cush which
now feels safe. The people of Cush will
tremble with fear when Egypt is punished. And that time is sure to come.
¹⁰"This is what the Lord God says:
I will destroy great numbers of people
in Egypt.
I will do it through Nebuchadnezzar
king of Babylon.

¹¹Nebuchadnezzar and his army
are the cruelest army of any
nation.
They will be brought in to destroy
the land.
They will pull out their swords against
Egypt.
They will fill the land with those
they kill.
¹²I will make the streams of the Nile
River become dry land.
Then I will sell the dry land to evil
people.
I will destroy the land and everything
in it.
I will do it through the power
of strangers.

I, the Lord, have spoken.

EGYPT'S IDOLS ARE DESTROYED

¹³"This is what the Lord God says:
I will destroy the idols.
And I will take away the statues of
false gods from the city of
Memphis.
There will no longer be a leader in
Egypt.
And I will spread fear through the
land of Egypt.
¹⁴I will make southern Egypt empty.
I will start a fire in Zoan.
I will punish Thebes.
¹⁵And I will pour out my anger against
Pelusium,
the strong place of Egypt.
I will destroy great numbers of
people in Thebes.
¹⁶I will set fire to Egypt.
Pelusium will be in great pain.
The walls of Thebes will be broken
open.
And Memphis will have troubles
every day.
¹⁷The young men of Heliopolis and
Bubastis
will fall dead in war.
And the people will be taken away
as captives.

[18]In Tahpanhes the day will be dark
    when I break Egypt's power.
A cloud will cover Egypt.
    And her villages will be captured
        and taken away.
[19]So I will punish Egypt.
    And they will know I am the Lord.'"

EGYPT BECOMES WEAK

[20]It happened in the eleventh year of our captivity, in the first month. It was on the seventh day of the month. The Lord spoke his word to me. He said: [21]"Human being, I have broken the powerful arm of the king of Egypt. It has not been tied up so it will not get well. It has not been wrapped with a bandage. So his arm will not be strong enough to hold a sword in war. [22]So this is what the Lord God says: I am against the king of Egypt. I will break his arms. I will break both the strong arm and the broken arm. I will make the sword fall from his hand. [23]I will scatter the Egyptians among the nations. And I will spread them among the countries. [24]I will make the arms of the king of Babylon strong. I will put my sword in his hand. But I will break the arms of the king of Egypt. Then he will cry out in pain as a wounded man cries out. [25]So I will make the arms of the king of Babylon strong. But the arms of the king of Egypt will fall. Then they will know that I am the Lord. I will put my sword into the hand of the king of Babylon. And he will use the sword in war against Egypt. [26]Then I will scatter the Egyptians among the nations. And I will spread them among the countries. And they will know that I am the Lord."

A CEDAR TREE

31 It happened in the eleventh year of our captivity, in the third month. It was on the first day of the month. The Lord spoke his word to me. He said: [2]"Human being, say to the king of Egypt and his people:

'No one was like you in your greatness.
[3]Assyria was once like a cedar tree in
    Lebanon.
    It had beautiful branches that
        shaded the forest.
It was very tall.
    Its top was among the clouds.
[4]Much water made the tree grow.
    The deep springs of water made
        the tree tall.
Rivers flowed
    around the bottom of the tree.
They sent their streams
    to all other trees of the field.
[5]So the tree was taller
    than all the other trees of the field.
Its branches became long and big
    because of so much water.
[6]All the birds of the sky
    made their nests in the tree's
        branches.
And all the wild animals
    gave birth under the tree's branches.
All great nations
    lived in the tree's shade.
[7]So the tree was great and beautiful,
    with its long branches.
Its roots reached down to many
    waters.
[8]The cedar trees in the garden of God
    were not as great as it was.
The pine trees
    did not have such great branches.
The plane trees
    did not have such branches.
No tree in the garden of God
    was as beautiful as this tree.
[9]I made it beautiful
    with many branches.
And all the trees of Eden in the garden
    of God
    wanted to be like it.

[10]"'So this is what the Lord God says: The tree has grown tall. Its top has reached the clouds. And it has become proud of its height. [11]So I have let a mighty ruler of the nations take care of the tree. The ruler will surely punish the tree. Because it is evil I will get rid of it. [12]The

cruelest foreign nation cut it down and left it. The tree's branches fell on the mountains and in all the valleys. Its broken branches were in all the ravines of the land. All the nations of the earth left the shade of that tree. ¹³The birds of the sky live on the fallen tree. The wild animals live among the tree's fallen branches. ¹⁴Then the trees that grow by the water will not be proud to be tall. They will not put their tops among the clouds. None of the trees that are watered well will grow that tall. They all are meant to die and go under the ground. They will be with those who have died and have gone down to where the dead are.

¹⁵"'This is what the Lord God says: On the day when the tree went down to where the dead are, I made people cry loudly. I covered the deep springs and held back their rivers. And the great waters stopped flowing. I made Lebanon cry loudly for the great tree. All the trees of the field dried up and died. ¹⁶I made the nations shake with fear at the sound of the tree falling. I brought the tree down to where the dead are. It went with those who go down to the grave. Then trees of Eden and the best trees of Lebanon were comforted. All the well-watered trees were comforted in the earth below. ¹⁷But these trees also went down with the great tree to the place where the dead are. They went to join those who were killed in war. They had lived under the great tree's shade. They were its friends among the nations.

¹⁸"'So no tree in Eden is equal to you in greatness and honor. But you will go down with the trees of Eden to the earth below. You will lie among unclean*ᵈ* people who were killed in war.

"'This will happen to the king of Egypt and all his people, says the Lord God.'"

A FUNERAL SONG

32 It happened in the twelfth year, in the twelfth month of our captivity. It was on the first day of the month.

The Lord spoke his word to me. He said: ²"Human being, sing a funeral song about the king of Egypt. Say to him:

'You are like a young lion among the nations.
You are like a crocodile in the seas.
You splash around in your streams.
And you stir up the waters with your feet.
You make the rivers muddy.

³"'This is what the Lord God says:
I will spread my net over you.
And I will use a large group of people
to pull you up in my net.
⁴Then I will throw you on the land.
I will toss you into the open field.
I will let the birds of the sky rest on you.
And I will let the animals of the earth eat you until they are full.
⁵I will scatter your flesh on the mountains.
And I will fill the valleys with what is left of you.
⁶I will drench the land with your flowing blood.
I will soak the mountains,
and the ravines will be full of your flesh.
⁷I will make you disappear.
And I will cover the sky and make the stars dark.
I will cover the sun with a cloud.
And the moon will not shine.
⁸I will make all the shining lights in the sky
become dark over you.
I will bring darkness over your land,
says the Lord God.
⁹I will cause many people to be afraid
when I have another nation destroy you.
Nations you have not known will be afraid because of you.

¹⁰I will cause people to be shocked
   about you.
      Their kings will tremble with fear
         because of you
      when I swing my sword before
         them.
   They will shake every moment
      on the day you fall.
      Each king will be afraid for his own
         life.

   ¹¹"'So this is what the Lord God says:
   The sword of the king of Babylon
      will come on you.
¹²I will cause your people to fall
      by the swords of mighty soldiers.
      They are the most terrible of all the
         nations.
   They will destroy the pride of Egypt.
      All Egypt's people will be destroyed.
¹³I will also destroy all Egypt's cattle
      which live alongside many waters.
   The foot of man will not stir the
      waters.
      And the hoofs of cattle will not
         muddy them anymore.
¹⁴So I will let the Egyptians' waters
      become quiet.
   I will cause their rivers to run as
      smoothly as olive oil,
      says the Lord God.
¹⁵I will make the land of Egypt empty.
   I will take everything that is in the
      land.
   I will destroy all those who live in
      Egypt.
      Then they will know that I am the
         Lord.'

¹⁶"This is the funeral song people will
sing for Egypt. The women of the nations
will sing it for Egypt. They will sing a
funeral song for Egypt and all its people,
says the Lord God."

EGYPT TO BE DESTROYED

¹⁷It happened in the twelfth year of
our captivity. It was on the fifteenth day
of the month. The Lord spoke his word
to me. He said: ¹⁸"Human being, cry for
the people of Egypt. Bring down Egypt,
together with the women of the powerful
nations. Bring them down to the earth
below. Bring them down with those who
go to the place of the dead. ¹⁹Say to them:
'Are you more beautiful than others? Go
lie down in death with those who are unclean.'ᵈ ²⁰The Egyptians will fall among
those killed by war. Egypt is going to be
killed by the sword. The enemy will drag
her and all her people away. ²¹The leaders
of the mighty ones will speak from the
place of death. They will say about the
king of Egypt and the nations which help
him: 'The king and the nations which
help him have come down here. They lie
killed by the sword among those who are
unclean.'

²²"Assyria and all its army lie dead
there. The graves of their soldiers are all
around. All were killed in war. ²³Assyria's
grave was put in the deep parts of the
place where the dead are. And its army
lies around its grave. When they lived,
they frightened people in the land of the
living. But now all of them have been
killed in war.

²⁴"The nation of Elam is there. And all
its army is around its grave. All of them
were killed in war. They had frightened
people on earth and were unclean. So
they went down to the lowest parts of the
place where the dead are. And they must
carry their shame with those who go
down to the place where the dead are.
²⁵A bed is made for Elam with all those
killed in war. They will be in the place
where the dead are. The graves of her
soldiers are all around her. Elam's people
are unclean. So they have been killed in
war. They also scared people who live on
earth. But they must also carry their
shame with those who go down to where
the dead are. Their graves are with the
rest who were killed.

²⁶"Meshech and Tubal are there. The
graves of all their soldiers surround
them. All of them are unclean. So they

have been killed in war. They also frightened people who live on earth. [27]But they are not buried with the other unclean soldiers who have been killed in battle. They are not with those who went where the dead are with their weapons of war. These soldiers had their swords laid under their heads and their shields on their bodies. People who live on earth used to be afraid of these mighty soldiers. [28]"You, king of Egypt, will be broken and lie among those who are unclean. You will be with those who were killed in war.

[29]"Edom is there also. Its kings and all its leaders are there. They were mighty. But now they lie in death with those killed in war. They will lie with those who are unclean. And they will be with those who go down to where the dead are.

[30]"All the rulers of the north are there. And all the Sidonians are there. Their strength frightened people. These rulers of the north and the Sidonians have gone down in shame with those who were killed. They are unclean, lying with those killed in war. They have carried their shame with those who go down to where the dead are.

[31]"The king of Egypt and his army will see these who have been killed in war. Then the king and all his army will be comforted for all his soldiers killed in war, says the Lord God. [32]I made people who live on earth afraid of the king of Egypt. But he and his people will lie among those who are unclean. They will lie with those who were killed by the sword, says the Lord God."

EZEKIEL IS WATCHMAN FOR ISRAEL

33 The Lord spoke his word to me. He said: [2]"Human being, speak to your people. Say to them: 'I might bring a war against a land. The people of the land may choose one of their men. They may make him their watchman. [3]This watchman might see the enemy coming to attack the land. And he blows the trumpet and warns the people. [4]A person might hear the sound of the trumpet, but do nothing. Then the enemy will come and kill him. That person will be responsible for his own death. [5]He heard the sound of the trumpet. But he did not do anything. So he is to blame for his own death. If he had done something, he would have saved his own life. [6]But the watchman might see the enemy coming to attack and not blow the trumpet. So the people are not warned. Then the enemy comes and kills one of them. That person has died because of his own sin. But I will punish the watchman for the person's death.'

[7]"As for you, human being, I have made you a watchman for Israel. If you hear a message from me, you must warn them for me. [8]I might say to the wicked person: 'Wicked man, you will surely die.' But you might not speak to warn the evil person to stop doing evil. Then he will die while still a sinner. But I will punish you for his death. [9]But you might warn a wicked person to stop doing evil. If he does not stop, he will die while still a sinner. But you have saved your life.

[10]"So you, human being, say to Israel: 'You have said: Surely our law-breaking and sins are hurting us. They will kill us. What can we do so we will live?' [11]Say to them: 'The Lord God says: As surely as I live, this is true. I do not want a wicked person to die. I want him to stop doing evil and live. Turn back! Turn back from your wicked ways! You don't want to die, people of Israel.'

[12]"And you, human being, say to your people: 'The goodness of a good person will not save him when he sins. The evil of the wicked person will not cause him to be punished if he turns from it. A good person will not be able to live by the good he did earlier if he sins.' [13]I might tell the good person, "You will surely live." But he might think he has done enough good and then do evil. Then none of the good

things he did will be remembered. He will die because of the evil he has done. ¹⁴Or, I might say to the wicked person, "You will surely die." But he might turn from his sin and do what is right and honest. ¹⁵He returns what somebody gave him as a promise to repay a loan. He pays back what he stole. He lives by the rules that give life. He does not sin. Then that one will surely live. He will not die. ¹⁶He will not be punished for any of his sins. He now does what is right and fair. He will surely live.

¹⁷"But your people say: 'The way of the Lord is not fair.' But it is their own way that is not fair. ¹⁸The good person might turn from his goodness and do evil. Then he will die for his evil. ¹⁹But the wicked person might stop doing evil and do what is right and fair. Then he will live. ²⁰You still say: 'The way of the Lord is not fair.' Israel, I will judge each of you by his own ways."

THE FALL OF JERUSALEM EXPLAINED

²¹It happened in the twelfth year of our captivity. It was on the fifth day of the tenth month. A person who had escaped from Jerusalem came to me. He said, "Jerusalem has been defeated." ²²Now I had felt the power of the Lord on me the evening before. The Lord had made me able to talk again. He did this before the person came to me in the morning. I could speak. I was not without speech anymore.

²³Then the Lord spoke his word to me. He said: ²⁴"Human being, people who live in the ruins in the land of Israel are saying: 'Abraham was only one person. Yet he was given the land as his own. Surely the land has been given to us, who are many, as our very own.' ²⁵So say to them: 'This is what the Lord God says: You eat meat with the blood still in it. You ask your idols for help. You murder people. Should you then have the land as your very own? ²⁶You depend on your sword. You do terrible things which I

hate. Each of you has sexual relations with his neighbor's wife. So should you have the land?'

²⁷"Say to them: 'This is what the Lord God says: As surely as I live, this is true. Those who are among the city ruins in Israel will be killed in war. Those who live in the country will be eaten by wild animals. People hiding in the strong places and caves will die of disease. ²⁸I will make the land an empty desert. The people's pride in the land's power will end. The mountains of Israel will become empty. No one will pass through them. ²⁹They will know that I am the Lord when I make the land an empty desert. This is because of the things they have done that I hate.'

³⁰"But as for you, human being, your people talk against you. They talk by the walls and in the doorways of houses. They say to each other: 'Come now, and hear the message from the Lord.' ³¹So they come to you as if they are still my people. They sit before you. They hear your words. But they will not do them. With their mouths they tell me they love me. But their hearts desire their selfish profits. ³²To your people you are nothing more than a singer who sings love songs. You are like one who has a beautiful voice. You are like one who plays a musical instrument well. They hear your words, but they will not do them.

³³"This will come true. It will surely happen. Then the people will know that a prophet*d* has been among them."

THE LEADERS ARE LIKE SHEPHERDS

34 The Lord spoke his word to me. He said: ²"Human being, prophesy*d* against the leaders of Israel, who are like shepherds. Prophesy and say to them: 'This is what the Lord God says: How terrible it will be for the shepherds of Israel who feed only themselves! Why don't the shepherds feed the flock? ³You eat the milk curds from the sheep. You clothe yourselves with the wool from the sheep. You kill the fat sheep. But you do not feed the flock. ⁴You have not made the weak strong. You have not healed the sick. You have not put bandages on those that were hurt. You have not brought back those who strayed away. You have not searched for the lost. You ruled the sheep with cruel force. ⁵The sheep were scattered because there was no shepherd. Then they became food for every wild animal. ⁶My flock wandered over all the mountains and on every high hill. They were scattered over all the face of the earth. And no one searched or looked for them.

⁷"So, you shepherds, hear the word of the Lord. This is what the Lord God says: ⁸As surely as I live, my flock has been caught. It has become food for all the wild animals. This is because the flock has no shepherd. The shepherds did not search for my flock. No, they fed themselves instead of my flock. ⁹So, you shepherds, hear the word of the Lord. ¹⁰This is what the Lord God says: I am against the shepherds. I will blame them for what has happened to my sheep. I will not let them tend the flock anymore. Then the shepherds will stop feeding themselves. And I will take my flock from their mouths. My sheep will no longer be their food.

¹¹"This is what the Lord God says: I, myself, will search for my sheep. I will take care of them. ¹²A shepherd will take care of his scattered flock when it is found. In the same way I will take care of my sheep. I will save them from all the places where they are scattered. I will do this on a cloudy and dark day. ¹³I will bring them out from the nations. I will gather them from the countries. I will bring them to their own land. I will pasture them on the mountains and in the ravines of Israel. And I will feed them in all the places where people live in the land. ¹⁴I will feed them in a good pasture. They will eat grass on the high mountains of Israel. They will lie down on

good ground where they eat grass. They will eat in rich grassland on the mountains of Israel. ¹⁵I will feed my flock and lead them to rest, says the Lord God. ¹⁶I will search for the lost. I will bring back those that were scattered. I will put bandages on those that were hurt. I will make the weak strong. I will destroy those sheep that are fat and strong. I will tend the sheep with fairness.

¹⁷"This is what the Lord God says: And as for you, my flock, I will judge between one sheep and another. I will judge between the male sheep and the male goats. ¹⁸Is it not enough for you to eat grass in the good land? Must you crush the rest of the grass with your feet? Is it not enough for you to drink clear water? Must you make the rest of the water muddy with your feet? ¹⁹Must my flock eat what you crush? And must they drink what you make muddy with your feet?

²⁰"So this is what the Lord God says to them: I, myself, will judge between the fat sheep and the thin sheep. ²¹You push with your side and with your shoulder. You knock down all the weak sheep with your horns. You do this until you have forced them away. ²²So I will save my flock. They will not be hurt anymore. I will judge between one sheep and another. ²³Then I will put one shepherd over them, my servant David. He will feed them. He will tend them and will be their shepherd. ²⁴Then I, the Lord, will be their God. And my servant David will be a ruler among them. I, the Lord, have spoken.

²⁵"And I will make an agreement of peace with my sheep. I will remove harmful animals from the land. Then the sheep will live safely in the desert. And they will sleep in the woods without danger. ²⁶I will bless them and let them live around my hill. I will cause the rains to come when it is time for them. There will be showers to bless them. ²⁷Also the trees of the field will give their fruit. The land will give its harvest. And the sheep will

be safe on their land. Then they will know that I am the Lord. I will break the bars of their captivity. And I will save them from the power of those who made them slaves. [28]They will not be led captive by the nations again. The wild animals will not eat them. But they will live safely. No one will make them afraid. [29]I will give them a place famous for its good crops. Then they will no longer suffer from hunger in the land. They will not suffer the insults of other nations anymore. [30]Then they will know that I, the Lord their God, am with them. The nation of Israel will know that they are my people, says the Lord God. [31]And you, my sheep, are the sheep of my pasture. You are my people and I am your God, says the Lord God.'"

PROPHECY AGAINST EDOM

35 The Lord spoke his word to me. He said: [2]"Human being, look toward Mount Edom and prophesy[d] against it. [3]Say to it: 'This is what the Lord God says: I am against you, Mount Edom. I will stretch out my hand against you. And I will make you an empty desert. [4]I will destroy your cities. And you will become empty. Then you will know that I am the Lord.

[5]"'This is because you have always been an enemy of Israel. You let them be defeated in war when they were in trouble. It was the time of their final punishment. [6]So the Lord God says, As surely as I live, I will let you be murdered. Murder will chase you. You did not hate murdering people, so murder will chase you. [7]And I will make Mount Edom an empty ruin. And I will destroy everyone who goes in or comes out of it. [8]I will fill its mountains with those who are killed. Those killed in war will fall on your hills. They will fall in your valleys and in all your ravines. [9]I will make you a ruin forever. No one will live in your cities. Then you will know that I am the Lord.

[10]"'You said, "These two nations, Israel and Judah, and these two lands will be ours. We will take them for our own." But the Lord was there. [11]So this is what the Lord God says: As surely as I live, this is true. I will treat you just as you treated them. When you were angry and jealous, you acted hatefully against them. I will punish you. And that is how I will show the Israelites who I am. [12]Then you will know that I, the Lord God, have heard all your insults. Those insults were against the mountains of Israel. You said, "They have been ruined. They have been given to us to eat." [13]You have not stopped your proud talk against me. I have heard you. [14]This is what the Lord God says: All the earth will be happy when I make you an empty ruin. [15]You were happy when the land of Israel was ruined. But I will do the same thing to you. Mount Edom and all Edom, you will become an empty ruin. Then you will know that I am the Lord God.'"

ISRAEL TO COME HOME

36 "Human being, prophesy[d] to the mountains of Israel and say: 'Mountains of Israel, hear the word of the Lord. [2]This is what the Lord God says: The enemy has said this against you: "Now the old places to worship false gods have become ours."' [3]So prophesy and say: 'This is what the Lord God says: They have made you an empty ruin. They have crushed you from all around. You belonged to the other nations. People talked and whispered against you. [4]So, mountains of Israel, hear the word of the Lord God. The Lord God speaks to the mountains, hills, ravines and valleys. And he speaks to the empty ruins and abandoned cities that have been robbed and laughed at by the other nations. [5]This is what the Lord God says: I have spoken in hot anger against the other nations. I have spoken against Edom. The Edomites took my land for themselves. They did this with joy and with hate in their hearts. They forced out the people and took their pastureland.' ⁶So prophesy about the land of Israel. Say to the mountains, hills, ravines and valleys: 'This is what the Lord God says: I speak in my jealous anger. This is because you have suffered the insults of the nations. ⁷So this is what the Lord God says: I promise that the nations around you will also have to suffer insults.

⁸"But you, mountains of Israel, you will grow branches and fruit for my people. My people will soon come home. ⁹I am concerned about you. I am for you. You will be plowed, and seed will be planted in you. ¹⁰I will multiply the people who live on you. All the people of Israel will come. The cities will have people living in them. The ruins will be rebuilt. ¹¹I will make the people and animals living on you increase in number. They will grow and be fruitful. You will have people living on you as you did before. I will make you better off than at the beginning. Then you will know that I am the Lord. ¹²I will cause my people Israel to walk on you. Then they will take you, and you will belong to them. You will never again take their children away from them.

¹³"This is what the Lord God says: People say about you: "You eat people and take children from your nation." ¹⁴You will not destroy people anymore. You will not make your nation stumble anymore, says the Lord God. ¹⁵I will not make you listen to insults from the nations anymore. You will not suffer shame from them anymore, says the Lord God.'"

THE LORD ACTS FOR HIMSELF

¹⁶The Lord spoke his word to me again. He said: ¹⁷"Human being, the nation of Israel was living in their own land. But they made it unclean*d* by their ways and the things they did. Their ways were like a woman's uncleanness in her time of monthly bleeding. ¹⁸So I poured out my anger against them. I did it because of the murders they did in the land. And I did it because they made the land unclean with their idols. ¹⁹I scattered them among the nations. And they were spread through all the countries. I punished them for how they lived and the things they did. ²⁰They dishonored my holy name in the nations where they went. The nations said about them: 'These are the people of the Lord. But they had to leave the land which he gave them.' ²¹But I felt bad about my holy name. The nation of Israel had dishonored it among the nations where they went.

²²"So say to the people of Israel, 'This is what the Lord God says: Israel, I am going to act, but not for your sake. Israel, I will do something to help my holy name. You have dishonored it among the nations where you went. ²³I will prove the holiness of my great name. It has been dishonored among the nations. You have dishonored it among these nations. But the nations will know that I am the Lord. I will prove myself holy before their eyes, says the Lord God.

²⁴"I will take you from the nations. I will gather you out of all the lands. And I will bring you back into your own land. ²⁵Then I will sprinkle clean water on you, and you will be clean. I will cleanse you from all your uncleanness and your idols. ²⁶Also, I will teach you to respect me completely. I will put a new way to think inside you. I will take out the stubborn heart like stone from your bodies. And I will give you an obedient heart of flesh. ²⁷I will put my Spirit*d* inside you. And I will help you live by my rules. You will be careful to obey my laws. ²⁸Then you will live in the land I gave to your ancestors. So you will be my people, and I will be your God. ²⁹Also, I will save you from all your uncleanness. I will command the grain to come and grow. I will not allow a time of hunger to hurt you. ³⁰I will multiply the harvest of the field. You

will never again suffer shame among the nations because of hunger. [31]And you will remember your evil ways and the things you did that were not good. Then you will hate yourselves because of your sins and terrible acts that I hate. [32]I want you to know that I am not doing this for your sake, says the Lord God. Be ashamed and embarrassed about your ways, Israel.

[33]"This is what the Lord God says: This is what will happen on the day I cleanse you from all your sins: I will cause the cities to have people living in them again. And the destroyed places will be rebuilt. [34]The empty land will be plowed. It will no longer be a ruin for everyone who passes by to see. [35]They will say: "This land was ruined. Now it has become like the garden of Eden. The cities were destroyed. They were empty and ruined. But now they are protected and have people living in them." [36]Then those nations still around you will know. They will know that I, the Lord, have rebuilt what was destroyed. And I have planted what was empty. I, the Lord, have spoken. And I will do it.'

[37]"This is what the Lord God says: I will again be asked by the people of Israel to do this thing for them. I will make their people grow to be as many as a flock of sheep. [38]They will be like the flocks brought to Jerusalem during her holy feasts. Her ruined cities will be filled with flocks of people. Then they will know that I am the Lord."

THE VISION OF DRY BONES

37 I felt the power of the Lord was on me. He brought me out by the Spirit[d] of the Lord. And he put me down in the middle of a valley. It was full of bones. [2]The Lord led me around among the bones. There were many bones on the bottom of the valley. I saw the bones were very dry. [3]Then he asked me, "Human being, can these bones live?"

I answered, "Lord God, only you know."

[4]The Lord said to me, "Prophesy[d] to these bones. Say to them, 'Dry bones, hear the word of the Lord. [5]This is what the Lord God says to the bones: I will cause breath to enter you. Then you will live. [6]I will put muscles on you. I will put flesh on you. I will cover you with skin. Then I will put breath in you, and you will live. Then you will know that I am the Lord.'"

[7]So I prophesied as I was commanded. While I prophesied, there was a noise and a rattling. The bones came together, bone to bone. [8]I looked and saw muscles come on the bones. Flesh grew, and skin covered the bones. But there was no breath in them.

[9]Then the Lord said to me, "Prophesy to the wind.[n] Prophesy, human being, and say to the wind: 'This is what the Lord God says: Wind, come from the four winds. Breathe on these people who were killed so they can live again.'" [10]So I prophesied as the Lord commanded me. And the breath came into them, and they came to life. They stood on their feet. They were a very large army.

[11]Then the Lord said to me: "Human being, these bones are like all the people of Israel. They say, 'Our bones are dried up, and our hope has gone. We are destroyed.' [12]So, prophesy, and say to them: 'This is what the Lord God says: My people, I will open your graves. And I will cause you to come up out of your graves. Then I will bring you into the land of Israel. [13]This is how you, my people, will know that I am the Lord. I will open your graves and cause you to come up from them. [14]And I will put my Spirit inside you. You will come to life. Then I will put you in your own land. And you will know that I, the Lord, have spoken and done it, says the Lord.'"

37:9 wind This Hebrew word could also mean "breath" or "spirit."

JUDAH AND ISRAEL BACK TOGETHER

¹⁵The Lord spoke his word to me. He said, ¹⁶"Human being, take a stick of wood. Write on it, 'For Judah and all the Israelites with him.' Then take another stick of wood. Write on it, 'The stick of Ephraim, for Joseph and all the Israelites with him.' ¹⁷Then join them together into one stick. Then they will be one in your hand.

¹⁸"Your people will say to you, 'Explain to us what you mean by this.' ¹⁹Tell them, 'This is what the Lord God says: I will take the stick which is for Joseph and the tribes^d of Israel with him. This stick is in the hand of Ephraim. Then I will put it with the stick of Judah. And I will make them into one stick. And they will be one in my hand.' ²⁰Hold the sticks of wood on which you wrote these names. Hold them in your hands so the people can see them. ²¹Say to the people: 'This is what the Lord God says: I will take the people of Israel from among the nations where they have gone. I will gather them from all around. I will bring them into their own land. ²²I will make them one nation in the land, on the mountains of Israel. One king will rule all of them. They will never again be two nations. They will not be divided into two kingdoms anymore. ²³They will not continue to make themselves unclean^d by their idols, their statues of gods which I hate or their sins. But I will save them from all the ways they sin and turn against me. And I will make them clean. Then they will be my people. And I will be their God.

²⁴"'And my servant David will be their king. They will all have one shepherd. They will live by my rules and obey my laws. ²⁵They will live on the land I gave to my servant Jacob. It is the land in which your ancestors lived. They will all live on the land forever: they, their children and their grandchildren. David my servant will be their king forever. ²⁶And I will make an agreement of peace with them. It will be an agreement that continues forever. I will put them in their land. I will make them grow in number. Then I will put my Temple^d among them forever. ²⁷The place where I live will be with them. I will be their God, and they will be my people. ²⁸When my Temple is among them forever, the nations will know that I, the Lord, make Israel holy.'"

PROPHECY AGAINST GOG

38 The Lord spoke his word to me. He said: ²"Human being, turn toward Gog of the land of Magog. He is the chief ruler of the nations of Meshech and Tubal. Prophesy^d against him. ³Say, 'The Lord God says this: I am against you, Gog, chief ruler of Meshech and Tubal. ⁴I will turn you around. I will put hooks in your jaws. And I will bring you out with all your army, horses and horsemen. All of them will be finely dressed. They will be a large army with large and small shields. All of them will have swords. ⁵Persia, Cush and Put will be with them. All of them will have shields and helmets. ⁶There will also be Gomer with all its troops. And there will be the nation of Togarmah from the far north. It will have all its troops. There will be many other nations with you.

⁷"'Be prepared. Be prepared, you and all the armies that have come together to make you their commander. ⁸After many days you will be called for service. After many years you will come into a land that has been rebuilt from war. The people in the land will be gathered from many nations to the mountains of Israel. Those mountains were empty for a long time. These people were brought out from the nations. They will all be living in safety. ⁹And you will go up like a storm. You will be like a cloud covering the land. It will be you, all your troops and many nations with you.

¹⁰"'This is what the Lord God says: At that time ideas will come into your mind.

You will think up an evil plan. [11]You will say, "I will march against a land of towns without walls. I will attack those who are at rest and live in safety. All of them live without city walls. They have no gate bars or gates. [12]I will capture valuable things and take good things. I will turn my power against the rebuilt ruins that now have people living in them. I will go against these people who have been gathered from the nations. They have become rich with farm animals and property. They live at the center of the world." [13]Sheba, Dedan and the traders of Tarshish, with all its villages, will say this to you: "Did you come to capture valuable things? Did you bring your troops together to take things? Did you bring them to carry away silver and gold? Did you bring them to take away farm animals and property?"'

[14]"So prophesy, human being, and say to Gog: 'This is what the Lord God says: Now that my people Israel are living in safety, you will know about it. [15]You will come from your place in the far north. And many people will be with you. All of them will ride on horses. You will be a large group with a mighty army. [16]You will come against my people Israel like a cloud that covers the land. This will happen in the days to come. I will bring you against my land. Gog, then the nations will know me. They will see me show my greatness by what I do through you.

[17]"'This is what the Lord God says: You are the one about whom I spoke in past days. I spoke through my servants the prophets of Israel. These prophets of Israel prophesied for many years. They said that I would bring you against them. [18]This is what will happen: On the day Gog comes against the land of Israel, my anger will become very great, says the Lord God. [19]With jealousy and great anger I tell you this. At that time there will surely be a great earthquake in Israel.

[20]The fish of the sea and the birds of the sky will shake with fear before me. The wild animals and everything that crawls on the ground will shake with fear. And all the people on the earth will shake with fear before me. Also the mountains will be thrown down. And the cliffs will fall. Every wall will fall to the ground. [21]And I will call for a war against Gog on all my mountains, says the Lord God. Every man's sword will be against his brother. [22]I will punish Gog with disease and death. I will send a heavy rain, with hailstones and burning sulfur on Gog. I will send it on his army and on the many nations with him. [23]Then I will show how great I am. I will show my holiness. And I will make myself known to the many nations that watch. Then they will know that I am the Lord.'

THE DEATH OF GOG AND HIS ARMY

39 "Human being, prophesy[d] against Gog and say: 'This is what the Lord God says: I am against you, Gog, chief ruler of Meshech and Tubal. [2]I will turn you around and lead you. I will bring you from the far north. I will send you to attack the mountains of Israel. [3]I will knock your bow out of your left hand. I will throw down your arrows from your right hand. [4]You will fall dead on the mountains of Israel. You, all your troops and the nations with you will fall dead. I will let you be food for every bird that eats meat and every wild animal. [5]You will die in the country. I have spoken, says the Lord God. [6]I will send fire on Magog and those who live in safety on the coastlands. Then they will know that I am the Lord.

[7]"'And I will make myself known among my people Israel. I will not let myself be dishonored anymore. Then the nations will know that I am the Lord. They will know I am the Holy One in Israel. [8]It is coming! It will happen, says the Lord God. The day I talked about is coming.

⁹"'Then those who live in the cities of Israel will go out. They will make fires with the enemy's weapons and burn them. They will burn both large and small shields. They will burn bows and arrows, war clubs and spears. They will use the weapons to burn in their fires for seven years. ¹⁰They won't need to take wood from the field or chop firewood from the forests. This is because they will make fires with the weapons. They will take the valuable things of those who took their valuable things. They will grab the things of those who grabbed their things, says the Lord God.

¹¹"'On that day I will give Gog a place to be buried in Israel. It will be the Valley of the Travelers, east of the Dead Sea.^{d} It will block the road for travelers. This is because Gog and all his army will be buried there. People will call it The Valley of Gog's Army.

¹²"'The people of Israel will be burying them for seven months to make the land clean^d again. ¹³All the people of the land will bury them. The people of Israel will be honored on the day of my victory, says the Lord God.

¹⁴"'They will choose men to work through the land to make it clean. With others they will bury Gog's soldiers still lying dead on the ground. After the seven months are finished, they will still search. ¹⁵They will go through the land. If one person sees a human bone, he will put a marker by it. The sign will stay there until the gravediggers come. They will bury the bone in The Valley of Gog's Army. ¹⁶A city will be there named Hamonah. So they will make the land clean again.'

¹⁷"Human being, this is what the Lord God says: Speak to every kind of bird and wild animal: 'Come together, come! Come together from all around to my sacrifice. I will prepare it for you. It is a great sacrifice on the mountains of Israel. Then you can eat flesh and drink blood. ¹⁸You will eat the flesh of mighty men.

You will drink the blood of the rulers of the earth. You will do it as people eat all the fat animals from Bashan: male sheep, lambs, goats and bulls. ¹⁹You will eat and drink from my sacrifice which I have made ready for you. So you will eat fat until you are full. You will drink blood until you are drunk. ²⁰At my table you will eat until you are full of horses and riders and all kinds of soldiers,' says the Lord God.

²¹"And I will show my greatness among the nations. All the nations will feel my power when I punish them. ²²From that day on the people of Israel will know that I am the Lord their God. ²³And the nations will know Israel was taken away captive because they turned against me. So I turned away from them. And I let their enemies defeat them. All of them died in war. ²⁴I punished them for their uncleanness^d and their sins. I turned away from them.

²⁵"So this is what the Lord God says: Now I will bring the people of Jacob back from captivity. I will have mercy on the whole nation of Israel. I will not let them dishonor me. ²⁶The people will forget their shame. And they will forget how they rejected me. They will live in safety on their own land. No one will make them afraid. ²⁷I will bring the people back from other lands. I will gather them from the lands of their enemies. That is how I will show that I am holy through my people. And many nations will see that I am holy. ²⁸Then my people will know that I am the Lord their God. This is because I sent them into captivity among the nations. But then I brought them back to their own land. And I didn't leave any behind. ²⁹I will not turn away from them anymore. I will put my Spirit^d into the people of Israel, says the Lord God."

THE NEW TEMPLE

40 It was the twenty-fifth year of our captivity. It was at the beginning of the year, on the tenth day of the month. It was in the fourteenth year after Jerusalem was defeated. On that same day I felt the power of the Lord. He brought me to Jerusalem. [2]In the visions of God he brought me into the land of Israel. He put me on a very high mountain. On the south of the mountain there were some buildings that looked like a city. [3]The Lord took me closer to the buildings. I saw a man who looked as if he were made of bronze. He was standing in the gateway. He had a cord made of linen and a stick in his hand, both for measuring. [4]The man said to me, "Human being, look with your eyes and hear with your ears. And pay attention to all that I will show you. That's why you have been brought here. Tell the people of Israel all that you see."

THE EAST GATE

[5]I saw a wall that surrounded the Temple.[d] The measuring stick in the man's hand was $10^1/_2$ feet long. So the man measured the wall. It was $10^1/_2$ feet thick and $10^1/_2$ feet high.

[6]Then the man went to the east gate. He went up its steps and measured the opening of the gate. It was more than $10^1/_2$ feet wide. [7]There were rooms for the guards. They were $10^1/_2$ feet long and $10^1/_2$ feet wide. The walls that came out between the guards' rooms were about 9 feet thick. And there was a gate next to the porch that faced the Temple. The opening of this gate was $10^1/_2$ feet wide.

[8]Then the man measured the porch of the gate. [9]It was about 14 feet deep. And its doors were $3^1/_2$ feet thick. The porch of the gate faced the Temple.

[10]There were three little rooms on each side of the last gate. These three rooms measured the same on each side. The walls between each room were the same thickness. [11]The man measured the width of the entrance to the gateway. It was $17^1/_2$ feet wide. The length of the gate was about 23 feet. [12]And there was a low wall about 21 inches high in front of each room. The rooms were $10^1/_2$ feet on each side. [13]The man measured the gateway from the roof of one room to the roof of the opposite room. It was about 44 feet from one door to the opposite door. [14]The man also measured the porch. It was about 35 feet wide. The courtyard was around the porch. [15]From the front of the outer side of the gate to the front of the porch of the inner side of the gate was $87^1/_2$ feet. [16]The rooms and porch had small windows on all sides. The windows were narrower on the side facing the gateway. Carvings of palm trees were on each inner wall of the rooms.

THE OUTER COURTYARD

[17]Then the man brought me into the outer courtyard. I saw rooms and a pavement of stones. Thirty rooms were along the edge of the paved walkway. [18]The pavement ran alongside the gates. It was as long as the gates were wide. This was the lower pavement. [19]Then the man measured from the outer wall to the inner wall. The outer court between these two walls was 175 feet on the east and on the north.

THE NORTH GATE

[20]The man measured the length and width of the gate leading to the outer courtyard. It faced north. [21]It had three rooms on each side. Its inner walls and its porch measured the same as the first gate. It was $87^1/_2$ feet long. And it was 44 feet wide. [22]Its windows, porch and carvings of palm trees measured the same as the east gate. Seven steps went up to the gate. And the gate's porch was opposite them. [23]The inner courtyard had a gate across from the northern gate like the one on the east. The man measured it and found it was 175 feet from inner gate to outer gate.

THE SOUTH GATE

[24]Then the man led me south. I saw a gate facing south. He measured its inner walls and its porch. They measured the same as the other gates. [25]The gate and

its porch had windows all around like the other gates. It was 87¹/₂ feet long and 44 feet wide. ²⁶Seven steps went up to this gate. Its porch was in front of them. It had carvings of palm trees on its inner walls. ²⁷A gate was on the south side of the inner courtyard. The man measured from gate to gate on the south side. It was 175 feet.

THE INNER COURTYARD

²⁸Then the man brought me through the south gate to the inner courtyard. The inner south gate measured the same as the gates in the outer wall. ²⁹The inner southgate's rooms, inner walls and porch measured the same as the gates in the outer wall. There were windows all around the gate and its porch. The gate was 87¹/₂ feet long and 44 feet wide. ³⁰Each porch of each inner gate was about 44 feet long and about 9 feet wide. ³¹The inner south gate's porch faced the outer courtyard. Carvings of palm trees were on its inside walls. Its stairway had eight steps.

³²The man brought me into the inner courtyard on the east side. He measured the inner east gate. It measured the same as the other gates. ³³The inner east gate's rooms, inside walls and porch measured the same as the other gates. Windows were all around the gate and its porch. The inner east gate was 87¹/₂ feet long and 44 feet wide. ³⁴Its porch faced the outer courtyard. Carvings of palm trees were on its inner walls on each side. Its stairway had eight steps.

³⁵Then the man brought me to the inner north gate. He measured it. It measured the same as the other gates. ³⁶Its rooms, inner walls and porch measured the same as the other gates. Windows were all around the gate. It was 87¹/₂ feet long and 44 feet wide. ³⁷Its porch faced the outer courtyard. Carvings of palm trees were on its inner walls on each side. And its stairway had eight steps.

ROOMS FOR PREPARING SACRIFICES

³⁸There was a room with a door that opened onto the porch of the inner north gate. In this room the priests washed animals for the burnt offerings. ³⁹There were two tables on each side of the room. Animals for burnt offerings, sin offerings and penalty offerings were killed on these tables. ⁴⁰On each side of the porch, outside the door to the room, were two tables. ⁴¹So four tables were on one side of the gate. And four tables were on the other side of the gate. In all there were eight tables on which the priests killed animals for sacrifices. ⁴²There were four tables of cut stone for the burnt offering. These tables were about 3 feet long and 3 feet wide. And they were about 2 feet high. On these tables the priests put their tools. They used the tools to kill animals for burnt offerings and the other sacrifices. ⁴³Double hooks 3 inches long were put up on all the walls. The flesh for the offering was put on the tables.

THE PRIESTS' ROOMS

⁴⁴There were two rooms in the inner courtyard. One was beside the north gate. It faced south. The other room was beside the south gate. It faced north. ⁴⁵The man said to me, "The room which faces the south is for the priests. They serve in the Temple.ᵈ ⁴⁶And the room that faces north is for the priests who serve at the altar. These priests are descendantsᵈ of Zadok. They are the only descendants of Levi who can come near the Lord to serve him."

⁴⁷The man measured the Temple courtyard. It was a perfect square. It was 175 feet long and 175 feet wide. The altar was in front of the Temple.

THE TEMPLE PORCH

⁴⁸The man brought me to the porch of the Temple.ᵈ And he measured each wall of the porch. It was about 9 feet on each side. The gate was 24¹/₂ feet wide. The walls of the gate were about 5 feet on each side. ⁴⁹The porch was 35 feet long

and 21 feet wide. Ten steps went up to the porch. Pillars were by the walls, one on each side of the entrance.

THE HOLY PLACE OF THE TEMPLE

41 The man brought me to the Holy Place. He measured its walls. They were $10^1/_2$ feet wide on each side. [2]The entrance was $17^1/_2$ feet wide. The walls alongside the entrance were about 9 feet wide on each side. The man measured the Holy Place. It was 70 feet long and 35 feet wide.

[3]Then the man went inside. And he measured the walls of the doorway. Each was $3^1/_2$ feet wide. The doorway was $10^1/_2$ feet wide. The walls next to it were more than 12 feet thick. [4]Then the man measured the room at the end of the Holy Place. It was 35 feet long and 35 feet wide. The man said to me, "This is the Most Holy Place."

[5]Then the man measured the wall of the Temple.[d] It was $10^1/_2$ feet wide. The side rooms were 7 feet wide all around the Temple. [6]The side rooms were on three different stories, each above the other. There were 30 rooms on each story. The side rooms had ledges on the wall all around. The rooms rested on the ledges but were not attached to the walls. [7]The side rooms around the Temple were wider on each higher story. So rooms were wider on the top story. A stairway went up from the lowest story to the highest through the middle story.

[8]I also saw that the Temple had a raised base all around. It was the foundation for the side rooms and was $10^1/_2$ feet thick. [9]The outer wall of the side rooms was about 9 feet thick. There was an open area between the side rooms of the Temple [10]and the priests' rooms. It was 35 feet wide and went all around the Temple. [11]The doors of the side rooms led to a paved base around the outside of the Temple. One door faced north. And the other door faced south. The paved base was about 9 feet wide all around.

[12]There was a building facing the Temple courtyard at the west side. It was $122^1/_2$ feet wide. The wall of the building was about 9 feet thick all around. It was $157^1/_2$ feet long.

[13]Then the man measured the Temple. The Temple was 175 feet long. This included the courtyard with the building and its walls. It was all 175 feet long. [14]Also the eastern front of the Temple and its courtyard was 175 feet wide.

[15]The man measured the length of the building facing the courtyard on the west side, including its side rooms. Its walls from one side to the other were 175 feet.

The Holy Place, the Most Holy Place and the porch of the courtyard [16]had wood panels on the walls. By the doorway, the Temple had wood panels on the walls. The wood covered all the walls from the floor up to the windows. The windows were covered with crossed strips of wood.

[17]In the space above the entrance to the Most Holy Place there were carvings. And on the outside and all the walls around the Most Holy Place and the Holy Place were carvings. [18]The carvings were of creatures with wings and palm trees. A palm tree was between each carved creature. Every creature had two faces. [19]One was a man's face looking toward the palm tree on one side. The other was a lion's face looking toward the palm tree on the other side. They were carved all around the Temple wall. [20]This was from the floor to above the door. Palm trees and creatures with wings were carved on all the walls of the Holy Place. [21]The walls of the Holy Place were square. In front of the Most Holy Place was something that looked like [22]an altar of wood. It was more than 5 feet high and 3 feet wide. Its corners, base and sides were wood. The man said to me, "This is the table that is in the presence of the Lord." [23]Both the Holy Place and the Most Holy Place had double doors. [24]Each of the doors had

two pieces that would swing open. [25]Palm trees and creatures with wings were also carved on the doors of the Holy Place. They were like those carved on the walls. And there was a wood roof on the front Temple porch. [26]There were windows and palm trees on both side walls of the porch. The side rooms of the Temple were also covered by a roof.

THE PRIESTS' ROOM

42 Then the man led me north out into the outer courtyard. He led me to the rooms across from the Temple[d] courtyard. The outer wall was north of these rooms. [2]The building on the north side was 175 feet long and 87$\frac{1}{2}$ feet wide. [3]There was 35 feet of the Temple courtyard between this building and the Temple. On the other side, this building faced the stone pavement of the outer courtyard. The building had rooms and balconies on three stories. [4]There was a hallway on the north side of the rooms. It was 17$\frac{1}{2}$ feet wide and 175 feet long. Doors led into the rooms from this hallway. [5]The top rooms were narrower. This was because the balconies took more space from them. The rooms on the first and second stories of the building were wider. [6]The rooms were on three stories. They did not have pillars like the pillars of the courtyards. So the top rooms were farther back than those on the first and second stories. [7]There was a wall outside parallel to the rooms and to the outer courtyard. It ran in front of the rooms for 87$\frac{1}{2}$ feet. [8]The row of rooms along the outer courtyard was 87$\frac{1}{2}$ feet long. The rooms that faced the Temple were about 175 feet long. [9]The lower rooms had an entrance on the east end of the building. This was so a person could enter them from the courtyard.

[10]There were rooms on the south side, parallel to the wall of the outer courtyard. They faced the Temple courtyard. [11]These rooms had a hallway in front of them. They were like the rooms on the north. They had the same length and width. And the doors were the same. [12]The doors of the south rooms were like the doors of the north rooms. There was a door at the east end of a hall. This hall went to all the rooms.

[13]The man said to me, "The north and south rooms across from the Temple courtyard are holy rooms. There the priests who go near the Lord will eat the most holy offerings. There they will put the most holy offerings: the grain offerings, sin offerings and the penalty offerings. [14]The priests who enter the Holy Place must leave their serving clothes there. Then they may go into the outer courtyard. This is because these clothes are holy. The priests must put on other clothes. Then they may go to the part of the Temple which is for the people."

THE OUTSIDE OF THE TEMPLE

[15]The man finished measuring inside the Temple.[d] Then he brought me out through the east gate. He measured the area all around. [16]The man measured the east side with the measuring stick. It was 875 feet by the measuring stick. [17]He measured the north side. It was 875 feet by the measuring stick. [18]He measured the south side. It was 875 feet by the measuring stick. [19]He went around to the west side. And it measured 875 feet by the measuring stick. [20]So he measured the Temple on all four sides. The Temple had a wall all around it. It was 875 feet long and 875 feet wide. It separated the holy from that which is not holy.

THE LORD AMONG HIS PEOPLE

43 The man led me to the outer east gate. [2]And I saw the greatness of the God of Israel coming from the east. God's voice was like the roar of rushing water. His greatness made the earth shine. [3]I saw a vision. It was like the vision I had seen when the Lord came to destroy the city. It was also like the vision I had seen by the Kebar River.

I bowed facedown on the ground. [4]The greatness of the Lord came into the Temple[d] through the east gate.

[5]Then the Spirit[d] picked me up. And he brought me into the inner courtyard. There the Lord's greatness filled the Temple. [6]The man stood at my side. I heard someone speaking to me from inside the Temple. [7]The voice from the Temple said to me, "Human being, this is my throne. And this is the place my feet rest. I will live here among the Israelites forever. The people of Israel will not make my holy name unclean[d] again. Neither the people nor their kings will make it unclean by their sexual sins. Nor will they make it unclean with the dead bodies of their kings. [8]They made my name unclean by putting their doorway next to my doorway. And they put their doorpost next to my doorpost. Only a wall separated me from them. When they did their acts that I hate, they made my holy name unclean. So I destroyed them in my anger. [9]Now let them stop their sexual sins. And let them take the dead bodies of their kings far away from me. Then I will live among them forever.

[10]"Human being, tell the people of Israel about the Temple. Then they will be ashamed of their sins. Let them think about the plan of the Temple. [11]Then they will be ashamed of all they have done. Let them know the design of the Temple. Let them know how it is built. Show them its exits and entrances. Show them all its designs, all its rules and all its teachings. And write the rules as they watch. Do this so they can obey all the Temple's teachings and rules. [12]This is the teaching of the Temple: All the area around the top of the mountain is most holy. This is the teaching of the Temple.

THE ALTAR

[13]"And these are the measurements of the altar, using the measuring stick. It is 21 inches long. The altar's base is 21 inches high and 21 inches long. Its rim is about 9 inches around its edge. And the altar is this tall: [14]From the ground up to the lower ledge, it measures $3^1/2$ feet. It is 21 inches wide. It measures 7 feet from the smaller ledge to the larger ledge and is 21 inches wide. [15]The place where the sacrifice is burned on the altar is 7 feet high. The four corners are shaped like horns and reach up above it. [16]It is square. It is 21 feet long and 21 feet wide. [17]The upper ledge is also square, $24^1/2$ feet long and $24^1/2$ feet wide. The border around it is $10^1/2$ inches wide. Its base is 21 inches around. Its steps are on the east."

[18]Then the man said to me, "Human being, this is what the Lord God says: These are the rules for the altar. When it is built, use these rules to offer burnt offerings and sprinkle blood on it. [19]You must give a young bull as a sin offering to the priests. These priests are the Levites from the family of Zadok. They come near me to serve me, says the Lord God. [20]Take some of the bull's blood and put it on the altar's four corners. Put it also on the four corners of the ledge. And put it on the border all around. This is how you will make the altar pure and ready for God's service. [21]Then take the bull for the sin offering and burn it in the proper place in the Temple[d] area. It will be outside the Holy Place.

[22]"On the second day offer a male goat. It must have nothing wrong with it. It will be for a sin offering. The priests will make the altar pure and ready for God's service. They will do it the same way they did with the young bull. [23]When you finish making the altar pure and ready, offer a young bull and a male sheep from the flock. They must also have nothing wrong with them. [24]You must offer them before the Lord. The priests will throw salt on them. Then they will offer them as a burnt offering to the Lord.

[25]"You must prepare a goat every day for seven days as a sin offering. Also, you must prepare a young bull and male

sheep from the flock. They must have nothing wrong with them. ²⁶For seven days the priests will make the altar pure and ready for God's service. Then the priests will give the altar to God. ²⁷After these seven days, on the eighth day, the priests must present your offerings. They must offer your burnt offerings and your fellowship offerings on the altar. Then I will accept you, says the Lord God."

THE OUTER EAST GATE

44 Then the man brought me back to the outer east gate of the Temple*d* area. The gate was shut. ²The Lord said to me, "This gate will stay shut. It will not be opened. No one may enter through it. This is because the Lord God of Israel has entered through it. So it must stay shut. ³Only the ruler himself may sit in the gateway to eat bread before the Lord. He must enter through the porch of the gateway and go out the same way."

⁴Then the man brought me through the outer north gate. He brought me to the front of the Temple. I looked and saw the greatness of the Lord. It was filling the Temple of the Lord. I bowed face-down on the ground.

⁵The Lord said to me, "Human being, pay attention. See this with your eyes. And hear this with your ears. See and hear everything I tell you about all the rules and teachings of the Temple of the Lord. Pay attention to the entrance to the Temple and to all the exits from the Temple area. ⁶Then speak to those who refuse to obey. Say to the people of Israel, 'This is what the Lord God says: Stop doing all your acts that I hate, Israel! ⁷You brought foreigners into my Holy Place. They were not circumcised*d* in the flesh. They had not given themselves to serving me. You dishonored my Temple when you offered me food, fat and blood. You broke my agreement by all your ways that I hate. ⁸And you have not taken care of my holy things. You put foreigners in charge of my Temple. ⁹This

is what the Lord God says: Foreigners who are not circumcised in flesh and who do not give themselves to serving me may not enter my Temple. Even a foreigner living among the people of Israel may not enter.

¹⁰"'Some Levites stopped obeying me when Israel left me and followed their idols. These Levites must be punished for their sin. ¹¹These Levites are to be servants in my Holy Place. They may guard the gates of the Temple. They may serve in the Temple. They may kill the animals for the burnt offering and the sacrifices for the people. They may stand before the people to serve them. ¹²But these Levites helped the people worship their idols and caused the people of Israel to fall. So I have made this promise: They will be punished for their sin, says the Lord God. ¹³They will not come near me to serve as priests. They will not come near any of my holy things or the most holy offerings. But they will be ashamed of the things they did that I hate. ¹⁴But I will make them take care of the Temple. They will take care of everything that must be done in it.

¹⁵"'But this is not true for priests who are Levites and descendants*d* of Zadok. They took care of my Holy Place when Israel left me. They may come near to serve me. They may stand in my presence. They will offer me the fat and blood of the animals they sacrifice, says the Lord God. ¹⁶They are the only ones who may enter my Holy Place. They may come near my table to serve me. They may take care of the things I gave them.

¹⁷"'When they enter the gates of the inner courtyard, they must wear linen robes. They must not wear wool to serve at the gates of the inner courtyard or in the Temple. ¹⁸They will wear linen turbans on their heads and linen underclothes. They will not wear anything that makes them perspire. ¹⁹At times they will go out into the outer courtyard to

the people. But before they go, they must take off their serving clothes. They must put these clothes away in the holy rooms. And they must put on other clothes. Then they will not let their holy clothes hurt the people.

20"'They must not shave their heads or let their hair grow long. They must keep the hair of their heads trimmed. 21None of the priests may drink wine when they enter the inner courtyard. 22The priests must not marry a widow or a divorced woman. They may marry only virgins*d* from the people of Israel. Or they may marry a widow of a priest. 23They must teach my people the difference between what is holy and what is not holy. They must help my people know what is unclean*d* and what is clean.

24"'In court they will act as judges. When they judge, they will follow my teachings. They must obey my laws and my rules at all my special feasts. They must keep my Sabbaths*d* holy.

25"'They must not go near a dead person, making themselves unclean.*d* But they are allowed to make themselves unclean if the dead person is a relative. It might be his father, mother, son, daughter, brother or a sister who has not married. 26After the priest has been made clean again, he must wait seven days. 27Then he may go into the inner courtyard to serve in the Temple. But he must offer a sin offering for himself, says the Lord God.

28"'These are the rules about the priests and their property: They will have me instead of property. You will not give them any land to own in Israel. I am what they will own. 29They will eat the grain offerings, sin offerings and penalty offerings. Everything Israel offers will be theirs. 30And the best fruits of all the first harvests will be for the priests. And they will have all the special gifts offered to me. You will also give to the priests the first part of your grain

that you grind. This will cause a blessing to come on your house. 31The priests must not eat any bird or animal that died a natural death. And they must not eat one that has been torn by wild animals.

THE LAND IS DIVIDED

45 "'Divide the land for the Israelite tribes*d* by throwing lots.*d* At that time you will give a part of the land to belong to the Lord. It will be about 7 miles long and about 6 miles wide. All of this land will be holy. 2An area of 875 feet square will be for the Temple.*d* There will be an open space around the Temple that is 87½ feet wide. 3In the holy area you will measure a part about 7 miles long and 3 miles wide. The Most Holy Place will be in this holy area. 4This holy part of the land will be for the priests who serve in the Temple. This is where they come near to serve the Lord. It will be a place for the priests' houses. And it will be the place for the Temple. 5Another area will be about 7 miles long and more than 3 miles wide. It will be for the Levites, who serve in the Temple. It will belong to them so they will have cities in which to live.

6"'And you will give the city an area that is about 1½ miles wide and about 7 miles long. It will be along the side of the holy area. It will belong to all the people of Israel.

7"'The ruler will have land on both sides of the holy area and the city. On the west of the holy area, his land will reach to the Mediterranean Sea. On the east of the holy area, his land will reach to the eastern border. It will be as long as the land given to each tribe. 8This land will be the ruler's property in Israel. So my rulers will not be cruel to my people anymore. But they will give land to each tribe in the nation of Israel.

9"'This is what the Lord God says: You have gone far enough, you rulers of Israel! Stop being cruel and hurting people. Do what is right and fair. Stop forcing my people out of their homes, says the Lord God. [10]You must have honest scales, an honest dry measurement and an honest liquid measurement. [11]The dry measure and the liquid measure will be the same: The liquid measure will always be a tenth of a homer.[n] The ephah will always be a tenth of a homer. The measurement they follow will be the homer. [12]The shekel[n] will be worth 20 gerahs. A mina will be worth 60 shekels.

OFFERINGS AND HOLY DAYS

[13]"'This is the gift you will offer: a sixth of an ephah from a homer of wheat; a sixth of an ephah from a homer of barley. [14]The amount of oil you are to offer is a tenth of a bath from each cor. (Ten baths make a homer and also make a cor.) [15]You should give 1 sheep from each flock of 200 from the watering places of Israel. They are to be offered with the grain offerings, burnt offerings and fellowship offerings. These offerings are to remove sins so you will belong to God, says the Lord God. [16]All people in the land will give this special offering for the ruler of Israel. [17]It will be the ruler's responsibility to supply the burnt offerings, grain offerings and drink offerings. These offerings will be given at the feasts and at the New Moons.[d] They will also be given on the Sabbaths[d] and at all the other feasts of Israel. The ruler will supply the sin offerings, grain offerings and fellowship offerings. These offerings are to pay for the sins of Israel.

[18]"'This is what the Lord God says: On the first day of the first month take a young bull that has nothing wrong with it. Use it to make the Temple[d] pure and ready for God's service. [19]The priest will take some of the blood from the sin offering. And he will put it on the door-posts of the Temple. He will put it on the four corners of the ledge of the altar. And he will put it on the posts of the gate of the inner courtyard. [20]You will do the same thing on the seventh day of the month. You will do it for anyone who has sinned by accident or without knowing it. This is how you make the Temple pure and ready for God's service.

PASSOVER FEAST OFFERINGS

[21]"'On the fourteenth day of the first month you will celebrate the Feast[d] of Passover. It will be a feast of seven days when you eat bread made without yeast. [22]On that day the ruler must offer a bull for himself and for all the people of the land. The bull will be a sin offering. [23]During the seven days of the feast the ruler must offer seven bulls. And he must offer seven male sheep. The bulls and sheep must have nothing wrong with them. They will be burnt offerings to the Lord. The ruler will offer them every day of the seven days of the feast. He must also offer a male goat every day as a sin offering. [24]The ruler must give as a grain offering a half bushel for each bull and a half bushel for each sheep. He must give a gallon of olive oil for each half bushel.

[25]"'Beginning on the fifteenth day of the seventh month, you will celebrate the Feast[d] of Shelters. During the feast, the ruler will do the same things for seven days. He will supply the sin offering, burnt offering, grain offering and the olive oil.

RULES FOR WORSHIP

46 "'This is what the Lord God says: The east gate of the inner courtyard will be shut on the six working days. But it will be opened on the Sabbath[d] day. And it will be open on the day of the New Moon.[d] [2]The ruler will

---

45:11 homer The Hebrew word means "donkey-load." It measured about 5 dry bushels or 175 liquid quarts. So an ephah was about one-half bushel. And a bath was about 18 quarts.
45:12 shekel In Ezekiel's time a shekel weighed about two-fifths of an ounce.

enter through the porch of the gateway. He will enter from outside and stand by the gatepost. Then the priests will offer the ruler's burnt offering and fellowship offerings. The ruler will worship at the entrance of the gate. Then he will go out. But the gate will not be shut until evening. ³The people of the land will worship at the entrance of that gateway. They will worship there in the presence of the Lord on the Sabbaths and New Moons. ⁴This is the burnt offering the ruler will offer to the Lord on the Sabbath day. It will be six male lambs that have nothing wrong with them. And it will be a male sheep that has nothing wrong with it. ⁵He must give a half bushel grain offering with the male sheep. But he can give as much grain offering with the lambs as he pleases. He must also give a gallon of olive oil for each half bushel of grain. ⁶On the day of the New Moon he must offer a young bull. It must have nothing wrong with it. He must also offer six lambs and a male sheep. They also must have nothing wrong with them. ⁷The ruler must give a half bushel grain offering with the bull. And he must give the same with the male sheep. With the lambs, he can give as much grain as he pleases. But he must give a gallon of olive oil for each half bushel of grain. ⁸And when the ruler enters, he must go in through the porch of the gateway. He must go out the same way.

⁹"The people of the land must come before the Lord at the special feasts. Anyone who enters through the north gate to worship must go out through the south gate. Anyone who enters through the south gate must go out through the north gate. No one will return the same way he entered. Each person will go out straight ahead. ¹⁰When the people go in, the ruler will go in with them. When they go out, the ruler will go out.

¹¹"At the feasts and regular times of worship a half bushel of grain must be offered. It will be offered with a young bull. And a half bushel of grain must be offered with a male sheep. But with an offering of lambs, the ruler may give as much grain as he pleases. He should give a gallon of olive oil for each half bushel of grain. ¹²The ruler may give an offering as a special gift to the Lord. It may be a burnt offering or fellowship offering. When he gives it to the Lord, the inner east gate will be opened for him. He must offer his burnt offering and his fellowship offerings as he does on the Sabbath*ᵈ* day. Then he will go out. After he has gone out, the gate will be shut.

¹³"Every morning you will give a year-old lamb that has nothing wrong with it. It will be for a burnt offering to the Lord every day. ¹⁴Also, you must offer a grain offering with the lamb every morning. With it you will give three and a third quarts of grain and one and a third quarts of olive oil. This is to make the fine flour moist. It will be a grain offering to the Lord. This is a rule that must be kept from now on. ¹⁵So they must always give the lamb, the grain offering and the olive oil every morning as a burnt offering.

RULES FOR THE RULER

¹⁶"This is what the Lord God says: The ruler might give a gift from his land to one of his sons. Then that land will belong to that son's children. It is their property from their family. ¹⁷But the ruler might give a gift from his land to one of his slaves. That land will belong to the slave only until the year of freedom. Then the land will go back to the ruler. Only the ruler's sons may keep a gift of land from the ruler. ¹⁸The ruler must not take any of the people's land. He must not force them out of their land. He must give his sons land from his own land. Then my people will not be scattered out of their own land.'"

THE SPECIAL KITCHENS

[19]The man led me through the entrance at the side of the gateway. He led me to the priests' holy rooms that face north. There I saw a place at the west end. [20]The man said to me, "This is where the priests will boil the meat of the penalty offering and sin offering. There the priests will bake the grain offering. Then they will not need to bring these offerings into the outer courtyard. That would hurt the people."

[21]Then the man brought me out to the outer courtyard. He led me to its four corners. In each corner of the courtyard was a smaller courtyard. [22]Small courtyards were in the four corners of the courtyard. Each small courtyard was 70 feet long and 52$\frac{1}{2}$ feet wide. All four corners measured the same. [23]A stone wall was around each of the four small courtyards. Places for cooking were built in each of the stone walls. [24]The man said to me, "These are the kitchens. The Temple[d] priests will boil the sacrifices for the people here."

THE RIVER FROM THE TEMPLE

47 The man led me back to the door of the Temple.[d] I saw water coming out from under the doorway that faces east. (The Temple faced east.) The water flowed down from the south end of the Temple. It was south of the altar. [2]The man brought me out through the outer north gate. And he led me around outside to the outer east gate. The water was coming out on the south side of the gate.

[3]The man went toward the east with a line in his hand. He measured about a third of a mile. Then he led me through water that came up to my ankles. [4]The man measured about a third of a mile again. Then he led me through water that came up to my knees. Then he measured about a third of a mile again. And he led me through water up to my waist. [5]The man measured about a third of a mile again. But it was now a river

that I could not cross. The water had risen too high. It was deep enough for swimming. It was a river that no one could cross. [6]The man asked me, "Human being, do you see this?"

Then the man led me back along the bank of the river. [7]As I went back, I saw many trees on both sides of the water. [8]The man said to me, "This water will flow toward the eastern areas. It will go down into the Jordan Valley. When the water enters the Dead Sea,[d] it will become fresh. [9]And everywhere the river goes, there will be many animals and fish. Wherever this water goes the Dead Sea will become fresh. So where the river goes there will be many living things. [10]Fishermen will stand by the sea. From En Gedi all the way to En Eglaim will become a place to spread fishing nets. There will be many kinds of fish in the Dead Sea. There will be as many kinds of fish as there are in the Mediterranean Sea. [11]But the swamps and marshes will not become fresh. They will be left for salt. [12]All kinds of fruit trees will grow on both banks of the river. Their leaves will not dry and die. The trees will have fruit every month because the water for them comes from the Temple. The fruit from the trees will be for food. And their leaves will be for medicine."

BORDERS OF THE LAND

[13]This is what the Lord God says: "These are the borders to divide the land among the 12 tribes[d] of Israel. Joseph will have two parts of land. [14]You will divide the land equally. I promised to give it to your ancestors. So this land will belong to you from your family.

[15]"This will be the border line of the land.

"On the north side it will start at the Mediterranean Sea. It will go by the Hethlon Road. This is where the road turns toward Lebo Hamath. And it will go to the cities of Zedad, [16]Berothah and Sibraim. Sibraim is on the border between Damascus and Hamath. And it will go on to the city of Hazer Hatticon on the border of the country of Hauran. ¹⁷So the border line will go from the Mediterranean Sea east to the city of Hazar Enan. This is on the northern border of Damascus. And the country of Hamath will be on the north side of the border.

¹⁸"On the east side the border runs south from a point between Hauran and Damascus. It will go along the Jordan between Gilead and the land of Israel. It will continue to the city of Tamar on the Dead Sea.ᵈ This will be the east side of the land.

¹⁹"On the south side the border line will go east from Tamar. It will go all the way to the waters of Meribah Hadesh. Then it will run along the brook of Egypt to the Mediterranean Sea. This will be the south side of the land.

²⁰"On the west side the Mediterranean Sea will be the border line. It will go to a place across from Lebo Hamath. This will be the west side of your land.

²¹"So you will divide this land among the tribes of Israel. ²²You will divide it as a property for yourselves. And it will be for you and for the foreigners who live and have children among you. These foreigners will be like people born in Israel. You will divide some land for them among the tribes of Israel. ²³In whatever tribe the foreigner lives, you will give him some land," says the Lord God.

DIVIDING THE LAND

48 "These are the names of the tribes.ᵈ Dan will have one share. It will begin at the northern border. It will go from the sea and over the Hethlon Road. It will follow the road to Lebo Hamath. It will go all the way to Hazar Enan. This is on the northern border of Damascus. It will stop there next to Hamath. This will be Dan's northern border from the east side to the Mediterranean Sea on the west side.

²"South of Dan's border, Asher will have one share. It will go from the east side to the west side.

³"South of Asher's border, Naphtali will have one share. It will go from the east side to the west side.

⁴"South of Naphtali's border, Manasseh will have one share. It will go from the east side to the west side.

⁵"South of Manasseh's border, Ephraim will have one share. It will go from the east side to the west side.

⁶"South of Ephraim's border, Reuben will have one share. It will go from the east side to the west side.

⁷"South of Reuben's border, Judah will have one share. It will go from the east side to the west side.

⁸"South of Judah's border will be the holy area which you are to give. It will be about 7 miles wide. It will be as long and wide as one of the tribes' shares. It will run from the east side to the west side. The Templeᵈ will be in the middle of this area.

⁹"The share which you will give the Lord will be about 7 miles long and 3 miles wide. ¹⁰The holy area will be divided among these people. For the priests on the north side, the land will measure about 7 miles. It will be 3 miles wide on the west side and 3 miles wide on the east side. It will be about 7 miles on the south side. The Temple of the Lord will be in the middle of it. ¹¹This land is for the priests who are given to serve the Lord. They are the descendantsᵈ of Zadok who did my work. They did not leave me. The other Levites left me when Israel did. ¹²This share from the holy portion of the land will be a gift for these priests. It will be next to the land of the Levites.

¹³"Alongside the land for the priests, the Levites will have a share. It will be about 7 miles long and 3 miles wide. Its full length will be about 7 miles. And its full width will be about 3 miles. ¹⁴The

Levites are not to sell or trade any of this land. They will not sell any of this best part of the land. It belongs to the Lord.

CITY PROPERTY

[15]"The rest of the land will be an area about 1¹/₂ miles wide and 7 miles long. It will be for the other people's use. It will be for the city, for homes and for pastures. The city will be in the middle of it. [16]These are the city's measurements: the north side will be about a mile. The south side will be about a mile. The east side will be about a mile. And the west side will be about a mile. [17]The city's land for pastures will be about 437 feet on the north, 437 feet on the south, 437 feet on the east and 437 feet on the west. [18]Alongside the length of the holy area there will be left 3 miles on the east and 3 miles on the west. It will be used to grow food for the city workers. [19]The city workers will plow this land. The workers will be from all the tribes[d] of Israel. [20]This whole area will be square, 7 miles by 7 miles. You shall give to the Lord the holy share along with the city property.

[21]"Land that is left over on both sides of the holy area and city property will belong to the ruler. That land will extend east of the holy area to the eastern border. And it will extend west of it to the Mediterranean Sea. Both of these areas run the length of the lands of the tribes. They belong to the ruler. The holy area with the Holy Place of the Temple[d] will be in the middle. [22]The Levites' land and the city property will be between the lands belonging to the ruler. The ruler's land will be between Judah's border and Benjamin's border.

THE OTHER TRIBES' LAND

[23]"Here is what the rest of the tribes will receive: Benjamin will have one share. It will go from the east side to the Mediterranean Sea on the west side.

[24]"South of Benjamin's land, Simeon will have one share. It will go from the east side to the west side.

[25]"South of Simeon's land, Issachar will have one share. It will go from the east side to the west side.

[26]"South of Issachar's land, Zebulun will have one share. It will go from the east side to the west side.

[27]"South of Zebulun's land, Gad will have one share. It will go from the east side to the west side.

[28]"The southern border of Gad's land will go east from Tamar on the Dead Sea[d] to the waters of Meribah Kadesh. Then it will run along the brook of Egypt to the Mediterranean Sea.

[29]"This is the land you will divide among the tribes of Israel. These are to be their shares," says the Lord God.

THE GATES OF THE CITY

[30]"These will be the outside borders of the city: The north side will measure more than a mile. [31]There will be three gates facing north. They are Reuben's Gate, Judah's Gate and Levi's Gate. The city's gates will be named for the tribes[d] of Israel.

[32]"The east side will measure more than a mile. There will be three gates facing east. They are Joseph's Gate, Benjamin's Gate and Dan's Gate.

[33]"The south side will measure more than a mile. There will be three gates facing south. They are Simeon's Gate, Issachar's Gate and Zebulun's Gate.

[34]"The west side will measure more than a mile. There will be three gates facing west. They are Gad's Gate, Asher's Gate and Naphtali's Gate.

[35]"The city will measure about six miles around. From then on the name of the city will be The Lord God Is There."

THE BOOK OF
DANIEL

DANIEL TAKEN TO BABYLON

1 Nebuchadnezzar king of Babylon came to Jerusalem and surrounded it with his army. This happened during the third year that Jehoiakim was king of Judah. ²The Lord allowed Nebuchadnezzar to capture Jehoiakim king of Judah. Nebuchadnezzar also took some of the things from the Temple*d* of God. He carried them to Babylonia and put them in the temple of his gods.

³Then King Nebuchadnezzar gave an order to Ashpenaz, his chief officer. He told Ashpenaz to bring some of the men from Judah into his house. He wanted them to be from important families. And he wanted those who were from the family of the king of Judah. ⁴King Nebuchadnezzar wanted only healthy, young, Israelite men. These men were not to have anything wrong with their bodies. They were to be handsome and well educated. They were to be able to learn and understand things. He wanted those who were able to serve in his palace. Ashpenaz was to teach them the language and writings of the Babylonians. ⁵The king gave the young men a certain amount of food and wine every day. That was the same kind of food that the king ate. They were to be trained for three years. Then the young men would become servants of the king of Babylon. ⁶Among those young men were some from the people of Judah. These were Daniel, Hananiah, Mishael and Azariah.

⁷Then Ashpenaz, the chief officer, gave them Babylonian names. Daniel's new name was Belteshazzar. Hananiah's was Shadrach. Mishael's was Meshach. And Azariah's new name was Abednego.

⁸Daniel decided not to eat the king's food and wine because that would make him unclean.*d* So he asked Ashpenaz for permission not to make himself unclean in this way.

⁹God made Ashpenaz want to be kind and merciful to Daniel. ¹⁰But Ashpenaz said to Daniel, "I am afraid of my master, the king. He ordered me to give you this food and drink. If you don't eat this food, you will begin to look worse than other young men your age. The king will see this. And he will cut off my head because of you."

¹¹Ashpenaz had ordered a guard to watch Daniel, Hananiah, Mishael and Azariah. ¹²Daniel said to the guard, "Please give us this test for ten days: Don't give us anything but vegetables to eat and water to drink. ¹³Then after ten days compare us with the other young men who eat the king's food. See for yourself who looks healthier. Then you judge for yourself how you want to treat us, your servants."

¹⁴So the guard agreed to test them for ten days. ¹⁵After ten days they looked very healthy. They looked better than all of the young men who ate the king's food. ¹⁶So the guard took away the king's special food and wine. He gave Daniel, Hananiah, Mishael and Azariah vegetables instead.

¹⁷God gave these four men wisdom and the ability to learn. They learned many kinds of things people had written and studied. Daniel could also understand all kinds of visions and dreams.

¹⁸The end of the three years came. And Ashpenaz brought all of the young men to King Nebuchadnezzar. ¹⁹The king talked to them. He found that none of the young men were as good as Daniel, Hananiah, Mishael and Azariah. So those four young men became the king's servants. ²⁰Every time the king asked them about something important, they showed much wisdom and understanding. He found they were ten times better than all the fortune-tellers and magicians in his kingdom. ²¹So Daniel

continued to be the king's servant until the first year Cyrus was king.

NEBUCHADNEZZAR'S DREAM

2 During Nebuchadnezzar's second year as king, he had some dreams. Those dreams bothered him, and he could not sleep. ²So the king called for his fortune-tellers, magicians, wizards and wise men. The king wanted those men to tell him what he had dreamed. So they came in and stood in front of the king. ³Then the king said to them, "I had a dream that bothers me. I want to know what the dream means."

⁴Then the wise men answered the king in the Aramaic language. They said, "Our king, live forever! We are your servants. Please tell us your dream. Then we will tell you what it means."

⁵Then King Nebuchadnezzar said to them, "No! You must tell me the dream. And then you must tell me what it means. If you don't do these things, I will have you torn apart. And I will turn your houses into piles of stones. ⁶But if you tell me my dream and its meaning, I will reward you. I will give you gifts and great honor. So tell me the dream, and tell me what it means."

⁷Again the wise men said to the king, "Please, tell us the dream. And we will tell you what it means."

⁸King Nebuchadnezzar answered, "Now I know that you are trying to get more time. You know that I meant what I said. ⁹If you don't tell me my dream, you will be punished. You have all agreed to tell me lies and wicked things. You are hoping things will change. Now, tell me the dream. Then I will know you can tell me what it really means!"

¹⁰The wise men answered the king. They said, "No one on earth can do what the king asks! Not even a great and powerful king has ever asked the fortune-tellers, magicians or wise men to do this. ¹¹The king is asking something that is too hard. Only the gods could tell the king this. But the gods do not live among people."

¹²When the king heard that, he became very angry. He gave an order for all the wise men of Babylon to be killed. ¹³So King Nebuchadnezzar's order was announced. All the wise men were to be put to death. Men were sent to look for Daniel and his friends to kill them.

¹⁴Arioch was the commander of the king's guards. He was going to put to death the wise men of Babylon. But Daniel spoke to him with wisdom and skill. ¹⁵Daniel asked, "Why did the king order such a terrible punishment?" Then Arioch explained everything to Daniel. ¹⁶When Daniel heard the story, he went to King Nebuchadnezzar. Daniel asked him to give him some more time. Then he would tell the king what he had dreamed and what it meant.

¹⁷So Daniel went to his house. He explained the whole story to his friends Hananiah, Mishael and Azariah. ¹⁸Daniel asked his friends to pray to the God of heaven. Daniel asked them to pray that God would show them mercy and help them understand this secret. Then Daniel and his friends would not be put to death with the other wise men of Babylon.

¹⁹During the night God explained the secret to Daniel in a vision. Then Daniel praised the God of heaven. ²⁰Daniel said:

"Praise God forever and ever.
    He has wisdom and power.
²¹He changes the times and seasons of
        the year.
    He takes away the power of kings.
    And he gives their power to new
        kings.
    He gives wisdom to people so they
        become wise.
    And he helps people learn and
        know things.
²²He makes known secrets that are deep
        and hidden.
    He knows what is hidden in
        darkness,
    and light lives with him.

²³I thank you and praise you, God of my
> ancestors.
> You have given me wisdom and
> power.
> You told me what we asked of you.
> You told us about the king's dream."

THE MEANING OF THE DREAM

²⁴Then Daniel went to Arioch. King
Nebuchadnezzar had chosen Arioch to
put to death the wise men of Babylon.
Daniel said to Arioch, "Don't put the
wise men of Babylon to death. Take me
to the king. I will tell him what his dream
means."

²⁵So very quickly Arioch took Daniel
to the king. Arioch said to the king, "I
have found a man among the captives
from Judah. He can tell the king what his
dream means."

²⁶The king asked Daniel (also called
Belteshazzar) a question. He asked, "Are
you able to tell me what I dreamed and
what it means?"

²⁷Daniel answered, "No person can
explain to the king the secret he has
asked about. No wise man, magician or
fortune-teller can do this. ²⁸But there is a
God in heaven who explains secret
things. God has shown King Nebuchadnezzar what will happen at a later time.
This is your dream. This is the vision you
saw while lying on your bed: ²⁹My king,
as you were lying there, you thought
about things to come. God, who can tell
people about secret things, showed you
what is going to happen. ³⁰God also told
this secret to me. It is not because I have
greater wisdom than other men. It is so
that you, my king, may know what it
means. In that way you will understand
what went through your mind.

³¹"My king, in your dream you saw a
large statue in front of you. It was huge,
shiny and frightening. ³²The head of the
statue was made of pure gold. Its chest
and arms were made of silver. Its middle
and the upper part of its legs were made
of bronze. ³³The lower part of the legs

were made of iron. Its feet were made
partly of iron and partly of baked clay.
³⁴While you were looking at the statue,
you saw a rock cut free. But no human
being touched the rock. It hit the statue
on its feet of iron and clay and smashed
them. ³⁵Then the iron, clay, bronze, silver
and gold broke to pieces at the same
time. They became like chaff^d on a
threshing^d floor in the summertime. The
wind blew them away, and there was
nothing left. Then the rock that hit the
statue became a very large mountain. It
filled the whole earth.

³⁶"That was your dream. Now we will
tell the king what it means. ³⁷My king,
you are the greatest king. God of heaven
has given you a kingdom. He has given
you power, strength and glory. ³⁸God
has given you power over people, wild
animals and birds. Wherever they live,
God has made you ruler over them all.
King Nebuchadnezzar, you are the head
of gold on that statue.

³⁹"Another kingdom will come after
you. But that kingdom will not be as
great as yours. Next a third kingdom will
rule over the earth. That is the bronze
part. ⁴⁰Then there will be a fourth
kingdom, strong as iron. Iron crushes
and smashes things to pieces. In the same
way the fourth kingdom will smash and
crush all the other kingdoms.

⁴¹"You saw that the statue's feet and
toes were partly baked clay and partly
iron. That means the fourth kingdom
will be a divided kingdom. It will have
some of the strength of iron in it. As you
saw, iron was mixed with clay. ⁴²The
toes of the statue were partly iron and
partly clay. So the fourth kingdom will
be partly strong like iron and partly
breakable like clay. ⁴³You saw the iron
mixed with clay. But iron and clay don't
mix completely together. In the same
way the people of the fourth kingdom
will be a mixture. Those people will not
be united as one people.

⁴⁴"During the time of those kings, the God of heaven will set up another kingdom. It will never be destroyed. And it will not be given to another group of people. This kingdom will crush all the other kingdoms. It will bring them to an end. But that kingdom itself will continue forever.

⁴⁵"King Nebuchadnezzar, you saw a rock cut from a mountain. But no human being touched it. The rock broke the iron, bronze, clay, silver and gold to pieces. In this way the great God showed you what will happen. The dream is true, and you can trust this explanation."

⁴⁶Then King Nebuchadnezzar fell facedown on the ground in front of Daniel. The king honored him. He ordered that an offering and incense*d* be presented to Daniel. ⁴⁷Then the king said to Daniel, "Truly I know your God is the greatest of all gods. And he is the Lord of all the kings. He tells people about things they cannot know. I know this is true. You were able to tell these secret things to me."

⁴⁸Then the king gave Daniel an important position in his kingdom. And he gave many gifts to Daniel. Nebuchadnezzar made him ruler over the whole area of Babylon. And he put Daniel in charge of all the wise men of Babylon. ⁴⁹Daniel asked the king to make Shadrach, Meshach and Abednego important leaders over the area of Babylon. And the king did as Daniel asked. Daniel himself became one of the important people who stayed at the royal court.

THE GOLD IDOL AND BLAZING FURNACE

3 Now King Nebuchadnezzar had a gold statue made. That statue was 90 feet high and 9 feet wide. He set up the statue on the plain of Dura in the area of Babylon. ²Then the king called the important leaders: the governors, assistant governors, captains of the soldiers, people who advised the king, keepers of the treasury, judges, rulers and all other officers in his kingdom. He wanted these men to come to the special service for the statue he had set up. ³So they all came for the special service. And they stood in front of the statue that King Nebuchadnezzar had set up. ⁴Then the man who made announcements for the king spoke in a loud voice. He said, "People, nations and men of every language, this is what you are commanded to do: ⁵You will hear the sound of the horns, flutes, lyres,*d* zithers,*n* harps, pipes and all the other musical instruments. When this happens, you must bow down and worship the gold statue. This is the one King Nebuchadnezzar has set up. ⁶Everyone must bow down and worship this gold statue. Anyone who doesn't will be quickly thrown into a blazing furnace."

⁷Now people, nations and men who spoke every language were there. And they heard the sound of the horns, flutes, lyres, zithers, pipes and all the other musical instruments. So they bowed down and worshiped the gold statue that King Nebuchadnezzar had set up.

⁸Then some Babylonians came up to the king. They began speaking against the men of Judah. ⁹They said to King Nebuchadnezzar, "Our king, live forever! ¹⁰Our king, you gave a command. You said that everyone would hear the horns, lyres, zithers, harps, pipes and all the other musical instruments. Then they would have to bow down and worship the gold statue. ¹¹Anyone who wouldn't do this was to be thrown into a blazing furnace. ¹²Our king, there are some men of Judah who did not pay attention to your order. You made them important officers in the area of Babylon. Their

---

3:5 zithers Musical instruments with 30 to 40 strings.

names are Shadrach, Meshach and Abednego. They do not serve your gods. And they do not worship the gold statue you have set up."

[13]Nebuchadnezzar became very angry. He called for Shadrach, Meshach and Abednego. So those men were brought to the king. [14]And Nebuchadnezzar said, "Shadrach, Meshach and Abednego, is it true that you do not serve my gods? And is it true that you did not worship the gold statue I have set up? [15]Now, you will hear the sound of the horns, flutes, lyres, zithers, harps, pipes and all the other musical instruments. And you must be ready to bow down and worship the statue I made. That will be good. But if you do not worship it, you will be thrown quickly into the blazing furnace. Then no god will be able to save you from my power!"

[16]Shadrach, Meshach and Abednego answered the king. They said, "Nebuchadnezzar, we do not need to defend ourselves to you. [17]You can throw us into the blazing furnace. The God we serve is able to save us from the furnace and your power. If he does this, it is good. [18]But even if God does not save us, we want you, our king, to know this: We will not serve your gods. We will not worship the gold statue you have set up."

[19]Then Nebuchadnezzar was furious with Shadrach, Meshach and Abednego. He ordered the furnace to be heated seven times hotter than usual. [20]Then he commanded some of the strongest soldiers in his army to tie up Shadrach, Meshach and Abednego. The king told the soldiers to throw them into the blazing furnace.

[21]So Shadrach, Meshach and Abednego were tied up and thrown into the blazing furnace. They were still wearing their robes, trousers, turbans and other clothes. [22]The king was very angry when he gave the command. And the furnace was made very hot. The fire was so hot that the flames killed the strong soldiers

who took Shadrach, Meshach and Abednego there. [23]Firmly tied, Shadrach, Meshach and Abednego fell into the blazing furnace.

[24]Then King Nebuchadnezzar was very surprised and jumped to his feet. He asked the men who advised him, "Didn't we tie up only three men? Didn't we throw them into the fire?"

They answered, "Yes, our king."

[25]The king said, "Look! I see four men. They are walking around in the fire. They are not tied up, and they are not burned. The fourth man looks like a son of the gods."

[26]Then Nebuchadnezzar went to the opening of the blazing furnace. He shouted, "Shadrach, Meshach and Abednego, come out! Servants of the Most High God, come here!"

So Shadrach, Meshach and Abednego came out of the fire. [27]When they came out, the princes, assistant governors, governors and royal advisers crowded around them. They saw that the fire had not harmed their bodies. Their hair was not burned. Their robes were not burned. And they didn't even smell like smoke.

[28]Then Nebuchadnezzar said, "Praise the God of Shadrach, Meshach and Abednego. Their God has sent his angel and saved his servants from the fire! These three men trusted their God. They refused to obey my command. And they were willing to die rather than serve or worship any god other than their own. [29]So I now make this law: The people of any nation or language must not say anything against the God of Shadrach, Meshach and Abednego. Anyone who does will be torn apart. And his house will be turned into a pile of stones. No other god can save his people like this." [30]Then the king promoted Shadrach, Meshach and Abednego in the area of Babylon.

NEBUCHADNEZZAR'S DREAM OF A TREE

4 King Nebuchadnezzar sent a letter. It went to the people, nations and those who speak every language in all the world. The letter said:

I wish you great wealth!

[2]The Most High God has done miracles[d] and wonderful things for me. I am happy to tell you about these things.

[3]The things he has done are great.
His miracles are mighty.
His kingdom continues forever.
His rule will continue for all time.

[4]I, Nebuchadnezzar, was at my palace. I was happy and successful. [5]I had a dream that made me afraid. As I was lying on my bed, I saw pictures and visions in my mind. Those things made me very afraid. [6]So I gave an order. All the wise men of Babylon were to be brought to me. I wanted them to tell me what my dream meant. [7]The fortune-tellers, magicians and wise men came. I told them about the dream. But those men could not tell me what it meant.

[8]Finally, Daniel came to me. (I called him Belteshazzar to honor my god. The spirit of the holy gods is in him.) I told my dream to Daniel. [9]I said, "Belteshazzar, you are the most important of all the fortune-tellers. I know that the spirit of the holy gods is in you. I know there is no secret that is too hard for you to understand. This was what I dreamed. Tell me what it means. [10]These are the visions I saw while I was lying in my bed: I looked, and there in front of me was a tree. It was standing in the middle of the earth. The tree was very tall. [11]The tree grew large and strong. The top of the tree touched the sky. It could be seen from anywhere on earth. [12]The leaves of the tree were beautiful. It had plenty of good fruit on it. On the tree was food for everyone. The wild animals found shelter under the tree. And the birds lived in its branches. Every animal ate from it.

[13]"I was looking at those things in the vision while lying on my bed. And then I saw a holy angel coming down from heaven. [14]He spoke very loudly. He said, 'Cut down the tree, and cut off its branches. Strip off its leaves. Scatter its fruit around. Let the animals that are under the tree run away. Let the birds that were in its branches fly away. [15]But let the stump and its roots stay in the ground. Put a band of iron and bronze around it. Let it stay in the field with the grass around it.

"'Let the man become wet with dew. Let him live among the animals and plants of the earth. [16]Let him not think like a man any longer. Let him have the mind of an animal for seven years.

[17]"'Messengers gave this command. The holy ones declared the sentence. This is so all the people may know that the Most High God rules over the kingdoms of men. God gives those kingdoms to anyone he wants. And he chooses people to rule them who are not proud.'

[18]"That is what I, King Nebuchadnezzar, dreamed. Now Daniel, called Belteshazzar, tell me what the dream means. None of the wise men in my kingdom can explain it to me. But you can, because the spirit of the holy gods is in you."

DANIEL EXPLAINS THE DREAM

[19]Then Daniel (also called Belteshazzar) was very quiet for a while. His thoughts made him afraid. So the king said, "Belteshazzar, do not let the dream or its meaning make you afraid."

Then Daniel, called Belteshazzar, answered the king. He said, "My master, I wish the dream were about your enemies. And I wish its meaning

were for those who are against you!
20You saw a tree in your dream. The tree grew large and strong. Its top touched the sky. It could be seen from all over the earth. 21Its leaves were beautiful, and it had plenty of fruit. The fruit gave food for everyone. It was a home for the wild animals. And its branches were nesting places for the birds. That is the tree you saw. 22My king, you are that tree! You have become great and powerful. You are like the tall tree that touched the sky. And your power reaches to the far parts of the earth.

23"My king, you saw a holy angel coming down from heaven. He said, 'Cut down the tree and destroy it. But leave the stump and its roots in the ground. Put a band of iron and bronze around it. Leave it in the field with the grass. Let him become wet with dew. He will live like a wild animal for seven years.'

24"This is the meaning of the dream, my king. The Most High God has commanded these things to happen to my master the king: 25You will be forced away from people. You will live among the wild animals. People will feed you grass like an ox. And dew from the sky will make you wet. Seven years will pass, and then you will learn this lesson: The Most High God is ruler over the kingdoms of men. And the Most High God gives those kingdoms to anyone he wants.

26"The stump of the tree and its roots were to be left in the ground. This means your kingdom will be given back to you. This will happen when you learn that heaven rules your kingdom. 27So, my king, please accept my advice. I advise you to stop sinning and do what is right. Stop doing wicked things and be kind to poor people. Then you might continue to be successful."

THE KING'S DREAM COMES TRUE

28All these things happened to King Nebuchadnezzar. 29Twelve months after the dream, King Nebuchadnezzar was walking on the roof[n] of his palace in Babylon. 30And he said, "Look at Babylon. I built this great city. It is my palace. I built this great place by my power to show how great I am."

31The words were still in his mouth when a voice came from heaven. The voice said, "King Nebuchadnezzar, these things will happen to you: Your royal power has been taken away from you. 32You will be forced away from people. You will live with the wild animals. You will be fed grass like an ox. Seven years will pass before you learn this lesson: The Most High God rules over the kingdoms of men. And the Most High God gives those kingdoms to anyone he wants."

33Those things happened quickly. Nebuchadnezzar was forced to go away from people. He began eating grass like an ox. He became wet from dew. His hair grew long like the feathers of an eagle. And his nails grew long like the claws of a bird.

34Then at the end of that time, I, Nebuchadnezzar, looked up toward heaven. And I could think correctly again. Then I gave praise to the Most High God. I gave honor and glory to him who lives forever.

God's rule is forever.
His kingdom continues for all time.
35People on earth
are not truly important.
God does what he wants
with the powers of heaven
and the people on earth.

4:29 roof In Bible times houses were built with flat roofs. The roof was used for drying things such as flax and fruit. And it was used as an extra room, as a place for worship and as a place to sleep in the summer.

No one can stop his powerful hand.
No one can question the things he
does.

³⁶So, at that time I could think correctly again. And God gave back my
great honor and power as king. The
people who advise me and the royal
family came to me for help again. I
became king again. And I became
even greater and more powerful than
before. ³⁷Now I, Nebuchadnezzar,
give praise and honor and glory to the
King of heaven. Everything he does is
right. He is always fair. And he is able
to make proud people humble.

THE WRITING ON THE WALL

5 King Belshazzar gave a big banquet
for 1,000 royal guests. And he drank
wine with them. ²As Belshazzar was
drinking his wine, he gave an order to
his servants. He told them to bring the
gold and silver cups that his ancestor
Nebuchadnezzar had taken from the
Temple*d* in Jerusalem. King Belshazzar
wanted his royal guests to drink from
those cups. He also wanted his wives
and his slave women*d* to drink from
them. ³So they brought the gold cups.
They had been taken from the Temple of
God in Jerusalem. And the king and his
royal guests, his wives and his slave
women drank from them. ⁴As they were
drinking, they praised their gods. Those
gods were made from gold, silver,
bronze, iron, wood and stone.

⁵Then suddenly a person's hand appeared. The fingers wrote words on the
plaster on the wall. This was near the
lampstand in the royal palace. The king
watched the hand as it wrote.

⁶King Belshazzar was very frightened.
His face turned white, and his knees
knocked together. He could not stand up
because his legs were too weak. ⁷The
king called for the magicians and wise
men to be brought to him. He said to the
wise men of Babylon, "I will give a reward

to anyone who can read this writing and
explain it. I will give him purple clothes
fit for a king. I will put a gold chain
around his neck. And I will make him
the third highest ruler in the kingdom."

⁸So all the king's wise men came in.
But they could not read the writing. And
they could not tell the king what it meant.
⁹King Belshazzar became even more
afraid. His face became even whiter. His
royal guests were confused.

¹⁰Then the king's mother came into
the banquet room. She had heard the
voices of the king and his royal guests.
She said, "My king, live forever! Don't be
afraid! Don't let your face be white with
fear! ¹¹There is a man in your kingdom
who has the spirit of the holy gods in
him. In the days of your father, this man
showed understanding, knowledge and
wisdom. He was like the gods in these
things. Your father, King Nebuchadnezzar, put this man in charge of all the
wise men. He ruled over all the fortune-
tellers, magicians and wise men. ¹²The
man I am talking about is named Daniel.
The king gave him the name Belte-
hazzar. He was very wise, and he had
knowledge and understanding. He could
explain dreams and secrets. He could
answer very hard problems. Call for
Daniel. He will tell you what the writing
on the wall means."

¹³So they brought Daniel to the king.
The king said to him, "Is your name
Daniel? Are you one of the captives my
father the king brought from Judah? ¹⁴I
have heard that the spirit of the gods is
in you. And I have heard that you are
very wise and have knowledge and
understanding. ¹⁵The wise men and
magicians were brought to me to read
this writing on the wall. I wanted those
men to explain to me what it means. But
they could not explain it. ¹⁶I have heard
that you are able to explain what things
mean. And you can find the answers to
hard problems. Read this writing on the

wall and explain it to me. If you can, I will give you purple clothes fit for a king. And I will put a gold chain around your neck. And you will become the third highest ruler in the kingdom."

[17]Then Daniel answered the king, "You may keep your gifts for yourself. Or you may give those rewards to someone else. I will read the writing on the wall for you. And I will explain to you what it means.

[18]"My king, the Most High God made your father Nebuchadnezzar a great, important and powerful king. [19]God made him very important. So all the people, nations and those who spoke every language were very afraid of Nebuchadnezzar. If he wanted a person to die, he put that person to death. And if he wanted a person to live, he let that person live. If he wanted to promote a person, he promoted him. And if he wanted a person to be unimportant, he made him unimportant.

[20]"But Nebuchadnezzar became too proud and stubborn. So he was taken off his royal throne. His glory was taken away. [21]Then Nebuchadnezzar was forced away from people. His mind became like the mind of an animal. He lived with the wild donkeys and was fed grass like an ox. He became wet with dew. These things happened to him until he learned his lesson: The Most High God rules over the kingdoms of men. And the Most High God sets anyone he wants over those kingdoms.

[22]"But, Belshazzar, you already knew these things. You are a descendant[d] of Nebuchadnezzar. But still you have not been sorry for what you have done. [23]Instead, you have turned against the Lord of heaven. You ordered the drinking cups from the Temple of the Lord to be brought to you. Then you and your royal guests drank wine from them. Your wives and your slave women also drank wine from them. You praised the gods of

silver, gold, bronze, iron, wood and stone. They are not really gods. They cannot see or hear or understand anything. But you did not honor God. He is the One who has power over your life and everything you do. [24]So God sent the hand that wrote on the wall.

[25]"These are the words that were written on the wall: 'Mene, mene, tekel, parsin.'

[26]"This is what these words mean: Mene: God has counted the days until your kingdom will end. [27]Tekel: You have been weighed on the scales and found not good enough. [28]Parsin: Your kingdom is being divided. It will be given to the Medes and the Persians."

[29]Then Belshazzar gave an order for Daniel to be dressed in purple clothes. A gold chain was put around his neck. And he was announced to be the third highest ruler in the kingdom. [30]That very same night Belshazzar, king of the Babylonian people, was killed. [31]A man named Darius the Mede became the new king. Darius was 62 years old.

DANIEL AND THE LIONS

6 Darius thought it would be a good idea to choose 120 governors. They would rule through all of his kingdom. [2]And he chose three men as supervisors over those 120 governors. Daniel was one of these three supervisors. The king set up these men so that he would not be cheated. [3]Daniel showed that he could do the work better than the other supervisors and the governors. Because of this, the king planned to put Daniel in charge of the whole kingdom. [4]So the other supervisors and the governors tried to find reasons to accuse Daniel. But he went on doing the business of the government. And they could not find anything wrong with him. So they could not accuse him of doing anything wrong. Daniel was trustworthy. He was not lazy and did not cheat the king. [5]Finally these men said, "We will never find any reason to accuse Daniel. But we must find something to complain about. It will have to be about the law of his God."

[6]So the supervisors and the governors went as a group to the king. They said: "King Darius, live forever! [7]The supervisors, assistant governors, governors, the people who advise you and the captains of the soldiers have all agreed on something. We think the king should make this law that everyone would have to obey: No one should pray to any god or man except to you, our king. This should be done for the next 30 days. Anyone who doesn't obey will be thrown into the lions' den. [8]Now, our king, make the law. Write it down so it cannot be changed. The laws of the Medes and Persians cannot be canceled." [9]So King Darius made the law and had it written.

[10]When Daniel heard that the new law had been written, he went to his house. He went to his upstairs room. The windows of that room opened toward Jerusalem. Three times each day Daniel got down on his knees and prayed. He prayed and thanked God, just as he always had done.

[11]Then those men went as a group and found Daniel. They saw him praying and asking God for help. [12]So they went to the king. They talked to him about the law he had made. They said, "Didn't you write a law that says no one may pray to any god or man except you, our king? Doesn't it say that anyone who disobeys during the next 30 days will be thrown into the lions' den?"

The king answered, "Yes, I wrote that law. And the laws of the Medes and Persians cannot be canceled."

[13]Then those men spoke to the king. They said, "Daniel is one of the captives from Judah. And he is not paying attention to the law you wrote. Daniel still prays to his God three times every day." [14]The king became very upset when he heard this. He decided he had to save Daniel. He worked until sunset trying to think of a way to save him.

[15]Then those men went as a group to the king. They said, "Remember, our king, the law of the Medes and Persians. It says that no law or command given by the king can be changed."

[16]So King Darius gave the order. They brought Daniel and threw him into the lions' den. The king said to Daniel, "May the God you serve all the time save you!" [17]A big stone was brought. It was put over the opening of the lions' den. Then the king used his signet[d] ring to put his special seal[d] on the rock. And he used the rings of his royal officers to put their seals on the rock also. This showed that no one could move that rock and bring Daniel out. [18]Then King Darius went back to his palace. He did not eat that night. He did not have any entertainment brought to entertain him. And he could not sleep.

[19]The next morning King Darius got up at dawn. He hurried to the lions' den. [20]As he came near the den, he was worried. He called out to Daniel. He said, "Daniel, servant of the living God! Has your God that you always worship been able to save you from the lions?"

[21]Daniel answered, "My king, live forever! [22]My God sent his angel to close the lions' mouths. They have not hurt me, because my God knows I am innocent. I never did anything wrong to you, my king."

[23]King Darius was very happy. He told his servants to lift Daniel out of the lions' den. So they lifted him out and did not find any injury on him. This was because Daniel had trusted in his God. [24]Then the king gave a command. The men who had accused Daniel were brought to the lions' den and thrown into it. Their wives and children were also thrown into it. The lions grabbed them before they hit the floor of the den. And the lions crushed their bones.

25Then King Darius wrote a letter. It was to all people and all nations, to those who spoke every language in the world:

I wish you great wealth.

26I am making a new law. This law is for people in every part of my kingdom. All of you must fear and respect the God of Daniel.

Daniel's God is the living God.
He lives forever.
His kingdom will never be destroyed.
His rule will never end.
27God rescues and saves people.
God does mighty miracles[d]
in heaven and on earth.
God saved Daniel
from the power of the lions.

28So Daniel was successful during the time that Darius was king. This was also the time that Cyrus the Persian was king.

DANIEL'S DREAM ABOUT FOUR ANIMALS

7 In Belshazzar's first year as king of Babylon, Daniel had a dream. He saw visions as he was lying on his bed. Daniel wrote down what he had dreamed. 2Daniel said: "I saw my vision at night. In the vision the wind was blowing from all four directions. These winds made the sea very rough. 3I saw four huge animals come up from the sea. Each animal was different from the others.

4"The first animal looked like a lion. But it had wings like an eagle. I watched this animal until its wings were torn off. It was lifted from the ground so that it stood up on two feet like a man. And it was given the mind of a man.

5"And then I saw a second animal before me. It looked like a bear. It was raised up on one of its sides. And it had three ribs in its mouth between its teeth. It was told, 'Get up and eat all the meat you want!'

6"After that, I looked, and there before me was another animal. This animal looked like a leopard. And the leopard had four wings on its back. The wings looked like a bird's wings. This animal had four heads. It was given power to rule.

7"After that, in my vision at night I continued looking. There in front of me was a fourth animal. This animal looked cruel and terrible and very strong. It had large iron teeth. It crushed and ate what it killed. Then it walked on whatever was left. This fourth animal was different from all the animals I had seen before it. It had ten horns.

8"While I was thinking about the horns, another horn grew up among them. It was a little horn. It had eyes like a person's eyes. It also had a mouth. And the mouth was bragging. The little horn pulled out three of the other horns.

9"As I looked,
thrones were put in their places.
And God, the Eternal One, sat on
his throne.
His clothes were white like snow.
And the hair on his head was white
like wool.
His throne was made from fire.
And the wheels of his throne were
blazing with fire.
10A river of fire was flowing
from in front of him.
Many thousands of angels were
serving him.
Millions of angels stood before him.
Court was ready to begin.
And the books were opened.

11"I kept on looking because the little horn was bragging. I kept watching until finally the fourth animal was killed. Its body was destroyed, and it was thrown into the burning fire. 12(The power and rule of the other animals had been taken from them. But they were permitted to live for a certain period of time.)

13"In my vision at night I looked. There in front of me was someone who looked like a human being. He was coming with clouds in the sky. He came near God, who has been alive forever. And he was led to God. [14]The one who looked like a human being was given the power to rule. He was also given glory and royal power. All peoples, nations and men who spoke every language will serve him. His rule will last forever. His kingdom will never be destroyed.

THE MEANING OF THE DREAM

[15]"I, Daniel, was worried. The visions that went through my mind frightened me. [16]I came near one of those standing there. I asked him what all this meant.

"So he told me. He explained to me what these things meant. [17]He said, 'The four great animals are four kingdoms. Those four kingdoms will come from the earth. [18]But the people who belong to the Most High God will receive the power to rule. And they will have the power to rule forever. They will have it from now on.'

[19]"Then I wanted to know what the fourth animal meant. It was different from all the other animals. It was very terrible. It had iron teeth and bronze claws. It was the animal that crushed and ate what it killed. And it walked on whatever was left. [20]I also wanted to know about the ten horns on its head. And I wanted to know about the little horn that grew there. It had pulled out three of the other ten horns. It looked greater than the others. And it had eyes and a mouth that kept bragging. [21]As I watched, the little horn began making war against God's people. And the horn kept killing them [22]until God, who has been alive forever, came. He judged in favor of the people who belong to the Most High God. And the time came for them to receive the power to rule.

[23]"And he explained this to me: 'The fourth animal is a fourth kingdom that will come on the earth. It will be different from all the other kingdoms. It will destroy people all over the world. It will walk on and crush the whole earth. [24]The ten horns are ten kings who will

come from this fourth kingdom. After those ten kings are gone, another king will come. He will be different from the kings who ruled before him. He will defeat three of the other kings. [25]This king will say things against the Most High God. And he will hurt and kill God's people. He will try to change times and laws that have already been set. The people that belong to God will be in that king's power for three and one-half years.

[26]"'But the court will decide what should happen. And the power of the king will be taken away. His kingdom will be completely destroyed. [27]Then the people who belong to the Most High God will have the power to rule. They will rule over all the kingdoms under heaven with power and greatness. Their power to rule will last forever. And people from all the other kingdoms will respect and serve them.'

[28]"And that was the end of the dream. I, Daniel, was very afraid. My face became very white from fear. But I kept everything to myself."

DANIEL'S VISION

8 During the third year Belshazzar was king, I saw this vision. This was after the other one. [2]In this vision I saw myself in the capital city of Susa. Susa is in the area of Elam. I was standing by the Ulai River. [3]I looked up, and I saw a male sheep standing beside the river. It had two long horns. But one horn was longer than the other. The long horn was newer than the other horn. [4]I watched the male sheep charge to the west. He also charged to the north and the south. No animal could stand before him. And none could save another animal from his power. He did whatever he wanted. And he became very powerful.

[5]While I was thinking about this, I saw a male goat come from the west. This goat had one large horn that was easy to see. It was between his eyes. He crossed over the whole earth. But his feet did not touch the ground.

⁶That goat charged the male sheep with the two horns. This was the male sheep I had seen standing by the river. The goat was very angry. ⁷I watched the goat attack the male sheep. It broke the sheep's two horns. The sheep could not stop it. The goat knocked the sheep to the ground. Then the goat walked all over him. No one was able to save the sheep from the goat. ⁸So the male goat became very great. But when he was strong, his big horn broke off. Then four horns grew in place of the one big horn. Those four horns were easy to see. They pointed in four different directions.

⁹Then a little horn grew from one of those four horns. It became very big. It grew to the south and the east and toward the beautiful land of Judah. ¹⁰That little horn grew until it reached to the sky. It even threw some of the army of heaven to the ground. And it walked on them. ¹¹That little horn became very strong against God, the commander of heaven's armies. It stopped the daily sacrifices that were offered to the commander. The place where people worshiped the commander was pulled down. ¹²There was a turning away from God. Because of this the people stopped the daily sacrifices. It was like throwing truth down to the ground. The horn was successful in everything it did.

¹³Then I heard one angel speaking. Another angel asked the first one, "How long will the things in this vision last? The vision is about the daily sacrifices. It is about the turning away from God that brings destruction. It is about the Temple*d* being pulled down. It is about the army of heaven being walked on."

¹⁴He said to me, "This will happen for 2,300 evenings and mornings. Then the holy place will be repaired."

¹⁵I, Daniel, saw this vision. And I tried to understand what it meant. Then someone who looked like a man suddenly stood before me. ¹⁶And I heard a man's voice calling from the Ulai River: "Gabriel, explain the vision to this man."

¹⁷Gabriel came to where I was standing. When he came close to me, I was very afraid. I bowed facedown on the ground. But Gabriel said to me, "Human being, understand that this vision is about the time of the end."

¹⁸While Gabriel was speaking, I fell into a deep sleep. My face was on the ground. Then he touched me and lifted me to my feet. ¹⁹He said, "Now, I will explain the vision to you. I will tell you what will happen later, in the time of God's anger. Your vision was about the set time of the end.

²⁰"You saw a male sheep with two horns. Those horns are the kings of Media and Persia. ²¹The male goat is the king of Greece. The big horn between its eyes is the first king. ²²After that horn broke, four horns grew in its place. Those four horns are four kingdoms. Those four kingdoms will come from the nation of the first king. But they will not be as strong as the first king.

²³"When the end comes near for those kingdoms, a bold and cruel king will come. This king will tell lies. This will happen when many people have turned against God. ²⁴This king will be very powerful. But his power will not come from himself. He will cause terrible destruction. He will be successful in everything he does. He will destroy powerful people and even God's people. ²⁵This king will use his wisdom to make lies successful. He will think that he is very important. He will destroy many people without warning. He will try to fight even God, the Prince of princes! But that cruel king will be destroyed. And it will not be human power that destroys him.

²⁶"The vision that has been shown to you about those times is true. But seal up the vision. Those things won't happen for a long time."

[27]I, Daniel, became very weak. I was sick for several days after that vision. Then I got up and went back to work for the king. But I was very upset about the vision. I didn't understand what it meant.

DANIEL'S PRAYER

9 These things happened during the first year Darius son of Xerxes was king. He was a descendant[d] of the Medes. [2]During Darius' first year as king, I, Daniel, was reading the Scriptures.[d] In them I saw what the Lord told Jeremiah. He said Jerusalem would be an empty desert for 70 years.

[3]Then I turned to the Lord God. I prayed to him and asked him for help. I did not eat any food. To show how sad I was I put on rough cloth and sat in ashes. [4]I prayed to the Lord my God. I told him about all of my sins. I said, "Lord, you are a great God. You cause fear and wonder. You keep your agreement of love with all who love you and obey your commands.

[5]"But we have sinned and done wrong. We have been wicked and turned against you. We have not obeyed your commands and laws. [6]We did not listen to your servants, the prophets. They spoke for you to our kings, our leaders and our ancestors. They spoke to all the people of the land.

[7]"Lord, you are good and right. But we are full of shame today. The people of Judah and Jerusalem and all the people of Israel are ashamed. People near and far whom you scattered among many nations are ashamed. We were not loyal to you. [8]Lord, we are all ashamed. Our kings and leaders and our fathers are ashamed. This is because we have sinned against you.

[9]"But, Lord our God, you show us mercy. You forgive us even though we have turned against you. [10]We have not obeyed the Lord our God. We have not obeyed the teachings he gave us through his servants, the prophets. [11]All the people of Israel have disobeyed your teachings. They all have turned away and refused to obey you. So you brought on us the curses and promises of punishment written in the Teachings of Moses, the servant of God. These things have happened to us because we sinned against you.

[12]"God said these things would happen to us and our leaders. And he made them happen. You brought on us a great disaster. Nothing has ever been done here on earth like what was done to Jerusalem. [13]All this disaster came to us just as it is written in the Teachings of Moses. But we still have not stopped sinning. We still do not pay attention to your truth. [14]The Lord was ready to bring the disaster on us. This is because he is right in everything he does. But we still have not obeyed him.

[15]"Lord our God, you used your power and brought us out of Egypt. Because of that, your name is known even today. Lord, we have sinned. We have done wrong. [16]Lord, you do the right things. So do not be angry with Jerusalem. Jerusalem is your city on your holy hill. All this has happened because of our sins and the evil things done by our ancestors. So now people all around insult and make fun of Jerusalem and your people.

[17]"Now, our God, hear my prayers. I am your servant. Listen to my prayer for help. Do good things for your holy place that is in ruins. Do this for your sake. [18]My God, pay attention and hear me. Open your eyes and see all the terrible things that have happened to us. See what has happened to the city that is called by your name. We do not ask these things because we are good. We ask because of your mercy. [19]Lord, listen! Lord, forgive! Lord, hear us and do something! For your sake, don't wait! Your city and your people are called by your name."

GABRIEL'S EXPLANATION

[20]I was saying those things in my prayer to the Lord, my God. I was confessing my

sins and the sins of the people of Israel. I was praying for God's holy hill. ²¹While I was still praying, Gabriel came to me. Gabriel was the person I had seen in my last vision. He came flying quickly to me about the time of the evening sacrifice. ²²Gabriel said to me, "Daniel, I have come to give you wisdom and to help you understand. ²³When you first started praying, an answer was given. And I came to tell you, because God loves you very much. So think about the message and understand the vision.

²⁴"God has ordered 490 years for your people and your holy city. These years are ordered for these reasons: to stop people from turning against God; to put an end to sin; to take away evil; to bring in goodness that continues forever; to make the vision and prophecy^d come true; and to appoint a most holy place.

²⁵"Learn and understand these things. A command will come to rebuild Jerusalem. The time from this command until the appointed leader comes will be 49 years and 434 years. Jerusalem will be rebuilt with streets and a trench around it. But it will be built in times of trouble. ²⁶After the 434 years the appointed leader will be killed. He will have nothing. The people of the leader who is to come will destroy the city. They will also destroy the holy place. That end will come like a flood. War will continue until the end. God has ordered that place to be completely destroyed. ²⁷That leader will make an agreement with many people for 7 years. He will put a stop to offerings and sacrifices after 3¹/₂ years. And the horrible thing that destroys will be placed on the highest point of the Temple.^d But God has ordered him to be destroyed!"

DANIEL'S VISION OF A MAN

10 During Cyrus' third year as king of Persia, Daniel learned about these things. (Daniel's other name is Belteshazzar.) The message was true. It was about a great war. But Daniel understood it, because it was explained to him in a vision.

²At that time I, Daniel, was very sad for three weeks. ³I did not eat any fancy food. I did not eat any meat or drink any wine. I did not use any perfumed oil. I did not do any of these things for three weeks.

⁴On the twenty-fourth day of the first month, I was standing beside the great Tigris River. ⁵While standing there, I looked up. And I saw a man dressed in linen clothes. A belt made of fine gold was wrapped around his waist. ⁶His body was like shiny yellow quartz. His face was bright like lightning, and his eyes were like fire. His arms and legs were shiny like polished bronze. His voice sounded like the roar of a crowd.

⁷I, Daniel, was the only person who saw the vision. The men with me did not see it. But they were badly frightened. They were so afraid they ran away and hid. ⁸So I was left alone, watching this great vision. I lost my strength. My face turned white like a dead person, and I was helpless. ⁹Then I heard the man in the vision speaking. As I listened, I fell into a deep sleep. My face was on the ground.

¹⁰Then a hand touched me and set me on my hands and knees. I was so afraid that I was shaking. ¹¹The man in the vision said to me, "Daniel, God loves you very much. Think very carefully about the words I will speak to you. Stand up because I have been sent to you." And when he said this, I stood up. I was still shaking.

¹²Then the man said to me, "Daniel, do not be afraid. Some time ago you decided to try to get understanding. You wanted to be humble before God. Since that time God has listened to you. And I came to you because you have been praying. ¹³But the prince of Persia has been fighting against me for 21 days. Then Michael, one of the most important

angels, came to help me. He came because I had been left there with the king of Persia. [14]Now I have come to you, Daniel. I will explain to you what will happen to your people. The vision is about a time in the future."

[15]While he was speaking to me, I bowed facedown. I could not speak. [16]Then one who looked like a man touched my lips. I opened my mouth and started to speak. I said to the one standing in front of me, "Master, I am upset and afraid. It is because of what I saw in the vision. I feel helpless. [17]Master, I am Daniel your servant. How can I talk with you! My strength is gone, and it is hard for me to breathe."

[18]The one who looked like a man touched me again. And he gave me strength. [19]He said, "Daniel, don't be afraid. God loves you very much. Peace be with you. Be strong now, be strong."

When he spoke to me, I became stronger. Then I said, "Master, speak, since you have given me strength."

[20]So then he said, "Daniel, do you know why I have come to you? Soon I must go back to fight against the prince of Persia. When I go, the prince of Greece will come. [21]But before I go, I must first tell you what is written in the Book of Truth. No one stands with me against them except Michael. He is the angel ruling over your people.

11 "In the first year Darius the Mede was king, I stood up to support Michael. I supported him in his fight against the prince of Persia.

KINGDOMS OF THE SOUTH AND NORTH

[2]"Now then, Daniel, I tell you the truth: Three more kings will rule in Persia. Then a fourth king will come. He will be much richer than all the kings of Persia before him. He will use his riches to get power. And he will stir up everyone against the kingdom of Greece. [3]Then a mighty king will come. He will rule with great power. He will do anything he

wants. [4]After that king has come, his kingdom will be broken up. It will be divided out toward the four parts of the world. His kingdom will not go to his descendants.[d] And it will not have the power that he had. This is because his kingdom will be pulled up and given to other people.

[5]"The king of the South will become strong. But one of his commanders will become even stronger. He will begin to rule his own kingdom with great power. [6]Then after a few years, the king of the South and the commander will become friends. The daughter of the king of the South will marry the king of the North. She will do this to bring peace. But she will not keep her power. And his family will not last. She, her husband, her child and those who brought her to that country will be killed.

[7]"But a person from her family will become king of the South. He will attack the armies of the king of the North. He will go into that king's strong, walled city. He will fight and win. [8]He will take their gods and their metal idols. He will also take their valuable things made of silver and gold. He will take those things to Egypt. Then he will not bother the king of the North for a few years. [9]Next, the king of the North will attack the king of the South. But he will be beaten back to his own country.

[10]"The sons of the king of the North will prepare for war. They will get a large army together. That army will move through the land very quickly, like a powerful flood. Later, that army will come back and fight. They will fight all the way to the strong, walled city of the king of the South. [11]Then the king of the South will become very angry. He will march out to fight against the king of the North. The king of the North will have a large army. But he will lose the battle. [12]The soldiers will be carried away. So the king of the South will be very proud.

And he will kill thousands of soldiers from the northern army. But he will not continue to be successful. ¹³The king of the North will gather another army. That army will be larger than the first one. After several years he will attack. That army will be very large, and it will have plenty of weapons.

¹⁴"In those times many people will be against the king of the South. Some of your own people who love to fight will turn against the king of the South. They will think it is time for God's promises to come true. But it will not be the time yet. And they will fail. ¹⁵Then the king of the North will come. He will build dirt roads to the tops of the city walls. And he will capture a strong, walled city. The southern army will not have the power to fight back. Even their best soldiers will not be strong enough to stop the northern army. ¹⁶The king of the North will do whatever he wants. No one will be able to stand against him. He will gain power and control in the beautiful land of Israel. And he will have the power to destroy it. ¹⁷The king of the North will decide to use all his power to fight against the king of the South. He will make an agreement with the king of the South. The king of the North will give one of his daughters as a wife to the king of the South. He will do that so he can defeat the king of the South. But those plans will not succeed or help him. ¹⁸Then the king of the North will turn his attention to other places. He will take many cities along the coast of the Mediterranean Sea. But a commander will put an end to the pride of the king of the North. The commander will turn that pride back on him. ¹⁹After that happens the king of the North will go back to the strong, walled cities of his own country. But he will lose his power. That will be the end of him.

²⁰"The next king of the North will send out a tax collector. He will then have plenty of money. In a few years that ruler will be killed. But he will not die in anger or in a battle.

²¹"That ruler will be followed by a very cruel and hated man. He will not have the honor of being from a king's family. He will attack the kingdom when the people feel safe. He will take power by lying to the people. ²²He will sweep away in defeat large and powerful armies. He will even defeat a prince who made an agreement. ²³Many nations will make agreements with that cruel and hated ruler. But he will lie to them. He will gain much power. But only a few people will support him. ²⁴The richest areas will feel safe. But that cruel and hated ruler will attack them. And he will succeed where his ancestors did not. He will take things from the countries he defeated. And he will give those things to his followers. He will plan to defeat and destroy strong cities. He will be successful, but only for a short time.

²⁵"That very cruel and hated ruler will have a large army. He will use it to stir up his strength and courage. He will attack the king of the South. The king of the South will get a large and very powerful army and get ready for war. But the people who are against him will make secret plans. And the king of the South will be defeated. ²⁶There were people who were supposed to be good friends of the king of the South. But they will try to destroy him. His army will be swept away in defeat. Many of his soldiers will be killed in battle. ²⁷Those two kings will want to hurt each other. They will sit at the same table and lie to each other. But it will not do either one any good. This is because God has set a time for their end to come. ²⁸The king of the North will go back to his own country with much wealth. Then he will decide to go against the holy agreement. He will do what he planned. Then he will go back to his own country.

²⁹"At the right time the king of the North will attack the king of the South again. But this time he will not be successful as he was before. ³⁰Ships from the west will come and fight against the king of the North. He will see those ships coming and be afraid. Then he will return and show his anger against God's people who obey the holy agreement. He will be good to those who have stopped obeying the holy agreement.

³¹"The king of the North will send his army. They will make the Temple*d* in Jerusalem unclean.*d* They will stop the people from offering the daily sacrifice. Then they will set up the horrible thing that destroys. ³²The king of the North will tell lies to God's people. Those who have not obeyed God will be ruined. But there will be some who know God and obey him. They will be strong and fight back.

³³"Those who are wise will help the others understand what is happening. But some of them will be killed with swords. Some will be burned or taken captive. Some of them will have their homes and things taken away. These things will continue for many days. ³⁴When the wise ones are suffering, they will get a little help. Many who join the wise ones will not love God. ³⁵Some of the wise ones will be killed. But the hard times must come. This is so they can be made stronger and purer. They will be without faults until the time of the end comes. Then, at the right time the end will come.

THE KING WHO PRAISES HIMSELF

³⁶"The king of the North will do whatever he wants. He will brag about himself. He will praise himself and think he is even better than a god. He will say things against the God of gods that no one has ever heard. He will be successful until all the bad things have happened. What God has planned to happen will happen. ³⁷That king of the North will not care about the gods his ancestors worshiped. He won't care about the god that women worship. He won't care about any god. Instead, he will make himself more important than any god. ³⁸The king of the North will worship power and strength. His ancestors did not love power as he will. He will honor the god of power with gold and silver, expensive jewels and gifts. ³⁹That king will attack strong, walled cities. He will do it with the help of a foreign god. He will give much honor to the people who join him. He will make them rulers in charge of many other people. He will make those rulers pay him for the land they rule.

⁴⁰"At the time of the end, the king of the South will fight a battle against the king of the North. The king of the North will attack him. He will attack with chariots and soldiers on horses and many large ships. He will invade many countries and sweep through their lands like a flood. ⁴¹The king of the North will attack the beautiful land of Judah. He will defeat many countries. But Edom, Moab and the leaders of Ammon will be saved from him. ⁴²The king of the North will show his power in many countries. Egypt will not escape. ⁴³The king will get treasures of gold and silver. And he will get all the riches of Egypt. The Libyan and Nubian people will obey him. ⁴⁴But the king of the North will hear news from the east and the north. And it will make him afraid and angry. He will go to destroy completely many nations. ⁴⁵He will set up his royal tents. They will be between the sea and the beautiful mountain where the Temple*d* is built. But, finally, his end will come. There will not be anyone to help him when he dies.

THE TIME OF THE END

12 "Daniel, at that time Michael, the great prince, will stand up. (He is the one who protects your people.) There will be a time of much trouble. It will be the worst time since nations have been on earth. But your people will be saved.

Everyone whose name is written in God's book will be saved. ²Many people who have already died will live again. Some of them will wake up to have life forever. But some will wake up to find shame and disgrace forever. ³The wise people will shine like the brightness of the sky. Those who teach others to live right will shine like stars forever and ever.

⁴"But you, Daniel, close up the book and seal it. These things will happen at the time of the end. Many people will go here and there to find true knowledge."

⁵Then I, Daniel, looked, and I saw two other men. One was standing on my side of the river. And the other was standing on the far side. ⁶The man who was dressed in linen was standing over the water in the river. One of the two men spoke to him. He asked, "How long will it be before these amazing things come true?"

⁷The man dressed in linen who stood over the water raised his hands toward heaven. And I heard him make a promise. He used the name of God who lives forever. He said, "It will be for three and one-half years. The power of the holy people will finally be broken. Then all these things will come true."

⁸I heard the answer, but I did not really understand. So I asked, "Master, what will happen after all these things come true?"

⁹He answered, "Go your way, Daniel. The message is closed up and sealed until the time of the end. ¹⁰Many people will be made clean,ᵈ pure and spotless. But the wicked will continue to be wicked. And those wicked people will not understand these things. But the wise people will understand them.

¹¹"The daily sacrifice will be stopped. There will be 1,290 days from that time. Then the horrible thing that destroys will be set up. ¹²Those who wait for the end of the 1,335 days will be happy.

¹³"As for you, Daniel, go your way till the end. You will get your rest when you die. And at the end you will rise from the dead to get your reward."

THE BOOK OF
HOSEA

1 The Lord spoke his word to Hosea son of Beeri. This was during the time that Uzziah, Jotham, Ahaz and Hezekiah were kings of Judah. During part of this time Jeroboam son of Jehoash was king of Israel.

HOSEA'S WIFE AND CHILDREN

[2]The Lord said to him, "Go, and marry a woman who will be unfaithful to you. She will give you children whose fathers are other men. Do this because people in this country have acted like an unfaithful wife toward the Lord." [3]So Hosea married Gomer daughter of Diblaim. Gomer became pregnant and gave birth to Hosea's son.

[4]The Lord said to Hosea, "Name him Jezreel. This is because soon I will punish the family of Jehu for the people they killed at Jezreel. Then I will put an end to the kingdom of Israel. [5]And I will also break the power of Israel's army in the Valley of Jezreel."

[6]Gomer became pregnant again and gave birth to a daughter. The Lord said to Hosea, "Name her Lo-Ruhamah.[n] This is because I will not pity Israel anymore. I will no longer forgive them. [7]But I will show pity to the people of Judah. I will save them. I will not use bows or swords, horses or horsemen, or weapons of war to save them. I, the Lord their God, will save them."

[8]After Gomer had finished nursing Lo-Ruhamah, she became pregnant again. And she gave birth to another son. [9]The Lord said, "Name him Lo-Ammi[n] because you are not my people. And I am not your God.

GOD'S PROMISE TO ISRAEL

[10]"But the people of Israel will become like the grains of sand of the sea. You cannot measure or count them. Now it is said to Israel, 'You are not my people.' But later they will be called 'children of the living God.' [11]Then the people of Judah and Israel will be joined together again. They will choose one leader for themselves. And again they will grow in their land. The day of Jezreel, when God plants, will be truly great.

2 "Your brothers and your sisters will be called 'my people' and 'you have been shown love.'

GOD SPEAKS ABOUT ISRAEL

[2]"Plead with your mother.[n]
   Plead with her because she no
      longer acts like a wife to me.
   And I am not treated like her
      husband.
   Tell her to stop acting like a
      prostitute.[d]
   Tell her to stop behaving like an
      unfaithful wife.
[3]If she refuses, I will strip her naked.
   I will leave her bare like the day she
      was born.
   I will make her dry like a desert.
   I will make her like a land without
      water.
   I will kill her with thirst.
[4]I will not take pity on her children.
   They are the children of an
      unfaithful wife.
[5]Their mother has acted like a
      prostitute.
   The one who became pregnant with
      them has acted disgracefully.
   She said, 'I will chase after my lovers.[n]
   They give me food and water.
   They give me wool and linen.
   They give me wine and olive oil.'

1:6 Lo-Ruhamah This name in Hebrew means "not pitied."
1:9 Lo-Ammi This name in Hebrew means "not my people."
2:2 mother This refers to the nation of Israel here.
2:5 lovers This refers to the nations surrounding Israel, who led Israel to worship false gods.

⁶So I will block her road with
　　thornbushes.
　I will build a wall around her
　　so she cannot find her way.
⁷She will run after her lovers.
　But she won't catch up to them.
She will look for them.
　But she won't find them.
Then she will say, 'I will go back to my
　　first husband.'ⁿ
　Life was better for me then than it is
　　now.'
⁸But she has not accepted that I was
　　the one
　who gave her grain, wine and oil.
I gave her much silver and gold.
　But she used it to make statues of
　　Baal.^d

⁹"So I will take away my grain at
　　harvest time.
　And I will take away my wine when
　　it is ready.
I will take back my wool and linen.
　I gave her those things to cover her
　　nakedness.
¹⁰So I will show her nakedness to her
　　lovers.
　No one will save her from my
　　punishment.
¹¹I will put an end to all her
　　celebrations:
　her yearly festivals, her New Moon^d
　　festivals and her Sabbaths.^d
　I will stop all of her special feasts.
¹²I will destroy her vines and fig trees.
　She said they were her pay from her
　　lovers.
I will turn them into a forest.
　Wild animals will eat those plants.
¹³I will punish her for all the times
　she burned incense^d to the Baals.
She put on her rings and jewelry.
　Then she went chasing after her
　　lovers.

But she has forgotten me!"
　says the Lord.

¹⁴"So I am going to attract her.
　I will lead her into the desert
　　and speak tenderly to her.
¹⁵Then I will give her back her
　　vineyards.
　And I will make the Valley of
　　Achorⁿ a door of hope.
Then she will respond as when she
　　was young,
　as when she came out of Egypt."

¹⁶The Lord says, "Then she will call me
　　'my husband.'
　She will no longer call me 'my baal.'ⁿ
¹⁷I will never let her say the names of
　　Baal again.
　Then people won't use their names
　　anymore.
¹⁸At that time I will make an agreement
　　for them.
　It will be with the wild animals, the
　　birds and the crawling things.
I will remove from the land
　the bow and the sword and the
　　weapons of war.
　Then my people will live in safety.
¹⁹And I will make you my promised
　　bride forever.
　I will be good and fair.
　I will show you my love and mercy.
²⁰I will be true to you as my promised
　　bride.
　Then you will accept that I am the
　　Lord.

²¹"And at that time I will answer you,"
　　says the Lord.
　"I will speak to the skies.
　And they will give rain to the
　　earth.
²²The earth will produce grain, wine
　　and oil.

2:7 husband This refers to God here.
2:15 Achor This name in Hebrew means "trouble." It refers here to punishment as the way to blessing.
2:16 baal Another Hebrew word for husband. But it was the same word as the false god Baal.

Much will grow because my people
   are called Jezreel—God plants.
[23]I will plant my people in the land.
   I will show pity to the one I had
      called 'not shown pity.'
I will say, 'You are my people'
   to those I had called 'not my
      people.'
And they will say to me, 'You are
   our God.'"

HOSEA BUYS GOMER BACK

3 The Lord said to me, "Go, show your
love to your wife again. She has had
other lovers and has been unfaithful to
you. But you must keep on loving her the
way the Lord loves the people of Israel.
This is true even though the Israelites
worship other gods. They love to eat the
raisin cakes."[n]

[2]So I bought Gomer for six ounces of
silver and about ten bushels of barley.
[3]Then I told her, "You must wait for me
for many days. You must not be a prostitute.[d] You must not be any other man's
lover. I, in turn, will wait for you."

[4]In the same way Israel will live many
days without a king or leader. They will
not have sacrifices or holy stone pillars.
They will be without the holy vest[d] or an
idol. [5]After this, the people of Israel will
return to the Lord their God. They will
follow the Lord and the king from David's family. In the last days they will
come to the Lord. And he will bless them.

THE LORD'S WORD AGAINST ISRAEL

4 People of Israel, listen to the Lord's
message.
The Lord says he has this
against you who live in this country:
"The people are not true, not loyal to
      God.
They do not even know him.
[2]They curse. They lie. They kill. They
   steal.
They are guilty of adultery.[d]

They break all my laws.
   One murder follows another.
[3]Because of this the land dries up,
   and all its people are dying off.
Even the wild animals are dying.
   Even the birds of the air and the
      fish of the sea are dying.

GOD'S CASE AGAINST THE PRIESTS

[4]"No one should accuse
   or blame another person.
Don't blame the people, you priests,
   when they quarrel with you.
[5]You will be ruined one of these days.
   And your prophets[d] will be ruined
      with you one of these nights.
I will also destroy your mother, the
   nation of Israel.
[6]My people will be destroyed
   because they have no knowledge.
You priests have refused to learn.
   So I will refuse to let you be priests
      to me.
You have forgotten the teachings of
   your God.
   So I will reject your children.
[7]The more priests there are,
   the more they sin against me.
I will take away their honor
   and give them nothing but shame.
[8]The priests live off the sin offerings of
   the people.
   So they want the people to sin more
      and more.
[9]The priests are as wrong as the
   people.
I will punish them both for what
   they have done.
I will repay them for the wrong they
   have done.

[10]"They will eat
   but not have enough.
They will have sexual relations with
   the prostitutes.[d]
But they will not have children.
This is because they left the Lord.

3:1 raisin cakes This food may have been used in the feasts that honored false gods.

GOD'S CASE AGAINST THE PEOPLE

11"Sexual sins, old wine and new wine
  take away my people's ability to
  understand.
12My people ask wooden idols for advice.
  They ask those sticks of wood to
    advise them!
Like prostitutes, they have chased
    after other gods.
They have left their own God.
13They make sacrifices on the tops of
    the mountains.
  They burn offerings on the hills,
under oaks, poplars and other trees.
  They think the shade under those
    trees is nice.
So your daughters become prostitutes.
  And your daughters-in-law are
    guilty of adultery.[d]

14"But I will not punish your daughters
    when they become prostitutes.
I will not punish your daughters-in-law
    for their sins of adultery.
I will not punish them
  because you yourselves have sexual
    relations with prostitutes.
You offer sacrifices with the temple
    prostitutes.
  You foolish people are destroying
    yourselves.

15"Israel, you act like a prostitute.
  But don't let Judah be guilty.
Don't go to sacrifice at Gilgal.
  Don't go up to give offerings at Beth
    Aven.[n]
Don't use the Lord's name to make
    promises.
  Don't say, 'As surely as the Lord
    lives . . .'
16The people of Israel are stubborn
    like a stubborn young cow.
How then can the Lord feed them
    like lambs in a meadow?
17Israel has chosen to worship idols.
  So, let them.

18Her rulers get drunk.
  Then they give themselves to being
    prostitutes.
  They love these disgraceful things.
19They will be swept away as by a
    whirlwind.
  Their sacrifices will bring them only
    shame.

THE LORD'S WORD AGAINST THE LEADERS

5 "Listen, you priests.
  Pay attention, people of Israel.
Listen, royal family.
  You will all be judged.
You have been like a trap at Mizpah.
  You have been like a net spread out
    at Mount Tabor.
2You have done many bad things.
  So I will punish you all.
3I know all about Israel.
  What they have done is not hidden
    from me.
They all act like prostitutes.[d]
  Israel has made itself unclean.[d]

4"And those bad things they have done
  keep them from returning to their
    God.
They are determined to be unfaithful
    to me.
  They do not know the Lord.
5Israel's pride testifies against them.
  The people of Israel will stumble
    because of their sin.
  The people of Judah will also
    stumble with them.
6The people will come to worship the
    Lord.
  They will come with their sheep and
    cattle.
But they will not be able to find him,
    because he has left them.
7They have not been true to the Lord.
  Their children do not belong to
    him.
So their false worship
  will destroy them and their land.

4:15 Gilgal . . . Beth Aven Cities in Israel where people worshiped false gods.

8"Blow the horn in Gibeah.
  Blow the trumpet in Ramah.
Give the warning at Beth Aven.
  Be first into battle, people of
    Benjamin.
9A time of punishment is coming.
  Israel will be destroyed.
I warn the tribes[d] of Israel
  that this will surely happen.
10The leaders of Judah are like thieves.
  They try to steal the property of
    others.
My punishment will overwhelm them
  like a flood of water.
11Israel will be crushed by the
    punishments,
  because they decided to follow idols.
12I will destroy Israel
  as a moth destroys clothing.
I will destroy Judah
  as rot destroys wood.

13"Israel saw how weak she was.
  Judah saw the wounds she suffered.
So Israel turned to Assyria for help.
  She sent to the great king of Assyria
    for help.
But he cannot heal you.
  He cannot cure your wound.
14I will be like a lion to Israel.
  I will be like a young lion to Judah.
I will attack them
  and tear them to pieces.
I will drag them off,
  and no one will be able to save
    them.
15Then I will go back to my place
  until the people admit they are
    guilty.
At that time they must look for me.
  In their trouble they must turn to
    me."

THE PEOPLE ARE NOT FAITHFUL

6 You people say,
  "Come, let's go back to the Lord.
He has hurt us, but he will heal us.

He has wounded us, but he will
  bandage our wounds.
2In a short while he will put new life
    in us.
We will not have to wait long for
  him to raise us up.
Then we may live in his presence.
3Let's learn about the Lord.
  Let's try hard to know who he is.
He will come to us
  as surely as the dawn comes.
The Lord will come to us like the rain,
  like the spring rain that waters the
    ground."

4The Lord says, "Israel, what should
    I do with you?
Judah, what should I do with you?
Your faithfulness is like a morning
    mist.
  It lasts only as long as the dew in
    the morning.
5I have warned you by my prophets[d]
  that I will kill you and destroy you.
My judgments will flash forth like
  lightning against you.
6I want faithful love
  more than I want animal sacrifices.
I want people to know me
  more than I want burnt offerings.
7But you have broken the agreement as
    Adam did.
  You have been unfaithful to me.
8Gilead is full of people who do evil.
  It is covered with bloody footprints.
9Some of the priests are like
  robbers waiting in ambush.
They murder people on the way to
    Shechem.[n]
  They do wicked crimes.
10I have seen horrible things in Israel.
  The people are unfaithful to God,
  and Israel has become unclean.[d]

11"Judah, I have set a time to punish
  you also.

6:9 **Shechem** A city of safety where men could go for protection.

"I would like to give my people back
   their riches.

7 I would like to heal Israel.
   But their sin can be seen by
      everyone.
   The wickedness of Israel is too
      well-known.
They cheat one another.
   They break into other peoples'
      houses.
   There are robberies in the streets.
²It never enters their minds
   that I remember all their wicked
      deeds.
   The bad things they do are all around,
   and I can see their sins clearly.

ISRAEL DESTROYS HER RULERS

³"They make the king happy with their
      wickedness.
   They make their rulers glad with
      their lies.
⁴But all of them are traitors.
   They are like an oven heated by a
      baker.
While he mixes the dough,
   he does not stir up the flame.
⁵They hold a festival day for the king.
   On that day the rulers become
      drunk with wine.
   The king joins in with those who
      had made evil plans.
⁶They approach him with murder in
      mind.
   Their hearts are like a hot oven.
All night long its fire is low.
   When morning comes, it is fanned
      into flame.
⁷So all these people are as hot as an
      oven.
   Like a fire they destroy their rulers.
Their kings fall one after another.
   And no one calls on me.

ISRAEL AND THE OTHER NATIONS

⁸"Israel mixes with other nations.
   Israel is useless like a pancake
      cooked only on one side.

⁹Foreign nations are using up Israel's
      strength.
   And Israel doesn't even know it.
Israel is weak and feeble, like an old
      man.
   And they don't even know it.
¹⁰Israel's pride will cause their defeat.
   They have had many troubles.
But they still do not turn to the Lord
      their God.
   They do not look to him for help.
¹¹Israel has become like a silly pigeon.
   The people have no understanding.
First they call to Egypt for help.
   Then they run for help to Assyria.
¹²When they go, I will catch them
   as men catch birds in a net.
Then I will punish them
   as I have warned them.
¹³How terrible for them because they
      left me!
   They will be destroyed because they
      turned against me.
I want to save them.
   But they have spoken lies against me.
¹⁴They do not call to me from their
      hearts.
   They just lie on their beds and cry.
They come together to ask for grain
      and new wine.
   But they really turn away from me.
¹⁵I trained them and gave them
      strength.
   But they have made evil plans
      against me.
¹⁶They did not turn to the Most High God.
   They are like a crooked bow that
      does not shoot straight.
Their leaders brag about their
      strength.
   But they will be killed with swords.
Then the people in Egypt
   will laugh at them.

ISRAEL HAS TRUSTED WRONG THINGS

8 "Put the trumpet to your lips and
      give the warning!
   The enemy swoops down on my
      people like an eagle.

The Israelites have broken my
  agreement.
They have turned against my
  teachings.
²They cry out to me,
  'Our God, we in Israel know you!'
³But Israel has rejected what is good.
  So the enemy chases them.
⁴They chose their own kings
  without asking my permission.
They chose their own leaders,
  men I did not know.
They made their silver and gold into
  idols.
For all this they will be destroyed.
⁵I hate that calf-shaped idol.
  I am very angry with the people.
How long will they remain unclean?ᵈ
⁶The idol is something a craftsman
  made.
It is not God.
Israel's calf-shaped idol
  will surely be smashed to pieces.

⁷"Israel's foolish plans are like planting
  the wind.
But they will harvest a whirlwind.
Her plans are like a stalk with no head
  of grain.
It produces nothing.
Even if it produces something,
  other nations would eat it.
⁸Israel is destroyed.
The people are mixed among the
  other nations.
They have become useless to me.
⁹Like a wild donkey,
  Israel has run to Assyria.
Israel has hired other nations to
  protect her.
¹⁰Although Israel is mixed among the
  nations,
I will gather them together.
They will become weaker and weaker
  as they suffer under the great king
  of Assyria.

¹¹"The more altars Israel built to
  remove sin,

the more they have become altars
  for sinning.
¹²They reject the many teachings I have
  written for them.
They act as if the teachings were
  strange and foreign to them.
¹³The Israelites offer sacrifices to me
  and eat the meat.
But the Lord is not pleased with them.
He remembers the evil they have
  done.
And he will punish them for their sins.
They will be slaves again as they
  were in Egypt.
¹⁴The people of Israel have forgotten
  their Maker.
They trust in the palaces they have
  built.
And Judah trusts in her many
  strong, walled cities.
But I will send fire on their cities
  and destroy their strong towers."

ISRAEL'S PUNISHMENT

9 Israel, do not rejoice.
  Don't celebrate as the other nations
  do.
You have been unfaithful to your God.
  You love the grain on your
  threshingᵈ floors.
So you worship the gods who
  supposedly gave it.
²But there won't be enough grain to
  feed the people.
And there won't be enough wine to
  go around.
³The Israelites will not stay in the
  Lord's land.
Israel will return to being captives
  as they were in Egypt.
In Assyria they will eat food that
  they are not allowed to eat.
⁴The Israelites will not give offerings of
  wine to the Lord.
Their sacrifices will not please him.
Their sacrifices will be like food that is
  eaten at a funeral.
It is unclean,ᵈ and everyone who
  eats it becomes unclean.

Their food will only satisfy their
hunger.
They cannot sacrifice it in the
Temple.[d]
[5]What will you do then on the day of
feasts
and on the festival days of the Lord?
[6]Even if the people are not destroyed,
Egypt will take them as captives.
They will be buried in Memphis.[n]
Weeds will grow over their silver
treasures.
Thorns will grow over their houses.
[7]Let Israel know this.
The time of punishment has come.
The time to pay for your sins has
come.
You have sinned very much,
and your hatred is great.
You think the prophet[d] is a fool.
You say the spiritual man is crazy.
[8]The prophet is God's watchman
to warn Israel of danger.
But everywhere he goes you set traps
for him.
You treat him as an enemy in God's
own land.
[9]The men of Israel have become as
sinful
as the men of Gibeah[n] were.
The Lord will remember the evil
things they have done.
He will punish them for their sins.

[10]"When I found Israel,
it was like finding grapes in the
desert.
Your ancestors were like
finding the first figs on the tree.
But when they came to Baal Peor,
they began worshiping an idol.
They became as disgusting as the
thing they worshiped.
[11]Israel's glory will fly away like a bird.
There will be no more pregnancies,
no more births, no more babies.

[12]But even if the Israelites bring up
children,
I will take them all away.
How terrible it will be for them
when I turn away from them!
[13]I have seen Israel, like Tyre,
given a pleasant place.
But the people of Israel will soon
bring out
their children to be killed."

[14]Lord, give them what they should have.
What will you give them?
Make their women unable to have
children.
Give them breasts that cannot feed
their babies.

[15]"The Israelites were wicked in Gilgal,
so I began to hate them there.
Because of the sinful things they have
done,
I will force them to leave my land.
I will no longer love them.
Their leaders have turned against
me.
[16]Israel is like a sick plant.
Its root is dying, and it has no fruit.
So the people will have no more
children.
And if they did, I would kill the
children they love."

[17]God will reject them,
because they have not obeyed him.
They will wander among the
nations.

ISRAEL WILL PAY FOR SIN

10 Israel is like a vine
that produced plenty of fruit.
As the people became richer,
they built more altars for idols.
As their land became better,
they put up better stone pillars to
honor false gods.
[2]Their heart was false.
Now they must pay for their guilt.

9:6 Memphis A city in Egypt famous for its tombs.
9:9 Gibeah The sins of the men of Gibeah caused a civil war. See Judges 19–21.

The Lord will break down their altars.
He will destroy their holy stone
pillars.

³Then the Israelites will say, "We have
no king,
because we didn't honor the Lord.
But even if we had one,
he couldn't do anything for us."
⁴They make many false promises.
They make agreements they don't
keep.
So people sue each other in court.
They are like poisonous weeds
growing in a plowed field.
⁵The people from Israel are worried
about
the calf-shaped idol at Beth Aven.
The people and the priests will cry
because their glorious idol is gone.
⁶It will be carried off as a payment that
was demanded
to the great king of Assyria.
Israel will be disgraced.
The people will be ashamed of
trusting that idol.
⁷The king of Israel will be carried off
like a chip of wood floating on the
water.
⁸The places of worship at Beth Aven
will be destroyed.
They are where Israel sins.
Thorns and weeds will grow up
and cover their altars.
Then they will say to the mountains,
"Cover us!"
And they will say to the hills, "Fall
on us!"

⁹"Israel, you have sinned since the
time of Gibeah.ⁿ
The people there have continued
sinning.
But war will surely overwhelm them,
because of the evil they have done
there.
¹⁰When I am ready,
I will come to punish them.

Armies will come together against
them.
They will be punished for their
many sins.
¹¹Israel is like a well-trained young cow
that likes to threshᵈ grain.
But I will put a yokeᵈ on her neck.
I will make Israel work hard in the
field.
Judah will plow.
Israel will break up the ground.
¹²I said, 'Break new ground.
Plant what is right.
Then you will harvest good things
from your loyalty to me.
It is time for you to turn back to me,
the Lord.
Do it until I come and pour out my
goodness on you.'
¹³But you have planted evil.
So you have harvested trouble.
You have trusted in your own power
and your many soldiers.
Now you must live with the result of
your lies.
¹⁴So your armies will hear the noise of
battle.
And all your strong, walled cities
will be destroyed.
It will be like the time King Shalman
destroyed Beth Arbel in battle.
Mothers and children were crushed
to the ground together.
¹⁵The same will happen to you, people
of Bethel,
because you did so much evil.
When that time comes,
the king of Israel will die.

GOD'S LOVE FOR ISRAEL

11 "When Israel was a child,
I loved him.
And I called my son out of Egypt.
²But the more I called to the people
of Israel,
the further they went from me.

10:9 Gibeah The sins of the men of Gibeah caused a civil war. See Judges 19–21.

They offered sacrifices to the Baals.[d]
  They burned incense[d] to the idols.
[3]But it was I who taught Israel to walk.
  I took them by the arms.
But they did not understand
  that I had healed them.
[4]I led them with cords of human
    kindness,
  with ties of love.
I lifted the yoke[d] from their neck.
  I bent down and fed them.

[5]"The Israelites will become captives
    again, as they were in Egypt.
  The king of Assyria will become
    their king.
  This is because they refuse to turn
    to God.
[6]War will sweep through their cities.
  It will destroy them,
  because of their wicked plans.
[7]My people have made up their minds
    to turn away from me.
The prophets[d] call them to turn to me.
  But none of them honors me at all.

[8]"Israel, I don't want to give you up.
  I don't want to go away and leave
    you.
I don't want to make you like
    Admah.
  I don't want to treat you like
    Zeboiim.[n]
My heart beats for you.
  My love for you stirs up my pity.
[9]I won't punish you in my anger.
  I won't destroy Israel again.
I am God and not man.
  I am the Holy One, and I am among
    you.
  I will not come against you in
    anger.
[10]I will call for my people like
    a lion calling for its young.
My children will come and follow me.
  They will hurry to me from the
    west.

[11]They will come swiftly
  like birds from a captivity like
    Egypt was,
  and like doves from Assyria.
I will settle them again in their
    homes,"
  says the Lord.

THE LORD IS AGAINST ISRAEL

[12]Israel has surrounded me with lies.
  The people of Israel have made
    their secret plans.
And Judah turns against God,
  the faithful Holy One.

12 What Israel does is as useless
    as chasing the wind,
  as dangerous as being in a
    windstorm.
They tell more and more lies
  and do more and more violence.
They make agreements with Assyria,
  and they send a gift of olive oil to
    Egypt.
[2]The Lord also has some things against
    Judah.
  He will punish Israel for what they
    have done.
  He will give them what they deserve.
[3]Their ancestor Jacob held on to his
    brother's heel
  while the two of them were being
    born.
When Jacob grew to be a man,
  he wrestled with God.
[4]He wrestled with the angel and won.
  Jacob cried and asked for his
    blessing.
Later, God met with him at Bethel
  and spoke with him there.
[5]He is the Lord God of heaven's armies.
  He wants to be remembered as the
    Lord.
[6]Like Jacob you must return to him.
  You must be loyal and true to him.
You must do what is honest and just.
  You must always trust in him as
    your God.

11:8 **Admah...Zeboiim** Two other cities destroyed when God destroyed Sodom and Gomorrah.

7The merchants use dishonest scales.
    They like to cheat people.
8The people of Israel brag that they are
    rich.
    They think that because they are rich
    no one will learn about their sins.

9"But I am the Lord your God.
    I brought you out of Egypt.
I will make you live in tents again
    as you used to do in the desert.
10I spoke to the prophets*d*
    and gave them many visions.
    Through them, I taught my lessons
    to you."

11The people of Gilead are evil.
    They are worth nothing.
    People sacrifice bulls at Gilgal.
    But their altars will become like
    piles of stone in a plowed field.
12Your ancestor Jacob fled to Northwest
    Mesopotamia.
    There he worked to get a wife.
    He tended sheep to pay for her.
13Later the Lord used a prophet
    to bring Jacob's descendants*d* out of
    Egypt.
    The Lord used a prophet
    to take care of the Israelites.
14But the Israelites made the Lord
    angry.
    They killed other people.
    They deserve to die for their crimes.
    The Lord will make them pay
    for the disgraceful things they have
    done.

THE FINAL WORD AGAINST ISRAEL

13 People used to fear the tribe*d*
        of Ephraim.
    They were important people in
    Israel.
    But they sinned by worshiping Baal.*d*
    So they must die.
2But they keep on sinning more and
    more.
    They make idols of their silver.
    Those idols are cleverly made.
    They are the work of a craftsman.

Yet the people of Israel say to each
    other,
    "Kiss those calf idols and sacrifice
    to them."
3So those people will be like the
    morning dew.
    They will disappear like the
    morning mist.
    They will be like chaff*d* blown from
    the threshing*d* floor.
    They will vanish away like smoke
    rising from a chimney.

4"I have been the Lord their God
    since they were in the land of Egypt.
    They have really known no other God
    except me.
    I am the one who has saved them.
5I cared for them in the desert
    where it was hot and dry.
6I gave them food, and they became
    full and satisfied.
    But then they became proud and
    forgot me.
7That is why I will be like a lion to
    them.
    I will be like a leopard waiting by
    the road.
8I will attack like a bear robbed of her
    cubs.
    I will rip their bodies open.
    I will devour them like a lion.
    I will tear them apart like a wild
    animal.

9"Israel, I will destroy you
    for turning against me, your helper.
10What good are your kings and your
    leaders now?
    Can they save you in any of your
    towns?
    You asked for them, saying,
    'Give us a king and leaders.'
11So I gave you kings, but only in anger.
    And I took them away in my great
    anger.
12The sins of Israel are on record.
    They are filed away, waiting for
    punishment.

13Israel has a chance to live again,
    but the people are too foolish to
        take it.
They are like an unborn baby
    who won't come out of its mother's
        womb.
14So I will not save them from the place
        where the dead are.
I will not rescue them from death.
I will call on death to hurt them.
I will call on the place where the
    dead are to destroy them.
I will show them no mercy.
15Israel has become important among
        the nations.
But the Lord will send a destroyer
        from the east.
He will come like a wind from the
        desert
    that dries up all the springs and
        wells of water.
He will destroy all their treasures,
    everything of value.
16The nation of Israel will be punished,
    because it fought against God.
The people of Israel will die by the
        sword.
    Their children will be torn to pieces.
    And their pregnant women will be
        ripped open."

ISRAEL RETURNS TO GOD

14 Israel, return to the Lord your
        God.
    Your sins have caused your ruin.
2Come back to the Lord
    and say these words to him:
"Take away all our sin
    and kindly receive us.
Then we will give you the praise we
    promised you.

3Assyria cannot save us.
    We will not trust in our horses.
We will not say again, 'Our gods,'
    to the things our hands have made.
    You show mercy to us, who are like
        orphans."

4The Lord says,
    "I will forgive them for leaving me.
    I will love them freely.
    I am not angry with them anymore.
5I will be like the dew to Israel.
    It will blossom like a lily.
Like the cedar trees in Lebanon,
    its roots will be firm.
6The people will be like spreading
        branches.
    They will be like the beautiful olive
        trees.
    They will be like the sweet-smelling
        cedars in Lebanon.
7The people of Israel will again live
        under my protection.
    They will grow like the grain.
They will bloom like a vine.
    They will be as famous as the wine
        of Lebanon.
8Israel, have nothing to do with idols.
    I, the Lord, am the one who
        answers your prayers.
    I am the one who watches over you.
I am like a green pine tree.
    Your blessings come from me."

9A wise person will know these things.
    An understanding person will take
        them to heart.
The Lord's ways are right.
    Good people live by following them,
    but those who turn against God die
        because of them.

JOEL

LOCUSTS DESTROY THE CROPS

1 The Lord spoke his word to Joel son of Pethuel:

²Elders, listen to this message.
Listen to me, all you people who
live in the land.
Nothing like this has ever happened
during your lifetime.
Nothing like this has ever happened
during your fathers' lifetimes.
³Tell your children about these things.
And let your children tell their
children.
And let your grandchildren tell
their children.
⁴What the cutting locusts have not
eaten,
the swarming locusts have eaten.
And what the swarming locusts have
left,
the hopping locusts have eaten.
And what the hopping locusts have
left,
the destroying locusts[n] have eaten.

⁵Drunks, wake up and cry!
All of you people who drink wine,
cry!
Cry because your sweet wine
has been taken away from you.
⁶A powerful nation has come into my
land.
It has too many soldiers to count.
It has teeth like a lion.
And it has fangs like a female lion.
⁷That army has eaten my grapevines.
It has destroyed my fig trees.
It has eaten the bark off my trees
and left the branches white.

⁸Cry as a young woman cries
when the man she was going to
marry is killed.
⁹There will be no more grain or drink
offerings
to offer in the Temple[d] of the Lord.
Because of this, the priests,
the servants of the Lord, cry.
¹⁰The fields are ruined.
Even the ground is dried up.
The grain is destroyed.
The new wine is dried up.
And the olive oil runs out.
¹¹Be sad, farmers.
Cry loudly, you who grow grapes.
Cry for the wheat and the barley.
Cry because the harvest in the field
is lost.
¹²The vines have become dry.
And the fig trees are dying.
The pomegranate[d] trees, the date
palm trees and the apple trees
have dried up.
All the trees in the field have died.
And the happiness of the people has
died, too.
¹³Priests, put on your rough cloth and
cry to show your sadness.
Servants of the altar, cry out loud.
Servants of my God,
sleep in your rough cloth to show
your sadness.
Cry because there will be no more
grain or drink offerings
to offer in the Temple of your God.
¹⁴Call the people together.
Tell them there will be a time to
give up food.
Bring together the elders
and everyone who lives in the land.
Bring them to the Temple of the Lord
your God.
And cry out to the Lord.
¹⁵This will be a terrible day!
The Lord's day of judging is near.

1:4 cutting ... locusts These are different names for an insect like a large grasshopper. The locust can quickly destroy trees, plants and crops. In this destruction by locusts, Joel sees a warning. God will cause this type of destruction when he punishes his people.

At that time punishment will come
  like an attack from God All-Powerful.

¹⁶Our food is taken away
  while we watch.
Joy and happiness are gone
  from the Temple of our God.
¹⁷We planted seeds,
  but they lie dry and dead in the dirt.
Our barns are empty and falling
    down.
  The storerooms for grain have been
    broken down.
  This is because the grain has dried
    up.
¹⁸The animals are hungry and groaning!
  The herds of cattle wander around
    confused.
  They have no grass to eat.
  Even the flocks of sheep suffer.
¹⁹Lord, I am calling to you for help.
  Fire has burned up the open
    pastures.
  Flames have burned all the trees in
    the field.
²⁰Wild animals also need your help.
  The water in the streams has dried
    up.
  Fire has burned up the open
    pastures.

THE COMING DAY OF JUDGMENT

2 Blow the trumpet in Jerusalem.
  Shout a warning on my holy
    mountain.
Let all the people who live in the land
  shake with fear.
The Lord's day of judging is
  coming.
The Lord's day of judging is near.
²It will be a dark, gloomy day.
  It will be a cloudy and black day.
Like the light at sunrise,
  the great and powerful army will
    spread over the mountains.
There has never been anything like it
  before.
  And there will never be anything
    like it again.

³The army destroys the land
  like a burning fire.
The land in front of them is like the
  garden of Eden.
  The land behind them is like an
    empty desert.
  Nothing will escape them.
⁴They look like horses.
  They run like war horses.
⁵Listen to them!
It is like the noise of chariots
  rumbling over the mountains.
It is like the noise of crackling flames
  burning dry stalks.
They are like a powerful army lined
  up for battle.
⁶Before this army, nations shake with
  fear.
  Their faces become pale.

⁷The army charges ahead like soldiers.
  They climb over the walls like
    warriors.
  They all march straight ahead.
  They do not move off their path.
⁸They do not run into each other.
  Each one walks in line.
  They charge through all efforts to stop
    them
  and stay in line.
⁹They run into the city.
  They run along the tops of the walls.
  They climb into the houses.
  They enter through windows like a
    thief.

¹⁰Before them, earth and sky shake.
  The sun and the moon become dark,
  and the stars stop shining.
¹¹The Lord calls out orders loudly
  as he leads his army.
That army obeys his commands.
  It is very large and powerful.
The Lord's day of judging
  is an overwhelming and terrible day.
  No one can stand up against it.

CHANGE YOUR HEARTS
¹²The Lord says, "Now, come back to
  me with all your heart.
  Go without food, and cry and be sad."

¹³Tearing your clothes is not enough to
   show you are sad.
Let your heart be broken.
Come back to the Lord your God.
He is kind and shows mercy.
He doesn't become angry quickly.
He has great love.
He would rather forgive than punish.
¹⁴Who knows? Maybe the Lord will
   change his mind
   and leave behind a blessing for you.
Then you may give grain and drink
   offerings
   to the Lord your God.

¹⁵Blow the trumpet in Jerusalem.
   Call for a special time of going
      without food.
   Call for a special meeting.
¹⁶Bring the people together.
   Make the meeting holy for the Lord.
   Bring together the elders.
   Bring together the children,
   even babies that still feed at their
      mothers' breasts.
The bridegroom should come from
   his room.
The bride should come from her
   bedroom.
¹⁷The priests, the Lord's servants,
   should cry.
   They should cry between the altar
      and entrance to the Temple.*d*
   They should say, "Lord, have mercy
      on your people.
   Don't let them be put to shame.
   Don't let other nations make fun of
      them.
   Don't let people in other nations ask,
      'Where is their God?'"

THE LORD RESTORES THE LAND
¹⁸Then the Lord became concerned
   about his land.
   He felt sorry for his people.
¹⁹The Lord said to them:

"I will send you grain, wine and
   olive oil.
You will have plenty.
No more will I shame you
   among the nations.
²⁰I will force the army from the north to
   leave your land.
I will force them into a dry, empty
   land.
Their soldiers in front will be forced
   into the Dead Sea.*d*
And those in the rear will be forced
   into the Mediterranean Sea.
Their bodies will rot and stink
   because they did horrible things."

²¹But, land, don't be afraid.
   Be happy and full of joy
   because the Lord has begun to do
      wonderful things.
²²Wild animals, don't be afraid.
   The open pastures will grow grass.
   The trees will grow fruit.
   The fig trees and the vines will grow
      much fruit.
²³So be happy, people of Jerusalem.
   Be joyful in the Lord your God.
   He will do what is right
      and will give you rain.
   He will send the early rain
      and the late rain for you, as before.
²⁴And the threshing*d* floors will be full
   of wheat.
   And the barrels will overflow with
      wine and olive oil.

THE LORD SPEAKS
²⁵"I sent my great army against you.
   Those swarming locusts and the
      hopping locusts,
   the destroying locusts and the
      cutting locusts*n* ate your crops.
   But I will pay you back
      for those years of trouble.
²⁶Then you will have plenty to eat.
   You will be full.

2:25 swarming . . . locusts These are different names for an insect like a large grasshopper. The locust can quickly
destroy trees, plants and crops. In this destruction by locusts, Joel sees a warning. God will cause this type of
destruction when he punishes his people.

You will praise the name of the Lord
    your God.
He has done miracles[d] for you.
My people will never again be
    shamed.
27Then you will know that I am among
    the people of Israel.
You will know that I am the Lord
    your God.
There is no other God.
My people will never be shamed
    again.

28"After this,
    I will give my Spirit[d] freely to all
        kinds of people.
Your sons and daughters will
    prophesy.[d]
Your old men will dream dreams.
Your young men will see visions.
29At that time I will give my Spirit
    even to servants, both men and
    women.
30I will show miracles
    in the sky and on the earth:
    blood, fire and thick smoke.
31The sun will become dark.
    The moon will become red as blood.
    And then the Lord's overwhelming
        and terrible day of judging will
        come.
32Then anyone who asks the Lord for
    help
    will be saved.
Even on Mount Zion[d] and in Jerusalem
    there will be people who will be
    saved.
This will happen just as the Lord has
    said.
Those left alive after the day of
    punishment
    are the people whom the Lord called.

PUNISHMENT FOR JUDAH'S ENEMIES

3 "In those days and at that time,
I will give Judah and Jerusalem
back their riches.
2I will also gather all the nations
together.

I will bring them down into the
    Valley Where the Lord Judges.
And there I will judge them.
Those nations scattered my own
    people, Israel.
They forced my people to live in
    other nations.
They divided up my land.
3They threw lots[d] for my people.
They traded boys for prostitutes.[d]
    And they sold girls to buy wine to
    drink.

4"Tyre and Sidon and all of you regions of Philistia! What do you have against me? Are you punishing me for something I did? Or are you doing something to hurt me? Then I will quickly do to you what you have done to me. 5You took my silver and gold. You took my precious treasures and put them in your temples. 6You sold the people of Judah and Jerusalem to the Greeks. That way you could send them far from their land.

7"You sent my people to that faraway place. But I will bring them back. And I will do to you what you have done to them. 8I will sell your sons and daughters to the people of Judah. Then they will sell them to the Sabean people far away." The Lord said this.

GOD JUDGES THE NATIONS

9Announce this among the nations:
    Prepare for war!
Wake up the soldiers!
    Let all the men of war come near
        and attack.
10Make your plows into swords.
    Make spears from your hooks for
        trimming trees.
Let the weak say,
    "I am strong."
11All of you nations, hurry.
    Come together in that place.
Lord, send your strong soldiers
    to gather the nations.
12"Wake up, nations.

Come to the Valley Where the Lord
Judges.
There I will sit to judge
all the nations on every side.
¹³Cut them down like grain
because the harvest is ripe with sin.
Come, walk on them as you would
walk on grapes,
because the winepress^d is full.
The barrels are full of their sins and
spilling over.
These people are so evil!"

¹⁴There are many people
in the Valley of Decision.^{n}
The Lord's day of judging is near
in the Valley of Decision.
¹⁵The sun and the moon will become
dark.
The stars will stop shining.
¹⁶The Lord will roar like a lion from
Jerusalem.
His loud voice will sound like a
growl from Jerusalem.
And the sky and the earth will shake.
But the Lord will be a safe place for
his people.
He will be a strong place of safety
for the people of Israel.

¹⁷"Then you will know that I am the
Lord your God.
I stay in my holy Mount Zion.^{d}
Jerusalem will become holy.
Strangers will never take over that
city again.

A NEW LIFE PROMISED FOR JUDAH

¹⁸"On that day the mountains will be
covered with grapes for sweet
wine.
The hills will be covered with cows
to give milk.
And water will flow through all the
ravines of Judah.
A fountain will flow from the Temple^d
of the Lord.
It will give water to the valley of
acacia trees.
¹⁹But Egypt will become empty.
And Edom will become an empty
desert.
This is because they were cruel to the
people of Judah.
They killed innocent people in the
land of Judah.
²⁰But there will always be people living
in Judah.
And people will live in Jerusalem
from now on.
²¹Egypt and Edom killed my people.
So I will definitely punish them."

The Lord lives in Jerusalem!

3:14 Valley of Decision This is like the name "the Valley Where the Lord Judges" in 3:2 and 3:12.

THE BOOK OF
AMOS

1 Amos was one of the shepherds from the town of Tekoa. God showed him this vision about Israel. It was at the time Uzziah was king of Judah and Jeroboam son of Jehoash was king of Israel. This happened two years before the earthquake.
²Amos said,

"The Lord will roar like a lion from Jerusalem.
His loud voice will sound like a growl from Jerusalem.
The green pastures of the shepherds will become dry.
Even Mount Carmel will dry up."

ISRAEL'S NEIGHBORS ARE PUNISHED

The People of Aram

³This is what the Lord says:
"For the many crimes Damascus is doing,
I will punish them.
They beat the people of Gilead
with threshing^d boards that had iron teeth.
⁴So I will send fire upon the house of Hazael.
That fire will destroy the strong towers of Ben-Hadad.
⁵I will break down the gate of Damascus.
I will destroy the king who is in the Valley of Aven.
I will also destroy the king of Beth Eden.
The people of Aram will be taken captive to the country of Kir,"
says the Lord.

The People of Philistia

⁶This is what the Lord says:
"For the many crimes Gaza is doing,
I will punish them.
They sold all the people of one area as slaves to Edom.

⁷So I will send a fire on the walls of Gaza.
That fire will destroy the city's strong towers.
⁸I will destroy the king of the city of Ashdod.
I will destroy the king of the city of Ashkelon.
Then I will turn against the people of the city of Ekron.
I will punish the Philistines until they are all dead," says the Lord God.

The People of Phoenicia

⁹This is what the Lord says:
"For the many crimes Tyre is doing,
I will punish them.
They sold all the people of one area as slaves to Edom.
They forgot the brotherly agreement they had made with Israel.
¹⁰So I will send fire on the walls of Tyre.
That fire will destroy the city's strong towers."

The People of Edom

¹¹This is what the Lord says:
"For the many crimes Edom is doing,
I will punish them.
They hunted down their brothers, the Israelites, with the sword.
They showed them no mercy.
The people of Edom were continually angry.
And they did not hold back their great anger.
¹²So I will send fire on the city of Teman.
That fire will even destroy the strong towers of Bozrah."^n

The People of Ammon

¹³This is what the Lord says:
"For the many crimes Ammon is doing,
I will punish them.
They ripped open the pregnant women in Gilead.

1:12 **Teman . . . Bozrah** Teman was in northern Edom, and Bozrah was in southern Edom. So this means the whole country will be destroyed.

They did this so they could take
over that land
and make their own country larger.
[14]So I will send fire on the walls of
Rabbah.
That fire will destroy the city's
strong towers.
It will come during a day of battle.
There will be strong winds on a
stormy day.
[15]Then their king and leaders will be
captured.
They will all be taken away together,"
says the Lord.

The People of Moab

2 This is what the Lord says:
"For the many crimes Moab is
doing,
I will punish them.
They burned the bones of the king
of Edom into lime.
[2]So I will send fire on Moab.
And it will destroy the strong
towers of the city of Kerioth.
The people of Moab will die in a great
noise.
They will die in the middle of
sounds of war and trumpets.
[3]So I will bring an end to the king of
Moab.
And I will kill all its leaders with
him," says the Lord.

The People of Judah

[4]This is what the Lord says:
"For the many crimes Judah is doing,
I will punish them.
They rejected the teachings of the
Lord.
They did not keep his commands.
Their ancestors followed false gods.
And Judah followed those same
gods.
[5]So I will send fire on Judah.
It will destroy the strong towers of
Jerusalem."

ISRAEL IS PUNISHED

[6]This is what the Lord says:

"For the many crimes Israel is doing,
I will punish them.
For silver they sell people who have
done nothing wrong.
They sell poor people for the price
of a pair of sandals.
[7]They walk on poor people
as if they were dirt.
They refuse to be fair to those who
are suffering.
Fathers and sons have sexual
relations with the same woman.
By doing this they ruin my holy
name.
[8]As they worship at their altars,
they lie down on clothes taken from
poor people.
They make people pay money as
punishment.
With that money they buy wine to
drink in the house of their god.

[9]"But it was I who destroyed the
Amorites before them.
The Amorites were tall like cedar
trees and as strong as oaks.
But I destroyed them completely.
[10]It was I who brought you from the
land of Egypt.
For 40 years I led you through the
desert.
I led you so I could give you the
land of the Amorites.
[11]I made some of your sons to be
prophets.[d]
I made some of your young men to
be Nazirites.[d]
People of Israel, isn't this true?" says
the Lord.
[12]"But you made the Nazirites drink
wine.
You told the prophets not to
prophesy my message.
[13]Now I will crush you
as a wagon loaded with grain
crushes anything beneath it.
[14]No one will escape, not even the
fastest runner.

Strong men will not be strong
    enough.
Warriors will not be able to save
    themselves.
¹⁵Soldiers with bows and arrows will
    not stand and fight.
Even soldiers who run quickly will
    not get away.
Soldiers on horses will not escape
    alive.
¹⁶At that time even the bravest warriors
    will run away without their armor,"
    says the Lord.

WARNING TO ISRAEL

3 Listen to this message that the Lord
    has spoken against you, people of
Israel. The message is against the whole
nation the Lord brought out of Egypt.
²"I have chosen only you
    out of all the families of the earth.
So I will punish you
    for all your sins."

³Two people will not walk together
    unless they have agreed to do this.
⁴A lion in the forest will roar
    when he has caught an animal.
He does not growl in his den
    when he has caught nothing.
⁵A bird will not fall into a trap
    where there is no bait.
The trap will not spring shut
    if there is nothing to catch.
⁶When a trumpet blows a warning,
    the people tremble.
When trouble comes to a city,
    the Lord has caused it.
⁷Before the Lord God does anything,
    he tells his servants the prophets.ᵈ
⁸The lion has roared!
    Who wouldn't be afraid?
The Lord God has spoken,
    and I must prophesy his message.

⁹Announce this to the strong towers of
    Ashdod.
Announce it to the strong cities of
    Egypt:
"Come to the mountains of Samaria.

There you will see great confusion.
You will see people hurting others."
¹⁰"The people don't know how to do
    what is right," says the Lord.
"Their strong cities are filled with
    treasures they took by force from
    others."
¹¹So this is what the Lord God says:
"An enemy will take over the land.
He will pull down your strong
    towers.
He will take the treasures you hid in
    your strong cities."

¹²This is what the Lord says:
"A shepherd might save from a lion's
    mouth
only two leg bones or a scrap of an
    ear of his sheep.
In the same way only a few Israelites
    will be saved.
These people now sit on their beds
    in Samaria.
They sit on their couches."

¹³"You nations, listen to what I say
against the family of Israel. You are my
witnesses against them," says the Lord
God, the God of heaven's armies.

¹⁴"The people of Israel sinned,
    and I will punish them.
I will also destroy the altars at
    Bethel.
The corners of the altar will be cut off,
    and they will fall to the ground.
¹⁵I will tear down the winter house,
    together with the summer house.
The houses decorated with ivory will
    be destroyed.
And the great houses will come to
    an end," says the Lord.

ISRAEL WILL NOT RETURN

4 Listen to this message, you rich
    women on the Mountain of
Samaria.
You take things from the poor
    and crush people who are in need.

You tell your husbands,
   "Bring us money so we can drink!"
[2]The Lord God has promised this:
   "It is certain that I am a holy God.
So it is certain that the time will come
   when some of you will be taken
   away by hooks.
The rest of you will be taken away
   with fishhooks.
[3]You will go straight out of the city
   through holes in the walls.
And you will be thrown on the
   garbage dump," says the Lord.

[4]"Go to the city of Bethel and sin.
   Go to Gilgal and sin even more.
Offer your sacrifices every morning.
   Bring one-tenth of your crops on
   the third day.
[5]Offer bread made with yeast as a
   sacrifice to show your thanks.
And brag about the offerings you
   bring to show thanks to the Lord.
Brag about these things, Israelites.
   This is what you love to do," says
   the Lord God.

[6]"I did not give you any food to eat.
   There was not enough food in any
   of your towns.
But you did not come back to me,"
   says the Lord.
[7]"I held back the rain from you
   three months before harvest time.
Then I let it rain on one city
   but not on another.
Rain fell on one field,
   but another field got none and
   dried up.
[8]People weak from thirst went from
   town to town for water.
But they could not get enough
   water to drink.
But you still did not come back to
   me," says the Lord.
[9]"I made your crops die from disease
   and mildew.[d]

I destroyed your gardens and your
   vineyards.
Locusts[d] ate your fig trees and olive
   trees.
But you still did not come back to
   me," says the Lord.
[10]"I sent disasters against you,
   as I did to Egypt.
I killed your young men with swords.
   I also killed your horses.
I made you smell the stink from all
   the dead bodies.
But you still did not come back to
   me," says the Lord.
[11]"I destroyed some of you
   as I destroyed Sodom and
   Gomorrah.
You were like a burning stick pulled
   from a fire.
But you still have not come back to
   me," says the Lord.

[12]"So this is what I will do to you, Israel.
   And because I will do this to you,
   get ready to meet your God, Israel."

[13]He is the one who makes the
   mountains.
He creates the wind.
He makes his thoughts known to
   man.
He changes the dawn into darkness.
He walks over the mountains of the
   earth.
His name is the Lord God of
   heaven's armies.

ISRAEL NEEDS TO REPENT

5 Listen to this funeral song that I sing
   about you, people of Israel.
[2]"Israel has fallen.
   It will not rise up again.
It was left alone in the land.
   There is no one to lift it up."

[3]This is what the Lord God says:
"If 1,000 soldiers leave a city,
   only 100 will return.
If 100 soldiers leave a city,
   only 10 will return."

[4]This is what the Lord says to the nation of Israel:
"Come to me and live.
[5]　But do not look in Bethel.
Do not go to Gilgal,
　and do not go down to Beersheba.
The people of Gilgal will be taken
　away as captives.
And Bethel will become nothing."
[6]Come to the Lord and live.
If you don't, he will destroy the
　descendants[d] of Joseph as a fire
　would.
The fire will burn.
But there will be no one to put it out
　for Bethel.
[7]You change the justice of the courts
　into something unfair.
You reject what is right.

[8]God is the one who made the star
　groups Pleiades and Orion.
He changes darkness into the
　morning light.
And he changes the day into the
　dark night.
He calls for the waters of the sea
　to pour out on the earth.
The Lord is his name.
[9]He destroys the protected city.
And he ruins the strong, walled city.

[10]You hate those who speak in court
　against evil.
And you hate those who tell the
　truth.
[11]You walk on poor people.
You force them to give you grain.
You have built fancy houses of cut
　stone.
But you will not live in them.
You have planted beautiful vineyards.
But you will not drink the wine
　from them.
[12]It is because I know your many crimes.
I know your terrible sins.
You hurt people who do right.
You accept money to do wrong.
You keep the poor from getting
　justice in court.

[13]In such times the wise man will keep
　quiet,
　because it is a bad time.

[14]Try to do good, not evil.
Then you will live.
And the Lord God of heaven's armies
　will be with you
　just as you say he is.
[15]Hate evil and love good.
Be fair in the courts.
Maybe the Lord God of heaven's
　armies will be kind
　to the people of Joseph who are left
　alive.

[16]This is what the Lord, the Lord God
of heaven's armies, says:
"People will be crying in all the public
　places.
They will be saying, 'Oh, no!' in the
　streets.
They will call the farmers to come
　and weep.
They will pay people to cry out loud
　for them.
[17]People will be crying in all the
　vineyards.
This is because I will pass among
　you to punish you," says the Lord.

THE LORD'S DAY OF JUDGING

[18]How terrible it will be for you who want
　the Lord's day of judging to come.
Why do you want that day to come?
It will bring darkness for you, not
　light.
[19]It will be like a man who runs from a
　lion
　and meets a bear.
It will be like him going into his house
　and putting his hand on the wall.
And then a snake bites him.
[20]So the Lord's day of judging will bring
　darkness, not light.
It will be a time of sadness, not joy.

[21]The Lord says, "I hate and reject your
　feasts.
I cannot stand your religious
　meetings.

²²You offer me burnt offerings and
   grain offerings.
But I won't accept them.
You bring the best fellowship offerings.
But I will ignore them.
²³Take the noise of your songs away
   from here!
I won't listen to the music of your
   harps.
²⁴But let justice flow like a river.
Let goodness flow like a
   never-ending stream.

²⁵"People of Israel, you did not bring
   me sacrifices and offerings
while you traveled in the desert for
   40 years.
²⁶But now you will have to carry with you
   your king, the false god Sakkuth,
   and Kaiwan your idol
and the idols of your other star
   gods you have made.
²⁷This is because I will send you away
   as captives beyond Damascus,"
says the Lord. His name is God of
   heaven's armies.

ISRAEL WILL BE DESTROYED

6 How terrible it will be for you who
      have it easy in Jerusalem.
How terrible for you who live on
   Mount Samaria and feel safe.
You think you are important people
   of the best nation in the world.
The Israelites come to you for help.
²Go look at the city of Calneh.
From there go to the great city
   Hamath.
Go down to Gath of the Philistines.
Are you better than these kingdoms?
Are their lands larger than yours?
³You put off the day of punishment.
But you bring near the day when
   you can do evil to others.
⁴You lie on beds decorated with ivory.
You stretch out on your couches.
You eat tender lambs
   and fattened calves.

⁵You play your harps.
Like David, you compose songs on
   musical instruments.
⁶You drink wine by the bowlful.
You use the best perfumed lotions.
But you are not sad over the ruin of
   Israel, Joseph's descendants.ᵈ
⁷So you will be some of the first ones
   taken as slaves.
Your feasting and lying around will
   come to an end.
⁸The Lord God made this promise.
The Lord God of heaven's armies says:
"I hate the pride of the people of Israel.
I hate their strong towers.
So I will let the enemy take the city
   and everything in it."

⁹At that time there might be ten
people left alive in a house. But they will
also die. ¹⁰A relative and one who is to
prepare bodies for burial may come to
get the bodies. One of them will take the
bodies out to burn them. He will call to
the other and ask, "Are there any other
dead bodies with you?"

That person will answer, "No."

Then the one who asked will say,
"Hush! We must not speak the name of
the Lord."

¹¹The Lord has given the command.
The large house will be broken into
   pieces.
And the small house will be broken
   into bits.
¹²Horses do not run on rocks.
People do not plow rocks with oxen.
But you have changed fairness into
   poison.
You have changed what is right into
   something wrong.
¹³You are happy that the town of Lo
   Debarⁿ was taken.
You say, "We have taken Karnaimⁿ
   by our own strength."

6:13 **Lo Debar** This name means "nothing at all."
6:13 **Karnaim** This name means "horns," a symbol of strength.

[14]The Lord God of heaven's armies says,
    "Israel, I will bring a nation against
        you.
It will bring trouble for you from Lebo
        Hamath in the north
    to the valley south of the Dead Sea."[d]

THE VISION OF LOCUSTS

7 This is what the Lord God showed me: He was forming a swarm of locusts.[d] This was after the king had taken his share of the first crop. The second crop had just begun growing. [2]The locusts ate all the crops in the country. After that I said, "Lord God, forgive us, I beg you! No one in Israel could live through this. Israel is too small already!"

[3]So the Lord felt sorry about this. "This will not happen," said the Lord.

THE VISION OF FIRE

[4]This is what the Lord God showed me: The Lord God was calling for fire to come to punish. The fire dried up the deep water and destroyed the land. [5]Then I cried out, "Lord God, stop, I beg you! No one in Israel could live through this. Israel is too small already."

[6]So the Lord felt sorry about this. "This will not happen either," said the Lord God.

THE VISION OF THE PLUMB LINE

[7]This is what the Lord showed me: The Lord stood by a straight wall. He had a plumb line[d] in his hand. [8]The Lord said to me, "Amos, what do you see?"

I said, "A plumb line."

Then the Lord said, "See, I will put a plumb line among my people Israel to show how crooked they are. I will not feel sorry for them any longer.

[9]"The places where Isaac's
        descendants[d] worship will be
        destroyed.
    Israel's holy places will be turned
        into ruins.
    And I will attack King Jeroboam's
        family with the sword."

AMAZIAH AND AMOS

[10]So Amaziah, a priest at Bethel, sent this message to Jeroboam king of Israel: "Amos is making evil plans against you with the people of Israel. He has been speaking so much that this land can't hold all his words. [11]Amos has said this:

'Jeroboam will die by the sword,
    and the people of Israel will be
        taken as captives
    out of their own country.'"

[12]Then Amaziah said to Amos, "Seer,[d] go, run away to Judah. Do your prophesying[d] and earn your living there. [13]But don't prophesy anymore here at Bethel. This is King Jeroboam's holy place. This is Israel's temple."

[14]Then Amos answered Amaziah, "I do not make my living as a prophet. And I am not a member of a group of prophets. I make my living as a shepherd. And I take care of sycamore trees. [15]But the Lord took me away from tending the sheep. He said to me, 'Go, prophesy to my people, the Israelites.' [16]So listen to the Lord's message. You tell me,
    'Don't prophesy against Israel.
    And stop prophesying against the
        descendants of Isaac.'

[17]"Because you have said this, the Lord says:
'Your wife will become a prostitute[d] in
        the city.
    Your sons and daughters will be
        killed with swords.
Other people will take your land and
        divide it among themselves.
    And you will die in a foreign
        country.
The people of Israel will definitely be
        taken
    from their own land as captives.'"

THE VISION OF RIPE FRUIT

8 This is what the Lord showed me: a basket of ripe fruit. [2]The Lord said to me, "Amos, what do you see?"

I said, "A basket of fruit from the end of the harvest."

Then the Lord said to me, "An end has come for my people, the Israelites. I will not overlook their sins anymore.

³"On that day the palace songs will become funeral songs," says the Lord God. "There will be dead bodies thrown everywhere! Silence!"

⁴Listen to me you who walk on helpless people.
  You are trying to destroy the poor people of this country.
⁵Your businessmen say,
"When will the New Moon^d Festival be over
  so we can sell grain?
When will the Sabbath^d be over
  so we can bring out wheat to sell?
We can charge them more
  and give them less.
We can change the scales to cheat the people.
⁶We will buy poor people for silver.
  And we will buy needy people for the price of a pair of sandals.
We will even sell the wheat that was swept up from the floor."

⁷The Lord used his name, the Pride of Jacob, to make a promise. He said, "I will never forget what these people did.
⁸The whole land will shake because of it.
  Everyone who lives in the land will cry for those who died.
The whole land will rise like the Nile.
  It will be shaken, and then it will fall like the Nile River in Egypt."

⁹The Lord God says:
"At that time I will cause the sun to go down at noon.
I will make the earth dark on a clear day.
¹⁰I will change your festivals into days of crying for the dead.

All your songs will become songs of sadness for the dead.
I will make all of you wear rough cloth to show your sadness.
You will shave your heads to show sadness.
I will make that day like the crying for the death of an only son.
Its end will be very painful."

¹¹The Lord God says: "The days are coming
  when I will cause a time of hunger in the land.
The people will not be hungry for bread or thirsty for water.
But they will be hungry for words from the Lord.
¹²People will wander from the Mediterranean Sea to the Dead Sea.^d
They will wander from the north to the east.
They will search for the word of the Lord.
But they won't find it.
¹³At that time the beautiful young women and the young men
  will become weak from thirst.
¹⁴They made promises by the idol in Samaria.
They said, 'As surely as the god of Dan lives . . .'
And they said, 'As surely as the god of Beershebaⁿ lives, we promise . . .'
So they will fall
  and never get up again."

ISRAEL WILL BE DESTROYED

9 I saw the Lord standing by the altar. He said:
"Smash the top of the pillars
  so that even the bottom of the doors will shake.
Make the pillars fall on the people's heads.
Anyone left alive I will kill with a sword.

8:14 Dan . . . Beersheba Dan was the city farthest north in Israel, and Beersheba was the city farthest south.

Not one person will get away.
No one will escape.
²If they dig down as deep as where the
dead are,
I will pull them up from there.
If they climb up into the skies,
I will bring them down from there.
³If they hide at the top of Mount Carmel,
I will find them and take them away.
If they try to hide from me at the
bottom of the sea,
I will command a snake to bite them.
⁴If they are captured and taken away
by their enemies,
I will command the sword to kill
them.
I will keep watch over them.
But I will keep watch to give them
trouble, not to do them good."

⁵The Master, the Lord of heaven's
armies, will touch the land.
And the land will shake.
Then everyone who lives in the land
will cry for the dead.
The whole land will rise like the Nile
River.
It will fall like the river of Egypt.
⁶The Lord built his upper rooms above
the skies.
He sets their foundations on the
earth.
He calls for the waters of the sea.
He pours them out on the land.
The Lord is his name.

⁷The Lord says this:
"Israel, you are no different to me
than the people of Cush.
I brought Israel out of the land of Egypt.
I also brought the Philistines from
Crete
and the Arameans from Kir.
⁸I, the Lord God, am watching the
sinful kingdom Israel.
I will destroy Israel
from the earth's surface.
But I will not completely destroy
Jacob's descendants,"ᵈ says the Lord.
⁹"I am giving the command
to scatter the nation of Israel
among all nations.

It will be like someone sifting flour.
A person shakes flour through a
sifter.
The good flour falls through, but
not the bad clumps.
¹⁰Sinners among my people
will die by the sword.
All of them say,
'Nothing bad will happen to us.'

THE LORD PROMISES TO RESTORE ISRAEL

¹¹"The kingdom of David is like a fallen
tent.
But in that day I will set it up again
and mend its broken places.
I will rebuild its ruins.
I will rebuild it as it was before.
¹²Then Israel will take over what is left
of Edom
and the other nations that belong to
me,"
says the Lord.
And he will make it happen.

¹³The Lord says, "The time is coming
when there will be plenty of food.
A person will still be harvesting his
crops
when it's time to plow again.
A person will still be taking the juice
from his grapes
when it's time to plant again.
Sweet wine will drip from the
mountains.
And it will pour from the hills.
¹⁴I will bring my people Israel back
from captivity.
They will build the ruined cities
again.
And they will live in them.
They will plant vineyards and drink
the wine from them.
They will plant gardens and eat
their fruit.
¹⁵I will plant my people on their land.
And they will not be pulled out
again
from the land which I have given
them,"
says the Lord your God.

OBADIAH

THE LORD WILL PUNISH THE EDOMITES

[1]This is the vision of Obadiah.

This is what the Lord God says about Edom:[n]
We have heard a message from the Lord.
A messenger has been sent among the nations, saying
"Let's go attack Edom!"

THE LORD SPEAKS TO THE EDOMITES

[2]"Look, I have made you only a small nation.
Others do not respect you.
[3]But your pride has fooled you.
You live in the hollow places of the cliff.
Your home is up high.
And you say to yourself,
'No one can bring me down to the ground.'
[4]You fly high like the eagle.
You make your nest among the stars.
But I will bring you down from there," says the Lord.
[5]"You will really be ruined!
It would be better if thieves come to you,
if robbers come by night.
They would steal only enough for themselves.
Workers come and pick the grapes from your vines.
But they would leave a few grapes behind.
[6]But you, Edom, will really lose everything!
People will find even your hidden treasures!
[7]All the people who are your friends will force you out of the land.
The people who are at peace with you will trick you and defeat you.

They eat your bread with you now.
But they are planning a trap for you.
And you will not notice it."

[8]The Lord says, "On that day
I will surely destroy the wise men from Edom.
I will destroy these men of understanding from the mountains of Edom.
[9]Then, city of Teman, your mighty men will be afraid.
And everyone from the mountains of Edom will be killed.
[10]You did violence against your relatives, the people of Israel.
So you will be covered with shame.
You will be destroyed forever.
[11]You stood aside without helping while strangers carried Israel's treasures away.
Foreigners entered Israel's city gate.
They threw lots[d] to decide what part of Jerusalem they would take.
At that time you were like one of those foreigners.

COMMANDS THAT EDOM BROKE

[12]"Do not laugh at your brothers' trouble.
Do not be happy when people destroy Judah.
Do not brag about the cruel things done to them.
[13]Do not enter the city gate of my people in their time of trouble.
Do not laugh at their problems in their time of trouble.
Do not take their treasures in their time of trouble.
[14]Do not stand at the crossroads to destroy those who are trying to escape.
Do not capture those who escape alive in a time of trouble.

---

1 Edom The Edomites were the people who came from Esau, Jacob's twin brother. They were enemies of the Israelites.

THE NATIONS WILL BE JUDGED

15"The Lord's day of judging is coming
　　soon
　　　to all the nations.
You did evil things to other people.
　　Those same things will happen to
　　　you.
　　They will come back upon your
　　　own head.
16Because you joined the nations in
　　robbing my Temple,*d*
　　you drank my anger.
So all the nations will drink my anger.
　　They will be punished so much that
　　　they will disappear.
17But on Mount Zion*d* some will be left
　　alive.
　　The mountain will be a holy place.
The people of Jacob will take back
　　their land.
　　They will take it from those who
　　　took it from them.
18The people of Jacob, the Israelites, will
　　be like a fire.
　　And the people of Joseph will be
　　　like a flame.
But the people of Esau, the Edomites,
　　will be like dry stalks.
　　The people of Jacob will set these
　　　stalks on fire.
They will burn up the Edomites.

Then there will be no one left of the
　　people of Esau."
This will happen because the Lord has
　　said it.

19Then God's people will regain
　　southern Judah from Edom,
　　the mountain of Esau.
They will take back the western
　　mountain slopes
　　from the Philistines.
They will regain the lands of Ephraim
　　and Samaria.
　　And Benjamin will take over Gilead.
20People from Israel once were forced to
　　leave their homes.
　　But at that time they will take the
　　　land of the Canaanites.
　　They will take it all the way to
　　　Zarephath.
People from Judah were once forced
　　to leave Jerusalem
　　and live in Sepharad.
But at that time they will take back
　　the cities of southern Judah.
21Powerful warriors will go up on
　　Mount Zion.
　　There they will rule the people
　　　living on Edom's mountain.
　　And the kingdom will belong to the
　　　Lord.

JONAH

GOD CALLS AND JONAH RUNS

1 The Lord spoke his word to Jonah son of Amittai: ²"Get up, go to the great city of Nineveh and preach against it. I see the evil things they do."

³But Jonah got up to run away from the Lord. He went to the city of Joppa. There he found a ship that was going to the city of Tarshish. Jonah paid for the trip and went aboard. He wanted to go to Tarshish to run away from the Lord.

⁴But the Lord sent a great wind on the sea. This wind made the sea very rough. So the ship was in danger of breaking apart. ⁵The sailors were afraid. Each man cried to his own god. The men began throwing the cargo into the sea. This would make the ship lighter so it would not sink.

But Jonah had gone down into the ship to lie down. He fell fast asleep. ⁶The captain of the ship came and said, "Why are you sleeping? Get up! Pray to your god! Maybe your god will pay attention to us. Maybe he will save us!"

⁷Then the men said to each other, "Let's throw lots*ᵈ* to see who caused these troubles to happen to us."

So the men threw lots. The lot showed that the trouble had happened because of Jonah. ⁸Then the men said to Jonah, "Tell us what you have done. Why has this terrible thing happened to us? What is your job? Where do you come from? What is your country? Who are your people?"

⁹Then Jonah said to them, "I am a Hebrew. I fear the Lord, the God of heaven. He is the God who made the sea and the land."

¹⁰Then the men were very afraid. They asked Jonah, "What terrible thing did you do?" They knew Jonah was running away from the Lord because Jonah had told them.

¹¹The wind and the waves of the sea were becoming much stronger. So the men said to Jonah, "What should we do to you to make the sea calm down?"

¹²Jonah said to them, "Pick me up, and throw me into the sea. Then it will calm down. I know it is my fault that this great storm has come on you."

¹³Instead, the men tried to row the ship back to the land. But they could not. The wind and the waves of the sea were becoming much stronger.

JONAH'S PUNISHMENT

¹⁴So the men cried to the Lord, "Lord, please don't let us die because of taking this man's life. Please don't think we are guilty of killing an innocent man. Lord, you have caused all this to happen. You wanted it this way." ¹⁵Then the men picked up Jonah and threw him into the sea. So the sea became calm. ¹⁶Then they began to fear the Lord very much. They offered a sacrifice to the Lord. They also made promises to him.

¹⁷And the Lord caused a very big fish to swallow Jonah. Jonah was in the stomach of the fish three days and three nights.

2 While Jonah was in the stomach of the fish, he prayed to the Lord his God. Jonah said,

²"I was in danger.
　So I called to the Lord,
　and he answered me.
I was about to die.
　So I cried to you,
　and you heard my voice.
³You threw me into the sea.
　I went down, down into the deep sea.
The water was all around me.
　Your powerful waves flowed over
　　me.
⁴I said, 'I was driven out of your
　presence.
But I hope to see your Holy
　Temple*ᵈ* again.'
⁵The waters of the sea closed over me.
　I was about to die.

The deep sea was all around me.
  Seaweed wrapped around my head.
⁶I went down to where the mountains
    of the sea start to rise.
  I thought I was locked in this prison
    forever.
  But you saved me from death,
    Lord my God.

⁷"When my life had almost gone,
    I remembered the Lord.
  Lord, I prayed to you.
    And you heard my prayers in your
      Holy Temple.

⁸"People who worship useless idols
    give up their loyalty to you.
⁹Lord, I will praise and thank you
    while I give sacrifices to you.
  I will make promises to you.
    And I will do what I promise.
  Salvation comes from the Lord!"

¹⁰Then the Lord spoke to the fish. And the fish spit Jonah out of its stomach onto the dry land.

GOD CALLS AND JONAH OBEYS

3 Then the Lord spoke his word to Jonah again. The Lord said, ²"Get up. Go to the great city Nineveh. Preach against it what I tell you."

³So Jonah obeyed the Lord. He got up and went to Nineveh. It was a very large city. It took a person three days just to walk across it. ⁴Jonah entered the city. When he had walked for one day, he preached to the people. He said, "After 40 days, Nineveh will be destroyed!"

⁵The people of Nineveh believed in God. They announced they would stop eating for a while. They put on rough cloth to show how sad they were. All the people in the city wore the cloth. People from the most important to the least important did this.

⁶When the king of Nineveh heard this news, he got up from his throne. He took off his robe. He covered himself with rough cloth and sat in ashes to show how upset he was.

⁷He made an announcement and sent it through the city. The announcement said:

By command of the king and his important men: No person or animal should eat anything. No herd or flock will be allowed to taste anything. Do not let them eat food or drink water. ⁸But every person and animal should be covered with rough cloth. People should cry loudly to God. Everyone must turn away from his evil life. Everyone must stop doing harm. ⁹Maybe God will change his mind. Maybe he will stop being angry. Then we will not die.

¹⁰God saw what the people did. He saw that they stopped doing evil things. So God changed his mind and did not do what he had warned. He did not punish them.

GOD'S MERCY MAKES JONAH ANGRY

4 But Jonah was very unhappy that God did not destroy the city. He was angry. ²He complained to the Lord and said, "I knew this would happen. I knew it when I was still in my own country. It is why I quickly ran away to Tarshish. I knew that you are a God who is kind and shows mercy. You don't become angry quickly. You have great love. I knew you would rather forgive than punish them. ³So now I ask you, Lord, please kill me. It is better for me to die than to live."

⁴Then the Lord said, "Do you think it is right for you to be angry?"

⁵Jonah went out and sat down east of the city. There he made a shelter for himself. And he sat there in the shade. He was waiting to see what would happen to the city. ⁶The Lord made a plant grow quickly up over Jonah. This made a cool place for him to sit. And it helped him to be more comfortable. Jonah was very pleased to have the plant for shade. ⁷The next day the sun rose. And God sent a worm to attack the plant. Then the plant died.

⁸When the sun was high in the sky, God sent a hot east wind to blow. The sun became very hot on Jonah's head. And he became very weak. He wished he were dead. Jonah said, "It is better for me to die than to live."

⁹But God said this to Jonah: "Do you think it is right for you to be angry because of the plant?"

Jonah answered, "It is right for me to be angry! I will stay angry until I die!"

¹⁰And the Lord said, "You showed concern for that plant. But you did not plant it or make it grow. It appeared in the night, and the next day it died. ¹¹Then surely I can show concern for the great city Nineveh. There are many animals in that city. And there are more than 120,000 people living there. Those people simply do not know right from wrong!"

THE BOOK OF
MICAH

SAMARIA AND ISRAEL TO BE PUNISHED

1 Jotham, Ahaz and Hezekiah were kings of Judah. During the time they were kings, the word of the Lord came to Micah, who was from Moresheth. He saw these visions about Samaria and Jerusalem.

[2] Hear this, all you nations.
Listen, all you who live on the earth.
The Lord God will come from his Holy Temple.[d]
He will come as a witness against you.
[3] See, the Lord is coming out of his place in heaven.
He is coming down to walk on the tops of the mountains.
[4] The mountains will melt under him like wax in a fire.
The valleys will crack open as if split by water raging down a mountain.
[5] This is because of Jacob's sin.
It is because of the sins of the nation of Israel.
Who is responsible for Jacob's sin? Samaria!
Who is responsible for Judah's worshiping idols? Jerusalem!

THE LORD SPEAKS

[6] "So I will make Samaria a pile of ruins in the open country.
It will be like a place for planting vineyards.
I will pour Samaria's stones down into the valley.
And I will destroy her down to her foundations.
[7] All her idols will be broken into pieces.
All the gifts to her idols will be burned with fire.
I will destroy all her idols.
This is because Samaria earned her money by being unfaithful to me.
So this money will be carried off by other people who are not faithful to me."

MICAH'S GREAT SADNESS

[8] I will moan and cry because of this evil.
I will go around barefoot and without clothes.
I will cry loudly like the wild dogs.
I will cry like the ostriches.
[9] I will do this because Samaria's wound cannot be healed.
Her destruction will spread to Judah.
It will reach the city gate of my people.
It will come all the way to Jerusalem.
[10] Don't tell it in Gath.[n]
Don't cry in Acco.[n]
Cry and roll in the dust at Beth Ophrah.[n]
[11] Pass on your way, naked and ashamed,
you who live in Shaphir.[n]
Those who live in Zaanan[n] won't come out to help you.
The people in Beth Ezel[n] will cry.
But they will not give you any support.
[12] Those who live in Maroth[n] will be anxious for good news to come.

1:10 **Gath** This name sounds like the Hebrew word for "tell."
1:10 **Acco** This name sounds like the Hebrew word for "cry."
1:10 **Beth Ophrah** This name means "house of dust."
1:11 **Shaphir** This name means "beautiful."
1:11 **Zanaan** This name sounds like the Hebrew word for "come out."
1:11 **Beth Ezel** This name means "house by the side of another," suggesting help or support.
1:12 **Maroth** This name sounds like the Hebrew word for "sad" or "miserable."

This is because trouble will come
from the Lord.
It will come all the way to the gate
of Jerusalem.
[13]You people living in Lachish,[n]
harness the fastest horse to the
chariot.
Jerusalem's sins started in you.
This is because you followed in
Israel's sins.
[14]So you must give farewell gifts
to Moresheth[n] in Gath.
The houses in Aczib[n] will be false help
to the kings of Israel.
[15]I will bring an enemy against you
who live in Mareshah.[n]
He will take what you own.
The leaders Israel brags about
will hide in the cave at Adullam.
[16]Cut off your hair to show you are sad.
Cry for the children you love.
Make yourself bald like the eagle,
because your children will be forced
to live in a foreign land.

THE EVIL PLANS OF PEOPLE

2 How terrible it will be for people
who plan wickedness.
They lie on their beds and make evil
plans.
When the morning light comes, they
do the things they planned.
They do them just because they
have the power to do so.
[2]They want fields; so they take them.
They want houses; so they take
them.
They cheat a man and take his house.
They cheat a man and take his
property.

[3]That is why the Lord says:
"Look, I am planning trouble against
such people.

You won't be able to save yourselves.
You will no longer walk proudly,
because it will be a terrible time.
[4]At that time people will make fun of
you.
They will sing this sad song about
you:
'We are completely ruined.
The Lord has taken away our land.
Yes, he has taken our land away from
us.
He has divided our fields among
our enemies!'"
[5]So you will have no land for people to
measure.
They will not throw lots[d] to divide
the land among the Lord's people.

MICAH IS ASKED NOT TO PROPHESY
[6]People say, "Don't prophesy[d] to us!
Don't say those bad things about us!
Nothing like that will happen to us!"
[7]But I must say this, people of Jacob.
The Lord is becoming angry about
what you have done.
If you lived right,
I could say nice words to you.
[8]But recently, my people have become
my enemy.
You take the coats from people who
pass by.
They think they are safe.
But you rob them
as if they were prisoners of war.
[9]You've forced the women of my people
from their nice houses.
You've taken my glory
from their children forever.
[10]Get up and leave.
This is not your promised place of
rest anymore.
You have made this place unclean.[d]
It is doomed to destruction.

1:13 Lachish This name sounds like the Hebrew word for "horses."
1:14 Moresheth This may be a wordplay on the word "engaged," referring to a farewell gift to a bride.
1:14 Aczib This name means "lie" or "trick."
1:15 Mareshah This name sounds like the Hebrew word for a person who captures other cities and lands.

11But you people want a false prophet
who will tell you nothing but lies.
You want one who promises to
prophesy good things for you
if you give him wine and beer.
He's just the prophet for you.

THE LORD PROMISES TO RESCUE HIS PEOPLE

12"Yes, people of Jacob, I will bring all
of you together.
I will bring together all those left
alive in Israel.
I'll put them together like sheep in a
pen,
like a flock in its pasture.
Then the place will be filled with
many people.
13Someone will open the way and lead
the people out.
The people will break through the
gate and leave the city where they
were held captive.
Their king will go out in front of them.
The Lord will lead his people."

THE LEADERS OF ISRAEL ARE GUILTY OF EVIL

3 Then I said,
"Listen, leaders of the people of
Jacob.
Listen, you rulers of the nation of
Israel.
You should know how to decide cases
fairly.
2 But you hate good and love evil.
You skin my people alive.
You tear the flesh off their bones.
3You are destroying my people.
You skin them and break their bones.
You chop them up in pieces
like meat to put in the pot.
4Then you will pray to the Lord.
But he won't answer you.
He will hide his face from you,
because you have done evil."

5The Lord says this about the prophetsd
who teach his people the wrong way of
living:

"If someone gives these prophets food
to eat,
they shout, 'Peace!'
But if he doesn't give them food,
they prepare for war against him.
6So it will become like night to the
prophets.
They won't have any visions from
the Lord.
It will become dark for them.
They won't be able to tell what will
happen in the future.
The sun is about to set for the prophets.
Their days will become dark.
7The seersd will be ashamed.
The people who see the future will
be embarrassed.
Yes, all of them will cover their
mouths.
This is because there will be no
answer from God."

MICAH IS AN HONEST PROPHET OF GOD

8But the Lord's Spiritd has filled me
with power and strength to preach
fairness.
I will tell the people of Jacob how they
have turned against God.
I will tell the people of Israel how
they have done wrong.
9Leaders of Jacob and rulers of Israel,
listen to me.
You hate fairness.
You destroy what is right.
10You build Jerusalem by murdering
people.
You build it with the sins you do.
11The judges in Jerusalem take money
to decide who wins in court.
The priests in Jerusalem only teach
for pay.
The prophetsd only look into the
future when they get paid.
But yet those leaders say,
"The Lord is with us.
Nothing bad will happen to us."
12Because of you,
Jerusalem will be plowed like a
field.

Jerusalem will become a pile of rocks.
The hill on which the Temple[d] stands
will be covered with bushes.

THE MOUNTAIN OF THE LORD

4 In the last days
the mountain on which the Lord's
Temple[d] stands
will become the most important of
all mountains.
It will be raised above the hills.
People from other nations will
come streaming to it.
²Many nations will come and say,
"Come, let us go up to the
mountain of the Lord.
Let us go to the Temple of the God
of Jacob!
Then God will teach us his ways.
And we will obey his teachings."
The Lord's teachings will go out from
Jerusalem.
The word of the Lord will go out
from Jerusalem.
³The Lord will settle arguments among
many nations.
He will decide between strong
nations that are far away.
Then the nations will make their
swords into plows.
They will make their spears into
hooks for trimming trees.
Nations will no longer fight other
nations.
They will not even train for war
anymore.
⁴Everyone will sit under his own vine
and fig tree.
No one will make him afraid.
This is because the Lord of heaven's
armies has said it.
⁵All other nations follow their own gods.
But we will follow the Lord our God
forever and ever.

⁶The Lord says, "At that time,
I will bring back to me the crippled.

I will bring back to Jerusalem those
who were sent away.
I will bring back to me those who
were hurt.
⁷I will keep alive those who were
crippled.
I will make a strong nation of those
who were sent away.
The Lord will be their king in Mount
Zion[d] forever.
⁸And you, watchtower of the flocks,[n]
strong city of Jerusalem,
you will be a kingdom as in the
past.
Jerusalem, the right to rule will
come again to you."

WHY THE ISRAELITES MUST GO TO BABYLON

⁹Now, why do you cry so loudly?
Is your king gone?
Have you lost your leader?
You are in pain like a woman trying
to give birth.
¹⁰People of Jerusalem, be in pain.
Be like a woman trying to give
birth.
Now you must leave the city
and live in the field.
You will go to Babylon.
But you will be saved from that
place.
The Lord will go there
and take you back from your
enemies.

¹¹But now many nations
have come to fight against you.
They say, "Let's destroy Jerusalem
and be proud we have defeated
her."
¹²But they don't know
what the Lord is thinking.
They don't understand his plan for
them.
He will crush them like a bundle of
grain on the threshing[d] floor.

4:8 watchtower ... flocks This probably means a part of Jerusalem. The leaders would be like shepherds in a
tower watching their sheep.

[13]"Get up and crush them, people of
      Jerusalem.
   I will make you strong as if you had
      horns of iron.
   I will make you strong as if you had
      hoofs of bronze.
   You will beat many nations into
      small pieces.
   You will give their wealth to the Lord.
   You will give their treasure to the
      Lord of all the earth."

5 So, strong city, gather your soldiers
      together.
   We are surrounded and attacked.
   The enemy will swing his club.
   He will hit the leader of Israel in the
      face.

THE RULER TO BE BORN IN BETHLEHEM

[2]"But you, Bethlehem Ephrathah,
      are one of the smallest towns in
      Judah.
   But from you will come one who will
      rule Israel for me.
   He comes from very old times,
      from days long ago."

[3]The Lord will leave his people in
      Babylon
   until Jerusalem, who is in labor,
      gives birth to her children.
   Then his brothers who are in captivity
      will return.
   They will come back to the people
      of Israel living in Judah.
[4]Then the ruler of Israel will stand
      and take care of his people.
   He will lead them with the Lord's
      power.
   He will lead them in the wonderful
      name of the Lord his God.
   They will live in safety.
   And his greatness will be known all
      over the earth.
[5] He will bring peace.

RESCUE AND PUNISHMENT

   The Assyrian army will come into our
      country.
   They will destroy our large houses.

   But we will choose seven or eight
      leaders.
   They will shepherd our people.
[6]They will destroy the Assyrians with
      their swords.
   They will conquer the land of
      Assyria with their swords drawn.
   The Assyrians will come into our
      land.
   They will come within our borders.
   But the leaders of Israel
      will save us from them.

[7]Then the people of Jacob who are left
      alive
   will be like dew from the Lord to
      many people.
   They will be like rain which does not
      wait for man.
   They will be like showers which do
      not wait for human beings.
[8]Those left alive of Jacob's people
      will be scattered among the nations.
   They will be among many peoples.
   They will be like a lion among the
      animals of the forest.
   They will be like a young lion going
      through the flock.
   He steps on what is in his way.
      No one can save the nations from
      God's people.
[9]So you will raise your fist in victory
      over your enemies,
   and you will destroy them.

[10]The Lord says, "At that time,
   I will take your horses from you.
   I will destroy your chariots.
[11]I will destroy the walled cities in your
      country.
   I will tear down all your defenses.
[12]You will no longer be able to do
      witchcraft.[d]
   You will not have anyone who can
      tell the future.
[13]I will destroy your statues of false
      gods.
   I will tear down the stone pillars
      you worship.

You will no longer worship
   what your hands have made.
[14]I will destroy the Asherah[d] idols.
   I will destroy your cities.
[15]Some people won't obey me.
   I will show my anger and punish
      them."

THE LORD'S COMPLAINT

6 Now hear what the Lord says:
   "Get up; plead your case in front
      of the mountains.
   Let the hills hear your story.
[2]Mountains, listen to the Lord's
      complaint.
   Foundations of the earth, listen to
      the Lord.
   The Lord has a complaint against his
      people.
   He will prove that Israel is wrong."

[3]The Lord says, "My people, did I do
      something wrong to you?
   How did I make you tired of me?
      Tell me.
[4]I brought you from the land of Egypt.
   I freed you from slavery.
   I sent Moses, Aaron and Miriam to
      you.
[5]My people, remember
   the evil plans of Balak king of
      Moab.
   Remember what Balaam son of
      Beor told Balak.
   Remember what happened from
      Acacia to Gilgal.
   Then you will know the Lord does
      what is right!"

[6]You say, "What can I bring with me
      when I come before the Lord?
   What can I bring
      when I bow before God on high?
   Should I come before the Lord with
      burnt offerings,
   with year-old calves?
[7]Will the Lord be pleased with 1,000
      male sheep?
   Will he be pleased with 10,000
      rivers of oil?

Should I give my first child for the evil
      I have done?
   Should I give my very own child for
      my sin?"
[8]The Lord has told you what is good.
   He has told you what he wants from
      you:
   Do what is right to other people.
   Love being kind to others.
   And live humbly, trusting your
      God.

[9]The voice of the Lord shouts to the
      city.
   The wise person honors the Lord.
   So pay attention to the rod of
      punishment.
   Pay attention to the One who
      threatens to punish.
[10]Can the Lord forget that the wicked
      still hide
   treasures they have stolen?
   Do they still cheat others?
   I curse their false measure!
[11]Can I forgive people who cheat others
      with wrong weights and scales?
[12]The rich men in the city
      still do cruel things.
   The people still tell lies.
   They do not tell the truth.
[13]So I have started to punish you.
   I will destroy you because of your
      sins.
[14]You will eat, but you won't become
      full.
   You will still be hungry and empty.
   You will store up but save nothing.
   What you store up the sword will
      destroy.
[15]You will plant,
      but you won't harvest.
   You will squeeze your olives.
   But you won't get any oil from them
      to put on your skin.
   You will crush the grapes.
   But you will not drink the wine.
[16]This is because you obey the wicked
      laws of King Omri.

You do all the evil that Ahab's
    family does.
You follow their teachings.
So I will let you be destroyed.
    The people in your city will be
        laughed at.
    Other nations will make fun of you.

MICAH IS UPSET AT THE EVIL THAT PEOPLE DO

7 Poor me! I am like a hungry man.
    And all the summer fruit has been
        picked.
There are no grapes left to eat.
    There are none of the early figs I
        love.
[2] All of the faithful people are gone.
    There is not one good person left in
        this country.
Everyone is waiting to kill someone.
    Everyone is trying to trap his
        brother.
[3] People are good at doing evil with
        both hands.
Rulers ask for money.
    And judges' decisions are bought
        for a price.
Rich people make their wishes
        known.
    They all join in their evil plans.
[4] Even the best of them is like a
        thornbush.
    Even the nicest of them is worse
        than a thornbush.
Your watchmen[n] warned you about
        this day.
    Now it has come.
Now you will be punished.
    Your punishment will amaze you.
[5] Don't trust your neighbor.
    Don't even trust a friend.
Be careful what you say,
    even to your wife.
[6] A son will not honor his father.
    A daughter will turn against her
        mother.

A daughter-in-law will fight with her
        mother-in-law.
    A person's enemies will be
        members of his own family.

THE LORD'S KINDNESS

[7] Israel says, "I will look to the Lord for
        help.
    I will wait for God to save me.
    My God will hear me.
[8] Enemy, don't laugh at me.
    I have fallen, but I will get up again.
I sit in the shadow of trouble now.
    But the Lord will be a light for me.
[9] I sinned against the Lord.
    So he was angry with me.
But he will defend my case in court.
    He will do what is right for me.
Then he will bring me out into the
        light.
    I will see him set things right.
[10] Then my enemies will see this,
    and they will be ashamed.
My enemies said to me,
    'Where is the Lord your God?'
Now I will laugh at them.
    They will fall down defeated, like
        the mud people walk on."

THE JEWS TO RETURN

[11] The time will come when your walls
        will be built again.
    At that time your country will grow.
[12] Your people will come back to your
        land.
    They will come from Assyria and
        the cities of Egypt.
They will come from the countries
        between the river of Egypt and the
        Euphrates River.
They will come from the countries
        between the Mediterranean Sea in
        the west and the mountains in
        the east.
[13] The rest of the earth will be ruined.
    This is because of what the people
        who lived in it did.

7:4 **watchmen** Another name for a prophet. The prophets were like guards who stood on a city's wall. They
    watched for trouble coming from far away.

A PRAYER TO GOD

[14]So shepherd your people with your
    stick.
  Tend the flock of people who
    belong to you.
  That flock now lives alone in the
    desert.
  But there is fertile pasture nearby.
  Let them feed in Bashan and Gilead
  as they did long ago.

[15]The Lord says, "I did many miracles[d]
    when I brought you out of Egypt.
  I will show you more miracles like
    that."

[16]The nations will see those miracles.
  Then they will no longer brag about
    their power.
  They will be amazed and put their
    hands over their mouths.
  They will refuse to listen.
[17]They will crawl in the dust like a
    snake.
  They will shake with fear.

They will crawl on the ground
  like insects crawling from their
    holes.
They will come trembling to you, Lord
    our God.
  They will tremble in fear before you.
[18]There is no God like you.
  You forgive people who are guilty of
    sin.
You don't look at the sins of your
    people
  who are left alive.
You, Lord, will not stay angry forever.
  You enjoy being kind.
[19]Lord, you will have mercy on us
    again.
  You will conquer our sins.
You will throw away all our sins
  into the deepest sea.
[20]You will be true to the people of Jacob!
  You will be kind to the people of
    Abraham.
You will do what you promised
  to our ancestors long ago.

NAHUM

1 This is the message for the city of Nineveh.[n] This is the vision of Nahum, who was from the town of Elkosh.

THE LORD IS ANGRY WITH NINEVEH

2The Lord is a jealous God who gives punishment.
The Lord punishes wicked people and is filled with anger.
The Lord punishes those who are against him.
He stays angry with his enemies.
3The Lord does not become angry quickly.
His power is great.
The Lord will not let the guilty go unpunished.
Where the Lord goes, whirlwinds and storms show his power.
The clouds are the dust that his feet kick up.
4The Lord speaks to the sea and makes it dry.
He dries up all the rivers.
The areas of Bashan and Carmel dry up.
And the flowers of Lebanon die.
5He shakes the mountains
and makes the hills melt away.
The earth trembles when he comes.
The world and all who live in it shake with fear.
6No one can stay alive when the Lord is angry with him.
No one can survive his strong anger.
His anger is poured out like fire.
He smashes rocks that are in his path.

7The Lord is good.
He gives protection in times of trouble.
He knows who trusts in him.

8But he will completely destroy the city of Nineveh.
An army will come like a rushing flood.
The Lord will chase his enemies until he kills them.
9The Lord will completely destroy the plans that are made against him.
Trouble will not come a second time.
10Those people will be like tangled thorns
or like people drunk from their wine.
They will be destroyed quickly like dry weeds.
11Someone has come from Nineveh.
He makes evil plans against the Lord.
And he gives wicked advice.

12This is what the Lord says:
"Assyria is strong and has many people.
But it will be defeated and brought to an end.
Judah, I have punished you, my people.
But I will punish you no more.
13Now I will free you from their control.
And I will tear away the chains with which they hold you."

14The Lord has given you this command, Nineveh:
"You will not have descendants[d] to carry on your name.
I will destroy the idols and metal images
that are in the temple of your gods.
I will dig your grave
because you are wicked."

1:1 **Nineveh** The capital city of the country of Assyria. Nahum uses Nineveh to stand for all of Assyria.

[15]Look, there on the hills,
    someone is bringing good news!
    He is announcing peace!
Celebrate your feasts, people of Judah.
    And do what you promised to God.
The wicked will not attack you again.
    They have been completely
        destroyed.

NINEVEH WILL BE DEFEATED

2 The destroyer[n] is coming to attack
    you, Nineveh.
    Guard the defenses.
    Watch the road.
    Get ready.
    Gather all your strength!
[2]Destroyers have destroyed God's
        people
    and ruined their vines.
But the Lord will make the people of
        Jacob
    and the people of Israel great again.

[3]The shields of the soldiers are red.
    The army is dressed in red.
The metal on the chariots flashes
    when they are ready to attack.
    Their horses are excited.
[4]The chariots race through the streets.
    They rush back and forth through
        the city squares.
    They look like torches.
    They run like lightning.

[5]He[n] calls his officers.
    But they fall down on the way.
    They hurry to the city wall.
    The shield is put into place.
[6]The river gates are thrown open.
    And the palace is destroyed.
[7]It has been announced that the people
        of Nineveh
    will be captured and carried away.
    The slave girls moan like doves.
    They beat their breasts because
        they are sad.

[8]Nineveh is like a pool.
    And its water is draining away.
"Stop! Stop!" the people yell.
    But no one turns back.
[9]Take the silver!
    Take the gold!
There is no end to the treasure.
    There is wealth of every kind.
[10]Nineveh is robbed, ruined and
        destroyed.
    The people lose their courage. Their
        knees knock with fear.
    Stomachs ache. And everyone's face
        grows pale from fright.

[11]Where is the lions'[n] den?
    Where do they feed their young?
Where did the lion, lioness and cubs
        go?
    Where were they not afraid?
[12]The lion killed enough for his cubs.
    He killed it for his mate.
He filled his cave with the animals he
        caught.
    He filled his den with what he had
        killed.

[13]"I am against you, Nineveh,"
    says the Lord of heaven's armies.
"I will burn up your chariots in
        smoke.
    And I will kill your young lions with
        a sword.
    I will stop you from hunting down
        others on the earth.
Your messengers' voices
    will no longer be heard."

IT WILL BE TERRIBLE FOR NINEVEH

3 How terrible it will be for the city
    which has killed so many.
    It is full of lies.
It is full of stolen things from other
        countries.
    It is always hurting or killing
        somebody.

2:1 **destroyer** The Babylonians, the Scythians and the Medes destroyed Nineveh.
2:5 **He** This probably means the king of Assyria.
2:11 **lions'** The symbol of Assyria was the lion.

²Hear the sound of whips.
  Listen to the wheels.
Hear horses galloping
  and chariots bouncing along!
³Soldiers on horses are charging.
  Their swords are shining.
  Their spears are gleaming!
There are many bodies.
  Dead people are piled up.
There are too many to count.
  People fall over the dead bodies.
⁴The city was like a prostitute.ᵈ
  She was charming and a lover of
    magic.
She made nations slaves with her evil
    ways
  and her witchcraft.ᵈ

⁵"I am against you, Nineveh," says the
    Lord of heaven's armies.
  "I will pull your dress up over your
    face.
I will show the nations your
    nakedness.
  And I will show the kingdoms your
    shame.
⁶I will throw dirt on you.
  I will make a fool of you.
People will see you and make fun of
    you.
⁷Everyone who sees you will run away
    and say,
  'Nineveh is in ruins. Who will cry
    for her?'
Nineveh, I cannot find anyone to
    comfort you."

⁸Nineveh, you are no better than
    Thebes.ⁿ
  She sits by the Nile River
    with water all around her.
The river was her defense.
  The waters were like a wall around
    her.
⁹Cush and Egypt gave her endless
    strength.
  Put and Libya supported her.

¹⁰But Thebes was captured.
  And she went into captivity.
Her small children were beaten to
    death
  at every street corner.
Lotsᵈ were thrown for her important
    men.
  And all of her leaders were put in
    chains.

¹¹Nineveh, you will be drunk, too.
  You will hide.
You will look for a place safe from
    the enemy.
¹²All your defenses are like fig trees
    with ripe fruit.
  When the tree is shaken, the figs fall
    into the mouth of the eater.
¹³Look at your soldiers.
  They are all women!
The gates of your land
  are wide open for your enemies.
  Fire has burned the bars of those
    gates.

¹⁴Get enough water before the attack
    begins.
  Make your defenses strong!
Make the bricks.
  Mix the mortar.
  Repair the wall!
¹⁵There the fire will burn you up.
  The sword will kill you.
  Like grasshoppers eating crops,
    the battle will completely destroy
    you.
Grow in number like hopping locusts.ᵈ
  Grow in number like swarming
    locusts!
¹⁶Your traders are more than the stars
    in the sky.
  But like locusts, they strip the land
    and then fly away.
¹⁷Your guards are like locusts.
  Your officers are like swarms of
    locusts
    that settle in the walls on a cold day.

3:8 Thebes A great city in Egypt.

But when the sun comes up they fly
away.
And no one knows where they have
gone.
¹⁸King of Assyria, your rulers are asleep.
Your important men lie down to rest.
Your people have been scattered on
the mountains.

And there is no one to bring them
back.
¹⁹Nothing can heal your wound.
Your injury will not heal.
Everyone who hears about you
applauds
because everyone has felt your
endless cruelty.

HABAKKUK

1 This is the message that was given to Habakkuk the prophet.^d

HABAKKUK COMPLAINS

²Lord, I continue to ask for help.
How long will you ignore me?
I cry out to you about violence,
but you do not save us!
³Why do you let me see wrong things?
Why do you put up with evil?
People are destroying things and
hurting others while I am
looking.
They are arguing and fighting.
⁴People are not forced to obey the
teachings.
No one receives a fair trial.
Evil people gain while good people
lose.
The judges no longer make fair
decisions.

THE LORD ANSWERS

⁵"You and your people, look at the
nations!
Watch them and be amazed.
I will do something in your lifetime
that will amaze you.
You won't believe it even when you
are told about it.
⁶I will use the Babylonian people to
punish the evil people.
The Babylonians are cruel and
powerful fighters.
They march across the earth.
They take lands that don't belong to
them.
⁷The Babylonians frighten other
people.
They do what they want to do.
They are good only to themselves.
⁸Their horses are faster than leopards
and more cruel than wolves at
sunset.
Their horse soldiers attack quickly.
They come from places that are far
away.

They attack quickly, like an eagle
swooping down for food.
⁹ They all come to fight.
Their armies march quickly like a
whirlwind in the desert.
Their prisoners are as many as the
grains of sand.
¹⁰The Babylonian soldiers laugh at
kings.
They make fun of rulers.
They laugh at all the strong, walled
cities.
They build dirt roads up to the top
of the walls.
They capture the cities.
¹¹Then they leave like the wind and
move on.
They are guilty of worshiping their
own strength."

HABAKKUK COMPLAINS AGAIN

¹²Lord, you are the Lord who lives
forever.
You are my God, my holy God.
You will not let those who trust you
die.
Lord, you have chosen the
Babylonians to punish people.
Our Rock,^d you created them to
punish the people.
¹³Your eyes are too good to look at evil.
You cannot stand to see people do
wrong.
So how can you put up with those evil
people?
How can you be quiet when wicked
people defeat people who are
better than they are?
¹⁴You treat people like fish in the sea.
You treat them like sea animals
without a leader.
¹⁵The enemy catches all of them with
hooks.
He catches them in his net.
He drags them in.
He is glad that he has caught them.

[16]The enemy offers sacrifices to his net.
He burns incense[d] to worship it.
This is because his net lets him live
like a rich man.
His net lets him enjoy the best food.
[17]Will he keep on taking riches with his
net?
Will he go on destroying people
without showing mercy?

2 I will stand like a guard to watch.
I will stand on the tower.
I will wait to see what the Lord will
say to me.
I will wait to learn how to answer
his complaint.

THE LORD ANSWERS

[2]The Lord answered me:
"Write down what I show you.
Write it clearly on stone tablets
so whoever reads it can run to tell
others.
[3]It is not yet time for the message to
come true.
But that time is coming soon.
The message will come true.
It may seem like a long time before it
happens.
But be patient and wait for it.
These things will happen.
They will not be delayed.
[4]See, the nation that is evil and trusts
in itself will fail.
But those who do right because
they trust in God will live.

[5]"Wine can trick a person.
In the same way the Babylonians
are fooled by their pride.
Their desire for wealth is like a grave's
desire for death.
They always want more and more.
And, like death, they collect other
nations for themselves.
They make them their own people.
[6]But all the nations the Babylonians
have hurt will laugh at them.
They will make fun of the
Babylonians.

They will say, 'How terrible it will be
for the nation that steals many
things.
How long will that nation get rich
by forcing others to pay them?'

[7]"One day the people you have taken
money from will turn against you.
They will realize what is happening
and make you shake with fear.
Then they will hurt you.
[8]You have stolen from many nations.
So the people who are left will take
much from you.
This is because you have killed many
people.
You have destroyed countries and
cities and everyone in them.

[9]"How terrible it will be for the nation
that becomes rich by doing
wrong.
They do those things to live in a
safe place.
They think they will be safe from
harm.
[10]You have made plans to destroy many
people.
This has made your own houses
ashamed of you.
Because of it, you will lose your
lives.
[11]The stones of the walls will cry out
against you.
Even the wooden boards that
support the roof will agree that
you are wrong.

[12]"How terrible it will be for the nation
that kills people to build a city.
How terrible for that nation that
wrongs others to start a town.
[13]The Lord of heaven's armies will send
fire
to destroy what those people have
built.
All the nations' work will be for
nothing.

¹⁴Then people everywhere will know the
Lord's greatness.
This news will spread like water
covering the sea.

¹⁵"How terrible for the nation that
becomes angry and makes others
suffer.
In anger they knock other people to
the ground.
And they treat them as if they are
naked and drunk.
¹⁶You Babylonians will receive the
Lord's anger, not respect.
This anger will be like a cup of
poison in the Lord's right
hand.
You will taste this anger and fall to the
ground like a drunk person.
You will drink from this cup.
You will receive disgrace, not
respect.
¹⁷You hurt many people in Lebanon.
Now you will be hurt.
You killed many animals there.
And now you must be afraid.
You will be afraid because of what you
did
to those cities and the people who
lived in them.

THE MESSAGE ABOUT IDOLS
¹⁸"An idol does no good, because a man
made it.
It is only a statue that teaches lies.
The person who made it expects his
own work to help him.
But it can't even speak!
¹⁹How terrible it will be for the nation
that says to a wooden statue,
'Come to life!'
How terrible it will be when this
nation says to a stone that
cannot speak, 'Get up!'
These things cannot tell them what
to do.

That idol is only a statue covered
with gold and silver.
There is no life in it.
²⁰The Lord is in his Holy Temple.ᵈ
So all the earth should be silent in
his presence."

HABAKKUK'S PRAYER
3 This is the prayer of Habakkuk the
prophet,ᵈ on shigionoth.ᵈ

²Lord, I have heard the news about
you.
Lord, I am amazed at the powerful
things you have done.
Do great things once again in our
time.
Make those things happen again in
our own days.
Even when you are angry,
remember to be gentle with us.

³God is coming from Teman in the
south.
The Holy One comes from Mount
Paran.ⁿ   Selahᵈ
The Lord's greatness covers the
heavens.
His praise fills the earth.
⁴He is like a bright light.
Rays of light shine from his hand.
And there he hides his power.
⁵Sickness goes before him,
and fever follows behind him.
⁶The Lord stands and shakes the earth.
He looks, and the nations shake
with fear.
The mountains, which stood for ages,
break into pieces.
The old hills fall down.
God has always done this.

⁷I saw that the tents of Cushan were in
trouble.
The tents of Midian trembled.
⁸Lord, were you angry at the rivers?
Were you angry at the streams?
Were you angry with the sea

3:3 Teman ... Paran God is seen as again coming from the direction of Mount Sinai. He came from Sinai when he
rescued his people from Egypt.

when you rode your horses and
chariots to victory?[n]
9 You uncovered your bow.
You commanded many arrows to
be brought to you.   *Selah*
You split the earth with rivers.
10 The mountains saw you and shook
with fear.
The rushing water flowed by.
The sea made a loud noise,
and its waves rose high.
11 The sun and moon stood still in the
sky.
They stopped when they saw the
flash of your flying arrows.
They stopped when they saw the
gleam of your shining spear.
12 In anger you marched on the earth.
In anger you punished the nations.
13 You came to save your people.
You came to save your chosen one.
You crushed the leader of the wicked
ones.
You took everything away from
them.   *Selah*
14 With the enemy's own spear you
stabbed the leader of his army.
His soldiers rushed out like a storm
to scatter us.
They were happy as if
they were robbing the poor people
in secret.

15 But you marched through the sea with
your horses,
stirring the great waters.

16 I hear these things, and my body
trembles.
My lips tremble when I hear the
sound.
My bones feel weak.
My legs shake.

But I will wait patiently for the day of
disaster.
That day is coming to the people
who attack us.
17 Fig trees may not grow figs.
There may be no grapes on the
vines.
There may be no olives growing on
the trees.
There may be no food growing in
the fields.
There may be no sheep in the pens.
There may be no cattle in the barns.
18 But I will still be glad in the Lord.
I will rejoice in God my Savior.
19 The Lord God gives me my strength.
He makes me like a deer, which
does not stumble.
He leads me safely on the steep
mountains.

For the director of music. On my
stringed instruments.

3:8 sea ... victory This is probably talking about the Israelites crossing the Red Sea.

ZEPHANIAH

1 This is the message of the Lord that came through Zephaniah. It came while Josiah son of Amon was king of Judah. Zephaniah was the son of Cushi, who was the son of Gedaliah. Gedaliah was the son of Amariah, who was the son of Hezekiah.

THE LORD'S JUDGMENT

2"I will destroy everything
on earth," says the Lord.
3"I will destroy the people and animals.
I will destroy the birds in the air
and the fish of the sea.
I will ruin the evil people.
I will remove all the people from the
earth," says the Lord.

THE FUTURE OF JUDAH

4"I will punish Judah
and all the people living in
Jerusalem.
I will remove from this place
all signs of Baal[d] and his priests.
5I will destroy those who worship
the stars from the roofs.[n]
I will destroy those who worship and
make promises
by both the Lord and the god
Molech.[d]
6I will destroy those who turned away
from the Lord.
They quit following the Lord and
consulting him.
7Be silent before the Lord God.
His day for judging people is
coming soon.
The Lord has prepared to sacrifice
Judah.
He has appointed the invited guests
to feast on Judah.
8On that day the Lord will sacrifice
Judah.

I, the Lord, will punish the princes
and the king's sons.
And I will punish all
those who wear foreign clothes.
9On that day I will punish those who
worship Dagon.[d]
I will punish those who hurt others
and tell lies in the temples of their
gods.

10"On that day this will happen," says
the Lord.
"A cry will be heard at the Fish Gate.
A wail will come from the new area
of the city.
A loud crash will echo from the
hills.
11The people living in the market area
will wail.
All the merchants will be dead.
All the silver traders will be gone.
12At that time I, the Lord, will search
Jerusalem with lamps.
I will punish those who are settled
and satisfied with themselves.
They are like wine left to settle.
They think, 'The Lord never does
anything.
He won't help us or punish us.'
13Their wealth will be stolen.
Their houses will be destroyed.
They may build houses,
but they will never live in them.
They may plant vineyards,
but they will never drink any wine
from them.

THE LORD'S DAY OF JUDGING

14"The Lord's day of judging is coming
soon.
That great day is near and coming
fast.
The cry will be very sad on that day.
Even soldiers will cry.

1:5 roofs In Bible times houses were built with flat roofs. The roof was used for drying things such as flax and fruit. And it was used as an extra room, as a place for worship and as a place to sleep in the summer.

¹⁵That day will be a day of anger.
  It will be a day of terror and
    trouble.
  It will be a day of destruction and
    ruin.
  It will be a day of darkness and
    gloom.
  It will be a day of clouds and
    blackness.
¹⁶It will be a day of alarms and battle
    cries.
  'Attack the strong, walled cities!
  Attack the corner towers!'
¹⁷I will make life hard on the people.
  They will walk around like blind
    men.
  This is because they have sinned
    against the Lord.
  Their blood will be poured out like
    dust.
  And their bodies will be dumped
    like trash.
¹⁸On that day God will show his anger.
  Then neither their silver nor gold
    will save them.
  The Lord's anger will be like fire.
  And the whole world will be burned
    up.
  Suddenly he will bring an end
    to everyone on earth."

GOD ASKS PEOPLE TO CHANGE

2 Gather together,
    you unwanted people.
²Do it before it's too late.
  Do it before you are blown away
    like chaff.ᵈ
  Do it before the Lord's terrible anger
    reaches you.
  Do it before the day of the Lord's
    anger comes to you.
³All you who are not proud, come to
    the Lord.
  You who obey his laws, come to
    him.
  Do what is right. Learn to be humble.
  Maybe you will escape

on the day the Lord shows his
  anger.

PHILISTIA WILL BE PUNISHED

⁴No one will be left in the city of Gaza.
  The city of Ashkelon will be
    destroyed.
  Ashdod will be empty by noon.
  And the people of Ekron will be
    chased away.
⁵How terrible it will be for you who live
    by the Mediterranean Sea,
  you Philistines!
  This message from the Lord is for you,
    people of Canaan, land of the
    Philistines.

"I will destroy you.
  No one will be left."
⁶You live in the land by the
    Mediterranean Sea.
  It will be a place for shepherds and
    sheep.
⁷Your land will belong to the
    descendantsᵈ of Judah who are
    left alive.
  There they will let their sheep eat
    grass.
  At night they will sleep
    in the houses of Ashkelon.
  The Lord their God will come to be
    with them.
  He will give them back their riches.

MOAB AND AMMON WILL BE PUNISHED

⁸"I heard the country of Moab insult
    my people.
  The country of Ammon threatened
    to take their land."
⁹So the Lord of heaven's armies, the
    God of Israel, says,
  "As surely as I live,
  Moab will be destroyed like Sodom.
  Ammon will be destroyed like
    Gomorrah."ⁿ
  Their land will be covered with weeds
    and salt.
  It will be destroyed forever.

2:9 Sodom . . . Gomorrah Two cities God destroyed because the people were so evil.

Those of my people who are left alive
will take whatever they want
from them.
Those who are left from my nation
will take their land."

¹⁰This is what Moab and Ammon get
for being proud.
This will happen because they
insulted and made fun of the
people of the Lord of heaven's
armies.
¹¹Those people will be afraid of the Lord.
He will destroy all the gods of the
earth.
Then those people in faraway places
will worship the Lord in their own
countries.

CUSH AND ASSYRIA WILL BE DESTROYED

¹²"You Cushites also
will be killed by my sword."
¹³Then the Lord will turn against the
north
and punish Assyria.
He will destroy Nineveh.
It will be dry like a desert.
¹⁴Sheep and goats will lie down there.
Wild animals will live there.
The owls and crows will sit
on the stone pillars that are left
standing.
Their calls will be heard through the
windows.
Trash will be in the doorways.
The wooden boards of the buildings
will be gone.
¹⁵This is the happy and safe city.
It thinks there is no one else as
strong as it is.
But that city will be destroyed.
Only animals will stay there.
Those who pass by will make fun
and shake their fists.

JERUSALEM WILL BE PUNISHED

3 How terrible it will be for Jerusalem
that hurts its own people.
It's a wicked, stubborn city.
²Her people don't listen.

They can't be taught to do right.
They don't trust the Lord.
They don't worship their God.
³Their officers are like roaring lions.
Their rulers are like hungry wolves
that attack in the evening.
In the morning nothing is left of
those they attacked.
⁴Their prophets[d] are proud.
They cannot be trusted.
Their priests don't respect holy things.
They break God's teachings.
⁵But the Lord is good, and he is there
in that city.
He does no wrong.
Every morning he governs the people
fairly.
Every day he can be trusted by his
people.
But evil people are not ashamed of
the bad things they do.

⁶"I have destroyed other nations.
Their towers have fallen.
I made their streets empty.
No one goes there anymore.
Their cities are ruined.
No one lives there anymore.
⁷I said, 'Maybe now Jerusalem will
respect me.
Maybe now my people will let me
teach them to do right.'
Then the place where they lived would
not be destroyed.
Then I would not have punished
them.
They got up early in order to do evil.
Everything they did was bad.
⁸Just wait," says the Lord.
"Some day I will hold court and be
the judge.
I will gather nations.
I will assemble kingdoms.
I will pour out my anger on them.
My anger will be very strong.
My anger will be like fire.
And the whole world will be burned
up.

A NEW DAY FOR GOD'S PEOPLE

9"Then I will make the people of all
    nations speak a pure language.
  All of them will speak the name of
    the Lord.
  And they will worship me together.
10People will come from where the Nile
    River begins.
  My scattered people will come with
    gifts for me.
11Then Jerusalem will not be ashamed
  of the wrongs done against me.
  I will remove from this city
    those who like to brag.
  There will never be any more proud
    people
  on my holy mountain in Jerusalem.
12Only the meek and humble will
    stay in my city.
  And they will trust in the Lord.
13Those who are left alive of Israel won't
    do wrong.
  They won't tell lies.
  They won't trick people with their
    words.
  They will be like sheep that eat and lie
    down.
  No one will bother them."

A HAPPY SONG

14Sing, Jerusalem.
  Israel, shout for joy!
Jerusalem, be happy.
  Rejoice with all your heart.
15The Lord has stopped punishing you.

He has sent your enemies away.
The King of Israel, the Lord, is with you.
  You will never again be afraid of
    being harmed.
16On that day Jerusalem will be told,
  "Don't be afraid, city of Jerusalem.
  Don't be so discouraged that you
    can't do anything.
17The Lord your God is with you.
  The mighty One will save you.
  The Lord will be happy with you.
  You will rest in his love.
  He will sing and be joyful about you."

18"I will take away the sadness planned
    for you.
  It would have made you very
    ashamed.
19At that time I will punish
    all those who harmed you.
  I will save my people who are hurt.
  I will gather my people who are
    scattered.
  I will give them praise and honor
    in every place where they were
    disgraced.
20At that time I will gather you.
  At that time I will bring you back
    home.
  I will give you honor and praise
    from people everywhere.
  That will happen when I give you back
    your riches.
  You will see this with your own
    eyes," says the Lord.

THE BOOK OF
HAGGAI

IT IS TIME TO BUILD THE TEMPLE

1 The prophet[d] Haggai spoke the word of the Lord to Zerubbabel and to Joshua. Zerubbabel son of Shealtiel was governor of Judah. Joshua son of Jehozadak was high priest. This message came in the second year that Darius was king of Persia. It came on the first day of the sixth month of that year. This was the message:

²"This is what the Lord of heaven's armies says: 'The people say the right time has not come to rebuild the Temple[d] of the Lord.'"

³Then Haggai the prophet spoke the word of the Lord: ⁴"The Temple is still in ruins. Is it right for you to be living in fancy houses?"

⁵This is why the Lord of heaven's armies says: "Think about what you have done. ⁶You have planted much, but you harvest little. You eat, but you do not become full. You drink, but you are still thirsty. You put on clothes, but you are not warm enough. You earn money, but then you lose it all. It is as if you put it into a purse full of holes."

⁷This is what the Lord of heaven's armies says: "Think about what you have done. ⁸Go up to the mountains. Bring back wood and build the Temple. Then I will be pleased with it and be honored," says the Lord. ⁹The Lord of heaven's armies says: "You look for much, but you find little. When you bring it home, I destroy it. Why? Because you are busy working on your own houses. But my house is still in ruins! ¹⁰Because of what you have done, the sky holds back its rain. And the ground holds back its crops. ¹¹I have called for a dry time in the land. There will be no rain in the mountains for the grain, new wine and olive oil. It will be a dry time for the plants which the earth produces. It will be a dry time for men and farm animals. The dry time will make your hard work useless."

¹²Zerubbabel was the son of Shealtiel. And Joshua, the high priest, was the son of Jehozadak. Zerubbabel and Joshua obeyed the Lord their God. And they obeyed the message from Haggai the prophet. All the rest of the people who were left alive also obeyed. This was because they realized that the Lord their God had sent Haggai. And they feared the Lord.

¹³The Lord sent a message to Haggai, the Lord's messenger. Haggai gave this message to the people. He said: "The Lord says, 'I am with you.'" ¹⁴The Lord made Zerubbabel and Joshua excited about building the Temple. Zerubbabel? son of Shealtiel was the governor of Judah. Joshua son of Jehozadak was the high priest. The Lord made all the rest of the people who were left alive excited, too. They came and worked on the Temple of their God, the Lord of heaven's armies. ¹⁵They began on the twenty-fourth day of the sixth month. This was in the second year that Darius was king of Persia.

THE BEAUTY OF THE TEMPLE

2 The Lord spoke his word through Haggai the prophet[d] on the twenty-first day of the seventh month. This is what the Lord said: ²"Speak to Zerubbabel son of Shealtiel, governor of Judah. Speak also to Joshua son of Jehozadak, the high priest. And speak to the rest of the people who were left alive. Say: ³'Do any of you who are still alive remember how beautiful the Temple[d] was before it was destroyed? What does it look like now? The truth is it means nothing to you!' ⁴But the Lord says: 'Zerubbabel, be brave. Joshua son of Jehozadak, the high priest, be brave. And all you people who live in the land, be brave,' says the Lord. 'Work, because I am with you,' says the

Lord of heaven's armies. ⁵'I made a promise to you when you came out of Egypt. My Spirit*d* is still with you. So don't be afraid.'

⁶"This is what the Lord of heaven's armies says: 'In a short time I will shake the heavens and earth once again. And I will shake the sea and the dry land. ⁷I will shake all the nations. All the nations will bring their wealth. Then I will fill this Temple with glory,' says the Lord of heaven's armies. ⁸'The silver is mine, and the gold is mine,' says the Lord of heaven's armies. ⁹'The new Temple will be more beautiful than the one that was destroyed,' says the Lord of heaven's armies. 'And in this place I will give peace to the people,' says the Lord of heaven's armies."

¹⁰The Lord spoke his word to Haggai the prophet. This was on the twenty-fourth day of the ninth month. It was in the second year that Darius was king of Persia. This is what the Lord said: ¹¹"This is what the Lord of heaven's armies says: 'Ask the priests what the teachings say. ¹²A person might carry meat made holy for the Lord in the fold of his clothes. And that fold might touch bread, cooked food, wine, olive oil or some other food. Will the thing the fold touches be made holy for the Lord, too?'"

The priests answered, "No."

¹³Then Haggai said, "A person who touches a dead body will become unclean.*d* If he touches any of these foods, will it become unclean, too?"

The priests answered, "Yes. It would become unclean."

¹⁴Then Haggai answered, "The Lord says this: 'This is also true for the people of this nation. They are unclean, and everything they do with their hands is unclean to me. If these people offer something at the altar to me, it is also unclean.

¹⁵"'Think about this from now on! Think about how it was before you started piling stones on top of stones. Think about how it was before you started building the Temple of the Lord. ¹⁶A person used to come to a pile of grain expecting to find 20 basketfuls. But there were only 10. And a person used to come to the wine vat to take out 50 jarfuls. But only 20 were there. ¹⁷I destroyed your work with diseases, mildew*d* and hail. But you still did not come to me.' The Lord says this. ¹⁸'It is the twenty-fourth day of the ninth month. On this day the people finished working on the foundation of the Temple of the Lord. From now on, think about these things: ¹⁹Do you have seeds for your crops already in the barn? No! Your vines and trees are not giving fruit yet, either. You don't have any figs, pomegranates*d* or olives yet. But from now on I will bless you!'"

THE LORD MAKES A PROMISE TO ZERUBBABEL

²⁰Then the Lord spoke his word a second time to Haggai. It was on the twenty-fourth day of the month. This is what the Lord said: ²¹"Tell Zerubbabel, the governor of Judah: 'I am going to shake the heavens and the earth. ²²I will destroy the foreign kingdoms. I will take away the power of the kingdoms of the nations. I will destroy the chariots and their riders. The horses will fall with their riders. People will kill each other with swords.' ²³The Lord of heaven's armies says this: 'On that day I will take you, Zerubbabel son of Shealtiel, my servant.' The Lord says this: 'I will make you important like my signet*d* ring. This is because I have chosen you!' says the Lord of heaven's armies."

ZECHARIAH

THE LORD CALLS HIS PEOPLE BACK

1 It was the eighth month of the second year Darius was king of Persia. The Lord spoke his word to the prophet[d] Zechariah son of Berekiah. Berekiah was the son of Iddo. The Lord said:

²"The Lord was very angry with your ancestors. ³So tell the people: This is what the Lord of heaven's armies says: 'Return to me, and I will return to you.' ⁴Don't be like your ancestors. In the past the prophets spoke to them. They said: This is what the Lord of heaven's armies says: 'Stop your evil ways and evil actions.' But they wouldn't listen or pay attention to me, says the Lord. ⁵Your ancestors are dead. And those prophets didn't live forever. ⁶I commanded my words and laws to my servants the prophets. They preached to your ancestors, who returned to me. They said, 'The Lord of heaven's armies did as he said he would. He punished us for the way we lived and for what we did.'"

THE VISION OF THE HORSES

⁷It was on the twenty-fourth day of the eleventh month, which is called Shebat. It was Darius's second year as king. The Lord spoke his word to the prophet[d] Zechariah son of Berekiah. Berekiah was the son of Iddo.

⁸During the night I had a vision. I saw a man riding a red horse. He was standing among some myrtle trees in the ravine. Behind him were red, brown and white horses.

⁹I asked, "What are these, sir?"

The angel who was talking with me answered. He said, "I'll show you what they are."

¹⁰Then the man standing among the myrtle trees explained. He said, "They are the ones the Lord sent through all the earth."

¹¹Then they spoke to the Lord's angel. He was standing among the myrtle trees.

They said, "We have gone through all the earth. Everything is calm and quiet."

¹²Then the Lord's angel asked, "Lord of heaven's armies, how long before you show mercy to Jerusalem and the cities of Judah? You have been angry with them for 70 years now." ¹³Then the Lord answered the angel who was talking with me. His words were comforting and good.

¹⁴Then the angel told me, "Announce this: This is what the Lord of heaven's armies says: 'I have a strong love for Jerusalem. ¹⁵And I am very angry with the nations that feel so safe. I was only a little angry, but they made things worse for my people.'

¹⁶"So this is what the Lord says: 'I will return to Jerusalem with mercy. My Temple[d] will be rebuilt,' says the Lord of heaven's armies. 'And the measuring line will be used to rebuild Jerusalem.'

¹⁷"Also announce: This is what the Lord of heaven's armies says: 'My towns will be rich again. I will comfort Jerusalem again. I will still choose Jerusalem.'"

THE VISION OF THE HORNS

¹⁸Then I looked up and saw four animal horns. ¹⁹I asked the angel who was talking with me, "What are these?"

He said, "These are the strong nations that scattered the people of Judah, Israel and Jerusalem."

²⁰Then the Lord showed me four craftsmen. ²¹I asked, "What are they coming to do?"

He answered, "They have come to scare and throw down the horns. Those horns scattered the people of Judah. No one could even lift up his head. The horns stand for the strong nations that attacked the people of Judah and scattered them."

THE VISION OF THE MEASURING LINE

2 Then I looked up. And I saw a man holding a line for measuring things. ²I asked him, "Where are you going?"

He said to me, "I am going to measure Jerusalem. I will see how wide and how long it is."

³Then the angel who was talking with me left. And another angel came out to meet him. ⁴The second angel said to him, "Run and tell that young man this: 'Jerusalem will become a city without walls because there will be so many people and cattle in it. ⁵I will be a wall of fire around it,' says the Lord. 'And I will be the glory within it.'

⁶"Hurry! Run away from Babylon. I have scattered you in all directions," says the Lord.

⁷"Hurry, people of Jerusalem! Escape from Babylon." ⁸This is what the Lord of heaven's armies says: "Whoever hurts you hurts what is precious to me."

So the Lord will honor me. And he will send me to speak against those nations who scattered you. ⁹"I will raise my hand against them. Their slaves will rob them."

Then you will know that the Lord of heaven's armies sent me.

¹⁰"Shout and be glad, Jerusalem. I am coming, and I will live among you," says the Lord. ¹¹"At that time people from many nations will come to the Lord. And they will become my people. I will live among you. And you will know that the Lord of heaven's armies has sent me to you. ¹²Judah will be the Lord's special part of the holy land. And Jerusalem will be his chosen city again. ¹³Be silent, everyone. The Lord is coming out of the holy place where he lives."

THE VISION OF THE HIGH PRIEST

3 Then he showed me Joshua the high priest. He was standing in front of the Lord's angel. And Satan was standing by Joshua's right side to accuse him. ²The Lord said to Satan, "The Lord says you are guilty, Satan. The Lord who has chosen Jerusalem says you are guilty. This man was like a burning stick pulled from the fire."

³Joshua was standing in front of the angel. And Joshua was wearing dirty clothes. ⁴Then the angel spoke to those standing near him. He said, "Take those dirty clothes off Joshua."

Then the angel said to Joshua, "Look, I have taken away your sin. And I am giving you new clothes."

⁵Then I said, "Put a clean turban on his head." So they put a clean turban on his head. They also dressed him while the Lord's angel stood there.

⁶Then the Lord's angel said to Joshua, "This is what the Lord of heaven's armies says: ⁷'Do as I tell you and serve me. Then you will be in charge of my Temple.ᵈ You will take care of my courtyards. And I will let you be with these angels who are standing here.

⁸"'Listen, high priest Joshua and the people with you. You stand for things that will happen. I am going to bring my servant called the Branch. ⁹Look, I put this stone in front of Joshua. The stone has seven sides. I will carve a message on it,' says the Lord of heaven's armies. 'And in one day I will take away the sin of this land.'

¹⁰"'The Lord of heaven's armies says, 'In that day, each of you will invite your neighbor to join you. And you will sit together under your own grapevine and under your own fig tree.'"

THE VISION OF THE LAMPSTAND

4 Then the angel who was talking with me came back. He woke me up as if I had been asleep. ²He asked me, "What do you see?"

I said, "I see a solid gold lampstand. There is a bowl at the top. And there are seven lamps. There are also seven places for wicks. ³There are two olive trees by it. One is on the right of the bowl. And one is on the left."

⁴I asked the angel who talked with me, "Sir, what are these?"

⁵The angel said, "Don't you know what they are?"

"No, sir," I said.

6Then he told me, "This is the message from the Lord to Zerubbabel: 'You will not succeed by your own strength or by your own power. The power will come from my Spirit,'*d* says the Lord of heaven's armies.

7"No mountain can stand in Zerubbabel's way. It will be flattened. Then he will bring out the topmost stone. There will be shouts of 'It's beautiful! It's beautiful!'"

8Then the Lord spoke his word to me again. He said: 9"Zerubbabel has laid the foundation of this Temple.*d* He will also complete it. Then you will know that the Lord of heaven's armies has sent me to you.

10"The people should not think that small beginnings are unimportant. They will be happy when they see Zerubbabel with tools, building the Temple.

"(These seven lamps stand for the eyes of the Lord. They look back and forth across the earth.)"

11Then I asked the angel, "What are the two olive trees on the right and left of the lampstand?"

12I also asked him, "What are the two branches full of olives? The olive oil flows through the two gold pipes to the lamps."

13He answered, "Don't you know what they are?"

"No, sir," I said.

14So he said, "They stand for two men. They have been appointed to serve the Lord of all the earth."

THE VISION OF THE FLYING SCROLL

5 I looked up again. And I saw a flying scroll.

2The angel asked me, "What do you see?"

I answered, "I see a flying scroll. It is 30 feet long and 15 feet wide."

3And he said to me, "This is the curse that will go all over the land. One side says every thief will be sent away. The other side says everyone who makes false promises will be sent away. 4The Lord of heaven's armies says, 'I will send it to the houses of thieves. I will also send it to those who use my name to make false promises. The scroll will stay in that person's house. And it will destroy the house with its wood and stones.'"

THE VISION OF THE WOMAN

5Then the angel who was talking with me came forward. He said to me, "Look up and see what is coming."

6I asked, "What is it?"

He answered, "It is a measuring basket." He also said, "It stands for the people's sins in all the land."

7Then the lid made of lead was raised. There was a woman sitting in the basket. 8The angel said, "The woman stands for wickedness." Then he pushed her back into the basket. And he put the lid back down.

9Then I looked up. I saw two women. They had wind in their wings. Their wings were like those of a stork. They lifted up the basket into the sky.

10I spoke to the angel who was talking with me. I asked, "Where are they taking the basket?"

11He answered, "They are going to Babylonia. They will build a temple for it. When the temple is ready, they will set the basket there in its place."

THE VISION OF THE FOUR CHARIOTS

6 I looked up again. I saw four chariots coming from between two mountains. They were mountains of bronze. 2Red horses pulled the first chariot. Black horses pulled the second chariot. 3White horses pulled the third chariot. And strong, spotted horses pulled the fourth chariot. 4I spoke to the angel who was talking with me. I asked, "What are these, sir?"

5He said, "These are going to the four directions on earth. They have just come from the presence of the Lord of the whole world. 6The chariot pulled by the black horses will go north. The white horses will go west. And the spotted horses will go south."

⁷The powerful horses were trying to go through all the earth. So he said, "Go through all the earth." And they did.

⁸Then he called to me, "Look. The horses that went north have calmed the Lord's anger that came from there to punish."

A CROWN FOR JOSHUA

⁹The Lord spoke his word to me. He said: ¹⁰"Heldai, Tobijah and Jedaiah were captives in Babylon. Get silver and gold from them. Go that same day to the house of Josiah son of Zephaniah. ¹¹Make the silver and gold into a crown. And put it on the head of Joshua son of Jehozadak. Joshua is the high priest. ¹²Tell him this is what the Lord of heaven's armies says: 'There is a man whose name is the Branch. He will branch out from where he is. He will build the Temple*d* of the Lord. ¹³One man*n* will build the Temple of the Lord. And the other*n* will receive the honor of a king. One man will sit on his throne and rule. And the other will be a priest on his throne. And these two men will work together in peace.' ¹⁴The crown will be kept in the Temple of the Lord. It will remind Heldai, Tobijah, Jedaiah and Josiah son of Zephaniah of God's king. ¹⁵People living far away will come and build the Temple of the Lord. Then you will know the Lord of heaven's armies has sent me to you. This will happen if you completely obey the Lord your God."

THE PEOPLE SHOULD SHOW MERCY

7 It was the fourth year of King Darius's rule. It was on the fourth day of the ninth month, which is called Kislev. The Lord spoke his word to Zechariah. ²The city of Bethel sent Sharezer, Regem-Melech and their men to ask the Lord a question. ³They went to the prophets*d* and priests. They were at the Temple*d* of the Lord of heaven's armies. The men said, "For years the fifth month of each year has been a special time for us. We have shown our sadness and gone without food in this month. Should we continue to do this?"

⁴The Lord of heaven's armies spoke his word to me. He said, ⁵"Tell the priests and the people in the country this: 'For 70 years you went without food and cried in the fifth and seventh months. But that was not really for me. ⁶And when you ate and drank, it was really for yourselves. ⁷The Lord used the earlier prophets to say the same thing. Jerusalem and the surrounding towns were at peace and wealthy then. People lived in the southern area and the western mountain slopes.'"

⁸And the Lord spoke his word to Zechariah again: ⁹"This is what the Lord of heaven's armies says: 'Do what is right and fair. Be kind and merciful to each other. ¹⁰Don't hurt widows and orphans, foreigners or the poor. Don't even think of doing evil to somebody else.'

¹¹"But they refused to pay attention. They were stubborn and would not listen. ¹²They made their hearts as hard as rock. They would not listen to the teachings of the Lord of heaven's armies. And they would not hear his words through the earlier prophets. So the Lord of heaven's armies became very angry.

¹³"The Lord of heaven's armies says, 'When I called to them, they would not listen. So when they called to me, I would not listen. ¹⁴I scattered them like a hurricane to other countries. These were countries they did not know. This good land was left so ruined that no one could live there.'"

THE LORD WILL BLESS JERUSALEM

8 The Lord of heaven's armies spoke his word to me again. ²This is what the Lord of heaven's armies says: "I have

---

6:13 **One man** This probably refers to Zerubbabel.
6:13 **other** This probably refers to Joshua.

a very strong love for Jerusalem. My strong love for her is like a fire burning in me."

³This is what the Lord says: "I will return to Jerusalem. I will live in Jerusalem. Then it will be called the City of Truth. And the mountain of the Lord of heaven's armies will be called the Holy Mountain."

⁴This is what the Lord of heaven's armies says: "Old men and old women will again sit along Jerusalem's streets. Each will carry a cane because of his age. ⁵And the streets will be filled with boys and girls playing."

⁶This is what the Lord of heaven's armies says: "Those who are left alive then may think it is too difficult to happen. But it is not too difficult for me," says the Lord of heaven's armies. ⁷This is what the Lord of heaven's armies says: "I will save my people from countries in the east and west. ⁸I will bring them back. And they will live in Jerusalem. They will be my people. And I will be their good and loyal God."

⁹This is what the Lord of heaven's armies says: "Be strong, you who are hearing these words today. The prophets spoke these words when the foundation was laid for the building of the Temple.ᵈ ¹⁰Before that time there was no money to hire men or animals. People could not safely come and go because of the enemies. I had turned everyone against his neighbor. ¹¹But I will not do to these people who are left alive what I did in the past," says the Lord of heaven's armies.

¹²"Their seeds will come up. Their grapevines will have fruit. The ground will give good crops. And the sky will send rain. I will give all this to those who are left alive. ¹³Judah and Israel, your names have been used as curses. But I will save you. And you will be a blessing. So don't be afraid. Be strong."

¹⁴This is what the Lord of heaven's armies says: "Your ancestors made me angry. So I planned to punish you. I had no mercy," says the Lord of heaven's armies. ¹⁵"But now I am planning to do good to Jerusalem and Judah. So don't be afraid. ¹⁶But do these things: Tell each other the truth. In the courts judge with truth and complete fairness. ¹⁷Do not make plans to hurt your neighbors. And don't make false promises. I hate all these things," says the Lord.

¹⁸The Lord of heaven's armies spoke his word to me again. ¹⁹This is what the Lord of heaven's armies says: "You have special days when you give up eating. These days are in the fourth, fifth, seventh and tenth months. Those days will become good, joyful, happy feasts in Judah. But you must love truth and peace."

²⁰This is what the Lord of heaven's armies says: "Many people from many cities will still come to Jerusalem. ²¹People from one city will say to those from another city, 'We are going to pray to the Lord. We want to ask the Lord of heaven's armies for help. Come and go with us.' ²²Many people and powerful nations will come to Jerusalem. They will worship the Lord of heaven's armies. They will pray to the Lord."

²³This is what the Lord of heaven's armies says: "At that time, ten men from different countries with different languages will come. They will take hold of one Jew by his coat. They will say to him, 'Let us go with you. We have heard that God is with you.'"

PUNISHMENT ON ISRAEL'S ENEMIES

9 This message is the word of the Lord.

The message is against the land of
    Hadrach.
  And it is against the city of
    Damascus.
The tribesᵈ of Israel and all people
  belong to the Lord.

²The Lord's message is also against the city of Hamath, which is on the border of the land of Hadrach.
The Lord's message is against Tyre and Sidon, with their skill.
³Tyre has built a strong, walled city.
The people have piled up silver like dust.
They have as much gold as mud in the streets.
⁴But the Lord will take away all she has.
He will destroy her power on the sea.
That city will be destroyed by fire.
⁵The city of Ashkelon will see it and be afraid.
The people of Gaza will shake with fear.
And the people of Ekron will lose hope.
No king will be left in Gaza.
And no one will live in Ashkelon anymore.
⁶Foreigners will live in Ashdod.
And I will destroy the pride of the Philistines.
⁷I will stop them from drinking blood.
They will not eat any other forbidden food.
Those left alive will belong to God.
They will be leaders in Judah.
And Ekron will become part of my people like the Jebusites.
⁸I will protect my Temple*d*
from armies who come and go.
No one will hurt my people again because now I am guarding it.

THE KING IS COMING

⁹Rejoice, people of Jerusalem.
Shout for joy, people of Jerusalem.
Your king is coming to you.
He does what is right, and he saves.
He is gentle and riding on a donkey.
He is on the colt of a donkey.
¹⁰I will take away the chariots from Ephraim
and the horses from Jerusalem.

The bows used in war will be broken.
The king will talk to the nations about peace.
His kingdom will go from sea to sea, and from the Euphrates River to the ends of the earth.

¹¹My people, I made an agreement with you
and sealed it with the blood of sacrifices.
Because of this, I will set your prisoners free from captivity,
which is like a dry pit.
¹²You prisoners who have hope, return to your place of safety.
Today I am telling you
that I will give you back twice as much as before.
¹³I will use Judah like a bow.
And Ephraim will be like the arrows.
Jerusalem, I will use your men
to fight the men of Greece.
I will make you like the sword of a warrior.
¹⁴Then the Lord will appear to them.
He will shoot his arrows like lightning.
The Lord God will blow the trumpet.
And he will march in the storms of the south.
¹⁵The Lord of heaven's armies will protect them.
They will destroy the enemy with slingshots.
They will drink and shout like drunk men.
They will be filled like a bowl
used for sprinkling blood at the corners of the altar.
¹⁶On that day the Lord their God will save them
as if his people were sheep.
They will shine in his land
like jewels in a crown.
¹⁷They will be so pretty and beautiful.

The young men will grow strong on
the grain.
And the young women will grow
strong on new wine.

THE LORD'S PROMISES

10 Ask the Lord for rain in the
springtime.
The Lord makes the clouds.
He sends the showers.
And he gives everyone green fields.
²Idols tell lies.
Fortune-tellers see false visions.
They tell about false dreams.
The comfort they give is worth
nothing.
So the people are like lost sheep.
They are abused because there is no
shepherd.

³The Lord says, "I am angry at my
shepherds.
I will punish the leaders.
I, the Lord of heaven's armies, will
care
for my flock, which is the people of
Judah.
I will make them like my proud war
horses.
⁴From Judah will come the
cornerstone[d]
and the tent peg.
From him will come the battle bow.
From him will come every ruler.
⁵They will be like soldiers
marching to battle through muddy
streets.
The Lord is with them.
So they will fight and defeat the
horsemen.

⁶"I will strengthen the people of Judah.
And I will save the people of Joseph.
I will bring them back
because I care for them.
It will be as though
I had never left them.
I am the Lord their God,

and I will answer their calls for help.
⁷The people of Ephraim will be strong
like soldiers.
They will be glad as when they have
drunk wine.
Their children will see it and rejoice.
They will be happy in the Lord.
⁸I will call my people
and gather them together.
I will save them.
And there will be as many of them
as there used to be.
⁹I have scattered them among the
nations.
But in those faraway places, they
will remember me.
They and their children will live and
return.
¹⁰I will bring them back from Egypt.
I will gather them from Assyria.
I will bring them to Gilead and
Lebanon.
There won't be enough room in the
land for them all.
¹¹They will come through their sea of
trouble.
The waves of the sea will be calm.
And the Nile River will dry up.
I will defeat Assyria's pride.
I will destroy Egypt's power over
other countries.
¹²I will make my people strong.
And they will live as I say," says the
Lord.

11 Lebanon, open your gates
so fire may burn your cedar
trees.[n]
²Cry, pine trees, because the cedar has
fallen.
The tall trees are ruined.
Cry, oaks in Bashan,
because the mighty forest has been
cut down.
³Listen to the shepherds crying.
Their rich pastures are destroyed.

11:1 **trees** In this poem, trees, bushes and animals stand for leaders of countries around Judah.

Listen to the lions roaring.
The thick bushes near the Jordan
River are ruined.

⁴This is what the Lord my God says: "Feed the sheep that are about to be killed. ⁵Their buyers kill them and are not punished. Those who sell them say, 'Praise the Lord. I am rich.' Even the shepherds don't feel sorry for their sheep. ⁶Even I don't feel sorry anymore for the people of this country," says the Lord. "I will let everyone be under the power of his neighbor and king. They will bring trouble to the country. And I will not stop them."

⁷So I fed the sheep about to be killed, particularly the weakest ones. Then I took two sticks. I called one Favor. I called the other Union. And I fed the sheep. ⁸In one month I got rid of three shepherds. The flock hated me, and I got impatient with them. ⁹I said, "I will no longer take care of you like a shepherd. Let those that are dying die. Let those that are to be destroyed be destroyed. Let those that are left eat each other."

¹⁰Then I broke the stick named Favor. This broke the agreement God made with his people. ¹¹That day it was broken. Those weak sheep were watching me. They knew this message was from the Lord.

¹²Then I said, "If you want to pay me, then pay me. If not, then don't." So they paid me 30 pieces of silver.

¹³The Lord said to me, "Throw the money to the potter." That is how little they thought I was worth.*ⁿ* So I threw the money to the potter in the Temple*ᵈ* of the Lord.

¹⁴Then I broke the second stick named Union. This broke the tie between Judah and Israel.

¹⁵Then the Lord said to me, "Become a foolish shepherd again. ¹⁶I am going to get a new shepherd for the country. He will not care for the dying sheep. He will not look for the young ones. He will not heal the injured ones. He will not feed the healthy. But he will eat the best sheep and tear off their hoofs.

¹⁷"How terrible it will be for the useless shepherd.
He abandoned the flock.
May war destroy his power and wisdom.
May his power become useless.
May his wisdom be taken away."

JERUSALEM WILL BE SAVED

12 This message is the word of the Lord to Israel. The Lord stretched out the skies. He laid the foundations of the earth. He put man's spirit in him. And the Lord says this: ²"I will make Jerusalem like a cup of poison to the nations around her. They will come and attack Jerusalem and Judah. ³One day all the nations on earth will come together to attack Jerusalem. But I will make Jerusalem like a heavy rock. Anyone who tries to move it will get hurt. ⁴At that time I will scare every horse. And its rider will panic," says the Lord. "I will watch over Judah. But I will blind all the horses of the enemies. ⁵Then the leaders of Judah will say to themselves, 'The people of Jerusalem are strong. This is because the Lord of heaven's armies is their God.'

⁶"At that time I will make the leaders of Judah like a fire burning a stack of wood. They will be like a fire burning straw. They will destroy all the people around them left and right. But Jerusalem will remain safe.

⁷"The Lord will save the people of Judah first. Then the people in Jerusalem, David's city, won't have more honor than Judah. ⁸At that time the Lord will protect the people in Jerusalem. Then

---

11:13 worth This was a small amount. It was about the price paid for a slave.

even the weakest of them will be strong like David. And the family of David will be like God. They will be like an angel of the Lord leading the people. ⁹At that time I will go to destroy all the nations that attack Jerusalem.

CRYING FOR THE ONE THEY STABBED

¹⁰"I will give David's family and people in Jerusalem a spirit of kindness and mercy. They will look at me, the one they have stabbed. And they will cry like someone crying over the death of an only child. They will be as sad as someone who has lost a firstborn*d* son. ¹¹At that time there will be much crying in Jerusalem. It will be like the crying for Hadad Rimmon in the plain of Megiddo. ¹²The land will cry. Each family will cry alone. The family of David and their wives will cry. The family of Nathan and their wives will cry. ¹³The family of Levi and their wives will cry. The family of Shimei and their wives will cry. ¹⁴And all the rest of the families and their wives will cry.

13 "At that time a fountain will be opened. It will be for David's descendants*d* and for the people of Jerusalem. It will cleanse them of their sins and wrongs."

²The Lord of heaven's armies says, "At that time I will get rid of the names of the idols from the land. No one will remember them anymore. I will also remove the prophets*d* and unclean*d* spirits. ³A person might continue to prophesy. If he does, his own father and mother will tell him, 'You have told lies using the Lord's name. So you must die.' When he prophesies, his own parents should stab him.

⁴"At that time the prophets will be ashamed of their visions and prophecies. They won't wear the prophet's clothes made of hair to trick people. ⁵They will say, 'I am not a prophet. I am a farmer. I have been a farmer since I was young.' ⁶But someone will ask, 'What are the deep cuts on your body?' And he will answer, 'I was hurt at my friend's house.'

THE SHEPHERD IS KILLED

⁷"Sword, hit the shepherd.
　Attack the man who is my friend,"
　says the Lord of heaven's armies.
"Kill the shepherd,
　and the sheep will scatter.
　I will punish the little ones."
⁸The Lord says, "Two-thirds of the
　people
　through all the land will die.
　And one-third will be left.
⁹I will test the ones left with fire.
　I will purify them like silver.
　I will test them like gold.
Then they will call on me.
　And I will answer them.
I will say, 'You are my people.'
　And they will say, 'The Lord is our
　God.'"

THE DAY OF PUNISHMENT

14 The Lord's day of judging is coming. The wealth you have taken will be divided among you.

²I will bring all the nations together to fight Jerusalem. They will capture the city and rob the houses. The women will be attacked. Half the people will be taken away as captives. But the rest won't be taken from the city.

³Then the Lord will go to war against those nations. He will fight as in a day of battle. ⁴On that day he will stand on the Mount of Olives,*d* east of Jerusalem. The Mount of Olives will split in two. A deep valley will run east and west. Half the mountain will move north. And half will move south. ⁵You will run through this mountain valley to the other side. You will run as you ran from the earthquake. That was when Uzziah was king of Judah. Then the Lord my God will come. And all the holy ones will be with him.

⁶On that day there will be no light, cold or frost. ⁷There will be no other day like it. The Lord knows when it will come.

There will be no day or night. Even at evening it will still be light.

8At that time fresh water will flow from Jerusalem. Half of it will flow east to the Dead Sea.*d* And half of it will flow west to the Mediterranean Sea. It will flow summer and winter.

9Then the Lord will be king over the whole world. At that time there will be only one Lord. And his name will be the only name.

10All the land south of Jerusalem from Geba to Rimmon will be turned into a plain. Jerusalem will be raised up. But it will stay in the same place. The city will reach from the Benjamin Gate to the First Gate to the Corner Gate. It will go from the Tower of Hananel to the king's winepresses.*d* 11People will live there. It will never be destroyed again. Jerusalem will be safe.

12But the Lord will punish the nations that fought against Jerusalem. He will bring a terrible disease on them. Their flesh will rot away while they are still standing up. Their eyes will rot in their sockets. And their tongues will rot in their mouths. 13At that time the Lord will cause panic. Everybody will grab his neighbor. They will attack each other. 14The people of Judah will fight in Jerusalem. And the wealth of the nations around them will be collected. There will be much gold, silver and clothes. 15A similar disease will strike the horses, mules, camels and donkeys. All the animals in the camps will have the disease.

16Some of the people who came to fight Jerusalem will be left alive. They will come back to Jerusalem year after year. They will come to worship the King, the Lord of heaven's armies. They will celebrate the Feast*d* of Shelters. 17Some people from the nations might not go to Jerusalem. They might not worship the King, the Lord of heaven's armies. Then rain will not fall on their land. 18The Egyptians might not go to Jerusalem. They might not celebrate the Feast of Shelters. Then the Lord will send them the same terrible disease the other nations got. 19This will be the punishment. It will be for Egypt and any nation which does not go to celebrate the Feast of Shelters.

20At that time the horses' bells will have written on them: Holy to the Lord. The cooking pots in the Temple*d* of the Lord will be like the holy altar bowls. 21Every pot in Jerusalem and Judah will be holy to the Lord of heaven's armies. And everyone who offers sacrifices will be able to cook in them. At that time there will not be any traders in the Temple of the Lord of heaven's armies.

MALACHI

1 This message is the word of the Lord. It is given to Israel through Malachi.

GOD LOVES ISRAEL

²The Lord said, "I love you."

But you ask, "How have you loved us?"

The Lord said, "Esau and Jacob were brothers. I loved Jacob, ³but I hated Esau. I destroyed his mountain country. I left his land to the wild dogs of the desert."

⁴The people of Edom might say, "We were destroyed. But we will go back and rebuild the ruins."

But the Lord of heaven's armies says, "If they rebuild them, I will destroy them. People will say, 'Edom is the Wicked Country. The Lord is always angry with the Edomites.' ⁵You will see these things with your own eyes. You will say, 'The Lord is great, even outside the borders of Israel!'"

THE PRIESTS DON'T RESPECT GOD

⁶The Lord of heaven's armies says, "A son honors his father. A servant honors his master. I am a father. So why don't you honor me? I am a master. So why don't you respect me? You priests do not respect me.

"But you ask, 'How have we shown you disrespect?'

⁷"You have shown it by bringing unclean^d sacrifices to my altar.

"But you ask, 'What makes them unclean?'

"They are unclean because you don't show respect for my altar. ⁸You bring blind animals as sacrifices, and that is wrong. You bring crippled and sick animals. That is wrong. Try giving them to your governor. Would he be pleased with you? He wouldn't accept you," says the Lord of heaven's armies.

⁹"Now ask God to be kind to you. But he won't accept you with such offerings," says the Lord of heaven's armies.

¹⁰"I wish one of you would close the Temple^d doors. Then you would not light useless fires on my altar! I am not pleased with you. I will not accept your gifts," says the Lord of heaven's armies. ¹¹"From the east to the west I will be honored among the nations. Everywhere they will bring incense^d and clean offerings to me. I will be honored among the nations," says the Lord of heaven's armies.

¹²"But you don't honor me. You say about the Lord's altar, 'It is unclean. The food has no worth.' ¹³You say, 'We are tired of doing this.' And you sniff at it in disgust," says the Lord of heaven's armies.

"And you bring hurt, crippled and sick animals. You bring them as gifts. But I won't accept them from you," says the Lord. ¹⁴"The cheat will be cursed. He has an animal in his flock. He promises to offer it. But then he offers me an animal that has something wrong with it. I am a great king," says the Lord of heaven's armies. "I am feared by all the nations.

RULES FOR PRIESTS

2 "Priests, this command is for you. ²Listen to me. Pay attention to what I say. Honor my name," says the Lord of heaven's armies. "If you don't, I will send a curse on you. I will curse your blessings. I have already cursed them because you don't pay attention to what I say.

³"I will punish your descendants.^d I will smear your faces with the garbage from your feasts. And you will be thrown away with it. ⁴Then you will know why I am giving you this command. It is so that my agreement with Levi will continue," says the Lord of heaven's armies. ⁵"My agreement for priests was with the tribe^d of Levi. I promised them life and peace. And I gave these to them so they would honor me. They did honor me and fear me. ⁶They taught the true teachings. They

spoke no lies. With peace and honesty they did what I said they should do. They kept many people from sinning.

[7]"A priest should teach what he knows. People should learn the teachings from him because he is the messenger of the Lord of heaven's armies. [8]But you priests have stopped obeying me. With your teachings you have caused many people to do wrong. You have broken the agreement with the tribe[d] of Levi!" says the Lord of heaven's armies. [9]"You have not been careful to do what I say. You take sides in court cases. So I have caused you to be hated and disgraced in front of everybody."

JUDAH WAS NOT LOYAL TO GOD

[10]We all have the same father. The same God made us. So why do people break their promises to each other? They don't respect the agreement that our ancestors made with God. [11]The people of Judah have broken their promises. They have done something God hates in Israel and Jerusalem. The people of Judah did not respect the Temple[d] that the Lord loves. The men of Judah married the women who worship foreign gods. [12]The man who does this might bring offerings to the Lord of heaven's armies. But the Lord will still separate him from the community of Israel.

[13]This is another thing you do. You cover the Lord's altar with your tears. You cry and moan because the Lord does not accept your offerings. He is not pleased with what you bring. [14]You ask, "Why?" It is because the Lord sees how you treated the wife you married when you were young. You broke your promise with her. She was your partner. You promised yourself to her. [15]God made husbands and wives to become one body and one spirit for his purpose. This is so they would have children who are true to God. So be careful. Do not break your promise with the wife you married when you were young.

[16]The Lord God of Israel says, "I hate divorce. And I hate people who do cruel things as easily as they put on clothes," says the Lord of heaven's armies. So be careful. And do not break your trust.

THE SPECIAL DAY OF JUDGING

[17]You have tired the Lord with what you say.

You ask, "How have we tired him?"

You did it by saying, "God thinks anyone who does evil is good. And he is pleased with them." Or you asked, "Where is the God who is fair?"

3 The Lord of heaven's armies says, "I will send my messenger. He will prepare the way for me to come. Suddenly, the Lord you are looking for will come to his Temple.[d] The messenger of the agreement, whom you want, will come." [2]No one can live through that time. No one can survive when he comes. He will be like a purifying fire. He will be like laundry soap. [3]He will be like someone who heats and purifies silver. He will purify the Levites. He will make them pure like gold and silver. Then they will bring offerings to the Lord in the right way. [4]And he will accept the offerings from Judah and Jerusalem. It will be as it was in the past. [5]The Lord of heaven's armies says, "Then I will come to you and judge you. I will testify against those who take part in evil magic, adultery[d] and lying. I will testify against those who cheat workers of their pay and who cheat widows and orphans. And I will testify against those who are unfair to foreigners. These people do not respect me.

STEALING FROM GOD

[6]"I am the Lord. I do not change. So you descendants[d] of Jacob have not been destroyed. [7]Like your ancestors before you, you have disobeyed my rules. You have not kept them. Return to me. Then I will return to you," says the Lord of heaven's armies.

"But you ask, 'How can we return?'

⁸"Should a man rob God? But you rob me.

"You ask, 'How have we robbed you?'

"You have robbed me in your offerings and the tenth of your crops. ⁹So a curse is on you because the whole nation has robbed me. ¹⁰Bring to the storehouse a tenth of what you gain. Then there will be food in my house. Test me in this," says the Lord of heaven's armies. "I will open the windows of heaven for you. I will pour out more blessings than you have room for. ¹¹I will stop the insects so they won't eat your crops. The grapes won't fall from your vines before they are ready to pick," says the Lord of heaven's armies. ¹²"All the nations will call you blessed. You will have a pleasant country," says the Lord of heaven's armies.

THE LORD'S PROMISE OF MERCY

¹³The Lord says, "You have said terrible things about me.

"But you ask, 'What have we said about you?'

¹⁴"You have said, 'It is useless to serve God. It did no good to obey his laws. And it did no good to show the Lord of heaven's armies that we are sorry for what we did. ¹⁵So we say that proud people are happy. Evil people succeed. They challenge God and get away with it.'"

¹⁶Then those who honored the Lord spoke with each other. The Lord listened and heard them. The names of those who honored the Lord and respected him were written in a book. The Lord will remember them.

¹⁷The Lord of heaven's armies says, "They belong to me. On that day they will be my very own. A father shows mercy to his son who serves him. In the same way I will show mercy to my people. ¹⁸You will again see the difference between good and evil people. You will see the difference between those who serve God and those who don't.

THE DAY OF THE LORD'S JUDGING

4 "There is a day coming that will be like a hot furnace. All the proud and evil people will be like straw. On that day they will be completely burned up. Not a root or branch will be left," says the Lord of heaven's armies. ²"But for you who honor me, goodness will shine on you like the sun. There will be healing in its rays. You will jump around, like calves freed from their stalls. ³Then you will crush the wicked. They will be like ashes under your feet. I will do this on that day," says the Lord of heaven's armies.

⁴"Remember the teaching of Moses my servant. I gave those laws and rules to him at Mount Sinai. They are for all the Israelites.

⁵"But I will send Elijah the prophet[d] to you. He will come before that great and terrible day of the Lord's judging. ⁶Elijah will help fathers love their children. And he will help the children love their fathers. Otherwise, I will come and put a curse on the land."

THE NEW TESTAMENT

MATTHEW

THE FAMILY HISTORY OF JESUS

1 This is the family history of Jesus Christ. He came from the family of David. David came from the family of Abraham.

[2] Abraham was the father[n] of Isaac.

Isaac was the father of Jacob.

Jacob was the father of Judah and his brothers.

[3] Judah was the father of Perez and Zerah.

(Their mother was Tamar.)

Perez was the father of Hezron.

Hezron was the father of Ram.

[4] Ram was the father of Amminadab.

Amminadab was the father of Nahshon.

Nahshon was the father of Salmon.

[5] Salmon was the father of Boaz.

(Boaz's mother was Rahab.)

Boaz was the father of Obed.

(Obed's mother was Ruth.)

Obed was the father of Jesse.

[6] Jesse was the father of King David.

David was the father of Solomon.

(Solomon's mother had been Uriah's wife.)

[7] Solomon was the father of Rehoboam.

Rehoboam was the father of Abijah.

Abijah was the father of Asa.[n]

[8] Asa was the father of Jehoshaphat.

Jehoshaphat was the father of Jehoram.

Jehoram was the ancestor of Uzziah.

[9] Uzziah was the father of Jotham.

Jotham was the father of Ahaz.

Ahaz was the father of Hezekiah.

[10] Hezekiah was the father of Manasseh.

Manasseh was the father of Amon.

Amon was the father of Josiah.

[11] Josiah was the grandfather of Jehoiachin[n] and his brothers.

(This was at the time that the people were taken to Babylon.)

[12] After they were taken to Babylon:

Jehoiachin was the father of Shealtiel.

Shealtiel was the grandfather of Zerubbabel.

[13] Zerubbabel was the father of Abiud.

Abiud was the father of Eliakim.

Eliakim was the father of Azor.

[14] Azor was the father of Zadok.

Zadok was the father of Akim.

Akim was the father of Eliud.

[15] Eliud was the father of Eleazar.

Eleazar was the father of Matthan.

Matthan was the father of Jacob.

[16] Jacob was the father of Joseph.

Joseph was the husband of Mary, and Mary was the mother of Jesus. Jesus is called the Christ.[d]

[17] So there were 14 generations from Abraham to David. And there were 14 generations from David until the time when the people were taken to Babylon. And there were 14 generations from the time when the people were taken to Babylon until Christ was born.

THE BIRTH OF JESUS CHRIST

[18] The mother of Jesus Christ was Mary. And this is how the birth of Jesus came about. Mary was engaged to marry Joseph. But before they married, she learned that she was going to have a baby. She was pregnant by the power of the Holy Spirit.[d] [19] Mary's husband, Joseph, was a good man. He did not want to disgrace her in public, so he planned to divorce her secretly.

[20] While Joseph thought about this, an angel of the Lord came to him in a dream. The angel said, "Joseph, descendant[d] of David, don't be afraid to take Mary as your wife. The baby in her is from the

---

1:2 father "Father" in Jewish lists of ancestors can sometimes mean grandfather or more distant relative.
1:7 Asa Some Greek Copies read "Asaph," another name for Asa (see 1 Chronicles 3:10).
1:11 Jehoiachin The Greek reads "Jeconiah," another name for Jehoiachin (see 2 Kings 24:6 and 1 Chronicles 3:16).

Holy Spirit. [21]She will give birth to a son. You will name the son Jesus.[n] Give him that name because he will save his people from their sins."

[22]All this happened to make clear the full meaning of what the Lord had said through the prophet:[d] [23]"The virgin[d] will be pregnant. She will have a son, and they will name him Immanuel."[n] This name means "God is with us."

[24]When Joseph woke up, he did what the Lord's angel had told him to do. Joseph married Mary. [25]But he did not have sexual relations with her until she gave birth to the son. And Joseph named the son Jesus.

WISE MEN COME TO VISIT JESUS

2 Jesus was born in the town of Bethlehem in Judea during the time when Herod was king. After Jesus was born, some wise men from the east came to Jerusalem. [2]They asked, "Where is the baby who was born to be the king of the Jews? We saw his star in the east. We came to worship him."

[3]When King Herod heard about this new king of the Jews, he was troubled. And all the people in Jerusalem were worried too. [4]Herod called a meeting of all the leading priests and teachers of the law. He asked them where the Christ[d] would be born. [5]They answered, "In the town of Bethlehem in Judea. The prophet[d] wrote about this in the Scriptures:[d]

[6]'But you, Bethlehem, in the land of
    Judah,
    you are important among the rulers
    of Judah.
A ruler will come from you.
He will be like a shepherd for my
    people, the Israelites.'" *Micah 5:2*

[7]Then Herod had a secret meeting with the wise men from the east. He learned from them the exact time they first saw

the star. [8]Then Herod sent the wise men to Bethlehem. He said to them, "Go and look carefully to find the child. When you find him, come tell me. Then I can go worship him too."

[9]The wise men heard the king and then left. They saw the same star they had seen in the east. It went before them until it stopped above the place where the child was. [10]When the wise men saw the star, they were filled with joy. [11]They went to the house where the child was and saw him with his mother, Mary. They bowed down and worshiped the child. They opened the gifts they brought for him. They gave him treasures of gold, frankincense,[d] and myrrh.[d] [12]But God warned the wise men in a dream not to go back to Herod. So they went home to their own country by a different way.

JESUS' PARENTS TAKE HIM TO EGYPT

[13]After they left, an angel of the Lord came to Joseph in a dream. The angel said, "Get up! Take the child and his mother and escape to Egypt. Herod will start looking for the child to kill him. Stay in Egypt until I tell you to return."

[14]So Joseph got up and left for Egypt during the night with the child and his mother. [15]Joseph stayed in Egypt until Herod died. This was to make clear the full meaning of what the Lord had said through the prophet.[d] The Lord said, "I called my son out of Egypt."[n]

HEROD KILLS THE BABY BOYS

[16]When Herod saw that the wise men had tricked him, he was very angry. So he gave an order to kill all the baby boys in Bethlehem and in all the area around Bethlehem who were two years old or younger. This was in keeping with the time he learned from the wise men. [17]So what God had said through the prophet[d] Jeremiah came true:

1:21 **Jesus** The name Jesus means "salvation."
1:23 **"The virgin . . . Immanuel."** Quotation from Isaiah 7:14.
2:15 **"I called . . . Egypt."** Quotation from Hosea 11:1.

[18]"A sound was heard in Ramah.
It was painful crying and much
sadness.
Rachel cries for her children,
and she cannot be comforted,
because her children are dead."

Jeremiah 31:15

JOSEPH AND MARY RETURN

[19]After Herod died, an angel of the Lord came to Joseph in a dream. This happened while Joseph was in Egypt. [20]The angel said, "Get up! Take the child and his mother and go to Israel. The people who were trying to kill the child are now dead."

[21]So Joseph took the child and his mother and went to Israel. [22]But he heard that Archelaus was now king in Judea. Archelaus became king when his father Herod died. So Joseph was afraid to go there. After being warned in a dream, he went to the area of Galilee. [23]He went to a town called Nazareth and lived there. And so what God had said through the prophets[d] came true: "He will be called a Nazarene."[n]

THE WORK OF JOHN THE BAPTIST

3 About that time John the Baptist[d] came and began preaching in the desert area of Judea. [2]John said, "Change your hearts and lives because the kingdom of heaven is coming soon." [3]John the Baptist is the one Isaiah the prophet[d] was talking about. Isaiah said:

"This is a voice of a man
who calls out in the desert:
'Prepare the way for the Lord.
Make the road straight for him.'"

Isaiah 40:3

[4]John's clothes were made from camel's hair. He wore a leather belt around his waist. For food, he ate locusts[d] and wild honey. [5]Many people went to hear John preach. They came from Jerusalem and all Judea and all the area around the Jordan River. [6]They told of the sins they had done, and John baptized them in the Jordan River.

[7]Many of the Pharisees[d] and Sadducees[d] came to the place where John was baptizing people. When John saw them, he said: "You are snakes! Who warned you to run away from God's anger that is coming? [8]You must do the things that show that you have really changed your hearts and lives. [9]And don't think that you can say to yourselves, 'Abraham is our father.' I tell you that God could make children for Abraham from these rocks. [10]The ax is now ready to cut down the trees. Every tree that does not produce good fruit will be cut down and thrown into the fire.[n]

[11]"I baptize you with water to show that your hearts and lives have changed. But there is one coming later who is greater than I am. I am not good enough to carry his sandals. He will baptize you with the Holy Spirit[d] and with fire. [12]He will come ready to clean the grain. He will separate the good grain from the chaff.[d] He will put the good part of the grain into his barn. And he will burn the chaff with a fire that cannot be put out."[n]

JESUS IS BAPTIZED BY JOHN

[13]At that time Jesus came from Galilee to the Jordan River. He came to John and wanted John to baptize him. [14]But John tried to stop him. John said, "Why do you come to me to be baptized? I should be baptized by you!"

[15]Jesus answered, "Let it be this way for now. We should do all things that are right." So John agreed to baptize Jesus.

2:23 Nazarene A person from the town of Nazareth. Matthew may be referring to Isaiah 11:1, where the Hebrew word translated "branch" sounds like "Nazarene."

3:10 The ax . . . fire. This means that God is ready to punish his people who do not obey him.

3:12 He will . . . out. This means that Jesus will come to separate the good people from the bad people, saving the good and punishing the bad.

[16]Jesus was baptized and came up out of the water. Heaven opened, and he saw God's Spirit[d] coming down on him like a dove. [17]And a voice spoke from heaven. The voice said, "This is my Son and I love him. I am very pleased with him."

THE TEMPTATION OF JESUS

4 Then the Spirit[d] led Jesus into the desert to be tempted by the devil. [2]Jesus ate nothing for 40 days and nights. After this, he was very hungry. [3]The devil came to Jesus to tempt him. The devil said, "If you are the Son of God, tell these rocks to become bread."

[4]Jesus answered, "It is written in the Scriptures,[d] 'A person does not live only by eating bread. But a person lives by everything the Lord says.'"[n]

[5]Then the devil led Jesus to the holy city of Jerusalem. He put Jesus on a very high place of the Temple.[d] [6]The devil said, "If you are the Son of God, jump off. It is written in the Scriptures,

'He has put his angels in charge of you.
    They will catch you with their
        hands.
And you will not hit your foot on a
    rock.'"   *Psalm 91:11-12*

[7]Jesus answered him, "It also says in the Scriptures, 'Do not test the Lord your God.'"[n]

[8]Then the devil led Jesus to the top of a very high mountain. He showed Jesus all the kingdoms of the world and all the great things that are in those kingdoms. [9]The devil said, "If you will bow down and worship me, I will give you all these things."

[10]Jesus said to the devil, "Go away from me, Satan! It is written in the Scriptures, 'You must worship the Lord your God. Serve only him!'"[n]

[11]So the devil left Jesus. And then some angels came to Jesus and helped him.

JESUS BEGINS WORK IN GALILEE

[12]Jesus heard that John had been put in prison. So Jesus went back to Galilee. [13]He left Nazareth and went and lived in Capernaum, a town near Lake Galilee. Capernaum is in the area near Zebulun and Naphtali. [14]Jesus did this to make true what the prophet[d] Isaiah said:

[15]"Land of Zebulun and land of Naphtali
    are on the way to the sea.
They are along the Jordan River.
    This is Galilee where the non-Jewish
        people live.
[16]These people who live in darkness
    will see a great light.
They live in a place that is very dark.
    But a light will shine on them."
          Isaiah 9:1-2

JESUS CHOOSES SOME FOLLOWERS

[17]From that time Jesus began to preach, saying, "Change your hearts and lives, because the kingdom of heaven is coming soon."

[18]Jesus was walking by Lake Galilee. He saw two brothers, Simon (called Peter) and Simon's brother Andrew. The brothers were fishermen, and they were fishing in the lake with a net. [19]Jesus said, "Come follow me. I will make you fishermen for men." [20]At once Simon and Andrew left their nets and followed him.

[21]Jesus continued walking by Lake Galilee. He saw two other brothers, James and John, the sons of Zebedee. They were in a boat with their father Zebedee, preparing their nets to catch fish. Jesus told them to come with him. [22]At once they left the boat and their father, and they followed Jesus.

JESUS TEACHES AND HEALS PEOPLE

[23]Jesus went everywhere in Galilee. He taught in the synagogues[d] and preached the Good News[d] about the kingdom of heaven. And he healed all the people's

---

4:4 'A person . . . says.' Quotation from Deuteronomy 8:3.
4:7 'Do . . . God.' Quotation from Deuteronomy 6:16.
4:10 'You . . . him!' Quotation from Deuteronomy 6:13.

diseases and sicknesses. [24]The news about Jesus spread all over Syria, and people brought all the sick to him. These sick people were suffering from different kinds of diseases and pain. Some were suffering very great pain, some had demons,[d] some were epileptics,[n] and some were paralyzed. Jesus healed all of them. [25]Many people followed him. They came from Galilee, the Ten Towns,[n] Jerusalem, Judea, and the land across the Jordan River.

JESUS TEACHES THE PEOPLE

5 Jesus saw the crowds who were there. He went up on a hill and sat down. His followers came to him. [2]Jesus taught the people and said:

[3]"Those people who know they have
    great spiritual needs are happy.
The kingdom of heaven belongs to
    them.
[4]Those who are sad now are happy.
    God will comfort them.
[5]Those who are humble are happy.
    The earth will belong to them.
[6]Those who want to do right more than
    anything else are happy.
    God will fully satisfy them.
[7]Those who give mercy to others are
    happy.
    Mercy will be given to them.
[8]Those who are pure in their thinking
    are happy.
    They will be with God.
[9]Those who work to bring peace are
    happy.
    God will call them his sons.
[10]Those who are treated badly for doing
    good are happy.
The kingdom of heaven belongs to
    them.

[11]"People will say bad things about you and hurt you. They will lie and say all kinds of evil things about you because you follow me. But when they do these things to you, you are happy. [12]Rejoice and be glad. You have a great reward waiting for you in heaven. People did the same evil things to the prophets[d] who lived before you.

YOU ARE LIKE SALT AND LIGHT

[13]"You are the salt of the earth. But if the salt loses its salty taste, it cannot be made salty again. It is good for nothing. It must be thrown out for people to walk on.

[14]"You are the light that gives light to the world. A city that is built on a hill cannot be hidden. [15]And people don't hide a light under a bowl. They put the light on a lampstand. Then the light shines for all the people in the house. [16]In the same way, you should be a light for other people. Live so that they will see the good things you do. Live so that they will praise your Father in heaven.

THE IMPORTANCE OF THE LAW

[17]"Don't think that I have come to destroy the law of Moses or the teaching of the prophets.[d] I have not come to destroy their teachings but to do what they said. [18]I tell you the truth. Nothing will disappear from the law until heaven and earth are gone. The law will not lose even the smallest letter or the smallest part of a letter until all has happened. [19]Whoever refuses to obey any command and teaches other people not to obey that command will be the least important in the kingdom of heaven. But whoever obeys the law and teaches other people to obey the law will be great in the kingdom of heaven. [20]I tell you that you must do better than the teachers of the law and the Pharisees.[d] If you are not better than they are, you will not enter the kingdom of heaven.

JESUS TEACHES ABOUT ANGER

[21]"You have heard that it was said to our people long ago, 'You must not

---

4:24 epileptics People with a disease that causes them sometimes to lose control of their bodies, and maybe faint, shake strongly, or not be able to move.
4:25 Ten Towns In Greek, called "Decapolis." It was an area east of Lake Galilee that once had ten main towns.

murder anyone.[n] Anyone who murders another will be judged.' [22]But I tell you, if you are angry with your brother,[n] you will be judged. And if you say bad things to your brother, you will be judged by the Jewish council. And if you call your brother a fool, then you will be in danger of the fire of hell.

[23]"So when you offer your gift to God at the altar, and you remember that your brother has something against you, [24]leave your gift there at the altar. Go and make peace with him. Then come and offer your gift.

[25]"If your enemy is taking you to court, become friends with him quickly. You should do that before you go to court. If you don't become his friend, he might turn you over to the judge. And the judge might give you to a guard to put you in jail. [26]I tell you that you will not leave that jail until you have paid everything you owe.

JESUS TEACHES ABOUT SEXUAL SIN

[27]"You have heard that it was said, 'You must not be guilty of adultery.'[n] [28]But I tell you that if anyone looks at a woman and wants to sin sexually with her, then he has already done that sin with the woman in his mind. [29]If your right eye causes you to sin, then take it out and throw it away. It is better to lose one part of your body than to have your whole body thrown into hell. [30]If your right hand causes you to sin, then cut it off and throw it away. It is better to lose one part of your body than for your whole body to go into hell.

JESUS TEACHES ABOUT DIVORCE

[31]"It was also said, 'Anyone who divorces his wife must give her a written divorce paper.'[n] [32]But I tell you that anyone who divorces his wife is causing his wife to be guilty of adultery.[d] The only reason for a man to divorce his wife is if she has sexual relations with another man. And anyone who marries that divorced woman is guilty of adultery.

MAKE PROMISES CAREFULLY

[33]"You have heard that it was said to our people long ago, 'When you make a promise, don't break your promise. Keep the promises that you make to the Lord.'[n] [34]But I tell you, never make an oath. Don't make an oath using the name of heaven, because heaven is God's throne. [35]Don't make an oath using the name of the earth, because the earth belongs to God. Don't make an oath using the name of Jerusalem, because that is the city of the great King. [36]And don't even say that your own head is proof that you will keep your oath. You cannot make one hair on your head become white or black. [37]Say only 'yes' if you mean 'yes,' and say only 'no' if you mean 'no.' If you must say more than 'yes' or 'no,' it is from the Evil One.

DON'T FIGHT BACK

[38]"You have heard that it was said, 'An eye for an eye, and a tooth for a tooth.'[n] [39]But I tell you, don't stand up against an evil person. If someone slaps you on the right cheek, then turn and let him slap the other cheek too. [40]If someone wants to sue you in court and take your shirt, then let him have your coat too. [41]If a soldier forces you to go with him one mile, then go with him two miles. [42]If a person asks you for something, then give it to him. Don't refuse to give to a person who wants to borrow from you.

5:21 You ... anyone. Quotation from Exodus 20:13; Deuteronomy 5:17.
5:22 brother Some Greek copies continue, "without a reason."
5:27 'You ... adultery.' Quotation from Exodus 20:14; Deuteronomy 5:18.
5:31 'Anyone ... divorce paper.' Quotation from Deuteronomy 24:1.
5:33 'When ... Lord.' Quotation from Leviticus 19:12; Numbers 30:2; Deuteronomy 23:21.
5:38 'An eye ... tooth.' Quotation from Exodus 21:24; Leviticus 24:20; Deuteronomy 19:21.

LOVE ALL PEOPLE

43"You have heard that it was said, 'Love your neighbor[n] and hate your enemies.' 44But I tell you, love your enemies. Pray for those who hurt you.[n] 45If you do this, then you will be true sons of your Father in heaven. Your Father causes the sun to rise on good people and on bad people. Your Father sends rain to those who do good and to those who do wrong. 46If you love only the people who love you, then you will get no reward. Even the tax collectors do that. 47And if you are nice only to your friends, then you are no better than other people. Even people without God are nice to their friends. 48So you must be perfect, just as your Father in heaven is perfect.

JESUS TEACHES ABOUT GIVING

6 "Be careful! When you do good things, don't do them in front of people to be seen by them. If you do that, then you will have no reward from your Father in heaven.

2"When you give to the poor, don't be like the hypocrites.[d] They blow trumpets before they give so that people will see them. They do that in the synagogues[d] and on the streets. They want other people to honor them. I tell you the truth. Those hypocrites already have their full reward. 3So when you give to the poor, give very secretly. Don't let anyone know what you are doing. 4Your giving should be done in secret. Your Father can see what is done in secret, and he will reward you.

JESUS TEACHES ABOUT PRAYER

5"When you pray, don't be like the hypocrites.[d] They love to stand in the synagogues[d] and on the street corners and pray loudly. They want people to see them pray. I tell you the truth. They already have their full reward. 6When you pray, you should go into your room and close the door. Then pray to your Father who cannot be seen. Your Father can see what is done in secret, and he will reward you.

7"And when you pray, don't be like those people who don't know God. They continue saying things that mean nothing. They think that God will hear them because of the many things they say. 8Don't be like them. Your Father knows the things you need before you ask him. 9So when you pray, you should pray like this:

'Our Father in heaven,
we pray that your name will always be
    kept holy.
10We pray that your kingdom will come.
We pray that what you want will be
    done,
    here on earth as it is in heaven.
11Give us the food we need for each day.
12Forgive the sins we have done,
    just as we have forgiven those who
        did wrong to us.
13Do not cause us to be tested;
    but save us from the Evil One.'
    [The kingdom, the power, and the
        glory are yours forever. Amen.][n]
14Yes, if you forgive others for the things they do wrong, then your Father in heaven will also forgive you for the things you do wrong. 15But if you don't forgive the wrongs of others, then your Father in heaven will not forgive the wrong things you do.

JESUS TEACHES ABOUT WORSHIP

16"When you give up eating,[n] don't put on a sad face like the hypocrites.[d] They

---

5:43 **Love your neighbor** Quotation from Leviticus 19:18.
5:44 **you** Some Greek copies continue, "Bless those who curse you, do good to those who hate you." Compare Luke 6:28.
6:13 **The . . . Amen.** Some Greek copies do not contain the bracketed text.
6:16 **give up eating** This is called "fasting." The people would give up eating for a special time of prayer and worship to God. It was also done to show sadness.

make their faces look strange to show people that they are giving up eating. I tell you the truth, those hypocrites already have their full reward. [17]So when you give up eating, comb your hair and wash your face. [18]Then people will not know that you are giving up eating. But your Father, whom you cannot see, will see you. Your Father sees what is done in secret, and he will reward you.

GOD IS MORE IMPORTANT THAN MONEY

[19]"Don't store treasures for yourselves here on earth. Moths and rust will destroy treasures here on earth. And thieves can break into your house and steal the things you have. [20]So store your treasure in heaven. The treasures in heaven cannot be destroyed by moths or rust. And thieves cannot break in and steal that treasure. [21]Your heart will be where your treasure is.

[22]"The eye is a light for the body. If your eyes are good, then your whole body will be full of light. [23]But if your eyes are evil, then your whole body will be full of darkness. And if the only light you have is really darkness, then you have the worst darkness.

[24]"No one can be a slave to two masters. He will hate one master and love the other. Or he will follow one master and refuse to follow the other. So you cannot serve God and money at the same time.

DON'T WORRY

[25]"So I tell you, don't worry about the food you need to live. And don't worry about the clothes you need for your body. Life is more important than food. And the body is more important than clothes. [26]Look at the birds in the air. They don't plant or harvest or store food in barns. But your heavenly Father feeds the birds. And you know that you are worth much more than the birds. [27]You cannot add any time to your life by worrying about it.

[28]"And why do you worry about clothes? Look at the flowers in the field. See how they grow. They don't work or make clothes for themselves. [29]But I tell you that even Solomon with his riches was not dressed as beautifully as one of these flowers. [30]God clothes the grass in the field like that. The grass is living today, but tomorrow it is thrown into the fire to be burned. So you can be even more sure that God will clothe you. Don't have so little faith! [31]Don't worry and say, 'What will we eat?' or 'What will we drink?' or 'What will we wear?' [32]All the people who don't know God keep trying to get these things. And your Father in heaven knows that you need them. [33]The thing you should want most is God's kingdom and doing what God wants. Then all these other things you need will be given to you. [34]So don't worry about tomorrow. Each day has enough trouble of its own. Tomorrow will have its own worries.

BE CAREFUL ABOUT JUDGING OTHERS

7 "Don't judge other people, and you will not be judged. [2]You will be judged in the same way that you judge others. And the forgiveness you give to others will be given to you.

[3]"Why do you notice the little piece of dust that is in your brother's eye, but you don't notice the big piece of wood that is in your own eye? [4]Why do you say to your brother, 'Let me take that little piece of dust out of your eye'? Look at yourself first! You still have that big piece of wood in your own eye. [5]You are a hypocrite![d] First, take the wood out of your own eye. Then you will see clearly enough to take the dust out of your brother's eye.

[6]"Don't give holy things to dogs. Don't throw your pearls before pigs. Pigs will only trample on them. And the dogs will only turn to attack you.

ASK GOD FOR WHAT YOU NEED

[7]"Continue to ask, and God will give to you. Continue to search, and you will

find. Continue to knock, and the door will open for you. [8]Yes, everyone who continues asking will receive. He who continues searching will find. And he who continues knocking will have the door opened for him.

[9]"What would you do if your son asks for bread? Which of you would give him a stone? [10]Or if your son asks for a fish, would you give him a snake? [11]Even though you are bad, you know how to give good gifts to your children. So surely your heavenly Father will give good things to those who ask him.

THE MOST IMPORTANT RULE

[12]"Do for other people the same things you want them to do for you. This is the meaning of the law of Moses and the teaching of the prophets.[d]

THE WAY TO HEAVEN IS HARD

[13]"Enter through the narrow gate. The road that leads to hell is a very easy road. And the gate to hell is very wide. Many people enter through that gate. [14]But the gate that opens the way to true life is very small. And the road to true life is very hard. Only a few people find that road.

PEOPLE KNOW YOU BY YOUR ACTIONS

[15]"Be careful of false prophets.[d] They come to you and look gentle like sheep. But they are really dangerous like wolves. [16]You will know these people because of the things they do. Good things don't come from bad people, just as grapes don't come from thornbushes. And figs don't come from thorny weeds. [17]In the same way, every good tree produces good fruit. And bad trees produce bad fruit. [18]A good tree cannot produce bad fruit. And a bad tree cannot produce good fruit. [19]Every tree that does not produce good fruit is cut down and thrown into the fire. [20]You will know these false prophets by what they produce.

[21]"Not everyone who says 'You are my Lord' will enter the kingdom of heaven. The only people who will enter the kingdom of heaven are those who do the things that my Father in heaven wants. [22]On the last day many people will say to me, 'You are our Lord! We spoke for you. And through you we forced out demons[d] and did many miracles.'[d] [23]Then I will tell them clearly, 'Get away from me, you who do evil. I never knew you.'

TWO KINDS OF PEOPLE

[24]"Everyone who hears these things I say and obeys them is like a wise man. The wise man built his house on rock. [25]It rained hard and the water rose. The winds blew and hit that house. But the house did not fall, because the house was built on rock. [26]But the person who hears the things I teach and does not obey them is like a foolish man. The foolish man built his house on sand. [27]It rained hard, the water rose, and the winds blew and hit that house. And the house fell with a big crash."

[28]When Jesus finished saying these things, the people were amazed at his teaching. [29]Jesus did not teach like their teachers of the law. He taught like a person who had authority.

JESUS HEALS A SICK MAN

8 When Jesus came down from the hill, great crowds followed him. [2]Then a man sick with a harmful skin disease came to Jesus. The man bowed down before him and said, "Lord, you have the power to heal me if you want."

[3]Jesus touched the man and said, "I want to heal you. Be healed!" And immediately the man was healed from his skin disease. [4]Then Jesus said to him, "Don't tell anyone about what happened. But go and show yourself to the priest.[n] And offer the gift that Moses commanded[n] for people who are made

---

8:4 show ... priest The law of Moses said a priest must say when a Jew who had a harmful skin disease was well.
8:4 Moses commanded Read about this in Leviticus 14:1-32.

well. This will show people that you are healed."

JESUS HEALS A SOLDIER'S SERVANT

[5]Jesus went to the city of Capernaum. When he entered the city, an army officer came to Jesus and begged for help. [6]The officer said, "Lord, my servant is at home in bed. He can't move his body and is in much pain."

[7]Jesus said to the officer, "I will go and heal him."

[8]The officer answered, "Lord, I am not good enough for you to come into my house. All you need to do is command that my servant be healed, and he will be healed. [9]I myself am a man under the authority of other men. And I have soldiers under my command. I tell one soldier, 'Go,' and he goes. I tell another soldier, 'Come,' and he comes. I say to my servant, 'Do this,' and my servant obeys me."

[10]When Jesus heard this, he was amazed. He said to those who were with him, "I tell you the truth. This man has more faith than any other person I have found, even in Israel. [11]Many people will come from the east and from the west. They will sit and eat with Abraham, Isaac, and Jacob in the kingdom of heaven. [12]And those people who should have the kingdom will be thrown outside into the darkness. In that place people will cry and grind their teeth with pain."

[13]Then Jesus said to the officer, "Go home. Your servant will be healed just as you believed he would." And at that same time his servant was healed.

JESUS HEALS MANY PEOPLE

[14]Jesus went to Peter's house. There Jesus saw that Peter's mother-in-law was in bed with a high fever. [15]Jesus touched her hand, and the fever left her. Then she stood up and began to serve Jesus.

[16]That evening people brought to Jesus many who had demons.[d] Jesus spoke and the demons left them. Jesus healed all the sick. [17]He did these things to make come true what Isaiah the prophet[d] said:

"He took our suffering on him.
    And he felt our pain for us."
                          Isaiah 53:4

PEOPLE WANT TO FOLLOW JESUS

[18]When Jesus saw the crowd around him, he told his followers to go to the other side of the lake. [19]Then a teacher of the law came to Jesus and said, "Teacher, I will follow you any place you go."

[20]Jesus said to him, "The foxes have holes to live in. The birds have nests to live in. But the Son of Man[d] has no place where he can rest his head."

[21]Another man, one of Jesus' followers, said to Jesus, "Lord, let me go and bury my father first."

[22]But Jesus said to him, "Follow me, and let the people who are dead bury their own dead."

JESUS STOPS A STORM

[23]Jesus got into a boat, and his followers went with him. [24]A very bad storm arose on the lake. The waves covered the boat. But Jesus was sleeping. [25]The followers went to Jesus and woke him. They said, "Lord, save us! We will drown!"

[26]Jesus answered, "Why are you afraid? You don't have enough faith." Then Jesus got up and gave a command to the wind and the sea. The wind stopped, and the sea became very calm.

[27]The men were amazed. They said, "What kind of man is this? Even the wind and the sea obey him!"

JESUS HEALS TWO MEN WITH DEMONS

[28]Jesus arrived at the other side of the lake in the country of the Gadarene[n] people. There, two men came to Jesus. They had demons[d] in them. These men lived in the burial caves. They were so

---

8:28 Gadarene From Gadara, an area southeast of Lake Galilee. The exact location is uncertain and some Greek copies read "Gergesene"; others read "Gerasene."

dangerous that people could not use the road by those caves. [29]The two men came to Jesus and shouted, "What do you want with us, Son of God? Did you come here to punish us before the right time?"

[30]Near that place there was a large herd of pigs feeding. [31]The demons begged Jesus, "If you make us leave these men, please send us into that herd of pigs."

[32]Jesus said to them, "Go!" So the demons left the men and went into the pigs. Then the whole herd of pigs ran down the hill into the lake and were drowned. [33]The men who were caring for the pigs ran away and went into town. They told about all of this and what had happened to the men who had demons. [34]Then the whole town went out to see Jesus. When they saw him, they begged him to leave their area.

JESUS HEALS A PARALYZED MAN

9 Jesus got into a boat and went back across the lake to his own town. [2]Some people brought to Jesus a man who was paralyzed. The man was lying on his mat. Jesus saw that these people had great faith, so he said to the paralyzed man, "Be happy, young man. Your sins are forgiven."

[3]Some of the teachers of the law heard this. They said to themselves, "This man speaks as if he were God—that is blasphemy!"[n]

[4]Jesus knew what they were thinking. So he said, "Why are you thinking evil thoughts? [5]Which is easier: to tell this paralyzed man, 'Your sins are forgiven,' or to tell him, 'Stand up and walk'? [6]But I will prove to you that the Son of Man[d] has power on earth to forgive sins." Then Jesus said to the paralyzed man, "Stand up. Take your mat and go home." [7]And

the man stood up and went home. [8]The people saw this and were amazed. They praised God for giving power like this to men.

JESUS CHOOSES MATTHEW

[9]When Jesus was leaving, he saw a man named Matthew. Matthew was sitting in the tax office. Jesus said to him, "Follow me." And Matthew stood up and followed Jesus.

[10]Jesus had dinner at Matthew's house. Many tax collectors and "sinners" came and ate with Jesus and his followers. [11]The Pharisees[d] saw this and asked Jesus' followers, "Why does your teacher eat with tax collectors and 'sinners'?"

[12]Jesus heard the Pharisees ask this. So he said, "Healthy people don't need a doctor. Only the sick need a doctor. [13]Go and learn what this means: 'I want faithful love more than I want animal sacrifices.'[n] I did not come to invite good people. I came to invite sinners."

JESUS IS NOT LIKE OTHER JEWS

[14]Then the followers of John[n] came to Jesus. They said to Jesus, "We and the Pharisees[d] often give up eating.[n] But your followers don't. Why?"

[15]Jesus answered, "The friends of the bridegroom are not sad while he is with them. But the time will come when the bridegroom will leave them. Then his friends are sad, and they will give up eating.

[16]"When someone sews a patch over a hole in an old coat, he never uses a piece of cloth that is not yet shrunk. If he does, the patch will shrink and pull away from the coat. Then the hole will be worse. [17]Also, people never pour new wine into old leather bags for holding wine. If they do, the old bags will break. The wine will

---

9:3 blasphemy Saying things against God.
9:13 'I want . . . sacrifices.' Quotation from Hosea 6:6.
9:14 John John the Baptist, who preached to people about Christ's coming (Matthew 3, Luke 3).
9:14 give up eating This is called "fasting." The people would give up eating for a special time of prayer and worship to God. It was also done to show sadness.

spill, and the wine bags will be ruined. But people always pour new wine into new wine bags. Then the wine and the wine bags will continue to be good."

JESUS GIVES LIFE TO A DEAD GIRL AND HEALS A SICK WOMAN

¹⁸While Jesus was saying these things, a ruler of the synagogue[d] came to him. The ruler bowed down before Jesus and said, "My daughter has just died. But come and touch her with your hand, and she will live again."

¹⁹So Jesus stood up and went with the ruler. Jesus' followers went too.

²⁰Then a woman who had been bleeding for 12 years came behind Jesus and touched the edge of his coat. ²¹She was thinking, "If I can touch his coat, then I will be healed."

²²Jesus turned and saw the woman. He said, "Be happy, dear woman. You are made well because you believed." And the woman was healed at once.

²³Jesus continued along with the ruler and went into the ruler's house. Jesus saw people there who play music for funerals. And he saw many people there crying. ²⁴Jesus said, "Go away. The girl is not dead. She is only asleep." But the people laughed at Jesus. ²⁵After the crowd had been put outside, Jesus went into the girl's room. He took her hand, and she stood up. ²⁶The news about this spread all around the area.

JESUS HEALS MORE PEOPLE

²⁷When Jesus was leaving there, two blind men followed him. They cried out, "Show kindness to us, Son of David!"[d]

²⁸Jesus went inside, and the blind men went with him. He asked the men, "Do you believe that I can make you see again?"

They answered, "Yes, Lord."

²⁹Then Jesus touched their eyes and said, "You believe that I can make you see again. So this will happen." ³⁰Then the men were able to see. But Jesus warned them very strongly, saying, "Don't tell anyone about this." ³¹But the blind men left and spread the news about Jesus all around that area.

³²When the two men were leaving, some people brought another man to Jesus. This man could not talk because he had a demon[d] in him. ³³Jesus forced the demon to leave the man. Then the man who couldn't talk was able to speak. The crowd was amazed and said, "We have never seen anything like this in Israel."

³⁴But the Pharisees[d] said, "The leader of demons is the one that gives him power to force demons out."

³⁵Jesus traveled through all the towns and villages. He taught in their synagogues[d] and told people the Good News[d] about the kingdom. And he healed all kinds of diseases and sicknesses. ³⁶He saw the crowds of people and felt sorry for them because they were worried and helpless. They were like sheep without a shepherd. ³⁷Jesus said to his followers, "There are many people to harvest, but there are only a few workers to help harvest them. ³⁸God owns the harvest. Pray to him that he will send more workers to help gather his harvest."[n]

JESUS SENDS OUT HIS APOSTLES

10 Jesus called his 12 followers together. He gave them power to drive out evil spirits and to heal every kind of disease and sickness. ²These are the names of the 12 apostles:[d] Simon (also called Peter) and his brother Andrew; James son of Zebedee, and his brother John; ³Philip and Bartholomew; Thomas and Matthew, the tax collector; James son of Alphaeus, and Thaddaeus; ⁴Simon the Zealot[d] and Judas Iscariot. Judas is the one who turned against Jesus.

⁵These 12 men he sent out with the following order: "Don't go to the non-Jewish people. And don't go into any town where

9:37-38 "There are . . . harvest." As a farmer sends workers to harvest the grain, Jesus sends his followers to bring people to God.

the Samaritans*d* live. ⁶But go to the people of Israel. They are like sheep that are lost. ⁷When you go, preach this: 'The kingdom of heaven is coming soon.' ⁸Heal the sick. Give dead people life again. Heal those who have harmful skin diseases. Force demons*d* to leave people. I give you these powers freely. So help other people freely. ⁹Don't carry any money with you—gold or silver or copper. ¹⁰Don't carry a bag. Take for your trip only the clothes and sandals you are wearing. Don't take a walking stick. A worker should be given the things he needs.

¹¹"When you enter a city or town, find some worthy person there and stay in his home until you leave. ¹²When you enter that home, say, 'Peace be with you.' ¹³If the people there welcome you, let your peace stay there. But if they don't welcome you, take back the peace you wished for them. ¹⁴And if a home or town refuses to welcome you or listen to you, then leave that place. Shake its dust off your feet.*n* ¹⁵I tell you the truth. On the Judgment Day it will be worse for that town than for the towns of Sodom and Gomorrah.*n*

JESUS WARNS HIS APOSTLES

¹⁶"Listen! I am sending you out, and you will be like sheep among wolves. So be as smart as snakes. But also be like doves and do nothing wrong. ¹⁷Be careful of people. They will arrest you and take you to court. They will whip you in their synagogues.*d* ¹⁸Because of me you will be taken to stand before governors and kings. You will tell them and the non-Jewish people about me. ¹⁹When you are arrested, don't worry about what to say or how you should say it. At that time you will be given the things to say. ²⁰It will not really be you speaking. The Spirit of your Father will be speaking through you.

²¹"Brothers will turn against their own brothers and give them over to be killed. Fathers will turn against their own children and give them to be killed. Children will fight against their own parents and have them killed. ²²All people will hate you because you follow me. But the person who continues strong until the end will be saved. ²³When you are treated badly in one city, go to another city. I tell you the truth. You will not finish going through all the cities of Israel before the Son of Man*d* comes.

²⁴"A student is not better than his teacher. A servant is not better than his master. ²⁵A student should be satisfied to become like his teacher. A servant should be satisfied to become like his master. If the head of the family is called Beelzebul,*d* then the other members of the family will be called worse names!

FEAR GOD, NOT PEOPLE

²⁶"So don't be afraid of those people. Everything that is hidden will be shown. Everything that is secret will be made known. ²⁷I tell you these things in the dark, but I want you to tell them in the light. I speak these things only to you, but you should tell them to everyone. ²⁸Don't be afraid of people. They can only kill the body. They cannot kill the soul. The only one you should fear is the One who can destroy the body and the soul in hell. ²⁹When birds are sold, two small birds cost only a penny. But not even one of the little birds can die without your Father's knowing it. ³⁰God even knows how many hairs are on your head. ³¹So don't be afraid. You are worth much more than many birds.

TELL PEOPLE ABOUT YOUR FAITH

³²"If anyone stands before other people and says he believes in me, then I will say that he belongs to me. I will say this before my Father in heaven. ³³But if

---

10:14 Shake . . . feet. A warning. It showed that they were finished talking to these people.
10:15 Sodom and Gomorrah Two cities that God destroyed because the people were so evil.

anyone stands before people and says he does not believe in me, then I will say that he does not belong to me. I will say this before my Father in heaven.

³⁴"Don't think that I have come to bring peace to the earth. I did not come to bring peace, but a sword. ³⁵I have come to make this happen:

'A son will be against his father,
    a daughter will be against her
        mother,
a daughter-in-law will be against her
    mother-in-law.
³⁶ A person's enemies will be
        members of his own family.'

Micah 7:6

³⁷"Whoever loves his father or mother more than he loves me is not worthy to be my follower. Whoever loves his son or daughter more than he loves me is not worthy to be my follower. ³⁸Whoever is not willing to die on a cross and follow me is not worthy of me. ³⁹Whoever tries to hold on to his life will give up true life. Whoever gives up his life for me will hold on to true life. ⁴⁰Whoever accepts you also accepts me. And whoever accepts me also accepts the One who sent me. ⁴¹Whoever meets a prophet*ᵈ* and accepts him will receive the reward of a prophet. And whoever accepts a good man because that man is good will receive the reward of a good man. ⁴²Whoever helps one of these little ones because they are my followers will truly get his reward. He will get his reward even if he only gave my follower a cup of cold water."

JESUS AND JOHN THE BAPTIST

11 Jesus finished telling these things to his 12 followers. Then he left there and went to the towns in Galilee to teach and preach.

²John the Baptist*ᵈ* was in prison, but he heard about the things the Christ was doing. So John sent some of his followers to Jesus. ³They asked Jesus, "Are you the man who John said was coming, or should we wait for another one?"

⁴Jesus answered, "Go back to John and tell him about the things you hear and see: ⁵The blind can see. The crippled can walk. People with harmful skin diseases are healed. The deaf can hear. The dead are raised to life. And the Good News*ᵈ* is told to the poor. ⁶The person who does not lose faith because of me is blessed."

⁷As John's followers were leaving, Jesus began talking to the people about John. Jesus said, "What did you go out to the desert to see? A reed*ⁿ* blown by the wind? No. ⁸Really, what did you go out to see? A man dressed in fine clothes? No. Those people who wear fine clothes live in kings' palaces. ⁹So what did you go out to see? A prophet?*ᵈ* Yes, and I tell you, John is more than a prophet. ¹⁰This was written about John in the Scriptures:*ᵈ*

'I will send my messenger ahead
    of you.
He will prepare the way for you.'

Malachi 3:1

¹¹I tell you the truth: John the Baptist is greater than any other man who has ever lived. But even the least important person in the kingdom of heaven is greater than John. ¹²Since the time John the Baptist came until now, the kingdom of heaven has been going forward in strength. People using force have been trying to take the kingdom. ¹³All the prophets and the law of Moses spoke until the time John came. They told about the things that would happen. ¹⁴And if you will believe the things the law and the prophets said, then you will believe that John is Elijah. The law and the prophets said he would come. ¹⁵Let those with ears use them and listen!

¹⁶"What can I say about the people who live today? What are they like? They are like children sitting in the marketplace. One group calls to the other,

---

11:7 reed It means that John was not weak like grass blown by the wind.

[17]"We played music for you, but you did not dance;

we sang a sad song, but you did not cry.'

[18]John came, and he did not eat like other people or drink wine. And people say, 'He has a demon.'[d] [19]The Son of Man[d] came, eating and drinking wine, and people say, 'Look at him! He eats too much and drinks too much. He is a friend of tax collectors and "sinners."' But wisdom is proved to be right by the things it does."

JESUS WARNS UNBELIEVERS

[20]Then Jesus criticized the cities where he did most of his miracles.[d] He criticized them because the people there did not change their lives and stop sinning. [21]Jesus said, "How terrible for you, Korazin! How terrible for you, Bethsaida! I did many miracles in you. If those same miracles had happened in Tyre and Sidon,[n] then the people there would have changed their lives a long time ago. They would have worn rough cloth and put ashes on themselves to show that they had changed. [22]But I tell you, on the Judgment Day it will be worse for you than for Tyre and Sidon. [23]And you, Capernaum,[n] will you be lifted up to heaven? No. You will be thrown down to the depths. I did many miracles in you. If those same miracles had happened in Sodom,[n] its people would have stopped sinning, and it would still be a city today. [24]But I tell you it will be worse for you on the Judgment Day than for Sodom."

JESUS OFFERS REST TO PEOPLE

[25]Then Jesus said, "I thank you, Father, Lord of heaven and earth. I praise you because you have hidden these things from the people who are wise and smart. But you have shown them to those who are like little children. [26]Yes, Father, this is what you really wanted.

[27]"My Father has given me all things. No one knows the Son—only the Father knows the Son. And no one knows the Father—only the Son knows the Father. And the only people who will know about the Father are those whom the Son chooses to tell.

[28]"Come to me, all of you who are tired and have heavy loads. I will give you rest. [29]Accept my work and learn from me. I am gentle and humble in spirit. And you will find rest for your souls. [30]The work that I ask you to accept is easy. The load I give you to carry is not heavy."

JESUS IS LORD OF THE SABBATH

12 About that same time, Jesus was walking through some fields of grain on a Sabbath[d] day. His followers were with him, and they were hungry. So they began to pick the grain and eat it. [2]The Pharisees[d] saw this, and they said to Jesus, "Look! Your followers are doing something that is against the Jewish law to do on the Sabbath day."

[3]Jesus answered, "Have you not read what David did when he and the people with him were hungry? [4]David went into God's house. He and those with him ate the bread that was made holy for God. It was against the law for them to eat that bread. Only the priests were allowed to eat it. [5]And have you not read in the law of Moses that on every Sabbath day the priests in the Temple[d] break this law about the Sabbath day? But the priests are not wrong for doing that. [6]I tell you that there is something here that is greater than the Temple. [7]The Scripture[d] says, 'I want faithful love more than I want animal sacrifices.'[n] You don't really know what those words mean. If you

---

11:21 **Tyre and Sidon** Towns where wicked people lived.
11:21-23 **Korazin . . . Bethsaida . . . Capernaum** Towns by Lake Galilee where Jesus preached to the people.
11:23 **Sodom** City that God destroyed because the people were so evil.
12:7 **'I . . . sacrifices.'** Quotation from Hosea 6:6.

understood them, you would not judge those who have done nothing wrong.

8"The Son of Man[d] is Lord of the Sabbath day."

JESUS HEALS A MAN'S CRIPPLED HAND

9Jesus left there and went into their synagogue.[d] 10In the synagogue, there was a man with a crippled hand. Some Jews there were looking for a reason to accuse Jesus of doing wrong. So they asked him, "Is it right to heal on the Sabbath[d] day?"[n]

11Jesus answered, "If any of you has a sheep, and it falls into a ditch on the Sabbath day, then you will take the sheep and help it out of the ditch. 12Surely a man is more important than a sheep. So the law of Moses allows people to do good things on the Sabbath day."

13Then Jesus said to the man with the crippled hand, "Let me see your hand." The man put his hand out, and the hand became well again, the same as the other hand. 14But the Pharisees[d] left and made plans to kill Jesus.

JESUS IS GOD'S CHOSEN SERVANT

15Jesus knew what the Pharisees[d] were doing, so he left that place. Many people followed him, and he healed all who were sick. 16But Jesus warned the people not to tell who he was. 17He did these things to make come true what Isaiah the prophet[d] had said:

18"Here is my servant whom I have chosen.
    I love him, and I am pleased with him.
    I will put my Spirit[d] in him.
    Then he will tell how I will judge all people fairly.
19He will not argue or shout.
    No one will hear his voice in the streets.
20He will not break a crushed blade of grass.

    He will not put out even a weak flame.
He will continue until he makes fair judgment win the victory.
21   In him will the nations find hope."
                                        Isaiah 42:1-4

JESUS' POWER IS FROM GOD

22Then some people brought a man to Jesus. This man was blind and could not talk, because he had a demon.[d] Jesus healed the man, and the man could talk and see. 23All the people were amazed. They said, "Perhaps this man is the Son of David!"[d]

24The Pharisees[d] heard the people saying this. The Pharisees said, "Jesus uses the power of Beelzebul[d] to force demons out of people. Beelzebul is the ruler of demons."

25Jesus knew what the Pharisees were thinking. So he said to them, "Every kingdom that is fighting against itself will be destroyed. And every city that is divided will fall. And every family that is divided cannot succeed. 26So if Satan forces out his own demons, then Satan is divided, and his kingdom will not continue. 27You say that I use the power of Satan when I force out demons. If that is true, then what power do your people use when they force out demons? So your own people prove that you are wrong. 28But if I use the power of God's Spirit[d] to force out demons, this shows that the kingdom of God has come to you.

29"If anyone wants to enter a strong man's house and steal his things, first he must tie up the strong man. Then he can steal the things from the strong man's house.

30"If anyone is not with me, then he is against me. He who does not work with me is working against me. 31So I tell you, people can be forgiven for every sin they do. And people can be forgiven for every bad thing they say. But if anyone speaks

---

12:10 "Is it right ... day?" It was against Jewish law to work on the Sabbath day.

against the Holy Spirit, then he will not be forgiven. [32]Anyone who says things against the Son of Man[d] can be forgiven. But anyone who says things against the Holy Spirit will not be forgiven. He will not be forgiven now or in the future.

PEOPLE KNOW YOU BY YOUR WORDS

[33]"If you want good fruit, you must make the tree good. If your tree is not good, then it will have bad fruit. A tree is known by the kind of fruit it produces. [34]You snakes! You are evil people! How can you say anything good? The mouth speaks the things that are in the heart. [35]A good person has good things in his heart. And so he speaks the good things that come from his heart. But an evil person has evil in his heart. So he speaks the evil things that come from his heart. [36]And I tell you that people will have to explain about every careless thing they have said. This will happen on the Judgment Day. [37]The words you have said will be used to judge you. Some of your words will prove you right, but some of your words will prove you guilty."

THE LEADERS ASK FOR A MIRACLE

[38]Then some of the Pharisees[d] and teachers of the law answered Jesus. They said, "Teacher, we want to see you work a miracle[d] as a sign."

[39]Jesus answered, "Evil and sinful people are the ones who want to see a miracle for a sign. But no sign will be given to them. The only sign will be what happened to the prophet[d] Jonah. [40]Jonah was in the stomach of the big fish for three days and three nights. In the same way, the Son of Man[d] will be in the grave three days and three nights. [41]And on the Judgment Day the men from Nineveh[n] will stand up with you people who live today. They will show that you are guilty because

when Jonah preached to them, they were sorry and changed their lives. And I tell you that someone greater than Jonah is here! [42]On the Judgment Day, the Queen of the South[n] will stand up with you people who live today. She will show that you are guilty because she came from far away to listen to Solomon's wise teaching. And I tell you that someone greater than Solomon is here!

PEOPLE TODAY ARE FULL OF EVIL

[43]"When an evil spirit comes out of a man, it travels through dry places looking for a place to rest. But it finds no place to rest. [44]So the spirit says, 'I will go back to the home I left.' When the spirit comes back to the man, the spirit finds the home still empty. The home is swept clean and made neat. [45]Then the evil spirit goes out and brings seven other spirits even more evil than it is. Then all the spirits go into the man and live there. And that man has even more trouble than he had before. It is the same way with the evil people who live today."

JESUS' TRUE FAMILY

[46]While Jesus was talking to the people, his mother and brothers stood outside. They wanted to talk to him. [47]Someone told Jesus, "Your mother and brothers are waiting for you outside. They want to talk to you."[n]

[48]He answered, "Who is my mother? Who are my brothers?" [49]Then he pointed to his followers and said, "See! These people are my mother and my brothers. [50]My true brothers and sisters and mother are those who do the things that my Father in heaven wants."

A STORY ABOUT PLANTING SEED

13 That same day Jesus went out of the house and sat by the lake. [2]Large crowds gathered around him. So

---

12:41 **Nineveh** The city where Jonah preached to warn the people. Read Jonah 3.
12:42 **Queen of the South** The Queen of Sheba. She traveled 1,000 miles to learn God's wisdom from Solomon. Read 1 Kings 10:1-13.
12:47 **Someone . . . you.** Some Greek copies do not have verse 47.

Jesus got into a boat and sat, while the people stayed on the shore. [3]Then Jesus used stories to teach them many things. He said: "A farmer went out to plant his seed. [4]While he was planting, some seed fell by the road. The birds came and ate all that seed. [5]Some seed fell on rocky ground, where there wasn't enough dirt. That seed grew very fast, because the ground was not deep. [6]But when the sun rose, the plants dried up because they did not have deep roots. [7]Some other seed fell among thorny weeds. The weeds grew and choked the good plants. [8]Some other seed fell on good ground where it grew and became grain. Some plants made 100 times more grain. Other plants made 60 times more grain, and some made 30 times more grain. [9]Let those with ears use them and listen!"

WHY JESUS USED STORIES TO TEACH

[10]The followers came to Jesus and asked, "Why do you use stories to teach the people?"

[11]Jesus answered, "Only you can know the secret truths about the kingdom of heaven. Other people cannot know these secret truths. [12]The person who has something will be given more. And he will have all he needs. But the person who does not have much, even what he has will be taken from him. [13]This is why I use stories to teach the people: They see, but they don't really see. They hear, but they don't really understand. [14]So they show that the things Isaiah said about them are true:

'You will listen and listen, but you will
    not understand.
You will look and look, but you will
    not learn.
[15]For these people have become
    stubborn.
They do not hear with their ears.
And they have closed their eyes.

Otherwise they might really understand
    what they see with their eyes
    and hear with their ears.
They might really understand in their
    minds.
If they did this, they would come
    back to me and be forgiven.'
                                    Isaiah 6:9-10

[16]But you are blessed. You understand the things you see with your eyes. And you understand the things you hear with your ears. [17]I tell you the truth. Many prophets[d] and good people wanted to see the things that you now see. But they did not see them. And many prophets and good people wanted to hear the things that you now hear. But they did not hear them.

JESUS EXPLAINS THE SEED STORY

[18]"So listen to the meaning of that story about the farmer. [19]What is the seed that fell by the road? That seed is like the person who hears the teaching about the kingdom but does not understand it. The Evil One comes and takes away the things that were planted in that person's heart. [20]And what is the seed that fell on rocky ground? That seed is like the person who hears the teaching and quickly accepts it with joy. [21]But he does not let the teaching go deep into his life. He keeps it only a short time. When trouble or persecution comes because of the teaching he accepted, then he quickly gives up. [22]And what is the seed that fell among the thorny weeds? That seed is like the person who hears the teaching but lets worries about this life and love of money stop that teaching from growing. So the teaching does not produce fruit[n] in that person's life. [23]But what is the seed that fell on the good ground? That seed is like the person who hears the teaching and understands it. That person grows and produces fruit, sometimes 100 times more, sometimes 60 times more, and sometimes 30 times more."

13:22 produce fruit To produce fruit means to have in your life the good things God wants.

A STORY ABOUT WHEAT AND WEEDS

²⁴Then Jesus told them another story. He said, "The kingdom of heaven is like a man who planted good seed in his field. ²⁵That night, when everyone was asleep, his enemy came and planted weeds among the wheat. Then the enemy went away. ²⁶Later, the wheat grew and heads of grain grew on the wheat plants. But at the same time the weeds also grew. ²⁷Then the man's servants came to him and said, 'You planted good seed in your field. Where did the weeds come from?' ²⁸The man answered, 'An enemy planted weeds.' The servants asked, 'Do you want us to pull up the weeds?' ²⁹The man answered, 'No, because when you pull up the weeds, you might also pull up the wheat. ³⁰Let the weeds and the wheat grow together until the harvest time. At harvest time I will tell the workers this: First gather the weeds and tie them together to be burned. Then gather the wheat and bring it to my barn.'"

STORIES OF MUSTARD SEED AND YEAST

³¹Then Jesus told another story: "The kingdom of heaven is like a mustard seed. A man plants the seed in his field. ³²That seed is the smallest of all seeds. But when it grows, it is one of the largest garden plants. It becomes a tree, big enough for the wild birds to come and make nests in its branches."

³³Then Jesus told another story: "The kingdom of heaven is like yeast that a woman mixes into a big bowl of flour. The yeast makes all the dough rise."

³⁴Jesus used stories to tell all these things to the people. He always used stories to teach people. ³⁵This is as the prophet*ᵈ* said:

"I will speak using stories;
    I will tell things that have been
        secret since the world was made."
                            Psalm 78:2

JESUS EXPLAINS ABOUT THE WHEAT AND WEEDS

³⁶Then Jesus left the crowd and went into the house. His followers came to him and said, "Explain to us the meaning of the story about the weeds in the field."

³⁷Jesus answered, "The man who planted the good seed in the field is the Son of Man.*ᵈ* ³⁸The field is the world. And the good seed are all of God's children in the kingdom. The weeds are those people who belong to the Evil One. ³⁹And the enemy who planted the bad seed is the devil. The harvest time is the end of the age. And the workers who gather are God's angels.

⁴⁰"The weeds are pulled up and burned in the fire. It will be this way at the end of the age. ⁴¹The Son of Man will send out his angels. They will gather out of his kingdom all who cause sin and all who do evil. ⁴²The angels will throw them into the blazing furnace. There the people will cry and grind their teeth with pain. ⁴³Then the good people will shine like the sun in the kingdom of their Father. Let those with ears use them and listen!

STORIES OF A TREASURE AND A PEARL

⁴⁴"The kingdom of heaven is like a treasure hidden in a field. One day a man found the treasure, and then he hid it in the field again. The man was very happy to find the treasure. He went and sold everything that he owned to buy that field.

⁴⁵"Also, the kingdom of heaven is like a man looking for fine pearls. ⁴⁶One day he found a very valuable pearl. The man went and sold everything he had to buy that pearl.

A STORY OF A FISHING NET

⁴⁷"Also, the kingdom of heaven is like a net that was put into the lake. The net caught many different kinds of fish. ⁴⁸When it was full, the fishermen pulled the net to the shore. They sat down and put all the good fish in baskets. Then they threw away the bad fish. ⁴⁹It will be this way at the end of the age. The angels will come and separate the evil people from the good people. ⁵⁰The angels will throw the evil people into the blazing

furnace. In that place the people will cry and grind their teeth with pain."

[51]Jesus asked his followers, "Do you understand all these things?"

They answered, "Yes, we understand."

[52]Then Jesus said to them, "So every teacher of the law who has been taught about the kingdom of heaven is like the owner of a house. He has both new things and old things saved in his house. And he brings out both those new things and old things."

JESUS GOES TO HIS HOMETOWN

[53]When Jesus finished teaching with these stories, he left there. [54]He went to the town where he grew up. He taught the people in the synagogue,[d] and they were amazed. They said, "Where did this man get this wisdom and this power to do miracles?[d] [55]He is only the son of the carpenter. And his mother is Mary. His brothers are James, Joseph, Simon and Judas. [56]And all his sisters are here with us. So where does this man get all these things?" [57]And the people refused to accept Jesus.

But Jesus said to them, "A prophet[d] is honored everywhere except in his own town or in his own home."

[58]The people there did not believe in Jesus. So Jesus did not do many miracles there.

HOW JOHN THE BAPTIST WAS KILLED

14 At that time Herod, the ruler of Galilee, heard the reports about Jesus. [2]So Herod said to his servants, "Jesus is really John the Baptist.[d] He has risen from death. That is why he is able to do these miracles."[d]

[3]Sometime before this, Herod had arrested John, tied him up, and put him into prison. Herod did this because of Herodias. Herodias was the wife of Philip, Herod's brother. [4]Herod arrested John because he told Herod: "It is not right for you to have Herodias." [5]Herod wanted to kill John, but he was afraid of the

people. They believed that John was a prophet.[d]

[6]On Herod's birthday, the daughter of Herodias danced for Herod and his guests. Herod was very pleased with her, [7]so he promised he would give her anything she wanted. [8]Herodias told her daughter what to ask for. So she said to Herod, "Give me the head of John the Baptist here on a platter." [9]King Herod was very sad. But he had promised to give her anything she wanted, and the people eating with him had heard his promise. So Herod ordered that what she asked for be done. [10]He sent men to the prison to cut off John's head. [11]And the men brought John's head on a platter and gave it to the girl. She took it to her mother, Herodias. [12]John's followers came and got his body and buried it. Then they went and told Jesus what happened.

MORE THAN 5,000 PEOPLE FED

[13]When Jesus heard what happened to John, Jesus left in a boat. He went to a lonely place by himself. But when the crowds heard about it, they followed him on foot from the towns. [14]When Jesus arrived, he saw a large crowd. He felt sorry for them and healed those who were sick.

[15]Late that afternoon, his followers came to Jesus and said, "No one lives in this place. And it is already late. Send the people away so they can go to the towns and buy food for themselves."

[16]Jesus answered, "They don't need to go away. You give them some food to eat."

[17]The followers answered, "But we have only five loaves of bread and two fish."

[18]Jesus said, "Bring the bread and the fish to me." [19]Then he told the people to sit down on the grass. He took the five loaves of bread and the two fish. Then he looked to heaven and thanked God for the food. Jesus divided the loaves of bread. He gave them to his followers, and they gave the bread to the people. [20]All the people ate and were satisfied. After they finished eating, the followers filled 12

baskets with the pieces of food that were not eaten. [21]There were about 5,000 men there who ate, as well as women and children.

JESUS WALKS ON THE WATER

[22]Then Jesus made his followers get into the boat. He told them to go ahead of him to the other side of the lake. Jesus stayed there to tell the people they could go home. [23]After he said good-bye to them, he went alone up into the hills to pray. It was late, and Jesus was there alone. [24]By this time, the boat was already far away on the lake. The boat was having trouble because of the waves, and the wind was blowing against it.

[25]Between three and six o'clock in the morning, Jesus' followers were still in the boat. Jesus came to them. He was walking on the water. [26]When the followers saw him walking on the water, they were afraid. They said, "It's a ghost!" and cried out in fear.

[27]But Jesus quickly spoke to them. He said, "Have courage! It is I! Don't be afraid."

[28]Peter said, "Lord, if that is really you, then tell me to come to you on the water."

[29]Jesus said, "Come."

And Peter left the boat and walked on the water to Jesus. [30]But when Peter saw the wind and the waves, he became afraid and began to sink. He shouted, "Lord, save me!"

[31]Then Jesus reached out his hand and caught Peter. Jesus said, "Your faith is small. Why did you doubt?"

[32]After Peter and Jesus were in the boat, the wind became calm. [33]Then those who were in the boat worshiped Jesus and said, "Truly you are the Son of God!"

[34]After they crossed the lake, they came to the shore at Gennesaret. [35]The people there saw Jesus and knew who he was. So they told people all around there that Jesus had come. They brought all their sick to him. [36]They begged Jesus to let them just touch the edge of his coat to be healed. And all the sick people who touched it were healed.

OBEY GOD'S LAW NOT MEN'S

15 Then some Pharisees[d] and teachers of the law came to Jesus from Jerusalem. They asked him, [2]"Why do your followers not obey the rules given to us by the great people who lived before us? Your followers don't wash their hands before they eat!"

[3]Jesus answered, "And why do you refuse to obey God's command so that you can follow those rules you have? [4]God said, 'Honor your father and mother.'[n] And God also said, 'Anyone who says cruel things to his father or mother must be put to death.'[n] [5]But you say that a person can tell his father or mother, 'I have something I could use to help you. But I will not use it for you. I will give it to God.' [6]You teach that person not to honor his father. You teach that it is not important to do what God said. You think that it is more important to follow the rules you have. [7]You are hypocrites![d] Isaiah was right when he spoke about you:

[8]"These people show honor to me with
　　words.
But their hearts are far from me.
[9]Their worship of me is worthless.
　The things they teach are nothing
　　but human rules they have
　　　memorized.'"   *Isaiah 29:13*

[10]Jesus called the crowd to him. He said, "Listen and understand what I am saying. [11]It is not what a person puts into his mouth that makes him unclean.[d] It is what comes out of his mouth that makes him unclean."

[12]Then his followers came to Jesus and asked, "Do you know that the Pharisees are angry because of what you said?"

15:4 'Honor ... mother.' Quotation from Exodus 20:12; Deuteronomy 5:16.
15:4 'Anyone ... death.' Quotation from Exodus 21:17.

[13]Jesus answered, "Every plant that my Father in heaven has not planted himself will be pulled up by the roots. [14]Stay away from the Pharisees. They are blind leaders.[n] And if a blind man leads another blind man, then both men will fall into a ditch."

[15]Peter said, "Explain the story to us."

[16]Jesus said, "You still have trouble understanding? [17]Surely you know that all the food that enters the mouth goes into the stomach. Then that food goes out of the body. [18]But what a person says with his mouth comes from the way he thinks. And these are the things that make him unclean. [19]Out of his mind come evil thoughts, murder, adultery,[d] sexual sins, stealing, lying, and saying bad things against other people. [20]These things make a person unclean. But eating with unwashed hands does not make him unclean."

JESUS HELPS A NON-JEWISH WOMAN

[21]Jesus left that place and went to the area of Tyre and Sidon. [22]A Canaanite woman from that area came to Jesus. The woman cried out, "Lord, Son of David,[d] please help me! My daughter has a demon,[d] and she is suffering very much."

[23]But Jesus did not answer the woman. So the followers came to Jesus and begged him, "Tell the woman to go away. She is following us and shouting."

[24]Jesus answered, "God sent me only to the lost sheep, the people of Israel."

[25]Then the woman came to Jesus again. She bowed before him and said, "Lord, help me!"

[26]Jesus answered, "It is not right to take the children's bread and give it to the dogs."

[27]The woman said, "Yes, Lord, but even the dogs eat the pieces of food that fall from their masters' table."

[28]Then Jesus answered, "Woman, you have great faith! I will do what you asked

me to do." And at that moment the woman's daughter was healed.

JESUS HEALS MANY PEOPLE

[29]Then Jesus left that place and went to the shore of Lake Galilee. He went up on a hill and sat there.

[30]Great crowds came to Jesus. They brought their sick with them: the lame, the blind, the crippled, the dumb and many others. They put them at Jesus' feet, and he healed them. [31]The crowd was amazed when they saw that people who could not speak were able to speak again. The crippled were made strong again. Those who could not walk were able to walk again. The blind were able to see again. And they praised the God of Israel for this.

MORE THAN 4,000 PEOPLE FED

[32]Jesus called his followers to him and said, "I feel sorry for these people. They have been with me three days, and now they have nothing to eat. I don't want to send them away hungry. They might faint while going home."

[33]His followers asked him, "Where can we get enough bread to feed all these people? We are far away from any town."

[34]Jesus asked, "How many loaves of bread do you have?"

They answered, "We have seven loaves and a few small fish."

[35]Jesus told the people to sit on the ground. [36]He took the seven loaves of bread and the fish and gave thanks to God for the food. Then Jesus divided the food and gave it to his followers. They gave the food to the people. [37]All the people ate and were satisfied. After this, the followers filled seven baskets with the pieces of food that were not eaten. [38]There were about 4,000 men there who ate, besides women and children. [39]After they ate, Jesus told the people to go home. He got into the boat and went to the area of Magadan.

15:14 **leaders** Some Greek copies continue, "of blind people."

THE LEADERS ASK FOR A MIRACLE

16 The Pharisees[d] and Sadducees[d] came to Jesus. They wanted to trap him. So they asked him to show them a miracle[d] to prove that he was from God.

[2]Jesus answered,[n] "When you see the sunset, you know what the weather will be. If the sky is red, then you say we will have good weather. [3]And in the morning if the sky is dark and red, then you say that it will be a rainy day. You see these signs in the sky, and you know what they mean. In the same way, you see the things that are happening now. But you don't know their meaning. [4]Evil and sinful people ask for a miracle as a sign. But they will have no sign—only the sign of Jonah."[n] Then Jesus left them and went away.

GUARD AGAINST WRONG TEACHINGS

[5]Jesus and his followers went across the lake. But the followers forgot to bring bread. [6]Jesus said to them, "Be careful! Guard against the yeast of the Pharisees[d] and the Sadducees."[d]

[7]The followers discussed the meaning of this. They said, "Did Jesus say this because we forgot to bring bread?"

[8]Jesus knew that they were talking about this. So he asked them, "Why are you talking about not having bread? Your faith is small. [9]You still don't understand? Remember the five loaves of bread that fed the 5,000 people? And remember that you filled many baskets with bread after the people finished eating? [10]And remember the seven loaves of bread that fed the 4,000 people? Remember that you filled many baskets then also? [11]So I was not talking to you about bread. Why don't you understand that? I am telling you to be careful and guard against the yeast of the Pharisees and the Sadducees." [12]Then the followers understood what Jesus meant. He was not telling them to guard against the yeast used in bread. He was telling them to guard against the teaching of the Pharisees and the Sadducees.

PETER SAYS JESUS IS THE CHRIST

[13]Jesus went to the area of Caesarea Philippi. He said to his followers, "I am the Son of Man.[d] Who do the people say I am?"

[14]They answered, "Some people say you are John the Baptist.[d] Others say you are Elijah. And others say that you are Jeremiah or one of the prophets."[d]

[15]Then Jesus asked them, "And who do you say I am?"

[16]Simon Peter answered, "You are the Christ,[d] the Son of the living God."

[17]Jesus answered, "You are blessed, Simon son of Jonah. No person taught you that. My Father in heaven showed you who I am. [18]So I tell you, you are Peter.[n] And I will build my church on this rock. The power of death will not be able to defeat my church. [19]I will give you the keys of the kingdom of heaven. The things you don't allow on earth will be the things that God does not allow. The things you allow on earth will be the things that God allows." [20]Then Jesus warned his followers not to tell anyone that he was the Christ.

JESUS SAYS THAT HE MUST DIE

[21]From that time on Jesus began telling his followers that he must go to Jerusalem. He explained that the Jewish elders, the leading priests, and the teachers of the law would make him suffer many things. And he told them that he must be killed. Then, on the third day, he would be raised from death.

[22]Peter took Jesus aside and began to criticize him. Peter said, "God save you

---

16:2 answered Some Greek copies do not have the rest of verse 2 and verse 3.
16:4 sign of Jonah Jonah's three days in the big fish are like Jesus' three days in the tomb. The story about Jonah is in the book of Jonah.
16:18 Peter The Greek name "Peter," like the Aramaic name "Cephas," means "rock."

from those things, Lord! Those things will never happen to you!"

²³Then Jesus said to Peter, "Go away from me, Satan!ⁿ You are not helping me! You don't care about the things of God. You care only about things that men think are important."

²⁴Then Jesus said to his followers, "If anyone wants to follow me, he must say 'no' to the things he wants. He must be willing even to die on a cross, and he must follow me. ²⁵Whoever wants to save his life will give up true life. And whoever gives up his life for me will have true life. ²⁶It is worth nothing for a man to have the whole world if he loses his soul. He could never pay enough to buy back his soul. ²⁷The Son of Manᵈ will come again with his Father's glory and with his angels. At that time, he will reward everyone for what he has done. ²⁸I tell you the truth. There are some people standing here who, before they die, will see the Son of Man coming with his kingdom."

JESUS WITH MOSES AND ELIJAH

17 Six days later, Jesus took Peter, James, and John the brother of James up on a high mountain. They were all alone there. ²While they watched, Jesus was changed. His face became bright like the sun. And his clothes became white as light. ³Then two men were there, talking with him. The men were Moses and Elijah.ⁿ

⁴Peter said to Jesus, "Lord, it is good that we are here. If you want, I will put three tents here—one for you, one for Moses, and one for Elijah."

⁵While Peter was talking, a bright cloud covered them. A voice came from the cloud. The voice said, "This is my Son and I love him. I am very pleased with him. Obey him!"

⁶The followers with Jesus heard the voice. They were so frightened that they fell to the ground. ⁷But Jesus went to them and touched them. He said, "Stand up. Don't be afraid." ⁸When the followers looked up, they saw Jesus was now alone.

⁹When Jesus and the followers were coming down the mountain, Jesus commanded them, "Don't tell anyone about the things you saw on the mountain. Wait until the Son of Manᵈ has been raised from death. Then you may tell."

¹⁰The followers asked Jesus, "Why do the teachers of the law say that Elijah must come first, before the Christᵈ comes?"

¹¹Jesus answered, "They are right to say that Elijah is coming. And it is true that Elijah will make everything the way it should be. ¹²But I tell you, Elijah has already come. People did not know who he was. They did to him everything they wanted to do. It will be the same with the Son of Man. Those same people will make the Son of Man suffer." ¹³Then the followers understood that Jesus was talking about John the Baptist.ᵈ

JESUS HEALS A SICK BOY

¹⁴Jesus and his followers went back to the crowd. A man came to Jesus and bowed before him. ¹⁵The man said, "Lord, please help my son. He has epilepsyⁿ and is suffering very much. He often falls into the fire or into the water. ¹⁶I brought him to your followers, but they could not cure him."

¹⁷Jesus answered, "You people have no faith. Your lives are all wrong. How long must I stay with you? How long must I continue to be patient with you? Bring the boy here." ¹⁸Jesus gave a strong command to the demonᵈ inside the boy. Then the demon came out, and the boy was healed.

16:23 **Satan** Name for the devil, meaning "the enemy." Jesus means that Peter was talking like Satan.
17:3 **Moses and Elijah** Two of the most important Jewish leaders in the past.
17:15 **epilepsy** A disease that causes a person sometimes to lose control of his body, and maybe faint, shake strongly, or not be able to move.

[19]The followers came to Jesus when he was alone. They said, "Why couldn't we force the demon out?"

[20]Jesus answered, "You were not able to drive out the demon because your faith is too small. I tell you the truth. If your faith is as big as a mustard seed,[n] you can say to this mountain, 'Move from here to there.' And the mountain will move. All things will be possible for you." [21][That kind of spirit comes out only if you use prayer and give up eating.][n]

JESUS TALKS ABOUT HIS DEATH

[22]Later, the followers met together in Galilee. Jesus said to them, "The Son of Man[d] will be given into the control of some men. [23]They will kill him, but on the third day he will be raised from death." And the followers were filled with sadness.

JESUS TALKS ABOUT PAYING TAXES

[24]Jesus and his followers went to Capernaum. There some men came to Peter. They were the men who collected the Temple[d] tax. They asked, "Does your teacher pay the Temple tax?"

[25]Peter answered, "Yes, Jesus pays the tax."

Peter went into the house where Jesus was. Before Peter could speak, Jesus said to him, "The kings on the earth collect different kinds of taxes. But who are the people who pay the taxes? Are they the king's children? Or do others pay the taxes? What do you think?"

[26]Peter answered, "Other people pay the taxes."

Jesus said to Peter, "Then the children of the king don't have to pay taxes. [27]But we don't want to make these tax collectors angry. So go to the lake and fish. After you catch the first fish, open its mouth. Inside its mouth you will find a coin. Take that coin and give it to the tax collectors. That will pay the tax for you and me."

WHO IS THE GREATEST?

18 At that time the followers came to Jesus and asked, "Who is greatest in the kingdom of heaven?"

[2]Jesus called a little child to him. He stood the child before the followers. [3]Then he said, "I tell you the truth. You must change and become like little children. If you don't do this, you will never enter the kingdom of heaven. [4]The greatest person in the kingdom of heaven is the one who makes himself humble like this child.

[5]"Whoever accepts a little child in my name accepts me. [6]If one of these little children believes in me, and someone causes that child to sin, then it will be very bad for that person. It would be better for him to have a large stone tied around his neck and be drowned in the sea. [7]How terrible for the people of the world because of the things that cause them to sin. Such things will happen. But how terrible for the one who causes them to happen. [8]If your hand or your foot causes you to sin, cut it off and throw it away. It is better for you to have only part of your body but have life forever. That is much better than to have two hands and two feet but be thrown into the fire that burns forever. [9]If your eye causes you to sin, take it out and throw it away. It is better for you to have only one eye but have life forever. That is much better than to have two eyes but be thrown into the fire of hell.

A LOST SHEEP

[10]"Be careful. Don't think these little children are worth nothing. I tell you that they have angels in heaven who are always with my Father in heaven. [11][The Son of Man came to save lost people.][n]

[12]"If a man has 100 sheep, but 1 of the sheep gets lost, he will leave the other 99 sheep on the hill. He will go to look for

---

17:20 mustard seed This seed is very small, but the plant grows taller than a man.
17:21 That ... eating. Some Greek copies do not contain the bracketed text.
18:11 The ... people. Some Greek copies do not contain the bracketed text.

the lost sheep. [13]And if he finds it, he is happier about that 1 sheep than about the 99 that were never lost. I tell you the truth. [14]In the same way, your Father in heaven does not want any of these little children to be lost.

WHEN A PERSON SINS AGAINST YOU

[15]"If your brother sins against you,[n] go and tell him what he did wrong. Do this in private. If he listens to you, then you have helped him to be your brother again. [16]But if he refuses to listen, then go to him again and take one or two other people with you. 'Every case may be proved by two or three witnesses.'[n] [17]If he refuses to listen to them, then tell it to the church. If he refuses to listen to the church, then treat him as you would one who does not believe in God. Treat him as if he were a tax collector.

[18]"I tell you the truth. The things you don't allow on earth will be the things God does not allow. The things you allow on earth will be the things that God allows.

[19]"Also, I tell you that if two of you on earth agree about something, then you can pray for it. And the thing you ask for will be done for you by my Father in heaven. [20]This is true because if two or three people come together in my name, I am there with them."

AN UNFORGIVING SERVANT

[21]Then Peter came to Jesus and asked, "Lord, when my brother sins against me, how many times must I forgive him? Should I forgive him as many as 7 times?"

[22]Jesus answered, "I tell you, you must forgive him more than 7 times. You must forgive him even if he does wrong to you 70 times 7.

[23]"The kingdom of heaven is like a king who decided to collect the money his servants owed him. [24]So the king began to collect his money. One servant owed him several million dollars. [25]But the servant did not have enough money to pay his master, the king. So the master ordered that everything the servant owned should be sold, even the servant's wife and children. The money would be used to pay the king what the servant owed.

[26]"But the servant fell on his knees and begged, 'Be patient with me. I will pay you everything I owe.' [27]The master felt sorry for his servant. So the master told the servant he did not have to pay. He let the servant go free.

[28]"Later, that same servant found another servant who owed him a few dollars. The servant grabbed the other servant around the neck and said, 'Pay me the money you owe me!'

[29]"The other servant fell on his knees and begged him, 'Be patient with me. I will pay you everything I owe.'

[30]"But the first servant refused to be patient. He threw the other servant into prison until he could pay everything he owed. [31]All the other servants saw what happened. They were very sorry. So they went and told their master all that had happened.

[32]"Then the master called his servant in and said, 'You evil servant! You begged me to forget what you owed. So I told you that you did not have to pay anything. [33]I had mercy on you. You should have had the same mercy on that other servant.' [34]The master was very angry, and he put the servant in prison to be punished. The servant had to stay in prison until he could pay everything he owed.

[35]"This king did what my heavenly Father will do to you if you do not forgive your brother from your heart."

JESUS TEACHES ABOUT DIVORCE

19 After Jesus said all these things, he left Galilee. He went into the area of Judea on the other side of the Jordan River. [2]Large crowds followed Jesus, and he healed them there.

18:15 **against you** Some Greek copies do not have "against you."
18:16 **'Every . . . witnesses.'** Quotation from Deuteronomy 19:15.

[3]Some Pharisees[d] came to Jesus and tried to trick him. They asked, "Is it right for a man to divorce his wife for any reason he chooses?"

[4]Jesus answered, "Surely you have read in the Scriptures:[d] When God made the world, 'he made them male and female.'[n] [5]And God said, 'So a man will leave his father and mother and be united with his wife. And the two people will become one body.'[n] [6]So the two are not two, but one. God joined the two people together. No person should separate them."

[7]The Pharisees asked, "Why then did Moses give a command for a man to divorce his wife by giving her divorce papers?"

[8]Jesus answered, "Moses allowed you to divorce your wives because you refused to accept God's teaching. But divorce was not allowed in the beginning. [9]I tell you that anyone who divorces his wife and marries another woman is guilty of adultery.[nd] The only reason for a man to divorce and marry again is if his first wife has sexual relations with another man."

[10]The followers said to him, "If that is the only reason a man can divorce his wife, then it is better not to marry."

[11]Jesus answered, "Not everyone can accept this truth about marriage. But God has made some able to accept it. [12]There are different reasons why some men cannot marry. Some men were born without the ability to become fathers. Others were made that way later in life by other people. And other men have given up marriage because of the kingdom of heaven. But the person who can marry should accept this teaching about marriage."[n]

JESUS WELCOMES CHILDREN

[13]Then the people brought their little children to Jesus so that he could put his hands on them[n] and pray for them. When his followers saw this, they told the people to stop bringing their children to Jesus. [14]But Jesus said, "Let the little children come to me. Don't stop them, because the kingdom of heaven belongs to people who are like these children." [15]After Jesus put his hands on the children, he left there.

A RICH YOUNG MAN'S QUESTION

[16]A man came to Jesus and asked, "Teacher, what good thing must I do to have life forever?"

[17]Jesus answered, "Why do you ask me about what is good? Only God is good. But if you want to have life forever, obey the commands."

[18]The man asked, "Which commands?"

Jesus answered, "'You must not murder anyone. You must not be guilty of adultery.[d] You must not steal. You must not tell lies about your neighbor in court. [19]Honor your father and mother.'[n] Love your neighbor as you love yourself.'"[n]

[20]The young man said, "I have obeyed all these things. What else do I need to do?"

[21]Jesus answered, "If you want to be perfect, then go and sell all the things you own. Give the money to the poor. If you do this, you will have a treasure in heaven. Then come and follow me!"

[22]But when the young man heard this, he became very sad because he was very rich. So he left Jesus.

[23]Then Jesus said to his followers, "I tell you the truth. It will be very hard for

---

19:4 'he made . . . female.' Quotation from Genesis 1:27 or 5:2.
19:5 'So . . . body.' Quotation from Genesis 2:24.
19:9 adultery Some Greek copies continue, "And anyone who marries a divorced woman is guilty of adultery." Compare Matthew 5:32.
19:12 But . . . marriage. This may also mean, "The person who can accept this teaching about not marrying should accept it."
19:13 put his hands on them Showing that Jesus gave special blessings to these children.
19:18-19 'You . . . mother.' Quotation from Exodus 20:12-16; Deuteronomy 5:16-20.
19:19 'Love . . . yourself.' Quotation from Leviticus 19:18.

a rich person to enter the kingdom of heaven. [24]Yes, I tell you that it is easier for a camel to go through the eye of a needle than for a rich person to enter the kingdom of God."

[25]When the followers heard this, they were very surprised. They asked, "Then who can be saved?"

[26]Jesus looked at them and said, "For men this is impossible. But for God all things are possible."

[27]Peter said to Jesus, "We left everything we had and followed you. So what will we have?"

[28]Jesus said to them, "I tell you the truth. When the new age comes, the Son of Man[d] will sit on his great throne. And all of you who followed me will also sit on 12 thrones. And you will judge the 12 tribes[d] of Israel. [29]And everyone who has left houses, brothers, sisters, father, mother,[n] children, or farms to follow me will get much more than he left. And he will have life forever. [30]Many who are first now will be last in the future. And many who are last now will be first in the future.

A STORY ABOUT VINEYARD WORKERS

20 "The kingdom of heaven is like a man who owned some land. One morning, he went out very early to hire some people to work in his vineyard. [2]The man agreed to pay the workers one silver coin[n] for working that day. Then he sent them into the vineyard to work. [3]About nine o'clock the man went to the marketplace and saw some other people standing there, doing nothing. [4]So he said to them, 'If you go and work in my vineyard, I will pay you what your work is worth.' [5]So they went to work in the vineyard. The man went out again about twelve o'clock and again at three o'clock. Both times he hired people to work in his vineyard. [6]About five o'clock the man went to the marketplace again.

He saw others standing there. He asked them, 'Why did you stand here all day doing nothing?' [7]They answered, 'No one gave us a job.' The man said to them, 'Then you can go and work in my vineyard.'

[8]"At the end of the day, the owner of the vineyard said to the boss of all the workers, 'Call the workers and pay them. Start by paying the last people I hired. Then pay all of them, ending with the workers I hired first.'

[9]"The workers who were hired at five o'clock came to get their pay. Each worker received one silver coin. [10]Then the workers who were hired first came to get their pay. They thought they would be paid more than the others. But each one of them also received one silver coin. [11]When they got their silver coin, they complained to the man who owned the land. [12]They said, 'Those people were hired last and worked only one hour. But you paid them the same as you paid us. And we worked hard all day in the hot sun.' [13]But the man who owned the vineyard said to one of those workers, 'Friend, I am being fair to you. You agreed to work for one silver coin. [14]So take your pay and go. I want to give the man who was hired last the same pay that I gave you. [15]I can do what I want with my own money. Are you jealous because I am good to those people?'

[16]"So those who are last now will someday be first. And those who are first now will someday be last."

JESUS TALKS ABOUT HIS OWN DEATH

[17]Jesus was going to Jerusalem. His 12 followers were with him. While they were on the way, Jesus gathered the followers together and spoke to them privately. He said to them, [18]"We are going to Jerusalem. The Son of Man[d] will be turned over to the leading priests and

---

19:29 mother Some Greek copies continue, "or wife."
20:2 silver coin A Roman denarius. One coin was the average pay for one day's work.

the teachers of the law. They will say that he must die. [19]They will give the Son of Man to the non-Jewish people. They will laugh at him and beat him with whips, and then they will kill him on a cross. But on the third day after his death, he will be raised to life again."

A MOTHER ASKS JESUS A FAVOR

[20]Then the wife of Zebedee came to Jesus. Her sons were with her. The mother bowed before Jesus and asked him to do something for her.

[21]Jesus asked, "What do you want?"

She said, "Promise that one of my sons will sit at your right side in your kingdom. And promise that the other son will sit at your left side."

[22]But Jesus said, "You don't understand what you are asking. Can you accept the kind of suffering that I must suffer?"[n]

The sons answered, "Yes, we can!"

[23]Jesus said to them, "Truly you will suffer the same things that I will suffer. But I cannot choose who will sit at my right side or my left side. Those places belong to those for whom my Father has prepared them."

[24]The other ten followers heard this and were angry with the two brothers.

[25]Jesus called all the followers together. He said, "You know that the rulers of the non-Jewish people love to show their power over the people. And their important leaders love to use all their authority. [26]But it should not be that way among you. If one of you wants to become great, then he must serve the rest of you like a servant. [27]If one of you wants to become first, then he must serve the rest of you like a slave. [28]So it is with the Son of Man.[d] The Son of Man did not come for other people to serve him. He came to serve others. The Son of Man came to give his life to save many people."

JESUS HEALS TWO BLIND MEN

[29]When Jesus and his followers were leaving Jericho, a great many people followed Jesus. [30]There were two blind men sitting by the road. The blind men heard that Jesus was going by, so they shouted, "Lord, Son of David,[d] please help us!"

[31]All the people criticized the blind men. They told them to be quiet. But the blind men shouted more and more, "Lord, Son of David, please help us!"

[32]Jesus stopped and said to the blind men, "What do you want me to do for you?"

[33]They answered, "Lord, we want to be able to see."

[34]Jesus felt sorry for the blind men. He touched their eyes, and at once they were able to see. Then the men followed Jesus.

JESUS ENTERS JERUSALEM AS A KING

21 Jesus and his followers were coming closer to Jerusalem. But first they stopped at Bethphage at the hill called the Mount of Olives.[d] From there Jesus sent two of his followers into the town. [2]He said to them, "Go to the town you can see there. When you enter it, you will find a donkey tied there with its colt. Untie them and bring them to me. [3]If anyone asks you why you are taking the donkeys, tell him, 'The Master needs them. He will send them back soon.'"[4]This was to make clear the full meaning of what the prophet[d] said:

[5]"Tell the people of Jerusalem,
  'Your king is coming to you.
He is gentle and riding on a donkey.
He is on the colt of a donkey.'"

Isaiah 62:11; Zechariah 9:9

[6]The followers went and did what Jesus told them to do. [7]They brought the donkey and the colt to Jesus. They laid their coats on the donkeys, and Jesus sat on them. [8]Many people spread their coats on the road before Jesus. Others

---

20:22 accept ... suffer Literally, "drink the cup that I must drink." Jesus used the idea of drinking from a cup to mean accepting the terrible things that would happen to him.

cut branches from the trees and spread them on the road. [9]Some of the people were walking ahead of Jesus. Others were walking behind him. All the people were shouting,

"Praise[n] to the Son of David![d]

God bless the One who comes in the name of the Lord!   *Psalm 118:26*

Praise to God in heaven!"

[10]Then Jesus went into Jerusalem. The city was filled with excitement. The people asked, "Who is this man?"

[11]The crowd answered, "This man is Jesus. He is the prophet from the town of Nazareth in Galilee."

JESUS GOES TO THE TEMPLE

[12]Jesus went into the Temple.[d] He threw out all the people who were buying and selling there. He turned over the tables that belonged to the men who were exchanging different kinds of money. And he upset the benches of those who were selling doves. [13]Jesus said to all the people there, "It is written in the Scriptures,[d] 'My Temple will be a house where people will pray.'[n] But you are changing God's house into a 'hideout for robbers.'"[n]

[14]The blind and crippled people came to Jesus in the Temple, and Jesus healed them. [15]The leading priests and the teachers of the law saw that Jesus was doing wonderful things. They saw the children praising him in the Temple. The children were saying, "Praise[n] to the Son of David."[d] All these things made the priests and the teachers of the law very angry.

[16]They asked Jesus, "Do you hear the things these children are saying?"

Jesus answered, "Yes. Haven't you read in the Scriptures, 'You have taught children and babies to sing praises'?"[n]

[17]Then Jesus left and went out of the city to Bethany, where he spent the night.

THE POWER OF FAITH

[18]Early the next morning, Jesus was going back to the city. He was very hungry. [19]He saw a fig tree beside the road. Jesus went to it, but there were no figs on the tree. There were only leaves. So Jesus said to the tree, "You will never again have fruit!" The tree immediately dried up.

[20]His followers saw this and were amazed. They asked, "How did the fig tree dry up so quickly?"

[21]Jesus answered, "I tell you the truth. If you have faith and do not doubt, you will be able to do what I did to this tree. And you will be able to do more. You will be able to say to this mountain, 'Go, mountain, fall into the sea.' And if you have faith, it will happen. [22]If you believe, you will get anything you ask for in prayer."

LEADERS DOUBT JESUS' AUTHORITY

[23]Jesus went to the Temple.[d] While he was teaching there, the leading priests and the elders of the people came to Jesus. They said to him, "Tell us! What authority do you have to do these things? Who gave you this authority?"

[24]Jesus answered, "I will ask you a question, too. If you answer me, then I will tell you what authority I have to do these things. [25]Tell me: When John baptized people, did that come from God or from man?"

The priests and the leaders argued about Jesus' question. They said to each other, "If we answer, 'John's baptism was from God,' then Jesus will say, 'Then why didn't you believe John?' [26]But if we say, 'It was from man,' we are afraid of what

---

21:9, 15 **Praise** Literally, "Hosanna," a Hebrew word used at first in praying to God for help. At this time it was probably a shout of joy used in praising God or his Messiah.
21:13 **'My Temple . . . pray.'** Quotation from Isaiah 56:7.
21:13 **'hideout for robbers.'** Quotation from Jeremiah 7:11.
21:16 **'You . . . praises'** Quotation from the Septuagint (Greek) version of Psalm 8:2.

the people will do because they all believe that John was a prophet."[d]

[27]So they answered Jesus, "We don't know."

Then Jesus said, "Then I won't tell you what authority I have to do these things!

A STORY ABOUT TWO SONS

[28]"Tell me what you think about this: There was a man who had two sons. He went to the first son and said, 'Son, go and work today in my vineyard.' [29]The son answered, 'I will not go.' But later the son decided he should go, and he went. [30]Then the father went to the other son and said, 'Son, go and work today in my vineyard.' The son answered, 'Yes, sir, I will go and work.' But he did not go. [31]Which of the two sons obeyed his father?"

The priests and leaders answered, "The first son."

Jesus said to them, "I tell you the truth. The tax collectors and the prostitutes[d] will enter the kingdom of God before you do. [32]John came to show you the right way to live. And you did not believe him. But the tax collectors and prostitutes believed John. You saw this, but you still refused to change and believe him.

GOD SENDS HIS SON

[33]"Listen to this story: There was a man who owned a vineyard. He put a wall around the vineyard and dug a hole for a winepress.[d] Then he built a tower. He leased the land to some farmers and left for a trip. [34]Later, it was time for the grapes to be picked. So the man sent his servants to the farmers to get his share of the grapes. [35]But the farmers grabbed the servants, beat one, killed another, and then killed a third servant with stones. [36]So the man sent some other servants to the farmers. He sent more servants than he sent the first time. But the farmers did the same thing to the servants that they had done before. [37]So the man

decided to send his son to the farmers. He said, 'The farmers will respect my son.' [38]But when the farmers saw the son, they said to each other, 'This is the owner's son. This vineyard will be his. If we kill him, then his vineyard will be ours!' [39]So the farmers grabbed the son, threw him out of the vineyard, and killed him. [40]So what will the owner of the vineyard do to these farmers when he comes?"

[41]The priests and leaders said, "He will surely kill those evil men. Then he will lease the vineyard to some other farmers. They will give him his share of the crop at harvest time."

[42]Jesus said to them, "Surely you have read this in the Scriptures:[d]

'The stone that the builders did not
    want
    became the cornerstone.[d]
The Lord did this,
    and it is wonderful to us.'
                          Psalm 118:22-23

[43]"So I tell you that the kingdom of God will be taken away from you. It will be given to people who do the things God wants in his kingdom. [44]The person who falls on this stone will be broken. But if the stone falls on him, he will be crushed."[n]

[45]The leading priests and the Pharisees[d] heard these stories that Jesus told. They knew he was talking about them. [46]They wanted to arrest him. But they were afraid of the people, because the people believed that Jesus was a prophet.[d]

A STORY ABOUT A WEDDING FEAST

22 Jesus used stories to tell other things to the people. He said, [2]"The kingdom of heaven is like a king who prepared a wedding feast for his son. [3]The king invited some people to the feast. When the feast was ready, the king sent his servants to tell the people to come. But they refused to come to the feast.

[4]"Then the king sent other servants. He said to them, 'Tell those who have

---

21:44 **The . . . crushed.** Some Greek copies do not have verse 44.

been invited that my feast is ready. I have killed my best bulls and calves for the dinner. Everything is ready. Come to the wedding feast.'

5"But the people refused to listen to the servants. They went to do other things. One went to work in his field, and another went to his business. 6Some of the other people grabbed the servants, beat them, and killed them. 7The king was very angry. He sent his army to kill the people who had killed his servants. And the army burned their city.

8"After that, the king said to his servants, 'The wedding feast is ready. I invited those people, but they were not worthy to come. 9So go to the street corners and invite everyone you see. Tell them to come to my feast.' 10So the servants went into the streets. They gathered all the people they could find, both good and bad. And the wedding hall was filled with guests.

11"Then the king came in to see all the guests. He saw a man there who was not dressed in the right clothes for a wedding. 12The king said, 'Friend, how were you allowed to come in here? You are not wearing the right clothes for a wedding.' But the man said nothing. 13So the king told some servants, 'Tie this man's hands and feet. Throw him out into the darkness. In that place, people will cry and grind their teeth with pain.'

14"Yes, many are invited. But only a few are chosen."

THE PHARISEES TRY TO TRAP JESUS

15Then the Pharisees[d] left the place where Jesus was teaching. They made plans to trap Jesus with a question. 16They sent some of their own followers and some men from the group called Herodians.[n] These men said, "Teacher, we know that you are an honest man. We know that you teach the truth about God's way. You are not afraid of what other people think about you. All men are the same to you. 17So tell us what you think. Is it right to pay taxes to Caesar[d] or not?"

18But Jesus knew that these men were trying to trick him. So he said, "You hypocrites![d] Why are you trying to trap me? 19Show me a coin used for paying the tax." The men showed him a silver coin.[n] 20Then Jesus asked, "Whose picture is on the coin? And whose name is written on the coin?"

21The men answered, "Caesar's."

Then Jesus said to them, "Give to Caesar the things that are Caesar's. And give to God the things that are God's."

22The men heard what Jesus said, and they were amazed. They left him and went away.

SADDUCEES TRY TO TRICK JESUS

23That same day some Sadducees[d] came to Jesus. (Sadducees believe that no person will rise from death.) The Sadducees asked Jesus a question. 24They said, "Teacher, Moses told us that a married man might die without having children. Then his brother must marry the widow and have children for him. 25There were seven brothers among us. The first one married but died. He had no children. So his brother married the widow. 26Then the second brother also died. The same thing happened to the third brother and all the other brothers. 27The woman was last to die. 28But all seven men had married her. So when people rise from death, whose wife will she be?"

29Jesus answered, "You don't understand because you don't know what the Scriptures[d] say. And you don't know about the power of God. 30When people rise from death, there will be no marriage. People will not be married to each other. They will be like the angels in heaven. 31Surely you have read what God said to you about the rising from death? 32God said, 'I am the God of Abraham,

22:16 **Herodians** A political group that followed Herod and his family.
22:19 **silver coin** A Roman denarius. One coin was the average pay for one day's work.

the God of Isaac, and the God of Jacob.'[n] God is the God of living people, not dead people."

[33]All the people heard this. They were amazed at Jesus' teaching.

THE MOST IMPORTANT COMMAND

[34]The Pharisees[d] learned that the Sadducees[d] could not argue with Jesus' answers to them. So the Pharisees met together. [35]One Pharisee was an expert in the law of Moses. That Pharisee asked Jesus a question to test him. [36]The Pharisee asked, "Teacher, which command in the law is the most important?"

[37]Jesus answered, "'Love the Lord your God with all your heart, soul and mind.'[n] [38]This is the first and most important command. [39]And the second command is like the first: 'Love your neighbor as you love yourself.'[n] [40]All the law and the writings of the prophets[d] depend on these two commands."

JESUS QUESTIONS THE PHARISEES

[41]While the Pharisees[d] were together, Jesus asked them a question. [42]He asked, "What do you think about the Christ?[d] Whose son is he?"

The Pharisees answered, "The Christ is the Son of David."[d]

[43]Then Jesus said to them, "Then why did David call him 'Lord'? David was speaking by the power of the Holy Spirit.[d] David said,

[44]'The Lord said to my Lord:
    Sit by me at my right side,
until I put your enemies under your
    control.'   *Psalm 110:1*
[45]David calls the Christ 'Lord.' So how can he be David's son?"

[46]None of the Pharisees could answer Jesus' question. And after that day no one was brave enough to ask Jesus any more questions.

JESUS ACCUSES THE LEADERS

23 Then Jesus spoke to the crowds and to his followers. Jesus said, [2]"The teachers of the law and the Pharisees[d] have the authority to tell you what the law of Moses says. [3]So you should obey and follow whatever they tell you. But their lives are not good examples for you to follow. They tell you to do things, but they don't do the things themselves. [4]They make strict rules and try to force people to obey them. But they themselves will not try to follow any of those rules.

[5]"The reason they do good things is so other people will see them. They make the boxes[n] of Scriptures[d] that they wear bigger and bigger. And they make their special prayer clothes very long so that people will notice them. [6]Those Pharisees and teachers of the law love to have the most important seats at the feasts. And they love to have the most important seats in the synagogues.[d] [7]They love people to show respect to them in the marketplaces. And they love to have people call them 'Teacher.'

[8]"But you must not be called 'Teacher.' You are all brothers and sisters together. You have only one Teacher. [9]And don't call any person on earth 'Father.' You have one Father. He is in heaven. [10]And you should not be called 'Master.' You have only one Master, the Christ.[d] [11]He who serves you as a servant is the greatest among you. [12]Whoever makes himself great will be made humble. Whoever makes himself humble will be made great.

[13]"How terrible for you, teachers of the law and Pharisees! You are hypocrites![d] You close the door for people to enter the kingdom of heaven. You yourselves don't enter, and you stop others who are

---

22:32 **'I am ... Jacob.'** Quotation from Exodus 3:6.
22:37 **'Love ... mind.'** Quotation from Deuteronomy 6:5.
22:39 **'Love ... yourself.'** Quotation from Leviticus 19:18.
23:5 **boxes** Small leather boxes containing four important Scriptures. Some Jews tied these to the forehead and left arm, probably to show they were very religious.

trying to enter. [14][How terrible for you, teachers of the law and Pharisees. You are hypocrites. You take away widows' houses, and you make long prayers so that people can see you. So you will have a worse punishment.][n]

[15]"How terrible for you, teachers of the law and Pharisees! You are hypocrites! You travel across land and sea to find one person who will follow your ways. When you find that person, you make him more fit for hell than you are.

[16]"How terrible for you, teachers of the law and Pharisees! You guide the people, but you are blind. You say, 'If anyone swears by the Temple[d] when he makes a promise, that means nothing. But if anyone swears by the gold that is in the Temple, then he must keep that promise.' [17]You are blind fools! Which is greater: the gold or the Temple? The Temple makes that gold holy. [18]And you say, 'If anyone swears by the altar when he makes a promise, that means nothing. But if he swears by the gift on the altar, then he must keep his promise.' [19]You are blind! Which is greater: the gift or the altar? The altar makes the gift holy. [20]The person who swears by the altar is really using the altar and also everything on the altar. [21]And the person who uses the Temple to make a promise is really using the Temple and also everything in the Temple. [22]The person who uses heaven to make a promise is also using God's throne and the One who sits on that throne.

[23]"How terrible for you, teachers of the law and Pharisees! You are hypocrites! You give to God one-tenth of everything you earn—even your mint, dill, and cummin.[n] But you don't obey the really important teachings of the law—being fair, showing mercy, and being loyal.

These are the things you should do, as well as those other things. [24]You guide the people, but you are blind! You are like a person who picks a fly out of his drink and then swallows a camel![n]

[25]"How terrible for you, teachers of the law and Pharisees! You are hypocrites! You wash the outside of your cups and dishes. But inside they are full of things that you got by cheating others and pleasing only yourselves. [26]Pharisees, you are blind! First make the inside of the cup clean and good. Then the outside of the cup can be truly clean.

[27]"How terrible for you, teachers of the law and Pharisees. You are hypocrites! You are like tombs that are painted white. Outside, those tombs look fine. But inside, they are full of the bones of dead people, and all kinds of unclean things are there. [28]It is the same with you. People look at you and think you are good. But on the inside you are full of hypocrisy and evil.

[29]"How terrible for you, teachers of the law and Pharisees! You are hypocrites! You build tombs for the prophets.[d] You show honor to the graves of people who lived good lives. [30]And you say, 'If we had lived during the time of our fathers, we would not have helped them kill the prophets.' [31]But you give proof that you are children of those people who murdered the prophets. [32]And you will complete the sin that your fathers started!

[33]"You are snakes! A family of poisonous snakes! You will not escape God. You will all be judged guilty and be sent to hell! [34]So I tell you this: I am sending to you prophets and wise men and teachers. You will kill some of these people. You will nail some of them to crosses. You will beat some of them in your synagogues. You will chase them from town to town.

23:14 How ... punishment. Some Greek copies do not contain the bracketed text.
23:23 mint, dill, and cummin Small plants grown in gardens and used for spices. Only very religious people would be careful enough to give a tenth of these plants.
23:24 You ... camel! Meaning, "You worry about the smallest mistakes but commit the biggest sin."

[35]So you will be guilty for the death of all the good people who have been killed on earth. You will be guilty for the murder of that good man Abel. And you will be guilty for the murder of Zechariah[n] son of Berakiah. He was murdered when he was between the Temple and the altar. [36]I tell you the truth. All of these things will happen to you people who are living now.

JESUS FEELS SORRY FOR JERUSALEM

[37]"Jerusalem, Jerusalem! You kill the prophets[d] and kill with stones those men God sent to you. Many times I wanted to help your people! I wanted to gather them together as a hen gathers her chicks under her wings. But you did not let me. [38]Now your home will be left completely empty. [39]I tell you, you will not see me again until that time when you will say, 'God bless the One who comes in the name of the Lord.'"[n]

THE TEMPLE WILL BE DESTROYED

24 Jesus left the Temple[d] and was walking away. But his followers came to show him the Temple's buildings. [2]Jesus asked, "Do you see all these buildings? I tell you the truth. Every stone will be thrown down to the ground. Not one stone will be left on another."

[3]Later, Jesus was sitting on the Mount of Olives.[d] His followers came to be alone with him. They said, "Tell us when these things will happen. And what will happen to show us that it is time for you to come again and for the world to end?"

[4]Jesus answered: "Be careful that no one fools you. [5]Many people will come in my name. They will say, 'I am the Christ.'[d] And they will fool many people. [6]You will hear about wars and stories of wars that are coming. But don't be afraid. These things must happen before the end

comes. [7]Nations will fight against other nations. Kingdoms will fight against other kingdoms. There will be times when there is no food for people to eat. And there will be earthquakes in different places. [8]These things are like the first pains when something new is about to be born.

[9]"Then men will arrest you and hand you over to be hurt and kill you. They will hate you because you believe in me. [10]At that time, many who believe will lose their faith. They will turn against each other and hate each other. [11]Many false prophets[d] will come and cause many people to believe false things. [12]There will be more and more evil in the world. So most people will stop showing their love for each other. [13]But the person who continues to be strong until the end will be saved. [14]The Good News[d] about God's kingdom will be preached in all the world, to every nation. Then the end will come.

[15]"Daniel the prophet spoke about 'the horrible thing that destroys.'[n] You will see this terrible thing standing in the holy place." (You who read this should understand what it means.) [16]"At that time, the people in Judea should run away to the mountains. [17]If a person is on the roof[n] of his house, he must not go down to get anything out of his house. [18]If a person is in the field, he must not go back to get his coat. [19]At that time, it will be hard for women who are pregnant or have nursing babies! [20]Pray that it will not be winter or a Sabbath[d] day when these things happen and you have to run away. [21]This is because at that time there will be much trouble. There will be more trouble than has ever happened since the beginning of the world. And nothing as bad as that will ever happen again. [22]God has decided to

---

23:35 **Abel ... Zechariah** In the Hebrew Old Testament, the first and last men to be murdered.
23:39 **'God ... Lord.'** Quotation from Psalm 118:26.
24:15 **'the horrible ... destroys.'** Mentioned in Daniel 9:27; 12:11 (cf. Daniel 11:31).
24:17 **roof** In Bible times houses were built with flat roofs. The roof was used for drying things such as flax and fruit. And it was used as an extra room, as a place for worship and as a place to sleep in the summer.

make that terrible time short. If that time were not made short, then no one would go on living. But God will make that time short to help the people he has chosen. ²³At that time, someone might say to you, 'Look, there is the Christ!' Or another person might say, 'There he is!' But don't believe them. ²⁴False Christs and false prophets will come and perform great things and miracles.ᵈ They will do these things to the people God has chosen. They will fool them, if that is possible. ²⁵Now I have warned you about this before it happens.

²⁶"If people tell you, 'The Christ is in the desert'—don't go there. If they say, 'The Christ is in the inner room'—don't believe it. ²⁷When the Son of Manᵈ comes, he will be seen by everyone. It will be like lightning flashing in the sky that can be seen everywhere. ²⁸Wherever there is a dead body, there the vultures will gather.

²⁹"Soon after the trouble of those days, this will happen:

'The sun will grow dark.

And the moon will not give its light.

The stars will fall from the sky.

And everything in the sky will be

    changed.'   *Isaiah 13:10; 34:4*

³⁰"At that time, there will be something in the sky that shows the Son of Man is coming. All the peoples of the world will cry. They will see the Son of Man coming on clouds in the sky. He will come with great power and glory. ³¹He will use a loud trumpet to send his angels all around the earth. They will gather his chosen people from every part of the world.

³²"The fig tree teaches us a lesson: When its branches become green and soft, and new leaves begin to grow, then you know that summer is near. ³³So also, when you see all these things happening, you will know that the time is near, ready to come. ³⁴I tell you the truth. All these

things will happen while the people of this time are still living! ³⁵The whole world, earth and sky, will be destroyed, but the words I have said will never be destroyed!

WHEN WILL JESUS COME AGAIN?

³⁶"No one knows when that day or time will be. Even the Sonⁿ and the angels in heaven don't know. Only the Father knows. ³⁷When the Son of Manᵈ comes, it will be the same as what happened during Noah's time. ³⁸In those days before the flood, people were eating and drinking. They were marrying and giving their children to be married. They were still doing those things until the day Noah entered the boat. ³⁹They knew nothing about what was happening. But then the flood came, and all those people were destroyed. It will be the same when the Son of Man comes. ⁴⁰Two men will be working together in the field. One man will be taken and the other left. ⁴¹Two women will be grinding grain with a hand mill.ⁿ One woman will be taken and the other will be left.

⁴²"So always be ready. You don't know the day your Lord will come. ⁴³Remember this: If the owner of the house knew what time a thief was coming, then the owner would be ready for him. The owner would watch and not let the thief enter his house. ⁴⁴So you also must be ready. The Son of Man will come at a time you don't expect him.

⁴⁵"Who is the wise and trusted servant? The master trusts one servant to give the other servants their food at the right time. ⁴⁶When the master comes and finds the servant doing his work, the servant will be very happy. ⁴⁷I tell you the truth. The master will choose that servant to take care of everything the master owns. ⁴⁸But what will happen if the servant is evil and thinks his master will not

---

24:36 Even the Son Some Greek copies do not have this phrase.
24:41 mill Two large, round, flat rocks used for grinding grain to make flour.

come back soon? [49]Then that servant will begin to beat the other servants. He will feast and get drunk with others like him. [50]And the master will come when the servant is not ready and is not expecting him. [51]Then the master will punish that servant. He will send him away to be among the hypocrites.[d] There people will cry and grind their teeth with pain.

A STORY ABOUT TEN GIRLS

25 "At that time the kingdom of heaven will be like ten girls who went to wait for the bridegroom. They took their lamps with them. [2]Five of the girls were foolish and five were wise. [3]The five foolish girls took their lamps, but they did not take more oil for the lamps to burn. [4]The wise girls took their lamps and more oil in jars. [5]The bridegroom was very late. All the girls became sleepy and went to sleep.

[6]"At midnight someone cried out, 'The bridegroom is coming! Come and meet him!' [7]Then all the girls woke up and got their lamps ready. [8]But the foolish girls said to the wise, 'Give us some of your oil. Our lamps are going out.' [9]The wise girls answered, 'No! The oil we have might not be enough for all of us. Go to the people who sell oil and buy some for yourselves.'

[10]"So the five foolish girls went to buy oil. While they were gone, the bridegroom came. The girls who were ready went in with the bridegroom to the wedding feast. Then the door was closed and locked.

[11]"Later the others came back. They called, 'Sir, sir, open the door to let us in.' [12]But the bridegroom answered, 'I tell you the truth, I don't know you.'

[13]"So always be ready. You don't know the day or the time the Son of Man[d] will come.

A STORY ABOUT THREE SERVANTS

[14]"The kingdom of heaven is like a man who was going to another place for a visit. Before he left, he talked with his servants.

The man told them to take care of his things while he was gone. [15]He decided how much each servant would be able to care for. He gave one servant five bags of money. He gave another servant two bags of money. And he gave a third servant one bag of money. Then the man left. [16]The servant who got five bags went quickly to invest the money. The five bags of money earned five more. [17]It was the same with the servant who had two bags of money. He invested the money and earned two more. [18]But the servant who got one bag of money went out and dug a hole in the ground. Then he hid his master's money in the hole.

[19]"After a long time the master came home. He asked the servants what they did with his money. [20]The servant who got five bags of money brought five more bags to the master. The servant said, 'Master, you trusted me to care for five bags of money. So I used your five bags to earn five more.' [21]The master answered, 'You did well. You are a good servant who can be trusted. You did well with small things. So I will let you care for much greater things. Come and share my happiness with me.'

[22]"Then the servant who got two bags of money came to the master. The servant said, 'Master, you gave me two bags of money to care for. So I used your two bags to earn two more.' [23]The master answered, 'You did well. You are a good servant who can be trusted. You did well with small things. So I will let you care for much greater things. Come and share my happiness with me.'

[24]"Then the servant who got one bag of money came to the master. The servant said, 'Master, I knew that you were a hard man. You harvest things you did not plant. You gather crops where you did not sow any seed. [25]So I was afraid. I went and hid your money in the ground. Here is the bag of money you gave me.' [26]The master answered, 'You are a bad

and lazy servant! You say you knew that I harvest things I did not plant, and that I gather crops where I did not sow any seed? ²⁷So you should have put my money in the bank. Then, when I came home, I would get my money back with interest.'

²⁸"So the master told his other servants, 'Take the bag of money from that servant and give it to the servant who has ten bags of money. ²⁹Everyone who uses what he has will get more. He will have much more than he needs. But the one who does not use what he has will have everything taken away from him.' ³⁰Then the master said, 'Throw that useless servant outside, into the darkness! There people will cry and grind their teeth with pain.'

THE KING WILL JUDGE ALL PEOPLE

³¹"The Son of Man*d* will come again in his great glory. All his angels will come with him. He will be King and sit on his great throne. ³²All the people of the world will be gathered before him. Then he will separate them into two groups as a shepherd separates the sheep from the goats. ³³The Son of Man will put the sheep, the good people, on his right and the goats, the bad people, on his left.

³⁴"Then the King will say to the good people on his right, 'Come. My Father has given you his blessing. Come and receive the kingdom God has prepared for you since the world was made. ³⁵I was hungry, and you gave me food. I was thirsty, and you gave me something to drink. I was alone and away from home, and you invited me into your house. ³⁶I was without clothes, and you gave me something to wear. I was sick, and you cared for me. I was in prison, and you visited me.'

³⁷"Then the good people will answer, 'Lord, when did we see you hungry and give you food? When did we see you thirsty and give you something to drink? ³⁸When did we see you alone and away from home and invite you into our house?

When did we see you without clothes and give you something to wear? ³⁹When did we see you sick or in prison and care for you?'

⁴⁰"Then the King will answer, 'I tell you the truth. Anything you did for any of my people here, you also did for me.'

⁴¹"Then the King will say to those on his left, 'Go away from me. God has said that you will be punished. Go into the fire that burns forever. That fire was prepared for the devil and his helpers. ⁴²I was hungry, and you gave me nothing to eat. I was thirsty, and you gave me nothing to drink. ⁴³I was alone and away from home, and you did not invite me into your house. I was without clothes, and you gave me nothing to wear. I was sick and in prison, and you did not care for me.'

⁴⁴"Then those people will answer, 'Lord, when did we see you hungry or thirsty? When did we see you alone and away from home? Or when did we see you without clothes or sick or in prison? When did we see these things and not help you?'

⁴⁵"Then the King will answer, 'I tell you the truth. Anything you refused to do for any of my people here, you refused to do for me.'

⁴⁶"These people will go off to be punished forever. But the good people will go to live forever."

THE PLAN TO KILL JESUS

26 After Jesus finished saying all these things, he told his followers, ²"You know that the day after tomorrow is the day of the Passover*d* Feast. On that day the Son of Man*d* will be given to his enemies to be killed on a cross."

³Then the leading priests and the Jewish elders had a meeting at the palace of the high priest. The high priest's name was Caiaphas. ⁴At the meeting, they planned to set a trap to arrest Jesus and kill him. ⁵But they said, "We must not do it during the feast. The people might cause a riot."

A WOMAN WITH PERFUME FOR JESUS

[6]Jesus was in Bethany. He was at the house of Simon, who had a harmful skin disease. [7]While Jesus was there, a woman came to him. She had an alabaster[d] jar filled with expensive perfume. She poured this perfume on Jesus' head while he was eating.

[8]His followers saw the woman do this and were upset. They asked, "Why waste that perfume? [9]It could be sold for a great deal of money, and the money could be given to the poor."

[10]But Jesus knew what happened. He said, "Why are you troubling this woman? She did a very beautiful thing for me. [11]You will always have the poor with you. But you will not always have me. [12]This woman poured perfume on my body to prepare me for burial. [13]I tell you the truth. The Good News[d] will be told to people in all the world. And in every place where it is preached, what this woman has done will be told. And people will remember her."

JUDAS BECOMES AN ENEMY OF JESUS

[14]Then 1 of the 12 followers went to talk to the leading priests. This was the follower named Judas Iscariot. [15]He said, "I will give Jesus to you. What will you pay me for doing this?" The priests gave Judas 30 silver coins. [16]After that, Judas waited for the best time to give Jesus to the priests.

JESUS EATS THE PASSOVER FEAST

[17]On the first day of the Feast[d] of Unleavened Bread, the followers came to Jesus. They said, "We will prepare everything for you to eat the Passover[d] Feast. Where do you want to have the feast?"

[18]Jesus answered, "Go into the city to a certain man. Tell him that the Teacher says, 'The chosen time is near. I will have the Passover Feast with my followers at your house.'" [19]The followers did what Jesus told them to do, and they prepared the Passover Feast.

[20]In the evening Jesus was sitting at the table with his 12 followers. [21]They were all eating. Then Jesus said, "I tell you the truth. One of you 12 will turn against me."

[22]This made the followers very sad. Each one said to Jesus, "Surely, Lord, I am not the one who will turn against you. Am I?"

[23]Jesus answered, "The man who has dipped his hand with me into the bowl is the one who will turn against me. [24]The Son of Man[d] will die. The Scriptures[d] say this will happen. But how terrible it will be for the person who gives the Son of Man to be killed. It would be better for him if he had never been born."

[25]Then Judas said to Jesus, "Teacher, surely I am not the one. Am I?" (Judas is the one who would give Jesus to his enemies.)

Jesus answered, "Yes, it is you."

THE LORD'S SUPPER

[26]While they were eating, Jesus took some bread. He thanked God for it and broke it. Then he gave it to his followers and said, "Take this bread and eat it. This bread is my body."

[27]Then Jesus took a cup. He thanked God for it and gave it to the followers. He said, "Every one of you drink this. [28]This is my blood which begins the new[n] agreement that God makes with his people. This blood is poured out for many to forgive their sins. [29]I tell you this: I will not drink of this fruit of the vine[n] again until that day when I drink it new with you in my Father's kingdom."

[30]They sang a hymn. Then they went out to the Mount of Olives.[d]

JESUS' FOLLOWERS WILL ALL LEAVE HIM

[31]Jesus told the followers, "Tonight you will lose your faith because of me. It is written in the Scriptures:[d]

26:28 **new** Some Greek copies do not have this word. Compare Luke 22:20.
26:29 **fruit of the vine** Product of the grapevine; this may also be translated "wine."

'I will kill the shepherd,
   and the sheep will scatter.'
                              Zechariah 13:7
[32]But after I rise from death, I will go ahead of you into Galilee."

[33]Peter said, "All the other followers may lose their faith because of you. But I will never lose my faith."

[34]Jesus said, "I tell you the truth. Tonight you will say you don't know me. You will say this three times before the rooster crows."

[35]But Peter said, "I will never say that I don't know you! I will even die with you!" And all the other followers said the same thing.

JESUS PRAYS ALONE

[36]Then Jesus went with his followers to a place called Gethsemane. He said to them, "Sit here while I go over there and pray." [37]He told Peter and the two sons of Zebedee to come with him. Then Jesus began to be very sad and troubled. [38]He said to Peter and the two sons of Zebedee, "My heart is full of sorrow and breaking with sadness. Stay here with me and watch."

[39]Then Jesus walked a little farther away from them. He fell to the ground and prayed, "My Father, if it is possible, do not give me this cup[n] of suffering. But do what you want, not what I want." [40]Then Jesus went back to his followers and found them asleep. Jesus said to Peter, "You men could not stay awake with me for one hour? [41]Stay awake and pray for strength against temptation. Your spirit wants to do what is right. But your body is weak."

[42]Then Jesus went away a second time. He prayed, "My Father, if it is not possible for this painful thing to be taken from me, and if I must do it, then I pray that what you want will be done."

[43]Then Jesus went back to the followers. Again he found them asleep, because their eyes were heavy. [44]So Jesus left them and went away one more time and prayed. This third time he prayed, he said the same thing.

[45]Then Jesus went back to the followers and said, "You are still sleeping and resting? The time has come for the Son of Man[d] to be given to sinful people. [46]Get up. We must go. Here comes the man who has turned against me."

JESUS IS ARRESTED

[47]While Jesus was still speaking, Judas came up. Judas was 1 of the 12 followers. He had many people with him. They had been sent from the leading priests and the elders of the people. They carried swords and clubs. [48]Judas had planned to give them a signal. He had said, "The man I kiss is Jesus. Arrest him." [49]At once Judas went to Jesus and said, "Greetings, Teacher!" Then Judas kissed him.

[50]Jesus answered, "Friend, do the thing you came to do."

Then the men came and grabbed Jesus and arrested him. [51]When that happened, one of Jesus' followers reached for his sword and pulled it out. The follower struck the servant of the high priest with the sword and cut off his ear.

[52]Jesus said to the man, "Put your sword back in its place. All who use swords will be killed with swords. [53]Surely you know I could ask my Father, and he would give me more than 12 armies of angels. [54]But this thing must happen this way so that it will be as the Scriptures[d] say."

[55]Then Jesus said to the crowd, "You came to get me with swords and clubs as if I were a criminal. Every day I sat in the Temple[d] teaching. You did not arrest me there. [56]But all these things have happened so that it will be as the prophets[d] wrote." Then all of Jesus' followers left him and ran away.

26:39 cup Jesus is talking about the bad things that will happen to him. Accepting these things will be very hard, like drinking a cup of something that tastes very bitter.

JESUS BEFORE THE LEADERS

⁵⁷Those men who arrested Jesus led him to the house of Caiaphas, the high priest. The teachers of the law and the Jewish elders were gathered there. ⁵⁸Peter followed Jesus but did not go near him. He followed Jesus to the courtyard of the high priest's house. He sat down with the guards to see what would happen to Jesus.

⁵⁹The leading priests and the Jewish council tried to find something false against Jesus so that they could kill him. ⁶⁰Many people came and told lies about him. But the council could find no real reason to kill Jesus. Then two people came and said, ⁶¹"This man said, 'I can destroy the Temple*ᵈ* of God and build it again in three days.'"

⁶²Then the high priest stood up and said to Jesus, "Aren't you going to answer? Don't you have something to say about their charges against you?" ⁶³But Jesus said nothing.

Again the high priest said to Jesus, "You must swear to this. I command you by the power of the living God to tell us the truth. Tell us, are you the Christ,*ᵈ* the Son of God?"

⁶⁴Jesus answered, "Yes, I am. But I tell you, in the future you will see the Son of Man*ᵈ* sitting at the right hand of God, the Powerful One. And you will see him coming in clouds in the sky."

⁶⁵When the high priest heard this, he was very angry. He tore his clothes and said, "This man has said things that are against God! We don't need any more witnesses. You all heard him say these things against God. ⁶⁶What do you think?"

The people answered, "He is guilty, and he must die."

⁶⁷Then the people there spit in Jesus' face and beat him with their fists. Others slapped Jesus. ⁶⁸They said, "Prove to us that you are a prophet,*ᵈ* you Christ! Tell us who hit you!"

PETER SAYS HE DOESN'T KNOW JESUS

⁶⁹At that time, Peter was sitting in the courtyard. A servant girl came to him and said, "You were with Jesus, that man from Galilee."

⁷⁰But Peter said that he was never with Jesus. He said this to all the people there. Peter said, "I don't know what you are talking about."

⁷¹Then he left the courtyard. At the gate, another girl saw him. She said to the people there, "This man was with Jesus of Nazareth."

⁷²Again, Peter said that he was never with Jesus. Peter said, "I swear that I don't know this man Jesus!"

⁷³A short time later, some people standing there went to Peter. They said, "We know you are one of those men who followed Jesus. We know this because of the way you talk."

⁷⁴Then Peter began to curse. He said, "May a curse fall on me if I'm not telling the truth. I don't know the man." After Peter said this, a rooster crowed. ⁷⁵Then he remembered what Jesus had told him: "Before the rooster crows, you will say three times that you don't know me." Then Peter went outside and cried painfully.

JESUS IS TAKEN TO PILATE

27 Early the next morning, all the leading priests and elders of the people decided to kill Jesus. ²They tied him, led him away, and turned him over to Pilate, the governor.

JUDAS KILLS HIMSELF

³Judas saw that they had decided to kill Jesus. Judas was the one who gave Jesus to his enemies. When Judas saw what happened, he was very sorry for what he had done. So he took the 30 silver coins back to the priests and the leaders. ⁴Judas said, "I sinned. I gave you an innocent man to be killed."

The leaders answered, "What is that to us? That's your problem, not ours."

[5]So Judas threw the money into the Temple.[d] Then he went off and hanged himself.

[6]The leading priests picked up the silver coins in the Temple. They said, "Our law does not allow us to keep this money with the Temple money. This money has paid for a man's death." [7]So they decided to use the coins to buy a field called Potter's Field. This field would be a place to bury strangers who died while visiting Jerusalem. [8]That is why that field is still called the Field of Blood. [9]So the thing came true that Jeremiah the prophet[d] had said: "They took 30 silver coins. That is how little the Israelites thought he was worth. [10]They used those 30 silver coins to buy the potter's field, as the Lord commanded me."[n]

PILATE QUESTIONS JESUS

[11]Jesus stood before Pilate the governor. Pilate asked him, "Are you the King of the Jews?"

Jesus answered, "Yes, I am."

[12]When the leading priests and the elders accused Jesus, he said nothing. [13]So Pilate said to Jesus, "Don't you hear these people accusing you of all these things?"

[14]But Jesus said nothing in answer to Pilate. Pilate was very surprised at this.

PILATE TRIES TO FREE JESUS

[15]Every year at the time of Passover[d] the governor would free one person from prison. This was always a person the people wanted to be set free. [16]At that time there was a man in prison who was known to be very bad. His name was Barabbas.[n] [17]All the people gathered at Pilate's house. Pilate said, "Which man do you want me to free: Barabbas,[n] or Jesus who is called the Christ?"[d] [18]Pilate knew that they gave Jesus to him because they were jealous.

[19]Pilate said these things while he was sitting on the judge's seat. While he was sitting there, his wife sent a message to him. The message said, "Don't do anything to that man. He is not guilty. Today I had a dream about him, and it troubled me very much."

[20]But the leading priests and elders told the crowd to ask for Barabbas to be freed and for Jesus to be killed.

[21]Pilate said, "I have Barabbas and Jesus. Which do you want me to set free for you?"

The people answered, "Barabbas!"

[22]Pilate asked, "What should I do with Jesus, the one called the Christ?"

They all answered, "Kill him on a cross!"

[23]Pilate asked, "Why do you want me to kill him? What wrong has he done?"

But they shouted louder, "Kill him on a cross!"

[24]Pilate saw that he could do nothing about this, and a riot was starting. So he took some water and washed his hands[n] in front of the crowd. Then he said, "I am not guilty of this man's death. You are the ones who are causing it!"

[25]All the people answered, "We will be responsible. We accept for ourselves and for our children any punishment for his death."

[26]Then Pilate freed Barabbas. Pilate told some of the soldiers to beat Jesus with whips. Then he gave Jesus to the soldiers to be killed on a cross.

[27]Pilate's soldiers took Jesus into the governor's palace. All the soldiers gathered around Jesus. [28]They took off his clothes and put a red robe on him. [29]Then the soldiers used thorny branches to make a crown. They put this crown of thorns on Jesus' head. They put a stick in his right hand. Then the soldiers bowed

---

27:9-10 "They . . . commanded me." See Zechariah 11:12-13 and Jeremiah 32:6-9.
27:16, 17 Barabbas Some Greek copies read "Jesus Barabbas."
27:24 washed his hands He did this as a sign to show that he wanted no part in what the people did.

before Jesus and made fun of him. They said, "Hail, King of the Jews!" [30]They spit on Jesus. Then they took his stick and hit him on the head many times. [31]After they finished making fun of Jesus, the soldiers took off the robe and put his own clothes on him again. Then they led Jesus away to be killed on a cross.

JESUS IS KILLED ON A CROSS

[32]The soldiers were going out of the city with Jesus. They forced another man to carry the cross to be used for Jesus. This man was Simon, from Cyrene. [33]They all came to the place called Golgotha. (Golgotha means the Place of the Skull.) [34]At Golgotha, the soldiers gave Jesus wine to drink. This wine was mixed with gall.[n] He tasted the wine but refused to drink it. [35]The soldiers nailed Jesus to a cross. They threw lots[d] to decide who would get his clothes.[n] [36]The soldiers sat there and continued watching him. [37]They put a sign above Jesus' head with the charge against him written on it. The sign read: "THIS IS JESUS THE KING OF THE JEWS." [38]Two robbers were nailed to crosses beside Jesus, one on the right and the other on the left. [39]People walked by and insulted Jesus. They shook their heads, [40]saying, "You said you could destroy the Temple[d] and build it again in three days. So save yourself! Come down from that cross, if you are really the Son of God!"

[41]The leading priests, the teachers of the law, and the Jewish elders were also there. These men made fun of Jesus [42]and said, "He saved other people, but he can't save himself! People say he is the King of Israel! If he is the King, then let him come down now from the cross. Then we will believe in him. [43]He trusts in God. So let God save him now, if God

really wants him. He himself said, 'I am the Son of God.'" [44]And in the same way, the robbers who were being killed on crosses beside Jesus also insulted him.

JESUS DIES

[45]At noon the whole country became dark. This darkness lasted for three hours. [46]About three o'clock Jesus cried out in a loud voice, "Eli, Eli, lama sabachthani?" This means, "My God, my God, why have you left me alone?"

[47]Some of the people standing there heard this. They said, "He is calling Elijah."

[48]Quickly one of them ran and got a sponge. He filled the sponge with vinegar and tied it to a stick. Then he used the stick to give the sponge to Jesus to drink from it. [49]But the others said, "Don't bother him. We want to see if Elijah will come to save him."

[50]Again Jesus cried out in a loud voice. Then he died.

[51]Then the curtain in the Temple[n] split into two pieces. The tear started at the top and tore all the way down to the bottom. Also, the earth shook and rocks broke apart. [52]The graves opened, and many of God's people who had died were raised from death. [53]They came out of the graves after Jesus was raised from death. They went into the holy city, and many people saw them.

[54]The army officer and the soldiers guarding Jesus saw this earthquake and everything else that happened. They were very frightened and said, "He really was the Son of God!"

[55]Many women were standing at a distance from the cross, watching. These were women who had followed Jesus from Galilee to care for him. [56]Mary Magdalene,

---

27:34 **gall** Probably a drink of wine mixed with drugs to help a person feel less pain.
27:35 **clothes** Some Greek copies continue, "So what God said through the prophet came true, 'They divided my clothes among them, and they threw lots for my clothing.'"
27:51 **curtain in the Temple** A curtain divided the Most Holy Place from the other part of the Temple. That was the special building in Jerusalem where God commanded the Jews to worship him.

and Mary the mother of James and Joseph, and the mother of James and John were there.

JESUS IS BURIED

[57]That evening a rich man named Joseph came to Jerusalem. He was a follower of Jesus from the town of Arimathea. [58]Joseph went to Pilate and asked to have Jesus' body. Pilate gave orders for the soldiers to give it to Joseph. [59]Then Joseph took the body and wrapped it in a clean linen cloth. [60]He put Jesus' body in a new tomb that he had cut in a wall of rock. He rolled a very large stone to block the entrance of the tomb. Then Joseph went away. [61]Mary Magdalene and the other woman named Mary were sitting near the tomb.

THE TOMB OF JESUS IS GUARDED

[62]That day was the day called Preparation[d] Day. The next day, the leading priests and the Pharisees[d] went to Pilate. [63]They said, "Sir, we remember that while that liar was still alive he said, 'After three days I will rise from death.' [64]So give the order for the tomb to be guarded closely till the third day. His followers might come and steal the body. Then they could tell the people that he has risen from death. That lie would be even worse than the first one."

[65]Pilate said, "Take some soldiers and go guard the tomb the best way you know." [66]So they all went to the tomb and made it safe from thieves. They did this by sealing the stone in the entrance and then putting soldiers there to guard it.

JESUS RISES FROM DEATH

28 The day after the Sabbath[d] day was the first day of the week. At dawn on the first day, Mary Magdalene and another woman named Mary went to look at the tomb.

[2]At that time there was a strong earthquake. An angel of the Lord came down from heaven. The angel went to the tomb and rolled the stone away from the entrance. Then he sat on the stone. [3]He was shining as bright as lightning. His clothes were white as snow. [4]The soldiers guarding the tomb were very frightened of the angel. They shook with fear and then became like dead men.

[5]The angel said to the women, "Don't be afraid. I know that you are looking for Jesus, the one who was killed on the cross. [6]But he is not here. He has risen from death as he said he would. Come and see the place where his body was. [7]And go quickly and tell his followers. Say to them: 'Jesus has risen from death. He is going into Galilee. He will be there before you. You will see him there.'" Then the angel said, "Now I have told you."

[8]The women left the tomb quickly. They were afraid, but they were also very happy. They ran to tell Jesus' followers what had happened. [9]Suddenly, Jesus met them and said, "Greetings." The women came up to Jesus, took hold of his feet, and worshiped him. [10]Then Jesus said to them, "Don't be afraid. Go and tell my brothers to go on to Galilee. They will see me there."

THE SOLDIERS REPORT TO THE JEWISH LEADERS

[11]The women went to tell Jesus' followers. At the same time, some of the soldiers who had been guarding the tomb went into the city. They went to tell the leading priests everything that had happened. [12]Then the priests met with the Jewish elders and made a plan. They paid the soldiers a large amount of money. [13]They said to the soldiers, "Tell the people that Jesus' followers came during the night and stole the body while you were asleep. [14]If the governor hears about this, we will satisfy him and save you from trouble." [15]So the soldiers kept the money and obeyed the priests. And that story is still spread among the Jews even today.

JESUS TALKS TO HIS FOLLOWERS

[16]The 11 followers went to Galilee. They went to the mountain where Jesus told them to go. [17]On the mountain they saw

Jesus and worshiped him. But some of them did not believe that it was really Jesus. [18]Then Jesus came to them and said, "All power in heaven and on earth is given to me. [19]So go and make followers of all people in the world. Baptize them in the name of the Father and the Son and the Holy Spirit.[d] [20]Teach them to obey everything that I have told you. You can be sure that I will be with you always. I will continue with you until the end of the world."

MARK

MARK TELLS ABOUT JESUS THE SUFFERING MESSIAH

JOHN PREPARES FOR JESUS

1 This is the beginning of the Good News[d] about Jesus Christ, the Son of God,[n] ²as the prophet[d] Isaiah wrote:

"I will send my messenger ahead
    of you.
He will prepare your way."

Malachi 3:1

³"There is a voice of a man who
    calls out in the desert:
'Prepare the way for the Lord.
    Make the road straight for him.'"

Isaiah 40:3

⁴John was baptizing people in the desert. He preached a baptism of changed hearts and lives for the forgiveness of sins. ⁵All the people from Judea and Jerusalem were going out to John. They told about the sins they had done. Then they were baptized by him in the Jordan River. ⁶John wore clothes made from camel's hair and had a leather belt around his waist. He ate locusts[d] and wild honey. ⁷This is what John preached to the people: "There is one coming later who is greater than I. I am not good enough even to kneel down and untie his sandals. ⁸I baptize you with water. But the one who is coming will baptize you with the Holy Spirit."[d]

JESUS IS BAPTIZED

⁹At that time Jesus came from the town of Nazareth in Galilee to the place where John was. John baptized Jesus in the Jordan River. ¹⁰When Jesus was coming up out of the water, he saw heaven open. The Holy Spirit[d] came down on him like a dove. ¹¹A voice came from heaven and said: "You are my Son and I love you. I am very pleased with you."

¹²Then the Spirit sent Jesus into the desert alone. ¹³He was in the desert 40 days and was there with the wild animals. While he was in the desert, he was tempted by Satan. Then angels came and took care of Jesus.

JESUS CHOOSES SOME FOLLOWERS

¹⁴After John was put in prison, Jesus went into Galilee and preached the Good News[d] from God. ¹⁵Jesus said, "The right time has come. The kingdom of God is near. Change your hearts and lives and believe the Good News!"

¹⁶When Jesus was walking by Lake Galilee, he saw Simon[n] and Simon's brother, Andrew. They were fishermen and were throwing a net into the lake to catch fish. ¹⁷Jesus said to them, "Come and follow me. I will make you fishermen for men." ¹⁸So Simon and Andrew immediately left their nets and followed him.

¹⁹Jesus continued walking by Lake Galilee. He saw two more brothers, James and John, the sons of Zebedee. They were in their boat, preparing their nets to catch fish. ²⁰Their father Zebedee and the men who worked for him were in the boat with the brothers. When Jesus saw the brothers, he called them to come with him. They left their father and followed Jesus.

JESUS REMOVES AN EVIL SPIRIT

²¹Jesus and his followers went to Capernaum. On the Sabbath[d] day Jesus went to the synagogue[d] and began to teach. ²²The people there were amazed at his teaching. He did not teach like their teachers of the law. He taught like a person who had authority. ²³While he was in the synagogue, a man was there who had an evil spirit in him. The man shouted, ²⁴"Jesus of Nazareth! What do you want with us? Did you come to destroy us? I know who you are—God's Holy One!"

1:1 **the Son of God** Some Greek copies do not have this phrase.
1:16 **Simon** Simon's other name was Peter.

25Jesus said strongly, "Be quiet! Come out of the man!" 26The evil spirit made the man shake violently. Then the spirit gave a loud cry and came out of him.

27The people were amazed. They asked each other, "What is happening here? This man is teaching something new. And he teaches with authority. He even gives commands to evil spirits, and they obey him." 28And the news about Jesus spread quickly everywhere in the area of Galilee.

JESUS HEALS MANY PEOPLE

29Jesus and his followers left the synagogue.d They all went at once with James and John to the home of Simonn and Andrew. 30Simon's mother-in-law was sick in bed with a fever. The people there told Jesus about her. 31So Jesus went to her bed, took her hand, and helped her up. Immediately the fever left her, and she was healed. Then she began serving them. 32That night, after the sun went down, the people brought to Jesus all who were sick. They also brought those who had demonsd in them. 33The whole town gathered at the door of the house. 34Jesus healed many who had different kinds of sicknesses. He also forced many demons to leave people. But he would not allow the demons to speak, because they knew who he was.

35Early the next morning, Jesus woke and left the house while it was still dark. He went to a place to be alone and pray. 36Later, Simon and his friends went to look for Jesus. 37They found him and said, "Everyone is looking for you!"

38Jesus answered, "We should go somewhere else, to other towns around here. Then I can preach there too. That is the reason I came." 39So he traveled everywhere in Galilee. He preached in the synagogues and forced demons to leave people.

JESUS HEALS A SICK MAN

40A man who had a harmful skin disease came to Jesus. The man fell to his knees and begged Jesus, "I know that you can heal me if you will."

41Jesus felt sorry for the man. So he touched him and said, "I want to heal you. Be healed!" 42At once the disease left the man, and he was healed.

43Jesus told the man to go at once. But Jesus warned him strongly, 44"Don't tell anyone about what I did for you. But go and show yourself to the priest. And offer a gift to God because you have been healed. Offer the gift that Moses commanded.n This will show the people that you are healed." 45The man left there, but he told everyone he saw that Jesus had healed him. So the news about Jesus spread. That is the reason Jesus could not enter a town if people saw him. He stayed in places where nobody lived. But people came from all the towns to wherever he was.

JESUS HEALS A PARALYZED MAN

2 A few days later, Jesus came back to Capernaum. The news spread that he was home. 2So many people gathered to hear him preach that the house was full. There was no place to stand, not even outside the door. Jesus was teaching them. 3Some people came, bringing a paralyzed man to Jesus. Four of them were carrying the paralyzed man. 4But they could not get to Jesus because of the crowd. So they went to the roof above Jesus and made a hole in the roof. Then they lowered the mat with the paralyzed man on it. 5Jesus saw that these men had great faith. So he said to the paralyzed man, "Young man, your sins are forgiven."

6Some of the teachers of the law were sitting there. They saw what Jesus did, and they said to themselves, 7"Why does this man say things like that? He is saying things that are against God. Only God can forgive sins."

1:29 Simon Simon's other name was Peter.
1:44 Moses commanded Read about this in Leviticus 14:1-32.

[8]At once Jesus knew what these teachers of the law were thinking. So he said to them, "Why are you thinking these things? [9]Which is easier: to tell this paralyzed man, 'Your sins are forgiven,' or to tell him, 'Stand up. Take your mat and walk'? [10]But I will prove to you that the Son of Man[d] has authority on earth to forgive sins." So Jesus said to the paralyzed man, [11]"I tell you, stand up. Take your mat and go home." [12]Immediately the paralyzed man stood up. He took his mat and walked out while everyone was watching him.

The people were amazed and praised God. They said, "We have never seen anything like this!"

[13]Jesus went to the lake again. A crowd followed him there, and he taught them. [14]While he was walking beside the lake, he saw a tax collector named Levi son of Alphaeus. Levi was sitting in the tax office. Jesus said to him, "Follow me." And Levi stood up and followed Jesus.

[15]Later that day, Jesus ate at Levi's house. There were many tax collectors and "sinners" eating there with Jesus and his followers. Many people like this followed Jesus. [16]The teachers of the law who were Pharisees[d] saw Jesus eating with the tax collectors and "sinners." They asked his followers, "Why does he eat with tax collectors and sinners?"

[17]Jesus heard this and said to them, "Healthy people don't need a doctor. It is the sick who need a doctor. I did not come to invite good people. I came to invite sinners."

JESUS' FOLLOWERS ARE CRITICIZED

[18]One day the followers of John[n] and the Pharisees[d] were giving up eating.[n] Some people came to Jesus and said, "John's followers and the followers of the Pharisees give up eating. But your followers don't. Why?"

[19]Jesus answered, "When there is a wedding, the friends of the bridegroom are not sad while he is with them. They do not give up eating while the bridegroom is still there. [20]But the time will come when the bridegroom will leave them. Then the friends will be sad and will give up eating.

[21]"When a person sews a patch over a hole on an old coat, he never uses a piece of cloth that is not yet shrunk. If he does, the patch will shrink and pull away from the coat. Then the hole will be worse. [22]Also, no one ever pours new wine into old leather bags for holding wine. If he does, the new wine will break the bags, and the wine will be ruined along with the bags for the wine. People always put new wine into new leather bags."

JESUS IS LORD OF THE SABBATH

[23]On the Sabbath[d] day, Jesus was walking through some grainfields. His followers were with him and picked some grain to eat. [24]The Pharisees[d] saw this and said to Jesus, "Why are your followers doing what is not lawful on the Sabbath?"

[25]Jesus answered, "You have read what David did when he and those with him were hungry and needed food. [26]It was during the time of Abiathar the high priest. David went into God's house and ate the bread that was made holy for God. The law of Moses says that only priests may eat that bread. But David also gave some of the bread to those who were with him."

[27]Then Jesus said to the Pharisees, "The Sabbath day was made to help people. They were not made to be ruled by the Sabbath day. [28]The Son of Man[d] is Lord even of the Sabbath."

JESUS HEALS A MAN'S CRIPPLED HAND

3 Another time when Jesus went into a synagogue,[d] a man with a crippled

---

2:18 **John** John the Baptist who preached to the Jews about Christ's coming (Mark 1:4-8).
2:18 **giving up eating** This is called "fasting." The people would give up eating for a special time of prayer and worship to God. It was also done to show sadness.

hand was there. ²Some people there wanted to see Jesus do something wrong so they could accuse him. They watched him closely to see if he would heal the man on the Sabbath*d* day.

³Jesus said to the man with the crippled hand, "Stand up here in front of everyone."

⁴Then Jesus asked the people, "Which is right on the Sabbath day: to do good, or to do evil? Is it right to save a life or to destroy one?" But they said nothing to answer him.

⁵Jesus was angry as he looked at the people. But he felt very sad because they were stubborn. Then he said to the man, "Let me see your hand." The man put his hand out for Jesus, and it was healed. ⁶Then the Pharisees*d* left and began making plans with the Herodians*n* about a way to kill Jesus.

MANY PEOPLE FOLLOW JESUS

⁷Jesus left with his followers for the lake. A large crowd from Galilee followed him. ⁸Also many people came from Judea, from Jerusalem, from Idumea, from the lands across the Jordan River, and from the area of Tyre and Sidon. They came because they had heard about all the things Jesus was doing. ⁹Jesus saw the crowds. So he told his followers to get a boat ready for him. He wanted the boat so that the many people would not crowd themselves against him. ¹⁰He had healed many people. So all the sick were pushing toward him to touch him. ¹¹Some had evil spirits in them. When the evil spirits saw Jesus, they fell down before him and shouted, "You are the Son of God!" ¹²But Jesus strongly commanded the spirits not to tell who he was.

JESUS CHOOSES HIS 12 APOSTLES

¹³Then Jesus went up on a hill and called some men to come to him. These were the men Jesus wanted, and they went up to him. ¹⁴Jesus chose 12 men and called them apostles.*nd* He wanted these 12 to be with him, and he wanted to send them to other places to preach. ¹⁵He also wanted them to have the power to force demons*d* out of people. ¹⁶These are the 12 men he chose: Simon (Jesus gave him the name Peter); ¹⁷James and John, the sons of Zebedee (Jesus gave them the name Boanerges, which means "Sons of Thunder"); ¹⁸Andrew, Philip, Bartholomew, Matthew, Thomas, James the son of Alphaeus, Thaddaeus, Simon the Zealot,*d* ¹⁹and Judas Iscariot. Judas is the one who gave Jesus to his enemies.

PEOPLE SAY JESUS HAS A DEVIL

²⁰Then Jesus went back home. But again a crowd gathered. There were so many people that Jesus and his followers could not eat. ²¹His family heard about all these things. They went to get him because people were saying that Jesus was out of his mind.

²²And the teachers of the law from Jerusalem were saying, "Beelzebul*d* is living inside him! He uses power from the ruler of demons*d* to force demons out."

²³So Jesus called the people together and used stories to teach them. He said, "Satan will not force his own demons out of people. ²⁴A kingdom that fights against itself cannot continue. ²⁵And a family that is divided cannot continue. ²⁶And if Satan is against himself and fights against his own people, then he cannot continue. And that is the end of Satan. ²⁷If a person wants to enter a strong man's house and steal his things, first he must tie up the strong man. Then the thief can steal the things from the strong man's house. ²⁸I tell you the truth. All sins that people do can be forgiven. And all the bad things people say against God can be forgiven. ²⁹But any person who says bad things against the Holy

---

3:6 Herodians A political group that followed Herod and his family.
3:14 and called them apostles Some Greek copies do not have this phrase.

Spirit[d] will never be forgiven. He is guilty of a sin that continues forever."

[30]Jesus said this because the teachers of the law said that Jesus had an evil spirit inside him.

JESUS' TRUE FAMILY

[31]Then Jesus' mother and brothers arrived. They stood outside and sent someone in to tell him to come out. [32]Many people were sitting around Jesus. They said to him, "Your mother and brothers[n] are waiting for you outside."

[33]Jesus asked, "Who is my mother? Who are my brothers?" [34]Then Jesus looked at those sitting around him. He said, "Here are my mother and my brothers! [35]My true brother and sister and mother are those who do the things God wants."

A STORY ABOUT PLANTING SEED

4 Another time Jesus began teaching by the lake. A great crowd gathered around him. So he got into a boat and went out on the lake. All the people stayed on the shore close to the water. [2]Jesus used many stories to teach them. He said, [3]"Listen! A farmer went out to plant his seed. [4]While the farmer was planting, some seed fell by the road. The birds came and ate all that seed. [5]Some seed fell on rocky ground where there wasn't much dirt. The seed grew very fast there because the ground was not deep. [6]But when the sun rose, the plants withered. The plants died because they did not have deep roots. [7]Some other seed fell among thorny weeds. The weeds grew and choked the good plants. So those plants did not make grain. [8]Some other seed fell on good ground. In the good ground, the seed began to grow. It grew and made a crop of grain. Some plants made 30 times more grain, some 60 times more grain, and some 100 times more grain."

[9]Then Jesus said, "Let those with ears use them and listen!"

JESUS TELLS WHY HE USED STORIES

[10]Later, when Jesus was alone, the 12 apostles[d] and others around him asked him about the stories.

[11]Jesus said, "Only you can know the secret truth about the kingdom of God. But to other people I tell everything by using stories. [12]I do this so that:

'They will look and look, but they will
    not learn.
They will listen and listen, but they
    will not understand.
If they did learn and understand,
    they would come back to me and be
    forgiven.'"   *Isaiah 6:9-10*

JESUS EXPLAINS THE SEED STORY

[13]Then Jesus said to the followers, "Do you understand this story? If you don't, then how will you understand any story? [14]The farmer is like a person who plants God's teaching in people. [15]Sometimes the teaching falls on the road. This is like some people. They hear the teaching of God. But Satan quickly comes and takes away the teaching that was planted in them. [16]Others are like the seed planted on rocky ground. They hear the teaching and quickly accept it with joy. [17]But they don't allow the teaching to go deep into their lives. They keep it only a short time. When trouble or persecution comes because of the teaching, they quickly give up. [18]Others are like the seed planted among the thorny weeds. They hear the teaching. [19]But then other things come into their lives: worries, the love of money, and wanting all kinds of other things. These things stop the teaching from growing. So that teaching does not produce fruit[n] in their lives. [20]Others are like the seed planted in the good ground. They hear the teaching and accept it. Then they grow and produce fruit—

3:32 brothers Some Greek copies continue, "and sisters."
4:19 produce fruit To produce fruit means to have in your life the good things God wants.

sometimes 30 times more, sometimes 60 times more, and sometimes 100 times more."

USE WHAT YOU HAVE

²¹Then Jesus said to them, "Do you hide a lamp under a bowl or under a bed? No! You put the lamp on a lampstand. ²²Everything that is hidden will be made clear. Every secret thing will be made known. ²³Let those with ears use them and listen!

²⁴"Think carefully about the things you hear. The way you give to others is the way God will give to you. But God will give you more than you give. ²⁵The person who has something will be given more. But the person who does not have much, even what he has will be taken from him."

JESUS USES A STORY ABOUT SEED

²⁶Then Jesus said, "The kingdom of God is like a man who plants seed in the ground. ²⁷The seed comes up and grows night and day. It doesn't matter whether the man is asleep or awake; the seed still grows. The man does not know how it grows. ²⁸Without any help, the earth produces grain. First the plant grows, then the head, and then all the grain in the head. ²⁹When the grain is ready, the man cuts it. This is the harvest time."

A STORY ABOUT MUSTARD SEED

³⁰Then Jesus said, "How can I show you what the kingdom of God is like? What story can I use to explain it? ³¹The kingdom of God is like a mustard seed. The mustard seed is the smallest seed you plant in the ground. ³²But when you plant this seed, it grows and becomes the largest of all garden plants. It produces large branches. Even the wild birds can make nests in it and be protected from the sun."

³³Jesus used many stories like these to teach them. He taught them all that they could understand. ³⁴He always used stories to teach them. But when he and his followers were alone together, Jesus explained everything to them.

JESUS STOPS A STORM

³⁵That evening, Jesus said to his followers, "Come with me across the lake." ³⁶He and the followers left the people there. They went in the boat that Jesus was already sitting in. There were also other boats with them. ³⁷A very strong wind came up on the lake. The waves began coming over the sides and into the boat. It was almost full of water. ³⁸Jesus was at the back of the boat, sleeping with his head on a pillow. The followers went to him and woke him. They said, "Teacher, do you care about us? We will drown!"

³⁹Jesus stood up and commanded the wind and the waves to stop. He said, "Quiet! Be still!" Then the wind stopped, and the lake became calm.

⁴⁰Jesus said to his followers, "Why are you afraid? Do you still have no faith?"

⁴¹The followers were very afraid and asked each other, "What kind of man is this? Even the wind and the waves obey him!"

A MAN WITH DEMONS INSIDE HIM

5 Jesus and his followers went across the lake to the region of the Gerasene[n] people. ²When Jesus got out of the boat, a man came to him from the caves where dead people were buried. This man, who lived in the caves, had an evil spirit living in him. ³No one could tie him up, not even with a chain. ⁴Many times people had used chains to tie the man's hands and feet. But he always broke the chains off. No one was strong enough to control him. ⁵Day and night he would wander around the burial caves and on the hills, screaming and cutting himself with stones. ⁶While Jesus was still far away, the man saw him. He

---

5:1 Gerasene From Gerasa, an area southeast of Lake Galilee. The exact location is uncertain and some Greek copies read, "Gergesene"; others read "Gadarene."

ran to Jesus and knelt down before him. [7-8]Jesus said to the man, "You evil spirit, come out of that man."

But the man shouted in a loud voice, "What do you want with me, Jesus, Son of the Most High God? I beg you, promise God that you will not punish me!"

[9]Then Jesus asked the man, "What is your name?"

The man answered, "My name is Legion,[n] because I have many spirits in me." [10]The man begged Jesus again and again not to send the spirits out of that area.

[11]A large herd of pigs was eating on a hill near there. [12]The evil spirits begged Jesus, "Send us to the pigs. Let us go into them." [13]So Jesus allowed them to do this. The evil spirits left the man and went into the pigs. Then the herd of pigs rushed down the hill into the lake and were drowned. There were about 2,000 pigs in that herd.

[14]The men who took care of the pigs ran away. They went to the town and to the countryside, telling everyone about this. So people went out to see what had happened. [15]They came to Jesus and saw the man who had had the many evil spirits. The man was sitting there, clothed and in his right mind. The people were frightened. [16]Some people were there who saw what Jesus had done. They told the others what had happened to the man who had the demons[d] living in him. And they also told about the pigs. [17]Then the people began to beg Jesus to leave their area.

[18]Jesus was getting ready to leave in the boat. The man who was freed from the demons begged to go with him. [19]But Jesus would not allow the man to go. Jesus said, "Go home to your family and friends. Tell them how much the Lord has done for you and how he has had mercy on you." [20]So the man left and told the people in the Ten Towns[n] about the great things Jesus had done for him. All the people were amazed.

JESUS GIVES LIFE TO A DEAD GIRL AND HEALS A SICK WOMAN

[21]Jesus went in the boat back to the other side of the lake. There, a large crowd gathered around him. [22]A ruler from the synagogue,[d] named Jairus, came to that place. Jairus saw Jesus and bowed before him. [23]The ruler begged Jesus again and again. He said, "My little daughter is dying. Please come and put your hands on her. Then she will be healed and will live." [24]So Jesus went with the ruler, and many people followed Jesus. They were pushing very close around him.

[25]A woman was there who had been bleeding for the past 12 years. [26]She had suffered very much. Many doctors had tried to help her. She had spent all the money she had, but she was not improving. She was getting worse. [27]When the woman heard about Jesus, she followed him with the people and touched his coat. [28]The woman thought, "If I can even touch his coat, that will be enough to heal me." [29]When she touched his coat, her bleeding stopped. She could feel in her body that she was healed.

[30]At once Jesus felt power go out from him. So he stopped and turned around. Then he asked, "Who touched my clothes?"

[31]The followers said, "There are so many people pushing against you! And you ask, 'Who touched me?'"

[32]But Jesus continued looking around to see who had touched him. [33]The woman knew that she was healed. So she came and bowed at Jesus' feet. Shaking with fear, she told him the whole story. [34]Jesus said to the woman, "Dear woman, you are made well because you believed. Go in peace. You will have no more suffering."

5:9 Legion Means very many. A legion was about 5,000 men in the Roman army.
5:20 Ten Towns In Greek, called "Decapolis." It was an area east of Lake Galilee that once had ten main towns.

³⁵Jesus was still speaking to her when some men came from the house of Jairus, the synagogue ruler. The men said, "Your daughter is dead. There is now no need to bother the teacher."

³⁶But Jesus paid no attention to what the men said. He said to the synagogue ruler, "Don't be afraid; only believe."

³⁷Jesus let only Peter, James, and John the brother of James go with him to Jairus's house. ³⁸They came to the house of the synagogue ruler, and Jesus found many people there crying loudly. There was much confusion. ³⁹Jesus entered the house and said to the people, "Why are you crying and making so much noise? This child is not dead. She is only asleep." ⁴⁰But they only laughed at Jesus. He told all the people to leave. Then he went into the room where the child was. He took the child's father and mother and his three followers into the room with him. ⁴¹Then he took hold of the girl's hand and said to her, "Talitha, koum!" (This means, "Little girl, I tell you to stand up!") ⁴²The girl stood right up and began walking. (She was 12 years old.) The father and mother and the followers were amazed. ⁴³Jesus gave the father and mother strict orders not to tell people about this. Then he told them to give the girl some food.

JESUS GOES TO HIS HOMETOWN

6 Jesus left there and went back to his hometown. His followers went with him. ²On the Sabbath*ᵈ* day he taught in the synagogue.*ᵈ* Many people heard him and were amazed. They said, "Where did this man get these teachings? What is this wisdom that has been given to him? And where did he get the power to work miracles?*ᵈ* ³He is only the carpenter. His mother is Mary. He is the brother of James, Joseph, Judas, and Simon. And

his sisters are here with us." The people did not accept Jesus.

⁴Jesus said to them, "Other people give honor to a prophet.*ᵈ* But in his own town with his own people and in his own home, a prophet does not receive honor." ⁵Jesus was not able to work many miracles there. The only miracles he did were to heal some sick people by putting his hands on them. ⁶Jesus was amazed that they had no faith.

Then Jesus went to other villages in that area and taught. ⁷He called the 12 followers together and sent them out in groups of 2. He gave them authority over evil spirits. ⁸This is what Jesus told them: "Take nothing for your trip except a walking stick. Take no bread, no bag, and no money in your pockets. ⁹Wear sandals, and take only the clothes you are wearing. ¹⁰When you enter a house, stay there until you leave that place. ¹¹If any town refuses to accept you or its people refuse to listen to you, then leave that town. Shake its dust off your feet.*ⁿ* This will be a warning to them."*ⁿ*

¹²The followers went out and preached to the people to change their hearts and lives. ¹³The followers forced many demons*ᵈ* out and poured olive oil on many sick people and healed them.

HOW JOHN THE BAPTIST WAS KILLED

¹⁴King Herod heard about Jesus, because Jesus was now well known. Some people said,*ⁿ* "He is John the Baptist.*ᵈ* He is risen from death. That is the reason he can work these miracles."*ᵈ*

¹⁵Others said, "He is Elijah."*ⁿ*

Other people said, "Jesus is a prophet.*ᵈ* He is like the prophets who lived long ago."

¹⁶Herod heard all these things about Jesus. He said, "I killed John by cutting off

---

6:11 Shake . . . feet. A warning. It showed that they were finished talking to these people.

6:11 them Some Greek copies continue, "I tell you the truth, on the Judgment Day it will be better for the towns of Sodom and Gomorrah than for the people of that town." See Matthew 10:15.

6:14 Some people said Some Greek copies read "He said."

6:15 Elijah A man who spoke for God. He lived hundreds of years before Christ.

his head. Now he has been raised from death!"

[17]Herod himself had ordered his soldiers to arrest John, and John was put in prison. Herod did this to please his wife, Herodias. Herodias was the wife of Philip, Herod's brother. But then Herod married her. [18]John told Herod that it was not lawful for him to be married to his brother's wife. [19]So Herodias hated John and wanted to kill him. But she could not because of Herod. [20]Herod was afraid to kill John because he knew John was a good and holy man. So Herod protected John. Also, Herod enjoyed listening to John preach. But John's preaching always bothered him.

[21]Then the perfect time came for Herodias to cause John's death. It happened on Herod's birthday. Herod gave a dinner party for the most important government leaders, the commanders of his army, and the most important people in Galilee. [22]The daughter of Herodias[n] came to the party and danced. When she danced, Herod and the people eating with him were very pleased.

So King Herod said to the girl, "I will give you anything you want." [23]He promised her, "Anything you ask for I will give to you. I will even give you half of my kingdom."

[24]The girl went to her mother and asked, "What should I ask the king to give me?"

Her mother answered, "Ask for the head of John the Baptist."[d]

[25]Quickly the girl went back to the king. She said to him, "Please give me the head of John the Baptist. Bring it to me now on a platter."

[26]The king was very sad. But he had promised to give the girl anything she wanted. And the people eating there with him had heard his promise. So Herod could not refuse what she asked. [27]Immediately the king sent a soldier to bring John's head. The soldier went and cut off John's head in the prison [28]and brought it back on a platter. He gave it to the girl, and the girl gave it to her mother. [29]John's followers heard about what happened. So they came and got John's body and put it in a tomb.

MORE THAN 5,000 PEOPLE FED

[30]The apostles[d] that Jesus had sent out to preach returned. They gathered around him and told him about all the things they had done and taught. [31]Crowds of people were coming and going. Jesus and his followers did not even have time to eat. He said to them, "Come with me. We will go to a quiet place to be alone. There we will get some rest."

[32]So they went in a boat alone to a place where there were no people. [33]But many people saw them leave and recognized them. So people from all the towns ran to the place where Jesus was going. They got there before Jesus arrived. [34]When he landed, he saw a great crowd waiting. Jesus felt sorry for them, because they were like sheep without a shepherd. So he taught them many things.

[35]It was now late in the day. Jesus' followers came to him and said, "No one lives in this place. And it is already very late. [36]Send the people away. They need to go to the farms and towns around here to buy some food to eat."

[37]But Jesus answered, "You give them food to eat."

They said to him, "We can't buy enough bread to feed all these people! We would all have to work a month to earn enough money to buy that much bread!"

[38]Jesus asked them, "How many loaves of bread do you have now? Go and see."

When they found out, they came to him and said, "We have five loaves and two fish."

[39]Then Jesus said to the followers, "Tell all the people to sit in groups on the green grass." [40]So all the people sat in groups.

6:22 The . . . Herodias Some Greek copies read "His daughter Herodias."

They sat in groups of 50 or groups of 100. [41]Jesus took the five loaves and two fish. He looked up to heaven and thanked God for the bread. He divided the bread and gave it to his followers for them to give to the people. Then he divided the two fish among them all. [42]All the people ate and were satisfied. [43]The followers filled 12 baskets with the pieces of bread and fish that were not eaten. [44]There were about 5,000 men there who ate.

JESUS WALKS ON THE WATER

[45]Then Jesus told his followers to get into the boat and go to Bethsaida on the other side of the lake. Jesus said that he would come later. He stayed there to tell the people they could go home. [46]After sending them away, he went into the hills to pray.

[47]That night, the boat was in the middle of the lake. Jesus was alone on the land. [48]He saw the followers working hard to row the boat because the wind was blowing against them. At some time between three and six o'clock in the morning, Jesus came to them, walking on the water. He continued walking until he was almost past the boat. [49]But when his followers saw him walking on the water, they thought he was a ghost and cried out. [50]They all saw him and were terrified. But Jesus spoke to them and said, "Have courage! It is I! Do not be afraid." [51]Then he got into the boat with them. And the wind became calm. The followers were greatly amazed. [52]They had seen Jesus make more bread from the five loaves. But they did not understand what it meant. Their minds were closed.

[53]When they had crossed the lake, they came to shore at Gennesaret. They tied the boat there. [54]When they got out of the boat, the people saw Jesus and immediately recognized him. [55]They ran to tell others everywhere in that area that Jesus was there. They brought sick people on mats to every place Jesus went. [56]Jesus went into towns and cities and farms around that area. And everywhere he went, the people brought the sick to the marketplaces. They begged him to let them just touch the edge of his coat. And all who touched him were healed.

OBEY GOD'S LAW NOT MEN'S

7 Some Pharisees[d] and some teachers of the law came from Jerusalem. They gathered around Jesus. [2]They saw that some of Jesus' followers ate food with hands that were not clean.[d] ("Not clean" means that they did not wash their hands in the way the Pharisees said people must. [3]The Pharisees and all the Jews never eat before washing their hands in this special way. They do this to follow the teaching given to them by their great people who lived before them. [4]And when the Jews buy something in the market, they never eat it until they wash it in a special way. They also follow other rules of their great people who lived before them. They follow rules about the washing of cups, pitchers, and pots.[n])

[5]The Pharisees and the teachers of the law said to Jesus, "Your followers don't follow the rules given to us by our great people who lived before us. Your followers eat their food with hands that are not clean. Why do they do this?"

[6]Jesus answered, "You are all hypocrites![d] Isaiah was right when he spoke about you. Isaiah wrote,

'These people show honor to me with
    words.
But their hearts are far from me.
[7]Their worship of me is worthless.
The things they teach are nothing
    but human rules they have
    memorized.'   *Isaiah 29:13*
[8]You have stopped following the commands of God. Now you only follow the teachings of men."[n]

7:4 pots Some Greek copies continue, "and dining couches."
7:8 teachings of men Some Greek copies continue, "You wash pitchers and jugs and do many other such things."

[9]Then Jesus said to them: "You think you are clever! You ignore the commands of God so that you can follow your own teachings! [10]Moses said, 'Honor your father and mother.'[n] Then Moses also said, 'Anyone who says cruel things to his father or mother must be put to death.'[n] [11]But you teach that a person can say to his father or mother, 'I have something I could use to help you. But I will not use it for you. I will give it to God.' [12]You are telling that person that he does not have to do anything for his father or mother. [13]So you are teaching that it is not important to do what God said. You think that it is more important to follow your own rules, which you teach people. And you do many things like that."

[14]Jesus called the people to him again. He said, "Every person should listen to me and understand what I am saying. [15]There is nothing a person puts into his body that makes him unclean. A person is made unclean by the things that come out of him." [16][Let those with ears use them and listen.][n]

[17]When Jesus left the people and went inside, his followers asked him about this story. [18]Jesus said, "Do you still have trouble understanding? Surely you know that nothing that enters a man from the outside can make him unclean. [19]Food does not go into a person's mind. Food goes into his stomach. Then that food goes out of his body." (When Jesus said this, he meant that there is no food that is unclean for people to eat.)

[20]And Jesus said, "The things that come out of a man are the things that make him unclean. [21]All these evil things begin inside a person, in his mind: evil thoughts, sexual sins, stealing, murder, adultery,[d] [22]selfishness, doing bad things to other people, lying, doing sinful things, jealousy, saying bad things about people, pride, and foolish living. [23]All these evil things come from within a person. These things make a person unclean."

JESUS HELPS A NON-JEWISH WOMAN

[24]Jesus left that place and went to the area around Tyre.[n] He went into a house and did not want anyone to know he was there. But Jesus could not stay hidden. [25]A woman heard that he was there. Her little daughter had an evil spirit in her. So the woman quickly came to Jesus and fell at his feet. [26]She was not Jewish. She was Greek, born in Phoenicia, in Syria. She begged Jesus to force the demon[d] out of her daughter.

[27]Jesus told the woman: "It is not right to take the children's bread and give it to the dogs. First let the children eat all they want."

[28]She answered, "That is true, Lord. But the dogs under the table can eat the pieces of food that the children don't eat."

[29]Then Jesus said, "That is a very good answer. You may go. The demon has left your daughter."

[30]The woman went home and found her daughter lying in bed. The demon was gone.

JESUS HEALS A DEAF MAN

[31]Then Jesus left the area around Tyre. He went through Sidon to Lake Galilee, to the area of the Ten Towns.[n] [32]While he was there, some people brought a man to him. This man was deaf and could not talk. The people begged Jesus to put his hand on the man to heal him.

[33]Jesus led the man away from the crowd, to be alone with him. Jesus put his fingers in the man's ears. Then Jesus spit and touched the man's tongue.

7:10 'Honor ... mother.' Quotation from Exodus 20:12; Deuteronomy 5:16.
7:10 'Anyone ... death.' Quotation from Exodus 21:17.
7:16 Let ... listen. Some Greek copies do not contain the bracketed text.
7:24 Tyre Some Greek copies continue, "and Sidon."
7:31 Ten Towns In Greek, called "Decapolis." It was an area east of Lake Galilee that once had ten main towns.

[34]Jesus looked up to heaven and took a deep breath. He said to the man, "Ephphatha!" (This means, "Be opened.") [35]When Jesus did this, the man was able to hear. He was also able to use his tongue, and he spoke clearly.

[36]Jesus commanded the people not to tell anyone about what happened. But the more he commanded them, the more they told about it. [37]They were really amazed. They said, "Jesus does everything well. He makes the deaf hear! And those who can't talk—Jesus makes them able to speak."

MORE THAN 4,000 PEOPLE FED

8 Another time there was a great crowd with Jesus. They had nothing to eat. So Jesus called his followers to him. He said, [2]"I feel sorry for these people. They have been with me for three days, and now they have nothing to eat. [3]I cannot send them home hungry. If they leave without eating, they will faint on the way home. Some of them live a long way from here."

[4]Jesus' followers answered, "But we are far away from any towns. Where can we get enough bread to feed all these people?"

[5]Jesus asked, "How many loaves of bread do you have?"

They answered, "We have seven loaves."

[6]Jesus told the people to sit on the ground. Then he took the seven loaves and gave thanks to God. Jesus divided the bread and gave the pieces to his followers. He told them to pass out the bread to the people, and they did so. [7]The followers also had a few small fish. Jesus gave thanks for the fish and told his followers to give the fish to the people. [8]All the people ate and were satisfied. Then the followers filled seven baskets with the pieces of food that were not eaten. [9]There were about 4,000 men who ate. After they had eaten, Jesus told them to go home. [10]Then he went in a boat with his followers to the area of Dalmanutha.

THE LEADERS ASK FOR A MIRACLE

[11]The Pharisees[d] came to Jesus and asked him questions. They wanted to trap him. So they asked Jesus to do a miracle[d] to show that he was from God. [12]Jesus sighed deeply. He said, "Why do you people ask for a miracle as proof? I tell you the truth. No miracle will be given to you." [13]Then Jesus left the Pharisees. He went in the boat to the other side of the lake.

GUARD AGAINST WRONG TEACHINGS

[14]The followers had only one loaf of bread with them in the boat. They had forgotten to bring more bread. [15]Jesus warned them, "Be careful! Guard against the yeast of the Pharisees[d] and the yeast of Herod."

[16]Among themselves, his disciples discussed the meaning of this. They said, "He said this because we have no bread."

[17]Jesus knew what his followers were talking about. So he asked them, "Why are you talking about having no bread? You still don't see or understand? Are your minds closed? [18]You have eyes, but you don't really see. You have ears, but you don't really listen. Remember what I did before, when we did not have enough bread? [19]I divided five loaves of bread for 5,000 people. Remember how many baskets you filled with pieces of food that were not eaten?"

They answered, "We filled 12 baskets."

[20]"And remember that I divided seven loaves of bread for 4,000 people. Remember how many baskets you filled with pieces of food that were not eaten?"

They answered, "We filled 7 baskets."

[21]Then Jesus said to them, "You remember these things I did, but you still don't understand?"

JESUS HEALS A BLIND MAN

[22]Jesus and his followers came to Bethsaida. Some people brought a blind

man to Jesus and begged him to touch the man. [23]So Jesus took the blind man's hand and led him out of the village. Then he spit on the man's eyes. He put his hands on the blind man and asked, "Can you see now?"

[24]The man looked up and said, "Yes, I see people, but they look like trees walking around."

[25]Again Jesus put his hands on the man's eyes. Then the man opened his eyes wide. His eyes were healed, and he was able to see everything clearly. [26]Jesus told him to go home, saying, "Don't go into the town."[n]

PETER SAYS JESUS IS THE CHRIST

[27]Jesus and his followers went to the towns around Caesarea Philippi. While they were traveling, Jesus asked them, "Who do people say I am?"

[28]They answered, "Some people say you are John the Baptist.[d] Others say you are Elijah.[n] And others say that you are one of the prophets."[d]

[29]Then Jesus asked, "Who do you say I am?"

Peter answered, "You are the Christ."[d]

[30]Jesus ordered his followers, "Don't tell anyone who I am."

[31]Then Jesus began to teach them that the Son of Man[d] must suffer many things. He taught that the Son of Man would not be accepted by the Jewish elders, the leading priests, and the teachers of the law. He taught that the Son of Man must be killed and then rise from death after three days. [32]Jesus told them plainly what would happen. Then Peter took Jesus aside and began to criticize him. [33]But Jesus turned and looked at his followers. Then he criticized Peter and said, "Go away from me, Satan![n] You don't care about the things of God.

You care only about things men think are important."

[34]Then Jesus called the crowd to him, along with his followers. He said, "If anyone wants to follow me, he must say 'no' to the things he wants. He must be willing to die on a cross, and he must follow me. [35]Whoever wants to save his life will give up true life. But whoever gives up his life for me and for the Good News[d] will have true life forever. [36]It is worth nothing for a person to have the whole world, if he loses his soul. [37]A person could never pay enough to buy back his soul. [38]The people who live now are living in a sinful and evil time. If anyone is ashamed of me and my teaching, then I will be ashamed of him. I will be ashamed of him when I come with the glory of my Father and the holy angels."

9 Then Jesus said to the people, "I tell you the truth. Some of you standing here will see the kingdom of God come with power before you die."

JESUS WITH MOSES AND ELIJAH

[2]Six days later Jesus took Peter, James, and John and went up on a high mountain. They were all alone there. While these followers watched, Jesus was changed. [3]His clothes became shining white, whiter than any person could make them. [4]Then two men appeared, talking with Jesus. The men were Moses and Elijah.[n]

[5]Peter said to Jesus, "Teacher, it is good that we are here. We will put three tents here—one for you, one for Moses, and one for Elijah." [6]Peter did not know what to say, because he and the others were so frightened.

[7]Then a cloud came and covered them. A voice came from the cloud. The

---

8:26 town Some Greek copies continue, "Don't even go and tell anyone in the town."
8:28 Elijah A man who spoke for God. He lived hundreds of years before Christ.
8:33 Satan Name for the devil meaning "the enemy." Jesus means that Peter was talking like Satan.
9:4 Moses and Elijah Two of the most important Jewish leaders in the past.

voice said, "This is my Son, and I love him. Obey him!"

[8]Then Peter, James, and John looked around, but they saw only Jesus there alone with them.

[9]As Jesus and his followers were walking back down the mountain, he commanded them, "Don't tell anyone about the things you saw on the mountain. Wait till the Son of Man[d] rises from death. Then you may tell."

[10]So the followers obeyed Jesus and said nothing about what they had seen. But they discussed what Jesus meant about rising from death.

[11]They asked Jesus, "Why do the teachers of the law say that Elijah must come first?"

[12]Jesus answered, "They are right to say that Elijah must come first. Elijah makes all things the way they should be. But why does the Scripture[d] say that the Son of Man will suffer much and that people will treat him as if he were nothing? [13]I tell you that Elijah has already come. And people did to him whatever they wanted to do. The Scriptures said this would happen to him."

JESUS HEALS A SICK BOY

[14]Then Jesus, Peter, James, and John went to the other followers. They saw a great crowd around them. The teachers of the law were arguing with them. [15]But when the crowd saw Jesus, they were surprised and ran to welcome him.

[16]Jesus asked, "What are you arguing about with the teachers of the law?"

[17]A man answered, "Teacher, I brought my son to you. He has a spirit from the devil in him. This spirit stops him from talking. [18]The spirit attacks him and throws him on the ground. My son foams at the mouth, grinds his teeth, and becomes very stiff. I asked your followers to force the evil spirit out, but they couldn't."

[19]Jesus answered, "You people don't believe! How long must I stay with you?

How long must I go on being patient with you? Bring the boy to me!"

[20]So the followers brought him to Jesus. As soon as the evil spirit saw Jesus, it attacked the boy. He fell down and rolled on the ground, foaming from his mouth.

[21]Jesus asked the boy's father, "How long has this been happening?"

The father answered, "Since he was very young. [22]The spirit often throws him into a fire or into water to kill him. If you can do anything for him, please have pity on us and help us."

[23]Jesus said to the father, "You said, 'If you can!' All things are possible for him who believes."

[24]Immediately the father cried out, "I do believe! Help me to believe more!"

[25]Jesus saw that a crowd was running there to see what was happening. So he spoke to the evil spirit, saying, "You deaf and dumb spirit—I command you to come out of this boy and never enter him again!"

[26]The evil spirit screamed and caused the boy to fall on the ground again. Then the spirit came out. The boy looked as if he were dead. And many people said, "He is dead!" [27]But Jesus took hold of the boy's hand and helped him to stand up.

[28]Jesus went into the house. His followers were alone with him there. They said, "Why couldn't we force that evil spirit out?"

[29]Jesus answered, "That kind of spirit can only be forced out by prayer."

JESUS TALKS ABOUT HIS DEATH

[30]Then Jesus and his followers left that place and went through Galilee. Jesus did not want anyone to know where he was [31]because he wanted to teach his followers alone. He said to them, "The Son of Man[d] will be given to men who will kill him. After three days, he will rise from death." [32]But the followers did not understand what Jesus meant. And they were afraid to ask.

WHO IS THE GREATEST?

³³Jesus and his followers went to Capernaum and went into a house there. Then Jesus said to them, "What were you arguing about on the road?" ³⁴But the followers did not answer, because their argument on the road was about which one of them was the greatest.

³⁵Jesus sat down and called the 12 apostles[d] to him. He said, "If anyone wants to be the most important, then he must be last of all and servant of all."

³⁶Then Jesus took a small child and had him stand among them. He took the child in his arms and said, ³⁷"If anyone accepts children like these in my name, then he is also accepting me. And if he accepts me, then he is also accepting the One who sent me."

ANYONE NOT AGAINST US IS FOR US

³⁸Then John said, "Teacher, we saw a man using your name to force demons[d] out of a person. We told him to stop, because he does not belong to our group."

³⁹Jesus said, "Don't stop him. Anyone who uses my name to do powerful things will not say evil things about me. ⁴⁰He who is not against us is with us. ⁴¹I tell you the truth. If anyone helps you by giving you a drink of water because you belong to the Christ,[d] then he will truly get his reward.

⁴²"If one of these little children believes in me, and someone causes that child to sin, then it will be very bad for him. It would be better for him to have a large stone tied around his neck and be drowned in the sea. ⁴³If your hand causes you to sin, cut it off. It is better for you to lose part of your body but have life forever. That is much better than to have two hands and go to hell. In that

place the fire never goes out. ⁴⁴[In hell the worm does not die; the fire is never stopped.][n] ⁴⁵If your foot causes you to sin, cut it off. It is better for you to lose part of your body but have life forever. That is much better than to have two feet and be thrown into hell. ⁴⁶[In hell the worm does not die; the fire is never stopped.][n] ⁴⁷If your eye causes you to sin, take it out. It is better for you to have only one eye but have life forever. That is much better than to have two eyes and be thrown into hell. ⁴⁸In hell the worm does not die; the fire is never stopped. ⁴⁹Every person will be salted with fire.

⁵⁰"Salt is good. But if the salt loses its salty taste, then you cannot make it salty again. So, be full of goodness. And have peace with each other."

JESUS TEACHES ABOUT DIVORCE

10 Then Jesus left that place. He went into the area of Judea and across the Jordan River. Again, crowds came to him. And Jesus taught them as he always did.

²Some Pharisees[d] came to Jesus and tried to trick him. They asked, "Is it right for a man to divorce his wife?"

³Jesus answered, "What did Moses command you to do?"

⁴They said, "Moses allowed a man to write out divorce papers and send her away."[n]

⁵Jesus said, "Moses wrote that command for you because you refused to accept God's teaching. ⁶But when God made the world, 'he made them male and female.'[n] ⁷"So a man will leave his father and mother and be united with his wife.[n] ⁸And the two people will become one body.'[n] So the people are not two, but one. ⁹God has joined the two people together. So no one should separate them."

9:44 In . . . stopped. Some Greek copies do not contain the bracketed text.
9:46 In . . . stopped. Some Greek copies do not contain the bracketed text.
10:4 "Moses . . . away." Quotation from Deuteronomy 24:1.
10:6 'he made . . . female.' Quotation from Genesis 1:27.
10:7 and . . . wife Some Greek copies do not have this phrase.
10:7-8 'So . . . body.' Quotation from Genesis 2:24.

[10]Later, the followers and Jesus were in the house. They asked Jesus again about the question of divorce. [11]He answered, "Anyone who divorces his wife and marries another woman is guilty of adultery[d] against her. [12]And the woman who divorces her husband and marries another man is also guilty of adultery."

JESUS ACCEPTS CHILDREN

[13]Some people brought their small children to Jesus so he could touch them. But his followers told the people to stop bringing their children to him. [14]When Jesus saw this, he was displeased. He said to them, "Let the little children come to me. Don't stop them. The kingdom of God belongs to people who are like these little children. [15]I tell you the truth. You must accept the kingdom of God as a little child accepts things, or you will never enter it." [16]Then Jesus took the children in his arms. He put his hands on them and blessed them.

A RICH YOUNG MAN'S QUESTION

[17]Jesus started to leave, but a man ran to him and fell on his knees before Jesus. The man asked, "Good teacher, what must I do to get the life that never ends?"

[18]Jesus answered, "Why do you call me good? No one is good except God alone. [19]You know the commands: 'You must not murder anyone. You must not be guilty of adultery.[d] You must not steal. You must not tell lies about your neighbor in court. You must not cheat. Honor your father and mother.'"[n]

[20]The man said, "Teacher, I have obeyed all these commands since I was a boy."

[21]Jesus looked straight at the man and loved him. Jesus said, "There is still one more thing you need to do. Go and sell everything you have, and give the money to the poor. You will have a reward in heaven. Then come and follow me."

[22]He was very sad to hear Jesus say this, and he left. The man was sad because he was very rich.

[23]Then Jesus looked at his followers and said, "How hard it will be for those who are rich to enter the kingdom of God!"

[24]The followers were amazed at what Jesus said. But he said again, "My children, it is very hard[n] to enter the kingdom of God! [25]And it will be very hard for a rich person to enter the kingdom of God. It would be easier for a camel to go through the eye of a needle!"

[26]The followers were even more amazed and said to each other, "Then who can be saved?"

[27]Jesus looked straight at them and said, "For people this is impossible. But for God all things are possible."

[28]Peter said to Jesus, "We left everything to follow you!"

[29]Jesus said, "I tell you the truth. Everyone who has left his home, brothers, sisters, mother, father, children, or fields for me and for the Good News[d] [30]will get a hundred times more than he left. Here in this world he will have more homes, brothers, sisters, mothers, children, and fields. And with those things, he will also suffer for his belief. But in this age he will have life forever. [31]Many who are first now will be last in the future. And those who are last now will be first in the future."

JESUS TALKS ABOUT HIS OWN DEATH

[32]Jesus and the people with him were on the road to Jerusalem. Jesus was leading the way. The followers were amazed, but those who followed behind them were afraid. Jesus took the 12 apostles[d] aside and talked with them alone. He told them what would happen in Jerusalem. [33]He said, "We are going to Jerusalem. The Son of Man[d] will be given

10:19 'You ... mother.' Quotation from Exodus 20:12-16; Deuteronomy 5:16-20.
10:24 hard Some Greek copies continue, "for those who trust in riches."

to the leading priests and teachers of the law. They will say that he must die. They will give him to the non-Jewish people, [34]who will laugh at him and spit on him. They will beat him with whips and kill him. But on the third day after his death, he will rise to life again."

TWO FOLLOWERS ASK JESUS A FAVOR

[35]Then James and John, sons of Zebedee, came to Jesus. They said, "Teacher, we want to ask you to do something for us."

[36]Jesus asked, "What do you want me to do for you?"

[37]They answered, "You will have glory in your kingdom. Let one of us sit at your right, and let one of us sit at your left."

[38]Jesus said, "You don't understand what you are asking. Can you drink the cup that I must drink? And can you be baptized with the same kind of baptism that I must have?"[n]

[39]They answered, "Yes, we can!"

Jesus said to them, "You will drink the same cup that I will drink. And you will be baptized with the same baptism that I must have. [40]But I cannot choose who will sit at my right or my left. These places are for those for whom they are prepared."

[41]The ten followers heard this. They began to be angry with James and John. [42]Jesus called all the followers together. He said, "The non-Jewish people have men they call rulers. You know that those rulers love to show their power over the people. And their important leaders love to use all their authority. [43]But it should not be that way among you. If one of you wants to become great, then he must serve you like a servant. [44]If one of you wants to become the most important, then he must serve all of you like a slave. [45]In the same way, the Son of Man[d] did not come to be served. He came to serve. The Son of Man came to give his life to save many people."

JESUS HEALS A BLIND MAN

[46]Then they came to the town of Jericho. As Jesus was leaving there with his followers and a large crowd, a blind beggar named Bartimaeus (son of Timaeus) was sitting by the road. [47]He heard that Jesus from Nazareth was walking by. The blind man cried out, "Jesus, Son of David,[d] please help me!"

[48]Many people scolded the blind man and told him to be quiet. But he shouted more and more, "Son of David, please help me!"

[49]Jesus stopped and said, "Tell the man to come here."

So they called the blind man. They said, "Cheer up! Get to your feet. Jesus is calling you." [50]The blind man stood up quickly. He left his coat there and went to Jesus.

[51]Jesus asked him, "What do you want me to do for you?"

The blind man answered, "Teacher, I want to see again."

[52]Jesus said, "Go. You are healed because you believed." At once the man was able to see again, and he followed Jesus on the road.

JESUS ENTERS JERUSALEM AS A KING

11 Jesus and his followers were coming closer to Jerusalem. They came to the towns of Bethphage and Bethany near the Mount of Olives.[d] There Jesus sent two of his followers. [2]He said to them, "Go to the town you see there. When you enter it, you will find a colt tied which no one has ever ridden. Untie it and bring it here to me. [3]If anyone asks you why you are doing this, tell him, 'The Master needs the colt. He will send it back soon.'"

[4]The followers went into the town. They found a colt tied in the street near the door of a house, and they untied it. [5]Some people were standing there and asked, "What are you doing? Why are you

---

10:38 Can you . . . have? Jesus was asking if they could suffer the same terrible things that would happen to him.

untying that colt?" [6]The followers answered the way Jesus told them to answer. And the people let them take the colt.

[7]The followers brought the colt to Jesus. They put their coats on the colt, and Jesus sat on it. [8]Many people spread their coats on the road. Others cut branches in the fields and spread the branches on the road. [9]Some of the people were walking ahead of Jesus. Others were following him. All of them were shouting,

"Praise[n] God!
God bless the One who comes in the
name of the Lord!   *Psalm 118:26*
[10]God bless the kingdom of our father
David!
   That kingdom is coming!
Praise to God in heaven!"

[11]Jesus entered Jerusalem and went into the Temple.[d] When he had looked at everything, and since it was already late, he went out to Bethany with the 12 apostles.[d]

[12]The next day as Jesus was leaving Bethany, he was hungry. [13]He saw a fig tree in leaf. So he went to the tree to see if it had any figs on it. But he found no figs, only leaves. It was not the right season for figs to grow. [14]So Jesus said to the tree, "May no one ever eat fruit from you again." Jesus' followers heard him say this.

JESUS GOES TO THE TEMPLE

[15]Jesus returned to Jerusalem and went into the Temple.[d] He began to throw out those who were buying and selling things there. He overturned the tables that belonged to the men who were exchanging different kinds of money. And he turned over the benches of the men who were selling doves.

[16]Jesus refused to allow anyone to carry goods through the Temple courts. [17]Then Jesus taught the people. He said, "It is written in the Scriptures,[d] 'My Temple will be a house where people from all nations will pray.'[n] But you are changing God's house into a 'hideout for robbers.'"[n]

[18]The leading priests and the teachers of the law heard all this. They began trying to find a way to kill Jesus. They were afraid of him because all the people were amazed at his teaching. [19]That night, Jesus and his followers[n] left the city.

THE POWER OF FAITH

[20]The next morning, Jesus was passing by with his followers. They saw the fig tree, and it was dry and dead, even to the roots. [21]Peter remembered the tree and said to Jesus, "Teacher, look! Yesterday, you cursed the fig tree. Now it is dry and dead!"

[22]Jesus answered, "Have faith in God. [23]I tell you the truth. You can say to this mountain, 'Go, mountain, fall into the sea.' And if you have no doubts in your mind and believe that the thing you say will happen, then God will do it for you. [24]So I tell you to ask for things in prayer. And if you believe that you have received those things, then they will be yours. [25]When you are praying, and you remember that you are angry with another person about something, then forgive him. If you do this, then your Father in heaven will also forgive your sins." [26][But if you don't forgive other people, then your Father in heaven will not forgive your sins.][n]

LEADERS DOUBT JESUS' AUTHORITY

[27]Jesus and his followers went again to Jerusalem. Jesus was walking in the

---

11:9 Praise Literally, "Hosanna," a Hebrew word used at first in praying to God for help, but at this time it was probably a shout of joy used in praising God or his Messiah.
11:17 'My Temple . . . pray.' Quotation from Isaiah 56:7.
11:17 'hideout for robbers.' Quotation from Jeremiah 7:11.
11:19 his followers Some Greek copies mention only Jesus here.
11:26 But . . . sins. Some Greek copies do not contain the bracketed text.

Temple.[d] The leading priests, the teachers of the law, and the older Jewish leaders came to him. [28]They said to him, "Tell us! What authority do you have to do these things? Who gave you this authority?"

[29]Jesus answered, "I will ask you one question. You answer it. Then I will tell you whose authority I use to do these things. [30]Tell me: When John baptized people, was that from God or from man? Answer me!"

[31]They argued about Jesus' question. They said to each other, "If we answer, 'John's baptism was from God,' then Jesus will say, 'Then why didn't you believe John?' [32]But if we say, 'From man,' then the people will be against us." (These leaders were afraid of the people. All the people believed that John was a prophet.[d])

[33]So the leaders answered Jesus, "We don't know."

Jesus said, "Then I will not tell you what authority I use to do these things."

GOD SENDS HIS SON

12 Jesus used stories to teach the people. He said, "A man planted a vineyard. He put a wall around it and dug a hole for a winepress.[d] Then he built a tower. He leased the vineyard to some farmers and left for a trip. [2]Later, it was time for the grapes to be picked. So the man sent a servant to the farmers to get his share of the grapes. [3]But the farmers grabbed the servant and beat him. They sent him away with nothing. [4]Then the man sent another servant. They hit him on the head and showed no respect for him. [5]So the man sent another servant. They killed this servant. The man sent many other servants. The farmers beat some of them and killed others.

[6]"The man had one person left to send, his son whom he loved. He sent him last of all, saying, 'The farmers will respect my son.'

[7]"But they said to each other, 'This is the owner's son. This vineyard will be his. If we kill him, then it will be ours.' [8]So they took the son, killed him, and threw him out of the vineyard.

[9]"So what will the man who owns the vineyard do? He will go to the vineyard and kill those farmers. Then he will give the vineyard to other farmers. [10]Surely you have read this Scripture:[d]

'The stone that the builders did not
    want
    became the cornerstone.[d]
[11]The Lord did this,
    and it is wonderful to us.'"
                            Psalm 118:22-23

[12]The Jewish leaders knew that the story was about them. So they wanted to find a way to arrest Jesus, but they were afraid of the people. So the leaders left him and went away.

THE LEADERS TRY TO TRAP JESUS

[13]Later, the Jewish leaders sent some Pharisees[d] and some men from the group called Herodians[n] to Jesus. They wanted to catch Jesus saying something wrong. [14]They came to him and said, "Teacher, we know that you are an honest man. You are not afraid of what other people think about you. All men are the same to you. And you teach the truth about God's way. Tell us: Is it right to pay taxes to Caesar?[d] Should we pay them, or not?"

[15]But Jesus knew what these men were really trying to do. He said, "Why are you trying to trap me? Bring me a silver coin. Let me see it." [16]They gave Jesus a coin, and he asked, "Whose picture is on the coin? And whose name is written on it?"

They answered, "Caesar's."

[17]Then Jesus said to them, "Give to Caesar the things that are Caesar's. And give to God the things that are God's." The men were amazed at what Jesus said.

12:13 **Herodians** A political group that followed Herod and his family.

SADDUCEES TRY TO TRICK JESUS

[18]Then some Sadducees[d] came to Jesus. (Sadducees believe that no person will rise from death.) The Sadducees asked Jesus a question. [19]They said, "Teacher, Moses wrote that a man's brother might die. He leaves a wife but no children. Then that man must marry the widow and have children for the dead brother. [20]There were seven brothers. The first brother married but died. He had no children. [21]So the second brother married the widow. But he also died and had no children. The same thing happened with the third brother. [22]All seven brothers married her and died. None of the brothers had any children. The woman was last to die. [23]But all seven brothers had married her. So at the time people rise from death, whose wife will the woman be?"

[24]Jesus answered, "Why did you make this mistake? Is it because you don't know what the Scriptures[d] say? Or is it because you don't know about the power of God? [25]When people rise from death, there will be no marriage. People will not be married to each other but will be like angels in heaven. [26]Surely you have read what God said about people rising from death. In the book in which Moses wrote about the burning bush,[n] it says that God told Moses this: 'I am the God of Abraham, the God of Isaac, and the God of Jacob.'[n] [27]God is the God of living people, not dead people. You Sadducees are wrong!"

THE MOST IMPORTANT COMMAND

[28]One of the teachers of the law came to Jesus. He heard Jesus arguing with the Sadducees[d] and the Pharisees.[d] He saw that Jesus gave good answers to their questions. So he asked Jesus, "Which of the commands is most important?"

[29]Jesus answered, "The most important command is this: 'Listen, people of Israel! The Lord our God, he is the only Lord. [30]Love the Lord your God. Love him with all your heart, all your soul, all your mind, and all your strength.'[n] [31]The second most important command is this: 'Love your neighbor as you love yourself.'[n] These two commands are the most important commands."

[32]The man answered, "That was a good answer, Teacher. You were right when you said these things. God is the only Lord, and there is no other God besides him. [33]One must love God with all his heart, all his mind, and all his strength. And one must love his neighbor as he loves himself. These commands are more important than all the animals and sacrifices we offer to God."

[34]Jesus saw that the man answered him wisely. So Jesus said to him, "You are close to the kingdom of God." And after that, no one was brave enough to ask Jesus any more questions.

[35]Jesus was teaching in the Temple.[d] He asked, "Why do the teachers of the law say that the Christ[d] is the son of David? [36]David himself, speaking by the Holy Spirit,[d] said:

'The Lord said to my Lord:
  Sit by me at my right side,
  until I put your enemies under your
    control.'   Psalm 110:1

[37]David himself calls the Christ 'Lord.' So how can the Christ be David's son?" The large crowd listened to Jesus with pleasure.

[38]Jesus continued teaching. He said, "Beware of the teachers of the law. They like to walk around wearing clothes that look important. And they love for people to show respect to them in the marketplaces. [39]They love to have the most

---

12:26 burning bush Read Exodus 3:1-12 in the Old Testament.
12:26 'I am . . . Jacob.' Quotation from Exodus 3:6.
12:29-30 'Listen . . . strength.' Quotation from Deuteronomy 6:4-5.
12:31 'Love . . . yourself.' Quotation from Leviticus 19:18.

important seats in the synagogues.[d] And they love to have the most important seats at the feasts. [40]They cheat widows and steal their homes. Then they try to make themselves look good by saying long prayers. God will punish these people terribly."

TRUE GIVING

[41]Jesus sat near the Temple[d] money box where people put their gifts. He watched the people put in their money. Many rich people gave large sums of money. [42]Then a poor widow came and gave two very small copper coins. These coins were not worth even a penny.

[43]Jesus called his followers to him. He said, "I tell you the truth. This poor widow gave only two small coins. But she really gave more than all those rich people. [44]The rich have plenty; they gave only what they did not need. This woman is very poor. But she gave all she had. And she needed that money to help her live."

THE TEMPLE WILL BE DESTROYED

13 Jesus was leaving the Temple.[d] One of his followers said to him, "Look, Teacher! This Temple has beautiful buildings with very big stones."

[2]Jesus said, "Do you see all these great buildings? Every stone will be thrown to the ground. Not one stone will be left on another."

[3]Later, Jesus was sitting on the Mount of Olives.[d] He was alone with Peter, James, John, and Andrew. They could all see the Temple. They asked Jesus, [4]"Tell us, when will all these things happen? And what will show us that the time has come for them to happen?"

[5]Jesus said to them: "Be careful that no one fools you. [6]Many people will come and use my name. They will say, 'I am the One.' And they will fool many. [7]You will hear about wars and stories of wars

that are coming. But don't be afraid. These things must happen before the end comes. [8]Nations will fight against other nations. Kingdoms will fight against other kingdoms. There will be times when there is no food for people to eat. And there will be earthquakes in different places. These things are like the first pains when something new is about to be born.

[9]"You must be careful. People will arrest you and take you to court. They will beat you in their synagogues.[d] You will be forced to stand before kings and governors, to tell them about me. This will happen to you because you follow me. [10]But before these things happen, the Good News[d] must be told to all people. [11]When you are arrested and judged, don't worry about what you should say. Say the things God gives you to say at that time. It will not really be you speaking. It will be the Holy Spirit.[d]

[12]"Brothers will turn against their own brothers and give them over to be killed. Fathers will turn against their own children and give them over to be killed. Children will fight against their own parents and cause their parents to be killed. [13]All people will hate you because you follow me. But the person who continues to be strong until the end will be saved.

[14]"You will see 'the horrible thing that destroys.'[n] You will see this thing standing in the place where it should not be." (You who read this should understand what it means.) "At that time, the people in Judea should run away to the mountains. [15]If a person is on the roof[n] of his house, he must not go down to take anything out of his house. [16]If a person is in the field, he must not go back to get his coat. [17]At that time, it will be hard for women who are pregnant or have nursing babies. [18]Pray that these things will not

---

13:14 'the horrible . . . destroys.' Mentioned in Daniel 9:27; 12:11 (cf. Daniel 11:31).

13:15 roof In Bible times houses were built with flat roofs. The roof was used for drying things such as flax and fruit. And it was used as an extra room, as a place for worship and as a place to sleep in the summer.

happen in winter. [19]This is because those days will be full of trouble. There will be more trouble than there has ever been since the beginning, when God made the world. And nothing as bad will ever happen again. [20]God has decided to make that terrible time short. If that time were not made short, then no one would go on living. But God will make that time short to help his special people whom he has chosen. [21]At that time, someone might say to you, 'Look, there is the Christ!'[d] Or another person might say, 'There he is!' But don't believe them. [22]False Christs and false prophets[d] will come and perform great wonders and miracles.[d] They will do these things to the people God has chosen. They will do these things to try to fool them, if that is possible. [23]So be careful. For I have warned you about all this before it happens.

[24]"During the days after this trouble comes,

'The sun will grow dark.

And the moon will not give its light.

[25]The stars will fall from the sky.

And everything in the sky will be changed.'   *Isaiah 13:10; 34:4*

[26]"Then people will see the Son of Man[d] coming in clouds with great power and glory. [27]The Son of Man will send his angels all around the earth. They will gather his chosen people from every part of the earth.

[28]"The fig tree teaches us a lesson: When its branches become green and soft, and new leaves begin to grow, then you know that summer is near. [29]So also when you see all these things happening, then you will know that the time is near, ready to come. [30]I tell you the truth. All these things will happen while the people of this time are still living. [31]The whole world, earth and sky, will be destroyed, but the words I have said will never be destroyed.

[32]"No one knows when that day or time will be. The Son and the angels in heaven don't know. Only the Father knows. [33]Be careful! Always be ready![n] You don't know when that time will be. [34]It is like a man who goes on a trip. He leaves his house and lets his servants take care of it. He gives each servant a special job to do. One servant has the work of guarding the door. The man tells this servant always to be watchful. This is what I am now telling you. [35]You must always be ready. You don't know when the owner of the house will come back. He might come in the evening, or at midnight, or in the early morning, or when the sun rises. [36]He might come back quickly. If you are always ready, then he will not find you sleeping. [37]I tell you this, and I say this to everyone: 'Be ready!'"

THE PLAN TO KILL JESUS

14 It was now only two days before the Passover[d] and the Feast[d] of Unleavened Bread. The leading priests and teachers of the law were trying to find a way to use some trick to arrest Jesus and kill him. [2]But they said, "We must not do it during the feast. The people might cause a riot."

A WOMAN WITH PERFUME FOR JESUS

[3]Jesus was in Bethany. He was at dinner in the house of Simon, who had a harmful skin disease. While Jesus was there, a woman came to him. She had an alabaster[d] jar filled with very expensive perfume, made of pure nard.[d] The woman opened the jar and poured the perfume on Jesus' head.

[4]Some of those who were there saw this and became angry. They complained to each other, saying, "Why waste that perfume? [5]It was worth a full year's work. It could be sold, and the money could be given to the poor." They spoke to the woman sharply.

13:33 ready Some Greek copies continue, "and pray."

⁶Jesus said, "Don't bother the woman. Why are you troubling her? She did a beautiful thing for me. ⁷You will always have the poor with you. You can help them anytime you want. But you will not always have me. ⁸This woman did the only thing she could do for me. She poured perfume on my body. She did this before I die to prepare me for burial. ⁹I tell you the truth. The Good News*d* will be told to people in all the world. And in every place it is preached, what this woman has done will be told. And people will remember her."

JUDAS BECOMES AN ENEMY OF JESUS

¹⁰One of the 12 followers, Judas Iscariot, went to talk to the leading priests. Judas offered to give Jesus to them. ¹¹The leading priests were pleased about this. They promised to pay Judas money. So he waited for the best time to give Jesus to them.

JESUS EATS THE PASSOVER FEAST

¹²It was now the first day of the Feast*d* of Unleavened Bread. This was a time when the Jews always sacrificed the Passover*d* lambs. Jesus' followers came to him. They said, "We will go and prepare everything for the Passover Feast. Where do you want to eat the feast?"

¹³Jesus sent two of his followers and said to them, "Go into the city. A man carrying a jar of water will meet you. Follow him. ¹⁴He will go into a house. Tell the owner of the house, 'The Teacher asks that you show us the room where he and his followers can eat the Passover Feast.' ¹⁵The owner will show you a large room upstairs. This room is ready. Prepare the food for us there."

¹⁶So the followers left and went into the city. Everything happened as Jesus had said. So they prepared the Passover Feast.

¹⁷In the evening, Jesus went to that house with the 12. ¹⁸While they were all eating, Jesus said, "I tell you the truth. One of you will give me to my enemies— one of you eating with me now."

¹⁹The followers were very sad to hear this. Each one said to Jesus, "I am not the one, am I?"

²⁰Jesus answered, "The man who is against me is 1 of the 12. He is the one who dips his bread into the bowl with me. ²¹The Son of Man*d* must go and die. The Scriptures*d* say this will happen. But how terrible it will be for the person who gives the Son of Man to be killed. It would be better for that person if he had never been born."

THE LORD'S SUPPER

²²While they were eating, Jesus took some bread. He thanked God for it and broke it. Then he gave it to his followers and said, "Take it. This bread is my body."

²³Then Jesus took a cup. He thanked God for it and gave it to the followers. All the followers drank from the cup.

²⁴Then Jesus said, "This is my blood which begins the new*n* agreement that God makes with his people. This blood is poured out for many. ²⁵I tell you the truth. I will not drink of this fruit of the vine*n* again until that day when I drink it new in the kingdom of God."

²⁶They sang a hymn and went out to the Mount of Olives.*d*

JESUS' FOLLOWERS WILL ALL LEAVE HIM

²⁷Then Jesus told the followers, "You will all lose your faith in me. It is written in the Scriptures:*d*

'I will kill the shepherd,
    and the sheep will scatter.'
                          Zechariah 13:7
²⁸But after I rise from death, I will go ahead of you into Galilee."

²⁹Peter said, "All the other followers may lose their faith. But I will not."

³⁰Jesus answered, "I tell you the truth. Tonight you will say you don't know me.

14:24 new Some Greek copies do not have this word. Compare Luke 22:20.
14:25 fruit of the vine Product of the grapevine; this may also be translated "wine."

You will say this three times before the rooster crows twice."

[31]But Peter answered strongly, "I will never say that I don't know you! I will even die with you!" And all the other followers said the same thing.

JESUS PRAYS ALONE

[32]Jesus and his followers went to a place called Gethsemane. He said to his followers, "Sit here while I pray." [33]Jesus told Peter, James, and John to come with him. Then Jesus began to be very sad and troubled. [34]He said to them, "I am full of sorrow. My heart is breaking with sadness. Stay here and watch."

[35]Jesus walked a little farther away from them. Then he fell on the ground and prayed. He prayed that, if possible, he would not have this time of suffering. [36]He prayed, "Abba,[n] Father! You can do all things. Let me not have this cup[n] of suffering. But do what you want, not what I want."

[37]Then Jesus went back to his followers. He found them asleep. He said to Peter, "Simon, why are you sleeping? You could not stay awake with me for one hour? [38]Stay awake and pray that you will not be tempted. Your spirit wants to do what is right, but your body is weak."

[39]Again Jesus went away and prayed the same thing. [40]Then he went back to the followers. Again he found them asleep because their eyes were very heavy. And they did not know what to say to Jesus.

[41]After Jesus prayed a third time, he went back to his followers. He said to them, "You are still sleeping and resting? That's enough! The time has come for the Son of Man[d] to be given to sinful people. [42]Get up! We must go. Here comes the man who has turned against me."

JESUS IS ARRESTED

[43]While Jesus was still speaking, Judas came up. Judas was 1 of the 12 followers. He had many people with him. They were sent from the leading priests, the teachers of the law, and the Jewish elders. Those with Judas had swords and clubs.

[44]Judas had planned a signal for them. He had said, "The man I kiss is Jesus. Arrest him and guard him while you lead him away." [45]So Judas went to Jesus and said, "Teacher!" and kissed him. [46]Then the men grabbed Jesus and arrested him. [47]One of the followers standing near drew his sword. He struck the servant of the high priest with the sword and cut off his ear.

[48]Then Jesus said, "You came to get me with swords and clubs as if I were a criminal. [49]Every day I was with you teaching in the Temple.[d] You did not arrest me there. But all these things have happened to make the Scriptures[d] come true." [50]Then all of Jesus' followers left him and ran away.

[51]A young man, wearing only a linen cloth, was following Jesus. The people also grabbed him. [52]But the cloth he was wearing came off, and he ran away naked.

JESUS BEFORE THE LEADERS

[53]The people who arrested Jesus led him to the house of the high priest. All the leading priests, the Jewish elders, and the teachers of the law were gathered there. [54]Peter followed far behind and entered the courtyard of the high priest's house. There he sat with the guards, warming himself by the fire.

[55]The leading priests and all the Jewish council tried to find something that Jesus had done wrong so they could kill him. But the council could find no proof against him. [56]Many people came and told false things about him. But all said different things—none of them agreed.

14:36 **Abba** Name that a child called his father.
14:36 **cup** Jesus is talking about the bad things that will happen to him. Accepting these things will be very hard, like drinking a cup of something that tastes very bitter.

57Then some men stood up and lied about Jesus. They said, 58"We heard this man say, 'I will destroy this Temple*d* that men made. And three days later, I will build another Temple—a Temple not made by men.'" 59But even the things these men said did not agree.

60Then the high priest stood before them and said to Jesus, "Aren't you going to answer the charges these men bring against you?" 61But Jesus said nothing. He did not answer.

The high priest asked Jesus another question: "Are you the Christ,*d* the Son of the blessed God?"

62Jesus answered, "I am. And in the future you will see the Son of Man*d* sitting at the right side of the Powerful One. And you will see the Son of Man coming on clouds in the sky."

63When the high priest heard this, he was very angry. He tore his clothes and said, "We don't need any more witnesses! 64You all heard him say these things against God. What do you think?"

They all said that Jesus was guilty and should be killed. 65Some of the people there spit at Jesus. They covered his eyes and hit him with their fists. They said, "Prove that you are a prophet!"*d* Then the guards led Jesus away and beat him.

PETER SAYS HE DOESN'T KNOW JESUS

66Peter was still in the courtyard when a servant girl of the high priest came there. 67She saw Peter warming himself at the fire. She looked closely at him.

Then the girl said, "You were with Jesus, that man from Nazareth."

68But Peter said that he was never with Jesus. He said, "I don't know or understand what you are talking about." Then Peter left and went toward the entrance of the courtyard.*n*

69The servant girl saw Peter there. Again she said to the people who were standing there, "This man is one of those who followed Jesus." 70Again Peter said that it was not true.

A short time later, some people were standing near Peter. They said, "We know you are one of those who followed Jesus. You are from Galilee, too."

71Then Peter began to curse. He said, "I swear that I don't know this man you're talking about!"

72As soon as Peter said this, the rooster crowed the second time. Then Peter remembered what Jesus had told him: "Before the rooster crows twice, you will say three times that you don't know me." Then Peter was very sad and began to cry.

PILATE QUESTIONS JESUS

15 Very early in the morning, the leading priests, the Jewish elders, the teachers of the law, and all the Jewish council decided what to do with Jesus. They tied him, led him away, and turned him over to Pilate, the governor.

2Pilate asked Jesus, "Are you the king of the Jews?"

Jesus answered, "Yes, I am."

3The leading priests accused Jesus of many things. 4So Pilate asked Jesus another question. He said, "You can see that these people are accusing you of many things. Why don't you answer?"

5But Jesus still said nothing. Pilate was very surprised at this.

PILATE TRIES TO FREE JESUS

6Every year at the Passover*d* time the governor would free one person from prison. He would free any person the people wanted him to free. 7At that time, there was a man named Barabbas in prison. He was a rebel and had committed murder during a riot. 8The crowd came to Pilate and asked him to free a prisoner as he always did.

9Pilate asked them, "Do you want me to free the king of the Jews?" 10Pilate knew that the leading priests had given

14:68 Verse 68 Many Greek copies add: "And the rooster crowed."

Jesus to him because they were jealous of Jesus. [11]And the leading priests had persuaded the people to ask Pilate to free Barabbas, not Jesus.

[12]Pilate asked the crowd again, "So what should I do with this man you call the king of the Jews?"

[13]They shouted, "Kill him on a cross!"

[14]Pilate asked, "Why? What wrong has he done?"

But they shouted louder and louder, "Kill him on a cross!"

[15]Pilate wanted to please the crowd. So he freed Barabbas for them. And Pilate told the soldiers to beat Jesus with whips. Then he gave Jesus to the soldiers to be killed on a cross.

[16]Pilate's soldiers took Jesus into the governor's palace (called the Praetorium). They called all the other soldiers together. [17]They put a purple robe on Jesus. Then they used thorny branches to make a crown. They put it on his head. [18]Then they called out to him, "Hail, King of the Jews!" [19]The soldiers beat Jesus on the head many times with a stick. They also spit on him. Then they made fun of him by bowing on their knees and worshiping him. [20]After they finished making fun of him, the soldiers took off the purple robe and put his own clothes on him again. Then they led Jesus out of the palace to be killed on a cross.

JESUS IS KILLED ON A CROSS

[21]There was a man from Cyrene coming from the fields to the city. The man was Simon, the father of Alexander and Rufus. The soldiers forced Simon to carry the cross for Jesus. [22]They led Jesus to the place called Golgotha. (Golgotha means the Place of the Skull.) [23]At Golgotha the soldiers tried to give Jesus wine to drink. This wine was mixed with myrrh.[d] But he refused to drink it. [24]The soldiers nailed Jesus to a cross. Then they divided his clothes among themselves. They threw lots[d] to decide which clothes each soldier would get.

[25]It was nine o'clock in the morning when they nailed Jesus to the cross. [26]There was a sign with the charge against Jesus written on it. The sign read: "THE KING OF THE JEWS." [27]They also put two robbers on crosses beside Jesus, one on the right, and the other on the left. [28][And the Scripture came true that says, "They put him with criminals."][n] [29]People walked by and insulted Jesus. They shook their heads, saying, "You said you could destroy the Temple[d] and build it again in three days. [30]So save yourself! Come down from that cross!"

[31]The leading priests and the teachers of the law were also there. They made fun of Jesus just as the other people did. They said among themselves, "He saved other people, but he can't save himself. [32]If he is really the Christ,[d] the king of Israel, then let him come down from the cross now. We will see this, and then we will believe in him." The robbers who were being killed on the crosses beside Jesus also insulted him.

JESUS DIES

[33]At noon the whole country became dark. This darkness lasted for three hours. [34]At three o'clock Jesus cried in a loud voice, "Eloi, Eloi, lama sabachthani." This means, "My God, my God, why have you left me alone?"

[35]Some of the people standing there heard this. They said, "Listen! He is calling Elijah."

[36]One man there ran and got a sponge. He filled the sponge with vinegar and tied it to a stick. Then he used the stick to give the sponge to Jesus to drink from it. The man said, "We should wait now and see if Elijah will come to take him down from the cross."

[37]Then Jesus cried in a loud voice and died.

15:28 And . . . criminals. Some Greek copies do not contain the bracketed text which quotes from Isaiah 53:12.

[38]When Jesus died, the curtain in the Temple[n] split into two pieces. The tear started at the top and tore all the way to the bottom. [39]The army officer that was standing there before the cross saw what happened when Jesus died.[n] The officer said, "This man really was the Son of God!"

[40]Some women were standing at a distance from the cross, watching. Some of these women were Mary Magdalene, Salome, and Mary the mother of James and Joseph. (James was her youngest son.) [41]These were the women who followed Jesus in Galilee and cared for him. Many other women were also there who had come with Jesus to Jerusalem.

JESUS IS BURIED

[42]This was Preparation[d] Day. (That means the day before the Sabbath[d] day.) It was becoming dark. [43]A man named Joseph from Arimathea was brave enough to go to Pilate and ask for Jesus' body. Joseph was an important member of the Jewish council. He was one of the people who wanted the kingdom of God to come. [44]Pilate wondered if Jesus was already dead. Pilate called the army officer who guarded Jesus and asked him if Jesus had already died. [45]The officer told Pilate that he was dead. So Pilate told Joseph he could have the body. [46]Joseph bought some linen cloth, took the body down from the cross and wrapped it in the linen. He put the body in a tomb that was cut in a wall of rock. Then he closed the tomb by rolling a very large stone to cover the entrance. [47]And Mary Magdalene and Mary the mother of Joseph saw the place where Jesus was laid.

JESUS RISES FROM DEATH

16 The day after the Sabbath[d] day, Mary Magdalene, Mary the mother of James, and Salome bought some sweet-smelling spices to put on Jesus' body. [2]Very early on that day, the first day of the week, the women were on their way to the tomb. It was soon after sunrise. [3]They said to each other, "There is a large stone covering the entrance of the tomb. Who will move the stone for us?"

[4]Then the women looked and saw that the stone was already moved. The stone was very large, but it was moved away from the entrance. [5]The women entered the tomb and saw a young man wearing a white robe. He was sitting on the right side, and the women were afraid.

[6]But the man said, "Don't be afraid. You are looking for Jesus from Nazareth, the one who was killed on a cross. He has risen from death. He is not here. Look, here is the place they laid him. [7]Now go and tell his followers and Peter, 'Jesus is going into Galilee. He will be there before you. You will see him there as he told you before.'"

[8]The women were confused and shaking with fear. They left the tomb and ran away. They did not tell anyone about what happened, because they were afraid.[n]

SOME FOLLOWERS SEE JESUS

[9]Jesus rose from death early on the first day of the week. He showed himself first to Mary Magdalene. One time in the past, he had forced seven demons[d] to leave Mary. [10]After Mary saw Jesus, she went and told his followers. They were very sad and were crying. [11]But Mary told them that Jesus was alive. She said that she had seen him, but the followers did not believe her.

[12]Later, Jesus showed himself to two of his followers while they were walking in the country. But Jesus did not look the same as before. [13]These followers went back to the others and told them what

---

15:38 curtain in the Temple A curtain divided the Most Holy Place from the other part of the Temple. That was the special building in Jerusalem where God commanded the Jews to worship him.
15:39 when Jesus died Some Greek copies read "when Jesus cried out and died."
16:8 Verse 8 Some early Greek copies end the book with verse 8.

had happened. Again, the followers did not believe them.

JESUS TALKS TO THE APOSTLES

[14]Later Jesus showed himself to the 11 followers while they were eating. He criticized them because they had little faith. They were stubborn and refused to believe those who had seen him after he had risen from death.

[15]Jesus said to the followers, "Go everywhere in the world. Tell the Good News[d] to everyone. [16]Anyone who believes and is baptized will be saved. But he who does not believe will be judged guilty. [17]And those who believe will be able to do these things as proof: They will use my name to force demons[d] out of people. They will speak in languages they never learned. [18]They will pick up snakes without being hurt. And they will drink poison without being hurt. They will touch the sick, and the sick will be healed."

[19]After the Lord Jesus said these things to the followers, he was carried up into heaven. There, Jesus sat at the right side of God. [20]The followers went everywhere in the world and told the Good News to people. And the Lord helped them. The Lord proved that the Good News they told was true by giving them power to work miracles.[d]

LUKE

LUKE TELLS ABOUT JESUS THE SAVIOR FOR ALL PEOPLE

LUKE WRITES ABOUT JESUS' LIFE

1 To Theophilus:
Many have tried to give a history of the things that happened among us. [2]They have written the same things that we learned from others—the people who saw those things from the beginning and served God by telling people his message. [3]I myself studied everything carefully from the beginning, your Excellency.[n] I thought I should write it out for you. So I put it in order in a book. [4]I write these things so that you can know that what you have been taught is true.

ZECHARIAH AND ELIZABETH

[5]During the time Herod ruled Judea, there was a priest named Zechariah. He belonged to Abijah's group.[n] Zechariah's wife came from the family of Aaron. Her name was Elizabeth. [6]Zechariah and Elizabeth truly did what God said was good. They did everything the Lord commanded and told people to do. They were without fault in keeping his law. [7]But Zechariah and Elizabeth had no children. Elizabeth could not have a baby; and both of them were very old.

[8]Zechariah was serving as a priest before God for his group. It was his group's time to serve. [9]According to the custom of the priests, he was chosen to go into the Temple[d] of the Lord and burn incense.[d] [10]There were a great many people outside praying at the time the incense was offered. [11]Then, on the right side of the incense table, an angel of the Lord came and stood before Zechariah. [12]When he saw the angel, Zechariah was confused and frightened. [13]But the angel said to him, "Zechariah, don't be afraid. Your prayer has been heard by God. Your wife, Elizabeth, will give birth to a son. You will name him John. [14]You will be very happy. Many people will be happy because of his birth. [15]John will be a great man for the Lord. He will never drink wine or beer. Even at the time John is born, he will be filled with the Holy Spirit.[d] [16]He will help many people of Israel return to the Lord their God. [17]He himself will go first before the Lord. John will be powerful in spirit like Elijah. He will make peace between fathers and their children. He will bring those who are not obeying God back to the right way of thinking. He will make people ready for the coming of the Lord."

[18]Zechariah said to the angel, "How can I know that what you say is true? I am an old man, and my wife is old, too."

[19]The angel answered him, "I am Gabriel. I stand before God. God sent me to talk to you and to tell you this good news. [20]Now, listen! You will not be able to talk until the day these things happen. You will lose your speech because you did not believe what I told you. But these things will really happen."

[21]Outside, the people were still waiting for Zechariah. They were surprised that he was staying so long in the Temple. [22]Then Zechariah came outside, but he could not speak to them. So they knew that he had seen a vision in the Temple. Zechariah could not speak. He could only make signs to them. [23]When his time of service as a priest was finished, he went home.

[24]Later, Zechariah's wife, Elizabeth, became pregnant. She did not go out of her house for five months. Elizabeth said, [25]"Look what the Lord has done for me! My people were ashamed[n] of me, but now the Lord has taken away that shame."

1:3 Excellency This word was used to show respect to an important person like a king or ruler.
1:5 Abijah's group The Jewish priests were divided into 24 groups. See 1 Chronicles 24.
1:25 ashamed The Jews thought it was a disgrace for women not to have children.

THE VIRGIN MARY

²⁶⁻²⁷During Elizabeth's sixth month of pregnancy, God sent the angel Gabriel to a virgin*d* who lived in Nazareth, a town in Galilee. She was engaged to marry a man named Joseph from the family of David. Her name was Mary. ²⁸The angel came to her and said, "Greetings! The Lord has blessed you and is with you."

²⁹But Mary was very confused by what the angel said. Mary wondered, "What does this mean?"

³⁰The angel said to her, "Don't be afraid, Mary, because God is pleased with you. ³¹Listen! You will become pregnant. You will give birth to a son, and you will name him Jesus. ³²He will be great, and people will call him the Son of the Most High. The Lord God will give him the throne of King David, his ancestor. ³³He will rule over the people of Jacob forever. His kingdom will never end."

³⁴Mary said to the angel, "How will this happen? I am a virgin!"

³⁵The angel said to Mary, "The Holy Spirit*d* will come upon you, and the power of the Most High will cover you. The baby will be holy. He will be called the Son of God. ³⁶Now listen! Elizabeth, your relative, is very old. But she is also pregnant with a son. Everyone thought she could not have a baby, but she has been pregnant for six months. ³⁷God can do everything!"

³⁸Mary said, "I am the servant girl of the Lord. Let this happen to me as you say!" Then the angel went away.

MARY'S VISIT

³⁹Mary got up and went quickly to a town in the mountains of Judea. ⁴⁰She went to Zechariah's house and greeted Elizabeth. ⁴¹When Elizabeth heard Mary's greeting, the unborn baby inside Elizabeth jumped. Then Elizabeth was filled with the Holy Spirit.*d* ⁴²She cried out in a loud voice, "God has blessed you more than any other woman. And God has blessed the baby which you will give birth to. ⁴³You are the mother of my Lord, and you have come to me! Why has something so good happened to me? ⁴⁴When I heard your voice, the baby inside me jumped with joy. ⁴⁵You are blessed because you believed what the Lord said to you would really happen."

MARY PRAISES GOD

⁴⁶Then Mary said,

"My soul praises the Lord;
⁴⁷   my heart is happy because God is
       my Savior.
⁴⁸I am not important, but God has
       shown his care for me, his
       servant girl.
From now on, all people will say that
       I am blessed,
⁴⁹   because the Powerful One has done
       great things for me.
       His name is holy.
⁵⁰God will always give mercy
       to those who worship him.
⁵¹God's arm is strong.
       He scatters the people who are
       proud
       and think great things about
       themselves.
⁵²God brings down rulers from their
       thrones,
       and he raises up the humble.
⁵³God fills the hungry with good things,
       but he sends the rich away with
       nothing.
⁵⁴God has helped his people Israel who
       serve him.
       He gave them his mercy.
⁵⁵God has done what he promised to
       our ancestors,
       to Abraham and to his children
       forever."

⁵⁶Mary stayed with Elizabeth for about three months and then returned home.

THE BIRTH OF JOHN

⁵⁷When it was time for Elizabeth to give birth, she had a boy. ⁵⁸Her neighbors

and relatives heard how good the Lord was to her, and they rejoiced.

[59]When the baby was eight days old, they came to circumcise[d] him. They wanted to name him Zechariah because this was his father's name. [60]But his mother said, "No! He will be named John."

[61]The people said to Elizabeth, "But no one in your family has this name!" [62]Then they made signs to his father, "What would you like to name him?"

[63]Zechariah asked for something to write on. Then he wrote, "His name is John." Everyone was surprised. [64]Then Zechariah could talk again. He began to praise God. [65]And all their neighbors became alarmed. In all the mountains of Judea people continued talking about all these things. [66]The people who heard about these things wondered about them. They thought, "What will this child be?" They said this because the Lord was with him.

ZECHARIAH PRAISES GOD

[67]Then Zechariah, John's father, was filled with the Holy Spirit.[d] He told the people what would happen:

[68]"Let us thank the Lord, the God of Israel.

God has come to help his people and has given them freedom.

[69]God has given us a powerful Savior from the family of God's servant David.

[70]God said that he would do this.

He said it through his holy prophets[d] who lived long ago.

[71]God will save us from our enemies and from the power of all those who hate us.

[72]God said he would give mercy to our ancestors.

And he remembered his holy promise.

[73]God promised Abraham, our father,

[74]   that he would free us from the power of our enemies,

so that we could serve him without fear.

[75]We will be righteous and holy before God as long as we live.

[76]"Now you, child, will be called a prophet of the Most High God.

You will go first before the Lord to prepare the people for his coming.

[77]You will make his people know that they will be saved.

They will be saved by having their sins forgiven.

[78]With the loving mercy of our God, a new day from heaven will shine upon us.

[79]God will help those who live in darkness,

in the fear of death.

He will guide us into the path that goes toward peace."

[80]And so the child grew up and became strong in spirit. John lived away from other people until the time when he came out to preach to Israel.

THE BIRTH OF JESUS

2 At that time, Augustus Caesar[d] sent an order to all people in the countries that were under Roman rule. The order said that they must list their names in a register. [2]This was the first registration[n] taken while Quirinius was governor of Syria. [3]And everyone went to their own towns to be registered.

[4]So Joseph left Nazareth, a town in Galilee. He went to the town of Bethlehem in Judea. This town was known as the town of David. Joseph went there because he was from the family of David. [5]Joseph registered with Mary because she was engaged to marry him. (Mary was now pregnant.) [6]While Joseph and Mary were in Bethlehem, the time came for her to have the baby. [7]She gave birth

---

2:2 **registration** Census. A counting of all the people and the things they own.

to her first son. There were no rooms left in the inn. So she wrapped the baby with cloths and laid him in a box where animals are fed.

SOME SHEPHERDS HEAR ABOUT JESUS

[8]That night, some shepherds were in the fields nearby watching their sheep. [9]An angel of the Lord stood before them. The glory of the Lord was shining around them, and suddenly they became very frightened. [10]The angel said to them, "Don't be afraid, because I am bringing you some good news. It will be a joy to all the people. [11]Today your Savior was born in David's town. He is Christ,[d] the Lord. [12]This is how you will know him: You will find a baby wrapped in cloths and lying in a feeding box."

[13]Then a very large group of angels from heaven joined the first angel. All the angels were praising God, saying:
[14]"Give glory to God in heaven,
    and on earth let there be peace to
        the people who please God."[n]

[15]Then the angels left the shepherds and went back to heaven. The shepherds said to each other, "Let us go to Bethlehem and see this thing that has happened. We will see this thing the Lord told us about."

[16]So the shepherds went quickly and found Mary and Joseph. [17]And the shepherds saw the baby lying in a feeding box. Then they told what the angels had said about this child. [18]Everyone was amazed when they heard what the shepherds said to them. [19]Mary hid these things in her heart; she continued to think about them. [20]Then the shepherds went back to their sheep, praising God and thanking him for everything that they had seen and heard. It was just as the angel had told them.

[21]When the baby was eight days old, he was circumcised,[d] and he was named Jesus. This name had been given by the angel before the baby began to grow inside Mary.

JESUS IS PRESENTED IN THE TEMPLE

[22]The time came for Mary and Joseph to do what the law of Moses taught about being made pure.[n] They took Jesus to Jerusalem to present him to the Lord. [23]It is written in the law of the Lord: "Give every firstborn[d] male to the Lord."[n] [24]Mary and Joseph also went to offer a sacrifice, as the law of the Lord says: "You must sacrifice two doves or two young pigeons."[n]

SIMEON SEES JESUS

[25]A man named Simeon lived in Jerusalem. He was a good man and very religious. He was waiting for the time when God would help Israel. The Holy Spirit[d] was in him. [26]The Holy Spirit told Simeon that he would not die before he saw the Christ[d] promised by the Lord. [27]The Spirit led Simeon to the Temple.[d] Mary and Joseph brought the baby Jesus to the Temple to do what the law said they must do. [28]Then Simeon took the baby in his arms and thanked God:
[29]"Now, Lord, you can let me, your
        servant,
    die in peace as you said.
[30]I have seen your Salvation[n] with my
        own eyes.
[31]   You prepared him before all people.
[32]He is a light for the non-Jewish people
        to see.
    He will bring honor to your people,
        the Israelites."

[33]Jesus' father and mother were amazed at what Simeon had said about him.

2:14 and . . . God Some Greek copies read "and on earth let there be peace and goodwill among people."
2:22 pure The law of Moses said that 40 days after a Jewish woman gave birth to a baby, she must be cleansed by a ceremony at the Temple. Read Leviticus 12:2-8.
2:23 "Give . . . Lord." Quotation from Exodus 13:2.
2:24 "You . . . pigeons." Quotation from Leviticus 12:8.
2:30 Salvation Simeon was talking about Jesus. The name Jesus means "salvation."

³⁴Then Simeon blessed them and said to Mary, "Many in Israel will fall and many will rise because of this child. He will be a sign from God that many people will not accept. ³⁵The things they think in secret will be made known. And the things that will happen will make your heart sad, too."

ANNA SEES JESUS

³⁶Anna, a prophetess,ᵈ was there at the Temple.ᵈ She was from the family of Phanuel in the tribeᵈ of Asher. Anna was very old. She had once been married for seven years. ³⁷Then her husband died and she lived alone. She was now 84 years old. Anna never left the Temple. She worshiped God by going without food and praying day and night. ³⁸She was standing there at that time, thanking God. She talked about Jesus to all who were waiting for God to free Jerusalem.

JOSEPH AND MARY RETURN HOME

³⁹Joseph and Mary finished doing everything that the law of the Lord commanded. Then they went home to Nazareth, their own town in Galilee. ⁴⁰The little child began to grow up. He became stronger and wiser, and God's blessings were with him.

JESUS AS A BOY

⁴¹Every year Jesus' parents went to Jerusalem for the Passoverᵈ Feast. ⁴²When Jesus was 12 years old, they went to the feast as they always did. ⁴³When the feast days were over, they went home. The boy Jesus stayed behind in Jerusalem, but his parents did not know it. ⁴⁴Joseph and Mary traveled for a whole day. They thought that Jesus was with them in the group. Then they began to look for him among their family and friends, ⁴⁵but they did not find him. So they went back to Jerusalem to look for him there. ⁴⁶After three days they found him. Jesus was sitting in the Templeᵈ with the religious teachers, listening to them and asking them questions. ⁴⁷All

who heard him were amazed at his understanding and wise answers. ⁴⁸When Jesus' parents saw him, they were amazed. His mother said to him, "Son, why did you do this to us? Your father and I were very worried about you. We have been looking for you."

⁴⁹Jesus asked, "Why did you have to look for me? You should have known that I must be where my Father's work is!" ⁵⁰But they did not understand the meaning of what he said.

⁵¹Jesus went with them to Nazareth and obeyed them. His mother was still thinking about all that had happened. ⁵²Jesus continued to learn more and more and to grow physically. People liked him, and he pleased God.

THE PREACHING OF JOHN

3 It was the fifteenth year of the rule of Tiberius Caesar.ᵈ These men were under Caesar: Pontius Pilate was the ruler of Judea. Herod was the ruler of Galilee. Philip, Herod's brother, was the ruler of Iturea and Trachonitis. And Lysanias was the ruler of Abilene. ²Annas and Caiaphas were the high priests. At this time, a command from God came to John son of Zechariah. John was living in the desert. ³He went all over the area around the Jordan River and preached to the people. He preached a baptism of changed hearts and lives for the forgiveness of their sins. ⁴As it is written in the book of Isaiah the prophet:ᵈ

"This is a voice of a man
　who calls out in the desert:
'Prepare the way for the Lord.
　Make the road straight for him.
⁵Every valley should be filled in.
　Every mountain and hill should be
　　made flat.
Roads with turns should be made
　straight,
　and rough roads should be made
　　smooth.
⁶And all people will know about the
　salvation of God!'"　　*Isaiah 40:3-5*

[7]Crowds of people came to be baptized by John. He said to them, "You poisonous snakes! Who warned you to run away from God's anger that is coming? [8]You must do the things that will show that you really have changed your hearts. Don't say, 'Abraham is our father.' I tell you that God can make children for Abraham from these rocks here. [9]The ax is now ready to cut down the trees. Every tree that does not produce good fruit will be cut down and thrown into the fire."[n]

[10]The people asked John, "What should we do?"

[11]John answered, "If you have two shirts, share with the person who does not have one. If you have food, share that too."

[12]Even tax collectors came to John to be baptized. They said to John, "Teacher, what should we do?"

[13]John said to them, "Don't take more taxes from people than you have been ordered to take."

[14]The soldiers asked John, "What about us? What should we do?"

John said to them, "Don't force people to give you money. Don't lie about them. Be satisfied with the pay you get."

[15]All the people were hoping for the Christ[d] to come, and they wondered about John. They thought, "Maybe he is the Christ."

[16]John answered everyone, "I baptize you with water, but there is one coming later who can do more than I can. I am not good enough to untie his sandals. He will baptize you with the Holy Spirit[d] and with fire. [17]He will come ready to clean the grain. He will separate the good grain from the chaff.[d] He will put the good part of the grain into his barn. Then he will burn the chaff with a fire that cannot be put out."[n] [18]And John continued to preach the Good News,[d] saying many other things to encourage the people.

[19]But John spoke against Herod, the governor, because of his sin with Herodias, the wife of Herod's brother. John also criticized Herod for the many other evil things Herod did. [20]So Herod did another evil thing: He put John in prison.

JESUS IS BAPTIZED BY JOHN

[21]When all the people were being baptized by John, Jesus also was baptized. While Jesus was praying, heaven opened and [22]the Holy Spirit[d] came down on him. The Spirit was in the form of a dove. Then a voice came from heaven and said, "You are my Son and I love you. I am very pleased with you."

THE FAMILY HISTORY OF JESUS

[23]When Jesus began to teach, he was about 30 years old. People thought that Jesus was Joseph's son.

Joseph was the son[n] of Heli.
[24]Heli was the son of Matthat.
Matthat was the son of Levi.
Levi was the son of Melki.
Melki was the son of Jannai.
Jannai was the son of Joseph.
[25]Joseph was the son of Mattathias.
Mattathias was the son of Amos.
Amos was the son of Nahum.
Nahum was the son of Esli.
Esli was the son of Naggai.
[26]Naggai was the son of Maath.
Maath was the son of Mattathias.
Mattathias was the son of Semein.
Semein was the son of Josech.
Josech was the son of Joda.
[27]Joda was the son of Joanan.
Joanan was the son of Rhesa.
Rhesa was the son of Zerubbabel.
Zerubbabel was the grandson of Shealtiel.
Shealtiel was the son of Neri.

3:9 The ax . . . fire. This means that God is ready to punish his people who do not obey him.
3:17 He will . . . out. This means that Jesus will come to separate the good people from the bad people, saving the good and punishing the bad.
3:23 son "Son" in Jewish lists of ancestors can sometimes mean grandson or more distant relative.

[28]Neri was the son of Melchi.
Melchi was the son of Addi.
Addi was the son of Cosam.
Cosam was the son of Elmadam.
Elmadam was the son of Er.
[29]Er was the son of Joshua.
Joshua was the son of Eliezer.
Eliezer was the son of Jorim.
Jorim was the son of Matthat.
Matthat was the son of Levi.
[30]Levi was the son of Simeon.
Simeon was the son of Judah.
Judah was the son of Joseph.
Joseph was the son of Jonam.
Jonam was the son of Eliakim.
[31]Eliakim was the son of Melea.
Melea was the son of Menna.
Menna was the son of Mattatha.
Mattatha was the son of Nathan.
Nathan was the son of David.
[32]David was the son of Jesse.
Jesse was the son of Obed.
Obed was the son of Boaz.
Boaz was the son of Salmon.[n]
Salmon was the son of Nahshon.
[33]Nahshon was the son of Amminadab.
Amminadab was the son of Admin.
Admin was the son of Arni.
Arni was the son of Hezron.
Hezron was the son of Perez.
Perez was the son of Judah.
[34]Judah was the son of Jacob.
Jacob was the son of Isaac.
Isaac was the son of Abraham.
Abraham was the son of Terah.
Terah was the son of Nahor.
[35]Nahor was the son of Serug.
Serug was the son of Reu.
Reu was the son of Peleg.
Peleg was the son of Eber.
Eber was the son of Shelah.
[36]Shelah was the son of Cainan.
Cainan was the son of Arphaxad.
Arphaxad was the son of Shem.

Shem was the son of Noah.
Noah was the son of Lamech.
[37]Lamech was the son of Methuselah.
Methuselah was the son of Enoch.
Enoch was the son of Jared.
Jared was the son of Mahalalel.
Mahalalel was the son of Kenan.
[38]Kenan was the son of Enosh.
Enosh was the son of Seth.
Seth was the son of Adam.
Adam was the son of God.

JESUS IS TEMPTED BY THE DEVIL

4 Jesus, filled with the Holy Spirit,[d] returned from the Jordan River. The Spirit led Jesus into the desert [2]where the devil tempted Jesus for 40 days. Jesus ate nothing during that time. When those days were ended, he was very hungry.

[3]The devil said to Jesus, "If you are the Son of God, tell this rock to become bread."

[4]Jesus answered, "It is written in the Scriptures:[d] 'A person does not live only by eating bread.'"[n]

[5]Then the devil took Jesus and showed him all the kingdoms of the world in a moment of time. [6]The devil said to Jesus, "I will give you all these kingdoms and all their power and glory. It has all been given to me, and I can give it to anyone I wish. [7]If you worship me, all will be yours."

[8]Jesus answered, "It is written in the Scriptures: 'You must worship the Lord your God. Serve only him!'"[n]

[9]Then the devil led Jesus to Jerusalem and put him on a high place of the Temple.[d] He said to Jesus, "If you are the Son of God, jump off! [10]It is written in the Scriptures:

'He has put his angels in charge of you.
    They will watch over you.'
                                    Psalm 91:11
[11]'They will catch you with their hands.
    And you will not hit your foot on a
    rock.'"   *Psalm 91:12*

3:32 Salmon Some Greek copies read "Sala."
4:4 'A person . . . bread.' Quotation from Deuteronomy 8:3.
4:8 'You . . . him!' Quotation from Deuteronomy 6:13.

[12]Jesus answered, "But it also says in the Scriptures: 'Do not test the Lord your God.'"[n]

[13]After the devil had tempted Jesus in every way, he went away to wait until a better time.

JESUS TEACHES THE PEOPLE

[14]Jesus went back to Galilee with the power of the Holy Spirit.[d] Stories about Jesus spread all through the area. [15]He began to teach in the synagogues,[d] and all the people praised him.

[16]Jesus traveled to Nazareth, where he had grown up. On the Sabbath[d] day he went to the synagogue as he always did. Jesus stood up to read. [17]The book of Isaiah the prophet[d] was given to him. He opened the book and found the place where this is written:

[18]"The Spirit of the Lord is in me.
This is because God chose me to tell the Good News[d] to the poor.
God sent me to tell the prisoners of sin that they are free,
and to tell the blind that they can see again.   *Isaiah 61:1*
God sent me to free those who have been treated unfairly,   *Isaiah 58:6*
[19] and to announce the time when the Lord will show kindness to his people."   *Isaiah 61:2*

[20]Jesus closed the book, gave it back, and sat down. Everyone in the synagogue was watching Jesus closely. [21]He began to speak to them. He said, "While you heard these words just now, they were coming true!"

[22]All the people praised Jesus. They were amazed at the beautiful words he spoke. They asked, "Isn't this Joseph's son?"

[23]Jesus said to them, "I know that you will tell me the old saying: 'Doctor, heal yourself.' You want to say, 'We heard about the things you did in Capernaum. Do those things here in your own town!'"

[24]Then Jesus said, "I tell you the truth. A prophet is not accepted in his own town. [25]What I say is true. During the time of Elijah it did not rain in Israel for three and a half years. There was no food anywhere in the whole country. And there were many widows in Israel during that time. [26]But Elijah was sent to none of those widows. He was sent only to a widow in Zarephath, a town in Sidon. [27]And there were many with a harmful skin disease living in Israel during the time of the prophet Elisha. But none of them were healed except Naaman, who was from the country of Syria."

[28]When all the people in the synagogue heard these things, they became very angry. [29]They got up and forced Jesus out of town. The town was built on a hill. They took Jesus to the edge of the hill and wanted to throw him off. [30]But Jesus walked through the crowd and went on his way.

JESUS REMOVES AN EVIL SPIRIT

[31]Jesus went to Capernaum, a city in Galilee. On the Sabbath[d] day, Jesus taught the people. [32]They were amazed at his teaching, because he spoke with authority. [33]In the synagogue[d] there was a man who had an evil spirit from the devil inside him. The man shouted in a loud voice, [34]"Jesus of Nazareth! What do you want with us? Did you come here to destroy us? I know who you are— God's Holy One!"

[35]But Jesus warned the evil spirit to stop. He said, "Be quiet! Come out of the man!" The evil spirit threw the man down to the ground before all the people. Then the evil spirit left the man and did not hurt him.

[36]The people were amazed. They said to each other, "What does this mean? With authority and power he commands

---

4:12 'Do . . . God.' Quotation from Deuteronomy 6:16.

evil spirits, and they come out." [37]And so the news about Jesus spread to every place in the whole area.

JESUS HEALS MANY PEOPLE

[38]Jesus left the synagogue[d] and went to Simon's[n] house. Simon's mother-in-law was very sick with a high fever. They asked Jesus to do something to help her. [39]He stood very close to her and commanded the fever to leave. It left her immediately, and she got up and began serving them.

[40]When the sun went down, the people brought their sick to Jesus. They had many different diseases. Jesus put his hands on each sick person and healed every one of them. [41]Demons[d] came out of many people. The demons would shout, "You are the Son of God." But Jesus gave a strong command for the demons not to speak. They knew Jesus was the Christ.[d]

[42]At daybreak, Jesus went to a place to be alone, but the people looked for him. When they found him, they tried to keep him from leaving. [43]But Jesus said to them, "I must tell the Good News[d] about God's kingdom to other towns, too. This is why I was sent."

[44]Then Jesus kept on preaching in the synagogues[d] of Judea.[n]

JESUS' FIRST FOLLOWERS

5 One day Jesus was standing beside Lake Galilee. Many people were pressing all around him. They wanted to hear the word of God. [2]Jesus saw two boats at the shore of the lake. The fishermen had left them and were washing their nets. [3]Jesus got into one of the boats, the one which belonged to Simon.[n] Jesus asked Simon to push off a little from the land. Then Jesus sat down in the boat and continued to teach the people on the shore.

[4]When Jesus had finished speaking, he said to Simon, "Take the boat into deep water. If you will put your nets in the water, you will catch some fish."

[5]Simon answered, "Master, we worked hard all night trying to catch fish, but we caught nothing. But you say to put the nets in the water; so I will." [6]The fishermen did as Jesus told them. And they caught so many fish that the nets began to break. [7]They called to their friends in the other boat to come and help them. The friends came, and both boats were filled so full that they were almost sinking. [8-9]The fishermen were all amazed at the many fish they caught. When Simon Peter saw what had happened, he bowed down before Jesus and said, "Go away from me, Lord. I am a sinful man!" [10]James and John, the sons of Zebedee, were amazed too. (James and John were Simon's partners.)

Jesus said to Simon, "Don't be afraid. From now on you will be fishermen for men." [11]When the men brought their boats to the shore, they left everything and followed Jesus.

JESUS HEALS A SICK MAN

[12]One time Jesus was in a town where a very sick man lived. The man was covered with a harmful skin disease. When he saw Jesus, he bowed before Jesus and begged him, "Lord, heal me. I know you can if you want to."

[13]Jesus said, "I want to. Be healed!" And Jesus touched the man. Immediately the disease disappeared. [14]Then Jesus said, "Don't tell anyone about what happened. But go show yourself to the priest.[n] And offer a gift to God for your healing as Moses commanded.[n] This will prove to everyone that you are healed."

[15]But the news about Jesus was spreading more and more. Many people

---

4:38; 5:3 **Simon** Simon's other name was Peter.
4:44 **Judea** Some Greek copies read "Galilee."
5:14 **show . . . priest** The law of Moses said a priest must say when a Jew with a harmful skin disease was well.
5:14 **Moses commanded** Read about this in Leviticus 14:1-32.

came to hear Jesus and to be healed of their sicknesses. [16]But Jesus often slipped away to other places to be alone so that he could pray.

JESUS HEALS A PARALYZED MAN

[17]One day Jesus was teaching the people. The Pharisees[d] and teachers of the law were there, too. They had come from every town in Galilee and from Judea and Jerusalem. The Lord was giving Jesus the power to heal people. [18]There was a man who was paralyzed. Some men were carrying him on a mat. They tried to bring him in and put him down before Jesus. [19]But because there were so many people there, they could not find a way to Jesus. So the men went up on the roof and made a hole in the ceiling. They lowered the mat so that the paralyzed man was lying right before Jesus. [20]Jesus saw that these men believed. So he said to the sick man, "Friend, your sins are forgiven."

[21]The Jewish teachers of the law and the Pharisees thought to themselves, "Who is this man? He is saying things that are against God! Only God can forgive sins."

[22]But Jesus knew what they were thinking. He said, "Why do you have thoughts like that in your hearts? [23]Which is easier: to tell this paralyzed man, 'Your sins are forgiven,' or to tell him, 'Stand up and walk'? [24]But I will prove to you that the Son of Man[d] has authority on earth to forgive sins." So Jesus said to the paralyzed man, "I tell you, stand up! Take your mat and go home."

[25]Then the man stood up before the people there. He picked up his mat and went home, praising God. [26]All the people were fully amazed and began to praise God. They were filled with much respect and said, "Today we have seen amazing things!"

LEVI FOLLOWS JESUS

[27]After this, Jesus went out and saw a tax collector named Levi sitting in the tax office. Jesus said to him, "Follow me!" [28]Levi got up, left everything, and followed Jesus.

[29]Then Levi gave a big dinner for Jesus. The dinner was at Levi's house. At the table there were many tax collectors and other people, too. [30]But the Pharisees[d] and the men who taught the law for the Pharisees began to complain to the followers of Jesus. They said, "Why do you eat and drink with tax collectors and 'sinners'?"

[31]Jesus answered them, "Healthy people don't need a doctor. It is the sick who need a doctor. [32]I have not come to invite good people. I have come to invite sinners to change their hearts and lives!"

JESUS ANSWERS A QUESTION

[33]They said to Jesus, "John's followers often give up eating[n] and pray, just as the Pharisees[d] do. But your followers eat and drink all the time."

[34]Jesus said to them, "When there is a wedding, you cannot make the friends of the bridegroom give up eating while he is still with them. [35]But the time will come when he will be taken away from them. Then his friends will give up eating."

[36]Jesus told them this story: "No one takes cloth off a new coat to cover a hole in an old coat. If he does, he ruins the new coat, and the cloth from the new coat will not be the same as the old cloth. [37]People never pour new wine into old leather bags for holding wine. If they do, the new wine will break the bags, and the wine will spill out. Then the leather bags for holding wine will be ruined. [38]People always put new wine into new leather bags. [39]No one after drinking old wine wants new wine because he says, 'The old wine is better.'"

5:33 give up eating This is called "fasting." The people would give up eating for a special time of prayer and worship to God. It was also done to show sadness.

JESUS IS LORD OVER THE SABBATH

6 One Sabbath[d] day Jesus was walking through some grainfields. His followers picked the heads of grain, rubbed them in their hands, and ate them. [2]Some Pharisees[d] said, "Why are you doing that? It is against the law of Moses to do that on the Sabbath day."

[3]Jesus answered, "Haven't you read about what David did when he and those with him were hungry? [4]David went into God's house. He took the bread that was made holy for God and ate it. And he gave some of the bread to the people with him. This was against the law of Moses. It says that only priests can eat that bread." [5]Then Jesus said to the Pharisees, "The Son of Man[d] is Lord of the Sabbath day."

JESUS HEALS A MAN'S CRIPPLED HAND

[6]On another Sabbath[d] day Jesus went into the synagogue[d] and was teaching. A man with a crippled right hand was there. [7]The teachers of the law and the Pharisees[d] were watching to see if Jesus would heal on the Sabbath day. They wanted to see Jesus do something wrong so that they could accuse him. [8]But he knew what they were thinking. He said to the man with the crippled hand, "Get up and stand before these people." The man got up and stood there. [9]Then Jesus said to them, "I ask you, which is it right to do on the Sabbath day: to do good, or to do evil? Is it right to save a life or to destroy one?" [10]Jesus looked around at all of them. He said to the man, "Let me see your hand." The man stretched out his hand, and it was completely healed.

[11]The Pharisees and the teachers of the law became very angry. They said to each other, "What can we do to Jesus?"

JESUS CHOOSES HIS APOSTLES

[12]At that time Jesus went off to a mountain to pray. He stayed there all night, praying to God. [13]The next morning, Jesus called his followers to him. He chose 12 of them, whom he named "apostles."[d] They were [14]Simon (Jesus named him Peter) and Andrew, Peter's brother; James and John, Philip and Bartholomew; [15]Matthew, Thomas, James son of Alphaeus, and Simon (called the Zealot[d]), [16]Judas son of James and Judas Iscariot. This Judas was the one who gave Jesus to his enemies.

JESUS TEACHES AND HEALS

[17]Jesus and the apostles[d] came down from the mountain. Jesus stood on level ground where there was a large group of his followers. Also, there were many people from all around Judea, Jerusalem, and the seacoast cities of Tyre and Sidon. [18]They all came to hear Jesus teach and to be healed of their sicknesses. He healed those who were troubled by evil spirits. [19]All the people were trying to touch Jesus, because power was coming from him and healing them all!

[20]Jesus looked at his followers and said,

"Poor people, you are happy,
    because God's kingdom belongs to
    you.
[21]You people who are now hungry are
    happy,
    because you will be satisfied.
You people who are now crying are
    happy,
    because you will laugh with joy.

[22]"You are happy when people hate you and are cruel to you. You are happy when they say that you are evil because you belong to the Son of Man.[d] [23]At that time be full of joy, because you have a great reward in heaven. Their fathers were cruel to the prophets[d] in the same way these people are cruel to you.

[24]"But how terrible it will be for you
    who are rich,
    because you have had your easy life.
[25]How terrible it will be for you who are
    full now,
    because you will be hungry.

How terrible it will be for you who are
laughing now,
because you will be sad and cry.

²⁶"How terrible when all people say
only good things about you. Their fathers
always said good things about the false
prophets.

LOVE YOUR ENEMIES

²⁷"I say to you who are listening to me,
love your enemies. Do good to those who
hate you. ²⁸Ask God to bless those who
say bad things to you. Pray for those who
are cruel to you. ²⁹If anyone slaps you on
one cheek, let him slap the other cheek
too. If someone takes your coat, do not
stop him from taking your shirt. ³⁰Give to
everyone who asks you. When a person
takes something that is yours, don't ask
for it back. ³¹Do for other people what
you want them to do for you. ³²If you
love only those who love you, should you
get some special praise for doing that?
No! Even sinners love the people who
love them! ³³If you do good only to those
who do good to you, should you get
some special praise for doing that? No!
Even sinners do that! ³⁴If you lend things
to people, always hoping to get something back, should you get some special
praise for that? No! Even sinners lend to
other sinners so that they can get back
the same amount! ³⁵So love your enemies. Do good to them, and lend to them
without hoping to get anything back. If
you do these things, you will have a great
reward. You will be sons of the Most
High God. Yes, because God is kind even
to people who are ungrateful and full of
sin. ³⁶Show mercy just as your father
shows mercy.

LOOK AT YOURSELVES

³⁷"Don't judge other people, and you
will not be judged. Don't accuse others of
being guilty, and you will not be accused
of being guilty. Forgive other people, and
you will be forgiven. ³⁸Give, and you will
receive. You will be given much. It will

be poured into your hands—more than
you can hold. You will be given so much
that it will spill into your lap. The way
you give to others is the way God will
give to you."

³⁹Jesus told them this story: "Can a
blind man lead another blind man? No!
Both of them will fall into a ditch. ⁴⁰A
student is not better than his teacher.
But when the student has fully learned
all that he has been taught, then he will
be like his teacher.

⁴¹"Why do you notice the little piece of
dust that is in your brother's eye, but you
don't see the big piece of wood that is in
your own eye? ⁴²You say to your brother,
'Brother, let me take that little piece of
dust out of your eye.' Why do you say
this? You cannot see that big piece of
wood in your own eye! You are a hypocrite!ᵈ First, take the piece of wood out
of your own eye. Then you will see clearly
to take the dust out of your brother's eye.

TWO KINDS OF FRUIT

⁴³"A good tree does not produce bad
fruit. Also, a bad tree does not produce
good fruit. ⁴⁴Each tree is known by its
fruit. People don't gather figs from thornbushes. And they don't get grapes from
bushes. ⁴⁵A good person has good things
saved up in his heart. And so he brings
good things out of his heart. But an evil
person has evil things saved up in his
heart. So he brings out bad things. A
person speaks the things that are in his
heart.

TWO KINDS OF PEOPLE

⁴⁶"Why do you call me, 'Lord, Lord,'
but do not do what I say? ⁴⁷Everyone who
comes to me and listens to my words
and obeys ⁴⁸is like a man building a
house. He digs deep and lays his foundation on rock. The floods come, and the
water tries to wash the house away. But
the flood cannot move the house, because the house was built well. ⁴⁹But the
one who hears my words and does not

obey is like a man who builds his house on the ground without a foundation. When the floods come, the house quickly falls down. And that house is completely destroyed."

JESUS HEALS A SOLDIER'S SERVANT

7 When Jesus finished saying all these things to the people, he went to Capernaum. [2]In Capernaum there was an army officer. He had a servant who was so sick he was nearly dead. The officer loved the servant very much. [3]When the officer heard about Jesus, he sent some Jewish elders to him. The officer wanted the leaders to ask Jesus to come and heal his servant. [4]The men went to Jesus and begged him saying, "This officer is worthy of your help. [5]He loves our people, and he built us a synagogue."[d]

[6]So Jesus went with the men. He was getting near the officer's house when the officer sent friends to say, "Lord, you don't need to come into my house. I am not good enough for you to be under my roof. [7]That is why I did not come to you myself. You only need to say the word, and my servant will be healed. [8]I, too, am a man under the authority of other men. And I have soldiers under my command. I tell one soldier, 'Go,' and he goes. And I tell another soldier, 'Come,' and he comes. And I say to my servant, 'Do this,' and my servant obeys me."

[9]When Jesus heard this, he was amazed. He turned to the crowd following him and said, "I tell you, this is the greatest faith I have seen anywhere, even in Israel."

[10]The men who had been sent to Jesus went back to the house. There they found that the servant was healed.

JESUS BRINGS A MAN BACK TO LIFE

[11]The next day Jesus went to a town called Nain. His followers and a large crowd were traveling with him. [12]When he came near the town gate, he saw a funeral. A mother, who was a widow, had lost her only son. A large crowd from the town was with the mother while her son was being carried out. [13]When the Lord saw her, he felt very sorry for her. Jesus said to her, "Don't cry." [14]He went up to the coffin and touched it. The men who were carrying it stopped. Jesus said, "Young man, I tell you, get up!" [15]And the son sat up and began to talk. Then Jesus gave him back to his mother.

[16]All the people were amazed. They began praising God. They said, "A great prophet[d] has come to us! God is taking care of his people."

[17]This news about Jesus spread through all Judea and into all the places around there.

JOHN ASKS A QUESTION

[18]John's followers told him about all these things. He called for two of his followers. [19]He sent them to the Lord to ask, "Are you the One who is coming, or should we wait for another?"

[20]So the men came to Jesus. They said, "John the Baptist[d] sent us to you with this question: 'Are you the One who is coming, or should we wait for another?'"

[21]At that time, Jesus healed many people of their sicknesses, diseases, and evil spirits. He healed many blind people so that they could see again. [22]Then Jesus said to John's followers, "Go tell John the things that you saw and heard here. The blind can see. The crippled can walk. People with a harmful skin disease are healed. The deaf can hear, and the dead are given life. And the Good News[d] is told to the poor. [23]The person who does not lose faith is blessed!"

[24]When John's followers left, Jesus began to tell the people about John: "What did you go out into the desert to see? A reed[n] blown by the wind? [25]What did you go out to see? A man dressed in fine clothes? No. People who have fine

---

7:24 **reed** It means that John was not weak like grass blown by the wind.

clothes live in kings' palaces. [26]But what did you go out to see? A prophet?[d] Yes, and I tell you, John is more than a prophet. [27]This was written about John:

'I will send my messenger ahead of you.
He will prepare the way for you.'
                                    Malachi 3:1

[28]I tell you, John is greater than any other man ever born. But even the least important person in the kingdom of God is greater than John."

[29](When the people heard this, they all agreed that God's teaching was good. Even the tax collectors agreed. These were people who were already baptized by John. [30]But the Pharisees[d] and teachers of the law refused to accept God's plan for themselves; they did not let John baptize them.)

[31]Then Jesus said, "What shall I say about the people of this time? What are they like? [32]They are like children sitting in the marketplace. One group of children calls to the other group and says,

'We played music for you, but you did not dance.
We sang a sad song, but you did not cry.'

[33]John the Baptist came and did not eat like other people or drink wine. And you say, 'He has a demon[d] in him.' [34]The Son of Man[d] came eating like other people and drinking wine. And you say, 'Look at him! He eats too much and drinks too much wine! He is a friend of the tax collectors and "sinners"!' [35]But wisdom is shown to be right by the things it does."

SIMON THE PHARISEE

[36]One of the Pharisees[d] asked Jesus to eat with him. Jesus went into the Pharisee's house and sat at the table. [37]A sinful woman in the town learned that Jesus was eating at the Pharisee's house. So she brought an alabaster[d] jar of perfume. [38]She stood at Jesus' feet, crying, and began to wash his feet with her tears. She

dried his feet with her hair, kissed them many times and rubbed them with the perfume. [39]The Pharisee who asked Jesus to come to his house saw this. He thought to himself, "If Jesus were a prophet,[d] he would know that the woman who is touching him is a sinner!"

[40]Jesus said to the Pharisee, "Simon, I have something to say to you."

Simon said, "Teacher, tell me."

[41]Jesus said, "There were two men. Both men owed money to the same banker. One man owed the banker 500 silver coins.[n] The other man owed the banker 50 silver coins. [42]The men had no money; so they could not pay what they owed. But the banker told the men that they did not have to pay him. Which one of the two men will love the banker more?"

[43]Simon, the Pharisee, answered, "I think it would be the one who owed him the most money."

Jesus said to Simon, "You are right." [44]Then Jesus turned toward the woman and said to Simon, "Do you see this woman? When I came into your house, you gave me no water for my feet. But she washed my feet with her tears and dried my feet with her hair. [45]You did not kiss me, but she has been kissing my feet since I came in! [46]You did not rub my head with oil, but she rubbed my feet with perfume. [47]I tell you that her many sins are forgiven. This is clear because she showed great love. But the person who has only a little to be forgiven will feel only a little love."

[48]Then Jesus said to her, "Your sins are forgiven."

[49]The people sitting at the table began to think to themselves, "Who is this man? How can he forgive sins?"

[50]Jesus said to the woman, "Because you believed, you are saved from your sins. Go in peace."

7:41 silver coins A Roman denarius. One coin was the average pay for one day's work.

THE GROUP WITH JESUS

8 The next day, while Jesus was traveling through some cities and small towns, he preached and told the Good News[d] about God's kingdom. The 12 apostles[d] were with him. [2]There were also some women with him who had been healed of sicknesses and evil spirits. One of the women was Mary, called Magdalene, from whom seven demons[d] had gone out. [3]Also among the women were Joanna, the wife of Chuza (Herod's helper), Susanna, and many other women. These women used their own money to help Jesus and his apostles.

A STORY ABOUT PLANTING SEED

[4]A great crowd gathered. People were coming to Jesus from every town. He told them this story:

[5]"A farmer went out to plant his seed. While he was planting, some seed fell beside the road. People walked on the seed, and the birds ate all this seed. [6]Some seed fell on rock. It began to grow but then died because it had no water. [7]Some seed fell among thorny weeds. This seed grew, but later the weeds choked the good plants. [8]And some seed fell on good ground. This seed grew and made 100 times more grain."

Jesus finished the story. Then he called out, "Let those with ears use them and listen!"

[9]Jesus' followers asked him, "What does this story mean?"

[10]Jesus said, "You have been chosen to know the secret truths of the kingdom of God. But I use stories to speak to other people. I do this so that:

'They will look, but they may not see.
They will listen, but they may not
    understand.'   *Isaiah 6:9*

[11]"This is what the story means: The seed is God's teaching. [12]What is the seed that fell beside the road? It is like the people who hear God's teaching, but then the devil comes and takes it away from their hearts. So they cannot believe the teaching and be saved. [13]What is the seed that fell on rock? It is like those who hear God's teaching and accept it gladly. But they don't have deep roots. They believe for a while, but then trouble comes. They stop believing and turn away from God. [14]What is the seed that fell among the thorny weeds? It is like those who hear God's teaching, but they let the worries, riches, and pleasures of this life keep them from growing. So they never produce good fruit. [15]And what is the seed that fell on the good ground? That is like those who hear God's teaching with a good, honest heart. They obey God's teaching and patiently produce good fruit.

USE WHAT YOU HAVE

[16]"No one lights a lamp and then covers it with a bowl or hides it under a bed. Instead, he puts the lamp on a lampstand so that those who come in will have enough light to see. [17]Everything that is hidden will become clear. Every secret thing will be made known. [18]So be careful how you listen. The person who has something will be given more. But to the person who has nothing, this will happen: Even what he thinks he has will be taken away from him."

JESUS' TRUE FAMILY

[19]Jesus' mother and brothers came to see him. There was such a crowd that they could not get to him. [20]Someone said to Jesus, "Your mother and your brothers are standing outside. They want to see you."

[21]Jesus answered them, "My mother and my brothers are those who listen to God's teaching and obey it!"

JESUS STOPS A STORM

[22]One day Jesus and his followers got into a boat. He said to them, "Come with me across the lake." And so they started across. [23]While they were sailing, Jesus fell asleep. A big storm blew up on the lake. The boat began to fill with water, and they were in danger.

[24]The followers went to Jesus and woke him. They said, "Master! Master! We will drown!"

Jesus got up and gave a command to the wind and the waves. The wind stopped, and the lake became calm. [25]Jesus said to his followers, "Where is your faith?"

The followers were afraid and amazed. They said to each other, "What kind of man is this? He commands the wind and the water, and they obey him!"

A MAN WITH DEMONS INSIDE HIM

[26]Jesus and his followers sailed across the lake from Galilee to the area where the Gerasene[n] people live. [27]When Jesus got out of the boat, a man from the town came to Jesus. This man had demons[d] inside him. For a long time he had worn no clothes. He lived in the burial caves, not in a house. [28]When he saw Jesus, he cried out and fell down before him. The man said with a loud voice, "What do you want with me, Jesus, Son of the Most High God? Please don't punish me!" [29]He said this because Jesus had commanded the evil spirit to come out of him. Many times it had taken hold of him. He had been kept under guard and chained hand and foot. But he had broken his chains and had been driven by the demon out into the desert.

[30]Jesus asked him, "What is your name?"

The man answered, "Legion."[n] (He said his name was "Legion" because many demons were in him.) [31]The demons begged Jesus not to send them into eternal darkness.[n] [32]On the hill there was a large herd of pigs eating. The demons begged Jesus to allow them to go into the pigs. So Jesus allowed them to do this. [33]Then the demons came out of the man and went into the pigs. The herd of pigs ran down the hill and into the lake. All the pigs drowned.

[34]The men who took care of the pigs ran away. They told about this in the town and the countryside. [35]And people went to see what had happened. They came to Jesus and found the man sitting there at Jesus' feet. The man was clothed and in his right mind because the demons were gone. But the people were frightened. [36]The men who saw these things happen told the others all about how Jesus had made the man well. [37]All the people of the Gerasene country asked Jesus to go away. They were all very afraid. So Jesus got into the boat and went back to Galilee.

[38]The man that Jesus had healed begged to go with him. But Jesus sent him away, saying, [39]"Go back home and tell people what God did for you." So the man went all over town telling how much Jesus had done for him.

JESUS GIVES LIFE TO A DEAD GIRL AND HEALS A SICK WOMAN

[40]When Jesus got back to Galilee, a crowd welcomed him. Everyone was waiting for him. [41]A man named Jairus came to Jesus. Jairus was a ruler of the synagogue.[d] He bowed down at Jesus' feet and begged him to come to his house. [42]Jairus had only one daughter. She was 12 years old, and she was dying.

While Jesus was on his way to Jairus' house, the people were crowding all around him. [43]A woman was there who had been bleeding for 12 years. She had spent all her money on doctors, but no doctor was able to heal her. [44]The woman came up behind Jesus and touched the edge of his coat. At that moment, her bleeding stopped. [45]Then Jesus said, "Who touched me?"

All the people said they had not touched Jesus. Peter said, "Master, the people are all around you and are pushing against you."

8:26 Gerasene From Gerasa, an area southeast of Lake Galilee. The exact location is uncertain and some Greek copies read "Gadarene"; others read "Gergesene."

8:30 "Legion" Means very many. A legion was about 5,000 men in the Roman army.

8:31 eternal darkness Literally, "the abyss," something like a pit or a hole that has no end.

46But Jesus said, "Someone did touch me! I felt power go out from me." 47When the woman saw that she could not hide, she came forward, shaking. She bowed down before Jesus. While all the people listened, she told why she had touched him. Then, she said, she was healed immediately. 48Jesus said to her, "Dear woman, you are healed because you believed. Go in peace."

49While Jesus was still speaking, someone came from the house of the synagogue ruler and said to the ruler, "Your daughter has died! Don't bother the teacher now."

50When Jesus heard this, he said to Jairus, "Don't be afraid. Just believe, and your daughter will be well."

51Jesus went to the house. He let only Peter, John, James, and the girl's father and mother go inside with him. 52All the people were crying and feeling sad because the girl was dead. But Jesus said, "Don't cry. She is not dead; she is only sleeping."

53The people laughed at Jesus because they knew that the girl was dead. 54But Jesus took her by the hand and called to her, "My child, stand up!" 55Her spirit came back into her, and she stood up immediately. Jesus said, "Give her something to eat." 56The girl's parents were amazed. Jesus told them not to tell anyone about what happened.

JESUS SENDS OUT THE APOSTLES

9 Jesus called the 12 apostles*d* together. He gave them power to heal sicknesses and power over all demons.*d* 2Jesus sent the apostles out to tell about God's kingdom and to heal the sick. 3He said to them, "When you travel, don't take a walking stick. Also, don't carry a bag, or food, or money. Take for your trip only the clothes you are wearing. 4When you go into a house, stay there until it is time to leave. 5If the people in

the town will not welcome you, go outside the town and shake the dust off of your feet.*n* This will be a warning to them."

6So the apostles went out. They traveled through all the towns. They told the Good News*d* and healed people everywhere.

HEROD IS CONFUSED ABOUT JESUS

7Herod, the governor, heard about all these things that were happening. He was confused because some people said, "John the Baptist*d* is risen from death." 8Others said, "Elijah has come to us." And still others said, "One of the prophets*d* from long ago has risen from death." 9Herod said, "I cut off John's head. So who is this man I hear these things about?" And Herod kept trying to see Jesus.

MORE THAN 5,000 PEOPLE FED

10When the apostles*d* returned, they told Jesus all the things they had done on their trip. Then Jesus took them away to a town called Bethsaida. There, Jesus and his apostles could be alone together. 11But the people learned where Jesus went and followed him. Jesus welcomed them and talked with them about God's kingdom. He healed those who needed to be healed.

12Late in the afternoon, the 12 apostles came to Jesus and said, "No one lives in this place. Send the people away. They need to find food and places to sleep in the towns and countryside around here."

13But Jesus said to them, "You give them something to eat."

They said, "We have only five loaves of bread and two fish. Do you want us to go buy food for all these people?" 14(There were about 5,000 men there.)

Jesus said to his followers, "Tell the people to sit in groups of about 50 people."

15So the followers did this, and all the people sat down. 16Then Jesus took the five loaves of bread and two fish. He

---

9:5 shake...feet A warning. It showed that they were finished talking to these people.

looked up to heaven and thanked God for the food. Then Jesus divided the food and gave it to the followers to give to the people. ¹⁷All the people ate and were satisfied. And there was much food left. Twelve baskets were filled with pieces of food that were not eaten.

JESUS IS THE CHRIST

¹⁸One time when Jesus was praying alone, his followers came together there. Jesus asked them, "Who do the people say I am?"

¹⁹They answered, "Some say you are John the Baptist.ᵈ Others say you are Elijah.ⁿ And others say you are one of the prophetsᵈ from long ago who has come back to life."

²⁰Then Jesus asked, "And who do you say I am?"

Peter answered, "You are the Christᵈ from God."

²¹Jesus warned them not to tell anyone. Then he said, ²²"The Son of Manᵈ must suffer many things. He will be rejected by the Jewish elders, the leading priests, and the teachers of the law. The Son of Man will be killed. But after three days he will be raised from death."

²³Jesus went on to say to all of them, "If anyone wants to follow me, he must say 'no' to the things he wants. Every day he must be willing even to die on a cross, and he must follow me. ²⁴Whoever wants to save his life will lose it. And whoever gives his life for me will save it. ²⁵It is worth nothing for a man to have the whole world, if he himself is destroyed or lost. ²⁶If anyone is ashamed of me and my teaching, then Iⁿ will be ashamed of him. I will be ashamed of him at the time I come with my glory and with the glory of the Father and the holy angels. ²⁷I tell you the truth. Some of you people standing here will see the kingdom of God before you die."

JESUS WITH MOSES AND ELIJAH

²⁸About eight days after Jesus said these things, he took Peter, James, and John and went up on a mountain to pray. ²⁹While Jesus was praying, his face was changed, and his clothes became shining white. ³⁰Then two men were talking with Jesus. The men were Moses and Elijah.ⁿ ³¹They appeared in heavenly glory, talking with Jesus about his death which would happen in Jerusalem. ³²Peter and the others were asleep. But they woke up and saw the glory of Jesus. They also saw the two men who were standing with him. ³³When Moses and Elijah were about to leave, Peter said, "Master, it is good that we are here. We will put three tents here—one for you, one for Moses, and one for Elijah." (Peter did not know what he was saying.)

³⁴While Peter was saying these things, a cloud came down all around them. Peter, James, and John became afraid when the cloud covered them. ³⁵A voice came from the cloud. The voice said, "This is my Son. He is the One I have chosen. Obey him."

³⁶When the voice finished speaking, only Jesus was there. Peter, James, and John said nothing. At that time they told no one about what they had seen.

JESUS HEALS A SICK BOY

³⁷The next day, Jesus, Peter, James, and John came down from the mountain. A large crowd met Jesus. ³⁸A man in the crowd shouted to Jesus, "Teacher, please come and look at my son. He is the only child I have. ³⁹An evil spirit comes into my son, and then he shouts. He loses control of himself, and he foams at the mouth. The evil spirit keeps on hurting him and almost never leaves him. ⁴⁰I begged your followers to make the evil spirit leave my son, but they could not do it."

9:19 Elijah A man who spoke for God. He lived hundreds of years before Christ.
9:26 I Literally, "the Son of Man."
9:30 Moses and Elijah Two of the most important Jewish leaders in the past.

⁴¹Jesus answered, "You people who live now have no faith. Your lives are all wrong. How long must I be with you and be patient with you?" Then Jesus said to the man, "Bring your son here."

⁴²While the boy was coming, the demon*d* threw him on the ground. The boy lost control of himself. But Jesus gave a strong command to the evil spirit. Then the boy was healed, and Jesus gave him back to his father. ⁴³All the people were amazed at the great power of God.

JESUS TALKS ABOUT HIS DEATH

The people were all wondering about the things Jesus did. But he said to his followers, ⁴⁴"Don't forget the things I tell you now: The Son of Man*d* will be handed over into the control of men." ⁴⁵But the followers did not understand what Jesus meant. The meaning was hidden from them so that they could not understand it. But they were afraid to ask Jesus about what he said.

THE MOST IMPORTANT PERSON

⁴⁶Jesus' followers began to have an argument about which one of them was the greatest. ⁴⁷Jesus knew what they were thinking. So he took a little child and stood the child beside him. ⁴⁸Then Jesus said, "If anyone accepts a little child like this in my name, then he accepts me. And when he accepts me, he accepts the One who sent me. He who is least among you all—he is the greatest."

ANYONE NOT AGAINST US IS FOR US

⁴⁹John answered, "Master, we saw someone using your name to force demons*d* out of people. We told him to stop because he does not belong to our group."

⁵⁰Jesus said to him, "Don't stop him. If a person is not against you, then he is for you."

A SAMARITAN TOWN

⁵¹The time was coming near when Jesus would leave and be taken to heaven. He was determined to go to Jerusalem ⁵²and sent some men ahead of him. The men went into a town in Samaria to make everything ready for Jesus. ⁵³But the people there would not welcome him because he was going toward Jerusalem. ⁵⁴James and John, the followers of Jesus, saw this. They said, "Lord, do you want us to call fire down from heaven and destroy those people?"*n*

⁵⁵But Jesus turned and scolded them. [And Jesus said, "You don't know what kind of spirit you belong to. ⁵⁶The Son of Man did not come to destroy the souls of men but to save them.]*n* Then he and his followers went to another town.

FOLLOWING JESUS

⁵⁷They were all going along the road. Someone said to Jesus, "I will follow you any place you go."

⁵⁸Jesus answered, "The foxes have holes to live in. The birds have nests to live in. But the Son of Man*d* has no place to rest his head."

⁵⁹Jesus said to another man, "Follow me!"

But the man said, "Lord, first let me go and bury my father."

⁶⁰But Jesus said to him, "Let the people who are dead bury their own dead! You must go and tell about the kingdom of God."

⁶¹Another man said, "I will follow you, Lord, but first let me go and say goodbye to my family."

⁶²Jesus said, "Anyone who begins to plow a field but keeps looking back is of no use in the kingdom of God."

JESUS SENDS THE 72 MEN

10 After this, the Lord chose 72*n* others. He sent them out in pairs.

9:54 **people** Some Greek copies add: ". . . as Elijah did."
9:55-56 **And . . . them.** Some Greek copies do not contain the bracketed text.
10:1 **72** Some Greek copies read "70."

He sent them ahead of him into every town and place where he planned to go. [2]He said to them, "There are a great many people to harvest. But there are only a few workers to harvest them. God owns the harvest. Pray to God that he will send more workers to help gather his harvest. [3]You can go now. But listen! I am sending you, and you will be like sheep among wolves. [4]Don't carry a purse, a bag, or sandals. Don't stop to talk with people on the road. [5]Before you go into a house, say, 'Peace be with this house.' [6]If a peaceful man lives there, your blessing of peace will stay with him. If the man is not peaceful, then your blessing of peace will come back to you. [7]Stay in the same house. Eat and drink what the people there give you. A worker should be given his pay. Don't move from house to house. [8]If you go into a town and the people welcome you, eat what they give you. [9]Heal the sick who live there. Tell them, 'The kingdom of God is soon coming to you!' [10]But if you go into a town, and the people don't welcome you, then go out into the streets of that town. Say to them, [11]'Even the dirt from your town that sticks to our feet we wipe off against you.[n] But remember that the kingdom of God is coming soon.' [12]I tell you, on the Judgment Day it will be worse for the people of that town than for the people of Sodom.[n]

JESUS WARNS UNBELIEVERS

[13]"How terrible for you, Korazin! How terrible for you, Bethsaida! I did many miracles[d] in you. If those same miracles had happened in Tyre and Sidon,[n] those people would have changed their lives and stopped sinning long ago. They would have worn rough cloth and put ashes on themselves to show that they had changed. [14]But on the Judgment Day

it will be worse for you than for Tyre and Sidon. [15]And you, Capernaum,[n] will you be lifted up to heaven? No! You will be thrown down to the depths!

[16]"He who listens to you is really listening to me. He who refuses to accept you is really refusing to accept me. And he who refuses to accept me is refusing to accept the One who sent me."

SATAN FALLS

[17]When the 72[n] men came back from their trip, they were very happy. They said, "Lord, even the demons[d] obeyed us when we used your name!"

[18]Jesus said to the men, "I saw Satan falling like lightning from the sky. [19]Listen! I gave you power to walk on snakes and scorpions. I gave you more power than the Enemy has. Nothing will hurt you. [20]You should be happy, but not because the spirits obey you. You should be happy because your names are written in heaven."

JESUS PRAYS TO THE FATHER

[21]Then the Holy Spirit[d] made Jesus rejoice. He said, "I thank you, Father, Lord of heaven and earth, because you have hidden these things from the people who are wise and smart. But you have shown them to those who are like little children. Yes, Father, you did this because this is what you really wanted.

[22]"My Father has given me all things. No one knows the Son—only the Father knows. And only the Son knows the Father. The only people who will know about the Father are those whom the Son chooses to tell."

[23]Then Jesus turned to his followers and said privately, "You are blessed to see what you now see! [24]I tell you, many prophets[d] and kings wanted to see what

---

10:11 **dirt ... you** A warning. It showed that they were finished talking to these people.
10:12 **Sodom** City that God destroyed because the people were so evil.
10:13 **Tyre and Sidon** Towns where wicked people lived.
10:13-15 **Korazin ... Bethsaida ... Capernaum** Towns by Lake Galilee where Jesus preached to the people.
10:17 **72** Some Greek copies read "70."

you now see. But they did not see these things. And many prophets and kings wanted to hear what you now hear. But they did not hear these things."

THE GOOD SAMARITAN

25Then a teacher of the law stood up. He was trying to test Jesus. He said, "Teacher, what must I do to get life forever?"

26Jesus said to him, "What is written in the law? What do you read there?"

27The man answered, "Love the Lord your God. Love him with all your heart, all your soul, all your strength, and all your mind."[n] Also, "You must love your neighbor as you love yourself."[n]

28Jesus said to him, "Your answer is right. Do this and you will have life forever."

29But the man wanted to show that the way he was living was right. So he said to Jesus, "And who is my neighbor?"

30To answer this question, Jesus said, "A man was going down the road from Jerusalem to Jericho. Some robbers attacked him. They tore off his clothes and beat him. Then they left him lying there, almost dead. 31It happened that a Jewish priest was going down that road. When the priest saw the man, he walked by on the other side of the road. 32Next, a Levite[n] came there. He went over and looked at the man. Then he walked by on the other side of the road. 33Then a Samaritan[n] traveling down the road came to where the hurt man was lying. He saw the man and felt very sorry for him. 34The Samaritan went to him and poured olive oil and wine[n] on his wounds and bandaged them. He put the hurt man on his own donkey and took him to an inn.

At the inn, the Samaritan took care of him. 35The next day, the Samaritan brought out two silver coins[n] and gave them to the innkeeper. The Samaritan said, 'Take care of this man. If you spend more money on him, I will pay it back to you when I come again.'"

36Then Jesus said, "Which one of these three men do you think was a neighbor to the man who was attacked by the robbers?"

37The teacher of the law answered, "The one who helped him."

Jesus said to him, "Then go and do the same thing he did!"

MARY AND MARTHA

38While Jesus and his followers were traveling, Jesus went into a town. A woman named Martha let Jesus stay at her house. 39Martha had a sister named Mary. Mary was sitting at Jesus' feet and listening to him teach. 40Martha became angry because she had so much work to do. She went in and said, "Lord, don't you care that my sister has left me alone to do all the work? Tell her to help me!"

41But the Lord answered her, "Martha, Martha, you are getting worried and upset about too many things. 42Only one thing is important. Mary has chosen the right thing, and it will never be taken away from her."

JESUS TEACHES ABOUT PRAYER

11 One time Jesus was praying in a place. When he finished, one of his followers said to him, "John taught his followers how to pray. Lord, please teach us how to pray, too."

2Jesus said to them, "When you pray, say:

10:27 "Love . . . mind." Quotation from Deuteronomy 6:5.
10:27 "You . . . yourself." Quotation from Leviticus 19:18.
10:32 **Levite** Levites were men from the tribe of Levi who helped the Jewish priests with their work in the Temple. Read 1 Chronicles 23:24-32.
10:33 **Samaritan** Samaritans were people from Samaria. These people were part Jewish, but the Jews did not accept them as true Jews. Samaritans and Jews hated each other.
10:34 **olive oil and wine** Oil and wine were used like medicine to soften and clean wounds.
10:35 **silver coins** A Roman denarius. One coin was the average pay for one day's work.

'Father, we pray that your name will
always be kept holy.
We pray that your kingdom will come.
[3]Give us the food we need for each day.
[4]Forgive us the sins we have done,
because we forgive every person
who has done wrong to us.
And do not cause us to be tested.'"[n]

CONTINUE TO ASK

[5-6]Then Jesus said to them, "Suppose
one of you went to your friend's house at
midnight and said to him, 'A friend of
mine has come into town to visit me. But
I have nothing for him to eat. Please loan
me three loaves of bread.' [7]Your friend
inside the house answers, 'Don't bother
me! The door is already locked. My children and I are in bed. I cannot get up
and give you the bread now.' [8]I tell you,
maybe friendship is not enough to make
him get up to give you the bread. But he
will surely get up to give you what you
need if you continue to ask. [9]So I tell you,
continue to ask, and God will give to you.
Continue to search, and you will find.
Continue to knock, and the door will open
for you. [10]Yes, if a person continues asking,
he will receive. If he continues searching,
he will find. And if he continues knocking,
the door will open for him. [11]What would
you fathers do if your son asks you for[n] a
fish? Would any of you give him a snake?
[12]Or, if your son asks for an egg, would
you give him a scorpion? [13]Even though
you are bad, you know how to give good
things to your children. So surely your
heavenly Father knows how to give the
Holy Spirit[d] to those who ask him."

JESUS' POWER IS FROM GOD

[14]One time Jesus was sending a demon[d]
out of a man who could not talk. When
the demon came out, the man was able
to speak. The people were amazed. [15]But
some of them said, "Jesus uses the power

of Beelzebul[d] to force demons out of
people. Beelzebul is the ruler of demons."
[16]Other people wanted to test Jesus.
They asked him to give them a sign from
heaven. [17]But Jesus knew what they were
thinking. So he said to them, "Every kingdom that is divided and fights against
itself will be destroyed. And a family that
fights against itself will break apart. [18]So
if Satan is fighting against himself, then
how will his kingdom last? You say that I
use the power of Beelzebul to force out
demons. [19]But if I use the power of Beelzebul to force out demons, then by what
power do your people force out demons?
So your own people prove that you are
wrong. [20]But if I use the power of God to
force out demons, the kingdom of God
has come to you!

[21]"When a strong man with many weapons guards his own house, then the
things in his house are safe. [22]But suppose a stronger man comes and defeats
him. The stronger man will take away
the weapons that the first man trusted to
keep his house safe. Then the stronger
man will do what he wants with the first
man's things.

[23]"If anyone is not with me, he is
against me. He who does not work with
me is working against me.

THE EMPTY MAN

[24]"When an evil spirit comes out of a
person, it travels through dry places,
looking for a place to rest. But that spirit
finds no place to rest. So it says, 'I will go
back to the home I left.' [25]When the spirit
comes back to that person, it finds that
home swept clean and made neat. [26]Then
the evil spirit goes out and brings seven
other spirits more evil than itself. Then
all the evil spirits go into that person and
live there. And he has even more trouble
than he had before."

11:2-4 'Father ... tested.' Some Greek copies include phrases from Matthew's version of this prayer (Matthew 6:9-13).
11:11 for Some Greek copies include the phrase "for bread? Would any of you give him a stone? Or if he asks you
for ..." and continue to verse 12.

PEOPLE WHO ARE TRULY BLESSED

[27]When Jesus was saying these things, a woman in the crowd spoke out. She said to Jesus, "Your mother is blessed because she gave birth to you and nursed you."

[28]But Jesus said, "Those who hear the teaching of God and obey it—they are the ones who are truly blessed."

GIVE US PROOF!

[29]The crowd grew larger. Jesus said, "The people who live today are evil. They ask for a miracle[d] as a sign from God. But they will have no sign—only the sign of Jonah.[n] [30]Jonah was a sign for those people who lived in Nineveh. In the same way the Son of Man[d] will be a sign for the people of this time. [31]On the Judgment Day the Queen of the South[n] will stand up with the men who live now. She will show that they are guilty because she came from far away to listen to Solomon's wise teaching. And I tell you that someone greater than Solomon is here! [32]On the Judgment Day the men of Nineveh will stand up with the people who live now. And they will show that you are guilty, because when Jonah preached to those people, they changed their hearts and lives. And I tell you that someone greater than Jonah is here!

BE A LIGHT FOR THE WORLD

[33]"No one takes a light and puts it under a bowl or hides it. Instead, he puts the light on a lampstand so that the people who come in can see. [34]Your eye is a light for the body. If your eyes are good, then your whole body will be full of light. But if your eyes are evil, then your whole body will be full of darkness. [35]So be careful! Don't let the light in you become darkness. [36]If your whole body is full of light, and none of it is dark, then you will shine bright, as when a lamp shines on you."

JESUS ACCUSES THE PHARISEES

[37]After Jesus had finished speaking, a Pharisee[d] asked Jesus to eat with him. So Jesus went in and sat at the table. [38]But the Pharisee was surprised when he saw that Jesus did not wash his hands[n] before the meal. [39]The Lord said to him, "You Pharisees clean the outside of the cup and the dish. But inside you are full of greed and evil. [40]You are foolish. The same One who made what is outside also made what is inside. [41]So give what is in your cups and dishes to the poor. Then you will be fully clean. [42]But how terrible for you Pharisees! You give God one-tenth of even your mint, your rue, and every other plant in your garden. But you forget to be fair to other people and to love God. These are the things you should do. And you should also continue to do those other things—like giving one-tenth. [43]How terrible for you Pharisees, because you love to get the most important seats in the synagogues.[d] And you love people to show respect to you in the marketplaces. [44]How terrible for you, because you are like hidden graves. People walk on them without knowing it."

JESUS TALKS TO TEACHERS OF THE LAW

[45]One of the teachers of the law said to Jesus, "Teacher, when you say these things, you are insulting us, too."

[46]Jesus answered, "How terrible for you, you teachers of the law! You make strict rules that are very hard for people to obey. But you yourselves don't even try to follow those rules. [47]How terrible for you, because you build tombs for the prophets.[d] But these are the prophets that your fathers killed! [48]And now you show that you approve of what your fathers

---

11:29 **sign of Jonah** Jonah's three days in the big fish are like Jesus' three days in the tomb.
11:31 **Queen of the South** The Queen of Sheba. She traveled 1,000 miles to learn God's wisdom from Solomon. Read 1 Kings 10:1-3.
11:38 **wash his hands** This was a Jewish religious custom that the Pharisees thought was very important.

did. They killed the prophets, and you build tombs for the prophets! [49]This is why in his wisdom God said, 'I will send prophets and apostles[d] to them. Some of my prophets and apostles will be killed, and others will be treated cruelly.' [50]So you who live now will be punished for the deaths of all the prophets who were killed since the beginning of the world. [51]You will be punished for the killing of Abel and for the killing of Zechariah.[n] Zechariah was killed between the altar and the Temple.[d] Yes, I tell you that you people who live now will be punished for them all.

[52]"How terrible for you, you teachers of the law. You have hidden the key to learning about God. You yourselves would not learn, and you stopped others from learning, too."

[53]When Jesus was leaving, the teachers of the law and the Pharisees[d] began to give him trouble, asking him questions about many things. [54]They were trying to catch Jesus saying something wrong.

DON'T BE LIKE THE PHARISEES

12 Many thousands of people had gathered. There were so many people that they were stepping on each other. Before Jesus spoke to them, he said to his followers, "Be careful of the yeast of the Pharisees.[d] They are hypocrites.[d] [2]Everything that is hidden will be shown. Everything that is secret will be made known. [3]The things you say in the dark will be told in the light. The things you have whispered in an inner room will be shouted from the top of the house."

FEAR ONLY GOD

[4]Then Jesus said to the people, "I tell you, my friends, don't be afraid of people. People can kill the body, but after that they can do nothing more to hurt you. [5]I will show you the One to fear. You should fear him who has the power to kill you and also to throw you into hell. Yes, he is the One you should fear.

[6]"When five sparrows are sold, they cost only two pennies. But God does not forget any of them. [7]Yes, God even knows how many hairs you have on your head. Don't be afraid. You are worth much more than many sparrows.

DON'T BE ASHAMED OF JESUS

[8]"I tell you, if anyone stands before others and says that he believes in me, then I will say that he belongs to me. I will say this before the angels of God. [9]But if anyone stands before others and says he does not believe in me, then I will say that he does not belong to me. I will say this before the angels of God.

[10]"If a person says something against the Son of Man,[d] he can be forgiven. But a person who says bad things against the Holy Spirit[d] will not be forgiven.

[11]"When men bring you into the synagogues[d] before the leaders and other important men, don't worry about how to defend yourself or what to say. [12]At that time the Holy Spirit will teach you what you must say."

JESUS WARNS AGAINST SELFISHNESS

[13]One of the men in the crowd said to Jesus, "Teacher, tell my brother to divide with me the property our father left us."

[14]But Jesus said to him, "Who said that I should be your judge or decide how to divide the property between you two?" [15]Then Jesus said to them, "Be careful and guard against all kinds of greed. A man's life is not measured by the many things he owns."

[16]Then Jesus used this story: "There was a rich man who had some land, which grew a good crop of food. [17]The rich man thought to himself, 'What will I do? I have no place to keep all my crops.' [18]Then he said, 'I know what I will do. I will tear down my barns and build bigger

---

11:51 Abel...Zechariah In the Hebrew Old Testament, the first and last men to be murdered.

ones! I will put all my grain and other goods together in my new barns. ¹⁹Then I can say to myself, I have enough good things stored to last for many years. Rest, eat, drink, and enjoy life!'

²⁰"But God said to that man, 'Foolish man! Tonight you will die. So who will get those things you have prepared for yourself?'

²¹"This is how it will be for anyone who stores things up only for himself and is not rich toward God."

DON'T WORRY

²²Jesus said to his followers, "So I tell you, don't worry about the food you need to live. Don't worry about the clothes you need for your body. ²³Life is more important than food. And the body is more important than clothes. ²⁴Look at the birds. They don't plant or harvest. They don't save food in houses or barns. But God takes care of them. And you are worth much more than birds. ²⁵None of you can add any time to your life by worrying about it. ²⁶If you cannot do even the little things, then why worry about the big things? ²⁷Look at the wild flowers. See how they grow. They don't work or make clothes for themselves. But I tell you that even Solomon, the great and rich king, was not dressed as beautifully as one of these flowers. ²⁸God clothes the grass in the field like that. That grass is living today, but tomorrow it will be thrown into the fire. So you know how much more God will clothe you. Don't have so little faith! ²⁹Don't always think about what you will eat or what you will drink. Don't worry about it. ³⁰All the people in the world are trying to get those things. Your Father knows that you need them. ³¹The thing you should seek is God's kingdom. Then all the other things you need will be given to you.

DON'T TRUST IN MONEY

³²"Don't fear, little flock. Your Father wants to give you the kingdom. ³³Sell the things you have and give to the poor. Get for yourselves purses that don't wear out. Get the treasure in heaven that never runs out. Thieves can't steal it in heaven, and moths can't destroy it. ³⁴Your heart will be where your treasure is.

ALWAYS BE READY

³⁵"Be ready! Be dressed for service and have your lamps shining. ³⁶Be like servants who are waiting for their master to come home from a wedding party. The master comes and knocks. The servants immediately open the door for him. ³⁷Those servants will be blessed when their master comes home, because he sees that his servants are ready and waiting for him. I tell you the truth. The master will dress himself to serve and tell the servants to sit at the table. Then the master will serve them. ³⁸Those servants might have to wait until midnight or later for their master. But they will be happy when he comes in and finds them still waiting.

³⁹"Remember this: If the owner of the house knew what time a thief was coming, then the owner would not allow the thief to enter his house. ⁴⁰So you also must be ready! The Son of Man*d* will come at a time when you don't expect him!"

WHO IS THE TRUSTED SERVANT?

⁴¹Peter said, "Lord, did you tell this story for us or for all people?"

⁴²The Lord said, "Who is the wise and trusted servant? Who is the servant the master trusts to give the other servants their food at the right time? ⁴³When the master comes and finds his servant doing the work he gave him, that servant will be very happy. ⁴⁴I tell you the truth. The master will choose that servant to take care of everything the master owns. ⁴⁵But what will happen if the servant is evil and thinks that his master will not come back soon? That servant will begin to beat the other servants, men and women. He will eat and drink and get

drunk. [46]Then the master will come when that servant is not ready. It will be a time when the servant is not expecting him. Then the master will cut him in pieces and send him away to be with the others who don't obey.

[47]"The servant who knows what his master wants but is not ready or does not do what the master wants will be beaten with many blows! [48]But the servant who does not know what his master wants and does things that should be punished will be beaten with few blows. Everyone who has been given much will be responsible for much. Much more will be expected from the one who has been given more."

JESUS CAUSES DIVISION

[49]Jesus continued speaking, "I came to set fire to the world. I wish it were already burning! [50]I must be baptized with a different kind of baptism.[n] I feel very troubled until it is over. [51]Do you think that I came to give peace to the world? No! I came to divide the world! [52]From now on, a family with five people will be divided, three against two, and two against three. [53]A father and son will be divided: The son will be against his father. The father will be against his son. A mother and her daughter will be divided: The daughter will be against her mother. The mother will be against her daughter. A mother-in-law and her daughter-in-law will be divided: The daughter-in-law will be against her mother-in-law. The mother-in-law will be against her daughter-in-law."

UNDERSTANDING THE TIMES

[54]Then Jesus said to the people, "When you see clouds coming up in the west, you say, 'It's going to rain.' And soon it begins to rain. [55]When you feel the wind begin to blow from the south, you say, 'It will be a hot day.' And you are right. [56]Hypocrites![d] You can understand the weather. Why don't you understand what is happening now?

SETTLE YOUR PROBLEMS

[57]"Why can't you decide for yourselves what is right? [58]When someone is suing you, and you are going with him to court, try hard to settle it on the way. If you don't settle it, he may take you to the judge. The judge might turn you over to the officer. And the officer might throw you into jail. [59]You will not get out of there until they have taken everything you have."

CHANGE YOUR HEARTS

13 At that time some people were there with Jesus. They told him about what had happened to some people from Galilee. Pilate[n] killed those people while they were worshiping. He mixed their blood with the blood of the animals they were sacrificing to God. [2]Jesus answered, "Do you think this happened to them because they were more sinful than all others from Galilee? [3]No, they were not! But if all of you don't change your hearts and lives, then you will be destroyed as they were! [4]What about those 18 people who died when the tower of Siloam fell on them? Do you think they were more sinful than all the others who live in Jerusalem? [5]They were not! But I tell you, if you don't change your hearts and lives, then you will all be destroyed too!"

THE USELESS TREE

[6]Jesus told this story: "A man had a fig tree planted in his vineyard. He came looking for some fruit on the tree, but he found none. [7]So the man said to his servant who took care of his vineyard, 'I have been looking for fruit on this tree for three years, but I never find any. Cut it down! Why should it waste the ground?' [8]But the servant answered, 'Master, let the tree have one more year to produce

---

12:50 I . . . baptism. Jesus was talking about the suffering he would soon go through.
13:1 Pilate Pontius Pilate was the Roman governor of Judea from A.D. 26 to A.D. 36.

fruit. Let me dig up the dirt around it and put on some fertilizer. [9]Maybe the tree will produce fruit next year. If the tree still doesn't produce fruit, then you can cut it down.'"

JESUS HEALS ON THE SABBATH

[10]Jesus was teaching in one of the synagogues[d] on the Sabbath[d] day. [11]In the synagogue there was a woman who had an evil spirit in her. This spirit had made the woman a cripple for 18 years. Her back was always bent; she could not stand up straight. [12]When Jesus saw her, he called her over and said, "Woman, your sickness has left you!" [13]Jesus put his hands on her. Immediately she was able to stand up straight and began praising God.

[14]The synagogue leader was angry because Jesus healed on the Sabbath day. He said to the people, "There are six days for work. So come to be healed on one of those days. Don't come for healing on the Sabbath day."

[15]The Lord answered, "You people are hypocrites![d] All of you untie your work animals and lead them to drink water every day—even on the Sabbath day! [16]This woman that I healed is our Jewish sister. But Satan has held her for 18 years. Surely it is not wrong for her to be freed from her sickness on a Sabbath day!" [17]When Jesus said this, all the men who were criticizing him were ashamed. And all the people were happy for the wonderful things Jesus was doing.

STORIES OF MUSTARD SEED AND YEAST

[18]Then Jesus said, "What is God's kingdom like? What can I compare it with? [19]God's kingdom is like the seed of the mustard plant.[n] A man plants this seed in his garden. The seed grows and becomes a tree. The wild birds build nests on its branches."

[20]Jesus said again, "What can I compare God's kingdom with? [21]It is like yeast that a woman mixes into a big bowl of flour. The yeast makes all the dough rise."

THE NARROW DOOR

[22]Jesus was teaching in every town and village. He continued to travel toward Jerusalem. [23]Someone said to Jesus, "Lord, how many people will be saved? Only a few?"

Jesus said, [24]"Try hard to enter through the narrow door that opens the way to heaven! Many people will try to enter there, but they will not be able. [25]A man gets up and closes the door of his house. You can stand outside and knock on the door. You can say, 'Sir, open the door for us!' But he will answer, 'I don't know you! Where did you come from?' [26]Then you will say, 'We ate and drank with you. You taught in the streets of our town.' [27]But he will say to you, 'I don't know you! Where did you come from? Go away from me! All of you do evil!' [28]You will see Abraham, Isaac, Jacob, and all the prophets[d] in God's kingdom. But you will be thrown outside. Then you will cry and grind your teeth with pain. [29]People will come from the east, west, north, and south. They will sit down at the table in the kingdom of God. [30]Those who are last now will be first in the future. And those who are first now will be last in the future."

JESUS WILL DIE IN JERUSALEM

[31]At that time some Pharisees[d] came to Jesus and said, "Go away from here! Herod wants to kill you!"

[32]Jesus said to them, "Go tell that fox Herod, 'Today and tomorrow I am forcing demons[d] out of people and finishing my work of healing. Then, on the third day, I will reach my goal.' [33]Yet I must be on my way today and tomorrow and the next day. Surely it cannot be right for a prophet[d] to be killed anywhere except in Jerusalem.

13:19 mustard plant The seed is very small, but the plant grows taller than a man.

[34]"Jerusalem, Jerusalem! You kill the prophets. You kill with stones those men that God has sent you. Many times I wanted to help your people. I wanted to gather them together as a hen gathers her chicks under her wings. But you did not let me. [35]Now your home will be left completely empty. I tell you, you will not see me again until that time when you will say, 'God bless the One who comes in the name of the Lord.'"[n]

IS IT RIGHT TO HEAL ON THE SABBATH?

14 On a Sabbath[d] day, Jesus went to the home of a leading Pharisee[d] to eat with him. The people there were all watching Jesus very closely. [2]A man with dropsy[n] was brought before Jesus. [3]Jesus said to the Pharisees and teachers of the law, "Is it right or wrong to heal on the Sabbath day?" [4]But they would not answer his question. So Jesus took the man, healed him, and sent him away. [5]Jesus said to the Pharisees and teachers of the law, "If your son[n] or ox falls into a well on the Sabbath day, will you not pull him out quickly?" [6]And they could not answer him.

DON'T MAKE YOURSELF IMPORTANT

[7]Then Jesus noticed that some of the guests were choosing the best places to sit. So Jesus told this story: [8]"When someone invites you to a wedding feast, don't take the most important seat. The host may have invited someone more important than you. [9]And if you are sitting in the most important seat, the host will come to you and say, 'Give this man your seat.' Then you will begin to move down to the last place. And you will be very embarrassed. [10]So when you are invited, go sit in a seat that is not important. Then the host will come to you and say, 'Friend, move up here to a more important place!' Then all the other guests will respect you.

[11]Everyone who makes himself great will be made humble. But the person who makes himself humble will be made great."

YOU WILL BE REWARDED

[12]Then Jesus said to the man who had invited him, "When you give a lunch or a dinner, don't invite only your friends, brothers, relatives, and rich neighbors. At another time they will invite you to eat with them. Then you will have your reward. [13]Instead, when you give a feast, invite the poor, the crippled, the lame and the blind. [14]Then you will be blessed, because they cannot pay you back. They have nothing. But you will be rewarded when the good people rise from death."

A STORY ABOUT A BIG BANQUET

[15]One of the men sitting at the table with Jesus heard these things. The man said to Jesus, "The people who will eat a meal in God's kingdom are blessed."

[16]Jesus said to him, "A man gave a big banquet and invited many people. [17]When it was time to eat, the man sent his servant to tell the guests, 'Come! Everything is ready!'

[18]"But all the guests said they could not come. Each man made an excuse. The first one said, 'I have just bought a field, and I must go look at it. Please excuse me.' [19]Another man said, 'I have just bought five pairs of oxen; I must go and try them. Please excuse me.' [20]A third man said, 'I just got married; I can't come.' [21]So the servant returned. He told his master what had happened. Then the master became angry and said, 'Go at once into the streets and alleys of the town. Bring in the poor, the crippled, the blind, and the lame.' [22]Later the servant said to him, 'Master, I did what you told me to do, but we still have places for more people.' [23]The master said to the servant,

---

13:35 'God . . . Lord.' Quotation from Psalm 118:26.
14:2 dropsy A sickness that causes the body to swell larger and larger.
14:5 son Some Greek copies read "donkey."

'Go out to the roads and country lanes. Tell the people there to come. I want my house to be full! [24]None of those men that I invited first will ever eat with me!'"

YOU MUST FIRST PLAN

[25]Large crowds were traveling with Jesus. He turned and said to them, [26]"If anyone comes to me but loves his father, mother, wife, children, brothers, or sisters more than he loves me, then he cannot be my follower. A person must love me more than he loves himself! [27]If anyone is not willing to die on a cross when he follows me, then he cannot be my follower. [28]If you wanted to build a tower, you would first sit down and decide how much it would cost. You must see if you have enough money to finish the job. [29]If you don't do that, you might begin the work, but you would not be able to finish. And if you could not finish it, then all who would see it would laugh at you. [30]They would say, 'This man began to build but was not able to finish!' [31]"If a king is going to fight against another king, first he will sit down and plan. If the king has only 10,000 men, he will plan to see if he is able to defeat the other king who has 20,000 men. [32]If he cannot defeat the other king, then he will send some men to speak to the other king and ask for peace. [33]In the same way, you must give up everything you have to follow me. If you don't, you cannot be my follower!

DON'T LOSE YOUR INFLUENCE

[34]"Salt is a good thing. But if the salt loses its salty taste, then it is worth nothing. You cannot make it salty again. [35]It is no good for the soil or for manure. People throw it away.

"Let those with ears use them and listen!"

A LOST SHEEP AND A LOST COIN

15 Many tax collectors and "sinners" came to listen to Jesus.
[2]The Pharisees[d] and the teachers of the law began to complain: "Look! This man welcomes sinners and even eats with them!"

[3]Then Jesus told them this story: [4]"Suppose one of you has 100 sheep, but he loses 1 of them. Then he will leave the other 99 sheep alone and go out and look for the lost sheep. The man will keep on searching for the lost sheep until he finds it. [5]And when he finds it, the man is very happy. He puts it on his shoulders [6]and goes home. He calls to his friends and neighbors and says, 'Be happy with me because I found my lost sheep!' [7]In the same way, I tell you there is much joy in heaven when 1 sinner changes his heart. There is more joy for that 1 sinner than there is for 99 good people who don't need to change.

[8]"Suppose a woman has ten silver coins,[n] but she loses one of them. She will light a lamp and clean the house. She will look carefully for the coin until she finds it. [9]And when she finds it, she will call her friends and neighbors and say, 'Be happy with me because I have found the coin that I lost!' [10]In the same way, there is joy before the angels of God when 1 sinner changes his heart."

THE SON WHO LEFT HOME

[11]Then Jesus said, "A man had two sons. [12]The younger son said to his father, 'Give me my share of the property.' So the father divided the property between his two sons. [13]Then the younger son gathered up all that was his and left. He traveled far away to another country. There he wasted his money in foolish living. [14]He spent everything that he had. Soon after that, the land became very dry, and there was no rain. There was not enough food to eat anywhere in the country. The son was hungry and needed money. [15]So he got a job with one of the citizens there. The man sent the son into the fields to

---

15:8 silver coins A Roman denarius. One coin was the average pay for one day's work.

feed pigs. [16]The son was so hungry that he was willing to eat the food the pigs were eating. But no one gave him anything. [17]The son realized that he had been very foolish. He thought, 'All of my father's servants have plenty of food. But I am here, almost dying with hunger. [18]I will leave and return to my father. I'll say to him: Father, I have sinned against God and against you. [19]I am not good enough to be called your son. But let me be like one of your servants.' [20]So the son left and went to his father.

"While the son was still a long way off, his father saw him coming. He felt sorry for his son. So the father ran to him, and hugged and kissed him. [21]The son said, 'Father, I have sinned against God and against you. I am not good enough to be called your son.'[n] [22]But the father said to his servants, 'Hurry! Bring the best clothes and put them on him. Also, put a ring on his finger and sandals on his feet. [23]And get our fat calf and kill it. Then we can have a feast and celebrate! [24]My son was dead, but now he is alive again! He was lost, but now he is found!' So they began to celebrate.

[25]"The older son was in the field. As he came closer to the house, he heard the sound of music and dancing. [26]So he called to one of the servants and asked, 'What does all this mean?' [27]The servant said, 'Your brother has come back. Your father killed the fat calf to eat because your brother came home safely!' [28]The older son was angry and would not go in to the feast. So his father went out and begged him to come in. [29]The son said to his father, 'I have served you like a slave for many years! I have always obeyed your commands. But you never even killed a young goat for me to have a feast with my friends. [30]But your other son has wasted all your money on prostitutes.[d] Then he comes home, and you kill the

fat calf for him!' [31]The father said to him, 'Son, you are always with me. All that I have is yours. [32]We had to celebrate and be happy because your brother was dead, but now he is alive. He was lost, but now he is found.'"

TRUE WEALTH

16 Jesus also said to his followers, "Once there was a rich man. He had a manager to take care of his business. Later, the rich man learned that his manager was cheating him. [2]So he called the manager in and said to him, 'I have heard bad things about you. Give me a report of what you have done with my money. You can't be my manager any longer!' [3]Later, the manager thought to himself, 'What will I do? My master is taking my job away from me! I am not strong enough to dig ditches. I am too proud to beg. [4]I know! I'll do something so that when I lose my job, people will welcome me into their homes.'

[5]"So the manager called in everyone who owed the master any money. He said to the first man, 'How much do you owe my master?' [6]The man answered, 'I owe him 800 gallons of olive oil.' The manager said to him, 'Here is your bill; sit down quickly and make the bill less. Write 400 gallons.' [7]Then the manager said to another man, 'How much do you owe my master?' The man answered, 'I owe him 1,000 bushels of wheat.' Then the manager said to him, 'Here is your bill; you can make it less. Write 800 bushels.' [8]Later, the master praised the dishonest manager for being smart. Yes, worldly people are smarter with their own kind than spiritual people are.

[9]"I tell you, make friends for yourselves using worldly riches. Then, when those things are gone, you will be welcomed in that home that continues forever. [10]Whoever can be trusted with small things can also be trusted with large

---

15:21 son Some Greek copies continue, "But let me be like one of your servants" (see verse 19).

things. Whoever is dishonest in little things will be dishonest in large things too. [11]If you cannot be trusted with worldly riches, then you will not be trusted with the true riches. [12]And if you cannot be trusted with the things that belong to someone else, then you will not be given things of your own.

[13]"No servant can serve two masters. He will hate one master and love the other. Or he will follow one master and refuse to follow the other. You cannot serve both God and money."

GOD'S LAW CANNOT BE CHANGED

[14]The Pharisees[d] were listening to all these things. They made fun of Jesus because they all loved money. [15]Jesus said to them, "You make yourselves look good in front of people. But God knows what is really in your hearts. The things that are important to people are worth nothing to God.

[16]"God wanted the people to live by the law of Moses and the writings of the prophets.[d] But ever since John[n] came, the Good News[d] about the kingdom of God is being told. Now everyone is trying hard to get into the kingdom. [17]Even the smallest part of a letter in the law cannot be changed. It would be easier for heaven and earth to pass away.

DIVORCE AND REMARRIAGE

[18]"If a man divorces his wife and marries another woman, he is guilty of adultery.[d] And the man who marries a divorced woman is also guilty of adultery."

THE RICH MAN AND LAZARUS

[19]Jesus said, "There was a rich man who always dressed in the finest clothes. He lived in luxury every day. [20]There was also a very poor man named Lazarus, whose body was covered with sores. Lazarus was often placed at the rich man's gate. [21]He wanted to eat only the small pieces of food that fell from the rich man's table. And the dogs would come and lick his sores! [22]Later, Lazarus died. The angels took Lazarus and placed him in the arms of Abraham.[d] The rich man died, too, and was buried. [23]But he was sent to where the dead are and had much pain. The rich man saw Abraham far away with Lazarus in his arms. [24]He called, 'Father Abraham, have mercy on me! Send Lazarus to me so that he can dip his finger in water and cool my tongue. I am suffering in this fire!' [25]But Abraham said, 'My child, remember when you lived? You had all the good things in life, but all the bad things happened to Lazarus. Now Lazarus is comforted here, and you are suffering. [26]Also, there is a big pit between you and us. No one can cross over to help you. And no one can leave there and come here.' [27]The rich man said, 'Then please send Lazarus to my father's house on earth! [28]I have five brothers. Lazarus could warn my brothers so that they will not come to this place of pain.' [29]But Abraham said, 'They have the law of Moses and the writings of the prophets[d] to read; let them learn from them!' [30]The rich man said, 'No, father Abraham! If someone came to them from the dead, they would believe and change their hearts and lives.' [31]But Abraham said to him, 'No! If your brothers won't listen to Moses and the prophets, then they won't listen to someone who comes back from death.'"

SIN AND FORGIVENESS

17 Jesus said to his followers, "Things will surely happen that cause people to sin. But how terrible for the one who causes them to happen. [2]It would be better for him to be thrown into the sea with a large stone around his neck than to cause one of these weak people to sin. [3]So be careful!

16:16 John John the Baptist, who preached to people about Christ's coming (Matthew 3, Luke 3).

"If your brother sins, tell him he is wrong. But if he is sorry and stops sinning, forgive him. [4]If your brother sins against you seven times in one day, but he says that he is sorry each time, then forgive him."

HOW BIG IS YOUR FAITH?

[5]The apostles[d] said to the Lord, "Give us more faith!"

[6]The Lord said, "If your faith is as big as a mustard seed,[n] then you can say to this mulberry tree, 'Dig yourself up and plant yourself in the sea!' And the tree will obey you.

BE GOOD SERVANTS

[7]"Suppose one of you has a servant who has been plowing the ground or caring for the sheep. When the servant comes in from working in the field, would you say, 'Come in and sit down to eat'? [8]No, you would say to your servant, 'Prepare something for me to eat. Then get yourself ready and serve me. When I finish eating and drinking, then you can eat.' [9]The servant does not get any special thanks for doing what his master told him to do. [10]It is the same with you. When you do everything you are told to do, you should say, 'We don't deserve any special thanks. We have only done the work we should do.'"

BE THANKFUL

[11]Jesus was on his way to Jerusalem. Traveling from Galilee to Samaria, [12]he came into a small town. Ten men met him there. These men did not come close to Jesus, because they all had a harmful skin disease. [13]But they called to him, "Jesus! Master! Please help us!"

[14]When Jesus saw the men, he said, "Go and show yourselves to the priests."[n] While the ten men were going, they were healed. [15]When one of them saw that he was healed, he went back to Jesus. He praised God in a loud voice. [16]Then he bowed down at Jesus' feet and thanked him. (This man was a Samaritan.[d]) [17]Jesus asked, "Ten men were healed; where are the other nine? [18]Is this Samaritan the only one who came back to thank God?" [19]Then Jesus said to him, "Stand up and go on your way. You were healed because you believed."

GOD'S KINGDOM IS WITHIN YOU

[20]Some of the Pharisees[d] asked Jesus, "When will the kingdom of God come?"

Jesus answered, "God's kingdom is coming, but not in a way that you will be able to see with your eyes. [21]People will not say, 'Look, God's kingdom is here!' or, 'There it is!' No, God's kingdom is within you."

[22]Then Jesus said to his followers, "The time will come when you will want very much to see one of the days of the Son of Man.[d] But you will not be able to see it. [23]People will say to you, 'Look, there he is!' or, 'Look, here he is!' Stay where you are; don't go away and search.

WHEN JESUS COMES AGAIN

[24]"The Son of Man[d] will come again. On the day he comes he will shine like lightning, which flashes across the sky and lights it up from one side to the other. [25]But first, the Son of Man must suffer many things and be rejected by the people of this time. [26]When the Son of Man comes again, it will be as it was when Noah lived. [27]In the time of Noah, people were eating, drinking, and getting married even on the day when Noah entered the boat. Then the flood came and killed all the people. [28]It will be the same as during the time of Lot. Those people were eating, drinking, buying, selling, planting, and building. [29]They were doing these things even on the day Lot left Sodom.[n] Then fire and sulfur

---

17:6 **mustard seed** This seed is very small, but the plant grows taller than a man.
17:14 **show ... priests** The law of Moses said a priest must say when a Jew with a harmful skin disease became well.
17:29 **Sodom** City that God destroyed because the people were so evil.

rained down from the sky and killed them all. [30]This is exactly how it will be when the Son of Man comes again.

[31]"On that day, if a man is on his roof, he will not have time to go inside and get his things. If a man is in the field, he cannot go back home. [32]Remember what happened to Lot's wife?[n] [33]Whoever tries to keep his life will give up true life. But whoever gives up his life will have true life. [34]At the time when I come again, there may be two people sleeping in one bed. One will be taken and the other will be left. [35]There may be two women grinding grain together. One will be taken and the other will be left. [36][Two men will be in the same field. One man will be taken, but the other man will be left behind.]"[n]

[37]The followers asked Jesus, "Where will this be, Lord?"

Jesus answered, "People can always find a dead body by looking for the vultures."

GOD WILL ANSWER HIS PEOPLE

18 Then Jesus used this story to teach his followers that they should always pray and never lose hope. [2]"Once there was a judge in a town. He did not care about God. He also did not care what people thought about him. [3]In that same town there was a widow who kept coming to this judge. She said, 'There is a man who is not being fair to me. Give me my rights!' [4]But the judge did not want to help the widow. After a long time, he thought to himself, 'I don't care about God. And I don't care about what people think. [5]But this widow is bothering me. I will see that she gets her rights, or she will bother me until I am worn out!'"

[6]The Lord said, "Listen to what the bad judge said. [7]God's people cry to him night and day. God will always give them

what is right, and he will not be slow to answer them. [8]I tell you, God will help his people quickly! But when the Son of Man[d] comes again, will he find those on earth who believe in him?"

BEING RIGHT WITH GOD

[9]There were some people who thought that they were very good and looked down on everyone else. Jesus used this story to teach them: [10]"One day there was a Pharisee[d] and a tax collector. Both went to the Temple[d] to pray. [11]The Pharisee stood alone, away from the tax collector. When the Pharisee prayed, he said, 'God, I thank you that I am not as bad as other people. I am not like men who steal, cheat, or take part in adultery.[d] I thank you that I am better than this tax collector. [12]I give up eating[n] twice a week, and I give one-tenth of everything I earn!'

[13]"The tax collector stood at a distance. When he prayed, he would not even look up to heaven. He beat on his chest because he was so sad. He said, 'God, have mercy on me. I am a sinner!' [14]I tell you, when this man went home, he was right with God. But the Pharisee was not right with God. Everyone who makes himself great will be made humble. But everyone who makes himself humble will be made great."

WHO WILL ENTER GOD'S KINGDOM?

[15]Some people brought their small children to Jesus so that he could touch them. When the followers saw this, they told the people not to do this. [16]But Jesus called the little children to him and said to his followers, "Let the little children come to me. Don't stop them, because the kingdom of God belongs to people who are like these little children. [17]I tell you the truth. You must accept God's kingdom like a little child, or you will never enter it!"

17:32 Lot's wife A story about what happened to Lot's wife is found in Genesis 19:15-17, 26.

17:36 Two . . . behind. Some Greek copies do not contain the bracketed text.

18:12 give up eating This is called "fasting." The people would give up eating for a special time of prayer and worship to God. It was also done to show sadness.

A RICH MAN'S QUESTION

[18]A Jewish leader asked Jesus, "Good Teacher, what must I do to get the life that continues forever?"

[19]Jesus said to him, "Why do you call me good? Only God is good. [20]You know the commands: 'You must not be guilty of adultery.[d] You must not murder anyone. You must not steal. You must not tell lies about your neighbor in court. Honor your father and mother.'"[n]

[21]But the leader said, "I have obeyed all these commands since I was a boy!"

[22]When Jesus heard this, he said to him, "But there is still one more thing you need to do. Sell everything you have and give the money to the poor. You will have a reward in heaven. Then come and follow me!" [23]But when the man heard this, he became very sad because he was very rich.

[24]When Jesus saw that the man was sad, he said, "It will be very hard for rich people to enter the kingdom of God! [25]It would be easier for a camel to go through the eye of a needle than for a rich person to enter the kingdom of God!"

WHO CAN BE SAVED?

[26]When the people heard this, they asked, "Then who can be saved?"

[27]Jesus answered, "The things impossible for men are possible for God."

[28]Peter said, "Look, we left everything we had and followed you!"

[29]Jesus said, "I tell you the truth. Everyone who has left his house, wife, brothers, parents, or children for God's kingdom [30]will get much more than he left. He will receive many times more in this life. And after he dies, he will live with God forever."

JESUS WILL RISE FROM DEATH

[31]Then Jesus talked to the 12 apostles[d] alone. He said to them, "Listen! We are going to Jerusalem. Everything that God told the prophets[d] to write about the Son of Man[d] will happen! [32]He will be turned over to the non-Jewish people. They will laugh at him, insult him, and spit on him. [33]They will beat him with whips and then kill him. But on the third day after his death, he will rise to life again." [34]The apostles tried to understand this, but they could not; the meaning was hidden from them.

JESUS HEALS A BLIND MAN

[35]Jesus was coming near the city of Jericho. There was a blind man sitting beside the road, begging for money. [36]When he heard the people coming down the road, he asked, "What is happening?"

[37]They told him, "Jesus, the one from Nazareth, is coming here."

[38]The blind man cried out, "Jesus, Son of David![d] Please help me!"

[39]The people who were in front, leading the group, told the blind man to be quiet. But the blind man shouted more and more, "Son of David, please help me!"

[40]Jesus stopped and said, "Bring the blind man to me!" When he came near, Jesus asked him, [41]"What do you want me to do for you?"

He said, "Lord, I want to see again."

[42]Jesus said to him, "Then see! You are healed because you believed."

[43]At once the man was able to see, and he followed Jesus, thanking God. All the people who saw this praised God.

ZACCHAEUS

19 Jesus was going through the city of Jericho. [2]In Jericho there was a man named Zacchaeus. He was a wealthy, very important tax collector. [3]He wanted to see who Jesus was, but he was too short to see above the crowd. [4]He ran ahead to a place where he knew Jesus would come. He climbed a sycamore tree so he could see Jesus. [5]When Jesus came

18:20 'You . . . mother.' Quotation from Exodus 20:12-16; Deuteronomy 5:16-20.

to that place, he looked up and saw Zacchaeus in the tree. He said to him, "Zacchaeus, hurry and come down! I must stay at your house today."

⁶Zacchaeus came down quickly. He was pleased to have Jesus in his house. ⁷All the people saw this and began to complain, "Look at the kind of man Jesus stays with. Zacchaeus is a sinner!"

⁸But Zacchaeus said to the Lord, "I will give half of my money to the poor. If I have cheated anyone, I will pay that person back four times more!"

⁹Jesus said, "Salvation has come to this house today. This man truly belongs to the family of Abraham. ¹⁰The Son of Man*d* came to find lost people and save them."

A STORY ABOUT THREE SERVANTS

¹¹Jesus traveled closer to Jerusalem. Some of the people thought that God's kingdom would appear soon. ¹²Jesus knew that the people thought this, so he told them this story: "A very important man was preparing to go to a country far away to be made a king. Then he planned to return home and rule his people. ¹³So the man called ten of his servants together. He gave a bag of money*n* to each servant. He said, 'Do business with this money till I get back.' ¹⁴But the people in the kingdom hated the man. So they sent a group to follow him and say, 'We don't want this man to be our king!'

¹⁵"But the man became king. When he came home, he said, 'Call those servants who have my money. I want to know how much they earned with it.'

¹⁶"The first servant came and said, 'Sir, I earned ten bags of money with the one bag you gave me!' ¹⁷The king said to the servant, 'Fine! You are a good servant. I see that I can trust you with small things. So now I will let you rule over ten of my cities.'

¹⁸"The second servant said, 'Sir, with your one bag of money I earned five bags!' ¹⁹The king said to this servant, 'You can rule over five cities.'

²⁰"Then another servant came in. The servant said to the king, 'Sir, here is your bag of money. I wrapped it in a piece of cloth and hid it. ²¹I was afraid of you because you are a hard man. You even take money that you didn't earn and gather food that you didn't plant.' ²²Then the king said to the servant, 'You evil servant! I will use your own words to condemn you. You said that I am a hard man. You said that I even take money that I didn't earn and gather food that I didn't plant. ²³If that is true, then you should have put my money in the bank. Then, when I came back, my money would have earned some interest.'

²⁴"Then the king said to the men who were watching, 'Take the bag of money away from this servant and give it to the servant who earned ten bags of money.' ²⁵They said to the king, 'But sir, that servant already has ten bags of money!' ²⁶The king said, 'The one who uses what he has will get more. But the one who does not use what he has will have everything taken away from him. ²⁷Now where are my enemies who didn't want me to be king? Bring them here and kill them before me.'"

JESUS ENTERS JERUSALEM AS A KING

²⁸After Jesus said this, he went on toward Jerusalem. ²⁹Jesus came near Bethphage and Bethany, towns near the hill called the Mount of Olives.*d* Then he sent out two of his followers. ³⁰He said, "Go into the town you can see there. When you enter it, you will find a colt tied there. No one has ever ridden this colt. Untie it, and bring it here to me. ³¹If anyone asks you why you are taking it, say, 'The Master needs it.'"

19:13 bag of money One bag of money was a Greek "mina." One mina was enough money to pay a person for working three months.

³²The two followers went into town. They found the colt just as Jesus told them. ³³The followers untied it, but the owners of the colt came out. They asked the followers, "Why are you untying our colt?"

³⁴The followers answered, "The Master needs it." ³⁵So they brought it to Jesus. They threw their coats on the colt's back and put Jesus on it. ³⁶As Jesus rode toward Jerusalem, the followers spread their coats on the road before him.

³⁷Jesus was coming close to Jerusalem. He was already near the bottom of the Mount of Olives. The whole crowd of followers was very happy. They began shouting praise to God for all the powerful works they had seen. They said,

³⁸"God bless the king who comes in the
     name of the Lord!
There is peace in heaven and glory to
     God!"   Psalm 118:26

³⁹Some of the Pharisees*d* said to Jesus, "Teacher, tell your followers not to say these things!"

⁴⁰But Jesus answered, "I tell you, if my followers don't say these things, then the stones will cry out."

JESUS CRIES FOR JERUSALEM

⁴¹Jesus came near Jerusalem. He saw the city and began to cry for it. ⁴²Jesus said to Jerusalem, "I wish you knew today what would bring you peace! But you can't know it, because it is hidden from you. ⁴³A time is coming when your enemies will build a wall around you and will hold you in on all sides. ⁴⁴They will destroy you and all your people. Not one stone of your buildings will be left on another. All this will happen because you did not know the time when God came to save you."

JESUS GOES TO THE TEMPLE

⁴⁵Jesus went into the Temple.*d* He began to throw out the people who were selling things there. ⁴⁶He said, "It is written in the Scriptures,*d* 'My Temple will be a house where people will pray.'*n* But you have changed it into a 'hideout for robbers'!"*n*

⁴⁷Jesus taught in the Temple every day. The leading priests, the teachers of the law, and some of the leaders of the people wanted to kill Jesus. ⁴⁸But all the people were listening closely to him and were interested in all the things he said. So the leading priests, the teachers of the law, and the leaders did not know how they could kill him.

THE LEADERS QUESTION JESUS

20 One day Jesus was in the Temple,*d* teaching the people and telling them the Good News.*d* The leading priests, teachers of the law, and Jewish elders came up to talk with him. ²They said, "Tell us! What authority do you have to do these things? Who gave you this authority?"

³Jesus answered, "I will ask you a question too. Tell me: ⁴When John baptized people, did that come from God or from man?"

⁵The priests, the teachers of the law, and the Jewish leaders all talked about this. They said to each other, "If we answer, 'John's baptism was from God,' then Jesus will say, 'Then why did you not believe John?' ⁶But if we say, 'John's baptism was from man,' then all the people will kill us with stones because they believe that John was a prophet."*d* ⁷So they answered, "We don't know the answer."

⁸So Jesus said to them, "Then I will not tell you by what authority I do these things!"

GOD SENDS HIS SON

⁹Then Jesus told the people this story: "A man planted a vineyard. The man leased the land to some farmers. Then he

19:46 'My Temple ... pray.' Quotation from Isaiah 56:7.
19:46 'hideout for robbers' Quotation from Jeremiah 7:11.

went away for a long time. [10]Later, it was time for the grapes to be picked. So the man sent a servant to those farmers to get his share of the grapes. But they beat the servant and sent him away with nothing. [11]Then he sent another servant. They beat this servant too. They showed no respect for him and sent him away with nothing. [12]So the man sent a third servant. The farmers hurt this servant badly and threw him out. [13]The owner of the vineyard said, 'What will I do now? I will send my son whom I love very much. Maybe they will respect him!' [14]When they saw the son, they said to each other, 'This is the owner's son. This vineyard will be his. If we kill him, then it will be ours!' [15]So the farmers threw the son out of the vineyard and killed him.

"What will the owner of this vineyard do? [16]He will come and kill those farmers! Then he will give the vineyard to other farmers."

The people heard this story. They said, "No! Let this never happen!"

[17]But Jesus looked at them and said, "Then what does this verse mean:

'The stone that the builders did not want
        became the cornerstone'?[d]

                                    Psalm 118:22

[18]Everyone who falls on that stone will be broken. If that stone falls on you, it will crush you!"

[19]The teachers of the law and the priests heard this story that Jesus told. They knew the story was about them. So they wanted to arrest Jesus at once. But they were afraid of what the people would do.

THE LEADERS TRY TO TRAP JESUS

[20]So they waited for the right time to get Jesus. They sent some spies who acted as if they were good men. They wanted to trap Jesus in what he said so they could hand him over to the authority and power of the governor. [21]So the spies asked Jesus, "Teacher, we know that what you say and teach is true. You teach the same to all people. You always teach the truth about God's way. [22]Tell us, is it right that we pay taxes to Caesar[d] or not?"

[23]But Jesus knew that these men were trying to trick him. He said, [24]"Show me a coin. Whose name is on the coin? And whose picture is on it?"

They said, "Caesar's."

[25]Jesus said to them, "Then give to Caesar the things that are Caesar's. And give to God the things that are God's."

[26]The men were amazed at his answer. They could say nothing. They were not able to trap Jesus in anything he said before the people.

SADDUCEES TRY TO TRICK JESUS

[27]Some Sadducees[d] came to Jesus. (Sadducees believe that people will not rise from death.) They asked, [28]"Teacher, Moses wrote that a man's brother might die. He leaves a wife but no children. Then that man must marry the widow and have children for his dead brother. [29]One time there were seven brothers. The first brother married, but died. He had no children. [30]Then the second brother married the widow, and he died. [31]And the third brother married the widow, and he died. The same thing happened with all the other brothers. They all died and had no children. [32]The woman was the last to die. [33]But all seven brothers married her. So when people rise from death, whose wife will the woman be?"

[34]Jesus said to the Sadducees, "On earth, people marry each other. [35]But those who will be worthy to be raised from death and live again will not marry. [36]In that life they are like angels and cannot die. They are children of God, because they have been raised from death. [37]Moses clearly showed that the dead are raised to life. When Moses wrote about the burning bush,[n] he said

20:37 burning bush Read Exodus 3:1-12 in the Old Testament.

that the Lord is 'the God of Abraham, the God of Isaac, and the God of Jacob.'[n] [38]God is the God of living people, not dead people. All people are alive to God."

[39]Some of the teachers of the law said, "Teacher, your answer was good." [40]No one was brave enough to ask him another question.

IS THE CHRIST THE SON OF DAVID?

[41]Then Jesus said, "Why do people say that the Christ[d] is the Son of David?[d] [42]In the book of Psalms, David himself says:

'The Lord said to my Lord:
   Sit by me at my right side,
[43]   until I put your enemies under your control.'[n]   Psalm 110:1

[44]David calls the Christ 'Lord.' But the Christ is also the son of David. How can both these things be true?"

JESUS ACCUSES THE LEADERS

[45]While all the people were listening, Jesus said to his followers, [46]"Be careful of the teachers of the law. They like to walk around wearing clothes that look important. And they love for people to show respect to them in the marketplaces. They love to have the most important seats in the synagogues[d] and at the feasts. [47]But they cheat widows and steal their houses. Then they try to make themselves look good by saying long prayers. God will punish these men very much."

TRUE GIVING

21 Jesus saw some rich people putting their gifts into the Temple[d] money box.[n] [2]Then Jesus saw a poor widow. She put two small copper coins into the box. [3]He said, "I tell you the truth. This poor widow gave only two small coins. But she really gave more than all those rich people. [4]The rich have plenty; they gave only what they did not need. This woman is very poor, but she gave all she had. And she needed that money to live on."

THE TEMPLE WILL BE DESTROYED

[5]Some of the followers were talking about the Temple[d] and how it was decorated with beautiful stones and gifts offered to God.

[6]But Jesus said, "The time will come when all that you see here will be destroyed. Every stone will be thrown down to the ground. Not one stone will be left on another!"

[7]Some followers asked Jesus, "Teacher, when will these things happen? What will show us that it is time for them to take place?"

[8]Jesus said, "Be careful! Don't be fooled. Many people will come using my name. They will say, 'I am the Christ'[d] and, 'The right time has come!' But don't follow them. [9]When you hear about wars and riots, don't be afraid. These things must happen first. Then the end will come later."

[10]Then he said to them, "Nations will fight against other nations. Kingdoms will fight against other kingdoms. [11]There will be great earthquakes, sicknesses, and other terrible things in many places. In some places there will be no food for the people to eat. Fearful events and great signs will come from heaven.

[12]"But before all these things happen, people will arrest you and treat you cruelly. They will judge you in their synagogues[d] and put you in jail. You will be forced to stand before kings and governors. They will do all these things to you because you follow me. [13]But this will give you an opportunity to tell about me. [14]Don't worry about what you will say. [15]I will give you the wisdom to say things so that none of your enemies will be able to show that you are wrong. [16]Even your

---

20:37 **'the God of . . . Jacob'** These words are taken from Exodus 3:6.
20:43 **until . . . control** Literally, "until I make your enemies a footstool for your feet."
21:1 **money box** A special box in the Jewish place for worship where people put their gifts to God.

parents, brothers, relatives and friends will turn against you. They will kill some of you. [17]All people will hate you because you follow me. [18]But none of these things can really harm you. [19]You will save yourselves by continuing strong in your faith through all these things.

JERUSALEM WILL BE DESTROYED

[20]"When you see armies all around Jerusalem, then you will know that it will soon be destroyed. [21]At that time, the people in Judea should run away to the mountains. The people in Jerusalem must get out. If you are near the city, don't go in! [22]These are the days of punishment to make come true all that is written in the Scriptures.[d] [23]At that time, it will be hard for women who are pregnant or have nursing babies! Great trouble will come upon this land, and God will be angry with these people. [24]Some will be killed by the sword and taken as prisoners to all nations. Jerusalem will be crushed by non-Jewish people until their time is over.

DON'T FEAR

[25]"Amazing things will happen to the sun, moon, and stars. On earth, nations will be afraid because of the roar and fury of the sea. They will not know what to do. [26]People will be so afraid they will faint. They will wonder what is happening to the whole world. Everything in the sky will be changed. [27]Then people will see the Son of Man[d] coming in a cloud with power and great glory. [28]When these things begin to happen, don't fear. Look up and hold your heads high because the time when God will free you is near!"

MY WORDS WILL LIVE FOREVER

[29]Then Jesus told this story: "Look at the fig tree and all the other trees. [30]When their leaves appear, you know that summer is near. [31]In the same way, when you see all these things happening, then you will know that God's kingdom is coming very soon.

[32]"I tell you the truth. All these things will happen while the people of this time are still living! [33]The whole world, earth and sky, will be destroyed; but the words I have said will never be destroyed!

BE READY ALL THE TIME

[34]"Be careful! Don't spend your time feasting and drinking. Or don't be too busy with worldly things. If you do that, you will not be able to think straight. And then that day might come when you are not ready. [35]It will close like a trap on all people on earth. [36]So be ready all the time. Pray that you will be strong enough to escape all these things that will happen. And pray that you will be able to stand before the Son of Man."[d]

[37]During the day, Jesus taught the people in the Temple.[d] At night he went out of the city and stayed on the Mount of Olives.[d] [38]Every morning all the people got up early to go to the Temple to listen to him.

PLANS TO KILL JESUS

22 It was almost time for the Jewish Feast[d] of Unleavened Bread, called the Passover[d] Feast. [2]The leading priests and teachers of the law were trying to find a way to kill Jesus. But they were afraid of the people.

[3]One of Jesus' 12 apostles[d] was named Judas Iscariot. Satan entered Judas, and he went to [4]the leading priests and some of the soldiers who guarded the Temple.[d] He talked to them about a way to give Jesus to them. [5]They were pleased and promised to give Judas money. [6]Judas agreed. Then he waited for the best time to turn Jesus over to them without the crowd knowing it.

PREPARATION OF THE PASSOVER MEAL

[7]The Day of Unleavened[d] Bread came. This was the day the Passover[d] lambs had to be sacrificed. [8]Jesus said to Peter and John, "Go and prepare the Passover meal for us to eat."

[9]They asked, "Where do you want us to prepare it?"

Jesus said to them, [10]"Listen! After you go into the city, you will see a man carrying a jar of water. Follow him into the house that he enters. [11]Tell the person who owns that house, 'The Teacher asks that you please show us the room where he and his followers may eat the Passover meal.' [12]Then he will show you a large room upstairs. This room is ready for you. Prepare the Passover meal there."

[13]So Peter and John left. Everything happened as Jesus had said. So they prepared the Passover meal.

THE LORD'S SUPPER

[14]When the time came, Jesus and the apostles[d] were sitting at the table. [15]He said to them, "I wanted very much to eat this Passover[d] meal with you before I die. [16]I will never eat another Passover meal until it is given its true meaning in the kingdom of God."

[17]Then Jesus took a cup. He gave thanks to God for it and said, "Take this cup and give it to everyone here. [18]I will not drink again from the fruit of the vine[n] until God's kingdom comes."

[19]Then Jesus took some bread. He thanked God for it, broke it, and gave it to the apostles. Then Jesus said, "This bread is my body[n] that I am giving for you. Do this to remember me." [20]In the same way, after supper, Jesus took the cup and said, "This cup shows the new agreement that God makes with his people. This new agreement begins with my blood which is poured out for you."

WHO WILL TURN AGAINST JESUS?

[21]Jesus said, "One of you will turn against me. His hand is by my hand on the table. [22]The Son of Man[d] will do what God has planned. But how terrible it will be for that man who gives the Son of Man to be killed."

[23]Then the apostles[d] asked each other,

"Which one of us would do that to Jesus?"

BE LIKE A SERVANT

[24]Then the apostles[d] began to argue about which one of them was the most important. [25]But Jesus said to them, "The kings of the world rule over their people. Men who have authority over others are called 'very important.' [26]But you must not be like that. The greatest among you should be like the youngest, and the leader should be like the servant. [27]Who is more important: the one sitting at the table or the one serving him? You think the one at the table is more important. But I am like a servant among you!

[28]"You men have stayed with me through many struggles. [29]My Father has given me the power to rule. I also give you authority to rule with me. [30]You will eat and drink at my table in my kingdom. You will sit on thrones and judge the 12 tribes[d] of Israel.

DON'T LOSE YOUR FAITH!

[31]"Satan has asked to test all of you as a farmer tests his wheat. Simon, Simon, [32]I have prayed that you will not lose your faith! Help your brothers be stronger when you come back to me."

[33]But Peter said to Jesus, "Lord, I am ready to go to prison with you. I will even die with you!"

[34]But Jesus said, "Peter, before the rooster crows tonight, you will say you don't know me. You will say this three times!"

BE READY FOR TROUBLE

[35]Then Jesus said to the apostles,[d] "When I sent you out without money, a bag, or sandals, did you need anything?"

They said, "No."

[36]He said to them, "But now if you have money or a bag, carry that with you. If you don't have a sword, sell your coat and buy one. [37]The Scripture[d] says, 'He was

---

22:18 fruit of the vine Product of the grapevine; this may also be translated "wine."
22:19 body Some Greek copies do not have the rest of verse 19 or verse 20.

treated like a criminal.'[n] This scripture must have its full meaning. It was written about me, and it is happening now."

[38]The followers said, "Look, Lord, here are two swords!"

He said to them, "That's enough."

JESUS PRAYS ALONE

[39-40]Jesus left the city and went to the Mount of Olives.[d] His followers went with him. (Jesus went there often.) He said to his followers, "Pray for strength against temptation."

[41]Then Jesus went about a stone's throw away from them. He kneeled down and prayed, [42]"Father, if it is what you want, then let me not have this cup[n] of suffering. But do what you want, not what I want." [43]Then an angel from heaven appeared to him to help him. [44]Jesus was full of pain; he prayed even more. Sweat dripped from his face as if he were bleeding. [45]When he finished praying, he went to his followers. They were asleep. (Their sadness had made them very tired.) [46]Jesus said to them, "Why are you sleeping? Get up and pray for strength against temptation."

JESUS IS ARRESTED

[47]While Jesus was speaking, a crowd came up. One of the 12 apostles[d] was leading them. He was Judas. He came close to Jesus so that he could kiss him.

[48]But Jesus said to him, "Judas, are you using the kiss to give the Son of Man[d] to his enemies?"

[49]The followers of Jesus were standing there too. They saw what was happening. They said to Jesus, "Lord, should we use our swords?" [50]And one of them did use his sword. He cut off the right ear of the servant of the high priest.

[51]Jesus said, "Stop!" Then he touched the servant's ear and healed him.

[52]Those who came to arrest Jesus were the leading priests, the soldiers who guarded the Temple,[d] and the Jewish elders. Jesus said to them, "Why did you come out here with swords and sticks? Do you think I am a criminal? [53]I was with you every day in the Temple. Why didn't you try to arrest me there? But this is your time—the time when darkness rules."

PETER SAYS HE DOESN'T KNOW JESUS

[54]They arrested Jesus and took him away. They brought him into the house of the high priest. Peter followed them, but he did not go near Jesus. [55]The soldiers started a fire in the middle of the courtyard and sat together. Peter sat with them. [56]A servant girl saw Peter sitting there near the light. She looked closely at Peter's face and said, "This man was also with him!"

[57]But Peter said this was not true. He said, "Girl, I don't know him."

[58]A short time later, another person saw Peter and said, "You are also one of them."

But Peter said, "Man, I am not!"

[59]About an hour later, another man insisted, "It is true! This man was with him. He is from Galilee!"

[60]But Peter said, "Man, I don't know what you are talking about!"

Immediately, while Peter was still speaking, a rooster crowed. [61]Then the Lord turned and looked straight at Peter. And Peter remembered what the Lord had said: "Before the rooster crows tonight, you will say three times that you don't know me." [62]Then Peter went outside and cried with much pain in his heart.

THE PEOPLE LAUGH AT JESUS

[63-64]Some men were guarding Jesus. They made fun of him like this: They covered his eyes so that he could not see

---

22:37 'He . . . criminal.' Quotation from Isaiah 53:12.

22:42 cup Jesus is talking about the bad things that will happen to him. Accepting these things will be hard, like drinking a cup of something that tastes very bitter.

them. Then they hit him and said, "Prove that you are a prophet,[d] and tell us who hit you!" [65]The men said many cruel things to Jesus.

JESUS BEFORE THE LEADERS

[66]When day came, the elders of the people, the leading priests, and the teachers of the law came together. They led Jesus away to their highest court. [67]They said, "If you are the Christ,[d] then tell us that you are!"

Jesus said to them, "If I tell you I am the Christ, you will not believe me. [68]And if I ask you, you will not answer. [69]But beginning now, the Son of Man[d] will sit at the right hand of the powerful God."

[70]They all said, "Then are you the Son of God?"

Jesus said to them, "Yes, you are right when you say that I am."

[71]They said, "Why do we need witnesses now? We ourselves heard him say this!"

GOVERNOR PILATE QUESTIONS JESUS

23 Then the whole group stood up and led Jesus to Pilate.[n] [2]They began to accuse Jesus. They told Pilate, "We caught this man telling things that were confusing our people. He says that we should not pay taxes to Caesar.[d] He calls himself the Christ,[d] a king."

[3]Pilate asked Jesus, "Are you the king of the Jews?"

Jesus answered, "Yes, that is right."

[4]Pilate said to the leading priests and the people, "I find nothing wrong with this man."

[5]They said again and again, "But Jesus is making trouble with the people! He teaches all around Judea. He began in Galilee, and now he is here!"

PILATE SENDS JESUS TO HEROD

[6]Pilate heard this and asked if Jesus was from Galilee. [7]If so, Jesus was under Herod's authority. Herod was in Jeru-

salem at that time; so Pilate sent Jesus to him. [8]When Herod saw Jesus, he was very glad. He had heard about Jesus and had wanted to meet him for a long time. Herod was hoping to see Jesus work a miracle.[d] [9]Herod asked Jesus many questions, but Jesus said nothing. [10]The leading priests and teachers of the law were standing there. They were shouting things against Jesus. [11]Then Herod and his soldiers made fun of Jesus. They dressed him in a kingly robe and then sent him back to Pilate. [12]In the past, Pilate and Herod had always been enemies. But on that day they became friends.

JESUS MUST DIE

[13]Pilate called all the people together with the leading priests and the Jewish leaders. [14]He said to them, "You brought this man to me. You said that he was making trouble among the people. But I have questioned him before you all, and I have not found him guilty of the things you say. [15]Also, Herod found nothing wrong with him; he sent him back to us. Look, he has done nothing for which he should die. [16]So, after I punish him, I will let him go free." [17][Every year at the Passover Feast, Pilate had to release one prisoner to the people.][n]

[18]But all the people shouted, "Kill him! Let Barabbas go free!" [19](Barabbas was a man who was in prison because he started a riot in the city. He was guilty of murder.)

[20]Pilate wanted to let Jesus go free. So he told this to the crowd. [21]But they shouted again, "Kill him! Kill him on a cross!"

[22]A third time Pilate said to them, "Why? What wrong has he done? I can find no reason to kill him. So I will have him punished and set him free."

[23]But they continued to shout. They demanded that Jesus be killed on the

---

23:1 **Pilate** Pontius Pilate was the Roman governor of Judea from A.D. 26 to A.D. 36.
23:17 **Every . . . people.** Some Greek copies do not contain the bracketed text.

cross. Their yelling became so loud that [24]Pilate decided to give them what they wanted. [25]They wanted Barabbas to go free, the man who was in jail for starting a riot and for murder. Pilate let Barabbas go free and gave Jesus to them to be killed.

JESUS IS KILLED ON A CROSS

[26]The soldiers led Jesus away. At that time, there was a man coming into the city from the fields. His name was Simon, and he was from the city of Cyrene. The soldiers forced Simon to carry Jesus' cross and walk behind him.

[27]A large crowd of people was following Jesus. Some of the women were sad and crying. [28]But Jesus turned and said to them, "Women of Jerusalem, don't cry for me. Cry for yourselves and for your children too! [29]The time is coming when people will say, 'Happy are the women who cannot have children! Happy are the women who have no babies to nurse.' [30]Then people will say to the mountains, 'Fall on us!' And they will say to the hills, 'Cover us!' [31]If they act like this now when life is good, what will happen when bad times come?"[n]

[32]There were also two criminals led out with Jesus to be killed. [33]Jesus and the two criminals were taken to a place called the Skull. There the soldiers nailed Jesus to his cross. They also nailed the criminals to their crosses, one beside Jesus on the right and the other beside Jesus on the left. [34]Jesus said, "Father, forgive them. They don't know what they are doing."[n]

The soldiers threw lots[d] to decide who would get his clothes. [35]The people stood there watching. The leaders made fun of Jesus. They said, "If he is God's Chosen One, the Christ,[d] then let him save himself. He saved other people, didn't he?"

[36]Even the soldiers made fun of him. They came to Jesus and offered him some vinegar. [37]They said, "If you are the king of the Jews, save yourself." [38](At the top of the cross these words were written: "THIS IS THE KING OF THE JEWS.")

[39]One of the criminals began to shout insults at Jesus: "Aren't you the Christ? Then save yourself! And save us too!"

[40]But the other criminal stopped him. He said, "You should fear God! You are getting the same punishment as he is. [41]We are punished justly; we should die. But this man has done nothing wrong!" [42]Then this criminal said to Jesus, "Jesus, remember me when you come into your kingdom!"

[43]Then Jesus said to him, "Listen! What I say is true: Today you will be with me in paradise!"[n]

JESUS DIES

[44]It was about noon, and the whole land became dark until three o'clock in the afternoon. [45]There was no sun! The curtain in the Temple[n] was torn into two pieces. [46]Jesus cried out in a loud voice, "Father, I give you my life." After Jesus said this, he died.

[47]The army officer there saw what happened. He praised God, saying, "I know this was a good man!"

[48]Many people had gathered there to watch this thing. When they saw what happened, they returned home. They beat their chests because they were so sad. [49]Those who were close friends of Jesus were there. Some were women who had followed Jesus from Galilee. They all stood far away from the cross and watched.

JOSEPH OF ARIMATHEA

[50-51]A man from the Jewish town of Arimathea was there, too. His name was Joseph. He was a good, religious man. He wanted the kingdom of God to come.

23:31 If ... come? Literally, "If they do these things in the green tree, what will happen in the dry?"
23:34 Jesus ... doing. Some Greek copies do not have this part of verse 34.
23:43 paradise A place where good people go when they die.
23:45 curtain in the Temple A curtain divided the Most Holy Place from the other part of the Temple. This was the special building in Jerusalem where God commanded the Jews to worship him.

Joseph was a member of the Jewish council, but he had not agreed when the other leaders decided to kill Jesus. [52]Joseph went to Pilate to ask for the body of Jesus. [53]So Joseph took the body down from the cross and wrapped it in cloth. Then he put Jesus' body in a tomb that was cut in a wall of rock. This tomb had never been used before. [54]This was late on Preparation[d] Day. When the sun went down, the Sabbath[d] day would begin.

[55]The women who had come from Galilee with Jesus followed Joseph. They saw the tomb and saw inside where the body of Jesus was laid. [56]Then the women left to prepare perfumes and spices.

On the Sabbath day they rested, as the law of Moses commanded.

JESUS RISES FROM DEATH

24 Very early on the first day of the week, the women came to the tomb where Jesus' body was laid. They brought the spices they had prepared. [2]They found that the stone had been rolled away from the entrance of the tomb. [3]They went in, but they did not find the body of the Lord Jesus. [4]While they were wondering about this, two men in shining clothes suddenly stood beside them. [5]The women were very afraid; they bowed their heads to the ground. The men said to the women, "Why are you looking for a living person here? This is a place for the dead. [6]Jesus is not here. He has risen from death! Do you remember what he said in Galilee? [7]He said that the Son of Man[d] must be given to evil men, be killed on a cross, and rise from death on the third day." [8]Then the women remembered what Jesus had said.

[9]The women left the tomb and told all these things to the 11 apostles[d] and the other followers. [10]These women were Mary Magdalene, Joanna, Mary the mother of James, and some other women. The women told the apostles everything that had happened at the tomb. [11]But they did not believe the women. It sounded like nonsense. [12]But Peter got up and ran to the tomb. He looked in, but he saw only the cloth that Jesus' body had been wrapped in. Peter went away to be alone, wondering about what had happened.

ON THE ROAD TO EMMAUS

[13]That same day two of Jesus' followers were going to a town named Emmaus. It is about seven miles from Jerusalem. [14]They were talking about everything that had happened. [15]While they were discussing these things, Jesus himself came near and began walking with them. [16](They were not allowed to recognize Jesus.) [17]Then he said, "What are these things you are talking about while you walk?"

The two followers stopped. Their faces were very sad. [18]The one named Cleopas answered, "You must be the only one in Jerusalem who does not know what just happened there."

[19]Jesus said to them, "What are you talking about?"

The followers said, "It is about Jesus of Nazareth. He was a prophet[d] from God to all the people. He said and did many powerful things. [20]Our leaders and the leading priests gave him up to be judged and killed. They nailed him to a cross. [21]But we were hoping that he would free the Jews. It is now the third day since this happened. [22]And today some women among us told us some amazing things. Early this morning they went to the tomb, [23]but they did not find his body there. They came and told us that they had seen a vision of angels. The angels said that Jesus was alive! [24]So some of our group went to the tomb, too. They found it just as the women said, but they did not see Jesus."

[25]Then Jesus said to them, "You are foolish and slow to realize what is true. You should believe everything the prophets said. [26]They said that the Christ[d] must suffer these things before he enters his glory." [27]Then Jesus began to explain

everything that had been written about himself in the Scriptures.[d] He started with Moses, and then he talked about what all the prophets had said about him.

28They came near the town of Emmaus, and Jesus acted as if he did not plan to stop there. 29But they begged him, "Stay with us. It is late; it is almost night." So he went in to stay with them. 30Jesus sat down with them and took some bread. He gave thanks for the food and divided it. Then he gave it to them. 31And then, they were allowed to recognize Jesus. But when they saw who he was, he disappeared. 32They said to each other, "When Jesus talked to us on the road, it felt like a fire burning in us. It was exciting when he explained the true meaning of the Scriptures."

33So the two followers got up at once and went back to Jerusalem. There they found the 11 apostles[d] and others gathered. 34They were saying, "The Lord really has risen from death! He showed himself to Simon."

35Then the two followers told what had happened on the road. They talked about how they recognized Jesus when he divided the bread.

JESUS APPEARS TO HIS FOLLOWERS

36While the two followers were telling this, Jesus himself stood among those gathered. He said to them, "Peace be with you."

37They were fearful and terrified. They thought they were seeing a ghost. 38But Jesus said, "Why are you troubled? Why do you doubt what you see? 39Look at my hands and my feet. It is I myself! Touch me. You can see that I have a living body; a ghost does not have a body like this."

40After Jesus said this, he showed them his hands and feet. 41The followers were amazed and very happy. They still could not believe it. Jesus said to them, "Do you have any food here?" 42They gave him a piece of cooked fish. 43While the followers watched, Jesus took the fish and ate it.

44He said to them, "Remember when I was with you before? I said that everything written about me must happen—everything in the law of Moses, the books of the prophets,[d] and the Psalms."

45Then Jesus opened their minds so they could understand the Scriptures.[d] 46He said to them, "It is written that the Christ[d] would be killed and rise from death on the third day. 47-48You saw these things happen—you are witnesses. You must tell people to change their hearts and lives. If they do this, their sins will be forgiven. You must start at Jerusalem and preach these things in my name to all nations. 49Listen! My Father has promised you something; I will send it to you. But you must stay in Jerusalem until you have received that power from heaven."

JESUS GOES BACK TO HEAVEN

50Jesus led his followers out of Jerusalem almost to Bethany. He raised his hands and blessed them. 51While he was blessing them, he was separated from them and carried into heaven. 52They worshiped him and then went back to the city very happy. 53They stayed in the Temple[d] all the time, praising God.

JOHN

JOHN TELLS ABOUT JESUS THE SON WHO REVEALS THE FATHER

CHRIST COMES TO THE WORLD

1 Before the world began, there was the Word.[n] The Word was with God, and the Word was God. [2]He was with God in the beginning. [3]All things were made through him. Nothing was made without him. [4]In him there was life. That life was light for the people of the world. [5]The Light shines in the darkness. And the darkness has not overpowered[n] the Light.

[6]There was a man named John[n] who was sent by God. [7]He came to tell people about the Light. Through him all people could hear about the Light and believe. [8]John was not the Light, but he came to tell people about the Light. [9]The true Light was coming into the world. The true Light gives light to all.

[10]The Word was in the world. The world was made through him, but the world did not know him. [11]He came to the world that was his own. But his own people did not accept him. [12]But some people did accept him. They believed in him. To them he gave the right to become children of God. [13]They did not become his children in the human way. They were not born because of the desire or wish of some man. They were born of God.

[14]The Word became a man and lived among us. We saw his glory—the glory that belongs to the only Son of the Father. The Word was full of grace and truth. [15]John told about him. He said, "This is the One I was talking about. I said, 'The One who comes after me is greater than I am. He was living before me.'"

[16]The Word was full of grace and truth. From him we all received more and more blessings. [17]The law was given through Moses, but grace and truth came through Jesus Christ. [18]No man has ever seen God. But God the only Son is very close to the Father.[n] And the Son has shown us what God is like.

JOHN TELLS PEOPLE ABOUT JESUS

[19]The Jews in Jerusalem sent some priests and Levites to John.[n] The Jews sent them to ask, "Who are you?"

[20]John spoke freely and did not refuse to answer. He said clearly, "I am not the Christ."[d]

[21]So they asked him, "Then who are you? Are you Elijah?"[n]

He answered, "No, I am not Elijah."

Then they asked, "Are you the Prophet?"[n]

He answered, "No, I am not the Prophet."

[22]Then they said, "Who are you? Give us an answer to tell those who sent us. What do you say about yourself?"

[23]John told them in the words of the prophet Isaiah:

"I am the voice of a man
    calling out in the desert:
'Make the road straight for the Lord.'"

Isaiah 40:3

[24]In the group of Jews who were sent, there were some Pharisees.[d] [25]They said to John: "You say you are not the Christ. You say you are not Elijah or the Prophet. Then why do you baptize people?"

[26]John answered, "I baptize people with water. But there is one here with you that you don't know. [27]He is the One who

---

1:1 **Word** The Greek word is "logos," meaning any kind of communication. It could be translated "message." Here, it means Christ. Christ was the way God told people about himself.
1:5 **overpowered** This can also be translated, "understood."
1:6, 19 **John** John the Baptist, who preached to people about Christ's coming (Matthew 3, Luke 3).
1:18 **But . . . Father.** This could be translated, "But the only God is very close to the Father." Also, some Greek copies read "But the only Son is very close to the Father."
1:21 **Elijah** A man who spoke for God. He lived hundreds of years before Christ.
1:21 **Prophet** They probably meant the prophet that God told Moses he would send (Deuteronomy 18:15-19).

comes after me. I am not good enough to untie the strings of his sandals."

28This all happened at Bethany on the other side of the Jordan River. This is where John was baptizing people.

29The next day John saw Jesus coming toward him. John said, "Look, the Lamb of God.*n* He takes away the sins of the world! 30This is the One I was talking about. I said, 'A man will come after me, but he is greater than I am, because he was living before me.' 31Even I did not know who he was. But I came baptizing with water so that the people of Israel could know who he is."

32-33Then John said, "I did not know who the Christ was. But God sent me to baptize with water. And God told me, 'You will see the Spirit*d* come down and rest on a man. That man is the One who will baptize with the Holy Spirit.'" John said, "I saw the Spirit come down from heaven. The Spirit looked like a dove and rested on him. 34I have seen this happen. So I tell people: 'He is the Son of God.'"*n*

THE FIRST FOLLOWERS OF JESUS

35The next day John*n* was there again with two of his followers. 36He saw Jesus walking by and said, "Look, the Lamb of God!"*n*

37The two followers heard John say this. So they followed Jesus. 38Jesus turned and saw them following him. He asked, "What do you want?"

They said, "Rabbi, where are you staying?" ("Rabbi" means "Teacher.")

39Jesus answered, "Come with me and you will see." So the two men went with Jesus. They saw the place where Jesus was staying and stayed there with him that day. It was then about four o'clock.

40These two men followed Jesus after they heard about him from John. One of the men was Andrew. He was Simon Peter's brother. 41The first thing Andrew did was to find his brother, Simon. He said to Simon, "We have found the Messiah." ("Messiah" means "Christ."*d*)

42Then Andrew took Simon to Jesus. Jesus looked at Simon and said, "You are Simon son of John. You will be called Cephas." ("Cephas" means "Peter."*n*)

43The next day Jesus decided to go to Galilee. He found Philip and said to him, "Follow me." 44Philip was from the town of Bethsaida, where Andrew and Peter lived. 45Philip found Nathanael and told him, "Remember that Moses wrote in the law about a man who was coming, and the prophets*d* also wrote about him. We have found him. He is Jesus, the son of Joseph. He is from Nazareth."

46But Nathanael said to Philip, "Nazareth! Can anything good come from Nazareth?"

Philip answered, "Come and see."

47Jesus saw Nathanael coming toward him. He said, "Here is truly a person of Israel. There is nothing false in him."

48Nathanael asked, "How do you know me?"

Jesus answered, "I saw you when you were under the fig tree. That was before Philip told you about me."

49Then Nathanael said to Jesus, "Teacher, you are the Son of God. You are the King of Israel."

50Jesus said to Nathanael, "You believe in me because I told you I saw you under the fig tree. But you will see greater things than that!" 51And Jesus said to them, "I tell you the truth. You will all see heaven open. You will see 'angels of God going up and coming down'*n* on the Son of Man."*d*

1:29, 36 Lamb of God Name for Jesus. Jesus is like the lambs that were offered for a sacrifice to God.
1:34 the Son of God Some Greek copies read "God's Chosen One."
1:35 John John the Baptist, who preached to people about Christ's coming (Matthew 3, Luke 3).
1:42 Peter The Greek name "Peter," like the Aramaic name "Cephas," means "rock."
1:51 'angels . . . down' These words are from Genesis 28:12.

THE WEDDING AT CANA

2 Two days later there was a wedding in the town of Cana in Galilee. Jesus' mother was there. [2]Jesus and his followers were also invited to the wedding. [3]When all the wine was gone, Jesus' mother said to him, "They have no more wine."

[4]Jesus answered, "Dear woman, why come to me? My time has not yet come."

[5]His mother said to the servants, "Do whatever he tells you to do."

[6]In that place there were six stone water jars. The Jews used jars like these in their washing ceremony.[n] Each jar held about 20 or 30 gallons.

[7]Jesus said to the servants, "Fill the jars with water." So they filled the jars to the top.

[8]Then he said to them, "Now take some out and give it to the master of the feast."

So the servants took the water to the master. [9]When he tasted it, the water had become wine. He did not know where the wine came from. But the servants who brought the water knew. The master of the wedding called the bridegroom [10]and said to him, "People always serve the best wine first. Later, after the guests have been drinking a lot, they serve the cheaper wine. But you have saved the best wine till now."

[11]So in Cana of Galilee, Jesus did his first miracle.[d] There he showed his glory, and his followers believed in him.

JESUS IN THE TEMPLE

[12]Then Jesus went to the town of Capernaum with his mother, brothers and his followers. They all stayed in Capernaum for a few days. [13]But it was almost time for the Jewish Passover[d] Feast. So Jesus went to Jerusalem. [14]In the Temple[d] he found men selling cattle, sheep, and doves. He saw others sitting at tables, exchanging money. [15]Jesus made a whip out of cords. Then he forced all these men, with the sheep and cattle, to leave the Temple. He turned over the tables and scattered the money of the men who were exchanging it. [16]Then he said to those who were selling pigeons, "Take these things out of here! Don't make my Father's house a place for buying and selling!"

[17]When this happened the followers remembered what was written in the Scriptures:[d] "My strong love for your Temple completely controls me."[n]

[18]The Jews said to Jesus, "Show us a miracle[d] for a sign. Prove that you have the right to do these things."

[19]Jesus answered, "Destroy this temple, and I will build it again in three days."

[20]The Jews answered, "Men worked 46 years to build this Temple! Do you really believe you can build it again in three days?"

[21](But the temple Jesus meant was his own body. [22]After Jesus was raised from death, his followers remembered that Jesus had said this. Then they believed the Scripture[d] and the words Jesus said.)

[23]Jesus was in Jerusalem for the Passover Feast. Many people believed in him because they saw the miracles he did. [24]But Jesus did not believe in them because he knew them all. [25]He did not need anyone to tell him about people. Jesus knew what was in a person's mind.

JESUS AND NICODEMUS

3 There was a man named Nicodemus who was one of the Pharisees.[d] He was an important Jewish leader. [2]One night Nicodemus came to Jesus. He said, "Teacher, we know that you are a teacher

---

2:6 washing ceremony The Jews washed themselves in special ways before eating, before worshiping in the Temple, and at other special times.
2:17 "My . . . me." Quotation from Psalm 69:9.

sent from God. No one can do the miracles[d] you do, unless God is with him."

[3]Jesus answered, "I tell you the truth. Unless you are born again, you cannot be in God's kingdom."

[4]Nicodemus said, "But if a man is already old, how can he be born again? He cannot enter his mother's body again. So how can he be born a second time?"

[5]But Jesus answered, "I tell you the truth. Unless you are born from water and the Spirit,[d] you cannot enter God's kingdom. [6]A person's body is born from his human parents. But a person's spiritual life is born from the Spirit. [7]Don't be surprised when I tell you, 'You must all be born again.' [8]The wind blows where it wants to go. You hear the wind blow. But you don't know where the wind comes from or where it is going. It is the same with every person who is born from the Spirit."

[9]Nicodemus asked, "How can all this be possible?"

[10]Jesus said, "You are an important teacher in Israel. But you still don't understand these things? [11]I tell you the truth. We talk about what we know. We tell about what we have seen. But you don't accept what we tell you. [12]I have told you about things here on earth, but you do not believe me. So surely you will not believe me if I tell you about the things of heaven! [13]The only one who has ever gone up to heaven is the One who came down from heaven—the Son of Man.[nd]

[14]"Moses lifted up the snake in the desert.[n] It is the same with the Son of Man. The Son of Man must be lifted up too. [15]Then everyone who believes in him can have eternal life.

[16]"For God loved the world so much that he gave his only Son. God gave his Son so that whoever believes in him may not be lost, but have eternal life. [17]God did not send his Son into the world to judge the world guilty, but to save the world through him. [18]He who believes in God's Son is not judged guilty. He who does not believe has already been judged guilty, because he has not believed in God's only Son. [19]People are judged by this fact: I am the Light from God that has come into the world. But men did not want light. They wanted darkness because they were doing evil things. [20]Everyone who does evil hates the light. He will not come to the light because it will show all the evil things he has done. [21]But he who follows the true way comes to the light. Then the light will show that the things he has done were done through God."

JESUS AND JOHN THE BAPTIST

[22]After this, Jesus and his followers went into the area of Judea. There Jesus stayed with his followers and baptized people. [23]John was also baptizing in Aenon, near Salim, because there was plenty of water there. People were going there to be baptized. [24](This was before John was put into prison.)

[25]Some of John's followers had an argument with a Jew about religious washing.[n] [26]So they came to John and said, "Teacher, remember the man who was with you on the other side of the Jordan River, the one you spoke about? He is baptizing, and everyone is going to him."

[27]John answered, "A man can get only what God gives him. [28]You yourselves heard me say, 'I am not the Christ.[d] I am only the one God sent to prepare the way for him.' [29]The bride belongs only to the bridegroom. The friend who helps the bridegroom waits and listens for him. He is glad when he hears the bridegroom's

---

3:13 **the Son of Man** Some Greek copies continue, "who is in heaven."

3:14 **Moses . . . desert.** The people of Israel were dying from snake bites. God told Moses to put a bronze snake on a pole. The people who looked at the snake were healed (Numbers 21:4-9).

3:25 **religious washing** The Jews washed themselves in special ways before eating, before worshiping in the Temple, and at other special times.

voice. That is the same pleasure I have. And my time of joy is now here. [30]He must become greater. And I must become less important.

THE ONE WHO COMES FROM HEAVEN

[31]"The One who comes from above is greater than all. He who is from the earth belongs to the earth and talks about things on the earth. But the One who comes from heaven is greater than all. [32]He tells what he has seen and heard, but no one accepts what he says. [33]The person who accepts what he says has proven that God is true. [34]God sent him, and he tells the things that God says. God gives him the Spirit[d] fully. [35]The Father loves the Son and has given him power over everything. [36]He who believes in the Son has eternal life. But he who does not obey the Son will never have that life. God's anger stays with him."

JESUS AND A SAMARITAN WOMAN

4 The Pharisees[d] heard that Jesus was making and baptizing more followers than John. [2](But really Jesus himself did not baptize people. His followers did the baptizing.) Jesus knew that the Pharisees had heard about him. [3]So he left Judea and went back to Galilee. [4]On the way he had to go through the country of Samaria.

[5]In Samaria Jesus came to the town called Sychar. This town is near the field that Jacob gave to his son Joseph. [6]Jacob's well was there. Jesus was tired from his long trip. So he sat down beside the well. It was about noon. [7]A Samaritan[d] woman came to the well to get some water. Jesus said to her, "Please give me a drink." [8](This happened while Jesus' followers were in town buying some food.)

[9]The woman said, "I am surprised that you ask me for a drink. You are a Jew and I am a Samaritan." (Jews are not friends with Samaritans.[n])

[10]Jesus said, "You don't know what God gives. And you don't know who asked you for a drink. If you knew, you would have asked me, and I would have given you living water."

[11]The woman said, "Sir, where will you get that living water? The well is very deep, and you have nothing to get water with. [12]Are you greater than Jacob, our father? Jacob is the one who gave us this well. He drank from it himself. Also, his sons and flocks drank from this well."

[13]Jesus answered, "Every person who drinks this water will be thirsty again. [14]But whoever drinks the water I give will never be thirsty again. The water I give will become a spring of water flowing inside him. It will give him eternal life."

[15]The woman said to him, "Sir, give me this water. Then I will never be thirsty again. And I will not have to come back here to get more water."

[16]Jesus told her, "Go get your husband and come back here."

[17]The woman answered, "But I have no husband."

Jesus said to her, "You are right to say you have no husband. [18]Really you have had five husbands. But the man you live with now is not your husband. You told the truth."

[19]The woman said, "Sir, I can see that you are a prophet.[d] [20]Our fathers worshiped on this mountain. But you Jews say that Jerusalem is the place where people must worship."

[21]Jesus said, "Believe me, woman. The time is coming when you will not have to be in Jerusalem or on this mountain to worship the Father. [22]You Samaritans worship what you don't understand. We Jews understand what we worship. Salvation comes from the Jews. [23]The time is coming when the true worshipers will worship the Father in spirit and truth. That time is now here. And these are the

---

4:9 Jews . . . Samaritans. This can also be translated "Jews don't use things that Samaritans have used."

kinds of worshipers the Father wants. [24]God is spirit. Those who worship God must worship in spirit and truth."

[25]The woman said, "I know that the Messiah is coming." (Messiah is the One called Christ.[d]) "When the Messiah comes, he will explain everything to us."

[26]Then Jesus said, "He is talking to you now. I am he."

[27]Just then his followers came back from town. They were surprised because they saw Jesus talking with a woman. But none of them asked, "What do you want?" or "Why are you talking with her?"

[28]Then the woman left her water jar and went back to town. She said to the people, [29]"A man told me everything I have ever done. Come see him. Maybe he is the Christ!" [30]So the people left the town and went to see Jesus.

[31]While the woman was away, the followers were begging him, "Teacher, eat something!"

[32]But Jesus answered, "I have food to eat that you know nothing about."

[33]So the followers asked themselves, "Did somebody already bring Jesus some food?"

[34]Jesus said, "My food is to do what the One who sent me wants me to do. My food is to finish the work that he gave me to do. [35]You say, 'Four more months to wait before we gather the grain.' But I tell you, open your eyes. Look at the fields that are ready for harvesting now. [36]Even now, the one who harvests the crop is being paid. He is gathering crops for eternal life. So now the one who plants can be happy along with the one who harvests. [37]It is true when we say, 'One person plants, but another harvests the crop.' [38]I sent you to harvest a crop that you did not work for. Others did the work, and you get the profit from their work."[n]

[39]Many of the Samaritans in that town believed in Jesus. They believed because of what the woman said: "He told me everything I have ever done." [40]The Samaritans came to Jesus and begged him to stay with them. So he stayed there two days. [41]Many more believed because of the things he said.

[42]They said to the woman, "First we believed in Jesus because of what you told us. But now we believe because we heard him ourselves. We know that this man really is the Savior of the world."

JESUS HEALS AN OFFICER'S SON

[43]Two days later, Jesus left and went to Galilee. [44](Jesus had said before that a prophet[d] is not respected in his own country.) [45]When Jesus arrived in Galilee, the people there welcomed him. They had seen all the things he did at the Passover[d] Feast in Jerusalem. They had been at the Passover Feast, too.

[46]Jesus went to visit Cana in Galilee again. This is where Jesus had changed the water into wine. One of the king's important officers lived in the city of Capernaum. This man's son was sick. [47]The man heard that Jesus had come from Judea and was now in Galilee. He went to Jesus and begged him to come to Capernaum and heal his son. His son was almost dead. [48]Jesus said to him, "You people must see signs and miracles[d] before you will believe in me."

[49]The officer said, "Sir, come before my child dies."

[50]Jesus answered, "Go. Your son will live."

The man believed what Jesus told him and went home. [51]On the way the man's servants came and met him. They told him, "Your son is well."

[52]The man asked, "What time did my son begin to get well?"

They answered, "It was about one o'clock yesterday when the fever left him."

4:35-38 Look at ... their work. As a farmer sends workers to harvest grain, Jesus sends his followers out to bring people to God.

[53]The father knew that one o'clock was the exact time that Jesus had said, "Your son will live." So the man and all the people of his house believed in Jesus.

[54]That was the second miracle that Jesus did after coming from Judea to Galilee.

JESUS HEALS A MAN AT A POOL

5 Later Jesus went to Jerusalem for a special Jewish feast. [2]In Jerusalem there is a pool with five covered porches. In the Jewish language[n] it is called Bethzatha.[n] This pool is near the Sheep Gate. [3]Many sick people were lying on the porches beside the pool. Some were blind, some were crippled, and some were paralyzed [and they waited for the water to move. Sometimes an angel of the Lord came down to the pool and stirred up the water. After the angel did this, the first person to go into the pool was healed from any sickness he had.][n] [5]There was a man lying there who had been sick for 38 years. [6]Jesus saw the man and knew that he had been sick for a very long time. So Jesus asked him, "Do you want to be well?"

[7]The sick man answered, "Sir, there is no one to help me get into the pool when the water starts moving. I try to be the first one into the water. But when I try, someone else always goes in before I can."

[8]Then Jesus said, "Stand up. Pick up your mat and walk." [9]And immediately the man was well. He picked up his mat and began to walk.

The day all this happened was a Sabbath[d] day. [10]So the Jews said to the man who had been healed, "Today is the Sabbath. It is against our law for you to carry your mat on the Sabbath day."

[11]But he answered, "The man who made me well told me, 'Pick up your mat and walk.'"

[12]Then they asked him, "Who is the man who told you to pick up your mat and walk?"

[13]But the man who had been healed did not know who it was. There were many people in that place, and Jesus had left.

[14]Later, Jesus found the man at the Temple.[d] Jesus said to him, "See, you are well now. But stop sinning or something worse may happen to you!"

[15]Then the man left and went back to the Jews. He told them that Jesus was the one who had made him well.

[16]Jesus was doing this on the Sabbath day. So the Jews began to do bad things to him. [17]But Jesus said to them, "My Father never stops working. And so I work, too."

[18]This made the Jews try harder to kill him. They said, "First Jesus was breaking the law about the Sabbath day. Then he said that God is his own Father! He is making himself equal with God!"

JESUS HAS GOD'S AUTHORITY

[19]But Jesus said, "I tell you the truth. The Son can do nothing alone. The Son does only what he sees his Father doing. The Son does whatever the Father does. [20]The Father loves the Son, and the Father shows the Son all the things he himself does. But the Father will show the Son greater things than this to do. Then you will all be amazed. [21]The Father raises the dead and gives them life. In the same way, the Son gives life to those he wants to. [22]Also, the Father judges no one. But the Father has given the Son power to do all the judging. [23]God did this so that all people will respect the Son the same way they respect the Father. He who does not respect the Son does not respect the Father. The Father is the One who sent the Son.

[24]"I tell you the truth. Whoever hears what I say and believes in the One who

---

5:2 **Jewish language** Aramaic, the language of the Jews in the first century.
5:2 **Bethzatha** Also called Bethsaida or Bethesda, a pool of water north of the Temple in Jerusalem.
5:3 **and . . . had** Some Greek copies do not contain all or most of the bracketed text.

sent me has eternal life. He will not be judged guilty. He has already left death and has entered into life. ²⁵I tell you the truth. The time is coming and is already here when the dead will hear the voice of the Son of God. And those who hear will have life. ²⁶Life comes from the Father himself. So the Father has allowed the Son to give life. ²⁷And the Father has given the Son the approval to judge because he is the Son of Man.ᵈ ²⁸Don't be surprised at this. A time is coming when all who are dead and in their graves will hear his voice. ²⁹Then they will come out of their graves. Those who did good will rise and have life forever. But those who did evil will rise to be judged guilty.

JESUS IS GOD'S SON

³⁰"I can do nothing alone. I judge only the way I am told, so my judgment is right. I don't try to please myself. I try to please the One who sent me.

³¹"If I tell people about myself, then they will not accept what I say about myself. ³²But there is another who tells about me. And I know that the things he says about me are true.

³³"You have sent men to John. And he has told you about the truth. ³⁴But I don't need a man to tell about me. I tell you this so that you can be saved. ³⁵John was like a burning and shining lamp. And you were happy to enjoy his light for a while.

³⁶"But I have a proof about myself that is greater than that of John. The things I do are my proof. These are the things my Father gave me to do. They show that the Father sent me. ³⁷And the Father who sent me has given proof about me himself. You have never heard his voice. You have never seen what he looks like. ³⁸His teaching does not live in you because you don't believe in the One that the Father sent. ³⁹You carefully study the Scripturesᵈ because you think that they give you eternal life. Those are the same Scriptures that tell about me! ⁴⁰But you refuse to come to me to have that life.

⁴¹"I don't want praise from men. ⁴²But I know you—I know that you don't have God's love in you. ⁴³I have come from my Father—I speak for him. But you don't accept me. But when another person comes, speaking only for himself, you will accept him. ⁴⁴You like to have praise from each other. But you never try to get the praise that comes from the only God. So how can you believe? ⁴⁵Don't think that I will stand before the Father and say that you are wrong. Moses is the one who says that you are wrong. And he is the one that you hoped would save you. ⁴⁶If you really believed Moses, you would believe me because Moses wrote about me. ⁴⁷But you don't believe what Moses wrote. So how can you believe what I say?"

MORE THAN 5,000 PEOPLE FED

6 After this, Jesus went across Lake Galilee (or, Lake Tiberias). ²Many people followed him because they saw the miraclesᵈ he did to heal the sick. ³Jesus went up on a hill and there sat down with his followers. ⁴It was almost the time for the Jewish Passoverᵈ Feast.

⁵Jesus looked up and saw a large crowd coming toward him. He said to Philip, "Where can we buy bread for all these people to eat?" ⁶(Jesus asked Philip this question to test him. Jesus already knew what he planned to do.)

⁷Philip answered, "Someone would have to work almost a year to buy enough bread for each person here to have only a little piece."

⁸Another follower there was Andrew. He was Simon Peter's brother. Andrew said, ⁹"Here is a boy with five loaves of barley bread and two little fish. But that is not enough for so many people."

¹⁰Jesus said, "Tell the people to sit down." This was a very grassy place. There were about 5,000 men who sat down there. ¹¹Then Jesus took the loaves of bread. He thanked God for the bread

and gave it to the people who were sitting there. He did the same with the fish. He gave them as much as they wanted.

[12]They all had enough to eat. When they had finished, Jesus said to his followers, "Gather the pieces of fish and bread that were not eaten. Don't waste anything." [13]So they gathered up the pieces that were left. They filled 12 large baskets with the pieces that were left of the five barley loaves.

[14]The people saw this miracle that Jesus did. They said, "He must truly be the Prophet[n] who is coming into the world." [15]Jesus knew that the people planned to come and take him by force and make him their king. So he left and went into the hills alone.

JESUS WALKS ON THE WATER

[16]That evening Jesus' followers went down to Lake Galilee. [17]It was dark now and Jesus had not yet come to them. The followers got into a boat and started across the lake to Capernaum. [18]By now a strong wind was blowing, and the waves on the lake were getting bigger. [19]They rowed the boat about three or four miles. Then they saw Jesus walking on the water, coming toward the boat. The followers were afraid. [20]But Jesus said to them, "Don't be afraid. It is I." [21]Then they were glad to take him into the boat. At once the boat came to land at the place where they wanted to go.

THE PEOPLE SEEK JESUS

[22]The next day came. Some people had stayed on the other side of the lake. They knew that Jesus had not gone in the boat with his followers but that they had left without him. And they knew that only one boat had been there. [23]But then some boats came from Tiberias. They landed near the place where the people had eaten the bread after the Lord had given thanks. [24]The people saw that Jesus and his followers were not there now. So they got into boats and went to Capernaum. They wanted to find Jesus.

JESUS, THE BREAD OF LIFE

[25]The people found Jesus on the other side of the lake. They asked him, "Teacher, when did you come here?"

[26]Jesus answered, "Are you looking for me because you saw me do miracles?[d] No! I tell you the truth. You are looking for me because you ate the bread and were satisfied. [27]Earthly food spoils and ruins. So don't work to get that kind of food. But work to get the food that stays good always and gives you eternal life. The Son of Man[d] will give you that food. God the Father has shown that he is with the Son of Man."

[28]The people asked Jesus, "What are the things God wants us to do?"

[29]Jesus answered, "The work God wants you to do is this: to believe in the One that God sent."

[30]So the people asked, "What miracle will you do? If we can see a miracle, then we will believe you. What will you do? [31]Our ancestors ate the manna[d] in the desert. This is written in the Scriptures:[d] 'God gave them bread from heaven to eat.'[n]

[32]Jesus said, "I tell you the truth. Moses was not the one who gave you bread from heaven. But my Father gives you the true bread from heaven. [33]God's bread is the One who comes down from heaven and gives life to the world."

[34]The people said, "Sir, give us this bread always."

[35]Then Jesus said, "I am the bread that gives life. He who comes to me will never be hungry. He who believes in me will never be thirsty. [36]But as I told you before, you have seen me, and still you don't believe. [37]The Father gives me the people who are mine. Every one of them

---

6:14 Prophet They probably meant the prophet that God told Moses he would send (Deuteronomy 18:15-19).
6:31 'God gave . . . eat.' Quotation from Psalm 78:24.

will come to me, and I will always accept them. [38]I came down from heaven to do what God wants me to do. I did not come to do what I want to do. [39]I must not lose even one of those that God has given me, but I must raise them up on the last day. This is what the One who sent me wants me to do. [40]Everyone who sees the Son and believes in him has eternal life. I will raise him up on the last day. This is what my Father wants."

[41]The Jews began to complain about Jesus. They complained because he said, "I am the bread that comes down from heaven." [42]The Jews said, "This is Jesus. We know his father and mother. He is only Joseph's son. How can he say, 'I came down from heaven'?"

[43]But Jesus answered, "Stop complaining to each other. [44]The Father is the One who sent me. No one can come to me unless the Father draws him to me. And I will raise him up on the last day. [45]It is written in the prophets,[d] 'God will teach all the people.'[n] Everyone who listens to the Father and learns from him comes to me. [46]No one has seen the Father except the One who is from God. Only he has seen the Father. [47]I tell you the truth. He who believes has eternal life. [48]I am the bread that gives life. [49]Your ancestors ate the manna in the desert. But still they died. [50]Here is the bread that comes down from heaven. If anyone eats this bread, he will never die. [51]I am the living bread that came down from heaven. If anyone eats this bread, he will live forever. This bread is my flesh. I will give my flesh so that the people in the world may have life."

[52]Then the Jews began to argue among themselves. They said, "How can this man give us his flesh to eat?"

[53]Jesus said, "I tell you the truth. You must eat the flesh of the Son of Man. And you must drink his blood. If you don't do

this, then you won't have real life in you. [54]He who eats my flesh and drinks my blood has eternal life. I will raise him up on the last day. [55]My flesh is true food. My blood is true drink. [56]Whoever eats my flesh and drinks my blood lives in me, and I live in him. [57]The Father sent me. The Father lives, and I live because of the Father. So he who eats me will live because of me. [58]I am not like the bread our ancestors ate. They ate that bread, but still they died. I am the bread that came down from heaven. He who eats this bread will live forever." [59]Jesus said all these things while he was teaching in the synagogue[d] in Capernaum.

THE WORDS OF ETERNAL LIFE

[60]The followers of Jesus heard this. Many of them said, "This teaching is hard. Who can accept it?"

[61]Jesus knew that his followers were complaining about this. So he said, "Does this teaching bother you? [62]Then will it also bother you to see the Son of Man[d] going back to the place where he came from? [63]It is not the flesh that gives a person life. It is the spirit that gives life. The words I told you are spirit, and so they give life. [64]But some of you don't believe." (Jesus knew who did not believe. He knew this from the beginning. And he knew who would turn against him.) [65]Jesus said, "That is the reason I said, 'If the Father does not let a person come to me, then he cannot come.'"

[66]After Jesus said this, many of his followers left him. They stopped following him.

[67]Jesus asked the 12 followers, "Do you want to leave, too?"

[68]Simon Peter answered Jesus, "Lord, who would we go to? You have the words that give eternal life. [69]We believe in you. We know that you are the Holy One from God."

6:45 'God ... people.' Quotation from Isaiah 54:13.

[70]Then Jesus answered, "I chose all 12 of you. But 1 of you is a devil."

[71]Jesus was talking about Judas, the son of Simon Iscariot. Judas was 1 of the 12. But later he was going to turn against Jesus.

JESUS AND HIS BROTHERS

7 After this, Jesus traveled around Galilee. He did not want to travel in Judea, because the Jews there wanted to kill him. [2]It was time for the Jewish Feast[d] of Shelters. [3]So Jesus' brothers said to him, "You should leave here and go to Judea. Then your followers there can see the miracles[d] you do. [4]Anyone who wants to be well known does not hide what he does. If you are doing these things, show yourself to the world." [5](Even Jesus' brothers did not believe in him.)

[6]Jesus said to his brothers, "The right time for me has not yet come. But any time is right for you. [7]The world cannot hate you. But it hates me, because I tell about the evil things it does. [8]So you go to the feast. I will not go now. The right time for me has not yet come." [9]After saying this, Jesus stayed in Galilee.

[10]So Jesus' brothers left to go to the feast. When they had gone, Jesus went, too. But he did not let people see him. [11]At the feast the Jews were looking for him. They said, "Where is that man?"

[12]There was a large crowd of people there. Many of them were whispering to each other about Jesus. Some said, "He is a good man."

Others said, "No, he fools the people." [13]But no one was brave enough to talk about Jesus openly. They were afraid of the Jews.

JESUS TEACHES AT THE FEAST

[14]The feast was about half over. Then Jesus went to the Temple[d] and began to teach. [15]The Jews were amazed. They said, "This man has never studied in school. How did he learn so much?"

[16]Jesus answered, "The things I teach are not my own. My teaching comes from him who sent me. [17]If anyone chooses to do what God wants, then he will know that my teaching comes from God. He will know that this teaching is not my own. [18]He who teaches his own ideas is trying to get honor for himself. But he who tries to bring honor to the one who sent him—that person speaks the truth. There is nothing false in him. [19]Moses gave you the law,[n] but none of you obey that law. Why are you trying to kill me?"

[20]The people answered, "A demon[d] has come into you. We are not trying to kill you."

[21]Jesus said to them, "I did one miracle,[d] and you are all amazed. [22]Moses gave you the law about circumcision.[d] (But really Moses did not give you circumcision. Circumcision came from our ancestors.) And yet you circumcise a baby boy on a Sabbath[d] day. [23]This shows that a baby boy can be circumcised on a Sabbath day to obey the law of Moses. So why are you angry at me for healing a person's whole body on the Sabbath day? [24]Stop judging by the way things look! Be fair, and judge by what is really right."

IS JESUS THE CHRIST?

[25]Then some of the people who lived in Jerusalem said, "This is the man they are trying to kill. [26]But he is teaching where everyone can see and hear him. And no one is trying to stop him. Maybe the leaders have decided that he really is the Christ.[d] [27]But we know where this man is from. Yet when the real Christ comes, no one will know where he comes from."

[28]Jesus was still teaching in the Temple.[d] He cried out, "Yes, you know me, and you know where I am from. But I have not come by my own authority. I was sent by the One who is true. You

---

7:19 law Moses gave God's people the law that God gave him on Mount Sinai (Exodus 34:29-32).

don't know him. [29]But I know him. I am from him, and he sent me."

[30]When Jesus said this, they tried to seize him. But no one was able to touch him. It was not yet the right time. [31]But many of the people believed in Jesus. They said, "When the Christ comes, will he do more miracles[d] than this man has done?"

SOME LEADERS TRY TO ARREST JESUS

[32]The Pharisees[d] heard the crowd whispering these things about Jesus. So the leading priests and the Pharisees sent some Temple[d] guards to arrest him. [33]Then Jesus said, "I will be with you a little while longer. Then I will go back to the One who sent me. [34]You will look for me, but you will not find me. And you cannot come where I am."

[35]The Jews said to each other, "Where will this man go so we cannot find him? Will he go to the Greek cities where our people live? Will he teach the Greek people there? [36]This man says, 'You will look for me but you will not find me.' He also says, 'You cannot come where I am.' What does this mean?"

JESUS TALKS ABOUT THE SPIRIT

[37]The last day of the feast came. It was the most important day. On that day Jesus stood up and said in a loud voice, "If anyone is thirsty, let him come to me and drink. [38]If a person believes in me, rivers of living water will flow out from his heart. This is what the Scripture[d] says." [39]Jesus was talking about the Holy Spirit.[d] The Spirit had not yet been given because Jesus had not yet been raised to glory. But later, those who believed in Jesus would receive the Spirit.

THE PEOPLE ARGUE ABOUT JESUS

[40]The people heard these things that Jesus said. Some of them said, "This man really is the Prophet."[n]

[41]Others said, "He is the Christ."[d]

Still others said, "The Christ will not come from Galilee. [42]The Scripture[d] says that the Christ will come from David's family. And the Scripture says that the Christ will come from Bethlehem, the town where David lived." [43]So the people did not agree with each other about Jesus. [44]Some of them wanted to arrest him, but no one was able to touch him.

THE LEADERS WON'T BELIEVE

[45]The Temple[d] guards went back to the leading priests and the Pharisees.[d] The priests and the Pharisees asked, "Why didn't you bring Jesus?"

[46]The Temple guards answered, "The things he says are greater than the words of any man!"

[47]The Pharisees answered, "So Jesus has fooled you too! [48]Have any of the leaders or the Pharisees believed in him? No! [49]But those people, who know nothing about the law, are under God's curse!"

[50]But Nicodemus was there in that group. He was the one who had gone to see Jesus before.[n] Nicodemus said, [51]"Our law does not judge a man without hearing him. We cannot judge him until we know what he has done."

[52]They answered, "Are you from Galilee too? Study the Scriptures.[d] You will learn that no prophet[d] comes from Galilee."

[53]And everyone left and went home.[n]

THE WOMAN CAUGHT IN ADULTERY

8 Jesus went to the Mount of Olives.[d] [2]But early in the morning he went back to the Temple.[d] All the people came to Jesus, and he sat and taught them. [3]The teachers of the law and the Pharisees[d] brought a woman there. She had been caught in adultery.[d] They forced the woman to stand before the people. [4]They said to Jesus, "Teacher, this woman was

---

7:40 Prophet They probably meant the prophet that God told Moses he would send (Deuteronomy 18:15-19).
7:50 But Nicodemus . . . before. The story about Nicodemus going and talking to Jesus is in John 3:1-21.
7:53 Verse 53 Some of the earliest surviving Greek copies do not contain 7:53–8:11.

caught having sexual relations with a man who is not her husband. ⁵The law of Moses commands that we kill with stones every woman who does this. What do you say we should do?" ⁶They were asking this to trick Jesus so that they could have some charge against him.

But Jesus knelt down and started writing on the ground with his finger. ⁷They continued to ask Jesus their question. So he stood up and said, "Is there anyone here who has never sinned? The person without sin can throw the first stone at this woman." ⁸Then Jesus knelt down again and wrote on the ground.

⁹Those who heard Jesus began to leave one by one. The older men left first, and then the others. Jesus was left there alone with the woman. She was standing before him. ¹⁰Jesus stood up again and asked her, "Woman, all of those people have gone. Has no one judged you guilty?"

¹¹She answered, "No one has judged me, sir."

Then Jesus said, "So I also don't judge you. You may go now, but don't sin again."

JESUS IS THE LIGHT OF THE WORLD

¹²Later, Jesus talked to the people again. He said, "I am the light of the world. The person who follows me will never live in darkness. He will have the light that gives life."

¹³But the Pharisees*ᵈ* said to Jesus, "When you talk about yourself, you are the only one to say these things are true. We cannot accept these things you say."

¹⁴Jesus answered, "Yes, I am saying these things about myself, but they are true. I know where I came from. And I know where I am going. You don't know where I came from or where I am going. ¹⁵You judge me the way you would judge any man. I don't judge anyone. ¹⁶But if I judge, I judge truthfully. When I judge, I am not alone. The Father who sent me is with me. ¹⁷Your own law says that when two witnesses say the same thing, then you must accept what they say. ¹⁸I am one of the witnesses who speaks about myself. And the Father who sent me is my other witness."

¹⁹They asked, "Where is your father?"

Jesus answered, "You don't know me or my Father. But if you knew me, then you would know my Father, too." ²⁰Jesus said these things while he was teaching in the Temple.*ᵈ* He was near the place where the money that the people give is kept. But no one arrested him. The right time for Jesus had not yet come.

THE PEOPLE MISUNDERSTAND JESUS

²¹Again, Jesus said to the people, "I will leave you. You will look for me, but you will die in your sins. You cannot come where I am going."

²²So the Jews asked, "Will he kill himself? Is that why he said, 'You cannot come where I am going'?"

²³But Jesus said, "You people are from here below. But I am from above. You belong to this world, but I don't belong to this world. ²⁴So I told you that you would die in your sins. Yes, you will die in your sins if you don't believe that I am he."

²⁵They asked, "Then who are you?"

Jesus answered, "I am what I have told you from the beginning. ²⁶I have many things to say about you and to judge you for. But I tell people only the things I have heard from the One who sent me. And he speaks the truth."

²⁷The people did not understand that Jesus was talking to them about the Father. ²⁸So Jesus said to them, "You will lift up the Son of Man.*ᵈ* Then you will know that I am he. You will know that these things I do are not by my own authority. You will know that I say only what the Father has taught me. ²⁹The One who sent me is with me. I always do what is pleasing to him. So he has not left me alone." ³⁰While Jesus was saying these things, many people believed in him.

FREEDOM FROM SIN

[31]So Jesus said to the Jews who believed in him, "If you continue to obey my teaching, you are truly my followers. [32]Then you will know the truth. And the truth will make you free."

[33]They answered, "We are Abraham's children. And we have never been slaves. So why do you say that we will be free?"

[34]Jesus answered, "I tell you the truth. Everyone who lives in sin is a slave to sin. [35]A slave does not stay with a family forever, but a son belongs to the family forever. [36]So if the Son makes you free, then you will be truly free. [37]I know you are Abraham's children. But you want to kill me because you don't accept my teaching. [38]I am telling you what my Father has shown me. But you do what your father has told you."

[39]They answered, "Our father is Abraham."

Jesus said, "If you were really Abraham's children, you would do[n] the things that Abraham did. [40]I am a man who has told you the truth which I heard from God. But you are trying to kill me. Abraham did nothing like that. [41]So you are doing the things that your own father did."

But they said, "We are not like children who never knew who their father was. God is our Father. He is the only Father we have."

[42]Jesus said to them, "If God were really your Father, you would love me. I came from God and now I am here. I did not come by my own authority. God sent me. [43]You don't understand what I say because you cannot accept my teaching. [44]Your father is the devil. You belong to him and want to do what he wants. He was a murderer from the beginning. He was against the truth, for there is no truth in him. He is a liar, and he is like the lies he tells. He is the father of lies.

[45]But I speak the truth. That is why you don't believe me. [46]Can any of you prove that I am guilty of sin? If I am telling the truth, why don't you believe me? [47]He who belongs to God accepts what God says. But you don't accept what God says, because you don't belong to God."

JESUS AND ABRAHAM

[48]The Jews answered, "We say you are a Samaritan![d] We say a demon[d] has come into you. Are we not right?"

[49]Jesus answered, "I have no demon in me. I give honor to my Father, but you dishonor me. [50]I am not trying to get honor for myself. There is One who wants this honor for me, and he is the judge. [51]I tell you the truth. If anyone obeys my teaching, he will never die."

[52]The Jews said to Jesus, "Now we know that you have a demon in you! Even Abraham and the prophets[d] died. But you say, 'Whoever obeys my teaching will never die.' [53]Do you think that you are greater than our father Abraham? Abraham died. And the prophets died, too. Who do you think you are?"

[54]Jesus answered, "If I give honor to myself, that honor is worth nothing. The One who gives me honor is my Father. And you say that he is your God. [55]But you don't really know him. I know him. If I said I did not know him, then I would be a liar as you are liars. But I do know him, and I obey what he says. [56]Your father Abraham was very happy that he would see my day. He saw that day and was glad."

[57]The Jews said to him, "What? You have never seen Abraham! You are not even 50 years old!"

[58]Jesus answered, "I tell you the truth. Before Abraham was born, I am!" [59]When Jesus said this, the people picked up stones to throw at him. But Jesus hid himself, and then he left the Temple.[d]

8:39 If ... do Some Greek copies read "If you are really Abraham's children, you will do."

JESUS HEALS A MAN BORN BLIND

9 As Jesus was walking along, he saw a man who had been born blind. [2]His followers asked him, "Teacher, whose sin caused this man to be born blind—his own sin or his parents' sin?"

[3]Jesus answered, "It is not this man's sin or his parents' sin that made him blind. This man was born blind so that God's power could be shown in him. [4]While it is daytime, we must continue doing the work of the One who sent me. The night is coming. And no one can work at night. [5]While I am in the world, I am the light of the world."

[6]After Jesus said this, he spit on the ground and made some mud with it. He put the mud on the man's eyes. [7]Then he told the man, "Go and wash in the Pool of Siloam." (Siloam means Sent.) So the man went to the pool. He washed and came back. And he was able to see.

[8]Some people had seen this man begging before. They and the man's neighbors said, "Look! Is this the same man who always sits and begs?"

[9]Some said, "Yes! He is the one." But others said, "No, he's not the same man. He only looks like him."

So the man himself said, "I am the man."

[10]They asked, "What happened? How did you get your sight?"

[11]He answered, "The man named Jesus made some mud and put it on my eyes. Then he told me to go to Siloam and wash. So I went and washed and came back seeing."

[12]They asked him, "Where is this man?"

The man answered, "I don't know."

PHARISEES QUESTION THE HEALING

[13]Then the people took to the Pharisees[d] the man who had been blind. [14]The day Jesus had made mud and healed his eyes was a Sabbath[d] day. [15]So now the Pharisees asked the man, "How did you get your sight?"

He answered, "He put mud on my eyes. I washed, and now I can see."

[16]Some of the Pharisees were saying, "This man does not keep the Sabbath day. He is not from God!"

Others said, "But a man who is a sinner can't do miracles[d] like these." So they could not agree with each other.

[17]They asked the man again, "What do you say about him? It was your eyes he opened."

The man answered, "He is a prophet."[d]

[18]The Jews did not believe that he had been blind and could now see again. So they sent for the man's parents [19]and asked them, "Is this your son? You say that he was born blind. Then how does he see now?"

[20]His parents answered, "We know that this is our son, and we know that he was born blind. [21]But we don't know how he can see now. We don't know who opened his eyes. Ask him. He is old enough to answer for himself." [22]His parents said this because they were afraid of the Jews. The Jews had already decided that anyone who said that Jesus was the Christ[d] would be put out of the synagogue.[d] [23]That is why his parents said, "He is old enough. Ask him."

[24]So for the second time, they called the man who had been blind. They said, "You should give God the glory by telling the truth. We know that this man is a sinner."

[25]He answered, "I don't know if he is a sinner. But one thing I do know. I was blind, and now I can see."

[26]They asked, "What did he do to you? How did he make you see again?"

[27]He answered, "I have already told you that. But you would not listen to me. Why do you want to hear it again? Do you want to become his followers, too?"

[28]Then they insulted him and said, "You are his follower. We are followers of Moses. [29]We know that God spoke to Moses. But we don't even know where this man comes from!"

[30]The man answered, "This is a very

strange thing. You don't know where he comes from, and yet he opened my eyes. [31]We all know that God does not listen to sinners. But God listens to anyone who worships and obeys him. [32]Nobody has ever heard of anyone giving sight to a man born blind. [33]If this man were not from God, he could do nothing."

[34]They answered, "You were born full of sin! Are you trying to teach us?" And they threw the man out.

SPIRITUAL BLINDNESS

[35]Jesus heard that they had thrown him out. So Jesus found him and said, "Do you believe in the Son of Man?"[d]

[36]He asked, "Who is the Son of Man, sir? Tell me, so I can believe in him!"

[37]Jesus said to him, "You have already seen him. The Son of Man is the one talking with you now."

[38]He said, "Yes, Lord, I believe!" Then the man bowed and worshiped Jesus.

[39]Jesus said, "I came into this world so that the world could be judged. I came so that the blind[n] could see and so that those who see will become blind."

[40]Some of the Pharisees[d] were near Jesus. When they heard him say this, they asked, "What? Are you saying that we are blind, too?"

[41]Jesus said, "If you were really blind, you would not be guilty of sin. But now that you say you can see, your guilt remains."

THE SHEPHERD AND HIS SHEEP

10 Jesus said, "I tell you the truth. The man who does not enter the sheepfold by the door, but climbs in some other way, is a thief and a robber. [2]The one who enters by the door is the shepherd of the sheep. [3]The man who guards the door opens it for him. And the sheep listen to the voice of the shepherd. He calls his own sheep, using their names, and he leads them out. [4]He brings all of his sheep out. Then he goes ahead of them and leads them. They follow him because they know his voice. [5]But they will never follow a stranger. They will run away from him because they don't know his voice." [6]Jesus told the people this story, but they did not understand what it meant.

JESUS IS THE GOOD SHEPHERD

[7]So Jesus said again, "I tell you the truth. I am the door for the sheep. [8]All the people who came before me were thieves and robbers. The sheep did not listen to them. [9]I am the door. The person who enters through me will be saved. He will be able to come in and go out and find pasture. [10]A thief comes to steal and kill and destroy. But I came to give life—life in all its fullness.

[11]"I am the good shepherd. The good shepherd gives his life for the sheep. [12]The worker who is paid to keep the sheep is different from the shepherd who owns them. So when the worker sees a wolf coming, he runs away and leaves the sheep alone. Then the wolf attacks the sheep and scatters them. [13]The man runs away because he is only a paid worker. He does not really care for the sheep.

[14]"I am the good shepherd. I know my sheep, and my sheep know me, [15]just as the Father knows me, and I know the Father. I give my life for the sheep. [16]I have other sheep that are not in this flock here. I must bring them also. They will listen to my voice, and there will be one flock and one shepherd. [17]The Father loves me because I give my life. I give my life so that I can take it back again. [18]No one takes it away from me. I give my own life freely. I have the right to give my life, and I have the right to take it back. This is what my Father commanded me to do."

[19]Again the Jews did not agree with

9:39 blind Jesus is talking about people who are spiritually blind, not physically blind.

each other because of these words Jesus said. [20]Many of them said, "A demon[d] has come into him and made him crazy. Why listen to him?"

[21]But others said, "A man who is crazy with a demon does not say things like this. Can a demon open the eyes of the blind?"

[22]The time came for the Feast[d] of Dedication at Jerusalem. This was during the winter. [23]Jesus was walking in the Temple[d] in Solomon's Porch.[d] [24]The Jews gathered around him and said, "How long will you make us wonder about you? If you are the Christ,[d] then tell us plainly."

JESUS IS THE SON OF GOD

[25]Jesus answered, "I told you already, but you did not believe. I do miracles[d] in my Father's name. Those miracles show who I am. [26]But you don't believe because you are not my sheep. [27]My sheep listen to my voice. I know them, and they follow me. [28]I give them eternal life, and they will never die. And no person can steal them out of my hand. [29]My Father gave my sheep to me. He is greater than all, and no person can steal my sheep out of my Father's hand. [30]The Father and I are one."

[31]Again the Jews picked up stones to kill Jesus. [32]But Jesus said to them, "I have done many good works from the Father. Which of these good works are you killing me for?"

[33]The Jews answered, "We are not killing you for any good work you did. But you say things that are against God. You are only a man, but you say you are the same as God!"

[34]Jesus answered, "It is written in your law that God said, 'I have said you are gods!'[n] [35]This Scripture[d] called those people gods, the people who received God's message. And Scripture is always true. [36]So why do you say that I speak against God because I said, 'I am God's Son'? I am the one God chose and sent

into the world. [37]If I don't do what my Father does, then don't believe me. [38]But if I do what my Father does, even though you don't believe in me, believe what I do. Then you will know and understand that the Father is in me and I am in the Father."

[39]They tried to take Jesus again, but he escaped from them.

[40]Then Jesus went back across the Jordan River to the place where John had first baptized. Jesus stayed there, [41]and many people came to him. They said, "John never did a miracle. But everything John said about this man is true." [42]And in that place many believed in Jesus.

THE DEATH OF LAZARUS

11 There was a man named Lazarus who was sick. He lived in the town of Bethany, where Mary and her sister Martha lived. [2]Mary is the woman who later put perfume on the Lord and wiped his feet with her hair. Mary's brother was Lazarus, the man who was now sick. [3]So Mary and Martha sent someone to tell Jesus, "Lord, the one you love is sick."

[4]When Jesus heard this he said, "This sickness will not end in death. It is for the glory of God. This has happened to bring glory to the Son of God." [5]Jesus loved Martha and her sister and Lazarus. [6]But when he heard that Lazarus was sick, he stayed where he was for two more days. [7]Then Jesus said to his followers, "Let us go back to Judea."

[8]The followers said, "But Teacher, the Jews there tried to kill you with stones. That was only a short time ago. Now you want to go back there?"

[9]Jesus answered, "Are there not 12 hours in the day? If anyone walks in the daylight, he will not stumble because he can see by this world's light. [10]But if anyone walks at night he stumbles

---

10:34 **'I . . . gods.'** Quotation from Psalm 82:6.

because there is no light to help him see."

[11]After Jesus said this, he added, "Our friend Lazarus has fallen asleep. But I am going there to wake him."

[12]The followers said, "But Lord, if he can sleep, he will get well."

[13]Jesus meant that Lazarus was dead. But Jesus' followers thought that he meant Lazarus was really sleeping. [14]So then Jesus said plainly, "Lazarus is dead. [15]And I am glad for your sakes that I was not there so that you may believe. But let us go to him now."

[16]Then Thomas (the one called Didymus) said to the other followers, "Let us go, too. We will die with him."

JESUS IN BETHANY

[17]Jesus arrived in Bethany. There he learned that Lazarus had already been dead and in the tomb for four days. [18]Bethany was about two miles from Jerusalem. [19]Many Jews had come there to comfort Martha and Mary about their brother.

[20]Martha heard that Jesus was coming, and she went out to meet him. But Mary stayed at home. [21]Martha said to Jesus, "Lord, if you had been here, my brother would not have died. [22]But I know that even now God will give you anything you ask."

[23]Jesus said, "Your brother will rise and live again."

[24]Martha answered, "I know that he will rise and live again in the resurrection[n] on the last day."

[25]Jesus said to her, "I am the resurrection and the life. He who believes in me will have life even if he dies. [26]And he who lives and believes in me will never die. Martha, do you believe this?"

[27]Martha answered, "Yes, Lord. I believe that you are the Christ,[d] the Son of God. You are the One who was coming to the world."

JESUS CRIES

[28]After Martha said this, she went back to her sister Mary. She talked to Mary alone. Martha said, "The Teacher is here and he is asking for you." [29]When Mary heard this, she got up quickly and went to Jesus. [30]Jesus had not yet come into the town. He was still at the place where Martha had met him. [31]The Jews were with Mary in the house, comforting her. They saw Mary stand and leave quickly. They followed her, thinking that she was going to the tomb to cry there. [32]But Mary went to the place where Jesus was. When she saw him, she fell at his feet and said, "Lord, if you had been here, my brother would not have died."

[33]Jesus saw that Mary was crying and that the Jews who came with her were crying, too. Jesus felt very sad in his heart and was deeply troubled. [34]He asked, "Where did you bury him?"

"Come and see, Lord," they said.

[35]Jesus cried.

[36]So the Jews said, "See how much he loved him."

[37]But some of them said, "If Jesus healed the eyes of the blind man, why didn't he keep Lazarus from dying?"

JESUS RAISES LAZARUS

[38]Again Jesus felt very sad in his heart. He came to the tomb. The tomb was a cave with a large stone covering the entrance. [39]Jesus said, "Move the stone away."

Martha said, "But, Lord, it has been four days since he died. There will be a bad smell." Martha was the sister of the dead man.

[40]Then Jesus said to her, "Didn't I tell you that if you believed, you would see the glory of God?"

[41]So they moved the stone away from the entrance. Then Jesus looked up and said, "Father, I thank you that you heard me. [42]I know that you always hear me. But I said these things because of the

---

11:24 resurrection Being raised from death to live again.

people here around me. I want them to believe that you sent me." ⁴³After Jesus said this, he cried out in a loud voice, "Lazarus, come out!" ⁴⁴The dead man came out. His hands and feet were wrapped with pieces of cloth, and he had a cloth around his face.

Jesus said to them, "Take the cloth off of him and let him go."

THE LEADERS PLAN TO KILL JESUS

⁴⁵There were many Jews who had come to visit Mary. They saw what Jesus did. And many of them believed in him. ⁴⁶But some of them went to the Pharisees.ᵈ They told the Pharisees what Jesus had done. ⁴⁷Then the leading priests and Pharisees called a meeting of the Jewish council. They asked, "What should we do? This man is doing many miracles.ᵈ ⁴⁸If we let him continue doing these things, everyone will believe in him. Then the Romans will come and take away our Templeᵈ and our nation."

⁴⁹One of the men there was Caiaphas. He was the high priest that year. Caiaphas said, "You people know nothing! ⁵⁰It is better for one man to die for the people than for the whole nation to be destroyed. But you don't realize this."

⁵¹Caiaphas did not think of this himself. He was high priest that year. So he was really prophesyingᵈ that Jesus would die for the Jewish nation ⁵²and for God's scattered children. This would bring them all together and make them one.

⁵³That day they started planning to kill Jesus. ⁵⁴So Jesus no longer traveled openly among the Jews. He left there and went to a place near the desert. He went to a town called Ephraim and stayed there with his followers.

⁵⁵It was almost time for the Jewish Passoverᵈ Feast. Many from the country went up to Jerusalem before the Passover. They went to do the special things to make themselves pure. ⁵⁶The people looked for Jesus. They stood in the Temple and were asking each other, "Is he coming to the Feast? What do you think?" ⁵⁷But the leading priests and the Pharisees had given orders about Jesus. They said that if anyone knew where Jesus was, he must tell them. Then they could arrest Jesus.

JESUS WITH FRIENDS IN BETHANY

12 Six days before the Passoverᵈ Feast, Jesus went to Bethany, where Lazarus lived. (Lazarus is the man Jesus raised from death.) ²There they had a dinner for Jesus. Martha served the food. Lazarus was one of the people eating with Jesus. ³Mary brought in a pint of very expensive perfume made from pure nard.ᵈ She poured the perfume on Jesus' feet, and then she wiped his feet with her hair. And the sweet smell from the perfume filled the whole house.

⁴Judas Iscariot, one of Jesus' followers, was there. (He was the one who would later turn against Jesus.) Judas said, ⁵"This perfume was worth an entire year's wages. It should have been sold and the money given to the poor." ⁶But Judas did not really care about the poor. He said this because he was a thief. He was the one who kept the money box, and he often stole money from it.

⁷Jesus answered, "Let her alone. It was right for her to save this perfume for today—the day for me to be prepared for burial. ⁸The poor will always be with you, but you will not always have me."

THE PLOT AGAINST LAZARUS

⁹A large crowd of Jews heard that Jesus was in Bethany. So they went there to see not only Jesus but also Lazarus. Lazarus was the one Jesus raised from death. ¹⁰So the leading priests made plans to kill Lazarus, too. ¹¹Because of Lazarus many Jews were leaving them and believing in Jesus.

JESUS ENTERS JERUSALEM

¹²The next day a great crowd in Jerusalem heard that Jesus was coming there. These were the people who had come to

the Passover[d] Feast. [13]They took branches of palm trees and went out to meet Jesus. They shouted,

"Praise[n] God!
God bless the One who comes in the name of the Lord!
God bless the King of Israel!"
Psalm 118:25-26

[14]Jesus found a colt and sat on it. This was as the Scripture[d] says,

[15]"Don't be afraid, people of Jerusalem!
Your king is coming.
He is sitting on the colt of a donkey."   *Zechariah 9:9*

[16]The followers of Jesus did not understand this at first. But after Jesus was raised to glory, they remembered that this had been written about him. And they remembered that they had done these things to him.

PEOPLE TELL ABOUT JESUS

[17]There had been many people with Jesus when he raised Lazarus from death and told him to come out of the tomb. Now they were telling others about what Jesus did. [18]Many people went out to meet Jesus, because they had heard about this miracle.[d] [19]So the Pharisees[d] said to each other, "You can see that nothing is going right for us. Look! The whole world is following him."

JESUS TALKS ABOUT HIS DEATH

[20]There were some Greek people, too, who came to Jerusalem to worship at the Passover[d] Feast. [21]They went to Philip. (Philip was from Bethsaida, in Galilee.) They said, "Sir, we would like to see Jesus." [22]Philip told Andrew. Then Andrew and Philip told Jesus.

[23]Jesus said to them, "The time has come for the Son of Man[d] to receive his glory. [24]I tell you the truth. A grain of wheat must fall to the ground and die. Then it makes many seeds. But if it never dies, it remains only a single seed.

[25]The person who loves his life will give up true life. But the person who hates his life in this world will keep true life forever. [26]Whoever serves me must follow me. Then my servant will be with me everywhere I am. My Father will honor anyone who serves me.

[27]"Now I am very troubled. What should I say? Should I say, 'Father, save me from this time'? No, I came to this time so that I could suffer. [28]Father, bring glory to your name!"

Then a voice came from heaven, "I have brought glory to it, and I will do it again."

[29]The crowd standing there heard the voice. They said it was thunder.

But others said, "An angel has spoken to him."

[30]Jesus said, "That voice was for you, not for me. [31]Now is the time for the world to be judged. Now the ruler of this world will be thrown down. [32]I will be lifted up from the earth. And when this happens, I will draw all people toward me." [33]Jesus said this to show how he would die.

[34]The crowd said, "We have heard from the law that the Christ[d] will live forever. So why do you say, 'The Son of Man must be lifted up'? Who is this 'Son of Man'?"

[35]Then Jesus said, "The light will be with you for a little longer. So walk while you have the light. Then the darkness will not catch you. He who walks in the darkness does not know where he is going. [36]So believe in the light while you still have it. Then you will become sons of light." When Jesus had said this, he left and hid himself from them.

SOME DON'T BELIEVE IN JESUS

[37]Though Jesus had done many miracles[d] before the people, they still did not believe in him. [38]This was to make clear

---

12:13 Praise Literally, "Hosanna," a Hebrew word used at first in praying to God for help, but at this time it was probably a shout of joy used in praising God or his Messiah.

the full meaning of what Isaiah the prophet[d] said:

"Lord, who believed the things we
    told them?
Who has seen the Lord's power?"

Isaiah 53:1

[39]This is why the people could not believe: Isaiah also said,

[40]"He has blinded their eyes.
He has closed their minds.
This is so that they will not see with
    their eyes
nor understand in their minds.
This is so they will not
    come back to me and be forgiven."

Isaiah 6:10

[41]Isaiah said this because he saw Jesus' glory and spoke about him.

[42]But many people believed in Jesus, even many of the leaders. But because of the Pharisees,[d] they did not say that they believed in him. They were afraid that they would be put out of the synagogue.[d] [43]They loved praise from men more than praise from God.

[44]Then Jesus cried out, "He who believes in me is really believing in the One who sent me. [45]He who sees me sees the One who sent me. [46]I have come as light into the world. I came so that whoever believes in me would not stay in darkness. [47]"If anyone hears my words and does not obey them, I do not judge him. For I did not come to judge the world, but to save the world. [48]There is a judge for the one who refuses to believe in me and does not accept my words. The word I have taught will be his judge on the last day. [49]The things I taught were not from myself. The Father who sent me told me what to say and what to teach. [50]And I know that eternal life comes from what the Father commands. So whatever I say is what the Father told me to say."

JESUS WASHES HIS FOLLOWERS' FEET

13 It was almost time for the Jewish Passover[d] Feast. Jesus knew that it was time for him to leave this world and go back to the Father. He had always loved those who were his own in the world, and he loved them all the way to the end.

[2]Jesus and his followers were at the evening meal. The devil had already persuaded Judas Iscariot to turn against Jesus. (Judas was the son of Simon.) [3]Jesus knew that the Father had given him power over everything. He also knew that he had come from God and was going back to God. [4]So during the meal Jesus stood up and took off his outer clothing. Taking a towel, he wrapped it around his waist. [5]Then he poured water into a bowl and began to wash the followers' feet. He dried them with the towel that was wrapped around him.

[6]Jesus came to Simon Peter. But Peter said to Jesus, "Lord, are you going to wash my feet?"

[7]Jesus answered, "You don't understand what I am doing now. But you will understand later."

[8]Peter said, "No! You will never wash my feet."

Jesus answered, "If I don't wash your feet, then you are not one of my people."

[9]Simon Peter answered, "Lord, after you wash my feet, wash my hands and my head, too!"

[10]Jesus said, "After a person has had a bath, his whole body is clean. He needs only to wash his feet. And you men are clean,[d] but not all of you." [11]Jesus knew who would turn against him. That is why Jesus said, "Not all of you are clean."

[12]When he had finished washing their feet, he put on his clothes and sat down again. Jesus asked, "Do you understand what I have just done for you? [13]You call me 'Teacher' and 'Lord.' And this is right, because that is what I am. [14]I, your Lord and Teacher, have washed your feet. So you also should wash each other's feet. [15]I did this as an example for you. So you should do as I have done for you. [16]I tell you the truth. A servant is not greater than

his master. A messenger is not greater than the one who sent him. [17]If you know these things, you will be happy if you do them.

[18]"I am not talking about all of you. I know those I have chosen. But what the Scripture[d] said must happen: 'The man who ate at my table has now turned against me.'[n] [19]I am telling you this now before it happens. Then when it happens you will believe that I am he. [20]I tell you the truth. Whoever accepts anyone I send also accepts me. And whoever accepts me also accepts the One who sent me."

JESUS TALKS ABOUT HIS DEATH

[21]After Jesus said this, he was very troubled. He said openly, "I tell you the truth. One of you will turn against me."

[22]The followers all looked at each other. They did not know whom Jesus was talking about. [23]One of the followers was sitting[n] next to Jesus. This was the follower Jesus loved. [24]Simon Peter made signs to him to ask Jesus who it was that he was talking about.

[25]That follower leaned closer to Jesus and asked, "Lord, who is it that will turn against you?"

[26]Jesus answered, "I will dip this bread into the dish. The man I give it to is the man who will turn against me." So Jesus took a piece of bread. He dipped it and gave it to Judas Iscariot, the son of Simon. [27]As soon as Judas took the bread, Satan entered him. Jesus said to Judas, "The thing that you will do—do it quickly!" [28]None of the men at the table understood why Jesus said this to Judas. [29]He was the one who kept the money box. So some of the followers thought that Jesus was telling Judas to buy what was needed for the feast. Or they thought that Jesus wanted Judas to give something to the poor.

[30]Judas accepted the bread Jesus gave him and immediately went out. It was night.

[31]When Judas was gone, Jesus said, "Now the Son of Man[d] receives his glory. And God receives glory through him. [32]If God receives glory through him,[n] then God will give glory to the Son through himself. And God will give him glory quickly."

[33]Jesus said, "My children, I will be with you only a little longer. You will look for me. And what I told the Jews, I tell you now: Where I am going you cannot come.

[34]"I give you a new command: Love each other. You must love each other as I have loved you. [35]All people will know that you are my followers if you love each other."

PETER WILL SAY HE DOESN'T KNOW JESUS

[36]Simon Peter asked Jesus, "Lord, where are you going?"

Jesus answered, "Where I am going you cannot follow now. But you will follow later."

[37]Peter asked, "Lord, why can't I follow you now? I am ready to die for you!"

[38]Jesus answered, "Will you really die for me? I tell you the truth. Before the rooster crows, you will say three times that you don't know me."

JESUS COMFORTS HIS FOLLOWERS

14 Jesus said, "Don't let your hearts be troubled. Trust in God. And trust in me. [2]There are many rooms in my Father's house. I would not tell you this if it were not true. I am going there to prepare a place for you. [3]After I go and prepare a place for you, I will come back. Then I will take you to be with me so that you may be where I am. [4]You know the way to the place where I am going."[n]

13:18 'The man . . . me.' Quotation from Psalm 41:9.
13:23 sitting Literally, "lying." The people of that time ate lying down and leaning on one arm.
13:32 If . . . him Some Greek copies do not have this phrase.
14:4 You . . . going. Some Greek copies read "You know where I am going and the way to the place I am going."

[5]Thomas said to Jesus, "Lord, we don't know where you are going. So how can we know the way?"

[6]Jesus answered, "I am the way. And I am the truth and the life. The only way to the Father is through me. [7]If you really knew me, then you would know my Father, too. But now you do know him, and you have seen him."

[8]Philip said to him, "Lord, show us the Father. That is all we need."

[9]Jesus answered, "I have been with you a long time now. Do you still not know me, Philip? He who has seen me has seen the Father. So why do you say, 'Show us the Father'? [10]Don't you believe that I am in the Father and the Father is in me? The words I say to you don't come from me. The Father lives in me, and he is doing his own work. [11]Believe me when I say that I am in the Father and the Father is in me. Or believe because of the miracles[d] I have done. [12]I tell you the truth. He who believes in me will do the same things that I do. He will do even greater things than these because I am going to the Father. [13]And if you ask for anything in my name, I will do it for you. Then the Father's glory will be shown through the Son. [14]If you ask me for anything in my name, I will do it.

THE PROMISE OF THE HOLY SPIRIT

[15]"If you love me, you will do the things I command. [16]I will ask the Father, and he will give you another Helper.[n] He will give you this Helper to be with you forever. [17]The Helper is the Spirit[d] of truth. The world cannot accept him because it does not see him or know him. But you know him. He lives with you and he will be in you.

[18]"I will not leave you all alone like orphans. I will come back to you. [19]In a little while the world will not see me anymore, but you will see me. Because I live, you will live, too. [20]On that day you will know that I am in my Father. You will know that you are in me and I am in you. [21]He who knows my commands and obeys them is the one who loves me. And my Father will love him who loves me. I will love him and will show myself to him."

[22]Then Judas (not Judas Iscariot) said, "But, Lord, why do you plan to show yourself to us, but not to the world?"

[23]Jesus answered, "If anyone loves me, then he will obey my teaching. My Father will love him, and we will come to him and make our home with him. [24]He who does not love me does not obey my teaching. This teaching that you hear is not really mine. It is from my Father, who sent me.

[25]"I have told you all these things while I am with you. [26]But the Helper will teach you everything. He will cause you to remember all the things I told you. This Helper is the Holy Spirit whom the Father will send in my name.

[27]"I leave you peace. My peace I give you. I do not give it to you as the world does. So don't let your hearts be troubled. Don't be afraid. [28]You heard me say to you, 'I am going, but I am coming back to you.' If you loved me, you should be happy that I am going back to the Father because he is greater than I am. [29]I have told you this now, before it happens. Then when it happens, you will believe. [30]I will not talk with you much longer. The ruler of this world is coming. He has no power over me. [31]But the world must know that I love the Father. So I do exactly what the Father told me to do.

"Come now, let us go.

JESUS IS LIKE A VINE

15 "I am the true vine; my Father is the gardener. [2]He cuts off every branch of mine that does not produce fruit. And he trims and cleans every branch that produces fruit so that it will

---

14:16 Helper "Counselor," or "Comforter." Jesus is talking about the Holy Spirit.

produce even more fruit. ³You are already clean[d] because of the words I have spoken to you. ⁴Remain in me, and I will remain in you. No branch can produce fruit alone. It must remain in the vine. It is the same with you. You cannot produce fruit alone. You must remain in me.

⁵"I am the vine, and you are the branches. If a person remains in me and I remain in him, then he produces much fruit. But without me he can do nothing. ⁶If anyone does not remain in me, then he is like a branch that is thrown away. That branch dies. People pick up dead branches, throw them into the fire, and burn them. ⁷Remain in me and follow my teachings. If you do this, then you can ask for anything you want, and it will be given to you. ⁸You should produce much fruit and show that you are my followers. This brings glory to my Father. ⁹I loved you as the Father loved me. Now remain in my love. ¹⁰I have obeyed my Father's commands, and I remain in his love. In the same way, if you obey my commands, you will remain in my love. ¹¹I have told you these things so that you can have the same joy I have. I want your joy to be the fullest joy.

¹²"This is my command: Love each other as I have loved you. ¹³The greatest love a person can show is to die for his friends. ¹⁴You are my friends if you do what I command you. ¹⁵I don't call you servants now. A servant does not know what his master is doing. But now I call you friends because I have made known to you everything I heard from my Father. ¹⁶You did not choose me; I chose you. And I gave you this work, to go and produce fruit. I want you to produce fruit that will last. Then the Father will give you anything you ask for in my name. ¹⁷This is my command: Love each other.

JESUS WARNS HIS FOLLOWERS

¹⁸"If the world hates you, remember that it hated me first. ¹⁹If you belonged to the world, then it would love you as it loves its own. But I have chosen you out of the world. So you don't belong to it. That is why the world hates you. ²⁰Remember what I told you: A servant is not greater than his master. If people did wrong to me, they will do wrong to you, too. And if they obeyed my teaching, they will obey yours, too. ²¹They will do all this to you because of me. They don't know the One who sent me. ²²If I had not come and spoken to them, they would not be guilty of sin. But now they have no excuse for their sin. ²³He who hates me also hates my Father. ²⁴I did works among them that no one else has ever done. If I had not done those works, they would not be guilty of sin. But now they have seen what I did, and yet they have hated both me and my Father. ²⁵But this happened so that what is written in their law would be true: 'They hated me for no reason.'[n]

²⁶"I will send you the Helper[n] from the Father. He is the Spirit of truth who comes from the Father. When he comes, he will tell about me. ²⁷And you also must tell people about me because you have been with me from the beginning.

16 "I have told you these things to keep you from giving up. ²People will put you out of their synagogues.[d] Yes, the time is coming when whoever kills you will think that he is offering service to God. ³They will do this because they have not known the Father and they have not known me. ⁴I have told you these things now. So when the time comes, you will remember that I warned you.

THE WORK OF THE HOLY SPIRIT

"I did not tell you these things at the beginning, because I was with you then.

15:25 'They . . . reason.' These words could be from Psalm 35:19 or Psalm 69:4.
15:26 Helper "Counselor," or "Comforter." Jesus is talking about the Holy Spirit.

[5]Now I am going back to the One who sent me. But none of you asks me, 'Where are you going?' [6]Your hearts are filled with sadness because I have told you these things. [7]But I tell you the truth. It is better for you that I go away. When I go away I will send the Helper[n] to you. If I do not go away, then the Helper will not come. [8]When the Helper comes, he will prove to the people of the world the truth about sin, about being right with God, and about judgment. [9]He will prove to them about sin, because they don't believe in me. [10]He will prove to them that I am right with God, because I am going to the Father. You will not see me anymore. [11]And the Helper will prove to them the truth about judgment, because the ruler of this world is already judged.

[12]"I have many more things to say to you, but they are too much for you now. [13]But when the Spirit[d] of truth comes he will lead you into all truth. He will not speak his own words. He will speak only what he hears and will tell you what is to come. [14]The Spirit of truth will bring glory to me. He will take what I have to say and tell it to you. [15]All that the Father has is mine. That is why I said that the Spirit will take what I have to say and tell it to you.

SADNESS WILL BECOME HAPPINESS

[16]"After a little while you will not see me. And then after a little while you will see me again."

[17]Some of the followers said to each other, "What does Jesus mean when he says, 'After a little while you will not see me, and then after a little while you will see me again'? And what does he mean when he says, 'Because I am going to the Father'?" [18]They also asked, "What does he mean by 'a little while'? We don't understand what he is saying."

[19]Jesus saw that the followers wanted to ask him about this. So Jesus said to the followers, "Are you asking each other what I meant when I said, 'After a little while you will not see me. And then after a little while you will see me again'? [20]I tell you the truth. You will cry and be sad, but the world will be happy. You will be sad, but your sadness will become joy. [21]When a woman gives birth to a baby, she has pain, because her time has come. But when her baby is born, she forgets the pain. She forgets because she is so happy that a child has been born into the world. [22]It is the same with you. Now you are sad. But I will see you again and you will be happy. And no one will take away your joy. [23]In that day you will not ask me for anything. I tell you the truth. My Father will give you anything you ask for in my name. [24]You have never asked for anything in my name. Ask and you will receive. And your joy will be the fullest joy.

VICTORY OVER THE WORLD

[25]"I have told you these things, using words that hide the meaning. But the time will come when I will not use words like that to tell you things. I will speak to you in plain words about the Father. [26]In that day you will ask the Father for things in my name. I am saying that I will not need to ask the Father for you. [27]No! The Father himself loves you. He loves you because you have loved me. And he loves you because you have believed that I came from God. [28]I came from the Father into the world. Now I am leaving the world and going back to the Father."

[29]Then the followers of Jesus said, "You are speaking clearly to us now. You are not using words that are hard to understand. [30]We can see now that you know all things. You can answer a person's question even before he asks it. This makes us believe that you came from God."

[31]Jesus answered, "So now you believe?

16:7 Helper "Counselor," or "Comforter." Jesus is talking about the Holy Spirit.

³²Listen to me. A time is coming when you will be scattered. Each of you will be scattered to your own home. That time is now here. You will leave me. I will be alone. But I am never really alone. Why? Because the Father is with me.

³³"I told you these things so that you can have peace in me. In this world you will have trouble. But be brave! I have defeated the world!"

JESUS PRAYS FOR HIS FOLLOWERS

17 After Jesus said these things he looked toward heaven. Jesus prayed, "Father, the time has come. Give glory to your Son so that the Son can give glory to you. ²You gave the Son power over all people so that the Son could give eternal life to all those people you have given to him. ³And this is eternal life: that men can know you, the only true God, and that men can know Jesus Christ, the One you sent. ⁴I finished the work you gave me to do. I brought you glory on earth. ⁵And now, Father, give me glory with you. Give me the glory I had with you before the world was made.

⁶"You gave me some men from the world. I have shown them what you are like. Those men belonged to you, and you gave them to me. They have obeyed your teaching. ⁷Now they know that everything you gave me comes from you. ⁸I gave these men the teachings that you gave me. They accepted those teachings. They know that I truly came from you. ⁹I pray for them now. I am not praying for the people in the world. But I am praying for those men you gave me, because they are yours. ¹⁰All I have is yours, and all you have is mine. And my glory is shown through these men. ¹¹Now I am coming to you. I will not stay in the world now. But these men are still in the world. Holy Father, keep them safe. Keep them safe by the power of your name (the name you gave me), so that they will be one, the same as you and I are one. ¹²While I was with them, I kept them safe. I kept them safe by the power of your name—the name you gave me. I protected them. And only one of them, the one who is going to hell, was lost. He was lost so that what was said in the Scripture*ᵈ* would happen.

¹³"I am coming to you now. But I pray these things while I am still in the world. I say these things so that these men can have my joy. I want them to have all of my joy. ¹⁴I have given them your teaching. And the world has hated them. The world hated these men, because they don't belong to the world, the same as I don't belong to the world. ¹⁵I am not asking you to take them out of the world. But I am asking that you keep them safe from the Evil One. ¹⁶They don't belong to the world, the same as I don't belong to the world. ¹⁷Make them ready for your service through your truth. Your teaching is truth. ¹⁸I have sent them into the world, the same as you sent me into the world. ¹⁹I am making myself ready to serve. I do this for them so that they can truly be ready for your service.

²⁰"I pray for these men. But I am also praying for all people who will believe in me because of the teaching of these men. ²¹Father, I pray that all people who believe in me can be one. You are in me and I am in you. I pray that these people can also be one in us, so that the world will believe that you sent me. ²²I have given these people the glory that you gave me. I gave them this glory so that they can be one, the same as you and I are one. ²³I will be in them and you will be in me. So they will be completely one. Then the world will know that you sent me. And the world will know that you loved these people the same as you loved me.

²⁴"Father, I want these people that you have given me to be with me in every place I am. I want them to see my glory. This is the glory you gave me because you loved me before the world was made. ²⁵Father, you are the One who is

good. The world does not know you, but I know you. And these people know that you sent me. [26]I showed them what you are like. And again I will show them what you are like. Then they will have the same love that you have for me. And I will live in them."

JESUS IS ARRESTED

18 When Jesus finished praying, he left with his followers. They went across the Kidron Valley. On the other side there was a garden of olive trees. Jesus and his followers went there.

[2]Judas knew where this place was, because Jesus met there often with his followers. Judas was the one who turned against Jesus. [3]So Judas led a group of soldiers to the garden. Judas also brought some guards from the leading priests and the Pharisees.[d] They were carrying torches, lanterns, and weapons.

[4]Jesus knew everything that would happen to him. Jesus went out and asked, "Who is it you are looking for?"

[5]The men answered, "Jesus from Nazareth."

Jesus said, "I am Jesus." (Judas, the one who turned against Jesus, was standing there with them.) [6]When Jesus said, "I am Jesus," the men moved back and fell to the ground.

[7]Jesus asked them again, "Who is it you are looking for?"

They said, "Jesus of Nazareth."

[8]Jesus said, "I told you that I am he. So if you are looking for me, then let these other men go." [9]This happened so that the words Jesus said before might come true: "I have not lost any of the men you gave me."

[10]Simon Peter had a sword. He took out the sword and struck the servant of the high priest, cutting off his right ear. (The servant's name was Malchus.) [11]Jesus said to Peter, "Put your sword back. Shall I not drink of the cup[n] the Father has given me?"

JESUS IS BROUGHT BEFORE ANNAS

[12]Then the soldiers with their commander and the Jewish guards arrested Jesus. They tied him [13]and led him first to Annas. Annas was the father-in-law of Caiaphas, the high priest that year. [14]Caiaphas was the one who had told the Jews that it would be better if one man died for all the people.

PETER SAYS HE DOESN'T KNOW JESUS

[15]Simon Peter and another one of Jesus' followers went along after Jesus. This follower knew the high priest. So he went with Jesus into the high priest's courtyard. [16]But Peter waited outside near the door. The follower who knew the high priest came back outside. He spoke to the girl at the door and brought Peter inside. [17]The girl at the door said to Peter, "Aren't you also one of that man's followers?"

Peter answered, "No, I am not!"

[18]It was cold, so the servants and guards had built a fire. They were standing around it and warming themselves. Peter was standing with them, warming himself.

THE HIGH PRIEST QUESTIONS JESUS

[19]The high priest asked Jesus questions about his followers and his teaching. [20]Jesus answered, "I have spoken openly to everyone. I have always taught in synagogues[d] and in the Temple,[d] where all the Jews come together. I never said anything in secret. [21]So why do you question me? Ask the people who heard my teaching. They know what I said."

[22]When Jesus said this, one of the guards standing there hit him. The guard said, "Is that the way you answer the high priest?"

[23]Jesus answered him, "If I said something wrong, then say what was wrong.

18:11 **cup** Jesus is talking about the bad things that will happen to him. Accepting these things will be very hard, like drinking a cup of something that tastes very bitter.

But if what I said is true, why do you hit me?"

²⁴Then Annas sent Jesus to Caiaphas, the high priest. Jesus was still tied.

PETER SAYS AGAIN HE DOESN'T KNOW JESUS

²⁵Simon Peter was standing and warming himself. They said to him, "Aren't you one of that man's followers?"

Peter denied it and said, "No, I am not."

²⁶One of the servants of the high priest was there. This servant was a relative of the man whose ear Peter had cut off. The servant said, "Didn't I see you with him in the garden?"

²⁷Again Peter said it wasn't true. Just then a rooster crowed.

JESUS IS BROUGHT BEFORE PILATE

²⁸Then they led Jesus from Caiaphas' house to the Roman governor's palace. It was early in the morning. The Jews would not go inside the palace. They did not want to make themselves unclean,ⁿ because they wanted to eat the Passoverᵈ meal. ²⁹So Pilate went outside to them. He asked, "What charges do you bring against this man?"

³⁰They answered, "He is a criminal. That is why we brought him to you."

³¹Pilate said to them, "Take him yourselves and judge him by your own law."

They answered, "But we are not allowed to put anyone to death." ³²(This happened so that what Jesus had said about how he would die would come true.)

³³Then Pilate went back inside the palace. He called Jesus to him and asked, "Are you the king of the Jews?"

³⁴Jesus said, "Is that your own question, or did others tell you about me?"

³⁵Pilate answered, "I am not a Jew. It was your own people and their leading priests who brought you before me. What have you done wrong?"

³⁶Jesus said, "My kingdom does not belong to this world. If it belonged to this world, my servants would have fought to keep me from being given over to the Jewish leaders. But my kingdom is from another place."

³⁷Pilate said, "So you are a king!"

Jesus answered, "You say that I am a king. That is true. I was born for this: to tell people about the truth. That is why I came into the world. And everyone who belongs to the truth listens to me."

³⁸Pilate said, "What is truth?" After he said this, he went out to the Jews again. He said to them, "I can find nothing to charge against this man. ³⁹But it is your custom that I free one prisoner to you at the time of the Passover. Do you want me to free this 'king of the Jews'?"

⁴⁰They shouted back, "No, not him! Let Barabbas go free!" (Barabbas was a robber.)

19 Then Pilate ordered that Jesus be taken away and whipped. ²The soldiers used some thorny branches to make a crown. They put this crown on Jesus' head and put a purple robe around him. ³Then they came to Jesus many times and said, "Hail, King of the Jews!" They hit Jesus in the face.

⁴Again Pilate came out and said to them, "Look! I am bringing Jesus out to you. I want you to know that I find nothing I can charge against him." ⁵Then Jesus came out, wearing the crown of thorns and the purple robe. Pilate said to the Jews, "Here is the man!"

⁶When the leading priests and the guards saw Jesus they shouted, "Kill him on a cross! Kill him on a cross!"

But Pilate answered, "Take him and nail him to a cross yourselves. I find nothing I can charge against him."

⁷The Jews answered, "We have a law that says he should die, because he said he is the Son of God."

18:28 unclean Going into a non-Jewish place would make them unfit to eat the Passover Feast, according to Jewish law.

[8]When Pilate heard this, he was even more afraid. [9]He went back inside the palace and asked Jesus, "Where are you from?" But Jesus did not answer him. [10]Pilate said, "You refuse to speak to me? Don't you know that I have power to set you free and power to have you killed on a cross?"

[11]Jesus answered, "The only power you have over me is the power given to you by God. The man who gave me to you is guilty of a greater sin."

[12]After this, Pilate tried to let Jesus go free. But the Jews cried out, "Anyone who makes himself king is against Caesar. If you let this man go free, you are not Caesar's friend."

[13]Pilate heard what the Jews were saying. So he brought Jesus out to the place called The Stone Pavement. (In the Jewish language[n] the name is Gabbatha.) Pilate sat down on the judge's seat there. [14]It was about six o'clock in the morning on Preparation[d] Day of Passover[d] week. Pilate said to the Jews, "Here is your king!"

[15]They shouted, "Take him away! Take him away! Kill him on a cross!"

Pilate asked them, "Do you want me to kill your king on a cross?"

The leading priests answered, "The only king we have is Caesar!"

[16]So Pilate gave Jesus to them to be killed on a cross.

JESUS IS KILLED ON A CROSS

The soldiers took charge of Jesus. [17]Carrying his own cross, Jesus went out to a place called The Place of the Skull. (In the Jewish language[n] this place is called Golgotha.) [18]There they nailed Jesus to the cross. They also put two other men on crosses, one on each side of Jesus with Jesus in the middle. [19]Pilate wrote a sign and put it on the cross. It read: "JESUS OF NAZARETH, THE KING OF THE JEWS." [20]The sign was written in the Jewish language, in Latin, and in Greek. Many of the Jews read the sign, because this place where Jesus was killed was near the city. [21]The leading Jewish priests said to Pilate, "Don't write, 'The King of the Jews.' But write, 'This man said, I am the King of the Jews.'"

[22]Pilate answered, "What I have written, I have written!"

[23]After the soldiers nailed Jesus to the cross, they took his clothes. They divided them into four parts. Each soldier got one part. They also took his long shirt. It was all one piece of cloth, woven from top to bottom. [24]So the soldiers said to each other, "We should not tear this into parts. We should throw lots[d] to see who will get it." This happened to give full meaning to the Scripture:[d]

"They divided my clothes among them.
   And they threw lots[d] for my
       clothing."   *Psalm 22:18*

So the soldiers did this.

[25]Jesus' mother stood near his cross. His mother's sister was also standing there, with Mary the wife of Clopas, and Mary Magdalene. [26]Jesus saw his mother. He also saw the follower he loved standing there. He said to his mother, "Dear woman, here is your son." [27]Then he said to the follower, "Here is your mother." From that time on, this follower took her to live in his home.

JESUS DIES

[28]After this, Jesus knew that everything had been done. To make the Scripture[d] come true, he said, "I am thirsty."[n] [29]There was a jar full of vinegar there, so the soldiers soaked a sponge in it. Then they put the sponge on a branch of a hyssop plant and lifted it to Jesus' mouth. [30]Jesus tasted the vinegar. Then he said, "It is finished." He bowed his head and died.

[31]This day was Preparation[d] Day. The next day was a special Sabbath[d] day. The

---

19:13, 17 **Jewish language** Aramaic, the language of the Jews in the first century.
19:28 **"I am thirsty."** Read Psalms 22:15; 69:21.

Jews did not want the bodies to stay on the cross on the Sabbath day. So they asked Pilate to order that the legs of the men be broken[n] and the bodies be taken away. [32]So the soldiers came and broke the legs of the first man on the cross beside Jesus. Then they broke the legs of the man on the other cross beside Jesus. [33]But when the soldiers came to Jesus, they saw that he was already dead. So they did not break his legs. [34]But one of the soldiers stuck his spear into Jesus' side. At once blood and water came out. [35](The one who saw this happen has told about it. The things he says are true. He knows that he tells the truth. He told about it so that you also can believe.) [36]These things happened to make the Scripture come true: "Not one of his bones will be broken."[n] [37]And another Scripture said, "They will look at the one they have stabbed."[n]

JESUS IS BURIED

[38]Later, a man named Joseph from Arimathea asked Pilate if he could take the body of Jesus. (Joseph was a secret follower of Jesus, because he was afraid of the Jews.) Pilate gave his permission. So Joseph came and took Jesus' body away. [39]Nicodemus went with Joseph. Nicodemus was the man who earlier had come to Jesus at night. He brought about 75 pounds of spices. This was a mixture of myrrh[d] and aloes.[d] [40]These two men took Jesus' body and wrapped it with the spices in pieces of linen cloth. (This is how the Jews bury people.) [41]In the place where Jesus was killed, there was a garden. In the garden was a new tomb where no one had ever been buried. [42]The men laid Jesus in that tomb because it was near, and the Jews were preparing to start their Sabbath[d] day.

JESUS' TOMB IS EMPTY

20 Early on the first day of the week, Mary Magdalene went to the tomb. It was still dark. Mary saw that the large stone had been moved away from the tomb. [2]So Mary ran to Simon Peter and the other follower (the one Jesus loved). Mary said, "They have taken the Lord out of the tomb. We don't know where they have put him."

[3]So Peter and the other follower started for the tomb. [4]They were both running, but the other follower ran faster than Peter. So the other follower reached the tomb first. [5]He bent down and looked in. He saw the strips of linen cloth lying there, but he did not go in. [6]Then following him came Simon Peter. He went into the tomb and saw the strips of linen lying there. [7]He also saw the cloth that had been around Jesus' head. The cloth was folded up and laid in a different place from the strips of linen. [8]Then the other follower, who had reached the tomb first, also went in. He saw and believed. [9](These followers did not yet understand from the Scriptures[d] that Jesus must rise from death.)

JESUS APPEARS TO MARY MAGDALENE

[10]Then the followers went back home. [11]But Mary stood outside the tomb, crying. While she was still crying, she bent down and looked inside the tomb. [12]She saw two angels dressed in white. They were sitting where Jesus' body had been, one at the head and one at the feet.

[13]They asked her, "Woman, why are you crying?"

She answered, "They have taken away my Lord. I don't know where they have put him." [14]When Mary said this, she turned around and saw Jesus standing there. But she did not know that it was Jesus.

19:31 broken The breaking of the men's bones would make them die sooner.
19:36 "Not one ... broken." Quotation from Psalm 34:20. The idea is from Exodus 12:46; Numbers 9:12.
19:37 "They ... stabbed." Quotation from Zechariah 12:10.

[15]Jesus asked her, "Woman, why are you crying? Whom are you looking for?"

Mary thought he was the gardener. So she said to him, "Did you take him away, sir? Tell me where you put him, and I will get him."

[16]Jesus said to her, "Mary."

Mary turned toward Jesus and said in the Jewish language,[n] "Rabboni." (This means Teacher.)

[17]Jesus said to her, "Don't hold me. I have not yet gone up to the Father. But go to my brothers and tell them this: 'I am going back to my Father and your Father. I am going back to my God and your God.'"

[18]Mary Magdalene went and said to the followers, "I saw the Lord!" And she told them what Jesus had said to her.

JESUS APPEARS TO HIS FOLLOWERS

[19]It was the first day of the week. That evening Jesus' followers were together. The doors were locked, because they were afraid of the Jews. Then Jesus came and stood among them. He said, "Peace be with you!" [20]After he said this, he showed them his hands and his side. His followers were very happy when they saw the Lord.

[21]Then Jesus said again, "Peace be with you! As the Father sent me, I now send you." [22]After he said this, he breathed on them and said, "Receive the Holy Spirit.[d] [23]If you forgive anyone his sins, they are forgiven. If you don't forgive them, they are not forgiven."

JESUS APPEARS TO THOMAS

[24]Thomas (called Didymus) was not with the followers when Jesus came. Thomas was 1 of the 12. [25]The other followers told Thomas, "We saw the Lord."

But Thomas said, "I will not believe it until I see the nail marks in his hands. And I will not believe until I put my finger where the nails were and put my hand into his side."

[26]A week later the followers were in the house again. Thomas was with them. The doors were locked, but Jesus came in and stood among them. He said, "Peace be with you!" [27]Then he said to Thomas, "Put your finger here. Look at my hands. Put your hand here in my side. Stop doubting and believe."

[28]Thomas said to him, "My Lord and my God!"

[29]Then Jesus told him, "You believe because you see me. Those who believe without seeing me will be truly happy."

WHY JOHN WROTE THIS BOOK

[30]Jesus did many other miracles[d] before his followers that are not written in this book. [31]But these are written so that you can believe that Jesus is the Christ,[d] the Son of God. Then, by believing, you can have life through his name.

JESUS APPEARS TO SEVEN FOLLOWERS

21 Later, Jesus showed himself to his followers by Lake Galilee.[n] This is how it happened: [2]Some of the followers were together. They were Simon Peter, Thomas (called Didymus), Nathanael from Cana in Galilee, the two sons of Zebedee, and two other followers. [3]Simon Peter said, "I am going out to fish."

The other followers said, "We will go with you." So they went out and got into the boat. They fished that night but caught nothing.

[4]Early the next morning Jesus stood on the shore. But the followers did not know that it was Jesus. [5]Then he said to them, "Friends, have you caught any fish?"

They answered, "No."

[6]He said, "Throw your net into the water on the right side of the boat, and you will find some." So they did this. They caught so many fish that they could not pull the net back into the boat.

[7]The follower whom Jesus loved said to Peter, "It is the Lord!" When Peter heard

---

20:16 **Jewish language** Aramaic, the language of the Jews in the first century.
21:1 **Lake Galilee** Literally, "Sea of Tiberias."

him say this, he wrapped his coat around himself. (Peter had taken his clothes off.) Then he jumped into the water. [8]The other followers went to shore in the boat, dragging the net full of fish. They were not very far from shore, only about 100 yards. [9]When the followers stepped out of the boat and onto the shore, they saw a fire of hot coals. There were fish on the fire, and there was bread.

[10]Then Jesus said, "Bring some of the fish that you caught."

[11]Simon Peter went into the boat and pulled the net to the shore. It was full of big fish. There were 153. Even though there were so many, the net did not tear. [12]Jesus said to them, "Come and eat." None of the followers dared ask him, "Who are you?" They knew it was the Lord. [13]Jesus came and took the bread and gave it to them. He also gave them the fish.

[14]This was now the third time Jesus showed himself to his followers after he was raised from death.

JESUS TALKS TO PETER

[15]When they finished eating, Jesus said to Simon Peter, "Simon son of John do you love me more than these?"

He answered, "Yes, Lord, you know that I love you."

Jesus said, "Take care of my lambs."

[16]Again Jesus said, "Simon son of John do you love me?"

He answered, "Yes, Lord, you know that I love you."

Jesus said, "Take care of my sheep."

[17]A third time he said, "Simon son of John do you love me?"

Peter was hurt because Jesus asked him the third time, "Do you love me?" Peter said, "Lord, you know everything. You know that I love you!"

He said to him, "Take care of my sheep. [18]I tell you the truth. When you were younger, you tied your own belt and went where you wanted. But when you are old, you will put out your hands and someone else will tie them. They will take you where you don't want to go." [19](Jesus said this to show how Peter would die to give glory to God.) Then Jesus said to Peter, "Follow me!"

[20]Peter turned and saw that the follower Jesus loved was walking behind them. (This was the follower who had leaned against Jesus at the supper and had said, "Lord, who will turn against you?") [21]When Peter saw him behind them he asked Jesus, "Lord, what about him?"

[22]Jesus answered, "Perhaps I want him to live until I come back. That should not be important to you. You follow me!"

[23]So a story spread among the brothers that this follower would not die. But Jesus did not say that he would not die. He only said, "Perhaps I want him to live until I come back. That should not be important to you."

[24]That follower is the one who is telling these things. He is the one who has now written them down. We know that what he says is true.

[25]There are many other things that Jesus did. If every one of them were written down, I think the whole world would not be big enough for all the books that would be written.

THE ACTS
OF THE APOSTLES

LUKE WRITES ANOTHER BOOK

1 To Theophilus,
The first book I wrote was about everything that Jesus did and taught. [2]I wrote about the whole life of Jesus, from the beginning until the day he was taken up into heaven. Before this, Jesus talked to the apostles[d] he had chosen. With the help of the Holy Spirit,[d] Jesus told them what they should do. [3]After his death, he showed himself to them and proved in many ways that he was alive. The apostles saw Jesus during the 40 days after he was raised from death. He spoke to them about the kingdom of God. [4]Once when he was eating with them, he told them not to leave Jerusalem. He said, "The Father has made you a promise which I told you about before. Wait here to receive this promise. [5]John baptized people with water, but in a few days you will be baptized with the Holy Spirit."

JESUS IS TAKEN UP INTO HEAVEN

[6]The apostles[d] were all together. They asked Jesus, "Lord, are you at this time going to give the kingdom back to Israel?"

[7]Jesus said to them, "The Father is the only One who has the authority to decide dates and times. These things are not for you to know. [8]But the Holy Spirit[d] will come to you. Then you will receive power. You will be my witnesses—in Jerusalem, in all of Judea, in Samaria, and in every part of the world."

[9]After he said this, as they were watching, he was lifted up. A cloud hid him from their sight. [10]As he was going, they were looking into the sky. Suddenly, two men wearing white clothes stood beside them. [11]They said, "Men of Galilee, why are you standing here looking into the sky? You saw Jesus taken away from you into heaven. He will come back in the same way you saw him go."

A NEW APOSTLE IS CHOSEN

[12]Then they went back to Jerusalem from the Mount of Olives.[d] (This mountain is about half a mile from Jerusalem.) [13]When they entered the city, they went to the upstairs room where they were staying. Peter, John, James, Andrew, Philip, Thomas, Bartholomew, Matthew, James son of Alphaeus, Simon (known as the Zealot[d]), and Judas son of James were there. [14]They all continued praying together. Some women, including Mary the mother of Jesus, and Jesus' brothers were also there with the apostles.

[15]During this time there was a meeting of the believers. (There were about 120 of them.) Peter stood up and said, [16-17]"Brothers, in the Scriptures[d] the Holy Spirit[d] said through David that something must happen. The Spirit was talking about Judas, one of our own group, who served together with us. The Spirit said that Judas would lead men to arrest Jesus. [18](Judas bought a field with the money he got for his evil act. But Judas fell to his death, his body burst open, and all his intestines poured out. [19]Everyone in Jerusalem learned about this. This is why they named the field Akeldama. In their language Akeldama means "field of blood.") [20]In the book of Psalms, this is written:

'May his place be empty.
Leave no one to live in it.'
Psalm 69:25

And it is also written:

'Let another man replace him as
leader.' *Psalm 109:8*

[21-22]"So now a man must join us and become a witness of Jesus' being raised from death. He must be one of the men who were part of our group during all the time the Lord Jesus was with us. He must have been with us from the time John began to baptize people until the day when Jesus was taken up from us to heaven."

23They put the names of two men before the group. One was Joseph Barsabbas, who was also called Justus. The other was Matthias. 24-25The apostles prayed, "Lord, you know the minds of everyone. Show us which one of these two you have chosen to do this work. Judas turned away from it and went where he belongs. Lord, show us which one should take his place as an apostle!"d 26Then they used lotsd to choose between them, and the lots showed that Matthias was the one. So he became an apostle with the other 11.

THE COMING OF THE HOLY SPIRIT

2 When the day of Pentecostd came, they were all together in one place. 2Suddenly a noise came from heaven. It sounded like a strong wind blowing. This noise filled the whole house where they were sitting. 3They saw something that looked like flames of fire. The flames were separated and stood over each person there. 4They were all filled with the Holy Spirit,d and they began to speak different languages. The Holy Spirit was giving them the power to speak these languages.

5There were some religious Jews staying in Jerusalem who were from every country in the world. 6When they heard this noise, a crowd came together. They were all surprised, because each one heard them speaking in his own language. 7They were completely amazed at this. They said, "Look! Aren't all these men that we hear speaking from Galilee?n 8But each of us hears them in his own language. How is this possible? We are from different places: 9Parthia, Media, Elam, Mesopotamia, Judea, Cappadocia, Pontus, Asia, 10Phrygia, Pamphylia, Egypt, the areas of Libya near Cyrene, Rome 11(both Jews and those who had become Jews), Crete and Arabia. But we hear these men telling in our own languages about the great things God has done!" 12They were all amazed and confused. They asked each other, "What does this mean?"

13But others were making fun of them, saying, "They have had too much wine."

PETER SPEAKS TO THE PEOPLE

14But Peter stood up with the 11 apostles.d In a loud voice he spoke to the crowd: "My fellow Jews, and all of you who are in Jerusalem, listen to me. Pay attention to what I have to say. 15These men are not drunk, as you think; it is only nine o'clock in the morning! 16But Joel the prophetd wrote about what is happening here today:
17'God says: In the last days
　I will give my Spiritd freely to all
　　kinds of people.
　Your sons and daughters will
　　prophesy.d
　　Your old men will dream dreams.
　　Your young men will see visions.
18At that time I will give my Spirit
　　even to my servants, both men and
　　women.
　　And they will prophesy.
19I will show miraclesd
　　in the sky and on the earth:
　　blood, fire and thick smoke.
20The sun will become dark.
　　The moon will become red as
　　blood.
　　And then the great and glorious day
　　of the Lord will come.
21Then anyone who asks the Lord for help
　　will be saved.'　　　*Joel 2:28-32*
22"Men of Israel, listen to these words: Jesus from Nazareth was a very special man. God clearly showed this to you by the miracles,d wonders, and signs God did through him. You all know this, because it happened right here among you. 23Jesus was given to you, and you killed him. With the help of evil men you nailed him to a cross. But God knew all this would happen. This was God's plan

---

2:7 from Galilee The people thought men from Galilee could speak only their own language.

which he had made long ago. ²⁴God raised Jesus from death. God set him free from the pain of death. Death could not hold him. ²⁵For David said this about him:

'I keep the Lord before me always.
Because he is close by my side,
I will not be hurt.
²⁶So I am glad, and I rejoice.
Even my body has hope.
²⁷This is because you will not leave me in the grave.
You will not let your Holy One rot.
²⁸You will teach me God's way to live.
Being with you will fill me with joy.'

Psalm 16:8-11

²⁹"Brothers, I can tell you truly about David, our ancestor. He died and was buried. His grave is still here with us today. ³⁰David was a prophet*ᵈ* and knew what God had said. God had promised David that he would make a person from David's family a king just as he was.*ⁿ* ³¹David knew this before it happened. That is why he said:

'He was not left in the grave.
His body did not rot.'

David was talking about the Christ*ᵈ* rising from death. ³²So Jesus is the One who God raised from death! And we are all witnesses to this. ³³Jesus was lifted up to heaven and is now at God's right side. The Father has given the Holy Spirit*ᵈ* to Jesus as he promised. So now Jesus has poured out that Spirit. This is what you see and hear. ³⁴David was not the one who was lifted up to heaven. But he said:

'The Lord said to my Lord:
Sit by me at my right side,
³⁵   until I put your enemies under your control.'*ⁿ*   *Psalm 110:1*

³⁶"So, all the people of Israel should know this truly: God has made Jesus both Lord and Christ. He is the man you nailed to the cross!"

³⁷When the people heard this, they were sick at heart. They asked Peter and the other apostles, "What shall we do?"

³⁸Peter said to them, "Change your hearts and lives and be baptized, each one of you, in the name of Jesus Christ for the forgiveness of your sins. And you will receive the gift of the Holy Spirit. ³⁹This promise is for you. It is also for your children and for all who are far away. It is for everyone the Lord our God calls to himself."

⁴⁰Peter warned them with many other words. He begged them, "Save yourselves from the evil of today's people!" ⁴¹Then those people who accepted what Peter said were baptized. About 3,000 people were added to the number of believers that day. ⁴²They spent their time learning the apostles' teaching. And they continued to share, to break bread,*ⁿ* and to pray together.

THE BELIEVERS SHARE

⁴³The apostles*ᵈ* were doing many miracles*ᵈ* and signs. And everyone felt great respect for God. ⁴⁴All the believers stayed together. They shared everything. ⁴⁵They sold their land and the things they owned. Then they divided the money and gave it to those people who needed it. ⁴⁶The believers met together in the Temple*ᵈ* every day. They all had the same purpose. They broke bread in their homes, happy to share their food with joyful hearts. ⁴⁷They praised God, and all the people liked them. More and more people were being saved every day; the Lord was adding those people to the group of believers.

PETER HEALS A CRIPPLED MAN

3 One day Peter and John went to the Temple.*ᵈ* It was three o'clock in the afternoon. This was the time for the daily

---

2:30 **God . . . was.** See 2 Samuel 7:13; Psalm 132:11.

2:35 **until . . . control** Literally, "until I make your enemies a footstool for your feet."

2:42 **break bread** This may mean a meal as in verse 46, or the Lord's Supper, the special meal Jesus told his followers to eat to remember him (Luke 22:14-20).

prayer service. [2]There, at the Temple gate called Beautiful Gate, was a man who had been crippled all his life. Every day he was carried to this gate to beg. He would ask for money from the people going into the Temple. [3]The man saw Peter and John going into the Temple and asked them for money. [4]Peter and John looked straight at him and said, "Look at us!" [5]The man looked at them; he thought they were going to give him some money. [6]But Peter said, "I don't have any silver or gold, but I do have something else I can give you: By the power of Jesus Christ from Nazareth—stand up and walk!" [7]Then Peter took the man's right hand and lifted him up. Immediately the man's feet and ankles became strong. [8]He jumped up, stood on his feet, and began to walk. He went into the Temple with them, walking and jumping, and praising God. [9-10]All the people recognized him. They knew he was the crippled man who always sat by the Beautiful Gate begging for money. Now they saw this same man walking and praising God. The people were amazed. They could not understand how this could happen.

PETER SPEAKS TO THE PEOPLE

[11]The man was holding on to Peter and John. All the people were amazed and ran to Peter and John at Solomon's Porch.[d] [12]When Peter saw this, he said to them, "Men of Israel, why are you surprised? You are looking at us as if it were our own power that made this man walk. Do you think this happened because we are good? No! [13]The God of Abraham, Isaac and Jacob, the God of our ancestors, gave glory to Jesus, his servant. But you gave him up to be killed. Pilate decided to let him go free. But you told Pilate you did not want Jesus. [14]He was pure and good, but you said you did not

want him. You told Pilate to give you a murderer[n] instead of Jesus. [15]And so you killed the One who gives life! But God raised him from death. We are witnesses to this. [16]It was the power of Jesus that made this crippled man well. This happened because we trusted in the power of Jesus. You can see this man, and you know him. He was made completely well because of trust in Jesus. You all saw it happen!

[17]"Brothers, I know you did those things to Jesus because you did not understand what you were doing. Your leaders did not understand either. [18]God said this would happen. He said through the prophets[d] that his Christ[d] would suffer and die. And now God has made these things come true in this way. [19]So you must change your hearts and lives! Come back to God, and he will forgive your sins. [20]Then the Lord will give you times of spiritual rest. He will give you Jesus, the One he chose to be the Christ. [21]But Jesus must stay in heaven until the time comes when all things will be made right again. God told about this time long ago when he spoke through his holy prophets. [22]Moses said, 'The Lord your God will give you a prophet like me. He will be one of your own people. You must obey everything he tells you. [23]Anyone who does not obey him will die, separated from God's people.'[n] [24]Samuel, and all the other prophets who spoke for God after Samuel, told about this time now. [25]You have received what the prophets talked about. You have received the agreement God made with your ancestors. He said to your father Abraham, 'Through your descendants[d] all the nations on the earth will be blessed.'[n] [26]God has raised up his servant and sent him to you first. He sent Jesus to bless

---

3:14 **murderer** Barabbas, the man the Jews asked Pilate to let go free instead of Jesus (Luke 23:18).
3:22-23 **'The Lord ... people.'** Quotation from Deuteronomy 18:15, 19.
3:25 **'Through ... blessed.'** Quotation from Genesis 22:18; 26:24.

you by turning each of you away from doing evil things."

PETER AND JOHN AT THE COUNCIL

4 While Peter and John were speaking to the people, a group of men came up to them. There were Jewish priests, the captain of the soldiers that guarded the Temple,*d* and some Sadducees.*d* ²They were upset because the two apostles*d* were teaching the people. Peter and John were preaching that people will rise from death through the power of Jesus. ³The Jewish leaders grabbed Peter and John and put them in jail. It was already night, so they kept them in jail until the next day. ⁴But many of those who heard Peter and John preach believed the things they said. There were now about 5,000 men in the group of believers.

⁵The next day the Jewish rulers, the Jewish elders, and the teachers of the law met in Jerusalem. ⁶Annas the high priest, Caiaphas, John, and Alexander were there. Everyone from the high priest's family was there. ⁷They made Peter and John stand before them. The Jewish leaders asked them: "By what power or authority did you do this?"

⁸Then Peter was filled with the Holy Spirit.*d* He said to them, "Rulers of the people and you elders, ⁹are you questioning us about a good thing that was done to a crippled man? Are you asking us who made him well? ¹⁰We want all of you and all the Jewish people to know that this man was made well by the power of Jesus Christ from Nazareth! You nailed him to a cross, but God raised him from death. This man was crippled, but he is now well and able to stand here before you because of the power of Jesus! ¹¹Jesus is

'the stone*n* that you builders did not want.

It has become the cornerstone.'*d*

Psalm 118:22

¹²Jesus is the only One who can save

people. No one else in the world is able to save us."

¹³The Jewish leaders saw that Peter and John were not afraid to speak. They understood that these men had no special training or education. So they were amazed. Then they realized that Peter and John had been with Jesus. ¹⁴They saw the crippled man standing there beside the two apostles. They saw that the man was healed. So they could say nothing against them. ¹⁵The Jewish leaders told them to leave the meeting. Then the leaders talked to each other about what they should do. ¹⁶They said, "What shall we do with these men? Everyone in Jerusalem knows that they have done a great miracle!*d* We cannot say it is not true. ¹⁷But we must warn them not to talk to people anymore using that name. Then this thing will not spread among the people."

¹⁸So they called Peter and John in again. They told them not to speak or to teach at all in the name of Jesus. ¹⁹But Peter and John answered them, "What do you think is right? What would God want? Should we obey you or God? ²⁰We cannot keep quiet. We must speak about what we have seen and heard." ²¹⁻²²The Jewish leaders could not find a way to punish them because all the people were praising God for what had been done. (This miracle was a proof from God. The man who was healed was more than 40 years old!) So the Jewish leaders warned the apostles again and let them go free.

THE BELIEVERS' PRAYER

²³Peter and John left the meeting of Jewish leaders and went to their own group. They told them everything that the leading priests and the Jewish elders had said to them. ²⁴When the believers heard this, they prayed to God with one purpose. They prayed, "Lord, you are the One who made the sky, the earth, the

4:11 **stone** A symbol meaning Jesus.

sea, and everything in the world. ²⁵Our father David was your servant. With the help of the Holy Spirit*d* he said:

'Why are the nations so angry?
Why are the people making useless plans?
²⁶The kings of the earth prepare to fight.
Their leaders make plans together against the Lord
and against his Christ.'*d* *Psalm 2:1-2*

²⁷These things really happened when Herod, Pontius Pilate, the non-Jewish people, and the Jewish people all came together against Jesus here in Jerusalem. Jesus is your holy Servant. He is the One you made to be the Christ. ²⁸These people made your plan happen; it happened because of your power and your will. ²⁹And now, Lord, listen to what they are saying. They are trying to make us afraid! Lord, we are your servants. Help us to speak your word without fear. ³⁰Help us to be brave by showing us your power; make sick people well, give proofs, and make miracles*d* happen by the power of Jesus, your holy servant."

³¹After they had prayed, the place where they were meeting was shaken. They were all filled with the Holy Spirit,*d* and they spoke God's word without fear.

THE BELIEVERS SHARE

³²The group of believers were joined in their hearts, and they had the same spirit. No person in the group said that the things he had were his own. Instead, they shared everything. ³³With great power the apostles*d* were telling people that the Lord Jesus was truly raised from death. And God blessed all the believers very much. ³⁴They all received the things they needed. Everyone that owned fields or houses sold them. They brought the money ³⁵and gave it to the apostles. Then each person was given the things he needed.

³⁶One of the believers was named Joseph. The apostles called him Barnabas. (This name means "one who encourages.") He was a Levite, born in Cyprus.

³⁷Joseph owned a field. He sold it, brought the money, and gave it to the apostles.

ANANIAS AND SAPPHIRA

5 A man named Ananias and his wife Sapphira sold some land. ²But he gave only part of the money to the apostles.*d* He secretly kept some of it for himself. His wife knew about this, and she agreed to it. ³Peter said, "Ananias, why did you let Satan rule your heart? You lied to the Holy Spirit.*d* Why did you keep part of the money you received for the land for yourself? ⁴Before you sold the land, it belonged to you. And even after you sold it, you could have used the money any way you wanted. Why did you think of doing this? You lied to God, not to men!" ⁵⁻⁶When Ananias heard this, he fell down and died. Some young men came in, wrapped up his body, carried it out, and buried it. And everyone who heard about this was filled with fear.

⁷About three hours later his wife came in. She did not know what had happened. ⁸Peter said to her, "Tell me how much money you got for your field. Was it this much?"

Sapphira answered, "Yes, that was the price."

⁹Peter said to her, "Why did you and your husband agree to test the Spirit of the Lord? Look! The men who buried your husband are at the door! They will carry you out." ¹⁰At that moment Sapphira fell down by his feet and died. The young men came in and saw that she was dead. They carried her out and buried her beside her husband. ¹¹The whole church and all the others who heard about these things were filled with fear.

PROOFS FROM GOD

¹²The apostles*d* did many signs and miracles*d* among the people. And they would all meet together on Solomon's Porch.*d* ¹³None of the others dared to stand with them. All the people were saying good things about them. ¹⁴More

and more men and women believed in the Lord and were added to the group of believers. [15]As Peter was passing by, the people brought their sick into the streets. They put their sick on beds and mats so at least Peter's shadow might fall on them. [16]Crowds came from all the towns around Jerusalem. They brought their sick and those who were bothered by evil spirits. All of them were healed.

THE APOSTLES OBEY GOD

[17]The high priest and all his friends (a group called the Sadducees[d]) became very jealous. [18]They took the apostles[d] and put them in jail. [19]But during the night, an angel of the Lord opened the doors of the jail. He led the apostles outside and said, [20]"Go and stand in the Temple.[d] Tell the people everything about this new life." [21]When the apostles heard this, they obeyed and went into the Temple. It was early in the morning, and they began to teach.

The high priest and his friends arrived. They called a meeting of the Jewish leaders and all the important older men of the Jews. They sent some men to the jail to bring the apostles to them. [22]When the men went to the jail, they could not find the apostles. So they went back and told the Jewish leaders about this. [23]They said, "The jail was closed and locked. The guards were standing at the doors. But when we opened the doors, the jail was empty!" [24]Hearing this, the captain of the Temple guards and the leading priests were confused. They wondered, "What will happen because of this?"

[25]Then someone came and told them, "Listen! The men you put in jail are standing in the Temple. They are teaching the people!" [26]Then the captain and his men went out and brought the apostles back. But the soldiers did not use force, because they were afraid that the people would kill them with stones.

[27]The soldiers brought the apostles to the meeting and made them stand before the Jewish leaders. The high priest questioned them. [28]He said, "We gave you strict orders not to go on teaching in that name. But look what you have done! You have filled Jerusalem with your teaching. You are trying to make us responsible for this man's death."

[29]Peter and the other apostles answered, "We must obey God, not men! [30]You killed Jesus. You hung him on a cross. But God, the same God our ancestors had, raised Jesus up from death! [31]Jesus is the One whom God raised to be on his right side. God made Jesus our Leader and Savior. God did this so that all Jews could change their hearts and lives and have their sins forgiven. [32]We saw all these things happen. The Holy Spirit[d] also proves that these things are true. God has given the Spirit to all who obey him."

[33]When the Jewish leaders heard this, they became very angry and wanted to kill them. [34]A Pharisee[d] named Gamaliel stood up in the meeting. He was a teacher of the law, and all the people respected him. He ordered the apostles to leave the meeting for a little while. [35]Then he said to them, "Men of Israel, be careful of what you are planning to do to these men! [36]Remember when Theudas appeared? He said that he was a great man, and about 400 men joined him. But he was killed. And all his followers were scattered. They were able to do nothing. [37]Later, a man named Judas came from Galilee at the time of the registration.[n] He led a group of followers, too. He was also killed, and all his followers were scattered. [38]And so now I tell you: Stay away from these men. Leave them alone. If their plan comes from men, it will fail. [39]But if it is from God, you will not be able to stop them. You might even be fighting against God himself!"

5:37 registration Census. A counting of all the people and the things they own.

The Jewish leaders agreed with what Gamaliel said. [40]They called the apostles in again. They beat the apostles and told them not to speak in the name of Jesus again. Then they let them go free. [41]The apostles left the meeting full of joy because they were given the honor of suffering disgrace for Jesus. [42]The apostles did not stop teaching people. Every day in the Temple and in people's homes they continued to tell the Good News—that Jesus is the Christ.[d]

SEVEN MEN ARE CHOSEN

6 More and more people were becoming followers of Jesus. But during this same time, the Greek-speaking followers had an argument with the other Jewish followers. The Greek-speaking Jews said that their widows were not getting their share of the food that was given out every day. [2]The 12 apostles[d] called the whole group of followers together. They said, "It is not right for us to stop our work of teaching God's word in order to serve tables. [3]So, brothers, choose seven of your own men. They must be men who are good. They must be full of wisdom and full of the Spirit.[d] We will put them in charge of this work. [4]Then we can use all our time to pray and to teach the word of God."

[5]The whole group liked the idea. So they chose these seven men: Stephen (a man with great faith and full of the Holy Spirit), Philip,[n] Procorus, Nicanor, Timon, Parmenas, and Nicolas (a man from Antioch who had become a Jew). [6]Then they put these men before the apostles. The apostles prayed and laid their hands on[n] the men.

[7]The word of God was reaching more and more people. The group of followers in Jerusalem became larger and larger. A great number of the Jewish priests believed and obeyed.

STEPHEN IS ARRESTED

[8]Stephen was richly blessed by God. God gave him the power to do great miracles[d] and signs among the people. [9]But some Jews were against him. They belonged to a synagogue[d] of Free Men[n] (as it was called). (This synagogue was also for Jews from Cyrene and from Alexandria.) Jews from Cilicia and Asia were also with them. They all came and argued with Stephen.

[10]But the Spirit[d] was helping him to speak with wisdom. His words were so strong that they could not argue with him. [11]So they paid some men to say, "We heard him say things against Moses and against God!"

[12]This upset the people, the Jewish elders, and the teachers of the law. They came to Stephen, grabbed him and brought him to a meeting of the Jewish leaders. [13]They brought in some men to tell lies about Stephen. They said, "This man is always saying things against this holy place and the law of Moses. [14]We heard him say that Jesus from Nazareth will destroy this place. He also said that Jesus will change the things that Moses told us to do." [15]All the people in the meeting were watching Stephen closely. His face looked like the face of an angel.

STEPHEN'S SPEECH

7 The high priest said to Stephen, "Are these things true?"

[2]Stephen answered, "Brothers and fathers, listen to me. Our glorious God appeared to Abraham, our ancestor. Abraham was in Mesopotamia before he lived in Haran. [3]God said to Abraham, 'Leave your country and your relatives. Go to the land I will show you.'[n] [4]So Abraham left the country of Chaldea and went to live in Haran. After Abraham's father died, God sent him to this place

---

6:5 **Philip** Not the apostle named Philip.
6:6 **laid their hands on** Here, doing this showed that these men were given a special work of God.
6:9 **Free Men** Jews who had been slaves or whose fathers had been slaves, but were now free.
7:3 **'Leave ... you.'** Quotation from Genesis 12:1.

where you now live. [5]God did not give Abraham any of this land, not even a foot of it. But God promised that he would give him and his descendants[d] this land. (This was before Abraham had any descendants.) [6]This is what God said to him: 'Your descendants will be strangers in a land they don't own. The people there will make them slaves. And they will do cruel things to them for 400 years. [7]But I will punish the nation where they are slaves. Then your descendants will leave that land. Then they will worship me in this place.'[n] [8]God made an agreement with Abraham; the sign for this agreement was circumcision.[d] And so when Abraham had his son Isaac, Abraham circumcised him when he was eight days old. Isaac also circumcised his son Jacob. And Jacob did the same for his sons, the 12 ancestors[n] of our people.

[9]"These sons became jealous of Joseph. They sold him to be a slave in Egypt. But God was with him. [10]Joseph had many troubles there, but God saved him from all those troubles. The king of Egypt liked Joseph and respected him because of the wisdom that God gave him. The king made him governor of Egypt. He put Joseph in charge of all the people in his palace.

[11]"Then all the land of Egypt and of Canaan became so dry that nothing would grow there. This made the people suffer very much. The sons could not find anything to eat. [12]But when Jacob heard that there was grain in Egypt, he sent his sons, our ancestors, there. This was their first trip to Egypt. [13]Then they went there a second time. This time, Joseph told his brothers who he was. And the king learned about Joseph's family. [14]Then Joseph sent some men to invite Jacob, his father, to come to Egypt. He also invited all his relatives (75 persons altogether). [15]So Jacob went down to Egypt, where he and his sons died. [16]Later their bodies were moved to Shechem and put in a grave there. (It was the same grave that Abraham had bought in Shechem from the sons of Hamor for a sum of money.)

[17]"The number of people in Egypt grew large. There were more and more of our people there. (The promise that God made to Abraham was soon to come true.) [18]Then a new king began to rule Egypt. He did not know who Joseph was. [19]This king tricked our people and was cruel to our ancestors. He forced them to put their babies outside to die. [20]This was the time when Moses was born. He was a fine child. For three months Moses was cared for in his father's house. [21]When they put Moses outside, the king's daughter took him. She raised him as if he were her own son. [22]The Egyptians taught Moses all the things they knew. He was a powerful man in the things he said and did.

[23]"When Moses was about 40 years old, he thought it would be good to visit his brothers, the people of Israel. [24]Moses saw an Egyptian doing wrong to a Jew. So he defended the Jew and punished the Egyptian for hurting him. Moses killed the Egyptian. [25]Moses thought that his fellow Jews would understand that God was using him to save them. But they did not understand. [26]The next day, Moses saw two Jewish men fighting. He tried to make peace between them. He said, 'Men, you are brothers! Why are you hurting each other?' [27]The man who was hurting the other man pushed Moses away. He said, 'Who made you our ruler and judge? [28]Are you going to kill me as you killed the Egyptian yesterday?'[n]

7:6-7 'Your descendants . . . place.' Quotation from Genesis 15:13-14 and Exodus 3:12.
7:8 12 ancestors Important ancestors of the Jews; the leaders of the 12 Jewish tribes.
7:27-28 'Who . . . yesterday?' Quotation from Exodus 2:14.

²⁹When Moses heard him say this, he left Egypt. He went to live in the land of Midian where he was a stranger. While Moses lived in Midian, he had two sons.

³⁰"After 40 years Moses was in the desert near Mount Sinai. An angel appeared to him in the flames of a burning bush. ³¹When Moses saw this, he was amazed. He went near to look closer at it. Moses heard the Lord's voice. ³²The Lord said, 'I am the God of your ancestors. I am the God of Abraham, Isaac and Jacob.'ⁿ Moses began to shake with fear and was afraid to look. ³³The Lord said to him, 'Take off your sandals. You are standing on holy ground. ³⁴I have seen the troubles my people have suffered in Egypt. I have heard their cries. I have come down to save them. And now, Moses, I am sending you back to Egypt.'ⁿ

³⁵"This Moses was the same man the Jews said they did not want. They had said to him, 'Who made you our ruler and judge?'ⁿ Moses is the same man God sent to be a ruler and savior, with the help of an angel. This was the angel Moses saw in the burning bush. ³⁶So Moses led the people out of Egypt. He worked miracles^d and signs in Egypt, at the Red Sea,^d and then in the desert for 40 years. ³⁷This is the same Moses that said to the Jewish people: 'God will give you a prophet^d like me. He will be one of your own people.'ⁿ ³⁸This is the same Moses who was with the gathering of the Jews in the desert. He was with the angel that spoke to him at Mount Sinai, and he was with our ancestors. He received commands from God that give life, and he gave those commands to us.

³⁹"But our fathers did not want to obey Moses. They rejected him. They wanted to go back to Egypt again. ⁴⁰They said to Aaron, 'Moses led us out of Egypt. But we don't know what has happened to him. So make us gods who will lead us.'ⁿ ⁴¹So the people made an idol that looked like a calf. Then they brought sacrifices to it. The people were proud of what they had made with their own hands! ⁴²But God turned against them. He did not try to stop them from worshiping the sun, moon and stars. This is what is written in the book of the prophets: God says,

'People of Israel, you did not bring me
    sacrifices and offerings
  while you traveled in the desert for
    40 years.
⁴³But now you will have to carry with
  you
  the tent to worship the false god
    Molech^d
  and the idols of the star god Rephan
    that you made to worship.
This is because I will send you away
    beyond Babylon.'   *Amos 5:25-27*

⁴⁴"The Holy Tent^d where God spoke to our fathers was with the Jews in the desert. God told Moses how to make this Tent. He made it like the plan God showed him. ⁴⁵Later, Joshua led our fathers to capture the lands of the other nations. Our people went in, and God drove the other people out. When our people went into this new land, they took with them this same Tent. They received this Tent from their fathers and kept it until the time of David. ⁴⁶God was very pleased with David. He asked God to let him build a house for him, the God of Jacob.ⁿ ⁴⁷But Solomon was the one who built the Temple.^d

⁴⁸"But the Most High does not live in houses that men build with their hands.

7:32 **'I am . . . Jacob.'** Quotation from Exodus 3:6.
7:33-34 **'Take . . . Egypt.'** Quotation from Exodus 3:5-10.
7:35 **'Who . . . judge?'** Quotation from Exodus 2:14.
7:37 **'God . . . people.'** Quotation from Deuteronomy 18:15.
7:40 **'Moses . . . us.'** Quotation from Exodus 32:1.
7:46 **the God of Jacob** Some Greek copies read "the house of Jacob." This means the people of Israel.

This is what the prophet says:
⁴⁹"Heaven is my throne.
The earth is my footstool.
So do you think you can build a house
   for me? says the Lord.
There is no place where I need to rest.
⁵⁰Remember, I made all these things!'"

Isaiah 66:1-2

⁵¹Stephen continued speaking: "You stubborn Jewish leaders! You have not given your hearts to God! You won't listen to him! You are always against what the Holy Spirit*ᵈ* is trying to tell you. Your ancestors were like this, and you are just like them! ⁵²Your fathers tried to hurt every prophet who ever lived. Those prophets said long ago that the Righteous One would come. But your fathers killed them. And now you have turned against the Righteous One and killed him. ⁵³You received the law of Moses, which God gave you through his angels. But you don't obey it!"

STEPHEN IS KILLED

⁵⁴When the leaders heard Stephen saying all these things, they became very angry. They were so mad that they were grinding their teeth at Stephen. ⁵⁵But Stephen was full of the Holy Spirit.*ᵈ* He looked up to heaven and saw the glory of God. He saw Jesus standing at God's right side. ⁵⁶He said, "Look! I see heaven open. And I see the Son of Man*ᵈ* standing at God's right side!"

⁵⁷Then they all shouted loudly. They covered their ears with their hands and all ran at Stephen. ⁵⁸They took him out of the city and threw stones at him until he was dead. The men who told lies against Stephen left their coats with a young man named Saul. ⁵⁹While they were throwing stones, Stephen prayed, "Lord Jesus, receive my spirit!" ⁶⁰He fell on his knees and cried in a loud voice, "Lord, do not hold this sin against them!" After Stephen said this, he died.

8 Saul agreed that the killing of Stephen was a good thing.

TROUBLE FOR THE BELIEVERS

²⁻³Some religious men buried Stephen. They cried very loudly for him. On that day people began trying to hurt the church in Jerusalem and make it suffer. Saul was also trying to destroy the church. He went from house to house. He dragged out men and women and put them in jail. All the believers, except the apostles,*ᵈ* went to different places in Judea and Samaria. ⁴And everywhere they were scattered, they told people the Good News.*ᵈ*

PHILIP PREACHES IN SAMARIA

⁵Philip*ⁿ* went to the city of Samaria and preached about the Christ.*ᵈ* ⁶The people there heard Philip and saw the miracles*ᵈ* he was doing. They all listened carefully to the things he said. ⁷Many of these people had evil spirits in them. But Philip made the evil spirits leave them. The spirits made a loud noise when they came out. There were also many weak and crippled people there. Philip healed them, too. ⁸So the people in that city were very happy.

⁹But there was a man named Simon in that city. Before Philip came there, Simon had practiced magic. He amazed all the people of Samaria with his magic. He bragged and called himself a great man. ¹⁰All the people—the least important and the most important—paid attention to what Simon said. They said, "This man has the power of God, called 'the Great Power'!" ¹¹Simon had amazed them with his magic tricks so long that the people became his followers. ¹²But Philip told them the Good News*ᵈ* about the kingdom of God and the power of Jesus Christ. Men and women believed Philip and were baptized. ¹³Simon himself believed and was baptized. He stayed very close to Philip. When he saw the

8:5 **Philip** Not the apostle named Philip.

miracles and the very powerful things that Philip did, Simon was amazed.

[14]The apostles[d] were still in Jerusalem. They heard that the people of Samaria had accepted the word of God. So they sent Peter and John to them. [15]When Peter and John arrived, they prayed that the Samaritan believers might receive the Holy Spirit.[d] [16]These people had been baptized in the name of the Lord Jesus. But the Holy Spirit had not yet entered any of them. [17]Then, when the two apostles began laying their hands on[n] the people, they received the Holy Spirit.

[18]Simon saw that the Spirit was given to people when the apostles laid their hands on them. So he offered the apostles money. [19]He said, "Give me also this power so that when I lay my hands on a person, he will receive the Holy Spirit."

[20]Peter said to him, "You and your money should both be destroyed! You thought you could buy God's gift with money. [21]You cannot share with us in this work. Your heart is not right before God. [22]Change your heart! Turn away from this evil thing you have done. Pray to the Lord. Maybe he will forgive you for thinking this. [23]I see that you are full of bitter jealousy and ruled by sin."

[24]Simon answered, "Both of you pray for me to the Lord. Pray that the things you have said will not happen to me!"

[25]Then the two apostles told the people the things they had seen Jesus do. And after the apostles had given the message of the Lord, they went back to Jerusalem. On the way, they went through many Samaritan towns and preached the Good News to the people.

PHILIP TEACHES AN ETHIOPIAN

[26]An angel of the Lord spoke to Philip.[n] The angel said, "Get ready and go south. Go to the road that leads down to Gaza from Jerusalem—the desert road." [27]So Philip got ready and went. On the road he saw a man from Ethiopia, a eunuch.[d] He was an important officer in the service of Candace, the queen of the Ethiopians. He was responsible for taking care of all her money. He had gone to Jerusalem to worship, and [28]now he was on his way home. He was sitting in his chariot and reading from the book of Isaiah, the prophet.[d] [29]The Spirit[d] said to Philip, "Go to that chariot and stay near it."

[30]So Philip ran toward the chariot. He heard the man reading from Isaiah, the prophet. Philip asked, "Do you understand what you are reading?"

[31]He answered, "How can I understand? I need someone to explain it to me!" Then he invited Philip to climb in and sit with him. [32]The verse of Scripture[d] that he was reading was this:

"He was like a sheep being led to be killed.

He was quiet, as a sheep is quiet while its wool is being cut.

He said nothing.

[33]   He was shamed and was treated unfairly.

He died without children to continue his family.

His life on earth has ended."

Isaiah 53:7-8

[34]The officer said to Philip, "Please tell me, who is the prophet talking about? Is he talking about himself or about someone else?" [35]Philip began to speak. He started with this same Scripture and told the man the Good News[d] about Jesus.

[36]While they were traveling down the road, they came to some water. The officer said, "Look! Here is water! What is stopping me from being baptized?" [37][Philip answered, "If you believe with all your heart, you can." The officer said, "I believe that Jesus Christ is the Son of God."][n] [38]Then the officer commanded

---

8:17 **laying their hands on** Here, doing this showed that these men were given a special work of God.
8:26 **Philip** Not the apostle named Philip.
8:37 **Philip . . . God.** Some Greek copies do not contain the bracketed text.

the chariot to stop. Both Philip and the officer went down into the water, and Philip baptized him. [39]When they came up out of the water, the Spirit of the Lord took Philip away; the officer never saw him again. The officer continued on his way home, full of joy. [40]But Philip appeared in a city called Azotus and preached the Good News in all the towns on the way from Azotus to Caesarea.

SAUL IS CONVERTED

9 In Jerusalem Saul was still trying to frighten the followers of the Lord by saying he would kill them. So he went to the high priest [2]and asked him to write letters to the synagogues[d] in the city of Damascus. Saul wanted the high priest to give him the authority to find people in Damascus who were followers of Christ's Way. If he found any there, men or women, he would arrest them and bring them back to Jerusalem.

[3]So Saul went to Damascus. As he came near the city, a bright light from heaven suddenly flashed around him. [4]Saul fell to the ground. He heard a voice saying to him, "Saul, Saul! Why are you doing things against me?"

[5]Saul said, "Who are you, Lord?"

The voice answered, "I am Jesus. I am the One you are trying to hurt. [6]Get up now and go into the city. Someone there will tell you what you must do."

[7]The men traveling with Saul stood there, but they said nothing. They heard the voice, but they saw no one. [8]Saul got up from the ground. He opened his eyes, but he could not see. So the men with Saul took his hand and led him into Damascus. [9]For three days Saul could not see, and he did not eat or drink.

[10]There was a follower of Jesus in Damascus named Ananias. The Lord spoke to Ananias in a vision, "Ananias!"

Ananias answered, "Here I am, Lord."

[11]The Lord said to him, "Get up and go to the street called Straight Street. Find the house of Judas.[n] Ask for a man named Saul from the city of Tarsus. He is there now, praying. [12]Saul has seen a vision. In it a man named Ananias comes to him and lays his hands on him. Then he sees again."

[13]But Ananias answered, "Lord, many people have told me about this man and the terrible things he did to your people in Jerusalem. [14]Now he has come here to Damascus. The leading priests have given him the power to arrest everyone who worships you."

[15]But the Lord said to Ananias, "Go! I have chosen Saul for an important work. He must tell about me to non-Jews, to kings, and to the people of Israel. [16]I will show him how much he must suffer for my name."

[17]So Ananias went to the house of Judas. He laid his hands on Saul and said, "Brother Saul, the Lord Jesus sent me. He is the one you saw on the road on your way here. He sent me so that you can see again and be filled with the Holy Spirit."[d] [18]Immediately, something that looked like fish scales fell from Saul's eyes. He was able to see again! Then Saul got up and was baptized. [19]After eating some food, his strength returned.

SAUL PREACHES IN DAMASCUS

Saul stayed with the followers of Jesus in Damascus for a few days. [20]Soon he began to preach about Jesus in the synagogues,[d] saying, "Jesus is the Son of God!"

[21]All the people who heard him were amazed. They said, "This is the man who was in Jerusalem. He was trying to destroy those who trust in this name! He came here to do the same thing. He came here to arrest the followers of Jesus and take them back to the leading priests."

[22]But Saul became more and more powerful. His proofs that Jesus is the

---

9:11 Judas This is not either of the apostles named Judas.

Christ[d] were so strong that the Jews in Damascus could not argue with him.

SAUL ESCAPES FROM DAMASCUS

23After many days, the Jews made plans to kill Saul. 24They were watching the city gates day and night. They wanted to kill him, but Saul learned about their plan. 25One night some followers of Saul helped him leave the city. They lowered him in a basket through an opening in the city wall.

SAUL IN JERUSALEM

26Then Saul went to Jerusalem. He tried to join the group of followers, but they were all afraid of him. They did not believe that he was really a follower. 27But Barnabas accepted Saul and took him to the apostles.[d] Barnabas told them that Saul had seen the Lord on the road. He explained how the Lord had spoken to Saul. Then he told them how boldly Saul had preached in the name of Jesus in Damascus.

28And so Saul stayed with the followers. He went everywhere in Jerusalem, preaching boldly in the name of Jesus. 29He would often talk and argue with the Jews who spoke Greek. But they were trying to kill him. 30When the brothers learned about this, they took Saul to Caesarea. From there they sent him to Tarsus.

31The church everywhere in Judea, Galilee, and Samaria had a time of peace. With the help of the Holy Spirit,[d] the group became stronger. The believers showed that they respected the Lord by the way they lived. Because of this, the group of believers grew larger and larger.

PETER HEALS AENEAS

32As Peter was traveling through all the area, he visited God's people who lived in Lydda. 33There he met a paralyzed man named Aeneas. Aeneas had not been able to leave his bed for the past eight years. 34Peter said to him, "Aeneas, Jesus Christ heals you. Stand up and make your bed!" Aeneas stood up immediately. 35All the people living in Lydda and on the Plain of Sharon saw him. These people turned to the Lord.

PETER IN JOPPA

36In the city of Joppa there was a follower named Tabitha. (Her Greek name, Dorcas, means "a deer.") She was always doing good and helping the poor. 37While Peter was in Lydda, Tabitha became sick and died. Her body was washed and put in a room upstairs. 38The followers in Joppa heard that Peter was in Lydda. (Lydda is near Joppa.) So they sent two men to Peter. They begged him, "Hurry, please come to us!" 39Peter got ready and went with them. When he arrived, they took him to the upstairs room. All the widows stood around Peter, crying. They showed him the shirts and coats that Tabitha had made when she was still alive. 40Peter sent everyone out of the room. He kneeled and prayed. Then he turned to the body and said, "Tabitha, stand up!" She opened her eyes, and when she saw Peter, she sat up. 41He gave her his hand and helped her up. Then he called the saints[d] and the widows into the room. He showed them Tabitha; she was alive! 42People everywhere in Joppa learned about this, and many believed in the Lord. 43Peter stayed in Joppa for many days with a man named Simon who was a leatherworker.

PETER AND CORNELIUS

10 At Caesarea there was a man named Cornelius. He was an officer in the Italian group of the Roman army. 2Cornelius was a religious man. He and all the other people who lived in his house worshiped the true God. He gave much of his money to the poor and prayed to God often. 3One afternoon about three o'clock, Cornelius saw a vision clearly. In the vision an angel of God came to him and said, "Cornelius!"

4Cornelius stared at the angel. He

became afraid and said, "What do you want, Lord?"

The angel said, "God has heard your prayers. He has seen what you give to the poor. And God remembers you. [5]Send some men now to Joppa to bring back a man named Simon. Simon is also called Peter. [6]Simon is staying with a man, also named Simon, who is a leatherworker. He has a house beside the sea." [7]Then the angel who spoke to Cornelius left. Cornelius called two of his servants and a soldier. The soldier was a religious man who worked for Cornelius. [8]Cornelius explained everything to these three men and sent them to Joppa.

[9]The next day as they came near Joppa, Peter was going up to the roof[n] to pray. It was about noon. [10]Peter was hungry and wanted to eat. But while the food was being prepared, he had a vision. [11]He saw heaven opened and something coming down. It looked like a big sheet being lowered to earth by its four corners. [12]In it were all kinds of animals, reptiles, and birds. [13]Then a voice said to Peter, "Get up, Peter; kill and eat."

[14]But Peter said, "No, Lord! I have never eaten food that is unholy or unclean."[d]

[15]But the voice said to him again, "God has made these things clean. Don't call them 'unholy'!" [16]This happened three times. Then the sheet was taken back to heaven.

[17]While Peter was wondering what this vision meant, the men Cornelius sent had found Simon's house. They were standing at the gate. [18]They asked, "Is Simon Peter staying here?"

[19]Peter was still thinking about the vision. But the Spirit[d] said to him, "Listen! Three men are looking for you. [20]Get up and go downstairs. Go with them and don't ask questions. I have sent them to you."

[21]So Peter went down to the men. He said, "I am the man you are looking for. Why did you come here?"

[22]They said, "A holy angel spoke to Cornelius, an army officer. He is a good man; he worships God. All the Jewish people respect him. The angel told Cornelius to ask you to his house so that he can hear what you have to say." [23]Peter asked the men to come in and spend the night.

The next day Peter got ready and went with them. Some of the brothers from Joppa joined him. [24]On the following day they came to Caesarea. Cornelius was waiting for them. He had called together his relatives and close friends. [25]When Peter entered, Cornelius met him. He fell at Peter's feet and worshiped him. [26]But Peter helped him up, saying, "Stand up! I too am only a man." [27]Peter went on talking with Cornelius as they went inside. There Peter saw many people together. [28]He said, "You people understand that it is against our Jewish law for a Jew to associate with or visit anyone who is not a Jew. But God has shown me that I should not call any person 'unholy' or 'unclean.' [29]That is why I did not argue when I was asked to come here. Now, please tell me why you sent for me."

[30]Cornelius said, "Four days ago, I was praying in my house. It was at this same time—three o'clock in the afternoon. Suddenly, there was a man standing before me wearing shining clothes. [31]He said, 'Cornelius! God has heard your prayer. He has seen what you give to the poor. And God remembers you. [32]So send some men to Joppa and ask Simon Peter to come. Peter is staying in the house of a man, also named Simon, who is a leatherworker. His house is beside the sea.' [33]So I sent for you immediately, and it was very good of you to come. Now we

---

10:9 roof In Bible times houses were built with flat roofs. The roof was used for drying things such as flax and fruit. And it was used as an extra room, as a place for worship and as a place to sleep in the summer.

are all here before God to hear everything the Lord has commanded you to tell us."

PETER'S SPEECH

[34]Peter began to speak: "I really understand now that to God every person is the same. [35]God accepts anyone who worships him and does what is right. It is not important what country a person comes from. [36]You know that God has sent his message to the people of Israel. That message is the Good News[d] that peace has come through Jesus Christ. Jesus is the Lord of all people! [37]You know what has happened all over Judea. It began in Galilee after John[n] preached to the people about baptism. [38]You know about Jesus from Nazareth. God made him the Christ[d] by giving him the Holy Spirit[d] and power. You know how Jesus went everywhere doing good. He healed those who were ruled by the devil, for God was with Jesus. [39]We saw all the things that Jesus did in Judea and in Jerusalem. But they killed him by nailing him to a cross. [40]Yet, on the third day, God raised Jesus to life and caused him to be seen. [41]But he was not seen by all the people. Only the witnesses that God had already chosen saw him, and we are those witnesses. We ate and drank with him after he was raised from death. [42]He told us to preach to the people and to tell them that he is the one whom God chose to be the judge of the living and the dead. [43]Everyone who believes in Jesus will be forgiven. God will forgive his sins through Jesus. All the prophets[d] say this is true."

NON-JEWS RECEIVE THE HOLY SPIRIT

[44]While Peter was still saying this, the Holy Spirit[d] came down on all those who were listening. [45]The Jewish believers who came with Peter were amazed that the gift of the Holy Spirit had been given even to the non-Jewish people. [46]These Jewish believers heard them speaking in different languages and praising God. Then Peter said, [47]"Can anyone keep these people from being baptized with water? They have received the Holy Spirit just as we did!" [48]So Peter ordered that they be baptized in the name of Jesus Christ. Then they asked Peter to stay with them for a few days.

PETER RETURNS TO JERUSALEM

11 The apostles[d] and the believers in Judea heard that non-Jewish people had accepted God's teaching too. [2]But when Peter came to Jerusalem, some Jewish believers argued with him. [3]They said, "You went into the homes of people who are not Jews and are not circumcised![d] You even ate with them!"

[4]So Peter explained the whole story to them. [5]He said, "I was in the city of Joppa. While I was praying, I had a vision. In the vision, I saw something which looked like a big sheet coming down from heaven. It was being lowered to earth by its four corners. It came down very close to me, and [6]I looked inside it. I saw animals, wild beasts, reptiles, and birds. [7]I heard a voice say to me, 'Get up, Peter. Kill and eat.' [8]But I said, 'No, Lord! I have never eaten anything that is unholy or unclean.'[d] [9]But the voice from heaven answered again, 'God has made these things clean. Don't call them unholy!' [10]This happened three times. Then the whole thing was taken back to heaven. [11]Right then three men came to the house where I was staying. They were sent to me from Caesarea. [12]The Spirit[d] told me to go with them without doubting. These six believers here also went with me. We went to the house of Cornelius. [13]He told us about the angel he saw standing in his house. The angel said to him, 'Send some men to Joppa and invite Simon Peter to come. [14]He will speak to you. The things

---

10:37 John John the Baptist, who preached to people about Christ's coming (Matthew 3, Luke 3).

he will say will save you and all your family.' [15]When I began my speech, the Holy Spirit came on them just as he came on us at the beginning. [16]Then I remembered the words of the Lord. He said, 'John baptized in water, but you will be baptized in the Holy Spirit!' [17]God gave to them the same gift that he gave to us who believed in the Lord Jesus Christ. So could I stop the work of God? No!"

[18]When the Jewish believers heard this, they stopped arguing. They praised God and said, "So God is allowing the non-Jewish people also to turn to him and live."

THE GOOD NEWS COMES TO ANTIOCH

[19]Many of the believers were scattered by the terrible things that happened after Stephen was killed. Some of them went to places as far away as Phoenicia, Cyprus, and Antioch. They were telling the message to others, but only to Jews. [20]Some of these believers were men from Cyprus and Cyrene. When they came to Antioch, they spoke also to Greeks,[n] telling them the Good News[d] about the Lord Jesus. [21]The Lord was helping the believers. And a large group of people believed and turned to the Lord.

[22]The church in Jerusalem heard about all of this, so they sent Barnabas to Antioch. [23-24]Barnabas was a good man, full of the Holy Spirit[d] and full of faith. When he reached Antioch and saw how God had blessed the people, he was glad. He encouraged all the believers in Antioch. He told them, "Never lose your faith. Always obey the Lord with all your hearts." Many people became followers of the Lord.

[25]Then Barnabas went to the city of Tarsus to look for Saul. [26]When he found Saul, he brought him to Antioch. And for a whole year Saul and Barnabas met with the church. They taught many people there. In Antioch the followers

were called Christians for the first time.

[27]About that time some prophets[d] came from Jerusalem to Antioch. [28]One of them was named Agabus. He stood up and spoke with the help of the Holy Spirit. He said, "A very hard time is coming to the whole world. There will be no food for people to eat." (This happened when Claudius ruled.) [29]The followers all decided to help their brothers who lived in Judea. Each one planned to send them as much as he could. [30]They gathered the money and gave it to Barnabas and Saul, who brought it to the elders[d] in Judea.

HEROD AGRIPPA HURTS THE CHURCH

12 During that same time King Herod began to do terrible things to some who belonged to the church. [2]He ordered James, the brother of John, to be killed by the sword. [3]Herod saw that the Jews liked this, so he decided to arrest Peter, too. (This happened during the time of the Feast[d] of Unleavened Bread.) [4]After Herod arrested Peter, he put him in jail and handed him over to be guarded by 16 soldiers. Herod planned to bring Peter before the people for trial after the Passover[d] Feast. [5]So Peter was kept in jail. But the church kept on praying to God for him.

PETER LEAVES THE JAIL

[6]The night before Herod was to bring him to trial, Peter was sleeping. He was between two soldiers, bound with two chains. Other soldiers were guarding the door of the jail. [7]Suddenly, an angel of the Lord stood there. A light shined in the room. The angel touched Peter on the side and woke him up. The angel said, "Hurry! Get up!" And the chains fell off Peter's hands. [8]The angel said to him, "Get dressed and put on your sandals." And so Peter did this. Then the angel said, "Put on your coat and follow me." [9]So the angel went out, and Peter

---

11:20 Greeks Some Greek copies read "Hellenists," non-Greeks who spoke Greek.

followed him. Peter did not know if what the angel was doing was real. He thought he might be seeing a vision. [10]They went past the first and the second guard. They came to the iron gate that separated them from the city. The gate opened itself for them. They went through the gate and walked down a street. And the angel suddenly left him.

[11]Then Peter realized what had happened. He thought, "Now I know that the Lord really sent his angel to me. He rescued me from Herod and from all the things the Jewish people thought would happen."

[12]When he realized this, he went to the home of Mary. She was the mother of John. (John was also called Mark.) Many people were gathered there, praying. [13]Peter knocked on the outside door. A servant girl named Rhoda came to answer it. [14]She recognized Peter's voice, and she was very happy. She even forgot to open the door. She ran inside and told the group, "Peter is at the door!"

[15]They said to her, "You are crazy!" But she kept on saying that it was true. So they said, "It must be Peter's angel."

[16]Peter continued to knock. When they opened the door, they saw him and were amazed. [17]Peter made a sign with his hand to tell them to be quiet. He explained how the Lord led him out of the jail. And he said, "Tell James and the other believers what happened." Then he left to go to another place.

[18]The next day the soldiers were very upset. They wondered what had happened to Peter. [19]Herod looked everywhere for Peter but could not find him. So he questioned the guards and ordered that they be killed.

THE DEATH OF HEROD AGRIPPA

Later Herod moved from Judea and went to the city of Caesarea, where he stayed for a while. [20]Herod was very angry with the people of Tyre and Sidon. But the people of those cities all came in a group to Herod. They were able to get Blastus, the king's personal servant, on their side. They asked Herod for peace because their country got its food from his country.

[21]On a chosen day Herod put on his royal robes. He sat on his throne and made a speech to the people. [22]They shouted, "This is the voice of a god, not a man!" [23]Herod did not give the glory to God. So an angel of the Lord caused him to become sick. He was eaten by worms and died.

[24]God's message continued to spread and reach more and more people.

[25]After Barnabas and Saul finished their task in Jerusalem, they returned to Antioch. John, also called Mark, was with them.

BARNABAS AND SAUL ARE CHOSEN

13 In the church at Antioch there were these prophets[d] and teachers: Barnabas, Simeon (also called Niger), Lucius (from the city of Cyrene), Manaen (who had grown up with Herod, the ruler) and Saul. [2]They were all worshiping the Lord and giving up eating.[n] The Holy Spirit[d] said to them, "Give Barnabas and Saul to me to do a special work. I have chosen them for it."

[3]So they gave up eating and prayed. They laid their hands on[n] Barnabas and Saul and sent them out.

BARNABAS AND SAUL IN CYPRUS

[4]Barnabas and Saul were sent out by the Holy Spirit.[d] They went to the city of Seleucia. From there they sailed to the island of Cyprus. [5]When they came to Salamis, they preached the Good News[d] of God in the Jewish synagogues.[d] John Mark was with them to help.

13:2 giving up eating This is called "fasting." The people would give up eating for a special time of prayer and worship to God. It was also done to show sadness.
13:3 laid their hands on Here, this was a sign to show that these men were given a special work of God.

⁶They went across the whole island to Paphos. In Paphos they met a Jew who was a magician. His name was Bar-Jesus. He was a false prophet,[d] ⁷who always stayed close to Sergius Paulus, the governor. Sergius Paulus was a smart man. He asked Barnabas and Saul to come to him, because he wanted to hear the message of God. ⁸But Elymas, the magician, was against them. (Elymas is the name for Bar-Jesus in the Greek language.) He tried to stop the governor from believing in Jesus. ⁹But Saul was filled with the Holy Spirit. (Saul's other name was Paul.) He looked straight at Elymas ¹⁰and said, "You son of the devil! You are an enemy of everything that is right! You are full of evil tricks and lies. You are always trying to change the Lord's truths into lies! ¹¹Now the Lord will touch you, and you will be blind. For a time you will not be able to see anything—not even the light from the sun."

Then everything became dark for Elymas. He walked around, trying to find someone to lead him by the hand. ¹²When the governor saw this, he believed. He was amazed at the teaching about the Lord.

PAUL AND BARNABAS LEAVE CYPRUS

¹³Paul and those with him sailed away from Paphos. They came to Perga, in Pamphylia. But John Mark left them and returned to Jerusalem. ¹⁴They continued their trip from Perga and went to Antioch, a city in Pisidia. On the Sabbath[d] day they went into the synagogue[d] and sat down. ¹⁵The law of Moses and the writings of the prophets[d] were read. Then the leaders of the synagogue sent a message to Paul and Barnabas: "Brothers, if you have any message that will encourage the people, please speak!"

¹⁶Paul stood up. He raised his hand and said, "Men of Israel and you other people who worship God, please listen! ¹⁷The God of the people of Israel chose our ancestors. He made the people great during the time they lived in Egypt. He brought them out of that country with great power. ¹⁸And he was patient with them[n] for 40 years in the desert. ¹⁹God destroyed seven nations in the land of Canaan and gave the land to his people. ²⁰All this happened in about 450 years.

"After this, God gave them judges until the time of Samuel the prophet. ²¹Then the people asked for a king. God gave them Saul son of Kish. Saul was from the tribe[d] of Benjamin. He was king for 40 years. ²²After God took him away, God made David their king. This is what God said about him: 'I have found David son of Jesse. He is the kind of man I want. He will do all that I want him to do.' ²³So God has brought one of David's descendants[d] to Israel to be their Savior.[d] That descendant is Jesus. And God promised to do this. ²⁴Before Jesus came, John[n] preached to all the people of Israel. He told them about a baptism of changed hearts and lives. ²⁵When he was finishing his work, he said, 'Who do you think I am? I am not the Christ.[d] He is coming later. I am not worthy to untie his sandals.'

²⁶"Brothers, sons in the family of Abraham, and you non-Jews who worship God, listen! The news about this salvation has been sent to us. ²⁷Those who live in Jerusalem and their leaders did not realize that Jesus was the Savior. They did not understand the words that the prophets wrote, which are read every Sabbath[d] day. But they made them come true when they said Jesus was guilty. ²⁸They could not find any real reason for Jesus to die, but they asked Pilate to have him killed. ²⁹They did to him all that the Scriptures[d] had said. Then they took

him down from the cross and laid him in a tomb. [30]But God raised him up from death! [31]After this, for many days, the people who had gone with Jesus from Galilee to Jerusalem saw him. They are now his witnesses to the people. [32]We tell you the Good News[d] about the promise God made to our ancestors. [33]We are their children, and God has made this promise come true for us. God did this by raising Jesus from death. We read about this also in Psalm 2:

'You are my Son.

Today I have become your Father.'
Psalm 2:7

[34]God raised Jesus from death. He will never go back to the grave and become dust. So God said:

'I will give you the holy and sure blessings

that I promised to David.'
Isaiah 55:3

[35]But in another place God says:

'You will not let your Holy One

rot in the grave.' *Psalm 16:10*

[36]David did God's will during his lifetime. Then he died and was buried with his fathers. And his body did rot in the grave! [37]But the One God raised from death did not rot in the grave. [38-39]Brothers, you must understand what we are telling you: You can have forgiveness of your sins through Jesus. The law of Moses could not free you from your sins. But everyone who believes is free from all sins through him. [40]Be careful! Don't let what the prophets said happen to you:

[41]'Listen, you people who doubt!

You can wonder, and then die.

I will do something in your lifetime

that will amaze you.

You won't believe it even when you

are told about it!'" *Habakkuk 1:5*

[42]While Paul and Barnabas were leaving the synagogue, the people asked them to tell them more about these things on the next Sabbath. [43]After the meeting, many Jews followed Paul and Barnabas from that place. With the Jews there were many who had changed to the Jewish religion and worshiped God. Paul and Barnabas were persuading them to continue trusting in God's kindness.

[44]On the next Sabbath day, almost all the people in the city came to hear the word of the Lord. [45]Seeing the crowd, the Jews became very jealous. They said insulting things and argued against what Paul said. [46]But Paul and Barnabas spoke very boldly. They said, "We must speak the message of God to you first. But you refuse to listen. You are judging yourselves not worthy of having eternal life! So we will now go to the people of other nations! [47]This is what the Lord told us to do. The Lord said:

'I have made you a light for the

non-Jewish nations.

You will show people all over the

world the way to be saved.'"
Isaiah 49:6

[48]When the non-Jewish people heard Paul say this, they were happy. They gave honor to the message of the Lord. And many of the people believed the message. They were the ones chosen to have life forever.

[49]And so the message of the Lord was spreading through the whole country. [50]But the Jews stirred up some of the important religious women and the leaders of the city against Paul and Barnabas. They started trouble against Paul and Barnabas and drove them out of their area. [51]So Paul and Barnabas shook the dust off their feet[n] and went to Iconium. [52]But the followers were filled with joy and the Holy Spirit.[d]

PAUL AND BARNABAS IN ICONIUM

14 In Iconium, Paul and Barnabas went as usual to the Jewish synagogue.[d] They spoke so well that a great

---

13:51 **shook ... feet** A warning. It showed that they were finished talking to these people.

many Jews and Greeks believed. [2]But some of the Jews who did not believe excited the non-Jewish people and turned them against the believers. [3]But Paul and Barnabas stayed in Iconium a long time and spoke bravely for the Lord. The Lord showed that their message about his grace was true by giving them the power to work miracles[d] and signs. [4]But some of the people in the city agreed with the Jews. Others believed the apostles.[d] So the city was divided.

[5]Some non-Jewish people, some Jews, and some of their rulers wanted to harm Paul and Barnabas by killing them with stones. [6]When Paul and Barnabas learned about this, they went to Lystra and Derbe, cities in Lycaonia, and to the areas around those cities. [7]They announced the Good News[d] there, too.

PAUL IN LYSTRA AND DERBE

[8]In Lystra there sat a man who had been born crippled; he had never walked. [9]This man was listening to Paul speak. Paul looked straight at him and saw that the man believed God could heal him. [10]So he cried out, "Stand up on your feet!" The man jumped up and began walking around. [11]When the crowds saw what Paul did, they shouted in their own Lycaonian language. They said, "The gods have become like men! They have come down to us!" [12]And the people began to call Barnabas "Zeus."[n] They called Paul "Hermes,"[n] because he was the main speaker. [13]The temple of Zeus was near the city. The priest of this temple brought some bulls and flowers to the city gates. The priest and the people wanted to offer a sacrifice to Paul and Barnabas. [14]But when the apostles,[d] Barnabas and Paul, understood what they were about to do, they tore their clothes in anger.

Then they ran in among the people and shouted, [15]"Men, why are you doing these things? We are only men, human beings like you! We are bringing you the Good News.[d] We are telling you to turn away from these worthless things and turn to the true living God. He is the One who made the sky, the earth, the sea, and everything that is in them. [16]In the past, God let all the nations do what they wanted. [17]Yet he did things to prove he is real: He shows kindness to you. He gives you rain from heaven and crops at the right times. He gives you food and fills your hearts with joy." [18]Even with these words, they were barely able to keep the crowd from offering sacrifices to them.

[19]Then some Jews came from Antioch and Iconium. They persuaded the people to turn against Paul. And so they threw stones at Paul and dragged him out of town. They thought that they had killed him. [20]But the followers gathered around him, and he got up and went back into the town. The next day, he and Barnabas left and went to the city of Derbe.

THE RETURN TO ANTIOCH IN SYRIA

[21]Paul and Barnabas told the Good News[d] in Derbe and many became followers. Paul and Barnabas returned to Lystra, Iconium, and Antioch. [22]In those cities they made the followers of Jesus stronger. They helped them to stay in the faith. They said, "We must suffer many things to enter God's kingdom." [23]They chose elders[d] for each church, by praying and giving up eating.[n] These elders were men who had trusted the Lord. So Paul and Barnabas put them in the Lord's care.

[24]Then they went through Pisidia and came to Pamphylia. [25]They preached the message in Perga, and then they went

14:12 **"Zeus"** The Greeks believed in many gods. Zeus was their most important god.
14:12 **"Hermes"** The Greeks believed he was a messenger for the other gods.
14:23 **giving up eating** This is called "fasting." The people would give up eating for a special time of prayer and worship to God. It was also done to show sadness.

down to Attalia. [26]And from there they sailed away to Antioch. This is where the believers had put them into God's care and had sent them out to do this work. And now they had finished the work.

[27]When they arrived in Antioch, they gathered the church together. Paul and Barnabas told them all about what God had done with them. They told how God had made it possible for the non-Jews to believe! [28]And they stayed there a long time with the followers.

THE MEETING AT JERUSALEM

15 Then some men came to Antioch from Judea. They began teaching the non-Jewish brothers: "You cannot be saved if you are not circumcised.[d] Moses taught us to do this." [2]Paul and Barnabas were against this teaching and argued with the men about it. So the group decided to send Paul, Barnabas, and some other men to Jerusalem. There they could talk more about this with the apostles[d] and elders.[d]

[3]The church helped the men leave on the trip. They went through the countries of Phoenicia and Samaria, telling all about how the non-Jewish people had turned to God. This made all the believers very happy. [4]When they arrived in Jerusalem, the apostles, the elders, and the church welcomed them. Paul, Barnabas, and the others told about all the things that God had done with them. [5]But some of the believers who had belonged to the Pharisee[d] group came forward. They said, "The non-Jewish believers must be circumcised. We must tell them to obey the law of Moses!"

[6]The apostles and the elders gathered to study this problem. [7]There was a long debate. Then Peter stood up and said to them, "Brothers, you know what happened in the early days. God chose me from among you to preach the Good News[d] to the non-Jewish people. They heard the Good News from me, and they believed. [8]God, who knows the thoughts of all men, accepted them. He showed this to us by giving them the Holy Spirit,[d] just as he did to us. [9]To God, those people are not different from us. When they believed, he made their hearts pure. [10]So now why are you testing God? You are putting a heavy load around the necks of the non-Jewish brothers. It is a load that neither we nor our fathers were able to carry. [11]But we believe that we and they too will be saved by the grace of the Lord Jesus!"

[12]Then the whole group became quiet. They listened to Paul and Barnabas speak. Paul and Barnabas told about all the miracles[d] and signs that God did through them among the non-Jewish people. [13]After they finished speaking, James spoke. He said, "Brothers, listen to me. [14]Simon has told us how God showed his love for the non-Jewish people. For the first time he has accepted them and made them his people. [15]The words of the prophets[d] agree with this too:

[16]'After these things I will return.

The kingdom of David is like a
    fallen tent.
But I will rebuild it.
    And I will again build its ruins.
    And I will set it up.
[17]Then those people who are left alive
    may ask the Lord for help.
And all people from other nations
    may worship me,
says the Lord.
    And he will make it happen.
[18]   And these things have been known
    for a long time.'　　*Amos 9:11-12*

[19]"So I think we should not bother the non-Jewish brothers who have turned to God. [20]Instead, we should write a letter to them. We should tell them these things: Do not eat food that has been offered to idols. (This makes the food unclean.[d]) Do not take part in any kind of sexual sin. Do not taste blood. Do not eat animals that have been strangled. [21]They should not do these things, because

there are still men in every city who teach the law of Moses. For a long time the words of Moses have been read in the synagogue[d] every Sabbath[d] day."

LETTER TO NON-JEWISH BELIEVERS

[22]The apostles,[d] the elders,[d] and the whole church decided to send some of their men with Paul and Barnabas to Antioch. They chose Judas Barsabbas and Silas, who were respected by the believers. [23]They sent the following letter with them:

From the apostles and elders, your brothers.

To all the non-Jewish brothers in Antioch, Syria and Cilicia:

Dear Brothers,

[24]We have heard that some of our men have come to you and said things that trouble and upset you. But we did not tell them to do this! [25]We have all agreed to choose some men and send them to you. They will be with our dear friends Barnabas and Paul— [26]men who have given their lives to serve our Lord Jesus Christ. [27]So we have sent Judas and Silas with them. They will tell you the same things. [28]It has pleased the Holy Spirit[d] that you should not have a heavy load to carry, and we agree. You need to do only these things: [29]Do not eat any food that has been offered to idols. Do not taste blood. Do not eat any animals that have been strangled. Do not take part in any kind of sexual sin. If you stay away from these things, you will do well.

Good-bye.

[30]So the men left Jerusalem and went to Antioch. There they gathered the church and gave them the letter. [31]When they read it, they were very happy because of the encouraging letter. [32]Judas and Silas were also prophets,[d] who said many things to encourage the believers and make them stronger. [33]After some time Judas and Silas were sent off in peace by the believers. They went back to those who had sent them. [34][But Silas decided to remain there.][n]

[35]But Paul and Barnabas stayed in Antioch. They and many others preached the Good News[d] and taught the people the message of the Lord.

PAUL AND BARNABAS SEPARATE

[36]After some time, Paul said to Barnabas, "We preached the message of the Lord in many towns. We should go back to all those towns to visit the believers and see how they are doing."

[37]Barnabas wanted to take John Mark with them too. [38]But John Mark had left them at Pamphylia; he did not continue with them in the work. So Paul did not think it was a good idea to take him. [39]Paul and Barnabas had a serious argument about this. They separated and went different ways. Barnabas sailed to Cyprus and took Mark with him. [40]But Paul chose Silas and left. The believers in Antioch put Paul into the Lord's care. [41]And he went through Syria and Cilicia, giving strength to the churches.

TIMOTHY GOES WITH PAUL AND SILAS

16 Paul came to Derbe and Lystra. A follower named Timothy was there. Timothy's mother was Jewish and a believer. His father was a Greek. [2]The brothers in Lystra and Iconium respected Timothy and said good things about him. [3]Paul wanted Timothy to travel with him. But all the Jews living in that area knew that Timothy's father was Greek. So Paul circumcised[d] Timothy to please the Jews. [4]Paul and the men with him traveled from town to town. They gave the decisions made by the apostles[d] and elders[d] in Jerusalem for the people to obey. [5]So the churches became stronger in the faith and grew larger every day.

15:34 But . . . there. Some Greek copies do not contain the bracketed text.

PAUL IS CALLED OUT OF ASIA

[6]Paul and the men with him went through the areas of Phrygia and Galatia. The Holy Spirit[d] did not let them preach the Good News[d] in Asia. [7]When they came near the country of Mysia, they tried to go into Bithynia. But the Spirit of Jesus did not let them. [8]So they passed by Mysia and went to Troas. [9]That night Paul had a vision. In the vision, a man from Macedonia came to him. The man stood there and begged, "Come over to Macedonia. Help us!" [10]After Paul had seen the vision, we immediately prepared to leave for Macedonia. We understood that God had called us to tell the Good News to those people.

LYDIA BECOMES A CHRISTIAN

[11]We left Troas in a ship, and we sailed straight to the island of Samothrace. The next day we sailed to Neapolis.[n] [12]Then we went by land to Philippi, the leading city in that part of Macedonia. It is also a Roman colony.[n] We stayed there for several days.

[13]On the Sabbath[d] day we went outside the city gate to the river. There we thought we would find a special place for prayer. Some women had gathered there, so we sat down and talked with them. [14]There was a woman named Lydia from the city of Thyatira. Her job was selling purple cloth. She worshiped the true God. The Lord opened her mind to pay attention to what Paul was saying. [15]She and all the people in her house were baptized. Then Lydia invited us to her home. She said, "If you think I am truly a believer in the Lord, then come stay in my house." And she persuaded us to stay with her.

PAUL AND SILAS IN JAIL

[16]Once, while we were going to the place for prayer, a servant girl met us. She had a special spirit[n] in her. She earned a lot of money for her owners by telling fortunes. [17]This girl followed Paul and us. She said loudly, "These men are servants of the Most High God! They are telling you how you can be saved!"

[18]She kept this up for many days. This bothered Paul, so he turned and said to the spirit, "By the power of Jesus Christ, I command you to come out of her!" Immediately, the spirit came out.

[19]The owners of the servant girl saw this. These men knew that now they could not use her to make money. So they grabbed Paul and Silas and dragged them before the city rulers in the marketplace. [20]Here they brought Paul and Silas to the Roman rulers and said, "These men are Jews and are making trouble in our city. [21]They are teaching things that are not right for us as Romans to do."

[22]The crowd joined the attack against them. The Roman officers tore the clothes of Paul and Silas and had them beaten with rods again and again. [23]Then Paul and Silas were thrown into jail. The jailer was ordered to guard them carefully. [24]When he heard this order, he put them far inside the jail. He pinned down their feet between large blocks of wood.

[25]About midnight Paul and Silas were praying and singing songs to God. The other prisoners were listening to them. [26]Suddenly, there was a big earthquake. It was so strong that it shook the foundation of the jail. Then all the doors of the jail broke open. All the prisoners were freed from their chains. [27]The jailer woke up and saw that the jail doors were open. He thought that the prisoners had already escaped. So he got his sword and was about to kill himself.[n] [28]But Paul shouted, "Don't hurt yourself! We are all here!"

[29]The jailer told someone to bring a light. Then he ran inside. Shaking with fear, he fell down before Paul and Silas.

16:11 Neapolis City in Macedonia. It was the first city Paul visited on the continent of Europe.
16:12 Roman colony A town begun by Romans with Roman laws, customs and privileges.
16:16 spirit This was a spirit from the devil. It caused her to say she had special knowledge.
16:27 kill himself He thought the leaders would kill him for letting the prisoners escape.

30Then he brought them outside and said, "Men, what must I do to be saved?" 31They said to him, "Believe in the Lord Jesus and you will be saved—you and all the people in your house." 32So Paul and Silas told the message of the Lord to the jailer and all the people in his house. 33At that hour of the night the jailer took Paul and Silas and washed their wounds. Then he and all his people were baptized immediately. 34After this the jailer took Paul and Silas home and gave them food. He and his family were very happy because they now believed in God.

35The next morning, the Roman officers sent the police to tell the jailer, "Let these men go free!" 36The jailer said to Paul, "The officers have sent an order to let you go free. You can leave now. Go in peace." 37But Paul said to the police, "They beat us in public without a trial, even though we are Roman citizens.[n] And they threw us in jail. Now they want to make us go away quietly. No! Let them come themselves and bring us out!" 38The police told the Roman officers what Paul said. When the officers heard that Paul and Silas were Roman citizens, they were afraid. 39So they came and told Paul and Silas they were sorry. They took Paul and Silas out of jail and asked them to leave the city. 40So when they came out of the jail, they went to Lydia's house. There they saw some of the believers and encouraged them. Then they left.

PAUL AND SILAS IN THESSALONICA

17 Paul and Silas traveled through Amphipolis and Apollonia and came to Thessalonica. In that city there was a Jewish synagogue.[d] 2Paul went into the synagogue as he always did. On each Sabbath[d] day for three weeks, Paul talked with the Jews about the Scriptures.[d] 3He explained and proved that the Christ[d]

must die and then rise from death. He said, "This Jesus I am telling you about is the Christ." 4Some of the Jews were convinced and joined Paul and Silas. Many of the Greeks who worshiped the true God and many of the important women joined them.

5But the Jews became jealous. They got some evil men from the marketplace, formed a mob and started a riot. They ran to Jason's house, looking for Paul and Silas. The men wanted to bring Paul and Silas out to the people. 6But they did not find them. So they dragged Jason and some other believers to the leaders of the city. The people were yelling, "These men have made trouble everywhere in the world. And now they have come here too! 7Jason is keeping them in his house. All of them do things against the laws of Caesar.[d] They say that there is another king called Jesus." 8When the people and the leaders of the city heard these things, they became very upset. 9They made Jason and the others put up a sum of money. Then they let the believers go free.

PAUL AND SILAS GO TO BEREA

10That same night the believers sent Paul and Silas to Berea. There Paul and Silas went to the Jewish synagogue.[d] 11These Jews were better than the Jews in Thessalonica. They were eager to hear the things Paul and Silas said. These Jews in Berea studied the Scriptures[d] every day to find out if these things were true. 12So, many of them believed. Many important Greek men and women also believed. 13But when the Jews in Thessalonica learned that Paul was preaching the word of God in Berea, they came there, too. They upset the people and made trouble. 14So the believers quickly sent Paul away to the coast. But Silas and Timothy stayed in Berea. 15The men who took Paul went with him to Athens.

16:37 Roman citizens Roman law said that Roman citizens must not be beaten before they had a trial.

Then they carried a message from Paul back to Silas and Timothy. It said, "Come to me as soon as you can."

PAUL IN ATHENS

[16]Paul was waiting for Silas and Timothy in Athens. He was troubled because he saw that the city was full of idols. [17]In the synagogue,[d] he talked with the Jews and the Greeks who worshiped the true God. He also talked every day with people in the marketplace.

[18]Some of the Epicurean and Stoic philosophers[n] argued with him. Some of them said, "This man doesn't know what he is talking about. What is he trying to say?" Paul was telling them the Good News[d] of Jesus' rising from death. They said, "He seems to be telling us about some other gods." [19]They got Paul and took him to a meeting of the Areopagus.[n] They said, "Please explain to us this new idea that you have been teaching. [20]The things you are saying are new to us. We want to know what this teaching means." [21](All the people of Athens and those from other countries always used their time talking about all the newest ideas.)

[22]Then Paul stood before the meeting of the Areopagus. He said, "Men of Athens, I can see that you are very religious in all things. [23]I was going through your city, and I saw the things you worship. I found an altar that had these words written on it: "TO A GOD WHO IS NOT KNOWN." You worship a god that you don't know. This is the God I am telling you about! [24]He is the God who made the whole world and everything in it. He is the Lord of the land and the sky. He does not live in temples that men build! [25]This God is the One who gives life, breath, and everything else to people. He does not need any help from them. He has everything he needs. [26]God began by making one man. From him came all the different people who live everywhere in the world. He decided exactly when and where they must live. [27]God wanted them to look for him and perhaps search all around for him and find him. But he is not far from any of us: [28]'By his power we live and move and exist.' Some of your own poets have said: 'For we are his children.' [29]We are God's children. So, you must not think that God is like something that people imagine or make. He is not like gold, silver, or rock. [30]In the past, people did not understand God, but God ignored this. But now, God tells everyone in the world to change his heart and life. [31]God has decided on a day that he will judge all the world. He will be fair. He will use a man to do this. God chose that man long ago. And God has proved this to everyone by raising that man from death!"

[32]When the people heard about Jesus being raised from death, some of them laughed. They said, "We will hear more about this from you later." [33]So Paul went away from them. [34]But some of the people believed Paul and joined him. One of those who believed was Dionysius, a member of the Areopagus. Also a woman named Damaris and some others believed.

PAUL IN CORINTH

18 Later, Paul left Athens and went to Corinth. [2]Here he met a Jew named Aquila. Aquila was born in the country of Pontus. But Aquila and his wife, Priscilla, had recently moved to Corinth from Italy. They left Italy because Claudius[n] commanded that all Jews must leave Rome. Paul went to visit

---

17:18 Epicurean and Stoic philosophers Philosophers were those who searched for truth. Epicureans believed that pleasure, especially pleasures of the mind, were the goal of life. Stoics believed that life should be without feelings of joy or grief.
17:19 Areopagus A council or group of important leaders in Athens. They were like judges.
18:2 Claudius The emperor (ruler) of Rome, A.D. 41-54.

Aquila and Priscilla. [3]They were tent-makers, just as he was. He stayed with them and worked with them. [4]Every Sabbath[d] day he talked with the Jews and Greeks in the synagogue.[d] Paul tried to persuade these people to believe in Jesus.

[5]Silas and Timothy came from Macedonia and joined Paul in Corinth. After this, Paul used all his time telling people the Good News.[d] He showed the Jews that Jesus is the Christ.[d] [6]But they would not accept Paul's teaching and said some evil things. So he shook off the dust from his clothes.[n] He said to them, "If you are not saved, it will be your own fault! I have done all I can do! After this, I will go to non-Jewish people!" [7]Paul left the synagogue and moved into the home of Titius Justus. It was next to the synagogue. This man worshiped the true God. [8]Crispus was the leader of that synagogue. He and all the people living in his house believed in the Lord. Many others in Corinth also listened to Paul. They too believed and were baptized.

[9]During the night, Paul had a vision. The Lord said to him, "Don't be afraid! Continue talking to people and don't be quiet! [10]I am with you. No one will hurt you because many of my people are in this city." [11]Paul stayed there for a year and a half, teaching God's word to the people.

PAUL IS BROUGHT BEFORE GALLIO

[12]Gallio became the governor of the country of Southern Greece. At that time, some of the Jews came together against Paul and took him to the court. [13]They said to Gallio, "This man is teaching people to worship God in a way that is against our law!"

[14]Paul was about to say something, but Gallio spoke to the Jews. Gallio said, "I would listen to you Jews if you were complaining about a crime or some wrong. [15]But the things you are saying are only questions about words and names—arguments about your own law. So you must solve this problem yourselves. I don't want to be a judge of these things!" [16]Then Gallio made them leave the court. [17]Then they all grabbed Sosthenes. (Sosthenes was now the leader of the synagogue.[d]) They beat him there before the court. But this did not bother Gallio.

PAUL RETURNS TO ANTIOCH

[18]Paul stayed with the believers for many more days. Then he left and sailed for Syria. Priscilla and Aquila went with him. At Cenchrea, Paul cut off his hair.[n] This showed that he had made a promise to God. [19]Then they went to Ephesus, where Paul left Priscilla and Aquila. While Paul was there, he went into the synagogue[d] and talked with the Jews. [20]When they asked him to stay with them longer, he refused. [21]He left them, but he said, "I will come back to you again if God wants me to." And so he sailed away from Ephesus.

[22]Paul landed at Caesarea. Then he went and gave greetings to the church in Jerusalem. After that, Paul went to Antioch. [23]He stayed there for a while and then left and went through the countries of Galatia and Phrygia. He traveled from town to town in these countries, giving strength to all the followers.

APOLLOS IN EPHESUS AND CORINTH

[24]A Jew named Apollos came to Ephesus. He was born in the city of Alexandria. He was an educated man who knew the Scriptures[d] well. [25]He had been taught about the Lord. He was always very excited when he spoke and taught the truth about Jesus. But the only baptism that Apollos knew about was the baptism that John[n] taught. [26]Apollos began to speak very boldly in the synagogue,[d] and Priscilla and Aquila heard

---

18:6 **shook . . . clothes** This was a warning. It showed that Paul was finished talking to the Jews.
18:18 **cut . . . hair** Jews did this to show that the time of a special promise to God was finished.
18:25 **John** John the Baptist, who preached to people about Christ's coming (Matthew 3, Luke 3).

him. So they took him to their home and helped him better understand the way of God. ²⁷Now Apollos wanted to go to the country of Southern Greece, so the believers helped him. They wrote a letter to the followers there, asking them to accept him. These followers had believed in Jesus because of God's grace. When Apollos went there, he helped them very much. ²⁸He argued very strongly with the Jews before all the people. Apollos clearly proved that the Jews were wrong. Using the Scriptures, he proved that Jesus is the Christ.ᵈ

PAUL IN EPHESUS

19 While Apollos was in Corinth, Paul was visiting some places on the way to Ephesus. There he found some followers. ²Paul asked them, "Did you receive the Holy Spiritᵈ when you believed?"

They said, "We have never even heard of a Holy Spirit!"

³So he asked, "What kind of baptism did you have?"

They said, "It was the baptism that Johnⁿ taught."

⁴Paul said, "John's baptism was a baptism of changed hearts and lives. He told people to believe in the One who would come after him. That One is Jesus."

⁵When they heard this, they were baptized in the name of the Lord Jesus. ⁶Then Paul laid his hands on them,ⁿ and the Holy Spirit came upon them. They began speaking different languages and prophesying.ᵈ ⁷There were about 12 men in this group.

⁸Paul went into the synagogueᵈ and spoke out boldly for three months. He talked with the Jews and persuaded them to accept the things he said about the kingdom of God. ⁹But some of the Jews became stubborn and refused to believe. These Jews said evil things about the Way of Jesus. All the people heard these things. So Paul left them and took the followers with him. He went to a place where a man named Tyrannus had a school. There Paul talked with people every day ¹⁰for two years. Because of his work, every Jew and Greek in Asia heard the word of the Lord.

THE SONS OF SCEVA

¹¹God used Paul to do some very special miracles.ᵈ ¹²Some people took handkerchiefs and clothes that Paul had used and put them on the sick. When they did this, the sick were healed and evil spirits left them.

¹³⁻¹⁴But some Jews also were traveling around and making evil spirits go out of people. The seven sons of Sceva were doing this. (Sceva was a leading Jewish priest.) These Jews tried to use the name of the Lord Jesus to force the evil spirits out. They would say, "By the same Jesus that Paul talks about, I order you to come out!"

¹⁵But one time an evil spirit said to these Jews, "I know Jesus, and I know about Paul, but who are you?"

¹⁶Then the man, who had the evil spirit in him, jumped on these Jews. He was much stronger than all of them. He beat them and tore their clothes off, so they ran away from the house. ¹⁷All the people in Ephesus, Jews and Greeks, learned about this. They were filled with fear. And the people gave great honor to the Lord Jesus. ¹⁸Many of the believers began to confess openly and tell all the evil things they had done. ¹⁹Some of them had used magic. These believers brought their magic books and burned them before everyone. Those books were worth about 50,000 silver coins.ⁿ

19:3 John John the Baptist, who preached to people about Christ's coming (Matthew 3, Luke 3).
19:6 laid his hands on them Here, doing this was a sign to show that Paul had God's authority or power to give these people special powers of the Holy Spirit.
19:19 50,000 silver coins Probably drachmas. One coin was enough to pay a man for working one day.

²⁰So in a powerful way the word of the Lord kept spreading and growing.

PAUL PLANS A TRIP

²¹After these things, Paul made plans to go to Jerusalem. He planned to go through the countries of Macedonia and Southern Greece, and then on to Jerusalem. He said, "After I have been to Jerusalem, I must also visit Rome." ²²Paul sent Timothy and Erastus, two of his helpers, ahead to Macedonia. He himself stayed in Asia for a while.

TROUBLE IN EPHESUS

²³But during that time, there was some serious trouble in Ephesus about the Way of Jesus. ²⁴There was a man named Demetrius, who worked with silver. He made little silver models that looked like the temple of the goddess Artemis.ⁿ The men who did this work made much money. ²⁵Demetrius had a meeting with these men and some others who did the same kind of work. He told them, "Men, you know that we make a lot of money from our business. ²⁶But look at what this man Paul is doing! He has convinced and turned away many people in Ephesus and in almost all of Asia! He says the gods that men make are not real. ²⁷There is a danger that our business will lose its good name. But there is also another danger: People will begin to think that the temple of the great goddess Artemis is not important! Her greatness will be destroyed. And Artemis is the goddess that everyone in Asia and the whole world worships."

²⁸When the men heard this, they became very angry. They shouted, "Artemis, the goddess of Ephesus, is great!" ²⁹The whole city became confused. The people grabbed Gaius and Aristarchus. (These two men were from Macedonia and were traveling with Paul.) Then all the people ran to the theater. ³⁰Paul wanted to go in and talk to the crowd, but the followers did not let him. ³¹Also, some leaders of Asia were friends of Paul. They sent him a message, begging him not to go into the theater. ³²Some people were shouting one thing, and some were shouting another. The meeting was completely confused. Most of the people did not know why they had come together. ³³The Jews put a man named Alexander in front of the people. Some of them had told him what to do. Alexander waved his hand because he wanted to explain things to the people. ³⁴But when they saw that Alexander was a Jew, they all began shouting the same thing. They continued shouting for two hours: "Great is Artemis of Ephesus!"

³⁵Then the city clerk made the crowd be quiet. He said, "Men of Ephesus, everyone knows that Ephesus is the city that keeps the temple of the great goddess Artemis. All people know that we also keep her holy stoneⁿ that fell from heaven. ³⁶No one can say that this is not true. So you should be quiet. You must stop and think before you do anything. ³⁷You brought these men here, but they have not said anything evil against our goddess. They have not stolen anything from her temple. ³⁸We have courts of law, and there are judges. Do Demetrius and the men who work with him have a charge against anyone? They should go to the courts! That is where they can argue with each other! ³⁹Is there something else you want to talk about? It can be decided at the regular town meeting of the people. ⁴⁰I say this because some people might see this trouble today and say that we are rioting. We could not explain this because there is no real reason for this meeting." ⁴¹After the city clerk said these things, he told the people to go home.

19:24 **Artemis** A Greek goddess that the people of Asia Minor worshiped.
19:35 **holy stone** Probably a meteorite or stone that the people thought looked like Artemis.

PAUL IN MACEDONIA AND GREECE

20 When the trouble stopped, Paul sent for the followers to come to him. He encouraged them and then told them good-bye. Paul left and went to the country of Macedonia. [2]He said many things to strengthen the followers in the different places on his way through Macedonia. Then he went to Southern Greece. [3]He stayed there three months. He was ready to sail for Syria, but some Jews were planning something against him. So Paul decided to go back through Macedonia to Syria. [4]Some men went with him. They were Sopater son of Pyrrhus, from the city of Berea; Aristarchus and Secundus, from the city of Thessalonica; Gaius, from Derbe; and Timothy; and Tychicus and Trophimus, two men from Asia. [5]These men went first, ahead of Paul, and waited for us at Troas. [6]We sailed from Philippi after the Feast[d] of Unleavened Bread and we met them in Troas five days later. We stayed there seven days.

PAUL'S LAST VISIT TO TROAS

[7]On the first day of the week,[n] we all met together to break bread.[n] Paul spoke to the group. Because he was planning to leave the next day, he kept on talking till midnight. [8]We were all together in a room upstairs, and there were many lamps in the room. [9]A young man named Eutychus was sitting in the window. As Paul continued talking, Eutychus was falling into a deep sleep. Finally, he went sound asleep and fell to the ground from the third floor. When they picked him up, he was dead. [10]Paul went down to Eutychus. He knelt down and put his arms around him. He said, "Don't worry. He is alive now." [11]Then Paul went upstairs again, broke bread, and ate. He spoke to them

a long time, until it was early morning. Then he left. [12]They took the young man home alive and were greatly comforted.

THE TRIP FROM TROAS TO MILETUS

[13]We sailed for the city of Assos. We went first, ahead of Paul. He wanted to join us on the ship there. Paul planned it this way because he wanted to go to Assos by land. [14]When he met us at Assos, we took him aboard and went to Mitylene. [15]The next day, we sailed from Mitylene and came to a place near Chios. The next day, we sailed to Samos. A day later, we reached Miletus. [16]Paul had already decided not to stop at Ephesus. He did not want to stay too long in Asia. He was hurrying to be in Jerusalem on the day of Pentecost,[d] if that was possible.

THE ELDERS FROM EPHESUS

[17]Now from Miletus Paul sent to Ephesus and called for the elders[d] of the church. [18]When they came to him, he said, "You know about my life from the first day I came to Asia. You know the way I lived all the time I was with you. [19]The Jews plotted against me. This troubled me very much. But you know that I always served the Lord. I never thought of myself first, and I often cried. [20]You know I preached to you, and I did not hold back anything that would help you. You know that I taught you in public and in your homes. [21]I warned both Jews and Greeks to change their lives and turn to God. And I told them all to believe in our Lord Jesus. [22]But now I must obey the Holy Spirit[d] and go to Jerusalem. I don't know what will happen to me there. [23]I know only that in every city the Holy Spirit tells me that troubles and even jail wait for me. [24]I don't care about my own life. The most important thing is that I complete my mission. I want to finish

---

20:7 first day of the week Sunday, which for the Jews began at sunset on our Saturday. But if in this part of Asia a different system of time was used, then the meeting was on our Sunday night.

20:7 break bread Probably the Lord's Supper, the special meal that Jesus told his followers to eat to remember him (Luke 22:14-20).

the work that the Lord Jesus gave me—to tell people the Good News*d* about God's grace.

[25]"And now, I know that none of you will ever see me again. All the time I was with you, I was preaching the kingdom of God. [26]So today I can tell you one thing that I am sure of: If any of you should be lost, I am not responsible. [27]This is because I have told you everything God wants you to know. [28]Be careful for yourselves and for all the people God has given you. The Holy Spirit gave you the work of caring for this flock. You must be like shepherds to the church of God.*n* This is the church that God bought with his own death. [29]I know that after I leave, some men will come like wild wolves and try to destroy the flock. [30]Also, men from your own group will rise up and twist the truth. They will lead away followers after them. [31]So be careful! Always remember this: For three years I never stopped warning each of you. I taught you night and day. I often cried over you.

[32]"Now I am putting you in the care of God and the message about his grace. That message is able to give you strength, and it will give you the blessings that God has for all his holy people. [33]When I was with you, I never wanted anyone's money or fine clothes. [34]You know that I always worked to take care of my own needs and the needs of those who were with me. [35]I showed you in all things that you should work as I did and help the weak. I taught you to remember the words of Jesus. He said, 'It is more blessed to give than to receive.'"

[36]When Paul had said this, he knelt down with all of them and prayed. [37-38]And they all cried because Paul had said that they would never see him again. They put their arms around him and kissed him. Then they went with him to the ship.

PAUL GOES TO JERUSALEM

21 We all said good-bye to them and left. We sailed straight to Cos island. The next day, we reached Rhodes, and from Rhodes we went to Patara. [2]There we found a ship that was going to Phoenicia. We went aboard and sailed away. [3]We sailed near the island of Cyprus. We could see it to the north, but we sailed on to Syria. We stopped at Tyre because the ship needed to unload its cargo there. [4]We found some followers in Tyre, and we stayed with them for seven days. Through the Holy Spirit*d* they warned Paul not to go to Jerusalem. [5]When we finished our visit, we left and continued our trip. All the followers, even the women and children, came outside the city with us. We all knelt down on the beach and prayed. [6]Then we said good-bye and got on the ship. The followers went back home.

[7]We continued our trip from Tyre and arrived at Ptolemais. We greeted the believers there and stayed with them for a day. [8]We left Ptolemais and went to the city of Caesarea. There we went into the home of Philip and stayed with him. Philip had the work of telling the Good News.*d* He was one of the seven helpers.*n* [9]He had four unmarried daughters who had the gift of prophesying.*d* [10]After we had been there for some time, a prophet named Agabus arrived from Judea. [11]He came to us and borrowed Paul's belt. Then he used the belt to tie his own hands and feet. He said, "The Holy Spirit says, 'This is how the Jews in Jerusalem will tie up the man who wears this belt. Then they will give him to the non-Jewish people.'"

[12]We all heard these words. So we and the people there begged Paul not to go to Jerusalem. [13]But he said, "Why are you crying and making me so sad? I am ready to be tied up in Jerusalem. And I am ready to die for the Lord Jesus!"

20:28 of God Some Greek copies read "of the Lord."
21:8 helpers The seven men chosen for a special work described in Acts 6:1-6.

¹⁴We could not persuade him to stay away from Jerusalem. So we stopped begging him and said, "We pray that what the Lord wants will be done."

¹⁵After this, we got ready and started on our way to Jerusalem. ¹⁶Some of the followers from Caesarea went with us. They took us to the home of Mnason, a man from Cyprus. Mnason was one of the first followers. They took us to his home so that we could stay with him.

PAUL VISITS JAMES

¹⁷In Jerusalem the believers were glad to see us. ¹⁸The next day, Paul went with us to visit James. All the elders[d] were there, too. ¹⁹Paul greeted them and told them everything that God had done among the non-Jewish people through him. ²⁰When they heard this, they praised God. Then they said to Paul, "Brother, you can see that many thousands of Jews have become believers. But they think it is very important to obey the law of Moses. ²¹These Jews have heard about your teaching. They heard that you tell the Jews who live among non-Jews to leave the law of Moses. They heard that you tell them not to circumcise[d] their children and not to obey Jewish customs. ²²What should we do? The Jewish believers here will learn that you have come. ²³So we will tell you what to do: Four of our men have made a promise to God. ²⁴Take these men with you and share in their cleansing ceremony.[n] Pay their expenses. Then they can shave their heads.[n] Do this and it will prove to everyone that what they have heard about you is not true. They will see that you follow the law of Moses in your own life. ²⁵We have already sent a letter to the non-Jewish believers. The letter said: 'Do not eat food that has been offered to idols. Do not taste blood. Do not eat animals that have been strangled. Do not take part in any kind of sexual sin.'"

²⁶Then Paul took the four men with him. The next day, he shared in the cleansing ceremony. Then he went to the Temple.[d] Paul announced the time when the days of the cleansing ceremony would be finished. On the last day an offering would be given for each of the men.

²⁷The seven days were almost over. But some Jews from Asia saw Paul at the Temple. They caused all the people to be upset, and they grabbed Paul. ²⁸They shouted, "Men of Israel, help us! This is the man who goes everywhere teaching things that are against the law of Moses, against our people, and against this Temple. And now he has brought some Greek men into the Temple. He has made this holy place unclean!"[d] ²⁹(The Jews said this because they had seen Trophimus with Paul in Jerusalem. Trophimus was a man from Ephesus. The Jews thought that Paul had brought him into the Temple.)

³⁰All the people in Jerusalem became very upset. They ran and took Paul and dragged him out of the Temple. The Temple doors were closed immediately. ³¹The people were about to kill Paul. Now the commander of the Roman army in Jerusalem learned that there was trouble in the whole city. ³²Immediately he ran to the place where the crowd was gathered. He brought officers and soldiers with him, and the people saw them. So they stopped beating Paul. ³³The commander went to Paul and arrested him. He told his soldiers to tie Paul with two chains. Then he asked, "Who is this man? What has he done wrong?" ³⁴Some in the crowd were yelling one thing, and some were yelling another. Because of all this confusion and shouting, the commander could not learn what had happened. So he ordered the soldiers to take Paul to the army building. ³⁵⁻³⁶The whole

---

21:24 **cleansing ceremony** The special things Jews did to end the Nazirite promise.
21:24 **shave their heads** The Jews did this to show that their promise was finished.

mob was following them. When the soldiers came to the steps, they had to carry Paul. They did this because the people were ready to hurt him. They were shouting, "Kill him!"

[37]The soldiers were about to take Paul into the army building. But he spoke to the commander, "May I say something to you?"

The commander said, "Do you speak Greek? [38]I thought you were the Egyptian who started some trouble against the government not long ago. He led 4,000 killers out to the desert."

[39]Paul said, "No, I am a Jew from Tarsus in the country of Cilicia. I am a citizen of that important city. Please, let me speak to the people."

[40]The commander gave permission, so Paul stood on the steps. He waved with his hand so that the people would be quiet. When there was silence, Paul spoke to them in the Jewish language.[n]

PAUL SPEAKS TO THE PEOPLE

22 Paul said, "Brothers and fathers, listen to me! I will make my defense to you." [2]When the Jews heard him speaking the Jewish language,[n] they became very quiet. Paul said, [3]"I am a Jew. I was born in Tarsus in the country of Cilicia. I grew up in this city. I was a student of Gamaliel.[n] He carefully taught me everything about the law of our ancestors. I was very serious about serving God, just as are all of you here today. [4]I hurt the people who followed the Way of Jesus. Some of them were even killed. I arrested men and women and put them in jail. [5]The high priest and the whole council of Jewish elders can tell you that this is true. These leaders gave me letters to the Jewish brothers in Damascus. So I was going there to arrest these people and bring them back to Jerusalem to be punished.

[6]"But something happened to me on my way to Damascus. It was about noon when I came near Damascus. Suddenly a bright light from heaven flashed all around me. [7]I fell to the ground and heard a voice saying, 'Saul, Saul, why are you doing things against me?' [8]I asked, 'Who are you, Lord?' The voice said, 'I am Jesus from Nazareth. I am the One you are trying to hurt.' [9]The men who were with me did not understand the voice. But they saw the light. [10]I said, 'What shall I do, Lord?' The Lord answered, 'Get up and go to Damascus. There you will be told about all the things I have planned for you to do.' [11]I could not see, because the bright light had made me blind. So the men led me into Damascus.

[12]"There a man named Ananias came to me. He was a religious man; he obeyed the law of Moses. All the Jews who lived there respected him. [13]Ananias came to me, stood by me, and said, 'Brother Saul, see again!' Immediately I was able to see him. [14]Ananias told me, 'The God of our fathers chose you long ago. He chose you to know his plan. He chose you to see the Righteous One and to hear words from him. [15]You will be his witness to all people. You will tell them about the things you have seen and heard. [16]Now, why wait any longer? Get up, be baptized, and wash your sins away. Do this, trusting in him to save you.'

[17]"Later, I returned to Jerusalem. I was praying in the Temple,[d] and I saw a vision. [18]I saw the Lord saying to me, 'Hurry! Leave Jerusalem now! The people here will not accept the truth about me.' [19]But I said, 'Lord, they know that in every synagogue[d] I put the believers in jail and beat them. [20]They also know that I was there when Stephen, your witness, was killed. I stood there and agreed that they should kill him. I even held the

---

21:40; 22:2 **Jewish language** Aramaic, the language of the Jews in the first century.
22:3 **Gamaliel** A very important teacher of the Pharisees, a Jewish religious group (Acts 5:34).

coats of the men who were killing him!' [21]But the Lord said to me, 'Leave now. I will send you far away to the non-Jewish people.'"

[22]The crowd listened to Paul until he said this. Then they began shouting, "Get rid of him! A man like this doesn't deserve to live!" [23]They shouted and threw off their coats.[n] They threw dust into the air.[n]

[24]Then the commander ordered the soldiers to take Paul into the army building and beat him. The commander wanted to make Paul tell why the people were shouting against him like this. [25]So the soldiers were tying him up, preparing to beat him. But Paul said to an officer there, "Do you have the right to beat a Roman citizen[n] who has not been proven guilty?"

[26]When the officer heard this, he went to the commander and told him about it. The officer said, "Do you know what you are doing? This man is a Roman citizen!"

[27]The commander came to Paul and said, "Tell me, are you really a Roman citizen?"

He answered, "Yes."

[28]The commander said, "I paid a lot of money to become a Roman citizen."

But Paul said, "I was born a citizen."

[29]The men who were preparing to question Paul moved away from him immediately. The commander was frightened because he had already tied Paul, and Paul was a Roman citizen.

PAUL SPEAKS TO JEWISH LEADERS

[30]The next day the commander decided to learn why the Jews were accusing Paul. So he ordered the leading priests and the Jewish council to meet. The commander took Paul's chains off.

Then he brought Paul out and stood him before their meeting.

23 Paul looked at the Jewish council and said, "Brothers, I have lived my life in a good way before God up to this day." [2]Ananias,[n] the high priest, heard this and told the men who were standing near Paul to hit him on his mouth. [3]Paul said to Ananias, "God will hit you too! You are like a wall that has been painted white! You sit there and judge me, using the law of Moses. But you are telling them to hit me, and that is against the law."

[4]The men standing near Paul said to him, "You cannot talk like that to God's high priest! You are insulting him!"

[5]Paul said, "Brothers, I did not know this man was the high priest. It is written in the Scriptures,[d] 'You must not curse a leader of your people.'"[n]

[6]Some of the men in the meeting were Sadducees,[d] and others were Pharisees.[d] So Paul shouted to them, "My brothers, I am a Pharisee and my father was a Pharisee! I am on trial here because I hope that people will rise from death!"

[7]When Paul said this, there was an argument between the Pharisees and the Sadducees. The group was divided. [8](The Sadducees believe that after people die, they cannot live again. The Sadducees also teach that there are no angels or spirits. But the Pharisees believe in them all.) [9]So there was a great uproar. Some of the teachers of the law, who were Pharisees, stood up and argued, "We find nothing wrong with this man! Maybe an angel or a spirit did speak to him."

[10]The argument was beginning to turn into a fight. The commander was afraid that the Jews would tear Paul to pieces.

22:23 **threw off their coats** This showed that the Jews were very angry at Paul.
22:23 **threw dust into the air** This showed even greater anger.
22:25 **Roman citizen** Roman law said that Roman citizens must not be beaten before they had a trial.
23:2 **Ananias** This is not the same man named Ananias in Acts 22:12.
23:5 **'You ... people.'** Quotation from Exodus 22:28.

So the commander told the soldiers to go down and take Paul away and put him in the army building.

[11] The next night the Lord came and stood by Paul. He said, "Be brave! You have told people in Jerusalem about me. You must do the same in Rome also."

[12] In the morning some of the Jews made a plan to kill Paul. They made a promise that they would not eat or drink anything until they had killed him. [13] There were more than 40 Jews who made this plan. [14] They went and talked to the leading priests and the Jewish elders. They said, "We have made a promise to ourselves that we will not eat or drink until we have killed Paul! [15] So this is what we want you to do: Send a message to the commander to bring Paul out to you. Tell him you want to ask Paul more questions. We will be waiting to kill him while he is on the way here."

[16] But Paul's nephew heard about this plan. He went to the army building and told Paul about it. [17] Then Paul called one of the officers and said, "Take this young man to the commander. He has a message for him."

[18] So the officer brought Paul's nephew to the commander. The officer said, "The prisoner, Paul, asked me to bring this young man to you. He wants to tell you something."

[19] The commander led the young man to a place where they could be alone. The commander asked, "What do you want to tell me?"

[20] The young man said, "The Jews have decided to ask you to bring Paul down to their council meeting tomorrow. They want you to think that they are going to ask him more questions. [21] But don't believe them! There are more than 40 men who are hiding and waiting to kill Paul. They have all made a promise not to eat or drink until they have killed him! Now they are waiting for you to agree."

[22] The commander sent the young man away. He said to him, "Don't tell anyone that you have told me about their plan."

PAUL IS SENT TO CAESAREA

[23] Then the commander called two officers. He said to them, "I need some men to go to Caesarea. Get 200 soldiers ready. Also, get 70 horsemen and 200 men with spears. Be ready to leave at nine o'clock tonight. [24] Get some horses for Paul to ride. He must be taken to Governor Felix safely." [25] And he wrote a letter that said:

[26] From Claudius Lysias.

To the Most Excellent Governor Felix:

Greetings.
[27] The Jews had taken this man, and they planned to kill him. But I learned that he is a Roman citizen, so I went with my soldiers and saved him. [28] I wanted to know why they were accusing him. So I brought him before their council meeting. [29] I learned that the Jews said Paul did some things that were wrong. But these charges were about their own laws. And no charge was worthy of jail or death. [30] I was told that some of the Jews were planning to kill Paul. So I sent him to you at once. I also told those Jews to tell you what they have against him.

[31] So the soldiers did what they were told. They took Paul and brought him to the city of Antipatris that night. [32] The next day the horsemen went with Paul to Caesarea. But the other soldiers went back to the army building in Jerusalem. [33] The horsemen came to Caesarea and gave the letter to the governor. Then they turned Paul over to him. [34] The governor read the letter. Then he asked Paul, "What area are you from?" He learned that Paul was from Cilicia. [35] He said, "I will hear your case when those who are against you come here too." Then the governor gave orders for Paul to be kept

under guard in the palace. (This building had been built by Herod.)

THE JEWS ACCUSE PAUL

24 Five days later Ananias, the high priest, went to the city of Caesarea. With him were some of the Jewish elders and a lawyer named Tertullus. They had come to make charges against Paul before the governor. [2]Paul was called into the meeting, and Tertullus began to accuse him, saying: "Most Excellent Felix! Our people enjoy much peace because of you, and many wrong things in our country are being made right through your wise help. [3]We accept these things always and in every place. And we are thankful for them. [4]But I do not want to take any more of your time. I beg you to be kind and listen to our few words. [5]This man is a troublemaker. He makes trouble among the Jews everywhere in the world. He is a leader of the Nazarene[d] group. [6]Also, he was trying to make the Temple[d] unclean,[d] but we stopped him. [And we wanted to judge him by our own law. [7]But the officer Lysias came and used much force to take him from us. And Lysias commanded his people to come to you to accuse us.][n] [8]You can decide if all these things are true. Ask him some questions yourself." [9]The other Jews agreed and said that all of this was true.

[10]The governor made a sign for Paul to speak. So Paul said, "Governor Felix, I know that you have been a judge over this nation for a long time. So I am happy to defend myself before you. [11]I went to worship in Jerusalem only 12 days ago. You can learn for yourself that this is true. [12]Those who are accusing me did not find me arguing with anyone in the Temple. I was not stirring up the people. And I was not making trouble in the Temple or in the synagogues[d] or in the city. [13]They cannot prove the things they are saying against me now. [14]But I will tell you this: I worship the God of our ancestors as a follower of the Way of Jesus. The Jews say that the Way of Jesus is not the right way. But I believe everything that is taught in the law of Moses and that is written in the books of the Prophets.[d] [15]I have the same hope in God that they have—the hope that all people, good and bad, will be raised from death. [16]This is why I always try to do what I believe is right before God and men.

[17]"I was away from Jerusalem for several years. I went back there to bring money to my people and to offer sacrifices. [18]I was doing this when they found me in the Temple. I had finished the cleansing ceremony. I had not made any trouble; no people were gathering around me. [19]But some Jews from Asia were there. They should be here, standing before you. If I have really done anything wrong, they are the ones who should accuse me. [20]Or ask these Jews here if they found any wrong in me when I stood before the Jewish council in Jerusalem. [21]But I did say one thing when I stood before them: 'You are judging me today because I believe that people will rise from death!'"

[22]Felix already understood much about the Way of Jesus. He stopped the trial and said, "When commander Lysias comes here, I will decide about your case." [23]Felix told the officer to keep Paul guarded. But he told the officer to give Paul some freedom and to let his friends bring what he needed.

PAUL SPEAKS TO FELIX AND HIS WIFE

[24]After some days Felix came with his wife, Drusilla, who was a Jew. He asked for Paul to be brought to him. He listened to Paul talk about believing in Christ Jesus. [25]But Felix became afraid when Paul spoke about things like right living, self-control, and the time when

---

24:6-8 And . . . us. Some Greek copies do not contain the bracketed text.

God will judge the world. He said, "Go away now. When I have more time, I will call for you." [26]At the same time Felix hoped that Paul would give him some money. So he sent for Paul often and talked with him.

[27]But after two years, Porcius Festus became governor. Felix was no longer governor, but he had left Paul in prison to please the Jews.

PAUL ASKS TO SEE CAESAR

25 Three days after Festus became governor, he went from Caesarea to Jerusalem. [2]There the leading priests and the important Jewish leaders made charges against Paul before Festus. [3]They asked Festus to do something for them; they wanted him to send Paul back to Jerusalem. (They had a plan to kill Paul on the way.) [4]But Festus answered, "No! Paul will be kept in Caesarea. I will return there soon myself. [5]Some of your leaders should go with me. They can accuse the man there in Caesarea, if he has really done something wrong."

[6]Festus stayed in Jerusalem another eight or ten days. Then he went back to Caesarea. The next day he told the soldiers to bring Paul before him. Festus was seated on the judge's seat [7]when Paul came into the room. The Jews who had come from Jerusalem stood around him. They started making serious charges against Paul. But they could not prove any of them. [8]This is what Paul said to defend himself: "I have done nothing wrong against the Jewish law, against the Temple,[d] or against Caesar!"[d]

[9]But Festus wanted to please the Jews. So he asked Paul, "Do you want to go to Jerusalem? Do you want me to judge you there on these charges?"

[10]Paul said, "I am standing at Caesar's judgment seat now. This is where I should be judged! I have done nothing

wrong to the Jews; you know this is true. [11]If I have done something wrong and the law says I must die, I do not ask to be saved from death. But if these charges are not true, then no one can give me to them. No! I want Caesar to hear my case!"

[12]Festus talked about this with the people who advised him. Then he said, "You have asked to see Caesar; so you will go to Caesar!"

PAUL BEFORE KING AGRIPPA

[13]A few days later King Agrippa and Bernice came to Caesarea to visit Festus. [14]They stayed there for some time, and Festus told the king about Paul's case. Festus said, "There is a man that Felix left in prison. [15]When I went to Jerusalem, the leading priests and the Jewish elders there made charges against him. They wanted me to sentence him to death. [16]But I answered, 'When a man is accused of a crime, Romans do not hand him over just to please someone. The man must be allowed to face his accusers and defend himself against their charges.' [17]So these Jews came here to Caesarea for the trial. And I did not waste time. The next day I sat on the judge's seat and commanded that the man be brought in. [18]The Jews stood up and accused him. But they did not accuse him of any serious crime as I thought they would. [19]The things they said were about their own religion and about a man named Jesus. Jesus died, but Paul said that he is still alive. [20]I did not know much about these things; so I did not ask questions. But I asked Paul, 'Do you want to go to Jerusalem and be judged there?' [21]But he asked to be kept in Caesarea. He wants a decision from the Emperor.[n] So I ordered that Paul be held until I could send him to Caesar[d] in Rome."

[22]Agrippa said to Festus, "I would like to hear this man, too."

25:21 Emperor The ruler of the Roman Empire, which was almost all the world.

Festus said, "Tomorrow you will hear him!"

²³The next day Agrippa and Bernice appeared. They dressed and acted like very important people. Agrippa and Bernice, the army leaders, and the important men of Caesarea went into the judgment room. Then Festus ordered the soldiers to bring Paul in. ²⁴Festus said, "King Agrippa and all who are gathered here with us, you see this man. All the Jewish people, here and in Jerusalem, have complained to me about him. They shout that he should not live any longer. ²⁵When I judged him, I could find nothing wrong. I found no reason to order his death. But he asked to be judged by Caesar. So I decided to send him. ²⁶But I have nothing definite to write the Emperor about him. So I have brought him before all of you—especially you, King Agrippa. I hope that you can question him and give me something to write. ²⁷I think it is foolish to send a prisoner to Caesar without telling what the charges are against him."

PAUL DEFENDS HIMSELF

26 Agrippa said to Paul, "You may now speak to defend yourself."

Then Paul raised his hand and began to speak. ²He said, "King Agrippa, I will answer all the charges that the Jews make against me. I think it is a blessing that I can stand here before you today. ³I am very happy to talk to you, because you know so much about all the Jewish customs and the things that the Jews argue about. Please listen to me patiently.

⁴"All the Jews know about my whole life. They know the way I lived from the beginning in my own country and later in Jerusalem. ⁵They have known me for a long time. If they want to, they can tell you that I was a good Pharisee.ᵈ And the Pharisees obey the laws of the Jewish religion more carefully than any other group of Jewish people. ⁶Now I am on trial because I hope for the promise that God made to our ancestors. ⁷This is the promise that the 12 tribesᵈ of our people hope to receive. For this hope the Jews serve God day and night. My king, the Jews have accused me because I hope for this same promise! ⁸Why do any of you people think it is impossible for God to raise people from death?

⁹"I too thought I ought to do many things against Jesus from Nazareth. ¹⁰And in Jerusalem I did many things against God's people. The leading priests gave me the power to put many of them in jail. When they were being killed, I agreed that it was a good thing. ¹¹In every synagogue,ᵈ I often punished them. I tried to make them say evil things against Jesus. I was so angry against them that I even went to other cities to find them and punish them.

¹²"One time the leading priests gave me permission and the power to go to Damascus. ¹³On the way there, at noon, I saw a light from heaven. The light was brighter than the sun. It flashed all around me and the men who were traveling with me. ¹⁴We all fell to the ground. Then I heard a voice speaking to me in the Jewish language.ⁿ The voice said, 'Saul, Saul, why are you doing things against me? You are only hurting yourself by fighting me.' ¹⁵I said, 'Who are you, Lord?' The Lord said, 'I am Jesus. I am the One you are trying to hurt. ¹⁶Stand up! I have chosen you to be my servant. You will be my witness—you will tell people the things that you have seen and the things that I will show you. This is why I have come to you today. ¹⁷I will not let your own people hurt you. And I will keep you safe from the non-Jewish people too. These are the people I am sending you to. ¹⁸I send you to open their eyes that they may turn away from

---

26:14 **Jewish language** Aramaic, the language of the Jews in the first century.

darkness to the light. I send you that they may turn away from the power of Satan and turn to God. Then their sins can be forgiven and they can have a place with those people who have been made holy by believing in me.'

[19]"King Agrippa, after I had this vision from heaven, I obeyed it. [20]I began telling people that they should change their hearts and lives and turn to God. I told them to do things to show that they really had changed. I told this first to those in Damascus, then in Jerusalem and in every part of Judea, and also to the non-Jewish people. [21]This is why the Jews took me and were trying to kill me in the Temple.[d] [22]But God helped me and is still helping me today. With God's help I am standing here today and telling all people what I have seen. But I am saying nothing new. I am saying what Moses and the prophets[d] said would happen. [23]They said that the Christ[d] would die and be the first to rise from death. They said that the Christ would bring light to the Jewish and non-Jewish people."

PAUL TRIES TO PERSUADE AGRIPPA

[24]While Paul was saying these things to defend himself, Festus said loudly, "Paul, you are out of your mind! Too much study has driven you crazy!"

[25]Paul said, "Most Excellent Festus, I am not crazy. My words are true. They are not the words of a foolish man. [26]King Agrippa knows about these things. I can speak freely to him. I know that he has heard about all of these things. They did not happen off in a corner. [27]King Agrippa, do you believe what the prophets[d] wrote? I know you believe!"

[28]King Agrippa said to Paul, "Do you think you can persuade me to become a Christian in such a short time?"

[29]Paul said, "Whether it is a short or a long time, I pray to God that not only you but every person listening to me today would be saved and be like me—except for these chains I have!"

[30]Then King Agrippa, Governor Festus, Bernice, and all the people sitting with them stood up [31]and left the room. They were talking to each other. They said, "There is no reason why this man should die or be put in jail." [32]And Agrippa said to Festus, "We could let this man go free, but he has asked Caesar[d] to hear his case."

PAUL SAILS FOR ROME

27 It was decided that we would sail for Italy. An officer named Julius, who served in the Emperor's[n] army, guarded Paul and some other prisoners. [2]We got on a ship and left. The ship was from the city of Adramyttium and was about to sail to different ports in Asia. Aristarchus, a man from the city of Thessalonica in Macedonia, went with us. [3]The next day we came to Sidon. Julius was very good to Paul. He gave Paul freedom to go visit his friends, who took care of his needs. [4]We left Sidon and sailed close to the island of Cyprus because the wind was blowing against us. [5]We went across the sea by Cilicia and Pamphylia. Then we came to the city of Myra, in Lycia. [6]There the officer found a ship from Alexandria that was going to Italy. So he put us on it.

[7]We sailed slowly for many days. We had a hard time reaching Cnidus because the wind was blowing against us. We could not go any farther that way. So we sailed by the south side of the island of Crete near Salmone. [8]We sailed along the coast, but the sailing was hard. Then we came to a place called Safe Harbors, near the city of Lasea.

[9]But we had lost much time. It was now dangerous to sail, because it was already after the Day of Cleansing.[n] So

---

27:1 Emperor The ruler of the Roman Empire, which was almost all the world.
27:9 Day of Cleansing An important Jewish holy day in the fall of the year. This was the time of year that bad storms happened on the sea.

Paul warned them, [10]"Men, I can see there will be a lot of trouble on this trip. The ship and the things in the ship will be lost. Even our lives may be lost!" [11]But the captain and the owner of the ship did not agree with Paul. So the officer did not believe Paul. Instead, the officer believed what the captain and owner of the ship said. [12]And that harbor was not a good place for the ship to stay for the winter. So most of the men decided that the ship should leave. The men hoped we could go to Phoenix. The ship could stay there for the winter. (Phoenix was a city on the island of Crete. It had a harbor which faced southwest and northwest.)

THE STORM

[13]Then a good wind began to blow from the south. The men on the ship thought, "This is the wind we wanted, and now we have it!" So they pulled up the anchor. We sailed very close to the island of Crete. [14]But then a very strong wind named the "Northeaster" came from the island. [15]This wind took the ship and carried it away. The ship could not sail against it. So we stopped trying and let the wind blow us. [16]We went below a small island named Cauda. Then we were able to bring in the lifeboat, but it was very hard to do. [17]After the men took the lifeboat in, they tied ropes around the ship to hold it together. The men were afraid that the ship would hit the sandbanks of Syrtis.[n] So they lowered the sail and let the wind carry the ship. [18]The next day the storm was blowing us so hard that the men threw out some of the cargo. [19]A day later they threw out the ship's equipment. [20]For many days we could not see the sun or the stars. The storm was very bad. We lost all hope of staying alive—we thought we would die.

[21]The men had gone without food for a long time. Then one day Paul stood up before them and said, "Men, I told you not to leave Crete. You should have listened to me. Then you would not have all this trouble and loss. [22]But now I tell you to cheer up. None of you will die! But the ship will be lost. [23]Last night an angel from God came to me. This is the God I worship. I am his. [24]God's angel said, 'Paul, do not be afraid! You must stand before Caesar.[d] And God has given you this promise: He will save the lives of all those men sailing with you.' [25]So men, be cheerful! I trust in God. Everything will happen as his angel told me. [26]But we will crash on an island."

[27]On the fourteenth night we were floating around in the Adriatic Sea.[n] The sailors thought we were close to land. [28]They threw a rope into the water with a weight on the end of it. They found that the water was 120 feet deep. They went a little farther and threw the rope in again. It was 90 feet deep. [29]The sailors were afraid that we would hit the rocks, so they threw four anchors into the water. Then they prayed for daylight to come. [30]Some of the sailors wanted to leave the ship, and they lowered the lifeboat. These sailors wanted the other men to think that they were throwing more anchors from the front of the ship. [31]But Paul told the officer and the other soldiers, "If these men do not stay in the ship, your lives cannot be saved!" [32]So the soldiers cut the ropes and let the lifeboat fall into the water.

[33]Just before dawn Paul began persuading all the people to eat something. He said, "For the past 14 days you have been waiting and watching. You have not eaten. [34]Now I beg you to eat something. You need it to stay alive. None of you will lose even one hair off your heads." [35]After

---

27:17 **Syrtis** Shallow area in the sea near the Libyan coast.
27:27 **Adriatic Sea** The sea between Greece and Italy, including the central Mediterranean.

he said this, Paul took some bread and thanked God for it before all of them. He broke off a piece and began eating. [36]All the men felt better. They all started eating too. [37](There were 276 people on the ship.) [38]We ate all we wanted. Then we began making the ship lighter by throwing the grain into the sea.

THE SHIP IS DESTROYED

[39]When daylight came, the sailors saw land. They did not know what land it was, but they saw a bay with a beach. They wanted to sail the ship to the beach, if they could. [40]So they cut the ropes to the anchors and left the anchors in the sea. At the same time, they untied the ropes that were holding the rudders. Then they raised the front sail into the wind and sailed toward the beach. [41]But the ship hit a sandbank. The front of the ship stuck there and could not move. Then the big waves began to break the back of the ship to pieces.

[42]The soldiers decided to kill the prisoners so that none of them could swim away and escape. [43]But Julius, the officer, wanted to let Paul live. He did not allow the soldiers to kill the prisoners. Instead he ordered everyone who could swim to jump into the water and swim to land. [44]The rest used wooden boards or pieces of the ship. And this is how all the people made it safely to land.

PAUL ON THE ISLAND OF MALTA

28 When we were safe on land, we learned that the island was called Malta. [2]It was raining and very cold. But the people who lived there were very good to us. They made us a fire and welcomed all of us. [3]Paul gathered a pile of sticks for the fire. He was putting them on the fire when a poisonous snake came out because of the

heat and bit him on the hand. [4]The people living on the island saw the snake hanging from Paul's hand. They said to each other, "This man must be a murderer! He did not die in the sea, but Justice[n] does not want him to live." [5]But Paul shook the snake off into the fire. He was not hurt. [6]The people thought that Paul would swell up or fall down dead. The people waited and watched him for a long time, but nothing bad happened to him. So they changed their minds about Paul. Now they said, "He is a god!"

[7]There were some fields around there owned by a very important man on the island. His name was Publius. He welcomed us into his home and was very good to us. We stayed in his house for three days. [8]Publius' father was very sick with a fever and dysentery.[n] But Paul went to him and prayed. Then he put his hands on the man and healed him. [9]After this, all the other sick people on the island came to Paul, and he healed them, too. [10-11]The people on the island gave us many honors. We stayed there three months. When we were ready to leave, they gave us the things we needed.

PAUL GOES TO ROME

We got on a ship from Alexandria. The ship had stayed on the island during the winter. On the front of the ship was the sign of the twin gods.[n] [12]We stopped at Syracuse for three days and then left. [13]From there we sailed to Rhegium. The next day a wind began to blow from the southwest, so we were able to leave. A day later we came to Puteoli. [14]We found some believers there, and they asked us to stay with them for a week. Finally, we came to Rome. [15]The believers in Rome heard that we were there. They came out as far as the Market of Appius[n] and the

---

28:4 **Justice** The people thought there was a god named Justice who would punish bad people.
28:8 **dysentery** A sickness like diarrhea.
28:10-11 **twin gods** Statues of Castor and Pollux, gods in old Greek tales.
28:15 **Market of Appius** A town about 27 miles from Rome.

Three Inns[n] to meet us. When Paul saw them, he was encouraged and thanked God.

PAUL IN ROME

[16]Then we arrived at Rome. There, Paul was allowed to live alone. But a soldier stayed with him to guard him.

[17]Three days later Paul sent for the Jewish leaders there. When they came together, he said, "Brothers, I have done nothing against our people. I have done nothing against the customs of our fathers. But I was arrested in Jerusalem and given to the Romans. [18]The Romans asked me many questions. But they could find no reason why I should be killed. They wanted to let me go free, [19]but the Jews there did not want that. So I had to ask to come to Rome to have my trial before Caesar.[d] But I have no charge to bring against my own people. [20]That is why I wanted to see you and talk with you. I am bound with this chain because I believe in the hope of Israel."

[21]The Jews answered Paul, "We have received no letters from Judea about you. None of our Jewish brothers who have come from there brought news about you or told us anything bad about you. [22]We want to hear your ideas. We know that people everywhere are speaking against this religious group."

[23]Paul and the Jews chose a day for a meeting. On that day many more of the Jews met with Paul at the place he was staying. Paul spoke to them all day long, explaining the kingdom of God to them. He tried to persuade them to believe these things about Jesus. He used the law of Moses and the writings of the prophets[d] to do this. [24]Some of the Jews believed what Paul said, but others did not. [25]So they argued, and the Jews were ready to leave. But Paul said one more thing to them: "The Holy Spirit[d] spoke the truth to your fathers through Isaiah the prophet. He said,

[26]'Go to this people and say:
You will listen and listen, but you will not understand.
You will look and look, but you will not learn.
[27]For these people have become stubborn.
They don't hear with their ears.
And they have closed their eyes.
Otherwise, they might really understand
what they see with their eyes
and hear with their ears.
They might really understand in their minds.
If they did this, they would come back to me and be forgiven.'
Isaiah 6:9-10

[28]"I want you Jews to know that God has also sent his salvation to the non-Jewish people. They will listen!" [29][After Paul said this, the Jews left. They were arguing very much with each other.][n]

[30]Paul stayed two full years in his own rented house. He welcomed all people who came and visited him. [31]He preached about the kingdom of God and taught about the Lord Jesus Christ. He was very bold, and no one stopped him.

28:15 **Three Inns** A town about 30 miles from Rome.
28:29 **After . . . other.** Some Greek copies do not contain the bracketed text.

ROMANS

1 From Paul, a servant of Christ Jesus. God called me to be an apostle[d] and chose me to tell the Good News.[d]

[2]God promised this Good News long ago through his prophets.[d] That promise is written in the Holy Scriptures.[d] [3-4]The Good News is about God's Son, Jesus Christ our Lord. As a man, he was born from the family of David. But through the Spirit[d] of holiness he was declared to be God's Son with great power by rising from death. [5]Through Christ, God gave me the special work of an apostle. This was to lead people of all nations to believe and obey. I do this work for Christ. [6]And you who are in Rome are also called to belong to Jesus Christ.

[7]This letter is to all of you in Rome whom God loves and has called to be his holy people.

May God our Father and the Lord Jesus Christ show you kindness and give you peace.

A PRAYER OF THANKS

[8]First I want to say that I thank my God through Jesus Christ for all of you. I thank God because people everywhere in the world are talking about your great faith. [9-10]God knows that every time I pray I always mention you. God is the One I serve with my whole heart by telling the Good News[d] about his Son. I pray that I will be allowed to come to you, and this will happen if God wants it. [11]I want very much to see you, to give you some spiritual gift to make you strong. [12]I mean that I want us to help each other with the faith that we have. Your faith will help me, and my faith will help you. [13]Brothers, I want you to know that I planned many times to come to you. But this has not been possible. I wanted to come so that I could help you grow spiritually. I wanted to help you as I have helped the other non-Jewish people.

[14]I must serve all people—Greeks and non-Greeks, the wise and the foolish. [15]That is why I want so much to preach the Good News to you in Rome.

[16]I am not ashamed of the Good News. It is the power God uses to save everyone who believes—to save the Jews first, and then to save the non-Jews. [17]The Good News shows how God makes people right with himself. God's way of making people right with him begins and ends with faith. As the Scripture[d] says, "The person who is made right with God by faith will live forever."[n]

ALL PEOPLE HAVE DONE WRONG

[18]God's anger is shown from heaven against all the evil and wrong things that people do. By their own evil lives they hide the truth. [19]God shows his anger because everything that may be known about God has been made clear. Yes, God has clearly shown them everything that may be known about him. [20]There are things about God that people cannot see—his eternal power and all the things that make him God. But since the beginning of the world those things have been easy to understand. They are made clear by what God has made. So people have no excuse for the bad things they do. [21]They knew God. But they did not give glory to God, and they did not thank him. Their thinking became useless. Their foolish minds were filled with darkness. [22]They said they were wise, but they became fools. [23]They gave up the glory of God who lives forever. They traded that glory for the worship of idols made to look like earthly people. They traded God's glory for things that look like birds, animals, and snakes.

1:17 "The person . . . forever." Quotation from Habakkuk 2:4.

²⁴People were full of sin, wanting only to do evil. So God let them go their sinful way. They became full of sexual sin, using their bodies wrongly with each other. ²⁵They traded the truth of God for a lie and worshiped and served things that were made by man. But they did not worship and serve the God who made those things. God should be praised forever. Amen.

²⁶Because people did those things, God left them and let them do the shameful things they wanted to do. Women stopped having natural sex and started having sex with other women. ²⁷In the same way, men stopped having natural sex and began wanting each other. Men did shameful things with other men. And in their bodies they received the punishment for those wrongs.

²⁸People did not think it was important to have a true knowledge of God. So God left them and allowed them to have their own worthless thinking. And so those people do the things that they should not do. ²⁹They are filled with every kind of sin, evil, selfishness, and hatred. They are full of jealousy, murder, fighting, lying, and thinking the worst about each other. They gossip ³⁰and say evil things about each other. They hate God. They are rude and conceited and brag about themselves. They invent ways of doing evil. They do not obey their parents. ³¹They are foolish, they do not keep their promises, and they show no kindness or mercy to other people. ³²They know God's law says that those who live like this should die. But they continue to do these evil things. And they also feel that those who do these things are doing right.

YOU PEOPLE ALSO ARE SINFUL

2 If you think that you can judge others, then you are wrong. You too are guilty of sin. You judge people, but you do the same bad things they do. So when you judge them, you are really judging yourself guilty. ²God judges those who do wrong things. And we know that God's judging is right. ³You judge those who do wrong, but you do wrong yourselves. Do you think you will be able to escape the judgment of God? ⁴God has been very kind to you, and he has been patient with you. God has been waiting for you to change. But you think nothing of his kindness. Perhaps you do not understand that God is kind to you so that you will change your hearts and lives. ⁵But you are hard and stubborn and refuse to change. So you are making your own punishment greater and greater on the day God shows his anger. On that day all people will see God's right judgments. ⁶God will reward or punish every person for what he has done. ⁷Some people live for God's glory, for honor, and for life that has no end. They live for those things by always continuing to do good. God will give life forever to them. ⁸But other people are selfish and refuse to follow truth. They follow evil. God will give them his punishment and anger. ⁹He will give trouble and suffering to everyone who does evil—to the Jews first and also to the non-Jews. ¹⁰But God will give glory, honor, and peace to everyone who does good—to the Jews first and also to the non-Jews. ¹¹For God judges all people in the same way.

¹²People who have God's law and those who have never heard of the law are all the same when they sin. Those who do not have the law and are sinners will be lost. And, in the same way, people who have the law and are sinners will be judged by the law. ¹³Hearing the law does not make people right with God. The law makes people right with God only if they obey what the law says. ¹⁴(The non-Jews do not have the law. But when they freely do things that the law commands, then they are the law for themselves. This is true even though

they do not have the law. [15]They show that in their hearts they know what is right and wrong, just as the law commands. And they also show this by the way they feel about right and wrong. Sometimes their thoughts tell them they did wrong. And sometimes their thoughts tell them they did right.) [16]All these things will happen on the day when God will judge the secret thoughts of people's hearts. The Good News[d] that I preach says that God will judge everyone through Christ Jesus.

THE JEWS AND THE LAW

[17]What about you? You call yourself a Jew. You trust in the law of Moses and brag that you are close to God. [18]You know what God wants you to do. And you know the things that are important because you have learned the law. [19]You think you are a guide for the blind and a light for those who are in darkness. [20]You think you can show foolish people what is right and teach those who know nothing. You have the law; so you think you know everything and have all truth. [21]You teach other people. So why don't you teach yourself? You tell others not to steal. But you yourselves steal. [22]You say that others must not take part in adultery.[d] But you yourselves are guilty of that sin. You hate idols. But you steal from temples. [23]You brag about having God's law. But you bring shame to God by breaking his law. [24]It is written in the Scriptures:[d] "The non-Jews speak against God's name because of you Jews."[n]

[25]If you follow the law, then your circumcision[d] has meaning. But if you break the law, then it is as if you were never circumcised. [26]The non-Jews are not circumcised. But if they do what the law says, then it is as if they were circumcised. [27]You Jews have the written law and circumcision, but you break the law. So those who are not circumcised in

their bodies, but still obey the law, will show that you are guilty.

[28]A person is not a true Jew if he is only a Jew in his physical body. True circumcision is not only on the outside of the body. [29]A person is a true Jew only if he is a Jew inside. True circumcision is done in the heart by the Spirit,[d] not by the written law. Such a person gets praise from God, not from other people.

3 So, do Jews have anything that other people do not have? Is there anything special about being circumcised? [2]Yes, of course, there is in every way. The most important thing is this: God trusted the Jews with his teachings. [3]It is true that some Jews were not faithful to God. But will that stop God from doing what he promised? [4]No! God will continue to be true even when every person is false. As the Scriptures[d] say:

"So your words may be shown to be right.
    You are fair when you judge me."
                                    Psalm 51:4

[5]When we do wrong, that shows more clearly that God is right. So can we say that God is wrong to punish us? (I am talking as men might talk.) [6]No! If God could not punish us, then God could not judge the world.

[7]A person might say, "When I lie, it really gives God glory, because my lie shows God's truth. So why am I judged a sinner?" [8]It would be the same to say, "We should do evil so that good will come." Some people find fault with us and say that we teach this. Those who say such things about us are wrong, and they should be punished.

ALL PEOPLE ARE GUILTY

[9]So are we Jews better than others? No! We have already said that Jews and non-Jews are the same. They are all guilty of sin. [10]As the Scriptures[d] say:
"There is no one without sin. None!

2:24 "The non-Jews . . . Jews." Quotation from Isaiah 52:5; Ezekiel 36:20.

¹¹ There is no one who understands.
    There is no one who looks to God
        for help.
¹²All have turned away.
    Together, everyone has become
        evil.
  None of them does anything good."
                                Psalm 14:1-3
¹³"Their throats are like open graves.
    They use their tongues for telling
        lies."   *Psalm 5:9*
  "Their words are like snake's poison."
                                Psalm 140:3
¹⁴ "Their mouths are full of cursing
        and hate."   *Psalm 10:7*
¹⁵"They are always ready to kill people.
¹⁶ Everywhere they go they cause ruin
        and misery.
¹⁷They don't know how to live in
        peace."   *Isaiah 59:7-8*
¹⁸ "They have no fear of or respect for
        God."   *Psalm 36:1*
¹⁹The law commands many things.
We know that those commands are for
those who are under the law. This stops
all excuses and brings the whole world
under God's judgment, ²⁰because no one
can be made right with God by following
the law. The law only shows us our sin.

HOW GOD MAKES PEOPLE RIGHT

²¹But God has a way to make people
right with him without the law. And God
has now shown us that way which the
law and the prophets*ᵈ* told us about.
²²God makes people right with himself
through their faith in Jesus Christ. This is
true for all who believe in Christ, because
all are the same. ²³All people have sinned
and are not good enough for God's glory.
²⁴People are made right with God by his
grace, which is a free gift. They are made
right with God by being made free from
sin through Jesus Christ. ²⁵God sent him
to die in our place to take away our sins.
We receive forgiveness through faith.

And all of this is because of the blood of
Jesus' death. This showed that God always
does what is right and fair. God was right
in the past when he was patient and did
not punish people for their sins. ²⁶And
God gave Jesus to show today that God
does what is right. God did this so that
he could judge rightly and also make
right any person who has faith in Jesus.

²⁷So do we have a reason to brag about
ourselves? No! And why not? It is the
way of faith that stops all bragging, not
the way of following the law. ²⁸A person
is made right with God through faith,
not through what he does to follow the
law. ²⁹Is God only the God of the Jews? Is
he not also the God of the non-Jews? ³⁰Of
course he is, for there is only one God.
He will make Jews right with him by
their faith. And he will also make non-
Jews right with him through their faith.
³¹So do we destroy the law by following
the way of faith? No! Faith causes us to
be what the law truly wants.

THE EXAMPLE OF ABRAHAM

4 So what can we say about Abraham,*ⁿ*
the father of our people? What did
he learn about faith? ²If Abraham was
made right by the things he did, then he
had a reason to brag. But he could not
brag before God. ³The Scripture*ᵈ* says,
"Abraham believed God. And that faith
made him right with God."*ⁿ*

⁴When a person works, his pay is not
given to him as a gift. He earns the pay
he gets. ⁵But a person cannot do any
work that will make him right with God.
So he must trust in God. Then God
accepts his faith, and that makes him
right with God. God is the One who can
make even those who are evil right in his
sight. ⁶David said the same thing. He
said that a person is truly blessed when
God does not look at what he has done
but accepts him as good:

4:1 Abraham Most respected ancestor of the Jews. Every Jew hoped to see Abraham.
4:3 "Abraham . . . God." Quotation from Genesis 15:6.

[7]"Happy are they
    whose sins are forgiven,
    whose wrongs are pardoned.
[8]Happy is the person
    whom the Lord does not consider
        guilty."   *Psalm 32:1-2*
[9]Is this blessing only for those who are circumcised?[d] Or is it also for those who are not circumcised? We have already said that God accepted Abraham's faith, and that faith made him right with God. [10]So how did this happen? Did God accept Abraham before or after he was circumcised? God accepted him before his circumcision. [11]Abraham was circumcised later to show that God accepted him. His circumcision was proof that he was right with God through faith before he was circumcised. So Abraham is the father of all those who believe but are not circumcised. He is the father of all believers who are accepted as being right with God. [12]And Abraham is also the father of those who have been circumcised. But it is not their circumcision that makes him their father. He is their father only if they live following the faith that our father Abraham had before he was circumcised.

GOD KEEPS HIS PROMISE

[13]Abraham[n] and his descendants[d] received the promise that they would get the whole world. But Abraham did not receive that promise through the law. He received it because he was right with God through his faith. [14]If people could receive what God promised by following the law, then faith is worthless. And God's promise to Abraham is worthless, [15]because the law can only bring God's anger. But if there is no law, then there is nothing to disobey.
[16]So people receive God's promise by having faith. This happens so that the promise can be a free gift. And if the promise is a free gift, then all of Abraham's children can have that promise. The promise is not only for those people that live under the law of Moses. It is [17]for anyone who lives with faith like Abraham. He is the father of us all. [17]As it is written in the Scriptures:[d] "I am making you a father of many nations."[n] This is true before God. Abraham believed in God—the God who gives life to the dead and decides that things will happen that have not yet happened.
[18]There was no hope that Abraham would have children. But Abraham believed God and continued hoping. And that is why he became the father of many nations. As God told him, "Your descendants will also be too many to count."[n] [19]Abraham was almost 100 years old, much past the age for having children. Also, Sarah could not have children. Abraham thought about all this. But his faith in God did not become weak. [20]He never doubted that God would keep his promise. Abraham never stopped believing. He grew stronger in his faith and gave praise to God. [21]Abraham felt sure that God was able to do the thing that God promised. [22]So, "God accepted Abraham's faith, and that made him right with God."[n] [23]Those words ("God accepted Abraham's faith") were written not only for Abraham. [24]They were written also for us. God will accept us also because we believe. We believe in the One who raised Jesus our Lord from death. [25]Jesus was given to die for our sins. And he was raised from death to make us right with God.

RIGHT WITH GOD

5 We have been made right with God because of our faith. So we have[n]

4:13 **Abraham** Most respected ancestor of the Jews. Every Jew hoped to see Abraham.
4:17 **"I . . . nations."** Quotation from Genesis 17:5.
4:18 **"Your . . . count."** Quotation from Genesis 15:5.
4:22 **"God . . . God."** Quotation from Genesis 15:6.
5:1 **we have** Some Greek copies read "let us have."

peace with God through our Lord Jesus Christ. [2]Through our faith,[n] Christ has brought us into that blessing of God's grace that we now enjoy. And we are happy because of the hope we have of sharing God's glory. [3]And we also have joy with our troubles because we know that these troubles produce patience. [4]And patience produces character, and character produces hope. [5]And this hope will never disappoint us, because God has poured out his love to fill our hearts. God gave us his love through the Holy Spirit,[d] whom God has given to us.

[6]Christ died for us while we were still weak. We were living against God, but at the right time, Christ died for us. [7]Very few people will die to save the life of someone else. Although perhaps for a good man someone might possibly die. [8]But Christ died for us while we were still sinners. In this way God shows his great love for us.

[9]We have been made right with God by the blood of Christ's death. So through Christ we will surely be saved from God's anger. [10]I mean that while we were God's enemies, God made us his friends through the death of his Son. Surely, now that we are God's friends, God will save us through his Son's life. [11]And not only that, but now we are also very happy in God through our Lord Jesus Christ. Through Jesus we are now God's friends again.

ADAM AND CHRIST

[12]Sin came into the world because of what one man did. And with sin came death. And this is why all men must die—because all men sinned. [13]Sin was in the world before the law of Moses. But God does not judge people guilty of sin if there is no law. [14]But from the time of Adam to the time of Moses, everyone had to die. Adam died because he sinned by not obeying God's command. But

even those who did not sin in the same way had to die.

Adam was like the One who was coming in the future. [15]But God's free gift is not like Adam's sin. Many people died because of the sin of that one man. But the grace that they received from God was much greater. Many people received God's gift of life by the grace of the one man, Jesus Christ. [16]After Adam sinned once, he was judged guilty. But the gift of God is different. God's free gift came after many sins. And the gift makes people right with God. [17]One man sinned, and so death ruled all people because of that one man. But now some people accept God's full grace and the great gift of being made right with him. They will surely have true life and rule through the one man, Jesus Christ.

[18]So one sin of Adam brought the punishment of death to all people. But in the same way, one good act that Christ did makes all people right with God. And that brings true life for all. [19]One man disobeyed God, and many became sinners. But in the same way, one man obeyed God, and many will be made right. [20]The law came to make people have more sin. But when people had more sin, God gave them more of his grace. [21]Sin once used death to rule us. But God gave people more of his grace so that grace could rule by making people right with him. And this brings life forever through Jesus Christ our Lord.

DEAD TO SIN BUT ALIVE IN CHRIST

6 So do you think that we should continue sinning so that God will give us more and more grace? [2]No! We died to our old sinful lives. So how can we continue living with sin? [3]Did you forget that all of us became part of Christ when we were baptized? We shared his death in our baptism. [4]So when we were baptized, we were buried with Christ and

---

5:2 Through our faith Some Greek copies do not include this phrase.

shared his death. We were buried with him so that we could live a new life, just as Christ was raised from death by the wonderful power of the Father.

[5]Christ died, and we have been joined with Christ by dying too. So we will also be joined with him by rising from death as he did. [6]We know that our old life died with Christ on the cross. This was so that our sinful selves would have no power over us, and we would not be slaves to sin. [7]Anyone who has died is made free from sin's control.

[8]If we died with Christ, we know that we will also live with him. [9]Christ was raised from death. And we know that he cannot die again. Death has no power over him now. [10]Yes, when Christ died, he died to defeat the power of sin one time—enough for all time. He now has a new life, and his new life is with God. [11]In the same way, you should see yourselves as being dead to the power of sin and alive with God through Christ Jesus.

[12]So, do not let sin control you in your life here on earth. You must not be ruled by the things your sinful self makes you want to do. [13]Do not offer the parts of your body to serve sin. Do not use your bodies as things to do evil with, but offer yourselves to God. Be like people who have died and now live. Offer the parts of your body to God to be used for doing good. [14]Sin will not be your master, because you are not under law but under God's grace.

SLAVES OF RIGHTEOUSNESS

[15]So what should we do? Should we sin because we are under grace and not under law? No! [16]Surely you know that when you give yourselves like slaves to obey someone, then you are really slaves of that person. The person you obey is your master. You can follow sin, or obey God. Sin brings spiritual death. But obeying God makes you right with him. [17]In the past you were slaves to sin—sin controlled you. But thank God, you fully

obeyed the things that were taught to you. [18]You were made free from sin, and now you are slaves to goodness. [19]I use this example because this is hard for you to understand. In the past you offered the parts of your body to be slaves to sin and evil. You lived only for evil. In the same way now you must give yourselves to be slaves of goodness. Then you will live only for God.

[20]In the past you were slaves to sin, and goodness did not control you. [21]You did evil things, and now you are ashamed of them. Those things only bring death. [22]But now you are free from sin and have become slaves of God. This brings you a life that is only for God. And this gives you life forever. [23]The payment for sin is death. But God gives us the free gift of life forever in Christ Jesus our Lord.

AN EXAMPLE FROM MARRIAGE

7 Brothers, all of you understand the law of Moses. So surely you know that the law rules over a person only while he is alive. [2]For example, a woman must stay married to her husband as long as he is alive. But if her husband dies, then she is free from the law of marriage. [3]But if she marries another man while her husband is still alive, the law says she is guilty of adultery.[d] But if her husband dies, then the woman is free from the law of marriage. So if she marries another man after her husband dies, she is not guilty of adultery.

[4]In the same way, my brothers, your old selves died, and you became free from the law through the body of Christ. Now you belong to someone else. You belong to the One who was raised from death. We belong to Christ so that we can be used in service to God. [5]In the past, we were ruled by our sinful selves. The law made us want to do sinful things. And those sinful things we wanted to do controlled our bodies, so that the things we did were only bringing us death. [6]In the past, the law held us like prisoners.

But our old selves died, and we were made free from the law. So now we serve God in a new way, not in the old way with written rules. Now we serve God in the new way, with the Spirit.[d]

OUR FIGHT AGAINST SIN

[7]You might think that I am saying that sin and the law are the same thing. That is not true. But the law was the only way I could learn what sin meant. I would never have known what it means to want something wrong if the law had not said, "You must not want to take your neighbor's things."[n] [8]And sin found a way to use that command and cause me to want every kind of wrong thing. So sin came to me because of that command. But without the law, sin has no power. [9]I was alive without the law before I knew the law. But when the law's command came to me, then sin began to live. [10]And I died because of sin. The command was meant to bring life, but for me that command brought death. [11]Sin found a way to fool me by using the command. Sin used the command to make me die.

[12]So the law is holy, and the command is holy and right and good. [13]Does this mean that something that is good brought death to me? No! Sin used something that is good to bring death to me. This happened so that I could see what sin is really like. The command was used to show that sin is something very evil.

THE WAR WITHIN MAN

[14]We know that the law is spiritual. But I am not spiritual. Sin rules me as if I were its slave. [15]I do not understand the things I do. I do not do the good things I want to do. And I do the bad things I hate to do. [16]And if I do not want to do the bad things I do, then that means that I agree that the law is good. [17]But I am not really the one who is doing these bad

things. It is sin living in me that does these things. [18]Yes, I know that nothing good lives in me—I mean nothing good lives in the part of me that is earthly and sinful. I want to do the things that are good. But I do not do them. [19]I do not do the good things that I want to do. I do the bad things that I do not want to do. [20]So if I do things I do not want to do, then I am not the one doing those things. It is sin living in me that does those bad things.

[21]So I have learned this rule: When I want to do good, evil is there with me. [22]In my mind, I am happy with God's law. [23]But I see another law working in my body. That law makes war against the law that my mind accepts. That other law working in my body is the law of sin, and that law makes me its prisoner. [24]What a miserable man I am! Who will save me from this body that brings me death? [25]God will. I thank him for saving me through Jesus Christ our Lord!

So in my mind I am a slave to God's law. But in my sinful self I am a slave to the law of sin.

LIFE IN THE SPIRIT

8 So now, those who are in Christ Jesus are not judged[n] guilty. [2]I am not judged guilty because in Christ Jesus the law of the Spirit[d] that brings life made me free. It made me free from the law that brings sin and death. [3]The law was without power, because the law was made weak by our sinful selves. But God did what the law could not do. He sent his own Son to earth with the same human life that others use for sin. He sent his Son to be an offering to pay for sin. So God used a human life to destroy sin. [4]He did this so that we could be right as the law said we must be. Now we do not live following our sinful selves, but we live following the Spirit.

7:7 **"You . . . things."** Quotation from Exodus 20:13, 15-17.
8:1 **judged** Some Greek copies continue, "guilty, those who do not live in the power of their sinful selves, but in the power of the Spirit."

⁵Those who live following their sinful selves think only about things that their sinful selves want. But those who live following the Spirit are thinking about the things that the Spirit wants them to do. ⁶If a person's thinking is controlled by his sinful self, then there is death. But if his thinking is controlled by the Spirit, then there is life and peace. ⁷This is true because if a person's thinking is controlled by his sinful self, then he is against God. He refuses to obey God's law. And really he is not able to obey God's law. ⁸Those people who are ruled by their sinful selves cannot please God.

⁹But you are not ruled by your sinful selves. You are ruled by the Spirit, if that Spirit of God really lives in you. But if anyone does not have the Spirit of Christ, then he does not belong to Christ. ¹⁰Your body will always be dead because of sin. But if Christ is in you, then the Spirit gives you life, because Christ made you right with God. ¹¹God raised Jesus from death. And if God's Spirit is living in you, then he will also give life to your bodies that die. God is the One who raised Christ from death. And he will give life through[n] his Spirit that lives in you.

¹²So, my brothers, we must not be ruled by our sinful selves. We must not live the way our sinful selves want. ¹³If you use your lives to do the wrong things your sinful selves want, then you will die spiritually. But if you use the Spirit's help to stop doing the wrong things you do with your body, then you will have true life.

¹⁴The true children of God are those who let God's Spirit lead them. ¹⁵The Spirit that we received is not a spirit that makes us slaves again to fear. The Spirit that we have makes us children of God. And with that Spirit we say, "Father, dear Father."[n] ¹⁶And the Spirit himself joins with our spirits to say that we are God's children. ¹⁷If we are God's children, then we will receive the blessings God has for us. We will receive these things from God together with Christ. But we must suffer as Christ suffered, and then we will have glory as Christ has glory.

OUR FUTURE GLORY

¹⁸We have sufferings now. But the sufferings we have now are nothing compared to the great glory that will be given to us. ¹⁹Everything that God made is waiting with excitement for the time when God will show the world who his children are. The whole world wants very much for that to happen. ²⁰Everything that God made was changed to become useless. This was not by its own wish. It happened because God wanted it. But there was this hope: ²¹that everything God made would be set free from ruin. There was hope that everything God made would have the freedom and glory that belong to God's children.

²²We know that everything God made has been waiting until now in pain, like a woman ready to give birth. ²³Not only the world, but we also have been waiting with pain inside us. We have the Spirit[d] as the first part of God's promise. So we are waiting for God to finish making us his own children. I mean we are waiting for our bodies to be made free. ²⁴We were saved, and we have this hope. If we see what we are waiting for, then that is not really hope. People do not hope for something they already have. ²⁵But we are hoping for something that we do not have yet. We are waiting for it patiently.

²⁶Also, the Spirit helps us. We are very weak, but the Spirit helps us with our weakness. We do not know how to pray as we should. But the Spirit himself speaks to God for us, even begs God for

8:11 through Some Greek copies read "because of."
8:15 "Father, dear Father." Literally, "Abba, Father." Jewish children called their fathers "Abba."

us. The Spirit speaks to God with deep feelings that words cannot explain. [27]God can see what is in people's hearts. And he knows what is in the mind of the Spirit, because the Spirit speaks to God for his people in the way that God wants.

[28]We know that in everything God works for the good of those who love him.[n] They are the people God called, because that was his plan. [29]God knew them before he made the world. And God chose them to be like his Son. Then Jesus would be the firstborn[n] of many brothers. [30]God planned for them to be like his Son. And those he planned to be like his Son, he also called. And those he called, he also made right with him. And those he made right, he also glorified.

GOD'S LOVE IN CHRIST JESUS

[31]So what should we say about this? If God is for us, then no one can defeat us. [32]God let even his own Son suffer for us. God gave his Son for us all. So with Jesus, God will surely give us all things. [33]Who can accuse the people that God has chosen? No one! God is the One who makes them right. [34]Who can say that God's people are guilty? No one! Christ Jesus died, but that is not all. He was also raised from death. And now he is on God's right side and is begging God for us. [35]Can anything separate us from the love Christ has for us? Can troubles or problems or sufferings? If we have no food or clothes, if we are in danger, or even if death comes—can any of these things separate us from Christ's love? [36]As it is written in the Scriptures:[d]

"For you we are in danger of death all the time.
People think we are worth no more than sheep to be killed."

Psalm 44:22

[37]But in all these things we have full victory through God who showed his love for us. [38-39]Yes, I am sure that nothing can separate us from the love God has for us. Not death, not life, not angels, not ruling spirits, nothing now, nothing in the future, no powers, nothing above us, nothing below us, or anything else in the whole world will ever be able to separate us from the love of God that is in Christ Jesus our Lord.

GOD AND THE JEWISH PEOPLE

9 I am in Christ, and I am telling you the truth. I do not lie. My feelings are ruled by the Holy Spirit,[d] and they tell me that I am not lying. [2]I have great sorrow and always feel much sadness for the Jewish people. [3]I wish I could help my Jewish brothers, my people. I would even wish that I were cursed and cut off from Christ if that would help them. [4]They are the people of Israel. They were God's chosen children. They have the glory of God and the agreements that God made between himself and his people. God gave them the law of Moses and the right way of worship. And God gave his promises to them. [5]They are the descendants[d] of our great ancestors, and they are the earthly family of Christ. Christ is God over all. Praise him forever![n] Amen.

[6]I do not mean that God failed to keep his promise to them. But only some of the people of Israel are truly God's people.[n] [7]And only some of Abraham's[n] descendants are true children of Abraham. But God said to Abraham: "The descendants I promised you will be from Isaac."[n]

8:28 We ... him. Some Greek copies read "We know that everything works together for good for those who love God."
8:29 firstborn Here this probably means that Christ was the first in God's family to share God's glory.
9:5 Christ ... forever! This can also mean, "May God, who rules over all things, be praised forever!"
9:6 God's people Literally, "Israel," the people God chose to bring his blessings to the world.
9:7 Abraham Most respected ancestor of the Jews. Every Jew hoped to see Abraham.
9:7 "The descendants ... Isaac." Quotation from Genesis 21:12.

[8]This means that not all of Abraham's descendants are God's true children. Abraham's true children are those who become God's children because of the promise God made to Abraham. [9]God's promise to Abraham was this: "At the right time I will return, and Sarah will have a son."[n] [10]And that is not all. Rebekah also had sons. And those sons had the same father, our father Isaac. [11-12]But before the two boys were born, God told Rebekah, "The older will serve the younger."[n] This was before the boys had done anything good or bad. God said this before they were born so that the one chosen would be chosen because of God's own plan. He was chosen because he was the one God wanted to call, not because of anything he did. [13]As the Scripture[d] says, "I loved Jacob, but I hated Esau."[n]

[14]So what should we say about this? Is God unfair? In no way. [15]God said to Moses, "I will show kindness to anyone I want to show kindness. I will show mercy to anyone I want to show mercy."[n] [16]So God will choose the one he decides to show mercy to. And his choice does not depend on what people want or try to do. [17]The Scripture says to the king of Egypt: "I made you king so I might show my power in you. In this way my name will be talked about in all the earth."[n] [18]So God shows mercy where he wants to show mercy. And he makes stubborn the people he wants to make stubborn.

[19]So one of you will ask me: "If God controls the things we do, then why does he blame us for our sins? Who can fight his will?" [20]Do not ask that. You are only human. And human beings have no right to question God. An object cannot tell the person who made it, "Why did you make me like this?" [21]The man who makes a jar can make anything he wants to make. He can use the same clay to make different things. He can make one thing for special use and another thing for daily use.

[22]It is the same way with what God has done. God wanted to show his anger and to let people see his power. But God patiently stayed with those people he was angry with—people who were ready to be destroyed. [23]God waited with patience so that he could make known his rich glory. He wanted to give that glory to the people who receive his mercy. He has prepared these people to have his glory, and [24]we are those people whom God called. He called us from the Jews and from the non-Jews. [25]As the Scripture says in Hosea:

"I will say, 'You are my people'
    to those I had called 'not my people.'
And I will show my love
    to those people I did not love."
                                    Hosea 2:1, 23
[26]"Now it is said to Israel,
    'You are not my people.'
But later they will be called
    'children of the living God.'"
                                    Hosea 1:10
[27]And Isaiah cries out about Israel:
"There are so many people of Israel.
    They are like the grains of sand by
    the sea.
But only a few of them will be saved.
[28]   For the Lord will quickly and
        completely punish the people on
        the earth."   *Isaiah 10:22-23*
[29]It is as Isaiah said:
"The Lord of heaven's armies
    allowed a few of our descendants
    to live.

9:9 "At ... son." Quotation from Genesis 18:10, 14.
9:11-12 "The older ... younger." Quotation from Genesis 25:23.
9:13 "I ... Esau." Quotation from Malachi 1:2-3.
9:15 "I ... mercy." Quotation from Exodus 33:19.
9:17 "I ... earth." Quotation from Exodus 9:16.

Otherwise we would have been
   completely destroyed
like the cities of Sodom and
   Gomorrah."[n]   *Isaiah 1:9*
[30]So what does all this mean? It means
this: the non-Jews were not trying to
make themselves right with God. But
they were made right with God because
of their faith. [31]And the people of Israel
tried to follow a law to make themselves
right with God. But they did not succeed,
[32]because they tried to make themselves
right by the things they did. They did not
trust in God to make them right. They
fell over the stone that causes people to
fall. [33]As it is written in the Scripture:

"I will put in Jerusalem a stone that
   causes people to stumble.
It is a rock that makes them fall.
Anyone who trusts in him will not be
   disappointed."   *Isaiah 8:14; 28:16*

10 Brothers, the thing I want most
is for all the Jews to be saved.
That is my prayer to God. [2]I can say this
about them: They really try to follow
God. But they do not know the right way.
[3]They did not know the way that God
makes people right with him. And they
tried to make themselves right in their
own way. So they did not accept God's
way of making people right. [4]Christ
ended the law, so that everyone who
believes in him may be right with God.

[5]Moses writes about being made right
by following the law. He says, "A person
who does these things will have life forever because of them."[n] [6]But this is what
the Scripture says about being made
right through faith: "Don't say to yourself, 'Who will go up into heaven?'" (That
means, "Who will go up to heaven to get
Christ and bring him down to earth?")

[7]"And do not say, 'Who will go down
into the world below?'" (That means,
"Who will go down to get Christ and
bring him up from death?") [8]This is what
the Scripture says: "God's teaching is
near you; it is in your mouth and in your
heart."[n] That is the teaching of faith that
we tell. [9]If you declare with your mouth,
"Jesus is Lord," and if you believe in
your heart that God raised Jesus from
death, then you will be saved. [10]We
believe with our hearts, and so we are
made right with God. And we declare
with our mouths to say that we believe,
and so we are saved. [11]As the Scripture
says, "Anyone who trusts in him will
never be disappointed."[n] [12]That Scripture
says "anyone" because there is no difference between Jew and non-Jew. The
same Lord is the Lord of all and gives
many blessings to all who trust in him.
[13]The Scripture says, "Anyone who asks
the Lord for help will be saved."[n]

[14]But before people can trust in the
Lord for help, they must believe in him.
And before they can believe in the Lord,
they must hear about him. And for them
to hear about the Lord, someone must
tell them. [15]And before someone can go
and tell them, he must be sent. It is
written, "How beautiful is the person
who comes to bring good news."[n]

[16]But not all the Jews accepted the good
news. Isaiah said, "Lord, who believed
what we told them?"[n] [17]So faith comes
from hearing the Good News.[d] And
people hear the Good News when
someone tells them about Christ.

[18]But I ask: Didn't people hear the Good
News? Yes, they heard—as the Scripture
says:

9:29 Sodom and Gomorrah Two cities that God destroyed because the people were so evil.
10:5 "A person ... them." Quotation from Leviticus 18:5.
10:8 "Don't ... heart." Quotations from Deuteronomy 9:4; 30:12-14; Psalm 107:26.
10:11 "Anyone ... disappointed." Quotation from Isaiah 28:16.
10:13 "Anyone ... saved." Quotation from Joel 2:32.
10:15 "How ... news." Quotation from Isaiah 52:7.
10:16 "Lord ... them?" Quotation from Isaiah 53:1.

"Their message went out through all
the world.
It goes everywhere on earth."

Psalm 19:4

[19]Again I ask: Didn't the people of Israel
understand? Yes, they did understand.
First, Moses says:

"I will use those who are not a nation
to make you jealous.
I will use a nation that does not
understand to make you angry."

Deuteronomy 32:21

[20]Then Isaiah is bold enough to say:

"I was found by those who were not
asking me for help.
I made myself known to people
who were not looking for me."

Isaiah 65:1

[21]But about Israel God says,

"All day long I stood ready to accept
people who disobey and are
stubborn." *Isaiah 65:2*

GOD SHOWS MERCY TO ALL PEOPLE

11 So I ask: Did God throw out his
people? No! I myself am an Israelite. I am from the family of Abraham,
from the tribe[d] of Benjamin. [2]God chose
the Israelites to be his people before they
were born. And God did not leave his
people. Surely you know what the
Scripture[d] says about Elijah, how he
prayed to God against the people of
Israel. Elijah said, [3]"They have killed
your prophets,[d] and they have destroyed
your altars. I am the only prophet left.
And now they are trying to kill me, too."[n]
[4]But what answer did God give Elijah?
He said, "But I have left 7,000 people in
Israel. Those 7,000 have never bowed
down before Baal."[n] [5]It is the same now.
There are a few people that God has
chosen by his grace. [6]And if God chose
them by grace, then it is not for the
things they have done. If they could be
made God's people by what they did,

then God's gift of grace would not really
be a gift.

[7]So this is what has happened: The
people of Israel tried to be right with God.
But they did not succeed. But the ones God
chose did become right with him. The
others became hard and refused to listen
to God. [8]As it is written in the Scriptures:[d]

"God gave the people a dull mind so
they could not understand."

Isaiah 29:10

"God closed their eyes so they could
not see,
and God closed their ears so they
could not hear.
This continues until today."

Deuteronomy 29:4

[9]And David says:

"Let their own feasts trap them and
cause their ruin.
Let their feasts cause them to sin
and be paid back.
[10]Let their eyes be closed so they cannot
see.
Let their backs be forever weak
from troubles." *Psalm 69:22-23*

[11]So I ask: When the Jews fell, did that
fall destroy them? No! But their failure
brought salvation to the non-Jews. This
took place to cause the Jews to be
jealous. [12]The Jews' failure brought rich
blessings for the world. And what the
Jews lost brought rich blessings for the
non-Jewish people. So surely the world
will get much richer blessings when
enough Jews become the kind of people
God wants.

[13]Now I am speaking to you who are
not Jews. I am an apostle[d] to the non-
Jews. So while I have that work, I will do
the best I can. [14]I hope I can make my
own people jealous. That way, maybe I
can help some of them to be saved.
[15]God turned away from the Jews. When
that happened, God became friends with

11:3 "They ... too." Quotation from 1 Kings 19:10, 14.
11:4 "But ... Baal." Quotation from 1 Kings 19:18.

the other people in the world. So when God accepts the Jews, then surely that will bring to them life after death.

[16]If the first piece of bread is offered to God, then the whole loaf is made holy. If the roots of a tree are holy, then the tree's branches are holy too.

[17]Some of the branches from an olive tree have been broken off, and the branch of a wild olive tree has been joined to that first tree. You non-Jews are the same as that wild branch, and you now share the strength and life of the first tree, the Jews. [18]So do not brag about those branches that were broken off. You have no reason to brag. Why? You do not give life to the root. The root gives life to you. [19]You will say, "Branches were broken off so that I could be joined to their tree." [20]That is true. But those branches were broken off because they did not believe. And you continue to be part of the tree only because you believe. Do not be proud, but be afraid. [21]If God did not let the natural branches of that tree stay, then he will not let you stay if you don't believe.

[22]So you see that God is kind, but he can also be very strict. God punishes those who stop following him. But God is kind to you, if you continue following in his kindness. If you do not continue following him, you will be cut off from the tree. [23]And if the Jews will believe in God again, then God will accept the Jews back again. God is able to put them back where they were. [24]It is not natural for a wild branch to be part of a good tree. But you non-Jews are like a branch cut from a wild olive tree. And you were joined to a good olive tree. But those Jews are like a branch that grew from the good tree. So surely they can be joined to their own tree again.

[25]I want you to understand this secret truth, brothers. This truth will help you understand that you do not know everything. The truth is this: Part of Israel has been made stubborn. But that will change when many non-Jews have come to God. [26]And that is how all Israel will be saved. It is written in the Scriptures:

"The Savior will come from Jerusalem;
he will take away all evil from the
family of Jacob.[n]
[27]And I will make this agreement with
those people
when I take away their sins."

Isaiah 59:20-21; 27:9

[28]The Jews refuse to accept the Good News,[d] so they are God's enemies. This has happened to help you non-Jews. But the Jews are still God's chosen people, and God loves them very much. He loves them because of the promises he made to their ancestors. [29]God never changes his mind about the people he calls and the things he gives them. [30]At one time you refused to obey God. But now you have received mercy, because those people refused to obey. [31]And now the Jews refuse to obey, because God showed mercy to you. But this happened so that they also can[n] receive mercy from God. [32]All people have refused to obey God. God has given them all over to their stubborn ways, so that God can show mercy to all.

PRAISE TO GOD

[33]Yes, God's riches are very great! God's wisdom and knowledge have no end! No one can explain the things God decides. No one can understand God's ways. [34]As the Scripture[d] says,

"Who has known the mind of the Lord?
Who has been able to give the Lord
advice?" *Isaiah 40:13*
[35]"No one has ever given God anything
that he must pay back." *Job 41:11*
[36]Yes, God made all things. And everything continues through God and for

---

11:26 **Jacob** Father of the 12 family groups of Israel, the people God chose to be his people.
11:31 **can** Some Greek copies read "can now."

God. To God be the glory forever! Amen.

GIVE YOUR LIVES TO GOD

12 So brothers, since God has shown us great mercy, I beg you to offer your lives as a living sacrifice to him. Your offering must be only for God and pleasing to him. This is the spiritual way for you to worship. [2]Do not be shaped by this world. Instead be changed within by a new way of thinking. Then you will be able to decide what God wants for you. And you will be able to know what is good and pleasing to God and what is perfect. [3]God has given me a special gift. That is why I have something to say to everyone among you. Do not think that you are better than you are. You must see yourself as you really are. Decide what you are by the amount of faith God has given you. [4]Each one of us has a body, and that body has many parts. These parts all have different uses. [5]In the same way, we are many, but in Christ we are all one body. Each one is a part of that body. And each part belongs to all the other parts. [6]We all have different gifts. Each gift came because of the grace that God gave us. If one has the gift of prophecy,[d] he should use that gift with the faith he has. [7]If one has the gift of serving, he should serve. If one has the gift of teaching, he should teach. [8]If one has the gift of encouraging others, he should encourage. If one has the gift of giving to others, he should give freely. If one has the gift of being a leader, he should try hard when he leads. If one has the gift of showing kindness to others, that person should do so with joy.

[9]Your love must be real. Hate what is evil. Hold on to what is good. [10]Love each other like brothers and sisters. Give your brothers and sisters more honor than you want for yourselves. [11]Do not be lazy but work hard. Serve the Lord with all your heart. [12]Be joyful because you have hope. Be patient when trouble comes. Pray at all times. [13]Share with God's people who need help. Bring strangers in need into your homes.

[14]Wish good for those who do bad things to you. Wish them well and do not curse them. [15]Be happy with those who are happy. Be sad with those who are sad. [16]Live together in peace with each other. Do not be proud, but make friends with those who seem unimportant. Do not think how smart you are.

[17]If someone does wrong to you, do not pay him back by doing wrong to him. Try to do what everyone thinks is right. [18]Do your best to live in peace with everyone. [19]My friends, do not try to punish others when they wrong you. Wait for God to punish them with his anger. It is written: "I am the One who punishes; I will pay people back,"[n] says the Lord. [20]But you should do this:

"If your enemy is hungry, feed him;
  if your enemy is thirsty, give him a
    drink.
Doing this will be like pouring
  burning coals on his head."
                Proverbs 25:21-22

[21]Do not let evil defeat you. Defeat evil by doing good.

CHRISTIANS SHOULD OBEY THE LAW

13 All of you must obey the government rulers. No one rules unless God has given him the power to rule. And no one rules now without that power from God. [2]So if anyone is against the government, he is really against what God has commanded. And so he brings punishment on himself. [3]Those who do right do not have to fear the rulers. But people who do wrong must fear them. Do you want to be unafraid of the rulers? Then do what is right, and the ruler will praise you. [4]He is God's servant to help you. But if you do wrong, then be afraid. The ruler has the power to punish; he is

12:19 "I ... back" Quotation from Deuteronomy 32:35.

God's servant to punish those who do wrong. [5]So you must obey the government. You must obey not only because you might be punished, but because you know it is the right thing to do.

[6]And this is also why you pay taxes. Rulers are working for God and give their time to their work. [7]Pay everyone, then, what you owe him. If you owe any kind of tax, pay it. Show respect and honor to them all.

LOVING OTHERS

[8]Do not owe people anything. But you will always owe love to each other. The person who loves others has obeyed all the law. [9]The law says, "You must not be guilty of adultery.[d] You must not murder anyone. You must not steal. You must not want to take your neighbor's things."[n] All these commands and all others are really only one rule: "Love your neighbor as you love yourself."[n] [10]Love never hurts a neighbor. So loving is obeying all the law.

[11]I say this because we live in an important time. Yes, it is now time for you to wake up from your sleep. Our salvation is nearer now than when we first believed. [12]The "night"[n] is almost finished. The "day"[n] is almost here. So we should stop doing things that belong to darkness and take up the weapons used for fighting in the light. [13]Let us live in a right way, like people who belong to the day. We should not have wild parties or get drunk. There should be no sexual sins of any kind, no fighting or jealousy. [14]But clothe yourselves with the Lord Jesus Christ. Forget about satisfying your sinful self.

DO NOT CRITICIZE OTHER PEOPLE

14 Do not refuse to accept into your group someone who is weak in faith. And do not argue with him about opinions. [2]One person believes that he can eat all kinds of food.[n] But if another man's faith is weak, then he believes he can eat only vegetables. [3]The one who knows that he can eat any kind of food must not feel that he is better than the one who eats only vegetables. And the person who eats only vegetables must not think that the one who eats all foods is wrong. God has accepted him. [4]You cannot judge another man's servant. His own master decides if he is doing well or not. And the Lord's servant will do well because the Lord helps him do well.

[5]One person thinks that one day is more important than another. And someone else thinks that every day is the same. Each one should be sure in his own mind. [6]The person who thinks one day is more important than other days is doing that for the Lord. And the one who eats all kinds of food is doing that for the Lord. Yes, he gives thanks to God for that food. And the man who refuses to eat some foods does that for the Lord, and he gives thanks to God. [7]For we do not live or die for ourselves. [8]If we live, we are living for the Lord. And if we die, we are dying for the Lord. So living or dying, we belong to the Lord.

[9]That is why Christ died and rose from death to live again. He did this so that he would be Lord over both the dead and the living. [10]So why do you judge your brother in Christ? And why do you think that you are better than he is? We will all stand before God, and he will judge us all. [11]Yes, it is written in the Scriptures:[d]

"Everyone will bow before me;
    everyone will say that I am God.

13:9 "You . . . things." Quotation from Exodus 20:13-15, 17.
13:9 "Love . . . yourself." Quotation from Leviticus 19:18.
13:12 "night" This is used as a symbol of the sinful world we live in. This world will soon end.
13:12 "day" This is used as a symbol of the good time that is coming, when we will be with God.
14:2 all . . . food The Jewish law said there were some foods Jews should not eat. When Jews became Christians, some of them did not understand they could now eat all foods.

As surely as I live, these things will happen, says the Lord."

Isaiah 45:23

[12]So each of us will have to answer to God for what he has done.

DO NOT CAUSE OTHERS TO SIN

[13]So we should stop judging each other. We must make up our minds not to do anything that will make a Christian brother sin. [14]I am in the Lord Jesus, and I know that there is no food that is wrong to eat. But if a person believes that something is wrong, then that thing is wrong for him. [15]If you hurt your brother's faith because of something you eat, then you are not really following the way of love. Do not destroy his faith by eating food that he thinks is wrong. Christ died for him. [16]Do not allow what you think is good to become what others say is evil. [17]In the kingdom of God, eating and drinking are not important. The important things are living right with God, peace, and joy in the Holy Spirit.[d] [18]Anyone who serves Christ by living this way is pleasing God and will be accepted by other people.

[19]So let us try to do what makes peace and helps one another. [20]Do not let the eating of food destroy the work of God. All foods are all right to eat, but it is wrong to eat food that causes someone else to sin. [21]It is better not to eat meat or drink wine or do anything that will cause your brother to sin.

[22]Your beliefs about these things should be kept secret between you and God. A person is blessed if he can do what he thinks is right without feeling guilty. [23]But if he eats something without being sure that it is right, then he is wrong because he did not believe that it was right. And if he does anything without believing that it is right, then it is a sin.

15 We who are strong in faith should help those who are weak. We should help them with their weaknesses, and not please only ourselves. [2]Let each of us please his neighbor for his good, to help him be stronger in faith. [3]Even Christ did not live to please himself. It was as the Scriptures[d] said: "When people insult you, it hurts me."[n] [4]Everything that was written in the past was written to teach us, so that we could have hope. That hope comes from the patience and encouragement that the Scriptures give us. [5]Patience and encouragement come from God. And I pray that God will help you all agree with each other the way Christ Jesus wants. [6]Then you will all be joined together, and you will give glory to God the Father of our Lord Jesus Christ. [7]Christ accepted you, so you should accept each other. This will bring glory to God. [8]I tell you that Christ became a servant of the Jews. This was to show that God's promises to the Jewish ancestors are true. [9]And he also did this so that the non-Jews could give glory to God for the mercy he gives to them. It is written in the Scriptures:

"So I will praise you among the
    non-Jewish people.
I will sing praises to your name."

Psalm 18:49

[10]The Scripture also says,

"Be happy, you non-Jews, together
    with God's people."

Deuteronomy 32:43

[11]Again the Scripture says,

"All you non-Jews, praise the Lord.
    All you people, sing praises to him."

Psalm 117:1

[12]And Isaiah says,

"A new king will come from Jesse's
    family.[n]
He will come to rule over the
    non-Jews;

15:3 "When . . . me." Quotation from Psalm 69:9.
15:12 Jesse's family Jesse was the father of David, king of Israel. Jesus was from their family.

and the non-Jews will have hope
     because of him."   *Isaiah 11:10*
[13]I pray that the God who gives hope
will fill you with much joy and peace
while you trust in him. Then your hope
will overflow by the power of the Holy
Spirit.[d]

PAUL TALKS ABOUT HIS WORK

[14]My brothers, I am sure that you are
full of goodness. I know that you have all
the knowledge you need and that you
are able to teach each other. [15]But I have
written to you very openly about some
things that I wanted you to remember. I
did this because God gave me this special gift: [16]to be a minister of Christ Jesus
to the non-Jewish people. I served God
by teaching his Good News,[d] so that the
non-Jewish people could be an offering
that God would accept—an offering
made holy by the Holy Spirit.[d]

[17]So I am proud of what I have done
for God in Christ Jesus. [18]I will not talk
about anything I did myself. I will talk
only about what Christ has done through
me in leading the non-Jewish people to
obey God. They have obeyed God because
of what I have said and done. [19]And they
have obeyed God because of the power
of miracles[d] and the great things they
saw, and the power of the Holy Spirit. I
preached the Good News from Jerusalem all the way around to Illyricum.
And so I have finished that part of my
work. [20]I always want to preach the
Good News in places where people have
never heard of Christ. I do this because I
do not want to build on the work that
someone else has already started. [21]But
it is written in the Scriptures:[d]

"Those who were not told about him
     will see,
and those who have not heard
     about him will understand."
               Isaiah 52:15

PAUL'S PLAN TO VISIT ROME

[22]That is why many times I was
stopped from coming to you. [23]Now I
have finished my work here. Since for
many years I have wanted to come to
you, [24]I hope to visit you on my way to
Spain. I will enjoy being with you, and
you can help me on my trip. [25]Now I am
going to Jerusalem to help God's people.
[26]The believers in Macedonia and
Southern Greece were happy to give
their money to help the poor among
God's people at Jerusalem. [27]They were
happy to do this, and really they owe it to
them. These non-Jews have shared in
the Jews' spiritual blessings. So they
should use their material possessions to
help the Jews. [28]I must be sure that the
poor in Jerusalem get the money that
has been given for them. After I do this,
I will leave for Spain and stop and visit
you. [29]I know that when I come to you, I
will bring Christ's full blessing.

[30]Brothers, I beg you to help me in my
work by praying for me to God. Do this
because of our Lord Jesus and the love
that the Holy Spirit[d] gives us. [31]Pray that
I will be saved from the non-believers in
Judea. And pray that this help I bring to
Jerusalem will please God's people there.
[32]Then, if God wants me to, I will come
to you. I will come with joy, and together
you and I will have a time of rest. [33]The
God who gives peace be with you all.
Amen.

GREETINGS TO THE CHRISTIANS

16 I recommend to you our sister
Phoebe. She is a helper[n] in the
church in Cenchrea. [2]I ask you to accept
her in the Lord in the way God's people
should. Help her with anything she
needs because she has helped me and
many other people too.

[3]Give my greetings to Priscilla and
Aquila, who work together with me in
Christ Jesus. [4]They risked their own lives

16:1 **helper** Literally, "deaconess." This might mean the same as one of the special women helpers in 1 Timothy 3:11.

to save my life. I am thankful to them, and all the non-Jewish churches are thankful to them as well. [5]Also, greet for me the church that meets at their house.

Greetings to my dear friend Epenetus. He was the first person in Asia to follow Christ. [6]Greetings to Mary, who worked very hard for you. [7]Greetings to Andronicus and Junias, my relatives, who were in prison with me. The apostles feel they are very important. They were believers in Christ before I was. [8]Greetings to Ampliatus, my dear friend in the Lord. [9]Greetings to Urbanus. He is a worker together with me for Christ. And greetings to my dear friend Stachys. [10]Greetings to Apelles. He was tested and proved that he truly loves Christ. Greetings to all those who are in the family of Aristobulus. [11]Greetings to Herodion, my relative. Greetings to all those in the family of Narcissus who belong to the Lord. [12]Greetings to Tryphena and Tryphosa. Those women work very hard for the Lord. Greetings to my dear friend Persis. She also has worked very hard for the Lord. [13]Greetings to Rufus who is a special person in the Lord. Greetings to his mother, who has been a mother to me also. [14]Greetings to Asyncritus, Phlegon, Hermes, Patrobas, Hermas, and all the brothers who are with them. [15]Greetings to Philologus and Julia, Nereus and his sister, and Olympas. And greetings to all God's people with them. [16]Greet each other with a holy kiss. All of Christ's churches send greetings to you.

[17]Brothers, I ask you to look out for those who cause people to be against each other and who upset other people's faith. They are against the true teaching you learned. Stay away from them. [18]For such people are not serving our Lord Christ. They are only doing what pleases themselves. They use fancy talk and fine words to fool the minds of those who do not know about evil. [19]All the believers have heard that you obey. So I am very happy because of you. But I want you to be wise in what is good and innocent in what is evil.

[20]The God who brings peace will soon defeat Satan and give you power over him.

The grace of our Lord Jesus be with you.

[21]Timothy, a worker together with me, sends greetings, as well as Lucius, Jason, and Sosipater, my relatives.

[22]I am Tertius, and I am writing this letter from Paul. I send greetings to you in the Lord.

[23]Gaius is letting me and the whole church here use his home. He also sends greetings to you, as do Erastus and our brother Quartus. Erastus is the city treasurer here. [24][The grace of our Lord Jesus Christ be with all of you. Amen.][n]

[25]Glory to God! God is the One who can make you strong in faith by the Good News[d] that I tell people and by the message about Jesus Christ. The message about Christ is the secret truth that was hidden for long ages past, but is now made known. [26]It has been made clear through the writings of the prophets.[d] And by the command of the eternal God it is made known to all nations, that they might believe and obey.

[27]To the only wise God be glory forever through Jesus Christ! Amen.

16:24 The . . . Amen. Some Greek copies do not contain the bracketed text.

CORINTHIANS

1 From Paul. I was called to be an apostle[d] of Christ Jesus because that is what God wanted. Also from Sosthenes, our brother in Christ.

²To the church of God in Corinth, to those people who have been made holy in Christ Jesus. You were called to be God's holy people with all people everywhere who trust in the name of the Lord Jesus Christ—their Lord and ours:

³Grace and peace to you from God our Father and the Lord Jesus Christ.

PAUL GIVES THANKS TO GOD

⁴I always thank my God for you because of the grace that God has given you in Christ Jesus. ⁵In Jesus you have been blessed in every way, in all your speaking and in all your knowledge. ⁶The truth about Christ has been proved in you. ⁷So you have every gift from God while you wait for our Lord Jesus Christ to come again. ⁸Jesus will keep you strong until the end. He will keep you strong, so that there will be no wrong in you on the day our Lord Jesus Christ comes again. ⁹God is faithful. He is the One who has called you to share life with his Son, Jesus Christ our Lord.

PROBLEMS IN THE CHURCH

¹⁰I beg you, brothers, in the name of our Lord Jesus Christ. I beg that all of you agree with each other, so that you will not be divided into groups. I beg that you be completely joined together by having the same kind of thinking and the same purpose. ¹¹My brothers, some people from Chloe's family have told me that there are arguments among you. ¹²This is what I mean: One of you says, "I follow Paul"; another says, "I follow Apollos"; another says, "I follow Peter"; and another says, "I follow Christ." ¹³Christ cannot be divided into different groups! Did Paul die on the cross for you? No! Were you baptized in the name of Paul? No! ¹⁴I am thankful that I did not baptize any of you except Crispus and Gaius. ¹⁵I am thankful, because now no one can say that you were baptized in my name. ¹⁶(I also baptized the family of Stephanas. But I do not remember that I myself baptized any others.) ¹⁷Christ did not give me the work of baptizing people. He gave me the work of preaching the Good News,[d] and he sent me to preach the Good News without using words of worldly wisdom. If I used worldly wisdom to tell the Good News, the cross[n] of Christ would lose its power.

CHRIST IS GOD'S POWER AND WISDOM

¹⁸The teaching about the cross seems foolish to those who are lost. But to us who are being saved it is the power of God. ¹⁹It is written in the Scriptures:[d]

"I will cause the wise men to lose their
    wisdom.
I will make the wise men unable to
    understand."   *Isaiah 29:14*

²⁰Where is the wise person? Where is the educated person? Where is the philosopher[n] of our times? God has made the wisdom of the world foolish. ²¹The world did not know God through its own wisdom. So God chose to use the message that sounds foolish to save those who believe it. ²²The Jews ask for miracles[d] as proofs. The Greeks want wisdom. ²³But we preach Christ on the cross. This is a big problem to the Jews. And it seems foolish to the non-Jews. ²⁴But Christ is the power of God and the wisdom of God to those people God has called—Jews and Greeks. ²⁵Even the foolishness of

---

1:17 cross Paul uses the cross as a picture of the gospel, the story of Christ's death and rising from death to pay for men's sins. The cross, or Christ's death, was God's way to save men.
1:20 philosopher Philosophers were those who searched for truth.

God is wiser than men. Even the weakness of God is stronger than men.

[26]Brothers, look at what you were when God called you. Not many of you were wise in the way the world judges wisdom. Not many of you had great influence. Not many of you came from important families. [27]But God chose the foolish things of the world to shame the wise. He chose the weak things of the world to shame the strong. [28]And he chose what the world thinks is not important. He chose what the world hates and thinks is nothing. He chose these to destroy what the world thinks is important. [29]God did this so that no man can brag before him. [30]It is God who has made you part of Christ Jesus. Christ has become wisdom for us from God. Christ is the reason we are right with God and have freedom from sin; Christ is the reason we are holy. [31]So, as the Scripture[d] says, "If a person brags, he should brag only about the Lord."[n]

THE MESSAGE OF CHRIST'S DEATH

2 Dear brothers, when I came to you, I did not come as a proud man. I preached God's truth, but not with fancy words or a show of great learning. [2]I decided that while I was with you I would forget about everything except Jesus Christ and his death on the cross. [3]When I came to you, I was weak and shook with fear. [4]My teaching and my speaking were not with wise words that persuade people. But the proof of my teaching was the power that the Spirit[d] gives. [5]I did this so that your faith would be in God's power, not in the wisdom of a man.

GOD'S WISDOM

[6]Yet I speak wisdom to those who are mature. But this wisdom is not from this world or of the rulers of this world. (These rulers are losing their power.) [7]But I speak God's secret wisdom, which he has kept hidden. God planned this wisdom for our glory, before the world began. [8]None of the rulers of this world understood it. If they had, they would not have killed the Lord of glory on a cross. [9]But as it is written in the Scriptures:[d]

"No one has ever seen this.
No one has ever heard about it.
No one has ever imagined
what God has prepared for those
who love him."   *Isaiah 64:4*

[10]But God has shown us these things through the Spirit.[d]

The Spirit knows all things, even the deep secrets of God. [11]It is like this: No one knows the thoughts that another person has. Only a person's spirit that lives in him knows his thoughts. It is the same with God. No one knows the thoughts of God. Only the Spirit of God knows God's thoughts. [12]We did not receive the spirit of the world, but we received the Spirit that is from God. We received this Spirit so that we can know all that God has given us. [13]When we speak, we do not use words taught to us by the wisdom that men have. We use words taught to us by the Spirit. We use spiritual words to explain spiritual things. [14]A person who is not spiritual does not accept the gifts that come from the Spirit of God. That person thinks they are foolish. He cannot understand the Spirit's gifts, because they can only be judged spiritually. [15]But the spiritual person is able to judge all things. Yet no one can judge him. The Scripture says:

[16]"Who has known the mind of the Lord?
Who has been able to teach him?"
Isaiah 40:13

But we have the mind of Christ.

FOLLOWING MEN IS WRONG

3 Brothers, in the past I could not talk to you as I talk to spiritual people. I had to talk to you as I would to people of the world—babies in Christ. [2]The teaching I gave you was like milk, not

---

1:31 "If ... Lord." Quotation from Jeremiah 9:24.

solid food. I did this because you were not ready for solid food. And even now you are not ready. [3]You are still not spiritual. You have jealousy and arguing among you. This shows that you are not spiritual. You are acting like people of the world. [4]One of you says, "I follow Paul," and another says, "I follow Apollos." When you say things like this, you are acting like worldly people.

[5]Is Apollos important? No! Is Paul important? No! We are only servants of God who helped you believe. Each one of us did the work God gave us to do. [6]I planted the seed of the teaching in you, and Apollos watered it. But God is the One who made the seed grow. [7]So the one who plants is not important, and the one who waters is not important. Only God is important, because he is the One who makes things grow. [8]The one who plants and the one who waters have the same purpose. And each will be rewarded for his own work. [9]We are workers together for God. And you are like a farm that belongs to God.

And you are a house that belongs to God. [10]Like an expert builder I built the foundation of that house. I used the gift that God gave me to do this. Others are building on that foundation. But everyone should be careful how he builds. [11]The foundation has already been built. No one can build any other foundation. The foundation that has already been laid is Jesus Christ. [12]Anyone can build on that foundation, using gold, silver, jewels, wood, grass, or straw. [13]But the work that each person does will be clearly seen, because the Day[n] will make it plain. That Day will appear with fire, and the fire will test every man's work. [14]If the building that a man puts on the foundation still stands, he will get his reward.

[15]But if his building is burned up, he will suffer loss. The man will be saved, but it will be as if he escaped from a fire.

[16]You should know that you yourselves are God's temple. God's Spirit[d] lives in you. [17]If anyone destroys God's temple, God will destroy him, because God's temple is holy. You yourselves are God's temple.

[18]Do not fool yourselves. If anyone among you thinks he is wise in this world, he should become a fool. Then he can become truly wise, [19]because the wisdom of this world is foolishness to God. It is written in the Scriptures,[d] "He catches wise men in their own clever traps."[n] [20]It is also written in the Scriptures, "The Lord knows what people think. He knows they are just a puff of wind."[n] [21]So you should not brag about men. All things are yours: [22]Paul, Apollos and Peter; the world, life, death, the present, and the future—all these things are yours. [23]And you belong to Christ, and Christ belongs to God.

APOSTLES OF CHRIST

4 This is what people should think about us: We are servants of Christ. We are the ones God has trusted with his secret truths. [2]A person who is trusted with something must show that he is worthy of that trust. [3]I do not care if I am judged by you or if I am judged by any human court. I do not even judge myself. [4]I know of no wrong that I have done. But this does not make me innocent. The Lord is the One who judges me. [5]So do not judge before the right time; wait until the Lord comes. He will bring to light things that are now hidden in darkness. He will make known the secret purposes of people's hearts. Then God will give everyone the praise he should get.

3:13 **Day** The day Christ will come to judge all people and take his people home to live with him.
3:19 **"He . . . traps."** Quotation from Job 5:13.
3:20 **"The Lord . . . wind."** Quotation from Psalm 94:11.

[6]Brothers, I have used Apollos and myself as examples. I did this so that you could learn from us the meaning of the words, "Follow only what is written in the Scriptures."[d] Then you will not be proud of one man and hate another. [7]Who says that you are better than others? Everything you have was given to you. And if this is so, why do you brag as if you got these things by your own power?

[8]You think you have everything you need. You think you are rich. You think you have become kings without us. I wish you really were kings! Then we could be kings together with you. [9]But it seems to me that God has given me and the other apostles[d] the last place. We are like men sentenced to die. We are like a show for the whole world to see—angels and people. [10]We are fools for Christ's sake. But you think you are very wise in Christ. We are weak, but you think you are strong. You receive honor, but we are hated. [11]Even now we still do not have enough to eat or drink or enough clothes. We are often beaten. We have no homes. [12]We work hard with our own hands for our food. People curse us, but we bless them. They hurt us, and we accept it. [13]They say evil things against us, but we say only kind things to them. Even today, we are treated as though we are the garbage of the world—the dirt of the earth.

[14]I am not trying to make you feel ashamed. I am writing this to give you a warning as if you were my own dear children. [15]For though you may have 10,000 teachers in Christ, you do not have many fathers. Through the Good News[d] I became your father in Christ Jesus. [16]So I beg you, please be like me. [17]That is why I am sending Timothy to you. He is my son in the Lord. I love Timothy, and he is faithful. He will help you remember the way I live in Christ

Jesus. This way of life is what I teach in all the churches everywhere.

[18]Some of you have become proud, thinking that I will not come to you again. [19]But I will come very soon if the Lord wants me to. Then I will see what those who are proud can do, not what they say. [20]I want to see this because the kingdom of God is not talk but power. [21]Which do you want: that I come to you with punishment, or that I come with love and gentleness?

WICKEDNESS IN THE CHURCH

5 Now, it is actually being said that there is sexual sin among you. And it is of such a bad kind that it does not happen even among those who do not know God. A man there has his father's wife. [2]And still you are proud of yourselves! You should have been filled with sadness. And the man who did that sin should be put out of your group. [3]My body is not there with you, but I am with you in spirit. And I have already judged the man who did that sin. I judged him just as I would if I were really there. [4]Meet together as the people of our Lord Jesus. I will be with you in spirit, and you will have the power of our Lord Jesus with you. [5]Then give this man to Satan, so that his sinful self[n] will be destroyed. And then his spirit can be saved on the day of the Lord.

[6]Your bragging is not good. You know the saying, "Just a little yeast makes the whole batch of dough rise." [7]Take out all the old yeast so that you will be a new batch of dough. And you really are new dough without yeast. For Christ, our Passover[d] lamb, was killed to cleanse us. [8]So let us continue our feast, but not with the bread that has the old yeast. That old yeast is the yeast of sin and wickedness. But let us eat the bread that has no yeast. This is the bread of goodness and truth.

5:5 sinful self Literally, "flesh." This could also mean his body.

[9]I wrote to you in my letter that you should not associate with those who take part in sexual sin. [10]But I did not mean that you should not associate with the sinful people of this world. People of the world do take part in sexual sin, or they are selfish and they cheat each other, or they worship idols. But to get away from them you would have to leave this world. [11]I am writing to tell you that the person you must not associate with is this: anyone who calls himself a brother in Christ but who takes part in sexual sin, or is selfish, or worships idols, or lies about others, or gets drunk, or cheats people. Do not even eat with someone like that.

[12-13]It is not my business to judge those who are not part of the church. God will judge them. But you must judge the people who are part of the church. The Scripture[d] says, "You must get rid of the evil person among you."[n]

JUDGING PROBLEMS AMONG CHRISTIANS

6 When one of you has something against a brother in Christ, why do you go to the judges in the law courts? Those people are not right with God. So why do you let them decide who is right? You should be ashamed! Why do you not let God's people decide who is right? [2]Surely you know that God's people will judge the world. So if you are to judge the world, then surely you are able to judge small things as well. [3]You know that in the future we will judge angels. So surely we can judge things in this life. [4]So if you have disagreements that must be judged, why do you take them to those who are not part of the church? They mean nothing to the church? [5]I say this to shame you. Surely there is someone among you wise enough to judge a complaint between two brothers in Christ.

[6]But now one brother goes to court against another brother. And you let men who are not believers judge their case!

[7]The lawsuits that you have against each other show that you are already defeated. It would be better for you to let someone wrong you! It would be better for you to let someone cheat you! [8]But you yourselves do wrong and cheat! And you do this to your own brothers in Christ!

[9-10]Surely you know that the people who do wrong will not receive God's kingdom. Do not be fooled. These people will not receive God's kingdom: those who sin sexually, or worship idols, or take part in adultery,[d] or men who have sexual relations with other men, or steal, or are selfish, or get drunk, or lie about others, or cheat. [11]In the past, some of you were like that. But you were washed clean. You were made holy. And you were made right with God in the name of the Lord Jesus Christ and by the Spirit of our God.

USE YOUR BODIES FOR GOD'S GLORY

[12]"I am allowed to do all things." But not all things are good for me to do. "I am allowed to do all things." But I must not do those things that will make me their slave. [13]"Food is for the stomach, and the stomach for food." Yes. But God will destroy them both. The body is not for sexual sin. The body is for the Lord, and the Lord is for the body. [14]By God's power God raised the Lord Jesus from death. And God will also raise us from death. [15]Surely you know that your bodies are parts of Christ himself. So I must never take parts of Christ and join them to a prostitute![d] [16]It is written in the Scriptures,[d] "The two people will become one body."[n] So you should know that a man who joins himself with a prostitute becomes one with her in body. [17]But the one who joins himself with the Lord is one with the Lord in spirit.

5:12-13 "You ... you." Quotation from Deuteronomy 17:7; 19:19; 22:21, 24; 24:7.
6:16 "The two ... body." Quotation from Genesis 2:24.

[18]So run away from sexual sin. Every other sin that a man does is outside his body. But the one who sins sexually sins against his own body. [19]You should know that your body is a temple for the Holy Spirit.[d] The Holy Spirit is in you. You have received the Holy Spirit from God. You do not own yourselves. [20]You were bought by God for a price. So honor God with your bodies.

ABOUT MARRIAGE

7 Now I will discuss the things you wrote to me about. It is good for a man not to marry. [2]But sexual sin is a danger. So each man should have his own wife. And each woman should have her own husband. [3]The husband should give his wife all that she should have as his wife. And the wife should give her husband all that he should have as her husband. [4]The wife does not have power over her own body. Her husband has the power over her body. And the husband does not have power over his own body. His wife has the power over his body. [5]Do not refuse to give your bodies to each other. But you might both agree to stay away from sexual relations for a time. You might do this so that you can give your time to prayer. Then come together again. This is so that Satan cannot tempt you in your weakness. [6]I say this to give you permission. It is not a command. [7]I wish everyone were like me. But each person has his own gift from God. One has one gift, another has another gift.

[8]Now for those who are not married and for the widows I say this: It is good for them to stay single as I am. [9]But if they cannot control their bodies, then they should marry. It is better to marry than to burn with sexual desire.

[10]Now I give this command for the married people. (The command is not from me; it is from the Lord.) A wife should not leave her husband. [11]But if she does leave, she must not marry again. Or she should go back to her husband. Also the husband should not divorce his wife.

[12]For all the others I say this (I am saying this, not the Lord): A brother in Christ might have a wife who is not a believer. If she will live with him, he must not divorce her. [13]And a woman might have a husband who is not a believer. If he will live with her, she must not divorce him. [14]The husband who is not a believer is made holy through his believing wife. And the wife who is not a believer is made holy through her believing husband. If this were not true, then your children would not be clean.[d] But now your children are holy.

[15]But if the person who is not a believer decides to leave, let him leave. When this happens, the brother or sister in Christ is free. God called us[n] to a life of peace. [16]Wives, maybe you will save your husband; and husbands, maybe you will save your wife. You do not know now what will happen later.

LIVE AS GOD CALLED YOU

[17]But each one should continue to live the way God has given him to live—the way he was when God called him. This is a rule I make in all the churches. [18]If a man was already circumcised[d] when he was called, he should not change his circumcision. If a man was without circumcision when he was called, he should not be circumcised. [19]It is not important if a man is circumcised or not circumcised. The important thing is obeying God's commands. [20]Each one should stay the way he was when God called him. [21]If you were a slave when God called you, do not let that bother you. But if you can be free, then become free. [22]The person who was a slave when the Lord called him is free in the Lord. He belongs to the

---

7:15 **us** Some Greek copies read "you."

Lord. In the same way, the one who was free when he was called is now Christ's slave. ²³You all were bought for a price. So do not become slaves of men. ²⁴Brothers, in your new life with God each one of you should continue the way you were when you were called.

QUESTIONS ABOUT GETTING MARRIED

²⁵Now I write about people who are not married. I have no command from the Lord about this, but I give my opinion. And I can be trusted, because the Lord has given me mercy. ²⁶This is a time of trouble. So I think that it is good for you to stay the way you are. ²⁷If you have a wife, then do not try to become free from her. If you are not married, then do not try to find a wife. ²⁸But if you decide to marry, this is not a sin. And it is not a sin for a girl who has never married to get married. But those who marry will have trouble in this life. And I want you to be free from this trouble.

²⁹Brothers, this is what I mean: We do not have much time left. So starting now, those who have wives should use their time to serve the Lord as if they had no wives. ³⁰Those who are sad should live as if they are not sad. Those who are happy should live as if they are not happy. Those who buy things should live as if they own nothing. ³¹Those who use the things of the world should live as if those things are not important to them. You should live like this, because this world, the way it is now, will soon be gone.

³²I want you to be free from worry. A man who is not married is busy with the Lord's work. He is trying to please the Lord. ³³But a man who is married is busy with things of the world. He is trying to please his wife. ³⁴He must think about two things—pleasing his wife and pleasing the Lord. A woman who is not married or a girl who has never married is busy with the Lord's work. She wants to give herself fully—body and soul—to the Lord. But a married woman is busy with things of the world. She is trying to please her husband. ³⁵I am saying this to help you. I am not trying to limit you. But I want you to live in the right way. And I want you to give yourselves fully to the Lord without giving your time to other things.

³⁶A man might think that he is not doing the right thing with the girl he is engaged to. The girl might be almost past the best age to marry. So he might feel that he should marry her. He should do what he wants. They should get married. It is no sin. ³⁷But another man might be more sure in his mind. There may be no need for marriage, so he is free to do what he wants. If he has decided in his own heart not to marry, he is doing the right thing. ³⁸So the man who marries his girl does right. And the man who does not marry does even better.

³⁹A woman must stay with her husband as long as he lives. If the husband dies, she is free to marry any man she wants. But she must marry another believer. ⁴⁰The woman is happier if she does not marry again. This is my opinion, and I believe that I have God's Spirit.

ABOUT FOOD OFFERED TO IDOLS

8 Now I will write about meat that is sacrificed to idols. We know that "we all have knowledge." Knowledge puffs you up with pride, but love builds up. ²Whoever thinks he knows something does not yet know anything as he should. ³But he who loves God is known by God.

⁴So this is what I say about eating meat sacrificed to idols: We know that an idol is really nothing in the world. And we know that there is only one God. ⁵It is really not important if there are things called gods, in heaven or on earth. (And there are many things that people call "gods" and "lords.") ⁶But for us there is only one God. He is our Father. All things came from him, and we live for him. And there is only one Lord—Jesus Christ. All

things were made through Jesus, and we also have life through him.

⁷But not all people know this. Until now, some people have had the habit of worshiping idols. So now when they eat meat, they still feel as if it belongs to an idol. They are not sure that it is right to eat this meat. When they eat it, they feel guilty. ⁸But food will not make us closer to God. Refusing to eat does not make us less pleasing to God. And eating does not make us better in God's sight.

⁹But be careful with your freedom. Your freedom may cause those who are weak in faith to fall into sin. ¹⁰Suppose one of you who has knowledge eats in an idol's temple.ⁿ Someone who is weak in faith might see you eating there. This would encourage him to eat meat sacrificed to idols. But he really thinks it is wrong. ¹¹So this weak brother is ruined because of your "knowledge." And Christ died for this brother. ¹²When you sin against your brothers in Christ like this and cause them to do what they feel is wrong, you are also sinning against Christ. ¹³So if the food I eat makes my brother fall into sin, I will never eat meat again. I will stop eating meat, so that I will not cause my brother to sin.

PAUL IS LIKE THE OTHER APOSTLES

9 I am a free man. I am an apostle.ᵈ I have seen Jesus our Lord. You people are all an example of my work in the Lord. ²Others may not accept me as an apostle, but surely you accept me. You are proof that I am an apostle in the Lord.

³Some people want to judge me. So this is the answer I give them: ⁴Do we not have the right to eat and drink? ⁵Do we not have the right to bring a believing wife with us when we travel? The other apostles, the Lord's brothers, and Peter all do this. ⁶And are Barnabas and I the only ones who must work to earn our living? ⁷No soldier ever serves in the army and pays his own salary. No one ever plants a vineyard without eating some of the grapes himself. No person takes care of a flock of sheep without drinking some of the milk himself.

⁸This is not only what men think. God's law says the same thing. ⁹Yes, it is written in the law of Moses: "When an ox is working in the grain, do not cover its mouth and keep it from eating."ⁿ When God said this, was he thinking only about oxen? No. ¹⁰He was really talking about us. Yes, that Scriptureᵈ was written for us. The one who plows and the one who works in the grain should hope to get some of the grain for their work. ¹¹We planted spiritual seed among you. So we should be able to harvest from you some things for this life. Surely this is not asking too much. ¹²Other men have the right to get something from you. So surely we have this right, too. But we do not use this right. No, we put up with everything ourselves so that we will not stop anyone from obeying the Good Newsᵈ of Christ. ¹³Surely you know that those who work at the Templeᵈ get their food from the Temple. And those who serve at the altar get part of what is offered at the altar. ¹⁴It is the same with those who tell the Good News. The Lord has commanded that those who tell the Good News should get their living from this work.

¹⁵But I have not used any of these rights. And I am not writing this now to get anything from you. I would rather die than to have my reason for bragging taken away. ¹⁶Telling the Good News is not my reason for bragging. Telling the Good News is my duty—something I must do. And how bad it will be for me if I do not tell the Good News. ¹⁷If I preach because it is my own choice, I should get

---

8:10 idol's temple Building where a false god is worshiped.
9:9 "When an ox ... eating." Quotation from Deuteronomy 25:4.

a reward. But I have no choice. I must tell the Good News. I am only doing the duty that was given to me. [18]So what reward do I get? This is my reward: that when I tell the Good News I can offer it freely. In this way I do not use my right to be paid in my work for the Good News.

[19]I am free. I belong to no man. But I make myself a slave to all people. I do this to help save as many people as I can. [20]To the Jews I became like a Jew. I did this to help save the Jews. I myself am not ruled by the law. But to those who are ruled by the law I became like a person who is ruled by the law. I did this to help save those who are ruled by the law. [21]To those who are without the law I became like a person who is without the law. I did this to help save those people who are without the law. (But really, I am not without God's law—I am ruled by Christ's law.) [22]To those who are weak, I became weak so that I could help save them. I have become all things to all people. I did this so that I could save some of them in any way possible. [23]I do all this because of the Good News. I do it so that I can share in the blessings of the Good News.

[24]You know that in a race all the runners run. But only one gets the prize. So run like that. Run to win! [25]All those who compete in the games use strict training. They do this so that they can win a crown. That crown is an earthly thing that lasts only a short time. But our crown will continue forever. [26]So I do not run without a goal. I fight like a boxer who is hitting something—not just the air. [27]It is my own body that I hit. I make it my slave. I do this so that I myself will not be rejected after I have preached to others.

DON'T BE LIKE THE JEWS

10 Brothers, I want you to know what happened to our ancestors who followed Moses. They were all under the cloud, and they all went through the sea. [2]They were all baptized as followers of Moses in the cloud and in the sea. [3]They all ate the same spiritual food. [4]And they all drank the same spiritual drink. They drank from that spiritual rock that was with them. That rock was Christ. [5]But God was not pleased with most of them. They died in the desert.

[6]And these things that happened are examples for us. They should stop us from wanting evil things as those people did. [7]Do not worship idols, as some of them did. It is written in the Scriptures:[d] "The people sat down to eat and drink. Then they got up and sinned sexually."[n] [8]We should not take part in sexual sins, as some of them did. In one day 23,000 of them died because of their sins. [9]We should not test the Lord as some of them did. They were killed by snakes. [10]And do not complain as some of them did. They were killed by the angel that destroys.

[11]The things that happened to those people are examples. And they were written down to be warnings for us. For we live in a time when all these things of the past have reached their goal. [12]So anyone who thinks he is standing strong should be careful not to fall. [13]The only temptations that you have are the temptations that all people have. But you can trust God. He will not let you be tempted more than you can stand. But when you are tempted, God will also give you a way to escape that temptation. Then you will be able to stand it.

[14]So, my dear friends, stay away from worshiping idols. [15]I am speaking to you, as to reasonable people; judge for yourselves what I say. [16]We give thanks for the cup of blessing.[n] It is a sharing in the blood of Christ's death. And the bread that we break is a sharing in the body of Christ. [17]There is one loaf of bread. And

10:7 "The people ... sexually." Quotation from Exodus 32:6.
10:16 cup of blessing The cup of the fruit of the vine that Christians thank God for and drink at the Lord's Supper.

we are many people. But we all share from that one loaf. So we are really one body.

[18]Think about the people of Israel: Do not those who eat the sacrifices share in the altar? [19]I do not mean that the food sacrificed to an idol is something important. And I do not mean that an idol is anything at all. [20]But I say that what is sacrificed to idols is offered to demons,[d] not to God. And I do not want you to share anything with demons. [21]You cannot drink the cup of the Lord and the cup of demons, too. You cannot share in the Lord's table and the table of demons, too. [22]Do we want to make the Lord jealous? We are not stronger than he is, are we?

HOW TO USE CHRISTIAN FREEDOM

[23]"We are allowed to do all things." Yes. But not all things are good for us to do. "We are allowed to do all things." Yes. But not all things help others grow stronger. [24]No one should try to do what will help only himself. He should try to do what is good for others.

[25]Eat any meat that is sold in the meat market. Do not ask questions about the meat to see if it is something you think is wrong to eat. [26]You can eat it, "because the earth and everything on it belong to the Lord."[n]

[27]Someone who is not a believer may invite you to eat with him. If you want to go, eat anything that is put before you. Do not ask questions about it. [28]But if anyone says to you, "That food was offered to idols," then do not eat it. Do not eat it because of that person who told you and because eating it would be something that might be thought wrong. [29]I don't mean that you think it is wrong. But the other person might think it is wrong. My own freedom should not be judged by what someone else thinks. [30]I eat the meal with thankfulness. And I do

not want to be criticized because of something I thank God for.

[31]So if you eat, or if you drink, or if you do anything, do everything for the glory of God. [32]Never do anything that might make others do wrong—Jews, Greeks, or God's church. [33]I do the same thing. I try to please everybody in every way. I am not trying to do what is good for me. I try to do what is good for the most people. I do this so that they can be saved.

11 Follow my example, as I follow the example of Christ.

BEING UNDER AUTHORITY

[2]I praise you because you remember me in everything. You follow closely the teachings that I gave you. [3]But I want you to understand this: The head of every man is Christ. And the head of a woman is the man.[n] And the head of Christ is God. [4]Every man who prophesies[d] or prays with his head covered brings shame to his head. [5]But every woman who prays or prophesies should have her head covered. If her head is not covered, she brings shame to her head. She is the same as a woman who has her head shaved. [6]If a woman does not cover her head, it is the same as cutting off all her hair. But it is shameful for a woman to cut off her hair or to shave her head. So she should cover her head. [7]But a man should not cover his head, because he is made like God and is God's glory. But woman is man's glory. [8]Man did not come from woman, but woman came from man. [9]And man was not made for woman. Woman was made for man. [10]So that is why a woman should have her head covered with something to show that she is under authority. And also she should do this because of the angels.

[11]But in the Lord the woman is important to the man, and the man is important to the woman. [12]This is true because

---

10:26 "because ... Lord" Quotation from Psalms 24:1; 50:12; 89:11.
11:3 the man This could also mean "her husband."

woman came from man, but also man is born from woman. Really, everything comes from God. [13]Decide this for yourselves: Is it right for a woman to pray to God without something on her head? [14]Even nature itself teaches you that wearing long hair is shameful for a man. [15]But wearing long hair is a woman's honor. Long hair is given to the woman to cover her head. [16]Some people may still want to argue about this. But I would add that neither we nor the churches of God accept any other practice.

THE LORD'S SUPPER

[17]In the things I tell you now I do not praise you. Your meetings hurt you more than they help you. [18]First, I hear that when you meet together as a church you are divided. And I believe some of this. [19](It is necessary for there to be differences among you. That is the way to make it clear which of you are really doing right.) [20]When you all come together, you are not really eating the Lord's Supper.[n] [21]This is because when you eat, each person eats without waiting for the others. Some people do not get enough to eat, while others have too much to drink. [22]You can eat and drink in your own homes! It seems that you think God's church is not important. You embarrass those who are poor. What should I tell you? Should I praise you for doing this? I do not praise you.

[23]The teaching that I gave you is the same teaching that I received from the Lord: On the night when Jesus was handed over to be killed, he took bread [24]and gave thanks for it. Then he broke the bread and said, "This is my body; it is[n] for you. Do this to remember me." [25]In the same way, after they ate, Jesus took the cup. He said, "This cup shows the new agreement from God to his people. This new agreement begins with the blood of my death.

When you drink this, do it to remember me." [26]Every time you eat this bread and drink this cup, you show others about the Lord's death until he comes.

[27]So a person should not eat the bread or drink the cup of the Lord in a way that is not worthy of it. If he does he is sinning against the body and the blood of the Lord. [28]Everyone should look into his own heart before he eats the bread and drinks the cup. [29]If someone eats the bread and drinks the cup without recognizing the body, then he is judged guilty by eating and drinking. [30]That is why many in your group are sick and weak. And some of you have died. [31]But if we judged ourselves in the right way, then God would not judge us. [32]But when the Lord judges us, he disciplines us to show us the right way. He does this so that we will not be destroyed along with the world.

[33]So my brothers, when you come together to eat, wait for each other. [34]If anyone is too hungry, he should eat at home. Do this so that your meeting together will not bring God's judgment on you. I will tell you what to do about the other things when I come.

GIFTS FROM THE HOLY SPIRIT

12 Now, brothers, I want you to understand about spiritual gifts. [2]You remember the lives you lived before you were believers. You let yourselves be influenced and led away to worship idols—things that have no life. [3]So I tell you that no one who is speaking with the help of God's Spirit says, "Jesus be cursed." And no one can say, "Jesus is Lord," without the help of the Holy Spirit.[d]

[4]There are different kinds of gifts; but they are all from the same Spirit. [5]There are different ways to serve; but all these ways are from the same Lord. [6]And there

11:20 Lord's Supper The meal Jesus told his followers to eat to remember him (Luke 22:14-20).
11:24 it is Some Greek copies read "it is broken."

are different ways that God works in people; but all these ways are from the same God. God works in us all in everything we do. [7]Something from the Spirit can be seen in each person, to help everyone. [8]The Spirit gives one person the ability to speak with wisdom. And the same Spirit gives another the ability to speak with knowledge. [9]The same Spirit gives faith to one person. And that one Spirit gives another gifts of healing. [10]The Spirit gives to another person the power to do miracles,[d] to another the ability to prophesy.[d] And he gives to another the ability to know the difference between good and evil spirits. The Spirit gives one person the ability to speak in different kinds of languages and to another the ability to interpret those languages. [11]One Spirit, the same Spirit, does all these things. The Spirit decides what to give each person.

THE BODY OF CHRIST

[12]A person's body is one thing, but it has many parts. Yes, there are many parts to a body, but all those parts make only one body. Christ is like that too. [13]Some of us are Jews, and some of us are Greeks. Some of us are slaves, and some of us are free. But we were all baptized into one body through one Spirit.[d] And we were all made to share in the one Spirit.

[14]And a person's body has more than one part. It has many parts. [15]The foot might say, "I am not a hand. So I am not part of the body." But saying this would not stop the foot from being a part of the body. [16]The ear might say, "I am not an eye. So I am not part of the body." But saying this would not make the ear stop being a part of the body. [17]If the whole body were an eye, the body would not be able to hear. If the whole body were an ear, the body would not be able to smell anything. [18-19]If each part of the body were the same part, there would be no body. But truly God put the parts in the

body as he wanted them. He made a place for each one of them. [20]And so there are many parts, but only one body.

[21]The eye cannot say to the hand, "I don't need you!" And the head cannot say to the foot, "I don't need you!" [22]No! Those parts of the body that seem to be weaker are really very important. [23]And the parts of the body that we think are not worth much are the parts that we give the most care to. And we give special care to the parts of the body that we want to hide. [24]The more beautiful parts of our body need no special care. But God put the body together and gave more honor to the parts that need it. [25]God did this so that our body would not be divided. God wanted the different parts to care the same for each other. [26]If one part of the body suffers, then all the other parts suffer with it. Or if one part of our body is honored, then all the other parts share its honor.

[27]All of you together are the body of Christ. Each one of you is a part of that body. [28]And in the church God has given a place first to apostles,[d] second to prophets,[d] and third to teachers. Then God has given a place to those who do miracles,[d] those who have gifts of healing, those who can help others, those who are able to lead, and those who can speak in different languages. [29]Not all are apostles. Not all are prophets. Not all are teachers. Not all do miracles. [30]Not all have gifts of healing. Not all speak in different languages. Not all interpret those languages. [31]But you should truly want to have the greater gifts.

LOVE

And now I will show you the best way of all.

13 I may speak in different languages of men or even angels. But if I do not have love, then I am only a noisy bell or a ringing cymbal. [2]I may have the gift of prophecy;[d] I may understand all the secret things of God and all knowledge; and I may have faith so great that I can move mountains. But even with all these things, if I do not have love, then I am nothing. [3]I may give everything I have to feed the poor. And I may even give my body as an offering to be burned.[n] But I gain nothing by doing these things if I do not have love.

[4]Love is patient and kind. Love is not jealous, it does not brag, and it is not proud. [5]Love is not rude, is not selfish, and does not become angry easily. Love does not remember wrongs done against it. [6]Love takes no pleasure in evil, but rejoices over the truth. [7]Love patiently accepts all things. It always trusts, always hopes, and always continues strong.

[8]Love never ends. There are gifts of prophecy,[d] but they will be ended. There are gifts of speaking in different languages, but those gifts will end. There is the gift of knowledge, but it will be ended. [9]These things will end, because this knowledge and these prophecies we have are not complete. [10]But when perfection comes, the things that are not complete will end. [11]When I was a child, I talked like a child; I thought like a child; I made plans like a child. When I became a man, I stopped those childish ways. [12]It is the same with us. Now we see as if we are looking into a dark mirror. But at that time, in the future, we shall see clearly. Now I know only a part. But at that time I will know fully, as God has known me. [13]So these three things continue forever: faith, hope and love. And the greatest of these is love.

SPIRITUAL GIFTS

14 Love, then, is what you should try for. And you should truly want to have the spiritual gifts. And the gift you should want most is to be able to prophesy.[d] [2]I will explain why. One who has the gift of speaking in a different language is not speaking to people. He is speaking to God. No one understands him—he is speaking secret things through the Spirit.[d] [3]But one who prophesies is speaking to people. He gives people strength, encouragement, and comfort. [4]The one who speaks in a different language is helping only himself. But the one who prophesies is helping the whole church. [5]I would like all of you to have the gift of speaking in different kinds of languages. But more, I want you to prophesy. The person who prophesies is greater than the one who can only speak in different languages—unless someone is there who can explain what he says. Then the whole church can be helped.

[6]Brothers, will it help you if I come to you speaking in different languages? No! It will help you only if I bring you a new truth or some knowledge, or some prophecy, or some teaching. [7]It is the same as with non-living things that make sounds—like a flute or a harp. If different musical notes are not made clear, you will not know what song is being played. Each note must be played clearly for you to be able to understand the tune. [8]And in a war, if the trumpet does not sound clearly, the soldiers will not know it is time to prepare for fighting. [9]It is the same with you. The words you speak with your tongue must be clear. Unless you speak clearly, no one can understand what you are saying. You will be talking in the air! [10]It is true that there are many kinds of speech in the world. And they all have meaning. [11]So unless I understand the meaning of what someone says to me, we will be like strangers to each other. [12]It is the same with you. You want spiritual gifts very much. So try most to have the gifts that help the church grow stronger.

[13]The one who has the gift of speaking in a different language should pray that

---

13:3 **give . . . burned** Other Greek copies read "hand over my body in order that I may brag."

he can also interpret what he says. [14]If I pray in a different language, my spirit is praying, but my mind does nothing. [15]So what should I do? I will pray with my spirit, but I will also pray with my mind. I will sing with my spirit, but I will also sing with my mind. [16]You might be praising God with your spirit. But a person there without understanding cannot say "Amen"[n] to your prayer of thanks. He does not know what you are saying. [17]You may be thanking God in a good way, but the other person is not helped.

[18]I thank God that my gift of speaking in different kinds of languages is greater than any of yours. [19]But in the church meetings I would rather speak five words that I understand than thousands of words in a different language. I would rather speak with my understanding, so that I can teach others.

[20]Brothers, do not think like children. In evil things be like babies. But in your thinking you should be like full-grown men. [21]It is written in the Scriptures:[d]

"I will use strange words and foreign
    languages
to speak to these people.
But even then they will not listen."

                 Isaiah 28:11-12

That is what the Lord says.

[22]So the gift of speaking in different kinds of languages is a sign for those who do not believe, not for those who believe. And prophecy is for people who believe, not for those who do not believe. [23]Suppose the whole church meets together and everyone speaks in different languages. If some people come in who are without understanding or do not believe, they will say you are crazy. [24]But suppose everyone is prophesying and someone comes in who does not believe or is without understanding. If everyone is prophesying, his sin will be shown to him, and he will be judged by all that he hears. [25]The secret things in his heart will be made known. So he will bow down and worship God. He will say, "Truly, God is with you."

MEETINGS SHOULD HELP THE CHURCH

[26]So, brothers, what should you do? When you meet together, one person has a song. Another has a teaching. Another has a new truth from God. Another speaks in a different language, and another person interprets that language. The purpose of all these things should be to help the church grow strong. [27]When you meet together, if anyone speaks in a different language, then it should be only two, or not more than three, who speak. They should speak one after the other. And someone should interpret what they say. [28]But if there is no interpreter, then anyone who speaks in a different language should be quiet in the church meeting. He should speak only to himself and to God.

[29]And only two or three prophets[d] should speak. The others should judge what they say. [30]And if a message from God comes to another person who is sitting, then the first speaker should stop. [31]You can all prophesy one after the other. In this way all the people can be taught and encouraged. [32]The spirits of prophets are under the control of the prophets themselves. [33]God is not a God of confusion but a God of peace.

This is true in all the churches of God's people. [34]Women should keep quiet in the church meetings. They are not allowed to speak. They must be under control. This is also what the law of Moses says. [35]If there is something the women want to know, they should ask their own husbands at home. It is shameful for a woman to speak in the church meeting. [36]Did God's teaching come from you? Or are you the only ones who have received that teaching?

14:16 "Amen" When a person says "Amen," it means he agrees with the things that were said.

37If anyone thinks that he is a prophet or that he has a spiritual gift, then he should understand that what I am writing to you is the Lord's command. 38If that person does not know this, then he is not known by God.

39So my brothers, you should truly want to prophesy. And do not stop people from using the gift of speaking in different kinds of languages. 40But let everything be done in a way that is right and orderly.

THE GOOD NEWS ABOUT CHRIST

15 Now, brothers, I want you to remember the Good News*d* I brought to you. You received this Good News, and you continue strong in it. 2And you are saved by this Good News. But you must continue believing what I told you. If you do not, then you believed for nothing.

3I passed on to you what I received. And this was the most important: that Christ died for our sins, as the Scriptures*d* say; 4that he was buried and was raised to life on the third day as the Scriptures say; 5and that he showed himself to Peter and then to the twelve apostles.*d* 6After that, Jesus showed himself to more than 500 of the believers at the same time. Most of them are still living today. But some have died. 7Then Jesus showed himself to James and later to all the apostles. 8Last of all he showed himself to me—as to a person not born at the normal time. 9All the other apostles are greater than I am. This is because I persecuted the church of God. And this is why I am not even good enough to be called an apostle. 10But God's grace has made me what I am. And his grace to me was not wasted. I worked harder than all the other apostles. (But I was not really the one working. It was God's grace that was with me.) 11So then it is not important if I preached to you or if the other apostles preached to you. We all preach the same thing, and this is what you believed.

WE WILL BE RAISED FROM DEATH

12It is preached that Christ was raised from death. So why do some of you say that people will not be raised from death? 13If no one will ever be raised from death, then Christ was not raised from death. 14And if Christ was not raised, then our preaching is worth nothing. And your faith is worth nothing. 15And also, we will be guilty of lying about God. Because we have preached about him by saying that he raised Christ from death. And if people are not raised from death, then God never raised Christ from death. 16If the dead are not raised, Christ has not been raised either. 17And if Christ has not been raised, then your faith is for nothing; you are still guilty of your sins. 18And also, those in Christ who have already died are lost. 19If our hope in Christ is for this life only, we should be pitied more than anyone else in the world.

20But Christ has truly been raised from death—the first one and proof that those who are asleep in death will also be raised. 21Death comes to everyone because of what one man did. But the rising from death also happens because of one man. 22In Adam all of us die. In the same way, in Christ all of us will be made alive again. 23But everyone will be raised to life in the right order. Christ was first to be raised. When Christ comes again, those who belong to him will be raised to life. 24Then the end will come. Christ will destroy all rulers, authorities, and powers. And he will give the kingdom to God the Father. 25Christ must rule until God puts all enemies under Christ's control. 26The last enemy to be destroyed will be death. 27The Scripture*d* says, "God put all things under his control."*n* When it says that "all things" are put under him, it is clear that this does not include God himself. God is the one putting everything under

---

15:27 "God put ... control." Quotation from Psalm 8:6.

Christ's control. [28]After everything has been put under Christ, then the Son himself will be put under God. God is the One who put all things under Christ. And Christ will be put under God, so that God will be the complete ruler over everything.

[29]If the dead are never raised, then what will people do who are baptized for those who have died? If the dead are not raised at all, why are people baptized for them?

[30]And what about us? Why do we put ourselves in danger every hour? [31]I die every day. That is true, brothers, just as it is true that I brag about you in Christ Jesus our Lord. [32]If I fought wild animals in Ephesus only for human reasons, I have gained nothing. If the dead are not raised, then, "Let us eat and drink, because tomorrow we will die."[n]

[33]Do not be fooled: "Bad friends will ruin good habits." [34]Come back to your right way of thinking and stop sinning. I say this to shame you—some of you do not know God.

WHAT KIND OF BODY WILL WE HAVE?

[35]But someone may ask, "How are the dead raised? What kind of body will they have?" [36]Those are stupid questions. When you plant something, it must die in the ground before it can live and grow. [37]And when you plant it, what you plant does not have the same "body" that it will have later. What you plant is only a seed, maybe wheat or something else. [38]But God gives it a body that he has planned for it. And God gives each kind of seed its own body. [39]All things made of flesh are not the same kinds of flesh: People have one kind of flesh, animals have another kind, birds have another, and fish have another. [40]Also there are heavenly bodies and earthly bodies. But the beauty of the heavenly bodies is one

kind. The beauty of the earthly bodies is another kind. [41]The sun has one kind of beauty. The moon has another beauty, and the stars have another. And each star is different in its beauty.

[42]It is the same with the dead who are raised to life. The body that is "planted" will ruin and decay. But that body is raised to a life that cannot be destroyed. [43]When the body is "planted," it is without honor. But it is raised in glory. When the body is "planted," it is weak. But when it is raised, it has power. [44]The body that is "planted" is a physical body. When it is raised, it is a spiritual body.

There is a physical body. And there is also a spiritual body. [45]It is written in the Scriptures:[d] "The first man became a living person."[n] But the last Adam became a spirit that gives life. [46]The spiritual man did not come first. It was the physical man who came first; then came the spiritual. [47]The first man came from the dust of the earth. The second man came from heaven. [48]People belong to the earth. They are like the first man of earth. But those people who belong to heaven are like the man of heaven. [49]We were made like the man of earth. So we will[n] also be made like the man of heaven.

[50]I tell you this, brothers: Flesh and blood cannot have a part in the kingdom of God. A thing that will ruin cannot have a part in something that never ruins. [51]But listen, I tell you this secret: We will not all die, but we will all be changed. [52]It will only take a second. We will be changed as quickly as an eye blinks. This will happen when the last trumpet sounds. The trumpet will sound and those who have died will be raised to live forever. And we will all be changed. [53]This body that will ruin must clothe itself with something that will never ruin. And

---

15:32 "Let us ... die." Quotation from Isaiah 22:13; 56:12.
15:45 "The first ... person." Quotation from Genesis 2:7.
15:49 So we will Some Greek copies read "So let us."

this body that dies must clothe itself with something that will never die. ⁵⁴So this body that ruins will clothe itself with that which never ruins. And this body that dies will clothe itself with that which never dies. When this happens, then this Scripture will be made true:

"Death is destroyed forever in
     victory."   *Isaiah 25:8*
⁵⁵"Death, where is your victory?
     Death, where is your power to
          hurt?"   *Hosea 13:14*
⁵⁶Death's power to hurt is sin. The power of sin is the law. ⁵⁷But we thank God! He gives us the victory through our Lord Jesus Christ.

⁵⁸So my dear brothers, stand strong. Do not let anything move you. Always give yourselves fully to the work of the Lord. You know that your work in the Lord is never wasted.

THE GIFT FOR OTHER BELIEVERS

16 Now I will write about the collection of money for God's people. Do the same thing that I told the Galatian churches to do: ²On the first day of every week, each one of you should put aside as much money as you can from what you are blessed with. You should save it up, so that you will not have to collect money after I come. ³When I arrive, I will send some men to take your gift to Jerusalem. These will be men who you all agree should go. I will send them with letters of introduction. ⁴If it seems good for me to go also, these men will go along with me.

PAUL'S PLANS

⁵I plan to go through Macedonia. So I will come to you after I go through there. ⁶Maybe I will stay with you for a time. I might even stay all winter. Then you can help me on my trip, wherever I go. ⁷I do not want to come to see you now, because I would have to leave to go other places. I hope to stay a longer time with you if the Lord allows it. ⁸But I will stay at Ephesus until Pentecost.*ᵈ* ⁹I will stay, because a good opportunity for a great and growing

work has been given to me now. And there are many people working against me.

¹⁰Timothy might come to you. Try to make him feel comfortable with you. He is working for the Lord just as I am. ¹¹So none of you should refuse to accept Timothy. Help him on his trip in peace, so that he can come back to me. I am expecting him to come back with the brothers.

¹²Now about our brother Apollos: I strongly encouraged him to visit you with the other brothers. But he was sure that he did not want to go now. But when he has the opportunity, he will go to you.

PAUL ENDS HIS LETTER

¹³Be careful. Continue strong in the faith. Have courage, and be strong. ¹⁴Do everything in love.

¹⁵You know that the family of Stephanas were the first believers in Southern Greece. They have given themselves to the service of God's people. I ask you, brothers, ¹⁶to follow the leading of people like these and anyone else who works and serves with them.

¹⁷I am happy that Stephanas, Fortunatus, and Achaicus have come. You are not here, but they have filled your place. ¹⁸They have given rest to my spirit and to yours. You should recognize the value of men like these.

¹⁹The churches in the country of Asia send greetings to you. Aquila and Priscilla greet you in the Lord. Also the church that meets in their house greets you. ²⁰All the brothers here send greetings. Give each other a holy kiss when you meet.

²¹I am Paul, and I am writing this greeting with my own hand.

²²If anyone does not love the Lord, then let him be separated from God— lost forever!

Come, O Lord!

²³The grace of the Lord Jesus be with you.

²⁴My love be with all of you in Christ Jesus.

CORINTHIANS

1 From Paul, an apostle[d] of Christ Jesus. I am an apostle because that is what God wanted.

Also from Timothy our brother in Christ.

To the church of God in Corinth, and to all of God's people in the whole country of Southern Greece:

[2]Grace and peace to you from God our Father and the Lord Jesus Christ.

PAUL GIVES THANKS TO GOD

[3]Praise be to the God and Father of our Lord Jesus Christ. God is the Father who is full of mercy. And he is the God of all comfort. [4]He comforts us every time we have trouble, so that we can comfort others when they have trouble. We can comfort them with the same comfort that God gives us. [5]We share in the many sufferings of Christ. In the same way, much comfort comes to us through Christ. [6]If we have troubles, it is for your comfort and salvation. If we have comfort, then you also have comfort. This helps you to accept patiently the same sufferings that we have. [7]Our hope for you is strong. We know that you share in our sufferings. So we know that you also share in the comfort we receive.

[8]Brothers, we want you to know about the trouble we suffered in the country of Asia. We had great burdens there that were greater than our own strength. We even gave up hope for life. [9]Truly, in our own hearts we believed that we would die. But this happened so that we would not trust in ourselves. It happened so that we would trust in God, who raises people from death. [10]God saved us from these great dangers of death. And he will continue to save us. We have put our hope in him, and he will save us again.

[11]And you can help us with your prayers. Then many people will give thanks for us—that God blessed us because of their many prayers.

THE CHANGE IN PAUL'S PLANS

[12]This is what we are proud of, and I can say with all my heart that it is true: In all the things we have done in the world, we have done everything with an honest[n] and pure heart from God. And this is even more true in what we have done with you. We did this by God's grace, not by the kind of wisdom the world has. [13]For we write to you only what you can read and understand. And I hope that [14]as you have understood some things about us, you may come to know everything about us. Then you can be proud of us, as we will be proud of you on the day our Lord Jesus Christ comes again.

[15]I was very sure of all this. That is why I made plans to visit you first. Then you could be blessed twice. [16]I planned to visit you on my way to Macedonia. Then I planned to visit you again on my way back. I wanted to get help from you for my trip to Judea. [17]Do you think that I made these plans without really thinking? Or maybe you think I make plans as the world does, so that I say "Yes, yes," and at the same time "No, no."

[18]But since you can believe God, then you can believe that what we tell you is never both "Yes" and "No." [19]The Son of God, Jesus Christ, that Silas and Timothy and I preached to you, was not "Yes" and "No." In Christ it has always been "Yes." [20]The "Yes" to all of God's promises is in Christ. And that is why we say "Amen"[n] through Christ to the glory of God. [21]And God is the One who makes you and us strong in Christ. God made us his chosen

---

1:12 honest Some Greek copies read "holy."
1:20 "Amen" When a person says "Amen," it means he agrees with the things that were said.

people. [22]He put his mark on us to show that we are his. And he put his Spirit[d] in our hearts to be a guarantee for all he has promised.

[23]I tell you this, and I ask God to be my witness that this is true: The reason I did not come back to Corinth was that I did not want to punish or hurt you. [24]I do not mean that we are trying to control your faith. You are strong in faith. But we are workers with you for your own happiness.

2 So I decided that my next visit to you would not be another visit to make you sad. [2]If I make you sad, who will make me happy? Only you can make me happy—you whom I made sad. [3]I wrote you a letter for this reason: that when I came to you I would not be made sad by the people who should make me happy. I felt sure of all of you. I felt sure that you would share my joy. [4]When I wrote to you before, I was very troubled and unhappy in my heart. I wrote with many tears. I did not write to make you sad, but to let you know how much I love you.

FORGIVE THE SINNER

[5]Someone there among you has caused sadness. He caused this not to me, but to all of you—I mean he caused sadness to all in some way. (I do not want to make it sound worse than it really is.) [6]The punishment that most of you gave him is enough for him. [7]But now you should forgive him and comfort him. This will keep him from having too much sadness and giving up completely. [8]So I beg you to show him that you love him. [9]This is why I wrote to you. I wanted to test you and see if you obey in everything. [10]If you forgive someone, I also forgive him. And what I have forgiven—if I had anything to forgive—I forgave it for you, and Christ was with me. [11]I did this so that Satan would not win anything from us. We know very well what Satan's plans are.

PAUL'S CONCERN IN TROAS

[12]I went to Troas to preach the Good News[d] of Christ. The Lord gave me a good opportunity there. [13]But I had no peace because I did not find my brother Titus there. So I said good-bye and went to Macedonia.

VICTORY THROUGH CHRIST

[14]But thanks be to God, who always leads us in victory through Christ. God uses us to spread his knowledge everywhere like a sweet-smelling perfume. [15]Our offering to God is this: We are the sweet smell of Christ among those who are being saved and among those who are being lost. [16]To those who are lost, we are the smell of death that brings death. But to those who are being saved, we are the smell of life that brings life. So who is able to do this work? [17]We do not sell the word of God for a profit as many other people do. But in Christ we speak the truth before God. We speak as men sent from God.

SERVANTS OF THE NEW AGREEMENT

3 Are we starting to brag about ourselves again? Do we need letters of introduction to you or from you, like some other people? [2]You yourselves are our letter, written on our hearts. It is known and read by everyone. [3]You show that you are a letter from Christ that he sent through us. This letter is not written with ink, but with the Spirit[d] of the living God. It is not written on stone tablets.[n] It is written on human hearts.

[4]We can say this, because through Christ we feel sure before God. [5]I do not mean that we are able to say that we can do this work ourselves. It is God who makes us able to do all that we do. [6]God made us able to be servants of a new agreement from himself to his people. This new agreement is not a written law. It is of the Spirit. The written law brings death, but the Spirit gives life.

3:3 stone tablets Meaning the law of Moses that was written on stone tablets (Exodus 24:12; 25:16).

[7]The law that brought death was written in words on stone. It came with God's glory. Moses' face was so bright with glory that the people of Israel could not continue to look at his face. And that glory later disappeared. [8]So surely the new way that brings the Spirit has even more glory. [9]That law judged people guilty of sin, but it had glory. So surely the new way that makes people right with God has much greater glory. [10]That old law had glory. But it really loses its glory when it is compared to the much greater glory of this new way. [11]If that law which disappeared came with glory, then this new way which continues forever has much greater glory.

[12]We have this hope, so we are very brave. [13]We are not like Moses. He put a covering over his face so that the people of Israel would not see it. The glory was disappearing, and Moses did not want them to see it end. [14]But their minds were closed. Even today that same covering hides the meaning when they read the old agreement. That covering is taken away only through Christ. [15]But even today, when they read the law of Moses, there is a covering over their minds. [16]But when a person changes and follows the Lord, that covering is taken away. [17]The Lord is the Spirit. And where the Spirit of the Lord is, there is freedom. [18]Our faces, then, are not covered. We all show the Lord's glory, and we are being changed to be like him. This change in us brings more and more glory. And it comes from the Lord, who is the Spirit.

PREACHING THE GOOD NEWS

4 God, with his mercy, gave us this work to do. So we don't give up. [2]But we have turned away from secret and shameful ways. We use no trickery, and we do not change the teaching of God. We teach the truth plainly. This is how we show everyone who we are. And this is how they can know in their hearts what kind of people we are before God. [3]The Good News[d] that we preach may be hidden. But it is hidden only to those who are lost. [4]The devil who rules this world has blinded the minds of those who do not believe. They cannot see the light of the Good News—the Good News about the glory of Christ, who is exactly like God. [5]We do not preach about ourselves. But we preach that Jesus Christ is Lord; and we preach that we are your servants for Jesus. [6]God once said, "Let the light shine out of the darkness!" And this is the same God who made his light shine in our hearts. He gave us light by letting us know the glory of God that is in the face of Christ.

SPIRITUAL TREASURE IN CLAY JARS

[7]We have this treasure from God. But we are only like clay jars that hold the treasure. This shows that this great power is from God, not from us. [8]We have troubles all around us, but we are not defeated. We do not know what to do, but we do not give up. [9]We are persecuted, but God does not leave us. We are hurt sometimes, but we are not destroyed. [10]We carry the death of Jesus in our own bodies, so that the life of Jesus can also be seen in our bodies. [11]We are alive, but for Jesus we are always in danger of death. This is so that the life of Jesus can be seen in our bodies that die. [12]So death is working in us, but life is working in you.

[13]It is written in the Scriptures,[d] "I believed, so I spoke."[n] Our faith is like this, too. We believe, and so we speak. [14]God raised the Lord Jesus from death. And we know that God will also raise us with Jesus. God will bring us together with you, and we will stand before him. [15]All these things are for you. And so the grace of God is being given to more and more people. This will bring more and more thanks to God for his glory.

4:13 "I . . . spoke." Quotation from Psalm 116:10.

LIVING BY FAITH

[16]So we do not give up. Our physical body is becoming older and weaker, but our spirit inside us is made new every day. [17]We have small troubles for a while now, but they are helping us gain an eternal glory. That glory is much greater than the troubles. [18]So we set our eyes not on what we see but on what we cannot see. What we see will last only a short time. But what we cannot see will last forever.

5 We know that our body—the tent we live in here on earth—will be destroyed. But when that happens, God will have a house for us to live in. It will not be a house made by men. It will be a home in heaven that will last forever. [2]But now we are tired of this body. We want God to give us our heavenly home. [3]It will clothe us, and we will not be naked. [4]While we live in this body, we have burdens, and we complain. We do not want to be naked. We want to be clothed with our heavenly home. Then this body that dies will be fully covered with life. [5]This is what God made us for. And he has given us the Spirit[d] to be a guarantee for this new life.

[6]So we always have courage. We know that while we live in this body, we are away from the Lord. [7]We live by what we believe, not by what we can see. [8]So I say that we have courage. And we really want to be away from this body and be at home with the Lord. [9]Our only goal is to please God. We want to please him whether we live here or there. [10]For we must all stand before Christ to be judged. Each one will receive what he should get—good or bad—for the things he did when he lived in the earthly body.

BECOMING FRIENDS WITH GOD

[11]We know what it means to fear the Lord. So we try to help people accept the truth. God knows what we really are. And I hope that in your hearts you know, too. [12]We are not trying to prove ourselves to you again. But we are telling you about ourselves, so you will be proud of us. Then you will have an answer for those who are proud about things that can be seen. They do not care about what is in the heart. [13]If we are out of our minds, it is for God. If we have our right mind, then it is for you. [14]The love of Christ controls us. Because we know that One died for all. So all have died. [15]Christ died for all so that those who live would not continue to live for themselves. He died for them and was raised from death so that they would live for him.

[16]From this time on we do not think of anyone as the world does. It is true that in the past we thought of Christ as the world thinks. But we no longer think of him in that way. [17]If anyone belongs to Christ, then he is made new. The old things have gone; everything is made new! [18]All this is from God. Through Christ, God made peace between us and himself. And God gave us the work of bringing everyone into peace with him. [19]I mean that God was in Christ, making peace between the world and himself. In Christ, God did not hold the world guilty of its sins. And he gave us this message of peace. [20]So we have been sent to speak for Christ. It is as if God is calling to you through us. We speak for Christ when we beg you to be at peace with God. [21]Christ had no sin. But God made him become sin. God did this for us so that in Christ we could become right with God.

6 We are workers together with God. So we beg you: Do not let the grace that you received from God be for nothing. [2]God says,

"I heard your prayers at the right time,
    and I gave you help on the day of
        salvation."   Isaiah 49:8

I tell you that the "right time" is now. The "day of salvation" is now.

[3]We do not want anyone to find anything wrong with our work. So we do nothing that will be a problem for anyone. [4]But in every way we show that we

are servants of God: in accepting many hard things, in troubles, in difficulties, and in great problems. [5]We are beaten and thrown into prison. Men become upset and fight us. We work hard, and sometimes we get no sleep or food. [6]We show that we are servants of God by living a pure life, by our understanding, by our patience, and by our kindness. We show this by the Holy Spirit,[d] by true love, [7]by speaking the truth, and by God's power. We use our right living to defend ourselves against everything. [8]Some people honor us, but other people shame us. Some people say good things about us, but other people say bad things. Some people say we are liars, but we speak the truth. [9]We are not known, but we are well-known. We seem to be dying, but look—we continue to live. We are punished, but we are not killed. [10]We have much sadness, but we are always rejoicing. We are poor, but we are making many people rich in faith. We have nothing, but really we have everything.

[11]We have spoken freely to you in Corinth. We have opened our hearts to you. [12]Our feelings of love for you have not stopped. It is you that have stopped your feelings of love for us. [13]I speak to you as if you were my children. Do to us as we have done—open your hearts to us.

WARNING ABOUT NON-CHRISTIANS

[14]You are not the same as those who do not believe. So do not join yourselves to them. Good and bad do not belong together. Light and darkness cannot share together. [15]How can Christ and Belial, the devil, have any agreement? What can a believer have together with a non-believer? [16]The temple of God cannot have any agreement with idols. And we are the temple of the living God. As God said: "I will live with them and walk with them. And I will be their God. And they will be my people."[n]

[17]"Leave those people,
and make yourselves pure, says the Lord.
Touch nothing that is unclean,[d]
and I will accept you."

Isaiah 52:11; Ezekiel 20:34, 41

[18]"I will be your father,
and you will be my sons and daughters,
says the Lord All-Powerful."

2 Samuel 7:14; 7:8

7 Dear friends, we have these promises from God. So we should make ourselves pure—free from anything that makes body or soul unclean. We should try to become perfect in the way we live, because we respect God.

PAUL'S JOY

[2]Open your hearts to us. We have not done wrong to anyone. We have not ruined the faith of any person, and we have cheated no one. [3]I do not say this to blame you. I told you before that we love you so much that we would live or die with you. [4]I feel very sure of you. I am very proud of you. You give me much comfort. And in all of our troubles I have great joy.

[5]When we came into Macedonia, we had no rest. We found trouble all around us. We had fighting on the outside and fear on the inside. [6]But God comforts those who are troubled. And God comforted us when Titus came. [7]We were comforted by his coming and also by the comfort that you gave him. Titus told us about your wish to see me. He told us that you are very sorry for what you did. And he told me about your great care for me. When I heard this, I was much happier.

[8]Even if the letter I wrote you made you sad, I am not sorry I wrote it. I know it made you sad, and I was sorry for that. But it made you sad only for a short time. [9]Now I am happy, but not because

---

6:16 "I . . . people." Quotation from Leviticus 26:11-12; Jeremiah 32:38; Ezekiel 37:27.

you were made sad. I am happy because your sorrow made you change your hearts. You became sad in the way God wanted you to. So you were not hurt by us in any way. [10]Being sorry in the way God wants makes a person change his heart and life. This leads to salvation, and we cannot be sorry for that. But the kind of sorrow the world has will bring death. [11]You had the kind of sorrow God wanted you to have. Now see what this sorrow has brought you: It has made you very serious. It made you want to prove that you were not wrong. It made you angry and afraid. It made you want to see me. It made you care. It made you want the right thing to be done. You proved that you were not guilty in any part of the problem. [12]I wrote that letter, but not because of the one who did the wrong. And it was not written because of the person who was hurt. But I wrote the letter so that you could see, before God, the great care that you have for us. [13]That is why we were comforted.

We were very comforted. And we were even happier to see that Titus was so happy. All of you made him feel much better. [14]I bragged to Titus about you. And you showed that I was right. Everything that we said to you was true. And you have proved that what we bragged about to Titus is true. [15]And his love for you is stronger when he remembers that you were all ready to obey. You welcomed him with respect and fear. [16]I am very happy that I can trust you fully.

CHRISTIAN GIVING

8 And now, brothers, we want you to know about the grace that God gave the churches in Macedonia. [2]They have been tested by great troubles. And they are very poor. But they gave much because of their great joy. [3]I can tell you that they gave as much as they were able.

They gave even more than they could afford. No one told them to do it. [4]But they asked us again and again—they begged us to let them share in this service for God's people. [5]And they gave in a way that we did not expect: They first gave themselves to the Lord and to us. This is what God wants. [6]So we asked Titus to help you finish this special work of grace. He is the one who started this work. [7]You are rich in everything—in faith, in speaking, in knowledge, in truly wanting to help, and in the love you learned from us.[n] And so we want you to be rich also in this gift of giving.

[8]I am not commanding you to give. But I want to see if your love is true love. I do this by showing you that others really want to help. [9]You know the grace of our Lord Jesus Christ. You know that Christ was rich, but for you he became poor. Christ did this so that by his being poor you might become rich.

[10]This is what I think you should do: Last year you were the first to want to give. And you were the first who gave. [11]So now finish the work that you started. Then your "doing" will be equal to your "wanting to do." Give from what you have. [12]If you want to give, your gift will be accepted. Your gift will be judged by what you have, not by what you do not have. [13]We do not want you to have troubles while other people are at ease. We want everything to be equal. [14]At this time you have plenty. What you have can help others who are in need. Then later, when they have plenty, they can help you when you are in need. Then all will be equal. [15]As it is written in the Scriptures,[d] "The person who gathered more did not have too much. The person who gathered less did not have too little."[n]

TITUS AND HIS COMPANIONS

[16]I thank God because he gave Titus

8:7 in . . . us Some Greek copies read "in your love for us."
8:15 "The person . . . little." Quotation from Exodus 16:18.

the same love for you that I have. [17]Titus accepted what we asked him to do. He wanted very much to go to you. This was his own idea. [18]We are sending with him the brother who is praised by all the churches. This brother is praised because of his service in preaching the Good News.[d] [19]Also, this brother was chosen by the churches to go with us when we deliver this gift of money. We are doing this service to bring glory to the Lord and to show that we really want to help.

[20]We are being careful so that no one will criticize us about the way we are handling this large gift. [21]We are trying to do what is right. We want to do what the Lord accepts as right and also what people think is right.

[22]Also, we are sending with them our brother who is always ready to help. He has proved this to us in many ways. And he wants to help even more now because he has much faith in you.

[23]Now about Titus—he is my partner who is working with me to help you. And about the other brothers—they are sent from the churches, and they bring glory to Christ. [24]So show these men that you really have love. Show them why we are proud of you. Then all the churches can see it.

HELP FOR FELLOW CHRISTIANS

9 I really do not need to write to you about this help for God's people. [2]I know that you want to help. I have been bragging about this to the people in Macedonia. I have told them that you in Southern Greece have been ready to give since last year. And your wanting to give has made most of them here ready to give also. [3]But I am sending the brothers to you. I do not want our bragging about you in this to be for nothing. I want you to be ready, as I said you would be. [4]If any of the people from Macedonia come with me and find that you are not ready, we will be ashamed. We will be ashamed that we were so sure of you. (And you will be ashamed, too!) [5]So I thought that

I should ask these brothers to go to you before we come. They will finish getting in order the gift you promised. Then the gift will be ready when we come, and it will be a gift you wanted to give—not a gift that you hated to give.

[6]Remember this: The person who plants a little will have a small harvest. But the person who plants a lot will have a big harvest. [7]Each one should give, then, what he has decided in his heart to give. He should not give if it makes him sad. And he should not give if he thinks he is forced to give. God loves the person who gives happily. [8]And God can give you more blessings than you need. Then you will always have plenty of everything. You will have enough to give to every good work. [9]It is written in the Scriptures:[d]

"He gives freely to the poor.
The things he does are right and
will continue forever." *Psalm 112:9*

[10]God is the One who gives seed to the farmer. And he gives bread for food. And God will give you all the seed you need and make it grow. He will make a great harvest from your goodness. [11]God will make you rich in every way so that you can always give freely. And your giving through us will cause many to give thanks to God. [12]This service that you do helps the needs of God's people. It is also bringing more and more thanks to God. [13]This service you do is a proof of your faith. Many people will praise God because of it. They will praise God because you follow the Good News[d] of Christ—the gospel you say you believe. They will praise God because you freely share with them and with all others. [14]And when they pray, they will wish they could be with you. They will feel this because of the great grace that God has given you. [15]Thanks be to God for his gift that is too wonderful to explain.

PAUL DEFENDS HIS MINISTRY

10 I, Paul, am begging you with the gentleness and the kindness of

Christ. Some people say that I am easy on you when I am with you and strict when I am away. [2]They think that we live in a worldly way. I plan to be very strict against them when I come. I beg you that when I come I will not need to use that same strictness with you. [3]We do live in the world. But we do not fight in the same way that the world fights. [4]We fight with weapons that are different from those the world uses. Our weapons have power from God. These weapons can destroy the enemy's strong places. We destroy men's arguments. [5]And we destroy every proud thing that raises itself against the knowledge of God. We capture every thought and make it give up and obey Christ. [6]We are ready to punish anyone there who does not obey. But first we want you to obey fully.

[7]You must look at the facts before you. If anyone feels sure that he belongs to Christ, then he must remember that we belong to Christ just as he does. [8]It is true that we brag freely about the authority the Lord gave us. But he gave us this authority to strengthen you, not to hurt you. So I will not be ashamed of the bragging we do. [9]I don't want you to think that I am trying to scare you with my letters. [10]Some people say, "Paul's letters are powerful and sound important. But when he is with us, he is weak. And his speaking is nothing." [11]They should know this: We are not there with you now, so we say these things in letters. But when we are there with you, we will show the same authority that we show in our letters.

[12]We do not dare to put ourselves in the same group with those who think that they are very important. We do not compare ourselves to them. They use themselves to measure themselves, and they judge themselves by what they themselves are. This shows that they know nothing. [13]But we will not brag about things outside the

work that was given us to do. We will limit our bragging to the work that God gave us. And this work includes our work with you. [14]We are not bragging too much. We would be bragging too much if we had not already come to you. But we have come to you with the Good News[d] of Christ. [15]We limit our bragging to the work that is ours. We do not brag in the work other men have done. We hope that your faith will continue to grow. And we hope that you will help our work to grow much larger. [16]We want to tell the Good News in the areas beyond your city. We do not want to brag about work that has already been done in another man's area. [17]But, "If a person brags, he should brag only about the Lord."[n] [18]It is not the one who says he is good who is accepted but the one that the Lord thinks is good.

PAUL AND THE FALSE APOSTLES

11 I wish you would be patient with me even when I am a little foolish. But you are already doing that. [2]I am jealous over you. And this jealousy comes from God. I promised to give you to Christ. He must be your only husband. I want to give you to Christ to be his pure bride. [3]But I am afraid that your minds will be led away from your true and pure following of Christ. This might happen just as Eve was tricked by the snake with his evil ways. [4]You are very patient with anyone who comes to you and preaches a different Jesus than the one we preached. You are very willing to accept a spirit or Good News that is different from the Spirit[d] and Good News[d] that you received from us.

[5]I do not think that those "great apostles" are any better than I am. [6]I may not be a trained speaker, but I do have knowledge. We have shown this to you clearly in every way.

[7]I preached God's Good News to you without pay. I made myself unimportant

10:17 "If . . . Lord." Quotation from Jeremiah 9:24.

to make you important. Do you think that was wrong? [8]I accepted pay from other churches. I took their money so that I could serve you. [9]If I needed something when I was with you, I did not trouble any of you. The brothers who came from Macedonia gave me all that I needed. I did not allow myself to depend on you in any way. And I will never depend on you. [10]No one in Southern Greece will stop me from bragging about that. I say this with the truth of Christ in me. [11]And why do I not depend on you? Do you think it is because I do not love you? No. God knows that I love you.

[12]And I will keep on doing what I am doing now. I will continue because I want to stop those people from having a reason to brag. They would like to say that the work they brag about is the same as ours. [13]Such men are not true apostles.[d] They are workers who lie. And they change themselves to look like apostles of Christ. [14]This does not surprise us. Even Satan changes himself to look like an angel of light.[n] [15]So it does not surprise us if Satan's servants also make themselves look like servants who work for what is right. But in the end they will be punished for the things they do.

PAUL TELLS ABOUT HIS SUFFERINGS

[16]I tell you again: No one should think that I am a fool. But if you think that I am a fool, then accept me as you would accept a fool. Then I can brag a little, too. [17]I brag because I feel sure of myself. But I am not talking as the Lord would talk. I am bragging like a fool. [18]Many people are bragging about their lives in the world. So I will brag, too. [19]You are wise, so you will gladly be patient with fools! [20]You are even patient with someone who orders you around and uses you! You are patient with those who trick you, or think they are better than you, or

hit you in the face! [21]It is shameful to me to say this, but we were too "weak" to do those things to you!

But if anyone else is brave enough to brag, then I also will be brave and brag. (I am talking like a fool.) [22]Are they Hebrews?[n] So am I. Are they Israelites? So am I. Are they from Abraham's family? So am I. [23]Are they serving Christ? I am serving him more. (I am crazy to talk like this.) I have worked much harder than they. I have been in prison more often. I have been hurt more in beatings. I have been near death many times. [24]Five times the Jews have given me their punishment of 39 lashes with a whip. [25]Three different times I was beaten with rods. One time they tried to kill me with stones. Three times I was in ships that were wrecked, and one of those times I spent the night and the next day in the sea. [26]I have gone on many travels. And I have been in danger from rivers, from thieves, from my own people, the Jews, and from those who are not Jews. I have been in danger in cities, in places where no one lives, and on the sea. And I have been in danger with false brothers. [27]I have done hard and tiring work, and many times I did not sleep. I have been hungry and thirsty. Many times I have been without food. I have been cold and without clothes. [28]Besides all this, there is on me every day the load of my concern for all the churches. [29]I feel weak every time someone is weak. I feel upset every time someone is led into sin.

[30]If I must brag, I will brag about the things that show I am weak. [31]God knows that I am not lying. He is the God and Father of the Lord Jesus Christ, and he is to be praised forever. [32]When I was in Damascus, the governor under King Aretas wanted to arrest me. So he put guards around the city. [33]But my friends

---

11:14 angel of light Messenger from God. The devil fools people so that they think he is from God.
11:22 Hebrews A name for the Jews that some Jews were very proud of.

put me in a basket. Then they put the basket through a hole in the wall and lowered me down. So I escaped from the governor.

A SPECIAL BLESSING IN PAUL'S LIFE

12 I must continue to brag. It will do no good, but I will talk now about visions and revelations[n] from the Lord. [2]I know a man in Christ who was taken up to the third heaven. This happened 14 years ago. I do not know whether the man was in his body or out of his body. But God knows. [3-4]And I know that this man was taken up to paradise.[n] I don't know if he was in his body or away from his body. But he heard things he is not able to explain. He heard things that no man is allowed to tell. [5]I will brag about a man like that. But I will not brag about myself, except about my weaknesses. [6]But if I wanted to brag about myself, I would not be a fool. I would not be a fool, because I would be telling the truth. But I will not brag about myself. I do not want people to think more of me than what they see me do or hear me say.

[7]But I must not become too proud of the wonderful things that were shown to me. So a painful problem[n] was given to me. This problem is a messenger from Satan. It is sent to beat me and keep me from being too proud. [8]I begged the Lord three times to take this problem away from me. [9]But the Lord said to me, "My grace is enough for you. When you are weak, then my power is made perfect in you." So I am very happy to brag about my weaknesses. Then Christ's power can live in me. [10]So I am happy when I have weaknesses, insults, hard times, sufferings, and all kinds of troubles. All these things are for Christ. And I am happy, because when I am weak, then I am truly strong.

PAUL'S LOVE FOR THE CHRISTIANS

[11]I have been talking like a fool. But you made me do it. You are the ones who should say good things about me. I am worth nothing, but those "great apostles" are not worth any more than I am! [12]When I was with you, I did what proves that I am an apostle[d]—signs, wonders, and miracles.[d] And I did these things with much patience. [13]So you received everything that the other churches have received. Only one thing was different: I was not a burden to you. Forgive me for this!

[14]I am now ready to visit you the third time. And I will not be a burden to you. I want nothing from you, I only want you. Children should not have to save up to give to their parents. Parents should save to give to their children. [15]So I am happy to give everything I have for you. I will even give myself for you. If I love you more, will you love me less?

[16]It is clear that I was not a burden to you. But you think that I was tricky and used lies to catch you. [17]Did I cheat you by using any of the men I sent to you? No, you know I did not. [18]I asked Titus to go to you. And I sent our brother with him. Titus did not cheat you, did he? No, you know that Titus and I did the same thing and with the same spirit.

[19]Do you think that we have been defending ourselves to you all this time? We have been speaking in Christ and before God. You are our dear friends. And everything that we do is to make you stronger. [20]I do this because I am afraid that when I come, you will not be what I want you to be. And I am afraid that I will not be what you want me to be. I am afraid that among you there may be arguing, jealousy, anger, selfish fighting, evil talk, gossip, pride, and confusion. [21]I am afraid that when I come to you again,

---

12:1 **revelations** Revelation is making known a truth that was hidden.
12:3-4 **paradise** A place where good people go when they die.
12:7 **painful problem** Literally, "thorn in the flesh."

my God will make me ashamed before you. I may be saddened by many of those who have sinned. I may be saddened because they have not changed their hearts and have not turned away from their sexual sins and from the shameful things they have done.

FINAL WARNINGS AND GREETINGS

13 I will come to you for the third time. And remember, "Every case must be proved by two or three witnesses."[n] [2]When I was with you the second time, I gave a warning to those who had sinned. Now I am away from you, and I give a warning to all the others. When I come to you again, I will not be easy with them. [3]You want proof that Christ is speaking through me. My proof is that he is not weak among you, but he is powerful. [4]It is true that he was weak when he was killed on the cross. But he lives now by God's power. It is true that we are weak in Christ. But for you we will be alive in Christ by God's power.

[5]Look closely at yourselves. Test yourselves to see if you are living in the faith. You know that Christ Jesus is in you—unless you fail the test. [6]But I hope you will see that we ourselves have not failed the test. [7]We pray to God that you will not do anything wrong. It is not important to see that we have passed the test. But it is important that you do what is right, even if it seems that we have failed. [8]We cannot do anything against the truth, but only for the truth. [9]We are happy to be weak, if you are strong. And we pray that you will grow stronger and stronger. [10]I am writing this while I am away from you. I am writing so that when I come I will not have to be harsh in my use of authority. The Lord gave me this authority to use to make you stronger, not to destroy you.

[11]Now, brothers, I say good-bye. Live in harmony. Do what I have asked you to do. Agree with each other, and live in peace. Then the God of love and peace will be with you.

[12]Give each other a holy kiss when you greet each other. [13]All of God's holy people send greetings to you.

[14]The grace of the Lord Jesus Christ, the love of God, and the fellowship of the Holy Spirit[d] be with you all.

13:1 "Every . . . witnesses." Quotation from Deuteronomy 19:15.

GALATIANS

1 From Paul, an apostle.[d] I was not chosen to be an apostle by men. I was not sent from men. It was Jesus Christ and God the Father who made me an apostle. God is the One who raised Jesus from death.

[2] This letter is also from all the brothers who are with me.

To the churches in Galatia.[n]

[3] I pray that God our Father and the Lord Jesus Christ will be good to you and give you peace. [4] Jesus gave himself for our sins to free us from this evil world we live in. This is what God the Father wanted. [5] The glory belongs to God forever and ever. Amen.

THE ONLY GOOD NEWS

[6] A short time ago God called you to follow him. He called you by his grace that came through Christ. But now I am amazed at you! You are already turning away and believing something different than the Good News.[d] [7] Really, there is no other Good News. But some people are confusing you and want to change the Good News of Christ. [8] We preached to you the Good News. So if we ourselves, or even an angel from heaven, preach to you something different than the Good News, he should be condemned! [9] I said this before. Now I say it again: You have already accepted the Good News. If anyone tells you another way to be saved, he should be condemned!

[10] Do you think I am trying to make people accept me? No! God is the One I am trying to please. Am I trying to please men? If I wanted to please men, I would not be a servant of Christ.

PAUL'S AUTHORITY IS FROM GOD

[11] Brothers, I want you to know that the Good News[d] I preached to you was not made by men. [12] I did not get it from men, nor did any man teach it to me. Jesus Christ showed it to me.

[13] You have heard about my past life. I belonged to the Jewish religion. I hurt the church of God very much and tried to destroy it. [14] I was becoming a leader in the Jewish religion. I did better than most other Jews of my age. I tried harder than anyone else to follow the old rules. These rules were the customs handed down by our ancestors.

[15] But God had special plans for me even before I was born. So he called me through his grace that I might [16] tell the Good News about his Son to the non-Jewish people. So God showed me about his Son. When God called me, I did not get advice or help from any man. [17] I did not go to Jerusalem to see those who were apostles[d] before I was. But, without waiting, I went away to Arabia and later went back to Damascus.

[18] After three years I went to Jerusalem to meet Peter and stayed with him for 15 days. [19] I met no other apostles, except James, the brother of the Lord. [20] God knows that these things I write are not lies. [21] Later, I went to the areas of Syria and Cilicia.

[22] In Judea the churches in Christ had never met me. [23] They had only heard this about me: "This man was trying to hurt us. But now he is preaching the same faith that he once tried to destroy." [24] And these believers praised God because of me.

OTHER APOSTLES ACCEPTED PAUL

2 After 14 years, I went to Jerusalem again, this time with Barnabas. I also took Titus with me. [2] I went because God showed me that I should go. I met with those men who were the leaders of the believers. When we were alone, I told

---

1:2 **Galatia** Probably the same country where Paul preached and began churches on his first missionary trip. Read the book of Acts, chapters 13 and 14.

them the Good News[d] that I preach to the non-Jewish people. I did not want my past work and the work I am now doing to be wasted. [3]Titus was with me. But Titus was not forced to be circumcised,[d] even though he was a Greek. [4]We talked about this problem because some false brothers had come into our group secretly. They came in like spies to find out about the freedom we have in Christ Jesus. They wanted to make us slaves. [5]But we did not agree with anything those false brothers wanted! We wanted the truth of the Good News to continue for you.

[6]Those men who seemed to be important did not change the Good News that I preach. (It doesn't matter to me if they were "important" or not. To God all men are the same.) [7]But these leaders saw that God had given me special work, just as he had to Peter. God gave Peter the work of telling the Good News to the Jews. But God gave me the work of telling the Good News to the non-Jewish people. [8]God gave Peter the power to work as an apostle[d] for the Jewish people. But he also gave me the power to work as an apostle for those who are not Jews. [9]James, Peter, and John, who seemed to be the leaders, saw that God had given me this special grace. So they accepted Barnabas and me. They said, "Paul and Barnabas, we agree that you should go to the people who are not Jews. We will go to the Jews." [10]They asked us to do only one thing—to remember to help the poor. And this was something that I really wanted to do.

PAUL SHOWS THAT PETER WAS WRONG

[11]When Peter came to Antioch, I was against him because he was wrong. [12]This is what happened: When Peter first came to Antioch, he ate with the non-Jewish people. But then some Jewish men were sent from James. When they arrived, Peter stopped eating with the non-Jewish people and separated himself from them. He was afraid of the Jews who believe

that all non-Jewish people must be circumcised.[d] [13]So Peter was a hypocrite.[d] The other Jewish believers joined with him and were hypocrites, too. Even Barnabas was influenced by what these Jewish believers did. [14]I saw what they did. They were not following the truth of the Good News.[d] So I spoke to Peter in front of them all. I said: "Peter, you are a Jew, but you are not living like a Jew. You are living like the non-Jewish people. So why do you now try to force the non-Jewish people to live like Jews?"

[15]We were not born as non-Jewish "sinners," but we were born as Jews. [16]Yet we know that a person is not made right with God by following the law. No! It is trusting in Jesus Christ that makes a person right with God. So we, too, have put our faith in Christ Jesus, that we might be made right with God. And we are right with God because we trusted in Christ—not because we followed the law. For no one can be made right with God by following the law.

[17]We Jews came to Christ to be made right with God. So it is clear that we were sinners too. Does this mean that Christ makes us sinners? No! [18]But I would really be wrong to begin teaching again those things of the Law of Moses that I gave up. [19]I stopped living for the law. It was the law that put me to death. I died to the law so that I can now live for God. I was put to death on the cross with Christ. [20]I do not live anymore—it is Christ living in me. I still live in my body, but I live by faith in the Son of God. He loved me and gave himself to save me. [21]This gift is from God, and it is very important to me. If the law could make us right with God, then Christ did not have to die.

BLESSING COMES THROUGH FAITH

3 You people in Galatia were told very clearly about the death of Jesus Christ on the cross. But you were very foolish. You let someone trick you. [2]Tell me this one thing: How did you receive the Holy Spirit?[d] Did you receive the Spirit by following the law? No! You received the Spirit because you heard the Good News[d] and believed it. [3]You began your life in Christ by the Spirit. Now do you try to continue it by your own power? That is foolish. [4]You have experienced many things. Were all those experiences wasted? I hope not! [5]Does God give you the Spirit because you follow the law? No! Does God work miracles[d] among you because you follow the law? No! God gives you his Spirit and works miracles among you because you heard the Good News and believed it.

[6]The Scriptures[d] say the same thing about Abraham: "Abraham believed God, and God accepted Abraham's faith, and that faith made him right with God."[n] [7]So you should know that the true children of Abraham are those who have faith. [8]The Scriptures told what would happen in the future. They said that God would make the non-Jewish people right through their faith. This Good News was told to Abraham beforehand, as the Scripture says: "All nations will be blessed through you."[n] [9]Abraham believed this, and because he believed, he was blessed. It is the same today. All who believe today are blessed just as Abraham was blessed. [10]But those who depend on following the law to make them right are under a curse because the Scriptures say, "Anyone will be cursed who does not always obey what is written in the Book of the Law!"[n] [11]So it is clear that no one can be made right with God by the law. The Scriptures say, "He who is right with God by faith will live." [12]The law does not use faith. It says, "A person who does these things will live forever because of them."[n] [13]So the law put a curse on us, but Christ took away that curse. He changed places with us and put himself under that curse. It is written in the Scriptures, "Everyone whose body is displayed on a tree[n] is cursed." [14]Christ did this so that God's blessing promised to Abraham might come to the non-Jews. This blessing comes through Jesus Christ. Jesus died so that we could have the Spirit that God promised and receive this promise by believing.

THE LAW AND THE PROMISE

[15]Brothers, let me give you an example: Think about an agreement that a person makes with another person. After that agreement is accepted by both people, no one can stop that agreement or add anything to it. [16]God made promises to Abraham and his descendant.[d] God did not say, "and to your descendants." That would mean many people. But God said, "and to your descendant." That means only one person; that person is Christ. [17]This is what I mean: God had an agreement with Abraham and promised to keep it. The law, which came 430 years later, cannot change God's promise to Abraham. [18]Can following the law give us what God promised? No! If this is so, it is not God's promise that brings us the blessings. Instead God freely gave his blessings to Abraham through the promise he had made.

[19]So what was the law for? The law was given to show the wrong things people do. It continued until the special descendant of Abraham came. God's promise was about this descendant. The law was

---

3:6 "Abraham . . . God." Quotation from Genesis 15:6.
3:8 "All . . . you." Quotation from Genesis 12:3.
3:10 "Anyone . . . Law!" Quotation from Deuteronomy 27:26.
3:11 "He . . . live." Quotation from Habakkuk 2:4.
3:12 "A person . . . them." Quotation from Leviticus 18:5.
3:13 displayed on a tree Deuteronomy 21:22-23 says that when a person was killed for doing wrong, his body was hung on a tree to show shame. Paul means that the cross of Jesus was like that.

given through angels who used Moses for a mediator[n] to give the law to men. [20]But a mediator is not needed when there is only one side. And God is only one.

THE PURPOSE OF THE LAW OF MOSES

[21]Does this mean that the law is against God's promises? Never! If there were a law that could give men life, then we could be made right by following that law. [22]But this is not true, because the Scriptures[d] showed that the whole world is bound by sin. This was so that the promise would be given through faith. And it is given to people who believe in Jesus Christ.

[23]Before this faith came, we were all held prisoners by the law. We had no freedom until God showed us the way of faith that was coming. [24]So the law was our master until Christ came. After Christ came, we could be made right with God through faith. [25]Now the way of faith has come, and we no longer live under the law.

[26-27]You were all baptized into Christ, and so you were all clothed with Christ. This shows that you are all children of God through faith in Christ Jesus. [28]Now, in Christ, there is no difference between Jew and Greek. There is no difference between slaves and free men. There is no difference between male and female. You are all the same in Christ Jesus. [29]You belong to Christ. So you are Abraham's descendants.[d] You get all of God's blessings because of the promise that God made to Abraham.

4 I want to tell you this: While the one who will inherit his father's property is still a child, he is no different from a slave. It does not matter that the child owns everything. [2]While he is a child, he must obey those who are chosen to care for him. But when the child reaches the age set by his father, he is free. [3]It is the same for us. We were once like children. We were slaves to the useless rules of this world. [4]But when the right time came, God sent his Son. His Son was born of a woman and lived under the law. [5]God did this so that he could buy freedom for those who were under the law. His purpose was to make us his children.

[6]And you are God's children. That is why God sent the Spirit of his Son into your hearts. The Spirit[d] cries out, "Father, dear Father."[n] [7]So now you are not a slave; you are God's child, and God will give you what he promised, because you are his child.

PAUL'S LOVE FOR THE CHRISTIANS

[8]In the past you did not know God. You were slaves to gods that were not real. [9]But now you know the true God. Really, it is God who knows you. So why do you turn back to those weak and useless rules you followed before? Do you want to be slaves to those things again? [10]You still follow teachings about special days, months, seasons, and years. [11]I am afraid for you. I fear that my work for you has been wasted.

[12]Brothers, I was like you; so I beg you to become like me. You were very good to me before. [13]You remember that I came to you the first time because I was sick. That was when I preached the Good News[d] to you. [14]Though my sickness was a trouble for you, you did not hate me or make me leave. But you welcomed me as an angel from God, as if I were Jesus Christ himself! [15]You were very happy then. Where is that joy now? I remember that you would have taken out your eyes and given them to me if that were possible. [16]Now am I your enemy because I tell you the truth?

[17]Those people[n] are working hard to persuade you. But this is not good for you. They want to persuade you to turn against us. They want you to follow only them. [18]It

---

3:19 mediator A person who helps one person talk to or give something to another person.
4:6 "Father, dear Father" Literally, "Abba, Father." Jewish children called their fathers "Abba."
4:17 Those people They are the false teachers who were bothering the believers in Galatia (Galatians 1:7).

is good for people to show interest in you, but only if their purpose is good. This is always true. It is true when I am with you and when I am away. [19]My little children, again I feel pain for you as a mother feels when she gives birth. I will feel this until you truly become like Christ. [20]I wish I could be with you now. Then maybe I could change the way I am talking to you. Now I do not know what to do about you.

THE EXAMPLE OF HAGAR AND SARAH

[21]Some of you people still want to be under the law of Moses. Tell me, do you know what the law says? [22]The Scriptures[d] say that Abraham had two sons. The mother of one son was a slave woman. The mother of the other son was a free woman. [23]Abraham's son from the slave woman was born in the normal human way. But the son from the free woman was born because of the promise God made to Abraham.

[24]This makes a picture for us. The two women are like the two agreements between God and men. One agreement is the law that God made on Mount Sinai.[n] The people who are under this agreement are like slaves. The mother named Hagar is like that agreement. [25]She is like Mount Sinai in Arabia and is a picture of the earthly Jewish city of Jerusalem. This city is a slave, and all its people are slaves to the law. [26]But the heavenly Jerusalem which is above is like the free woman. She is our mother. [27]It is written in the Scriptures:

"Be happy, Jerusalem.
    You are like a woman who never
        gave birth to children.
Start singing and shout for joy.
    You never felt the pain of giving
        birth to children.
But you will have more children
    than the woman who has a
        husband."   *Isaiah 54:1*

[28]My brothers, you are God's children because of his promise, as Isaac was then. [29]The son who was born in the normal way treated the other son badly. It is the same today. [30]But what does the Scripture say? "Throw out the slave woman and her son! The son of the free woman will receive everything his father has. But the son of the slave woman will receive nothing."[n] [31]So, my brothers, we are not children of the slave woman. We are children of the free woman.

KEEP YOUR FREEDOM

5 We have freedom now because Christ made us free. So stand strong. Do not change and go back into the slavery of the law. [2]Listen! I am Paul. I tell you that if you go back to the law by being circumcised,[d] then Christ is no good for you. [3]Again, I warn every man: If you allow yourselves to be circumcised, then you must follow all the law. [4]If you try to be made right with God through the law, then your life with Christ is over—you have left God's grace. [5]But we hope to be made right with God through faith, and we wait for this hope anxiously with the Spirit's[d] help. [6]When we are in Christ Jesus, it is not important if we are circumcised or not. The important thing is faith—the kind of faith that works through love.

[7]You were running a good race. You were obeying the truth. Who stopped you from following the true way? [8]Whatever way he used did not come from the One who chose you. [9]Be careful! "Just a little yeast makes the whole batch of dough rise." [10]But I trust in the Lord that you will not believe those different ideas. Someone is confusing you with such ideas. And he will be punished, whoever he is. [11]My brothers, I do not teach that a man must be circumcised. If I teach circumcision, then why am I still being treated badly? If I still taught circumcision, my preaching about the cross would

---

4:24 Mount Sinai Mountain in Arabia where God gave his laws to Moses (Exodus 19 and 20).
4:30 "Throw . . . nothing." Quotation from Genesis 21:10.

not be a problem. [12]I wish the people who are bothering you would castrate[n] themselves!

[13]My brothers, God called you to be free. But do not use your freedom as an excuse to do the things that please your sinful self. Serve each other with love. [14]The whole law is made complete in this one command: "Love your neighbor as you love yourself."[n] [15]If you go on hurting each other and tearing each other apart, be careful! You will completely destroy each other.

THE SPIRIT AND HUMAN NATURE

[16]So I tell you: Live by following the Spirit.[d] Then you will not do what your sinful selves want. [17]Our sinful selves want what is against the Spirit. The Spirit wants what is against our sinful selves. The two are against each other. So you must not do just what you please. [18]But if you let the Spirit lead you, you are not under the law.

[19]The wrong things the sinful self does are clear: being sexually unfaithful, not being pure, taking part in sexual sins, [20]worshiping false gods, doing witchcraft,[d] hating, making trouble, being jealous, being angry, being selfish, making people angry with each other, causing divisions among people, [21]having envy, being drunk, having wild and wasteful parties, and doing other things like this. I warn you now as I warned you before: Those who do these things will not be in God's kingdom. [22]But the Spirit gives love, joy, peace, patience, kindness, goodness, faithfulness, [23]gentleness, self-control. There is no law that says these things are wrong. [24]Those who belong to Christ Jesus have crucified their own sinful selves. They have given up their old selfish feelings and the evil things they wanted to do. [25]We get our new life from the Spirit. So we should follow the

Spirit. [26]We must not be proud. We must not make trouble with each other. And we must not be jealous of each other.

HELP EACH OTHER

6 Brothers, someone in your group might do something wrong. You who are spiritual should go to him and help make him right again. You should do this in a gentle way. But be careful! You might be tempted to sin, too. [2]Help each other with your troubles. When you do this, you truly obey the law of Christ. [3]If anyone thinks that he is important when he is really not important, he is only fooling himself. [4]He should not compare himself with others. Each person should judge his own actions. Then he can be proud for what he himself has done. [5]Each person must be responsible for himself.

[6]Anyone who is learning the teaching of God should share all the good things he has with his teacher.

LIFE IS LIKE PLANTING A FIELD

[7]Do not be fooled: You cannot cheat God. A person harvests only what he plants. [8]If he plants to satisfy his sinful self, his sinful self will bring him eternal death. But if he plants to please the Spirit,[d] he will receive eternal life from the Spirit. [9]We must not become tired of doing good. We will receive our harvest of eternal life at the right time. We must not give up! [10]When we have the opportunity to help anyone, we should do it. But we should give special attention to those who are in the family of believers.

PAUL ENDS HIS LETTER

[11]I am writing this myself. See what large letters I use. [12]Some men are trying to force you to be circumcised.[d] They do these things so that the Jews will accept them. They are afraid that they will be treated badly if they follow only the cross

---

5:12 castrate To cut off part of the male sex organ. Paul uses this word because it is similar to "circumcision." Paul wanted to show that he is very upset with the false teachers.
5:14 "Love . . . yourself." Quotation from Leviticus 19:18.

of Christ.*ⁿ* ¹³Those who are circumcised do not obey the law themselves, but they want you to be circumcised. Then they can brag about what they forced you to do. ¹⁴I hope I will never brag about things like that. The cross of our Lord Jesus Christ is my only reason for bragging. Through the cross of Jesus my world was crucified and I died to the world. ¹⁵It is not important if a man is circumcised or not circumcised. The important thing is being the new people God has made. ¹⁶Peace and mercy to those who follow this rule—to all of God's people.

¹⁷So do not give me any more trouble. I have scars on my body. These show*ⁿ* I belong to Christ Jesus.

¹⁸My brothers, I pray that the grace of our Lord Jesus Christ will be with your spirit. Amen.

6:12 cross of Christ Paul uses the cross as a picture of the gospel, the story of Christ's death and rising from death to pay for men's sins. The cross, or Christ's death, was God's way to save men.

6:17 These show Many times Paul was beaten and whipped by people who were against him because he was teaching about Christ. The scars were from these beatings.

EPHESIANS

1 From Paul, an apostle[d] of Christ Jesus. I am an apostle because that is what God wanted.

To God's holy people living in Ephesus,[n] believers in Christ Jesus.

[2]Grace and peace to you from God our Father and the Lord Jesus Christ.

SPIRITUAL BLESSINGS IN CHRIST

[3]Praise be to the God and Father of our Lord Jesus Christ. In Christ, God has given us every spiritual blessing in heaven. [4]In Christ, he chose us before the world was made. In his love he chose us to be his holy people—people without blame before him. [5]And before the world was made, God decided to make us his own children through Jesus Christ. That was what he wanted and what pleased him. [6]This brings praise to God because of his wonderful grace. God gave that grace to us freely, in Christ, the One he loves. [7]In Christ we are set free by the blood of his death. And so we have forgiveness of sins because of God's rich grace. [8]God gave us that grace fully and freely. God, with full wisdom and understanding, [9]let us know his secret purpose. This was what God wanted, and he planned to do it through Christ. [10]His goal was to carry out his plan when the right time came. He planned that all things in heaven and on earth would be joined together in Christ as the head.

[11]In Christ we were chosen to be God's people. God had already chosen us to be his people, because that is what he wanted. And God is the One who makes everything agree with what he decides and wants. [12]We are the first people who hoped in Christ. And we were chosen so that we would bring praise to God's glory. [13]So it is with you. You heard the true teaching—the Good News[d] about your salvation. When you heard it, you believed in Christ. And in Christ, God put his special mark on you by giving you the Holy Spirit[d] that he had promised. [14]That Holy Spirit is the guarantee that we will get what God promised for his people. This will bring full freedom to the people who belong to God, to bring praise to God's glory.

PAUL'S PRAYER

[15-16]That is why I always remember you in my prayers and always thank God for you. I have always done this since the time I heard about your faith in the Lord Jesus and your love for all God's people. [17]I always pray to the God of our Lord Jesus Christ—to the glorious Father. I pray that he will give you a spirit that will make you wise in the knowledge of God—the knowledge that he has shown you. [18]I pray that you will have greater understanding in your heart. Then you will know the hope that God has chosen to give us. I pray that you will know that the blessings God has promised his holy people are rich and glorious. [19]And you will know that God's power is very great for us who believe. That power is the same as the great strength [20]God used to raise Christ from death and put him at his right side in heaven. [21]God made Christ more important than all rulers, authorities, powers, and kings. Christ is more important than anything in this world or in the next world. [22]God put everything under his power. And God made him the head over everything for the church. [23]The church is Christ's body. The church is filled with Christ, and Christ fills everything in every way.

FROM DEATH TO LIFE

2 In the past your spiritual lives were dead because of your sins and the

---

1:1 **in Ephesus** Some Greek copies do not have this phrase.

things you did wrong against God. [2]Yes, in the past you lived the way the world lives. You followed the ruler of the evil powers that are above the earth. That same spirit is now working in those who refuse to obey God. [3]In the past all of us lived like them. We lived trying to please our sinful selves. We did all the things our bodies and minds wanted. We should have suffered God's anger because we were sinful by nature. We were the same as all other people.

[4]But God's mercy is great, and he loved us very much. [5]We were spiritually dead because of the things we did wrong against God. But God gave us new life with Christ. You have been saved by God's grace. [6]And he raised us up with Christ and gave us a seat with him in the heavens. He did this for those of us who are in Christ Jesus. [7]He did this so that for all future time he could show the very great riches of his grace. He shows that grace by being kind to us in Christ Jesus. [8]I mean that you have been saved by grace because you believe. You did not save yourselves. It was a gift from God. [9]You cannot brag that you are saved by the work you have done. [10]God has made us what we are. In Christ Jesus, God made us new people so that we would do good works. God had planned in advance those good works for us. He had planned for us to live our lives doing them.

ONE IN CHRIST

[11]You were born non-Jews. You are the people the Jews call "uncircumcised."[n] Those who call you "uncircumcised" call themselves "circumcised."[d] (Their circumcision is only something they themselves do on their bodies.) [12]Remember that in the past you were without Christ. You were not citizens of Israel. And you had no part in the agreements[n] with the promise that God made to his people. You had no hope, and you did not know God. [13]Yes, at one time you were far away from God. But now in Christ Jesus you are brought near to God through the blood of Christ's death. [14]Because of Christ we now have peace. Christ made both Jews and non-Jews one people. They were separated as if there were a wall between them. But Christ broke down that wall of hate by giving his own body. [15]The Jewish law had many commands and rules. But Christ ended that law. Christ's purpose was to make the two groups of people become one new people in him. By doing this Christ would make peace. [16]Through the cross Christ ended the hatred between the two groups. And after Christ made the two groups to be one body, he wanted to bring them back to God. Christ did this with his death on the cross. [17]Christ came and preached peace to you non-Jews who were far away from God. And he preached peace to those Jews who were near to God. [18]Yes, through Christ we all have the right to come to the Father in one Spirit.[d]

[19]So now you non-Jews are not visitors or strangers. Now you are citizens together with God's holy people. You belong to God's family. [20]You believers are like a building that God owns. That building was built on the foundation of the apostles[d] and prophets.[d] Christ Jesus himself is the most important stone[n] in that building. [21]That whole building is joined together in Christ. And Christ makes it grow and become a holy temple in the Lord. [22]And in Christ you, too, are being built together with the Jews. You are being built into a place where God lives through the Spirit.

PAUL'S WORK FOR THE NON-JEWS

3 So I, Paul, am a prisoner of Christ Jesus. I am a prisoner for you who

---

2:11 **uncircumcised** People not having the mark of circumcision as the Jews have.
2:12 **agreements** The agreements that God gave to his people in the Old Testament.
2:20 **most important stone** Literally, "cornerstone." The first and most important stone in a building.

are not Jews. ²Surely you know that God gave me this work to tell you about his grace. ³God let me know his secret plan. He showed it to me. I have already written a little about this. ⁴And if you read what I wrote, then you can see that I truly understand the secret truth about the Christ.^d ⁵People who lived in other times were not told that secret truth. But now, through the Spirit,^d God has shown that secret truth to his holy apostles^d and prophets.^d ⁶This is that secret truth: that the non-Jews will receive what God has for his people, just as the Jews will. The non-Jews are together with the Jews as part of the same body. And they share together in the promise that God made in Christ Jesus. The non-Jews have all of this because of the Good News.^d

⁷By God's special gift of grace, I became a servant to tell that Good News. God gave me that grace through his power. ⁸I am the least important of all God's people. But God gave me this gift—to tell the non-Jewish people the Good News about the riches of Christ. Those riches are too great to understand fully. ⁹And God gave me the work of telling all people about the plan for God's secret truth. That secret truth has been hidden in God since the beginning of time. God is the One who created everything. ¹⁰His purpose was that through the church all the rulers and powers in the heavenly world will now know God's wisdom, which has so many forms. ¹¹This agrees with the purpose God had since the beginning of time. And God carried out his plan through Christ Jesus our Lord. ¹²In Christ we can come before God with freedom and without fear. We can do this through faith in Christ. ¹³So I ask you not to become discouraged because of the sufferings I am having for you. My sufferings bring honor to you.

THE LOVE OF CHRIST

¹⁴So I bow in prayer before the Father.

¹⁵Every family in heaven and on earth gets its true name from him. ¹⁶I ask the Father in his great glory to give you the power to be strong in spirit. He will give you that strength through his Spirit.^d ¹⁷I pray that Christ will live in your hearts because of your faith. I pray that your life will be strong in love and be built on love. ¹⁸And I pray that you and all God's holy people will have the power to understand the greatness of Christ's love. I pray that you can understand how wide and how long and how high and how deep that love is. ¹⁹Christ's love is greater than any person can ever know. But I pray that you will be able to know that love. Then you can be filled with the fullness of God.

²⁰With God's power working in us, God can do much, much more than anything we can ask or think of. ²¹To him be glory in the church and in Christ Jesus for all time, forever and ever. Amen.

THE UNITY OF THE BODY

4 I am in prison because I belong to the Lord. God chose you to be his people. I tell you now to live the way God's people should live. ²Always be humble and gentle. Be patient and accept each other with love. ³You are joined together with peace through the Spirit.^d Do all you can to continue together in this way. Let peace hold you together. ⁴There is one body and one Spirit. And God called you to have one hope. ⁵There is one Lord, one faith, and one baptism. ⁶There is one God and Father of everything. He rules everything. He is everywhere and in everything.

⁷Christ gave each one of us a special gift. Each one received what Christ wanted to give him. ⁸That is why it says in the Scriptures,^d

"When he went up to the heights,
he led a parade of captives.
And he gave gifts to people."
                              Psalm 68:18

[9]When it says, "He went up," what does it mean? It means that he first came down to the earth. [10]So Jesus came down, and he is the same One who went up. He went up above all the heavens. Christ did that to fill everything with himself. [11]And Christ gave gifts to men—he made some to be apostles,[d] some to be prophets,[d] some to go and tell the Good News,[d] and some to have the work of caring for and teaching God's people. [12]Christ gave those gifts to prepare God's holy people for the work of serving. He gave those gifts to make the body of Christ stronger. [13]This work must continue until we are all joined together in the same faith and in the same knowledge about the Son of God. We must become like a mature person—we must grow until we become like Christ and have all his perfection.

[14]Then we will no longer be babies. We will not be tossed about like a ship that the waves carry one way and then another. We will not be influenced by every new teaching we hear from men who are trying to fool us. Those men make plans and try any kind of trick to fool people into following the wrong path. [15]No! We will speak the truth with love. We will grow up in every way to be like Christ, who is the head. [16]The whole body depends on Christ. And all the parts of the body are joined and held together. Each part of the body does its own work. And this makes the whole body grow and be strong with love.

THE WAY YOU SHOULD LIVE

[17]In the Lord's name, I tell you this. I warn you: Do not continue living like those who do not believe. Their thoughts are worth nothing. [18]They do not understand. They know nothing, because they refuse to listen. So they cannot have the life that God gives. [19]They have lost their feeling of shame. And they use their lives for doing evil. More and more they want

to do all kinds of evil things. [20]But the things you learned in Christ were not like this. [21]I know that you heard about him, and you are in him; so you were taught the truth. Yes, the truth is in Jesus. [22]You were taught to leave your old self—to stop living the evil way you lived before. That old self becomes worse and worse because people are fooled by the evil things they want to do. [23]But you were taught to be made new in your hearts. [24]You were taught to become a new person. That new person is made to be like God—made to be truly good and holy.

[25]So you must stop telling lies. Tell each other the truth because we all belong to each other in the same body.[n] [26]When you are angry, do not sin. And do not go on being angry all day. [27]Do not give the devil a way to defeat you. [28]If a person is stealing, he must stop stealing and start working. He must use his hands for doing something good. Then he will have something to share with those who are poor.

[29]When you talk, do not say harmful things. But say what people need—words that will help others become stronger. Then what you say will help those who listen to you. [30]And do not make the Holy Spirit[d] sad. The Spirit is God's proof that you belong to him. God gave you the Spirit to show that God will make you free when the time comes. [31]Do not be bitter or angry or mad. Never shout angrily or say things to hurt others. Never do anything evil. [32]Be kind and loving to each other. Forgive each other just as God forgave you in Christ.

LIVING IN THE LIGHT

5 You are God's children whom he loves. So try to be like God. [2]Live a life of love. Love other people just as Christ loved us. Christ gave himself for us—he was a sweet-smelling offering and sacrifice to God.

4:25 Tell . . . body. Quotation from Zechariah 8:16.

[3]But there must be no sexual sin among you. There must not be any kind of evil or greed. Those things are not right for God's holy people. [4]Also, there must be no evil talk among you. You must not speak foolishly or tell evil jokes. These things are not right for you. But you should be giving thanks to God. [5]You can be sure of this: No one will have a place in the kingdom of Christ and of God if he does sexual sins, or does evil things, or is greedy. Anyone who is greedy is serving a false god.

[6]Do not let anyone fool you by telling you things that are not true. These things will bring God's anger on those who do not obey him. [7]So have no part with them. [8]In the past you were full of darkness, but now you are full of light in the Lord. So live like children who belong to the light. [9]Light brings every kind of goodness, right living, and truth. [10]Try to learn what pleases the Lord. [11]Do not do the things that people in darkness do. That brings nothing good. But do good things to show that the things done in darkness are wrong. [12]It is shameful even to talk about what those people do in secret. [13]But the light makes all things easy to see. [14]And everything that is made easy to see can become light. This is why it is said:

"Wake up, sleeper!
    Rise from death,
and Christ will shine on you."

[15]So be very careful how you live. Do not live like those who are not wise. Live wisely. [16]I mean that you should use every chance you have for doing good, because these are evil times. [17]So do not be foolish with your lives. But learn what the Lord wants you to do. [18]Do not be drunk with wine. That will ruin you spiritually. But be filled with the Spirit.[d] [19]Speak to each other with psalms, hymns, and spiritual songs. Sing and make music in your hearts to the Lord. [20]Always give thanks to God the Father for everything, in the name of our Lord Jesus Christ.

WIVES AND HUSBANDS

[21]Be willing to obey each other. Do this because you respect Christ.

[22]Wives, be under the authority of your husbands, as of the Lord. [23]The husband is the head of the wife, as Christ is the head of the church. The church is Christ's body—Christ is the Savior of the body. [24]The church is under the authority of Christ. So it is the same with you wives. You should be under the authority of your husbands in everything.

[25]Husbands, love your wives as Christ loved the church. Christ died for the church [26]to make it belong to God. Christ used the word to make the church clean by washing it with water. [27]Christ died so that he could give the church to himself like a bride in all her beauty. He died so that the church could be pure and without fault, with no evil or sin or any other wrong thing in it. [28]And husbands should love their wives in the same way. They should love their wives as they love their own bodies. The man who loves his wife loves himself. [29]No person ever hates his own body, but feeds and takes care of it. And that is what Christ does for the church, [30]because we are parts of his body. [31]The Scripture says, "So a man will leave his father and mother and be united with his wife. And the two people will become one body."[n] [32]That secret truth is very important—I am talking about Christ and the church. [33]But each one of you must love his wife as he loves himself. And a wife must respect her husband.

CHILDREN AND PARENTS

6 Children, obey your parents the way the Lord wants. This is the right thing to do. [2]The command says, "Honor

---

5:31 "So ... body." Quotation from Genesis 2:24.

your father and mother."[n] This is the first command that has a promise with it. [3]The promise is: "Then everything will be well with you, and you will have a long life on the earth."[n]

[4]Fathers, do not make your children angry, but raise them with the training and teaching of the Lord.

SLAVES AND MASTERS

[5]Slaves, obey your masters here on earth with fear and respect. And do that with a heart that is true, just as you obey Christ. [6]You must do more than obey your masters to please them only while they are watching you. You must obey them as you are obeying Christ. With all your heart you must do what God wants. [7]Do your work, and be happy to do it. Work as if you were serving the Lord, not as if you were serving only men. [8]Remember that the Lord will give a reward to everyone, slave or free, for doing good.

[9]Masters, in the same way, be good to your slaves. Do not say things to scare them. You know that the One who is your Master and their Master is in heaven. And that Master treats everyone alike.

WEAR THE FULL ARMOR OF GOD

[10]Finally, be strong in the Lord and in his great power. [11]Wear the full armor of God. Wear God's armor so that you can fight against the devil's evil tricks. [12]Our fight is not against people on earth. We are fighting against the rulers and authorities and the powers of this world's darkness. We are fighting against the spiritual powers of evil in the heavenly world. [13]That is why you need to get God's full armor. Then on the day of evil you will be able to stand strong. And when you have finished the whole fight, you will still be standing. [14]So stand strong, with the belt of truth tied around your waist. And on your chest wear the protection of right living. [15]And on your feet wear the Good News[d] of peace to help you stand strong. [16]And also use the shield of faith. With that you can stop all the burning arrows of the Evil One. [17]Accept God's salvation to be your helmet. And take the sword of the Spirit[d]—that sword is the teaching of God. [18]Pray in the Spirit at all times. Pray with all kinds of prayers, and ask for everything you need. To do this you must always be ready. Never give up. Always pray for all God's people.

[19]Also pray for me. Pray that when I speak, God will give me words so that I can tell the secret truth of the Good News without fear. [20]I have the work of speaking that Good News. I am doing that now, here in prison. Pray that when I preach the Good News I will speak without fear, as I should.

FINAL GREETINGS

[21]I am sending to you Tychicus, our brother whom we love. He is a faithful servant of the Lord's work. He will tell you everything that is happening with me. Then you will know how I am and what I am doing. [22]That is why I am sending him. I want you to know how we are. I am sending him to encourage you.

[23]Peace and love with faith to you from God the Father and the Lord Jesus Christ. [24]God's grace to all of you who love our Lord Jesus Christ with love that never ends.

6:2 "Honor ... mother." Quotation from Exodus 20:12; Deuteronomy 5:16.
6:3 "Then ... earth." Quotation from Exodus 20:12; Deuteronomy 5:16.

PHILIPPIANS

1 From Paul and Timothy, servants of Jesus Christ.

To all of God's holy people in Christ Jesus who live in Philippi. And to your overseers[d] and deacons.[d]

[2]Grace and peace to you from God our Father and the Lord Jesus Christ.

PAUL'S PRAYER

[3]I thank God every time I remember you. [4]And I always pray for all of you with joy. [5]I thank God for the help you gave me while I preached the Good News.[d] You helped from the first day you believed until now. [6]God began doing a good work in you. And he will continue it until it is finished when Jesus Christ comes again. I am sure of that.

[7]And I know that I am right to think like this about all of you. I am sure because I have you in my heart. All of you share in God's grace with me. You share in God's grace with me while I am in prison, while I am defending the Good News, and while I am proving the truth of the Good News. [8]God knows that I want to see you very much. I love all of you with the love of Christ Jesus.

[9]This is my prayer for you: that your love will grow more and more; that you will have knowledge and understanding with your love; [10]that you will see the difference between good and bad and choose the good; that you will be pure and without wrong for the coming of Christ; [11]that you will be filled with the good things produced in your life by Christ to bring glory and praise to God.

PAUL'S TROUBLES HELP THE WORK

[12]Brothers, I want you to know that what has happened to me has helped to spread the Good News.[d] [13]I am in prison because I am a believer in Christ. All the palace guards and everyone else knows this. [14]I am still in prison, but most of the believers feel better about it now. And so they are much braver about telling the Good News about Christ.

[15]It is true that some preach about Christ because they are jealous and bitter. But others preach about Christ because they want to help. [16]They preach because they have love, and they know that God gave me the work of defending the Good News. [17]But others preach about Christ because they are selfish. Their reason for preaching is wrong. They want to make trouble for me in prison.

[18]But I do not care if they make trouble for me. The important thing is that they are preaching about Christ. They should do it for the right reasons. But I am happy even if they do it for wrong reasons. And I will continue to be happy. [19]You are praying for me, and the Spirit of Jesus Christ helps me. So I know that this trouble will bring my freedom. [20]The thing I want and hope for is that I will not fail Christ in anything. I hope that I will have the courage now, as always, to show the greatness of Christ in my life here on earth. I want to do that if I die or if I live. [21]To me the only important thing about living is Christ. And even death would be profit for me. [22]If I continue living in the body, I will be able to work for the Lord. But what should I choose—living or dying? I do not know. [23]It is hard to choose between the two. I want to leave this life and be with Christ. That is much better. [24]But you need me here in my body. [25]I know that you need me, and so I know that I will stay with you. I will help you grow and have joy in your faith. [26]You will be very happy in Christ Jesus when I am with you again.

[27]Be sure that you live in a way that brings honor to the Good News of Christ. Then whether I come and visit you or am away from you, I will hear good things about you. I will hear that you continue strong with one purpose and that you

work together as a team for the faith of the Good News. ²⁸And you will not be afraid of those who are against you. All of these things are proof from God that you will be saved and that your enemies will be lost. ²⁹God gave you the honor both of believing in Christ and suffering for Christ. Both these things bring glory to Christ. ³⁰When I was with you, you saw the struggles I had. And you hear about the struggles I am having now. You yourselves are having the same kind of struggles.

2 Does your life in Christ give you strength? Does his love comfort you? Do we share together in the Spirit?ᵈ Do you have mercy and kindness? ²If so, make me very happy by having the same thoughts, sharing the same love, and having one mind and purpose. ³When you do things, do not let selfishness or pride be your guide. Be humble and give more honor to others than to yourselves. ⁴Do not be interested only in your own life, but be interested in the lives of others.

BE UNSELFISH LIKE CHRIST

⁵In your lives you must think and act like Christ Jesus.
⁶Christ himself was like God in
    everything.
He was equal with God.
But he did not think that being
    equal with God was something to
    be held on to.
⁷He gave up his place with God and
    made himself nothing.
He was born as a man
and became like a servant.
⁸And when he was living as a man,
he humbled himself and was fully
    obedient to God.
He obeyed even when that caused
    his death—death on a cross.
⁹So God raised Christ to the highest
    place.
God made the name of Christ
    greater than every other name.

¹⁰God wants every knee to bow to
    Jesus—
everyone in heaven, on earth, and
    under the earth.
¹¹Everyone will say, "Jesus Christ is
    Lord"
and bring glory to God the Father.

BE THE PEOPLE GOD WANTS YOU TO BE

¹²My dear friends, you have always obeyed. You obeyed God when I was with you. It is even more important that you obey now while I am not with you. Keep on working to complete your salvation, and do it with fear and trembling. ¹³Yes, God is working in you to help you want to do what pleases him. Then he gives you the power to do it.

¹⁴Do everything without complaining or arguing. ¹⁵Then you will be innocent and without anything wrong in you. You will be God's children without fault. But you are living with crooked and mean people all around you. Among them you shine like stars in the dark world. ¹⁶You offer to them the teaching that gives life. So when Christ comes again, I can be happy because my work was not wasted. I ran in the race and won.

¹⁷Your faith makes you offer your lives as a sacrifice in serving God. Perhaps I will have to offer my own blood with your sacrifice. But if that happens, I will be happy and full of joy with all of you. ¹⁸You also should be happy and full of joy with me.

TIMOTHY AND EPAPHRODITUS

¹⁹I hope in the Lord Jesus to send Timothy to you soon. I will be happy to learn how you are. ²⁰I have no other person like Timothy. He truly cares for you. ²¹Other people are interested only in their own lives. They are not interested in the work of Christ Jesus. ²²You know the kind of person Timothy is. You know that he has served with me in telling the Good News,ᵈ as a son serves his father. ²³I plan to send him to you quickly when

I know what will happen to me. [24]I am sure that the Lord will help me to come to you soon.

[25]Epaphroditus is my brother in Christ. He works and serves with me in the army of Christ. When I needed help, you sent him to me. I think now that I must send him back to you [26]because he wants very much to see all of you. He is worried because you heard that he was sick. [27]Yes, he was sick, and nearly died. But God helped him and me too, so that I would not have more sadness. [28]So I want very much to send him to you. When you see him, you can be happy. And I can stop worrying about you. [29]Welcome him in the Lord with much joy. Give honor to people like Epaphroditus. [30]He should be honored because he almost died for the work of Christ. He put his life in danger so that he could help me. This was help that you could not give me.

THE IMPORTANCE OF CHRIST

3 My brothers, be full of joy in the Lord. It is no trouble for me to write the same things to you again, and it will help you to be more ready. [2]Be careful of those who do evil. They are like dogs. They demand to cut[n] the body. [3]But we are the ones who are truly circumcised.[d] We worship God through his Spirit.[d] We are proud to be in Christ Jesus. And we do not trust in ourselves or anything we can do. [4]Even if I am able to trust in myself, still I do not. If anyone thinks that he has a reason to trust in himself, he should know that I have greater reason for trusting in myself. [5]I was circumcised eight days after my birth. I am from the people of Israel and the tribe[d] of Benjamin. I am a Hebrew, and my parents were Hebrews. The law of Moses was very important to me. That is why I became a Pharisee.[d] [6]I was so enthusiastic that I tried to hurt the church. No

one could find fault with the way I obeyed the law of Moses. [7]At one time all these things were important to me. But now I think those things are worth nothing because of Christ. [8]Not only those things, but I think that all things are worth nothing compared with the greatness of knowing Christ Jesus my Lord. Because of Christ, I have lost all those things. And now I know that all those things are worthless trash. This allows me to have Christ [9]and to belong to him. Now that I belong to Christ, I am right with God and this being right does not come from my following the law. It comes from God through faith. God uses my faith in Christ to make me right with him. [10]All I want is to know Christ and the power of his rising from death. I want to share in Christ's sufferings and become like him in his death. [11]If I have those things, then I have hope that I myself will be raised from death.

CONTINUING TOWARD OUR GOAL

[12]I do not mean that I am already as God wants me to be. I have not yet reached that goal. But I continue trying to reach it and to make it mine. Christ wants me to do that. That is the reason Christ made me his. [13]Brothers, I know that I have not yet reached that goal. But there is one thing I always do: I forget the things that are past. I try as hard as I can to reach the goal that is before me. [14]I keep trying to reach the goal and get the prize. That prize is mine because God called me through Christ to the life above.

[15]All of us who have grown spiritually to be mature should think this way, too. And if there are things you do not agree with, God will make them clear to you. [16]But we should continue following the truth we already have.

[17]Brothers, all of you should try to follow my example and to copy those who live the way we showed you. [18]Many people live like enemies of the cross of

---

3:2 cut The word in Greek is like the word "circumcise," but it means "to cut completely off."

Christ. I have often told you about them, and it makes me cry to tell you about them now. [19]The way they live is leading them to destruction. Instead of serving God, they do whatever their bodies want. They do shameful things, and they are proud of it. They think only about earthly things. [20]But our homeland is in heaven, and we are waiting for our Savior, the Lord Jesus Christ, to come from heaven. [21]He will change our humble bodies and make them like his own glorious body. Christ can do this by his power. With that power he is able to rule all things.

WHAT THE CHRISTIANS ARE TO DO

4 My dear brothers, I love you and want to see you. You bring me joy and make me proud of you. Continue following the Lord as I have told you.

[2]I ask Euodia and Syntyche to agree in the Lord. [3]And because you serve faithfully with me, my friend, I ask you to help these women to do this. They served with me in telling people the Good News.[d] They served together with Clement and others who worked with me. Their names are written in the book of life.[n]

[4]Be full of joy in the Lord always. I will say again, be full of joy.

[5]Let all men see that you are gentle and kind. The Lord is coming soon. [6]Do not worry about anything. But pray and ask God for everything you need. And when you pray, always give thanks. [7]And God's peace will keep your hearts and minds in Christ Jesus. The peace that God gives is so great that we cannot understand it.

[8]Brothers, continue to think about the things that are good and worthy of praise. Think about the things that are true and honorable and right and pure and beautiful and respected. [9]And do what you learned and received from me. Do what I told you and what you saw me do. And

the God who gives peace will be with you.

PAUL THANKS THE CHRISTIANS

[10]I am very happy in the Lord that you have shown your care for me again. You continued to care about me, but there was no way for you to show it. [11]I am telling you this, but it is not because I need anything. I have learned to be satisfied with the things I have and with everything that happens. [12]I know how to live when I am poor. And I know how to live when I have plenty. I have learned the secret of being happy at any time in everything that happens. I have learned to be happy when I have enough to eat and when I do not have enough to eat. I have learned to be happy when I have all that I need and when I do not have the things I need. [13]I can do all things through Christ because he gives me strength.

[14]But it was good that you helped me when I needed help. [15]You people in Philippi remember when I first preached the Good News[d] there. When I left Macedonia, you were the only church that gave me help. [16]Several times you sent me things I needed when I was in Thessalonica. [17]Really, it is not that I want to receive gifts from you. But I want you to have the good that comes from giving. [18]And now I have everything, and more. I have all I need because Epaphroditus brought your gift to me. Your gift is like a sweet-smelling sacrifice offered to God. God accepts that sacrifice, and it pleases him. [19]My God will use his wonderful riches in Christ Jesus to give you everything you need. [20]Glory to our God and Father forever and ever! Amen.

[21]Greet each of God's people in Christ. God's people who are with me send greetings to you. [22]All of God's people greet you. And those believers from the palace of Caesar[d] greet you, too.

[23]The grace of the Lord Jesus Christ be with you all.

4:3 **book of life** God's book that has the names of all God's chosen people (Revelation 3:5; 21:27).

1 From Paul, an apostle[d] of Christ Jesus. I am an apostle because that is what God wanted.

Also from Timothy, our brother.

[2] To the holy and faithful brothers in Christ that live in Colosse. Grace and peace from God our Father.[n]

[3] In our prayers for you we always thank God, the Father of our Lord Jesus Christ. [4] We thank God because we have heard about the faith you have in Christ Jesus and the love you have for all of God's people. [5] You have this faith and love because of your hope, and what you hope for is saved for you in heaven. You learned about this hope when you heard the true teaching, the Good News[d] [6] that was told to you. Everywhere in the world that Good News is bringing blessings and is growing. This has happened with you, too, since you heard the Good News and understood the truth about the grace of God. [7] You learned about God's grace from Epaphras, whom we love. Epaphras works together with us and is a faithful servant of Christ for us.[n] [8] He also told us about the love you have from the Holy Spirit.[d]

[9] Since the day we heard this about you, we have continued praying for you. We ask God that you will know fully what God wants. We pray that you will also have great wisdom and understanding in spiritual things. [10] Then you will live the kind of life that honors and pleases the Lord in every way. You will produce fruit in every good work and grow in the knowledge of God. [11] Then God will strengthen you with his own great power. And you will not give up when troubles come, but you will be patient. [12] Then you will joyfully give thanks to the Father. He has made you[n] able to have all that he has prepared for his people who live in the light. [13] God made us free from the power of darkness, and he brought us into the kingdom of his dear Son. [14] The Son paid for our sins,[n] and in him we have forgiveness.

THE IMPORTANCE OF CHRIST

[15] No one has seen God, but Jesus is exactly like him. Christ ranks higher than all the things that have been made. [16] Through his power all things were made—things in heaven and on earth, things seen and unseen, all powers, authorities, lords, and rulers. All things were made through Christ and for Christ. [17] Christ was there before anything was made. And all things continue because of him. [18] He is the head of the body. (The body is the church.) Everything comes from him. And he is the first one who was raised from death. So in all things Jesus is most important. [19] God was pleased for all of himself to live in Christ. [20] And through Christ, God decided to bring all things back to himself again—things on earth and things in heaven. God made peace by using the blood of Christ's death on the cross.

[21] At one time you were separated from God. You were God's enemies in your minds because the evil deeds you did were against God. [22] But now Christ has made you God's friends again. He did this by his death while he was in the body, that he might bring you into God's presence. He brings you before God as people who are holy, with no wrong in you, and with nothing that God can judge you guilty of. [23] And Christ will do this if you

---

1:2 **Father** Some Greek copies continue, "and the Lord Jesus Christ."
1:7 **for us** Some Greek copies read "for you."
1:12 **you** Some Greek copies read "us."
1:14 **sins** Some Greek copies continue, "with his blood."

continue to believe in the Good News[d] you heard. You must continue strong and sure in your faith. You must not be moved away from the hope that Good News gave you. That same Good News has been told to everyone in the world. I, Paul, help in preaching that Good News.

PAUL'S WORK FOR THE CHURCH

[24]I am happy in my sufferings for you. There are many things that Christ must still suffer through his body, the church. I am accepting my part of these things that must be suffered. I accept these sufferings in my body. I suffer for his body, the church. [25]I became a servant of the church because God gave me a special work to do that helps you. My work is to tell fully the teaching of God. [26]This teaching is the secret truth that was hidden since the beginning of time. It was hidden from everyone, but now it is made known to God's holy people. [27]God decided to let his people know this rich and glorious truth which he has for all people. This truth is Christ himself, who is in you. He is our only hope for glory. [28]So we continue to preach Christ to all men. We use all wisdom to warn and to teach everyone. We are trying to bring each one into God's presence as a mature person in Christ. [29]To do this, I work and struggle, using Christ's great strength that works so powerfully in me.

2 I want you to know that I am trying very hard to help you. And I am trying to help those in Laodicea and others who have never seen me. [2]I want them to be strengthened and joined together with love. I want them to be rich in the strong belief that comes from understanding. I mean I want you to know fully God's secret truth. That truth is Christ himself. [3]And in him all the treasures of wisdom and knowledge are safely kept.

[4]I say this so that no one can fool you by arguments that seem good, but are false. [5]I am not there with you, but my heart is with you. I am happy to see your good lives and your strong faith in Christ.

CONTINUE TO LIVE IN CHRIST

[6]As you received Christ Jesus the Lord, so continue to live in him. [7]Keep your roots deep in him and have your lives built on him. Be strong in the faith, just as you were taught. And always be thankful.

[8]Be sure that no one leads you away with false ideas and words that mean nothing. Those ideas come from men. They are the worthless ideas of this world. They are not from Christ. [9]All of God lives fully in Christ (even when Christ was on earth). [10]And in him you have a full and true life. He is ruler over all rulers and powers.

[11]In Christ you had a different kind of circumcision.[d] That circumcision was not done by hands. I mean, you were made free from the power of your sinful self. That is the kind of circumcision Christ does. [12]When you were baptized, you were buried with Christ and you were raised up with Christ because of your faith in God's power. That power was shown when he raised Christ from death. [13]You were spiritually dead because of your sins and because you were not free from the power of your sinful self. But God made you alive with Christ. And God forgave all our sins. [14]We owed a debt because we broke God's laws. That debt listed all the rules we failed to follow. But God forgave us that debt. He took away that debt and nailed it to the cross. [15]God defeated the spiritual rulers and powers. With the cross God won the victory and defeated them. He showed the world that they were powerless.

DON'T FOLLOW PEOPLE'S RULES

[16]So do not let anyone make rules for you about eating and drinking or about a religious feast, a New Moon[d] Festival, or a Sabbath[d] day. [17]In the past, these things were like a shadow of what was to come. But the new things that were coming are found in Christ. [18]Some enjoy acting as if they were humble and love to

worship angels. They are always talking about the visions they have seen. Do not let them tell you that you are wrong. They are full of foolish pride because of their human way of thinking. [19]They do not keep themselves under the control of Christ, the head. The whole body depends on Christ. Because of him all the parts of the body care for each other and help each other. This strengthens the body and holds it together. And so the body grows in the way God wants.

[20]You died with Christ and were made free from the worthless rules of the world. So why do you act as if you still belong to this world? I mean, why do you follow rules like these: [21]"Don't handle this," "Don't taste that," "Don't touch that thing"? [22]These rules are talking about earthly things that are gone as soon as they are used. They are only human commands and teachings. [23]These rules seem to be wise. But they are only part of a human religion. They make people pretend not to be proud and make them punish their bodies. But they do not really control the evil desires of the sinful self.

YOUR NEW LIFE IN CHRIST

3 You were raised from death with Christ. So aim at what is in heaven, where Christ is sitting at the right hand of God. [2]Think only about the things in heaven, not the things on earth. [3]Your old sinful self has died, and your new life is kept with Christ in God. [4]Christ is your[n] life. When he comes again, you will share in his glory.

[5]So put all evil things out of your life: sexual sinning, doing evil, letting evil thoughts control you, wanting things that are evil, and always selfishly wanting more and more. This really means living to serve a false god. [6]These things make God angry.[n] [7]In your evil life in the past, you also did these things.

[8]But now put these things out of your life: anger, bad temper, doing or saying things to hurt others, and using evil words when you talk. [9]Do not lie to each other. You have left your old sinful life and the things you did before. [10]You have begun to live the new life. In your new life you are being made new. You are becoming like the One who made you. This new life brings you the true knowledge of God. [11]In the new life there is no difference between Greeks and Jews. There is no difference between those who are circumcised[d] and those who are not circumcised, or people that are foreigners, or Scythians.[n] There is no difference between slaves and free people. But Christ is in all believers. And Christ is all that is important.

[12]God has chosen you and made you his holy people. He loves you. So always do these things: Show mercy to others; be kind, humble, gentle, and patient. [13]Do not be angry with each other, but forgive each other. If someone does wrong to you, then forgive him. Forgive each other because the Lord forgave you. [14]Do all these things; but most important, love each other. Love is what holds you all together in perfect unity. [15]Let the peace that Christ gives control your thinking. You were all called together in one body[n] to have peace. Always be thankful. [16]Let the teaching of Christ live in you richly. Use all wisdom to teach and strengthen each other. Sing psalms, hymns, and spiritual songs with thankfulness in your hearts to God. [17]Everything you say and everything you do should all be done for Jesus your

---

3:4 **your** Some Greek copies read "our."
3:6 **These . . . angry.** Some Greek copies continue, "against the people who do not obey God."
3:11 **Scythians** The Scythians were known as very wild and cruel people.
3:15 **body** The spiritual body of Christ, meaning the church or his people.

Lord. And in all you do, give thanks to God the Father through Jesus.

YOUR NEW LIFE WITH OTHER PEOPLE

[18]Wives, be under the authority of your husbands. This is the right thing to do in the Lord.

[19]Husbands, love your wives, and be gentle to them.

[20]Children, obey your parents in all things. This pleases the Lord.

[21]Fathers, do not nag your children. If you are too hard to please, they may want to stop trying.

[22]Slaves, obey your masters in all things. Do not obey just when they are watching you, to gain their favor. But serve them honestly, because you respect the Lord. [23]In all the work you are doing, work the best you can. Work as if you were working for the Lord, not for men. [24]Remember that you will receive your reward from the Lord, which he promised to his people. You are serving the Lord Christ. [25]But remember that anyone who does wrong will be punished for that wrong. And the Lord treats everyone the same.

4 Masters, give the things that are good and fair to your slaves. Remember that you have a Master in heaven.

WHAT THE CHRISTIANS ARE TO DO

[2]Continue praying and keep alert. And when you pray, always thank God. [3]Also pray for us. Pray that God will give us an opportunity to tell people his message. Pray that we can preach the secret truth that God has made known about Christ. I am in prison because I preach this truth. [4]Pray that I can speak in a way that will make it clear as I should.

[5]Be wise in the way you act with people who are not believers. Use your time in the best way you can. [6]When you talk, you should always be kind and wise. Then you will be able to answer everyone in the way you should.

NEWS ABOUT THE PEOPLE WITH PAUL

[7]Tychicus is my dear brother in Christ. He is a faithful minister and servant with me in the Lord. He will tell you all the things that are happening to me. [8]That is why I am sending him. I want you to know how we are. I am sending him to encourage you. [9]I send him with Onesimus. Onesimus is a faithful and dear brother in Christ. He is one of your group. They will tell you all that has happened here.

[10]Aristarchus greets you. He is a prisoner with me. And Mark, the cousin of Barnabas, also greets you. (I have already told you what to do about Mark. If he comes, welcome him.) [11]Jesus, who is called Justus, also greets you. These are the only Jewish believers who work with me for the kingdom of God. They have been a comfort to me.

[12]Epaphras also greets you. He is a servant of Jesus Christ. And he is from your group. He always prays for you. He prays that you will grow to be spiritually mature and have everything that God wants for you. [13]I know that he has worked hard for you and the people in Laodicea and in Hierapolis. [14]Demas and our dear friend Luke, the doctor, greet you.

[15]Greet the brothers in Laodicea. And greet Nympha and the church that meets in her house. [16]After this letter is read to you, be sure that it is also read to the church in Laodicea. And you read the letter that I wrote to Laodicea. [17]Tell Archippus, "Be sure to do the work the Lord gave you."

[18]I, Paul, greet you and write this with my own hand. Remember me in prison. God's grace be with you.

1 From Paul, Silas, and Timothy.
To the church in Thessalonica, the church in God the Father and the Lord Jesus Christ. May God's grace and peace be yours.

THE FAITH OF THE THESSALONIANS

²We always remember you when we pray and thank God for all of you. ³When we pray to God our Father, we always thank him for the things you have done because of your faith. And we thank him for the work you have done because of your love. And we thank him that you continue to be strong because of your hope in our Lord Jesus Christ.

⁴Brothers, God loves you. And we know that he has chosen you to be his. ⁵We brought the Good News*d* to you. But we did not use only words. We brought the Good News with power, with the Holy Spirit,*d* and with sure knowledge that it is true. Also you know how we lived when we were with you. We lived that way to help you. ⁶And you became like us and like the Lord. You suffered much, but still you accepted the teaching with the joy that comes from the Holy Spirit. ⁷So you became an example to all the believers in Macedonia and Southern Greece. ⁸The Lord's teaching spread from you in Macedonia and Southern Greece. And your faith in God has become known everywhere. So we do not need to say anything about your faith. ⁹People everywhere are telling about the good way you accepted us when we were there with you. They tell about how you stopped worshiping idols and changed to serving the living and true God. ¹⁰And you changed to wait for God's Son to come from heaven. God raised that Son from death. He is Jesus, who saves us from God's angry judgment that is sure to come.

PAUL'S WORK IN THESSALONICA

2 Brothers, you know that our visit to you was not a failure. ²Before we came to you, we suffered in Philippi. People there insulted us. You know about that. And when we came to you, many people were against us. But our God helped us to be brave and to tell you his Good News.*d* ³Our message was a message to encourage you. We were not trying to lie. We had no evil plan. We were not trying to trick you. ⁴But we speak the Good News because God tested us and trusted us to do it. When we speak, we are not trying to please men. But we are trying to please God, who tests our hearts. ⁵You know that we never tried to influence you by saying nice things about you. We were not trying to get your money. We had no selfishness to hide from you. God knows that this is true. ⁶We were not looking for praise from you or anyone else. We are apostles*d* of Christ. When we were with you, we could have used our authority to make you do things. ⁷But we were very gentle with you.*n* We were like a mother caring for her little children. ⁸Because we loved you, we were happy to share God's Good News with you. But not only that, we were also happy to share even our own lives with you. ⁹Brothers, I know that you remember how hard we worked. We worked night and day so that we would not burden any of you while we preached God's Good News to you.

¹⁰When we were with you, we lived in a holy and right way, without fault. You know that this is true, and God knows that this is true. ¹¹You know that we treated each of you as a father treats his own children. ¹²We strengthened you, we comforted you, and we told you to live good lives for God. It is God who calls you to his glorious kingdom.

2:7 But ... you. Some Greek copies read "But we were like infants among you."

13Also, we always thank God because of the way you accepted his message. You heard his message from us, and you accepted it as the word of God, not the words of men. And it really is God's message. And that message works in you who believe. 14Brothers, you have been like God's churches in Christ that are in Judea.ⁿ God's people suffered bad things from the other Jews there. And you suffered the same bad things from the people of your own country. 15Those Jews killed both the Lord Jesus and the prophets.^d And they forced us to leave that country. They do not please God. They are against all people. 16They try to stop us from teaching the non-Jews so that they may be saved. But those Jews are adding more and more sins to the sins they already have. The anger of God has come to them at last.

PAUL WANTS TO VISIT THEM AGAIN

17Brothers, we were separated from you for a short time, but our thoughts were still with you. We wanted very much to see you, and tried very hard to do so. 18I, Paul, tried to come many times, but Satan stopped us. 19For you are our hope, our joy, and the crown we will be proud of when our Lord Jesus Christ comes. 20Truly you are our glory and our joy.

3 We could not come to you, but it was very hard to wait any longer. So we decided to stay in Athens alone 2and send Timothy to you. Timothy is our brother, who works with us for God. He helps us tell people the Good News^d about Christ. We sent Timothy to strengthen and comfort you in your faith. 3We sent him so that none of you would be upset by these troubles we have now. You yourselves know that we must have these troubles. 4Even when we were with you, we told you that we all would have to suffer. And you know that it has happened the way we said. 5This is why I sent Timothy to you, so that I could know about your faith. I sent him when I could not wait any longer. I was afraid that the devil had tempted you, and perhaps our hard work would have been wasted.

6But Timothy now has come back to us from you and has brought us good news about your faith and love. He told us that you always remember us in a good way. He told us that you want to see us just as much as we want to see you. 7So, brothers, we are comforted about you, because of your faith. We have much trouble and suffering, but still we are comforted. 8For our life is really full if you stand strong in the Lord. 9We have so much joy before our God because of you, and we thank him for you. But we cannot thank him enough for all the joy we feel. 10And we continue praying with all our heart for you night and day. We pray that we can see you again and give you all the things you need to make your faith strong.

11We pray that our God and Father and our Lord Jesus will prepare the way for us to come to you. 12We pray that the Lord will make your love grow more and more for each other and for all people. We pray that you will love others as we love you and 13that your hearts will be made strong. Then you will be holy and without fault before our God and Father when our Lord Jesus comes with all his holy people.

A LIFE THAT PLEASES GOD

4 Brothers, now I have some other things to tell you. We taught you how to live in a way that will please God. And you are living that way. Now we ask you and encourage you in the Lord Jesus to live that way more and more. 2You know what we told you to do by the authority of the Lord Jesus. 3God wants you to be holy and to stay away from sexual sins. 4He wants each one of you to

---

2:14 **Judea** The Jewish land where Jesus lived and taught and where the church first began.

learn how to take a wife[n] in a way that is holy and honorable. [5]Don't use your body for sexual sin. The people who do not know God use their bodies for that. [6]So do not wrong your brother or cheat him in this way. The Lord will punish people who do those things. We have already told you and warned you about that. [7]God called us to be holy and does not want us to live in sin. [8]So the person who refuses to obey this teaching is refusing to obey God, not man. And God is the One who gives us his Holy Spirit.[d]

[9]We do not need to write to you about having love for your brothers and sisters in Christ. God has already taught you to love each other. [10]And truly you do love the brothers in all of Macedonia. Brothers, now we encourage you to love them more and more.

[11]Do all you can to live a peaceful life. Take care of your own business. Do your own work. We have already told you to do these things. [12]If you do, then people who are not believers will respect you. And you will not have to depend on others for what you need.

THE LORD'S COMING

[13]Brothers, we want you to know about those who have died. We do not want you to be sad as others who have no hope. [14]We believe that Jesus died and that he rose again. So, because of Jesus, God will bring together with Jesus those who have died. [15]What we tell you now is the Lord's own message. We who are living now may still be living when the Lord comes again. We who are living at that time will be with the Lord, but not before those who have already died. [16]The Lord himself will come down from heaven. There will be a loud command with the voice of the archangel[n] and with the trumpet call of God. And those who have died and were in Christ will rise

first. [17]After that, those who are still alive at that time will be gathered up with them. We will be taken up in the clouds to meet the Lord in the air. And we will be with the Lord forever. [18]So comfort each other with these words.

BE READY FOR THE LORD'S COMING

5 Now, brothers, we do not need to write to you about times and dates. [2]You know very well that the day the Lord comes again will be a surprise like a thief that comes in the night. [3]People will say, "We have peace and we are safe." At that time they will be destroyed quickly, as pains come quickly to a woman having a baby. And those people will not escape. [4]But you, brothers, are not living in darkness. And so that day will not surprise you like a thief. [5]You are all people who belong to the light. You belong to the day. We do not belong to the night or to darkness. [6]So we should not be like other people. We should not be sleeping, but we should be awake and have self-control. [7]Those who sleep, sleep at night. Those who get drunk, get drunk at night. [8]But we belong to the day; so we should control ourselves. We should wear faith and love to protect us. And the hope of salvation should be our helmet. [9]God did not choose us to suffer his anger, but to have salvation through our Lord Jesus Christ. [10]Jesus died for us so that we can live together with him. It is not important if we are alive or dead when Jesus comes. [11]So comfort each other and give each other strength, just as you are doing now.

FINAL INSTRUCTIONS AND GREETINGS

[12]Now, brothers, we ask you to respect those people who work hard with you, who lead you in the Lord and teach you. [13]Respect them with a very special love because of the work they do with you.

Live in peace with each other. [14]We

4:4 learn . . . wife This might also mean "learn to control your own body."
4:16 archangel The leader among God's angels or messengers.

ask you, brothers, to warn those who do not work. Encourage the people who are afraid. Help those who are weak. Be patient with every person. [15]Be sure that no one pays back wrong for wrong. But always try to do what is good for each other and for all people.

[16]Always be happy. [17]Never stop praying. [18]Give thanks whatever happens. That is what God wants for you in Christ Jesus.

[19]Do not stop the work of the Holy Spirit.[d] [20]Do not treat prophecy[d] as if it were not important. [21]But test everything. Keep what is good. [22]And stay away from everything that is evil.

[23]We pray that God himself, the God of peace, will make you pure, belonging only to him. We pray that your whole self—spirit, soul, and body—will be kept safe and be without wrong when our Lord Jesus Christ comes. [24]The One who calls you will do that for you. You can trust him.

[25]Brothers, please pray for us. [26]Give all the brothers a holy kiss when you meet. [27]I tell you by the authority of the Lord to read this letter to all the brothers.

[28]The grace of our Lord Jesus Christ be with you.

1 From Paul, Silas, and Timothy. To the church in Thessalonica in God our Father and the Lord Jesus Christ.

²Grace and peace to you from God the Father and the Lord Jesus Christ.

PAUL TALKS ABOUT GOD'S JUDGMENT

³We must always thank God for you. And we should do this because it is right. It is right because your faith is growing more and more. And the love that every one of you has for each other is also growing. ⁴So we brag about you to the other churches of God. We tell them about the way you continue to be strong and have faith. You are being treated badly and are suffering many troubles, but you continue with strength and faith.

⁵This is proof that God is right in his judgment. God wants you to be worthy of his kingdom. Your suffering is for that kingdom. ⁶And God will do what is right. He will give trouble to those who trouble you. ⁷And he will give peace to you people who are troubled and to us also. God will give us this help when the Lord Jesus is shown to us from heaven with his powerful angels. ⁸He will come from heaven with burning fire to punish those who do not know God. He will punish those who do not obey the Good News*d* of our Lord Jesus Christ. ⁹Those people will be punished with a destruction that continues forever. They will not be allowed to be with the Lord, and they will be kept away from his great power. ¹⁰This will happen on the day when the Lord Jesus comes to receive glory with his holy people. And all the people who have believed will be amazed at Jesus. You will be in that group of believers because you believed what we told you.

¹¹That is why we always pray for you. We ask our God to help you live the good way that he called you to live. The goodness you have makes you want to do good, and the faith you have makes you work. We pray that with his power God will help you do these things more and more. ¹²We pray all this so that the name of our Lord Jesus Christ can have glory in you. And you can have glory in him. That glory comes from the grace of our God and the Lord Jesus Christ.

EVIL THINGS WILL HAPPEN

2 Brothers, we have something to say about the coming of our Lord Jesus Christ. We want to talk to you about that time when we will meet together with him. ²Do not become easily upset in your thinking or afraid if you hear that the day of the Lord has already come. Someone may have said this in a prophecy*d* or in a message. Or you may read it in a letter that someone tells you came from us. ³Do not let any person fool you in any way. That day of the Lord will not come until the turning away from God happens. And that day will not come until the Man of Evil*n* appears. He belongs to hell. ⁴He is against any so-called god or anything that people worship. And the Man of Evil puts himself above anything called God or anything that people worship. And that Man of Evil even goes into God's Temple*d* and sits there. Then he says that he is God.

⁵I told you when I was with you that all this would happen. Do you not remember? ⁶And you know what is stopping that Man of Evil now. He is being stopped now so that he will appear at the right time. ⁷The secret power of evil is already working in the world now. But there is one who is stopping that power. And he will continue to stop it until he is

2:3 **Man of Evil** Some Greek copies read "Man of Sin."

taken out of the way. [8]Then that Man of Evil will appear. And the Lord Jesus will kill him with the breath that comes from his mouth and will destroy him with the glory of his coming. [9]The Man of Evil will come by the power of Satan. He will have great power, and he will do many different false miracles,[d] signs, and wonders. [10]He will use every kind of evil to trick those who are lost. They are lost because they refused to love the truth. (If they loved the truth, they would be saved.) [11]But they refused to love the truth; so God sends them something powerful that leads them away from the truth. He sends them that power so they will believe something that is not true. [12]So all those who do not believe the truth will be judged guilty. They did not believe the truth, and they enjoyed doing evil.

YOU ARE CHOSEN FOR SALVATION

[13]Brothers, the Lord loves you. God chose you from the beginning[n] to be saved. So we must always thank God for you. You are saved by the Spirit[d] that makes you holy and by your faith in the truth. [14]God used the Good News[d] that we preached to call you to be saved. He called you so that you can share in the glory of our Lord Jesus Christ. [15]So, brothers, stand strong and continue to believe the teachings we gave you. We taught you those things in our speaking and in our letter to you.

[16-17]We pray that the Lord Jesus Christ himself and God our Father will comfort you and strengthen you in every good thing you do and say. God loved us. Through his grace he gave us a good hope and comfort that continues forever.

PRAY FOR US

3 And now, brothers, pray for us. Pray that the Lord's teaching will continue to spread quickly. And pray that people will give honor to that teaching, just as happened with you. [2]And pray that we will be protected from bad and evil people. (Not all people believe in the Lord.)

[3]But the Lord is faithful. He will give you strength and protect you from the Evil One. [4]The Lord makes us feel sure that you are doing the things we told you. And we know that you will continue to do those things. [5]We pray that the Lord will lead your hearts into God's love and Christ's patience.

THE DUTY TO WORK

[6]Brothers, by the authority of our Lord Jesus Christ we command you to stay away from any believer who refuses to work. People who refuse to work are not following the teaching that we gave them. [7]You yourselves know that you should live as we live. We were not lazy when we were with you. [8]And when we ate another person's food, we always paid for it. We worked and worked so that we would not be a trouble to any of you. We worked night and day. [9]We had the right to ask you to help us. But we worked to take care of ourselves so that we would be an example for you to follow. [10]When we were with you, we gave you this rule: "If anyone will not work, he will not eat."

[11]We hear that some people in your group refuse to work. They do nothing. And they busy themselves in other people's lives. [12]We command those people to work quietly and earn their own food. In the Lord Jesus Christ we beg them to do this. [13]Brothers, never become tired of doing good.

[14]If anyone does not obey what we tell you in this letter, then remember who he is. Do not associate with him. Then maybe he will feel ashamed. [15]But do not treat him as an enemy. Warn him as a brother.

FINAL WORDS

[16]We pray that the Lord of peace will

2:13 God . . . beginning Some Greek copies read "God chose you as the firstfruits of the harvest."

give you peace at all times and in every way. May the Lord be with all of you.

[17] I am Paul, and I end this letter now in my own handwriting. All my letters have this to show they are from me. This is the way I write.

[18] May our Lord Jesus Christ show all of you his grace.

TIMOTHY

1 From Paul, an apostle*d* of Christ Jesus, by the command of God our Savior and Christ Jesus our hope.

²To Timothy, a true son to me because you believe.

Grace, mercy, and peace from God the Father and Christ Jesus our Lord.

WARNING AGAINST FALSE TEACHING

³I want you to stay in Ephesus. I asked you to do that when I went into Macedonia. Some people there in Ephesus are teaching false things. Stay there so that you can command them to stop. ⁴Tell them not to spend their time on stories that are not true and on long lists of names in family histories. These things only bring arguments; they do not help God's work. God's work is done by faith. ⁵The purpose of this command is for people to have love. To have this love they must have a pure heart, they must do what they know is right, and they must have true faith. ⁶Some people have wandered away from these things. They talk about things that are worth nothing. ⁷They want to be teachers of the law, but they do not know what they are talking about. They do not even understand what they say they are sure about.

⁸We know that the law is good if a man uses it right. ⁹We also know that the law is not made for good men. The law is made for people who are against the law and for those who refuse to follow the law. It is for people who are against God and are sinful, who are unholy and ungodly, who kill their fathers and mothers, who murder, ¹⁰who take part in sexual sins, men who have sexual relations with other men, those who sell slaves, who tell lies, who speak falsely, and who do anything against the true teaching of God. ¹¹That teaching is part of the Good News*d* that God gave me to tell. That glorious Good News is from the blessed God.

THANKS FOR GOD'S MERCY

¹²I thank Christ Jesus our Lord because he trusted me and gave me this work of serving him. And he gives me strength. ¹³In the past I spoke against Christ and persecuted him and did all kinds of things to hurt him. But God showed mercy to me because I did not know what I was doing. I did those things when I did not believe. ¹⁴But the grace of our Lord was fully given to me. And with that grace came the faith and love that are in Christ Jesus.

¹⁵What I say is true, and you should fully accept it: Christ Jesus came into the world to save sinners. And I am the worst of those sinners. ¹⁶But I was given mercy. I was given mercy so that in me Christ Jesus could show that he has patience without limit. And he showed his patience with me, the worst of all sinners. Christ wanted me to be an example for those who would believe in him and have life forever. ¹⁷Honor and glory to the King that rules forever! He cannot be destroyed and cannot be seen. Honor and glory forever and ever to the only God. Amen.

¹⁸Timothy, you are like a son to me. I am giving you a command that agrees with the prophecies*d* that were given about you in the past. I tell you this so that you can follow those prophecies and fight the good fight of faith. ¹⁹Continue to have faith and do what you know is right. Some people have not done this. Their faith has been destroyed. ²⁰Hymenaeus and Alexander are men who have done that. I have given them to Satan so that they will learn not to speak against God.

SOME RULES FOR MEN AND WOMEN

2 First, I tell you to pray for all people. Ask God for the things people need, and be thankful to him. ²You should pray for kings and for all who have authority.

Pray for the leaders so that we can have quiet and peaceful lives—lives full of worship and respect for God. ³This is good, and it pleases God our Savior. ⁴God wants all people to be saved. And he wants everyone to know the truth. ⁵There is only one God. And there is only one way that people can reach God. That way is through Jesus Christ, who is also a man. ⁶Jesus gave himself to pay for the sins of all people. Jesus is proof that God wants all people to be saved. And that proof came at the right time. ⁷That is why I was chosen to tell the Good News*d* and was chosen to be an apostle.*d* (I am telling the truth. I am not lying.) I was chosen to teach the non-Jewish people to believe and to know the truth.

⁸I want men everywhere to pray. These men who lift up their hands in prayer must be holy. They must not be men who become angry and have arguments.

⁹I also want women to wear clothes that are right for them. They should dress with respect and right thinking. They should not use fancy braided hair or gold or pearls or expensive clothes to make themselves beautiful. ¹⁰But they should make themselves beautiful by doing good deeds. Women who say they worship God should make themselves beautiful in that way.

¹¹A woman should learn by listening quietly and being fully ready to obey. ¹²I do not allow a woman to teach a man or to have authority over a man. She must remain silent. ¹³For Adam was made first; Eve was made later. ¹⁴Also, Adam was not the one who was tricked by the devil. It was the woman who was tricked and became a sinner. ¹⁵But women will be saved through having children. They will be saved if they continue in faith, love, holiness, and self-control.

LEADERS IN THE CHURCH

3 What I say is true: If anyone wants to become an overseer,*d* he is wanting a good work. ²An overseer must be so good that people cannot rightly criticize him. He must have only one wife. He must have self-control and be wise. He must be respected by other people and must be ready to help people by accepting them into his home. He must be a good teacher. ³He must not drink too much wine, and he must not be a man who likes to fight. He must be gentle and peaceful. He must not love money. ⁴He must be a good leader of his own family so that his children obey him with full respect. ⁵(If a man does not know how to be a leader over his own family, he will not be able to take care of God's church.) ⁶But an elder must not be a new believer. A new believer might be too proud of himself. Then he would be judged guilty for his pride just as the devil was. ⁷An elder must also have the respect of people who are not in the church. Then he will not be criticized by others and caught in the devil's trap.

HELPERS IN THE CHURCH

⁸In the same way, deacons*d* must be men that people can respect. They must not say things they do not mean. They must not use their time drinking too much wine, and they must not be men who are always trying to get rich by cheating others. ⁹They must follow the faith that God made known to us and always do what they know is right. ¹⁰You should test those men first. If you find nothing wrong in them, then they can serve as deacons. ¹¹In the same way, the women*n* must have the respect of other people. They must not be women who repeat evil gossip about other people. They must have self-control and be women who can be trusted in everything.

3:11 women This might mean the wives of the deacons, or it might mean women who serve in the same way as deacons.

¹²Deacons must have only one wife. They must be good leaders of their children and their own families. ¹³Those who serve well as deacons are making an honorable place for themselves. And they will feel very sure of their faith in Christ Jesus.

THE SECRET OF OUR LIFE

¹⁴I hope I can come to you soon. But I am writing these things to you now. ¹⁵Then, even if I cannot come soon, you will know about the things that people must do in the family of God. That family is the church of the living God, the support and foundation of the truth. ¹⁶Without doubt, the secret of our life of worship is great:

He[n] was shown to us in a human body,
   proved right by the Spirit,[d]
and seen by angels.

He was preached to the nations,
believed in by the world,
   and taken to heaven in glory.

A WARNING ABOUT FALSE TEACHERS

4 The Holy Spirit[d] clearly says that in the later times some people will stop believing the true faith. They will obey spirits that lie and will follow the teachings of demons.[d] ²Such teachings come from hypocrites,[d] men who cannot see what is right and what is wrong. It is as if their understanding were destroyed by a hot iron. ³They tell people that it is wrong to marry. And they tell people that there are some foods that must not be eaten. But God made those foods, and the people who believe and who know the truth can eat those foods with thanks. ⁴Everything that God made is good. Nothing that God made should be refused if it is accepted with thanks to God. ⁵Everything God made is made holy by what God has said and by prayer.

BE A GOOD SERVANT OF CHRIST

⁶Tell these things to the brothers. This will show that you are a good servant of Christ Jesus. You will show that you are made strong by the words of faith and good teaching that you have been following. ⁷People tell silly stories that do not agree with God's truth. Do not follow what those stories teach. But teach yourself only to serve God. ⁸Training your body helps you in some ways, but serving God helps you in every way. Serving God brings you blessings in this life and in the future life, too. ⁹What I say is true, and you should fully accept it. ¹⁰For this is why we work and struggle:[n] We hope in the living God. He is the Savior of all people. And in a very special way, he is the Savior of all who believe in him.

¹¹Command and teach these things. ¹²You are young, but do not let anyone treat you as if you were not important. Be an example to show the believers how they should live. Show them with your words, with the way you live, with your love, with your faith, and with your pure life. ¹³Continue to read the Scriptures[d] to the people, strengthen them, and teach them. Do these things until I come. ¹⁴Remember to use the gift that you have. That gift was given to you through a prophecy[d] when the group of elders[d] laid their hands on[n] you. ¹⁵Continue to do those things. Give your life to doing them. Then everyone can see that your work is progressing. ¹⁶Be careful in your life and in your teaching. Continue to live and teach rightly. Then you will save yourself and those people who listen to you.

RULES FOR LIVING WITH OTHERS

5 Do not speak angrily to an older man, but talk to him as if he were your father. Treat younger men like brothers. ²Treat older women like mothers, and

---

3:16 **He** Some Greek copies read "God."
4:10 **struggle** Some Greek copies read "suffer."
4:14 **laid their hands on** A sign to show that Timothy was being given a special work of God.

younger women like sisters. Always treat them in a pure way.

³Take care of widows who are all alone. ⁴But if a widow has children or grandchildren, the first thing they need to learn is to do their duty to their own family. When they do this, they will be repaying their parents or grandparents. That pleases God. ⁵If a widow is all alone and without help, then she puts her hope in God and prays night and day for God's help. ⁶But the widow who uses her life to please herself is really dead while she is still living. ⁷Tell the believers there to do these things so that no one can say they are doing wrong. ⁸A believer should take care of his own relatives, especially his own family. If he does not do that, he has turned against the faith. He is worse than a person who does not believe in God.

⁹To be on your list of widows, a woman must be 60 years old or older. She must have been faithful to her husband. ¹⁰She must be known as a woman who has done good works. By this, I mean good works such as raising her children, accepting visitors in her home, washing the feet of God's people, helping those in trouble, and using her life to do all kinds of good deeds.

¹¹But do not put younger widows on that list. After they give themselves to Christ, they are often pulled away from him by their physical desires. And then they want to marry again. ¹²And they will be judged for not doing what they first promised to do. ¹³Also, those younger widows begin to waste their time going from house to house. They begin to gossip and busy themselves with other people's lives. They say things that they should not say. ¹⁴So I want the younger widows to marry, have children, and take care of their homes. If they do this,

then no enemy will have any reason to criticize them. ¹⁵But some of the younger widows have already turned away to follow Satan.

¹⁶If any woman who is a believer has widows in her family, then she should care for them herself. The church should not have to care for them. Then the church will be able to care for the widows who have no living family.

¹⁷The elders[d] who lead the church well should receive great honor. Those who work hard by speaking and teaching especially should receive great honor. ¹⁸For the Scripture[d] says, "When an ox is working in the grain, do not cover its mouth to keep it from eating."[n] And the Scripture also says, "A worker should be given his pay."[n]

¹⁹Do not listen to someone who accuses an elder, unless there are two or three other persons who say he did wrong. ²⁰Tell those who keep on sinning that they are wrong. Do this in front of the whole church so that the others will have a warning.

²¹Before God and Jesus Christ and the chosen angels, I command you to do these things. Be careful to do them without showing favor to anyone.

²²Think carefully before you lay your hands on[n] anyone for the Lord's service. Do not share in the sins of others. Keep yourself pure.

²³Timothy, you stop drinking only water and drink a little wine. This will help your stomach, and you will not be sick so often.

²⁴The sins of some people are easy to see even before they are judged. But the sins of others are seen only later. ²⁵So also good deeds are easy to see. But even when they are not easy to see, they cannot stay hidden.

5:18 **"When … eating."** Quotation from Deuteronomy 25:4.
5:18 **"A worker … pay."** Quotation from Luke 10:7.
5:22 **lay your hands on** A sign of giving authority or power to another person.

6 All who are slaves should show full respect to their masters. Then no one will speak against God's name and our teaching. ²Some slaves have masters who are believers. This means they are all brothers. But the slaves should not show their masters any less respect. They should serve their masters even better, because they are helping believers they love.

FALSE TEACHING AND TRUE RICHES

You must teach and preach these things. ³If anyone has a different teaching, he does not accept the true teaching of our Lord Jesus Christ. And that teaching shows him the true way to serve God. ⁴The person who teaches falsely is full of pride and understands nothing. He is sick with a love for arguing and fighting about words. And that brings jealousy, making trouble, insults, and evil mistrust. ⁵And that also brings arguments from men who have evil minds. They have lost the truth. They think that serving God is a way to get rich.

⁶It is true that serving God makes a person very rich, if he is satisfied with what he has. ⁷When we came into the world, we brought nothing. And when we die, we can take nothing out. ⁸So, if we have food and clothes, we will be satisfied with that. ⁹Those who want to become rich bring temptation to themselves. They are caught in a trap. They begin to want many foolish things that will hurt them, things that ruin and destroy people. ¹⁰The love of money causes all kinds of evil. Some people have left the true faith because they want to get more and more money. But they have caused themselves much sorrow.

SOME THINGS TO REMEMBER

¹¹But you are a man of God. So you should stay away from all those things. Try to live in the right way, serve God, have faith, love, patience, and gentleness.

¹²Keeping your faith is like running a race. Try as hard as you can to win. Be sure you receive the life that continues forever. You were called to have that life. And you confessed the great truth about Christ in a way that many people heard. ¹³Before God and Christ Jesus I give you a command. Christ Jesus confessed that same great truth when he stood before Pontius Pilate. And God gives life to everything. Now I tell you: ¹⁴Do the things you were commanded to do. Do them without wrong or blame until the time when our Lord Jesus Christ comes again. ¹⁵God will make that happen at the right time. He is the blessed and only Ruler. He is the King of all kings and the Lord of all lords. ¹⁶God is the only One who never dies. He lives in light so bright that men cannot go near it. No one has ever seen God, or can see him. May honor and power belong to God forever. Amen.

¹⁷Give this command to those who are rich with things of this world. Tell them not to be proud. Tell them to hope in God, not their money. Money cannot be trusted, but God takes care of us richly. He gives us everything to enjoy. ¹⁸Tell the rich people to do good and to be rich in doing good deeds. Tell them to be happy to give and ready to share. ¹⁹By doing that, they will be saving a treasure for themselves in heaven. That treasure will be a strong foundation. Their future life can be built on that treasure. Then they will be able to have the life that is true life.

²⁰Timothy, God has trusted you with many things. Keep those things safe. Stay away from people who say foolish things that are not from God. Stay away from those who argue against the truth. They use something they call "knowledge," but it is really not knowledge. ²¹They say that they have that "knowledge," but they have left the true faith.

God's grace be with you.

TIMOTHY

1 From Paul, an apostle[d] of Christ Jesus by the will of God. God sent me to tell about the promise of life that is in Christ Jesus.

[2]To Timothy, a dear son to me. Grace, mercy, and peace to you from God the Father and Christ Jesus our Lord.

ENCOURAGEMENT FOR TIMOTHY

[3]I always remember you in my prayers, day and night. And I thank God for you in these prayers. He is the God my ancestors served. And I serve him, doing what I know is right. [4]I remember that you cried for me. And I want very much to see you so that I can be filled with joy. [5]I remember your true faith. That kind of faith first belonged to your grandmother Lois and to your mother Eunice. And I know that you now have that same faith. [6]That is why I remind you to use the gift God gave you. God gave you that gift when I laid my hands on[n] you. Now let it grow, as a small flame grows into a fire. [7]God did not give us a spirit that makes us afraid. He gave us a spirit of power and love and self-control.

[8]So do not be ashamed to tell people about our Lord Jesus. And do not be ashamed of me. I am in prison for the Lord. But suffer with me for the Good News.[d] God gives us the strength to do that. [9]God saved us and made us his holy people. That was not because of anything we did ourselves but because of what he wanted and because of his grace. That grace was given to us through Christ Jesus before time began. [10]It was not shown to us until our Savior Christ Jesus came. Jesus destroyed death. And through the Good News, he showed us the way to have life that cannot be destroyed. [11]I was chosen to tell that Good News and to be an apostle[d] and a teacher. [12]And I suffer now because I tell the Good News. But I am not ashamed. I know Jesus, the One I have believed in. And I am sure that he is able to protect what he has trusted me with until that Day.[n] [13]Follow the true teachings you heard from me. Follow them as an example of the faith and love we have in Christ Jesus. [14]Protect the truth that you were given. Protect it with the help of the Holy Spirit[d] who lives in us.

[15]You know that everyone in Asia has left me, even Phygelus and Hermogenes. [16]I pray that the Lord will show mercy to the family of Onesiphorus. He has often helped me and was not ashamed that I was in prison. [17]When he came to Rome, he looked for me until he found me. [18]I pray that the Lord will allow Onesiphorus to have mercy from the Lord on that Day. You know how many ways Onesiphorus helped me in Ephesus.

A LOYAL SOLDIER OF CHRIST JESUS

2 Timothy, you are like a son to me. Be strong in the grace that we have in Christ Jesus. [2]You and many others have heard what I have taught. You should teach the same thing to some people you can trust. Then they will be able to teach it to others. [3]Share in the troubles that we have. Accept them like a true soldier of Christ Jesus. [4]A soldier wants to please his commanding officer, so he does not waste his time doing the things that most people do. [5]If an athlete is running a race, he must obey all the rules in order to win. [6]The farmer who works hard should be the first person to get some of the food that he grew. [7]Think about these things that I am saying. The Lord will give you the ability to understand all these things.

1:6 laid my hands on A sign to show that Paul had power from God to give Timothy a special blessing.
1:12 Day The day Christ will come to judge all people and take his people to live with him.

[8]Remember Jesus Christ. He is from the family of David. After Jesus died, he was raised from death. This is the Good News[d] that I preach, [9]and I am suffering because of that Good News. I am even bound with chains like a criminal. But God's teaching is not in chains. [10]So I patiently accept all these troubles. I do this so that those whom God has chosen can have the salvation that is in Christ Jesus. With that salvation comes glory that never ends.

[11]This teaching is true:

If we died with him,
 then we will also live with him.
[12]If we accept suffering,
 then we will also rule with him.
If we say we don't know him,
 then he will say he doesn't know us.
[13]If we are not faithful,
 he will still be faithful,
 because he must be true to who he is.

A WORKER PLEASING TO GOD

[14]Continue teaching these things. And warn people before God not to argue about words. Arguing about words does not help anyone, and it ruins those who listen. [15]Do the best you can to be the kind of person that God will approve, and give yourself to him. Be a worker who is not ashamed of his work—a worker who uses the true teaching in the right way. [16]Stay away from those who talk about useless worldly things. That kind of talk will lead a person more and more away from God. [17]Their evil teaching will spread like a sickness inside the body. Hymenaeus and Philetus are men like that. [18]They have left the true teaching. They say that the rising from death of all men has already taken place. And those two men are destroying the faith of some people. [19]But God's strong foundation continues to stand. These words are written on that foundation: "The Lord knows those who belong to

him."[n] And also these words are written on that foundation, "Everyone who says that he believes in the Lord must stop doing wrong."

[20]In a large house there are things made of gold and silver. But also there are things made of wood and clay. Some things are used for special purposes, and others are made for ordinary jobs. [21]If anyone makes himself clean[d] from evil things, he will be used for special purposes. He will be made holy, and the Master can use him. He will be ready to do any good work.

[22]Stay away from the evil desires of youth. Try hard to live right and to have faith, love, and peace. Work for these things together with those who have pure hearts and who trust in the Lord. [23]Stay away from foolish and stupid arguments. You know that such arguments grow into bigger arguments. [24]And a servant of the Lord must not quarrel! He must be kind to everyone. He must be a good teacher. He must be patient. [25]The Lord's servant must gently teach those who do not agree with him. Maybe God will let them change their hearts so that they can accept the truth. [26]The devil has trapped them and causes them to do what he wants. But maybe they can wake up and free themselves from the devil's trap.

THE LAST DAYS

3 Remember this! There will be many troubles in the last days. [2]In those times people will love only themselves and money. They will brag and be proud. They will say evil things against others. They will not obey their parents. People will not be thankful or be the kind of people God wants. [3]They will not have love for others. They will refuse to forgive others and will speak bad things. They will not control themselves. They will be cruel and will hate what is good.

2:19 "The Lord . . . him." Quotation from Numbers 16:5.

⁴In the last days, people will turn against their friends. They will do foolish things without thinking. They will be conceited and proud. They will love pleasure. They will not love God. ⁵They will continue to act as if they serve God, but they will not really serve God. Stay away from those people. ⁶Some of them go into homes and get control of weak women who are full of sin. They are led to sin by the many evil desires they have. ⁷Those women always try to learn new teachings, but they are never able to understand the truth fully. ⁸Just as Jannes and Jambres were against Moses, these people are against the truth. They are people whose thinking has been confused. They have failed in trying to follow the faith. ⁹But they will not be successful in what they do. Everyone will see that they are foolish. That is what happened to Jannes and Jambres.

OBEY THE TEACHINGS

¹⁰But you know all about me. You know what I teach and the way I live. You know my goal in life. You know my faith, my patience, and my love. You know that I never stop trying. ¹¹You know how I have been hurt and have suffered. You know all that happened to me in Antioch, Iconium, and Lystra. You know the hurts I suffered in those places. But the Lord saved me from all those troubles. ¹²Everyone who wants to live the way God wants, in Christ Jesus, will be persecuted. ¹³People who are evil and cheat other people will go from bad to worse. They will fool others, but they will also be fooling themselves.

¹⁴But you should continue following the teachings that you learned. You know that these teachings are true. And you know you can trust those who taught you. ¹⁵You have known the Holy Scriptures*d* since you were a child. The Scriptures are able to make you wise. And that wisdom leads to salvation through faith in Christ Jesus. ¹⁶All Scripture is inspired by God and is useful for teaching and for showing people what is wrong in their lives. It is useful for correcting faults and teaching how to live right. ¹⁷Using the Scriptures, the person who serves God will be ready and will have everything he needs to do every good work.

4 Before God and Jesus Christ I give you a command. Christ Jesus is the One who will judge all who are living and all who have died. Jesus has a kingdom, and he is coming again. So I give you this command: ²Preach the Good News.*d* Be ready at all times. Tell people what they need to do, tell them when they are wrong, and encourage them. Do these things with great patience and careful teaching. ³The time will come when people will not listen to the true teaching. They will find more and more teachers who are pleasing to them, teachers who say the things they want to hear. ⁴They will stop listening to the truth. They will begin to follow the teaching in false stories. ⁵But you should control yourself at all times. When troubles come, accept them. Do the work of telling the Good News. Do all the duties of a servant of God.

⁶My life is being given as an offering to God. The time has come for me to leave this life. ⁷I have fought the good fight. I have finished the race. I have kept the faith. ⁸Now, a crown is waiting for me. I will get that crown for being right with God. The Lord is the judge who judges rightly, and he will give me the crown on that Day.*n* He will give that crown not only to me but to all those who have waited with love for him to come again.

PERSONAL WORDS

⁹Do your best to come to me as soon as you can. ¹⁰Demas loved this world

---

4:8 Day The day Christ will come to judge all people and take his people to live with him.

too much. He left me and went to Thessalonica. Crescens went to Galatia. And Titus went to Dalmatia. [11]Luke is the only one still with me. Get Mark and bring him with you when you come. He can help me in my work here. [12]I sent Tychicus to Ephesus.

[13]When I was in Troas, I left my coat there with Carpus. So when you come, bring it to me. Also, bring my books, particularly the ones written on parchment.[n]

[14]Alexander the metalworker did many harmful things against me. The Lord will punish him for the things he did. [15]You should be careful that he does not hurt you too. He fought strongly against our teaching.

[16]The first time I defended myself, no one helped me. Everyone left me. I pray that God will forgive them. [17]But the Lord stayed with me. He gave me strength so that I could fully tell the Good News[d] to the non-Jews. The Lord wanted all the non-Jews to hear it. So I was saved from the lion's mouth. [18]The Lord will save me when anyone tries to hurt me. The Lord will bring me safely to his heavenly kingdom. Glory forever and ever be the Lord's. Amen.

FINAL GREETINGS

[19]Greet Priscilla and Aquila and the family of Onesiphorus. [20]Erastus stayed in Corinth. And I left Trophimus sick in Miletus. [21]Try as hard as you can to come to me before winter.

Eubulus sends greetings to you. Also Pudens, Linus, Claudia, and all the brothers in Christ greet you.

[22]The Lord be with your spirit. Grace be with you.

4:13 **parchment** Something like paper made from the skins of sheep and used for writing on.

1 From Paul, a servant of God and an apostle[d] of Jesus Christ. I was sent to help the faith of God's chosen people. I was sent to help them to know the truth. And that truth shows people how to serve God. [2]That faith and that knowledge come from our hope for life forever. God promised that life to us before time began, and God does not lie. [3]At the right time God let the world know about that life through preaching. He trusted me with that work, and I preached because God our Savior commanded me to.

[4]To Titus. You are like a true son to me in the faith we share.

Grace and peace to you from God the Father and Christ Jesus our Savior.

TITUS' WORK IN CRETE

[5]I left you in Crete so that you could finish doing the things that still needed to be done. I left you there also so that you could choose men to be elders[d] in every town. [6]To be an elder, a man must not be guilty of doing wrong. He must have only one wife. His children must be believers. They must not be known as children who are wild and who do not obey. [7]An overseer has the job of taking care of God's work. So he must not be guilty of doing wrong. He must not be a man who is proud and selfish or who becomes angry quickly. He must not drink too much wine. He must not be a person who likes to fight. And he must not be a person who always tries to get rich by cheating people. [8]An overseer must be ready to help others by accepting them into his home. He must love what is good. He must be wise. He must live right. He must be holy. And he must be able to control himself. [9]An overseer must faithfully follow the truth just as we teach it. He must be able to help people by using true and right teaching. And he must be able to show those who are against the true teaching that they are wrong.

[10]There are many people who refuse to obey—people who talk about worthless things and lead others into the wrong way. I am talking mostly about those who insist on circumcision to be saved.[d] [11]These people must be stopped from talking. They are destroying whole families by teaching things that they should not teach. They teach them only to cheat people and make money. [12]Even one of their own prophets from Crete said, "Cretan people are always liars. They are evil animals and lazy people who do nothing but eat." [13]The words that prophet said are true. So tell those people that they are wrong. You must be strict with them. Then they will become strong in the faith [14]and stop accepting Jewish stories. And they will stop following the commands of others who do not accept the truth. [15]To those who are pure, all things are pure. But to those who are full of sin and do not believe, nothing is pure. The thinking of those people has become evil and their knowledge of what is right has been ruined. [16]They say they know God, but the evil things they do show that they do not accept God. They are terrible people, they refuse to obey, and they are useless for doing anything good.

FOLLOWING THE TRUE TEACHING

2 You must tell everyone what they must do to follow the true teaching. [2]Teach older men to have self-control, to be serious, and to be wise. They should be strong in faith, strong in love, and strong in patience.

[3]Also, teach older women to be holy in the way they live. Teach them not to speak against others or have the habit of drinking too much wine. They should teach what is good. [4]In that way they can

teach younger women to love their husbands and children. ⁵They can teach younger women to be wise and pure, to take care of their homes, to be kind, and to obey their husbands. Then no one will be able to criticize the teaching God gave us.

⁶In the same way, tell young men to be wise. ⁷You should do good deeds to be an example in every way for young men. When you teach, be honest and serious. ⁸And when you speak, speak the truth so that you cannot be criticized. Then anyone who is against you will be ashamed because there is nothing bad that he can say against us.

⁹And tell slaves to obey their masters at all times. They should try to please them and not argue with them. ¹⁰They should not steal from them. And they should show their masters that they can be trusted. Slaves should do these things so that in everything they do, they will show that the teaching of God our Savior is good.

¹¹That is the way we should live, because God's grace has come. That grace can save every person. ¹²It teaches us not to live against God and not to do the evil things the world wants to do. That grace teaches us to live in the present age in a wise and right way—a way that shows that we serve God. ¹³We should live like that while we are waiting for the coming of our great God and Savior Jesus Christ. He is our great hope, and he will come with glory. ¹⁴He gave himself for us; he died to free us from all evil. He died to make us pure people who belong only to him—people who are always wanting to do good things.

¹⁵Tell everyone these things. You have full authority. So use that authority to strengthen the people and tell them what they should do. And do not let anyone treat you as if you were not important.

THE RIGHT WAY TO LIVE

3 Remind the believers to do these things: to be under the authority of rulers and government leaders, to obey them and be ready to do good, ²to speak no evil about anyone, to live in peace with all, to be gentle and polite to all people.

³In the past we were foolish people, too. We did not obey, we were wrong, and we were slaves to many things our bodies wanted and enjoyed. We lived doing evil and being jealous. People hated us and we hated each other. ⁴But then the kindness and love of God our Savior was shown. ⁵He saved us because of his mercy, not because of good deeds we did to be right with God. He saved us through the washing that made us new people. He saved us by making us new through the Holy Spirit.ᵈ ⁶God poured out to us that Holy Spirit fully through Jesus Christ our Savior. ⁷We were made right with God by His grace. And God gave us the Spirit so that we could receive the life that never ends. That is what we hope for.

⁸This teaching is true. And I want you to be sure that the people understand these things. Then those who believe in God will be careful to use their lives for doing good. These things are good and will help all people.

⁹Stay away from those who have foolish arguments, who talk about useless family histories, who make trouble and fight about what the law of Moses teaches. Those things are worth nothing and will not help anyone. ¹⁰If someone causes arguments, then give him a warning. If he continues to cause arguments, warn him again. If he still continues causing arguments, then do not be around him. ¹¹You know that such a person is evil and sinful. His sins prove that he is wrong.

SOME THINGS TO REMEMBER

¹²I will send Artemas and Tychicus to you. When I send them, try hard to come to me at Nicopolis. I have decided to stay

there this winter. ¹³Zenas the lawyer and Apollos will be traveling from there. Do all that you can to help them on their way. Be sure that they have everything they need. ¹⁴Our people must learn to use their lives for doing good deeds.

They should do good to those in need. Then our people will not have useless lives.

¹⁵All who are with me greet you. Greet those who love us in the faith.

Grace be with you all.

PHILEMON

[1]From Paul, a prisoner of Jesus Christ, and from Timothy, our brother.

To Philemon, our dear friend and worker with us; [2]to Apphia, our sister; to Archippus, a worker with us; and to the church that meets in your home.

[3]Grace and peace to you from God our Father and the Lord Jesus Christ.

PHILEMON'S LOVE AND FAITH

[4]I remember you in my prayers. And I always thank my God for you. [5]I hear about the love you have for all God's holy people and the faith you have in the Lord Jesus. [6]I pray that the faith you share will make you understand every blessing that we have in Christ. [7]My brother, you have shown love to God's people. You have made them feel happy. This has given me great joy and comfort.

ACCEPT ONESIMUS AS A BROTHER

[8]There is something that you should do. And because of your love in Christ, I feel free to order you to do it. [9]But because I love you, I am asking you instead. I, Paul, am an old man now, and a prisoner for Christ Jesus. [10]I am asking you a favor for my son Onesimus. He became my son while I was in prison. [11]In the past he was useless to you. But now he has become useful for both you and me.

[12]I am sending him back to you, and with him I am sending my own heart. [13]I wanted to keep him with me to help me while I am in prison for the Good News.[d] By helping me he would be serving you. [14]But I did not want to do anything without asking you first. Then any favor you do for me will be because you want to do it, not because I forced you to do it.

[15]Onesimus was separated from you for a short time. Maybe that happened so that you could have him back forever— [16]not to be a slave, but better than a slave, to be a loved brother. I love him very much. But you will love him even more. You will love him as a man and as a brother in the Lord.

[17]If you think of me as your friend, then accept Onesimus back. Welcome him as you would welcome me. [18]If Onesimus has done anything wrong to you, charge that to me. If he owes you anything, charge that to me. [19]I, Paul, am writing this with my own hand. I will pay back anything Onesimus owes. And I will say nothing about what you owe me for your own life. [20]So, my brother, I ask that you do this for me in the Lord. Comfort my heart in Christ. [21]I write this letter, knowing that you will do what I ask you and even more.

[22]Also, please prepare a room for me to stay in. I hope that God will answer your prayers and I will be able to come to you.

FINAL GREETINGS

[23]Epaphras is a prisoner with me for Christ Jesus. He sends greetings to you. [24]And also Mark, Aristarchus, Demas, and Luke send greetings. They are workers together with me.

[25]The grace of our Lord Jesus Christ be with your spirit.

THE LETTER TO THE
HEBREWS

GOD SPOKE THROUGH HIS SON

1 In the past God spoke to our ancestors through the prophets.[d] He spoke to them many times and in many different ways. [2]And now in these last days God has spoken to us through his Son. God has chosen his Son to own all things. And he made the world through the Son. [3]The Son reflects the glory of God. He is an exact copy of God's nature. He holds everything together with his powerful word. The Son made people clean from their sins. Then he sat down at the right side of God, the Great One in heaven. [4]The Son became much greater than the angels. And God gave him a name that is much greater than theirs.

[5]This is because God never said to any of the angels,

"You are my Son.
Today I have become your Father." *Psalm 2:7*

Nor did God say of any angel,

"I will be his Father,
and he will be my Son." *2 Samuel 7:14*

[6]And when God brings his firstborn Son into the world, he says,

"Let all God's angels worship him."[n] *Psalm 97:7*

[7]This is what God said about the angels:

"God makes his angels become like winds.
He makes his servants become like flames of fire." *Psalm 104:4*

[8]But God said this about his Son:

"God, your throne will last forever and ever.
You will rule your kingdom with fairness.
[9]You love what is right and hate evil.

So God has chosen you to rule those with you.
Your God has given you much joy." *Psalm 45:6-7*

[10]God also says,

"Lord, in the beginning you made the earth.
And your hands made the skies.
[11]They will be destroyed, but you will remain.
They will all wear out like clothes.
[12]You will fold them like a coat.
And, like clothes, you will change them.
But you never change.
And your life will never end." *Psalm 102:25-27*

[13]And God never said this to an angel:

"Sit by me at my right side
until I put your enemies under your control."[n] *Psalm 110:1*

[14]All the angels are spirits who serve God and are sent to help those who will receive salvation.

OUR SALVATION IS GREAT

2 So we must be more careful to follow what we were taught. Then we will not be pulled away from the truth. [2]The teaching that God spoke through angels was shown to be true. And anyone who did not follow it or obey it received the punishment he earned. [3]The salvation that was given to us is very great. So surely we also will be punished if we live as if this salvation were not important. It was the Lord himself who first told about this salvation. And those who heard him proved to us that this salvation is true. [4]God also proved it by using wonders, great signs, and many kinds of miracles.[d] And he proved it by giving people gifts through the Holy Spirit,[d] just as he wanted.

1:6 "Let … him." These words are found in Deuteronomy 32:43 in the Septuagint, the Greek version of the Old Testament, and in a Hebrew copy among the Dead Sea Scrolls.
1:13 until … control Literally, "until I make your enemies a footstool for your feet."

CHRIST BECAME LIKE MEN

⁵God did not choose angels to be the rulers of the new world that was coming. It is that future world we have been talking about. ⁶It is written somewhere in the Scriptures,*d*

"Why is man important to you?
   Why do you take care of the son
      of man?*n*
⁷For a short time you made him lower
      than the angels.
   But you crowned him with glory
      and honor.
⁸   You put all things under his
      control."   *Psalm 8:4-6*

If God put everything under his control, there was nothing left that he did not rule. But we do not yet see him ruling over everything. ⁹But we see Jesus! For a short time he was made lower than the angels. But now we see him wearing a crown of glory and honor because he suffered and died. Because of God's grace, he died for everyone.

¹⁰God is the One who made all things. And all things are for his glory. God wanted to have many sons share his glory. So God made perfect the One who leads people to salvation. He made Jesus a perfect Savior through Jesus' suffering. ¹¹Jesus, who makes people holy, and those who are made holy are from the same family. So he is not ashamed to call them his brothers. ¹²He says,

"Then, I will tell my fellow Israelites
      about you.
   I will praise you when your people
      meet to worship you."
                              Psalm 22:22

¹³He also says,

"I will trust in God."   *Isaiah 8:17*

And he also says,

"I am here. And with me are the
      children that God has given me."
                              Isaiah 8:18

¹⁴These children are people with physical bodies. So Jesus himself became like them and had the same experiences they have. He did this so that, by dying, he could destroy the one who has the power of death. That one is the devil. ¹⁵Jesus became like men and died so that he could free them. They were like slaves all their lives because of their fear of death. ¹⁶Clearly, it is not angels that Jesus helps, but the people who are from Abraham.*n* ¹⁷For this reason Jesus had to be made like his brothers in every way. He became like men so that he could be their merciful and faithful high priest in service to God. Then Jesus could bring forgiveness for their sins. ¹⁸And now he can help those who are tempted. He is able to help because he himself suffered and was tempted.

JESUS IS GREATER THAN MOSES

3 So all of you, holy brothers, should think about Jesus. You were all called by God. God sent Jesus to us, and he is the high priest of our faith. ²And Jesus was faithful to God as Moses was. Moses did everything God wanted him to do in God's family. ³A man who is the head of a family receives more honor than others in the family. It is the same with Jesus. Jesus should have more honor than Moses. ⁴Every family has its head, but God is the head of everything. ⁵Moses was faithful in God's family as a servant. He told what God would say in the future. ⁶But Christ is faithful as a Son who is the head of God's family. And we are God's family if we hold on to our faith and are proud of the great hope we have.

WE MUST CONTINUE TO FOLLOW GOD

⁷So it is as the Holy Spirit*d* says:

"Today listen to what he says.
⁸   Do not be stubborn as in the past
      when you turned against God.

2:6 son of man This can mean any, but the name "Son of Man" is often used to mean Jesus. When Jesus became a man, he showed what God planned for all people to be.
2:16 Abraham Most respected ancestor of the Jews. Every Jew hoped to see Abraham.

There you tested God in the desert.

9 For 40 years in the desert your
    ancestors saw the things I did.
But they tested me and my patience.
10I was angry with them.
I said, 'They are not loyal to me.
They have not understood my ways.'
11So I was angry and made a promise.
'They will never enter my land of
    rest.'"n   *Psalm 95:7-11*

12So brothers, be careful that none of you has an evil, unbelieving heart. This will stop you from following the living God. 13But encourage each other every day. Do this while it is "today."n Help each other so that none of you will become hardened because of sin and its tricks. 14We all share in Christ. This is true if we keep till the end the sure faith we had in the beginning. 15This is what the Scriptured says:

"Today listen to what he says.
Do not be stubborn as in the past
    when you turned against God."
                 Psalm 95:7-8

16Who heard God's voice and was against him? It was all those people Moses led out of Egypt. 17And whom was God angry with for 40 years? He was angry with those who sinned, who died in the desert. 18And whom was God talking to when he promised that they would never enter and have his rest? He was talking to those who did not obey him. 19So we see that they were not allowed to enter and have God's rest because they did not believe.

4 Now God has left us that promise that we may enter and have his rest. Let us be very careful, then, so that none of you will fail to get that rest. 2The Good Newsd was preached to us just as it was to them. But the teaching they heard did not help them. They heard it but did not accept it with faith.n 3We who have believed are able to enter and have God's rest. As God has said,

"So I was angry and made a promise.
'They will never enter my land of
    rest.'"   *Psalm 95:11*

But God's work was finished from the time he made the world. 4Somewhere in the Scripturesd he talked about the seventh day of the week: "And on the seventh day God rested from all his work."n 5And again in the Scripture God said, "They will never enter my land of rest."

6It is still true that some people will enter and have God's rest. But those who first heard the way to be saved did not enter. They did not enter because they did not obey. 7So God planned another day, called "today." He spoke about that day through David a long time later. It is the same Scripture used before:

"Today listen to what he says.
Do not be stubborn."   *Psalm 95:7-8*

8We know that Joshuan did not lead the people into that rest. We know this because God spoke later about another day. 9This shows that the seventh-day restn for God's people is still coming. 10For anyone who enters and has God's rest will rest from his work as God did. 11So let us try as hard as we can to enter God's rest. We must try hard so that no one will be lost by following the example of those who refused to obey.

12God's word is alive and working. It is sharper than a sword sharpened on both

---

3:11 **rest** A place of rest God promised to give his people.

3:13 **"today"** This word is taken from verse 7. It means that it is important to do these things now.

4:2 **They . . . faith.** Some Greek copies read "They did not share the faith of those who heard it."

4:4 **"And . . . work."** Quotation from Genesis 2:2.

4:8 **Joshua** After Moses died, Joshua became leader of the Jewish people. Joshua led them into the land that God promised to give them.

4:9 **seventh-day rest** Literally, "sabbath rest," meaning a sharing in the rest that God began after he created the world.

sides. It cuts all the way into us, where the soul and the spirit are joined. It cuts to the center of our joints and our bones. And God's word judges the thoughts and feelings in our hearts. [13]Nothing in all the world can be hidden from God. Everything is clear and lies open before him. And to him we must explain the way we have lived.

JESUS IS OUR HIGH PRIEST

[14]We have a great high priest who has gone into heaven. He is Jesus the Son of God. So let us hold on to the faith we have. [15]For our high priest is able to understand our weaknesses. He was tempted in every way that we are, but he did not sin. [16]Let us, then, feel free to come before God's throne. Here there is grace. And we can receive mercy and grace to help us when we need it.

5 Every high priest is chosen from among men. He is given the work of going before God for them. He must offer gifts and sacrifices for sins. [2]He himself is weak. So he is able to be gentle with those who do not understand and who are doing wrong things. [3]Because he is weak the high priest must offer sacrifices for his own sins. And then he offers sacrifices for the sins of the people.

[4]To be a high priest is an honor. But no one chooses himself for this work. He must be called by God as Aaron[n] was. [5]So also Christ did not choose himself to have the honor of being a high priest. But God chose him. God said to him,

"You are my Son;
    today I have become your Father."
                                    Psalm 2:7

[6]And in another Scripture[d] God says,

"You are a priest forever,
    a priest like Melchizedek."[n]
                                    Psalm 110:4

[7]While Jesus lived on earth, he prayed to God and asked God for help. He prayed with loud cries and tears to the One who could save him from death. And his prayer was heard because he left it all up to God. [8]Even though Jesus was the Son of God, he learned to obey by what he suffered. [9]And he became our perfect high priest. He gives eternal salvation to all who obey him. [10]And God made Jesus high priest, a priest like Melchizedek.

WARNING AGAINST FALLING AWAY

[11]We have much to say about this. But it is hard to explain because you are so slow to understand. [12]You have had enough time so that by now you should be teachers. But you need someone to teach you again the first lessons of God's message. You still need the teaching that is like milk. You are not ready for solid food. [13]Anyone who lives on milk is still a baby. He knows nothing about right teaching. [14]But solid food is for those who are grown up. They are mature enough to know the difference between good and evil.

6 So let us go on to grown-up teaching. Let us not go back over the beginning lessons we learned about Christ. We should not start over again with teaching about turning from acts that lead to death and about believing in God. [2]We should not return to the teaching of baptisms,[n] of laying on of hands,[n] of the raising of the dead and eternal judgment. [3]And we will go on to grown-up teaching if God allows.

[4]Some people cannot be brought back again to a changed life. They were once in God's light. They enjoyed heaven's gift, and they shared in the Holy Spirit.[d] [5]They found out how good God's word is, and they received the powers of his

---

5:4 Aaron Moses' brother and the first Jewish high priest.
5:6 Melchizedek A priest and king who lived in the time of Abraham. (Read Genesis 14:17-24.)
6:2 baptisms The word here may refer to Christian baptism, or it may refer to the Jewish ceremonial washings.
6:2 laying on of hands Putting the hands on people showed that they were being given some special work or some spiritual gift or blessing.

new world. [6]And then they fell away from Christ! It is not possible to keep on bringing them back to a changed life again. For they are nailing the Son of God to a cross again and are shaming him in front of others.

[7]Some people are like land that gets plenty of rain. The land produces a good crop for those who work it, and it receives God's blessings. [8]Other people are like land that grows thorns and weeds and is worthless. It is about to be cursed by God. It will be destroyed by fire.

[9]Dear friends, we are saying this to you. But we really expect better things from you that will lead to your salvation. [10]God is fair. He will not forget the work you did and the love you showed for him by helping his people. And he will remember that you are still helping them. [11]We want each of you to go on with the same hard work all your lives. Then you will surely get what you hope for. [12]We do not want you to become lazy. Be like those who have faith and patience. They will receive what God has promised.

[13]God made a promise to Abraham. And as there is no one greater than God, he used himself when he swore to Abraham. [14]He said, "I will surely bless you and give you many descendants."[n] [15]Abraham waited patiently for this to happen. And he received what God promised.

[16]People always use the name of someone greater than themselves when they swear. The oath proves that what they say is true. And this ends all arguing about what they say. [17]God wanted to prove that his promise was true. He wanted to prove this to those who would get what he promised. He wanted them to understand clearly that his purposes never change. So God proved his promise by

also making an oath. [18]These two things cannot change. God cannot lie when he makes a promise, and he cannot lie when he makes an oath. These things encourage us who came to God for safety. They give us strength to hold on to the hope we have been given. [19]We have this hope as an anchor for the soul, sure and strong. It enters behind the curtain in the Most Holy Place in heaven. [20]Jesus has gone in there ahead of us and for us. He has become the high priest forever, a priest like Melchizedek.[n]

THE PRIEST MELCHIZEDEK

7 Melchizedek[n] was the king of Salem and a priest for the Most High God. He met Abraham when Abraham was coming back after defeating the kings. When they met, Melchizedek blessed Abraham. [2]And Abraham gave Melchizedek a tenth of everything he had brought back from the battle. First, Melchizedek's name means "king of goodness." Also, he is king of Salem, which means "king of peace." [3]No one knows who Melchizedek's father or mother was.[n] No one knows where he came from. And no one knows when he was born or when he died. Melchizedek is like the Son of God; he continues being a priest forever.

[4]You can see that Melchizedek was very great. Abraham, the great father, gave Melchizedek a tenth of everything that Abraham won in battle. [5]Now the law says that those in the tribe[d] of Levi who become priests must get a tenth from the people. The priests collect it from their own people, even though the priests and the people are both from the family of Abraham. [6]Melchizedek was not from the tribe of Levi. But he got a tenth from Abraham. And he blessed Abraham, the man who had God's promises. [7]And

---

6:14 "I . . . descendants." Quotation from Genesis 22:17.
6:20; 7:1 **Melchizedek** A priest and king who lived in the time of Abraham. (Read Genesis 14:17-24.)
7:3 **No . . . was.** Literally, "Melchizedek was without father, without mother, without genealogy."

everyone knows that the more important person blesses the less important person. [8]Those priests get a tenth, but they are only men who live and then die. But Melchizedek, who got a tenth from Abraham, continues living, as the Scripture[d] says. [9]It is Levi who gets a tenth from the people. But we might even say that when Abraham paid Melchizedek a tenth, then Levi also paid it. [10]Levi was not yet born. But Levi was in the body of his ancestor Abraham when Melchizedek met Abraham.

[11]The people were given the law[n] concerning the system of priests from the tribe of Levi. But they could not be made spiritually perfect through that system of priests. So there was a need for another priest to come. I mean a priest like Melchizedek, not Aaron. [12]And when a different kind of priest comes, the law must be changed, too. [13]We are saying these things about Christ. He belonged to a different tribe. No one from that tribe ever served as a priest at the altar. [14]It is clear that our Lord came from the tribe of Judah. And Moses said nothing about priests belonging to that tribe.

JESUS IS LIKE MELCHIZEDEK

[15]And this becomes even more clear. We see that another priest comes, who is like Melchizedek.[n] [16]He was not made a priest by human rules and laws. He became a priest through the power of his life, which continues forever. [17]In the Scriptures,[d] this is said about him:

"You are a priest forever,
    a priest like Melchizedek."

Psalm 110:4

[18]The old rule is now set aside because it was weak and useless. [19]The law of Moses could not make anything perfect. But now a better hope has been given to us.

And with this hope we can come near to God.

[20]Also, it is important that God made an oath when he made Jesus high priest. When the others became priests, there was no oath. [21]But Christ became a priest with God's oath. God said:

"The Lord has made a promise
    and will not change his mind.
'You are a priest forever.'"

Psalm 110:4

[22]So this means that Jesus is the guarantee of a better agreement[n] from God to his people.

[23]Also, when one of the other priests died, he could not continue being a priest. So there were many priests. [24]But Jesus lives forever. He will never stop serving as priest. [25]So he is always able to save those who come to God through him. He can do this, because he always lives, ready to help those who come before God.

[26]So Jesus is the kind of high priest that we need. He is holy; he has no sin in him. He is pure and not influenced by sinners. And he is raised above the heavens. [27]He is not like the other priests. They had to offer sacrifices every day, first for their own sins, and then for the sins of the people. But Christ does not need to do that. He offered his sacrifice only once and for all time. Christ offered himself! [28]The law chooses high priests who are men with all their weaknesses. But the word of God's oath came later than the law. It made God's Son to be the high priest. And that Son has been made perfect forever.

JESUS IS OUR HIGH PRIEST

8 Here is the point of what we are saying: We do have a high priest who sits on the right side of God's throne in heaven. [2]Our high priest serves in the

---

7:11 **The . . . law** This refers to the people of Israel who were given the law of Moses.
7:15 **Melchizedek** A priest and king who lived in the time of Abraham. (Read Genesis 14:17-24.)
7:22 **agreement** God gives a contract or agreement to his people. For the Jews, this agreement was the law of Moses. But now God has given a better agreement to his people through Christ.

Most Holy Place. He serves in the true place of worship that was made by God, not by men.

[3]Every high priest has the work of offering gifts and sacrifices to God. So our high priest must also offer something to God. [4]If our high priest were now living on earth, he would not be a priest. I say this because there are already priests here who follow the law by offering gifts to God. [5]The work that they do as priests is only a dim copy of what is in heaven. For when Moses was ready to build the Holy Tent,[d] God warned him: "Be very careful to make everything by the plan I showed you on the mountain."[n] [6]But the priestly work that has been given to Jesus is much greater than the work that was given to the other priests. In the same way, the new agreement that Jesus brought from God to his people is much greater than the old one. And the new agreement is based on promises of better things.

[7]If there was nothing wrong with the first agreement,[n] there would be no need for a second agreement. [8]But God found something wrong with his people. He says:[n]

"The time is coming, says the Lord,
  when I will make a new agreement.
It will be with the people of Israel
  and the people of Judah.
[9]It will not be like the agreement
  I made with their ancestors.
That was when I took them by the
    hand
  to bring them out of Egypt.
But they broke that agreement,
  and I turned away from them, says
    the Lord.
[10]In the future I will make this
    agreement

with the people of Israel, says the
    Lord.
I will put my teachings in their minds.
  And I will write them on their
    hearts.
I will be their God,
  and they will be my people.
[11]People will no longer have to teach
    their neighbors and relatives to
    know the Lord.
This is because all will know me,
  from the least to the most
    important.
[12]I will forgive them for the wicked
    things they did.
  I will not remember their sins
    anymore."   Jeremiah 31:31-34

[13]God called this a new agreement, so he has made the first agreement old. And anything that is old and worn out is ready to disappear.

WORSHIP UNDER THE OLD AGREEMENT

9 The first agreement[n] had rules for worship. And it had a place on earth for worship. [2]The Holy Tent[d] was set up for this. The first area in the Tent was called the Holy Place. In it were the lamp and the table with the bread that was made holy for God. [3]Behind the second curtain was a room called the Most Holy Place. [4]In it was a golden altar for burning incense.[d] Also there was the Holy Box[d] that held the old agreement. The Holy Box was covered with gold. Inside this Holy Box was a golden jar of manna[d] and Aaron's rod—the rod that once grew leaves. Also in it were the stone tablets of the old agreement. [5]Above the Holy Box were the creatures with wings that showed God's glory. The wings of the creatures reached over the lid. But we cannot tell everything about these things now.

8:5 "Be . . . mountain." Quotation from Exodus 25:40.
8:7 **first agreement** The contract God gave the Jewish people when he gave them the law of Moses.
8:8 **But . . . says** Some Greek copies read "But God found something wrong and says to his people."
9:1 **first agreement** The contract God gave the Jewish people when he gave them the law of Moses.

[6]Everything in the Tent was made ready in this way. Then the priests went into the first room every day to do their worship. [7]But only the high priest could go into the second room, and he did that only once a year. He could never enter the inner room without taking blood with him. He offered that blood to God for himself and for the people's sins. These were sins people did without knowing that they were sinning. [8]The Holy Spirit[d] uses this to show that the way into the Most Holy Place was not open. This was while the system of the old Holy Tent was still being used. [9]This is an example for the present time. It shows that the gifts and sacrifices offered cannot make the worshiper perfect in his heart. [10]These gifts and sacrifices were only about food and drink and special washings. They were rules for the body, to be followed until the time of God's new way.

WORSHIP UNDER THE NEW AGREEMENT

[11]But Christ has come as the high priest of the good things we now have.[n] The tent he entered is greater and more perfect. It is not made by men. It does not belong to this world. [12]Christ entered the Most Holy Place only once—and for all time. He did not take with him the blood of goats and calves. His sacrifice was his own blood. He entered the Most Holy Place and set us free from sin forever. [13]The blood of goats and bulls and the ashes of a cow are sprinkled on the people who are unclean[d] and this makes their bodies clean again.

[14]How much more is done by the blood of Christ. He offered himself through the eternal Spirit[n] as a perfect sacrifice to God. His blood will make our hearts clean from useless acts. We are made pure so that we may serve the living God.

[15]So Christ brings a new agreement from God to his people. Those who are called by God can now receive the blessings that God has promised. These blessings will last forever. They can have those things because Christ died so that the people who lived under the first agreement could be set free from sin.

[16]When there is a will,[n] it must be proven that the man who wrote that will is dead. [17]A will means nothing while the man is alive. It can be used only after he dies. [18]This is why even the first agreement could not begin without blood to show death. [19]First, Moses told all the people every command in the law. Next he took the blood of calves and mixed it with water. Then he used red wool and a branch of the hyssop plant to sprinkle the blood and water on the book of the law and on all the people. [20]He said, "This is the blood which begins the agreement that God commanded you to obey."[n] [21]In the same way, Moses sprinkled the blood on the Holy Tent[d] and over all the things used in worship. [22]The law says that almost everything must be made clean by blood. And sins cannot be forgiven without blood to show death.

CHRIST'S DEATH TAKES AWAY SINS

[23]So the copies of the real things in heaven had to be made clean[d] by animal sacrifices. But the real things in heaven need much better sacrifices. [24]For Christ did not go into the Most Holy Place made by men. It is only a copy of the real one. He went into heaven itself. He is there now before God to help us. [25]The high priest enters the Most Holy Place once every year. He takes with him blood that is not his own blood. But Christ did not go into heaven to offer himself many

---

9:11 good . . . have Some Greek copies read "good things that are to come."
9:14 Spirit This refers to the Holy Spirit; to Christ's own spirit; or to the spiritual and eternal nature of his sacrifice.
9:16 will A legal document that shows how a person's money and property are to be distributed at the time of his death. This is the same word in Greek as "agreement" in verse 15.
9:20 "This . . . obey." Quotation from Exodus 24:8.

times. [26]Then he would have had to suffer many times since the world was made. But Christ came only once and for all time. He came at just the right time to take away all sin by sacrificing himself. [27]Everyone must die once. After a person dies, he is judged. [28]So Christ was offered as a sacrifice one time to take away the sins of many people. And he will come a second time, but not to offer himself for sin. He will come again to bring salvation to those who are waiting for him.

10 The law is only an unclear picture of the good things coming in the future. It is not a perfect picture of the real things. The people under the law offered the same sacrifices every year. These sacrifices can never make perfect those who come near to worship God. [2]If the law could make them perfect, the sacrifices would have already stopped. The worshipers would be made clean, and they would no longer feel guilty for their sins. [3]These sacrifices remind them of their sins every year, [4]because it is not possible for the blood of bulls and goats to take away sins.

[5]So when Christ came into the world, he said:

"You do not want sacrifices and offerings.
But you have prepared a body for me.
[6]You do not ask for burnt offerings and offerings to take away sins.
[7]Then I said, 'Look, I have come.
It is written about me in the book.
My God, I have come to do what you want.'"   *Psalm 40:6-8*

[8]In this Scripture[d] he first said, "You do not want sacrifices and offerings. You do not ask for burnt offerings and offerings to take away sins." (These are all sacrifices that the law commands.) [9]Then he said, "Here I am. I have come to do what

you want." So God ends the first system of sacrifices so that he can set up the new system. [10]Jesus Christ did what God wanted him to do. And because of this, we are made holy through the sacrifice of his body. Christ made this sacrifice only once, and for all time.

[11]Every day the priests stand and do their religious service. Again and again they offer the same sacrifices. But those sacrifices can never take away sins. [12]But Christ offered one sacrifice for sins, and it is good forever. Then he sat down at the right side of God. [13]And now Christ waits there for his enemies to be put under his power. [14]With one sacrifice he made perfect forever those who are being made holy.

[15]The Holy Spirit[d] also tells us about this. First he says:
[16]"In the future I will make this
        agreement[n]
    with the people of Israel, says the
        Lord.
I will put my teachings in their hearts.
    And I will write them on their
        minds."   *Jeremiah 31:33*
[17]Then he says:
"Their sins and the evil things they
        do—
    I will not remember anymore."
                        Jeremiah 31:34

[18]And when these have been forgiven, there is no more need for a sacrifice for sins.

CONTINUE TO TRUST GOD

[19]So, brothers, we are completely free to enter the Most Holy Place. We can do this without fear because of the blood of Jesus' death. [20]We can enter through a new way that Jesus opened for us. It is a living way. It leads through the curtain— Christ's body. [21]And we have a great priest over God's house. [22]So let us come near to God with a sincere heart and a sure faith.

10:16 agreement God gives a contract or agreement to his people. For the Jews, this agreement was the law of Moses. But now God has given a better agreement to his people through Christ.

We have been cleansed and made free from feelings of guilt. And our bodies have been washed with pure water. 23Let us hold firmly to the hope that we have confessed. We can trust God to do what he promised.

24Let us think about each other and help each other to show love and do good deeds. 25You should not stay away from the church meetings, as some are doing. But you should meet together and encourage each other. Do this even more as you see the Day[n] coming.

26If we decide to go on sinning after we have learned the truth, there is no longer any sacrifice for sins. 27There is nothing but fear in waiting for the judgment and the angry fire that will destroy all those who live against God. 28Any person who refused to obey the law of Moses was found guilty from the proof given by two or three witnesses. He was put to death without mercy. 29So what do you think should be done to a person who does not respect the Son of God? He looks at the blood of the agreement, the blood that made him holy, as no different from other men's blood. He insults the Spirit[d] of God's grace. Surely he should have a much worse punishment. 30We know that God said, "I will punish those who do wrong. I will repay them."[n] And he also said, "The Lord will judge his people."[n] 31It is a terrible thing to fall into the hands of the living God.

32Remember those days in the past when you first learned the truth. You had a hard struggle with many sufferings, but you continued strong. 33Sometimes you were hurt and persecuted before crowds of people. And sometimes you shared with those who were being treated that way. 34You helped the prisoners. And you even had joy when all that you owned was taken from you. You were joyful because you knew that you had something better and more lasting.

35So do not lose the courage that you had in the past. It has a great reward. 36You must hold on, so you can do what God wants and receive what he has promised. 37For in a very short time,

"The One who is coming will come.

He will not be late.
38The person who is right with me

will have life because of his faith.

But if he turns back with fear,

I will not be pleased with him."

Habakkuk 2:3-4

39But we are not those who turn back and are lost. We are people who have faith and are saved.

FAITH

11 Faith means being sure of the things we hope for. And faith means knowing that something is real even if we do not see it. 2People who lived in the past became famous because of faith.

3It is by faith we understand that the whole world was made by God's command. This means that what we see was made by something that cannot be seen.

4It was by faith that Abel offered God a better sacrifice than Cain did. God said he was pleased with the gifts Abel offered. So God called Abel a good man because of his faith. Abel died, but through his faith he is still speaking.

5It was by faith that Enoch was taken to heaven. He never died. He could not be found, because God had taken him away. Before he was taken, the Scripture[d] says that he was a man who truly pleased God. 6Without faith no one can please God. Anyone who comes to God must believe that he is real and that he rewards those who truly want to find him.

10:25 Day The day Christ will come to judge all people and take his people to live with him.
10:30 "I . . . them." Quotation from Deuteronomy 32:35.
10:30 "The Lord . . . people." Quotation from Deuteronomy 32:36; Psalm 135:14.

[7]It was by faith Noah heard God's warnings about things that he could not yet see. He obeyed God and built a large boat to save his family. By his faith, Noah showed that the world was wrong. And he became one of those who are made right with God through faith.

[8]It was by faith Abraham obeyed God's call to go to another place that God promised to give him. He left his own country, not knowing where he was to go. [9]It was by faith that he lived in the country God promised to give him. He lived there like a visitor who did not belong. He lived in tents with Isaac and Jacob, who had received that same promise from God. [10]Abraham was waiting for the city[n] that has real foundations—the city planned and built by God.

[11]He was too old to have children, and Sarah was not able to have children. It was by faith that Abraham was made able to become a father. Abraham trusted God to do what he had promised.[n] [12]This man was so old that he was almost dead. But from him came as many descendants as there are stars in the sky. They are as many as the grains of sand on the seashore that cannot be counted.

[13]All these great men died in faith. They did not get the things that God promised his people. But they saw them coming far in the future and were glad. They said that they were like visitors and strangers on earth. [14]When people say such things, then they show that they are looking for a country that will be their own country. [15]If they had been thinking about that country they had left, they could have gone back. [16]But those men were waiting for a better country—a heavenly country. So God is not ashamed to be called their God. For he has prepared a city for them.

[17]It was by faith that Abraham offered his son Isaac as a sacrifice. God made the promises to Abraham. But God tested him. And Abraham was ready to offer his own son as a sacrifice. [18]God had said, "The descendants I promised you will be from Isaac."[n] [19]Abraham believed that God could raise the dead. And really, it was as if Abraham got Isaac back from death.

[20]It was by faith that Isaac blessed the future of Jacob and Esau. [21]It was by faith that Jacob blessed each one of Joseph's sons. He did this while he was dying. Then he worshiped as he leaned on the top of his walking stick.

[22]It was by faith that Joseph spoke about the Israelites leaving Egypt while he was dying. He told them what to do with his body.

[23]It was by faith that Moses' parents hid him for three months after he was born. They saw that Moses was a beautiful baby. And they were not afraid to disobey the king's order.

[24]It was by faith that Moses, when he grew up, refused to be called the son of the king of Egypt's daughter. [25]He chose to suffer with God's people instead of enjoying sin for a short time. [26]He thought that it was better to suffer for the Christ[d] than to have all the treasures of Egypt. He was looking only for God's reward. [27]It was by faith that Moses left Egypt. He was not afraid of the king's anger. Moses continued strong as if he could see the God that no one can see. [28]It was by faith that Moses prepared the Passover[d] and spread the blood on the doors. It was spread so that the one who brings death would not kill the firstborn[d] sons of Israel.

[29]It was by faith that the people crossed the Red Sea as if it were dry land. The

---

11:10 city The spiritual "city" where God's people live with him. Also called "the heavenly Jerusalem." (See Hebrews 12:22.)
11:11 It . . . promised. Some Greek copies refer to Sarah's faith, rather than Abraham's.
11:18 "The descendants . . . Isaac." Quotation from Genesis 21:12.

Egyptians also tried to do it, but they were drowned.

³⁰It was by faith that the walls of Jericho fell. They fell after the people had marched around the walls of Jericho for seven days.

³¹It was by faith that Rahab, the prostitute,ᵈ welcomed the spies and was not killed with those who refused to obey God.

³²Do I need to give more examples? I do not have time to tell you about Gideon, Barak, Samson, Jephthah, David, Samuel, and the prophets.ᵈ ³³Through their faith they defeated kingdoms. They did what was right and received what God promised. They shut the mouths of lions, ³⁴stopped great fires and were saved from being killed with swords. They were weak, and yet were made strong. They were powerful in battle and defeated other armies. ³⁵Women received their dead relatives raised back to life. Others were tortured and refused to accept their freedom. They did this so that they could be raised from death to a better life. ³⁶Some were laughed at and beaten. Others were tied and put into prison. ³⁷They were killed with stones and they were cut in half.ⁿ They were killed with swords. Some wore the skins of sheep and goats. They were poor, abused, and treated badly. ³⁸The world was not good enough for them! They wandered in deserts and mountains, living in caves and holes in the earth.

³⁹All these people are known for their faith. But none of them received what God had promised. ⁴⁰God planned to give us something better. Then they would be made perfect, but only together with us.

FOLLOW JESUS' EXAMPLE

12 So we have many people of faith around us. Their lives tell us what faith means. So let us run the race that is before us and never give up. We should remove from our lives anything that would get in the way. And we should remove the sin that so easily catches us. ²Let us look only to Jesus. He is the one who began our faith, and he makes our faith perfect. Jesus suffered death on the cross. But he accepted the shame of the cross as if it were nothing. He did this because of the joy that God put before him. And now he is sitting at the right side of God's throne. ³Think about Jesus. He held on patiently while sinful men were doing evil things against him. Look at Jesus' example so that you will not get tired and stop trying.

GOD IS LIKE A FATHER

⁴You are struggling against sin, but your struggles have not yet caused you to be killed. ⁵You have forgotten his encouraging words for his sons:

"My son, don't think the Lord's
    discipline of you is worth
    nothing.
And don't stop trying when the
    Lord corrects you.
⁶The Lord corrects those he loves.
And he punishes everyone he
    accepts as his child."

Proverbs 3:11-12

⁷So accept your sufferings as if they were a father's punishment. God does these things to you as a father punishing his sons. All sons are punished by their fathers. ⁸If you are never punished (and every son must be punished), you are not true children and not really sons. ⁹We have all had fathers here on earth who punished us. And we respected our fathers. So it is even more important that we accept punishment from the Father of our spirits. If we do this, we will have life. ¹⁰Our fathers on earth punished us for a short time. They punished us the way they thought was best. But God punishes us to help us, so that we can become holy as he is. ¹¹We do not enjoy punishment. Being punished is

---

11:37 they were cut in half Some Greek copies also include, "and they were tested."

painful at the time. But later, after we have learned from being punished, we have peace, because we start living in the right way.

BE CAREFUL HOW YOU LIVE

[12]You have become weak. So make yourselves strong again. [13]Keep on the right path so the weak will not stumble but rather be strengthened.

[14]Try to live in peace with all people. And try to live lives free from sin. If anyone's life is not holy, he will never see the Lord. [15]Be careful that no one fails to get God's grace. Be careful that no one becomes like a bitter weed growing among you. A person like that can ruin all of you. [16]Be careful that no one takes part in sexual sin. And be careful that no person is like Esau and never thinks about God. Esau was the oldest son, and he would have received everything from his father. But Esau sold all that for a single meal. [17]You remember that after Esau did this, he wanted to get his father's blessing. He wanted this blessing so much that he cried. But his father refused to give him the blessing, because Esau could find no way to change what he had done.

[18]You have not come to a mountain that can be touched and that is burning with fire. You have not come to darkness, sadness and storms. [19]You have not come to the noise of a trumpet or to the sound of a voice. When the people of Israel heard the voice, they begged not to have to hear another word. [20]They did not want to hear the command: "If anything, even an animal, touches the mountain, it must be put to death with stones."[n] [21]What they saw was so terrible that

Moses said, "I am shaking with fear."[n]

[22]But you have not come to that kind of place. The new place you have come to is Mount Zion.[n] You have come to the city of the living God, the heavenly Jerusalem. You have come to thousands of angels gathered together with joy. [23]You have come to the meeting of God's firstborn[n] children. Their names are written in heaven. You have come to God, the judge of all people. And you have come to the spirits of good people who have been made perfect. [24]You have come to Jesus, the One who brought the new agreement from God to his people. You have come to the sprinkled blood[n] that has a better message than the blood of Abel.[n]

[25]So be careful and do not refuse to listen when God speaks. They refused to listen to him when he warned them on earth. And they did not escape. Now God is warning us from heaven. So it will be worse for us if we refuse to listen to him. [26]When he spoke before, his voice shook the earth. But now he has promised, "Once again I will shake not only the earth but also the heavens."[n] [27]The words "once again" clearly show us that everything that was made will be destroyed. These are the things that can be shaken. And only the things that cannot be shaken will remain.

[28]So let us be thankful because we have a kingdom that cannot be shaken. We should worship God in a way that pleases him. So let us worship him with respect and fear, [29]because our God is like a fire that burns things up.

13 Keep on loving each other as brothers in Christ. [2]Remember to welcome strangers into your homes.

12:20 "If ... stones." Quotation from Exodus 19:12-13.
12:21 "I ... fear." Quotation from Deuteronomy 9:19.
12:22 **Mount Zion** Another name for Jerusalem, here meaning the spiritual city of God's people.
12:23 **firstborn** The first son born in a Jewish family was given the most important place in the family and received special blessings. All of God's children are like that.
12:24 **sprinkled blood** The blood of Jesus' death.
12:24 **Abel** The son of Adam and Eve, who was killed by his brother Cain (Genesis 4:8).
12:26 "Once ... heavens." Quotation from Haggai 2:6, 21.

Some people have done this and have welcomed angels without knowing it. ³Do not forget those who are in prison. Remember them as if you were in prison with them. Remember those who are suffering as if you were suffering with them.

⁴Marriage should be honored by everyone. Husband and wife should keep their marriage pure. God will judge guilty those who take part in sexual sins. ⁵Keep your lives free from the love of money. And be satisfied with what you have. God has said,

"I will never leave you;
  I will never abandon you."
                    Deuteronomy 31:6
⁶So we can feel sure and say,
"I will not be afraid because the Lord
  is my helper.
People can't do anything to me."
                        Psalm 118:6
⁷Remember your leaders. They taught God's message to you. Remember how they lived and died, and copy their faith. ⁸Jesus Christ is the same yesterday, today, and forever.

⁹Do not let all kinds of strange teachings lead you into the wrong way. Your hearts should be strengthened by God's grace, not by obeying rules about foods. Obeying such rules does not help anyone. ¹⁰We have a sacrifice. But the priests who serve in the Holy Tent*d* cannot eat from it. ¹¹The high priest carries the blood of animals into the Most Holy Place. There he offers this blood for sins. But the bodies of the animals are burned outside the camp. ¹²So Jesus also suffered outside the city. He died to make his people holy with his own blood. ¹³So let us go to Jesus outside the camp. We should accept the same shame that Jesus had.

¹⁴Here on earth we do not have a city that lasts forever. But we are looking for the city that we will have in the future. ¹⁵So through Jesus let us always offer our sacrifice to God. This sacrifice is our praise, coming from lips that speak his name. ¹⁶Do not forget to do good to others. And share with them what you have. These are the sacrifices that please God.

¹⁷Obey your leaders and be under their authority. These men are watching you because they are responsible for your souls. Obey them so that they will do this work with joy, not sadness. It will not help you to make their work hard.

¹⁸Continue praying for us. We feel sure about what we are doing, because we always want to do the right thing. ¹⁹And I beg you to pray that God will send me back to you soon.

²⁰⁻²¹I pray that the God of peace will give you every good thing you need so that you can do what he wants. God is the One who raised from death our Lord Jesus, the Great Shepherd of the sheep. God raised him because of the blood of his death. His blood began the agreement that God made with his people. And this agreement is eternal. I pray that God, through Christ, will do in us what pleases him. And to Jesus Christ be glory forever and ever. Amen.

²²My brothers, I beg you to listen patiently to this message I have written to encourage you. This letter is not very long. ²³I want you to know that our brother Timothy has been let out of prison. If he arrives soon, we will both come to see you.

²⁴Greet all your leaders and all of God's people. Those from Italy send greetings to you.

²⁵God's grace be with you all.

THE LETTER OF
JAMES

1 From James, a servant of God and of the Lord Jesus Christ. To all of God's people who are scattered everywhere in the world:

Greetings.

FAITH AND WISDOM

[2]My brothers, you will have many kinds of troubles. But when these things happen, you should be very happy. [3]You know that these things are testing your faith. And this will give you patience. [4]Let your patience show itself perfectly in what you do. Then you will be perfect and complete. You will have everything you need. [5]But if any of you needs wisdom, you should ask God for it. God is generous. He enjoys giving to all people, so God will give you wisdom. [6]But when you ask God, you must believe. Do not doubt God. Anyone who doubts is like a wave in the sea. The wind blows the wave up and down. [7-8]He who doubts is thinking two different things at the same time. He cannot decide about anything he does. A person like that should not think that he will receive anything from the Lord.

TRUE RICHES

[9]If a believer is poor, he should take pride that God has made him spiritually rich. [10]If he is rich, he should take pride that God has shown him that he is spiritually poor. The rich person will die like a wild flower in the grass. [11]The sun rises and becomes hotter and hotter. The heat makes the plants very dry, and the flower falls off. The flower was beautiful, but now it is dead. It is the same with a rich person. While he is still taking care of his business, he will die.

TEMPTATION IS NOT FROM GOD

[12]When a person is tempted and still continues strong, he should be happy. After he has proved his faith, God will reward him with life forever. God promised this to all people who love him.

[13]When someone is being tempted, he should not say, "God is tempting me." Evil cannot tempt God, and God himself does not tempt anyone. [14]It is the evil that a person wants that tempts him. His own evil desire leads him away and holds him. [15]This desire causes sin. Then the sin grows and brings death.

[16]My dear brothers, do not be fooled about this. [17]Every good action and every perfect gift is from God. These good gifts come down from the Creator of the sun, moon, and stars. God does not change like their shifting shadows. [18]God decided to give us life through the word of truth. He wanted us to be the most important of all the things he made.

LISTENING AND OBEYING

[19]My dear brothers, always be willing to listen and slow to speak. Do not become angry easily. [20]Anger will not help you live a good life as God wants. [21]So put out of your life every evil thing and every kind of wrong you do. Don't be proud but accept God's teaching that is planted in your hearts. This teaching can save your souls.

[22]Do what God's teaching says; do not just listen and do nothing. When you only sit and listen, you are fooling yourselves. [23]A person who hears God's teaching and does nothing is like a man looking in a mirror. [24]He sees his face, then goes away and quickly forgets what he looked like. [25]But the truly happy person is the one who carefully studies God's perfect law that makes people free. He continues to study it. He listens to God's teaching and does not forget what he heard. Then he obeys what God's teaching says. When he does this, it makes him happy.

THE TRUE WAY TO WORSHIP GOD

[26]A person might think he is religious. But if he says things he should not say, then he is just fooling himself. His

"religion" is worth nothing. [27]Religion that God accepts is this: caring for orphans or widows who need help; and keeping yourself free from the world's evil influence. This is the kind of religion that God accepts as pure and good.

LOVE ALL PEOPLE

2 My dear brothers, you are believers in our glorious Lord Jesus Christ. So never think that some people are more important than others. [2]Suppose someone comes into your church meeting wearing very nice clothes and a gold ring. At the same time a poor man comes in wearing old, dirty clothes. [3]You show special attention to the one wearing nice clothes. You say, "Please, sit here in this good seat." But you say to the poor man, "Stand over there," or "Sit on the floor by my feet!" [4]What are you doing? You are making some people more important than others. With evil thoughts you are deciding which person is better.

[5]Listen, my dear brothers! God chose the poor in the world to be rich with faith. He chose them to receive the kingdom God promised to people who love him. [6]But you show no respect to the poor man. And you know that it is the rich who are always trying to control your lives. And they are the ones who take you to court. [7]They are the ones who say bad things against Jesus, who owns you.

[8]One law rules over all other laws. This royal law is found in the Scriptures:[d] "Love your neighbor as you love yourself."[n] If you obey this law, then you are doing right. [9]But if you are treating one person as if he were more important than another, then you are sinning. That royal law proves that you are guilty of breaking God's law. [10]A person might follow all of God's law. But if he fails to obey even one command, he is guilty of breaking all the commands in that law. [11]God said, "You must not be guilty of adultery."[dn] The same God also said, "You must not murder anyone."[n] So if you do not take part in adultery, but you murder someone, then you are guilty of breaking all of God's law. [12]You will be judged by the law that makes people free. You should remember this in everything you say and do. [13]Yes, you must show mercy to others, or God will not show mercy to you when he judges you. But the person who shows mercy can stand without fear when he is judged.

FAITH AND GOOD WORKS

[14]My brothers, if someone says he has faith, but does nothing, his faith is worth nothing. Can faith like that save him? [15]A brother or sister in Christ might need clothes or might need food. [16]And you say to him, "God be with you! I hope you stay warm and get plenty to eat." You say this, but you do not give that person the things he needs. Unless you help him, your words are worth nothing. [17]It is the same with faith. If faith does nothing, then that faith is dead, because it is alone.

[18]Someone might say, "You have faith, but I do things. Show me your faith! Your faith does nothing. I will show you my faith by the things I do." [19]You believe there is one God. Good! But the demons[d] believe that, too! And they shake with fear.

[20]You foolish person! Must you be shown that faith that does nothing is worth nothing? [21]Abraham is our father. He was made right with God by the things he did. He offered his son Isaac to God on the altar. [22]So you see that Abraham's faith and the things he did worked together. His faith was made perfect by what he did. [23]This shows the full meaning of the Scripture[d] that says:

2:8 "Love . . . yourself." Quotation from Leviticus 19:18.
2:11 "You . . . adultery." Quotation from Exodus 20:14 and Deuteronomy 5:18.
2:11 "You . . . anyone." Quotation from Exodus 20:13 and Deuteronomy 5:17.

"Abraham believed God, and God accepted Abraham's faith, and that faith made him right with God."[n] And Abraham was called "God's friend."[n] 24So you see that a person is made right with God by the things he does. He cannot be made right by faith only.

25Another example is Rahab, who was a prostitute.[d] But she was made right with God by something she did: She helped the spies for God's people. She welcomed them into her home and helped them escape by a different road.

26A person's body that does not have a spirit is dead. It is the same with faith. Faith that does nothing is dead!

CONTROLLING THE THINGS WE SAY

3 My brothers, not many of you should become teachers. You know that we who teach will be judged more strictly than others. 2We all make many mistakes. If there were a person who never said anything wrong, he would be perfect. He would be able to control his whole body, too. 3We put bits into the mouths of horses to make them obey us. We can control their whole bodies. 4It is the same with ships. A ship is very big, and it is pushed by strong winds. But a very small rudder controls that big ship. The man who controls the rudder decides where the ship will go. The ship goes where the man wants. 5It is the same with the tongue. It is a small part of the body, but it brags about doing great things.

A big forest fire can be started with only a little flame. 6And the tongue is like a fire. It is a whole world of evil among the parts of our bodies. The tongue spreads its evil through the whole body. It starts a fire that influences all of life. The tongue gets this fire from hell. 7People can tame every kind of wild animal, bird, reptile, and fish, and they have tamed them. 8But no one can tame the tongue. It is wild and evil. It is full of poison that can kill. 9We use our tongues to praise our Lord and Father, but then we curse people. And God made them like himself. 10Praises and curses come from the same mouth! My brothers, this should not happen. 11Do good and bad water flow from the same spring? 12My brothers, can a fig tree make olives? Can a grapevine make figs? No! And a well full of salty water cannot give good water.

TRUE WISDOM

13Is there anyone among you who is truly wise and understanding? Then he should show his wisdom by living right. He should do good things without being proud. A wise person does not brag. 14But if you are selfish and have bitter jealousy in your hearts, you have no reason to brag. Your bragging is a lie that hides the truth. 15That kind of "wisdom" does not come from God. That "wisdom" comes from the world. It is not spiritual. It is from the devil. 16Where there is jealousy and selfishness, there will be confusion and every kind of evil. 17But the wisdom that comes from God is like this: First, it is pure. Then it is also peaceful, gentle, and easy to please. This wisdom is always ready to help those who are troubled and to do good for others. This wisdom is always fair and honest. 18When people work for peace in a peaceful way, they receive the good result of their right-living.

GIVE YOURSELVES TO GOD

4 Do you know where your fights and arguments come from? They come from the selfish desires that make war inside you. 2You want things, but you do not have them. So you are ready to kill and are jealous of other people. But you still cannot get what you want. So you argue and fight. You do not get what you want because you do not ask God. 3Or when you ask, you do not receive because

---

2:23 "Abraham . . . God." Quotation from Genesis 15:6.
2:23 "God's friend" These words about Abraham are found in 2 Chronicles 20:7 and Isaiah 41:8.

the reason you ask is wrong. You want things only so that you can use them for your own pleasures.

⁴So, you people are not loyal to God! You should know that loving the world is the same as hating God. So if a person wants to be a friend of the world, he makes himself God's enemy. ⁵Do you think the Scripture*d* means nothing? It says, "The Spirit*d* that God made to live in us wants us for himself alone."*n* ⁶But God gives us even more grace, as the Scripture says,

"God is against the proud,
  but he gives grace to the humble."
                                    Proverbs 3:34

⁷So give yourselves to God. Stand against the devil, and the devil will run away from you. ⁸Come near to God, and God will come near to you. You are sinners. So clean sin out of your lives. You are trying to follow God and the world at the same time. Make your thinking pure. ⁹Be sad, cry, and weep! Change your laughter into crying. Change your joy into sadness. ¹⁰Humble yourself before the Lord, and he will honor you.

YOU ARE NOT THE JUDGE

¹¹Brothers, do not say bad things about each other. If you say bad things about your brother in Christ or judge him, then you are saying bad things about the law he follows. You are also judging the law he follows. And when you are judging the law, you are not a follower of the law. You have become a judge! ¹²God is the only One who makes laws, and he is the only Judge. He is the only One who can save and destroy. So it is not right for you to judge your neighbor.

LET GOD PLAN YOUR LIFE

¹³Some of you say, "Today or tomorrow we will go to some city. We will stay there a year, do business, and make money." ¹⁴But you do not know what will happen

tomorrow! Your life is like a mist. You can see it for a short time, but then it goes away. ¹⁵So you should say, "If the Lord wants, we will live and do this or that." ¹⁶But now you are proud and you brag. All of this bragging is wrong. ¹⁷And when a person knows the right thing to do, but does not do it, then he is sinning.

A WARNING TO THE RICH

5 You rich people, listen! Cry and be very sad because of the trouble that will come to you. ²Your riches will rot, and your clothes will be eaten by moths. ³Your gold and silver will rust, and rust will be a proof that you were wrong. It will eat your bodies like fire. You saved your treasure for the last days. ⁴Men worked in your fields, but you did not pay them. They harvested your crops and are crying out against you. Now the Lord of heaven's armies has heard their cries. ⁵Your life on earth was full of rich living. You pleased yourselves with everything you wanted. You made yourselves fat, like an animal ready to be killed. ⁶You showed no mercy to the innocent man. You murdered him. He cannot stand against you.

BE PATIENT

⁷Brothers, be patient until the Lord comes again. A farmer is patient. He waits for his valuable crop to grow from the earth. He waits patiently for it to receive the first rain and the last rain. ⁸You, too, must be patient. Do not give up hope. The Lord is coming soon. ⁹Brothers, do not complain against each other. If you do not stop complaining, you will be judged guilty. And the Judge is ready to come! ¹⁰Brothers, follow the example of the prophets*d* who spoke for the Lord. They suffered many hard things, but they were patient. ¹¹We say they are happy because they were able to do this. You have heard about Job's patience.

4:5 "The Spirit . . . alone." These words may be from Exodus 20:5.

You know that after all his trouble, the Lord helped him. This shows that the Lord is full of mercy and is kind.

BE CAREFUL WHAT YOU SAY

[12]My brothers, it is very important that you not use an oath when you make a promise. Don't use the name of heaven, earth, or anything else to prove what you say. When you mean yes, say only "yes." When you mean no, say only "no." Do this so that you will not be judged guilty.

THE POWER OF PRAYER

[13]If one of you is having troubles, he should pray. If one of you is happy, he should sing praises. [14]If one of you is sick, he should call the church's elders.[d] The elders should pour oil on him[n] in the name of the Lord and pray for him. [15]And the prayer that is said with faith will make the sick person well. The Lord will heal him. And if he has sinned, God will forgive him. [16]Confess your sins to each other and pray for each other. Do this so that God can heal you. When a good man prays, great things happen. [17]Elijah was a man just like us. He prayed that it would not rain. And it did not rain on the land for three and a half years! [18]Then Elijah prayed again. And the rain came down from the sky, and the land grew crops again.

SAVING A SOUL

[19]My brothers, one of you may wander away from the truth. And someone may help him come back. [20]Remember this: Anyone who brings a sinner back from the wrong way will save that sinner's soul from death. By doing this, that person will cause many sins to be forgiven.

5:14 pour oil on him Oil was used like medicine, so that is probably how the believers used it.

1 From Peter, an apostle[d] of Jesus Christ.

To God's chosen people who are away from their homes. You are scattered all around Pontus, Galatia, Cappadocia, Asia, and Bithynia. [2]God planned long ago to choose you by making you his holy people. Making you holy is the Spirit's[d] work. God wanted you to obey him and to be made clean by the blood of the death of Jesus Christ. Grace and peace be yours more and more.

A LIVING HOPE

[3]Praise be to the God and Father of our Lord Jesus Christ. God has great mercy, and because of his mercy he gave us a new life. He gave us a living hope because Jesus Christ rose from death. [4]Now we hope for the blessings God has for his children. These blessings are kept for you in heaven. They cannot be destroyed or be spoiled or lose their beauty. [5]God's power protects you through your faith, and it keeps you safe until your salvation comes. That salvation is ready to be given to you at the end of time. [6]This makes you very happy. But now for a short time different kinds of troubles may make you sad. [7]These troubles come to prove that your faith is pure. This purity of faith is worth more than gold. Gold can be proved to be pure by fire, but gold will ruin. But the purity of your faith will bring you praise and glory and honor when Jesus Christ comes again. [8]You have not seen Christ, but still you love him. You cannot see him now, but you believe in him. You are filled with a joy that cannot be explained. And that joy is full of glory. [9]Your faith has a goal, to save your souls. And you are receiving that goal—your salvation.

[10]The prophets[d] searched carefully and tried to learn about this salvation. They spoke about the grace that was coming to you. [11]The Spirit[d] of Christ was in the prophets. And the Spirit was telling about the sufferings that would happen to Christ and about the glory that would come after those sufferings. The prophets tried to learn about what the Spirit was showing them. They tried to learn when those things would happen and what the world would be like at that time. [12]It was shown to them that their service was not for themselves. It was for you. They were serving you when they told about the truths you have now heard. The men who preached the Good News[d] to you told you those things. They did it with the help of the Holy Spirit that was sent from heaven. These are truths that even the angels want very much to know about.

A CALL TO HOLY LIVING

[13]So prepare your minds for service and have self-control. All your hope should be for the gift of grace that will be yours when Jesus Christ comes again. [14]In the past you did not understand, so you did the evil things you wanted. But now you are children of God who obey. So do not live as you lived in the past. [15]But be holy in all that you do, just as God is holy. God is the One who called you. [16]It is written in the Scriptures:[d] "You must be holy, because I am holy."[n]

[17]You pray to God and call him Father. And this Father judges each man's work equally. So while you are here on earth, you should live with respect for God. [18]You know that in the past you were living in a worthless way. You got that way of living from the people who lived before you. But you were saved from

---

1:16 **"You must be . . . holy."** Quotation from Leviticus 11:45; 19:2; 20:7.

that useless life. You were bought, but not with something that ruins like gold or silver. [19]You were bought with the precious blood of the death of Christ, who was like a pure and perfect lamb. [20]Christ was chosen before the world was made. But he was shown to the world in these last times for you. [21]You believe in God through Christ. God raised Christ from death and gave him glory. So your faith and your hope are in God.

[22]Now you have made yourselves pure by obeying the truth. Now you can have true love for your brothers. So love each other deeply with all your heart. [23]You have been born again. This new life did not come from something that dies, but from something that cannot die. You were born again through God's living message that continues forever. [24]The Scripture says,

"All people are like the grass.
    And all their strength is like the
        flowers of the field.
The grass dies and the flowers fall.
[25]But the word of the Lord will live
    forever."   *Isaiah 40:6-8*
And this is the word that was preached to you.

JESUS IS THE LIVING STONE

2 So then, get rid of all evil and all lying. Do not be a hypocrite.[d] Do not be jealous or speak evil of others. Put all these things out of your life. [2]As newborn babies want milk, you should want the pure and simple teaching. By it you can mature in your salvation. [3]For you have already examined and seen how good the Lord is.

[4]The Lord Jesus is the "stone"[n] that lives. The people of the world did not want this stone. But he was the stone God chose. To God he was worth much. So come to him. [5]You also are like living stones. Let yourselves be used to build a spiritual temple—to be holy priests who offer spiritual sacrifices to God. He will accept those sacrifices through Jesus Christ. [6]The Scripture[d] says:

"I will put a stone in the ground in
    Jerusalem.
Everything will be built on this
    important and precious rock.
Anyone who trusts in him
    will never be disappointed."
                  Isaiah 28:16
[7]This stone is worth much to you who believe. But to the people who do not believe, he is

"the stone that the builders did not
    want.
It has become the cornerstone."[d]
                Psalm 118:22
[8]To people who do not believe, he is
"a stone that causes people to stumble.
It is a rock that makes them fall."
               Isaiah 8:14
They stumble because they do not obey what God says. This is what God planned to happen to them.

[9]But you are chosen people. You are the King's priests. You are a holy nation. You are a nation that belongs to God alone. God chose you to tell about the wonderful things he has done. He called you out of darkness into his wonderful light. [10]At one time you were not God's people. But now you are his people. In the past you had never received mercy. But now you have received God's mercy.

LIVE FOR GOD

[11]Dear friends, you are like visitors and strangers in this world. So I beg you to stay away from the evil things your bodies want to do. These things fight against your soul. [12]People who do not believe are living all around you. They might say that you are doing wrong. So live good lives. Then they will see the good things you do, and they will give glory to God on the day when Christ comes again.

2:4 **"stone"** The most important stone in God's spiritual temple or house (his people).

OBEY EVERY HUMAN AUTHORITY

[13]Obey the people who have authority in this world. Do this for the Lord. Obey the king, who is the highest authority. [14]And obey the leaders who are sent by the king. They are sent to punish those who do wrong and to praise those who do right. [15]So when you do good, you stop foolish people from saying stupid things about you. This is what God wants. [16]Live as free men. But do not use your freedom as an excuse to do evil. Live as servants of God. [17]Show respect for all people. Love the brothers and sisters of God's family. Respect God. Honor the king.

FOLLOW CHRIST'S EXAMPLE

[18]Slaves, accept the authority of your masters. Do this with all respect. You should obey masters who are good and kind, and you should obey masters who are bad. [19]A person might have to suffer even when he has done nothing wrong. But if he thinks of God and bears the pain, this pleases God. [20]If you are punished for doing wrong, there is no reason to praise you for bearing punishment. But if you suffer for doing good, and you are patient, then that pleases God. [21]That is what you were called to do. Christ suffered for you. He gave you an example to follow. So you should do as he did.

[22]"He did no sin.

He never lied." *Isaiah 53:9*

[23]People insulted Christ, but he did not insult them in return. Christ suffered, but he did not threaten. He let God take care of him. God is the One who judges rightly. [24]Christ carried our sins in his body on the cross. He did this so that we would stop living for sin and start living for what is right. And we are healed because of his wounds. [25]You were like sheep that went the wrong way. But now you have come back to the Shepherd and Overseer of your souls.

WIVES AND HUSBANDS

3 In the same way, you wives should accept the authority of your husbands. Then, if some husbands have not obeyed God's teaching, they will be persuaded to believe. You will not need to say a word to them. They will be persuaded by the way their wives live. [2]Your husbands will see the pure lives that you live with your respect for God. [3]It is not fancy hair, gold jewelry, or fine clothes that should make you beautiful. [4]No, your beauty should come from within you— the beauty of a gentle and quiet spirit. This beauty will never disappear, and it is worth very much to God. [5]It was the same with the holy women who lived long ago and followed God. They made themselves beautiful in this way. They accepted the authority of their husbands. [6]Sarah obeyed Abraham, her husband, and called him her master. And you women are true children of Sarah if you always do what is right and are not afraid.

[7]In the same way, you husbands should live with your wives in an understanding way. You should show respect to them. They are weaker than you. But God gives them the same blessing that he gives you—the grace that gives true life. Do this so that nothing will stop your prayers.

SUFFERING FOR DOING RIGHT

[8]Finally, all of you should live together in peace. Try to understand each other. Love each other as brothers. Be kind and humble. [9]Do not do wrong to a person to pay him back for doing wrong to you. Or do not insult someone to pay him back for insulting you. But ask God to bless that person. Do this, because you yourselves were called to receive a blessing. [10]The Scripture[d] says,

"A person must do these things
    to enjoy life and have many, happy
    days.
He must not say evil things.
    He must not tell lies.
[11]He must stop doing evil and do good.

He must look for peace and work
for it.
[12]The Lord sees the good people.
He listens to their prayers.
But the Lord is against
those who do evil."   *Psalm 34:12-16*
[13]If you are always trying to do good,
no one can really hurt you. [14]But you
may suffer for doing right. Even if that
happens, you are blessed.
"Don't be afraid of the things they fear.
Do not dread those things.
[15]But respect Christ as the holy Lord in
your hearts."   *Isaiah 8:12-13*
Always be ready to answer everyone who
asks you to explain about the hope you
have. [16]But answer in a gentle way and
with respect. Always feel that you are
doing right. Then, those who speak evil
of your good life in Christ will be made
ashamed. [17]It is better to suffer for doing
good than for doing wrong. Yes, it is
better, if that is what God wants. [18]Christ
himself died for you. And that one death
paid for your sins. He was not guilty, but
he died for those who are guilty. He did
this to bring you all to God. His body was
killed, but he was made alive in the
spirit. [19]And in the spirit he went and
preached to the spirits in prison. [20]These
were the spirits who refused to obey God
long ago in the time of Noah. God was
waiting patiently for them while Noah
was building the boat. Only a few
people—eight in all—were saved by
water. [21]That water is like baptism that
now saves you—not the washing of dirt
from the body, but the promise made to
God from a good heart. And this is
because Jesus Christ was raised from
death. [22]Now Jesus has gone into heaven
and is at God's right side. He rules over
angels, authorities, and powers.

CHANGED LIVES

4 Christ suffered while he was in his
body. So you should strengthen
yourselves with the same way of thinking Christ had. The person who has suffered in his body is finished with sin.

[2]Strengthen yourselves so that you will
live your lives here on earth doing what
God wants, not doing the evil things that
people want. [3]In the past you wasted too
much time doing what the non-believers
like to do. You were guilty of sexual sins
and had evil desires. You were getting
drunk, you had wild and drunken parties, and you did wrong by worshiping
idols. [4]Non-believers think it is strange
that you do not do the many wild and
wasteful things that they do. And so they
insult you. [5]But they will have to explain
about what they have done. They must
explain to God who is ready to judge the
living and the dead. [6]The Good News[d]
was preached to those who are now
dead. By their dying, they were judged
like all men. But the Good News was
preached to them so that they could live
in the spirit as God lives.

USE GOD'S GIFTS WISELY

[7]The time is near when all things will
end. So keep your minds clear, and control yourselves. Then you will be able to
pray. [8]Most importantly, love each other
deeply. Love has a way of not looking at
others' sins. [9]Open your homes to each
other, without complaining. [10]Each of
you received a spiritual gift. God has
shown you his grace in giving you different gifts. And you are like servants
who are responsible for using God's
gifts. So be good servants and use your
gifts to serve each other. [11]Anyone who
speaks should speak words from God.
The person who serves should serve
with the strength that God gives. You
should do these things so that in everything God will be praised through Jesus
Christ. Power and glory belong to him
forever and ever. Amen.

SUFFERING AS A CHRISTIAN

[12]My friends, do not be surprised at
the painful things you are now suffering.
These things are testing your faith. So do

not think that something strange is happening to you. [13]But you should be happy that you are sharing in Christ's sufferings. You will be happy and full of joy when Christ comes again in glory. [14]When people insult you because you follow Christ, then you are blessed. You are blessed because the glorious Spirit,[d] the Spirit of God, is with you. [15]Do not suffer for murder, theft, or any other crime, nor because you trouble other people. [16]But if you suffer because you are a Christian, then do not be ashamed. You should praise God because you wear that name. [17]It is time for judgment to begin, and it will begin with God's family. If that judging begins with us, what will happen to those people who do not obey the Good News[d] of God?

[18]"It is very hard for a good person to
be saved.
Then the wicked person and
the sinner will surely be lost!"[n]

[19]So then those who suffer as God wants them to should trust their souls to him. God is the One who made them, and they can trust him. So they should continue to do what is right.

THE FLOCK OF GOD

5 Now I have something to say to the elders[d] in your group. I am also an elder. I myself have seen Christ's sufferings. And I will share in the glory that will be shown to us. I beg you to [2]take care of God's flock, his people, that you are responsible for. Watch over it because you want to, not because you are forced to do it. That is how God wants it. Do it because you are happy to serve, not because you want money. [3]Do not be like a ruler over people you are responsible for. Be good examples to them. [4]Then when Christ, the Head Shepherd, comes, you will get a crown. This crown will be glorious, and it will never lose its beauty.

[5]In the same way, younger men should be willing to be under older men. And all of you should be very humble with each other.

"God is against the proud,
but he gives grace to the humble."

Proverbs 3:34

[6]So be humble under God's powerful hand. Then he will lift you up when the right time comes. [7]Give all your worries to him, because he cares for you.

[8]Control yourselves and be careful! The devil is your enemy. And he goes around like a roaring lion looking for someone to eat. [9]Refuse to give in to the devil. Stand strong in your faith. You know that your Christian brothers and sisters all over the world are having the same sufferings you have.

[10]Yes, you will suffer for a short time. But after that, God will make everything right. He will make you strong. He will support you and keep you from falling. He is the God who gives all grace. He called you to share in his glory in Christ. That glory will continue forever. [11]All power is his forever and ever. Amen.

FINAL GREETINGS

[12]I wrote this short letter with the help of Silas. I know that he is a faithful brother in Christ. I wrote to comfort and encourage you. I wanted to tell you that this is the true grace of God. Stand strong in that grace.

[13]The church in Babylon sends you greetings. They were chosen the same as you. Mark, my son in Christ, also greets you. [14]Give each other a kiss of Christian love when you meet.

Peace to all of you who are in Christ.

4:18 **"It . . . lost!"** Quotation from Proverbs 11:31 in the Septuagint, the Greek version of the Old Testament.

PETER

1 From Simon Peter, a servant and apostle[d] of Jesus Christ.

To you who have received a faith as valuable as ours. You received that faith because our God and Savior Jesus Christ is fair and does what is right.

[2]Grace and peace be given to you more and more. You will have grace and peace because you truly know God and Jesus our Lord.

GOD HAS GIVEN US BLESSINGS

[3]Jesus has the power of God. His power has given us everything we need to live and to serve God. We have these things because we know him. Jesus called us by his glory and goodness. [4]Through his glory and goodness, he gave us the very great and rich gifts he promised us. With those gifts you can share in God's nature. And so the world will not ruin you with its evil desires.

[5]Because you have these blessings, you should try as much as you can to add these things to your lives: to your faith, add goodness; and to your goodness, add knowledge; [6]and to your knowledge, add self-control; and to your self-control, add the ability to hold on; and to your ability to hold on, add service for God; [7]and to your service for God, add kindness for your brothers and sisters in Christ; and to this kindness, add love. [8]If all these things are in you and are growing, they will help you never to be useless. They will help your knowledge of our Lord Jesus Christ make your lives better. [9]But if anyone does not have these things, he cannot see clearly. He is blind. He has forgotten that he was made clean from his past sins.

[10]My brothers, God called you and chose you to be his. Try hard to show that you really are God's chosen people. If you do all these things, you will never fall. [11]And you will be given a very great welcome into the kingdom of our Lord and Savior Jesus Christ. That kingdom continues forever.

[12]You know these things, and you are very strong in the truth. But I will always help you to remember these things. [13]I think it is right for me to help you remember while I am still living here on earth. [14]I know that I must soon leave this body. Our Lord Jesus Christ has shown me that. [15]I will try the best I can to help you remember these things always. I want you to be able to remember them even after I am gone.

WE SAW CHRIST'S GLORY

[16]We have told you about the powerful coming of our Lord Jesus Christ. What we told you were not just smart stories that someone invented. But we saw the greatness of Jesus with our own eyes. [17]Jesus heard the voice of God, the Greatest Glory. That was when Jesus received honor and glory from God the Father. The voice said, "This is my Son, and I love him. I am very pleased with him." [18]We heard that voice. It came from heaven while we were with Jesus on the holy mountain.

[19]This makes us more sure about the message the prophets[d] gave. And it is good for you to follow closely what they said. Their message is like a light shining in a dark place. That light shines until the day begins and the morning star rises in your hearts. [20]Most of all, you must understand this: No prophecy in the Scriptures[d] ever comes from the prophet's own interpretation. [21]No prophecy ever came from what a man wanted to say. But men led by the Holy Spirit[d] spoke words from God.

FALSE TEACHERS

2 There used to be false prophets[d] among God's people, just as there are now. And you will have some false teachers in your group. They will secretly teach things that are wrong—teachings that will cause people to be lost. They will even refuse to accept the Master, Jesus, who bought their freedom. And so they will quickly destroy themselves. [2]Many will follow their evil ways and say evil things about the Way of truth. [3]Those false teachers only want your money. So they will use you by telling you what is not true. But God has already judged them guilty. And they will not escape the One who will destroy them.

[4]When angels sinned, God did not let them go free without punishment. God sent them to hell and put them in caves[n] of darkness. They are being held there to be judged. [5]And God punished the evil people who lived long ago. He brought a flood to the world that was full of people who were against him. But God saved Noah and seven other people with him. Noah was a man who preached about being right with God. [6]And God also punished the evil cities of Sodom and Gomorrah.[n] He burned those cities until there was nothing left but ashes. He made those cities an example to show what will happen to those who are against God. [7]But God saved Lot from those cities. Lot, a good man, was troubled because of the dirty lives of evil people. [8](Lot was a good man, but he lived with evil people every day. His good heart was hurt by the evil things that he saw and heard.) [9]And so the Lord knows how to save those who serve him. He will save them when troubles come. And the Lord will hold evil people and punish them, while waiting for the Judgment Day. [10]That punishment is especially for those who live by doing the evil things their sinful selves want, and for those who hate the Lord's authority.

These false teachers do anything they want and brag about it. They are not afraid to say bad things about the glorious angels. [11]The angels are much stronger and more powerful than false teachers. But even the angels do not accuse them with insults before[n] the Lord. [12]But these men say bad things about what they do not understand. They are like animals that act without thinking. These animals are born to be caught and killed. And, like wild animals, these false teachers will be destroyed. [13]They have caused many people to suffer; so they themselves will suffer. That is their pay for what they have done. They take pleasure in doing evil things openly. So they are like dirty spots and stains among you. They bring shame to you in the meals that you eat together. [14]Every time they look at a woman they want her. Their desire for sin is never satisfied. They lead weak people into the trap of sin. They have taught their hearts to be selfish. God will punish them. [15]These false teachers left the right road and lost their way. They followed the way that Balaam went. Balaam was the son of Beor, who loved being paid for doing wrong. [16]But a donkey told Balaam that he was sinning. And the donkey is an animal that cannot talk. But the donkey spoke with a man's voice and stopped the prophet's crazy thinking.

[17]Those false teachers are like rivers that have no water. They are like clouds blown by a storm. A place in the blackest darkness has been kept for them. [18]They brag with words that mean nothing. By their evil desires they lead people into the trap of sin. They lead away people who are just beginning to escape from other people who live in error. [19]They promise them freedom, but they themselves are not free. They are slaves of things that will

---

2:4 **caves** Some Greek copies read "chains."
2:6 **Sodom and Gomorrah** Two cities that God destroyed because the people were so evil.
2:11 **before** Some Greek copies read "from."

be destroyed. For a person is a slave of anything that controls him. [20]They were made free from the evil in the world by knowing our Lord and Savior Jesus Christ. But if they return to evil things and those things control them, then it is worse for them than it was before. [21]Yes, it would be better for them to have never known the right way. That would be better than to know the right way and then to turn away from the holy teaching that was given to them. [22]What they did is like this true saying: "A dog eats what it throws up."[n] And, "After a pig is washed, it goes back and rolls in the mud."

JESUS WILL COME AGAIN

3 My friends, this is the second letter I have written to you. I wrote both letters to you to help your honest minds remember something. [2]I want you to remember the words that the holy prophets[d] spoke in the past. And remember the command that our Lord and Savior gave us through your apostles.[d] [3]It is important for you to understand what will happen in the last days. People will laugh at you. They will live doing the evil things they want to do. [4]They will say, "Jesus promised to come again. Where is he? Our fathers have died. But the world continues the way it has been since it was made." [5]But they do not want to remember what happened long ago. God spoke and made heaven and earth. He made the earth from water and with water. [6]Then the world was flooded and destroyed with water. [7]And that same word of God is keeping heaven and earth that we have now. They are being kept to be destroyed by fire. They are being kept for the Judgment Day and the destruction of all who are against God.

[8]But do not forget this one thing, dear friends: To the Lord one day is as a thousand years, and a thousand years is as one day. [9]The Lord is not slow in doing what he promised—the way some people understand slowness. But God is being patient with you. He does not want anyone to be lost. He wants everyone to change his heart and life.

[10]But the day the Lord comes again will be a surprise, like a thief. The skies will disappear with a loud noise. Everything in the skies will be destroyed by fire. And the earth and everything in it will be exposed.[n] [11]In that way everything will be destroyed. So what kind of people should you be? You should live holy lives and serve God. [12]You should wait for the day of God and look forward to its coming. When that day comes, the skies will be destroyed with fire, and everything in the skies will melt with heat. [13]But God made a promise to us. And we are waiting for what he promised—a new heaven and a new earth where goodness lives.

[14]Dear friends, we are waiting for this to happen. So try as hard as you can to be without sin and without fault. Try to be at peace with God. [15]Remember that we are saved because our Lord is patient. Our dear brother Paul told you the same thing when he wrote to you with the wisdom that God gave him. [16]Paul writes about this in all his letters. Sometimes there are things in Paul's letters that are hard to understand. And some people explain these things falsely. They are ignorant and weak in faith. They also falsely explain the other Scriptures.[d] But they are destroying themselves by doing that.

[17]Dear friends, you already know about this. So be careful. Do not let those evil people lead you away by the wrong they do. Be careful so that you will not fall from your strong faith. [18]But grow in the grace and knowledge of our Lord and Savior Jesus Christ. Glory be to him now and forever! Amen.

2:22 "A dog . . . up." Quotation from Proverbs 26:11.
3:10 And . . . exposed. Some Greek copies read "And everything in it will be burned up."

JOHN

1 We write you now about something that has always existed.
We have heard.
We have seen with our own eyes.
We have watched,
and we have touched with our hands.
We write to you about the Word[n] that gives life. [2]He who gives life was shown to us. We saw him, and we can give proof about it. And now we tell you that he has life that continues forever. The one who gives this life was with God the Father. God showed him to us. [3]Now we tell you what we have seen and heard because we want you to have fellowship with us. The fellowship we share together is with God the Father and his Son, Jesus Christ. [4]We write this to you so that we may be full of joy.[n]

GOD FORGIVES OUR SINS

[5]Here is the message we have heard from God and now tell to you: God is light,[n] and in him there is no darkness at all. [6]So if we say that we have fellowship with God, but we continue living in darkness, then we are liars. We do not follow the truth. [7]God is in the light. We should live in the light, too. If we live in the light, we share fellowship with each other. And when we live in the light, the blood of the death of Jesus, God's Son, is making us clean from every sin.

[8]If we say that we have no sin, we are fooling ourselves, and the truth is not in us. [9]But if we confess our sins, he will forgive our sins. We can trust God. He does what is right. He will make us clean from all the wrongs we have done. [10]If we say that we have not sinned, then we make God a liar. We do not accept God's true teaching.

JESUS IS OUR HELPER

2 My dear children, I write this letter to you so that you will not sin. But if anyone does sin, we have Jesus Christ to help us. He is the Righteous One. He defends us before God the Father. [2]Jesus died in our place to take away our sins. And Jesus is the way that all people can have their sins taken away, too.

[3]If we obey what God has told us to do, then we are sure that we truly know God. [4]If someone says, "I know God!" but does not obey God's commands, then he is a liar. The truth is not in him. [5]But if someone obeys God's teaching, then God's love has truly arrived at its goal in him. This is how we know that we are following God: [6]Whoever says that God lives in him must live as Jesus lived.

THE COMMAND TO LOVE OTHERS

[7]My dear friends, I am not writing a new command to you. It is the same command you have had since the beginning. It is the teaching you have already heard. [8]But I am writing a new command to you. This command is true; you can see its truth in Jesus and in yourselves. The darkness is passing away, and the true light is already shining.

[9]Someone says, "I am in the light."[n] But if he hates his brother, he is still in the darkness. [10]Whoever loves his brother lives in the light, and there is nothing in him that will cause him to do wrong. [11]But whoever hates his brother is in darkness. He lives in darkness and does not know where he is going. The darkness has made him blind.

[12]I write to you, dear children,
because your sins are forgiven
through Christ.

1:1 Word The Greek word is "logos," meaning any kind of communication. It could be translated "message." Here, it means Christ. Christ was the way God told people about himself.
1:4 so . . . joy Some Greek copies read "so that you may be full of joy."
1:5; 2:9 light This word is used to show what God is like. It means goodness or truth.

[13]I write to you, fathers,
>   because you know the One who
>   existed from the beginning.
> I write to you, young men,
>   because you have defeated the Evil
>   One.
[14]I write to you, children,
>   because you know the Father.
> I write to you, fathers,
>   because you know the One who
>   existed from the beginning.
> I write to you, young men,
>   because you are strong;
>   the word of God lives in you,
>   and you have defeated the Evil One.

[15]Do not love the world or the things in the world. If anyone loves the world, the love of the Father is not in him. [16]These are the evil things in the world: wanting things to please our sinful selves, wanting the sinful things we see, being too proud of the things we have. But none of those things comes from the Father. All of them come from the world. [17]The world is passing away. And everything that people want in the world is passing away. But the person who does what God wants lives forever.

REJECT THE ENEMIES OF CHRIST

[18]My dear children, the end is near! You have heard that the Enemy of Christ[d] is coming. And now many enemies of Christ are already here. So we know that the end is near. [19]Those enemies of Christ were in our group. But they left us. They did not really belong with us. If they were really part of our group, then they would have stayed with us. But they left. This shows that none of them really belonged with us.

[20]You have the gift[n] that the Holy One gave you. So you all know the truth.[n] [21]Why do I write to you? Do I write because you do not know the truth? No, I write this letter because you do know the

truth. And you know that no lie comes from the truth.

[22]So who is the liar? It is the person who says Jesus is not the Christ. A person who says Jesus is not the Christ is the enemy of Christ. He does not believe in the Father or in his Son. [23]If anyone does not believe in the Son, he does not have the Father. But whoever accepts the Son has the Father, too.

[24]Be sure that you continue to follow the teaching that you heard from the beginning. If you continue in that teaching, you will stay in the Son and in the Father. [25]And this is what the Son promised to us—life forever.

[26]I am writing this letter about those people who are trying to lead you the wrong way. [27]Christ gave you a special gift. You still have this gift in you. So you do not need any other teacher. The gift he gave you teaches you about everything. This gift is true, not false. So continue to live in Christ, as his gift taught you.

[28]Yes, my dear children, live in him. If we do this, we can be without fear on the day when Christ comes back. We will not need to hide and be ashamed when he comes. [29]You know that Christ is righteous. So you know that all who do what is right are God's children.

WE ARE GOD'S CHILDREN

3 The Father has loved us so much! He loved us so much that we are called children of God. And we really are his children. But the people in the world do not understand that we are God's children, because they have not known him. [2]Dear friends, now we are children of God. We have not yet been shown what we will be in the future. But we know that when Christ comes again, we will be like him. We will see him as he really is. [3]Christ is pure. And every person who has this hope in Christ keeps himself pure like Christ.

2:20 gift This might mean the Holy Spirit. Or it might mean teaching or truth as in verse 24.
2:20 So ... truth. Some Greek copies read "So you know all things."

[4]When a person sins, he breaks God's law. Yes, sinning is the same as living against God's law. [5]You know that Christ came to take away sins. There is no sin in Christ. [6]So the person who lives in Christ does not go on sinning. If he goes on sinning, he has never really understood Christ and has never known him.

[7]Dear children, do not let any person lead you the wrong way. Christ is righteous. To be like Christ, a person must do what is right. [8]The devil has been sinning since the beginning. Anyone who continues to sin belongs to the devil. The Son of God came for this purpose: to destroy the devil's work.

[9]When God makes someone his child, that person does not go on sinning. The new life God gave that person stays in him. So he is not able to go on sinning, because he has become a child of God. [10]So we can see who God's children are and who the devil's children are. Those who do not do what is right are not children of God. And anyone who does not love his brother is not a child of God.

WE MUST LOVE EACH OTHER

[11]This is the teaching you have heard from the beginning: We must love each other. [12]Do not be like Cain who belonged to the Evil One. Cain killed his brother. He killed his brother because the things Cain did were evil, and the things his brother did were good.

[13]Brothers, do not be surprised when the people of this world hate you. [14]We know that we have left death and have come into life. We know this because we love our brothers in Christ. Whoever does not love is still in death. [15]Everyone who hates his brother is a murderer.[n] And you know that no murderer has eternal life in him. [16]This is how we know what real love is: Jesus gave his life for us. So we should give our lives for our brothers. [17]Suppose a believer is rich enough to have all that he needs. He sees his brother in Christ who is poor and does not have what he needs. What if the believer does not help the poor brother? Then the believer does not have God's love in his heart. [18]My children, our love should not be only words and talk. Our love must be true love. And we should show that love by what we do.

[19-20]This is the way we know that we belong to the way of truth. When our hearts make us feel guilty, we can still have peace before God. God is greater than our hearts, and he knows everything. [21]My dear friends, if we do not feel that we are doing wrong, we can be without fear when we come to God. [22]And God gives us the things we ask for. We receive these things because we obey God's commands, and we do what pleases him. [23]This is what God commands: that we believe in his Son, Jesus Christ, and that we love each other, just as he commanded. [24]The person who obeys God's commands lives in God. And God lives in him. How do we know that God lives in us? We know because of the Spirit[d] whom God gave us.

WARNING AGAINST FALSE TEACHERS

4 My dear friends, many false prophets[d] are in the world now. So do not believe every spirit. But test the spirits to see if they are from God. [2]This is how you can know God's Spirit:[d] One spirit says, "I believe that Jesus is the Christ who came to earth and became a man." That Spirit is from God. [3]Another spirit refuses to say this about Jesus. That spirit is not from God but is the spirit of the Enemy of Christ. You have heard that the Enemy of Christ is coming. And now he is already in the world.

[4]My dear children, you belong to God. So you have defeated them because God's

---

3:15 Everyone . . . murderer. If a person hates his brother in Christ, then in his mind he has killed his brother. Jesus taught about this sin to his followers (Matthew 5:21-26).

Spirit, who is in you, is greater than the devil, who is in the world. [5]And they belong to the world. What they say is from the world, and the world listens to them. [6]But we are from God, and those who know God listen to us. But those who are not from God do not listen to us. That is how we know the Spirit that is true and the spirit that is false.

LOVE COMES FROM GOD

[7]Dear friends, we should love each other, because love comes from God. The person who loves has become God's child and knows God. [8]Whoever does not love does not know God, because God is love. [9]This is how God showed his love to us: He sent his only Son into the world to give us life through him. [10]True love is God's love for us, not our love for God. God sent his Son to die in our place to take away our sins.

[11]That is how much God loved us, dear friends! So we also must love each other. [12]No one has ever seen God. But if we love each other, God lives in us. If we love each other, God's love has reached its goal. It is made perfect in us.

[13]We know that we live in God and God lives in us. We know this because God gave us his Spirit.[d] [14]We have seen that the Father sent his Son to be the Savior of the world. That is what we teach. [15]If someone says, "I believe that Jesus is the Son of God," then God lives in him. And he lives in God. [16]And so we know the love that God has for us, and we trust that love.

God is love. Whoever lives in love lives in God, and God lives in him. [17]If God's love is made perfect in us, then we can be without fear on the day God judges us. We will be without fear, because in this world we are like him. [18]Where God's love is,

there is no fear, because God's perfect love takes away fear. It is punishment that makes a person fear. So love is not made perfect in the person who has fear.

[19]We love because God first loved us. [20]If someone says, "I love God," but hates his brother, he is a liar. He can see his brother, but he hates him. So he cannot love God, whom he has never seen. [21]And God gave us this command: Whoever loves God must also love his brother.

FAITH IN THE SON OF GOD

5 Everyone who believes that Jesus is the Christ[d] is God's child. The person who loves the Father also loves the Father's children. [2]How do we know that we love God's children? We know because we love God and we obey his commands. [3]Loving God means obeying his commands. And God's commands are not too hard for us. [4]Everyone who is a child of God has the power to win against the world. It is our faith that wins the victory against the world. [5]So the one who conquers the world is the person who believes that Jesus is the Son of God.

[6]Jesus Christ is the One who came with water[n] and with blood.[n] He did not come by water only. He came by both water and blood. And the Spirit[d] says that this is true. The Spirit is the truth. [7]So there are three witnesses:[n] [8]the Spirit, the water, and the blood. These three witnesses agree. [9]We believe people when they say something is true. But what God says is more important. And he has told us the truth about his own Son. [10]Anyone who believes in the Son of God has the truth that God told us. Anyone who does not believe makes God a liar. He does not believe what God told us about his Son. [11]This is what God

---

5:6 water This probably means the water of Jesus' baptism.
5:6 blood This probably means the blood of Jesus' death.
5:7 So . . . witnesses A few very late Greek copies and the Latin Vulgate continue, "in heaven: the Father, the Word, and the Holy Spirit, and these three witnesses agree. [8]And there are three witnesses on earth."

told us: God has given us eternal life, and this life is in his Son. [12]Whoever has the Son has life. But the person who does not have the Son of God does not have life.

WE HAVE ETERNAL LIFE NOW

[13]I write this letter to you who believe in the Son of God. I write so that you will know that you have eternal life now. [14]We can come to God with no doubts. This means that when we ask God for things (and those things agree with what God wants for us), then God cares about what we say. [15]God listens to us every time we ask him. So we know that he gives us the things that we ask from him.

[16]Suppose someone sees his brother in Christ sinning (sin that does not lead to eternal death). That person should pray for his brother who is sinning. Then God will give the brother life. I am talking about people whose sin does not lead to eternal death. There is sin that leads to death. I do not mean that a person should pray about that sin. [17]Doing wrong is always sin. But there is sin that does not lead to eternal death.

[18]We know that anyone who is God's child does not continue to sin. The Son of God keeps him safe, and the Evil One cannot hurt him. [19]We know that we belong to God. But the Evil One controls the whole world. [20]And we know that the Son of God has come and has given us understanding. Now we can know God, the One who is true. And our lives are in that true God and in his Son, Jesus Christ. He is the true God, and he is eternal life. [21]So, dear children, keep yourselves away from false gods.

[1]From the Elder.[n]

To the chosen lady[n] and to her children: I love all of you in the truth.[n] Also, all those who know the truth love you. [2]We love you because of the truth—the truth that lives in us and will be with us forever.

[3]Grace, mercy, and peace will be with us from God the Father and from his Son, Jesus Christ. And may we have these blessings in truth and love.

[4]I was very happy to learn about some of your children. I am happy that they are following the way of truth, as the Father commanded us. [5]And now, dear lady, I tell you: We should all love each other. This is not a new command. It is the same command we have had from the beginning. [6]And loving means living the way he commanded us to live. And God's command is this: that you live a life of love. You have heard this command from the beginning.

[7]Many false teachers are in the world now. They refuse to say that Jesus Christ came to earth and became a man. Anyone who refuses to say this is a false teacher and an enemy of Christ. [8]Be careful! Do not lose the reward that you[n] have worked for. Be careful, so that you will receive your full reward.

[9]A person must continue to follow only the teaching of Christ. If he goes beyond Christ's teaching, then he does not have God. But if he continues following the teaching of Christ, then he has both the Father and the Son. [10]If someone comes to you, but does not bring this teaching, then do not accept him into your house. Do not welcome him. [11]If you accept him, you are helping him with his evil work.

[12]I have much to say to you, but I do not want to use paper and ink. Instead, I hope to come visit you. Then we can be together and talk. That will make us very happy. [13]The children of your chosen sister[n] send you their love.

---

1 **Elder** This is probably John the apostle. "Elder" means an older man. It can also mean a special leader in the church (as in Titus 1:5).

1 **lady** This might mean a woman. Or, in this letter, it might mean a church. If it is a church, then "her children" would be the people of the church.

1 **truth** The truth or "Good News" about Jesus Christ that joins all believers together.

8 **you** Some Greek copies read "we."

13 **sister** Sister of the "lady" in verse 1. This might be another woman or another church.

JOHN

[1]From the Elder.[n]

To my dear friend Gaius whom I love in the truth:[n]

[2]My dear friend, I know your soul is doing well. I pray that you are doing fine in every way and that your health is good. [3]Some brothers in Christ came and told me about the truth in your life. They said that you are following the way of truth. This made me very happy. [4]It always gives me the greatest joy when I hear that my children are following the way of truth.

[5]My dear friend, it is good that you continue to help the brothers. You are helping those that you do not even know! [6]These brothers told the church about the love you have. Please help them to continue their trip. Help them in a way that will please God. [7]They started out on their trip to serve Christ. They did not accept any help from those who are not believers. [8]So we should help these brothers. And when we do, we share in their work for the truth.

[9]I wrote a letter to the church. But Diotrephes will not listen to what we say. He always wants to be their leader. [10]When I come, I will talk about what Diotrephes is doing. He lies and says evil things about us. But that is not all he does. He refuses to help those who are working to serve Christ. He also stops those who want to help the brothers and puts them out of the church.

[11]My dear friend, do not follow what is bad; follow what is good. He who does what is good is from God. But he who does evil has never known God.

[12]Everyone says good things about Demetrius. And the truth agrees with what they say. Also, we say good about him. And you know that what we say is true.

[13]I have many things I want to tell you, but I do not want to use pen and ink. [14]I hope to visit you soon. Then we can be together and talk. [15]Peace to you. The friends here with me send their love. Please give our love to each one of the friends there.

---

1 **Elder** This is probably John the apostle. "Elder" means an older man. It can also mean a special leader in the church (as in Titus 1:5).

1 **truth** The truth or "Good News" about Jesus Christ that joins all believers together.

JUDE

¹From Jude, a servant of Jesus Christ and a brother of James.

To all who have been called by God. God the Father loves you, and you have been kept safe in Jesus Christ. ²All mercy, peace, and love be yours.

GOD WILL PUNISH SINNERS

³Dear friends, I wanted very much to write to you about the salvation we all share together. But I felt the need to write to you about something else: I want to encourage you to fight hard for the faith that God gave his holy people. God gave this faith once, and it is good for all time. ⁴Some people have secretly entered your group. They have already been judged guilty for the things they are doing. Long ago the prophets[d] wrote about these people. They are against God. They have used the grace of our God in the wrong way—to do sinful things. They refuse to accept Jesus Christ, our only Master and Lord.

⁵I want to remind you of some things that you already know: Remember that the Lord[n] saved his people by bringing them out of the land of Egypt. But later the Lord destroyed all those who did not believe. ⁶And remember the angels who had power but did not keep it. They left their own home. So the Lord has kept these angels in darkness. They are bound with everlasting chains, to be judged on the great day. ⁷Also remember the cities of Sodom and Gomorrah[n] and the other towns around them. They acted as the angels who did not obey God. Their towns were full of sexual sin and men having sexual relations with men. They suffer the punishment of eternal fire, as an example for all to see.

⁸It is the same with these people who have entered your group. They are guided by dreams. They make themselves dirty with sin. They reject God's authority and say bad things against the glorious angels. ⁹Not even the archangel[n] Michael did this. He argued with the devil about who would have the body of Moses. Michael did not dare to accuse the devil with insults. He said, "The Lord punish you." ¹⁰But these people say bad things about what they do not understand. They do understand some things. But they understand them not by thinking, but by feeling, the way dumb animals understand things. And these are the very things that destroy them. ¹¹It will be bad for them. They have followed the way that Cain went. To make money, they have given themselves to doing the wrong that Balaam did. They have fought against God as Korah did. And like Korah, they will be destroyed. ¹²They are like dirty spots in the special meals you share together. They eat with you and have no fear. They take care of only themselves. They are clouds without rain. The wind blows them around. They are trees that have no fruit when it is time and are pulled out of the ground. So they are dead two times. ¹³They are like wild waves in the sea. These people do shameful things in the same way waves make foam. They are like stars that wander in the sky. A place in the blackest darkness has been kept for them forever.

¹⁴Enoch, the seventh descendant[d] from Adam, said this about these people: "Look, the Lord is coming with thousands and thousands of his holy angels. ¹⁵The Lord will judge every person. He is coming to judge everyone and to punish

---

5 the Lord Some Greek copies read "Jesus."
7 Sodom and Gomorrah Two cities that God destroyed because the people were so evil.
9 archangel The leader among God's angels or messengers.

all who are against God. He will punish them for all the evil they have done against him. And he will punish the sinners who are against God. He will punish them for all the evil things they have said against him."

[16]These people always complain and blame others. They always do the evil things they want to do. They brag about themselves. The only reason they say good things about other people is to get what they want.

A WARNING AND THINGS TO DO

[17]Dear friends, remember what the apostles[d] of our Lord Jesus Christ said before. [18]They said to you, "In the last times there will be people who laugh about God. They will do only what they want to do—things that are against God." [19]These are the people who divide you. They do only what their sinful selves want. They do not have the Spirit.[d]

[20]But dear friends, use your most holy faith to build yourselves up strong. Pray with the Holy Spirit. [21]Keep yourselves in God's love. Wait for the Lord Jesus Christ with his mercy to give you life forever.

[22]Show mercy to people who have doubts. [23]Save them. Take them out of the fire. Show mercy mixed with fear to others. Hate even their clothes which are dirty from sin.

PRAISE GOD

[24]God is strong and can help you not to fall. He can bring you before his glory without any wrong in you and give you great joy. [25]He is the only God. He is the One who saves us. To him be glory, greatness, power, and authority through Jesus Christ our Lord for all time past, now, and forever. Amen.

THE REVELATION
OF JESUS CHRIST

JOHN TELLS ABOUT THIS BOOK

1 This is the revelation[n] of Jesus Christ. God gave this revelation to Jesus, to show his servants what must soon happen. And Jesus sent his angel to show it to his servant John. [2]John has told everything that he has seen. It is the truth that Jesus Christ told him; it is the message from God. [3]The one who reads the words of God's message is happy. And the people who hear this message and do what is written in it are happy. The time is near when all of this will happen.

JESUS' MESSAGE TO THE CHURCHES

[4]From John,

To the seven churches in Asia:

Grace and peace to you from the One who is and was and is coming, and from the seven spirits before his throne, [5]and from Jesus Christ. Jesus is the faithful witness. He is first among those raised from death. He is the ruler of the kings of the earth.

He is the One who loves us. And he is the One who made us free from our sins with the blood of his death. [6]He made us to be a kingdom of priests who serve God his Father. To Jesus Christ be glory and power forever and ever! Amen.

[7]Look, Jesus is coming with the clouds! Everyone will see him, even those who stabbed him. And all peoples of the earth will cry loudly because of him. Yes, this will happen! Amen.

[8]The Lord God says, "I am the Alpha and the Omega.[n] I am the One who is and was and is coming. I am the All-Powerful."

[9]I am John, and I am your brother in Christ. We are together in Jesus, and we share in these things: in suffering, in the kingdom, and in patience. I was on the island of Patmos[n] because I had preached God's message and the truth about Jesus. [10]On the Lord's day the Spirit[d] took control of me. I heard a loud voice behind me that sounded like a trumpet. [11]The voice said, "Write what you see and send that book to the seven churches: to Ephesus, Smyrna, Pergamum, Thyatira, Sardis, Philadelphia, and Laodicea."

[12]I turned to see who was talking to me. When I turned, I saw seven golden lampstands. [13]I saw someone among the lampstands who was "like a Son of Man."[n] He was dressed in a long robe. He had a gold band around his chest. [14]His head and hair were white like wool, as white as snow. His eyes were like flames of fire. [15]His feet were like bronze that glows hot in a furnace. His voice was like the noise of flooding water. [16]He held seven stars in his right hand. A sharp two-edged sword came out of his mouth. He looked like the sun shining at its brightest time.

[17]When I saw him, I fell down at his feet like a dead man. He put his right hand on me and said, "Do not be afraid! I am the First and the Last. [18]I am the One who lives. I was dead, but look: I am alive forever and ever! And I hold the keys of death and where the dead are. [19]So write the things you see, what is now and what will happen later. [20]Here is the hidden meaning of the seven stars that you saw in my right hand and the seven golden lampstands that you saw: The seven lampstands are the seven churches. The seven stars are the angels of the seven churches.

1:1 **revelation** A making known of truth that has been hidden.
1:8 **the Alpha and the Omega** The first and last letters in the Greek alphabet. This means "the beginning and the end."
1:9 **Patmos** A small island in the Aegean Sea, near the coast of Asia Minor (modern Turkey).
1:13 **"like ... Man"** "Son of Man" is a name Jesus called himself. It showed he was God's Son, but he was also a man. See dictionary.

TO THE CHURCH IN EPHESUS

2 "Write this to the angel of the church in Ephesus:

"The One who holds the seven stars in his right hand and walks among the seven golden lampstands says this to you. [2]I know what you do. You work hard, and you never give up. I know that you do not accept evil people. You have tested those who say that they are apostles[d] but really are not. You found that they are liars. [3]You continue to serve me. You have suffered troubles for my name, and you have not given up.

[4]"But I have this against you: You have left the love you had in the beginning. [5]So remember where you were before you fell. Change your hearts and do what you did at first. If you do not change, I will come to you. I will take away your lampstand from its place. [6]But there is something you do that is right: You hate what the Nicolaitans[n] do, as much as I.

[7]"Every person who has ears should listen to what the Spirit[d] says to the churches. To him who wins the victory I will give the right to eat the fruit from the tree of life. This tree is in the garden of God.

TO THE CHURCH IN SMYRNA

[8]"Write this to the angel of the church in Smyrna:

"The One who is the First and the Last says this to you. He is the One who died and came to life again. [9]I know your troubles. I know that you are poor, but really you are rich! I know the bad things that some people say about you. They say they are Jews, but they are not true Jews. They are a synagogue[d] that belongs to Satan. [10]Do not be afraid of what will happen to you. I tell you, the devil will put some of you in prison to test you. You will suffer for ten days. But be faithful, even if you have to die. If you are faithful, I will give you the crown of life.

[11]"Everyone who has ears should listen to what the Spirit[d] says to the churches. He who wins the victory will not be hurt by the second death.

TO THE CHURCH IN PERGAMUM

[12]"Write this to the angel of the church in Pergamum:

"The One who has the sharp two-edged sword says this to you. [13]I know where you live. You live where Satan has his throne. But you are true to me. You did not refuse to tell about your faith in me even during the time of Antipas. Antipas was my faithful witness who was killed in your city. Your city is where Satan lives.

[14]"But I have a few things against you: You have some there who follow the teaching of Balaam. Balaam taught Balak how to cause the people of Israel to sin. They sinned by eating food offered to idols and by taking part in sexual sins. [15]You also have some who follow the teaching of the Nicolaitans.[n] [16]So change your hearts and lives! If you do not, I will come to you quickly and fight against them with the sword that comes out of my mouth.

[17]"Everyone who has ears should listen to what the Spirit[d] says to the churches!

"I will give the hidden manna[d] to everyone who wins the victory. I will also give him a white stone with a new name written on it. No one knows this new name except the one who receives it.

TO THE CHURCH IN THYATIRA

[18]"Write this to the angel of the church in Thyatira:

"The Son of God is saying these things. He is the One who has eyes that blaze like fire and feet like shining bronze. He says this to you: [19]I know what you do. I know about your love,

---

2:6, 15 **Nicolaitans** This is the name of a religious group that followed false beliefs and ideas.

your faith, your service, and your patience. I know that you are doing more now than you did at first. [20]But I have this against you: You let that woman Jezebel do what she wants. She says that she is a prophetess.[d] But she is leading my people away with her teaching. Jezebel leads them to take part in sexual sins and to eat food that is offered to idols. [21]I have given her time to change her heart and turn away from her sin. But she does not want to change. [22]And so I will throw her on a bed of suffering. And all those who take part in adultery[d] with her will suffer greatly. I will do this now if they do not turn away from the wrongs she does. [23]I will also kill her followers. Then all the churches will know that I am the One who knows what people feel and think. And I will repay each of you for what you have done.

[24]"But others of you in Thyatira have not followed her teaching. You have not learned what some call Satan's deep secrets. This is what I say to you: I will not put any other load on you. [25]Only continue the way you are until I come.

[26]"I will give power to everyone who wins the victory and continues to the end to do what I want. I will give him power over the nations:
[27]'You will make them obey you by
    punishing them with an iron rod.
You will break them into pieces like
    pottery.'   Psalm 2:9
[28]This is the same power I received from my Father. I will also give him the morning star. [29]Everyone who has ears should listen to what the Spirit[d] says to the churches.

TO THE CHURCH IN SARDIS

3 "Write this to the angel of the church in Sardis:

"The One who has the seven spirits and the seven stars says this to you. I know what you do. People say that you are alive, but really you are dead. [2]Wake up! Make yourselves stronger while you still have something left and before it dies completely. I have found that what you are doing is not good enough for my God. [3]So do not forget what you have received and heard. Obey it. Change your hearts and lives! You must wake up, or I will come to you and surprise you like a thief. And you will not know when I will come. [4]But you have a few there in Sardis who have kept themselves clean. They will walk with me. They will wear white clothes, because they are worthy. [5]He who wins the victory will be dressed in white clothes like them. I will not take away his name from the book of life. I will say that he belongs to me before my Father and before his angels. [6]Everyone who has ears should listen to what the Spirit[d] says to the churches.

TO THE CHURCH IN PHILADELPHIA

[7]"Write this to the angel of the church in Philadelphia:

"The One who is holy and true says this to you. He holds the key of David. When he opens something, it cannot be closed. And when he closes something, it cannot be opened. [8]I know what you do. I have put an open door before you, and no one can close it. I know that you have a little strength. But you have followed my teaching. And you were not afraid to speak my name. [9]Listen! There is a synagogue[d] that belongs to Satan. Those in this synagogue say they are Jews, but they are liars. They are not true Jews. I will make them come before you and bow at your feet. They will know that I have loved you. [10]You have followed my teaching about not giving up. So I will keep you from the time of trouble that will come to the whole world. This trouble will test those who live on earth.

[11]"I am coming soon. Continue the way you are now. Then no one will take away your crown. [12]I will make the one who wins the victory a pillar in the temple of my God. He will never have to leave it. I

will write on him the name of my God and the name of the city of my God. This city is the new Jerusalem.[n] It comes down out of heaven from my God. I will also write on him my new name. [13]Every person who has ears should listen to what the Spirit[d] says to the churches.

TO THE CHURCH IN LAODICEA

[14]"Write this to the angel of the church in Laodicea:

"The Amen[n] is the One who is the faithful and true witness. He is the ruler of all that God has made. He says this to you: [15]I know what you do. You are not hot or cold. I wish that you were hot or cold! [16]But you are only warm—not hot, not cold. So I am ready to spit you out of my mouth. [17]You say you are rich. You think you have become wealthy and do not need anything. But you do not know that you are really miserable, pitiful, poor, blind, and naked. [18]I advise you to buy gold from me—gold made pure in fire. Then you can be truly rich. Buy from me clothes that are white. Then you can cover your shameful nakedness. Buy from me medicine to put on your eyes. Then you can truly see.

[19]"I correct and punish those whom I love. So be eager to do right. Change your hearts and lives. [20]Here I am! I stand at the door and knock. If anyone hears my voice and opens the door, I will come in and eat with him. And he will eat with me.

[21]"He who wins the victory will sit with me on my throne. It was the same with me. I won the victory and sat down with my Father on his throne. [22]Everyone who has ears should listen to what the Spirit[d] says to the churches."

JOHN SEES HEAVEN

4 After this I looked, and there before me was an open door in heaven.

And I heard the same voice that spoke to me before. It was the voice that sounded like a trumpet. The voice said, "Come up here, and I will show you what must happen after this." [2]Then the Spirit[d] took control of me. There before me was a throne in heaven. Someone was sitting on the throne. [3]The One who sat on the throne looked like precious stones, like jasper and carnelian. All around the throne was a rainbow the color of an emerald. [4]Around the throne there were 24 other thrones. There were 24 elders[n] sitting on the 24 thrones. The elders were dressed in white, and they had golden crowns on their heads. [5]Lightning flashes and noises of thunder came from the throne. Before the throne there were seven lamps burning. These lamps are the seven spirits of God. [6]Also before the throne there was something that looked like a sea of glass. It was clear like crystal.

Around the throne, on each side, there were four living things. These living things had eyes all over them, in front and in back. [7]The first living thing was like a lion. The second was like a calf. The third had a face like a man. The fourth was like a flying eagle. [8]Each of these four living things had six wings. The living things were covered all over with eyes, inside and out. Day and night they never stop saying:

"Holy, holy, holy is the Lord God
        All-Powerful.

    He was, he is, and he is coming."

[9]These living things give glory and honor and thanks to the One who sits on the throne. He is the One who lives forever and ever. And every time the living things do this, [10]the 24 elders bow down before the One who sits on the throne. The elders worship him who lives forever and ever. They put their crowns down before the throne and say:

3:12 **Jerusalem** This name is used to mean the spiritual city God built for his people.
3:14 **Amen** Used here as a name for Jesus, it means to agree fully that something is true.
4:4 **24 elders** Elder means "older." Here the elders probably represent God's people.

11"Our Lord and God! You are worthy
to receive glory and honor and
power.
You made all things.
Everything existed and was made
because you wanted it."

5 Then I saw a scroll in the right hand
of the One sitting on the throne. The
scroll had writing on both sides. It was
kept closed with seven seals. ²And I saw
a powerful angel. He called in a loud
voice, "Who is worthy to break the seals
and open the scroll?" ³But there was no
one in heaven or on earth or under the
earth who could open the scroll or look
inside it. ⁴I cried and cried because there
was no one who was worthy to open the
scroll or look inside. ⁵But one of the elders said to me, "Do not cry! The Lion*ⁿ*
from the tribe*ᵈ* of Judah has won the victory. He is David's descendant.*ᵈ* He is able
to open the scroll and its seven seals."

⁶Then I saw a Lamb standing in the
center of the throne with the four living
things around it. The elders were also
around the Lamb. The Lamb looked as if
he had been killed. He had seven horns
and seven eyes. These are the seven
spirits of God that were sent into all the
world. ⁷The Lamb came and took the
scroll from the right hand of the One sitting on the throne. ⁸After he took the
scroll, the four living things and the 24
elders bowed down before the Lamb.
Each one of them had a harp. Also, they
were holding golden bowls full of incense.*ᵈ* These bowls of incense are the
prayers of God's holy people. ⁹And they
all sang a new song to the Lamb:

"You are worthy to take the scroll
and to open its seals,
because you were killed;
and with the blood of your death
you bought men for God
from every tribe, language, people,
and nation.

10You made them to be a kingdom of
priests for our God.
And they will rule on the earth."

11Then I looked, and I heard the voices
of many angels. The angels were around
the throne, the four living things, and
the elders. There were thousands and
thousands of angels—there were 10,000
times 10,000. ¹²The angels said in a loud
voice:

"The Lamb who was killed is worthy
to receive power, wealth, wisdom and
strength,
honor, glory, and praise!"

13Then I heard every living thing in
heaven and on earth and under the earth
and in the sea. I heard every thing in all
these places, saying:

"All praise and honor and glory and
power
forever and ever
to the One who sits on the throne
and to the Lamb!"

14The four living things said, "Amen!"
And the elders bowed down and worshiped.

6 Then I watched while the Lamb
opened the first of the seven seals. I
heard one of the four living things speak
with a voice like thunder. It said,
"Come!" ²I looked and there before me
was a white horse. The rider on the horse
held a bow, and he was given a crown.
And he rode out, defeating the enemy.
He rode out to win the victory.

³The Lamb opened the second seal.
Then I heard the second living thing say,
"Come!" ⁴Then another horse came out.
This was a red horse. Its rider was given
power to take away peace from the
earth. He was given power to make
people kill each other. And he was given
a big sword.

⁵The Lamb opened the third seal.
Then I heard the third living thing say,
"Come!" I looked, and there before me

5:5 **Lion** Here refers to Christ.

was a black horse. Its rider held a pair of scales in his hand. ⁶Then I heard something that sounded like a voice. It came from where the four living things were. The voice said, "A quart of wheat for a day's pay. And three quarts of barley for a day's pay. And do not damage the olive oil and wine!"

⁷The Lamb opened the fourth seal. Then I heard the voice of the fourth living thing say, "Come!" ⁸I looked, and there before me was a pale horse. Its rider was named death. Hades[n] was following close behind him. They were given power over a fourth of the earth. They were given power to kill people by war, by starving them, by disease, and by the wild animals of the earth.

⁹The Lamb opened the fifth seal. Then I saw some souls under the altar. They were the souls of those who had been killed because they were faithful to God's message and to the truth they had received. ¹⁰These souls shouted in a loud voice, "Holy and true Lord, how long until you judge the people of the earth and punish them for killing us?" ¹¹Then each one of these souls was given a white robe. They were told to wait a short time longer. There were still some of their brothers in the service of Christ who must be killed as they were. They were told to wait until all of this killing was finished.

¹²Then I watched while the Lamb opened the sixth seal. There was a great earthquake. The sun became black like rough black cloth. The full moon became red like blood. ¹³The stars in the sky fell to the earth like figs falling from a fig tree when the wind blows. ¹⁴The sky disappeared. It was rolled up like a scroll. And every mountain and island was moved from its place.

¹⁵Then all people hid in caves and behind the rocks on the mountains. There were the kings of the earth, the rulers, the generals, the rich people and the powerful people. Everyone, slave and free, hid himself. ¹⁶They called to the mountains and the rocks, "Fall on us. Hide us from the face of the One who sits on the throne. Hide us from the anger of the Lamb! ¹⁷The great day for their anger has come. Who can stand against it?"

THE 144,000 PEOPLE OF ISRAEL

7 After this I saw four angels standing at the four corners of the earth. The angels were holding the four winds of the earth. They were stopping the wind from blowing on the land or on the sea or on any tree. ²Then I saw another angel coming from the east. This angel had the seal of the living God. He called out in a loud voice to the four angels. These were the four angels that God had given power to harm the earth and the sea. He said to the four angels, ³"Do not harm the land or the sea or the trees before we put the sign on the people who serve our God. We must put the sign on their foreheads." ⁴Then I heard how many people were marked with the sign. There were 144,000. They were from every tribe[d] of the people of Israel.

⁵From the tribe of Judah 12,000 were marked with the sign,

from the tribe of Reuben 12,000,
from the tribe of Gad 12,000,
⁶from the tribe of Asher 12,000,
from the tribe of Naphtali 12,000,
from the tribe of Manasseh 12,000,
⁷from the tribe of Simeon 12,000,
from the tribe of Levi 12,000,
from the tribe of Issachar 12,000,
⁸from the tribe of Zebulun 12,000,
from the tribe of Joseph 12,000,
from the tribe of Benjamin 12,000.

THE GREAT CROWD

⁹Then I looked, and there was a great number of people. There were so many

---

6:8 **Hades** The unseen world where the dead are.

people that no one could count them. They were from every nation, tribe,*d* people, and language of the earth. They were all standing before the throne and before the Lamb. They wore white robes and had palm branches in their hands. [10]They were shouting in a loud voice, "Salvation belongs to our God, who sits on the throne, and to the Lamb." [11]The elders*n* and the four living things were there. All the angels were standing around them and the throne. The angels bowed down on their faces before the throne and worshiped God. [12]They were saying, "Amen! Praise, glory, wisdom, thanks, honor, power, and strength belong to our God forever and ever. Amen!"

[13]Then one of the elders asked me, "Who are these people in white robes? Where did they come from?"

[14]I answered, "You know who they are, sir."

And the elder said, "These are the people who have come out of the great suffering. They have washed their robes*n* with the blood of the Lamb. Now they are clean and white. [15]And they are before the throne of God. They worship God day and night in his temple. And the One who sits on the throne will protect them. [16]Those people will never be hungry again. They will never be thirsty again. The sun will not hurt them. No heat will burn them. [17]For the Lamb at the center of the throne will be their shepherd. He will lead them to springs of water that give life. And God will wipe away every tear from their eyes."

THE SEVENTH SEAL

8 The Lamb opened the seventh seal. Then there was silence in heaven for about half an hour. [2]And I saw the seven angels who stand before God. They were given seven trumpets.

[3]Another angel came and stood at the altar. This angel had a golden pan for incense.*d* The angel was given much incense to offer with the prayers of all God's holy people. The angel put this offering on the golden altar before the throne. [4]The smoke from the incense went up from the angel's hand to God. It went up with the prayers of God's people. [5]Then the angel filled the incense pan with fire from the altar and threw it on the earth. There were flashes of lightning, thunder and loud noises, and an earthquake.

THE SEVEN ANGELS AND TRUMPETS

[6]Then the seven angels who had the seven trumpets prepared to blow them.

[7]The first angel blew his trumpet. Then hail and fire mixed with blood was poured down on the earth. And a third of the earth and all the green grass and a third of the trees were burned up.

[8]The second angel blew his trumpet. Then something that looked like a big mountain burning with fire was thrown into the sea. And a third of the sea became blood. [9]And a third of the living things in the sea died, and a third of the ships were destroyed.

[10]The third angel blew his trumpet. Then a large star, burning like a torch, fell from the sky. It fell on a third of the rivers and on the springs of water. [11]The name of the star is Wormwood.*n* And a third of all the water became bitter. Many people died from drinking the water that was bitter.

[12]The fourth angel blew his trumpet. Then a third of the sun and a third of the moon and a third of the stars were hit. So a third of them became dark. A third of the day was without light.

[13]While I watched, I heard an eagle that was flying high in the air. The eagle said

---

7:11 **elders** Elder means "older." Here the elders probably represent God's people.
7:14 **washed their robes** This means they believed in Jesus so that their sins could be forgiven by Christ's blood.
8:11 **Wormwood** Name of a very bitter plant, used here to give the idea of bitter sorrow.

with a loud voice, "Trouble! Trouble! Trouble for those who live on the earth! The trouble will begin with the sounds of the trumpets that the other three angels are about to blow."

9 Then the fifth angel blew his trumpet. And I saw a star fall from the sky to the earth. The star was given the key to the deep hole that leads down to the bottomless pit. ²Then it opened the bottomless pit. Smoke came up from the hole like smoke from a big furnace. The sun and sky became dark because of the smoke from the hole. ³Then locusts*ᵈ* came down to the earth out of the smoke. They were given the power to sting like scorpions.*ⁿ* ⁴They were told not to harm the grass on the earth or any plant or tree. They could harm only the people who did not have the sign of God on their foreheads. ⁵These locusts were given the power to cause pain to the people for five months. But they were not given the power to kill anyone. And the pain they felt was like the pain that a scorpion gives when it stings a person. ⁶During those days people will look for a way to die, but they will not find it. They will want to die, but death will run away from them.

⁷The locusts looked like horses prepared for battle. On their heads they wore things that looked like crowns of gold. Their faces looked like human faces. ⁸Their hair was like women's hair, and their teeth were like lions' teeth. ⁹Their chests looked like iron breastplates. The sound their wings made was like the noise of many horses and chariots hurrying into battle. ¹⁰The locusts had tails with stingers like scorpions. The power they had to hurt people for five months was in their tails. ¹¹The locusts had a king who was the angel of the bottomless pit. His name in the Hebrew language is Abaddon. In the Greek language his name is Apollyon.*ⁿ*

¹²The first great trouble is past. There are still two other great troubles that will come.

¹³The sixth angel blew his trumpet. Then I heard a voice coming from the horns on the golden altar that is before God. ¹⁴The voice said to the sixth angel who had the trumpet, "Free the four angels who are tied at the great river Euphrates." ¹⁵These four angels had been kept ready for this hour and day and month and year. They were freed to kill a third of all people on the earth. ¹⁶I heard how many troops on horses were in their army. There were 200,000,000.

¹⁷In my vision I saw the horses and their riders. They looked like this: They had breastplates that were fiery red, dark blue, and yellow like sulfur. The heads of the horses looked like heads of lions. The horses had fire, smoke, and sulfur coming out of their mouths. ¹⁸A third of all the people on earth were killed by these three terrible things coming out of the horses' mouths: the fire, the smoke, and the sulfur. ¹⁹The horses' power was in their mouths and also in their tails. Their tails were like snakes that have heads to bite and hurt people.

²⁰The other people on the earth were not killed by these terrible things. But they still did not change their hearts and turn away from what they had made with their own hands. They did not stop worshiping demons*ᵈ* and idols made of gold, silver, bronze, stone, and wood— things that cannot see or hear or walk. ²¹These people did not change their hearts and turn away from murder or evil magic, from their sexual sins or stealing.

THE ANGEL AND THE LITTLE SCROLL

10 Then I saw another powerful angel coming down from heaven.

9:3 **scorpions** A scorpion is an insect that stings with a bad poison.
9:11 **Abaddon ... Apollyon** Both names mean "Destroyer."

He was dressed in a cloud and had a rainbow around his head. His face was like the sun, and his legs were like poles of fire. [2]The angel was holding a small scroll open in his hand. He put his right foot on the sea and his left foot on the land. [3]He shouted loudly like the roaring of a lion. When he shouted, the voices of seven thunders spoke. [4]The seven thunders spoke, and I started to write. But then I heard a voice from heaven. The voice said, "Do not write what the seven thunders said. Keep these things secret."

[5]Then the angel I saw standing on the sea and on the land raised his right hand to heaven. [6]He made a promise by the power of the One who lives forever and ever. He is the One who made the skies and all that is in them. He made the earth and all that is in it, and he made the sea and all that is in it. The angel said, "There will be no more waiting! [7]In the days when the seventh angel is ready to blow his trumpet, God's secret plan will be finished. This plan is the Good News[d] God told to his servants, the prophets."[d]

[8]Then I heard the same voice from heaven again. The voice said to me, "Go and take the open scroll that is in the angel's hand. This is the angel that is standing on the sea and on the land."

[9]So I went to the angel and asked him to give me the little scroll. He said to me, "Take the scroll and eat it. It will be sour in your stomach. But in your mouth it will be sweet as honey." [10]So I took the little scroll from the angel's hand and I ate it. In my mouth it tasted sweet as honey. But after I ate it, it was sour in my stomach. [11]Then I was told, "You must prophesy[d] again about many peoples, nations, languages, and kings."

THE TWO WITNESSES

11 Then I was given a measuring stick like a rod. I was told, "Go and measure the temple[n] of God and the altar, and count the number of people worshiping there. [2]But do not measure the yard outside the temple. Leave it alone. It has been given to the people who are not Jews. They will walk on the holy city for 42 months. [3]And I will give power to my two witnesses to prophesy[d] for 1,260 days. They will be dressed in rough cloth to show how sad they are."

[4]These two witnesses are the two olive trees and the two lampstands that stand before the Lord of the earth. [5]If anyone tries to hurt the witnesses, fire comes from their mouths and kills their enemies. Anyone who tries to hurt them will die like this. [6]These witnesses have the power to stop the sky from raining during the time they are prophesying. They have power to make the waters become blood. They have power to send every kind of trouble to the earth. They can do this as many times as they want.

[7]When the two witnesses have finished telling their message, the beast will fight against them. This is the beast that comes up from the bottomless pit. He will defeat them and kill them. [8]The bodies of the two witnesses will lie in the street of the great city. This city is named Sodom[n] and Egypt. These names for the city have a special meaning. It is the city where the Lord was killed. [9]Men from every race of people, tribe,[d] language, and nation will look at the bodies of the two witnesses for three and a half days. They will refuse to bury them. [10]People who live on the earth will be happy because these two are dead. They will have parties and send each other gifts. They will do these things because these

---

11:1 temple God's house—the place where God's people worship and serve him. Here, John sees it pictured as the special building in Jerusalem where God commanded the Jews to worship him.
11:8 Sodom City that God destroyed because the people were so evil.

two prophets brought much suffering to those who live on the earth.

11But after three and a half days, God put the breath of life into the two prophets again. They stood on their feet. Everyone who saw them was filled with fear. 12Then the two prophets heard a loud voice from heaven say, "Come up here!" And they went up into heaven in a cloud. Their enemies watched them go.

13At that same time there was a great earthquake. A tenth of the city was destroyed. And 7,000 people were killed in the earthquake. Those who did not die were very afraid. They gave glory to the God of heaven.

14The second great trouble is finished. The third great trouble is coming soon.

THE SEVENTH TRUMPET

15Then the seventh angel blew his trumpet. And there were loud voices in heaven. The voices said:

"The power to rule the world
now belongs to our Lord and his
Christ.d
And he will rule forever and ever."

16Then the 24 eldersn bowed down on their faces and worshiped God. These are the elders who sit on their thrones before God. 17They said:

"We give thanks to you, Lord God
All-Powerful.
You are the One who is and who
was.
We thank you because you have used
your great power
and have begun to rule!
18The people of the world were angry;
but now is the time for your anger.
Now is the time for the dead to be
judged.
It is time to reward your servants the
prophetsd

and to reward your holy people,
all who respect you, great and small.
It is time to destroy those who destroy
the earth!"

19Then God's templen in heaven was opened. The Holy Boxd that holds the agreement that God gave to his people could be seen in his temple. Then there were flashes of lightning, noises, thunder, an earthquake, and a great hailstorm.

THE WOMAN AND THE DRAGON

12 And then a great wonder appeared in heaven: There was a woman who was clothed with the sun. The moon was under her feet. She had a crown of 12 stars on her head. 2The woman was pregnant. She cried out with pain because she was about to give birth. 3Then another wonder appeared in heaven: There was a giant red dragon. He had seven heads with seven crowns on each head. He also had ten horns. 4The dragon's tail swept a third of the stars out of the sky and threw them down to the earth. The dragon stood in front of the woman who was ready to give birth to a baby. He wanted to eat the woman's baby as soon as it was born. 5The woman gave birth to a son. He will rule all the nations with an iron scepter.d But her child was taken up to God and to his throne. 6The woman ran away into the desert to a place God prepared for her. There she would be taken care of for 1,260 days.

7Then there was a war in heaven. Michaeln and his angels fought against the dragon. The dragon and his angels fought back. 8But the dragon was not strong enough. He and his angels lost their place in heaven. 9He was thrown down out of heaven. (The giant dragon is that old snake called the devil or Satan. He leads

11:16 24 elders Elder means "older." Here the elders probably represent God's people.
11:19 temple God's house—the place where God's people worship and serve him. John sees the heavenly temple pictured to be like the Temple of God's people in the Old Testament.
12:7 Michael The archangel—leader among God's angels or messengers (Jude 9).

the whole world the wrong way.) The dragon with his angels was thrown down to the earth.

[10]Then I heard a loud voice in heaven say:

"The salvation and the power and the
　　kingdom of our God
and the authority of his Christ[d]
　　have now come.
They have come because the accuser
　　of our brothers has been thrown
　　out.
He accused our brothers day and
　　night before our God.
[11]And our brothers defeated him
　　by the blood of the Lamb's death
　　and by the truth they preached.
They did not love their lives so much
　　that they were afraid of death.
[12]So be happy, you heavens
　　and all who live there!
But it will be terrible for the earth and
　　the sea,
because the devil has come down to
　　you!
He is filled with anger.
　　He knows that he does not have
　　much time."

[13]The dragon saw that he had been thrown down to the earth. So he hunted down the woman who had given birth to the son. [14]But the woman was given the two wings of a great eagle. Then she could fly to the place that was prepared for her in the desert. There she would be taken care of for three and a half years. There she would be away from the snake. [15]Then the snake poured water out of its mouth like a river. He poured the water toward the woman, so that the flood would carry her away. [16]But the earth helped her. The earth opened its mouth and swallowed the river that came from the mouth of the dragon. [17]Then the dragon was very angry at the woman. He went off to make war against all her other children. Her children are those who obey God's commands and have the truth that Jesus taught.

[18]And the dragon[n] stood on the seashore.

THE TWO BEASTS

13 Then I saw a beast coming up out of the sea. It had ten horns and seven heads. There was a crown on each horn. A name against God was written on each head. [2]This beast looked like a leopard, with feet like a bear's feet. He had a mouth like a lion's mouth. The dragon gave the beast all of his power and his throne and great authority. [3]One of the heads of the beast looked as if it had been wounded and killed. But this death wound was healed. The whole world was amazed and followed the beast. [4]People worshiped the dragon because he had given his power to the beast. And they also worshiped the beast. They asked, "Who is as powerful as the beast? Who can make war against him?"

[5]The beast was allowed to say proud words and words against God. He was allowed to use his power for 42 months. [6]He used his mouth to speak against God. He spoke against God's name, against the place where God lives, and against all those who live in heaven. [7]He was given power to make war against God's holy people and to defeat them. He was given power over every tribe,[d] people, language, and nation. [8]All who live on earth will worship the beast. These are all the people since the beginning of the world whose names are not written in the Lamb's book of life. The Lamb is the One who was killed.

[9]If anyone has ears, he should listen:
[10]If anyone is to be a prisoner,
　　then he will be a prisoner.
If anyone is to be killed with the sword,
　　then he will be killed with the
　　sword.

12:18 the dragon Some Greek copies read "I."

This means that God's holy people must have patience and faith.

¹¹Then I saw another beast coming up out of the earth. He had two horns like a lamb, but he talked like a dragon. ¹²This beast stands before the first beast and uses the same power that the first beast has. He uses this power to make everyone living on earth worship the first beast. The first beast was the one that had the death wound that was healed. ¹³The second one does great miracles.ᵈ He even makes fire come down from heaven to earth while people are watching. ¹⁴This second beast fools those who live on earth. He fools them by the miracles he has been given the power to do. He does these miracles to serve the first beast. The second beast ordered people to make an idol to honor the first beast. This was the one that was wounded by the sword but did not die. ¹⁵The second beast was given power to give life to the idol of the first one. Then the idol could speak and order all who did not worship it to be killed. ¹⁶The second animal also forced all people, small and great, rich and poor, free and slave, to have a mark on their right hand or on their forehead. ¹⁷No one could buy or sell without this mark. This mark is the name of the beast or the number of his name. ¹⁸Whoever has understanding can find the meaning of the number. This requires wisdom. This number is the number of a man. His number is 666.ⁿ

THE SONG OF THE SAVED

14 Then I looked, and there before me was the Lamb. He was standing on Mount Zion.ⁿ There were 144,000 people with him. They all had his name and his Father's name written on their foreheads. ²And I heard a sound from heaven like the noise of flooding water and like the sound of loud thunder. The sound I heard was like people playing harps. ³And they sang a new song before the throne and before the four living things and the elders.ⁿ The only ones who could learn the new song were the 144,000 who had been saved from the earth. No one else could learn the song. ⁴These 144,000 are the ones who did not do sinful things with women. They kept themselves pure. They follow the Lamb every place he goes. These 144,000 were saved from among the people of the earth. They are the first people to be offered to God and the Lamb. ⁵They were not guilty of telling lies. They are without fault.

THE THREE ANGELS

⁶Then I saw another angel flying high in the air. The angel had the eternal Good Newsᵈ to preach to those who live on earth—to every nation, tribe,ᵈ language, and people. ⁷The angel said in a loud voice, "Fear God and give him praise. The time has come for God to judge all people. Worship God. He made the heavens, the earth, the sea, and the springs of water."

⁸Then the second angel followed the first angel and said, "She is destroyed! The great city of Babylon is destroyed! She made all the nations drink the wine of her adulteryᵈ and of God's anger."

⁹A third angel followed the first two angels. This third angel said in a loud voice: "It will be bad for the person who worships the beast and his idol and gets the beast's mark on the forehead or on the hand. ¹⁰He will drink the wine of God's anger. This wine is prepared with all its strength in the cup of God's anger. He will be put in pain with burning sulfur before the holy angels and the Lamb. ¹¹And the smoke from their

13:18 666 Some Greek copies read "616."
14:1 Mount Zion Another name for Jerusalem, here meaning the spiritual city of God's people.
14:3 elders Elder means "older." Here the elders probably represent God's people.

burning pain will rise forever and ever.
There will be no rest, day or night, for
those who worship the beast and his idol
or who get the mark of his name." [12]This
means that God's holy people must be
patient. They must obey God's commands and keep their faith in Jesus.

[13]Then I heard a voice from heaven. It
said, "Write this: From now on, the dead
who were in the Lord when they died are
happy."

The Spirit[d] says, "Yes, that is true.
They will rest from their hard work. The
reward of all they have done stays with
them."

THE EARTH IS HARVESTED

[14]I looked and there before me was a
white cloud. Sitting on the white cloud
was One who looked like a Son of Man.[n]
He had a gold crown on his head and a
sharp sickle[n] in his hand. [15]Then another
angel came out of the temple. This angel
called to the One who was sitting on the
cloud, "Take your sickle and gather
from the earth. The time to harvest has
come. The fruit of the earth is ripe." [16]So
the One that was sitting on the cloud
swung his sickle over the earth. And the
earth was harvested.

[17]Then another angel came out of the
temple in heaven. This angel also had a
sharp sickle. [18]And then another angel
came from the altar. This angel has
power over the fire. This angel called to
the angel with the sharp sickle. He said,
"Take your sharp sickle and gather the
bunches of grapes from the earth's vine.
The earth's grapes are ripe." [19]The angel
swung his sickle over the earth. He gathered the earth's grapes and threw them
into the great winepress[d] of God's anger.
[20]The grapes were crushed in the winepress outside the city. And blood flowed

out of the winepress. It rose as high as
the heads of the horses for a distance of
200 miles.

THE LAST TROUBLES

15 Then I saw another wonder in
heaven. It was great and amazing.
There were seven angels bringing seven
troubles. These are the last troubles, because after these troubles God's anger is
finished.

[2]I saw what looked like a sea of glass
mixed with fire. All of those who had won
the victory over the beast and his idol
and over the number of his name were
standing by the sea. They had harps that
God had given them. [3]They sang the song
of Moses, the servant of God, and the
song of the Lamb:

"You do great and wonderful things,
                              Psalm 111:2
Lord God, the God of heaven's
    armies.   *Amos 3:13*
Everything the Lord does is right and
    true,   *Psalm 145:17*
King of the nations."[n]
[4]Everyone will respect you, Lord.
                           Jeremiah 10:7
They will honor you.
Only you are holy.
All people will come
    and worship you.   *Psalm 86:9, 10*
This is because he is a faithful God
    who does no wrong.
He is right and fair."
                      Deuteronomy 32:4
[5]After this I saw the temple (the Tent[d]
of the Agreement) in heaven. The temple
was opened. [6]And the seven angels
bringing the seven troubles came out of
the temple. They were dressed in clean,
shining linen. They wore golden bands
tied around their chests. [7]Then one of
the four living things gave seven golden
bowls to the seven angels. The bowls

14:14 Son of Man "Son of Man" is a name Jesus called himself. It showed he was God's Son, but he was also a
    man. See dictionary.
14:14 sickle A farming tool with a curved blade. It was used to harvest grain.
15:3 King . . . nations Some Greek copies read "King of the ages."

were filled with the anger of God, who lives forever and ever. [8]The temple was filled with smoke from the glory and the power of God. No one could enter the temple until the seven troubles of the seven angels were finished.

THE BOWLS OF GOD'S ANGER

16 Then I heard a loud voice from the temple. The voice said to the seven angels, "Go and pour out the seven bowls of God's anger on the earth."

[2]The first angel left. He poured out his bowl on the land. Then ugly and painful sores came upon all those who had the mark of the beast and who worshiped his idol.

[3]The second angel poured out his bowl on the sea. Then the sea became blood like that of a dead man. Every living thing in the sea died.

[4]The third angel poured out his bowl on the rivers and the springs of water. And they became blood. [5]Then I heard the angel of the waters say to God:

"Holy One, you are the One who is
     and who was.
You are right to decide to punish
     these evil people.
[6]They have spilled the blood of your
     holy people and your prophets.[d]
Now you have given them blood to
     drink as they deserve."

[7]And I heard the altar say:

"Yes, Lord God All-Powerful,
the way you punish evil people is
     right and fair."

[8]The fourth angel poured out his bowl on the sun. The sun was given power to burn the people with fire. [9]They were burned by the great heat, and they cursed the name of God. God is the One who had control over these troubles. But the people refused to change their hearts and lives and give glory to God.

[10]The fifth angel poured out his bowl on the throne of the beast. And darkness covered the beast's kingdom. People bit their tongues because of the pain. [11]They cursed the God of heaven because of their pain and the sores they had. But they refused to change their hearts and turn away from the evil things they did.

[12]The sixth angel poured out his bowl on the great river Euphrates. The water in the river was dried up. This prepared the way for the kings from the east to come. [13]Then I saw three evil spirits that looked like frogs. They came out of the mouth of the dragon, out of the mouth of the beast, and out of the mouth of the false prophet.[d] [14]These evil spirits are the spirits of demons.[d] They have power to do miracles.[d] They go out to the kings of the whole world. They go out to gather the kings for battle on the great day of God All-Powerful.

[15]"Listen! I will come as a thief comes! Happy is the person who stays awake and keeps his clothes with him. Then he will not have to go without clothes and be ashamed because he is naked."

[16]Then the evil spirits gathered the kings together to the place that is called Armageddon[n] in the Hebrew language.

[17]The seventh angel poured out his bowl into the air. Then a loud voice came out of the temple from the throne. The voice said, "It is finished!" [18]Then there were flashes of lightning, noises, thunder, and a big earthquake. This was the worst earthquake that has ever happened since people have been on earth. [19]The great city split into three parts. The cities of the nations were destroyed. And God did not forget to punish Babylon the Great. He gave that city the cup filled with the wine of his terrible anger. [20]Every island disappeared, and there were no more mountains. [21]Giant hailstones fell on people from the sky. The hailstones weighed about 100 pounds each. People cursed God because of the hail. This trouble was a terrible thing.

16:16 **Armageddon** This word means "Hill of Megiddo," where many battles were fought long ago.

THE WOMAN ON THE ANIMAL

17 One of the seven angels came and spoke to me. This was one of the angels that had the seven bowls. He said, "Come, and I will show you the punishment that will be given to the famous prostitute.*d* She is the one sitting over many waters. ²The kings of the earth sinned sexually with her. And the people of the earth became drunk from the wine of her sexual sin."

³Then the angel carried me away by the Spirit*d* to the desert. There I saw a woman sitting on a red beast. He was covered with names against God written on him. He had seven heads and ten horns. ⁴The woman was dressed in purple and red. She was shining with the gold, jewels, and pearls she was wearing. She had a golden cup in her hand. This cup was filled with evil things and the uncleanness of her sexual sin. ⁵She had a title written on her forehead. This title has a hidden meaning. This is what was written:

THE GREAT BABYLON
MOTHER OF PROSTITUTES
AND THE EVIL THINGS OF THE EARTH

⁶I saw that the woman was drunk. She was drunk with the blood of God's holy people. She was drunk with the blood of those who were killed because of their faith in Jesus.

When I saw the woman, I was fully amazed. ⁷Then the angel said to me, "Why are you amazed? I will tell you the hidden meaning of this woman and the beast she rides—the one with seven heads and ten horns. ⁸The beast that you saw was once alive. He is not alive now. But he will be alive and come up out of the bottomless pit and go away to be destroyed. The people who live on earth will be amazed when they see the beast. They will be amazed because he was once alive, is not alive now, but will come again. These are the people whose names have never been written in the book of life since the beginning of the world.

⁹"You need a wise mind to understand this. The seven heads on the beast are the seven hills where the woman sits. They are also seven kings. ¹⁰Five of the kings have already died. One of the kings lives now. And the last king is coming. When he comes, he will stay only a short time. ¹¹The beast that was once alive but is not alive now is an eighth king. This eighth king also belongs to the first seven kings. And he will go away to be destroyed.

¹²"The ten horns you saw are ten kings. These ten kings have not yet begun to rule. But they will receive power to rule with the beast for one hour. ¹³All ten of these kings have the same purpose. And they will give their power and authority to the beast. ¹⁴They will make war against the Lamb. But the Lamb will defeat them, because he is Lord of lords and King of kings. He will defeat them with his chosen and faithful followers—the people that he has called."

¹⁵Then the angel said to me, "You saw the water where the prostitute sits. These waters are the many peoples, the different races, nations, and languages. ¹⁶The beast and the ten horns you saw will hate the prostitute. They will take everything she has and leave her naked. They will eat her body and burn her with fire. ¹⁷God made the ten horns want to carry out his purpose: They agreed to give the beast their power to rule. They will rule until what God has said is completed. ¹⁸The woman you saw is the great city that rules over the kings of the earth."

BABYLON IS DESTROYED

18 Then I saw another angel coming down from heaven. This angel had great power. The angel's glory made the earth bright. ²The angel shouted in a powerful voice:

"The great city of Babylon is destroyed!

She has become a home for
  demons.[d]
She has become a city for every evil
  spirit,
  a city for every unclean[d] and hated
  bird.
[3]All the peoples of the earth have
  drunk
  the strong wine of her sexual sin.
The kings of the earth have sinned
  sexually with her,
  and the businessmen of the world
  have grown rich from the great
  wealth of her luxury."

[4]Then I heard another voice from
heaven say:
"Come out of that city, my people,
  so that you will not share in her sins.
  Then you will not receive the terrible
  things that will happen to her.
[5]The city's sins are piled up as high as
  the sky.
God has not forgotten the wrongs
  she has done.
[6]Give that city the same as she gave to
  others.
Pay her back twice as much as she
  did.
Prepare wine for her that is twice as
  strong
  as the wine she prepared for others.
[7]She gave herself much glory and rich
  living.
Give her that much suffering and
  sadness.
She says to herself, 'I am a queen
  sitting on my throne.
I am not a widow; I will never be
  sad.'
[8]So these terrible things will come to
  her in one day:
  death, crying, and great hunger.
She will be destroyed by fire,
  because the Lord God who judges
  her is powerful."
[9]The kings of the earth who sinned
sexually with her and shared her wealth

will see the smoke from her burning.
Then they will cry and weep because of
her death. [10]They will be afraid of her
suffering and stand far away. They will
say:
"Terrible! How terrible, great city,
  powerful city of Babylon!
Your punishment has come in one
  hour!"

[11]And the businessmen of the earth
will cry and weep for her. They will be sad
because now there is no one to buy the
things they sell. [12]They sell gold, silver,
jewels, pearls, fine linen cloth, purple
cloth, silk, and red cloth. They sell all
kinds of citron wood and all kinds of
things made from ivory, expensive wood,
bronze, iron, and marble. [13]They also sell
cinnamon, spice, incense,[d] myrrh,[d]
frankincense,[d] wine, and olive oil; fine
flour, wheat, cattle, sheep, horses, and
carriages. They sell the bodies and souls
of men.
[14]They will say,
"Babylon, the good things you wanted
  are gone from you.
All your rich and fancy things have
  disappeared.
You will never have them again."
[15]The businessmen will be afraid of her
suffering and stand far away from her.
These are the men who became rich
from selling those things to her. The
men will cry and be sad. [16]They will say:
"Terrible! How terrible for the great
  city!
She was dressed in fine linen,
  purple and red cloth.
She was shining with gold, jewels,
  and pearls!
[17]All these riches have been destroyed
  in one hour!"

Every sea captain, all those who travel
on ships, the sailors, and all the people
who earn money from the sea stood far
away from Babylon. [18]They saw the
smoke from her burning. They said
loudly, "There was never a city like this

great city!" [19]They threw dust on their heads and cried to show how sad they were. They said:

"Terrible! How terrible for the great
　city!
All the people who had ships on the sea
　became rich because of her wealth!
But she has been destroyed in one
　hour!
[20]Be happy because of this, heaven!
　Be happy, God's holy people and
　　apostles[d] and prophets![d]
God has punished her because of
　what she did to you."

[21]Then a powerful angel picked up a stone like a large stone for grinding grain. The angel threw the stone into the sea and said:

"That is how the great city of Babylon
　will be thrown down.
The city will never be found again.
[22]The music of people playing harps
　and other instruments, flutes
　and trumpets,
will never be heard in you again.
No workman doing any job
　will ever be found in you again.
The sound of grinding grain
　will never be heard in you again.
[23]The light of a lamp
　will never shine in you again.
The voices of a bridegroom and bride
　will never be heard in you again.
Your businessmen were the world's
　great men.
All the nations were tricked by your
　magic.
[24]She is guilty of the death
　of the prophets and God's holy people
　and of all who have been killed on
　earth."

PEOPLE IN HEAVEN PRAISE GOD

19 After this I heard what sounded like a great many people in heaven. They were saying:

"Hallelujah![n]
Salvation, glory, and power belong to
　our God.
[2]　His judgments are true and right.
Our God has punished the prostitute.[d]
　She is the one who made the earth
　evil with her sexual sin.
God has punished the prostitute to
　pay her for the death of his
　servants."
[3]Again they said:
"Hallelujah!
She is burning, and her smoke will
　rise forever and ever."

[4]Then the 24 elders[n] and the four living things bowed down. They worshiped God, who sits on the throne. They said:

"Amen, Hallelujah!"
[5]Then a voice came from the throne:
"Praise our God, all you who serve him!
Praise our God, all you who honor
　him, both small and great!"

[6]Then I heard what sounded like a great many people. It sounded like the noise of flooding water and like loud thunder. The people were saying:

"Hallelujah!
　Our Lord God rules. He is the All-
　　Powerful.
[7]Let us rejoice and be happy
　and give God glory!
Give God glory, because the wedding
　of the Lamb has come.
And the Lamb's bride has made
　herself ready.
[8]Fine linen was given to the bride for
　her to wear.
The linen was bright and clean."
(The fine linen means the good things done by God's holy people.)

[9]Then the angel said to me, "Write this: Those who are invited to the wedding meal of the Lamb are happy!" Then the angel said, "These are the true words of God."

19:1 **Hallelujah** This means "Praise God!"
19:4 **24 elders** Elder means "older." Here the elders probably represent God's people.

[10]Then I bowed down at the angel's feet to worship him. But he said to me, "Do not worship me! I am a servant like you and your brothers who have the truth of Jesus. Worship God! Because the truth about Jesus is the spirit that gives all prophecy."[d]

THE RIDER ON THE WHITE HORSE

[11]Then I saw heaven open. There before me was a white horse. The rider on the horse is called Faithful and True. He is right when he judges and makes war. [12]His eyes are like burning fire, and on his head are many crowns. He has a name written on him, but he is the only one who knows the name. No other person knows the name. [13]He is dressed in a robe dipped in blood. His name is the Word of God. [14]The armies of heaven were following him on white horses. They were dressed in fine linen, white and clean. [15]A sharp sword comes out of the rider's mouth. He will use this sword to defeat the nations. He will rule them with a scepter[d] of iron. He will crush out the wine in the winepress[d] of the terrible anger of God All-Powerful. [16]On his robe and on his leg was written this name: "KING OF KINGS AND LORD OF LORDS."

[17]Then I saw an angel standing in the sun. The angel called with a loud voice to all the birds flying in the sky, "Come together for the great feast of God. [18]Come together so that you can eat the bodies of kings and generals and famous men. Come to eat the bodies of the horses and their riders and the bodies of all people—free, slave, small, and great."

[19]Then I saw the beast and the kings of the earth. Their armies were gathered together to make war against the rider on the horse and his army. [20]But the beast was captured and with him the false prophet.[d] This false prophet was the one who did the miracles[d] for the beast. The false prophet had used these miracles to trick those who had the mark of the beast and worshiped his idol. The false prophet and the beast were thrown alive into the lake of fire that burns with sulfur. [21]Their armies were killed with the sword that came out of the mouth of the rider on the horse. All the birds ate the bodies until they were full.

THE 1,000 YEARS

20 I saw an angel coming down from heaven. He had the key to the bottomless pit. He also held a large chain in his hand. [2]The angel grabbed the dragon, that old snake who is the devil. The angel tied him up for 1,000 years. [3]Then he threw him into the bottomless pit and closed it and locked it over him. The angel did this so that he could not trick the people of the earth anymore until the 1,000 years were ended. After 1,000 years he must be set free for a short time.

[4]Then I saw some thrones and people sitting on them. They had been given the power to judge. And I saw the souls of those who had been killed because they were faithful to the truth of Jesus and the message from God. They had not worshiped the beast or his idol. They had not received the mark of the beast on their foreheads or on their hands. They came back to life and ruled with Christ for 1,000 years. [5](The others that were dead did not live again until the 1,000 years were ended.) This is the first raising of the dead. [6]Blessed and holy are those who share in this first raising of the dead. The second death has no power over them. They will be priests for God and for Christ. They will rule with him for 1,000 years.

[7]When the 1,000 years are over, Satan will be set free from his prison. [8]He will go out to trick the nations in all the earth—Gog and Magog. Satan will gather them for battle. There will be so many people that they will be like sand on the seashore. [9]And Satan's army marched across the earth and gathered around the camp of

God's people and the city that God loves. But fire came down from heaven and burned them up. [10]And Satan, who tricked them, was thrown into the lake of burning sulfur with the beast and the false prophet.[d] There they will be punished day and night forever and ever.

PEOPLE OF THE WORLD ARE JUDGED

[11]Then I saw a great white throne and the One who was sitting on it. Earth and sky ran away from him and disappeared. [12]And I saw the dead, great and small, standing before the throne. And the book of life was opened. There were also other books opened. The dead were judged by what they had done, which was written in the books. [13]The sea gave up the dead who were in it. Death and Hades[n] gave up the dead who were in them. Each person was judged by what he had done. [14]And Death and Hades were thrown into the lake of fire. This lake of fire is the second death. [15]And if anyone's name was not found written in the book of life, he was thrown into the lake of fire.

THE NEW JERUSALEM

21 Then I saw a new heaven and a new earth. The first heaven and the first earth had disappeared. Now there was no sea. [2]And I saw the holy city coming down out of heaven from God. This holy city is the new Jerusalem.[n] It was prepared like a bride dressed for her husband. [3]I heard a loud voice from the throne. The voice said, "Now God's home is with men. He will live with them, and they will be his people. God himself will be with them and will be their God.[n] [4]He will wipe away every tear from their eyes. There will be no more death, sadness, crying, or pain. All the old ways are gone."

[5]The One who was sitting on the throne said, "Look! I am making everything new!" Then he said, "Write this, because these words are true and can be trusted."

[6]The One on the throne said to me: "It is finished! I am the Alpha and the Omega,[n] the Beginning and the End. I will give free water from the spring of the water of life to anyone who is thirsty. [7]Anyone who wins the victory will receive this. And I will be his God, and he will be my son. [8]But those who are cowards, who refuse to believe, who do evil things, who kill, who sin sexually, who do evil magic, who worship idols, and who tell lies—all these will have a place in the lake of burning sulfur. This is the second death."

[9]One of the seven angels came to me. This was one of the angels who had the seven bowls full of the seven last troubles. He said, "Come with me. I will show you the bride, the wife of the Lamb." [10]The angel carried me away by the Spirit[d] to a very large and high mountain. He showed me the holy city, Jerusalem. It was coming down out of heaven from God. [11]It was shining with the glory of God. It was shining bright like a very expensive jewel, like a jasper. It was clear as crystal. [12]The city had a great high wall with 12 gates. There were 12 angels at the gates. On each gate was written the name of 1 of the 12 tribes[d] of Israel. [13]There were three gates on the east, three on the north, three on the south, and three on the west. [14]The walls of the city were built on 12 foundation stones. On the stones were written the names of the 12 apostles[d] of the Lamb.

[15]The angel who talked with me had a measuring rod made of gold. He had this

---

20:13 **Hades** Where the dead are.
21:2 **new Jerusalem** The spiritual city where God's people live with him.
21:3 **and . . . God** Some Greek copies do not have this phrase.
21:6 **the Alpha and the Omega** The first and last letters in the Greek alphabet. This means "the beginning and the end."

rod to measure the city, its gates, and its wall. [16]The city was built in a square. Its length was equal to its width. The angel measured the city with the rod. The city was 1,500 miles long, 1,500 miles wide, and 1,500 miles high. [17]The angel also measured the wall. It was 216 feet high, by man's measurement. That was the measurement the angel was using. [18]The wall was made of jasper. The city was made of pure gold, as pure as glass. [19]The foundation stones of the city walls had every kind of jewel in them. The first cornerstone was jasper, the second was sapphire, the third was chalcedony, the fourth was emerald, [20]the fifth was onyx, the sixth was carnelian, the seventh was chrysolite, the eighth was beryl, the ninth was topaz, the tenth was chrysoprase, the eleventh was jacinth, and the twelfth was amethyst. [21]The 12 gates were 12 pearls. Each gate was made from a single pearl. The street of the city was made of pure gold. The gold was clear as glass.

[22]I did not see a temple in the city. The Lord God All-Powerful and the Lamb are the city's temple. [23]The city does not need the sun or the moon to shine on it. The glory of God is its light, and the Lamb is the city's lamp. [24]By its light the people of the world will walk. The kings of the earth will bring their glory into it. [25]The city's gates will never be shut on any day, because there is no night there. [26]The greatness and the honor of the nations will be brought into it. [27]Nothing unclean[d] will ever enter the city. No one who does shameful things or tells lies will ever go into it. Only those whose names are written in the Lamb's book of life will enter the city.

22 Then the angel showed me the river of the water of life. The river was shining like crystal. It flows from the throne of God and of the Lamb [2]down the middle of the street of the city. The tree of life was on each side of the river. It produces fruit 12 times a year, once each month. The leaves of the tree are for the healing of all people. [3]Nothing that God judges guilty will be in that city. The throne of God and of the Lamb will be there. And God's servants will worship him. [4]They will see his face, and his name will be written on their foreheads. [5]There will never be night again. They will not need the light of a lamp or the light of the sun. The Lord God will give them light. And they will rule like kings forever and ever.

[6]The angel said to me, "These words are true and can be trusted. The Lord is the God of the spirits of the prophets.[d] He sent his angel to show his servants the things that must happen soon."

[7]"Listen! I am coming soon! He who obeys the words of prophecy in this book will be happy."

[8]I am John. I am the one who heard and saw these things. When I heard and saw them, I bowed down to worship at the feet of the angel who showed these things to me. [9]But the angel said to me, "Do not worship me! I am a servant like you and your brothers the prophets. I am a servant like all those who obey the words in this book. Worship God!"

[10]Then the angel told me, "Do not keep secret the words of prophecy in this book. The time is near for all this to happen. [11]Whoever is doing evil, let him continue to do evil. Whoever is unclean, let him continue to be unclean. Whoever is doing right, let him continue to do right. Whoever is holy, let him continue to be holy."

[12]"Listen! I am coming soon! I will bring rewards with me. I will repay each one for what he has done. [13]I am the Alpha and the Omega,[n] the First and the Last, the Beginning and the End.

[14]"Those who wash their robes[n] will be blessed. They will have the right to eat

---

22:13 **the Alpha and the Omega** The first and last letters in the Greek alphabet. This means "the beginning and the end."
22:14 **wash their robes** This means they believed in Jesus so that their sins could be forgiven by Christ's blood.

the fruit from the tree of life. They may go through the gates into the city. [15]Outside the city are the evil people, those who do evil magic, who sin sexually, who murder, who worship idols, and who love lies and tell lies.

[16]"I, Jesus, have sent my angel to tell you these things for the churches. I am the descendant[d] from the family of David. I am the bright morning star."

[17]The Spirit[d] and the bride say, "Come!" Everyone who hears this should also say, "Come!" If anyone is thirsty, let him come; whoever wishes it may have the water of life as a free gift.

[18]I warn everyone who hears the words of the prophecy of this book: If anyone adds anything to these words, God will give him the troubles written about in this book. [19]And if anyone takes away from the words of this book of prophecy, God will take away his share of the tree of life and of the holy city, which are written about in this book.

[20]Jesus is the One who says that these things are true. Now he says, "Yes, I am coming soon."

Amen. Come, Lord Jesus!

[21]The grace of the Lord Jesus be with all. Amen.

DICTIONARY

A

Aaron (AIR-ohn) was the older brother of Moses. He often spoke for Moses. Only men from Aaron's family could be priests. (Exodus 4–40; Numbers 1–25)

Abba (AB-uh) was a child's word for "father" in the Aramaic language. Early Christians used this word in speaking to God. This shows how close we can feel to him. (Mark 14:36; Romans 8:15; Galatians 4:6)

Abib (ah-BEEB) means "young ears of grain." It is the first month of the Jewish calendar and about the time of year as our March or April. It is also called Nisan. (Exodus 13:4; 34:18; Deuteronomy 16:1)

Abraham (AY-brah-ham) was the most respected man in the Jewish nation. The Jews called him "father Abraham." He was known for his great faith. (Genesis 12–25; John 8:39; Romans 4:1, 16; Hebrews 11:11-12)

Adam (AD-um) means "out of the earth." He was the first man God created. He was made from the dust of the ground. (Genesis 1–4; 1 Corinthians 15:45)

adultery (ah-DUL-ter-ee) is breaking a marriage promise by having sexual relations with someone other than your husband or wife. (Exodus 20:14; Mark 10:11-12; John 8:3-5)

agreement (uh-GREE-ment) is a contract or promise. It is sometimes called a covenant. God made agreements with his people. One agreement was the "law of Moses." God has given a new agreement to his people through Christ in the New Testament. Hebrews 8–10 explains the differences between the two agreements. (Genesis 9:9-17; Hebrews 9:15-22)

Agrippa (uh-GRIP-pah) See "Herod Agrippa II."

alabaster (AL-a-bas-ter) is a bright-colored stone with streaks or stripes through it. Perfume was often kept in beautiful containers made of alabaster. (Matthew 26:7; Luke 7:37)

alamoth (AL-a-moth) was probably a musical word. It may mean "like a flute" or "high-pitched." (Psalm 46)

aloes (AL-ohs) were oils from sweet-smelling sap of certain trees. They were used for perfume, medicine and to prepare bodies for burial. (Numbers 24:6; John 19:39)

altar (ALL-ter) was a place where sacrifices, gifts or prayers were offered to God. Altars were often made of dirt, grass or rocks piled up in the shape of a table on which the gift could be placed. (Genesis 8:20; 22:9; 1 Kings 18:30-35; Matthew 5:23-24; James 2:21)

amen (AY-MEN or AH-MEN) is a Hebrew word for "that is right." A person says "amen" to show he agrees with what has been said. (1 Chronicles 16:36; Nehemiah 5:13; 8:6; Psalm 106:48; 1 Corinthians 14:16; Revelation 7:11-12)

Anak/Anakites (A-nak/AN-uh-kites) The Anakites were named for their ancestor Anak. They were a group of people who lived in Canaan when the Israelites arrived. They were known as large, mean, fighting people. (Numbers 13:22, 28, 33; Deuteronomy 1:28; 2:10-11; 9:2; Joshua 11:21-22)

Andrew (AN-droo) was a fisherman and the brother of the apostle Peter. Andrew was also 1 of the 12 apostles of Jesus. (Mark 1:16-18; 3:14-19; John 1:40-44; Acts 1:13)

angel (AIN-jel) is a Greek word that means "messenger." Angels are heavenly beings. They can sometimes look like people. God used angels to help his people and to announce important events. (Genesis 21:17; 22:11-15;

Matthew 25:41; Luke 2:8-15; Hebrews 1:14; 12:22; 13:2; 2 Peter 2:4)

Annas (AN-us) was a high priest of the Jews during Jesus' lifetime. He served as the high priest in Jerusalem from A.D. 7 to 14. (Luke 3:2; John 18:12-23; Acts 4:6) See also "priest."

apostle (uh-POS-'l) is a Greek word that means "someone who is sent off." Jesus gave the name to the 12 men he chose as his special followers. He sent them to tell the good news about him to the whole world. Later, after Judas killed himself, Matthias became an apostle. Paul was also called an apostle. (Matthew 10:1-4; Mark 3:14-19; Acts 1:2-26; 1 Corinthians 15:8-10)

Aquila (AK-wi-lah) was a Jewish Christian from the city of Rome. He and his wife Priscilla (or Prisca) worked as tentmakers and traveled with Paul. When they were at home in Rome or working in Ephesus, the Christians worshiped in their home. (Acts 18:2-3, 18, 26; Romans 16:3-5; 1 Corinthians 16:19)

Aramaic (AIR-uh-MAY-ik) was the language of the people in the nation of Aram. The Jews in the country of Palestine started speaking Aramaic when they were taken as slaves by the Babylonian people. Jesus probably spoke Aramaic. (2 Kings 18:26-28; John 19:20)

ark, Noah's In this Bible it is called Noah's boat. (Genesis 6:13-14; 1 Peter 3:20)

Ark of the Covenant See "Box of the Agreement with the Lord."

Asherah (ah-SHIR-ah) was the name of a false goddess of the people of Canaan. She was thought to be the wife of the false god Baal. (Judges 3:7; 1 Kings 15:13; 2 Kings 21:7; 2 Chronicles 15:16)

Ashtoreth (ASH-toh-reth) was the name of a false goddess of the Canaanites. (Judges 2:13; 1 Samuel 7:3; 12:10; 1 Kings 11:5, 33)

Augustus Caesar (aw-GUS-tus SEE-zer) or Caesar Augustus was the first Roman emperor. He was the ruler when Jesus was born. He was a nephew to the famous Julius Caesar. (Luke 2:1-2)

B

Baal was a false god of the Canaanites. (1 Kings 18:17-40; Jeremiah 11:13)

Babylonians (bab-e-LONE-e-unz) were the people from Babylonia. This was a land east of Israel. Their largest city was Babylon. When Nebuchadnezzar was their king, they took many of the people of Judah to Babylonia as captives. The Babylonians were sometimes called Chaldeans. (2 Kings 25:4-26; 2 Chronicles 36; Daniel 1-4)

balm was an oil from a plant used as a medicine to comfort and heal sore skin. (Genesis 37:25; Jeremiah 51:8)

Baptist (BAP-tist) means "someone who baptizes." John, a relative of Jesus, was called this because he baptized many people. (Matthew 3:11)

baptize (BAP-tize) is from a Greek word that in New Testament times meant to dip or immerse. Baptism as practiced by Christians was in water. Baptism reminds us of Jesus' death, burial and rising to live again. It shows our death to sin and our being raised to new life with Christ. (Acts 2:38, 41; 8:36-39; 10:47; 16:15, 33; 18:8; Romans 6:3-4)

Barabbas (bah-RAB-us) means "son of a father." He was a robber who had murdered someone in Jerusalem. He was in jail when Jesus was on trial. It was the time of year when a criminal would be freed from prison. The people cried out to have Barabbas freed and Jesus killed on the cross. Pilate, the Roman governor, did as they demanded. (Matthew 27:16-26; Mark 15:6-11)

Barnabas (BAR-nah-bus) means "one who encourages." The apostles gave this name to Joseph because he helped others. Barnabas, who was from Cyprus, often traveled with Paul to teach about Jesus. The journeys of Barnabas with Paul are told in Acts 13–15. (Acts 4:36-37; 11:22-26)

Bartholomew (bar-THOL-oh-mew) was 1 of the 12 apostles of Jesus. He may also have been called Nathanael. (Matthew 10:2-3; Luke 6:13-15; John 1:43-50)

beatitude (bee-AT-i-tyood) means "blessed" or "happy." This name is often used for Jesus' teaching in Matthew 5:3-12 and Luke 6:20-22. In these verses Jesus described a blessed or happy person.

Beelzebul (bee-EL-ze-bull), also spelled Beelzebub, came from the name Baal-Zebub. This was the name of the false god of the Philistines. In the New Testament, Beelzebul is a name sometimes used for the devil. (Matthew 12:24; Mark 3:22-23)

Bel was a false god of the Babylonians. (Jeremiah 50:2)

believers (be-LEE-vers) is a word used in the New Testament to describe the followers of Jesus. (Acts 2:41-47; 5:14)

Bethlehem (BETH-le-hem) means "house of bread." It is a small town five miles from Jerusalem in the country of Judea. It was the hometown of King David in the Old Testament. Jesus was born there. (1 Samuel 16:4; Matthew 2:1; Luke 2:15-18)

Bible (BY-bul) means "the book." The Bible is a group of books and letters that Christians accept as the word of God. It is divided into two parts. The Old Testament contains 39 books, and the New Testament contains 27 books. See also "Scriptures."

blasphemy (BLAS-feh-mee) is saying things against God. Jesus was often accused of blasphemy because he said he was the Son of God. The people who accused him did not understand

that he really was God's Son. (Matthew 9:3; 26:65; John 10:36)

blessing (BLES-ing) is a good gift from God to his people. (Luke 6:28; 24:50-51; Acts 3:26; Hebrews 6:7; 1 Peter 3:9)

Box of the Agreement with the Lord or **Holy Box** is often called Ark of the Covenant. It was a special box made of acacia wood and gold. Gold creatures with wings covered the top. Inside were the stone tablets where the Ten Commandments were written. Later, a pot of manna and Aaron's walking stick were also put into the Box. It was to remind the people of Israel of God's promise to be with them. In this Bible it is also called the Holy Box or the Holy Box of God. (Exodus 25:10-22; 26:34; Joshua 3:1-17; 2 Chronicles 35:3; Hebrews 9:4)

bread that shows we are in God's presence is also called Bread of the Presence, or showbread. It was a group of 12 loaves of bread that were kept on the table in the Holy Tent and later in the Temple. This special bread reminded the people that they were always in God's presence. (Exodus 25:30; Leviticus 24:5-9; Luke 6:1-4)

C

Caesar (SEE-zer) was the name of a famous Roman family. In New Testament times it was used as the title of the Roman emperors. (Luke 2:1; 3:1; 20:22-25) See "Augustus Caesar."

Caiaphas (KAY-uh-fus) was the Jewish high priest from A.D. 18 to 36. He was one of those who planned to kill Jesus. (Matthew 26:57-68; John 11:49-53; 18:12-28)

calamus (KAH-lah-mus) is a sweet-tasting plant stalk probably like sugar cane. (Exodus 30:23; Jeremiah 6:20; Ezekiel 27:19)

capital is the top of a pillar. This top part of the pillar was usually decorated with beautiful carvings. (1 Kings 7:16-20; 2 Kings 25:17; Amos 9:1)

cassia (CASH-ah) is a pleasant-smelling powder. Its odor is like that of the cinnamon plant. (Exodus 30:24; Psalm 45:8)

centurion (sen-TUR-ree-un) was a Roman army officer who commanded 100 soldiers. (Matthew 8:5; 7:12)

Cephas (SEE-fus) See "Peter."

chaff (CHAF) is the husk of a head of grain. Farmers must separate it from the good part of the grain. In Bible times they tossed the grain and chaff together into the air. Since the chaff is lighter, the wind blew it away and the good grain fell back to the threshing floor. (Job 21:18; Psalms 1:4; 35:5; Isaiah 29:5; 41:2) See "threshing."

chariot (CHAIR-e-ut) was a fast, two-wheeled cart usually pulled by two horses. It was used for battles, traveling and parades. (Genesis 46:29; Exodus 14:6; Acts 8:28-31)

Chemosh (KEE-mosh) was the name of a false god of the Moabites. (Numbers 21:29; Jeremiah 48:46)

Christ (KRYST) means "anointed (or chosen) one" in Greek. In Hebrew the word is "Messiah." Jesus is the Christ. He was chosen by God to save people from their sins. (Mark 8:29; 14:61-62; Luke 23:2; Acts 2:36; 17:3; 18:28)

Christian (KRIS-chun) means "belonging to Christ." Christ's followers are called Christians. (Acts 11:26; 26:28; 1 Peter 4:16)

church in the New Testament means a group of Christians. In those times the church often met in someone's home. (Matthew 16:18; Acts 2:47; 14:27; Romans 16:5)

circumcision (SIR-kum-SIH-zhun) This means to cut off the foreskin of the male sex organ. Each Jewish baby boy was circumcised on the eighth day after he was born. This act was done as a sign of the agreement God had made with his people, the Jews. Because of this, the Jews sometimes are called "the circumcision" and non-Jews are called "the uncircumcision." (Leviticus 12:3; John 7:22; Acts 7:8)

clean is used to describe the state of a person, animal or action that is pleasing to God. God called some animals clean and said they could be eaten. People who had not touched or eaten anything God said was unclean were called clean. Or, if they did not have a disease that made them unclean, they were called clean. They could live and serve God normally. (Genesis 7:2; Leviticus 20:25; Deuteronomy 14:3-20) See "unclean."

Cleansing, Day of is also called the Day of Atonement. It was the most special day of the year for the Israelites. No one worked or ate on that day. This was the one day of the year when the high priest could go into the Most Holy Place. Animals were sacrificed for the sins of the people. This was a sign to the people that they were cleansed from their sins for a year. Jews still celebrate this day today. It is called Yom Kippur. (Leviticus 16:1-34; 25:9)

confess (kun-FES) means to admit that something is true. The New Testament teaches a believer to confess that Jesus is the Son of God. Christians are also told to confess their sins, to admit that they have done wrong. (Romans 10:9-10; Philippians 2:11; 1 John 1:9)

coral (KOR-al) is a type of limestone that forms in the ocean. Coral is usually a rich red or deep pink color. It is used to make jewelry. (Job 28:18; Ezekiel 27:16)

cornerstone This was the most important stone at a corner in the base of a building. The cornerstone had to be perfect so the building's walls would be straight. The other stones were fitted against the cornerstone. Jesus is called the cornerstone of the new law. (Joshua 6:26; Job 38:6; Ephesians 2:20)

council (KOWN-s'l), or meeting, was the highest Jewish court in the days of Jesus. Its proper name was the "Sanhedrin." The men of the council sat in a half circle to hear the people who came to speak to them. The trials of Jesus and Stephen were held in front of this council. (Matthew 26:57-68; Acts 6:13-15)

covenant (KUV-eh-nant) See "agreement."

cross refers to a cruel way of killing criminals in New Testament times. The person was tied or nailed to two rough beams of wood nailed together in the shape of an "x" or a "t." Then, he was left hanging in a public place to die. Jesus was killed by the Roman soldiers this way. In the New Testament the word "cross" is often used to remind us that Christ's death on the cross was God's way of saving us from our sins. (John 19:17-31; 1 Corinthians 1:18-25; Galatians 6:12; Ephesians 2:15-16)

cud An animal that chews the cud chews its food and swallows it. Then it chews it a second time. (Leviticus 11:3)

D

Dagon (DAY-gon) was one of the false gods of the Philistines. (Judges 16:23; 1 Samuel 5:2-7; 1 Chronicles 10:10)

Daniel (DAN-yel) was a Hebrew captive taken to Babylon as a young man. He told Nebuchadnezzar what his dream meant. God also made him able to tell Belshazzar what the strange handwriting on the wall meant. When he was about 80 years old, Daniel was put in the lions' den by King Darius. But God saved him. (Daniel 1–6)

David (DAY-vid) was Israel's greatest king. Jesus is called the "Son of David" because he was born to members of David's family. (1 Samuel 1:16-31; Luke 1:69; 2:4; 18:38; Acts 2:29-31; 13:22)

deacon (DEE-kun) is a Greek word meaning "servant." Deacons are people

chosen to serve the church in special ways. The men named in Acts 6:1-6 may have been the first deacons. Deacons are described in 1 Timothy 3:8-13.

Dead Sea is a large lake at the south end of the Jordan River. The Jordan and several small streams flow into it. But it has no outlet. And it is so salty that nothing lives in it. It is about 50 miles long and 10 miles wide. In Bible days it was often called the Salt Sea, the Eastern Sea or the Sea of the Arabah. (Genesis 14:3; Numbers 34:3, 12; Joshua 3:16)

demon (DEE-mun) was an evil spirit from the devil. Sometimes a demon lived in a person. But Jesus has more power than demons and could make them come out of people. (Deuteronomy 32:17; Psalm 106:37; Matthew 12:22; Luke 8:26-39)

descendants (de-SEN-dants) are family members who are born to a person and his children. They would include grandchildren, great-grandchildren, great-great-grandchildren and so on. (Genesis 12:7; Leviticus 21:21; Romans 4:18)

devil (DEV-'l) means "one who accuses." In the New Testament, the devil is often called Satan or Beelzebul. He is a spirit and the enemy of God and man. (Matthew 4:1-11; John 13:2; Ephesians 4:27; 6:10-17) See "Beelzebul."

disciple (dih-SYE-p'l) See "follower."

E

Edom (E-dum) means "red." Edom was also called Esau, the older son of Isaac. The land where Esau's descendants lived was named Edom. It was south of the Dead Sea. Seir is another name for the land of Edom. (Genesis 25:30; 36:8; 2 Samuel 8:14; Psalm 137:7; Ezekiel 25:12-14; Obadiah 10-14)

elder (EL-der) means "older." In the Old Testament this Bible uses elders, older leaders, to describe a special group of men who led God's people. In the New Testament elders are appointed leaders in the church. (Numbers 11:16; Acts 20:17-38; 1 Timothy 3:1-7; 1 Peter 5:1-4)

Elijah (e-LIE-juh) was a man who spoke for God in the Old Testament. He was a prophet about 800 years before Jesus was born. (1 Kings 17–21; 2 Kings 1; 2; Matthew 16:14; 17:3-4; 27:47; Luke 1:17; James 5:17)

ephod (EF-ahd) See "vest, holy."

epistle (e-PIS-'l) is a Greek word meaning "letter." Many books of the New Testament were actually letters written to Christians in various cities. Some of these letters are Ephesians, Galatians, Romans, 1 and 2 Corinthians, Philippians and Colossians. (Colossians 4:16; 1 Thessalonians 5:27; 2 Thessalonians 3:17; 2 Peter 3:16)

Esau (E-saw) See "Edom."

eternal life (e-TER-nul LIFE) is the new kind of life promised to those who follow Jesus. It is living with a new help from God. It is also life that will never end. (John 3:16; 4:14; Galatians 2:20; 1 John 5:11-15)

eunuch (U-nuk) is a man who cannot have sexual relations. In the Bible eunuchs were often high officers in royal palaces or armies. (2 Kings 9:32; Esther 2:3; Isaiah 56:3-5; Acts 8:26-40)

Eutychus (YOU-ti-cus) means "lucky." Eutychus was a young man in the city of Troas. As he was sitting in an upstairs window listening to Paul preach, he went to sleep. He fell out of the window and died. But Paul, by God's power, brought him back to life. (Acts 20:7-12)

Ezra (EZ-ra) was the leader of a group of Israelites who were allowed to return to Jerusalem from Babylon. He taught them to worship and serve God correctly. (Ezra 7–10; Nehemiah 8; 9)

F

faith (FAYTH) is belief and trust. People who have great faith in God do what he says to do, even when they do not understand why. They do it because they believe in him and trust him. Faith in Jesus means believing he is the Son of God and trusting in him. (2 Chronicles 20:20; Isaiah 7:9; Habakkuk 2:4; Matthew 8:10; Luke 8:24-25; Romans 4:16-22; 5:1-2; Ephesians 4:13; Hebrews 11)

fasting (FAST-ing) means giving up food for a while. People sometimes fast during a special time of prayer and worship to God. Jesus fasted for 40 days before he began preaching. It was also done to show sadness. (2 Samuel 12:16-22; Ezra 8:23; Matthew 4:1-11; 6:16-18; 9:14-15; Acts 12:2-3; 14:23)

feast (FEEST) is a special meal and celebration for a certain purpose. There were many different feasts in Bible times.

Feast of Dedication was an eight-day celebration for the Jews. It was a way of being thankful that the Temple had been cleansed again. This was done in 164 B.C. after the Greeks had spoiled and ruined it. The celebration is called Hanukkah today by the Jews. (John 10:22)

Feast of Harvest See "Feast of Weeks."

Feast of Shelters is also called the Feast of Booths or Feast of Tents. The people gathered fruit and lived in tent-like shelters for a week. This feast reminded them of how God had taken care of them when the Israelites left Egypt and lived in tents in the wilderness. (Exodus 23:14-17; Deuteronomy 16:13-17)

Feast of Unleavened Bread was also called Passover. It was held to remember how God helped the Israelites in Egypt. He saved them from the one that brings death that passed over their families. And God led them out of slavery. For seven days they ate bread made without yeast and did only certain types of work. (Exodus 12:14-20; Numbers 28:16-25; Deuteronomy 16:1-8) See "Passover Feast."

Feast of Weeks was also called Pentecost, the Feast of Harvest and the Day of Firstfruits. It was held seven weeks and one day after Passover. This was a feast of thanksgiving for the summer harvest. (Exodus 34:22; Leviticus 23:15-22; Numbers 28:26-31; Deuteronomy 16:9-12; Acts 2) See "Pentecost."

Felix (FEE-lix) was the Roman governor of Judea from A.D. 52 to 54. He was a cruel ruler. He kept the apostle Paul in prison for two years to please the Jews who hated Jesus and Paul. His full name was Marcus Antonius Felix. (Acts 23:24–24:27)

fellowship (FEL-o-ship) is sharing friendship and love with others. Christians have a very special fellowship with God and his people. (Acts 2:42; 1 John 1:3-7)

Festus (FES-tus) was the governor of Judea after Felix. His full name was Porcius (POR-shus) Festus. He allowed Paul to go to Rome to be tried by Caesar. (Acts 24:27–25:27; 26:24-32)

firstborn (FIRST-born) is the oldest child in a family. The son born first to a Jewish family received a double share of his father's wealth. Then he became the leader of the family when his father died. The Israelite people were called God's firstborn because he gave them special privileges. Jesus was also called God's firstborn Son. He is now ruling over all creation. (Genesis 35:23; Exodus 4:22; Psalm 89:27; Romans 8:29; Colossians 1:18; Hebrews 1:6)

firstfruits (FIRST-fruits) were the first and best crops and animals the Israelites raised. They were to give these to God. This showed that they knew

everything really belonged to God. (Exodus 34:22-26; Leviticus 23:9-21; Numbers 28:26; Deuteronomy 18:4)

flax (FLAKS) is a plant used to make clothing and ropes. The inside of the plant was combed and spun into thread. Then it was woven into cloth. (Exodus 9:31; Joshua 2:6; Proverbs 31:13; Isaiah 19:9)

follower (FAHL-o-wer) is a person who is learning from someone. Jesus' followers are those who believe and obey his teaching. Another word for "follower" is "disciple." During his ministry, Jesus chose 12 special followers and made them his apostles. (Matthew 15:32-39; John 19:38; Acts 6:1-7; 11:26)

forgiveness (for-GIV-ness) means to be pardoned and not punished for a wrong thing done. A sinner who is sorry for his sin and stops doing that sin will be forgiven when he comes to God. That person will not be punished. Christians are also to forgive others for wrong things done to them. (Genesis 50:17; Psalms 19:12; 32:1-5; 51:1-17; Matthew 6:12-15; 9:2-8; 18:21-22; Acts 8:22; Romans 4:7; 1 John 1:9)

frankincense (FRANK-in-sense) is a very expensive, sweet-smelling perfume. It comes from inside the terebinth tree that grows in the country of Arabia. Some wise men gave frankincense to Jesus when he was born. (Exodus 30:34; Matthew 2:11; Revelation 18:13)

G

Gabriel (GAY-bree-el) is God's angel who announced that John the Baptist and Jesus would be born. (Luke 1:11-20, 26-35)

Galilee (GAL-i-lee) was the country between the Jordan River and the Mediterranean Sea. It had lots of water and trees, and the land was good for growing grains like wheat and barley. Jesus grew up in the city of

Nazareth in Galilee and, so, was often called "the Galilean." (Matthew 4:23-25; 21:11; John 2:1-2; 7:1, 9, 41)

Galilee, Lake (GAL-i-lee) is also called the "Sea of Galilee." It is really a lake 13 miles long and about 8 miles wide. Storms often come up very quickly on this lake. Jesus spent much time around Lake Galilee. (Matthew 4:18-22; 8:23-27; 14:22-36; John 6:1-2, 16-21)

gazelle (guh-ZEL) is an animal of the antelope family. It is known for its beauty and speed. It is usually about two feet tall and three feet long. (Deuteronomy 12:15, 22; 2 Samuel 2:18; Proverbs 6:5)

Gentiles (JEN-tiles) means "nations." The Jews called anyone who was not a Jew a Gentile. The Jews thought all non-Jewish people were enemies. The Good News of Jesus is for all people, both Jews and non-Jewish people. (Acts 10:44-48; 11:18; 13:46-48; Romans 1:5; 11:11-13; Ephesians 3:6-8)

Gethsemane (geth-SEM-uh-nee) was a garden of olive trees just outside Jerusalem. It was at the bottom of the Mount of Olives. The night before Jesus was killed, he prayed in this garden. Jesus was there when Judas brought the soldiers to arrest him. (Matthew 26:36-50; Mark 14:32)

gittith (GIT-tith) is probably a musical word and may be a kind of musical instrument. (Psalms 8; 81; 84)

God is the One who made the world and everything in it. He is a spirit and does not have a body as man does. But people can know what God is like because he sent Jesus into the world to show them. God hates evil, but he loves his people so much that he let his Son die for them. God is the wisest and most powerful being in the universe. He has always been alive, and he will always be alive. He is love. Christians are called "children of God" because they have been given a spirit like God.

(Genesis 1:1; Psalm 139:7-12; Isaiah 44:6; Matthew 5:9; John 4:24; 14:9; Romans 1:18; 5:8-11; 8:16; 11:36; Hebrews 1:1-4; 1 John 4:7-12)

Golgotha (GOL-guh-thuh) is an Aramaic word meaning "skull." The Latin word for it is "Calvary." This is the hill where Jesus was killed on the cross by the Roman soldiers. It may have been called "the place of the skull" because many people died there. Or it may have been called that because the hill looks like a giant skull. (Matthew 27:32-35; Mark 15:22-24; John 19:17-18)

Good News is also called the gospel. In the New Testament, the Good News is that Jesus died for us on the cross, was buried in a tomb and came back to life. Because he did these things for us, we can be saved. That is good news. (Mark 1:1; Acts 20:24; Colossians 1:21-23; 2 Timothy 1:10) See "gospel."

gospel (GOS-p'l) means "good news." It refers to Jesus' life, death and rising to live again. The first four books of the New Testament are called the Gospels because they tell the good news of what Jesus has done for us. (Philippians 1:5, 7, 12; 2 Thessalonians 1:8) See "Good News."

grace is God's kindness and love shown to us, even though we do not deserve them. Part of God's grace is his forgiveness. He forgives us for the wrong things we do. He even let Jesus take the punishment for our sins. (John 1:14; Acts 15:11; Romans 5:1-2, 8; 1 Corinthians 15:10; 2 Corinthians 6:1-2; Ephesians 2:4-5, 8; Titus 3:3-7; Hebrews 4:16)

Greek is the language of the people of Greece. The New Testament was first written in the Greek language. Also, a person from the country of Greece is called a Greek. (John 19:20; Acts 14:1; 16:1, 3; 21:37; Colossians 3:11)

H

Hades (HAY-deez) is where the dead, both good and bad, are. (Acts 2:27, 31; Revelation 1:18)

heart in the Bible usually means the mind or feelings. It is not talking about the physical heart that pumps blood through the body. (Deuteronomy 30:10-17; Psalm 26:2; Proverbs 15:13-15; Mark 12:30; Luke 2:19; 6:45; 12:34; Acts 2:46)

heaven (HEV-'n) is the home of God. In the New Testament it is said to be a place where there is no pain, no crying, no sadness, no night and no death. Jesus showed us his love by leaving heaven and coming to earth to die on a cross. God's people will live in heaven with him forever. (John 3:13; 6:38-40; Acts 7:56; 2 Corinthians 5:1-10; 1 Peter 1:4; Revelation 21:4)

Hebrews (HEE-brooz) is another name for the Jewish people. The book of Hebrews is a letter written to Jewish Christians. (2 Corinthians 11:22; Philippians 3:5; Hebrews)

heir (AIR) is the person who is supposed to inherit what belongs to a relative. The heir usually receives these things when the relative dies. Because through Christ we can be adopted children of God, Christians are heirs of God's riches. (Genesis 15:3-4; 2 Samuel 14:7; Galatians 4:1)

hell is the home of the devil. It is the place of punishment forever for those who turn against God. Hell is described in the New Testament as a place of fire, pain, sorrow and sadness. (Matthew 23:33; 25:41; 2 Peter 2:4, 9; Revelation 20:14-15; 21:8)

Herod (HEH-rud) was the name of four different rulers in the New Testament: **Herod I** (Herod the Great) was king of the country of Palestine from the year 40 B.C. until about 4 B.C. He tried to kill the baby Jesus because Jesus was called a "king." Herod thought Jesus was an earthly king and would take away his throne. (Matthew 2:1-16; Luke 1:5)

Herod Antipas was the son of Herod I. He had John the Baptist's head cut off. Later, Jesus was sent to this man for trial. He ruled from the year 4 B.C. to about A.D. 39. (Matthew 14:1; Mark 6:14; Luke 23:6)

Herod Agrippa I was the king of Palestine for about three years (A.D. 41-44). He was the grandson of Herod I. He had the apostle James killed and the apostle Peter arrested. He did it to please the Jews who hated Jesus' followers. Later, this man was eaten by worms and died because he let the people treat him like a god. (Acts 12:1-21)

Herod Agrippa II was king of Palestine from the year A.D. 48 to 93. He was a great-grandson to Herod I. He heard the apostle Paul speak. He sent Paul to Caesar for trial. (Acts 25:13, 26; 26:1-32)

higgaion (hig-GI-on) is probably a musical word. It seems to mean "to meditate." So it may mean a time to think quietly during a song. (Psalm 9:16)

high priest was the most important religious leader of the Jewish people. He was often as important as the king. Caiaphas was the high priest when Jesus was killed. Annas was another high priest at that time. (Matthew 26:3, 57; Acts 23:2-5)

holy (HO-lee) means pure, belonging to and willing to serve God. God's people are called "holy people." (Exodus 3:5; 22:31; 31:13; 1 Corinthians 1:2; Ephesians 1:4; Philemon 4; 1 Peter 1:15-16)

Holy Place This was a room in the Holy Tent and the Temple. The priests came to this room every day to burn candles and incense to the Lord. Each week fresh loaves of bread were placed on the table there. A curtain separated the Holy Place from the Most Holy Place. (Exodus 26:31-35; 31:11; Leviticus 6:30) See "bread that shows we are in God's presence."

Holy Spirit (HO-lee SPIH-rit) is one of the three persons of God. The other two persons are God the Father and God the Son (Jesus). The Holy Spirit helped the apostles do miracles. He led men to write God's word. The Holy Spirit lives in Christians today. He is also called the Spirit of Christ, the Spirit of God, and the Comforter. (Genesis 1:2; John 3:5-8; 16:13; Acts 2:1-4; 5:32; Romans 5:5; 8:9-16; 2 Peter 1:20-21)

Holy Tent See "Meeting Tent."

hypocrite (HIP-oh-krit) comes from the word for an actor on a stage. In the Bible it is a person who acts as if he is good but isn't. (Matthew 6:2, 5, 16; 7:3-5; Luke 13:15-17)

I

idol (EYE-d'l) is a false god. The non-Jewish people often worshiped statues they made from wood, stone or metal. They worshiped these idols instead of the true God of heaven. (Leviticus 19:4; 2 Kings 17:12-17; Acts 7:40-43; 17:16-23; 1 Thessalonians 1:9)

incense (IN-senz) was a spice burned to make a sweet smell. This was done by the priests in the Meeting Tent and the Temple. A special altar was used to burn incense as worship to God. Since the smoke seemed to go up to God, this reminded people of prayer. (Exodus 30:1-10, 34-38; Psalm 141:2; Luke 1:9; Revelation 8:3-4)

Isaac (EYE-zak) means "laughter." He was the son of Abraham and Sarah. He was named Isaac because Sarah laughed when the angel told her she would have a baby. She thought she was too old. God tested Abraham by asking him to offer Isaac as a sacrifice

on an altar. When God saw that Abraham would obey him, he saved Isaac's life. (Genesis 21–26; Mark 12:26; Hebrews 11:17-20)

Isaiah (i-ZAY-uh) was one of the great prophets of the Old Testament. He often gave God's message to King Hezekiah. (2 Kings 19; 20; Isaiah 6–9; 53)

Israel (IZ-rah-el) is a Hebrew word that means "he who wrestles with God." When Jacob struggled with an angel at Bethel, God named him Israel. The 12 tribes of the Jewish nation were descendants of Jacob. They were called Israelites. (Exodus 3:16-18; Psalm 73:1; Luke 1:68; Acts 2:36; 5:33-36)

J

Jacob (JAY-cub) was one of the sons of Isaac. He was the father of the 12 tribes of God's chosen people. He had 12 sons, and each son was the head of a tribe. (Genesis 25–36; Matthew 1:2; 8:11; John 4:6)

Jacob's Portion (JAY-cubs POR-shun) is a name for God. It means that God cares for Jacob's people, the Israelites. (Jeremiah 10:16; 51:19)

James was the name of several men in the New Testament:
James, the son of Zebedee, was an apostle of Jesus and a brother of the apostle John. He was killed by Herod Agrippa I. (Matthew 10:2; Mark 10:35, 41; Acts 12:2)
James, the son of Alphaeus, was also one of Jesus' apostles. He may have been a cousin to Jesus. (Matthew 10:3)
James, the brother of Jesus, was a respected leader in the church in Jerusalem. He probably wrote the book of James in the New Testament. (Matthew 13:55; John 7:5; Acts 12:17; 21:18; Galatians 1:19)

Jeremiah (jer-eh-MY-ah) was a prophet who warned the people of Judah. He told them they were disobeying God and would be punished. He had a very difficult life, but he stayed faithful to God. He lived to see Jerusalem destroyed and the people taken to Babylon. (2 Chronicles 35:25; 36:21-22; Jeremiah 1; 2; 20:1-6; 28:5; 36-40)

Jerusalem (jeh-ROO-suh-lem) is sometimes called "Zion" or the "City of David." It was the greatest city of the country of Palestine. It was the center of the Jewish religion because the Temple was there. Jesus was killed on the cross near Jerusalem. The city was destroyed by the Roman army in the year A.D. 70. Later, it was rebuilt in the same place by the Moslems and is a great city today in the Middle East. (2 Samuel 5:5-6; 2 Chronicles 36:14, 19; Ezra 1:1-11; Luke 2:22-45; 13:34; 24:13, 18, 33, 47, 49; Acts 2:5, 14) See "Zion."

Jesus (JEE-zus) means "savior." He is the Son of God. He was born to Mary, a young Jewish woman. Mary was told by the angel Gabriel that she would have a baby boy. She was to name him "Jesus" because he would save his people from their sins. He is also called "Christ" and "Messiah." He lived a perfect life and never sinned. But he was killed by Roman soldiers on a cross near Jerusalem. Then, he came back to life and now lives in heaven with his father, God. He is one of the three persons of God. The other two persons are God the Father, and God the Holy Spirit. (Matthew 1:21; Luke 2:21; 3:23; John 20:19; Acts 1:19, 36; 4:10; Philippians 2:10-11) See "Christ" and "Messiah."

Jesus was a common name among Jewish people, so there were other less important men in the New Testament named Jesus, too. (Colossians 4:11)

Jew (JOO) at first meant someone from the tribe of Judah. Judah was 1 of Jacob's 12 sons and the head of 1 of the 12 tribes of Israel. Later, the word Jew meant any person in any of the 12 tribes (Hebrews 1-13). A person who is not a Jew is called a Gentile or non-Jew. Jesus was a Jew. (Ezra 4:12; Matthew 2:2; 28:11-15; Acts 2:5; Romans 1:16; 10:12)

John was the name of several men in the New Testament:

John the Baptist was Jesus' relative and the son of Elizabeth and Zechariah the priest. He lived in the desert and ate locusts and wild honey. He preached that the Savior, Jesus, was coming soon. Jesus came to John the Baptist to be baptized in the Jordan River. Herod Antipas had John killed by cutting off his head. (Matthew 3:1-17; 11:11-13; 14:3-12; Luke 1:13-17)

John, the apostle, was one of the sons of Zebedee. He and his brother James were fishermen. He wrote the Gospel of John, the books of 1, 2 and 3 John and probably Revelation. He is sometimes referred to as "the one Jesus loved." John, Peter and James were Jesus' closest friends. (Mark 1:19-20; 9:2; 14:33-34; Acts 3:1-11; Revelation 1:1-4, 9)

John Mark See Mark.

Jordan (JOR-d'n) is the only large river in the country of Palestine. It runs about 75 miles from Mount Hermon to the Dead Sea. It also makes two lakes–Lake Huleh and Lake Galilee. Jesus was baptized in the Jordan River near the city of Jericho. (Joshua 3:11-17; 2 Kings 5:10, 14; Matthew 3:5-17)

Joseph (JOZ-uf) was the name of several men in the Bible.

Joseph, the son of Jacob, was 1 of the 12 sons of Israel. His two sons, Ephraim and Manasseh, each started a tribe. (Genesis 37-50; Exodus 1:5-8; 13:19; Acts 7:10-14)

Joseph of Nazareth was the husband of Mary, Jesus' mother. He was a carpenter. He may have died when Jesus was a young man because he is not mentioned after Jesus' childhood. The

New Testament says he was "a good man." (Matthew 1:18-24; 2:13-23)

Joseph of Arimathea took the body of Jesus down from the cross and buried it in a tomb he had dug for himself. He was a member of the Jewish religious court called the Sanhedrin. He was probably a Christian. (Matthew 27:57-60; Mark 15:43-46)

Jubilee (JOO-bih-lee) was a Jewish celebration that took place every fifty years. Israelites were to do three things: (1) give the soil a rest and not farm, (2) free Israelite slaves, and (3) return land and houses to the first owners or their children. (Leviticus 25)

Judas Iscariot (JOO-dus is-CARE-ee-ut) was the apostle who turned against Jesus and handed him over to the Roman soldiers to be killed. For this he was paid only 30 pieces of silver, the price of a slave. Later, Judas killed himself. (Matthew 26:47-50; 27:3-5; John 13:26-30)

Jude (JOOD) was possibly a brother of Jesus and James. In Jesus' early ministry, Jude did not believe Jesus was the Son of God. Later, he believed and became a leader in Christ's church. He wrote the book of Jude in the New Testament. (John 7:5; Jude)

Judea (joo-DEE-uh) was the land of the Jews. It was a district in the country of Palestine. Both Jerusalem and Bethlehem were cities in Judea. John the Baptist began his preaching in the desert of Judea. (Matthew 2:1; Luke 1:5; 2:4; Acts 1:8)

judges (JUHG-es) were the leaders of Israel before Israel had kings. A judge decided who was guilty in court, led the army in battle and was in charge of the government, like a governor. Israel had 15 judges in all. (Judges 2:16-19; 1 Samuel 7:15-17)

Judgment Day (JUJ-ment DAY) is the day Christ will judge all people. He will take his followers to live with him

forever in heaven. Those who have followed the devil will be sent to live with him in hell forever. (Matthew 11:20-24; Hebrews 9:27-28; 2 Peter 2:9-10; 3:7)

L

lamb (LAM) is an animal that the Jews often offered as a sacrifice (gift) to God. Since Jesus died as a sacrifice for us, he is called the Lamb of God that takes away the sins of the world. (Genesis 4:4; 22:7; Exodus 12:3-13; John 1:29, 36; 1 Corinthians 5:7)

Lazarus (LAZ-uh-rus) was the name of two men in the New Testament:

Lazarus of Bethany was a brother to Mary and Martha. He was also a very dear friend of Jesus. When he died, Jesus brought him back to life. (John 11:1-45; 12:1-11)

Lazarus, the beggar, was the name of a person in a story Jesus told his followers. (Luke 16:19-31)

leprosy (LEH-prah-see) is a name for some bad skin diseases. A person with leprosy was called a leper and had to live outside the city. When other people came by, the lepers had to warn them by crying out, "Unclean! Unclean!" (Leviticus 13:45-46; 2 Kings 5:1-27; 2 Chronicles 26:19-23; Matthew 8:1-3; Luke 17:11-19)

Leviathan (lee-VI-ah-than) was the name for a sea creature; exact identity unknown. (Job 3:8; 41:1; Psalm 74:14; Isaiah 27:1)

Levites (LEE-vites) were descendants of Levi, one of Jacob's sons. The priests all came from this tribe. But not all Levites were priests. Those who were not priests worked in the Meeting Tent or Temple in other ways. (Exodus 32:25-29; Numbers 1:47-53; 8:5-26; Deuteronomy 10:8-9; 18:1-8; 1 Kings 12:31; Luke 10:32)

lid on the Holy Box is also called the mercy seat. This was the beautiful gold lid on the Box of the Agreement. It had a gold creature with wings on each end of it. This Holy Box was kept in the Most Holy Place of the Meeting Tent and later in the Temple. (Exodus 25:17-22; 26:34; Leviticus 16:2, 14-16; Hebrews 9:5)

locust (LO-cust) is an insect that looks like a grasshopper. Locusts travel in large groups. They eat crops and other green plants. Locusts were sometimes eaten as food. (Exodus 10:4-19; Deuteronomy 28:38-42; Joel 1:4; Matthew 3:4)

lord means "master" or one who is in control. Jesus is called Lord because he rules over all the world and universe. Christians let Jesus be the Lord of their lives. (Acts 2:36; 21:12-14; Romans 10:9; 1 Corinthians 6:11; Colossians 3:17-24)

Lord's Prayer is the name often given to the model prayer Jesus taught his followers. (Matthew 6:9-13; Luke 11:1-4)

Lord's Supper is the meal Jesus' followers eat to remember how he died for them. The bread reminds us of his body. The fruit of the vine reminds us of his blood. The Lord's Supper also shows that Jesus came back to life and now lives in heaven with God. (Matthew 26:26-30; Luke 22:14-20; 1 Corinthians 10:17; 11:23-32)

lots were sticks, stones or pieces of bone thrown like dice to decide something. Often God controlled the result of the lots to let the people know what he wanted them to do. (Numbers 26:55-56; Proverbs 18:18; Jonah 1:7; Luke 1:9; 23:34; Acts 1:26)

Luke was a non-Jewish doctor who often traveled with the apostle Paul. He was a very educated man. He wrote the books of Luke and Acts in the New Testament. Luke tells many acts of Jesus that are not told in the other three Gospels. (Colossians 4:14; 2 Timothy 4:11)

lyre (LIRE) is a musical instrument with strings. It is similar to a harp, but smaller. (2 Samuel 6:5; 1 Chronicles 15:16-28; Psalms 33:2; 144:9; 150:3)

M

mahalath (mah-HAY-lath), or mahalath leannoth, was probably a musical word. It may have been the name of a tune, or it may mean to dance and shout. (Psalms 53; 88)

manna (MAN-ah) means "what is it?" It was the white, sweet-tasting food God gave the people of Israel in the wilderness. It appeared on the ground during the night so they could gather it in the morning. (Exodus 16:13-35; Numbers 11:7-9; Joshua 5:12; Hebrews 9:4)

Marduk (MAR-dook) was a false god of the Babylonians. (Jeremiah 50:2)

Mark, sometimes called John Mark, was a cousin to Barnabas. Mark traveled with Paul and Barnabas on part of their first missionary journey. He also wrote the Gospel of Mark. Christians met in the home of Mark's mother, Mary, to pray for Peter to be freed from prison. (Acts 12:12, 25; 13:5, 13; 15:36-41; Colossians 4:10; 2 Timothy 4:11)

Martha (MAR-thuh) was the sister of Mary and Lazarus. They lived in the village of Bethany, which is very near Jerusalem. Jesus often stayed in their home when he was in that area. Martha and her brother and sister loved Jesus very much. (Luke 10:38-41; John 11:1-39; 12:12)

martyr (MAR-ter) is a Greek word that means "witness." Being a witness means telling what you know about something. Later, martyr came to mean a person who was killed for being a witness. Stephen was the first Christian martyr. He was killed because he told people that Jesus is the Son of God. It is believed that all the apostles, except one, were martyrs for being witnesses about Jesus. (Acts 7:54-60; 12:2; 22:20; Revelation 2:13)

Mary is the name of several women in the New Testament:

Mary, the mother of Jesus, was a Jewish woman whom God chose to give birth to his only Son. This was a great honor and blessing from God. She married a man named Joseph. Mary stood at the foot of the cross when Jesus was killed. (Matthew 1:18-25; Luke 1:27-45; John 19:25-27)

Mary Magdalene was from the town of Magdala. She was a follower of Jesus. She watched the men put Jesus' body in the tomb. She was the first person to see Jesus after he came back to life. (Matthew 27:56, 61; Mark 15:40, 47; 16:1, 9; John 20:1-18)

Mary of Bethany was the sister of Martha and Lazarus. She was a dear friend of Jesus. Mary sat at Jesus' feet and listened to him teach. One time she poured some expensive perfume on his feet and dried them with her hair. (Luke 10:39-42)

maskil (MAS-kil) is probably a description of the kind of song that some of the Psalms were. It appears with 13 of the Psalms. (Psalms 32; 42; 44; 45)

Matthew (MATH-you), also called Levi, was a tax collector. He was 1 of Jesus' 12 apostles. He wrote the Gospel of Matthew. (Matthew 9:9-10; 10:3)

medium (MEED-ee-um) means "go-between." This is a person who tries to help living people talk to the spirits of dead people. (Leviticus 19:31; Deuteronomy 18:11; 1 Samuel 28:3-9; 2 Kings 23:24; Isaiah 8:19-20)

Meeting Tent is often called the Tabernacle or Holy Tent. This was the special tent where the Israelites worshiped God. It was used from the time they left Egypt until Solomon built the Temple in Jerusalem. This tent was kept in the middle of their camp to remind them that God was always with them.

(Exodus 25-27; 39:32-40:36; Numbers 8; 2 Chronicles 1:3-13; 5:5)

Melchizedek (mel-KIZ-ih-dek) means "king of righteousness." He was a priest and king who worshiped God in the time of Abraham. Jesus is now the Christian's king and high priest. In this way, Jesus is a priest and a king like Melchizedek. (Genesis 14:17-24; Hebrews 5:4-10; 7:1-17)

mercy (MUR-see) is kindness and forgiveness. God had mercy on us. He sent his only Son, Jesus, to die on the cross for our sins. We, too, are taught to have mercy on other people. God says he will be as merciful to us as we are to others. (Genesis 43:14; 2 Samuel 24:14; Matthew 5:7; Romans 11:32; James 2:13; 5:11; 1 Peter 2:10)

mercy seat See "lid on the Holy Box."

Messiah (muh-SYE-uh) is a Hebrew word for "appointed one" or "one chosen by God." The Greek word for Messiah is "Christ." Christians believe that Jesus is the Messiah or Christ. (John 1:41; 4:25)

miktam (MIK-tam) is probably a description of what kind of song some of the Psalms were. It may mean that it is a sad song or a song about danger. (Psalms 16; 56-60)

mildew (MIL-doo) is a growth that appears on things that have been damp for a long time. (Leviticus 13:47-59; 14:33-54)

minister (MIN-i-ster) means "servant." It also means one who lives serving God and others. Christians are taught to minister to each other and to non-Christians. (Romans 15:16)

miracle (MEER-ih-k'l) is a Latin word that means "wonderful thing." It is a great event which can be done only by God's help. Miracles are special signs to show God's power. In the Old Testament God used miracles to rescue his people. Jesus did miracles to prove that he was God's Son. The

Bible tells us of many miracles. The sick were healed, the blind were given sight, the crippled were able to walk and people could speak languages they had never studied. Sometimes people were even brought back to life after they had died. The best miracle was Jesus' coming back to life after he was killed on the cross. (Nehemiah 9:17; Psalm 77:11, 14; Matthew 28:5-7; Luke 23:8; John 2:1-11; 3:2; 20:30-31; Acts 4:16-22; 8:13)

Molech (MO-lek) was a false god of the Canaanite people. Those who worshiped Molech often sacrificed their own children to him by burning them on altars. (Leviticus 18:21; 20:1-5; 2 Kings 23:10; Jeremiah 32:35)

mortar (MORE-tar) has two meanings:

It can be a stone bowl where grain is ground into flour by pounding. Manna was ground up this way. (Numbers 11:8; Proverbs 27:22)

Mortar is also the sticky material that holds bricks together. It was often made of mud or clay. (Genesis 11:3; Exodus 1:14; Isaiah 41:25)

Moses (MO-zez) in Hebrew means "saved from the water." Moses led God's people out of the land of Egypt where they had been slaves for 400 years. Moses wrote the first five books of the Old Testament. On Mount Sinai God gave to Moses the law for the Israelite people. It is called "the law of Moses." (Exodus 2–40; Numbers 1–26; Deuteronomy 27–34; John 1:17, 45; 3:14; Hebrews 11:23-24; Revelation 15:3)

Most Holy Place was the inner and most special room in the Meeting Tent and the Temple. The Box of the Agreement was kept here. Only the high priest could come into this room, and he could enter only once a year. This was when he sprinkled blood on the lid of the Holy Box to remind the people that their sins needed to be forgiven.

(Exodus 26:33-34; Leviticus 16:2-20; 1 Kings 6:16-35; Hebrews 9:3-25)

Mount of Olives is a hill covered with olive trees near Jerusalem. The garden of Gethsemane is on one side of the Mount of Olives. Jesus was praying there when the Roman soldiers came to arrest him. Some of the same olive trees that were in the garden when Jesus was on earth may still be there today. (2 Samuel 15:30; Luke 22:39-52; Acts 1:12)

Mount Zion (ZI-on) at first meant one of the hills on which Jerusalem was built. Later Zion became another name for the whole city of Jerusalem. In the New Testament, Zion is also used as a name for heaven. (Psalms 48:2, 11; 74:2; 78:68; Obadiah 17; Hebrews 12:22)

myrrh (MUR) was a sweet-smelling liquid taken from certain trees and shrubs. It was used as a perfume and as a pain reliever. It was one of the gifts the wise men gave Jesus when he was born. (Genesis 37:25; 43:11; Proverbs 7:17; Matthew 2:11; Mark 15:23; John 19:39)

N

nard was an expensive perfume. It cost so much because it had to be imported from India. (Song of Solomon 4:13; Mark 14:3; John 12:3)

Nazarene (NAZ-uh-reen) is a person from the town of Nazareth. Jesus grew up in Nazareth and was called a Nazarene. Sometimes Christians also were called Nazarenes, since they followed Jesus. (Matthew 2:23; Acts 24:5)

Nazirite (NAZ-e-rite) was a Jewish person who made a special promise to God. He was to serve God by following special rules. Samson and Samuel were Nazirites. (Numbers 6:1-21; Judges 13:7; 16:17)

Nebo (NEE-boh) was the name of a Babylonian god. He was thought to be the god of writing and the son of Bel. (Isaiah 46:1)

Nebo was also the name of the mountain where Moses died, as well as a town nearby. (Numbers 32:3; Deuteronomy 34:1; Isaiah 15:2)

Nehemiah (nee-uh-MY-uh) was a servant of King Artaxerxes I of Persia. He got permission to take a group of Jews back to Jerusalem to rebuild its walls. Nehemiah was such a good leader that they finished the job even though they had many difficulties. (Nehemiah 1–12)

Nephilim (NEF-eh-lim) were a group of people who were famous for being large and strong. The ten spies who were afraid to enter Canaan had seen the Nephilim who lived there. (Genesis 6:4; Numbers 13:33)

New Moon was a Jewish feast held on the first day of the month. It was celebrated with animal sacrifices and the blowing of trumpets. It was a way for the Israelites to dedicate the month to the Lord. (Numbers 10:10; 28:14; 1 Samuel 20:5, 24; Psalm 81:3; Ezekiel 46:3-6; Colossians 2:16)

Noah (NO-uh) and his family were the only people of their time who served God. So God told them about the great flood that was coming. They built a large boat (often called an ark) about 450 feet long. Noah's family and every kind of animal were saved to start the world all over again. (Genesis 6–9; 1 Peter 3:20)

P

parable (PARE-uh-b'l) is a story that teaches a lesson by comparing two things. Jesus often used parables to teach the people. Some examples of parables can be found in Mark 12:1-12; Luke 10:29-37 and Luke 15:1-31.

Passover Feast (PASS-o-ver FEEST) was an important holy day for the Jews in the spring of each year. They ate a special meal on this day to remind

them that God had freed them from being slaves in Egypt. Jesus was killed at Passover time. (Exodus 12:27; Numbers 9; Joshua 5:10; Matthew 26:2, 17-19)

Paul is the Roman name for "Saul." Saul was a Jew, born in the city of Tarsus. He studied under Gamaliel, a famous teacher of God's law. At first, Paul tried to destroy Christ's church by putting Christians in jail and killing them. But Jesus appeared to him and changed his life completely. He was then called Paul. And he became an apostle and a great servant of God. He traveled to many countries, teaching about Jesus. Paul wrote many of the books of the New Testament as letters to Christians in different cities, such as Romans, Colossians and Corinthians. (Acts 7:58-60; 9:1-31; Philippians 3:5-7)

Pentecost (PEN-tee-cost) means "fifty." Pentecost was a Jewish feast day celebrating the summer harvest. It took place 50 days after the Passover Feast. The apostles began telling the Good News on Pentecost after Jesus died. (Acts 2; 20:16; 1 Corinthians 16:8)

persecute (PUR-seh-cute) means to hurt people. Christians in the New Testament times were often persecuted. Saul persecuted Christians by dragging them from their homes, putting them in jail and killing them. (Matthew 5:11-12; Acts 8:1-4; Galatians 6:12; 1 Peter 3:13-15)

Peter (PEE-ter) was a fisherman. He and his brother, Andrew, were the first two apostles Jesus chose. He was first named Simon, but Jesus changed his name to Cephas, which means "rock" in Aramaic. In Greek the name is Peter. Peter, James and John were Jesus' closest friends. Peter was the first to tell the Good News of Jesus to the non-Jewish people. Later in his life Peter wrote the New Testament books of 1 and 2 Peter. He probably died as a martyr for Christ. (Matthew 14:25-33; 16:13-18; Mark 14:27-39; Luke 22:54-62; John 20:1-6; Acts 3:1-26; 10:1-48)

pharaoh (FAY-row) was the title given to the kings of Egypt. The word first meant "great house," meaning the palace where the king lived. Later it became the title of the king who lived in the great house. Pharaoh is also called "king of Egypt." (Genesis 40–47; Exodus 1–14; 2 Kings 23:29)

Pharisees (FARE-uh-seez) means "the separate people." They were a Jewish religious group who followed the religious laws and customs very strictly. Jesus often spoke against the Pharisees for their religious teachings and traditions. Many of the Pharisees did not like Jesus because he did not follow all of their rules. (Matthew 5:20; 23:23-36; Mark 7:1-13; Luke 18:9-14)

Philip (FIL-ip) was the name of several men in the New Testament:

Philip, the apostle, was from the city of Bethsaida and was a friend of Peter and Andrew. He brought Nathanael to Jesus. (Matthew 10:2-3; John 1:43-48; 12:21; 14:8-9)

Philip, the evangelist, was a Greek-speaking Jew. He was one of the seven men chosen to serve in the church in Jerusalem. Later, he preached the Good News in many places. (Acts 6:1-6; 8:5-40; 21:8-9)

Philip, the tetrarch (ruler), was the son of Herod I and Cleopatra. He built the city of Caesarea Philippi. (Luke 3:1)

Philistines (FIL-ih-steens) were Israel's enemies for many years. They had five strong cities near the Mediterranean Sea: Ashdod, Ashkelon, Ekron, Gath and Gaza. They worshiped several false gods. They were finally defeated by the Egyptians. (Judges 15; 16; 1 Samuel 4:1-10; 6; 7; 17; 18; 1 Chronicles 18:1)

plumb line (PLUM LINE) is a string with a rock or other weight on one end. People used it to see if a wall was straight. The plumb line was sometimes used to mean that God was checking to see if his people were living right. This is just as they checked to see if a wall was built right. (2 Kings 21:13; Amos 7:7-8)

pomegranate (PAHM-gran-it) is a red fruit about the size of an apple. It has many seeds. Each seed has a pocket of sweet juice around it. (Exodus 28:33; 39:24; Numbers 13:23; Deuteronomy 8:8; 1 Samuel 14:2)

Pontius Pilate (PON-shus PIE-lut) means "armed with a spear." Pilate was the Roman governor of Judea from A.D. 26 to 36. The Jews who wanted Jesus killed brought him to Pilate. He did not find Jesus guilty of any crime. But Pilate allowed the Jews to crucify Jesus because he was afraid of the people. (Luke 13:1; 23:1-52; Acts 3:13; 4:27; 1 Timothy 6:13)

Preparation Day (prep-a-RAY-shun-DAY) was the day before the Sabbath day. On that day the Jews prepared or got everything ready for the Sabbath. (Luke 23:54; John 19:14, 31)

priest (PREEST) in the Old Testament was a servant of God who worked in the Meeting Tent or Temple. Priests helped the people offer their gifts and sacrifices to God. Jesus is the Christian's high priest. He brings man and God together. Because of this all Christians are now priests. (Leviticus 21; 22; Hebrews 7:26-28; 1 Peter 2:5, 9; Revelation 1:5-6) See "high priest."

Priscilla (prih-SIL-uh) See "Aquila."

prophecy (PRAH-feh-see) means "message." It is God speaking through chosen people called prophets. The Old Testament has many prophecies about the Savior who was to come into the world. Jesus was the answer to these prophecies. (Ezekiel 12:26-28; 2 Peter 1:20-21; Revelation 22:18-19) See "prophet."

prophesy (PRAH-fes-sy) is to speak a prophecy. See "prophecy."

prophet (PRAH-fet) means "messenger" or one who speaks for someone else. With God's help, a prophet was able to tell the people God's message correctly. Sometimes prophets told what would happen in the future. A woman who spoke God's message was called a prophetess (2 Kings 22:14; Luke 2:36). Several books of the Old Testament were written by prophets, including Jeremiah, Amos, Jonah and Micah. (2 Kings 6:12-16; 17:12-13; Matthew 2:5-6; Luke 16:29-31; 24:25-27; Romans 1:2; 1 Corinthians 12:28-29; 1 Peter 1:10-12)

prophetess See "prophet."

prostitute (PRAH-sti-toot) is a person who sells his or her body for sexual relations with someone to whom he or she is not married. This is a sin. In the Old Testament God's people often worshiped other gods. God said this was acting like a prostitute. (Genesis 38:15; Exodus 34:15-16; Proverbs 23:27; Jeremiah 3:1-6; Hosea 3:3; 1 Corinthians 6:15)

proverbs (PRAH-verbs) are wise sayings. They are usually short so they can be easily remembered. The Old Testament book of Proverbs contains many wise sayings. They tell how to live a good and happy life. (book of Proverbs)

psalm (SAHM) means "song." The book of Psalms is like a songbook. The Jews sang many of these psalms, particularly at special times. There are many musical directions in the Psalms, such as the tune or the instruments to be used. (book of Psalms)

Q

Queen Goddess is another name for Ishtar, a goddess of the Babylonians. During Jeremiah's time some of the Israelites worshiped her. (Jeremiah 7:18; 44:17-25)

R

Rahab (RAY-hab) was the name of a make-believe dragon. In a well-known story, Rahab looked strong but was defeated. Egypt was sometimes called Rahab to show that it would be defeated as Rahab was. (Job 9:13; 26:12; Psalms 87:4; 89:10; Isaiah 30:7; 51:9)

Rahab was also the name of a woman in Jericho. She hid the Israelite spies and helped them escape. (Joshua 2:1-3; 6:17-25; Matthew 1:5; Hebrews 11:31; James 2:25)

Rapha (RAY-fa) was a leader of a group of people in Canaan. They may have been giants. The descendants of Rapha are called Rephaites. (Genesis 14:5; Deuteronomy 2:11; 2 Samuel 21:16-22)

Red Sea is sometimes called the Sea of Reeds. It is a large body of water between Africa and Arabia. At the northern end it has two parts, one on each side of the Sinai Peninsula. God used a miracle to divide these waters on the northern end on the west side. Then the Israelites could walk across on dry land and escape from Egypt. (Exodus 13:17–15:22; Joshua 2:10; 4:23; Psalm 106:7-22)

repent (ree-PENT) means being sorry for doing something wrong and not continuing to do that wrong thing. To repent is to "change your heart and life." (2 Chronicles 32:26; Matthew 3:2; 4:17; Mark 1:15; Luke 15:7, 10; Acts 2:38; 3:19)

Rephaites See "Rapha."

resurrection (REZ-uh-REK-shun) is a dead person's coming back to life. In the New Testament several people came back to life with God's help. Some of them were Lazarus (John 11:38-45), Tabitha (Acts 9:36-42), the widow's son in the town of Nain (Luke 7:11-17), and Eutychus (Acts 20:8-12). Jesus, the Son of God, came back to life after being dead three days. This was the most important resurrection. His resurrection from death means we can be saved and live in heaven forever. (Matthew 28:1-10; 1 Corinthians 15; 1 Peter 3:21-22)

revelation (rev-uh-LAY-shun) means to show plainly something that has been hidden. The last book in the New Testament is called the Revelation of Jesus Christ. God showed the apostle John what to write to Christians to give them hope and faith even though they were being persecuted. (2 Corinthians 12:1; Revelation 1:1-3)

Rock is often used as a name for God. A large rock is strong and a good place to hide. God is strong and protects us from our enemies. (Genesis 49:24; Deuteronomy 32:4, 15, 18, 30; 2 Samuel 22:32, 47; Psalm 18:2, 31, 46)

S

Sabbath (SAB-uth) means "rest." It was the seventh day of the Jewish week, their day of worship to God. The Jews were not allowed to work on this day. Some Jews became angry with Jesus because he healed people on the Sabbath. They thought this was breaking the Old Testament law of the Sabbath. (Exodus 16:23-30; 20:8-11; Matthew 12:9-14; Luke 6:1-11; Acts 18:4; Colossians 2:16-17)

Sadducees (SAD-you-seez) were a Jewish religious group. They were rich and important men. They believed that only the first five books of the Old Testament were true. They did not believe in angels or life after death (resurrection). The Sadducees lost their power and importance after Jerusalem was destroyed by the Romans about the year A.D. 70. (Matthew 22:23-33; Acts 4:1-2; 5:17-18; 23:6-9)

safety, city of is sometimes called City of Refuge. In Bible times, someone who had accidentally killed another person could go to a city of safety for protection. As long as the person was in a city of safety, the dead person's relative could not punish him. There were six cities of safety. (Numbers 35:6-34; Joshua 20)

saffron (SAF-ron) is a purple flower. Parts of it are used as a spice. (Song of Solomon 4:14)

saint is another word for Christian. God has set Christians apart to serve him. They live to please God and be like him—pure and holy. (Acts 9:13, 32, 41; 26:10; Romans 1:7; 1 Corinthians 1:2; Ephesians 1:1)

Samaritan (suh-MEHR-ih-t'n) was a person from the area of Samaria in Palestine. Samaria was between Galilee and Judea. These people were only part Jewish, so the Jews did not accept them. They hated the Samaritans. But Jesus showed love and concern for the Samaritans. One story that Jesus told is known as the story of "the good Samaritan." (Luke 10:30-37; John 4:1-42)

Samuel (SAM-you-el) was the last judge in Israel. God used him to choose both Saul and David as kings. (1 Samuel 1-3; 7-16)

Sanhedrin (san-HEE-drin) See "council."

Satan (SAY-t'n) in Hebrew means "enemy." It is a name for the devil, the enemy of God and man. (1 Chronicles 21:1; Job 1:6-9; Matthew 4:10; Luke 10:18-19; Acts 5:3; 26:18) See "devil."

Saul (SAWL) in the Old Testament was the first king of Israel (1 Samuel 9–31). Saul in the New Testament was a man whose name was changed to Paul. See "Paul."

savior (SAVE-yor) is someone who saves people from danger. The name Jesus means "savior." Jesus is the Savior of the people of this world. His life, death and resurrection made it possible for people to be saved from death and punishment for their sins. (Luke 2:11; John 4:42; Ephesians 5:23; Philippians 3:20; Titus 1:4; 1 John 4:14)

scepter (SEP-tur) is a wand or a rod that the king holds. It is a sign of his power. Some are long and thin. Others are short and flat like a paddle. Some of them are highly decorated with gold. (Esther 4:11; 5:2; 8:4; Psalm 2:9)

scribe is a Hebrew word that means to write, to count and to put in order. In New Testament times scribes were men who wrote copies of the Scriptures. They were very careful when they copied the words of God. To be sure they had not made a mistake in copying, they would count the number of letters on each line they wrote. Scribes were educated, and some of them served as secretaries, royal assistants and teachers. (Nehemiah 8:1; Jeremiah 36:26; Matthew 7:29; 15:1-9; 23:1-36; Luke 22:2)

Scriptures (SCRIP-churs) means "writings." They are the special writings of God's word for man. When the word "Scriptures" is used in the New Testament, it usually means the Old Testament. Later, it came to mean the whole Bible. (Daniel 9:2; Luke 24:27, 32, 45; Acts 8:32-35; 17:2, 11; 2 Timothy 3:16; 2 Peter 1:20; 3:16) See "Bible."

scroll is a long roll of paper used for writing. In Bible times books were written on scrolls. These scrolls were rolled up from each end to the middle. They were made of papyrus (a plant) or parchment (an animal skin). Some scrolls were as long as 35 feet. (Numbers 5:23; Isaiah 8:1; Jeremiah 36; Luke 4:17-20; 2 Timothy 4:13; Revelation 5:1-5)

Sea of Galilee See "Galilee, Lake."

seal was a tool with a design or picture carved on it. Kings pressed this seal into wax which would be placed on important papers to close them. It was like a person's signature. If the seal was broken, it showed that someone else had looked at the papers. A seal also showed who owned something.

Sometimes these seals were worn as rings. (1 Kings 21:8; Esther 8:8; 2 Corinthians 1:22) See "signet ring."

seer was another name for prophet. (1 Samuel 9:9) See "prophet."

Selah (SEE-lah) is probably a musical direction and is used in the Psalms. It may mean to pause. The word was not intended to be spoken when reading the Psalm. (Psalms 3; 4; 9; 24)

sheminith (SHEM-e-nith) means "on the eighth." It is probably a musical word in the Psalms that means an octave. It may mean to use an instrument with eight strings. (1 Chronicles 15:21; Psalms 6; 12)

shepherd (SHEP-'rd) is a person who cares for and protects sheep. A shepherd loves his sheep and gives them food and water. He guides them to a quiet place to rest. He protects the sheep from wolves and other wild animals. A good shepherd will even die trying to protect his sheep.

Jesus is called the Good Shepherd because he loves and cares for his followers who are often called sheep. Jesus was willing to die for his followers to save them. (Psalm 23; Mark 6:34; John 10:1-30; 1 Peter 2:25; 5:4)

shiggaion/shigionoth (shi-GY-on/shi-gi-O-noth) could be musical words meaning a sad song. (Psalm 7; Habakkuk 3:1)

signet ring (SIG-net ring) was a ring worn by a king or other important person. It had his seal on it. He would stamp things with this ring to show that he owned them. The stamp was like a signature. (Genesis 41:42; Esther 3:10; 8:2-10; Daniel 6:17) See "seal."

Silas (SY-lus) is sometimes called Silvanus. He was a teacher in the church in Jerusalem who often traveled with Paul. He became one of Paul's most trusted helpers. He may have written down some of Peter and Paul's letters for them. (Acts 15:22,

30–17:16; 18:5; 1 Thessalonians 1:1; 1 Peter 5:12)

Simeon (SIM-ee-un) is a name that means "God has heard." He was 1 of the 12 sons of Israel. (Genesis 29:33; 35:23)

Another Simeon was a godly man who lived in Jerusalem. When he saw the baby Jesus in the Temple, he knew that this child would save his people from their sins. He held the baby Jesus in his arms and said a prayer of thanks to God. (Luke 2:25-35)

Simon (SY-mun), sometimes called Simeon, is a name that means "God has heard." The apostle Peter was first named Simon. Other men named Simon are also mentioned in the New Testament:

Simon of Cyrene carried the cross of Jesus to the hill of Calvary. (Matthew 27:32)

Simon, the magician, tried to buy the power of the Holy Spirit to do miracles. (Acts 8:9-24)

Simon, the Zealot, was 1 of the 12 apostles. (Matthew 10:4)

Simon, the brother of Jesus (Matthew 13:55)

sin is a word, thought or act against the law of God. Sin is doing something God said not to do, or it could be not doing something he said to do. Jesus came to save us from being punished for our sins. (Psalm 32:2; Romans 3:23; 5:12; 1 Corinthians 15:3; Galatians 1:4; Hebrews 4:15-16; 1 John 1:8-10; 2:1-2)

Solomon (SOL-o-mon) was a son of David. He took his father's place as king. He was famous for his wisdom and for building the Temple in Jerusalem. (1 Kings 1–11; 2 Chronicles 1–11)

Solomon's Porch (SOL-o-mon's PORCH) was a covered courtyard on the east side of the Temple. People gathered here to sell animals and exchange money. Others met to discuss the Law of Moses. (1 Kings 7:6; John 10:23; Acts 3:11; 5:12)

Son of David was a name the Jews used for the Christ who was to save the world. This was because the Savior was to come from the family of King David. Jesus was the "Son of David." (Matthew 9:27; 20:30; 21:9)

Son of Man was a name Jesus called himself. It showed that he was God's Son, but he was also a man. This title for Jesus comes from "one who looked like a human being" in Daniel 7:13-14. There Daniel prophesies about Jesus. (Matthew 24:30; 26:64; Mark 13:26; 14:62; Luke 21:27; 22:69)

sorcery (SOR-sir-ee) means trying to put magical spells on people or harming them by some kind of magic. The Bible warns against doing this. (Leviticus 19:26; Deuteronomy 18:14; 2 Kings 17:17)

soul (SOLE) is what makes a person alive. Sometimes the Bible writers used words like heart and soul to mean a person's whole being or the person himself. (Deuteronomy 4:29; Psalm 108:1; Matthew 10:28)

Spirit See "Holy Spirit."

spirit (SPIH-rit) is the part of man that was made to be like God because God is spirit. The New Testament also talks about evil spirits. (Isaiah 26:9; John 4:23-24; James 2:24-26) See "demons," "Holy Spirit" and "soul."

Stephen (STEE-ven) was one of the seven men chosen to serve the church in Jerusalem. The New Testament says he was a man who had much faith. He was able to do miracles. Stephen was the first martyr for Christ. The Jews killed him by throwing stones at him because he taught that Jesus was the Son of God. (Acts 6:5-15; 7:54-60; 22:20)

synagogue (SIN-uh-gog) is a Greek word that means "a meeting." By the first century, the Jews met in synagogues to read and study the Scriptures. The building was also used as the Jewish court and as a school. Both Jesus and Paul often went to the Jewish synagogues to teach and discuss the Scriptures. (Matthew 4:23; Luke 4:16-17; Acts 15:21; 17:1, 10)

Syria (SEER-ee-uh) is a Hebrew word that means "plain." In New Testament times, it was the area north of Galilee and east of the Mediterranean Sea. Damascus was its capital city. In Old Testament times, this country was called Aram. (1 Kings 11:25; 2 Kings 5:1; Matthew 4:24; 15:23)

T

tabernacle (TAB-er-NAK'l) See "Meeting Tent."

tambourine (tam-buh-REEN) is a musical instrument that is beaten to keep rhythm. (Exodus 15:20; 1 Samuel 18:6; Psalm 81:2)

tax collector was a Jew hired by the Romans to collect taxes. Most people did not like tax collectors because they worked for the Romans and often cheated people. The apostle Matthew was a tax collector before he became an apostle. Zacchaeus was also a tax collector. (Matthew 9:10-11; 10:3; Luke 5:27; 19:1-8)

temple (TEM-p'l) is a building where people worship their gods. God told the Jewish people to worship him at the Temple in Jerusalem. This Temple had been built by King Solomon. It was later destroyed by the Babylonians. It was rebuilt by Zerubbabel. This Temple was destroyed by a Roman general, Pompey. Herod built a third Temple which was used in Jesus' time. (2 Chronicles 2–7; Ezra 3:10-12; Mark 11:15-17; Acts 7:47; 19:27)

The New Testament also speaks of a Christian's body as a temple. That is because God's Spirit lives in the Christian. (Acts 7:48; 19:27; 1 Corinthians 6:19)

temptation (temp-TAY-shun) is the devil's trying to get us to do something wrong. God has promised to help us when we are tempted, so we can choose to do the right thing. (Matthew 4:1-11; 1 Corinthians 10:13; Hebrews 2:18; 4:15-16; James 1:12-14)

Tent See "Meeting Tent."

testament (TES-tuh-ment) See "agreement."

Thaddaeus (THAD-ee-us) was 1 of the 12 apostles. Little else is known about him. (Matthew 10:3; Mark 3:18)

Thomas (TOM-us), or Didymus, is a name that means "twin." He was 1 of Jesus' 12 apostles. His courage and love for Jesus are shown in John 11:16. Sometimes people call him "doubting Thomas." The other apostles told him Jesus had been raised from death. But Thomas did not believe it until he saw Jesus himself. (John 14:5-7; 20:24-29; 21:2)

threshing floor was a place where farmers separated grain from chaff. This was done by beating the stalks on the hard ground. Then they would throw it in the air and let the wind blow the chaff away. (Genesis 50:10; Judges 6:11; 2 Samuel 24:16-24) See "chaff."

Thummim (THUM-im) The Urim and Thummim were something attached to the holy vest of the high priest. They may have been gems. They were used in some way to find out what God wanted the Israelites to do. (Exodus 28:30; Leviticus 8:8; Deuteronomy 33:8)

Tiberius Caesar (tie-BEER-ee-us SEE-zur) was the Roman emperor during the last half of Jesus' life. He ruled from A.D. 14 to 37. The city of Tiberias was named for him. (Luke 3:1)

Timothy (TIM-oh-thee) means "one who honors God." Timothy was a close friend and helper of the apostle Paul. He was the son of a Greek father and Jewish Christian mother. His mother Eunice and his grandmother Lois taught him the Scriptures. Paul wrote two letters, called 1 and 2 Timothy, to him. (Acts 16:1-3; 17:13-16; 1 Corinthians 4:17; 1 Thessalonians 3:1-6; 2 Timothy 1:2-5)

tithe (TIETH) means "tenth." In the Old Testament the Jewish people were told to give one-tenth of what they earned to God. (Leviticus 27:30-32; Malachi 3:8; Luke 11:42; 18:12)

Titus (TIE-tus) was a trusted friend and helper of the apostle Paul. He often traveled with or for Paul. Paul wrote the book of Titus to him while Titus was on the island of Crete. (2 Corinthians 2:13; 7:6-7, 13-15; 8:6, 16, 23; Titus 1:4-5)

tomb (TOOM) is a place where a dead person's body is buried. Some tombs were underground. More often, in biblical times they were dug out of the side of a huge rock or mountain. A large stone was then rolled in front of the tomb to seal it. (Genesis 50:5; Luke 23:53-55; 24:1-2; John 20:1-9; 11:38-41)

transfiguration (tranz-fig-you-RAY-shun) means "to change." Jesus was transfigured in front of Peter, James and John. Jesus had taken them up on a mountain with him. There his face and clothes began to shine brightly. God spoke to the apostles. He said that Jesus is his Son and that they should obey only him. (Matthew 17:1-9)

tribe was all the descendants of a certain person. The 12 tribes of Israel were the descendants of the 12 sons of Jacob, who was later named Israel. (Genesis 49:28; Joshua 3:12; 7:14)

U

uncircumcised See "circumcision."

unclean is used to describe the state of a person, animal or action that was not pleasing to God. In the Old Testament God said certain animals were unclean. They were not to be eaten. If a person disobeyed this (or some other rule about being clean), that person was called unclean. He could not serve God until he was made clean again. (Genesis 7:2; Leviticus 11-15; Romans 14:14) See "clean."

unleavened bread (un-LEV-'nd bread) is bread made without yeast. This kind of bread is like a flat, thin cracker because it does not rise when it is baked. God told the Jews to use unleavened bread for the Passover Feast. (Exodus 12:20; Matthew 26:17-29; Mark 14:12-25)

Unleavened Bread, Day of was the first day of the Feast of Unleavened Bread or Passover. (Luke 22:7)

Urim (YOUR-im) See "Thummim."

V

vest, holy is often called the "ephod." This was a special type of clothing for the priests in the Old Testament. The holy vest for the high priest had gold and gems on it. The Urim and Thummim were attached to the holy vest. (Exodus 25; 28; 39) See "Thummim."

virgin (VUR-jin) is a woman or girl who has not had sexual relations. (Genesis 24:16; Deuteronomy 22:15-28; Isaiah 7:14; Matthew 1:23; Luke 1:34)

vision (VIZ-zhun) is like a dream. A vision may come to a person when he is awake or asleep. God used visions to tell people what he wanted them to do, to teach them something or to let them know something that was going to happen. Peter had a vision of a sheet filled with animals. (Genesis 15:1; Daniel 2:19; Acts 9:10-12; 10:3-19; 11:5; 16:9-10; 18:9)

W

winepress was a pit where grapes were mashed to get the juice out. People stepped on the grapes. The juice ran out into another container. The winepress is sometimes used to describe how God will punish people. When they sinned terribly, God would allow enemy armies to defeat them as if they were grapes crushed in a winepress. (Deuteronomy 15:14; Judges 6:11; Lamentations 1:15)

wise men, or "magi," was a name for men who studied the stars. Some wise men followed a star from the East and brought gifts to Jesus when he was born. (Matthew 2:1-12)

witchcraft means using the power of the devil to do magic. (Deuteronomy 18:10; 2 Chronicles 33:6; Galatians 5:20)

witness (WIT-ness) is someone who tells what he has seen or what he knows. The apostles were witnesses for Christ because they told people that Jesus is the Son of God. (Acts 1:8, 22; 2:32; 22:14-15)

woman, slave is also called a concubine. She was a woman who may have been captured by a man during a war. Or he may have bought her as a slave. She was like a second-class wife whose main purpose was to have children for him. (Genesis 36:12; 2 Chronicles 11:21)

word in the Bible often means God's message to us in the Scriptures. (1 Peter 1:24-25; 1 John 2:14) Jesus is called the "Word" because he shows us what God is like. (John 1:1-5, 14)

Y

yoke is a wooden frame that fits on the necks of animals to hold them together while working. Two oxen were often yoked together to pull a farmer's plow. The word yoke is also used to mean the work a person is to do. (Deuteronomy 21:3; 2 Chronicles 10:4-11; Matthew 11:29)

Z

Zealots (ZEL-ots) were a group of Jewish men who were also called "Enthusiasts." They hated the Romans for controlling their home country and planned to force them out. Simon, the apostle, was a Zealot. (Luke 6:15; Acts 1:13)

Zion (ZY-on) was a hill inside the city of Jerusalem. Later, the name Zion, or Sion, was used to mean all of Jerusalem. In the New Testament, Mount Zion is sometimes even used as a name for heaven. (Hebrews 12:22; Revelation 14:1)

WHERE DO I FIND IT?

Abraham
  God Calls Abraham, *Genesis 12:1-9*
  Abraham Offers Isaac, *Genesis 21:1-8; 22:1-19*

Advice to Children, *Proverbs 3:1-8*
Babel (The Tower), *Genesis 11:1-9*
Balaam and His Donkey, *Numbers 22:21-34*
Battle of Jericho, *Joshua 6:1-27*
The Beatitudes, *Matthew 5:3-12*
Cain and Abel, *Genesis 4:1-15*

Creation
  God Made Our World, *Genesis 1:1-25*
  Adam and Eve, *Genesis 1:26–2:25*
  Garden of Eden, *Genesis 2:8-14*
  The Big Mistake, *Genesis 2:15-17; 3:1-19*
  The First Brothers, *Genesis 4:1-15*

Daniel
  The Blazing Furnace, *Daniel 3:1-30*
  Writing on the Wall, *Daniel 5:1-31*
  Daniel in the Lion's Den, *Daniel 6:1-28*

David
  David and Goliath, *1 Samuel 17:4-51*
  David and Jonathan, *1 Samuel 20:1-42*
  David Becomes King, *2 Samuel 5:1-5*
  David and Bathsheba, *2 Samuel 11:1–12:25*

Elijah
  Elijah and the Prophets of Baal, *1 Kings 18:1-40*
  Elijah Is Taken to Heaven, *2 Kings 2:1-12*

Esther Saves Her People, *Esther 2:1–8:8*
The Excellent Wife, *Proverbs 31:10-31*
The Faith Chapter, *Hebrews 11:1-39*
Gideon's Brave 300, *Judges 6:33–8:3*

Paul and Barnabas Sent to Preach, *Acts 13:4-5*
Paul's First Missionary Journey, *Acts 13:1–14:28*
Paul's Second Missionary Journey, *Acts 15:36–18:22*
Paul and Silas in Jail, *Acts 16:16-40*
Paul's Third Missionary Journey, *Acts 18:22–21:16*
Paul Sails to Rome, *Acts 27:1–28:15*

Peter
Peter Tries to Walk on Water, *Matthew 14:28-31*
Peter Lies About Knowing Jesus, *Matthew 26:69-75*
Peter's First Sermon, *Acts 2:14-36*
Peter and John Heal a Crippled Man, *Acts 3:1-10*
Peter Freed from Prison, *Acts 12:6-19*

Philip Teaches a Man from Ethiopia, *Acts 8:26-40*
The Prodigal Son, *Luke 15:11-32*

The Promised Land
The Twelve Spies, *Numbers 13:1–14:35*
A Talking Donkey, *Numbers 22:1-34*
Rahab Helps the Spies, *Joshua 2:1-21; 6:22-25*
The Sun Stands Still, *Joshua 10:5-14*

The Rich Young Man's Question, *Matthew 19:16-30*
Rules for Children, *Ephesians 6:1; Colossians 3:20*
Rules for Leaders, *1 Timothy 3:1-13*
Rules for Parents, *Proverbs 22:6; 23:13; Ephesians 6:4*
Rules for Wives and Husbands, *Ephesians 5:21-33*
Ruth, *Ruth 1:1–4:22*
Samson and Delilah, *Judges 16:4-22*
The Sermon on the Mount, *Matthew 5:1–7:29*
Shadrach, Meshach and Abednego, *Daniel 3:1-30*
Solomon's Wisdom, *1 Kings 3:5-28; 4:29-34*
Stephen, the First Deacon, *Acts 6:1–8:1*
The Sun Stands Still, *Joshua 10:5-14*
The Ten Commandments, *Exodus 20:1-17*
The Tower of Babel, *Genesis 11:1-9*
Twelve Apostles, *Luke 6:12-16*
Twelve Tribes, *Exodus 1:1-5*
The Valley of Dry Bones, *Ezekiel 37:1-14*
The Wasteful Son, *Luke 15:11-32*
A Widow's Great Gift, *Mark 12:41-44; Luke 21:1-4*

WHAT GOD
PROMISES ABOUT . . .

The Bible contains many wonderful promises that God has made to us. Below are just a few of them. You might want to see what other promises you can find. One reason God's promises are special is that "the Lord will keep his promises" (Psalm 145:13).

Doing Good

We must not become tired of doing good. We will receive our harvest of eternal life at the right time. We must not give up!
Galatians 6:9

You are young, but do not let anyone treat you as if you were not important. Be an example to show the believers how they should live. Show them with your words, with the way you live, with your love, with your pure life. . . . Then you will save yourself and those people who listen to you.
1 Timothy 4:12, 16

Forgiveness

If we confess our sins, he will forgive our sins. We can trust God. He does what is right. He will make us clean from all the wrongs we have done.
1 John 1:9

Giving

God loves the person who gives happily. And God can give you more blessings than you need. Then you will always have plenty of everything.
2 Corinthians 9:7-8

Helping Me

God is our protection and our strength:
He always helps in times of trouble.
Psalm 46:1

The Lord is close to the brokenhearted.
He saves those whose spirits have been crushed.
Psalm 34:18

You can be sure that I will be with you always. I will continue with you until the end of the world.
Matthew 28:20

The Lord is my shepherd.
I have everything I need.
Psalm 23:1

Remember the Lord in everything you do.
And he will give you success.
Proverbs 3:6

With God's power working in us, God can do much, much more than anything we can ask or think of.
Ephesians 3:20

Yes, God is working in you to help you want to do what pleases him. Then he gives you the power to do it.
Philippians 2:13

I can do all things through Christ
because he gives me strength.
Philippians 4:13

My Faith

Remember that I commanded you
to be strong and brave. So don't be
afraid. The Lord your God will be
with you everywhere you go.
Joshua 1:9

I tell you the truth. If your faith is as
big as a mustard seed, you can say to
this mountain, "Move from here to
there." And the mountain will move.
All things will be possible for you.
Matthew 17:20

Jesus said to her, "I am the resurrection and the life. He who believes in
me will have life even if he dies. And
he who lives and believes in me will
never die."
John 11:25-26

In Christ we can come before God
with freedom and without fear. We
can do this through faith in Christ.
Ephesians 3:12

Everyone who is a child of God has
the power to win against the world.
It is our faith that wins the victory
against the world. So the one who
wins against the world is the person
who believes that Jesus is the Son of
God.
1 John 5:4-5

My Happiness

Do what the Lord says is good and
right. Then things will go well for you.
Deuteronomy 6:18

Those people who know they have
great spiritual needs are
happy.
The kingdom of heaven belongs
to them.
Those who are sad now are happy.
God will comfort them.
Those who are humble are happy.
The earth will belong to them.
Those who want to do right more
than anything else are happy.
God will fully satisfy them.
Those who give mercy to others
are happy.
Mercy will be given to them.
Those who are pure in their
thinking are happy.
They will be with God.
Those who work to bring peace are
happy.
God will call them his sons.
Those who are treated badly for
doing good are happy.
The kingdom of heaven belongs
to them.
Matthew 5:3-10

My Obedience

Honor your father and your mother.
Then you will live a long time in the
land.
Exodus 20:12

Jesus said, "Those who hear the
teaching of God and obey it—they
are the ones who are truly blessed."
Luke 11:28

Children, obey your parents the way
the Lord wants. This is the right
thing to do. . . . . "Then everything

will be well with you, and you will have a long life on the earth."
Ephesians 6:1, 3

My Prayers

The Lord listens when I pray to him.
Psalm 4:3

When a good man prays, great things happen.
James 5:16

Salvation

God will soon save those who respect him.
And his greatness will be seen in our land.
Psalm 85:9

For God loved the world so much that he gave his only Son. God gave his Son so that whoever believes in him may not be lost, but have eternal life.
John 3:16

Jesus said, "Don't let your hearts be troubled. Trust in God. And trust in me. There are many rooms in my Father's house. . . . I am going there to prepare a place for you. After I go and prepare a place for you, I will come back. Then I will take you to be with me so that you may be where I am."
John 14:1-3

Wisdom

The Lord says, "I will make you wise. I will show you where to go.
I will guide you and watch over you."
Psalm 32:8

Listen to advice and accept correction.
Then in the end you will be wise.
Proverbs 19:20

But if any of you needs wisdom, you should ask God for it. God is generous. He enjoys giving to all people, so God will give you wisdom.
James 1:5

MEMORY VERSES FOR MY LIFE

Always be humble and gentle. Be patient and accept each other with love.
Ephesians 4:2

A friend loves you all the time.
Proverbs 17:17

But I tell you, love your enemies. Pray for those who hurt you.
Matthew 5:44

Do what is right to other people.
Love being kind to others.
And live humbly, trusting your God.
Micah 6:8

Do for other people what you want them to do for you.
Luke 6:31

Depend on the Lord.
Trust him, and he will take care of you.
Psalm 37:5

Being afraid of people can get you into trouble.
But if you trust the Lord, you will be safe.
Proverbs 29:25

Do not worry about anything. But pray and ask God for everything you need.
Philippians 4:6

My child, do not reject the Lord's discipline.
And don't become angry when he corrects you.
The Lord corrects those he loves just as a father corrects the child that he likes.
Proverbs 3:11-12

Give all your worries to him, because he cares for you.
1 Peter 5:7

A gentle answer will calm a person's anger.
But an unkind answer will cause more anger.
Proverbs 15:1

Children, obey your parents the way the Lord wants. This is the right thing to do.
Ephesians 6:1

Those who work to bring peace are happy.
God will call them his sons.
Matthew 5:9

Serve the Lord with joy.
Come before him with singing. . . .
Come into his city with songs of thanksgiving.
Come into his courtyards with songs of praise.
Thank him, and praise his name.
Psalm 100:2, 4

If someone does wrong to you, do not pay him back by doing wrong to him. Try to do what everyone thinks is right. Do your best to live in peace with everyone.
Romans 12:17-18

Praise the Lord!
> Thank the Lord because he is
> good.
> His love continues forever.
>> *Psalm 106:1*

Do not be bitter or angry or mad. Never shout angrily or say things to hurt others. Never do anything evil. Be kind and loving to each other. Forgive each other just as God forgave you in Christ.
> *Ephesians 4:31-32*

Happy is the person
> whose sins are forgiven,
> whose wrongs are pardoned.
>> *Psalm 32:1*

Be happy with those who are happy.
> *Romans 12:15*

Wait for the Lord's help.
> Be strong and brave
> and wait for the Lord's help.
>> *Psalm 27:14*

Be full of joy in the Lord always. I will say again, be full of joy.
> *Philippians 4:4*

But the people who trust the Lord
> will become strong again.
They will be able to rise up as an
> eagle in the sky.
> They will run without needing
> rest.
> They will walk without becoming
> tired.
>> *Isaiah 40:31*

Come to me, all of you who are tired and have heavy loads. I will give you rest.
> *Matthew 11:28*

Finally, be strong in the Lord and in his great power.
> *Ephesians 6:10*

Those who want to do right more
> than anything else are happy.
> God will fully satisfy them.
>> *Matthew 5:6*

If you love me, you will do the things I command.
> *John 14:15*

Do not let evil defeat you. Defeat evil by doing good.
> *Romans 12:21*

Your word is like a lamp for my feet
> and a light for my way.
>> *Psalm 119:105*

The only temptations that you have are the temptations that all people have. But you can trust God. He will not let you be tempted more than you can stand. But when you are tempted, God will also give you a way to escape that temptation. Then you will be able to stand it.
> *1 Corinthians 10:13*

When a person is tempted and still continues strong, he should be happy. After he has proved his faith, God will reward him with life forever. God promised this to all people who love him.
> *James 1:12*

Dear children, do not let any person lead you the wrong way. Christ is righteous. To be like Christ, a person must do what is right.
> *1 John 3:7*

You must choose for yourselves today. You must decide whom you will serve. . . . As for me and my family, we will serve the Lord.
Joshua 24:15

We know that in everything God works for the good of those who love him. They are the people God called, because that was his plan.
Romans 8:28

We have troubles all around us, but we are not defeated. We do not know what to do, but we do not give up.
2 Corinthians 4:8

The Lord is kind and shows mercy.
He does not become angry
quickly but is full of love.
Psalm 145:8

[Jesus] said to them, "Let the little children come to me. Don't stop them. The kingdom of God belongs to people who are like these little children."
Mark 10:14

God, examine me and know my
heart.
Test me and know my thoughts.
See if there is any bad thing in me.
Lead me in the way you set long
ago.
Psalm 139:23-24

I showed you in all things that you should work as I did and help the weak. I taught you to remember the words of Jesus. He said, "It is more blessed to give than to receive."
Acts 20:35

Always remember what you have
been taught.
Don't let go of it.
Keep safe all that you have learned.
It is the most important thing in
your life.
Proverbs 4:13

Love is patient and kind. Love is not jealous, it does not brag, and it is not proud.
1 Corinthians 13:4

Continue to ask, and God will give to you. Continue to search, and you will find. Continue to knock, and the door will open for you.
Matthew 7:7

All people have sinned and are not good enough for God's glory.
Romans 3:23

I give you a new command: Love each other. You must love each other as I have loved you. All people will know that you are my followers if you love each other.
John 13:34-35

I can do all things through Christ because he gives me strength.
Philippians 4:13

Forget about the wrong things people do to you. You must not try to get even. Love your neighbor as you love yourself.
Leviticus 19:18

Everything you say and everything you do should all be done for Jesus your Lord. And in all you do, give thanks to God the Father through Jesus.
Colossians 3:17

Love the Lord your God with all your heart, soul and strength.

Deuteronomy 6:5

Be kind and loving to each other. Forgive each other just as God forgave you in Christ.

Ephesians 4:32

But if we confess our sins, he will forgive us our sins. We can trust God. He does what is right. He will make us clean from all the wrongs we have done.

1 John 1:9

May the Lord bless you and keep you.
May the Lord show you his kindness.
May he have mercy on you.
May the Lord watch over you and give you peace.

Numbers 6:24-26

MY FAVORITE THINGS

FAVORITE COLORS

_____

_____

_____

_____

_____

FAVORITE FOODS

_____

_____

_____

_____

_____

FAVORITE PETS

_____

_____

_____

_____

_____

FAVORITE BIBLE SONGS

_____

_____

_____

_____

_____

FAVORITE GAMES

_____
_____
_____
_____

FAVORITE BIBLE VERSES

_____
_____
_____
_____

FAVORITE FAMILY MEMORIES

_____
_____
_____
_____
_____
_____
_____
_____
_____
_____
_____
_____

PRAYER REQUESTS

NOTES

Caspian Sea

Persian Gulf

Mount Ararat?

Nuzi

Nineveh

Tigris River

Babylon

Erech

Ur

Mari

Euphrates River

Haran

MESOPOTAMIA

Carchemish

Ebla

Ugarit

PADAN ARAM

Damascus

Hazor

Dothan

Shechem

Dead Sea

HITTITES

CANAAN

Beersheba

Mediterranean Sea

Mount Sinai

Red Sea

Memphis

On

EGYPT

ABRAHAM'S JOURNEY

Possible route
that Abraham followed.

THE DESERT WANDERINGS

Jordan River

Mediterranean Sea

Jericho
Heshbon

Dead Sea

Rameses
Baal Zephon
Zilu
Succoth

DESERT OF SHUR

EDOM

GOSHEN

Kadesh Barnea

Bitter Lakes

EGYPT

DESERT OF PARAN

Ezion Geber

Marah
Elim

DESERT OF SIN

Hazeroth

Red Sea

Dophkah

Rephidim

Gulf of Aqaba

Mount Sinai

MIDIAN

Possible route of
the desert wanderings.